U0838366

澳门基金会
※
北京外国语大学
中国海外汉学研究中心
※
大象出版社

合作项目

卫三畏文集
Selected Works of Samuel Wells Williams

汉英韵府
（卷上）

Syllabic Dictionary of the Chinese Language

[美]
卫三畏　编著
Samuel Wells Williams

中原出版传媒集团
大地传媒

大象出版社
·郑州·

图书在版编目(CIP)数据

汉英韵府 / (美) 卫三畏 (Williams, S. W.) 编著.— 郑州 : 大象出版社, 2015. 7
(卫三畏文集)
ISBN 978-7-5347-8444-6

Ⅰ. ①汉⋯ Ⅱ. ①卫⋯ Ⅲ. ①英语—词典②词典—汉、英 Ⅳ. ①H316

中国版本图书馆 CIP 数据核字(2015)第 149974 号

卫三畏文集
汉英韵府
卫三畏 编著

出 版 人	王刘纯
责任编辑	李光洁
责任校对	钟 骄
封面设计	意拓设计
版式设计	凌 青

出版发行	大象出版社(郑州市开元路 16 号 邮政编码 450044)
	发行科 0371-63863551 总编室 0371-65597936
网 址	www.daxiang.cn
印 刷	北京汇林印务有限公司
经 销	各地新华书店经销
开 本	787mm×1092mm 1/16
印 张	84.5
字 数	1800 千字
版 次	2016 年 12 月第 1 版 2016 年 12 月第 1 次印刷
定 价	265.00 元(上、下卷)

若发现印、装质量问题,影响阅读,请与承印厂联系调换。
印厂地址 北京市大兴区黄村镇南六环磁各庄立交桥南 200 米(中轴路东侧)
邮政编码 102600 电话 010-61264834

主编序言

陶德民　张西平　吴志良

2008年8月8日，在北京奥运会开幕的当天，新落成的美国驻华使馆举行了剪彩仪式。美国国务院历史文献办公室为此发行了纪念图册，题为《共同走过的日子——美中交往两百年》，其中把1833年抵达广州的卫三畏(Samuel Wells Williams, 1812—1884)称扬为美国“来华传教第一人”，虽然他并非是第一个来到中国的美国传教士。图册对卫三畏在促进美中两国人民的相互了解方面所作的贡献作了这样的概括和评价：“传教士成为介绍中国社会与文化的重要信息来源，因为他们与大部分来华经商的外国人不一样，这些传教士学习了中文。例如，美国传教士卫三畏就会说流利的广东话和日语。他曾参与编辑英文期刊《中国丛报》，供西方传教士及时了解中国的最新动态，方便在美国的读者了解中国人的生活。卫三畏还编辑出版了《汉英拼音字典》（即《汉英韵府》——序者）和分为上下两卷的历史巨著《中国总论》。时至今日，他依然被公认为对19世纪的中国生活认识得最为精透的观察家。”

图册中也提到“蒲安臣于1862年成为第一个常驻北京的美国代表，在促进中国的国际关系上扮演了更为积极的角色。蒲安臣迅速结识了一批清政府的主要改革派官员，其中就包括咸丰皇帝的弟弟，设立了中国第一个外务部（应为总理各国事务衙门—序者）的恭亲王奕訢，”以及他1867年辞去驻华公使后作为清朝使节率团访问欧美，与当时的美国国务卿签订《蒲安臣条约》一事。“该条约扩展了中美两国的往来领域。条约规定，两国人民享有在彼此国家游历、居住的互惠权，并可入对方官学；中国领事在美国口岸享有完全的外交权利；鼓励华工移民美国；美国政府支持中国的领土主权。”其实，蒲安臣的卓有成效的外交活动及其维护正义的外交主张，与当时担任使馆秘书兼翻译的卫三畏的鼎力相助是分不开的。卫三畏的儿子卫斐列后来倾注极大热忱为蒲安臣撰写传记，其重要原因之一也在于此。

今天，当我们出版这部文集以纪念卫三畏诞辰200周年，并重新探讨其经历和成就之际，有必要思考这样一个问题，即卫三畏一生所体现的诸多志趣和倾向之中，什么是值得我们加以特别关注的呢？虽然这是一个“仁者见仁，智者见智”的问题，多数人恐怕都不会对以下见解持有异议，即卫三畏在对华态度上所发生的“从教化到对话”的某种转变可以说是他留给后世的最重要的精神遗产之一。而这恰恰可以从耶鲁大学校园里留存至今的两件文物上得到印证。

第一件文物是该校公共大食堂 (Commons Dining Hall) 墙上的卫三畏肖像画，它其实是设在纽约的美国圣经协会所藏同一油画的一个复本。如所周知，卫三畏的在华生涯大抵分为两个阶段，作为传教士的前 22 年 (1833—1855) 和作为外交官的后 20 年 (1856—1876)。在前 22 年的最后一段时间里，他还作为首席翻译官随同佩里将军的舰队两次远征日本，在改变日本锁国政策的外交谈判过程中发挥了重要作用。佩里将军对其语言天赋和交涉手腕的赏识，无疑是卫三畏转而步入为期 20 年的外交生涯的一个契机。1877 年辞职回国后不久，他受聘为耶鲁大学的中国语言文学讲座教授。1881 年春被遴选为美国圣经协会会长后，他便提出希望有才华的画家制作自己的肖像画，并将其献给圣经协会。结果，由耶鲁大学艺术学院的韦约翰教授制作的油画所呈现的是这样一个形象：等身大的卫三畏站立在放有纸、笔和一个中国式花瓶的桌子边上，目视前方，手持 1858 年《中美天津条约》的文本。

很显然，这样的构图反映了卫三畏本人的意思：他一直把基督教传教自由的条款得以列入 1858 年《中美天津条约》看作自己毕生的最大成就。这是因为当时负责谈判的美国公使列卫廉对是否要在条约中加入该条款并不经意，只是在卫三畏的坚持之下才获得了最后的成功。此一事实，不仅可见于耶鲁大学斯德龄纪念图书馆附属档案馆所藏卫三畏的亲笔日记，也可以由当时协助他进行谈判工作的丁韪良牧师后来所写的《花甲忆记》得到证实："那份现在成为条约荣耀之处的条款是卫三畏博士提出的。"在预定签约的 6 月 18 日即"决定命运的那天早上，卫三畏博士告诉我他一夜未眠，一直在考虑这份宽容条款。现在他想到了一种新的形式，可能会被对方接受。他写了下来，我建议我们应当马上坐轿子直接奔赴中方官邸解决这个问题。……中方代表接见了我们，他们当中的负责人稍作修改，就接受了卫三畏博士的措辞"(详见陶德民《从卫三畏档案看 1858 年中美之间的基督教弛禁交涉——写在〈基督教传教士传记丛书〉问世之际》)。1876 年夏天，美国国务院接受卫三畏的辞呈，在正式解职通知中对他赞扬有加："您对中国人的性格与习惯的熟悉，对该民族及其政府愿望与需求的了解，对汉语的精通，以及您对基督教与文明进步事业的贡献，都使您有充分的理由自豪。您无与伦比的中文字典与有关中国的诸多著作已为您赢得科学与文学领域内相应的崇高地位。更为重要的是，宗教界不会忘记，尤其多亏了您，我们与中国订立的条约中才得以加入自由传教这一条。"而卫三畏则在复信中坦承，这一嘉许是"最最让他感动与满意的"(见卫斐列著，顾钧、江莉译《卫三畏生平及书信——一位美国来华传教士的心路历程》)。顺便提到，在 1858 年 6 月 19 日，亦即《中美天津条约》签订的第二天，美国驻日总领事哈里斯便与德川幕府的代表签订了《美日修好通商条约》。卫三畏闻讯后，又不失时机地向美国的新教诸团体提出派遣牧师赴日传教的建议，并得到了切实的响应。所以，对美国基督教会的东亚传教事业来说，卫三畏确实是一位有功之臣。

那么，卫三畏是基于一种什么样的信念而企图以基督教义来教化东亚的所谓异教徒的呢？试举一个例子。1853 年 7 月 16 日，在佩里将军初访日本，成功向日方递交美国总统国书一周之后，卫三畏曾从停泊在江户湾的军舰上给他在土耳其传教的弟弟 W. F. 威廉斯写了一封长信，其中指出："佩里告诉日本官员，他将在次年率领一支更大的舰队以求得到他们对所提要求的回答，即所有前来访问或遇难流落日本海岸的美国人应得到善待，美国汽船在一个日本港口得到煤炭以及有关物资的补给。这些是我们花费巨大开支和派出强大舰队到日本水域的表面上的理由，而真正的理由是为了提高我们民族的名誉和得到称扬我们自己的材料。在这些理由的背后并通过这些理由，存有上帝的目的，即将福音传达给所有国家，并将神旨和责任送达这个至今为止只是在拙劣地模仿耶稣之真的民族。我十分确信，东亚各民族的锁国政策决非根据上帝的善意安排，其政府必须在恐怖和强制之下将之改变，尔后其人民或可自由。朝鲜人、中国人、琉球人和日本人必须承认这唯一活着的和真实的上帝，他们的锁国之墙必将为我们所拆除，而我们西方的太平洋沿岸城市正开始派出船队前往大洋的彼岸。”从卫三畏对佩里访日使命的解读来看，他固然赞成打开东亚各国的大门，但更重视把上帝的福音传入各国人们的心扉，期盼由此引发一系列的变革。因为他认定上帝所代表的真善美的品格和力量是美国等基督教国家所拥有的绝对优势和无比强势的源泉（详见陶德民《十九世纪中叶美国对日人权外交的启示——写在日本开国150周年之际》）。

然而，卫三畏在以后长期驻节北京的岁月里，逐步加深了对中国的悠久历史和深厚文化传统的了解，使他在对华态度上开始发生“从教化到对话”的某种转变。而这一点可以耶鲁校园里的另一件艺术杰作来作为象征，那就是在卫三畏于1884年2月16日去世两周之后，在举行其丧礼的巴特尔教堂（Battell Chapel）东北角中心位置安装的一块非常别致的彩色纪念玻璃。玻璃的中央写有《论语》中的七个汉字：“敏则有功，公则说。”（意思大体为，勤勉能积成事功，公道则众人心悦诚服。）玻璃的下方用英文记载了卫三畏的名字、生卒年份以及他一生所扮演的角色与身份，即“传教士、学者、外交官、耶鲁学院中文教授”。这块玻璃由纽约的路易斯·第法尼公司（Louis C. Tiffany & Co.）负责制作，其别出心裁的设计显然是出于卫三畏生前的授意。

卫三畏选用孔子的话作为自己一生的概括，可谓恰如其分。勤勉能积成事功的道理，可以从他孜孜不倦编纂而成的《中国丛报》、《中国总论》以及《汉英韵府》等多种刊物和名著得到了解。公道则众人心悦诚服的道理，则充分体现在了他辞职回国之际所受到的各界朋友的赞扬。他在信中告诉他的妻子，“临行前威妥玛于周六、西华于周一为我举办了两次特别宴会，我见到了北京的所有名流，并受到了他们的盛赞。然后，似乎是为了区别于外交聚会，丁韪良、艾约瑟、怀定先后请我吃饭。我告诉过你，我在丁韪良家见到了所有的传教士，那真是一次令人难忘的聚会”。“接连不断的登门送别者中有三四位是总理衙门的官员，京城中最位高权重的大官也来为我送行。除了亲王之外，我都是在办公室里会见他们，彼此依依惜别。九位官员每人赠我一柄折扇作为纪念，这充分显示了中国人的友善”。不仅北京的新教传教士们发给他一封送别信以示友谊与敬意，上海的同仁也发给他一封相似的信，恰如其分地总结了他在中国的生活：“您长期担任美国使馆秘书、翻译，九次代理公使的职务，这些工作给了您许多重要的机遇，使您得以把知识、经验用于为中国人造福、为您自己的国家谋利，尤其是为基督教在中国的传播效力。对您工作中表现出的高度责任感，我们不胜钦佩。”对这些热情洋溢的赞美之辞，卫三畏则表示自己的所作所为只不过是在执行上帝的旨意，“我在传教过程中与同伴们相处融洽、身体健康、工作愉快，为此我要虔诚地赞美造物主”。

在某种意义上说，卫三畏选用孔子的话来概括自己的一生，也显示了他对中国文化传统的敬重之意。而这种敬重之意，可以由1879年他为反对加州的排华风潮而撰写的《中国移民》中的一节得到佐证：“当加州的法庭想用立法来反对中国人时，它将中国人等同于印第安人的简单态度是颇为古怪的。生理学家查尔斯·匹克林将中国人和印第安人归为蒙古的成员，但加州的最高法院却认为‘印第安族包括汉族和蒙古族’。这样在概念错误的同时，它还支持了一种错误的观点。它把现存最古老国度的臣民和一个从未超越部落关系的种族相提并论；把这样一个民族——它的文学早于《诗篇》和《出埃及记》，并且是用一种如果法官本人肯于学习就不会叫作印第安语的语言写就，而它的读者超过了其他任何民族的作品——与最高的写作成就仅是一些图画和牛皮上的符号的人群混为一谈；把勤奋、谨慎、技艺、学识、发明等所有品质和全部保障人类生命和财产安全的物品等同于猎人和游牧民族的本能和习惯。它诋毁了一个教会我们如何制作瓷器、丝绸、火药，给予我们指南针，展示给我们茶叶的用处，启迪我们采用考试选拔官员的制度的民族；把它和一个轻视劳动，没有艺术、学校、贸易的种族归为同类，后者的一部分现在还混迹于加州人中间，满足于以挖草根过活。”虽然卫三畏在赞扬中国人的同时，也表达了他对印第安人的歧视态度，他的观点还是得到当时耶鲁学院全体教授的同情，他们纷纷签名支持他起草的请愿书，呼吁海斯总统否决1879年的反移民法，其中包含这样的警告：如果我们的政府首先改变条约的规定，中国政府也可以根据国际法取消治外法权，致使美国在华公民失去领事的保护。此外，1878年中国北方发生大饥荒时，身处太平洋彼岸的卫三畏利用他对美国在华传教士和商社的影响，不遗余力地推动救灾。他还试图劝说国会归还1859年中方赔款余额的一部分来帮助缓解灾区的困境。而早在1860年，他就曾建议国务院用这笔赔款余额在中国建立一所美中学院，以培养中方的翻译、通商和外交人才。这个建议得到了新上任的总统林肯的同意，只因为当时的国会未予批准而搁浅。卫三畏这个未能实现的建议完全可以称之为后来退回庚款吸引中国学生留美的先驱性方案。

卫三畏还对亲眼目睹的中国同时代的缓慢而确凿的变化做了一定的正面评价。1883年7月，即辞世的半年多之前，卫三畏在儿子的帮助下终于完成了《中国总论》这一巨著的修订工作，在增补版的序言中他写下了如下字句：“我在1833年到达广州时，和另外两位美国人作为‘番鬼’向行商经官正式报告，在他的监护之下才得以生存。1874年，我作为美国驻北京公使馆秘书，跟随艾忭敏公使觐见同治皇帝，美国使节站在与‘天子’完全平等的地位呈上国书。由于一生之中的这两次遭遇，并念念不忘在思想和道德上的重大进步是使一个孤傲的政府从强加于人的姿态改而听从他人所必需的，毫不足怪的是，我确信汉人的子孙有着伟大的未来，不过，唯有纯正基督教的发展才是能使这一成长过程中的各个冲突因素免于互相摧残的充分条件。无论如何，这个国家已经度过被动时期，这是肯定无疑的。中国不可能再安于懒散隔绝—像过去那样，以过于自负的态度俯视其他国家，就像面对她所无需劳神的星星一样。”

如果说，17世纪的礼仪之争最后是以天主教士在康熙禁令之下被逐出中国告终的，那么，这场可谓19世纪的礼仪之争则是以“天朝上国”在第二次鸦片战争之后所做出的巨大让步来结局的，包括废除以夷相称、公使驻京、平身觐见皇帝而不必行三跪九叩之礼。卫三畏的字里行间所透露的，既有在礼仪上争得与最古老“中央王国”之“天子”平等地位的自豪，又有从其所信奉的上帝的立场针砭这个王国“懒散隔绝”和“过于自负”的高傲。联系到上述1853年他给在土耳其传教的弟弟W. F. 威廉斯的长信，可见这时的卫三畏虽然在其对华态度上开始了“从教化到对话”的转变，但并未把“异教徒”放在完全对等的位置上，特别是在道德和精神的层面上。在这个意义上说，自以为占据着道德精神的制高点，只有基督教可以拯救中国的卫三畏也难免“过于自负”的诟病。这就是笔者在前文中提到其转变时，始终不忘加上“某种”一词来予以限定的缘故。

尽管如此，卫三畏在序言中宣称，修订版“坚持初版序言中所述的观点——为中国人民及其文明洗刷掉古怪的、模糊不清的可笑印象”。卫三畏相信，在传教“事业取得成功的基础上，中国作为一个民族，在道义和政治两方面，将会得到拯救。这一成功有可能和人民的需要同步前进。他们将会变得适应于自己着手处理问题，并且和外国文明以多种活动形式结合起来。不久，将会引进铁路、电报和制造业，随之而来的是中国人民中成百万地受到启发，无论在宗教、政治和家庭生活的每一方面”。这种力图呈现中国文明及民族的美好品质和衷心期待中国在对外交往中日益开放进步的善意态度，自然是应该予以充分肯定的。

从卫三畏的例子不难联想到，身处所谓“轴心文明”（主要以几大世界性宗教作为标识）的人们往往患有“老子天下第一”的自恋症，而以“居高临下”的态度傲视其他人，难以免俗和根治。反观我们自己，历代国人的“华夷之辨”又何尝不是如此？而时至今日，仍不乏“宅兹中国”的自尊和输出“天下体系”的自负。但也不必悲观，因为这个五彩缤纷的世界本来就是由形形色色、各有偏好的人们构成的。他们之间有相辅相成的关系，也有相反相成的因素。虽然各派宗教和文化的代表自以为有“替上帝传教”或“替天行道”的使命，谁都无法垄断真理和剥夺他人的信仰，也不能指望按照自己的面貌来彻底改造他人。其出于宗教或政治动机的种种努力的后果，客观上会推动各国和各民族之间的交往和融合，并推动人类文明的进步和升华，则是毫无疑义的。从这一点来看，卫三畏一生的变化过程所显示的方向对我们建构今日地球村的和平共处规则还是不乏启迪作用的，那就是要逐渐学会把“老子化胡”的心态改为“相敬如宾”的心理，对异民族、异文化和异文明采取更加宽容、尊重和善于调适的态度，以便用文明对话来取代文明对抗，从而把亨廷顿认为不可避免的“文明冲突”消弭于萌芽状态和无形之间。

同治甲戌年鐫

衛三畏廉士甫編譯

漢英韻府

滬邑美華書院銅板梓行

A

SYLLABIC DICTIONARY

OF THE

CHINESE LANGUAGE;

ARRANGED ACCORDING TO THE WU-FANG YUEN YIN,

WITH THE

PRONUNCIATION OF THE CHARACTERS AS HEARD IN PEKING, CANTON, AMOY, AND SHANGHAI.

By S. WELLS WILLIAMS, LL.D.

取之精而用之宏誠哉斯語茲集諸書大旨以成是書無非翔爲博雅君子之一助爾

"Very true it is, that a careful selection of expressions must precede their extensive use remembering this, and in the hope of affording some aid to scholars, the purport of many books has been here brought together into one."

SHANGHAI:
AMERICAN PRESBYTERIAN MISSION PRESS.
1896.

STEREOTYPED AT THE PRESBYTERIAN MISSION PRESS FOUNDRY.

PREFACE.

FIFTY-TWO years ago, Dr. MORRISON ended his labors on his Chinese Dictionary with the sentence, "Thanks to Heaven's gracious Providence, Canton, April 9, 1822," as the expression of his thankfulness that he had been enabled to bring the seven years' toil to a close; and in his own copy, presented to me in 1834 by his son John, he had written underneath it, "Glory be to God on high, Nov. 12, 1828; R.M."—as if the recollection of the day on which the first sentence was printed, had only deepened the satisfaction he felt after six years at having seen it through the press. That work will ever remain a monument of his industry and scholarship; and its publication in six quarto volumes by the East India Company at an outlay of $60,000 was a just appreciation of its merits.

Since then, many similar works have been published, dictionaries both of the general language and its chief dialects; but their editions were small, and during a course of years they have either become exhausted, or are very scarce, while the number of students has increased tenfold. Thus the works of MEDHURST, BRIDGMAN, CALLERY, and GONÇALVES, are now almost unknown; and the only lexicons available for the use of Chinese students have been the reprint of MORRISON's Syllabic Dictionary, MACLAY's Fuhchau, DOUGLAS' Amoy, and LOBSCHEID's Canton, Vernacular Dictionaries.

These considerations led me to regard the preparation of a Dictionary on the syllabic plan, as the way in which I could best facilitate the study of the language. My first plan was to reärrange my Tonic Dictionary of the Canton Dialect, and fit it for general use; but I soon saw that its incompleteness required an entire revision. I accordingly commenced in 1863, and took the *Wu-fang Yuen Yin* as the basis for arranging the characters, instead of following MORRISON, to whom this vocabulary seems to have been unknown. It was easier and safer to adopt a native arrangement of the syllables, than to undertake to make a new one as he had done, and this Dictionary, therefore, follows that work almost exactly. Though its pronunciation differs probably from that heard at any one place where the *kwan hwa* is spoken, it is probably nearer to the general average of the spoken language, as heard north of the Yang-tsz' River, than it would have been to reduce it to the speech of a single city or prefecture, as Peking for instance. In a work intended for general use, this approximation is better in one point, that it allows every student to mark the variations from this standard as heard in his own region; moreover, it is what the natives themselves look for in their own dictionaries. We can hardly expect anything nearer than this general approach to a uniform pronunciation of Chinese.

I have consulted all the works of my predecessors which I could get, and have examined each character in MORRISON'S Syllabic Part, in GONÇALVES' *Diccionario China-Portuguez*, in DE GUIGNES' *Dictionnaire Chinois*, and in my Canton Dictionary. Dr. MEDHURST'S translation of the *K'anghi Tsz'tien* has been much used, but the principal source for definitions has been its original, which, imperfect as it is according to our ideas of a lexicon, is still the most convenient work of the kind in the language. The etymological definitions are drawn from the *Selected Characters Carefully Examined* 埶文備覽, a dictionary published in 1787, and furnishing good definitions of all the common characters, whose ancient forms are explained.

The end aimed at has been to give the meanings of a word, and to illustrate them with phrases, adding the colloquial uses where they could be ascertained. The limited extent to which I have carried this part, has only served to show more strikingly how much there is still to do, and how many collaborators are needed to do it effectually. When local dictionaries of the leading dialects have been published like those issued in the Canton, Amoy, and Fuhchau dialects, it will be possible to compare the local usages of characters, and learn their differences from the authorized definitions. Many expressions now regarded as unwritten will probably then be found to have once had proper characters since forgotten.

In such a comparison of dialects the natives have done nothing; for few or none of the colloquial meanings are given in the local dictionaries of those three cities, though one would have supposed that their principal object and benefit would be to illustrate the local usages of words. The literati, however, despise all such inroads upon classical usage, and except in the *kwan hwa*, the colloquial has never received their attention. This is not to be wondered at, and probably it has been the only way to maintain the purity, if not the sense, of the written character and language; for confusion would soon arise by using local characters instead of authorized ones. When the knowledge of books increases, and men can rapidly pass and repass across the country, the *kwan hwa* will, perhaps, become more uniformly and widely used, and the local dialects, like those once current in parts of England and France, gradually give way to it; or else, the wider diffusion of knowledge will compel the people speaking one dialect to reduce it to an alphabetic form, discard the complex characters, and crystallize their speech into a separate tongue.

Mr. MARSH says the distinction between the written and spoken languages in Europe was once far greater than at present, and has diminished as education has advanced:—

"It is difficult for Englishmen and Anglo-Americans, who habitually speak much as they write, and write much as they speak, to conceive of the co-existence of two dialects in a people, one almost uniformly employed in conversation, the other almost as exclusively in writing. Yet such was the state of things in England, from the Conquest at least till the middle of the XIVth century, and such is the case in a large part of Europe at this day. In Italy, for instance, there is almost everywhere a popular speech, commonly employed by all classes in familiar oral intercourse, and so far cultivated that it can be, though it rarely is, written; while, at the same time, the *lingua commune d'Italia*, or, as it is often called, the Tuscan dialect, is known to all as the language of books, of journals, and of correspondence, and is also employed as the medium of religious and scholastic instruction. But this literary tongue, at least in those parts of Italy where dialects widely different from it are habitually spoken, always remains to the Italians themselves essentially a foreign language. This fact BIONDELLI states in stronger terms than a prudent stranger would venture to do upon the testimony of his own observation, in his *Saggio sui Dialetti Gallo-Italici, X.*

"There is a similar discrepancy between the written and spoken language in many parts of Germany, though the diffusion of literary culture in that country has made the dialect of books more universally familiar than in most European nations. The oriental traveler SEETZEN, whose journals have lately been published, sometimes makes entries in them in the Platt-Deutsch of his native province, and states expressly that he uses that dialect, in order that those passages may not be understood by strangers, into whose hands his papers might chance to fall."—G. P. MARSH, *Early Literature of the English Language*, page 337.

If these differences still remain in those civilized countries, much more are they seen among the half-educated people of Asia, where the literary classes have tried rather to encumber the road to knowledge than to help the student over its difficulties; who is compelled, as it were, to waste most of his energy in sharpening his ax before he can cut down the tree.

The plan of a Chinese lexicon to satisfy all the needs of a foreigner, should comprise the general and vernacular pronunciations, with the tones used in various places, and the sounds given to each character as its meanings vary. The history and composition of the character, its uses in various epochs, and its authorized and colloquial meanings should be explained and illustrated by suitable examples. All this knowledge should be methodically arranged so as to be accessible with the least possible trouble. But even when arranged and ready, the foreigner would find it to be incomplete for all his purposes by reason of the local usages, as another extract from Mr. MARSH shows:—

"I may here notice a widely-diffused error, which it may be hoped the lexicographical criticism of the present day may dispel. I refer to the opinion that words, individually and irrespectively of syntactical relations, and combinations in phrases, have one or more inherent, fixed, and limited meanings, which are capable of logical definition, and of expression in other descriptive terms of the same language. This may be true of artificial words—that is, words invented for, or confined to the expression of arbitrary distinctions and technical notions in science or its practical applications, and also of the names of material objects and of the sensuous qualities of things; but of the vocabulary of the passions and the affections, which grows up and is informed with living meaning by the natural, involuntary processes to which all language but that of art owes its being, it is wholly untrue. Such words live and breathe only in mutual combination and interdependence with other words. They change their force with every new relation into which they enter; and consequently, their meanings are as various and exhaustless as the permutations and combinations of the ten digits. To teach, therefore, the meaning of a great proportion of the words which compose the vocabulary of every living speech, by formal definition, is as impossible as to convey by description a notion of the shifting hues of the pigeon's neck."—*Second Course*, page 383.

If this be true of English or German, it is still more applicable to the Chinese language, whose painstaking students have quoted a vast number of phrases in their two great lexicons, *viz.*, the *Treasury of Good Sentences* 佩文韻府 in 110 volumes, and the *Classification of Dissyllables* 駢字類編 in 120 volumes. In these their aim has been to show the different uses of the same word, but the variety of material bewilders the student, and he soon despairs of finding any connection between their meanings. But there are other difficulties in the way of making a complete Anglo-Chinese lexicon. There is, as a preliminary, the vast extent of the literature to become familiar with, which demands much and protracted study. Neither is it easy to find exact equivalents for single Chinese words in English; and to render their combinations into corresponding phrases requires long practice in writing and speaking. If concrete terms like 書, 筆, or 墨, are so unlike as to require some explanation when rendering them by *book*, *pen*, or *ink*; much more unlike are abstract terms like those relating to mental or religious exercises. This every one knows who has tried to teach our ideas of *sin*, *righteousness*, or *salvation* by 罪, 義, or 救, their nearest equivalents. Then again, the native scholars who help us are trained in a different school, and their ignorance, carelessness, and deceit have all to be guarded against. They do not like to appear ignorant before a foreigner on any subject, and are usually ready with an answer, whether to give the name of a flower, to render a distich, or to state the location of a town; trusting, perhaps, that their pupil will never inquire into the matter. In my own case, hundreds of questions could not be revised by cross-questioning others, and errors have probably crept in which will require more time to correct than it did to make them. The subjects to be explained comprise all branches of knowledge, too, some of which are not very familiar, and on this account, accuracy, which is the thing most wanted, is especially difficult of attainment. Added to this, the effort to find the meaning of a sentence originally written wrong, has not unfrequently perplexed both teacher and pupil. Chinese books are very rich in misprints and misuse of characters, and having no stops or punctuation, and no capital letters to denote proper names, a phrase is easily misread or misunderstood.

The early associations of the native with the language and its literature are wanting to the foreigner, and he often fails to relish an allusion because he is ignorant of the incident, or appreciate a metaphor, because he cannot tell what object is referred to. I have tried to ascertain as near as possible the names of natural objects, for which I have consulted the Chinese *Herbal* 本草綱目, the *Book of Nature* 三才圖, and the *Names and Pictures of Vegetables*, 植物名實圖考; but in religious, medical, legal, and mercantile terms, much remains to be done. The common uses of many words in all these departments are unlike in different parts of China; and this confusion can only be removed by further comparison. The book word for a flower or a disease often differs from the common name, which itself changes in remote parts of the country. We are not yet acquainted with the botany, zoölogy, mineralogy, or nosology of China well enough to recognize in the poor descriptions of native authors the objects of our inquiry. For instance, the *jasmine* is called 茉莉花 in Canton, but this name denotes the *four-o'-clock* in Peking; in one city the 木瓜 is the *papaya*, while in the other it is the *quince*. Again, the *panda* of Nipal (*Ailurus refulgens*) is probably intended by the 貔; but one would need to know well this animal's habitat and appearance to recognize it under the description of "a sprightly animal like a small bear, with short hair, but yellowish."

The misuse of words in passing from one dialect to another can be illustrated by the name given to the people of Swatow. This was *hok-lò*, 福佬 *i.e.* people from Fuhkien; but when the Cantonese heard *hok-lò*, they wrote it as they heard the sound, 學佬 being now the name given to the people of that prefecture, and the Cantonese of the present day puzzle themselves to know why it was applied to them. No Chinese scholar has examined these dialectical changes, which are an ample source of many colloquialisms in every dialect.

I have followed EITEL'S *Hand-book of Buddhism*, F. P. SMITH'S *Materia Medica*, and HOBSON'S *Medical Vocabulary*, for terms in those branches. Mr. WADE'S *Category of T'ien* and his *Course of Colloquial Chinese*, EDKINS' *Grammar of the Shanghai Dialect* and his *Progressive Lessons in the Chinese Spoken Language*, MACLAY and BALDWIN'S *Dictionary of the Foochow Dialect*, LEGGE'S *Translation of the Chinese Classics*, and BRIDGMAN'S *Chrestomathy*, have all furnished their quotas. I have not, however, mentioned my authorities in the body of the work, lest I should cumber it. The examples and phrases number about 53,000, and are not repeated when it could be avoided; nor is their pronunciation added, for as the work is intended for students in all the dialects, each will read them in the one he is learning. A space is left under each character, if one wishes to write the local sound beside the Pekingese, which has been carefully revised by Rev. CHAUNCEY GOODRICH. The colloquial use of a character is placed by itself. MACLAY'S Dictionary is the authority for the few given in the Fuhchau dialect, and my Canton Dictionary for that dialect. For the Shanghai dialect, I am indebted to Miss LYDIA M. FAY, of the American Episcopal Mission; and also for the Shanghai sounds given in the Index, and — what involved far more work, — a careful oversight of the manuscript before it went into the printer's hands. The Amoy sounds in the Index were furnished by Rev. W. S. SWANSON and Rev. W. MCGREGOR. The long list of surnames owes most of its accuracy and extent to Rev. Dr. BLODGET of Peking; and the careful revision of the proof-sheets of the Introduction and Index by Mr. A. WYLIE has contributed everything to their accuracy. Other friends have aided in whatever way they could, by whom during the progress of the work many points have been cleared up.

The number of characters in this work is 12,527, contained in 10,940 articles, and placed under 522 syllables, which follow each other alphabetically, aspirated syllables coming after the unaspirated. Those syllables which begin with *ts*, on account of their number, are placed by themselves after *tw'an*. When a character is described as unauthorized, it merely means that it does not occur in K'anghi, for several of those thus designated are in good use. The edition of the *Wu-fang Yuen Yin*, which I have followed, has 10,486 characters, including scores of duplicates; but the full edition contains 41,247 words, or nearly as many as are in K'anghi's Dictionary. I have brought together all the sounds and meanings of a word under its most common sound, in order to avoid repeating the character. The characters in MORRISON'S Dictionary are arranged under 411 syllables, (not distinguishing between aspirated and unaspirated sounds,) and their total number, including hundreds of duplicates, is 12,674. In DE GUIGNES' Dictionary there are 13,933, of which 1040 are duplicated forms; in the Canton Dictionary, 7850; in the Fuhchau Dictionary, 9390; and in GONÇALVES, 7670.

The tables scattered through the book will serve to elucidate many points occurring in the course of study, and save reference to other works. They are placed as follows:—

The Introduction is designed to furnish some explanations respecting the scope of the work, the orthography employed, the construction of characters, and such hints and helps in commencing the study of the language as practice has proved to be useful. Those paragraphs respecting the affinities between the general spoken language and the south-eastern dialects, are short and imperfect compared with the subject, but may lead to something fuller. The whole subject of comparison of dialects has not been worked out, because there are not sufficient data on which to found either reasoning or deductions. The short lists of dialectical sounds prefixed to each syllable, may furnish starting points to students at various parts, to mark the local differences from the *Wu-fang Yuen Yin.*

In concluding these remarks, I have the satisfaction of feeling that the labor spent upon this work during the past eleven years, in the intervals of official duties, will now be available for students in acquiring the Chinese language. Its deficiencies will be hereafter supplied by others who will build upon their predecessors as I have done; for the field is too vast to be explored or exhausted by even many laborers. The stimulus to past effort, and the hope that it would not be in vain, both sprang from the desire to aid the labors of those who are imparting truth in any branch to the sons of Han, especially those religious and scientific truths whose acquisition and practice can alone Christianize and elevate them. At the end of the forty years spent in this country in these pursuits, I humbly thank the good Lord for all the progress I have been permitted to see in this direction, and implore His blessing upon this effort to aid their greater extension.

UNITED STATES LEGATION,
Peking, June, 1874.

S. W. W.

INTRODUCTION.

SECT. I. —THE MANDARIN DIALECT AS EXHIBITED IN THE WU-FANG YUEN YIN.

THE speech of the great body of the educated classes among the Chinese, called by them the *kwan hwa* 官話 or Official Language, and known as the Court or Mandarin Dialect, is spoken throughout the regions north of the Yangtsz' River, without much variation in its idiom and grammatical construction, and very extensively in the provinces south of it, except in Fuhkien and Kwangtung, to such a degree as to make it the prevailing speech in sixteen of the provinces. In most parts of the two above-named provinces, the vernacular presents so many variations from it in those two respects, that educated men are obliged to specially learn to speak the *kwan hwa*, in addition to the general study of the characters, in order to carry on oral intercourse with their educated countrymen at the north. This peculiarity of the Chinese language,—that of having many sounds for the same symbol, like the different names of the Arabic numerals among European nations, probably at first attached also to the Egyptian symbols; but the phonetic element there triumphed at last over the symbolic, and the Egyptian became finally an alphabetic language. Not so with the Chinese written language; this still maintains its ideographic character, and is now used as the written medium for the intercourse of more human beings than any other. The forms and significations of the symbols, too, have altered so slightly that inscriptions a thousand years old are read without difficulty, and books written thirty centuries ago are daily quoted as good authority both for style and for precept.

It is not surprising, perhaps, that such an ideographic language as this was invented; for the first thought of one who tries to write an idea, is more likely to be to picture it than to attempt to express the sounds by which it is spoken. The greater wonder is that it should have lasted so lóng, and exerted such an influence in perpetuating and unifying the people who use it. Nations who wrote in alphabetic languages were, it may be, not near enough, or civilized enough, to influence the very early Chinese, so as to fairly place the question before them of adopting an alphabetic language instead of their own; but after the introduction of Budhism, and the extension of the Imperial power of Han as far west as the Caspian Sea, this point must have presented itself to many minds. But no trace can be found of any serious effort on the part of native Chinese, to discard the characters and reduce their own speech to an alphabetic form in Devanagari, Persian, or any other character. In the ages succeeding the introduction of Budhism down to the present, this symbolic language has maintained itself intact. This is owing, more than any other one cause, to the difficulty that minds, long trained to associate ideas with separate pictorial symbols, find in associating them with combined symbols or letters, expressing only sounds. Educated Chinese are ready to acknowledge that other nations can write down their speech by letters, and understand it perfectly; but they have been trained so thoroughly to trust chiefly to the eye, to obtain the full meaning of an expression, that nothing else will serve. The laconism and energy of their written language over their spoken, tends too to confirm them in this habit, and prevent a fair trial of an easier mode of conveying thought. To a true disciple of Confucius, the notion that his teachings can be conveyed in any other form than the very characters he wrote them in, is almost preposterous ;—it is stronger than the feeling among Mohammedans that Arabic is the only language fit for the Koran, and has more to support it. But in these days, this question will come to the front with increased power; and the difficulty of using such a cumborous medium to introduce new ideas on every subject, among millions of ignorant people, will force a solution. At present, their language seems to be the greatest intellectual obstacle to the advancement of the Chinese; but naturally, they will not reject it until they themselves see the need of another and easier; and vital Christianity alone can furnish the stimulus, guide, and reward of such a change.

It is not designed here to enter into a disquisition on the many interesting points connected with the origin, construction, and modifications of these characters; or to discuss the inception and growth of the great variety of sounds now given to the same character in various parts of the land. The present object is to furnish the student with such explanations as will facilitate his use of this Dictionary, and aid his progress in acquiring the written and spoken language.

The Chinese have adopted three modes of arranging the characters in their dictionaries, each of which has its special advantages. These are, the *natural method*, in which words of a similar meaning are grouped under leading heads;—the *analytic method*, by which words are arranged under certain determinatives called keys or radicals;—and the *syllabic* or rhyming *method*, by which words fall into certain classes according to their terminations.

Of the first kind, the 爾雅 or *Ready Guide*, is the best known, and first in age of philological works extant in any language. This ancient relic is usually ascribed to Cheu Kung, about B.C. 1100, but it was completed by Tsz'hia, a disciple of Confucius, nearly seven hundred years after; and remodeled into its present shape by Kwoh P'oh, about A.D. 280. It is still in constant use, and its quaint illustrations and archaic expressions illustrate both the ancient manners and language of the Chinese. It is divided into nineteen sections, some having several subdivisions, containing for the most part a natural arrangement of characters under the sixteen heads of kindred, houses, utensils, music, heaven, earth, mounds, hills, waters, plants, trees, insects, fishes, birds, and wild and domestic animals. These are preceded by a more strictly philological part in three sections, explaining ancient terms, words, and phrases. The first section gives the first, and almost the only attempt at a treatise on synonyms in the Chinese language, but it is too meager to be useful to the foreigner. For instance, the character 告 is defined by the following group of words, 命, 令, 禧, 畛, 祈, 請, 謁, 訴, and 誥, each of them in certain cases having the meaning of announcing, enjoining on, &c.; but there are no examples of their use. The work is now reckoned as the last of the Thirteen Classics.

It has had many imitations, which, though much modified, have generally assumed the form of encyclopedias of greater or less extent. One of the most useful of these classified dictionaries is the valuable 三才圖會 or *Pictorial Book of Nature*, published in the Ming Dynasty in 106 chapters; wherein various objects belonging to Heaven, Earth and Man, are treated of under sections like those in the *Ready Guide*, and every article has its own picture and explanatory letterpress. Useful as this class of books is to furnish materials for the lexicographer, the cumbersome arrangement forbids their general use as definers of characters.

The second, or *analytic* plan has grown out of the construction of the characters. When a writer wishes to express a new term, the genius of the language leads him to unite a symbol denoting *sense*, with another expressing *sound* rather than quality; though *sound* and *quality* are sometimes both attended to in the composition of the new symbol, the phonetic part not being used simply or altogether for its sound. It has also a signification of its own, and is sometimes so chosen that that shall furnish part of the idea to be conveyed by the new character; though this remark has many exceptions. For instance, in Pekingese, 鼻 the *nose*, joined to 囊 a *bag*, means the nose stopped up by a cold; it is read *nang'*, in a different tone from ˓*nang*, its primitive, but evidently alluding to it. As the number of characters increased, they were grouped by their natural or most prominent feature; thus the names of stones, birds, or armor, were ranged under the symbols 石, or 鳥, or 戈, these being common characters for those things already in use.

The earliest work on this principle is the 說文 or *Discourse on Meaning of Words*, published about A.D. 100, wherein the characters are arranged in 514 groups. They were reärranged by Ku Yé-wang of the Sui dynasty (A.D. 543), under 542 radicals; and again in the Sung dynasty by another writer under 544. In the Ming dynasty, the compiler of the 六書本義 or Origin of of the Six Modes of Writing, reduced them to 360; and about a century after, they were fixed at their present number of 214 in the 字彙 or Classification of Characters. This method of grouping characters, and arranging those placed under each radical by the number of their strokes, has proved to be so convenient, that no alteration has since been made in their order or number. It was adopted in the 正字通 or Explanations of Authorized Characters, the 康熙字典 or Emperor K'anghi's Dictionary, and the 埶文備覽, or Selected Characters Carefully Examined, three of the most common dictionaries now in use.

The third, the *syllabic* or rhyming plan of arranging characters by their finals and tones, was adopted later than the analytic, but has been more extensively used. The confusion and diversity found amidst the works in each of these three classifications, prove the inherent difficulty of the attempt; but the readiness with which general and local rhyming vocabularies are made, proves too, their adaptability to meet a want, and the tendency of the language towards an alphabetic arrangement. The number of finals, at first 206 in the T'ang dynasty, was reduced to 160 in the Sung, and the initials were thirty-six. Subsequently these were reärranged and reduced by various authors, but all adhered to the mode of combining initials and finals brought from India by the Budhist priests Shăn-yoh 沈約 and Shăn-kung 神珙, during the Liang dynasty, A.D. 510. The 佩文韻府, probably the largest dictionary in any language of the world, is arranged on this rhyming principle, and all the local vocabularies.

It is very difficult for us, who are habituated to the use of letters, and their combinations into syllables to express the words in our Western languages, to appreciate the perplexities and difficulties of a Chinese scholar when he tries to represent the sounds and tones of his own language. In doing so, he can only employ other characters; but each one of these, too, having no inherent sound, perhaps, in its turn requires to be more accurately sounded, by comparing it with a third. To him the words 理 or 風 are indivisible simple sounds or names, as *a* or *o* are to us; but we describe them as *li* or *fung* — words of two or four letters. If an Englishman finds himself at fault in trying to read Spanish or Welsh correctly, because he pronounces the words according to his own letters;—and those people are still more perplexed, perhaps, when they try to read English according to their own letters, while all use a common alphabet to express elementary sounds;—how much more awkward does the Chinese philologist find it to express unknown syllables by known syllables. The plan now adopted is to express the sound by taking parts of two other words and combining them. For instance, the sound of 扮 is expressed by uniting 父 and 吻 to make 扮, *i.e.* *f*-u and w-*ăn* to make *făn*, or as we should express it, dropping two out of the five letters, and uniting the rest to form the new word. But as the sounds of all three characters may be unlike in different parts of the country, the next thing is to quote another character of the same sound, as 憤, to indicate this one. This difficulty of accurately exhibiting the sound is seen in the variety of characters quoted in K'anghi's Dictionary, which have been used by lexicographers to combine and express the sound of the characters they were defining; and this new sound, in its turn, is sometimes used to express the very sound of those characters used in writing its own. The following directions for the native student to find a character in the *Wu-fang Yuen Yin* will illustrate the dilemma both teacher and scholar feel in this respect, and in order to show it more clearly, only the tones are given, and not the pronunciation of the characters.

"Suppose a man wishes to find the character ꜀方; he runs the word through the five tones, ꜀方 ꜁房, '倣 放', which as it has the same final with ꜀央, ꜁羊, '養, 樣', enables him to perceive that it is to be looked for under the ꜁羊 final. Turning then to the table of initials, he sees that it belongs to the light-lip sounds (經 唇 音), and runs it over, saying ꜀方, '倣, 放', 縛, ꜀風, and ascertains that it comes under the initial ꜀風. Now this character ꜀風 as an initial, is known because it is derived from ꜀江; by coalescing them in spelling, as ꜀風 ꜀江; we thus get ꜀風, ꜀分, ꜀翻, ꜀方, [all under the same initial, and the last one] ꜀方 ꜁房 '倣 放', 縛, has all the five tones complete. This is the warp (經) way, and it can also be called the lengthwise (縱) rule.

"But if one wishes a shorter way to find this same character [꜀方]; let him run over the sounds ꜀邦, ꜀鎊, ꜀牻, ꜀方, ꜁郎, and he will immediately perceive that it comes under the sound ꜁羊, the fourth of the finals; looking there he will see it arranged among the characters under ꜀風, the first one in the *shang p'ing* tone. This is the woof (緯) way, or it can also be called the cross-wise (橫) rule. This warp and woof way is certain, and there is no more convenient and direct manner of ascertaining the sounds of characters than by thus following them along and across. All other sounds can be ascertained in the same way."

It would be just as impossible for a Chinese, able only to *speak* his own language, to learn how to find a character from these directions if he desired to learn to read, as it would be for a foreigner who had just landed, and could not *speak* a word. Both of them must learn the sounds of the characters from a living voice; both must, so to speak, be introduced *viva voce* to the acquaintance and name of the character, as they would to the name of a visitor, or a row of flowers. The impossibility of writing foreign sounds with Chinese characters, so that native scholars can thereby read the words and study the books of other languages, is thus seen in its full difficulty; no doubt, it has had much to do with the isolation of this race, and the formation of their national character. The student in every other civilized nation can study foreign languages through his own; but however well a Chinese may read or speak the English language, for example, he cannot open its treasures to his countrymen by a grammar or praxis, so that one of them could, otherwise unaided, read or learn it. The Budhists tried to introduce the prayers of their religion from India to their fellow-disciples in China, using the Chinese characters; the result was only a rude transliteration of the Sanscrit sounds, to which the meanings were originally given; these sounds are still recited but their sense is mostly lost. It is safe to say that their symbolic language has shut out the people of this land from mental intercourse with their fellow-men more than any other one cause.

Foreigners have also arranged their dictionaries on three different plans. One is the *analytic* mode, under the 214 radicals, as has been done by De Guignes, Morrison, Medhurst, and Lobscheid; or according to an abridged series of radicals, as elaborated by Gonçalves. Another is the *phonetic*, adopted only by Callery in the Systema Phoneticum, in which he grouped characters by their primitives. The third is the *syllabic*, in which the characters follow one another alphabetically, as has been done by Morrison, Medhurst in his Hokkëen Dictionary, Maclay and Baldwin, Goddard, Douglas, and Williams.

It is the plan followed in the present work, and is on the whole the most useful to the foreign student, for it brings together homophonous characters, arranged in the order of their tones. Such are most frequently interchanged and mistaken by the people themselves, and those which a foreigner has most need of discriminating

He is certain in speaking, at first, to confound words of different tones, but written with the same letters, as ꜀yen 烟 *smoke*; ꜀yen 言 *words*; yen' 燕 a *swallow*, which are widely separated by their construction. A native also usually confuses characters having the same tone; and if all such are grouped together, their similarities and distinctions are more readily seen. Another advantage is the facility thereby afforded to the foreigner, who is learning the language with the help of a native teacher, to find the word he hears, which he knows not yet in its written form, or may not have had correctly given to him.

Further, the synonymous forms of the same character, which are sometimes alike as to their primitive, as 斵 and 斷 and 㫁; or perhaps, more frequently occur under the same radical, as 瞬, 眴, 瞤, 瞚, can, in the syllabic arrangement, all be seen at once. The addition of an index where every character is placed under its proper radical and stroke, furnishes all the aid required to find it, when the spelling is not known. The Chinese have never added a radical index to any of their syllabic dictionaries, for such a help would be quite useless, unless to indicate the page on which a character occurred. The native who wishes to examine the local vocabulary in another dialect must, therefore, first learn the system of initials and finals on which it is planned, or trust to a native of the locality where it is used.

The groundwork of the present Dictionary is the *Wu-fang Yuen Yin* 五方元音 or Original Sounds of the Five Regions, *i.e.* North, South, East, West and Center, which denote all the land. It is a vocabulary of the Court Dialect much used in Central and Northern China. It was first published in 1700, about the same date that the literati employed by K'anghi had finished the Thesaurus and Lexicon which reflect so much credit on his reign; and, perhaps, was suggested by the former of those works. The editions have been numerous and all exhibit slight variations in the arrangement of certain characters. An earlier work of the same sort had, however, appeared in the 13th century,—the 中原音韻 or Original Sounds and Finals in Chinese, in which the characters are arranged under nineteen finals; and it would have been better if the compiler of the present work had followed it in this respect. A third book, the 中州全韻 or Complete Finals for Central China, presents the characters arranged according to the several organs of the voice, as dental, lingual, palatal, guttural, &c.; but, as this system involves more attention to the initial than the others, it has not obtained so wide a circulation.

The definitions given in the *Wu-fang Yuen Yin* seldom consist of even a score of words; but this brevity was indispensable for the general usefulness of the manual, where only the principal meanings were needed. A translation of the preface of the edition of 1710 is here inserted; but it gives no information about the reasons for the work, or to what part of the empire it is applicable. It is a fair sample of the style of prefaces to Chinese books, wherein one looks in vain for information or practical directions.

PREFACE TO THE EDITION OF 1710.

Those who heretofore engaged in the preparation of dictionaries did, as they should, carefully learn and go through the classics and all the miscellaneous writings of noted scholars. The number of these works, advantageous to learners, is not easy to reckon; some of them are still preserved, and others have been quite lost; the former are, to this day constantly in the hands of learners, but the latter are, to the great regret of all, gone utterly, and cannot be described. Of these the 字學 or Study of Characters is one. Books of this kind are not of equal worth, but among those which have of late years been in use, and are still regarded by all scholars as precious as an officer's signet, the 字彙 or Classification of Characters stands preëminent. In this work the characters are arranged in classes according to their strokes, and when one has ascertained the number, he can then find the one he seeks. No one can do without it; the venerable professor and old student, as well as the tyro and young learner, each and all need it.

But these persons still do not all know that the book called *Wu-fang Yuen Yin*, a work in which the combination of the [initial and final] sounds can be seen at a glance is even superior in some respects to the 字彙. Its compiler is Fan Tăng-fung 樊騰鳳 of Yao-shan 堯山 in the district of T'ang-shan 唐山縣 in the south of Chihli. This book not being often seen in the shops, I rather unexpectedly met with it. On looking it over closely, and examining its plan and execution, I was surprised at the carefulness displayed. The plan of the 字彙 depends on the number of strokes in a character, but this on their sounds.

There is besides the plan on which [this manual is arranged], that followed in the 六書, *viz.*, grouping together things belonging to heaven, both single and in pairs, but not going beyond the dual powers and the five elements, so that the five elements are under the head of heaven, the five regions under that of earth, and the five tones under that of sounds. Such a work only requires the redundancies to be removed and the four or five tones to be carefully indicated to make it complete. But then this arrangement [of the 六書] is really a natural one, and not one which man made out (or can alter).

In this work the author has selected the twelve finals 韻目 with reference to the twelve musical pitch-pipes, and the five fundamental tones of voice; and these with the twenty initials 字母 he has chosen, make the warp and the woof, the lengthwise and the crosswise; by combining these according to his rules, one can find the sound of any character. If one wishes to practice the combination of sounds, and counts over the 36 finals on his fingers, he will find the plan here adopted very much easier; it is like an essay in which only the ideas are wanted, or an agreement which has only the bare stipulations. In the Canon of Shun it is said, "Notes depend on prolonging the utterance, and they are harmonized among themselves by the pitch-pipes." If one will carefully examine this work, they will find that this principle has been observed. Original sounds may without doubt properly be called those produced by harmonizing the pitch-pipes of nature with the sounds of nature.

Those who may daily use this work will at a glance so readily see the mode of combining the initials and finals, that they can have no need of rules. But how then is one to find out characters when only the number of their strokes is known? I myself really regret the number of those books which have been lost, leaving only the 字彙 Classification of Characters preserved.

In the spare moments of my public business, I have got out a revised edition of this work for the booksellers; and perhaps it will thus get a wide circulation; but those scholars who carefully use it will most certainly find many things to add to it.

September, 1710. Written by Nien Hi-yao of Kwang-ning, a district in Manchuria.

This same man, Nien Hi-yao, afterwards enlarged the book until he had introduced nearly all the characters in the language. He published it in 1728, in four thin volumes, and several editions have since been printed; its extensive list of characters makes it a useful manual. In the preface he says that, when compared with the first edition, he has "added five out of every ten characters, and expunged one out of every ten."

In arranging the initials and finals, the compilers of the *Wu-fang Yuen Yin* sacrificed accuracy to brevity, and hindered the ready search for a character, in order, apparently, to make a short list of finals for the memory. Its twenty initials are actually thirty-six, and the twelve finals expand to twenty-nine in the table of sounds; or to thirty-eight if those in the *juh-shing* be reckoned separately. The characters in this tone, which in Cantonese all come under the first four finals, are here transferred to the last six finals; "because," says the compiler, with truly Chinese logic, "the first six finals (*ien, ăn, ung, ang, iu,* and *ao*) are light and clear like heaven, and it is not suitable to mix with them the heavy and gross sounds of the *juh-shing*, which are therefore scattered among the last six finals (*u, o, é, a, ai,* and *i*), these being gross and thick like earth, and assimilated to the *juh-shing*, which therefore are distributed among them."

LIST OF TWELVE FINALS.

The finals are represented by the following twelve characters, which include fourteen others, and twelve in the *juh-shing*, making thirty-eight, according to our mode of writing.

1. T-*ien* 天 includes t-*an* 丹 and k-*üen* 圈.
2. J-*ăn* 人 includes p-*in* 賓.
3. L-*ung* 龍 includes l-*ing* 靈 and l-*ăng* 冷.
4. Y-*ang* 羊 includes k-*iang* 江.
5. N-*iu* 牛 includes ch-*eu* 周.
6. Ng-*ao* 獒 includes n-*iao* 鳥.
7. H-*u* 虎 includes h-*uh* 斛.
8. T-*o* 駝 includes t-*oh* 脫, and l-*ioh* 略.
9. Sh-*é* 蛇 includes h-*üé* 鞾, y-*eh* 葉, y-*üeh* 月, and k-*ieh* 結.
10. M-*a* 馬 includes p-*ah* 八.
11. Ch-*ai* 豺 includes k-*iai* 皆.
12. T-*i* 地 includes t-*ui* 堆, ts-*ü* 聚, *sz'* 思, '*rh* 而 and w-*éi* 惟, with t-*eh* 德, y-*uh* 玉, l-*ih* 力, and k-*üh* 曲.

LIST OF TWENTY INITIALS.

The initials are represented by the following twenty characters, which are subdivided into thirty-six by separating those having a medial vowel.

1. *P*-ang 梆.
2. *P'*-ao 匏.
3. *M*-uh 木.
4. *F*-ung 風.
5. *T*-eu 斗 and *tw*-an 短.
6. *T'*-u 土 and *tw'*-an 湍.
7. *N*-iao 鳥 and *nw*-an 暖.
8. *L*-éi 雷 and *lw*-an 亂.
9. *Ch*-uh 竹 and *chw*-ang 莊.
10. *Ch'*-ung 虫 and *chw'*-ang 創.
11. *Sh*-ih 石 and *shw*-ang 爽.
12. *J*-ih 日 and *jw*-an 軟.
13. *Ts*-ien 剪 and *tsw*-an 纂.
14. *Ts'*-ioh 鵲 and *tsw'*-an 竄.
15. *S*-z' 系 and *sw*-an 算.
16. *Y*-un 雲.
17. *K*-in 金 and *kw*-a 瓜.
18. *K'*-iao 橋 and *kw'*-a 誇.
19. *Hw*-o 火 and *h*-ao 好.
20. *W*-a 蛙 and *ng*-an 安 and the suppressed initial, as in ai 挨 or uh 屋.

If all the possible combinations of these initials and finals existed in the *kwan hwa*, there would be 1368 syllables, exclusive of tonal variations, to be written with our letters; but the actual number of groups is 460, and of these several are almost undistinguishable. There is some difficulty about dividing words having the terminations *wa*, *wan*, and *wang*, for the Chinese regard them as finals; and some other deviations from the native rules are also required by the exigencies of an alphabetic system when applied to their spelling. Some of them are caused by the medial vowel *i* as *shen* for *shien* 扇,—(spelled 尸連 *sh*-i l-*ien*); and others by the imperfect vowels, as *tsz'* for *tsi* 子, to distinguish it from *tsi* 齊, but in this, the greater accuracy of alphabetic writing is seen.

The following table includes the combinations of initials and finals in the *Wu-fang Yuen Yin*, with a leading character under each syllable, and also shows the *juh shing* in separate columns, making 532 words in all. The actual variations in speech from the given sounds in this manual are almost endless; but it is as needless as it is impossible to ascertain and try to express them all. Each student will learn them for himself.

TABLE OF INITIALS AND FINALS, WITH

FINALS.		CH	CH‘	CHW	CHW‘	F	H	HW	J	JW	K	K‘	KW	KW‘	L	LW	M
A	...	楂 cha	茶 ch‘a	撾 chwa	...	...	...	花 hwa	....	[illegible] jwa	....	....	瓜 kwa	誇 kw‘a	藞 la	....	馬 ma
AH	....	扎 chah	察 ch‘ah	....	....	髮 fah	....	....	....	....	....	....	刮 kwah	....	臘 lah	....	帓 man
AI	挨 ai	齋 chai	柴 ch‘ai	....	揣 chw‘ai	....	海 hai	淮 hwai	....	....	該 kai	開 k‘ai	乖 kwai	快 kw‘ai	來 lai	....	埋 mai
AN	....	斬 chan	攙 ch‘an	....	....	番 fan	寒 han	歡 hwan	然 jan	軟 jwan	干 kan	坎 k‘an	官 kwan	寬 kw‘an	闌 lan	亂 lwan	滿 man
ĂN	....	眞 chăn	陳 ch‘ăn	....	....	分 făn	很 hăn	....	人 jăn	....	根 kăn	懇 k‘ăn	....	....	....	...	門 măn
ANG	盎 ang	張 chang	昌 ch‘ang	莊 chwang	創 chw‘ang	方 fang	杭 hang	黃 hwang	讓 jang	....	岡 kang	康 k‘ang	光 kwang	狂 kw‘ang	郎 lang	....	芒 mang
ĂNG	....	爭 chăng	撐 ch‘ăng	....	....	....	亨 hăng	....	仍 jăng	....	庚 kăng	坑 k‘ăng	....	....	冷 lăng	....	萌 măng
AO	....	昭 chao	超 ch‘ao	....	....	....	蒿 hao	....	饒 jao	....	高 kao	考 k‘ao	....	....	勞 lao	....	毛 mao
É	....	者 ché	車 ch‘é	...	....	....	....	....	惹 jé	....	....	瘸 k‘ié	....	....	....	....	咩 mé
EH	....	折 cheh	徹 ch‘eh	....	....	....	....	....	熱 jeh	....	....	....	....	....	勒 leh	....	蔑 meh
ÉI	....	....	....	....	....	肥 féi	....	....	....	....	....	....	歸 kwéi	虧 kw‘éi	雷 lei	....	梅 méi
EN	....	占 chen	纏 ch‘en	專 chwen	川 chw‘en	....	....	...	....	....	....	....	....	....	....	....	....
EU	....	周 cheu	抽 ch‘eu	....	....	浮 feu	侯 heu	....	柔 jeu	....	勾 keu	口 k‘eu	....	....	樓 leu	....	謀 meu
I	衣 i	之 chi	池 ch‘i	....	....	...	希 hi	而 ’rh	....	....	幾 ki	溪 k‘i	....	....	理 li	....	米 mi
IA	....	....	....	....	....	....	遐 hia	...	....	....	加 kia	跒 k‘ia	....	....	....	....	....
IAI	....	...	....	....	....	....	鞋 hiai	...	....	....	皆 kiai	揩 k‘iai	....	....	....	....	....
IANG	....	....	....	....	....	...	香 hiang	....	....	....	江 kiang	羌 k‘iang	....	....	良 liang	....	....
IAO	....	....	....	....	....	....	曉 hiao	....	....	....	交 kiao	蹻 k‘iao	....	....	遼 liao	....	苗 miao
IEH	....	....	....	....	....	....	頡 hieh	....	....	....	結 kieh	挈 k‘ieh	....	....	列 lieh	....	滅 mieh
IEN	....	....	....	....	....	....	賢 hien	....	....	....	堅 kien	鉗 k‘ien	....	....	連 lien	....	面 mien
IH	....	汁 chih	尺 ch‘ih	....	....	....	檄 hih	....	....	....	吉 kih	乞 k‘ih	....	....	力 lih	....	覓 mih
IN	....	....	....	....	....	....	欣 hin	....	....	....	巾 kin	禽 k‘in	....	....	林 lin	....	民 min
ING	....	貞 ching	城 ch‘ing	....	....	....	興 hing	....	....	....	京 king	卿 k‘ing	....	....	靈 ling	....	明 ming
IOH	....	....	....	....	....	....	學 hioh	....	弱 joh	....	角 kioh	却 k‘ioh	....	....	畧 lioh	....	....
IU	....	....	....	....	....	....	休 hiu	....	....	....	九 kiu	求 k‘iu	....	....	留 liu	....	謬 miu
IÜN	....	....	....	....	....	....	熏 hiün	....	...	....	君 kiün	群 k‘iün	....	....	....	....	....
IÜNG	....	....	....	....	....	....	兄 hiüng	....	....	....	....	穹 k‘iüng	....	....	....	....	....
O	阿 o	....	....	....	....	....	河 ho	火 hwo	....	....	個 ko	科 k‘o	戈 kwo	....	羅 lo	...	麽 mo
OH	....	着 choh	趠 ch‘oh	....	....	縛 foh	喝 hoh	鑊 hwoh	....	....	閣 koh	客 k‘oh	國 kwoh	廓 kw‘oh	絡 loh	....	莫 moh
SZ’	....	....	....	....	....	....	....	....	....	....	....	...	....	....	....	....	....
U	....	朱 chu	除 ch‘u	....	....	夫 fu	湖 hu	....	....	....	古 ku	苦 k‘u	....	...	盧 lu	....	母 mu
Ü	....	....	....	....	....	....	虛 hü	....	如 jü	....	居 kü	墟 k‘ü	....	....	閭 lü	....	....
ÜÉ	....	....	....	....	....	....	靴 hüé	....	....	....	....	....	....	....	....	....	....
ÜEH	....	....	....	....	....	....	血 hüeh	....	....	....	厥 küeh	缺 k‘üeh	....	....	劣 lüeh	....	....
ÜEN	....	....	....	....	....	....	玄 hüen	....	....	....	捐 küen	圈 k‘üen	...	...	戀 lüen	....	....
UH	....	竹 chuh	出 ch‘uh	....	....	福 fuh	斛 huh	忽 hwuh	入 juh	...	谷 kuh	哭 k‘uh	....	....	六 luh	....	木 muh
ÜH	....	...	....	....	....	....	....	....	....	....	局 küh	曲 k‘üh	....	....	律 lüh	....	....
UI	...	追 chui	吹 ch‘ui	....	....	....	....	灰 hwui	蕊 jui	....	....	....	....	....	....	....	....
UN	....	准 chun	春 ch‘un	....	....	....	....	昏 hwun	閏 jun	....	....	....	崑 kwun	坤 kw‘un	論 lun	....	....
UNG	....	中 chung	充 ch‘ung	....	....	風 fung	紅 hung	....	戎 jung	....	公 kung	空 k‘ung	....	....	隆 lung	....	蒙 mung

CHARACTERS TO ILLUSTRATE THE SYLLABLES. xvii.

N	NG	NW	P	P‘	S	SH	SHW	SW	T	T‘	TS	TS‘	TSW	TSW‘	TW	TW‘	W	Y
拿 na	....	....	巴 pa	琶 p‘a	....	沙 sha	....	....	打 ta	他 t‘a	咱 tsa	....	....	....	....	....	蛙 wa	牙 ya
納 nah	....	....	八 pah	....	撒 sah	殺 shah	刷 swah	....	笪 tah	塔 t‘ah	匝 tsah	擦 ts‘ah	....	....	....	....	韈 wah	押 yah
乃 nai	艾 ngai	....	拜 pai	牌 p‘ai	腮 sai	曬 shai	帥 shwai	....	戴 tai	台 t‘ai	在 tsai	才 ts‘ai	...	....	....	....	歪 wai	涯 yai
男 nan	安 ngan	暖 nwan	班 pan	盤 p‘an	三 san	山 shan	拴 shwan	算 swan	丹 tan	貪 t‘an	讚 tsan	蠶 ts‘an	纂 tswan	竄 tsw‘an	端 twan	湍 tw‘an	灣 wan	...
....	恩 ngăn	....	本 păn	盆 p‘ăn	....	森 shăn	....	....	....	....	怎 tsăn	....	....	....	....	....	文 wăn	....
囊 nang	....	....	邦 pang	傍 p‘ang	桑 sang	商 shang	爽 shwang	....	當 taug	湯 t‘ang	葬 tsang	倉 ts‘ang	....	....	....	....	王 wang	羊 yang
能 năng	....	....	崩 păng	朋 p‘ăng	僧 săng	生 shăng	....	....	等 tăng	籐 t‘ăng	增 tsăng	曾 ts‘ăng	....	....	....	....	翁 wăng	....
鬧 nao	敖 ngao	....	包 pao	抛 p‘ao	騷 sao	少 shao	....	....	刀 tao	桃 t‘ao	早 tsao	曹 ts‘ao	....	....	....	....	....	要 yao
....	....	....	....	....	些 sié	蛇 shé	....	....	爹 tié	....	借 tsié	且 ts‘ié	...	....	....	....	....	野 yé
....	..	....	....	....	色 seh	舌 sheh	....	...	得 teh	特 t‘eh	則 tseh	拆 ts‘eh	....	....	....	....	....	葉 yeh
內 néi	....	....	悲 péi	丕 p‘éi	....	....	....	....	....	....	....	....	....	....	....	....	威 wéi	....
....	....	....	....	....	....	扇 shen	....	....	....	....	....	....	....	....	....	....	....	烟 yen
耨 neu	偶 ngeu	....	....	剖 p‘eu	搜 seu	手 sheu	....	....	兜 teu	偷 t‘eu	走 tseu	愁 ts‘eu	....	....	....	....	....	....
你 ni	....	....	比 pi	披 p‘i	西 si	是 shi	....	....	地 ti	提 t‘i	祭 tsi	妻 ts‘i	....	....	....	....	未 wi	....
....	....	....	....	....	....	....	....	....	....	....	....	....	....	....	....	....	....	....
....	....	....	....	....	....	....	....	....	....	....	....	....	....	....	....	....	....	....
娘 niang	....	....	....	....	相 siang	....	....	....	....	....	將 tsiang	槍 ts‘iang	....	....	....	....	....	....
鳥 niao	....	....	標 piao	漂 p‘iao	消 siao	....	....	....	雕 tiao	挑 t‘iao	焦 tsiao	悄 ts‘iao	....	....	....	....	....	....
聶 nieh	....	....	別 pieh	撆 p‘ieh	屑 sieh	....	....	....	耋 tieh	帖 t‘ieh	節 tsieh	切 ts‘ieh	....	....	....	....	....	....
年 nien	....	....	扁 pien	偏 p‘ien	線 sien	....	....	....	典 tien	天 t‘ien	煎 tsien	千 ts‘ien	....	....	....	....	....	....
匿 nih	....	....	璧 pih	疋 p‘ih	惜 sih	十 shih	....	....	的 tih	踢 t‘ih	疾 tsih	七 ts‘ih	....	....	....	....	....	益 yih
您 nin	....	....	禀 pin	品 p‘in	心 sin	....	....	....	....	....	津 tsin	親 ts‘in	....	....	....	....	....	因 yin
寧 ning	....	....	兵 ping	平 p‘ing	星 sing	聖 shing	....	....	丁 ting	聽 t‘ing	精 tsing	青 ts‘ing	....	....	....	....	....	英 ying
虐 nioh	....	....	....	....	削 sioh	....	....	....	....	....	爵 tsioh	鵲 ts‘ioh	....	....	....	....	....	....
牛 niu	....	....	彪 piu	....	羞 siu	....	....	....	丟 tiu	....	酒 tsiu	秋 ts‘iu	....	....	....	....	....	憂 yiu
....	....	....	....	....	旬 siün	....	....	....	....	....	....	竣 ts‘iün	....	....	....	....	....	...
....	....	....	....	....	....	....	....	....	....	....	....	....	....	....	....	....	....	....
糯 no	鵝 ngo	....	波 po	婆 p‘o	梭 so	....	....	....	多 to	妥 t‘o	左 tso	搓 ts‘o	....	....	....	....	窩 wo	....
諾 noh	鶚 ngoh	....	薄 poh	珀 p‘oh	索 soh	朔 shoh	說 shwoh	....	奪 toh	脫 t‘oh	作 tsoh	娖 ts‘oh	...	....	....	....	蠖 woh	約 yoh
....	....	....	....	....	思 sz’	....	....	....	....	....	子 tsz’	此 ts‘z’	....	....	....	....	....	....
奴 nu	....	....	補 pu	普 p‘u	穌 su	書 shu	....	....	都 tu	土 t‘u	祖 tsu	醋 ts‘u	....	....	...	....	烏 wu	....
女 nü	....	....	....	....	須 sü	....	....	....	....	....	沮 tsü	取 ts‘ü	....	....	....	....	....	魚 yü
....	....	....	....	....	....	....	....	....	....	....	....	....	....	....	....	....	....	....
....	....	....	....	....	雪 süeh	....	....	....	....	....	絕 tsüeh	....	....	....	...	....	....	月 yüeh
....	....	....	....	....	宣 süen	....	....	....	....	....	鐫 tsüen	全 ts‘üen	....	....	....	....	....	圓 yüen
....	....	....	卜 puh	咄 p‘uh	俗 suh	叔 shuh	....	....	毒 tuh	禿 t‘uh	卒 tsuh	促 ts‘uh	...	....	....	....	....	玉 yuh
....	....	....	....	....	恤 süh	....	....	....	....	....	....	....	....	....	....	....	....	....
....	....	....	....	....	雖 sui	水 shui	....	....	對 tui	退 t‘ui	醉 tsui	催 ts‘ui	....	....	....	....	....	....
嫩 nun	....	....	....	....	孫 sun	順 shun	....	....	盾 tun	吞 t‘un	尊 tsun	村 ts‘un	...	....	....	....	....	孕 yun
農 nung	....	....	....	....	松 sung	舂 shung	....	....	東 tung	通 t‘ung	宗 tsung	聰 ts‘ung	...	....	....	....	....	用 yung

In the Canton dialect, according to the local vocabulary, there are 53 finals and 23 initials, producing only 707 different words to be written in an alphabetic list, including those ending in the *juh shing*.

In the Fuhchau dialect, there are only 33 finals and 15 initials enumerated. But the real number of finals is increased by remarkable inflections of words falling in the upper and lower *juh shing*, so that Maclay and Baldwin's Dictionary enumerates 90 finals, and gives 928 syllables, of which scores are colloquial.

The dialect spoken in and about Changcheu, near Amoy, is exhibited in the 十五音 or Fifteen [initial] Sounds. It has 15 initials and 50 finals, which produce 846 syllables, including the modifications of the *juh shing;* the number of distinct enunciations in that dialect including all tonal modifications, is not far from 2500, according to Medhurst; and this is nearly the number spoken in Fuhchau. According to Douglas' Amoy Dictionary, the variations heard in the two prefectures of Changchau and Tsüenchau much exceed this number.

In the Swatow dialect, and that heard in the southeastern part of Kwangtung, which has much affinity with the Amoy, the number of separate syllables, as given in Mr. Goddard's Manual is 674, less than either of the three preceding. The dialect known as the Hakka dialect, spoken best in Kia-ying cheu, has not been so much studied as those, but it has marked peculiarities, and approaches nearer to the *kwan hwa* than either of them.

The speech heard at Shanghai and Ningpo, and throughout Kiangsu and Chehkiang, assimilates still more to the *kwan hwa* in its idiom and pronunciation, which is probably the reason why no native vocabulary has been published in it. The Rev. C. Keith, of the American Episcopal Mission had prepared a copious vocabulary of the Shanghai dialect ready for printing, but it was lost. A carefully prepared list of syllables in the Shanghai dialect, by the late Dr. Jenkins, contains 660 words; and he reckons 33 initials and 44 finals as competent to combine all the sounds in it. The speech heard at Suchau and Hangchau differs but little from that at Shanghai and Ningpo.

The *kwan hwa* spoken at Peking, and indeed with inconsiderable variations in the provinces of Chihli and Shantung, has received much attention from Mr. Wade. In the *Hsin Ching Lu* he enumerates 25 initials and 43 finals, and places the number of distinct syllables at 397; in the *Tzŭ-erh-chi*, he has retained the initials and finals, and increased the syllables to 420; which probably includes nearly all the distinct words used by the people. It is much less than in any of the preceding dialects, and not one half of the variety heard at Fuhchau, which is to be ascribed chiefly to the suppression of the *juh shing*. The number of initials given by Mr. Wade is 25 instead of 36 as in the preceding table, as he follows more strictly the Chinese mode in the arrangement of words in the initials *chw*, *kw*, *hw*, &c., putting them under the finals beginning with *u;* which thereby correspondingly increases their number. It is not easy to decide which is the best way in an alphabetic arrangement.

SECT. II.—SYSTEM OF ORTHOGRAPHY.

If the difficulties of illustrating and analyzing the sounds in their language are almost insurmountable to Chinese philologists, the results of the various attempts of foreigners to do so have not the less proved the inherent difficulties of the attempt; and a comparison of their various systems does not encourage the hope that anything like uniformity will ever be attained. In addition to the different powers given to vowels and consonants by English, French, and Portuguese sinologues, when used to express the same Chinese sound, each in their own tongue, as *wu*, *ou*, and *u* for 五; or *wun*, *ouen*, and *ven* for 文, we have a most troublesome discrepancy in the modes of writing the same sound in the same language, especially in English, in which more has been written than in all the others. Not to quote many instances of strange spelling, as *tadge-in* for 大人 *ta-jin;* *see-ue* for 羞 *siu;* *hiouĕ* for 血 *hüĕ;* *taa-mau* for 大馬 *ta ma;* *czzi cio* for 橘果 *küeh-kwo;* *tar-garn* for 大安 *ta-ngan*, &c., the more elaborate systems devised for writing the sounds in the mandarin and local dialects, present a series of perplexing anomalies and variations hard to understand, and which renders it difficult for a person who has studied one dialect to learn the sounds in another. The Protestant missionaries at Amoy and Ningpo have published thousands of volumes in those dialects in a romanized colloquial, which they teach in their schools; but a native of Ningpo, able to read it with ease and understanding, would find himself completely nonplussed if he tried to read the Amoy colloquial according to the sounds he had learned at home. The natives of the two cities are unable to converse with each other in any case, but previous consultation among the missionaries would, perhaps, have led them to adopt a similar mode of writing the vowels, diphthongs, and consonants common to both, before these beginnings of new alphabetic languages had been laid.

The embarrassments of recognizing the Chinese characters when written in alphabetic letters, were noticed by De Guignes in 1813, before they had reached their present diversity. Speaking in his Dictionary of his changes in P. Basile's system of orthography, he remarks, "I have just explained the reasons which have led me to suppress certain letters and to simplify the orthography, and now add a table to show the changes, so that readers can recognize the same words in different authors. I refer only to works written by the missionaries, and not to those issued by other Europeans; the mode of pronouncing our letters not being uniform, in Europe it is impossible to give a general rule. In the account of Lord Macartney's Voyage, for instance, what the missionaries write *Kien-long-ta-ouang-ty* the English write *Tchien-lung-ta-whang-tee.* The letter *k* is certainly aspirated, but it has not the sound of *tch* in English; the vowel *u* of the word *lung* is sometimes pronounced *o* in English, but it is then short, and it is long in *long,* when it has the meaning it has in this phrase now quoted; the letter *h* is needless in *whang,* for the word *ouang* is not aspirated. I will say nothing about *tee,* for such an orthography is fit only for an Englishman."

In this Dictionary, an attempt has been made to apply one system of spelling to five different dialects, and though the result has not been entirely satisfactory, it has shown that their discrepancies can be reduced to something like a classification, and their vowels and diphthongs assimilated much more than has hitherto been supposed possible. To this end, it is necessary to permit some latitude to the value of the simple vowels according to the consonants which precede and follow them; diphthongs, too, must have some freedom as influenced by various consonants. For instance, in *lun* 倫 and *sun* 孫, the value of the final *un* is altered a little by the initial; and when a medial vowel is inserted, as in *lüen* 戀, and *süen* 宣, it is desirable to indicate the change if possible, by a differently marked vowel. Such diversities as this, however, cannot all be noted by any system.

In words ending in some diphthongs, a change in the initial will throw the syllable into a new class in one dialect and not in another; thus, *léi* 雷 and *méi* 梅 in mandarin keep the older forms of *lúi* and *múi* in Cantonese; but at Fuh-chau, one is read *lòi* and the other *múi.* This final *éi,* unknown in both those cities, in the north inclines to *éi* and *ui* according to the initial, but both never have the same initial, as *téi* and *tui*, *péi* and *pui.* The diversities and analogies of this kind among the several dialects will no doubt in time receive more careful study than has yet been given to them, but the materials are at present not sufficient to lay down rules or adduce comparisons. But I think that this list is adequate to express all their sounds with sufficient precision.

The system of writing the sounds now employed is nearly the same as that formerly followed in the Tonic Dictionary of the Canton Dialect, as far as that is applicable to *kwan hwa.* In order to diminish the use of accented letters, the long *a* in *father* is written *a* instead of *á*; and this involved the change of the short *a* in *quota* to *ă*; and of *áu*, as *ow* in *howl,* to *ao*; the diphthong *ai*, or the English *i*, is altered to *ei*, because the *ai* represented the broad sound as in *aisle*; the terminations *iá*, *iáng*, *iái*, and *iáh*, have also all dropped their accents. Other ways adopted by previous writers to express the same sounds are added, so as to facilitate reference to their modes of spelling.

VOWELS.

1.—*a* as in *father*; written *á* by Bridgman, Goddard, Jenkins; *ä* by Yates.

2.—*ă* as in *quota, variable*; written *ă* by Bridgman; *ă* and *u* by Morrison; *u* by Edkins, Bonney; *ĕ* by Maclay; *u* by Goddard; *e* by De Guignes, Callery; *ê* by Wade; *ā* and *e* by Gonçalves.

3.—*e* as in *men*; written *ĕ* and *ë* by Medhurst; *é* by Maclay; *è* by Callery.

4.—*é* as in *grey*, or *a* in *say*; written *e* by Gonçalves, De Guignes, Maclay, Douglas; *ay* by Morrison, Medhurst; *ei* by Wade.

5.—*è* as in *there*, or *a* in *fan, hat;* written *á* by Maclay; *à* by Goddard; *ă* by Yates; *a* by Edkins; ɛ by Douglas.

6.—*i* as in *pin*, and never occurs as a final; written *e* and *i* by Morrison; *í* by Maclay; *ï* by Douglas; *i* and *c* by De Guignes, who writes *y* when it is the medial vowel.

7.—*í* as in *machine*, and left unmarked [*i*] when a final; written *c* by Morrison, Medhurst; *y* by De Guignes when final; *i* by Wade, Maclay, Douglas; *ĕe* by Bonney.

8.—*o* as in *long*, or *aw* in *law*; written *ó* by Bridgman, Maclay; *ŏ* by Gonçalves; *â* by Jenkins; *aw* by Bonney; *au* by Edkins, Yates; o· by Doty; ȯ by Douglas.

9.—*ò* as in *no, crow;* written *ow* by Morrison; *ō* by Bonney; *ou* by Gonçalves; *o* by Maclay, Douglas, Goddard; *o* and *ō* by Yates.

10.—*ö* as in *könig*, a German sound; written *o* and ô by Callery; *ê* by Wade.

11.—*u* as in *put, bull,* and seldom heard as a final; written *oo* and *u* by Morrison; *ue* by Callery; *ô* by De Guignes, Gonçalves.

12.—*ú* as *oo* in *fool*, or *o* in *move*, and left unmarked [*u*] when a final; written *oo* by Morrison, Medhurst; *ū* by Gonçalves; *ou* and *o* by De Guignes; *u* by Wade, Douglas.

13.—*ü* as in *June, abuse;* written *ói* by Gonçalves; *eu* by Morrison; *u* by De Guignes.

14.—*ù* as in *turn* or *ea* in *learn*; written *eu* by Edkins, Yates; *ë* by Maclay.

DIPHTHONGS.

1.—*ai* as in *aisle*; written *ái* by Bridgman; *ae* by Morrison, Medhurst; *ay* by De Guignes.

2.—*ao* like *ow* in *howl*, prolonged; written *aou* by Morrison; *au* by Gonçalves; *áu* by Bridgman; *ow* by Bonney.

3.—*au* as *ow* in *now*; written *ow* by Bonney.

4.—*ei* as in *height*, or *i* in *sigh*; written *ai* by Douglas, Bridgman; *ī* and *ïe* by Bonney; *ei* and *ai* by Gonçalves.

5.—*éi* as *eyi* in *greyish*; written *eï* by Morrison, Wade; *oei* and *ei* by Gonçalves.

6.—*eu* as *ou* in *souse*, shorter than No. 3; written *ow* by Morrison; *eu* by Callery; *ou* by Gonçalves, Wade.

7.—*éu* as *au* in *Capernaum*; *eu* by Maclay; *ay-u* by Bonney; *ea* by Gonçalves; *eo* and *ao* by Devan.

8.—*ia* as in *piastre*, or *ya* in *yard*; written *ea* by Morrison, Gonçalves.

9.—*iai* and *iao*, each letter sounded; written *eae* and *eaou* by Morrison; *èau* by Gonçalves.

10.—*ie* as in *siesta*; written *ëe* by Morrison, Medhurst.

11.—*ié* as *ea* in *fealty*; written *íe* by Jenkins.

12.—*io* as *yaw* in *yawn*; written *eo* and *eŏ* by Morrison.

13.—*iu* as *ew* in *pew*; written *iú* by Bridgman; *ew* by Morrison; *ieou* by De Guignes; *ieu* by Gonçalves, Maclay; *ee-ue* by Bonney.

14.—*iü* like *ew* in *chewing* prolonged; written *io* by De Guignes.

15.—*oí* as in *boil*; written *oy* by Morrison; *oe* by Douglas.

16.—*òi* as *owi* in *knowing*; written *oi* by Maclay.

17.—*ua* as in *Mantua*, each vowel sounded; written *oa* by Douglas, De Guignes.

18.—*üe* as in *duet*; it runs into *üé* when a final.

19.—*ui* as *ewy* in *dewy*, or *oui* in *Louis*; written *ouy* by De Guignes; *uy* by Morrison; *oei* by Gonçalves.

20.—*üi* as *ooi* in *cooing*; written *uéi* by Gonçalves; *uy* by Morrison, Bonney.

ANOMALOUS VOWELS.*

21.—*'m*, a sound like *hm* with closed lips, as a suppressed cough; written *m* by Medhurst, Douglas.

22.—*'ng*, a nasal made by closing the nose, a whining sound; written *ng* by Douglas, Goddard.

23.—^{n}, a nasal in the middle of a word as *ki*^{n}*a*, or oftener at the end, as *pi*^{n}; more distinct usually than in the French *vin*; written *n* by Edkins.

* The late T. T. Meadows objected to the term *Imperfect Vowels* for the sounds here brought together, saying that "an *imperfect vowel* is really an impossibility." In this he was strictly correct, perhaps, but still they resemble suppressed vowels, and by grouping them, may be better illustrated.

24.—*sz'*, *tsz'*, a peculiar sibilant; the first can be made by changing *di* in *dizzy* to *s*, and speaking it quickly; written *sze* by Morrison; *sŭ* by Gonçalves; *ssŭ* and *tzŭ* by Wade; *sï* by Edkins; *ss* by De Guignes; *se* by Callery.

25.—*ch'* and *sh'*, like the preceding but softer; they are often uttered by a person who stutters, as if in speaking *chin* or *shin*, he could not get out the *n*; or like the sound made when chiding a child for making a noise; written *chih* and *shih* by Wade.

26.—*'rh*, like the word *err*; written *olr* by Gonçalves; *êrh* by Wade; *urh* by Morrison; *eul* by De Guignes; *ell* by Callery; *ŭr* by Jenkins; *rh* by Edkins.

CONSONANTS.

Of these, only *h*, *k*, *m*, *n*, *ng*, *p*, and *t*, occur as final letters.

1.—*b* as in *bar*.

2.—*ch* as in *church*; written *tch* by De Guignes.

3.—*ch'* the same sound aspirated.

4.—*d* as in *dun*.

5.—*dj* as in *djezzar*, or *j* in *judge*; written *j* by Yates, Douglas, Goddard.

6.—*dz* as in *adze*.

7.—*f* as in *farm*.

8.—*g* as in *gag*.

9.—*h* as in *hung*; as a final it is nearly suppressed.

10.—*h'* before *i* and *ü*, a sibilant sound resembling an affected lisp, and easily confounded with *sh*; written *hs* by Wade, *h'* by Edkins, *sh* by Jenkins.

11.—*j* as in the French *jamais*.

12.—*k* as in *king*, *kick*; written *c* by Gonçalves.

13.—*k'* nearly the same sound, but softened and aspirated.

14.—*l* as in *lion*.

15.—*m* as in *man*, *ham*.

16.—*n* as in *nun*.

17.—*ng* as in *singing*; written *g* as an initial and *m* as a final by Gonçalves; *ñg* initial and *m* final by Callery; *gn* by Medhurst; *gh* by De Guignes as initial.

18.—*p* as in *pot*, *lop*.

19.—*p'* the same sound aspirated.

20.—*s* as in *sand*; before *i*, it closely resembles No. 10.

21.—*sh* as in *shall*; written *ch* by De Guignes; *x* by Gonçalves, Callery.

22.—*t* as in *top*, *lot*.

23.—*t'* the same sound aspirated.

24.—*ts* as in *wits*; written *ch* and *ç* by Gonçalves; *z* by De Guignes.

25.—*ts'* the same sound aspirated.

26.—*v* as in *vine*.

27.—*w* as in *want*, *wo*; when it follows another consonant, as *chw*, *hw*, *kw*, &c., it shortens as the two coalesce; for this position Wade and Goddard use *u*, and Douglas *o*; written *v* by Gonçalves; *v* and *ou* by De Guignes.

28.—*y* as in *yard;* written *i* by Callery, Gonçalves.
29.—*z* as in *zone.*
30.—*zh* as *z* in *azure.*

One object kept in view in this system has been to abridge the use of accented letters, to do without which altogether has by all writers been found to be impracticable, consistently with accuracy; and another has been to adapt the spelling to the use of English readers. How far these objects have been attained, practice alone will show; but it is not an unimportant thing to the student, how a word is written, for the spelling insensibly affects his pronunciation. For example, the word 絨 is sounded like *jung,* or *zhung,* or *rung* or *zung,* by different persons in Peking; and constantly reading it in one of these modes confirms him in that pronunciation, while another mode will influence another person.

The present attempt to harmonize the sounds of the five dialects by one system of spelling, has this element of error, that I have not been able to consult natives of Fuhchau or Amoy, and hear their pronunciation. In the brief list of corresponding sounds given at the head of every syllable in the Dictionary, there are no doubt both errors and deficiencies, owing to this disadvantage. Heretofore, each dialect has been spelled without reference to the sounds in other dialects, and this has caused needless discrepancies, which become apparent when a comparison is instituted. For instance, the *o* in *note* is not heard in the north, where the *o* in *long* prevails; while in the south, this last is rather unusual, and has been the one usually marked with an accent, though taking the whole country together it is by far the most common, and the *o* in *note* ought to be marked. In the north, no word like *kím* occurs, with *í* (as in *machine*) in the middle; and in the south, no guttural *ng* begins a word; but the short *i* in *pin* is a thousand times the commonest, and should be left unaccented. These peculiarities render it difficult to adapt one system to all the dialects, and not employ many accented letters in some of them; but the thing is not impossible, and with a good degree of accuracy too. The greater difficulty is to get those who have become accustomed to their own modes of writing to adopt another more generally applicable. A few remarks on the preceding lists of vowels and consonants will explain the changes they undergo in various positions.

VOWELS.

1. *a.*—This occurs in all the dialects; it is never to be sounded as in English *fan, hat.*

2. *ă.*—The common use of *u* in English as in *sun,* to represent this sound has made it a perplexing one to write; and the phrase, "The mother bird flutters o'er her young," shows that in that language it is very differently written. I prefer *ă* to *a, e, ë, ê,* or *u* of other authors, chiefly because it is less liable to be mispronounced by the general reader, except the last. But that letter is needed to write another sound.

3. *e.*—Along the southern coasts, this vowel is heard alone before consonants, as *meng, kek, veh,* but northward it is usually preceded by *i,* as in *lien;* when followed by *n* it constantly inclines to the sound of *a* in *man,* and even that of *a* in far. When used in *teh, seh,* it often changes its quality according to the succeeding word into *ö* or *é.*

4. *é.*—This vowel occasionally occurs at Fuhchau in the middle of a word, as in *héng, ték,* before a decided consonant; and at Shanghai and Swatow, in nasalized words, as *kné, pén;* but it is almost always a final, as *ché, mé,* or succeeding *i* or *ü,* as *tié, hüé.*

5. *è.*—This is rarely heard in the north or at Canton, but in Kiangsu and southward it is common alone, as in *lèn, sèh, pèn;* or more commonly preceded by *i* as in *pièt, pièn, sièk, lièng;* in all these words its tendency is to broaden out into *liang, sian,* as at Amoy and Swatow.

6. *i.*—This vowel is always written in the middle of a word, as *ming, kik, lih;* in the latter class of words it apparently ends them, but even then the vowel approaches the next [*í*], so that *tih* and *pih* become *ti* and *pi.* As a medial vowel in diphthongs like *ia, ie,* it is one of the commonest sounds in the language, and undergoes very little alteration.

7. *í.*—This vowel occurs only at the end of words in the *kwan hwa;* but is often heard in their middle in the southern dialects, as *pín, líng, kít,* &c., where it will be more likely to be pronounced aright if accented. I have, therefore, written it like the last vowel (*i*) when it is a final, in order to reduce the number of accented letters, as the final *i* in English is usually written *y* as in *mighty,* and there is little danger of confusion. Mr. Wade uses *i* for both the sounds in *tree* and *trim,* apparently to save accents, and they do run into each other; Maclay transposes *i* and *í,* as I write them, to *í* and *i,* for the same reason; but in those southern dialects the medial vowel in the dipthongs *ia, iu, iau,* is always short, and thus two sounds are given to one symbol, which is undesirable.

8. *o.*—This is the only sound of the vowel in mandarin, and almost always as a final; but after *b, f* and *p,* in the southern dialects, it often runs into the next, where it also occurs in the middle, as *song, loi, kok.*

9. *ò.*—This sound, as in *note,* is not heard in mandarin, but, from Shanghai southward, it is so common that it has usually been left unmarked; at Fuhchau it is common in *yòng, siòng, lòi,* &c., occurring in many words which have an *a* at the north. At Amoy and Canton it is less frequent. To mark such words seems to be more likely to insure their proper pronunciation, than to expect the English reader to pronounce *tong* and *toi,* as *towng* and *towy;* though, on the other hand *to* and *pok* are more like to be sounded like *toe* and *poke,* than like *taw* and

pawk. It is a choice of difficulties, but the argument in favor of writing *o* and *ò* as in *long* and *lo*, is not a little strengthened by the vast preponderance of the first sound throughout China.

10. *ö.*—This sound is not often heard in the southern dialects, but is common in Kiangsu and northward, chiefly as a final; the *é* in *ché*, *a* in *tsan*, *o* in *toh*, and *u* in *tu*, each and all run into it in one place or another; in Chihli, it characterizes words which have a tendency to become guttural.

11. *u.*—A difficult sound to express uniformly, as it is so much modified by the letters before and after it, and runs into the next; it is never heard as a final, but unites with *a* as a medial, as is noticed under *ua* and *w* (Nos. 17 and *Consonants* 27). Maclay writes the sounds *u* and *ú* alike, but they are not the same, and especially in Cantonese are kept clearly distinct as in *sun*, *sut*, shorter sounds than *soon*, *soot*; while *kún*, *kút* are like *coon*, *coot*; in the word *sung*, the vowel is evidently a prolongation of *sun* rather than of *kún*. Common readers will no doubt often mispronounce such words, until they hear the right sound.

12. *ú.*—The frequent use of this vowel as a final makes it desirable to reduce the number of accented words by leaving it unmarked when in that position, or in the *juh shing*, as *tu*, *tuh*, where alone it occurs in mandarin, and marking it in the middle as *mún*, *fút*. In Canton and places north of it, there is a tendency to sound this final as *ò* before certain initials, as *mò*, *pò*, for *mu*, *pu*.

13. *ü.*—This vowel sound occurs in all the dialects in the middle and end of words, as *chü*, *shün*, *püt*, *ngüng*, *ük*, &c., or following the vowels *i*, *a*, *e*, and *é*, suffering different modifications with each of them; its tendency is to run into *u* (No. 11), but the changes are slight. It has been generally written in this way.

14. *ù.*—This is not found in mandarin, and is not a common sound. It runs into *ö* and *é* when preceding a consonant; it is a common final in Shanghai, and in Swatow and that region; in Fuhchau it also precedes other vowels as *chùü*, *sùuh*, *ngùung*; but these combinations are limited to a small district. Some would perhaps, write it *ă*, which it nearly resembles, had it not been prolonged as if followed by an *r*, as in the English words *turn*, *bird*, *her*.

DIPHTHONGS.

1, 2, 3. *ai*, *ao*, *au.*—These three are almost everywhere heard only as finals, and the two first form, when preceded by *i*, the common triphthongs, *iai* and *iao*. In Fuhchau, they are followed by *h* or *k*, as in *paih*, *pauk*. The third sound is written *ou* by Wade, but the risk of mispronouncing words thus written as *soo*, *hoo*, and not *sow*, *how*, owing to the common use of *ou* by the French to express a final *u*, renders *au* or *eu* preferable; the English *ow* for *au* is also liable to confusion, as seen in the sentence, "The *row* of *flowers now flowed* to the *tow*-line." Morrison used *ow* to express both *au* and *ò* (*i.e. now* and *no*) in two of his works.

4. *ei.*—This final sound, unknown in mandarin, is common in Cantonese, where it is carefully distinguished from *ái*, but the two seem to run into each other further north, or *ei* is changed to *í*, and No. 5, *éi*.

6. *eu.*—It is doubtful whether the distinction between this final and No. 3 is sufficiently clear to authorize two forms of writing them; at the North the pronunciation of characters like 州 *cheu*, 勾 *keu*, 手 *sheu*, is usually quicker than the pronunciation of the same words *chau*, *kau*, *shau*, in Cantonese and other southern dialects. They are very much alike, however, and the chief reason for separating them was to indicate this diversity, which is not a fanciful one.

7. *éu.*—This sound is rarely heard as a final, and is most common at Canton; at Fuhchau the second vowel is often prolonged in *ü*, as *séüng*, while at Canton it is also shortened into *ă*, and forms one of the most characteristic sounds in that dialect.

10. *ie.*—This diphthong is unknown at Canton, where the *í* take its place, as in *sín* for *sien*, but reäppears as one goes north. When followed by *n* or *m*, it turns into *ièm* or *iam*, *ièn* or *ián* at Swatow and Amoy, and *ieng* at Fuhchau; at Ningpo and Shanghai it is again superseded by *ín* and *í*ⁿ. In all words having this diphthong before *n*, there is difficulty at the south in distinguishing *ie* from *iè*; but at the north this difficulty is mostly confined to those words where the *i* is merged in the other vowel.

11, 12. *ié*, *io.*—These two have some affinity, but they do not run into each other; both are oftenest found in the *juh shing*, and their variations from the mandarin into other dialects are so capricious as to be irreducible to any rules which would be useful.

13, 14. *iu*, *iü.*—The first of these occurs mostly as a final in all the dialects, but it is also heard in mandarin before *n* in a few words; the second occurs only in the middle of words, and then is rather a prolongation of *iu*; it is hardly ever heard in Fuhkien or Kwangtung.

15, 16. *oi*, *òi.*—Both these diphthongs are confined to the extreme south, and the latter seems to be peculiar to Fuhchau; they are easily distinguished.

17. *ua.*—The distinct sounds of both vowels are often heard at Swatow and Amoy, like *too-an*, *loo-an*; but elsewhere *wa* (see *Consonants* No. 27), better represents this diphthong to the English reader than *oa* or *ua*, as they are liable to be too much separated.

18. *üé*, *üe.*—The first of these two is most easily distinguished from the other in those words which are in the three first tones, but as most of the words are in the *juh shing*, and followed by the

h, they are in practice nearly alike in sound.

19, 20. *ui*, *úi*.—The second of these is distinctly marked in the Cantonese under initials like *k*, *t*, and *ts*, but they everywhere glide into each other and into *éi*. In Fuhchau, they run into *i* and *òi*, and at Shanghai into *é*, both of them being everywhere heard as finals.

ANOMALOUS VOWELS.

21, 22. *'m*, *'ng*.—These two words are heard from Shanghai southwards in the colloquial; they are really vowel sounds, and at Amoy they occur preceded by a consonant, as *s'ng*, *h'm* or *hm*.

23. *ⁿ*.—This nasal sound is unknown at Canton or Fuhchau, but occurs at Swatow and Amoy, and more frequently at Shanghai; though hardly so marked, and not found in the middle of a word; the raised *ⁿ* is probably its fittest mark, though in the romanized Ningpo dialect it is undistinguished.

24. *sz'*, *tsz'*, *dz'*, *zz'*.—These four are the only forms of this sibilant; the first two are common in mandarin and at Canton, but all are entirely unheard between Swatow and Fuhchau. The last two are heard mostly at Shanghai, and the regions of Kiangsu and Chehkiang.

25. *ch'*, *sh'*.—The characters spoken with these peculiar vowels get their full sounds of *chi*, *ch'i*, and *shi* as one goes south from the Yangtsz' River. The apocopated form is unknown at Canton or at Fuhchau. The *Wu-fang Yuen Yin* indicates the full sound of *chi* and *shi* as the standard, and in this work they have, therefore, been all arranged under those syllables, while the contracted form is placed under each character. It is probable, that of the two forms *chi*, *shi*, and *ch'*, *sh'*, the latter is most generally heard.

26. *'rh*.—This sound is seldom heard south of the Méiling, and its pronunciation is uniform; the many foreign modes of writing it show the difficulty of expressing it satisfactorily. In Peking, it is often heard as if preceded by a consonant, as *mi'rh*, *w'rh*, *f'rh*, &c., which is caused by the elision of an intermediate final, the full sound being *ming 'rh* 明而, *wăn 'rh* 聞而, *făng 'rh* 風而, &c.

CONSONANTS.

1. *b*.—A common initial at Swatow and Amoy, but unknown at Canton or Fuhchau; it reäppears at Shanghai in many of the words so spelled at Amoy.

2, 3. *ch*, *ch'*.—This initial and *ts*, *ts'*, are interchanged so much and so irregularly all over the country, that it is impossible to follow their variations. In Canton, they are used as initials very nearly according to the spelling of the *K'anghi Tsz'tien* and *Wu-fang Yuen Yin*, but as one goes north, they mingle in a greater or less degree, and many natives cannot tell them apart. At Swatow and Amoy, *ts* is heard doubtfully only before *a*, *o*, and *u*; but on reaching Fuhchau, it is altogether merged in *ch*; both reäppear at Shanghai, but mostly applied to a different set of characters, and this interchange continues more or less along the valley of the Yangtsz' River.

4, 6, 11, 5. *d*, *dz*, *j*, *dj*.—The first two of these initials are very common around Shanghai; the last is also heard there and at Swatow and Amoy, but none of them at Canton or at Fuhchau, where such words begin with *t* or *y*. The digraph *dj* is preferable to the single *j* for writing it, since it is a harsh form of the soft *j* so common in mandarin, and not so likely to be mispronounced as the simple *j* is. At Peking, *d* is often heard before *a* and *u*, and the initial *t* often becomes *d*, and the *j* runs into *r*; as *da* for *ta*, and *răn* for *jăn*.

7. *f*.—This common initial is unheard from Swatow to Fuhchau, *h* almost everywhere taking its place; it occurs in all other dialects.

8. *g*.—This initial easily runs into *ng*, and their differences are sometimes imperceptible. At Swatow, Amoy and Shanghai, both *ng* and *g* are clearly heard as initials; at Canton and Fuhchau, the *ng* is just as plainly spoken in all words, and none begin with *g*. Morrison and Medhurst wrote *g* alone for the mandarin, but *ng* is more nearly correct.

9. *h*.—This, at the beginning of words, is the same initial aspirate as in the English words *hung*, *holy*; but to extend the use of the letter and make it entirely silent in words beginning with an aspirated *d*, *p* or *t* as consonant, as Medhurst and Douglas have done, is injudicious, owing to the sounds which *ph* and *th* have in English, and which will always mislead when the uninitiated read them. But to those who have been long accustomed to the use of *h* final, as the best sign for expressing the indistinct *juh shing*, Wade's application of it for a few of the Pekingese sounds in other tones is still more perplexing and needless. The characters to which he often applies it as 是 *shih*, 界 *chieh*, 爺 *yeh*, &c., are never heard in the *juh shing*, while he leaves it off in 的 *ti*, 屋 *u*, 得 *tê*, &c. Such use, therefore, tends to mislead those who are not acquainted with the local patois, and even to them it is a perplexity.

10. *h'*.—This sound is not heard in the four coast dialects, in which it drops the sibilant sound, or takes an initial *y*, or more rarely an *s*; it is common at Shanghai. The digraph *hs* adopted by Meadows and Wade does not exactly express it, for there is no proper *s* in the sound, and *sh* is too much; if one puts the finger between the teeth, and tries to speak *hing* or *hü*, he will probably nearly express this sibilant initial. The Spanish *x*, as in *Quixote*, comes near it, and would be much the best symbol, if it were not that it would be mispronounced by the common reader, as in *xiang* 香, *xin* 忻, &c.

12, 13. *k*, *k'*.—As a final, from Shanghai to Canton this consonant always indicates the *juh shing* of those words whose other tones end in *ng*, as *ping*, *pik*; *hang*, *hak*. In Kiangsu, it is often doubtful whether the word ends abruptly enough for an *h*, or should be written *h*. The aspirated initial *k* before *i* and *u* is one of the difficult sounds in the mandarin, and is often heard like *kt*, *ch* or *ks*, and still unlike all these.

14. *l*.—Along the southern coast this initial is often pronounced as *n* before *a* and *i*; not so frequently before *í*, *o*, or *u*; but all over China there is a curious interchange of the two letters, which perplexes the foreigner. At Amoy, *l* often approximates the sound of *d*.

15. *m*.—This letter occurs as a final from Canton to Amoy, in those words which end in *n* in the *kwan hwa*; but there seems to be no general rule guiding the change, as many retain the *n*. It is unheard at Fuhchau and northward, but reäppears in Kiangsi. As an initial, *m* often changes into *b* at Amoy and Swatow.

16. 17. *n*, *ng*.—These two liquids are employed as finals in every part of China; but in Amoy and Shanghai, they often take a nasalized form. As initials, *n* often interchanges with *l*; and *ng* in the mandarin is elided into a guttural *ă* or *ö*, as *^{ng}ăn*, *^{ng}ö*, especially in Chihli; but this initial is the most capricious of all, and its changes are irreducible to a general rule.

18. 19. *p*, *p'*.—As a final, this letter only occurs in many parts of the coast provinces south of the Yang-tsz' River, in the *juh shing* of those words whose other tones end in *m* in Cantonese, as *kim*, *kip*. In mandarin such words always end in *n*. As a final, *p* is unknown from Fuhchau northward, but as an initial it generally follows the mandarin, except in Kiangsu, where it alters into *b* in some of the tones before certain vowels.

20. 21. *s*, *sh*.—These two initials play the same part among the Chinese as they seem to have done among the ancient Israelites, and form a true *shibboleth* by which a man's native place can be detected. They are used at Canton at the beginning of nearly the same words which divide them in the *Wu-fang Yuen Yin*; but from that city going coastwise to Shanghai, the *sh* nearly everywhere turns into *s* or *z*, and reäppears generally when further north; there are, however, many exceptions over this wide range. Between Canton and Macao, for instance, the *sh* is changed in many words, as *shui* 水 becomes *sui*; and just the same difference exists between Peking and Tientsin; yet in Sz'hwui hien, a district west of Macao, most of the words which at Canton begin with *s* take the *sh*.

22. 23. *t*, *t'*.—This letter occurs as a final in the same regions with *p*; and as *p* always follows words ending with *m*, so the *t* shows the *juh shing* of words ending in *n* in the other tones; the modes of variation from the fourth tone in mandarin into the abrupt consonants *k*, *p* and *t*, in the three southern dialects, have not been traced sufficiently to lay down any rules; at Fuhchau, the finals *p* and *t* are not heard. As an initial, *t* becomes *d* in certain tones in those parts of Kiangsu near the Yangtsz' River.

24. 25. *ts*, *ts'*.—These are much interchanged everywhere in China with *ch*, *ch'*; and, in consequence, many words in this Dictionary will be sought for under one of them which have been placed under the other. In the regions from Swatow to Fuhchau, it is entirely superseded by *ch*, and in Shanghai is mostly used in those words which at Canton and Peking begin with *ch*.

26. *v*.—This initial is heard chiefly in the Yangtsz' valley, where it begins words elsewhere commencing with *f* or *w*. It is unknown at Canton or Peking, and the regions around those cities.

27. *w*, *wa*, *hwa*.—This letter is employed as an initial consonant in this work, as in *wang*, *wăn*. The Chinese spell words beginning with *kw*, *sw*, &c., as *ku-wang* for *kwang*, *su-wan* for *swan*, &c., where the medial vowel is so closely joined with the initial, that it is more distinct for us to make the initial out of both. Others, however, treat them as separate. Wade and Goddard use *u* as in *shuo* 說, *suan* 算, &c.; De Guignes and Douglas use *o*, as *hoang* 黃, *hoat* 發, &c.; but the general method has been to use *w*, and regard the letters *shw* or *hw* as the initial. The medial vowel is itself modified by the preceding consonant, and after *t* or *p* it is much more distinct than after *k* or *h*; but an Englishman is less likely to misread a word written *lwan* or *gwat*, than if it be written *luan* or *loan*, *guat* or *goat*. Besides which, as stated above, the diphthong *ua* is more distinctly heard at Amoy and Swatow in many words ending with a vowel as *sua*, *p^{n}ua*. In Fuhchau and Amoy, the initials *ch^{g}*, *h*, *k*, *l*, *m*, *n*, *ng*, *p* and *s* are followed by *w*; *i.e.* by this medial vowel, making this class of initial more frequent there than elsewhere; at Canton, *kw* is the only initial of this kind, and *gw*, *hw* and *kw* at Shanghai. Though the Chinese divide by the initial consonant, as 多官 *to-kwan* for 端 *twan*, their ignorance of alphabetic writing makes their practice no guide to our mode of expressing such sounds; and the use of *w* is attended with the least risk of mispronunciation.

28. *y*.—This letter is used only as a consonant in this work. De Guignes used *y* to express the final *í* and *i*, as in *ky* 記 and *tsay* 再; and some others write the short *i* in the diphthongs *ie*, *ia*, &c., with it. At Ningpo it has been thus employed, and when the *i* is doubled, as in *niing*, *niih*, the use of *y*, as in *nying*, *nyih*, is perhaps preferable. In Peking, some words beginning with *y* change it into *r* before *u* and *ă*, as *rung* 容 for *yung*, *rueh* for 月 *yueh*; but it is an exceptional deviation.

29. 30. *z*, *zh*.—The initial *z* begins many words at Shanghai and Ningpo which elsewhere begin with *ts* or *s*, and forms a marked feature of the speech of that region; it is unknown in Fuhkien, and is limited in other directions as in Kiangsi and Nganhwui. The initial *zh* is a change from *j* in Peking and its vicinity, but does not extend very far, as it is unknown in Shantung.

SECT. III.—ASPIRATES.

These words which commence with *ch*, *chw*, *k*, *kw*, *p*, *t*, *tw*, *ts*, *tsw*, are, according to our spelling, divided into aspirated and unaspirated characters, but the Chinese philologists see no connection between them. Indeed they have no well-understood name for a hard breathing like an aspirate, and the usual term 噴氣 is of foreign origin, which no native scholar can understand without explanation. In alphabetic writing, when the aspirate begins the word, as *hang* 杭, *hwang* 黄, it is plainly marked by the letter *h* alone, which distinguishes *ang* from *hang*, and *wang* from *hwang*. But if this letter be written after other consonants, especially *p* or *t*, the word is liable to be mispronounced as *phing* (*fing*) 平, or *thing* 聽, at least by Englishmen. De Guignes used it in words like *khoueng* 誇, *tchhouang* 創, *thsiouan* 泉; but a Frenchman would not err in this way. He was followed by Medhurst, who in order to avoid the mispronunciation of words like *thing* 廳 wrote it *t'hing*, placing an aspirate before the *h*; Douglas omits the aspirate, as in *thau* 透, *phi*, 皮; but there is such a risk of confusion, that they have not been followed elsewhere.

The Greek spiritus asper [ʽ] is now generally regarded as a sufficient and easily-written sign, to indicate the aspirated words under the above nine initials; but in cases where a printing-office does not afford a proper aspirate [ʽ], an inverted comma ['] must take its place. In this Dictionary, the aspirated characters immediately follow the unaspirated, and are not all placed in a new series by themselves, as is done in Maclay's Fuhchau, and Douglas' Amoy Dictionary. There are 136 aspirated syllables in the *Wu-fang Yuen Yin*, not including those under the initials *h* and *hw*, which number 41. In Cantonese, there are 157 of the former and 40 of the latter; but Medhurst in his Hokkëen Dictionary enumerates 281 aspirated syllables in all, many of which are colloquial. There are fewer aspirated words in the Fuhchau dialect, and their number appears to decrease as one goes north.

Aspirated words have been classed as surds, to distinguish them from the unaspirated, or sonants, but this distinction seems to be inapplicable in relation to Chinese. Such words are continually changed from one class to the other by the compilers of general and local native vocabularies, even when the initial consonant does not change. If we compare two or three dialects with each other, we find that the aspirated and unaspirated words are not fixed; one drops, and another takes an aspirate, especially under the initials *k* and *h*. Learning the aspirate is an important subject to the student, who will find it beneficial to read over lists of characters of both kinds with a teacher, so as to distinguish them.

In some respects they are harder to learn than the tones, as the distinction is very delicate to our ears, and is more a matter of memory than of imitation.

SECT. IV.—*SHING* OR TONES.

It would be better, for many reasons, to introduce the term *shing* into philological works upon Chinese, than to try to explain the foreign word *tone* when it denotes the curious feature of Chinese words by which their meaning is changed according to the inflexion of voice used in speaking them. In English we speak of a whining tone, a guttural tone, a hoarse or harsh accent, but the *shing* of the Chinese are quite different from such modulations of voice, which affect only the sound of a sentence or important word, and not its meaning. There are cases in all languages where accent and emphasis alter the meaning of particular words, and some may choose to call such modulations the tone, and compare them to the *shing* of the Chinese, but the two are hardly comparable. In the Burmese, Siamese, Shan and Assamese languages, there are remains of the same system of *shing* which prevails in Chinese; but in those countries the *shing* are not found in every word, nor do they involve their meanings to an equal degree.

The *shing* in the Chinese language really partake of the nature of vowels; and as the vowels in western languages are constantly undergoing local changes which give rise to particular patois, so have these delicate modulations suffered various changes in different parts of China, till they are involved in a perfect maze of obscurity and contrariety.

The mode of representing the *shing* in an alphabetic language, must of course be entirely arbitrary, but only three methods have been adopted. The earliest was that of Fourmont, De Guignes, Morrison, Medhurst, Douglas and others, of marking the vowels with different accents. De Guignes employed five, as *yūn*, *yûn*, *yùn*, *yún* and *yŭh*, to indicate the differences in the sounds of 氳, 雲, 隕, 運, 聿, and this series of tonal accents has attained a wide use since his dictionary was published in 1813. Dr. Morrison employed only four marks, as *chāng*, *chàng*, *cháng*, *chăh*, to represent 張, 塲, 漲, 帳, 札, where the upper and lower *pʽing shing* are indicated by the same sign; he left the aspirate unmarked. This mode was adopted in form by Medhurst in his Mandarin Dictionary, but altered in fact by dropping the accent for the upper *p'ing shing* and writing *cháng* for the lower *p'ing shing*. In his Hokkëen Dictionary, he increased the four marks of Morrison to seven, but altered their application in order to distinguish the seven tones in the Amoy dialect; in this Douglas follows him. These were written *kwun, kwún, kwùn, kwut, kwûn, kwūn, kwŭn, kwut*, to show the local differences between the sounds of the characters 君, 滾, 棍, 骨, 群, 滾, 郡, 滑, thus using only five accents to show seven *shing*, and these not in the same way as De Guignes had employed them.

The strongest objection against using marks at all over vowels to denote the *shing*, is that they materially interfere with those marks which show the power of those vowels. In De Guignes' Dictionary, the aspirate, tone and vowel marks are all put over the word; and Medhurst was obliged in the same way to write *këén, keăóuh, këê*, where one sign is for the prosody, and the other for the *shing*. At present, in Amoy, where the missionaries have adopted his system of marks in their romanized books, they have contrived to eliminate all prosodical marks affecting the vowels, except that of *o* in *no*, and *o* in *long*, the latter being written *o̤*. No tones are marked in the romanized books published at Ningpo, and of the two, this is the best way.

A second mode, employed by Gonçalves, is that of marking the *shing* by a figure after the word, as 1, 2, 3, 4, to represent the same five *shing* which De Guignes denoted by five accents; but it is difficult to understand why he did not write them 1, 2, 3, 4, 5, at once, and not use an inverted period for the *p'ing shing*. The following sentence,—*we are his comrades*, 我們是他的夥計 is written *uo*2 *men*1 *xe*3 *t'a*˙ *ti*4 *hŏ*2 *ki*3 by Gonçalves in his orthography and tones, where the mark for the *p'ing shing* in the fourth word *t'a*˙ would easily be overlooked. He applied the same five signs to indicate the eight *shing* in the Canton dialect, which necessarily mixed them up so, that no reader could possibly decide what the figures meant, and get the right tone. Meadows recommended four figures too, to represent the two *p'ing shing* and the two *tseh shing*, and he has been followed by Wade, because it is the simplest. So it would be, if there was only one system all over China. Wade applies the figures 1, 2, 3, 4, to the upper and lower *p'ing shing, shang shing* and *k'ü shing*, so that each one represents a different tone from that denoted by Gonçalves. The sentence above quoted would be written in the Peking dialect, *wo*³ *mên*¹ *shih*¹ *t'a*¹ *ti*¹ *'huo*³ *chi*⁴ by him, and this comparison shows the confusion which would ensue, if the use of figures was extended to the various dialects, and their number run up to seven or eight. In his *Grammar of the Shanghai Dialect*, Mr. Edkins has contrived to eliminate all tonal marks except an apostrophe ['] and a comma ['], as *'lau* 老 for the *shang shing* and *tau'* 道 for the *k'ü shing*; but they are entirely insufficient for general use, and rather confusing in his work. The capabilities of the printing-office probably influenced his adoption of such queer signs.

The third mode, which was begun in Bridgman's Chrestomathy, and has been adopted by Yates, Lobscheid, Goddard and Baldwin, is a modification of the native mode of indicating the tones. Chinese authors do not usually indicate the *shing*; but in certain cases where a word has two tones, with two corresponding significations, they mark the tone by a semicircle on the corner of the characters as *oh* 惡, and *u* ˛惡, or *tu* 度 and *toh* 度˛; in these cases, the second signification is the one marked. This mode has this advantage over the other two, that the marks are easily understood by the natives, and are applicable alike to all dialects without risk of confusion. Though all modes of denoting the *shing* must be alike conventional to the foreign reader, only the native method can be used for both Chinese and English with equal ease. Thus the sentence ***I** wish to go and do it*,—˛*ngo yao*' '*tseu* ˛*ts'ien k'ü*' *tso*', '我要' '走˛前去' 做', is read ˜*ngo iu*' '*tsau* ˛*ts'in hü*' *tsò*˙ '我要' '走˛前去' 做' in the Cantonese, and the different tones of the first and last characters are as accurately and easily indicated in one language as in the other, but could not easily be so by means of figures or accents appended to the characters. If figures are used, there ought to be a double series, employing 1, 2, 3, 4, for the upper *p'ing, shang, k'ü*, and *juh*, and 5, 6, 7, 8, for the lower *p'ing, shang, k'ü* and *juh*, so as to make them applicable alike to all dialects; otherwise, as in the example cited above from Gonçalves and Wade, they fail of being read correctly. Native scholars always call the tones by their names, and do not number them.

It is a great help to the learner to have the tones marked on the word, and several years practice has proved the ease with which the native marks are recognized. In writing the names of persons and places for foreigners, no one adds marks to designate the tones, but in a work designed for the beginner, the tones can easily be distinguished.

Every character in this Dictionary is marked with its proper tone for the *nan hwa*, according to the *Wu-fang Yuen Yin*. They follow each other in the order of that work, *shang p'ing, hia p'ing, shang shing* and *k'ü shing*; words in the *juh shing* being placed by themselves. Underneath each is given the Peking pronunciation in its tone in that city, with a blank space for the student to insert the sound in any other dialect. The five tones of the *nan hwa* and the four tones of the

Pekingese, are marked according to the same system adopted in my Tonic Dictionary of the Canton Dialect; in which the whole eight are given as in the following series.

1	2	3	4	5	6	7	8
上	上	上	上	下	下	下	下
平	聲	去	入	平	上	去	入
[꜀]	[‘]	[’]	[꜆]	[꜁]	[꜂]	[꜄]	[꜇]
shang	*shang*	*shang*	*shang*	*hia*	*hia*	*hia*	*hia*
p'ing	*shing*	*k'ü*	*juh*	*p'ing*	*shang*	*k'ü*	*juh*
꜀温	‘穩	慍’	屈꜆	꜁雲	꜂尹	混꜄	核꜇

In Peking, the tones of these eight characters are easily marked by the same set of signs;—

꜀温 ‘穩 慍’ ꜀屈 ꜁雲 ‘尹 混’ ꜀核

In all the southern dialects, the *shing* are commonly divided into 上聲 and 下聲, or an upper and lower series. They are also more generally called 平聲 and 仄聲; the first term denoting the two even tones, the second all the others, grouped as the deflected tones. East of Canton to Fuhchau, the second and sixth or upper and lower *shang shing*, coalesce in exactly the same sound. In the region around Shanghai, the two series are subjected to other modifications, according to Edkins, who enumerates twelve modulations heard in the *shing* of words, and enters very fully into the subject, illustrating each one with examples.

The names which have been given to the *shing* by foreigners, have usually had more or less reference to their native names. For instance, the 上平 and 下平聲 have been called the *upper* and *lower monotone*, *primary* and *secondary smooth* tone, *upper acute* and *lower even* tone, and *high* and *low even*. Other tones have also received many names, but as soon as the learner begins to perceive their real nature by talking them with the natives, he naturally uses their names as the ones which most accurately describe them.

As this work is chiefly intended to aid in learning the written language, the student is referred to other treatises* for general and particular descriptions and illustrations of the *shing* in the various dialects. After reading the authors referred to in the note, it is probable that the student will agree with Edkins, that the Chinese terms 平上去入 "do not in the majority of cases, represent the actual effect of the sound on the ear. When first adopted they must have represented the tones of the dialect spoken by the writer who selected them; but when applied according to universal practice, to the sounds given to the same characters in other parts of the empire, they convey no idea of the actual pronunciation."

Yet the characteristics of the *shing* are alike in all parts of the country. They are not, strictly speaking, either tones, accents, modulations, brogue or emphasis, as these terms are used in European languages; but perhaps more nearly resemble musical notes, and are best illustrated by the variations of pitch and time in an instrument. Mr. Hartwell says, "the *shing* have five elements, *viz.*, pitch, quality of voice, inflection, stress, and time," and he has neatly explained those heard at Fuhchau by comparing them with musical intervals and their variations on the staff, taking the middle line of the staff as the key-note of the speaker's voice. The note **G** struck successively on a violin, an organ, and a flute, for example, strikes the ear very differently, just as the voices of a child or a man do; yet the three sounds are the same on the gamut, and the note chords on all the instruments. But let **G** sharp be struck on one of them, and we feel the discord; it is not the note at all. So in respect to Chinese *shing*; if the right *shing* be not spoken, the right word is not spoken, it is some other word. For instance if a person says *ku*' instead of ꜀*ku* 孤 an *orphan*, he does not say the word for *orphan* at all, he says that for 故' *old*, or 固' *firm*, or 顧' *to hire*, or some other word, equally unlike it in meaning. The *shing* constitutes an integral part of the word, and has nothing to do with stress or emphasis; they always retain their peculiar force, whether at the beginning or end of a sentence, whether asking or replying to a question, whispering or scolding, soothing or menacing,—they remain ever the same. A native seldom or never thinks whether he has the right tone or not, but speaks as he learned it from his infancy; just as an Englishman has no difficulty in uttering the words *that thing* is *thoroughly thrashed*, which to a Frenchman or Dutchman is well nigh impossible.

If one has a quick and imitative ear, he will learn the tones while learning characters and expressions, and by mixing with the people his ear will unconsciously catch the right sound. Let him not be perplexed as to their nature, which has nothing mysterious, but imitate the *sounds* as well as the *words* of the sentences he hears, as he would learn a tune, or when trying to mimic another, and not try to find out certain rules by which he must train his voice. The full exercises given by Mr. Wade

---

* Prefaces to Morrison's *Dictionary*, Vol. I, to Medhurst's *Hokkeën Dictionary* and Douglas' *Dictionary of Amoy Vernacular*, Dyer's *Vocabulary of the Fuhkien Dialect*, Maclay's *Dictionary of the Fuhchau Dialect*, Williams' *English and Chinese Vocabulary*, and his *Easy Lessons in Chinese*, pp. 48-55, Callery's *Systema Phoneticum* pp. 68-72, and *Chinese Repository*, Vol. III, pp. 26—28, Vol. IV, p. 172, Vol. VI, p. 579, Vol. VII, p. 87; but the fullest description and critical examination of the tones are to be found in Edkins' *Shanghai Grammar*, pp. 6-70, and in Wade's *Course*, where exercises on them are given.

in his *Course*, or the sets of examples drawn out by Edkins in his *Shanghai Grammar*, or similar exercises made by the student for the particular dialect he is learning, as is recommended in the *Canton Tonic Dictionary*, and in Medhurst's *Hokkëen Dictionary*, can profitably be read over and over until the ear is trained to the tones. It is not difficult for a foreigner to be understood in Chinese, even if he does misapply the *shing* of many words; but one is almost sure to imitate and learn the correct tone of the commonest words as he becomes familiar with them, if he pays a little attention to them at the outset, and feels that a vicious pronunciation will be harder to correct, than it is to learn a good one at first.

The unchangeable nature of the written character has probably had a powerful influence, in forcing the people of China to pay close attention to their sounds, in order to avoid the confusion which would ensue in speaking dozens and scores of homophonous words. It is absolutely necessary that a language so very meager in vocables, should have some contrivance to supplement this paucity, and natural that its speakers should endeavor to qualify their sounds and vary the modulations of their words, if thereby they could facilitate intercourse and render speech less liable to confusion. The set phrases in which the Chinese usually convey their thoughts, tend to enlarge this paucity of sounds, and it is easier to learn the right tones of such dissyllabic compounds than of single words.

One chief difficulty which is met at the outset in this study, is the strangeness of having a different modulation for every word. It is as if one were made to talk up and down the gamut, and apply *do, re, mi, fa, sol, la,* to all his words. Such delicate differences and modulations would never be retained in an alphabetic language, as is shown by the Japanese losing them in those words adopted from the Chinese; and in the Burmese, Shan and Siamese languages, where they are heard more distinctly in many words, they are not general, and cause little trouble. Practice in speaking, with careful attention at first to the right *shing* will soon make a habit that will gradually become easy; if the student does not learn them in this way, no rules will materially help him.

SECT. V.—OLD SOUNDS OF THE CHINESE CHARACTERS.

The Rev. Joseph Edkins has prepared this section, to explain the principles adopted by the early Chinese philologists, in spelling and writing the sounds of their language; and to give the sources from which he made out the lists of old sounds placed at the beginning of each syllable.

1. *K'anghi's Dictionary.*—The first source of this old pronunciation of the characters is the *K'anghi Tsz'-tien*, where it is registered in the most convenient way. The system of spelling therein used, called *fan ts'ieh* 反切, can be illustrated by the character *sin* 心, which is spelled *sik-lim* 昔林, and the reader is directed to take the initial *s* of the first word, and the vowel *i* and final *m* of the second, and call the word *sim* in the *p'ing shing*. *Fah* 乏 is spelled *bong-pap* 房法, to be read *bap* in the *juh shing*. *Ch'eu* 怞 is spelled *dék-yu* 直祐, to be read *du* in the *p'ing shing*. *Kih* 急 is spelled *kü-lip* 居立, to be read *kip* or *kip*. *Ma* 馬 is spelled *moh-hia* 莫下, to be read *ma*. *Tich* 跌 is spelled *do-kiet* 徒結, to be read *diet*.

From these examples it is seen, how the two characters are combined in each case to indicate the sound; the first giving the initial only, the other the medial vowel, the final vowel or consonant, and the tone.

The books from which the spelling is quoted, are the *Kwang Yun* 廣韻, *T'ang Yun* 唐韻, and other works chiefly of the T'ang and Sung dynasties, in which the spelling of a thousand years ago is registered. The remaining specimens of the oldest mandarin literature date from the later Sung of Hangchau. The pronunciation of the Mongol dynasty of Yuen is known from the Bashpa monuments. A comparison shows that the modern mandarin pronunciation was then in a state of formation, and fully preserved the letter *m* among the finals.

The present *kwan hwa* cannot be taken, therefore, as a guide in reading the phonetic signs of the *fan ts'ieh*, but they must be derived from the values furnished by the Sanscrit alphabet, as employed in the formation of the 等韻, or *Sorted Finals*, a volume found among the introductions to K'anghi's Dictionary.

The thirty-six initials there used are to be read with their corresponding values in the Sanscrit alphabet, in the following manner.

見 k	溪 k'	郡 g	疑 ng		
端 t	透 t'	定 d	泥 n		
知 ch, t	徹 ch', t'	澄 dj, d	娘 ni		
幫 p	滂 p'	並 b	明 m		
非 f, p	敷 f, p'	奉 v, b	微 v, b, m		
精 ts	清 ts'	從 dz	心 s	邪 z	
昭 ch, ts	穿 ch', ts'	牀 dj, dz	審 sh	禪 zh	
景 yy	曉 hh	喻 y	匣 h	來 l	日 j.

The emperor's preface and decree following it dated 1710, should be regarded as proof that the pronunciation of Shăn Yoh 沈約 is to be taken as the standard in his dictionary. This involves three things:—1st. That the pronunciation of the old middle dialect, as still spoken in Hangchau, Suchau, and the adjoining region, furnishes the initials. 2nd. The dialects of Canton and south-western Fuhkien, and partially the old middle dialect, furnish the medial vowels and finals. 3rd. The standard of comparison for ascertaining and verifying the old pronunciation as preserved in dialects, is found in the Sanscrit alphabets and in the old dictionaries.

It should be remembered too, that Shăn Yoh, who framed the syllabic spelling with the assistance of Hindoo Budhists, lived in Kiangnan, when the court was at Nanking, and when Budhism was in its most flourishing condition. The transcription of names in Julien's "*Methode*" proves plainly that the thirty-six initials are to be read as in the old middle dialect, checked and verified by the Sanscrit alphabet.

In reference to the second particular, the value of the finals is known by comparing the local vocabularies of the Canton and Amoy dialects with the tonic dictionaries used by scholars in all parts of the country. For example, the 詩韻, or *Poetical Rhymes*, gives the finals much as they are pronounced in the south-eastern dialects, though the latter must yield when at variance with the tonic dictionaries, as being the older authority. Thus, 法 is *fap* or *pap*, not *hwat* as at Amoy, or *fat* as at Canton, or *hwak* as at Fuhchau.

In further elucidation of the above particulars, the usage of Japan, Corea and Cochin-China may be appealed to; for the transcription of Chinese sounds anciently made in those countries, is an index to the contemporary sounds as employed by the natives of north and south China. It may be known at once from these three transcriptions, that the true final of 法 was *p* and not *t*. From all this it can be fairly inferred that the present mandarin is as modern in its sounds as it is in its idioms and syntax. The 上平 and 下平 consist of the old 平聲 split in two; the surds and aspirates go to make up the 上平, and the sonants, liquids and nasals, the 下平. In regard to the other tones, the surds and sonants have united in the 上聲 and 去聲; and in the mandarin heard at Nanking, in the 入聲; in that spoken in the northern provinces, the 入聲 has become irregularly distributed among the other tone groups, but a critical ear can still easily recognize it, although its name is altered.

In the Canton and other dialects, the sonant initials *g, d, b,* have hardened into *k, p, t,* and are distinguished from the old surd series by tones and difference in pitch. For example, *ti* 帝 (formerly *té*) is distinguished from *ti* 地 (formerly *dé*) by tone at Canton into 帝ʾ and 地ʾ, as well as change of finals into *teiʾ* and *tiʾ*; at Shanghai they are *ti* and *di*, the initials being changed; but in *kwan hwa*, both are read *tiʾ*

Method of finding the eld sound of a word in K'anghi.—Look in the tables of rhymes, for the value of the phonetic signs used to spell it in the *fan ts'ich*. For instance, *wang* 忘 is spelt with *mo-pong* 武方, and is to be read *꜀mong*; for 武 is in the tables under the initial 遇 in the column 明 and 微 for *m*; and under the final *tang* 宕 in the column 幫 and 非 for *p*.

The old sound of *pʿing* 馮 is spelled with *bé-pang* 皮氷, and is to be called *꜀bang*. That of *kuh* 骨 is spelled with *ko-hot* 古忽, and is called *kot꜇*. In these two cases, *bé* 皮 is found under *b* in the tables of rhymes, and *ko* 古 under *k*.

The old sound of *kia* 駕 is spelled with *kü-nga* 居迓, and is to be called *kaʾ*. The surd initial *k* is found by noticing the place of 居 under 見 in page 12 of the second series of tables of rhymes, and the final *a* is obtained from the position of 迓 in page 1 in the second division.

In regard to these tables of rhymes, the second and fuller series is the most useful in helping a foreigner to determine the ancient sound. The first and briefest is intended as a guide in fixing the tones, and does not give information on the final consonants, *m, k, p, t.* It is useful for natives who speak the *kwan hwa*, and require tables of sounds in a transition state from the old to the new, but foreigners should use the second series.

The second series of tables of rhymes can be consulted to determine the initial letters, whether *p* or *b*, *t* or *d*, *k* or *g*, &c.; also to discover the ancient tone, which often differs from the modern, as in *dé* 弟 which was at first *꜂dé*, but is now nearly everywhere heard *tiʾ*; and lastly, to learn whether *ng, n, m, k, p* or *t* is the final consonant, although there are many irregularities in the last three finals. But for the vowels, the information given in K'anghi is not sufficient, for they have undergone greater changes than would be readily understood from the tables.

The student must not expect to find in the *Tăng Yun* all the words employed in the body of K'anghi in spelling sounds. These words are quoted from older dictionaries, and are too numerous to be all embraced in the tables, though quite enough of them are registered.

On the initials.—The reason that there are two groups beginning with *ch*, is that in some varieties of the old middle dialect, words in the first group are distinctly heard *ch, ch', dj*, while those of the second are heard *ts, ts', dz*. In certain cities, on the other hand, all are alike pronounced *ch, ch', dj*.

The reason that in the series under *f*, there is an aspirated *fʿ*, is not that the old pronunciation had two *f*s, but that *f* came from an older *p* and *pʿ*. The compilers of the tables, finding that in certain dialects, both *f* and *p* existed as the initials of some characters, and *f* and *p*ʻ as the initials of others, separated them in the tables. It may be that *f* was then the reading sound, and *p*, *p*ʻ the colloquial. In modern times along the southern coasts east of Canton, the *f* is usually changed to *h*.

Initial *b* occurs in three places. In the *p* series, it is the mandarin *p* as applied to words whose initial was formerly *b*. In the sonant division of the *f* series, it is applied to words now having *f* in mandarin, but which formerly had *v*, and before that *b*. In the nasal division of the *f* series, it is attached to words now pronounced with *w*, formerly with *m*, and in certain dialects with ***b***.

The existence of a double ***h*** series, is explained by the fact of a former strong and weak aspirated initial, as is still found in the old middle dialect.

The initial *j* or *r* should really be *ni*, as it is given in the list of old sounds subjoined.

On the finals and medial vowels.—It will be convenient for the student to write the final consonants and vowels in the margin of his copy of Kʻanghi's, Dictionary opposite the tables. In the first page headed *ka* 果, the first division reads *ka, ka, ka, kak;* the second, *kia, kia, kia, kiat;* the third *kie, kiet;* the fourth *kiet* or *kit*. In the fifteenth page, the first division is *kam, kam, kam, kap;* the second *kiam, kiam, kiam, kiap*. The southern dialects retain the old final letters, and their local vocabularies may therefore be used, to get the needed letters thus to be put in the margin.

The approximate values of the sixteen classes in the second series of rhyming tables are here given:—

1.—*ka, kak, kia, kat, kiet, kwa, kwak, kiüet.*
2.—*keng, kʻeh, king, kik, kung, kok, kiüng, kiok.*
3.—*keng, kek, king, kik, kiüng, kwok.*
4.—*kung, kok, kiüng, kiok.*
5.—*pei, pek, ki, kit, kwʻei, kút.*
6.—*kai, kat, kiai, kiat, ki, kit, kwei, kwat.*
7.—*ku, kuk, kü, kʻok.*
8.—*kan, kat, kien, kiet, kwan, kwat, kiüen, kiüet.*
9.—*kam, kiam, kiap.*
10.—*tsem, kim, kip.*
11.—*ken, ket, kin, kit, kwan, kút, kiün, kiüet.*
12.—*kong, kok.*
13.—*kiong, kiok, kwong, kwok.*
14.—*kau, kok, kiau, kiok.*
15.—*keu, kieu.*
16.—*ko, kok, kiok, kak.*

2.—The *Kwang Yun* 廣韻. This dictionary has been recently reprinted, and is readily to be obtained; it dates from the seventh century, and is one of those most commonly quoted in Kʻanghi as authority for old sounds. In it, all words having the same initial and final are placed under one heading, so that it is in fact a syllabic dictionary. The principle of arrangement is, however, tonic, all words in the *pʻing shing* being first registered, and then those in the *shang shing, kʻü shing* and *juh shing*, following each other in this order; those words falling under the *pʻing shing* are divided into two parts, owing to their number. The *Kwang Yun*, like other tonic dictionaries, is syllabic, though its arrangement appears to be according to the tones. The words are, of course, not placed in the order of our alphabet, but begin with *꜀tung* 東, *tung* 冬, an order which has since been adopted with variations in some other tonic dictionaries. It seems to have been invented by the compilers of the *Kwang Yun*, as it is there first found. The *Wu-fang Yuen Yin* and the Canton *Făn Yun* begin with the final *ien*.

The sounds given as *Old sounds* at the head of each syllable in this Dictionary were ascertained by a skilled native, who compared each character under that syllable, one by one with the *Kwang Yun*. So far as the two vocabularies were found to be identical he wrote out the words. After this list was prepared, the old pronunciation was added, following chiefly the authority of the *Kwang Yun*. The old prounciation thus ascertained agrees in most essential points with that of Kʻanghi's Dictionary, but the variations caused by vowels are much more complex. During the formation of the present *kwan hwa*, the variations of the syllables became much fewer; but it is hopeless, probably, to try to restore exactly the sounds as they were used by the compilers of the *Kwang Yun*.

We can only draw an outline expressing the chief features. The simple syllables used by the Budhists to transcribe Sanscrit words can be correctly ascertained, but more complex syllables cannot be restored. Vowels are the most evanescent parts of words, easily become modified, and an exact orthographic representation of their nicer shades cannot be obtained. The following changes have taken place in their value:—the modern *o* is from *a*, *eu* from *u*, *u* from *o*, *i* from *é*, *iau* from *au*, *ieu* from *u*, *éi* from *i*, the imperfect vowel in *sz'* from *i* or *a*, *i* from *ei* or *ui*, *ya* from *o*, *a* from *é* or *o*, *ă* from *i*.

3.—*Old Poetry.—Phonetics.* The complete merging of *f* in an older *p*, and of *h* in an older *k*, takes us back to an age contemporaneous with the old poetry. A great narrowing of the range of the hissing letters *s*, *z*, *ts*, *sh*, &c., is a mark of the same period. At that time, *ch* was probably lost entirely in *t*, and *dj* in *d*. The researches of native scholars, and the existence of dialects like the Amoy and Swatow, without an *f*, and with a contracted *ch* and *s*, tend to this conclusion.

To that earlier era in the history of the Chinese

language, belongs the dropping of final letters from a host of words spelled in the *Kwang Yun* with vowel finals only. The rhymes of the old poetry require that many words now spoken in the *k'ü shing* and other tones, should be read in the *juh shing*; which implies that such words once ended in a consonant.

In the list of *old sounds*, the words are arranged somewhat as they apply to the characters found under that syllable in this Dictionary, but it was impossible, without risk of confusion, to give the sound opposite each character with the Pekingese. They represent only partially the changes that have taken place in the old Chinese pronunciation, through the elision of the final consonants from words now referred to other tones. The sounds are therefore chiefly from the *Kwang Yun*, and not more than 1200 years old. Perhaps when the phonetic characters have been fully examined, and all the lost consonants restored, it may be possible to carry this inquiry farther, and restore the language to the form it had when the phonetic characters were made

SECT. VI.—RANGE OF DIALECTS.

The peculiar nature of the written language makes it necessary to explain the use of the word *dialect*, which has been objected to as not applicable to the various forms of local speech heard over this wide land. Some assert that they rise to the dignity of a language, like the Spanish, Italian, and other offshoots from the Latin; while others regard them as more like the patois heard in various parts of Spain itself, where each, amidst its local expressions, retains the idioms and laws of the Castilian. The essential unlikeness between the variations heard in speaking those alphabetical languages, and the greater discrepancies between the sounds given to the ideographic characters, will explain the wider use of the term in Chinese, but certainly does not elevate them into the rank of separate languages.

The differences between the speech heard at Canton and that at Shanghai, are indeed far greater than those between any of the local dialects heard in Spain, for they affect the idioms of the language; yet both are still so intimately connected with each other and the mandarin in the meaning and tones of their words, and laws of their syntax, that they cannot properly be called anything but *dialects*, although three persons speaking them are mutually unintelligible. A *dialect* is defined by Webster, — "The form of speech of a limited region or people, as distinguished from others nearly related to it;" and this is applicable to the Chinese dialects. It is also defined a *patois*, but this term as well as *brogue*, is far too contracted to describe the differences between the speech of Kwangtung and Kiangsu provinces. The word *patois* is more applicable to the varieties of a dialect, like those heard at Shanghai, Ningpo, Hangchau, and the interjacent cities, where one can generally be understood at each place, if he speaks the other vernacular correctly.

The fundamental fact, that no character has an inherent sound, has tended to make and perpetuate these dialects throughout the country; and the general ignorance of the written language by the people at large, has helped to multiply and modify them still further. It, however, entirely misleads to describe any one of these as "no mere dialectic variety of some other language, but a distinct language;" for until a new sense be given to the word, such a description conveys a misconception of the relation between the spoken and written languages. So varied are the sounds heard even in one province, as Fuhkien or Nganhwui, that if it were not for the bond of the same written medium, the people would probably long ago have crystallized into separate nations through their inability to understand each other. It is also an error to term the written language a dead language, and say, as Dr. Douglas does, that it "is not *spoken* in any place whatever under any form of pronunciation," and that "learned men never employ it as a means of ordinary oral communication even among themselves." The exercises in Wade's *Course* and the *Hung Leu Măng* or "Dreams of the Red Chamber," are proof enough that the *kwan hwa* can be, and is written and spoken like any other language. The conversation of the officials in Peking, too, can all be written in proper characters without any difficulty. No one will dispute the remark that no two Chinese pronounce their words alike, even in any one dialect; but this does not weaken the remarkable power of their written language to maintain the solidarity of the people.

The extent to which a dialect is spoken, is therefore a point varying according to one's ideas of what is a *dialect*; but some general notion in regard to the matter can be obtained. Native scholars give us no information on this point, for they are unable to compare local sounds by means of characters which their readers will pronounce differently; for instance, how can a man in Peking tell his readers that 外 is read *ngoi*[2] at Canton, *gwa'* at Swatow, *ngwoi*[2] at Fuhchau, and *'nga* at Shanghai? The *kwan hwa* ought perhaps, not to be called a *dialect*, but rather to be regarded as the Chinese spoken language, of which the provincial speech in Canton or Fuhkien is a dialect. The fact that it is unintelligible in those cities, does not invalidate the statement, that it is understood generally in fifteen of the eighteen provinces, and is everywhere spoken by those who pretend to a polite education. Mr. Edkins regards Peking, Nanking and Ch'ingtu, as the centers of its three marked varieties, and the wide separation of these cities, whose inhabitants, as a whole, have no intercommunication with each other, and yet can orally converse, all the more proves its claim to be the Chinese spoken language.

In this wide area, the Nanking, called 南官話 and 正音 or true pronunciation, is probably the most used, and described as 通行的話, or the speech everywhere understood. The Peking, however, also known as 北官話 or 京話 is now most fashionable and courtly, and like the English spoken in London, or the French in Paris, is regarded as the accredited court language of the empire. The two most striking differences between them, consist in the change of the initial *k* before *i* and *ü* into *ch* or *ts*, and the distribution of words in the *juh shing* among the other tones. In Peking itself, words are constantly clipped in speaking, and the finals *n* and *ng* often coalesce with their next syllables, as *tsien 'rh* 前而 into *tsi'rh;* but such variations and peculiarities are endless, and do not constitute dialectical differences.

So far as is yet known, the range of mountains dividing the basins of the Min river in Fuhkien, the Pearl river in Kwangtung and others in southern China from the Yangtsz' kiang, forms the chief dividing line of a series of local dialects, in which the frequency of abrupt final consonants and nasal sounds strike the ear. Neither of the local vocabularies issued at Canton, Changchau or Fuhchau, give one any idea of the extent of country over which those dialects prevail; but probably they are not spoken in any considerable degree of purity by even one half of the inhabitants of the two provinces south of the Méi-ling. Their divergences from the general language and from each other are almost endless, but their peculiar syntax, and the limits of their use, have only been partially investigated. It is this feature of a different idiom which has attracted the attention of native philologists, and they therefore speak of the dialects of Kwangtung and Fuhkien as unlike the speech of Honan and the north.

There are four well-marked dialects in the whole province of Kwangtung, but that called the Canton dialect is probably spoken by more people than any of the others. Next to it is the Hak-ka 客家 dialect, which has its center at Kia-ying cheu, prevails in the northern and eastern part of Kwangtung, and is—owing to the wandering habits of the emigrants from that region, — said to be more widely understood. It is the usual form of Chinese heard in Borneo. The Cantonese called 白話 or plain talk by the people, is marked by the rarity of the medial *i*, from the *kwan hwa* and the Fuhkien dialects. Words like *lien* 連, *liang* 頁, *hia* 下, *kiah* 甲, *hioh* 學, *hiu* 休, *hiüng* 兄, *kiai* 皆, &c. become *lín*, *léung*, *ka*, *kap*, *hok*, *yau*, *hing*, *kai*, &c.; the only exception to this rule is in the final *iao* of the mandarin, which uniformly ends in *iu*, as *liu* for *liao* 了, *hiu* for *hiao* 曉. Another feature is the frequent change of aspirated words beginning with *h* or *k*, into a breathing or labial consonant; for instance, *k'i* 氣, *hwan* 歡, *k'o* 科, *k'eu* 口, *k'oh*, 渴, *k'ang* 康, &c., change into *hi*, *fún*, *fo*, *hau*, *hot*, *hong*, &c. A very few words, unaspirated in mandarin, take an aspirate in Cantonese, as *hi* 携 becomes *kw'ei*, and *hoh* 貉 becomes *k'ok*. No such alteration takes place under other initials, but there is a tendency to drop the aspirate. One feature in which this dialect, particularly around the city of Canton, corresponds to Pekingese, is the regularity with which it retains the initials *ch* and *ts*, and their affiliated sounds *sz'* and *tsz'* and the final *ng*, though in the intervening region of nearly two thousand miles, these initials and sounds are frequently changed, altered, and interchanged in a most perplexing manner.

In Cantonese, the initials *chw*, *hw*, *h'*, *j*, *lw*, *nw*, *sw*, *shw*, *tsw*, and *tw* of the *kwan hwa*, and the initials *d*, *dz*, *v*, and *z*, heard along the Yangtsz', are all unknown. No word begins with *dj* as at Amoy, but south and east of Canton there is a tendency to add *ng* before words beginning with a vowel, as *i* 二 becomes *ngi;* and to substitute *s* for *sh*.

Compared with the dialects of Swatow and Amoy, the Cantonese like the *kwan hwa*, has no nasal sounds, nor does it ever change the initial *m* to *b*, or alter the finals *n* and *ng* into contracted nasals, as *ching* 貞 into *ch^{n}é* or *chien* 錢 into *chw^{n}a*. Unlike the dialects in Kiangsi, Chehkiang and Fuhkien, it has only one sound for a character in speaking or reading, and the number of unwritten words in the colloquial is probably not one tenth as many as at Amoy or Ningpo. This peculiarity of a reading and colloquial sound for hundreds of common characters, the two running parallel to each other something like the two sides of a railway, forms a great addition to the labor of learning to speak and read those dialects; but in Cantonese, as in Pekingese, there is nothing of the kind.

The Cantonese dialect has only 17 among its 33 finals, which make the *juh shing* in *k*, *p*, *t*. These are grouped in the *Wu-fang Yuen Yin* under the first four finals *t'ien*, *jăn*, *lung* and *yang*, which there have no *juh shing*. In the latter work, words ending in *u*, *a*, *o*, *é*, *ai*, and *i* form this tone, but in Cantonese none are heard under these six finals. For instance, the series ꜀登 ꜂等 凳꜄ 德꜆ is read ꜀*tăng*, ꜂*tăng*, *tăng*꜄, *tăk*꜆ at Canton; but in the north, the series ꜀都 ꜂覩 杜꜄ 突꜆, is read ꜀*tu*, ꜂*tu*, *tu*꜄, *tuh*꜆, where the last word would, at Canton, be found under the series ꜀*tăn*, ꜂*tăn*, *tăn*꜄, *tăt*꜆. The terminations in the *juh shing* at Canton follow one rule. Words ending in *ng*, have it in *k*, as ꜀*king*, ꜂*king*, *king*꜄ *kik*꜆; those ending in *m* have it in *p*, as ꜀*lam*, ꜂*lam*, *lam*꜄, *lap*꜆; and those in *n* have it in *t*, as ꜀*kon*, ꜂*kon*, *kon*꜄, *kot*꜆. This holds good at Swatow, but at Amoy they are all sounded gently, and *p* and *t* often lapse into *h*, as if dropping back into the mandarin. At Fuhchau they are softened to *h*, which prevails further north, but the *k* is retained, and the *m* vanishes.

Of all the dialects thus far examined, the Cantonese is among the most regular. No words are clipped, no character has two sounds, and the variants in the 33 finals are few in proportion to the regular sounds. Many books have been written in it by Protestant Missionaries which are easily understood by the common people. It is spoken westerly and southerly from the city even into Kwangsi, but its northerly limits are undefined; eastward the Swatow and Hakka dialects soon supplant it, though the people of Hwuichau fu 惠州府 use the *Făn Wăn* as the Cantonese do.

The dialect spoken in Ch'aochau fu 潮州府 (locally read *Tiéchiu hu*), in the eastern part of Kwangtung, and in the adjacent parts of Fuhkien, is less widely understood than the Cantonese, and is closely affiliated to the Amoy in its general character. The people of the two regions can understand each other without much difficulty. It is spoken along the coast of Hainan I., and is almost the only dialect of Chinese heard in Siam. A Cantonese, on hearing it, notices that the medial *i* reäppears, and that it is used perhaps rather more than in mandarin, as in *liap*꜆ 粒 for *lih*꜆, *tiat*, 姪 for *chih*, &c. It has many nasal sounds, and changes *n* and *ng* into such, as *k*ⁿ*é* 更 for *kăng*; or *tw*ⁿ*a* 壇 for *tan*; and often drops the final *k* where the Cantonese retain it. The initials *b*, *g*, *chw*, *dj*, *mw*, *ngw*, *pw*, are frequently heard, and indicate its affinities with the Fuhchau dialect; as the absence of *sh*, *ts*, *sz'*, *tsz'* and *f*, show its separation from that of Canton. Of these, *sh* usually becomes *s*, *sz'* becomes *sù*, and *ts* becomes *ch*, aspirated *ch'* turns into *t*, and *f* is divided between *h* and *p*. No sibilant *h*, *j*, *v* or *d*, occur in this dialect, as at Shanghai.

No native vocabulary has appeared in it, but a small word-book has been published by Mr. Goddard, and a beginner's *Lessons* by Dr. Dean. The former, referring to the differences between the reading and colloquial sounds of characters, says that the colloquial sound accords largely with the reading, and that the two are interchanged in a great number of words; while in others, the reading sound is heard only when chanting the classics. In reading aloud, all use the colloquial sound, and hearers expect no other; and the explanations made are rather of the thought than of the words. Characters having a reading and a spoken sound, however, seem to be much less in proportion to the whole mass than in the Amoy vernacular. In the reading sounds, the nasal disappears, and there is a tendency to keep the *m* instead of the *b*, *y* instead of *ng*, *y* and *w* instead of *g*, and other forms of the mandarin. There are only seven tones, as is the case further east; but the *k'ü shing* is inflected into three modulations called *shang k'ü* 上去, *k'ü shing* 去聲, and *hia k'ü* 下去, of which the middle one is confined chiefly to the spoken language, as the characters thus pronounced are mostly *read* in the *shang p'ing*.

The dialect spoken at Amoy is heard throughout the two departments of Changchau 漳州 and Tsüenchau 泉州, and by the Chinese settlers in the Island of Formosa, who went from those regions. The general features of its changes are given in the 十五音 or *Fifteen* [*Initial*] *Sounds*, which formed the basis of Medhurst's Dictionary, though strictly applicable only to Changpu hien 漳浦縣 lying south-west of Amoy. Its spoken vocabulary is fully illustrated in Douglas' Dictionary of the Amoy Vernacular. He estimates that it is spoken by eight or ten millions of people, including its cognate variations. In the *Fifteen Sounds*, the reading and colloquial pronunciation of characters with the tones are carefully distinguished. The colloquial used by the people of this region differs widely from the style in which books are written, — as much perhaps as anywhere in China. They substitute other words or dissyllabic phrases for the single terms used in books, and vary the inflection of even common words; giving them a nasal or contracted ending, or changing their sound and tone altogether. The greatest part of them are earlier forms of what is now accepted as the authorized reading sound, which has gradually become assimilated to the mandarin; but some are manifestly derived from characters which have dropped out of use, and some perhaps from an older aboriginal speech. A more thorough examination of the written characters, and their gradual changes in sound, would probably detect their originals in many cases, as I have ascertained in the Canton dialect in several words.

Medhurst classifies the changes which words undergo in their finals and initials, as they pass into the colloquial of Changchau, and has given the reading sounds and colloquial enlargement of every quotation in his dictionary. This difference is so great, that a person only acquainted with the reading sound, is not able to understand a conversation in the vulgar tongue; nor can a person proficient in the latter make out the meaning of any passage recited from a book not previously familiar to him. This is in striking contrast with the more precise Cantonese, though the differences in that dialect between a phrase in the colloquial and in the terser book style are not small.

The Fuhchau dialect, which is fully illustrated in Baldwin and Maclay's Dictionary, is more circumscribed in its range than either of the preceding; it is not easily understood out of the prefecture, and is not spoken accurately beyond a radius of forty miles from the city. Comparing it with those already described, its most marked features are, the absence of the abrupt finals *p* and *t*, the universal change of the liquid finals *m* and *n* into *ng*, the absence of all nasal sounds, and the prevalence of initials with a medial *u* or *w*, as *pwi, ngwoh, mwang, lwok*, &c. over those with a medial *i*, as *chiu, hièng, miòng*, &c., though the two are constantly interchanged. The final *k* is heard plainly from this point northerly to Shanghai; and, as it is elsewhere in the south, is the completion of the series in the *juh shing*, of words ending in *ng*. There are several curious and peculiar anomalies in the tables of tonal finals; as *꜀tăng, ʻtăng, téung꜄, téuk꜀*; *꜀kòng, ʻkòng, kaung꜄, kauk꜀* &c. In comparison with the Amoy dialect, the reading and spoken sounds of the Fuhchau probably assimilate more closely. It is not difficult to write the Fuhchau vernacular in the character, so as to be read intelligibly by persons making no pretension to classical learning. This is done, as it is at Canton, by selecting characters without reference to their meaning, to express the colloquial sound; to indicate such words, the Cantonese usually prefix 口 *mouth* to a character, as 嗻꜄ for *place;* and Fuhchau people add 人 *man* as 仈 to *know*. In the Amoy or Tʻiéchiu dialects, the colloquial cannot be so satisfactorily written perhaps, but even with all drawbacks, such attempts to simplify the dialect, seem to be preferable to the romanized books made in Amoy and Ningpo colloquial. These completely cut off the pupil from his native literature, and his labor is lost so far as helping him to read that, while those written in the character do much to introduce him to the knowledge of his own language, as has been proved at Canton. The total failure in India of the attempt to supplant its thirteen languages, by a uniform system of romanizing them, does not encourage one to try to supersede the Chinese character in the same way.

The speech heard throughout Chehkiang and Kiangsu shows its affinity to the *kwan hwa* in its grammatical idioms, absence of the finals *m, p, t*, and a general softness of tone, in marked contrast to the abrupt finals noticeable in Fuhkien and Kwangtung. But it is almost as unintelligible to a Peking or Sz'ch'uen man, owing to the numerous changes in the initials *ch* and *ts*, *s* and *sh*, *n* and *y*, the prevalence of *b, v, dz, zz* and *z*, and an almost unlimited variation in final vowels and nasals. Mr. Edkins has carefully traced its variations and laws over a large part of this area, in his *Shanghai Grammar*, and tried to show that the ancient sounds of the Chinese language are still retained in many places within the three provinces. His remarks are directed toward the search he was making after traces of the old sounds given in the *Kwang Yun* 廣韻 and the *Kʻanghi Tsz'tien;* but as they are applicable to the present subject, that of examining the range of dialects, I here quote them with some abridgment of details.

"Nowhere do we find such an accurate general correspondence with the tables given in Kʻanghi, as in the pronunciation of the central provinces. The tones are such, that the dictionary system is seen at once to apply to them accurately. The alphabetical peculiarities of the native tables are found with one or two doubtful exceptions, to be embraced throughout the following region. In the north, the thick series of consonants, *g, z*, &c. marking the lower series of words in tones 5—8, makes its appearance in Nan Tʻungchau 南通州, a prefecture near the northern bank of the Yangtsz' River where it enters the ocean. The transition from the *d*, &c. heard at Shanghai to the *t*, &c., where the region of the northern mandarin is approached, is marked by the introduction of the aspirate. Thus 地 changes to *tʻi*꜄ from *di*꜄, before it does to *ti*꜄. At Chinkiang, the two pronunciations are mixed; and there the five tones of the *kwan hwa* cross the river and extend to Nanking. All round Hangchau Bay, the two correlate series of consonants and the four-tone system, mark the colloquial; Chusan, Ningpo and Hangchau on the south, are at one with Sungkiang, Suchau and Chʻangchau on the north; and probably the whole of Chehkiang province has substantially the same speech.

"Passing west from the point where the three provinces, Fuhkien, Kiangsi and Chehkiang meet, we find that the thick consonants partially prevail in Kwangsin fu and Kienchʻang fu, near the borders of Fuhkien; but at Fuhchau fu 撫州府, a little further west, they disappear and are replaced by aspirates. Instead of *di*꜄ 地 the people say *tʻi*꜄; instead of *꜁bing* 病, they say *꜁pʻing*, &c., through all words beginning with *k, p, t*, in the lower series. The same peculiarity marks the speech of Kiaying chau in the heart of Kwangtung. At the capital of Kiangsi, the aspirates are heard only in the *hia pʻing*, where they should properly be; and in the other lower tones the words are distinguished from the upper tones, only by the tone, and not by a change in the initial. North of this city, on both sides of the Pʻoyang lake, the broad consonants occur again. Through Nganhwui, a connecting chain of dialects links the broad pronunciation of this region with the similar system extending over Chehkiang and most of Kiangsu. This line extends through Ningkwoh fu 寧國府, but does not reach the Yangtsz' River on the north, nor Hwuichau fu 徽州府 on the south; in this city two patois are heard; in one of them, two sets of tones are heard, those used in talking being distinct from those in reading, and independent of the different pronunciation of the reading and spoken sounds, which seems here to reach its maximum. In one district hereabouts, three dialects are heard, so rapidly does the speech vary. West of the Pʻoyang lake, the initials *g, d, b*, are heard around the Tungtʻing lake in Hunan, showing the same system of pronunciation as at Suchau in Kiangsu, which goes to prove that the native tables of sounds given in Kʻanghi are founded on what is now a provincial system. Of the three abrupt consonants, *k* only is heard at Shanghai; but at Fuchau 撫州 *t* and *p* are heard with their correlates *m* and *n*, but no *k* final; at Nankʻang fu 南康府, west of the Pʻoyang lake, *p* and *m* are represented, but no *k* or *t*, and the finals *n* and *ng* are confounded."

The Japanese learned their first use of Chinese characters from this region, about A. D. 250; and that language may still be quoted for many original sounds of that period; they call them *Gò-on* 吳音 *i.e.* 吳國音 "sounds of the Kingdom of Wu," and by means of their *kana* or syllables, have probably nearly retained the first pronunciation. For instance, 昨晚 is read *saku-ban* by them, while it is *chòk-bwan* in Amoy, and *tsok-man* at Canton; 詐病 is *saku-biyo* in one, and *ché-péng* and *cha-ping* in the other two; 作文 is *saku-ban, chòk-bún* and *tsok-măn* respectively. The second phrase has altered most of these three, and the 詐 appears now to have lost it *juh shing* and abrupt final in China. The variations in Japanese are however often so anomalous, that their pronunciation cannot now be accepted as conclusive for ancient Chinese.

As distinguished from mandarin, the Shanghai vernacular has no *sh, ch* or *j;* and changes *s, sh, ch* and *ts,* with the sibilant *h,* into *dj, z* or *dz,* but not uniformly; *y* and *j* easily run into *n* or *ni;* the *k* is retained in many words where the medial *i* follows it, and sometimes lengthens it, as *king* 經 becomes *kiăng; f* and *w* often become *v, t* becomes *d,* the final *k* is soft and easily confounded with the *juh shing* in *h,* and the final *n* often turns into a slight nasal. These few peculiarities may serve to mark the most prominent dissimilarities. The eight tones in the Shanghai dialect are divided into two series of four each as in Cantonese; but unlike that dialect, characters otherwise written with the same letters in the different tones in Canton, change their initials in the Shanghai to correspond to the tone. Thus the initials *k, t, p,* and *k', p', t', f, s, sz, ts, tsz,* and *ts', tsz'* and *h'* indicate the word to be in the upper series; while *g, b, d, b', v, z, zz, dj, dz, l, 'rh, m, ni, ng* and *n* show it to be in the lower series. These distinctions are so marked, that in writing the dialect in alphabetic letters, only the *shang shing* and *k'ü shing* need to be denoted by signs. No such influence on the initial is noticeable in the southern dialects nor in mandarin, but it facilitates their distinction to a foreign student.

Attempts have been made to write the Shanghai dialect (called *t'u bak* 土白 or local plain [talk]) in the character, and the success was such as to warrant the publication of a variety of religious works in it. They are not hard to learn, even by children, though the proportion of colloquial characters is greater than at Canton. It has been romanized too, and on a different plan of spelling from that used at Amoy and Ningpo; but the trial which Mr. Keith began in 1860, has not been prosecuted to any large extent.

Rev. Messrs. Pearcy and Crawford published an ingenious mode of writing this dialect, by devising a system of symbols or letters for the initials, finals, tones and aspirates, which could be neatly combined into a logotype, to denote the sound of the words. The writing somewhat resembles Corean in its general appearance, and is not difficult to learn. A few books have been printed in it, but it has never been adopted by others, and has far less to recommend it as a substitute for Chinese than the roman letters.

The Ningpo dialect has, it is said, a much greater proportion of unwritten sounds than the Shanghai, and no attempt has been made to write the colloquial in the character. The dialect in that city differs less from mandarin than the Shanghai, which is perhaps ascribable somewhat to the greater literary reputation of the region. At Ningpo, the initials *z, dz* and *t,* for *s, sh, ch, h',* are unknown, and no final *k* is heard; the frequent use of the initial *ni* and final *ò,* and change of *é* for *a,* also mark the southern city. Its idioms are often unlike those heard at Shanghai, and more nearly approach the pure *kwan hwa.*

The differences of speech among the people in various parts of the central, western and north-western provinces have not yet been studied minutely, and cannot usefully be analysed until more data have been obtained by those living at places remote enough to form suitable stations for comparison.

The anomalies and variations in pronunciation and tones found at the points now noticed, are very great and perplexing; but better knowledge of the intermediate regions would probably enable us to classify them. For instance, the tones called *shang p'ing* and *hia p'ing* at Hankow, are just the opposite in actual sound to those so called at Tientsin; the *juh shing* is retained in name at the former place, but it is not perceptibly different there from the *hia p'ing,* while at Nanking the two are unlike. The comparisons now made are therefore imperfect,—perhaps erroneous too in some points,—and are chiefly done to point out what has been ascertained, and the nature of the diversities.

In order the better to compare these dialects now noticed, the reading sounds in eight of them, given to the characters of a portion of the Emperor Yungching's discourse on Filial Duty in the 聖諭廣訓 or Sacred Commands of K'anghi, are here arranged in parallel columns. The first column contains the sounds of the *Wu-fang Yuen Yin;* and the others have been kindly furnished by friends who are familiar with the vernacular of each place, and probably fairly represent the main peculiarities of the reading sounds over the greater part of seven provinces. It is plain from this table, that though the characters are not primarily designed to express sound, their early sounds have been wonderfully preserved by means of the binary mode of spelling brought from India twelve centuries ago.

PRONUNCIATION OF AN EXTRACT FROM THE SACRED COMMANDS IN EIGHT DIALECTS.

	MANDARIN.	PEKING.	HANKOW.	SHANGHAI.	NINGPO.	FUHCHAU.	AMOY.	SWATOW.	CANTON.
夫	꜀fu	꜀fu	꜀fu	꜀vu	꜀vu	꜁hu	꜁hu	꜀hu	꜁fu
孝	hiao’	hʻiao’	hiao’	hio’	hiao’	hau’	hau’	hau^{2}	hao’
者	‘ché	‘chö	‘tsé	‘tsé	‘tsié	‘chia	‘chia	‘chia	‘ché
天	꜀tʻien	꜀tʻien	꜀tʻien	꜀tʻī^{n}	꜀tʻī^{n}	꜀tʻiéng	tʻien	꜀t^{n}i	꜀tʻín
之	꜀chi	꜀ch’	꜀tsz’	꜀ts	꜀tsz’	꜀chi	꜀chi	꜀chù	꜀chi
經	꜀king	꜀ching	꜀kin	꜀kiăng	꜀kying	꜀kíng	꜀keng	꜀k^{n}ia	꜀king
地	ti’	ti’	ti’	di’	di’	té^{2}	té^{2}	ti’	ti^{2}
之	꜀chi	꜀ch’	꜀tsz’	꜀ts	꜀tsz’	꜀chi	꜀chi	꜀chù	꜀chi
義	i’	i’	i’	ni’	i’	ngié^{2}	gi^{2}	ngi^{2}	i^{2}
民	꜀min	꜀min	꜁min	꜀ming	꜀ming	꜁míng	꜁bin	꜁min	꜁măn
之	꜀chi	꜀ch’	꜀tsz’	꜀ts	꜀tsz’	꜀chi	꜀chi	꜀chù	꜀chi
行	hing’	hʻing’	꜁hin	yăng’	hʻing’	haing^{2}	heng^{2}	heng^{2}	hăng^{2}
也	‘yé	‘yé	‘yé	‘ʻa	‘yé	ya’	‘ya	‘ya	ya’
人	꜁jăn	꜀zhăn	꜁lăn	꜀niăng	꜁jăn	꜁íng	꜁jin	꜁nang	꜁yăn
不	puh,	pu’	pu,	peh,	peh,	pòk,	pút,	pút,	păt,
知	꜀chi	꜀ch’	꜀tsz’	꜀ts	꜀ch’	꜀ti	꜀ti	chai’	꜀chi
孝	hiao’	hʻiao’	hiao’	hio’	hiao’	hau’	hau’	hau^{2}	hao’
父	fu’	fu’	fu’	vu’	vu’	hò^{2}	hu^{2}	pé^{2}	fu^{2}
母	‘mu	‘mu	‘mung	‘mu	‘méu	‘mu	‘bo	‘bò	‘mò
獨	tuh,	꜁tu	teu,	tòk,	doh,	túk,	tòk$_{2}$	tok$_{2}$	tòk,
不	puh,	pu’	pu,	peh,	peh,	pòk,	pút,	pút,	păt,
思	꜀sz’	꜀sz’	꜀sz’	꜀sz	꜀sz’	꜀sü	꜀su	sù’	꜀sz’
父	fu’	fu’	fu’	vu’	vu’	hò^{2}	hu^{2}	pé^{2}	fu^{2}
母	‘mu	‘mu	‘mung	‘mu	‘méu	‘mu	‘bo	‘bò	‘mò
愛	ngai’	ai’	ngai’	é’	ai’	ai’	ai’	a^{n}i^{2}	oi’
子	‘tsz’	‘tsz’	‘tsz’	‘ts	‘tsz’	‘chü	‘chu	‘chŭ	‘tsz’
之	꜀chi	꜀ch’	꜀tsz’	꜀ts	꜀tsz’	꜀chi	꜀chi	꜀chù	꜀chi
心	꜀sin	꜀sin	꜀hin	꜀sing	꜀sin	꜀síng	꜀sím	꜀sim	꜀săm
乎	꜀hu	꜀hu	꜀hu	꜀u	꜀wu	꜁hu	꜁ho	꜀hu	꜁u
方	꜀fang	꜀fang	꜀fang	꜀fong	꜀fong	꜀hwòng	꜀hong	hwang’	꜀fong
其	꜁kʻi	꜁chʻi	꜁chʻi	꜁ji	꜁djʻi	꜁ki	꜁ki	꜁kʻi	꜁kʻi
未	wéi’	wéi’	wéi’	vi’	vi’	é^{2}	bi^{2}	bué’	mi^{2}
離	꜁li	꜁li	꜁li	꜁li	꜁li	lié^{2}	li^{2}	꜁li	li’
懷	꜁hwai	꜁hwai	꜁hwai	꜁wé	꜁wé	꜁hwai	꜁hwai	꜁hwai	꜁wai
抱	pao’	pao’	pʻao’	po’	bao’	po^{2}	pʻau^{2}	pʻo	‘pʻò
饑	꜀ki	꜀chi	꜀ki	꜀ki	꜀dji	꜀ki	꜀ki	꜀ki	꜀kï
不	puh,	pu’	pu,	peh,	peh,	pòk,	put.	pút,	păt,
能	꜁năng	꜁năng	꜁lăn	꜁năng	꜀năng	꜁néng	꜁leng	꜁neng	꜁năng

	MANDARIN.	PEKING.	HANKOW.	SHANGHAI.	NINGPO.	FUHCHAU.	AMOY.	SWATOW.	CANTON.
自	tsz’’	tsz’’	tsz’’	z’	sz’’	chùü^{2}	chu^{2}	chù^{2}	tsz’^{2}
哺	‘pu	‘pu	pu’	‘pu	‘bu	pwò^{2}	po^{2}	‘pu	꜀pò
寒	꜁han	꜁han	꜁han	꜁hö^{n}	꜁bè^{n}	꜁hang	꜁han	꜁han	꜁hon
不	puh,	pu’	pu,	peh,	peh,	pòk,	pút,	pút,	pat,
能	꜁nǎng	꜁nǎng	꜀lǎn	꜁nǎng	꜀nǎng	꜁néng	꜁leng	꜁neng	꜁nǎng
自	tsz’’	tsz’’	tsz’’	z’	sz’’	chùü^{2}	chu’	chù^{2}	tsz’^{2}
衣	꜀i	꜀i	꜀i	꜀i	꜀i	é’	i’	i’	i’
爲	꜁wéi	꜁wéi	꜁wéi	꜁wé	꜁wé	꜁ui	꜁úi	꜁úi	꜁wei
父	fu’	fu’	fu’	vu’	vu’	hò^{2}	hu^{2}	pé^{2}	fu^{2}
母	‘mu	‘mu	‘mung	‘mu	‘méu	‘mu	‘bo	‘bò	‘mò
者	‘ché	‘chö	‘tsé	‘tsé	‘tsié	‘chia	‘chia	‘chia	‘ché
審	‘shǎn	‘shǎn	‘sǎn	‘sǎng	‘sing	‘síng	‘sím	‘sím	‘shǎm
音	꜀yin	꜀yin	꜀yin	꜀yǎng	꜀ing	꜀íng	꜀ím	꜀ím	꜀yǎm
聲	꜀shing	꜀shǎng	꜀sǎn	꜀sǎng	꜀sing	꜀síng	꜀seng	s^{n}ia’	꜀shing
察	chʻah,	꜁chʻa	tsʻa,	tsʻah,	tsʻah,	chʻak,	tsʻat,	chʻat,	chʻat,
形	꜁hing	꜁hʻing	꜁hin	꜀yǎng	꜁ying	꜁híng	꜁heng	꜁heng	꜁ying
色	seh,	seh’	sé,	sǎh,	seh,	saik,	sek,	sek,	shik,
笑	siao’	siao’	hiao’	sio’	‘siao	chʻiu’	siau’	chʻié	siu’
則	tseh,	꜁tsö	tsé,	tsǎh,	tseh,	chaik,	chek,	chek,	tsǎk,
爲	wéi’	wéi’	wéi’	‘wé’	wé’	꜁úi	꜁úi	꜁úi	꜁wei
之	꜀chi	꜀ch’	꜀tsz’	꜀ts	꜀tsz’	꜀chi	꜀chi	꜀chù	꜀chi
喜	‘hi	‘hʻi	‘hi	‘hi	‘hʻi	‘hi	‘hi	‘hi	‘hi
啼	꜁tʻi	꜁tʻi	꜁ti	꜁di	꜁di	꜁tʻè	꜁tʻé	꜁tʻi	꜁tʻei
則	tseh,	꜁tsö	tsé,	tsǎh,	tseh,	chaik,	chek,	chek,	tsak,
爲	wéi’	wéi’	꜁wéi	‘wé’	wé’	꜁úi	꜁úi	꜁úi	꜁wei
之	꜀chi	꜀ch’	꜀tsz’	꜀ts	꜀tsz’	꜀chi	꜀chi	꜀chù	꜀chi
憂	꜀yiu	꜀yiu	꜀yù	꜀yù	꜀iu	꜀iu	꜀iu	꜀iu	꜀yau
行	꜁hing	꜁hʻing	꜁hin	꜁yǎng	꜁hang	꜁héng	꜁heng	꜁k^{n}ia	꜁hǎng
動	tung’	tung’	tung’	‘dung	dung’	tòng^{2}	tong^{2}	tong^{2}	tung^{2}
則	tseh,	꜀tsö	tsé,	tsǎh,	tseh,	chaik,	chek,	chek,	tsǎk,
跬	꜁kwʻéi	꜀kwʻéi	‘kwʻéi	꜀kwʻé	꜀kwo	꜀kié	‘chi	꜀wa	‘kwʻei
步	pu’	pu’	pu’	pu’	bu’	pwò^{2}	po^{2}	pò’	pò^{2}
不	puh,	pu’	pu,	peh,	peh,	pòk,	pút,	pút,	pat,
離	꜀li	꜁li	꜁li	꜁li	꜀li	꜁lié	li^{2}	꜁li	꜁li
疾	tsih,	tsi’	ki,	dsih,	dsih,	chík,	chek$_{2}$	chit$_{2}$	tsǎt,
痛	tʻung’	tʻung’	tʻung’	tʻung’	tʻung’	tʻòng’	tʻong’	tʻ^{n}ia’	tʻung’
則	tseh,	꜁tsö	tsé,	tsǎh,	tseh,	chaik,	chek,	chek,	tsǎk,
寢	‘tsʻin	‘tsʻin	‘chʻin	‘tsʻing	‘tsʻíng	‘chʻíng	‘chʻím	‘chʻim	‘tsʻǎm
食	shih,	꜁shih	sz’,	zǒk,	sih,	sík,	sit$_{2}$	chia$_{2}$	shik,
俱	꜀kü	꜀chü	꜀kü	꜀kü	꜀chü	kùü^{2}	ku^{2}	ku^{2}	꜀kü

	MANDARIN.	PEKING.	HANKOW.	SHANGHAI.	NINGPO.	FUHCHAU.	AMOY.	SWATOW.	CANTON.
廢	féiʾ	féiʾ	féiʾ	fíʾ	fiʾ	hiéʾ	hoéʾ	kúi^2	feiʾ
以	ʿi	ʿi	ʿi	ʿí	ʿi	ʿi	ʿi	ʿi^n	ʿi
養	ʿyang	ʿyang	ʿyang	ʿyang	ʿyang	ʿyòng	ʿyong	ʿyang	ʿyéung
以	ʿi	ʿi	ʿi	ʿi	ʿi	ʿi	ʿi	ʿi^n	ʿi
教	kiaoʾ	chiaoʾ	kiaoʾ	kioʾ	kiaoʾ	kauʾ	kauʾ	ka^2	kaoʾ
至	chiʾ	chʾʾ	tszʾʾ	tsʾ	tszʾʾ	chéʾ	chiʾ	chi^2	chiʾ
於	꜁yü	꜁yü	꜁ü	꜁ü	꜀ü	꜀ü	꜁u	iʾ	꜀ü
成	꜁chʿing	꜁chʿăng	꜁tsʿăn	꜁zăng	꜁dzing	꜁síng	꜁seng	꜁seng	꜁shing
人	꜀jăn	꜁jăn	꜁lăn	꜀niăng	꜀jăn	꜁ʹng	꜁jin	꜁jin	꜁yăn
復	fuh,	꜁fu	fu,	vòk,	vauh,	húk$_2$	hiuʾ	꜁h^{n}iu	fòk$_2$
爲	wéiʾ	wéiʾ	꜁wéi	wéʾ	wéʾ	꜁úi	꜁úi	꜁úi	꜁wei
授	sheuʾ	sheuʾ	sùʾ	dzùʾ	siuʾ	séu^2	siu^2	siu^2	shau^2
家	꜀kia	꜀chia	꜀kia	꜀kia	꜀chio	꜀ka	꜀ka	꜀kia	꜀ka
室	shih,	shihʾ	szʾ,	săk,	sheh,	sék,	sek,	sit,	shăt,
謀	꜀meu	꜁meu	꜁mù	꜀mù	꜁meu	꜁méu	꜁bo	mongʾ	꜁mau
生	꜀shăng	꜀shăng	꜀săn	꜀săng	꜀săng	꜀seng	꜀seng	꜀s^{n}é	꜀shăng
理	ʿli	ʿli	ʿli	ʿli	ʿli	ʿli	ʿli	ʿli	ʿli
百	poh,	ʿpai	pé,	pak,	pah,	paik,	pek,	pé,	pak,
計	kiʾ	chiʾ	kiʾ	kiʾ	kiʾ	kiéʾ	kéʾ	koi^2	keiʾ
經	꜀king	꜀ching	꜀kin	꜀kiăng	꜀kying	꜀kíng	꜀keng	꜀keng	꜀king
營	꜁ying	꜁ying	꜁yin	꜀yăng	꜁ying	꜁ʹng	꜁eng	꜁yong	꜁ying
心	꜀sin	꜀sin	꜀hin	꜀sing	꜀sin	꜁síng	꜀sím	꜀sím	꜀săm
力	lih,	liʾ	li,	lih,	lih,	lik$_2$	lek$_2$	lat$_2$	lik$_2$
俱	꜀kü	꜀chü	꜀kü	꜀kü	꜀chü	kùü^2	ku^2	ku^2	꜀kü
瘁	tsʿuiʾ	tsʿuiʾ	tsʿuiʾ	dzüéʾ	zéʾ	choi^2	chui^2	chʿui	sui^2
父	fuʾ	fuʾ	fuʾ	vuʾ	vuʾ	bò^2	hu^2	pé^2	fu^2
母	ʿmu	ʿmu	ʿmung	ʿmu	ʿméu	ʿmu	ʿbò	ʿbò	ʿmò
之	꜀chi	꜀chʾ	꜀tszʾ	꜀ts	꜀tszʾ	꜀chi	꜀chi	꜀chù	꜀chi
德	teh,	꜁tö	té,	tăh,	teh,	taik,	tek,	tek,	tăk,
實	shih,	shiʾ	szʾ,	zeh,	shih,	sík,	sit,	sit$_2$	shăt,
同	꜀tʿung	꜁tʿung	꜁tʿung	꜁dung	꜁dung	꜁tung	꜁tong	꜁tang	꜁tʿung
昊	haoʾ	haoʾ	ʿhao	ʿo	haoʾ	ho^2	hò^2	꜀hau	hao^2
天	꜀tʿien	꜀tʿien	꜀tʿien	꜀tʿí^n	꜀tʿí^n	꜀tʿiĕng	꜀tʿien	꜁tʿien	꜀tʿín
罔	ʿwang	ʿwang	ʿwang	ʿvong	ʿvong	ʿwòng	ʿbong	ʿbwang	ʿmong
極	kih,	꜁chih	ki,	jăk,	kieh,	kik$_2$	kek$_2$	kek$_2$	kik$_2$
人	꜀jăn	꜁jăn	꜁lăn	꜀niăng	꜀jăn	꜁ʹng	꜁jin	꜁nang	꜁yăn
子	ʿtszʾ	ʿtszʾ	ʿtszʾ	ʿts	ʿtszʾ	ʿchü	ʿchu	ʿchù	ʿtszʾ
欲	yuh,	꜁yü	yù,	yòk,	yoh,	ük$_2$	yok$_2$	auï^2	yòk$_2$
報	paoʾ	paoʾ	paoʾ	poʾ	paoʾ	poʾ	pòʾ	pò^2	pòʾ
親	꜀tsʿin	꜀tsʿin	꜀chʿin	꜀tsʿing	꜀tsʿin	꜀chʿíng	꜀chʿin	chʿin	꜀tsʿăn

	MANDARIN.	PEKING.	HANKOW.	SHANGHAI.	NINGPO.	FUHCHAU.	AMOY.	SWATOW.	CANTON.
恩	꜀ngăn	꜀ngăn	꜀ngăn	꜀ăng	꜀ăn	꜀òng	꜀ùn	ùn꜄	꜀yăn
于	꜀yü	꜀yü	꜁ü	꜀ü	꜀ü	꜀ü	꜁u	꜀i	꜀ü
萬	wan꜄	wan꜄	wan꜄	mèn꜄	vèn꜄	wang꜅	ban꜅	꜀bwan	man꜅
一	yih꜆	꜀yih	i꜆	ih꜆	yih꜆	ék꜆	it꜆	chek꜆	yăt꜆
自	tsz’꜄	tsz’꜄	tsz’꜄	z꜄	tsz’꜄	chùü꜅	chu꜅	chù꜅	tsz’꜅
當	꜀tang	꜀tang	꜀tang	꜀tong	꜀tong	꜀tòng	꜀tong	꜀tung	꜀tong
內	néi꜄	néi꜄	léi꜄	né꜄	né꜄	noi꜅	loé꜅	lai꜅	noi꜅
盡	tsin꜄	tsin꜄	kin꜄	dzing꜄	zing꜄	chéng꜅	chín꜅	chín꜅	tsun꜅
其	꜁kʻi	꜁chʻi	꜁chʻi	꜁ji	꜁djʻi	꜁ki	꜁ki	꜁kʻi	꜁kʻi
心	꜀sin	꜀sin	꜀hin	꜀sing	꜀sin	꜀sing	꜀sím	꜀sím	꜀sam
外	wai꜄	wai꜄	wai꜄	nga꜄	wé꜄	ngwoi꜅	goé꜅	꜂gwa	ngoi꜅
竭	kieh꜆	꜁chié	kʻié꜆	jih꜆	djìeh꜆	kiek꜇	kiet꜇	kiet꜇	kʻít꜆
其	꜁kʻi	꜁chʻi	꜁chʻi	꜁ji	꜁djʻi	꜁ki	꜁ki	꜁kʻi	꜁kʻi
力	꜃lih꜆	li꜄	li꜆	lih꜆	lih꜆	lík꜇	lek꜇	lat꜇	lik꜇
謹	꜂kin	꜂chin	꜂kin	kiăng꜄	꜃king	꜃kíng	꜂kín	꜃kùn	꜃kăn
身	꜀shăn	꜀shăn	꜀săn	꜀săng	꜀sing	꜀síng	꜀sín	꜀sín	꜀shăn
節	tsieh꜆	꜁tsié	kié꜆	tsih꜆	tsih꜆	chièk꜆	chièt꜆	chat꜆	tsít꜆
用	yung꜄	yung꜄	yung꜄	yung꜄	yung꜄	ùüng꜅	yong꜅	eng꜄	yung꜅
以	꜂i	꜂i	꜂i	꜂i	꜃i	꜃i	꜂i	꜃i^{n}	꜃i
勤	꜁kʻin	꜁chʻin	꜁chʻin	꜀kiăng	꜁djing	꜁kʻüng	꜁kʻùn	꜁kʻùn	꜁kʻăn
服	fuh꜆	꜁fu	fu꜆	vòk꜆	voh꜆	húk꜇	hòk꜇	hok꜇	fòk꜇
勞	꜁lao	꜁lao	꜁lao	꜀lo	꜁lao	꜁lo	꜁lò	꜁lau	꜁lò
以	꜂i	꜂i	꜂i	꜃i	꜃i	꜃i	꜃i	꜃i^{n}	꜃i
隆	꜀lung	꜀lung	꜁lung	꜀lung	꜀lung	꜁lüng	꜁liong	꜁long	꜁lung
孝	hiao꜄	hʻiao꜄	hiao꜄	hio꜄	hʻiao꜄	hau꜄	hau꜄	hau꜄	hao꜄
養	꜂yang	꜂yang	꜂yang	꜃yang	꜃yang	yòng꜅	꜂yóng	꜂yang	yéung꜅
毋	꜀wu	꜁wu	꜁wu	꜀vu	꜁vu	꜁u	꜁bu	꜁bò	꜁mò
博	poh꜆	poh꜄	po꜆	pòk꜆	poh꜆	pauk꜆	pʻòk꜆	pak꜆	pok꜆
奕	yih꜆	yi꜄	i꜆	yăh꜆	yih꜆	ík꜇	ek꜇	ek꜇	yik꜇
飲	꜂yin	꜂yin	꜂yin	꜃yăng	꜂ying	꜃íng	꜂ím	꜂ím	꜂yăm
酒	꜂tsiu	tsiu	꜃kiu	꜃tsiù	꜂tsiu	꜂chíu	꜂chiu	꜂chiu	꜃tsau
毋	꜀wu	꜁wu	꜁wu	꜀vu	꜁vu	꜁u	꜁bu	꜁bò	꜁mò
好	hao꜄	hao꜄	hao꜄	ho꜄	hao꜄	ho꜄	ho^{n}꜄	hau꜅	hò꜄
勇	꜂yung	꜂yung	꜂yung	꜂yung	꜂yung	꜂üng	꜂yong	꜂yong	꜂yung
鬬	teu꜄	teu꜄	tù	dù꜄	teu꜄	tsiú꜄	tò꜄	tò꜅	tau꜄
很	꜂hăn	꜂hăn	꜂hăn	꜃hăng	꜃hăn	꜂kʻòng	꜂hún	꜃hùn	꜃hăn
毋	꜀wu	꜁wu	꜁wu	꜀vu	꜁vu	꜁u	꜁bu	꜁bò	꜁mò
好	hao꜄	hao꜄	hao꜄	ho꜄	hao꜄	ho꜄	ho^{n}꜄	hau꜅	hò꜄
貨	hwo꜄	hwo꜄	ho꜄	hu꜄	heu꜄	hwò꜄	ho^{n}꜄	hué꜅	fo꜄
財	꜁tsʻai	꜁tsʻai	꜁tsʻai	꜁zé	꜁dzé	꜁chai	꜁tsai	꜁chʻai	꜁tsʻoi

	MANDARIN.	PEKING.	HANKOW.	SHANGHAI.	NINGPO.	FUHCHAU.	AMOY.	SWATOW.	CANTON.
私	꜀sz	꜀sz’	꜀sz’	꜀sz’	꜀sz’	꜀sü	꜀su	sai’	꜀sz’
妻	꜀tsʻi	tsʻi	꜀chʻi	꜀tsʻi	꜀tsʻi	꜀chʻè	꜀chʻé	꜀chʻi	꜀tsʻai
子	꜂tsz’	꜂tsz’	꜂tsz’	꜂ts	꜂tsz	꜂chü	꜂tsu	꜂chù	꜂tsz’
縱	꜂tsung	꜂tsung	tsung’	tsung’	꜂tsung	chùüng’	chiong’	chong^{2}	tsung’
使	꜂shi	꜂sh’	꜂sz’	꜂sz	꜂sz’	꜂sü	꜂su	꜂sai	꜂shei
儀	꜁i	꜁i	꜁i	꜁i	꜁ni	꜁ngi	꜁gi	꜁ngi	꜁i
文	꜁wăn	꜁wăn	꜁wăn	꜁văng	꜁văn	꜁ung	꜁bún	꜁bún	꜁măn
未	wéi’	wéi	wéi’	vi’	vi’	é^{2}	bi^{2}	꜀bué	mi^{2}
備	pi’	pi’	péi’	bé’	bé’	pé^{2}	pi^{2}	pi^{2}	pi^{2}
而	꜁’rh	꜁’rh	꜁’rh	꜀’rh	꜀’rh	꜁i	꜁ji	꜁jù	꜁i
誠	꜁chʻing	꜁chʻăng	꜁tsʻăn	꜀dzăng	꜁dzing	꜁síng	꜁seng	꜁seng	꜁shing
慤	kʻioh꜆	chʻüé’	chʻio꜆	chièk꜆	chʻoh꜆	kʻauk꜆	kʻak꜆	kok꜆	kʻéuk꜆
有	꜂yiu	꜂yiu	꜂yù	꜂yù	꜂yiu	꜂iu	꜂iu	u^{2}	꜂yau
餘	꜁yü	꜁yü	꜁ü	꜁ü	꜁ü	꜁ü	꜁u	꜁ù	꜁ü
推	꜀tʻui	꜀tʻui	꜀tʻéi	꜀tsüé	꜀tʻé	꜀chwʻi	꜀tsʻui	꜀chʻiu	꜀tʻúi
而	꜁’rh	꜁’rh	꜁’rh	꜀’rh	꜁’rh	꜁i	꜁ji	꜁jù	꜁i
廣	꜂kwang	꜂kwang	꜂kwang	꜂kwong	꜂kwong	꜂kwòng	꜂kong	꜂kwang	꜂kwong
之	꜀chi	꜀ch’	꜀tsz’	꜀ts	꜀tsz’	꜀chi	꜀chi	꜀chù	꜀chi
如	꜁jü	꜁zhu	꜁ü	꜁zü	꜁zh’	꜁ü	꜁ju	꜁ju	꜁ü
曾	꜀tsăng	꜀tsăng	꜀tsăn	꜀tsăng	꜀tsăng	꜀chéng	꜀cheng	꜀cheng	꜀tsăng
子	꜂tsz’	꜂tsz’	꜂tsz’	꜂ts	꜂tsz’	꜂chü	꜂tsu	꜂chù	꜂tsz’
所	꜂su	so’	꜂so	꜂su	꜂so	꜂su	꜂sò	꜂sò	꜂sho
謂	wéi’	wéi’	wéi’	wé’	wé’	oi^{2}	úi^{2}	úi^{2}	wei^{2}
居	꜀kü	꜀chü	꜀kü	꜀kü	꜀chü	꜀kü	꜀ku	꜀kù	꜀kü
處	꜂chʻü	꜂chʻü	꜂tsʻu	꜂tsʻü	꜂ch’	꜂chʻü	꜂tsʻu	꜂chʻu	꜂chʻü
不	puh꜆	pu’	pu꜆	peh꜆	peh꜆	pòk꜆	pút꜆	pút꜆	păt꜆
莊	꜀chwang	꜀chwang	꜀tswang	꜀tsong	꜀tsong	꜀chòng	꜀tsong	chang’	꜀chong
非	꜀féi	꜀fé	꜀féi	꜀fi	꜀fi	꜀hi	꜀húi	꜀húi	꜀fi
孝	hiao’	hʻiao’	hiao’	hio’	hʻiao’	hau’	hau’	hau^{2}	hao’
事	shi’	sh’’	sz’’	zs’	zz’’	sùü^{2}	su^{2}	sù^{2}	sz’^{2}
君	꜀kiün	꜀chiün	꜀kiün	꜀kiün	꜀kiün	꜀kung	꜀kún	꜀kún	꜀kwăn
不	puh꜆	pu’	pu꜆	peh꜆	peh꜆	pòk꜆	pút꜆	pút꜆	păt꜆
忠	꜀chung	꜀chung	꜀tsung	꜀tsung	꜀chung	꜀tüng	꜀tiong	꜀tong	꜀chung
非	꜀féi	꜀fé	꜀féi	꜀fi	꜀fi	꜀hi	꜀húi	꜀húi	꜀fi
孝	hiao’	hʻiao’	hiao’	hio’	hʻiao’	hau’	hau’	hau^{2}	hao’
涖	li’	li’	li’	li’	li’	lé^{2}	li^{2}	꜁li	li^{2}
官	꜀kwan	꜀kwan	꜀kwan	꜀kwé^{n}	꜀kwú^{n}	꜀kwang	꜀kwan	꜀kw^{n}a	꜀kún
不	puh꜆	pu’	pu꜆	peh꜆	peh꜆	pòk꜆	pút꜆	pút꜆	păt꜆
敬	king’	ching’	kin’	kiăng’	kying’	keng’	keng’	keng^{2}	king’
非	꜀féi	꜀fé	꜀féi	꜀fi	꜀fi	꜀hi	꜀húi	꜀húi	꜀fi

	MANDARIN.	PEKING.	HANKOW.	SHANGHAI.	NINGPO.	FUHCHAU.	AMOY.	SWATOW.	CANTON.
孝	hiaoʾ	hʻiaoʾ	hiaoʾ	hioʾ	hʻiaoʾ	hauʾ	hauʾ	hau^{2}	haoʾ
朋	꜀pʻăng	꜀pʻăng	꜀pung	ˏbăng	꜀bàn	꜀peng	꜀peng	꜀pʻeng	꜀pʻăng
友	ʻyiu	ʻyiu	ʻyù	ʻyù	ʻyiu	ʻiu	ʻiu	ʻiu	ʻyau
不	puhˎ	puʾ	puˎ	pehˎ	pehˎ	pòkˎ	pútˎ	pútˎ	pătˎ
信	sinʾ	sinʾ	hinʾ	singʾ	sing	sengʾ	sínʾ	sín^{2}	sunʾ
非	ˏféi	ˏfé	ˏféi	ˏfi	ˏfi	ˏhi	ˏhúi	ˏhúi	ˏfi
孝	hiàoʾ	hʻiaoʾ	hiaoʾ	hioʾ	hʻiaoʾ	hauʾ	hauʾ	hauʾ.	haoʾ
戰	chenʾ	chanʾ	tsanʾ	tsèⁿ·	tsíⁿʾ	chiéngʾ	chienʾ	chùn^{2}	chín^{2}
陣	chʻănʾ	chʻănʾ	tsănʾ	dzăngʾ	dzingʾ	teng^{2}	tin^{2}	tinʾ	chăn^{2}
無	꜀wu	꜀wu	꜀wu	꜀vu	꜀vu	꜀u	꜀bu	꜀bò	꜀mò
勇	ʻyung	ʻyung	ʻyung	ʻyung	ʻyung	ʻüng	ʻyong	ʻyong	ʻyung
非	ˏféi	ˏfé	ˏféi	ˏfi	ˏfi	ˏhi	ˏhúi	ˏhúi	ˏfi
孝	hiaoʾ	hʻiaoʾ	hiaoʾ	hioʾ	hʻiaoʾ	hauʾ	hauʾ	hau^{2}	haoʾ
皆	ˏkiai	ˏchié	ˏkai	ˏkia	ˏkié	ˏkai	ˏkai	ˏkai	ˏkai
孝	hiaoʾ	hʻiaoʾ	hiaoʾ	hioʾ	hʻiaoʾ	hauʾ	hauʾ	hau^{2}	haoʾ
子	ʻtszʼ	ʻtszʼ	ʻtszʼ	ʻts	ʻtszʼ	ʻchü	ʻtsu	ʻchù	ʻtszʼ
分	fănʾ	făn	fănʾ	văngʾ	vănʾ	hòng^{2}	hún^{2}	ˏhun	ʻfăn
內	néiʾ	néiʾ	léiʾ	néʾ	néʾ	noi^{2}	lọé^{2}	lai^{2}	noi^{2}
之	ˏchi	ˏchʼ	ˏtszʼ	ˏts	ˏtszʼ	ˏchi	ˏchi	ˏchù	ˏchi
事	shiʾ	shʼ	szʼʾ	ˏszʾ	zzʼʾ	sùü^{2}	su^{2}	sù^{2}	szʼ^{2}
也	ʻyé	yé	ʻyé	ʻa	ʻyé	yaʾ	ʻya	ʻya	yaʾ

TRANSLATION OF THE ABOVE EXTRACT.

Now filial piety is a statute of heaven, a principle of earth, and an obligation of mankind. Do you, who are void of filial piety, ever reflect on the natural affection of parents for their children? Even before you left the maternal bosom, if hungry, you could not have fed yourselves; or if cold, you could not have put on your own clothes. A father or a mother judge by the voice, or look at the features of their children, whose smiles make them joyful, or whose weeping excites their grief. When trying to walk, they leave not their steps; and when sick or in pain, they can neither sleep nor eat in comfort, in order that they may nurture and teach them. When [their children] reach man's estate, they see to their marriage, and scheme for their livelihood by a hundred plans, in which they weary their minds and spend their strength. Parental virtue is truly as limitless as high heaven!

A man who desires to recompense one in a myriad of the loving acts of his parents, must really devote to them his whole heart at home, and exert all his strength abroad. He must care well for his body and be frugal in his expenses, in order that he may diligently labor for them. To enable him to fully and filially nurture them, he must neither gamble nor get drunk, he must neither love to quarrel, nor desire to hoard wealth for the use of his wife and children. Though his manners and accomplishments may be defective, yet his heart must, at any rate, be thoroughly sincere.

Let us enlarge a little on this principle. Tsăngtsz' speaks thus respecting it:—"It is unfilial to move and act without dignity; it is unfilial to serve one's prince disloyally; it is unfilial to fill an office without reverential care; it is unfilial to act insincerely towards a friend; [and finally], to turn a coward in battle is unfilial." All these things are involved in the duty of a filial son

The same extract from the Sacred Commands has been written out in the colloquial of the same dialects, except that of the Amoy; but the example given in the Swatow will serve somewhat to illustrate it. The teachers at Amoy declared themselves unable to write their colloquial intelligibly. The colloquial characters used in one dialect are not of course understood elsewhere, for the reason that they are sounded differently, and none of them would be used by an educated native anywhere in writing even a common letter. It is, however, a difference in degree only in the Chinese, and not in kind, from what is the case in every cultivated language in the world, and its great extent is owing mostly to the peculiar nature of this written language.

The differences between the style called **文理** or book style, and **俗話** or colloquial in Chinese are not easily described; but these seven examples will help the student to perceive them, and mark the alterations good written Chinese undergoes when it is spoken in the local patois. Only in the first two columns, containing examples from Peking and Hankow, are all the characters used in their proper signification. The variety of words exhibited in these examples, is not so great as a portion of some other work would have been;—the **千字文** or Millenary Classic for instance; but this popular essay on Filial Piety suits the spirit of the colloquial better, and the benefits of this comparison do not depend on the range of sounds.

COLLOQUIAL FORM OF THE EXTRACT IN SEVEN DIALECTS.

TEXT	京 PEKING	漢 HANK.	滬 SHANG.	寧 NINGPO	福 FUHCH.	汕 SW'TAU	廣 CANTON
夫孝者天之經地之義民之行也人不	那孝是什麼就是天上的常道地上的定理人間所應當奉行的呵人若不	這個孝是天地間常存的道理百姓們頂大的德行人不	講到孝末是天个常經地个道義人个好行爲也人若然勿	這孝順个道理是天个綱常地个道義人个行爲一个人弗	孝順是天其大經地其至義仈仈其根本仈㑚賣	大凡行孝個事天理之常人情之正百姓之行爲也做子不	個的孝道乃係天嘅常經地嘅定理人嘅德行呀世人唔

TEXT	京 PEKING	漢 HANK.	滬 SHANG.	寧 NINGPO	福 FUHCH.	汕 SW'TAU	廣 CANTON
知孝父母獨不思父母愛子之心乎方	曉得孝順父母先不用講別的獨不想一想父毋疼愛兒子的心腸麼當	曉得孝順爹娘不是單把爹娘疼愛兒子的心腸沒有想嗎	曉得孝順爺娘啥勿想到爺娘愛妮子个心腸呀比方纔起始	曉的孝順大人也弗忖忖大人愛惜兒子个心嗎	曉的孝順罷奶都伓想做罷奶愛仔其心是生箬樣呢當	曉行孝爹娘做年不想着爹娘惜子兒個心性乎許	知孝敬父母獨唔想吓父母愛仔個點心咩當

TEXT	京 PEKING	漢 HANK.	滬 SHANG.	寧 NINGPO	福 FUHCH.	汕 SW'TAU	廣 CANTON
其未離懷抱饑不能自哺寒不能自衣爲父母者察音聲	他沒有離開父母懷抱的時候餓了自己不能吃冷了自己不能穿作父母的揣度他的聲音	小娒們沒有離開懷抱的時候餓了不會自己吃飯冷了不會自己穿衣做爹娘的過細聽兒子的聲音	小干勿曾離開手裏抱拉胸膛頭个辰光肚裏餓之末自家勿會去吃身上冷之末自家勿會去着做爺娘个末聽聽伊个聲音	其在抱手个時候肚飢兒自叉弗會吃冷兒自叉弗會穿做大人个聽其聲音	仔手上抱時候腹老饑自家賣儈天寒自家賣穿藉罷奶查察聲音	幼時未放開胸前抱在手時肚困儹得交己食身寒儹得交己穿做爹娘個人聽子個音語聲說	佢未曾離開襟懷保抱個時肚餓唔噲自己揾食身冷唔噲自己揾著做父母嘅聽佢聲音

TEXT	京 PEKING	漢 HANK.	滬 SHANG.	寧 NINGPO	福 FUHCH.	汕 SW'TAU	廣 CANTON
察形色笑則爲之喜啼則爲之憂行動則跬步不離疾痛則	察看他的氣色他若嬉笑就爲他歡喜他若啼哭就爲他愁煩他一行走就連半步也不肯離開他有病痛就	過細看兒子的臉色或是笑就喜懽或是哭就憂愁或是走動就一步的不肯離開或是病痛	看看伊个面色笑之末就快活哭之末就憂愁走走末寸步當心生之病末爺娘	看其相貌若是笑兒大人就歡喜起來若是叫兒大人就弗爽快會走个時候大人步步跟着其有病个時候大人	辨別形色儺笑罷奶就歡喜㑚啼罷奶就苦行止舉動步步罷奶毛離身邊務喇心苦病疼罷奶	看子個様相歡喜就兒子懽喜啼哭就兒子煩惱行走舉動爹娘脚步不敢行開病痛爹娘	睇佢形像面色笑就替佢歡喜喊就替佢最慮初學行就寸步唔敢離開有病痛就

TEXT	京 PEKING	漢 HANK.	滬 SHANG.	寧 NINGPO	福 FUHCH.	汕 SW'TAU	廣 CANTON
寢食俱廢以養以教至于成人復爲授家室謀生理	連睡覺吃飯也都廢掉從他小時候就拿衣食養活他拿詩書教訓他直到他長大成人的時候又給他娶媳婦謀事業	睡同吃都丢了一路養活他教訓他到了成人還要替他配親謀個養生的方法	睏也睏勿着吃也吃勿落養活伊咾教訓伊直到大要討娘子拉伊謀生意拉伊	日弗安夜弗眠養其教其到拉成人長大又替其娶一房家小謀一行事業	飡伓像飡困伓像困哺伊伺候伊至成人長大仅着替伊討親拍算做生意	⿰口鬱食全儨用飯飼大用規矩教示到能得偺就做人再該伊母子嬷致房室尋事業	唔瞓得唔食得一自養一自教至到長大成人個時又替佢娶妻子謀生意
百計經營心力俱瘁父母之德實同昊天罔極人子	千方百計替他打算把心機氣力都用得勞困這樣看來父母的恩典實在如同那廣大的天無窮無盡了爲人子的	百般的打算安排心也想碎了力也用盡了爹娘的恩典實在像天一樣沒有極處做兒子的	千方百計廢盡心機想想爹娘个恩典大來像天能做妮子个	百樣打算費了多少心機用了多少氣力大人个恩惠寔在像天介大兒子	成百樣苦心廢盡箬価心力罷奶其德實在比天故大做仔伲	百樣計算思想心事磨力全抨艱苦爹娘個功勞眞親像大天無底止做人個子	百樣計較打算心共力都孜倦咯父母嘅恩德眞係同理至大嘅天咁無窮盡噃做人仔嘅

TEXT	京 PEKING	漢 HANK.	滬 SHANG.	寧 NINGPO	福 FUHCH.	汕 SW'TAU	廣 CANTON
欲報親恩於萬一自當內盡其心外竭其力謹身節用	若思想父母的恩典要在萬分裏頭報答一分自然應當裏面盡心志外面竭盡力量又要保守身體省儉用度爲得	要報爹娘的恩典在萬分中的一分自然應該裏面盡心外面竭力身體要謹慎費用要節儉	要報答爺娘个恩典萬分之一自然應該裏向末盡伊个心外面末盡伊个力當心伊身體咾省儉伊个用頭	要想萬分裡頭報其一分自然當該盡心竭力保重自个身體省束自个用度	欲報罷奶其恩內伓通假意外着勉力保身爲重莫花奢務世乇	欲報答爹娘功勞於萬分中行一分交己應該在家盡子個心在外兌苦子個力惜身體儉銀錢	想報答父母恩典萬份之一就應該裏頭盡自己嘅心外便盡自己嘅力謹慎個身減省使用

TEXT	京 PEKING	漢 HANK.	滬 SHANG.	寧 NINGPO	福 FUHCH.	汕 SW'TAU	廣 CANTON
以勤服勞以隆孝養毋博弈飲酒毋好勇鬭狠毋好貨財	是可以勤勤謹謹的服事他可以豐豐盛盛的奉養他不可賭錢下棋喝酒鬧事不可好勇逞強忿怒爭鬥不可貪愛錢財	如此替他們殷勤勞苦好好的孝順養活他們不可賭博喝酒不可行兇打架不可賺積銀錢	認眞服侍伊大大裏孝順咾養伊勿許賭銅錢着棋吃酒勿許愛用氣力同別人相打勿許貪錢財賺來	服事其要勤力供飲其要豐富弗要戲賭吃酒弗要逞勇造孽弗要單貪銅錢銀子	代着替伊勤苦加倍孝敬伊伓通好賭嗜酒伓通藉勇共仈相拍仅伓通私積錢財	應該兌苦代父兄勞力應該滂沛孝敬吃爹娘食不可跋錢着碁食酒不可好抖力相刣相爭不可貪心物件錢財	嚟服事佢買的好飲食孝敬佢唔好賭博飲酒唔好恃勇力打鬭唔好貪財物

TEXT	京 PEKING	漢 HANK.	滬 SHANG.	寧 NINGPO	福 FUHCH.	汕 SW'TAU	廣 CANTON
私妻子縱使儀文未備而誠慤有餘推	偏疼妻子果能這樣卽或外面的禮節稍有不足却是內裏的眞誠已經有餘孝的根本算是立住了從此再推開了	私下把倒妻子用雖然外面的禮貌不齊備確誠實敬意有餘呵推	私底下撥拉娘子就是規矩勿周到咾十分老實末是好第个上推	弗要只顧老婆兒囡如此做法雖即外頭个禮節有點弗到然而裡頭个眞心實在有餘推單	乞姆仔就禮貌不及眞實其心是務再進	私心嬷子雖然是外面禮貌未到足而孝心着實有多多推論到	厚待妻子即使外便禮文唔得齊備但係眞實嘅心有餘剩噉樣推潤

TEXT	京 PEKING	漢 HANK.	滬 SHANG.	寧 NINGPO	福 FUHCH.	汕 SW'TAU	廣 CANTON
而廣之如曾子所謂居處不莊非孝事君不忠非孝	往寬廣裏講這孝道就如曾子所說的平日在家裏住着若不端方穩重的就算不得孝事奉君王若不誠寔盡心的也算不得孝	開了來講像曾子說過的爲人不莊重不是孝服事皇上不忠心不是孝	廣開來恰得曾夫子話歇个話咾坐立勿端正末勿是孝服事皇帝勿忠心勿算孝	開去像曾夫子所話住在屋裡弗守規矩算弗得是孝服事皇上無得忠心算弗得是孝	一層想學曾子所講其在家賣沈靜伓算是孝事君賣忠伓算是孝	曠曠大大個孝道親像姓曾孔子弟子所呾大家做𠱸不正即不是行孝服事王家不盡忠即不是行孝	開嚟好似曾子所講坐立唔端正唔係孝服事人君唔盡心唔係孝

TEXT	京 PEKING	漢 HANK.	滬 SHANG.	寧 NINGPO	福 FUHCH.	汕 SW'TAU	廣 CANTON
蒞官不敬非孝朋友不信非孝戰陣	臨民作官若不小心慎重的也算不得孝交朋友若沒有信實的也算不得孝出兵打仗	做官不小心不是孝結交朋友不信實不是孝打仗	做官勿恭敬勿是孝朋友相交勿老實勿好算孝衝鋒打仗	出仕做官辦事弗敬算弗得是孝朋友來往言而無信算弗得是孝出兵打仗臨陣	做官賣淸怀算是孝朋友賣取信戰陣	做官不敬畏即不是行孝朋友無信實即不是行孝相刣個地場	做官唔謹慎唔係孝交朋友唔信實唔係孝打仗

TEXT	京 PEKING	漢 HANK.	滬 SHANG.	寧 NINGPO	福 FUHCH.	汕 SW'TAU	廣 CANTON
無勇非孝皆孝子分內之事也	若不能奮勇爭先的也算不得孝這所說的都是孝子本分以內的事呵	不奮勇不是孝這都是孝子分內應該做的事	勿上前勿好算孝攏總个話頭禿是孝順个妮子名分裏應該做个事體	退縮算弗得是孝這些都是孝子分內个事干	禮毛胆略都賣算的是孝孝是做仔分內其代就是郎罷	無出力即不是行孝攏總孝道人子本等心內個事也	唔出力唔係孝一的都係孝子本分嘅事呀

SECT. VII.—THE RADICALS.

When a foreigner commences the study of the Chinese written language, the characters appear to be so intricate and senseless, that he is liable to be discouraged at the apparently endless, wearisome task of learning so many unmeaning marks. A further examination, however, discloses both order and use; and although the study is a slow and difficult one, there are methods of prosecuting it so as greatly to reduce the labor. One of these methods is to call to the student's aid as much as possible, the principle of combination which regulates the formation of the mass of characters, and by means of which he can link together form, sound and signification. The knowledge of all these is indispensable to every one who wishes to become a Chinese scholar, and the first point,—form, is that on which he must bestow the most pains.

Early associations invest the symbols of his language with beauty as well as sense to a native, who has never learned any other mode of expressing ideas; and there are no doubt a few points in which the Chinese characters are superior to the alphabetic letters of the West. A foreigner begins by degrees to appreciate their picturesque symbolism, as he becomes familiar with them; and as sight is quicker than sound, ideas conveyed through the eye often flash on his mind with a force and distinctness superior to the slower process of sound. As no grammatical inflections are used, the unaided characters serve as pictures to imprint their meanings on the mind; and fancy helping the memory to store itself with these changing forms, each idea gradually comes to be clothed in its own appropriate embroidery. Associations of this kind between the shape of a character and its meaning, can be greatly developed by special attention, and in time will become a series of links which will facilitate their ready use. The short etymological paragraphs prefixed to many characters in this Dictionary, furnish some material in this respect, and will help the student to remember them.

An examination into the origin and changes in the Chinese characters, an account of their construction, classification, and analysis, with examples of the six styles of writing, and the development or contraction of different words, each and all offer attractive subjects for illustration, and are interesting studies to the antiquarian etymologist. Much has been written upon all these topics by Chinese philologists; and foreigners have elucidated them to some extent. A reference to the works of the latter* is all that is necessary here, and a recommendation to read them carefully. The information there given cannot be repeated here, but it will materially assist the learner of the language.

Every character may be divided, for convenience, into two parts, called the *radical* and the *primitive*. Though native etymologists have not dissected them in this way, the terms serve to distinguish the two portions; and if we except the two thousand radicals and primitives themselves, are applicable to far the largest part of the words in the language. The people never learn their characters by any dissection or classification, but depend upon their constant use to imprint them on the memory, just as we learn our numerals. Few, perhaps none, of their scholars ever learn the radicals by rote, and they are often at a loss to find a word in the dictionary. When the radical is obscure, as in 以, 業 or 卒, they depend on the list of difficult characters given in that work, to point out its proper radical.

The terms *formative*, *determinative* and *key*, have all also been used, because the radicals indicate the general meaning of a large portion of the characters. These names are in some respects more accurate than *radical*, but have not come into general use. Their number has been fixed at 214 for about four centuries; and those who selected them out of the previous collections of 544 and 360, probably deemed it necessary to reduce them to a manageable number. In doing so, the natural order yielded to the artificial, so that a few incongruous groups like those under 亠, 大, 一, 儿, &c., could not be avoided.

The Rev. J. A. Gonçalves, in his *Diccionario China-Portuguez*, further reduced the number to 127, but this diminution has proved to be only an additional labor to all who use that book. His plan also involved an alphabetic arrangement, by which radicals having the same number of strokes, were arranged in a regular sequence. He made the letters, by taking the nine component parts of the character 永, which the Chinese regard as combining in itself all the strokes used in writing, and making them into the following series 丶 一 ㇆ 丿 乙 丨 亅 ㇀ ㇏. Characters having altogether the same number of strokes, are arranged in this system, so that their first stroke is one of these letters. Thus among characters having four strokes, 斗, 夫, 引, 爿, 中, would follow each other in this order. The last three strokes never occurring at the beginning of a character, reduces the whole practically to six letters.

In the *Arte China*, he has classified 1412 of the commonest characters in this manner, adding the radical to each; but the plan nearly breaks down even in this small number, and if extended to the whole language, would prove to be quite impracticable. This ingenious mode of arrangement is perfectly artificial; and in this respect inferior to that by radicals, as it hides the natural grouping which results from using them, and the student loses that important aid to learning the characters.

The native name for radicals is 字部 or Class characters; and a reference to the classified list on page 1153 will show the general groups selected as classes. The student is strongly recommended to commit them, so as to repeat them in their proper order and write them correctly, as the first thing he does. It is not necessary to learn them by their number, any more than it is the letters of an alphabet; but it is well to divide them into groups by the number of their strokes. Mr. Wade sorts them into 137 colloquial, 30 classical, and 47 obsolete radicals;—rather a fanciful division, which has reference chiefly to the very useful exercises he gives to make them familiar; the obsolete ones are nearly the same as those marked with a C in the list on pages 1151—53. A rearrangement of some groups would improve them, no doubt; and a few new radicals, as 丹 *red*, 束 a *faggot*, 桑 *mulberry*, or 枲 *hemp*, might be added; but long usage, and their adop-

---

* Introduction to Morrison's Quarto *Dictionary;* Callery's *Systema Phoneticum*, one of the best works on the subject; Williams' *Easy Lessons in Chinese; Chinese Repository*, vol. iii, p. 14; vol. ix, pp. 518, 587; Rémusat's *Grammaire Chinoise;* Edkins' *China's Place in Philology*.

tion in K'anghi, compels one to take them as they now stand.

It appears from researches into the cuneiform language, that it also possessed something like the Chinese radicals. "Certain classes of words," says Rawlinson, speaking of the language of the Assyrians, "have a sign prefixed or suffixed to them, more commonly the former, by which their general character is indicated. The names of gods, of men, of cities, of tribes, of wild animals, of domestic animals, of metals, of months, of the points of the compass, and of dignities, are thus accompanied. The sign prefixed or suffixed may have originally represented a word, but when used in the way here spoken of, it is believed that it was not sounded, but served simply to indicate to the reader the sort of word which was placed before him. Thus a single perpendicular wedge 𒁹 indicates that the next word will be the name of a man; and a wedge preceded by two horizontal ones ≫𒁹 tells us to expect the appellative of a god; while other more complicated combinations are used in the remaining instances. There are ten or twelve characters of this description."—*Rawlinson's Five Ancient Monarchies*, Vol. I., page 270.

It may be surmised, that the use of such signs arose at a time, when the written language of the Assyrians was in a transition state between the symbolical and the alphabetic; and if they had been neighbors of the Chinese, they might have adopted the former.

Chinese philologists have looked upon the radicals chiefly as expedients to facilitate the arrangement and search for characters; and have applied their efforts rather to illustrate the composition and origin of the characters themselves. In the 説文, they are arranged in six classes, and under each class, the supposed number of characters belonging to it is stated, with much information about their origin and changes.

1. Imitative symbols or 象形 like 月 moon, 608.
2. Indicative symbols or 指事 like 三 three, 107.
3. Symbols combining ideas or 會意 like 泪 tears, 740.
4. Inverted symbols or 轉註 like 正 standing, 372.
5. Syllabic symbols or 形聲 like 鯉 a carp, 21,810.
6. Metaphoric symbols or 假借 like 心 mind, 598.

It may be inferred, therefore, that the 2425 characters comprised in five of these classes, include nearly or quite all the ancient and original characters in the language; and that it is by the combination of a radical and phonetic, that the vast majority of the words in the language have been formed. The introduction of printing and the compilation of dictionaries, have given more uniformity and certainty to the characters, and there is now no difficulty in ascertaining the correct forms. In a few cases, slight variations, as 凡 and 丸, constitute different words; in other cases, a change in the arrangement of the parts, as 帕 and 帛, makes two different words. The radicals rarely indicate the sounds of the characters placed under them, but usually refer to their meanings, and are generally quite conspicuous. Their position, contractions and interchanges, are described in the following list, in which this analysis is confined to those points which are of the most service to the student. The interchange of radicals without altering the signification of the character, as 坭 and 泥, or 徧 and 遍 &c., occurs mostly when the two are analogous. Thus, the radicals 心 *heart* and 石 *stone* would never be interchanged; but the last might naturally be altered to 玉 *gem* or 瓦 *tile*, and the first to 人 *man*. As a rule, the primitives interchange most frequently, but the alterations in radicals are most perplexing.

The different position of the two parts sometimes alters the meaning and sound of the word; this is seen in *li* 砯 to step on stones in crossing water; *tăn* 泵 to thump, as a vessel (a Canton word); *t'oh* 沰 to drip; and *tsah* 沓 an old form of 淋 water dashing against stones. In other cases, as in *lah* 翋 and *yih* 翊 the sounds of the characters alter by the transposition of their component parts, while their meaning, *to fly, to soar*, does not alter; but *yih* 翌 to-morrow, differs in both sound and sense. These and other changes are among the curiosities of the language.

As the characters selected for radicals, comprise only a small portion of the original characters of the language, the rest must be distributed under these radicals. When the radical constitutes an integral part of a character, as in 愛, 今, 亞, 事, &c., it is said to be in *combination;* for if it be taken away, the remainder has no meaning. When it is formed of a radical and a primitive, as in 俔, 訃 or 親, the two are described as in *composition*.

When the radicals have been learned, it is a good practice to make them familiar by constructing sentences, such as are furnished in Wade's *Course*, or Williams' *Easy Lessons*. In doing so, the benefit of writing them repeatedly cannot be too much insisted on; for our habit, when learning western languages, to pay attention chiefly to *sounds* as expressing ideas, makes us soon weary in learning complex forms like the Chinese ideographs. Some persons gradually give up studying the written language, and content themselves with speaking only, and thus by degrees lose even their acquaintance with books.

In the following list, the contractions, and the C prefixed to those radicals which are used only in combination, are not inserted, as they are given in the Index list. The word *primitive* is here used merely with reference to the list in the next section; and the application of the remarks on each radical can be best seen, by referring to the General Index.

TABLE OF RADICALS.

Showing the position, changes and influence of each on its compounds, with an analysis of each group.

ONE STROKE.

一 1 *Yih,* Of this incongruous group of characters, about a dozen are primitives; this and the next seven groups contain many original forms.

丨 2 *‹Kwun* This radical passes through the middle of the other strokes in most of the characters, which have no similarity of meaning.

丶 3 *‹Chu* This radical is rather prominent; but of the characters only two are in common use.

丿 4 *P'ieh,* This radical is the first stroke in nearly all its incongruous compounds, most of the common ones being primitives.

乙 5 *Yih,* This is usually found on the right side like a hook, as in 乳; but there is no relationship in meaning among the compounds.

亅 6 *Küeh,* This leads the most incongruous group in the language; it contains 予, 事 and 了, which are common primitives; in others, their little use renders the difficulty of finding them less important.

TWO STROKES.

二 7 *'Rh'* All the common characters are primitives; it sometimes incloses the other strokes as 亘, or is put below as in 些, or on the left as in 况.

亠 8 *‚T'eu* This radical is placed on top, as 交; it was adopted merely to group together several incongruous and early forms, as the lower half never forms another radical.

人 9 *‚Jăn* This group, with the exception of a few primitives, as in 令 and 仄, &c., is a natural one; the compounds denote the actions, &c. of man; the radical is usually contracted on the left side, as 信; in others astride as 今; it is described as 企人邊 and 單立人, or single-stand man, to distinguish it from No. 60 彳.

儿 10 *‚Jăn* This is placed underneath, as 兄, &c., and is distinguished from No. 16 by a separation of the strokes; its compounds are not readily recognized, the upper part being another radical in a few, or else in combination as 兎; they have no likeness of meaning.

入 11 *Juh,* This and No. 9 are distinguished by this being placed on top as 全, or in the middle as 兩; the meanings are incongruous, and all the common characters are primitives.

八 12 *Pah,* This radical is placed above as in 兼, or below as in 典; some practice is required to recognize it in the compounds, which have no common significance.

冂 13 *‚K'iüng* The largest part of this group is really under its compound 冃 a *cap*, which being similar to 日 *day*, renders it difficult to distinguish 杲 and 果; in many others, as 冓 and 冊, it is in combination.

冖 14 *Mih,* This radical called 禿寶蓋, or bald-precious cover, lies over the other strokes, and does not envelope them like the last; there is some relationship to its meaning in a part of the characters.

冫 15 *‚Ping* This is usually placed on the left, and all its compounds refer to cold, wintry, &c., forming a natural group; it is described as 兩點水 *i.e.* two-dot water, and several characters are interchanged with No. 85.

几 16 *‹Ki* This is distinguished from No. 10 儿 by its inclosing the other strokes in about half the compounds; in the rest it is underneath, or on the right.

凵 17 *‹K'an* Here the radical incloses and supports the other strokes, the opposite of No. 13; the characters have no likeness of meaning, and their place is not at first easily recognized.

刀 18 *‚Tao* The contracted form, called 側刀旁 knife at-side, is always placed on the right side, as in 到; but the regular form is placed below, as in 分; the group has reference to cutting, severity, and uses of weapons, forming a natural collection.

力 19 *Lih,* In a few cases, as 勞, this radical is put below, but it is easily distinguished from the last by not being contracted; the compounds relate to strength, fatigue, violence, &c.; several hybrid characters, as 勰 occur among them.

勹 20 *‚Pao* In nearly every character, *pao* incloses all the right side of the other strokes as 勻; they refer mostly to ideas of enveloping, bending, &c.

匕 21 *‹Pi* An incongruous group, both in form and meaning; the radical is usually on the right side, but sometimes on top; the most common characters are primitives.

匚 22 *‚Fang* The upper stroke is detached and shorter than in the next; in both groups the primitive is inclosed within the radical, which depicts a place in which things can be concealed; it is called 框欄兒 or the picket-fence; the compounds denote chests, coffers, or drawers.

匸 23 *‹Hi* The upper stroke in this radical projects; the compounds mostly mean to store, and many of them are in common use.

十 24 *Shih,* Nearly all the common characters under this radical are primitives, and it is placed in all parts; the meanings are unlike, therefore, and some practice is needed to find them.

卜 25 *Puh,* This radical is mostly found on top as 占, or on the right side; the group contains many ancient forms, and all partake somewhat of its meaning.

卩 26 *Tsieh,* This radical, when on the right side as in most cases, resembles No. 163, as in 卿; when at the bottom, it is like No. 49 as 卷; most of its common compounds are primitives.

厂 27 *Han'* Some likeness is seen among the characters here, which refer to protection, shelter, &c.; it is known as 禿偏閃, or the bald side dodge, alluding to No. 53 广, with which it is often interchanged.

厶 28 *‚Sz'* In this group, the radical is in combination as in 去, or repeated as in 參, and not placed uniformly; the compounds are unusual and heterogeneous.

又 29 *Yiu'* This occurs usually on the right side as 友, or underneath; the common characters are primitives, showing traces of its meaning, and several have 殳 for their radical, making many hybrid forms now obsolete.

THREE STROKES.

口 30 *'K'eu* This is usually found on the left side; when it is at the bottom or in combination, as 合, 啓 or 咸, the character is probably an original one; it is employed to indicate that the character is used phonetically, as 咖 啡 for *coffee*, and many words under it in Kanghi's Dictionary are of this kind; voice, names, actions of the mouth, &c. are the general meanings; many are onomatapoetic.

囗 31 *Hwui* In this group, the radical incloses the primitive, as 圍; the compounds mostly allude to surrounding, shutting in, &c.

土 32 *'T'u* *T'u* is placed on the left or underneath; the group generally relates to things and kinds of earth; several characters are interchanged with No. 150 谷 and No. 170 阜, a few with No. 85 水 and No. 112 石; the radical is called 踢土邊 kicking-earth at-side, in allusion to its shape.

士 33 *Sz'* This has a long upper stroke, and is placed at the top as in 壽, by which it can be distinguished from the preceding; the group is incongruous, and the common words are all primitives.

夂 34 *Chi'* This also is found on the top, and its transverse stroke begins within the left one, which distinguishes it from the next.

夊 35 *Sui* The transverse stroke projects, and it is placed underneath as in 夏; the characters are mostly obsolete.

夕 36 *Sih,* More than half these characters are formed of another radical 多, as 够; their meanings are incongruous, though ideas of number appear in a large proportion.

大 37 *Ta'* This radical enters so much into combination that its compounds are rather puzzling, as 天, and 奏; they have little affinity in meaning, and a large part are primitives; it is mostly placed on the top.

女 38 *'Nü* Usually found on the left, as 婢, or underneath, or in combination as 妻; the group relates to females, beauty, intrigue, lewdness, &c.

子 39 *'Tsz'* *Tsz'* is placed underneath and on the side; it is tripled in a few as 孱, and combined as 孝; the compounds mostly refer to children, and to scholars, learning, &c.,

宀 40 *Mien* This radical, called 宀字頭 and 寶蓋頭, alluding to the head and shoulders of a man, and *lăm pung t'au* in Canton, covers the other strokes; but when they form another radical, it is not certain under which half the character is to be looked for; about twenty of the compounds are formed of 寐 contracted, as 寤, all of which refer to sleeping; with these exceptions, the meanings relate to shelter, houses, &c.

寸 41 *Ts'un'* In this group, which is a miscellaneous one, the radical is placed underneath or on the right; most of the common words are primitives.

小 42 *'Siao* Nearly half of this group is formed of the character 少 as the radical, as 尠, and show traces of its meaning; the others form rather a natural assemblage of ideas.

尢 43 *Wang* This radical is usually on the left side, and its compounds are about equally divided between two of its forms, except 就, which is used more than all the others put together.

尸 44 *Shi* Except in a few old words, this radical covers the other strokes on the left; its compounds relate chiefly to the parts and secretions of the body, &c.; it is interchanged with 骨 in a few cases; about twenty characters relate to shoes, all having 履 for their real radical.

屮 45 *Ch'eh,* This, called 半草 or half the grass radical, is on top, or in combination as in 屯; few of them are in use.

山 46 *Shan* This group is remarkably uniform in its meanings, which relate to the shape, parts, and names of mountains; *shan* is placed on three sides of characters, and when on top resembles No. 40 宀 a little; it is interchanged with No. 32 土 and No. 150 谷 in a few cases.

巛 47 *Chw'en* This radical occurs in combination as 州 or 巠, but is mostly found on top; many characters refer to streams; one name for it is 三拐 or the three staves.

工 48 *Kung* All the common compounds are primitives, in which *kung* is found in combination, as 差, or 巨 or 巫; their meanings bear no resemblance to the radical.

己 49 *'Ki* *Ki* usually occurs underneath, when it resembles No. 26, as in 卷; the three words *ki* 己, *i* 已, and *sz'* 巳, are often confounded in writing.

巾 50 *Kin* A natural group, relating to cloth, sash, flag, &c.; *kin* is usually found on the left or at the bottom, or in combination, as 師; in a few cases, it is interchanged with No. 120 糸; it is spoken of as 大巾旁 or great-napkin at-side.

干 51 *Kan* All the common characters in this group are primitives, and the radical is in combination, as 平 or 幸 or 年; their meanings are very unlike.

幺 52 *Yao* This collection contains really two radicals, 幺 and 丝, both alike in sense; 幻 and 幾 are examples; the meanings exhibit traces of their influence.

广 53 *'Yen* The characters in this group refer to buildings, protection, &c.; in several the radical is interchanged with No. 27 厂, and always found on the left; it is called 偏閃 or the side dodge.

廴 54 *'Yin* This radical and No. 162 are used synonymously, but also sometimes wrongly, as 廻 for 迴, and 延 for 延, &c.; it supports the other strokes, and most of the characters relate to walking.

廾 55 *'Kung* *Kung* is placed underneath; in many cases it is altered like No. 37 大, and a few words are found under both, of which 奕 and 弈 is one.

弋 56 *Yih,* This is easily confounded with No. 62 戈, and is interchanged in a few characters; the radical is on the right, and its compounds usually refer to it.

弓 57 *Kung* The radical is on the left, or combined as 弟 or 弔, or underneath; the regular compounds mostly refer to its meanings, directly or figuratively.

彐 58 *Ki'* This is placed on the top as 彘, or at the bottom as 彗; the radical influences the meanings but little; it is sometimes called 橫山部 overturned hill radical.

彡 59 *San* Most of these compounds refer to stripes, plumage, &c.; the radical is usually on the right, or in combination, as 彧.

彳 60 *Ch'ih,* This radical is on the left, and known as 雙企人 or 雙立人, referring to the apparent doubling of 亻 *man* in it; it resembles No. 144 行, under which and

No. 162 辵 are many synonyms; the group contains ideas of walking, advancement, &c.

FOUR STROKES.

心 61 ˏSin These characters mostly refer to the feelings, passions, mind, &c.; it is called 小心邊, or 佳心邊, or 豎心旁, upright-heart side; the contracted form is always on the left as 情, and the other beneath, as 恭; the regular form is usually beneath.

戈 62 ˏKwo *Kwo* covers the other strokes as 或, or combines with them as 我, and then it is not so easily detected; it resembles No. 56 弋, and is interchanged with No. 18 刀 in a few cases.

戶 63 Hu˒ This radical is placed over the other strokes; most of the characters refer to the uses or parts of a door, and a few are interchanged with No. 169 門.

手 64 ˊSheu The contracted form, called 才手邊 and 提手旁, is placed on the left, as 操; and the full form elsewhere, as 掌; the group is a natural one, acts and motions of the hand, ability, and power being the prominent meanings.

支 65 ˏChi This radical is never contracted, which distinguishes it from the next; there are some erroneous forms of the two following in the group, which is a miscellaneous one.

攴 66 P'uh˒ The contracted form of the radical, called 昂文邊 and 反文旁 to distinguish it from the next, is on the right side, and is used in the common characters; the others (about one half of all) have the regular form, as 敍, but are seldom met.

文 67 ˏWăn The contracted form is seldom used, and the radical is placed variously; the compounds generally refer to streaks, variegated, mixed, &c.

斗 68 ˊTeu Ideas of measuring, &c., run through this group, in which the radical is usually on the right or beneath; a few variants occur.

斤 69 ˏKin Ideas of division are prominent in this natural group, in which the radical is on the right side, except a few like 斧; the primitive is seldom another radical.

方 70 ˏFang This group has two radicals, and 方 has only eighteen compounds under it as 於; the other is 㫃 a *flag*, as written in 旗; these compounds refer to the shape or color of banners, making a natural collection.

无 71 ˏWu The common character under this radical 旣 has no likeness to it in meaning, and the rest seldom occur.

日 72 Jih˒ This natural group refers to the sun, time, luminous, &c.; the radical is usually on the left, and when on top it resembles the next, as 晏; some of these latter are like others under No. 13 冂, as 晟 or 冕; sometimes the next radical and No. 134 臼 are wrongly written like it.

曰 73 Yueh˒ A miscellaneous group; 更 forms the real radical of several in it, and all the common characters are primitives, rendering their search difficult; a few of them properly would fall under the last radical.

月 74 Yueh˒ Some reference to the moon or time is seen in most compounds under this radical, which is usually on the left; it is then like the contracted form of No. 130 肉, but practice will distinguish them; others having it on the right or at the bottom, as 期 or 有, are easily known.

木 75 Muh˒ A natural group, referring to trees and fruits, wood and wooden things; the radical is usually on the left, but also at the top or bottom, and in combination, as 本 and 東.

欠 76 K'ien This is easily confounded with No. 66 攴, as in 欹 and 攲; it and Nos 30 口 and 149 言 have several interchangeable forms; in this group, the characters refer to the tones, condition, and force of the voice,—on the whole a natural collection.

止 77 ˊChi When this radical is on the left as 歧, there is an allusion to its meaning; but when in combination as 正 or 歸, or underneath as 武, no likeness is apparent; it is interchanged with No. 60 彳 and No. 157 足, and rarely with other radicals.

歹 78 ˊTai The proper radical of this group is 歺 *a rotten bone*, contracted to 歹 in the compounds, all of which refer to whatever is dead, offensive, &c.; *tai* is also interchanged with No. 104 疒, and is generally placed on the left side, or underneath as 死, which last is the radical of ten other compounds under it.

殳 79 ˏShu When *shu* is used as a radical, the primitive is never another radical; it is placed on the right; characters like 縠 which appear to be under this, have their radical on the left side, the rest being 㱿 an *empty skin*; a dozen characters are also formed of 殸 *sound*, with a primitive, so that there are really three radicals instead of one in the group.

毋 80 ˏWu In this small group the radical is underneath the other strokes, as in 毒 or 每, most of the characters being primitives.

比 81 ˊPi Two radicals are here combined, of which *pi* heads one half as 毖; and 㲋 *a hare* the others, as 毚; none of them are much used, but the latter are most alike.

毛 82 ˏMao Most of these characters relate to uses and state of hair, fur, or feathers; the radical is found oftenest on the left, also on the right or beneath.

氏 83 Shi˒ The three primitives in this group 氏, 民 and 氐, are all found as radicals of some characters under it, which consequently show no likeness in their meanings.

气 84 K'i˒ These few characters all bear some relationship to their radical, which covers the other strokes.

水 85 ˊShui Some reference to the properties or the appearance of water is found in nearly all these words, making it a natural group; several are interchanged with No. 32 土 and No. 112 石; the radical is called 三點水 or three-dot water, when placed on the left, as in 海; it is also found beneath as 汞, and more rarely in combination as 泰 or 求.

火 86 ˊHwo This group indicates the appearance and effects of fire, &c.; the radical is called 四點脚 four-dot foot, and in most of the compounds occurs on the side, or in about one third of the whole, as 照, it is underneath.

爪 87 ˊChao In about one half of the characters, *chao* is contracted on top, as 爭; in the rest it is found on the left; it is easily distinguished from No. 97 瓜 by the dot.

父 88 Fu˒ This small collection is very natural; *fu* is placed on top, and its compounds refer to a father, and his different appellations.

爻 89 ˊHiao Two primitives 爽 and 爾 are the common characters in this group, which all show slight affinity to the radical.

爿 90 ˎch'wang This is a contraction of 牀 *a bed*, and most of its compounds refer to the parts and forms of a couch; it is placed on the left.

片 91 P'ien' Some allusion to a plank, board, or parts of a house, is observed in most of these characters, whose radical is always on the left.

牙 92 ˎYa An unimportant, though natural group; the radical imparts some of its meaning to all under it.

牛 93 ˎNiu The compounds refer to the ages, colors, uses, and nurture of bovine animals; the radical, called 提牛旁 or the goring-ox, is placed on the left, and seldom underneath.

犬 94 ʿK'üen The contracted form is always placed on the left; elsewhere it is the full form, which then may be wrongly written 犬; the former is called 反犬旁 turned-round-dog; and in Canton *lai kau pin* or dog-looking-backward; it refers to wild beasts, fierce, lying, crafty, &c.; some words under it, and Nos. 152 豕 and 153 豸, are interchanged.

FIVE STROKES.

玄 95 ˎHüen A sacred character, and therefore seldom written with the final point; it occurs in combination in 率, one of its common derivatives.

玉 96 Yuh, The complete form is only used underneath, and leads the meanings of all its compounds, which relate to gems and music; the contraction is the character 王, described as 斜玉旁 or 玉王邊; it is also interchanged with No. 112 石 and No. 167 金.

瓜 97 ˎKwa This radical is placed on the sides, thus helping to distinguish it from No. 87 爪; the compounds all refer to melons, gourds, &c.

瓦 98 ʿWa Under this radical, which usually occurs on the right or bottom, are found the names of tiles, earthenware, &c.; it is interchanged with No. 108 皿, No. 32 土, and No. 112 石.

甘 99 ˎKan There is one primitive 甚, in this group; the rest are unusual, but resemble their radical in meaning.

生 100 ˎShăng One primitive 產 occurs under this; in the others the radical is easily recognized, and all the compounds partake of its meaning.

用 101 Yung' No bond of connection pervades the meanings of these compounds; the primitives 甫 and 甬 are the most common.

田 102 ˎT'ien Words hereunder mostly refer to land, cultivation, &c.; it is usually on the left, and when placed above or below as 畏 or 畜, is usually a primitive, of which there are about twenty in the group; several are interchanged with No. 32 土 and others.

疋 103 P'ih, The common characters in this group are primitives, as 疐 and 疑, and all are very diverse in meaning.

疒 104 Nih, This is perhaps the most natural collection of characters in the language, as all refer to ailments; the radical is on top, and called 疾病頭 or disease head.

癶 105 Poh, The radical is placed on top; the three common characters under it have no uniformity of meaning.

白 106 Poh, In most cases, *poh* is placed on the left, in others on top or underneath; the meanings usually indicate brightness, light; No. 132 自 and No. 109 目 are both like it, and No. 72 日 is interchanged in a few cases.

皮 107 ˎP'i This radical is placed variously, but is easily seen; the uses and parts of skin are the common ideas.

皿 108 ˎMing Some reference to the radical, called 器皿部, or dish radical, is observed in nearly all the compounds; it is at the bottom, and in a few cases may be mistaken for No. 143 血.

目 109 Muh, These relate to the eye and vision; their radical is usually found on the left, and when underneath resembles No. 132 自; the contracted form, as in 罿, is like No. 122 网 as in 羅, but such are few; in the primitives 眞 or 直, it is in combination.

矛 110 ˎMeu This and No. 115 禾 are somewhat alike; it is placed on the left, and its compounds give the names and describe uses of lances.

矢 111 ʿShi A large proportion of this group indicates a connection with 短 *short*; the others chiefly refer to arrows, and have the radical on the left.

石 112 Shih, This radical is on the left or underneath, and conveys something of its meaning to all its compounds; it is interchanged with No. 32 土 or No. 98 瓦; also with No. 96 玉 or No. 46 山 in many cases.

示 113 Shi' This is placed on the left or underneath; the contracted form 礻 is not used in books, but resembles that of No. 145 衣, as in 袪 and 祛; it is hence called 禮衣旁, in allusion to this similarity; the group contains words of a religious nature.

内 114 ʿJeu These few characters are mostly primitives, as 禽 or 禹; they slightly resemble the radical in meaning.

禾 115 ˎHwo The appearance, uses, &c., of grain, especially rice, are leading ideas in these words; the radical is on the left, or in combination as 秉; several are interchanged with No. 113 示, chiefly from the use made of grain in sacrifices; it is described as 禾木旁, from its resemblance to the 75th radical.

穴 116 Hüeh, This can only be mistaken for No. 40 宀, but it is not always easy to tell whether the upper or lower radical determines the place in the dictionary, as in 窅 or 窨; hollowness, boring, and darkness, are prominent ideas in the group.

立 117 Lih, The radical is at top, or on the right, or below; several are primitives, and most of the characters allude to the radical.

SIX STROKES.

竹 118 Chuh, This is on top, and called 竹花頭 or bamboo-flower top; its compounds denote the kinds and utensils of bamboo, with a few referring to writing.

米 119 ʿMi This is placed on the left, and occasionally elsewhere; some of the characters interchange with No. 115 禾, and nearly all refer to rice in the grain, or made into cakes, spirit, flour, &c.

糸 120 Mih, This natural group relates to the kinds and modes of raising and making silk; the radical is described as 繳絲邊 or wind-silk at-side, and is usually found on the left or beneath, rarely on the right as 縣, or in combination as 繭.

缶 121 ʿFeu Kinds and uses of jars are the leading ideas; the radical is interchanged with No. 98 瓦 or No. 75 木; in a few cases it is often written like No. 167 金, unlike as the two are.

网 122 ‘*Wang* This radical is on top, and called 四字部 or the letter-four radical, from the resemblance; it is also contracted as in 罕; a few like 罔 suggest Nos. 13 冂 and 14 冖; the meanings refer to nets and traps.

羊 123 ˛*Yang* This is often contracted as in 羔 and 羞, or written in the old form as 芺; it is usually on the right or beneath, and several are interchanged with No. 198 鹿; the ages or colors of sheep, &c., are common meanings.

羽 124 ‘*Yü* This conveys something of its meaning to its compounds; it is found on all sides, and in combination as 翰; several are primitives.

老 125 ‘*Lao* Terms for age are the common meanings in this small group, but in nearly all the words the radical is contracted, as 者 or 考, so as to puzzle the beginner.

而 126 ˛*'Rh* This group is increased by many characters as 耍 and 耎 which should have been properly placed under the other radical, as this one gives their sound.

耒 127 *Lei*’ This resembles No. 115 禾; it is placed on the left, and the characters denote the uses and parts of ploughs, harrows, &c.

耳 128 ‘*'Rh* This and No. 109 目 are often written so much alike as to be confounded; its compounds mostly relate actually or figuratively to the ear; it is placed on the left, on the top, or in combination as 聚, and underneath.

聿 129 *Yuh*, Placed on the right, or in combination, as in 肅, the radical adds nothing of its meaning to its common compounds.

肉 130 *Juh*, The contracted form and No. 74 月 are written alike, as in 服 and 肺, but this group is the largest; and many characters like 勝, which would be searched for here, come under the other radical; those under *juh* have it on three sides, and the full form is usually found underneath.

臣 131 ˛*Ch'ăn* This is placed on the left, or in combination as in 臧; an incongruous group.

自 132 *Tsz*’ This is easily confounded with No. 106 白, and occasionally wrongly used for it; it is mostly found on top, as in 臭, which itself is again the radical of a dozen compounds referring to putrid smells.

至 133 *Chi*’ This small group has no common idea running through it; the radical is underneath as 臺, or on the left.

臼 134 ‘*Kiu* This is easily mistaken for No. 106 白; it occurs in combination as in 輿 or 舆, or is placed underneath.

舌 135 *Sheh*, This radical is on the left, as 舒, and the ideas of licking or sucking predominate, making it a natural though but little-used group.

舛 136 ‘*Ch'wen* In these characters the radical is found underneath, but it does not influence their meaning.

舟 137 ˛*Cheu* A natural group, referring to the parts, uses, and positions of boats; the radical is on the left; it is interchanged with No. 75 木 and No. 85 水 in a few characters, but in some others erroneously with No. 130 肉, as 艕 for 勝, in which 力 is the radical.

艮 138 *Kăn*’ In this, the smallest group, its radical is in combination as 艮, or on the right.

色 139 *Seh*, The conditions of color are the leading ideas in this small group; *seh* is placed on the right, and must not be confounded with No. 163 邑, which resembles it.

艸 140 ‘*Ts'ao* This radical in its contracted form on top, as in 芝, is called 草花頭 or 草字頭; it is the largest group and one of the most natural, comprising the names and condition of plants, vegetables, grasses, &c.; it is interchanged with No. 75 木 or No. 115 禾, and others.

虍 141 ˛*Hu* This radical, or its commonest compound 虎, affects the meaning of its derivatives, which relate to tigers and leopards, showing how common they must once have been; it covers the other strokes, or is placed on the side, as 號.

虫 142 ˛*Ch'ung* This natural group includes snakes, insects, reptiles, &c., having characters interchanged with No. 195 魚 and No. 208 鼠; the radical is usually on the left, but when doubled it is underneath, as 蝨, which makes scores of synonyms.

血 143 *Hüeh*, This resembles No. 108 皿, and is known as 血堆部 to distinguish it; the radical is mostly on the left.

行 144 ˛*Hing* This radical incloses the primitive, as in 衎; the left half is the same as No. 60 彳; the characters relate to going or to lanes, and metaphors derived therefrom.

衣 145 ˛*I* This radical conveys a meaning to most of its compounds; its contracted form is only on the left, as 衫, and the full form at the bottom as 裘, or divided as 裏; the contracted form of No. 113 示 resembles that of this radical.

襾 146 *Hia*’ This radical is on top, and does not influence many of its compounds; it is ususally called 西字部 *i.e.* west radical, from its common derivative.

SEVEN STROKES.

見 147 *Kien*’ Uses of the eye, and emotions of the mind, are the principal ideas of this group, some of whose characters interchange with No. 109 目; the radical is chiefly on the right side, and sometimes underneath.

角 148 *Kioh*, In this group, the uses, ages, and appearance of horns are the leading ideas; the radical is usually on the left or underneath.

言 149 ˛*Yen* Words in this natural group express emotions, and ideas pertaining to conversation, letters, &c.; the radical is usually on the left or underneath; some characters are interchanged with No. 30 口, and a few with No. 61 心.

谷 150 *Kuh*, Words in this group interchange with No. 46 山, No. 85 水 and No. 170 阜, all referring to valleys; it looks a little like No. 135 舌 when written badly.

豆 151 *Teu*’ This group contains two radicals, one of which leads the meaning of those referring to pulse and sacrificial vessels, as 豇 or 登; the other is a contraction of No. 207 鼓, and most of its compounds refer to drums.

豕 152 ‘*Shi* This is interchanged with the next and No. 94 犬, all relating to wild beasts; it is found mostly on the left or underneath, and in composition, as 象; the group is natural.

豸 153 ‘*Chai* This group is like the last, both containing many synonymous forms; *chai* occurs only on the left.

貝 154 *Pei*’ This occurs on the left or at the bottom, and in combination as 貞; the prevailing ideas in the group are of property, trade or honors, making a somewhat natural collection; the radical is sometimes called 具貝邊 from the similarity of these two characters.

赤 155 *Ch'ih,* Most of the characters convey some idea of redness, applied to earth or to the face; the radical is found on the left.

走 156 *ʻTseu* This radical supports the other strokes as 起, and conveys somewhat of its meaning to the compounds; they are frequently interchanged with the next and with No. 162 辵 and others; only a small proportion of the whole are now used.

足 157 *Tsuh,* This usually occurs on the left; the group resembles the last, and many characters are interchanged with it and No. 162 辵; the forms and uses of the foot are the leading ideas.

身 158 *ˌShăn* This radical is on the left; it is interchanged with No. 130 肉, No. 128 耳, No. 132 自, and No. 188 骨; a small and natural group.

車 159 *ˌChé* This natural collection refers to vehicles; the radical is on the left, but in a few, as 軍, it is beneath, or as in 輿 inside.

辛 160 *ˌSin.* In many of the compounds, the radical is doubled as 辦; in others, as 宰, it is beneath or on either side; their meanings have some similarity.

辰 161 *ˎCh'ăn* As a radical or in combination, as in the common words 辱 or 農, this imparts no meaning to most of the characters under it; No. 168 長 resembles it.

辵 162 *Choh,* The contracted form on the left is by some called 撑船邊 poling-boat at-side, from a fancied resemblance; this and the groups under No. 170 走, No. 60 彳 and No. 157 足, all have some characters in common.

邑 163 *ˉYih,* Except in a few cases, as 邕, the contracted form of this radical, described as 雙耳朶 two-lobed ear, is placed on the right side, as in 都, by which alone its compounds are distinguished from No. 170 阜; they mostly refer to land, places, inclosures, &c.

酉 164 *ʻYiu* This is placed usually on the left, but others occur like 醫 or 酒 or 釁; the characters mostly refer to pickles or spirits, and their effects.

釆 165 *Pien'* This group is very heterogeneous and irregular; the radical is often confounded with its compound 采, the only character much in use.

里 166 *ʻLi* This is placed underneath, on the left, or in composition, as 重; making a miscellaneous group.

金 167 *ˌKin* This group refers to metals, their uses, shapes, &c.; the radical is usually placed on the left or underneath as 釜, it is interchanged with No. 112 石 and No. 75 木 in a few cases.

長 168 *ˌCh'ang* The contracted form is on the left side; the derivatives are little used; most of them refer to lengths, but others to hair, showing that the radical is a contraction of No. 190 髟, and not originally this one.

門 169 *ˎMăn* This radical covers the primitive as in 問, forming a symmetrical group, most of which refer to doors, entrances, &c.; it is sometimes used as a contraction of No. 191 鬥, because it is easier to write.

阜 170 *Feu'* This is placed on the left, as 防, in its contracted form, which is sometimes called 耳斗邊 alluding to a water bucket; the characters mostly refer to places, hills, mounds, &c.

隶 171 *Tai'* These few characters are obsolete, though mostly referring to their radical, which is placed on the right side.

隹 172 *ˌChui* This stands on the right as 雅, or beneath as 雀, but in a few as 艧 or 巂 it is obscure; it is often interchanged with No. 196 鳥, and most of the words denote kinds or acts of birds.

雨 173 *ʻYü* A natural group referring to rain, dew, mist, and their times, forces, and appearances; the radical is on top, but there are many compounds as [illegible] in which 雲 is the real radical.

青 174 *ˌTs'ing* This is placed on either side as in 靜 or 靖 and imparts a shade of its meaning to the compounds, and its sound too to most of them.

非 175 *ˌFei* The radical is really the primitive to a large portion of this group, the other moiety of the character imparting the meaning.

NINE STROKES.

面 176 *Mien'* The form, condition, and expression of the face are described in this natural group; the radical is on the left or at bottom.

革 177 *Koh,* This is on the left or beneath, as 鞏; it is often interchanged with the next; the uses and articles of leather are described.

韋 178 *ˎWei* This is usually on the left, though 韙 and a few others are exceptions; the group describes the uses, garments, &c., of leather.

韭 179 *ʻKiu* This small and unused group is incongruous in its meanings; the radical is usually beneath as 韲, and looks like No. 175 非.

音 180 *ˌYin* This imparts a shade of its meaning to nearly all its compounds; it is found on the left or beneath, as 響, and on the right.

頁 181 *Hieh,* The motions, parts, and appearances of the head and face are here given; the radical is usually on the right, but [illegible] is an exception; it originally was a form of No. 180 首, and has nearly superseded it.

風 182 *ˌFung* Motions and effects of the wind are described in this group; the radical is found on the right, but oftener it is on the left.

飛 183 *ˌFei* The radical is the only word in common use; its compounds mostly refer to flying.

食 184 *Shih,* This is usually on the left as 飾, but otherwise in a few cases as 養; in some unusual characters it is interchanged with No. 130 肉, No. 119 米, and No. 30 口; the words mostly refer to sorts of food, appetite, eating, &c.

首 185 *ʻSheu* The compounds are unusual, and in several *sheu* is interchanged with No. 181 頁 and No. 190 髟; the radical occurs on all sides of the primitive.

香 186 *ˌHiang* The radical affects the meaning of all its compounds, which are seldom used; it is usually placed on the left.

TEN STROKES.

馬 187 *ʻMa* The characters all refer to the ages, colors, uses, &c. of horses, and metaphors taken from them.

骨 188 *Kuh,* This large and rather natural group describes the names and condition of bones; the radical is on the left, and is interchanged with No. 181 頁 and No. 130 肉 in a few cases.

高 189 *ˌKao* The radical is the only word in common use; nearly half of the compounds have *kao* for their radical, while 稾 leads the rest, and its compounds describe the condition of walls, and are now mostly found under No. 32

土; in combination it is contracted, as in 亭 or 京, and does not serve as a radical.

髟 190 *Piao* This group describes the condition and uses of the beard or hair; it has many interchangeable characters, and the radical is always on top; some of its real compounds are contracted under No. 168 長

鬥 191 *Teu* This covers the primitive as in 鬧, and is frequently written wrongly like No. 169 門, which it resembles.

鬯 192 *Ch'ang* The only character 鬱 in common use in this group has no reference to its meaning; and many of the compounds are duplicate forms.

鬲 193 *Lih* This is the radical of about half of its compounds, which mostly refer to boilers; the other radical is 鬳 *a steaming vase*, as in 鬻, whose derivatives refer chiefly to steaming or boiling, and gruel.

鬼 194 *Kwéi* This is found mostly on the left, and is readily recognized; the number of compounds might be indefinitely increased, for cabalistic sentences are often made, to all whose characters this is added; the names of spirits, demons, stars, &c., occur in this group, which contains much to illustrate the idolatry of the Chinese.

ELEVEN STROKES.

魚 195 *Yü* This is usually on the left, though 魯 and others are exceptions; it is also interchanged both with No. 205 黽 and No. 142 虫, but the group is unusually natural.

鳥 196 *Niao* In this natural group a few characters are interchanged with No. 172 隹; the radical is mostly on the right; there are many duplicate forms.

鹵 197 *Lu* These characters pertain to the taste and uses of salt, making a small, natural group.

鹿 198 *Luh* This is interchanged with No. 123 羊 in some characters; it is usually placed on top, and conveys ideas relating to cervine animals.

麥 199 *Meh* Characters in this group refer to cakes and other things made from wheat; few of them are in use.

麻 200 *Ma* Some of the characters found here ought to have been placed elsewhere, as 麼 and 麿; very few of those properly coming under this radical are used.

TWELVE STROKES.

黃 201 *Hwang* This is nearly an obsolete though a natural group; the shades of yellow are the leading definitions, and in this, as in a few other groups, one wonders how so many characters were needed upon such a subject.

黍 202 *Shu* This is usually on the left, except in 黎; in some it is interchanged with No. 119 米; the characters mostly denote kinds of millet, paste, &c.

黑 203 *Hoh* Ideas of shades and combinations of black, vileness, &c., belong to this group; the radical is on the left as in 點 or underneath as in 黨, in which cases the character appears as if belonging to No. 86 火.

黹 204 *Chi* This small, natural group has the radical on the left of the characters.

THIRTEEN STROKES.

黽 205 *Min* Several characters in the group are interchanged with No. 195 魚, No. 142 虫 and No. 213 龜; they mostly refer to reptilia.

鼎 206 *Ting* These few unusual words refer to tripods and braziers; the radical is generally underneath.

鼓 207 *Ku* This is usually found above, as 鼕, which will prevent its compounds being looked for under No. 66 攴; a few words as 鼖 really belonging to it, are found under No. 151 豆, because their right half is omitted; they denote sizes and sounds of drums.

鼠 208 *Shu* The names of rodents form most of these characters; it is occasionally interchanged with No. 142 虫 and No. 153 豸, though in the main a natural group.

FOURTEEN STROKES.

鼻 209 *Pi* Words describing the uses, forms, and diseases of the nose, &c., are comprised in this group.

齊 210 *Ts'i* These words derive their sound from the radical, which is properly the phonetic, and the real radical is contained within the lower part, as 齋; many similarly formed compounds are distributed among other radicals, the whole making a phonetic collection.

FIFTEEN STROKES.

齒 211 *Ch'i* The forms, uses, and diseases of the teeth and gums are described; a few unusual characters are interchanged with No. 92 牙 and No. 30 口.

SIXTEEN STROKES.

龍 212 *Lung* Like 210, many characters here should have been placed elsewhere, as only a few of those with *lung* refer to a dragon, which really acts as the phonetic.

龜 213 *Kwéi* A natural group referring to tortoises, &c.; the radical is also interchanged with No. 205 黽 and No. 142 虫, in a few instances.

SEVENTEEN STROKES.

龠 214 *Yoh* In this small group, several characters are interchanged with No. 76 欠 and No. 118 竹; the word 龥 is more used than all the others.

SECT. VIII.—THE PRIMITIVES.

That part of a character which is not the radical, has no name among the Chinese, but foreigners have termed it the *primitive* or *phonetic*. Neither of these names is entirely suitable, for that part of a character which is not the radical cannot always be said to have been formed first, any more than that it always imparts its sound to the united symbol. For instance, in the character 台, the combination of the radicals 口 *mouth* and 厶 *selfish*, to form the word for *exalted*, is etymologically speaking only apparent, since the upper half is really a contraction of 以 *by*, which having now lost its full form, has become simply 厶 to the learner. In this case, one half is just as much a primitive as the other, and neither of them imparts its sound to the character. Not so with the 35 derivatives in which this symbol *t'ai* 台 occurs, where it unites with the radicals 手 *hand*, 心 *heart*, 水 *water*, 冫 *ice*, &c. to make common words like 抬 to carry, 怡 concord, 治 to rule, 冶 to melt, &c.; for in such it is properly a primitive, in so far that in all of them it was a full character before combining with those radicals. Yet it is not strictly their phonetic; for these four are now read *t'ai*, *i*, *chi* and *yé*. Such combined words probably take their present sound from this part in rather more than one half of the total number of characters in the language, whatever they may have done in earlier times. Still it misleads the learner so often to call it the *phonetic*, if he looks to it to get the sound, that Marshman's term *primitive* is preferable. When the primitive does give its sound, as under 方 and its 33 derivatives, and was evidently taken to express it, the term *phonetic* is proper; and both words are useful in describing characters.

Dr. Marshman was the first who investigated the composition of Chinese characters in this manner. He made a complete classification of all those in Kanghi's Dictionary, so that their construction could be seen according to their *primitives*. He applied this term to that portion of a character which is left after its radical is removed; and used the word *derivatives* to express the compound formed by the union of a radical and a primitive. He found that the language contains 3867 of such primitives, that is, characters which combine at least once with a radical to form a third. He added the 214 radicals themselves, most of which also combine as primitives with other radicals, and thus estimated that about 4081 characters out of the 41,000 in the dictionary, should be classed as primitives. The greatest number which spring from any one is 74, but the average is less than ten.

Of this total number, he ascertained that 1726 combine only once with a radical to form a third character, and as they are all derivatives themselves, they may for all practical purposes be excluded from the list. Such a character is the derivative formed of 宀 and 龍 read *chung* 寵 which afterwards combines with 人 to make 儱, and with nothing else; another example is an old or erroneous form of 籌 with 心 underneath, a mere synonymous variety of itself.

There are also 452 others, formed, generally speaking, in the same manner from other derivatives, each of which produces only two philological shoots, and may be discarded for the same reason, their great rarity. These together make 2178 characters, which as they are the parents of only 2630 derivatives, and are themselves mostly included under simpler forms, can have little influence on the great mass of characters, and may all be dropped from the reckoning.

There are then about 1689 primitives in the language, from which, by the addition of 214 of their own number, are formed at least seven-eighths of all the characters in the Chinese language. This for all practical purposes is equivalent to the whole. This number of primitives can be reduced still more without injury, by striking off those whose derivatives form only three unusual characters, and those which are obsolete or synonymous, by referring them as sub-groups under their more conspicuous primitives. In describing them they may be arranged for convenience into the following five classes, according to the relation they bear to the radicals.

I.—*The 214 radicals themselves, when used as primitives.*—There are only 127 of them included in Callery's list, but these are of frequent occurrence. When two combine side by side, as 嗎, 坊, 視, 樚, &c., the one which imparts the sound is usually made the primitive by its location in Kanghi's Dictionary, and the character should be sought for first under the other radical. When they are placed one above the other, as 昌, 員, 李, 沓, &c., the signification of the word has mostly guided its position in the dictionary, but no rules can be laid down; most of the characters so formed are themselves primitives. Under the radical 水 *water* there are 117 compounds, which are made by combining it with another radical, of which 59 follow its sound, and 58 do not, or are primitives. Out of 115 similar characters under 木 *wood*, as many as 72 are sounded like their phonetic, and about 20 of the remainder as 槀, 杏, 呆, &c., are primitives. Out of 101 such derivatives under 艸 *plants*, as many as 78 retain the sound of the primitive radical. Out of the 333 derivatives of this sort under these three common radicals, only one 樢 has the sound of the radical *muh*, and that is wrongly placed, seeing it is a sort of bird, and *muh* is really the primitive. The compilers of the dictionary were occasionally careless in this respect, and have distributed characters erroneously, according to their own rules; as for instance 靟 fine hair, is found under 非, and not under 毛 its proper radical. It is useful to know this arrangement, in order the sooner to know where to look for a character in Kanghi's Dictionary.

II.—*Primitives formed of a radical, by an addition which is of itself unmeaning.*—When the radicals were reduced from 544 to their present number, the compilers of the 字彙 were likely to distribute such of them as were not important enough to use as radicals, wherever they could most easily be found, without regard to their meaning. For instance, 重 and 然, are placed under 里 and 火; but the remaining strokes possess no meaning when it is removed, nor have those three characters any reference to *bow*, *mile* or *fire*. All such are among the most ancient and common characters in the language, and number more than four hundred in all.

Most of them are contained in the list of difficult characters given after the Index on page 1239.

III.—*Primitives formed of two radicals, or which can be separated into two complete radicals.*—Some which come under this class, when analysed, have only a stroke or two as one of its radicals, as 必, 丁, 千, 壬, 仄, &c.; but most of them as 尾, 吉, 如, 相, &c. are readily divisible into two common ones, and are most easily learned by remembering their component parts. A few, are composed of a radical repeated, as 多, 圭, 林, 朋, 賏, &c., which are readily noticed. The number of both these kinds of primitives is over two hundred.

IV.—*Primitives formed of three or four-radicals.*—They are fewer in number than the preceding, and when their radical is removed, the rest is not usually a complete character, but is divisible into two radicals. Such are 京, 聖, 質, 坐, 來, &c., which are much easier learned and remembered as integral primitives than by their component parts. About thirty characters in the language are formed by the triplication of single radicals, as 劦, 畾, 森, 聶, 惢, &c., of which only five are common primitives. The last three classes together compose about half of the 1689 primitives, and most of the elementary Chinese characters.

V.—*Primitives formed from a derivative by the addition of another radical*, or by the combination of two derivatives. This class is, so to speak, of the third generation, and one of its parts will therefore be found in one of the preceding classes. Thus, 忽, 易 and 昜 may all be regarded as flowing from 勿, however little connection they may have with it in meaning; and each of them is joined again to several radicals as primitives. Such is also the case with 各, 尙, and 合, whose progeny as 路, 略 and 洛, or 黨, 常 and 敞, with 弇, 答 and 翕, and others, all combine with radicals to form new derivatives. A few of this class are composed of two derivatives, as 哥, 兢, 棘, which form a small collection easily recognized. The language contains many characters of this kind, which in classifying them by their primitives as Callery has done, must be left out; but when arranged by a radical, can be easily assorted. They are not very common indeed, as [illegible], 嚭, 顛, &c., but this dilemma of either rejecting them altogether, or making the index table too cumbersome to use, indicates the imperfection of this plan for general arrangement. What the student is most concerned with is to find a character quickly, and he soon sees that the practical point to be decided is whether to have 214 or 1689 keys to help him in his search. There can be no hesitation about the relative facilities of the two sets of determinatives for this special purpose, and that the 214 radicals demand the most careful study of the two.

This combination of a radical and primitive to form the great mass of the Chinese characters, whether the latter half is used as a mere phonetic as in 搡, or to aid the sense of the derivative, as in 駟, is such an important part of the language, that the student will derive advantage from examining the primitives to this end. The essay of Marshman, contained in his *Clavis Sinica*, shows the fascination that such an analysis of the characters had over him. An acquaintance with the general principles which the Chinese have followed in combining them, will doubtless assist in remembering the characters, and whatever diminishes this labor is advantageous. No one who means to read and talk Chinese can avoid the drudgery of learning its characters. I have, therefore, made an analysis of the groups found under each of the primitives given by Callery, in the belief that a careful study of it will repay the student, who wishes to become familiar with the written language.

The number of primitives in his list is 1040, or about two-thirds of the number collected by Marshman; but the derivatives from the remaining 649 are proportionately very few. Callery has defined only the most important of the words under each primitive, and the total mumber of characters contained in his *Systema* is 12,753. The highest number of derivatives is 74 under No. 285 合, of which he gives only 33; under No. 1040 靈 he gives only 9 of the 30 which actually occur; but his selection comprises all that are in common use.

The primitives of the same number of strokes are arranged in the following list under the six letters contrived by Gonçalves, and described in the last section; and if their application be learned, it will not be difficult to find each character. I have followed his order and list, because it will render reference to his work easy; but his mode of arrangement seems to have only one advantage, *viz.*, that it shows the possibility of such an alphabetic device. If they had been arranged by their radicals, it would have rendered them more accessible. It will be easy, however, for the student to mark the number of each primitive in the general index, and that will then serve as a guide to find them by their proper radical. This list has been reprinted in Doolittle's *Vocabulary*, Part III., page 455–478, where the common derivatives under each are given.

LIST OF 1040 PRIMITIVES.

According to Callery's Systema Phoneticum; with the common sounds, and an analysis of the respective groups under each.

TWO STROKES.

乙 1 *Yih,* *Rad.* 5.—The sounds under this primitive are *yih, chah, wah, yah,* and *kiu;* the characters placed under it as a radical might also be reckoned; it is a contraction, as in 礼 for 禮, and reäppears in No. 150 札 and No. 88 乞.

丂 2 *K'ao* *Afflatus.*—This group is read *k'ao* and *hiu;* the primitive is found in No. 194 号, and perhaps also in No. 241 考; it is never used alone.

十 3 *Shih,* *Rad.* 24.—This character has modified the meanings of some of its compounds, which are read *shih, ki, chin* and *hieh.*

丁 4 *Ting* *A man.*—This phonetic gives the sound to nearly all its derivatives, the others being read *chăng* and *ta;* it is used as a contraction for No. 841 登, and No. 513 亭 flows from it.

刀 5 *Tao* *Rad.* 18.—The half-score of characters under this are read *tao,* except one or two read *ch'u,* and their meanings are not influenced by it perceptibly; it is not the same as No. 34 刃, though the two are often written alike.

力 6 *Lih,* *Rad.* 19.—The derivatives here are read *lih* and *lieh* or *lüeh;* an offshoot 劦 *hieh* produces a sub-group in No. 659 脅, having no affinity with it.

㔾 7 *Tsieh,* *Rad.* 26.—This resembles No. 32 己, and reäppears in No. 66 厄 and No. 267 危; the compounds are read *fan, pien* and *yuen,* and in some of them it is a contraction of No. 127 氾.

乃 8 *Nai* *Is.*—This group is read *nai, jăng* and *yin;* there is no similarity in the meanings of the characters.

几 9 *Ki* *Rad.* 16.—This occurs more frequently as a primitive than a radical, and is often used as a contraction for No. 856 幾; one or two are read *fu* and *kiuh,* all the others *ki.*

九 10 *Kiu* *Nine.*—This and the last are easily confounded, and No. 16 丩 is interchanged in a few cases; the leading sound is *kiu,* the others are *kwéi, kao* and *süh.*

匕 11 *Pi* *Rad.* 21.—From this proceeds No. 108 比, with which one of this group 北 is easily confounded; the sounds are *pi, pin, tsin* and *yü.*

人 12 *Jăn* *Rad.* 9.—Two of the compounds, 囚 and 閃, give rise to a few derivatives; the sounds are *jăn, sin, shen* and *wo,* and the significations are equally unlike.

八 13 *Pah,* *Rad.* 12.—This is readily distinguished from the last as a primitive; the compounds are all read *pa* or *pah* except 扒 *pai.*

乂 14 *I* *To regulate.*—The contracted form of 五 five is written like this primitive, which is seldom met except in combination one of its derivatives is read *ngai,* the others *i.*

又 15 *Yiu* *Rad.* 29.—This occurs as a contraction for 田 in 叠, for 丵 in 对, and 萬 in 难; the compounds are read *yiu, yu,* and *nih.*

丩 16 *Kiu* *To involve.*—This is occasionally interchanged with No. 10 九, and several of its compounds exhibit some affinity in meaning; they are read *kiu, kiao* and *sheu.*

卜 17 *Puh,* *Rad.* 25.—This is sometimes interchanged with No. 869 菐; its derivatives are read *puh poh. fu,* and *wai;* it is not readily confused with itself when a radical.

THREE STROKES.

亡 18 *Wang* *To die.*—This reäppears in No. 217 巟 and No. 488 罔, and a common derivative 芒 is often interchanged with it, and regarded almost as a synonym; the sounds are *wang, mang,* and *mung.*

亏 19 *Yü* *In.*—This is now a synonym of No. 21 于, but was originally distinguished, and in those compounds read *wu,* it is usually retained; others are read *hwa.*

干 20 *Kan* *Rad.* 51.—The largest part of this group is read *kan;* others are *han, ngan, hien, kien* and *kieh;* No. 364 旱 flows from it, and it is sometimes confounded with No. 40 千 and the next.

于 21 *Yü* *In.*—It is interchanged with No. 19 亏 in several characters; its sounds are all *yü* and *hü,* but the significations vary greatly.

兀 22 *Wuh,* *A plateau.*—The sounds here are like the primitive, except 軏 *yueh;* their meanings are not influenced by it.

大 23 *Ta* *Rad.* 37.—This primitive is sometimes wrongly written like No. 72 犬 as 駄 for 馱, and also 太; its derivatives are read *to, tai* and *ti.*

丈 24 *Chang* *A staff.*—This character is also written 丈, partly to distinguish it from the last; the compounds all read *chang,* and exhibit some reference to the meaning of their phonetic.

弋 25 *Yih,* *Rad.* 56.—This and No. 75 戈 are liable to be confounded; its compounds are mostly read *yih,* others being *yuen* and *teh,* the last 忒 making a sub-group.

下 26 *Hia* *Below.*—These few characters are read *hia* or *sha* and *teh;* they show no trace of the primitive in their meaning; No. 57 卞 might sometimes be taken for it.

工 27 *Kung* *Rad.* 48.—This primitive has a large sub-group under No. 646 貢, and smaller ones under *kiüng* 邛, No. 250 巩 and No. 384 空; its derivatives are mostly read *kung* and *hung,* then *kang, kiang* and *kiüng.*

土 28 *T'u* *Rad.* 32.—This group is read *t'u, mu* and *shié;* its characters indicate no affinity with its meaning, and one of them 杜 leads a few derivatives.

寸 29 *Ts'un* *Rad.* 41.—This must not be confounded with the next; it is used as a contraction for 壽 by rapid penmen; its derivatives are read *tsün, sheu, cheu* and *tao;* 紂 and 守 both lead off several others.

才 30 *Ts'ai* *Talented.*—This group contains many common words; all but one (閉 *pi*) are read like it, and their meanings differ greatly.

弓 31 ꜀Kung — *Rad.* 57.—This character imparts none of its meanings to its derivatives, which are read *kung*, and *kiüng*; two of them 躬 and 穹, lead sub-groups of five or six characters, and No. 156 弘 may come from it.

己 32 ꜂Ki — *Rad.* 49.—This and the next might, as primitives, be joined in one, for they are seldom accurately written; this group is read *ki* mostly, also *pi*, *péi* and *kai*; one sub-group under No. 331 忌 is large.

巳 33 ꜂Sz' — *The tenth hour.*—The characters in this group follow the phonetic, but their meanings have no likeness to it or each other.

刃 34 Jan꜄ — *Sword.*—This and No. 5 刀 are similar in sense, but their groups differ in sound, this being read *jăn* throughout; No. 332 忍 comes from this, but the form 刅 is a contraction of 創 ꜀chwang.

也 35 ꜂Yé — *Also.*—This reäppears in No. 510 施, and No. 165 匜 and other sub-groups; the derivatives are read *i*, *ti*, *chi*, *shi* and *to*, none of them like itself either in sound or sense.

子 36 ꜂Tsz' — *Rad.* 39.—The derivatives all follow their leading sound in this group, and also show an unusual affinity with its meaning.

孑 37 Kieh꜆ — *Orphan.*—This is easily confounded with the last, but it is seldom met; the sounds of the derivatives are like it, but their meanings differ.

乞 38 Kih꜆ — *To beg.*—This primitive appears like an offshoot from No. 1 乙, but its affinities are with No. 664 氣 and the 84th radical 气, with which it is interchanged; its compounds are read *hih*, *yih*, *kih*, *hoh*, *koh*, *kuh* and *kien*.

乇 39 ꜀To — *A sprout.*—The sub-group under No. 210 宅 is the only important one; the compounds are read *toh*, *cha*, *tsih* and *tu*; and are unlike in sense.

千 40 ꜀Ts'ien — *A thousand.*—This and No. 20 干 are often mistaken for each other, but this is the least used; its compounds are all read *ts'ien*.

勺 41 Choh꜆ — *A ladle.*—This primitive affects the meaning of a few characters under it; their sounds are mostly *choh* and *tih*, with *poh*, *yoh*, *tiao* and *liao*; 的 and 灼 both lead two or three compounds.

夕 42 Sih꜆ — *Rad.* 36.—This character reäppears in a large sub-group, No. 265 多; its few unimportant compounds are read *sih* and *to*.

彡 43 ꜀Shan — *Rad.* 59.—A homophonous group, in which it is sometimes difficult to decide the office of the primitive as a radical or a phonetic.

久 44 ꜂Kiu — *Long.*—This gives its sound to all under it except 畂 *liu*; their meanings are various, and one 匛 forms a group of three.

凡 45 Fan꜄ — *All.*—This and No. 49 卂 are much alike, and the next group resembles both of them; these derivatives are read *fan*, except one contraction 芃 *păng*.

丸 46 ꜀Hwan — *A pill.*—Its derivatives are all read *hwan* or *wan*, and some of them partake of its meaning; this and the last group are alike in form.

叉 47 Cha꜄ — *Forked.*—The sounds of the compounds in this group are *cha* and *chai*, and the primitive evidently affects the meaning of its derivatives.

川 48 ꜀Chw'en — *Rad.* 47.—The characters in this group are read *ch'wen*, *shun*, *hiün*, *siün* and *tsai*, and their meanings have very little in common.

卂 49 Sin꜄ — *Rapid.*—This primitive is an altered form of No. 45 凡; its compounds are like it in sound except *wéi* 䫻, but differ in their meaning.

女 50 ꜂Nü — *Rad.* 38.—The derivatives of 女 as a primitive are read *jü*, but they are seldom met with, and have diverse meanings.

口 51 ꜂K'eu — *Rad.* 30.—The few characters in which this is used as a primitive are read *k'eu*; the groups under No. 287 如, No. 268 后 and No. 169 句 come from it, but show no affinity in sense or sound.

山 52 ꜀Shan — *Rad.* 46.—The few characters in this group are read *shan* or *sien*; most of them are in common use.

FOUR STROKES.

斗 53 ꜂Teu — *Rad.* 68.—This group is homophonous except 料 and 炓 *liao*; the compounds are diverse in their meanings.

方 54 ꜀Fang — *Rad.* 70.—A large and nearly homophonous group, a few only being read *pang*; the characters exhibit traces of the phonetic in their meanings

亢 55 ꜀Hang — *The nape.*—This character flows from No. 9 儿 only in appearance; its derivatives are read *hang*, *kang* and *kăng*, and some of them are like it in meaning.

文 56 ꜀Wăn — *Rad.* 67.—Some of the characters in this group are read *min* and *lin*, but more than half are *wăn*; one of them, No. 830 閔, leads a small sub-group.

卞 57 Pien꜄ — *Agile.*—This unimportant group is uniform in its sound; the phonetic is derived from No. 17 卜 and not from No. 26 下, which it resembles.

冘 58 ꜀Yin — *Walking.*—This primitive is also written 宂 or 冗, though the two characters are unlike; the sounds are *chin*, *shăn* and *tan*, and their meanings are very dissimilar.

火 59 ꜂Hwo — *Rad.* 86.—The compounds are all read *hwo*, and one or two partake of the meaning of their phonetic.

心 60 ꜀Sin — *Rad.* 61.—The sound *sin* or *tsin* pertains to all in this group, except 恥 another form of 耻 *chi*; the meanings have no noticeable resemblance; No. 403 忝 shows the other form of the radical.

元 61 ꜀Yuen — *Origin.*—This is easily written so as to resemble No. 55 亢, and from it flows No. 294 完; its derivatives are read *yuen* or *wan*.

井 62 ꜂Tsing — *A well.*—Some of the characters are somewhat like their phonetic in meaning; they are read *tsing* and *kăng*.

夫 63 ꜀Fu — *A husband.*—This primitive resembles No. 163 失; its compounds are homophonous throughout, and careful search might bring to light a little resemblance in their meanings to the phonetic.

云 64 ꜀Yun — *To speak.*—Three or four derivatives are read *hwun*, the others are *yun*; none of them alike in their meanings.

王 65 ꜀Wang — *Rad.* 96.—The characters under this phonetic are all read like it; it reäppears in No. 223 匡 and No. 353 狂, besides groups under 汪 and 往 of three or four words.

厄 66 Ngoh꜆ — *Unfortunate.*—This properly flows from No. 7 㔾; it occurs again in No. 267 危 and is often written 戹; its derivatives are mostly read *ngoh* and *ngai* or *yai*.

仄 67 Tsieh꜆ — *Oblique.*—This small group presents traces of the primitive in its meanings, and is like it in sound.

反 68 ꜂Fan — *Contrary.*—This primitive resembles the last in form; its compounds are read *pan* and *fan*, and many of them partake of its leading idea of opposition.

尤 68 ꜀Yiu *Rad.* 43.—The sounds of these compounds follow their primitive, but it has had no perceptible influence on their meaning.

厷 70 ꜀Kung *The forearm.*—The derivatives are mostly read *hung*, and this primitive is often interchanged with No. 156 弘; the meanings of many of them allude to a twang or vibration.

不 71 Puh, *Not.*—The sounds in this group are *puh*, *peu*, *feu* and *péi*, and the meanings of the characters show no resemblance; No. 138 丕 is often interchanged with it, and No. 308 否 is derived from it.

犬 72 ꜂K'iüen *Rad.* 94.—This and No. 23 大 are often wrongly interchanged; this group is read *k'üen* and *féi*; and the compound 吠 is a good example of ideographic writing.

互 73 Hu' *Mutual.*—The derivatives are identical with the sounds of their phonetic, but their meanings show slight resemblance; No. 228 亙 is sometimes wrongly written like this, and it is interchanged with 彑 in many cases.

切 74 Tsieh, *To cut off.*—The sounds in this group are *tsieh* and *tsi*, both which the phonetic has; the meanings are very unlike.

戈 75 ꜀Kwo *Rad.* 62.—As a primitive, this gives none of its meaning to the compounds, which are read *hwa*, *chao*, *hwan* and *hwo*; No. 437 戔 flows from it.

牙 76 ꜀Ya *Rad.* 92.—The compounds in this group mostly follow their leading sound; others are read *hia*, *kia* and *chwen*; No. 424 亞 is interchanged with it in several characters.

巿 77 Féi' *A short dress.*—This and *shi'* 市 a market, are nearly alike in form, but this is the phonetic, and half the compounds follow it; others are read *pei* and *tseh*; the sub-group of five under 市 is read *shi.*

支 78 ꜀Chi *Rad.* 65.—The group under this as a primitive is more important than that under it as a radical, and it is not easy to draw the line; the sounds are *chi* and *ki* in equal proportions, with three read *kwéi.*

丏 79 Mien' *Obscure.*—This resembles 丐; its compounds follow its sound, and in several of them 面 takes its place from mere identity of sound.

木 80 Muh, *Rad.* 75.—The few compounds under this primitive are read *muh*, *hiu*, *hiao* and *sung*, of which No. 278 休 and 梟 form sub-groups.

予 81 Yü' *To give.*—This group is read *yü*, *sü*, *shu*, *chu* and *yé*; in combination the primitive is often written like No. 36 子; and one or two of the compounds have a few derivatives.

引 82 ꜂Yin *To lead on.*—The compounds under this character partake slightly of its meanings; their sounds are *yin*, *shăn* and *chăn.*

丑 83 ꜂Ch'eu *The second hour.*—The derivatives are read *ch'eu* and *niu*; their meanings show no similarity to it or each other.

夬 84 Kwai' *A chord.*—This often occurs written 叏 in obsolete forms, and resembles No. 200 央; the compounds are read *kwai*, *küĕh*, *h'üeh*, *yüeh* and *méi*, a miscellaneous group.

叒 85 Muh, *Not.*—This character is easily confounded with No. 103 殳, but it seldom occurs in combination; its sounds are all like the primitive.

巴 86 ꜀Pa *Would that.*—This group regularly follows its phonetic throughout; the compounds show no resemblance in signification to it or each other.

乏 87 Fah, *Deficient.*—The sounds under this primitive, which resembles 之, are *fah*, *fan* and *pien*; their meanings are still more diverse.

毛 88 ꜀Mao *Rad.* 82.—This group is read *mao*, with the exception of three read *hao* and *muh*; the meanings of the characters are unlike.

午 89 ꜂Wu *Noon.*—The compounds are read *wu*, *ch'u* and *hü*; one of them 許 leads off three or four in a sub-group.

牛 90 ꜀Niu *Rad.* 93.—The few words in this group are read *niu*, *lao* and *kien*; they have no similarity of meaning.

夭 91 ꜂Yao *Fair.*—This primitive resembles 天 heaven, but that forms no derivatives; its sounds, are *yao*, *ngao*, *hiao*, *yu* and *uh*; one 芺 leads a small sub-group.

攵 92 Puh, *Rad.* 66.—The forms of the radical and primitive differ a little, but this resembles No. 78 支 in some cases; the dervatives are read *muh*, *méi.*

丹 93 ꜀Tan *Cinnabar.*—The primitive gives its sound to five compounds, the rest being read *chen*, *nan*, and *tung*; it might have itself been elevated to be a radical.

匀 94 ꜀Yun *Uniform.*—An unusual similarity runs through the meanings of this group, which is read *yun*, *kiun* and *tsin*; one derivative 均 has three under it.

月 95 Yüeh, *Rad.* 74.—This gives its sound to all its derivatives, and traces of its meanings can be detected in two or three.

勿 96 Wuh, *Do not.*—The sounds in this group are *wuh*, *hwuh*, *muh* and *wăn*; from one of the characters proceeds No. 466 忽, and there are other small sub-groups.

及 97 Kih, *Up to.*—About half of this group is read *kih*; the rest are *chah*, *hih* and *sah*, suggesting a contraction from other forms to explain the sounds.

欠 98 K'ien' *Rad.* 76.—The sounds of *k'ien*, *hien*, *kan*, *yin* and *chui*, occur in this group; in many of the characters, it is not easy to decide whether 欠 is the radical or primitive.

斤 99 ꜀Kin *Rad.* 69.—No similarity in meaning is seen in these derivatives, which are read *kin*, *hin*, *yin*, *k'i*, *tsiang* and *so.*

升 100 ꜀Shing *To ascend.*—These compounds resemble their primitive in sound and sense; and one of them 坓 is often substituted for it.

戶 101 Hu' *Rad.* 63.—More than usual uniformity appears among the derivatives, most of them being read *hu*, with *ku* and *tu*; No. 769 扈 is derived from it, and 雇 and 戽 both have a few followers.

爪 102 ꜂Chao *Rad.* 87.—The compounds are similar to the primitive in sound, and some of them partake of its sense.

殳 103 ꜀Shu *Rad.* 79.—This primitive is a little like No. 85 叒; the derivatives are read *sheh*, *shau*, *teu*, *ku* and *yih*, and show a few sub-groups; some of the compounds properly belong to the radical.

屯 104 ꜀T'un *To sprout.*—Half of the derivatives are read *tun*; others are *chwen*, *tsüen* and *shun*; there are two or three small sub-groups.

化 105 Hwa' *To transform.*—The compounds of this group are read *hwa* and *wo*, and several of them are modified by the meaning of the primitive.

氏 106 Shi' *Rad.* 83.—The sounds vary much among these derivatives, but their meanings are even more dissimilar; it is not the same as No. 174 氐.

卬 107 ꜀Ang *To look up.*—This is not the same as No. 175 卯; the sounds are *ang*, *ying* and *yang*, and the sense of the primitive appears in many of the compounds.

比 108 ‹Pi — *Rad.* 81.—This primitive comes from No. 11 匕, and gives its sound to all under it, but no trace of its meaning; No. 354 毕 and No. 685 皀 are connected with it.

凶 109 ˏHiüng — *Cruel.*—Some likeness of sound appears in this group; it is sometimes written 㐫 and 囟 or 匈.

今 110 ˏKin — *Now.*—The compounds are read *kin* and *king*, but none of them follow the meaning of the phonetic.

兮 111 ˏHi — *Sign of admiration.*—This and the next are easily distinguished; the group is small, and nearly uniform in sound.

分 112 ˏFăn — *To divide.*—The idea of expansion or division runs through the words in this large group, two-thirds of which follow the sound of the primitive; the rest are *păn*, *pan* and *pin*.

介 113 Kiai› — *Confines.*—Much uniformity in sound, as *kiai* and *hiai* pervades this group, but only a few of its words resemble the primitive in sense.

父 114 Fu› — *Rad.* 88.—No trace of the meaning of the primitive is seen in the compounds, but all of them agree with it in sound; 釜 is an example of a modified radical.

爻 115 ˏHiao — *Rad.* 89.—This group is nearly uniform in sound; the primitive affects the meanings of only one or two.

公 116 ˏKung — *Equal.*—The sounds of these compounds are unlike, and in many cases they follow No. 434 松, with which some are interchanged.

允 117 ‹Yun — *To permit.*—Much dissimilarity in pronunciation occurs in this group, and the meanings have no reference to the primitive.

丬 118 ˏChw'ang — *Rad.* 90.—This rules the sounds of only a part of the compounds, the rest being *tsiang*; and imparts its meaning to none.

止 119 ‹Chi — *Rad.* 77.—This group agrees in sound with its phonetic, and a trace of its meaning is seen in several of the compounds.

日 120 Jih, — *Rad.* 72.—An incongruous group in both sound and signification; 馹 is regarded as a contraction of 驛 by many.

内 121 Néi› — *Within.*—This imparts its own sound to none of the compounds, which read *nah*, or *jui*› or *noh*,; nor are their meanings like it.

中 122 ˏChung — *Middle.*—This gives the sound to all its compounds, and traces of its meaning appear in all the common ones.

少 123 ‹Shao — *Few.*—The sounds *chao*, *miao* and *sha* appear in this group; their significations show little influence from the primitive; 12 characters occur under the radical 小, having this for their radical, and partaking of its meaning.

FIVE STROKES.

宁 124 ‹Chu — *A vestibule.*—One sound runs through this group, but its meanings are incongruous; it is contracted to 宀 in some characters.

它 125 ˏT'o — *To carry on the back.*—A group nearly uniform in sound, but diverse in its meanings; some of them are interchanged with No. 35 也.

穴 126 Hüeh, — *Rad.* 116.—A trace of the meaning of the primitive appears in many of the compounds, most of which are like it in sound.

氾 127 Fan› — *Waves rising.*—This is derived from No. 7 巳, but while the sounds are alike, the meanings of the derivatives show no affinity with it.

立 128 Lih, — *Rad.* 117.—An incongruous group in sound, as *lih*, *lah*, *sah*; and their meanings show even more diversity.

主 129 ‹Chu — *Lord.*—A group uniform in sound, and one where the sense of many characters shows the influence of the primitive; 往 is another form of 㞷, which is found under No. 65 王, from which this flows.

玄 130 ˏHuen — *Rad.* 95.—This affects the sounds of all its compounds; which are more numerous and common than those in which it is a radical.

永 131 ‹Yung — *Always.*—The sounds in this group are nearly uniform, but their meanings show no trace of the primitive.

必 132 Pih, — *Must.*—This leads the sounds as *pi* or *pih*; and No. 708 密 heads a sub-group of one of its derivatives.

平 133 ˏP'ing — *Peace.*—The sounds in this group are *p'ing* and *păng*; the meanings are various; 秤 is nearly the same as 稱 ˏch'ing.

未 134 Wi› — *Not yet.*—This and the next need to be distinguished; its sounds are *wi* or *méi*, and its meanings often indicate incompleteness.

末 135 Muh, — *End.*—The sounds here are uniform, and there is a trace of the primitive in the meanings of most of the words.

左 136 ‹Tso — *The left.*—This gives its sound to the group; No. 522 脊 and No. 629 差 flow from it.

犮 137 Pah, — *To pull out.*—The sounds of *pah* or *poh*, *fah* or *fuh* are common in this group, whose characters have no reference to the primitive in their meanings.

丕 138 ˏP'éi — *Great.*—This is a derivative from No. 71 不; its sounds follow the primitive, but not its meanings.

右 139 Yiu› — *Right.*—This has some affinity to No. 231 有 in sound and form; its derivatives are all sounded alike.

石 140 Shih, — *Rad.* 112.—This group has no reference in meaning to the primitive, and the sounds are very unlike.

布 141 Pu› — *Cloth.*—These characters agree in sound, and 飾 is modified in its form, and may be of a different origin.

正 142 Ching› — *Correct.*—Uniform in sound; only a few of the characters indicate affinity with the meaning of the primitive, which seems to proceed from No. 119 止.

去 143 K'ü› — *To depart.*—These characters are read *k'ü*, *kieh* and *fah*; the primitive influences the meaning of very few of them.

巨 144 Kü› — *Vast.*—A group nearly uniform in sound, but various in its meanings; it resembles No. 248 臣 and the radical 匚 in form.

可 145 ‹Ko — *Able.*—These characters derive their various sounds of *ko*, *ho* and *ngo* from the primitive, but their meanings show little analogy to it; No. 446 阿 and No. 650 哥 flow from it.

丙 146 ‹Ping — *Cyclic term.*—No similarity in meaning appears in this group, but all follow it in their sounds.

匝 147 Tsah, — *To bind.*—The sounds of this group are uniformly like their phonetic; it is often contracted to 帀.

朮 148 Shuh, — *A medicine.*—The meaning of the primitive affects none of the compounds, but their sounds *chuh* and *shuh* resemble it.

本 149 ‹Păn — *Origin.*—These characters mostly denote rudeness; they are read *păn* and *poh*, and No. 528 奔 is probably derived from it.

札 150 Chah, — *A tablet.*—The sounds of this group are uniform, but their meanings have no similarity.

甘 151 ˏKan — *Rad.* 99.—The pronunciation is *kan*, *han* and *kien*; and a trace of the meaning of the primitive is observable in this group.

世 152 *Shi'* — *The age.*—The sounds here are *shi*, *i* and *sieh;* their significations vary much; it is sometimes interchanged with No. 289 曳, and No. 542 枼 is an offshoot.

古 153 *'Ku* — *Ancient.*—This group is read *ku* and *hu*, but their meanings differ widely; No. 497 固 and No. 544 胡 are derived from it.

戉 154 *Yueh,* — *An ax.*—This group is similar in its sounds, but not otherwise; the primitive must not be written like 戊 a cyclic character.

弗 155 *Fuh,* — *Not so.*—The sounds here are *fuh*, and *féi'*, but no likeness to the primitive can be traced in their meanings.

弘 156 *˛Hung* — *To extend.*—The primitive gives its sound to the compounds; it is perhaps derived from No. 31 弓.

尼 157 *˛Ni* — *A nun.*—The sounds here follow the primitive; the meanings are incongruous.

司 158 *˛Sz'* — *An official.*—One sound pervades this group, which yet exhibits no likeness in its meanings; 嗣 is a hybrid.

民 159 *˛Min* — *The people.*—Uniform in sound, with the exception of 眠 *mien;* in some of the compounds 昏 is improperly interchanged with it.

召 160 *'Chao* — *To call.*—The compounds are read *tiao*, *choo* and *shao;* their meanings are diverse; it is contracted to 刁 in some cases.

加 161 *˛Kia* — *To add.*—The sounds in this group are *kia*, with a few *ho* and *kié;* the meanings however show few traces of its meaning.

乎 162 *˛Hu* — *Ah!*—The sounds follow the primitive, which itself recurs in No. 784 虖 in a small group.

失 163 *Shih,* — *To lose.*—The words here are read *cheh*, *tieh* and *i;* their meanings indicate little affinity with each other.

生 164 *˛Shăng* — *Rad.* 100.—More resemblance exists in this group to the sound than the sense of the primitive; No. 595 is one of them.

㐌 165 *˛I* — *Mountaineer.*—This is derived from No. 35 也; the characters are read *t'o* and *i*, and few of them are common.

乍 166 *Cha,* — *Suddenly.*—The primitive gives its sound to nearly half the group, the rest being *tsoh*, *tsieh* and *tsu;* No. 611 窄 is one of its compounds.

禾 167 *˛Hwo* — *Rad.* 115.—The characters, not like the primitive in their sounds, are read *su;* their meanings are all unlike it.

包 168 *˛Pao* — *To embrace in.*—Much uniformity of sound appears in this group; many characters resemble the primitive in sense.

句 169 *Kü'* — *A phrase.*—The compounds are read *kü*, *keu* and *heu* or *hü;* it is sometimes written 勾, but not correctly.

皮 170 *˛P'i* — *Rad.* 107.—Besides the regular sound *p'i*, a few are read *po*, or *péi;* the meaning of skin appears in only three or four.

斥 171 *Cheh,* — *To reprimand.*—The sounds of this group are *cheh*, *su* and *toh;* several of them refer to breaking; it has no affinity with No. 99 斤.

瓜 172 *˛Kwa* — *Rad.* 97.—Words in this group are read *kwa*, *ku* or *hu*, but none of them relate to melons.

冬 173 *˛Tung* — *Winter.*—The sounds in this group are *tung*, *t'ang* and *chung*, and a few of the characters refer to cold.

氐 174 *'Ti* — *Bottom.*—About half of these derivatives are read *ti*, and the rest *chi;* in some of the latter 至 is interchanged with 氏 the primitive, which is not the same as No. 106. 氏.

卯 175 *'Mao* — *Morning hour.*—This group is read *mao*, *liao* and *liu;* its significations are incongruous; 卵 an egg is aberrant, and No. 673 留 leads a large group.

代 176 *Tai'* — *An age.*—These sounds are uniform, and a trace of the primitive is seen in several of the compounds.

丘 177 *˛K'iu* — *A hill.*—This group is mostly read like the primitive, but few of them show its influence in their meaning.

付 178 *Fu'* — *To give.*—This is uniformly sounded *fu*, and in many of the compounds something of the primitive is apparent.

白 179 *Poh,* — *Rad.* 106.—All except three read *pa*, follow the primitive in their pronunciation; only two or three resemble its meaning.

弟 180 *'Tsz'* — *To stop one's-self.*—The sounds are nearly uniform in this group; it is sometimes confounded with No. 301 弟.

半 181 *Pan'* — *Half.*—The primitive imparts its sound to all the derivatives, and its meaning to a large proportion.

令 182 *Ling'* — *To order.*—A uniform group; the primitive is sometimes used as a contraction of No. 1040 靈.

㐱 183 *˛Chăn* — *Thick hair.*—All the compounds but two follow its sound, but only one or two of them its meaning; No. 780 參 comes from it.

㕣 184 *˛Yuen* — *A marsh.*—These characters differ in sound and sense from the primitive, which is also written 㕣.

弁 185 *Pien'* — *A casque.*—Half of this group is pronounced *pien* and half is *fan;* the primitive is sometimes written 弃, but not correctly.

台 186 *˛Tai* — *A terrace.*—A variety of sounds as *i*, *tai*, *chi*, *si*, *ye* and *shi* occur in this group; it is often a contraction of No. 945 臺, in those read *tai*.

毋 187 *˛Mu* — *Mother.*—An incongruous group, for part of them are compounded of the radical 毋 not, and part of 毌 to string on; No. 340 每 flows from it.

奴 188 *˛Nu* — *A slave.*—The sounds here vary from *nu* into *nao*, *na* and *t'ang;* there is no similarity in sense among the derivatives.

幼 189 *Yeu'* — *Young.*—The sounds here are nearly uniformly *yeu* or *yao*, but their meanings do not resemble the phonetic.

占 190 *˛Chen.* — *To divine.*—Among its compounds some are read *nien*, *tien*, *tieh* and *shen;* one of them is No. 387 沾 making a sub-group; it and No. 153 古 are often misprinted for each other.

此 191 *'Ts'z'* — *This.*—A few are read *chai*, but the other derivatives are uniform in sound with it.

旦 192 *Tan'* — *The dawn.*—About half a dozen of this group are read *tah;* in some the primitive is often contracted to No. 901 詹, because of the sameness of sound.

且 193 *'Tsie* — *Furthermore.*—This much resembles the last; the sounds *tsü*, *cha*, *chu*, *tsu* and *tsié* occur under it; No. 370 助 flows from it.

号 194 *Hao'* — *A signal.*—Some derivatives are read *hiao*, but their significations vary much; it is deemed to be derived from No. 2 丂.

甲 195 *Kiah,* — *A scale.*—The compounds are read *kiah*, *hiah*, *chah* or *yah;* they show no trace of the primitive in their meanings.

申 196 *˛Shăn* — *To report to.*—The characters here are nearly uniform in pronunciation, and have a slight resemblance in meaning; this and the last must not be confounded.

叧 197 *˛Kwa* — *To scrape off.*—This small group is incongruous, and the primitive is often written 另 erroneously.

兄 198 ˏHiüng *Elder brother.*—None of the compounds are read like it, and none of them exhibit any traces of its meaning.

只 199 ʿChi *Only.*—All the compounds are read like it, but their meanings vary much.

央 200 ˏYang *Middle.*—Most of these follow the primitive in sound; four are read *ying*, and one derivative No. 588 英 leads a group.

田 201 ˏT'ien *Rad.* 102.—All but one of this group are read like it, and they all refer more or less to its meaning.

由 202 ˏYiu *From, by.*—This group is read *siu, chu, tih, cheu* and *yiu*, but in none does the meaning of the primitive appear.

冉 203 ʿYen *Gradually.*—One sound runs through this group, but nothing of the primitive comes out in the meanings.

册 204 Tsieh, *Catalogue.*—*Shan* is the most common sound in these few characters, which are incongruous in meaning.

四 205 Sz'ʾ *Four.*—A similarity of sound pervades this group; the primitive is often printed to resemble 匹 a piece.

冋 206 ʿKiüng *A desert.*—All these are read nearly alike, and in a large part there is some allusion to space; No. 291 回 and No. 293 同 are like it.

出 207 Ch'uh, *To go out.*—Besides *ch'uh*, the sounds *kiüh, tuh* and *choh* occur; the meanings are very diverse.

以 208 ʿI *Therefore.*—The sounds are *i* and *tsz*; the primitive is changed to the old form 㠯 in some cases.

SIX STROKES.

字 209 Tsz'ʾ *A letter.*—The sounds here are uniform, but the characters do not take after the primitive, itself derived from No. 36 子.

宅 210 Cheh, *A house.*—These compounds are read *ch'a*, but they are not uniform in meaning; it is itself derived from No. 39 乇.

安 211 ˏNgan *Peace.*—Nearly uniform in sound; the primitive is parted in 宴 to feast with.

亦 212 Yih, *Also.*—Usually read *yih*, but none of the compounds resemble it in meaning; No. 1024 緐 is often contracted to this, especially in those characters where it is placed over the radical.

衣 213 ˏI *Rad.* 145.—Uniformly read *i*, but nothing of its signification appears in the compounds.

交 214 ˏKiao *To join.*—The sounds *hiao* and *yao* occur in a few cases, and a trace of the primitive is often seen in the derivatives.

充 215 ˏCh'ung *To fill.*—The sounds here are uniform, with one exception; it is often written 克 in formal books.

亥 216 Haiʾ *The tenth hour.*—This group is read *kai, hiai, kiai, koh* and *hai*, but the primitive affects none of the meanings.

巟 217 Hwang *Ample.*—These follow one sound, and traces of the primitive reäppear in some of the compounds; it flows from No. 18 亡, and 荒 makes another form of it.

羊 218 ˏYang *Rad.* 123.—Besides *yang*, many of these are read *siang*, and three or four of them refer to the primitive.

龹 219 ʿKüen This group is uniformly read *küen*; the primitive is not in use, and reäppears in No. 453 卷 and No. 666 朕; it was anciently a radical.

米 220 ʿMi *Rad.* 119.—The sounds are alike in this group, with one exception; the compounds show no meaning of the phonetic; one of them forms a sub-group, No. 631 迷, of four.

次 221 ˏTsz' *A series.*—These all follow the sounds of the phonetic, and No. 578 咨 is a compound which leads a few others.

刑 222 ˏHing *Punishment.*—This group is uniform in sound, but has none in signification; it is perhaps derived from No. 62 井.

匡 223 ˏKw'ang *To aid.*—One sound runs through all these characters, and some of them slightly indicate the meaning of the primitive.

戎 224 ˏJung *Martial.*—A few of these are read *sung*; one derivative 賊 forms two further compounds itself; No. 154 戉, No. 233 成, and No. 235 戌 are easily confounded with it.

式 225 Sheh, *A model.*—These generally follow their primitive in sound, but it does not influence their meanings.

夷 226 ˏI *A foreigner.*—This group is read *i* and *t'i*; the phonetic is sometimes wrongly interchanged with 弟 No. 301.

灰 227 ˏHwui *Ashes.*—The sounds here are *hwui, kwei* and *tan*; a few show something of the primitive in their meaning.

亙 228 Kăngʾ *Constant.*—Two of these are read *hăng*; the primitive is sometimes written like No. 73 亙 and No. 245 亘, but there is a clear distinction between them.

列 229 Lieh, *To arrange.*—The sounds are *lieh* and *li*, but none of the compounds show much trace of the primitive.

百 230 Poh, *A hundred.*—This group is read *poh* and *moh*, and in one or two some influence of the phonetic appears.

有 231 ʿYiu *To have.*—Besides *yiu*, others are read *hwui, wéi* and *yü*; a few show traces of the meaning of the primitive.

而 232 ˏ'Rh *Rad.* 126.—Most of the sounds are *'rh, nai* or *nuh*, being aberrant; from it flow No. 527 耎 and No. 936 需, two small groups.

成 233 ˏCh'ing *To complete.*—Two are read *shing*, as exceptions to *ch'ing*; their meanings sometimes partake of its own; it is not the same as No. 224 戎 or No. 235 戌.

存 234 ˏTs'un *To preserve.*—About half are read *tsien* and *ts'un*; none exhibit any decided trace of the primitive in their meanings.

戌 235 Süh, *The eighth hour.*—This primitive is not to be written 戍 which nearly resembles it; the sounds are incongruous.

夸 236 ˏKw'a *To brag.*—With *kw'a*, the sounds of *k'u* and *hu* also occur; in many compounds some ideas of bragging or grandeur are noticed.

至 237 Chi' *Rad.* 133.—Half a dozen words are read *tieh*; the others are *chi*, but their meanings are dissimilar.

耳 238 ʿ'Rh *Rad.* 128.—The sounds in this group are *'rh* or *ni*; few of them relate to the meaning of the phonetic.

圭 239 ˏKwéi *A baton.*—Much diversity of sound exists here, as *kwa, wa, kwéi, hiai* and *kiai*; No. 421 卦 is derived from it.

寺 240 Sz'ʾ *A temple.*—In this group all differ from the primitive, the sounds *shi, chi, t'ang* and *tai* being common; No. 697 時 flows from it.

考 241 ʿK'ao *To examine.*—A small uniformly-sounded group, but with very dissimilar meanings.

𢦏 242 ˏTsai *To wound.*—All but one are read *tsai*; the primitive is not in use, but most of the compounds show traces of its meaning.

吉 243 Kih, *Fortunate.*—Modifications of the sound *kih*, as *kieh, hieh, hiah* and *kiah*, occur in this group, which is very incongruous.

亘 ...

老 244 Lao — Rad. 125.—Most of these are uniform in sound, but have no common bond in their meaning.

亘 245 Süen — *To publish.*—The sounds *hwan* and *yuen* prevail under this primitive, which is much like No. 228 亙 and flows into No. 503 宣.

吏 246 Li — *An official.*—The compounds are read *shi*, and have apparently got their sounds from 史 a history.

西 247 Si — *Rad.* 146.—This is also used as a contraction of 麗 in 洒 and 晒 and others; the sounds are *si*, *shai*, *tsien* and *shin*.

𦣞 248 I — *The chin.*—These are sounded *i*, with one exception, but their meanings vary much; it differs from 臣 a statesman.

朿 249 Tsz' — *A thorn.*—Besides *tsz'* the sounds *tsieh* or *shih* occur; this is liable to be confounded with its derivative No. 323 束, and the two are often miswritten.

巩 250 K'ung — *Within.*—Two of this group are read *k'iüng*, but their meanings indicate nothing of the primitive; a sub-group appears in No. 836 筑.

共 251 Kung — *Altogether.*—Those not read *kung*, are read *hung*, and a few exhibit traces of the signification of the phonetic.

聿 252 Yuh — *Rad.* 129.—Most of these are read *lüh*; others are *tsin*, *pih* and *yuh*, and their meanings are equally diverse; No. 569 律 is a sub-group.

艮 253 Kăn — *Rad.* 138.—In this group *kan* runs into *hăn*, *yin*, *yen* and *k'ien*; one derivative No. 300 良 gives rise to others, as No. 624 郎.

羽 254 Yü — *Rad.* 124.—The sounds in this small group change from the primitive into *hü* and *i*; No. 948 翟 heads a large sub-group.

丞 255 Ch'ing — *To aid.*—A group uniform in sound, and from one of the compounds comes No. 660 烝; the character 承 is much like it.

㓞 256 Kieh — *To separate.* The sounds are mostly *kieh*, *kiah* and *yeh*; the primitive alters a little in composition; two sub-groups, No. 567 契 and No. 809 絜 are important.

耒 257 Léi — *Rad.* 127.—Uniform in sound, this group is diverse in meaning; No. 409 來 is often contracted like it.

缶 258 Feu — *Rad.* 121.—All but one, *sie*, read like the primitive, which also gives its meaning to one or two derivatives.

朱 259 Chu — *Red.*—In a few words *chu* runs into *shu*, but the group is nearly homophonous, and several show traces of its meaning.

先 260 Sien — *First.*—Considerable diversity of sound exists in this group, as *si* and *shăng* are applied even to the same character.

幵 261 Kien — *Equally.*—The sound *kien* runs into *yen*, *hing* and *ki*; it is often contracted to 开, and the contraction of No. 435 其 is 亓, which is sometimes confounded with it.

舌 262 Sheh — *Rad.* 135.—The sounds *kwah*, *hwa*, *koh*, *hoh* and *tien*, show the variations in this group; the meanings are very diverse.

朶 263 Tŏ — *A bouquet.*—Uniform in sound, this group shows no similiarity in its meanings; 朵 is another form of it.

旬 264 Süun — *A decade.*—A few of these read *h'iün* for *siün*, and the primitive is occasionally written as No. 359 夋 and No. 565 盾 from likeness of sound; 𦥯 leads a few other derivatives.

多 265 To — *Many.*—The sounds *to*, *ché* and *i* are heard in these compounds, which are unlike the primitive in meaning; it is also used as a radical under 夕 the evening.

名 266 Ming — *Name.*—This group is uniform in sound, while the significations indicate no affinity with the phonetic in meaning.

危 267 Wéi — *Dangerous.*—The sound *wéi* alters into *kwéi* in most of the characters, some of which resemble it in meaning.

后 268 Heu — *Empress.*—*Heu* and *keu* are the sounds in this group, but none of them show the sense of the primitive.

𠂢 269 P'ai — *Rivulet.*—*Pai*, *mih* and *moh* are the sounds; the meanings show little likeness to the primitive, which is altered to No. 131 永 in badly-written characters.

行 270 Hing — *Rad.* 144.—The compounds are read *hăng*, but few of them show any traces of its meaning.

夅 271 Kiang — *To descend upon.*—The sound *kiang* varies into *hiang*, *hung* and *pang*; the primitive is not used alone, and differs from No. 348 夆 slightly.

各 272 Koh — *Each.*—The most part of this group is read *loh*, then *hoh*, *koh*, *lioh* and *lu*; from it flows No. 504 客 and No. 865 路.

舟 273 Cheu — *Rad.* 137.—All the compounds read like their phonetic, but none of them have its meaning.

兆 274 Chao — *A sign.*—The sounds *yao*, *tiao*, *tao*, *chao* and *fu* are found here, but the meaning of the primitive does not appear.

旨 275 Chi — *Will.*—These are read *i* and *chi*, but their meanings show no reference to it.

伏 276 Fuh — *To prostrate.*—These are uniform in sound, but not in sense; it is easily distinguished from No. 278 休 and No. 72 犬, from which it flows.

伐 277 Fah — *To fight.*—All agree with their phonetic in sound at least; it must be distinguished from No. 176 代 and No. 345 我

休 278 Hiu — *To desist.*—The sounds are uniform in this group; one of the compounds 烋 is sometimes used for itself.

伊 279 I — *He.*—A small group, uniform in sound, but diverse in meaning; the right half is used also as a synonymous form.

向 280 Hiang — *Towards.*—*Hiang* runs into *shang* in some of these; it is to be distinguished from No. 206 冋 and No. 291 同

血 281 Hüeh — *Rad.* 143.—The sound of *hüeh* glides into *süh* in many of these characters, and one is read *si*.

任 282 Jin — *An official charge.*—With one exception this group is read *jin*; the primitive is sometimes abbreviated to 壬 in composition, which is seen also in No. 373 呈.

州 283 Cheu — *A district.*—One sound runs through all these, but their meanings show no similarity.

全 284 Ts'üen — *Altogether.*—The sounds of *ts'üen* and *shwan* run through this group; No. 478 金 is somewhat like it in form.

合 285 Hoh — *To join.*—Besides *hoh*, the sounds *koh*, *hiah*, *kiah*, *shih* and *kéh* occur; it reäppears in Nos. 579 弇 and 837 答; several words bear traces of the meaning of the primitive.

牟 286 Meu — *To bellow.*—The group is uniform in sound, but the derivatives bear no affinity with the meaning of their phonetic.

如 287 Jü — *As, if.*—Most of these follow their leader, *shu* and *sü* being exceptions; it is somewhat like No. 188 奴.

光 288 *Kwang* *Light.*—A group nearly uniform in sound, one only being read *kung*, but showing little analogy to it in meaning; No. 699 晃 is derived from it.

曳 289 *I* *To draw.*—The sound *i* prevails, but *yeh* and *sieh* are also heard; some of the derivatives interchange it with No. 152 世.

因 290 *Yin* *Because.*—*Yin* is altered to *yen* in four instances, but the meanings of the words show no affinity; it is interchanged with No. 536 垔 in some of them.

同 291 *Tung* *Same.*—A group uniform in sound; many of the derivatives contain an allusion to tubular things; it is like No. 206 冋 and No. 293 回 in its shape.

曲 292 *K'üh* *Crooked.*—This small group is unlike in sound and sense, one being pronounced *küng*.

回 293 *Hwéi* *To revolve.*—These characters are uniform in sound, and many of them preserve something of the primitive in their meanings.

完 294 *Wan* *To finish.*—*Hwan*, *kwan*, *wan* and *yuen* are the sounds of these derivatives, in which no similarity of meaning appears.

沙 295 *Sha* *Sand.*—*Sha* and *so* divide these characters, and in a few a meaning like a sandy color or roughness can be traced; No. 123 少 is the origin of this primitive.

辛 296 *Sin* *Rad.* 160.—These characters have no similarity in sound or sense, and might be properly referred to the radical; the real group is under No. 933 辡.

言 297 *Yen* *Rad.* 149.—These words might have been properly referred to the radical *yen*, as their meanings partake of it.

㐬 298 *Liu* *An expanse of water.*—This resembles No. 217 巟; *liu* and *sho* are the sounds, and the derivative 疏 becomes a primitive in 蔬 pulse.

亨 299 *Hăng* *Pervading.*—*Hăng* and *păng* are the sounds, but in none of the compounds is the influence of the primitive to be seen.

良 300 *Liang* *Conscientious.*—*Liang*, *lang* and *niang* are the sounds; it much resembles No. 253 艮, and is sometimes interchanged with No. 624 郎, one of its derivatives.

弟 301 *Ti* *Brother.*—Uniform in sound with their primitive, several of the characters show traces of its meanings; it is sometimes written like No. 226 夷 making a few synonyms.

辰 302 *Shăn* *Rad.* 161.—The sounds are all *chün* and *shun*, and the primitive is liable to be mistaken for No. 402 長.

戒 303 *Kiai* *A precept.*—*Kiai* and *hiai* are the only sounds; and several words exhibit some analogy to the primitive in their meaning.

夾 304 *Kiah* *To compress.*—The largest part are read *kieh*, others are *kiah*, *hiah*, *hieh* and *tsieh*; 陝 is read *shen*; and, unlike 陜 *hieh*, the primitive is interchanged with No. 285 合 and No. 521 匧 in a few.

巫 305 *Wu* *Incantation.*—The characters exhibit traces of the primitive, from which they differ in sound; one (筮) becomes a primitive.

吾 306 *Wu* *I.*—*Wu*, *yü* and *ya* are the sounds; the idea of forcibly stopping is found in half of the derivatives.

尨 307 *Mang* *A hound.*—Uniform in sound, the group is diverse in meaning, and contains no word in common use.

否 308 *Feu* *Not.*—These derivatives are read *péi* and *pi*; it is derived from No. 71 不, and resembles that group in meaning.

克 309 *Koh* *To overcome.*—These are read *koh* and *k'ing*; two common derivatives are synonyms.

巠 310 *King* *A rivulet.*—This group is read *king*, *hing* and *kăng*; it is often contracted to 圣 in rapid writing.

邪 311 *Sié* *Illicit.*—All are read *yé*; and the primitive is probably contracted from 耶, with which half of the derivatives are still written, as 椰 a cocoa-nut.

孛 312 *Poh* *To turn pale.*—These are divided between *poh*, *puh* and *péi*; but there is no similarity of meaning among them.

志 313 *Chi* *Will.*—All are read like the primitive, but they have no likeness to it in meaning.

耴 314 *Cheh* *Pendulous ears.*—This resembles No. 417 取, but is not properly interchanged with it; nearly all are read *cheh*.

弄 315 *Lung* *To handle.*—These characters all follow their phonetic, but not in its meaning.

孝 316 *Hiao* *Filial duty.*—All except one (酵 *kiao*) are sounded *hiao*, but no connection in their meanings can be traced.

却 317 *Kioh* *To refuse.*—This is often written 卻 and 郄, but not quite correctly; the characters are read alike, but are seldom used.

走 318 *Tseu* *Rad.* 156.—The derivatives are unlike in sound and sense; and only one of them (徒 *tu*) is much used.

豆 319 *Teu* *Rad.* 151.—*Teu* is the common sound; others are read *jü*, *shu* and *twan*; but no reference to the primitive appears in its derivatives.

車 320 *Ché* *Rad.* 159.—Besides those read *ché*, two are read 陣 *chăn* and 庫 *k'u*, which show a reference to the meaning of the primitive; it is tripled in one aberrant form 轟 *hăng*.

更 321 *Kăng* *To change*—All but two, 硬 and 鞕 *ying* are read *kăng*, but no similarity of sense appears in any of them; No. 573 便 is derived from this.

甫 322 *Fu* *To begin.*—In this group, *fu* and *pu* are only sounds; No. 648 尃 is formed from it.

束 323 *Shuh* *To bind.*—Three are read *sung*, the others are *shuh*, *suh* and *shoh*; it is often confounded with No. 249 朿 even in well-printed books.

酉 324 *Yiu* *Rad.* 164.—Four are read *yiu*; two do not really belong to the group, though they (*tsiu* 酒 and 遒) cannot well be placed elsewhere in this system.

求 325 *K'iu* *To ask.*—All these are alike in sound, but their senses differ greatly; many are common characters.

折 326 *Cheh* *To break.*—Out of this group only two (逝 and 誓 *shi*) vary in sound, but there is no general connection between them in meaning.

甬 327 *Yung* *To promenade.*—Most are read *yung*, and the others are *tung* and *sung*; some of them are interchanged with 勇 or No. 720 庸.

𠬶 328 *Tsin* This group is nearly uniform in its sound of *tsin*, one being read *sien*; no similarity in signification appears.

君 329 *Kiun* *A prince.*—These characters are read *kiun* and *hiun*; none of them show any allusion to the phonetic in their meanings.

局 330 *Küh* *A storehouse.*—All here are read *küh*, but are rarely used; the primitive itself more than they all.

忌 331 *Ki* *To shun.*—All here agree with the primitve in sound, and some slightly in meaning; none of them are much in use.

忍 332 ʿJăn *Patience.*—This sub-group comes from No. 34 刃 and is read *nien, no, jăn* or *jăng;* the primitive is sometimes badly written like No. 466 忽.

那 333 ˏNo *That.*—All are read *no* and *na*, like the primitive, but they resemble it only in sound.

寽 334 Lieh, *A pinch.*—All agree with its sound *lieh*, except two read *lai;* it is like the next.

孚 335 Feu *Trustful.*—The last and next are liable to be confounded with this; all under it are read *fu* or *feu, jü* or *piao*, but their meanings show no agreement.

妥 336 T'oʾ *Stable.*—These characters are read *sui, no, néi* and *t'o*, and their senses vary much; it is not often confounded with No. 457 委, which it resembles.

坐 337 Tsoʾ *To sit.*—All these are read like the primitive, and four of them show traces of its meaning.

谷 338 Kuh, *Rad.* 150.—This group is read *luh, kih, yuh* and *suh;* one character 欲 reäppears in 慾 with the same sound and the sense intensified.

邦 339 ˏPang *A kingdom.*—These follow the primitive only in their sound; it resembles No. 256 切 a little.

每 340 ʿMéi *Each.*—More than half are read like the phonetic, the others are *hwéi, hai*, and one (敏 *min*,) reäppears in 慜 *min* and 繁 *fan*.

廷 341 ˏTing *A pavilion.*—This is occasionally written 廷, but it is often confounded with No. 350 延; the group is uniformly read *t'ing*, and the idea of elongation runs through their meanings.

告 342 ʿKao *To announce.*—*Kuh, huh, kao* and *hao* are the sounds in this group; the character 嚳 shows the integration of two ancient characters.

秀 343 ʿSiu *Adorned.*—This group is read *siu, yiu* and *teu*, and a common character is found under each sound; the primitive resembles 秃 bald, which forms 痜 *tuh* and 頹 *tui*, and this last again forms 穨; but this small group is not worth separating.

利 344 ʿLi *Advantage.*—The characters are uniform in sound, but exhibit no likeness in sense; it is altered to 𥝢, but not in good usage.

我 345 Ngoʾ *I.*—This collection is sounded *wo* and *ngo*, but no trace of the primitive appears in the significations.

角 346 Kioh, *Rad.* 148.—These characters are all read *kioh;* one of those put among them 魟 properly belongs to No. 27.

免 347 ʿMien *To refrain.*—This group is read *mien* and *wan*, with *méi* and *wăn;* it closely resembles 兔 a rabbit, which forms a few derivatives.

夆 348 ˏFung *To meet.*—This group is read *fung* and *pung;* the primitive is derived from 丰 luxuriant; it is not unlike No. 271 夅 and even No. 401 奉, but cannot be thus written; a large sub-group occurs under No. 774 逢.

位 349 Wéiʾ *A dignity.*—The compounds are read *li*, a small group much in use.

延 350 ˏYen *To delay.*—Most are read *yen*, and others *tan, shen* and *sien;* this primitive is so nearly like No. 341 廷 that they are often confounded, and this one is wrongly numbered with eight strokes.

攸 351 ˏYiu *Contented.*—More than half of these are read *tiao* from 條 one of its derivatives; the others are read *yiu, siu* and *siao;* the radical is usually placed in the right corner, as in 倐; the form 條 reäppears in 滌 to wash, and seven other characters.

狄 352 Tih, *Nomads.*—This group is pronounced like its primitive, but their significations show little resemblance to it.

狂 353 Kw'ang *Insensate.*—This is derived from No. 65 王, and its combinations are read *kw'ang;* the primitive is sometimes improperly altered to No. 223 匡.

坒 354 ʿPi *Joined.*—This is a sub-group of No. 108 比, and its sounds are all *pi*, but their meanings are unlike in all respects.

余 355 ˏYü *I.*—The sounds here are *yü, tu, sü, chu* and *shé;* the primitive is often written 佘 wrongly, and a compound 除 reäppears in a sub-group of three or four.

含 356 ˏHan *To contain.*—This group follows its leading sound, and some have tried to find traces of its meaning in them; it resembles No. 182 令 when written badly.

希 357 ˏHi *To hope.*—A group read *hi, ch'i* and *hiu*, but showing no similarity to the primitive in sense.

兌 358 Tuiʾ *To barter.*—The sounds of *tui* and *shui*, with those of *jui, shwoh, toh* and *yueh*, are heard, most of them common characters.

夋 359 Siünʾ *Elated.*—This group is sounded *tsun, tswan, tsü* and *so*, showing the uncertainty of the phonetic element; the forms of this and the next are to be carefully noted.

矣 360 ʿI *Certainly*—This group is mostly read *ngai* and *ai*, with *i* and *si;* three of the derivatives are like the primitive, an interjection.

壯 361 Chwangʾ *Robust.*—These characters are read like their primitive, which is itself derived from No. 118 爿; none of them indicate any affinity in meaning.

𡿧 362 Nih, *Flowing water.*—This small group is read *tsah*, or *tsan* in some dialects; the primitive is sometimes written 甾, like No 483, and oftener 㚔, neither of them accurately.

步 363 Puʾ *A step.*—This group is read *pu*, except two that are pronounced *cheh* or *sheh*.

旱 364 ʿHan *Dry.*—Four characters are read *kan*, the rest are *han;* they are derived from No. 20 干, and many derivatives in the two groups are synonymous; 早 is like it in form.

臬 365 Nieh, *To close.*—This is also written 臯, but the briefer form is also correct; the compounds are read like it, and the two mean much the same.

見 366 Kienʾ *Rad.* 147.—Most of these are read *hien*, others *kien, yen* and *tien;* it is a natural group and easily distinguished from those under the radical.

貝 367 Péiʾ *Rad.* 154.—All are read *péi* or *pai;* it is not always easy to discriminate between this and No. 490 具, especially in badly-printed books.

甹 368 ˏPing *Quickly.*—*Ping* and *ching* are the sounds in this small group; three of them relate to marriage contracts.

里 369 ʿLi *Rad.* 166.—All are read *li*, except 埋 *mai* and 悝 *kwei*, but none of them derive their meanings from it.

助 370 Chuʾ *To help.*—This is derived from No. 193 且, and the group follows its sound; their meanings are different, but one may force a connection in 鋤, and say it is the *iron* which *helps* the farmer.

別 371 Pieh, *To divide.*—These words are read *pieh* and *pah*, and a little ingenuity can discover traces of the meaning of *pieh* in most of them.

邑 372 Yih, *Rad.* 163.—All are read *yih* or *yeh;* but the meanings of the derivatives differ entirely from the primitive.

呈 373 ˏChing *To report to.*—This group is read *ch'ing*, except 郢 *ying*, but the meanings vary according to the radical; 聖 reappears in the sub-group No. 886.

肙 374 Yuen˒ *To twist.*—This is contracted to 肙 in common books; its similarity to No. 703 員 often leads to mistakes; most are read *küen*, others are *yüen* and *hüen*.

呂 375 ˋLu *A vertebra.*—This is often written without the connecting line, with six strokes; most of the characters are read *lü*, two are read *kü*, and 宮 forms a sub-group of three.

足 376 Tsuh˒ *Rad.* 157.—The few compounds in which this serves as a primitive are mostly read *choh*, with *tsoh* or *tsuh*, but none refer to its meaning very clearly.

困 377 K'wăn *Wearied.*—All this group follows its leading sound, but none of them its signification; it is easily confounded with No. 499 囷, and care is required to distinguish them.

吳 378 ˏWu *To cry aloud.*—All are read *wu* or *yü*, but their diversity of meanings shows that the primitive has had no effect upon them.

岑 379 ˏCh'ăn *High.*—This group is read *tsin*, *chăn* or *chin*; its meanings bear no affinity to the primitive.

肖 380 Siao˒ *Like.*—About half of these are read *siao*; others are *shao*, *tsiao* and *chao*; a sub-group is found under No. 658 屑.

EIGHT STROKES.

宗 381 ˏTsung *Ancestors.*—These are pronounced *tsung* and *chung*; there are several synonyms, and the phonetic is often exchanged with 悤 and with No. 582 㚇.

定 382 Ting˒ *To fix.*—*Ting*, *chan* and *tien* are the common sounds, but the diversity in meanings is greater.

宛 383 ˋYuen *To environ.*—About half of this group is read *yuen*, and the others *wan*; the primitive is now and then contracted to 夗, as 盌 and 盌 a plate.

空 384 ˏK'ung *Empty.*—This primitive is derived from No. 27 工, as that sound is heard in three-fourths of the characters, others being read *k'iang*; many of them, too, are like it in meaning.

宜 385 ˏI *Right.*—All of this group are read *i*, but most of the characters are unlike the phonetic in meaning; it is written like 冝 very often.

官 386 ˏKwan *An officer.*—Some of this group vary their sounds from *kwan* into *wan* and *kien*, but show no indication that the primitive has influenced their meanings.

沾 387 ˏChen *To moisten.*—This is derived from No. 190 占, and follows it in sound.

妾 388 Tsieh˒ *A concubine.*—*Tsieh* and *sah* are the only sounds under this primitive, which has two or three ideographic derivatives.

咅 389 ˏPéi *To spit.*—This can be mistaken for No. 508 音, but it is never used by itself, the sounds are *péi*, *feu*, *peu*, *teu* and *pu*, and their meanings are still more unlike.

卒 390 Tsuh˒ *A soldier.*—The compounds in the *juh shing* are sounded *tsuh* or *suh*; those in the *k'ü shing* are *tsui* and *sui*.

庚 391 ˏKăng *Age.*—This group is uniformly read *kăng*, but the primitive is used more than all its compounds.

於 392 ˏYü *In, at.*—All in this group are read *yü*, except two; the primitive is changed to 扵 but this form is rarely seen in the compounds.

府 393 ˋFu *A prefecture.*—This is derived from No. 178 付, which has three sub-groups, but they are seldom interchanged with this; their pronunciation is like the primitive.

夜 394 Yé˒ *Night.*—Half the compounds are read *yih*; the rest *yé*, one of which 㖡 denotes the *night voice* of a bird.

育 395 Yuh˒ *To nourish.*—These are read like the primitive, and one of the compounds is a synonym of it.

享 396 ˋHiang *To enjoy.*—This is to be distinguished from No. 299 亨; it makes two sub-groups, Nos. 727 郭 and 728 孰; *chun*, *tun* and *shun* are the only sounds in it.

京 397 ˏKing *A metropolis.*—Most of the compounds are read *liang*, then *king*, *lioh* and *kiang*; No. 863 景 and No. 803 就 form two sub-groups.

罙 398 ˏShan Only two of this group are in common use, one of which is read *tan*; the primitive is not used.

羌 399 ˏKiang *Strong.*—These characters are all read *kiang*; the primitive is written 羗 and 羗 in most cases.

炎 400 ˏYen *A flame.*—Most of the derivatives are read *tan*, others are *yen*, *shan*, *piao* and *huh*, and a few of them refer to it in their meanings.

奉 401 Fung˒ *To offer.*—*Fung*, *pung* and *pang* are the sounds in this group; the primitive is often wrongly written like No. 348 夆, in consequence of the similarity of sound.

長 402 ˏCh'ang *Rad.* 168.—These characters are all read *chang*; the derivatives are more used than those under the radical; it is sometimes miswritten like No. 302 镸.

忝 403 ˋT'ien *To defame.*—This is also written 忝, and there seems to be no difference between the two; they both look like 恭 *kung*, which has no derivatives; the sounds are uniformly *t'ien*.

武 404 ˋWu *Military.*—This group is mostly read *wu*, the derivative 賦 *pin* being the chief exception.

妻 405 ˏTs'i *A wife.*—All are read *ts'i*, but in none of them can any trace of the primitive be seen.

疌 406 Nieh˒ *A treddle.*—This is often written 疌, apparently to show the radical plainly; the sounds of *tsieh*, *tieh*, *sheh* and *sha* are heard.

肩 407 ˏKien *The shoulder.*—This group reads like its phonetic, but none of the characters are much used.

奇 408 ˏKi *Surprising.*—The sounds *i* and *ki* are the only ones in this most numerous group under one primitive; three or four of its compounds as 旖 waving, 猗 flourishing and 寄 to send, form sub-groups.

來 409 ˏLai *To come on.*—This group follows the phonetic; the primitive is sometimes written 来 when it resembles No. 257 耒.

厓 410 ˏYai *A cliff.*—These characters are read *yai* and *ngai*, but only one of them has any reference to its meaning.

直 411 Chih˒ *Straight.*—The sounds *chih* and *sheh* are the chief ones; No. 674 眞 is derived from it, and care is necessary to distinguish the two.

豖 412 Chuh˒ *A pig fettered.*—The sounds in this group are *chuh*, *chung*, *choh* and *tuh*; it is derived from the radical 豕 a pig, and is often carelessly written without the crossed line.

奄 413 ˋYen *Suddenly.*—The sounds in this collection range between *yen* and *ngan*, *yeh* and *ngoh*.

奈 414 Nai' *How.*—The sounds here are *nah* and *noh*, as well as *nai*, but only one word is in common use.

到 415 Tao' *To reach.*—This sub-group is derived from No. 237 至, and is uniformly read *tao*.

幸 416 'Hing *Happily.*—This primitive differs from No. 296 辛 and is sometimes written 㚔 in pedantic or ancient style; the derivatives are mostly read *hing*, and half of them mean to note; it reäppears in No. 927 睪.

取 417 'Tsu *To take.*—This resembles No. 314 耴; about one-half of the characters change into *tseu* and *cheu*; No. 864 最 forms a sub-group.

表 418 'Piao *To show out.*—From the similarity in sound, this is sometimes interchanged with No. 752 票; the derivatives are read *piao*.

毒 419 Tuh, *Poisonous.*—This group is read *tuh*, except 瑇 *tai*, but has no unity of meaning; the incorrect form 毐 is occasionally seen.

青 420 ,Tsing *Rad.* 174.—Some confusion exists in these derivatives, many of which properly come under the radical; all are read *tsing*, except 猜 *chai*, and many of them relate to color.

卦 421 Kwa' *Augury.*—A sub-group from No. 239 圭; its characters mostly refer to suspension, and are read *kwa* and *hwa*.

坴 422 Luh, *A road.*—These are mostly read *lüh*, with *müh* and *kwéi*; their meanings seldom have reference to the primitive.

夌 423 ,Ling *An eminence.*—This resembles the preceding, but is never interchanged with it; the characters are read *ling* or *lăng*.

亞 424 Ya' *Second to.*—The prevailing sounds are *ngoh* and *ya*; this primitive forms sub-groups under 壼 and 壺 and No. 819 惡.

東 425 ,Tung *East.*—This resembles No. 532 柬 in poorly-printed books; the compounds are read *tung* except 陳 *chăn*, but their meanings have no likeness.

事 426 Shi' *Affair.*—Uniform in sound with the primitive, but showing no affinity to its meaning.

亟 427 Kih, *Extreme.*—The compounds of this phonetic follow its sound, and it is almost a synonym of 極, its most common character.

画 428 Hwah, *To limn.*—This is regarded as a contraction of 畫, and the full form is also found in well-printed books; the characters are mostly read *hwoh*.

臤 429 ,Kien *Robust.*—This resembles 取, and its full form 堅 seems to have been often intended in the compounds; No. 946 監 and No. 995 覽 form two sub-groups; *kien*, *hien*, *shu*, *kin*, *shăn* and *kăng* are the sounds under it.

或 430 Hwoh, *Perhaps.*—This group is read *kwoh*, *hwoh* or *yuh*; there are sub-groups under No. 794 國 and 彧 elegant.

兩 431 'Liang *Two.*—The sounds in this group are all *liang*, and a tinge of its meaning is seen in several of them.

林 432 ,Lin *A forest.*—The sounds *lan*, *lin*, *shăn* and *pin* occur under this primitive; it is not the same as 𣏟, with which it is occasionally confounded.

析 433 Sih, *To cleave.*—This is derived from No. 99 斤, and the group is uniformly sounded *sih*, but the compounds show nothing of its meaning.

松 434 ,Sung *A pine.*—This is derived from No. 116 公, of which it is a sub-group; all are read *sung*, but have no likeness of meaning.

其 435 ,K'i *This.*—A large and homophonous group; three small sub-groups flow from it, as 基 a foundation, No. 284 斯 that, and 綦 bluish.

昔 436 Sih, *Anciently.*—The sounds *sih*, *tsih*, *tsoh* and *tsioh*, in the *juh shing*, and *cha*, *tso* and *tsié* in the *shang shing* occur; one derivative No. 950 措 heads a small sub-group.

戔 437 ,Tsan *Light.*—The sounds of *tsien*, *chan* and *tsan* are common in this group; some sub-groups are formed from it.

帚 438 'Cheu *To sweep.*—*Sao* and *fu* are the sounds; one derivative 掃 is another form of the primitive, which is not in use.

門 439 ,Măn *Rad.* 169.—Two are read *wăn*, and the others *măn*; some of them properly belong to 門 as a radical.

隶 440 'Tai *Rad.* 171.—This group mostly belongs to 隶 as a radical, and it is impossible to decide under which class to look for a character.

居 441 K'ü, *To dwell.*—Regular in its form and sound, and three or four of the group show some analogy to the primitive in their signification.

屈 442 Küih, *To bend.*—The sounds are *küih*, *kuh*, *küeh* and *huh*; the primitive comes from No. 207 出, with which it is occasionally interchanged.

叕 443 Choh, *To connect.*—The sound of these characters is mostly *choh*, then *chui*, *toh* and *ti*; an idea of continuity is often seen in their meanings.

函 444 ,Han *A letter.*—The sounds here are uniformly *han*, but the significations are unlike.

孟 445 Măng' *First.*—A small collection, read *măng*; the derivatives are of trifling importance.

阿 446 ,Ngo *A particle.*—The compounds are *ngo* or *o*; it is one of several sub-groups derived from No. 145 可.

受 447 Sheu' *To receive.*—All but one 閺 *wăn* of this collection are read *sheu*, and that is rarely used.

㸒 448 ,Yin *To approach.*—This group is read *yin*; there are few common characters except 婬 and 淫, the last of which reäppears in 霪 a soaking rain.

采 449 'Ts'ai *Ornamental.*—One of this group is read *kwéi*, an exception to the usual sound of *ts'ăi*; four or five are common characters.

爭 450 ,Chăng *To dissent.*—This group is read *chăng* and *tsing*; some of the words affect the meaning as well as the sound of the primitive; it is interchanged with No. 420 青.

非 451 ,Fei *Rad.* 175.—Most of this group read *féi*, the others are read *pai* and *péi*; the distinction between it as a phonetic and a radical is dubious.

幷 452 ,Ping *United.*—The sounds of *ping*, *pung* and *p'ien* occur in this group; the primitive is often contracted to 并, and may be sought for under six strokes.

卷 453 Küen' *A roll.*—These are all read *küen*, and a trace of its meaning is perceptible in many of the derivatives; where the radical is placed underneath, 劵 is sometimes contracted to No. 219 共, which thus becomes a synonym.

知 454 ,Chè *To know.*—Uniformly read *chi*, this group has no similarity in meaning.

制 455 Chi' *A law.*—This collection of characters is read *chi*, but their meanings are very diverse.

垂 456 ˏChui *Pendent.*—The sounds *chui*, *to*, *shui* and *yue* occur in the group, in which no affinity of meaning is seen.

委 457 ʿWéi *To depute.*—The sound *wéi* varies into *wo*, *jui*, *jwa*, *néi* and *ngai*; this primitive is like No. 336 妥, and the two are often written wrongly.

匊 458 Küh˒ *A pinch.*—The sounds of this group follow the primitive, and in many of the characters some glimpses of its meaning are seen.

肥 459 ˏFéi *Fat.*—All are read *féi*, and one or two show some analogy to the primitive, as 痱 *ill from obesity*; it is interchanged with 巴 in one instance.

朋 460 ˏPăng *A friend.*—This group is read *păng*, with one or two read *ping*; a sub-group of nine characters is formed from 崩, many of them synonymous forms of it.

服 461 Fuh˒ *To subdue.*—All are sounded *fuh* or *puh*; this group is properly derived from 𠬝 to govern, under which are found 報 to recompense, 赧 to blush, and others.

戾 462 Li˒ *Crime.*—These are sounded *li* and *léi*; their meanings differ widely from the primitive.

𢼄 463 ʿKi *To open.*—One character 肇 *chao* is peculiar in its sound, and the primitive always covers the radical.

周 464 ˓Cheu *Around.*—So many in this group are read *tiao*, that the more usual sound *cheu* is made doubtful; their meanings have no affinity.

匋 465 ˏT'ao *A kiln.*—This group is all read *t'ao*; the primitive is derived from No. 258 缶, and the two have many synonyms.

忽 466 Hwuh˒ *Suddenly.*—Nearly alike in sound, as *hwuh* or *uh*, these characters also present many analogies in their meanings; the primitive proceeds from No. 96 勿, and is not the same as No. 563 忽.

臽 467 Hien˒ *A pit.*—This character proceeds from 臼 a mortar, and its compounds are read *hien*, *yen*, *han*, *kan*, *tan*, *chan* and *kiah*; ideas alluding to cavities occur in several.

欣 468 ˓Hin *Joyful.*—Many of this group are synonyms with those under No. 99 斤, and resemble their primitive in sound and sense.

咎 469 Kiu˒ *A fault.*—These differ wholly in sound and sense, and no analogy can be traced; the primitive 朁 *tsan* resembles it; 僭 噆 and 撍 are all its derivatives.

兒 470 ˏ'rh *A child.*—This is often erroneously written 皃 *mao*; the group is read *'rh*, *i* or *ni*, a few varying, and many show a trace of the primitive.

臾 471 ˏYü *An instant.*—This is often contracted to 臾, and like No. 467 臽 and No. 953 與, is derived from 臼 a mortar; its compounds are all read *yü*.

隹 472 ˓Chui *Rad.* 172.—As a primitive, this is confounded with *kia* 佳, and must be regarded as the same; a sub-group is formed from 雀 a sparrow, which then resembles No. 626 崔; the sounds *shui*, *sui*, *tui*, *hwéi*, *wéi* and *chun* occur under it.

帛 473 Poh˒ *Taffety.*—This group is read *poh*, *mien* and *kin*, and one of them 綿 has two derivatives.

阜 474 ʿFeu *Rad.* 170.—The derivatives are all read *feu* except 埠 *pu*, but their meanings are unlike; in some characters it is contracted to No. 208 𠂤, when the radical is under.

卑 475 ˓Pi *Despicable.*—This group is mostly read *pi*, then *péi* and *pai*; it is often incorrectly written like No. 498 畀.

昏 476 Hwun *Obscure.*—This character is altered to 昬 in those which are read *min*, apparently to indicate their difference from those read *hwun*, which more resemble the primitive.

念 477 Nien˒ *To think on.*—The sounds *nien*, *nieh*, *yen*, *jăn*, *tien* and *shăn* occur in this group, but none of the characters assimilate to the meaning of the primitive.

金 478 ˓Kin *Rad.* 167.—As a phonetic, this gives the sound of *kin* to nine, the others being read *yin* and *chao*; 欽 forms a sub-group of three.

肴 479 ˏHiao *Food.*—This group is uniformly read *hiao*, but no likeness is traceable in its meanings; it is made of No. 115 爻 placed above 肉 flesh.

侖 480 ˏLun *To join.*—*Lun*, the usual sound, rarely runs into *lüen*; the meanings do not correspond.

舍 481 Shié˒ *A cottage.*—This is derived from No. 262 舌, with which it has some synonyms; in 舖 and 舘 it is altered from the radicals 金 and 食.

彔 482 Luh˒ *To carve.*—The compounds are read *luh* and *poh*; No. 584 彖 is much like this in appearance.

甾 483 ˓Tsz *Wild land.*—These are often read *chi*; the primitive is also written 甾, but is not interchanged with No. 362 巛.

叔 484 Shuh˒ *A younger uncle.*—The sounds here are *shuh*, *tsuh*, *tuh*, *tsih* and *tsiao*; their meanings are quite unlike.

肯 485 ʿK'ăng *Willing.*—This group is read *kang* and *shih*; the primitive is a little like No. 479 肴.

卓 486 Choh˒ *To excel.*—The sound *choh* varies into *chao* in nearly half, others being read *tao* and *tiao*; it must not be written 𠦝, as that is used only as part of No. 826 朝.

虎 487 ʿHu *A tiger.*—This is regarded as another form of Rad. 141 虍, and all the compounds are so read; No. 672 虒 and 處, each make a small sub-group.

罔 488 ʿWang *None of.*—This group is sounded *wang*; the primitive is sometimes contracted to 网, which more easily distinguishes it from the next.

岡 489 ʿKang *A peak.*—These compounds are all read *kang*, but have no resemblance in meaning; 岡 is altered to 罡 in some of them; this and the last are easily confounded.

具 490 Kü˒ *To prepare.*—This group is read *kü*; the phonetic is often written like No. 367 貝, with which it has nothing in common.

㝵 491 Ngai˒ *An obstacle.*—The half of these are read *ngai* and the rest *teh*; the primitive has some relation to No. 240 寺 in some of the synonyms.

果 492 ʿKwo *Fruit.*—About two-thirds of this group agree in the sound *kwo*, but the others, read *hwo*, *lo*, *wo*, *hwa* and *kwan*, are so much in use, that the primitive is no guide to the sound.

明 493 ˏMing *Bright.*—One of this small group is read *măng*, the others *ming*; there is no resemblance in the meanings.

易 494 Yih˒ *To alter.*—Most of these derivatives are read *tih*, others *i*, *yih*, *sih*, *tsz'* and *sing*; the primitive is similar to No. 592 昜 light.

昆 495 ˓Kwun *Like.*—*Hwun* takes the place of *kwun* in about one-third of this group; in badly-printed books the primitive resembles No. 685 皀 clear.

昌 496 Ch'ang *Distinguished.*—All are read *ch'ang* in this group, and the primitive is shadowed forth in the meanings of many; its form resembles No. 597 冒.

固 497 Ku *Stable.*—This flows from No. 153 古, and the group is nearly uniformly sounded, *ku*, *ko* and *hoh* being variants.

畀 498 Pi *To give.*—This primitive differs from No. 475 卑, though confounded with it; the group is regularly sounded *pi*.

囷 499 K'iun *A granary.*—This and No. 377 困 are easily confounded, and the similarity of their sounds *kiun* and *k'wăn* is a reason for particular care.

典 500 T'ien *A law.*—This group follows the phonetic *tien;* one variant is read *t'un;* in some cases, No. 953 與 is badly written like this.

尙 501 Shang *Still.*—This group is read *shang*, *chang* and *tang;* similarity of sound may lead beginners to confound this and No. 715 商; several sub-groups flow from it, as No. 870 敞, No. 1032 黨 No. 786 堂, No. 914 當, No. 858 棠 and others.

沓 502 Tah *Heavy.*—This group is read *tah*; in a few of the compounds it is interchanged with No. 698 㬰 from identity of sound.

NINE STROKES.

宣 503 Siün *To publish.*—This flows from No. 245 亘, but it has little in common except sound; most of the words are read *hüen;* No. 555 爰 is interchanged with it.

客 504 Koh *A guest.*—This offshoot of No. 272 各 differs from it in sound, *kiah* being most common.

突 505 Tuh *Suddenly.*—One sound, *tuh* guides this group, but no ingenuity can detect any uniformity in the significations.

恒 506 Hăng *Constant.*—This group somewhat resembles No. 503, but it is a sub-group from No. 228 亙, and all the characters are read *kăng;* none are much used.

帝 507 Ti *A sovereign.*—In combination this is occasionally interchanged with No. 755 帶 and altered to 啇, but the group is nearly uniform in sound and form; *shò* 啻 is an anomaly.

音 508 Yin *Rad.* 180.—The use of this character as a phonetic or a radical is often perplexing; most are read *ngan*, the rest *yin*, *yen* and *k'in*; some of them are good examples of ideographic writing, as 䪦 *sick in sound* for drunk.

斿 509 Yiu *A pennon.*—This is also correctly written 斿; the sounds are all *yin*, but the meanings are unlike; it resembles the next in its form.

施 510 Shi *To concede.*—This appears to be derived from No. 35 也 and is often contracted to 㐌 in common books; the compounds are read *i* and *shi.*

度 511 Tu *A measure.*—The sounds here are *tu*, *toh* and *tuh;* it resembles, but is not likely to be confounded with *sih* 席 a mat, as that forms no compounds.

彥 512 Yen *Wise.*—A group nearly all read *yen* and *ngan*; the correct form is contracted to 彦 in well-printed books.

亭 513 T'ing *An arbor.*—This sub-group arises from No. 4 丁, and is sounded *t'ing;* the primitive varies into 亭 at all times.

复 514 Fuh *To revert to.*—The primitive has been superseded by one of its compounds, No. 849 復, which leads a sub-group; the sounds are *fuh* and *pih*, and many characters show traces of the primitive in their meaning.

軍 515 Kiün *An army.*—The sounds in this group are *kiün*, *hiün*, *yun*, *hwun*, *kwăn* and *hwéi*, but in only a few cases is there any hint of the meaning of the primitive.

首 516 Sheu *Rad.* 185.—Of this group, only two of the four come under it, which are read *tao.*

前 517 Tsien *Before.*—A homophonous collection read *tsien*, but only one or two of them show traces of the primitive in their signification.

咨 518 Tsz' *To report to.*—This might properly have remained a sub-group of No. 221 次, with which it agrees in sound.

奏 519 Tseu *To memorialize.*—These characters vary from *tseu* to *cheu* in a few cases; the primitive is easily confounded with No. 633 秦 unless care is taken.

春 520 Ch'un *The spring.*—This group is read *ch'un* nearly throughout; No. 732 舂 is sometimes confounded with it, by being contracted to this form.

匧 521 Kieh *A coffer.*—This flows from No. 304 夾, of which it is a derivative; the groups resemble each other in sense and sound.

育 522 To *To fall.*—The compounds are read *to;* the primitive is otherwise written 隋 without altering its sense; the sub-group No. 833 flows from 隨, but the others are unused.

威 523 Wéi *Majestic.*—This is sounded *wéi*, but the characters are unusual, nor liable to be confounded with those under No. 233 成 if care be used.

咸 524 Hien *All.*—The sound *hien* varies into *kien*, *chen*, *han* and *kan*, and one derivative 感 originates the few under No 884.

頁 525 Hieh *Rad.* 181.—Many of the derivatives of this primitive when used as a radical, show the difficulty of deciding where to put them; 須 reappears in No. 847; the sounds are *sü* and *fan.*

面 526 Mien *Rad.* 176.—The similarity of sound has ruled this group, which in many cases decides whether to put it here or under the radical; the meanings are incongruous.

耎 527 Jwan *Tender.*—The sounds in this group are *jwan*, *no* and *nwan;* the meanings in several cases exhibit traces of the primitive.

奔 528 Păn *To hasten.*—One character is read *făn*, and the others *păn;* the form of this primitive suggests some affinity to No. 149 本.

奓 529 Cha *Great.*—This flows from No. 265 多; the sounds are mostly *cha* and a few *na;* they bear no resemblance in meaning.

封 530 Fung *To seal.*—The derivatives which have this primitive on the side are read *fung*, those with it on the top are mostly read *pang.*

者 531 Ché *This.*—Most of these characters are read *chu*, and others are read *tu*, *ché* and *sü;* three small sub-groups occur under 著 *chu*, 署 *shu* and 諸 *chu*, and a fourth under No. 812 奢 still larger.

柬 532 Kien *To select.*—This primitive is often carelessly written like No. 425 東; one compound reappears in No. 1 0 0 闌; most of the characters are read *lien*, and a few *kien.*

匽 533 ʻYen *To conceal.*—This is really a sub-group of 晏 *yen*, but that has only one or two compounds; nearly all are read *yen*; *yah* and *an* being the exceptions.

畐 534 ʻFu *Happy.*—Most of this group are sounded *fu* or *fuh*, the rest are *pih*; 富 forms a sub-group of four characters.

剌 535 Lah˒ *Cruel.*—This group is read *lah*; the primitive resembles a compound of No. 249 刺, but the two are easily distinguished.

垔 536 ˛Yin *To wall up.*—The prevailing sound *yin* alters to *yen* and *kien* in a few cases; the phonetic often interchanges with No. 290 因

要 537 ˛Yao *To desire.*—This resembles the character 耍 *shwa*, but that forms no compounds; the sounds are uniformly *yao*.

相 538 ˛Siang *Mutual.*—A nearly homophonous group read *siang* and *shwang*; and the meanings are totally dissimilar; under No. 1007 霜 is a small sub-group.

査 539 ˛Ch'a *To examine.*—This primitive resembles No. 785 虘 in sound, and both may be derived from No. 192 且; its sounds are all *cha*.

甚 540 Shinʼ *Excessive.*—*Shăn*, *chăn*, *tan*, *kan*, *săn* and *chan*, are the sounds in this group; their meanings are even more diverse.

某 541 ʻMeu *Certain.*—Most of this group are read *méi*; only two follow the primitive in sound, and none in meaning.

枼 542 Yeh˒ *A leaf.*—The numerous sounds here are read *yeh*, *sieh*, *tieh*, *cheh* and *sheh*, and in several its meaning can be traced.

南 543 ˛Nan *South.*—A uniform group in sound, but unlike in meanings.

胡 544 ˛Hu *How.*—Apparently derived from No. 153 古, but its etymology shows a different source; its sounds are all *hu*, but its meanings diverse.

柔 545 ˛Teu *Soft.*—These are read *jau* and *nao*; a large number exhibit traces of the meaning of the primitive.

敄 546 Meuʼ *Strong.*—The radical is usually placed under the primitive, as in 務 *wu*; this group is read *meu*, *mu* and *muh*.

建 547 Kienʼ *To build.*—The derivatives are all read *kien*, but almost none of them exhibit its meaning.

屋 548 Wuh˒ *A dwelling.*—The characters in this group are read *wuh* or *uh*, but none of the meanings of the primitive enter into them.

叚 549 Kiaʼ *Illusory.*—This resembles No. 572 段, and some care is necessary to distinguish the two; the sounds are *kia* and *hia*.

韋 550 ˛Wéi *Rad.* 178.—It is sometimes doubtful in this group which should belong to the primitive and which to the radical; *wéi* is altered to *hwéi* and *i* in a few cases.

負 551 Fuʼ *To carry.*—These derivatives are sounded *fu*, but their meanings are incongruous; it is allied to No. 367 貝.

奐 552 Hwanʼ *Beautiful.*—*Hwan* is the usual sound in this group, except one or two read *twan*; the meanings are sometimes like the phonetic.

胥 553 ˛Sü *All.*—These are all read *sü* or *si*; their meanings have no relation to that of the primitive.

眉 554 ˛Méi *Eyebrows.*—A group read *méi* throughout; the old form of the phonetic 睂 is often used.

爰 555 Yuenʼ *Up to.*—About half are read *yuen*, the rest are *nwan*, *hwan* and *hüen*; the primitive is interchanged with No. 928 睘 and No. 527 奐 in a few cases.

爯 556 Chingʼ *To elevate.*—The sounds are *ching* or *chăng*; but their meanings are incongruous; it is often written 再 under eight strokes.

癸 557 ʻKwéi *To return.*—These compounds are read *kwéi*, except *küeh*; the group is very diverse in its meanings.

重 558 ʻChung *Heavy.*—About six are read *t'ung* or *hüeh*, the others are all *chung*; two (動 and 董) reäppear in sub-groups of three each.

臿 559 Chah˒ *To hull.*—A uniform group under *chah*, except a few read *shah* or *hiah*; the compounds show no affinity in meaning.

秋 560 ˛Ts'iu *Autumn.*—The usual sound of *ts'iú* varies into *tsiao* and *cheu* in half a dozen instances; some find traces of the phonetic in several characters.

香 561 ˛Hiang *Rad.* 186.—These compounds are alike in sound, but have not much similarity in meaning.

訇 562 ˛Hung *A crash.*—This group is mostly read *hung*, one being sounded *küh*, in which it is evidently interchanged with No. 458 匊, as some of the others are with 旬.

怱 563 ˛Ts'ung *Hastily.*—This is written 悤 and 息, or contracted to 匆, but has no connection with No. 466 忽; the sound *ts'ung* varies into *chw'ăng* in two cases.

盈 564 ˛Ying *Full.*—One of this small group occasionally varies into *chăng*, but it is read *ying* in all common words.

盾 565 ʻTun *A shield.*—*Tun*, *shun*, *siün* and *chwen* are found in this group; the meanings are very unlike.

扁 566 ʻPien *A slip.*—Nearly all of this group are read *pien*, which alters into *pin* and *pan* in two or three cases; traces of the primitive are seen in several words.

契 567 K'iʼ *A deed.*—This is derived from No. 256 刧, of which No. 809 絜 forms another sub-group; its sounds are unlike, varying into *hi*, *kieh*, *hieh* and *sieh*.

衍 568 ʻYen *To inundate.*—Out of this group of *yen*, one character is pronounced *k'ien*; the primitive itself is ideographic.

律 569 Lüh˒ *A law.*—A derivative from No. 252 聿; the meanings in the group are unlike, though their sounds are all *lüh*.

皆 570 ˛Kiai *All.*—All of this number are read *kiai* or *hiai*; some of them indicate an influence of the primitive in their meanings.

風 571 ˛Fung *Rad.* 182.—Most of this group are read *fung*, then *fan* or *lan*; the significations are sometimes ideographic, as 颾 a soughing.

段 572 Twanʼ *A fragment.*—This is very similar to No. 549 叚, but their dissimilarity in sound helps to distinguish them, as each group follows its leader.

便 573 Pienʼ *Convenient.*—A sub-group derived from No. 321 更, uniformly sounded *pien*, but incongruous in meaning.

皇 574 ˛Hwang *Emperor.*—One sound *hwang* names these derivatives, but their meanings have little analogy to their phonetic.

卽 575 Tsih˒ *Also.*—These are all sounded *tsih*; the primitive is written like No. 624 郎 in poorly-printed books, and No. 974 節 flows from it.

矦 576 ˛Heu *A prince.*—This and 候 are evidently the same primitive, but this form is mostly used in the compounds, which are sounded *heu* or *keu*.

禹 577 ʻYü *An old Emperor.*—This and No. 598 禺 are similar in form, and many derivatives under both are sounded alike; half of these are read *kü*.

保 578 ˛Pao *To protect.*—A homophonous group read *pao*, into whose meanings the primitive does not enter to any perceptible degree.

弇 579 Yen *To conceal.*—The sounds of *yen* and *ngan* occur in these characters; this is a sub-group from No. 285 合, but the two have no analogy.

俞 580 Yü *To assent.*—The sounds are *yü*, *shu* and *teu*, mostly the former; this and No. 517 前 may hastily be confused.

酋 581 Ts'eu *A leader.*—Half are read *ts'eu*, the others *yiu* and *siu*; it proceeds from No. 324 酉, but the analogy between them is undiscoverable.

㚇 582 Tsung *Gay.*—This group is entirely homophonous; in many of the compounds it is interchanged with 從 and 宗.

飛 583 Fei *Rad.* 183.—This group is quite unnecessary, as the characters under the radical contain all but one.

彖 584 Tw'an *To explain.*—This is similar both to No. 482 彔 and No. 412 豖; most of the derivatives are read *chwan*, then *twan*, *yuen* and *hwei*.

𡿺 585 Nao *Brains.*—This group is all read *nao*; its meanings occasionally allude to the primitive.

貞 586 Ching *Virginity.*—All the compounds are read *ching*, but their meanings bear no likeness to the primitive.

若 587 Joh *If.*—This group is read *joh*, *jé*, *noh* and *ch'oh*; it is derived from No. 139 右, but their meanings are diverse.

英 588 Ying *Flowery*—This group is read *ying*, and its phonetic is derived from No. 200 央, but the compounds seldom take after it in signification.

苗 589 Miao *Sprouts.*—A few in this collection change *miao* into *mao* and *nao*, but none indicate any affinity with the primitive.

昱 590 Yuh *Light.*—This group is read *yuh*, and one derivative has supplanted the primitive.

則 591 Tseh *Law.*—Most of these words are read *tseh* or *tsi*; and none indicate that the primitive has perceptibly influenced their meanings.

昜 592 Yang *The sky.*—This resembles No. 494 易, and in many cases is confused with it; Nos. 767 昜 and No. 798 湯 form sub-groups; the sounds are *yang*, *t'ang*, *tang*, *chang* and *shang*.

是 593 Shi *To be.*—The sounds *shi* and *ti* about equally divide this group, one of the easiest to recognize.

眇 594 Miao *Mysterious.*—Uniform in its sound *miao*, this is derived from No. 123 少, with which its meanings have the most affinity.

星 595 Sing *A star.*—This group is read *sing* and *tăng*; the primitive is derived from No. 164, 生, and one or two derivatives are like it.

曷 596 Hoh *Who?*—A large group sounded *hoh*, *ngoh*, *koh*, *hieh*, *yeh*, *kieh*, *hiah* and *ai*; 歇 is often used for its primitive, and 謁 leads a small sub-group.

冒 597 Mao *Illicit.*—The sound of *mao* changes into *méi*, *fung* and *suh* in some characters; this primitive is often contracted to 冐 in combination.

禺 598 Yü *Alone.*—*Yü*, *yung*, *ngeu* and *yeu* are the sounds; it somewhat resembles No. 577 禹, and reäppears in No. 921 萬.

咠 599 Tsih *To flatter.*—Uniformly sounded *tsih*; the derivative 戢 has three under it, but they are not common.

思 600 Sz' *To think.*—This is like 恩 favor, whose four compounds are rarely met; this group is sounded *sz'*, *si*, *sai* and *tsai*.

畏 601 Wéi *To fear.*—A group read *wéi*, and similar in form and sound to the next, but presenting no likeness in sense.

胃 602 Wéi *Stomach.*—This primitive resembles 胄 a helmet, but that forms no compounds; these are read *wéi* and *kwéi*.

咢 603 Ngoh *To frighten.*—This phonetic is like No. 994 噩, with which it is often interchanged; the words in this group are all pronounced *ngoh*.

廻 604 Hwéi *To curve.*—This flows from No. 293 回, with which it is often interchanged, and agrees entirely in its sounds.

咼 605 Kwa *A wry mouth.*—These derivatives are sounded *kwa*, *ko*, *kwo*, *ho* and *wo*; the primitive is not in use, and one compound 過 reäppears in No. 924.

耑 606 Twan *Beginning.*—The sounds *twan*, *chwen*, *jui*, *chui* and *shwan*, occur in this group, whose primitive is a contracted form of 專 singly.

TEN STROKES.

宰 607 Tsai *To rule.*—This, a sub-group of No. 296 辛, is read *tsai*, *tsz'* and *hai*; the primitive exerts no influence on the sense.

𡨄 608 Hia *To fill a crack.*—The primitive is regarded as an old form of 塞, and covers the radical; the sub-groups are No. 1004 蹇, with 搴 and 褰; the sounds are *kien*, *hien*, *seh*, *chai* and *sai*.

家 609 Kia *A household.*—These derivatives are all read *kia*; it is not a sub-group of No. 412 豕, nor should it be confounded with No. 623 冢.

害 610 Hai *To injure.*—The sounds are *hai*, *hiah*, *koh* and *hoh*; several of the characters are not unlike it in signification.

窄 611 Cha *Narrow.*—This is derived from No. 166 乍, with which it is sometimes interchanged; the sounds are all *cha*.

窊 612 Wa *A hollow.*—A sub-group from No. 172 瓜; the derivatives are uniformly read *wa*.

容 613 Yung *Patient.*—A group having little in common in the meanings of its characters, which are uniformly read *yung*.

𤇾 614 Ying This has now become an imperfect character, often contracted to 苂 in common books; No. 806 勞 forms a sub-group; the sounds are *ying*, *yung*, *king*, *lao*, *loh*, *liao* and *kiüng*.

旁 615 Pang *The side.*—An offshoot from No. 54 方; the derivatives are like the primitive in sound, but show little likeness in their meaning; a small sub-group occurs under 滂.

疾 616 Tsih *Urgent.*—These compounds are read *tsih*, but their meanings are very incongruous.

唐 617 T'ang *Great.*—These derivatives are read *t'ang*, and most of them are in common use; it is not likely to be confounded with No. 720 庸.

衮 618 Kwăn *Royal robes.*—Alike in their sound *kwan*, these compounds show no affinity with their phonetic.

兹 619 Tsz' *This.*—A group read *tsz* or *tsi*, and having two small sub-groups; the primitive is properly written 茲, but contracted to 玆 and 兹.

畜 620 Chuh *To rear.*—All the compounds are read *chuh*, and a remarkable similarity is to be seen in their meanings.

衰 621 Shwai *Ruined.*—This primitive resembles No. 647 袁 and still more 哀, to compassionate; the derivatives are sounded *so*, *tsui* and *shwai*, and are in common use.

高 622 ˓Kao Rad. 189.—In composition this is often contracted a little, as seen in No. 935 豪 and 毫; the sounds are *kao, hao, kiao, hiao, hoh* and *sung*.

冡 623 ˓Mung *Obscure.*—This primitive is more frequently written 蒙, to distinguish it more easily from No. 625 冢 and No. 609 家; its compounds are all read *mung*.

郎 624 ˓Lang *A man.*—An offshoot from No. 300 艮, and easily confounded with No. 575 卽 in badly-printed books; the sounds are uniformly *lang*.

冢 625 ˓Chung *Great.*—The compounds all read *chung*, are few and not much used, so that they are less likely to be mistaken for those under No. 623 冡.

隺 626 Hoh˒ *Eminent.*—A variety of this primitive, written 寉 with eleven strokes, is considered to be more correct; this and No. 796 雈 are unlike; *hoh* and *kioh* are the common sounds in this group.

冥 627 ˓Ming *Obscure.*—*Ming* is changed to *mih* and *mien* in a few cases; this group has many characters exhibiting a trace of their primitive.

羔 628 ˓Kao *A lamb.*—*Kao* and *yao* are the only sounds; the primitive is derived from No. 218 羊 but its compounds show no affinity with either.

差 629 ˓Cha *To differ.*—The complicated form 𢀩 is sometimes met with in the compounds; their sounds are *cha, so, tsié* and *tso*, the last showing the influence of No. 136 左.

朔 630 Soh˒ *New moon.*—This primitive shows some affinity with 欮 to hiccup, the source of No. 810 厥, but only in appearance; the sounds are *soh* and *su*.

迷 631 ˓Mi *To bewitch.*—This is a sub-group of No. 220 米, and the compounds exhibit traces of the primitive in their meanings.

脊 632 Tsih˒ *Backbone.*—This group is read *tsih*, and one or two of the derivatives show some analogy to the phonetic.

秦 633 ˓Ts'in *A kingdom.*—This group is sounded *tsin* and *chin* or *chăn*; the primitive resembles 泰 *t'ai*, which makes no compounds, and there is less likelihood therefore of confounding the two.

素 634 Su˒ *Simple.*—A group read *su*, whose phonetic is very similar to No. 641 索, both of them relating to silk.

冓 635 Keu˒ *To link.*—A group whose original sound *keu* varies into *kiang* in four characters;—an unusual change.

辱 636 Juh˒ *Disgrace.*—Most of the derivatives are read *juh*, others *nuh* and *neu*; they often show a trace of the primitive.

原 637 ˓Yuen *Origin.*—These are generally read *yuen*; one is *tsüen*, and the characters show little reference to the primitive.

夏 638 Hia˒ *Summer.*—*Hia* and *sha* are the sounds; the primitive looks a little like No. 971 憂 contracted, but they are totally distinct.

致 639 Chi˒ *To effect.*—These characters form a sub-group under No. 237 至, and many are like those in meaning; they all follow the leading sound *chi*.

晉 640 Tsin˒ *To increase.*—This is contracted to 晋, which is similar to the aberrant character 普 everywhere; its usual sound *tsin* becomes *tsien* in some cases.

索 641 Soh˒ *A cord.*—Nearly all are read *soh*, others are *sheh* or *sih*; the primitive resembles No. 634 素 in form and meaning.

馬 642 ˋMa *Rad.* 187.—This group is mostly read *ma*, the others are *chăn*; the derivatives have no likeness in meaning to their phonetic.

㱿 643 Koh˒ *A shell.*—This primitive was originally 殸, now altered to accommodate the radical on the left, as in 穀; their sounds are *koh, keu, kuh, huh, kioh* and *hioh*.

耆 644 ˓K'i *A sexagenarian.*—This primitive flows from No. 244 老, but the meanings in this group are unlike either; most of them are read *shi*, not *k'i*.

盍 645 Hoh˒ *How?*—This primitive is also written 盇 and 蓋, but in the compounds the correct form is generally followed; their sounds are *hoh, koh, ngoh, yeh, kai* and *ngai*.

貢 646 Kung˒ *Tribute.*—The sound *kung* in this group shows an affinity with No. 27 工, and the whole character reäppears in No. 1039 贛; *kung* runs into *lung* and *hung*.

袁 647 ˓Yuen *A robe.*—This resembles No. 618 衺, and is contracted to 表 in writing and common books; No. 928 睘 flows from it; the sounds are *yuen*.

尃 648 ˓Fu *To publish.*—This and No. 748 專 are very easily confounded; 溥 forms a sub-group; the sounds are *fu, foh, pu* and *poh*, the last being most common.

鬲 649 Kih˒ *Rad.* 193.—This primitive has two sounds; the compounds read *kih, koh* and *hoh*, show considerable uniformity of meaning with its less usual signification of division.

哥 650 ˓Ko *Elder brother.*—A derivative from No. 145 可; the characters are all read *ko*.

栗 651 Lih˒ *A chestnut.*—This phonetic rules the group under it; the character 粟 is very similar, and has seven derivatives; the two are easily mistaken unless care is taken.

葡 652 Pi˒ *To prepare.*—This primitive is often written 𤰈, and incorrectly 俻, both of which lead one astray when searching for it; *pi, pai* and *péi* are the sounds.

𠦝 653 Kan˒ *Surmise.*—The radical is placed on the right in these characters as in 翰; one sub-group occurs under No. 895 幹; the sounds are *kan, han* and *wah*.

退 654 Tui˒ *To recede.*—This is interchanged with No. 682 追 in a few characters; one alone is read *tun*.

弱 655 Joh˒ *Weak.*—This group has the sounds *nioh, joh, nao, nih* and *niao*; the primitive has little influence on the meanings.

犀 656 ˓Si *Late.*—This is also written like 犀 a rhinoceros, under eleven strokes, and both forms are correct; the sounds vary from *si* to *ts'z'* and *chi*.

展 657 ˋChen *To expand.*—These characters follow the sound of their primitive with two or three exceptions, some being read both *chen* and *nien*.

屑 658 Sieh˒ *Fragments.*—This appears like a sub-group under No. 380 肖, with which it shows no connection in sense or sound; all its characters are read *sieh*.

脅 659 Hieh˒ *Ribs.*—Similar in sound, these characters are unlike in form, a few being written 劦, which are regarded as synonyms.

烝 660 ˓Ching *To steam.*—This flows from No. 255 丞 and has influenced many of its compounds, all of which are read *ching*.

孫 661 ˓Sun *Grandson.*—This primitive resembles 係 to join, and each of them form sub-groups; these are all read *sun*, but have no similarity of meaning.

舀 662 ˋYao *To lade out.*—In this group the compounds all differ in sound from their primitive, which resembles No. 467 臽 in shape; all being read *t'ao*.

奚 663 ˏ*Hi* *How ?*—These characters are read *hi*, *kʻi* and *hiai* in nearly equal proportions; several sub-groups occur.

氣 664 *Kʻi*ˀ *Air.*—These characters are mostly read *hi*, but show little affinity with the meaning of their primitive; which is an offshoot of No. 38 乞, varied in form.

乘 665 ˏ*Ching* *To mount.*—These characters are read *ching*, *shing* or *shăng*, but none show much affinity in meaning with the primitive, which resembles No. 456 垂 in its old form.

朕 666 ˏ*Tăng* A derivative of No. 219 关, resembling 朕 emperor; it is a contracted character, and the radical is placed on its right side, as 媵 &c.; the sounds *tăng*, *shing*, *ying* and *ching* occur; two or three sub-groups occur.

芻 667 ˏ*Tseu* *Fodder.*—Formed like 艸 from two sprouts, this primitive imparts its meaning to few or none of its compounds, which are read *tseu*, *tsiu* and *chu*.

䍃 668 ˏ*Yao* *Pottery.*—This primitive, which is an offshoot of No. 258 缶, is also written 䍃; the compounds are all read *yao*, like it.

桀 669 *Kieh*ˀ *A brave.*—This primitive, No. 838 舜 and No. 844 舞, all contain the same radical; this group bears no affinity to it, and its sounds *kieh* and *tsieh* are unlike.

般 670 ˏ*Pʻan* *A manner.*—This group is read *pan*, but is not connected in its meanings; its compounds are in common use.

扇 671 *Shen*ˀ *A fan.*—Uniformly sounded *shen*, the primitive in this group imparts its meaning to none of its compounds.

虒 672 ˏ*Sz'* *A horned tiger.*—This occurs interchanged with No. 507 帝; the primitive is also read *ti*, and the sounds *si*, *i* and *chi* are heard, but *ti* most of all.

留 673 ˏ*Liu* *To detain*—Other forms are 畱 and 畄, which puzzle the student, but this is most correct; the derivatives are all read *liu*.

眞 674 ˏ*Chăn* *True.*—A derivative from No. 411 直, for which it can be mistaken; the common sound *chăn* becomes *tien* and *shăn* in many cases; No. 1029 顛 forms a large sub-group.

叟 675 ʿ*Seu* *Aged.*—These characters are read *seu*, *sheu*, *sao* and *siao*; the primitive has no perceptible influence on them.

息 676 *Sih*ˀ *To pity.*—This and the next two resemble each other; these characters are sounded *sih*.

臭 677 *Chʻeu*ˀ *Fetid.*—Many of these compounds are like their primitive, which resembles the next; they are read *cheu*, *kʻeu*, and *heu* or *hiu*.

臬 678 *Nieh*ˀ *A target.*—The compounds differ from their phonetic in meaning; part of them are read *yao*.

皋 679 ˏ*Kao* *An eminence.*—This is also written 皐 and 臯, with 11 and 12 strokes, which perplexes the search for its compounds, which are read *hao* and *kao*.

烏 680 ˏ*Wu* *Black.*—This primitive and No. 775 鳥 are easily mistaken, but the greater use of this as a phonetic and that as a radical will help to distinguish the two.

射 681 *Shé*ˀ *To dart.*—The derivatives are in common use, and their sounds *shé* or *tsié* are analogous.

追 682 ˏ*Chui* *To pursue.*—A few in this group are pronounced *tui*, and interchanged with No. 654 退, but the greater part are read *chui*.

師 683 ˏ*Shi* *A preceptor.*—The sounds are *shi* and *shai*; the primitive has no analogy with the perceding.

鬼 684 ʿ*Kwéi* *Rad.* 194.—*Kwéi* is the common sound, with *hwai*, *kwai*, *wéi*, *chʻeu* and *sheu*; it is sometimes difficult to decide whether a character belongs to the phonetic or the radical.

毘 685 ˏ*Pi* *To help.*—This group is read *pi*; the phonetic is sometimes incorrectly written 昆 or 皆, both of which mislead in searching for it.

蚤 686 ʿ*Tsao* *A flea.*—The compounds are read *sao*, and show no likeness of meaning to their primitive.

倉 687 ˏ*Tsʻang* *A granary.*—Most of these characters are read *tsiang*, others are *chwang* or *tsʻang*; but their meanings are quite unlike.

兼 688 ʿ*Kien* *Together.*—This primitive is contracted to 𠔉 and 秉; its usual sound *kien* is changed to *hien*, *lien* and *chan* in one third of the derivatives.

益 689 *Yih*ˀ *Advantage.*—The sound *yih* or *i* changes to *ai*, *ngai* or *ngoh* in a few words; no uniformity of meaning appears in the group.

翁 690 ˏ*Wăng* *An elder.*—Nearly uniform in their sound *wăng* or *ung*, most of these words have no sympathy with the meaning of the primitive.

桑 691 ˏ*Sang* *Mulberry.*—These compounds all read *sang*, but their meanings show no reference to a mulberry.

能 692 ˏ*Năng* *Able.*—The sounds *năng*, *nai*, *tai* and *lăng* are all found in this group; No. 986 罷 flows from it.

蚩 693 ˏ*Chi* *Stupid.*—This is occasionally contracted to 蚩, but without authority; the sounds of *chao* and *cheu* take the place of *chi* in some of the compounds.

茸 694 ˏ*Jung* *Hartshorn.*—The phonetic gives its name to all these compounds, few of which are in use.

茶 695 ˏ*Chʻa* *Tea.*—This group is uniformly read *chʻa*; the primitive resembles No. 355 余 a little.

草 696 ʿ*Tsʻao* *Plants.*—This resembles No. 667 芻 in its meaning, both being regarded similar to the radical 艸; its compounds are read *tsʻao*.

時 697 ˏ*Shi* *Time.*—This is a derivative of No. 240 寺; its compounds are all read *shi*, and most of them remotely refer to its meaning.

𦐇 698 *Tah*ˀ *To fly.*—This is continually interchanged with No. 853 翕, and the compounds all have the sound *tah*.

晃 699 ʿ*Hwang* *Brilliant.*—This is derived from No. 288 光; the characters are read *hwang*, but their meanings differ greatly.

骨 700 *Kuh*ˀ *Rad.* 188.—This group can be easily distinguished from that under the radical; the sound *kuh* becomes *huh* and *hwah* in one half.

畟 701 *Tsih*ˀ *To increase.*—These derivatives are read *tsih* and *suh*; they are incongruous in their meanings.

圂 702 *Hwun*ˀ *A sty.*—This is easily discerned from No. 499 困; the phonetic gives its sound *hwun* to the compounds.

員 703 ˏ*Yuen* *An officer.*—This is often contracted to 貟, even in well-printed books; it is like No. 374 目 in form; the sounds *yuen*, *yun* and *sun* are found.

昷 704 ˏ*Wăn* *Warm.*—This is also written 𥁕 with nine strokes; the sounds of the characters vary from *wăn* to *yun*, *wuh* and *ngao*; and most of them are in common use.

眔 705 *Tah*ˀ *A sight of.*—Part of these compounds are read *tah* and part *kwan*; a sub-group is found under 遝; the primitive bears resemblance to No. 852 衆.

豈 706 'K'i *How?*—The sound *k'i* changes into *ngai, hai* and *kai* in most of the derivatives, whose meanings are more incongruous than their sounds.

貨 707 'So *Fragments.*—This primitive resembles No. 782 巢, and is often written 貨; so is the common sound of the derivatives whose meanings refer to communication.

ELEVEN STROKES.

密 708 Mih, *Secret.*—This is a sub-group under No. 132 必 through 宓 one of its compounds, which also forms other groups, all of which are sounded *mi* or *mih.*

寇 709 Keu' *A robber.*—This is often written like 冠 a cap; the compounds are all read *keu.*

寅 710 ˏYin *To venerate.*—The primitive gives its sound *yin* to most of this group, the exceptions being read *yen.*

宿 711 Suh, *To lodge at.*—*Shuh, suh,* and *siu* are the sounds; a glimpse of the primitive appears in some of them.

章 712 ˏChang *Adorned.*—The primitive regularly gives its sound to all its compounds, but its meaning to almost none of them.

竟 713 King' *A border.*—Most of this group are read *king;* an errant sound *kiang* is heard in a few, enough to render all uncertain.

啇 714 Tih, *A root.*—This is easily confounded with the next, but their sounds are unlike, these being read *tih, tsieh* and *sheh;* 適 forms a small sub-group.

商 715 ˏShang *To consult.*—Similar to the last, it is less frequently found in combination, and all the characters follow the sound of *shang.*

旋 716 ˏSüen *To revert to.*—This and the next resemble each other; the sounds of the derivatives are all *süen,* and their meanings have considerable affinity with it.

族 717 Tsuh, *Kindred.*—Similar to the preceding in form, its sounds are unlike it, following the primitive *tsuh,* except in one or two cases.

庶 718 Shu' *Many.*—The compounds are read *ché* and *cheh;* one (遮) forms a sub-group, but the primitive imparts nothing to their meanings.

麻 719 ˏMa *Rad.* 200.—The Chinese found some difficulty in assorting these characters, whose sounds are *ma, mo, mi* and *măn;* as many now under the radical, should have been placed under the primitive; No. 1025 靡 makes a sub-group.

庸 720 ˏYung *Common.*—Part of this group is read *jung* and others *yung;* the primitive is contracted to 庁, and often interchanged with No. 327 甬.

康 721 ˏK'ang *Tranquil.*—These derivatives follow their leader *k'ang* in sound but not in sense; this primitive and No. 391 庚 resemble each other in form and sound.

鹿 722 Luh, *Rad.* 198.—This group and that under the radical are quite unlike; these are all read *luh* but one, 麈 *chin,* which forms two compounds.

產 723 'Ch'an *Productions.*—Uniformly like the phonetic *ch'an* in sound, this group shows no likeness of meaning in the characters.

离 724 ˏLi *To separate.*—Part are read *chi,* but more are *li;* one derivative 離 leads a sub-group of 12 characters, most of them synonymous forms.

牽 725 ˏK'ien *To drag.*—These few characters are alike sounded *k'ien,* and the meaning of the primitive appears in each.

率 726 Shwai' *A leader.*—This primitive has four sounds itself; its compounds are read *lüh, soh* and *shwai,* none of them bearing much likeness to it in meaning.

郭 727 Kwoh, *A suburb.*—This is derived from No. 396 享, with which some of its compounds are interchanged; they are read *kwoh;* its shape resembles No. 802 敦 and the next.

孰 728 Shuh, *Who?*—This, like the last, is derived from No. 396, and resembles No. 744 埶 and No. 742 執; its compounds are read *shuh.*

羕 729 ˏYang *Great.*—This group is all read *yang,* but the number do not all retain a trace of their primitive.

羞 730 ˏSiu *Ashamed.*—This resembles No. 629 差, but it occurs less frequently; the sounds are all *siu,* and the meanings unlike the primitive.

雩 731 ˏYü *Rainbow.*—This heads a sub-group under No. 19 亐, none of which bear much likeness to it in meaning, and the sounds are *yü, shu* and *hu.*

舂 732 ˏShung *To triturate.*—This and No. 520 春 look much alike, but this is the least common; most of the compounds are read *chwang, ch'ung* and *shwang.*

彗 733 Sui' *A besom.*—The sounds here are *hwui, sui* and *süeh;* those read *hwui* often interchange with No. 820 惠, from similarity of sound.

規 734 ˏKwéi *A rule.*—Most of the characters in this group are read *kwéi,* others are *hwéi;* their meanings sometimes show traces of the primitive.

責 735 Tseh, *To blame.*—The sound *tseh* changes into *tsih, tsz'* and *chai* in a large proportion of the derivatives, whose meanings exhibit little affinity with each other.

𠩺 736 ˏLi *To split.*—This is an obsolete character, which gives its sound *li* to most of the compounds, though its meaning to none.

殹 737 I' *An echo.*—A homophonous group read *i;* many of the characters exhibit the idea of blackness.

戚 738 Tsih, *Troubled.*—This group is read *tsih* and *tsuh,* and many words in it are allied to the primitive in sense as well as sound.

爽 739 'Shwang *Lively.*—These compounds are all read *chw'ang* or *shwang,* but none show the influence of their primitive.

焉 740 ˏYen *How?*—A group where the phonetic *yen* leads the sounds of the compounds, but does not influence their meaning.

敖 741 Ngao' *Proud.*—Nearly uniform in its sound *ngao,* the others are read *ao* or *yao* and *chui;* a few resemble the primitive in sense.

執 742 Chih, *To take.*—This is like No. 744 埶 and No. 728 孰, but occurs more frequently; most of the words are read *chih* or *chi,* and others *tien.*

殸 743 King' *Sounding stones.*—The sounds are *king, hing* and *shing;* this character is obsolete, and often contracted to 声 for its compound 磬.

埶 744 I' *Apt.*—These derivatives are read *i, sieh, jeh* and *shi;* it closely resembles No. 742 執, and the two are often confounded even by natives.

匿 745 Nih, *Hidden.*—This group is read *nih,* with the exception of 慝 *teh;* the compounds show some traces of the phonetic in their meaning.

連 746 ˏLien *To connect.*—A group whose compounds follow their phonetic *lien,* but none of them resemble it in meaning.

斬 747 'Chan *To decapitate.*—The sounds here vary from *chen* to *tsan* and *tsien;* 漸 leads a sub-group of three.

專 748 ˏChwen *Solely.*—This and No. 648 叀 are frequently confounded in poorly-printed books; the group is read *chwen* and *twan.*

區 749 ˓K'ü *A place.*—The sounds here change from *k'ü* into *yü*, *kèu*, *ngao* and *ch'u*; their meanings are altogether diverse.

欶 750 Shuh˒ *To respire.*—This is often incorrectly written 敕, which is another form of 勅 *ch'ih*; the compounds are read *suh*, *seu* and *nwan*.

曹 751 ˓Ts'ao *Dignity.*—All the compounds are read *ts'ao*, like their phonetic, though few are influenced by it in their signification.

票 752 ˓Piao *To signalize.*—A large and regular group in its uniform sound of *piao*; a few compounds, as 剽 and 漂, lead small sub-groups.

署 753 ˓Sien *To mount.*—About half the compounds are read *sien* like their primitive, the others *ts'ien*.

桼 754 Tsih˒ *Varnish.*—This primitive resembles the radicals 麥 wheat and 黍 millet, but those do not occur as phonetics; this group is read *tsih* and *sih*.

帶 755 Tai˒ *A girdle.*—The sounds here are *chai*, *tai*, *ti* and *chi*; some traces of the primitive appears, which is interchanged with No. 507 帝 in many cases.

堇 756 Han˒ Nearly all are read *han*, others are *nan* and *tan*; the primitive is not used; No. 1027 難 is a sub-group.

堇 757 ˓Kin *A few.*—The primitive gives its sound *kin* to most of the compounds; 勤 leads a small sub-group.

㒼 758 ˓Man *Equal.*—This somewhat resembles 兩 a couple, or altered to 𦍌; the coumpounds are read *man* and *măn*.

强 759 ˓K'iang *Violent.*—The phonetic gives its sound *k'iang* to all under it; the form 强 is commonly used, but is still reckoned as having only eleven strokes.

尉 760 Wéi˒ *To console.*—This gives its sound to most of its compounds; they are read *wéi* or *yuh*.

屚 761 Leu˒ *To leak.*—A small group, uniformly read *leu*, and many of its characters analogous to the primitive, which is contracted to 扁 in poor books.

習 762 Sih˒ *To practice.*—This group is read *sih* and *cheh*; the meanings are unlike the primitive.

翏 763 Liu˒ *To fly high.*—The leading sound is *liu*, but *liao*, *lao*, *luh*, *kiao*, *kiu*, *miu* and *cheu* are also heard, rendering them all doubtful to a beginner.

侌 764 ˓Yin *Dark.*—The right half of this character is an earlier form of itself, traces of which are to be detected in the compounds; the sounds are uniformly *yin*.

悉 765 Sih˒ *To know.*—The few derivatives are read *sih*, but their meanings are totally different.

造 766 Tsao˒ *To make.*—This sub-group comes from No. 342 告; its derivatives are uniformly sounded *tsao*.

昜 767 ˓Shang An offshoot from No. 592 易, and an idea of injury runs through the group; the sounds are *shang*, then *tsiang* and *tang*.

祭 768 Tsi˒ *To sacrifice.*—About half of this group is read *tsi*, and the others *chi*, *chai*, *tsai*, *si* and *chah*; a sub-group of seven comes under 察 *chah*.

扈 769 Hu˒ *To follow.*—These few characters are read *hu*, like their phonetic; but are unlike it in meaning, and not much in use.

斛 770 Huh˒ *A bushel.*—These characters are read *huh*, but their meanings are dissimilar.

從 771 ˓Ts'ung *To follow.*—This and the two next are similar; half of this group follow the sound *ts'ung*, others are read *sung* and *chwang*.

御 772 Yü˒ *Imperial.*—A small group, read *yü*, whose words show some affinity in the meanings with the primitive.

徙 773 ˓Si *To transport.*—The derivatives are read *si* and *sien*; the primitive is like No. 771 從, but it does not influence the meaning of the words.

逢 774 ˓Fung *To meet.*—This flows from No. 348 夆, with which its compounds agree in sound, and often in sense; nearly one half are read *fung*, the rest *pung*.

鳥 775 ˓Niao *Rad.* 196.—The sounds vary to *tiao*, *ming* and *niao*; this and No. 680 烏 resemble each other.

旣 776 Ki˒ *Already.*—The compounds in this group are read *ki*, *kai* and *keu*; the primitive resembles No. 575 卽, but is more used.

兜 777 ˓Teu *A helmet.*—The few derivatives under this primitive have no affinity with its meaning, but are all sounded *teu*.

殺 778 Shah˒ *To kill.*—The compounds are read *sah* and *shah*, and the original meaning crops out in some of them.

貪 779 ˓T'an *To covet.*—An unimportant group, uniform in its sound of *t'an*, but showing no affinity in meaning.

參 780 ˓Ts'an *A counsellor.*—This is occasionally interchanged with No. 813 晉, and altered to 叅 and 参; the compounds are read *tsan*, *san*, *shan*, *shăn* and *chăn*, and most of them have some reference to confusion.

貫 781 Kwan˒ *Accustomed.*—The derivatives follow the phonetic *kwan*, except 實 *shih*, and some of them partake of its meaning.

巢 782 ˓Ch'ao *A nest.*—This resembles No. 707 貨; the characters mostly follow their leading sound *ch'ao*, *tsiao* and *sao* being the variants.

將 783 ˓Tsiang *A leader.*—The derivatives take the sound of *tsiang*, and the primitive, in a few cases is interchanged with No. 687 倉 from their similarity of sound.

虖 784 ˓Hu *A groan.*—This is a sub-group from No. 162 乎, and the characters follow its sound *hu* with a few exceptions which are read *h'ia*.

虘 785 ˓Tso *A tiger.*—This primitive is sometimes written like No. 857 虛, but more often 虘, which is allowable; the compounds are read *cha*, *ts'ü* and *tso*.

堂 786 ˓T'ang *A hall.*—One of the sub-groups under No. 501 尙; most of its members are read *t'ang* and a few *chăng*.

鹵 787 ˓Lu *Rad.* 197.—All the derivatives with one exception, *king*, are read *lu*, and the primitive conveys its meaning to only one of them.

莫 788 Moh˒ *Not.*—The radical is usually written beneath the primitive, and in a few cases as 摸 and 摹, 謨 and 摹 its position varies the sense; the derivatives are read *moh*, *mu* and *ma*.

婁 789 ˓Leu *Poor.*—This group is mostly read *leu*; others are *lü*, and one 數 *shu*, forms a sub-group No. 984.

曼 790 ˓Man *Long.*—The phonetic gives its sound *man* to this group, but no clue to the meanings, except in one or two cases.

畢 791 Pih˒ *Finished.*—All these compounds are read *pih*, but their primitive does not influence their meanings at all.

異 792 I˒ *Remarkable.*—The sounds in this group are *i*, *yih*, *făn* and *chih*; 翼 leads a sub-group of four; in K'anghi's Dictionary this character is reckoned under twelve strokes.

累 793 ˓Léi *To involve.*—About one half of this group is read *lo*, the rest are *léi* and *tah*; the primitive is akin to No. 881 雷 and No. 985 畾, with which it is sometimes interchanged.

國 794 Kwoh, *A kingdom.*—Derived from No. 430 或; the compounds in this group are mostly read *kwoh* like the phonetic, with whose meaning they have no affinity.

患 795 Hwan' *Sorrow.*—*Hwan*, *wan* and *chan* are the only sounds; the primitive is sometimes wrongly written for No. 928 睘.

崔 796 ꜀Tsui *A peak.*—This is very similar to No. 626 隺, and the two are not carefully separated in books; it is like 雀 a bird, which is made from No. 472 隹.

TWELVE STROKES.

渠 797 K'ü *A gutter.*—The sound of this is given by No. 144 巨 with which it has no other affinity.

湯 798 ꜀Tang *To scald.*—This is derived from No. 592 昜, and all its compounds follow its sound *tang* but not its sense.

戠 799 Chih, *To burn.*—This has become obsolete and is sometimes pedantically written 戠 with thirteen strokes; the sounds are *chih*, *chi* and *shih*.

童 800 ꜀T'ung *A youth.*—The sounds are *t'ung*, *chung* and *chwang*; its sound and form resemble No. 558 重, with which it is never interchanged.

散 801 Cheh, This is now obsolete, and its derivatives are read *cheh* and *sah*; it resembles No. 825 散 and is still less like No. 815 敢.

敦 802 ꜀Tun *Sincere.*—This heads the largest sub-group under No. 396 享, of which No. 727 郭 and No. 728 孰 are two others; the sounds are *tun* and *tui*.

就 803 Tsiu' *Then.*—This is derived from No. 397 京, but has no likeness to it in sound or sense; the words are *tsiu* and *tsuh*.

善 804 ꜂Shen *Good.*—This phonetic gives its sound ꜂*shen*, but has no appreciable influence on the sense of the compounds; it differs from No. 818 喜.

粦 805 ꜀Lin *Will-o'-wisp.*—This guides to the sounds of all its compounds except three read *lien*; and an idea of frangibility runs through many of them.

勞 806 ꜀Lao *Fatigue.*—This is a derivative from No. 614 𤇾; the compounds all follow its sound, but rarely its signification.

惢 807 ꜂Jui *To suspect.*—This is also written 甤 in most of its compounds, but the second form alone is a synonym of 澀 *sih*; *jui* is the common sound.

貳 808 'Rh' *Two.*—This comes secondarily from No. 25 弋, under which 弍 is a simpler form of this character; this group is read *'rh*, *ni* and *ch'i*.

絜 809 Kieh, *Pure.*—This and No. 567 契 are derived from No. 256 丯; its compounds are mostly read *kieh*, and some of them are akin in meaning.

厥 810 Küeh, *That.*—This is derived from 欮, which unites with three radicals, one of them forming this sub-group, which is read *küeh* and *kwéi*.

尞 811 ꜂Liao *To light.*—A group whose members are read *liao* and *lao*, but their meanings vary indefinitely.

奢 812 ꜀Shé *Prodigal.*—This is derived from No. 531 者, which sends off four or five sub-groups, of which this is the largest; its compounds are read *ché* and *cha*, and are written sometimes with No. 529 奓.

朁 813 ꜀Tsan *Impious.*—This is often interchanged with No. 780 參 and No. 1028 贊; it is also incorrectly written 朁, which itself leads a group of three; the compounds are read *tsan*, *tsien*, *chăn* and *ti*.

壹 814 Yih, *One.*—This group is sounded *yih*, *i* and *ngai*; the words exhibit no likeness in meaning.

敢 815 ꜂Kan *To dare.*—The sounds here vary from *kan* to *han* and *hien*; its nearest resemblances are No. 801 散 and No. 825 散.

堯 816 ꜀Yao *Virtuous.*—This gives its sound to a few derivatives, the others being read *jao*, *kiao*, *hiao*, *nao* and *shao*.

彭 817 ꜀P'ăng *A tambourine.*—These compounds are read *p'ang* like their phonetic, but show no trace of its meaning.

喜 818 ꜂Hi *Joy.*—This resembles No. 804 善; the sounds are all *hi*, except two or three read *ch'i*.

惡 819 Ngoh, *Evil.*—This, derived from No. 424 亞, is read both *wu* and *ngoh*; its compounds are found under both sounds, and partake of its meaning.

惠 820 Hwui' *Grace.*—This group frequently interchanges its phonetic with 慧 a sub-group of No. 733 彗; the sounds are *hwéi* and *sui*.

棥 821 ꜀Fan *A hedge.*—These are all read *fan*, as well as the larger sub-group under 樊, to which belong eight compounds.

覃 822 ꜀T'an *Ample.*—This differs from No. 867 單, though they are interchanged; besides the sound *t'an*, a few are read *tien* and *sin*.

斯 823 ꜀Sz' *This.*—Apparently derived from No. 435 其, this primitive exhibits no likeness in sound or sense to it; a few are read *si*, but most of them *sz'*.

黃 824 ꜀Hwang *Rad.* 201.—The derivatives are mostly read *hwang*, and others *hăng*; No. 996 廣 is a sub-group.

散 825 San' *To scatter.*—This is so much like No. 801 散 that some notice is desirable of their differences; *sah*, *sien* and *san* are the sounds.

朝 826 ꜀Chao *Morning.*—Most of the derivatives are read *chao*, 廟 *miao* being the only exception.

項 827 Hiang' *A sort.*—This group follows the sound of its primitive, which resembles 頃 *k'iung*, a word that has four derivatives, 傾 and 潁 being the most common.

矞 828 Yuh, *To deceive.*—The sounds here are *yuh*, *küeh*, *hüeh* and *küh*, and modifications of these; the meanings are incongruous.

尋 829 ꜀Sin *To seek.*—These compounds are read *sin* and *t'an*; none of them indicate any influence of the primitive on their meanings.

閔 830 ꜂Min *Pity.*—This group is alike read *min*; the primitive is derived from No. 56 文 rather than No. 439 門.

閏 831 Jun' *Intercalary moon.*—These characters are read both *jun* and *jwan*, the primitive has both sounds; its form resembles the last and the next.

閒 832 ꜀Hien *Leisure.*—As a primitive, this is also written 間 and 閑, though these three forms are not wholly synonymous; the sounds are about equally *hien* and *kien*.

孱 833 ꜀Chw'en *Weak.*—The compounds, which are mostly read *ch'an*, show no influence of the primitive, which is sometimes interchanged with No. 437 戔.

巽 834 Sun' *To concede.*—This group has many sounds, as *sun*, *siün*, *chwen*, *tsüen* and *tswan*; the meanings have nothing in common.

隆 835 ˓*Lung* *Opulent.*—In some of these derivatives simply 夆 is written, but the full form is better; the group is read *lung*.

筑 836 *Chuh*˓ *A guitar.*—This derivative from No. 250 巩 is incorrectly written without the dot; most of the compounds are arranged in Kanghi's Dictionary under the 竹 radical.

答 837 *Tah*˓ *To reply.*—This is often contracted to 荅 in the compounds, which are read *tah* and *chah;* it is derived from No. 285 合, being one of its five sub-groups.

舜 838 *Shun*˒ This group furnishes one character read *chwen*, and the others are *shun;* all are in common use.

爲 839 *Wéi*˒ *To be.*—The sound of *wéi* is heard in nearly half of this group, the others being read *hwéi*, *wo* and *kwéi;* 蔿 forms a small sub-group.

番 840 ˓*Fan* *Foreign.*—This is sometimes improperly written 畨; some of its compounds are read *shin*, *fan*, *pan* and *p'o;* No. 963 審 leads a sub-group.

登 841 ˓*Tăng* *To ascend.*—This resembles 豋 *tăng* a vase, which forms only one or two compounds; this group is mostly read *tăng*, others are *chăng* and *ching*.

發 842 *Fah*˓ *To issue.*—This group is read *fah*, *féi* and *poh* or *puh;* 廢 leads a sub-group of four read *féi* like itself.

毳 843 *Ts'ui*˒ *Down.*—Half of these are read *tsui* or *chui*, and the rest *chwen* and *kiao;* no influence of the primitive on their meanings is perceptible.

無 844 ˓*Wu* *None.*—This is occasionally interchanged with No. 404 武; its compounds are read *wu*, *hu* and *fu*, and some of them as 蕪 and 膴 lead others; a character like this 舞 also heads a group of six, read *wu*.

喬 845 ˓*K'iao* *Grand.*—This character, derived from No. 622 高, influences many of its compounds, indicating lofty, noble, &c; the common sound *k'iao* is changed to *kioh* in a few.

然 846 ˓*Jan* *Certainly.*—About half of this group is read *jen*, and the others *nien;* this and No. 997 燕 are somewhat alike.

須 847 ˓*Sü* *Necessary.*—This is derived from No. 525 頁, and all its compounds follow its sound *sü*.

象 848 *Siang*˒ *Elephant.*—Only one of these, read *shang*, differs in sound from the primitive, which bears a resemblance to No. 852 衆.

復 849 *Fuh*˓ *Repeating.*—One of this group is read *li*, and the others *fuh;* the primitive comes from No. 514 复, with which it is interchanged in a few cases.

焦 850 ˓*Tsiao* *Scorched.*—This may be regarded as derived from No. 472 隹, and its derivatives are all read *tsiao;* their significations have a little affinity with it.

集 851 *Tsih*˓ *To congregate.*—These are read *tsah* and *tsih*, and one of the three is a synonym of the primitive.

衆 852 *Chung*˒ *A crowd.*—Traces of the meaning of the phonetic, which gives its sound *chung* to all the derivatives, occur in several of them.

翕 853 *Hih*˓ *United.*—Like No. 837 答, this is derived from No. 285 合; it may easily be confounded with No. 698 翯; the compounds are read *hih*.

尊 854 ˓*Tsun* *Illustrious.*—This group follows the primitive in its sound *tsun*, but not at all in meaning; it resembles No. 748 尃.

曾 855 ˓*Ts'ăng* *Already.*—This and No. 912 會 are easily mistaken, and this is usually written 曽 to diminish their likeness; the derivatives are read *tsăng* and *săng*.

幾 856 ˓*Ki* *Several.*—This regularly follows its phonetic *ki;* in a few cases, like 譏 the primitive is abbreviated, but oftener to 几, as 机 for 機, &c.

虛 857 ˓*Hü* *Empty.*—This is sometimes written like No. 785 虗, and seldomer like No. 784 虖; the derivatives are read *k'ü* and *hü*.

牚 858 ˓*Ch'ăng* *A prop.*—This is one of the offshoots from No. 501 尚, and is also written 棠 and 掌 in some of the derivatives; their sounds vary from *chăng* to *chang*.

觜 859 ˓*Tsui* *A beak.*—This group is pronounced *tsui* like its phonetic, which influences the meanings of the compounds.

華 860 ˓*Hwa* *Flowery.*—This is often contracted to ten strokes 華 as it is a sound character, but the dictionaries place the words under twelve; they are read *hwa*, *yeh* or *yih* and *wéi*.

莽 861 ˓*Mang* *Flourishing.*—This word is troublesome to find, for it is contracted to 莾 and 𦬸, but the dictionaries place such under twelve strokes; they are read *mang*.

黑 862 *Heh*˓ *Rad.* 203.—One of this class, 墨, forms a sub-group of eight, and another 默 of four derivatives; the compounds are read *heh*, *méi* and *moh*, chiefly the latter.

景 863 ˓*King* *A prospect*—This like No. 803 就 is an offshoot of No. 397 京; the sounds under it vary into *ying*, *kiüng*, *hung* and *hao*.

最 864 *Tsui*˒ *Important.*—This is a derivative from No. 417 取; the compounds are read *tsoh*, *chwai* and *tsui*.

路 865 *Lu*˒ *A road.*—This is derived from No. 272 各, and the characters are all read *lu* like the phonetic, of whose meaning there is no trace in them.

貴 866 *Kwéi*˒ *Honored.*—Two derivatives under this, 匱 and 遺, form sub-groups, and the former is often interchanged with it; they are mostly read *kwéi*, others are *tui*, *i* and *wai*.

單 867 ˓*Tan* *Alone.*—This is not unlike No. 822 覃 in form and sound; the compounds are mostly read *tan*, then *chen*, *shen*, *toh* and *i*.

買 868 *Mai*˒ *To buy.*—This phonetic leads the sounds of all its derivatives, and one of them No. 973 賣 heads a large sub-group, though some etymologists separate them.

菐 869 *Puh*˓ *Thicket.*—This and No. 930 業 resemble each other; the compounds here are all read *puh* or *poh*.

敞 870 ˓*Ch'ang* *Spacious.*—This offset from No. 501 尚 has a few characters under it which follow its sound *ch'ang;* it is easily confounded with the next.

敝 871 *Pi*˒ *Broken.*—This is like the last and more common; most of the characters are read *pieh*, then *pi*, and ideas of injury pervade most of them.

THIRTEEN STROKES.

意 872 *I*˒ *Intention.*—The group of characters which flow from this primitive are all read *i* or *yih*, and many of them partake of its meaning.

廌 873 ˓*Chai* *A griffon.*—This resembles No. 839 爲 a little, but it and its derivatives are seldom met; they are read *chai* and *tsien*.

䧹 874 ˓*Ying* *A hawk.*—This is easily mistaken for 雁 a wild goose, but the latter seldom occurs; its derivatives are all read *ying*, and 應 leads a sub-group.

廉 875 ꜀Lien *Frugality.*—A derivative of No. 688 兼, with which it is rarely interchanged; this primitive gives its sound *lien* to all but two of its compounds read *chan* and *tswan*, but its meaning to none.

雍 876 ꜀Yung *Concord.*—This is also written 邕 and 雝, but these forms are not common; their sounds are *yung* and *wăng*.

𣎆 877 ꜂Lo An obsolete character, where the radical is found between the lower parts, as 羸; the characters are read *lo*, *lei* and *ying*.

稟 878 ꜂Pin *To state to.*—This group derives its sound from *lin* 㐭 a granary, and the two are considred the same primitive; the derivatives are read *lin* and *lan*.

亶 879 ꜂Tan *Grand.*—This is often interchanged with No. 867 單 from the similarity of sound; these are read *tan*, *shen* and *chen*.

義 880 I꜄ *Right.*—This group is read *i* throughout, and some of the characters show affinity with the meaning of the primitive.

雷 881 ꜀Léi *Thunder.*—This and No. 985 畾 resemble each other in sound; this group is read *léi*, and the derivatives occasionally intimate the meaning of the primitive.

韰 882 Tsah꜄ *Sordid.*—This is derived from Rad. 179 韭; its compounds are read *tsah* and *sah*, and partake somewhat of its meaning.

遀 883 ꜀Sui *To follow.*—This sub-group under No. 522 有, is frequently interchanged with it, and its derivatives are read *sui*; one of them 隨 has six flowing from it.

感 884 ꜂Kan *To excite.*—A derivative from No. 524 咸; the characters in this group are read *kan* and *han*, and many of them partake of the sense of their phonetic.

達 885 Tah꜄ *To perceive.*—This is not an offshoot from No. 416 幸, but from 羍 altered; all its compounds are read *tah*.

聖 886 Shing꜄ *Holy.*—This is a sub-group under No. 373 呈, and is often contracted to 圣; its derivatives are read *ch'ing* or *ch'ăng*.

賁 887 Făn꜄ *Bold.*—This is apparently derived from 卉 plants, but the sound indicates No. 528 奔 as its origin; the sounds *păn* and *făn* are curiously confused in the group.

𢧜 888 Tieh꜄ *Sharp.*—This was at first written 戜, but this is now the proper form, and is also contracted as in 鉄; all are read *tieh*.

毄 889 Kih꜄ *To strike.*—The compounds in this group are read *kih* and *hi*; they have little likeness of meaning.

畺 890 ꜀Kiang *A border.*—Occasionally interchanged with No. 759 强, and most of the compounds are sounded *kiang*; 疆 leads three or four derivatives.

賈 891 ꜂Kia *Trader.*—The compounds are also read *kia*, and are in common use.

禁 892 Kin꜄ *To prohibit.*—This group comes from No. 432 林, with which it has little affinity; the compounds are read *kin*, and look a little like the next.

楚 893 ꜂Ch'u *Grievous.*—These characters sound like their phonetic, which resembles the preceding; they all contain the idea of suffering.

嗇 894 Sheh꜄ *Avaricious.*—This is contracted to 啬, and its compounds are read *sheh*, *seh* and *ts'iang*; several of them partake of its meaning.

幹 895 Kan꜄ *Ability.*—This forms one of three sub-groups under No. 653 倝; its derivatives are read *kan* and *hwan*.

肅 896 Suh꜄ *Serious.*—This properly has thirteen strokes, but the characters are placed under twelve in the dictionaries; they are read *suh*, *siu* and *siao*; 蕭 forms a sub-group of eight.

殿 897 Tien꜄ *A palace.*—This group is read *tien* and *tun*; the characters are not much used.

辟 898 Pih꜄ *A model.*—The meaning of this phonetic appears in several of its compounds, which are read *pi*, *pih*, *poh* and *mih*; the group is easily distinguished from No. 1014 薛.

歰 899 Sheh꜄ *Rough.*—In the dictionaries, this is counted with twelve strokes, while it really has fourteen, and this discrepancy causes some difficulty in finding it; the compounds partake of its meaning and are sounded *seh* and *sah*.

愛 900 Ngai꜄ *To love.*—This group is uniformly read *ngai* or *ai*; most of its characters have the idea of obscurity.

詹 901 ꜀Chen *To direct.*—*Chen* is the common sound, and *tan*, *yen* and *shen* are the others; their meanings are quite unlike.

解 902 Kiai꜄ *To explain.*—This group is about equally divided between *kiai* and *hiai*; the primitive is merely a phonetic.

𢼸 903 ꜀Wéi *Minute.*—This can be easily mistaken for No. 977 徵; its compounds are read *wéi* or *wi*, and a few of them are like it in meaning.

雋 904 ꜂Tsüen *Fat.*—This group contains the sounds *tswan*, *tsui*, *tsüen*, and *tsun*; No. 1003 嶲 forms a sub-group.

𦥯 905 Hioh꜄ An imperfect character, to which No. 953 與 bears most likeness; the compounds are read *hioh*, *kioh*, *hoh* and *hung*; it is often contracted, as 斈 for 學 in poorly-printed books.

毀 906 ꜂Hwéi *To break.*—This leads the sounds of its compounds, and traces of its meaning are seen in several of them.

敫 907 Kih꜄ *To respect.*—The four sounds of this primitive reäppear in its compounds, as *kih*, *yao*, *hih*, *hoh*, *kioh* and *kiao*, the last the commonest; this and No. 741 敖 look alike.

奧 908 Ngao꜄ *Obscure.*—The derivatives in this group are read *ngao* and *yuh*; it resembles 粤, which has only three derivatives read *yueh*.

禽 909 ꜀K'in *Birds.*—This group is read *k'in*; its meanings have no likeness; this and No. 724 离 resemble each other.

遂 910 Sui꜄ *To follow.*—This is sometimes mistaken for 逐 which has itself seven derivatives read *chuh* like it; these are all read *sui*.

僉 911 ꜀Ts'ien *All.*—The sounds under this primitive are *tsien*, *sien*, *yen*, *hien*, *kien* and *lien*, of which the last preponderates.

會 912 Hwui꜄ *To assemble.*—This and No. 855 曾 are liable to be confounded; half of the characters in this group are read *kwéi*; the others *hwui*, *wéi* and *kwai*.

鄉 913 ꜀Hiang *A village.*—A small group read *hiang*, whose phonetic is liable to be mistaken for 卿 *k'ing*, but that has no derivatives.

當 914 ꜀Tang *Ought.*—This is a sub-group under No. 501 尚; it is frequently contracted to 当 in cheap books; all the compounds are read *tang*, but their meanings follow their radicals.

豦 915 Kü꜄ *Fighting.*—This primitive which resembles 處 a place, gives its sound to most of its compounds, of which others are read *kioh* and *kih*; two of them lead two or three derivates each.

虛 916 ˏHi *A vase.*—This phonetic is similar to No. 785 虗 and No. 857 虐; the compounds are all read *hi*, and the most common one 戲 leads thirteen derivatives also read *hi*.

虜 917 ʿLu *To captivate.*—This primitive, No. 981 慮 and No. 999 盧 resemble each other in sound and form; the group is read *lu* throughout.

粲 918 Tsʻanʾ *Fresh.*—This is rather a sub-group of *tsan* 奴, which leads four other derivatives as 餐 and 粲; not many of either group are in common use.

歲 919 Suiʾ *A year.*—The sounds in this group are *kwéi*, *hwui*, *wéi* and *yueh*; the primitive is contracted to 歩 and other forms.

敬 920 Kingʾ *To respect.*—This group is read *king*, and most of the charracters are in common use; it looks a little like No. 870 敞.

萬 921 Wanʾ *A myriad.*—This offshoot from No. 598 禺, itself reäppears in a sub-group, No. 970 厲; its derivatives are read *wan*, *tun* and *mai*.

黽 922 ʿMin *Rad.* 205.—This group is read *min*, *yin*, *ying* and *shing* or *shăng*; it is easily to be distinguished from that under the radical.

喿 923 Saoʾ *Birds singing.*—In this group, the compounds are read *sao*, *tsiao* and *tsao*, mostly the latter; the idea of discord appears in many of them.

過 924 Kwoʾ *Overpassing.*—This comes from No. 605 咼, and imparts its sound *kwo* to half of its derivatives, the others being read *chwa*.

農 925 ˏNung *To farm.*—This group is mostly read *nung*, then *nang* and *nao*; many of the characters relate to density or thickening.

豊 926 Liʾ *A vase.*—This is used as a contracted form of No. 1021 豐, but as a phonetic has no likeness to it, all the derivatives being read *li* or *tʻi*.

睪 927 Yih, *To direct.*—This is derived indirectly from No. 416 幸, and one compound 擇 has three or four under it; the sounds are *yih*, *i*, *shih*, *tseh* and *tŏh*.

睘 928 ˏKiüng *Delicate.*—This and No. 555 爰 are sometimes interchanged; its compounds are read *hwan*, *hüen*, *pien*, *yuen*, *shwan* and *süen*; some of them have one or two derivatives.

蜀 929 Shuh, *An insect.*—The characters in this group are read *chuh*, *choh*, *tuh* and *shuh*; No. 1037 屬 is an offset, and one or two other sub-groups are found.

業 930 Yeh, *Patrimony.*—This resembles No. 869 美, and is comparatively a small group, whose members are read both *yeh* and *nieh* in some parts of the country.

FOURTEEN STROKES.

寧 931 ˏNing *Happy.*—This being a sacred character is contracted to 寍 with ten strokes; its compounds are read *ning* and *năng* in equal proportions.

賓 932 ˏPin *A guest.*—This is often changed to 賔 as being more easily written; the words are read *pin* or *pien*.

辡 933 ʿPien *Recrimination.*—This is derived from No. 296 辛 by duplication; its compounds are read *pien* and *pan*, and most of them are placed under the 160th radical.

齊 934 ˏTsi *Rad.* 210.—Many of the characters which properly come under this phonetic are placed under the radical in Kanghi's Dictionary; the derivatives here are read *tsi* and *chai*.

豪 935 ˏHao *Heroic.*—The characters in this group are read *hao*; the primitive flows from No. 622 高, and is somewhat like it.

需 936 ˏSü *Necessary.*—This primitive, also written 需, is sometimes interchanged with No. 847 須, which it resembles in sound and sense; it flows from No. 527 耎, and the compounds are read *jü*, *'rh*, *neu* and *sü*.

爾 937 ˏRh *You.*—This is contracted to 尔 in composition; the derivatives are read *'rh*, *lo*, *mi*, *nai*, *ni*, *ching*, *nieh*, *si* and *sien*; 彌 has six derivatives.

臧 938 ˏTsang *Just.*—One derivative under this 藏 has four under it, which and the others are all read *tsang*.

厭 939 ˏYen *To dislike.*—This is read both *yen* and *yeh*, and its compounds are read *yen*, *yeh* and *yah*, chiefly the first; their meanings show some traces of the primitive.

疐 940 Chʻiʾ *An obstacle.*—A small group whose compounds are read *chʻi* and *ti*.

聚 941 Tsüʾ *To congregate.*—This is occasionally interchanged with No. 417 取, and looks like No. 852 衆; the derivatives are read *tsü*, *tsung*, *cheu* and *chung*.

壽 942 Sheuʾ *Longevity.*—This group contains the sounds *cheu*, *tao* and *chu*, but none *sheu*; the primitive is written in many ways.

截 943 Tsieh, *Intercepted.*—This resembles No. 1010 鐵 and is also written 㦰; its derivatives are all read *tsieh*.

赫 944 Hoh, *Glistening.*—Formed by duplicating Rad. 155 赤, whose meaning it has partially kept; the words are read *hoh* and *hia*.

臺 945 ˏTai *A terrace.*—This group follows the sound *tai* of its phonetic, which is often contracted to No. 186 台, and also to 臺 with thirteen strokes.

監 946 ˏKien *To examine.*—An offshoot from No. 429 臤, this primitive has affinity with its derivative No. 995 覽; the sounds are *kien*, *yen*, *hien*, but chiefly *lan*.

盡 947 Tsinʾ *Completed.*—All but one [illegible] *nai* of this group are read *tsin*, and there is much affinity with the primitive in their meanings.

翟 948 Tih, *Plumagery.*—This primitive, an offshoot from No. 254 羽, does not affect the sense of its derivatives, which are read *tih*, *tiao*, *yoh*, *yao*, *chao* and *choh*.

㥯 949 ʿYin *Diligent.*—This is often interchanged with 隱 one of its derivatives, the two being regarded as synonyms; their sounds are *yin* and *wăn*.

耤 950 Tsih, *To cultivate.*—This is derived from No. 436 昔, and its compounds are all read *tsih*.

熏 951 ˏHiün *Steam.*—The compounds under this character are read *hiün* and *hüen*; it has no affinity with No. 558 重, nor will No. 1032 黨 be taken for it.

疑 952 ˏI *Suspicion.*—This conveys its own sound *i* to about half its compounds, the rest being read *ngai*, *ying*, *chi* and *hai*, and some having two or three sounds.

與 953 ˏYü *To give.*—This resembles No. 905 舁, but still more the word 興 *hing*, which has four derivatives read like it; this group is read *yu*, *kü* and *sü*.

獄 954 Yuh, *A prison.*—The derivatives are here read both *yoh* and *yuh* in different places; one is a synonym of its primitive.

㡭 955 Kiʾ *To connect.*—Part of these characters are read *ki*, and others *twan*; some of them are like the primitive. which is contracted to 迷.

睿 956 *Jui*ˀ *Sagacious.*—This is often contracted in writing to 叡 under twelve strokes; the compounds are read *jui* and *siün.*

蒦 957 *Hwoh*, *To measure.*—This flows from 隻 *chih*, which has also 雙 *shwang* as one derivative, and No. 1033 矍 as another; 艸 is frequently wrongly written so as to cover the whole characters as 䕶; the sounds are *hwoh* and *woh*, *hu* and *hwa.*

夢 958 *Mung*ˀ *Dreaming.*—This perplexes one by its varied forms, in which 瞢 and 曹 predominate; the group is read *mung* and *măng.*

賏 959 *Ying*ˀ *A necklace.*—This is formed of *Rad.* 154 貝 repeated, and has its derivative in No. 1015 嬰; they are all read *ying.*

㬎 960 ˎ*Hien* *Manifest.*—This has been superseded by its common derivative 顯, which itself has a few offshoots; the sounds under it are *hien*, *shih*, *sih* and *ngan.*

遣 961 ˋ*K'ien* *To send.*—This primitive resembles No. 682 追, but is not an offset from it; the derivatives are all read *kien*, but show no likeness in sense to the primitive.

對 962 *Tui*ˀ *To match.*—This is constantly contracted to 对; all the compounds are as much used as their leader, whose sound *tui* they follow.

FIFTEEN STROKES.

審 963 ˋ*Shăn* *To judge.*—This flows from No. 840 番, and its derivatives are read *shăn.*

寫 964 ˋ*Sié* *To write.*—This group is read *sié*; its characters are little in use.

廚 965 ˏ*Ch'u* *A kitchen.*—This and No. 817 彭 both come from 壴 *chu*, a band of music; 尌 has also three or four common derivatives, read *chu* and *shu*; this primitive is very often written 厨 under 14 strokes.

廣 966 ˋ*Kwang* *Broad.*—This comes from No. 824 黃, and its compounds are read *kwang*, *kung* and *kwoh*; one or two exhibit some analogy to it.

麃 967 ˏ*Piao* *Iridescent.*—This seems to flow from No. 722 鹿; in composition it interchanges with 票 and 表 in a few cases, and all the derivatives are read *piao.*

廛 968 ˏ*Ch'en* *A shop.*—This is often wrongly written, as if the lower part was 墨 ink, but the two are unlike; this group is read *chăn* and *chĕn.*

養 969 ˏ*Yang* *To nourish.*—This group is read *yang*, but its members indicate no likeness to their phonetic, which flows from No. 218 羊.

厲 970 *Li*ˀ *Severe.*—This is derived from No. 921 萬, but resembles it neither in sense nor sound; the characters are read *li.*

憂 971 ˏ*Yiu* *Afflicted.*—This is sometimes contracted to 忧, but only in poorly-printed books; the compounds are read *yiu* and *jao.*

頡 972 *Hieh*, *To mount.*—This comes from No. 243 吉; its compounds are few and infrequent, and all follow its sound *hieh.*

賣 973 *Mai*ˀ *To sell.*—This comes from No. 868 買, but its sounds are not so uniform as that; most of them are *tuh*, then *yuh*, *shuh*, *teu*, *tih* and *mai*; their meanings vary greatly.

節 974 *Tsieh*, *A joint.*—This derivative from No. 575 即 leads a few common characters read *tsieh*; it is contracted to 节 by rapid penmen.

質 975 *Chih*, *Essential.*—This leads the sounds of its derivatives, a few changing from *chih* to *chi*; it is contracted to 貭 even in good printing.

魯 976 ˋ*Lu* *Rustic.*—The derivatives here follow the sound *lu* except one read *lü*; they have no likeness in meaning.

徵 977 ˎ*Ching* *To prove.*—This is sometimes contracted to 敳 in combination, and resembles No. 903 微; the derivatives are read *ching* and *chi.*

樂 978 *Loh*, *Pleasure.*—The characters in this group are read *loh*, *yoh* and *shoh*, but mostly *lih*; their meanings often refer to splendor; 藥 leads three derivatives.

鄭 979 *Ching*ˀ *Prudent.*—This primitive does not give its sound, as the derivatives are read *chih*; No. 854 尊 suggests it in part.

巤 980 *Lieh*, *Bristles.*—The derivatives in this group are read *lieh* and *lah*; in common books it is contracted, as 蜡 for 蠟 and one or two others.

慮 981 *Lü*ˀ *To reflect.*—This primitive resembles No. 917 虜 and No. 999 盧 in its general form, and shows some affinity in sound with them both.

蔑 982 *Mieh*, *To exterminate.*—Some of these derivatives show a little affinity with their primitive; most of them are read *mieh* and *wah.*

暴 983 *Pao*ˀ *Cruel.*—This gives its sound *pao* to half of its compounds, and the others are read *poh*; they frequently show some trace of its many meanings.

數 984 ˏ*Shu*ˀ *Number.*—This is an offshoot of No. 789 婁; its compounds are read *shu*, *seu* and *soh*, and show no similarity to the meaning of either.

畾 985 ˏ*Léi* *Fields.*—This group and those under No. 793 累 and No. 881 雷 are alike read *léi*, and their compounds are often interchanged; 纍 has 12 derivatives, and 壘 has six, beside others; 田 is contracted often to 又 as 叒, even in well-printed books.

罷 986 *Pa*ˀ *To stop.*—This flows from No. 692 能, and is often contracted to 罢 in common books; its sounds are *pa*, *pi*, *péi* and *pai.*

SIXTEEN STROKES.

憲 987 *Hien*ˀ *Grandees.*—This primitive somewhat resembles No. 872 意, but the group is quite unlike; one character is read *hin*, and the others *hien.*

親 988 ˏ*Ts'in* *Near.*—Half of this character is sometimes wrongly written 辛, which is a synonym of 榛 the hazel; the derivatives are read *c'hăn* throughout.

龍 989 ˏ*Lung* *Rad.* 212.—The group placed under this radical contains many in which it is properly phonetic; the prevailing sound is *lung*, with a few read *chung*, *pang*, *sih* and *cheh.*

褱 990 ˏ*Hwai* *To embosom.*—This character is contracted to 褱 in composition; its derivatives are read *hwai*, and 壞 leads a group of three.

滕 991 ˏ*Tăng* *To ascend.*—This flows from No. 219 关, and in sound is like No. 666 朕, and seems to be a contraction of one of its compounds; the group is read *tăng* throughout.

霍 992 *Hoh*, *Sudden.*—This group resembles No. 626 隺 in sound, and No. 948 翟 in appearance; it is read *hoh*, but the compounds are not much used.

歷 993 *Lih*, *Generations.*—This is often written 歷 under 14 strokes, but the dictionaries follow this form; it is also contracted to 厤 as in 歷, when the radical is underneath; all are read *lih*.

噩 994 *Ngoh*, *Simple.*—This is constantly interchanged with No. 603 咢, both forms being regarded as correct; the sounds are all *ngoh*.

覽 995 ‹*Lan* *To observe.*—This primitive is derived from No. 946 監, but in practice the latter is contracted to 臤, nearly like No. 429 臤, as in 欖 olive; the sounds are all *lan*.

賴 996 *Lai*› *To trust.*—This is often contracted in composition to No. 535 剌, and the right side is also written like 頁; its derivatives are read *lai*, *lah*, *tah* and *lan*.

燕 997 *Yen*› *A swallow.*—This and No. 846 然 are often taken for each other; the words in this group are read *yen* like the phonetic.

穌 998 ‹*Su* *To resuscitate.*—This group is sounded *su* throughout; the characters are seldom met.

盧 999 ‹*Lu* *Black.*—Many derivatives under this character partake of its meaning, and all but three read *lü* follow its sound; it resembles No. 917 虜 and No. 981 慮 in form and sound.

諧 1000 *Hiai*› *Courageous.*—This group conforms in its sound *hiai* to its phonetic; the characters seldom occur and are diverse in meaning.

頻 1001 ‹*Pin* *Often.*—The derivatives from this phonetic are all read *pin*; few of them are much in use.

縣 1002 *Hien*› *Suspend.*—These characters are read *hüen*, one of the sounds of the primitive, of which one of the three is a synonym.

雟 1003 ‹*Hi* *A law.*—This is an offshoot from No. 904 雋, but the lower half of the primitive is often altered; the compounds are read *hi* and *hoh*.

SEVENTEEN STROKES.

蹇 1004 ‹*Kien* *Impediment.*—This primitive comes from No. 608 寒, and its derivatives are often interchanged with those; all are read *kien*.

襄 1005 ‹*Siang* *To encourage.*—This is contracted to 襄 in common books; the sounds under it are mostly *jang* or *yang* with *siang*, *niang* and *nang*.

羲 1006 ‹*Hi* *A victim.*—This resembles No. 880 義, but occurs less frequently; its compounds are all read *hi*.

霜 1007 ‹*Shwang* *Hoar-frost.*—A derivative from No. 538 相, the sounds are uniformly *shwang*; it is frequently interchanged with No. 739 爽.

聯 1008 ‹*Lien* *To connect.*—This flows from 絲, which itself has a few other derivatives as 關 and 聯; this group is read *lien* and *lin*.

闌 1009 ‹*Lan* *A barricade.*—These characters are uniformly read *lan*, and from one of them 蘭 flow six derivatives; the primitive is an offshoot from No. 532 柬.

韱 1010 ‹*Tsien* *Minced.*—This can be mistaken for No. 943 截, from which it differs in sound; the derivatives are read *tsien*, *chan*, *tsan* and *sien*.

毚 1011 ‹*Ch'an* *A leveret.*—This primitive is often contracted to 毚 in common books; its derivatives are read *chan* and *tsan*, and one in common use is *tsai*.

鮮 1012 ‹*Sien* *Fresh.*—A homophonous group read *sien*; the primitive is not unlike No. 998 穌 in form but not in sound.

龠 1013 *Yoh*, *Rad.* 214.—The characters with this in it as a radical resemble each other in sense, and those under it as a phonetic are alike in sound, except *yü*; 籥 has four derivatives.

薛 1014 *Sieh*, *A fault.*—These characters are read *sieh* and *yeh*; the primitive is not derived from No. 898 辥 which resembles it in construction.

嬰 1015 ‹*Ying* *An infant.*—This is one of the derivatives from No. 959 賏; its compounds are all read *ying*, but their meanings have no connection.

EIGHTEEN STROKES.

竄 1016 *Ts'wan*› *To conceal.*—The characters in this group are all read *tsw'an*; they must not be confounded with those under No. 980 巤 read *lah*.

雜 1017 *Tsah*, *Mixed.*—This is indirectly derived from No. 851 集, and is a little like No. 1027 難; its compounds are all read *tsah*.

聶 1018 *Nieh*, *To whisper.*—This imparts a trace of its meaning to some of its derivatives, which are read *nieh*, *cheh* and *sheh*.

爵 1019 *Tsioh*, *A nobleman.*—The characters in this group are read *shwoh*, *tsiao* and *tsioh*, but show no likeness in meaning to their primitive.

歸 1020 ‹*Kwei* *To return.*—This primitive leads its small company with its own sound *kwei*, but gives none of them any of its meaning.

豐 1021 ‹*Fung* *Abundant.*—This and No. 926 豊 are constantly interchanged with each other, but not quite correctly; the sounds *fung* and *yen* are the usual ones in this group.

雚 1022 *Kwan*› *An iris.*—About one half of these characters have the sound *kwan*, the rest are *hwan*; it is contracted to 萑 in rapid writing.

瞿 1023 *Kü*› *To dread.*—This and No. 1034 矍 differ a little in form, and altogether in sound, this group being read *kü* throughout.

NINETEEN STROKES.

䜌 1024 ‹*Lüen* *To bind.*—In some of the common derivatives, this primitive is contracted to No. 212 as 恋 for 戀; the sounds are chiefly *lüen* or *lwan*, then *wan*, *man*, *shwan* and *pien*; two or three small sub-groups are formed from it.

靡 1025 ‹*Mi* *Without.*—This is an offshoot from No. 719 麻, and some of its derivatives are interchanged with those; all here are read *mi*.

麗 1026 *Li*› *Elegant.*—This is derived from No. 722 鹿; in some characters it is contracted to No. 247 西 or No. 724 离 and even to 丽 the upper half; the compounds are read *li*, *si*, *sz* and *shai*.

難 1027 ‹*Nan* *Difficult.*—This is in form an offshoot from No. 756 堇, the derivatives are read *nan*, *no*, *ni* and *tan*, some of them having two sounds.

贊 1028 *Tsan*› *To help.*—This is also written 賛 and 賛, which perplexes the student as to the proper number of strokes; the last contraction resembles No. 813 朁, with which it is sometimes interchanged; this group is read *tsan*, *tswan* and *tsah*.

顛 1029 ‹*Tien* *Summit.*—This is derived from No. 674 眞, and agrees with it in sound; the compounds are read *tien*, and show a little likeness in signification.

邊 1030 ꜀Pien *Side.*—This is properly a sub-group of 臱, which itself has six derivatives, some under both being interchangeable, and all read *pien*.

羅 1031 ꜀Lo *A net.*—This group is read *lo*, and some of the characters partake of its meaning.

黨 1032 ʻT'ang *A clan.*—The sound *t'ang* shows this group to be a derivative of No. 501 尚, and not of No. 862 黑; its meanings are unlike either.

獻 1033 Hien' *Offering.*—This is contracted to 献 even in well-printed books; the sounds of the compounds are *hien, yen, hwan* and *yah*.

矍 1034 Kioh, *To fear.*—This comes from No. 1023 瞿, and somewhat resembles No. 957 蒦; the characters are read *kioh* or *koh* and *hoh*.

嚴 1035 ꜀Yen *Severe.*—This primitive may be regarded as derived from No. 815 敢, with which it has no likeness in sound or sense; a few derivatives are read *ngan*, most of them *yen*.

TWENTY-ONE STROKES.

霸 1036 ʻPa *To oppress.*—The few derivatives in this group are read *pa;* their meanings often indicate pressure, and the complicated primitive is sometimes contracted.

屬 1037 Shuh, *Appertaining.*—This flows from No. 929 蜀, and is often contracted to 属; the derivatives are read *chuh* and *shuh*.

TWENTY-TWO STROKES.

囊 1038 ꜀Nang *A bag.*—This primitive appears to be derived from No. 1005 襄, and is often abbreviated in writing; its compounds are all read *nang*.

TWENTY-FOUR STROKES.

贛 1039 Kung' *To donate.*—This primitive seems to come from No. 646 貢, but its derivatives are read *kung, kan* and *chwang*, and its parts contracted to 贑 in some cases.

靈 1040 ꜀Ling *Spirit.*—This is contracted to No. 182 令 and 霝 or 零, but not indiscriminately; the derivatives are read *ling*.

Those who are curious to follow the manner in which these primitives unite to form groups and sub-groups of derivatives, will easily be able to do so by running one or two through the radicals. It will soon be perceived how far they really serve as phonetics now, and how cautious one must be in deducing the sound from the primitive, especially of words in the *juh shing*. This combination of radicals and primitives is easily paralleled in other languages, especially in Greek and German, whose facility of compounding and decompounding roots and prefixes gives them such power and variety of expression. If there was a possibility or use in a universal language, in which mankind could convey their thoughts irrespective of the sound of the symbols, the Chinese seems to be the best fitted for it, inasmuch as the system of combination here explained is susceptible of infinite development to express almost any name or idea.

Out of this whole number 106 characters are either imperfect, contracted forms, not in use, or such as are rarely met with, leaving 934 common characters, most of which occur as often as any of their compounds. One advantage of learning this list, is the readiness it gives the student in reckoning the number of strokes in a character. When it has only a few strokes as 抽, 供 or 鉊, there is no hesitation in the search; but when their number is over twelve, as in 嚀, 驛 or 攝, it saves much time to know at sight, that they are to be found under 14, 13, or 21 strokes respectively. It is easy to ascertain the strokes by inspection, after becoming familiar with their construction, and is more rapid than to count them. For instance, 嚼 is composed of 口 *mouth* joined to 封 the 256th primitive, and 齒 the 211th radical, making 21 strokes, under which number it is placed. In others, like 携, or 彌, or 劉, where the component parts are not so easily separable, to know by sight that the characters occur under 12, 14, and 17 strokes respectively, is worth all the previous labor spent upon learning the primitives, in the time it saves.

Callery has given a score of pages containing sentences constructed out of the primitives, in order to assist in learning them. It will be worth more to the student to make and write sentences himself, out of the characters contained in the two preceding lists, and thereby familiarize himself with their use. The practice of repeatedly writing the characters, is the best way to imprint them on the memory; but it may be made more serviceable, by trying to form them into sentences. The proper manner of forming a character can best be learned by imitating a native as he writes, and it is the only way to produce well-shaped characters. It is not worth while to spend much time in using the Chinese pencil, for we are more familiar with the pen; and to make an accurate character is more important than to write an elegant one.

A

SYLLABIC DICTIONARY 韻分

OF

THE CHINESE LANGUAGE.

AI.

See also under the syllables YAI *and* NGAI. *Old sounds*, a, ap, ak, *and* at. *In Canton*, oi *and* ai; — *in Amoy*, ai *and* ó; — *in Fuhchau*, a *and* ai; — *in Shanghai*, a, é, ya, *and* yih; — *in Chifu*, ai.

挨 ˛ai From *hand* and *really* as the phonetic; it is interchanged with ˛yai 捱 to defer.

To rely on, to trust to; to push away; to carry on the back; to place alongside; to force, to crowd, as with the elbows; to graft; to strike on the back; to be the object of, to suffer, and thus it becomes the sign of the passive; next, near, contiguous.

相 丨 to be next to each other; to lean on.

有大山丨靠 he has powerful friends.

丨保 a student's surety.

丨門丨戶 to go from door to door, as a beggar; to gad about.

丨背 back to back.

丨不進去 I can't get in, — for the crowd.

丨打 or 丨了打 to be beaten; I was thrashed, or struck.

丨晚 towards evening; late in the afternoon.

丨肩弟兄 brothers nearly the same age.

丨了一年 I have waited already a year.

丨延過日 to procrastinate day by day, to delay till the time has passed.

In *Cantonese*. To lounge, to lean against; to lie down; an interjection of surprise, sorrow, or pain; to beg or ask.

丨下的 lie down a little.

丨呢邊 lean it here, as against a wall.

丨得去 it will answer.

丨求你 I intreat you.

丨吔 oh dear! whew! an exclamation also written as below, and in other ways.

哎 ˛ai An interjection of surprise, mixed with regret or self-reproach.

丨呀 haiya! it indicates more distress than our heigh-ho; alas! alack!

丨喲我錯了 oh dear! I've made a mistake.

丨我纔知道了 ah! I only just now knew it.

靄 ˋai From *rain* and *to visit* as the phonetic.

The heavens covered and adorned with clouds; a cloudy but bright sky; obscured.

祥雲丨丨 the beautiful clouds are scattered about.

丨氣 fair clouds.

嵐丨 cloudy hill-tops.

靉 ˋai From *clouds* and *to desire*; like the last.

Cloudy, obscure; sky covered with clouds; murky.

丨靆 dull or cloudy; applied to spectacles, as they can relieve sight; said to have been brought from Malacca in the Yuen dynasty.

藹 ˋai From *plants* and *to visit*.

Beautiful and luxuriant vegetation; shady, flourishing; fine, graceful, stylish, pleasing.

丨丨王多吉士 the many accomplished officers in the king's employ.

和丨 dignified and courteous.

翠丨 a rich emerald color, as of a lawn or grassy bank.

幽丨 shady groves.

壒 ˋai From *earth* and *to cover*.

Dust rising in the air; obscured, as in a dust storm.

不丨水 clear, pellucid water.

泥化輕丨 the mud turned into light dust.

軼挨丨之混濁 to get beyond the defilements of this dusty world, — as when becoming a priest.

矮 / 躷 *ai'* From *dark* or *body*, and to *send*. The second form is unusual, and confined to stature.

Low of stature; diminutive, short, squat; to lower.

丨子 or 丨人 or 丨仔 a pigmy, a little man, a dwarf.

丨丨的身量 of rather low stature.

丨胖子 a short fat man.

丨墩墩的 too low; squat, dumpy.

丨下去 make it lower, as a door.

丨得狠 too low; very diminutive.

睚 *ai'* From *eye* and a *bank;* very often read ˏ*ai*.

The outer corner of the eye; to raise the eye and stare at.

丨目 to look at fixedly.

丨眥 to glance at angrily, to look at aside threateningly.

隘 *ai'* From a *place* and *advantage;* the primitive is regarded by some rather as a contraction of 冓 a great number; it is interchanged with *ngoh*, 阨 dangerous.

A pass, a defile; in difficulties, straits; narrow, confined, straitened; urgent, exacting, stern; distressed; narrow-minded, low-lived, illiberal; impeded, as a path.

狹丨 narrow, as a pass; *met.* contracted, as one's views.

丨巷 a narrow lane.

丨口 a defile; the approach, as to a fortress.

貧丨 poor and distressed, as from calamity.

險丨 a dangerous pass, as a mountain path; *met.* unjust.

急若窘丨之中 appalled or excited, as if in perilous straits.

餲 *ai'* From to *eat* and *how*.

Cooked rice which has turned sour; moldiness on food; a kind of cake.

食至于丨 when the food has become sour.

食饐而丨 the food was sour and moldy.

㦬 *ai'* Sparing, niggardly.

呃 *ai'* From *mouth* and a *knot;* it is also interchanged with 呝 the crow of a cock.

An uneven or unnatural tone of voice; to chirp, as birds; to cackle; to hiccough.

丨喔 to belch, from wind in the stomach.

ANG.

A part of these characters are also pronounced NGANG. *Old sounds,* ngung *and* yung. *In Canton,* ong *and* ngong;—*in Amoy and Fuhchau,* ngang *and* yang;—*in Shanghai,* ngong;—*in Chifu,* ang.

𧲣 ˏ*ang* In Shantung, the raccoon dog 貉 was once called 丨貏 by the people.

昂 ˏ*ang* From *sun* and *high;* to be distinguished from 昴 ˊ*mao*.

To rise higher and higher, as the sun; to issue; to elevate; grand, stately, as a house; lofty, imposing; dear, as a price.

丨首 to carry the head high.

丨貴 exorbitant; the price is rising.

志氣丨丨 self-possessed; not afraid of men; satisfied and elated.

高丨 tall, imposing; proud, haughty.

丨然而入 he entered in a dignified manner.

丨丨氣像 a pompous manner.

卬 / 卬 ˏ*ang* The original form is composed of 匕 *even* and 卩 a *seal;* the second form is most common, and must not be confounded with 卯 *mao*, or 邛 *kiung;* it is like the last.

Great, high, to raise the head, as an attitude of expectation; used by speakers for I; high priced; strenuous.

物價低丨 the prices vary; they are now cheap and now dear.

意慷慨而自丨 public spirited and energetic, yet still self-possessed.

不丨自恤 I do not pity myself.

𣘻 ˏ*ang* The turned-up eaves of a Chinese roof, called 飛簷 and 飛丨; when the gable or ridge-pole is turned up, it is called 喜鵲尾 or magpie's tail at Peking; and 金鷄頭 or golden pheasant's head at Canton.

枊 ˏ*ang* Also read *yih*,. A horse-post is 馬丨. Also hard, strong.

䭹 ˏ*ang* An angry horse is 丨丨 one who throws up his head; startled and prancing.

Read ˏ*liu*. A horse with a white belly.

丨丨千里駒 a swift courser that can go a thousand *li* in one day.

胦 *ang'* The navel.

脖丨 the navel.

脖丨風疼 a windy colic.

盎 *ang'* A basin, a dish; a gurglet; a water jug; a sort of tureen; an earthen vessel for beating time on; overflowing; sleek.

瓦丨 a water ewer; broken pottery; potsherds. *(Cantonese.)*

丨於背 his good keeping is seen on his back, as a fat man.

湯丨 a soup-tureen; water-coolers, a vessel to cool things in a well. *(Cantonese.)*

丨丨 rich and abundant, like a spring.

丨齊 an ancient name for old spirits, generous and rich flavor.

CHA.

Old sounds, ta, tat, tap, tak, da, dat, *and* dak. *In Canton,* cha; — *in Swatow,* cha; — *in Amoy,* ché *and* t'a; — *in Fuhchau,* cha; — *in Shanghai,* tsò, sò, zò; — *in Chifu,* tsa.

樝 槎 ꜀cha. From *wood* and *fierce tiger* or *raft;* the second form is commonest for the fruit, and is also used for ꜀ch'a 槎 a raft.

A sour red fruit of the size of a cherry, a species of hawthorn (*Cratœgus cuneata* and *pinnatifida*), common throughout China; the fruit is called 紅菓子 and 山裡紅 at Peking; and 山丨 elsewhere; the acid is much esteemed.

山丨糕 a sweetmeat or jam made from the haw.

丨丨 the cry of magpies;

柤 ꜀cha From *wood* and *to obstruct;* used sometimes for the preceding, and for ꜀tsz 滓 sediment.

To put wood in the way to post the passage; to lie near to; conterminous and opposing; name of a place.

喳 ꜀cha An unauthorized character.

The sound of indistinct utterances; a lisp.

丨丨的亂叫 [the sparrows] are twittering and calling to each other.

喊喊丨丨 whispering together.

In *Cantonese.* A final particle, implying a short time.

等吓丨 wait a moment!

飲茶丨 just take a cup of tea.

渣 ꜀cha From *water* and *to examine* as the phonetic.

Sediment, refuse, lees, dregs, grounds, settlings; the residuum left after expressing the juice; the garbles of an article.

丨滓 feculence, leavings, siftings.

八角丨 broken star-aniseed.

紫梗丨 shell-lac.

藥丨 the refuse left after preparing drugs; a second decoction.

Read *cha'.* Name of a stream in the south of Shensi.

戱 ꜀cha To place the finger on a thing, for the purpose of selecting it; to take, to press down, to feel.

瘡 ꜀cha The scab on a healing sore.

痂丨 a cicatrix, a scar.

穞 ꜀cha Red upland rice called 赤丨 by some authors; the term is local.

皻 皶 齄 ꜀cha The third form is properly used only for pimples on the nose.

Discolorations or cracks of the skin, supposed to arise from the obstructed perspiration; a pimple, a blotch; pustules.

皵丨 chapped; a cracked and rough skin.

酒丨鼻 wine blossoms on the nose, sometimes called 粉刺 or flour thorns, from the pus in them.

齇 ꜀cha Irregular teeth; uneven, distorted teeth, sometimes called snaggle-teeth.

奓 ꜀cha From *great* above *many,* and is regarded by the etymologists as a contracted form of 奢; it is sometimes written 侈 but not quite correctly.

To open out, to stretch open; to bluster; to extend or display, as, a cause.

丨言 to boast.

丨戶 to open the door.

心丨體泰 a vain disposition and unwieldy person.

二儀丨闊 the two original powers are vastly spread out, as at the creation.

膠 ꜀cha Not close grained, said of some kinds of meat; a scar; to adhere, to stick, as paste; cohering, close together.

觰 ꜀cha Broad, spreading horns, such as are largest at the base; to strike an ox across the horns.

張丨 expanded horns.

譇 謯 ꜀cha From *words* and *to boast;* the second form is obsolete.

To speak hesitatingly, not straightforward; afraid to speak out, reticent; angry, disturbed in mind.

丨詉 incoherent talk, like that of one confused and afraid.

摣 揸 ꜀cha Also read ꜀chwa; the second, and most common form at Canton, is unauthorized, and has no doubt been altered from the first.

To take up, as by the fingers; to seize or take, as animals; to grasp, to clutch, to grab; take firmly, to hold fast; to work, as a bellows; to squeeze; a handful.

丨得穩 I've got it safe; hold it steady.

丨風箱 to work a bellows.

丨一大丨 grab a big handful.

丨攤 to keep a gambling-table.

丨水猪肉 water-sogged pork; it is sometimes watered to increase the weight.

丨火筒 to blow the fire-pipe; to act as a scullion.

有丨手 I have security for it.

丨着印柄 he holds the power.

丨緊 hold it tight; I've got it fast.

無丨拏 there is nothing to hold on by, no security for him; also, a nickname for a Budhist priest.

丨拳頭 to double up the fist.

丨爛 to crush to pieces.

挓 ꜀cha To open; to widen out.

丨挱 to expand; to come out, as flowers; to spread out, as the embroidered plaits of a Chinese lady's skirt.

丨開五指 to open out the fingers.

謯 ꜀cha An exclamation of regret and surprise; to chant or sing. Read tsü'. To curse or scold at.

鮓 ꜀cha Sometimes written 鲊, but not quite correctly; see also under 蛇 ch'a'.

A condiment of fish, prepared by finely hashing it with rice and salt, and setting it aside till fermented.

丨魚 a species of edible Acalepha, or perhaps a Medusa; it is described as red like coagulated blood, and draws crabs after it.

丨答 a general term for biliary and other calculi; bezoar stones found in animals; this term is probably a foreign word imitated.

苲 ꜀cha A water plant, called ground hemp; the ancient name of a district near the present Kia-hing fu in the north of Chehkiang.

筹 ꜀cha Also read ꜁tsz'. Tones of a pipe. A basket for charcoal is called ꜀cha, at Changsha in Hunan; a basket with a bale.

篸丨 bamboos growing irregularly; uneven; also to play on a flageolet.

踏 ꜀cha An unauthorized character; also read ꜁chá.

To tread on, to walk through; to step on.

丨一脚泥 I got my feet covered with mud.

丨雨 to walk through the rain and mud.

乍 cha꜄ The original form is composed of 亾 *lost* or *forgotten*, and 一 *one* inserted in it; as if on going out, a man should get one and then stop.

At first; for a moment; a while; unexpectedly, inadvertently; now, at this juncture; hastily, quickly, on a sudden; hesitating, as if something was in the way.

丨涼丨熱 now it is cold and then it is warm; very fitful, as the weather.

丨然 abruptly, at once.

丨見 I happened to see it; it was suddenly seen.

丨斷 by sudden stops.

痄 cha' A running sore; a chronic, severe disease.

丨腮 scrofulous sores under the ears, running sores on the neck; in Canton, the mumps is so called.

丨瘂 severe sickness.

咋 cha' A loud rude noise; the noise of crunching, as of hogs when eating; for a moment; a loud noise.

丨舌 to run out the tongue, as when surprised or alarmed.

In *Cantonese*. A particle, implying doubt, it may be so; also a final sound, denoting it is so; I see it.

詐 cha' From *words* and *suddenly* as the phonetic.

To deceive, to impose upon; to feign, to make believe; artful, cunning, false; fraudulent, underhand, pretending.

知者丨愚 he knew but pretended to be foolish; a wise man acting as a fool.

訛丨 to extort by false promises.

奸丨 to delude, designing, treacherous.

丨僞 supposititious, false; counterfeit.

丨老實 to feign to be honest.

丨敗 to sham defeat; to skulk from the enemy.

巧丨 clever at imposing on one.

丨睡 to feign to be asleep.

騙丨 to cozen, to cheat out of.

丨匿 to disguise; to pretend to be hid away.

勒丨 to force out of, to exact, as taxes; to falsely demand, as a debt.

變丨 protean, changeable, fickle.

榨 醡 cha' From *wood* or *spirits* and *narrow;* the verb is often written 搾 at Canton, but incorrectly; the second form is usually employed as the verb.

A press for extracting oil or sugar; a press for spirits; to press in order to extract the juice, as from fruit or sugar-cane; to squeeze, to press down hard.

丨房 a house or shed where oil or bean-cake is pressed.

油丨 an oil-press.

酒丨 a spirit vat; a press for pressing the mash.

唶 cha' A sigh; groaning; a loud noise, as when calling one.

丨丨 the cries of birds.

丨吮 to suck wounds.

禚 蜡 cha' From to *worship* or *insect* and *ancient;* the second form is used as a contraction of 蠟 beeswax so often, that it is not much used in this connection.

The imperial thanksgiving made to earth at the end of the year for the crops, was called 大丨 in the Cheu dynasty; the allusion was to the binding up or hybernation of things at that season.

灹 cha' From *fire* and *leaflet;* it is interchanged with 炸 chah꜇.

A crackling sound, as of a clap of thunder or burning thorns; a discharge, as of a gun.

丨雷 a sharp clap of thunder.

溠 cha' One of the small branches of the River Han near Sui chau in the north of Hupeh; this name is also given to four other streams in the empire.

磋 cha' Careless about; not arranged in the middle, or nicely.

作事磊丨 to do work in a slovenly, heedless manner,—alluding to the disorder in a heap of stones; the phrase, however, is variously written.

CH'A.

Old sounds, mostly *t'a*, *t'ap*, and *t'ak*, with one or two in *do* and *dot*. In Canton, *ch'a*, with two or three in *t'so*;— in Amoy, *ch'a ch'è*, and *té*; and nearly the same in Swatow;—in Fuhchau *ch'a*, and a few in *ta*;— in Shanghai, *dsô*;—in Chifu, *ts'a*.

叉 *ˏch'a* The fingers crossing each other, which the character is supposed to represent; it is also interchanged with 杈 and 岔 *ch'a'*.

To cross the arms, to interlace the fingers; to fold the hands, as in bowing; diverging; a crotch; a place where roads diverge; a prong, a fork; cross-roads.

禾丨 a pitchfork; 銀丨 a silver fork; 魚丨 fish-grains.

三丨 a trident; also, a trivium.

丨燒 to roast or toast on a fork.

丨手躬身 to interlace the fingers and make a bow.

飛丨 the play of throwing up tridents and catching them.

扠 *ˏch'a* To fork up; to nip; to seize with pincers or a fork; a fish-prong or grains; to take up with the fingers; to drive out; to pitch out.

丨出去 turn him out.

丨上去 fork it up;—as when putting a thing on a high nail.

衩 *ˏch'a* From *clothes* and *crotch*; it is also read *ch'a'*.

The skirt of a robe; the flaps of the skirt.

裙丨 the opening of a petticoat, where it is not sewed to the bottom.

丨褲 the upper half or seat of a pair of trowsers, worn by ditchers and workmen.

靫 *ˏch'a* A quiver, called usually 箭袋 or arrow bag.

差 *ˏch'a*, *ˏch'ai* From 左 the *left* or wrong, and 𠂹 uneven *branches* contracted; also explained as things done in two ways, *i. e.* things wrongly done, which cannot be straightened

To err, to mistake, to miss the mark; error, fault, difference; a discrepancy; an excess; unassorted, unlike.

丨不多 not much unlike, nearly the same.

丨得遠 very different, dissimilar; you are quite mistaken,

丨錯 a mistake; 丨錯脚 to step wrong; a blunder, a faux-pas.

丨一點兒 differs a little; they are very much the same.

若其酒醴之丨 respecting the different sorts of wines.

丨樣兒 in *Pekingese*; extraordinary, unusual, as a lusus naturæ.

丨着 differing; they are unlike.

Read *ˏch'ai*. To send, as an envoy; to commission, to act for, to manage vicariously; a minister, a legate, an envoy; an official messenger.

丨使 a bailiff, an agent.

當丨 official messengers, who serve in turn.

丨事 governmental business.

解丨 the escort or guard which conducts a criminal.

丨役 a policeman, an official underling.

放大欽丨 to send a chancellor to hold an examination.

報京丨 or 快丨 a government courier; the first is one who goes to Peking.

聽丨 an attendant, an official servant.

Read *ˏts'z'*. Uneven, projecting irregularly; discrepancies; to make a distinction; to go wrong, to act differently.

參丨 not uniform, unequal; not to do as one was expected.

各有丨等 every one has his own peculiarities.

罔丨有辭 no difference being shown to the excusable or the less guilty.

嗏 *ˏch'a* A final sound used in chanting, to prolong the line; a euphonic particle, like Oh!

⿰差刂 *ˏch'a* From *knife* and *sent*.

To take up a thing with a fork or a bodkin; a small javelin.

用叉子丨肉 to stick a fork into a bit of meat and take it up.

仛 *ˏch'a* A young girl, for which 奼 *ˏch'a* is also used; an easy, retired life of leisure and respect.

Read *toh*, Another; that one.

茶 *ˏch'a* The character 荼 *ˏtu* was once used instead of this, showing that the use of tea dates from earliest times; it was afterwards changed by dropping a line, so that it became, as one etymologist analyzes it, a 艸人木 or plant for man, the shrub itself was once called 檟, and the last gathering 茗; it must not be confounded with 恭 to respect.

The tea plant; the name also includes the genus Camellia, and forms part of the names of many plants which are infused, or which resemble tea; the earliest gathering of the leaves; a tea, an infusion of any kind.

綠丨 green tea; 黑丨 black tea.

丨餅 and 丨磚 tea pressed into cakes and brick tea; there are many forms of each.

丨葉 cured tea, the tea leaf; but leaf tea is 毛丨 intimating that it looks unprepared.

飲丨 or 喝丨 or 嗑丨 to drink tea.

倒丨來 bring in tea; used sometimes as a polite request to stop and take a cup.

獻丨 to hand tea to visitors.

傑丨or 倣丨or 起丨or 閅丨 to draw tea; to prepare and bring in tea.

丨壺 a tea-pot.

丨杯 or 丨盅 a tea-cup; 丨碟 or 丨船 a saucer; the latter gets its name from its boat-shape.

丨几 a small side-table or stand; a teapoy.

丨館 or 丨居 a tea saloon; a restaurant.

丨舖 or 丨林 a tea-shop, a tea dealer's store.

上品丨 first rate tea.

丨錢 a bakshish; a fee, bonus, or privilege.

炒丨 to fire tea, as in curing it.

丨師 a tea-inspector.

丨末 or 碎丨 broken tea, refuse tea, stems and leaves mingled.

丨花 the flower of tea; also, the Camellia plant, especially the *C. japonica;* the *C. oleifera* produces the 丨油 or tea oil.

搽 ˏch'a From *hand* and *tea* as the phonetic; it is an unauthorized character.

To rub on, to smear; to daub, to spread over; to cross out, as in a writing.

丨粉 to paint with cosmetics.

丨藥 to spread a plaster.

丨瘡 to rub ointment on sores.

丨花口面 to disguise one's face.

丨白鼻哥 to whiten his nose; *i. e.* to flatter, to agree with.

In *Pekingese*, read ˋch'a. To mix together, as sand and lime, or mud and mortar; to get jammed, as carts in a gateway.

秅 ˏch'a A mode of reckoning grain when reaped, one ˏch'a being equal to four hundred ˋping 秉 or handfuls.

烏丨 name of a part of ancient Bactria.

詫 ˏch'a Deep and retired, as the further rooms in a mansion.

兩目詫丨 his two eyes are very sunken.

㢉 ˏch'a A house injured, and ready to tumble down.

丨屋之下不可坐也 don't sit under a decayed, rotten roof.

艖 **舣** ˏch'a The first is also read ˏts'o; occurs used with the next.

A skiff, a long shallop called 小㢉 or small bottom, in Hunan on the River Siang.

鹽丨 salt boat; a scow to transport salt.

丨頭鯿 a fish, described as like a skiff in shape; it is probably one of the carp family.

槎 ˏch'a To fell trees, to hew, to chop; drift wood for a float; a raft, in which it is interchanged with the next.

仙丨 the fairy raft, refers to a story of *Ho-sien-ku,* one of the eight genii.

乘丨 to ride a raft; to sail on a ship, to take a voyage.

丨枒 wood cut unevenly.

查 ˏch'a From 木 *wood* and 旦 *morning* under it; it was originally the same with 柤 an obstruction; and in combination is often changed to 㢉 without altering the meaning.

A raft, for which the last is now used.

To examine officially; to inquire into; to look up or over, as records; it appears that, I have learned, having ascertained, &c., and much used in dispatches, when commencing a statement.

巨丨 or 貫月丨 the great raft, which in the days of Yao floated twelve years around the globe; it is thought by some, without any evidence, to refer to Noah's ark.

訪丨 to ask about especially, as when there is 差丨 a police search.

丨察 to examine, to scrutinize.

丨街 to patrol the streets, as the 丨夜官 or night guard does.

丨收 I find it has been received.

丨數 to audit accounts.

厏 ˋch'a Also read *cheh*ˎ.

Disagreeing, not fitting.

丨厊 incongruous, not corresponding.

奼 **姹** ˋch'a Much the same as 侘 ˏch'a.

A handsome young lady, an elegant girl.

嬰兒丨女 a fine boy and a beautiful girl.

丨女 a Taoist name for vermilion, or for the fairy which springs out when oxidizing quicksilver.

吒 **咤** ch'aˋ From *mouth* and to *rely on* or *dwell;* it is like the next.

To vociferate, as when angry; to sputter, to talk thick; to grind the teeth; to grumble at; to disdainfully upbraid; to pity.

The first is read ˏcha in 哪丨太子 the name of a god fabled to have been a son of 李靖, born about B. C. 1200, in a ball of flesh. He is the Chinese form of the Indian *vajza* or god of the thunderbolt; and is pictured as riding on two fire-wheels through the sky, wielding the lightning.

Read ˏ*ta,* in the Sanscrit word 阿丨丨 *atata,* the third frozen hell, whose damned can only say *atata,* because their lips are stiffened.

Read *tu*ˋ. To set down a cup at a sacrifice.

In *Fuhchau.* To trouble, to interfere with.

拍丨 to cause a failure.

詫 ch'aˋ Like the last. To talk extravagantly, to vaunt, to talk big; to deceive by brag and talk.

誇丨 to vaunt one's self.

丨異 strange, incredible; hard to believe, amazing.

蛇 ch'aˋ From *insect* and *dwelling;* it is a synonym of 鮓 ˋch'a.

The large sea-blubber or jelly fish *(Medusa)* that floats on the ocean; it is described as like a sheep's stomach, but having no belly, body of a dull white color, eyes red as clots of blood, and drawing crabs with it; another name is 水母 water mother; it is sometimes eaten.

䶪 An unauthorized character.
ch'a' A shred, a fragment of pottery is 瓦 ㄧ 兒 in Peking; when used as a verb, to split off, it is pronounced *ₑch'a*; as 齊 各 ㄧ 兒 to break or snap off even.

汊 A stream dividing up into streamlets.
ch'a' 三 ㄧ 河 a river in Liaotung, and one in Hanyang fu in Hupeh.
三 ㄧ 水 the union of three streams.

岔 From *hill* and *divided*; this and the next occur used for *ₑch'a* 叉 a fork.
ch'a' The place where roads meet; divergent paths.
ㄧ 道 a place where the road forks. a town at the head of Nankow Pass.
三 ㄧ 路口 a trivium, or meeting of three roads.

In *Pekingese*. Wrong, as going astray; pained.
走 ㄧ 了 you are going wrong.
ㄧ 了 氣 了 a pain in the side, as physicians say.
旁 ㄧ 的 話 a digression, an episode; irrelevant talk.

杈 From *tree* and *fork*; used with the last.
ch'a' Divergent branches; crotch of a tree; a fish-prong; a kind of rake, a pitchfork.
春 來 嶺 樹 共 生 ㄧ the forests on the hills send out their branches in spring.
ㄧ 杖 a pronged stick.
ㄧ 雞 賊 a pickpocket who slips an arm out of his sleeve.

In *Pekingese*. An offense; a flaw in the conduct.
出 了 ㄧ 兒 something unlucky has happened.
找 ㄧ 兒 to seek a fault in one; to criticize others.

CHAH.

Old sounds, *tat* and *tap*, with a few in *dap*. In Canton, *chat*, *chap*, and one or two in *tsò*; — in Amoy, *chap*, *chah*, and *chwat*; — in Fuhchau, *chak*, *chwok*, and *cha*; — in Shanghai, *tsah*; — in Chifu, *tsah*.

札 From *wood* and a *slip*.
ₑcha A thin wooden tablet, anciently used for writing; a thin slip of wood; a paddle; a letter; often interchanged with 劄 writings, documents; a direction from a superior to a subordinate a little below him; plates or folds of armor; a severe epidemic.
ㄧ 文 orders from a superior officer.
簡 ㄧ writing tablets; blocks cut for books.
華 ㄧ your letter, your esteemed favor.
鴈 ㄧ a letter, so called because one was fabled to have been taken by a wild goose.
ㄧ 委 an order received; similar to
來 ㄧ the letter under reply.
夭 ㄧ an untimely death.

紮 From *silk* and a *slip of wood*.
ₑcha To bind the arch of a bow; to tuck in; to wind around and bind up; to tie in a bundle; to make secure; a bundle.
一 ㄧ 花 a nosegay, a bouquet.
ㄧ 縛 to tie up, as in a roll.
ㄧ 營 to set a camp, to intrench.
ㄧ 脚 to bind the feet of girls.
ㄧ 帳 to hook or tie open the bed curtains.
ㄧ 緊 tie it up tight; as when one ㄧ 帶 tightens his girdle.

扎 From *hand* and a *slip*; it is interchanged with 劄 to stab; also used for the last.
ₑcha To pull up, as weeds; to make or cut out paper images; to prick, to pierce; to bind or fasten, as the slips in a wattled fence.
ㄧ 得 像 cut out to the life.
ㄧ 花 to embroider a certain design.
刀 ㄧ to stick with a knife.
ㄧ 豬 to stick a pig.
ㄧ 掙 不 住 I cannot exert myself; I am too weak to do it.

蚻 A small species of cicada,
ₑcha striped and marked on its wings, which leaps far; it is also called 麥 ㄧ or wheat locust.

吽 螞 ㄧ a kind of Truxalis of green grasshopper, which makes a dull noise; the name is applied to a chatterbox, a woman whose clack never stops.

鷟 A water bird, with a long bill
ₑcha and plumage of a lark, common in Chehkiang; it is probably a sort of sandpiper (*Tringa*) or dunlin; the 水 ㄧ as described, include water birds like plover, snipe, redshank, or lapwing.
雀 兒 ㄧ red-breasted plover of Chihli.
葦 ㄧ 子 the eastern reed sparrow (Calamo, *dyta orientalis*.)
大 水 ㄧ woodcock (*scolopax*.)

劄 From to *answer* and a *knife*; the
ₑcha composition of the word alludes to the old way of cutting writings on bamboos. The word *chop*, so much used by foreigners, is derived from this through the Cantonese pronunciation *chap*. Occurs interchanged with 札, but this and 劄 *tah*, are different words.

To prick, to puncture; to stitch in, to embroider; a document, a paper; a particular kind of paper for dispatches; a contract; a diploma; an order from a superior officer; a warrant or patent; to write out, as a list of prices or items.

紙 丨 a stationer's shop.

丨 子 anciently a memorial to the throne; now an order from an officer to one under him.

監 丨 a diploma purchased by a *Kiensăng*.

丨 落 部 charge it in account;—a Cantonese phrase.

丨 單 a contract for goods.

丨 貨 to settle for goods to arrive.

丨 價 錢 to agree upon the price.

住 丨 to lodge at, as in traveling; to be an officer at a place, the one holding the post.

丨 支 an order from government.

茁, ˓cha From *grass* and *issuing* as the phonetic.

Sprouts and shoots appearing above ground; animals growing stronger and larger; to sprout.

蘭 丨 其 芽 the orchid puts out its sprouts.

俄 丨 丨 俄 亭 亭 first it sprouts, then it grows up high, — and lastly it decays; said of plants.

牛 羊 丨 壯 長 the oxen and sheep grow strong and large.

Read *ch'uh*, A sort of herb; a dandelion is called 苦 丨 菜 in Chihli.

霅, ˓cha From *rain* and *words*.

Pattering of rain or flashes of lightning; a multitude of voices; name of a place and river in Chehkiang.

電 丨 丨 flashes of lightning.

雨 丨 丨 the rain patters down.

公 庭 丨 丨 the hall was full of loud talking.

Read *sah*, Suddenly.

丨 爾 霅 落 the hail poured suddenly down.

紮, ˓cha To sew and hem; to sew together, as strips of cloth.

詀, ˓cha From *words* and to *hull grain*.

Verbose; to talk much; to mutter unintelligibly.

丨 讘 to grumble at with muttering; incoherent words.

褔, ˓cha A double hem or border on a robe; to bind the loins.

丨 袋 a sheath or a fan, worn in ceremonial dresses.

牐, ch'a' To shut a city gate; the board or gate which shuts off a sluice or flume; to stop a door by a board.

下 丨 板 put up the front-boards; *i. e.* to close the shop at evening.

排 丨 a kind of tester or framework over a brick bed, on which clothes are hung.

閘, ˓cha From a *gate* and a *scale*; similar to the last.

A flood-gate, a water-gate; a lock in a canal; a dam; any thing placed to impede progress; a barrier, a guarded gate; a turnstile; a gate in a stockade; a barricade of posts; to shut a gate. In Fuhchau, applied to the front curtain of a sedan.

丨 卡 a guard-house at a barrier.

關 丨 a pass; a barrier, like that formerly at Macao; to shut the gate.

水 丨 an aqueduct; a sluice; a waste-weir with gates.

街 丨 street gates, common in Chinese cities; they serve to prevent the assemblage of mobs, to divide off the wards, and aid the police in arresting thieves.

丨 門 a guard-gate; to bar a gate.

看 守 丨 門 to stand guard at the passes.

開 丨 open the barrier; take up the portcullis.

看 丨 or 丨 夫 a gate-keeper.

丨 河 the Grand Canal is so called in some parts of its course.

眨, ˓cha chan˒ To wink; to move the eyes about.

哎 丨 巴 眼 兒 Ah, see how he winks!

丨 目 to wink the eyes.

丨 眼 兒 的 工 夫 in the twinkling of an eye, in a very short time.

不 開 口 丨 眼 會 意 to intimate one's wishes by a wink without speaking.

煠, 炸, 灹, ˓cha From *fire* and *leaf*; but the unauthorized forms are the most common; the meanings of this character vary in different parts of the country.

To fry food; to boil in fat or oil; to scald by pouring on water.

丨 熟 to boil thoroughly; to fry.

丨 肉 丸 to fry meat balls.

丨 蔴 花 to fry crullers.

丨 香 椿 to scald Ailantus leaves, they are eaten when tender.

In *Pekingese*. The second is also read *cha'*; coal broken up into fragments; bits; to blow up, to burst.

丨 子 nut coal, or coal in bits.

丨 煤 coal of any kind.

丨 炮 a bomb or mortar.

炮 丨 the gun burst in pieces.

哳, ˓cha The crowing of a bird.

嘲 丨 the mournful crowing of a jungle fowl or pheasant.

鍘, ˓cha From *metal* and to *chop*; it is commonly but erroneously contracted to 鈒 in Canton.

A heavy pair of shears working on a rivet as a fulcrum at the end; it is used to cut up fodder, money, slips of sheet iron, and such things; to slice or cut open.

丨 草 to cut grass fine.

丨 刀 a grass-cutter

劕, ˓cha Also read *tsan* or *tswan*, and used with the preceding.

To cut up or chop; the noise of cutting fine.

CH'AH.

Old sounds, *t'at* and *t'ap*. In Canton, *ch'at* and *ch'ap*; — in Swatow, *ch'at*, *sat*, *k'ip*, and *ch'ah*; — in Amoy, *ch'at*, *ch'ap*, and *ch'ak*; — in Fuhchau, *ch'ak* and *sak*; — in Shanghai, *ts'ah*; — in Chifu, *ts'ah*.

察, *ch'a* From 宀 a *cover* and 祭 to *sacrifice*, intimating that when human efforts were unavailing to find out a cause, then sacrifice was the best thing.

To examine, to get at the truth, to inquire into judicially, to act as a censor; to criticise, to observe closely, to scrutinize, to learn the particulars; to sacrifice; to survey.

審丨or 查丨 to examine carefully, especially as an officer, like the 按丨司 provincial judge, does.

丨情 to ascertain the circumstances.

丨奪 to examine and decide, as a case.

苛丨 a vexatious questioning.

省丨 to make a self-examination.

丨丨 unsullied, as a reputation.

辨丨其微 he examined the minutest points.

明丨無屈于庶子 to candidly examine an affair, so that the people feel no sense of injustice.

丨出 to ferret out; to search and find, as a detective does.

詧, *ch'a* Similar to the last, and often employed as a synonymous form.

To inquire into every particular; name of a statesman in the Liang dynasty, A.D. 540.

刹, *ch'a* From 刀 *knife* and 殺 to *kill* contracted.

A pillar or spire on the top of a dagobah or shrine, from which to hang streamers; a tope covering the ashes of priests; a Budhist monastery.

寶丨 your convent; said to a priest.

梵丨 a temple of Budha.

上丨 to visit a temple.

丨竿 a staff for banners before a temple.

丨帝利 the *kshatriyas*, one of the Indian castes.

丨那 in Sanscrit *kshana*, the 90th part of a thought, reckoned to be the 4500th part of a minute.

臿, *ch'a* Form a *pestle* in a *mortar*; occurs used with 插 and 鍤, to which it gives part of its own meaning.

To hull wheat; to deprive grain of its husk.

築丨 a beetle to pound adobie walls.

畚丨 agricultural implements in general.

扱, *ch'a* From *hand* and *up to*; it is sometimes wrongly used for the next.

To receive; to take or gather; to raise up; to help; to lead; to bow with the hands nearly touching the ground,—the salutation of a woman; to tuck the skirt under the girdle.

丨引高賢 to introduce good people to the great.

收丨 to get or collect.

走勞無丨 to labor without adequate reward.

丨地 to bow very low, as the Japanese do.

插, *ch'a* From *hand* and to *hull wheat* as the phonetic; it is interchanged with the last two and the next.

To insert; to pierce, to drive into or stick in, as a pole in the ground, or flowers in the hair; to thrust into; to set in a socket; to interfere, to meddle with; to insert, as stuffing in a fowl; an iron pointed pole or crow-bar.

丨秧 to transplant rice-shoots.

丨票 to stick in a label or mark.

丨手落去 to meddle officiously, to want a share in.

八擡八丨 eight bearers and eight out-riders.

丨掙 to make an effort to get in.

丨耳遊營 to stick flags in the ears, when [whipping a man] through the camp.

丨贜 to furtively secrete in another's room, so as to implicate him.

丨柳成陰 set out willows, and you will have a shade; — diligence will get its reward.

丨口 or 丨嘴 to interrupt, to put in a word.

丨旗子 to put out a flag, as an auctioneer.

丨草賣身 to put grass in his hair and sell him, as the poor are obliged to do with their children in distress.

匙丨 a narrow purse for keys.

安丨 to find a place for one, to get one a situation.

丨翼難飛 he cannot get away, even if he gets a pair of wings.

丨燒 to put in stuffing for roasting; in Canton, a concubine's child is so called in sport.

鍤, *ch'a* Sometimes used for the last. A spade or pick for turning up the ground; a large pin or skewer for fastening the outer garments; a flat hairpin, ornamented with feathers; a carrying beam; a sort of crow-bar.

扛丨 to carry a pick; *met.* a farmer, a field-hand.

香匙丨 a little spatula for incense.

䰈, *ch'a* The name of demons 羅丨 which bring pestilence; they are the *rakshas* of the Hindu mythology, the agents of evil; also written 羅刹 by many persons. Also used as the name of a foreign country.

侘, *ch'a* Irresolute; to boast; to be diverted from one's purpose is 丨傺, said of disappointed aims.

CHAI.

Old sounds *tai*, *dai*, *dat*, and *dak*, with one or two in *tak*, *tat* and *dan*. In Canton, *chai*; — in Swatow and Amoy, *chai* and *chè*; — in Fuhchau, *chè* and *chai*; — in Shanghai, *tsa* and *sa*; — in Chifu, *tsai*.

齋 斋 齊 *꜀chai* *꜀ch'* From 齊 *even* and 示 *to worship*; the third form is used in the classics, and the contraction is common in cheap books.

To respect, to reverence; to abstain from; to guard against, to purify, as by fasting or penance; pure, serious, reverential; a study, a closet; a retiring room; a fine shop, as for the sale of medicines; lenten fare.

打 〡 to perform services for releasing a soul.

打 〡 鶴 paper storks on which the soul flits to heaven; *met.* a pander.

清 〡 he has only vegetable food.

〡 戒 to fast and not kill animals.

不入 〡 戒 [onions] are not regarded as proper food for fast days.

〡 期 fasting days.

〡 醮 to fast on the Budhist festival of All-souls.

〡 公 a pilgrim—to a Taoist shrine.

食 〡 to fast on vegetables.

閒 〡 a study; a library-room.

書 〡 a student's room.

雅 〡 elegant leisure.

〡 居 to live at ease.

〡 莊 respectful, modest.

Read *꜀tsz'*. A mourning dress for parents.

In *Cantonese*. A particle, implying that it is so, it was said.

乜人話 〡 who dared to say so?

好似佢話 〡 it is just as he said.

[广齊] *꜀chai* Like the preceding, but restricted to a dwelling of thatch, a hut; while the last is a more substantial edifice.

梩 *꜀chai* From *wood* and to *bury*.

Suckers springing from the roots of a decayed tree; dead, rotten wood in the roots.

債 *chai'* From *man* and to *blame*.

To owe money; to bear a burden; a debt, an obligation; freight or passage-money, so called by the ship-owners.

欠 〡 to owe a debt.

〡 主 a creditor.

〡 人 (or 〡 仔 in *Cantonese* a debtor.

還 〡 to pay up, to settle a debt.

償 〡 to honor one's endorsement.

討 〡 to collect a debt; whence 討 〡 鬼 a term for the spirit of a son who died before he could recompense his parents; and of an unpaid creditor which torments the debtor.

放 〡 to lend money, shave notes; it indicates usurious lending.

〡 精 a miserable debtor, one over head and ears in debt.

酒 〡 a tavern score.

花 〡 to spend riotously.

威逼 〡 折 to force one to pay up, as by intimidation.

錢 〡 細故 the debt is of little consequence.

寃孽 〡 a revenge due for an injury received in a former life.

寨 砦 *chai'* From *wood* and to *fill a crevice*; both of these are regarded as aberrant forms of 柴 a faggot.

A stockade for defense; a palisade; a hold, a guarded retreat, like a hold, a guarded retreat, like a Maori *pah*; a cantonment or encampment, a military station; a pen for animals, a corral; a brothel.

營 〡 barracks; a military post, a cantonment.

山 〡 a temporary defense hastily thrown up; a hill fortress, like the New Zealand *pahs*.

刼 〡 to plunder a post.

賊 〡 a bandit's hold; and 〡 主 is the wife of the bandit chief.

鹿角 〡 a stockade guarded by cheveaux-de-frise.

柵 〡 a log-house fort.

老舉 〡 in *Cantonese*, a bagnio; and 打 〡 is to frequent one.

豸 廌 *chai'* *꜀ch'* The original form is thought to represent a crawling beast, and resembles the second character; the first is the 153d radical of a group of characters referring to feline beasts, of which the second is the obsolete, pedantic form.

To discriminate; a fabulous monster called 獬 〡, having one horn; others picture it more like a deer; it can discriminate right and wrong, and eats fire in its ravenous fury, even to its own destruction; it is drawn like a tiger on the wall which screens a *yamun*, as a warning to rulers against extortion; provincial judges and censors once wore it as their insignia; and are designated 〡 史, a term also applied now to district magistrates in respect.

獬 〡 冠 an ancient name for an executioner's cap.

Read *꜀chi*. A worm or grub; reptiles without feet.

꜂長行 〡 progressing like a caterpillar.

貏 〡 a sloping hill-side; to descend gradually.

子逞其志庶有 〡 乎 if you carry out your purpose, Sir, do you think it will be quiet?

[酉責] *chai'* A press for pressing the mash in making spirits; a kind of strainer.

瘵 *chai'* From *disease* and to *worship*.

A wasting disease; weakness, like marasmus, distress, trouble, care.

勞 〡 a debilitating disease, slow consumption of the energies.

自 〡 to bring disease on one's self.

〡 凋 atrophy of the bodily powers.

CHʻAI.

Old sounds, *tʻai, tʻap, tʻat,* running into *dʻai dʻat* and *dʻak.* In Canton, *chʻai;*—in Amoy, *chʻai, chʻa, tʻé,* and *ban;* with slight changes in Swatow;—in Fuhchau, *chai, chʻai, cha chʻa* and *twʻang;*—in Shanghai, *dza;*—in Chifu, *tsʻai.*

釵 *ₛchʻai* From *metal* and a *fork.*
A hair-pin, broad and curved, so that it will lie across the occiput: *met.* females.
卜 丨 to divine by a hair-pin.
群 丨 a bevy of women.
裙 丨 a maid-servant.
荆 丨 a thorn hair-pin; *met.* miserably poor, because she cannot buy a metallic pin.
丨 環 耀 目 her hair-pins and ear-rings dazzle one.
鳳 頭 丨 a pin with a phœnix.
金 丨 石 斛 a kind of medicine, the stem of an epiphytic orchid of the genus Dendrobium, whose dried yellow stalks are likened to hair-pins, and look like liquorice roots.

膗 *ₛchai* Strips of meat dried in the north wind, called 丨 脵 were anciently prepared for winter provision.
Read *ₛtsʻo.* Rumbling in the belly; flatulent.

柴 *ₛchʻai* From *wood* and *this;* when officers went into the wilds, they stockaded their lodges; 寨 *chaiʻ* is now used in this last sense.
Brushwood; faggots, firewood, fuel; to stop up; to screen, to protect; like the next, to make a burnt-offering to Heaven, as Shun did on the mountains.
一 把 丨 a faggot of firewood.
打 丨 的 a woodcutter, a lumberer.
劈 丨 firewood split up for use.
丨 頭 a knotty stick.
破 丨 to split wood.
丨 花 kindling wood.
丨 把 or 丨 擔 a quantity of firewood, or faggots.
丨 火 fuel, wood.
丨 門 my cottage, my humble abode.
水 流 丨 drifted timber, or that which has been rafted.
乾 丨 近 火 if dry sticks are put near the fire,—they will ignite; *met.* don't go too near temptation.
廢 丨 a poor stick, a useless fellow.
瘦 丨 lean as a lath.
丨 魚 an empty pated fellow.
丨 望 秩 于 山 川 [Shun] sacrificed burnt offerings in order to the mountains and streams.

祡 *ₛchʻai* Originally written like the last.
To burn faggots in sacrifice; the firewood used in a sacrifice to Heaven.
燒 丨 以 祭 天 神 to worship the gods by burning a heap of wood.

茈 *ₛchʻai* A kind of sudorific medicine, 丨 葫, otherwise called mouse-ear; 柴 胡 is another mode of writing it.

喍 *ₛchʻai* A dog whining for his food; 丨 啀 dogs snarling over their food.

豺 犲 *ₛchʻai* From *beast* and *talent,* but the combination is said to allude to its leanness, as like a stick of wood; the second form is not so correct as the other.
A lean and tawny beast akin to the dog; it loves rapine and destruction; the wolf; *met.* wicked, wolfish, truculent.
丨 狼 a wolf (*canis lupus*); in ancient times two animals were here designated, of which the first was the common wolf, the other a smaller species, or a hyena or lynx, to which the description answers better; 狼 子 it now denotes the wolf alone, and 丨 狼 includes the jackal; *met.* evil beings who tempt man.
丨 狼 當 道 a wolf stops the road, —said of bad rulers.
丨 狗 a jackal, or a wild dog.
瘦 如 丨 lean as a wolf.
其 心 如 虎 其 面 如 丨 he has a tiger's heart and a wolf's face; —the latter is said to smile on seeing a man.

儕 *ₛchʻai* From *man* and *even* together.
A class, a company, persons of the same sort; a sign of the plural.
我 丨 or 吾 丨 we; ourselves; we together.
伍 丨 we comrades, all of us chums; persons of the same rank or age.
同 丨 the same kind or class.
丨 偶 good fellows, comrades.

踹 踊 *ʻchʻai chwʻaiʾ* From *foot* and *single;* it is also read *ₛchwʻen,* but more commonly read *chwʻaiʾ;* the second form is vulgar, and often pronounced *ʻtsʻai,* while both are synonyms of 跐 *ₛtsʻzʼ* which itself also occurs read *ₛchʻai.*
To tread on, to put the heel on; to stamp, to trample on; to raze, to destroy.
丨 實 step on it firmly.
足 丨 the heel; to tread on.
丨 一 脚 泥 stepped into the mud over my foot.
丨 西 瓜 皮 tread on the water-melon skin; *i.e.* to trip one up; to delude you.
丨 住 他 tread on it.
丨 高 脚 to walk on stilts.
馬 丨 芳 草 to take a ride over the fragrant grass,—a spring ramble.
丨 足 而 怒 to stamp angrily.
丨 輭 索 to tread on a slack rope, an acrobat; also a thief, who uses rope ladders.
丨 破 營 盤 he has destroyed the camp; to remain victorious.
丨 成 肉 漿 trampled to a jelly, as in a crowd.

蠆 *chʻaiʾ* From *insect* and *myriad;* but the ancient form resembles a squirming scorpion.
A sting in the tail, as in the hornet or scorpion.
蜂 丨 a bee's sting.
卷 髮 如 丨 to wind the hair like a scorpion's tail.

CHAN.

Old sounds, *tam* and *dam*. In Canton, *chan* and *cham*; — in Swatow, *cham*, *chw^{n}a*, *t^{n}ia*, *chié* and *chan*; — in Amoy, *cham*, *ch'an*, *chien* and *tam*; — in Fuhchau, *chang* and *tang*; — in Shanghai, *tsè^n*; — in Chifu, *tsan*.

詀 *ˏchan* From *words* and to *incroach*; it is also read *cheh*,

To talk and gabble; to joke with, as children; guileful, artful talk; incoherent; to convey one's words; occurs used for *tswan'* 譧 to be hoaxed.

丨讘 to whisper in a friendly way.

丨謔 piquant raillery; sarcastic.

斬 *ˋchan* From *chariot* and *ox*, alluding to a battle field, or to an ancient military execution by destroying a criminal between two chariots.

To sunder, to cut in two; to decapitate by public execution; to cut off, to root up; to sever, as intercourse; temporary, shortly; furiously, bravely; faded, forgotten.

丨首 to decollate, as is done in cases of 丨罪 or capital crimes.

丨伐 to subjugate [a refractory state]; to destroy; to prune trees.

丨開 to cleave or cut open.

腰丨 to cut [a criminal] in twain.

監丨 to oversee an execution.

丨祀 his posterity is all cut off, as of a great rebel.

丨斷路 to break off all intercourse with.

丨釘截鐵 to cut an iron nail; *met.* decided, certain, fixed.

丨關截氣 to sever the influences and aura, — as in geomancy.

丨關而入 [the troops] forced the defenses and carried the place.

琖 *ˋchan* Used with the last. A wine cup made of jade, deeper than the lamp-cup.

玉丨 fine, beautiful cups.

盞 *ˋchan* From *dish* and *small*.

A shallow cup for oil; a wine saucer; a classifier of lamps and glasses of wine.

一丨燈 one lamp.

燈丨 a cup for a water-lamp.

銅丨聲聲喚賣冰 the brass cups of the ice-venders are rattling briskly to invite purchasers.

醆 *ˋchan* Formerly used for the last in 酒丨 a wine goblet; it is now applied to spirits, which beginning to clear itself is allowed to remain over winter.

丨酒 turbid liquor not yet settled.

㹽 *ˋchan* To fly swift and powerfully like a falcon is 丨丨, referring to its darting here and there for its prey.

Read *ˏtsien*. Martial; 丨丨 warlike.

棧 *chan'* From *wood* and *small*.

A covered loft; a scaffold, a terrace; a way made along a cliff, a pathway or bridge in narrow, steep places; a bearse; a bamboo tumbril, for which the next is also used; the body of a cart; a storehouse, a ware-room; a workshop; a pen or corral surrounded with stakes or boards; a small bell; a kind of fragrant wood.

丨房 a warehouse, a go-down.

丨租 storage; the price paid for storing.

丨齴 a path over and along a steep cliff.

馬丨 a horse-pen or stable; a corral.

貯丨 to put into store.

丨道 a plank road, a corduroy way.

輚 轏 *chan'* A carriage arranged for sleeping in, used by army officers.

丨輅 a sort of ambulance; also, a kind of hearse.

丨車 a military chariot.

䍀 *chan'* A sheep-cote, or a pen staked around to guard sheep.

虥 *chan'* A striped cat, perhaps a species allied to the tiger cat.

丨貓 a tiger shedding its hair, or having lost most of its hair.

綻 *chan'* From *silk* and *to secure*.

A seam which has opened; to rip, to rend, to come apart; cracked, split as bark; a hint, an inkling.

破丨 a slight defect; a hint, a slight idea of.

丨裂 ripped; to rip open seams.

花丨 the corol of a flower, or the separate petals.

打丨 to calk, to pay the seams in a boat.

米色未能飽丨 the rice did not look plump, but shriveled.

䘺 *chan'* Like the last. An opened seam in a garment.

補丨 to sew or patch a seam; to mend clothes.

湛 *tsan'* From *water* and *very*.

Deep, clear, tranquil, as water; calm, serene, as placid moonlight; to sink, to immerse; to soak in, to imbibe, as a sponge; to steep, to moisten; to receive, as benefits; excessive, as in dissipation, addicted to dregs.

丨河 an affluent on the north of the Yellow River, in Hwai-king fu in Honan.

丨恩 imbued with favor, said of the Emperor's kindness.

丨露 or 丨丨露斯 a heavy dew.

丨新的 bran new.

蘸 *chan'* To dip, as a morsel in sauce; this character has been used by some Protestant missionaries for baptizing by immersion.

丨筆 to put the pencil in ink.

丨濕 to soak; to dip and wet through.

站 From to *stand* and *incroaching* as the phonetic.

chan' To stand up; to stand still; stopping, standing; a stage, a fixed governmental post; a journey, a day's travel.

驛 丨 the distance between post-houses; at the end is the 丨 頭 or stage-house.

一 丨 路 one stage; it is about one league or ten *li* in length.

丨 住 stand still; stop!

丨 立 on his feet; standing.

丨 開 stand off a little.

丨 起 來 stand up; get up.

包 丨 to engage to make the stages, as cartmen are often hired to do.

賺 賺 䝼 From *pearl* and *together with* or *frugal*; the last character is sometimes read *wan'*, and the first also *tswan'* and *tsan'*.

chwan' To impede, to interfere with, as by underselling; to sell at a profit, to gain; to palm off, as poor goods; to overcharge, to ask an exorbitant price; to mistake; to earn, to be in the receipt of.

丨 錢 to make a profit.

丨 得 多 it has been very profitable.

加 倍 丨 to double the cost.

丨 得 作 I had the work for my profit; *i. e.* I got nothing but bother for my pains.

丨 食 to get just a living.

丨 詐 to palm off on one.

丨 辛 苦 to reap disappointment and sorrow.

沒 有 丨 or 丨 不 着 I made nothing on it; there is no gain in it.

壥 From *earth* and *wily*.

chan' To border or dyke which defines the limit of a grave; the bounds of an altar.

CH'AN.

Old sounds, *t'am, dam, t'an, shan* and *ts'im*. In Canton, *ch'am, ts'am* and *ch'an*; — in Swatow, *ch'am, cham, swⁿa, chien, siam, ch'iam* and *ch'an*; — in Amoy, *ch'am, san*, and *swⁿa*; — in Fuhchau, *chang, sang, ch'ang*, and *ch'iang*; — in Shanghai, *ts'an*, and *za"*; — in Chifu, *ts'an*.

攙 From *hand* and *wily*.

ˌch'an To stab or prick; to sustain, to push, to support by the hand; to supply what is wanted, to repair, to make up; to divide with, to foist in; to wedge in; to pull out; sharp; pointed.

丨 扶 to uphold, to support and lead, as a cripple.

丨 多 一 份 make another share; as when stock is to be increased.

丨 罅 to fill a crack.

丨 嘴 to interrupt another, to take the word out of his mouth.

丨 銀 器 a local name for plated-ware.

力 丨 傾 危 to get help for the feeble and tottering.

丨 雜 不 純 to put inferior sorts in, to dilute, to foist in, to mix.

丨 和 着 吃 mix them all properly for eating.

劖 To cut off; to cut into, as when testing the purity of sycee.

ˌch'an

丨 斷 to cut apart.

鑱 Used for the last. A chisel; a bore for cutting or piercing; to cut out, to engrave deeply.

ˌch'an

犁 丨 coulter of a plow.

藥 丨 a boiler for seething and decocting medicine.

丨 字 為 記 he carved on the characters for a memento.

欃 A tree called 丨 檀 which grew near Confucius' tomb, having hard whitish wood and large flowers; it was perhaps a magnolia; sharp pointed; a water-gate.

ˌch'an

丨 槍 or 天 丨 terms for a comet, referring to its tail; the first is also applied to a rebel leader.

毚 Formed of *hare* and an animal described to be like the muntjak; several of the combinations under this primitive, which seldom occurs by itself, embody its leading idea.

ˌch'an

A crafty hare full of dodges; artful, wily, cunning.

丨 兔 a crafty rabbit, which has several holes to its burrow.

讒 From *words* and *wily* as the phonetic.

ˌts'an To humor, to flatter; to misrepresent, to gloss over; to traduce, to asperse, to detract; to insinuate bad motives, or conceal good traits; cozening, slandering, fawning.

丨 鼎 name of an ancient tripod.

丨 佞 to cajole and then malign.

丨 謗 to grumble at.

丨 諂 to intrigue against.

丨 人 a traducer; to asperse people.

丨 言 惹 禍 calumny brings trouble on one.

丨 口 交 加 he is everywhere vilified.

君 子 信 丨 our sovereign listens to slanders.

瀺 The rippling sound of water is 丨 灂; applied also to the sportive leaping of fish; perspiration of the hands and feet; water gurgling through a hole.

ˌch'an

饞 嚵 ꜀ch'an — To gourmandize, to love good eating; greedy, gluttonous. The second form also means to sip or taste; to peck at.
口丨 voracious, gluttonous.
嘴不丨 not particular about one's food, not fastidious; not much appetite.

巉 嶃 嶄 ꜀ch'an — A cliff; a high peak, a summit that rises above the clouds; the first form is commonest.
丨巖 a craggy, steep ascent; rocks piled up, high precipices.

獑 ꜀ch'an — Also read ꜀tsan. A kind of monkey, found in Yunnan, the 丨猢, whose description allies it to the duoc; its swiftness on the trees is said to be like that of the flight of a bird.

產 ꜂ch'an — From 生 *to bear*, and 彥 *eminent* contracted.
To produce, to breed, to bear; the increase of anything; a birth, a parturition; productions or resources of a country; the natives; an estate, a patrimony; an occupation, livelihood; a sort of flageolet or large reed with three holes.
丨業 real estate, a property.
置丨業 to found or buy an estate.
分家丨 to divide the estate.
傾家蕩丨 the estate is totally lost or dissipated.
輸淸家丨 wasted all his patrimony, as by gambling.
土丨 or 本丨 the productions of a region.
恒丨 constant occupation, means of living, a regular income.
生丨 to increase; to bear a child.
難丨 difficult labor, as from malformation or wrong presentation.
扶丨 a midwife.
補丨 a tonic for pregnant women.
小丨 an abortion.
丨門 the vagina, a medical term; it also means accoucheurs, and 丨科 is the art of midwifery.

犍 ꜂ch'an — To breed domestic animals.

嵼 ꜂ch'an — Windings among hills.
巙丨 a devious path among hills, a goat-path.

滻 ꜂ch'an — Name of a small stream, a league east of Si-ngan fu in Shensi, a branch of the R. Pa 灞河, which flows through the 藍田 Blue Field.
丨丨 waters bursting out.

蹍 ꜂ch'an — To put a shoe or patten on the bare foot.

鏟 剷 ꜂ch'an — From *metal* and *to produce*; the second is an old and unusual form; used with the next.
A thin iron plate; a shovel, a spade; a plane or shaving tool, like a spoke-shave, to cut and pare; to smooth, to level off. In Fuhchau, to shell off or scale, as the plaster from a wall with a chisel.
鑊丨 or 飯丨 a rice shovel, used by cooks.
丨山 to scarp hill-sides, to dig into hills.
一副丨鉗 a set of tongs and shovel.
丨草除根 to root up plants; to extirpate root and branch.

刬 剗 ꜂ch'an — Interchanged with the last. To spade up, to level off; to trim, to pare down; to cut grain; to cut with a weapon or edge-tool.
丨刀 to plane or sharpen a razor by shaving the edge.
花丨 or 丨香 a dark fragrant wood, or sandal-wood shavings, burned for perfume.
丨削 to smooth off.
丨傷 to wound, as with an ax slipping.

樼 ꜂ch'an — A sort of tree growing in Nganhwui, which produces a fruit shaped like a peach, nearly two inches long, of a yellow color; when cured by salt it tastes like a plum.
Read ꜂shan. A mattress.

羼 ꜂ch'an — Composed of three 羊 *sheep* and 屋 *house* contracted, to represent sheep huddling under a shelter.
Sheep crowding as each one tries to get out first; to put in confusion, as records or books disarranged.

驏 ꜂ch'an — To ride a horse barebacked.
丨騎着馬 to ride without a saddle.

丳 ꜂ch'an ꜂chw'an — Intended to represent a spit or gridiron for roasting flesh, and the meat on it.
如以肉貫丨 like a joint of meat skewered on a spit.

㦃 ch'an꜄ — Complete virtue, as shown in one's life well spent in good actions; a company, a group of people.

懺 ch'an꜄ — To regret, to repent; among Budhists and Rationalists, a class of ritualistic works, which are intended to be used as manuals.
丨悔自新 to reform and do right, as submissive insurgents.

㹌 ch'an꜄ — A dog crunching his food; gnawing, crushing between the teeth.
In *Cantonese*. A word of indignation; to devour.
俾你丨 here then, eat it!
你丨淸我的野 you've clean gobbled up all my dinner! — said to an importunate sorner.

甗 ch'an꜄ — An earthen pitcher for boiling.
瓦丨 a sort of jug for making congee, common at Cantor.

CHĂN.

Old sounds, *tin*, *tim*, and *dim*. In Canton, *chăn*, *chăm*, and *tsun*; — in Swatow, *chin*, *chim*, *tién*, *tiam*, *cham*, *chién*, and *tim*; — in Amoy, *tim*, *chin*, *chim*, and *chim*; — in Fuhchau, *ching*, *ting*, *chéng*, *tòng*, and *téng*; — in Shanghai, *tsăng*, with a few in *dzăng*; — in Chifu, *chin*.

眞 真 ꜀*chăn* From 直 *upright* and 八 *man* underneath, but its present composition is explained to be from 目 the *eye*, 匕 for 化 to *change*, and 乚 for 隱 *hidden*, referring to the power of genii to change and ascend to heaven.

To change the corporeal into its pure essence, to become one of the genii; among Taoists, it means divinity, immortality, no dross, essence; true, real, sincere, unfeigned; to act as the soul prompts; genuine, unadulterated; authoritative, as a classic; spiritual, pure, ethereal; in reality, truly, no mistake, in fact; a likeness or portrait; actual, not secondary.

丨正 truly, indeed, actually is so.
丨係 it is really so.
說丨 it is true; he says the truth.
不知丨假 I don't know whether it be true or false.
丨容 the true image, as seen in a glass.
丨不堪 utterly unworthy of trust.
丨心 true hearted, ingenuous.
丨理 true, orthodox principles.
認丨 throughly do a thing; earnest to get at the truth of it.
丨贓 his veritable property, as a stolen thing proven when claimed.
丨宰 the true ruler; Heaven; a Moslem word for God.
天丨 heavenly endowments, referring to temper and heart.
丨人 a phantom of a man, is one who 含丨 possesses divinity, and therefore can become invisible.
寫丨 or 傳丨 to draw portraits.
本丨 original source or vocation; first condition, said of persons or things; but 丨本 is the real cost of a thing.
四丨 are the four great disciples of Laotsz'; named Chwang-tsz' 莊子, Wăn-tsz' 文子, Lieh-tsz' 列子, and K'ang-sang-tsz' 庚桑子; they are worshiped with him.

禛 ꜀*chăn* From *worship* and *truth*.

To be blessed because of truth in worship or prayer.

瞋 ꜀*chăn* Dropsical swelling, like anasarca; a puffy swelling of the legs.

甄 ꜀*chăn* From *tile* and a *kiln*; it is also read ꜀*kien*.

To mold; to model, as a potter does the clay; to act on, to fashion, to mold another's mind, to make like; influenced, guided; to examine, to distinguish; to act on reciprocally; in epitaphs used for alarm, or whatever horrifies; to avoid; plain; a potter, a modeler in clay.

丨陶萬類 to fashion and guide all things, as God does.
丨別人才 to discern men of talents.

蘣 ꜀*chăn* A bright blue orchid, the 蒴丨 which grows in the south of China; other names are 地松 ground fir, and 蟾蜍蘭 toad orchid.

珍 珎 ꜀*chăn* From 玉 *gem* and 㐱 *bushy hair* contracted; the second is a vulgar form.

Whatever is noble, precious, or beautiful; rare, important; excellent; a prize, a rarity, a delicacy; to prize, to esteem.

丨珠 pearls; 丨珠粉 pearl sago, named from its pearly look; 丨珠花 the Spiræa or meadow-sweet, from its white corymb; and 丨珠米 one of the names for maize;—all refer to their resemblance to pearls.
丨寶 precious things.
丨味 a delicious, savory taste.
丨饈 a dainty.
丨奇 precious and rare.
丨瑞 an auspicious token, as a just statesman in a reign.
見丨入世者 the things which are prized by mankind.
命世丨 the first man of the age.
丨重 to esteem very highly, to be careful of; to treat with great formalty; ceremonious.
如掌上丨 like a pearl in the palm, said of a daughter.
八丨豈所敢望 how can I hope to have all the delicacies! — the *eight pearls* are kinds of game at Peking, *viz.*, venison, wild boar, pheasant, gazelle, bear's paw, &c.

鍼 針 ꜀*chăn* From *metal* and *all* or *ten*; the second is the common form.

A needle; a pin; a sharp probe, a cauterizing needle; a sting, any sharp, thorny thing; to probe, to prick; pine leaves.

穿丨 or 紉丨 or 引丨 to thread a needle.
丨黹工 embroidery, fine needle-work.
丨脚稀 the stitches are coarse.
乞巧丨 to beg for excellent needle-work; *met.* she is very skillful.
鷄頭丨 a hair-pin used in Canton.
鼓鎚丨 a drumstick needle — a Cantonese name for a pin.
如坐丨氈 like sitting on a cushion of needles,—is a troublesome or unsatisfactory affair.
丨法 rules for the acupuncture.
丨灸 to cauterize; to probe.
風雨丨 a barometer.
寒暑丨 a thermometer.
丨對 exactly opposite, like two needles; *i. e.* their ideas are just the same; exactly in point; diamond cut diamond.
丨皮削鐵 mean, petty, close, *lit.* one who saves by sewing skins and scraping iron.

箴 Interchanged with the last. A probe, a needle; to pierce; to warn, to exhort, to urge a reform, to expostulate; admonition, appeals to reform; maxims warning people; pointed, cautionary.
ˏchăn

石丨 or 丨砭 surgeon's probes, formerly made of stone.

丨言 or 丨規 warning words, admonitions.

丨銘 restraining laws.

丨疵 to criticise defects, to probe another's faults, to satirize.

丨尹 an ancient officer, like a censor.

鱵 The *needle fish*, as the character imports; it is described as a slim, small fish like the *Leucosoma*, or Chinese white-bait, and noted for the extension of the snout like a bodkin; it is the *Hemiramphus intermedius*, called 長短丨 (or 鱘) at Canton; *i.e.* the long-short bodkin; in Kiangnan, it is known as the 罵婆魚 or scolding old-wife.
ˏchăn

斟 From *peck* and *very*; giving the sound.
ˏchăn To pour from or into, to empty out, to ladle; to add to; a ladle or cup; to deliberate, to adjust, to arrange.

丨酌爲佳 it will be better to consult about it.

丨茶 to pour out tea.

丨妥了 it is all well settled.

細丨 carefully talk it over.

丨議 to discuss, to settle by consultation.

椹 A kind of wood good for arrows; it is probably one of the conifers, like a larch or juniper; a target.
chăn'

丨菌 a mushroom or fungus found on this tree.

丨質 a target; to kill criminals by making a target of them.

Read *shăn'*, a synonym of 葚 the mulberry fruit, also called 桑丨 mulberry seeds.

帪 An old name for the bag tied to a horse's head when baiting him, now called 馬篼囊 or horse bucket-bag.
ˏchăn

砧 From *stone* and *to incroach*; used with the next.
ˏchăn A block on which to beat clothes; a square stone or block; an anvil; a stone with which athletes exercise their strength by lifting and pitching it.

丨板 a board used by butchers; a chopping-board.

石丨 a horse-block; a stone to which criminals are chained.

抽丨 to lift the weight, as soldiers do, to test their strength, like throwing the discus.

稾丨 a straw anvil, or stone to beat plants on; also, an old term for my husband; as if he were a block for me to beat on.

碪 Constantly used for the last, with which it is nearly synonymous.
ˏchăn

Read *ˏhan*. Peaked, like an upright stone; hilly.

丨碍於青霄 the lofty peaks pierced the sky.

左右石丨碍立 the stones were piled up like pillars on both sides [of the dyke.]

霹靂丨 a name in the Păn Tsao for a meteoric stone from Luicheu fu on the mainland north of Hainan I.

臻 From *extreme* and *to enter*.
ˏchăn The utmost, the highest degree; extremely; to reach; a multitude, many; to collect.

百福駢丨 may all blessings settle here; a phrase put on doors.

澤丨四表 his bounty reached everywhere.

蓁 Also read *ˏts'in*. Abundant, exuberant herbage; bushy trees; accumulated, a collection of; to wear on the head.
ˏchăn

其葉丨丨 how abundant is the foliage [of this peach!]

丨頭巾 the kerchiefs worn on the head by the boatwomen at Macao.

榛 亲 The Chinese hazel or filbert is 丨子 (*Corylus heterophylla*) shaped like the pekan nut; it grows in the northern provinces, is smaller than the European nut and more oily; a thorny tree, like those in quickset hedges, whose spines were once used for mourning hair-pins.
ˏchăn

丨丨 overgrown with thorns and brushwood.

溱 One of the small headwaters of the R. Hwai in Honan; also, a river in Hupeh; to reach.
ˏchăn

丨丨 abundant, as a crop; thickly placed, as houses; loose, easy, comfortable.

顲 To hang the head, as when weak or sleepy; a peaked head.
ˋchăn

枕 From *wood* and *walking*.
ˋchăn A pillow; a rest for the back in a carriage; a stake to fasten cattle; to use as a pillow; to lean on, to pillow on; to lie on the side; contiguous, conterminous, adjacent.

丨頭 a pillow; 耳丨 a kind with an ear hole.

丨伴 a bedfellow.

丨着 in bed, asleep; while asleep.

丨骨 the occiput; the neck bone in fishes.

後丨候 your occiput is thick,—*met.* your friends are strong.

門丨 the socket of the door-hinge.

丨邊 in bed; in private, secretly; a wife.

曲肱而丨 he pillowed his head on his bended arm.

安丨無憂 now I can sleep without anxiety.

丨簟難安 cares disturb his rest.

輾轉伏丨 turning and rolling on my pillow — restless.

丨上死 to die of old age, to die in one's bed.

木丨墻 the stick leans against the wall.

丨冷衾寒 insufficient bed-clothes; *met.* a poor man.

高丨而寐 he sleeps quietly, he has no cares.

頂 ʿchăn As if composed of 項 and 枕, meaning the *neck pillow*, or the *sleeping bone; i.e.* the occiput, that bone of the head on which one rests in sleeping; or to droop the head.

Read ʿ*tan.* Filthy.

Read ˏ*tăn.* Silly, in the phrase 丨顉 foolish looking.

眕 ʿchăn Bright, clear as a gem; transparent.

畛 ʿchăn From 田 *field* and 珍 *pearl* contracted, as the phonetic.

Raised paths between fields; dykes over drains; a border; to come before the gods; to announce to the Terminalia that the Emperor is coming to visit the border; the origin; to terminate, as life.

丨域 a frontier.

畦丨相接 the dykes were contiguous.

田丨 paths for landmarks.

紾 ʿchăn To twist a cord around, to bind; to revolve, to turn; a revolution; a single thin garment, for which the next is most used; crooked, obstinate.

丨戾 crabbed, mulish.

丨轉 to go around.

袗 ʿchăn Plain, dark garments; summer clothes of one thickness; border of a dress; a figured garment.

丨絺綌 single grasscloth or linen.

兄弟丨玄 the brothers all wore black.

疹 胗 ʿchăn From *disease* or *flesh*, and *pearl* contracted, referring to their form; *ch'an*ʾ 疢 is sometimes wrongly used for it.

Pustules of any kind, a rash; eruptions, pimples, sore lips or fever sores; fever breaking out in sores; measles;—to remove which, the 痧神娘娘 is worshiped.

痘丨 small-pox pustules.

瘢丨 a sort of carbuncle.

出丨子 to have the measles or scarlet fever.

癮丨 small pimples, as in measles.

診 ʿchăn To ascertain the state of; to verify, to examine, as when a disease shows itself.

丨脈 to feel the pulse.

丨夢 to interpret a dream.

眹 ʿchăn From 目 *eye* and a contraction of *fire* 火 and *hands joined* 廾 as in 朕, which is not the same as this character, though sometimes miswritten for it.

The pupil of the eye, the want of which makes one blind.

兆丨 the subtle germs of good and bad things;—used in this phrase wrongly for 朕ʾ incipient.

軫 ʿchăn From *cart* and *bushy hair* contracted for the phonetic.

To turn, to revolve; to move; to act in behalf of; a cross-board to lean upon in a carriage; *met.* a carriage; distressed, sorrowing; cramped; pegs for cords in a lute; the last of the 28 constellations, including the stars $\beta\,\delta\,\eta\,\nu$ in Corvus.

輿丨 wains and carriages.

丨轉其道 the carriage went rolling on its way, or revolving in its rut.

士卒殷丨 military carriages in numbers.

丨懷 compassionating; kind feelings towards one.

丨念 kind thoughts of, to think of and do something for.

紾丨 curbed, discontented, as in a treadmill sort of life, where one is kept down by power.

鬒 参 ʿchăn The second character is intended to represent streaming hair; as a primitive, its meaning in most cases is lost.

Bushy, thick hair; black and abundant hair.

丨髮如雲 his bushy hair was like a cloud.

黰 ʿchăn Similar to the last.

Beautiful black and glossy hair, shining like a mirror; black.

Read ˏ*yin.* To dye black.

縝 ʿchăn To tie; black and thick, as hair; close-woven, thick.

丨密 fine and close, as cloth.

誰丨不變 whose black hair will not change its color?

丨黑 black, a deep black.

眕 ʿchăn To restrain rising anger and not show it in the eye; to keep one's equanimity by a strong effort.

憾而能丨者鮮矣 few and remarkable are those who can be angry and not show it.

鎮 chănʾ From *metal* and *true* as the phonetic.

To press down; to repress, to keep in subjection; to guard, to keep in order, as a pass; to protect and oversee; to restrain or forestall evil influence, as pagodas or peaked hills do; a mart, called 大丨飢, a great manufacturing place, of which there are four in China; in the days of the 五代 Wu Tai, it seems to have designated certain cities or palatinates, whose rulers had superior privileges from their power and subordinate territory.

丨服 to maintain superior power over things which 丨壓 repress evil, as charms on a door linted do noxious influences.

丨星 a name for the planet Saturn.

遊丨 an idolatrous procession to quiet demons.

丨物 charms, spells; magic.
丨宅 to invite the gods to come to a house to protect it.
丨驚 to quiet the fears; to repress breels.
丨市 an êntrepôt, a trading-mart.
丨店 a fair; a town more important than a village, but less than a district.
威丨海內 to awe the whole land into peace.
丨守 to guard, to keep watch and ward
總丨 provincial rulers, both civil and military, who 丨撫 guard and soothe the whole people.
丨臺 a brigadier-general, a military officer next under a 副都統 or major-general; there is at least one in each province.

朕 *chăn'* Originally written with 舟 *boat* (altered to 月 *moon* 火 *fire*, and 廾 *hands joined*, now contracted; the combined idea refers to the virtue of light and limits of man's power.

In early times a common word for I, me; but appropriated by Ts'in Chi-hwangti, B.C. 221, for the royal We, Ourself; subtle, incipient.
丨躬 our royal self, our Imperial Majesty.
丨德 our virtue.
丨安 We are well;—the reply written on the cards sent to court by high provincial officers to ask after the Emperor's health.
兆丨 the incipient springs of the germ not yet acted on; the first idea of; a protoplasm.

鴆 酖 *chăn'* From *bird* or *spirits* and *walking*. A bird like the secretary falcon, also called 同力鳥, with a long, black neck and red bill; it eats snakes, and is supposed to be so noxious that fish die where it drinks, the grass around its nest withers, and its feathers steeped in spirits make a virulent poison; in this sense, the second from is used; some parts of this description accord better with the bittern, as its voice is noticed as remarkable; a poison; virulent, venemous; mortal, deadly.
丨酒 poisoned wine.
丨毒 destructive, poisonous.
飲丨卒 he drank poison and died.
宴安丨毒 dissipation is like a deadly poison.

栚 *chăn'* The head of a beetle or mallet; a plant, whose leaves when burned, furnish a mordant for fixing colors; it is probably a kind of saltwort or *Salsola*.

震 *chăn'* From *rain* and to *shake* or excite; occurs used with the next.

To shake, as thunder does; to quiver, to tremble, to strike with lightning; to awe, to move; impressed by, startled; to quicken, as a fœtus; to alarm, to intimidate, to arouse; thunder; thundering, terrible; marvelous; surprisingly.
地丨 an earthquake.
雷丨 struck or killed by lightning.
丨雷 the rattling sound of thunder.
一丨 one outcry, one shake.
丨驚 terrified; to scare terribly.
丨怒 incensed, irate.
丨威 to strike with awe.
丨破了 shattered by the concussion or noise.
丨動 to move, to disturb; to act on, as the vernal sun on nature.
丨卦 the fourth of the eight diagrams; it refers to the quickening movements of nature.
莫不丨懼其威 all trembled with fear at his awful presence.
爗爗丨電 brilliant are the thunder and lightning.
薄言丨之莫不丨疊 not one but regards his movements with tremulous awe.
丨旦 a Budhist name for China, the last word being intended for the Sanscrit *stan*, a country.

振 *chăn'* From *hand* and to *shake*; similar to the last.

To move, to joggle; to stir up the energies; to excite, to stimulate; to issue forth; to rescue, to save; to restore, to put in order, to repair; to flap, as wings; to terrify; to uphold; to receive, to contain; to stop; to call back; from; unsteady, trembling; ancient; many.
丨動 to set about a work, to be up and doing.
丨救 to save from danger.
丨作 to encourage; diligent.
丨拔 to pull up or out of, to raise up or from.
丨作有爲 to animate the mind to obtain an object.
威丨四海 he is one who can arouse the country.
丨衣 to shake the dress.
丨古如茲 from of old it has been so.
丨怖 to alarm.
丨興 to go on prosperingly, to flourish.
手丨 the hand unsteady, trembling.
大丨家聲 his great eneryg has made his family famous.
丨丨鷺 [like] egrets on the wing.
丨起精神 to stir one's self up to exertion.
丨埋一團 cuddled up in a heap, as a scared child. (*Cantonese.*)

Read *ˌchăn*. Numerous; plentiful; honored, noble; 宜爾子孫丨丨兮 it is right that your descendants, should be in [like] flocks.

侲 *chăn'* A lad of ten or twelve years; a good boy.
丨童 gentle lads, such as play a part in idolatrous processions; a horse-boy, a hostler.

賑 *chăn'* Liberal; rich, affluent; to give, to relieve; a largess, a charity; bounty, supplies.
丨濟 to aid the distressed.
丨餓 to feed the hungry.
丨恤 to commisserate and assist.

揕 *chăn'* To strike or stab; the noise of felling wood.

CH'ĂN.

Old sounds, *dín* and *t'in*, with some in *t'ím*, *dím* and *dam*. In Canton, *ch'ăn*, *ch'ăm*, and *shăn*; — in Swatow, *tien*, *ngím*, *tím*, *tín*, *sin*, and *chien*; — in Amoy, *chin*, *tin*, *t'ím*, *sin*, *t'an* and *tien*; — in Fuhchau, *ching*, *ting*, *t'íng*, *t'éng*, *sing* and *ch'aing*; — in Shanghai, *ts'ăng*, *dzăng*, *tsé*ⁿ and *yang*; — in Chifu, *ch'in*.

嗔 *ch'ăn* To get angry, to rail at; passionate; scolding.
生丨 or 丨怪 to get very angry.
並不丨着 he never scolded him at all.
他不尋丨你來 he does not seek to irritate you.

Read *t'ien*. To bluster, to bully.
怒氣丨胸 anger filled his breast.

瞋 *ch'ăn* From *eye* and *true*. To glare at; to stare angrily at a person.
丨怒無度 incensed beyond all bounds.
丨大眼 set his eye on him in anger.

琛 䞶 *ch'ăn* *From gem or pearl*, and 㓞 *sombre* abbreviated; the second form is unusual. A beautiful precious stone; a rarity, such as tribute bearers bring.
天丨氷怪 beautiful gems and natural curiosities.

郴 *ch'ăn* From *city* and *forest*. A superior district in the south of Hunan, on the headwaters of the R. Siang; it extends along the northern slopes of the Nan-ling.

綝 *ch'ăn* To stop; good, set in order, as trappings or attire.
丨纚 a sort of feather or hair flounce, which was apparently sewn along the hem, somewhat like the fringe on the ancient Persian dress.

嵾 *ch'ăn* Uneven; 丨嵳 irregular, as the peaks of mountains or the tops of trees.

鎧 抻 *ch'ăn* The second of these is also read *t'ien*. To stretch a thing out; to pull out, as an elastic band.
丨麪 to pull and work the dough, as a baker does.

陳 陣 陣 *ch'ăn* From 阜 *a place*, and 木 *wood*, joined with 申 *going*; the etymology refers to the virtue of the element *wood* in the state of China; the surname *ch'ăn* is only written in the first form, the two last are mostly read *ch'ăn*.

To arrange, to set in regular order, to spread out; to dispense; to diffuse; to state, to express carefully, to lay before, as an officer; to reply; what has been stored long; a long time, of old; stale, not fresh; turned, as eggs or fruit; dried up, worn out; many, all; path leading up to the hall; a feudal state of the Cheu dynasty, lying southeast of the present capital of Honan, comprising also Ch'ăn-cheu fu; it existed from about B.C. 1100 to 477; thirteen princes are enumerated.
伸丨 or 申丨 to state to a superior officer; the phrase is employed by consuls when addressing a governor.
布丨 or 丨列 to seat or rank in due order.
丨腐 spoiled, as grain; obsolete, out of date, inapplicable.
丨人兒 one long in the employ, an old hand; a veteran.
丨設 to arrange in place.
丨情表 a statement or plaint to the Emperor.
丨粟 the old grain in the granary.
在丨絕粮 to lack food in *Ch'ăn*; *met.* to be short of supplies.
丨皮 dried orange peel, — lit. "old skin."
丨案 a case of long standing.
鋪丨錦帳 to spread out the embroidered tester; *met.* the wedding-day.
年丨日久 old and antique, out of date, as curiosities.

Read *ch'ăn*. A rank or file of soldiers; a battalion; an army, troops, forces; to place in rank, to set in array, to marshal; a battle, a fight; as a classifier, used to denote a gust, blast, burst, or time, a shower, a short space; transitory, a little while.
丨上 in the fight.
上丨 to go into battle.
排丨 to deploy or post troops.
打頭丨 the van, the front troop; the front of the battle.
敗丨 defeated the army.
丨勢 the force of the army; valiant, martial.
冲鋒陷丨 he braved the enemy and rushed on the foe.
擺女人丨 get a woman to start the quarrel.
迷魂丨 besotted with, infatuated, to act silly about.
樓丨 sleepers for the floor.
一丨丨冷 it is growing colder and colder.
一丨雨 a passing shower.
一丨烟 a puff of smoke.
一丨明一丨不明 one while you know, and then you don't know.
一丨火粉 one explosion of fireworks.

蔯 *ch'ăn* A medicinal herb, regarded as good for rheumatism; the 茵丨 or 茵丨蒿, a fragrant plant (*Artemisia abrotanum*), from whose leaves a decoction is made for fever patients to drink.

塵 From *earth* and *deer*, as these animals raise a dust when herding.
ˏch'ăn
Dust, small particles; molecules, atoms, exhalations; traces, example; to make one's self dusty; *met.* the dusty world, the age; worldly vice and pleasures; confused and troublous days; in *Budhism*, fleshly perceptions of the senses, as the 六丨 six *baya ayatana*, or outward conceptions.
丨埃 dust, dirt.
拂丨 to dust things.
丨封起來 covered with dust.
丨垢 grimed in; dirty, as a beggar's face.
丨土大 a cloud of dust.
洗丨 to wash down the dust,—to feast a friend on his return.
步後丨 to follow another's example, to walk in his dust.
紅丨 or 丨世 or 凡丨 the toils and vexations of this world; a Budhist idea, designed to extol asceticism.
心丨 passions, evil desires.
惹丨 it shows the dust, as black cloth.
清丨 the dust cleaner,—a poetical term for the wind.
無一點丨 it is perfectly clean.

臣 The original character is supposed to represent a man bending low; it forms the 131st radical of a few miscellaneous characters.
ˏch'ăn
An attendant, one who is subject to another; a vassal; a minister, a courtier who can speak to his sovereign, a statesman; to serve in office; to bend before; to rule, to act the lord over; only Chinese statesman use it for I in their memorials.
君丨 prince and minister, one of the five social relations.
忠丨 a loyal officer.
群丨 or 諸丨 the officers at court; statesmen.
文丨 civilians.
武丨 military officers.
萬國丨服 all nations submitted.
本大丨 I, the high officer, used only by the highest grades of officials.
莫非王丨 the king's power and officers reached everywhere.
素有不丨之心 he never had the feelings of an officer.
不丨 a rebellious or contumacious officer.
丨妾 my chamberlains and concubines, *i.e.* my imperial household; it is also used by these people when speaking to their master.
樸雖小天下不敢丨 though the body [of Reason] be small, the universe cannot sway it.

沈 沉 From *water* and *walking*; but some derive it from 水 *water* and 酖 *dregs;* the first is read *ʻshăn* when used as a surname.
ˏch'ăn
To sink, to immerse, to put under the water; to quash, to suppress; lost, destroyed, depraved, ruined; muddy; deep, dull, as colors; a bass or subdued note; confused; a lake, a tarn.
丨淪 lost, irretrievably ruined, as the lost in hell.
丨溺 drowned; doting on; victimized.
丨案 to quash a case.
丨沒 to stifle or crush, as an affair.
十丨九浮 nine to ten it will sink; the odds are rather against it.
病丨重 he is very sick.
丨底 sunk to the bottom.
丨沫 lost, sunk, gone down; no hope for it.
丨香 the garu-wood, agila, or lign-aloes (*Aquilaira agallochum*), prized for its fragrance; the 土丨香 is a sort of Agave, deemed to resemble it.
丨天 the eighth heaven, or epicycle of the Budhists.
丨國 a small feudal state in the Cheu dynasty, now 丨邱縣 on the River Sha in Ch'ăn-cheu fu in the east of Honan.
丨水 a river in Ch'ing-tu fu in Sz'chw'en.
In *Pekingese*. Heavy, a synonym of *ˏchung* 重 weighty.
分兩丨 excessively heavy.

魫 The roe of fish; the parts of this character are sometimes wrongly transposed in Canton; and perhaps the character *ˏch'un* 鰆 eggs, commonly used there, is derived from it.
ˏch'ăn

霃 Long continued, rainy dark weather.
ˏch'ăn
陰陰丨丨 dull, lowering; it looks like rain.

麎 The female of the 麋 elk; as the sexes of this animal have separate names, it is to be inferred that it was once common.
ˏch'ăn

挋 Similar to *chăn'* 振 to shake. To rub, to wipe clean; to give; to adjust, to contract; to shake and cleanse.
ˏch'ăn
丨衣 to brush clothes.
丨約 to arrange firmly.
丨刷 shake and brush—the coat.

敐 Hilarity exhibited in action, as by children capering.
ˏch'ăn
輷輷丨丨 hopping and dancing about from joy.

辰 The original form is supposed to represent sprouting plants transformed by heaven; it forms the 161st radical of a small, incongruous group of characters.
ˏch'ăn
To excite to action, to move, to influence; a day, a time; times, hours, seasons; a Chinese hour or one twelfth of a day, but especially the time from 7 to 9 A.M.; heavenly bodies which mark the times, and especially the sun and moon; applied as in 大丨 to the planet Mercury; the fifth of the twelve stems, over which the dragon rules; spots in the sky where no stars are seen; the elements.
一個時丨 an hour of the Chinese day.

星｜ the heavenly bodies; the zodiacal spaces where the sun and moon meet in conjunction.
北｜ the north star.
三｜ sun, moon and stars.
時｜香 long incense sticks, designed to mark time as they burn.
我生不｜ I was born out of time, my natal day was ill-starred; unlucky.
好日｜ a birthday, a lucky day; as 生｜ is one's birthday.
百工惟時撫于五｜ all officers will perform their duties in time, in accordance with the seasons; *i. e.* the five elements will harmonize with the four seasons.

晨 Composed of 日 *day*, or 晶 *clear* contracted, and 辰 *time*.
˛ch'ăn The sun beaming forth; morning, dawn; clear.
鷄司｜ the cock heralds the dawn.
良｜ a lucky day.
明｜ to-morrow morning.
｜昏顚倒 to turn day into night.
｜早到 I came at daylight.
｜昏一炷香 burn a pastille from morning till evening.

宸 From a *cover* and *time* as the phonetic.
˛ch'ăn Retired rooms where the Emperor dwells.
楓｜ the maple rooms; *met.* the palace, the Emperor.
｜垣 the capital, the imperial city; the name indicates its seclusion within the inclosing walls.

岑 An isolated peak, like an aiguelle, tapering and lofty; a steep bank.
˛ts'ăn
ˊch'ăn 黃｜ a medicine, probably the 黃芩 Scuttellaria or skull-cap, but written wrongly.
巒｜ the sharp peaks; the old name of a small feudatory in Honan.

涔 A river in Han-chung fu in Shensi, a branch of the R. Han; also called *Hwang Shui* or Yellow Water; pure, limped; mountain rills; to soak; stagnant; puddles in ruts and tracks; to get fish out of a fish-pool.
ˊch'ăn
雨｜｜ long drizzling rain.
｜｜淚下 the falling tears came fast.
蹄｜ footsteps filled with water.

磣 Sand mixed in things, as in grain or dishes.
ˊch'ăn 牙｜ grittiness in the food which hurts the teeth.

In *Pekingese*. Offensive; 含｜ vulgar, not in good taste; sordid, grimed.

顜 Interchanged with the last. Ugly, deformed.
ˊch'ăn 頩｜ to hang the head in confusion and shame.

醦 Vinegar-like, sour.
ˊch'ăn ｜酢 vinegar; also very drunk.

墋 Dirty, dusty; turbid water; obscure, as when the sky is filled with dust.
ˊch'ăn ｜黷 dirty, begrimed, covered with filth.

紖 From *silk* and *to lead*; also read *ˊyin*.
ˊch'ăn A rope by which cattle are led, drawn through the cartilege of the nose.
執｜ to hold the ropes of a pall or catafalque, as is done by the bearers.

趁 趂 From 走 *to go*, and 㐱 *bushy hair*, or 爾 *you* contracted, for the primitive.
ch'ănˋ To follow, to come up behind; to avail of, to embrace, to improve, as an opportunity; to go to, as a fair; or to frequent, for which the second form is most used; as a preposition, at the time of; by, through.
去｜市 go and learn the state of the market.
｜墟 to go to market.
｜行 to learn the secrets of another's art or trade.
｜願 just as I wished.
｜時候 to improve the time or occasion.
｜機會 to take advantage of the chance or opportunity.
｜風揚帆 when there's a wind, hoist sail.
｜勢而爲 you did it when you had the power.
｜洋 to go on a trading voyage.
｜着這陣雨 avail yourself of this shower.

闖 From a *door* out of which a *horse* is going.
ˊchw'ang To thrust out the head, to appear; to bolt out or in; rudely, suddenly; forcibly to push ahead, and against etiquette; lawlessly.
｜關 to slip by the pass, to disregard the customs' regulations.
｜出頭 to put out the head; to distinguish one's self.
亂｜進來 to rush in, to rudely intrude.
｜轅門 to force open the office door; to rush into a *yamun*.
｜道 to rush across [an officer's] pathway.
｜然而出 he rushed out violently.
｜亮的 a thief, *i. e.* one who rushes in at daybreak.
｜禍 to induce calamities.
李｜王 an epithet for the rebel Li Tsz'ch'ing, who overthrew the Ming dynasty, A.D. 1643.

疢 From *disease* and *fire*; it must not be confounded with 疹 *ˊchăn* with which however it is often interchanged.
ˊch'ăn A fever which breaks out in sores; a febrile feeling; a fastidious appetite, longing for delicacies.
心之憂矣｜如疾首 the sadness of my heart makes me feverish like a throbbing head.

襯 儭 ch'ăn' From *dress* or *man* and *personal;* the second form is obsolete.

Inner garments next the body; ornamental but not necessary; to give effect, to show off; to make a largess, to dotate, to assist; to patronize, to befriend.

丨僧 to help the priests by alms.

丨巾 a handkerchief carried in the girdle.

丨袋 girdle fobs, as those for fan, chopsticks, &c.

丨紙 a fly-leaf in books.

丨色 to beautify the person; to allure by meretricious arts.

添丨 put on for effect.

陪丨 to bring forward in illustration, to explain by figures.

帮丨 to give custom to; to assist in any way, as to a support; to give strength to; to toady.

䞋 䞋 ch'ăn' To donate, especially to Budhist priests for religious purposes.

達丨 the recompense received by donors for gifts, in being led to heaven.

櫬 ch'ăn' The *wood next* to the body; *i.e.* a coffin, especially the inner one; to gather faggots.

棺丨 a coffin, often detained in a 棺丨屋 or mortuary-shed near the grave before interment.

丨梧 one name for the *Elæococca cordifolia*, the favorite tree of the Chinese.

Read *kwan'*. A water bucket.

齔 ch'ăn' To shed milk teeth, usually at the age of seven years, as the composition of the character indicates.

CHANG.

Old sounds *tung* and *dung*. In Canton, *chéung;* — in Swatow, *tⁿié*, *chⁿié* and *chiêng;* — in Amoy, *chiong* and *tiong;* — in Fuhchau, *tiŏng*, *t'iŏng*, and *chiŏng;* — in Shanghai, *tsang;* — in Chifu, *chang*.

張 ˌchang' From *bow* and to *lengthen*.

To draw a bow; to extend, to stretch, to open; to draw up, as a list; to increase; to state, to proclaim to, to publish abroad; to grant to; to appoint or set out, to display for sale; to make much of; displayed, adjusted; to string a lyre; to boast of; a classifier of things which show much surface, as a table or bed, paper, a proclamation, a chair, &c.

丨掛 to hang up for display, as festoons.

開丨 to open out, as goods; to set up a business; to sell; to re-open, as at new-year's.

今天沒開丨 I've sold nothing to-day.

丨開 to open wide, as a door.

亮丨三天 to have a brilliant [shop] opening for three days.

鋪丨華麗 to make a parade, to show off, to put one's house in the best of trim.

丨大 to make much of.

誇丨 self-laudatory, boastful.

乖丨 cross-grained, unreasonable.

戾氣方丨 impetuous, incroaching, unscrupulous; to burst out angrily.

丨仙 a demi-god who protects children from harm, much worshiped by the Manchus.

丨揚 to make widely known.

主丨 to lord it over; but 不主丨 is rather not to agree with, to let alone; no way to bring it about.

沒有主丨 I have no idea as to how it is; I cannot decide the point.

一丨椅 or 椅子一丨 one chair.

丨三李四 Chang the third brother and Li the fourth; *scil.* two common surnames used, as John Doe and Richard Roe.

丨狂 wildly, furiously.

丨羅故陷 to cast a net to inveigle others.

犬怒丨耳 the surly dog pricked up his ears.

丨惶敗露 to spoil an affair by sudden fright.

丨皇六師 maintain fully your six armies in good order.

章 ˌchang' From 音 *sound* and 十 *ten*, referring to the finishing of a strain in music; as a primitive it usually gives the idea of a barrier; it occurs used for 樟 and 獐 and others of its compounds.

A piece of music; a character or section; an essay written according to strict syntax; a pattern; a statement; statutes, institutes, rules, items; clear, beautiful, as the Milky Way; variegated; to polish, to decorate; courteous, elegant, as blazoury on a flag, or a piece of weaving; a display; a grove; a classifier of documents; name of a small state in the Cheu dynasty, an old name for a maternal uncle.

書丨 a chapter; an article or paper.

丨句 sections and paragraphs.

數丨 many documents; several papers or statements.

作文丨 to write essays, such as are presented at examinations.

丨甫 an ancient style of cap in the Shang dynasty.

成丨 a complete affair, a finished thing,—referring to a finished composition, as 不成丨 means an inelegant essay; *met.* confused, in disorder.

采丨 adorned, variegated; the 五丨 were emblematic figures on ancient robes.

丨程 regulations, rules of action, directions; bye-laws.

擇日丨 guide for selecting lucky days.

奏丨 a memorial to the Throne.

憲丨 orders issued by the magistrates.

丨京 the under-secretary of the General Council, who receives decrees from the Throne and transmits them to the Inner Council.

圖丨 or 印丨 a seal, the instrument to stamp orders.

丨歲 the metonic cycle of nineteen years.

品物咸丨 every article is well arranged or disposed.

丨魚 or 丨舉 the poulpe or large cuttle-fish; large sized ones are caught along the coasts.

粻 *ˎchang* Food, particularly fine white rice for the table.

以峙其丨 he laid up the rice, or supplies, like a hill.

餦 *ˎchang* Cakes made of flour.

丨餭 a general name for buns, sweet cakes, biscuit, &c.

嫜 *ˎchang* A husband's father; while 姑丨 denotes both his parents.

兄丨 a husband's brother.

傽 *ˎchang* Interchanged with the last and the next.

Fear; in the phrase 丨偟 terror-struck, alarmed, horrified.

慞 *ˎchang* Terrified; 丨惶 scared out of one's wits.

獐 *ˎchang* To go fast; 丨徨 to walk in a great hurry, and as when alarmed; to proceed awkwardly.

彰 *ˎchang* From *feathers* and *elegant*.

The variegated pelage of animals or plumage of birds; beautiful, adorned; to exhibit, to show; to give distinction to; to make manifest; plainly.

丨明 clearly exhibited.

昭丨 luminously displayed.

嘉言孔丨 his excellent sayings were very impressive.

丨其德威 exhibiting his virtue and dignity.

丨信兆民 by his display [of liberality and humanity,] the people all trusted in him.

樟 *ˎchang* The camphor tree (*Laurus camphora,*) said to be so named from *yü-chang* 豫章 the ancient and classic name for Kiangsi, because the tree grew there.

丨木 camphor-timber,

丨腦 gum-camphor.

香丨 camphorated; a camphor odor.

漳 *ˎchang* A large tributary of the R. Wei in the northeast of Honan and south of Chihli, called the 衡丨 or Cross-flowing Chang, from its course of west to east; it has two main branches, the clear and the muddy Chang; part of its waters join the Pei-ho, and part reach the ocean through other channels.

丨縣 a district in Kung-chang fu in the southeast of Kansuh.

丨州府 in the southwest of Fuhkien, about 35 miles west of Amoy.

璋 *ˎchang* A kind of ancient stone ornament like a flat ruler, used in state ceremonies; a jade plaything.

左右奉丨 the attendants presented the batons.

弄丨 to bear a son, because this thing was anciently given a boy to play with.

鄣 *ˎchang* An ancient feudal state, now part of Tai-ngan fu in central Shantung; also an ancient city in 莒 Kü in Shantung; name of a large province in the Ts'in dynasty comprising the south of Nganhwui, where Hwui-chau fu lies.

鞝 *ˎchang* The housings of a saddle.

丨泥 (or 障泥) spatter-dashes, an outer flap attached to a saddle to protect the rider's dress.

麞 *ˎchang* A hornless deer or muntjak (*Hydropotes inermis*) akin to the musk, known as the river deer, common in Kiangsu, with long tusks; it is a graceful and elegant animal, as the composition of the character intimates; other small deer are popularly so called.

銀丨 the silver or white chevrotain,—which appears when a good king reigns.

丨麑 [fragrant as] the musk and roebuck; the terms 麑子 and 麑鹿 are specially applied to the roebuck.

四眼丨 a Formosan deer (*Cervus Swinhoii*), so called from two spots near its eyes.

鱆 *ˎchang* A bird belonging to the waders; another name is 水鴒 water-hen, and it is perhaps a bird akin to the 青丨 a book name for the heron, called 青莊 in Chihli jacana or rail.

掌 *ˋchang* From *hand* and *constantly* as the phonetic.

The palm of the hand, the sole; a webbed foot; a hoof; to grasp; to slap with the hand; to rule, to control; a jurisdiction, what is under one's hand.

手丨 the palm.

拍丨 to clap the hands.
看丨文 to scrutinize the hand; palmistry.
丨櫃 the book-keeper, a chief manager, the boss; an accountant.
打一巴丨 to slap once.
釘馬丨 to shoe a horse.
合丨 to join the hands, as Budhists do in prayer.
丨握兵權 to command the forces.
職丨 to administrate a post; the control of an officer.
丨事 to direct a matter.
丨管人 an overseer, a director.
丨教 to teach and direct, as a class of graduates; *ex cathedrá* teaching.
丨史 a department in a yamun.
易'如反丨 [he ruled the empire] as easy as turning over the palm.
鞅丨 bewildered, unmannerly, as from fuming and bustling; from he has lost his balance.
熊丨 a bear's paw.
仙人丨 the cactus, more especially the flat leaved kinds.

鞝 ‹*chang* The piece of leather used for soles on Chinese shoes; a part of a saddle; a patch.
打皮丨 to put on a sole.
打個丨子 to put on a patch,—either cloth or leather, on shoes.

仉 ‹*chang* The family name of Mencius' mother, and still retained in this form in honor of her; his own private given name was 軻 ˏK'o.

帳 *chang*› From a *cloth* and *extended*; it is interchanged with the next in some senses.

A curtain, a canopy, a screen; a tent; *met.* an abode, a a dwelling; a plan, a reason; to calculate, to spread out; an account, for which the next is now substituted; to reckon, as an account; occurs used for 障 to screen.
布丨 or 丨子 an awning, a screen.
丨簾 a hanging screen, before a door.
將軍丨 an awning, as over a court; a great awning.
設丨 to pitch one's tent; to open a school, to turn teacher.
丨頂 a tester, the top fringe of a bed-curtain.
混丨 unreasonable, incoherent, stupid, muddled.
營丨 a soldier's tent.
壽丨 a scroll given to old people on their birthdays.
銷金丨 a scroll in gold letters, sent to mourners.
圍丨 or 幃丨 a screen; a curtain hung around a bed or *kang*› for protection or concealment.
白雲丨望 the white clouds screen the view.
錦丨一佳人 a beautiful bride.

賬 *chang*› An unauthorized character in general use for the last; it affords a good example of the power of the radical in relation to its influence on the meaning.

An account; a debt, a claim, a charge; to reckon, to sum up.
計丨 or 算丨 to estimate gains; to reckon or settle with.
不算丨 don't charge that in my account; it's none of my business; I'll not allow that item.
收丨 to collect accounts.
丨目 accounts; 丨單 a bill.
丨房 the counting room, where the 丨簿 or 丨部 account books are kept; also, the counter in an inn.
淸丨 or 完丨 to clear off, to pay 丨尾 or balance of an account.
欠丨 to owe debts.
丨務絆身 to be embarrassed with debts.
放丨 to let out money, to shave notes; to give credit.
開花丨 to charge articles not really bought, to foist in fancy items.
倒丨 to transfer the accounts and debts to another, to make an assignment; to fail.

In *Cantonese.* A synonym of ‹*tang* 躺 a time, an occasion.
來過一丨 I came here once.

脹 **瘨** *chang*› From *flesh* or *disease* and *to increase*; the first is also read ˏ*ch'ang*, the intestines.

A swelled belly; a tumefaction, a swelling of any kind; pot-bellied; dropsical, puffy, tense; to swell up; to grow big, as a boil.
水丨 dropsy in the abdomen, ascites.
飽丨 puffed, a sense of fullness, as from indigestion or repletion.
腫丨 or 丨肚 swollen.
消丨 to relieve the swelling.
丨滿 the belly hard and puffed.
丨氣 flatulency.
丨數 to charge interest on credit sales. (*Fuhchau*).

瘬 *chang*› Like the last. Dropsical swellings, presenting puffy, hard places.

漲 *chang*› The *extension* of *water;* an overflow, a freshet; to inundate, to swell and wash over, as the bank; to expand, as iron by heat; applied also to prices advancing,— a use common along the coast.
水'丨 or 丨起 the flood is rising, the water advances.
丨潮 or 潮丨 the tide is coming in.
丨溢 or 丨滿 an overflow, bursting of the bank, a crevasse.
丨滿了 filled with water; up to the banks.
丨破了 swelled and burst, as a jug by the water in it freezing.
春日丨雲岑 the clouds in spring cover the peaks.
價錢要丨 the price will advance.
流質丨力 the elasticity of a fluid, — a term in mechanics.
丨海 a name for the Gulf of Tonquin.

瘴 *chang*› From *disease* and *section* as the phonetic.

Malaria, iasma, pestilent vapors; noxious exhalations that cause general sickness.

烟 丨 an unhealthy climate.

氣 丨 miasmatic, malarious.

丨 癘 a plague, an epidemic arising from malaria.

嵐 丨 noxious gases; vapors rising on hills, which are deemed to be injurious.

墇 chang' A dyke, an embankment; to separate, as by a bank, to stop up.

障 chang' From *place* and *section*. To separate so as to screen or protect; to divide off, to shut up inside, to include; to embank; to raise a dyke; an intervening distance that serves as a protection; a barricade, trench, or dyke, that divides or protects; a terminus; a screen, as of cloth, serving as a nominal defense.

丨 衛 an intrenched camp.

保 丨 a defense; to defend the barriers; *met.* a capable minister.

板 丨 a wooden partition.

丨 塞 whatever stops the onset or path.

丨 閉 to close against ingress.

築 丨 to throw up defenses.

遮 丨 to screen off, to rail off.

境 丨 a protection on the border or frontier.

錦 丨 a brocade screen.

嶂 chang' A steep cliff, a range of peaks. 峰 丨 a line of steep hills that serve as a limit.

青 丨 green hills.

山 丨 遠 重 疊 the steep peaks rise one above the other in the distance.

屏 丨 青 螺 the green paths wind up the intervening hills.

瞕 chang' A cataract forming, as the composition of the character, a *screen* in the *eye*, indicates.

丨 翳 or 丨 瞖 a cataract, more usually called 綠水灌瞳人 meaning green water poured into the pupil.

丈 chang' The original form is a combination of 又 *hand* grasping 十 *ten*. A line of ten *ch'ih* or feet, reckoned in the tariff to be 141 English inches; but it varies according to the foot used, to even less than 120 inches in some parts of China; to measure; an elder, a senior; one worthy of respect.

丨 量 to measure off, as land or a room.

丨 堪 to verify a measurement, as by officials.

有 丨 量 its measure has been made or taken.

丨 尺 有 數 the measurement can be ascertained.

一 丨 長 ten feet long.

岳 丨 a wife's father.

國 丨 the Emperor's father-in-law.

丨 夫 a (or my) husband; a man, one who acts his part; a son.

丨 人 a wife's father, often applied also to other elderly people.

丨 母 or 丨 母 娘 a wife's mother.

大 丨 夫 a man of ability, one fit to manage; a capable man.

方 丨 the abbot of a Budhist monastery; a monastery.

老 丨 an old gentleman.

仗 chang' From *man* and a *measure;* interchanged with the next. Weapons of war, sharp weapons; to fight, to come to blows; to rely on, to look up to; to depend on, as a man on his wealth or influence.

打 勝 丨 to get the victory.

敗 丨 or 打 敗 丨 defeated, vanquished,

接 丨 to join battle, as armies do.

打 丨 or 對 丨 to fight, to go into action.

丨 勢 欺 人 to insult people because one has power (or friends).

得 丨 to get an ally.

委 丨 to confide a responsible office to one.

仰 丨 to look to, to implore aid from a superior.

兵 丨 military arms.

丨 人 之 力 to trust on a human arm.

內 丨 a palace guard.

倚 丨 or 憑 丨 to trust to, to rely on.

杖 chang' From 木 *wood* and 仗 to *rely on* contracted; used with the last. A staff, a cane; a cudgel, a club, a shillelah; shaft of a lance; one who leans on a staff, an old man, aged; to lean on; to beat, as a criminal in a court; to bamboo.

拐 丨 an old man's staff, hence the term 丨 者 an old man.

丨 于 鄉 a village elder, one over sixty years of age.

丨 信 to confidently rely on.

朋 友 相 交 所 丨 者 信 mutual confidence is the bond of friendship.

執 丨 "staff holders," denote the chief mourners for a parent in a funeral.

操 丨 以 戰 to drill in order to be ready for war.

錫 丨 or 禪 丨 an abbot's staff or crosier, usually made of tutenague; it is supposed to have power to open the gates of hell, and let souls out of misery, and is therefore carried when masses for the dead are made; it stands for the Sanscrit *kakkurma*, the staff of begging priests; aged women wear a hair-pin having a Budha's hand, called by the same name.

丨 一 百 inflict a hundred blows — on the prisoner.

丨 責 八 十 gave him eighty blows.

笞 丨 to beat, as with rattans or green bamboos; there is a difference in the severity of these two punishments, the second being the heaviest.

行 丨 or 丨 打 a bambooing; to beat a criminal.

丨 枷 to beat and then expose in the cangue.

In *Fuhchau.* A classifier of sugar-cane.

CH'ANG.

Old sounds, *t'ung, dung, dzung* and *zhung*. In Canton, *ch'éung* and a few *shéung*; — in Swatow, *ch'iang, tiang, s"ié* and *t"ié*; — in Amoy, *ch'iong, tiong, t'iong* and *siong*; — in Fuhchau, *ch'iòng, t'iòng* and a few *siòng*; — in Shanghai, *ts'ang, dz'ang* and a few *ts'ong*; — in Chifu, *ch'ang*.

昌 *ch'ang* From the 日 *sun* and 曰 to *say*, referring to sunlight; as a primitive, it exhibits some of its meaning in many of the compounds.

The light of the sun; effulgent; flourishing, prosperous; fine-looking, elegant, beauteous; suitable, as just words; increasing in wealth or peace in which sense it is used in shop names; powerful, affluent; to illuminate, crowded; prosperity.

丨盛 abundantly; prosperous; having many descendants.

吉丨 well off, lucky.

光丨 splendid, brilliant.

順天者丨 he prospers who obeys Heaven.

其兆必丨 it is really a lucky sign.

丨盡必殃 ill luck follows after good fortune is exhausted.

克丨厥後 it insures prosperity to your descendant.

百丨 plants of all kinds; all things, the world.

文丨 the six stars of the Dipper; others give only the three stars $\phi\ \mu\ \vartheta$ in the Great Bear; and others only the star Dubhe.

禹拜丨言 Yü bowed when he heard good instructions.

幅 裮 *ch'ang* To throw a cloak or other garment loosely over one, and not to fasten it with the girdle.

猖 *ch'ang* A herd of animals fleeing.

丨狂 mad, ravenous, like dogs; insubordinate, boisterous, seditious.

丨摩神 violent, acting like mad, possessed.

娼 *ch'ang* From *woman* and *elegant*; it is constantly interchanged with 倡 to lead.

A singing woman; her children cannot enter the examinations.

丨妓 or 丨婦 a courtesan, a prostitute, a strumpet.

窩丨 to keep a brothel; to keep a house of assignation.

當丨 to be a whore.

丨們 public women.

菖 *ch'ang* The *elegant plant*; the sweet flag, much liked by Wăn Wang; applied to other water plants like it.

丨蒲 the calamus (*Acorus terrestris*); its leaves are hung on door lintels on the 5th of the 5th moon to ward off evil influences; a water Iris is sometimes wrongly so named.

閶 *ch'ang* From *door* and *elegant*.

The gate of heaven, called 丨闔, kept by Kwan-ti or the Chinese Mars; it is also applied to the emperor's palace gates, and to the west wind, which is a cool wind.

丨門 one of the gates of Su-chau.

倀 *ch'ang* From *man* and *long*; it is also read *chăng*.

Groping about, not knowing the road; madly; blindly; to fall down.

丨鬼 the lares of a person who has been eaten by a tiger, and leads the beast to seize others; *met.* a tempter, an evil adviser.

丨丨然 bewildered, undecided.

丨薅 a rash man, a blunderer.

丨丨乎其何之 going here and there without any particular rule, as one who has no home.

蜣 *ch'ang* The *long insect*, as the character indicates; it denotes a worm of the centipede family.

丨蠼 an old name for the millepede (*Julus*), supposed to get into people's ears.

場 塲 *ch'ang* From *earth* and *laid out*; the first form is correct, but the second is most used.

An area of level ground set apart, an open waste plat; a field, a lot; an arena for any purpose, as drill, gaming, theatricals, or executions; and extended to study and examinations; a scacrificial ground; a thrashing-floor; a kitchen garden; a company of, the society; a classifier of affars, a fit, a spell; and in some places of a job of work.

較丨 a parade-ground, a field for reviews.

屋丨 a building lot.

丨院 a court-yard; a lawn.

官丨中 among the officers; the official style of things.

通丨 all are alike, as a uniform set or body.

戰丨 the field of battle.

法丨 an execution-ground.

文丨 the tripos, the hall; as 進丨 to enter the examination as a candidate, either civil or military.

開攤丨 to open a gambling-shop.

賭博丨 dice-houses, gambling tables or hells.

禾丨 or 穀丨 a thrashing-floor.

好住丨 a commodious residence; a respectable neighborhood.

監丨 to oversee a literary examination.

大夢一丨 [this life is like] one great dream.

佛丨 a Budhist festival.

不知丨面 he is unacquainted with etiquette.

丨中作興 to raise a disturbance during the performance; to make a little excitement at the fête.

壇丨 an altar in the open air; the ground about it.

是非丨 a place where a man is criticised.

腸 From *flesh* and *expanded*.
꜀*ch'ang* The intestines, the bowels; they are divided into the 大丨 the large or lower intestines and colon, which the Chinese suppose connect with the lungs; and the 小丨 the urinary intestines, which join the heart and bladder; *met.* feelings, affections.

臟丨 or 丨肚 the bowels, the inwards, the viscera.

直丨 the rectum.

釀猪丨 to stuff pork sausages.

羊丨路 a serpentine, winding road.

好心丨 kindly disposed; tender feeling for another.

絞丨痧 griping pains, as in cholera; spasms and gripes.

自有肺丨 he has his own lungs and bowels;—opinionated, self-poised.

償 From *man* and *reward*.
꜀*ch'ang* To restore, to indemnify; to pay back; to forfeit, to atone; to retaliate; to make amends, to replace; an indemnity; restitution.

賠丨 to make compensation, as for property destroyed.

丨心願 my desires are gratified; to pay a vow.

殺人丨命 a murderer forfeits his life.

塡丨 to pay up the indemnity.

丨還 to pay back, to replace; to restore, as lost things.

要我抵丨 he wants me to indemnify for the loss—as of life.

夙願難丨 it will be hard to fulfill his old wish, as for an old man to get a degree.

嘗 **甞** From 旨 the *will* and 尙 to *manifest;* and the second, with 甘 *sweet*, refers to tasting; the first form is the best.
꜀*ch'ang* To taste, to test; to essay, to prove; to deliberate; when preceding another verb, it denotes past time; usually, formerly, ever; the autumnal offering of first fruits to ancestors.

他丨尋過吊 he once tried to hang himself.

丨一丨 or 先丨之 first try it; taste it once.

丨一些 taste a little of this.

丨業 hereditary property.

丨試 I have tasted it; 試丨 to try, to attempt.

未丨 not yet occurred; I never knew of it; I have had no experience in it.

丨聞 I have ever heard; it is usually the case; and 思丨 is similar—I have thought, it is commonly supposed; these phrases are opening expressions in an essay.

烝丨 entailed property, whose proceeds are applied to ancestral sacrifices.

何丨 who has tested it?—nobody knows of such a thing, it never happened; 何丨不是 how can it be otherwise?

實未丨於該船有所稽留 I really have not been the one who detained this ship.

長 One original form indicates a *man* appearing *above* his *dress;* as a primitive it serves chiefly as a phonetic; it forms the 168th radical of a few characters, most of which relate to hair, as this radical is regarded as a contraction of the 190th radical 髟 long locks.
꜀*ch'ang*

Long in time or distance; ball; constantly, regularly, always; used to, skilled; grand, much used; direct, straight; to excel; to make profit; often occurs in names of places.

丨生 "long life"—a euphuism for a coffin, in order to avoid a direct allusion to death.

丨生不老 a green, old age, denotes the physical immortality of the Taoists.

丨久 a long time, from of old; enduring.

丨氣 long-winded, as a great talker.

丨歸 the long return or home, a Budhist term for the soul's abode.

出丨紅 to issue a notification or report, as by a neighborhood at Canton.

使丨 spent more than the limit.

丨短 the length of a thing; traits of character, the long and short of, the pros and cons, merits of; often answers to expediency, trimming to circumstances; also, a turn in affairs.

論人所丨 to speak of what men excel in.

門丨關 the door is constantly shut.

各有所丨 in what each one excels.

丨遠 durable, lasting.

一無所丨 changeable, no perseverance, vacillating.

計丨三千兩 the profit was reckoned at 3000 taels.

黃丨虫 a common snake (*Elaphis*) near Peking.

Read ᶜ*chang*. Old, senior; superior, greater; an elder; one who ranks; able to lead; to excel; to increase, to grow; to cause increase, to prosper; to think highly of, to elevate; too heavy, as in weighing; to swell, as wood, or a boil.

家丨 head of a family, the paterfamilias.

丨子 the eldest son.

我比你丨 I am older than you.

貴庚多丨 how old are you?

尊丨 or 年丨 a senior, a venerable person.

丨房 family of the oldest brother, especially when he lives on the estate.

保丨 a constable, a headman.

大丨 to grow larger, to swell, to develop.

不丨進 he does not improve—in his studies.

君子道丨 the good man's ways prosper.

然後來見丨者乎 will he then come to see the elders?

丨蟲 it bred worms.

生丨 born and brought up; trained, reared.

丨他人志氣 he praised the other's good qualities.

丨人聰明 it makes men wise.

此風不可丨 this custom (or practice) cannot be suffered.

百夫丨 a centurion.

萇 ˏchʻang A pleasant fruit called 丨楚, the carambola or bilimbi (*Averrhoa*), known as the 楊桃 or willow peach at Canton.

烏丨國 a country called Udyana, which Budha visited, in North-western India, along the River Subhavastu, noted for its forests; the Greeks called it Suastene.

丨弘 name of a musician 太史 whom Confucius visited.

敞 ʻchʻang From 攴 a *blow* and 尙 *usual* as the phonetic.

High, level land; a plateau, from which can be had a wide view; open, spacious; to disclose or display; to rub bright, to burnish.

高丨 a high spot, like a terrace.

寬丨 or 闊丨 broad, ample, as a mansion; spacious.

一片丨地 a broad, open space of ground.

處險不丨 a dangerous, contracted spot.

事還丨着口兒呢 the business still requires some further discussion; it is not yet finished.

ʻ廠 ʻ厰 ʻchʻang From *shelter* and *spacious*; the second and unauthorized form is most common.

A shed, a covered place not walled in; a temporary erection; a dépôt, a depository; a storehouse; wholesale stores; an extensive workshop, a manufactory of government stores; a place to receive taxes; a street of workshops; occurs used for a mine, as of silver.

煤炭丨 a coal dépôt; a coal shed.

篷丨 a mat shed, erected for a temporary use.

鑄錢丨 a mint for casting cash.

標丨 an office for selling lottery tickets.

草丨 a thatched shed.

關丨 a customs' or tidewaiter's shed.

ʻ惝 ʻ⿰忄敞 ʻchʻang Alarmed; 丨怳 nervous and discomposed; apprehensive, disturbed.

ʻ昶 ʻchʻang From *day* and *ever;* occurs interchanged with *chʻang*ˀ 暢 joyous.

A long day; remote; bright; pervious, as when a ray shines through; extended, filled; clearly perceived.

日丨 a long day.

ʻ氅 ʻ⿱敞鳥 ʻchʻang The downy fearthers of a crane or other long legged bird, used in trimming fine dresses.

丨衣 a kind of cloak or gown without sleeves, worn by women; a shroud.

鶴丨 down of the crane, used in adorning dresses; a robe with wide sleeves and facings, worn by actors.

淌ˀ chʻangˀ Great billows, raging waves.

Read ʻtʻang. To leak, as a roof; to run as water in a gully; to drip; to perspire.

丨眼淚 to shed many tears.

丨水 the water runs down, as from a roof.

丨出水來 the water drips down.

丨汗 to drip with perspiration.

丨溝 an eaves-gutter; a water channel.

唱ˀ ⿰龠昌ˀ chʻangˀ From *mouth* or *pipe* and *elegant;* the second is obsolete.

To lead, as in singing; to go before; to act as a coryphеus; the leader or master of ceremonies; to sing, to carol; to give or pass the word; to crow; anciently applied to a division of a night watch, equal to one fifth of it.

淸丨 to sing and play quietly, as amateurs who 丨曲 sing songs.

丨名 to call out one's name, as at a levee.

丨二簧 to sing slowly; and 丨梆子 to sing rapidly; are terms used by theatrical singers, derived from the wind instruments used by them.

丨隨 to follow in singing, to join the chorus.

丨戲 to sing pays, theatrical performances.

彈丨 to thrum and sing, to accompany an instrument with the voice.

鳴鑼丨道 to beat the gong and clear the road.

丨禮 to give orders at a ceremony.

丨飯 to call out rice [to the corpse];—a usage in some parts of China, accompanied with a plaintive cry.

倡ˀ chʻangˀ From *man* and *elegant* as the phonetic.

A fine looking person; a leader, an example, a guide; to introduce; to induce, to lead, to seduce; to start, as a tune.

丨率 to lead on, as a reconnoitering party.

丨亂 to head a riot.

丨言 to speak first; to lead, as a precentor.

丨隨 to lead and follow, as a husband and wife.

首丨 an inventor, one who 丨始 invents, or takes the lead in starting.

丨一陣 to lead a troop.

Read ˏ*chʻang;* and interchanged with 娼, meaning a singing girl; to sing; also occurs used for 猖 ravenous.

丨優 hired singers and actors, both boys and girls.

畼ˀ chʻangˀ From *field* and *increasing;* it is the original form of the next, but the two are now distinguished.

A broad barren plot of ground or country; name of a place in the old feudatory of Wêi 衛, now the north of Honan.

丨畝荒涼 the waste and neglected fields—have no inhabitants.

暢' Originally like the last.
ch'ang' The inner qualities developing; joyous, contented, in good spirits; exhilirating, as home music; penetrating, thorough; spreading, filling.

丨膽 bold, hardy; presumptuous.
丨懷 gratified, happy.
快丨 delighted, as children.
丨敘 pleasant conversation.
丨飲 social feasting.
丨月 the eleventh moon.
丨遂 according to one's wishes.
通丨 or 丨達 going through; perspicuous, as a style; clearly expressed.

脹' *ch'ang'* Losing one's senses, acting as if giddy; large eyes.
In *Pekingese.* The eyes blurred and swollen.
眼睛發丨 the eye has swollen greatly.

悵' *ch'ang'* Disappointed in one's hopes; vexed; dissatisfied.
丨丨然 lamentable and provoking too.
丨望而不見 I looked for it longingly, but never saw it; I was utterly disappointed.

韔' *ch'ang'* A case for a bow; to put up a bow in the cover.
虎丨 a sheath for a bow.

鬯' *ch'ang'* Originally formed of 凵 *a vessel* in which 米 *grain* is fermenting, and 匕 a *spoon* underneath; it forms the 192d radical of a few obsolete characters.
Sacrificial spirits made by fermenting millet and fragrant herbs, one of which was turmeric; to put a bow in its case; the case.
丨酒 mixed wine.
秬丨 odoriferous spirits made from millet, which it was thought caused the gods to draw near.
丨草 aromatic herbs.
抑丨弓忌 he puts up his bow.
主丨 one who prepares libations.
丨茂 luxuriant, as plants growing vigorously.

CHĂNG.

Old sounds are *tang, tăng, ding* and *ting.* In Canton, *chăng, chang* and *t'ong;* — in Swatow, *chⁿé* and *chéng;* — in Amoy, *chéng, téng,* and *tong;* — in Fuhchau, *chéng,* and *chang;* — in Shanghai, *tsang;* — in Chifu, *ching.*

爭 争 *˓chăng* The original form is composed of 爪 *claws* and two 又 *hands* pulling; as a primitive, its influence is apparent in several of its compounds; the second form is a common contraction.
To wrangle, to contest, to litigate; to emulate, to strive for precedence; to debate; to differ; used with *chăng'* 諍 to reprove, to expostulate with.

相丨 quarrelsome.
丨氣 petulant, unforgiving.
丨先 striving to excel, contentious.
丨訟 to go to law; litigious.
丨功 to laud one's own deeds; to emulate merit.
丨奪 to seize by force or process of law.
丨奈 howbeit, still, nevertheless.
丨執 obstinate, pig-headed.
丨競 to squable and wrangle.
丨鬪 to come to blows, in consequence of 丨口 or 丨鬧, getting into a dispute and angry.
丨拗 self opinionated.
難與丨鋒 it's not easy to measure lances with him.
丨有限 the difference is very little.
丨的上'當' I came very near being gulled by him. (*Cantonese.*)

猙 *˓chăng* A fabulous griffon like a leopard, having five tails and a horn; others describe it as like a flying fox.
丨獰 horrid, repulsive, hideous.

睜 *˓chăng* To open the eyes.
睖丨 to look at angrily, displeased at the sight of.
丨着一隻眼 to open one eye; keep a watch over the thing.

箏 *˓chăng* From *bamboo* and *wrangling.*
A sort of virginal or harpsichord, having twelve brass strings, and played with a plectrum.
風丨 jingling stones hung in porches, or under the eaves; they are attached to kites, and hence 放風丨 is to fly kites, especially singing ones.
彈丨 to thrum a virginal.
丨丨 shrill piercing sounds.

錚 *˓chăng* The clanging jangle of metals struck together; a small cymbal or gong.
鼓丨 the din of drums.
丨丨之士豈易'多得 do you imagine that such famous scholars are easily to be got?

竳 *˓chăng* Broad, open; the echo in a wide house; painted silk;
丨宖 ample, expansive.

瞪 瞠 *tăng'* The second form is not much used, but is probably more correct than the first, which is also read *tăng'.*
To sit and doggedly look at; to fix the eye on; to gaze at in a supercilious way.
睖丨 the vacant stare of one just awaked from sleep, before his thoughts are collected.

掙 *chăng'* To pierce, to stab; to file; to amass, as property; to collect; to nerve one's self.
丨塞 to block up the way.
丨牙 to get something between the teeth.
硬丨 determined; energetic.
丨家 to take care of a family.
丨開 to break away, as a horse from his halter.
灑丨 to embroider tambours.
丨了錢 to make money, to get rich.
丨脫 to get rid of one.
In *Cantonese*. To wedge in; to calk.

丨砂鷄 to stuff a fowl with san d (*Cantonese*).
打丨 to calk seams.

諍 *chăng'* From *words* and *wrangling*; it occurs interchanged with its primitive.
To remonstrate with; to try to stop oppression by expostulating with the ruler.
諫丨 to reprove and warn; to oppose arbitrary power.
議丨 to debate, to discuss faithfully with one; to dispute.
天子之前丨論可否 is it allowable to dispute one in the imperial presence?

丨人 a race of pigmies, described as being seven inches high.

弸 *chăng'* To draw a bow; to press open anything so as to inspect it.

鋥 棖 *chăng'* To burnish, to rub metal bright. The second character also means to stop up.
磨丨 to furbish a sword so as to see one's face in it.
丨牙 minium or red lead.

幬 *chăng'* To unroll a painting or scroll, so as to display it.

CH'ĂNG.

Old sounds, t'ang, djang, *and* dang. *In Canton*, ch'ang *and* ch'ăng; — *in Swatow*, ch'éng, tⁿé, *and* téng; — *in Amoy*, t'éng, chong, chóng, *and* ch'éng; — *in Fuhchau*, ch'éng, chéng, *and* téng; — *in Shanghai*, ts'ang, tsang, *and* dzang; — *in Chifu*, ts'ăng.

牚 *˛ch'ăng* The original form of the next two, now used in combination as a primitive.
A prop, something to shore up; a post out of the perpendicular.

撐 撑 *˛ch'ăng* From *hand* and to *prop*; used with the next.
To prop, to shore up; to distend; to fasten open, as with a stretcher; to pole, to push off; to buttress; to open out; to adjoin, bordering on; to run up, as a firth into the land; to prop, a fulcrum, a stay, a leaning post.
丨船 to pole a boat,—which a generous man can do in his belly; a metaphor for his liberal views.
丨渡 to push across the ferry; *met.* to intrigue with officials.
充丨 to curry favor with one.
烟霧丨天 the mist rises upward.

丨不來 I can't help you much — with the officers.
丨持 to curtail, as one's expenses.
能彀支丨得住 I am quite able to stand up under it.

橕 *˛ch'ăng* Like the preceding.
A branch stretching out; a fulcrum, a prop; a horizontal strip to support the frame, as the slats on a bedstead.
丨柱 a bracket or truss to support a beam.
丨開窗門 stretch open the window.
彎丨 a crooked brace.
In *Cantonese*. To expel, to turn out.
丨佢出去 kick or turn him out.
丨牙較 to prop up the jaw;— *i. e.* to praise one's self.

饓 *˛ch'ăng* To eat much.
丨餩 to gormandize, to eat to excess.

鬇 *˛ch'ăng* Often read *˛tsăng.*
The hair in disorder and standing up.
丨鬡 untrimmed hair, short and not combed smooth; applied often to the beard.

崢 *˛ch'ăng* *˛ts'ăng* From *hill* and *wrangling.*
To rise high; overtopping, excelling; conspicuous, as a peak.
霄丨特立 [like] standing alone on the airy peak.
丨嶸 dignified, high; used by physiognomists as 頭角丨嶸 he has a noble brow; eminent; lofty, as a character.

棦 *˛ch'ăng* A thorn on a tree; sometimes rendered a fagot, a bundle, from the similarity or misprinting of 朿 and 束, in dictionaries.

琤 *˛ch'ăng* The tinkling sound of gems or sonorous glasses striking together.
琮丨 tinkling; a phrase intended to imitate the sound.

傖 From *man* and *granary* as the phonetic.
'ts'ăng A reckless fellow, a son of Belial; a profligate; so the people of Wu 吳 or Kiangsu anciently called those of Chung-cheu 中州 or Honan.
丨父 an old reprobate.
無端逐饑丨 he drove off the hungry wretches without any cause.

棖 From *wood* and *long*; it is often wrongly used for the next.
ˌch'ăng A prop, a stay; the two door-posts; a rule; to follow or comply with.
丨柱 a side post or column; also to make one follow after.
杖丨 a staff.
申丨 one of Confucius' minor disciples, whom he said was under the power of his lusts.
企門丨 standing in the doorway on the sill.
In *Cantonese*. The threshold.

橙 The common orange (*Citrus aurantium*), or coolie orange,
ˌch'ăng poetically termed 金球 the golden ball; the shaddock is also called by this name in some parts of Fuhkien.
甜丨 sweet oranges from Sin-hwui, a district southwest of Canton.
丨皮 dried orange skin.
丨糖 and 丨膏 orange sweetmeats; marmalade.
山丨 a wild fruit of the dogbane family (*Melodinus*) like an orange in shape and color, growing on a vine, found in Kwangtung; used for a deobstruent.

棠 A perch for fowls; a prop; to straighten or pull out, to
ˌch'ăng tread on; to roost.
維角丨之 the ends [of the bow] should be straightened out.

CHAO.

Several of these characters are heard as if sounded CHIAO. *Old sounds,* to, tok, do, *and* dok *or* dot. *In Canton,* chiu, chau, *and* shiu; —*in Swatow,* chio, chié, jiò, tiò, siò, tau, chau *and* tié; —*in Amoy,* chiau, tiau, chau, *and* tau; —*in Fuhchau,* tiu, chau, chiu, *and* chwa; —*in Shanghai,* tsao, dzao, *and* dao; —*in Chifu,* tsao.

昭 From *day* and to *call*.
ˌchao The brightness of the sun; bright, luminous, refulgent, splendid; manifested; to show forth, to display; shrined on the left in the hall.
丨言 intelligible; perspicuous.
丨明 bright; to fully understand.
丨著 clear, evident, plainly shown.
丨顯 famous, renowned.
丨陽宮 the empress' palace.
耳目丨彰 well known to all the world, universally heard.
左丨右穆 the row on the right and the row on the left, *i. e.* in the order of age or nearness and precedence; used only for the arrangement of imperial ancestral tablets in the temple, by which the proper generation of each person is designated.
天眼丨丨 the eye of Heaven is clear; heaven is clear-sighted.
丨然如揭 plain as when the cover has been taken off.
其音丨丨 his reputation is illustrious.
丨君套 the fillet of Queen Chao of the Han dynasty, now worn by the Chinese; it somewhat resembles a small havelock.

招 From *hand* and to *call*.
ˌchao To beckon, to motion to, to hail with the hand; to let people know; to invite, to induce, as by proclamation or handbills; to entangle, to provoke, to annoy, to excite; to raise, as troops; to confess, to assume; self-crimination; a sign-board; a placard; a signal, a wave of the hand.
丨呼 to call and beckon to; to wait on.
丨安 to proclaim an amnesty; to invite rebels to submit.
丨充 engaged to serve, as a clerk.
丨帖 a handbill, a poster for sale of goods; a shop-card.
不許丨帖 "Stick no bills here."
丨工 or 丨募工人 to engage or advertise for laborers.
丨郎入舍 to bring a son-in-law into one's house.
丨牌 a sign-board.
肯丨認 he owns to the charge; he becomes responsible for it.
丨鄉民 or 丨兵 to enlist volunteers, to recruit; to raise a troop.
自丨 to bring on one's self.
丨搖撞騙 to excite or beguile people,—and then rob them.
丨接客 to entertain guests.
丨丨舟子 calling and beckoning is that boatman.
丨引 to introduce, to bring in, as a convert or attaché.
丨架不住 unequal to resist him; I can't fend off.
不丨惹他 don't entangle yourself with him; don't provoke him.
丨財童子 the lad who causes profit; *i. e.* the God of Wealth.
丨魂 to call home the soul — of a man who died abroad.
丨潮 poetical name for a crab, which seems to call for the tide to come up by moving its palpi

丨認口供 he confessed his crime by his evidence.

丨租 to offer a house to let.

嘲 ˛chao To ridicule another, to jest upon; to laugh and joke with; railing, sportive allusions.

白丨 a pasquinade.

丨笑 to jeer at; gibes and jokes.

丨罵 to rail at sarcastically, to abuse and ridicule.

執蝘蜓而丨龜龍 he held up a moth and a dragon-fly, and laughed at the tortoise and dragon, — for they could neither of them fly, big as they were.

啁 ˛chao Interchanged with the last, but some say not properly. To boast; to talk much.

丨噍 or 丨丨聲 the chirping and bickering of birds.

Read ˛tao, in the phrase 嘐丨 talkative, verbose.

抓 ˛chao ˛chwa From *hand* and *claws;* it is usually pronounced ˛chaw in Peking, and often written 抓, but wrongly.

To scratch, to tickle, to titillate; to tear with the claws; to please, to cajole.

丨住 to clutch, as a hawk; to pounce upon, as tidewaiters do on smugglers.

丨破臉 scratched his face so that it bled.

丨頭 or 丨首 to scratch the head, as when in perplexity.

丨鬮 to draw lots.

丨替身 to pester another — till he commits suicide, as is believed to be done by the spirits of suicides to their enemies.

樔 ˛chao Similar to ˛ch'ao 巢 a nest. A raised lodge erected in a marsh to watch the crop; a kind of grass creel for catching fish; to drag a net.

Read *tsiao*, and used for 剿 to execute.

命丨絕而不長 he ordered them to be exterminated, and not suffered to live.

鉊 ˛chao A large bill-hook or sickle, was so called in the region of the River Hwai during the feudal times.

皽 ˛chao The white skin which grows over a scar, called 皽膜 or shadow cuticle.

朝 **晁** ˛chao ˛ch'ao From 倝 *sunrise* and 舟 *a boat* contracted to 月 *moon;* the second, meaning a *sign* of the *sun*, is a pedantic form.

The dawn, the opposite of *sih*, 夕 eve; morning; early.

丨夕 or 丨晚 morning and evening; early and late.

一丨 in a morning, in a trice; suddenly, quickly.

丨丨來 he comes every morning.

用丨(or 早)飯沒有 have you breakfasted? — a polite morning salutation.

明丨 to-morrow morning; sometimes used indefinitely.

三丨湯餅會 the merrymaking on the third day — after a birth.

花丨 the 10th of the 2d moon, when all the flowers are supposed to open in northern China.

靡有丨矣 I never took a morning's [leisure].

丨鮮 name for Corea given by Wu Wang when made a fief of Ki-tsz' 箕子; the rulers prefer it to 高麗, and use it in official papers; its meaning refers to its eastern position, where the *fresh morning* comes.

Read ˛ch'ao. A court, so called because held in early morning; the imperial palace or court; to have an audience, to go to court; to show fealty; to hold a levee; an imperial audience; a dynasty; a reign; the government; courtly, fashionable; to visit a father or elder; as a *preposition*, towards, facing; fronting.

丨見 or 上丨 to go to court; to see his Majesty.

坐丨 his Majesty holding court.

臨丨 to take the reins of government.

侍丨 the high officers who support or stand near the sovereign at such times.

本丨 Our dynasty; also called 天丨 the heavenly or celestial dynasty; its present style 丨號 or dynastic name, is *Ts'ing Chao* 淸丨 the Pure dynasty.

轉丨 to change the dynasty.

丨馬 to ride on horseback into the Forbidden City; — a mark of high favor conferred on grandees.

丨房 or 丨燕 an antechamber of the audience-room.

丨服 a court-dress.

丨考 examination for conferring the Hanlin degree.

整頓丨綱 to reform and strengthen the government.

一丨天子一丨臣 each monarch has his own set of ministers.

三丨元老 a high grandee of three reigns.

一品當丨 the first rank sees the emperor's face.

丨上坡子走 to go up the hill.

志心丨禮 the devout heart fixedly performs the ritual, — said of priests when at worship.

丨前一點兒 move forward a little, as when sitting back in a cart.

丨聘 to invite one to court, as was done in old times by presents.

丨斗姆 to worship the Goddess of the Dipper — for long life.

The following list of the dynasties which have swayed China, is made out from the *Lih-tai Ti-wang nien Piao* 歷代帝王年表 Digest of the Reigns of Emperors and Kings; in this work there is a historical synopsis of the leading events of each year from the Han dynasty to the beginning of the Manchu sway.

ABSTRACT OF THE CHINESE DYNASTIES.

WU TI KI 五帝紀 RECORD OF THE FIVE RULERS.	BEGAN B.C.	REIGNED.
T'ai Hao 太皞 commonly known as 伏羲氏 Fui-hi shi.	2852	115
Yen Ti 炎帝, commonly known as 神農氏 Shin-nung shi.	2737	140
Hwang Ti 黃帝, also called 軒轅氏 Hien-yuen shi.	2697	100
Chinese historians commence their chronology with the 61st year of this reign or B.C. 2637, which is 518 years after the deluge, and 82 years after the death of Arphaxad, according to Hales' chronology.		
Shao-hao 少皞, named 金天氏 Kin-t'ien shi.	2597	84
Chwen-hüh 顓頊, named 高陽氏 Kao-yang shi.	2513	78
Ti Küh 帝嚳, named 高辛氏 Kao-sin shi.—Ti Chi 帝摯 his son, included in the next reign.	2435	78
Ti Yao 帝堯, named 陶唐氏 T'ao-t'ang shi.	2357	102
Ti Shun 帝舜, named 有虞氏 Yiu-yü shi.	2255	50

NAME OF DYNASTY.	NUMBER OF SOVEREIGNS.	BEGAN B.C.	ENDED B.C.	DURATION.
1. Hia 夏	Seventeen, averaging 26 years to each monarch's reign.	2205	1766	439
2. Shang 商	Twenty-eight, averaging 23 years.	1766	1122	644
3. Cheu 周	Thirty-four, averaging 25½ years.	1122	255	867
4. Ts'in 秦	Two, one reigned 37 years, and one 3 years.	255	206	40
	The beginning of Ts'in Chi Hwang-ti's reign is placed at B.C. 221, and the end of the Cheu dynasty at B.C 249; for 28 years—天下無天子 the empire had no emperor. Some writers divide this dynasty, making the After Ts'in endure 46 years.			
5. Han 漢	Fourteen, averaging 16½ years.	206	A.D. 25	231
6. Tung Han 東漢	Twelve, averaging 16⅓ years.	A.D. 25	221	196
7. Heu Han 後漢	Two, one 2 years, the other 41 years.	221	264	43
	The San Kwoh 三國 which divided China during this period were the Han 漢, Wei 魏, and Wu 吳.			
8. Tsin 晋	Four, averaging 14¼ years.	265	322	57
9. Tung Tsin 東晋	Eleven, averaging about 9½ years.	323	419	106
10. Sung 宋	Eight, averaging 7¼ years.	420	478	58
11. Ts'i 齊	Five, averaging 4⅗ years.	479	502	23
12. Liang 梁	Four, one 48 years, and three 7 years in all.	502	556	54
13. Ch'ăn 陳	Five, averaging about 6½ years.	557	589	32
	The four last dynasties are known by the collective name of Nan-peh ch'ao 南北朝 Northern and Southern Dynasties; the 魏 Wei dynasty divided the country with them from A.D. 420 to 550, under fifteen princes.			
14. Sui 隋	Three, one reigned 16, and another 12 years.	589	619	30
15. T'ang 唐	Twenty, averaging 14⅓ years,	620	907	287
16. Heu Liang 後梁	Two, one 8 years, and one 7 years.	907	923	16
17. Heu T'ang 後唐	Four, averaging 3¼ years.	923	936	13
18. Heu Tsin 後晋	Two, one 7 years, and one 3 years.	936	946	10
19. Heu Han 後漢	Two, one 3 years, and one 1 year.	947	951	4
20. Heu Cheu 後周	Three, averaging 3 years.	951	960	9
	The last five shortlived dynasties are collectively known as the Wu Tai 五代 Five Dynasties; they had 13 monarchs in 54 years.			
21. Sung 宋	Nine, averaging 18½ years.	960	1127	167
22. Southern Sung 南宋	Nine, averaging 17 years.	1127	1280	153
23. Yuen 元	Nine, averaging 9⅔ years.	1280	1368	88
24. Ming 明	Sixteen, averaging 17 years	1368	1644	276
25. Ts'ing 清	Seven rulers up to 1861, 217 years, averaging 31 years.	1644	—	—

From Ta Yu, B.C. 2205 to T'ung-chi, A.D. 1862, are 4067 years, during which time 236 sovereigns reigned, each about 17 years.

爪 叉 ꜀chao — The original form represents three talons; it forms the 87th radical of a small group of characters relating to clawing; sometimes written like 抓 as a verb; the second and antique form represents the nails growing on the hand.

Claws of animals; the talons of birds; to scratch, to claw; to hold in the claws; to grasp with the fingers; *met.* an agent, a minion, a runner for, an aid.

丨爛 or 丨破 to tear in pieces, to dissever.
裹丨 to bind a girl's feet.
丨牙 or 丨翼 agents, emissaries servants.
狐丨皮 fox-claws' skin, a kind of fur of inferior sort.
買辦丨 a comprador's claws, one who buys for him; a purveyor's assistant, a market-man.
鷹丨花 a name for the hawk's claw, (*Artabotrys odoratissimus*) at Canton.
一丨蕉 a bunch of plantains.
丨搲 to scratch.
虎丨 a kind of shears.

找 ꜂chao — From *hand* and *spear*; it must be distinguished from ꜂ngo 我 I.

To supply what is deficient, to make up; to pay a balance; to seek, to look for; to exchange, as money; to barter; settled, as an account.

丨數尾 to pay off the balance of the account.
丨尋 to seek for, to search.
丨換 to exchange, as silver into cash or bills.
丨門路 to seek for employment.
丨足其數 make up the number; return the full sum.
丨補 supply the deficiency.
丨票子 to change a bank note.
丨出來 he has changed it, as a bill.
丨不着 I cannot find it.

Read ꜀hwa, and used for ꜀hwa. 划 a boat, for which it seems to have been miswritten.

沼 ꜀chao — A fish-pond; an irregular tank, a pool.
蓮丨 a water-lily pond.
池丨 pools and tanks in parks.
靈丨 a celebrated, fine fish-pond of Wăn Wang.

帊 ꜀chao — To cover the head.
丨頭巾 a turban or cloth to wrap around the head, as the Fuhkien sailors do.

趙 chao꜄ — From to *go* and *resembling*.

To hasten to, to visit a suzerain, as very small fiefs did; a few; acute; a long time; to pierce; an ancient feudal state in the south of Chihli and Shansi; its capital was the present Chao-chʻing hien 丨城縣 a town on the R. Făn.

丨州 a prefecture in the southwest of Chihli; and also a district in the west of Yunnan, south of Ta-li Lake.
丨久 a good while.
趨丨 to hasten, quick traveling.
明日奉丨 I will return it tomorrow, as a borrowed book.

笊 chao꜄ — From *bamboo* and *claw* as the phonetic.

A bamboo skimmer; a ladle; a nest in a cave or under a shelter, as distinguished from one on a tree.

丨籬 a wire ladle.

櫂 棹 chao꜄ — The first is also read *chuh*, branches growing up straight, as in a cypress. The second is also read *choh*, a table. The first is derived from 木 *wood* and 濯 to *wash* contracted.

An oar, a scull; a long, steering oar projecting from the bow; to row with an oar (its only use at Canton, where it is sometimes wrongly written 掉 to denote the verb); to shoot, as an arrow; to throw away;— these uses are confined to southern dialects.

丨槳 to row an oar.
出力丨 row harder.
丨出街 throw it into the street
丨過海 rowed across the river—at Canton.
丨中꜄ to hit, as a target.

罩 箌 chao꜄ — A basket for snaring fish by covering them in the mud; to catch, to cover over, to shade, to protect, as a vail or cover does; a protection from dust or wind; to envelop, to surround, as by a cloud.

丨魚 to entrap fish in a basket creel.
鷄丨 a basket for fowls.
轎丨 a cover to keep the dust off a sedan.
燈丨 a lamp-shade or globe.
棺丨 a sort of catafalque over a bier; a pall of any kind.
丨面巾 a vail, such as foreign ladies wear.
丨衣 a sort of cloak or hood.
烝然丨丨 how full the net was—of barbel!

箌 chao꜄ — Great, large; rank, high, as grass; erroneously used for 倬, which is the correct character; and also for the last.

焯 chao꜄ — To fry at a fire; a blazing fire; the crust left on a pan after boiling or frying.
油丨 to fry in fat.
丨到脆 fried to a crisp.

兆 㸒 chao꜄ — The original form represents the lines on a tortoise-shell, after roasting to prepare it for divination; the second form is not common.

An omen, a prognostic; the border of a grave or altar, for which the next is used; a million, used chiefly in Budhistic writings.

一丨 a million; as 億丨 is millions and millions, a vast indefinite number.

丨民 the people, the mass of the people, the million.

億丨之衆 the multitnde of his men.

敗丨 a bad sign; rather ominous.

丨頭 a sign of; as 雪花飛六出先丨豐年 it is a sign of a good year when the snow flakes have six sides.

吉丨 a good prognostic.

預先之丨 a foreshadowing omen.

京丨 the capital; a great city, a vast mart; its magistrate is 京丨尹; he is now only found in Peking.

垗 chao' The bank around a grave; a border, limit, or bound.

宅丨 the boundary of a grave.

旐 chao' From *banner* and *omen*.

A flag inscribed with snakes and tortoises, one of four kinds used of old in the army.

丨旝 banners and scrolls in funerals or other processions.

設此丨矣 raise on high this battle flag.

卲 chao' From *to divine* and *to cite*.

To prognosticate, to inquire by auguries, to divine.

肇 肈 chao' The second form is very common, but not so correct.

To commence, to lay a foundation, to institute; to project, to devise; at first, the beginning; to rectify; to strike; to extend; capable, intelligent.

丨慶府 the city of Chao-k'ing fu, lying west of Canton; it was once the provincial capital.

丨十有二州 there were twelve provinces at first.

丨緒 the clue or rationale of a thing.

丨端 the oriroinal institution; the first plans.

德丨其昌 [his forefather's] virtue laid the foundation of his prosperity.

釗 chao From *metal* and *knife*.

To pare, to lop off; to trim an excrescence; bright, clear; a catch on a crossbow; to encourage; to visit, to wait on.

丨勉 to incite, to urge on.

召 chao From *mouth* and *knife*, alluding to the incisiveness of the citation; its meaning appears in several of its compounds.

To call by words; to summon, to cite; to require a subordinate to appear; to invoke.

丨見 or 宣丨 to be called to court.

寵丨 your gracious summons;— a phrase in a note of thanks.

父丨無諾 do not delay when your father calls.

乃丨六卿 to convoke the six presidents.

丨請 to invite [the ghosts to their feast,] — as priests do.

徵丨使來 to send for an officer to appear at court.

Read *shao'* when used for 邵, an old city in Jü-ning fu in Honan; the appanage of 丨伯 lying in the present 絳州 in Shansi.

詔 chao' From *words* and *to summon*; it occurs interchanged with the last.

To proclaim, to announce, to declare, as a king; to instruct by decree or order, as a sovereign does, a usage that began with the Han dynasty; to animate, to encourage; a royal proclamation, a mandate; name of a small state of the Laos people in the southwest of China, A. D. 850, called 南丨, now Tsun-i fu, situated in the north of Kwéi-cheu.

恩丨 a gracious proclamation, as a pardon.

丨命 or 王丨 a royal mandate.

丨告 to proclaim; and 降丨 is to issue the proclamation.

皇丨 or 敕丨 or 鳳丨 an Imperial mandate.

丨對 to consult with the Emperor.

丨旨 a rescript from the monarch to his cabinet.

丨令奏議 mandates, orders, and memorials; *i. e.* official records of every kind.

頒丨天下 to issue a decree from the Throne; to make an imperial announcement over the empire.

丨子以義方 he taught his sons the principles of justice.

待丨 a petty officer in the Hanlin Academy who makes poetry.

遺丨 the Emperor's will, which is afterwards 白丨 proclaimed to the people.

丨導 to give orders about, to direct.

照 chao' From *fire* and *bright*, *i. e.* the light of fire illumining.

To enlighten, to shine on; to regard, to care for, to oversee; to patronize; to front towards; to accord with, as a precedent; as, like, accordding to, same as; light, the reflection of light; as an initial word, it often answers to whereas, seeing that; something given or referred to as evidence, in which cases it is often used elliptically to include much that has gone before; a permit, a pass, a release.

丨鏡 to look in a glass; but 丨身鏡 means a pier-glass.

丨顧 to pay attention to; to buy of, to patronize.

火丨 a blaze; fire, flame.

高丨 large candles or lanterns used in temples or processions, probably named from the phrase 吉星高丨 may a lucky star shine down on you; a candlestick and candle are called a 手丨 or hand-light.

正丨 or 反丨 denote the direct ray and the reflected ray.

丨樣作 do it like the pattern.

丨抄 copy it so.

丨你說 as you say.

丨算 according to the account or number; the number tallies.

丨臨下土 shine over the world.

丨明 to manifest, to consider.

存 ㅣ to keep as evidence; a part cut off to be retained as a tally or proof.

心肝 ㅣ 見 I see into his designs.

ㅣ 着他 light him; give him a light, as to one going home by night.

心 ㅣ to understand thoroughly, as a friend.

ㅣ 管 to oversee, or look after.

垂 ㅣ to regard kindly, to look down on.

ㅣ 會 a communication between foreign and native officers of equal rank; to inform officially.

晚 ㅣ evening, the evening sunlight.

執 ㅣ or 護 ㅣ a passport, a safe warrant, a paper that protects.

江 ㅣ a river-pass.

ㅣ 應 to look after, to be interested in; to intercede for; to oversee, to regulate.

ㅣ 得 be it known; whereas, referring to;—used in official papers.

台 ㅣ for you, Sir, to look at;—a phrase on a bill of goods.

燭 ㅣ or 電 ㅣ illumine it, lighten it; *i. e.* please cast your eye on this etition or paper.

ㅣ 像 or ㅣ 日像 to take photograph likenesses.

ㅣ 影畫 photograph pictures.

炤 *chao*ʾ Another form of the last.

Bright; visible.

螢夜 ㅣ the *Sampyris noctiluca* or fire-fly.

ㅣ ㅣ clearly seen and understood.

亦孔之 ㅣ still are clearly seen.

堢 *chao*ʾ To spade the ground to get out bad soil; to open up a fallow field; a bank, a boundary.

ㅣ 壁 a wall to divide or screen off.

CHʻAO.

Several of these characters are heard *chʻiao*. Old sounds, *tʻo, do, tʻok, dok, tʻio, djio, tʻiok* and *diop*. In Canton, *chʻao* and *chʻiu*;—in Swatow, *tié, chʻiò, chʻau tʻiò, swa*, and *chʻa*;—in Amoy, *chʻiau, tiau, chʻau, chau* and *chʻa*;—in Fuhchau, *chʻieu, tieu, chʻau*, and *chau*;—in Shanghai, *tsʻao dzao*, and *tsiao*;—in Chifu, *tsʻao*.

超 ˛*chʻao* From to *go* and to *cite*.

To step over, to leap over; to vault; to go before; to excel, to surpass; to promote, to raise; to bring up, or release from purgatory, as Budhists do.

ㅣ 群 above the average; or ㅣ 常 better than the common run.

ㅣ 卓 very clever; fine looking and accomplished.

ㅣ 越 excelling, singular.

天生 ㅣ 性 a heaven-born genius, one of rare talents.

ㅣ 拔 or ㅣ 升 to promote over others, to overslaugh other officials.

ㅣ 生 [as if] restored to life; to save from death; also to cause one to be reborn into another life; similar to ㅣ 渡 or ㅣ 幽 to leap the ford or abyss, *i.e.* to release souls from suffering.

ㅣ 北海 [like] leaping over the northern sea; *met.* impossible.

ㅣ 等 one in the first rank of *siu-tsʻai* or *kŭjin* graduates.

弨 ˛*chʻao* The recoil of the bow after the arrow leaves it; a bow unbent.

大 ㅣ a large bow.

彤弓 ㅣ 兮 the red bows all unstrung.

怊 ˛*chʻao* To be grieved; extravagant.

ㅣ 悵 grieved, as a child mourning for his mother; disheartened.

抄 ˛*chʻao* From *hand* and *few*; it is much interchanged with *chʻao*ʾ 鈔 a bill.

To seize a little, to take some; to search, to hunt up; to lade out; to transcribe, to engross; to confiscate, to escheat, to sequestrate.

攻 ㅣ to attack from behind, to come on an enemy unaware.

ㅣ 錄 or ㅣ 寫 or ㅣ 謄 to transcribe, to copy; as ㅣ 案 to write off the records of a case.

ㅣ 白 copy it out fair, as from a 手 ㅣ or manuscript copy.

ㅣ 批語 to copy an official decision

ㅣ 化 to beg, said only of mendicant priests.

ㅣ 家 to search and seal up a house, as when confiscated.

ㅣ 錢用 to embezzle money intrusted to one.

京 ㅣ the Peking Gazette; in the provinces it is often copied out.

匙 ㅣ to take out with a spoon.

ㅣ 覽本 to copy other's compositions, as at the examinations.

In *Pekingese*. Near, as a crosscut; to fold up.

走 ㅣ 道 go by the nearest road.

ㅣ 手 to put the hands in the sleeves, and sit idle.

耖 ˛*chʻao* To harrow ground over after ploughing; a harrow with long teeth to break clods; to scatter seed.

譟 ˛*chʻao* To speak for another, to state a case in behalf of another.

巢 ˏch'ao The original form represents a 臼 *nest* on a 木 *tree* under *leaves.*

A nest on a tree, distinguished from ˏk'o 窠 one on the ground; a lurking-place, a haunt, a retreat, a den; used to designate the holds or camps of an enemy or rebels; to nestle; to make a nest; a sort of pandean pipe; a small ancient state, now Ch'ao hien 丨縣 in Lü-cheu fu in Ngan-hwui, north of Wuhu on the Yangtsz' River; it was here in Nan Ch'ao 南丨 that T'ang imprisoned Kieh, the last sovereign of the Hia dynasty, B. C. 1766.

雀丨 or 丨窩 a bird's nest.

百鳥歸丨 the birds have gone to roost; *met.* a wooded, rural region, the resort of birds.

丨居 to lodge, to sojourn at a house.

賊丨 a resort of robbers; the enemy's (who are always deemed to be rebels) camp.

毁丨 to rout out the robbers.

丨父 a sage in the days of Shun, who when asked to take high office, washed his ears to remove the defilement.

無丨穴 houseless, beggared, destitute.

丨穴 to skulk in, as a brigand.

In *Cantonese.* Crumpled, wrinkled; rough, like a piece of coarse paper; shriveled, as dried fruit.

好似亞婆皮咁丨 as wrinkled as a granny's face.

丨䁯䁯 wrinkled, creased, rumpled.

漅 ˏch'ao A lake in Hoh-fi hien 合肥縣 in Nganhwui, which produces gold fish; its name, meaning *nest water*, has probably a reference to its position.

轈 ˏch'ao From *chariot* and *nest*, referring to the form and use.

A turret or lookout place on a war-chariot, from which to observe the foe.

潮 ˏch'ao From *water* and *morning;* referring to the notion that the water every morning returns to the sea.

The early tide; flood tide; a tide, called 地之喘息者 "the breathing of the earth;" moist, damp.

乘丨 to avail one's self of the tide.

順丨 a fair tide.

逆丨 a head tide.

丨ʻ長 and 丨退 the tide is rising, the tide is falling.

丨蒸 to become damp and heated, as grain.

丨濕 damp, as ground or a thing; said too of 丨田 tidal grounds.

反丨 becoming damp again.

丨氣 damp, miasmatic exhalations; *met.* stupid.

丨水滿了 the tide is now at high water; same as 丨平 water is at its level.

丨州府 a prefecture in southeast of Kwangtung, whence 丨腦 means camphor in the north of China, as it comes from there.

鼂 ˏch'ao A marine animal, called 匽丨, said to sing in the night and go into the sea by day; the animal here referred to is perhaps the lamantin, found in the Indian Archipelago.

僬 ʻch'ao Tall, as a man; small.

丨丨 stately, tall.

丨長大漢 a fine looking tall man.

傭丨宇而處焉 he rented a small lodging and lived therein.

炒 燭 鬻 ʻch'ao From *fire* and *few;* the second and third forms have gone out of use.

To roast in a pan; to fry in oil or butter till dry; to pop, as is done with kernels of rice or maize.

乾丨 to fry brown, to roast to dryness.

丨茶 to roast or fire tea-leaves.

丨米 to roast or brown rice.

丨栗子 or 丨風栗 to roast chestnuts.

丨賣 to fry and sell, as a traveling cook or huckster.

煎丨 fry it in fat.

丨熟 to roast thoroughly.

麵 ʻch'ao Dried provisions taken for a journey, as wheaten cakes.

吵 ʻch'ao From *mouth* and *few;* it is nearly synonymous with the next.

A clamor, an uproar, a hubbub; to wrangle, to quarrel; to disturb, to annoy, to interrupt.

丨鬧 a violent altercation; loud scolding; a brawl.

相丨 quarreling together.

嘈丨 to make a noise and a row.

丨人耳 to make a din in one's ears, as the clang of cymbals.

大丨一塲 a great hubbub.

作丨 to raise a rumpus, as evil fellows do.

Read *miao*ʾ. The cry of pheasants or other fowls.

訬 ʻch'ao Used for the last. To annoy; graceful, light, nimble; rapid; strong; cunning, deceitful.

丨擾 to disturb; to trouble another.

丨輕 troublesome and flippant.

丨婧 graceful; 丨婡 high.

鈔 ch'aoʾ From *metal* and a *few;* or ˏ抄 contracted, with which it is constantly interchanged.

A document, a voucher, a government paper; a receipt; a passport, warrant, or similar official paper; paper-money; to take up, as with pincers, or a pinch in the fingers; to copy, for which ˏch'ao 抄 is most correct; a little.

丨錢 paper money, of which those under 1000 cash were called 小丨 small bills; and larger ones 大丨 great bills.

丨票局 a Government bank, a bank of issue.

丨關 an office for stamping duty receipts on goods; a douane.
船丨 tonnage-dues; port charges on ships.
放丨 to burn paper money to Neptune.
攻丨 to force people to pay taxes.
費丨 to waste money, lavish.

吏丨 historical readings; studies in history.
稅丨 transit dues; duties.

耖 *ch'ao'* To plough or harrow the ground.
丨田 to cultivate the land.
帶水三丨 when the water is on rake it thrice.

艸 *ch'ao'* A vessel rolling and tossing on the water; uneasy and pitching.
風狂舟丨 the vessel rolls when the wind is high.

趠 *ch'ao'* Occurs used with *ch'oh*, 踔 to stride.
To limp, to walk lamely.

CHÉ.

Old sound, ta, tak, *and* tat. *In Canton,* ché; —*in Swatow,* chia, ché, *and* su; —*in Amoy,* chia *and* gan; —*in Fuhchau,* chie *and* chié; —*in Shanghai,* tsé *and* tsò; —*in Chifu,* ché.

遮 *ˏchö* From 辵 to *go* and 庶 *people.* To cover, to screen, to shade, to veil; to cut short, to intercept; to shut off, as light; to protect from; and hence the thing that protects, as an umbrella, a parasol; to care for.
丨掩 to hide from view; to hush up, to conceal.
丨羞 to veil what modesty requires; to parry, to evade, as an accusation.
丨飾 to disguise, to excuse, to throw dust in one's eyes.
丨灰 to screen from the dust.
丨攔 to fence off; to protect by an inclosure.
一把丨 a sun-shade or parasol.
雨丨 an umbrella. (*Cantonese.*)
丨太陽 to shade from the sun.
丨不得 it will not cover it; it can't be concealed.
丨蓋 cover it over; to cloak.
丨蔽 to hide, to conceal.
丨擋 to stand between, to take the part of; to impede.
丨醜 to hide one's shame; thoroughly mortified.
周丨 loquacious; great, discursive, as talk.

傶 *ˏchö* Firm.
丨儸 firm, but not virtuous; one says, artful, clever at schemes; and another defines it, unauthenticated, unproven.

嗻 *ˏchö* To screen; loquacious, babbling.
囉丨 garrulous; to vociferate, as an excited crowd.

謶 *ˏchö* Used with the preceding.
To reprimand, to abuse; to hope for; to deceive.
費周丨 to talk much and not to convince.

者 *ˋchö* Said to be formed of 自 *self* contracted to 白 *white,* and 旅 a *stranger* contracted to resemble 老 *old;* others make it from 多 *many* and 白 *white; q. d.* one distinguished among *many,* one having *éclat.*

A *pronoun,* this, that, it, which, what; when it is the subject of the proposition, it comes at the end of the entire sentence, and thus differs from 所, which comes before the verb; as 不得而能至丨未之有也 of those who succeed without laboring, there are none; as a relative pronoun, 這 is now colloquially used instead.

When following verbs, it forms sometimes the concrete, and sometimes marks the person after a verbel phrase; as 行丨 a walker; 冠丨 he who has been capped; 觀丨 the observer; he who looks.

As a disjunctive *particle* it is preceded by 也; as 中也丨天下之大本也 a just medium—that is the real basis of a country.

After nouns it indicates a class as 愚丨 the foolish; 死丨 the dead; 賢丨 worthies; 無情丨 people without affection; 先死丨後死丨 we who shall die first, you who will die last.

It also puts the noun it follows in the abstract, as 誠丨 perfection; 誠之丨 he who is perfect; 性丨 nature; 元丨 the origin; 駕以行丨 whatever is for riding in; 中也丨 this midst of which we speak.

It is often used in this way between single words or phrases, and puts them in apposition; 天丨理也 heaven—a principle; 仁丨愛也 humanity [consists in] love; 德丨本也 virtue, that is the basis; 仁丨樂山 benevolent people delight in hills; 居丨處也 the word *kü* 居 means to dwell at (or in) a place.

As an adverbial particle, or to arrest attention; 啟丨 to commence; —though at the beginning of a letter, this should be rendered, I who commence; 昔丨 formerly; 或丨 perhaps; 曩丨 recently; 一丨 once, this time only 今丨一逝丨 now—then, hereafter.

不爲丨與不能丨之形何以異 what is the difference between those who do not, and those who cannot act?

仁丨安仁智丨利仁 humanity makes man happy, wisdom profits him.

赭 'chĕ From *reddish* and *that which*. An ochre color; a reddish brown or carnation, like nankeen.

丨石 ochrey stone, used as a coarse paint; it is hæmatite iron ore, and one sort, called 代丨石 is brought from Taicheu fu in Shansi.

丨衣 a felon's dress, which is often made of nankeen.

丨其山 made the hill brown — by clearing it of trees.

這 这 这 迠 chĕ' From to *go* and *words*; it was originally read *yen'*; the contracted forms are common in cheap books.

To meet, to receive; a demonstrative pronoun or particle; this, the nearest; here; now; this thing.

丨裏 here; 丨個 this.

丨樣 so, thus, this way.

丨等 such, this sort.

丨兒的人 people of this place.

丨時候 now, at this time.

丨麼下雨不止 such an incessant rain.

丨件事情 this affair, this matter.

丨還了得 that beat's all!

In *Cantonese*. An adverb of time, placed at the end of a sentence; just now; shortly; momentarily; a form of the subjunctive.

打過丨 let me whip you.

等吓丨 stop a moment.

蔗 藷 樜 chĕ' The first is the form given in the dictionary, but the second is most common; the third occurs very seldom.

The sugar cane (*Saccharum officinarum*) grown in southern provinces, called 甘丨 sweet cane, or 竹丨 bamboo cane, and 竿丨 reed cane; 鉄丨 dark or reddish cane;

丨寮 sugaring sheds.

刻丨 or 榨丨 to extract the juice.

熱丨 boiled cane, hawked about for sucking.

丨渣 and 丨粕 the refuse after grinding, cane shreds.

丨尾 the cane slips for planting.

丨合 tuft of top leaves.

柘 chĕ' Sometimes used for the last. Also a small tree, having oval, acuminate leaves, on which wild silkworms feed; the Quercus or silkworm oak of China; the trunk is straight, bows are made from the wood, and the root furnishes a dye, once used for making the imperial yellow.

拏丨 a small, thorny sort, on which silkworms also feed; resembling a scrub oak.

鷓 chĕ' The common partridge or 丨鴣; the grouse and francolin are probably included under this term in some parts of the country.

䗪 chĕ' A sort of grasshopper; also an insect found in rat holes, flat like a turtle and scaly; it is probably a sort of land *Isopoda*, or wood-louse; or perhaps a large species of Porcellio; another name is 土鼈 ground turtle.

丨蛛 a sort of serpent.

CH'É.

Old sounds, *t'a*, *t'ap*, and *t'at*. In Canton, *ch'é*; — in Swatow, *ch'ia*, *chi*, and *chⁿi*; — in Amoy, *ch'ia*, *ch'é* and *ku*; — in Fuhchau, *ch'iè*, *kü*, and *ch'ie*; — in Shanghai, *ts'ò* and *ts'a*; — in Chifu, *ch'é*.

車 'ch'ö The original form is intended to depict the body, wheels, and axle of a carriage; it forms the 159th radical of a large natural group of characters relating to vehicles.

A wheeled carriage; a cart, barrow, coach; a frame with wheels in it, as an irrigating trough or lathe; to turn a wheel, to turn over; a frame-work.

丨輪 or 丨轆轤 a cart-wheel.

一輛丨 one cart.

丨夫 or 赶丨的 a cartman; a charioteer, a cart-boy.

敢扳丨駕 I presume to arrest your carriage, — to invite a guest.

轎丨 or 單套丨 a one horse cart.

丨圍 the covering on a cart-top.

丨脚 or 丨價 or 丨錢 cart-hire.

丨棚 an awning over the horse; the calash of a carriage.

風丨 a windmill; a whirligig.

旋丨光 to polish on a 丨牀 or 丨架 a turner's lathe.

滑丨 a pulley; and 滑丨架 a pulley-block.

大丨 or 長丨 a baggage cart.

指南丨 an old name for the mariner's compass.

小丨 a wheelbarrow.

丨過 turn it over

丨剝 to exact usury (*Fuhchau*.)

天丨 an elevator.

下丨伊始未及周知 he has just reached his jurisdiction, and is not yet conversant with everything.

丨前草 the cart-way grass, the plantain, (*Plantago major*) used as a diuretic.

丨玉 to work gems, to cut jade.

三丨 the three carriages, a Budhist term for three modes of crossing *sansara* to *nirvana*, as if drawn by sheep, oxen, or deer, which shadow forth the three degrees of saintship; this term (*triyana*) is also written 三丨之教 and

三乘 three vehicles, and is further used for three developments of Budhist doctrine.

Read ꜀*kü*, and used for large vehicles; but both this sound and ꜀*ch'é* are given it in sentences without any real distinction in sense.

The chariot in Chinese chess; its powers resemble those of the queen; the black piece is distinguished from the white by being written 俥, with 人 at the side; a wheel in mechanics.

兵丨 war chariots.

公丨 a public office.

丨馬臨門 carriage and horses at the door; *met.* a rich man.

一丨兩馬 two horses to a chariot.

牙丨 or 丨頰骨 the jaw-bone.

砗 ꜀*ch'ö* An aluminous mineral, 丨磲 with pearly luster, and veined; the opaque white official buttons for the sixth grade are made of it; it is brought from Yunnan; the name seems to have been given from the veining resembling that in the 車渠 or mother-o'-pearl shell; it is a kind of pyrophyllite.

撦 扯 ꜀*ch'ö* From *hand* and *to spread open;* the second is a common but vulgar form.

To tear open, to rive, to pull apart; to tear away; to pull up or on; to haul, to drag; to track.

丨上 haul it up on top; hoist!

丨開 to pull apart.

丨篷拉縴 to hoist sail and haul the tow-line.

住丨 haul it fast, as from sliding.

丨住降驢 to pull an obstinate donkey.

尋丨 to gather up the thread of.

丨破 or 丨碎 to tear in pieces.

丨衣衿 to hold on by the lappel, as a child.

In *Cantonese.* To abscond; to clear out; to scud, to skedaddle; to send off; to go.

我丨咯 I'm off!

丨住 to detain, to keep back.

丨埋 pull it close up.

哆 ꜀*ch'ö* To open the mouth wide, to gape; to loll the lip, a drooping lip.

丨然 with one consent, the popular wish.

CHEH.

Old sounds, *tit* and *tip*. In Canton, *chip*, *chit*, and *ship*; — in Swatow, *chi*, *chiet*, *tiet*, *niap* and *sip*; — in Amoy, *chiat*, *sék*, *liap*, *siap* and *chih*; — in Fuhchau, *chiek*, *niek*, and *tiek*; — in Shanghai, *tseh* and *seh*; — in Chifu, *cheh*.

折 *chö*꜆ ꜁*shö* From *hand* and *ax*; explained by a reference to frozen plants snapping in two; it must be distinguished from *ts'eh*, 拆 to tear.

To sunder, to snap in two, to break off in the middle; to annul; to fold; to oppress, to repress; to decide or discriminate between; to deduct; to stop; to reprehend; to injure; to lose one's heir; to exchange or lose in trade; to make amends for, to set over against; to break and then rejoin; to abate, to lower; part of a coffin, a matted frame laid above it to receive the dirt; act of a play; to be deprived of one's future peace by dying unmarried, the succession being lost.

丨損 to injure, to break.

丨獄 to decide causes, clear the docket; to make a jail delivery.

打丨了 broken or snapped off.

丨節下交 to condescend to all classes.

每疋丨量二石 each piece was reckoned at two stone of corn.

將功丨罪 to atone for error by future merit, as officials do.

曲丨 to twine and bend; to allude to.

面丨 to reprimand personally; to take to task, as an elder brother has the right to do.

丨價 to abate the price.

丨扣 or 扣丨 a discount.

丨服 to induce rebels to yield, as by a defeat.

丨不得 it won't break.

幾成丨還 what dividend will you pay?

丨福 to lose one's mercies; to waste things.

工人丨算賬目 to mortgage one's labor to pay a debt.

丨對證 to decide as umpire or referee.

丨兌 to sell cheaper; to retail.

丨中 to decide equitably; broken in the middle.

蟾宮丨桂 to obtain the honor of a *küjin* from the emperor; the phrase refers to a legend connected with the moon.

凶短丨 an untimely and disastrous shortening — as of life.

丨餉 or 丨席 a money equivalent for rations.

丨磨 greatly afflicted, as if broken and ground to powder.

丨墮 reduced to extremities.

In *Cantonese.* To tickle; to spatter at; to spurt, as from a hose.

㯰 *chö*꜆ To join a seam; to cut or engrave.

丨縫 to join or rabbet planks together; to sew a seam.

蜇, 蜥, chŏ' To sting; a sting, or whatever insects use to wound their enemies.

丨吻 to sting the lips.

海丨 or 丨皮 the dried skins of various sorts of jelly-fish or sea-blubber, known as 水母 when alive. The last form is most commonly used for this meaning; it also denotes a kind of swimming crab, which is edible.

哲, 喆, 悊, ₍chŏ From *mouth* and to *snap*; the last two forms are seldom used.

Wise, sage, perspicacious; to know intuitively; discerning; versed in, fully aware of.

明丨 sagacious, shrewd, knowing.

濬丨 judicial clearness; said of the emperor Shun.

聖丨 intuitive wisdom, as of the sages; said of the emperor.

浙, chŏ' From *water* and to *break*.

A stream in Chehkiang, a feeder of the Ts'ien-t'ang River, from which the province 丨江 derives its name; it is said to mean the bore or *eagre*, which often breaks at the embouchure; also a river in the west of Honan; the province of Chehkiang; to scour rice; to rain.

門對丨江潮 the door [of the temple] looked out on the tidal bore in the Chehkiang.

慴, chŏ' From *heart* and *listening* to whispers.

Afraid, agitated; to subdue, to influence, to bring under; pusillanimous, disheartened.

丨服人心 to win people's hearts.

丨慴 cowardly, afraid.

欇, ₍chŏ The branches of a tree swaying in the wind; a sort of vine that climbs trees, like the Glycine.

丨丨 the waving of trees, as 楓丨丨 the waving, fluttering maple.

丨虎藟 a trailing plant that runs over trees.

襵, ₍chŏ This is sometimes made synonymous with *t'ieh*, 褶, but the two are different.

A fold in garments made when ironing; a tuck; gathers, plaits, or flounces, like those in a Chinese lady's skirt; plaited, puckered.

打丨子 to fold, to plait; to lap over, as when tightening the dress.

百丨裙 an embroidered and plaited skirt.

丨被 to fold up bed-clothes.

摺, ₍chŏ From *hand* and to *practise* as the phonetic.

To injure, to destroy; to fold, to double together; to rumple; to pile up; a fold, a doubling; a paper properly folded, as an official document; the paper itself.

丨紙 to fold paper.

丨子 a document for government.

奏丨 a memorial to the Throne.

丨腰 to bend the body.

丨足申謝 to thank one with a graceful curtesy.

丨疊 to pile or fold up, as garments.

跑丨子 a fleet courier.

丨角 to turn down the corner, to make dog's ears.

丨畧 a written digest, a précis.

手丨 a paper for memoranda.

不要丨兒 you need not fold it.

丨人來 to induce one to give in or come in.

遞遺丨 the last will — of a statesman; it is sent up for the Emperor's inspection after the testator's death.

豨, chŏ' An old name for a hog in Honan and southwards; a term given to fat ones.

輒, 輙, chŏ' From *cart* and *long ears*, or to *take*; both forms are used.

The sides of a chariot, where the arms are carried; unceremoniously, abruptly; directly, without permission; a disease of the feet.

丨敢 I must forthwith presume; — an apologetic phrase.

丨然 hastily, suddenly, forthwith.

專丨 to reduce to one.

丨足長坐 to sit all day with benumbed feet.

耴, chŏ' Supposed to represent long ears, which are considered to be a sign of wisdom; it is now used only as a primitive, seldom conveying any meaning to the compounds.

讋, chŏ' To take up other's words; to quote or mimic what others say; verbose, talkative.

牒, chŏ' From *flesh* and a *slip*.

To slice off meat; to mince, to hash meat; a hash of mutton, beef and fish.

鞢, chŏ' A scabbard, a case for a knife; one author defines it soft leather.

CH'EH.

Old sounds, *t'it* and *t'ak*. In Canton, *ch'it* and *ch'ak*; — in Swatow, *t'iet*, *ch'é*, and *chek*; — in Amoy, *t'iat* and *ch'ők*; — in Fuhchau, *t'iek*, *ch'ah*, *ch'aik* and *chak*; — in Shanghai, *ts'eh*, *ts'ak* and *săk*; — in Chifu, *ch'eh*.

徹, *ch'ö'* From 彳 to *step* and 攴 to *tap*, with 育 to *rear* between them; it is often interchanged with the next two.

Pervious; discerning, perspicacious; to penetrate, to go through; to remove; to peel off, to skin; to cultivate during the Cheu dynasty, a tithe; on a share system of rental; mutual division of crop; a road, a bye-way; to destroy.

慣丨 or 通丨 to penetrate, to fully understand.

丨底查明 to sift and investigate to the bottom.

丨田爲糧 he alloted the revenue on the land.

不透丨 superficial, not taking pains with, careless.

丨始丨終 to understand thoroughly, from first to last.

丨饌 to remove the dishes—when the band played at sacrifices.

丨侯 an order of merit instituted by Kao-ti, B. C. 201.

丨法 the rule for tithing.

撤, *ch'ö'* Similar to the preceding and easily confounded with it.

To remove from or to one; to recall; to send off, to reject, to set aside; to flay.

被風丨去 the wind whisked it away.

丨開 to remove; to peel; to take off, as a wrapping.

丨回 to withdraw or cancel, as a license; to recall, as an officer from his post; to do away with.

丨任丨委 to supersede an officer by sending another.

酒丨子 a syphon, used to decant liquor.

不丨薑食 [Confucius] never omitted to eat ginger at meals.

丨災 to remove calamity.

丨席散枱 to clear off and leave the table.

丨去 to carry off the [table] things; to remove, as a shed.

澈, *ch'ö'* Occurs wrongly used for 徹 thoroughly.

Pellucid clear water, through which the bottom can be seen; water exhausted, run out, as in a channel; to search out.

澄丨 clear, pure; *met.* sincere in heart.

丨底根究 to thoroughly search a matter to the bottom.

轍, *ch'ö'* From 車 *carriage* and 徹 *thorough* contracted.

A rut, the track of a wheel; precedent, example; to follow a precedent.

仍蹈前丨 to follow in the old track; he acts as badly as ever.

涸丨 a dried-up rut; *i. e.* at the last gasp, used by borrowers.

丨可循 this precedent can be followed.

依丨而行 follow on in the old paths.

屮, *ch'ö'* The original form represents a plant sprouting; below is the root, with the culm shooting up and two plumules on its sides; it is only used as the 45th radical of a few miscellaneous characters, some of which refer to springing plants.

册, *ts'ö'* The form of the character is intended to represent a number of *slips* containing decrees tied together.

A slip, a memorandum with writing on it; to record on tablets; a register, a list, an inventory; a volume, especially one with a hard or board cover; records; a census; a patent or commission; to plan; to choose, to appoint.

塡丨 to enrol one's name in a list; to write in a list.

烟戶丨 or 丁丨 or 戶口丨 a list of the population, a census.

門牌丨 a door register, giving a list of the family.

造丨 to make a list of people or things.

丨封 a book sealed in an envelope.

黃丨 an imperial register of population.

丨爲王 he was promoted to be a king; to make a man a king, and give him the patent or invest him.

一本丨 one register.

書丨 and 丨卷 books, documents, archives, law-papers, &c.

史乃丨祝曰 the historiographer then recorded the prayer, saying.

柵, *ts'ö'* *cha'* From *wood* and *slips*; also read *shan'*; nearly synonymous with 閘 *ch'ah,*.

A palisade; posts of a stockade; a railing of posts; window-bars; moveable upright slats that serve for a door.

門丨 a sort of turnstile, a doorway railing.

丨欄 or 丨櫪 or 丨閘 a street stockade, or gateway of posts, used to divide the wards in a city.

連營立丨 the whole force raised a stockade.

看丨 the guard at a stockade.

籬丨 a fence, a line of posts.

丨棧 an inclosure of posts, as in a corral.

暮飽眠深丨愳愧主人恩 having plenty to eat and a wide park to sleep in, [the deer] might feel ashamed at its keeper's kindness.

硩, *ch'ö'* From *stone* and to *break*-off as the phonetic.

To drive off an ill-omened bird, which is building its nest near.

丨鳥巢 to destroy the nest of such a bird with a pole, or by stoning.

CHEN.

Old sounds, *tiam, tian*, and *tan*. In Canton, *chím* and *chín*; — in Swatow, *chiam*, *chⁿi*, *chian*, and *tian*; — in Amoy, *chiam, tiam, chian*, and *tian*; — in Fuhchau, *chieng*; — in Shanghai, *tsé*ⁿ, *sé*ⁿ and *dzé*ⁿ; — in Chifu, *chen*.

占 *chan* From 卜 to *divine* and 口 *mouth*; *q.d.* asking by sortilege; also read *chen'*, and used with 佔 to usurp.

To divine by casting lots; to observe signs, to wait for a verification; to look towards, as an augury; divination, sortilege; a lot.

丨卦 or 丨卜 to cast lots; the first is usually restricted to divining by the diagrams, or by the dried carapace of tortoises.

丨不靈 a false prediction or sortilege; — the reverse of a 丨驗 or 丨應 a verified lot.

丨算 consult the fates.

丨口卦 to predict by what one first hears; to tell fortunes merely by word of mouth; it is also written 口丨 to guess events, and have the words recorded.

童女丨燈花 a girl guessing fortunes by the lampwick.

丨斷 to decide a thing by sortilege, as in bibliomancy.

丨候 to foretell the weather, as farmers wish to do.

丨兆 to see a sign of; to discern the omens.

遺丨 a posthumous command, an order left behind one.

丨城國 Cambodia or Chiampa; the second name is an imitation.

沾 *chan* From *water* and to *divine*.

To moisten, to tinge; to receive benefits, to enjoy; to participate in, to be a recipient; obliged, benefited; infected with; affected by, imbued with.

丨恩 to receive favors; I have enjoyed kindness.

丨光 got it through your favor; also, to make some profit on, as a shopman does through a customer.

丨染世情 corrupted by bad company.

丨病 to catch a disease.

汗丨背 the perspiration wet his back.

苦樂均丨 sorrow and joy are equally divided.

丨着 soiled; influenced; infected; it usually means 丨污 defiled; made turbid, dirtied, — literally and metaphorically.

丨丨自喜 very well satisfied, conceited.

柳汁丨衣 the willow drops have soaked his clothes [blue]; *met.* he has become a *siutś'cai*.

深丨惠澤 I am deeply sensible of your great favor.

Read *tien'*. The old name of Loh-ping hien 樂平縣 in Ping-ting cheu in the east of Shansi.

Read *ˏt'ien*. A small stream in 壺關縣 in the south-east of Shansi, a branch of the River Chang.

霑 *chan* Interchanged with the last. A drizzling, soaking rain; to wet, to soak; pattering; soaked; to moisten; to bestow favors.

丨醉 dead drunk.

丨濕 wet through, — by the rain.

丨漬 or 丨潤 soaked through; moistened — by your kindness.

丨體 wet to the skin.

衣濕丨體 clothes are so wet as to cleave to the skin.

仁恩丨洽 imbued with your favors and goodness.

其丨其足 when [the ground] is thoroughly soaked.

氈 氊 *chan* From *hair* and *faithful*; the contracted form is common.

Felt of any kind; coarse fabrics, rough and nappy, as rugs, carpets blankets, felted hats.

丨帽 a felt hat.

丨包 a carpet bag.

丨子 a rug; if large, it is 地丨 a carpet.

塞坐幷肩丨 to huddle together on the rug in winter.

洋丨 a blanket; a carpet.

五彩丨子 a flowered rug; a Turkish carpet.

如坐針丨 [uneasy] as if you was sitting on needles.

邅 𨓸 *chan* The second form is unusual, and also means to hide away.

To turn around; to remove; to follow; to run; — unable to advance is 迍丨, usually referring to want of success in life, unfortunate in one's plans.

蹇丨 lame, halting in one's walk.

鸇 *chan* A kestrel or sparrow-hawk, with light grayish plumage, and swift and strong of flight in pursuit of its prey.

丨陰 ancient name of a place in Kansuh.

如鷹如丨 like hawks and kites.

鱣 *chan* From *fish* and *faithful* as the phonetic.

A large sea-monster, the sturgeon, described as 20 or 30 feet long, and weighing a thousand catties; the mouth opens below the muzzle, and a row of spines run along the back and belly; the body is scaleless, and the flesh yellow; it is also called 蠟魚 wax fish; 皇魚 imperial fish; and 黃丨 yellow fish.

丨鯨 sturgeons and whales; — to which unscrupulous men are likened.

饘 飦 *chan* Congee or gruel that has been thoroughly boiled, thick and rich.

丨粥 watery congee and thick porridge.

旜 Much the same as the next.
chan A silken banner of a reddish color, plain and triangular, used in the olden time to announce the prince's order or approach, because he had no emblazonry.

建醮丨壇 to set out and arrange an altar for worship; it is especially done by the Taoists when honoring Yuh-hwang Shangti.

旃 From 㫃 a *flag* and 丹 *crimson*, used with the last.
chan A silken banner; a staff bent at the top to allow the banner to hang well; it was used to call or to signalize a high officer; used for 之 as a final particle; attentive.

丨表 a signal flag.

戒丨 to respect or keep aloof from.

丨蒙 a term for the five years in the cycle having 乙 in them.

上愼丨哉 may he be careful.

舍丨 take it away; reject it, as a story.

栴 A red, hard, close-grained wood found in western China,
chan called 丨檀 in imitation of the Sanskrit *chandana* or sandal wood, but including too the Pterocarpus and Styrax trees; the wood is used for carvings, fine furniture, and boxes.

詹 Composed of 产 *high* 八 for 分 to *divide* and 言 *words; q.d.*
chan to talk high and unreasonably; as a primitive, its meaning seldom appears in the compounds.

Verbose, tattling; for which the next is preferable; at such a time; to oversee, to direct; excellent; a government augur in old times; to reach; sufficient, more than enough.

丨事府 the bureau which manages the households of the empress and heir-apparent; its officers are chiefly Manchus.

小言丨丨 the sound of low, unmeaning talk; gabbling; loquacious.

謹丨 to carefully provide.

譫 Talkative; nonsensical, wild or prattling talk.
chan 丨語 delirious talk of a sick man; heady, incoherent talk.

發丨話 or 打丨語 to talk like a fool or crazy person.

瞻 From *eye* and to *oversee* as the phonetic.
chan To look up, to reverence, to regard very respectfully; to revere.

丨視 to regard, look up to.

仰丨膝下 these children look up to you.

丨仰 to look up adoringly, as to a sovereign; to have an audience.

失觀丨 to make mistakes in public ceremonies.

民具爾丨 all people have their eyes fixed on you.

丨望 to long for, to anticipate, as if with bated breath.

丨彼日月 I look at that sun and moon; *i. e.* upon my troth, I am as true; a kind of asseveration.

顧丨 to look at thoughtfully.

丨禮 ceremonies of an audience, ritual forms; the term 丨禮日 has been used to denote the Sabbath, and 丨禮一 then means Monday, and so on.

丨國 name of a portion of Annam in the T'ang dynasty.

驙 A heavily laden horse; a white horse with a black
chan back; a unicorn.

颭 From *wind* and to *divine* as the phonetic.
'chan Anything moved off by the wind, especially the water when raised in waves.

風亂丨 the blast raises the waves.

招丨 to shake, as things in a tempest.

展 The original form is composed of 尸 *body* and 工 *workman* repeated four times, showing united action.
'chan

To open out, to unroll and inspect; to expand; to exhibit; to stretch out at one's ease; to judge of, to look into; to prolong; something great attained; true, sincere; cheerful, pleasant.

丨笑 to laugh.

丨眉 to raise the eye-brows, to look cheerful.

丨放 to blossom out; to open.

丨開 to open, as a book; to spread out, as a map.

丨看 to display for a sight; to inspect.

丨限 to extend, as the time.

丨發 to exhibit.

丨舒 gratified, at ease.

玉丨 may you open this—a phrase put on the address of a letter.

大丨奇才 to develop rare abilities.

丨幣 to display a bridal trousseau.

搌 To bind up; one says, to wipe away, as tears. This
'chan character is wrongly read *'nien* by many, in the sense of to twist, to curl, to twine; as 丨繩子 to twist thread; 丨錢 to take or pay a quota; but 捻 is more correct.

丨搭 stretched as wide as possible.

丨布 a duster to wipe a table.

輾 From *carriage* and to *open out*; it is also read *'ch'ăn*; and inter
'chan changed with *'nien* 碾 a roller.

To turn half over, to roll over on the side.

丨轉 to revolve; back and forth; over and over; to and fro.

丨轉難忘 continually thinking on, unable to forget.

水丨 a water mill.

Read *'nien*. To roll on.

車丨一道轍 the barrow has rolled (or made) one rut.

軆 ʻ*chan* From *body* and *faithful* as the phonetic.
Naked, nude; without any covering; to strip.
丨身赤體 stark naked and exposed.
丨清衣服 stripped off his clothes.

皽 ʻ*chan* To tear off, as a placard; to peel off, as a scab; the scurf skin, the epidermis; a scab; skin peeling off.
皮開肉丨 [beaten till] his skin broke and the flesh flayed off.

Read *tan*ʾ. The skin of the face chapped and sore.

顫 *chan*ʾ The head awry; shivering, chilled through; trembling, shaking; unsteady, as the hand.
四肢丨凍 the limbs shaking with cold.
寒丨 shivering; and 發丨 trembling, either from weakness or cold.
心驚肉丨 so terrified that the flesh creeps, as when in view of danger.
丨微微 a child blubbering or shivering, as when afraid.

Read ˏ*shen*. To smell.

穜 *chan*ʾ From *grain* and *faithful* as the phonetic.
A sheaf of grain; grain bound up in any way after it has been cut.

驏 *chan*ʾ From *horse* and *to roll*.
A horse rolling himself in the dust, commonly called 打滾兒 or 滾砂 making a whirl or boiling the dust.

贍 *chan*ʾ From *property* and a *shop*.
To scheme how to get the property of others by fraud or robbery.

檀 *chan*ʾ A kind of white veined wood, well fitted for making combs and spoons.

佔 **占** *chan*ʾ From *man* and *to divine*; this form is rather modern, and some etymologists call it erroneous; it is commonly employed to distinguish the two tones and meanings of the second form, which is also read ˏ*chen*. It is used for ˏ*ch'en* 覘 to see.

To usurp, to seize by force; to arrogate, to take a liberty, to assume; to possess; to trespass upon; to take improper precedence of.
覇丨 to invade and possess, as 糧田 fields for sowing.
丨先 to presume; to rudely take or go first; to push forward.
丨便宜 to take what one likes; to peculate, to take some profit or advantage; not considerate of others.
丨踞 to forcibly occupy.
丨多 to demand or covet more than one's share.
丨地步 to incroach a little, to make a grievance.
侵丨 to trespass on; to appropriate.
丨人妻女 to wheedle and get other people's wises.

Read ˏ*tien*. Careless, superficial; low; trifling; to skim.
丨侸 light, trifling; as 勿學丨侸 don't slight your lessons.
丨畢呫唔 to hum, to read in a low tone, as one turns over a book.

In *Pekingese*. To pay close heed to; to do faithfully.

丨身分ʾ to attend diligently to one's business.

戰 *chan*ʾ From *weapon* and *single*; others derive it from 戈 *weapon* and 獸 wild *beast* contracted.

Alarmed, terrified; fearful; to join battle, to fight with numbers; a battle; war, hostilities; military, pertaining to war; anxious dread caused by rumors of war.
對丨 or 步丨 or 相丨 to join battle, to fight.
丨陣 drawn up in battle array, on the 丨塲 battle-field.
丨死 or 丨沒 died in battle, as a 丨士 soldier.
血丨 or 酣丨 a long and severe battle; a bloody fight, as in a prize-ring.
丨勝 victorious.
丨鼓 drums sounding.
打冷丨 terrified, scared, as one going into the mêlée; to shiver, as with cold.
丨慄 or 丨懼 paralyzed, trembling with fright.
丨丨兢兢 frightened, quaking with consternation.
下丨書 to send a challenge, to declare war.
好ʾ丨鬭 pugnacious, given to quarreling.
焉有不丨而勝者乎 who ever yet got a victory without having to fight for it?
拇丨 to play the game of morra at a feast.
丨船 a war-junk; a man-of-war.
久丨 a veteran, one used to war; a long war.
免丨牌 a flag of truce, made of board with these three characters on it.

CH'EN.

Old sounds, *t'iam, t'ian, dian* and *t'am.* In Canton, *ch'ím, ch'ín* and *shín;* — in Swatow, *chiam, ch'ien,* and *t'ien;* — in Amoy, *ch'iam, ch'ian, tian* and *t'ian;* — in Fuhchau, *chieng, tieng,* and *ch'ieng;* — in Shanghai, *ts'éⁿ, tséⁿ* and *dzéⁿ;* — in Chifu, *ch'en.*

裧 *‚ch'an* A bordered curtain on a lady's cart, in which sense it is like the next two; a coverlet.

婦車有丨 a lady's chariot has curtains.

共轄有丨 the hearse had a fringe or curtain.

Read *‚tan.* Felt clothes.

襜 裣 *‚ch'an* From *clothes* and to *oversee;* the second form is least used.

An apron or flap; the skirt of a robe, which shakes when walking; a covering for the knees; to adjust the dress; flapping.

丨裧 or 前丨 an apron.

丨蔽 a screen, a covering.

丨丨 nice and trim, as a robe; a skirt flapping.

不盈一丨 not enough to fill one apron.

丨如也 neatly dressed.

幨 幓 *‚ch'an* Similar to the last; the second form is commonly used for valance.

The curtain of a carriage stretched along its sides; a screen on an entrance; the lappel that hides a seam; to break or snap off.

牀丨 a bed-curtain fringe or valance.

泪滿前丨 his tears bedewed his apron.

惉 *‚ch'an* Also written 怗 in this sense. Discord; a jarring noise.

丨懘 the discord of notes, harsh sounds that grate on the ear.

五音不亂則無丨懘之音 when the five notes do not confuse each other, there is no discord.

覘 *‚ch'an* From *to see* and *to divine.*

To spy, to peep; to glance at.

丨候 to wait in hope for;

窺丨 to have a sly look at.

梴 *‚ch'an* Long, slender, as a stick of timber; the pivot on which a rice beater works.

松桷有丨 the cedar rafters should be slender.

廛 壥 *‚ch'an* Composed of 广 *dwelling,* 里 *a village,* 八 *eight,* and 土 *ground,* to represent the 1½ *meu* which was allotted to each yeoman in a village; the second form is unusual.

A dwelling-lot assigned to a retainer; a shop, a stall; a square for a market; a town residence.

丨市 a bazaar; a market-place.

巡行丨肆 to inspect the shops and markets.

纏 *‚ch'an* From *silk* and *shop* as the phonetic.

To bind up, to wrap, to bandage; to entwine, to cling to; to implicate; to molest, to bother; intricate, involved; twining about; swathed.

丨脚 to bind up the feet.

丨腰 to lace the waist.

手丨 hindered; to impede one's acts or movements.

丨頭 to put on a turban; but 丨頭費 is the hire of a harlot.

丨袋 a waist-bag for carrying money or things.

丨累 to implicate, to get around one.

丨絆 to trip, as by a rope; involved, obscure, as a meaning.

丨綿 bound by many ties, involved with; to entwine; *met.* interminable; protracted, as illness.

丨繞 wound round and round; to bind about; to cord; implicate.

丨不清 he never stops, or gets done troubling me.

丨緊 to importune, to bother.

難丨 it is hard to get rid of his importunity.

延丨 delayed, hampered, as from circumstances; slow, as in recovery.

瀍 *‚ch'an* A small branch of the R. Loh, mentioned in the Shu King; it rises in Măng-tsin hien, and flows south by the city of Honan fu, near the entrance of the R. I into the R. Loh; and is about twenty-nine miles long; also, an affluent of the R. Han in Kuh-ch'ing hien 穀城縣 in the north of Hupeh.

躔 *‚ch'an* From *foot* and *market* as the phonetic.

To tread in, to follow in order; to revolve; the motion of the sun in his fixed orbit; a course; a trodden path, a rut.

日運爲丨 the sun moves in his orbit.

星丨 or 丨次 the courses of the stars.

丨度 the path of a star; the zodiac

丨迹 or 丨蹊 to follow a precedent, to tread in the old paths.

闡 *shan'* From *door* and *single.*

To open; to spread out, to enlarge from the original condition; to expand, as by instruction; manifest, plain.

丨明 to state clearly.

丨註 to illustrate, to comment on.

丨達 to make one to know.

丨拜天下 to enlarge the empire.

丨幽 to explain what is obscure.

丨邑 a city of Tsi, now Ning-yang hien 寧陽縣 in south of Shantung.

幝 ʽch'an An old carriage altogether worn out; the canopy of a carriage.
檀車丨丨 the ebony carriage is quite ruined.

譂 ʽch'an Incoherent talk, as of one in a fever; irregular and incorrect expressions.

諂 讇 ʽch'an From *words*, and *pitfall*, or an inner *gate;* the second form has become antiquated.
To flatter, to cajole; to lie to one by flattering, to worship a god, or praise a man, beyond what is due to them; to pander, to fawn, to court; adulation, sycophancy; gratifying to one's feelings.
貧而無丨 poor and yet no flatterer.
丨媚 sycophantic; to cajole, to play the lickspittle.
丨諛取容 to praise one, in order to get his favor.
丨笑 to laugh and joke with, in order to please.
丨人可鄙 the flatterer is despicable.

淫聲丨耳 wanton music tickles the ear.
丨佞 specious flattery.
上交不丨 meet your superiors without sycophancy.

囅 ʽch'an To laugh loudly.
丨然而笑 to laugh and smile with one.

蕆 ʽch'an Etymologists derive this character from 去 to *leave* and 貨 or 貝 *property* changed and combined.
To command, to order; to prepare; to release.
丨武以禦敵 to keep ready military means so as to meet the foe.
丨兵 to muster troops out of service.
丨備 to prepare, to get ready for.
丨事 to end an affair.

鏟 ʽch'an Also read ꜀ch'an. To pull or extend anything, to attempt steadily and persistently.
丨長了他 stretch it out longer, as cloth.
丨着辦 try it on if he won't give any more; make the attempt to get it.

搌 ʽch'an To strike, to beat.

嘬 ʽch'an The foolish look of a simpleton is 丨嗖; — a gaping, gawky look, as of a bumpkin.

韂 韉 ch'an' From *hide* and to *oversee;* the second form is rarely used.
A flap to protect the dress or the horse from the mud when riding; spatterdashes; a skirt to cover the dress.
鞍丨 saddle-cloths, housings; they are made of thin leather.
花驄錦丨 the piebald courser's gay housings.

簷 ch'an' Small sticks resting on the plate, on which to support and extend the eaves beyond the wall.

驂 ch'an' A horse traveling very fast; a rapid canter.

闖 ch'an' To open a door a little in order to peep; to obtain.
闚丨 to spy through a crevice.

貼 ch'an' Like the last; it is also read ꜀tien.
To spy or peep; to look at sideways; to eye another privily.
窺丨 to furtively spy at.

CHEU.

Old sounds, tu, t'út, du, dút, dju, tòk, *and* dòk. *In Canton*, chau; — *in Swatow*, chiu *and* tiu; — *in Amoy*, chiu, tiu, *and* liu; — *in Fuhchau*, chiu, ch'iu, tiu, tóu, *and* chéu; — *in Shanghai*, tseù *and* zeù; — *in Chifu*, chiu.

周 ꜀cheu Composed of 口 *mouth* and 用 to *use;* the three next derivatives are interchanged with it; as a primitive it usually conveys an idea of everywhere, if it influences the sense of the compound at all.
To provide for, to supply; to extend everywhere, to make a circuit; to environ; plenty, enough; secret, deep; subtle; a curve, a bend; open, honest, the opposite of 比 ʽpi; to the end, extreme; entirely; close, fine.
丨備 everything is ready.
丨密 secret; crowded, close together; well arranged, satisfactory; definite and particular; no defect.
丨朝 the famous feudal dynasty of Cheu which lasted from B. C. 1022 to 255, under thirty-four sovereigns; it was so called because the emperor's power reached everywhere.
丨旋 to treat friends cordially; to make a circuit; circulating, as the winds do.

丨全 to bring about a thing, to remove ill feeling, to carry through; everyway complete.

丨道 a broad road; but 道丨 means the windings of the road.

丨圍 or 丨匝 universal, everywhere, all around.

丨知 let all know; universal knowledge.

丨而不比 public and open, without selfish ends; nothing left undone or slighted.

丨納 give him the whole duty or tax.

夢見丨公 I was dreaming that I saw Duke Chen, *i. e.* I was asleep; said by Confucius, who admired him.

岐丨 a place in the south-west of Shansi, now K'i-shan 岐山, where 太王 planned the overthrow of the Shang dynasty.

待客不丨到 to fail to treat a guest properly; 不丨 also denotes a deficiency, "not enough to go round."

週 *ˎcheu* Frequently used for the last. To revolve, to circulate; to inform the people; a year.

丨年旺相 may the whole year be prosperous.

丨流不息 flows unceasingly, as the blood.

一丨 one turn or revolution; as 一丨遭 all the way around it.

丨圍百里 a hundred *li* around it.

丨時一樣 he is ever the same.

對丨 return of the year.

徟 *ˎcheu* Hurried; 丨徫 to walk in an irregular manner; fluttered and impatient; bustling.

賙 *ˎcheu* From *wealth* and *everywhere*. To bestow, as alms; to give; and usually intimates a free gift.

丨恤 beneficent, liberal.

丨濟 to relieve the poor; help the distressed people.

丨給 to give to.

禮物不丨 the offering or present is inadequate.

輈 *ˎcheu* A heavily laden cart; a wain overloaded in front; heavy; low.

椆 *ˎcheu* Interchanged with *ˎt'ao* 檮 in this sense.

An evergreen found in Hunan, furnishing a hard, tough wood, good for presses, thills, carts or poles; the bark of one sort furnishes a coarse paper; a tree like the Styrax; a pole for poling boats; name of a river.

In *Fuhchau.* A closet, cupboard, or cabinet.

舟 *ˎcheu* The original form depicted a *canoe,* three cross boads and a turned-up bow; it is the 137th radical, and the characters under it form a natural group.

A vessel, a boat of any sort, a "dug-out;" to go in a boat; to transport; if the people are likened to a water, the prince is the boat; a stand for a cup; to carry in the girdle.

丨牧 the captain of a boat, or a flotilla; 丨子 a ferryman.

何以丨之 what did he carry at his girdle?

丨載 cargo of a vessel; to transport.

丨次 on board a vessel; a landing-place; 丨次大沽 the boats are lying at Taku.

一葉扁丨 one punt, one dingey; a wherry.

丨車並途 the water and land routes are parallel.

丨之 to boat it; to take a thing with one.

丨山 or Chusan I., so called from its shape being thought to resemble a boat.

侜 *ˎcheu* To cover close; to shade and conceal; a veil, a shade.

誰丨予美 who has deluded my beautful one?

丨張 false; to deceive.

輖 *ˎcheu* A square frame or dash-board in front of a carriage, supporting and protecting the driver's seat, and covering the thills.

梁丨 bended poles at the end of the thills.

鵃 *ˎcheu* From *bird* and *boat.*

A sort of crested lark or bob-o'-link, called 鶻丨 or 鶻鳩 whose song is heard in the morning; native writers liken it to the magpie.

丨了 a narrow, long boat.

州 *ˎcheu* The original form represents three *mounds,* around which the *water* flows; as a primitive, it is used chiefly to impart its sound.

An islet, a place in the water where men dwelt, for which the next is now used; a political district, ranking next to a *fu* or prefecture; anciently comprised 2500 families; of old a grand division of the empire; a continent; a dwelling; a horse's rump; a region, a spot, a place; a time.

丨里 a neighborhood, a hamlet.

知丨 a district magistrate of the highest grade, having a 丨同 for his deputy, and a 丨判 for his assistant judge or syndic.

九丨 the nine divisions of China in the days of Yü; *met.* the world.

丨吏目 or 丨目 the city jailer; an inspector of roads.

神丨 a poetical name for China.

洲 *ˎcheu* From *region* and *water;* occurs written *ˎcheu* 州, in old books.

An islet, one small enough to be seen at once; a place where men and birds collect and dwell; the term is chiefly used on the southern coasts, 島 is more common on the northern; in *Budhism,* a *dwipa* or continent; 勝神丨 is the continent of "those who conquer the spirit" (*Purva-Videha*); or 離體丨 "those who leave the body," the great continent on the east, whose inhabitants have semicircular faces; and 勝 丨 "the superior continent," is the northern continent of *kuru-dwipa* or *uttara-kuru* 俱盧 丨 where the inhabitants have square faces.

沙 丨 a low island; a bank awash in a river or sea.

丨 田 alluvial fields; made lands.

九 丨 the Nine Islands near Macao.

盩 ˓cheu To strike; to pluck out; the winding lines of hills; a place called Cheu-chih 丨 厔 in Si-ngan fu in Shensi, south of the R. King, is so termed from its winding valleys.

譸 ˓ch'eu From *words* and *long life* as the phonetic.

Hurried, bustling; to impose upon, to hoodwink.

丨 張 爲 幻 to deceive; to delude by misstatements; to make a lying representation.

帚 箒 ˋch'eu The original form represents a 又 *hand* holding a 巾 *cloth* in the 冂 *house;* the second form with *bamboo* is most used.

To sweep up dirt; a besom of twigs; a broom,—written only with the second form.

執 箕 丨 the sieve and broom holder,—a term for a concubine.

掃 丨 菜 a species of goose-foot (*Chenopodium* [*Kochia*] *scoparia*), whose tender leaves are eaten; it is cultivated in Chihli for besoms and coarse brushes, which are prepared by simply drying and trimming the whole plant; the book name of 地 膚 is perhaps identical with it.

犸 ˋch'eu A kind of gibbon or macacus found in Sz'ch'uen, and said to be as large as an ass; it is the female of the *kioh* 玃, and perhaps denotes a species which has not yet been described; or it may be the dusky gibbon (*Hylobates funereus*).

抐 ˋch'eu To grasp, as a fan.

丨 扇 to flirt or hold a fan.

肘 ˋch'eu From *flesh* and *inch*, referring to the pulse at the elbow.

The elbow, the joint of the fore-arm, and also includes the wrist or fore-arm sometimes; a fore quarter of meat; to conceal, to hold in the elbow; to take by the wrist; an old measure of 2 or 1½ *chih*,—probably a cubit, or the length from the elbow to the finger-tip; the Budhists say it is the 16,000th part of a *yodjana*, or the 1000th part of a mile.

丨 腋 相 交 as near as the elbow to the side;—a dear friend, a near relative.

猪 丨 a fore shoulder of pork.

手 丨 the elbow; the wrist.

捉 丨 to hold one by the wrist.

欲 去 被 丨 when he starts it sticks to him.

交 着 丨 to fold the arms.

製 丨 之 虞 the dangers of a bare arm,—*i.e.* of want or exposure, referring to a sleeve that reaches only to the elbow.

酎 ch'eu' From *spirits* and *an inch.*

New, ripe liquor; pure, strong spirits, thrice distilled, and enjoined to be drunk by the sovereign in summer; it was prepared for the libations and feasts in the ancestral temple, and was made in the first moon so as to become mellow by the eighth moon, when it was wanted.

丨 金 or wine money, was a vail paid to chamberlains at a banquet by feudal princes.

坐 丨 punished for having vile spirits.

紂 ch'eu' A trace in a harness; the crupper of a saddle, which is made of wood and passes across the haunches; it is now superseded by the next.

丨 辛 or 丨 王 the infamous monarch, whose crimes caused the ruin of the Shang dynasty, B. C. 1122.

鞦 ch'eu' Used with the last. The crupper of a harness, called 丨 棍 on pack-animals; it is now usually merely a stick across the rump, fastened to the saddle by the ends.

胄 ch'eu' From 肉 *flesh* and to 由 *proceed;* not the same as the next.

Descendants, posterity; said only of the families of grandees.

丨 子 the oldest son.

丨 裔 posterity.

貴 丨 the sons of high statesmen.

世 丨 generations.

冑 伷 ch'eu' From 冃 *cap* and 由 to *proceed;* it is often confounded with the last, and with *wéi*' 胃 stomach; the second form occurs in the classics as a synonym, but is usually read *yiu*'.

A helmet, formerly made of rhinoceros' skin; it seems occasionally to denote a visor.

甲 丨 morions and cuirasses; defensive armor worn by warriors.

宙 ch'eu' From a *shelter* and to *proceed.*

To hold, as the earth does; all ages, past, present, and future; from remote antiquity till now.

宇 丨 之 江 山 不 改 yet the hills and rivers in the world do not change.

咒 說 ch'eu' From two 口 *mouths* over 儿 *man;* the first *mouth* was altered to *words*, in order to denote the verb; it was at first the same as 祝 to bless, but was subsequently employed by the Budhists for the *dharani*, a charm or magic formulas, which are defined 眞 言 true words.

To curse, to imprecate; to recite over spells; an incantation, an imprecation, a charm to hurt another; a litany, such as priests recite, and for which sense they employ mostly the form 咒 as a technic, using it only as a noun.

念｜or 誦｜ to recite prayers or incantations.

大悲｜ the charms addressed to Kwanyin.

｜罵 to curse, to blackguard.

賭｜ to invoke imprecations on one.

｜詛 to rail and curse one.

｜他死 may he die! curse him dead!

詶 *ch'eu'* To ask blessings on; to bless, to pray for; a man's name, a statesman during the T'ang dynasty.

籀 *cheu'* The seal character, called ｜書 or ｜文 from Ch'eu ｜ 太史, a high officer of Süen-wang of the Cheu dynasty B. C. 800, who invented this form of the character; to study.

晝 *cheu'* From 日 *day* and 畫 to *divide* contracted.

Daytime, daylight; half of the twenty-four hours.

｜夜不息 or 不舍｜夜 going on day and night; unceasingly.

｜爾于茅 in the day, collect your rushes [and reeds for the thatch].

白｜ broad daylight; openly.

｜寢 a siesta.

俾｜作夜 to turn day into night, as rakes do.

咮 *cheu'* To peck, as a bird; birds twittering; a star in Hydra.

鳥｜ the bill of a bird.

不濡其｜ [the pelican] never even wets his bill.

Also read *chu*. Talkative.

譸｜ loquacious, garrulous.

噣 *cheu'* Considered by some to be the same as the last.

To peck; the bill of a bird; a large bird with a crooked beak which eats its young.

CH'EU.

Old sounds, t'u, t'út, du, dút, dòk *and* t'òk. *In Canton*, ch'au; — *in Swatow*, ch'iu *and* t'iu; — *in Amoy*, tiu, siu, hiu, *and* t'iu; — *in Fuhchau*, t'iu, ch'éu, *and* siu; — *in Shanghai*, dzeù, ts'eù *and* zeù; — *in Chifu*, ch'iu.

抽 搊 *ch'eu* Composed of 手 *hand* and 由 *from*, which is a contraction of 留 to *detain*, as the phonetic; the second form is not common.

To take out with the hand; to lift; to take out, as a dividend; to levy or assess, as duty; to select, to draw, as a lot; to expand, as the plants in spring; to utter aloud; to raise water; to pluck up; to receive one's portion; to whip; a tenth, a fee.

｜收 to levy duty on.

｜頭 or ｜水 to take a fee or percentage; a commission.

｜起來 lift it up.

｜出 reject it; take it out.

草｜新綠漸知春 when the plants throw out green shoots, we know spring is coming.

｜筋 spasms or cramp; but ｜脚筋 is an old punishment of pulling out the tendon achilles.

｜一陣瘋 convulsed by spasms; quivering from a fit.

｜剎 to extort; to exact illegal fees.

拿鞭｜他 drive him off with a whip; 我｜你 I'll whip you!

加一｜ to add a tenth.

｜身 to go out, as on a visit.

｜身不暇 I've no spare time.

不能｜身 I cannot take the time; also, I cannot release or free myself, as from a visit.

｜身跑 he took himself off; he ran away.

｜閒 or ｜空兒 to take a little leisure or vacation.

｜份 to lay by a percentage, as for expenses.

｜實 lift it carefully.

｜砧 to weight or heft the stone — a martial test.

｜底 lift it by the bottom.

｜稅 to levy taxes, but not to include 私｜ illegal rates or fees.

｜案卷 to abstract the papers of a case from court.

In *Fuhchau*. To miss; ｜絲 to drop a thread in weaving.

In *Pekingese*. To smoke; it is also wrongly used for 縮 to shrink, to contract.

｜屜 a drawer in a table.

｜烟 to smoke a pipe.

惆 *ch'eu* Vexed, annoyed.

｜悵 dissatisfied, disappointed in one's wishes.

瘳 *ch'eu* From *disease* and to *fly high*.

To be healed, to cure; convalescent; to reform, as by teaching; remedy; an injury.

云胡不｜ does he say he is not yet well?

不｜ incurable.

病｜ healed; well; cured.

儔 *ch'eu* From *man* and *long life*; occurs used with the next.

A company of four, a party; a class, a sort; a comrade, a mate; fellows, friends; who? to cover, to screen.

｜類 a circle of friends.

匹 丨 a partner, a match.
丨 侶 a band of fellows.
丨 黨 a clique, a ring, a camarilla.
丨 爲'爲之 who will do this for him?
鶯 丨 a young bride; the phrase alludes to the oriole's voice.

疇 ꜀ch'eu From *field* and *long life*; used with the last.
A cultivated field, particularly a field of hemp; to till; to continue successively; to classify; a mate, a class; who; formerly; to aid.
故 丨 or 丨 昔 heretofore; time past, previously.
易其田 丨 to cultivate the arable fields.
丨 隴膏腴 the diked fields are rich and fertile.
九 丨 the nine fields, denote the divisions of Yü's Great Plan in the Book of Records.
丨 咨 who asked about it?

籌 ꜀ch'eu From *bamboo* and *long life* as the phonetic.
To calculate, to compute; to devise, to arrange, to plan; a time; a lot, a tally; a ticket, a tillot; an ancient division of a night watch, about fifteen minutes.
讀幾 丨 書 how many times have you read it?
攢 丨 or 執 丨 to draw a lot or tally.
꜀更 丨 to strike the hours, as a watchman; a clepsydras.
派 丨 to give out tickets, as to a soup kitchen.
丨 矢 to pitch reeds into a jar; name of an old game.
運 丨 幃幄 to plan strategy in his tent; *met.* a high general.
丨 策 or 丨 謀 to devise, to scheme; to set a trap for, to plan.
丨 畫 to settle and arrange, as a way of action.
丨 碼 a counter in play.
通盤 丨 算 to calculate the whole thing at once.
竹 丨 a tally or bamboo billet.

一 丨 莫展 he never proposed one plan; he has no cleverness.

躊 ꜀ch'eu Embarrassed.
丨 躇 irresolute, undecided; unable to get on, wavering.

酬 醻 酧 ꜀ch'eu From *spirits* and *region* as the phonetic; the other forms are unusual.
To pledge a guest; to urge him to drink, or toast him in return for his bumper; to recompense, to make a return; to repay, to requite.
丨 還 to pay, as a vow.
丨 酢 pledging, as a host and guest.
一 丨 一酢都非偶 even the interchange of wine-cups is not a fortuitous thing.
丨 謝 to return thanks, especially by a return present.
丨 愿 to make a thank-offering.
丨 神 or 丨 答天恩 to thank the gods; to acknowledge heaven's favor, as in being saved from fire or death.
應 丨 大 at a great expense, as for entertaining.
丨 金 a gratuity for services, as when one 丨 勞 requites for trouble.
丨 客 to return an invitation.

詶 ꜀ch'eu Occurs used with the last, and for *cheu'* 詋 to revile.
To answer, to respond.
丨 對 to reply to.

裯 ꜀ch'eu A single coverlet; a bed-curtain; to cover, as with bedclothes; an under-shirt.
衾 丨 coverlets and sheets.
丨 帳 a curtain.
Read ꜀*tao*. The sleeve of a coat.

怞 ꜀ch'eu From *heart* and *from*; also read *yiu'*.
Grieving, sorrowful; cast down and anxious.
憂心且 丨 a sorrowing and anxious heart.
丨 丨 careworn; weary and sad looking.

蓨 ꜀ch'eu A medicinal plant with a bitterish root, called 丨 蔯 and 地榆 the ground elm; it is a species of *Hedysarum*.

稠 ꜀ch'eu From *grain* and *everywhere*.
Grain growing rank and close; thickset, crowded; a crowd; dense, close together; viscid, stiff; thick, as paste.
人煙 丨 密 people closely crowded.
丨 人廣衆 a very great crowd.
恐 丨 人中迷失 lest they should lose each other in the crush.
丨 的稀的 there is both thick [soup] and thin.

綢 ꜀ch'eu From *silk* and *everywhere* as the phonetic; used with the next and last.
Thin silk; wash silks, like pongee, senshaw, or levantine; to bind; to wrap around, to twine; to hang with ornaments; thick; stiff.
生 丨 stiff or raw pongee.
熟 丨 soft or boiled silk.
丨 緞 silks and satins; a general term for silk goods.
紡 丨 reeled pongee.
綿 丨 silk and cotton mixture.
繭 丨 coarse serge of wild silk; raw crape or punjam.
丨 繆 to wrap around, to intertwine, to wreath; to hold consultation with.
線 丨 a kind of silk or thread camlet.
丨 ꜀行 a quilting needle.
丨 緻 fine, close woven, beautiful.

紬 ꜀ch'eu Used with the last when denoting pongee.
To draw out threads for weaving; a clue, a thread; to arrange the details of; to search, as a cause; to try the tone of a string.
丨 繹 to investigate the causes of.
織 丨 to wind off threads, as for weaving.

讐 讎 ꜀ch'eu } From *words* and two *birds;* the first is also used for ꜀ch'eu 酬 to pledge, and both are contracted to the next.

To contradict, to oppose in argument; to recriminate; to abhor, to hate; to compare and verify, to collate; to revenge, to pay off, to requite; an enemy, a competitor; dislike, enmity; to class; a sort, a match for or pair.

丨匹 or 丨對 or 丨類 the same kind; to class; to pair; an opponent, a rival.

寃丨 a wrong, a cause for revenge.

含丨 to cherish a grudge, for which one must 報丨 get revenge; it usually means blood revenge.

丨敵 an enemy, an opponent.

口丨 to asperse, to blackguard.

恨丨極 to hate, to detest; I cannot endure him.

隨價丨直 to get the real market price.

恩將丨報 to return evil for good.

仇 ꜀ch'eu An abbreviated form of the last. An enemy; to draw spirits and pledge a guest; proud; to unite; a pair; a companion.

丨人 my opponent.

宿丨 two men urged on by their unappeased dead ancestors to destroy each other.

與子同丨 I will be your comrade.

手丨 to hand up or draw spirits.

成丨 an appeased blood feud.

丨丨 mortal enemies; very proud, haughty.

Read ꜀kiu. A great portrait painter, named Kiu Ying 丨英, of the Ming dynasty, also known as Shih Cheu 石洲 Stone Island.

雔 讐 ꜀ch'eu } A brace of birds; the altercations of birds; to wrangle, to bicker; a silkworm found on the Ailantus tree.

犨 ꜀ch'eu The panting or grunting of an ox; to go out, to issue from; an old district in Honan.

丨牛 an old name for the yak.

丑 ꜂ch'eu The original form resembles a hand holding things; others say it is like 十 *ten* inside of 二 *two,* because the twelfth moon is called 丨月 ꜂ch'eu yueh,

The second of the twelve horary characters or branches; the second hour of the day from 1 to 3 o'clock A.M. or the fourth watch; it is denoted by the ox, and astrologers say that persons born in this hour are likely to be dull.

小丨兒 the merry-andrews in a play, the jesters; also called 丨脚; they paint their faces.

白丨 seeds of the morning glory (*Pharbites nil*), used as a purgative.

醜 ꜂ch'eu From *spirit* and *demon.*

Abominable, ugly, deformed, vile; disagreeable, disgraceful, shameful, ashamed; to dislike; shamefaced; ashamed of; to act violently; to compare, to bear a likeness to; a sort, a group.

命丨 an unhappy fate or lot.

貌丨 or 丨樣 ill-looking, as an ugly face.

不知丨 brazen-faced, hardened.

見丨 ashamed for — or of.

可丨 shameful.

怕丨 bashful, timid, maidenish.

丨類 scamps, vagabonds, hoodlums.

比物丨類 compare one sort with the other.

家丨 a disgrace to the family.

丨惡˒脾氣 a vile disposition; ungrateful; impertinent and impracticable.

小丨 a miscreant; a mean wretch.

丨事 or 丨行 disgraceful conduct.

繆丨 to presume and act rudely.

其實丨之 the reality is its reproach.

好丨 and 美丨 are opposites, good and evil; handsome and ugly.

臭 ch'eu˒ From *self* and *dog,* alluding to the scent; several characters under the radical 自 have this primitive in combination, to which it gives a hue of its meaning.

The scent of a track followed by a dog; to scent out; an odor, a smell, now confined to bad ones; effluvia, stench, putridity; disreputable, unsavory; to stink, to rot: heretical doctrines.

丨名 a bad reputation.

丨蟲 bed-bugs; *met.* foul-mouthed fellows.

丨氣 a bad breath; a stink; — not so noisome as 穢丨 putridity.

他們早就丨了 they will soon come to a quarrel.

遺丨萬年 to leave a perpetual reproach — upon one's name.

口丨 a foul breath; high priced, exorbitant; — a Peking phrase.

丨銅 "stinking copper," denotes a hardfisted miser, and an officer who bought his post.

丨腥 noisome, rank; putrid, as fish.

丨語難聽 vile talk ought not to be listened to.

丨東西 worthless, as a corrupt thing, or a scamp.

Read hiu˒. Fragrance; to smell; to injure.

丨之 smell it.

善丨 a pleasant smell.

胡丨亶時 how fragrant and in good season.

魗 ch'eu˒ To discard, to reject; bad, disagreeable, in which sense it is like the last.

無我丨兮 I don't wish you to cast me off.

趠 ch'eu˒ To go as if weary; to walk.

In *Cantonese.* To sprain, as the ankle.

丨親脚 I sprained my foot.

溴 ch'eu˒ Name of a stream which joins the Yellow River in Măng hien 孟縣 in the north of Honan; it is about fifty miles long; the effluvia of water.

CHI.

Old sounds, tei, tai, dai, ti, tat, dat, zhat, tít, dík *and* dít. *In Canton*, chi *and* chei; — *in Swatow*, ti, chi, chei, *and* si; — *in Amoy*, chi, si, ti, chu, *and* ché; — *in Fuhchau*, chi, ti, té, chie, chai, *and* ché; — *in Shanghai*, tsz,' sz' *and* dsz'; — *in Chifu*, chi.

知 ˓*chʻ* From *dart* and *mouth*, indicating the rapidity with which knowledge is communicated; it occurs interchanged with *chi*˒ 智 sagacity.

To know, to perceive; sensible of, to appreciate; to manage, as one who knows; to be acquainted with; to tell, to inform; an intimate friend, a fellow; knowledge, wisdom; to remember; healed.

聞 ｜ I heard so.

｜ 覺 to notice, to advert to.

有 ｜ 覺 self-conscious, having emotions, intelligent.

足 ｜ contented, satisfied.

｜ 識 or ｜ 曉 knowledge, information; to comprehend, to fully know.

｜ 過必改 you should reform when you see your faults.

誰 ｜ who knew it? *i. e.* nobody knows it; unexpected.

｜ 心 or ｜ 己朋友 an intimate friend, one who knows you.

｜ 道了 Ourself knows it; the thing is known to Us; used by the Emperor as a reply to reports and memorials.

｜ 風聲 aware of it; I have heard of it already.

故 ｜ an old friend.

｜ 確 I am sure of it; I know it certainly.

不 ｜ 底細 I do not know it thoroughly, or the reason for it.

明 ｜ 故犯 a misprision of treason; accessory before the fact.

無 ｜ 之徒 the doltish; ignorant fellows; uneducated rascals.

｜ 府 a prefect; *i. e.* one who knows the prefecture.

一 ｜ 半解 a moderate scholar, not well informed.

預 ｜ 子 a fortune-teller, a sight-seer.

不 ｜ ignorant of, unaware; unconsciously; unacquainted with.

｜ 事 a private or confidential clerk; also, a sub-abbot or sub-prior, a *karmadana* one who looks after the food, guests, buildings, &c., in a monastery.

｜ 政 to manage public affairs.

先 ｜ the old-time sages; 先 ｜ 者 a foreign term for a prophet.

｜ 遇 a patron, one who recommends another to office.

｜ 會 or ｜ 照 to tell to, to communicate; to inform in a semi-official or private manner.

茹 ˓*chʻ* A plant called ｜ 母 which appears to belong to Verbenaceæ; its seeds are used as a cooling medicine and expectorant.

蜘 ˓*chʻ* An insect, the ｜ 蛛 or a spider, applied to all the Araneæ or spider family; the etymolgy of the name is 知誅 *i. e.* the insect that *knows* how to *kill*.

｜ 蛛瘡 a ring worm.

之 ˓*chʻ* The original form represented a plant issuing from the ground, afterwards gradually altered to its present shape.

To go to, to progress; towards; for, in regard to; to pass from one state to another; the sign of the *genitive*, when placed between two nouns; after the subject of a verb, it becomes an expletive particle or like a partitive; as a *pronoun* in the accusative,—it, him, them; which, what; and in these cases shows the action of the preceding active verb; occurs used like ˊ*ché* 者 after a noun to make the abstract; or as a relative this, that; or to denote nouns in opposition; in most cases it must be construed with the preceding word; to leave behind.

聽 ｜ ｜ 人 the person who hears it.

天 ｜ 明命 heaven's plain decree.

如 ｜ 何 then how will it be?

如 ｜ 奈何 if so, how then?

未 ｜ 有也 there is no such thing.

未 ｜ 聞也 I have not heard of it.

心 ｜ 所 ｜ that to which the mind inclines.

｜ 子于歸 this same child (*i. e.* bride) went to her home.

天命 ｜ heaven orders it.

不知 ｜ ｜ 路 he did not know the road there.

行而不至者有 ｜ to go and not arrive at their destination, is not uncommon.

有三年 ｜ those who were three years old.

將何 ｜ where are you going?

無 ｜ nothing of it; impossible.

死 ｜ was killed or died; here it is a sign of the past tense.

有德 ｜ 人 a virtuous man.

大而化 ｜ ｜ 謂聖 [virtue] which is great and influential is called holy or sage.

鳥 ｜ 將死其鳴也哀 when the bird is dying, its note is sad indeed.

天后 ｜ 神 Tʻienheu that goddess, *i. e.* the goddess Tʻienheu.

｜ 死矢靡他 I swear to be faithful till death.

芝 ˓*chʻ* A plant, often drawn in the mouth of deers, and regarded as felicitous from its durability; six varieties of different colors are noticed; the preserved specimens, or wooden gilded models of it are common in temples; it is a sort of branching boletus, called 靈 ｜ 草 or 瑞 ｜ in allusion to its supposed power to prolong life; the *Polyporus igniarus*, or similar sorts of fungus; bringing good luck;

vivifying; a flower like an orchid.

丨蔴 the sesamum, which produces an oil, called 香油 from its fragrance, it is the *til* or *jingili* oil of the Hindus; the white seeds are used in cooking, and are sprinkled on cakes, whence speckled things are likened to them, as the 丨蔴貂 or Corean sable, from the white hairs in it.

丨蘭之室 the house of the Epidendrum,—a beautiful mansion; *met.* to be intimate with the good.

丨顏 your happy face, 丨宇 your house.

華丨 the ornamental orchid, refers to a state umbrella.

丨栭 a species of agaricus.

丨田 fields of sesamum—in fairy land, *i. e.* Mt. Meru.

支 *ch'* The original form represents a *hand* breaking a bamboo *sprig*; it is the 65th radical of a small group of incongruous characters.

A branch, for which the next is used; those that branch off, as posterity; to diverge; to hold, to withstand; to pay out,—and politely, that the one who asks may receive or draw out; to advance, as on goods; to succor, to prop; posterity, descendants; a sept, a tribe; subordinate, secondary; divergent, parting; to attend to; to bear up, to stand firm; to measure.

丨更 a watchman.

丨用 or 丨給 to give out, as 丨工銀 to pay wages; and 日中丨用 the daily outlay.

丨派 descendants; a tribe of.

宗丨 of the same clan or surname

近丨 nearly allied to, blood relatives.

横丨 a collateral branch of a family.

丨子 a child of.

丨裔 descendants.

丨離 irrelavent, vague, evasive, lying.

凡事丨吾 he delays in everything he undertakes; he is unwilling to do anything.

丨借 to lend.

丨消 to expend; expenses, outlay; receipts and disbursements, as given in by a steward.

本丨 root and branches; father and sons; the original stock and collateral branches.

病體莫丨 a weakened, ailing body is not equal to such work.

濫丨帑銀 to waste the public money.

分丨賬 an agreement or contract.

丨那 occurs in Budhist books for China; and 丨提 for the Sanscrit word *chaitya*, a tope or building that contains no relic.

停丨 to refuse advances; to suspend payment.

候丨 to gradually redeem [its paper]; to pay instalments.

地丨 or 十二丨 the twelve horary characters, given in the following table.

USES OF THE TWELVE HORARY CHARACTERS.

The application of the Twelve Branches to the hours of the day dates from before the time of the construction of the Sexagenary Cycle (B.C. 2637), and is ascribed to the Celestial Sovereign. They are also called *Ti Chi* 地支 Earthly Branches, and the animal which represents each branch is supposed to have great iufluence upon the destiny of the person born during the hour it rules; the Mongols, Coreans, Japanese, Siamese and Annamese apply these animals to the same signs; and the combination of the animal with the hours, and then with the zodiacal constellations, on through the points of compass, and the elements, all furnish the groundwork for the astrologer's skill and influence. To express European hours it is enough to prefix *kiao* 交 and *ching* 正 to the characters; thus, *ching-tsz'* 正子 is midnight, 交丑 is 1 o'clock A.M. and so throughout. Each Chinese hour is divided into eight *k'oh* 刻 of fifteen minutes each.

TWELVE BRANCHES.		SYMBOLICAL ANIMALS.	ZODIACAL SIGNS.	POETICAL NAMES.	CORRESPONDING HOURS.	POINTS OF COMPASS.
Tsz'	子	Shu 鼠 a rat.	Aries.	困敦	11 to 1 A. M. is 三更 3d watch.	NORTH.
Ch'eu	丑	Niu 牛 an ox.	Taurus.	赤奮若	1—3 is 四更 4th watch.	N.N.E. $\frac{3}{4}$ E.
Yin	寅	Hu 虎 a tiger.	Gemini.	攝提格	3—5 is 五更 5th watch.	E.N.E. $\frac{3}{4}$ N.
Mao	卯	T'u 兎 a hare.	Cancer.	單閼	5—7	EAST.
Sh'ăn	辰	Lung 龍 a dragon.	Leo.	執徐	7—9	E.S.E. $\frac{3}{4}$ E.
Sz'	巳	Shé 蛇 a serpent.	Virgo.	大荒落	9—11 is 上午 forenoon.	S.S.E. $\frac{3}{4}$ E.
Wu	午	Ma 馬 a horse.	Libra.	敦牂	11—1 P. M. is 正午 noon.	SOUTH.
Wĕi	未	Yang 羊 a sheep.	Scorpio.	協洽	1—3 is 下午 afternoon.	S.S.W. $\frac{3}{4}$ W.
Shăn	申	Heu 猴 a monkey.	Sagittarius	涒灘	3—5	W.S.W. $\frac{3}{4}$ S.
Yiu	酉	Ki 雞 a cock.	Capricornus.	作噩	5—7	WEST.
Süh	戌	K'üen 犬 a dog.	Aquarius.	閹茂	7—9 is 初更 1st watch.	W.N.W. $\frac{3}{4}$ N.
Hai	亥	Chu 猪 a boar.	Pisces.	大淵獻	9—11 is 二更 2d watch.	N.N.W. $\frac{3}{4}$ W.

枝 ˎch' From *wood* and to *diverge*; it is interchanged with the last.

A branch, a twig; a slender upright post, while a leaning post is called 梧; to branch, to scatter; a tributary, as of a river; a classifier of slender things, as pencils, pens, flowers, arrows, spears, coral, &c.

一丨花 a flower, *met.* a pretty girl.
一丨軍 a detachment of troops.
丨榦 trunk and branches.
丨棲 to roost on a branch; *met.* to get a post or literary position; a sinecure.
丨葉 leaves and branches.
其辭丨 to leave the subject, to branch off to another topic.
丨指 an extra finger or toe.
別生丨節 other shoots will sprout; disorders will spread; other contingencies may arise.
莫敢丨梧 he did not venture to become a pillar; *met.* to take the management.

肢 **胑** ˎch' From *flesh* and to *diverge*; the second form is vulgar.

The limbs.
四丨 the four limbs.
丨體 the body.
腰丨嬝娜 slim, small waisted, said of young girls.
丨解 to cut into four quarters; to quarter.

祇 ˎch' From *worship* and *reaching* to; not to be confounded with ˏk'i 祇 sacrifice, though the two are said to be mere variants.

A disjunctive conjunction, only, but, not only, yet; to invocate; to respect, as when seeing the gods; awe, regard; reverently; to attend to reverently.
丨敬 to venerate.
丨領 or 丨承 to reverently receive, as from the Emperor.
罔顧于天顯民丨 he did not regard the bright principles of Heaven, or the awfulness of the people.
丨可 however; still it can be.
丨望 to expect.
丨有一樣 there is only one sort.
丨丨 to revere what is reverend.
丨此 only this.

胝 ˏch' From *flesh* and *reaching* as the phonetic.

A thick, indurated skin on the hands or feet; a wart or callosity on the knuckles, said to proceed from eating too much pickled food.
手足胼丨 horny and callous hands and feet.

秖 ˎch' Grain when first ripe, or beginning to ripen; to transplant rice.

脂 ˎch' From *flesh* and *excellent* as the phonetic.

Horned animals of all kinds, whose fat is firm; fat, lard, suet, grease; viscid juices or dried gums of plants; applied to mineral bole and soapstone; to grease, to daub; wealth; glory.
胭丨 cosmetics, rouge; though 丨粉 is the white cosmetic, and by *met.* the fair sex, the girls.
民丨 the fat of the people, their money.
出泥入丨 to get out of disgrace or poverty into honors or wealth.
丨膏 greasy matter; unctuous; *met.* wealth.
丨飾 to paint — the face.
花丨 juice of flowers.
赤石丨 a red bole, used in making certain ointments; aluminous or unctuous earth.
丨車秣馬 he greased the cart and fed the horses.
龍骨木丨 a gum obtained from a species of Euphorbiaceæ.

卮 ˏch' The character is supposed to represent 人 a *man* with 卩 a *seal* underneath.

A cup to measure meat and drink; a goblet holding four gills; a syphon.
漏丨 a syphon to decant liquor; *met.* to waste, to run out at the spiggot.
玉丨 a jade or precious goblet.

梔 ˎch' From *tree* and *goblet*.

A plant whose seeds are used to dye yellow, the *Gardenia floribunda* and *radicas*, called 丨子 or 黃丨, the becho nut; when roasted it is the 黒丨, and is exhibited in fevers.
山丨 a small kind (*Gardenia florida*), of which the blossoms of some varieties are used to scent tea.
紅丨子 the *Gardenia rubra*.
丨榴爭妍 the jasmine and pomegranate contend as to their goodness.

鳷 ˎch' From *bird* and to *diverge* as the phonetic.

A lucky bird, referred to as the harbinger of joy.
丨鵲 supposed to be a bird akin to the magpie, whence the 丨鵲觀, a fine monastery in Shansi, built about A. D. 40 by Wu-ti, of the Han, derived its name.

吱 ˎch' In *Cantonese*. A particle indicating certainty; also that the act was immaterial.
丨丨係 certainly it is so.
丨丨聲 the buzzing of bees.

毸 ˎch' Light down, like that growing under the feathers; a soft kind of felt or plush.

搘 ˎch' A stone plinth which supports a tablet, called 丨捂, the socket; to prop, to shore up.
丨起窗戶 prop up (or open) the window, referring to such as have hinges at the top.

榰 ˎch' The base or plinth of a pillar when made of wood; the use of stone for bases and pedestals has now become general.

夂 ꜀ch' The original form rudely delineates a person coming behind another; its only use is as the 34th radical of a dozen unusual characters; most of which are themselves primitives, and relate to progressing.

止 ꜀ch' The original form represents plants growing on a border, which they define; it forms the 77th radical of characters, chiefly relating to stopping, modes of progress, &c.

To halt, to be stopped, as by the edge of a lot of land; to cease from, to desist; to be still; to remain, to wait; right deportment; to dwell, to lodge at; an object, that which the mind rests satisfied in; stopped, as a cough; hindered, detained; as a prisoner; a final expletive; as an *adverb*, but, only, however, not to stop at; but after a negative, it often makes a neat climax; — as 愛之如身不丨如子 he loved him not as a son merely, but as himself; used by the Budhists for ten trillions.

丨是 only is.

丨得 merely can.

不丨三個 not merely three, *i. e.* there are more than that.

丨血 to stanch blood.

知丨 he knows when to stop; sagacious.

丨息 to desist from; it came to a stop.

丨不住 will not, or cannot be stopped.

容丨 deportment, air; — but 口容丨 means not to talk at improper times, to keep the door of the lips.

丨怒 pacified; to calm down; appeased.

禁丨 to forbid; prohibitions.

可以丨則丨 stop when you like (or must); *i. e.* there is no help for it.

無丨之徒 a rascal who stops at nothing, a reckless fellow.

民所丨 whither the people tend, the national center or capital.

無定丨 no fixed purpose.

舉丨 or 行丨 deportment, bearing; acts, conduct, doings

丨渴 to quench thirst.

舉丨 to raise the foot — *met.* to go a plowing.

趾 ꜀ch' Interchanged with the last two, and used for the last.

The toes; the foot; a hoof; to stop; a foundation.

丨高氣揚 to step high or daintily and look pompous.

左丨 the left leg.

玉丨惠臨 let your feet condescend to come here; — used in invitations or notes to superiors.

請袵何丨 please say which way you wish to turn your mat — for sleeping on?

麟丨呈祥 the unicorn's hoof is given as a prognostic.

址 ꜀ch' From *earth* and *to stop*; it is also written like the next.

A foundation; the limits of a lot; fundamental; one's country.

基丨 a basis, as of a wall; a dependence.

住丨 a dwelling-place; a lodging.

地丨 a lot, a plot of land.

四丨 the area of a lot.

故丨 old ruins, substructions.

阯 ꜀ch' Like the last, and nearly synonymous with it.

The base of a wall.

略基丨 the foundation of a city wall.

交丨 Cochin-china; the first half of this name is a transcript of this old Chinese name, and said to have been given because in that land men and women bathed together; the other part was added by foreigners, apparently because the people used the Chinese language.

訨 ꜀ch' To accuse to one's face; to reprove boldly; to impeach.

芷 ꜀ch' From *plant* and *to stop* as the phonetic.

A fragrant plant but bitter, used for a carminative; it resembles orris root and is the root of a fleur-de-lis (*Iris florentina*), of which the tincture is employed; 白丨 and 澤芬 and 芳香 are common names, but some of the roots so called may be derived from umbelliferous plants like the *Opoponax.*

丨陽 name in the Tsin dynasty of Si-ngan fu, now in Shensi.

沚 ꜀ch' From *water* and *to stop* as the phonetic.

A small islet or bank in a stream; to stop at, as at a watering-place or island in the sea.

于沼于丨 among the pools and islets.

祉 ꜀ch' From *worship* and to *stop* as the phonetic.

Happiness; enduring contentment; the satisfaction which comes from attaining one's end; to take pleasure in.

丨福 joy, blessedness.

頌日丨 or 時丨 or 蕃丨 may you have this day's joy, or daily joy, or abundant contentment; — forms of salutations in closing letters, denoting a desire for the reader's happiness.

受丨 to be blessed.

特候近丨 particularly anxious for present felicity.

君子如丨 if our prince would be happy — in the good.

紙 **帋** ʻch' From *silk* or *kerchief* and a *surname;* the second form is unusual; silk or cloth was used for writing before paper, which was invented by 蔡敬仲 Ts'ai King-chung, *alias* Ts'ai Lun, about A. D. 100, of the bark of the Broussonetia, old rags, and fishing-nets, all cut and rasped together.

Paper, stationery; a document; classifier of writings.

打 丨 牌 to play cards.
裱花 丨 to paper walls of rooms.
一 丨 書 one document, one letter.
丨 張 or 丨 聯 stationery; scroll paper; &c.
一張 丨 a sheet of paper.
丨 錢 stamped and scolloped pieces representing money, scattered along the way at funerals to buy the quiet of malicious spirits.
敬惜字 丨 respect written paper, — which is carefully gathered by scavengers, who are paid for their work as a meritorious deed, lest holy names become defiled.
京院 丨 a soft kind of cottony paper; it is found at Canton.
打燒 丨 to "burn the paper," a Canton phrase for torturing in prison.
別戳破這層 丨 兒 don't rip open that paper; *i. e.* don't divulge the secrets of the trade.
遞 丨 to hand in a petition.
金銀 丨 paper burnt in worship to represent gold and silver.
密香 丨 a sort mentioned as brought from Europe in A. D. 280, which seems to have been manufactured from the fiber of aloes.
鎮 丨 a brass rim to flatten paper when writing on it.
丨 帛 or 丨 扎 paper houses, animals, &c., burned at funerals to the dead.
丨 煤 the paper match; it retains the fire by thrusting it inside of a bamboo.
襯 丨 the fly-leaf of a book.

砥 ʿch' From *stone* and *downward*; it is also written 底 and read ʿti.

A whetstone; a fine grindstone; even; smooth, as a hone; to attend to one's conduct, to observe the rules of decorum; to level, to equalize.
丨 礪之資 [as a friend] who warns and polishes one.
扔石 丨 子 to swing stone weights, — a military practice.

中流 丨 柱 [like] a peak in the current, *i. e.* a patriot statesman an inflexible man; one unmoved at danger; the allusion is to the *Ti-chu* hill in Shen cheu 陝州 in the west of Honan, which interferes with the channel of the Yellow river.

枳 ʿch' From *tree* and *only*; also read chih˷; it was a contraction of *küh*, 橘 an orange, but the two are now distinguished.

A hedge-thorn or spinous shrub; a variety of orange like the pumelo, with a thick rind; hurtful, injurious, like thorns; a peccadillo, a trivial offense; an old name for 南川縣 in the southeast of Sz'chʿuen on the borders of Kwéicheu.
丨 殼 skin of the *Citrus fusca;* and 丨 實 denotes its dried seeds and skin.
丨 椇 the *Hovenia dulcis;* the enlarged stems are used to flavor spirits.
丨 棘 thorns, prickles.

In *Cantonese*. A plug, a stopper, a cork, a spiggot; to cork. Also used for 只 as a classifier of flowers, hanks of thread, or what is tied up in parcels.
罇 丨 a cork for a bottle.
丨 實 cork it tight.

咫 ʿch' From *only* and a *cubit*.

The foot measure of the Cheu dynasty, which was as long as a woman's fore-arm, or nearly the same as an English foot, divided into eight 寸 inches.
丨 尺之間 between a foot and a cubit, *i. e.* a very little; very near, close by.
丨 尺天顏 a near adviser of a monarch, denoting one who is a foot or two from his face.

軹 ʿch' From *carriage* and *only*.

The end of the axle which projects from the hub like a finger; the hole in the nave that keeps it in; forked, bifurcate; an old name for Tsi-yuen hien 濟源縣 in the north of Honan near to Shansi.
歧 丨 a cross-roads.
丨 首蛇 a monster of a double-headed snake, described by the Chinese.

疻 ʿch' A bruise; a swelling caused by a blow or knock, which does not break the skin.
丨 痏 a black and blue swelling.

旨 ʿch' This character is composed of 甘 *agreeable* contracted, below 匕 a *spoon;* as a primitive it is used phonetically.

Excellent, pleasant tasted, delicate; meaning, intention; purpose, design; scope, sense; the Emperor's will; an order; a decree, a ukase, a rescript.
奉 丨 to receive orders; always denotes the 聖 丨 or sacred will, for which officers 請 丨 request his Majesty's orders.
美 丨 or 丨 甘 fine flavored; delicious, as a dish.
丨 哉 how luscious!
丨 意 the import, the drift of; as 意 丨 深遠 this argument is very recondite, or far reaching.
一章之大 丨 an important remark; a synopsis.
禹惡' 丨 酒 Yü abhorred pleasant liquor.

指 ʿch' From *hand* and *excellent* as the phonetic.

A finger; its thickness is a common measure; a toe; 艮, the third of the eight diagrams, refers to the finger; to point out, to refer to; to teach, to command; to denote; a mode, a particular.
大 丨 or 巨 丨 or 手 丨 公 the thumb.
將 丨 or 中 丨 the middle finger.
無名 丨 the nameless finger, *i. e.* the ring finger

食丨 the forefinger.

三丨厚 the thickness of three fingers' breadth.

丨手畫足 to make gestures, to gesticulate.

丨點 to show one how; to reveal to.

丨示迷途 to point out the evil results of such a path.

丨東擊西 or 丨東丨西 to make a feint, as in battle; to point here and there, befooling one.

丨使 to employ; to direct, as a servant.

丨實 certain; surely.

丨不定 it is doubtful, I can't say certainly.

丨談風月 to talk about the weather.

丨揮 to signalize with the hand; title of a military officer of the rank of a captain.

彈丨間 in a trice, quick as a fillip; instantly.

丨証者 an informer.

瞭如丨掌 plain as your hand.

丨天誓日 to point to heaven and swear by the sun.

丨斥 or 丨摘 rebuke; to criticise sharply.

丨甲花 the henna flower (*Lawsonia inermis*); but the 丨甲草 denotes the *Impatiens* or balsam, both being used to dye the finger nails; the 山丨甲 is a species of *Symplocos* resembling the Lawsonia, and therefore confounded with it.

庤 ʿch' To provide in store; to have ready, as implements of husbandry.

丨乃錢鎛 the bills, hoes, and other tools were all provided.

峙 ʿch' From *hill* and *office* as a phonetic.

A high and isolated peak; to pile, as in a hillock; to lay up; provided with, as supplies.

供丨 to prepare stores, especially for public use.

丨糧 to collect provisions.

丨立不搖 firm and unmoved.

畤 ʿch' A terrace or tumulus on which the ancient emperors worshiped the five Shangti.

西丨 a place near Lohyang in Honan.

黹 ʿch' The original form is intended to represent the delicate lines in needlework, it is the 204th radical of a group of characters relating to embroidery.

To embroider; to adorn with braid or lace; braided; an embroidered cap used in sacrificing.

鍼丨 to sew, to do needlework.

智 ch'ʾ The original form was composed of 白 *clear*, 亏 *seriatim* contracted, and 知 *knowledge*, now reduced to the present form; it occurs interchanged with ˛chi 知 to know.

Wisdom, understanding; knowledge of all kinds; prudence; wise; sagacious, discreet; shrewd, sharp.

丨勇 brave and capable.

丨識 a good, clear judgment; intelligent wit.

丨慧 wise and discerning; in Budhist canons, the last and highest of the six virtues called *pradjna*, or intuitive wisdom; he who attains it passes on to *nirvana*.

可以爲丨士 he can become a prudent man.

無丨 indiscreet; no apprehension of.

一切丨 universal knowledge, the highest degree of intelligence (*sarvajna*) attainable, and is applied to every Budha.

彘 ch'ʾ Composed of 彑 a *pig's head*, 矢 a *dart*, and two 匕 *spoons* to represent the cloven feet.

A sow that wallows; swine; they are enumerated by Mencius in addition to pigs.

野丨 a wild boar.

二母丨 two brood sows — were given to each cultivator in the days of Wăn Wang.

人丨 a corpse cut in pieces; — it refers to a speech of a princess of the Han dynasty.

致 ch'ʾ From 至 to *reach* and 夂 to *come up behind*.

To go or cause to go, to convey to; to accompany; to visit; to intimate; to resign, to give over to; to induce, to bring on; to hazard; to regulate, to order; tending to; a sort; an aim, an end; when an auxiliary to a verb, it is a causative, that, in order to; as a *superlative*, the extreme, the highest degree; secret, minute.

丨于人 to tell a man; to send to one.

丨使他來 he came on that account; make him come.

是丨有此 it is done for this end.

以丨如此 in order that it may be so.

招丨 to induce one — to come.

委丨 to act for another.

丨意 to inform, to intimate one's wishes; to bow slightly, to nod assent.

丨仕 to resign office.

丨書 to send a dispatch; — used only for equals.

丨誠 the utmost sincerity.

不二丨 the two are not unlike.

風丨 the air, bearing, carriage of a man.

丨之 to send with, as a list.

轉丨 to send compliments (or a present) to one.

丨身 or 丨命 to risk one's life.

備物丨用 to provide whatever is needed.

丨師 to inspirit men — in the fight.

丨知 to apply knowledge to final causes.

一丨而百慮 each took a different method to reach the same end.

大丨 a resumé; in general.

緻 ch'ˋ From *silk* and to *cause*; occurs interchanged with the last.

To mend garments; to patch; soft, delicate; close, fine in texture; torn, tattered.

精 〡 beautiful, exquisite, fine, delicate.

柔 〡 soft, elegant.

縹 〡 handsome, suitable to.

細 〡 fine, minute and beautiful.

密 〡 虛 詞 a well planned, cunning falsehood.

制 ch'ˋ Composed of 刀 *knife* and 未 *incomplete* altered; it is interchanged with the next.

To cut and pare; to form; to govern, to regulate; to limit, to hinder, to prevent; to invent, to make; a rule; a practice, a law; mourning usages.

〡 作 to make, to do.

有 節 〡 I can only do so much; I am restrained by the rules.

法 〡 laws, rules, restrictions.

限 〡 to bring within rules.

〡 錢 fixed rate, as of land rent.

〡 度 to form rules; management, plans; to restrain and subdue.

禁 〡 prohibitions; to forbid.

監 〡 to restrain; to set a limit.

〡 書 an Imperial order.

〡 地 the Court, the seat of Government.

國 〡 the rule of a state; the Government or Administration.

品 〡 the etiquette of Court.

皇 帝 〡 日 his Majesty is pleased to say.

臨 朝 稱 〡 [an empress] ascending the throne is termed *ch'ˋ*.

〡 臺 a governor-general; he is addressed as 〡 軍 [your excellency] commanding the army.

自 〡 self-restraint; 自 〡 不 住 I don't care, I'll not be hampered.

守 〡 attending to mourning; this phrase is written on a son's visiting cards for nearly two years.

中 〡 in deep mourning; the phrase is put on doors to announce it to friends.

體 〡 government prestige or property; what is issued by public officers, or for public purposes.

士 死 〡 an officer dying for his loyalty.

製 ch'ˋ From *clothes* and to *form*; it is similar to the last.

To cut out, as garments; to invent, to make, to manufacture; to compound, as medicines; a mode, a pattern; a rain-cloak, a fur robe.

美 〡 well contrived, well done; handsomely dressed.

〡 造 to make, to manufacture.

裁 衣 之 形 〡 to make (or cut out) clothes after the fashion.

好 〡 法 a good prescription, either to 〡 藥 compound medicines; or to 〡 炮 decoct by boiling or using fire.

遵 古 法 〡 put up according to the old prescription.

御 〡 done by the Emperor, or for him.

狸 〡 a fox-skin garment.

鯯 ch'ˋ From *fish* and to *prepare* as the phonetic.

A fish whose head is esteemed a delicacy, and prepared by pickling.

〡 魚 子 the roe of a sort of perch eaten at Canton.

治 ch'ˋ From *water* and *venerable*; also read ˏ*ï* and ˏ*t'ai*.

Name of a small stream in south of Shantung promontory; and one in the southwest of Fuhkien in T'süen-cheu fu, called 〡 水 T'ai-shui; to govern, to rule well; to heal, to remedy; to oversee; to form; to try, as a legal cause; to compare; demanded or required by the nature of the case; practiced, experienced; fitted for ruling, talented; a prosperous or good government; the ruler's residence, or seat of his government; a retired room or the cloister of a Tao priest.

〡 下 者 subjects; those under his rule, the governed; those within the 〡 屬 official jurisdiction of a magistrate.

〡 喪 to attend to funeral rites.

〡 病 to practice medicine.

〡 家 to manage the family.

〡 心 to regulate one's desires.

無 法 可 〡 there's no way of managing him; it cannot be brought about.

一 〡 一 亂 at times the country is peaceful, and then it is disturbed.

〡 獄 to try causes.

ʻ處 〡 or 〡 罪 to try and punish crimes; to sentence or condemn prisoners.

女 所 〡 兮 it was your doing.

〡 理 天 下 to govern the empire.

政 〡 日 新 his rule daily improves.

平 〡 general tranquillity.

〡 世 之 才 fitted to rule the world.

府 〡 the prefect city.

〡 於 人 ruled by men, or by a man.

偫 ch'ˋ, 待 — The difference between these two probably arose from confounding their radicals.

To wait on; to store up and provide for.

儲 〡 to gather in readiness for a contingency, as food or stores.

値 ch'ˋ From *man* and *straight*.

To meet, to happen, to occur; to hold, as in the hand; to manage, to attend to; happened, chanced; a turn in course.

現 〡 or 適 〡 just then; just at this time; it so happened.

〡 其 事 之 紛 紜 it happened in the multitude of his affairs.

〡 日 the day on which the 當 〡 的 or certain officer is in charge.

相 〡 to meet rather unexpectedly.

〡 班 the class which comes on duty, or in turn.

Read *chih*, when used for *chih*, 直 the price of a thing; value, worth of.

丨不丨 is it cheap or not?

不丨一塊錢 it is not worth a cash.

價丨多少 what is the price of it?

不丨與他商量 it is not worth while to argue it with him.

置 寘 ch'ʾ From *net* and *straight*, but the primitive is however regarded as an equivalent of *pa*ʾ 罷 to *cease;* the second, from *cover* and *true*, is less used, and not always exactly identical with it.

To dismiss; to let go, to put aside and take another; to establish, to make firm, to place; to constitute, as a new district; to arrange, to employ; to determine, to judge, to decide; to buy, to lay in goods; when used before another verb, it often implies merely present action, as 均免丨議 neither [of the cases] need be made the subject of inquiry.

建丨 to build; to establish.

處丨 to decide; to sentence, as a criminal.

廢丨 to remove, as from office; to supersede.

丨辦 (or 丨買) 什物 to buy (or settle for) all things necessary.

本客自丨 we (in this shop) attend to buying or perparing our goods ourselves.

丨身事外 I'll have nothing to do with it.

丨身無地 no way of escape, no place to hide myself.

丨家 to take a wife.

丨業 to buy an estate.

丨予于懷 cherish me in your heart.

念念不丨 unceasingly thinking of him.

丨辭 to speak properly or accurately.

丨郵 a post-station.

丨已從之 to settle on what course one will follow.

滯 ch'ʾ From *water* and *belt*, perhaps with an allusion to a girdle crossing water.

Water congealed or impeded in any way; to obstruct, to stop; left behind, untouched; indigestible, disagreeing with one; discordant; to sprinkle; piled up; a hindrance, a stoppage; stagnated.

丨積 indigestion; a stagnant market, overstocked.

丨住 impeded; to restrain.

丨運 unprosperous; bad luck; he don't get on.

柀丨 or 沾丨 an old fogy, who cannot adapt himself to new ways.

阻丨 hindered, as a case in court; stopped.

丨隔 obstructed; prevented from doing or going.

氣丨 a stoppage in the fluids; the nervous system deranged; bilious; out of sorts.

凝丨 constipation, bowels bound up; stiffened or congealed.

食丨 indigestible; as 膩丨 fat, gross food.

消丨 to relieve repletion; to aid digestion.

留丨他鄉 to tarry long in other places.

五重丨 the "five serious hindrances;" a Budhist term for the *pantcha klesa*, or the 五鈍使 five dull messengers which oppose perfection, *viz* 貪 avarice. 嗔 anger, 痴 foolishness, 慢 irreverence, and 疑 doubt.

雉 ch'ʾ From *fowl* and *dart* as the phonetic.

A pheasant or a francolin, of which fourteen sorts are described; to hunt pheasants; an embrasure on a wall; a sort of curtain-wall; to rule, or arrange; it pertains to ˏ*li* 離 the sixth diagram, because of its plumage and cleverness.

丨鷂 the Tartar or longtailed Reeves' pheasant (*Syrmaticur*); also the common ringed pheasant (*Phasianus torquatus*).

黑丨 the eared pheasant (*Crossoptilon*).

越丨 a book term for partridge.

丨尾 the long tail feathers of the Argus, which are used by actors.

丨堞 a parapet wall.

丨門 the southern gate of the palace.

稚 稺 穉 穉 ch'ʾ From *grain* and a *phonetic;* the third and fourth forms are unusual.

Young grain; grain sown late or self-sowed; small; tender, young, delicate; self-conceited, haughty.

幼丨 young and tender.

丨子 or 童丨 a child; a youngster, a lad.

丨氣 gentle, immature; good natured as the young; child-like.

老丨 the old and the young.

痔 ch'ʾ From *disease* and *office* as the phonetic.

The piles; ulcers in the rectum, which gnaw it like insects.

內丨 and 外丨 internal and external piles; bleeding and blind piles.

穿腸丨 a fistula in ano.

丨瘡 sores in the rectum.

至 ch'ʾ The original form is designed to represent a bird flying down, the lower line indicating the earth which it has reached; it forms the 133d radical of a small group of miscellaneous characters.

To go or come to; to arrive, to reach; the end or summit, as in place, time or desire; as an *adverb* the greatest degree of, much, greatly; and forms the superlative, very, most highly; good; as a *preposition*, to, at, even till, up to; respecting as to, in order to; the solstices; a pulsation at the wrist.

自古丨今 from of old till now.

丨極 the very extreme.

先丨 to reach it first.

丨關緊要 of the highest importance.

丨誠 wholly sincere.

丨止 to get to the place to stop; reached it.
丨好 the best.
丨於 with respect to, as to.
丨此 on this account.
四丨 all around, the four sides.
丨不濟 at the very least.
即丨 he will be here soon.
丨不仁 inhuman, malevolent; most truculent.
不丨 not good, ordinary.
丨人 one who excels others.
丨所稱 in regard to what is said.
丨老奸邪 even to old age he was a vile intriguer.
丨期來 come here at that time, or on that day.
無所不丨 he goes everywhere, he is very wild; also omnipresent, universal.
丨日 that day; in the Yih King, it seems to refer to a Sabbath.

輊 *ch'* A carriage so built that the front is lower than the back, or turns down.
丨軒 to go forward and to retreat; to raise and depress; to despise and esteem; to regard one highly and slight another.

踸 *ch'* To walk hastily, to come in abruptly.
丨踱 to run in and out; to appear and disappear, as a servant does.

摯 *ch'* From *hand* and *to hold*; it is similar to the next.
To seize with the hand, to grasp; to hold in the hand when seeing a person; to present to a superior; to enter, to advance; to reach the edge; to break down, as trees from snow; to loosen, as ground.
丨到 to tumble down.
大丨 a superabundance, as of snow.
執丨 to hold firmly, as a bridle.
丨獻 to hold up and present.

贄 *ch'* From *pearl* and *to hold*; used with the last.
A present of homage given when visiting a superior, or requesting a favor of one, as alluded to in Proverbs xviii. 16; a fee when entering school;—gems, silks, birds, and fruit were given in ancient time.
丨儀 presents of ceremony and obeisance.
丨見 to visit with a present; bridal gifts.
出疆必載丨 presents must be taken when you cross the frontier.
丨敬 wedding presents by the female guests; gift to a teacher, especially the present annually sent by a *tsin-sz'* as long as he lives to the officers who passed him at the highest examination.

鷙 *ch'* From *bird* and *holding*.
Birds of prey, accipitrine birds; lawless, violent, hawk-like; to seize by violence.
丨鳥 a sort of harrier, which alights on cattle.
丨鳥不羣 hawks do not go in flocks; *met.* peerless, unequaled.
猛丨 valiant; ruthless.
無忿丨之師 soldiers who are contented.
Read *chih*, To doubt; to strike at with the talons.
卓丨 uneven places in a road.

驇 *ch'* A heavy laden horse; a horse with crooked legs, caused by overloading.
馬丨不能行 the horse was overladen and could not go.

志 *ch'* From 心 *heart* and 之 *to go* contracted.
That on which the mind determines; the will, the inclination; a resolve, a good determination; a fixed purpose; earnest thought; a sense of right; to record, to collect and digest data; statistical works; collected memoirs on various subjects, annals;—in which it is used with the next; an arrow-head.
丨意 a purpose; the will; a mind for, determination.
百丨 all one's aims.
丨向 inclination; wish, object.
大丨 high purposes, great thoughts.
心丨 good resolutions, hearty will.
出得丨 not to be turned from; conscious of power.
丨氣不墜 don't lose your courage, don't be disheartened.
無丨之人 a ne'er-do-well; a reckless, shiftless waif.
適丨而為 to follow one's whim; unsettled.
丨於此 my mind is fixed on this.
有丨竟成 I have a settled purpose to finish the work.
三國丨 Annals of the Three States; they succeeded the Han dynasty, A. D. 221 to 265.

誌 識 *ch'* *shʻ* From *word* and *purpose*; the second form is usually read *shih*, this use being confined to the classics. Used for the last.
To remember; to record for the purpose of remembering; to write in; a record; annals.
丨書 archives, records.
丨念 to keep in mind; to journalize.
多學而丨之 to study much and remember it too
以丨而不朽 an unfading memorial of, as a work of genius.
墓丨 an epitaph, a eulogy.

痣 *ch'* From *disease* and *purpose* as the phonetic.
Black or red spots on the body; a mole; a hair-mole.
面丨 spots on the face; freckles.
丨鬚 the hairs growing on a mole.
丨記 mark by which one is known.

𦭫 ch'' A medicinal plant from Shansi, called 遠丨 or 遠志, the roots of the *Polygala tenuifolia* and *P. sibirica* used in fevers; another sort from Yunnan is sweet, and is the root of a different plant.

銡 ch'' To record; to remember.
銘丨 to write or engrave, so as to be perpetual; to indelibly record; to cut, as in the rock.
丨于五內 it is written on my inwards.

覟 ch'' From *to see* and *record*.
To judge by inspection; to hold a survey on.

觶 ch'' A goblet of horn holding three *shing* 升 gills, anciently used by elders; a tankard; to fine one so many cups.
舉丨 to present the wine cup.

疐 ch'' Said to be derived from 叀 or 專 to bind and *lead*, and 止 to *stop*; as a horse led or stopped by his nose.
Prevented from acting or advancing, as a wolf stepping on his own tail when retreating; hindered, embarrassed; to stumble over.
載丨其尾 [see how the wolf] tripped on his own tail!

Read *ti'* The stem or peduncle of a fruit, especially of the date and pear; the place or scar of the stem.

懥 懫 ch'' Enraged, angry at; to be resentful; the second also means to stop, to desist from; to hate; cruel.
忿丨 incensed, enraged at, irritated.
叨丨日欽 he daily honored the covetous and irascible.

躓 ch'' From *foot* and *proof*.
To stumble at something tripping the feet; to put the foot on.
丨蹶 to stumble and fall.

夥 ch'' Many; this character is in common use in the south and west of Fuhkien.
丨多 numerous.
來日無丨 wanting a few days.

擿 ch'' To stab, to pierce; to plunder, to seize; to point with the finger; to reach to.

擿 ch'' To compare things together in order to see wherein they are alike; to try, to ascertain.
打丨子 to inquire the price.
丨丨這墻的長短 find out the measure of that wall.
丨水淺深 ascertain the depth of the water.

茎 ch'' The seeds of a plant resembling the gall-nut.
樞丨 a tree, otherwise called 刺榆 prickly elm.
芊丨 another name for the 牛膝 Achyranthes.

晢 ch'' Fine bright eyes; to pass before the eyes, to get a sight of.

晢 晣 ch'' From *sun* and *to snap*.
The light of the stars.
明星丨丨 how the bright stars twinkle and glow.
Read *cheh*, To illumine a little; perspicuous.
昭丨 a little bright; it is lighting up.
庭燎丨丨 the torch in the court is going out.
縷丨呈明 to make out and present a minute statement.

忮 ch'' Stubborn, froward; to dislike, injurious to others.
不丨不求 neither froward nor fawning.
丨懻 perversely obstinate.

CH'I.

Old sounds, t'ai, t'i, t'ít, t'ét, t'ap, dé, da, dap, di, dít *and* dík. *In Canton*, ch'i; — *in Swatow*, ch'i, t'i, chi, *and* li; — *in Amoy*, ch'i, ti, t'i, li, hi, *and* chi; — *in Fuhchau*, ch'i, ti, t'i, ch'ie, *and* lie; — *in Shanghai*, ts'z', dz', *and* ts'eh; — *in Chifu*, ch'i.

癡 痴 ch'i From *disease* and *doubt* or *knowledge*; the second form is least used.
Silly, foolish; inapt, simple, luckless; doting after, hankering, lustful; wandering, idiotic; out of one's head, daft after.
丨迷 doting on, an uncontrollable longing for.
丨獃 or 丨呆 heedless, stupid.
丨狂 mad after; besotted with.
丨愚 rude and stupid, as a blundering lout.
丨纏 bound up in, very fond of; set on.
嬌丨 afraid of, as timid childern are.
丨孩 childish, imbecile.
書丨 doting on books, unpractical, pedantic.
丨情 salacious, lusting after.
丨心妄想 the unfounded hopes of a fool; a silly notion.
丨男勝過巧女 a simple man is far better than a crafty woman.

不丨不聾曷作阿家翁 if I am not foolish or deaf, how can I manage the family?—I must overlook some things.

螭 ꜀c'h' From *insect* and *elfin;* also read ꜀*li.*
A dragon whose horns have not grown; a term applied to cruel men.
丨坳 or 丨頭 stone slabs with a dragon carved on them, placed between, or on the sides of steps leading up to palaces or temples.
丨紐 dragon handles on cups.

魑 ꜀c'h' A mountain elf, a brownie; an evil monster, with a man's face and a beast's body.
丨魅 a hobgoblin.

瞝 ꜀c'h' From *eye* and *elfin* as the phonetic.
To examine things in a series; to go from one country to another to examine its customs.

黐 穲 ꜀c'h' From *millet* or *rice* and *elfin.*
Glutinous, pasty, sticky; to stick on; to attach or glue on.
丨得實 it sticks tight.
丨鳥 to entrap birds with the 丨膠 birdlime.
丨脚 sticking feet; *i. e.* to sorn, to sponge on others for meals.

絺 ꜀c'h' From *silk* and *fine.*
The fine fibres of the *Dolichos bulbosus*, or of hemp; fine grasscloth used for napkins.
丨葛布 fine linen.
黼黻丨繡 finely embroidered linen.
丨綌 fine and coarse linen.

瓻 ꜀c'h' An ancient earthen jar or amphora for holding spirits; some of them held a stone or 12 gallons, others half that quantity; presents of wine were sent in them, especially when borrowing or returning books.

笞 ꜀c'h' From *bamboo* and *table; q. d.* bambooed before the bench.
To flog the hand, or beat the mouth with a rattan or a ferule; to bamboo, to bastinado, to scourge; to correct, so as to reform and make one ashamed of his bad conduct.
丨杖 the bamboos and sticks used in a *yamun* for beating.
丨責 to bamboo, to whip; to punish in the courts.
丨臀 to beat the buttocks.
丨四十 give him forty blows.
丨籐 to flog with rattans.
丨律 laws directing the degrees of bambooing.
捶丨 to beat with sticks.

蚩 ꜀c'h' Composed of 虫 *insect* under 一 the *earth*, and a 屮 *sprout;* as a primitive it sometimes gives the sense of *rude.*
A worm; ignorant, unpolished, rustic; to impose upon; to despise on account of ignorance.
丨民 the uneducated masses, the *ignobile vulgus;* plain people.
丨丨 stupid, unpolished, countrified.
丨眩 to contemn and use harshly.
妍丨自見 clever and dull people each think well of themselves.
丨尤作亂 Ch'i Yiu first raised rebellion B. C. 2637; a comet is sometimes called 丨尤旗 after him, because it foretells war.

嗤 ꜀c'h' Laughter; to laugh heartily, to laugh at.
笑丨丨 to laugh aloud.
含丨 laughing and smiling.
時人丨之 the people there laughed at him for—his odd dress.
自丨 to laugh at one's self, for one's blunders.

獶 ꜀c'h' A kind of dog, apparently from the Desert, called 獶丨 having long shaggy hair; it probably denotes the ferocious shepherd dogs of the Mongols.

媸 ꜀c'h' From *woman* and *rustic.*
A worthless, or ill-looking woman, one who acts ridiculously; a foolish woman; wanton.
丨奴 a harridan, a crone.
妍丨好'惡' to like or hate the handsome or plain.

鴟 ꜀c'h' From *bird* and to *revert.*
An owl, of which there are several kinds which prey on young birds; when used alone, the goshawk, or some of the smaller harriers, is denoted.
丨鵂 or 角丨 the white horned or eagle-owl (*Bubo maximus*).
怪丨 or 梟丨 a barn-owl; though the night-hawk seems to be sometimes meant.
丨張 to act violently and oppressively; deceived, imposed upon; artful, said of people's customs.
丨夷 a leathern bag.
以丨義而有其國 he held his sway by his reputation for stern justice.

鮐 ꜀c'h' The mackerel, at Canton is so called; two or three species of *Caranx* and *Auxis* are common there in the spring.

眵 ꜀c'h' Eyes diseased and dim; purulent or smegmatic eyes, sore at the corners.
兩目丨昏頭雪白 his eyes were blurred and running, and his head snowy white;—old and decrepid.

胵 ꜀c'h' The crop of a fowl; the entrails of a bird is 膍丨, applied also to the stomach of a bullock or sheep; tripe; the manyplus.

池 ꜀c'h' From 水 *water* and 地 *earth* contracted; *q. d.* where the earth is bored water collects.
A pool, a pond, a tank; a fosse, a ditch or stagnant water; a receptacle for liquids; the part of a lute where the nuts are; an ancient

ornamental cover or pall of woven bamboo; a prefecture east of Nganking in Nganhwui.

氷 丨 a tank, a reservoir.

魚 丨 a fish-pond.

城 丨 the city moat.

溝 丨 a great moat or canal.

丨 塘 pools and ponds.

湯 丨 a bath-room, the washing tank.

中 丨 the heart; and 玉 丨 the kidneys; are Taoist terms.

酒 丨 肉林 a tank of wine and a forest of meat; *i. e.* plenty.

泮 丨 the pool around the examination-hall in the Confucian temple.

亢 丨 four small stars near 大角 or Arcturus.

丨 中物 [I am not like a] thing in a pool.

硯 丨 the place for water on an inkstone.

差 丨 uneven, not of the same height or length 差 丨 其羽 how the [swallow's] wings flittered!

咸 丨 an ancient piece of sacrificial music; a star north of the stars ι κ λ in Virgo.

馳 ꜀chʻi A horse galloping; to go quickly, as a courser; far, spread abroad; fast, fleet; a courier.

丨 馬報 a rapid courier, a postman; by quick post.

丨 道 the imperial highway.

丨 馬 to race or gallop horses.

丨 口妄談 running here and there with wild stories and talk.

丨 鶩紛華 to earnestly strive, as for honors.

丨 驅 to drive fast; *met.* to act for another.

丨 驛 to ride post.

四遠 丨 名 the name has traveled everywhere; widespread, famous.

丨 逐 a great gathering of people.

衆生奔 丨 如影 men's toils pass away like a shadow; — we are soon forgotten.

彽 ꜀chʻi To go [illegible] and fro.

丨 徊 irresolute; running hither and thither.

蚳 ꜀chʻi Eggs or larvæ of ants.

丨 醢 condiment or pickle, in which they form a part.

坻 ꜀chʻi From *earth* and *reaching* to; also read ˋti.

An islet; a ledge of rocks in a stream; to bank in, to stop; an embankment; a place in a river dyked up, as a platform.

坡 丨 a slope down to the water; a levee.

如 丨 如京 [there will be grain enough] to make an islet or heap a mound.

墀 ꜀chʻi From *earth* and *rhinoceros.*

A porch, a court in front of a hall; a kind of open piazza or vestibule, and the steps leading up to it; the raised path leading from the gate to the palace.

丹 丨 the vermilion avenue, *i. e.* the emperor's palace, the court; it is also called 玉 丨 or perfect avenue; and other names.

堦 丨 the courtyard of the palace.

遲 ꜀chʻi From *to go* and *rhinoceros.*

Slow, dilatory; late, behind time, the opposite of ˋ*tsao* 早 early; not urgent; to delay, to walk leisurely; to procrastinate; to wait for, not to hurry; tardy; slowly and surely, by degrees; used for ˋ*nai* 乃, in the phrase 丨 令 then he ordered him.

來得 丨 he came too late, or after time.

丨 來不及 you'll be too late — to reach the boat.

窗外日 丨 丨 the sun is going down slowly out of doors.

是以 丨 丨 it was therefore delayed from time to time.

丨 一日 wait one day.

拖 丨 to put off continually, to defer; to cause delay.

疑 丨 irresolute; in doubt.

慢 丨 late, dilatory.

早 丨 揭楚 sooner or later I will settle all the account.

太 丨 too late, too slow altogether.

延 丨 to dawdle, to put off purposely; dilatory, slack.

委 丨 far off, remote.

天尙 丨 明 the sky is waiting for the dawn.

丨 一會兒 (or 丨 一吓 in (*Cantonese,*) wait a little, rest a space.

棲 丨 to sojourn; to rest a while; to wait for.

[illegible] ꜀chʻi Also read ˋ꜀*si; interchanged with* the last.

To cut open the skin; to dismember; to cut and cleanse a fish.

凌 丨 the ignominious slow punishment of cutting to pieces.

持 ꜀chʻi From *hand* and *office.*

To grasp, to seize hold of; to observe, to maintain, to direct with a firm hand; firm, resolute, decided; a classifier of fans.

把 丨 to manage, to take the direction of.

扶 丨 to uphold, to assist.

丨 法 to vindicate the laws.

丨 躬 to demean one's self with dignity.

丨 杯 to hand a cup of wine.

丨 意 obstinate, unconvinced.

挾 丨 甚大 very capable; having good administrative ability.

操 丨 權柄 to direct military affairs.

執 丨 to hold in the hand; — as 扇一 丨 one fan.

堅 丨 or 有 丨 守 a firm resolve, — as not to drink.

丨 身 to restrain the passions, to keep the body under.

可以支 丨 I will try hard to attend to the matter.

趍 ꜀chʻi A contracted form of 趨, to walk briskly; to approach or recede with a quick step.

丨 趄 lengthened in time.

篪 箎 A sort of bamboo flute with seven holes, whose sound resembles children's crying. 壎 丨 the earthen bell and flute, were two sacrifical instruments that were employed to regulate the ceremonies; *met.* fraternal love; brothers.

踟 Undecided; to step over. 丨 蹰 embarrassed, and not knowing what course to take.

褫 From *clothes* and a *horned tiger* as the phonetic.
To take off clothes, to disrobe, to undress; to take away official insignia; to put an end to; a fringe.
丨 脫 to strip off.
丨 氈 thick felt for sleeping; plush.
丨 革頂翎 to deprive one of his button and feather.
極禮而 丨 he laid aside his honors and insignia.

恥 耻 From *ear* and *heart*, because the ear reddens when a person is ashamed; the second form is common.
Disgraced, humbled, ashamed; to feel shame, to blush, to redden; shame, chagrin.
見羞 丨 to be ashamed; chagrined, mortified.
你不畏羞 丨 do you not dread being ashamed?
蒙 丨 covered with disgrace.
被人 丨 笑 to get laughed at.
丨 駡 afraid of a scolding.
無 丨 之徒 a brazen faced rascal.
無廉 丨 shameless, devoid of honor.
愧 丨 confused, mortified; crestfallen; — used in polite language when complimented.
丨 惡衣食 ashamed of poor clothes and food.
辱奴 丨 于主 the master is shamed by beating his servant.
丨 辱之 he was quite disgraced; 一君子 丨 之 the superior man abominates a shameful act.

恀 Also read *shi'*
To cling to, to depend on, as a child on its mother.
怙 丨 to entirely rely on.

侈 From *man* and *many*.
Extravagant, profuse; large, tending to expand; superfluous.
奢 丨 profuse, wasteful; as 奢 丨 繁華 making a great show, living high.
丨 服 extravagances of all kinds.
丨 用 a profuse outlay.
丨 談 or 丨 言 exaggeration; wild talk.
哆兮 丨 兮 divergent and small, like the stars of the sieve.

誃 Interchanged with 'ch'i 哆 gaping, opened out.
To separate, to part; diffused, spread out.
丨 別 sundered; separated, as friends.

姼 A pretty woman, but worthless and wanton; airy, trifling.
姡 丨 a playful, seductive girl.
Read *shi'* or *ti*. A local term in the state of Tsu for deceased parents.
考 丨 or 父 丨 a deceased father.

阤 A slide on a hill-side; a breaking away, the earth tumbling down; to loosen, to destroy; a slope or bank; a cliff.
登陂 丨 to go up the hillside.
綱紀頹 丨 the bonds of government and society were destroyed, as when anarchy prevailed.
崩 丨 to fall, as a hill-slide; to break away.

茝 Also read 'ch'ai.
A fragrant flower, called 蘭 丨 cultivated for its scent, and which serves as a term for fragrant flowers in general.

齒 The original form represented the teeth appearing in the open mouth; it forms the 211th radical of a natural group of characters relating to teeth.
The front teeth, especially the upper; the mouth; words; age, years; a sort, a class; associates, equals; serratures; to toothed, as a serrated leaf; to commence; to classify, as by years; to be reckoned among; to record, to write in.
年 丨 '長 old, elderly, advanced.
父之 丨 a father's equals and friends — are to be respected.
尊 丨 how old are you? what is your age? to which the reply is, 馬 丨 [or 賤 丨] 徒增 my days have vainly passed, &c.
雛 丨 young; undistinguished.
好 丨 音 fine elocution.
不 丨 don't speak of him.
切 丨 to gnash the teeth, in anger.
啓 丨 to begin to talk.
丨 言 specious, wordy.
入所不 丨 unendurable, like gravel in the teeth.
露 丨 open-mouthed; protruding teeth.
乳 丨 milk teeth.
丨 類 people of the same class.
生 丨 日繁 the population daily increases.
說話尖 丨 cutting talk; impudent; rude and sharp.
沒 丨 without teeth; *i. e.* dead, passed away; but the phrase 沒 丨 無怨言 means, to the day of his death he will have no angry words.
丨 座 the jaw; also, to seat people by seniorty, as at a feast.
鄉黨敘 丨 in the village meetings place people according to age.
丨 錄 the genealogical register of the *tsin-sz'* graduates of one examination; 不入人 丨 錄 he gives no handle for people's talk.
金 丨 gold teeth, the name of a tribe of aborigines in Yung-chang fu in Yunnan, whom Marco Polo calls *Zai-dandan*; they covered the teeth with thin plates of gold.

牙丨相打 his teeth chatter.
伶牙俐丨 eloquent; wordy.

齒 'c'h' From *plant* and *teeth*.
A weed, the 馬丨莧 or purslane (*Portulaca*); it is also known as 瓜子菜 or melon-seed greens; and 長命菜 or long-life greens.

熾 c'h' Fron 火 *fire* and 識 *to understand* contracted.
The blaze or flame of fire; glare, effulgence, splendor; a dazzle of lights; to burn, to catch, to spread; raging, as lust; numerous.
丨起 blazing up; *met.* imperious, ardent, as lusts.
勢丨 their power was fierce.
炎丨 firing up.
丨炭 to burn charcoal.
俾爾昌而丨 that you may be prosperous and glorious 丨盛 numerous, as descendants.
以油救火愈撲愈丨 as if one try to put out a blaze with oil, the more you put on the fiercer it burns.

幟 **織** c'h' The second form is unusual; occurs written 織 *chih*.
A pennon or streamer with a fringe, containing a motto or inscription; a banner, or flag, long and narrow, used as a marker; to fasten, as with cords; to tie on fringes; to make a minute of; to signalize.
旗丨 flags and pennons.
奪丨 to seize the flag, — to win the prize.
拔丨 to pull down the flag, — to conquer.
錦丨 a pennon woven in silk.

趼 c'h' To leap; to jump about or over; lame, a signification preserved in Kiangsu in the phrase 丨手 a maimed hand.

饕 c'h' From to *eat* and *break* off.
A noisome smell, such as is made by burnt hair, putrid meat, or noxious gas.

埴 c'h' From *earth* and *correct*.
Adhesive clay, suitable for the potter's use.
搏丨 to mold in clay
擿丨 to grope one's way with a pole, as a blind man does.

傺 c'h' To stop, to detain; once in use among the people of Tsu or Hunan.
侘丨 disappointed; irresolute or vexed, as when one is met by a sudden obstruction or delay.

掣 c'h' chö' From *hand* and to *limit*; it is also read *ch'eh*,
To obstruct, to embarrass, to hinder; to raise, to take up; to select; to draw, as lots; to pull; to grasp, to hold, as the hands.
丨簽 to draw lots; to pull out, as a ticket.
挾丨 to restrain, to hamper; to extort by intimidation.
飛丨 to call back, as a falcon.
丨肘 to grasp the elbow; to impede, to bother; rigid; cramped and disabled.
丨電 flashing; sparkling, as an electrical machine acts; scintillating.
牽丨 to compel, to drag with one; to clutch and haul.
丨籤 to draw lots, as officers do who are appointed to the same rank, and thus decide where each is to go.
丨住 to discourage, to throw cold water on. (*Cantonese*)

遵古法丨(or 製) to make up a prescription in the old way.
乍丨乍縱 now tight, now loose; twitching, as one in convulsions.

饎 **糦** From to *eat* or *rice* and *joy*
Food, victuals; meat and drink; wine and bread; to boil or dress food; sacrificial millet.
丨饌 meat and drink; food, living.
大丨是承 the large dishes of millet are thus borne in.
丨人 a cook.
丨爨 a kettle or pan, used by cooks.

翅 **翄** c'h' From *branch* and *plume*; the first is used for 啻 in the classics, also sometimes wrongly written 翨, which means a flock of birds flying.
A wing; a fin; in commerce, 魚丨 denotes the 鯊丨 or shark's fins.
丨翼 wings.
展丨 or 振丨 to flap the wings.
丨膀 a wing, wings; hence 生丨膀 is to be merry, to become hilarious.
抉丨 fowl's giblets are sometimes so called.
金丨 a brown colored finch, common at Peking.
丨排 ranged along; bristling, like the teeth of a comb, alluding to spinous dorsal fins.
丨丨 flying about; winging its way.
蜻蜓丨 the dragon-fly's wings,— a sort of fine gauze.
奚丨食重 why stop at regarding eating as the most important?

翨 c'h' The primary feathers of the wing; a pinion, a quill; strong, rapacious, as a hawk.

CHIH.

Old sounds, típ, tít, tík, díp *and* dit. *In Canton*, chăt, chăp, chak, chik, *and* shik; — *in Swatow*, tiet, chip, chap, chek, chi, tek, sip, sit, sek *and* tit; — *in Amoy*, chip, chiap, chi, chék, tít, chít, ék, sék, and tiat; — *in Fuhchau*, chék, chaik, chi, k'ék, t'ík, chiàh, chià, *and* ché; — *in Shanghai*, tseh, tsăk, dzeh, zeh, zuk, tsék, *and* dzék; — *in Chifu*, chih.

執 *chih* The original form is composed of two old characters, meaning a *hand seizing* and 羍 to *terrify*, here written like 幸 *happy*, and altered in combination.

To apprehend, to seize; to look after, to take in hand; to pick up, to lay hold of; to persecute; to bring and show; to retain, to keep; to hold as, to look upon; to maintain; to stop up; what is retained, as evidence; what is in the hand; obstinate, set; engaged in, attending to.

丨手 to take by the hand.

手丨 to keep, as evidence.

丨籌 to draw lots.

丨中 to maintain the just medium; candid.

偏丨 biassed, prejudiced.

拘丨 or 固丨 or 丨拗 pertinacious, set in his way; obstinate, not open to conviction.

丨之而已 keep (or take) it, and make the best of it, — as a bad coin.

回丨 a receipt, as of the reception of an official document.

丨會 to take bids among stockholders.

丨法 to maintain the law, to abide by the rule.

各丨一藝 each follows his own trade or profession.

丨事 a manager, to manage; the retinue of an officer, a procession; as 共無丨事人員 those who have nothing to do with the cortége; officers who have no retinue.

丨事單 schedule of a procession; a list of duties of official retainers.

丨字 or 丨活字 to set types.

丨筆 to hold the pen, as an amanuensis.

丨競 vigorous, brawny, forcible.

捕丨 to arrest, as a criminal.

丨友 a father's friend; and 父丨 a father's equal in age.

In *Cantonese* A heap, pile; a handful; a group.

住埋一丨 living together in one community.

一丨米 a handful of rice.

縶 *chih'* From *silk* and to *keep*.

To tie up or tether an animal; to connect, to secure; a cord; a fetter, a shackle.

丨維 to shackle; hampered or confined, as by duties or promises.

言授之丨以丨其馬 give him the ropes to bind his horses.

馽 *chih'* From *horse* and *middle*; like the last, and also read *shuh*.

To fetter a horse; a foot-rope; a restraint; a bond.

天脫馽丨 heaven has burst our bonds.

蟄 *chih'* *ₑchö* From *insect* and to *keep*.

To hybernate; stored, hid in quiet; insects or animals burrowing or becoming torpid; gone into darkness.

驚丨 the fifth of the 24 terms, from March 5th to 20th, when the "torpid are excited," and spring begins.

子孫丨丨兮 the pleasant gathering of children and grandchildren.

丨蟲 animals that become torpid.

慹 *chih'* To lose one's courage or firmness; to show the white feather; to give up, to submit.

豪强丨服 the brave man has succumbed and yielded.

汁 *ₑchih* From *water* and *ten*; *scil.* ten drops make a stillicidium.

Juice, gravy, drippings; slush; the expressed juice, the liquor or best part strained off; sleet, rain, and snow all falling together; delicate, pleasing to the taste.

丨液 juices; sap, exudation.

水丨 essence, juice.

菜丨 the pot liquor, left after boiling vegetables.

啜丨 to suck the juice.

雪丨 melting snow.

丨漿 gravy; *met.* pleasing to the taste.

葡萄丨 grape-juice or wine.

梹榔丨 betel-nut juice and saliva.

石灰丨子 a cake or crust of mortar hardend like stone; a Peking term.

只 *ʻchih* Represents the *mouth* with the *breath* issuing from it; much used as a contraction of *chih*, 隻 as a classifier, but not quite correctly.

A final particle or tone; a disjunctive *conjunction*, but, however, yet; as an *adverb*, merely, only; but just, just then.

丨宜 or 丨可 this will only be the right; this alone is proper.

丨管 merely for the present; on the spur of the moment, inconsiderately.

我丨是不要 but I don't want it; I just don't need it.

丨有 merely have.

丨有一件 there is only one thing or affair.

丨此而已 just this and no more.

丨見 just observed, only saw; it came to pass.

丨得 obliged to, no alternative; only can.

母也天丨 Oh, mother! Oh, heaven!

樂丨君子 they rejoiced in that he was an honorable man.

In *Fuhchau*. Used for 此 this; here.

質, 質, chih' } From 貝 *property* and 斦 two *taels* pledged for it; the abbreviated form is much like *tun'* 盾 a shield.

The substance, matter, or grosser nature of, as distinguished from the aura 氣 or subtle parts; to substantiate by evidence, to establish; to appear, as in court; to cross-examine, to confront, to set over against; to fix or settle; to perfect; opposite to, appearing in presence of; essential; plain, not figured; honest, sincere, true; firm, as a texture; a disposition, a habit.

氣 丨 or 地 丨 the natural disposition or parts; the mind; the constituents of a vapor.

體 丨 substance, elements of.

鴉片 丨 morphine.

品 丨 disposition, capabilities.

對 丨 to confront the parties, as for proof.

丨 訊 to cross-examine or confront, as in court.

苦 丨 a bitter principle.

好姿 丨 perspicacious, very clever.

丨 頁 a firm tint, said by dyers; a good disposition.

性 丨 直 an honest disposition.

丨 信 evidence of, something to go by, an earnest.

丨 樸 plain, unostentatious, not extravagant.

文 丨 elegant, delicate.

丨 之 於 人 I'll ask people about it, — so as to be sure.

文 and 丨 are opposites; plain and flowery; showy and real; elegant, polished and solid learning.

丨 爾 人 民 complete what concerns your officers and people.

美 丨 a good mind; brilliant, gifted.

Read *chi'* A witness; a pledge; an introductory present; a hostage; a large market-place.

交 丨 to exchange hostages or pledges.

丨 庫 or 丨 鋪 a pawn shop; it is less extensive and cheaper than the 當 鋪 or security shops.

丨 因 減 稅 I pawned it there to save the tax.

劕, chih' Used with the last.

A ticket; a token, passed as a pledge or security, when pawning.

丨 劑 a check cut from a register, as a ticket or share.

鑕, chih An ax or hatchet; an iron block or anvil used by smiths or artisans.

騭, 隲, chih } From *horse* and to *ascend* or to *step*; the first is the common form.

A stallion; to go up, as a hill; to cause to progress; to promote, to raise; to fix, to determine.

好陰 丨 that was a good deed, — meaning done from real love, a secret act, unostentatious benevolence.

陰 丨 下 民 [heaven] orders the melioration of mankind.

陰 丨 文 exhortations to benevolent acts.

侄, chih Often wrongly used for the next.

Firm, unbending; foolish.

丨 佗 not advancing, hindered by something.

姪, chih From *woman* and to *reach* as the phonetic.

The child of a brother; also called 內 丨, while 丨 子 is his son; a nephew.

丨 女 a niece, his daughter.

表 丨 a sister's child.

外 丨 a wife's nephew.

舍 丨 my nephew.

丨 婿 a niece's husband

眷 丨 young relatives, nephews and cousins.

年 丨 the sons of *küjin* or *tsin-sz'* alumni of the same year.

世 丨 a term used by one's self towards a father's chum or fellow graduate.

愚 丨 your "ignorant nephew," is the subscription of one writing to his friend's father.

晊, chih Luminous, splendid; great.

厔, 庢, chih } The turnings and windings of a mountain brook; derived from Cheu-chih hien 盩 丨 縣 a district in the south of Shensi near Singan fu, where the streams are much impeded in their courses among the hills.

挃, 秷, chih } The second form is unusual.

The rustling noise made when reaping grain is likened to 丨 丨, — in imitation of the sound.

擿 丨 to trill the fingers across the strings of a lute.

桎, chih From *wood* and *extreme* as the phonetic.

Fetters, handcuffs; stocks of wood or iron; to manacle, to shackle; to stab, to pierce; to stop; a thing to clog wheels; a spike.

丨 梏 manacles and gyves.

丨 械 而 不 問 fetter him but do not ask him questions.

丨 鎋 a linch-pin; a wheel-chock; *met.* a censor of manners, one who influences the tone of morals.

蛭, chih A leech.

水 丨 a bloodsucker, for which there are several local names.

郅, chih' From a *place* and *extreme* as the phonetic.

To go up, as a hill; flourishing, as an age; a superlative, very.

丨 隆 very prosperous.

郁 丨 an ancient name of Nganhwa hien 安 化 縣 in King-yang fu on the River King, in the east of Kansuh.

丨 治 a good government, one proved by the general prosperity.

窒 chih' To stop up; to close, to fill; to obstruct; solid; the moon in 庚 or nearly in opposition; to pare off.

氣丨 to hiccup.

丨手丨脚 difficult to manage; impeded in every way.

丨皇 a bedroom door; an old term for the entrance to a grave.

丨塞 to stop, to choke or fill the entrance of.

其內不無丨碍之處 there are no doubt some difficulties (or objections) in the way.

蛭 chih' From *insect* and *to stop* up. An insect that burrows, the 丨蟷 a sort of field-spider that weaves a tubular web on the ground; probably a sort of *Mygale* or *Atyphus;* it is also called 土蜘蛛 or ground spider.

銍 chih' From *metal* and *extreme* as the phonetic. A small sickle or toothed bill-hook; *met.* the grain which it reaps, which was the head cut off short; an old name of Suh cheu 宿州 near the River Hwai, in the north of Ngan-hwui, during the Han dynasty.

丨刈 to reap grain near the ear, leaving the straw.

禾丨 a sickle.

納丨 to pay in the grain due on the government land tax.

秩 chih' From *grain* and *to lose.* Orderly, regularly, in a series; to dispose in order; a station, a post, an office; usual, acquainted with; permanent; clear, explicit, as teaching; a decennium, or increase of ten years in one's life.

品丨 or 班丨 official rank or precedence.

序丨 or 丨次 a series, a rank.

德音丨丨 methodical, lucid instruction; an unsullied name.

丨丨其干 a graceful sloping bank.

祿丨 official salary or perquisites.

左右丨丨 the attendants were all in their places.

開七丨 entered his seventh decennary, as at 61 years.

天丨天敍 heaven's orderings and scheme, as the human relations, five virtues, &c.

散丨大臣 high ministers in the Household Guards; they are all noblemen and palace dignitaries.

帙 袠 chih' From *napkin* or *clothes* and *to lose;* the second character also means to sow; a period of ten years. A cloth or paper case to cover Chinese books; a book-wrapper; a satchel or bag used like an envelope; to arrange, as books; a classifier of letters.

卷丨 or 書丨 a book cover or wrapper; a large envelope.

公文一丨 one public dispatch.

紩 ˏchih To stitch, to seam; to sew.

丨衣 to mend or sew clothes.

隻 ˏchih From *bird* and *hand;* it is often erroneously contracted to *chih* 只, from the similarity of tone. A bird, one of a sort, not a pair; single, by itself; a classifier applied to ships, boats, gems, animals, birds, insects, &c.; also things in pairs or sets, when one is individualized, as legs, eyes, shoes, cups, saucers, spoons, &c.; and to things resting on a base or legs, as a table; following a noun, it denotes several of the kind; as 牛丨 several oxen.

丨丨有尾 each one has a tail.

一丨洋船 one foreign ship.

船丨到 many ships have arrived.

丨手不能遮天 one hand can not screen the sky;—one person is inadequate to do it.

形單影丨 one body makes only one shadow;—I am quite alone, solitary.

丨身 I myself alone; only one in it.

不過幾丨 only a few of them.

雙丨 duplicated or by twos; in pairs.

片紙丨字 [do n't despise this] slip of paper and one character; *i. e.* my brief note.

炙 ˏchih From 肉 *flesh* contracted over 火 *fire.* To roast flesh; to broil; to dry or toast before a fire; to cauterize; to be intimate with, to approach, to approximate; near; to simmer in honey, as dates are cured; warm, hot.

丨草 dried liquorice.

丨乾 to dry thoroughly; as 丨衣服 to dry clothes.

膾丨人口 hashed and fried for people's eating; pleasing all tastes.

親丨 very friendly with.

薰丨 injured, as by bad company.

炮丨 to parch in a boiler, as in preparing drugs.

焚丨 to cook or roast; to burn.

丨手 to warm the hands.

心火上丨 rising anger; also the internal heat coming out,—and parching the lips.

墌 ˏchih The base or foundation of a wall.

高丨城 a place in Sz'-ch'uen, noted for a battle.

摭 拓 ˏchih From *hand* and *people* or *stone;* the second is also read *t'oh,* a synonym of 托 to hold. To take up, to gather, to collect; to adopt; to improve, to brighten.

丨拾遺文 to collate (or gather) old books or phrases.

丨取 to quote or plagiarize others' words; to appropriate.

開丨 to flourish, like a city; to enlarge, as a place.

文氣開丨 his style improves.

丨落 not to get advancement; to fail of promotion.

蹠, ˏchih From *foot* and *people;* it is like the next.

To tread, on, to follow after; to stamp, to leap; the sole of the foot.

自無丨有 to pass or leap out of chaos or non-existence into being; now here and then gone.

盗丨 a leader of thieves, a sort of Robin Hood in early Chinese history; hence 舜丨之分 as unlike as Shun and Chih, *i. e.* as Peter and Judas.

跖, ˏchih Like the preceding.

The sole of the foot; the foot of birds.

丨足下 to tread under foot.

鷄丨 a fowl's foot.

戠, ˏchih From a *dart* and a *sound.*

A sword; others say, to gather, or a synonym of *shih*, 埴 or potter's clay; it is only used as a primitive, without conveying any meaning to its compounds.

織, ˏchih From 糸 *silk* and 職 *to govern* contracted; used for 幟 a flag.

To weave; woven; weaving.

丨機 a loom.

丨布 to weave cloth.

丨得精緻 woven very beautifully.

丨餘 weaver's thrums, ends of the threads.

丨文鳥章 the blazonry of birds on the flags.

丨紋 to weave figured fabrics.

促丨 a name for the cricket.

丨造 an officer in Kiangnan who attends to procuring silk and porcelain for the Court.

職, 軄, ˏchih From *ear* or *body* and a *sword;* the second form is pedantic and unusual.

To record events; to act officially; to govern, to oversee, having the direction of; to make a thing important or leading; official duty, title, office; used for I, when an officer speaks of himself, as 丨道 I, the Intendant; presents from other states; single; really, certainly; numerous, as duties.

丨守 to govern, to manage.

丨任 in office; its duties; the post itself.

加虛丨 to confer an honorary title or nominal office.

卑丨 I, the officer; those who are in the service, down to low officials, even when only titular, call themselves *chih*, and 俾丨 when addressing a superior.

丨員 an official title; an officer, either actual or titular, a functionary of any grade under a red button.

革丨 to deprive one of office or title.

受丨 to receive an office.

丨分' a title; official duties, of which once the 六丨 comprised the various departments.

丨丨 numerous, said of an officer's duties.

納丨 to pay tribute; *i. e.* the 丨貢 presents or customary offerings to the Crown.

世丨 hereditary office or title.

丨事 official duty; to specially manage an affair.

設官分丨 to institute a post and define its duties.

帶丨回家 a retired officer who is allowed to retain his titles.

膱, 脑, ˏchih These two characters are used in ancient rituals with the same meaning, though not altogether identical.

Pieces of jerked meat, a foot or more in length, formerly reckoned among betrothal presents; high, of not putrid meat; sticky, adhesive.

髮丨 pomatum.

陟, chih' From *place* and a *step.*

To ascend; to enter on a higher office; to mount, to go up to; advanced, promoted; to proceed.

丨梯 to go up a ladder or stairs.

丨臨 to behold from on high, as God does.

黜丨 to degrade and to advance; official changes.

丨降 to advance and retire, as to and from the altar.

丨彼高岡 ascend that high peak.

汝丨帝位 do you ascend the throne.

丨進聖域 to be admitted into the holy regions.

直, chih' Composed of 目 *eye*, 十 *ten*, and 隱 *hidden* contracted, for ten eyes can see a thing straight; it is used for 値 and the next; and is easily mistaken for *chin* 眞 true.

To look ahead; straight, direct; upright, blunt, outspoken, true; just, exactly; to be straight, in *writing*, a perpendicular stroke; to straighten, to proceed, to go direct; that which leads or directs; as an *adverb*, only, but, merely; stiff and straight; purposely; suitable; the price of.

正丨 just; the upright.

丨言不隱 to speak without reservation; to tell all.

曲 and 丨, and also 彎 and 丨 are opposites; crooked — straight; devious — upright.

丨道 self-evident doctrines.

丨去 he left immediately.

丨程去 go directly on, follow the straight road.

一丨入 go straight in; 一丨去 go straight on.

一丨走 go straight ahead.

丨來這裏 I came directly here.

打丨 pound it straight.

嘴丨 true, fearless, blunt; always speaking his opinions.

伸丨脚 stretch out your leg; *met.* stretched-out legs, *i.e.* dead; for which 丨一 is also used.

丨不百步 they only fled a hundred paces.

骾丨 or 骨丨 sturdy, stiff-necked, willful; honest, trusty.

舉丨錯枉 promote the men of integrity, remove the double-dealing.

其丨如矢 straight as an arrow.

傭丨 wages.

枉尺而丨尋 a crooked foot he wished to make a straight fathom; *i.e.* give him an inch, and he'll take an ell.

丨多少錢 how much is it worth?

丨隸省 Chihli province, *e.i.* the province which superinteuds the others; as a 丨隸州 is an inferior department, or a district whose magistrate is not under a prefect.

各丨省 all the provinces, the governing and all others.

莫信丨中丨 don't believe everything called true, or every strong asseveration.

植, ꜀*chih* From *tree* and *straight* as the phonetic.

To plant, to set out; to set up; erect, standing upright; to lean on, as a staff; to place, to lay down; a beater or mallet.

栽丨 or 樹丨 to set out trees.

丨其杖 he laid aside his staff.

戶丨 door-posts.

生丨 to produce plants.

丨黨 to form a party or cabal.

多蒙培丨 I am very thankful for you aid in setting me up—in life.

殖, ꜀*chih* To fatten, to enrich; to produce, to prosper, to grow; to be largely produced; to get rich, to amass; price, value; to raise the price of; to appoint, as to an office; to set upright, like the last, to plant, to cultivate.

封丨 to appoint to office; to hoard or store money.

丨丨 even, level; regular.

豐丨 abundant, prosperous.

不丨貨 do not be greedy of money, do not set your heart on riches; do not raise prices.

萬物蕃丨 all nature flourishes.

丨有禮 appoint upright men to office.

同姓不婚惡不丨也 people of the same surname must not intermarry, lest they do not increase.

我有田疇子產丨之 we have fields which Tsz'ch'an got for us;—who will do so, when he is dead?

稙, ꜀*chih* The grain first sown; the first grain that comes up; sometimes applied to the wife first married.

丨稺菽麥 first sow the pulse and then the wheat [for the next crop]

擲, *chih'* From *hand* and a *plain;* it occurs written 擿, but this last is more commonly read *t'ih,*

To throw down or at; to fling away, to reject; to waste, as time; to pitch, as quoits.

丨中 to hit the mark.

丨骰子 or 丨色 to throw dice.

丨下 or 抛丨 to throw down.

丨棄 to discard; to throw away.

丨回 or 丨還 to return, as a memorial to the writer.

丨光陰 or 虛丨 to throw away time; to idly spend it.

飛丨石礫 to throw stones and brickbats to and fro.

丨地金聲 [like] the sound of ringing brass striking on the ground,—so is this rhythmical composition.

丨九仔 to gamble (*Cantonese.*)

⿰虫鄭, ꜀*chih* A large green caterpillar, the 丨蠋 which feeds on the bean; it is perhaps the larva of a sphinx moth.

躑, *chih'* Embarrassed, bewildered.

丨躅 irresolute, unquiet; advancing and retreating, as dancers do, or as when venturing into a palace; also the name of the *Rhododendron indicum.*

CH'IH.

Old sounds, t'ak, tik *and* t'ik. *In Canton,* ch'ik *and* shik;—*in Swatow,* ch'ié, ch'ek, ch'ia, *and* t'ek;—*in Amoy,* ch'ék, t'ék, sek, *and* hwa;—*in Fuhchau,* ch'ók, ch'iòh, ch'iàh, t'ék *and* sék;—*in Shanghai,* ts'èk, ts'ăk, *and* sèk;—*in Chifu,* ch'ih.

尺, ꜂*ch'ih* From 尸 a *body* and 乙 to *understand* combined; it refers to the fingers, for when the hands were laid side by side and opened to their widest extent, the length seems to have been a popular measure for a foot; used for the next.

A cubit, or the Chinese foot of ten *ts'un';* it has in different dynasties been divided into 8, 9 and 10 *ts'un'* 寸, and the present variations in its length in different parts of China are equal to $1\frac{1}{2}$ *ts'un';* by treaty the length is fixed at 14.1 inches English, or 0.3581 metre French; the fifth note in the diatonic scale.

排田丨 or 足丨 is the tailor's foot at Canton of 14.8 inches; and the 迴通丨 is the mason's foot measure of 14.1 inches.

墨丨 a five foot measure.

曲丨 a carpenter's square.

丨寸有大小 there are different sorts and sizes of the article.

多少丨寸 what are its dimensions?

這是丨寸地方 that's a place where etiquette is to be observed, where you must mind your ps and qs.

不彀丨寸 not of full stature or dimensions.

六丨之孤 a minor reigning very soon after his father's death.

戒丨or 界丨 a ruler, a ferule.

量天丨 a sextant.

量幾丨 measure its length.

一丨之書 a brief epistle, a sharp note; the 一丨 was a name given in the Han dynasty to the tablets on which the Emperor wrote his orders.

有丨度 measurable; what is done by rule; one who works methodically.

三丨劍 the three foot blade — of the first emperor of the Han.

三丨孩童 a lad of three cubits, a stripling.

三丨法 imperial laws; so called in reference to the size of the paper used.

三丨帛綢 a three foot scarf, alludes to a bowstring or halter.

丨地 a circumscribed narrow spot; insufficient.

響丨 a two foot rule, struck at a funeral by the undertaker to call in the spirit.

蚇, *ch'ih'* From *insect* and a *foot;* used with the last.

Caterpillars of the family of the loopers, or *Geometridæ*, called 丨蠖 or foot measurers; hampered, repressed.

赤, **烾**, *ch'ih*, Composed of 大 *great* over 火 *fire*, as shown in the second and antique form; others say of 炎 and 土 *i. e. hot earth*, both referring to the dark skin of southern people; the south pertains to *fire* and *carnation;* it forms the 155th radical of a few characters, all relating to red.

The third of the five primary colors, a reddish carnation or cinnabar color; a purplish light red; color of a newborn infant; naked; poor, destitute, barren; to redden; to strip, to denude; any highly polished metal.

丨日 sultry; a very hot day.

丨帝 the god of Fire.

丨子 an infant; the emperor so calls his subjects, indicating his love.

丨道 the equator, the south road.

丨身 or 丨體 or 丨光 naked; stark, nude.

丨心 guileless, sincere; it is an appellation of Kwanti.

丨膽 a pure heart.

六丨 to throw aces and quatres, or the red faces of the dice.

丨口日 red mouthed days, are those on which the Cantonese avoid bargains.

打丨脚 to bare the feet.

丨手 empty handed.

丨地 unoccupied wastes; pampas; a steppe.

丨土國 the red earth country; an old name for Siam.

丨縣 an old name for China; 丨呢 is another name used by the Moslems.

紅丨 flushed from drink; red in the face; as 臉上一紅一丨的 his face turned red and then crimson, — on being detected.

斥, **㡿**, *ch'ih'* The second is the earliest form, composed of 广 a *shelter* and 屰 *perverse*, contracted to the first; the second also means to put a top to.

To expel, to drive far from, to turn out of the house; to scold; to strike or cuff, as with the fist; to pry into; to point out; reaching far, extending to; extensive, broad; salt or nitrous land.

丨逐 or 屛丨 to expel, to thrust out.

面丨 to reprimand, to speak severely to.

指丨 to point out faults.

明丨 to blame, plainly.

丨責 to blame, to reprimand.

丨法 to juggle; legerdemain.

丨放 to dismiss from office and banish.

揮丨 wandering, reckless; to motion one off.

賊匪充丨 the filchers and banditti are numerous.

丨革 to degrade, or take away a titular rank by a higher functionary.

不丨所格何物 it does not point out the peculiarities of things.

丨候 to spy another's conduct in order to find fault; to keep a watch on.

叱, *ch'ih'* From *mouth* and *seven*.

To cry out at, to scold, to hoot at; to blurt out; to angrily order another; to make mention of.

丨狗 to drive out a dog.

丨罵 or 呼丨 辱罵 to scold and abuse; to blackguard, to rail at.

訶丨 to breathe hard, to speak loud.

煩爲丨名致候 please mention my name, and present my respects — to your father.

勅, **敕**, **勑**, *ch'ih'* From *strength* and to *bind* or *order;* the third form is also read *ˏlai*.

To try, to attempt; an ordinance; an order, what is done by special command of the Emperor,—for which the next character is the verbal form; a charter, a special permit or precept from him; to carefully look after; to have charge; to give in charge, as to punish; to receive warning; the execution of a charge; steady; urgent.

丨書 credentials, letters-patent.

丨封 by Imperial appointment, a special title.

誡丨 royal orders, laws, precepts, prohibitions, &c.

丨贈 to bestow honors on an officer's dead parents.

丨行 the Emperor's mandate promulgated.

丨旨 or 丨命 an Imperial order; his Majesty's will.

丨令符 charms containing the "special orders" of a god; they are hung on the lapel.

飭, *ch'ih'* From to *eat*, *man*, and *strength*; it is often used for the last, and must not be confounded with *shih* 飾 to adorn.

To make a thing firm; reverent, careful, respectful; to enjoin on or instruct, as a superior does a subordinate; to direct, to command; to adjust, to make ready, to prepare to do; diligent; prepared.

丨差 to dispatch on public service.

申丨 to issue orders.

謹丨 to use care in doing.

嚴丨 to strictly charge.

仰丨 I hope you will do it.

整丨地方 to preserve order in a region.

丨躬齋戒 he fasted and kept under his body.

恭錄丨知 I have respectfully copied the orders for your information.

戎車既丨 the war-chariots were all ready.

丨力以長地財 use diligence to increase the productions of the soil.

丨知 to make orders known to an officer, that he may do them.

鳷, 鶒, *ch'ih'* From *bird* and *method*, because the cock and hen always walk in proper order.

A beautiful water bird, the 㶉丨 which has a broad and upright fan tail, described to be like a rudder; it is perhaps allied to the mandarin duck, though the muscovy duck or the pied duck, is rather more likely to be intended.

栻, *ch'ih'* From *tree* and *pattern*; it is also read *shih*,

Name of a tree; a thing used in divination, in connection with maple seeds and the heart wood of the Rhamnus date.

忯, *ch'ih'* To fear with respect and veneration.

丨丨 to regard with awe.

彳, *ch'ih'* The original form is intended to represent a short step, or the motion of the leg in walking; it forms the 60th radical of a natural group of characters relating to walking and regulations.

丨亍 the motion of walking; when joined they make the character *hing* 行 to walk.

埴, *ch'ih'* Hard ground, dried by the sun and caked; to enter the ground; one says, water appearing, the ground becoming damp, which is suggested by the parts of the character.

抶, *ch'ih'* To chastise, to flog; the sound of a thrashing or beating.

CHING.

Old sounds, ting, *and* ding *in one instance*. *In Canton*, ching, *and one or two* ch'ing; — *in Swatow*, cheng, teng, chín, chⁿia, *and* tⁿé; — *in Amoy*, chéng, *and one or two* chín and téng; — *in Fuhchau*, chíng, tíng, *and* chéng; — *in Shanghai*, tsăng, *and one or two* zăng; — *in Chifu*, ching.

貞 *chăn* Composed of 貝 *pearl* and 卜 to *divine*; or, as in an ancient form, of 鼎 a *tripod* and 卜 to *divine*.

To inquire by divination, either by cowrie shells, coins, or other things; chaste, pure, virtuous, undefiled, uncorrupted; moral, high principled; a term for the inner row of the 64 diagrams, the outer row is named 悔 *hwui'*

丨烈 chaste, even to death.

丨正 firm in the right.

丨諒 reliable, trustworthy, faithful.

丨潔 honest, chaste; undefiled, as a virgin.

冰丨玉潔 pure and unsullied, virgin purity.

丨固不搖 immovable, energetic in maintaining the right.

丨榦 the elementary parts.

丨節 a chaste widow, one who will not marry again; many 丨節坊 honorary gateways are found in China to their memories.

守丨 a betrothed girl, whose affianced died before the nuptials, and she refuses to marry.

楨 *chăn* The *chaste tree*, a common evergreen growing in northern China; it is the 女丨 or wax tree (*Ligustrum lucidum* and *L. obtusifolium*); it is also called 冬青, because it maintains its pure green color through all seasons; its seeds, called 女貞子, are much used as a tonic.

邦之丨 a high statesman, a stay of the realm.

丨榦 planks used in making adobie walls.

禎 *chăn* From *worship* and *pure*.

Lucky, felicitous; a good omen.

丨祥 auspicious; a sign indicative of heaven's approbation.

湞 *chăng* The name of an upper branch of the North River in Kwang-tung, whence 丨陽 was an old name for Wăng-yuen hien 翁源縣 in Shaocheu fu.

征 *chăng* From to *go* and *correct*; it is interchanged with 徵 in some senses.

To proceed, to get on; to pass; as time; to reduce, to chastise refractory states; to subjugate; to levy taxes, to take duty; to be in the army; to spy.

丨伐 to reduce [a feudal state] by force.

丨收 to collect taxes by force.

丨勦 or 丨誅 to exterminate, as seditious rebels.

出丨無道 to go to war against barbarians.

而月斯丨 and your months are also going.

汝徂丨 do you go and coerce them;—a punctive expedition.

丨討 to demand with authority.

丨量 to collect taxes on the land.

丨夫 imperial troops; an envoy and his suite.

丨比 a clerk of the taxes in a district magistrate's yamun.

客赴長丨 the travelers proceeded on their long journey.

怔 *chăng* Restless; afraid.

丨忪 or 丨忡 agitated, nervous; unable to sleep.

肅肅宵丨 to quietly pass the night.

脠 *chăng* To fry fish or flesh in a pan.

鉦 *chăng* From *metal* and *correct*.

Cymbals or small gongs set in a frame, used to sound a halt to troops; a brass tambourine used by priests; the place outside of a bell where it is struck.

神丨 the divine cymbal, a stone drum spoken of in ancient books.

樹頭掛銅丨 the brazen cymbal bangs in the tree; *i.e.* the sun is shining through its branches.

姃 *chăng* Name of a woman; a correct deportment, as the two parts intimate; reserved and modest, such demeanor as is proper for a woman.

烝 *chăng* The character is intended to represent *fire* under *vapor* ascending; it is used with the next.

Vapor made by fire, steam; mist, watery exhalations; to steam; to cook by steaming; to stew, to distil, to decoct; a multitude; to act as a prince; a winter sacrifice in the ancestral temple; to enter, to make progress; to bring forward; to set forth offerings; all; clouds of dust rising like vapor; to lie with or debauch superiors; liberal; generous; to lay down; an initial expletive.

丨熟 to steam thoroughly.

丨飯 to steam rice; the usual mode of cooking it is in a 丨籠 or steaming-basket.

丨民乃粒 all the people then had grain.

丨酒 to distil spirits.

丨丨皇皇 energetic and splendid.

丨丨乂 to gradually lead to self government.

丨水鑊 the boiler in a steamer.

丨進 to introduce into.

文王丨哉 how Wăn Wang rose to be a true prince!

蒸 *chăng* From *plants* and *steam* as the phonetic; it is interchanged with the last in some of its senses.

The twigs of hemp (*Sida*) used for fuel; small faggots; hemp torches; to rise, as steam; vapor; all, numerous.

天生丨民 heaven produced all men.

丨丨日上 daily rising better and higher, as a state, or when doing business.

冬丨 the winter sacrifice.

Read *ching'* The reflection of the sun; the sun striking on one; vapor rising through the sun's heat.

癥 *chăng* From *disease* and *steam*; it is sometimes written like the last.

A disease of the bones, with rheumatic pains; the 骨丨 a sort of syphilitic cachexy.

生乾丨 to eat but never grow fat.

乾丨 is applied to withered fruit, dried up while on the tree.

脀 *chăng* The cooked meat that fills a sacrificial basin, at an offering; swollen; doltish; to ascend.

徵 *chăng* From 微 *fine* and 王 *good* which is explained, that by acting right in small matters, the moving principle will appear.

To set in motion, to induce action; to act, and thus show the proof or power of; to testify, to witness, to make clear by proof; to be called, to summon, to cite; to complete; to seek, to hunt up, to inquire after; proof; verifications; fulfillment, as of a prayer or hope; to levy, as taxes; to raise or enlist, as troops; an old name for Ch'ing-ch'ing hien 澄城縣 in Shensi, near the elbow of the Yellow River.

丨歛 to gather, as the tribute.

有丨 verified; proof exists.

明丨 plain evidence.

丨驗 verified; we see its effects, as of a good medicine.

無丨之言 unfounded assertions.

丨兵 to enlist soldiers.

立丨據 to establish proof.

丨收賦稅 to collect taxes and duties.

丨召 an invitation by Government for good men to serve it.

丨聘 to induce by a present, as Balak did Balaam.

丨逐 to visit often, to seek continually; to hang around, as an idler; to weary by coming.

納丨 to send the betrothal presents.

貴丨 or 丨格 a noble bearing, a lucky look, alluding to the 八丨 eight evidences of good fortune which the physiognomists look for in one's face.

Read *'chi.* One of the five musical notes, regarded as corresponding to fire.

癥 From *disease* and *proof* as the phonetic.
ˏchăng A swelling or hardness of the abdomen, supposed to proceed from calculi or derangement of the pulse and viscera.
丨瘕 biliary calculus.
丨結 spasms from biliary calculi, or from obstructions in the colon.

整 Composed of 攴 to *rap* 束 a *sheaf*, and 正 to *straighten;* the allusion seems to be to the farmer's work.
ˋchăng To place evenly, to adjust; to do with, to work on; to repair, to put in order, to mend; to marshal to arrange, to make new, to trim up; the entire amount, the whole of.
丨齊 to put things to rights, to settle; to organize.
丨頓 to set in order, to repair.
丨丨齊齊 regular; in trim, like a dress; in due order, like a procession.
丨治 to oversee, to repair.
丨年和暖 it is warm all the year
丨橋修路 to mend bridges and repair roads.
丨隊 to lead on detachments in order.
丨肅軍容 grave, serious, precise deportment.
丨作 to make right.
丨天家 or 丨天的 the whole day, the livelong day.
丨吊給他 give him the whole bill.
丨理規模 to reform a usage.
丨束衣冠 to arrange one's dress carefully, as for worship.
丨的破的 the whole and the broken, those which are of first quality and the inferior.
丨表 to mend a watch.
丨壞 to spoil, as when trying to mend a thing.
丨好 or 丨翻 to make as before; to put in order.
丨詭馬 to set a catch for one.

晸 From *sun* and *regular.*
ˋchăng The sun rising, just appearing above the horizon.

宵雨初晴朝日丨 just as the night shower stopped, the sun rose on the earth.

拯 拼 From *hand* and an *aid* or *pint measure.*
ˋch'ăng To lift up, to raise; to pull out, as from a slough; to rescue, to deliver.
丨救 to save from danger; to rescue, as from hell.
丨民於水火之中 to deliver the people, as from fire and water.

正 From 止 to *stop* and 一 *one;* *q. d.* to hold on to one thing, to maintain uniformity; others derive it from 一 *one* and 足 *enough* used in the sense of to *stop.*
chăngˋ Correct, proper, legal, straight, right; not awry, erect; not incline nor deflected; exact, as a full-formed character; regular, constant, usual, proper; really, truly; orthodox, the opposite of 邪 depraved; genuine, as goods; the first, the principal, of two colleagues; to govern, to adjust; to rectify; what makes right; rule, government; to execute the laws, to punish capitally; to assume or enter on, as an office; just, while, at the time; a fair copy, not the first draft; in *mathematics*, plus, and *fu*ˋ 負 minus; an old term for a trillion.
丨中 put in the middle; the exact centre.
丨不丨呢 is it straight or not?
丨三百兩 exactly three hundred taels.
丨合時 just in good time.
丨要再問 just as I was asking him again.
撥丨 to put a thing straight; to set upright.
丨是 just is; is so; yes; that's it.
坐丨 to sit properly.
丨講 to speak literally or exactly.
丨貨 genuine goods.
正丨 a correct death, one for which all preparation has been made, also called 狐死 a fox's death.

丨當 all right; as it ought to be.
丨如所云 let it be as you say.
丨宗 the true rule; the true laws of a science.
不丨經 immoral, disregarding law; the opposite of 丨派人 a respectable, honest man.
丨堂 the main hall; the chief officer.
鄉丨 village elders.
先丨 upright men of olden time.
擬丨擬陪 to propose a primary and secondary; a candidate and his alternate.
丨南面 to sit facing the south; *i. e.* to be emperor.
朝丨 to have an audience.
丨從ˋ principal and secondary, as among the nine ranks; 正 and 子 sometimes also denote classes, as chief and subordinate; the tariff and transit duties are so distinguished in the customs rules.
丨大夫 heads of departments.
六丨 are six official virtues.
丨法 to put to death, as a criminal.
丨人君子 an upright man.
令丨 your wife.
寫丨字 write the characters out in full.
丨道功名 a degree earned by talent, not bought.
丨敎 the Mohammedan faith or sect
就丨於人 ask some person about it.
八丨門 or 八丨道 are the eight true entrance gates, or correct paths (*marga*) of the Budhists into *nirvana*, meaning thereby the rules of correct conduct in life, as 丨見 correct views, 丨命 pure life, &c.; that which will infallibly lead to beatitude.

Read ˏ*ching*. The center of a target; the frontage of a room to the sunlight; 丨月 first month of summer in the Cheu dynasty; now the first of the year, so applied by Duke Yin 隱公 of Lu, and confirmed by Ts'in Chi Hwangti, B.C. 221.

開丨 to resume business after new year.

來丨 in January next.

丨鵠 a target; it is made of cloth with a movable bull's eye called *tih* 的, which falls out if it be hit.

政 *chăng'* From 攴 to *strike* and 正 *correct* as the phonetic.

To rule; to render service to the government; a standard, that which regulates; government, administration; laws, regulations; the measures of a government, or its departments; a treatise, a guide to the knowledge of a subject.

丨事 politics, governmental affairs.

丨人 those who carry them on.

家丨 family regulations.

仁丨 or 虐丨, and 善丨 or 苛丨, are opposites; — a good rule, an oppressive rule; a merciful or a harsh government.

從丨 in official employ; under orders.

七丨 the seven regulators, *i. e.* the sun, moon, and five planets.

丨令 official orders.

丨教 official admonitions, exhorting the people to keep order.

議丨 a councillor of state.

論丨 to criticize government; to discuss politics.

農丨 a farmer's cyclopædia; also a supervisor of agriculture.

症 *chăng'* From *disease* and *correct*; it is unauthorized by Kanghi, but is in general use.

The causes of disease; a chronic malady, originating in organic disturbance.

外丨 external or unusual diseases.

內丨 functional or internal ailment.

紫痧丨 scarlet-fever.

病丨 or 丨候 a malady; as 急丨 and 惡丨 a dangerous or sudden attack.

順丨 and 反丨 a curable and incurable disease; an attack in the season, or out of season.

証 證 *chăng'* From *word* and *correct*, or to *ascend*; the first form is most used.

To inform truly; to prove, to testify, to substantiate; evidence, proof; legal testimony; to remonstrate with, a meaning which is confined to the first form, as in 諫丨 to take to task for, as a superior.

丨人 or 干丨 a witness.

丨見 to bear witness to what one has seen.

作見丨 an eye-witness.

丨驗 to verify, as by 丨據 testimony, evidence.

丨實 full, adequate proof.

丨佐 to prove, as by quoting authorities.

監丨 to take testimony, to get proof.

黲 *chăng'* Rice which has become black by damp, and thereby spoiled.

鄭 *chăng'* An important feudal state in the Cheu dynasty (B.C. 774 — 500). now the prefecture of 開封府 in Honan, of which province it occupied about a half; its capital was the present situated 丨州 lying southwest of K'ai-fung; the names of eighteen princes are recorded; a plain, a prairie.

丨重 earnest, prudent.

周丨交質 [the emperor of] Cheu and [the duke of] Ching exchanged pledges; — one restoring the land for the other's son.

CH'ING.

Old sounds, t'ing, ding, *and* zhing. *In Canton*, ch'ing, ch'eng *and* shing; — *in Swatow*, ch'ing, seng, sⁿia, t'eng *and* t'ⁿia; — *in Amoy*, ch'éng, t'éng, téng, séng *and* chéng; — *in Fuhchau*, ch'éng, t'éng, tíng, *and* t'íng; — *in Shanghai*, ts'ăng *and* dzăng; — *in Chifu*, ch'ing.

稱 穪 *ch'ăn* From *grain* and to *lift up*, alluding to the gradual lengthening of the blade when growing; the second form is obsolete.

To style, to designate, to call; to say, to talk about; to remark, or report, — in which sense it often indicates a quotation; to compliment, to commend; to plead an excuse, to feign; to take up; to weigh, to heft; an excuse; a name, an appellation.

丨讚 to praise, to laud; to eulogize.

丨揚 to speak in praise of to others; to commend.

丨呼 or 丨謂 termed, called; to designate, to style.

通丨 a general term for.

丨病 to feign sickness; to malinger.

丨說 to state; to say with care.

丨爾戈 to take up arms, to fight.

自丨其父曰家父 one styles his own father *kia-fu*.

報丨 to report to, to inform about.

丨人 to praise people.

丨斤 to find out the number of pounds.

Read *ch'ing'*. To weigh; to adjust; for which 秤 is mostly used; to compare things; a steelyard or dotchin (word corrupted through

Cantonese from 托稱); suitable, agreeable to one's wishes; corresponding to, satisfied with; compared with; a suit, as of clothes.

丨貨 to weigh goods.

丨物平施 to give good and fair weight.

丨價 a fair price.

壓丨 or 搭丨頭 to add for waste or tare, as in weighing goods.

丨人意 it suits one's notions; it agrees with men's ideas.

不丨 unfitting; as 衣不丨身 his dress does not fit him.

不丨其職 it dishonors his rank and station; I can't judge of his qualifications.

一丨公分 to divide with regard to equity.

可以相丨 symmetrical; they will counterbalance each other.

偵 ˓ch'ăn From *man* and *honest*.

To spy out, to explore; a spy, a scout, one sent to reconnoitre.

丨伺 a spy; one who 丨探 explores and searches.

遊丨 to go as a scout.

赬 經 ˓ch'ăn From *red* and *pure*; the second form is unusual; like the next.

A deep red color, made by twice dyeing; to dye red; *met.* wicked doings which flush one, or cause a blush.

丨顏自負 a guilty face discloses one's faults.

丨尾 red tail, refers to a notion that the bream's tail turns red when it is frightened.

竀 ˓ch'ăng From 穴 a *cave* and 視 to *see*; *i. e.* to look straight ahead, as one must when looking through a hole.

To look at; a carnation color, like the tail of a bream; dyed the second time.

瞠 ˓ch'ăng To stare at sternly; to look at in anger.

檉 ˓ch'ăng From *tree* and *sage*.

The tamarix (*Tamarix sinensis*) described as a willow with reddish bark, very graceful and delicate in shape; it fears neither snow nor hoar-frost, but is very sensitive, and indicates rain by its branches moving; it is called 丨柳, and 三春柳 or third spring willow, from its flowering late.

蟶 ˓ch'ăng From *insect* and *sage*.

A bivalve shell, the razor-sheath or Solen; the name also includes some narrow kinds of clams and mussels; it is reared on the southern coasts; 丨乾 and 鮮丨 are terms for dried clams and fresh cockles, and common shell-fish in various forms for sale.

丨紐 the muscle which holds the solen to its shell.

成 ˓ch'ăng Composed of 戊 a *stem*, denoting 茂 *flourishing* and 丁 *branch* or *man*; *q.d.* a 成丁 or *complete man*, one arrived at full age.

To finish, to effect, to complete; to do one's duty, to become, to fulfill one's part; to bring about, to make, to rise to; to accomplish, to terminate; to be completed; to assist; to pacify; entire, perfect, completed; determined on; whole, filled, overwhelming, full; completion; duties to be done; the results of; the quality of a thing, as of timber, metals, &c.; doubled; a compact or covenant; a rest in music; a tract of ten square *li*; a tenth; name of a district on the R. Wei in the south of Kan-suh.

丨不得 impracticable; unable to do.

丨就 to bring about; successful.

不丨句 it makes no sense.

丨何事體 what thing do you ever finish?

現丨 or 行丨 or 丨了 done, succeeded; it is carried out, or into effect; all finished.

丨始丨終 well done from first to last.

不丨器 incomplete, uneducated, unfitted for actual life.

丨了客 to act the visitor, reserved, formal.

丨親 married; consummated the nuptials.

丨病 he will (or has) get sick, as from grief.

丨人 thoroughly accomplished, a complete man; 不丨人 to act like a brute; incapable, careless.

丨人之美 to assist people in their good objects.

老丨 trustworthy, a sincere man.

收丨 a good harvest, to get in crops.

歲之丨 the last day of the year; the year's harvest.

丨百 a full hundred.

一丨數 one tenth of the number.

五丨 five tenths; one half.

幾丨 what percentage is taken?

丨疋 a whole piece of cloth.

丨日 the entire day.

守丨父業 to preserve one's patrimony.

落丨之喜 to congratulate one on getting into his new house.

求丨 to sue for peace or pardon.

難道哄你不丨 do I wish to cheat you?—here 不丨 forms the question.

丨空 void, vanished; to become nothing; to disappear, as paper when 丨灰 burned to ashes.

大丨 the Great Perfection; a title of Confucius.

城 ˓ch'ăng From *earth* and *completed*; *q.d.* a finished work of earth.

A citadel; a place walled in for the defense of the people; wall of a city; a city that has a wall; a provincial capital; in Peking, a municipality; a sepulchre; to wall in or fortify for protection; to mend, to repair; an encampment or lodge, as among free-masons; completed, done.

築 ǀ to build a wall.
ǀ 基 base of the wall; above it is the ǀ 根 or foot of the wall.
ǀ 樓 tower over a city gate.
ǀ 門口 at the city gate.
ǀ 上 or ǀ 頂 on the city walls.
一座 ǀ one citadel; one city or its wall; one fort.
上 ǀ or 進 ǀ or 入 ǀ to enter the city; to go to town.
閉 ǀ to bar the gates as on an enemy's approach.
守 ǀ to guard a fort or city.
困 ǀ or 衛 ǀ to beleaguer a city, to surround a fort.
紫禁 ǀ the Forbidden City, in which are the Imperial palaces in Peking.
崇 ǀ the Emperor's dwelling.
五 ǀ five municipalities of the city of Peking, under special officers, subordinate to the Censorate; their courts are called *ch'ing;* and to hold court is 坐 ǀ, to sit in the municipality.
萬里長 ǀ the Great Wall; *i.e.* the long rampart of ten thousand *li.*
佳 ǀ the happy city; *i.e.* a tomb or cemetery.
火 ǀ a great array of torches, as in a procession.
金 ǀ 湯池 the golden city has majestic moats; *i.e.* the imperial citadel is well guarded.
干 ǀ a great general.
難解愁 ǀ it is hard to open the castle of your grief.

宬 *꜀ch'ăng* From a *covering* and *completed* as the phonetic.
A house for storing records; an office where archives, books, and papers, are stored.

誠 *꜀ch'ăng* From *words* and *perfect;* it much resembles *kiai꜄* 誡 precept.
Guileless, sincere, honest, truthful, real; perfect in virtue, without falsity; unalloyed; to judge candidly; as an *adverb,* really, verily, certainly, in fact.
ǀ 敬 sincere regard, pure-minded reverence.
投 ǀ to return to allegiance.
ǀ 實 sincere; earnest about a thing.
克 ǀ capable of sincerity; disciplining one's self.
ǀ 心在乎人 sincerity of heart depends on a man himself.
著 ǀ 去僞 employ the upright and dismiss the treacherous.
ǀ 不知 I really am ignorant of it.
至 ǀ 感神 entire sincerity will move the gods.
中庸不外一 ǀ the inculcation of integrity is the whole object of the Due Medium.
虔 ǀ 再拜 devoutly repeat the worship.
輸 ǀ to be earnest in a work, to do it heartily.

郕 *꜀ch'ăng* The name of a small feudal state lying in the west of Shantung, included in the present 東平州 near the Grand Canal.
隰 ǀ an ancient town in the present Hwai-k'ing fu 懷慶府 in the north of Honan.

澄 *꜀ch'ăn* Clear, limpid; still, pure.
ǀ 清 pure, transparent.
月 ǀ 明 bright, as the clear moon.
ǀ 江 a limpid stream.
ǀ 州 an ancient region in the north of Kwangsi, in the present 柳州府 near the Willow River.
ǀ 城縣 a district in 同州府 in the east of Shensi, along the Yellow River.
ǀ 海縣 the district in Kwangtung in which Swatow lies.

瀓 *꜀ch'ăng* Like the preceding.
Still, limpid.
ǀ 江府 a prefecture in the east of Yunnan; its chief town lies on the north side of Sien Hu 仙湖 or Fairy Lake.

丞 *꜀ch'ăng* Composed of 卪 a *seal* over 山 a *hill,* and 廾 two *hands* reverencing, altered in combining them; *q. d.* small hills assist a higher peak; it is like the next.
To aid, to second; a deputy, a coadjutor, an assistant; used chiefly in official titles.
ǀ 相 a prime minister; — an ancient term.
縣 ǀ a deputy to a *chi-hien,* or district magistrate.
文 ǀ 武尉 the civilian premier and the military guardian, — are the names of door guardians written over doors as a charm.

承 *꜀ch'ăng* The original form is composed of 卪 a *seal* over 手 a *hand,* and 廾 two *hands* reverencing, as when receiving a seal of office; used with the last.
To receive, to accept; to succeed to a post, to exercise a function; to take a charge, to carry out a plan; to be honored; to take in hand; to catch, as water from a spout; to receive orders, as a shopman; to anticipate; to withstand; to go with, as an escort; to contest, to compete with; to assist, as a deputy; to support, to carry on; to uphold; in *rhetoric,* the opening up of a proposition; next, second to; to stop.
ǀ 繼 to adopt, to take an heir.
ǀ 接 to take in, as a job; to contract for.
ǀ 你責言 I hear your representations, or advice.
奉 ǀ adulation, flattery.
ǀ 定 to take a business off another's hands.
不克靈 ǀ 于旅 unskilled in dealing with the multitude.
今不 ǀ 于古 if we do not now accept the guidance of the ancients.
ǀ 受不起 he is inadequate to do the job; he cannot accomplish it.

丨載 to contain, as a ship's hold.

丨不起來 it cannot support, or bear up so much.

莫我敢丨 they will not dare to resist us.

這事我丨當起來 I will answer for that matter; I will bear the brunt.

石丨 a stone base or plinth.

子產爭丨 heirs disputing about the division of an estate.

丨發 to receive [a dispatch] and forward it; the officer in a Board who does this.

呈 ꜀ch'ăng From 口 *mouth* and 壬 *to flatter;* as a primitive, it sometimes imparts the idea of presuming on.

To state to a superior, to complain to a plea, a statement; to hand in a petition; to offer, to present to; to show, to discover.

丨上 to lay before a superior, as in a 丨子 plea, petition, or accusation.

丨露 it has come to light.

進丨 to present a plea to a high official; to memorialize.

卽丨 I now send this statement.

丨覽 or 丨電 this paper is for your inspection.

丨控 to put in a rejoinder or demurrer; to accuse a party in court.

丨瑞 signs of general prosperity.

丨遞 to send a letter or report to an equal.

丨政 to send [an essay] for revision, as to a teacher.

丨期 the days on which papers are received by a court, at the most six in a month.

程 ꜀ch'ăng From *grain* and a *statement.*

An order, a series; a minute measure, the hundredth part of an 寸 inch, now known as a 厘; a rule, a pattern; a regulation; a limit, a period; a task; an allowance; a measure, a percentage, a part; a touch in assaying silver; to measure, to estimate; to use as a pattern; a road, a post, a journey; to travel; a Taoist word for a leopard, which was its local name in the Tsin state, B. C. 300; an earldom in feudal times.

送丨儀 to give one for his traveling expenses.

起丨 to start on a journey.

限丨 a day's travel, a stage.

路丨 or 丨途 a road, a journey; the way gone; *met.* one's career or course in life.

不丨其力 I wrongly estimated his strength.

匪先民是丨 they do not pattern after the ancients.

快丨 to travel fast.

憶歸丨 I am thinking of the quickest road to get home.

兼丨走 to travel an extra distance; a forced journey.

一丨 a tenth.

九丨九可以 ninety-nine to a hundred it will do; — *i. e.* it is most probably so.

丨式 a form, a pattern to work by.

這一丨子好嗎 have you been well these few days (or lately)?

幾丨足 what touch is it?

丨數 a percentage on one's accounts; also the quality or meltage of silver.

工丨 a job of work, as in building.

各願前丨 each looks forward to his future preferment; whence 大多前丨 what rank do you now hold?

珵 ꜀ch'ăng A brilliant stone worn at the girdle; it will shine if it be buried six inches, and seems to denote a carbuncle or diamond.

豈丨美之能當 it cannot compare with the beauty of the diamond.

裎 ꜀ch'ăng To disrobe so as to leave part of the body naked; spreading garments; to carry in the girdle.

裸丨 half-naked.

丨衣 under-clothes, garments next to the skin.

酲 ꜀ch'ăng To drink till fuddled; half sobered, and ashamed of being tipsy; stupid from drink; a sickness arising from drink.

解丨 to get over a debauch.

憂心如丨 sorrowing so as to look like one stupid from drink.

埕 ꜀ch'ăng From *earth* and a *statement;* an authorized character used in the southern provinces.

An amphora or earthen jar of a pear shape, having no ears or handles, and with a small mouth; used to hold oil, spirits, or water.

水丨 a water jar.

一丨酒 a jar of spirits.

油丨 an oil biggen; it holds 30 catties.

In *Fuhchau*, used for ꜀*ch'ang* 場 A floor or arena for drying grain; an area before a house.

糞倒丨 a place for refuse, a compost-heap.

堘 ꜀
塍 ꜀ch'ăng } A dike or ridge between fields, made high and broad, on which the laborers can pass from one field to another.

盛夏丨田泛綠雲 in midsummer the diked fields look like clouds of waving green.

懲 ꜀
惩 ꜀ch'ăng } From *heart* and *proof;* the second contracted form is most used.

To repress, to correct, to curb, as officials do miscreants; to correct one's self; to punish; to reprimand, to reprove; a warning, a caution; punishment, as a corrective.

治丨 to govern strictly, just as the law requires.

丨忿 to restrain one's wrath.

小丨 an admonitory hint.

勸丨 to exhort and warn.

丨創 to keep in order; to train by good laws, as a teacher does.

從重丨辦 to strictly carry a sentence into execution.

定丨不貸 I certainly shall punish and not pardon them.

逞 *ˏch'ăng* From *progress* and a *plea*.

To act on an impulse, to act with effrontery; presuming, froward; relying on one's pretensions or power; to permeate; irascible, precipitate, hasty; to free from; to go to an extreme, to exhaust; pleased with.

不可億 丨 utterly inexhaustible.

乃可以 丨 this can be removed, as a misfortune.

不 丨 careless, desultory; displeased.

不 丨 之徒 a reckless fellow.

丨 其鬼蜮 acting simply for his own selfish ends.

丨 功能 confident in one's abilities, overweening.

自 丨 boastful, vaporing; to brag of one's self.

丨 兇 to murder one in a passion.

丨 威勢 relying on his power and intimidation.

丨 干戈 eager for battle.

丨 强壓鄉黨 to browbeat the villagers.

丨 惡行刧 to rob and pillage without restraint.

徎 *ˏch'ăng* A bye-path; to go in a path; a gulley or way worn by the rain.

騁 *ˋch'ăng* To gallop a horse; to hasten on, to press forward, as when defeated; animated, excited.

馳 丨 to ride on fast, to drive rapidly.

丨 懷 elated; hilarious, as one on a fleet horse.

丨 詞 an animated style; lively, forcible writing.

悜 *ˋch'ăng* Obscure, or half brought out, as a meaning or idea.

其言慏 丨 his words (or expressions) are difficult to be understood.

秤 *ch'ăngˋ* From *grain* and *even*; it is used for *ˏch'ing* 稱, but only in this tone.

To weigh; to adjust by weighing; a steelyard; a weight of 15 catties.

一把 丨 a steelyard.

丨 到準 it is weighed accurately.

丨 杆 the beam of a steelyard.

丨 鉈 the poise or weight.

丨 鈎 the hook.

司碼 丨 to weigh full weight, or 16 taels to a catty; the weights themselves.

丨 茶 to weigh teas.

心如 丨 the heart is like a balance — to discern right and wrong.

丨 平斗滿 even balances and full measures; — a just, honest dealer.

CHOH.

Many of these characters are heard pronounced like chioh. *Old sounds,* diok, dok, djak, dak, tak, tok, tet, *and* tot. *In Canton,* chéuk, t'éuk, chüt, chuk, *and* chok; — *in Swatow,* tió, chiet, chiak, chwat, chwak, to, *and* tòk; — *in Amoy,* chiòk, tiòk, tòk, chòk, *and* chwat; — *in Fuhchau,* chiòk, tiòh, ch'iòk, chwòk, chòk, *and* tauk; — *in Shanghai,* tsék, ts'eh, tsòk, *and* zòk; — *in Chifu,* tsoh.

着 *ˏchao* *ˏcho* Originally the same as 著 *chuˋ*; it has gradually been altered from that to denote the differences in their meanings.

To cover over; to put on, as clothes; to cause, to order, to send; to stick to; to place; at, in, present; must, ought; after a verb, it gives force to the meaning, and indicates a transition or completed action, as 遇 丨 I met one, I came across him; 洗 丨 having been washed; between two verbs it makes the present participle, as 溜 丨 走 gliding and going, *i. e.* gliding on; before a verb, it is an auxiliary, let, make, permit, as 丨 丁前赴天津辦事 let Ting proceed to T'ientsin to attend to the affair; when used in a reply, yes, so, truly, right, exactly so; a way, a manner; to add; a move in chess.

尋 丨 了 I have found it.

丨 實 certainly; entirely right.

丨 意 to give attention to.

睡不 丨 I could not sleep.

丨 他來 bring him here, tell him to come.

背 丨 面 he turned away his face.

丨 急 impatient, anxious.

不要 丨 忙 don't be discomposed.

三十六 丨 走爲上 丨 among all the moves [in playing chess], move forward your men is the one.

這事還沒 丨 落呢 this matter is not yet finished.

全無 丨 落 there's no remedy; it is all over with him; I can't find anything of him.

這麽 丨 that's the way; this is the sort.

丨 上些 add a little, as salt.

In *Cantonese*. Correct; suitable, useful.

丨 唔 丨 is it right or no? will it do?

丨 數 cheap, good for the price.

丨 用 useful; it will serve.

好 丨 it sets well, as a coat.

點遇得 丨 how shall I get it to him?

In *Fuhchau*. Seized, taken with, as a fit; to hit a mark.

丨 脉 I hit his pulse; — I shamed him completely.

燋, *ˌchao* To set fire to, to flare up, to blaze out.
一燒就 ㅣ it will catch fire presently.
點ㅣ了燈 he lighted up the lamps.
火ㅣ了 the fire has kindled.

勺, *ˌshao* From 勹 to *wrap* with a dot to denote something *solid* inside; occurs in Shi king for 芍 the pæony.
To dip or lade out with a spoon; a little, a spoonful; the tenth of a *hoh*, 合 or gill; a hymn of Duke Cheu's liturgy; to adopt, to follow.
一ㅣ之多 as much as a spoonful.
漏 ㅣ a colander; a skimmer.
水 ㅣ a ladle for dashing on water.
北斗似 ㅣ the Northern Peck resembles a ladle.
長 ㅣ at the age when a lad plays; *i. e.* ten years to sixteen; a place in Lu where Chwʻang kung gained a victory.
舞 ㅣ an ancient place in Lu where a great battle was fought in the Cheu dynasty.

杓, *shwoˀ* From *wood* and *ladle;* used for the last and 彴; also read ˌ*piao*.
A handle, as of a cup; a ladle, a spoon; to lead; to tie, to bind to.
斗ˌㅣ the handle of the Dipper.

灼, *shwoˀ* To burn; to cauterize with moxa; to singe; to overroast; clear, distinct.
明 ㅣ dazzling, glorious, lustrous; splendid.
ㅣ艾 to burn the moxa.
ㅣ ㅣ其華 the flowers are so exuberant.
ㅣ知ㅣ見 to perceive clearly at a glance.
ㅣ龜 to scorch a terrapin's (or *Emys*) shell to use in divination; this shell is selected because it has 28 segments, answering to the Chinese zodiacal signs.
ㅣ爛 raised a blister.

彴, *chwaˀ* Also read ʻ*pao*, and interchanged with the next.
A shooting star.
ㅣ約 a meteor that rushes across the sky.

彴, *shwoˀ* Used with the last.
A board or plank laid down to bridge a stream.
略 ㅣ 横 秋 木 the plank lies across the rushing creek.

妁, *shwoˀ* From *woman* and *ladle.*
A go-between; to consult concerning surnames, as a match-maker.
媒 ㅣ an intermediary for marriages.

酌, *ˌcho* From *wine* and *ladle;* used with *choh*, 勺 to ladle.
To pour out liquor, to fill a cup; a glass; wine, liquor; a feast, a party; to deliberate upon; to choose the right and act on it; to adopt, to imitate; to avail of.
薄 ㅣ my slight repast, — said by the host.
喜 ㅣ a marriage feast.
對 ㅣ to drink healths.
春 ㅣ a newyear's entertainment.
媒 ㅣ (or 苗 ㅣ in *Cantonese*,) the return feast given by the bridegroom.
薑 ㅣ a feast given on a birth; the 上ʾ ㅣ, the 中 ㅣ and the 下 ㅣ, are the main feast, the servants' course, and what is left for muleteers, &c.
ㅣ酒 to pour out wine; to entertain guests.
一酬一ㅣ都非偶 after this glass, we will be well acquainted.
參 ㅣ or ㅣ議 to consult about.
ㅣ量妥當 all is satisfactorily settled.
斟 ㅣ而行 they consulted about it and then acted.
ㅣ於民為政 to rule according to public sentiment; to hear the people's voice.
泂 ㅣ彼行潦 take water from the distant pool.

鼩, *ˌcho* From *rat* and a *spoon;* it is also read *paoˀ*
An animal described like a large marmot, the ㅣ鼠 found in Sz'chʻuen, also called 鼨鼠 and 鼫鼠 the great rat; it is most probably, the North China squirrel (*Sciurus Davidianus*) which lives in rocky hills and holes, and its hair is used for pencils; also an animal that can fly like the flying squirrel, or the *Anomalures* of Africa.

斫, *ˌchö* From *hatchet* and *stone;* used with the next.
To cut with a sword; to chop, to cut up fine; to amputate, to hew off.

斮, *ˌchö* To cut in twain.
ㅣ鱗 to scale fish.
ㅣ朝涉之脛 [Cheu-sin] cut off the shins of those who crossed the ford in early morning.

輟, *chʻohʾ* From *carriage* and *connected.*
To rest, to hold up, to stop; a carriage which has been repaired; to reunite, as a cart.
ㅣ工 to suspend work, to rest.
或作或 ㅣ now working and then resting.
讀書勿 ㅣ do not remit or interrupt your studies.
ㅣ業而嬉 to cease work and take a holiday.

穛, *ˌchao* Ancient name of a city in the state Tsi, now in Tsinan fu in Shantung.

惙, *chohʾ* Mournful, grieved; unsettled; out of breath.
憂心ㅣㅣ undecided; sorry.

頔, *chohʾ* From 頭 *head* contracted and 出 to *issue.*
The cheek-bones; the aspect of the face, as a physiognomist looks at it.
顴 ㅣ the cheek-bones.
隆 ㅣ high cheek-bones.

辵, 辶, *cho* From 彳 to *step out* and 止 to *stop*; it is used in the contracted form as the 162d radical of a large and homogeneous group of characters relating to travel.

Going on, and stopping; to run fast and stop.

卓, *cho'* Composed of 早 *early* and 匕 a *spoon* above.

To establish, to make firm; stable and lofty; to surpass; tall or raised above others in person or talents; eminent in; distant, profound; reached, as a time.

超丨 fine-looking, excelling all; supereminent in ability.

旂杆之丨立 [like] the stateliness of a flag-staff.

丨異 meritorious, as officials who are mentioned at the quinquennial examination.

丨然高堅也 [this doctrine] excels in profundity and difficulty.

丨越人群 superior to others in any way; tall, stately.

倬, *cho* From *man* and *to surpass*.

Tall, lofty; bright; to manifest, to exhibit; extensive.

明丨 clear, luminous.

有丨其道 there is a plain road.

丨彼雲漢 how brilliant is yon Milky Way!

棹, 桌, *cho* From *wood* and *surpassing*; the second form is least used; the first is also used for *chuo'* 櫂 an oar.

A table, a stand; name of a tree.

丨子 a table.

椅丨 chairs and tables.

倚丨 a low writing-stand.

吃獨丨 to eat by one's self.

橫頭丨 a side table; a sofa table, on which are placed flowers, &c.

夯丨面 to carry a table-top;—a euphemism in Peking for wearing the cangue.

八仙丨 the Eight Genii table, is one for eight sitters.

捉, *cho* From *hand* and *leg*, perhaps referring to the act of a policeman.

To seize, to arrest; to gripe, to lay hold of; to grasp; to catch.

丨獲 or 捕丨 to arrest a criminal; to catch, as a thief.

丨鼠 to catch rats, as a terrier does.

丨拿 to gripe firmly; to seize.

守丨 the subordinate troops who guard the frontier;—an old term.

In *Cantonese*. To guess accurately; to apprehend, to see through.

丨你用神 I can see all your thoughts.

猜丨意思 to guess the intention; to hit one's fancy, as in a gift.

浞, *cho* To soak; to steep in water a little, to dampen.

寒丨 a man of the Shang dynasty, famed for his power of slandering others.

In *Fuhchau*. Scurf on the hands; dirty crust on dishes.

鋜, *cho* From *metal* and *leg*.

To bind the feet with gyves; fetters; a hoe.

啄, *cho* From 口 *mouth* and 豕 a *pig* tied by two legs.

To peck, as a fowl; to preen or plume the feathers; a bird picking up food; in *penmanship*, a quick stroke to the left.

丨毛 to dress the plumage, as a duck does.

丨木鳥 the woodpecker; the 山丨木 or black woodpecker (*Dryocopus martius*) also called 火老鴉 great crow.

丨食 to eat, as birds do.

丨殼 to break its shell, as the inclosed chick does.

剝丨 to rap, as on a door, when coming in.

In *Cantonese* pronounced *téung*. To thump one's self with a brick, as beggars do.

丨頭殼 to pound one's skull.

啅, *cho* Sometimes used for the last.

A multitude of people disputing.

丨丨 the notes of a bird, probably of the magpie.

In *Cantonese*. To coax, to beguile one to do a thing.

琢, *cho* Used with the next.

To push; to beat; to peck or pierce wood; the sound of rapping; a reverberation.

丨門 to knock at the gate.

椓, *cho* Interchanged with the last.

To strike; to ram; to afflict; to castrate, for fornication in the palace; an old term for eunuchs.

丨之丁丁 rapping on it again and again; knock after knock.

涿, *cho* From *water* and a *pig* tied by two legs for the sound.

To drop, to trickle, to fall drop by drop, a stillicidum; to strike on the water; name of a stream southwest of Peking, which gives its name to 丨州 in Shun-t'ien fu; but Choh-luh 丨鹿, the capital of Hwangti (B. C. 2680), was the present 保安州 in Süen-hwa fu, northwest of Peking.

雨丨濕了衣服 the rain has wet my dress.

瀧丨 a dropping, as a spring trickling down the rocks; spattering and dripping.

琢, *cho* To work in gems; to cut, to carve, to dress up jewels; to work on; to choose, as good expressions.

雕丨 to cut and polish gems.

丨工 a lapidary.

如丨如磨 like cutting and polishing; *met.* the labor of making a fine composition.

玉不丨不成器 an unwrought gem is a useless thing, or cannot be put to any use.

修丨詩文 to improve and polish the style and rhythm.
敦丨其旅 he carefully selected his assistants.

諑, ˏcho To accuse, to report against, to vilify.
丨謠 to slander, to insinuate errors against one.

斲, 斵, ˏcho From 㔫 a *vessel* and 斤 the *ax*, which is to cut it out from the wood.
To cut to pieces, to hack, to chop, to hew; to hash, to mince; to rive; to carve out.
丨削 to hew and trim, as a log.
丨棺 to dig out a coffin — from a log.
方丨是虔 we carefully hewed them square.
丨爛 to chop in pieces.
丨肉圓 to make mince meat balls.

濁, ˏcho From *water* and *worm* as the phonetic.
Muddy, drumly, turbid; unstrained; thick, impure; vicious; dull, stupid; degenerate; name of one river in the east of Sz'ch'uen, and of other streams; another name for the Hyades.
丨 and 清 are opposites; foul and limpid; corrupt and pure.
世丨 a corrupt, wicked age.
丨氣 dull of apprehension; a foul smell, odorous.
丨流 a turbid stream; the rabble, the canaine, the unwashed.
丨酒 unstrained liquor.
丨到兒 dull but muscular; a rude, vigorous man, as a peasant.
重丨 what settles in turbid water.

鐲, ˏcho A sort of cymbals, or small bell plates, anciently used for stopping the drums in an army; a small brazier, a hand-stove; bracelets, wristlets.
丨子 or 手丨 ornaments for the wrist; armlets.

擢, ˏcho From *hand* and a *flabellum*.
To pull up; to select, to lead on, to raise; to promote, to employ in office; to excite; to remove; to reject, as good resolutions.
丨髮難數 [like] hairs that cannot be counted if one pull them out,—these cannot be numbered.
丨用 or 丨取 to select and use—for governmental employ; to recommend one for such use.
拔丨人材 to select men of real worth.
丨德 to quench one's scruples, to vitiate or restrain virtuous feelings.

濯, ˏcho To rinse, to dip; to wash; great, bright, as a fame; sleek, glossy; to drink; to ramble about; fat, as a deer.
丨湖 a small lake in Sin-ch'ang hien 新昌縣 in the northwest of Kiangsi.
洗丨 or 洒丨 to cleanse; to reform, as the heart.
丨丨 bare as a sandy hill; sleek, as a deer; bright, as trappings.
翩翩丨丨 graceful and clean, lithe and sleek, as a youth.
丨足萬里流 I've washed my feet [in the Yangtsz',] and the water has run a myriad *li*.

灂, ˏcho A heavy rain.
大雨丨丨 the rain came down most violently and copiously.

茁, ˏcho Grass starting; the budding forth of plants.
丨壯 growing lusty, fattening, as cattle.
草丨其芽 the grass is sprouting.

蚍, ˏcho A garden spider, the 丨蟱 which makes its web on the grass, and has a door to go in and out of it.
Read *k'uh*, and used for 蝠. A grub in timber.

拙, ˏcho From *hand* and to *issue* as the phonetic.
Stupid, unhandy, unskillful, the opposite of 巧 clever; a depreciatory term used by people of themselves; clumsy, unworkmanlike; bad, unsuccessful, as a speculation; gradually becoming worse.
丨子 my stupid son.
丨筆 my poor penmanship.
丨作 my rude composition.
丨嘴 an unskilled lip, *i. e.* a bad speaker, a slow or stupid fellow.
丨性 slow of apprehension.
守丨 or 藏丨 to keep mum, to pretend to be stupid or ignorant; to act the ninny.
丨笨之極 stupid in the extreme.
丨計 an unwise plan, a silly scheme.
丨算 a bad speculation, a losing adventure.

啜, 歠, 歡, ˏcho From *mouth* or to *blow*, and to *connect*; the last form is antiquated.
To drink with a noise; to taste; to sip, to suck; to kiss; to prate incessantly and praise people; to sob.
丨面 to kiss one's cheek.
留丨 to detain one to take a cup.
丨菽 to live on meager fare and simples.
流丨 to slobber in drinking, to swill down.
惧丨汁作漿 he hastily sucked the juice, thinking it was gin.
丨菽飲水 he ate pulse and drank water.
丨其泣矣 crying and weeping bitterly.

婑, ˏcho Noise of strife and scolding; angry, irate.
婠丨 good-looking, according to some authorities.

窽, ˏcho Looking out from a hole; coming out of a cave.

棳, 梲, ‹cho — From *wood* and *to connect* or *weigh out.*

A small king-post above the girder which connects with the upper tie-beam; a club, a cane.

丨杖 a shillelah, a cudgel.

揮丨而呼狗 swing the club and then call the dog—of course he will not come.

山節藻丨 he has painted his rafters and carved his joists; referring to a foolish parvenu.

Read *toh,* Used for 脫 to leave.

始乎丨成乎文終乎悅 commence [your writing] as a draft, finish it by careful polish, and end it with pleasure.

畷, ‹cho — From *field* and *to connect.*

Raised dykes, six feet wide, to go from one field to another, as is the case over southern China.

畛丨 pathways through the field and country.

醊, 餟, ‹cho — The wine or spirits used in libations; to worship by pouring out libations to the lares, or the gods, several times in succession.

奠丨 to offer libations.

錣, ‹cho — A needle or awl; sharp, like a needle; the sharp end of a staff; to offer, as a present.

䜵, ‹cho — The mouth stuffed with food when chewing; to eat fast or vulgarly.

CH'OH.

Several of these characters are heard pronounced ch'ioh. *Old sounds,* t'ok. *In Canton,* ch'éuk *and* ch'uk; —*in Swatow,* ch'iak *and* ch'òk; —*in Amoy,* ch'iòk, tòk, ch'òk, *and* chak; —*in Fuhchau,* ch'iòk, tauk, *and* chék; —*in Shanghai,* ts'èk *and* tsòk; —*in Chifu,* ts'oh.

綽, ch'o' ‹ch'ao — From *silk* and *excelling* as the phonetic.

Slow, leisurely; large, spacious; liberal, generous; indefinite, vague; many.

寬丨 not hurried, taking it easy; ample, wide, as a house; well versed in; to render liberal and generous.

丨丨然 ample room for; not used as it might be;—said of one capable of higher things; also, shadowy.

丨丨有裕 more than enough;—applied also to brotherly kindness.

丨號 a nickname; a pet or fancy name; to nickname.

苗條丨約 beautiful, delicate, as flowers or young girls.

丨態 guileless, pureminded, loving.

婥, ch'o' — A *woman* who *excels;* beautiful; used with the last.

丨約 delicate, shrinking, like a girl unacquainted with the world.

Read *tih,* A sick woman.

焯, ch'o' — From *fire* and *excelling;* it is interchanged with *choh,* 灼 to roast.

Light, bright; heat, caloric; one defines it, hot, boiling, as water.

丨爍 sparkling, glittering, as melted iron.

逴, ‹ch'o — Distant; going to a distance; to hasten, to walk fast; used with the next.

舶丨風 a spanking breeze—after a ten days' rain; —name of an ode of Su Tung-p'o.

Read *tiao'* To overpass; to step over.

踔, ‹ch'o — From *foot* and *excelling;* also read *chao'*

To stamp on with the foot; to jump over; to get ahead in running; to stride; to excel.

丨脚 to walk lamely.

丨遠 distant, as in walking far.

丨絕之能 unusual ability.

丨夭蟜 to writhe when trodden on; to stretch out, as when running.

婼, ‹ch'o — Disobedient, disobliging; the name of a statesman in the kingdom of Lu.

Read ‹'rh. A country.

丨羌 was one of thirty-six Turfan states, or tribes west of China.

擉, ‹ch'u — To pierce, as with a dart; to harpoon, to spear fish or turtles; used sometimes for *tsoh,* 撮 to take a pinch, to take up in the fingers; and also for *ch'uh,* 觸 to gore, to run against; to punch; a harpoon.

丨刅 a fishing-prong.

丨刺 to spear.

丨一丨 take a pinch, as of snuff.

鐵义丨鼈 he struck the turtle with the iron fork.

別用手丨破窓戶 don't burst the windows in with your hands.

戳, ‹ch'wo — From *spear* and *flabellum;* used with the next.

To stab; to punch, to stick into; to affix a stamp, to seal; a die, a stamp.

丨記 an official seal, such as is used by petty officers, or constables; the seal of a company or corporation.

蓋丨 to affix a stamp.

丨子 a stamp in common characters, not an official seal; as 名丨子 a name for cards.

丨頭機 to deceive one.

拿棍子丨 give it a punch with your cane.

錨齒丨損 the anchor's flukes ran [into the bow], and stove it in.

戳 ˓ch'wo To pierce; to dart through one, as a shooting pain; to build and beat an abobie wall; a fish-prong with a cross piece.

齪 ˓chwo From *tooth* and *foot;* an allusion perhaps to the harsh noise made.

To grate the teeth; an augur or tool to make a hole.

握丨 or 齷丨 pettish, ill-tempered, the latter also means dirty, vile, mean.

委瑣握丨 cross-grained, narrow-minded, discontented.

CHU.

Old sounds, té, tu, tot, dé du, djot, t'o, *and* t'ot. *In Canton,* chü, *and a few* cho; — *in Swatow,* chu, tù, *and* tu; — *in Amoy,* chu, cho, tu, *and* t'u; — *in Fuhchau,* chiò, chwò, chü, tu, t'ü, *and* tùü; — *in Shanghai,* tsö, tsü, tsz', dzö, tsu, *and* dzu; — *in Chifu,* chu.

朱 ˓chu Formed of 木 *wood* and 一 *one, i. e.* the *one tree,* referring to the heart-wood of the cedar, which is reddish or fiery.

Red, especially a vermilion color; it is considered a lucky color.

丨紅 scarlet.

丨提 silver, so called from the name of the mine.

共結丨陳 to make a contract of marriage.

丨雀 the scarlet bird, a fancy name of a position in geomancy.

丨門 the gentry, literary graduates; so called from an ancient custom of painting their doors red.

丨筆點頭 to dot the forehead [of an idol] red; this is supposed to vivify it with the god.

近丨者赤 he who comes near vermilion will get red; — like Prov. xiii. 20, He who walketh with wise men will be wise.

丨衣 the "red dressed,"—denotes the attendant of the God of Literature, or his star.

侏 ˓chu A pigmy is 丨儒, applied to men who are undersized.

丨柱 a sort of king-post, or short pillar in a roof-truss.

伶丨 name of an ancient musician.

株 ˓chu The trunk or bole of trees; a classifier of trees, posts, pillars, stumps, stalks of shrubs, &c.; low, degraded, kept down; in the lowest place.

桑樹七丨 there were seven mulberry plants.

丨枸 a tree broken off.

丨榦 a trunk of a tree.

丨守一隅 confined to one corner, as a clerk who cannot leave his home; *met.* kept in obscurity.

丨梜 a hard wood, good for naves.

丨林 a grove, a forest of large trees.

洙 ˓chu A small stream in Shantung flowing north from Tai-shan into the River Sz'.

丨泗之間 the region of the rivers Chu and Sz' where Confucius taught.

珠 ˓chu From *gem* and *red.*

A pearl; a bead; a string of beads; small and round like a pearl or bead; pearly, fine, excellent; round and bead-like; beaded.

一粒丨 or 一顆丨 one pearl.

丨江 the Pearl River, which flows by Canton; the application to the entire stream is not known to the people.

江丨 a name for amber.

假丨 or 礬丨 false pearls; while 眞丨 are real pearls; and the Budhists say 赤眞丨 the red-true pearl, for the ruby or spinelle, the Sanscrit *padmaraga.*

眼丨 pupil of the eye; but others say it denotes the crystalline lens.

有眼無丨 your eyes have no pearls; *i. e.* you're half blind; you can't distinguish things.

素丨 or 念丨 a Budhist rosary of 108 beads, referring probably to the 108 compartments in the *phrabat* or sacred foot of Budha, wherein are pictured his attributes and attendants.

朝丨 a necklace worn by officials.

丨寶 pearls, gems; jewelry, bijouterie.

一串丨 a necklace, a string of beads.

節菰丨 beads shaped like a flat squash, made from a sort of smooth, gray grass-seed, resembling those of Job's tears.

丨圓玉潤 pearly, fat-cheeked; handsome, elegant; polished, as a fine composition.

魚目混丨 mixing up fish-eyes and pearls; *i. e.* indiscriminating.

連丨砲 a continued firing, a cannonade.

東丨 or 夜明丨 the night-shining pearl, spoken of by Taoists; it may mean the pyrope or carbuncle; a brilliant gem, which the Emperor is said to possess, and shines like a lamp.

藥丨 seed pearls, used in making, the 丨珀散 or pearl powder sprinkled on ulcers.

火丨 a sun-glass to ignite moxa; it is made of crystal, and was early brought from India.

丨履三千客 three thousand rich men, who had pearls on their shoes.

硃 *chu* From *stone* and *red*; this is often incorrectly written *shu* 銖 a small weight.

Vermilion; made of vermilion; imperial, because the emperor uses red ink for his autograph in official writings.

銀丨 vermilion,—either the powdered preparation, the color, or the paint.

銀丨錠 a cake of red ink.

丨砂 cinnabar.

丨砂桔 the mandarin orange (*Citrus nobilis*), named from its vermilion colored skin.

丨筆 the Emperor's pencil, an imperial autograph.

丨批 the Emperor's approval; an official endorsement.

丨卷 the essays of graduates who are successful; so called because they are copied in red.

丨諭 the vermilion or autograph order.

朱 *chu* An unauthorized character, probably altered from one of the last two, used in Canton for the cheeks.

面丨墩 full rosy cheeks.

跦 *chu* To hop, as a wren; to get on by hops; used for 躕 in 踟丨 embarrassed, unable to get on, uncertain what to do.

丨丨 hopping about.

蛛 鼄 *chu* From *insect* or *frog*, and the next character contracted.

The spider; called in Peking 丨丨; whence a lazy, good for nothing fellow is called 土丨丨 the name of the burrowing spider or *Atyphus*.

蜘丨網 a spider's web.

丨絲 filaments of the web.

草蜘丨 ground spiders, like the *Epeira*.

蜘丨集而百事喜 everything prospers where there are plenty of spider's webs.

誅 *chu* From *words* and *red* as the phonetic.

To seek for in order to punish, to make judicial inquiry; to punish capitally, to put to death, to kill; to reprove; to involve for another's crime; to eradicate, to clear away.

丨累 to involve in punishment.

丨除 or 丨滅 to utterly exterminate, as a family or rebels.

丨戮 to cut off, to execute.

伏丨 to be decapitated; executed.

丨罰 to reduce to subjection, to punish.

丨其過 to expose and reprove his crime.

丨草 to dig up and clear off plants or grass.

丨求無厭 to desire inordinately; insatiable, as a conqueror.

以惠丨怨 to overcome hatred with kindness, or evil with good.

天丨 a divine judgment, as to be killed by lightning, or some remarkable casualty.

邾 *chu* Name of a feudal state which existed B. C. 700 to 469, under ten rulers; now the district of Tsau hien 鄒縣 in Yen-cheu fu in the south of Shantung; 小丨 was a small principality southwest of it, near the present Tăng hien 滕縣 in the same prefecture.

丨城 was a city to which the people of Chu 邾 were removed; it is near Hwang-cheu fu 黃州府 in Hupeh, on the Yangtsz' River.

祩 *chu* To curse.

呪丨 to imprecate evils on one.

袾 *chu* Red garments; to dress; elegant.

丨襦 short dresses, underjacktets.

丨冕 a red coronet, is a term given by one author.

茱 *chu* From *plant* and *red*.

A small tree, the 吳丨萸 *Boymia rutæcarpa*, allied to the Xanthoxylon, growing in the eastern provinces; its bitter seeds are used by the Chinese in coughs and tonic medicines; the ripe capsules are deep red, and the seeds black; which herbalists say should be gathered on the 9th day of the 9th moon to be most efficacious.

丨萸肉 is the fruit of the 山丨萸 a sort of dogwood, (*Cornus officinalis*) used as a vermifuge and in fevers.

諸 *chu* From *words* and *this*.

To discriminate, to distinguish; an *adjective* of number placed before its noun, not one only but many; all, every, several; as a *preposition*, it marks origin or place, to, in, respecting, in regard to; at, upon, from,—modified by the preceding verb; it stands for the pronoun at the end of a sentence; a final particle implying doubt or asking a question; it is sometimes introduced only for the rhythm; frequently occurs in names of places.

書丨紳 wrote it on his girdle.

遇丨路 I met him on the road.

人其捨丨 will men reject him?

丨事勞駕 I give you much trouble.
丨如此類 all are like this.
丨凡 all of, the whole.
丨位 or 丨君 all you gentlemen; you, Sirs.
視丨斯 look at it here.
惟求丨己 he only depends on or thinks of himself.
丨侯 feudal princes; a prince; the dignity or post of a prince.
王如改丨則必反予 if the king alters his mind, then he must recall me.
有丨 denotes a doubt whether it is so or not; as 不識有丨; 曰有之 I did not know whether there was a way; he said, there was.
文王之囿方七十里有丨 was not Wăn Wang's park 70 *li* square?
丨丨便便 of a ready wit; able to argue; quick and fluent.
其丨 before ꜀*yü* 與 denotes perhaps, or, probably; as 其丨此之謂與 this was probably what he wished to say.
日居月丨 days and months.
丨般 all sorts; every variety.
于丨 in this, going to this.
丨于 a certain robe worn by empresses in the Han dynasty.
丨生 *siuts'ai* graduates; *i. e.* the whole body of them.
丨子百家 all classes of authors.
丨蔗 or 甘蔗 are two old names in Annam for sugar-cane.
桃丨 or 梅丨 peaches or plums preserved either in sugar or salt; an ancient mode of preparation.

櫧 ꜀*chu* A kind of oak furnishing a durable timber, found in Honan; the acorns are sharp pointed, and acrid to the taste, whence they are called 苦丨子 bitter acorns; silkworms feed on the leaves; it is not improbable that a kind of oak is referred to by the same name in other parts.

猪 豬 ꜀*chu* From *dog* or *beast* and *that*; it is interchanged with the next when used as a verb.

A hog; any animal of the genus *Sus*; to dig a trench or pool.
丨子 or 丨隻 a pig.
丨母 or 丨牳 a sow; it is used for coarse in Fuhchau, as 丨牳針 coarse needles.
丨公 a boar.
山丨 a wild hog, differing perhaps from the 野丨, *Sus leucomystax*, common in China.
箭丨 a hedgehog.
豪丨 the porcupine, found in Shensi.
丨油 or 丨膏 pork-fat, lard.
丨毛 or 丨鬃 hog's bristles.
丨排骨 pork-chops.
丨脚凍 or 丨脚氷 pig's foot jelly.
丨籠草 the pig-basket plant, or pitcher plant, the *Nepenthes distillatoria*.
丨苓 a kind of China-root; or perhaps a *Lycoperdon* or puff-ball.
丨頭三牲 a boar's head, with a carp and a cock, — to worship Plutus.

潴 ꜀*chu* From *water* and *hog* as the phonetic.

A place where water stagnates; a pool or small lake, a puddle; to dig out, as when making a pool, or confining its limits.
丨河氷 an affluent of the Grand Canal in Tsi-ning cheu 濟寧州 in Shantung.
大野旣丨 the pools and marshes in the wilderness.
洿其宮而丨焉 to raze the palace, and dig a pool there—so as to obliterate it.
孟丨 a marsh in Kwéi-teh fu, near Yü-ch'ing hien 虞城縣, once drained or restrained by the Great Yü.

蠩 ꜀*chu* One says an edible worm or larva like a silkworm.
蟾丨 a term for a toad.

株 ꜀*chu* A dead tree still standing.
枯丨 dead, rotten trees.
衆木槁丨 all the trees are dead.

丶 ꜀*chu* ꜂*chu* The original form of this character, which is now used as the 3d radical of a small group of miscellaneous characters, originally represented a flame, as of a candle.

As fire appertains to the heart, this character has come to mean the ruling power of the will, or the clear intelligence of the heart, for which the next is now used.

A point, a dot, such as is put on the top of the character *wang* 王 to vivify the ancestral tablet; in *penmanship*, read ꜂*tien*, for 點 a dot.

主 ꜀*chu* ꜂*chu* The character originally represented a lamp-stand with the *flame* rising.

That which gives light; a ruler, a lord, a master; a host; the chief; the head; to rule, to make one the chief; to indicate, to show what is to be; certainly, with authority, as a lord's will.
丨人 the host; the head of the house; a master.
家丨 a pater-familias; used by children and domestics.
業丨 a landlord, the owner of real estate.
丨婚 the master of a wedding.
丨公 or 丨上 or 丨子 our sovereign; used in speaking of him.
君丨 or 國丨 the emperor; a sovereign; the chief ruler of a country.
上公丨 the emperor's sisters.
太上公丨 the emperor's aunt.
誰作丨 who is lord here? who manages this?
丨在你家 I'll make you my lord in your house; *i. e.* I am going to visit you.

丨顧 a patron, one who buys much.

有頭丨 she has a head; she is married; also used by traders, [the goods] are spoken for.

天丨 the Lord of Heaven; God is so called by the Roman Catholics, and 天丨教 is the name for their sect and the Greek church; but 主 and 眞丨, are both used for God by the Mohammedans.

天父恩丨 the heavenly Father and merciful Lord.

丨宰 the controler, the superintending power;—a term often applied to God.

丨日 a term for the Sabbath or Lord's day.

神丨 the ancestral tablet; intimating that the deified lord resides in it.

我不敢專丨 or 我不敢丨張 I can't venture to take the control; I dare not assume the direction.

丨意 the will, the fixed resolution.

丨意不在我 the decision is not with me.

有丨意 I have a plan.

丨張 to give directions, to manage; an overseer.

爲丨 to be or take the head, regarded as chief; it is of the greatest moment.

縣丨 a district magistrate.

正丨考 and 副丨考 the chief and deputy literary examiners at the *küjin* tripos.

丨守 to guard, to protect.

必丨得福 it will certainly bring you good luck.

丨下雨 it indicates rain.

丨治 to govern; to rule as an autocrat; a Budhist term for an abbot.

財丨 or 財丨老 a rich man.

自丨 free, voluntary; as I like.

施丨 a donor, as to a temple or a charity.

拄 ʿchu From *hand* and to *rule;* it occurs used for *chu'* 柱 a pillar.

A prop or post; to shore up; to pierce, to stick; to point sideways; to oppose.

丨楣 a prop or stretcher, as to an awning.

丨拐 or 丨棍 a crutch, a stick; to lean on a staff.

鞋 ʿchu A sort of overalls or leathern gaiters for the knees.

麈 ʿchu From *deer* and to *rule* as the phonetic.

A large beast like a deer, found in Tung-chʿwen fu in the north of Sz'chʿuen; he guides the herd, indicates their course by shaking his long tail, which brushes away the dust; if other deer see it, they follow his track. This animal has been identified by some with the Chinese elk or tailed deer (*Elaphurus Davideanus*); but a comparison of native books shows that it is more probably a general term for a large stag, the *ruler* of *deer*, and not any species; it is drawn with spots and having one stumpy horn; the large red deer of Mongolia (*cervus maral*) may be the one; a fly-whip or switch.

丨尾 a chowry, used by fairies; some authors suppose that the chowry from Tibet is furnished by a deer, instead of the yak.

拂丨而談 to converse while whisking away the flies.

揮丨無由停 unceasingly twirling the chowry — to drive off the musquitos.

祇聆丨談 I respectfully listen to your guiding remarks.

砫 祍 宔 ʿchu From *stone* or *worship* and *lord;* the third form is unusual.

A stone tablet dedicated to ancestors in the family temple.

丨祏 a stone shrine or niche, in which the tablet is placed.

神丨 the ancestral tablet.

渚 陼 ʿchu An islet; a low place, a wash in a river, a deposit appearing above the waters; an affluent of the R. Hwai in Honan near Hü cheu,

寶丨 the precious land, an ancient name for Ceylon (*Ratna-dwipa*, probably derived from its pearls and gems.

蓬萊之丨在海 the isles of fairies are far away in the sea.

江有丨 in the rivers are islets,—which were slowly formed; and so must you persevere.

煮 ʿchu To cook, to dress food; to boil in water; to steep, to decoct; boiled, cooked.

丨熟 boiled through; to cook thoroughly.

丨飯 or 丨菜 to dress a dinner, to prepare food.

丨茗 to make tea; to prepare an entertainment.

丨海爲鹽 to boil sea-water to get salt.

詛 ʿtsu From *words* and *further.*

To curse, to announce to the gods and implore calamities upon others; curses and oaths before the gods to bring punishment on others, or for evils suffered.

丨誓 oaths and curses.

丨盟 an imprecation sealed by blood.

口毒丨人 to curse and rail at others bitterly.

丨駡 cursing and railing.

丨盡嘴 to take a dreadful oath; lips filled with curses.

阻 ʿtsu From *place* and *further.*

A defile or torrent among hills which hinders progress; separated by obstacles; to hinder, to impede, to oppose, to discommode; to cause delay; dangerous from some impediment; to suspect, to doubt; to grieve.

丨止 to stop, prevent progress.
險丨 a hindrance, stumbling-block; something in the road.
隔丨 an impediment, as a hill; far separated and thus hindered.
丨碍 to prevent from accomplishing, to retard, to try to defeat.
丨難 hardships, straits; everything working against one.
丨攔 or 擋丨 to stand in the way of, to block, to oppose.
丨事情 to hinder business, as an untimely visitor does.
山川修丨 the hills and rivers sunder us widely;— as friends.
丨風于瓜步 a head wind detained me (Su Tung-p'o) at Kwapu.

In *Cantonese*. A sign of the past tense, used after other verbs.
去丨 he has gone; left.
拈丨來 he has brought it.

炷 ‘chu From *fire* and to *rule* as the phonetic.
That which guides the flame; a wick; a stick of incense; to light.
丨香 to burn incense sticks, to worship the gods; but 一丨香 is one incense stick.
燈丨 a lampwick.
三丨香 three incense-sticks; this number is usually lighted at once by worshipers in reference to the trinity of powers.

蛀 ‘chu Insects like the *Ptinus*, which eat books or clothes; moths in furs; insects like the carpenter beetle, especially referring to the fly; to eat, as such insects do; eaten, bored.
丨爛 spoiled by insects.
丨空 all eaten through.
虫丨了 it is all worm-eaten.

澍 ‘chu From *rain* and *flowing water*; like the next.
A seasonable rain, 丨霖 one which fills the channels, and starts the vegetation.

澍 ‘chu Like the last. Water running off in streamlets; moistened, well watered; to fertilize by rain.
丨生萬物 timely showers cause things to grow.
丨濡 saturated with water; enriched by favors.

駐 ‘chu From *horse* and to *rule* as the phonetic.
To rest one's horse; to stop, to sojourn, to live at for a while; a stopping-place, a hostelry.
丨足 to lodge, to tarry over, to put up at with one's carriage.
丨紮 or 丨劄 or 丨扎 to be stationed at, temporarily filling an office at a place; appointed to live at.
丨蹕 places where the Emperor halts in a progress.
丨防 to live on guard — in the provinces; applied to the Bannermen stationed out of the capital.

住 chu' From *man* and to *rule*; it is easily mistaken for ‘*wang* 往 to go.
To halt, to stop; to cease; to detain; to dwell; to live in; to endure, to erect; when following another verb, it usually forms the present tense, or shows that the action has just stopped, as 揸丨 hold it; 歇丨 rested a little; but it also forms the imperative, as 塞丨 stop it up; 停丨脚 stop walking, hold up your going,— according to the context; a classifier of birds.
守丨路口 keep guard over the passes.
丨步 stay your steps; stand there.
丨手 hold up; stay your hand.
忍不丨氣 I can't help being angry.
忍不丨 I am not equal to that, I can't endure it.
你在那裏丨 where do you live?
居丨 living at.

丨口 he ceased talking.
丨了哭 he stopped crying.
靠不丨 unreliable; an unsafe dependance.
丨持 a custodian of a temple; the resident or head-priest.

咮 chu' The noise of calling fowls; a distorted mouth; occurs used for *cheu'* 咮 the bill of a bird.
丨丨 to chuck for fowls when calling them.

柱 chu' From *wood* and to *rule* as the phonetic
A pillar, a post, a stanchion, a joist; a main dependance, a support; a statesman; a chief agent or manager in; to uphold; to rely on; a row or line, as in writing; clusters of stars in Auriga and in Centaur.
丨意 the leading ideas in a paper; the heads, as of a sermon.
丨墩 the base or plinth of a pillar.
五丨 at the South, denotes a house of five pillars.
國丨 or 砥丨 a high statesman.
擎天丨 one who bears up the state, the Atlas of his country.
丨廳 a hall supported on pillars, a pillared porch.
樑丨之材 the ability or service of beams and pillars; *i.e.* useful officers or statesmen.
丨工 the nuts of a lute.
珠丨 the red pillars; a poetical name for a 琴 lute.
丨後 a kind of official cap.

注 chu' From *water* and to *rule*; it is used with the next, and occasionally for *chu'* 著 to manifest.
Water flowing off in streamlets, or shooting over a ledge; to lead water in channels, to flow out; to soak, to saturate; to fix the mind on, to direct the thoughts to; to collect; to comment on, to record; to strike; belonging to.
丨念 to remember, to ponder.
丨意 attentive; to think on much
先丨于我心 I had that idea already

上丨 to fix the thoughts on heaven.

丨目 to set the eyes on; to gaze.

丨射 to hit the nail on the head, to describe exactly.

重勞關丨 I am extremely obliged for your thoughtful regard — for me.

大雨淋丨 the rain pours violently.

挹彼丨此 take it from this, and direct it that; to have one's hope realized, or design appreciated.

丨矢於弦 to set the arrow on the string.

仰承俯丨 look out above and mind what's below; pay heed to what goes before and comes after, as the arrangment of your sentences; regard the orders of the sovereign, and listen to the people.

註 *chu'* From *words* and *to rule* as the phonetic.

To define, to explain; to open out the sense; to write about, to record; an emendation or gloss; used in some cases for *ting'* 定 to determine; destined.

丨明 a clear explanation; written clearly and fully.

丨释 to illustrate the meaning of; notes.

丨解 an explanation.

丨記 to note particulars, to keep a record.

丨作 or 丨述 to write an essay on.

補丨 to add to the commentary.

丨疏 an open, full explanation, as of the classics.

丨生丨死 he fixes the day of birth and of death.

牏 *chu'* From *slip* and *yes*; it is also read *ˌt'eu* and *ˌyü*.

Short boards used in beating adobie walls; a wall to screen off a privy or a bath; a cess-pool; the receptacle of dirty water from a bath.

著 *chu'* From *plants* and *this*; it is the original form of *choh*, 着 to cause, and is interchanged with *chu'* 註 and *chu'* 注 to narrate.

Bright, clear; conspicuous; to set forth, to manifest; to write an account, to narrate; to fix, to settle; to publish, as a book; the space between the gate and the screen wall inside; the revolution of a year.

其名彰丨 his name is increasingly known.

丨述 or 標丨 to narrate in a record; to write occurrences, as in a journal; to write a history.

丨其善 to pretend to his goodness.

表丨 or 顯丨 to manifest, as Christ did the will of God.

箸 **筯** *chu'* From *bamboo* and *this* or *helpful*; the first also means a delicate sort of bamboo, and the second is defined the hermit-crab or its temporary abode.

Chopsticks; to take up food with them.

牙丨 ivory or bone chopsticks; the 比丨 are usually made of bamboo.

一雙丨 a pair of chopsticks.

架一丨 put down your chopsticks, — in pledge of a glass.

飯黍毋以丨 cooked millet cannot be taken up with the chopsticks.

不堪下丨 it is not worth putting the chopsticks into it; *i. e.* uneatable.

舉丨用菜 take up your chopsticks and begin — to eat.

玉杯象丨 he has jade cups and ivory chopsticks; *i. e.* he is very extravagant and lavish.

助 *chu'* *tsu'* From *strength* and *furthermore*.

To assist, to help; to succor; beneficial, strengthening.

帮丨 to succor, to aid.

丨成其事 helped him to finish the affair.

丨你一臂之力 I will lend you a helping hand.

資丨 or 樂丨 to cheerfully aid — by a donation.

丨威 a guard of honor, an escort.

隻身無丨 I can't do it by myself; I am not able to effect it alone.

丨紂為虐 whoever helps Cheusin (the Nero of China) will become truculent; *i.e.* a companion of the cruel becomes cruel.

翥 **翥** *chu'* From *feathers* or *to fly* and *this*; the second form is rather pedantic.

To fly upward; to soar into the sky, as a phœnix.

鳳丨 the phœnix soars on high; — denotes a bride going to her husband's house.

鳳丨鸞翔 a flying phœnix and soaring argus; — a newly married pair.

鑄 *chu'* From *metal* and *longevity* as the phonetic; occurs read *chuh*,

To cast, to fuse metal for running into molds, ancient name of a small feudal state in the present Shantung, north of the River Tsi; used for *chuh*, 祝 to wish happiness, to bless.

丨錢 to cast cash or coins.

冶工丨器 the founders cast vessels.

鎔丨 to found; to melt and cast, as a boiler.

聚鐵丨錯字 all the iron you could get would not suffice to cast your faults.

丨金事之 such virtues should be cast in gold — to preserve them.

馵 *chu'* A horse with the near hind leg white, or one having white knees; to ease one leg, as a horse does, by standing on three.

駕我騏丨 harness up my dappled lightfoot.

丨足 a name for *chăn'* 震 the fourth diagram, referring to the mode of shackling a horse's two legs to teach him to amble.

宁 chu' From a *shelter* and a *man*; but the original form represents a strong room to contain stores or preserve them, for which the next is now used; some of the compounds show traces of its meaning.

The space between the throne and the retiring door behind it, is called 朝 丨, where the attendants stand within call.

貯 chu' From *precious* and to *store* up as the phonetic.

To store up; to hoard; to lay by for safety; to put in its place; a store of, a hoard; an accumulation, a treasure.

積 丨 to keep in store, as the government does.

藏 丨 or 丨 棧 to warehouse; kept in the warehouse.

存 丨 無 幾 there's not much left.

丨 庫 it is put in the treasury.

丨 粟 to store up grain.

In *Fuhchau*. Containing; to hold; holding; contained in.

丨 水 it holds the water.

丨 苦 鼻 so full as to touch the nose, as a bowl of rice.

紵 chu' A coarse kind of hempen cloth; suitable only for bags and wrappers or poor clothes.

絺 丨 fine and coarse hemp.

眝 chu' From *eye* and to *store*; it is similar to *chu'* 注 to fix.

To stare at.

丨 目 to fix the eyes on, as when stupidly amazed.

羜 chu' A lamb five months old.

旣 有 肥 丨 the fatted lambs are ready.

詝 chu' That which is known; knowledge. This character is contracted to 訨 unless it is used for the personal name of the late Emperor Hienfung.

鉒 chu' To inter valuables with the dead; to temporarily place a thing; metals in their ores, which are to be known by the aspect of the surface soil, whether 丨 銀 or 丨 金 or 丨 銅 ores are beneath.

杼 chu' From 木 *wood* and 予 to give.

A shuttle; thin, as the wheels of a cart, which cut into the mire; long, said of the head; a low, scrubby oak, for which 栩 is another name, and 柔 another form; a water trough or flume.

豐 人 丨 首 long-lived people have long heads.

腹 丨 經 綸 he is full of learning as a filled shuttle.

丨 軸 其 空 the shuttle and reed are empty; a time of want; these two parts of a loom seem to have been once differently named, as the *chuh*, 軸 is said to be the shuttle, and the other the reed, and made of earthen.

孟 母 斷 丨 Mencius' mother cut the web in the loom, — in token of her grief and disappointment.

筀 chu' The nut to which the strings of a lute are fastened, and by which they are tuned.

CH'U.

Old sounds, t'é, t'u, t'ot, t'op, dé, du, *and* dot. *In Canton*, ch'ü, ch'o *and* shü; — *in Swatow*, ch'o, k'u, tù, ch'u, *and* tiu; — *in Amoy*, ch'u, ch'o, k'u, tu, *and* t'u; — *in Fuhchau*, ch'è, ch'u, kü, yü, *and* tü; — *in Shanghai*, ts'u, ts'ü, tsö, ts'ö dzü, dzu, *and* tsz'; — *in Chifu*, ch'u.

初 ꜀ch'u From *knife* and *garment*, alluding to the tailor's craft.

To cut out clothes, *i. e.* to begin the making of garments, which is the first step in civilization; to begin; the first; at first, the early part; incipient.

丨 丨 or 當 丨 when it began; at the first.

丨 發 市 to make a great show at opening the shop.

丨 來 a new comer; the first visit.

太 丨 at the beginning.

丨 開 天 地 at the creation.

丨 一 the first day of the moon.

丨 旬 or 丨 間 the first decade of a moon.

丨 幾 來 which day of the [first] decade did you come?

丨 學 to commence study.

出 丨 the first part of next moon.

人 之 丨 性 本 善 man's nature originally was good.

丨 次 the first-time.

丨 開 埠 to open a new port for trade; to found a mart, as Raffles did Singapore.

愼 厥 丨 be careful how you begin a work.

丨 生 the firstborn.

In *Cantonese*. A final particle; to stop or wait.

你 等 吓 丨 do you stop a while.

亞 丨 哥 a novice, a raw hand.

芻 蒭 ꜀ch'u ꜀ts'u The character is intended to represent 艸 *grass* bound in two 勹 *sheaves* or faggots; the second form is unused.

To cut grass; hay, dried grass for animals, fodder.

生 丨 一 束 a bundle of green grass.

飼 丨 fodder for cattle; to fodder them.

丨靈 a scarecrow, a straw man; effigies burned at a funeral.

丨蕘者 grass and reed cutters; *met.* the people.

丨豢 four domesticated animals which are reared, *viz.* the horse, sheep, ox, with the dog.

丨尼 a name for the magpie.

[口楚] ˓*ch'u* To scold people; a colloquial word, imitating the sound of scolding or reproving.

樞 ˓*shu* From *wood* and a *corner; q.d.* the stick that keeps the corner.

The wooden pivots on which a door turns; an axis, a center, that on which a thing hinges; what is indispensable, fundamental, cardinal; the source of power; a spinous tree like a buckthron, or hornbeam, called 刺楡 or thorny elm.

丨機 the controling power, as the boiler in a steamer; the moving spirit, the guiding mind.

丨機之位 the station of chief authority.

丨紐 or 丨要 the central part on which a machine works; the gist of an affair.

金丨 a term for the moon.

天丨 or heaven's pivot, is the star Dubhe *a* in Ursa Major.

丨密 the secret pivot; an old term for a general; in the Sung dynasty, 丨密院 denoted the privy council.

丨垣 the pivot's wall;—a name for the Censorate.

中丨 the powers or machine of government in the capital and provinces.

貙 ˓*shu* A feline animal called 丨虎, marked like a fox; it is big as a dog, and was once used in sacrifice; it is probably the cheetah or ounce, but may also denote the lynx.

[王雩] ˓*shu* A kind of stone, the 丨玗 whose description allies it to the jasper.

樗 ˓*shu* From *wood* and prayer for *rain.*

A tree with glossy bark and fetid leaves, whose timber is fit only to burn; it is another name for the *ch'eu*˒ ˓*ch'un* 臭椿 or fetid *Ailantus glandulosa*, common in northern China; it is also applied to the *Euscaphys*, or bladdernut of Japan.

丨櫟之材 useless material, as the ailantus and scrub oak, neither of which furnish very good timber;—a depreciatory phrase used by officers when speaking of themselves.

丨鷄 the ailantus hen, is a beetle with gray elytra and red wings, common on this tree; it makes a humming noise, and is called the 紅娘子 or red damsel; it seems to be a sort of Cerambyx.

摴 ˓*shu* Pleased, gratified; for which the next is also used.

丨蒱 to make antics and perform like mummers, for which slaves were once employed; it now means to play cards.

攄 ˓*shu* From *hand* and *anxiety* it is used with the last, and much resembles ˓*lu* 擄 to capture.

At ease, pleased; to scatter, to spread; to ascend, to mount as a carriage; to discuss and settle.

丨所見 to set forth one's views, to express one's ideas.

龍驤超丨 the dragon (*i. e.* fleet) courser distanced all the others.

丨頌六經 he fully understood and made known the six classics.

姝 ˓*shu* From *woman* and *carnation* as the phonetic.

A pretty woman; a beautiful, accomplished female; timid; to adorn, to dress up, as a woman does.

丨麗 beautiful; a bright face.

彼丨者子 that elegant, handsome man.

丨色 a pretty face, a handsome lady.

除 ˓*ch'u* From *place* and a *person.*

The steps going into a palace; the vestibule or porch; the space between the door and an inner screen; to take off, as a dress; to exclude, to root out, to remove; to divide or subtract; to do away with; to pass, as time; to take away; to be kept out; to exchange; to open; to vacate; as a *preposition*, besides, excepting, exclusive of; and is used in regimen with *wai*˒ 外 outside.

丨服 to lay aside mourning.

歸丨 or 丨起 to divide by one or more figures, as in division.

丨去 to eject, to push away.

丨病 to remove disease or its causes.

丨非 if, when, premising, thenceafter.

丨此之外 besides this; not including this.

丨下 take it down.

丨了皮 taking away the tare; not reckoning the case.

庭丨 the outer porch.

丨道 to cleanse or prepare a road.

丨官 to remove from office, to degrade.

丨收尚欠 besides what is now received, some is still owing.

日月其丨 the days and months glide by us.

丨害安良 to suppress the evil and quiet the good.

滁 ˓*ch'u* ˓*shu* A small branch of the Yangtsz' River that flows into it between Nanking and Iching, which gives its name to Ch'u cheu 丨州 a city and prefecture in the east of Nganhwui.

篨 ˓*ch'u* A mat rolled up.

籧丨 a coarse mat; a disease that makes one repulsive; a deformed person, a hunchback.

蒢 ꜀ch'u A small medicinal plant, 蕏 丨, otherwise called 地榆 or ground elm; it bears white flowers with a yellow center; it is perhaps allied to the *Hedysarum*.

蜍 蠩 ꜀ch'u From *insect* and *person* or *all*; the second form is little used, and also means a huge caterpillar.

A toad is called 蟾 丨; parts of it are used medicinally; it is seldom eaten, and sometimes grows to a huge size; it has many local names.

潴 ꜀ch'u Name of a small stream flowing from the Hăng shan 恒山 in Ta-tung fu in the north of Shansi, into the Sang-kan and Yung-ting Rivers, and thence into the Pei-ho at T'ientsin.

儲 ꜀ch'u From *man* and *all* as the phonetic.

To collect, to lay up for need; furnished with; to assist; to be second to.

丨貨 stored, bonded, warehoused.

丨積 accumulated, in store.

東丨 or 丨君 the heir-apparent.

丨胥 an imperial pleasure-ground.

廚 厨 ꜀ch'u From *shelter* and to *stand waiting*; the second is a common, but unauthorized form.

A place for killing and cooking animals; a kitchen; a case for holding books, clothes, crockery, &c.; a quiver.

丨人 or 丨子 or 丨官 a cook.

丨房 a kitchen.

幫丨 a scullion, a cook's mate.

丨店 a public cooking-shop, a restaurant.

庖丨 a large kitchen; with an abattoir attached.

碧紗丨 a gauze safe. (*Pekingese.*)

一口衣丨 a clothes-press; one wardrobe.

櫥 ꜀ch'u A screen which is put up to make a temporary kitchen.

躇 ꜀ch'u Undecided, as if one's feet were fettered.

躊丨 at a loss how to proceed; sometimes used to intimate a desire for advice, or for help to relieve one from perplexity.

躕 ꜀ch'u Similar to the last.

Puzzled, in a fix; uncertain what to do.

搔首踟丨 he scratched his head, uncertain what to do.

雛 鶵 ꜀ch'u From *fowl* and dried *grass*.

A chick which can pick its own food; a fledgeling; the callow young of birds; to rear a brood.

The second character also denotes the name of a bird, the 鵷丨, a variety of the peacock.

丨於其中 rears its brood inside of its hole, as the kingfisher.

丨鷄 a little chick.

丨得狠 the birds are very callow.

力不能勝一匹丨 his strength was not equal to lift one fledgeling, as of a duck.

鋤 鉏 ꜀ch'u From *metal* and *to help* or *furthermore*; the second form is not much used.

A hoe, a mattock; to cultivate the fields, to hoe and delve, and thus *assist* the growth.

丨頭 a hoe.

誅丨 or 丨地 to hoe up, as weeds; to hoe the ground.

强丨 a stout farmer.

犁丨之計 the business of agriculture, as of those who 扛丨把子的 shoulder the hoe.

帶經而丨 he took his classic and went off to his hoeing.

丨鋙難入 unfitted for each other, unsuitable, like putting a round handle into a square hole.

媰 ꜀ch'u From *woman* and dried *grass*.

A pregnant woman; a widow.

惠于丨孀 be kind to the widows.

蒭 ꜀ch'u The stalk of the small spiked millet; the straw of the panicled millet.

耡 ꜀ch'u From *plough* and to *assist*; *q.d.* the plowman aids the land.

A kind of corve or socage of the Shang dynasty, consisting of a certain number of day's work on the king's land as a way of paying rent, and thus assisting government; to assist in working land to pay taxes.

楮 ꜂ch'u A species of mullberry, 丨桑 the *Broussonetia papyfera*, from whose bark the Coreans and Japanese make paper; a coarse kind of cloth is also made of it by them, but the paper itself is much used for garments.

丨錢 paper money; such as is used in worship and then burned.

丨紙 paper from the mulberry.

丨片 a slip of paper, as that for notes.

丨儀 money given by friends for funerals.

特修寸丨 I specially send you this short note.

丨幣 bank-notes, paper bills; this term was common in the Yuen dynasty.

褚 ꜂ch'u A bag or satchel for holding clothes; a valise, a portmanteau; to cut out clothes; to pack away clothes.

丨幕 a high pall, or catafalque, over a bier.

杵 ꜂ch'u From *wood* and *noon*; *q. d.* the sound of the pestle heard at noontide.

A pestle; a beetle or beater with which to ram down earth; to beat with a pestle.

砧丨 a board or block, and the beater;—used by washermen.

秋山響丨 hear the washing boards resounding among the hills in autumn.

舂丨 to pound with a pestle.

丨碎 to beat very fine.

臼丨 a mortar and pestle; used as a metaphor for brothers, dear friends, married people.

金剛丨 the "diamond club," a Budhist term for the *vadjra* or scepter of Indra; name for a kind of mace used by priests when exorcising or praying, and as a symbol of the all conquering power of Budha, who overcomes sin by *pradjna* or wisdom.

楚 'ch'u — Originally composed of 林 a *coppice*, and 足 to *walk* in its center; *q. d.* it is hard to walk in a thicket.

A cluster or clump of trees, a bramble-bush; spinous, sharp; used with the next for painful, distressing; orderly, well-done, properly-finished; a large feudal state in the Cheu dynasty, existing from B. C. 740 to 330, under the rule of twenty princes; it occupied Hukwang and parts of Honan and Kiangsu, having K'ing-cheu fu on the R. Yangtsz' for its capital; the name is still applied to the two Lake Provinces.

丨丨 new and clean, as garments.

苦丨 suffering; distress, anguish.

辛丨 grievous, hard as work; toil and drudgery.

淸丨 perspicuous, as style; well-done, clear, fresh; spruced up, tidy.

夏丨 a ferule for punishing truants.

南丨 was the region about the Méi-ling, in the south of Hunan and Kiangsi.

In *Cantonese*. A form of the past tense, like 'yuen 完 done.

食丨飯 I have done eating.

整丨 the job is done; it's all made right.

憷 'ch'u — Interchanged with the last in the sense of grieved, miserable, pained.

礎 'ch'u — The base or plinth of a pillar; the stone on which it rests; a pedestal.

丨潤而雨 [a halo round the moon] and a moist plinth, are signs of rain.

佇 竚 'ch'u — From *man* or to *stand*, and to *store*; the first is rather the commonest.

To stand and wait a long time; to hope and wait for.

丨立 to stand near.

望丨 to hopefully expect, longing and waiting.

丨切 I wait on tiptoe; I eagerly look — for a reply.

倚欄丨眺 leaning on the railing and looking afar at it.

齼 'ch'u — The teeth set on edge, as by a very sour thing.

濋 'ch'u — Small streams which flow off aside, when a large river overflows its banks.

泞 'ch'u — Clear, limpid, as water; or spirits settled on its lees.

苧 'ch'u — From *plant* and to *store* up.

A plant like a nettle, the *Boehmeria nivea*, called *ramie*, *chuma*, *caloi*, and China grass; it is one of the hemps of China, of which ropes, grasscloth, coarse linen, and sackcloth (紵) are made.

丨根 hemp roots; they are ground with rice-flour to be used for food.

丨蔴 the nettle-hemp fibers, or plants, grown chiefly in the central provinces.

丨店 a grasscloth shop.

蔴丨裙衫鬓髮焦 their hempen garments were worn to rags and their hair unkempt; — a time of misery.

處 処 處 'ch'u — The second or abbreviated form is composed of 止 to *stop* and 几 a *seat*; *q.d.* one stops on reaching his seat; 虍 is added in the full form as the phonetic; it much resembles ꜀k'ien 虔 devout.

To be at, to rest, to dwell; to repress, or stop one's self; to be appeased, to rest from; to act, to occupy the place of; while in; to occupy as a country; to distinguish, to decide, to judge; to attend to, to do what is proper, to place; when preceding a verb, it sometimes denotes the past tense, or increases its force, as 丨斬 executed; or 丨治 to govern.

丨分 to judge one's abilities; to decide an officer's demerits.

丨士 an unemployed graduate.

丨女 or 丨子 a young lady, a maiden.

丨夫婦 when I was married; during my married life.

丨貧 to be poor.

怎麼丨 how? what could I do?

丨兩難 either course is hard.

丨暑 limit of hot weather; name of the 14th term, from August 23d to September 8th.

交部議丨 hand him over to the Board to decide his sentence.

難丨 not easy to judge.

相丨 friends living together.

丨君身 to be an officer near the emperor.

丨决 to sentence after trial.

丨置 placed, put safely.

丨置他 to manage, to do for one, to settle him; — implies a great difficulty in the case.

丨世 to enter on life.

丨不來 I can't bear him; I can't live, or get along, with him.

丨死 to visit with death; I mean to be the death of you; to compass one's death.

于時丨丨 here we had ample room to dwell in.

Read *ch'u'* A place, a spot; a circumstance, a condition, a point of a matter; used as a relative pronoun, as 兩丨之銀 the money of these two persons; when added to a noun, it sometimes makes the plural, as 大憲丨 the high authorities; and at other times denotes the concrete, as 正見他靈丨 we now see its spirituality.

別丨 elsewhere.

丨所 a location, a place; the spot referred to.

四丨 or 各丨 or 丨丨 everywhere; in all regions.

短丨 a failing, a shortcoming; an idiosyncrasy.

無丨不到 he went everywhere; he goes all about.

好丨 a good; in good circumstances; a benefit; an advantage.

有個去丨 he has a place where he hails from; he is not altogether a loafer.

本丨 I the officer,—said by those of low grade; I who write; the writer.

亦有可取丨 he has still some good points.

尊丨 and 敝丨 are terms in letters for *You* or *Sirs*, and *We*, when the names are not mentioned.

傗 *ch'u'* Rough, hispid; not smooth.

瘯 *ch'u'* From *sickness* and to *remove*.

A scar; scarred; stupid, not comprehending things.

癡丨不達 thick-skulled; not quickly taking the meaning of.

CHUH.

Old sounds, tok, dok, *and* t'ok. *In Canton,* chȯk;—*in Swatow,* tek, to, sȯk, chek, *and* tȯk;—*in Amoy,* tiok, chiok, chwat, *and* tek;—*in Fuhchau,* tùük, chùük, *and* tük;—*in Shanghai,* tsȯk *and* dzȯk;—*in Chifu,* chüh.

竹 *₍chu* The original form represented leaves drooping on two stalks, in which way the Chinese draw the bamboo; it is the 118th radical, called sometimes 丨花頭 *i. e.* bamboo flower top, and the characters under it mostly refer to kinds or articles of bamboo.

The bamboo, of which the Chinese reckon sixty varieties; musical instruments made of bamboo.

丨黃 tabasheer.

丨實 bamboo seeds, said to ripen mostly in years of famine.

丨竿 bamboo sticks or poles.

丨茹 the siliceous skin of the bamboo.

丨蘊 bamboo roots; whangees, or bamboo walking-sticks; umbrella-handles.

丨絲 bamboo splints or threads.

丨·瓤 shavings for cushions.

丨節樣 ribbed, ridged, corrugated, like bamboo joints.

南天丨 the *Nandina domestica*, much cultivated for its red seeds.

丨葉青 or 丨綠葉 a clear spirit in which bamboo leaves have been steeped; hence the 13th day of the 5th moon is called 丨醉日 because this liquor was drunk on that day.

丨布 a foreign name for Irish linen.

丨夫人 a long bamboo pillow.

淡丨 the spider-wort. (*Commelyna medica.*)

爆丨 large tubular fireworks; fire-crackers.

丨箭有筠 bamboo arrows have a hard skin; *met.* a person of clear mind and fixed purpose.

虛心丨有低頭葉 the lowly bamboo always bows its leafy head.

丨報 the "bamboo reporter," a poetical name for family letters, derived from a scholar in the Han dynasty, who always inquired about his bamboo grove.

竺 *₍chu* A sort of bamboo; the common name of India in Buddhist books, 天丨 or 西丨國 or 丨國, from the word *India;* this character was first altered from the last to designate a surname, and when adopted for *India* was read *tuh,* as a contraction of 篤 in the word 身篤 Shintuh or Scinde; it has also been written 身毒 or 捐毒 or 天篤 or 印度 and 天竺, all different forms of the same sound or name.

柮 *₍chu* Grieved; pain and distress manifested in the face.

憂心丨丨 sick at heart and cast down.

柷 *₍chu* From *wood* and the next character contracted.

An ancient musical instrument of wood used to start the band; it was made like a tub with a handle in the middle, or a chapper hung on the side that hit it when turned.

祝 *chu'* From to *worship* joined to *mouth of man; i.e.* to implore by words.

To help the master of ceremonies; to ask the gods for blessing, to pray for mercies; to supplicate the gods; to recite prayers; to be obliged for; to tie or bind; joined to, allied to, akin; to afflict, as by taking away one's friends; to cut off; to reiterate, to repeat as prayers; the origin; an ancient name of 禹城縣 in Tsinan fu in Shantung.

司丨官 an officer who recites the ritual.

無疆之丨 may your [Majesty] live for ever.

頌丨九如 to felicitate one every happiness, as when seventy.

丨告 or 丨禱 to say prayers, to implore, to ask the gods; to repeat 丨文 or forms of prayer.

丨福 to pray for blessings.

丨壽 to congratulate another on his birthday.

廟丨 an acolyte in a temple.

丨髮文身 to cut off the hair and tattoo the body.

厥口詛丨 he both cursed and prayed.

不必在彼遊歷爲丨 I beg of you not to wander or ramble about there.

丨融 a god of fire worshiped in summer; he is the deified son of 顓頊 an early monarch.

Read ꜀ch'eu. To curse.

侯作侯丨 they go on cursing still.

妯, ꜀chu Sisters-in-law call each other 丨娌, but not in direct address.

Read ꜀ch'eu. The mind not at ease; disquieted.

憂心且丨 sad and moved is my heart.

軸, ꜀cheu From 車 *carriage* and 抽 to *support* contracted; it is interchanged with 柚 in the last meaning.

That which supports the cart, the end of the axle; a pivot, that which turns as a center of power; the axis of motion; a catch, a bolt, a spring, whatever causes a thing to work; weak or crippled in walking; a roller, as of a map; a classifier of maps or pictures rolled up, — and often denotes the chart, map, or drawing itself, the reed of a loom.

車丨 or 丨子 an axle-tree.

丨兒 a catch, a bolt.

當丨 one who manages — the country, or an affair.

五人丨 a water-wheel turned by five men.

祭丨 a eulogistic scroll suspended near a coffin before its burial.

懸丨 the axis of suspension.

乾丨 or 坤丨 the heaven and the earth; their revolutions and movements as the axes of the universe.

卷丨 a roller, as for a map; rolls.

剪丨 the rivet of shears.

畫三丨 three mounted pictures, or on rollers.

千丨不如一書 a thousand drawings are not equal to one book — well studied.

舳 ꜀chu The after part of a vessel, the stern quarters where the steersman stands; the tiller or scull.

Read yiu. The bow of a vessel.

丨艫 a sort of scow for transport; the stem and stern of a vessel.

築, ꜀chu chu, From a *dulcimer* with *wood* under; occurs used for *chuh*, 妯 a sister-in-law.

To beat down hard as a thrashing-floor; to ram down the earth; to make chunam pavements or adobie walls; to raise, to erect; to build dykes or intrenchments; to gather; to flap the wings.

丨坭墻 to build mud walls.

丨馬頭 to make a jetty or landing-place.

丨石磡 to build stone piers, bunds, or sea-walls.

起丨砲臺 to raise a fort.

丨堤 to raise the banks.

修丨基圍 to strengthen and repair, the dykes or foundations.

筑, ꜀chu From *bamboo* and to *grasp*.

A kind of crooked dulcimer, shaped like a rude harp, having five strings; it was afterwards made with thirteen strings that were struck with hammers.

丨陽 the old name of Kuh-ch'ing hien 穀城縣 on the R. Han in the northwest of Hupeh.

貴丨縣 is the capital district in Kwéicheu province.

囑, 嘱, ꜀chu From *mouth* and *belonged to*; *shuh*, 屬 also occurs used for this; the second abbreviated form is common.

To bid, to order; to engage or ask another to do; to commit to another's charge by request or injunction; to enjoin upon.

丨咐 to charge one to do; to instruct.

丨托 to commission, to give in charge.

賄丨 to bribe, to fee in a case.

買丨 to suborn.

丨書 a will; a written injunction.

叮丨 or 叮嚀丨咐 to repeat an order, to reiterate it, to din it in the ears.

孎, ꜀chu The obedient and respectful deportment of a wife; a waiting attitude, as of one receiving instruction.

斸, ꜂chu To cut up the ground.

斫丨 to hoe and dig.

矚, ꜂chu To look earnestly; to fix the eyes on.

凝神遠丨 to gaze at from afar with earnest attention.

丨望 to look at from afar.

躅, ꜀chu From *foot* and *worm*.

To walk sedately; to limp or halt; a trace.

躑丨 to hesitate in walking; to pace off, to step haltingly.

躑丨 to amble, as a horse; to walk with a halting step.

踢丨 the rut of a wheel.

羊躑丨 a species of *Hyoscyamus*; the name probably alludes to its rejection by sheep.

In *Cantonese*. To knead with the feet, as in working or mixing things; to press on.

丨出腸 to crush out the bowels, as when trampled to death.

藸, ˏchu A kind of medicinal plant, called also 黃杜鵑 or yellow Azalea, and 老虎花 or tiger's flower; it is regarded as poisonous; it may belong to the *Apocyneæ* or oleander family.

燭, **烛**, ˏchu From *fire* and *worm;* the contracted form is also read ˏch'ung, to dry by the fire.

The illumination of torches; a candle; a torch; to light a candle; a light; to give or shed light upon, to illumine.

蠟丨 or 腊丨 a wax candle, a bougie; a tallow candle inclosed in wax.

硬油丨 hard candles, like those made from the tallow tree; harder than 牛油丨 tallow candles.

水蠟丨 or water candle, the *Typha* or cat-tail rush.

花丨 painted candles, such as are placed before shrines or used in worship; they are also made of wood, and called 看丨 or show candles.

丨花 a wick, when it is partly burned; its form is sometimes taken as an omen of luck.

丨斗 or 丨臺 or 丨插 a candlestick.

丨剪 snuffers.

坐花丨 refers to the part of a marriage ceremony when the pair are seated at the nuptial table before the candles.

洞房花丨夜 the lighted nuptial chamber.

小心火丨 take care lest you set the house on fire.

無微不丨 it shines everywhere; *met.* he sees the case clearly; he assists his relatives.

丨照無私 [the emperor's goodness is like the sun] which shines upon all without partiality.

風前之丨 [his life is as precarious as] a candle in the wind; said of old folks.

丨山 an iron frame for candles.

明丨 a clear understanding of.

燈丨光耀 the splendor of lamps and candles, an illumination.

丨星 an auspicious comet or bright star like a candle; one appeared B. C. 76 in the constellations 奎 and 婁 or Pisces and Aries, bright as Venus.

蠋, ˏchu A name for a short legged spider the 丨蝓, so called from its looking like a pigmy; a flea; the caterpillar of the sphinx moth.

粥, ˏchu ˏcheu Composed of 米 *rice* between what looks like *two bows*, but is intended to represent the steam of offerings; it is often described as 雙弓米 double-bowed rice. It forms a kind of sub-radical of many characters under *lih* 鬲 a boiler, with which this once was written.

Gruel, congee, mush, porridge; a thickened, decoction made of rice or millet boiled very soft.

煑丨 or 熬丨 or 煲丨 to boil congee.

猪肉丨 a kind of rice porridge with bits of pork.

荳丨 bean and rice porridge.

丨飲 the gruel of congee.

丨丨 humble, diffident.

茗丨 a preparation like the thickened fried tea of the Tibetans.

丨三碗飯也三碗 three bowls of congee and three of rice too; — the same rule for all.

喌, **啁**, ˏchu From 吅 to *call* and 州 *region;* the second and unusual form is also read ˏcheu.

To call fowls; the sound made when chucking fowls.

逐, ˏchu From 辵 to *walk* and 豚 a *pig* contracted.

To drive or push out; to expel; to order away; to fray away; to exorcise; to take up in order, as the heads of a discourse; to press, to urge, on, to hurry up; in earnest, sincere; successively.

丨出 or 丨去 to turn out, to drive away, to expel.

丨罵 to order off with abuse.

丨日 daily, day after day.

丨一丨二 or 丨個丨個 to take up one by one; to arrange orderly.

三仕三見丨 he held office thrice and was thrice dismissed.

朋友徵丨 to gad here and there, as companions urge or coax one.

丨細 minutely and carefully.

丨少而進 to advance step by step, to gradually become familiar with or learned in.

赶丨 to eject, to deport, to turn out by force, to evict.

其欲丨丨 he was really sincere in that; in this phrase it is also read *tih tih*.

瘃, ˏchu Sores arising from cold.

涷丨 chilblains on the hands or feet.

蓫, ˏchu A weed, called also 羊蹄 goat's hoof; it is difficult to extirpate, and seems to be a sort of *Rumex* or dock.

我行其野言采其丨 I went about the country gathering the docks.

豖, ˏchu From 豕 a *pig*, with a cross-mark to denote that two of its legs are tied; it is used only as a primitive, but conveys no meaning to most of the compounds.

丨丨 the appearance of a shackled pig trying to get on.

CH'UH.

Old sounds, t'ot *and* t'uk. *In Canton,* chòk, chut, *and* ch'ut; —*in Swatow,* ch'ut, tut, *and* tiòk; —*in Amoy,* ch'ut, t'ut t'iòk, ch'o, *and* chiok; —*in Fuhchau,* ch'ok, t'òk, hùük, *and* ch'öü; —*in Shanghai,* tseh, hiòk, *and* ts'òk; —*in Chifu,* ch'uh.

出, *ch'u* The original form represents stalks thrusting themselves out of the ground.

To go forth, to go out; the opposite of *juh,* 入 out—in; abroad—at home; to issue or manifest, to proceed from; to surpass; to eject; to leave finally; to spring from, to beget; its force is often modified by the next verb, and it frequently serves as an auxiliary verb to denote completion or progress of an act; as 丨賣 for sale; or 丨賃 to let; when joined to 不 after a verb, implies its negation.

丨來 to come out, as from the room; this phrase succeeds other verbs to denote the present tense, as 寫丨來 I am writing it.

你替我查丨來 do you examine it for me.

辨不丨來 they cannot be distinguished.

說不丨來 I can't express it well; I don't understand it clearly.

只走丨一半來 he will then have gone only half-way.

行丨來 to carry into practice; to bring forth fruit, as of a belief.

鬧丨事來 to create a disturbance.

丨頭 to act for others.

丨人頭地 to take the lead of others.

丨首人 an informer.

丨主意 to give directions about.

丨仕 to enter on public office.

丨身 to enter on life, to begin the world.

他做甚麼丨身 what did he spring from?

丨嫁 or 丨閣 to marry a husband.

丨家 to become a priest.

丨缺 to retire from a post, having filled the term.

人才丨衆 surpassing others in talent, preëminent.

丨沒無常 appears in a surprising degree; very unusual, inconstant.

想不丨 I cannot recall it to mind; it is inconceivable.

從心所丨 it was at first [my own] idea.

丨外 to travel abroad; to go out.

丨門 or 丨街 to go out of the house.

何時丨世 when were you born?

丨天花 or 丨痘 to have the small-pox.

丨恭 to retire respectfully,—to ease nature; 丨多少回恭呢 how often did the medicine operate?

丨將 and 入相 doors for entering and leaving the stage.

丨名 famous; 不丨名 do not let my name appear; incognito; sub rosa.

丨息 perquisites, extras; to fee for services; douceurs.

一位丨本一位丨身 one finds the capital, the other the service.

量入爲丨 reckon your income before you spend your money; estimate your expenses carefully.

百弊層丨 one cannot reckon up the defects; too many bad qualities to estimate.

言丨如山 his words are stable as the hills.

隨你丨心 do as you like about it.

丨貴 he brings honor—to the family.

丨聲 or 丨言 to speak out loud; to say something.

丨坭入脂 to get out of the mire into the fat; *i. e.* to rise from poverty to affluence.

露丨馬脚 to let the horse-hoof appear, to let the cat out of the bag.

丨氣 to fume, to fret; to avenge another's cause.

丨醜 to be despised; to draw odium on one.

黜, *ch'u* From *black* and to *issue* as the phonetic.

To degrade; to dismiss from office; to blame; to expel or drive away.

三丨 thrice dismissed from office—as 柳下惠 of Lu in the Cheu dynasty was, and then recalled.

丨陟幽明 to degrade the inefficient and promote the intelligent.

丨革 or 丨退 to cashier, to degrade, to dismiss officers.

丨辱 to expel dishonorably.

In *Cantonese.* To wrench or sprain.

丨着手 to sprain the wrist.

絀, *ch'u* Used for the last.

Crimson silk; to baste; to sew badly; to stitch coarsely; withdrawn, as notes from circulation; something in the way.

贏丨 to bend and to straighten; elevated, joyous, and then depressed, dull; uncertain.

支丨 or 短丨 short up for money.

財用之丨 impediments in the way of trade, as a want of capital, or banditti.

畜, *h'ü* *ch'ü* From *field* and *black,* referring to loamy soil good for pasturage; others say from 田 *field* and 玆 *increase* contracted; it is interchanged with the next.

To rear, to feed, to raise; to domesticate; to herd together; to entertain, as a guest; to bear with;

to restrain; to detain; to obey, as a child; cattle, domestic animals; to hoard; to store up.

丨君何尤 to restrain the prince from committing wrong.

丨生 you brute!

大丨 the 26th diagram, relating to wind.

丨養 to rear, as slaves, children, or animals; but 丨牧 is to pasture or rear only the 六丨 six domestic animals, which men use in sacrifice or food.

丨衆 to assist the people.

丨幸臣 to gather persons in a palace, as catamites.

丨德 to cultivate virtue.

難丨 hard to stand; not easy to serve, as an unjust prince.

蓄 ch'ü' Used with the last.

To collect; to lay up in store; to bring up; to rear, as vegetables.

丨積 or 丨聚 to accumulate, to hoard, to lay by.

丨力 to husband one's strength.

丨馬 to breed horses.

丨髮頭 to bring up slave girls.

丨疑 to strengthen suspicions.

我有旨丨 I have a good supply of vegetables — for winter.

丨意未釋 my anxious thoughts are not yet removed.

私丨 selfishly to lay up things — unknown to one's parents.

傗 ˏchʻu Bent down.

丨傶 unable to extricate one's self, compelled to stoop.

慉 ˏchʻu From *heart* and *to rear* as the phonetic.

To nourish; to foster; to hate; to excite.

丨驕 to encourage or develop pride.

丨怒 to stir up wrath; angry, wrathful.

不我能丨 he cannot (or does not) like me.

搐 chʻü' From *hand* and *to rear*.

To drag along by force; to shake rudely; a spasm or cramp of the tendons.

抽丨 to be taken with a cramp or numbness; convulsed.

滀 ˏchʻu Water flowing into a reservoir or pool; to flush from excitement.

丨漯 waters running together.

怵 ˏchʻu Afraid, timorous; to entice; to commisserate.

丨惕 apprehensive.

丨迫之徒 a wretch who is tempted on by avarice.

觸 chu' ˏchʻu From *horn* and *worm* as the phonetic.

To butt, to gore, to push with the horns; to run against; to oppose, to excite, to offend; stirred, moved, excited; to render one's self obnoxious; among the Budhists, denotes sensation, touch, perception.

丨怒 to irritate, to exasperate.

丨起 startling; to recollect suddenly.

頂丨 to butt, to run at each other, as rams.

丨犯 to insult; to sin wilfully.

丨山之力 vast, herculean strength.

牛丨角 the oxen are butting; also applied to fellows fighting.

丨機會 to suddenly meet a chance, — as for solving a doubt.

丨目驚心 interesting and startling, as a style or a narrative.

羝羊丨籓 the ram rushed against the fence, — and was caught by his horns.

丨類引伸 to single out one idea, and bring out — its bearings and results.

丨景生情 the circumstances excited his feelings, — as of joy or sorrow.

丨處洞然 when he attacked [a subject,] he mastered it.

丨寒 to take cold.

丨衣 a waistband used by ancient princesses.

歜 ˏchʻu Choked with anger; violent from raging passion; a man's name.

丨怒 filled with wrath.

叔丨國 a region beyond sea, to which Chwen-hiuh's son was appointed.

Read ʻtsʻan. A dish or platter on which square pieces of sweet flag were anciently served as a relish.

菖丨 a dish of sweet flag.

矗 ˏchʻu From *straight* thrice repeated.

Rising above others like an overtopping tree; lofty as a peak; luxuriant growth; straight and upright; to stand or set upright, as a pole.

丨然不誣 upright, without any deception.

崇山丨丨 the lofty hills rising like galleries.

直丨丨的 very straight like a flag-staff.

闎 ˏchʻu From *door* and three *men* inside; it is considered to be a Budhistic form of *chung'* 衆 a multitude.

A crowd standing in the doorway.

阿丨鞞 or 阿丨, or 阿丨婆 a fabulous Budha, called *Akchobhya* or 無動佛 the motionless, or impassive Budha; it is also defined as the kingdom of joy (*abhirati*), where this Budha dwelt; and a numerical term equal to one followed by seventeen cyphers.

亍 chʻö' The step with the right foot; 彳丨 first the left, then the right foot; this makes ˏhing 行 to walk; in these three characters there is an endeavor to depict the appearance of walking.

CHUI.

Old sounds, ti, tui, tut, tup, di *and* dut. *In Canton*, chui *and* ch'ui; —*in Swatow*, tui, chui *and* chué; —*in Amoy*, chui, tui, choé, sui *and* twat; —*in Fuhchau*, twi, tui, chwŏk, toi, chwoi, chw'i, *and* ch'oi; —*in Shanghai*, tsö, dzüé, *and* tsöⁿ; —*in Chifu*, tséi.

追 ˛*chui* From to *go* and a *mound* of earth.

To follow after, to pursue; to expel; to escort; to come up with, to overtake; to trace out, to follow to its source; to advert, to; to sue for; to reflect on, to look back on; retrospective; a wild ancient tribe.

丨趕 to chase, to try to overtake.

丨到 or 丨及 to catch up with.

丨他回來 hurry him back; run and call him back.

丨不到 I could not catch him.

丨悔 to feel remorse.

緊丨 a close chase.

愼終丨遠 carefully attend to those gone, and follow departed — ancestors.

丨封 to obtain posthumous honors for one's parents.

丨念 to reflect on.

丨非 to lay the blame on others.

丨債 or 丨討 to dun for debt.

銀不丨回 the money cannot be recovered.

遹丨來孝 he thus evidenced his inherited filial duty.

丨究 to sift to the bottom.

不丨論 let it drop; it need not be again spoken of.

來者猶可丨 future [evils] may perhaps be averted.

丨思往日 to recall past days.

丨兵 soldiers in pursuit.

Read ˛*tui*. To engrave; a graver.

丨琢其章 to engrave and carve the ornaments.

糙 ˛*chui* Also read ˛*tui*.

Flour cakes or dumplings; soft and sticky; adhesive; to adhere; in which sense it is used in Kiangsu. 勿丨住 it will not stick, as glue.

隹 ˛*chui* The original form rudely represents the short tail feathers of some birds; but must not be confounded with ˛*kia* 佳 excellent; it now only serves as the 172d radical of characters relating mostly to birds.

Short tailed birds, as pigeons, fowls, sparrows, &c.

翩翩者丨 the doves fly round and round.

Read ˛*tsui*. The wind waving the groves.

山林之畏丨 the wild woods dread the tempest.

鵻 ˛*chui* Used for the last.

A pigeon or turtle, noted for its filial, gentle temper; also called 鳺丨 or 䳕鳺, and many other names.

沙丨 the snipe.

錐 ˛*chu* The character 鉹 is sometimes used for this as another form.

An awl, a borer, a sharp pointed tool; the apex or tip; to bore, to pierce; a trifle; unimportant.

毛丨 a Chinese pencil.

毛丨子 a mere penman; a copyist, a hair-awl, one useful only to wield a pencil.

安用毛丨 why longer use the pencil? — the sword is better; a saying of Pau Ch'ao, who became a great general.

丨刀之末 an awl's tip, a small matter, a trifle.

無地立丨 not even a spot to stick an awl in; no land, not a foot of real estate; miserably poor.

丨鋩 the point of a weapon.

丨孔 or 丨眼兒 to bore a hole.

丨鑽不動 the awl wont go in.

丨捺底 to stitch shoe-soles.

丨牛不若雞豚 to stick a bullock is not equal to giving a cock or a pig; — referring to the one being offered to deceased, the other to living parents.

丨刺股 he pierced his thigh with an awl; said of Su Tsin, a diligent student of old.

丨處囊 the awl placed in the bag — cannot be kept down, but will work itself out; — a genius cannot be repressed.

鼦 ˛*chui* From *rat* and *awl* contracted, referring to its habit of boring and gnawing.

The common rat or mouse was formerly called ˛*chui* in Honan, and the name is retained in books.

騅 ˛*chui* A black horse with white and dark gray spots.

烏丨馬 a dark gray spotted horse, the charger of Hiang Yu 項羽 of Tsin, B.C. 220.

有丨有駓 there were gray and white spotted, with white and yellow spotted horses.

黄丨魚 a yellowish kind of carp.

捶 ˊ*ch'ui* From *hand* and *to hang down*; sometimes used for ˛*ch'ui* 搥 to beat, and for the next.

To beat with a staff; to cudgel; to torture by beating.

丨扑 to beat a criminal.

丨鉤 the bit of a bridle.

棰 *ch'ui* From *wood* and *to hang down*; similar to ˛*ch'ui* 椎 a mallet.

A cudgel, a club, a stick; to beat; to extort a confession by beating.

丨楚之下 in the agonies of torture.

Read ˊ*to*. Trees and shrubs growing exuberantly.

箠 'chui — From *bamboo* and *hanging down*. Drooping bamboos; joints of the bamboo; a riding switch; to punish with the bamboo, as in a yamun; to flog.

笞 丨 to bamboo.

鞭 丨 to whip and beat.

硾 chui' — To press things down, as with stones; to add weights on a thing; to pound; to ram down; to make a thing sag; sagged, loaded; hanging down.

丨之以石 keep it down with a stone.

秤 丨 a steelyard weight — is sometimes so written.

千斤 丨 a stone weight to press things down.

綴 chui' chŏ' — From *silk* and *to connect*; it is also read *choh*.

To baste or sew together; to connect; to carry on; to put a stop to; mixed; variegated.

丨衣 to mend or sew clothes; also, to oversee the robes of state; a kind of audience marquee of the ancient emperors.

補 丨 to sew a rip, to mend and patch.

丨旒 small flags or pendants hanging on a large flag.

禮以丨淫 propriety leads one to stop irregularities.

丨丨然 on good terms with; no estrangement.

丨之以祀 to connect them by sacrifices.

點 丨 to add surroundings, as when taking a photograph.

縋 chui' — From *silk* and *to pursue*.

A cord; to let down, as by a rope into a well; to suspend by a rope.

丨下水 let it down into the water.

夜丨而出 he was let down by night and got away.

丨城 to let down over the wall, as a letter.

膇 chui' — A swelling of the foot, as from rheumatism, or having been cramped, or from wet.

惴 chui' — Mournful, sorrowing; the moan of grief; in great straits.

丨惺 embarrassed, anxious.

丨丨其慄 he looked so terrified and sad to behold.

墜 隊 chui' — From *earth* and *falling*; the second form is oftener read *tui*'.

Grand, extravagant, wasteful; to settle down, to fall of itself; to slide, as earth; to sink, as into hell; to tumble into ruins; to crumble, to topple; pendents, as from a fan or a chatelain.

丨落 or 丨下 it fell down; it slid off.

丨底 to sink to the bottom.

累 丨 troublesome, unmanageable; difficult to arrange.

丨胎 a falling of the womb; a miscarriage.

善騎者必丨 it is the skillful riders who get the falls; *met.* presumptuous confidence.

丨跌 it all fell down, as from too great a strain.

未丨於地 [their designs] have not yet collapsed.

In *Fuhchau*. To mark a price on; at, after.

贅 chui' — From a *pearl* and to *place*.

To pledge, to pawn; hanging on, connected with; a wen, an excrescence; a useless appendage; a parasite; tautology, repetition; unsuitable, irrelevant; to obtain.

出 丨 to go from a father's to a father-in-law's house to live before marrying his daughter.

丨婿 a son-in-law who lives with his wife's parents.

招 丨 or 入 丨 to go and live at the house of a wife's father.

行 丨 to act improperly.

累 丨 reiterated, verbose.

多 丨 tiresome talk.

丨瀆 I am mortified with your importunity.

丨語 or 丨言 reiteration, verbiage.

再 丨 or 丨筆 or 丨及 a postscript; to add a postscript.

CH'UI.

Old sounds, t'i, t'ui, t'ut, di, dui, dup. *In Canton*, ch'ui *and* shui; — *in Swatow*, t'ui, ch'ui, ch'ué, *and* sui; — *in Amoy*, ch'ui, t'ui, *and* sui; — *in Fuhchau*, t'ui, sui, t'oi, *and* chw'i; *in Shanghai*, ts'z', dzüé, *and* tsö; — *in Chifu*, ts'éi.

吹 龡 'ch'ui — From *mouth* or *key* and *to gape*; the second form is antiquated; interchanged with the next.

To blow, as by the breath or wind; to play on wind instruments; to puff; to breathe, as fishes do; to speak in praise of, to puff up; a puff, a blast, a gust.

丨獎 to flatter, to magnify unduly.

丨筒 a sumpitan; a pitchpipe.

燈 丨 a blow-pipe.

丨滅 to extinguish, to blow out; as 丨燈 blow out the lamp.

丨水 to blow water into meat, as butchers sometimes do; to brag, to draw a long bow.

丨哨子 to whistle; whistling.

丨灰之力 [as easy as] to blow away the dust.

丨毛求疵 [why] blow aside the fur to find the scar? — nobody is perfect.

丨病 injured; — as by 丨風 the wind blowing on one.

丨壞 blown to tatters, as a flag by the wind.

風丨浪湧 the wind raises the waves high.

丨丨打打 the clangor of instruments; great huzzas and rejoicings.

丨嘘他 to recommend another.

Read *ch'ui'*. The wind; the noise of drums.

丨唱 playing and singing.

習丨 practicing on the drums.

鼓丨 the drums sounding, a band.

炊 *ch'ui* Used for the last.

To dress food; to cook, especially by steaming.

丨飯 to cook or steam rice.

晨丨 a very early meal.

丨爨 a boiler, a shallow kettle.

先丨 or 古丨 the manes of a mother.

丨餅 at *Peking*, to bake cakes.

林 *ch'ui* Two *streams* running from one fountain.

This character is now obsolete, but at Amoy its sound is retained in the colloquial word for *water*, for which 水 is written.

垂 **𠙽** *ch'ui* From *earth* below *pendent* leaves, which the second form represents.

To suspend, to hang down; to drop, to let fall, as the hands; to hand down, as from olden time; to reach to the future; to make known; to regard, to condescend to inferiors; to bow; nearly, presently, almost, near to in place; approaching in time; suspended; reaching to; a boundary, for which the next is properest; a lodge or station for a guard near the hall; an ancient place in Tsi (now northern Shantung,) and one in Honan.

丨下來 let it hang as a tassel.

丨手而得 drop the hands and get it; — to acquire a thing easily.

名丨後世 his name will reach to future ages.

丨顧 or 丨愛 to regard kindly; a condescending interest in.

丨老 becoming old.

丨法於後 to make one's example felt long after.

天丨雨露 heaven sends down rain and dew.

丨危 in great danger; imminent.

丨頭 to hang down the head.

丨憐 your kind compassion.

丨情 to pity, to feel for.

丨恩 your great favor; the Emperor's bounty.

丨拱而天下治 they let fall their robes and folded their hands, and the empire was governed; said of Yao and Shun's wise sway.

陲 *ch'ui* A frontier, a boundary, the line between two countries; a dangerous place, like the edge of a cliff.

邊丨 the frontier, the border.

遠丨 the remote marches.

丨命 dispatches from the frontier.

鎚 *ch'ui* This is often used with the next, but not rightly.

A hammer; a mallet, a club or thing beat with; to hammer; to pound.

打鉄丨 a sledge-hammer.

金瓜丨 "melon hammers," gilded balls carried in processions.

一雙銅丨 a pair of brass maces.

不丨我 don't beat me.

鐵丨對鐵砧 the iron hammer meets the iron anvil; *met.* two fierce bullies fighting.

Read *tui.* To work gems.

錘 *ch'ui* From *metal* and to *hang down*; interchanged with the last; some regard them as identical.

An ancient weight of twelve *liang*, or about a pound avoirdupois; the weight on a steelyard or in a clock; heavy; a forging hammer.

秤丨 or 稱丨 the poise or weight on a steelyard.

戥丨 the weight on a money yard.

丨煉 to work out wrought iron, as on an anvil.

槌 **椎** *ch'ui* Interchanged with the last and next; the first also means to reject.

A wooden mallet, a beetle; a blugdeon, a beater, a club; to beat, to pommel, to knock; a frame for silkworms to wind their cocoons on.

丨鼓 to drum with a 鼓丨 or drumstick.

硏丨 a muller.

打樁丨 a pile-hammer.

擂丨 a triturating pestle, such as apothecaries use; a term for large fingers.

搥 *ch'ui* Used for the last; and for *chui* 捶 to strike.

To beat, as a bell; to strike with the fist, to pommel; to throw at or away.

丨提仁義 to discard kindness and right.

丨石 to cast stones at.

丨背 to shampoo; to knead the back.

一丨打倒 knocked him down with a blow of his fist.

丨打一頓 give him a thump, hit him a settler. (*Pekingese.*)

丨魯 blockhead like, stupid.

擣枕丨床 to pound the pillow and beat the bed; *met.* so anxious as to be unable to sleep.

丨胸頓足 to pound the breast and stamp — in anger.

施丨楚于頑 give a good beating to the disobedient — boy.

丨金爲箔 to beat out gold-leaf.

倕 ˏch'ui Heavy.

Read *shui'*, and also written 垂. The name of a man, otherwise known as 共工, a clever maker of arrows in the time of Shun, who appointed him to be minister of works.

腄 ˏch'ui The large warts or splints on a horse's leg; a thick indurated scar; the buttocks; the spur or hallux on a cock.

丨縣 ancient name of Fuh-shan hien 福山縣 in Tăng-cheu fu on Shantung promontory, established by Ts'in Chi Hwang-ti.

鬌 ˏch'ui The front tresses of a maiden which are parted on the forehead, and fall down the temples, called 刷寒毛 or the cold-brushed hair.

高環雲髻不復丨髻 when the ringed and lofty coiffure has once been arranged, she cannot again let her tresses fall; *i. e.* a girl once married is fixed for life.

𩙪 ˏch'ui The wind blowing things over nearly to the ground.

弱柳受風丨 the pliable willow bends to the blast.

顀 䭲 ˏch'ui From *bone* and to *pursue*.

A projecting forehead.

項丨 the vertebræ on the neck; others say, those on the back.

竁 ts'ui' Also read ˏ*chwen*.

To dig and search for ore; to dig a hole in which to secrete things; noise of a mouse.

硾 chui' From 石 *stone* and 墜 to *fall* contracted; also read *shuh*ˏ.

To fall of itself, to come to the earth; to crash down.

星丨地 a star, or meteoric stone, fell to the earth.

CHUN.

Old sounds, tan, ton, dan *and* don. *In Canton*, chun; — *in Swatow*, chun *and* tun; — *in Amoy*, tun *and* chun; — *in Fuhchau*, tung; — *in Shanghai*, tsăng; — *in Chifu*, tsăn.

諄 ˏchun To inculcate, to teach carefully, to impress on one; to reiterate and enjoin; carefully, earnestly, really.

丨丨然命之乎 did Heaven thus impress its commands — on Shun?

叮嚀丨囑 to repeat and reiterate one's orders.

丨憎 mutual hatred.

丨丨的求雨 to pray for rain with earnest supplications.

誨爾丨丨 I taught you with unwearied care.

吨 ˏchun Incoherent babble, never ending nonsensical talk.

丨丨 maundering, driveling.

Read *t'un'*. Discontented, grumbling; the feelings restrained by fear.

窀 ˏchun From *cave* and to *sprout*.

To inter with respect.

丨穸 to lay a coffin away for the long night, *i. e.* to bury.

丨穸之敬 a douceur sent to help in a funeral.

肫 ˏchun The cheek-bones; flesh dried for winter's use; the flesh under the chin; a meat dumpling; occurs used for *tun'* 忳 honest, earnest.

丨丨其仁 his benevolence was undoubted.

丨誠 trustworthy, earnest in doing.

鳥丨朧 the offals of a bird.

迍 ˏchun Also read ˏ*t'un*, and used with ˏ*t'un* 屯 difficult.

Unable to progress; hard to get on.

命運丨邅 always baffled in life, never reaching one's aims.

衠 ˏchun True; unmixed, simple or uniform; right.

准 ʻchun From 冫 *ice* and 隹 *excellent*; originally the same as the next, but now usually distinguished, though often interchanged.

To permit; to approve; to allow, to grant one; to decide; to answer, as a petition; in official papers, to acknowledge, to receive, as a dispatch; on or upon, as a day.

丨狀 to grant the plea or demurrer.

稟丨 the petition is granted.

丨備 to prepare for.

丨行 to permit to be done; to confirm a decision.

丨以十日 to get permission for ten days.

丨期 to set a day.

案丨 the case has been decided.

丨此 and 不丨 received—rejected; allowed — dismissed; come to hand — not received.

前丨大人照會 when I previously received your Excellency's dispatch.

允 丨 pass by, wink at; condone, as sins.

沒有丨兒的 not at all certain; not sure; undecided.

旨 丨 We grant the request.

丨奏 his memorial is granted.

丨信 to rely upon; a certain or definite promise.

準 ʿchun From *water* and a *harrier hawk*; used with the last.

To equalize, to adjust; to level, to measure; that by which things are made even; a rule, a guage, a plumb-line, a water-level; a thing to mark time; exact, true, as a watch; even, just.

丨則 a rule, a mode; a right way.

丨繩 a marking line.

丨規 a regulator, as a dial; a fixed mode.

丨時刻 the proper time has come.

射到丨 he hit the target.

丨折多少 how much will you take off?—*i.e.* make an offset and settle the account.

丨不丨呢 is it exact or not? as the running of a watch.

一丨的 perfectly so; true every way, as a plan or machine.

兑丨完數 to compare (or equalize) the items, and settle the account.

探丨 to exactly learn—his haunts

瞧丨 to look carefully.

就定丨了 it will then be fixed.

較丨 to follow the measure or rule.

鼻丨 or 丨頭 end of the nose.

隆丨 a big or Roman nose, which Europeans are said to always have.

埻 ʿchun A target, a mark; a mound, a pile of earth; a park or place for archery.

稕 chunʾ A bundle of straw; grass or hay tied in faggots.

CHʿUN.

Old sounds, t'an, t'on, dan. *In Canton*, ch'un; — *in Swatow*, ch'un; — *in Amoy*, ch'un *and* t'un; — *in Fuhchau*, ch'ung; — *in Shanghai*, ts'ăng; — *in Chifu*, ts'ăn.

春 ˛chʿun The original form represents 日 the *sun* under 屮屮 *plants* contracted, denoting the quickening effects of the sun.

Spring, the beginning of the year, when all nature is excited; vernal; wanton, lustful; obscene; joyous, glad; prosperity; return to health; to rejuvenate; *met.* times, periods; budding, starting; wine, liquor.

新丨 new spring; *i.e.* a new year.

丨分 the vernal equinox,—the 4th of the 24 terms.

迎丨 going out to meet the spring by officials, accompanied by a 丨牛 clay ox, borne by men who afterwards break it in pieces.

丨色 cheering, delightsome, as a view or a gay procession.

丨秋高 springs and autumns eminent; *i.e.* advanced in years, about sixty.

青丨 the spring-time—of life, is applied to youths under twenty.

百病回丨 he can reprieve one from all diseases.

滿口丨風 mouth filled with the vernal breeze; *i.e.* persuasive in speech.

三丨柳綠 the bright green willow in spring.

丨王月 the first moon.

小陽丨 the tenth moon.

幾易丨秋 how old are you?

丨茗候光 I shall expect you to be at my spring feast.

丨心 or 丨意 lewd thoughts, lustful desires.

椿 ˛chʿun From *wood* and *spring*; not the same as ˛*chwang* 椿 a post.

A long-lived tree, and hence a symbol of a father; in northern China, the 香丨 denotes the *Cedrela odorata*, and 臭丨 the *Ailantus glandulosa*; silkworms feed on them, and the fragrant leaf-buds of the former are cooked for greens.

大丨 or 丨堂 your father.

丨萱並茂 may your parents both be vigorous.

靈丨未老 your respected father keeps his vigor well.

杶 檷 ˛chʿun Both these are regarded as synonymous with the last by some authors; the second form is least used.

A kind of tree like the sumac (*Rhus*) or *Augia*, producing a varnish or gum; the wood is used for musical instruments; the seeds are black and grow in a cyme; leaves turn red after frost; its common name is 野漆樹 wild varnish tree, to which class of plants (the *Anacardiaceæ*) it probably belongs.

鰆 ˛chʿun A salt water fish, with cirri, called 丨子 and 黃瓜 at Amoy, probably a species of mullet; at Canton, the 丨魚 is a sort of roach or *Leuciscus*.

輴 ˛chʿun Also written 楯 in some books.

A hearse used by great men in old times; the 龍丨 had dragons painted on it; a kind of mud shoe on which to slide over the ooze.

泥乘丨 a mud sledge or scow to get across mud flats.

㖭 ˏch'un — An unauthorized, ideographic character composed of 肉 *flesh*, 未 *not*, and 成 *perfected*; it is sometimes written 春, as a synonym.

In *Cantonese*. The eggs of crabs, the roe of fish, or bird's eggs.

雷公丨 "thunder-lord's eggs," are aerolites; others say, truffles.

鷄丨 hen's eggs.

蠢 ˋch'un — From *insects* and *spring*.

To crawl, to wriggle like worms; to move, to rise up against just rule; stupid, foolish; uncompliant, doltish, lumpish; rude, contrary.

丨才 inapt, foolish.

丨動爲惡 to stir up evil, to act insubordinately.

製丨 silly-looking.

丨鈍 doltish, dull, inapt.

愚丨 or 丨笨 heedless, unwise, headstrong.

賰 ˋch'un — Corpulent, fat.

踳 ˋch'un — From *foot* and *spring*.

Blended, mixed, as colors.

丨駮 obstinate, self-willed; mistaken and perverse.

偆 ˋch'un — From *man* and *spring*.

Rich; one in the enjoyment of life.

丨厚 substantial, well-off.

CHUNG

Old sounds, tong, dong, *and* t'ong. *In Canton*, chung and ch'ung; — *in Swatow*, tòng, chòng, teng, *and* cheng; — *in Amoy*, tiòng *and* chiòng; — *in Fuhchau*, tóüng, tüng, t'ung, chüng, chéüng, *and* ch'üng; — *in Shanghai*, tsung *and* dzung; — *in Chifu*, ts'ung.

中 ˏchung — Composed of 口 *mouth* to represent a square, with a passage through it to connect the sides.

The middle, the center; the heart or core of, in the middle of; half; within, in; inner; medium in size or quality; to accomplish, to fill; to estimate a quantity; complete, exact, undeviating.

不丨用 useless, inefficient, effete, unserviceable; often remarked by people of themselves.

內丨有 there are such; more are to be had.

丨年 middle aged.

丨道 halfway, incomplete; as 丨道而歿 died before he had completed it.

丨間 between, inside, among.

丨正 in the center; indifferent to.

丨等人材 common, mediocre, he has only ordinary abilities.

當丨 in the midst; while going on.

丨央 the center or heart of;

心丨 in my mind.

丨天景運 the noontide of prosperity had then come.

五丨 the viscera, the vital organs.

丨人 or 丨保人 an arbitrator or umpire; an agent; a daysman; an intercessor.

上丨 and 下丨 terms for goods; superior-middling and inferior-middling; better than ordinary, and worse than ordinary.

丨丨兒的 rather ordinary, not the best.

丨有二十石 I guess that there are twenty peculs.

丨州 ancient name for Honan.

丨山 an old name for Lewchew.

丨都 a name of Peking, used by the Mongols.

丨國 or 丨華, or 丨土, or 丨原 China, the Middle Kingdom; the first is also used by *met.* for the Government, the power or the people of China.

丨外 native and foreign; China and other countries; at home and abroad.

丨庸 the exact medium or Doctrine of the Mean; name of the Classic by Tsz'-sz' 子思, who was the grandson of Confucius.

Read *chung*ˀ To hit the center; struck by, as a fit; to attain, to accomplish; fit, suitable.

丨酒 to get drunk; affected or giddy from liquor.

丨寒 to catch cold.

丨暑 a sun-stroke.

丨肯 is fitly done; all right; it meets the exigency.

丨我意 it suits me; it is what I wanted; it is my wish.

高丨 to reach the high degrees, as 丨翰林 to become a Hanlin.

丨不得 unattainable.

丨風不語 struck with a paralysis.

猜丨 or 估丨 to guess aright.

量丨 guessed [the weight or size] correctly.

丨槍 hit by a bullet.

看丨了 approved (or guessed) at a glance.

丨計 to make a lucky hit; to succeed in a plan; to be taken in or deceived.

丨他的圈兒 I have been deluded, he has fooled me.

忠 ˓chung From *heart* and *center*.
Loyal, patriotic, faithful; devoted, sincere; attached to; sedate; to maintain one's integrity; unselfish, honest, earnest; upright.
丨臣 a loyal, devoted minister.
丨烈 faithful to the last.
丨厚 to be depended on.
丨義 faithful and upright.
丨言逆耳 sincere reproofs grate on the ear.
丨心耿耿 most faithful and true; an unchanging regard.
篤念丨藎 I recall his entire devotion.

衷 ˓chung Inner garments, which the character indicates; underclothes; the center; the heart or mind; rectitude, a right moral nature; goodness, sincerity; equity, a fair, just judgment, a full knowledge of, conversant with.
不丨 insincere.
無亢不丨 inflexibly upright; just.
言不由丨 your words are deceptive.
丨懷 the mind; to bear in mind; to cherish.
折丨 to distinguish justly; to weigh opinions.
皇上帝降丨于民 the High Shangti has conferred a discriminating heart on mankind.
丨曲所發 thoughts which arise; the train of thought.
和丨 accommodating, friendly; amicable.
丨腸 or 丨情 the feelings.
私丨 a desire or intention of benefiting one.

終 ˓chung From *silk* and *winter* as the phonetic.
The end of a cocoon or ball of silk; the end, the termination; a finis; a euphemism for death; to the last, all of; the utmost, extreme; to end one's days; *met.* dead, the deceased; a cycle of twelve years; a space of a thousand square *li*; before a negative, it is equivalent to never; as 始丨沒下雪 it never snowed at all.
丨未 not at all, none of, not the least.
丨然不聽 he paid not the least heed to it.
丨日 or 丨朝 the whole day.
丨食之間 during the time of a meal, an hour's time.
年丨 the end of the year.
始丨 the beginning and end, first and last.
丨止 to stop halfway, not to complete an undertaking.
丨身大事 the great affair of life,—usually refers to marriage.
丨古 through all ages; for ever.
臨丨 near his end.
壽丨 the end of one's days.
丨須 it is absolutely necessary; I must have it.
丨性難改 it is hard to change one's nature.
從一而丨 faithful to one [husband] to the last.
善丨 a happy death — is one of the five happinesses.
能丨天年 to fullfil one's natural life.
歡好不丨 they have disagreed at last; again have fallen out.
愼丨 to render the last dues to the dead, refers to a filial preparation for a parent's funeral.

螽 ˓chung A long-headed green grasshopper, the 丨斯 or *Truxalis*, called 禾米蜢 at Canton, and 青螞扎 at Nanking.
丨斯衍慶 may you children be numerous as the grasshoppers.

刣 ˓chung To scrape things; to oppose.
相丨 to fight and quarrel, to injure each other.
In *Fuhchau.* To kill; to behead, to execute.
丨賊 to kill a thief.
丨頭 to decapitate.

彸 伀 ˓chung The second form is unused.
An agitated, quick manner, resulting from awe or fear.
征丨 restless, nervous, fidgetty; explained as not knowing what to do with the hands and feet.

忪 ˓chung Like the last. The mind agitated with alarm.
宜爾惶丨 you should be impressed and startled.

鍾 ˓chung An ancient measure, equal to four 斗 or pecks; others say 34 斗, and others again to ten ˓*fu* 釜 or 640 gills; a small cup; to bring together; to bestow, to confer; gifted, endowed with, as a talent; heavy; weeping; to repeat; name of a small ancient state in the present Sü-cheu fu in the northwest of Kiangsu.
酒丨 a wine goblet.
丨情 ardent feeling, warm affections.
龍丨 imbecile, childish.
千丨電爵 he drained a thousand cups in a flash.
號丨 a kind of ancient lute.
所丨愛 whom I love best; a dearly beloved.
丨靈毓秀 a genius; one gifted with varied talents, like a prophet or sage; 丨靈 is also the luck of a grave, the distinguishing favor of heaven to a country or spot.

鐘 ˓chung From *metal* and *lad*.
A bell with a flaring mouth, generally without a tongue, and struck with a mallet; a clock; things hollow or sonorous are often so called.
打丨 or 敲丨 to strike or ring a bell.
丨表舖 a watchmaker's shop.
丨打一點 the clock has struck one.
時辰丨 a clock; usually denotes one that strikes the hours.
丨樓 a belfry.

搖丨子 to ring a hand-bell.

撞木丨 to knock a wooden bell; — to intrust business to a fool; to be disappointed; to demand extortionate prices or gratuity.

幽冥丨 the bell that sounds through hades; it is struck thrice hourly for a year to drive away demons.

鼨 ˏchung A sort of rodent found in western China, marked with spots like a leopard, and large as one's fist; it may be an animal allied to the *Jupaia* or banxring of Java.

蹱 ˏchung From *foot* and *child*; it is also read *ch'ung*ˀ.

To walk in a staggering way, head downwards, as if faint or tipsy; a shambling, uncertain gait; a toddling walk; to faint and halt as one goes, like a paralytic.

丨下水 to fall into the water.

丨下來 to fall head first.

行路亂丨 to go along staggering and nodding.

冢 ˋchung Composed of 勹 to *inclose* and 豖 a *pig tied*, as the primitive; this character is very often written like ˏmung 冡 dull, but the dictionaries distinguish them.

A tumulus or barrow, made high, as if it inclosed something, for which the next is now used; the peak of a hill; eminent, great; honorable; first.

丨宰 a high statesman; the premier, the president of the Board of Civil Office.

丨土 a mound or earth-altar on which to worship the powers of earth, or Ceres.

丨子 the eldest son; originally confined to a prince's heir.

丨君 an old term for a sovereign.

山丨崒崩 the crags on the hill-tops came crashing down.

丨碣 a stone erected to mark the limits of a grave or land.

塚 ˋchung Interchanged with the last, and made to restrict its meaning.

A sepulcher, a tomb; a barrow or mound, such as cover graves.

荒丨 an abandoned grave, at which no one worships.

挖丨 to rifle graves.

開丨 to dig a grave and prepare the tomb.

義丨 a public cemetery, which is open to all applicants.

明丨 a vaulted tomb, one that can be entered; it is made by some families to retain their coffins till lucky times.

墳丨 or 丨墓 a sepulcher; a burying-ground.

舂丨 to ram down the earth solid in the bottom of a grave.

古丨纍然 the old barrows are just like a row of hills.

嵸 ˋchung A small hill shaped like a tumulus over a grave; the last is sometimes wrongly written in this way.

煄 ˋchung Fire flaming up brightly; to kindle.

火丨 a coal to start the fire.

瘇 ˋchung From *disease* and *heavy*; it is like the next.

A swelled leg; a dropsical disease of the legs.

腫 **尰** ˋchung From *flesh* and *heavy*; the second is like the last; and also denotes a swelling of the legs arising from damp.

To swell, to tumefy; a boil, a swelling; inflated, swollen; boastful; the galls or protuberances on trees.

丨脹 to swell up.

癀丨 puffy, dropsical.

浮丨 a dropsical swelling.

丨傷 a bruise, a contusion.

丨起青黑 swollen up and turned black and blue.

丨疼 swollen and painful.

偅 ˋchung Also read *chung*ˀ.

Careless, reckless.

儱丨 never finishing anything, without foresight, heedless; — this phrase is written in many ways.

踵 **歱** ˋchung From *foot* or to *stop* and *heavy*; the second form is unusual.

The heel; to follow at one's heels; to imitate, to do after another; to act in the same way; to rule as a precedent; to reach; to visit.

丨貴國 reached your country.

丨門 to go to his door — on a visit.

丨跡 to follow one's steps or instructions.

接丨而至 they came on uninterruptedly; arriving successively.

丨事增華 in doing it he excelled the other in pomp (or brag).

種 ˋchung From *grain* and *heavy*.

A seed, a germ, a kernel; that which produces its second or double; a sort, a class, a kind; to select or use, as seed; ancient name of a small state near Tibet.

丨類 a kind, a description; a class.

播丨 to sow seed; such as 穀丨 grain, seed corn, rice or wheat.

打丨 to beget, to sire, as animals.

遺丨 to leave heirs or issue.

誕降嘉丨 he gave the people the best grains.

丨丨不合 everything went wrong; but 丨丨 also means short hair and careful.

傳丨 to propagate a kind, as fruit; to introduce a sort elsewhere; to transmit by descent.

雜丨 mixed kinds; illegitimate, in which sense it is used in reproach; a bastard.

禍丨 the source of misfortune and sorrow.

Read *chung'* To sow or plant seeds; to cultivate, to raise; to propagate; to spread abroad; to beget.

丨菜 to raise vegetables.

丨福 to bequeath happiness, *i. e.* to be a source of prosperity to one's descendants.

丨植 to set out trees.

布丨 to disseminate, as doctrines.

痘丨 vaccine virus, which is used to 丨痘 vaccinate with; also called 丨花兒 in Peking.

重 *chung'* Some say it is composed of 壬 inclosing 東 *east* as a phonetic, and explain it that *man* is the most important thing in the earth.

Heavy, weighty; the opposite of 輕 light; trifling; momentous; severe, heinous; decorous, grave; secluded, or peculiarly appropriated to government or imperial use; to regard as difficult, to consider as important; to honor, to give weight to; very; a sign of the comparative; crowded, near together.

丨人倫 to elevate the social relations.

丨罪 an aggravated offence.

自丨 to think much of one's self, self-respect.

丨大 grave, important.

丨好 still better; 更丨 heavier.

丨打 to beat severely.

丨位 an important post, a responsible office held by 丨臣 a high minister.

女丨 a chaste woman.

以丨其國 he therefore honored that state.

三丨 are three important things in government, *viz.* 議禮 settle the rites, 制度 make laws, and 考文 examine the literati.

丨憂 very sorry.

丨星 a name for the planet Jupiter.

武不可丨用 the sword must not always be appealed to.

丨用 to repose confidence in, to regard.

不丨虛詞 don't mind the unimportant expressions.

丨數 frequently; but 數丨 is a series; several layers.

不倚丨 not to rely on the basis, disregard the fundamental law; to discard trustworthy men.

丨十斤 it weighs ten catties.

三起丨船 three crowded fleets of vessels.

恩丨如山 his favors have been great as the hills.

丨地 reserved, secluded, or important spots, like palace-grounds not open to all; also dangerous places, as a gunpowder room.

以丨論 to be understood in the strictest sense, to be rigidly interpreted, as a law.

不足丨輕 the affair is of no importance; he is not much.

Read *ˏch'ung.* To double, to repeat, to do over; to add; a time; again; a thickness; a classifier of thicknesses or layers.

三丨 thrice; three thicknesses.

九丨 or 九丨殿 the nine-entrance palace—the Emperor's.

一丨一丨 laid one upon the other regularly.

打入丨圍 to break through the besieging army.

丨刋 a second set of blocks, a new edition.

丨複 duplicated; two at once.

丨疊 or 丨丨疊疊 reiterated; piling one on another, as mountain peaks; often, duplicated.

丨陽節 the double-odd festival on the 9th day of the 9th moon.

丨夫 a second husband; *i. e.* she will marry again.

抄丨 to write out a copy.

Read *ˏt'ung.* A variety of rice.

腫 *chung'* From *body* and *heavy*.

A woman with child.

諥 *chung'* To offend by harsh words; careful in speaking.

仲 *chung'* The second of three, the *man* in the *middle;* the second born of brothers; used for 中 in the second month in a season; inferior; a sort of musical instrument.

丨秋 the eighth moon, middle of autumn.

丨父 a father's younger brother; an old title, like chief adviser.

伯丨 the two oldest brothers; as 伯丨叔季 are terms for the four eldest brothers.

丨尼 the style of Confucius; he was regarded as the second brother, the hill *Ni* 尼山 being held as the elder, though Măng-p'i 孟皮 was really his brother.

衆 眾 乑 *chung'* From 目 *eye* and 人 *man* thrice repeated; the first is a corrupted form, and the third a very common contraction.

A company of at least three; a concourse, a majority, a quorum; a sign of the plural of persons; an adjective of number, much, many, all, and precedes the noun; a classifier of Budhist priests; the people, as apart from their rulers.

得丨 to get popular favor.

丨位 all you gentlemen; the company here.

公丨 or 丨人 the public; the crowd; mankind.

丨目所見 every eye saw it.

丨生 all living things; a Budhist term.

一丨僧 a priest; 幾丨僧 how many bonzes are there?

丨論 or 丨議 public opinion.

丨雨 copious showers.

丨盛 a great crowd and an abundance, said of a mart.

丨寡不敵 the few cannot withstand the many; we (the minority) are no match for them.

出丨 extra, not ordinary, no common thing or man.

丨約 at Canton, all the wards or neighborhoods.

丨多 a great many, a multitude.

CH'UNG.

Old sounds, t'ong, dong, *and* dzong. *In Canton*, ch'ung *and* shung; — *in Swatow*, t'òng, ch'òng, ch'eng, chan, t'ăng, *and* chòng; — *in Amoy*, ch'iòng, tiòng, *and* tòng; — *in Fuhchau*, ch'üng, tüng, *and* chung; — *in Shanghai*, ts'ung *and* dzung; — *in Chifu*, ts'ung.

充 兗 *ch'ung* From 人 *man* and 育 to *nourish* contracted; the second form is not common nor regarded as correct.

To fill; to fullfil, as a duty or station; to satiate; to satisfy, as hunger; to carry out, to continue; to stop up, to stuff full; to act in place of, or in the capacity of; high, long; sufficient, fine; extreme; to fatten.

承 丨 to fill an office.

丨 滿 to fill up, to gratify, said of things and desires, literally and figuratively.

仁義 丨 塞 to be imbued with principles of humanity and justice.

丨 足 or 丨 盈 well supplied, as soldiers with rations; in vigorous health; enough of.

丨 當 to fill a station; to act for another.

丨 實 overflowing; abundant, as resources; stuffed full.

丨 名冒籍 to use the name and residence of another — to deceive, as at the examination.

口外 丨 軍 banished to the frontiers or beyond the wall; such persons are often employed for camp-followers.

丨 耳盈聽 it fills the ear with melody.

丨 雜 to foist in, as poor goods in a lot.

丨 公 to become public property, to revert to the state.

丨 人 one who fattens animals.

大 丨 eaten to excess, injured by repletion.

褎如 丨 耳 noticed him as if their ears were stopped; — said of the coldness shown to the unfortunate.

假 丨 官長 to assume the style of an official.

丨 役 to be a policeman.

浺 *ch'ung* The murmuring of water is 丨 淙, spoken of a bubbling spring at the foot of a hill.

恍 *ch'ung* The mind excited; moved, perturbed.

忡 *ch'ung* Sorrowful, mourning.

憂心 丨 丨 grieved to the utmost, heart-broken.

沖 *ch'ung* A wide smooth expanse of water.

丨 瀜 沆 瀁 vast and deep, as the great lakes of China.

冲 沖 *ch'ung* From *ice* or *water* and *middle*; the first is most used.

To shake, to agitate; to collide; to strike against, as things do in the water; to dash against; to rush at; young, immature, delicate; peaceful; deep, hollow; used for the next, to rise in the air; to send, as a letter; to infuse or steep, by pouring on hot water.

丨 天 or 丨 霄 to fly or glance towards heaven.

怒氣 丨 天 or 氣 丨 斗牛 his wrath waxed furious, — as if it filled the sky; the second phrase refers to the Dipper.

丨 鋒陷陣 to rush on an enemy and break his ranks.

鑿冰 丨 丨 like the noise of cutting ice.

丨 丨 is also the tinkling noise of ornaments hitting each other; and the loose look of reins hanging down.

日子相 丨 the day will be unpropitious or untoward.

丨 和 on good terms, harmonious.

丨 撞 to disagree with, to beg to differ from, to offend in word; — a polite phrase.

出言 丨 撞 to talk rather impudently.

丨 年 or 丨 齡 young in years.

丨 人 a sovereign who is a minor.

丨 破 to defeat; ruined, collapsed, as an affair.

丨 遠 a rhetorical term for a wide digression in a discourse.

丨 煞 overpowering or malign, as in geomancy; to provoke the bad influences.

丨 郎 to precipitate over, as a fall or cascade.

某日 丨 sent [the letter off] on such a day.

丨 茶 to infuse tea.

翀 *ch'ung* From *wings* and *middle*; used with the last.

To fly up, to mount to the skies, as an eagle.

志可 丨 霄 his mind can reach the clouds; *i. e.* he has aspiring talents.

茺 *ch'ung* A labiate plant (*Leonurus sibirica?*) which has several names, as 丨 蔚 and 白益母; it is used in female complaints, and is common in Kiangsu and further south; more than one plant is probably designated by this name.

憧 *ch'ung* From *mind* and *lad*.

Unsettled, irresolute, disturbed.

丨 丨 往來 hesitating, wavering; many passing to and fro.

Read *chw.ang'*. Stupid looking.

衝 衝 *ch'ung* From to *go* and *heavy* or *lad*; the second form is unusual.

A common path, a thoroughfare; a place of great concourse; to move towards, to rise on or rush against; to sustain; to move; to excite; towards; abrupt; a machine employed in seiges to protect the sappers, probably a portable shed or mantlet.

水丨 a canal, a sluice; an open drain.

相丨 to meet, to collide, to rush against.

丨倒 to overthrow, to upset.

中丨 the pulse in the middle finger.

能折丨 it can be resisted; not impregnable.

折丨 an old name for a general.

丨突 to rush against.

丨撞 to butt against, to meet suddenly.

子午一丨 the characters *tsz'* and *wu* are opposed — the people whose horoscope has them had better not marry.

丨繁疲難 frequented, troublesome, wearisome, and difficult—are four terms applied to provincial posts to indicate the relative importance of the office.

丨要 a post much traveled, is applied to the first of these four.

丨撞馬頭 to run at the horse's head,—to impede the way, as a beggar might; to come in conflict, as with a bully.

罿 ˓chʻung From *net* and *lad;* also read ˓tʻung.

A spring-net to catch birds; others say a rabbit hutch, or a frame to entrap them.

雉離于丨 the pheasant shuns the snare.

虫 **蟲** ˓chʻung The original form represents a snake coiled up with its head projecting from the center; it is repeated thrice to intimate the great number of insects, and in many of the characters grouped under it, as the 142d radical, it is duplicated without change of meaning.

An ancient term for all animals with legs, whether 羽 feathery, 毛 hairy, 介 shelly, 鱗 scaly, or 倮 naked; there are supposed to be 360 species of each class; it now usually denotes the smaller sorts of animals, as snails, frogs, worms, insects, &c.; a person, a comrade, one of a craft; a demeaning term for a son.

丨類 or 丨部 comprises the order of entomology in Chinese zoology.

百丨 insects generally; all small animals.

長丨 a snake.

丨積 worms in the bowels.

一個小丨 one small bug;—an affected phrase for one's son.

雕丨小技 to carve worms with little skill;—to get one's living by light literature.

華丨 a pheasant; a poetical name.

桃丨 the peach bug, a name for a wren or the tailor-bird.

丨丨 the irritation of great heat, perhaps referring to prickly heat.

Read *chung'* To eat, as insects like moths and white ants do into things.

种 ˓chʻung Tender and sprouting, like the blade of grain; delicate.

幼丨 small and delicate.

盅 ˓chʻung From ··sh and *middle.*

A covered cup, such as tea is made in; a bowl, usually with a cover.

湯丨 a soup bowl.

牛油丨 in Canton, a butter-dish.

茶丨 a covered tea-cup, in which the tea is infused.

酒丨 a wine goblet.

寵 **寵** ˓chʻung From a *shelter* and a *dragon;* the second form is common but unauthorized.

To think much of, whether of one's self or others; to place high; kindness, grace, regard for; favor of superiors; to esteem, to prefer; to confer favors; to indulge unreasonably; doting on, as a wife or girl.

丨錫 a special favor, as of the king.

恩丨 loving-kindness, tender affection; the emperor's regard.

丨愛 to delight in; ardent love, for a concubine.

內丨 or 丨妾 a favorite concubine, who rules her husband; and hence 納丨 is to take a concubine.

得丨 to find grace in one's eyes; to win a husband's love.

承天丨 to receive favors from heaven or the emperor.

希惟丨臨 do me the honor of coming to see me.

毋啓丨納侮 don't give place to favorites and thus get contempt.

崇 ˓chʻung From *hill* and *honorable.*

High, eminent, lofty; estimable and honorable in the highest degree; greatly; noble, exalted; worthy of worship; to honor; to extol, to adore, to reverence, to approach with respect; to be made honorable or exalted; to collect; to go to; entire; a small ancient state, and since used in many proper names.

丨尙 to regard as preëminent.

丨拜 to worship.

敬丨 to reverence.

丨朝 early in the day, the entire morning, as before breakfast.

福祿來丨 may your prosperity be the very highest.

丨安 I wish you great peace, — a phrase in letters; it is also a district in Kien-ning fu in Fuhkien, famed for good tea.

欽丨 to regard with great respect, as if from the Throne; to revere.

丨山 a noted peak in Yung-ting hien in Hunan, west of Tung-ting Lake near the Li-shui, to which Hwan-teu was banished by Shun.

丨明縣 Chʻung-ming district, the island in the mouth of the Yang-tsz' River.

𨛱 *ₒchʻung* Name of a small feudal state, anciently written like the last, which lay in the present Hu hien 鄠縣 in the provincial prefecture of Shensi.

銃 *chʻungʾ* Hollowed out by an ax; bored; a sort of shell for firing balls, fired in the muzzle; a blunderbuss, a gingal; a mortar-gun, a petard; a pistol; small arms.

丨炮 cannon; fire-arms generally.

丨手 or 丨首 cannoniers; those who fire salutes from the 銕丨子 or petards in a yamun.

手丨 short guns, like a mortar; a kind of hand petard used in salutes.

丨了去 to peck, to chip off, as with a chisel.

三丨出巡 when three petards are fired, he goes on his circuit; — said of the municipal god.

揔 *chʻungʾ* To leap, to skip, to hop about.

In *Cantonese*. At once, altogether; to push, to hit.

丨䞋 to run upon, to thump against.

一丨三斗有 at a clip he has three pecks; *i. e.* I don't know why he is all at once so angry.

In *Shanghai*. To grab, to lift.

丨手 a pilferer, a shoplifter.

惷 *ₒchʻung* From *heart* and *to pound* in a mortar.

Simple, foolish; one naturally unteachable and obtuse; one not amenable to law.

丨笨 stupid, uneducated.

𪊓 *chʻungʾ* From *to rap on* and *collected*.

To come in upon one abruptly; to invite one's self to a meal; to nod.

𪊓丨 to come without an invitation.

直丨入 to bolt in on one.

丨食 to drop in at a meal, to sorn on one.

亂丨 to intrude on rudely.

跌跌丨丨 reeling, when tipsy.

丨着了 nodding, sleepy.

𨒫 *chʻungʾ* From to *go* and *many*.

Leisure, or at ease, without pressing occupation; in retirement.

揰 *chʻungʾ* From *hand* and *heavy*.

To push, as a stick into a rat-hole; to poke at.

丨通水渠 clear out the drain, as by running a pole into it.

丨落來 poke it down.

莫丨蜂竇 don't stir up a wasp's nest; — don't meddle with dangerous things.

CHWA.

Old sounds, ta, tap *and* tat. *In Canton*, cha; — *in Swatow*, kwa *and* cha; — *in Amoy*, kwa; — *in Fuhchau*, kwò; — *in Shanghai*, tsò; — *in Chifu*, tswa.

檛 *ₒchwa* From *wood* and *error*.

A switch, a horsewhip.

馬丨 a lash, a whip.

簻 *ₒchwa* Like the last.

A switch made of a twig, used when riding.

撾 *ₒchwa* To beat a drum with a pair of drumsticks; to knock on a bell.

丨婦翁 an old name for an orphaned girl.

打漁陽丨鼓 he struck the Yü-yang drum — thrice; alludes to a story of Tsʻao Tsao.

更鼓畏添丨 [on newyear's eve] the night-watchman dreads to add another tap, — because it makes another year.

髽 *ₒchwa* From *hair* and *to sit*.

To dress the hair, as women do; an ancient funeral coiffure, which originated in the state of Lu, when the women went out to receive the bodies of their countrymen killed in battle.

丨髻 in old times, a woman's mourning coiffure; now applied to the hair coiled hastily on the head, and not made into a bow.

丨而相弔 they disheveled their hair and mourned with each other.

膼 *ₒchwa* The thigh; the ham of an animal.

CHWʻAI.

Old sounds, tui. *In Canton*, chʻai, *and* chʻui; — *in Swatow*, chʻui *and* chui; — *in Amoy*, chui; — *in Fuhchau*, chʻoi; — *in Shanghai*, tsö[u]; — *in Chifu*, tswai.

搋 ˛chwʻai From *hand* and *for*.

To thump, to pommel with the fist; to pocket, to put into the breast pocket.

丨起來 put it in the bosom.

只宜肚飽不可懷丨 when you have eaten your fill, there's no need of pocketing anything.

丨麵 to knead dough, in making bread.

丨着一本書 to carry away a book.

丨一肚子的壞 in *Pekingese*, to cherish evil schemes, as a hypocrite does.

Read ˛chʻi. To split; to knock to pieces.

膗 ˛chwai To be distinguished from *hoh*, 膗 mince meat.

Ugly, repulsive; obese, gross, and therefore unable to stir about.

丨猪 an overfat hog.

丨肉 overfat pork.

是一塊丨 he is only a piece of fat, he is very gross and obese.

那人很胖是個膘丨 that man is too pursy, he is only a lump of fat.

揣 ʻchwʻai ʻchʻui From *hand* and *beginning*; it is also read ʻchʻui.

To estimate, to measure; to try to find the origin or cause of, to essay; to feel, to ascertain; to push away, to exclude; to detect, to ascertain.

丨度, or 丨摩 to feel after, to guess, to conjecture after much inquiry; to examine thoroughly.

不丨 unable to detect.

丨練 to study and imitate, as a good author.

丨測 to penetrate the meaning; to measure, as a hill.

嘬 chwʻai˒ From *mouth* and *extremely*.

To lap with the tongue; to taste, to sip; to suck, as flies do; to eat, to gnaw at; to swallow fast, without chewing.

丨血 to suck the blood, as gnats do.

禽獸同丨 birds and beasts eating together, as on a carcase of carrion.

蠅蚋蛄丨之 the flies, gnats, and mole-crickets ate it up.

膪 chwʻai˒ Also read *cha*˒, and much like 膗 gross.

Fat that is flabby and soft like a hog's; flesh that is soft like marrow or suet.

猪肉下丨 the fat along a hog's belly.

牝猪丨掃地 the sow's belly sweeps the ground.

CHWANG.

Old sounds, tung *and* dung. *In Canton*, chong, *and one* ngong; — *in Swatow*, cheng, tʻong, chung, chwang, chiang, *and* chang; — *in Amoy*, chòng, gòng, and tòng; — *in Fuhchau*, chòng, chʻung, maung, kòng, *and* taung; — *in Shanghai*, tsong *and* dzong; — *in Chifu*, tswang.

莊 ˛chwang From *grass* and *robust*; often contracted like the next.

Suckers sprouting vigorously; sedate, serious, stern; correct in conduct; used for 粧 highly dressed out; a farmstead, for which the next is also used; a thoroughfare, a high road.

丨嚴 grave, stern, as an officer is deemed to be.

端丨 a strict propriety, said of females; a close observance of etiquette.

丨整 dressed in the tip of fashion.

康丨大路 a level highway.

丨重 or 丨敬 serious and respectful.

色丨 hypocritical; put on.

柳丨 a prosperous appearance.

飯丨子 a large restaurant. (*Pekingese.*)

丨子 or 丨周 a famous philosopher of the Rationalists in the Cheu dynasty; he has the reputation of being a great sorcerer or magician.

庄 ˛chwang Much used for the last; it is properly read ˛*păng*, meaning even, level.

A cottage, a grange, a farmhouse; a work-shed, a place where rural labors are carried on; a place of business; a store, a dépôt; a firm or house; a deadhouse or public lararium; a division of a township like a parish; a hamlet, a village; in Kiangsu, occurs used as a classifier of affairs, as 一丨事體 one affair or enterprise.

丨戶 or 丨稼人 a farmer, a peasant.
丨丁 men on a farm, not the 丨客 or hired laborers.
茶丨 a tea dépôt in the hills, where the leaf is gathered.
寄丨 to store a coffin, as in a dead-house. (*Cantonese.*)
田丨 a farmstead.
布丨 a cotton warehouse.
丨子 or 村丨 a grange; a village.
丨口 a mercantile house, a firm.
作丨 a resident partner, one who manages the store or packs off the goods.

妝 粧 糚 ˓chwang From *woman* or *rice* and a phonetic; the second form is the most common.

To adorn the head and paint the eyes; to rouge; to feign, to appear in a disguise; to gloss; ornamented, dressed up.

梳丨 to arrange the hair; to dress up; the 梳丨盤 is a paper toilet burned on the 7th evening of the 7th moon to the Weaver.
丨扮 the style of dress; a costume; the fashion.
丨飾 dressed out, adorned; *met.* glossed over, falsified.
素丨 plainly dressed, not rouged.
丨奩 or 嫁丨 a bride's trousseau; a marriage portion.
丨次 or 丨臺 the place of dressing; *met.* your ladyship; used in letters.
濃丨 over-dressed, flaunting in colors, bedizened.
丨假 or 丨出來的 dressed in a character, as an actor.
外面丨作羊似的 dressed up to look like a sheep.
丨腔 pedantic, put on, as an actor; like 丨模作樣 he is pretending; he is playing a part.
慵丨 a dowdy looking coiffure.
賜丨 the gift dressing-case, was a name for a palace built for a concubine by an emperor.

裝 ˓chwang Used with the preceding, but that is confined chiefly to dressing the body.

To dress; to bind on, to tie; to busk, to prink; to put into, to pack, to load or store in; to catch, as rain in a tub; to receive, to contain; to imitate, to adopt; to pretend, to affect; to send or forward; style, costume, fashion.

行丨 traveling dress; equipage and baggage.
閒丨 in deshabille, common attire.
丨束好看 well-dressed, in good taste.
丨殮 or 丨裹 to enshroud a corpse.
丨載 to pack, as a cart; to stow, as cargo in a ship.
卸丨 to unload, as a boat.
丨鎗 to load a gun.
丨房 a store-room.
丨頭賣面 (or 盖面) to put the best goods on top to sell by; as 丨頭 is a style; a sort; a pattern of a thing.
扮作唐丨 to dress like a Chinese. (*Cantonese.*)
丨幌子 to counterfeit a trademark or sign; to carry the mark of the shop or calling, as a blacksmith his apron, or a groom the smell of the stable.
丨佯 to pretend not to know or hear.
丨不聽見 he pretended not to notice, or hear the man.
無天丨 there's no place for you to hide in.
丨整 or 丨潢 to put in order, to furnish up; the latter refers to the Milky Way, to which new things are likened.
丨神像 to make and dress up idols or images.
丨裱 to mount scrolls, to hang pictures.
丨箱 to pack a box; to arrange [paper] trunks — to burn to the spirits.
天然丨飾 [these spring flowers are] Heaven's dressing up.

椿 ˓chwang From *wood* and to *pound*; it is not the same as ˓chun 椿 the Ailantus.

A post to tie a horse to; a stake driven in the ground; a log, a stick; a club, a bludgeon; to strike; used with 庄 for ˓kien 件, a classifier of affairs.

打丨 to drive piles, as the 松丨 fir joists or piles.
丨其心 he beat his breast.
浮丨 a buoy.
半丨子 half a post, is a name for a boy of fifteen.
拴馬丨 a post to hitch a horse to.
一丨大事 an important affair.
獸醫丨子 a frame to strap a horse to shoe him.
拔丨 to pull up stakes; to have done with, to return home with one's things, to leave a service.
你牽牛我拔丨 you bring the ox and I'll pull up the stake; — I'll do the hardest part.
梅花丨 an abattis outside of the moat.
千斤丨 an upright windlass for hoisting boats up a lock.

褈 ˓chwang A short mean-looking dress; clothes unfit to appear in company.

蹖 ˓chwang To tread on; to step on, as a stool.

鶇 ˓chwang A bird allied to the cuckoo in its habits, called 蜀丨 or the Sz'ch'uen cuckoo; others describe it as more like a thrush; in Kiangnan the people say it appears in April, and sings 麥黃快割 the yellow wheat will soon be cut.

奘 ˓chwang˒ From *great* and *robust*, as the phonetic.

Large; powerful, as a robust horse; short and stout, as people; to make great.

丨的細的 some [of the sticks] are big and some are slender.

壯' *chwang'* From *scholar* and *splint* as the phonetic; one old form is 爿馬 referring especially to animals.

Stout, strong, robust, bold, hardy, healthy; full-grown, manly; manhood, at the age of thirty; fertile; full and flourishing; abundant; and hence a classical term for the eighth moon or harvest; to cauterize; to wound; to inspirit, to animate.

丨大 lusty, strong; like 丨盛, which is also applied to exuberant health.

丨旺 fat, vigorous; in its prime.

丨丁 an able-bodied man, one fit to serve for a soldier.

丨勇 volunteer troops; same as 丨民 the militia.

丨年 manhood; in strong health.

少丨 young and hearty.

丨健 a healthy, sound frame.

灸三丨 cauterized it three times.

肥丨 fat, as animals; in prime condition.

丨志 firm, set, willful, resolved; used in a good sense.

丨他膽 incite his courage, animate his heart.

大丨 name of the 34th diagram, which refers to thunder.

武丨 or 丨士 one accomplished in manly sports.

狀' *chwang'* From *dog* and a *splint* as the phonetic.

Form, appearance; to appear, to make plain; to declare in writing, to state, to accuse; a remonstrance, an accusation, a complaint; a certificate.

丨師 an attorney, a lawyer, a notary.

告丨 to indict, to accuse; to go to law; to bring a 丨詞 or indictment, or lay a plaint.

丨棍 a pettifoger, one who 具丨 prepares the complaint.

形丨 or 情丨 form, style, manner, arrangement.

丨貌非常 unusually engaging, a captivating manner.

無丨可名 it can be spoken of though it has no form; though it be so unsubstantial it can be described.

丨如 appearing like, as if.

體丨 the fashion of; an embodiment of.

丨元 the highest graduate of the Hanlin, the senior wrangler of the empire.

告御丨 to carry a case to the Throne through the Censorate.

毫無善丨 nothing goes right with me; I am utterly discontented.

戇' *chwang'* From *heart* and *rustic.*

Simple, stupid; doltish, unpolished; half crazy, half-witted.

粗丨 dull, obstinate, arising from a coarse, uneducated life.

丨喪' crazy like, acting wildly.

詐丨 to feign to be silly.

愚丨 half-idiotic, acting very stupidly.

莽丨 hasty, immethodical, quick but heedless.

丨佬 a rattle-brain, a mad-cap. (*Cantonese.*)

撞' *chwang'* From *hand* and *lad.*

To grasp in the hand and beat; to pound; to thump; to knock or run against, to dart upon; to tap on, as a hoop; to strike accidentally; to intrude; to cheat.

丨見 to meet unexpectedly.

相丨 or 丨着 to meet; to run against each other.

丨額 to thump foreheads, as two persons hitting each other in the dark; face to face, hob-a-nob; an intimate confab.

丨頭 to collide, to run into.

丨口卦 to hear an ominous word.

白丨 to go in on a pretense, as a thief into a yard to look about.

白丨雨 a sun-shower.

丨板 to strike the boards, *i. e.* to made a discord; disappointed; blundering; vexatious. (*Cantonese.*)

衝丨了 I beg pardon for my rudeness; a polite phrase.

丨騙 to swindle, to embezzle; to peculate.

丨門 to push at the door, to beat on it.

丨破 to break against each other.

丨着和尙 to meet a priest, a bad omen; as 丨鬼 to meet a ghost,—is worse; this last in Canton, means to meet a foreigner.

丨倒 knocked or pushed him over; he hit and upset it.

瞎丨 reckless, desperate, as a bird struggling to get out, or a blind man in a strange place.

獞' *chwang'* From *dog* and *lad.*

Savage people classed with the *yao* 猺 or satyrs, said to live near Hainan; they dress with leaves and feathers, and make huts; some of the Miao-tsz' or Laos tribes are probably intended by this contemptuous epithet.

䡴' *chwang'* A war chariot that rushes on the ranks of the enemy; it is used with the *chung* 衝, because it attacks the flanks.

CHWʻANG.

Old sounds, tʻung, dung, tong *and* shong. *In Canton*, chʻong, chʻéung *and* shong ; — *in Swatow*, chong, tʻeng, chʻüng, chang, chwang, tʻong, *and* swang ; — *in Amoy*, chʻòng *and* sòng ; — *in Fuhchau*, chʻòng, chʻaung, tung, *and* sòng ; — *in Shanghai*, tsʻong, zong, *and* song ; — *in Chifu*, tswʻang.

꜀窗 ꜀窓 ꜀牕 ꜀chwʻang } The original forms depict the lattices used for windows, of which there are several shapes ; the first form is composed of 穴 *hole* and 聰 *bright*, contracted.

An aperture to give light in a room ; a window ; a sash ; a blind, a shutter ; a school ; a student.

丨 戶 latticed paper windows ; glass sashes.

丨 門 a window that opens on hinges.

丨 帳 子 window curtains.

天 丨 a sky-light ; a dormar window.

十 年 丨 下 he was ten years at his studies.

同 丨 or 丨 友 or 丨 兄 弟 chums, fellow-students, classmates.

寒 丨 a poor student.

風 丨 子 an outer or double porch door to protect from cold ; common at Peking.

꜀囱 ꜀chwʻang The original form of the preceding ; it is also read ꜀tsʻung.

The vent or flue of a furnace or fireplace.

꜀摐 ꜀chwʻang From *hand* and *following*.

To beat, as a drum or gong ; to motion to.

丨 金 鼓 to sound the gong and drum.

꜀舂 ꜀chwʻang Composed of 臼 a *mortar*, with 廾 *two hands* grasping a 杵 *pestle* between them ; it is also read ꜁chʻung and ꜀shung, and is to be distinguished from ꜀chʻun 春 spring.

To pound paddy or millet with a pestle in a mortar to remove the husk or skin ; to beat or ram down firmly.

丨 米 to hull rice.

丨 墻 to make mud or adobie walls ; and 丨 灰 砂 is to pound chunam walks, as in Canton.

丨 容 手 大 篇 what an inordinate length this paper (or document) has !

丨 鋤 to pound and hoe,— a poetic name of the white egret heron, from its habit of bobbing its head when seeking its food.

꜀瘡 ꜀chwʻang From *sickness* and *granary*.

A sore, a boil, an ulcer, an abscess ; an eruption ; used for the next, a cut, a wound.

丨 穿 the boil has broken ; as a

火 釘 丨 a sore that comes to a head.

꜂長 丨 or 生 起 丨 to have a boil.

寄 丨 or 過 丨 to give away a sore, by means of a charm.

楊 梅 丨 a bubo ; venereal ulcers.

丨 痍 滿 目 the starved and wounded everywhere meet my eyes ; used by an emperor when speaking of the sufferings of the people.

丨 疤 or 丨 瘢 a scab, a scar.

刮 肉 成 丨 to scrape the flesh to make a sore ; — to meddle and cause a serious business.

꜀刅 ꜀戧 ꜀創 ꜀chʻang } From 刀 a *sword* and 一 *one cut* ; the third form is usually read chwʻang꜄, except in this sense.

A wound made by a knife or sword ; to wound ; cut, gashed ; a prop or inclined support, for which the second form is only used.

身 被 多 丨 he received many gashes.

丨 風 a side or baffling wind.

折 丨 走 to tack in sailing.

金 丨 a wound with a sharp weapon.

꜀爿 ꜀chʻang Supposed to be intended to represent the left half of a stick just split in two, but this and 片 are both regarded as derived from the lower half of 鼎 a tripod ; its phonetic power is taken from 牆 and 牀, and it forms the 90th radical of a few characters chiefly relating to walls and beds, or their connections.

In *Shanghai* read baⁿ, as if another form of 邊 a side. A preposition of place ; also used for ꜀pan 班 as a classifier of shops, firms, &c.

東 半 丨 on the eastern side.

一 丨 酒 店 a grog-shop.

꜁床 ꜁牀 ꜁chwʻang } From *covering* or *splinter* and *wood* ; *i. e.* something to recline on ; the first is the common form.

A bed, a couch ; a lounge, a sofa, a settee ; boards for a bed ; a well-curb ; a sled ; a framework ; a measure of eight cubits, *q.d.* as long as a bed ; a classifier of bed-clothes.

一 張 丨 a bedstead.

丨 鋪 the bed and bedding.

鋪 丨 to make up a bed.

丨 榻 a couch, a divan, a settle.

上 丨 to go to bed.

夾 丨 a double bedstead.

牙 丨 the jaw-bone ; also bedsteads inlaid with ivory.

東 丨 a son-in-law.

同 丨 bedfellows.

匟 丨 a couch or divan for guests in the hall.

停 了 丨 了 he is fixed on the bed ; he will surely die, they have given up hope for him.

拉 氷 丨 to draw an ice-sledge.

棉 一 丨 or 被 一 丨 one coverlet.

丨 笫 之 情 married life, conjugal affection.

羅漢 丨 a kind of dais or large divan in the hall, to receive guests in.

睡編 丨 to sleep in the twist-bed, a kind of punishment in prisons, done by squeezing numbers into a small place.

霷 ˓chwʻang From *rain* and *strong*; it is also synonymous with ˓tsʻung 淙 bubbling.

A great rain, sudden and heavy.

天沛然作 丨 the sky suddenly darkened, and there was a great shower.

幢 ˓chwʻang A curtain for a carriage, placed to screen the side windows; a sort of distinguishing pennant; streamers hung from the roof.

丨 幡 pendant scrolls of silk before a shrine.

海 丨 寺 the Honam temple opposite Canton.

Read ˓tʻung. Screening.

樹羽 丨 丨 he set up the shading curtains.

穜 ˓chwʻang To sow seed; to plant seed in the ground.

饞 ˓chwʻang To eat immoderately, to stuff.

丨 饞 to eat rudely, to gorge one's self regardless of decorum.

舂 ˓chwʻang Grain that is half grown or withered; one says, to cut the stalks of grain.

ʻ傸 ʻchwʻang Evil, wicked; to obstinately oppose with a wicked temper.

懷 丨 to harbor evil against one.

剏 chwʻangʾ To wound slightly.

丨 剮 to break the skin, as with a knife or a contusion.

丨 了肉了 to hurt or cut the skin.

悞爲棘 丨 I run a splinter into me by accident.

鏃 丨 the arrow-head hit him.

磢 chwʻangʾ To rub or wash things by sand or brick-dust, as by putting sand in a bottle to clean it.

覦 chwʻangʾ To see indistinctly; to look straight ahead.

創 刱 chwʻangʾ From *knife* and *granary*; one of the original forms represents a board cut in by a knife; the second unusual form is composed of 办 a *cut* and 井 a *pattern*.

To begin, to lay the foundation of; to create, to transform; to invent; to take measures for; to reprove; the first, commencement.

造 丨 to invent, to make first.

丨 始 to begin, to do first; at the beginning.

丨 事業 to found a family, to get an estate.

丨 藝精緻 a very clever invention, a beautiful contrivance.

丨 得狠好 to get on well, as in business.

開 丨 to found, as a state; to originate; to commence, as a settlement.

丨 世以來 from the first ages and afterwards.

懲 丨 to reprove, to reprimand; to punish, as a teacher does.

愴 chwʻangʾ Sad and wounded in heart.

悽 丨 to sorrow; to pity; sick at heart.

丨 惻 a distressed heart.

丨 怳 disappointed.

CHWAN.

Old sounds, tan, dan *and* zhan. *In Canton*, chün, chan, sün, *and* shan; — *in Swatow*, chwan; — *in Amoy*, chwan *and* twʻan; — *in Fuhchau*, chiòng, tiòng, *and* chwang; — *in Shanghai*, tsén *and* dzén; — *in Chifu*, tswen.

專 耑 ˓chwan The original form was 叀, composed of 幺 and 屮 *tender care* of, to which 寸 an *inch* has been added; the second form is common, but not well authorized, and was originally a form of 端 ˓twan.

One, single, only, particular; devoted to, attentive; bent on, to attend to one object; to take upon one, to engross, to assume, to presume; self-willed.

丨 呈 I specially address this....

丨 丨 的 he has only one occupation; he does that especially; I came purposely for that.

丨 一 devoted to one thing, particularly.

丨 門口眼 the speciality of an oculist.

丨 房 under the rule of one wife or concubine.

丨 擅 or 自 丨 to take upon one's self, in disregard of rule or place.

丨 權 having the sole power; to act without reference to others.

丨 差 sent specially, as on a mission.

丨 對 wise in council, ingenious, ready wit; one designated to a special agency, a referee.

受人丨責 engaged (or hired) for a single purpose.

丨 意來 I came for that very purpose.

不敢 丨 I would not dare to take the direction.

丨 心致志 a fixed resolve; a settled inflexible will.

甎 磚 *ˏchwan* } From *tile* or *stone* and *only*. A brick; a square tile, used for pavements or floors; a block or piece shaped like a brick, as 鐵 丨 pig iron; in the tea trade denotes brick tea, of which there are several sorts; pressed cakes; to cover with brick.

丨 窰 a brick-kiln.
石 丨 a stone tile or flag.
階 丨 square red tiles; or 方 丨 large tiles for flagging.
火 頭 丨 bricks burnt red.
大 坭 丨 you great brick or dolt! (*Cantonese*.)
城 丨 at Peking, the very large bricks with which the city wall is built.
桂 元 丨 cakes of the dried lung-yen fruit.
抛 丨 引 玉 throw him a brick to get back a gem;—said in compliment to literary persons who correct compositions, and of persons making a little present in hopes of a large reward.
青 丨 or 沙 板 丨 common or blue bricks.
青 丨 梨 a brick pear, — a local term for a niggard.
丨 地 a brick pavement.
滿 地 丨 to pave the ground.
金 丨 golden tiles, a poetic term for a rich man.
舂 坭 丨 to make adobie bricks in a mold.

嫥 *ˏchwan* Uniform; to be attached to only one; lovely, amiable.

丨 捖 to accord with; to blend; mild, unresisting.
嬌 丨 秀 媚 [these mountains] are so delicate and beautiful in their tints.

鄟 *ˏchwan* An ancient place situated in the present Wei-hwui fu in the east of Honan.

丨 門 an ancient city lying west of K'ai-fung fu in Honan.

鱄 *ˏchwan* A sort of large fish found in Tungting Lake, and sent as presents; the soup is excellent; a salmon-trout?

丨 諸 name of a brave man who tried to kill the king of Wu, B. C. 540, and put a poisoned dagger into the belly of this fish to do it with.

Read *ˏtw'an*. A kind of grunting-fish found in the southern seas, which betokens a drought; it may denote the drumming fish found about Hainan I.

顓 *ˏchwan* From *head* and *only*. To carry the head high; respectful, sedate; obscure, dull; only, alone.

丨 蒙 rude but respectful.
丨 頊 an early sovereign of China, a grandson of Hwangti, B. C. 2513–2435, so called to denote his ability and rectitude.
丨 臾 and ancient town, now called Mung-yin hien 蒙 陰 縣 lying in the southeast of Shantung.

踡 *ˏchwan* From *foot* and *whole*. To kick, to trample down; to bend the body, to cuddle up; to lie along; to crawl.

身 子 丨 着 to curl up the legs, as when lying on a short bed.
丨 莊 to crawl, as a baby.

剸 *ˋchwan* To cut flesh in pieces; to mutilate; to cut wood in two. Also read *ˏchwen*, in the sense of 專 to assume; and *ˏtw'an*, to cut out, as a tailor.

轉 *ˏchwan* From *carriage* and *single*. To turn, as a wheel; to revolve, to transmit, to shift, to turn over to; to forward; to transport, to carry; to circulate; to comprehend; to alter the condition of; to go back; to interpret.

丨 旗 turned his flag, he has left his party.
丨 了 土 音 to interpret the local dialect.
丨 曲 serpentine, winding, as a road.
丨 法 輪 the rule of the metempsychosis.
想 敎 丨 他 I will try to bring him round.
丨 運' to be in better luck; bettered; to transport, as goods.
丨 瞬 or 丨 眼 間 or 丨 息 間 in a twinkling, instantly.
我 心 匪 石 不 可 丨 也 my heart is not as a stone that can be rolled about.
丨 折 太 大 too much changing and confusion, very troublesome.
丨 賃 與 人 to sub-let to another.
丨 致 to convey a hint; to send a message.
丨 輪 骨 a ball-and-socket joint.
丨 稟 to petition by proxy.
丨 相 效 尤 they will then all act still more badly.
丨 語 to turn the subject.
丨 灣 兒 to turn a corner.
丨 風 the wind is veering.
丨 症 the crisis or turn of the disease.

Read *chw'en'*. A revolution, a turn; to move away; becoming more, still more; a disjunctive preposition having the force of — on the other hand, on the contrary; the middle term in a syllogism, the minor premise; the carpet of a carriage.

日 輪 一 丨 one revolution of the sun.
反 丨 to turn over, as a box.
丨 回 來 看 to look behind one.
丨 手 于 人 turn it over to somebody else to do.
連 軸 兒 丨 the axle turns too with the wheel; *i. e.* I have no leisure, I am driven day and night.

In *Pekingese*. To benumb; to finish a thing.

丨' 舌 (or 丨 條 利 in *Cantonese*. to deprive the tongue of taste, as by eating hot things.

弄不丨' I cannot bring it about; it can't be done.

囀' From *mouth* and *turning*.
chwan' Warbling voice, like a bird; delicate modulations; a tone, a note.

聲嬌丨 a sweet voice.
鶯丨 a nightingale's song.
黃鸝丨 the warbling of the mango bird.

篆' From *bamboo* and *pig*.
chwan' The square and involuted form of Chinese characters invented in the Cheu dynasty, called 丨字 or 丨書 or seal characters, from their use; any complicated form of characters, resembling birds, fishes, or other things; to engrave this kind of letters; to call or name; bands on bells.

接丨 to receive the seals.
丨章 a seal.
印丨 name on the seal.
葉大人丨名琛 his Excellency Yeh, named Ming-shăn.
署丨 at present styled.
丨烟徵 curling like rising smoke.
蝸牛丨 the slimy marks of a snail.

瑑' An ornament on the top of the tablets or badges held by courtiers in ancient times at an audience; it resembled a seal character; to engrave such ornaments.
chwan'

良玉不丨 fine gems ought not to be engraved.

瑑' To turn over the soil in ploughing; to plough together.
chwan'

撰' From *hand* and *mild*; interchanged with the next.
chwan' To regulate, to correct; to dispose in order; to compose, to record; to collect, as literary materials; to edit, to revise and publish; to grasp; a pattern, a law, a statute; a maxim; an act.

丨述 to narrate, as annals.
修丨 to indite the state records; —the duty of the Hanlin graduates.
著丨 to write a book.
丨制 to compose and prepare a work for the press.

Read *swan'*, and used for *swan'* 算. To reckon; to count; also used for *süen'* 選 to select.

譔' Used with the preceding.
chwan' To exhort by precept; to discourse in praise of.

丨文 to write an account of, as an obituary notice.
論丨 eulogy of a deceased man.
手丨 his own work or writing.

饌' } From *eat* and *mild*; the second form is nearly obsolete.
籑' } To feed persons; to provide for; dressed animal food; a meal; a relish, a delicacy.
chwan'

設丨 to set out a dinner.
盛丨 a banquet, a sumptuous feast.
殽丨 a delicacy; a well-dressed dish.
菜丨 vegetable and animal food.
有酒食'先生丨 give wine to your elders to sustain them.

Read *süen'*. An ancient weight or piece of silver of six taels.

籑' To provide and make ready a meal; to narrate, to detail, to particularize.
swan'

丨食堂 the dining-hall.
至孔子丨焉 he detailed all the points down to the days of Confucius.

Read *swan'*. A sort of bamboo platter used in worship, having carvings on it.

僎' From *man* and *mild*; also read ˏ*tsun*.
chwan' The governor or master at a village feast, in which sense it is analogous to ˏ*tsun* 尊 or 遵, the one who is honored or obeyed; to number, to arrange in place; tools; articles, gear.

丨爵 to give a banquet.
丨席 a feast.

瑑' Valuable.
chwan'

珍丨 precious; desirable, like a pearl.

縳' Also read *küen'* and sometimes ʿ*pang*, for 綁 to bind; it closely resembles *foh*ˎ 縛 to tie.
chwan'

A bright white color; to spin thrown silk or the floss silk sorted; to bind; a name given to a pack of ten bundles of a hundred feathers each; to roll, as paper; fine cotton cloth which is doubled when put up.

丨一隻猪 to bind a pig, as by the feet.
丨行囊 to strap one's bags and baggage.
丨腿 knee-pads, worn by women.
手無丨鷄之力 they have not strength enough to tie a hen; — said of the cowardly gentry by the people.

CHW'EN.

Old sounds, t'an, dan, *and* zhan. *In Canton*, ch'ün, shün, shan, *and* shun ; — *in Swatow*, chw'an, chun, hun, *and* ch'un ; — *in Amoy*, chw'an, ch'an, swan, *and* ch'un ; — *in Fuhchau*, sung, ch'iòng, chw'a, chw'ang, tiòng, *and* chw'òng ; — *in Shanghai*, ts'é^{n}, zé^{n} *and* dzé^{n} ; — *in Chifu*, tsw'an.

川 巛 *chw'an* — The second is the original form, and is intended to represent the course of rivulets blending to make a creek; it forms the 47th radical of a few incongruous characters.

A mountain runlet, a river's fountains; a stream; to run through the ground; to flow out; the province of Sz'chu'en, and often prefixed to goods, medicines, &c., from that region.

丨流不息 uninterrupted flow; continually going on.

山丨 hills and streams; the champagne, the country.

四丨 the province of Sz'chu'en, so called from the 泯江 Min River, the 沱江 To River, the 黑水 Black River, and the 白水 White River, four rivers in that region near each other.

三丨 or Three Rivers, a prefecture in Honan, during the T'ang dynasty, now Yung-tsih hien 滎澤縣 in K'ai-fung fu.

穿 *chw'an* — From *hole* and *tusk*, alluding to the gnawing of rats in boring through walls.

To perforate, to dig or bore through; to run on or through, as cash on a straw; to chisel a hole; worn through; to break, as a boil; to leak out, as a secret; to put garments on the body only, not on the head.

丨金戴銀 she dresses in gold and tires in silver; — elegantly dressed.

事情丨了 the matter has become known.

丨珠 to string beads.

丨房使喚 a maid of all work; an errand-boy.

丨窬 to bore into, as a wall, in order to steal.

丨出 went through, as a shot.

眼望丨 my eyes are bored through with looking — so long for him, as a wife for her husband.

丨衣服 to dress; to put on a garment.

丨插衙門 to be well acquainted in the public offices.

貫丨經傳 thoroughly conversant with the classics.

百步丨楊 at a hundred paces, [Hwang Chung] pierced the aspen leaf.

百丨 a poetical name for a beehive, from the cells.

丨山甲 the pangolin or scaly ant-eater, (*Manis tetradactyla*) regarded as a type of a crafty fellow.

丨鑿道理 to pervert the original principles of a doctrine, to corrupt the truth.

In *Fuhchau*. To stretch, as the hand.

孱 *chw'an* — From three *children* or orphans and *body*, here defined to mean a house.

Embarrassed; timid, weak, like a petty prince; sighing, groaning; unapt, unfit for.

丨弱 enervated, enfeebled.

丨陵 an old name for Hwa-yung hien 華容縣 just north of Tung-t'ing Lake.

丨劣不堪任事 inadequate to the management of affairs, superannuated.

丨顏 lofty, like a mountain peak.

潺 *chw'an* — Water murmuring; the sound of water; flowing tears; a river in the west of Sz'chu'en.

丨湲 a current; *met.* dropping tears.

In *Cantonese*. Saliva; phlegm.

口丨 phlegm.

吐丨 to expectorate.

丨涎 to slaver, to drool.

一身丨 the whole body is slimy, said of eels.

僝 *chw'an* — To scold, to rail at; to see, to manifest.

丨僽 to vilify, to scold.

椽 *chw'an* — From *wood* and a *pig* ; it is sometimes wrongly used for *yuen* 櫞 a citron.

A round beam or the plate which sustains the eaves; in the north, it denotes the small and short rafters which sustain the wide eaves; and the lathing which connects the large purlines, and supports the tiling; a classifier of houses.

數丨 several buildings or houses.

采丨 painted rafters.

丨料 lumber for rafters.

排丨 short rafters laid close.

屋丨 at *Canton*, the round plate.

傳 *chw'an* — From *man* and *single*.

To transmit, as doctrines; to deliver, as orders; to transfer; to hand down, to perpetuate; to promulgate, to propagate; to interpret or explain; to carry forward, as a balance; to narrate, to record; to send, as by an express; to send for, to subpœna.

丨授 to deliver to one.

丨教 to propagate doctrines, to missionate.

丨聞 to tell the news; to declare in one's hearing.

丨說 a rumor; a legend, tradition.

丨令 to issue a summons, to promulge orders.

丨他來 order him to come, as to a court.

丨言 to send a verbal message.
丨話 to transmit an order or information.
丨情 to give a hint, to intimate.
抗丨不到 he refused to come when summoned.
丨供 a sort of court crier, one who assists the magistrate in his examinations.
丨遞 to pass from one to another.
祖丨 received from one's ancestors or predecessors.
秘丨 secretly transmitted, as a recipe is 丨家 handed down in a family.
丨位 to transmit the throne.
丨世 to make known to mankind.
關丨 a sort of custom-house certificate.
丨臚 the fourth on the list of Hanlin graduates.
電理丨 or 通線丨 to send a a telegram.
丨鑼 to arouse or spread alarm by beating gongs.

Read *chwen*ʾ. A record of; precepts handed down; chronicles, traditions.
家丨 a family history; genealogical annals of a family.
文丨 a story of.
列丨 biographies, narratives of people.

In *Fuhchau*. To hand things; to move.

船 舡 ˏchwʿan From 舟 *boat* and 鉛 *lead* contracted for the phonetic; the abbreviated form is common.

A ship, boat, bark, junk, or whatever carries people on the water; a sort of apothecary's mortar; a long tea-saucer; to follow the stream; to drift, as a boat.
一隻丨 one vessel, one boat.
丨隻 ships, vessels.
一起丨 or 一幫丨 a squadron, a fleet.
下丨 or 落丨 to embark.
上丨 to go ashore; it also means to go on board, when used at the spot.
看風駛丨 look at the wind before you hoist sail.
丨家 the whole crew.
丨主 the captain.
丨戶 one sailor; sailors; a crew.
丨課 tonnage dues or taxes on native boats.
兵丨 or 戰丨 a man-of-war.
渡丨 a ferry-boat, a passenger-boat.
撐丨 or 刺丨 to pole a boat up stream.
官丨 a flag-ship; a ship with an officer in it.
巡丨 a revenue-cutter, a cruizer.
押丨 custom-house guard-boats.
三枝桅丨 a three-masted ship.
火輪丨 a steamer; either 明輪丨 a side-wheel vessel, or 暗輪丨 a propeller.
開丨 or 行丨 to weigh anchor; the second phrase also means, like 行丨手, to be a sailor.
丨駕不住風 the ship could not stand the wind.
夾板丨 or 篷丨 or 帆丨 a sailing vessel; the first term is the Malay word *kapal*, and has come into use through the Fuhkien traders.
天丨 the stars γ η in Perseus.
丨頭官 a harbor-master.
寄丨 to go with cargo, as a supercargo.
跑旱丨 a light frame made like a boat, in which a man is hidden, who plies it round and round to entertain people.

遄 ˏchwʿan From to *go* and *head* of.

To hurry; to go to and fro; to hasten, to walk rapidly.
丨往 to go quickly.
式丨其歸 to cause (or see that) he soon returns.
戎馬丨征 a troop of cavalry going out on an expedition.

喘 ʿchwʿan To pant, to breathe quick and short, as in asthma; the breath, the life.
丨丨氣兒 to rest and take breath, as when tired; but 氣丨 is panting from shortness of breath.
丨定了 the panting fit was over.
殘丨 my failing breath; my poor life; old, ready to depart.
丨吠 to wheeze and cough.
丨逆 hiccup, shortness of breath.
吳牛丨月 the buffaloes in Kiangnan [fearing the heat], pant when they see the moon; — *met.* imaginary fears.

舛 ʿchwʿan The original form represents *two men* sleeping back to back; it is the 136th radical of an insignificant group of characters.

Opposed to, contradictory; perverse, incongruous, incompatible.
丨午 or 乖丨 opposing; to be disobedient.
丨錯 erroneous, in disorder.
丨僕 or 煩丨 talkative and mistaken; either from heedlessness or many cares.
丨謬 to deceive purposely.
命途多丨 I've had a great many untoward haps in my life.

荈 ʿchwʿan The late and old leaves of the tea-plant, which require a strong drawing.
賜茶丨以當酒 send him some old tea instead of wine.

篡 tswʿanʾ From 算 to *calculate* and 厶 *perversely*.

To rebel against a sovereign and usurp his throne; to abolish a dynasty; to seize a criminal.
丨位 to seize the throne.
丨弒 to murder the ruler.
丨逆 to plot and rebel.
滴血成丨字 the drops of blood [from his tongue] formed the character *rebel*; said of 方孝如 a minister of Kien-wăn, whose tongue Yung-loh cut off (A. D. 1404), and this was his way of asserting his loyalty.

[算+攴]ʾ *chwʽanʾ* Properly read *fanʾ*.

A small mortar to hull grain.

In *Pekingese.* To husk rice in a mortar with a wooden pestle is 丨 米; it removes the chaff without breaking the grain, as a stone pestle does.

釧ʾ *chwʽanʾ* From *metal* and *rivulet.*

An armlet, a bracelet; an old name is 條 脫 or warder off.

釵 丨 pins and bangles; *i. e.* female ornaments.

玔ʾ *chwʽanʾ* A ring made of jade; this is now superseded by the last.

諯ʾ *chwʽanʾ* To number, to reckon; to mutually yield, as politeness requires.

串ʾ *chwʽanʾ* From two *mouths connected;* it is contracted from an older form of two mortars with a line drawn through them; interchanged with ˏ*chwʽen* 穿 to string.

To string together, as cash; to connect; leagued or banded for some evil end; a string of.

一 丨 錢 a string of cash.

丨 過 it is strung on.

丨 炮 a string of fire-crackers.

丨 同 作 弊 to band together to make disturbance.

丨 計 or 丨 謀 to join in swindling or entrapping one; a blackleg's crafty plan; to cabal.

丨 騙 to lay a scheme to swindle one.

文 理 貫 丨 the argument is well supported throughout.

不 丨 irrelevant, incoherent.

丨 合 to league together; to join, as forces.

In *Pekingese.* To miss a line in reading or copying.

書 念 丨 了 you have skipped a column in reading.

丨 門 子 to gad about, not to stay at home.

僢ʾ *chwʽanʾ* Used for 舛 in some cases.

To flow in opposite directions; to turn the feet inwards from the door, a usage among the Laos when dying; batons of office laid across each other.

鶨ʾ *chwʽanʾ* A bird, more commonly called 癡 鳥 the stupid bird, which seems to be allied to the wood-pecker; one says, a bird in a cage.

猭ʾ *chwʽanʾ* A hare running away through the grass; to scamper, like a rabbit.

FAH.

Old sounds, pat, pap, bat, *and* bap. *In Canton,* fat; — *in Swatow,* hwat *and* hwap: — *in Amoy,* hwat; — *in Fuhchau,* hwak; — *in Shanghai,* fĕh *and* vĕh; — *in Chifu,* fah.

髮ˎ ʽ*fa* From *hair* and to *eradicate.*

The hair on top of the human head; also applied to the hair-like feathers of some birds; numerous, as hairs; *met.* grass, reeds, moss, vegetation.

頭 丨 human hair.

一根 丨 or 一 條 丨 a single hair of the head.

削 丨 to shave the whole head.

丨 赤 red hair, *i. e.* a small child.

留 丨 to let the hair grow, said of girls or priests.

披 頭 散 丨 disheveled hair.

丨 落 to become bald.

石 丨 and 苔 丨 frog's spittle (*Confervæ*); applied to some kinds of mosses.

丨 菜 a kind of algæ used for food.

鬚 丨 皆 白 the hair and beard were all white.

結 丨 夫 婦 an old couple, a long married pair.

丨 網 a silk cap or net used by bald women.

合 人 丨 指 [his crimes are like] his hairs for number.

窮 丨 之 北 the desolate and bare northern regions.

毫 丨 不 爽 completely miserable, feeling very wretched.

束 丨 to bind up the hair in a knot called 丨 冠, such as is worn by a Taoist priest.

鬓 丨 斑 the temples are becoming grisly.

發ˎ ˏ*fa* Composed of 癶 to *straddle,* with 弓 *bow* and 矢 an *arrow;* others make it to consist of 癹 to *tread grass* and 弓 a *bow.*

To shoot an arrow; to send forth, to throw out; to issue, to start; to have, to show, as a disease, perspiration, &c.; to cause to go out, to dispatch; to expand, to prosper; to go to; to advance; to ferment, to rise; to leak out; to show forth; to manifest, to elevate; to pay out, as money; to attack and suppress; sometimes has a passive sense, as 丨 福 to be blest, *i. e.* he shows the effect of the blessing, meaning fat, in good liking; the spring, because then all things bud out; a shot, as of a bow.

丨起 to increase, as plants.

丨起來 to succeed, to get on; to rise, as dough.

丨財 to make money, to prosper; used as a wish, may you have good luck.

丨客 for customers; *i. e.* to sell 丨兌 by retail, or 丨行 by wholesale.

丨市 to have a customer.

丨誓 to take an oath.

丨潮 to get moldy, to become damp.

丨心 to give in charity, to show pity.

丨單 to give a bill of goods; to issue a permit; to advertise for.

丨丁 to have many descendants.

丨回 to return; to send back.

打丨 to send, as a messenger or a letter.

丨出 to send off, to dismiss.

丨怒 to get angry; irritated.

丨現 to display; to appear.

丨明 breaking of the dawn; to explain, to make clear.

丨兵 to march out troops.

丨科甲 you will be a *küjin* or *tsinsz'*; a form of a wish.

以財丨身 to buy one's way to office or promotion.

丨丨 or 觱丨 blustering, raw, as the wind.

要開丨兒 I want a present or baksheesh.

不要啓丨我 you'll get no wine-money out of me.

怎生丨落 what will be the end of it? what will come of it?

丨揚 to make a way for one's self, to become well-known.

Read *poh*, The motion of fishes struggling.

丨丨然 quick, perpetually moving, as a fish's tail.

橃, *˛fa* A large sea-going vessel, like a raft for size; an ark.

Read *˛fei*. A fruit resembling a pumelo; the end of the plate in a roof.

筏, **栰**, *˛fa* Interchanged with the preceding; the second form is not common.

A bamboo raft, or something similar, for crossing a river; a pontoon.

火丨 fire rafts.

紮丨子 to tie together a raft.

排丨 bamboo rafts with a bent stem.

伐, *fa'* From *man* and *lance*; to be distinguished from *tai'* 代 a generation.

To reduce a dependency to order, to chastise rebels; to destroy, to desolate; to cut down; to brag, to bring one's merit to notice; meritorious deeds; fine; to beat a drum; a midsman; the stars ι in Capricorn, and ι ν in Orion.

丨木 or 丨樹 to fell trees.

丨善 to boast of one's goodness.

丨罪 to punish an offense.

丨鼓 to drum, in order to call one.

殺丨利害 to kill recklessly; famous for prowess.

不自丨故有功 he was meritorious, because he did not brag of himself.

且旌君丨 to set forth our prince's deeds.

爲人作丨 to act as a go-between.

閥, *fa'* From *door* and *to reduce* as the phonetic.

The left-side door in a great palace gateway, or the left side of a gate.

丨閱 the leaves of a double door; degrees of merit; meritorious services, such as entitle one to pass through the gate.

丨閱之家 a distinguished family, one of the gentry; in the Mongol dynasty there was an order of nobility called 烏頭丨閱 from certain insignia which the members were allowed to show at their gateways.

垡, *fa'* To *subdue* the *ground*, which the composition of the character indicates.

耕丨 to plough, to turn over the clods and prepare the soil for seed.

挖丨子 people who build mud walls.

䑦, *fa'* From *mortar* and *market*.

To pound rice for the purpose of hulling it.

罰, *˛fa* Composed of 詈 to *rail* at and 刀 a *sword*, with which to stab; *q.d.* actions that deserve punishment.

A fault, a peccadillo, a petty offense; a crime; a slight punishment, a penalty commutable by money; a fine; to forfeit, to fine, to flog.

責丨 to reprimand, to find fault with, to punish corporeally, as a pupil or subaltern.

丨酒 to forfeit a glass of wine—by being made to drink it.

丨俸 to forfeit or be mulcted one's salary.

丨項 a fine; moneys accruing from fines.

賞 and 丨 are opposites;—to confer; to mulct.

刑丨 punishments of every grade.

丨量 or 丨米 to cut one's pay or rations, as a soldier.

恭行天丨 I (Wu Wang) will reverently execute Heaven's punishment.

受丨 cursed, punished; under disgrace.

我丨你 I'll punish you; *i. e.* you've offended me, you've not done it right.

乏, *˛fa* The original form is from 正 *correct* turned to the left, to denote its opposite.

To be in want of, defective empty, poor; exhausted, weary needing rest, and thus like the next; a temporary deficiency, embarrassed; to fail of; to injure; without, wanting; a leather screen to protect archers; a sort of shield.

困 丨 wearied, tired out.

丨 乂 照 應 few ministered to his wants.

窮 丨 or 空 丨 absolutely destitute, impoverished.

缺 丨 insufficient, unsupplied, out of.

不 敢 丨 事 I may not venture to impede this affair.

不 丨 乂 材 no want of clever men.

走 得 丨 了 I've walked till I am tired out.

疺 fa' Weary, without energy; lassitude, arising from heat; lean, lank.

姂 ˏfa From *woman* and *destitute*.

Handsome, beautiful, feminine; whatever is matronly and lady-like.

法, 灋 ˏfa From *water* and *to put away*, *i. e.* to reduce to a level, as water is; the second form has 廌 a fabulous benign animal that punishes the guilty, added to it, and occurs only in Budhist books.

A law, a statute, a rule, something that restrains one; a set of regulations, precepts; in scientific usage, the rules for, or science of; a legal infliction; a sect, a religion; an art; skill; the code of the Budhists, so called from the first syllable of *dharma* or law; the sect of Budhists; to follow a rule, to imitate an example; and hence, excellent, natural, like, accurate; a working factor in a sum.

國 丨 or 律 丨 the statutes of a country.

丨 網 the net or power of the laws.

刑 丨 penal laws.

禮 丨 a code of politeness.

方 丨 a means, a way, a style.

道 丨 無 邊 their doctrines and law are unlimited—in their application.

丨 國 or 丨 蘭 西 國 France; the French.

執 丨 如 山 to rigidly maintain the laws; 執 丨 also denotes an executor of the laws, a magistrate.

丨 度 or 丨 則 a set of rules; a plan; regulations, patterns.

符 丨 to lay a spell, to exorcise.

沒 丨 子 or 無 丨 no help, no remedy; it can't be helped.

丨 水 to spurt water by the mouth or asperge it; applied to the act of priests when they sprinkle a charm.

想 丨 子 think whether there's no other way, or no plan.

水 丨 hydraulics.

折 丨 to unravel; to relieve from danger, to plan a rescue; to solve a mystery.

丨 門 the Budhists.

丨 衣 a priestly or clerical dress.

丨 繪 accurate, life-like drawings.

丨 身 a spiritual, ethereal body that can pass through things; also an image of Budha.

丨 輪 a praying-machine, used by the Mongols to repeat prayers as it revolves by the wind; but 轉 丨 輪 also means to preach or hand down Budhist doctrines.

丨 術 rules or way of legerdemain, the black art.

現 身 說 丨 I will show you how to do it, as a flugelman does; it is used too by priests when they explain the tenets of their faith, which they exhibit in themselves.

珐 fa' An unauthorized character.

The enameled ware of the Chinese.

丨 琅 瓶 a cloisonnée or enameled jar

浟 fa' Chilly; to open sluices to let water upon fields.

丨 灌 to irrigate, to water.

FAN.

Old sounds, pan, pon, pam *and* bam. *In Canton*, fan; — *in Swatow*, hwan *and* hwam; — *in Amoy*, hun, hwan, hong, *and one* bwan; — *in Fuhchau*, hwang, *and a few* pang; — *in Shanghai*, fèⁿ *and* vèⁿ; — *in Chifu*, fan.

番 ˏfan Composed of 田 *field* and 釆 the *claws* of a beast, as it seems to be designed to represent their footsteps.

The tracks of a wild beast; a time, a turn; to repeat, to duplicate; to send, to dispatch to; to change; to reckon; an ancient tribe of Mongols or Huns near Kokonor beyond the frontier of China; aborigines of the country in the south, now applied to any uncivilized people, and in contempt along the southern coasts, to Europeans and other foreigners; in some ports, it means a dollar, alluding to the effigy.

丨 話 foreign talk.

丨 人 or 老 丨 at *Canton*, a foreigner.

銅 丨 a counterfeit or copper dollar.

土 丨 the native savages or people; the name *Turfan*, on foreign maps applied to the regions west of China as a proper name, is derived from this.

八 丨 eight tribes of Miaotsz' in Ting-fan cheu 定 丨 州 in Kwéi-chau province.

幾 丨 several times.

三丨兩次 times and times, repeatedly.
連丨 incessantly, continuously.
更丨 to alter.
往丨貿易 to go abroad to trade.

Read ꜀*po*. Warlike.
丨丨頁士 an old and courageous warrior, like John Hunyades.

Read ꜀*pan*. Name of a district.
丨禺縣 Pan-yü hien, which includes Whampoa and part of Canton city.
丨州 an old name of Kao-cheu fu 高州府 in the southwest of Kwangtung.

翻 ꜀*fan* From *wings* and to *repeat* as the phonetic; occurs used for ꜀*fan* 反 to turn back.

To fly to and fro, to flutter about; to return; to change, to turn over; to revise, as a case; wrongly used for the next, to translate; fickle, vacillating.
丨生 to resuscitate, to come to; to come back to life.
丨過來 turn it over.
丨案 to rejudge a case; an appeal.
丨覆 or 丨丨覆覆 to go to and fro, changeable, uncertain, unsettled, vacillating.
丨風大 a boisterous wind.
翩丨 to soar and sail, as a hawk.
丨飛 to flutter and flit.
丨臉 to change color, to get angry or blush.
丨觔斗 to turn somersaults, to perform gymnastics, as an acrobat.
丨騰東西 to turn things over and over, to throw into disorder.
奔走一丨 running about on your business; to attend to an affair.
丨轉 overturned; wrong side up.
弄丨了 turned it over; upset it, as by accident.
一丨雨過一丨風 at each dash of rain there's a gust of wind.

In *Pekingese*, often wrongly written 播 to show that it is colloquial, but this last is properly read *po*ʾ. To turn over, to toss about.
丨書 to turn over the leaves of a book, to count them, or see their contents.

繙 ꜀*fan* From *silk* and to *repeat* as the phonetic. Used with the last; it is also erroneously written 譒 from the power of the radical.

The wind fluttering a flag; to agitate, to display, to open out; to translate; to open out the meaning in the colloquial, to interpret; loose, easy; fluttering.
丨譯官 an official translator or interpreter.
打丨語 to speak foreign languages.

幡 ꜀*fan* From *napkin* and to *repeat;* used with the next.

A duster or cloth to wipe goblets; a marker or distinguishing pennant to signalize the presence of an officer; tripartite streamers hung in temples before the shrine, generally bearing legends, and beautifully embroidered; to return.
張丨一對 a pair of ornamental banners.
丨然改 forthwith (or suddenly) changed it.
丨纚 waving, fluttering; flying abroad.
打丨兒 to carry the white 三丨 or three-tier banner, on which the name of the defunct is written, to show its spirit the way to the grave, where it is burned.

旛 ꜀*fan* From *flag* and to *repeat*. Used with the last, and more frequently.

A streamer; a funeral flag or banner.
旗丨 flags and pennons; banners of all sorts.
招魂丨 the banner used to call spirits to their tombs or tablets, especially of those who died abroad.

立青丨 to hoist the green banner, refers to the same usage; this is simply a full leaved bamboo, which is waved over the family grave.

轓 ꜀*fan* A screen or hood for a cart, called 丨蔽, which keeps off the dust and mud; it appears to have been a sort of mat dashboard thrown over the front.

拚 ꜀*fan* From *hand* and *cap* ; it is interchanged with *pien*ʾ 抃 to pat.

Soaring; flying.
允彼桃蟲丨飛維鳥 it was then only a wren, but when it flew away it became a [big] bird.

Read *pien*ʾ. To brandish or clap the hands; to sweep clean, to brush off; to reject, to lightly regard.
丨除 to clear away; to reject, to ignore.
丨命 to risk life, as in rescuing one.

燔 ꜀*fan* From *fire* and to *repeat* as the phonetic.

To roast meat for sacrifices.
丨肉不至不稅冕而行 when the roasted flesh was not brought in, [Confucius] went away without taking off his cap.
或丨或炙 either roasted or grilled.
丨柴 an ancient kind of burnt offering on the great altar when worshiping Heaven.

膰 ꜀*fan* Meats used in sacrifices, and distributed by the emperors of Cheu to their kinsmen.
丨肉 sacrificial meats.

墦 ꜀*fan* A tomb or grave.
丨間之祭 the worship at the tombs; religious ceremonies at graves.

璠 ꜀*fan* A sort of precious stone found in Lu, called 璵丨, which Confucius admired; it was probably a veined agate.

蹯 *ˌfan* A plantigrade foot, like that of a badger; the paw of a bear, called 熊 丨, which is regarded as one of the 八珍 or eight delicacies.

蕃 *ˌfan* From *plants* and a *turn;* occurs used for the next.

Plants growing luxuriantly; flourishing; plenty; numerous; the increase of; to inclose, to fence in, to shield.

丨 盛 abundant, full.

丨 衍 numerous, as progeny.

丨 滋 or 丨 茂 flourishing, as a garden or field; to increase.

丨 庶 numerous, increasing population.

支系丨昌 his descendants are many and prospering.

四國于丨 [Fu and Shăn] are screens to the other states.

藩 *ˌfan* From *grass* and *spring of water;* it is also used for ˌ轓 a cart-cover.

A fence or hedge; a boundary, a frontier; to protect, to fend off; to inclose; in the Peh Sung 北宋 dynasties, applied to certain feudatories near the frontiers, which only rendered homage, but were regarded as Chinese subjects.

丨 維 a defense, an outlying jurisdiction or fief.

丨 籬 a wattle; a bamboo or hurdle fence.

丨 域 the frontier.

丨 垣 an inclosing wall.

丨 邦 a neighboring, allied, or feudatory state; Corea so calls herself.

丨 司 or 丨 臺 the fending-off commissioner; *i. e.* the treasurer of a province, so called to show the importance of the revenue.

价人維丨 serviceable men are as a fence — to the state.

丨 臣 officers near the throne; this, and 丨 屏 a screen, are also applied to a high officer who protects the throne, or defends the frontier.

籓 *ˌfan* A dust basket or fan to separate chaff; a refuse basket called 丨 籮, made somewhat like a sieve; to cover, to screen from view.

獢 *ˌfan* A very small sized deer, occurring among the mountains of Koko-nor, having a yellow belly, and called *kien-ʻrh* on the spot; the Păn Tsʻao regards it as a variety of the dzeron (*Antilope gutturosa*), but it is most probably another species.

煩 *ˌfan* From *fire* and *head.*

Heat and pain in the head; trouble, annoyance; perplexed, heated; important, not indifferent; to intrude on, to trouble, to ask; impertinent, urgent; grieved, sorry.

干 丨 to trouble one, as with an errand.

敢丨 or 丨勞 or 多丨你 I give you much trouble, or I will be obliged to you; *i. e.* please do this; I'll thank you to do this; — polite forms of request.

丨 悶 perplexed, vexed, grieved, annoyed.

丨 擾 to annoy, to interrupt.

丨 帶此信 please take this letter; — written on the envelop.

丨 瑣 or 丨 碎 troublesome, impertinent; vexed with trifles.

禮丨則亂 an excess of ceremony is confusing.

不耐丨 I can't bear to be troubled so.

怪丨的 very annoying; unusually troublesome.

薠 *ˌfan* An aquatic grass, on which wild geese feed, the 青 丨, probably a triquetrous sedge, like a *Carex* or *Cyperus.*

繁 *ˌfan* One form is composed of 糸 *silk* and 每 *each,* and defined to be an ornament placed on a horse's neck or mane.

Much, numerous; the opposite of ʻ*kien* 簡 limited; troublesome; thick, as grass; a variety of affairs; manifold, multitudinous.

丨 華 gaiety, pomp; extravagant show.

丨 冗 troublesome from excess.

丨 多 or 紛 丨 overburdened; confused; perplexed with cares.

丨 緒 harassed by many cares.

丨 費 expensive, costly, using more than is needed.

丨 難 and 丨 疲 troublesomely hard and troublesomely weary-ing, are terms aplied to certain district and prefectural posts.

Read ˌ*pʻan.* A saddle-girth.

蘩 *ˌfan* From *plants* and *troublesome* as the phonetic.

An edible kind of celery or borage, anciently called 白蒿, whose leaves are eaten when green, and pickled for winter; the leaves are fed to young silkworms, and a decoction sprinkled on their eggs hastens their hatching; some consider this plant to be a species of woolly *Artemisia,* but the uses and description seem to point out a more edible plant.

于以采丨 she collects the celery.

瀿 *ˌfan* Water thrown upon plants to cover their roots when first set out; to water plants.

丨 溢 to drip or run over.

棥 *ˌfan* From two *trees bound* and interlaced by branches, to form a hedge; it is now superseded by the next, and occurs only in combination.

A screen; a hedge; a fence.

樊 *ˌfan* Composed of *hedge* and *great,* but the original form is like the last.

A railing; an inclosed place, a spot hedged around; a cage; obstructed, hedged up; mixed.

丨 籠 a cage.

營營青蠅止於丨 the fitting green bottle-fly has stopped in the hedge.

礬 From *stone* and a *hedged plat* as the phonetic.

꜀fan Styptic mineral or metallic salts fit for dyeing or painting; alum; to dye with alum; to tan leather in lime and copperas.

白丨 alum; 丨石 alum shale.

皂丨 or 青丨 copperas, green vitriol, or sulphate of iron.

膽丨 or 紅丨 blue vitriol, or sulphate of copper.

綠丨 acetate of copper.

山丨 a tree in Honan, whose leaves furnish a dyeing salt.

丨紙 paper sized with alum.

丨皮店 a tanning-shop.

蠜 A small grasshopper, called 負丨, the common Gryllus. 氣丨 the cockroach, or perhaps a sort of *Cimex*, which stinks when it is struck; it is said to have been eaten.

꜀fan

凡 凢 The original form had 二 *two* inside to denote a pair, and was derived from an old form of 及 denoting to bring all together; others derive it from 乃 *thus* and 一 *one*; others from still different forms; the second is unauthorized, and mostly used by the Budhists.

꜀fan

All, everybody; common, vulgar, usual; generally, for the most part; among the Budhists, the world; laic; mortal, earthly, human.

丨人 men, people, mankind; used by Budhists as a demeaning term for the laity, the world, secular persons, who cannot attain to immortality like 仙人 ethereal men, or to high happiness like 聖人 holy ones.

丨間 the world; in secular life.

丨事 everything; all affairs.

大丨 whoever; in general.

諸丨 or 丨物 all, everything, everybody; altogether.

諸丨多勞 I give you much trouble about these things.

不知丨幾 I don't know how many there are altogether.

非丨 clever, not common, above the average.

丨夫 or 丨夫俗子 or 丨民 common sort of people, the vulgar.

下丨 to come into the world, as a divine being.

降丨 to descend from heaven to this world.

思丨 to think of leaving the priesthood and marrying; — said by priests.

大丨所有 people generally have it.

大丨人做好 whoever performs good deeds.

發丨起例 do the whole in the same way as the pattern.

脫丨尸 to shuffle off this mortal coil, to turn into a spirit, or go among the genii.

丨胎 of human origin, — *i. e.* not a god.

帆 From *kerchief* and *all* as the phonetic.

꜀fan A sail for vessels; canvas; to sail; sailing.

丨布 canvas, sail-cloth.

丨船 sailing vessels, not steamers.

揚丨 to spread sail, to set out on a voyage.

張雲丨 to hoist the lofty sails.

錦丨高掛 hoist high the gay sails.

借一丨風 to get another's help, to raise the wind; refers to a fair wind filling the sail.

石丨 a sort of laminated seaweed.

颿 From *wind* and *horse*; one form of the last when used as a verb.

꜀fan A horse racing; a boat sailing swiftly.

船丨丨而去 or 船丨行 a vessel sailing; the ships are sailing away.

驚丨 a horse frightened and running.

笲 An osier basket shaped like a fish-basket, with a small mouth and covered with silk; in olden times, brides placed millet and dates in one, and carried it on meeting their husbands.

꜀fan

杋 A large tree, whose bark is called 氷梓木 because it floats; one defines it to be the bark of firewood; it may be a kind of cork tree.

꜀fan

反 Composed of 厂 a *retreat* and 又 a *hand*; the hand is the agent in turning; interchanged with the next, and with 翻 to revert.

ˋfan

To turn back voluntarily; to return, to recur to; to turn, as the leaves of a book; to send back, to send for; to resume; to take back; in revenge for; perversity; a repetition; to be or act contrary, to rebel, to plot against; to revise; the reverse of; to turn around; again; as a *conjunction*, but, on the contrary, opposed to; used in dictionaries to denote the union of an initial and final when expressing a third sound.

相丨 discordant, unmatched.

照丨 to reflect light; refraction.

丨回 or 丨還 to turn back to, to revert to.

丨骨 to slander, to backbite.

作丨 to rebel, to excite sedition.

平丨 to reduce insurgents.

丨口 to retract, to disown, to deny one's words.

丨叛 rebels to government; the seditious.

丨胃噎食 the stomach rejects food.

丨轉 to turn over; turn it around.

丨轉面皮 to change countenance.

丨面 to turn a cold shoulder; the contrary idea.

丨倒 on the contrary; upset.

偪丨 to drive the people to revolt.

丨教 a renegade, a turncoat.

丨必自問 carefully ask your own heart.

禠來祿丨 uninterrupted blessings.

丨病 a relapse of an illness.

丨不如初 but now it is different from then.

丨爲不美 on the contrary it was disagreeable.

丨 and 正 are used in opposition, as a direct and indirect argument in logic; 丨論 is negative, adverse, ironical; 正論 is positive, favorable, serious, direct.

丨切 to spell or combine the sounds of characters, as 甫遠 *f*-u yu-*en*, which gives 反 *fan*.

丨覆 back and forth; to retract; tautological; over again.

丨語辭 a disjunctive particle.

丨風禾則盡起 by a contrary wind the grain all rose up.

返 From to *go* and *contrary*; used with the last.

ˎ*fan* To return, to go or come back; to revert to; but, on the other hand.

往丨幾日 how many days will you be gone?

丨之於天 refer it to Heaven.

丨程 [he left] on his return.

而丨受累 on the contrary, he suffered by it, or was involved.

丨旋 to return, as home, or from a visit; to revert to.

丨棹 to sail or row back; to back water in rowing.

坂 From *earth* and *contrary* as the phonetic.

ˎ*fan* A declivity, a hill-side; a bank; a dike.

坡丨 a terraced bank or slope.

蒲丨 the place where Shun built his capital, now Pu-cheu fu 蒲州府 in the southwest corner of Shansi.

阪 Used with the preceding, and occurs used for its primitive.

ˎ*fan* A bank, a dike; the steep rocky descent of hills.

丨田 hill-side terraces; fields banked up to retain the water.

隴丨 a plateau or level parterre in a valley.

飯 From *to eat* and *return* as the phonetic.

*fan*ˋ A meal; cooked rice, because it is the chief dish at every meal; food in general; the bottom of the thumb; to eat a meal.

吃丨食 or 丨用 or 丨 to eat, to take a meal; 丨後 after eating.

無丨食 poor, beggared; I have no food.

討丨的 a beggar, a needy person.

一頓丨 or 一餐丨 one meal.

吃過丨嗎 have you had your rice? — *i.e.* Are you well? How do you do? — to which the reply is, 有偏 or 偏過了 I've no need to inconvenience you; I've already eaten.

毋搏丨 do not grab the rice.

會ˋ丨 cooked millet.

丨疏食飲水 [Confucius said,] with my meal of coarse rice and with water to drink, I am happy.

米丨 or 白丨 rice ready to eat.

白丨魚 the southern name for the white-bait (*Leucosoma*), from its diaphanous body.

丨匙頭 the cobra de capello, so called from its spoon shaped head.

漂母一餐丨 [like] the bleaching woman's meal — given to Han Sin, which was nobly rewarded.

餐荳丨 to cook beans and glutinous rice for mourners; — a Cantonese custom.

丨鈒 rice shears; — a term for the molar teeth.

亞丨 in ancient times, the cook of the second meal of noblemen.

販 販 } From *pearl* or *to buy* and *to return*.

*fan*ˋ To turn a penny, to buy cheap and sell dear, to traffic, to deal in, to carry about for sale.

丨夫 or 丨仔 a peddler, a chapman, one who buys at night to sell in the morning.

丨客 to peddle, to retail; a peddler.

丨莊 a warehouse, a large shop.

丨賣人口 to deal in human beings, especially children.

人丨子 a broker in children.

拐丨 to kidnap people for sale.

丨牛馬 to trade in cattle, as a 馬丨子 jockey does.

丨家 house of a broker in women; a sort of marriage-broker; it is not a disreputable business.

忛 To regret; penitent; hasty, precipitate; wicked.

*fan*ˋ 丨悔 to regret an act.

㽹 From *disease* and *to turn*.

*fan*ˋ To vomit food; to faint and relieve the stomach; in Tso, bad people were so called.

畈 A plain, a field; in Honan, used in the sense of a farmstead, a hamlet.

*fan*ˋ 丨疇 fields and plats.

䣐 醉 } From *spirits* and an *officer*.

*fan*ˋ Liquor kept over night; newly distilled spirits; that which is made of refuse grain.

In *Cantonese*. Ill-luck, as upon children; ill starred; things or agencies that injure children.

起丨 to exorcise the demon which makes sickness.

丨着 to meet with misadventures that affect the fœtus.

丨神 elfins or gnomes which bring evil on a household.

梵 From *forest* and *all* as the phonetic.

*fan*ˋ A Hindu word denoting stillness or retirement, now used for the Sanscrit or Pali languages, as a contraction of 丨覽摩 Brahma; the country of Magadha whence Budha came.

丨咒 Budhist prayers and charms.

丨章 Brahma's chapter, is the syllabary in twelve parts, ascribed to him.

丨音 the sound of chanting; Sanscrit sounds.

丨字 or 丨書 or 丨言 Pali or Sanscrit (*i. e.* Brahma's) characters or writing; while 丨語 is Sanscrit word or speech.

丨刹 a Budhist monastery, in which the 丨宇 is the great hall of idols.

丨志 a Brahmin.

丨天王 or 大丨王 Brahma is so called by some Chinese Budhists; and 丨天 is Brahmaloka, the eighteen mansions in heaven.

Read ˏ*fung*. The soughing of wind through trees; to spread abroad widely.

氾 *fan'* From *water* and a *joint*.

Water overflowing; to inundate; agitated, in motion, like a flood; weak in mind, and unable to compose the thoughts; name of a river in Shantung and in Honan.

丨濫 an inundation, overflowing everything.

汎 泛 *fan'* Sometimes used for the preceding; it is also read ˏ*fung*; the second form is most used.

To float; driven to and fro by the wind; floating; to transport; unguided, reckless, careless, objectless; extensive, universal; to overflow; name of a river in Shensi.

浮丨 floating about; superficial.

丨漂 light, buoyant, as a cork or spume.

丨丨其流 drifting with the current.

丨常 customary; unacquainted with.

丨言 vague talk, untrustworthy.

丨舟 sailing or riding in a boat.

丨淫 excessive, as a flood.

丨洒 to sprinkle abundantly.

丨澾 the plunging and dashing of waves on a shore.

丨遊 to wander at will, purposeless.

丨丨的交情 a superficial acquaintance with; I only recently knew him.

Read ˊ*fung*. To throw, as a horse his rider.

丨駕之馬 a horse that spills his rider; *met.* a stubborn boy.

犯 *fan'* From *dog* and a *joint*.

To rush against; to offend, to transgress; to resist, to oppose, to violate; to invade, to attack a territory; to attack impudently, to assault unprovokedly; to encounter that which injures one; possessed by, as a spirit; to be exposed to; a criminal; a prisoner at the bar, a culprit, whether proven guilty or not; adverse; opposing.

丨罪 to transgress, to commit a crime; guilty.

丨法 to break the laws.

丨人 a criminal, one under arrest; a 囚丨 is one in custody.

侵丨 to invade, to incroach on.

有丨尊顏 I have offended you; — a polite phrase.

惑丨 to be exposed to; infected with, as mischief.

悮丨 an unintentional violation.

干丨 to offend, to resist law.

觸丨 an intentional offense, deliberate resistance.

丨上 impertinent to superiors.

衆怒難丨 it will be hard to stand their united wrath.

丨潮濕 to encounter malaria.

天是丨了潮了 the air is very damp.

丨諱 to improperly use the Emperor's personal name or that of Confucius.

丨不上 it won't pay; I can't afford to do it.

丨頭七 the whole thing is spoiled.

丨思量 to estimate the risks.

丨而不校 [Yen Hwui] never retaliated when assaulted.

河水不丨井水 river water does not run with well-water; — I want nothing to do with you, I have no quarrel with you.

范 *fan'* From *herb* and to *float*.

Plants, grass, herbage; a kind of wasp, having a sort of crown on its head, for which the next is also used.

丨冠 a sort of ancient cap.

蠦 *fan'* From 虫 *insect* and 範 a *rule* contracted, referring to the economy of a hive.

A bee or wasp.

丨則冠而蟬有緌 the bee has the cap of honor, the cicada has the fringe.

範 *fan'* From 車 *carriage* and 笵 a *rule* contracted; this last is also another form of this character.

A law, a rule, a pattern; a custom, standard, or usage; a mold; to imitate.

模丨 a founder's mold; a pattern, an exemplar.

洪丨 the great guide; — a chapter in the Book of Records.

丨常 a constant rule.

防丨 a rule for guarding or protecting.

風丨 a graceful, winning air.

丨圍不過 do not overpass the restraining law.

雅丨 or 尊丨 your good self, your person; — used in letters.

嬎 *fan'* From *female*, *hare* and *born*, — an instance of ideographic combination.

The young of rabbits, which the Chinese affirm are born at the mouth; to litter, as rabbits.

芝 *fan'* Plants floating on the water.

蘋藻丨溪 the *lemna* and *chara* float on the stream.

FĂN.

Old sounds, pún, bún, *and* p'ún. *In Canton*, făn ; — *in Swatow*, nun, pun, *and* p'un ; — *in Amoy*, hun ; — *in Fuhchau*, hung, hòng, *and* pwòng ; — *in Shanghai*, făng *and* văng ; — *in Chifu*, făn.

分 ꜀fan — From 刀 *knife* and 入 to *enter*, because the edge must go in to divide a thing ; it is also read *făn*꜆ and used with 份 a part.

To separate; to divide or sort out for distribution; to apportion, to part; to share, to partake with; often used for 吩 to order; to distinguish between; the second place for tenths in decimal notation; a nominal money, the tenth of a mace called a candareen; the tenth of a Chinese inch.

平丨 to divide alike.
丨開 to distinguish between; to separate, to open.
丨別 to discriminate apart or between; to divide.
丨派 to sort out for distribution.
丨散 utterly routed; scattered, dispersed.
丨作十分'就丨散 divide it into ten parts and it will then all be distributed.
丨手 to bid good-bye; to wave adieu.
丨心 purposeless, undetermined.
丨兵 to station troops.
丨業 or 丨家 to divide an estate.
幾丨指望 there is still some hope left.
丨肥 to give a gratuity; to pay a bonus.
坐地丨肥 (or 丨賍) to secretly receive ill gotten gains; to partake with a thief.
丨明 to clearly distinguish; plain, lucid.
丨發 sent off, as a petty officer to his post.
丨府 a magistrate deputed by a prefect; a sub-prefect in districts where there is a *chi-hien*.
丨辯是非 to argue a point.
一丨爲二 divided it will make two.
丨柑同味 the carpels of an orange all taste alike; *met.* friends of one mind.
丨憂 to condole with, to sympathize.
十丨好 exceedingly good; best.
得雨丨寸不等 the rain fell more or less everywhere.

紛 ꜀făn — From *silk* and *divided* as the phonetic.

A horsehair sheath; a variegated ribbon; mottled, as a cloud; confused, perplexed; many things at once; ill-assorted; hurry, bustle, excitement; to mix up.

丨丨多事 distracted by many cares.
丨紜 confused multiplicity.
丨亂 all in confusion; a hubbub, a crowd.
雨丨丨 a slow, drizzling rain.
丨丨然 disorderly, confusedly.
丨雜 mixed, unassorted.
丨華 gaiety, bustle; a gay time.
用志不丨 he is never confused, or diverted from his purpose; — said of a just or decided man.

帉 ꜀făn — Used with the last, denoting a large towel or napkin, called 丨帨, and hung in the left side of the girdle.

雰 ꜀făn — Misty, foggy; snowy.
雨雪丨丨 the sleety snow falls slowly and abundantly.

芬 ꜀făn — From *plant* and to *divide*, because a flower disperses fragrance.

Perfume of opening flowers; fragrance; numerous; amicable; used with 棼 confused.

丨丨 harmonious, joyous; fragrant.
氾丨 in confusion, as a state.
丨然 rising like impalpable dust.
丨芳 odoriferous.

氛 ꜀făn — Vapor, misty exhalations, miasma; ærial omens, shadowy signs, will-o'-the wisp; applied to rebels, which portend decay in the state.

丨氲 ærial, smoky, or misty vapors.
丨祲 dark portents, infelicitous omens; an apparition.
國丨 demagogues; seditious risings.
海丨 "sea-mist," *i. e.* pirates.
妖丨 portents, dreadful omens.
賊丨正熾 the rebel miasma then burned most furiously.

翂 ꜀făn — From *wings* and to *divide*.

To fly; 丨丨 flying and soaring.
翻丨 flying; the act or appearance of flying.

昐 ꜀făn — The light of the sun issuing forth.

毲 ꜀făn — The *hair* and to *part*.

The hair falling off is 丨丨, said of animals, or of the molting of birds.

吩 ꜀făn — To direct, to order.
丨附 to give orders to inferiors, to charge straitly; a command, a direction.

衯 ꜀făn — Long flowing robes.
丨丨裶裶 a full, wide skirt spreading gracefully.

梦 ˛*făn* From *forest* and *divide* as the phonetic; it is similar to 紛 to mix.

Double beams on the ridge of a roof; the ridge-pole; a hempen covering for a cart; confused, disordered; tangled, raveled.

泯泯丨丨 all in confusion; turbulent, riotous, as a country.

治絲而丨之 to hatchel the silk and tangle it; *met.* to manage badly, as state affairs.

鳻 ˛*făn* Birds flying in flocks; a kind of pie of a dark color, whose long tail feathers are used in soldiers' helmets.

Read *pan.* The wild pigeon is 丨鳩; its neck is iridescent.

饙 饎 ˛*făn* To cook or steam rice, and throw water on it when half done, so that the grains will separate; then steam it again.

丨饎 to half-cook the rice, leaving the grains hard.

釋之丨丨 wash and then steam it once and again.

汾 ˛*făn* The chief river of Shansi, the 丨水, which joins the Yellow River at Lung-măn in the southwest; it is about 250 miles long, and gives its name to several places in the province.

丨酒 spirits distilled in Fănchau from sorghum; it has a wide reputation.

丨陽王 was a petty ruler during the T'ang dynasty, named 郭, whose name is now synonymous with earthly happiness, as he lived to a great age and had numerous descendants; the phrase 丨陽點頭 the king of Fănyang in Honan nodding his head —because he did not know all his posterity,—is a birthday wish.

坋 ˛*făn* A hill of earth, rising steep and high.

登隱丨之邱 let us go up this steep hill.

枌 ˛*făn* From *wood* and *divide;* occurs used for 棼 a beam.

A lofty tree, a kind of elm, with small seeds and white bark; it is probably allied to the white elm.

東門之丨 the elm at the east gate.

丨榆社 a famous temple erected by the founder of the Han dynasty.

焚 ˛*făn* From 火 *fire* and 楙 a *hedge* contracted; used for 僨 to lose, in the phrase 丨其身 [elephants] lose their lives—for their tusks.

To burn a thing; to make preparations for consuming it; to set it on fire; to destroy utterly.

丨香 to light incense sticks.

丨修 cremation, now employed only in burning priests' corpses.

丨化 to burn up, as written paper.

丨書坑儒 [Tsin] burned the books and inhumed the scholars.

仲春毋丨山林 don't set the woods on fire in spring.

丨紙錢 to burn paper-money to the dead.

羒 ˛*făn* A ram; though some define it to mean a ewe.

棻 ˛*făn* From *wood* and *fragrant.*

A kind of wood burned for its perfume.

墳 坟 ˛*făn* From *earth* and *strenuous;* the contracted form is in constant use; occurs used for the next.

A grave; a tumulus or tomb; a heap; an embankment or water-dyke; a sprite; rich soil; loam; great.

丨地 a plot of ground for burials.

丨墓 the grave or mound.

掃丨 or 拜丨 to worship at the tomb, to sweep the grave.

丨院 a cemetery, the yard around the tomb.

荒丨 a neglected grave, no longer worshiped.

丨起 the mound is growing,—as a heap of refuse.

黒丨 black loamy soil.

丨壤 rich soil.

丨少爺 custodian of graves, who lives near them. (*Pekingese*)

三丨 the three powers,—heaven earth and man,—which 分 divide everything among them; also the monuments or records of the three first rulers, Fuh-hi, Shin-nung, and Hwangti.

羵 ˛*făn* This is regarded as another form of the last in its meaning of a sprite, shaped like a half-formed ram; a sheep with a big head.

牂羊丨首 a lean sheep with a big head.

蕡 ˛*făn* From *plants* and *strenuous.*

Trees or plants producing abundance of fruits; flowers growing together.

丨子 seeds of the hemp.

丨實 very fruitful.

濆 ˛*făn* A branch of the River Jü in Honan; small streamlets caused by the overflow of a river; the brink of a river.

鼖 鼓 ˛*făn* From *drum* contracted and *strenuous,* because such drums inspirit troops.

A bass drum, five or six feet long; one like it is now used at funerals.

馚 馩 ˛*făn* Aromatic; a perfume from opening flowers.

花丨香 flowers emitting their sweetness.

香丨丨 deliciously fragrant.

黂 ,făn The seeds of flax or hemp.

丨不類布而可以爲布 though the seeds of flax do not look at all like cloth, still cloth is made from them; — the roughest and most unlikely material may prove to be useful.

幩 ,făn The ornament on a bridle, like a pompon of hair, near the horse's mouth; also called 扇汗 a perspiration fan. 朱丨 the red tasseled bit, commonly called 踢胸 or kick-breast.

Read *făn'* A bag full of grain.

豶 ,făn A gelded pig or barrow; the Chinese generally geld hogs; to draw out or deprive.

丨豕之牙吉 it is lucky to break the tusks of hogs.

⿸疒賁 ,făn Pimples or boils caused by fever; fever sores.

丨脪 fever boils, which cause great itching and irritation.

粉 'făn From *rice* and to *divide* as the phonetic.

Rice broken to pieces; meal, flour, powder, of any kind; a pigment in powder; to adorn, as with pigment; to whitewash or color; sometimes applied to pus; in fragments, fine, comminuted.

米丨 rice-flour; 麵丨 a cosmetic.

丨絲, or 丨條, or 丨仔, or 丨皮, vermicelli.

丨袋 a tailor's chalk-bag.

塗脂抹丨 to rub on the rouge and daub the paint; said of a slatternly belle who dresses for an occasion; also of bad goods spruced up.

丨流 the pus is sloughing off.

涼丨子 a kind of jelly made from agar-agar.

丨碎 smashed to pieces; ground small.

丨紅 rouge; rosy, as cheeks.

丨板 or 丨牌 a painted board on which boys learn to write.

丨澤 adorned, beautified; painted, as a well-dressed lady.

研成丨 rub it to a powder, as paint-stuffs.

丨頭 a bad woman, implying a reference to her character.

丨牆 or 丨皮牆 to whitewash a wall.

丨飾 to paint and furbish up; *met.* specious, for appearance sake, as 丨飾太平 a pretended peace.

胭丨計 a trap to catch one with a pretty or lewd woman.

脂丨客 a gay rake, a dandified fellow.

黺 'făn Court robes embroidered in colors, as if spotted with grains.

畫丨 adorned with gay colors.

鼢 'făn A kind of mole or gopher, also called 犁鼠 the plough rat; and 田鼠 field rat; it is supposed to be transformed from the shrike; it is also called 隱鼠 or 偃鼠 the hiding rat, and 地老鼠 earth rat, from its well-known habits.

忿 făn' From *heart* and to *divide* as the phonetic.

Anger, resentment; irritated at; indignation.

丨怒 angry, wrathful.

一朝之丨 hasty wrath, sudden fury.

丨丨不消 implacable anger.

丨恨 deep malice, bitter hate.

丨疾 cross, displeased.

不丨 or 氣不丨 one cannot overlook it; cannot but be angry.

坌 } From *earth* and to *divide*; some writers make a distinction between these.
坋 } făn'

Dust; dust raised by the wind; others say, a bank of earth; to mix up; to bring together; to dig.

丨集京師 to collect the officers at the capital.

丨鬆 to dig the ground loose.

份 } The second form is the authentic one, and is sometimes marked to distinguish it from ,分, but
分 } făn' the first is much used; it is a synonym of ,*pin* 彬 neat, but has become obsolete in that sense.

A part, a portion, a share, a dividend; the duties of a post; its rank; the position of one in society, the part he acts, his lot; a sort, a kind.

身丨 the duties of one's station.

本丨 my duty, my office; my interest in.

三丨之一 one third of a thing.

丨兩大 a great portion; extra large, too many; it is very big.

,分丨 to divide the shares.

安丨 contented with his lot.

股丨 a share in a shop.

丨外 more than it should be; unusual.

丨承 to divide pro-rata, to pay proportionally.

一丨行貨一丨錢 each sort of goods has its own price.

丨子 or 名丨 a proper part; the lot coming to one.

緣丨 attached to, liking for.

一丨禮物 one lot of presents; one share of them.

越丨 to overstep one's place, to go beyond his functions.

僨 făn' Prostrate, fallen, as on one's back; to overturn, to ruin, to subvert; to move or excite.

一言丨事 one word can spoil an affair.

憤 făn' From *heart* and *strenuous*.

Impatient zeal; ardor; strong feeling; urgent impulses.

發丨 excited, aroused; to stimulate one's ardor.

丨力 or 丨興 to exert one's strength.

丨懥 perturbed, deep feeling.

鱝 *făn'* A species of thornback or skate, with spines in its long tail to defend itself; it is a kind of *Rhina* or *Myliobates* found on the southern coasts, and supposed to be transformed from the osprey.

糞 *făn'* From *rice* and *different*; but one out of the many different forms depicts carrying off refuse with both hands.

Ordure, filth, muck, dung; to manure; to remove dirt, to clean up; to hoe earth around plants; vile, bad, the offscouring.

丨厠 a necessary; a dung-hole.

丨門 the rectum or anus.

丨地 a manure yard, a jakes.

落丨 or 上丨 to manure.

丨料 poudrette prepared and dried for sale.

丨除 a dust-pan, a dust-hod.

丨草 refuse, sweepings.

錢財如丨土 to spend money as if it was dung.

丨池 a manure pit, as in fields; a cess-pool.

瀵 *făn'* The old name of a stream in Pu-cheu fu 蒲州府 in the southwest of Shansi, whose headwaters spout up as a fountain.

神丨 the vapors which rise, like a fountain, from valleys after rain.

奮 *făn'* From *field* and to *fly upward*.

Impetuous action, prompt, urgent, lively, spirited; to excite, to arouse, as thunder moves the earth; to press on to, to spread abroad; to remove or brush, as dust.

丨勇 undaunted, courageous to rashness.

丨力 energetic, putting forth all his strength.

丨武 martial, warlike.

丨衣 to shake and lift up the dress, in order to walk up.

丨飛 to fly rapidly; *met.* to put forth great effort.

丨至德之光 to diffuse the lustre (or knowledge) of great virtue.

丨志不懈 determined, active and unwearied.

丨興 or 丨氣 to rouse one's feelings, to exert one's energies.

㸋 *făn'* To fill a bag with grain till it bursts; the cord of a bow.

瞓 *făn'* An unauthorized word in Cantonese, written under the radical 目 and not 口; it seems to be derived from, or is another form of the Shanghai word *kwᵘng* 睏, to sleep.

To sleep; to feel sleepy.

合眼丨 to nod and doze.

你丨匀 you are half asleep.

FANG.

Old sounds, pung *and* bung. *In Canton*, fong; — *in Swatow*, hwang; — *in Amoy*, hong, *and one* pong; — *in Fuhchau*, hwòng *and* hòng; — *in Shanghai*, fong, bong *and* vong; — *in Chifu*, fang.

方 *fang* The original form is thought to resemble two boats lashed together; it is the 70th radical of characters mostly relating to flags, as iti s superseded in most of them by one of its compounds *yen'* 㫃 a banner.

Square or angular, not round; a region, a place; manner, art; a rule; a means; a way, a road; regular, correct, what pertains to a position; to compare, to lay together; to possess; to disregard, to disobey; as a *preposition*, towards, to; then, thereupon, in consequence of, in that case; to issue sideways; a prescription; occurs used for 妨 to oppose, to avoid doing; a list of vassals or retainers; a thin board; unfilled grain; great, correct; a classifier of cakes of ink, slices of meat, &c.; a center; used for 舫 to cross a stream.

四丨 square, rectangular; the four points of compass; everywhere, for which 萬丨 is also used; the vicinity.

五丨 the four quarters and the center.

丨位 a location; the aspect of, as a house; the bearings of.

丨向 direction of; towards.

丨正 correct, as deportment.

端丨 personal appearance; proper carriage, correct bearing.

叫地丨 call the local — officers, *i. e.* the police or constable.

丨略 a plan, a mode of action.

丨可 suitable; it will do.

相怨一丨 each dislikes the other, holding to his own view.

有丨法 there is a way; some plan or remedy can be found.

丨單 a description of a house or land; it usually accompanies the deed.

丨便 convenient; all ready; used to denote alms, as 行丨便 to to bestow charity; to consider others; to oblige; to do good to.

省丨 to examine the places.

良丨 a good prescription; the best remedy.

大丨 liberal, on a large scale; generous minded.

維鳩丨之 the pigeon occupies it, *i. e.* the other's nest.

丨纔 then, jnst at that moment; now

丨且 about to do; just then.

丨今 the present time, now-a-days.

丨寸 the heart, from its supposed size.

不能知丨 he does not know or appreciate what belongs to his post.

丨命 a polite phrase for declining. I must oppose your orders, I must excuse myself; as 只得丨命 we cannot but disregard the orders.

丨人 to compare or measure men's ability.

外丨人 foreigners; people from other provinces.

何丨人 where's the man from?

萬邦之丨 the focus of all the states.

以社以丨 this to the gods of the land, and this to those of the four points.

丨外 out of the bounds, in the streets, or in foreign parts, according to the scope.

修丨 to change the aspect, as of a grave.

開丨 to begin a course of life; to turn over a new leaf.

開牛丨 to become as an ox, *i. e.* reduced to miserable shifts.

墨一丨 one cake of ink.

一丨磚 in Peking, a solid mass of broken bricks, 9½ *chih* square by 2½ *chih* high, measuring 225¼ cubic *chih*.

上丨來的 this came from the imperial room or quarter.

多丨培植 [I am obliged to you] for many acts of kindness.

有義丨 she has her right portion, — as a mother like Mencius' had in his fame.

大丨家 a great teacher.

年丨多少 how old are you now?

丨程 equations; 立丨 cubic involution; and 丨田 plane mensuration; —are all mathematical terms.

坊 ˏ*fang* From *earth* and *place*; interchanged with 防 to guard.

A lane, an alley or short street, a wynd; a hamlet; a neighborhood; in Peking, a ward or subdivision of each of the five 城 or municipalities; a burgh, a country-house; an honorary portal; a small shop, where the things sold are made; a grocery; to guard; to impede; an obstruction.

丨社 the street altar to the gods of the land.

牌丨 an honorary monumental gateway.

丨里 a street; a neighborhood; villages, hamlets.

表丨 a model, a person or thing worthy of imitation.

便宜丨 a restaurant, an eating-shop.

堆丨 a store-room, a go-down.

書丨 a bookstore, a book-stall.

作丨 a workshop, an atelier.

春丨 the heir-apparent's palace, name of two honorary offices in the Chen-sz'-fu, conferred on members of the Hanlin Academy.

寶丨 your monastery; said to a priest.

僧丨 a Budhist term for a convent.

妨 ˏ*fang* From *woman* and *place* as the phonetic.

An impediment; to hinder, to oppose; to injure, to dislike.

丨碍 a difficulty, an obstacle; something to be afraid of, or which stops one.

小心丨害 lookout for yourself, don't get any damage.

不丨 or 無丨 harmless; no matter about that; it is all the same whether it be there or not.

丨賢 to envy worthy people; to malign the good.

枋 ˏ*fang* A wood used by cartwrights and in boats; the white board used to entice fish to leap into a boat; a frame for drying fish; a boat-builder.

丨子 a support; a strip of wood used to underpin and strengthen the girders in a roof.

丨木 scantling stuff, thin pieces; a general term for lathing and facings.

蘇丨木 a kind of sapan-wood or logwood.

肪 ˏ*fang* Fat, especially the grease or fat of a goose.

脂丨 the fat of meat.

邡 ˏ*fang* The ancient name for Wu-kang hien 武康縣 in the northwest of Chehkiang, is sometimes written 丨風氏, but 防風氏 is more correct.

什丨縣 a district in Sz'-ch'uen, north of the capital.

芳 ˏ*fang* Fragrant, odoriferous; beautiful, as flowers; agreeable, pleasant; virtuous, excellent.

丨芷 fragrant plants, used in perfumery.

丨草 sweet smelling plants; fresh.

丨名 a good name, a virtuous reputation.

流丨百世 to hand down a fair name to after years.

遺丨 to perpetuate the memory of.

丨蹤 the fragrant records, as of good men of old.

丨德 fragrant or great virtue.

鈁 ˏ*fang* A square bell, like a cow-bell, worn by camels; a sort of boiler or shallow kettle; name for a *fanam*, an old Madras coin, worth about one-tenth of a rupee, used in imitation of that word.

匚 ˏ*fang* An open basket with a bale or handle, holding about a peck, which the original form rudely represents; it is now written ˏ*k'wang* 筐, and this is only used for the 22d radical of a small group of characters, mostly relating to vessels and receptacles.

房 From *house* and *place* as the phonetic.

fang A room, a chamber; a dwelling; an office or bureau in a public court; the room where a particular department is carried on; a division of a government, as the Upper House, the Senate; one living in the same room, a wife or concubine; what is done in it, *i. e.* sexual intercourse; a branch of a family; in plants, a spathe, calyx, or receptacle; the nest or comb of a bee; the 11th of the zodiacal constellations, the stars $\beta\ \gamma\ \delta\ \sigma$ in Scorpio; it always marks a Sunday in the calendar.

一間丨 one division in a room, made by the framework; at the south it denotes a room.

丨間 or 丨屋 rooms, buildings, as in a single yard.

丨子 a house, of which 正丨 is the building facing the south or north in the court; and 照丨 the rear building or row of rooms.

盖丨子 to build a house.

耳丨 or 陪丨 small rooms at the ends of the main building.

內丨 the female apartments of a large building, where the 下丨 or women live; it is styled 上丨 in a yamun.

丨下有多少姬妾 how many women have you in your household?

丨東 the owner of a house.

門丨 or 號丨 the ante-room for visitors in a yamun; a porter's lodge or room.

六丨 six under-bureaus in a yamun; as the 銀丨, or 庫丨, the treasury.

賤丨 or 做丨 my wife, also termed 正丨; — as 偏丨, or 丨下 is a concubine.

同丨 to lie with a woman.

補丨 to take a second wife.

專丨之寵 the loved one of the room, the concubine who has won her husband's favor, the odalique.

長丨 or 二丨 the eldest and second brothers in a household, used after they have grown up or are married; also applied to very lucky or less lucky aspects of a grave.

防 From a *spot* and *square*.

fang A bank, a dyke, a levee; a defense, a screen, a protection; to keep off, to ward off, to protect from, to defend, to guard against; to repress, to forbid; to provide against; a match for.

丨備 or 豫丨 to be ready for, to prepare for; guarding; prepared; as 不丨 is unaware, not expecting.

丨荒 or 丨饑 to provide against dearth, or a bad year, by laying in stores.

隄丨 an embankment, or other obstruction.

丨禦 to watch against, to guard, as the captain of a picket.

丨風 remedy against colds or flatulency.

丨風氏 the name of an ancient state in Chehkiang, lying in the northwest part of the present Wu-kang hien.

分丨 and 海丨 are civil officers like a sub-prefect, in some of the provinces.

冷不丨 cold cannot be avoided; *i. e.* who could have guarded against it? suddenly, unforeseen.

百夫之丨 equal to (or a match for) a hundred braves.

魴 From 魚 *fish* and *fat* 肪 contracted, alluding to its delicate flesh.

fang A freshwater fish, also called 鯿魚 a kind of bream common in central China, about a foot long; some sorts have a red tail, or it is said to turn red from fear; another kind has long red dorsal rays, and the dorsal fin is like a bat's wing.

俚語云伊洛鯉丨美如牛羊 the village proverb says, The carp and bream out of the River I-loh taste as sweet as beef or mutton.

訪 From *words* and *place*.

fang To search out, to go and see about; to inquire into, to inform one's self, as an officer does; to ask advice, to consult; to learn the character of.

丨問 to inquire of, to ask.

丨聞 to hear of, to have or seek information of.

丨拿 to hunt up and seize, as a rascal.

丨予落止 on coming to the throne I take counsel.

丨察 to examine a matter officially.

採丨使 a special commissioner sent to learn the facts.

丨親 to learn the connections, &c., as of a girl for a wife; to inquire about one's relatives.

丨謁 to visit and ask, as a friend.

私行察丨 to go in disguise to search and learn the facts, as a detective.

昉 From *sun* and *place* as the phonetic.

fang The first light of the morning; bright; lucid, as a style; to appear, to begin; to occur; happening, just then.

丨亮 dawning, bright.

丨亮炮 the early morning gun.

丨於何時 when was [this invention] found out?

倣
仿 From *man* and to *liberate* or *place;* they are similar to the next.

fang To imitate; like, resembling; a model; to copy after.

相丨 much alike.

丨照 to like and then imitate; to make like.

丨樣 to follow the pattern; hence 寫丨字 is to line a copy-slip, by which boys learn to write.

丨古筆意 to delineate the scenes of the ancients.

丨圈 a brass circle or frame for laying on the paper to write within it.

彷 髣 From a *step* and *place*; the second form is obsolete, and both are interchanged with the last.

fang Like, resembling; seen but vaguely; indistinct; equivocal, seeming.

丨彿 somewhat like, not unlike; doubtful and still possible; — eight forms of writing this phrase are given in the native dictionary.

丨徨 timid, undecided; agitated, as insects are.

丨徉 roving, unsettled, doubtful.

昉 *fang* Indistinct.

丨昹 apparently similar, but which cannot be seen distinctly; looking alike.

兩下相丨 the two look exactly alike, as twins.

紡 *fang* To spin; to reel; to coil or twist into thread or ropes; the threads of a net; lines, cords; to tie up.

丨紗 to spin thread for weaving.

丨績 to twist hempen thread.

川丨 fine Sz'ch'uen pongee.

丨絲 to make silk or sewing thread.

丨綢 reeled pongee, well-woven and firm.

舫 From *vessel* and *square*; 方 occurs used for this.

fang Two boats or rafts lashed alongside like a double canoe; a pilot or steersman, who knows the channel; a galley to carry fifty men, square and clumsy.

畫丨 a handsomely furnished boat, a flower-boat.

輕丨如葉 the boat [floats] as lightly as a leaf.

採蓮丨 finely adorned pleasure boats.

丨中談飲 drinking and conversing in a boat.

瓬 旊 *fang* To mold and work clay into shape ready for the oven; sticky clay fit for the potter's use.

丨人爲簋豆 the potter makes the compote dishes.

丨陶 a potter, a worker in clay.

放 From to *part* and *place*.

fang To let go, to loosen, to liberate; to reject, to cast off; to banish, to send away; to stretch, to extend; to indulge, to relax; to lay down; to open out, to scatter; to emit, as light; to fire, as a gun; to fly, as a kite; to start; to let, as blood; to issue, as a permit.

丨縱 to give loose rein; to let others do as they list; heedless of rules.

丨鬆 to loosen somewhat, to slack off.

丨心 be easy about, unsolicitous; it is also used for a lost heart, one not able to resist evil.

丨手 hands off! let go! to have nothing to do with.

不丨手 don't part with it, keep tight hold; don't loosen it.

丨手不得 I can't let go of it.

丨肆 impudent, audacious; to cast off restraint.

丨蕩 willful, wild, extravagant.

發丨 to dischage, as a prisoner at the end of his term.

丨赦 to pardon and release.

丨生 to let living things go, a Budhist good work, for doing which there are 丨生會 "let live societies."

大丨王命 to disregard the royal commands.

丨下 lay it down; to let it down.

丨在這裏 put it down there.

丨言 to speak one's mind.

丨走 to let a culprit escape.

丨賬 to get on credit; and reckon the interest.

丨利 to shave notes.

毋丨飯 don't make a rude noise in eating.

丨乎四海 reaches quite to the ocean.

丨餤口 to get souls out of torment.

丨花 to let off fireworks.

丨膽 courageous, in good heart.

丨牌 to close or end an examination — as for *siuts'ai*.

丨路燈 to burn incense lamps in the road — on the full moon of the 7th month; in some places, the priests 丨水燈 burn floating lanterns instead.

丨差 sent as special commissioner from the capital, — usually to superintend the examinations.

丨出來了 he has let it out, as a caged bird; liberated, as a prisoner.

Read *fang*. To lay boats alongside; to imitate, to accord with. 若稽古帝堯曰放勳 looking into ancient records, the Emperor Yau was named Fang-hiun.

In *Fuhchau*. A last, a hat-block.

FÉI.

Old sounds, péi, p'i, bi, pit, *and* bit. *In Canton*, fi *and* fei ; — *in Swatow*, hui, púe, *and* hut ; — *in Amoy*, hui *and* hòé ; — *in Fuhchau*, p'i, hi, hie, pé, *and* hé ; — *in Shanghai*, fi *and* vi ; — *in Chifu*, fi.

飛 ˛fé The original rudely represents a bird soaring ; it is the 183d radical of a few characters all relating to flying.

To spread the wings and fly away ; to flit, to go swiftly ; to let fly ; flying, swift ; to act with dispatch ; sudden, quick, overtaking one in a moment ; airy, high up.

丨去 flown ; to fly away.

丨快 quick as possible.

丨騰之兆 a sign of his rapid advancement.

丨翔 to soar and sail, as a hawk.

丨報 hasten to announce ; a fleet messenger.

差丨馬 to send a fleet courier.

丨龍在天 the flying dragon in the sky ; *i. e.* the present emperor.

丨昇 to be taken on high ; an apotheosis.

丨鷹 to let loose a falcon.

丨簷走壁 fly over the eaves and run on the walls ; — an expert thief.

插翼難丨 I could not fly, even with a pair of wings.

雄雉于丨 the pheasant has flown.

丨災 sudden calamity, an unexpected trouble.

丨馳 to urge a racer to his utmost speed.

丨射士 flying bowmen.

丨廉 a fabulous bird, changed from a warrior who helped Cheu-sin, B. C. 1120, and is now regarded as the god of the Wind ; also, a kind of water plant or rush.

丨啓者 I write in great haste.

丨劍 to let fly a sword — out of the mouth, which sorcerers are said to do.

丨跑 to run as fast as possible ; fleet as an Asahel.

In *Cantonese*. Clever, shrewd.

蜚 ˛fé From *insect* and *not* ; occurs used for the next.

An offensive insect produced in moist places, which devours grain and clothes ; the cockroach and some sorts of *Cimex* are probably both included ; a fabulous monster indicative of pestilence.

丨零 an old name for the mason or ground bee.

非 ˛fé The original form is intended to represent the wings of a bird opposite each other, as it folds them ; it is the 175th radical of a few incongruous characters, most of which should have been arranged under their other radicals.

An *adverb* of negation, not so, not right ; when in regimen with another negative, it answers to without — not, and makes a strong assertion ; to turn the back on, opposed to good ; unreal ; shameless, vicious, low ; false, bad ; to blame, to reproach.

是丨 right and wrong ; yes and no ; pro and con.

一塲是丨 nothing worse than a little gossip.

不知是丨 I can't say whether it is so or not.

丨是 it is not so.

說人是丨 to talk of people's failings, to backbite.

丨禮 indecent, improper.

丨禮勿言丨禮勿動 neither speak nor act without observing propriety.

豈丨 is it not so ? — *i.e.* it is true.

必丨無因 it certainly must have a cause.

無丨 or 莫丨 really.

丨易 not so easy, rather difficult.

無丨無儀 neither doing wrong nor yet good ; said of a woman.

丨也 or 丨然 truly it is not so.

丨吃卽喝 if he is not eating he is drinking ; — a useless lout.

丨分'之事 it does not appertain to his functions.

不丨輕 it is rather a difficult matter.

本丨 unintentional.

丨愛寫字無奈手疼 it is not that I don't wish to write, but my hand pains me.

丨此則彼 if it is not this, then it is that.

裶 ˛fé A train trailing on the ground ; long robes dragging.

緋 ˛fé Dark red or purplish colored silk, of which officers of the fifth rank make their robes.

丨紫 a deep lilac color.

扉 ˛fé From leaf of a *door* and *not*.

A door with one leaf ; *met.* a rustic house.

依丨而待 waiting as she leans on the door.

柴丨 a kind of movable bars in a fence.

馡 ˛fé Aromatic.

丨丨 or 芳丨 fragrant and odoriferous.

郁郁丨丨 exceedingly sweet and fragrant.

霏 ˛fé From *rain* and *not* ; another old form is from 雨 *rain* and 飛 *to fly*.

Rain and snow driving along, filling the air.

雨'雪丨丨 the snow is falling in clouds.

騑 ˛fé From *horse* and *not*.

The outer horses of a team of four ; an extra horse fastened to the axle with long traces ; a colt three years old.

四牡丨丨 the four horses went on quietly, without stopping.

妃 ˏfé From *woman* and *self*, *q. d.* a woman made equal to one's self

A partner; the secondary wives or concubines of a monarch; royal women next the queen, called 后丨, and 皇貴丨, and other names; the heir-apparent's wife was also called 王丨, in olden times.

天丨 the goddess of sailors, the Amphitrite of Chinese mythology.

宮丨 imperial concubines.

嬪丨 a class of women like ladies in waiting.

奸丨 a crafty concubine; — a term of reproach.

丨子笑 Féi-tsz' laughed — to see the lichis come; — a legend of the Tang dynasty, whence this name is given to the fruit.

肥 ˏfé From 肉 *flesh* and 卩 a *limit*; *i. e* fleshiness should not become obesity.

Fat, fleshy, plump; the opposite of *sheu'* 瘦; oily, rich, unctuous; fertile; abundant, rich, as crops; manure, tilth; to fatten; to benefit one; fattened.

丨壯 robust; fat and stout.

亞丨 a fat person, a paunch-belly. (*Cantonese*)

丨大 corpulent

丨美 plump, in good liking.

策丨 to whip up the fat — horses; *met.* a rich man, one who keeps his carriage.

潤丨 fertile, rich as land.

丨胆 fat and rich, as meat.

丨甘 fat and sweet, as pork.

君瘦民丨 [let] the ruler be lean, so that the people be fat.

只顧已丨 he only looks to his own benefit.

上丨 or 落丨 to manure land.

私丨己 to enrich one's self, to line one's nest.

丨腯 fat as a pig; of which 丨豚 豚 is another form.

車馬輕丨 the carts are light and our horses are hearty; — a hostler's card.

丨皂 a sort of coarse native soap made from the 丨皂子 or soap berries, seeds of the *Gleditschia*.

丨國 a small feudatory lying in the present Yung-ping fu 永平府 in the extreme east of Chihli.

淝 ˏfé Name of an affluent of the Poyang Lake.

丨水 a small stream running into Lake Ch'ao by Lu-cheu fu in Nganhwui; also the old name of Mung-ching hien 蒙城縣 in the northwest of that province.

丨泉 streams diverging from one fountain.

蜰 ˏfé A stinking grub, like the Cimex; a sort of snake.

丨蠐 the large grubs of some kinds of beetles, found in compost heaps, also called 地蠶 or ground silkworms.

盧丨 a cockroach.

蟦 ˏfé The sea-qualm or Medusa, found in the northern sea; but others define it the Scarabeus or tumble-dung.

Read ˏ*pǎn*. A clam or large muscle found on the southern coast.

婓 ˏfé From *woman* and *not*.

To pace to and fro, as one in uncertainty.

丨丨遲遲 hesitating and lingering.

江丨 a water goddess or naiad; one who roams along the river banks.

腓 ˏfé The calf of the leg; to avoid, to skulk; to cover or hide each other, as animals do in a herd; diseased; to change; altered.

丨腸 the calf of the leg.

小人所丨 that which protects the men — or troops.

丨字之 to suckle, as a cow her calf.

百卉具丨 all the plants are changed, or diseased — from the frost.

厞 ˏfé The south corner of a room, where a table was spread with offerings, when it was not known where the god of the land was abiding; hence it means hidden, concealed; low, base.

斐 ˊfé From *marks* and *not* as the phonetic; occurs interchanged with the next.

Streaks, or veins; graceful, elegant, adorned, polished, applied to the deportment, or to a composition.

有丨君子中不可諼兮 one elegant accomplished prince can never be forgotten.

丨美 elegant, graceful, polished; said of things or persons.

丨然成章 truly it is a finished composition.

匪 ˊfé From a square *basket* and *not*; occurs interchanged with 非 not, and the last.

A bamboo square covered basket, for which the next is now used; the stately march of horses; a graceful gait; illegal; banditti, vagabonds, seditious, disorderly people, by which term officials stigmatize whoever opposes their rule; banded robbers, brigands, or oppressed people; no, not so, is not; without; variegated.

丨類 or 丨徒 vagabonds, wandering people, vagrants.

奸丨 insurgents, open rebels.

丨黨 a band of villains; a seditious club or cabal.

土丨 local robbers, a nest of thieves.

會丨 a party or association of seditious subjects.

捍丨 or 捻丨 filchers, marauders, highway robbers.

敪 丨 a brotherhood or clan of seditious, a sworn sect.

丨 我 愆 期 it is not I who protract the time.

丨 色 particolored, inharmonious colors.

丨 今 斯 今 it is not now, and yet it is as if it were now.

比 之 丨 人 凶 intimacy with bad men is disastrous.

Read ˛*făn*. The emperor making gifts to his officers.

丨 頒 imperial favors.

˓篚 *'fé* Bamboo baskets, round or oval, and having a cover and short legs.

筐 丨 baskets of all sorts.

˓剕 *'fé* To cut off the feet, an ancient punishment; others say, to cut off the knee-pan.

丨 辟, 疑 赦 when the penalty is to cut off the feet, set the fine for it.

˓菲 *'fé* A red marshy plant, the stem and roots are good for food if gathered at the right time; the plant belongs to the *Crucifera*, and has a large root like a turnip, which is acrid at certain times; the description seems to apply rather to a plant like the *Crambe tatarica*, or Hungarian bread, than to a sort of turnip or wild radish; pot-herbs, greens; sparing, frugal; trifling, unworthy, mean; fragrant; beautiful; sandals, in which sense it is used for the next.

丨 儀 a formal offering, a trifling present, said by one of his gift, which is also termed 丨 物 [only] a thing like a turnip.

丨 飲 食 coarse food and drink.

芳 ˛丨 exuberant, fragrant.

丨 丨 odoriferous; mixed, blended.

丨 惄 sad, in deep depression.

丨 悵 mournful.

丨 薄 poor, shabby, of no worth; — as one's present.

丨 敬 my poor respects; — written on a present of money.

采 葑 采 丨 無 以 下 體 when gathering the turnips do not throw them away because of their roots; *i.e.* do not reject the good because of the bad.

˓扉 *'fé* Interchanged with the last.

Coarse hempen or grass sandals or cheap shoes; they are poetically termed 不 借 *i. e.* not worth borrowing.

˓棐 ˓榧 *'fé* These characters are interchanged, but the first is properly applied to the tree and its timber, which is fit for furniture; and the second to the 丨 子 or long, hazel shaped nuts of the *Torreya nucifera*, a species of Taxineæ or yew, found in Northern China, and used by the people to cure the worms; the first also means a e piec of wood fastened to a bow to strengthen the center; to assist; to lean on; used for 篚 a basket.

篤 丨 to zealously assist.

以 丨 民 彝 in order to assist the people in their virtuous works.

丨 几 benches or stands made of the yew.

粗 丨 the *Cephalotaxus drupacea*, an evergreen tree like a yew.

˓悱 *'fé* Desirous of speaking, but unable to do so from trepidation, ignorance, or otherwise.

不 丨 不 發 he could not speak out, and the other therefore did not learn it.

憤 丨 the heart's anger repressed, indignant but silent.

˓誹 *'fé* From *words* and *not* as the phonetic.

To backbite, to slander; unjust, wicked aspersions; a slanderer.

怨 丨 to hate and slander another; angry defamation.

丨 譽 slander and flattery.

腹 丨 heart-burnings; malice in the heart.

丨 謗 to slander, to defame.

˓朏 *'fé* From *moon* and to *go out*.

The moon in a crescent form, five days old, and not yet very bright.

丨 明 the moon waxes brighter.

廢˒ *féi* From *covering* and to *issue*.

A house fallen in ruins; to throw aside, to abandon; to set aside, to depose; to destroy; to annul; to disinherit; to stop, to fail; void, null; spoiled, useless, corrupt; discarded, degraded; degenerated; come to nought; large.

丨 去 thrown aside.

殘 丨 or 丨 物 useless, worn out; a good for nothing fellow.

丨 時 to waste one's time.

半 途 而 丨 to turn back, to back out, to give up when half done.

丨 長 立 幼 to set aside the eldest, and place the younger on the throne.

不 豫 則 丨 things spoil if care be not taken with them.

國 政 丨 弛 the state is all going to ruin.

丨 事 lost his labor; he has missed his aim.

丨 墮 lazy, unthrifty.

丨 棄 to abandon, to discard.

丨 人 cripples, infirm people; superannuated.

癈˒ *féi* From *disease* and to *issue*; interchanged with the last in this sense.

An incurable disease.

丨 疾 a disability that unfits one for all labor; maimed or imperfect in body.

蕟˒ *féi* A mat made of rushes for spreading on beds or floors.

編 蘆 爲 丨 to weave rush grass into mats.

費 *fé*ˋ From *wealth* and *without*.

To scatter wealth; to use, to spend; to lavish; to hurt, to injure; expense, cost, outlay; wasteful, squandering; trouble, anxiety for, kindness to others; vast.

使 〡 or 〡 用 or 敷 〡 to lay out money, to spend on; what is needed.

過 〡 ["you go to] over much expense;" — politely said to a host; another phrase, 破 〡 "you have lost your outlay," is used when receiving a present.

〡 事 vexatious, fussy, troublesome; needless labor.

浪 〡 to waste foolishly, unnecessary outlay.

〡 力 to use effort.

甚 〡 手 very difficult to bring about.

〡 心 or 〡 勞 occupied your mind; I've put you to trouble; *i. e.* I thank you for your trouble.

小 〡 a douceur, a fee, a vail given to waiters.

盤 〡 traveling expenses.

耗 〡 extra expense; wasteful.

君子惠而不 〡 the princely man is kind but not wasteful.

〡 而隱 [doctrines are] wide and subtle too.

頗 〡 神 it requires great care, as a wearying job.

〡 時則有饑餧 if you pass the right time, then you will be hungry; like Proverbs xx. 4.

〡 唇舌 you've wasted your breath — in trying to convince him.

Read *p'i*. An ancient town, now P'i hien 〡 縣 a district in the southeast of Shantung.

疿 *fé*ˋ Small pimples, eruptions on the skin.

〡 子 or 熱 〡 prickly heat.

生 〡 or 長了 〡 子 to have prickly heat.

〡 驚瘡 prickly heat emulates boils.

沸 濆 *fé*ˋ From *water* and *not*; it is very frequently read *fuh*,

To bubble up, as gushing or boiling water; to rush over the rocks, as waves do; bubbling, perturbed; excited, angry; to sprinkle.

如 〡 如羹 like boiling water and gruel; said of a disturbed kingdom.

過三 〡 則老 if it bubbles more than thrice, [the tea] is bitter.

風浪 〡 騰 the raging waves were blown over the rocks;— applied to quarrelsome, noisy brawls.

水 〡 山崩 the water is bubbling, the hills are falling, — general anarchy.

鴻 〡 greatly raging, as waves.

〡 水 a stream in Shantung, whose waters are thought to lengthen life.

百 〡 水 boiling, bubbling water; — a medical term.

鼎 〡 the caldron is boiling; *met.* a country in rebellion.

Read *pi*ˋ. The name of Duke Tao of Ching, who ruled B. C. 586; and of a ruler of Lu. The second form alone is used in this sense.

狒 *fé*ˋ A kind of ape, the 〡 〡, found in Chin-India and the southwest of China, of which strange stories are told; it is probably a hairy variety of the *mia* or orang, of a black color, with very large lips; it is described as carniverous, and four or five feet high.

𩲃 *fé*ˋ From 内 a *paw* and four 又 *hands* clasping the 頭 *head*.

An old character, denoting an animal like the last, which was brought from India, B.C. 1100, said to be twelve feet high.

誹 *fé*ˋ To speak rapidly; to talk very fast and thick.

柿 *fé*ˋ From *wood* and a sort of *nettle*.

A chip or shaving; to plane or shave wood; a wooden case.

芾 *fé*ˋ From *grass* and a *market* which gives the sound.

To overshadow, as by luxuriant foliage.

蔽 〡 甘棠 the umbrageous flowering crab or service tree; — used as a simile for grateful remembrances.

〡 〡 exuberant, full of leaves.

Read *fuh*, A knee-pad worn when sacrificing.

朱 〡 斯皇 how royal-looking were the red knee-covers!

肺 *fé*ˋ From 肉 *flesh* and 市 a *market*, though others say the primitive is 巾 an *apron*.

One of the five *tsang* or organs, the lungs, "called 金臟 the metallic viscera, which rules the breath; they have altogether eight lobes, and are attached to the vertebræ; their office is to direct the motions of the body;" to plane or cut wood.

祭 〡 to sacrifice the lungs, as was done in the Cheu dynasty at autumn.

〡 家 the lungs, the lights.

〡 癰 an abscess in the lungs.

見其 〡 肝 I can see through his lungs and liver, I can look into his designs.

調理 〡 經 we must give medicine for the lungs.

〡 腑話 secret thoughts, private opinion on a subject.

〡 石 a reddish kind of jasper, anciently used in courts as a sort of ordeal stone to test plaintiffs.

自有 〡 腸 he keeps his own counsel.

Read *p'éi*ˋ Luxuriant.

其葉 〡 〡 the leaves were very abundant.

翡 *fé*ʾ From *feather* and *not*.

A beautiful bird, the cock bird of the 丨翠鳥 or blue-green kingfisher (*Halcyon smyrnensis* and H. *pileata*,) whose plumage is used in feather work.

丨翠玉 is applied to chrysoprase, green pyroxene or Sausserite, and even to malachite; but the precious 丨翠 is a silicate of aluminum, called *jadite*, and regarded as very valuable.

痱 *fé*ʾ A rheumatic sickness; a fiery swelling, an ulcer like a carbuncle; a dropsical swelling or fattiness in the feet.

茷 *fé*ʾ From *grass* and to *punish* refractory states; also read *fah*,

Luxuriant, as 茅丨 a plant covered with leaves.

Read *pai*. Regular, and in fine order, as banners.

吠 *fé*ʾ From *mouth* and *dog*; alluding to the cry of a dog.

The bark of a dog; to bark, to yelp, to howl, as canine animals do.

亂丨狗 a dog which barks at everybody.

跖之狗丨堯 Chih's dog barked at Yao; a simile for dissatisfied grumblers, who cannot discriminate between good and bad people.

FEU.

Old sounds, pu, bu, pút, *and* bút. *In Canton*, fau; — *in Swatow*, p'u, hu, hⁿò, *and* hui; — *in Amoy*, ho, *and one* hoⁿ; — *in Fuhchau*, p'éu, p'i *and* p'aiü; — *in Shanghai*, vù *and* fü; — *in Chifu*, fu.

罘 ˏ*fu* From *net* and *not*, but the primitive is properly a contraction of 否 whether.

A net to catch rabbits; a screen or intervening framework.

丨罳 a wooden screen within the outer gate.

芝丨 or 之丨頭 the port of Chifu in Shantung, the headland of this name is famous for a visit of Chi Hwangti, about B C. 220.

浮 ˏ*feu* ˏ*fu* From *water* and *trustworthy*.

To float, to drift; to float or cross a stream with gourds; to overflow, to exceed; to run over; light, unsteady, giddy, volatile; unsubstantial, fleeting; time gone by, clouds scudding by; a forfeit; excessive.

丨丨 abundant, like a rushing torrent; rising, like vapor; vain.

莫信丨言 don't trust reckless talk.

丨生若夢 [life] passes away like a dream.

丨記賬 acccounts put in the blotter

丨財 floating property, not fixed or certain, uncertain gains.

丨躁 light-minded, no stability or dignity.

雨雪丨丨 rain and snow in abundance.

丨丨汎汎 floating and unsteady; weak and giddy.

丨游在世 to roam about the world.

輕丨 levity, no steadiness; untrustworthy.

食丨於人 [the business or duties] are more than the men to do them.

丨橋 or 丨梁 a bridge of boats, or raft; a pontoon bridge.

丨額 an excess over the set number, more than the limit.

丨沉 floating and sinking, unsettled; *met.* alternately this and then that.

丨面皮兒 an insincere courteous manner; a heartless but decorous way.

泛宅丨家 having no settled residence.

丨頭兒的 the one on top, that one floating.

雪上丨凍 thin ice on the snow.

丨圖 or 丨屠 names for a dagoba, and a pagoda or tower, imitating the word *Budha*.

一丨太白 to take off a foaming bumper.

交情是丨的 their relations (or friendship) are not very cordial.

丨頭浪子 a child of the billow, an idle, thriftless unreliable man.

蜉 ˏ*feu* A kind of large ant.

丨蝣 gnats or ephemera produced from water; but the Pǎn Tsao describes them like a Scarabeus, with yellow-black elytra, slender and having a horn.

蚍丨撼樹可笑不自量 the ant pushed against the tree, and it was laughable to see its estimate of its strength.

烰 ˏ*feu* Steam or vapor ascending with a noise.

丨氣 steam.

丨人 one who steams food.

涪 ˏ*feu* A river in Sz'ch'uen, about 800 miles long, the 丨陵 or 丨江 or 黒今江 which joins the Yangtsz' River at Fu-cheu 丨州 as it is called on the spot.

丨漚 the bubbles on water; foam, spume.

苤 ˓feu The greater plantain, rib-grass, rib-wort, or ripple-grass, a common roadside herb.

丨 莒 the plantago, better known as 車前草 rut grass, and 牛舌草 cow's tongue, as it is said to spring up in cows' tracks; it is eaten as greens, and the mucilaginous seeds are used as a diuretic.

丨 醜山 a peak in Mih hien near K'ai-fung fu in Honan.

紑 ˓feu New and lustrous silk clothes; white garments.

絲衣其丨 his silken robes are clean and bright; such are now worn by the Empress when she worships the goddess of silk.

缶 缻 ˓feu The original form delineates an earthen vessel to contain spirits; it is the 121st radical of a natural group of characters referring to vases

Earthenware vessels in general; a wine-jar; a measure holding four *huh* 斛 or eight bushels? a vase on which the ancients marked time.

擊丨 or 鼓丨 to beat time on the vase.

瓦丨 earthenware in general.

懸丨 the hanging jar, a name for a poor man.

否 ˓feu From *mouth* and *not*, because "the thoughts are not discerned in the mouth."

To deny, to refuse; not, not so, ought not; at the end of a sentence, construes it into an alternative interrogative, whether or not? else, otherwise.

是丨 is it so?

王曰丨 the king said, It is not.

唯唯丨丨 yes, yes — no, no; undecided, as men; indefinite measures.

可丨 or 是丨可行 will it do or not?

Read ˓p'i. Closed, obstructed, which is the meaning of the 12th diagram; to bar the way; wicked, as mankind.

晦盲丨塞 disturbed and gloomy, like the world.

丨世 this evil world.

命丨 a hard lot, unsuccessful in life.

丨則威之 if it be bad, then frown it away.

以定然丨 you must decide whether it be yes or no.

曾丨 has it happened or not?

獻可替丨 will it do for you to offer it in my stead?

未知得收丨 I don't know whether they have been received or not.

臧丨人物 to praise and blame people.

阜 阝 feu˒ The original form represents a mound of earth; it is the 170th radical of a group of words relating to conditions or forms of places, and is in the contracted form always put on the left of the primitive; occurs used for the next.

A mound or tumulus of earth only; fertile, abundant; fat; to make rich, to increase in size; great.

物丨 plenty of things.

丨成兆民 to enrich and develop the condition of the unnumbered multitudes.

豐丨 abundant, as a harvest.

螽 feu˒ The 丨螽 is properly a gryllus, the small grasshopper of the fields, rather smaller than a locust.

喓喓草蟲趯趯丨螽 the locusts sing in the grass, and the grasshoppers leap and skip; the first of these is described as of a grass green color, which however is also applicable to the *Truxalis*.

丨成 full and complete.

香丨 a Budhist monastery, referring to the incense burned there.

駟驖孔丨 the two spans were very fat and large.

丨財解慍 [the people] increased in wealth, and this removed their complaints.

FOH.

Old sound, bok. *In Canton*, fok; — *in Swatow*, pak; — *in Amoy*, pòk; — *in Fuhchau*, pwoh; — *in Shanghai*, vok; — *in Chifu*, foh.

縛 ˓foh From *silk* and to *scatter*; it closely resembles *chwen*˒ 縳 spin.

To bind, as a sheaf; to tie up, to tie fast; to strap and secure; to roll up securely; a strap under the axle to drag another cart; a roll.

綑丨 to bind securely, as a prisoner.

丨在車下 hang it under the cart, as a basket.

丨緊 tie it tight, as when 丨帶 tightening the girdle.

纏丨甚 it is tied too tight.

鞭丨 to tie to a whipping post.

繩丨 ropes to bind things.

丨上一道箍 bind it with a hoop above.

丨束 a restricted rule, a fixed limit; impeded, as the circulation.

FU.

Old sounds, pu, bu, pút, bút *and* pok. *In Canton*, fu *and* pò ; — *in Swatow*, hu, pé, pò, *and* pu ; — *in Amoy*, hu, bu, *and* pau ; — *in Fuhchau*, hu, u, *and* hò ; — *in Shanghai*, fu *and* vu ; — *in Chifu*, fu.

夫 *꜀fu* From 大 *great* and 一 *one*, *q. d.* a man with a pin in his hair to show that he is of age ; — the 一 being a contraction of 丈 a pole of ten feet, intimating his full stature, or of 伩 to lean on.

One who can help; to assist; a husband; a man, a scholar, a distinguished man; a pronoun, denoting men; added to other noun, denotes a workman, a strong man, a fellow; as 水丨 a waterman; an artist; an exalted lady, an officer's wife.

丨婦 or 丨妻 husband and wife.

大丨 an old term for officials, now mostly used for a physician.

丨子 a sage, a rabbi, a great teacher; a hero.

丨君 my husband.

丨主 my deceased husband.

丨人 the wife of an officer of very high rank; Shakya's mother is so styled by the Budhists, and it is politely used when speaking of the wife of a gentleman.

如丨人 your concubine.

大丈丨 a great and good man, an eminent leader.

萬丨之ʻ長 the head of all men, the chief of all braves, — the sovereign.

挑丨 a porter, a coolie.

轎丨 a chair-bearer.

販丨 chapmen, peddlers.

車丨 a cartman.

馬丨 attendants, servitors of all kinds; a groom.

鄙丨 a mean fellow, a base man.

狂丨 a desperate man.

匹丨 a beast of a man, a low wretch.

百丨長 an old term for a centurion.

老丨 I the old worker; — used by common people.

萬丨之勇 one able to cope with ten thousand.

非丨人之爲慟而誰爲 if I am not moved on account of this man, what can move me?

丨星子息 husbands and children, — a fortune-teller's term.

獨丨受 this lonely isolated fellow Sheu.

Read ꜁*fu*. An adverbial initial particle; — now, therefore, forasmuch; however; an interjection.

且丨 moreover.

若丨 if then.

今丨 so, ah! now, then!

丨人之子 now, that man's son.

彼丨 that thing, therefore.

嗟丨 alas!

丨仁者 now, as to the humane man; now, concerning virtue.

袂 *꜀fu* From *clothes* and *help*.

The lapel which folds over the side; overalls or outer drawers.

丨襪 a case to protect a scabbard, made of coarse cloth.

砆 珐 *꜀fu* A reddish stone that looks like a gem, but inferior in beauty and value; a second class gem, like veined jasper or red-white cornelian.

碱丨亂玉 the pebbles are mingled in with gems, — the vile and the good are confounded.

鈇 *꜀fu* An ax used to decapitate high officers and princes.

丨鉞 a headsman's ax.

枎 *꜀fu* To spread out; name of a tree.

丨疎 to lay down or spread out in every part, as a mat on a floor.

丨栘 a sort of wild apple; the *Aronia*.

麩 *꜀fu* Bran of wheat; at Canton, 田丨 is the refuse cake of the ground-nut or hemp-seed, used for manure.

丨子 bran from grain.

丨料 horse-feed, as bran, beans, straw.

鹽丨子 fruit of the *Rhus semialata*, which produces the 五倍子 or gall-nuts.

孚 *꜀fu* From *claws* over a *child*, representing a bird brooding, as she sits on the nest.

To hatch, to brood on eggs; to trust to, depended on; trustworthy, because the time of hatching can be known; sincerely, truly; trust, confidence, belief; accordant; what is fully proved; fully established in.

交丨 mutual trust, as in trading.

作周丨先 be an example of loyalty (or trust) to the future statesmen of Cheu.

丨信 to rely on.

罔不是丨 every one reposed entire confidence in them.

丨甲 (also written 苻甲) the calyx, which bursts at flowering.

中丨 the 61st diagram, referring to confidence.

桴 *꜀fu* From *wood* and *trust*.

A float or raft; the ridge-pole in a roof; a drumstick; a barrow or hurdle to carry dirt.

乘丨浮于海 to float over the seas on a raft.

丨炭 floating charcoal; anything light.

丨思 a door-screen, or a door to screen from the street.

俘 ˛fu From *man* and *trust*.

A prisoner of war; to capture alive, to take prisoner; spoil taken in war.

丨囚 captives.

賤丨 I a poor prisoner.

丨掠 to take captive.

丨虜 to carry off spoil.

不相遺丨 [the princes] left no prisoners behind them.

莩 ˛fu From *herb* and *trust*; it occurs used for 殍 starved.

The white pellicle lining the culms of a water plant called 丨葭; a rush; *met.* related; friendly; the female hemp.

葭丨之親 distantly related; not intimate.

郛 ˛fu The outer purlieus of a city, especially the place where parades or trials of horsemanship are held; a border, a suburb.

五經爲衆說丨 all books are like the suburbs of the five Canonical Books.

稃 秿 ˛fu Bran of rice; the capsule or pericarp of a seed; the calyx or glumes of gramineous flowers.

跗 ˛fu The top or instep of the foot; top of the toes; occurs used for the next.

丨注 a sort of gaiters or stockings joining the trowsers.

蹶坭濘丨 to fall into the mud and dirty one's feet.

趺 ˛fu Used for the last.

To set in state, with the legs under one; to bow or curtsey.

丨丨然 the deep obeisance of a bride to her husband.

女丨坐 the women bowing low sat down.

跏丨 to sit crosslegged in a devotional attitude with the hands raised, when performing (*utkatu kasana*) the great meditation.

枹 ˛fu ˛feu From *tree* and *to wrap*.

A drumstick.

援丨 to take the drumstick.

執丨而鼓 to hold the stick and drum.

Read ˛pao. Bushy; plants growing thickly like a clump of canes.

丨罕 the ancient name of 河州 Ho-cheu in Kansuh.

柎 ˛fu From *tree* and to *give*.

The lower part of a railing; a calyx or receptacle of a flower; a raft to cross streams; handle of a knife; a sort of mat bran-bag used to drum with; to wash in lye and bleach.

丨栰 a raft; a scow, a ferry-boat.

罦 罳 ˛fu A spring-net, now called 翻車, shaped like the hood of a carriage, for trapping pheasants.

雉離于丨 the pheasants have got caught in the net.

怤 ˛fu To think on with pleasure; gratified, pleased with, as a friend.

鄜 ˛fu From *town* and *deer*.

A small department in the west of Shensi, bordering on Kansuh, anciently called 丨畤; it lies on the headwaters of the River Loh 洛河 in the mountains.

旉 ˛fu Original form of the next.

The fourth of the eight diagrams is 震 to tremble; and this character exhibits it; whence it means to display, to show the energy of spring in the budding or starting of plants.

敷 尃 ˛fu From to *spread* and *disperse*; the second composed of *inch* and *first*, is seldom used, and is also read *pu*ˀ with the same meaning.

To state to the sovereign or a superior; to lay, as a mat; to spread out, to diffuse; to disclose, as the feelings; to announce, to send out orders, to promulge; to show forth; to divide and arrange; to apply, as a plaster; extensively.

丨放 or 丨布 to distribute, to make known; to widely circulate, as news.

丨演經典 to make known or diffuse moral books, or exhortations to good habits.

不丨 or 不丨用 insufficient, not enough for the purpose.

丨敎 to spread abroad doctrines, to diffuse a religion.

丨奏 to memorialize the throne.

丨告 to proclaim, as the Emperor does.

丨藥 to put on, as a plaster or ointment.

丨求 to extend one's researches.

旻天疾威丨于下土 high Heaven's angry afflictions extend through this lower world.

膚 ˛fu From *flesh*, *tiger*, and *field*; the etymologists regard it as a contraction of ˛lu 臚 the skin.

The epidermis, the skin; the soft flesh, muscle; minced meat; pork; skin-deep, superficial; to skin, to flay; to receive; beautiful, admirable; large; the breadth of four fingers, or two 寸 *tsun*.

髮丨 hair and skin; *i. e.* the whole body.

肌丨 muscle, flesh.

丨文 superficial writing.

皮丨 the skin.

以奏丨功 to accomplish his great merit.

丨如凝脂 the flesh was like solid fat.

丨受 he personally received — the wound.

蘬 ₍fu An herb, the 地丨, used to make besoms; it is also called duck's tongue, and broom weed; the *Kochia scoparia.*

憋 ₍fu Hasty, urgent; occurs used for 怤 gratified.

憋丨 irascible, a hasty disposition.

符 ₍fu From *bamboo* and to *give* as the phonetic.

Bamboo slips in pairs, made to give one half to each party; a seal in two pieces, which when joined proves its genuineness by matching; the impression of such a seal; to correspond with, to agree with; to testify, to verify, to compare; a spell or charm to prevent evil, such as are often hung in 丨袋 or charm-bags on the lapel as amulets.

丨咒 written charms to exorcise spirits, to convey sores to others, to ward off infection, &c.; incantations, spells, amulets.

兵丨 a seal conferring unlimited military powers, which 兵丨在手 should always be at hand,—and the officer ready for his duty.

丨節 a warrant or commission, half of which is given the officer; credentials, a tally.

不相丨 the parts do not match; the circumstances disagree; there is a discrepancy between the statements.

字跡不丨 the writing does not tally; *i. e.* it is like a forgery.

畫丨 or 書丨 to write or draw spells or incantations.

丨瑞 favorable influences, as genial dews, springs, &c.

靈丨 an effectual charm.

不得恃游歷爲護丨 they cannot make a plea of traveling about, to screen themselves—from their wrong acts.

病丨 the demon of sickness; sickness, as defined by geomancers, including ill-luck, misfortune.

苻 ₍fu From *herb* and to *give*; occurs used for 莩 bursting.

A herbaceous plant with round and downy leaves, and red seeds shaped like ear-rings;—a Medicago?—it is also called 鬼目 a devil's eye.

Read ₍fu. A scale; buds bursting, as in the spring.

丨甲 the outer scale of a leaf or bud; a glume.

Read ₍pu, and used for 蒲 sweet flag. The name of a place.

甚于萑丨之可畏 more to be dreaded than [the robbers of] Hwan-p'u in Lu; this place being a fenny spot where bandits skulked.

泭 ₍fu From *water* and to *give*; it is used for 桴 a raft and the next.

A float made of boards for crossing streams by pushing it across, a thing smaller than a raft.

丨漚 bubbles on the water.

庶人乘丨 the common people got across on floats.

游 ₍fu Similar to the preceding.

To cross a stream on small floats fastened to each other.

鳧 ₍fu From *bird* and a *chair.*

A sheldrake, widgeon, or mallard, including some sorts with a crest; a small species near the Yangtsz' is called 冠丨 the capped duck; and another is named the 沉丨 the deep duck, from its habit of diving.

家丨 a poetical name for the common duck.

雙丨 a pair of shoes, in allusion to a man who stole a pair which had been offered to the goddess of the Little Orphan I. in the Yangtsz'.

丨鷖在涇 the ducks and widgeons are on the River King.

丨趨 to walk slow, like a duck.

泛若水丨 drifting along like a duck, as an idle useless lout; applied also to men of ability who prefer retirement to their duty to the state.

䒇 ₍fu From *herb* and *mallard*, as the phonetic.

An edible tuber, described as a variety of the water-chestnut or *Eleocharis*, called 丨茈, which people eat in times of scarcity.

芙 ₍fu A flower, the 丨蓉花 or *Hibiscus mutabilis*, common in southern China.

丨蓉江 a branch of the Wu (Black) Kiang in the north of Yunnan.

丨蓉面 a flowery (*i. e.* pretty) face of a girl;—a fancy name for a looking-glass.

阿丨蓉 the poppy, so called in imitation of the Arabic *ufyun* for opium, introduced into China about A. D. 800 by Arab traders.

丨蕖 the lotus flower.

蚨 ₍fu From *insect* and *man*; in Canton it is sometimes wrongly used for 蝴 a butterfly.

A species of water beetle like the Dytiscus, called 青丨 and 丨蟬; the popular notion is that it can recover its stolen young, and the mother and young always somehow rejoin each other; coins rubbed with their blood will also one day come together again; hence copper cash are often called 青丨, from their resemblance to the shape of the insect; and 花丨 by an extension of the idea, is sometimes used as a name for dollars, rupees, and other coins.

京丨四吊 two *tiao* or bills of Peking money.

扶 ₍fu From *hand* and *man* as the phonetic.

To lend a hand, to help one along; to aid, to assist; to uphold, to protect; to defend, to shield, as in days of calamity.

丨助 to aid, to succor, to help.
丨挾 to sustain, as one who is weak.
丨持 to uphold, to steady.
丨手 a support for the hand, as a cane; the 丨手板 is a board in a sedan to lean on.
丨杖 to lean on a staff; hence a poetical name for the adjutant is 丨老 the old man on a staff, because the bird has such an old bald head and looks so demure.
丨櫬 to return home with a coffin.
丨災 to bear up under calamity.
顛而不丨 though he had fallen, he would not help him up; — refused all assistance.
赤子丨丨 the young and helpless children.
丨桑國 described as the country where the sun rises, refers probably to Japan, and is regarded by the Japanese as an old Chinese name of their country.
山有丨蘇 the hills produce mulberries; this ancient name is probably the same as the last, as applied to Japan.

榑 ˏfu A sort of divine tree, said to grow where the sun rises, called 丨桑 a name indicating its affinity to the mulberry; the wood is excellent; the name is probably derived or altered from 扶桑國 or Japan.

颫 ˏfu A storm.
丨風 a great tempest.
丨飄 the wind blowing down from the sky in a sudden gust; the Budhists liken the ascent of the departing soul to it.

鼖 ˏfu From *drum* and to *give*.
The noisy clamor and joy of an army; joyful cries and drumming of soldiers.
前軍丨譟 the troops in front cheered and rejoiced.

府 ˊfu From a *shelter* and to *give* as the phonetic.
A library, a record-office; to collect, to store; a storehouse a treasury; *met.* a thesaurus or encyclopædia; a palace, the hall of a regulus or prince; and thus in polite phrase, a gentleman's house; department or office in government; the officer over such a department or bureau; a prefecture or subdivision of a province, first instituted in the T'ang dynasty; the officer placed over it, a prefect.
丨上 or 貴丨 or 尊丨 are polite terms for your residence, your mansion.
太丨 or 丨尊 his Honor the 知丨 or prefect; applied too to a 分丨 or sub-prefect.
王丨 a prince's palace in Peking.
宗人丨 the Board of the Imperial Clan.
丨庫 the treasury; a dépôt.
身居丨職 he is still in government employ.
六丨 the six treasuries are the five elements, grain, and all plants.

拊 ˊfu From *hand* and to *give*; occurs used for the next.
To pat, to slap, as in good humor; to quiet, to lay the hand on; to permit; the handle of things; a sort of drum.
丨心 lay your hand on your heart, — and ask yourself.
丨石 to tap the stone — in keeping time.
丨我畜我 [you, my parents,] indulged and reared me.
循丨 to pat and stroke, as a cat; to soothe.
搏丨琴瑟 to thrum and tap the lute and guitar.

撫 擄 ˊfu From *hand* and *without* or a *treasury*; the second form is not common; interchanged with the last.
To keep down with the hand, to hold; to quiet, to tranquilize, to soothe; to stroke, to pat, as a dog; to cherish, to provide for; to console, to cheer up; to manage, to control gently but firmly, as a good magistrate; to thrum, as a lute.
丨綏四方 to fully pacify the country.
安丨 or 摩丨 to gently manage.
丨養 to rear, as a child; to nurture, to educate.
丨養人材 to bring out men of ability.
丨臺 or 巡丨 or 丨院 the governor of a province.
丨劍 to draw the sword.
丨御 to manage and drive, as a span; — applied to a firm and gentle sway over the people.
丨左 and 丨右 the Governor's left and right — troop or escort.

腑 ˊfu From *flesh* and *treasury* as the phonetic.
The membranous or inferior viscera, called 六丨, are reckoned by the Chinese to be the stomach, gall-bladder, large and small intestines, bladder, and three functional passages.
肺丨 the lungs; *met.* the intentions, the real opinions.

腐 ˊfu This must be distinguished from the last.
Rotten, corrupt, spoiled; crushed to powder; carious, unsound; inert, inapt, slow.
丨肉 sloughing flesh; gangrenous; proud flesh.
丨氣 foolish, obstinate and doltish.
丨爛 putrid, as a sore; spoiled, as meat.
丨刑 the punishment of castration.
丨敗 an utter defeat.
丨儒 a learned fool, a vicious pedant.
荳丨 bean-curd; low policemen and underlings are nicknamed 荳丨官 because they live on and are no better than this curd; and also the teachers in low government schools.

去丨生肌 remove the proud flesh, and thus produce healthy.

丨乳 soured bean-curd.

奶荳丨 a Mongol name for cheese.

陳丨 an old saw, an ancient, worn-out proverb, not applicable to the present day.

ʻ俯 ʻ頫 ʻfu From *man* and *storehouse;* the second is also read *tʻiaoʼ;* it is rather obsolete.

To stoop, to bend down, to bow; to look down from a height, to condescend to, to regard the lowly, — said of superiors, and much used in prayers and petitions; to consider; unequal.

丨伏 to fall on the face; to bow and kneel.

丨准 to look graciously on.

丨 and 仰 are correlatives, to look down — to look up; a term for all ranks, as 丨仰皆寬 he treats everybody with kindness.

丨首無言 held down his head and kept silent.

丨察地理 to examine the lay of the land or its capabilities, as a strategist or geomancer.

ʻ弣 ʻfu The middle of a bow, where it is grasped; better known as 弓弝 the hold of the bow.

ʻ魊 ʻfu Stars in Ursa Major, especially one near δ Megrez in the square of the Dipper.

ʻ甫 ʻfu Composed of 用 to *use* and 父 *father* contracted.

To begin, the first; an appellation or style taken by men, by which their friends call them; it is also called their 大號 great designation, or 別字 the other name; large, fine, good; eminent, great; numerous; I, myself; a small lordship mentioned in the Shi King.

丨丨 all, every kind, all sizes.

請問台丨 what is your style, Sir?

年丨弱冠 he has just been capped, he is still a very young man; 年丨 is also a polite term for asking another's age.

丨及月 just a month from the time.

丨初 to begin; a beginning.

仲尼丨 the appellation of Confucius.

丨田 a large, wide field.

章丨 a grandee's coronet.

Read ʻ*pu*, and used for 圃 a garden.

丨草 field plants.

In *Cantonese*. A ward in the provincial city, of which there are eighteen; a league, as 十里爲一丨 ten *li* make one station or post, which are a league apart; some write 赴ʼ for this last sense.

ʻ盙 ʻ簠 ʻfu From *dish* and *great;* the second form with *bamboo* added is commonly used.

A sort of basket or hamper, square outside and round within, used to hold boiled grain in government worship.

丨簋 dishes of different shapes, used when adoring Confucius and ancestors.

ʻ輔 ʻfu From *cart* and *great.*

Poles attached to a cart to help it out of the mud, or to shore it up on a side-hill from oversetting; a cart; a rack on a cart, which extends over the sides; the jaw-bone; to help, to flank, to second; to succor and guide.

丨衛 to protect, as a guardian.

丨佐 or 丨助 to aid in carrying out; to succor, to assist.

丨相 to join and help, to cooperate, in government.

丨頬 the jawbone.

宰丨 a cabinet-minister.

丨㢸 high statesmen; in geomancy, hills or knolls which support or flank a spot.

以友丨仁 to be helped by one's friends in virtuous ways.

無棄爾丨 do not throw aside your props.

四丨 four officers anciently placed near the throne as supporters; applied to four stars in Camelopardalis near the pole.

ʻ黼 ʻfu From to *embroider* and *great.*

Embroidered garments used anciently to indicate high rank, having axes drawn on them in black and white; diversified.

丨黻 ancient sacrificial dresses embroidered with white lines or axes.

丨黻文章 elegant composition.

丨繡 finely embroidered.

常服丨冔 constantly appearing in their hatchet robes and state coronets.

ʻ脯 ʻfu From *flesh* and *great* as the phonetic.

Dried meat, like jerked meat; flesh or fruit dried for food.

丨鮓品 preserved meats or other preparations of food and fish.

脩丨 slices of dried meat formerly sent to teachers; hence it, or 束丨 a bundle of meat, now means the wages of a teacher taken to him by a pupil.

桃丨 dried peaches.

市丨不食 [Confucius] did not eat the dried meat sold in shops.

ʻ䰌 ʻfu From a *boiler* and *great;* nearly the same as the next.

A large ancient measure, holding about a kilderkin, or 6⅔ 斗 or pecks; a boiler for dressing food; a meal.

二丨不合 not having two meals — a day.

覆丨 rude huts like inverted kettles, in which people lived in marshy places after Yü's deluge.

釜 ˊfu From 金 metal and 父 *father* contracted.

A caldron or hemispherical boiler; a pot without feet; an old measure, nearly the same as the *huh*, 斛 or half-pecul, holding 6 斗 and 4 升, or rather more than 1½ bushel.

丨 甑 a boiler and vat.

丨 中 之 魚 [like] a fish in the kettle; — in imminent danger.

丨 底 游 魂 [like] a wandering ghost in the caldron; — alludes to hell torments.

與 之 丨 I gave him half a bushel of millet.

斧 ˊfu From *hatchet* and *father*.

An ax, a hatchet, a cleaver, all having short handles; to fell trees, to hack.

丨 依 or 丨 削 to prune; to correct, as composition.

丨 頭 or 丨 斤 or 丨 子 a hatchet; cleavers and axes for chopping.

打 丨 頭 to levy a percentage, to cheat in price. (*Cantonese.*)

丨 鉞 halberds and bills, like those used in battle.

資 丨 不 濟 there is not enough for his expenses.

㕮 ˊfu To bite and chew fine; to try the taste by chewing.

丨 咀 to ruminate, to think over a matter, — referring to chewing herbs.

父 fuˋ The original form represents a right *hand* raising a *rod*; it forms the 88th radical of a small group of natural characters.

A rule; one who is the rule of a family, and directs its instruction; a father; an ancestor; a senior; to act as a father; loving, paternal; fatherly.

丨 親 a father; 生 丨 my father, the one who begat me.

家 丨 our father.

先 丨 a deceased father.

伯 叔 丨 my paternal uncles.

丨 母 官 the local officers are occasionally so called; especially the *chi-hien*, who is spoken of as 老 丨 台 old father.

丨 王 my imperial father.

王 丨 a grandfather in the ancestral hall.

丨 兄 輩 superiors generally.

丨 老 village elders.

諸 丨 an old polite term for a feudal prince.

丨 執 my father's friends.

丨 丨 子 子 treating a father as a father, and son as a son.

Read ˊfu. A term for old people and peasants; when used after clan names it corresponds to our Mr.; and after a title to his Honor.

漁 丨 a fisherman.

傅 fuˋ From *man* and to *display*; it is often mistaken for ˏ*chuen* 傳 to transmit; occurs used for 附 to join.

To arrange; to superintend; once designated a high officer about the court, now a tutor, a teacher, a superintendent; a skilled workman, an artist; to teach, as a tutor; a function; to annex, to reach to; to receive; near; to lay on, as colors.

太 丨 the highest tutor; now an honorary title.

面 如 丨 粉 your face is white as if painted.

師 丨 a master workman.

師 丨 骨 a pedantic simpleton, a conceited ass. (*Cantonese.*)

丨 顏 色 to paint, to put on colors.

丨 訓 a teacher's instruction.

丨 會 to accord with the crowd; to yield one's views, to become unanimous.

丨 別 a sort of warrant or commission, of which the officer took only one half.

付 fuˋ From 人 a *man* and 寸 an *inch*, which in one form is altered into 又 a *hand* holding something to be presented.

To give to, to deliver over to another, to hand over; to send; to transfer; to let go; to engage or put into one's hands; to enjoin on, for which the next is now used.

交 丨 to transfer, as to a successor.

丨 來 sent to or back; received from.

過 丨 人 one who introduces parties to each other, as a common acquaintance.

寄 丨 to send by one, as a parcel.

丨 諸 東 流 let it go on the eastern streams; *i. e.* to be careless of a matter.

丨 淸 the account is all cleared off.

丨 託 to charge one with, to commission.

咐 fuˋ Commonly used for the last in 吩 丨 to order, to instruct, to enjoin on.

囑 丨 to give strict orders to.

Read ˏfu. To breathe on; to blow gently with the breath.

祔 fuˋ From *worship* and *near*; also written 祔 by some.

To worship ancestors recently buried, with those more remote, all in the same hall; to inter in the family tomb.

丨 葬 to bury together.

丨 食 to sacrifice to all, as when a new ancestor enters the hall.

升 丨 太 廟 gathered to his imperial ancestors in the great temple.

附 fuˋ From *mound* and to *give*.

To be next to, to lean on, to follow, as a satellite; near, about, approaching; to join; to attach one's self to; annexed, tributary, but not dependent; a supplement, an inclosure, an appendix; to inclose, as one letter in another.

丨和 to agree with another; to follow blindly.

不丨 insubmissive, incongruous; do not accord or accept.

丨會 to echo or adopt another's views.

丨近 adjacent, near, conterminous.

丨耳 to bend the ear — and listen; also, a satellite.

丨單 to inclose an account.

依丨 dependent.

丨益 to increase one's advantages, to better one's position.

被鬼丨身 possessed by a devil, crazed, out of his mind.

丨於其末 to put one's self after others, to be the last.

丨薦 to send one's ancestral tablets to a mass; to hire priests to pray for one's dead.

歸丨 to return to one's allegiance, to lay down arms.

丨生 a young *siuts'ai* graduate.

丨庸 in the Cheu dynasty, a title of nobility, a landed squire, whose possessor had a fief of fifty *li* or less, and no right of audience.

女蘿丨松 the cypress-vine clings to the pine, — as a wife to her husband.

蔀 *fu'* A medicinal herb, like wolf's bane (*Aconitum variegatum*), whose seeds called 丨子 or 附子 are pungent, poisonous, and bitterish, and taken for their tonic properties; the tubers are called 地雄 or 丨片, and are also used in medicine.

地丨子 the seeds of the *Kochia*, one of the *Chenopodiæ* or goose-foot family.

白丨子 a plant of the Arum family, brought as a medicine from Manchuria.

駙 *fu'* A subsidiary horse, harnessed by the wheel horse, to make the cart go quicker; to approach; near; rapid.

丨馬 a son-in-law of the emperor; he is called 額丨 by the Manchus; the name is derived from an office in the Han dynasty which the emperor's son-in-law held; in the Tsin dynasty, a princess was also called by this term.

鮒 *fu'* A freshwater fish resembling a perch, common in Tungting L., and by some considered to be the same as the 鯽魚; it is so called because it goes in pairs and schools, each pair being faithful to each other; also a sort of goby, which can crawl on land.

丨行 to go in shoals.

丨魚涸轍 [I am like] a goby thirsting in the rut — which will soon die if not watered; said by needy persons.

副 *fu'* From *knife* and *full*.

To aid, to second; to announce; to investigate, to examine; the correlative of 正 a principal, an assistant, a substitute, a vice, a deputy, or lieutenant, a secundus; an alternate; an ornament of braided hair worn by queens at worship; a classifier of suits or sets of things, as beads, tools, plates, buttons, ear-rings, &c.

丨使 the assistant or second commissioner.

丨將 a brigadier general; whence 丨爺 is a compellation for low military officers.

丨榜 or 丨車 an under-graduate (*kü-jin*), one who just missed getting his degree.

丨室 a second wife.

一丨心腸 the disposition, temperament; the habits and character of a person.

全丨執事 a procession wholly filled up; the whole set-out.

又是一丨臉色 he has quite a different countenance for such folks.

正的丨的 principal and vice; a chief and his deputy.

Read *fuh*, To rend, as in parturition.

不坼不丨 there was neither bursting nor rending.

富 *fu'* From a *shelter* and *full*.

Provided with in every respect; affluent, rich; abundant; supplied; learned; to enrich; to provide; to regard riches; the rich; wealth, riches.

丨貴 rich and noble; *met.* abundant and good.

年丨 in the prime of life, lusty.

丨豪 or 丨厚, or 丨足 wealthy, well off; affluent.

丨餘 an overplus, more than is needed.

丨翁 a rich man, a man of means.

丨家 or 丨戶 a wealthy family.

丨之 to enrich one; to benefit.

學丨者 universally learned.

非丨天下 he did not esteem the wealth of the empire.

丨而好禮 when he is rich he is fond of ceremony.

才詞辨丨 learned; every way accomplished and talented.

多文爲丨 great learning is riches.

葍 *fu'* This seems to be the same as *fuh*, 葍 in the name 葍萊 a wild vegetable, whose roots when white are sometimes eaten, and which seems to be allied to the pokeweed, (*Phytolacca*) a species of which is found in Chihli.

言采其丨 we went gathering pokeweed.

仆 *fu'* From *man* and to *divine*.

To fall over, to fall to the earth; overthrown.

丨倒 fallen down; a euphemism for deceased.

驚丨 fell down from fright.

眩丨 fell down from vertigo, or in a fit.

訃 *fu'* From 言 *words* and 赴 *to reach* contracted; it was once written like the next, and is often confounded with *poh*, 朴 to beat.

A son announcing the death of a parent or grandparent to his relatives and friends; to go to.

丨音 or 丨聞 or 丨報 the letter or card or messenger announcing a death; there is some difference in the usages; a small sum, called 香儀, is returned to aid in buying incense and candles.

聞丨丁憂 hearing of a parent's decease and resigning office.

赴 *fu'* To go to a place; to arrive at, to reach; to repair to speedily, to reach quickly, to hasten, and thus used in reports or visits to superior officers; to present; to attend.

丨任 to enter on the duties of a post.

丨命 to obey an order or a call.

丨約 to engage to meet one.

丨席 to go to a feast.

丨告 to present a petition.

切丨台前 I earnestly offer [this petition] to your Honor.

速丨 to hurry, to go there speedily.

丨蓬萊 to go to fairy land; *i. e.* to die.

丨會 to attend a meeting.

丨海 to leap into the sea—or water; *i. e.* to drown one's self.

丨湯蹈火 I would go into hot water and tread on fire—in your service.

In *Cantonese*. A league or ten *li*.

一丨路 a military post.

賻 *fu'* From *wealth* and to *display*.

To assist a friend to bury his dead by contributing towards the funeral expenses.

丨儀 the money given for this purpose.

賦 *fu'* From *wealth* and *martial*.

To exact, to demand, to levy, to require taxes; a tax of money or arms, but especially of service or villanage; tribute from fiefs; to receive from Heaven and bestow on men; to spread out, to arrange; to give; a kind of poetical composition having a metre of four or six feet in alternate lines, regarded as irregular compared with the *shi* 詩 or ode; a madrigal, an idyl; to spread abroad, as decrees.

丨貢 to apportion or levy taxes.

丨稅 to collect land tax; the impost.

丨役 to make a conscription; to draft troops.

丨納 to send up taxes.

丨畀之初 the moment of birth.

丨性 one's mind; the natural abilities.

丨質 one's native powers and talents.

薄丨輕徭 light taxes and easy rates.

丨斂之臣 an exactor and oppressive collector of the revenue, one who 重丨於民 exacts unjustly from the people.

詩丨 poems and ballads.

丨事陳詞 to take a theme and write out one's ideas in poetry.

婦 **媍** *fu'* From *woman* and *besom*, indicating her household duties; the second form is unusual.

A wife; a married woman who follows and is subject to a 夫 man, and includes both wife and concubine; a lady; a female; and is often an equivalent of Mrs. or Mistress; beautiful; female, pertaining to woman.

丨女 women; the sex.

丨人 a woman; in speaking, it is often used rather like granny, goodwife, a depreciatory term.

娶新丨 to get married, to take a wife with all the legal formalities.

丨德 female virtues.

丨道之家 a well-bred woman; female propriety.

賢丨 a virtuous woman.

潑丨 a pettish, captious woman, a termagant.

醜丨 a hag, a beldame, a harridan.

艷丨 a beautiful woman, a stylish, well-dressed lady.

命丨 a titled lady.

寺丨 a eunuch; an old term.

小丨 a concubine.

丨人長舌維厲之階 a woman's long tongue is the step by which misfortune enters the house.

同我丨子饁彼南畝 with our women and children we carry food to those working in the southern fields.

負 *fu'* Composed of *wealth* and *man*.

To carry on the back, to bear; to assume; to take a duty; to rely on, to depend on; to take refuge in; to disregard, to turn the back on; to requite evil; to slight; to refuse; to owe; to fail, to be defeated; a burden; a duty; ungrateful; in *mathematics*, a term for minus.

丨累 to involve, as an indorser by non-payment.

丨戴 to carry on the head.

丨屈 to suffer a wrong; to be deeply injured.

丨荷 to bear a burden—of care; a responsibility.

丨心 ungrateful, heartless.

丨心賊 you heartless thief; you jilt!

丨恩 to forget favors.

背丨 traitorous, ungrateful; to carry on the back.

丨苦 to endure hardness; to work for a living, as a laborer.

抱丨不凡 more learned and able than common men.

勝丨 to win or lose; to succeed or fail.

虧丨了他 I failed to treat him properly; I was unfair towards him.

丨欠 or 丨債 in debt.

襁丨其子 strapped her child on her back.

皇天不丨苦心人 high Heaven never turns away from the sorrowful in heart.

丨棋 to lose a game of chess.

丨主 to turn against one's master.

辜丨 unmindful of kindness; to render benefits conferred nugatory.

阿丨 or 丨耳 an old term for mother — from the manner of carrying children.

偩 *fu'* Also read *feu'*.
Like, resembling; to depend on.

禮樂丨天地之情 propriety and music are like the feelings of heaven and earth.

自丨其志 he trusts to his own determination.

蚹 *fu'* The scales on the belly of large serpents by which they progress.

蛇丨 a snake's scales along the belly.

丨蠃 a garden snail.

FUH.

Old sounds, pok, p'ok, bok, puk, p'uk, buk, pút, bút, *and* p'ut. *In Canton*, fuk *and* fát; — *in Swatow*, hok, pak, hut, *and* pwat; — *in Amoy*, hok *and* hut; — *in Fuhchau*, huk *and* hòk; — *in Shanghai*, fòk, vòk, *and* feh; — *in Chifu*, fuh.

畐 *,fu* Composed of 高 *high* and 厚 *generous* both contracted and placed one above the other; it is an ancient form of the next, and used only as a primitive.

To be full; to fill; a roll of cloth.

福 *,fu* From *worship* and *full*; this character is symbolized by the next.

Happiness, the felicity which attends divine protection; good fortune, blessing, prosperity, well provided for; favors; a blessing; to bless, to render happy; sacrificial meats; occurs meaning with; often stands for the province of Fuhkien.

近來納丨 have you been quite well lately?

丨善 to bless the good.

丨田 a blessed field; *i. e.* your ancestor's fortune.

樹丨田 a Budhist phrase for doing good works, giving alms, or worshiping often.

丨地 a lucky grave spot.

發丨 to grow fat.

丨晉 a Manchu word meaning the wife of a Manchu prince; she is addressed by this term.

有丨氣 or 丨分 a good-looking man; well off, successful in life.

添丨添壽 may you be happy and live long.

散丨 to distribute offerings among one's friends, after a sacrifice; they then 飲丨受胙 drink their happiness and get their flesh.

丨安 may you be happy;—written at the end of a letter.

五丨 the five blessings (represented by five bats) are long life, riches, sound body and serene mind, (others say honors,) love of virtue, and a peaceful end.

一路丨星 may a happy star [light] your way.

丨神 the happy gods, are the *lares rustici* and street gods.

有丨之人不在忙 lucky people never need be in a hurry.

厚德載丨 great virtue carries happiness with it.

Read *fu'* To store up, to lay up.

蝠 *,fu* The bat is called 蝙丨, but others think the 丨鼠 is a flying squirrel; the bat is frequently drawn as the emblem of *happiness* from the similar sounds of this and the preceding.

丨蛇 a scorpion; *met.* a malignant heart.

蝙丨荳 a kind of bean found in Yunnan.

幅 *,fu* From *cloth and full.*

A wide strip of cloth; a roll, as of paper; a selvedge or hem; a frontier, a border; a classifier of maps, rolls, pictures, scrolls, flags, leggings, strips of land, walls, &c.

四條丨 four scrolls,—like those for hanging on walls.

丨員 the area of a country, its extent.

邊丨 a hem, an edging; applied to the border or frontier, as the provinces on the south and west.

葍 *,fu* An edible wild vegetable, the 丨菜 having large veined leaves and roots like a finger; it is found in Shantung, and is a *Portulacca* or pokeweed; the same as the 蓄菜; it is regarded as a poor vegetable; a sort of rush.

輻, *ˌfu* From *carriage* and *full*.
The spoke of a wheel.
地輿丨輳 that place is one where they collect, — as the capital to which people resort.

复, *ˌfu* This is only used as a primitive.
To go back the old way, to retrace; now written like the next.
不丨從 not to do according to — a rule.

復, *ˌfu* From to *step* and to *retrace* a path; it is used for the next.
Again, reiterated; to go and come; to do the second time; to return; to reply, to report to, as that an order is performed; to recover; to restore, to repay; to recompense; to observe, as a promise; to recall the spirit of one who died from home; a hut like a kraal; the 24th diagram, meaning to repeat.
反丨 or 反反丨丨 repeatedly; troublesome from repetition.
丨音 an answer; but 丨信 is rather the reply to a letter.
丨來 returned; repeated.
丨又 to do over again, to recur, to repeat; again.
丨戰 to renew the battle.
丨興 to recover; to start again and prosper; to revive, as business after depression.
丨命 to report on, as a commission.
丨出為惡 on the contrary he waxes worse.
丨還 to repay, to requite, to revenge, to recompense.
丨仇 or 報丨 to revenge an enemy; to pay him off.
丨我諸兄 I will go back to my brothers.
是顧是丨 they are protected and promoted.
丨生 to revive, as from a swoon; a resurrection, to come to life.
仍丨如是 or 丨舊如初 to replace as it was at first; to restore, as at the beginning.
丨降在原 he descended again to the plains.
丨原 or 丨元 restored to health.

覆, *ˌfu* From to *cover* and *again*; often interchanged with the last, and must not be confounded with *hoh*, 覈 to investigate.
Back and forth; on the contrary; to and fro; unstable; to overthrow, to subvert; to defeat; to throw down, to upset, to prostrate; to reply to, to report on; to inquire into and judge; to do a second time; an ambush.
傾丨 overthrown, as a state; fallen, as a wall.
顛丨 tumbled down; ruined, reduced to poverty.
顛丨流連 reprobate (or unfortunate) and pursued everywhere; dispersed and scattered, as a troop; utterly helpless.
馬前丨水 [like] gathering the water poured before a horse, — so impossible will it be.
丨車之戒 the warning of the overturned cart [ahead]; *i. e.* to learn caution from others' troubles.
丨白 to report on clearly; to explain in a perspicuous manner.
射丨 to guess at things under a screen or cover.
全軍皆丨 the whole host was destroyed.
丨敗 discomfited, as an army.
丨逃 the *argumentum ad hominem* in rhetoric.
丨沒 lost and sunk, as a 丨舟 or sunken vessel.
查丨 to inquire and report on.
丨奏 to reply in a memorial.

Read *feu'* To cover, to overshadow; to brood, as a bird.
鳥丨翼之 the bird spread her wings over it.
天地無不丨載 there is nothing which is not covered by heaven or supported by earth.
丨蓋 to cover, as a dish.

腹, *ˌfu* From *flesh* and to *retrace* a path.
That which envelopes the viscera; the belly or abdomen; to carry in the arms; the seat of the mind; the middle of, as a hill; thick, substantial; intimate, dear; the earth, because it embraces all things.
丨肚 the belly.
小丨 below the navel.
丨結 constipated.
肚丨大 gluttonous; a big paunch.
為口丨 merely for a living, — not for favor or to do good.
坦丨之倚 the assistance of a son-in-law.
滿丨文章 a great scholar, a walking encyclopædia.
令人捧丨 to make one laugh till his sides shake.
丨心 beloved; dear, as a child.
丨心之靠 to depend on entirely.
膽丨之言 most reliable words.
水澤丨堅 the watery marsh is thick and hard — in winter.
口是丨非 specious, false; disingenuous.
遺丨子 a posthumous child.
指丨為婚 to betroth children before birth.
剖丨明心 you may search my inmost heart.
稿懷於丨 I composed the draft in my mind.
出入丨我 [you, my mother] never forgot me in all my ways.
剖丨藏珠 he cuts open his belly to hide pearls, — as one who sacrifices life for gain.

馥, *ˌfu* A fragrant smell; odors diffused around; the whirr of an arrow.
芬丨 odoriferous.
丨郁 beautiful and fragrant.

蝮, *ˌfu* From *insect* and *repeated*, referring to the viper's reputed habit of striking back.
A venemous serpent, 丨蛇 including the adder, viper, and cobra; poisonous, deadly.
丨虺 a huge serpent like a boa, found in the west of China.
蝝丨蜪 the wingless young of locusts.

複, ˏ*fu* — Double garments; wadded or lined garments; to double; the second.

丨道 a double or parallel road leading around a hill, one above and one below.

重丨 again, repeated.

丨襟 a double lapel.

敞丨提刀 to strap the dress tight and seize the sword — to fight.

輹, ˏ*fu* — The cord or band which is tied around the projecting sticks that clasp the body of a cart on the axle to prevent its slipping.

輿脫丨 the chariot has lost its axle band.

㙏, 𡐗, ˏ*fu* — To excavate a cave or hole in a bank for a residence, as is frequently the case in Shansi and elsewhere; a den where people can live in troublous times.

陶丨是也 just those kind of hill-side dwellings.

伏, ˏ*fu* — From *man* and *dog*; the combination perhaps intimates the subjection of the dog to man.

To lie or fall prostrate, to fall on the face; to humble, to subject; to hide, to conceal; to lie or place in ambush; to suppress, to keep hidden; subjected; hidden; silently, closely, secretly; villains who hide away; to acknowledge, to confess; received; — a sign of the passive; to brood, as a bird; when addressing a superior, used *adverbially* for humbly, earnestly, in my opinion, as 丨思 I humbly think; a sign of the ablative, as 邵丨誅駿卽位 Shao having been destroyed, Tsun then reigned.

丨罪 to own one's guilt.

丨望 I earnestly hope.

丨乞 or 丨祈 to earnestly beg or ask.

埋丨 to hide perdue; to keep out of sight.

輾轉丨枕 rolling and tossing as I hug my pillow.

丨誅 he suffered decapitation.

發奸擿丨 to make known the traitors and seize rascals.

丨兵 soldiers in ambush; to dispose troops in an ambush.

寑無丨 don't lie on your face when sleeping.

匍丨台堦 I would crawl up your Honor's steps.

丨卵 or 丨窩 to set on eggs; she is hatching.

旣丨其辜 they have suffered for their misdeeds.

潛丨 to quietly get away,

丨臘炎涼 the summer there is hot, and the winter very cold.

三丨 are three decades in the summer; the 初丨 commences July 19th; the 中丨 on July 29th; and the 末丨 on August 8th; — a month of hot weather, dog-days, when the 陰氣 is in the ascendant.

栿, ˏ*fu* — A strap or girder placed on a beam to strengthen it.

洑, ˏ*fu* — A return flow, as in water; name of an anchorage.

丨流 an eddy.

In *Pekingese*. Used sometimes for swimming, said of fishes.

茯, ˏ*fu* — From *grass* and to *hide*.

The medicine 丨苓, known as China root; it is the *Pachyma cocos*, a fungus-like substance found in the western provinces on the roots of fir-trees; some regard it as more like a puff-ball (*Lycoperdon*); the Chinese say it is the sap of the fir tree, which turns into *fuh-ling* in a thousand years, and then into amber in another millenium.

丨苓糕 a kind of cake made of this fungus.

土丨苓 the root of the *Smilax chinensis*, a medicine used in syphilis.

袱, ˏ*fu* — From *clothes* and to *hide*.

A square cloth.

包丨 a square strong cloth used for wrapping bedding and clothes.

手丨 a small wrapper or satchel, with one string.

服, 舩, ˏ*fu* — The first is the usual form, but it was originally formed of 舟 a *boat* and 𠬝 to *manage*, contracted to 𠬝 its present form.

To use, as one does a boat; to wait on, as an attaché does; attached to, as things are to a girdle; hence clothes, dress, apparel; a saddle-cloth; to dress; to fold; to yield to, to serve; to undergo; to go into mourning; to convince, to cause to submit; to subject, as animals; to effect or carry out; to accord with from fear; to think; to fold up; accustomed to, habituated, acclimated; to fullfil the duties of an office; a title; office; in old times, a tenure or domain; a quiver; an affair; the wheel horses, which bear up the carriage.

朝丨 or 公丨 court dresses.

丨官 to take the garb of an officer; *i. e.* to hold office.

有丨 or 着丨 in mourning.

五丨 five tenures of early times; the divisions of China in Yü's day; also five grades of 孝丨 or mourning apparel, called the 斬縗丨; the 齊縗丨 or 期丨; the 大功丨; the 小功丨, and 細麻丨, worn respectively for 12, 9, 7, 5, and 2 months after the death of relatives of the same surname; the 袒免丨 is nearly the same as the first.

衣丨 clothes, garments; a wardrobe; but 丨衣 is to put on a dress.

丨藥 to take medicine.

吃不丨 it does not agree with me, I cannot take it.

一丨藥 a dose of physic.

佩 丨 to hang on the dress; *met.* to accord with, to reverence, to follow with docility.

不 丨 老 unwilling to be regarded as old or infirm.

丨 事 to serve, to wait on, to obey orders, as an attendant.

不 丨 敎 headstrong, intractable.

水土不 丨 not acclimated; I am unused to the place.

欽 丨 complete submission; hearty accord.

丨 從 or 歸 丨 to follow obediently, to accord with.

以德 丨 人 to win men by virtue.

舒 丨 in good spirits, well, in health; contented.

無替厥 丨 do not (uselessly or) perfunctorily do the duties — of the post.

丨 休 丨 采 those who serve at ease, and those who serve actively; — cabinet and executive officers.

脱 丨 or 起 丨 to lay off mourning; to fullfil the period, and be able to resume office.

成 丨 去 [the officer] has gone into mourning.

荒 丨 之人 people from the outskirts of the land, half-savage or uncouth people.

箙, *꜀fu*

Used for the last.

A quiver made of shagreen or hide to hold both bow and arrows.

魚 丨 a quiver made of shagreen or fish-skin.

鰒, *꜀fu*

The *Haliotis* or ear-shell, called 丨 魚 and included among fishes; its anomalous form and manner of clinging to the rocks, leads people to gather both animal and shell for medicine; the name is applied to a sort of shark.

甶, *꜀fu*

The original form resembles a square with a pyramid above.

A devil's head; this character is used in Budhist prayers instead of *kwéi* 鬼, as 諸 丨 子等 all you demons.

菔, *꜀fu*

The seeds of a plant akin to the turnip, used as a medicine; also read *poh,* when applied to the turnip; the raw roots of the 蘆 丨, or white turnip, are eaten to remove the effects of sour bread and of coal-gas or charcoal smoke.

鵩, *꜀fu*

From *bird* and to *submit,* because the bird does not leave its habitat.

A sort of owl or goshawk called 鴞 丨, the size of a dove; it has a screeching cry and a short flight, and is regarded an ill-omened bird.

弗, *꜀fu*

Originally composed of 韋 *hide* contracted to 弓 *a bow,* havinn withes bound each side.

An *adverb* of prohibition, not; now rather used as a deprecatory word, not so, it should not be, not permissable; do not, will not, can not; distorted; to grasp; to leave.

丨 來 he will not come.

丨 乎 丨 乎 no, by no means.

雪 丨 如雨 the snow cannot be compared with the rain; *i. e.* it is not so beautiful.

丨 丨 gusty, like the wind.

以 丨 無子 thinking how to be no longer childless.

澤 丨 exceedingly, abundant.

佛, 僊, *꜀fo*

From man and *not;* the second ideographic form meaning the *man* of the *west country,* is used only by priests.

To see indistinctly when examining, and thus like the next; to bend down; great; opposed, unreasonable; to turn aside; bright; Budha, which is 丨 度 or 丨 陀 when written in full, in imitation of the Indian word; it is explained by 覺 prescience and intelligence; a Budha is considered by the Chinese to be radically distinct from *shăn* 神 a god or spirit.

丨 敎 Budhism, the sect of Budhists.

丨 法 the laws or doctrines of Budha; Budhist charms and spells; the power of Budha.

丨 國 India; also employed for the sphere of each Budha's influence.

丨 力 the energy of Budha.

丨 祖 or 丨 爺 my lord Budha or old Budha; a term for Gaudama himself as a god.

丨 性 placid, undisturbed, like Budha.

三寶 丨 the three perfect Budhas; they are 釋迦牟尼 Shakyamuni; 阿彌陀 丨 Amida Budha or Amitabha, and explained by 無量壽 the boundless age; and 彌勒尊 丨 the honorable Melih Budha; there are others; the phrase also denotes *Budha, Dharma* and *Sangaya, i. e.* Intelligence, Law, and Union, applied to Budha, the assembly of the faithful, and the priests.

阿彌陀 丨 不要寃屈他 for Budha's sake, don't implicate him, — in which the second name is used as an invocation.

丨 口蛇心 a villainous hypocrite.

激惱 丨 [you are enough] to make even Budha angry.

丨 頭 Budha's head is often applied to prominent hills; the large beads in a rosary which lie on the neck.

我 丨 慈悲 our Budha's kindness.

丨 甲草 the houseleek. (*Sempervivens.*)

丨 眼相看 he has treated him as the apple of his eye.

Read *pih,* and synonymous with 弼 to guide. Great; to help, to support.

丨 時仔肩 to help the throne in bearing its great duties.

彿, *꜀fu*

Like, as if; indistinct.

彷 丨 for example; as it were; resembling.

髴, ˎfu Used for the last; also read *féi*.
Disheveled hair; ornaments on a head-dress; like, nearly.

艴, fo' The countenance changing through anger.
丨然不悅 he turned pale and showed his displeasure.

Read *puh*, Full, flushed.
色丨如也 his face flushed and changed color — as from rage.

怫, ˎfu Like the last.
Sorry; anxious; excited and disappointed.
丨然作色 he changed color from vexation.
丨鬱 disquieted and grieving.
丨而不釋 unable to remove one's anxiety.

刜, ˎfu To chop, to hew; to cut in two; to beat.
丨鐘無聲 he clave the bell without making it sound; *i.e.* great talents make little parade in doing their work.

第, ˎfu The bamboo screen or curtain at the back door of a carriage; to trim an arrow or dart.
簟丨 an ornamented carriage screen, worked out in checkers.

颰, ˎfu A light breeze.
飄風丨丨 the gentle zephyrs now and then come.
惠風丨我 your kindness [has been like] a gentle breeze to me.

咈, fo' To oppose, to refuse; to object to; contrary to.
吁丨哉 Oh no! let it not be so.
罔丨百姓 do not oppose the people's wishes.
從諫弗丨 hear good advice and don't act perversely.
丨其耇長 to oppose the old men and elders.

拂, ˎfu From *hand* and *do not* as the phonetic.
To shake off, to wave to and fro; to brush or push away; to expel; used with the last, to oppose, to contradict; to wipe, to dust; perverse; proud; used for 彿 like; a brush, a duster; a sort of mummer or pantomime, accompanying recitative plays.
丨袖 shook his sleeve — and left.
丨塵 to brush off the dust.
丨拭 to clean and wipe; to make tidy.
丨人性 to thwart people's wishes.
勿丨吾意 don't oppose my plans.
丨蠅 a fly whip.
丨手 a small duster.
互相題丨 mutual aid and countenance; log-rolling.
丨戾 or 丨逆 perverse, mulish.
丨菻 a name for the Roman Empire, supposed to be a transcript of the word πόλιν, or city, applied to Constantinople; the word seems to have been used also for other cities, as 波斯丨菻 in one author denotes Persepolis.

綍, ˎfu From *silk* and *to oppose*; it nearly resembles the next.
The lines which are used to lift or carry the coffins of a grandee, or to drag the bier; a rope; weighty, powerful, applied to the emperor's words.
王言如綸其出如丨 the king's words are like silk thread, but they grow [to be strong] as ropes.

紼, ˎfu Tangled or raveled silk; the tape or cord which sustains a seal; a trace for dragging a bier; to bind on.
丨縴 a cord, a rope.
執丨 to lay hold of the hearse ropes; *i. e.* to attend a funeral.

茀, ˎfu Occurs used for the last and for 福 happiness.
Luxuriant, tangled vegetation that conceals the path; to screen; a vail; a carriage screen; ornaments for the hair; to open, to clear away, as weeds.
丨祿 official income.
臨衝丨丨 he went into battle, lusty and nerved for the strife.
丨草 to remove grass, to pull up the weeds.
婦喪其丨 the woman lost her head coverings.

紱, ˎfu Used for the two last.
A ribbon or tape to hold a seal; a sash.
朱丨方來 the red sashes (*i. e.* the gentry) then came.

犮, 犮, ˎfu From 犬 *dog* and 丿 to *reach*, as a dog who is dragged along; the two forms are now only used in combination as a phonetic or primitive, and the second is the most common.
To prick a dog to make him go.

冹, ˎfu Cold, wintry wind; icy.
一之日滭丨 the icy winds of the eleventh moon.

帗, ˎfu A wand called 丨舞, ornamented or covered with variegated silk, and held by mummers; a handkerchief.
丨縷 fringes on these wands.

祓, fo' From *worship* and a phonetic; occurs used for 茀 happiness.
To remove evil, to deprecate sickness; to disperse or drive off; to cleanse impurity, to wash away; a sort of Budhist baptism employed to obtain blessings.
丨除釁浴 to ward off evil by washing away all sins.
祝丨 to beg for cleansing.
丨飾厥文 remove all ornaments and begin anew; — said in a moral sense.

黻, ˏfu Colored in black and blue stripes, which was one of the symbols anciently embroidered on the lower of the emperor's sacrificial robes; elegant; an embroidered knee-pad or apron.
丨紩 an ornamented skirt.
畫丨 embroidered figures.
丨衣繡裳 his embroidered robe bore the symbol.

韍, ˏfu Like the next.
A knee-pad of leather; a cap or crown used in worship.
璽丨 the strap to secure a signet or seal.

袚, ˏfu A knee-pad, or covering for the shin, used by men; buskins or breeches, anciently worn by the southern tribes.
朱丨 red knee-pads.
丨褲 or 丨膝 garter pads; they are usually of embroidered silk.

FUNG.

Old sounds, pong, p'ong *and* bong. *In Canton*, fung; — *in Swatow*, hong *and* pong; — *in Amoy*, hong; — *in Fuhchau*, hung, hòng, *and* p'ung; — *in Shanghai*, fung *and* vung; — *in Chifu*, fung *and* făng.

風, ˓făng Composed of 凡 *all* and 虫 *insects* or living things, because when the mind moves all things live; it forms the 182d radical of a group of characters relating to storms, winds, &c.; occurs used for 諷 to ridicule.

The wind; a gust, gale, or breeze; air, or as the Chinese define it, "the eructations or gusts of the dual principles, the envoy of heaven and earth;" breath, spirit, in which sense the term 聖丨 has sometimes been used for the Holy Ghost; the voice of; manner, deportment, style; the humors or operations of the body, as influenced by the weather; fashion, example; administration, usage, policy; influence, reformation, instruction; fame, reputation; temper; to effect by example; to enjoy the breeze; function or habit; fleet, swift, as the wind; lust; heat in animals; to scatter, as wind does.
順丨 a fair wind.
逆丨 or 迎丨 or 頂頭丨 a head wind.
由上丨飛至 coming up fast with a fair wind.
鬼頭丨 a strong gust of hot wind.
大丨 a gale, a high wind; a tyfoon, — a word derived from the Cantonese sound of this phrase.
閃山丨 a gust from the hills; a wind squall.
寒丨 a cold wind.
横丨 a side wind.
清丨 a grateful breeze.
涼丨 to take the air; it is also a poetical name for the North wind; as 谷丨 is for the East wind; 凱丨 for the South wind; and 泰丨 for the West wind.
融丨 a northeast wind.
丨聲 the noise of a blast; a rumor; influence; fame.
丨流 gaiety, folly, vice, dissipation.
丨俗 usages, manners of a place.
丨化 effects of the wind; *met.* influence or example.
淫丨 wanton, lascivious, as a courtesan.
民丨 character or usage of a people; national character.
文丨 a literary spirit or fame.
好' 丨月 to love dissipation.
愛丨月 to attract attention, to play seductive wiles.
丨烈得很 irascible, quick tempered, fault-finding.
聞丨而洮 they heard [of Sié Ngan's 謝安] fame and ran; said of a hundred thousand opposing troops.
丨氣 the temper or general feeling, as of a community.
看丨水 to study the aspect of a place, as for geomancy.
丨水先生 one who professes to know the luck of a place or grave.
吹出丨去 to make one declaration, to say it once.
聞丨捉影 to listen to idle rumors and guesses, a newsmonger, a talebearer; to gossip.
耳傍丨 it was a side-ear wind; *i. e.* I did not hear.
頗有丨味 it has a relish; it is well-cooked.
甘拜下丨 I willingly acknowledge your influence.
中丨不語 struck down speechless, as by apoplexy.
傷丨 I have caught a cold; rheumatic pains.
丨濕 damp and chilly, as a room; malarious; rheumatic.
國丨 the ballads of a country.
馬牛丨 the cattle have gone to roam.
或出入丨'議 some go about ridiculing and satirizing others.
丨馬無關 they have nothing to do with each other; *i. e.* the two persons are no more connected than the wind and a horse.
露丨 to expose to the air; *met.* to divulge.
那陣丨兒吹得你來了 what lucky wind blew you here!

丨乎舞雩 to enjoy the breeze among the rustic altars.

接丨酒 to give a feast to greet a friend.

丨言丨語的 to spread idle rumors; a newsmonger.

吹丨 or 颳丨 the wind blows.

丨神 the god of the wind, Æolus; also, the style, bearing, or demeanor of a man.

晨丨 a name for the falcon, alluding to its flight against the wind.

楓 *fʻăng* From *wood* and *wind*.

The maple (*Acer*), of which two or three species are common in northern China; in the southern provinces, it includes the liquidambar; in some places, as in Nganhwui, the plane tree is intended, and also a sort of sycomore; while the tallow tree is sometimes wrongly so called, probably from the likeness of its leaf to the maple; and one Chinese author says the people of Kiangnan thus call any tree with deeply trifid leaves and a balsamic odor.

丨香 the gum of the liquidambar, said to turn into amber in ages.

丨宸 the palace, because an emperor of the Han dynasty planted many maples in his grounds.

丹丨 the maple, alluding to its autumnal leaves.

霜染江丨醉 the plane tree turns red when the hoarfrost dyes the river's banks.

大丨子 lucrabau or chaulmugra seeds of the *Gynocardia odorata*, brought from Siam as a remedy for leprosy and itch.

瘋 *fʻăng* From *disease* and *wind*.

In the south of China, leprosy, scrofula, and their kindred diseases; in the north, where leprosy is uncommon, it signifies insane, deranged; also palsied, paralyzed.

發丨 to exhibit signs of leprosy; leprous.

痳丨 the leprosy.

頭丨 a snapping headache.

丨狗咬了他 a mad dog has bitten him.

丨院 a lazar-house; a lazaretto.

丨癲 or 丨狂 mad, deluded, silly; acting strangely; such a person is called 丨魔 a possessed imp, or 丨子 a maniac.

丰 *fʻăng* The original form was intended to represent a vigorous plant rising above the ground; contracted from 生 to *grow* and 逹 *roots* striking down.

Luxuriant; plump, good-looking, easy; graceful, fine; mellow, as sound.

丨采 graceful, as a dress; plump, fresh.

丨格 an easy carriage, said of men.

丨情瀟灑 very pleasing and animated.

丨姿 or 丨神 fair, handsome; sylph-like, fairy.

子兮丨兮 your fine bearing, Sir.

丨韻 mellow, sweet, as music.

丨茸 luxuriant grass.

丨雅 accomplished, elegant and learned.

妦 *fʻăng* Light and trifling, as the way of a flirt.

夆 *fʻăng* Mutual opposition; to butt, to push, as cattle do; to pull and drag; to meet and clash.

峯 *fʻăng* From *hill* and *opposing*; occurs used for *fung* 犎 the zebu.

The peak or top of a hill; a summit, an apex; the hump on a camel or zebu.

丨巒 ridges and peaks.

高丨 a lofty summit; as 最高丨 a noted hill south of the Yangtsz' River, between Nanking and Chinkiang.

玉丨 a fine green, grassy peak.

孤丨 a solitary lofty height.

鼻丨 a high bridge of the nose.

夏雲多奇丨 what beautiful peaks are seen in the summer clouds!

烽 *fʻăng* From *fire* and *opposing* as the phonetic.

A fire-place of brick of a conical shape to light beacon fires on, so as to notify an enemy's approach.

丨烟 a beacon fire.

燒丨火 light the fire in the beacon.

𥉼 *fʻăng* From 目 *eye* and 縫 *crack* contracted, to describe the malady.

The eyelids drawn together from disease or otherwise, so that they open slightly.

眯丨眼 a sleepy eye.

眼都合丨了 your eyes are blinking and nodding.

蜂 **蠭** *fʻăng* From *insect* and the next character contracted; the first form is the common one.

Insects of the family of *Vespidæ*, as bees, hornets, wasps, sphex, &c.; also large flies similar to them; to swarm, to multiply; to fill the land, said of rebels, who thus, so to speak, sting the state.

蜜丨 a honey bee.

丨王 the queen bee.

馬丨 a gad-fly, a horse-fly.

丨窩 or 丨房 or 丨衙 a bee's nest.

黃丨 a wasp, a hornet.

土丨 a ground or humble-bee.

吳丨 a large blue-bottle fly.

丨針 or 丨蠆 or 丨釘 a wasp's sting.

盜賊丨起 the robbers arose in swarms.

丨媒蝶使 a go-between, a match-maker; the reference is to the bee and butterfly sucking flowers.

丨擁而上 a great crowd gathered; a rabble ran together.

鋒 ˓făng The sharp point of a weapon or tool; a spear, a lance; the tip; bristling, like a line of bayonets; to rise up, as spears; turbulent; the van of a troop.

交丨 to join battle; to attack.

丨鋩 the tip of a spear.

丨刃交加 in the crossing of swords and spears, *i. e.* in actual battle.

前丨 or 先丨 the front, the vanguard.

丨快的刀 a sharp, keen knife or blade.

及丨而試 try when the knife is sharp; *met.* use your powers at their prime.

不合他碰丨 it is not best to hit against the spears; *i. e.* do not run into temptation.

爭丨 bitter strife and rivalry, as for a woman.

同他答答機丨 to try her powers of repartee and conversation.

犎 ˓făng A humped animal of the ox kind, which is perhaps intended for the brahminee bull (*Bos indicus*) or zebu of India.

封 ˓făng Originally composed of 守 to *guard*, and 之 to *go*, with 土 *land* under it, denoting the tenures granted to nobles; others derive it from 圭 a *baton* and 守 to *guard*, referring to the duties of a vassal prince.

The appanage of a lord; a domain, a tenure; to grant a fief to one; to invest a noble with rule over it; to appoint to office; to give a patent of nobility; to seal, to stamp; to press, to taboo, to appropriate for government use; to close, as a letter; to cover or fill, as a crack; boundaries; great; affluent; to enrich; to be avaricious for gain; mercenary; to heap up earth; to raise a tumulus; to get dusty; an envelope; a classifier of letters or things sealed up; the contents of such parcels, a present; occurs used for the last.

一丨信 one letter; 公文一總丨 an envelope containing several inclosures.

一丨銀子 a parcel of money, say 20 or 25 taels.

丨誥 to ennoble an officer's parents; the patents of such a dignity.

丨爵 to confer a rank of nobility.

賞丨 to give a largess; to make a present of money.

丨禁 to prohibit and seal up, as a mine.

丨船 to impress a boat.

門丨 a douceur to a porter.

丨舖 to seal up a shop, as on a failure; which is called 丨鎖, when affixed to a criminal's house; the strips pasted across the door are called 丨皮, and bear the title of the officers; a government seal.

丨神 to deify a person, as is done by the emperor.

丨疆大臣 the high provincial officers.

丨筒 or 丨套 an envelope.

釘ʾ丨 a "nailed-up dispatch," is a secret or important order from government; it is nailed between boards.

丨國 to confer a right to rule over a state, as is now done to Lewchew.

丨建 to establish a fief for one.

丨印開印 to close and open public offices, as at new-year.

丨密 seal it close; glue it tight.

素丨之家 a very rich family.

塵丨舊 old and dirty from dust.

崶 ˓făng A hill with a terrific gorge, (thought to be in Shansi,) on which the great carp ascended, and became a dragon; it is also called 龍門 dragon gate, and frequent allusions to it occur in literary efforts and contests.

葑 ˓făng An old name for a sort of cultivated *Crucifera*, allied to the mustard, and having various names in different places, of which the most common now is 蕪菁; its sprouts, stalks, and roots were successively eaten in the four seasons.

丨非 cheap vegetables; *met.* poor and unavailable; trifling, unworthy.

爰采丨矣 I am going to gather the mustard salad.

豐 ˓făng The character is intended to represent a 豆 *goblet* filled or heaped up with things; it is often contracted to 豊 when used alone, but not correctly.

A large goblet, a full cup; abundant, plenteous, as a crop; copious, affluent; exuberant, fertile, prolific; plenty, the opposite of *k'ien'* 歉 scarcity; rich in talents, property, or friends.

丨年 a plenteous year, when 五穀丨登 the grain fills the granaries, and is copiously piled up.

丨盛 or 丨盈 prosperous, increasing in everything.

丨足 ample, growing rich, well supplied.

丨熟 ripe, full grown, as grain.

丨京 a term for the ancient capital of Wăn Wang, situated near the 丨水, and southerly from the present Si-ngan fu in Shensi.

丨本 a name for garlic.

丨厚 sumptuous, as a feast.

丨人 a fat, portly man.

丨席 a plenteous table.

面貌丨隆 a face with high cheek bones, like Han Kao-tsu the founder of the Han dynasty.

丨隆 is also the god of Thunder.

從丨 to give of the fullness; *i. e.* to make a present, to fork out, to pay the bill.

打抽丨 to scheme how to get a high price or a good return; as to present a peach and get a dollar.

檒 ˓*făng*

From *forest* and *wind* as the phonetic.

The wind swaying the tops of the trees; the maple or plane tree; the noise made by priests when chanting.

僼 ˓*făng*

Fairies, genii, called 偓 丨; a term used by the Taoists for immortals.

澧 ˓*făng*

A stream in the south of Shensi in Hu hien 鄠縣 in Si-ngan fu; it joins the R. Wei on the north, west of the River King.

酆 ˓*făng*

From *city* and *abundant*.

A modern way of writing 豐京 the old capital of Wăn Wang in the present Hu hien in Shensi.

丨都 a district on the Yangtsz' R. in Chung cheu in the east of Sz'ch'uen, where the fire-wells occur; it is used as a term for hell or Tophet, whose entrance is under the 沃焦石 placed there; in it is a 丨都城 the city of Yen-lo wang or Pluto, who is styled 丨都大帝 the great Ruler of Hades.

馮 ˓*făng*

From 馬 *horse* and 冰 *ice* contracted; occurs used for ˓*p'ing* 憑 evidence.

A horse running swiftly.

Read ˓*p'ing*. To mount, to ascend; to boast; to rely on, to trust; dissatisfied; to get over a stream without a boat; evidence, proof.

暴虎丨河 to attack a tiger or cross a river; — a brave reckless fellow would do it.

丨夷 a marine deity, the son of the Yellow Emperor, who drowned himself.

丨丨 the sound of beating walls.

丨氣 boastful, trusting in, as in riches.

渢 ˓*făng*

From *water* and *wind* as the phonetic.

The dashing, rippling sound of waves along the beach.

Read ˓*fan*, in the phrase 丨丨 an easy, gentle sound.

逢 ˓*făng*

From 辵 to *go* and 夆 *opposing*, but some say from 峯 a *peak* contracted.

To meet with one, to come across; to meet unexpectedly; to anticipate, to countenance, to run against; to occur; wide, flowing, as a robe.

丨着 I have just met him.

丨吉 to have good fortune; a turn of good luck.

相丨 the two met; to visit or see one; but 喜相丨 means mutual congratulations on a similar good fortune or promotion.

巧於丨迎 to be very attentive (or sycophantic) to people you meet.

難丨 hard to find; a difficulty in seeing, as a friend.

狹路相丨 we have met in a narrow path, — and which shall yield?

丨人便說 when you meet a man speak to him; he tells it to everybody he meets, as a tattler does.

每丨 whenever; every time; as 每丨三 whenever a third [day] occurs; *i. e.* on the 3d, 13th, and 23d of the moon.

時丨 just now met him (or occurs); it is the time of; seasonable.

丨掖之衣 the flowing robes of literati, such as Confucius wore.

丨君之惡 to meet or countenance a prince in his evil deeds.

Read ˓*păng*. The roll of drums.

鼉鼓丨丨 the lizard skin drums rattled their tattoo.

摓 ˓*făng*

Interchanged with the next.

To sew; to baste; to mend, as a rip.

丨衣服 to make clothes.

縫 ˓*făng* *făng*˒

From *silk* and to *meet*; used with the last.

To sew, to baste, to stitch; to unite, as by a seam.

裁丨 a tailor; to cut or sew clothes.

丨衣 to make clothes.

丨窮的 poor seamstresses who sit in the streets.

丨新 to make new garments.

丨密˓行 to quilt (or hem) finely.

彌丨 to mend or sew as one; *met.* to make up or rectify, as an error or blunder.

丨口 to sew a rent; to join or cover a seam.

丨上幾針 sewed it over several times.

Read *fung*˒ A seam, a crack, a chink, a cleft; a chance, an opportunity.

糊丨子 to paste up cracks.

齊丨 to seam or point, as bricks; to paste or join on another piece; to lengthen the sheet.

錯丨子 a mistake in doing things; a defect in character.

無地丨可鑽 not a place (or crack) where he can hide himself or escape.

綻了丨 the seam is ripped open.

漏丨 to lose; to let slip, as through the fingers.

漨 ˓*făng*

The name of river; a pool, a marsh.

丨浡 harassed, anxious, disturbed.

Read ˓*p'ăng*. The swirling eddies in a stream.

唪 *făng*˒

To recite prayers.

丨經 to chant the litany, as Budhists do the Pali text.

丨丨 very productive, as melons.

Read ˓*păng*. To laugh aloud; a loud voice.

覂 'făng From 襾 to *cover* and 乏 *wanting*; it is nearly synonymous with 泛 to reject; and is used also for 俸 to receive.

To return, to go back against one's wishes; to throw a rider; to be thrown from one's horse.

丨駕之馬 an unmanageable restive horse; disobedient, like fractious children.

捧 'făng From *hand* and to *receive*; similar to 抨 and frequently read 'p'ăng.

To hold up or receive in both hands; to scoop up; to offer, as to a superior; to present a handful; to hold in both hands.

丨讀 to hold [a book], and read it carefully.

一丨東西 a double handful.

雲丨日 clouds embosom the sun.

手丨子 wooden gyves, used like stocks on the feet.

丨着力 hold it firmly.

丨住 grasp it carefully; hold it by the rim.

丨水飲 to drink out of the hands.

奉 făng' Composed of 手 *hand* and 廾 *grasped* together, with 丰 *flourishing* as a phonetic; occurs used for the last.

To receive respectfully, as in both hands; to receive from a superior; to deliver or offer to him; to reverence; to serve, to escort; to praise; respectfully, obediently; to obey, to follow.

丨待 to attend to orders, to carry out commands.

丨養 to take care of one's parents.

丨教 to receive instruction; to become a convert; to enter a sect.

丨承 to receive kindly; to flatter.

丨賀 to congratulate and send presents to one.

丨事 to serve; to wait on.

丨命 to get orders.

丨天承運 intrusted by Heaven with the care of the empire; Mukten is called 丨天 in allusion to this idea.

趨丨君王 to cheerfully receive the prince's orders.

侍丨晨昏 to wait on and help [one's parents] morning and evening.

丨托 to respectfully undertake.

丨行故事 to follow the old custom, to imitate predecessors.

丨劄飭 I have received the despatch ordering me.

丨答天命 to reverently respond to Heaven's behest.

丨候 to go and offer congratulations; to wait to receive a visit.

丨烟丨茶 hand a cup of tea and a pipe.

丨旨 received the will — of the Emperor.

丨上 to present a gift to a superior.

實言丨告 I tell you with the utmost sincerity.

老供丨 I receive just that sum and no more; that is only the wages or salary, no perquisites.

非我一人丨德不康寧 it was not that I the sovereign deemed it to be my prerogative to make you uneasy.

鳳 făng' From 鳥 *bird* and 凡 *all*; *q. d.* the chief of all birds.

A fabulous and felicitous bird; the male of which is so termed, and the female 凰, usually called a phœnix; the type of this bird seems to have been the argus pheasant, which has been gradually embellished and exaggerated; it is poetically applied to the empress as incomparable and happy; the 龍 and 鳳 are referred to in marriage observances as the groom and bride; it often occurs in names of places, flowers, and officers; ornamented with phœnixes; imperial.

丨冠 a bride's coronet with pendents.

鳥中之丨 as the phœnix among birds; *q. d.* the chief, the cynosure, as an emperor.

龍肝丨髓 [like] a dragon's liver and a phœnix's marrow; *i.e.* a great delicacy; a rare dish.

龍丨之姿 an emperor's children.

丨眼 [like] the emperor's eye, a sign of good luck; it has certain striæ on the outer canthus.

俸 făng' From *man* and to *receive*.

Emoluments, salary, stipend; allowance, wages, or income, — usually from the state.

丨祿 or 丨米 salary paid an officer; some of it is paid in rice to military men.

薪丨 an official stipend.

額丨 a fixed salary.

丨修 government allowance.

罰丨 to forfeit the salary.

加丨 to increase the pay.

帶丨歸田 to retire from office on its income.

諷 făng' From *word* and *wind*; *q. d.* repartees are spread abroad by the wind; occurs interchanged with its primitive.

To rehearse or recite in a musical tone, or as when learning a lesson; to speak metaphorically; to satirize; to ridicule; to reprove by parables or inuendo; metaphor, allusion, irony, satire; pasquinade.

丨誦 to chant; to hum over, as a lesson.

譏丨 to ridicule, to quiz, to reflect on, to joke.

丨諫 to reprove, to remonstrate with, as by allusion or satire.

丨語 satire, irony; jokingly.

丨刺 a pointed gibe, a cutting quip.

詞丨 satirical ballads.

賵 făng' From *property* and to *cover*, referring to covering a corpse.

To give aid to a friend in preparing for a funeral, especially a horse and carriage.

丨賻 to give things, as money and clothes, to be interred.

HAI.

Old sounds, ha, hai, ka, gak, gat, *and* kai. *In Canton*, hoi; — *in Swatow*, hai; — *in Amoy*, hai; — *in Fuhchau*, hai; — *in Shanghai*, hé *and* ˊé; — *in Chifu*, hai.

咍 ˏhai From *mouth* and *pleased;* it is also read ˏsi, *hi*ˀ and *tai*.

A noise of laughing and joking; one says, the speechless terror of fright; to smile at; used also as an exclamation of astonishment.

孩 ˏhai From *son* and a horary character, or more likely the next contracted.

A child beginning to smile, children that need to be carried; a child; a youth, especially a boy; tender, just born.

嬰丨 a male infant, a baby lately born.

丨子 or 小丨子 children, bairns.

丨兒見識 he has no more wisdom than a child.

丨提之童 young children; babies in arms.

丨兒兵 a group of children playing boisterously.

丨兒面 a child's face, — a fancy name for the mowtan flower.

無殺丨蟲 don't kill newly hatched insects.

咳 ˏhai Like the last, but it is now usually read *k'oh*, a synonym of 欬 to cough.

A smile or prattle of a child.

丨嬰 a laughing infant, when it begins to return a parent's caress.

頦 ˏhai ˏk'ö From *head* and a *horary* character; also read *k'oh*.

The bones of the chin; to hold by the chin or neck, as an infant is dandled; under the chin.

手承丨 resting the chin on the hand.

丨皮 a furrier's name for pelage on the neck.

丨頷 or 丨頰 the chin, also called 頰巴丨子 in colloquial.

腨 ˏhai Tall and thin.

躴丨 a gaunt, lank man.

趩 ˏhai From to *go* and a *mite*.

Ready to start, and yet inclined to remain; uncertain about starting.

海 ˊhai From 水 *water* and 晦 *obscure* contracted.

The sea, *i. e.* nature's pool, which is the receptacle of all streams with their silt, — referring chiefly to the Yellow Sea; an arm of the ocean; a large river; marine, capacious; vast, as an encyclopædia; great, oceanic; that which comes from the sea; maritime; an expanse, as a desert; in *anatomy*, some spaces in the body.

四丨 the four seas, or 丨內 within the seas, old phrases for China, — now vaguely used for it alone, and for all the world too; no specific bodies of water were intended, for the outer borders of China were thought to reach the utmost seas on all sides; the phrase 四丨 often means free, at large, unconfined; great, big, vast; everywhere.

出去遊逛就四丨了 if we take a ramble, we shall be refreshed greatly.

人很四丨的 a clever, pleasant and good-looking man.

出丨 or 上丨 to voyage by sea; to travel.

丨賊 or 丨盜 pirate

丨邊 the sea-side.

丨外奇談 that strange story is from beyond the seas; a great exaggeration.

丨味 marine delicacies.

丨龍王 the Dragon Sea King, the Chinese Neptune.

丨量 he is able to drink a sea of wine.

過丨 over the seas; at *Canton*, it means to cross the river.

福如東丨 may your happiness be like the eastern sea.

丨巡 to watch against smugglers; to patrol the coasts.

丨角天涯 far off, remote regions; to the ends of the earth.

丨說 a long yarn, a sea-story.

丨蛇 sea-serpents; a sea-blubber like the Medusa is sometimes so called.

誇丨口 to talk grandly, to vapor and brag.

丨碗 a very big platter.

出外丨 gone over the seas.

西丨 sometimes refers to Kokonor, at others to the Aral or Caspian seas, and even to Lake Baikal.

丨市 a mirage; any strange unreal sight; imaginative.

苦丨 the bitter sea — of life; — a Budhist term for the world; as 生死大丨 the great sea of life and death (*Sangsara*), means mortal life subject to change.

丨澄公 the Duke who cleared the seas; — the title of Koxinga's lineal descendant.

陸丨 the arable rich regions; *i. e.* China.

In *Pekingese.* Fully, altogether; wildly, at random, all at sea.

院丨墁磚 the court was all paved.

跑丨車 a cart that goes anywhere for custom, or has no regular stand.

丨拏 to seize loosely; having no clue or order to arrest anybody.

盍 *ʿhai* A wine jar, 酒丨shaped like a gallipot, made of earthen or pewter; and containing 50 to 100 catties; an amphora.

榼 *ʿhai* Correct form of the last.

A wooden tub for holding spirits.

酒丨(also wrongly written 酒海) containing a hundred catties or more.

醢 *ʿhai* From *spirits* and a *jar*.

Minced and pickled meat, of crabs, fowls, fish, insects; &c.; to cut fine and put into brine with seasoning; the brine or pickle of these sauces or condiments; to simmer.

丨醬 pickled sauce or hash.

斲爲肉丨 may you be cut into hashed meat!

丨蝦 pickled crabs or shrimps.

毋歠丨 don't suck up the brine.

烹丨 or 煠丨 to fry hashed meat.

垓 *hai*ʾ Also written like the next.

To raise up.

豎丨 name of the god whom the Great Yü ordered to plan what land was to appear from the deluge.

亥 *hai*ʾ This ancient character is said to be made of *man* 人 above and 女 *woman* below, or of 二 *two* placed above 二 *two* below.

The last of the twelve branches, answering to the 猪 boar; it pertains to water, and denotes North on the compass-card.

丨月 the tenth moon.

巳丨一冲 *sz'* and *hai* countervail each other; — people born in those years may not wed.

丨年 are five years in the cycle (the 12th, 24th, 36th, 48th, and 60th, all referred to the boar,) which contain this branch.

丨時 the hour from 9 to 11 o'clock P. M.; 正丨 is 10 o'clock, and 交丨 is 9 o'clock.

丨市 a fair held late in the evening.

魯魚丨豕以己爲誰 [he mistakes characters, confounding] *lu* for *yü*, and *hai* for *shi*, and hardly knows who he is himself.

害 *hai*ʾ Composed of 宀 a *shelter* and 口 *mouth*, with 丰 between; another old form is composed of 宀 a *covering* and 炙 to *burn*.

To injure, to hurt, to prejudice; to receive injury; to offend; to damage; injurious, hurtful, calamitous; fearful of, anxious about, a sense or fear of, — for which the next is more correct; a dread produced by calamity; envious of; before a verb, becomes an adverb of intensity.

丨怕 much scared, terrified.

丨怕冷 excessively cold.

丨處因貪其利 these calamities have come on him because of his greed for gain.

那賊來燒得利丨 those robbers have burned a great deal.

丨病 taken very sick; he is dangerously sick.

傷丨 to injure and wound.

不丨羞 cares for nothing, brazen-faced.

丨人即丨己 you will only injure yourself by wronging others.

丨羞 entirely disgraced; sensitive to shame.

殺丨 or 戕丨 to injure deeply, to destroy property or wound.

殘丨 to injure recklessly.

有丨無丨 is it dangerous or not? — as opium smoking.

水丨 injury from water.

除丨 to remove danger or evil.

爲丨不淺 it has sustained no slight damage.

丨盈福謙 [the gods] bring down the arrogant and bless the humble.

心丨其能 envious of his power.

王其罔丨 the king will not be injured.

利已丨人 to benefit one's self at another's expense or injury.

要丨之地 important places, spots that need to be guarded; it is also read *hoh*, in this sense.

Read *hoh*, Who? why?

丨澣丨否 shall it be washed or not.

㤥 *hai*ʾ Sorrowful; depressed by fear of a worse illness.

丨病 I am afraid I am going to be sick.

丨眼 I think my eyes will be ailing.

妎 *hai*ʾ Envy; injurious jealousies, which it is said did not exist in primitive times; to suppress, to conceal, as envy.

髂 *hai*ʾ Bones.

髐骨丨 an ingrate, one who has no sense of gratitude or right.

嗐 *hai*ʾ An exclamation of regret or startling surprise.

丨可惜了 what a pity! Oh! how sad.

丨呀 Alack! oh! haiya! an exclamation which is written in many ways.

Read *hiah*, To gape, to open the mouth.

HAN.

Old sounds, han, ham, kam, kan, gan, *and* gam. *In Canton*, hon, hòm, *and* ham ; — *in Swatow*, ham, k'am, han, kwⁿa, *and* wⁿa ; — *in Amoy*, ham *and* han ; — *in Fuhchau*, hang, ; — *in Shanghai*, hėⁿ, yėⁿ, hėⁿ, hōⁿ *and* 'ōⁿ ; — *in Chifu*, han.

酣 ˏhan From *spirits* and *sweet*.
Exhilirated, merry, as from drink; jolly, tipsy; jocund, riant, as a landscape; deep, as sleep; fearless, determined, as a soldier.
丨暢 cheerful, excited; delightful, as a view; lively, as a style.
酒半丨 elevated, happy from a little drink.
丨歌 drinking and singing.
丨睡 a deep, sweet sleep.

蚶 魽 ˏhan From *insect* or *fish*, and *sweet*, alluding to its taste; the first form is commonest.
Bivalve shells with scolloped surfaces, crenulated or ribbed like the *Arca* or *Pecten*, are called 蝸丨; the spacies are numerous on this coast, the great *Chama* is one; one name for the common Arca is 瓦屋子 from its resemblance to Chinese tiling.

邯 ˏhan The district city of 丨鄲 in Kwang-ping fu in the south of Chihli, so called because it is said that the hilly country of Shantung ends there; it was the capital of the feudal state of Chao 趙 in the Cheu dynasty; abundant; the name of a river.

歛 ˏhan From *to sigh* and the *whole*; it differs from *lien* 斂 to enshroud.
To desire; to ask for a thing playfully; to pretend to beg.

憨 ˏhan From *heart* and to *presume*; one also reads it *hien'* meaning obstinate.
Foolish, silly; having the look and manner of an imbecile person.
丨癡 half idiotic; harebrained.
丨頭郎 a crazy loon, a half-cracked fellow.
半丨子 a half-witted chap.

顄 ˏhan A large face.
丨頟 bald-headed; a smooth pate.

鼾 ˏhan From *nose* and *shield*.
To snore.
鼻丨 or 丨齁 to snore.
臥榻之下豈容他人丨息 am I going to quietly let another man snore under my bed? — said by Tao-kwang in reference to foreigners' demands.

欿 ˏhan To smile under restraint; a suppressed laugh or smile; to desire.
丨笑 a forced laugh.

甗 ˏhan A water jar with ears by which to carry it.
丨空 a drain, a spout.
溝丨子 drain-pipes which fit into each other.
水丨 a water sluice, a flume, an aqueduct.

谽 ˏhan A wide opening; an adit.
丨谺 the mouth, as of a valley or cave; a wide and deep cavity.

含 ˏhan From *mouth* and *now* above it.
To hold something in the mouth the mouth; full; to contain, to embody; to cherish; to suffer, to tolerate, to put up with; to restrain; to put a gem or coin in a corpse's mouth.
丨容 or 丨忍 to be patient towards; to bear with, as a wayward scholar.
丨笑 to smile; whence the fragrant *Magnolia fuscata*, the 丨笑花 gets its name.
丨筆使鋒正 to suck or lick a pencil to a sharp point.
丨羞 to blush, to be ashamed.
包丨 to contain in; inclosed in; to be lenient, to endure wrong; magnanimous; to quell, as one's temper.
丨怒 to restrain the anger.
丨記 to bear in mind.
丨丨 or 丨糊 muttering, indistinct, reticent.
海丨 to bear with, to forgive.
丨垢忍辱 to patiently bear insult and obloquy.
丨德 to maintain one's principles.
丨弘光大 the vast and glorious canopy that embraces all.
阿丨 or 丨 alone, a Budhist term for *agama*, or four kinds of writings on minor subjects of philosophy.
嘴裏丨着 to hold in the mouth, as a sugar-plum.
丨淚 to restrain the tears.
丨混 or 丨糊 half asleep about a thing; careless as to how it is done; slovenly; immaterial, anyhow.
丨蓄 to smother one's resentments.

In *Pekingese*. Disgraceful.
丨碜 (or 丨塵) bad looking, incongruous, reproachful; to mortify, to cause disgrace.

In *Fuhchau*. Incomplete, confused; shabbily; to close, to shut to only partially; to cover, as a fire with ashes.

鋡 ˏhan A press or closet; armor.
丨甲 mail armor, for making which the 丨人, armorers or artisans of Yen 燕 or Chihli were celebrated of old.

函 函 函 ˓han — Said to be composed of 人 *man* and 臼 a *mortar*; it occurs used for the last; the first and unusual form is supposed to represent the space under the tongue, or the tongue lolling or thrust out; the third form much resembles *kih* 亟 extreme.

To infold, to contain, to envelop; to comprehend; what is contained in an envelope or a cover, such as enwraps Chinese books; a letter; a press; armor; liberal, capacious.

信丨 or 書丨 letters; a letter.

瑤丨 or 尊丨 or 吉丨 your valued favor.

華丨 an epistle.

丨人 an armorer, one who makes 丨甲 the mail plates; the preceding is also used for this sense.

丨容 patiently; generous, forbearing.

丨稱 declared in the letter; the dispatch says . . . .

丨丈之下 I who am your pupil, *i.e.* your obedient servant; derived from 丨丈 the name given to a teacher's table.

專丨 a letter written for a special purpose.

丨托 to request a favor by letter.

實丨斯活 the seeds held their vitality in them.

丨之如海 covered it like the sea.

丨谷關 a retired spot near the present Ling-pao hien 靈寶縣 in the northwest of Honan, where Laotsz' wrote his Taoteh King.

腦 頣 ˓han — The later form of the preceding, denoting the chin, or the space directly under the mouth.

涵 ˓han — From *water* and *contain*; occurs used for its primitive.

Water coming into a boat; to submerge; to steep, to soak; to contain; vast, capacious; to leak; marshy.

丨養 to keep one's temper; to cherish, as virtue; kindly, patient.

波浪丨天 the boisterous waves go as high as the sky.

丨沉 submerged, sunk.

丨洞 a sluice, a waste-weir, a draining channel.

海丨 indulgent, very ready to forgive.

椷 ˓han — A wooden bowl or trencher to hold liquids; a casket; a case; one defines it to plant trees.

裲 ˓han — A sleeve; a cloth to stuff the ear.

丨祿 a long sleeve.

邗 ˓han — Name of an ancient place, 丨溝 in the state of Wu 吳, now Kao-yiu cheu 高郵州 near Yang-cheu fu on the Grand Canal in Kiangsu, where was a canal; another name for the state of Yueh 越, lying south towards Hangcheu.

丨江 is a river near it, which is now applied to Chinkiang fu on the Yangtsz' R.

寒 ˓han — From 宀 a *shelter* and 人 *man* under it among 艸 *plants*.

Cold, wintry; shivering; chilled; simple, plain; poor, unsupplied, necessitous; a depreciating term for my, mine; discouraged.

丨冷 shivering with cold.

嚴丨 excessively cold.

一丨一暑 now cold and then warm.

丨素 plain, unpretending, not showy.

打丨戰 struck through with the cold.

傷丨 or 傷丨病 to take cold, sick with a cold.

丨涼藥 cooling medicines.

丨舍 or 丨門 my house, my family.

丨窓誦讀 to study hard in school.

丨族 our clan, our sept.

饑丨 very cold and starved; destitute, poor.

時丨 periodic colds or cattarhs.

丨苦人家的 a miserable wretch, a poor fellow.

膽丨 or 丨心 disheartened; to strike with fear.

丨儒 or 丨士 a poor scholar.

孤丨 alone, no relatives, without friends.

丨温 cold and warm; adversity and success.

丨食節 the first two or three days before Tsing-ming term, when cold provisions, called 丨具, are eaten while worshiping ancestors; an old custom.

韓 ˓han — A fence or wall around a lot; the star ζ in Ophiucus; a small ancient feudal state which existed from B. C. 403 to 273, occupying the north of Honan and south of Shensi; Ping-yang fu was the capital at the first, and was finally moved to Yangteh near K'ai-fung fu; only nine princes are named, the first of whom, King Heu 景侯, had been really the ruler of Tsin 晉 for years; the last three were styled *wang*.

丨范之勳 the valorous fame of Han Sin and Fan Tsăng, — two generals of the Han dynasty.

㰹 㶰 ˓han — A particle implying doubt, used by people in Honan; a *conjunction*, if, perhaps; uncertain.

丨糊不定 perhaps it is so; this phrase is more correctly written 含糊不定 at present.

暵 ˓han — From 日 *sun* and 漢 the *galaxy* contracted; interchanged with 熯 to roast.

Dry, heated air; to dry; to plow dry fields; parched, as by drought; crisp.

丨其乾矣 parched (or heated) it to dryness.

農夫耐丨而耘 the farmer must still weed even if it be hot.

罕 ʿhan From 网 a *net* and 干 a *shield*.

A net for birds; a snare for rabbits; rare, few, scarce, seldom, infrequent.

丨見 or 看希丨 rarely seen; seldom observed.

丨有 it is rare, as a fruit.

丨規 a strange peculiar custom.

叔發丨忌 few could rival Shuh in archery.

雲丨 a kind of ornamental flag.

丨車 eight stars in Hydra.

物以丨而見珍 whatever is rare is regarded as precious, or like a pearl.

頷 ʿhan From *head* and *to contain*.

To hold in the mouth, as a plum; the jaws, the chops,—likened, when sharp, to a 燕丨 swallow's chin; to contain; to hold down or shake the head; sallow, as from hunger.

頤丨 or 顒丨 the chin or chops, the under jaw; the last phrase also means to hold in the mouth.

丨下珠 [as hard to get as] the pearl under [a dragon's] chin.

下丨尖 a sharp or peaked jowl.

喊 ʿhan From *mouth* and *all*.

To call after, to vociferate, to halloo or bawl after; an angry scream, the noise of angry or loud calling; a call, a cry.

丨呼 to loudly cry to or call after one.

丨寃 to implore redress; to exclaim against wrongs.

丨救 to call on to rescue, to cry for help.

丨苦 bitter wailing.

丨殺連天 the din and clamor reached to heaven.

丨叫 the noise of pain or anger; crying out.

䦧 ʿ**闞** ʿhan This is most frequently written like the second, but the first form is more consonant to the meaning.

An angry growl of a beast, such as an irritated tiger makes; loud, angry voices.

丨如虓虎 looking as savage as a mad tiger.

焊 ʿhan From *plant*, *fire* and *drought*, as if to indicate its pungency.

A wild flower, found in Kiangsi, the 丨菜 or 辣米子, so called from its pungent taste; it is a Crucifera, resembling the cress, and is sometimes pickled as a condiment; this character is also applied to the nasturtium (*Tropæolum*).

菡 ʿhan From *plant* and *to contain*.

A flower not opened; the buds of the lotus, Hibiscus, and sweet flag, are all called 丨萏 as a poetical name.

依于丨萏 it swam by the opening lotuses.

漢 han' From 水 *water* and 難 *hardship* contracted.

The milky way; the large branch of the Yangtsz' River which joins it at 丨口 Hankow; a Chinese; relating to China; a fine fellow, a man in a good sense, and rather in commendation; and by synecdoche, used for form, stature, personal appearance.

好丨子 or 好丨相 a gentlemanly man, a fine fellow; lusty, stout.

大丨 a very tall man.

老丨 I, an old man; this old man.

好丨 a brave fellow, a chieftain; superior to 丨子 a rustic; a brave boaster, a bully.

丨人 a native of China; this use is most general north of the Yangtsz' River, and indicates that the person is not a Bannerman.

丨朝 the Han dynasty, which existed from B. C. 206 to A. D. 220, so called from its founder 丨公 Duke of Han; it was termed 東丨 the Eastern Han, after A. D. 25, when the capital was removed to Loh-yang; there were twelve sovereigns in each division, and two usurpers.

後丨朝 the After Han dynasty existed from A. D. 221 to 264, under two rulers; another of this name existed four years, A. D. 947 to 951, under two rulers.

丨滿 Chinese and Manchus.

丨軍 the naturalized Banner Force, *i.e.* Chinese incorporated under the eight Banners.

丨文 the Chinese language or characters.

壯丨 brave, robust, strong, lusty.

天丨 or 雲丨 or 銀丨 the Milky Way.

莊稼丨 a farmer, a peasant, a farm-hand.

熯 han' Also read *jen*, and interchanged with 暵 heated.

To roast, to dry over a fire; drying; to respect; exhausted, dried up.

莫丨乎火 nothing is more drying than fire.

我孔丨矣 I am exceedingly wearied out.

暵 han' Ploughed fields where wheat is sown.

旱 han' From *sun* and *shield*; not the same as *kan*' 旰 sunset.

Dry weather, drought; rainless; a sunny sky; to travel by land.

天丨 dry weather

丨天多雨勢 in drought it often looks like rain.

歲丨 a year of drought.

你丨路來 did you come by land?

丨雷 thunder without rain.

走丨 to take to the road, as after a voyage.

丨潦不收 neither in very dry or very wet seasons, will there be good crops.

丨歉米如珠 in droughts, rice is counted as pearls.

丨道兒 only a road — to get there, intimating that there is no way by water.

丨厘斤 what belongs to land tax, in distinction from the water-borne, as the imposts levied at the road douanes.

丨烟 native tobacco, such as is smoked in pipes, and not in hookahs.

垾 *han'* A small bank raised to protect a field; it is also regarded as a wrong form of *ngan'* 岸 a shore.

悍 *han'* From *heart* and *dry* as the phonetic.

Ardent; an energetic temperament; cruel, ruthless, violent; fearless; hasty, choleric.

丨急 fierce and rash; testy.

强丨 overbearing, imperious.

兇丨 irascible, passionate and violent.

丨婦 a virago, a Xanthippe.

睅 *han'* Protuberant eyes, such as near-sighted people often have.

丨其目 his large goggle eyes.

釬 銲 *han'* From *metal* and *shield* or *dry* as the phonetic; the second form is seldom seen.

Greaves; something to protect the arms of archers; to solder metals; hasty, too quick.

丨口 or 打丨 or 丨住 to solder.

丨料 or 丨藥 or 丨口錫 solder, the alloy used in soldering.

丨上他 solder it on — or together.

䩱 *han'* Leather coverings put over the sleeves when practicing archery.

駻 *han'* A vicious horse that bolts and shies; a horse six feet high; to rule a hasty tempered people with lax government, is like 無轡策御丨馬 driving and whipping a vicious horse without any bridle — to curb him.

捍 *han'* To grasp, to lift; to ward off, to defend; to move; to stop; to forbid.

丨禦 to watch against.

能丨大患則祀之 he who can prevent serious calamity should be sacrificed to — at the spring and autumn worship.

扞 *han'* From *hand* and *shield;* it is interchanged with the last.

To fend off with the hand; to guard, to escort; to defend, to desist; to environ; an obstacle, a hindrance, a shield.

丨衛 to set a guard around, to protect.

丨堅 strongly guarded.

丨關 to guard a pass; to keep a post.

丨格 an obstacle; impeded; to obstruct.

丨格不入 conflicting, irreconcileable, as ideas.

手丨 to defend with the hand.

丨禁 to prohibit.

汗 *han'* From *water* and *shield;* to be distinguished from *ₑwu* 汙 a pool; occurs used for the next.

Sweat, perspiration; long, as an expanse of water; bright; trouble, labor, which causes one to perspire.

心丨濁 a guileful heart; *lit.* one whose heart's sweat is dirty.

丨顏 to feel ashamed.

出丨 to perspire.

洗丨澡 to take a sweat bath — over a hot fire.

氣丨水 condensed steam.

發丨 produces sweat; as a 發丨藥 or sudorific.

丨衫 an undershirt; a shirt; a chemise.

丨瘢 white streaks in the skin, thought to be caused by obstructed perspiration.

丨馬功勞 toil and hardship in the wars.

無丨的 obtained without any trouble.

令無反丨 the orders cannot be rescinded, — as the sweat cannot reënter the skin.

香丨如珠 the fragrant sweat stood like pearls upon her.

丨丨 or 瀾丨 a vast expanse of ocean.

澔丨 the dazzling effect of colors; bright, dazzling.

盜丨 night sweats; much the same as 自丨 or involuntary sweating.

可丨 denotes a *khan*, or Tartar lord, in imitation of the Persian word.

丨海 the Desert of Shamo, for which the next character is more correct.

瀚 *han'* The northern sea, but now applied to that part of Gobi, the most arid and barren, which lies northwest of Kansuh, the 丨海, from its resembling a sea.

丨海石 petrified or silicified wood brought from the Desert.

波濤浩丨 the vast and boundless raging ocean.

閈 *han'* The gate of a village; a ward or street gate; a neighborhood; a wall, or what it incloses; to shut.

同丨 of the same village.

里丨 a village, hamlet, or town, which has a gate.

高其丨閎 he raised his gate very high.

諴 *han'* From *words* and *affected.*

Angry words.

詩 丨 indistinct words.

唅 *han'* Similar to 含 to containt

A grunt, a mere sound; to put something in the mouth.

哺 丨 to feed by hand, as a babe.

羹藜 丨 糗 to make a soup of weeds and eat broken rice.

豃 *han'* A hog running away.

豕 丨 則難獲 when the hogs run off, they are not easily caught.

矸 *han'* A stony hill with clean, bare rocks.

丨 白玉 white marble.

丹 丨 cinnabar, as in pills.

Read *˛kan.* To strike.

犴 豻 *han'* From *dog* and *shield,* because it guards from evil and foes.

A sort of black feline beast found on the confines of the Desert; it is described as a monstrous, terrific beast, scaly, and producing one horn in its old age. Some accounts ally it to the Tibetan mastiff, but the Pǎn Tsao makes it a synonym of the 貊 or Malacca tapir, to which, or the rhinoceros, it should probably be referred.

Read *ngan'* A village jail in ancient times.

丨 獄 a prison.

由不平以立繫丨 when people are discontented, it is necessary to open the jails.

皯 *han'* Black or dark spots on the face or head, thought to be caused by bad blood.

翰 *han'* From *feathers* and the *dawning light.*

A fabulous bird like a pheasant, with red plumage, which was brought to Chʻing wang of Cheu, B.C. 1110; to fly high; trunk or stem of a plant; a prop; a pencil; a plume or quill to write or draw with; writings; white; protracted.

丨 書 written with your hand.

華 丨 your esteemed letter.

丨 筆 a pencil; Chinese pencils.

丨 墨香 literary reputation; one who has become an Academician.

詞 丨 to write out a fine distich for hanging up.

點 丨 to be chosen an Academician.

丨 音 a cock; *i. e.* the bird which sounds among the stems.

文 丨 a good style; a learned classical expression.

維周之丨 [Duke Cheu] was the safeguard of the Cheu family.

丨 林院 the Pencil Forest office, or National Academy; the members are allowed to put up a tablet over their doors with 太史第 on it; when brothers reach this honor, they write 兄弟丨林; the first wrangler writes 狀元 the first, the coryphæus; the second 榜眼 eye of the list; the third 探花 he who has picked the [apricot] flower; and the fourth 傳臚 the one who makes known the series, as this man is designated to call off the names of the graduates.

鶾 *han'* A pheasant called 白丨 or 白翰, which seems to be only another name for the 白鷴 or silver pheasant (*Nyctopteron;*) it is also called 白雉 or white pheasant.

憾 *han'* From *heart* and *emotion.*

To feel hatred or remorse; mortified with one's self; moved to sorrow or vexation; to be dissatisfied at, to murmur at; vexed, as at a disappointment; resentful, regretful.

丨 恨 deep remorse.

無 丨 placid, forgiving.

抱 丨 終身 he regretted it all through life.

死而無丨 if I die, I would have nothing to regret.

人猶有所丨 all have something to be vexed at.

撼 *han'* To move, as waves do the stones; to brandish a thing at another; to surge against; shaking, trembling.

搖 丨 to be driven against; shaken by.

丨 風 the wind moves it.

丨 振人心 it startles people greatly.

丨 動 to shake, to make to quiver.

丨 山易丨岳家軍難 to move a mountain is easier than to repel the armies of Yoh Féi — of the Sung dynasty.

琀 *han'* Gems or other things put into the mouth of a corpse in former times; the usage is still continued, and is called 釘口 nailing the mouth — by a bit of silver.

厂 *han'* Intended to represent an overhanging cliff; it is now used only as the 27th radical of many characters referring to shelter, and is interchanged with 广 in some of them.

A cliff which projects; a stone on a hill-side, under which men can dig out a residence.

HĂN.

Old sounds, hăn *and* găn. *In Canton*, hăn ; — *in Swatow*, hun, kùn, *and* hùn ; — *in Amoy*, hun ; — *in Fuhchau*, haung, héng, *and* hong ; — *in Shanghai*, 'ng *and* hăng ; — *in Chifu*, hăn.

哏 *˛kăn* The noise of people quarreling; loud, angry tones and words.

痕 *˛hăn* From *disease* and *perverse*.

A scar, a cicatrix; a mark, a stain, a trace left; a flaw, as in glass; a crack, as in crockery.

淚 〡 traces of tears.

水 〡 stains from liquids as on clothes; traces of the action of water; marks or water lines, as in paper.

雨跡添來隔宿 〡 the traces of last night's rain are seen [upon these flowers] in their stains.

〡 跡 a trace of, as a footstep; a seam, as in glass.

露 〡 跡 the secret is out, the evidence is seen.

波 〡 gentle ripples.

瘢 〡 and 傷 〡 a scar, as of a wound; a pit, as from small-pox.

苔 〡 上 堦 綠 the moss grows green upon my steps; *i. e.* I prefer to retain my privacy.

In *Cantonese*. To itch; an itching.

好 〡 it itches much; very irritable, as a sore.

拫 *˛hăn* To pull along quickly, to drag; to forcibly place in order, to jerk into position; to stop another.

〡 挌 to turn out, to eject, to drag out.

〡 抑 to keep down, as a lot of feathers from blowing away.

引 繩 排 〡 to prevent people passing by stretching a rope across the way.

很 *˛hăn* From a *step* and *perverse*; this and the next are nearly synonymous.

Disobedient, sulky, refractory; stern, harsh; indisposed to listen to reason; quarrelsome; intractable, like a goat dragged by the horns; revengeful; a sign of the superlative; grievous, painful.

好' 勇 鬭 〡 fond of quarreling and fighting

〡 心 harsh; quarrelsome.

發 〡 to get angry; to became very wrathy.

〡 得 〡 dreadfully overbearing.

好 得 〡 exceedingly good.

〡 㥯 然 fine, new, splendid; elated, very happy.

In *Fuhchau*. To scowl, to look at angrily.

狠 *˛hăn* From *dog* and *perverse*; it is used with the last, and also read *˛wan*.

Dogs quarreling and snarling; turning on one when struck; desperate, out of all reason; to gnaw; a sign of the superlative; still more.

多 得 〡 very many; a multitude.

〡 是 very right.

賭 〡 empty threats.

〡 歪 very crooked.

不 怕 〡 I am not afraid of him.

〡 大 too large.

厥 心 疾 〡 his mind became frenzied.

恨 *hăn'* From *heart* and *perverse*.

Hatred, spite; indignation, dislike, resentment; regret, sorrow; vexed, sorry; to hate, to feel resentment; to bear malice against; to feel annoyed or reproached at one's conduct.

悔 〡 deep remorse; to bitterly regret.

〡 不 得 to desire greatly; would that! O for!

可 〡 detestable, odious; like 〡 極 very odious; it also means to hate greatly.

雪 〡 or 出 我 心 頭 之 〡 to wreak one's spite, to gratify one's revenge.

〡 怒 to hate, to be angry at.

惹 得 人 〡 to get people's ill-will; generally shunned.

遺 〡 or 〡 不 了 he could not finish or forget his hatred; unappeased; I regret my ill-luck.

〡 視 to look at angrily.

怨 〡 to bear a grudge against.

懷 〡 to cherish malice towards.

〡 世 人 不 肯 回 頭 [Kwanyin] hates men if they do not reform their ways.

長 〡 歌 the song of [Minghwang's] lasting resentment — at the death of Yang Kwéi-féi, in the T'ang dynasty.

抱 〡 終 身 cherished his hatred all his life.

無 人 〡 no one regrets him (*Cantonese*); elsewhere it means no one cares much for him any way.

HANG.

Old sounds, hung, kung, *and* gung. *In Canton,* hong ; — *in Swatow,* hang ; — *in Amoy,* hong *and* k'ong ; — *in Fuhchau,* hòng ; — *in Shanghai,* hong ; — *in Chifu,* hang.

碚 ꜀hang The rumbling noise of stones is 丨磅, as when they are rolling down; another says, to pave with stones; often used for 夯 as the verb, to ram down the earth; to drive piles.

丨歌 the cry of workmen driving piles.

狰 ꜀hang A sullen dog.

獬丨 a mulish dog which lies down and refuses to be led.

杭 ꜀hang A square boat or scow, for which the next is now used; to cross a stream.

丨州府 the capital of Chehkiang, and the metropolis of China during all the Southern Sung dynasty from A.D. 1127 to 1260; applied to goods brought from the province.

丨綢 Chehkiang silks.

天丨 the Milky Way.

一葦丨之 crossed the river on a bundle of reeds.

航 ꜀hang A square boat or two lashed together; a scow used at ferries and in floating bridges; to sail, to navigate.

採蓮丨 to pluck lilies in the boats; — to love dissipation.

普渡慈丨 all pass over in the merciful barge [to heaven,] — refers to the vessel in which Kwanyin carries souls to rest; it may allude originally to the Ark.

乘丨 to sail in a large boat, as the hong-boats at Canton.

梯山丨海 to scale hills and cross seas; — to travel.

趁丨船 or 搭丨船 to go in a passenger-boat.

衖 ꜀hang An old name 丨衖 for musicians; it has now become obsolete.

閤 ꜀hang To open a door; fragrance.

有丨無色有色無丨 fragrant flowers frequently have no beauty, and the finest flowers are scentless.

頏 ꜀hang From *head* and a *vertebra* of the neck; also read *hang'* and written with the radical 羽 *wings.*

To fly down.

頡丨 birds flying about, now down and then up.

Read ꜀*kang.* A man's name; the neck of a bird or of a man.

迒 ꜀hang The foot-tracks of a hare or other animal; the rut of a wheel; the path made by animals.

車丨 a rut; wheel-tracks.

筕 ꜀hang A coarse mat, called 丨篖, made of bamboo splints, to spread on the ground.

夯 頏 ꜀hang From *great* and *strength;* the second form is but little used.

The noise made in carrying burdens; to strain in lifting a weight; to pound earth, as when settling a foundation; a beater.

丨子 a beetle used to drive piles.

丨性 an obstinate temper.

打丨 to ram the ground firm for laying a wall.

丨藥 to pound gunpowder; also a name for a certain kind of powder.

骯 ꜂ang Fat; stiff, straight.

丨眞 right, sincere.

丨髒 noisome, dirty, filthy, as the sight of old bones decaying.

吭 hang꜄ Interchanged with 頏 the neck.

The gullet of a bird; the throat; to gulp down; an important pass in a country.

珠丨 a sweet melody, a bird's song.

鳥弄丨 the bird is trying its throat; — *i.e.* singing.

沆 hang꜄ Mist or fog rising from the sea; a vast expanse of water; to cross the waters.

莽丨 running water; like a vast stagnant pool.

丨瀁 deep and vast, as a great lake.

丨茫 a marshy waste, where the plants hide the water.

丨瀣 a dry smoky mist which is seen at night.

笐 統 hang꜄ Bamboo poles on which clothes are hung; a row of bamboos; a rude fiddle, made by raising the skin of the bamboo in strips, like those made in America from cornstalks. The second character also denotes a small tree found in Honan, having the leaves in threes, and yellow seeds like small peas, which are used as food.

憃 hang꜄ Violent.

丨憧 to look at angrily, to appear stern and angry; to show great wrath.

HĂNG.

Old sounds, heng, keng, *and* geng. *In Canton*, hăng, *sometimes prolonged to* hang; — *in Swatow*, heng, hwang, *and* keng; — *in Amoy*, heng; — *in Fuhchau*, héng *and* kéng; — *in Shanghai*, hăng, ăng, *and* yăng; — *in Chifu*, hˣng.

亨 ꜀hăng It is regarded as having the same origin as ꜀hiang 享 to enjoy, from which it is now distinguished.

To pervade, to influence throughout; going through with a thing; successful.

出入亅通 quite successful in the enterprise; having all things to your liking.

大亅天衢 a grand avenue and a fine prospect.

亅嘉 or 泰亅 prosperous, excellent, successful.

Read p'ăng. An ancient form of 烹 to cook.

七月亅葵及菽 in the seventh month they cook okras and pulse.

哼 ꜀hăng Frightened; having an antipathy to; looking foolish.

唅亅 looking aghast.

亅哈二將 the two ferocious gigantic guardians at temple doors.

In *Pekingese*. An interjection of pain or displeasure.

亅不是他麽 what! is not that he?

亅啊亅啊 a groan, as when carrying a load; or as a sick man cries out.

亅亅唧唧 groaning and moaning.

In *Cantonese*. Excessive.

臭亅亅 very horrid or loathsome; stinking.

In *Fuhchau*. To vociferate, to hoot, to scream at.

脝 ꜀hăng Puffed up; fat, obese.

膨亅 a swollen belly; bloated, like a swollen corpse.

鍧 ꜀hăng The combined sound of bells and drums mingled is 鏗亅, as when a great mass is performed.

衡 衜 ꜀hăng From 行 to *go*, having 角 a *horn*, with 大 *great* above, placed inside; the second form with 魚 *fish* between is a common but unauthorized alteration; occurs used for ꜀hung 横 crosswise.

A stick across an ox's horn to prevent his goring; a yoke; the frontal sinus or space between the eyebrows; a balance, that which adjusts weights; to weigh; to adjust, to get at the right of a thing; compared, balanced; a balustrade; the string of a cap; a forester; a weight of $1\frac{5}{8}$ catty; transverse.

亅量 to measure; to estimate, as one's ability.

亅平 a pair of scales.

鑑空亅平 to have a quick and clear perception of what is just; equitable.

亅情 to judge of the circumstances.

亅門之下 beneath my cross-laid door; *i. e.* in a scholar's cottage.

亅從其畝 the acres are to be plowed across and along.

抗亅 to dispute about precedence and resist rule.

阿亅 the name of I Yin 伊尹 the great minister in the Shang dynasty, though others regard it as a title, like Preceptor.

亅論 to discuss the reasons of.

玉亅 the gemmeous transverse, was a part of an astronomical instrument of Shun; it is applied to the star Alioth ε Ursa Major, which is thought to be the regulator of the stars.

亅星 the stars ν μ ϑ in Centaur.

亅山 the southern of the 五岳 five mountains, which lies in 亅州府 on the west side of the River Siang in Hunan; it is about 3000 feet high, and appears to be part of an ancient mountain range, whose summits only are visible at present, and formed the northern rim of a basin, in which coal measures and soft red sandstone predominate.

權亅指掌 to have the entire control of; *q. d.* the poise and scale are in his hands.

蘅 ꜀hăng A fragrant syngenesious flower, the *Ligularia*, called 杜亅, a marshy plant with large cordate leaves, and smelling like a rose; it is thought that horses fed on them travel fast.

微亅草 sweet vernal grass (?)

恆 恒 ꜀hăng From 心 *heart* and 舟 a *boat* between *two* banks; the second form is most common.

Constant, regular, perpetual; always according to rule; constancy; to make constant, to continue of the same mind; persevering; everywhere, extensively; the 32d of the diagrams, denoting continuance or perseverance; the moon nearly full.

亅常 accustomed to; permanent.

亅心 constant in purpose.

如月之亅 like the waxing moon.

有亅 or 有亅性 persevering in acts, laborious, assiduous.

亅產 a regular income; enduring possessions.

丨足 ever enough; always sufficient.

丨之秬秠 everywhere were the two kinds of millet sown.

丨河 old name of one the sources of the Yung-ting R., which rises in K'üh-yang hien 曲陽縣 in the southwest of Chihli; it is also applied to the Ganges, as in the comparison 丨河沙數 numerous as the sands of the Ganges; and written 丨迦 for Gunga, which is explained to mean 福水 or lucky water.

丨山 the northern of the 五岳 or Five Mountains, now considered to be a peak in Hwun-yuen cheu 渾源州 in Ta-t'ung fu in the north of Shansi; but others with more probability place it near the source of the River Hăng in Chihli.

緪 縆 ˓hăng — Also read k'ăng˒; the second form is seldom met with.

A large rope; a long string; hasty, quick.

丨梯 a rope ladder.

姮 ˓hăng — This is often read ˓chang.

A woman's name.

丨娥 one of the genii, the daughter of I, the prince of K'iüng, who once 偷食靈藥奔於月窟 stole the elixir of immortality, and fled to the moon palace; she is now called 嫦娥, and regarded as the goddess of the moon.

桁 ˓hăng — From *wood* and a *row;* also read *hang*˒ and ˓*yen.*

The purlines of a roof which support the rafters; a row of tiles; large boards for stocks; a plank to cross a stream; boards to support a coffin over the grave; a clothes-horse.

屋丨 at Canton, a row of tiles on a roof; as 闊幾丨 how many rows of tiles wide is the house? — the width of houses being measured by them in that city.

丨桷 purlines and rafters.

˓丨楊 a cangue — at Peking.

樹丨˒子 rows of trees, like looking through a long grove.

珩 ˓hăng — From *gem* and a *row* as the phonetic.

Gems hung at the lapel, or used in the girdle clasp, which have a play of colors, like the cat's eye; ancient ornaments or gems on a crown.

有瑲葱丨 his girdle-pendents tinkled.

丨紞紘綖 the gems, fringes, and bands of a coronet.

莖 ˓hăng — The culm or stalk of grasses and herbs, especially such as have no branches; rising straight up, like a stalk; a stem; hilt of a sword.

蓮丨 a lotus stalk.

一根丨 one culm or stalk.

玉丨 a medical term for the penis.

諱 hăng˒ — To speak angrily, to look at sternly; to berate; refractory words.

向他發丨 scolded him roundly.

HAO.

Old sounds, ho, ko, kok, gok *and* got. *In Canton,* hò; — *in Swatow,* kau, hau, *and* ho; — *in Amoy,* ò, hò, *and* koh; — *in Fuhchau,* ho *and* ko; — *in Shanghai,* ho, o, *and* hòk; — *in Chifu,* hao.

蒿 ˓hao — From *plant* and *high.*

Tall herbs; it is applied to several fragrant or aromatic plants, like the *Artemisia, Vitex, Pedicularis,* or *Amaranthus,* whose stalks or leaves are prized for their scent; tansy; to close the eyes; to reduce.

青丨 the wormwood or southern wood, of which the sort called 香丨 or 丨子 (*Artemisia*) is dried and coiled into ropes to burn, and drive off musketoes by its smoke.

黃花丨 a species of Ambrosia or amaranthus.

同丨菜 a sort of insipid celery cultivated at Peking.

塘丨 celery.

丨目 to screw up the eyes, as when filled with dust; because in time of affliction one has no desire to cleanse them.

焄丨 steam rising from things; the subtle odor or vapors arising from sacrifices offered.

蘆丨 a fragant edible plant found among rushes along the Yangtsz'.

嚆 ˓hao — Also read ˓hiao.

A whizzing sound like that of an arrow.

丨矢 the whirring dart.

山禽丨 the wild birds sing.

薅 拺 茠 ˓hao — From 蓐 *rowan grass* and 好 *good* contracted; the other forms are unusual, and seem to have been constructed from 休 *not,* with a reference to the sense.

To pull up weeds; to weed out grass from the field; to extirpate.

丨草 to weed.

丨頭毛來 to pull out the hair, as in a rage.

丨亂絲膠 to unloosen the sticky snarls of raw silk.

豪 ˏhao From 豕 a *boar* and 高 *high*; it occurs used for the next.

A kind of porcupine, 丨彘 armed with long skewer-like quills; eminent, excellent, superior; excelling, dominating other minds; martial, brave; a leader, a martial, overbearing man; imperial, as the emperor's flocks.

丨民 robust, martial people.

英雄丨傑 a hero and leader in military acts.

遴選英丨 to select a capable, energetic ruler.

土丨or 丨橫 a local tyrant, a village bully, a ruffian.

丨客 a rich, influential man.

丨俠 generous minded, open-spoken, having moral courage.

丨强 to act violently and oppressively.

丨馬 a fine, powerful horse, a Bucephalus, one fit for a king to ride.

丨光 a sudden flash, a dazzling glory like that at the transfiguration.

毫 ˏhao From *hair* and *high*, and regarded as altered from the last; when used for *dime* it is often contracted to 毛; it must be distinguished from *poh*, 亳 a place.

The down or pubescence on plants; long soft hair; a pencil's point; atoms, motes, anything very minute; a superlative; in regimen with a negative, it denotes the very least; lavish; in weights, the tenth of a mill, or the place next to a 厘 cash, the thousandth part of a tael; a dime, or ten cents

丨末事 petty, trifling affairs.

丨釐 a very little, a mere fraction.

丨無過犯 I've not overpassed my place; I have not offended in the least.

絲丨不錯 or 分丨不差 there is no error in it; it is perfectly exact; no difference at all.

含丨 to wet the pencil on the tongue, as when thinking what to write.

揮丨 to flourish the hair, *i.e.* to write.

秋丨 very minute, an autumn's down; the least bit, like the pappus of a thistle.

丨髮之多 [of no more importance] than a bit of hair.

丨不容情 I will not have the least temper shown; he has no patience at all.

白丨茶 Pecco tea, so called from the downy white leaves in it.

一丨私心 a little selfish feeling; some regard for his own interest.

壕 ˏhao From *earth* and *excelling*; used with the next.

The fosse or ditch around a city wall; this ditch, the 城丨 is not seldom quite dry.

丨塹架吊橋 let down the drawbridge over the moat.

石丨鎮 an old place near the Yellow River in Shen chen 陝州 in the west of Honan.

濠 ˏhao Interchanged with the last.

A moat with water in it; the city ditch.

丨州 old name of Fung-yang fu 鳳陽府 in Nganhwui, derived from the River Hao 丨河 running near it.

通丨 to clear out a moat.

溝丨 drains and sewers leading into the moat.

蠔 ˏhao An oyster.

丨殼 an oyster-shell.

丨山 oyster-spat.

丨豉 dried oysters.

丨塘 an oyster-bed.

丨油 oyster sauce — a native preparation.

丨墪 Second Bar near Whampoa, called from the oysters there.

擃 ˏhao To compare quantities and ascertain which is the greatest or fewest.

丨較 to estimate and compare.

In *Pekingese*. To pull out.

丨鬚 to pull out the beard.

譹 ˏhao Nearly synonymous with 號 to call loudly, and written like the next.

To cry out; to speak loud and gruffly.

嘷 ˏhao 嚎 ˏhao The second of these characters, though in common use, is regarded as erroneous.

The roaring of a tiger or a bear; noise of wild beasts; grunt of a wild boar; to howl as a dog; to bawl, to wail.

丨丨聲 a bawling noise.

兒子終日丨 the child wailed and moaned the whole day.

狼丨怪叫 the horrid, startling howl of wolves.

好 ˊhao hao˒ From *woman* and *child* or man, expressing the admiration or desire of women for men.

Good, right, excellent; the good; goodness, good deeds; peace; fit, arranged, proper for the purpose needed; fine, graceful; as an *adverb*, well, very; the highest degree of, extra, exceeding, superlative; recovered, in health; friendly.

丨得狠 first rate, exceeding good; exactly the thing.

丨丨兒的 very carefully; the best of thought upon it.

丨不丨 will it do? are you quite well?

丨不辛苦 extremely distressing.

丨不耐煩 I cannot stand it any longer, as an annoyance.

丨笑 very laughable.

丨久的 a very long time.

丨彩 successful, lucky, opportune, fortunate.

丨像你 it is very much like you.

你來的恰丨 you've come in the nick of time.

丨回話 to enable me to return an answer.

丨了沒有 is it ready yet?

丨是丨 it will do, but.

丨些 a little better, improving; also, very many, a good many, a good deal.

丨一些 getting on, rather better.

那麼丨些 such a large number.

修丨 or 行丨 to give in charity; *i. e.* cultivate or exercise your goodness or good deeds to please Budha; the act is called 丨事 a meritorious deed.

驕人丨丨勞人草草 the proud are delighted, and the weary are in sorrow.

永以爲丨 we always were good friends.

丨說 or 丨話 well said; I thank you; I am obliged; — used in reply to another's complimentary remark.

丨穢氣 very bad luck at dice.

Read *hao'*. To love, to be fond of, to like, the opposite of 惡'; to esteem good, to take pleasure in; addicted to; to wish for; the object of regard; a hole in a wall; beauty, grace.

丨酒的 a wine-bibber.

丨學 studious; a lover of books.

丨交 to love one's friends.

兩君之丨 the friendly meeting of two princes.

各有所丨 what every man likes; generally prized.

百姓心丨義 the people at heart love justice.

偏丨 to love with partiality.

昊' *hao'* From 日 *sun* and 夰 *luminous* contracted, alluding to the clear summer sky; used with the next.

A luminous, clear summer sky; vast, grand; the powers which rule in the sky.

丨天 the empyrean, the bright sky; whence 丨天上帝 the Shangti of the glorious Heaven.

丨天金闕 the golden palace of the heavens, where he dwells.

丨慈 Heaven's kind compassion.

有北不受投畀有丨 if the northern regions would not take them, then I would leave them with the Powers above.

晧' 顥' *hao'* From *white* and to *announce;* the second character is one of four unusual forms, and is only used for hoary.

The light of heaven, especially at the horizon; luminous, like the clear sky; bright, as the rising moon; resplendent, glistering; hoary, white.

丨首 a hoary head.

四丨 were four gray-beards in the Han dynasty, and probably albinos.

丨丨 shining, brilliant, as stones washed white; glittering, as the stars.

揚之水白石丨丨 the white rocks glisten through the fretted waters.

太丨 the firmament.

趁着丨月走路 to travel by moonlight.

光芒丨耀 brilliant and lustrous, like Venus or Sirius.

天丨 a star in Sagittarius.

Read *₍hwui*. The hair turning white and falling off.

皞' *hao'* Used with the two last.

Bright; reflecting light, brilliant.

丨丨如也 so numerous, happy and prosperous; said of a contented people.

太丨 and 少丨 are old terms for the first and ninth moons; and of their *ti* 帝' or rulers; the first is also a designation of Fuh-hi, and the second of Shao-hao, the son and successor of Hwang-ti, B. C. 2597; they are supposed to patronize these months.

熙熙丨丨之風 excellent and courteous manners, as one self-possessed at all times.

浩' *hao'* From *water* and to *proclaim.*

A vast expense, as of a deluge; great, swelling waters; immense, vast; affluent; an overplus; wide views, noble-minded.

丨丨乎 how grand! how vast.

丨然之氣 magnanimous; liberal-minded, of large conceptions.

丨然而去 to leave quickly, as a good man departs from a company of scorners.

丨丨蕩蕩 exceeding great, like God's glory.

丨繁 very perplexing, as duties or engagements; almost numberless, as people.

Read *kao'*. To dilute spirits.

灝' *hao'* The vast stretch of the ocean, boundless and magnificent; vast, unfathomable; the liquor in which pulse has been boiled, once used for washing the hair, and by the priests to wash Budha; traces of the custom still remain.

丨丨 deep, inscrutable, said of writings.

丨漾 a boundless waste, as of waters.

滈' *hao'* Ancient name of a river in Shensi, a branch of the R. Wéi near the capital; and also of a pool; a long dreary rain.

丨汗 fretted waters; rippling.

丨丨 the bright look of water when agitated; the bubbling of water.

鎬' *hao'* A warming stove; a hand-brazier; bright; the northern regions in the days of Hia.

丨京 the capital of Wu Wang of Cheu; it lay west of the present capital of Shensi, and the site was turned into a lake by Han Wu-ti; the city is often wrongly known as 豐丨, but the two places were about eight miles apart on two sides of the R. Fung.

鄗 hao' Used as another, but not very usual form of the last.

The name of a place belonging to Chao 趙 and seized by Tsi; now known as Kao-yih hien 高邑縣 in Chao cheu in the southwest of Chihli.

鰝 'kaó The large crawfish or *Palinurus*, common in Chinese and Japanese waters; also known as the 龍蝦 dragon shrimp and Chinese lobster.

悎 hao' Perturbation, fear; the mind greatly disturbed.

耗 秏 hao' From a *plow* or *grain* and *hair*; the second is rather an unusual form, and applied chiefly to a kind of fine grain.

A kind of fine rice; to diminish, to consume, to destroy through time or use; to lay out, to spend, to squander; to injure; to make void; vicious, bad.

捐 丨 destroyed or spoiled, as grain by mice.

鼠 丨 loss from rats, a grain-dealer's charge; whence 丨 子 has become a term for a rat.

黃 丨 子 a sort of marmot found in the north of Chihli.

丨 銀 色 the silver looks alloyed.

池 水 丨 去 一 寸 the water in the pond has gone down an inch.

加 丨 to add something for loss, to supply the extra expense.

虛 丨 國 帑 a useless outlay or waste of the country's resources.

丨 得 精 光 he spent till all was gone, he wasted everything.

煞 丨 injurious, said of the evil doings of spirits, elves, or malaria.

丨 磨 日 子 to waste and idle the time away.

丨 費 spent beyond the estimate; useless waste.

作 丨 to gambol, to play tricks, mischievous sport.

年 之 豐 丨 the year's supply, more or less.

息 丨 or 音 丨 news of, tidings, reports.

丨 散 元 氣 to waste one's energies or stamina, as by drink.

號 号 hao' From *tiger* and to *cry* out; the contracted form is common in cheap books.

A mark, a designation, a denomination; a description or class of; a label, a name, a *chop*, as that word is used in China; sign of a shop; a style or honorable appellation; an order or verbal command; a summons; a countersign, a signal; to put a mark on, to label or direct, as a box; to name, to style.

丨 令 a mandate, a word of command, an order.

字 丨 a mark; the sign or firm name of a shop.

你 寶 丨 what is your shop's name.

字 丨 貨 goods which are labeled; genuine wares.

放 丨 炮 to fire a salute or signal.

起 丨 to blow the horn or bugle; to make the signal.

暗 丨 a private signal or cry.

尊 丨 呀 what is your style.

別 丨 or 名 丨 is the virile style taken after marriage, or when entering office.

丨 房 the room in a yamun where visitors enter their names; a store-room, a depository.

混 丨 a nickname, an epithet indicating a man's bad character.

掌 起 雙 丨 the trumpeters who call troops to engage.

第 幾 丨 頭 what number is it? which mark?

丨 召 to summon.

丨 衣 a soldier's uniform, because his regiment is painted on the breast.

懺 佛 丨 to call on Budha, to say his name.

掛 丨 to put on a stamp, as at a custom-house.

丨 上 個 記 丨 mark a name on it, as on a box.

丨 呼 to signal one by a cry, as a boatswain by his whistle.

一 丨 買 賣 one class of traders, *i.e.* those who deal in the same article.

請 問 法 丨 please tell me your priestly name.

國 丨 the name of a dynasty.

年 丨 the style of a reign, the name by which its years are called,—as 大 清 道 光 the reign Tao-kwang of the Great Ts'ing dynasty; in the Han and later dynasties, the emperors often changed the style during their reigns, but the usage was dropped by the Ming dynasty.

Read ꜀*hao*. To scream, as a tiger; to bay, as a dog; to bawl, to cry after one, to yell; to crow.

丨 呼 to scream; to cry after.

丨 啼 a cock-crowing.

鬼 哭 神 丨 [like] demons wailing and spirits crying,—a dreadful clamor, as at a fight or a fire.

日 丨 泣 于 旻 天 he daily cried and wept before high Heaven.

HEU.

Old sounds, hu, ku, gu, kup *and* kút. *In Canton*, hau; — *in Swatow*, hò, hau, au, *and* kau; — *in Amoy*, ho, *and* hau; — *in Fuhchau*, héu, haiü, *and* hau; — *in Shanghai*, hù *and* hö; — *in Chifu*, hò.

齁 ꜀heu To snore, to breathe hard; one says, disease in the throat; in colloquial, a superlative often applied to tastes and smells.

丨鼾 to breathe hard through the nose, as one who has an obstruction; to test by the smell.

丨臭 it stinks here.

丨酸 excessively sour.

矦 ꜀heu From 人 *man* and 厂 a *shelter*, which denoted a spreading out, with 矢 an *arrow* underneath; it must be distinguished from 候 to wait.

A target ten feet square; beautiful, pretty; to be happy; as *a conjunction*, but, unless; how, in what it consisted; the second of the five orders of nobility, answering now to a marquis; anciently, a noble, a prince.

丨誰在矣 but who then is there?

丨于周服 however, he was [a prince] in the time of Cheu.

射丨 to shoot at the target.

封丨 to raise one to the rank of marquis; he is called 丨爺, but when written to he is styled 一等丨 premier marquis.

諸丨 a prince or feudal baron, when occupying his own realm; a nobleman.

丨服 the domain or tenure of a prince; an appanage; the principalities.

肆師丨禳 the priests invoked the good, and averted evil luck.

郈 ꜀heu An ancient place, called 丨田, belonging to the state of 晉 Tsin, lying in the present Wei-hwui fu 衛輝府 in Honan; it was a frontier town, and caused a quarrel.

喉 ꜀heu From *mouth* and *nobleman* as the phonetic.

The throat, the trachea; the gullet; guttural, as a sound.

咽丨 the windpipe.

丨嚨 denot s either of the passages, but properly the œsophagus; 硬丨 and 軟口 are other terms for them.

丨欖 or 結丨 adam's apple.

封丨 the throat stopped up.

丨嗓 the voice, the intonation

生鵝丨 to have the quinsy or diphtheria; he has a sore throat.

咽丨之地 (or 區) an important pass, a throat-gates, a Thermopyla.

潤丨 to quench thirst, to wet the whistle.

王之丨舌 a minister of state, *q. d.* the king's throat and tongue.

令人丨舌 to make people talk about you.

婉囀歌丨 delicate modulations of the warbling throat, — as of a fine singer.

糇 餱 ꜀heu From *rice* or *food* and a *nobleman*.

Dry provisions.

丨糧 food cooked for a journey.

猴 ꜀heu The monkey; it is common in the central provinces; the ninth branch 申 is denoted by it, and the hour from 3 to 5 P. M.

丨子 or 猻 丨 a monkey; the last is large and intractable; it is applied to people in contempt.

丨三兒 a droll name for the monkey.

硏丨 a small species of marmoset, said to rub ink, reared as a pet; it is found in Yunnan.

丨子戲 games with monkeys.

跳丨 to play monkeys; *met.* rascally, untrustworthy.

丨兒崽子 you villain! similar to the epithet, you puppy!

沐丨而冠 [you are no better than] a washed monkey with a cap on.

丨爪 the skins of monkeys' limbs.

孫丨兒 or 孫大聖 an elf, a bogie, transformed from a monkey, first into a *djin*, and then into a sort of Budha.

瘊 ꜀heu Warts, pimples, or such like excrescences of a small size, are called 丨子; in Canton they are known as 飯蕋 rice stamens, and elsewhere as 千日瘡 thousand-day sores.

睺 ꜀heu Half blind, as an old man, or when a cataract is forming.

羅丨羅 or Rahula, the eldest son of Sakya-muni, whose birth was impeded for six years by an *asura* or demon; hence the dog or demon who eats the moon in an eclipse has been called Rahula; it is the same as Rahu in Brahminical mythology, the god of the ascending node, represented as headless, and riding on a tortoise.

睺 ꜀heu An unauthorized character.

A constellation called 羅丨 by the horoscopists; it is regarded as very unlucky, and is probably somehow connected with the preceding.

篌 ꜀heu A musical instrument, with 25 strings, the 箜丨, which resembles a wide lute or harpischord.

媄 ˏheu A name of a woman.

In *Fuhchau.* Wanton, adulterous, gadding, whorish.

禠 ˏheu To pray for blessings; to offer sacrifices in order to obtain blessings.

鍭 ˏheu The iron barb or head of an arrow or dart; a feathered shaft with a barb.

四 丨 既 鈞 the four shafts have hit the target.

鯸 ˏheu A sort of Tetraodon, called 丨 鮧 or 丨 鮐 and regarded as poisonous; it is said to make a noise, and one name is 吹 肚 魚 belly-inflating fish, from its power of distension; several sorts are said to exist; some of the synonyms refer to a kind of river porpoise, which the name 丨 鮔 no doubt designates.

犼 ˋheu A fierce wolf found in Mongolia that devours men; an astrological term for the 16th constellation in Aries.

In *Pekingese.* The dragon's heads put on the ends of roofs on the ridge-pole; workmen who put up awnings are called 叫 天 丨 "people who call on the heavenly wolf," lest they get a fall.

吼 ˏheu From *mouth* and *hole*; used with the next.

The cries of animals, especially of cattle and feline beasts; the voice of anger.

咆 丨 如 雷 what a thundering noise he makes.

河 東 獅 丨 the lion is roaring on the east side of the river, — *i. e.* the old woman is scolding like a Xanthippe; applied to shrews.

㸃 ˋheu The lowing of an ox; in Shantung, an old name for a calf.

牛 丨 the ox is bellowing.

呞 ˋheu From *mouth* and *empress.*

The tone or voice of anger; to scold, to abuse.

郈 heuˋ Name of an ancient place in Lu, now in the southeast of Tung-ping cheu 東 平 州 in Tai-ngan fu in the center of Shantung.

后 ˋheu From 一 口 *one mouth* under 厂 a *shelter*, to give orders; occurs used for 後 afterwards.

A ruler; the sovereign; an empress or queen, the equal of the sovereign, one who succeeds to him, — but it can not properly be applied to a queen regnant; an ancestor of the sovereign; all the later rulers of the Hia dynasty are so styled, as 丨 泄 King Sieh; a feudal or dependant prince, so called when he went to court to serve the ruler, but at home he was a 侯 baronial prince.

元 丨 or 君 丨 the sovereign ruler.

皇 丨 or 國 丨 the empress, the queen.

皇 太 丨 or 太 丨 the empress dowager.

我 先 神 丨 之 勞 the toils of my predecessors, those divine sovereigns.

母 丨 our Imperial mother, said by the Emperor.

丨 土 a god of the land; in Kwangtung, worshiped behind graves, because the dead have, as it were, trespassed on his domain.

皇 天 丨 土 imperial heaven and earth, — are the deified powers of nature.

天 丨 or 天 丨 聖 母 the Queen of Heaven is the goddess of seamen, the Chinese Amphitrite; a girl of Fuhkien named Lin 林; she is also *Maritchi* or *Chundi* of the Brahmins, the personification of light; the Taoists say that she dwells in one of the stars of the Dipper, and call her 斗 姥 or Dipper Mother.

逅 heuˋ From to *go* and *empress.*

To meet; a pleasant and unexpected meeting.

邂 丨 相 逢 to meet unexpectedly and agreeably.

茩 heuˋ A medicinal plant, the 薢 丨, which appears to be allied to a *Hyoscyamus*, or one of that order; its seeds are reputed to cure inflamed eyes, and its tender leaves are edible.

後 heuˋ Composed of 彳 a *step*, 幺 *gently* and 夂 to *come up* behind.

After in time, late, subsequent; unavailing, too late; a future; behind in place; then, next, future; often a form of past time; an heir, successors, posterity, descendants; to regard as secondary, to put one's self after; to postpone; to be remiss in; to remain; the second; an attendant.

以 丨 or 丨 來 afterwards, then, subsequently.

丨 面 or 丨 頭 behind, in the rear.

丨 生 a young man.

丨 學 I, your pupil; I myself.

丨 世 after ages, futurity; posterity.

背 丨 on the back, as a papoose; the tail, the rear.

我 生 之 丨 in my latter days.

不 自 我 丨 they were not after me.

丨 天 or 丨 日 or 丨 兒 the day after to-morrow.

然 丨 therefore, then, in consequence; next.

隨 丨 就 到 I will come on after.

隨 在 丨 to push after behind.

自 丨 者 人 先 之 是 也 keep yourself back and put others foremost; this is right.

有 丨 無 丨 has he any sons or descendants?

末 丨 尾 the very last, the hindmost.

未 有 義 而 丨 其 君 者 也 no officer of integrity (or patriotism) ever neglects his prince.

候 heu' The original form was 𠊱 a *nobleman*, from which it is now distinguished by the central stroke.

To wait; to expect; to inquire; to visit, to wait on; to look after; a time or period; a period of five days; to pay a reckoning.

問 丨 to visit an equal, to inquire after, one's health, to send respects.

丨 駕 I wait for you, Sir! — said on invitation cards.

丨 補 an expectant for an office; a brevet rank.

等 丨 wait! to wait for one; stop awhile.

丨 叙 I shall await [your coming] to arrange [the guests]; — a phrase on an invitation card.

氣 丨 or 節 丨 the full time for, the period of.

過午不 丨 I shall not wait for you beyond noon.

善 丨 風 it knows well when there will be wind, as a gull.

伺 丨 to wait on and serve.

恭 丨 to come and salute one; a respectful visit.

丨 訊 kept for his trial, awaiting examination.

在此 丨 着 wait here; I am waiting.

我 丨 你們喫 I invite you all to a dinner.

我 丨 罷 let me settle the score for us all, — as at a café.

堠 heu' From *earth* and *prince* as the phonetic.

A terrace or flat mound by which distances were marked, and fire-signals placed in the Ming dynasty; every ten *li* a double mound was raised, and a single one every five *li*; they are now disused.

嚴斥 丨 rigorously examine the mounds for fire-signals.

厚 heu' Composed of 厂 a *shelter*, 曰 to *say*, and 子 a *son*; *q. d.* a large number of sons; but others say it is derived from 高 *high*, written as if laid on its side.

Thick, large; substantial, liberal, kind, generous; intimate, faithful; good; well, very; well-flavored, mellow; rich, as loam; to secure or cause plenty; to esteem.

丨 惠 a liberal donation.

丨 待 to treat kindly; gracious demeanor towards.

丨 道 kind, considerate, placable, generous.

丨 情 kind feelings; friendly.

丨 重 generous; dignified; fat and heavy, as a person.

丨 實 rich, well off.

丨 德 liberality, generosity.

丨 祿 a good salary.

忠 丨 honest-hearted, sincere.

丨 and 薄 are opposites — thick and thin, liberal and stingy; applied to degrees of civility or favor, to the relations of things, as 躬自 丨 薄責人 I judge myself closely and blame others moderately.

面皮 丨 shameless, brazenfaced.

丨 交 an intimate friend.

非能 丨 勝之 you will not be able to conquer him.

鱟 heu' The king-crab or 丨 魚, the horse-hoof (*Limulus longispina*) one of the Xiphosuræ, common on the southern coasts; its roe is used as food, and forms part of the offerings to ancestors.

丨 帆 the horse-hoof; the name intimates that it knows when a storm is coming, and to take in sail.

丨 殼 its dried shell, used for dippers and ladles.

HI.

Old sounds, hi, ki, gi, kuit, guit, git, hé, kó, gé, *and* gét. *In Canton*, hi, hei, ai, kw'ai; — *in Swatow*, hi, iⁿ, wa, *and* k'i; — *in Amoy*, hi, hé, k'é, *and* k'ai; — *in Fuhchau*, hi, hi², *and* hé; *in Shanghai*, hi, i, *and* yi; — *in Chifu*, h'i.

希 'h'i Originally composed of 爻 as if *thin* and far apart, and 巾 *tattered garments* contracted; it occurs used for the next two.

Few, rare, seldom, infrequent; to hope, to wait in expectation of, to anticipate; desirous, wishing; striving to be like, emulating; loose, not close or near; to thin out, as a bird's feathers in the molting season; to suspend, as music; to disburse, to scatter; deprived of sound, as Laotsz' says reason is; to molt, to shed.

丨 奇 or 丨 少 rare, curious, unusual.

丨 望 to look for, hoping; it often implies an order.

丨 罕 seldom, not common

丨 爲見復 I shall hope to get a reply.

丨 革 to shed hair.

丨 世之珍 there are few such men in the world.

鼓瑟 丨 a rest in playing the lute.

佇 丨 I humbly earnestly look for your aid.

知丨我貴 I honor those who are known to few.

睎 *hi* From *eye* and *few*.
To long for, to look afar to; to remember kindly; to look askance.
依丨 to see a thing indistinctly from its distance.

稀 *hi* From *grain* and *few*; occurs interchanged with its primitive.
Open, loose, apart; the opposite of *ch'eu* 稠 close; not near or thick; scattered here and there; sleazy, as cloth; thin, as gruel; spongy, light, as cake or bread; not joining; careless, remiss; very, fully; to become scattered or distant.
丨薄 sleazy; thin, unsubstantial.
丨疏 wide and open; sparse, as the large stars; bare, as leafless trees.
丨少 not many such; very few.
羮丨爛 cooked very thoroughly.
丨丨的 watery, as a porridge; coarse or thin, as cloth.
剁得丨泥爛 you've hashed it much too fine.
月朗星丨 when the moon is bright the stars seem few.
丨遠世路 he separated himself from the ways of the world.

俙 *hi* From *man* and *few* as the phonetic.
The heart and face disagreeing; pretending, simulating, like to; to counterfeit.
依丨 appearing as if.
僾丨 obscure; dimly.

晞 *hi* To dry; dried by the sun; break of day; a local word for boisterous.
東方未丨 the dawn does not yet show.
白露未丨 the dew has not dried up

悕 *hi* To consider, to reflect on and remember; to compassionate; to wish.

浠 *hi* Name of a small tributary of the Yang-tsz' River in Lo-tien hien 羅田縣 in the northwest part of Hupeh.

欷 *hi* To sob, to catch the breath in weeping; whimpering and timid.
丨歔流涕 to sigh and cry; blubbering and weeping, as a child.

郗 *hi* Ancient name of a city in the Cheu dynasty, now near or at the present Hwai-king fu, north of the Yellow River, in Honan.

豨 *hi* An old name for a hog, used in Kiangsu and westward; to call swine; the grunting of pigs.
丨丨 the noise of scampering pigs.
豬突丨勇 the swinish herd suddenly ran off as braves; said of the banditti who helped Wang Mang in the Han dynasty
封丨 a divine animal supposed to protect against snakes; also, the name of a star.

羲 *hi* Composed of 義 *right* and 兮 a *breath* or tone.
Breath, vapor; the family name of one of the chief astronomers of Yao and his successors.
伏丨 the reputed founder of the Chinese monarchy, B.C. 2952 to 2837; also called 丨皇 the Emperor Hi.

犧 *hi* Victims of a uniform color fit to be offered in sacrifice, as oxen, sheep, goats, or pigs; a sacrificial victim; spotless.
丨牲 animals offered in sacrifice.
丨牛 a bullock for an offering.
以我齊明與我丨羊 my vessels are full of clean millet, and I have a pure ram—to sacrifice.

曦 *hi* The light of day.
赫丨 the color or effulgence of the sun.

熙 熈 *hi* From *fire* and *joyful*; the second form is not correct, and seems to have come into use from a desire to thus mark the reign Kanghi, by putting the inner stroke outside.
Light, bright, splendid, intelligent; glorious, prospering; harmonious; extensive, ample; to enlarge, to consolidate; to fully discharge; lasting; to dry.
丨和之世 a prosperous and peaceful time.
咸丨 everything flourishing, general prosperity.
丨丨 how many people there are!
丨朝人瑞 a prosperous dynasty and fortunate people.
木丨 a play of rope-dancing.

Read *i*. Large and strong.

醯 *hi* Composed of 酉 *spirits*, 皿 *dishes*, and 鬻 *gruel* contracted.
Sour, acid, vinegar-like; condiments, pickles.
丨醬 pickled minced condiments.
丨鷄 the animalculæ in vinegar.
丨醢 minced meat pickled and seasoned.

虘 *hi* From *tiger* and a *vase*; it is now only used in combination as a primitive.
A description of ancient earthenware vase used in sacrifices.

巇 *hi* A gorge with beetling cliffs opposite, a cañon; a dangerous pass along a precipice; a crack; an occasion, a chance, as for quarreling.

嚱 *hi* A whistling sound; a shrill cry.
丨丨 noise, uproar.
嗚丨 Alas, Alas! — a cry of wailing or regret.

誒 *'hi* An interjection of abhorrence; to laugh violently; to giggle, like a silly person.

丨 丨 fie! tush! pshaw!

丨 笑 to laugh boisterously.

恀 *'hi* Contemptuous.

慴 丨 insulting, reproachful words.

娭 *'hi* Used with the next.

A depreciating epithet for a woman.

丨 婢 a slave girl, a handmaid.

戲 丨 to dally, to play with, to entertain with sports; childrens' games.

嬉 *'hi* From *woman* and *joy*; used with the last and next.

Pretty, handsome; pleasant sports; an excursion, a picnic; to ramble, to play, to enjoy one's self; to laugh, for which the next is correct.

遊 丨 a pleasure excursion.

水 丨 a boating trip.

丨 玩 or 丨 耍 games and plays, jolly sports; tricks and pastimes.

業荒于 丨 [to attend to] business as if it were play — will soon end in ruin.

婦子 丨 丨 終吝 a family which only seeks amusement will at last come to grief.

嘻 *'hi* An interjection expressing joy, and sometimes indignation; the sound of merriment; to laugh; pleased, delighted.

噫 丨 Alas! Oh! dreadful! — an interjection of surprise or grief.

丨 丨 呵呵 or 丨 丨 哈哈 tittering, laughing aloud.

僖 *'hi* Used for 喜 to feel joy; also to take particular care; cautious and fearful, as of danger; very strict about.

丨 樂 delighted, pleased.

歖 *'hi* Used with 喜 joyful, especially a sudden delight or extasy.

Read *'i*, in 丨 䶢 the braying of an ass.

譆 *'hi* The cry of one in pain; the scream of fear, or grief, or indignation.

丨 丨 咄咄 the wail of ghosts or demons, which are suffering for failure of worship and oblations.

熹 *'hi* From *fire* and *joy* as the phonetic.

To heat in any way; to roast, to toast; hot, bright, burning; light and heat together pervading; abundant, diversified; in epitaphs, denotes one who has merit and peace.

晨光之 丨 微 the warmth and freshness of the morning light.

熺 *'hi* Used for the last.

Lucky stars shining on their worshipers in old times; to worship a star; the glitter of a star; to roast.

禧 *'hi* Joy arising from divine blessings; happy, favored by the gods; to announce or pray to them.

鴻 丨 [may you have] great joy; or 迎 丨 meet with good luck; these phrases are often written on the wall opposite front doors, and are regarded as invocations.

恭賀新 丨 I respectfully congratulate you on this new joy, — written on newyear's cards.

奚 *'hi* Originally combined of 大 *great*, and an old form of 系 a *nerve*, meaning a big belly; used with the next.

An interrogative particle implying doubt; why? how? what? which? a page, a waiter; a maidservant; a domestic.

丨 不爲政 why do you not enter on office?

丨 爲後我 why are you so late? — or so long coming? *i. e.* I've been hoping to see you.

子以爲 丨 what do you think of it, Sir?

欣慰 丨 如 what could be more agreeable?

丨 可以與我友 how can he become my friend?

小 丨 奴 a servant, a young attendant.

傒 *'hi* Used with the last.

A waiter, one who stands at the right hand; a page or boy; to serve; name of an ancient tribe on the northeast of China.

丨 奴 a servant-boy.

嫨 *'hi* A waiting-maid; a slave girl in the service of an officer.

徯 *'hi* From to *walk* and a *page*; occurs used with the next.

To wait for or on; to expect and attend on; a narrow path, a goat-path.

丨 我后 waiting for (or on) my prince.

丨 待 to wait for one.

今雖遭此 丨 後毋咎 although we have met this difficulty, I hope there will be no trouble in future.

蹊 *'hi* A footpath; a road or track up a hill; a bridle-path, a narrow way; to go across, to penetrate where no path is made.

丨 徑 a narrow path on a hill-side.

山 丨 a mountain path.

丨 蹺古怪 very extraordinary; unusual, strange.

桃李無言只自成 丨 though the peach and plum cannot talk, yet paths form under them, — because people are attracted by their goodness; so with real virture.

曲逕丨磵 to follow the winding paths and cross the pretty bridges — in the country.

螇 *ˎhʻi* A noisy kind of green cicada, or a grasshopper with a note like its name, the 丨蚸 heard in hot weather.

Read *ˎkʻi*. A sort of bee which burrows its nest; the ground-bee.

鞵 *ˎhʻi* Shoes made of raw hide, or with hide soles; the sole.

女丨 or 坤丨 a Chinese lady's shoe.

紅繡丨 the red embroidered shoe, is a fancy name for the red bean.

鼷 *ˎhʻi* A sort of minute mouse which bites so gently as to give its victim no pain, but the bite is venemous; it is also called 甘口鼠 sweet mouthed rat, and may denote a kind of insect, but more probably refers to an animal like the tiny harvest mouse (*Mus messorius.*)

兮 *ˎhʻi* From 八 *eight* or divide, and 气 *breath, q. d.* the breath dividing or issuing forth.

An interjection of admiration, used in poetry alone, placed at the end of a line or cæsural pause, as if to take breath, and emphasize the expression, like *Selah;* but also of inquiry or doubt, if in the first part of it; it is a final expletive in many cases, to show that the sentence is poetical.

安且吉丨 fitting and tasteful, eh? — said of dress.

乃如之人丨 just that very man.

鳳丨鳳丨何德之衰 Oh Fung! Oh Fung! how your virtue has degenerated.

有美人丨天一方 I have a dear one, besure, but she is far off under her own sky.

燕笑語丨 how we did laugh and talk at the feast!

畦 *ˎhʻi* From *field* and *scepter*.

A field containing fifty *meu*, or between eight and nine acres; a parcel of ground; the labors of the fields.

菜丨 a kitchen garden.

病於夏丨 distressed by the summer's toil.

一丨菜 a row of growing vegetables.

Read *ˏkwéi*. A low wall around a field.

嵇 *ˎhʻi* From 山 *hill* and 稽 to *examine* contracted for the sound.

Name of a mountain in Poh cheu 亳州 in Ying-cheu fu in the north of Nganhwui; 丨康 Hi K'ang lived here, and gave it his name, which he had changed from 奚 to escape trouble.

巂 *ˎhʻi* Combined of 隹 a *pheasant*, with 屮 a *sprout* on top to represent the crest, and 冏 *splendid* for the phonetic.

A sort of bird classed among the swallows; a revolution.

子丨, a bird like a hoopoe, which the people of Sz'chʻuen say was transformed from a gentlewoman, the wife of his minister, whom the king having forced, died of grief; perhaps the crow-pheasant is the bird here referred to.

丨規 one revolution of a wheel.

Read *ˏsui*. An old name of Li-kiang fu 麗江府 in Yunnan, for which 嶲 is now the common form, and to which this character as a primitive is continually contracted.

酅 *ˎhʻi* An old town in the state Ki 紀 in the southeast of Shantung, but afterwards taken by the ruler of Tsi.

丨下 a place in the state Tsi north of the River Tsi, in the northwest of Shantung.

攜 携 *ˎhʻi* To lead by the hand, as a child or blind man; to go with, to conduct, to take along; to lock arms, as in walking; to carry off or take up in the hands; to leave; to lead apart.

提丨 to lead, to carry in the hand; to recommend.

丨眷 my family is with me.

丨帶 to take along with one; to sustain from falling.

丨手 to take another by the hand.

丨筐 to carry a basket on the arm.

丨失 carried off and lost.

左右丨僕 personal attendants.

丨持 or 丨起 to lift up and carry away.

如取如丨 if you take it up and carry it away.

扶老丨幼 support the aged and lead away the young, as Æneas did when escaping danger.

觿 *ˎhʻi* A sort of horn stiletto, or ivory bodkin hung at the girdle; it was used to untie knots.

童子佩丨 the lad wears a bodkin.

觜丨 a star λ in Orion; a large tortoise, for which the next is probably the correct form.

蠵 *ˎhʻi* A species of land tortoise, whose shell is rather fine; it is marbled and used in divination; name of a star.

丨龜 or 靈丨 the great tortoise found about the mouth of the Yellow River; it is said to make some kind of noise.

鑴 *ˎhʻi* A kind of tripod or boiler; a large basin; a large bell; the rays proceeding from the sun like darts, as it shines through the clouds; they are indicative of good luck, and describe the watery rays at sunset.

Read *ˏkwéi*. An awl.

黳 ꜀hi A mineral described as a beautiful black stone, and explained to be a mineral amber of a clear black color like lacker; a piece is mentioned that was large as a cart-wheel; it is said to come from Tibet or Turfan, and may denote a kind of jet, of which large fine specimens are found in that region.

喜 ꜀hi From 口 *mouth* and 壴 a *band of music;* it must not be confounded with *shen* 善 goodness.

Joy, delight; glad, joyful; to be pleased with; that which gives joy; to give joy to; to rejoice; to like.

丨氣 or 丨色 a joyful face; a happy look.

有丨色 gratified; it gives pleasure; I am greatly pleased.

丨悅 pleased with.

丨金 festival fees.

丨容 your portrait; pleasant looking.

甚丨 greatly pleased with.

丨歡 joyful, delighted.

丨事 or 丨慶 a joyful occasion, a festa.

辦丨事 to prepare for a merry time.

不勝之丨 exceeding great joy.

丨溢門庭 the whole house is alive with merriment.

新丨 a happy newyear to you! 恭丨 is more commonly used in the southern provinces.

夫人有丨了 your wife is with child; 有了丨了 is another form of the same congratulation.

道丨 to congratulate one upon anything.

丨愛 to delight in, to joy in.

丨樂 joy and delight; it is also a Budhist term (*tushita*) for the fourth heaven (*deva-loka*) where *bodhi-satwas* are reborn before they become Budhas on earth; it is often applied to monasteries.

雙丨 doubled joys, as when two happy events come together; this is also written 囍, and placed on walls as a wish that all joys may be doubled.

先否後丨 when things are very bad, then they must surely mend.

妹丨 a courtesan who aided Kwéi or Kieh in his orgies, and brought on the ruin of the Hia dynasty, B. C. 1765.

報丨 it foretokens good luck, as when the lampwick opens.

中心丨之 I like it with all my heart.

丨出望外 a pleasure exceeding all my hopes, a most unexpected joy.

丨雀 the magpie, from its merry-sounding chatter.

丨雀尾 magpie's tails, the perked-up things put at the ends of the ridge-pole on fine houses.

憙 ꜀hi To get the *heart's joy*; gratified, exultant at success; pleased, fond of doing.

丨改造 fond of altering and making.

欣丨 delighted at.

蟢 ꜀hi A small, long-legged red spider, called 丨子 or 喜子 the happy child, which suspends itself by the web from trees; the people who meet it carefully let it go, as it is supposed to denote good luck.

壁丨 a small flat-bodied spider.

唏 ꜀hi From *mouth* and *hopeful;* used for 欷 to sob, and the next.

To grieve and mourn without weeping; to be alarmed and whimper; to breathe hard in sleep; one defines it to laugh, to chuckle.

丨哈 surprising! dreadful!

齂 ꜀hi To snore in a loud manner; to blow the nose, to clean the nose.

狶 ꜀hi Occurs used for 豨 a sprite; the noise used in calling pigs.

匸 ꜀hi Intended to represent a *receptacle*, with a *lid* over it to hide things; it is the 23d radical, and is used only as such in a few characters relating to coffers; it nearly resembles ꜀*fang* 匚 a wild.

A case or coffer for storing things.

戲 hi꜄ From *weapon* and a sort of *dish*, referring to the wings of an army.

To fence with weapons; to play, to divert one's self; to joke; in jest; a play, a comedy, a mime, a theatrical performance; to make fun of; to dally with.

丨笑 to laugh at.

丨謔 to make sport or game of one, to play practical jokes.

調丨 to take liberties with, to dally with.

弄丨法 or 變丨法 to play tricks; juggling; to do sleight-of-hand tricks.

丨弄 to disturb one, to annoy, to make a fool of.

聽丨 or 睇丨 to go to the theater.

演丨 or 做丨 to act plays.

一班丨子 a company of actors.

丨檯 or 丨枱 the boards; also called 丨館 or 丨棚, a theater, a play-house or stand.

丨房 the green-room.

一齣丨 or 一軸丨 one act of a play.

丨舞 to play, as children or mummers.

鴨丨水 the gambols of ducks.

龍丨珠 the dragon playing with the pearl.

魚丨落花 the fish are nibbling at the fallen blossoms.

嘲丨 to ridicule, to make gibes at, to joke.

Read ꜀*hu*. An exclamation of regret.

於꜀丨前王不忘 Ah! the ancient kings are not forgotten.

繫ˀ *hi*ˀ From *silk* and to *connect*.

To tie, to bind, to fasten on; to continue; to hold on, to retain; to keep in mind; attached to; to recall, as something by association; as a title in some histories, denotes private or appended biographies.

丨舟 to fasten a boat.

提丨兒 a strap or cord to fasten by, as that which holds a button on a cap.

丨累 to implicate.

丨聯 results following; the consequences of an act.

丨戀 or 丨懷 to remember with affection; ardent love.

無庸丨念 don't be so anxious about him, as an absent friend.

丨上去 tie it on so that I can draw it up, as a hod of mortar.

丨辭 explanation of the prognostics.

丨春情 anxious thoughts come up — about my absent husband.

系ˀ *hi*ˀ From 糸 *silk* and 丿 a *stroke* or stem; it is used with the preceding, and some regard it as a contracted form.

The clue, connection, link, or passage, which joins things; a succession, as in a family; related to, succeeding; in *anatomy*, a nerve or connecting tube.

世丨 a genealogy; successive generations.

譜丨 a family record.

相丨 continuous, mutually joined.

胃丨 the æsophagus.

肝丨 a tube or duct which native physicians think connects the heart and liver; there are two others from the heart to the spleen and kidneys.

丨累無窮 an interminable succession, an infinite series.

不勝懸丨之至 the deepest anxiety and concern, as for another's safety.

丨出皖南 my ancestors came from Nganhwui.

係ˀ *hi*ˀ From *man* and to *connect*; used with the last two.

To connect with what is before; belonging to; attached to; to bind; the substantive verb, to be, is, are.

委丨 or 實丨 or 本丨 it is thus, it is truly so; the reply is 丨咯 or 果丨 that is the case.

丨都有 you have all here; there are all kinds.

丨屬 connected with; belongs to that.

丨麼 is it not so?

關丨重大 his responsibilities are great; the consequences are very serious.

他丨惡人 he is a bad man.

In *Cantonese*. A *preposition*, from, at, in; to remain, to stay at; a particle showing that all is done, no more, well so.

你重丨個處 do you still live here?

丨邊處來 where do you come from?

點丨呢 how will it be? how is it?

繫ˀ *hi*ˀ The pivot in a well-sweep on which it works; the name of a fruit like a plum.

禊ˀ *hi*ˀ From *worship* and to *join*.

A sacrifice or worship known in the Tsin 晉 dynasty, called 祓丨, observed in spring and autumn; it was designed to avert bad harvests and other evils.

褉ˀ *ch'i* A girdle; a sleeve; a slit; the opening or slit in a gown or dress robe at the bottom is 開丨; it enables the wearer to walk easily.

霼ˀ *hi*ˀ From *cloud* and *vapor*; interchanged with 俙 like.

Cloudy.

霎丨 indistinct; sun somewhat obscured, but the sky bright.

愾ˀ *hi*ˀ A long sigh, *q. d.* the *heart's breath*; to groan, to sigh.

丨然太息 one needs to sigh over it.

丨我寤歎 groaning aloud as I lie on my bed.

Read *k'ai*ˀ Angry, enraged at; to reach to.

破丨衝鋒 break their raging onset, and drive them back.

餼ˀ *hi*ˀ From to *eat* and *breath*.

Living cattle anciently offered to the gods or presented to princes, to give a banquet; provisions, food, grain, fruit.

丨羊 a living sheep, presented at the new moon.

馬丨 fodder for horses.

廩丨 allowances of rice given to *suits'ai*; it has become reduced till now it is about one half the original amount of a pecul per month.

In *Cantonese*. To feed animals.

丨猪 feed the pigs.

丨雀未曾 have you fed the bird?

咥ˀ *hi*ˀ From *mouth* and *reaching* to.

To laugh out; sneering laughter.

丨丨然 jolly, loud laughing.

兄弟不知丨其笑矣 my brothers will not know it, and will only laugh at me.

Read *tieh*, To bite, to gnaw.

履虎尾不丨人亨 it is lucky if you step on a tiger's tail that he don't bite you; — a fortuneteller's saw.

盻ˀ *hi*ˀ From *eye* and an *interjection*; it is not the same as *pan*ˀ 盼 to see.

To look at in anger.

丨丨然 wearied out, ceaseless toiling and moiling.

瞋目丨之 looked at him sternly.

殊深懸丨 in much anxious doubt.

屭 屓 *hí'* From *corse* and *precious*; the abbreviated form is not common.

The exertion of titanic strength; herculean, robustious; extraordinary, Samson-like strength; to lie down to rest.

贔 丨 a powerful being in the days of Yü, who is fabled to have opened a passage through a hill for a river to run; he is now represented by a tortoise, which is sculptured as a basis for stone tablets in temples and princely mausolea.

呬 *hí'* An old word used in the east of Shantung for breathing.

昆夷 丨 矣 savages breathe hard through the nose.

犔 *hí'* An ox dying from want of food; cattle starving; provender, fodder.

HIA.

Old sounds, ha, ka, ga, *and* hat. *In Cantonese*, ha, *and one* la *and* hăk; — *in Swatow*, hé, hia, *and* hu; — *in Amoy*, ha; — *in Fuhchau*, ha, hiă, *and* haik; — *in Shanghai*, 'a, ya, 'o, hön, *and* hak; — *in Chifu*, hia.

躽 *hia* Hunchbacked, the body bent over; to stoop.

丨 腰 to bow, to bend low.

丨 不下 腰 unwilling (or unable) to bow.

谺 *hia* From *valley* and *tooth*.

The opening of a valley.

谽 丨 the adit of a gorge, a desolate mouth of a ravine, or wady between hills. This phrase is written in many ways.

閜 *hia* From *door* and *tooth*; interchanged with the last.

To close a door, and yet leave a crack.

丨 着 門 不 要 關 上 close the door without shutting it.

歑 *hia* To open the mouth and breathe slowly, as when eating peppermint or ginger; to pant.

霞 *hia* From *rain* and *to borrow*.

Clouds tinged red, as at the coming dawn; vapor which looks lurid and lowering; a smoky red haze; flushed, bright.

雲 丨 cloudy red vapors.

開 作 臉 邊 丨 [the Althea] opens its flowers in emulation of a beauty's cheeks.

晚 丨 or 暮 丨 a bright ruddy sunset.

丨 背 a gentlewoman's mantle or robe.

餐 丨 "to dine on redness,"—*i. e.* to eat a watermelon.

莫 丨 霧 don't talk so confused; don't get flustered.

醉 流 丨 flushed with drink.

丨 光 萬 道 the bright rays shine in all directions, as the aureole over a god.

鰕 *hia* Crustaceans allied to the lobster and shrimp; a prawn, a crawfish, a crangon; it is also applied to the black fish from its leaps.

丨 子 or 子 母 丨 a shrimp.

明 丨 large yellow prawns.

龍 丨 the great crawfish or *Palinurus*.

銀 丨 small shrimps (*Palæmonidæ*), which when dried are called 丨 米 or shrimp rice.

丨 油 oil from prawns.

丨 shrimp sauce.

笋 丨 dry salted prawns.

丨 鬚 a shrimp's feelers; also a fancy name for finely woven door-screens of bamboo.

丨 𢭃 鈒 a skin-flint, *lit.* one who will cut a shrimp's egg in two. (*Cantonese.*)

蝦 *hia* Like the last, and mostly used for it.

A shrimp, a prawn.

丨 蛤 a sort of shell-fish.

丨 夷 the people of Yeso, so called because they were said to burrow like crabs or crayfish.

Read *hia* or *ha*. A frog.

丨 蟆 a sort of speckled frog with warts.

In *Cantonese*. Playful, skipping like a shrimp.

騢 *hia* A horse of a light rust color, likened to a topaze, or the hue of prawns.

有 駰 有 丨 there were both bay and grisly horses.

遐 *hia* Distant, remote, afar off; advanced in years; occurs used for *ho* 何 why.

丨 邇 皆 知 everybody knows it.

丨 邇 一 體 both those near and those far off; those here and far away are alike.

松 鶴 丨 齡 the fir and stork are long-lived; — they are both used as emblems of longevity.

丨 終 to remove away, to make an end of.

丨 荒 unknown, desert regions.

蕸 ˏhʻia The leaves of the water-lily or Nelumbium.

Read ʻkia Water rushes not yet in flower.

瑕 ˏhʻia A reddish stone; a blemish, flaw, or crack in a gem; a fault, a bad habit; distant, separated; how; severe.

烈假不丨 his great merits were without stain.

不丨有害 would not this act bring trouble?

丨病 a defect in a gem.

丨不謂矣 why have you not told me?

丨疵 a fault, a defect in character; a mistake, an oversight.

丨丘 an old name of Tsz'-yang hien 滋陽縣 the chief district of Yen-cheu fü in the south of Shantung.

乘丨則神 a very sprite in taking advantage of another's mistake; clever at seizing on a fault.

白玉無丨 white jade has no flaw; *met.* spotless purity.

嘏 ˏhʻia The throat, the gullet.

In *Cantonese.* To vex, to treat harshly, to intimidate.

丨霸人 to insult, to browbeat another.

叚 ˏhʻia To be distinguished from *twanʾ* 段 an affair, and used chiefly as a primitive.

A surname.

Read ʻkia, and used for 假 to borrow, to transfer to another.

閜 ʻhʻia To throw wide open as a door, and see a vacancy within; empty, vast; a large cup.

丨砢 to overthrow, as an enemy.

啁 ʻhʻia Same as 呵 to laugh aloud.

丨丨 a phrase in imitation of the sound of noisy laughter.

詬丨 to bluster; to bully one.

下 hʻiaʾ The character originally represented something *under* the *earth.*

Below, underneath; bottom, lower side, down; mean, low, vulgar; poor in quality, inferior; belonging to, as a banner; near; at the close of, as the year; next; a time, once; to lower, to descend; to fall as rain; to go down; to go from the capital; to lay, as an egg; to curb, to keep under; the person who is under or inferior; to imprison; the people, the lower classes; to sprinkle upon, as a powder; to place, as the hand; in *grammar*, what follows; as 函丨 the purport of the following; 起丨 a transition of the subject in hand; turn now to the next.

丨次 the next time.

丨月 the following moon.

一丨子 one rap, as on a drum.

在底丨 it is below; underneath.

丨民 the people, the multitude, the lower classes; but 丨流 denotes the baser sort, vicious people.

丨貨 to ship off goods.

丨船 to embark.

丨蘇州嗎 are you going to Suchau?

丨不去 discontented with, offended at; it will not do, it can't pass; I cannot stand it.

慮以丨人 he tries to think himself to be less than others.

手丨 dependants, aids; but 丨手 is to begin to act, to lay down the hand.

丨人 servants, attendants.

丨聲 a low tone, a low pitch.

丨便 the right hand or inferior side.

雨不丨來 it will not rain.

丨丨來 it does rain.

四丨裏 everywhere, all around, as in a house.

不恥丨問 do not hesitate to ask your inferiors.

不丨數千 not less than many thousands.

必先丨之 you must go to him first.

治丨 we who are under your control, said by the gentry or others to a local magistrate.

丨品 a poor sort, inferior.

丨氣 to repress, to curb anger.

丨找多少 how much did you exchange it for?

丨朝鮮 he invaded Corea; *i. e.* he descended on it.

丨戰書 to send a challenge to battle.

丨地 bottom lands, plains; also used for this lower world.

君能丨丨 a prince can condescend to his inferiors; it can also mean, your abilities, Sir, are very ordinary.

In *Pekingese.* An hour, the hour or stroke of the clock.

六丨半 half past six.

回來一丨多鐘 come back in about an hour.

In *Cantonese.* A little while.

等一丨 stop a minute.

一丨同去 I'll go with you presently.

夏 hʻiaʾ Formed of 夊 to *follow* and 頁 a *leaf* contracted; occurs used for the next.

Summer, the time when nature borrows largely and becomes great; mixed colors, variegated, large, expanding.

丨衣 summer dresses.

丨坐 a summer retreat, a Budhist term for a season of retirement and meditation in summer.

大丨 an old name for musical instruments.

丨楚 a ferule, a rod.

丨國 or 大丨 an old name for Bactria or part of it.

行丨之時 plant the fields at the right time.

丨天 or 丨季 the summer season.

丨至 the summer solstice.

炎丨 weather like the dog-days.

丨布 Chinese linen, grass-cloth.

功揚涵 丨 his merits are known throughout the country

綠樹陰濃 丨 日長 the dense shadows of the luxuriant trees lengthen out the summer's day.

丨 枯草 a labiate plant, resembling the Lophanthus in its habit, with a capitate inflorescence, which dries up in the summer.

丨 日可畏 dog-days are really to be dreaded.

丨 朝 the first great Chinese dynasty of Hia from B. C. 2205 to 1766; a list of seventeen sovereigns is given, who reigned during this period.

華 丨 or cultivated Hia, is still used for China, denoting the country not its government; while 諸 丨 for the same has become obsolete.

廈 廋 *h'ia'* From *shelter* and *summer*; the first form is most usual.

A great house, a mansion.

便 丨 a side-room; the smaller rooms on the sides of a court.

一木難支大 丨 you can't make a palace out of one stick.

大 丨 須異材 a great house demands a great variety of materials; — a great ruler needs many talents in his officers.

丨 門 Amoy.

望 丨 村 the village of Mongha near Macao, where the first American treaty was signed.

庌 *h'ia'* Regarded the same as the last in its meaning of rooms built against a wall; in Peking it is mostly used for the back of a house, where there is no verandah or porch.

前廊後 丨 a verandah before, and a flush wall behind.

半 丨 的廂房 a row of side-rooms built against the wall.

暇 *h'ia'* From *day* and to *borrow*.

Leisure, relaxation: unoccupied; self-indulgence; to wait.

偷 丨 to take a rest, to have a vacation.

稍 丨 when I have a little leisure.

未 丨 very busy, no time for it.

丨 逸 easy going, slow, moderate.

閒 丨 not much to do.

餘 丨 over-time, after the day's work is done.

不敢自 丨 I can't think of indulging myself.

須 丨 to wait patiently for, as an erring son to reform.

不 丨 深究 he did not take time to inquire into it fully.

丨 日 a day of leisure; a period of repose.

迨我 丨 矣 when we have a leisure day.

罅 墲 *h'ia'* From a *dish* and to *cry* out, because earthenware often cracks in baking; it is occasionally written with 金 as a radical instead of the right one, and more frequently with 土 earth.

Rent, cracked; a crevice, an opening; a fissure; a chance, an occasion, a pretext; yawning, gaping; to crack, as the earth in drought; *met.* foppish.

裂 丨 a split, a crack.

孔 丨 a cleft, a hole.

漏 丨 a leak, a crack where the water runs through.

莫ˏ教窻 丨 紙條鳴 don't let the cracks in the lattice go on singing that way.

彼此毫無 丨 隙 not the least grudge between them.

牆 丨 a hole in a wall.

巷 丨 a narrow alley.

丨 隙 a fissure, a crack; *met.* a cause of offen e, an occasion for strife.

Read ˏ*hu*, and used as another form of 呼 to summon.

In *Cantonese.* Dirty; a final particle indicating that a thing is done, or will do as it is.

做乜野 丨 what *have* you been doing.

丨 苴 foul, dirty, as linen.

睱 *h'ia'* To look at carefully and leisurely; to watch with interest, as a vessel maneuvering.

碬 *h'ia'* A stone split through; clefts in rocks.

丨 石爲魚穿 the fish go in and out through the rocky fissures.

疨 *h'ia'* From *disease* and to *descend* as the phonetic.

A diarrhea.

諕 *h'ia'* This is often incorrectly written like *hiah*, 瞎 blind.

Wild, reckless talk.

說 丨 話 to deceive, to tell untruths.

襾 *h'ia'* Composed of 冂 a *cover*, with 上 and 下 interwoven into it, to show its enveloping character; it is the 146th radical of a few common characters, and the Chinese dictionaries caution the reader not to confound it with *si* 西 west.

A cover, anything which overshadows.

HIAH.

Old sounds, hat, kat, gat, hap, *and* gap. *In Canton*, hăt, hap, *and* ap ; — *in Swatow*, hat, ap, kiap, *and* chiap ; — *in Amoy*, hat, gát, ah, ap, gap, hiap, k'iat, *and* kiap ; — *in Fuhchau*, hak, ak, hiek, *and* k'ak ; — *in Shanghai*, hèh, hè, 'èh, kiėk, kèh, *and* yèh ; — *in Chifu*, hiah..

匣 ꜀hʻia꜇ From a *case* and a *scale*. A chest, a trunk of a small size ; a coffer, a casket ; a press or escrutoire ; a case for books ; to inclose.

拜帖〡 a card-case.

箱〡 a box, a nicely made case.

花線〡 a lady's thread-case.

珠寶〡 a jewel-case, a casket.

〡劍圍燈 he incloses a sword and surrounds a lamp ; — said of a clever but plain-looking man.

柙 ꜀hʻia꜇ A pen for tigers or wild beasts ; a lock-up or pen for prisoners ; to cage ; a scabbard.

楓〡 name of a fragrant tree, perhaps the sassafras.

虎兕出於〡 the tigers and the rhinoceroses have got out of their cages ; *met.* the rulers are cruel or remiss, and the people rebel.

狎 ꜀hʻia꜇ From *dog* and a *scale*. A well trained dog ; to approach near ; familiar with, accustomed ; irreverent, disrespectful ; to desecrate, to contemn, to slight ; to change ; to caress.

〡愛 mutual attachment.

玩〡 to play with, to toy with, as a woman.

褻〡 to desecrate, to profane, to do indignity to.

輕〡 to disregard and slight.

侮〡 to annoy, to disturb, to treat irreverently.

未〡君政 I am not used to government affairs.

〡優 to entertain or see jugglers or actors.

〡習 intimate with ; expert at.

呷 ꜀hʻia꜇ To swallow, to gulp down ; to taste ; to inhale, as fishes do water.

噏〡 to sip, to drink.

〡一啖茶 take a drink of tea.

〡一口酒 sip a little wine.

嗅〡 the cry or hum of a crowd.

In *Cantonese*. To tuck up the sleeves or dress ; to turn up the skirts.

〡褲頭 to tuck up the trowsers.

〡艜 to strap the tiller, as when steering in a high wind.

怾 ꜀hʻia꜇ Pleased ; joy, delight.

瞎 ꜀hʻia꜇ From *eye* and *injury*. Blind of one or both eyes ; blindly, ignorantly ; benighted ; heedless, recklessly ; to do things blindly, to act as if blind.

〡子 a blind person ; used as an epithet, you blind lout !

〡七〡八 all in confusion.

〡一目 lost one eye ; such a person is called 〡虎 a blind tiger, a cyclops.

〡闖 to run against, like a blind man ; to be disappointed.

摸着〡兒 too dark to see ; *i. e.* it is time to light the lamps.

莫弄得黑燈〡火的 before the dark lamps and blind fires are used ; — before lamp-lighting.

〡子摸魚 like a blind man seeking a fish ; — *i. e.* I cannot find him ; also a name for the blindman's buff.

〡答譐 to answer like a blind man ; to mislead by one's replies ; to talk with wayfarers.

〡弄 to meddle with in a disorderly manner.

〡充掌櫃 to heedlessly advance money, to venture it blindly on a scheme.

兩個〡子作揖 [you are like] two blind people bowing to each other ; — neither of you know anything about it.

說〡話 (properly written 說譁話) to tell a falsehood ; to lie.

盲人騎〡馬 a blind man riding a blind horse ; *i. e.* running into danger heedlessly.

In *Shanghai*. Like, resembling.

〡像 or 〡替 like ; looks the same.

轄 鎋 舝 ꜀hʻia꜇ From *carriage* or *metal* and *injury* ; the third form is antique. The linch-pin, or iron ring on the nave, which keeps the wheel in its place ; the creaking or rumbling of a cart ; to govern, to rule ; to regulate or guide public morals, as a censor does ; to turn.

統〡 to direct generally, to oversee.

管〡 to control, to rule over.

萬世之桎〡 the controller of all ages — is filial piety.

受〡 to be under another's orders.

投〡留客 to take out the linch-pin and keep a friend ; — to urge a guest to stay.

左〡 and 右〡 names of stars $\alpha\ \beta\ \tau\ \eta$ Algorab in Corvus.

峽 hʻia꜄ Hills each side of a chasm or gorge, with a stream below ; the watershed of hills ; a rapid formed by an island in a stream, or by hills contracting it ; a narrow reach or gut ; a strait.

〡口 a pass in the hills.

水〡 a rapid, applied only where steep banks contract the stream.

丨州 an old name for I-chang fu on the Yangtsz' River.

來龍過丨 the dividing ridge of hills.

巫丨 and 三丨 are noted gorges and peaks in the east of Sz'-ch'uen.

硤 *h'ia'* Like the last.

The name of an ancient town, 丨石 in the province of Hupeh, near I-chang fu, where a battle took place B. C. 230; subsequently the place was known as 丨州, derived from the rapids in the Yangtsz' River.

狹 *h'ia* From *dog* and to *squeeze*; this and the next are constantly interchanged.

Narrow, strait, the opposite of 廣; mean, contracted, narrow-minded; to regard as petty; to treat as mean.

丨窄 narrow, as a boat; insufficient, cramped for room.

肚皮丨窄 niggardly; mean, stingy.

卑丨 or 丨志 contracted views, prejudiced; mean; low-live.

度量丨 sordid, petty; illiberal.

丨路相逢 they met in a narrow path; *i.e.* these enemies could not avoid each other.

無自廣以丨人 do not condemn other's straits by your freedom.

陜 *h'ia* Used with the last; it must not be confounded with *Shen* 陝 the province of Shensi.

A narrow defile.

丨隘 a narrow pass; a gorge, a defile; a confined place in a river; in straits.

丨門 a narrow door; *met.* the strait gate.

劼 *h'ia'* From *strength* and *happy*.

Firm, determined, energetic; diligent, careful.

丨毖 vigorous and earnest.

黠 *h'ia'* From *black* and *lucky*.

A deep, uniform black; crafty, wily, artful; or in a good sense, clever, intelligent.

奸丨 full of dodges, guileful.

狡丨 slippery, untrustworthy.

孰痴孰丨 which is the dolt, and which is the smart one?

圚 *'h'ia* The plaintive cry of the camel.

載重駝鳴丨 when loaded too heavily, the camel cries out.

鞈 *h'ia* A saddle-cloth.

紅葩丨韘 a horse's housings embroidered with red flowers.

洽 *h'ia'* From *water* and to *join*; it occurs used for its primitive.

To soak, as water into the ground; to instil, to imbue; to assemble; to permeate, to pervade; to blend, to harmonize with; to affect well; to supply, provided for; just, exactly; old name of a river, now called the 金河, on which Hoh-yang hien lies in the east of Sh nsi.

丨丨的纔去了 he has just this moment gone.

丨于民心 the people are well satisfied; it pleases the people greatly.

相丨 or 和丨 intimate, as friends; mutual liking; agreeable to, as two dispositions.

以丨百禮 to furnish everything for the ceremonies.

丨情合理 he has good sense and great ability.

恩丨 favors granted, as by government.

丨當 proper, agreeable, in order.

丨可 very well done, all right.

溥丨高論 to disseminate high, correct doctrine; true and exalted principles.

在丨之陽 on the north of the River Hiah.

教化浹丨 his doctrines pervade and reform, as the soul or world.

In *Cantonese*. To cover; to keep from the air, as a sore by a poultice; poor, neglected, dirty.

丨歪 spoiled, as by moldiness.

丨瘡 to poultice a sore.

丨丨脆 crackling, crisp, light, like pastry.

祫 *h'ia'* The *united sacrifice*, a general worship by relatives of their remote and near ancestors, made triennially by the emperor and princes; the smell of the sacrifices mingling in the temple.

大丨 the grand family sacrifice.

烚 *h'ia'* Fiery, blazing; at the south it means to provoke, to scold; to boil in water, to cook by boiling.

丨湯 to boil soup.

丨氣 to irritate.

偺 *h'ia'* Stout, vigorous, brawny.

丨不知懼 he is perfectly fearless.

垥 *h'ia'* Offal or rubbish heaped up.

埃丨 a high pile of dust and refuse..

HIAI.

Old sounds, ha, ka, kap, gap, *and* gak. *In Cantonese*, hai *and* hoi ; — *in Swatow*, hai, oi, hia, hoi *and* kiu ; — *in Amoy*, hai ; — *in Fuhchau*, hai, a, *and* ha ; — *in Shanghai*, yé, 'a, ya, *and* h'ié ; — *in Chifu*, hiai.

鞋 鞵 鞖 ˏh'ié — From *hide* and a *baton ;* the second form, though unauthorized, is common ; the third is antique, and is more frequently read ˏ*hi*.

Shoes ; a pump ; a slipper ; a gaiter ; a band or string.
一對丨 or 一雙丨 one pair of shoes.
氷丨 skates.
弓丨 a woman's shoe, worn by women with small feet.
水丨 wooden soled shoes for wet weather.
丨底 the sole of a shoe.
丨匠 a shoemaker.
丨抽 a shoe-horn.
丨金 fees paid to brokers.
踏拉丨兒 slippers without heels.
丨掌 a sole ; a strip of hide used to beat the mouth.
乍穿新丨高擡脚 one lifts his feet high when he has just put on a pair of new shoes ; — the man is not yet used to his new honors.

In *Cantonese*. Rough, hispid, harsh ; stingy, crabbed ; an interjection of disappointment, ah !
粗丨 coarse and rough.
佢甚丨 he is very mean.

諧 龤 ˏh'ié — From *words* or *reed* and *all* ; the second form is very unusual.

To harmonize, as musical instruments do ; to pair, to accord with ; consenting, accordant ; to agree, as upon a price ; to laugh at, to joke.
和丨 agreeing, of one mind.
白髮丨老 a hoar-headed, married pair ; a Darby and Joan.
事不丨了 the matter will brook no delay ; imminent, instant.
丨聲 harmonious tone or chords ; a grammatical term for characters whose primitive is a real phonetic, and rules the sound, as 案 is sounded like 安 ; or 妨 like 方, &c.
八音克丨 to make the notes to accord ; to harmonize the tones.
事無不丨 all is well arranged ; nothing is descordant.
丨笑 or 詼丨 to jest and laugh with ; to gibe, to sport with.

蟹 ˋh'ié — From *insect* and *to loosen* as the phonetic.

A crab.
丨羹 or 丨紛 crab soup.
膏丨 a large red species, fat and rich.
蟧丨 swimming sea crabs like the *Portunus ;* called 無腸公子 the young gentleman without bowels, from a popular notion.
黄油丨 a large swimming crab at Canton.
無脚丨似的 it is like a crab without legs ; *i. e.* the affair cannot be done, you can't get on.
快丨艇 at *Canton*, a rapid row-boat, so called from its oars, often as many as fifty or sixty.
扮丨 to tie a crab to take out its meat ; applied to a mode of tricing a man up by the hands and feet to make him confess.

駭 ˋh'ié — From *horse* and a *horary* character.

Suddenly alarmed, startled, terrified ; to change color from fear ; to disperse ; to beat the tattoo and arouse the army.
丨怕 to be scared, frightened.
驚丨 astonished, amazed.
丨愕 suddenly alarmed, startling.
丨羞 abashed, ashamed.
丨異 strange, frightful, horrid-looking.
丨形 he looks much scared.
不勝丨憤 excessively alarmed and angry at.

懈 h'ié˞ — From *heart* and *to loosen* as the phonetic.

Idle, remiss, negligent, inattentive ; slow.
丨惰 slow and idle, shiftless.
鬆丨 or 丨怠 lazy, inefficient in office.
夙夜匪丨 busy morning and night.
不丨 not to weaken, not allowed to diminish in vigor.

澥 h'ié˞ — From *water* and *to loosen*.

A creek or canal ; a cove or small inlet is 渤丨 ; it is applicable also to a large estuary.
漻丨 a rivulet.

In *Pekingese*. Thin, as congee or paste.
糨子丨了 the paste has turned to be watery, as from the weather.

嶰 h'ié˞ — A valley ; a low hill separated from a higher one ; name of a valley in the Kwănlun Mts.

獬 h'ié˞ — A fabulous animal, the 丨豸, half deer, half unicorn, also called 神羊 ; it dwells in the desert, and gores wicked men when it sees them ; the figure is used as the official embroidery of censors and intendants ; stern, firm, as this animal is thought to be.
丨冠 an ancient cap worn by judges.

邂 *k'ié'* To meet one unexpectedly; a pleasant accidental meeting.

丨逅 to come across unexpectedly, as a friend.

薢 *k'ié'* From *plant* and *to loosen* as the phonetic.

A woody climbing plant, the 萆丨 which has hooked spines and axillary tendrils, with large oval ribbed leaves, furnishing a tonic like sarsaparilla, of which the decoction is drank; some say it is the plant, while 土茯苓 is the root of the *Smilax China*, but this is unlikely, though the plant is most probably one of that genus, and in Kiangsi its root is used for food.

紅萆丨 has reddish flowers, and is probably a species of Asclepiadæ (a *Symphyoglossum*?)

Read *kiai*. A medicinal plant having yellow lance shaped leaves, reddish flowers, and round pepper like seeds; the 丨茩 seems to denote two plants, of which one is a sort of *Trapa*, the other resembles the *Hyoscyamus*.

丨寶葉 a plant growing near Macao (*Fallopia nervosa, Lour.*) whose leaves are dried for a tea.

丨草 a water plant (*Butomus umbellatus*) resembling a lily, whose rhizomes are eaten.

擨 *k'ié'* To take hold, to take up in the hand; to pass, as a dish at table; to bring to one.

丨茶來 bring the tea.

丨把刀仔 bring a penknife to me. (*Cantonese.*)

械 *k'ié'* From *wood* and *implement.*

Gyves, shackles, or manacles, whatever is used to fetter prisoners; military weapons, arms of all sorts; things carried by a grandee in his traveling equipage; a craft, an art.

軍丨 or 兵丨 weapons or spears, guns, artillery, swords, &c.

機丨 a curious contrivance, delicate machinery.

機丨變詐 a crafty, malicious scheme.

丨鬥 fights with weapons, usually refers to clan and village fights.

齘 *k'ié'* From *teeth* and *scaly plates.*

To gnash the teeth, as when angry; plates of mail arranged like teeth.

類丨 to exhibit a venomous hatred.

凡甲衣之欲其無丨也 whenever you dress in mail, it is important that the plates be even.

薤 *k'ié'* Composed of *plants*, *leeks* and *bad.*

A species of onion, the shallot or scallions (*Allium ascalonicum*), with fistular leaves, common in Hu-kwang; it is forbidden to those who fast; name of a mat.

丨薤 or 丨白 the bulbs of scallions.

山丨 a wild species of Allium without bulbs.

韰 *k'ié'* From *leek* and *broken;* it is used chiefly as a primitive, and is also written with the radical 人 added.

Courageous, bold, energetic; mean; hasty, urgent.

丨倮 daring, full of fight.

瀣 *ńié'* Mist or dewy vapor on the sea is 沆丨; also denotes night damps in northern regions. which are conducive to health, — an allusion, it may be, to the aurora.

師生沆丨一氣 the teacher and his pupils are all in a happy and pleasing accord.

HIANG.

Old sounds, hiung, kiung, *and* giung. *In Canton*, héung *and* hong; — *in Swatow*, hiàng, h^nié, *and* hang; — *in Amoy*, hiòng, kòng, hang, *and* k'iòng; — *in Fuhchau*, hiòng *and* hòng; — *in Shanghai*, hiāng *and* 'ong; — *in Chifu*, hiang.

香 *ₒhiang* Composed of 黎 *millet* and 甘 *sweet*, both contracted; it forms the 186th radical of a small and natural group of characters.

Fragrant, odoriferous, sweet; a fragrant or renowned name; reputable; the memory cherished for one's virtues; perfume, aroma, effluvia; incense; this word is much used in names of places.

丨氣 fragrance; sweet smell.

丨甜 sweet to the taste.

丨料 spicery, aromatics.

酒丨 the aroma of wine.

天丨 name for several fragrant orchids, like a Malaxis.

書丨 or 翰墨丨 a very literary reputation.

一炷丨 one stick of incense.

燒丨 or 拈丨 or 行丨 to worship, to burn incense; the last also means going to the temples.

丨爐 an incense jar or basin.

丨油 aromatic oils, as pomatum or bergamot; but in the north, it usually means sesamum oil.

丨案 an incense-table in a temple.

丨荷包 scent bags, small aromatic fobs for perfumes.

燒悶丨 to burn stupefying drugs.
丨客 worshipers, or visitors to temples.
丨珠 fragrant beads, made of lign-aloes and other woods.
丨烟冷落 the smoke of incense has ceased, as in a ruined temple.
安息丨 gum benjamin or benzoin.
木丨 putchuck, burned as an incense.

麘 ꜀*Hiang* The *fragrance* of the *deer*, *i. e.* the navel of the musk deer.
麝丨 musk.

鄉 ꜀*Hiang* From 邑 or 阝 *place* repeated back to back, with 皀 a *kernel* between them; it is not the same as *k'ing* 卿 a minister.

A village, the home whither people tend; a region; the country; in olden time five 州 made one 鄉 of 12,500 families; a neighborhood, a ward or part of a city; a great sound, as of rain; an entresol or place between flights of stairs; windows opposite; rude, rustic, country-like.
同丨 fellow townsmen.
住丨 or 落丨 in the village.
家丨 one's native country or place.
丨村 a village, a country town unwalled.
丨下 the country; at the village.
夢入白雲丨 he dreamed that he went to the cloudy halls.
老丨民 an elderly gentleman, an old man of sixty.
丨老 the village elder.
丨紳 a country gentleman.
丨黨 a village company, cabal, or society.
居國南丨 they dwell in the southern parts of the land.
丨科 or 丨試 the triennial examination for *küjin*.
丨愿 a hypocrite, a double-faced man.
異丨 a strange country, a distant region.

入醉丨 to frequent grog-shops and taverns.
打丨談 to speak a village brogue.
黒甜丨 to sleep soundly.
有丨隣 he has several neighbors near him.

Read *hiang'*, and used for 向, directed towards; time past, formerly.
丨' 導 to show the way, to guide, to pilot.
夜丨晨 the night draws on to the dawn.

薌 ꜀*Hiang* The fragrant smell of grain, as newly reaped millet; the odor of beef's tallow; used for the last.
微聞丨澤 to perceive a slight fragrance.
丨合 smell of a stack of millet.

膷 ꜀*Hiang* Soup or porridge made of beef hashed fine and boiled thoroughly; small ganglions found in the flesh of oxen or sheep.

舡 ꜀*Hiang* From *boat* and *work*; it is now chiefly used as a contraction for ꜁*chw'en* 船 vessel.

A sort of boat.
艅丨 a vessel or boat in the Wu country, an old name for the canal boats in Kiangsu.

亨 ꜀*Hiang* From 高 *high* and 日 *to speak*, both altered in combination; *q.d.* as when bringing in sacrifices to the gods; it differs now from 亨 successful, though originally like it.

To offer up with thanks, to present in sacrifice; to accept, as the gods do; to enjoy; to receive gratefully; to give enjoyment, to confer dignities; a dignity.
孝丨 filial offerings — to ancestors.
丨用 to enjoy the use of.
丨年多少歲 how long did he live?

福不可丨盡 it is not well to run through all your pleasures.
丨永遠福 to enjoy eternal happiness.
長丨 a long enjoyment.
丨國祚 to reign, to sit on the throne.
配丨 mating or equalizing the felicity, refers to the deification of the spirits of emperors, making them equal to Heaven and Earth.

饗 ꜀*Hiang* From to *eat* and *village*; occurs used for both the last and next.

To entertain a guest, to feast people; to offer in sacrifice; a banquet; a sacrifice; offerings.
一朝丨之 all the morning I will feast him.
宴丨賓客 to feast friends and guests, as at a 大丨 a state banquet or formal entertainment.
神丨 offerings for the gods.
祀丨 to present offerings of any kind.
尙丨 "still [come to] the sacrifice," — the usual end of a prayer to the gods.
上丨 a dinner to graduates.
丨糖 sugar figures carried at weddings.

響 ꜀*Hiang* From *sound* and *village* as the phonetic.

An echo, described as the "noise outside of the sound;" a noise, clamor, fracas; echoing, sounding, reverberating; jingling; used for an intensitive before adjectives.
丨亮 a loud, a distinct sound.
一聲丨 one word, one clap; a single sound.
水丨 the rippling of water, as by the side of a boat.
丨應 an echo, a reverberation; a response or general consent, popular coöperation.
丨晴天 a very clear sky, a cloudless day.

吹不丨 you can't make it sound, as a trumpet.

莫丨 silence! don't be so noisy.

影丨 shadow and echo, which like retribution, follow their cause.

影丨之談 mere idle rumor, gossip.

丨動兒 a noise of some sort, as a rustling or cry at night, that draws notice.

丨馬 jingling horses; *i. e.* a thief or highway robber, a bandit; a rebel leader.

磕丨頭 importunate; I beseech you earnestly; *i. e.* you can hear my head as it knocks.

ʿ响 *ʿhiang* An unauthorized and very common contraction for the last.

谷聲丨應 the valley repeats the echo.

In *Cantonese*. Used for 向 at or in a place.

你丨馬頭住呢 do you live at the landing-place?

ʿ餉 *ʿhiang* From *to eat* and *towards* as the phonetic.

The provisions given to husbandmen as part of their wages; rations for troops; taxes paid to government in kind; duties, excise; to give or send food; to provide an entertainment for one.

兵丨 pay and allowances of soldiers.

丨銀 revenue; moneys received for the land tax; commissariat funds.

納丨 to pay duties.

洋丨 maritime duties, imports.

丨單 an official receipt for duties.

婦丨于田 his wife took his food out to the field.

仇丨 he murdered those who supplied him with provisions; said of 葛伯 in the last days of the Hia dynasty.

饁丨 a boiled mess of greens and rice,—taken to the field-hands.

抽釐助丨 excise is collected here in aid of the revenue.

ʿ饟 *ʿhiang* Like the last.

To prepare food and take it out to the laborers in the fields.

其丨伊黍 they fed them with millet while at work.

ʿ蠁 *ʿhiang* From *insect* and *village*, but explained to be the insect that knows sound.

Larva which proceed from other caterpillars are 丨子, applied too, to the ichneumon flies which lay their eggs in them; grubs.

肸丨 may-flies or musketoes rising in swarms from damp grounds.

向ʾ *hiangʾ* From 口 *mouth* and 宀 *a cover*; *q.d.* an opening for ventilation; it is nearly synonymous with the next.

A window, an aperture; towards, facing, opposite to; from or to; to face; an object, an intention, a subject of study; formerly, hitherto, time past, heretofore; points of the compass; name of a small ancient feudatory in the present Ho-cheu 和州 in east of Ngan-hwui, near the Yangtsz' R.

丨日 on a former day, previously; towards the sun.

丨來 hitherto a while past.

一丨 for a while, formerly.

丨先走 going first.

方丨兒 the bearing, the aspect of, as a location.

丨北 northerly, facing the north.

志丨 the object of desire.

意丨 the intention; the scope of the idea.

丨他借銀 you can try to borrow money of him.

丨前去 to go ahead.

丨你說 I wish to speak to you.

丨我說 attend to what I say.

你丨那裏去 where are you going?

定個丨當 to settle the direction of, as a grave.

面面相丨 looking at each other, nonplussed.

二十四丨 the twenty-four points of compass; *met.* uneasy, as 你心二十四丨 your mind is quite bewildered.

心不丨 your mind is not on your work.

塞丨墐戶 close the [north] windows and stop up the doors.

嚮ʾ *hiangʾ* Used for the last.

Opposite; to incline to; to seek to attain; to approach; to show one's mind to; to guide; attractively, encouragingly.

天下丨應 the country relies on him, the empire turns to him.

丨背 backwards.

丨用五福 the settled or common use of every happiness.

丨于時夏 indicating the signs of the times to [the sovereigns of] Hia.

曏ʾ *hiangʾ* From *sun* and *village*.

A little while; formerly; lucid, plain, as evidence.

丨者 recently, a short time ago.

丨役之三月 I lately employed him for three months.

證丨今古 this is good proof for present and former times.

珦ʾ *hiangʾ* A kind of gem; some describe it as an ornament of stone worn by women as a girdle clasp.

巷ʾ *hiangʾ* The old form is composed of two 邑 *places* back to back, and 共 *public*, denoting the public thoroughfare in a place.

A side street, a crooked lane among the houses; an alley in a village; a bye-street; a wynd; a a narrow path or street of dwellings; a passage in a hareem.

在陋丨 in a wretched neighborhood.

柳 ㅣ brothels, called the willow lane, from their being found on watersides where those trees shade the paths.

火 ㅣ a narrow lane between adjacent buildings.

水 ㅣ a sluice to let in water.

永 ㅣ a row of side rooms behind the chief court of the palace, where female criminals were anciently confined.

ㅣ 口 entrance of a side street, or a 僻 ㅣ or bye-lane.

閭 ㅣ or 里 ㅣ a street, a neighborhood; a close or place.

ㅣ 戰 street brawls, a row.

ㅣ 議街談 street rumor, village gossip; a canard.

ㅣ 伯 a chief eunuch in a hareem; an old name.

閧 *k'iang'* A raised path between fields; to prepare, to make ready.

項 *k'iang'* From *head* and *work*.

The nape, the part which rests on the pillow; a sort, item, class, thing, or species of anything, but usually relates to money affairs; the effects from a cause; a source of income; funds, deposits; great; name of a small feudatory, now Hiang-ch'ing hien ㅣ 城縣 in Chăn-cheu fu in the east border of Honan.

ㅣ 帶 cap strings; a neck-ribbon.

頸 ㅣ the back of the neck, nearly the same as 脖 ㅣ, a common term for the throat.

款 ㅣ a deposit on interest.

公 ㅣ public funds; the general stock.

ㅣ 下未清 there are items (or charges) which are not yet cleared off.

欠 ㅣ debts; one's liabilities.

一 ㅣ 錢 one class of revenue or payments.

四牡 ㅣ 領 four steeds with long arched necks.

各 ㅣ 貨 each sort of goods.

別 ㅣ another kind.

ㅣ 圈 a neck ring of silver, a sort of torque worn by children.

來 ㅣ 兒 an income, the means of support.

指 ㅣ 兒 an uncertain income; a doubtful asset, as a bad debt.

這一 ㅣ 事情 this sort of thing, this kind of affair.

HIAO.

Old sounds, hio, kio, gio, kat, kak, *and* gat. *In Canton,* hiu, hao, *and* ngao; — *in Swatow,* ngao, hiò, *and* hau; — *in Amoy,* hiau, kau, ngau^{n}, *and* hau; — *in Fuhchau,* hiu, ngo, hau, *and* ngau; — *in Shanghai,* h'io *and* yo; — *in Chifu,* hiao.

囂 *‹h'iao* From four *mouths* around one *head; q.d.* the voice going above the head; it is also read *‹ngao.*

To vociferate; to cry out as when calling off; to scold, to rail at; clamor, hum, as in a market; a complaining or whining tone; contentious noise; name of a long-armed ape, a bird with a dogs tail; and a river.

讒口 ㅣ ㅣ to vilify with foul words, as the populace do.

聽我 ㅣ ㅣ you hear me with indifference and contempt.

民之 ㅣ ㅣ the people were dissatisfied with him.

民情浮 ㅣ the disposition of the populace is giddy and conceited.

ㅣ 陵人 to treat unfairly.

ㅣ 薄 impoverished, no resources, diminishing.

嘵 *‹h'iao* The querulous tone of complaint; the chattering of birds; to grieve, to mourn; fear dread.

ㅣ ㅣ 辯論 wearisome arguing and disputation.

嘮 ㅣ ㅣ garrulous, complaining.

予維音 ㅣ ㅣ I could only scream from dread.

In *Cantonese.* A corruption of *liao* 了, and used as a sign of the past tense.

做 ㅣ it is done.

寫 ㅣ written.

In *Shanghai,* pron. *‹nao,* though it is also written 喏 and 哪 in that dialect. See; to look at.

ㅣ 一星星 look! there is one star.

驍 *‹h'iao* From *horse* and *eminent.*

A gentle, good horse; strong, brave, courageous; skillful at pitching, as in quoits; to pitch at.

勇 ㅣ lusty, warlike, valorous.

ㅣ 騎校 an aid-de-camp to a general.

ㅣ 將 a brave general.

ㅣ 中' to hit the tag, as in pitch-farthing; to throw the rods into the jar, an old game.

熇 *‹h'iao* From *fire* and *high;* also read *koh, ‹hao,* and *‹tao,* in the same general sense of blazing.

To scorch, to burn or char; to roast, to toast; great heat.

ㅣ 乾 to dry before the fire.

多將 ㅣ ㅣ he has a raging fever.

Read *hoh*, Blazing.
丨丨 high flames.

呺 *'hiao* Vast, large.
丨然 empty, vast, boundless.

Read *'hao*. The noise of a blast; an angry sound; the voice of anger.

枵 *'hiao* A hollow root or stump of a tree; hollow, empty; famished; unfilled.

丨腹 an empty belly, hungry; *met.* ignorant.

丨耗 all has been wastefully spent.

丨元 a star in or near Aquarius.

丨腹從公 to do public duties without any salary.

鴞 *'hiao* From *birds* and to *cry out.*

A bird with a mournful voice, called 鴟丨 the white owl, or a similar species of the owl family; a fabulous animal.

青丨 a delicious tasted bird, good for soups or to roast.

丨獍 [like] owls and tigers — for fierceness; said of banditti.

梟 *'hiao* Composed of a *stick*, on which is the head of a *bird.*

A species of owl, called 土丨 which some say is the same as the preceding; it is used as an emblem of filial ingratitude, because it is said to eat its dam; Han Wu-ti served up a soup made of it on the 5th of the 5th moon; to expose the heads of criminals in cages in terrorem; brave, wicked, unscrupulous; a bandit.

丨首示衆 or 丨示 to expose heads in cages.

私丨 a smuggler; a lawless fellow.

丨騎 brave cavalry; hardy, moss-troopers.

丨雄 a wicked chieftain.

丨羹 an owl soup; — a figure for one who would kill even his kindred.

鹽丨 one who risks his head by smuggling or selling salt illegally.

庨 *'hiao* The lofty imposing effect of grand buildings.

丨豁 or 呀丨 grand and high, as a palace.

痚 *'hiao* Like the next and more correct; used in medical books.

A difficulty in breathing; asthmatic; coughing.

丨嗽 a hacking cough; irritation in the throat.

丨症 or 丨疾 the asthma.

哮 *'hiao* From *mouth* and *filial;* it is often used for the last, and is interchanged with the next.

To howl, to bellow; to scream, as a tiger; to roar, as beasts when angry or afraid; to grunt, as a boar; to pant, to gasp; to cough, to breathe hard.

咆丨怒罵 to angrily bluster and rail at.

丨瘕 short of breath.

丨喘 the asthma; to breathe with difficulty.

丨嚇 to frighten and scream at; to threaten, to browbeat.

唬 虓 猇 *'hiao* From *mouth* and *tiger;* also read *hia'* and occurs used for 諕 to intimidate; the third form also means the snarl of a dog; and the second is a synonym for a lion.

The scream or snarl of a tiger when about to spring; a growl, a roar; to alarm.

丨怒 very angry; irritated beyond bounds.

闞如丨虎 savage as a screaming tiger.

丨了一跳 he scared me dreadfully.

歊 *'hiao* From to *breathe* and *high.*

Vapor rising high; hot air ascending.

丨烝 hot mists, vapor like steam.

丨浮雲 the mist rises and floats off into clouds.

丨丨 hot air, like the summer-colt in dog days.

詨 *'hiao* To call one from a distance, to hail.

丨人 to halloo at, to call after.

骹 *'hiao* A sound, arising from cracking the joints; the shin-bone.

In *Fuhchau* used for 脚. The leg or foot; a classifier of one of a pair.

丨仔 a lackey, an attendant, a footman.

丨牛目 the ankles.

丨步 a step, a pace.

爻 *'yao* The original form is intended to represent the blending of things, referring to the diagrams; it forms the 89th radical of a few incongruous characters.

To mix, to intertwist; to lay crosswise; to imitate or change, referring to the mutations of things.

六丨 the six lines of a diagram as 豐; each line is called a *hiao*, and their meaning 丨象 or the diagram's *eidolon* or imagery.

卦丨 the eight original, or the sixty-four derived diagrams of Fuh-hi; the 世丨 refer to one's self, and the 應丨 to another, when casting a divination or charm.

丨辭 the explanation or occult end of each line in the diagram.

肴 *'yao* From *flesh* and to *blend;* like the next.

Savory viands; meats dressed for the table with the bones in; sacrificed meats; delicacies for a feast.

佳丨旨酒 delicate viands and sweet liquor; *i. e.* every luxury.

餚 *'yao* From to *eat* and savory *meats;* used with the last.

Meats; rich food; a feast; to taste.

燒丨 to roast meats.

丨饌 dressed meats, delicacies.

丨核 meats and fruits, as arranged for an offering.

殽 ˏyao — Used for the last and the next.

Mixed, blended; to mix, as metals; to confuse, to put into disorder; meat with the bones in it; pulse food or diet; to use as food; viands, sauces.

丨列 to set out in order, arranged properly.

混丨 all mixed up.

又有嘉丨 and they had their nice dishes too.

丨雜 miscellaneous; not perspicuous; muddy.

淆 ˏyao — Mixed, muddy, roiled; name of an affluent of the Yellow river in south of Shansi in Yangching hien 陽城縣 which runs across Honan.

丨亂 all in confusion.

淸濁混丨 the pure and turbid (*i. e.* the bad and the good) are all mixed up.

崤 ˏyao — Name of several hills in the western part of Honan province; a stream near them.

丨函關 a famous pass in Honan, not far from Wăn Wang's capital Fung-ching.

二丨山 two noted peaks in Min-chi hien in Honan fu.

膮 ˏh'iao — Soup made from pork cut up and boiled thoroughly; savory, fragrant.

丨羹 pork soup.

曉 ˋh'iao — From *day* and *eminent.*

Light, clear, as in the morning; early, the dawn; matins; luminous, perspicuous, plainly stated; intelligent, easy to perceive; to make to understand, to comprehend; to meet; gratified.

我丨得 I understand; I perceive it.

丨之 inform him; I see it clearly.

未丨何意 I don't catch the meaning.

明丨 clearly understood; a full perception of.

天將丨 it is getting to be light.

丨諭 a plain proclamation; to plainly command.

通丨 I fully understand it; it is very plain; — the opposite of 不知ˏ分丨 he does not understand it at all.

丨行夜宿 start early and stop late.

鷄報丨 the cock announces the dawn.

丨鐘 the matin bell — in a monastery.

皛 ˋh'iao — Composed of *white* thrice repeated

Three dishes, composed of turnips, rice, and sugar-candy, all of them white things, to which the character alludes, and called 丨飯; they were prepared by a man named Ts'ien, for his friend the poet Su Tung-p'o, but he answered it by a 毳飯 or downy meal, *i. e.* one out of empty dishes or 無飯; hence these two phrases denote a Barmacide feast

孝 h'iaoˀ — From 老 *old* contracted, with 子 *child* underneath; *q.d.* the child supporting the parent.

Duty, respect and obedience to parents and seniors; filial piety, which 百行丨爲先 is regarded as the chief of virtues, and is made to include loyalty, official dignity, confidence in friends, self-respect, and bravery in battle; the 經 line or warp of heaven, the 義 right of earth, and the 行 duty of man; time of mourning for parents; filial; mourning apparel; funeral.

丨子 a filial son.

穿丨 to put on the 丨服 or mourning dress for a parent; which is worn 27 months in different styles, till 丨滿 the mourning is ended, when 脫丨 it is laid aside.

丨順 dutiful and submissive to parents; to act filially.

忤逆不丨 he is an obstinate undutiful — son.

丨道 filial requirements; the logic of filial piety.

行丨 to obey a parent.

丨心 a filial heart.

謝丨 to visit and thank friends after a parent's funeral.

丨乎鬼神 to worship the ancestral spirits.

丨經 the Canon of Filial Duty, a work written about B. C. 475, by Tsăngtsz' 曾子 a disciple of Confucius.

丨廉 a term for a *küjin* graduate, intimating his loyalty and frugality.

神保是饗丨孫有慶 the deified [ancestors] enjoy the offerings, and their filial descendants are blessed.

効 h'iaoˀ — From *strength* and to *join*; it is much used where the next would be correctly employed.

To toil, to labor earnestly at, especially in the army; exertion in obedience to orders, or to reach an aim; to imitate; merit, exertions; meritorious results.

丨力 earnest efforts in a calling; in speaking of officers' punishments, as 丨力贖罪 to exert themselves to atone for their crimes, it denotes often that they are to remain in prison till the commutation money is paid, or the time of exile is up.

丨命疆埸 to valorously defend the imperial domains.

白丨勞 to moil for another without reward.

報丨 to recompense, as for a favor.

效 h'iaoˀ — Interchanged with the last and next.

To imitate, to learn, to copy; to fulfill, to verify; to require, as a charge; to give to; exertions, merits; effects, results; action, as of a medicine; efficacious; like, similar.

丨法 to follow, as a rule; to emulate, as a good man's life.

學丨or 丨放 to imitate, to strive after, to try to copy.

丨驗 the consequences of effort; effectual, prevailing; results of earnestness; verified.

功丨如神 divinely efficacious, as a pill.

功丨 merit earned by service; useful labors.

丨尤 to excel the pattern, as in doing evil.

前言已丨 the prediction has been verified.

服藥無丨 the medicine has produced no effect.

見丨 it has benefited me.

莫丨他 don't do as he does.

跟誰丨的 whom do you try to equal?

傚ˀ *h'iao'* From *man* and to *imitate*; used for the last.

To follow, to pattern after; to labor; effect.

倣丨 to do after, to copy.

君子是則是丨 the princely man regards it as his rule and pattern.

恔 *h'iao'* From *heart* and to *blend*.

Cheerful, as when in pleasant company; elated; hilarity, joy; jovial.

心丨 heartfelt pleasure.

於人心獨無丨乎 do you think that others are not also much delighted?

Read ʿ*kiao*. Wise, sagacious.

斆ˀ *h'iao'* Used as an old form of its primitive.

To imitate; to awaken, to arouse, to excite to effort; to learn.

丨鷄鳴 to imitate a cock's crowing.

丨悞 to startle one, as out of his indifference.

惟丨學半 to teach him was only one half of his labor.

Read ʿ*kiao*. Clever, intelligent, subtle wit; to perceive beforehand.

攪 *h'iao'* From *hand* and to *learn*.

To stir about; to mix up, to put in confusion.

HIEH.

Old sounds, hit, kit, gip, *and* git. *In Canton*, hit, hip, ip, *and one* lit; — *in Swatow*, hiap, hié, hia, hiat, *and* hat; — *in Amoy*, hiap, k'iat, íat, *and* giat; — *in Fuhchau*, hiek, hiȯk, *and* k'ik, — *in Shanghai*, yih, yėh, *and* hih; — *in Chifu*, hieh.

頡 ˛*chié* From *head* and *lucky*; occurs used for *kieh*, 竭 to exhaust.

To fly or soar up; a stiff or straight neck; to force to take less; rut of a wheel; to rob by violence; to diminish, to exclude.

丨滑 a double entendre, artful talk; difficult or involved; deceptive.

燕燕于飛丨之頏之 the swallows are flying about, up they go and down they come.

盜丨資糧 to rob and take people's goods.

挺丨就戮而不畏 if you should grab my neck with a threat to kill me, I would not be afraid.

倉丨 the name of the reputed inventor of Chinese characters in the reign of Hwangti.

襭 ˛*chié* The skirt of a dress; a lapel; to tuck the skirt in the girdle in order to put things into it; to carry in the lap or bosom.

薄言丨之 now tuck up your skirt.

敞丨以哺 she opened the bosom to suckle — her son.

纈 ˛*chié* To bind silk, as when dyeing it; tied up in skeins; to tie together; a knot; a joint, a knuckle; a quarrel, an altercation; a lawsuit.

打個丨 tie the knot.

老鼠丨 a slip-noose.

死丨 a hard knot.

核桃丨子 a knob on caps made of cord.

打實個丨 to embroil parties, to incite to quarrel.

擷 ˛*chié* From *hand* and to *soar*; used with the next.

To take up with the fingers and put in the lap or bosom, as when gleaning; to select.

頁 *yė'* The original form is derived from 首 a *head* over 儿 a *man*; it forms the 181st radical of a natural group of characters relating to the head, neck, &c.

The head; a classifier of the leaves of a book, a sheet, a door, a bundle of paper, a folio, a lobe of the liver, the layers in a cow's manyplus, and the slats in blinds.

一丨白摺子 the blank or fly leaf of a document.

冊丨 books bound with hard covers.

丨數 the number of sheets.

風翻書丨 the wind blows open the leaves of the book.

歇, *ₛhʻié* From to *breathe* and *why*; occurs used for the next.

To rest, to desist; to halt, to stop awhile; to discontinue; to keep silence, to hold up; to appease; to exhaust or let out; in some places used colloquially after verbs to show that they are completed.

丨住手 to rest from work; to let alone.

丨住口 to hold one's tongue; to stop eating.

丨嘴 stop talking; hold your tongue.

丨罷 hold up! stop! belay!

丨店 an inn; a rest-house; to stay at a hotel.

一丨 a moment; as 一丨大一丨 it seems greater every minute.

一丨丨工夫就來了 he will be here in a breath, — in a moment.

丨一宿 to stay over night.

丨工 to stop work, to take a holiday.

丨擔 to put down the load.

丨息 to cease work, to wait, to suspend operations.

丨夏 to pass the summer — in the country.

丨客 a guest at an inn.

不丨 uninterrupted, continuous.

丨一丨兒 take a rest, wait a spell; 丨丨 is often used as a question, Wont you rest a little? while at other times it means time after time, constantly.

脈丨至 the pulse is irregular.

丨業 to give up business.

帶丨人 to affect others.

猲, *ₛhʻié* A dog resembling the bull-dog in its short muzzle; to fear, to terrify.

丨狚 a great wolf.

載獫丨獢 he took in long nosed and snub-nosed dogs (greyhounds and mastiffs) with him.

恐丨頁民 I fear he will harass the peaceable people.

蠍, *ₛhʻié* From *insect* and to *rest*; it is often written 蝎, but not correctly.

A scorpion, the 丨子; its sting is 丨勾子; a sort of grub in wood, for which 蝎 is the correct form.

丨虎子 a house lizard is often thus written, but 蛇虎子 is the proper form.

搚, *ₛhʻié* From *hand* and united *strength*; unlike the next.

To fold, to double up; to drag or pull.

協, **叶**, *ₛhʻié* From *ten* denoting a multitude, and *strength* thrice repeated; the second unusual form alludes to the ten stems.

United in, to bring into accord; the united action of several; agreement, concord, unison; mutual help, both together; harmoniously; joint, assistant; to aid; to yield to cordially; to agree with; to help the right; to be brought into harmony.

同寅丨恭和衷哉 if they accord in respect for [these principles], do they not harmonize the moral nature of man?

丨力 combined strength.

打丨同 to join in with another officer; to coöperate, as in seizing a criminal, or executing a process.

丨和 to unite discordant parties; to bring about peace.

丨比ʼ讒言予一人 [do not you] form parties to defame me the One man.

丨時 a fortunate or favorable period.

衆情允丨 the hearts of all consent to union.

丨辦大學士 an assistant cabinet minister.

丨領 a brigadier-general among Bannermen.

丨守 or 丨台 or 丨鎮 a colonel, usually in charge of a garrison.

丨拜 the second bridesmaid, — a term known in Fuhkien.

叶, *ₛchié*, *ₛhʻié* From *ten* and *mouth*; an old form of, and used with the last.

To harmonize, to rhyme; to unite or coalesce, as an initial and final to denote the sound of a character; as 丨孔五切音苦 join the sounds of *kʻung* and *wu* to form *kʻu*.

丨時月 the day of the moon was exact.

丨韻 a forced rhyme of characters, when an unusual tone is given to one.

丨音 in harmony; [to sing] in tune or in parts; used for the last phrase as in 丨音制 it can be made to rhyme with *chi*ʼ

三多丨吉 may the three fortunate things (*viz.* happiness, long life, and sons) come to you.

脇, **脅**, *ₛhʻié* From *flesh* and united *effort*; the second form is not used in the figurative senses.

The part or space under the arms; the flanks, the sides; the ribs; to shrug; to intimidate, to reprimand; to take advantage of; to bring together.

短丨 the false ribs.

丨骨 or 兩丨 the ribs; it is said that 晋公子重耳 in the Cheu dynasty had 駢丨 a solid bone instead of ribs.

迫丨 to overawe; to force to do or to join, as a cabal.

丨權 to avail one's self of power.

威丨 to browbeat, to intimidate.

丨生 born between the ribs, as Laotsz' is fabled to have been.

被丨難民 the officers distressed the suffering people.

丨驅 a chock for a wheel.

爲賊裹丨 I was carried off by the rebels — when they took the town.

猶虎丨生翼 [they are now] like a tiger who has got wings.

丨肩諂笑 to shrug the shoulders and laugh with one, — as a sycophant.

勰, 恊, *hʻié* — From united *strength* and to *think* or *heart*; the second form is regarded as another form of 協 united.
Harmony of sentiment, union of purpose.
丨 謀 to consult upon jointly.

熁, *hʻié* — Vapor or heated air rising; fire heating or drying things fiercely.

愶, *hʻié* — To intimidate by a display of force or power; to overawe into submission.
假 威 力 以 相 丨 to pretend to awful power in order to terrify.

歙, *hʻié* — To inhale, to draw in, as a sip; one says, bones covered by the skin; *i. e.* nothing but skin and bone, lean.

襭, *hʻié* — Short garments.
修 丨 to wash the lapels of the coat on the 3d of the 3d moon to ward off misfortune; this refers to a custom in the 晋 Tsin dynasty, at the Lan-ting Pond 蘭 亭 池 in the northern part of Chehkiang.
丨 帖 a peculiar style of character used by one Wang in writing about this custom.

HIEN.

Old sounds, hien, hin, kin, han, kan, hon, kon, ham, kam, *and* gam. *In Canton*, ín, ím, hín, han, *and* ham; — *in Swatow*, hùn, hien, ham, kⁿoi, ⁿoi, kan, hⁿi, *and* kiam; — *in Amoy*, hian, ham, hiam, kian *and* lam; — *in Fuhchau*, hieng, hiòng, hang, kang, kʻang *and* lin; — *in Shanghai*, hʻiⁿ, chín, yiⁿ, yèⁿ, hèⁿ, kʻèⁿ, yüiⁿ, ʻèⁿ, *and* kʻèⁿ; — *in Chifu*, hien.

軒, *hʻüen* — From *carriage* and *shield*.
A sort of hood before a chariot; high officials in olden time had the roof of their carriage arched and the front high; a nobleman's carriage; a porch projecting beyond the eaves; a balcony or railed terrace; a fine or fancy shop; a side room, a boudoir, a lounging room; a saloon, a refectory.
書 丨 a study, a library.
茶 丨 a tea-shop, a restaurant.
舍 丨 an out-house, a side lodge; a pavilion used for study or other purposes.
鶴 乘 丨 he harnessed cranes to his coach.
丨 丨 然 well satisfied; gamboling, sporting.
丨 丨 自 得 much delighted, making merry.
丨 昂 lofty, dignified in manner; grand, as a palace.
丨 檻 a railed off room or recess.
犀 丨 a carriage with a rhinoceros' skin for a hood; it was ridden in by ladies, hence this and 魚 丨 are also used as terms for a lady.
丨 敞 a fine, spacious room.
臨 丨 對 月 let us go into the side-room and see the moon.
In *Shantung*. A covered mule-litter made like a sedan, the *shan tsz'* 丨 子; it is also otherwise written.

祆, *hʻien* — From *worship* and *heaven*.
A term for heaven or god among the Persians; in Sü's Geography, 火 丨 is explained as their fire worship; 胡 丨 or foreign worship, is used to denote the ritual of the Jews or Nestorians, but the author rather confuses the two; the character was probably formed to denote the Jewish worship.
丨 正 an officer in the Tʻang dynasty.

掀, *hʻien* — From *hand* and *joyful*.
To lift a little; to raise anything up, as a lid from a dish; to jerk up or aside; to pull out, as a wheel in the mud; to lay hold of; to whisk, as the wind does a leaf; high, proudly; to lead.
首 丨 to carry the head high.
丨 被 to pull the coverlet over one.
丨 帽 to lift the cap.
丨 簾 子 turn aside the door-curtain — and enter.
丨 引 to direct one.
丨 起 來 to raise; to turn over, as a leaf when reading.
木 丨 a wooden shovel used on thrashing-floors.

杴, *hʻien* — From *wood* and to *breathe*; interchanged with the next.
A wooden pole used by mummers; a trough or flume for leading off water.

忺, *hʻien* — An object of desire; pleasant, longed for, relished by the mind.
散 帙 揮 毫 總 不 丨 I have now no delight in spreading out my sheets and flourishing my pencil; *i. e.* literary pursuits afford me no more pleasure.

騫, *hʻien* — To fly and soar high.
騰 丨 or 高 丨 to fly on high, as the stork.

瀐 *ʿh'ien* From *disease* and *together.*
A disease resembling bronchitis, called 瘌 丨, which prevents breathing with ease, and is caused by tubercles.

蛝 *ʿh'ien* A flat bivalve shell, the 丨蛤, found off Shantung; it has a byssus growing on it, and is probably a kind of Pinna.

翻 *ʿh'ien* From to *fly* and *abundance.*
To fly.
丨翻 to wheel and soar in the air, as a hawk.

嫌 *ʿh'ien* From *woman* and *together with.*
To suspect; to dislike, to loath; to depreciate, to hold in slight regard, to have an aversion to; fastidious, prejudiced; jealous of; to consider.
小 丨 petty dislikes; querulous; antipathies.
丨小 he disdains it, thinks it is too little.
丨多 丨少 he disfavors much and little; he's hard to please.
丨棄 to reject with contempt.
丨氣 a dislike to; repugnant; jealous of.
丨醜 丨好 he depreciates good and bad too; talks at random about everything.
事避丨疑 a very suspicious affair.
挾丨 to take offense at; to keep up a grudge; to remember a wrong.
不畏丨怨 I'm not afraid of his enmity.

賢 **臤** *ʿh'ien* From *precious* added to its own old form, composed of *minister* and right *hand*; the second and unusual form, with 臤 a *loyal officer* above 貝 *precious*, further shows the same idea.
Moral, worthy, virtuous; one whose virtue, talents, power, and actions exceed others, but do not equal the 聖人, and he is still of the second grade; superior in moral excellence; to treat as worthy; a laudatory epithet, used often by a man to his wife; to surpass; to excel, as in archery.
丨才 or 丨能 good and clever; superior abilities.
鄉 丨 a village worthy.
丨弟 my good brother, — spoken to him.
丨妻 my worthy, faithful wife.
丨人 a trustworthy man.
自 丨 self-righteous.
彼丨於此 that one excels this in character.
大丨幾亞聖 the great worthies are second only to Mencius.
我從事勳丨 I was the only one who excelled in the business.
求丨若渴 to pant after virtue as for water when thirsty.
丨其丨 to regard as worthy what he deemed worthy.
丨德 exalted virtue, high moral character.

礥 *ʿh'ien* Difficult, hard; hard to bring forth.
陽氣微動動而丨 when the spring excites things but little, they seem to be hard (or slow) to come forth.

弦 *ʿh'ien* From *bow* and *somber.*
The string of a bow or fiddle; *met.* stringed instruments generally; the chord of an arc; the moon in her quarters on the 8th and 23d days; a crescent; the action of the pulse, from the idea that it is on a tendon.
通 丨 a chord; 正 丨 a sine.
餘 丨 a co-sine.
脈丨長 the pulse is hard and tense.
上 丨 and 下 丨 the first and third quarters — of the moon.
奏鼓丨歌 they beat the drums and sang to the sound of their stringed instruments.
丨國 was a small feudal state occupying the present Kwang cheu 光州 in the southeast corner of Honan.

絃 *ʿh'ien* From *silk* and *somber*; resembles the last.
The string of a lute, fiddle, or other stringed instrument of music; to play on such; *met.* a female, as she is taught to play on them.
一根丨 one string — of a lute.
三 丨 a three stringed guitar, a sort of virginal.
二 丨 a rebeck with two strings.
四 丨 a foreign fiddle; a guitar.
調 丨 or 理 丨 to tune the strings.
曉丨索 skilled in playing on stringed instruments.
聞丨歌之聲 I hear the sound of playing and singing.
彈 丨 to thrum and play the lute.
斷 丨 the guitar cord is broken; *i. e.* my wife is dead.
偏丨可續 you had better put on another string; — *i. e.* take another wife.

舷 *ʿh'ien* The side or gunwale of a vessel; the bulwarks; the gangway; the water-line of a ship.
採菱以扣丨 when picking the caltrops knock them on the boat's side.

蚿 *ʿh'ien* The gally-worm or millepede (*Julus*) of a dark purple color, common in dampish places and rotten wood; 馬 丨 and 刀環虫, as also 硬殼蟲 the hard-shell worm, and 百節 the hundred jointed, are other names of it; the second one refers to its habit of coiling itself up when disturbed.

痃 *ʿh'ien* Indigestion, dyspepsia accompanied with heart-burn.
丨癖 a sinking or faintness in the stomach, resulting from indigestion, or perhaps from a scirrhus stomach, for which garlic is recommended.
橫 丨 blind piles, a large extrusion of the intestines.

胘 From 肉 *flesh* and 弦 a *chord* contracted.
ˏh'ien

The stomach or manyplus of an ox.

牛 ㅣ tripe.

閒 From *door* and *moon; q.d.* the moonlight streaming in through a closed door; used with the next, but unlike *ˏkien* 間 between, for which it is often written.
ˏh'ien

Repose, leisure; private, of no importance; at ease, sauntering, unoccupied; idle, indolent; empty, vacant; unoccupied, as a place; a low tone of voice.

有 ㅣ or 得 ㅣ at leisure.

ㅣ不住 or 不 ㅣ or 不得 ㅣ busy, no spare time, not at leisure, much occupied.

ㅣ人 or ㅣ人兒 a loafer or intruder, an outsider, an intermeddler.

打 ㅣ兒的 a beggar. (*Pekingese.*)

ㅣ暇 unoccupied; no duty pressing.

ㅣ手 an idler, a lazy fellow.

ㅣ話 trifling chitchat, gossip; pleasant talk.

游手好ˀ ㅣ an idler loves to loaf about.

ㅣ近 proximate, adjoining.

虛 ㅣ to waste the time.

ㅣ地 void, roomy; a spare spot; vacant land.

抽 ㅣ to take time for.

淸 ㅣ nothing to do, indifferent to.

皇以 ㅣ之 [Heaven] made him ruler in his stead.

ㅣ居 living alone.

ㅣ居獨處 while I was quite alone.

ㅣ散 unsettled, as the thoughts uneasy; playing truant.

ㅣ門 a side or back door.

ㅣ事 private affairs, trifling matters.

ㅣ隙 slight cause of disagreement.

反 ㅣ計 I turned the tables on them; it was a ruse.

幽 ㅣ in privacy, *i. e.* not in office or busy life.

ㅣ是 ㅣ非 it is no business of mine; I'll take no responsibility for it.

忙裏偷 ㅣ seized a little leisure in the midst of his hurry.

閑 From *door* and *wood; q. d.* something in the doorway obstructing entrance; not seldom used for the last, and often wrongly.
ˏh'ien

A bar, a barrier, a fence; an inclosure; a fold or corral; to guard, to regulate by law; to close, to obstruct; to restrain, to forbid; to move about; to be trained, to display expertness; practiced, accustomed to; large.

ㅣ阻 to embarrass, to hinder,

ㅣ習 trained, as a horse; used to, broken in.

四馬旣 ㅣ his four horses show their training.

ㅣ闌 obstructed; headed off.

ㅣ邪存誠 to restrain vicious, and foster truthful or sincere —habits.

防 ㅣ to guard against.

ㅣ ㅣ兮 what crowds of people — are moving about!

馬 ㅣ a pen or paddock or corral for horses.

癇 From *disease* and *interval.*
ˏh'ien

Convulsions in children, like those arising from worms; epileptic fits, called in Canton 發羊吊 *i. e.* having sheep's leaps; of this disease, known as 癲 ㅣ, five sorts are enumerated, classified according to the animals whose voices are imitated.

驚 ㅣ spasms in children arising from terror.

痰 ㅣ convulsions caused by phlegm or worms.

風 ㅣ fits, convulsions.

嫺
h'ien

Elegant, accomplished; accustomed to; tasteful, refined; indolent, loving leisure.

ㅣ雅 polished, apt; of cultivated taste.

ㅣ熟 skilled in, as music.

ㅣ靜 understanding the proprieties of life, as an educated lady.

韜畧久 ㅣ he has long been skilled in all kinds of strategy.

ㅣ於禮 acquainted with etiquette; versed in the rites, as a courtier.

鷳 From *bird* and *leisure; q. d.* the bird that moves about leisurely.
ˏh'ien

The silver pheasant, the 白 ㅣ (*Euplocamus* [Phasianus] *nycthemerus*); black pheasants of this sort are mentioned.

白 ㅣ補服 the silver pheasant in the official embroidery — of civilians of the fifth rank, as a *chicheu* 知州, or those who wear crystal buttons.

咸 From 口 *mouth* and 戌 a horary character denoting *all,* and referred to the dog.
ˏh'ien

Together, all, jointly; totally, completely; always; reaching everywhere, around in; concord, suitable; hasty; the 31st diagram, referring to the whole of.

ㅣ漢 name of a northern star.

萬國 ㅣ寧 all countries are at peace.

不 ㅣ disagreeing; a discrepancy.

周邦 ㅣ喜 all the states of Cheu rejoiced at it.

ㅣ知 ㅣ聞 everybody has heard and knows it.

人物 ㅣ亨 men and things all prosperous; general good order.

ㅣ豐 general thriftiness or plenty; name of the reign Hien-fung, A. D. 1851-1862; also a district in the southwest corner of Hupeh.

鹹 From *saltish* and *wholly.*
ˏh'ien

One of the five tastes; saltish, like sea-water; preserved, salted, put in brine; bitter, said of the taste of the northern regions, which may refer to the nitrous land in Gobi desert, and the bad or brackish water of northern China.

丨菜 pickled cabbage, salted vegetables.

丨土 sour saltish land.

丨水 sea-water.

丨魚 pickled or salt fish.

丨酸 saltish-sour, a savory, decided flavor.

In *Cantonese*. Bitter, distressing, hard to bear.

受慣丨苦 he has been long familiar with suffering.

羬 ˏh'ien An animal of the cervine family, described as six feet high, small horns, and tail like the horse; its fat makes good candles; the animal intended is perhaps the *nilgaie* or *nyl-ghau* of northern India (*Portax pictus*,) to which the description is similar; or else an elk.

麙 ˏh'ien Some regard this as a synonym of the last, but the Păn Tsao makes it the same as the 羚 *Antilope crispa;* also the finest cubs of a tiger, or the strongest whelps of a bear.

諴 ˏh'ien From *words* and *wholly*.

Sincere, cordial, hearty; union, harmony, sincerity; to accord with, united.

至丨感神 earnest sincerity will move the gods.

其丕能丨于小民 let him wholly adapt himself (or harmonize) with the people.

銜 ˏh'ien From *metal* and to *go*; *q. d.* the metal that guides the horse in going.

A bit, a bridoon; to champ, to hold in the mouth, for which the next is used; to contain; to control or guide one's self; rank, official power or position; acting as, a brevet rank; affected by, moved, indignant.

頭丨 or 官丨 or 職丨 an official title; the address of an officer.

同知丨 a brevet sub-prefect.

會丨 several officers joined in a report or document.

丨命 to act upon orders received; I will attend to your request, said to a friend.

丨枚 to keep still; to hold from talking; to gag, to make one keep quiet.

唱丨 to cry out one's rank, as at a levee.

丨恨 to restrain one's anger.

人丨 one of the names of ginseng.

馬丨 a horse's bit; also the name of a sea god.

丨環以報 I champ the ring in order to repay your kindness; referring to a legend.

㘅 / 啣 ˏh'ien These forms are unauthorized by Kanghi's Dictionary; but are in use with the last character.

To hold in the mouth, to clasp; to receive, as an order.

口內丨 to hold in the mouth.

丨糖欖 to suck a sugared olive; *met.* pleased and silent; to shut his mouth.

丨鐵彈 [may you be condemned to] hold a hot iron ball — in hell, you liar!

燕子丨泥 the martin takes mud — to make its nest.

雀丨梅 the bird holds a rose in its bill.

鳳丨書 the phœnix has a scroll.

丨草壘巢 to carry grass to build a nest.

半山丨月 the high hill hides the moon.

精衛丨石塡海 the titmouse took up stones to fill the sea; — said of one who attempts impossible things, or uselessly vents his spite.

崡 ˏh'ien From *hill* and to *contain*; the radical has been added, and the sound changed in recent times.

The name of a mountain in the northwest of Honan very near the Yellow River, where is the 丨谷關, a celebrated defile.

㬎 ˊh'ien From 日 *sun* and 絲 *floss silk*, explained to be the motes and fibres seen floating in the sunlight, where alone they are visible; an old form of the next, and now used as a primitive.

Anything fine, volatile, minute, impalpable; having many orifices, reticulate; full of striæ or threads, fibrous; bright.

顯 / 顕 ˊh'ien From *head* and *manifested;* there is a reference in it to the nimbus or aureole of celestial beings; the second is a common form.

Light, manifest, apparent; conspicuous, clear; illustrious, glorious, effulgent; supernal; to be enlightened; to be held in regard; to make plain, to exhibit; to render illustrious; as if, appears to be, like as.

丨達 distinguished; famous.

丨者 those who are distinguished; high officers.

丨揚 generally known; notable, famous from one's father being an officer.

丨考 the illustrious completer of probation; *i. e.* a deceased father.

丨親 to shed honor on one's kindred.

天有丨道 the dealings of Providence are plain.

大丨其道 to disseminate his doctrines widely.

靈丨 a divine or spiritual glory.

丨著 manifest, as to the world; plainly seen, as objects in a microscope.

丨見供詞不實 his evidence appeared to be untrustworthy.

丨明 it seems to be clear or evident; to make plain.

丨手段 to show off one's skill; to brag of it.

丨然 how plain! it is even so.

神明丨聖 the god has shown his holiness or power.

不丨亦臨 when out of sight he acted as if seen by all.

丨丨令德 how illustrious is his virtue!

ʿ峴 From *hill* and to *see*.

ʿk'ien A steep isolated hill with a pleateau on top; a small butte.

京丨 a steep cliff in Tan-yang hien 丹陽縣 in Kiangsu.

丨山 a noted mountain in Siang-yang fu 襄陽府 in the north of Hupeh.

ʿ睍 From *eye* and to *see*; *q. d.* the eyes starting out.

ʿk'ien To look at with fear; protuberant eyes; to view slightly, to regard.

丨丨 a frightened look.

伈伈丨丨 cowed, terrified.

丨睆 charming; a pleasant, musical voice, as of an oriole.

ʿ幰 ʿk'ien A curtain which protects the front of a carriage from the sun, or conceals the rider; the screen of a sedan.

ʿ蜆 From 虫 *insect* and 睍 *brilliant* contracted, referring to the iridescent nacre in shells.

ʿk'ien A term for small, smooth bivalves, especially the thin shelled or lacustrine kinds, as *Tellinæ*, *Mytili*, *Unionidæ*, &c.; as a class they are smaller than the 蚌 or 蛤; a small black insect with a red head, the 縊女 which suspends itself when weaving its chrysalis.

丨肉 shelled mussels or clams.

丨蚧 raw clams seasoned.

黃沙丨 a kind of mussel common at Canton.

丨塘 a pond for rearing mussels.

丨殼字 *i. e.* clam-shell phrases, a Canton term for dissyllabic phrases which cannot be disjoined; they should properly belong to the same radical, as 窀穸 or 縹緲, but the term is not restricted to such.

ʿ㺝 From *dog* and *daring*.

ʿk'ien The yelp of a puppy or lap-dog; the bark of a little dog.

ʿ險 From a *mound* and *all*.

ʿk'ien An obstruction very difficult to surmount; a precipice, a cliff; an abyss; dangerous, insecure; in jeopardy; what brings one into danger, as corrupt or wicked ways; the point of danger, the key of the position.

丨些死了 I just escaped death; it was very hazardous.

丨得很 or 丨中 in the midst of danger; imminently dangerous.

危丨 a steep place; perilous; prejudicial.

終踰絕丨 you will finally get over the dangerous places.

丨阻 in straits; I can't get on; safely defended, as a city.

行丨道 to go in hazardous paths, to follow evil ways.

心丨 malignant feelings, a heart bent on evil plots.

丨傷 a dangerous wound.

丨症 a severe illness.

丨要 perilous, as a pass that can't be avoided.

行丨僥倖 reckless of danger; a dare-devil, a swashbuckler.

司丨 an officer whose duties resemble a hydrographer.

化丨爲夷 to change a danger into a comfort.

陰丨的人 a malicious, scheming fellow.

ʿ獮 ʿ獫 From *dog* and *strict* or *all*; the second is also read ʿ*lien*.

ʿk'ien A dog with a long nose like a pointer or greyhound.

丨狁 the name of a fierce horde of Huns, savage as dogs, who were notorious in the days of Confucius.

載丨歇驕 the pointer was very agile and sagacious.

ʿ僩 Interchanged with the next.

ʿk'ien Courageous, martial; depending on one's self, self-possessed; formidable, stern, liberal and candid.

瑟兮丨兮 dignified and stern.

ʿ撊 Like the last.

ʿk'ien Brave, valiant; angry, incensed; to suppress.

早已丨起來 she soon had suppressed her feelings.

執事丨然授兵登陴 the centurion in a sudden burst of anger gave him some troops to scale the wall.

ʿ憪 ʿk'ien Composed, contented; liberal; eager to help others; affected, aroused, as by remorse or meditation.

丨然 pleased, tranquil.

丨念人之非 to be affected by reflecting on the vices of others.

ʿ瞯 From *eye* and an *interval*.

ʿk'ien To watch narrowly, to spy or watch one; the sclerotica or white of the eye; the eyes turned so as to show their whites, as in convulsions; a wall-eyed horse.

白丨過睛 the sclerotica (cornea) covers the iris.

窺丨婦女 to take a peep at the women.

使人丨夫子 [the king] set a man to watch the sage (Mencius).

ʿ隒 ʿk'ien A stony path at the foot of a steep hill.

水丨 a steep, difficult river bank.

ʿ轞 From *carriage* and to *oversee*; occurs used for the next.

ʿk'ien The creaking of wagons; a carriage or van in which prisoners or wild beasts are carried.

大車丨丨 the great wains go lumbering along.

檻' From *wood* and to *oversee*; occurs used for *lan'* 濫 excessive.

k'ien' A baluster, a railing; a trellis; bars outside of a window; a parapet; a cage or pen for wild beasts; to cage.

圈丨 a railed inclosure or menagerie.

花 〡 a garden railing; a fence around flowers.

〡 送 京 師 cage him and send him to Peking, — as a criminal.

〡 車 a cart with a cage on it.

〡 泉 a fountain or jet-d'eau.

Read ʿ*kan*. A door-sill, which can be removed; a threshold.

〡 墻 子 a low wall, like the part under a window.

艦 *h'ien'* A war-junk, a vessel with strong bulwarks to defend its crew; used for large vessels, as a frigate; a protected turret or top for archers or marksmen.

戰 〡 a war vessel; national ships.

大 〡 a great ship of war.

縣 *h'ien'* From 系 *silk* and 首 *head* upside down; also read ˏ*hüen*.

To bind, to suspend, to hang before one, to show to, — in which senses ˏ*hüen* 懸 is now oftener used; a political division answering to a district, the subdivision of a 州 or 府, the fifth in order of territorial divisions, and sometimes called a county.

〡 城 the chief town of a district.

知 〡 a district magistrate; he is addressed as 太爺, and spoken of as 〡 令 or 〡 主; his deputy is 〡 丞 or 分 〡 but more usually called 左 堂 or left hall.

郡 〡 departments and districts.

〡 學 教 諭 the official tutor of a district.

扭 〡 賄 買 刑 逼 斃 命 dragged her to the magistrate's office, and by bribery had her punished so that she died.

繁 〡 and 簡 〡 are terms to distinguish important and unimportant district posts.

山 州 草 〡 a poor region.

不 同 〡 not of the same district.

ˏ〡 空 suspended in vacancy, as a balloon.

花 〡 name of the peach and plum flower, alluding to one Pan Yoh of the Tsin dynasty who declined presents, and told the people to plant peach trees; when he left his post, the trees all flowered in his honor.

憲 *h'ien'* Composed of 心 *heart*, 目 *eye*, and 害 *injurious* contracted.

To exhibit or uphold the laws so as to impress men with the dread of crime; to impose or publish laws, to govern; governmental; an example, law, or precept; to take as a pattern; a ruler, but strictly only officials above the fourth rank; the Censorate Board is also so termed; to follow; well-informed, intelligent; abundant.

大 〡 the high authorities; this term applies to all above an intendant; but 三 大 〡 denotes the three highest provincial officers.

〡 臺 your Honors, used in addressing them; and 仁 〡 is a complimentary term.

〡 禁 a governmental prohibition.

時 〡 書 the Imperial Calendar.

奉 〡 to receive orders from the provincial rulers.

成 〡 the perfect rules; *i. e.* the 〡 典 or statutes of the government.

文 武 是 〡 such examples as Wăn Wang and Wu Wang.

〡 〡 然 gratified, elated, pleased; taking things complacently, indifferent to.

献 獻 *h'ien'* From a *dog* and a *boiler* used in sacrificing; the contracted form is common in cheap books.

A fat dog fit for an offering; to offer in worship, to present to a superior; in polite language, to give, to hand up to; an offering; intelligent.

〡 縣 a district in Ho-kien fu in the east of Chihli.

進 〡 or 奉 〡 or 〡 上 to present, to offer to.

文 〡 不 足 intelligent officers are not to be had.

〡 城 歸 ˏ降 they surrendered the city, and returned to their allegiance.

〡 盤 red trays for sending presents to the bride's father-in-law and mother.

呈 〡 to send a present, as to a ruler.

〡 策 to proffer advice or a plan — to government.

〡 勤 sedulously offer respects or presents; — *i. e.* to curry favor.

〡 功 to exhibit meritorious acts; to show the evidences of skill or merit.

甗 *h'ien'* An earthen vessel without a bottom used in steaming; it was of various shapes, and some kinds had legs; a hole resembling this kind of vessel; old name of a place in north of the kingdom of Tsi, which is probably the same originally as the last.

現 *h'ien'* From *gem* and *to see*; occurs used for *kien'* 見 seeing.

The brilliancy of a jewel; to manifest, to display, to appear; to divulge, to show; to be seen now, at present, *de facto*; current; at once; plain, apparent; conspicuous.

〡 在 existing, now, here.

〡 今 at present, just now.

〡 刻 this instant.

〡 銀 or 〡 錢 ready money, cash in hand.

〡 錢 不 賒 no credit given.

明 〡 it comes out bright, as a color; a speedy recompence or retribution.

買 〡 成 to buy things ready made.

〡 出 to appear; to come out, as rash on the body.

〡 形 it shows its form; it becomes manifest.

屢 〡 人 目 it has often been seen.

一 天 一 個 〡 在 each day has its own want or duty.

丨世報 his retribution appears, his punishment is apparent.

丨了原形兒 he has shown his real feelings.

要丨罷 I must have the money in hand.

丨成物 the thing is on hand, as an article in a shop.

丨身説法 he was made manifest and explained the law, — as Budha.

哯 *h'ien'* To throw up, as infants do their milk; to vomit easily.

晛 *h'ien'* The *sun appearing* or coming out; the winter sun melting the snow; clear, warm sunlight.

見丨曰消 when the sun appears [the snow] straightway melts.

俔 *h'ien'* From *man* and *to see*; also read *'k'ien*, and used for 俔 craven.

Like; to liken, to compare; to spy out, to explore; a dog-vane, a weather-cock.

丨天之妹 like a celestial woman or fairy.

閒丨 a spy, a secret observer.

伈伈丨丨 craven, fearful; looking around affrighted.

丨如雲 like the clouds.

丨迎風而不定 the vane takes the wind, and so it cannot be quiet.

鋧 *h'ien'* A small chisel to cut holes, called 銑丨; a term also applied to a sort of javelin or spear.

莧 *h'ien'* Edible sorts of coarse greens; the southern-wood (*Artemisia*), the goosefoot or pigweed (*Chenopodium*), spinach (*Spinacia*), and even *Sedum*, are all called 丨菜, and distinguished by various adjectives; spinach is usually intended by the single name.

假丨菜 false spinach or pigweed; goosefoot (*Chenopodium*).

刺丨 prickly spinach, a sort of goosefoot.

馬齒丨 purslane (*Portulacca*); applied also to a sort of *Sedum*, and a long leaved spinach.

垷 *h'ien'* Mud, mire; a great embankment.

昡 *h'ien'* The bright sun or light.

世幽昧以丨曜兮 how the glorious sun illuminates this dark world! — applied also to sages.

臽 *h'ien'* This character originally represented 人 *man* over 臼 a *mortar*; it is now superseded by the next, and used chiefly as a primitive; also read *꜀k'an*, and to be distinguished from *'yao* 舀 to bale.

A pitfall in which to catch beasts; to insnare; a hole in the ground made to serve as a pestle.

坎丨 a pit, a trap for beasts.

虎丨 a tiger pit.

陷 *h'ien'* From *place* and *pitfall* as the phonetic.

To fall, as a wall; to sink; to drop into or descend; to throw into or pitch down; to capture, to pillage, to sack, as a besieged place; to take a city from the emperor; overwhelmed, betrayed, ruined; to involve, to beguile, to lead into sin.

丨害 implicated unjustly; led into a scrape.

丨阱 or 丨坑 a trap or pit.

丨阱之中 in the pit; *met.* sunk into the lowest vice.

坑丨 to entrap.

丨溺 whelmed, drowned; to pitch down and drown; reprobate, given over, lost.

崩丨 fell down, as a cliff.

丨人不義 to seduce men to do wrong.

丨沙河 to sink in the quicksands; they are very dangerous in Kicheu 蘄州 in Hupeh.

丨罪 to lead others into crime.

丨於李 it submitted to Li.

城丨 the city has fallen — to the rebels.

丨地獄 he will go to hell; may you be punished in hell!

低丨 the location is low.

車丨在泥 or 丨車 to mire a cart; to get into the mud.

剛健不丨 firm, unapproachable by craft.

餡 *h'ien'* From *to eat* and a *pitfall*.

The core of cakes or dumplings; the fruit, meat, or sugar put in pastry; *met.* a secret, a hidden thing.

餅丨 or 點心丨 pastry cakes with fruit, &c.

剁丨 to hash up and make these dumplings.

拌丨子 to mix up dumplings.

菓子丨 or 菓丨子 fruit pies.

肉丨餑餑 meat patties.

不知是什麼丨兒 I don't know what his intentions are; I can't tell what he is driving at.

露了丨兒 the fruit has come out — of the dough; the secret is out. (*Pekingese.*)

限 *h'ien'* From *place* and *perverse*; occurs used for the next.

A limit, a boundary; a restriction; an impediment, literal or metaphorical; a threshold; a few of; a short time; to limit, to impede; to set a time, to assign; to moderate, to restrain; to appoint, to contract for, to adjust.

有丨 a few, a limit; not very good or strong, as cloth; it is modified by what follows.

有丨的 not very dear; not enough, not many of them.

有丨的事 there are not many items, as in an account.

有丨時候 or 有丨辰光 there is yet a little time.

艱丨 it is hard to restrain him.

丨幾日 how many days do you set?

無 | 福澤 a wonderful run of luck, no end of his good fortune.
寬 | to extend the time.
過 | overpast the time.
| 定 a stint; an allowance.
| 碗 to limit one's eating; to diet.
| 度 a restricted, fixed measure.
| 期 to set a time; to place limits; to restrain.
大 | 將到 the great limit is near at hand; *i. e.* you are not likely to live long;—a fortune-teller's phrase.

| 制 a legal restriction; a restraint.
無 | illimitable; abundant, unlimited, exhaustless, infinite.
無 | 景緻 a vast variety of wonders and sights.

閬 扊 *han'* } From *door* and *perverse*; the first and common form is usually read *han'* and resembles *'lang* 閬 empty; both are interchanged with the last.

A threshold; it is often made half a foot or so high.

門 | the door-board, the sill.
君子立不踐 | the well-bred man does not stand or step on the door-way.
門 | 稅 a house tax once levied according to the number of doors.

㡉 㬎 *'hien* } From a *shelter* or *wood* and *perverse*; the second form is unusual.

A threshold; the high board forming the threshold of a door, which is movable in large gateways.

HIH.

Old sounds, kit, hip, hik, kip, *and* kik. *In Canton*, hät, k'äp, ngăp, ngăt, yăp, *and* sheng; — *in Swatow*, kio, hip, k'ip, ngŭt, *and* bu; — *in Amoy*, hék, gék, hip, k'ip, *and* gút; — *in Fuhchau*, hék, k'ik, k'ék, *and* ngék; — *in Shanghai*, hih and yăk; — *in Chifu*, hih.

檄 *chi* From *wood* and to *respect*.

A summons to war, anciently written on boards two feet long; it alluded to the sovereign's call to his vassals for aid against rebels; a proclamation calling to arms; to give orders to the people; haste, urgency; a reprimand to lower officials; a branchless tree.

| 文 a warning proclamation; an official summons; an exciting placard; irritating talk.
羽 | an urgent call, as to arms.
飛 | a flying dispatch, a pressing order.
長 | a sort of safe-warrant or passport.
討 | a declaration of war.
傳 | 而定 when the dispatches arrived, the thing was decided.
布 | 宣揚 to send out a pressing call, — as for troops.

虩 *hih* A tiger skulking from fear of man; alarmed, frightened; a sort of spider, called also 蠅虎 the fly tiger.

震來 | | awe-struck at the thunder.

覡 *chi* From to *see* and a *wizard*.

A witch, a sorceress, one who fasts and worships the gods to get their aid; a necromancer.

| 公 usually denotes a wizard.
信巫 | to believe in witches and seers.

赥 *hih* The sound of laughing; like the next.

| | 聲 the sound of merriment.

欯 *hih* From to *breathe* and *happy*.

To rejoice, to look pleased.
| | to laugh and be jolly.
| 嘆一堂 many persons laughing at once.

衋 *chi* From 血 *blood*, 百 repeated for 200, and 聿 *rule*, referring to the popular mind under a sense of wrong; but the primitive seems to be better explained as denoting a sound, as of people chafing at oppression.

Grief of heart at wrong, as of the people chafing at the tyranny of their rulers.

民罔不 | 傷心 the people were all sorely grieved at heart.

鬩 *hih* From to *wrangle* and a *child*.

Domestic quarrels, litigations; mutual contentions, animosities, resentments, incessant recriminations.

| 釁 causes of strife.
| 恨 mutual hatred.
脅 | sighing and grieving, under undeserved wrong.
| 訟 family litigations.
兄弟 | 于墻 brothers quarreling in the house.

吸 噏 *hih* } From *mouth* and *up to* or *to collect*; the second form is rare.

To draw in the breath, to inhale, to make an inspiration; to imbibe, to suck in; the second also means to attract, as a loadstone.

| 一口氣 draw in a long breath.
魚 | 水 the fishes breathe water.
| 去魂靈 to attract and lead one's heart — into vice.
| 露 to suck the dew, as a cicada or gryllus is thought to do.
禹門 | 浪 [may you soon] meet the waves from Neptune's Hall; — *i. e.* be a *kŭjin*.

丨露水 [nothing left me but] to drink dew, — so poor am I.

丨食烟 or 丨烟 to smoke tobacco or opium.

呼丨相通 their views all accord; *i. e.* the expirations and inspirations interchange; applied too to a telegraph.

In *Cantonese.* To talk at random; to rave, to wander, as when half delirious; worthless.

丨三丨四 to talk without aim.

丨錯句話 mistaken the sentence, as in reading.

二丨師傅 a second rate workman, a poor artisan.

歙, *h'i'* From *breath* and *united;* occurs used for the next.

To snuff at; to turn up the nose, as in disgust.

𭭸丨 the sound of waving trees.

丨絶 the brilliant crimson of evening clouds.

丨張 to collect and scatter; to gather and disperse; to shut and open.

Read *sheh,* The prefect city or head district of Hwui-cheu fu 徽州府 in the southwest of Nganhwui; the name has existed from the Cheu dynasty.

翕, *h'i'* From *wings* and *united.*

To collect, to reässemble, to unite; to raise; to harmonize; abounding, full

丨張 to shut and to open.

和丨 at peace, made up.

兄弟既丨 the brothers are all in accord.

𪖐丨北舌 only lolling out its tongue.

丨合 joined; reünited, as divergent streams.

潝, **滊,** *h'i* The noise of flowing water; running, murmuring, gurgling, as a brook; used with the last in 丨丨訾訾 now they agree, and now they defame one another.

熻, *h'i'* To heat, to burn; to roast.

丨死 to smother to death.

丨熟之肉 meat thoroughly roasted.

In *Fuhchau.* To steam; to cause warmth by covering, as when taking a sweat.

齂, *h'i'* Strong breathing through the nose; snoring or stertorous breathing.

肸, *h'i'* From 𦥑 to *agitate* and 十 *ten* or many.

Sounds spreading and prolonging, as that of bells, or a soughing among trees; buzz of gnats; reports going abroad.

佛丨 stalwart; the name of a man, Pih Hih, the commandant of Chung-meu in Tsin, in Confucius' time.

汔, *h'ih* From *water* and *air* altered; used for the next and for *ˏki* 幾 nearly.

Water dried up; to shed tears; dangerous.

迄, *h'i'* From 辵 to *travel* and 气 *air* altered; occurs interchanged with *hih,* 訖 to extend.

To reach in time; finally, even, till, up to, at last; to extend.

丨竟 after all, to the last.

丨今 or 丨於今 even till now, up to this day.

丨無成功 to the last he did not accomplish it.

肐, *h'i'* This is sometimes incorrectly used for *koh,* 胳 the arm-pit.

The sternum or breast-bone; one says, the body shaking from fear.

闟, *h'i'* From *door* and to *assemble.*

The spears or scythes, which in ancient times were fastened to war chariots; to contain; to stand in a menacing attitude; to shut a door.

丨然止睦然視 to stand firmly and look at attentively.

丨丨屋摧霤 the gargoyles spurt their drippings fast.

Read *t'ah,* Soft hair or down near the skin.

丨什 a valley in Shensi, where the river Han has its source.

HIN.

Old sounds, hin, kin, him, *and* kim. *In Canton,* yăn; — *in Swatow,* hien *and* hùn; — *in Amoy,* him *and* hûn; — *in Fuhchau,* hŭng, heŭng, *and* hing; — *in Shanghai,* hiáng; — *in Chifu,* hin.

欣, **忻,** *ˏh'in* From to *breathe* or *heart* and an *ax;* the first is most used; the second is the district.

Laughing from joy; delight, happiness; pleased at doing or getting something; merry, elated, jolly.

歡丨 joyful, glad.

丨從 to readily comply with.

丨暢 elated, jocund, happy.

丨慰 wholly satisfied; solaced, anxiety removed.

丨丨然 with pleasure, readily.

丨州 a department in the north of Shansi.

丨丨向榮 springing up vigorously, as flowers after a drought; or revived, as people from starvation.

丨逢佳節 a jolly festival.

無不丨悅 with the utmost alacrity.

炘 ꜀h'in The effulgent, burning sun; the garish heat of midday.

昕 ꜀h'in From *sun* and an *ax*.
The morn, the dawn; early daylight.
太 丨 too early to see plainly, yet dark.
大 丨 鼓 徵 the drum calls them at early dawn, as scholars.
丨 夕 從 公 morning and night he was diligent at his post.

脪 ꜀h'in An ulcer beginning to slough or show proud flesh; gangrene commencing in a wound; among *furriers*, used with 膁 to denote the fur on the neck.
金 銀 丨 a kind of fox-skin used for collars and jackets.

廞 ꜀h'in Also read ꜀k'in.
To dress up and prepare chariots for going out; to begin, as a tune by the band; a sort of musical instrument; to stop up, as a sewer.

歆 ꜀h'in From to *breathe* and *sound*.
The gods gratified with incense; to accept the fumes of sacrifice; to taste, to enjoy; to conceive, to quicken; to extol.
丨 饗 the grateful odors.
上 帝 居 丨 the High Ruler accepted the sacrifice.
丨 羨 to long for, to desire earnestly.
丨 享 to be pleased with, as an offering.
履 帝 武 敏 丨 she stepped on the Ruler's foot-print and was quickened.

盺 ꜀h'in To see indistinctly, as near-sighted persons when they look at anything fixedly; joyful.

釁 h'in꜄ From 酉 *spirits* under 興 to *arise*, here defined a sacrificial *vessel*, and 分 to *divide*; contracted like the next.
To offer blood in sacrifice; to smear the vessels with blood; to consecrate with blood; a flaw, a crevice; a cause of quarrel, an offense, a grievance; a wrong between nations, a pretext, a handle for a quarrel; a presage, an omen; to excite; to fumigate; to oil one's self for the ancestral worship.
起 丨 to give cause for offense, to irritate.
丨 隙 a pretext, a slight, a miff.
搆 丨 to stir up strife, to excite acrimony, to embroil, to foster trouble.
丨 浴 to perfume and wash, as enchanters do.
丨 端 or 瑕 丨 a defect; an offense, a charge against.
尋 丨 to seek occasion against.

衅 h'in꜄ From *blood* and *half*; much used for the preceding from its having fewer strokes.
To smear vessels used in sacrificing with blood; to cover arms with skin so as to protect them.

脪 h'in꜄ The flesh of an ulcer exserted and becoming proud flesh; to swell, as an ulcer, thought to arise from cold in it.

HING.

Old sounds, hing, hăng, king, kăng, *and* găng. *In Canton*, hing, ying, *and* hăng; — *in Swatow*, heng *and* kⁿé; — *in Amoy*, heng *and* keng; — *in Fuhchau*, hing, héng, haing, *and* kéng; — *in Shanghai*, yăng, h'iăng, *and* ăng; — *in Chifu*, hing.

興 hing꜄ Composed of 舁 to *lift up* in both hands, and 同 *united* inside; *q.d.* to do with united strength; it is easily confounded with ꜀yü 與 to give.
To raise, to elevate; to rise, to get up; rising, growing; flourishing, prospering, the opposite of 亡 when applied to a state; to make to prosper; to be in demand, fashionable; to move, to put in motion; to originate, to give rise to, to start; to maintain, as in office; promoted, expanding, abundant, in which sense it often forms part of names of places, peoples, and firms.
丨 走 to arise, to get on, to flourish.
丨 居 busy or resting; in active or private life; in motion or quiet.
丨 居 納 福 I hope you keep in good health and are prospering.
丨 工 to commence work.
丨 兵 to raise or move troops.
時 丨 in the fashion.
不 大 丨 rather out of date, not now in vogue.
我 友 敬 矣 讒 言 其 丨 if my friends were reverent, would these slanders arise?
新 丨 a new style, just come in fashion.
大 丨 土 木 a great bustle of masons and carpenters, — as when building.
丨 旺 or 丨 隆 prospering, successful, flourishing.
丨 作 to begin a thing or job.
勃 然 丨 how quickly it has started! — as the grass.

中丨 to repair, to renew, to fit up.

丨盛 flourishing, abundant, as a commerce.

丨發 to multiply, to issue forth.

以丨嗣歲 in order to begin the coming year.

'女丨是力 you employ them, which gives them power — to do wrong.

軍丨以來 since the army has been called out or employed.

國家將丨 the country is prosperous.

丨縣 a district in Tai-yuen fu in the center of Shansi.

Read *hing*' Joyful, elated; to take delight in; a resemblance; to desire; an appetite, a passion; excited, as a gambler by his evil habit; a furor or inspiration.

高丨 highly pleased with, in good spirits.

丨致兒 a passion for, mad on, addicted to.

有丨致 in fine spirits; eager.

作丨 complaisant in, pleased with.

父祖倘遺德丨 his ancestors' goodness has caused this prosperity.

丨頭 or 丨丨頭頭的 a joyful time, a merry-making; a great bustle.

喜丨 pleasurable, as an interview or party

起丨 risings of desire, sexual appetency.

沒丨 disappointed in, no joy with; disheartened.

馨 From 香 *fragrance* and 聲 *sound* contracted.

˛hing *˛hin* Odors perceived a long distance; the sweet incense of sacrifice.

丨香 sweet savor, incense; fumes of offerings; a good reputation; virtue.

芳丨 the perfume of flowers.

明德惟丨 [the gods regard] eminent virtue as the best incense.

弗惟德丨香祀 he never thought of presenting any virture as a sacrifice of sweet savor.

爾殽旣丨 your viands are fragrant; *i. e.* good enough for a sacrifice.

刑 From *sword* and *even*; occurs used with the next.

˛hing Punishment by officers, legal punishment; torture; to punish, to castigate; penal, criminal, as laws; inimical to, destructive of, as one's destiny; a law, an invariable rule; jurisprudence; behavior; a mold, a pattern; to imitate; to sacrifice victims.

丨問 or 丨訊 to examine by torture.

寬丨 a light punishment.

用丨嚇他 threaten him with the question.

非丨 or 酷丨 illegal punishment; to torture cruelly.

遊丨 to whip one through the streets.

行丨 or 加丨 to carry a sentence into effect, to punish.

丨部 the Board of Punishments.

丨房 the criminal bureau in the lower courts.

丨名先生 a sort of legal counsel in the local courts, who is applied to in criminal cases.

丨戮 capital punishment.

五丨 the five legal punishments; *viz.* bambooing under fifty blows and under a hundred, transportation under 500 *li*, exile for life, and death.

八字丨尅 the horoscope is inimical.

丨期無丨 would that there were no punishments! — as in the halcyon days of Yao.

丨牲 to kill the victims.

君子懷丨 the good man respects the laws.

儀丨足式 his conduct and habits all conform to the rules; — are such as one likes.

丨于寡妻 it will be imitated by my wife; — said by a prince.

型 From *earth* and *law*; occurs used with the last.

˛hing A mold of earth or sand; to mold; to serve as an example; a statute, a formulary.

典丨 a precedent, a law.

丨模 a mold used in casting metals.

儀丨裕後 his manners were a model to his descendants.

硎 A whetstone; a square stone for sharpening tools.

˛hing 發丨新試 to get out a whetstone and make a new trial.

丨谷 a valley wherein Tsin Chi Hwangti ordered melons to be grown in winter.

邢 Name of an ancient principality, now Hing-tai hien 丨臺縣 in the southwest of Chihli, near Shansi; it was given to Duke Cheu's son as a fief.

˛hing

凡蔣丨茅 all the grass or rushes in Tsiang and Hing.

鉶 A sort of jar resembling a skillet or tripod, in which to cook the 丨羹 or fragrant broth offered in sacrifice.

˛hing

設丨 set out the dishes.

丨鼎 a copper tripod used for the same purpose.

侀 From *man* and *law*; occurs used for the next.

˛hing A thing finally formed; a law which ought not to be changed; a figure, a form, a body.

形 From *pelage* and *even*; occurs used for the last.

˛hing Form, figure, shape, contour; the body, as distinct from the life or soul; material, bodily; manner, visage, air, style; site, aspect; a landscape; an apparition; to give form to, to imitate, to appear; to make manifest, to show, as the bones in a lean man.

丨貌 or 丨容 the countenance.

丨容之 to give shape to it.

丨容出來 [the actor] expresses that character well.

丨勢 the outline, as of hills; the aspect, as of graves; a display, as of troops.

丨體 or 丨像 the substance of, the resemblance, the person of; a likeness, an image.

丨家 geomancers.

有丨 and 無丨 are opposites, natural and supernatural; real and spiritual; evident and unfounded.

有影無丨 has a form without substance, as smoke.

丨影相弔 [only my] body and shadow to encourage each other; *met.* I am alone; friendless.

丨跡可疑 I am in doubt about his face and manner; I don't quite like his looks.

丨諸紙筆 its image is on the paper; *i. e.* it is written out.

原丨出現 the original form then appeared.

丨單 alone, one; solitary, by myself.

不拘丨迹 you need not grasp its shadow;—the thing is of no great importance.

喜怒不丨于色 neither joy nor anger appeared in his face; impassive, imperturbable.

誠中丨外 sincerity will surely manifest itself.

成丨 the exhibition of a form; their shapes are completed, as the hills.

丨者神之宅 the body is the tenement of the animal spirits or the soul.

忘丨之交 one who is intimate, as a friend with whom ceremony can be waived.

娙 ꜀hing — A tall, personable woman; stylish and handsome.

丨娥 was the name of an office held by women in the Han dynasty, A. D. 50, in reign of Wu-ti.

蛵 ꜀hing — A synonym of 蜻 the dragon fly, called 虰丨; it is known also as the 紗羊 or gauze sheep, from its wings; and 負勞 toil-bearer, from its untiring flight.

陘 ꜀hing — From *place* and *path*; it is also read *king*ʾ and used with 徑 a path.

A declivity in hills, an abrupt descent; a defile, a gorge, a pass; names of several hills, one of which is in Ping-yang fu 平陽府 in Shansi.

竈丨 a niche near the fire-place, a place where the kitchen god rests.

井丨 a noted hill and pass in Chehkiang.

井丨縣 a district in Ching-ting fu 正定府 in the south-west of Chihli south of the R. Hu-to.

行 ꜀hing — Composed of 彳 one *step* with the left foot, joined to 亍 one *step* with the right; it forms the 144th radical of a group of characters mostly relating to motion.

To step, to go, to walk; to act, to do, to direct, in which senses it can often be rendered by *let*, for it serves as an auxiliary to the next verb,— as 丨敎 to teach, 丨善 to do good; to transmit, to send off; denotes *imperial* when preceding a noun, showing that the thing is going or being carried on a journey by his Majesty; to appeal a legal case; a road, a way; a step, a manner; motion; in Budhism, a half year (*ayana*) or a march; also one of the *nidana* or causes of things denoting idea (*samskara*) or illusion.

五丨 the five elements which give motion are metal, wood, water, fire, and earth.

丨路 or 出丨 to go in the road, to travel, to go abroad.

丨不丨 will you do it or not? can it be done or not?

丨千步 to walk a mile, to walk to and fro.

步丨 to walk, to travel afoot.

丨人 a traveler; an envoy or special agent of government.

丨語 to tell to.

丨好心 to practice good works.

丨書 the running hand.

丨禮 to visit; to observe the etiquette; to salute.

丨清 to worship at the tombs in the spring.

遊丨 to travel, to journey.

丨宮 the Emperor's traveling lodges.

大丨皇帝 the Emperor who has just gone the great journey; *i. e.* the recently deceased sovereign.

大丨其道 the doctrine is widely speading; his great acts are known.

丨險 to follow illegal or dangerous courses.

丨令 or 丨飭 to trasmit orders to inferior officers.

丨走 to act in another function in addition to one's own official duties.

修丨無間 a ceaseless practice of asceticism, as the Budhists teach.

丨知 to inform [an equal] officially, by 丨文 sending him an official document.

作主施丨 I beg you will favor me by acting in the matter;—said at the end of a petition.

丨丨且止 interrupted, irregular.

丨 and 止 are opposites, as moving and resting; but when joined are synonymous with 丨爲 actions, conduct.

丨權 to do unwillingly; to submit to circumstances.

Read ꜀hang. A row, a line; a series or order; a class, a guild, a trade; a sort; a company of a hundred, or a squad of 25; in *Canton*, a store or warehouse of several divisions; a mercantile establishment, often called a *hong* by foreigners, from the Canton pronunciation.

丨 戶 a guild; a corporation; it has a 丨 ʻ長 or head manager, a chairman.

丨 用 the subscription to the guild; the funds of a corporation.

入 丨 to enter a company by paying the fee.

丨 貨 goods made for general market; ordinary.

同 丨 or 丨 家 of the same craft or firm.

丨 實 or 丨 情 the custom of the craft, the rate of exchange, the current price.

丨 情 光 expert in markets, sharp in dealing.

丨 規 the commission for selling.

發 丨 to sell by wholesale.

洋 丨 商 the hong-merchants, formerly at Canton.

丨 商 a trader in a guild.

他 是 甚 丨 當 呢 what calling or occupation has he?

ʻ上 丨 to commission goods to a firm for sale.

年 紀 長 成 自 然 在 丨 as he grows older he will doubtless become better versed in the rules of the guild.

內 丨 skillful, versed in, accustomed to.

外 丨 a bungler, a raw hand, a lubber.

丨 伍 a soldier; the army; a band.

丨 伍 出 身 rose or was promoted from the ranks.

一 丨 樹 one row of trees.

一 丨 雁 a row or flock of wild geese; but 雁 丨 wild-geese rows, also denotes a series, a succession.

排 丨 在 幾 or 丨 幾 which number [of your family of brothers] are you?

Read *hang*ʾ A firm manner; strong.

子 路 丨 丨 如 也 Tsz'-lu had a decided and energetic way.

Read *hing*ʾ. Actions, conduct; the motives of men.

言 丨 the words and acts of a man.

德 丨 good works, virtues.

品 丨 disposition, character, whether good or bad; a man's 素 丨 is his usual habit, his temper and ways.

道 丨 深 skilled in Taoist tricks; clever, experienced.

損 丨 to destroy the character.

短 丨 snappish, crusty, curt.

信 丨 honest, reliable, trustworthy.

丨 者 心 之 發 actions proceed from the heart.

邪 丨 to act perversely, dissipated; to act as if possessed.

In *Cantonese* read ˛*hong*. To support on, to rest on; to baste. Also read *hăng*ʾ Tense, taut, drawn tight, as an umbrella or a drum.

丨 高 的 raise it a little higher, as a box on a trestle.

丨 衣 服 to baste clothes.

䯒 ˛*hing* Defined to be the backbone of an ox near the rump; but the Păn Tsʻao makes it to be the femur of a bird, speaking of it in the pelican as good for pipes or horns.

擤 ʻ*hing* To blow the nose with the fingers.

丨 鼻 涕 clean the nose.

婞 ʻ*hing* Very, exceedingly.

丨 直 excessively precise and unbending; grouty, particular on trifles.

涬 ʻ*hing* A watery expanse.

溟 丨 a vivifying effluence, a vapor or aura which produces things.

丨 己 to draw on one's self.

悻 ʻ*hing* From *heart* and *lucky*.

Anger, vexation; much displeased; captious, quarrelsome.

丨 直 stiff, punctilious.

丨 丨 然 enraged, looking very cross; proud.

幸ʾ ʻ*hing* Originally composed of 屰 *opposing* and 夭 *ominous*; used with the next.

Fortunate, lucky, prospered beyond one's deserts; blessed; as an initial *adverb*, luckily, happily; to rejoice at; to love tenderly; to wait or hope for; an emperor doing something or visiting a place, which his acts or presence are supposed necessarily to bless; pleased.

丨 得 happily succeeded in.

是 丨 is well, I will be pleased; — a phrase used by shopmen in a bill.

家 門 不 丨 domestic affliction; family trouble, as the death of an eldest son.

算 得 萬 丨 I deemed myself to be very fortunate.

寵 丨 inordinate liking, as for a concubine or female.

何 丨 如 之 what could be more lucky than this!

丨 而 or 丨 虧 very lucky; a sudden good fortune.

不 丨 中 之 丨 cheerful amid sorrow and misfortune.

丨 未 致 命 luckily it did not involve life; — I was not quite killed.

榮 丨 glory, prosperity.

巡 丨 an emperor's progress.

貴 丨 the women in the Imperial hareem, of whom there are four ranks.

不 丨 短 命 死 矣 how sad that he (Yen-tsz') died so early!

丨 臣 an imperial minion, — usually intimates that the person is a eunuch.

倖ʾ ʻ*hing* From *man* and *lucky*; it is a modern alteration from the last.

Unusually fortunate, lucky; to get without any effort or right.

僥 丨 to get accidentally; a good chance, a windfall; a fortunate coincidence.

佞 丨 fawning, sycophantic.

丨 免 I fortunately escaped or avoided it.

莕 荇 k'ing' } An aquatic plant, called 丨菜 with peltate floating leaves, red beneath, and having slender stems, which are used to steep in spirits to improve the flavor; the roots are sometimes powdered and eaten; another name is 金蓮兒 golden lotus; it is probably a *Lemnanthemum* or marsh flower.

杏 k'ing' From 木 *tree* and 可 *can* contracted.

The apricot fruit is 丨兒, but the name includes the sorts of *Prunus* generally, almonds and plums; the flower is also called 及第花 *i. e.* flower of the Hanlin, from its beauty.

丨仁 almonds; also apricot pits from which the 丨仁茶 an emulgent, milk-like tea is made.

銀丨 "silver apricots," the nuts of the gingko or *Salisburia;* it is applied also to the tree.

丨壇 or "apricot altar," was the name of the place where Confucius had his school.

丨桃 a variety of plum like green gage, common at Tientsin.

丨梅 a sort of dark plum.

丨月 a poetical name for the second moon, when the apricots flower.

一色丨花紅十里 the apricot blossoms redden the country for miles.

丨眼桃腮 [she has] apricot eyes and peach cheeks; — a pretty girl.

脛 k'ing' From 肉 *flesh* and 巠 *culm* contracted, alluding to its thinness.

The shank or shin bone; the bone of the leg below the knee in animals and birds; the tarsus.

丨骨 the shin bone.

丨丨昂然 stiff; a commanding presence.

以杖叩其丨 [Confucius] rapped him on the shins with his staff — to teach him manners.

胻 k'ing' From *flesh* and *to rise.*

A painful swelling coming out on the body; to swell, as a boil.

瘡丨快破 the boil will soon discharge.

HIOH.

Old sounds, hak, kak, gak, *and* hiak. *In Canton,* hok *and* yéuk; — *in Swatow,* hak *and* ngiak; — *in Amoy,* hak *and* hiòk; — *in Fuhchau,* hok, oi, kauk, k'iòk, *and* ngiòk; — *in Shanghai,* òk, yòk, *and* kòk; — *in Chifu,* hioä.

學 斈 ˎh'io ˎh'iau } The original form was composed of 敎 to *teach* under 冖 a *waste* place where ignorance reigns, and 臼 a *mortar* as the phonetic, combined; at present the 攴 is omitted; the contracted form is common in cheap books, but not given in the dictionaries.

To learn, to receive instruction; to practice, to imitate; instruction, learning; a science, a study; the science of; the school of; doctrines, tenets; a school, a place of learning; as an *adjective,* like, similar.

丨問 to learn, to examine into, to ascertain; acquirements.

丨習 to practice an art, to carry out what has been learned.

進丨 or 入丨 to become a *siuts'ai.*

上丨 to enter school, at about seven years old, when the lad takes a 丨名 or 書名 by which he is known through life.

丨武 to learn tactics or military science.

數丨 the science of numbers, mathematics.

丨政 the tenets or school of a teacher; but 丨臺 or 丨政 or 丨院 is the title of the provincial literary chancellor.

丨生 a pupil, a scholar, an undergraduate.

丨堂 the school-room.

逃丨 to play truant.

鬧丨 to play tricks in school.

鄉丨 or 社丨 a private village school.

縣丨宮 a governmental school in a district.

遊丨 to travel for information.

博丨 versatile acquirements; very learned.

爲丨 learning; he is at his studies.

假道丨 a charlatan, not a thorough scholar.

大丨士 cabinet ministers, members of the 內閣 Inner Council, of whom there are four principal and two 協辦大丨士 secondary; the term is derived from the 大丨 or Great Learning, whose principles they are supposed to follow.

老道丨 a guide, a teacher who can instruct pupils; an old professor.

丨師 the teacher or guide of the undergraduates; he is under the 丨官 or superintendant of district schools.

我丨你作 I'll do it as you do; I'll follow your way.

丨老 at *Canton,* denotes a man from Swatau or Ch'ao-cheu fu.

義丨 a free school; they are mostly supported by the gentry.

丨而不厭 to study without disliking it; to love books.

壆 ˏhʻio Stiff hard clay or rocky strata; a hard-pan lying under the surface, which prevents the water percolating; bowlders on hills; a crack in a jar.

澩 ˏhʻio From *water* and to *learn* contracted.

A rivulet, dry in winter and running in the summer; the noise of a torrent; rivulets led off from the R. Wéi.

丨 漻 disturbance, confusion; angry, provoked.

鷽 ˏhʻio From *bird* and to *learn* contracted; it is also read *uh*ˎ

A small bird of the jay family, resembling the magpie in its contour; it has red legs and bill, a long tail and variegated plumage; it is reared for fighting, and can imitate the cry of hawks; if its song is heard early, the weather will be fair; if at eventide, rain will come; it may be the *Pica vagabunda*, but is more probably a sort of *Garrulax* or thrush.

丨 鳩 a small species of pigeon.

嗀 ˏhʻio To vomit; the sound of vomiting, which this word seems to imitate.

嘔 丨 vomiting.

謔 ˏhʻio From *words* and *cruel*.

To laugh at, to ridicule; to play and jest with, to make sport of, to mock, to trifle with.

戲 丨 to play tricks on; to haze.

笑 丨 to jest and frolic with.

丨 浪笑敖 with scornful words and jeering smiles.

劇 丨 sportive tricks.

丨 丨 然 trifling, jolly, mockingly.

善戲 丨 兮 how clever he is at a repartee and raillery.

狎 丨 profane or obscene talk.

善 丨 name of an important post on the R. Han in Nan-yang fu in the southwest of Honan.

翯 ˏhʻio From *feathers* and *high*.

The glistening white plumage of cranes and other birds, as they are seen flying; the reflection of the sunlight on water.

白鳥 丨 丨 the bright sheen of the white [egrets, or other] birds.

戄 ˏhʻio Dreading, as when suddenly brought face to face with danger.

驚 丨 startled, terrified.

Read *hwoh*ˎ Hastily, suddenly.

晏子 丨 然攝衣冠謝 Yen-tsz' hurriedly gathered up his dress and made an obeisance.

HIU.

Old sounds, hu *and* ku. *In Canton*, yau *and* hiu; — *in Swatow*, hiu *and* hⁿiu; — *in Amoy*, hiu; — *in Fuhchau*, hiu; — *in Shanghai*, hʻü; — *in Chifu*, hiu.

休 ˏhʻiu From *man* and *tree*; *q. d.* a man leaning against a tree and resting.

To rest, to cease for a while; to spare, to deal gently; to desist; to repudiate, as a wife; to resign; to enjoy; to congratulate, to commend, to praise; to release, to let off; excellent; prosperous; blessing, or a sign of prosperity; as a *negative*, stop, let that alone, don't, quit that.

丨 止 to desist from.

丨 息 to cease labor on, to rest.

丨 息在此 I live here now.

不肯就罷 丨 if you will not consent, then that finishes it.

丨 致 removed from office, but allowed to retain the rank.

丨 妻 to repudiate or divorce a wife, and give her a 丨 書 bill of separation.

告 丨 養 asked leave to resign on account of health.

我心則 丨 our hearts are now at rest.

丨 沐 to stop and wash, refers to an old usage of officials vacating their seats once in ten days to bathe, &c.

丨 徵 favorable verifications, such as show a good government.

丨 手 to leave off work.

丨 祥 or 丨 嘉 fortunate, excellent, propitious.

問 丨 咎 to ask what the luck will be.

自誓不干 丨 I swear that I will not cease — till I get the case.

丨 題起 don't mention the subject.

無疆之 丨 unbounded, unending, as happiness; may you have unlimited joy.

舊事 丨 題 don't rake up old sores.

丨 丨 frugal; to restrict outlay.

良士 丨 丨 the quite and serene scholar; a good officer.

丨 教走了 don't let him get away.

雖 丨 勿 丨 although he wished to rest, he would not.

丨 怕他 you need not fear him.

丨矣皇考以保明其身 be favorable, O Imperial ancestor, and preserve and enlighten my humble self.

不干丨 unceasing enmity.

至死方丨 only till death comes will I stop; but 無常一到萬事丨 when Wu-chang (death) comes, every affair then stops.

若是不肯丨想活命 if you refuse, you will risk your life.

In *Cantonese.* To move off, as a table; to hitch up, as a waistband.

丨開 to move away.

丨褲頭 pull up your trowsers.

庥 *‚h'iu* From a *shelter* and to *cease*; occurs used with the last.

Shade, shelter, which invites to rest; protection, kindness from superiors; to sustain, to protect.

鴻丨 your great favor.

神丨 divine care and aid.

聖丨 your holy favor, is said both of the gods and of the Emperor.

多蒙庇丨 I am deeply indebted for your protection.

用迓天丨 by these means to await the blessing of heaven [in sending snow]; *i. e.* by thanks and prayers.

履祉延丨 may your daily joys long continue; — a phrase used in closing a letter.

咻 *‚h'iu* To call out clamorously, as a crowd of people talking and crying confusedly when jeering at one; a shriek, a groan.

噢噢丨丨 the cry of agony.

衆楚人丨之 a crowd of Ts'u people laughed at him.

烋 *‚h'iu* Used with the two last, to praise and to clamor.

Excellent, beautiful; felicitous, happy; amiable; good; minute, fine; exhalations or steam.

Read *‚hiao.* To decoct, to boil; to fumigate.

炰丨 to swagger; to take on airs.

貅 *‚h'iu* A ferocious beast, the 貔丨, fabled to devour tigers; it is drawn like a leopard, of which it seems to be a variety; the term is applied to a valiant general or brave troops.

鵂 *‚h'iu* A sort of owl, whose hoot resembles laughter; the 鵋丨 or horned owl, which is regarded as a bird of evil omen, as it frequents ruins.

鎀 *‚h'iu* A fine war-steed, a charger; name of a famous horse.

髹 *‚h'iu* From *hair* and *wood;* this character was once wrongly written 捎 from a similarity in the pronunciation.

A varnish of a red or mauve color, approaching purple; to varnish a red color; to put on two coats of lacker.

丨漆器 lackered-ware of a dark red color.

朽 殀 *‘h'iu* From 木 *wood* or 歹 *bad* and 丂 *skilled* contracted; the second old form is uncommon.

Rotten wood; decayed, putrid, noisome, putrescent; failing, forgotten; out of mind; worn out, superannuated.

丨壞 or 丨爛 spoiled, decayed; rotten, as timber.

腐丨 putrid, decomposed.

老丨 I, a poor useless old man.

丨材 unserviceable, as an old or inert official; superannuated; emeritus.

丨木不可雕 decayed wood cannot be carved; — *met.* he is a worthless fellow.

名垂不丨 his name will endure.

德音不丨 his virtuous fame will never be forgotten.

萬古不丨 [real merit] is not forgotten in myriads of years.

死而不丨 [their words] die, but do not perish; — said of the ancients.

齅 *h'iu’* From *nose* and *stink;* nearly synonymous with the next.

To smell anything with particular care; to snuff up.

不丨驕君之耳 when near a proud man do not snuff at things.

嗅 *h'iu’* Also read *ch'eu’*; it is like the last.

The mournful note of birds; to smell, to scent, as dogs do.

三丨而作 [Confucius] smelt of it thrice and then rose.

丨丨看 to smell of anything (*Shanghai.*)

嘼 *h'iu’* Composed of 口 *mouth*, with a rude representation of the ears, head and legs, and tracks of a beast; it is now superseded by 畜 domestic animals.

Animals which put the mouth to the ground when feeding; domestic animals pasturing on the hills.

HIUN.

Old sounds, hún *and* kún. *In Canton*, făn ; — *in Swatow*, hùn *and* hún — *in Amoy*, hún ; — *in Fuhchau*, hŭng *and* hòng ; — *in Shanghai*, hiūng ; — *in Chifu*, hiūn.

熏 燻 *˛h'ün* Composed of 黑 *black* and 屮 to *sprout ;* the second and unusual form is also read *tung'* meaning a great smoke and blaze ; this and the next are interchanged.

The smoke issuing from fire; the fog ascending from hills; steam, smoke; exhalations, vapor, miasma; to scent, as tea with flowers; to fumigate; to smoke, as hams; to grill or broil; to heat, to parch; to offend, to becloud; evening time, dusk; balmy; agreeable.

丨風 a warm southeast wind.

丨丨 uneasy, fidgetty; pleased, harmonious.

丨乾 to dry at the fire.

憂心如丨 my heart is mournful, or unsteady as smoke.

丨黑 smoked black, as by lamp smoke.

丨炙 to cauterize.

丨鼠 to smoke out rats.

烟丨 soot; the smoke blackens it.

烝丨 to steam.

丨烝 steam, hot vapor rising up.

丨肉 to smoke pork previously boiled; a 丨籠 or smoking frame is sometimes used.

Read *hiün'* To suffocate; to injure by coal gas.

煤丨着了 he has been stifled (or made senseless) by coal gas.

丨死 suffocated, as by carbonic acid gas.

薰 *˛h'ün* From *plant* and *vapor ;* often interchanged with the last.

A fragrant labiate plant which opens a new flower every morning, and its savory smell is thought to expel noxious influences; fragrant plants; odor, perfume; to perfume things; fragrant; to cauterize; to embalm; to becloud.

丨香 fragrance of plants.

丨草 a general name for plants like lavendar, which are burned to expel miasma or insects.

丨衣裳 to put camphor or perfumed plants among clothes.

丨蕕 fragrant or stinking; — opposite terms used in speaking of plants.

利慾丨心 avarice and lust becloud the heart.

曛 *˛h'ün* From *sun* and *vapor.*

Twilight; the reflected light at sunset.

丨夕 the evening gloaming.

斜丨 reflected rays at sunset.

山涵丨映 the hills are tinged by the setting sun.

獯 *˛h'ün* A tribe of Scythians in the Hia dynasty, the 丨鬻 who invaded the dominions of T'ai Wang, and drove him south near the River King; they were afterwards known as *Hiung-nu.*

纁 *˛h'ün* A bright red produced by dipping the cloth thrice into the dye; a light scarlet tint, compared to the monthly rose.

丨裳純衣 [one with a] red robe and an elegant pelisse; — *met.* a gambler.

醺 *˛h'ün* Intoxicated, drunk; smelling of liquor.

醉丨丨的 foolishly tipsy.

丨丨然 jolly from drink; fuddled, boozy.

來燕丨丨 he came to the banquet and got drunk.

勳 勛 *˛h'ün* From *strong* and *vapor :* the contracted form is common.

Meritorious effort put forth for one's king; loyal merit; to acquire such fame.

丨臣 a patriotic statesman.

功丨衆著 everybody knew his great services.

丨業 or 丨勞 honors conferred for loyal and distinguished services.

奇丨 unparalleled services.

放丨 an epithet of Yao from his great acts.

丨猷素著 his honorable record is long and glorious.

開國元丨 one who aided in founding the dynasty, and therefore has 丨舊 long established merit; the last phrase also means that such services were formerly rewarded.

爾尙一乃心力其克有丨 do you all go on with one purpose of heart, and the work will surely be accomplished.

焄 *˛h'ün* From *fire* and *prince ;* it occurs used with ˛熏 vapor.

A blaze; odors from cooking flesh, whether fragrant or unsavory; fumes from sacrifices.

丨蒿悽愴 the savory odors and bad smells are very rank.

訓 *h'ün'* From *words* and a *stream ; q. d.* when teaching, words should flow like a stream.

To lead in the right way; to instruct, especially women; to teach and persuade; to caution; doctrine, instruction, precepts; definition; instructed in; explanations; to follow, as instruction; to approve; according.

教丨 to teach, to indoctrinate.

丨 練 to drill in the manual or any military art

皇天用丨厥道 Imperial Heaven approved their ways.

丨 誨 諄 諄 line upon line, precept upon precept; reiterated warnings.

出受傅丨 to go from home to get an education

古丨 the lessons of antiquity; tradition

丨 誨 to instruct, to bring up.

請丨示 I request direction, as an officer asks his superior.

丨 導 the second official superintendant of education in a prefecture

女丨 female education.

丨 詁 to explain; to comment on; a commentary.

丨 典 moral maxims, old and wise sayings.

In *Pekingese*. An adjective of comparison, an intensive adverb.

丨 甜 very sweet.

In *Cantonese* it is also written 瞓 to distinguish it as a colloquial word, but it may also be an alteration from 瞳 dull eyes. To sleep; to rest.

眼丨 sleepy.

你丨着 you are sleepy.

HIUNG.

Old sounds, hiong, kiong, *and* giong. *In Canton*, hung, hing, *and* k'ing; — *in Swatow*, hiòng, him, *and* hⁿia; — *in Amoy*, heng *and* hiòng; — *in Fuhchau*, hüng, hing, *and* hiàng; — *in Shanghai*, hiung *and* yung; — *in Chifu*, hiüng.

兄 *hiüng* From 儿 *man* and 口 *mouth* above it, *q. d.* as if the senior has the right to instruct; occurs used for *hwang* 怳 sorrow.

An elder brother; a senior; a superior; used after names as a term of respect, like Don, Señor, or Mr.; to act as an elder brother.

老丨 or 吾丨 or 丨臺 your honor; Sir; venerable Sir; — terms of direct and respectful address.

令丨 your elder brother.

丨長 my elders, is like 仁丨 my kind or respected friends; — both used in addressing any respectable person.

家丨 my elder brother, — used when speaking of him.

丨弟 my younger brother

堂丨弟 kindred of the same surname; 表丨弟 cousins of a different surname, whether on the father or mother's side

同胞丨弟 a uterine brother.

內丨 a wife's elder brother.

外丨 a sister's husband.

愚丨 I, your senior — tell you; said by an old man.

師丨 a fellow workman or priest who is older.

誰復丨丨 who could better treat him as a brother?

誼丨 or 如丨 an adopted brother, a sworn brother; the usage of the two terms is however unlike

王芝祥丨 [to] Mr. Wang Chi-siang; but when speaking to him, 芝丨 my brother Chi is proper.

大丨 great Sir, — is used chiefly in writing.

孔方丨 the brother with a square hole; *i. e.* a cash.

凶 *hiüng* Intended to depict 凵 a *pit* with something fallen into it; it is constantly written like the next.

Unfortunate, unlucky, the opposite of 吉; lugubrious, funeral; adverse, unhappy; calamitous, like a judgment on one; sad, unpromising; malignant, cruel, injurious, in which it is like the next.

鴉報丨 the crow croaks bad luck.

吉丨未知 I don't know whether it is lucky or not.

丨年 a bad year, as one of drought.

丨星 a baleful star.

丨德 an evil or unfavorable condition or aspect.

丨信 bad news, as of a death.

四丨 were four brigands in the days of Yao.

丨事 an unlucky affair; also mourning and funereal matters.

病狠丨險 this sickness is very dangerous

兇 *hiüng* From 儿 *man* and 凶 *unlucky*; *q. d.* one who has fallen into ruin; used with the last.

Malevolent, inhuman, cruel; malignant, desperate, truculent; harsh and unmerciful in treatment of others; to excite fear; fearful; a cry of terror.

丨惡 wickedly cruel, as a 丨惡棍徒 an unscrupulous villain.

丨橫 vicious, cross-grained, intractable.

丨暴 fierce, unscrupulous and cruel.

恃勢行丨 employed his power to act savagely; to act like a brigand.

丨頑 a cruel disposition.

丨手 a murderer, one who has compassed the death of a man, a homicide; one who 行丨霸道 acts cruelly and kills willfully in defiance of right

恟 *K'iung* Timorous, nervous; to start up frightened, as from a dream.

匈 胸 胷 *K'iung* From 月 *flesh* and 匈 the *breast;* the first and now obsolete form was intended to represent the thorax enveloping the heart; occurs used for the next.

The thorax; the breast, the bosom; the feelings, the heart; the affections; clamor; brawling.

丨 懷 the feelings, the affections.

丨 中 or 丨 次 near or in the breast; on the mind.

丨 隔 翳 滯 a stricture or weight in the diaphragm, indigestion, heart-burn.

丨 堂 the breast, the bosom, the front.

捶 丨 to beat the breast, as a beggar does.

丨 藏 錦 繡 silks and embroidery stored in the breast; *met.* learned and accomplished.

怒 氣 塡 丨 he is quite suffocated with rage.

丨 無 蔕 芥 not a mote in his breast; *i. e.* light of heart, inconsiderate, no anxiety.

小 人 丨 丨 little minded men are disputatious and clamorous.

鷄 丨 a protruding breast, caused by disease in the breast-bone.

丨 襟 闊 liberal-minded, magnanimous, considerate.

拊 丨 大 痛 to clasp the bosom in one's deep anguish.

丨 羅 武 庫 he carries an arsenal in his breast, — so brave is he.

寬 丨 be easy in your mind; a tranquil or liberal mind.

丨 奴 the Huns, *i. e.* the clamorous slaves; the name dates from about the Han dynasty.

訩 詾 *K'iung* From *words* and *breast;* the second form is least used; occurs written like the last.

To speak all at once; to brawl, to scold; to complain against; to litigate; full, as of trouble; a great clamor; threatenings.

天 下 丨 丨 everybody is railing.

降 此 鞠 丨 these disorders and miseries were sent on them — for their sins.

洶 *K'iung* From *water* and *breast.*

The forcible rush of water, as along a beach; the bubbling of a spring; tumultuous, clamorous, as a crowd.

丨 湧 the lashing of waves; the gurgling of a fountain.

丨 丨 the réveillé of drums; the din of men and instruments, as at an audience; *met.* excited, as 忿 丨 丨 幾 不 可 過 their anger became so very outrageous it could hardly be surpassed.

雄 *K'iung* From *bird* and the upper *arm.*

A cock bird, the "father bird;" the male of insects and small animals; the best; masculine, martial; brave, heroic.

丨 壯 burly and strong.

抖 起 丨 心 arouse yourself, screw your courage up.

丨 鷄 a fine cock.

丨 才 大 略 a master hand at strategy and schemes, a good contriver.

丨 兵 百 萬 legions of brave soldiers.

丨 霸 一 方 to seize a region by force.

丨 精 the purest part of 丨 黃 or hartall.

决 雌 丨 to test the leadership.

熊 *K'iung* From 炎 *flame* and 能 *able,* but the etymologists give no explanation.

The bear, called 蟄 獸 the hybernating animal; it is commended for its clean lair, notwithstanding its ugliness; clear white suet called 丨 白, envelopes the heart, a good medicine.

丨 掌 a bear's paw, considered to be a delicacy.

丨 膽 bear's gall, which it is said by the Chinese moves into the head, belly, and legs according to the season.

如 丨 如 羆 [brave] as brown and white bears.

丨 人 or 人 丨 the brown bear, much larger and fiercer than the 耍 狗 丨 or small, white-necked bear trained to perform feats.

丨 耳 山 a high peak near Lushi hien 盧 氏 縣 in Honan, where Yü began his survey; there are two high green pointed summits resembling bear's ears, whence the name, which is now extended to the range making the watershed between the Yellow River and the River Han.

其 光 丨 丨 the glare and brightness are very great.

吉 夢 維 丨 his lucky dream was all about a bear.

詗 *K'iung* From *words* and a *desert space.*

To give information about places; to spy about, to pry into and make intelligent observations upon; shrewd, clever.

丨 悟 sharp, quicksighted.

中 丨 a clever talebearer or gossip; a spy, one who 丨 探 seeks out and hunts up information.

窺 丨 時 事 to watch current events, to keep the run of.

夐 *K'iung'* Also read *hing'* and *hüen'.*

Preëminent, superior in abilities; to aim at high success; to scheme to reach; to go far away.

丨 哉 特 立 or 丨 乎 尙 矣 he stood alone and peerless! high and exalted he stood above all.

終 日 丨 丨 to struggle and labor the whole day.

丨 莫 與 京 there's no place comparable to the capital.

In *Cantonese.* A bunch, a cluster, a handful of flowers.

一 丨 蕉 a bunch of plantains.

HO.

Old sounds, ha, ka, *and* ga. *In Canton*, ho ; — *in Swatow*, ho *and* o ; — *in Amoy*, ò *and* hò ; — *in Fuhchau*, ho ; — *in Shanghai*, hu *and* u ; — *in Chifu*, hwoä.

呵 ˓*hö*. From *mouth* and *can* ; it is interchanged with ˓o 阿 and the next.

To expel the breath ; to scold, to get angry at ; to please ; to interrogate ; a final sound in assent.

打丨氣 to gape.

打丨 or 丨欠 the noise of yawning ; to yawn.

丨凍作字 warm [your fingers] with the breath to write easier.

不丨奉他 do not be too officious.

Read ˓*ha*. To laugh, in imitation of the sound.

丨丨 the sound of laughter.

丨丨大笑 a fit of loud laughing.

是個丨丨兒 it was only a forced laugh.

訶 ˓*hö*. From *words* and *can* ; *q. d.* to tell what one ought to do.

To blame, to speak harshly and reprove ; to upbraid, to talk loud to one ; to ridicule.

譏丨 to traduce by ridicule.

丨責 to blame, to find fault with, as a servant.

詆丨古人 to disparage and decry the ancients.

丨求責備 to find fault for trifles.

丨遣役卒 to browbeat and order about one's underlings.

丨子 or 丨黎革 an astringent nut of foreign origin (as the name rather indicates), used for the toothache ; the fruit of the *Terminalia chebula* or myrobalanus.

魺 ˓*hö*. A sort of sea-blubber. In Canton, the 洋梭丨 is a large fish resembling a sciæna, and shaped like a shuttle ; at Fuhchau, the name is applied to three or four kinds, one a small yellow sort, the 黃䱐丨 or yellow tough perch.

苛 ˓*hö*. From *plants* and *can* as the phonetic.

Small plants or grass ; petty, troublesome, vexatious ; small, trifling, minute ; unimportant, as an ailing ; to reprove, to criticize ; to vex, to annoy, as by interfering ; to molest uselessly.

丨刻 needlessly severe.

丨求 to tire one by asking.

丨疾 a dangerous disease, one which is critical.

丨政猛于虎 an inquisitive government is more savage than a tiger.

丨癢相關 even his trifling itching affects me ; *i. e.* I feel a sympathy for his small troubles.

不得偏狥丨縱 I cannot make a partial decision, being harsh to one and lenient to the other.

河 ˓*hö*. A river, defined as "that into which rivulets flow ;" when used alone, it denotes the 黃丨 or Yellow River ; it also occurs in many geographical names ; in the northern provinces rivers are generally called ˓*ho*, and ˓*kiang* 江 in the southern ; a canal ; a sort of wine-vessel ; in physiognomy, the mouth.

丨套 the great bend of the Yellow River in the Ortous country.

兩丨 denotes north and south of the Yellow River.

口如懸丨 his mouth is like a tumbling river ; *i. e.* he talks like a mill-race.

閘丨 and 御丨 are names for portions of the Imperial Canal.

一統山丨 the hills and rivers — of China ; *met.* the whole of a country.

梗丨 the stars ρ δ in Boötes.

丨間 and 丨中 the stars γ and β in Hercules.

丨沿上 along the river's bank.

蚵 ˓*hö*. Also read ˓*k'o*.

A sort of lizard, the 丨蠖 which frequents damp places.

丨蚑萊 a trailing plant resembling the honeysuckle, found near K'ai-fung fu, having yellow flowers ; the young plants are used for food.

何 ˓*hö*. From *man* and *able* ; also read ˓*ho*, and used for the next.

An interrogative *pronoun*, who which, what ; as an *adverb*, how, wherefore ; to bear, to endure.

如丨 in what way ?

丨故 wherefore ? why ?

丨事 what business have you ?

因丨 why, what is the reason ?

爲丨 for what reason ?

無幾丨 in no long time ; suddenly ; few of that sort.

無得奈我丨 he can do (or it is) nothing to me.

丨不早來 why did you not come earlier ?

丨解 what is the meaning or reason ?

丨必如此 what need is there of this ? *i. e.* it need not be so.

丨以 how can it be ? — implying a negative.

丨哉 why, pray !

如之丨則可 it can be, if that be so.

莫敢如丨 no one will dare to do that ; let him do as he likes.

誠是丨心哉 well, what are your real ideas ?

無丨 well then ; it is only for a moment.

無可奈丨 there is no help for it.

莫可誰丨 what help is there for it ?

丨不去也 why don't you go ?

汝意丨居 what is your opinion of it ?

擔˒丨 to bear, as an evil or a load.

丨有丨無 all the same; whether or no; rather immaterial.

無法奈丨 there's no resource now! what hope is there?

荷 ₍hŏ From *plants* and *what* as the phonetic.

The small leaved variety of the water-lily (*Nelumbium*); the name is also applied to some kinds of asters and mallows, from their resemblance to its flowers.

丨包 a purse, from its likeness to the shape of a lily leaf.

隰有丨華 in the marshes the lilies are in full blossom.

丨衣 the broad lotus leaf.

丨露 the water on a lotus leaf.

金絲丨葉 the marsh flower (*Limnanthemum*.)

丨葉 a door butt in Peking; and this leaf is often used as a name of things.

丨風 a pleasant breeze, especially a mild, south wind.

丨月 a poetical name for the sixth moon.

丨蘭國 a name for Holland.

丨蘭薯 Irish potatoes (*Cantonese*.)

Read ʿho. To bear, to sustain; to carry on the back, or hanging around the neck; competent; to be obliged for; indebted to, obtained of.

負丨 to carry; competent for.

欣丨 I am pleased to get.

丨笠 to wear a rain-hat.

背丨 to lift on the back.

丨蒙大恩 I am thankful for your great kindness.

感丨隆情 duly sensible of your great consideration.

是丨 for which I will thank you; — a closing phrase in letters.

賀 hòʾ From *precious* and to *add*.

To congratulate, to felicitate at festivals or other occasions; to send presents when wishing one joy; the presents thus sent; to carry.

恭丨 with my respectful congratulations; — often written on presents.

慶丨 to congratulate; as 丨年 denotes the new-year salutations.

奉丨 to send presents; as 丨禮 is a term for the articles sent.

丨喜 or 可喜可丨 joy be with you, as when a friend meets with success.

朝丨 a general levee, as at a coronation.

丨戟 to carry a spear, to escort.

四方來丨 felicitations will come from all quarters.

丨蘭山 the Ara-shan Mts., lying north of Kansuh.

HOH.

Old sounds, hat, gat, hak, kak, gak, hap, gap, hek, gek, hot, got, hiap, giap, ngap, *and* wap. *In Canton*, hot, hok, hăk, hăt, hòp, *and* hòk; — *in Swatow*, hat, hek, hiat, ho, k'ap, ap, hap, *and* ha; — *in Amoy*, hap, ap, hat, k'ap, hek, hòk, kek, giat, *and* gút; — *in Fuhchau*, hak, haik, kak, ak, hòk, *and* k'auk; — *in Shanghai*, hŏh, yŏh, heh, hăk, hòk, ngòk, hih, niăk, *and* ha; — *in Chifu*, hwoä, ho, *and* ka.

曷 ₍hŏ From 曰 to *speak* and 匃 to *beg*; as a primitive it seldom imparts any of its meaning to the compound; occurs used for the next.

An interrogative particle, why, wherefore? why not? to stop, as by a question; to intimidate; to hoot at.

丨之用 why not use it?

丨故 what is the reason?

丨可 it will not be proper.

丨虐朕民 why does he harass our people?

丨其奈何弗敬 why does he not treat him respectfully?

丨勝感戴 I shall certainly carry with me [the remembrance] of your kindness.

喝 ₍hŏ From *mouth* and *why*; interchanged with the last.

To call out aloud, to shout out, to grunt at; a reprimand, an exclamation of reproof; a gurgling, guttural, sobbing, or choking sound; to sip, to drink, in which sense it is synonymous with *k'oh*, 嗑, and is not spoken of animals drinking.

丨道 to clear the road, as lictors do; to bawl.

呼丨 to order about, to find fault.

丨醉了 to get drunk.

丨開 to separate people who are quarreling.

丨令 to set on, to egg on; to shout an order, as an underling does.

聞丨一聲 I heard a scream.

丨住 be quiet, stop your fighting! — as fellows in the street.

嘶丨 a sobbing wail of infants.

丨再 or 丨彩 to applaud; encore! fine!

丨西北風 [like a] sip of the northwest wind—are my wages.

吃丨嫖賭 to give one's self over to whoring and gambling.

蟬丨柳 the cicada chirps on the willow.

髷 ₍hŏ From *hair* and *why*; used with the next.

A felted woolen fabric like pilot cloth or coarse baize, called *darma* by the Mongols, and made in the northern provinces; embroidered or stitched leather; a light grayish color.

氈 丨 a sort of pilot cloth, coarse woolen stuff.

㲝 丨 worked or ornamented leather.

打 丨 燥 he has singed the baize; *i. e.* he is disappointed in attaining a degree.

褐 *ˏhŏ* Clothes made of pilot cloth; coarse woolen, such as the poor wear; hempen socks; poor, miserable; a gray color, like that of camel's hair or unbleached hemp.

衣' 丨 to wear coarse cloth; as a 丨 夫 poor man does.

釋 丨 to throw off country garments; *i. e.* to become an officer.

被 丨 振 裙 he put on his wrapper and threw his arms about.

車 丨 子 a cartman in Peking, where this coarse serge is worn.

無 衣 無 丨 何 以 卒 歲 without clothes and wrappers, how are we to get through the winter?

寓 眠 多 擁 丨 when traveling have plenty of wrappers.

鞨 *ˏhŏ* A stocking or shoe.

丨 巾 a kind of turban.

紅 丨 red buskins.

靺 丨 name of a tribe of nomads, whose country is said to produce gems as large as chestnuts.

鶡 *ˏhŏ* Composed of 鳥 *bird* and 褐 *gray* contracted, from the prevailing colors.

A variety of Reeves' pheasant (*Phasianus superbus*), considered to be a very pugnacious bird, and used as an emblem of courage; its long tail feathers are worn by actors; the plumage is black, yellow, and gray; it has a crest.

丨 冠 a plumed cap with 雉 鷄 尾 in them, as these pheasant's feathers are called; lictors in theaters, called 丨 冠 子 now wear them.

丨 鴠 or 丨 旦 a sort of thrush or nightingale, which sings at night as if calling for the dawn.

蝎 *ˏhŏ* From *insect* and *why*; this is often erroneously used for *hieh*ˎ 蠍 the scorpion.

A grub found in trees which bores them through; to eat like a grub; *met.* lusts which destroy one.

桑 丨 the mulberry grub.

丨 蠹 grubs and larvæ of all kinds.

丨 盛 則 木 朽 when grubs multiply the tree decays.

合 *ˏhŏ* From 口 *mouth* and 亼 the contracted form of 集 to *assemble.*

To shut the mouth; to join, to unite; to shut, to close; to fold up, as a pocket foot-rule does; to coalesce; to pair; to collect or convene; to deduce from, as an antecedent in logic; accordant, agreeable to, suitable; harmonious, in unison; joint; to preserve in harmony; the first note of the octave; to reply; to correspond, to match; to meet, as shear-blades; the whole; together, with; a pair; a classifier of diverging streams, of doorways, and other things made up of parts; a kind of millet.

丨 無 is it best? ought I to do so? if it be right.

丨 我 用 it is just what I needed.

丨 意 it suits me; agreeable.

丨 門 to close the door.

丨 做 生 意 in partnership.

相 丨 agreeing, fitting, corresponding.

配 丨 to betroth, to pair.

丨 年 生 to compare the horoscope of two children.

丨 樣 or 丨 式 like the pattern; suitable.

丨 口 to match the openings or lines.

不 丨 often intimates disapproval of a proposition or principle; as 不 丨 道 理 unreasonable, unjust.

不 丨 法 illegal.

立 丨 同 to settle an agreement; to make a contract.

丨 本 to join a stock in trade as 丨 夥 joint partners do.

丨 府 the whole prefecture.

丨 家 the entire family.

一 丨 流 北 一 丨 流 南 one branch of the river flows north, the other flows south.

丨 符 節 to agree and make out a contract.

天 作 之 丨 a match made in heaven.

保 丨 太 和 may [Heaven] bring great peace to all people.

妻 子 好' 丨 loving union with wife and children.

丨 攏 起 來 bring them together; to join, as a mortice and tenon, or persons in partnership.

丨 壁 side by side, as things.

丨 一 打 算 to calculate, to see if there be money enough.

窻 二 丨 two windows.

六 丨 are the four points of compass, with zenith and nadir, and thus denotes the empire, the whole land; which is also expressed by 丨 天 底 下 the covering sky over all below.

丨 共 or 共 丨 all, the sum total, the aggregate.

丨 埋 in *Cantonese*, to close up, to bring all together; like 丨 在 一 塊 兒 all at once.

丨 眼 瞓 to shut the eyes and doze.

In *Fuhchau.* Cheap; to break or snap.

Read *koh*ˎ A dry measure like a gill, the tenth of a *ˏshing* 升 or pint; it holds ten *choh*ˎ 勺 or spoons; in common use, the quantity one hand will scoop up.

姶 *ˏhŏ* A *woman* who is *agreeable*; fair, handsome.

美 丨 beautiful.

婤 丨 the concubine of Duke Siang, B.C. 540, in the state of Wéi.

哈 ˏhŏ A school of fishes; a fish's mouth; used with the next, a sip; to taste, to take a swallow.

丨飲 to drink by sipping.

打丨息 to gape.

Read ˏha or ˏhwo; as 丨丨笑 the sound of hearty laughter; a horse laugh.

Read ka' in 丨喇 for kara, i. e. black, and now used at the north to denote Russian woolen cloth.

丨密 Hamil or Khamil, a town near Barkoul in the west of Kansuh; it was once the capital of a kingdom of the Túrks.

欱 ˏhŏ To sip, to drink; to suck in, as fish; to take a mouthful or draught; to bring together.

口丨湯水 to take a sip of broth.

匌 ˏhŏ From to *envelop* and *united*.

To environ; everywhere.

匒丨 stones piled upon each other.

翕丨 a dull smoky atmosphere; a warm mist.

郃 ˏhŏ Name of 丨陽縣 a district in Tung-cheu fu adjoining the Yellow River in the east of Shensi; the name dates from the Han dynasty.

頜 hŏ' From *head* and to *join*; it is used with ʿhan 頷 the chin.

The bone under the ear; the end of the jaw, the jowl.

麧 ˏhŏ From *wheat* and to *beg* as a phonetic.

Wheat in the kernel, not yet ground; broken kernels found in chaff.

糠丨 bran or grits.

盒 ˏho From *dish* and to *unite*, alluding to the mode of construction.

A name for such boxes or dishes as have covers fitting on, as gallipots, hat or pill-boxes, caskets; they are often nearly spherical in shape; a covered platter; a case for articles, especially for sending presents.

一個丨 or 丨子 one box.

拜帖丨 a card-case.

鼻烟丨 a snuff-box.

全丨 a partition box for sweetmeats.

菓丨 a covered box to send fruit in; the bearers expect to receive 丨錢 a box gratuity.

一丨禮物 one box of ceremonial presents; it is fitted with trays.

盍 **盇** ˏho From *dish* and to *go*; it was anciently written like the second form to indicate a dish covered; it is not seldom erroneously used for kai' 蓋 a covering.

To unite in order to attain one purpose; to cover; an interrogation like hoh, 曷 why not? intimating an alternative.

丨各言爾志 why doesn't each of you speak his mind?

丨歸乎來 will it not be best to go home?

丨去 let us go.

丨稚 a depreciating term for one's self; *scil.* am I not a callow youth?

朋丨簪 to collect one's friends and ask them, as Haman did.

闔 ˏhŏ From *door* and a *cover*; used with the last.

A leaf of a folding or double door; a two leaved door; all within the doors, a family; to shut; used for hoh, 合 all, the whole; to unite all; occurs used as an interrogative why not? a thatch.

丨家大小 the entire establishment.

丨門 or 丨戶 to close the door; also, the whole household, all within the door.

剪丨 to trim a thatch.

丨郡公啓 the whole department unites in this public notice, — as to repair a temple.

丨廬 to close one's cottage; — to retire from public life.

丨潭均吉 I hope your excellent family is well.

閶丨風 a poetical term for a westerly wind, an evening breeze, supposed to blow from the gate of paradise.

嗑 ˏhŏ From *mouth* and to *cover*.

Loquacious; often used for 喝 to sip, to drink.

丨然 laughing, talking.

丨一杯茶 take a cup of tea.

丨丨 the noise of many persons conversing.

噬丨 the 21st diagram, which represents something crunched in the mouth as it is closed, and therefore the lot denotes eating or consuming.

黑 ˏhĕi hŏ' Originally composed of altered forms of 炎 *flame* and an old form of 囱 a *window*; q. d. flame and smoke blacken the openings; it forms the 203d radical of a natural group of words relating to black.

Black, a hue which was the lucky color in the Hia dynasty; it belongs to water and the north; sooty; dark, obscure, cloudy, dull; evening, dusk, night; wicked, malicious; dark designs.

漆丨 or 丨色 black.

丨家 by (or at) night.

丨白難分 good and bad are not easily distinguished; he has no fixed principles.

快丨 it will soon be dark.

丨下 it is dark now; while dark.

夜丨 in the night-time; a dark night.

丨暗 dark, not well lighted; dim, dusky.

摸着丨兒 feeling for it in the dark; hard to find.

丨子 a black spot, a mole; a little bit.

丨稿 an outline, a pencil sketch.

丨蒼蒼 very black, as hair; quite dark, as the hour.

丨股冬 or 丨股影 at early dawn, still dark; dark as a pocket. (*Pekingese.*)

丨良心 an unprincipled fellow.

丨心 villainous, black-hearted.

丨貨 opium; it is also called 丨土 black earth.

丨地升科 the unregistered lands are entered to pay taxes.

丨水 a river forming one of the headwaters of the River Yangtsz', the Murus-usu.

丨龍江 the Amoor river up to its junction with the Songari River; also the commandery of Tsi-tsi-har in Manchuria.

In *Pekingese.* To dote on, to long for, to desire.

眼睛丨上這個了 his eyes are fixed on this thing to have it.

赫, *hŏ'* Formed of 赤 *carnation* doubled; occurs used for the next.

Bright, luminous, gleaming like a red hot fire, as the composition of the character intimates; a red color; glorious, brilliant; elegant, clever; majestic; to glisten, to scorch; to frighten, to terrify.

丨怒 fearful anger.

丨耀 bright and glorious.

丨丨 bright, glorious, awful, as a manifestation of the gods; fiery, as the sky in a drought; great, as a fame.

丨奕 glorious, grand, as a general in his skill.

天子臨下有丨 when the emperor comes among the people it is with majesty.

丨如渥赭 [my face is] red (or flushed) as if I had been rouged.

顯丨 it is brightly manifested, as dignity or power.

丨顯 [the god] brilliantly manifested — his power; in Kiangsu, this phrase is also applied to lightning, in allusion to supernatural power.

Read *shih*, Quick, rapid.

嚇, *hia'* *hŏ'* From *mouth* and *illustrious* as the phonetic; it is also read *hia'* and used for the last.

Anger; angry tones; to threaten, to scare, to intimidate, to alarm; that which alarms; a superlative.

丨掉了魂 to scare the demon out of one.

丨死人 to scare people to death.

驚丨 to browbeat; frightened.

呼丨 to hoot at; to threaten.

丨勢 one who pretends to power, one who refers to authority to bully another.

丨詐 to alarm others deceitfully.

恐丨 to idly arouse one's fears.

丨着 well scared; terrified.

丨了一跳 it gave me a great fright; it scared him dreadfully.

丨殺 is a superlative, as 被財主丨殺 to be intimidated or browbeaten by a rich man.

窮苦來丨殺 extremely poor; (*Shanghai.*)

壑, *hŏ'* From 土 *earth* and 谷 *valley* with 叔 *to put on.*

A bed of a torrent, a deep gully or wady; a valley; a pit, a fosse; a conduit; a pool.

大丨 the ocean.

胸中邱丨 he has hills and ravines in his breast; *i. e.* he is obstinate in his notions.

溝丨 a ditch, a moat; a puddle.

布假山之邱丨 to arrange a hill and pool in fancy rockwork, as is done in fine gardens.

谿丨 a gully, a ravine, a valley.

崕巖絕丨 an abrupt precipice; a road impassible from gulches.

隺, *hŏ'* From 隹 a *bird* getting out into the 冂 *wilds;* its use as a primitive is mostly phonetic.

A bird flying high, as the crane does.

Read *kioh*, An aspiring, ambitious mind.

夫乾丨然 now, the first diagram *kien* 乾 denotes exaltation.

鶴, *hao* *hŏ'* From *bird* and *high*, because it carries its head so erect.

The crane, regarded as an emblem of longevity, from the notion that after 2000 years it turns black, whence 玄丨 means thousands of years; the name is applied to several species of waders, and often used in proper names.

白丨 the white egret (*Herodias modesta*), eaten at Canton; the district of Hoh-shan 丨山 in Shao-k'ing fu to the southwest of Canton gets its name from this bird.

朱頂丨 the red crowned crane.

仙丨 the Manchurian crane (*Grus montignesia*) called the fairy's crane, because paper images of it are carried at funerals, on which the departed spirit rides to heaven; it is the official insignia on the court robes of civilians of the first grade.

霧水丨 a sort of gray crane found about Canton.

丨筭同長 may your life be as long as the crane's.

丨髮童顏 he has hoar hairs but a youthful face.

丨立鷄群 [he excels them all] as a crane standing among chickens.

丨膝瘋 the crane's knee scrofula, is a swollen knee-joint.

陳兵丨列 troops drawn out in regular file, — as cranes fly.

丨骨松姿 [like] a crane's bone and a pine's figure; — very lean.

丨神 the god of cranes — is an unlucky god.

梅妻丨子 a poetical term for wife and sons, derived from a poet who chose the flowers and birds for his family.

丨鳴于九臯 the crane screams in the middle marsh.

丨頂 a long crane-shaped button worn by *siuts'ai* and *küjin* graduates.

臛, 矐, *hŏ'* Soup or broth made from meat, without any vegetables; meat tea. The second character also means to smoke with horse-dung; the smarting eye and obscure vision resulting.

涸, 㵑, *hŏ'* The first, from *water* and *firm*, alludes to the hard caked earth left when the water has dried off; the second form is pedantic and obsolete.

Dried up, run out, exhausted; in need, at extremity.

乾 丨 thirsty; parched by the sun, as land; *met.* needy, out of funds.

濟 丨 to help one in distress.

水始 丨 the water is drying up.

陰 丨 loss of virility.

無本之水 丨 可立待 when a stream has no lasting fountain, one can wait for it to dry up; — fame without merit is soon forgotten.

甦 丨 轍之魚 like giving life to a fish in a dry rut; help at the last gasp; alluding to the goby, which sometimes jumps on land.

謞, *hŏ'* From *words* and *high*; it is nearly synonymous with 熇 *hiao.*

To slander, to vilify.

多將 丨 丨 he is always backbiting and railing.

Read *hiao'* To bawl, to roar.

滈, *hŏ* Name of a small lake, called Hoh-hoh hu 合 丨 湖 in I-hing hien in Chang-cheu fu lying in the east of Kiangsu.

貉, *hŏ'* From a *beast* and *each*, because it is common.

An animal akin to the badger, but the description makes it also like the ratel; it burrows and sleeps much, gets its food by night, has a sharp nose and thick reddish fur; it occurs in Tibet.

丨 裘 badger's skin robes, though wolf skins are also included.

打 丨 睡 lethargic, sleepy.

一之日于 丨 in the first days [of the moon] the badger — is hunted.

狐 丨 之厚以居 when the fox and badger are intimate they can burrow together; — as thieves can associate.

Read *moh,* and confounded with 貊 the tapir. The name of a wild tribe in the north, whose speech Confucius said was rude; hence 丨 道 means the principles of savages; still; a raveled thread.

貈, *hŏ* An animal resembling the fox, prone to sleep, which some authors say is the same as the last, but it is probably nearer allied to the ratel; others confound it with the tapir.

莫 丨 a sort of mantis.

狢, *hŏ'* A sort of grass or grain resembling spiked millet, but smaller; it is probably a kind of panic grass.

垎, *hŏ'* Water drying off and showing the firm land.

郝, *hŏ'* *'hao* Name of an ancient place, called 丨 鄉 in T'ai-yuen fu in Shensi; and of another in Fu-fung hien 扶風縣 north of the River Wei in the west of Shensi; now used as a surname.

Read *shih,* To plough.

丨 丨 to turn up and loosen the soil.

翮, *kŏ* From *wing* and a *sacrificial vessel;* occurs used for 鬲 the hollow legs of a tripod.

The barrel or root of a feather; a quill; a pinion.

奮 丨 rapid pinions; *i. e.* high and firm resolution.

羽 丨 a quill-feather of the wing.

振 丨 高翔 [the roc] shook its pinions and went on high; — *met.* rapid promotion in office.

劾, *hŏ* From *strength* and a *horary* character.

To judge, to examine into; to search out the merit or otherwise of officials; to impeach, to prosecute or accuse one; to restrain; diligent in discharge of duty.

丨 叅 to impeach an official.

糾 丨 and 彈 丨 an impeachment and the reply to it.

考 丨 其實 to inquire (as a judge) into the real facts.

丨 奏 to accuse in a memorial.

自投 丨 狀 to accuse one's self of incapacity; this is sometimes done to stave off a trial.

丨 究 and 丨 問 to examine officially into cases; the second denotes a preliminary inquiry.

紇, *hŏ'* Also read *hiuh,*

The ends of a fringe; tassels.

丨 國 a tribe of the Ouigors, mentioned A.D. 757.

In *Pekingese* read *koh,* A knot.

死 丨 縺 a hard knot.

活 丨 縺 a bow knot.

齕, *hŏ'* To bite; to gnaw, as a rat; applied to the peculations of public property.

覈, *hŏ'* From to *cover* and to *beat;* its form somewhat resembles *fuh* 覆 to reply; and it is nearly synonymous with *huh,* 核 to search into.

To put aside all coverings and glosses, to learn the real condition of things; to examine thoroughly; to pare; to cut or engrave; the reality; truly, verily.

丨 驗 to verify, to search and see.

考 丨 or 審 丨 to inquire into an affair.

刻 丨 to question by torture.

糠 丨 wheat still covered, *i. e.* unthrashed.

綜 丨 名實 to ferret out the names and facts.

蠚, *hŏ'* The sting of an insect or its poison; the pain of a sting; to poison by stinging.

HU.

Old sounds, hu, ku, gu, wu, mo, ngo, kut, *and* gut. *In Canton*, u *and* fu; — *in Swatow*, hu, hò, hⁿò, o, *and* u; — *in Amoy*, ho *and* o; — *in Fuhchau*, hu, u, *and* hò; — *in Shanghai*, u, hu, *and* vu; — *in Chifu*, hu.

呼 *hu* From *mouth* and the *breath* going forth; occurs used for the next.

An expiration of the breath; to breathe out; to call out to, to address, to speak to; to blurt, to cry out loud; to invoke, to call upon.

丨吸 breathing.

一丨一吸 one expiration and one inspiration.

嗚丨哀哉了 alas! alas! how sad it is.

丨喚 to call out, as to a person some way off.

丨風喚雨 to call for wind and rain, as jugglers.

丨使 to call for, to order.

丨猫丨狗 [you think people will come and go, as when] calling a dog or a cat.

丨丨喝喝 calling and scolding, not pleased with anything.

丨喊 to bawl at, to call rudely.

丨來喊去 calling here and ordering there; inconsiderate, undecided.

丨門 to call out, at a door.

三丨已畢 the three salutes [to the emperor] being finished.

攘臂一丨 he waved his hand and cried out.

稱丨大人 he is styled or addressed as *ta-jin*.

丨丨 or 丨喚 the fourth hot hell (*raurava*) of the Budhists, where life lasts 4000 years, each day being 400 mundane years.

嘑 *hu* From *mouth* and to *roar*; it is nearly synonymous with the last, and also used for the next.

To menace, to howl at; to hoot.

口丨 to insult by a rude call, to bawl at.

丨旦 to call out the dawn, as Chanticleer does.

虖 *hu* From *tiger* and a *sigh*; it resembles the two last and 乎, and is occasionally used for them.

The scream of a tiger; an interjection of regret; a sigh or exclamation.

嗚丨 alas! alack! well now.

書不云丨 does not the Book of Records say so?

謼 *hu* Also read *hu'* and improperly used as another form of 諕 to intimidate; read *hiao* when used for 詨 to call.

To designate, to call out to; to sigh and lament one's sad fate.

鬼哭若丨 the demons wept as if calling on some one.

仰天大丨 looking upward he cried a bitter cry.

滹 *hu* The bank of a stream; name of a long river, the 丨沱河, which rises in the northeast of Shansi, flows southeast into Chihli and thence into North Lake, whence it runs northeast into the Pei-ho just above Tientsin; it receives the River Wéi 衛河 from the south of the province, and is itself sometimes called by that name.

歑 *hu* To blow with the breath, as when warming the hands; to breathe out strongly.

丨氣 to breathe on and warm.

膴 *hu* From *flesh* and *without* as the phonetic.

Meat dried in slices without bones; jerked meat.

祭丨 to offer a slice of meat; or as some say, a dried fish.

Read *'wu*. A rule, a law or guide; fertile; generous; large; many, numerous.

丨丨 fine, hearty; elegant; substantial, fat.

周原丨丨 at the beginning of the Chen dynasty the country was fertile.

民雖靡丨 though the people had no guide.

瑣瑣姻亞則無丨仕 his petty relatives could not be put in fat offices.

幠 *hu* From *napkin* and *without* as the phonetic; occurs used with *'wu* 憮 uncivil.

To cover over, as with a winding sheet; great; arrogant, rude to; large.

無丨無敖 do not be cross or arrogant — when playing.

虍 *hu* The original form rudely represents the stripes on a tiger; it is the 141st radical of a group of characters referring to the tiger and its attributes.

A tiger standing over its prey; the stripes on its body.

胡 *hu* From *flesh* and *old* as the phonetic; as a primitive it is chiefly a phonetic, and is not seldom wrongly used for some of its compounds.

The dewlap of an ox, and as the Chinese add, of an old wolf too; an *interrogative* particle, why, what, how; long, lasting; used in epitaphs for aged; distant; a term for the Mongols, Huns, or other tribes of Central Asia; foreign, Túrkish; often used erroneously for 糊 confusedly, — whence it has in some parts come to mean careless, reckless, lying.

丨混 a loafer, a ne'er-do-well, and yet not altogether a worthless fellow.

弗爲丨成 if you don't work at it, how can anything be accomplished?

丨爲如此 how is this so?

伊丨爲者 who is that person?

丨粉 a cosmetic of white lead.

丨人 the Tartars, the people of the West, as far as the Caspian Sea, whose writing is described as being horizontal.

丨語 the Tartar and Mongolian languages; barbarous tongues; unmeaning words.

東丨 Eastern Mongols or Tongusian tribes; 丨人 and 丨地 Mongols and Mongolia.

丨餅 cakes with flax seeds in them.

前丨 a tonic medicine, a shrub whose root tastes like ginseng.

柴丨 a bitterish sudorific resembling gentian.

丨福 eternal happiness.

丨戈 a sort of three pronged spear.

丨同 is often wrongly written for 衚衕 a side street or lane in Peking.

丨行亂走 to go on at any risk, irrespective of the hazard or bad road.

延宕丨底 when will this long delay come to an end?

瑚 ˏhu A vessel to hold grain in imperial sacrifices.

珊丨 fine pink coral, the precious kind, used for official buttons of the highest rank; a poetical name for summer.

假珊丨 false or imitation coral, used for beads.

七尺珊丨 a seven-foot piece of coral; *i. e.* a man's body; your worthy self.

猢 ˏhu An animal found in Yunnan and Annam, the 猢丨 which resembles the duoc monkey, but smaller; it is described as having a black body and belly with a band resembling a girdle; it probably belongs to the genus *Semnopithecus*.

蔛丨 a variety of it whose description assimilates it to the proboscis monkey.

葫 ˏhu From *plants* and *distant*; used with the next.

The bottle-gourd, the 丨蘆瓜, called also the calabash (*Lagenaria*), and everywhere cultivated; the large garlic.

丨蒜 garlic and leeks.

依樣畫丨蘆 imitate the gourd in its shape and marks; *i. e.* make it just like the pattern.

丨蔴 flax, also called 山西胡麻, as it grows only in northern China; the linseed oil is used by house painters.

丨荾 coriander seed.

你的丨蘆賣什麽藥 what medicines have you in your gourd for sale? *met.* what have you come here for?

瓠 ˏhu Used with the last. The calabash when dried is 丨蘆; there are several sorts; the dried shell is used for dippers, spoons, and ladles.

丨棚 a frame for growing gourds.

齒如丨犀 her teeth were like a row of seeds in a slice of melon.

湖 ˏhu A lake; a large pool; waters collected within an embankment.

走江丨 to travel much.

丨廣 the old province of Hukwang, now divided into 丨南 Hunan and 丨北 Hupeh, *i. e.* north and south of the Tung-t'ing Lake.

五丨 the five lakes, are the Po-yang 鄱陽 in Kiangsi; the Tung-t'ing 洞庭 and Ts'ing-tsao 青草 in Hunan; and the T'ai 太 and Tan-yang 丹陽 in Kiangsu; the Yuen topographers enumerated five different ones.

江丨子弟 a great traveler; applied too to strolling mountebanks.

江丨手 a brigand; a fortune-teller; a sailor; a jack of all trades.

西丨景 West Lake scenery, *i. e.* beautiful as around Hangcheu.

丨絲 Nanking raw silk; from Hu-cheu fu in Chehkiang.

五丨四海 all the empire.

五丨四海酒席 a small dinner with five bowls and four platters on the table.

丨牌 a sort of playing cards, perhaps first brought from Hukwang.

衚 ˏhu A side street at right angles with an avenue is called 丨衕 in Peking; the word is of Manchu origin, and its use is nearly confined to the capital.

死丨衕 a closed street, a blind alley, no thoroughfare.

糊 ˏhu Paste; sticky, glutinous preparations; to paste, to stick together; to seek a living, for which the next is also used; foolish, nonsensical, incoherent; careless, untrustworthy.

丨漿 or 糨丨 paste made of flour.

裱丨 to paste or mount, as pictures; to paper, as walls.

丨說亂道 foolish, ridiculous talk.

丨裏搭塗 careless, confused, foolish, addle-pated.

丨塗 or 丨丨塗塗 or 丨裏丨塗的 muddle-headed, doltish, reckless.

無以丨口 nothing to live on, no regular employment.

丨混 confused; not perspicuous.

模丨字板 the page (or printing) is obscure or blurred.

餬 ˏhu Interchanged with the last.

Congee, thick gruel, porridge; to seek a living.

丨口四方 to go about looking for a support.

丨饘 rich congee, rice gruel.

鞠 箶 ˏhu The second form is unusual.

A quiver made of hide is 丨簏; archers usually carry it under their left arm.

餬 ˏhu The oily scum which floats on boiling butter called 丨醍; it has a rich taste like that of butter; it is the quintessence of milk, or essential oil of butter.

聖德醍丨 [the emperor's] holy virtue is like the elaine of milk.

蝴 ˏhu A butterfly; the *Papilionidæ*, those which fly by day.

丨蝶 a butterfly; the name is applied to many flowers, as the fleur-de-lis, the Bauhinia, heart's-ease, &c.; also to things resembling it.

丨蝶鉸 broad butts or hinges.

丨蝶店 shops on each side, as of an arcade.

飛作白丨蝶 it has flown up like white butterflies; — said of burning paper money.

飛丨蝶 flown like a butterfly; *i. e.* sold off quickly. (*Shanghai.*)

鶘 ˏhu A web-footed bird, the 鵜丨 or pelican, which is expert at diving in deep water; it has a crest, and a long red bill with a pouch.

鷘丨 a fabulous sort of bird allied to the widgeon.

鬍 ˏhu From *hair* and *foreign*; the dictionaries do not sanction it, and its use is chiefly at the north.

The beard, especially that on the cheeks.

丨鬚 the whole beard.

薙丨 to shave the face.

有丨子 a man with a beard; whiskered.

淸奇丨臉 a very thin beard.

丨髯 the whiskers.

丨連鬢 a continuous, flowing full beard, not common among the Chinese.

五綹丨子 five patches of beard and mustache.

兩撇兒丨子 two whiskers on the face.

戲子丨子 an actor's beard; to deceive people or dress up.

煳 熩 ˏhu Both of these are unauthorized characters, and used in the north; they resemble ˏtsiao 焦 singed.

To burn food in cooking; the skin which sticks to the pan; burned, singed; blackened, because the fat or water is gone.

餅子炙丨了發苦 the cake has burned in toasting and is bad tasted.

燒丨的紙捻兒 roll an allumette and singe the end.

丨成炭了 it is quite burned to a coal.

粥罐丨底 the congee is burned to the bottom of the pan.

熬丨了 boiled dry, so that it has been blackened.

壺 ˏhu The original form rudely depicts a vase with a cover; it much resembles ˋkwʻun 壼 a corridor.

A pot, a jug, a tankard; a vase with or without a cover; one ancient kind was made with tubes each side of the mouth, and a common game called 投丨 was to pitch reeds into the three orifices; a cup made of a gourd; the calabash gourd.

酒丨 a wine-jug; a tankard.

唾丨 a spittoon, a cuspidor.

座丨 a hot-water tankard.

提丨 a wine-pot with a bale; a cup-bearer.

提丨斟酒 bring the pot and pour out a cup of wine.

茶丨 a tea-pot.

一丨茶 a pot of tea.

便丨 or 夜丨 a urinal, a chamber-pot.

玉丨冰淸 clear as ice in a gem cup; *met.* pure in heart; chaste; ingenuous.

淸酒百丨 a hundred jars of clear spirits.

淸夢落冰丨 your retired devotees are like people fallen into a jar of ice.

丨口 name of a gorge in Ping-yang fu through which the Yellow River rushes.

鋘 鋙 ˏhu A trowel, a tool to plaster walls; to daub, to plaster.

Read *hwa*ˀ A double edged hoe; two swords so made as to go into one scabbard.

弧 ˏhu From *bow* and *melon* as the phonetic.

A wooden bow; a stretcher on which a crescent shaped flag can be displayed; in *mathematics*, an arc; curved, arched.

蝥丨 a semicircular shaped flag.

懸丨 a natal day; so called from a custom of hanging a bow at the door when a son was born.

丨矢之利以威天下 the empire can be kept in awe only by the bow and dart.

丨三角 a spheric triangle.

丨矢 the stars $\delta\ \eta\ \kappa$ in Canis Major with some in Argo.

狐 ˏhu From *dog* and *melon*, but etymologists say the primitive is a contraction of 孤 an orphan, because this beast is always seen alone.

A canny animal that can change its own form, or be possessed by spirits, especially of women; the fox, which the Chinese believe to be rather a brownie or urchin than a wild beast; suspicious, mistrusting.

丨狸 the fox.

丨裘 fox skin robes.

丨狸精 or 妖丨 an elfin or urchin like a fox; he is addressed as 丨仙爺 my lord fox, and worshiped as a keeper of seals.

丨仙 as described, suggests the repentant peri or culprit fay, of western books.

丨媚 an enchantress; a bewitching woman.

莫赤匪丨 nothing about here but red foxes.

丨假虎威 the fox borrows the tiger's terror; — said of oppressive lictors and underlings.

兎死丨悲 the fox mourns when the hare is dead; *met.* hypocrisy, crocodile's tears.

灰丨皮 a sort of gray fur very thick and firm, from Kansuh.

丨惑 or 丨疑 suspicious, distrustful; to doubt, to mistrust.

乎 ʿhu The Shwoh Wăn describes this word as an alteration of 兮, which is an endeavor to depict a sigh or querulous tone of voice, the breath rising or extending; it is often printed so as to be taken for ʻpʻing 平 peace; as a primitive it imparts no special meaning.

A particle of varied uses; an interrogative adverb or interjection of doubt, admiration, or inquiry, placed at the end of a sentence; it is often a mere expletive; after nouns it denotes the vocative; after negatives and adjectives it forms the comparative degree; when it follows a verb, it becomes a preposition meaning to leave or reach a point, at, in, towards, to, from; in consequence of, or in quality of, and thus becomes a sign of the ablative.

孝丨鬼神 dutifully regard ancestral spirits and the gods; — or (in some connections) demons and gods.

可丨 can it be done? how then?

豈可得丨 can we possibly get it?

仁遠丨哉 can benevolence be so far off? — *i. e.* so difficult.

不亦樂丨 is it not very pleasant?

吾無隱丨爾 I have concealed nothing from you.

宜丨否丨 is it right to do so or not?

行丨富貴 to act as becomes a rich and honorable person.

庶丨其可矣 then it perhaps can be allowed; here 庶丨 answers to *I think.*

幾丨 about, nearly, probably.

合丨此 that agrees with this.

異丨此 it differs from this.

保丨民 to preserve the people.

莫高丨天 there's nothing higher (or greater) than heaven.

不敬莫大丨是 there is no greater indignity or disrespect than this.

之丨者也 eh! ah! so? it is used sometimes as a phrase, — it is all moonshine; bosh! it is useless to try; an idle effort; — these four particles having no meaning of themselves.

在丨 consists, is; that is its function.

不在丨此在丨彼 it does not consist in this but in that.

位丨上者 his place is on high; or, he who is on the high place.

勿在丨此 that's neither here nor there; regardless of expense; I don't mind.

於丨小子 alas, you poor boy!

似丨 for instance; fancy!

敢問夫子ˌ惡丨長 I venture to ask you, Sir, in what excellence consists?

衣食於是丨足 food and raiment thereupon became plenty.

洋洋丨 how vast! immense indeed!

知丨不知 do you understand or not?

ʿ虎 ʿhu From 虍 a *tiger's strips* and 儿 a *man's legs;* it is thought to represent the animal about to leap.

The tiger, called the 山獸之君 king of wild beasts; the wind accords with him; brave; fierce, awful; cruel, truculent; dreadful, it occurs in names of places and plants, and often used as a term of comparison for soldiers, and painted on their shields and accoutrements; it holds a high place in geomancy, and the bones and other parts are taken for medicine; a urinal; made of tiger skin; applied to some kinds of insects.

老丨 or 猛丨 a tiger; the fierce tiger.

丨政 a cruel government.

丨臣 or 丨將 dauntless officers, brave soldiers.

丨形 ferocious looking, stern.

雌老丨 an epithet for a meddlesome virago.

丨威 warlike; stern, dreadful.

丨視眈眈 to glare at fiercely.

紙糊頭老丨 a paper faced tiger; *i. e.* a braggart.

丨狼之性 a savage, wolfish disposition.

拔丨鬚 to seize a tiger's whiskers; or 丨頭捉虱 to catch a louse on a tiger's head; — courageous, daring, dangerous.

龍丨鬬 a savage quarrel, a furious fight between two persons.

丨頭軍 troops with tiger-faced helmets.

看家老丨 one who looks after a house or workman with careful scrutiny.

把家丨兒 to assume the responsibilities of the house.

丨賁百人 a hundred of the life-guards—in olden times; — their captain was called 丨臣 a tiger officer.

丨臂 a tiger's shoulder, denotes the right side of a grave.

燈丨兒 to guess riddles; to propound conundrums.

丨門 the Bocca Tigris at the entrance of the Canton River; so called from a hill, called 丨頭 the Tiger's Head, which bears a remarkable resemblance to an elephant.

白丨 the white tiger — on the right is very unlucky; a geomancer's rule.

丨牢關 a famous pass mentioned in the San Kwoh Chi, which was in Sz'shui hien 汜水縣 in Kʻaifung fu, south of the Yellow River.

ʿ琥 ʿhu From *gem* and *tiger.*

A signet shaped like a tiger, and made of veined stone; the 丨符 which gave its bearer power to levy troops; a kind of goblet.

丨珀 amber, said by the Chinese to be transformed from resin.

諕 唬 'hu From *words* or *mouth* and *tiger* as a phonetic.

To intimidate by boisterous talking; incoherent talk.

嚇 丨 to cry at in a loud violent tone, so as to alarm.

祜 'hu From *worship* and *ancient*.

The favor or protection of heaven; prosperity; liberality; it was the personal name of the emperor 安帝 of Han, A. D. 107.

受天之丨 blessed by heaven.

皇恩多丨 many are his Majesty's blessings.

滸 'hu From *water* and to *promise* as the phonetic.

The sloping bank of a river; a slope or easy descent to the water-side; an old name for the R. Hwai in Nganhwui, or for some of its headwaters.

丨墅關 a station near Suchau where is an excise office on silks.

戽 淴 hu' From a *door* and a *peck measure*; the verb is properly written in the second form.

To bale out water; to raise water by working a bucket in slings; a baling ladle.

丨水上田 to bale water upon the fields, a mode of irrigation.

丨斗 a bucket for lifting water; it is suspended between long ropes held by two men.

丨起 to bale out and float — a vessel.

戶 hu' The ancient form represents one leaf of a door, half of the character *măn* 門; it is the 62d radical of a small group of characters most of which relate to doors and spaces.

An inner door, a chamber door; a door having only one leaf; a hole, an opening; to screen, to protect; to stop progress; the master of a house, vessel, or shop; a person, an individual, who is in a certain calling; a household; the nidus of a larva.

大門丨 a distinguished family, a powerful house.

門丨 a family or household.

船丨 people who live afloat; boat-people.

店丨 or 舖丨 a shopman; also, the shop.

丨口 the population, the householders.

丨部 means the Board of Population and Revenue; and 丨籍 is the record of the census, the lists kept by the government.

查十家丨 to inquire into the people of ten households, as is done by the *chi-hien*; they are under the care of a 甲頭 who is responsible.

丨房 the revenue department in a prefect's *yamun*.

報大丨 report it to the rich families.

家家丨丨如是 every family and household does that way.

破落丨 a decayed, beggared family; a miserable spendthrift.

門丨相對 the two families are of equal rank, — and can intermarry.

蟄蟲啓丨 the dormant insects have come out of their chrysalides.

編丨 the poor, the common people; also called 住家丨們 the families with one door.

花丨 custodians of granaries, the underlings who deliver the grain. (*Pekingese.*)

鳸 hu' From *bird* and *door*; the next is another form of it.

A bird regarded by the Chinese as akin to the quail, and of which there are several varieties named according to the color of the bill; it feeds on insects; the 桑丨 is most common, and seems to be allied to the hawfinch or Java sparrow, but the others may all be varieties of the snipe or quail.

扈 hu' From *door* and a *city*.

To follow in a suite; a retinue, a cortége; to act waywardly or irregularly, as hunters do; a broad but not high hill; to cover over; name of a small state in the Hia dynasty in the present Hu hien 鄠縣 in Shensi on the R. Wéi near the Yellow River.

跋丨 to act violently, to behave improperly or rudely.

丨丨 broad, vast, extensive.

隨丨執事 followers in a procession or 丨從 retinue, such as accompany officers.

九丨 were nine farmers in ancient times.

桑丨 an insectiverous bird, apparently allied to a kind of hawfinch, that lives in mulberry groves; it is also called 青觜 green-beak and 竊脂 grease thief, but its affinities are not exactly known; its name is a term for a retired scholar.

帍 hu' A fine napkin.

丨表 a lady's neckerchief.

扈 hu' From *hand* and to *follow* as the phonetic.

To distribute; to impart to others liberally.

抪丨 to act perversely or recklessly; unreasonable.

彌綸布丨 you must give them out methodically.

滬 hu' From *water* and to *follow*, or perhaps from the next contracted.

To fish by stakes, or placing weirs in the tideway, which detain the fish as the tide runs out.

丨江 or 丨 a name for Shanghai, derived from the 玄丨 one of the branches of the Hwang-pu.

丨瀆宣猷 let us praise the equity of the river magistrate at Shanghai.

丨尾 town and stream of Hu-wéi at Tamsui in Formosa.

簄 hu' Fishing weirs made of bamboo, on which cords are strung so as to entrap the fish at turn of tide; they are common on the canals in Kiangsu.

鶘 hu' The 丨鵜 or pelican, so called because it scrapes around the marshes, and gets fishes into its bill; another name is 淘河 the searcher of rivers.

楛 hu' A red colored wood fit for arrows and darts, obtained from a thorny plant, probably one of the genus Cratægus; fragile and inferior articles.

丨矢 arrows made of buckthorn.

芐 hu' A medicinal plant, the *Rehmannia Chinensis* or foxglove, called 地黃 earth-yellow, or 地髓 earth-marrow, and other names; it is common about Peking, and is gathered for its roots.

怙 hu' From *heart* and *old*.

To look to for help; to rely or lean on, as a father; to have a support; to presume on; a father, a parent, a helper.

失丨 to lose a father.

丨終不改 even to the last he did not amend.

丨終賊刑 those who offend purposely and repeatedly, punish them as brigands; *i. e.* capitally.

西土惟時丨冒 through all the western regions they constantly relied on him.

父母何丨 what will our parents have to rely on?

丨惡凌人 to oppress people by arbitrary acts of power.

岵 hu' A hill covered with trees and vegetation; some define it to mean a barren, naked hill.

陟彼丨兮 let me ascend that wooded hill.

鄠 hu' Name of a district in Singan fu in Shensi, lying south of the R. King, formerly the small state of Hu 扈 in the Hia dynasty.

嫭 / **嫮** hu' Graceful, beautiful.

丨扒 handsome, good.

姿妒丨之難並兮 how hard it is for jealous and beautiful women to live together!

護 hu' From *words* and to *measure*.

To protect, to guard; to aid, to deliver, to save; to succor, as a god; to patronize; to convoy, to escort; and hence, the flank of an army, a division that supports a corps, a reserve; to act officially for, or attend to duties for another, and used chiefly for officers of a high grade.

保丨 to give protection, to guard; whence 丨照 the protecting evidence, *i. e.* a passport, a safe-warrant.

防丨 or 丨衛 to guard from danger, as a garrison or protecting spirit.

丨助 or 救丨 to rescue and help; to succor and save; to assist.

丨身符 a charm, an amulet, what will screen the body from harm.

丨身披 a powerful protector.

丨庇 to shelter, to screen.

丨封 safely sealed, — as a letter.

丨送 to escort, as with a guard; to accompany, as a 丨駕 chariot guard does the emperor.

丨軍 a covering or supporting detachment or corps, outposts.

袒秘丨短 to screen defaulters, to cover over others' shortcomings, to connive at wrong doing.

丨法 to countenance Budhism.

爺娘太丨 father and mother are the greatest screens — of what is done by their children.

丨衆 to be responsible for, as a head-servant for the rest.

丨城河 a city moat, the fosse.

丨領 a brigadier-general, among the Manchus.

丨書 an envelop for papers; a portfolio.

前丨理官 the officer recently in charge, the one who acted for the proper incumbent.

暫行丨理 temporarily acting for another.

互 hu' The original form represents the fingers interlocking; as a primitive it imparts somewhat of its meaning to several compounds.

Dovetailing or interlocking, as serrated edges or cog-wheels; fitting into each other; interchangeable, reciprocal, mutual, blended; responsive; with, together; a butcher's skewer or meat-hook.

交丨 blended, united; in *rhetoric*, a continued antithesis.

丨相愛 a mutual love; to cotton to each other.

丨物 interlocking animals, said of shells like the *Arca* with crenulated edges.

回丨 mutual regard, a common care for.

前後丨異 the former and latter do not tally.

彼此丨倚仗 that and this depend on each other.

丨較 to confront, as witnesses or the parties.

丨鄉 a region of bad repute, a bad neighborhood.

丨相交合 to dovetail together.

丨相來往 coming and going, constant intercourse.

丨相關照 they screen each other; mutual collusion, as in a ring.

笠 hu' From *bamboo* and *mutual*; originally used with the last.

A windle or reel on which to wind silk; a bamboo hook or skewer on which to hang meat.

丨筍 a sort of bamboo sprouts found in Nganhwui, which are prepared with fire and salted as a delicacy.

苙 *hu'* A sort of febrifuge, the 丨草 more commonly known as 常山, the name by which all such remedies are called; this kind is obtained from the woody roots which are sliced, and is exhibited in chills and fever as a tincture.

婟 *hu'* Covetous.

丨嫪 avaricious, greedy for bribes.

冱 沍 *hu'* From *ice* or *water* and *mutual*; the first is commonly used.

Frozen, congealed, ice-bound; chilly, cloudy, concealing the sun; a glassy, icy appearance.

固陰丨寒 cloudy, freezing weather.

川池暴丨 the rivers and pools suddenly froze.

枑 *hu'* Balustrades or a kind of tourniquet placed across the imperial roads, or near encampments, to prevent people intruding, called 梐丨; a kind of railed in circus, or corral.

跍 *hu'* To kneel on both knees.

丨跪 to kneel down to the ground.

行丨禮 to perform the ceremony of kneeling.

篧 *hu'* Also read *tsuh*.

A sort of creel, shaped like a cowl, used in Hunan for catching fish, woven of bamboo; when made of twigs, it is called 梵丨 or brier creel.

如入丨之魚不能復出 like a fish once in the basket, which then cannot make its escape from it.

HÜ.

Old sounds, hiu, kiu, kot, *and* kop. *In Canton*, hü; — *in Swatow*, hù *and* hu; — *in Amoy*, hu *and* u; — *in Fuhchau*, hü; — *in Shanghai*, hü; — *in Chifu*, hü.

虛 *ₑhü* Composed of 虍 *tiger's stripes* and 丘 a *tumulus* or barrow.

A neighborhood of 144 people; empty, vacant; untrue, not authentic; simulated; unsubstantial, inane, unsatisfactory; suspicious, sensitive; deficient, scant, as a measure; titular; humble, pure; emptied of passion and able to receive quiet; a vacant, abstracted, contemplative condition of the mind, such as Budhists aim to reach; space, the firmament.

空丨 empty, like the vault of heaven; deserted, unoccupied; in *rhetoric*, a hypothesis.

太丨 the great space, the heavens, also called 丨空 emptiness.

丨浮 nonsensical, vague.

丨誣 visionary.

丨話 unfounded, idle prating.

謙丨 humble-minded, unambitious.

丨心 unprejudiced, gracious to; but 心丨 means apprehensive, doubtful about.

情丨畏罪 he was conscious that he merited punishment.

丨負光陰 to waste one's time; otherwise called 丨度 a vain passing.

丨字 in *grammar*, particles, adverbs, &c., reckoned to be chiefly these seven, 之乎者也矣焉哉 though there are many more.

丨坐以待 a vacant seat awaits you.

並非子丨 there is really nothing true in it.

丨傳 a false account; a legend, a made-up story.

做賊人心丨 his guilty conscience ever fears danger.

丨無寂滅 to be absorbed into nothing, to enter nirvana.

丨名丨利 vain is fame, empty are riches; a Budhist proverb.

丨弱 weak, decrepid.

丨體 a delicate constitution.

不丨勞役 he does not exact his subjects' labor for nothing.

丨己下人 humbly to abase one's self below others.

如丨反坐 if what I say be false, let the penalty come on me.

六丨 the six quarters or spaces; — everywhere.

丨星 the eleventh of the 28 constellations, answering nearly to Aquarius; it always marks a Sunday in the calendar.

淸丨之府 the pure and empty palace; — the moon.

蝹 *ₑhü* A moth; others describe it as the silkworm just hatched.

丨子幺蠶 the young of the moth are tender silkworms.

嘘 歔 *ₑhü* To blow with the breath; to breathe softly; a respiration; to speak well of, to recommend; to puff.

丨水 to suck up water.

吹丨 to breathe on; to say a good word for.

丨氣 to expel the breath, to belch.

噫丨嘻 hiccuping and eructating.

歔 This is sometimes interchanged with the last and next.

ˏh'ü To blow with the breath; to warm a thing with the breath; to look smilingly or approvingly.

丨欣欣 to engage in a thing with satisfaction.

丨愉歡釋抃舞蹈溢 his beaming face showed his pleasure, and he began to dance about in his overflowing joy.

歔 To blow hard through the nose; to snuffle; to blow and snort, as animals do when afraid; alarmed.

ˏh'ü

丨欷 sighing and breathing hard; to sob and sniffle.

吁 From 口 the *mouth* and 亏 the *breath* going out.

ˏh'ü An interjection like *ugh!* expressive of dislike and disapprobation; and also of grief, alas; woe worth the day!

丨嗟 or 丨嗟乎 an exclamation of wonder and sorrow.

丨是何言也 fudge! why did you speak of it?

丨好出奇 alas! it is very strange.

王曰丨來有邦有土 the king said, Ah! come all you princes and fiefs.

長丨短歎 groans and sighs; a querulous man, a hypochondriac.

盱 From *eye* and *in;* also written 盻 but not commonly.

ˏh'ü To open the eyes wide, as in doubting wonder; to gaze at surprised; to raise the eyebrows; to hope for; doubtful; vexed; name of a river in Kiangsi.

恂丨 joyful, pleased.

睢丨 a twinkle of joy in a fool's eyes; to open the eyes wide; a stupid appearance.

丨眙縣 a district in the northeast of Nganhwui near Hung-tsih Lake in Sz' cheu.

丨丨 staring about, as if undetermined what to do.

丨衡當世 to have an inquiring and sagacious knowledge of the world.

訏 Occurs used for the last; also read *hü'* and to be distinguished from *kieh*, 訐 to reprove.

ˏh'ü To brag, to boast, to exaggerate; deceitful, vain boasting; large big.

丨誇 to glorify one's self.

丨謨定命 the important laws and fixed orders.

川澤丨丨 great streams and lakes.

Read ˏ*hu.* To cry and sing with outstretched mouth, as a bird.

許 From *words* and the *meridian hour.*

ˊh'ü To grant, to allow, to let; to acquiesce in, to permit; to accede to, to accord, to be content with; to promise; to betroth in marriage; to enter, to advance; to flourish, to revive, to emulate; more than, an excess; as an adverb, very; an ancient feudatory of Cheu, now 丨州 in the center of Honan.

爾之丨我 you promised it to me.

不過丨丨 only a promise; it is all talk.

丨多 very many.

丨久 a long time, unusually long.

丨信 to put faith in.

王丨之乎 did your Highness believe it?

可復丨乎 can you hope to equal him?

丨允 to accede, to yield, to make terms.

酒杯丨聘 to arrange a betrothal over one's cups.

少丨 a very little, as in giving medicine.

不丨他來 don't let him come here.

不丨 to disallow, to forbid, to refuse; "thou shalt not."

也丨有的 perhaps it can also be allowed or assented to.

丨約 to make an agreement with.

丨送鬼 a promise never intended to be fulfilled.

丨願 to make a vow.

丨配良緣 to assent to a felicitous or promising offer of betrothal; one whose horoscope is lucky.

面目如丨 their features are similar.

三千丨 more than three thousand.

丨諾 or 應丨 to promise certainly; to assent entirely.

丨神丨佛 to make vows to the gods or Budha; used ironically, don't break your promises to me, as you do your vows.

Read ˊ*hu.* The noise of falling trees.

伐木丨丨 like the cheering cries of woodchoppers.

In *Fuhchau.* That; so, thus.

詡 From *words* and *to fly.*

ˊh'ü High-flying, boasting talk; to talk of everything; widespread, generally known, as virtuous acts; to display; energetic, bold, full of activity.

奢麗誇丨 foppish and boasting; a vainglorious exaggeration.

德發揚丨萬物 the king's virtue will reach over his whole realm and influence all things.

和丨 moderate, mild.

遍丨 everywhere.

主丨 brave and gentle; one who can rule and be moderate.

栩 A sort of oak that bears a blackish, soft acorn called

ˊh'ü 皂斗 or black cup; it grows in Kiangnan; soft, pliable; flexible wood, easily bent.

肅肅鴇羽集於苞丨 how the feathers of the wild geese rustle as they settle on the oaks.

丨丨自得 pleased; happy in attaining one's wishes.

蝶舞丨丨 hopping and capering about; flitting here and there like a butterfly.

珝 ʿhü A sort of precious stone; name of two or three noted persons in history.

煦 ʿhü From *mouth* and *warm* steam.

To report to superiors; to blow or breathe; to smile upon, to soothe; to laugh; warm, genial.

吹丨 to puff and blow.

丨丨趄趄 smiling and chuckling.

丨之若子 he pacified them as if they were children; said of an emperor of the Tʻang dynasty.

昫 ʿhü Also read *hü*ˀ

The sun rising and diffusing his genial warmth and glow; warm, pleasant; an ancient name of a district in the present Hai cheu 海州 north of the mouth of the Yellow River in the northeast of Kiangsu.

煦 ʿhü From *fire* and the *sun's heat*; not the same as *chao*ˀ 照 to illuminate.

The genial, brooding, stimulating warmth of the sun; to boil, to heat; to mature; hot, vivifying, nutritive; kind, gracious; a red, carnation color.

和丨 genial, warm, as the weather; placid, kind.

温丨 to make warm.

丨日 a genial warm day; the warm sun.

丨嫗萬物 to vivify and stimulate nature.

丨丨爲仁 it is chiefly a pretense or assumption of benevolence; 丨丨 also means gracious.

冔 ʿhü From 冃 a *cap* contracted and 吁 a *breath*.

A sort of cap or literary bonnet worn in the Yin dynasty; it was flat topped like a Cantab's cap; to cover, as a cap.

常服黼丨 they constantly wore the hatchet-pictured robe and sacrificial cap.

姁 ʿhü Handsome; also used as a synonym of *yü*ˀ 嫗 a mother, but without good authority.

丨媮 elegant, graceful.

丨丨而笑 greatly delighted and laughing aloud, as two or three cronies meeting.

酗 hüˀ From *spirits* and *unlucky*; it is frequently pronounced ˏ*hiung*, from following the primitive.

Mad with drink; raving drunk.

沈丨于酒 dead drunk; he has the delirium tremens.

丨酒滋事 drunkards make great trouble, or produce confusion.

呴 hüˀ From *mouth* and a *sentence*; also read ˏ*hü*.

To breathe upon; to warm with the breath; to gasp for breath; to sputter and gasp, as fish do in shallow water; to call out.

丨丨 gentle, kind words; in some places it also denotes a rattling, wheezing sound, as from phlegm in the throat.

丨鏡迷容 to dim the mirror and obscure the real sight.

HÜÉ.

Old sounds, hwa *or* hwŏ. *In Canton*, hü; — *in Swatow*, hia; — *in Amoy*, hia; — *in Fuhchau*, kwʻŏ; — *in Shanghai*, hüé; — *in Chifu*, hüé.

靴 鞾 ˏhüé From *hide* and to *change* or *flowery*; the two are synonymous, but at first the second and ancient form was described to be a sort of boot-leggings or buskin now disused.

A boot, made of silk or leather; it is made to serve as a convenient pocket.

官丨 official boots; they are also called 方頭丨 square toed boots, and should always be 緞丨 or satin boots.

一對丨 or 一雙丨子 a pair of boots.

水丨 wet weather boots; the soles are often guarded by big nails.

壽丨 boots to put on a corpse; the soles are made of paper.

貼丨的 an aid or accomplice in swindling or forging.

丨子裏撲襪子 the boots can always fret the sock; — a master can always prove the servant to be in error.

布丨 mourning boots.

丨夾 or 丨掖子 a pocket-book for papers, because it is usually carried in the 丨桶 boot-barrel or loose top.

隔丨抓癢 [it will be as ineffectual as] scratching your sock through your boot.

破丨黨 he spoils [other people's] boots; — a cunning pettifogger; also used to dissuade from going to law.

HÜEH.

Old sounds, hiet, kiet, *and* giet. *In Canton*, hüt *and* üt; — *in Swatow*, huó, hiap, *and* hwat; — *in Amoy*, hiat; — *in Fuhchau*, haik *and* hiek; — *in Shanghai*, hüih *and* yöh; — *in Chifu*, hüćh *and* hićh.

血 *h'üe* *h'ie* From 皿 a *dish* and 丿 or 一 a *stroke*, representing something flowing into it, as the spurting blood of a victim held over it, to which the hissing sound of the character may further allude; it forms the 143d radical of a few characters relating to bloody things and uses of blood.

Blood, defined as 陰精所生 the essence of the *yin* principle by which life is kept; bloody; nearly related, ties of blood; *met.* money, property.

丨氣 the stamina, the constitution; the flesh, the animal feelings and desires.

丨氣之勇 mere brute force, insensible to reason or decency.

凡有丨氣者 all who have feelings, — *i. e.* reasonable beings.

破丨 to reduce the system; depletion.

出丨 bleeding, as by vomiting.

放丨 to bleed one.

丨餘 the hair of the head.

補丨 to strengthen the system; to take tonics.

衄丨 blood left in butcher's meat; coagulated blood.

瘀丨 extravasated blood in a bruise.

丨性 carefully, attentively; earnestly.

丨性漢子 a warm-hearted, enthusiastic person; one in earnest.

丨汗的錢 wages earned by the hardest toil.

丨書 a blood letter, — an application for relief at the last extremity.

丨弱 pale, white-livered.

泣丨 poignant distress; to weep blood, as at a parent's death; it is written on funeral cards.

丨脈 related by blood; race, stock.

地丨 a sort of borage that furnishes a red root like alkanet, called also 紫丹; it is used in small-pox, and is probably a species of *Tournefortia*.

情同骨丨 affectionate as own brothers.

心丨來潮 the heart's blood came to court; *i. e.* the thing came to mind suddenly.

丨竭 dragon's blood, a sort of dry red resin used as a pigment, obtained from the fruit of the *Dæmonorops* [Calamus] *draco*, a sort of palm found in Sumatra.

丨本 capital in trade.

丨戰得脫 after a bloody fight, he got off.

穴 *h'üe* Composed of 宀 a *shelter* and 八 to *enter*; it forms the 116th radical of a large group of characters mostly referring to pits and holes.

A cave; a hole in the earth or side of a hill,— they are used for dwellings; a den, a grotto, a cavern, a pit; an open grave; underground holes, a lurking place; in *anatomy*, a sinus in the body; to dig a hole, to dig through; empty; among geomancers, the location of a grave.

丨居 to live in the ground; troglodytes.

丨木而居 [this bee] bores into the tree and lives in the hole.

鑽丨 to bore a hole.

窟丨 to dig a hole.

孔丨 a cavity, a recess, a hole.

死同丨 they are buried in the same grave.

墓丨 the hole where the coffin is laid; a vault.

丨情好 a lucky grave-spot.

點丨 to point out a good burial spot.

一丨山 a single grave. (*Cantonese.*)

丨道 the underground channels and influences which affect the health and luck of a region; the spots for the acupuncture; a vital part of the body.

毁其巢丨 to destroy (or burn) their dens and nests, as robbers.

丨出 winds its way out, said of water running into springs.

吷 *h'üe* To sip, to make a noise when drinking; to whistle; to make a wheezing noise.

窩 *ch'üh* Empty, vacant, as the mind of an anchorite should be of worldly cares and desires.

丨丨如也 pure-minded, weaned from all passion.

泬 *h'üe* From *water* and *hole*; it may be easily confounded with *ch'ăn* 沈 deep.

A stream flowing rapidly from a hole.

丨寥 vast and void, like the empyrean.

回丨 dissipated, depraved and reckless.

眖 *h'üeh* Deep set eyes; to look or glance at, as a falcon after his prey; to spy about.

用眼丨了一丨 take a sharp look at it; use your eyes.

兩隻眼直丨東西 he was glancing around at the things,— as a pilferer or shoplifter.

HÜEN.

These characters are often heard pronounced hiüen. *Old sounds,* hiòn, kiòn, giòn, hín, *and* kín. *In Canton,* hün *and* ün ; — *in Swatow,* hien, hⁿui, *and* súan ; — *in Amoy,* hun, hian, *and* swan ; — *in Fuhchau,* hiòng, hüng, *and* hieng ; — *in Shanghai,* hüen, hün, yöⁿ, *and* hüen ; — *in Chifu,* hüen.

咺 ˓h'üen — From *mouth* and *to promulge*; it is interchanged with the next; also read *hwan*˒.

The incessant crying and wailing of infants; a glorious majestic character, as one of stern virtue; a holy man, whose appearance hushes men; to fear.

赫兮兮丨 how majestic, how dignified!

喧 ˓h'üen — From *mouth* and *to promulge*; it is nearly synonymous with the next.

Clamor, noise; the hubbub of many people talking; to vociferate; in Corea, the incessant crying of children.

丨嘩 brawling, confused noises, which are forbidden in public offices.

丨鬧 altercation; boisterous merriment or wrangling.

丨天振地 they mingled heaven and earth with their din.

諠 ˓h'üen — Used for the last in 丨呼 to bawl out to one; fallacious, deceitful, — in which sense it is the same as the next, and not much used.

丨駭 to frighten one with noise.

諼 ˓h'üen — Occurs used for the next two.

Deceitful, false; to impose on; to forget.

詐丨 lying impositions, cunning stratagems, sharp practice.

終不可丨兮 we shall never forget him; — our prince.

愋 ˓h'üen — Occurs interchanged with the last.

To forget; to dislike.

丨諒 wise and intelligent.

萱 蘐 ˓h'üen — From *plant* and *promulge* or *ruler*; the second form is unusual.

A species of day-lily, the *Hemerocallis graminea,* called 忘憂草 because it causes one to forget their sorrows; and 鹿葱花 or deer's onions; a mother, because it is said that if a woman carries it she will bear a son, whence another name for it is 宜男丨; there are several varieties.

丨堂 your mother; a polite dignified term.

椿丨並茂 both parents are in good health.

暄 ˓h'üen — Genial, pleasant, as the warm sunshine on a spring day.

日丨 warm sunshine; the sun warms.

寒谷成丨 the cold glens (or valleys) became warm.

晅 烜 ˓h'üen — Resembles the last; the first character is the most common.

The bright shining heat of the sun or a fire; to parch, to dry by either of them; clear, brilliant.

丨肉 to smoke or jerk meat.

丨魚 to smoke fish to cure them.

丨明衆著 splendor that all can see.

日以丨之 to dry a thing by the sun; the sun parches it.

貆 ˓h'üen — Another name for the ˓*hwan* 貛 or badger, which occurs throughout the northern provinces.

胡瞻爾庭有縣丨兮 how is it then that we see the badger's skin hanging in your hall?

塤 壎 ˓h'üen — An ancient wind instrument of music, shaped like an egg, made of porcelain; it had six or eight holes, and was blown through the apex, making a whistling sound.

如丨如篪 like a pipe and flute; *i. e.* loving brothers, which these two instruments symbolized.

伯氏吹丨 the seniors played on the porcelain conch.

蠉 ˓h'üen — The reddish larvæ of musketoes found in wells and pools called 蜎丨, which doubtless includes several species of larvæ, and probably some of the smaller leeches; an insect crawling.

嬛 ˓h'üen — A woman who is rather careless of her appearance, and yet careful of propriety; solitary.

丨丨在疚 alone I bear my sad distress.

玄 玄 ˓h'üen — The first form, being the personal name of the Emperor Kanghi, has now generally given place to the second, which has been substituted out of respect, even in compounds where it is a primitive; 元 in the sense of black, is also occasionally written for it; it forms the 96th radical of a few incongruous characters.

Dark, somber, like the deep ether in the sky; a blackish, dark color; dun; deep, still, silent; profound, abstruse, subtle; heaven; applied to names of gods to intimate that they deserve praise and worship; to manage, to direct.

上丨 heaven, the empyrean; a name for the heart.

丨色 blackish.
丨衣 black dresses.
丨鳥 an old term for the swallow.
丨妙 or 丨奥 abstruse, mysterious.
丨化 incorporeal.
丨酒 somber spirits, a quaint name for water.
丨月 the ninth moon.
丨帝 or 丨天上帝 the god of the somber heavens, the god of the North Pole.
丨圃 the still garden, a Taoist name for paradise; as 丨都 is for fairy land, a region in the north.
丨伎 a Taoist term for a level, good road.
丨機 a skillful contrivance.
丨 and 牝 are terms used by Lao-tsz' for immaterial spirits, and for heaven and earth.
丨明粉 glauber's salts, sulphate of soda.
丨默 silent and sedate, like an anchoret.

眩 ꜀*h'üen* From *eye* and *dark*; the verb is also read *hüen*ʾ; it is often wrongly used for 熏 to stifle by gas.

Confused vision, dizzy; eyes wandering here and there; out of order, in confusion; mistaken, deceived by, as one deluded by a mirage, or things at a distance; defective or distorted vision.
丨于名實 he confused the real and unreal, the nominal and the earnest.
丨疾 nervous from the effects of wind; made dizzy or distressed, as by medicine.
丨仆 fell down from vertigo.
瞑丨ʾ to confuse, to make dizzy.
眡丨 eyes swollen and sight blurred.
丨ʾ死 suffocated to death.

泫 ꜀*h'üen* From *water* and *somber*; also read ʿ*hüen*.

Glistening dewdrops, or the sparkle of dewdrops in the sun; falling tears; deep flowing water; name of a river in the south-east of Shansi, a branch of the River Tan in Kao-p'ing hien 高平縣 which flows into the Yellow River.
困丨 a vasty deep, a wide waste.
光ʿ丨 glittering dewdrops.
露丨花上 the dew sparkles on the flowers.
丨冥 a spirit of the water, an Undine; a naiad or nyx.
丨然流涕 the tears fell like dewdrops.

懸 ꜀*h'üen* From *heart* and *attached* to; occurs interchanged with its primitive.

To tie to and suspend; to hang in view, as a prize; to promise to; to be anxious; in suspense, undecided, precarious, insecure; anxiously; unlike.
丨絕 very unlike.
天地丨隔 as wide apart as heaven and earth.
丨斷 to summarily decide a case.
丨望 to anxiously hope for.
丨有重賞 I offered a great reward — for his capture.
丨揣之詞 double entendres, ambiguous expressions.
丨掛 to hang up, as charms to a lintel.
倒丨 to hang upside down; to be in suspense; an unfinished affair; a Budhist term for the suspended state of souls in hell who are waiting to be relieved by priestly prayers, as at the 盂蘭會 or All Souls' Festival.
猶解倒丨 like relieving one hung up by the heels; *i. e.* very joyful, greatly relieved of his anxiety.
頭丨樑 tied his head to a beam — as an ancient student did, lest he should fall asleep over his book.
丨得很 exceedingly doubtful, no certainty in it.
案丨不結 the case is still in doubt or not yet settled.
丨念 to bear in mind.
丨空 [it is as if] suspended in nothing; unfounded, no evidence.
丨丨乎我也 be very careful of me.
丨上 a placard, a broadsheet.
綢成本較緞丨殊 the cost of pongee, compared with that of satin, is very different.

鉉 ʿ*h'üen*ʾ Ears or rings on the side of a tripod by which it can be carried.

楦 楥 *h'üen*ʾ From *wood* and *to promulge*; the second form is unusual.

A last for making shoes or boots called 丨頭; to form on a last or mold; *met.* that which supports the external figure; to turn in a lathe.
丨鞋 to fit a shoe to the last.
丨圓 to turn or cut out round in a 丨床 or lathe, as a pipe mouth-piece.

揎 *h'üen*ʾ To strike.

Read ꜀*hung*. To wave off with the hand.

絢 *h'üen*ʾ From *silk* and a *decade* as the phonetic; occurs used with ꜀*siün* 紃 a tassel.

Silken pouches or fobs a foot long, hung at the girdle for ornament, and worn at levees; stylish, adorned; colored, variegated; fleet, quick.
丨彩 elegant and adorned; garnished.
花丨錦 flowered and colored.
丨練 to hasten, to hurry on.
素以爲丨兮 how finely the white sets off the coloring.

衒 *h'üen*ʾ From *to go* and *somber*; but the original form had 言 *words* in the middle; also read ꜀*hüen*.

To sell one's self; to brag of one's qualities; to display for sale; bragging, vain-glorious, vaunting.

丨女 a woman who seeks praise, a coquette.

自丨 to recommend or boast of one's self.

矜丨 self-laudation.

丨玉求售 to offer a gem for sale; *met.* seeking a market for one's talents.

丨鬻自信 to sell or pass one's self off as a trustworthy person.

炫ˀ *h'üen'* The brightness of fire; luminous, refulgent, shining; to dazzle, to lighten.

丨光 brilliant, splendid.

丨熿于道 the lights illuminated the road.

丨人耳目 to confuse people's senses; to make obscure.

丨耀於人 to throw a light on a man, as in the night.

袨ˀ *h'üen'* Good and elegant clothing.

丨服 fine raiment, either of a black or yellow color.

駽ˀ *h'üen'* A horse with a dark or iron gray mane.

駜彼乘丨 get on that strong horse with the iron gray mane.

HUH.

See also HWUH *for other similar words.* *Old sounds*, hok, gok, hút, gút, *and* mút. *In Canton*, hòk, hăt, *and* kwăt; — *in Swatow*, hek, hòk *and* kút; — *in Amoy*, hak, hút, *and* kút; — *in Fuhchau*, hăk, hòk, *and* pák; — *in Shanghai*, hòk, weh, *and* hweh; — *in Chifu*, hu *and* hai.

斛ˎ *ˏhu* From a *peck* measure and *horn;* occurs used for the next.

To measure; a dry measure shaped like the frustrum of a pyramid, the Chinese bushel, holding ten 斗 pecks or a picul, according to some authorities; but the common table makes it to measure 5 pecks or half a picul; at Peking it holds 25 large 升 pints, or 5 斗 pecks, and two of them make a 石 or picul; between Tientsin and the capital it varies more than a quart; its capacity is $51\frac{1}{2}$ litres according to the regular table, and this makes it equal to 90.64 pints or $2\frac{1}{2}$ bushels, which is rather larger than any; at Shanghai, the *huh* for rice holds only 2.05 pints, and that for peas 1.86 pint; the Budhists use it for a full picul of $133\frac{1}{3}$ *lbs.* av.; but the Hindu *drôna*, which the *huh* represents, weighs only 7 *lbs.* 11 *oz.* av.

較丨 to test the accuracy of the bushel measures.

丨手 a clever hand at giving bad measure.

斗丨 pecks and bushels; parasitic orchids are so called from a fancied resemblance in the shape of the flowers.

蔛ˎ *hu'* A small orchidaceous plant, with hexapetalous and white flowers of the habit of a Dendrobium, growing in Kiangsu and south thereof, for which the last is most used; the leaves are used in cooking fish, and the culms dried as a tonic for weak children.

石丨 a tonic medicine (*Dendrobium ceraia*) growing on the rocks in southern China; the name is applied to several similar orchids as the 木丨 and 金丨, which turn yellow when dried; the culms of other plants resembling this epiphyte are probably included under this term.

簛ˎ *ˏhu* A *bamboo bushel*, as the character indicates; a large box adapted for holding rice, called 箱丨 or bushel box.

槲ˎ *ˏhu* From *wood* and *bushel*, referring to the shape and cup of the fruit.

A small timber tree, a species of oak whose acorns have roughish cupules, and are used to dye black; the leaves are long, rather obovate, and deeply serrated; the wood is used for posts.

觳ˎ *ˏhu* From *horn* and a *hollow;* used for 斛 a bushel.

A kind of goblet with ears; a sort of quiver; the top of the foot; a hoof; unkind; trembling; insufficient, meager, poor, exhausted.

衣長及丨 the dress reached to his foot.

丨瘠 poor, emaciated from illness.

丨薄 thin, meager, lean.

Read *kioh*ˎ To compare, to match, to contend with.

强弱不丨力 the strong and the weak should not measure their strength.

欻ˎ *ˏhu* From *to blow* and a *flame.*

Suddenly, abruptly; moving, flitting, like a will-o'-wisp; to blow on, to snuff up.

奄丨 going to and fro, undecided.

丨丨聲 a roaring noise, as of the blast in a furnace.

丨丨而動 shaking, quivering.

丨吸 to breathe quickly, panting.

In *Pekingese*, pronounced *ˊchwˋa.* A gust of wind; an exclamation of dissatisfaction, as if one throws down a thing as useless; a sudden noise, as of bursting.

焀 ˏhu From *fire* and *valley* as the phonetic.

Flame; the blaze of fire.

丨丨 a flame crackling as it first catches.

火苗兒丨丨着 the furious flames shot upward.

核 ˏhu ˏhŏ From *wood* and a *horary* character; as a verb, *hoh*, 覈 is nearly synonymous.

The kernel or pit of fruits, the inner nut or seed; the seed as distinguished from its pod or pulp; hard lumps in a soft body, as ganglions in flesh, or nodules in clay; the nucleus; the facts, the real circumstances, the gist of, the pith; to inquire into the facts; to severely scrutinize a matter, as a judge; truly, thoroughly, earnestly, sincerely.

荔枝丨 lichi stones; and also of all 菓丨 fruit-stones, as the peach, walnut, &c.

生丨 to have a hard lump grow up, as on the neck.

刻丨太甚 an excessive scrutiny; to oppress by examining into details.

察丨 to thoroughly examine.

綜丨名實 investigate thoroughly, to ascertain the nominal and the real of a question.

丨與上年 it was examined last year.

丨奪 to examine and decide, as a case in court.

槅 ˏhu Like the last, and superseded by it.

The stone, pit, or kernel of fruit; a nodule, a lump, a ganglion.

杏丨兒 apricot stones.

鶻 ˏhu From *bird* and *bone*, as the phonetic.

A migratory bird, the 丨鵃 larger than, but resembling the crested lark; it has a short tail, black plumage, and a fine song; it appears in the spring; anciently designated an office; also a sort of glede or pigeon hawk, which is trained to seize birds.

出籠丨 let the hawk out of its cage.

鶉頭丨 a poetical name for the bamboo partridge. (*Bambusicola*).

鷹頭丨眼 a kite's head and hawk's eye; — *i. e.* a violent tempered man.

海丨 a sort of war-canoe anciently used in Kiangsu, which could not sink.

丨突而來 pounced down upon; he came here without knowing the reason why.

丨突過 going from one thing to another; desultory, careless.

In *Cantonese*. Dirty, filthy, grimed with dirt; — for which perhaps the next character is better.

搰 ˏhu To dig for; to muddy, to roil, to confuse, to mix; to exert one's strength.

丨丨然 with great force.

丨濁 to make turbid.

淈 ˏhu From *water* and *to dig*.

Dirty, muddy water; confused, disordered; exhausted.

丨丨 to open a channel for water.

曶 ˏhu To see obscurely, as on first awaking; early morning, at dawn.

丨丨 to behold.

眵曶丨 the secretion from the eye, smegmatic pus.

HUNG.

Old sounds, hong, kong, gong, hang, *and* gang. *In Canton*, hung, kwăng, wang, *and* wăng; — *in Swatow*, hong, wang, *and* hⁿuó; — *in Amoy*, hong, heng, eng, hian, *and* hang; — *in Fuhchau*, héng, éng, hăng, hung, hwang, *and* haing; — *in Shanghai*, hung, hwăng, wang, lung, *and* yung; — *in Chifu*, hung.

轟 ˏhung From three *chariots* racing, which then make much noise.

The rumbling of carriages, muttering of thunder, or roaring of cannon; to blast, to destroy with guns; to blurt out, to hoot at; any stunning noise.

雷丨 the crash of thunder.

丨石 to blast rocks.

烈烈丨丨的 very boisterous; a din, an uproar; irascible, apt to scold.

丨丨 roaring, deafening.

丨開狗 drive away the dog.

丨行天下 his fame echoed through the land.

放炮丨擊 to open upon it with artillery.

丨陷 blown to ruins, as by an explosion.

心裏丨的一聲 he blurted out his rage in loud tones.

丨塌了城 the wall came down with a crash.

In *Pekingese*. To whip up, to beat.

我給你丨 let me whip [the donkey] for you.

薨 ˏhung From 死 *to die* and 夢 *a dream* contracted.

The death of a prince or feudatory; to die; like a swarm, many, numerous, as descendants; quickly, suddenly.

丨逝 demise of, departed this life.

度之丨丨 many people laboring at a work.

丨丨 the hum or buzz of a swarm of insects, applied to descendants.

螽斯羽丨丨兮 [may your descendants] be as numerous as the flying locusts; — a wish like that of Laban, Gen. xxiv. 60.

烘 / **灴** ᶜhung — From *fire* and *all* or *work*; the first is most common.

A flash or flame; fire rising high; to bake, to roast; to dry at a fire, to kiln-dry.

卬丨于煁 I warmed myself at the brazier.

丨屋子 warm up the room.

丨爐 a portable furnace, a stove.

丨乾 to dry thoroughly.

丨彎 warped by the fire.

In *Cantonese*. To scorch, to burn or dry up in cooking; browned, burned.

燒到丨 done brown, done to a crisp.

丨起面 to look cross, to scowl.

吽 / **䜫** ᶜhung — From *mouth* and *work*; the second form, composed of *sound* and *all*, has become obsolete.

The bawling and din of a market-place.

丨丨聲 the clamor of a multitude.

訇 ᶜhung — From 言 *words* and 勻 *even* contracted; used with the next two; as a primitive, it imparts something of its meaning to most of the compounds.

A crashing, stunning noise as of drums or bells; the roar of a cataract; the stammering cry of fright.

丨然震動 trembling from the thundering sound.

⿰石訇 ᶜhung — Like the last. The noise of stones striking together in the water is 丨砰, as when a torrent rushes down a gorge.

渹 ᶜhung — The roaring sound of rushing waters.

丨丨 roar of a cataract; dashing of waters.

硡 ᶜhung — The sound of rocks falling is 丨礚, applied to such as are thrown down on people; or rolling from hills, as in a land slide.

⿰訇頁 ᶜhung — A ringing in the head is 丨丨, regarded as a sign of a cold or slight fever; a heaviness in the head.

紅 ᶜhung — From *silk* and *work* as the phonetic.

A red color; reddish, fiery; lucky, pleasant, because red or vermilion is now the fortunate color, and used for marriage sedans, highest official buttons, or official seals, and other things connected with rank; rosy, ruddy; gentle, pretty; the blood; the menses.

丨色 red; vermilion is the standard tint.

丨顏 ruddy, fair, as a girl.

當丨 rising, prosperous.

長丨 a public notice from the people, because all such papers are written on red paper.

出花丨 to issue a notice, as of a lost child; when it is found, 賞花丨 the reward is paid.

燒丨 heated to redness, red-hot.

想着丨嗎 do you think this is a fortunate thing?

狀元丨 the best red wine.

丨片 a visiting card, because it is on red paper.

丨白二事 a pleasant and a melancholy affair, usually denote a wedding and a funeral.

丨妝女 or 丨粉佳人 a young lady, so called from the rouge; one who exhibits herself to show her dress.

丨眼 or 丨了眼了 black and blue eyes; *met.* fisticuffs.

花丨色 scarlet.

銀丨 rose red, a light vermilion.

火丨 a deep red like sealing-wax.

丨日當天 the emperor is healthy; when the emperor was strong.

大丨花 the great red flower is the shoe-flower (*Hibiscus rosa-sinensis*) at Canton, where it is also known as 丨花, a name elsewhere applied to the saffron (*Crocus sativa*), and to the safflower (*Carthamus tinctoria*), both used as dyes; the latter is also known as 丨藍花 or red-blue flower; and the former as 臧丨花 or Tibetan red flower.

丨貨 or red goods; the term is sometimes given to red dye-stuffs.

流丨 or 落丨 to have a menstrual discharge.

丨頂大人 a grandee of the first rank.

看丨了眼 he is quite entranced with it — or her.

血點丨 to add red to blood; useless labor, unnecessary.

鮮丨的 fresh, ruddy, new.

Read ᶜkung. Female employments.

女丨 women's skill, women's work.

虹 ᶜhung — From *insect* and *work*; it is interchanged with 訌 to litigate; in *Peking*, it is pronounced *kiang*ᵓ and for it many write 蜂 an unauthorized character.

The rainbow, which 雨映日而見 is seen when the rain reflects the sun; it is supposed to be the result of the impure effluence of the vapors, and to be composed of minute insects; any colored halo or parhelion, or vapor on a hill-top; connected together; old name of a district in Fung-yang fu 鳳陽府 in Nganhwui.

天丨 or 丨霓 or 丨蝣 or 丨橋 the rainbow; the last refers to its bridge-like shape.

一道長丨 one full formed rainbow.

垂丨 a reverted rainbow, — is the reflected shadow of an arch.

心丨萬丈 a man of great abilities and merit.

丨洞 the vault of heaven.

天地丨洞 heaven and earth join.

宛丨a dragon.

洪 From *water* and *all*; occurs used for the next.

˳hung An inundation, a flood; the water rising; water rushing over rocks; a torrent overflowing its banks; great, vast, immense; but some authors define it not as an adjective, but as an exclamation of wonder when beginning a sentence; used by the Triad Society in a cabalistic way, referring to the Ming dynasty.

丨水 the deluge of Yü, B. C. 2200, regarded by most scholars as different from the Noachic deluge.

丨福 vast happiness.

丨惟我幼冲人 amazing! I only a mere child!

脈丨an irregular pulse.

寬丨大量 liberal-minded and very kind.

丨荒 vast and waste, as the world.

惟爾丨無度 but you were exceedingly lawless.

丨河 an important branch of the River Hwai, which joins it at Sin-tsai hien 新蔡縣 in the eastern part of Honan.

丨家 or the family of 丨武 the first emperor of the Ming dynasty, is a name for the 天地會 or Triad Society, still existing in the Southern provinces.

丨洞縣 a town on the River Făn north of P'ing-yang fu 平陽府 in Shansi.

鴻 From *bird* and *river*; *q. d.* the river bird, as it frequents marshes.

˳hung A swan or large sort of wild goose, considered to be of the same species as the 鴈 *yen*, but larger, and is perhaps really another bird; the 小丨 is smaller, has white plumage, and is more like a widgeon; *met.* a letter-carrier; as an *adjective*, immeasurable, large, vast; learned, profound; altogether.

丨鴈 the wild goose, also called 賓丨 the guest goose; from its migrations.

丨殺 strong, greedy for the whole.

日出丨濛 the sun rises through the vapors, — and dispels the darkness; the phrase denotes the confused mists of chaos.

丨啓 an expression on an envelop; *scil.* open this [in peace] from the postman; whence 丨便 means to send a letter by a friend.

丨禧 vast felicity, — two words placed opposite doors as a wish or prayer for all who pass through them.

𨸏 The name of the mountain Tsung-hung 從丨 in Yunnan which furnishes copper; it lies in the prefecture of

˳hung Yunnan.

葒 From *plants* and *red*.

˳hung A marshy plant, the 水丨, a sort of smart weed (*Polygonum amphibium*), or a kindred species of that genus, having reddish leaves and flowers.

黌 From 黃 *yellow* and 學 *to learn* contracted.

˳hung The 丨宇 was a college or gymnasium in the Han dynasty, A.D. 128, built by Shunti; it had 240 rooms and 1850 dormitories, and was designed to accommodate 30,000 students.

丨宮 students' rooms in ancient times near the temples to Confucius, now applied rather to the latter buildings, as the colleges are disused.

進丨宮 to enter college as a *siuts'ai.*

丨門秀士 a *siuts'ai*, one who has really earned his degree, and not bought it.

橫 From *wood* and *yellow*; it is also read *hung'* in some phrases.

˳hung A cross-bar, anything placed transversely or at a right angle to the main part; transverse, crosswise, athwart, the opposite of *shu'* 豎 upright; perverse, unreasonable, mulish; disagreeable, grim; unexpected, unlooked for; unlucky, untimely; disrespectful; to go athwart, to cross; to lie on, as clouds on the hills; the narrow width of a thing.

丨門 a side door; a back door.

丨生 a cross presentation at birth.

從丨 agreeing and disagreeing; by fair or foul means.

縱 and 丨 along and across; down and crosswise.

丨手買 to buy underhand through another.

丨禍 an unexpected calamity.

打丨做事 to perversely ruin an affair, to act mulishly.

丨行霸道 to act obstinately and oppress others, to force out of.

兇丨人 an evil, truculent fellow.

丨量 to measure across.

丨水渡 ferry-boats.

丨豎要過河 I must under any circumstances cross the river.

擺丨 to arrange things across — as a room.

丨住了 to bar, to withstand; to arrest; to stop, as a thief.

丨了三間 passed over three houses.

丨斜 criss-cross.

丨直 exactly at right angles.

丨抽 to levy blackmail, to take by violence.

丨財 sudden good luck, a windfall; underhand gains.

丨躲裏 a diagonal line across a square or rectangle. (*Shanghai.*)

雲丨秦嶺家何在 the clouds indeed rest on the Ts'in Mts., but where is my family? — I have none.

打丨 lay it crosswise.

丨'逆 or 豪丨' unbending, obstinate; imperious, arrogant, turbulent.

刁丨' violent and disobedient.

發丨' cross; to show a sudden dislike or perverseness.

丨心丨腸 cross, perverse, one with whom nobody can get along.

丨躺着 lay it crosswise.

天丨 eight stars in Cassiopeia or near it.

翃 ˏ*hung* To fly about.

丨丨 flying and buzzing about, as a swarm of flies; humming, flitting, as bees.

蚊虻丨聚 the musquitoes come in buzzing swarms.

竑 ˏ*hung* To measure, to judge of, to estimate.

故丨其輻雖重任而轂不折 you must make your felloes so thick that when the cart bears a heavy load the wheel will not break.

耾 ˏ*hung* From *ear* and *fore-arm* as the phonetic.

A noise or drumming in the ear; to speak into another's ear because of his deafness.

隱隱丨丨 a prolonged increasing sound, as of distant thunder.

閎 ˏ*hung* The gate across the entrance of a lane or its bar; applied to the gates of heaven; wide, vast; vacant, as a garden.

虛丨 vast, infinite, as the firmament.

丨廓 waste and limitless, as a steppe or prairie.

曾丨 the great gate, as of the palace.

騰九丨 to ascend to the heavens.

丨中肆外 to freely employ one's stores of learning for another's use and pleasure.

丨丨 beautiful and spacious, as a mansion and grounds.

紘 纮 ˏ*hung* The first character is commonest.

The cord or band which passes under the chin to keep the cap on the head; a string on which musical stones are hung in the wind; to connect, to fasten; the rope which springs the net upon birds.

八丨 the eight ties, which reach to all sides; everywhere.

丨纓 the band and tassels of a cap.

宖 ˏ*hung* Similar to the last.

A large mansion; a vast hall.

丨窨 a wide house in which there is an echo, a large hall.

宏 ˏ*hung* From a *shelter* and the *fore-arm*; interchanged with the next.

An echoing noise in a spacious hall; vast, large; ample; wide, as a prospect; to enlarge.

開張丨發 may we have great profits in our business; — a shopman's wish.

丨業 an extended business.

量丨 you are well able to drink; — a polite phrase.

丨遠 long standing, as a custom; very prosperous, as a firm.

大展丨才 fit for a high post.

丨父 title of an officer in the Chau dynasty, the Minister of Works who guarded the marches.

弘 ˏ*hung* From *bow* and *private*; also read ˏ*kwang*; this character is often used for the last, because it was the personal name of the emperor Yungching.

The twanging of a bowstring; flapping of curtains; large, vast, expanded; liberal, largely; to make great, to give full development to; to act generously and with large views.

含丨光大 vast and glorious, as the heavens.

人能丨道非道丨人 man can act according to the greatness of truth, but the truth will not enlarge for him; — *i. e.* truth is greater than its disciples.

喪'亂丨多 death and disorder everywhere increase.

丨大其業 he magnifies his office.

乃服惟丨王 it is yours to make the king great.

吰 ˏ*hung* The sound of a bell.

喤丨 the ringing of bells; the clamor of a market-place.

⿰口弘 ˏ*hung* The lowing of an ox is 嗡丨 intended probably to imitate the moaning of the animal.

泓 ˏ*hung* From *water* and *vast*.

Still and deep, like a clear pool; a stream near the site of a famous battle during the reign of Ching-kung of Sung, B. C. 638.

飛瀑落丨潭 the flying cascade comes down into the deep pool.

龍丨 is applied to two streams in Shensi.

美目如一丨秋水 her beautiful eyes were limpid as a clear pool in autumn.

⿰車厷 ˏ*hung* A movable board placed in front of a carriage for the rider to lean on as he stood.

以鞹爲丨以淺爲幭 cover the dash-board with leather, and make a cover of tiger's skin.

嶸 ˏ*hung* A *glorious*, lofty *hill*, as the character indicates; high, prominent; majestic, dignified in bearing.

山勢崢丨 the lofty peak seems to aspire to the sky; applied to imposing sights.

殿閣丨丨 a grand palatial edifice.

氣象崢丨 a dignified and imposing manner.

汞 From *water* and *work* as the phonetic.

ˊhung The ore from which quicksilver is obtained; quicksilver.

丨粉 or 水銀粉 calomel.

燒丹鍊丨 to smelt cinnabar and extract the quicksilver.

澒 Original form of the last.

ˊhung Also, a vast vapory appearance; whirling about; gyrating, as water in an eddy.

丨溶 limitless, as an ocean.

濛丨 chaos, the confusion before the vapors were divided.

丨洞 at the dawn of things, before created things were arranged.

吽 The lowing of an ox; but it is mostly used for the last

ˊhung syllable in the Chinese form of the Budhistic exorcising canticle *Om mani padmi hom.*

嗊 A song; to sing ballads; occurs used with the next.

ˊhung 囉丨 to sing and beat on cymbals in unison.

囉丨樓 a theatrical hall, a musical hall.

哄 From *mouth* and *all.*

ˊhung The hum or din of a crowd; the indistinct noise of singing; to intimidate; to cozen, to deceive; to falsify, to beguile, to tempt.

丨丨 a din, a clamor.

大笑丨堂 the laughter resounded through the hall.

丨佢來 induce him to come.

嚇丨 to scare by loud tones.

丨喝 to browbeat; to badger; to hoot at and turn one out.

丨誆 or 丨騙 or 丨弄 to cheat, to swindle one out of; to deceive, as in the price; to take one in.

丨鬧 playing and screaming, making a jolly uproar.

丨孩子 to soothe a child; to play tricks on a simple, verdant man.

丨慫他的東西 to trick him out of his things.

In *Cantonese.* To smell of; to test by the smell.

閧ˋ 衖ˋ From *door* or to *go* and *all;* the first is commonly used as a contraction of the next, but the dictionaries regard it as another form of *hiang*ˋ 閧 a lane.

hungˋ A road through a village; a narrow street in a city.

丨丨有十家八家 ten families live in every lane.

丨堂裏拜丈母 bows to his mother-in-law in every lane and hall; *i. e.* officiously polite, obsequious.

鬨ˋ From to *fight* and *all;* often contracted like the last.

hungˋ The noise of fighting; the yells of men entering battle; cries of a mob; to fight; wrangling.

丨鬥 the clamor of a quarrel or battle.

丨戰 a battle cry; a roaring fight.

丨兵之日 the day of the battle.

In *Pekingese* read ˏ*hung.* To brush flies from a horse with a chowry or fly switch; to push aside; a cry of ordering; a shout.

一ˏ丨而散 they scattered at one command.

ˏ丨開 to open out, as a crowd parts by ordering and pushing.

亂ˏ丨ˏ丨的 a confused noise; the din of many clamorous applicants.

ˏ丨出去 make them all go out.

訌ˋ From *words* and *work;* occurs written 虹 but wrongly.

hungˋ To denounce or implicate officials; to insinuate against persons to their damage; to litigate; to make confusion, as rebels do; domestic squabbles; internal discord, revolution.

丨亂 rebellious, seditious.

丨敗 a ruinous defeat.

蝨賊內丨 [they are like so many] devouring grubs which destroy men's minds.

外阻內丨 opposition from without and feuds within.

蕻 蕻 The second form is applied rather to the shrub and sprout.

hungˋ Flourishing; a vegetable that keeps green in the winter, called 雪裏丨, which may be a sort of moss; an old term in Chehkiang for budding and sprouting.

臭丨 a small shrub found in Honan like a honeysuckle in foliage, with the leaves in fives, and bearing white flowers.

HWA.

Old sounds, hwa, kwa, kap, kat, gat, *and* gap. *In Canton*, fa, wa, *and* wak; — *in Swatow*, húe, ho, úe, *and* hwa; — *in Amoy*, hwa, kwa, *and* k'o; — *in Fuhchau*, hwa, wa, hek, wah, kw'a, *and* hwòk; — *in Shanghai*, hwò, wò, *and* wah; — *in Chifu*, hwa.

花 From *plant* and to *transform*; the next was the original form.

hwa A flower, a blossom, a corolla; to make flowers, to carve; to spend, to lay out; variegated, flowered, ornamented; to exaggerate, to talk flowery; vice, pleasure; in trade, raw cotton; motes in the eyes, *muscæ volitantes*.

一朶丨 or 一枝丨 a single flower.

一綑丨 a nosegay, a bouquet of flowers.

丨蕊 or 丨鬚 the pistils and stamens of a blossom.

名丨 fine, ornamental flowers.

丨卉 flowers, plants, the vegetable world.

丨名 a nickname, an alias, a soubriquet; but 丨名冊 is a rollster of clerks and employés in a *yamun*, and the word here means miscellaneous.

閒丨費 needless expenditure; pin money.

丨費 or 丨散 to squander, to spend recklessly.

丨旦 an actor who personates women.

打丨面 to paint for acting.

好'丨 to love flowers; addicted to dissipation.

丨話 exaggeration; figures of speech.

丨丨公子 a spendthrift, a rake.

丨林 flowers and trees; *met.* a brothel.

烟丨柳巷 a place for dissipation, a brothel and smoking room.

丨錢 to spend money; expensive; to lay out funds.

丨丨世界 a thoughtless age.

丨街 an illuminated street; one dressed with flags and festoons.

丨子 or 老丨子 a beggar.

丨丨搭搭 chequered, irregular; higgledy-piggledy.

丨燈 ornamented lanterns.

丨縣 a district lying north of Canton city.

丨貌 or 丨容 fair, pretty, as a girl.

天丨亂墜 [he can talk till] the flowers come down from the sky.

天丨 the small pox; whence in some places 丨娘娘 denotes the goddess of the small-pox.

出丨兒 to have the small-pox.

丨布 colored cottons.

一包丨 a bale of raw cotton.

眼丨繚亂 obscurity of vision, arising from disease, or multiplicity of objects.

丨完了 the money is all spent.

閉月羞丨 the moon hides herself and the flowers blush — at her presence.

簪丨 to stick in the flowers denotes one who succeeds in his degree, or has married his betrothed, from a custom of putting flowers in his cap.

丨地 florist's grounds, public gardens.

丨兒匠 or 丨王 a florist.

筆丨 the pen of a good scholar; accomplished.

草丨 or 通枝丨 pith-paper or artificial flowers.

丨生 or 落丨生 the groundnut. (*Arachis.*)

華 蕐 The original form is designed to represent a plant covered with flowers; it is much interchanged with the last.

hwa The beauty or abundance of flowers; flowery, elegant, as a garden; splendor, glory; blooming, charming, beautiful; accomplished, virtuous; a term for China, intended to describe its civilization and literature; ornate; to divide a melon; the flowers or efflorescence of lead; often occurs in proper names.

榮丨 glory, grandeur, effulgence.

丨美 beautiful, showy.

年丨而老 his years are waxing old.

丨首 hoar-headed, white hair.

光丨 brilliant, fine, bright, as a show.

丨光 the god of Fire; at Canton, he is called 丨光大帝 the Effulgent Great Emperor, and worshiped with much pomp.

丨彩 finely colored, variegated.

鋪設丨麗 his sales' rooms are beautifully arranged.

丨瓜 to quarter a melon.

丨蓋 a term for a state umbrella; also four small stars between Cassiopeia and Camelopardalis, which are supposed to exercise an influence over people's fates; whence the phrase 命犯丨蓋 his fate has offended the flowery canopy, denotes becoming a priest, because unlucky people often turn priests, or devote their sons to the priesthood.

丨表柱 ornamented pillars before a grave; some of the finest resemble the triumphal pillars of the Romans.

中丨國 or 丨夏 China; it denotes rather the territory than the people or the government.

丨虫 an old poetical name of the pheasant, from its variegated plumage.

春丨秋實 flowers in the spring and fruit in the autumn; *i. e.* gradual progress.

丨州 a district south of the River King in the southeast of Shensi.

月丨明 bright moonlight.

不丨不朴 neither gaudy nor coarse, in good taste.

丨'山 one of the Five Mountains; it lies in Si-ngan fu in the southeast of Shensi.

丨皮 a bark from which withes can be made, probably a sort of birch.

鏵 ꜀hwa A spade used in making ditches; to open the ground, as a ploughshare does; a ploughshare.

丨鍫 a hoe or shovel.

驊 騧 ꜀hwa From *horse* and *fine*; the second form is unusual.

A fine, shapely chestnut colored steed.

丨騮 or Beauty, was the name of one of Muh-wang's eight famous horses, (B. C. 980,) which was harnessed on the right side.

划 ꜀hwa From *knife* and *spear.*

To pole a boat; a pinnace; a scow, such as soldiers use to cross streams; a bill-hook.

丨子 a scow, a punt, an open boat.

丨艇 a lorcha, such as are used at Macao.

拿丨子丨上岸 get a punt to go ashore on.

嘩 譁 ꜀hwa Clamor, noise, hubbub; the confused noise of a crowd talking and bickering; din-some, noisy.

禁止諠丨 all loud talking is strictly forbidden — in this *yamun*; a notice suspended at the door.

無丨 don't make such a noise.

丨然 a general hurrah.

諠丨 or 丨譟 a disturbance, a squabble of voices.

Read ꜀wa. To change.

丨湟 eggs not yet hatched.

踝 ꜂hwa From *foot* and *real.*

The ankle, the external malleolus, called 丨子骨, while 丨跟 denotes the heel.

丨丨忙行 to hurry on alone.

In *Fuhchau.* An irregular gait; to shuffle, to limp, a gait caused by a tight shoe, a boil, or similar cause.

化 hwa꜄ From 匕 the old form and 人 *man* prefixed, intimating that which influences man's actions.

To alter, to influence; to act upon mind, manners, or nature so as to change them; to transform; the operation of nature; to convert, to influence for good; to repent, to reform; to digest; to transmute, to melt; to pass into metempsychosis; to barter; to resolve doubts; transformed by; an alteration; mutation; metamorphosis.

氣丨 changes caused by the seasons or air.

消丨 digestion of food.

不丨 indigestible, disagreeing with one.

教丨 to instruct and improve; the good effects of example; a change of heart, for which 感丨 is also used.

風丨 good manners, improvement in morals and habits, by example or warning.

丨民 to reform the people.

丨生 produced by its own change, as the metamorphoses of insects; used by Budhists for birth without parents (*anupapadaka*), as Bodhisatwas are when they appear on earth.

造丨 the changes of nature, creation, production, and destruction; fate, nature.

好造丨 good luck.

王丨 royal civilization, the best of principles.

丨州 a district in the southwest of Kwangtung near the sea.

丨作沙門 he took the form of a Shaman.

德丨日新 his virtue daily increases.

形丨 a visible change in the appearance.

鎔丨 to melt metals; to dissolve, as by acids.

氷丨了 the ice has thawed.

丨工 the operations of nature in the seasons.

丨緣 or 募丨 to beg for Budhist temples or priests.

丨錢 or 丨紙 or 丨元寶 to burn paper and mock money at the tombs in spring.

丨命 a fate that cannot be resisted.

亡丨過了 transformed and gone; dead.

丨身 to burn a priest's corpse; it also expresses the power of transformation (*nirmanakaya*), which every Budha possesses, a sense which is also expressed by 應丨身 a body capable of transformation.

品性難丨 it is hard to go against nature.

丨日光天 as the sun lightens up the heavens, said of peaceful times.

話 譮 hwa꜄ From *words* and *tongue*; another form has 舌 the *tongue* thrice repeated; the second form, composed of *words joined, i. e.* to unite good words, is obsolete.

Words, discourse, speech, conversation; a language; to talk, to tell; to narrate, to speak well; to talk loud; to put to shame; to regulate.

説丨 now it is said, now let us say; — an initial phrase used in novels.

不懂丨 I don't understand the words, I am unacquainted with that language.

説丨長 it's a long story.

不在丨下 I will not speak of it.

丨不到此 don't speak of that now, don't bring that up.

他說甚麼 丨 what does he say?
丨不投機 you talk wild, you don't talk to the point.
丨別 a farewell; parting words.
大丨 a lie, a brag, a big story.
多丨 talkative, impertinent.
不成丨 it makes no sense.
不像丨 improper talk, blarney, billingsgate, balderdash.
丨中有丨 he does not yet tell it all out.
發丨 to grumble, to mutter at.
丨舊 to talk over old times.
說黑丨 ventriloquism.
一句丨 one expression, a phrase.
土丨 or 俗丨 local or vulgar talk; a patois; colloquial.
笑丨人 to laugh at one.
詭丨 innuendoes, whisperings.
丨緒叨 prosy talk, repetitions.
丨柄 or 丨把 a topic for conversation.
出丨不然 the words you speak are not to the point.
不識英丨 I do not know the English language.

In *Cantonese*. A rumor, an *on dit*; a final particle, expressing doubt.
好多賊丨 it is said there are many robbers.

畫ᐤ **画**ᐤ *hwa'* From 田 *a field* inclosed and 聿 *pencil; q. d.* a field that has been traced around; the contracted form is common in cheap books.

A picture, a drawing; a painting; a mark, a line; a division; painted; to map, to mark out a plan of.
一副丨 one picture or drawing.
山水丨 landscape drawings.
丨工 or 丨匠 painters, such as color walls; the first also means drawings, elaborate painting.
愛挂丨 to love to bedeck one's self; fond of fine clothes.
洋丨 foreign pictures, engravings.
日影丨 photographs, daguerreotypes.
山色如丨 the view is like a picture.
丨蛇添足 to draw a snake with legs, *i. e.* exaggeration.
今汝丨 you must now restrain yourself; or limit your desires.
丨眉 the gray thrush (*Leucodiopteron sinense*) a common song-bird in southern China; as is the 白丨眉 or white eye-brow thrush, a species of *Garrulax*.
丨師 a good painter, an artist.
主丨 a master schemer.
丨餅難充饑 picture cakes don't satisfy hunger; — promises are not enough.
丨押 or 丨號 to sign one's private mark or cypher.
丨虎丨皮難丨骨 a tiger's bones are not so easily painted as his skin; — it is easier to learn a man's face than his heart.

Read *hwah*, To draw a horizontal line; to mark, to limn; to line off, to divide by lines; to paint, to sketch; to draw a plan; to limit, to devise.
一丨 a line; in writing, a horizontal stroke of the pencil; also, to act by one rule.
不丨一 incongruous, not up to the mark.
丨地自限 to make a rule or limit for one's self.
丨策 to contrive, to lay a plan.
丨花 to draw flowers.
指丨 to designate, to point off; to trace with the finger.
丨止 to draw a line, to stop short, to go no further.
多少丨 how many strokes are there — in this character?

華 *hwa'* Frequently written without the radical on top.

The western of the five celebrated mountains in China, to and on which sacrifices were anciently made, lying in Hwa-yin hien, 華陰縣 southeast of the capital of Shensi; on its highest peak, called 白虎 White Tiger Mt., there is a pond or tarn where the longevity water-lily grows.

樺 *hwa'* From *wood* and *flowery* as the phonetic.

A tree found in Manchuria and Mongolia, a foot or more through, of whose thick, resinous bark links and bands for bows and caps are made; the wood is curled and takes a polish, and is employed in cabinet-ware; it appears to be akin to the birch; in Honan, another tree of this name furnishes a bark of which sheds and houses are rudely constructed.
丨皮局 a birch bark shop.

擭 *hwa'* From *hand* and *to measure*; it must not be confounded with *hwoh*, 獲 to seize.

A trap or pit in which to take animals; a gin; a noose laid over a pit to catch wolves.
丨陷阱之中 he fell into the pit.
罟丨 a spring-net for birds.
杜乃丨 shut up your gins.

Read *hwoh*, To seize or hold by the hand, to secure.

Read *hu'* To divide, to spread out.

鱯 *hwa'* Same as the *wéi* 鮠 or mud-fish; a large kind of silure or cat fish having cirri on the mouth, and a white protuberant belly.

HWAH.

Old sound, hwat *and* gwat. *In Canton,* wat *and* wak ; — *in Swatow,* kút ; — *in Amoy,* kút ; — *in Fuhchau,* hwak *and* kòk ; — *in Shanghai,* weh *and* wah ; — *in Chifu,* hwa.

滑, *ˌhwah* From *water* and *bone ;* occurs written like the next.

Smooth, slippery ; polished ; wet and sludgey ; soapy, glassy, glairy ; oily and shining ; cunning, knavish, flattering ; confused, as turbid water ; to slip up.

路 丨 a slippery (or wet) path.

丨路追人 [like] chasing a man on a slippery walk ; — you will not get your debt out of me.

丨了一交 slipped down once.

光 丨 bright, shining, lustrous, like a polished surface.

丨石 steatite, soapstone.

丨膩 glossy, as a rouged face.

丨縣 a district in the north of Honan on the River Wéi.

巧 丨 artful, cunning, tricky.

丨口 flattering, cajoling ; delusive, as talk ; to gloss over.

詭 丨 deceptive, to take one in.

溜 丨 的 slippery, as ice ; oily, soapy, glairy.

丨利 keen, sharp, deceitful.

丨棍 a knave, an unscrupulous fellow.

丨流 or 丨澤 slushy, muddy.

丨達達 or 丨流流 slippery, muddy, as the walking.

甜言丨舌 or 油嘴丨舌 a smooth-tongued fellow.

丨丨 the appearance of flowing water.

磨到 丨 grind (or rub) it smooth.

眼睛 丨 an observant eye.

足不把 丨 the feet do not have firm footing.

刁丨之徒 an unscrupulous rascal.

油頭丨面 bedizened and dressed up very gaily.

丨稽 fawning and sycophantic, as a flatterer.

丨擦 to rub smooth, to scrape clean.

In *Pekingese.* A pully, such as is used in drawing water ; to wrench, to turn, as a door-knob.

丨上他 turn the handle.

丨車 a bolt, a thing that acts by turning in a socket.

In *Fuhchau.* Free and easy ; to cook in boiling water like a roly-poly.

猾, *ˌhwa* From *dog* and *bone ;* it is often written like the last, to which it is similar.

Disorderly ; uncivilized, as barbarians ; artful, cunning, treacherous, unreliable ; clever, smart, lying, as children ; to disturb, to cause trouble, especially internal commotions ; the allusion is to the 丨子 a boneless animal which is fabled to get into tigers, and devour them.

狡 丨 impudent and tricky ; a sharper.

丨的很 he is very uncertain ; as a slippery knave.

奸 丨 traitorous, disloyal.

丨賊 a scamp, a glib rascal.

蠻夷丨夏 the southern savages disturb [the kingdom of] Hia.

磆, *ˌhwa* From 石 *stone* and 滑 *slippery* contracted ; sometimes used for its primitive.

A mineral, talcose slate or soapstone ; lard-stone, potstone, steatite.

丨石子 a kind of feldspathic mineral containing magnesia, used in the porcelain manufacture.

繣, *ˌhwa* Also read *hwoh,*

Obstinate, perverse, in which sense it is the same as 懂 ; stupid and mulish ; to mismatch ; a cord or rope.

緯 丨 disobedient, opposed to.

丨結 to tie together (or ally) what cannot agree, as a cow and a camel drawing a plow.

丨瓦解而氷銷 the tiles are broken and the ice is melted ; — all is over.

㦎, *ˌhwa* The noise of tearing silk.

丨的一聲 a ripping sound.

丨嘴 cut open his lip, as by a fall.

碰在釘拉 丨 he ran against a nail and ripped a hole in his skirt.

鯛, *ˌhwa* A reptile with four feet, described as found in marshes, resembling a snake and having wings, which feeds on fish ; this brief description may obscurely indicate an animal akin to the *Pterodactyl,* but the basilisk lizard is more probably intended ; it makes a noise like *ch'-yü.*

HWAI.

Old sounds, hwa *and* gwat. *In Canton*, wai; — *in Swatow*, hwai; — *in Amoy*, hwai; — *in Fuhchau*, hwai; — *in Shanghai*, wa *and* wé; — *in Chifu*, hwai.

懷 怀 ꜀hwai From *heart* and to *hide in*; the contracted form is common in cheap books and writing.

To cherish kindly in the heart, to dwell on, to think of; to embrace; to come to, as in returning to a parent; to cling to, as one's home; to put in the bosom; to carry in the womb; to comfort, to favor; to lay by, to board, to store up; to harbor, to bring on one's self; to remember against one; to be tranquil; tranquillity; the affections, the heart, the bosom, the lap; wounded feelings; selfish, private; occurs in the names of many places.

丨念 to think of, to long for.

丨德 to think upon virtue; to esteem virtue.

丨人 to remember one.

丨胎 or 丨孕 pregnant; to be with child.

開丨暢飲 to throw off care and take a jolly cup.

放丨 to relax the mind, to forget care.

丨我好音 letting us hear their fine notes; — an ironical phrase.

丨抱 to carry or hug, as a nurse does a babe.

抱在丨裏 to esteem, to cherish kindly.

丨私 to seek selfish ends.

三年免於父母之丨 at three years it can leave its parents' arms.

寘予于丨 you placed me in your breast.

丨其寶而迷其邦可謂仁乎 can he be called humane who keeps his pearl in his bosom, and lets the country go to ruin?

丨哉丨哉 perfect rest, sorrow all relieved.

願言則丨 I think of him and am grieved.

丨恨 to cherish resentment, to bear illwill towards.

身丨利刃 he carried (or concealed) a sharp knife.

心丨不軌 he cherishes evil designs.

有丨莫訴 I have nobody to unbosom myself to.

丨來 to reach, as home; to get back, as to a family.

何足掛丨 what's the use of thinking of him?

無不囊丨 there is nothing it does not embrace or contain.

頗中丨下丨 it measurably meets my views.

心丨 or 胸丨 the bosom, the feelings, the affections.

丨詭胎 to conceal a dreadful secret; to scheme evil.

望風丨想 I watch every wind, anxiously thinking — of your return.

褱 褢 ꜀hwai From 衣 *clothes* and 眔 *all* or 鬼 *demon*; they are both original forms and synonyms of the last; in their only use as primitives, they impart somewhat of their sense to several of the compound characters.

To carry in the sleeve, or hide in one's bosom; to hold under the arm; to wrap, to conceal; a sack, a fob.

蘹 ꜀hwai An umbelliferous plant, 丨香 of which the leaves are fragrant; it is a species of dill or *Anethum*, and also called 香絲菜 the sweet thread vegetable; it is also written 茴香, and in the Păn Ts'ao is described more like fennel (*Fœniculum*); probably both dill and fennel are included.

槐 ꜀hwai From *wood* and *devil*, but the phonetic is explained as denoting 懷 to cherish because this tree is remembered by people.

A leguminous tree, common in the northern provinces, a sort of locust (*Styphnolobium* [or Sophora] *Japonicum*) grown for its wood and shade; an ancient ruler heard complaints under it; the blossoms are used to dye imperial yellow, and mixed with other things to make a green; the seeds are enveloped in a juice, which preserves them from freezing, and the pods remain on the tree till the new leaves sprout; at Canton, this name is given to the *Cassia alata*, which resembles it in general appearance.

三丨 three officers in the Cheu dynasty.

丨檀 a tree whose wood is described as able to produce fire by friction, and therefore called the 丨火 the fire locust; perhaps a kind of ebony.

地丨 the *Robinia amara*, whose roots are used in dysentery.

丨月 a poetical name for the fourth moon.

丨花米 dried hops, so called in commerce.

丨花黃舉子忙 when the locust flowers, students are very busy — with their examination at the autumn tripos.

淮 ꜀hwai From *water* and *good*.

A large stream which drains the provinces of Honan and Nganhwui, flowing into Hung tsih lake; its waters now reach the Yangtsz' River through the Grand Canal; an even, equable flow, like this river.

丨夷來求 we came seeking the tribes on the Hwai.

兩丨 the region between the Yellow and the Yangtsz Rivers in Kiangsu and Nganhwai.

壞 *hwai'* From *earth* and *hiding*.
Going or gone to ruin; to spoil, to injure, to perish, to destroy; dilapidated, broken down of itself, fallen into ruins; injured, spoiled, rotten, useless; hence in Canton, sometimes heard as a slang word for dead.
學 丨 dissipated, vicious, gone to the bad.
破 丨 broken, useless, unusable.
丨 良 心 a depraved, seared conscience.
丨 了 spoiled; bad, as a worn out harness.
丨 子 or 丨 品 an ill-mannered child.
朽 丨 rotten, carious; dead-rot.
譬 彼 丨 木 I may be likened to this decayed tree.
肚 丨 a chronic diarrhea, an incurable bowel complaint.
損 丨 worn out, broken down; in ruins.
好 and 丨 are opposites, good, bad; useful, useless.
毀 丨 mildewed; broken down, utterly ruined.
你 丨 我 事 you have spoiled my affairs; you are a marplot.
弄 丨 to injure by meddling, to put out of order.
丨 行 or 丨 意 corrupt actions, evil thoughts; depraved.

{儈} *hwai'* Also read *wai'*
A wide room.
丨 丨 high and light, as a palace hall.

HWAN.

Old sounds, hwan, kwan, gwan, kon, *and* gon. *In Canton*, wan, fún, ún, *and* ün; — *in Swatow*, hwan, wan, hwam, man, *and* iⁿ; — *in Amoy*, hwan, wan, hian, *and* kw'an; — *in Fuhchau*, hwang, kwang, kw'ang, wang, wong, *and* hang; — *in Shanghai*, hwéⁿ, kwôⁿ, wéⁿ, *and* wêⁿ; — *in Chifu*, hwan *and* wan.

歡 *hwan* From a *breathing* and *flourishing;* it is nearly synonymous with *kw'an'* 懽 pleased.
Joy expressed by the voice; jolly, merry, glad, frolicksome, jocund; pleased, gratified; to rejoice, to gladden; pleased with.
合 丨 to entertain, to make merry with friends.
你 喜 丨 他 嗎 do you like him? how do you like it?
丨 心 a merry, gleeful heart.
丨 天 喜 地 extravagant joy and rejoicing.
丨 容 a happy face.
丨 暢 or 丨 樂 or 丨 娛 highly delighted, merry.
丨 伯 the Earl Joy; — a poetical name for wine.
馬 跑 丨 了 the horse runs very fast.
丨 奔 亂 跳 的 hopping and scampering about for joy.
不 丨 而 散 they are now not on speaking terms.

讙 *hwan* To bawl, to vociferate; to rouse, to stimulate by the voice or cheering words; pleasing, joyful tidings, in which it is like the last.
丨 鬧 the clamor of the market-place.
丨 悅 a cry of joy, a cheering cry.
丨 呼 道 左 to cheer and cry out to the passengers.
丨 囂 acclamations and greetings.

貛 貆 *hwan* A badger, the 狗 丨, which is found in Shansi, Sz'ch'uen, Chihli, and elsewhere; it has dun colored, coarse, long hair, and the skins are used for cushions.
猪 丨 a blackish colored, and perhaps another variety of the badger.
海 丨 a name applied to beaver skins, but the animal is not certain.
人 丨 an animal able to rise and fight on its haunches, which, when forced to do by its foes, the Indian badger (*Miles collaris*) will do.

驩 *hwan* A gentle, tractable horse; a horse frisking.
丨 虞 之 民 happy, peaceable people, — as they were in the days of Shun.
丨 兜 a noted criminal, *Hwan Teu*, who lived in the days of Shun.

獂 *hwan* A wild beast with claws, which has a row of bristles along the back like quills, the 丨 貐, a sort of porcupine found in Shensi, which the Chinese assert to be hermaphrodite.
丨 道 an old name of a district in the eastern part of Kansuh, among the nomads.

還 还 *hwan* *hai* From to *go* and to *stare at;* the contracted form is not sanctioned by the dictionaries; also read *han* and *hai*, when used as an adverb or conjunction.
To return, to revert to, to come back; to recompense; to repay, to cancel, as a debt; to regard, to look at, to give attention to; to look back; to surround, to revolve, a return; agile, light; as an *adverb*, still, furthermore, even to this; now, forthwith; as a *conjunction*, and, also; when repeated, answers to either — or.
丨 家 or 丨 鄉 to return home.
丨 手 to repay a blow, to strike back.
丨 神 to thank the gods.
賠 丨 or 償 丨 to indemnify, to make good a loss.

爾 〡 而 入 我 心 易 也 if you had come into my house on your return, my heart would have been relieved.
收 〡 I have received them back.
淸 〡 paid up in full.
天 打 〡 覆 陣 again another shower!
〡 要 三 個 three more are wanted.
〡 有 they are still here.
〡 不 來 嗎 why did you not come sooner? why has he not yet come?
王 曰 〡 歸 the king said, Let us go home.
〡 在 it is yet extant; he is still here.
是 這 樣 〡 是 那 樣 is it to be done this way or that way?
回 〡 to return whence he came.
子 之 〡 兮 what a nimble fellow you are?
〡 價 to give a price, to make an offer for.
〡 拜 to return a visit.
哥 哥 好 呢 〡 是 兄 弟 好 which do you prefer, the elder or younger brother?
答 〡 to answer, as a letter.
有 福 依 〡 在 I shall have better luck next time.
〡 車 言 邁 the return chariot will go on.
〡 欠 or 〡 賬 to pay up a debt.
〡 原 to verify a sum or account.
〡 不 來 he is very tardy, he still has not returned (or arisen).
心 病 〡 將 心 藥 醫 for heart ailments you must apply (or turn to) heart remedies.
〡 復 衣 服 double-dyed clothes.
無 所 〡 忌 nobody will ever regret him.
大 〡 and 小 〡 refer to the solstices.
〡 陽 or 〡 魅 過 來 restored to health; come back to life, as it were.

In *Fuhchau*. To bid, to offer a lower price for; to yield.

Read ˓*siüen*. To revolve.
周 〡 中 規 they revolve by their appointed rules; the first two characters referring to a circle.

環 ˓*hwan* From *gem* and to *stare*; it is often interchanged with ˓*wan* 灣 a beach, and occurs used for the last and next.

Originally a stone ring cut out for an armlet; a ring of any sort, a circlet, a bracelet; an open punctuation mark; a sandy beach; to encircle, to surround; to go around.
耳 〡 an ear-ring; as 三 連 〡 may be applied to an ear-ring of three links.
〡 繞 to encircle, to environ.
圓 轉 如 〡 round and well turned as a ring; — said of polished, courteous speech.
投 〡 to run into the noose, to hang one's self.
山 水 〡 抱 the hills and streams encircle the spot.
〡 視 to look around.
〡 縣 a district among the mountains in the east of Kansuh on a branch of the River King.
〡 珮 叮 噹 the ringing girdle or chatelaine ornaments; jingles.
九 連 〡 the chain and bar puzzle.
其 志 如 〡 不 解 his feelings (or heart) is like a ring, and will not alter.
天 理 循 〡 heaven's law works itself around in time; — *scil.* the mills of the gods grind slowly.

鐶 鍰 鐉 ˓*hwan* Like the preceding.
An iron or gold ring; a finger-ring; a link. The second form also means an ancient weight of 6⅔ taels, a 鋝 or ten 鈞, used in the Han dynasty; a hundred ˓*hwan* were at another time reckoned to weigh only three catties or 48 taels, which shows its variableness.

門 〡 a ring to close a door.
手 〡 bracelets, bangles.
金 指 〡 a gold finger-ring.
其 罰 百 〡 fined him a hundred ˓*hwan*,—about a rupee in weight.

圜 ˓*hwan* From a *circuit* and to *gaze*, as if referring to the canopy or body of the heavens; it is like the last two, and often read ˓*yuen*, and used for 圓 a ball.

To revolve; to encircle, to environ, to go around; to start, to look alarmed; a circle; a ball; round, complete.
〡 橋 門 he inclosed the bridge gate.
〡 土 a prison wall.
〡 轉 to circulate around a center, said of the stars.
〡 法 a term for a copper cash.
天 下 〡 視 而 起 the whole mass of people will rise and look around in dread.

寰 ˓*hwan* A wall around the palace; a circuit; the emperor's domain or park.
〡 宇 the world.
〡 內 in the emperor's jurisdiction.
宸 〡 the palace or its inclosing wall.
〡 州 an old name of Ma-yih hien 馬 邑 縣 in the northern part of Shansi in Ta-tung fu.

闤 ˓*hwan* A wall around a market place; the gate to it.
通 〡 帶 闠 throughout all the entrances and thoroughfares of the market.

儇 ˓*hwan* When read ˓*hüen*, the name of a state.
Ingenious, expert, nimble; clever at contrivances; in very early times, name of a fief or small state.
〡 性 expert, ready at.
〡 薄 alert, lively, nervous.
揖 我 謂 我 〡 兮 Ah, you wish to honor me as a smart fellow!

翾 ꜀hwan Like the last in the sense of hasty, quick; a short flight, like a sparrow's.

丨飛兮翠晉 see its quick jerks; how the kingfisher then flies off!

繯 ꜀hwan Anything to bind with; to bind around, to cord up, to tie; to environ or gird; the rope of a flag to tie it to the staff.

投丨自盡 he got into a noose and finished (hung) himself.

虹蜺爲丨 the rainbow encircles the heavens.

環 ꜀hwan A wall in front of one; an inclosing wall.

丨堵蕭然 the four walls are quietness itself; *met.* utter poverty, destitution.

鬟 ꜀hwan To dress the hair in a knot on the top of the head, as the ancient Chinese did, securing it with rings to the pin; a tuft, a knob, a knot, like a Tao priest; *met.* hill-tops.

烟丨 the distant misty hills.

翠丨 the bright green hills.

垂丨 falling tresses.

髻丨 a coiffure done up in style, as a lady's.

亞丨 a maid-servant who has been bought; a slave girl.

花丨 a flowery, ornamented coiffure.

潺 ꜀hwan Also read ꜀*yuen.*

The murmuring noise of a rapid current.

潺丨 the flow of a stream; water flowing, as in a sluice.

桓 ꜀wan From *wood* and to *fill;* occurs used for 槵 the soap-berry.

A tree having leaves like the willow and a white bark; the Sapindus, or its hard black seeds, used for beads; sign-boards upheld by stone posts before a hong; pillars or stone tablets before a grave; planks and posts put inside of a grave to prevent it caving in; posts to steady the coffin when lowering it; a title applied to defunct warriors and statesmen of renown, who had great power; mournful; name of a king of Tsi, B.C. 685, who reigned 43 years, and swayed the empire under the emperor Hwui wang 惠王 of the Cheu.

丨表 tablet pillars erected at the graves of great men.

丨丨 martial valor; sorrowful.

盤丨 to get on with difficulty; but 盤丨熟了 means conversant with, at home in.

盤丨幾天 remain a few days — and look about you; a Peking phrase, where it denotes resting, tarrying, to visit.

丨楹 supports for a prince's coffin when interring it; — an old custom.

峘 ꜀hwan A high hill, when compared with a small one near it, or as seen beyond it.

萓 ꜀hwan A vegetable allied to the celery, whose root or leaves are used in preparing a detergent to clean the face or hands.

瓛 ꜀wan From *gem* and to *offer.*

A sort of tablet or scepter anciently held by dukes as a badge of rank; trappings of a horse.

完 ꜀wan From a *covering* and *original;* as a primitive it is mostly used as a phonetic.

To finish, to conclude; completed, finished, done well, and thus often becomes merely a sign of the past tense, though it occasionally precedes the verb; paid up, settled; finally, wholly, entirely; used up, all gone.

丨固 well-made, strong.

丨人 an estimable, perfect man, a finished man.

丨備 all is made ready.

丨工 the work is done, the job is finished.

丨結 closed, settled, as a law case; similar to 丨訖 completed, not to be reöpened.

用丨 they are all used up.

丨全 all is brought to a conclusion.

丨數 the account is balanced.

丨了 done, ended, got through.

講丨 spoken; I've no more to say, I've done speaking.

短褐不丨 my clothes are short and worn out, I am in great distress.

In *Shanghai.* Used as an adverb of intensity when following an adjective.

容貌黃丨 his face is very pale.

未丨 disagreeable, as a person; unpleasant, as an affair.

垸 ꜀wan Lime and varnish mixed and ground up for lacker or paint; the name of an ancient implement for weighing.

馯 ꜀hwan From *horse* and *ten,* a combination which the etymologists say should mean a horse ten years old, and they therefore derive it from 馬 *horse* and 絆 to *fetter* contracted.

A colt one year old, or in its first year.

丸 ꜀wan To be distinguished from 凡 all, with which it was at first synonymous; the form refers to the ease with which round things are rolled about.

Anything spherical or that can be rolled; a pill, a pellet, a small ball; forced-meat balls; a bullet; a nodule.

藥丨 a medicinal pill.

吞丨 to swallow a pill.

蠟丨 pills inclosed in wax, as is done with those containing fragrance.

彈丨 a ball; whence 彈丨之地 a little region, a small spot, a mere dot.

搓丨子 or 摶成丨兒 to roll pills.

和丨 to concoct pills.

結丨 lumpy, concreted; to form lumps.

松柏丨丨 the pines and firs grow symmetrically, alluding to their boles as seen in a row.

汍 ₍wan To shed tears abundantly.

涙丨瀾而雨集 the tears coursed down like rivulets of rain.

紈 ₍wan From *silk* and a *pill* as the phonetic.

White; unsullied and lustrous, as white silk; plain, not figured; fine, close, as a fabric.

丨扇 silk fans or screens.

丨袴子弟 a fellow with white silk breeches, a rich fool.

氷丨 fine, evenly wove; — a weaver's term, alluding to the uniform texture of ice.

芄 ₍wan A sedgy plant, called 丨蘭, of whose leaves mats can be made; it seems to be allied to the Iris or Orchis, but is doubtless different from the next.

萑 ₍wan A tough kind of sedgy grass, fit for weaving into mats in the month of October; this and 莞 may denote the same plant, but this is probably rather a sort of *Juncus* or *Cyperus*, as it has no blossoms.

Read ₍*ch'ui.* Luxuriant foliage; applied also to a labiate plant.

唍 ʿhwan Another form of 莞 a mat-grass, but it is not much used.

To smile; looking pleased.

捖 ʿhwan From *hand* and to *finish* as the phonetic.

To rub or polish as gems; to work in stones; to strike, to beat.

浣 **澣** ʿhwan To wash and cleanse; to bathe; to purify one's self; a decade, because in the T'ang dynasty, this bath took place thrice a month; the feet; the first is specially the name of a stream where the beautiful Si-shi 西施 lived, the 丨紗溪 in Chehkiang; also of the smaller 丨花溪, and of another river in Sz'ch'uen.

丨衣 to wash clothes.

丨沐 to bathe.

丨滌 to purify, to cleanse the heart.

火丨布 asbestos cloth, which can be cleaned by fire.

中丨 the middle decade of the month.

睆 ʿwan Bright, as a star; arrived at maturity, as fruit; smooth, even, as a well-planed board; a fine rolling eye; to look around; beautifully formed or molded.

睍丨黃鳥 the clear, melodious warble, as of the oriole or mainah.

丨丨 to look at carefully.

丨彼牽牛 brilliant that Herd-boy shines!

有丨其實 [the russet pear] with its fruit so bright.

皖 ʿwan Like the preceding.

Bright, luminous, as a star; the ancient name of Nganking, the capital of Nganhwui; there was a small fief of this name during the Cheu dynasty, so called from a Mt. Hwan 丨山 near it; sometimes applied to the province, in the terms 丨南 and 丨北, which denote the region south and north the Yangtsz' River.

晥 ʿwan Nearly synonymous with the preceding.

Light, luminous; clear, pure, as water; also erroneously used with the last, as the designation of Nganhwui province.

緩 ʿhwan From *silk* and *connecting* as the phonetic.

Slow, tardy; leisurely, lax; easily, gradually, gently; in a safe or easy condition; to delay, to dawdle, to neglect, to let things take their own way; indifferent to; to retard; to tie things loosely.

丨 and 急 are opposites, slow — fast; adverse — prosperous; the good and the evil of.

丨急相通 helping one another in straits, as shopmen lending to each other.

不可丨 it admits of no delay; you must not put it off.

延丨 needless delay; procrastinating.

遲丨 remiss, late, behindhand.

莊稼丨 the crops are safe enough, *i. e.* will not be injured.

丨過來了 it is recovering slowly, it is reviving again.

怠丨 lazy, negligent.

舒丨 to feel easy, self-indulgent, not strict.

丨步當車 to walk slowly, and not tire yourself more than if you rode.

寬丨 not pressing, easy with; to act kindly towards, as a debtor.

丨丨而行 leisurely and carefully, as in walking.

丨兵之計 contrive to delay the approach of the troops; *met.* to gain by delay, as in paying a debt.

鯇 **鰀** ʿhwan From *fish* and *easy-going*, alluding to its sluggishness; the first form is commonest.

A species of tench, with dark green fins, and stout ventral and dorsal fins, the *Leuciscus idella.*

黑丨 another species (*Leuciscus piceus*), has no cirri, and the lateral line is white.

黑石丨 the red fin tench (*Leuciscus curriculus*), has jagged fins, a tapering head, and a green body; all these species are common at Canton.

患 *hwan'* From *heart* and to *string* on, as cash; but the etymologists give 吅, which is another form of 喧 *clamor*, as the primitive, referring to distress penetrating the heart; occurs used for the next.

Evil, tribulation; distress, misfortune, grief, affliction; sad; vexed; fearful; to sorrow for or with; to be afflicted, grieved for.

禍 丨 a calamity, an affliction.

後 丨 subsequent misfortune.

除後 丨 to escape future evil consequences.

丨 病 a distressing malady; to be taken sick.

丨 瘋病時 when the mad fit was on him.

避 丨 to escape impending evil, to avoid calamity.

丨 難之中 in the midst of difficulties.

丨 得 丨 失 hard to obtain it and hard to lose it, — as money.

心丨之 my heart sorrows for them.

何 丨 之有 why do you lament it?

養虎爲 丨 [like] rearing a tiger to make yourself trouble.

不 丨 無位 丨 所以位 don't sorrow because you have no rank, but because you have no fitness for it.

槵 *hwan'* From *wood* and *sorrow* as the phonetic.

Name of a tree, a species of soap-berry or *Sapindus*, whose black seeds are used for rosaries by priests to drive off demons, which are believed to fear its odor; their pulpy skin is used as a detergent.

無 丨 子珠 soap-berry beads.

宦 *hwan'* 偭 *hwan'* From a *shelter* and an *officer*; the second form is obsolete.

One who serves; a servant of the crown; a dignitary, either real or titular.

官 丨 officials; statesmen.

鄉 丨 one of the gentry, a village ruler.

丨家子弟 a scion or cadet of an honorable family.

閹 丨 or 丨 寺 or 丨 官 eunuchs, who are palace courtiers, chamberlains, or domestics.

丨 囊不敷 his official perquisites are insufficient.

仕 丨 行臺 the temporary residence of a government functionary.

丨 遊 an officer who goes from home to his post.

瘓 *hwan'* From *disease* and *excellent* as the phonetic; the dictionary reads it *twan'*, but the usage has changed.

Sick, ailing, looking ill.

癱 丨 partially palsied; numbness, as in torpid circulation; incipient paralysis, especially in the legs.

豢 *hwan'* From a *pig* and a *phonetic*.

To feed pigs and dogs with prepared grain; to bait; to befriend, to make presents in order to get friendly favor; to bribe.

丨 養 to rear; to support by charity, as foundlings; to help.

以利 丨 之 allured him with the hope of some advantage.

餽賂于隣是 丨 隣也 to give gifts and food to our neighbors is simply to support them — against ourselves.

芻 丨 grass and grain, *i.e.* domestic animals; the first word refers to horses and cattle which eat hay, the latter to pigs and dogs.

幻 *hwan'* It was originally supposed to represent two triangles interlocked.

Mutual deception; what imposes on one, sleight of hand; magic; a trick, a dream or apparition, whatever deludes the sight; deceit; deceptive, unreal; to transform so as to deceive; changeable.

虛 丨 empty appearances.

丨 術 magical arts, like table-turning.

夢 丨 visions, dreams; unrealities.

譸張爲 丨 to lie and brag is the part of a trickster; to impose on by tricks.

丨 象 changes, as of nature; signs, tokens, as of a storm.

丨 影 visionary things, like dissolving views.

丨 化 magical changes, metamorphoses.

世情變 丨 the world is as a changing show.

圂 *kwan'* From *inclosure* and a *pig* in it, referring to its use.

A sty; a privy, a retiring place.

逭 *hwan'* From to *go* and *officer* as the *phonetic*.

To flee, to escape from; to avoid.

丨 逃 to run away.

法無可 丨 you cannot elude the laws.

作孽不可 丨 you cannot escape [the just reward of] your misdeeds.

Read *kwan'* To go, to reach; to revolve, to change and turn around.

奐 *hwan'* Composed originally of 廾 to *raise* the *hands* placed under 夐 *preëminent* contracted; its use as a primitive is mostly as a phonetic.

Gradually growing larger; excellent; at ease, leisurely; colored, gay; to take one's pleasure.

明 丨 bright, lustrous.

美哉 丨 焉 how beautiful and accomplished, as a lady; how delightful! — as a garden.

伴 丨 爾游矣 ramble about when you are at leisure.

侖 丨 美富 a beautiful, spacious room, much ornamented.

喚 *hwan'* From *month* and *excellent*; the last was once used for it.

To call out, to hail one, to call for; to invite; to bid, to order, intimating a certain degree of authority; to name, to designate.

呼 丨 or 叫 丨 to call, to order.

使 丨 to send at a call, to employ.

鳩丨雨 the pigeon cries for the rain, as its cooing is greater before a shower.

丨頭 a barber's clang; it is a long steel fork made like pincers, and trilled with a nail.

使丨白人 a head-servant, a butler.

丨嬌娘 the beauty's call, is a hand-drum with rattles, which flower-peddlers twirl.

名丨三桃 her name is called San-t'ao.

丨他止住 tell him to stop.

丨醒迷途 to awaken men from their delusions and errors, as a preacher should.

奐 hwan' Elegant, colored.

丨爛 variegated, ornamented with colors, as an embroidered robe.

煥 hwan' Resplendent, brilliant; the brightness of fire.

明丨 brilliant, lustrous.

丨目 agreeable to the eye, view.

丨乎其有文章 how elegant it is! in fine style.

丨然一新 how new and fine it is! — as a new suit of clothes.

換 hwan' From *hand* and *excellent* as the phonetic.

To remove, to change about with the hand; to exchange, to interchange; to barter; to commute; to move and alter, as in arranging the things in a room.

丨轉 to transpose; to exchange.

丨季 altering for the season; *i. e.* changing the official uniform twice a year, about the first of May and November.

回丨 to send back, as bad silver.

對丨 to swap; to exchange even.

包丨 I agree to change it — if bad, as a dollar.

便丨 changed as wanted; a money-changer's sign.

無得丨 I'll not take it back.

出門不丨 or 不管丨 it will not be exchanged after you have taken it away.

金十五丨 gold is exchanged at fifteen — for silver.

金銀兌丨 to exchange gold and silver by weight.

丨錢 change [this dollar] into copper cash.

丨帖 to exchange cards — and become sworn friends.

丨骨 a thorough change in one, as at conversion.

改丨 to make in another style.

丨親 to make a betrothal, by exchanging horoscopes.

丨門道 to change one's profession or calling.

敗子回頭金不丨 gold cannot seduce the repentant prodigal to return to vice.

脘 hwan' The knee-joint.

丨骨 the bones under the knee-pan, the joint.

渙 hwan' A small upper branch of the R. Hwai in the east of Ho-nan, south from K'ai-fung fu, which flows first into the River Wo; to spread abroad, to expand, to dissipate; dispersed; swelling waters; the 59th diagram denoting dispersion, as of wind and water.

河水丨丨 the rivers are full.

方丨丨兮 their waters are broad and swelling.

丨爛 elegant, variegated.

繼猶判丨 the connection seems as if severed, referring to the prosperous omens of the dynasty.

擐 hwan' To put on armor; to brace on, as a helmet.

服兵丨甲 to prepare one's arms and put on mail.

Read *süen.* To strip.

丨衣出其臂脛 he rolled up his clothes and exposed his legs and arms.

轘 hwan' From 車 *carriage* and 環 *ring* contracted.

The punishment of pulling a criminal in pieces by chariots drawing him asunder; it was once used in China.

HWANG.

Old sounds, hung, kung, *and* gung. *In Canton*, wong *and* fong; — *in Swatow*, hwang, kw'ang, *and* kwang; — *in Amoy*, hông *and* k'ong; — *in Fuhchau*, hwòng *and* wòng; — *in Shanghai*, wong *and* hwong; — *in Chifu*, hwang.

巟 *hwang* From 巛 *streams* and 亡 *lost*; it is now merged in the next, and used chiefly as a primitive; it occurs interchanged with 慌 hurried.

A watery waste; to reach, to get to.

天作高山大王丨之 Heaven created a high mountain for Tai-wang to go and occupy, referring to his fief of Pin 邠 in Shensi.

荒 *hwang* From *plants* and a *watery waste* as the phonetic.

Wild, barren, waste; unproductive, deserted; neglected; without restraint, reckless, with neglect; very; empty, void; unripe, blasted; a jungle, a moor, wilds, heath; a famine, dearth of; to overshadow, to magnify; to nullify, to frustrate.

丨野 or 丨郊 a wilderness, a desert.

丨裔 aborigines, wild tribes.

丨蕪 bushy, overgrown with brushwood; weedy.

丨廢 to fall into disuse; to disregard; old, in desuetude; intermitted, as a business.

丢丨 out of practice, forgotten it.

丨唐 incoherent, incredible, untrustworthy, deceptive.

丨疎 obsolete; to neglect one's duty.

丨年 a year of scarcity, dearth.

不打饑丨 you need not be anxious about the means of living.

丨空 utterly empty, as a deserted, ruined house.

丨淫無度 to totally neglect public duties, as by hunting and following women.

大丨兒 in general, the purport of, a synopsis.

丨棄 to set aside, to frustrate.

業丨於嬉 he neglected his duties for his pleasures.

丨之 to make important.

洪丨之世 the times are [as peaceable] as the wastes were after the flood.

流連丨亡 year after year I am so unfortunate and ruined.

稐 穔 *hwang* Similar to the last.

Grain not ripening; it is immature and therefore empty-eared.

百菓皆丨 all the fruit is blasted; none has ripened — this season.

統 *hwang* From *silk* and a *waste* as the phonetic.

Silk tangled, which is to be drawn out to find the clue.

肓 *hwang* From *flesh* and to *die*.

The space between the heart and diaphragm; the vitals; it probably refers to the region of the aorta.

病入膏丨 the disease has entered the vitals; this expression usually indicates an incurable consumption.

衁 *hwang* Blood; it is used in connection with animals, an omen is mentioned of a sheep butchered that had no blood.

丨池 the blood-pool; — it may denote the aorta and vena cava.

皇 *hwang* Originally composed of 自 *self* and 王 to *rule*, meaning the self-ruler or first rulers, referring to the 三丨 three rulers, (Fuh-hi, Shin-nung and Hwangti) who ruled by their own virtue; it is now composed of 白 *white* and 王 *ruler*, and is defined by 煌 resplendent, as 成德煌煌 perfect virtue is gloriously resplendent; it occurs used for 遑 and the two next.

High, great, exalted; supreme, heaven-like, honorable; imperial, august; an autocrat, a sovereign, an emperor, who owes allegiance only to Heaven, as the Chinese think only their own ruler does; he alone combines in himself all power in civil, military, religious, and judicial matters, and there can in the nature of things be only one such vicegerent acknowledged on earth; it was assumed first by Tsin Chi Hwangti, B. C. 227; heaven; applied to deceased parents and to Budha; excellent, superior; to put to rights, to act right; to go and come; bright; rapid; grand, admirable.

丨帝 or 丨上 or 聖丨 or 天丨 His Majesty, not used in direct address.

丨天 high Heaven, the azure empyrean; often used as a petition, Good Heavens!

丨天上帝 the imperial Shangti, or 玉丨上帝 Yuh-hwang Shangti, the highest of the gods.

地丨 imperial Earth, — worshiped by the Emperor; also, the palace, the Forbidden City, inside of 丨都 Peking.

於丨 how imperial!

丨朝 this (or our) imperial dynasty.

丨考 and 丨妣 a deceased father and mother.

太上丨 the emperor's father, said when he is alive, as in Kienlung's case.

天丨大帝 a name for the north star, which is worshiped by the Taoists.

東 丨 a genial spring breeze.
穆穆 丨 丨 how vast and beautiful!
先祖是 丨 majestic are our ancestors.
丨 恩 imperial favor.
豈是冠冕堂 丨 的話 why have such unseemly talk? *i.e.* is this the right talk for coroneted men and courtiers?
四國是 丨 the four states all dread you — Wăn Wang and Wu Wang.

凰 ˓hwang The female of the phœnix or 鳳 丨, a fabulous bird whose appearance indicates great prosperity to the land.
鳳 丨 無寶不落 phœnixes alight only where jewels are found; *i. e.* he only comes where money is to be made.

惶 ˓hwang From *heart* and *emperor*; *q.d.* as if one was startled when he saw the monarch.
Fear, hesitation; respectful dread, tremor, apprehension, scared, terrified.
恐 丨 alarmed; fluttering.
丨 丨 fearing, trembling.
丨 惑 dreadful doubt, afraid to act.
丨 擾 perturbed, excited with great fear.

偟 ˓hwang From *man* and *emperor*; interchanged with the next two.
Agitated; in a state of uncertainty or consternation.
四海彷 丨 the whole country was confused and doubtful.
不 丨 no leisure; not at ease.

徨 ˓hwang Doubtful.
徬 丨 無家 in doubt where to go; no fixed place.
徊 丨 vacillating, going back and forth; irresolute.

遑 ˓hwang From to *go* and *emperor*, as the phonetic.
Leisure, vacant time; disengaged, indifferent to; to waste time in trifling.
不 丨 啓處 I have no time to take my ease.
莫敢或 丨 I dare not idle my time.
日昃不 丨 暇食 the day is closing and I am too busy even to eat.
胡爲乎 丨 丨 欲何之 why are you so much pressed? where do you wish to go?

煌 ˓hwang A great blaze; splendid, bright; luminous, as stars.
丨 丨 exceedingly resplendent, said of the emperor's virtue, or of the glittering stars.
輝 丨 於道 the street is shining brilliantly, as at an illumination.

餭 ˓hwang Dried pastry, cakes made of wheat flour and sugar, but having no meat or fruit.

艎 ˓hwang A kind of dispatch boat; a ferry boat.
艅 丨 a cutter or fast-sailing boat.

鰉 **鱑** ˓hwang From *fish* and *imperial* or *yellow*; the second form is not common.
The *fish* for the *emperor*, the sturgeon, which is found in the Yangtsz' of great size; it is brought frozen to Peking from the Amoor River, as a tribute or tax from those regions.
鱘 丨 魚 the sturgeon.
丨 花魚 a kind of gurnard found about Canton.

篁 ˓hwang Bamboo sprouts which are too old for eating; a sort of bamboo, very hard, with a whitish skin; the largest ones are used in building boats, and the smaller culms for fifes; a clump of bamboos.
幽 丨 a thick grove of bamboos.

媓 ˓hwang Name of a concubine of Yao in ancient times; an old term for mother in Hunan.

蝗 ˓hwang The locust; the god who is invoked to drive them away is called 劉猛將 or 丨 蝻將軍 in the central provinces.
旱 丨 drought and locusts.
丨 蟲爲災 the locusts have become a plague.
蚱 丨 the migratory locust, which appears at times in the southern provinces.

隍 **堭** ˓hwang From *place* or *ground* and *imperial*; the second form is unusual.
A dry moat or fosse under a city wall; a dry ditch.
城 丨 廟 the wall and moat temple is the municipal temple in every walled city, where officials worship the tutelar or palladial god, who is called the 都城 丨 and in the Chinese Hades, answers somewhat to Rhadamanthus of the Greeks.
城復于 丨 the walls were close to the moat.

湟 ˓hwang A river in Kansuh, a tributary of the Ta-t'ung and Yellow Rivers, that runs near Si-ning fu; whence a portion of the department was formerly called 丨 州 and 丨 中; also a branch of the North River in the northwest of Kwangtung, which joins at Fu-kang ting; cold water.
潏 丨 a turbulent torrent.

喤 ˓hwang The cry of children weeping; clamor; the ringing of bells.
其泣 丨 丨 their sobbing and weeping were distressing.
鐘鼓 丨 丨 the bells and drums rung out in concert.

鍠 ˓hwang Interchanged with the last.
Also a sort of triquetrous blade fastened at the end of a lance, and covered with tiger's skin when sheathed.
輿前儀 丨 the lances were borne before the chariot.
丨 丨 鎗鎗 clanging and ringing, like bells and drums.

黃 ˳hwang Originally composed of 田 a *field*, and an old form of 光 *bright*, to denote that the earth is yellow, which in fact is the hue of the loess that forms the soil of half of the country north of the Yellow River; it forms the 201st radical of a small natural group of characters relating to that color; as a primitive used phonetically, and interchanged with some of its compounds.

The color of earth, ochreous; it belongs to earth; yellow; the imperial color, nearly a lemon yellow; it is used by his Majesty, because it is the central color of the five, and sometimes when alone designates him; it doubtless has been derived from 丨帝 the Yellow Emperor, who is said to have ruled B. C. 2597, and was so called because he had affinity to, and ruled by the power of the element 土 earth; imperial; hurried; the harvest; applied also to lamas, one of the Manchu banner corps, and to those who are 丨帶子 yellow girdle sons, or connected with the imperial family; in medicine, used for biliary and other calculi from the color of cow-bezoar, the most common sort.

丨色 yellow; the standard color is 杏丨 apricot yellow.

牙丨 a light ivory yellow.

丨口孺子 a suckling child, an infant under four years, to which age women often nurse their young.

大丨 rhubarb; also a kind of cross-bow.

地丨 a medicinal root grown in Honan, perhaps allied to cumfrey (*Symphitum*), and used as a febrifuge.

丨犬 a Canton name for the earthworm; the mole-cricket is elsewhere so called.

丨道 the ecliptic; but 丨道日子 is a lucky day.

蛋丨 yolk of an egg.

丨瘦 cadaverous, jaundiced.

中丨 the emperor's private treasury or privy purse.

丨綾夾板 yellow silk boards in which imperial orders are forwarded.

貼丨 to cover a dispatch with a yellow envelop; it is also applied to the notices pasted at doors, showing that the person has obtained his degree.

丨門官 palace servants or eunuchs in the Han dynasty.

丨馬褂 a yellow tabard or jacket, — given to high officials as a mark of special honor.

丨髮 a very old man, his hair being often tinted yellow.

丨皮 the whampee or yellow skin (*Cookia punctata*), a fruit of Canton province.

丨魚 a kind of herring (*Chatoessus maculatus*) at Canton.

蛇丨 a medicinal name for nodular iron pyrites, thought to be vomited by snakes.

青丨不接 the green and the yellow have not yet joined, the new crop is not yet come in.

事情丨了 the affair has entirely miscarried; referring to the yellow color of the dying leaves.

倉丨無托 so irresolute that he can undertake nothing.

丨綿襖 the yellow cotton jacket — a poor man's name for the winter sun.

丨昏 the eventide, twilight.

丨河 the Yellow River, so called from the ochery color of its waters.

丨錢 three lucky papers hung on door lintels.

潢 ˳hwang From *water* and *yellow*.

A lake without an outlet; a pool; a dyke, a dam; water that sparkles, deep and pure.

銀丨 the milky way.

裝丨 the cushion on which jewelry is exhibited.

十分裝丨 mere outside show, living beyond one's means.

陂丨 a rivulet flowing down slopes.

丨河 the Sira-muren River, or River Liao, a large stream that drains the eastern slope of the mountains north of Chihli, and flows into the Gulf at Niuchwang.

天丨一派 of the same imperial generation, in which 天丨 denotes exclusively the emperor's family; the term is probably derived from 天丨星 the stars μ ϛ σ near γ in Auriga.

Read ˳hwang' To dye paper, mostly of a straw or light brown color.

丨' 瀁 the vast expanse of water.

癀 ˳hwang The *yellow disease*, the jaundice or icterus, also known as 發黃病 from the hue; forms of dropsy seem also to be included in this term.

黌 ˳hwang The yolk of an egg, which the component parts of the character, *yellow* and *husk*, somewhat indicate.

璜 ˳hwang A jade gem of a semicircular shape, hung up as an ornament, called 半璧 or half signet; it had two stones hung from it which tinkled when struck, and it was supposed to represent winter.

趪 ˳hwang To exert one's self, to bustle about.

丨丨 a brave, warlike appearance; to spread out things, to make a fine display, as in a shop.

簧 ˳hwang The metallic tongue in tubes of the *săng* or reed-organ; the reed of a clarinet, trombone, or melodeon; a spring, a catch in a lock; anything very delicate in a machine.

鎖丨 the wards of a lock.

君子陽陽左執丨 my lord is happy indeed, his left hand grasps his reed organ.

笙 丨 a reed-organ and its mouthpiece.

鼓 丨 drumming and fifing; to flatter with fair speeches; to excite by canards.

線 丨 the hair-spring of a watch.

巧言如丨顏之厚矣 their artful words, dulcet as a reed's notes, show how unblushing are their faces.

丨口言語 mumbling gibberish, like a witch's incantations.

磺 ˓hwang Its composition of *stone* and *yellow* evidently has had an influence in limiting this word to 硫丨 or sulphur, for which alone it is now used.

火丨孔 brimstone pits in Formosa, where the crude article is obtained.

採辦硝丨 to select and superintend the saltpetre for powder works.

Read ˓kw'ang. The ore or gangue of metal, especially iron in copper, for which ˓kw'ang 礦 is now commonly used; hard, obdurate.

蟥 ˓hwang A green beetle which makes a noise with its wings.

螞丨 the leech.

螞丨釘住鷺鷥脚 the leech fastens itself to the egret's legs; *met.* a lickspittle, a spiritless sycophant.

幌 ˓hwang From *napkin* and *bright.*

A curtain; a shop-sign of wood or other things, which particularly indicates the nature of the goods sold or occupation, and not a mere painted board; a sort of ornamented cap.

丨傘 a flabellum or screen to shield from the sun.

書丨 a screen in a school-room.

丨帷 curtains, screens.

錢丨 a money-changer's sign, a carved wooden string of cash.

挑丨子 take in the sign.

膏藥丨子 diamond shape, so called from the form of plasters drawn on a sign.

妝你的丨子 your sign is mere show; *i. e.* you are not fit to trade, you are a sharper.

In *Cantonese.* A gust; a whirl of wind.

旗 ˓hwang Similar to the last.

A sign denoting a tavern, which in former times was a flag or banner.

晃 ˓hwang From *sun* and *light* as the phonetic.

The full brightness of the sun; to dazzle, to come out bright; a flash, a ray of; quivering, as a sunbeam.

丨耀 bright sunshine; brilliant.

亮丨丨 glittering, as a sun-beam.

炫丨芬馥 bright and fragrant, like a flower garden.

一丨兒的工夫 in a moment, very quickly.

日光丨眼 the light dazzles my eyes.

電光一丨 a flash of dazzling lightning.

天氣丨開 the sun has come out bright again.

搖搖丨丨的 quivering, shimmering; glittering, like sunlight glancing on the water.

怳, **恍** ˓hwang The first is commonest; the second occurs written 兄 in the Book of Odes.

Wild, mad; disturbed, fluttered, unable to collect one's thoughts; sorrowful.

丨狂 delirious; out of one's head.

丨然 irresolute, unready, as when one has mislaid or lost something.

丨惚 or 丨丨惚惚 half right, not certain; confused, as a witness, under cross-examination.

聽丨惚了 I did not get the idea clearly, I did not get the right sense.

慌 ˓hwang From *heart* and a *waste;* interchanged with the last.

Apprehensive, nervous; obscure, indeterminate; to scare, to alarm; as a superlative, very, frightfully.

發丨 or 丨忙 agitated, lost his presence of mind.

驚丨 frightened, as at a sudden start.

心丨 or 丨張 trepidation.

不要丨 don't be in a hurry.

着丨 you frighten me; I'm quite alarmed.

跑得丨 he runs very fast.

In *Pekingese.* To shake, to toss the head, as a fop when he struts; to roll or waddle, as a heavily laden mule.

曂 ˓hwang Dry and hot, as in the midst of summer.

謊, **詤** ˓hwang From *words* and a *waste;* the first is commonest.

To talk in one's sleep; incoherent, raving; exaggeration, fibbing; to lie, to mislead by wild statements.

全是丨 it is all a lie.

撒丨 to scatter fibs; to deceive, to lie to.

丨言 nonsense, falsehoods, raving talk; legendary tales.

説丨 to deceive by falsehoods.

説丨獨怕對證 a liar only fears a truthful witness.

丨謬 untrue, mendacious, fabulous.

扯丨吊白 the whole is a made-up story.

很大的丨 you brag much; the price is exorbitant, you charge too dear.

愰 ˓hwang From *heart* and *bright* as the phonetic.

Clearness of mind; perspicacious.

丨懩 the mind unsettled.

丨丨兒 suddenly; at times.

況 From *water* and *elder brother*; now mostly superseded by the next two.

'hwang kw'ang' Cold, icy water; to lead; to compare; to overflow; then; to confer on, to bestow.

修丨 a sort of five-stringed lute or lyre, placed in the temples of Confucius.

來丨 to come to a place to make a judicial examination; to pay a visit.

况 From *two* (or *ice*) and *elder brother*; used for the last.

'hwang kw'ang' An adjective of comparison; more, moreover; now; furthermore; to come to; to bestow; to grow, as plants; a time, a period.

何丨 how much more!

丨兼 still more, in addition to.

丨然 suprisingly and wrongly.

丨且 or 丨復 still further, additionally.

丨係 it is just that.

景丨何如 how do times go with you? how do you like your work?

仁智周公未之盡也而丨於王乎 Duke Cheu did not fully exhibit the virtues of humanity and wisdom, how much more then our present ruler.

丨味 relish, taste, character of, savor, quality.

In *Cantonese*. To thrum.

丨琴 to play the lute.

貺 Used with the last.

hwang' kw'ang' To give, to bestow; to confer, as a largess or bounty.

丨施 to give freely.

丨賜 to grant to, to confer on.

天丨有德 virtue is the gift of heaven.

丨儀 a present; the recipient replies 荷蒙厚丨 I heartily thank you for your generous gift.

天丨節 the airing clothes' festival, on the 6th of the 6th moon.

睆 To look at; it is used frequently in proper names.

hwang' 丨視 to examine carefully.

纊 A cord; to cord, to tie with a string.

hwang' 丨繩 halliards, with which to hoist a flag, a sign-board, or a sail.

榥 A window screened with thin silk; a book-rack or lectern to

hwang' support a book when reading.

櫎 Similar to the last; it is also read *hwang* and used for 幌 a screen.

hwang' Something that will screen off or keep out the wind; a term for a passage, as a porch, a verandah, or door; a strip; to join things; to reel silk from the cocoon.

熀 The blaze of fire.

hwang' 煒丨 effulgent, blazing; a bright, dazzling light.

丨眼睛 dazzling to the eyes; it blinds my eyes.

滉 A bright expanse of water illuminated by the sun.

hwang'

鎤 The sound of bells.

hwang'

HWO.

Old sounds, ha, ka, ga, hwa, *and* kwa. *In Canton*, fo *and* wo; — *in Swatow*, hwa, hué, *and* ho; — *in Amoy*, hô, hôⁿ, *and* hé; — *in Fuhchau*, hwò *and* hwi; — *in Shanghai*, hwo, hu, *and* u; — *in Chifu*, hwoa.

禾 The original form is composed of 木 *tree* and 𠂹 *pendent* contracted, alluding to the bent appearance of ripe grain; it forms the 115th radical of a natural group of characters relating to grains and their uses.

꜀hŏ

Growing grain, especially paddy in the southern provinces, and wheat in the northern; grain, corn; crops; occurs used for the next.

丨苗 growing rice.

割丨 to reap the grain.

嘉丨 a fine crop of grain.

丨米 unhulled rice, paddy.

看丨 to watch the fields. (*Cantonese.*)

丨易長畝 the grain grows well over the acres.

一丨九穗 nine heads on one stalk — in a good year.

丨稈 the straw of grain.

早丨 the early or first crop at Canton; also, a grain that ripens early.

丨虫 a grub or worm like a Nereid, used for food at Canton.

和 龢 咊 From *mouth* or *musical pipe* and *grain*; the third is an antique and rather erroneous, but not unusual form.

꜀hŏ Harmony, union, concord, agreement; conciliation after a strife; to become mild; kindly, agreeing with, as a medicine; bells put on the cross-bar of a carriage; inclined to; to be at peace, to make friends; to fit, fitting; to work in and mix up; to unite, to harmonize; to compound, to hush up; to go with, to join, to conform to; as a *preposition*, with, together, to, — and thus becomes a sign of the accusative; a small reed; gate of a camp.

平丨 even, as a pulse; mild, as food.

心恬氣丨 cordial and gratified feelings.

一團丨氣 cordial harmony between them.

丨味 well-flavored, delicately seasoned.

丨鈴央央 the bells on the chariots tinkled merrily.

終丨且平 harmony and peace will be lasting.

樂旣丨奏 all the instruments perform in harmony.

太丨 peace generally prevails.

風雨調丨 the wind and rain come in their time.

丨睦 amicable relations.

做丨頭 to be a peacemaker.

丨頭 proper ingredients, as for a soup. (*Shanghai.*)

丨順 complaisant, accordant.

他們不相丨 they don't agree; incompatible.

丨顏悅色 a pleasant, benign countenance.

八音丨諧 the instruments all keep in tune.

丨約 a compact giving peace; a treaty of amity.

講丨 to treat of peace.

交丨 to make up a quarrel, to become reconciled, like two opposing armies which yet do not fight.

免傷丨氣 do not destroy the present harmony, do not wound good feelings.

人丨平 an even tempered man.

丨坭兒 to work over the mud, as a bricklayer does.

丨他說 speak to him.

丨碩 the transcription of the Manchu title *hwo-shwui*, meaning the officer who stands at the corner; used only by the highest princes.

我丨你去 we will both go.

私丨人命 to hush up a homicide, to secretly compensate for killing a man.

丨衣而睡 to sleep in one's clothes.

丨尙 or 丨闍 a Budhist priest, because he should be a peacemaker, as some natives assert; but the priests explain it by 親教師 a self-taught teacher; it is probably derived from the Sanscrit *upa-dhyaya*, of which the sound *hwah-shie* is the equivalent in Kashgar.

招君丨番 called a princess to pacify the tribe, — by marrying her to its Hunnish chief; done by an emperor of the Han.

Read *ho'*. To accord, to make rhymes with; to sing a second; to keep in tune and time; to mix, as tastes; to conciliate; assenting.

丨韻的詩 verses which have proper rhymes.

隨聲附丨 he always agrees to what one says.

丨勻 to mix properly, as a cook; well blended.

四樣對丨 mix in four equal parts.

一唱百丨 one sings, all follow; a leader of a band of music.

寡丨 few assented to it; *i. e.* only a few agreed.

夥 ʻ*hwo* From *many* and *real* as the phonetic; *q. d.* many men come together; interchanged with the next.

Numerous; a band, a company, a party; a comrade, a partner; colleague, accomplice, crony, or messmate; a classifier of bands of men.

丨計 a companion, a fellow; this phrase in Cantonese is the word *foky* or *fokee* by which foreigners often call all natives.

丨長 or 大丨 a name for the chief mate of a vessel; but 大丨兒 usually means one set, this company, all the fellows.

丨伴 a partner in business.

幾丨 how many? — as coolies or sailors.

小丨子 a young man, a youth, up to about 25 years.

合丨 a partner in, an associate, a pal.

丨盜 bandits, fellow-thieves.

一丨客人 a company of friends.

搭丨 to join a company or partnership.

供開同丨 to turn evidence, to tell of one's accomplices.

歸丨 or 丨連着 to start a company, to form a partnership.

案件甚丨 the [criminal] cases are very numerous.

合着丨兒 all are together; the whole posse.

丨騙 two or three concerting to cheat one.

做小丨 to trade, or act for one's self, when agent for another; to make something privately.

伙 ʻ*hwo* From *man* and *fire*; an unauthorized word, interchanged with the last and next, which seems to have been derived from the phrase 十人爲一火 ten men make one fire or mess.

Goods; furniture, household property, gear; a comrade.

傢丨 tools, articles, furniture; a set of things, a complete set out.

進丨 to move into a house.

丨食 stores, supplies; daily food for the table.

大丨 and 二丨 denote the chief and second mates in foreign ships; 丨長 mates.

好傢丨 in *Cantonese*, well-pleasing; but *ironically*, mean, badly done.

火 灬 ʻ*hwo* The character is intended to represent an ascending flame, and in combination is contracted to four dots; it forms the 86th radical of a large and natural group of characters relating to heat; names of boys are often selected from it.

Fire, flame; to burn, to consume, to annihilate by fire; among physicians, exciting humors, full habit, fever; one of the five elements belonging to the south; one of the six magazines of nature; urgent full speed; lustful.

丨燄 a flame; 丨花 a spark.

救丨 to put out a conflagration.

失丨 caught fire accidentally.

封丨 to cover or bank a fire, as with wet coal-dust.

丨鎗 or 軍丨 fire-arms and ammunition.

一把丨 a fire, a blaze, a tongue of flame.

丨之 burn it.

丨石粉 chalk powdered.

丨化 burned, as a priest's corpse; cremation.

丨家 those who burn corpses.

息丨 or 滅丨 the fire is out; to put out the fire, as in a stove.

如丨烈烈 like a blazing fire.

着丨 or 生丨 or 點丨 or 弄丨 to make or light a fire.

丨票 an urgent dispatch.

虛丨 feverish; febrile.

邪丨 bad humors.

丨氣 heat, caloric; temper, anger.

不要發丨氣 don't get angry.

丨氣大 testy, irascible, furious.

沒點丨性兒 you have no animation, as an opium smoker.

丨頭 a scullion. (*Cantonese.*)

不舉丨 they light no cooking fires, — but get their meals outside.

丨食多少 what are your table expenses?

丨速進兵 order the troops to advance quickly.

丨伴 a comrade; 一丨 was formerly the term for a mess of ten soldiers, whose cook was called 丨頭軍 soldiers' fire-boy.

心丨盛 or 心裏冒丨 his temper is up, he is fired with rage.

丨杖 a poker; 丨鉗 tongs.

丨引 a match, a sun-glass, or other thing to 打丨 strike a fire.

自來丨 a lucifer-match.

慾丨動 burning with lust.

丨星 the planet Mars; but the 星丨 in the Shu King denoted a star then near the heart of Scorpio, the culminating star at dusk on the summer solstice, but now the star *α* Hydra.

禍ʾ From to *worship* and a *wry mouth* as the phonetic.

*hwo*ʾ Evil, misery, the opposite of 福; calamity, suffering, adversity; woes, judgments, especially those beyond one's control; unhappy; to send down woes; to bring calamity on others; to curse, to injure.

避丨 to avoid calamity, to escape impending wrath.

惹丨 to bring on, or invite suffering.

丨患 or 丨災 calamities, adversities.

丨不單行 misfortunes never come singly.

誰爲此丨 which brought this calamity on me?

具丨以燼 all are destroyed by this burning.

丨福倚伏於其中 disgrace or promotion (sorrow or joy) will follow one of the two courses.

福善丨淫 [heaven] blesses with goodness and chastises with evil.

嫁丨于人 to implicate others in one's crimes.

丨害人 to injure people deeply.

丨亂之災 the horrors of civil war.

丨不遠矣 trouble is not far off.

丨積有日 he has been long laying up for these troubles.

創丨 to meet an unlucky thing.

闖窮丨 to run into mischief, to meddle to one's hurt.

In *Fuhchau.* Dropping, as of rain.

貨ʾ From *pearls* or *property* and to *change; q. d.* things for changing.

*hwo*ʾ Goods, wares, merchandize, whatever can be changed or bartered; to deal in goods; to bribe or fee.

丨物 goods, stock in trade; an article of merchandise.

丨財 produce, goods.

押丨 to go with, or escort goods.

丨賂 bribes to officials; 丨其左右 he bribed the attendants.

各樣丨色 all descriptions of goods.

囤丨 to monopolize an article, by buying it up.

一水丨 goods brought in the same trip; and 頭水丨 denotes their best quality.

道地的丨 genuine goods from that place.

視爲奇丨哞 do you fancy that these are first-rate goods?

落丨 and 上丨 to ship off and to land goods.

出丨 to take delivery of goods.

奇丨可居 it is a rare article; *met.* a remarkable man, a sort of wonder, an eccentric man.

脚丨 poorest kind of goods; the garblings.

賤丨 poor goods, cheaply made; *met.* an adulteress.

盉ʾ From *dish* and *grain* or harmony as the phonetic; it is used with 和ʾ to mix.

*hwo*ʾ To mix and season, as a cook; dishes for mixing food.

HWOH.

Old sounds, hak, kak, hiah, hwat, gwat, kwak, *and* gwak. *In Canton*, fok, wok, kʻüt, út, *and* wak ; — *in Swatow*, kʻak, wak, hu, wa, *and* hòk ; — *in Amoy*, hòk, ho, hwat, hek, *and* hat ; — *in Fuhchau*, hwòk, wak, kwak, hek, *and* hék ; — *in Shanghai*, hok *and* kwʻok ; — *in Chifu*, hwoa.

霍 ʻhwo From *rain* and *beautiful*, often interchanged for the next.

Speed, celerity ; fleet, agile ; the cholera.

飛 丨 to fly swiftly.

丨 然 suddenly, as when the clouds disperse.

揮 丨 extravagant, wasteful ; also frolicsome, gamboling, like birds or animals.

丨 山 a lofty peak in Hunan, same as the 衡 山, also called 天 柱 山 or Atlas of China.

丨 山 縣 a district in the west of Nganhwui on the River Pi.

丨 州 an inferior prefecture in the south of Shensi on the River Făn ; anciently the appanage of Chʻu, the brother of Wu Wang.

白 丨 a contemptuous look, a disdainful glance. (*Cantonese.*)

癨 hwo Mostly written like the last.

The *rapid disease*, the Asiatic cholera or 丨 亂 症, described as attended with vomiting, spasms of the tendons, gripes, and depression of spirits.

藿 hwoʼ Leaves of a legume used for fodder ; bean stalks which are fed to camels ; greens ; clover ; a fragrant plant of the mint family.

丨 香 betony or bishopwort (*Lophanthus rugosus*), used in headache and colic ; others apply the name to the *Betonica officinalis*.

食 我 塲 丨 [the colt] can eat the bean stalks on my fields.

淫 羊 丨 the spinous leaved aspen (*Populus spinosa*), found in Shantung.

豆 丨 wild legumes, pea vines.

藜 丨 之 羹 a soup of simples.

擢 hwoʼ To recall one with the hand ; to move a thing back, or as when using a fan ; to strike.

戲 丨 to make a fool of.

鞭 丨 to whip, as when driving off a crowd ; to flog.

丨 手 to motion off ; to gesticulate.

蒦 hwoʼ From 萑 a *sedge* grass and 又 the *hand*, meaning to measure with a reed ; also read *yoh* ; as a primitive it merely imparts its sound to the combined character.

To measure ; to calculate, especially the weal or woe of men ; a measure.

尺 者 丨 也 a foot-rule is for measuring.

矱 hwoʼ A measure ; a marking-line ; to adjust by a line, to get the dimensions by a rod.

準 繩 丨 a marking-line.

矩 丨 a square like a carpenter's.

穫 hwoʼ From *grain* and to *measure* as the phonetic ; this and the last look much alike.

To cut grain in the autumn ; to reap the crops ; a reaping ; harvest ; to treat harshly ; to gather the roots and stubble for fuel.

不 耕 而 丨 [the literati] do not plough, and yet they reap.

刈 丨 to reap, as pulse or grain.

彼 有 不 丨 穉 there shall be young grain unreaped.

是 丨 是 亂 [the crops] were reaped and stacked on the fields.

劐 hwoʼ Similar to the preceding and the next.

To split with a knife ; to rend, to separate ; to pry up.

丨 出 去 了 it is all known ; published generally ; to divide assets, as of an insolvent.

丨 着 幹 do it at any risk, fear nothing, go on.

丨 肚 子 to rip open woman with child.

丨 地 to dig up the ground, as when planting a tree.

劃 ˏhwa From *knife* and to *mark* ; it is nearly synonymous with the last.

To rive, to split open ; to dig ; to carve open flower work ; to engrave ; to cut glass ; to mark off ; to deface, as a writing ; a catch or mark in writing ; a burin, a stylus, a graving-tool.

丨 傷 to wound, to deface.

丨 開 cut it open ; mark it with a line or cut ; to carve out ; *met.* to digest one's ideas and set them forth.

丨 荻 to sharpen a reed — to write with.

丨 破 地 皮 just scratched open the skin.

丨 地 爲 牢 to mark the spot for a prison.

丨 補 to cut out and insert, as a patch in a garment, or a correction in a document.

指 甲 丨 了 一 下 made a crease with the finger-nail.

丨 一 不 二 I've said it once, I've not two — prices for the thing.

謀 爲 丨 策 to consider a matter ; to see if the ends will meet.

濩 hwoʼ From *water* and a *measure*.

To rain profusely ; water pouring down after a rain ; the dashing of water ; to cook, to boil.

濆 丨 dashing and rolling, as a torrent.

丨 澤 an old name of Yang-chʻing hien in the southwest of Shansi.

Read *hu'* To diffuse, as rain spreads itself over the land.

聲教布 丨 his instructions were universally diffused.

大 丨 a great joy to the empire, said of a sort of general festival of T'ang the Successful.

臒 *hwo'* The *vermilion measure*, a kind of vermilion or red ochre; it was a kind of mineral paint, probably prepared from cinnabar ore.

檴 *hwo'* A tree, the 丨 落, whose leaves are shaped like the elm; withes can be made from the bark, and dishes of the timber; it is a sort of birch.

無浸 丨 薪 do not soak the faggots of the birch.

嚄 *hwo'* To bawl out, as when in a fright.

丨 唶 loquacious, boisterous, talkative.

嚿 *hwo'* To bawl after, to cry aloud when calling for one.

鑊 *hwo'* From *metal* and a *measure* as the the phonetic.

A flat boiler shaped like the segment of a sphere, and generally without feet; a caldron; an iron pan; a graver; to bore or cut in.

丨 烹之刑 the punishment of boiling to death.

鼎 丨 a large caldron or boiler.

鉄 丨 an iron pan or boiler.

你會箍 丨 you are able to hoop a boiler; *i. e.* very smart; an ironical phrase.

丨 底這樣 [black] as a boiler's bottom.

粦大 丨 飯 to cook a great dinner; in Canton, it sometimes means to have a clan fight.

滚水 丨 a steamer's boiler.

車大 丨 to wheel a great pan, a tumbler's feat.

獲 *hwo'* *hu'* A kind of wild beast; to take in hunting; to catch, as a thief; to get, to obtain; to find opportunity; to receive; to hit, as the mark; an epithet for a slave.

丨 罪 to commit a crime; to sin.

大有所 丨 he has been very successful; gotten much.

拿 丨 arrested, apprehended.

丨 醜 he has seized the chief criminal.

丨 利 to make money.

迯犬 丨 之 it is caught by the hound.

丨 恩 to obtain favor.

實 丨 我心 he just suits my wishes.

不隕 丨 于貧賤 do not oppress and dishearten the poor and lowly.

先難後 丨 the attainment comes only after the toil; similar to *per aspera ad astra.*

漷 *hwo'* The noise of waters roaring and dashing.

Read *kw'oh,* A small stream which formed the border of the state Ch'u 邾 in olden time; it is a small branch of the River I in Tăng hien 滕縣 in the southeast of Shantung.

豁 *hwo* From *valley* and to *injure.*

A wide, open valley; to understand thoroughly; to penetrate the meaning; to open as a window; liberal, magnanimous, generous.

丨 達 intelligent, good tact, farseeing.

丨 然貫通 I thoroughly understand it.

丨 心眼 to expand the mind, as by travel.

空 丨 vast, empty, as a palatial hall or deep cañon.

丨 拳 to play at morra.

丨 免錢粮 to remit the land taxes.

這人狠開 丨 的 this is a remarkably intelligent man.

活 *hwo* From *water* and *tongue*; but the ancient form, instead of tongue, has 昏 to *stop* the *mouth.*

Name of one of the headwaters of the River Chang in the southeast of Shansi in Hu-kwan hien 壺關縣; running, bubbling, like water; living, lively, active; bright, cheerful; to live; to vivify; life, motion; the germ of life; open, as a thoroughfare; movable, not fastened; work, livelihood, occupation, a living; applied to some drugs to indicate their efficacy.

丨 了 reviving, resuscitated.

復 丨 to revive, to come to; a resurrection.

生 丨 alive; to be busy, employed; getting a living.

丨 神 the living God; a foreign term.

西天 丨 佛 a western living Budha; *met.* a merciful, generous man.

丨 字 a verb; it is also applied to movable types, and 丨 板 is being printed with them.

丨 龍 丨 現 I've just now seen a live dragon; — as an inventor of stories says.

快 丨 joyful, pleased, merry.

丨 計 an employment; *lit.* an ever-changing plan; a calling.

織布度 丨 he weaves for a living.

針線 丨 does needlework for a living.

丨 動 handy, loose, movable; spry, agile; good, as credit; active, as trade.

獨 丨 a kind of angelica root.

過 丨 daily expenses; bright, as prospects; constant outlay; one's living.

丨 脫兒 a living, striking resemblance; life-like.

丨 便纔好 better to adapt yourself to circumstances; it will be best to do as exigencies demand.

丨 絡話 ambiguous promises, slippery talk; double-tongued.

圓 丨 此事 let us accommodate this matter; be tractable.

圓 〡 that will easily turn.
河水洋洋北流 〡 〡 the ocean-like waters of the Ho flow northwards in their majestic course.
不知死 〡 heedless of consequences; reckless of life; he has no idea of things.
〡 潑 lively, as a fish; bustling, generous-hearted, kind to.
〡 世 giving life to people; said of physicians.
空 〡 了 or 白 〡 了 useless, unserviceable; said of people.
〡 現 apparent, as if alive; to manifest, as a ghost.
說得 〡 現 word painting; described to the life.
施水以 〡 我 give me some water to revive me.
〡 水 living or spring water; running streams.
做 〡 to work at a job.
散 〡 irregular work, odd jobs.
〡 該 results, consequences, effects of bad courses.
〡 口 an antagonist in a law-case; a defendant.

枓, *ˌhwo* To lade water with a bucket and pour it on fields; to take up refuse, to scrape up.

佸, *ˌhwo* To unite; to act with united strength; to tug at; to assemble, to collect; to include the whole; to reach.
〡 〡 tugging at altogether, as sailors at a hawser.
不日不月曷其有 〡 some day or month perhaps, but when then will it be done? *i. e.* it must be attended to now.

砉, *ˌhwo* The ripping sound heard when tearing the skin off an animal.

湱, *ˌhwo* Dashing waves are 㶁 〡, referring to the roaring of breaking billows.
瀫 〡 name of a stream issuing from a western valley.

或, *hwo'* Composed of *dart*, *mouth*, and *one* place, denoting a spot which needs to be guarded, or whose safety is in doubt; *yih*, 域 has since been used for it, and this occurs interchanged with the next.

Doubtful, uncertain; a preposition of doubt; moreover, perhaps, if, may, perchance; a certain person; often occurs in classic writers for 有 having, there is; when repeated, it forms contrasts, as either – or; now – then; here – there; some – others; this – that; when it follows negative adverbs it intimates a reservation in the assertion.
莫 〡 不難 never hesitate to admit the difficulty.
去抑 〡 不去呢 do you go or stay?
〡 曰 some one has said.
〡 往 〡 來 comes and goes; to and fro; unsteady.
間 〡 有之 see whether there are any?
〡 有人 perhaps there is some one.
〡 以其酒 if we serve them with wine.
時予乃 〡 言 whatsoever I have said.
〡 群 〡 友 here in groups, there in pairs.
卽 〡 如此 them perhaps it is so.
〡 問 some one made the inquiry.
〡 者 or 〡 是 perhaps, probably.
〡 然 〡 不然 it may be so or not.
無不爾 〡 承 may there never fail to you some to succeed.

惑, *hwo'* From *heart* and *doubting* as the phonetic.

To lead into errors, to delude, to blind the mind; to excite doubt, to unsettle other's opinions; suspicion, doubt, unbelief; blinded, led astray.
疑 〡 suspicious, in doubt of.
蠱 〡 人心 to dishearten by suspicions, to beguile out of the right way.
收 〡 imposed upon, fooled.
〡 世 to deceive mankind.
迷 〡 befooled; to inveigle into; to lead into evil.
魔 〡 instigated or possessed by the devil.
無 〡 乎 can you still doubt? there is no suspicion.
謠言 〡 衆 wild rumors lead astray the multitude.

掝, *hwo'* like the last.

Deluded.
〡 〡 a deception; guiles, tricks; the noise or act of splitting.

鰔, *ˌhwo* This is described like a species of lizard, which frequents the bamboo.
〡 魚 or 〡 頭 a common sort of perch at Canton (*Corvina grypota*), which is dried like stockfish.

魊, *ˌhwo* The ghost of an infant.
鬼 〡 a gust of wind propelled by demons, called 鬼旋風, which is supposed to wrench people's lips awry.

幗, *ˌhwo* A curtain to screen from the wind.
〡 〡 譽 slapping and flapping, as a flag in the breeze.

HWUI.

Some of these characters are heard HWÉI. *Old sounds,* hwé, gwé, kwé, két, gét, *and* kek. *In Canton,* fúi, úi, fei, *and* wei ; — *in Swatow,* húe *and* húi ; — *in Amoy,* hòe, húi, òe, *and* k'úi ; — *in Fuhchau,* hwi, hwi, húi, hwoi, *and* hoi ; — *in Shanghai,* hwé, kwé, *and* wé ; — *in Chifu,* hwéi.

灰 *hwui* Composed of 火 *fire* and 又 the *hand ; q. d.* fire which can be handled.

Ashes, embers ; ashy, ash color, gray ; soot ; lime ; dust ; to plaster ; to turn pale, to faint ; to sink from terror ; disheartened.

火 ┃ wood ashes ; ashes of any kind.

炭 ┃ charcoal dust or ashes.

石 ┃ stone lime.

┃ 牆 to plaster a wall.

檳榔 ┃ red betel-nut lime, eaten with the siri leaf ; it is burned from shells.

生 ┃ quicklime.

盡成 ┃ 燼 or 成 ┃ reduced quite to ashes, burned to a coal.

不 ┃ 爐 a fire-clay furnace.

黑 ┃ a sort of bitumen.

磨骨揚 ┃ may his bones be ground and their ashes scattered! — to appease my hate.

白 ┃ kaolin or quartz powder used in porcelain or glass-making.

┃ 土 or ┃ 塵 dust.

死 ┃ useless for making ashes.

槁木死 ┃ utterly dead to ; no inclination for, like a decayed tree which will produce no ashes.

牙 ┃ 色 an ivory or sepia color.

眼中流血心內成 ┃ his eyes ran blood and his heart turned to ashes ; in utter despair.

┃ 了心 or 心 ┃ disheartened ; no desire for.

心不 ┃ my heart's wish is not yet fulfilled.

劫 ┃ utter desolation, as after a rebellion.

牙 ┃ a white powder made by calcining paddy chaff ; it is used for sharpening knives and as a dentrifice.

黣 *hwui* An ashy color ; a light black color.

煇 *hwui* From *fire* and *army ;* interchanged with the next, which is more common.

The effulgence of fire or the sun ; bright, glorious ; light, as an illumination.

┃ 光 brilliant, lustrous, illuminated.

┃ 煌 bright, luminous, splendid.

┃ 德 distinguished virtue.

輝 *hwui* From an *army* and *bright ;* but one etymologist thinks the sound was derived from *wéi* 撝 to motion ; used with the last, and has rather superseded it.

Glorious, like the sun ; refulgent, glistering.

┃ 然 very happy ; spruced up.

┃ 耀 exceedingly glorious, very bright.

光 ┃ brilliant, refulgent.

敝舍生 ┃ [if you come,] my mean abode will be made brilliant.

暉 *hwui* Used with the last two.

Bright, splendid ; a ray of the sun.

日 ┃ sunlight.

斜 ┃ slanting beams.

流 ┃ a ray or stream of sunshine.

遙隔鈞 ┃ your pleasant face is far away.

揮 *hwui* From *hand* and *army.*

To move, to shake ; to rouse, to animate ; to move the hand briskly as in drawing ; to wield with skill ; to sprinkle, to scatter ; to throw away, as dregs.

┃ 淚 to brush away the tears.

┃ 金如土 to spend money like dirt.

┃ 春 to wield the spring [pencil], to write newyear's inscriptions.

┃ 毫 to flourish the brush ; same as ┃ 寫 to write.

┃ 灑 to spend liberally ; to sprinkle ; not constant at a thing.

大筆一 ┃ one dash of your fine pencil.

指 ┃ to point or direct with the hand ; title of an officer like a major in Peking.

┃ 散 to disperse ; to dismiss, as an assembly.

六爻發 ┃ the six lines [of this diagram] animate things.

┃ 軍前進 he motioned the troops to go forward.

Read *hwun.* Whole.

┃ 掄 entire, unbroken.

撝 *hwui* From *hand* and to *do ;* it is interchanged with the last.

To split, to rend ; to point out ; unassuming.

强 ┃ to order about roughly.

┃ 謙 to show quietly ; an unassuming, humble manner.

楎 *hwui* Also read *hwun.*

A peg to hang clothes on a wall ; an upright clothes-horse or shelf ; the crooked handle of a plow.

翬 *hwui* From 羽 *wings* and 揮 to *move* contracted.

To fly swiftly and with noise, as a pheasant does ; a powerful rapid flight ; colored, variegated.

┃ 雉 a name for the Tartar pheasant, on account of its beauty.

鼓翅 ┃ ┃ they clapped their wings and flew away swiftly.

如 ┃ 斯飛 beautiful as the flying pheasant.

麾 ˓hwui From *hemp* and *hair*.

A signal flag, a marker, a standard; to signalize, to beckon, to make motions with the hand, to wave off; quick, hasty.

旗丨 a signal flag, that intimates orders; it often had a leopard's tail on the staff.

丨之使去 he motioned to him to leave.

指丨 to direct with a flag.

丨之以肱 motioned to him with his arm.

丨斥來使 he waved off the messenger; — refused to receive the order.

丨下聽令 I hear your excellency's orders; — spoken to a high general or commander.

徽 ˓hwui From 微 *fine* and 糸 *silk*.

A cord of three strands; a string; garments worn by queens; honorable, excellent; beautiful, adorned; to beautify, to set forth the goodness of; the stops on a lute; the tone of an instrument; a sort of pennant.

丨音 sweet, plaintive music, as of a lute.

丨墨 ink from Hwui-cheu fu 丨州府 in the south of Nganhwui 安丨 province.

丨美 excellent, as one's thoughts.

丨猷 good services, high reputation.

丨婕 quick, urgent, as a horse ridden post.

上丨號 or 你丨號 what is your honorable style? said to old men; the 丨號 was a sort of flag.

隳 ˓hwui From 隋 *indifferent* to, 心 *heart* and 人 *man*; it is like 灰 in some of its senses.

To break or tear in pieces; to destroy, to overthrow, to throw down, as the defenses of a city; to dismantle; to raze.

丨廢 or 丨敗 come to nought; disused, obsolete; destroyed.

紀綱丨墮 the safeguards of law and morality are cast down.

一行丨而百行可疑 one faux-pas will make people suspect every act; like Ec. x: 1.

不作丨心 do nothing that can wound your honor.

我丨了心 I am rather mortified at my attempt.

倠 ˓hwui From *man* and *bird*.

Ugly, as an old hag.

仳丨 homely, ill-favored.

豗 ˓hwui The grunting sound of pigs rooting; the sound of quarreling.

喧丨 high words; altercation, bickering.

回 囬 囘 ˓hwui The character is intended to represent a thing revolving on an axis; the two last forms are fanciful.

To revert to, to revolve; to recoil, to go to its source; to turn back; to turn aside, as to error; to rebel, to disobey; repenting, returning, changing one's mind; a time, a turn, an effort, a revolution; a brochure, a livraison, a chapter in a novel; the Moslems; and hence in some places at the north, foreign.

丨信 or 丨書 a written answer.

此丨 this occasion.

上一丨 the previous time.

三丨五次 again and again, repeatedly.

丨轉 to turn around or back; to revolve.

奉丨 send it back, as a present.

丨心轉意 to relent; to change one's opinions.

風丨南 the wind is veering to the south.

其德不丨 his virtue was unimpeachable.

丨糖 lost its savor, said of over-ripe fruit. (*Cantonese.*)

退丨多少 how much [of the present] will you decline to take?

丨天意盡人力 endeavor to make Heaven favorable, and put forth all your own efforts.

丨答 or 丨音 a reply, an answer, either verbal or written.

丨拜 to return a visit.

丨門 the first visit of a bride to her parents.

丨字門口 a framed gateway, one with carved border.

丨味思量 the doctrine (or advice) seemed better on reflection.

丨祿 a fire, as of a house; the god of Fire.

來丨 coming and going; come and gone; there and back.

丨來 to return; in colloquial it also has the force of 然後 in many phrases; as 丨來再說 we will discuss that afterwards; 丨來去辦 settle that after going there; — at other times it is equivalent to presently, in a little while, as 丨來挪去 I'll move it away shortly.

追丨 to send for; to come or bring back.

低丨 or 丨想 to reflect on, to turn over in one's mind.

丨頭是岸 turn and there is the shore; — there's yet room for repentance.

周丨多少里 how many miles is it round there and back?

丨顧 to look behind; also *met.* to regret an action.

丨不脫 you cannot retract from the engagement now.

船隻丨空 the vessels have all gone away empty.

輪丨 transmigration (*sansara*), or human life as subject to it.

丨丨國 the Ouigours or Wigurs; applied also to all Moslem countries.

丨丨敎 or 丨敎 Mohammedanism, Islamism.

丨子 the Moslems.

丨樣子 in foreign style; — a northern phrase.

迴 迥 ˓hwui Interchanged with the last.

To curve, to bend around and return, as a stream; to double, as a fox; revolving; intricate involved, as a pattern or figure.

丨流水 an eddy.

丨避 get out of the way! retire aside! — a notice given to the crowd; to skulk, to avoid one's sight.

丨繞 surrounding, inclosing, as hills do a valley.

千丨百轉 continually revolving.

丨廊 a corridor or verandah on the outside of a range of rooms.

丨文詩 a kind of ode that requires the line to be read over and over, each time beginning with a new character, to get the full sense.

徊 ˓hwui From a *step* and a *turn*.

To pace to and fro, as if undecided; to hover about.

徘丨 irresolute; back and forth, not advancing.

洄 ˓hwui Water flowing round and round; a back current; an eddy, a whirlpool; name of a lake in the southeast of Honan; indistinct, as an eddying stream.

丨瀾 [the tide is] turning; the recoil of waves; an eddy in a stream, also called 丨注 a revolving pool.

溯丨從之 I was cogitating how best to reach you, he deliberated much how he could get at it.

鮰 ˓hwui An unauthorized character, though it is found in the Păn Ts'ao, and was perhaps changed from *yiu* 鮪 the mud sturgeon, to denote this variety.

A fish belonging to the salmon tribe, common in the Yangtsz' about three feet long, resembling a small sturgeon in its snout, transverse mouth, and four short barbels below it; the adipose fin is very large, and three large serrated spines protect the pectorals and first dorsal, which has six rays; the skin is smooth, slate colored on the back, and white underneath; the eyes are placed behind the mouth, and are the size of peas.

牙竹笋燒丨魚 when the bamboo is just sprouting, then cook the sturgeon with it.

痐 蚘 蛔 蛕 ˓hwui From *disease* or *insect* and *turn*; the third form is the commonest.

A long, intestinal worm, the tape-worm, common in northern China, and named 寸食虫 and 曹食虫 by the people; common intestinal worms seem to be also frequently referred to under this name, as they speak of 吐丨 vomiting worms.

The second form is also used for 尤 in the proper name of 蚩丨 Chi-yiu, an ancient rebel in the days of Hwang-ti, probably a mythical being.

誰是你肚子裏的丨蟲 who is the tape-worm in your belly? why have you not told me of this affair?

恛 ˓hwui From *heart* and *turning*.

Disordered; indistinct.

丨丨然從人也 he is in doubt which side to take.

茴 ˓hwui Fennel or caraway.

小丨香 a fragrant seed like dill (*Fenicula dulcis*).

大丨香 the star-aniseed.

栦 ˓hwui An unauthorized character.

A large tree found in Yunnan and Hunan, whose hard, heavy wood is used by boatbuilders for rudders; the fruit grows in clusters at the end of the branches and is red; the pod is triquetrous and pointed, containing many seeds shaped like orange seeds.

毀 ʿhwui From 土 *earth* and 毇 *rice broken in a mortar* contracted; used with the next.

To break down; to level, as a house; to shed, as teeth; ruined, broken, dilapidated, fallen; abolished; cast down; to slander, to vilify, to defame, — for which the next is better; to put away, to diminish; to deprecate calamities, as by prayer.

丨齒 to shed the teeth.

哀丨 sick and thin, as from grief.

折丨 or 丨棄 to pull down and clear away, as a building; to cast away.

丨滅 destroyed utterly.

丨壞 injured, defaced, worn out.

豈敢丨傷 how can I injure and wound — this body, which came from my parents?

丨了罷 destroy them all!

衰丨 failing in strength, as at the age of sixty.

聖言不丨 true doctrines are never lost.

詯 譭 ʿhwui From *words* and *broken*; interchanged with the last.

To slander, to vilify, to defame; to upbraid.

丨謗 to backbite, to blacken.

丨譽 to vituperate and to praise; to curse and to bless.

由嘴丨罵人 her mouth is always scolding and railing

燬 ʿhwui From *fire* and to *destroy*.

A fire, a blaze; flaming, blazing; bright, splendid.

烈丨 a furious fire.

王室如丨 the palace was splendid as a blaze.

燒丨 or 丨焚 burned up; quite consumed.

腲 ʿhwĕi Also read ʿtui.

To swell, to enlarge or bulge out.

腽丨 a boss; protuberances like those on the plates of a tortoise.

ˏ瘣 *hwui*ˀ Disease in trees which causes protuberances to grow on the trunk; woody knobs out of which no branches grow.

老樹生 丨 an old tree produces knobs.

ˏ虺 ˏ*hwui* This and ˏ*yuen* 蚖 seem to be confounded with each other by some authors.

A venomous serpent, which has a big head and small neck; to dream of it foretokens the birth of a daughter; jaded, ailing.

蝮 丨 a viper.

王 丨 a sort of boa found in Yunnan.

維丨維蛇 [my dreams were of] cobras and of snakes.

水丨 a sea-serpent.

丨隤 fagged; spavined, said of a horse.

丨丨其雷 the rumbling of distant thunder.

土 丨 蛇 a venomous snake in Kiangsu, which is said to have no eyes, and eject a web from the mouth to feel its way.

ˏ卉 ˏ芔 *hwui*ˀ From 屮屮 *plants* and 屮 *sprouting* or growing about; it is usually contracted to the first form.

A general term for plants, herbs, &c., especially small ones.

花 丨 flowers and plants.

百丨 all sorts of plants, the vegetable world.

丨木萋止 the plants and trees grow well.

萬 丨 爭春 all plants strive to come out in spring, — except the aster.

ˏ賄 *hwui*ˀ From *riches* and *having*.

Riches, wealth; cloths, silks, or whatever constitutes property; to give property, and thus bind people to do certain things; to bribe; hush-money.

受 丨 to take bribes.

送 丨 or 丨 賂 to bribe with money.

贓 丨 presents or douceurs; advantages afforded, instead of direct bribes.

囑 丨 or 丨 托 to bribe in order to get a thing through; to dictate or buy a favorable decision.

以爾車來以我丨遷 come with your carriages, and I will remove with my stuff.

ˏ匯 ˏ滙 *hwui*ˀ From *box* and *eddy* or *water* and *box*; the dictionaries favor the first, but the second unauthorized form is now most used.

A sort of vase or box; waters gurgling and eddying, running to one spot, — and referred especially to the swirling waters of the River Han where it joins the Yangtsz' at Hankow; a place to which people converge; to stagnate, as a pool; to deposit, as money; to advance money; a check, a draft, a letter of credit; to draw on, as for funds.

丨 源 a fountain.

沙 丨 quicksands, like those near Hangchau Bay.

東 丨 澤 爲 彭 蠡 on the east the streams unite to make the P'angli, — a part of Poyang Lake.

四 書 丨 叅 an edition of the Four Books with all the comments.

丨 劃 or 丨 單 or 丨 票 an order for money; a bank check; a letter of credit.

玆 丨 到 when this draft is presented.

有 路 丨 至 來 省 if you have any way of drawing an order on the provincial city.

丨 息 discount for cashing an order.

我 向 你 丨 一 千 兩 銀 子 I will draw you a draft for a thousand taels.

丨 銀 行 or 丨 兌 局 a bank; a discount office.

ˏ悔 ˏ*hwui* From *heart* and *each*.

To repent, to change; to be dissatisfied with one's conduct; indignant, repentant; grieved with.

丨 恨 remorse, contrition; vexed at one's ill luck.

丨 罪 to repent of sin.

反 丨 to recall one's promise.

丨 心 compunction, regret.

其 德 靡 丨 his virtue was not to be repented of.

丨 過 to acknowledge one's error.

丨 改 to reform, to amend.

追 丨 無 及 repentance will then be beyond your reach.

痛 丨 poignant sorrow for.

丨 後 遲 your repentance is now too late; — a phrase sometimes placed over prisons.

宜 無 丨 怒 they ought not to be thus angry.

𣧲 *hwui*ˀ From to *divine* and *each*; usually regarded as another form of the last.

To repent; a name for the 外 卦 or upper three lines in any one of the diagrams; the under three or 內 卦 are called 貞 or lucky.

ˏ晦 *hwui*ˀ The last day of the moon; night, obscure, dark; misty, as from fog; unpropitious; unusual.

丨 明 night and morning.

月 丨 dark nights, no moonlight.

昏 丨 obscure, dark; not clear, as a writing.

風 雨 丨 冥 obscured by the tempest.

時 丨 dark days; unprosperous times.

運 丨 unlucky; fortune is going against me.

丨 氣 an ill-omened fellow.

丨 氣 頭 how ill-starred that is! you are a bird of ill-luck. (*Cantonese.*)

丨 氣 星 進 命 born under an unlucky star.

眞丨氣子 really I was unlucky! I could get no redress.

丨得很 [this character] is very unusual.

背丨 not to use, to avoid; to keep dark about.

背丨爺娘 not to speak of one's parents' — affairs or names.

誨 *hwui'* From *words* and *constantly*.

To teach, to admonish; to reiterate words of instruction; to urge upon, to induce to; inviting, urging; instructive; counsel, instruction.

教丨 to instruct diligently.

丨人不倦 I am not weary of exhorting men.

丨爾諄諄 or 叮嚀丨之 I would instruct you constantly; give them line upon line.

訓丨 to inculcate upon.

納丨 to receive instruction.

冶容丨淫 ogling looks invite to wantonness.

惠 *hwui'* From 心 *heart* and 專 *single* contracted; *q.d.* the heart having one object.

Kind, gracious, forbearing; compliant, complaisant, accordant; benevolent, liberal; to give in charity; to give, to bestow; to sympathize, to be kind to; to adorn; to obey, to accord with; benefit, grace; presents, charities; in epitaphs denotes one who was gracious to the people; a triangular-headed halberd formerly carried before officers.

蒙丨 I am obliged for your kindness.

能保丨于庶民 he could kindly protect the people.

恩丨 grace, favor, mercy.

承蒙厚丨 thanks for your many great favors.

受丨 or 領丨 I am thankful for your compassion.

丨愛 benevolent, kind to all.

丨我良多 he has often been kind to me.

丨而不費 kindness need not be expensive.

盛丨 I am filled with your favor; many thanks, as for a letter received.

丨然肯來 you kindly agreed to come to me.

得實丨 to get some real aid; substantial help.

如蒙見丨不勝銘感 if you will kindly grant this, I shall be for ever obliged, — said by a borrower, or a shopkeeper when dunning.

虛丨 a mere show of kindness, empty promises.

憓 *hwui'* A synonym of the preceding.

Especially used for compliant; obedient, as to a ruler; loving.

義征不丨 they would not obey a just government when enforced.

譓 *hwui'* A clever mind, full of schemes and shifts; to examine closely; able to discriminate; sagacious; obedient, accommodating, in which it is like the last.

蟪 *hwui'* An insect, the 丨蛄, which lives but six months, and therefore only knows but one season; it appears to be a sort of cicada.

蕙 *hwui'* A fragrant species of marshy orchid, called 丨蘭, having many flowers on one stalk; the name probably includes several sorts, as Angræcum, Cymbidium, &c.

蘭丨齊芳 the flowers are alike fragrant; said of two brothers reaching degrees.

雪丨 the snow orchid of Yunnan; it flowers late.

會 *hwui'* Composed of 曾 to *add* and 亼, a contracted form of 集 to *assemble* over it; as a primitive its use is chiefly a phonetic, and it is easily confounded with *ₒtsăng* 曾 adding.

To collect, to convene, to assemble, to bring or meet together as equals; to visit; to make an agreement; to associate those of the same rank, views, or powers; to communicate with, to let all know; to understand after being informed, to know how, — and in this sense it becomes a sign of the future when preceding another verb; expert, skilled in; apt, likely to cause; joint, united; a blending; a junction, as of rivers or roads; an association for any purpose, a club, a union, a society, a fraternity, a cabal, — and hence discouraged by the Government; a church or congregation; a joint-stock company; an occasion, an annual reckoning; a meeting, a time; a seam in a cap.

拜丨 to visit and make up a quarrel; also used for 入丨 to become a 丨友 or member; to enter a society or organization.

丨客 to receive and see a guest; to visit.

丨齊 to assemble, to hold a meeting; the collective body.

僧丨 a meeting of Budhist priests.

丨過一面 I have seen him once.

文丨 a literary club.

以文丨友 friends uniting in some literary scheme.

丨兵 to assemble troops; to muster the forces.

燕丨賓客 to give an entertainment.

出丨 to get up a procession, usually idolatrous.

盂蘭勝丨 (or 烏藍婆 from Sanscrit *ulamba*) a kind of All Souls' day, a Budhist festival held on the 15th of the 7th moon for appeasing hungry ghosts; it was introduced into China about A.D. 733 by Amogha from Ceylon.

三合丨 the Triad Society existing in southern China.

開丨 and 收丨 to form a company and to wind it up.

丨首 or 丨頭 or 丨主 the manager of a club; a chairman.

丨匪 banditti; a junto; a clique of conspirators.

龍華佛丨 a festival held three days at full of the 3d moon in Shanghai, at which women pray for sons, or to be changed into men in the next life.

丨景 a gay procession.

好機丨 a good opportunity; a fine chance.

集戲丨 a sort of associated theatricals.

丨項 the funds or subscriptions to a company, for which 丨單 share tickets are given.

不期而丨 to meet unexpectedly.

鳴鑼丨衆 beat the gong and call them together.

丨意 to understand; a combined idea, as when the radical and primitive indicate the sense of a character.

韻丨 to combine an initial and final to make a third sound.

理丨 to comprehend; to manage.

丨要 and 丨典 are compilations of state regulations and records, made by Government for its officers.

不大丨兒 not a great while, presently.

一丨兒一丨兒 from time to time; now and then.

知丨 or 咨丨 to report to a super-ordinate officer.

竟丨如此 I hardly thought it would come to this pass.

丨水 to dive; also the junction of streams.

丨審 a joint examination, as of two officials.

省丨 a provincial capital.

丨作不丨作 do you know how to do it?

學丨 then learn how.

就丨下雨 it will then rain.

丨生病 it will probably make you sick.

In *Cantonese*. To simmer, to stew.

丨燕窩 stewed birdsnests.

Also read ˊ*hwui*, and sometimes written 膾 to distinguish it. Expert, skilled in; a sign of the future.

繪ˀ *hwui*ˀ From *silk* and to *assemble*; occurs used for the last.

To embroider or adorn in colors; to draw, to paint, to sketch; to make a plan; colored, painted; in conjunction, as the sun and moon.

丨畫 to draw and paint.

丨地圖 to draw a map.

丨像 to paint portraits.

丨事後素 the limning comes after the outline ground has been prepared.

暳ˀ *hwui*ˀ From *sun* and a *besom*; occurs used with the next.

Small stars which cannot be distinguished clearly; star-dust; fine, minute, but distinct.

嘒ˀ *hwui*ˀ A shrill, stridulous sound, as of a cicada; a soft, low melodious voice; a quick sound; in harmony or tune, as several voices or instruments; fine; delicate but distinct, as the stars.

丨丨和鳴 the two birds sing in concert.

丨彼小星 that pretty little star; said of a girl.

丨丨然 a sweet melody, as several flutes or small bells.

有丨其星 brilliant are its sparkling stars.

慧ˀ *hwui*ˀ From *heart* and a *comet* as the phonetic.

Perspicacious, intelligent; ingenious, clever, quickwitted; adroit, sharp; wisdom, sagacity; in epitaphs, denotes one who receives reproofs mildly.

敏丨 discerning, sagacious.

聰丨 or 靈丨 lucid; an instant perception of.

有丨性 he has a bright mind.

小丨 dextrous, skillful, handy.

美而丨 beautiful and witty.

丨根 in Budhism, the organ of wisdom in the soul (*pradj-nendrya*).

丨力 denotes its power (*pradjna-bala*).

恚ˀ *hwui*ˀ Rage, anger; to hate, to dislike; to be angry at; irritated, indignant, angry.

丨恨 angry and hating one.

丨怒 in a towering passion.

抵床而丨 he beat the bed in his anger.

⿰山廻ˀ *hwui*ˀ A hill bare of trees and grass; a barren, rocky hill.

潰ˀ *kwʻéi*ˀ From *water* and *honorable* as the phonetic; occurs used for the next.

A stream overflowing its banks, or rushing through a crevasse or waste-weir; to separate; dispersed, broken; a flight, a rout; defeated; driving surges; enraged, hasty.

丨濩 dashing waves.

丨敗 the river banks are burst; miscarried, unlucky; defeated.

丨敗決裂 the disagreement is irreconcileable.

紛紛丨散 completely routed.

淹丨 soaked, so as to be spoiled.

是用不丨于成 it will not meet your expectations if you use it.

丨亂 not in order; seditious; raging, as a mob.

頮ˀ **靧**ˀ *hwui*ˀ To wash the face; one adds, when dying.

王乃洮丨水 the prince then washed his face.

闠ˀ *hwui*ˀ From *gate* and *honorable*.

The outer gate of a market; the street leading to a bazaar.

通闤帶丨 the thoroughfares through the market.

嬇ʾ *hwuiʾ* A woman, 女丨 of ancient times who bore six sons by the parts being 坼剖 rent and cut open, by the Cæsarian operation; (?) she is said to have been the younger sister of 鬼方氏 of the Tsu country.

殨ʾ *hwuiʾ* To open a sore; broken, as an ulcer.
瘡丨 the boil has broken.
通身丨爛 the whole body is covered with running sores.

瞶ʾ *hwuiʾ* Eyes nearly gone, dull sighted; scarcely able to see, as very old people.
盲丨 sightless.
昏丨 dim vision, sight blurred and weak.

喙ʾ *hwuiʾ* From *mouth* and *pig*.
A beak, a bill; a snout; to pant, to breathe hurriedly.
丨息 to rest and breathe.
困丨 wearied, as a dog from running; panting, as from heat.
維其丨矣 startled and panting, — they fled.
無從置丨 there's no need of putting in your word; *i. e.* what can you say that will equal him?

諱ʾ *hwuiʾ* From *words* and *refractory* as the phonetic.
To shun; to deny; to avoid using from a sense of respect for, as the Jews did from mentioning the ineffable Name; to honor by concealing their faults; to hide from; to keep a respectful silence upon; name of the manes in the ancestral hall, given it by the eldest son, and used when the family sacrifices to their ancestors; forbidden, tabooed.
忌丨 prohibit or shun the use of sacred names.
犯丨 to heedlessly use sacred names.
丨名不丨姓 respect another's given name, but use his surname.
以丨事神 worship their manes by their posthumous titles.
爲親者丨 hide the errors of your relatives.
隱丨 to cover a fault by not bruiting it.
不丨 not dead, still living.
丨法 rules for applying names to deceased persons; sometimes made in great families.
請教官丨 I beg to ask your official or honored name?
直認不丨 don't deny, confess it all; make a full disclosure.
你先父尊丨 what is your father's temple style?
丨言 forbidden talk; not to be mentioned.
避丨 avoid sacred names, as the emperor's 聖丨 personal name; this is strictly observed, and often extends even to characters where it occurs as the primitive; this practice during the course of Chinese history has modified only a few characters, and most of them unusual, but it has altered the meanings of many which were substituted for the sacred name; when the dynasty is changed, this respect is no longer observed.

The following are the personal names of the eight Manchu sovereigns, with their changed forms, or the words which have been substituted; the first was formed of characters so much in use that they were left unaltered.

Shunchi, 福臨 was left unaltered.
Kanghi, 玄燁 was altered to 玄熀 or 元燁
Yungching, 胤禛 was altered to 亂禛 or 允禛
Kienlung, 宏曆 was altered to 宏歷
Kiak'ing, 顒琰 was altered to 顒琰 or 永琰
Taokwang, 旻寧 was altered to 旻寕 or 綿寕
Hienfung, 奕詝 was altered to 奕詝
Tungchi, 載淳 was altered to 載湻

噦ʾ 譓ʾ *hwuiʾ* From *mouth* or *words* and *year*; the first is usually read *yueh*, but is regarded as a synonym of the second when read *hwuiʾ*.
A prolonged sound, as of an approaching carriage; the hum of many people; spacious and light, as a mansion; one says the beard or the jaw.
丨丨 cries of pheasants, tinkling of horses' bells, rumbling of carriages, &c.
丨丨其冥 the farthest corners of the house were light.

翽ʾ *hwuiʾ* The sound of a phœnix; the noise of a flock of birds.
丨丨其羽 [the phœnix] clapped its wings.

HWUH.

See also HUH *for other similar sounds. Old sounds,* mot *and* mat. *In Canton,* făt ; — *in Swatow,* hút ; — *in Amoy,* hút *or* hwut ; — *in Fuhchau,* hwòk ; — *in Shanghai,* hweh, weh, *and* feh ; — *in Chifu,* hu.

忽 ˏhu From *heart* and *pennon ; q. d.* the mind like a fluttering streamer.

To forget, to disregard, to slight ; to exhaust, to terminate ; as an *adverb,* suddenly, unexpectedly, abruptly ; instantly, all at once ; in notation, the fifth place in fractions, the hundred thousandth, likened to the tenth part of a floss of silk.

丨有人來 just then a man came.

輕丨 to make little of ; to treat cavalierly, to slight.

是絕是丨 [its sacrifices were] abolished and its existence ended ; said of a state.

丨略 forgetful of ; careless.

丨然 or 丨然間 suddenly, in a moment.

丨丨一年 how quickly the year has come and gone.

丨明丨滅 it appeared and disappeared quickly.

丨必忘懷 totally careless and forgetful ; absent-minded.

絲丨之間 the minutest space ; an instant of time, a twinkling.

㧾 ˏhu From *hand* and *abruptly* as the phonetic.

To slap, to tap ; to bale out, to clean up ; to push.

丨水 to bale water, to dip it up.

丨斗 a dust-pan, a dirt-board.

惚 ˏhu Abstruse, inexplicable ; minute, preventing the mind from deciding, as a subtle point in metaphysics.

恍丨不能辨 anything fine and obscure, so that it cannot be discriminated ; the mind so startled that it cannot clearly discern and decide.

囫 ˏhu Round, entire ; whole, said of fruits.

丨圇 or 渾侖 complete in all its parts ; in syntax, the summation of an argument.

丨圇的衣服 a new, complete suit, such as a child first puts on.

丨圇吞下 he swallowed it whole, — as a date ; a careless, rough way of doing things.

笏 ˏhu From *bamboo* and *a square* with lines, afterward altered to *pennon.*

A tablet nearly three feet long, made of ivory, gem, wood, or bamboo, held before the breast by courtiers at audiences, even down to the Ming dynasty ; it was first designed for taking notes on.

執丨 or 正丨 to hold the tablet ; *i. e.* to be a statesman.

家無象丨 there is no ivory tablet in this family ; — we have never held office ; plebeian.

牙丨 ivory tablets used by Taoists.

In *Fuhchau.* A cake or block of ink ; 墨一丨 one cake of ink.

縠 huˀ Fine silk gauze or open-worked silk.

丨粟 a sort of woven gauze of corded thread, crossed and knotted, so as to resemble millet seeds on the surface.

春水丨紋生 the placid water ripples into silken lines.

紗丨 heavy gauze.

羅丨 thin, coarse law.

HWUN.

Old sounds, hwun, kwun, *and* gwun. *In Canton,* wăn *and* făn ; — *in Swatow,* hún ; — *in Amoy,* hún ; — *in Fuhchau,* hwòng *and* hung ; — *in Shanghai,* hwăng *and* wăng ; — *in Chifu,* hwun.

昏 ˏhwun From 日 *sun* and 氐 *descending* contracted to 氏 a name ; one old form is composed of 日 *sun* placed below 民 *people,* as if intimating cessation of a day's work.

Dusk, twilight, which is called 代明 or substituted brightness ; the sun below the horizon ; to be dark ; benighted ; evening ; obscure, confused, dull ; in disorder ; to oblige one to do ; to marry a wife, for which the next is used ; a wife ; affinity ; relatives ; to die before being married.

黃丨 the gloaming ; dusk.

說話不明猶如丨鏡 indefinite talk is like a misty mirror.

丨暗 dark ; late ; cloudy, dull.

丨亂 in confusion, as from a multiplicity of affairs ; dim, as the vision ; disordered.

定丨 or 丨夜 night ; very dark.

丨花 motes in the eyes ; *muscæ volitantes.*

丨碧 a despot, a tyrant ; a niggardly husband.

丨腦 addle-pated, dull ; disliking, vexed at, but saying nothing.

丨頭搭腦 muddled, forgetful.

丨昧 growing dark; unintelligible, as talk.

丨邁 very old, said of one who leans on a staff.

不丨作勞 don't exert yourself beyond your strength.

利令志丨 gain has blinded his better judgment.

利慾丨心 avarice and passion blind the heart.

宴爾新丨 I wish you joy on your marriage.

丨丨睡熟 sleeping soundly.

晨丨定省 morning and evening inquire after — your parents' health.

終日丨丨 drunk all day long.

婚 ˏhwun From *woman* and *dusk*; because anciently the wedding took place in the evening, when the bride came to the house.

A bridegroom, a husband; to marry a wife, the opposite of 嫁; a wife's connections; relatives.

丨姻 marriage; matrimonial affairs.

合丨, and 成丨, and 完丨, denote successively to compare the horoscopes, to exchange the presents, and to consummate the nuptials.

連丨 to marry relatives.

皇上大丨 an emperor's marriage.

丨書 the marriage contract, said of a girl whose first betrothed died.

後丨 or 後丨兒 a second wife, who is herself a widow.

賣丨 to purchase a marriage alliance; it is often merely to advance funds for the bride's trousseau.

結丨 or 丨配 or 同丨 to contract a marriage.

拴丨之大臣 an officer who arranges the Emperor's marriage and those of his immediate relatives.

指腹爲丨 to betroth children before birth; the practice is known in southern China.

惛 / **㥵** ˏhwun From *heart* and *obscure*; the second form is preferred.

The perceptions confused; stupid, forgetful, dull.

心丨 forgetful.

丨耄 lost his memory, old.

丨悶 grieved and vexed at, but unable to express one's self.

丨迷不醒 dull-headed; incoherent.

睧 ˏhwun Dull eyes; mind set on one object and unable to appreciate others.

莫丨於勢利 don't dote on power and gain.

閽 ˏhwun From *gate* and *dusk* as the phonetic.

To shut the door at eventide; a porter of the palace.

叩丨 to knock at the gate; *i. e.* to present an urgent petition.

丨人 a gate-keeper to a prince or grandee.

丨閹 or 丨寺 eunuchs who keep the palace harem.

晨丨啟閉 to open the gate at morning and shut it at even.

殙 ˏhwun The dimness of death coming on; dim-sighted; to kill by taking gold; to die without fame.

涽 ˏhwun Unsettled.

丨丨 unstable; also applied to muddy water.

葷 ˏhwun From *plant* and *army*; see the next.

Strong smelling vegetables, as onions, leeks, rue, garlic, &c., which, with five kinds of meat, *viz.*, that of the horse, dog, cow, goose, and pigeon, are all forbidden to those who fast; all meat or vegetable food not included in the list of fast-day dishes is so called, and 素 is the term for other kinds.

不茹丨 [when fasting,] do not eat meat.

丨腥 strong odors, as of cooked meat.

二丨鋪 small eating shops, little stalls for selling food.

大丨館 a restaurant for selling spirits, meats, &c.

那隻猫兒不吃丨 where's the cat that don't eat meat? — everybody seeks his own interest.

腪 ˏhwun Used with the preceding.

Meat which must not be eaten on fast days; strong flesh.

犬五丨 the five kinds of meats, that of the horse, ox, dog, pigeon, and wild goose, which are regarded as strong.

渾 ˏhwun From *water* and *army* as the phonetic; also interchanged with ˋhwun 混 in some senses.

A roaring torrent; the noise of many waters; vast; turbid, polluted; sordid, dirty, and used as a term of reproach; chaotic, confused, blended; the whole, the mass, entire; even, uniform.

丨天球 a celestial globe.

丨濁 turbid, foul; whence the Yung-ting R. near Peking gets its common name of 丨河 or Muddy River.

丨家 my wife; — a depreciating term.

丨厚人 one who feels his incompetency.

丨人 a stupid lout, an owl of a fellow.

丨身冷寒 my whole body is chilled through.

肧丨 undistinguishable, as a fœtus a month old; formless, undeveloped.

丨沌 confused, disordered.

丨敦 simple and unlearned, as the peasantry.

丨元之氣 confused vapors, as at the creation.

天下一丨 the empire was under one sway.

丨 淆 confused, mixed up, muddy.
丨 然 天 理 he is quite muddled, his mind is imbecile.
丨 然 一 新 all is now as if new; times will now prosper.
丨 化 careless, not paying much attention to.
丨 成 in the gross; lumping; no order or completeness.

Read *kw'un*. To circulate, as goods; to roll on continuously.
財 貨 丨 丨 如 泉 源 riches flowed in on him like a running fountain.

婫 *ˏhwun* An appellation of a woman.
丨 家 my wife, my good woman.

鼲 *ˏhwun* A sort of marmot (*Arctomys marmorta*), also called 黄 鼠 the yellow rat from its color, which sits before its burrow in warm weather; it rubs its neck on seeing people, and reënters its hole, from which habit it is called 拱 鼠 the bowing rat, and 禮 鼠 the polite rat.

琿 *ˏhwun* A fine stone, a pretty gem; this character is often used for given names.
碧 丨 a green serpentine.

餛 **餫** *ˏhwun* From *wood* and *mixed* or *army* as the phonetic.
Flat or round balls of pork called 丨 飩 which are fried in a gravy of fat, soy, and onions, then rolled in flour and steamed; a sort of fritter cakes; the second also means provisions for soldiers on a march; to present a sheep to one.
只 一 百 丨 飩 吃 過 九 十 九 還 勿 曉 得 葷 腥 素 [like a man who] eats all but one in a hundred fritters, and then asks what they are made of; — so is he who does a job, and then asks how; an incompetent, conceited man.

倱 *ˏhwun* Completed, brought to an end.
朕 實 不 明 以 丨 伯 父 We certainly do not see why Our uncle was so finished.

魂 *ˏhwun* From *demon* and *vapor*; the Taiping rebels changed this character into 伝 in order to purify its meaning and elevate the idea of soul.

The shade, the manes, the spiritual part of the ghost which ascends, and is supposed to proceed from the *yang* principle; the Taoists say that there are three ghosts 三 丨, proceeding from the feelings, the breath, and the spirits; the mind, the wits, the faculties.
丨 魄 the manes, the departed soul, which then becomes a 鬼 δαιμόν.
失 丨 he has lost his wits.
引 丨 or 招 丨 to invite the spirit to come; this is done when one dies abroad.
鈎 生 丨 to hook live ghosts, is to invoke demons; it also refers to a custom of placing a corked vase in a bridge when building to prevent it ever falling.
丨 夢 I dreamed of seeing a ghost.
靈 丨 the spiritual soul; — a foreign term.
丨 不 守 舍 or 丨 不 在 身 he is out of his mind; he is terrified out of his wits.
神 丨 出 現 his ghost has appeared.
丨 氣 無 不 至 the soul is not confined to any place.
游 丨 or 孤 丨 an orbate spirit, one which has no one left to worship it.
冤 丨 不 息 or 冤 丨 不 散 the unrevenged ghost will not be quiet; murder cries for vengeance.
回 丨 the soul returns to the tablet — before the 49th day.
嚇 掉 了 丨 兒 you have scared me out of my senses; a bogie to frighten children.
萬 物 之 丨 丨 the vast variety of created things.

忶 **惃** *ˏhwun* The mind full of sorrow; melancholy, vaporish, out of spirits.
丨 濁 悶 陵 a thick-headed dolt who has no feeling.

焜 *ʻhwun* From *fire* and *confused*; it is also read *ˏkwun*.
Fire, the flame of fire; bright.
丨 燿 blazing.
火 丨 丨 而 上 蒸 the lambent flame curled upwards.

混 *hwunʾ* From *water* and *confused*; it is often synonymous with *ˏhwun* 渾 and the next.
Turbid, roiled, as a torrent; a chaos of waters and sky; foul, mixed, ill-assorted; disorderly; heedlessly, promiscuously, dark, underhand.
丨 閙 confused clamor.
丨 世 界 a troublesome world; this and 丨 世 虫 also mean a fellow who does nothing for his living, a ne'er-do-well.
男 女 丨 雜 men and women mixed together.
丨 名 a nickname, an alias.
丨 沌 or 丨 丨 沌 沌 all confusion; unintelligible, irretrievably mixed up.
丨 手 子 or 丨 星 子 roughs, rowdies, loafers, street Arabs.
打 丨 to confuse; to do slightingly, to slur over.
丨 來 to do out of order, to intrude into another's duty or post.
丨 賬 東 西 you foolish thing! you piece of stupidity!
丨 說 a rigmarole; foolish talk.
畏 刑 丨 認 to confess anything from fear of torture.
丨 揑 to implicate others by false statements.
濛 丨 or 丨 充 to deceive, to throw dust in one's eyes; to simulate.
含 丨 inconsiderate, careless.
丨 堂 a bath-house where the great unwashed bathe.

丨着去 he went without an invitation.

丨元一氣 the three original powers unitedly acting.

In *Cantonese.* To make game of, to overreach, to diddle; to importune, to trouble.

莫丨我 don't play off your fun on me.

In *Pekingese.* To resist, to throw off, not to yield to; to work; to do.

丨睏兒 to strive against drowsiness.

咱們一塊兒丨事 we are engaged in work at the same place.

溷 *hwun'* From *water* and a *sty*; it is similar to the preceding.

Confused, dirty, turbid; unclean, as animals; filthy, foul, as a sewer; a privy, a jakes.

世丨濁 the times are in confusion.

丨餘 unclean animals, as dogs and hogs which eat garbage.

攪丨 to roil; muddied.

懵丨 disordered, confounded; obscure, as one's perceptions.

別丨插言 don't rudely interrupt people.

藩丨 a retiring-place, a spot fenced off.

搵 *hwun'* To push with the hand; to take up with tongs or pincers.

諢 *hwun'* From *words* and *army*; *q.d.* low army talk.

Vulgar mirth, low jests, broad allusions, sportive trifling.

打丨 to joke, to dally with.

丨衣 a harlequin dress, a robe with obscene drawings.

丨言 scurrilous jests.

優丨 a jester, a buffon, a court fool.

慁 慁 *hwun'* From *mind* and a *sty* as the phonetic.

To incommode, to excite, to disturb; to dishonor, to disgrace, to distress, to mortify, to bring reproach on one; grieved, ashamed, mortified.

造丨 to incommode.

不敢丨命 I dare not disobey his orders.

主不丨賓 the host must not mortify his guest.

心丨不釋 my grief is unbearable.

丨君 to dishonor one's ruler.

常常有之未始以爲丨也 common custom makes it to be regarded as not disgraceful.

掍 *hwun'* The same as, similar; to make alike; to inlay, as with ivory; to combine; to root up.

丨連 connected throughout, as a suite of buildings.

I.

Old sounds, i, it, ik, ngi, ngit, ip, ai, at, *and* ap. *In Canton*, i, ngei, wei, yei, yui, *and* ai; — *in Swatow*, i, iⁿ, úi, ngi, gi, goi, ngai, hia, *and* chi; — *in Amoy*, i, iⁿ, é, gi, ki, *and* ngaiⁿ; — *in Fuhchau*, i, é, ié, ngi, ngie, ngè, mi, yò *and* hé; — *in Shanghai*, i *and* ni; — *in Chifu*, i.

衣 衤 *i* The original form is designed to represent two *men* under a *cover*; it forms the 145th radical of a large and natural group of characters relating to garments; when written at the left side as in the second form, it resembles 礻 the contracted form of the 113th radical.

Clothes for the upper part of the body; garments; a cover, a husk, as on nuts; a case of any kind.

丨服 or 丨裳 garments; a dress.

一套 (or 一副) 丨服 one suit of clothes.

小丨 or 內丨 inner garments.

大丨 or 外丨 outer garments.

穿丨 or 着丨 to dress; to put on clothes.

丨繡夜行 in his embroidered robes he goes by night; — said of an over modest but thorough scholar.

睡丨 or 寢丨 sleeping clothes.

青丨 black jackets; a term for lictors and official runners.

白丨 commoners, scholars who have not yet graduated.

無丨食 beggared, suffering; wasteful, heedless.

丨冠 in full dress, cap and all; *i. e.* well-dressed.

成丨店 a tailor's shop.

丨冠禽獸 [you are no whit better than] a dressed up beast, — so cruel are you.

丨不稱體身之災也 garments which do not befit one are the body's misfortune; — clothes cannot adorn a villain.

號丨 a uniform; Chinese soldiers have characters on the breast and back to show their corps.

燒丨節 festival of Burning Clothes, the 冥丨, for wandering ghosts, is held three days on the middle of the 7th moon, when they are supposed to be thus rescued from suffering.

Read *i'* To dress; to wear; to cover another with garments.

解丨丨'之 take off your coat and put it on him.

丨'錦尙絅 to dress in brocade and over it a plain dress.

依 *ₒi* From *man* and *clothes; q. d.* clothes lean on the man.

To rely on, to trust to; to conform to, the opposite of 違; to accede to; as a *preposition*, according to, as; like; imagery, illustration.

違丨 compliant, willing.

不丨你 I cannot agree with you.

丨言 as you say; according to the expression.

丨然一式 in the same way, as usual, as before.

丨然故我 I am just in the same place; I am the same old fellow.

丨稀 similar; very nearly the same.

丨稀之間 shortly, in a little while; nearly exact.

丨稀彷彿 the resemblance is considerable.

無所丨 or 無丨無靠 nothing to depend on; no resource, as an orphan.

丨議 according to the consultation; let it be as it was discussed.

丨丨不'舍 unable to part from; I cannot let you go.

瞻丨膝下 fondly looking up to, as a child does to its mother.

不丨呈控 he did not care about complaining to the rulers.

丨生木下 its habitat is under trees, as a plant.

博丨 illustrations, metaphors.

惟德是丨 he regards nothing but his virtue.

思慕丨人 to fondly regard one.

楊柳丨丨 the swaying willows are young and green.

無憑丨 no evidence to go by, nothing to depend on.

丨實說 undoubted; the report can be relied on.

In *Cantonese*. An *adverb*, well, just.

丨喇 well then; supposing, if he likes.

伊 *ₒi* From *man* and *faithful;* occurs used for the next two.

A personal pronoun, he, she, it, that one, —mostly used along the valley of the Yangtsz'; occasionally used impersonally for I, the party speaking; an initial particle, because, that, only.

是丨勿是丨 is it he or not?

所謂丨人 that very man of whom I spake.

丨誰云何 what was it that man said?

丨等 they, those.

丨塊地方 that place. (*Shanghai.*)

丨年 that year.

與丨相好 [I tell you] I am quite intimate with him.

丨邇 presently, soon.

丨尹 I Yin, a famous minister of T'ang the Successful, B. C. 1760.

丨犂 the province of Ili or Chinese Turkestan.

洢 *ₒi* A stream, the 丨河 or 丨水 a branch of the River Loh, spoken of in the Shu King, which rises in Shen cheu, and flows northeast about a hundred miles, joining the main stream at Yen-shi hien 偃師縣 in Honan fu in the west of that province.

蛜 *ₒi* The sow-bug (*Oniscus*) found under stones and in damp places.

丨蝛在室 the sow-bugs have got into the house.

咿 **吚** *ₒi* The sound of giddy laughter is 丨啞; the first when read *hi*, means to moan.

喔丨嚅唲 forced laughter; dalliance, trifling with women.

丨唔不輟 his hum never stops; —he studies all the time.

丨唔哎呀 alack! alas! dreadful!

噫 *ₒi* The tone of regretful indignation, surprise, or pain; groaning, moaning; for shame, alas! to belch.

丨噎 to eructate.

丨嘻 admirable! used as a word of earnest exhortation, and also ironically.

大塊丨氣 the breathing of nature —is termed wind.

譩 *ₒi* Similar to the last.

To dislike; a cry of pain, grief, or anger.

丨譆 the name of a bird found in Hupeh, for which many synonyms are given, and whose brief description seems to denote a sort of goatsucker or night-hawk.

禕 *ₒi* Excellent; to admire a thing for its beauty; precious, rare, like a pearl.

堅 *ₒi* From *earth* and a *screen* as the phonetic.

Dirt, dust; particles of earth.

翳 *ₒi* From *feathers* and a *screen*, denoting the purpose and material; it occurs interchanged with the next.

A fan or screen made of peacock's or pheasant's feathers, a flabellum; to overshadow, to screen or intercept; a thing that intercepts, as an arbor; to seclude from observation; to keep close, to repress; to destroy; a dimness in the eyes, like that caused by pterygium; trees withering away; a gay colored bird like a phœnix.

蔭丨 a dense shade.

隱丨 to hide away.

障丨 to screen off.

一層丨子 a film over the eyes

媒丨 a target for archery practice.

In *Cantonese*. Feverish, hot; sultry; hurried or asthmatic breathing; a stricture across the lungs.

丨氣 hard of breathing.

身子丨熱 the body is hot and feverish.

曀 ꜀i From *sun* and *one*; it is also read *yeh*, and interchanged with the last.

The sun hidden by clouds; windy and cloudy; to obscure by clouds.

陰丨 obscure, gloomy.

夜丨 a gusty night.

終風且丨 the wintry winds are blowing and the sky is dark.

風雲丨日光 the windy clouds intercept the sunlight.

丨丨其陰 cloudy and dark is the sky.

醫 医 ꜀i From *spirits* and *screen*; it is very often wrongly contracted to the second form in cheap books.

To heal, to cure; a physician; healing; medical; to drink.

丨生 or 丨士 a doctor.

神丨 a skillful physician.

時丨 a fashionable doctor.

包丨 to promise or assure a cure.

丨藥 healing medicines.

庸丨殺人 charlatans kill people.

太丨院 the Medical Board; its head is the court physician, who is 丨師 a medical grandee.

丨治不效 the treatment produces no good results.

延丨罔效 to invite many docters will effect no cure.

丨家 or 丨門 the medical profession.

行丨 to practice medicine.

施丨院 or 丨館 a hospital.

行丨 to practice medicine.

世丨 a family of physicians.

獸丨 a veterinary doctor.

無藥丨 there's no medicine to heal — such a runagate.

丨不來 incurable.

繄 ꜀i From *silk* and *screen*.

In classsical use, an interjection; a reddish black or blue-black color; a case for a spear's head.

丨袼 a child's bib or apron.

爾有母遺丨我獨無 you have still a mother to nourish; alas! I have none left.

鷖 ꜀i From *bird* and *screen*.

A bird resembling the tern, with blue and white plumage, that frequents the shore, and foretokens a storm by flying inland; a sort of duck, which flies in flocks; used with 鷖, denoting a fabulous bird of great size and beauty.

鳧丨在涇 the ducks and widgeons are on the River King.

蠮 ꜀i The solitary wasp, the 丨螉 or sphex, probably so named from the hum of its wings; the Chinese have the idea that it rears its young from worms.

蘙 ꜀i Name of a plant.

丨薈 luxuriant herbage, as plants growing in a jungle.

欭 ꜀i The hesitating sound made by many speakers before saying the next word, half a stutter; a sigh, or short breath interrupting the word.

猗 欹 ꜀i From *dog* or to *breathe* and *remarkable*; it is a synonym of 兮, and the second form is unusual.

A fierce, robust dog; to depend on, or be near each other, as two horses drawing together; to pull aside; an interjection of pleasure, bravo! good! well! extended, continuous.

丨重較兮 behold the high banked chariot!

丨與那與 or 丨歟休哉 Ah! how fine that is! how complete and elegant!

丨嗟 an interjection, like alas for! ah!

丨氏縣 a district in Pu-cheu fu in the southwest of Shansi on the River Făn.

Read ꜀wo. Pliant, as the mulberry; limber, lithe.

丨儺其枝 he folded and bent the twigs.

綠竹丨丨 how beautiful and fresh are the green bamboos!

犄 ꜀i Also read ꜀k'i, and used for the last.

A large ox with divergent, awkward horns; to rely on, to help; long, extended; to bestow, to give.

丨角之勢 one side helps the other; they keep each other in countenance.

坐在丨角 sit in the corner.

漪 ꜀i The ripples or curling lines made on water by a breeze, which are compared to brocading it.

丨瀾漣漾 rippling and curling as it flows on.

旖 ꜀i The tremulous waving of a banner is 丨旎; also applied to the easy motion of a girl, or the sailing of clouds.

丨旎從風 the pennons flutter to the breeze.

陭 ꜀i Projecting, as a headland.

丨嶇 rugged, steep, like a cape.

丨氏阪 the dyke of the I family, a village in Yoh-yang hien 岳陽縣 in Ping-yang fu in Shansi.

黟 ꜀i From *black* and *many*.

Black and shining; a black sort of wood, probably a kind of ebony.

丨縣 a district north of Hwui-cheu fu in the south part of Nganhwui, famed for its ink.

宜 宐 ᶜi — This character was originally composed of 宀 a *covert* over 一 *one*, with 多 *many* between them; the second is a common form, and retains most of the original shape.

That which is of itself reasonable; fit and right; harmonious, accordant, compatible; proper, it meets the conditions, just suits; ought, should, and is often merely a form of the imperative mood; to order aright; to make fit; harmony, accord; name of a sacrifice to earth; occurs used for i² 誼 fit; frequent in proper names.

丨其家室 ordering well her house and home.

與子丨之丨言飲酒 I will dress them for you, and when well done, we will drink.

不丨有怨 let not angry passions rise.

便' 丨 or 便'當 convenient, serviceable; according to circumstances; at will, as in 便丨行事 to do as one pleases.

ᶜ便丨' cheap, low price.

貪小便丨' to covet little advantages, to want more than one's part.

丨乎不丨 is it right or not? will this do?

丨此 proper; fit for this use.

應丨恭敬 you ought to reverence him.

各得其丨 each one in his place.

不相丨 unsuitable, unfitting; not his place.

合丨 well done; just; suitable, as a dish for an invalid.

不合時丨 old fashioned; a fogy; behind the age.

丨其事也 [the day] is a lucky one for that affair.

花柳丨人 the [green] willows and flowers delight people.

丨春 may it always be spring weather, or genial times with you; — a phrase before doors.

妻封丨人 his wife has been made a lady of the fifth rank.

輗 ᶜi — From *carriage* and *child* as the phonetic.

The center of a yoke; a cross-bar to which the animals are fastened when drawing the carriage; this and the 軏 were similar in use, but the latter was the smallest; they served for the whipple-tree.

大車無丨 if a wain be without its cross-bar, — how can it be drawn?

猊 ᶜi ᶜni — From *dog* and *child*; in Fuhchau, this is used metaphorically for 倪 precise, excessively strict.

A fabulous beast like a lion, the 狻丨, which can devour even tigers, and go swiftly, 500 *li* at a jump; it has red eyes.

麑 ᶜi ᶜni — A fawn; the last is also written like this.

素衣丨裘 plain garments and deer-skin robes.

蜺 ᶜi ᶜni — An insect like the cicada, small, and of a greenish-black color; used for the next, because the rainbow is thought to be composed of insects, but strictly applied to the inner and secondary bow.

嬰丨 an insect that lodges in the ears of deer.

霓 ᶜi ᶜni — From *rain* and *child* as the phonetic; interchanged with the last.

Colored clouds shaped like a dragon; *i. e.* the rainbow, — specially the secondary one, called the female; variegated, colored.

虹丨 the rainbow.

有雲丨之望 [I long for your face,] as we hope for rain clouds — in times of drought.

彩丨 variegated, as the clouds.

丨現雨止 the rain stops when the rainbow is seen.

若大旱之望雲丨也 [it is as hopeless] as looking for a rainbow in dry weather.

霆丨 a clap of thunder.

丨裳羽衣 ornamented dresses worn by ancient court musicians in the T'ang dynasty; now applied to certain songs.

郳 ᶜi ᶜ'rh — A tributary state of the Cheu emperors, also known as 丨郲; it was situated in the present T'ăng hien in 滕縣 the south of Shantung near the Grand Canal; an envoy from its ruler came to court in the days of Confucius.

鯢 ᶜi ᶜni — From *fish* and *child*, because it is said to cry like a child.

A hairy marine animal, a species of dugong or lamantin, which the Chinese say can climb trees, and in times of drought hide itself in a nest near the bank to catch birds that come to drink; it is also called 人魚 the man-fish, from its likeness to human beings.

丨鮒 minnows, small fish.

鯨丨 a whale; *met.* an oppressor, a Verres, a big fish which swallows little ones.

倪 ᶜi ᶜni — From *man* and *child*; it occurs used for ᶜi 睨 to peep.

Little, feeble like children; the young and delicate; a limit, a verge, the edge; to benefit; to distinguish; to glance at.

俾丨 to look askance.

端丨 embryonic, the beginning of; the least point, strict to a hair, exacting; decorous, grave.

反其旄丨 he sent back the young and the decrepit.

天丨 the verge of heaven.

左丨右丨 he glanced to the right and left.

齯 ᶜi ᶜni — To cut teeth in old age.

黃髮丨齒 the hoary headed man has cut his second teeth.

酏 ꜀i Arrack; sweet spirits, clear and pure; to drink; a sort of broth strained from congee.

甘 | sweet wine.

粉 | cakes made from bean flour and fried.

移 ꜀i 迻 ꜀i From *grain* or to *go*, and *many*.

Shoots leaning on each other; to transplant; to move, to shift, to transpose; to change the place or direction of; to transmit, to dispatch; to convey, as an infection; to migrate, to remove; to graft; to praise; to display; great.

| 開 move it off; move aside.

| 近 or | 埋 move it nearer.

| 文 to forward a dispatch.

| 寬就近 to move nearer for convenience; to accommodate one with a timely loan.

挪 | to move elsewhere; also to borrow a thing.

| 玉 to invite a friend to an entertainment.

| 借 to get the loan of, to borrow money.

寸步難 | I cannot get away a step, — I am so busy.

不能更 | it cannot be altered.

| 花接木 to graft flowers on a tree.

| 禍他人 to shift a charge to another, to secretly lay a crime elsewhere.

| 風易俗莫善於樂 to improve the public morals, there is nothing better than music.

| 尸 to lay a corpse at another's door, — in order to involve him.

不延 | not a great while.

事莫 | 脫 don't neglect that affair.

一轉 | 間 to pay [a debt] over to a third through a second person.

遺臭萬年 it will take ten thousand years to wipe away the disgrace.

不 | 言 I will not alter a word, I adhere to what I said.

扅 ꜀i From *door* and *many;* occurs written like the last.

The bar of a gate, which is sometimes a great beam inserted into the walls.

烹伏雌炊扊 | 汝不記當時 do you forget when I boiled my last hen with the door-bar for firewood, — to give you a meal? said of Peh Li-hi's 百里奚 wife, after he had risen to office; it is now used as a metaphor for extreme poverty.

誃 ꜀i A side door by which people conveniently went in and out of a large court or palace; it had a covered porch.

| 門曲榭 a side gate and a winding passage.

栘 ꜀i A fruit tree with whitish bark, the 枎 | or 夫 | (*Aronia asiatica*); it is allied to the apple or crab, and grows in Nganhwui.

| 楊 a variety of the aspen or poplar; as 扶 | is the name of another kind, the *Populus tremula;* both are found in Hupeh.

匜 ꜀i From a *receptacle* and a *dish;* it was first the primitive alone, but that having come into use as a particle, the radical was added.

A wash-basin with a tubular handle to let the water run off; a dish with a partition into which the dirty water runs.

卮 | a vessel contrived for heating spirits; it is a sort of portable urn with fire beneath; a wine heater.

奉盤 | he presented the wash-basin.

盥 | a large wash-bowl.

訑 ꜀i An arrgoant self-sufficiency, like that of one who knows it all; shallow-minded; to look down on, to brag over, to insult; verbose.

| 自得 overbearing, assuming.

慢 | proud and mean.

| | 之聲音顏色 a tone and air of perfect satisfaction.

貤 ꜀i A gradation or series rising one above another, as of weights, hills, storeys, generations, &c.; to advance, to promote, to reward the worthy; to superimpose; to move; advantage.

| 贈 to present; gifts, as from the emperor.

分 | 各物 distribute the things according to rank.

益 | to increase by steps or seriatim.

一 | one grade; one strata.

| 封三代 ennobled his ancestors for three generations.

乺 ꜀i An obsolete word, used only as a primitive in combination.

It was originally applied to some of the wild aborigines of Kwangtung.

猗 | name of a king of Wei 魏 about A. D. 530, who reigned in Shensi.

迤 ꜀i To go at the side; to walk awkwardly; extending, reaching, as a road.

逶 | self-sufficient swagger.

| 邐千頃 to travel on, going along for thousands of acres.

| 南 going south; towards the south.

岮 ꜀i A long and low ridge is 崺 |, applied to it as one sees it from a distance.

暆 ꜀i From *sun* and to *change.*

The course of the sun in the heavens, as it begins to go down.

日行 | | the sun is now declining.

椸 ꜀i From *wood* and to *change* as the phonetic.

A clothes-horse or frame.

男女不同 | 架 the sexes must not use the same clothes-rack.

檠 | to put the night-lamp on the stand.

沂 ꜀i Name of a river in the southeast of Sangtung, which rises in 丨山 a part of the Tʻai-shan range near the center of the province, and runs south into Lake Loh-ma in Kiangsu, and thence into the sea.

丨州府 a prefecture in its valley, which was the scene of many historical events.

沶 ꜀i A small tributary of the River Han in I-ching hien 宜城縣 in the northwest of Hupeh.

Read *shiʾ* or *kʻiʾ* A town, 丨鄉 formerly in Yun-yang fu in Hupeh, now called Fang hien 房縣 lying on the River Făn, a branch of the River Han.

Read ꜀*chi.* A bank or dyke.

疑 ꜀i Composed of 子 a *child* placed above 止 *to stop*, and an old form of 矢 *dart* for the phonetic; *q.d.* children are often undecided.

To doubt, to suspect, to guess; to surmise; to fear; to dislike; doubtful of, hesitating; corrupt, perverse, tricky.

丨似 similar, perhaps the same; doubtful, unsettled.

狐丨 a fox's doublings, fearful; uncertain.

思丨 to suspect; suspicious, doubt.

避嫌丨 avoid suspicious acts.

丨惑 to suspect; in doubt of.

無丨 plain, undoubted.

丨病 irresolute, hesitating.

懷丨上控 to inform the authorities of one's suspicions about others.

因此致丨 it will therefore produce surmises.

丨難的事 a very mysterious and suspicious affair.

憂丨未解 his fears are not yet cleared up.

毫無丨意 there is not the least ground for hesitation.

析丨 to decide doubts, as by throwing the divining-blocks.

丨惚在他身上 my suspicions rest on him.

丨慮不決 my hesitancy is not removed.

南人多丨 southerners are rather suspicious.

嶷 ꜀i From *hill* and *doubtful.*

A name said to have been given to the 九丨山, on the west of Shansi, whose nine summits were so much alike as to be doubtful; they form part of the range between the Yellow River and Făn River, and are noted as the burial place of Shun.

其德丨丨 his eminent virtue is lofty as mountain peaks.

克岐克丨 ability and wit like a mountain top; said of a smart child.

貽 ꜀i From *precious* and *you;* it is nearly synonymous with the next.

To hand down, to bequeath; to leave, to communicate to posterity; to give to; to induce, to bring on one's self; caused by.

丨贈 to leave to, as a legacy; to make a parting present.

丨厥孫謀 to plan what will benefit one's posterity.

丨累 to involve others.

丨悞後人 to mislead after ages, to propagate error.

丨送知己 to give to an intimate friend.

丨笑大方 it would make even an expert laugh — to see such bad work.

丨遺 to transfer to those who follow.

神之弔矣丨爾多福 the gods come; they confer many blessings on you.

詒 ꜀i Like the last, and used with it.

Also to deceive; to ridicule; to act so as to be despised.

丨傳 to hand down, as one's good name or property.

千里丨情 to send remembrances [to friends] from afar.

饋丨 to send a delicacy, to present food.

自丨伊戚 he brought that evil on himself.

君子有穀丨孫子 may our prince maintain his goodness, and transmit it to his posterity.

Read *ʻtʻai.* To defraud.

欺丨 to insult.

骨肉相丨 relatives cheating each other.

Read ꜀*tai.* Weary of; remiss, negligent.

眙 ꜀i To look straight on, to gaze at fixedly.

目丨不禁 to stare at without stopping.

怡 ꜀i From *heart* and *you* as the phonetic; not the same as *taiʾ* 怠 idle.

Harmonious concord; mutual pleasure in each other, as among brothers or friends; joyful, satisfied.

丨悅 taking delight in, pleased at.

丨和 delightful harmony, true accord.

下氣丨色 to repress the feelings and appear happy, — as when a parent errs.

丨然自得 happy and satisfied.

丨丨如也 so delighted and cordial, as brothers.

飴 ꜀i Sweet cakes made of rice and fried; clarified sugar, comfits like barley sugar; a delicacy, a tidbit; to feed.

丨鹽 rock or mineral salt.

丨糖 or 甘丨 sugar-plums, sweetmeats.

甜言丨訓 smooth words and pleasant counsel.

石丨 wild honey.

苦丨 sorrows and joys.

含丨弄孫 feeding sugar-plums and playing with one's grandchild;— the pleasures of old age.

𦣝 ˛i This character originally rudely represented the face and projecting chin; it is now superseded by the next, and occurs only as a primitive; it nearly resembles ˛ch'in 臣 an officer.

The chin; the neck under the chin.

頤 ˛i The preceding was the original form, and the radical was added afterwards.

The chin, the jowl, the chops; name of the 27th diagram, denoting to feed; deep; an initial particle.

朵丨 red cheeks.

期丨 very old; a centenarian, who needs to be fed.

丨指如意 to order one by shaking the chin at him.

解人丨 to nod the head, as when assenting to a thing, or intimating that it is understood.

獨幽丨 to roll the head from side to side, as the Chinese often do when interested in talking, or in thinking what they shall write.

胰 **脃** ˛i The fat over the stomach or spleen; the caul or omentum; the flesh on the loins.

丨子 soap; the coarse kind used in northern China, made from the hog's caul.

丨皂鋪 a soap-chandler's shop.

鮧 ˛i The fresh water or white porpoise, the 鯸丨; it is also known as the 河豚 or river pig, and by other names; at Canton it is called 白丨, and avoided by the fishermen; its back is less white than the belly; "when angry it runs against things; its liver is deleterious;" it seems to be confounded with the trunk-fish (*Tetraodon*) by some native authors.

溰 **皚** ˛i Hoarfrost and snow covering the ground.

霜雪兮漼丨 how abundant is the frost and snow!

丨皚 snow white.

宧 ˛i The northeast corner of a house, where the food used to be stored; *met.* to nourish.

丨明 a hole in the lattice, where the sun shines in.

丨養 the genial stimulus of spring.

圯 ˛i From *earth* and *self*; it is not the same as ˋp'i 圮 to destroy.

A bridge; some say it is rather the bank that supports the bridge.

丨橋三進履 he thrice offered him the shoes under the bridge.

彝 ˛i Composed of 米 *rice* and 糸 *silk* placed above 廾 two *hands* raised, as if making offerings in the ancestral temple, with 彑 a *hog's head* above all for the phonetic.

Cups or vases of a cyathiform shape, used for libations; a constant rule, an invariable principle, assented to by all; regular, constant, usual, common; addicted to.

丨倫 the social relations.

民之秉丨 the moral sense of mankind, that which the conscience approves.

宗丨 sacrificial vessels, such as are used in the imperial temples.

是丨是訓進德無疆 direct yourself by this rule, and you will go on in the path of virtue to perfection.

螔 ˛i An insect.

丨蝓 a garden snail or slug.

Read ˛sz'. A reptile, the 丨蜈, resembling the iguana, which lives in marshes.

儀 ˛i From *man* and *right* as the phonetic.

The usages of mankind; a rule, a rite; etiquette, decorum, of which nine classes are recorded; presents or fees required by custom; form, figure; the external appearance or deportment; correct, proper, just, what ought to be; regular, decorous; to imitate, to study how to effect; to reckon, to judge; a principle, a power, as in nature; good, or to do good; a pair, a match; a machine that exhibits or measures a thing, as a globe, a sphere.

程丨 a present sent to one commencing a journey.

天體丨 an armillary sphere; an orrery, or whatever shows the movements of the heavens.

容丨 deportment, air; visage.

丨著 style, particular etiquette suitable to an office.

三丨 heaven, earth, and man, the three powers of nature.

兩丨 heaven and earth; also applied to the sun and moon.

威丨 a dignified carriage; an imposing escort.

代丨 a present of money.

丨制司 the master of ceremonies or the Bureau of Ceremonies, where usages and forms 丨制 are attended to.

五丨 the five ranks of nobility.

我丨圖之 when I try to understand it.

丨物 or 謝丨 a present; an acknowledgment of some service.

丨文 the style of one's house, furniture, or things.

丨註 rules of propriety.

平丨 etiquette among equals.

丨仗 imperial attendants; the out-riders; those who manage a cortège or procession.

丨門 the side-doors of the second entrance in a yamun.

奠丨, or 香丨, or 祭丨 money or offerings sent to mourners, to assist them in the expenses; the last kind consists of incense, &c.

無非無丨 neither doing wrong nor good; — said of a daughter.

夷 ˛i From 大 *great* and 弓 *bow* combined, referring to the weapon of the eastern tribes.

To squat; even, level; ordinary; to equalize, to arrange; to feel at ease; to wound; to kill, to destroy, to exterminate; to push out, as a shoot comes up; to cut, as grass; to class, to sort; good living; ample, contented, pacified; colorless, as the Taoists say reason is; enters into the appellatives of many gods; distant, remote, and therefore unacquainted with Chinese literature and decorum; a tribe on the east; name of a branch of the River Han in Hupeh.

東 丨 an old name for Corea.

丨 人 a foreigner or barbarian, *i. e.* one who is ignorant of Chinese literature and civilization, just as the Greeks used βάρβαροι to denote all who spoke other tongues; it is applied to tribes in Sz'ch'uen and towards Tibet, and has been extended to all foreigners.

丨 船 foreign ships.

陵 丨 gradually decaying, as an imperial tomb; and by *met.* the power of the state.

丨 九 族 he destroyed his whole race.

貴賤等 丨 nobles and plebeians of all grades.

云胡不 丨 he asked, Who would not be pleased?

丨 俟 to sit cross-legged; otherwise 乃 丨 居 he squats at ease, *i. e.* he shows no reverence.

旣有淫威降福孔 丨 having such great dignity, these great blessings would naturally come to him.

明 丨 the 36th diagram; it belongs to earth and fire.

大道甚 丨 the great road [of truth] is plain.

馮 丨 and 丨 女 are names of divinities; the latter is a goddess worshiped by sailors.

桋 ꜀i A tall timber tree found in Shansi; the wood is gnarled, tough, and reddish, and suitable for cart-wheels; the bark thick and whitish, the leaf oval and small; it is probably akin to the beach.

跠 ꜀i To sit on the heels, a common posture for all Asiatics; to crouch.

丨 踞 to squat down; it indicates contempt for one, if it be retained while another is speaking.

丨 俟 to sit and wait for one.

峓 ꜀i A noted hill, called 嵎 丨, lying towards sunrise, to which the Great Yü sent his astronomers; also written 嵎 夷, and said to be a peak in Tăng-cheu fu in Shantung, though others think it may be a mountain in Japan.

姨 ꜀i A wife's sister, distinguished as 大 丨 and 小 丨 for the elder and younger; maternal aunts are distinguished as 丨 母 or 丨 媽 or 丨 娘 for the elder, and 亞 丨 for the younger; a maid-servant.

蘇 州 娘 丨 a Suchau girl, a handsome woman or maid-servant.

堂 丨 a mother's female cousins.

丨 爹 or 丨 夫 or 丨 丈 an aunt's husband; 丨 表 his daughters.

亞 丨 不 上 姊 夫 門 a sister-in law should not live at her sisters house.

痍 ꜀i A wound or bruise made by a stick; an ulcer, a sore; to hurt, to wound.

瘡 丨 未 瘳 his bruises and sores are not healed.

恞 ꜀i Pleased, well satisfied.

我 心 則 丨 my heart is now fully gratified.

洟 ꜀i From *water* and *gratified* as the phonetic; it is also read *t'i'*, and interchanged with 涕 tears.

Snivel, mucus from the nose.

丨 涕 tears and snot.

不 敢 唾 丨 don't blow your nose in company.

温 丨 name of a marshy lake in Shansi.

侇 ꜀i A class; sign of the plural; a corpse.

儒 丨 the class of philosophers; the literary class.

丨 衾 the pall or shroud which is placed over a corpse before it is coffined.

遺 ꜀i From *to go* and that which gives *value;* occurs used for the next, and much resembles *k'ien* 遣 to send.

To leave, as at death; to will, to entail; to leave behind, to forget, to lose; to neglect; to emit, to lose unconsciously; plucked, as at an examination; escaped; to throw a largess to; a will; a residue, a surplus, leavings; supererogation; posthumous; a form of the passive.

丨 囑 dying commands.

丨 下 bequeathed; left to me.

丨 忘 forgotten; long out of mind.

丨 命 or 丨 言 his dying words, final orders.

丨 落 it was left behind; lost or dropped, as when walking.

丨 失 lost, gone, no trace of it.

丨 書 a testament, a will.

丨 體 the body given or handed down — by my parents.

丨 臭 of infamous memory; detested, as a Nero.

丨 念 兒 a souvenir, a memento, a remembrance.

上 古 丨 風 the memory of its goodness has come down.

下 丨 inferiors, attendants.

考 丨 才 to examine the scholars who entered once but did not pass.

遞 丨 摺 to hand up a father's dying or last memorial.

丨 餘 the overplus, what is left.

丨 丨 tortuous, as a road.

丨 溺 to urinate when asleep.

小 丨 a medical term for urine.

丨 下 一 子 he left one son behind him, a 丨 腹 子 posthumous son.

Read *wei'* and used for 贈 to give a present. To send a present.

⿰貝遺 ˏi To send presents to a friend; to exchange tokens of regard. 朋友餽丨 mutual gifts among friends.

鸃 ˏi A small species of pheasant, the 鵔丨; the bird is not clearly defined, and may perhaps denote a kind of jungle-fowl or grouse.

⿰口兮 ˏi Yes; it will do; let it go.

In *Cantonese*. Poor, inferior, ungarbled, deteriorated; not to speak out, timid; dumpy.

丨貨 a poor quality of goods; an inferior article.

以 㠯 ʿi Altered from the second form, which is composed of 已 *already* twice joined, to indicate the thought and action already done.

To serve one's self with, to use; to aid; to place; occurs for 有 to have, to possess; as a *preposition*, by, with, because, for, in; being, acting as; although; for that, to the end that; by means of, in order to; using, taking; and, next, at; according to, thus; when it precedes a verb, it marks the manner or instrument; and the result or intention, when it follows a verb; a reason, a cause; to do; to resemble; when preceded by 所, wherein, therefore, that by which, thereby; when followed by 爲, deeming, considering, by it make; to judge; preceded by 可, could, can be so, how; it is a synonym of 已 in 無丨 or else, if not so, — but this phrase also sometimes means a negative; a common sign of the accusative, from, to, in; as 丨仁存心 he cherishes humanity in his heart; or of the infinitive, as 丨洽百禮 to supply all the ceremonies; preceded by 自 from, 丨來 becomes a form of the pluperfect or denotes time past, as 自他死丨來 since the time of his death.

不敢丨告人 I will not presume to tell any one.

此身丨外 it is none of my business.

是丨 therefore, since.

必有丨也 there must be a reason.

于丨用之公侯之事 to be employed in the business of the prince.

何丨 how, by what? wherefore, whereby.

可丨使得 it can be used, it will do.

丨管窺天 looking at the sky through a tube.

登位丨前 before he mounted the throne.

視其所丨 mark what he does.

故丨 for this reason, wherefore.

無丨與之 I have nothing to give him; — implying, I decline to give him anything.

明丨誨他 use plain words in counseling him.

丨義爲利 get gain honestly.

丨爲成大功 they reckoned that they had done a great exploit.

不丨爲耻 he did not think it was shameful.

衆人丨上 rather above the common run of men.

丨直爲曲 to bend the crooked straight.

好鬬狠丨危父母 you jeopard your parents by your passion for quarreling and scrapes.

習習谷風丨陰丨雨 gently blows the east wind with clouds and rain.

不我丨歸 he did not take us back.

因你躭擱丨致我不成功 I can do nothing great because you hinder me.

苡 苢 ʿi Name of a plant.

芣丨 the plantago.

丨米 or 丨薏仁 pearl barley, which the Chinese make from the seeds of the Job's tears (*Coix*), and other kinds of grasses.

已 ʿi This character like ʿki 己, is supposed to represent that the breath or energy has all been expended; they were originally the same, and are now distinguished by the back of this being closed.

A verbal particle; used before a word implies when an act is past or finished, and thus serves as a sign of the perfect tense; it is also placed after the verb; yes; truly; as an *adverb*, now, already, just; to terminate; to decline, to have done with; to reject, to lay aside; when used as a *final* particle, it denotes an excess of, no more, enough.

業丨 (or 丨經) 寫了 it is written; the writing is finished.

丨去 he has gone off.

不得丨 I can't help it; inevitable; obliged to do.

丨後 hereafter, subsequent to.

丨甚 an extreme, too much; as 是皆丨甚 all that is far too overdone.

病之丨甚 he badly maltreated him.

丨而 that's all, it's all said; much the same as 丨矣乎 that's the end of it; alack! is that all?

三丨之 he thrice rejected him.

丨而不知其然 this is it, but I don't know its nature.

有不能自丨者也 I am not at liberty to deny him — or to yield the post.

丨過聲 it's all over; gone by; you are too late, as to see the show.

旣丨如此就照所論 it has come about just as you said it would.

异 ʿi From the *hands* raised and *already* as the phonetic.

To retire, to stop; to raise; an interjection expressive of doubt and wonder, how can it be! implying that the thing should be tried again.

何以丨哉 is it possible? is it so? well, but how can it be?

丨哉試可乃已 well then, try him, and that will be enough.

‘偯 ‘i Combined of 依 to *rely on* and 心 *heart* contracted to *mouth*.

The sobbing which follows a fit of weeping; the wail of condolence with mourners.

哭不丨 weep but wail not.

大功之哭三曲而丨 when weeping for a parent, the three kneelings and wailings should be done, — as a mourner enters.

‘矣 ‘i From 矢 a *dart* with 已 *done* altered for the phonetic; *q. d.* the thought has hit the mark.

A final particle denoting that the sense has been fully expressed, or that the intention is very strong.

禮則然丨 the mode is just that.

否丨 certainly not.

至丨盡丨 a superlative, meaning the very best or worst; nothing can exceed that.

而已丨 certainly so; and that's enough; nothing more.

樂甚者丨 what a jolly, happy thing he is!

‘迆 ‘i To walk awkwardly; awry, crooked; adjoining, connected; conterminous.

田畝丨邐 their fields lay next to each other.

欲其無丨 he wished them not to march obliquely.

‘㕈 ‘i To hide in the dress; to conceal, to screen, as woods do a house.

隱丨 to shelter from view.

‘倚 ‘i From *man* and *unusual*; it is a synonym of ˏ依 to lean.

To rely on, to lean against or on; trusting in, to depend on; to engage one to do; inclined, leaning; a support, a fulcrum.

丨賴 or 丨靠 to depend on, as on a husband.

斷無偏丨 quite impartial, not the least unfairness.

丨托 to engage one to do; to ask a favor of.

丨瑟而歌 to sing in time with a lute.

中立而不丨 he stands perfectly erect; *met.* candid, unprejudiced.

丨馬可待 immediately; *i. e.* while waiting on horseback.

丨住了 he held it fast; I held on firmly.

丨度, to carefully estimate.

丨角之勢 a body of troops in reserve.

丨憑 or 丨仗 to rely on; to show as evidence; to take advantage of, as an officer's servant to extort in his master's name.

笑丨攔杆暗點頭 he nodded assent as he smilingly leaned on the balustrade; *met.* pretended knowledge.

‘掎 ‘i From *hand* and *unusual*; it is also read ‘*ki*.

To drag an animal off by one leg, or lead it when tied up; to issue; to draw forth.

伐木丨矣 drag away the timber when it is cut.

機不虛丨 set the gin so that you will not draw it empty.

‘椅 ‘i A sort of wood suitable for cabinet-ware and furniture; the confusion in the synonyms of this tree is great, the conclusion being that the four names given denote the same tree, which is probably either a *Catalpa* or *Rottlera*; a chair, a seat, a couch, a fauteuil.

一張丨 or 一個丨子 one chair.

丨披 or 丨搭 a chair-cover; it is usually made of red cloth.

掛燈丨 a chair without arms.

虎皮褥蓋學士丨 a tiger's skin should cover a scholar's seat; — a metaphor for office.

太師丨 a grand state chair, one fit for a statesman.

馬叉丨 a camp-chair, a folding chair.

丨柅 pliant, lithe, as a switch.

‘錡 ‘i From *metal* and *unusual*; it is also read *i*’ and ˏ*k‘i*.

A spider or iron frying-pan having three legs; a boiler or pan; a stand for bows in an armory; a chisel; a pick to dig out holes.

崎丨 unquiet, unsteady, not standing firm.

蘭丨 stands for spears and bows.

維丨及釜 there were both kettles and pans.

缺我丨 we splintered our chisels.

‘𩡧 ‘i Fragrant, odoriferous.

丨香 an agreeable pleasant smell.

‘輢 ‘i The sides of a war chariot where the soldiers plant their spears in the sockets; the sides of a carriage.

‘扆 ‘i From *inner door* and *garment* as the phonetic.

A silken screen anciently placed in the audience chamber between the door and window, called 斧丨, because it was ornamented with hatchets or axheads.

‘艤 ‘檥 ‘i To moor or turn a boat's head to the bank; to run the bow on shore; to set up a pole as a signal.

試水客丨輕舟 the sailors tried to run their empty vessel ashore.

‘嶬 ‘i A high peak, irregular and steep.

山崎丨而重注 the waters are rushing down from the high steep hillsides.

‘蟻 ‘i From *insect* and *right*, "ants," as the Chinese say, "having the distinction of prince and minister."

The ant; it includes all the genus *Formica*, and a few other insects resembling the ant; a demeaning term used by the people when addressing their rulers, the same as, "we, the petitioners;" or "I, the suppliant;" the commonalty, the masses.

白 ㅣ the white ant. (*Termites.*)

螞 ㅣ an ant, a general term.

黃絲 ㅣ a small red ant.

ㅣ民 or ㅣ等 we, the people.

ㅣ聚 collected like ants, as banditti.

浮 ㅣ the scum of liquor, the spume on water.

麻冕 ㅣ裳 a hempen cap and a somber garment; — in mourning dress.

ㅣ頭, or ㅣ穴, or ㅣ丘, or ㅣ壤 an ant-hill.

ㅣ封穴 the ants close their hill, — as when the rain threatens.

飛 ㅣ flying or winged ants.

ㅣ陣 the lines of ants.

螘 'i Like the last, but specifically used for a large winged kind of black ant; though the account of its habits indicates that the name includes some kind of dung-bettle, if indeed it refers to an ant at all.

顗 'i A still and respectful manner; decorous, joyous; pleased and quietly happy.

擬 'i 'ni From *hand* and to *doubt* as the phonetic.

To compare, to consider; to guess; to decide as a judge on a trial, after full examination and sifting; to estimate; to intend, to purpose; figure, form; similar to, like.

相 ㅣ resembling each other.

ㅣ度, to think over, to form an opinion.

比 ㅣ to compare in order to a decision.

ㅣ軍罪 to sentence to transportation.

ㅣ奏 to sentence and report — the case to the throne.

ㅣ罪 to sentence, to fix the punishment.

ㅣ定 to determine; to decide, as a suit.

ㅣ舉何人 whom had we better promote to the place?

本 ㅣ the former trial, the original purpose.

儗 'i Interchanged with the last and with ˏ疑 to doubt.

To compare; to assort.

佁 ㅣ an obstinate, stupid manner.

Read *hai'* Foolish, in the phrase 儓 ㅣ a silly look.

薿 'i Flourishing, vigorous plants.

秀 ㅣ growing luxuriantly.

黍稷 ㅣ ㅣ the millet and sorghum are growing finely.

譺 'i To consult, to deliberate; to impose on, to consider doubtful; to delude one by pretending to consult; foolish, stupid.

睨 'i From *eye* and *child* as the phonetic.

The glancing of the eye; to look askance, to glance the eye, as monkeys do; the slanting rays of the sun.

日 ㅣ踈林 the sun's beams are streaming through the grove.

怒 ㅣ an angry look.

持璧 ㅣ柱 he held the baton to glance at the pillar — through the hole.

In *Fuhchau.* To examine closely; to scrutinize.

義 i' From 羊 *sheep*, which one says is a contraction of 善 *good*, above 我 *I*; *q. d.* I am a good man; it is often synonymous with ˏ宜 correct.

The rule of self-dignity and respect, "that which enables the heart to rule itself, and things to be in their places;" right, equity, that which is proper and just *per se*; it is reckoned as the second greatest virtue; righteousness, uprightness, high moral feeling, conforming to what the heart approves; common, free by public contribution or government appropriation, as ㅣ井 a public well; patriotism in defense of one's rights; public spirited, as ㅣ兵 or ㅣ勇 patriot volunteers; superior, surpassing, excellent, as ㅣ士 an eminent scholar; ㅣ犬 a faithful dog; — in place of, putative, as ㅣ父 an adopted father; made up, compounded of, as ㅣ墨 a composition ink; meaning, intention, as 同 ㅣ of the same meaning or synonymous; a cause which engages the aid of the people.

ㅣ戰 a fight for the right.

ㅣ倉 a public granary.

ㅣ僕 a faithful servant.

ㅣ氣 honorable, right-minded; ever the same.

ㅣ塚 or ㅣ山 a public or free burial-ground.

ㅣ重如山 his integrity is firm as the hills.

懷利非師長之 ㅣ a love of lucre is incompatible with a master's rectitude.

ㅣ不容辭 justice admits of no excuses.

仗 ㅣ踈財 he distributed (or used) his property in a good cause — or for worthy ends.

不 ㅣ惟君王 he deemed it unpatriotic to be king.

ㅣ意如何 what can he mean by that?

ㅣ髮 a false head-dress, a chignon.

ㅣ女 an adopted daughter; the term is applied to female slaves.

議 i' From *words* and *right*; it is often synonymous with ʿ擬 to decide.

To deliberate, to discuss in council; to consult in order to decide on the best course; to blame, to criticise, to find fault with; to arrange; to select; deliberation, consultation; laws, rules.

公丨 a public debate, a free discussion.
庶民不丨 the people must not discuss — politics.
而丨 a personal consultation.
丨論 to deliberate on.
論而不丨 to speak about and yet not criticise.
駁丨 to call in question, to discuss a decision.
會丨 to meet for discussion.
丨事廳 a council chamber; like the Senate House in Macao.
丨擇賢者 to seek to select the best men.
丨政王 a prince-regent — of the empire; it was applied to Prince Kung in 1862.
八丨 eight honorary ranks or privileges conferred on distinguished men, answering to the medals and crosses in the West; members of these ranks, called 應丨者 have special privileges.
依丨 to confirm a decision or opinion.
交部丨處 let the case be referred to the proper Board to consult upon and decide.
巷丨街談 street gossip, public rumor and notions.

誼 i' From *words* and *correct*; interchanged with the last two and ˓宜 right.

That which is suitable; right, proper or fit, for the time or person; the relations of things; friendly, acquainted; putative, in place of; adopted, as by the exchange of cards; goodness; order.
行' 丨 to act justly and right.
年丨 the year's acquaintance, as officers or friends; to exchange cards of amity, as by persons who graduated the same year.
世丨 sons of those persons who have thus adopted each other.
芝蘭之丨 friends adopted as brothers; a fraternal regard.
親丨 or 戚丨 relatives; kind regards paid to relatives.

医 i' From a *case* and *dart*; this character is much used as a contraction of ˓醫 medicine.

A case for arrows; a sort of quiver.

藙 i' A species of pepper tree (*Xanthoxylon*), the seeds of which are used in cooking mutton or beef, and to give soup a relish.
三牲用丨 in cooking the three meats (pork, beef, or mutton), use wild pepper; the people of Sz'ch'uen flavored spirits with the seeds.

易 i' From 日 *sun* and 勿 *pennon*, referring to the quick changes of the sun and the moon; others say it is formed of *sun* above *moon*, showing that as one goes the other comes; the original form is likened to a house lizard; it somewhat resembles *hoh*, 曷 who.

To dress a field, to clear waste land; easy, the opposite of 難; not difficult, done without care or nicety; remiss, indifferent to, negligent; disrespectful, inattentive; to deal lightly with; easy, at ease; pleased; minute attention to.
略丨 rather easier.
平丨 easy and plain, as wisdom is to sages.
容丨 not hard to do, easy, facile.
慢丨 or 輕丨 careless, disregardful, trifling with.
丨脫手 easy to rid out of hand, as saleable goods.
丨爲力 he will do it with help; it is not very hard.
君子居丨以俟命 the princely man is quiet and calm as he awaits his lot.
禾丨長畝 the grain is well tended over all the acres.
丨於變幻 changeable in sentiment, fickle-minded.
丨其田疇 to clear up the fields and lots.
丨信 credulous, trustful.
命不丨哉 [Heaven's] orders are not easily — preserved.

Read *yih*, The mutations or alternations in nature, as of the sun and moon; the theory of permutations and combinations shown by the sixty-four diagrams; to change; to barter, to exchange; a market.
卜丨 to cast lots.
不丨 immutable.
以此丨彼 change this for that.
變丨 to change and alter.
公平貿丨 a fair trade.
幾丨春秋 how easily the seasons slip by!
交丨 to exchange commodities.
無俾丨種 I will not let them perpetuate their seed.
丨卦 the symbols of the changes in nature, which constitute the 丨學 or the science of these combinations, which are given in the 丨經 or Book of Changes.
丨地則皆然 it will be just the same even if you change your location.
移風丨俗 to modify and better their manners.

敡 i' To change, to speak lightly of; to treat irreverently.
簡丨 to act rudely to one.
幻丨轉瞬 changeable, vacillating, rapidly altering.

異 i' Composed of 畀 to *confer on* contracted, in combination with 廾 two *hands*; *q.d.* presents are assorted according to the recipients, and superiors get theirs on a different day from inferiors.

To divide, to separate; different, diverse; not home-made, foreign; sundered; admirable, unusual, rare, extraordinary; perverse, bizarre, heterodox; to marvel at, to regard as foreign or strange; to oppose; a difference, the odds.
豈伊丨人 how can they be strangers?
丨姓 a different surname.
丨聞 special or unusual news.
丨日 another day.
勢不丨 I will not be forced to change; I dare not differ.

大同小丨 they are very much alike.
珍丨 rarities, curiosities.
怪丨 monstrous, as a lusus naturæ.
丨邦 foreign states.
殊丨乎公路 [but perhaps] very unlike what the Lord of the Roads should be.
何以丨于是 what difference is there between them?
丨道 sectarianism, heresy.
立丨爲高 to esteem what is strange as being superior on that account.
懷丨心 to cherish hard feelings; to bear a grudge.

殪 i' From *bad* and *once*; another form is composed of 死 and 壹, but it is unusual.

To kill by a single shot, to shoot dead at once; to exterminate; to prostrate, to overthrow; to overshadow, to overhang.
敵兵盡丨 the enemy was entirely cut off.
奔丨百餘里 they ran more than a hundred *li*.
丨此大兕 he shot this great rhinoceros.

饐 i' From to *eat* and *one*; it is interchanged with *yih*, 噎 to choke.

Cooked rice or other food which has become damp and moldy; a sour, harsh taste, such as spoiled food has; to gag with food; a sobbing; to catch the breath.
臭丨 it is altogether spoiled.
敗丨 moldy food, a sour dish.

膭 i' Lean, poor, cadaverous.

鷧 i' An old name for the fishing cormorant (*Phalacrocorax*); it is also known as the 老水鴉 or old water crow.

壇 i' The air full of dust; a dull murky atmosphere, arising from clouds.

瘞 i' From *earth* and *intermission of disease.*

A retired place; to throw on the ground, as in worshiping the dead; the gods of the streams or the moon; to gather up the sacrifices; fine.
奠丨 to pour out libations to the gods.

翳 i' From *eye* and a *quiver*.

A film in the eye, a cataract.
后生而丨一目 the empress had a cataract in one eye.
丨瞙 a cataract; a film over the sight.

勩 i' From *strength* and to *forgive*.

Labor, toil; affliction, distress; to be weary, to endure, to labor in.
莫知我丨 you don't know what I have endured.

泄 i' From *water* and *age*; it is also a synonym of *sich*, 洩 to leak.

A small tributary of the River Hwai in Nganhwui; to disperse, to spread abroad; to scatter; easy, graceful.
丨丨其羽 how graceful and slow is its flight! as a flying pheasant.
桑者丨丨兮 see the crowds picking the mulberries!
無然丨丨 do not be so leisurely in your movements.

呭 i' **詍** i' Occurs interchanged with the last; the first is the most common form.

Loquacious, garrulous; unceasing talk.
無然丨丨 there is no need for so much talking.

枻 i' A long oar.

Read *sich*, An utensil or gauge for adjusting a bow called 檠丨, a sort of frame for bending it.

鞢 i' To give a paper saddle for burning at a funeral.

Read *sieh*, The saddle flaps made of leather; a saddle-cloth; a strip of leather near the bit to lead the horse.

曳 i' **拽** i' The first is derived and altered from ˛*shăn* 申 to *issue*, and is least used; the second specially refers to taking in the hand; they are also read *yeh*ˏ; in colloquial, a difference is made in the second character, which when written 拽 is read *chwai*' and means to drag.

To trail, to drag after one; to pull; to leave a trace; to saunter along leisurely; to lead off, to take up by the hand; to raise up.
丨尾 to wag the tail.
軟丨 easy, flexible.
搖丨 to flirt, as a fan; shaking, as branches in the wind.
棄甲丨兵而走 he threw off his armor, and led away his troops.
拉丨 to drag along, as a vessel.
丨丨 an easy, slouching gait.
丨踵 to go on tiptoe; to drag the heels in walking.
拖丨 to trail after one, as a lady's train.
往前丨 he drags along the whole; said of a man who supports the whole family.
丨白卷 to put in a blank page by mistake in the essay sent to the examiner; to turn over two leaves instead of one.

秇 i' An old name for very white rice was 白丨; it is now disused.

意 i' From *heart* and *sound*; *q. d.* if you examine the words, you will know the thought.

A thought, intention, idea; the inclination, will; a sentiment, an opinion; the motive or purpose; the meaning, as of a word.
丨思 the feelings, the intention.

不好丨思 disreputable; disagreeable, as to refuse a favor; ashamed at.

什麽丨思 what does it mean? what does he wish about it?

何丨 what is the meaning of it?

沒主丨 undetermined; no decision.

借丨 and 反丨 metaphor and irony; comparison and double meaning.

曾是不丨 but this you have not thought of.

丨見 a sentiment, a view.

風以丨 to tell rumors about, to convey hints upon.

用丨 I am thinking about it; you must bear it in mind.

丨外 unexpected, not reckoned upon.

大丨了 careless, inconsiderate.

不丨中' unintentional.

得丨 got his wish, gratified.

好得丨 curious, cunning, odd, extraordinary; also used as an exclamation of admiration.

寫丨 a rough sketch.

固丨 obstinate, willful, opinionated.

誠丨正心 a fixed purpose and a guileless heart.

做生丨 to follow a business.

過丨不去 I can hardly take so much; I am vastly obliged to you.

專丨 or 着丨 a fixed intention, a strong desire, singleness of purpose.

勝丨 exceeding my wishes.

丨丨思思 I prefer not, I am rather unwilling to do it.

加丨 thoughtfully; special care about.

會丨 or 取丨 combined or taken meanings, a term given to characters whose component parts somewhat indicate their meaning.

不可以丨測 his design is inscrutable.

口丨 purport of one's remarks.

丨馬心猿 his will is like a horse's, and his heart like an ape's; *met.* inconstant and strong.

假丨 specious, pretending.

見財起丨 he thinks of stealing on seeing the goods.

事事如丨 may everything be as you wish.

薏 *i'* The seeds of a water lily, smaller than the common lotus.

苡丨米 pearl-barley from the *Coix*; sago is sometimes so called.

褹 *i'* The train of a dress which drags after one.

飄丨 streaming, like a pennon.

藝 埶 秇 蓺 *i'* The second is the original form, composed of a *clod* and to *grasp*, referring to agricultural pursuits; the additions in the first and common form were subsequent, and the other forms are seldom met.

Aptitude, skill in doing a thing; skilled, cunning; expert; ability in working; a craft, an art, a calling; an accomplishment; to cultivate the arts; to discriminate, as in articles; the last character particularly means to cultivate plants, to set out trees; a limit or extreme point.

六丨 the six liberal arts — are propriety 禮, music 樂, archery 射, charioteering 御, writing 書, and arithmetic 數.

文丨 literary pursuits.

丨文 an indenture to teach a craft.

才丨 or 能丨 ability, talent.

手丨 a handicraft.

好手丨 good workmanship; he is skillful.

手丨人 a clever artisan, a skilled workman.

技丨 skilled in a fine art, as painting or carving.

丨貢 to distinguish the sorts of presents.

學丨 to learn a trade.

武丨 tactics; all military accomplishments, as lifting weights, archery, &c.

樹丨五穀 to plant and till crops; agriculture.

百丨無如一丨精 better to be skilled in one art than to be a jack-at-all-trades.

洪丨 varied arts and accomplishments.

丨之荏菽 plant it with horse-beans.

貪欲無丨 his ambition is boundless.

曉機丨 acquainted with machinery; an engineer.

讛 *i'* To talk in one's sleep; to talk behind a covert, or in a retired place.

撒丨章 to murmur or talk in one's sleep.

囈 *i'* Like the preceding.

Talking and laughing; snoring and muttering in one's sleep.

唥丨呻呼 snoring and calling out.

槸 *i'* The rubbing of branches against each other by the wind.

褹 *i'* The sleeves of a robe; those of a lady's dress are wide and the cuff embroidered.

箭丨 the sleeves of a garment.

寱 *i'* Composed of a *cover*, a *bed* and a *law*.

To talk in one's sleep.

丨語 to speak when asleep.

羿 *i'* Name of I, the prince of Kiüng 有窮后丨 a famous rebel in the Hia dynasty, a mighty archer, who drove T'ai-k'ang beyond the Yellow River to T'ai-k'ang hien 太康縣 in Honan, about B. C. 2169, and kept the power till his death.

裔 齐 i' From *garments* and to *stutter*; or, as one says, from *garment* and a part to represent a skirt; the second form is obsolete.

The train or skirt of a robe; its lower hem; a border, a frontier; an extreme point; descendants, posterity.

四 丨 之 地 the remote borders, 4000 *li* from the capital.

後 丨 or 苗 丨 descendants; one's race or remote posterity.

的 丨 a direct descendant.

絕 丨 the family is extinct.

厥 丨 蕃 昌 his race is widely extended.

夷 丨 rude, wild bands or races.

丨 丨 flying or walking about.

魚 丨 丨 like the fry of fishes, as a crowd running together.

泓 宏 融 丨 a protracted sound.

淨 丨 a Budhist term for the Brahmins; it is a translation of *Brahmatchari.*

澮 i' The surface of water roughened by the wind.

溶 丨 water raised high by the wind, surging billows; a mob is likened to it.

毅 i' From *weapon* and an angry *boar*, that rushes at everything.

Undeterred, firm, resolute, intrepid; patient, enduring; forgetful of one's self; stern, wrathful; fortitude, resolution.

温 丨 gentle and brave.

丨 然 resolute, intrepid.

剛 丨 unappaled, not afraid of danger.

士不可以不弘 丨 a scholar cannot succeed without great resolution.

丨 力 enduring effort; unwearied.

果 丨 inflexible, fixed in purpose.

丨 勇 enduring and brave.

乂 i' The character is intended to represent the blades of shears; it is interchanged with the next.

To cut grass; to govern, to regulate; to bring into order; to aid; clever, able; orderly.

安 丨 at peace, as a country.

俊 丨 在 官 he had able and virtuous men to fill office.

康 丨 fully satisfied, as a people.

保 丨 有 殷 they preserved and regulated the empire of Yin.

刈 i' To cut grass, to mow; to reap; to kill, to cut off.

言 丨 其 茅 he then said, cut the stalk down.

丨 穫 to reap and get in crops.

帠 i' ni' From *napkin* and a *mortar*.

A law, a way.

又 何 丨 以 治 天 下 感 予 之 心 焉 now what mode have you to govern the country and influence my heart?

劓 臬 i' To cut off the nose, as the component parts of the character indicate; it was done in ancient times, but is now disused; to torture.

丨 滅 無 遺 he maimed or destroyed all, leaving none.

丨 割 夏 邑 he tortured and harried the people of Hia.

詣 i' From *word* and the emperor's *will*.

To reach a place, to repair to; to go, as to a tryst; to meet at a place; to wait for.

親 丨 I went there in person.

候 丨 or 玉 丨 I shall wait for you.

丨 謁 to make a visit, to repair to.

蛄 丨 a name for the mole-cricket.

造 丨 to make great proficiency in learning.

縊 i' From *silk* and *advantage*.

To strangle one's self; to die by hanging; to restrain or halter an animal; the wasp.

丨 頸 to put to death by strangling; to bowstring; to hang.

自 丨 suicide by hanging.

丨 阨 其 牛 he triced up the ox.

丨 殺 to kill by a halter.

懿 i' From *willful* and *one* as the phonetic.

Bent on one thing; mild, benign, virtuous; admirable, admired, esteemed, as an accomplished woman, and applied especially to an empress.

丨 德 eminently virtuous; excellence that is a part of the nature, as a good mother.

丨 旨 the virtuous will; *i. e.* her Majesty's commands.

丨 美 worthy of confidence and admiration.

丨 親 your accomplished relative.

丨 範 an example worthy of esteem

女 執 丨 筐 the girls take their pretty baskets.

嫕 i' Obedient, compliant, as a woman ought to be.

婉 丨 以 爲 德 yielding kindly is a woman's virtue.

肄 i' From a *stylus* and a final *particle* as the phonetic; this must be distinguished from *sz'* 肆 to spread.

To practice and become skilled in a profession; to accustom one's self; to serve assiduously; toil, distress; pain; tender sprouts that shoot up from a stump.

丨 業 to learn a profession or trade; resident graduates who live in the district college; now merely a nominal privilege.

丨 習 to practice, to get skillful.

條 丨 tender shoots or twigs.

莫 知 我 丨 you don't know what pains I have taken to learn it.

禩 i' From to *worship* and to *hope*; some regard it as an altered form of 祀, which is itself a synonym of *sz'* 祀 to sacrifice; but others consider it to be unauthorized.

The years of the emperor's life or reign.

國 丨 the emperor's reign.

奕 丨 great prosperity and duration, as of a dynasty.

願 貴 國 萬 丨 I wish your Majesty a long reign.

JAN

Old sound, nien. *In Canton*, in *and* im ; — *in Swatow*, jian and jiam ; — *in Amoy*, jian, jiam, *and* lam ; — *in Fuhchau*, yòng, yóng, *and* nieng ; — *in Shanghai*, zé *and* niⁿ ; — *in Chifu*, yen.

然 ˏzhan The original form was composed of 犬 *dog* and 肉 *flesh* to which 火 *fire* was afterwards added ; it is interchanged with ˏ*yen* 焉 in forming adverbs.

To simmer, to burn, for which the next is now used ; an adverbial particle, implying yes, certainly, truly, it is so ; when it comes after verbs or nouns, it turns them into an adverbial phrase ; as a disjunctive *conjunction*, but, if so, but then ; thus, in this way ; then ; however ; often used to add force to the sense by making a pause at a word.

未必丨 probably not so, very uncertain.

自丨而丨 it comes (or is so) of itself ; easily, readily, naturally ; underived, self-existent, as God.

卒丨or 或丨 suddenly, unpremeditatedly.

果丨 truly, certainly ; the name of the proboscis monkey, for which the next but one is better.

亦丨 thus, in like manner.

丨且 or 丨而 however, meanwhile.

丨也 just so ; well then.

不丨 on the contrary.

謂丨 plaintive ; mournfully.

丨後知其 we shall afterwards know that it is so.

所以丨的話 an explanation of a thing ; giving the reason.

其丨豈其丨乎 if that be so, how then can it be ?

如曰不丨 if he say it is not so.

惠丨肯來 he kindly consented to come.

當丨之理 its natural properties ; such a course is what ought to be by all means.

以爲丨否 will you regard it so or not ?

丨乎否乎 is it so or not ?

丨故民不困財 therefore this is the reason why the people do not want for resources.

無好˒無惡˒丨已乎 [the princely man] has neither love nor hate, and that is the whole of it.

將丨下雪 it will presently snow.

不期丨而丨 it came quite unexpectedly ; I had not hoped for it.

對曰丨 [the teacher] replied, saying, Yes ; he answered it was so.

燃 ˏzhan Interchanged with the last.

To burn, to light, to fire ; to boil, to simmer.

丨燒 it has caught, it is on fire.

丨眉之急 urgent ; in my utmost need, as if my eyebrows had caught fire ; — said by a needy borrower.

獼 ˏzhan A sort of monkey, 猓丨 the proboscis or long-nosed monkey (*Nasalis larvatus*), which constantly strokes its black beard, — or a variety of it with a recurved nose ; it is gregarious, and inhabits the forests of Siam and Yunnan ; the name is said to imitate the cry.

繎 ˏzhan Red silk ; that which has been dyed a bright crimson or scarlet ; silk threads all tangled together.

髯 ˏzhan From *hair* and to *advance* as the phonetic ; it is used with the next.

The hair on the face near the ears ; the whiskers ; the beard.

美丨公 the Lord with the Handsome Whiskers ; — a name for Kwanti, the god of War.

長丨 a long beard.

髭丨 a beard rather short and thin.

鬢丨俱斑 a grisly beard and hair.

頿 ˏzhan Like the last. The whiskers.

黑色而丨 a dark complexion and black whiskers.

蚺 ˏzhan From *insect* and *stealthy* ; others derive it from *insect* and the last, saying that it has hairs between the scales.

A large serpent found in southern China, described as fifty feet long, which can seize deer for food ; it has long teeth, and a bright variegated skin, which is cured for covering guitars ; it carries its head close to the ground, whence it is called 埋頭蛇 ; the gall is reputed to be useful in curing consumption ; this description doubtless refers to a sort of boa like that reported to be found in Hainan Island.

丨氏 a tribe of southern savages.

袡 ˏzhan A hem or broad band on a woman's dress, especially at the bottom ; a knee-pad or stuffed wrapper to protect the knee ; an old term for padding the knee.

婦人纁丨 black knee-pads for women

蚦 ˏzhan A caterpillar, like that of the tiger-moth, called 丨蜥, whose hairs inflame the skin when it crawls over it ; its chrysalis, called 雀甕 or the sparrow's jar, is found on the pomegranate and mowtan.

ˊ冉 ˊ冄 ˊzhan The character is intended to represent the hair just growing on the body; the first is the usual form and a little resembles tsai˒ 再 again; as a primitive it imparts only its sound to the compounds.

Tender, weak.

丨丨 a gradual, but imperceptible advance.

光陰丨丨 your suns are gradually going down, your years are passing away.

丨有 also called 丨子 a favorite disciple of Confucius, who died before him.

ˊ苒 ˊzhan From *plants* and *tender;* occurs used with the last.

Luxuriant, tender herbage; by turns; successively, gradually.

草色丨丨 the fresh, vigorous grass.

光陰荏丨日月如梭 light and darkness take turns, and the sun and moon follow each other like the swift shuttles.

ˊ染 ˊzhan From 杂 a twig or *petal* and 水 *water;* others say it is formed of 木 madder *wood* and 九 *nine*, because the dipping must be repeated nine times.

To dye, to tinge; to steep or dip in dye-stuffs; to taint, to infect; to catch, as a disease; to soil, to spot; to imbue; to vitiate, to render vile; soft, pliant; dirtied.

沾丨 or 丨色 to dye; to dip in the dye.

傳丨 to infect; infectious; to give a disease.

習丨 to learn vicious ways.

丨痘 to catch the small-pox.

丨店, or 丨坊, or 丨靛鋪 a dyer's shop; the third phrase means one who dyes blue.

彈丨 to dye by brushing, as fur dresses are served

丨耨 soft, yielding.

丨指 to stain the finger red; to taste by the fingers, as a cook; *met.* to stick to the fingers, as a perquisite.

丨污 to get a bad name; soiled, dirtied, as a dress.

點丨 to finish up and adorn, as a picture; to revise, as a composition; said of a present by its giver, that it is trifling.

與他有丨 there is some improper dalliance between them.

JĂN.

Old sounds, nin *and* nim. *In Canton*, yăn, yăm, ngăn, năm, *and* ying; — *in Swatow*, jin, jim, *and* nang; — *in Amoy*, jin, jim, *and* jiam; — *in Fuhchau*, ing, ning, sing, éng, *and* néng; — *in Shanghai*, zăng, niăng, *and* săng; — *in Chifu*, yin.

ˏ人 ˏ亻 ˏ儿 ˏzhăn The character represents the *legs* when opened; the second is the form it takes in combination on the left side of a character; and the third, representing the lower limbs of the body, is placed under the primitive; they form the ninth and tenth radicals of two groups of characters, the first of which relates to man, his names, conditions, and functions.

A man; human beings, the human race; the third of the three powers in the universe, defined by the phrase 天地之性 the spirit of heaven and earth; human, belonging to mankind; to make a man of; to ascribe personal existence to a thing; following other nouns, often denotes a laborer, an artist, in that occupation, as 工丨 a laborer; 農丨 a farmer.

一個丨 one person, whether a 男丨 male, or 女丨 a female.

凡丨 or 丨丨 everybody; all mankind; the world.

內丨 my wife.

尊夫丨 your wife.

一群丨 or 一干丨 or 一起丨 or 一夥丨, or 一叢丨 each denotes a crowd, a group, a party; a knot of people.

小丨 or 下丨 a boy, a waiting lad; official menials.

小丨不知道 the mean man does not understand the principles of human actions.

成丨˒長 he is now of age, *i. e.* over sixteen years.

沖丨 a prince who came to his sovereignty while yet a minor.

天生丨天養丨 heaven produces people and finds food for them.

丨材 men of ability, the talent in the country.

丨品 a man s disposition.

無競維丨 the great thing is to be a man.

無分於丨己 don't be partial to yourself over others; treat all fairly.

丨物 men, people; men of mark.

大家丨物 a family of cultivation and position.

丨生如夢 man's life is like a dream.

老丨家 venerable Sir; you, Sir.

你的老丨家 your respected father or mother.

彼何丨斯 what can he do? why mind that man?

豈能爲˒丨 how can he look after another man?

丨中 the upper lip or rather its raphis; the Chinese say, if it curl up, the person is likely to be shortlived.

爲丨君 to be an emperor.

丨家 people, folks, men, mankind, the world.

丨其丨 make men of these fellows; *i. e.* of priests who avoid their duties in society.

正可驚丨 is adapted to strike terror.

性不畏丨 he does not fear men; it is without fear, as a docile bird.

丨緣 a man's favorable presence or influence; the cause of his fate; his luck.

思慕伊丨 I always bear that man pleasantly in mind.

販賣丨口 to traffic in human beings, as girls.

安丨 the peaceful person, — the address of the wife of one who wears a red button.

予丨子 my sons, referring to those grown up.

上丨 my father, my mother.

成丨美 an excellent deed, a worthy action.

不成丨 to scold a man as a poor stick, a ne'er-do-well.

丨子 the Son of Man, Christ; — a foreign term.

In *Fuhchau*, 亻 is added to other characters to show that they are used phonetically, as 仈 *năng*, 亻食 *siàh*, or 伓 *'ng*, in which the radical indicates a change in the sound; this usage is known as far south of that city as Ch'ao-cheu fu in Kwangtung.

仁 ˓*zhăn* From *man* and *two*, because one ought to love another, or two persons united as one from both loving.

Humanity; regard for others, the first of the constant virtues; fulfilling one's social duties; "the foundation of right and the embodiment of regard for;" unselfish, having regard to the public weal; humane, benevolent, kind, merciful; a kernel, a pit; a small seed; paralyzed, numb.

丨德 charity, kindness; humane.

丨憲 a just judge.

丨慈 compassionating, tender-hearted.

丨義充塞 the fullness (or vast reach) of humanity and justice.

瞳丨 the pupil of the eye.

丨心 kindness out of a pure heart.

不丨甚矣 malevolent; no consideration for.

不丨 also denotes unkind, shortcoming; rude conduct; in medical use, palsied, stiff, no use of an organ, as 手足不丨 the limbs are insensible; stiff, paralyzed.

菓丨 the pit of a fruit; the seed inside the nut.

花丨 the seeds of a flower. (*Cantonese.*)

丨兄 or 丨台 kind Sir! used in addressing others.

親親而丨民丨民而愛物 if devoted to your parents, you will then regard the people kindly, and from that come to be considerate to animals and all things.

朲 ˓*zhăn* The rafters or laths on which the tiles are laid; one says, the spaces between them.

壬 ˓*zhăn* The character is defined as a 人 *man* standing on the 土 *earth*, the earth denoting the business of life; others say it represents the germ in the womb; it resembles *ting*ˀ 壬 in form, and as a primitive is often interchanged with 任 sincere.

The ninth of the ten stems; it is connected with the north and running water; great; full; to flatter, to adulate.

六丨 a book of magic respecting lucky days.

扭六丨 to lay a plot. (*Cantonese.*)

百禮既至有丨有林 when all the rites have been performed grandly and fully.

何畏乎巧言令色孔丨 why should he fear one of fair words, smooth face, and great artfulness?

妊 **姙** ˓*zhăn* From *woman* and *germ*; the second form is most in use.

Pregnant; used only of women.

身懷丨 to be with child.

有丨 to conceive.

魜 ˓*zhăn* A sort of *man-fish* or merman; it is described as resembling a human being in its head, with the addition of soft fur and long hair or mane; and probably refers to the dugong (*Halicore dugong*) of the Indian Archipelago.

忍 **㣼** ʻ*zhăn* From *heart* and a cutting *weapon*; the first form is commonest.

Fortitude; patience, endurance; moral hardihood, assurance in a bad sense; able to sustain; to bear or suffer patiently; to repress; to allow, to give way to, as anger; harsh, hard-hearted, severe, inflexible.

丨耐 patience, equanimity.

是可丨也 endurable.

丨性 patient; long endurance.

丨氣吞聲 restrain one's anger by not speaking.

丨而一下 wait awhile, don't fret.

丨笑 to keep one's countenance.

含丨 to curb one's feelings.

啞丨 to bear in silence.

丨不住 I cannot bear it.

不丨的 unendurable.

丨心害理 to harshly violate propriety.

丨辱報仇 bore the disgrace in order to revenge the insult, as a violated woman.

必有丨乃有濟 you must exercise patience before you can accomplish the object.

情懷丨丨 his feelings will not suffer it.

丨於言 to forbear speaking.

胡寧丨予 how can they endure to have me thus?

堅丨 resolute endurance, unflinching fortitude.

ʻ**腍** ʻzhăn The ancient name of a district called 朐丨縣 in the present Kwei-cheu fu in the eastern border of Sz'chʻuen, now Yun-yang hien 雲陽縣, so named from certain insects.

ʻ**飪** ʻ**肚** ʻzhăn To season and cook meats very thoroughly.
失丨不食 he would not eat overdone meat.
丨熟 cooked through, well roasted.
羹丨 rich soup and meats; *met.* a sumptuous entertainment.

ʻ**腍** zhăn' Like the last.
To gormandize; good tasted; thoroughly cooked; mellow, ripe.
丨熟 well-cooked.

In *Cantonese.* Soft; muggy, dampish, as weather; kind, good-natured, amiable.
丨善 very good-natured, placable, easy to be intreated.
丨丨的 a kind affable person.
天時丨 humid, damp.
唔濕丨 not soaked through.

ʻ**荏** ʻzhăn A kind of large oily bean, as big as Windsor beans; kindhearted, gentle; flexible; name of a place in the kingdom of Chao, probably the present Jăn-pʻing hien 丨平縣 in the west of Shantung.
丨菽 large beans.
桂丨 an oily seed of which ducks are fond, and gather in flocks to eat it when ripe.
丨苒至今 we have gradually come to this day.
色厲而內丨 he was stern-looking, but had a kind heart.
丨柔 tough and elastic.
丨桐 one name for the *Elæococca verrucosa*, whose seeds furnish a painter's oil.
丨染柔木君子樹之 wise men plant trees of soft wood, easily worked.

ʻ**棯** ʻzhăn A kind of jujube or date (*Rhamnus*), called 丨棗 whose taste is insipid and slightly acid.

In *Cantonese.* The carambola, called 三丨 and 番丨 is sometimes thus written.

Read ʻshăn. A kind of tree, probably the Pride of India (*Melia*).

ʻ**恁** ʻzhăn From *heart* and to *sustain*; it is also read *nin'*.
To dwell upon with satisfaction; to consider, to think; delightful; as an adverb, thus, so, in this way.
丨樣 in this way.
旣然丨的 since it is so.

ʻ**稔** ʻzhăn ʻshăn From *grain* and to *think* on as the phonetic.
Grain which is fully ripe; a harvest or season; a year; laid up, accumulated; matured, practiced in; familiar with.
歲丨 or 丨年 a good year.
五丨 five harvests.
積丨 hoarded up; great store, as of grain or provision.
丨惡 very bad, apt in wickedness.
丨熟 ripe and abundant harvest.
聞之丨矣 much spoken of.
暗丨財主 a rich man who has secret hoards.
丨頭 a northern term for sorghum which has the mildew or ergot.
一切丨悉 I know the whole affair thoroughly.

刃' **刄**' zhăn' The character represents a *sword* with a *stain* on the blade; the second form is not usual.
A strong and well-tempered weapon; edged weapons; the edge; a knife or sword at the end of a spear; sharp pointed; to kill, to slaughter.
乃手丨其子 killed her own child with her hand.
迎丨而解 [it will be as easy as] to open (or kill) it with a blade.
兵丨 warlike weapons.
丨牛 to slaughter and skin beeves.
刀丨兒 the edge of a sword.
花錢花在刀丨上 the outlay on a sword is at (or for) its edge; *met.* use your money chiefly for necessary things.
丨傷事主 wounded the chief man or leader.

仞' zhăn' From *man* and *weapon* as the phonetic.
A measure of eight cubits or about ten English feet; to fathom; full; to fill.
充丨其中 filled quite full.
高丨 high, tall, as a tree.
壁立千丨 the precipice is of vast height.

軔' zhăn' From *carriage* and *weapon*; it is interchanged with the last.
To block a wheel, to chock a carriage; a catch, an impediment; a length of eight cubits; to embarrass.
發丨 to remove the stop, as to a wheel; to unlatch, to start, to begin a thing.
掘井九丨 he dug the well more than nine fathoms deep.
以頭丨乘輿輪 he blocked the wheel of his Majesty's chariot with his head.

牣' zhăn' To stuff, to fill up; crammed full; the yellowish color of an old sword.
實丨 solid; stuffed hard.
於丨魚躍 oh! how full of fishes jumping about.

肕' zhăn' Tough, not brittle; strong but flexible, like tendons; tenacious, like wire.
軟丨 flexible and tough.
鐵丨 iron is tenacious.
丨皮 a piece of tough skin or hide.
筋丨骨強 tough sinews and hard bones.
丨心腸 an obdurate unfeeling disposition.

In *Cantonese.* A sediment; silt.
清水丨 let the sediment settle.

韌 } Similar to the last, but especially referring to hide; the second form is commonest.
靭 zhăn' ning' Soft but tough, like catgut.
堅丨 pliant but strong; soft and firm, like fine parchment.
他素常丨性 he is always just so crabbed and self-willed.

紉 zhan' To thread, as a needle; to join fibres together, and make a thread; to sew; to stitch.
丨一針 take a stitch.
丨秋蘭以爲佩 string on the autumn orchids as a memento.
丨絲 to make floss or silk fibres into thread.
縫丨 to mend or sew a rip; to sew on or together.

訒 zhăn' From *words* and a *sharp sword* as the phonetic.
Slow of speech, unready; to hesitate, lest one speak unadvisedly; cautious, well-considered remarks; not glib of tongue; benevolent.
丨頓 disjointed speech.
仁者其言也丨 the words of the humane man are carefully considered.
丨難 it cannot be readily expressed.
丨訥 slow of speech; stammering.

認 zhăn' From *words* and *patient;* the last is sometimes used for it.
To know well, to discriminate between; to recognize, to know again; to acknowledge, to confess; a mark, a criterion; a recognition.
丨罪 to confess one's fault; to apologize; to own up to a crime.
丨識他 I recognize him.
有識丨 it has a mark to know it by.
擔丨 a surety; to enter into recognizances.
你丨得這個字 do you know that character?
丨實 I know this very well.
冒丨 to pretend to know or claim.
丨眞 scrupulous care in one's conduct; to act in reference to the truth.
丨左了 to take one man for another.
丨不出來 I am not sure whether I know it or not.
丨不淸 or 丨不眞 I did not recognize it (or him) certainly.
招丨口供 to confess to a charge, to plead guilty.
錯丨水 a poetical name for spirits.
丨住他 have an eye on him.
丨得他 I know him well; I know that it is he.
而不丨 to give the cut direct, to see and not acknowledge.

絍 zhăn' To lay the warp of a piece; to wind off the threads for it; to weave; to make a pattern with threads.
織丨 to weave.
縷丨 the warp.

衽 } From *garment* and *to bear* as the phonetic; the second form is not much used.
袵 zhăn' The lappel or flap in front of a coat, which is buttoned under the right arm; the skirt; a single mat; fastenings on a coffin.
丨席之安 the pleasures and contentment of peace.
四丨齊 the four points of the skirt are even; *met.* to indulge in four kinds of excess.
端肅斂丨 I respectfully salute you; said by a woman.
登斯民於丨席之上 raise this people to the enjoyments of plenty and contentment.
四夷左丨 the four tribes whose jackets buttoned under their left arm.

In *Cantonese.* To dip; to rinse.
丨吓 souse it in, as a garment.

任 zhăn' From *man* and a *horary* character, which last gives its sound to all but one of the compounds, in which this primitive occurs.
Sincere, sure, trustworthy; trusted, relied on; a trust, an office; a duty; a burden; that which is imposed on one; friendly confidence; to bear, to sustain, to execute; to undertake, to be responsible for; the incumbent, the acting official.
丨用 to engage, to employ.
丨着意兒行 I hope all will turn out as you wish.
丨意 according to one's wish; may your desires be attained.
丨重 a responsible trust.
赴丨 or 上丨 to enter on an office; to reach the post.
革職留丨 to degrade and yet retain in a post; — sometimes done in order that the incumbent may repair his misdeeds.
接丨 to take the seals of an office.
信丨 to confide in one; close friendship.
保丨 to be security for.
現丨 the person now in office.
前丨 the former incumbent.
丨氣敢爲 to give loose to one's passion, to act recklessly.
負丨 to take upon one's self.
仁以爲已丨 humanity is to fulfill one's duties.
丨人家事 to become the head of a family.
責丨甚大 there are very important duties.
丨憑 to allow to be done, either from confiding in or impotence.
丨你是誰不能依從 I don't care if it is you, the thing cannot be done (or allowed).
丨性妄爲 to act recklessly in gratifying one's revenge.
才不勝丨 he is not fit for the post.

丨從你 do as you please.
免丨 to dismiss from office.

Read ˎ*jăn*. To be able to bear; equal to a duty; to endure; artful; name of a district in Shun-teh fu in the south of Chihli; occurs used for 姙 pregnant.

衆怒難丨 no one could stand their wrath.

丨邦 a name for Corea.

不敢與諸丨齒 I cannot equal myself to that man.

仲氏丨只 enduringly faithful was the Lady Chung.

我丨我輩 I take care of my own folks (or people).

丨恤 kind; sympathizing and charitable.

惇德允元而難丨人 honor the virtuous, trust the good, and discountenance the artful.

鵀 *zhăn*ˀ An ancient feathered or ornamented head-dress made from the crest or plumes of a bird of the same name, which by its description seems to refer to the hoopoe.

戴丨 to wear feathers on the head; these head-dresses, called 戴勝 were of several varieties, and seem to have been made in imitation of a hoopoe's crest.

JANG.

Old sound, niang. *In Canton*, yéung *and* séung; — *in Swatow*, jiàng *and* siàng; — *in Amoy*, jiòng *and* siòng; — *in Fuhchau*, yòng *and* nòng; — *in Shanghai*, zang, siang, *and* niang; — *in Chifu*, yang.

穰 ˏ*zhang* From *grain* and to *effect* as the phonetic.

The culm or stalk of grain; grain in fruit; luxuriant, abundant, fruitful; in *mathematics*, a term for ten billions.

福丨 the blessings of plenty.

降福丨丨 Heaven gave them unnumbered blessings.

盛丨 abundance; prosperous.

丨邑 the ancient name of Tăng cheu 鄧州, a small prefecture in the southwest of Honan.

攘 ˏ*zhang* From *hand* and to *effect*; it is also read *jang*ˀ and used for 讓 to cede.

To push to or from one with the hand; to appropriate, to seize without a clear right, to retain possession of; to reject, to expel; to bare, as the arms.

丨奪 to seize and hold on to.

丨臂 to bare the arms.

丨羊 to seize a stray sheep.

月丨一鷄 [he only] poached one hen in a month.

丨災 to drive off evil, as by incantations.

外丨夷狄 to expel the barbarians from the country.

Read ˋ*jang*. To stop; to embroil, to cause confusion.

天下擾ˋ丨 the country was thrown into disorder.

瀼 ˏ*zhang* From *water* and to *effect*; it is also read *nang*ˀ.

The name of a river in the eastern corner of Sz'chu'en; also the old name of a district in Nan-ning fu in the south of Kwangsi; an abundant, heavy dew; muddy water flowing, or water stopped in its flow because of silt.

涓流泱丨 the water flowed in a constant stream.

零露丨丨 the heavy dew stood in drops.

禳 ˏ*zhang* To fast and pray as the Taoists do in order to avert calamity; to deprecate evil.

丨禍 or 丨災 to seek to avert calamities.

丨除癘殃 to have prayers for averting pestilence.

丨星禮斗 intercede with one's natal star and reverence the Dipper, — for better luck.

儴 ˏ*zhang* An old form of ˏ*yin* 因 because, for; — now become obsolete.

勷 ˏ*zhang* Urgent; walking fast.

劻丨 in haste, hurried; to assist one in need.

瓤 ˏ*jang* From *melon* and to *effect*; also read ˏ*nang*.

The pulp of a squash or melon; the pith or whitish pulp of plants, as of the elder or pith-paper plant; the second film or coating; a corn-cob; the fleshy kernel or pit of nuts; the nasal cartilage.

核桃丨 walnut meats.

倒丨瓜 the melon's pulp is poured out; — emptied; exhausted, as one's energy.

東瓜丨 [like] the pulp of a squash; said of a flaw in a gem.

丨子 a letter or dispatch, as distinguished from the 皮 or envelop.

竹丨 the pellicle inside of the bamboo.

蘘 ˏ*zhang* A plant found in Kwéichau, growing in the shade of trees, called 丨荷, whose stem and leaves resemble ginger (*Zinziber mioga*); its root is aromatic and crisp and removes worms; the drawings and description assimilate it to the common ginger.

鬤 ˏ*zhang* The hair disheveled and uncombed.

鬇 丨 the hair in disorder from neglect; unkempt.

嚷 ʿ*zhang* The character is not authorized by the dictionaries.

To make a clamor, or cry out; to scold and bluster.

別 丨 don't bawl so, do not make such a noise.

山 丨 怪 叫 a great clamor and bawling.

吵 丨 甚 麽 what are you scolding about?

𢐧 ʿ*zhang* A bow bent and make ready for use.

壤 ʿ*zhang* Soft, loamy, rich earth without clods; mold, humus, soil; earth thrown up by moles; a place, a region; land; a country; a plat; productions; a mound, a billock; good, lovable, as a fine child; an ancient game; disarranged; sometimes used by the Budhists, for 穰 ten billions.

蓋 丨 the cover and ground; — heaven and earth.

三 丨 are the three qualities of soil which regulate the amount of tax laid on land.

外 丨 and 內 丨 the outer and inner limit of the sun in an eclipse.

蟻 丨 an ant-hill.

糞 丨 manure, poudrette.

沃 丨 a rich soil.

丨 子 a healthy, fat child; one doted on.

同 丨 of the same place.

接 丨 or 隣 丨 adjacent boundaries.

擊 丨 而 歌 to thump the clods and sing; *met.* a time of general peace; a sort of game is here referred to by thumping clods.

天 下 丨 丨 the crowds of people in the empire.

敢 執 丨 奠 we presume here to offer the production of our lands.

三 年 大 丨 a good harvest in three years.

讓 *zhang*ʾ From *words* and to *effect*; it occurs interchanged with ˏ攘 to push.

To cede, to yield, to give way to; to esteem others; to recede from one's rights, to waive them in favor of others; to reprove, to recriminate; to cheapen; complaisant, retiring, courteous; polite.

謙 丨 humble, unpresuming.

相 丨 each one yielding.

丨 位 to give up one's seat.

行者 丨 路 the travelers yielded the road.

責 丨 to blame one, to reprehend.

退 丨 retiring, refusing an honor.

揖 丨 而 升 he bowed and yielded the way, and then went in.

卑 丨 德 之 基 humility is the basis of virtue.

丨 多 少 how much will you take off the price?

受 爵 不 丨 don't decline to drink after receiving the cup.

爭 之 不 足 丨 之 有 餘 quarrelsome people are never satisfied, but the yielding have an overplus.

JĂNG.

Old sound, ning. *In Canton*, ying; — *in Swatow*, jéng *and* jiong; — *in Amoy*, jéng; — *in Fuhchau*, ing; — *in Shanghai*, sáng; — *in Chifu*, tsáng *and* láng.

仍 ˏ*zhăng* From *man* and *then*.

An *adverbial* particle, as, according to, as before; however, still, again; usual, ordinary; just so, in like manner, thus; in imitation of; a *conjunction*, and, and also.

丨 係 still is so.

丨 舊 as of old; usual, customary.

丨 然 yet is, still, the same as before.

丨 尙 往 彼 he still will go there.

丨 復 如 是 it is yet again so.

雲 丨 the son of a great grandson.

丨 蹈 前 轍 he continues at his old practices.

因 丨 苟 且 he is no better in his ways than before.

丨 丨 undecided; very bashful or hesitating.

丨 駐 勿 遽 回 省 let him stay there and not hasten his return to the provincial capital.

扔 ˏ*zhăng* To drag or lead along; to urge along; to toss, as a ball; to push, as a cart up-hill.

Read ˏ*jang*. To throw away, as a useless thing.

丨 石 to throw stones down.

丨 掉 了 he threw it away; he discarded the man.

丨 了 罷 throw it aside.

陾 ˏ*zhăng* The pattering sound made by pestles and beaters when rearing an adobie wall.

丨 丨 many, a crowd.

礽 ˏ*zhăng* Happiness; to approach to.

祈 天 百 丨 to implore every blessing from heaven.

艿 ˏ*zhăng* From 艸 *plants* and 仍 *as contracted.*

Old roots, stumps; plants cut down; shoots.

丨 草 當 夏 復 生 these old stumps will sprout again in the summer.

JAO.

Old sounds, nio, niok, no, nok, not. *In Canton*, iu *and* nao ; — *in Swatow*, jiò ; — *in Amoy*, jiao *and* giao ; — *in Fuhchau*, nieu, ngieu, *and* nao ; — *in Shanghai*, zo *and* nio ; — *in Chifu*, yao.

饒 ꜀zhao From to *eat* and *eminent* as the phonetic.

Plenty to eat; abundant, satisfied; affluent, an overplus, what is left; exceeding; liberal, indulgent; to throw in, as in a bargain; to favor in a sale; to excuse, to forbear, to spare; a region east of Poyang Lake where porcelain is made.

豐 〡 abounding in, ample.

富 〡 richly supplied.

寬 〡 to act leniently to criminals or prisoners.

我替你討 〡 I will intercede for your forgiveness.

〡 棋子 one or two chessmen given to an opponent.

〡 手 hold up, no more fighting; to let an adversary get the game.

〡 命 to spare life.

日月不相 〡 the sun and moon never yield (or delay) for each other.

告 〡 to own one's offenses, to beg pardon.

〡 裕 superabundant.

〡 舌 liberal-tongued, wrangling, disputatious.

〡 且不行 I surely am unable to assent, — how much less another one.

〡 了他 let him off this time; to forgive an offense.

白 〡 不值 the man throws in what is worth nothing, as pitching a bucket of water into the sea.

得 〡 人處且 〡 人 when you let a man off, then do it fully and frankly.

頌歲 〡 a most productive year.

〡 恕了罷 please do forgive me!

〡 一齣 to give an extra act in a play.

嬈 ꜀zhao From *woman* and *eminent*.

Pleasing, fascinating, witty, graceful; said of females.

嬌 〡 slender, airy, lady-like.

Read ˊniao. To make a disturbance; to play tricks with.

鬼 〡 the shade of a murdered man; imps who haunt a place.

橈 ꜀zhao From *wood* and *eminent*; it is as commonly read *nao*ʾ.

A short oar or paddle; to row; crooked, distorted; bigoted, prejudiced, unjust; to wrench, to pervert; weak, lithe, flexible, slim; to disperse, to disturb; to break.

〡 船 to paddle a boat.

〡 萬物 for scattering things — there's nothing like the wind.

柔 〡 骨體 a slender person, a graceful figure.

〡 敗 broken, ruined.

枉 〡 perverted, unjust, as a judgment.

蘭 〡 your fine oar; *i. e.* a pleasant row.

蕘 ꜀zhao Grass, rushes; stubble or thorns cut for fuel; to gather stubble.

火 〡 kindlings.

芻 〡 者 those who collect stubble for fuel.

薪 〡 faggots and grass, brushwood.

〡 花 a plant resembling the heath in habit, probably a *Passerina* or sparrow-wort.

襓 ꜀zhao The covering on a scabbard; it is made of cloth or strips wrapped around.

袂 〡 the covering of a sword more commonly called; it is 劍套 the sword's glove.

蟯 ꜀zhao Short worms found in the intestines; a squirming motion.

〡 蛔 worms like the tapeworm, which infest the bowels.

遶 zhaoʾ
繞 ꜀zhao
To wind around, to go about; to environ, to make the circuit of, to compass; to be entangled in.

圍 〡 to surround, as hills environ a town.

纏 〡 to cord up; to bind, as a vine does a tree.

山海週 〡 the sea and hills surround the place.

〡 路 or 〡 道走 to make a detour, to go round about.

〡 影壁 to play hide and seek, to have many wiles and tricks.

擾 ˊzhao From *hand* and *pitiful*.

To give or bring trouble to; to incommode, to embarrass; to confuse; to infest, as banditti do a region; to rear; to train to obedience, to pacify; mild, courteous, agreeable to.

煩 〡 to trouble needlessly, to bother.

騷 〡 or 〡 害地方 to disturb the peace of a country, as rebels do.

〡 亂 to make a region unsafe; to unsettle people's minds.

六 〡 the six domestic animals.

攪 〡 to disturb, to annoy.

〡 而毅 mild and yet brave.

〡 兆民 he pacified the people.

有 〡 有 〡 or 〡 飯 I've given you much trouble for this meal; — a polite phrase to a host.

陰人纏 〡 tormented by a devil-seer; or inveigled by a wench.

犪 ˊzhao A docile, tractable, well-trained ox; yielding, obliging, accommodating.

JÉ.

Old sounds, nia *and* niak. *In Canton*, yé *and* yui ; — *in Swatow*, jia *or* jé ; — *in Amoy*, jia *and* jiòk ; — *in Fuhchau*, niè ; — *in Shanghai*, za ; — *in Chifu*, yeh.

惹 ʿzhö From *heart* and *dried plants*.

To provoke, to irritate; to excite without an adequate cause; to produce, to elicit; to induce, to attract, to bring on one.

丨禍 to bring evil on one's self.

丨火燒身 [it is like] taking fire and burning myself.

丨我相思 it sets me pondering seriously.

不丨是非 do not excite needless trouble.

花丨蝶 the flowers draw the butterflies.

招丨 to provoke one another.

丨着 aggravating, irritating.

丨他不起 I am unwilling to provoke him.

丨事 to make trouble gratuitously.

引丨 to tempt, to incite to evil.

丨人笑 to mock at, to deride.

喏 ʿzhö Respectful language; a word used in replying to superiors, for which *noh*, 諾 is now commonly substituted as more correct.

唱丨 (used for 長揖) to make a profound reverence with the folded hands, in the Chinese manner.

偌 zhöʾ An exclamation used in light composition.

丨大 an expression of surprise, intimating a great size, a large, monstrous thing; the phrase is merely a phonetic one.

丨大的車 what a big carriage!

JEH.

Old sounds, niet *and* nit. *In Canton*, it *and* yat ; — *in Swatow*, jwa *or* jiet *and* jit ; — *in Amoy*, jiat *and* jit ; — *in Fuhchau*, yek *and* nik ; — *in Shanghai*, nih ; — *in Chifu*, i *and* yeh.

熱 爇 zhöʾ From *fire* and *skilled*, or *to grasp*; the first is the most common; it is liable to be confounded with *shuh*, 熟 ripe.

Hot; heat, caloric; feverish, restless; fever; ardent, energetic, warm-hearted; heated; to warm.

和和丨 or 温丨 tepid, lukewarm.

暑丨 or 炎丨 hot, fervid, as the sun.

發丨 feverish; having a dry skin, as when 丨病 a fever is coming on.

丨如坐甑 [I am as] hot as if I was sitting on a still.

丨氣烝人 the weather almost roasts one.

丨鬧 bustle of a fair or a feast; a hubbub; great excitement and show.

誰能執丨 who can take up a hot thing?

五心煩丨 I am very very anxious and nervous.

不分冷丨 it is quite indifferent to me; also, he cares neither for cold nor heat, — in his zeal.

丨心 or 丨心腸 warm-hearted; zealous; affectionate.

天時丨 hot weather.

悶丨 or 燥丨 sultry and humid weather; hot and close.

丨河 or Zhehol, the summer retreat of the Emperor northeast of Peking.

丨決 to have a sunstroke.

兩個人打得火丨 the two men are mad at each other, — have quarreled till the fire came.

日 ʒzhih The original form represents a *circle*, or what surrounds, with *one* inside of it, to denote that the sun is incomparably the greatest circle: it forms the 72d radical of a natural group of characters relating to the sun and time.

The sun, described as 太陽之精, the energy of the male power; worshiped in India as a god under the name *surya*, and as 丨天 regarded by the Budhists as the *deva* in the sun; a day; daily; days, times; daytime; in the time of; the day for a thing, as an anniversary; in casting lots, means the emperor, his palace, day, or reign, as in the phrase 丨下 under the sun, — *i. e.* near his throne, as if he was light.

一個丨子 one day, from morn till evening.

丨頭 the sun's light or heat; in the sunshine.

白丨 dawn, very early; by daylight; daytime.

連丨 or 丨丨 daily, every day; constantly.

別丨, or 異丨, or 他丨 on another day; in future; after this; by and by.

今丨 to-day.

昨丨 or 丨昨 yesterday, two or three days ago; recently.

無丨 or 不丨 erelong, in a few days; in less than a day; quickly.

丨輪 the sun's disk.

後丨 day after to-morrow.

明丨 to-morrow, *i.e.* the bright day.

往丨 or 昔丨 a while ago.

丨者 persons who divine for days.

丨用 or 丨給 daily needs or expenses.

丨子短 the days are short now.

丨落 or 丨平西 sunset; sun going to the west; it is getting late in the day.

丨重一丨 he is daily becoming worse.

何丨忘之 when can I forget them? — *i. e.* never can I forget.

丨對千金 a day is worth a thousand pieces of gold ;— time is priceless.

不丨有曀 before the day is over it clouds up again.

丨圍主水 a halo round the sun indicates rain.

丨蝕 a solar eclipse.

不丨不月 not for days nor for months; indefinitely, no time fixed.

丨課 a daily exercise or lesson.

捧丨心 to cherish loyal feelings, referring to the clouds which appear to bear up the sun.

丨新 daily renovated or improved.

瞻雲就丨 to look up to the clouds and approach the sun; — to draw near to the palace.

虛度時丨 I have idled away my days; life has been vainly spent.

後會有丨 we shall again meet another day.

丨角 the high protuberance seen on the crowns of some Budhist saints.

丨本國 Japan or Nippon.

丨國 is sometimes used for 日斯巴尼亚 Hispania or Spain.

黃道丨 a fortunate, lucky day; *lit.* an ecliptic day.

丨就月將 [work as] the sun and moon gradually rise; *i. e.* be diligent at your calling.

爇 ˎzhö From *fire* and *dead trees* as the phonetic.

To burn; to heat; to set over a blaze; to sear, as with an iron.

卜以明火丨燋 burn it (the tortoise-shell) before a bright fire to divine by it.

丨山林以逐豺狼 burn the underbrush to drive out the wolves.

丨茶 tea heated a second time.

衵 ˎzhih From *clothes* and *daily*.

The clothes which are worn every day; common garments.

Read *nih*, A woman's under garment, a chemise.

皆衷其丨服以戲於朝 she wore only her chemise to show her contempt for the court.

挼 ˎzhö To soak or dip in sauce or liquor; to sop, as in soy or vinegar.

丨于醢 dip it in the sauce or pickle.

Read ˏ*jwan*. To push; a synonym of ˏ*jwan* 撋 to move things.

JEU.

Old sounds, nio *and* net. *In Canton*, yau; — *in Swatow*, jiu *and* nui; — *in Amoy*, jiu; — *in Fuhchau*, iu *and* niu; — *in Shanghai*, zù; — *in Chifu*, yiu.

柔 ˏzheu From *wood* and *spear*; it occurs used for the next, and as a primitive exercises some influence on the compounds.

Flexible, elastic; pliant, like twigs; the opposite of 剛 stiff; tender, as budding plants; soft, yielding, as wool; fawning; mild, kind; soft, meek; limp; in *music*, a flat note; complaisant, condescending, bland to; to show kindness, to subdue by kindness, to act gently towards; to give rest to.

丨軟 mild, as speech; soft, as a feather-bed.

丨弱 gentle and weak.

無不丨嘉 never fail to act mildly and correctly.

剛丨並濟 temper firmness with gentleness.

丨遠人 be gracious to strangers, — and thus cause them to live quietly under you; — was the advice of Tsăng-tszʾ.

温丨敦厚 courteous and sincere.

懷丨百神 remember the duties owing to the gods.

德以丨中國 I subdued (or brought over) China by virtue.

體態丨情 a simpering, mincing gait and manner, as wanton women have.

揉 ˏzheu From *hand* and *pliant*; it is also read ʿnao, and interchanged with the preceding and the next.

To bend, to twist, to work about, to contort; to make pliable; to make wood supple by heat; to bring under one's sway.

丨搓 to rumple in the hand; to bully; to scold and lord it over roughly.

丨碎 to twist to pieces.

丨球 to roll a ball in the hand to keep the fingers supple; a common practice with elderly people.

丨此萬邦 to subdue all these countries.

丨捺 to yield to any usage; craven, fawning, helpless.

楺 ꜀zheu Like the last.

To bend wood by fire or steaming.

丨木爲耒 to bend a stick to make a plow-handle.

蹂 ꜀zheu From *foot* and *pliant* as the phonetic.

To tread out grain; to trample over, to tread down; to dampen grain in order to free it from chaff.

丨踐 trodden under foot, as in a rush.

丨躪 the crowded trampling of animals; *met.* oppressive and harassing exactions; the devastations of troops.

丨去粃糠 to winnow away the chaff.

輮 ꜀zheu Occurs used for the last two.

The felly of a wheel was once known in Shansi by this term.

行山者仄丨[in making carts] for traveling in the hills, put hard wood into the fellies.

坎爲矯丨 in the second diagram *kien*, the straight and the crooked alternate.

鞣 ꜀zheu Soft, well dressed leather, like chamois or wash-leather.

腬 ꜀zheu Good meat, fat and juicy; excellent, abundant; an affable, pleasing countenance.

煣 ꜂zheu Occurs interchanged with ꜀揉 to bend.

To bend wood by the application of fire or steam.

糅 ꜂zheu Mixed, as grain of different kinds, or as feathers; to eat.

同丨玉石 the gems and stones are all together.

禸 ꜂zheu The original character is intended to represent the impression of a rounded foot like a fox's, the upper part denoting the hind toe; in explanation it is said that wolves, badgers, and foxes are ashamed of their paws, and step lightly; it is used as the 114th radical of a few unusual characters.

A step, the track of an animal's paws; to track, to step.

JOH.

Old sound, nok. *In Canton*, yéuk; — *in Swatow*, jiak; — *in Amoy*, jiòk; — *in Fuhchau*, yòk *and* nioh; — *in Shanghai*, zak; — *in Chifu*, yòa.

弱 zho꜄ The character is thought to resemble the shape of crooked pelage, like the long curled hair of some lambs, represented by 彡 doubled on a body; others say that the character depicts two 象 *elephants* contracted.

Pliable, slender, fragile; weak, feeble, languishing; infirm of purpose; weakness; ruined, decayed; frail, fading, dead; to despise.

丨冠 a young man of twenty.

衰丨 decrepid, no stamina.

志氣丨 infirm of purpose.

軟丨 having no strength.

瘦丨 much wasted away.

丨質 weak, thin in substance; a gentle disposition; *met.* a young lady delicately reared.

嫵媚孅丨 lithe, graceful and sprightly, as a girl.

柔丨 pliable, like a twig.

懦丨 without energy; gross and weak, morose; imbecile minded.

丨水 a fluid between air and water, found in fairy land.

濟丨 help the weak.

春寒花丨 when the spring is cold, the flowers are stunted.

丨不勝衣 too weak to wear a coat.

勿爭强丨 what is the use of quarreling? let us have done.

蒻 zho꜄ A sort of water plant, the cat-tail rush (*Typha*), whose tender shoots, called 蒲丨 are good for food; mats are woven from the mature plants.

葯丨 a vegetable whose roots are eaten.

叒 zho꜄ Formed of *three hands*, referring to the ancient custom of joining hands to show their unity of heart, and principle, and mutual confidence.

Obedient, accommodating; united.

丨木 a divine, self-existing tree, which grows in Fu-sang 扶桑 the land where the sun rises.

鄀 zho꜄ A small feudal state, situated within the present district of I-ch'ing hien 宜城縣 in Siang-yang fu in the north of Hupeh.

若, *zho'* From *plants* and the *right hand* with which to select them.

To select plants, to pluck plants; to accord with, to follow; to arrive at; a *conjunction*, as, same as, like; followed by a noun or pronoun, then, as to; a conditional particle, if, perhaps, should it be, supposing; and; occurs used for 汝 you, the second person or the person spoken of; this, the one; as that; when duplicated, it answers to either — or; a euphonic particle; name of a marine deity.

如丨 if, as, since, it seems; — used as an initial phrase.

丨然來 supposing he comes.

莫丨, or 不丨, or 豈丨, it will be best; the better way is; nothing better than.

時寒丨 a seasonable cold; it is the cold usual at the season.

有丨無 to possess as if not having.

倘丨 if so, if it be.

丨輩 of such (or the same) sort.

相丨 similar to, probably.

猶丨 is like 猶然, still, it seems proper; he ought.

民猶丨不足 the people still have not enough.

丨民則喜 as to the people, they were pleased.

丨遲不及 if you delay, you will not be there in time.

丨何 how then? then what?

丨曰 it was reported; some one said.

丨老丨幼 of the old and young — scores died.

丨此何來 where then did you come from?

曾孫是丨 you are then my grandson.

匚讀丨方 the character ˏ*fang* is read like ˏ*fang*.

欽丨昊天 reverently comply with Heaven's orders.

邦國丨否仲山甫明之 whether the princes were obedient or not, Chung-Shan-fu understood them.

丨干 such a number, so many; indeterminate and yet large.

指不丨人 the finger is not worth the whole man; but 丨人 also means a certain man, this fellow, such a one.

自丨 truly, just so; self-collected.

君丨待於曲棘 Prince, wait in Kiüh-kih.

綏丨丨 the ends of the dispatch napkin hang down; it is wrapped in yellow silk and carried across the neck.

病未丨死 although sick, he is not yet dead.

杜丨 name of a plant like turmeric.

丨彼丨此皆可爲也 either this way or that will do.

丨乃雲開現日 now then, if the clouds clear off, we shall see the sun.

丨論 if we speak of this, &c.

丨是不好就不買 if it be not a good one, then don't buy it.

厎丨之人兮 ah! such a woman as this!

丨花丨月丨酒皆足移情 enjoying the fragrant flowers in the moonlight, and a cup of wine, surely ought to satisfy one's feelings.

Read *'jé*. Dried plants; hay; a Budhist word meaning clever.

波丨眼 the eye of Budha, which can see the heart and motives.

般丨 adroit; wise; imitation of the Sanscrit *pradjna* or wisdom, the highest virtue, which is the means of attaining to *nirvana*.

般若婆羅密多 the *Pradjna Paramita*, a classical work of the Mahayana school of Budhist philosophers.

蘭丨 a retired still place, fit for meditation; a hermit's cell.

箬, *zho'* From *bamboo* and *if* as the phonetic.

An old name for the cuticle of the bamboo; a slender variety of the bamboo about four feet high (*Bambusa latifolia*), much cultivated for its broad leaves; they are used to weave into boat-sails, and hats called 青丨笠; to wrap rice-balls in when boiled, or to line and cover tea chests; women put them in the soles of shoes; and in old time, people prepared them for writing on; the culms furnish pencil handles.

丨包船 a sort of gypsy-boat in Kiangsu, whose inmates have a bad reputation for kidnapping and thieving.

丨帽芒鞋 [I am now wearing] a leaf hat and rush sandals; — I am retired from office.

丨篷 mat sails of bamboo leaves, woven between splints.

In *Fuhchau*. Many, how many; an interrogative of quantity.

楉, *zho'* A kind of fruit called 丨榴, which resembles a plum or bullace; the unusual efficacy of all gigantic trees, which causes them to be worshiped.

JÜ.

Old sounds, no, not, *and* niok. *In Canton*, yü; — *in Swatow*, ju; — *in Amoy*, ju; — *in Fuhchau*, ü *and* sü; — *in Shanghai*, sö, sü, *and* na; — *in Chifu*, yü.

如 ˓zhu From *woman* and *mouth*, to denote that a daughter or wife attends to the orders of a father or husband; as a primitive its use is chiefly to give sound; occurs used for 汝 you.

A *conjunction* of comparison, as, like, as if, according to; if, perhaps, — and thereby has somewhat the force of a future in it; and, also; an initial word, regarding, but as to, then; seeming; to allow or permit; to become as, to equal; to go to; after adjectives, it often has only an intensive force, as an interjection; a personal pronoun, you.

丨此 thus; like this; also 有丨此 and this is its purport; — expressions closing an extract.

丨今 now, at this time.

二三丨六 two into three make six.

丨月 an old term for the second moon.

不丨 nothing like; 'tis the best way, it will be better; and cases occur where the negative being involved, 如 alone is used; — as 愛其二毛則丨服焉 if you like graybeards you had better follow them.

稱心丨意 may your heart's wish be accomplished; — in this phrase there is a reference to a common ornament, the 丨意 (*lit.* as you wish,) which is often given at marriages and to friends for good luck; it is of Budhistic origin, and is usually called a scepter from its probable early use as a mark of royalty in India; it is one of the *sapta ratna*, or seven precious things.

丨何 how; then how?

丨有 if there be, if any one has.

無丨之何 could nothing be done with him? — then there's no help for it.

空空丨也 really nothing at all.

縱意所丨 just where my thoughts go.

丨果這樣 if it be so.

其丨我何 well what are you going to do to me about it?

有女丨雲 the girls were numerous as clouds.

突丨其來 he suddenly came in.

雖有不丨無 if you have it, that's better than being without.

善丨爾之問也 ah! what a fine question you've asked.

丨來佛 the Thus-come Budha, is the translation of the Sanscrit *tată-gata*, one who exhibits perfect human nature, one whose coming and going accords with that of his predecessor; it is the highest appellation given to every Budha.

茹 ˓zhu From *plants* and *like* as the phonetic.

Intertwisted as roots; interlaced or entangled, as roots are with the stem; to receive, to take; to eat much, to gormandize; to covet; to feed, as cattle; pliant, flexible; putrid, as fish; dried, as vegetables for keeping; to die, to wither away; to conjecture, to deliberate.

貪丨 a great appetite.

拔茅連丨 to pull the roots up with the grass.

啜丨 to quaff greedily.

不可以丨 I cannot guess what it is.

丨毛飲血 to eat the hair and drink the blood, as savages do.

香丨 a fragrant plant (*Eschscholtzia cristata*), allied to the vervain.

丨魚驅蠅 stinking fish brings flies.

丨藘 a sort of madder (*Rubia*), grown for its dye.

不丨葷 don't eat gross food.

丨素念經 fasting and praying, as a good Budhist.

來咨來丨 consult about [the rules] and consider.

鴽 ˓zhu A bird resembling a quail, which is thought to be produced by transformation from a mole; it is also defined a pigeon, but it is probably allied to the quail, godwit, or stone-curlew.

箬 ˓zhu The tender epidermis or scurf skin of the bamboo; it is sometimes gathered to use as oakum in calking, and occasionally exhibited as a sudorific.

竹丨 bamboo oakum, used also to scour vessels.

儒 ˓zhu From *man* and *necessary* as the phonetic.

Persons who understand the principles of things, philosophers, literati, the learned; scholars, more especially those who pretend to follow the teachings of Confucius, in distinction from Budhists and Taoists; mild, accomplished, as a scholar should be.

丨教 Confucianists; the literary class.

丨者 or 丨士 or 丨生 a scholar, a man of letters.

寒丨 an indigent scholar.

大丨 or 名丨 or 宿丨 a celebrated scholar.

丨學 an officer, analogous to a director of graduates; there are two in each district over the *siutsʻai*.

腐丨 a made-up scholar, a pretentious pedant, a scholasticus.

丨醫 a learned physician.

小人丨 a hypocritical man, one who stickles at trifles in doctrine.

丨雅 elegant, stylish; lady-like.

濡 ˏzhu From *water* and *necessary*; it is also read ˏ'rh, ˏsü, no', nwan', and ˓jwan, in its various uses and names.

To immerse; to moisten; thick, viscid, sediment-like; damp, wet; glossy, fresh; mild, forbearing, patient, enduring; to urinate; to soak in.

丨鷄 to scald a fowl to remove the feathers.

羔裘如丨 soft as a lamb's wool coat.

含丨 patience; enduring.

無丨忍之心 I have no patience with him.

沾丨 soaked; to macerate, to immerse.

丨滯 obstructed, flowing slowly; embarrassed, undecided.

丨溺 immersed in; to dip, to souse in.

濟盈不丨軌 the ford though high will not wet the axle.

耳丨目染 he has soaked ears and tinted eyes; he is an expert, he knows all about it; a mellow scholar.

丨河 old name of a river in Yihcheu 易州 in Chihli, and another in the east of Kwangsi.

嚅 ˏzhu Chattering; the indistinct hum of conversation.

囁丨 much talking; querulous, a hesitating speech, as when one is afraid to tell out his sentiments.

襦 ˏzhu From *garment* and *necessary* as the phonetic.

A short coat; a soft, close fitting spencer; a jerkin.

單丨 an unquilted jacket, one without wadding.

汗丨 an under-shirt, an absorbing garment.

腰丨 a sort of round-about.

丨袴 jacket and trowsers.

醹 ˏzhu Generous, rich spirit.

酒醴維丨 new wine (or must) is rich and well tasted.

蕠 ˏzhu A sort of *Boletus*, or similar kind of fungus, known as 香丨 (or sometimes written 香茹草); the decoction is used in dog-days as a cooling drink, and a remedy in cholera; this medicine has been identified in northern China as the *Eschscholtzia cristata*, but probably two dissimilar plants are referred to by confounding two homophonous characters.

乳 ˊzhu Composed of 孚 to *incubate* and 乙 a *period*; the explanation given is that the 玄鳥 blackbird or swallow, as soon as it comes to its nesting ground in spring, prays to the plum flower for young.

Milk; milky; the breasts; the nipple,— Wăn Wang is said to have had four; to suck; to nurse; to brood upon eggs; to grind fine as paints; suckling; shaped like nipples.

丨汁 the milk.

丨母 a wet-nurse.

丨鉢 to triturate in a mortar.

丨金 liquid gold, used in painting.

羊羔跪丨 the lamb kneels to suck; quoted as a proof that nature herself teaches filial piety.

竹丨 tabasheer.

石鐘丨 stone-bell teats; *i. e.* stalactites, from their shape.

斷丨 to wean a babe.

牛丨餅 a cake of curd, a cheese-cake.

丨子 or 丨哺 to suckle; the first is an infant at the breast.

馬丨葡萄 mare's teat grape, the long white Isabella grape.

蠅於蠶身丨子 the fly lays her eggs in the caterpillar's body.

天丨星 the stars *a ω* in Serpens.

丨香 olibanum or incense; the gum resin obtained from the *Boswellia papyrifera*, and gum sandarach; the name alludes to the drops resembling nipples; both these gums are included under it, and both are often contained in the same mass.

汝 ˊzhu From *water* and *woman*; it is interchanged with *nü* 女 you.

The personal pronoun, your, you; name of two tributaries of the R. Hwai; one joins it above Ch'ăn-cheu fu; the small feudal state of this name is retained in the inferior department of Jü cheu 丨州 situated on the river near the center of Honan; the other and larger stream, whose basin includes the department of Jü ning fu 丨寧府 flows southeast of it, and joins the River Hwai below Sin-tsai hien 新蔡縣 near the border of the province.

是非丨所知也 you do not understand this thing.

丨其于予治 do you try to govern them for me.

致意丨主人 do you tell what I say to your master.

籹 ˊzhu Cakes baked of rice flour and honey, used for desserts, and made in many forms.

鞣 ˊzhu Shoes.

孺 ˊzhu From *child* and *necessary* as the phonetic.

A child still at the breast, a suckling; a tender or weaned child; attached to or dependant, as a child; intimate with.

黃口丨子 a child still nursing; used in reference to King Ching in the Book of Records.

丨子其朋 my young son, can you be partial?

和樂且丨 a pleasant friendship and attachment,— as the infant with its mother's breast.

丨人 wives of officials of the 7th rank; when a commoner's wife dies, her son worships her as if this rank had been conferred on her.

丨慕之私 these are my humble opinions;— used in letters.

擩 zhu' To stain, to dye; to dip, as into sauce; to put in brine; to hold up a thing in the hands as when worshiping; to raise; to rub the hands.

丨 噴 道 眞 when the heart is imbued with a subject the speech is sincere.

Read *neu'* in 擩 丨 not to understand an affair.

洳 zhu' From *water* and *like* as the phonetic.

To become moist, to soak in; to dampen.

丨 河 old name of a river in King-cheu fu 荆州府 in Hupeh, joining the Yangtsz'.

彼汾沮 丨 in those low, oozy banks of the River Făn.

霧 彌 衣 欲 丨 the dress soon becomes soaked in a heavy mist.

袽 zhu' Poor, worn-out garments, fit only for padding.

繻 有 衣 丨 they used the silk selvege — to stop the leaks in the boat.

帤 zhu' The wrapping which is wound on the ends of a bow to strengthen it; a large napkin; an ornamented streamer hung in houses.

JUH.

Old sounds, nip *and* nok. *In Canton*, yăp, yŏk, *and* ya; — *in Swatow*, jip, jŏk, *and* nek; — *in Amoy*, jip, jih, *and* jiŏk; — *in Fuhchau*, ík, ŭk, *and* nŭk; — *in Shanghai*, zeh, zŏk, niŏk, *and* nieⁿ; — *in Chifu*, yü *and* tsü.

入 zhu' The original form is intended to represent the junction of 上 and 下 going in and out; it forms the 11th radical of a small and incongruous group of characters; it resembles *pah*, 八 eight and *ˏjăn* 人 man, but their similarity causes more care in writing each.

To enter, to go into; to enter upon; to penetrate; to become a member of, as a sect; to enter a family; to incroach on, to usurp; to recede from view; to take in, to receive, as fees; to progress, as in a course of action; to put into; income, receipts; according to, in which sense it becomes an adjective; an entrance.

丨 口 貨 imports, goods arriving from sea.

眼 丨 色 the eye takes in objects.

收 丨 to have in hand, to receive.

無 丨 息 not making anything; no revenue or interest from it.

丨 熟 你 he wishes to make your acquaintance.

出 丨 outlay and expenditure; out and in; here and there; going and coming.

六 丨 the six organs of sensation (*shada-yatana*), the eye, ear, nose, tongue, body and mind; a Budhist term.

丨 章 to try for the *kü-jin* degree.

丨 人 頭 he is affable at first. (*Cantonese.*)

丨 夜 at night; night is approaching.

不 相 丨 incongruous; they do not match.

丨 數 put it in the account; reckon it in the number.

故 丨 人 罪 to charge a crime on one.

丨 伙 to become an affiliated member, as of a club.

莒 人 丨 向 the men of Kü came submitting themselves.

丨 理 reasonable, proper.

丨 官 to confiscate.

ˏ長 丨 a term given to courtiers who daily see the emperor.

丨 信 credible, worthy of trust.

丨 定 去 了 a Budhist priest engaged in his devotions.

我 丨 自 外 when I came home from abroad.

量 丨 以 爲 出 estimate your income in order to see what you can spend.

不 諫 亦 丨 he went on improving even without admonition.

丨 耳 之 言 excellent sayings, words of wisdom.

丨 彀 well enough; done well, as a piece of work; capable, adequate for.

辱 zhu' From 辰 *time* and 寸 an *inch* or rule, because the farmer who passed the proper time for sowing, was executed on the border.

To insult, to put to shame; to dishonor, to bring reproach on; to mortify; to rail at, to pour contempt on; to defile, to debauch; shamed, degraded, disgraced, defiled; used in polite phrase for, You have done me the honor, — but in so doing you have disgraced yourself.

丨 在 泥 塗 bedaubed with filth.

忍 丨 patient under obloquy.

舍 丨 偷 生 to save one's life disgracefully, as in battle.

一 番 羞 丨 he berated him shamefully.

丨 沒 了 他 you reproached him; you rather scolded him.

屈 丨 you have submitted to dishonor, — as a host says when another comes to visit him.

丨 臨 敝 舍 you have demeaned yourself to honor my hovel with your presence.

丨 還 答 you have honored me by an answer.

不 丨 君 命 not to reproach his prince's orders,—by doing aught dishonorable.

君 無 所 丨 命 the prince did not trouble himself to give me any orders.

玷 丨 to defile a gem; *i. e.* to violate a girl.

丨 身 to expose the person; disgraced himself; to do menial offices; sold to infamy.

喪師 丨 國 the army was demoralized and the country disgraced.

溽, *zhu'* Damp, muggy; vaporish; steaming, close; hot and reeking; rich, savory; name of a river where Muh wang 穆王 drank (B. C. 1000).

不 丨 poor fare, meager living.

飲食不 丨 don't eat or drink what is very rich.

丨 暑 humid, hot weather, as near the summer solstice.

丨 氣蒸騰 the muggy vapor steams upward.

林無不 丨 the woods are always damp.

嗕, *zhu'* To pity; name of a tribe of Scythians in the Han dynasty.

嚅 丨 a kind, compassionating look.

縟, *zhu'* Adorned, beautified with colors; gay, pretty; lustrous, as a gem; elegant, ornate; to reckon with, to collect together.

密采珍 丨 thickly studded with precious things.

繁 丨 gaily variegated, as a robe.

In *Cantonese*. Sleek, smooth.

油 丨 soft and fine, as fur.

褥, *zhu'* From *clothes* and to *disgrace*; the next is sometimes used for this.

A thick, stuffed mat; a felt or thick cover; a mattress, a cushion, a wadded seat; a palliasse.

丨 子 a mattress.

椅 丨 chair covers falling over the back.

棉 丨 a cotton mattress.

被 丨 a coverlet and bed.

馬 丨 a saddle-cloth to protect the horse's back.

裀 丨 a carriage-cushion.

床 丨 a bed mattress.

Read *no'* A child's dress.

蓐, *zhu'* Occurs used for the last.

Suckers, shoots; sprouts springing from an old root; rushes for making mats; a silkworm frame; name of an ancient petty state somewhere in the present Shantung.

竹 丨 a fungus growing on the bamboo.

丨 食 to eat while lying in bed.

秋物摧 丨 而可收也 rushes mature in autumn when they can be gathered; hence 丨 收 has become a term for harvest.

茵 丨 a thick greensward, a cushion of grass, a green lawn.

肉, 月, *zheu'* *zhu'* The original shape of this character is thought to represent a slice of meat; in combination it is usually contracted like *yueh*, 月 the moon, and resembles *ˊcheu* 舟 a boat; it forms the 130th radical of a large natural group of characters relating to meat and food.

Flesh; meat; in the southern provinces it usully denotes pork when used alone; the pulp or eatable part of fruits; the rim of a cash; fat, fleshy; corporeal, fleshly.

丨 丸 or 丨 圓 pork or meat balls.

牛 丨 beef; 羊 丨 mutton.

飛 丨 poultry, birds, game.

丨 片 slices of meat.

丨 案子 a butcher's stall.

長 丨 or 生 丨 fleshy; in season, as fruit or fish.

風入 丨 the wind chills me through.

骨豐 丨 潤 the strokes are vigorous and their lines broad, — said of well-formed characters.

剪 丨 焚香 [I would] cut off my flesh to burn as incense, — to show my gratitude.

不入 丨 [this wind] does not chill one; *met.* you don't spend anything; it's not a serious matter to you.

丨 食者鄙 a glutton is a despicable fellow; the epithet is often applied to officials in reproach because they eat meat.

骨 丨 bones and flesh; — *met.* brothers; children; sisters; blood relatives; 親骨 丨 refers only to parents and children.

一身 丨 obese, fat, corpulent.

丨 身 this mortal body.

丨 癢討打 your flesh itches for me to thrash you, — as an irate teacher exclaims.

土 丨 a marine animal like the *Medusa* or sea-anemone.

作爲熟 丨 treated him like a piece of cooked meat to get his money.

乾水 丨 pork not water-blown.

丨 眼無珠 a fleshy eye has no pupil; — used when one does not appreciate another.

瘠 丨 lean and fleshy.

丨 眼不識英雄 his fleshly (sordid) eyes cannot appreciate a real hero.

腐 丨 sloughing flesh; proud flesh.

裏 丨 and 柳 丨 tender-loin; the last is used at Canton, because it is tender like new willow leaves.

廿, 卄, *zhu'* Also read *nien'*; the second form is used in books.

Two tens combined making twenty; a score.

打 丨 板 beat him twenty strokes.

丨 多人 more than a score of people.

勿管三七 丨 一 he does not know that 3 times 7 make 21; — the silly fellow.

JUI.

Old sounds, nui, nai, nút, *and* nap. *In Canton*, yui ; — *in Swatow*, lui, jué, *and* jui ; — *in Amoy*, jui, sui, lui, *and* jòé ; — *in Fuhchau*, yò, wi, *and* lwi ; — *in Shanghai*, djüé *and* süé ; — *in Chifu*, yòh *and* tsui.

緌 ꜀sui — From *silk* and to *depute* ; some regard it as a synonym of *sui* 綏 a fringe.

A fringe which hangs from a cap on the back ; throat-band of a cap ; to bind ; a part of ancient bridal apparel, which was a band covering the sides of the face, to denote the wife's dependence on her husband ; anciently, a military standard made of yak's tails.

冠 丨 雙 止 a pair of throat-bands.

桵 ꜀sui — A low, thorny bush, called 白 丨 and *yuh*, 棫 whose fruit is edible, and likened in shape to an ear-pendent ; it seems to be a kind of scrubby date like the *Rhamnus utilis*.

甤 ꜀sui — From 生 to *bear* and 豨 a *hog* contracted.

Prolific like swine ; luxuriant, as flowers bearing much fruit.

蕤 ꜀sui — From *plants and prolific* ; occurs interchanged with the next.

Pendent twigs of trees, drooping leaves or flowers, as of air-plants ; ends of a fringe or band hanging down ; soft, delicate.

葳 丨 旗 a red flag or scroll hung among flowers on the 3d day of the 3d moon to encourage them to open.

布冠不 丨 a cloth cap has no fringe.

丨 賓 a metaphorical name for the fifth moon, meaning prolific guests, in allusion to its flowers.

芳 丨 the fragrant spikes of flowers.

萎 丨 also called 玉竹, an emulgent sweetish root, used in throat disease ; it looks like orris root ; the first term is applied also to a *Polygonum* or knot-grass.

惢 ꜀ **蕋** ꜀ ꜂zhui — From *plants* and *heart* or to *stop* repeated thrice ; the second form is unusual, and derived through the seal form.

The stamens or pistils of a flower, the pointals ; flowers in spikes or bushy heads, opening in succession ; a leaf-bud ; *met.* a virgin ; sap, juice.

發 丨 the buds are starting.

花 丨 the stamens of a flower.

花 丨 頭 an unopened bud.

石 丨 the common lichens on stone, as *Parmela* and *Lecidea*.

鴉片 丨 the juice of the poppy.

丨 汁 glutinous or viscid juices of plants, as of spurge. (*Euphorbia.*)

燭 丨 the lighted wick of a candle.

嫩 丨 方開蜂媒至問 when the tender bud is opening, then the wasp of a go-between comes asking for it.

蘂 ꜀ ꜂zhui — Like the preceding.

The inner organs of a flower ; plants growing thick and pendent.

玉 丨 花 one name for the passion-flower.

縈 ꜀ ꜂zhui — From *silk* and *stamens* as the phonetic.

Hanging down like the ends of the girdle, or the things attached to a fan.

芮 zhui꜄ — From *plants* and *within*.

Small plants budding ; springing ; a bank or brink ; the thongs of a shield.

丨 城 縣 a district in the department of Kiai cheu in the southwest of Shansi, the ancient feudal state of Jui ; there was a Baron of Jui 丨 伯 in the Cheu dynasty, whose fief is referred to Chao-yih hien 朝邑縣 near the capital of Shensi.

丨 丨 soft, small leaves, like those of some rocky plants, as the saxifrage.

丨 鞫 之 卽 in the region beyond the River Jui, — a branch of the River King in Shensi.

丨 草 or 蛇 丨 a species of knotweed. (*Polygonum multiflorum.*)

汭 zhui꜄ — From *water* and *within*, alluding to the junction of a small stream with a larger one.

Name of a branch of the River King in the southeast of Kansuh, near the town of Hwating hien 華亭縣 ; a bay, bight, or shallow part near the shore ; junction of two rivers ; north side of a stream ; winding of a stream.

沙 丨 beach of a bay.

涇 屬 渭 丨 junction of the rivers Wéi and King.

枘 zhui꜄ — The handle of a chisel ; the haft of an ax or cutting tool.

丨 鑿 不 入 the haft and the chisel, if separated, — are both unserviceable.

蚋 ꜄ **蜹** ꜄ zhui꜄ — A musquito, a gnat ; a kind of venemous snake.

蚊 丨 musquitoes or stinging flies ; water flies.

蠅 丨 flies that swarm upon corpses or sour things.

睿 ꜄ **叡** ꜄ zhui꜄ — Composed of 目 the *eye*, 𣦵 a *hollow* in a bone, and 谷 *valley* contracted placed between ; denoting that as the eye receives light and a valley echoes sound, so does the mind wisdom ; the second is most used, as the first is a sacred character.

Perspicacious, clever, bright and quick of perception ; shrewd, discreet, astute ; able to detect subtle causes ; the divine sagacity of sages ; profound.

丨智 intuitive wisdom.

聖丨 divine perception of things.

思曰丨丨作聖 reflection can be called wisdom, and this wisdom leads to an intuitive knowledge of things.

仁宗丨皇帝 our Humane Ancestor, the Emperor Discreet; his reign was called Kiak'ing; A.D. 1796-1820.

銳 *zhui'* From *metal* and to *change*.

Sharp-pointed, acute; peaked, piercing, lance-like; zealous, ardent; valiant; quickwitted, subtle, keen, shrewd; resolute, earnest in; small, insignificant, as a spear's point or a peccadillo.

丨兵 or 丨師 well drilled troops.

丨利 sharp and pointed, as a blade.

失丨 crestfallen; dull.

一人露晃執丨 one man with a conspicuous helmet took the front in the fight; — as Henry IV. at Ivry.

丨氣 ardent, fired up, ready for a fight.

精丨 skilled in, as a workman; ready at, as in repartee.

口丨 talkative, glib-tongued, pert.

尖丨 sharp-pointed; *met.* sarcastic, biting.

敏丨 keen, as in argument.

丨身去救人 a zealous man rushes forward to save another.

丨氣不可墮 the determined spirit never yields or fails.

諉 *zhui'* From *words* and to *bend*; it is also read *néi'* and *wéi'*.

To implicate others, to lay blame on one; to shirk one's work; to give over one's duty to another; to apologize and decline.

推丨 to evade and shove off; to retract, to draw back.

丨謝 to ceremoniously decline.

丨累 to implicate others.

何丨之拘 why do you demur at it so?

丨託 to intrust a thing to one; to devolve on another.

JUN.

Old sounds, non *and* nien. *In Canton,* yun; — *in Swatow,* jún; — *in Amoy,* jwan, lun, *and* jûn; — *in Fuhchau,* nòng *and* ö̀ung; — *in Shanghai,* zăng; — *in Chifu,* yuen.

瞤 *ˌzhun* From *eye* and *leap-moon* as the phonetic.

The eyes twitching from a nervous or muscular affection, which physiognomists carefully notice; a palpitation of the flesh.

Read *shun'* To wink; to blink frequently.

蝡 *ˋzhun* To move; to wriggle as a worm; to squirm.

丨動 the tortuous motion of insects.

丨蛇 a red snake found in southern regions.

閏 *zhun'* From *door* and *king*, because in olden time the king sat in the door of the ancestral temple in the intercalary moon.

The intercalary moon; something extra, as a sixth finger; to intercalate.

丨日 the intercalary day in leap year; — a foreign term.

五歲再丨 in five years there are two intercalations.

丨壽 a birthday coming in a leap moon.

添丨 add a little extra.

丨月 an intercalary moon.

七丨爲一章 seven intercalations make one Metonic cycle of 19 years, the *saros* of the Chaldeans.

潤 *zhun'* To moisten, to bedew; to enrich, to fatten; to benefit, to increase; the increase, the fat of, as the profits of a business; moist, rich, shining, sleek, in good liking; to imitate, to follow; name of two rivers.

澤丨羣生 to benefit or do good to the people.

丨滑 smooth, shining; slippery.

富丨屋德丨身 wealth benefits the house, virtue the person.

丨心養眼 to comfort and fatten one, — as with good cheer.

丨筆 a douceur for writing; a cup or feast given to wish a candidate success at the examination.

分丨 to share good things.

翻丨 [the weather has] turned to be moist.

珠圓玉丨 round as a pearl and polished as a gem; — a finished composition, a perfect article.

泡丨 soak it through.

水曰丨下 water is that which soaks or flows off.

按股分丨 divided the profits according to the shares.

丨州 an old name for Chin-kiang fu in Kiangsu.

丨着步兒來 follow me a little behind; also, to pattern after.

容顏滋丨 his complexion is fresh and florid.

土丨成暑 when the earth is soaked, hot weather is on us.

胸 *zhun'* A kind of wingless insect or grub, called 丨䏰 which once was found in such quantities in the present district of Yun-yang 雲陽縣 in the east of Sz'ch'uen, as to give its name to the region in the Han dynasty.

JUNG.

Old sounds, nung *and* niung. *In Canton*, yung *and* nung; — *in Swatow*, jòng; — *in Amoy*, jiòng, yòng, *and* lòng; — *in Fuhchau*, üng *and* nòng; — *in Shanghai*, zung, yung, *and* niung; — *in Chifu*, yung.

戎 *ˏzhung*, From 戈 a *spear* and 甲 *armor* contracted; as a primitive, it is mostly merged in its next compound.

A weapon, arms; soldiers; military, warlike; brutal, violent, like those who use weapons; great, respectable, — and used as an appellation of military officials; a war chariot; a personal pronoun, you or thou; to assist or pull out; ancient name of a region in the northwest of Yunnan and farther west.

丨行 the troops drawn out in line.

一丨衣 [it is as easy as putting on] a military dress or arming one's self.

肆丨疾不殄 even if he could not prevent some great disasters.

丨伍 or 軍丨 the army, the ranks.

五丨 all kinds of weapons.

每有良朋烝也無丨 the friends though good will not afford the least help.

丨功 distinguished for martial bravery.

總丨 his excellency the major-general.

元丨 a great or the leading chariot; *met.* a general.

丨車旣駕 the war-chariot is now yoked for going.

起丨 or 興丨 to begin hostilities.

丨成不退 war has done its work, yet he stays not—his hand from evil.

ˏ從丨 to join the army, to volunteer.

丨裝打扮 like troops drawn out for battle; martial array.

丨雖小子而式弘大 though you are as small children, your work is exceeding by great.

狄丨 or 西丨 the wild tribes in Turfan and west of China generally.

絨 *ˏzhung* From *silk* and *weapon* as the phonetic.

Floss, fine silk carded out; a nap, as on plush or velvet; punk; down, fine silken hair or feathers; egret or pubescence on plants; woolen cloth.

丨線鋪 a floss and thread shop.

回子丨 velvet, velveteen.

斜丨 twilled cloth, kerseymere.

丨車 a silk reel.

火丨 tinder, punk.

丨字 characters of velvet put on scrolls.

紮丨 to make artificial flowers of velvet.

小丨 flannel; spanish stripes; habit-cloth.

大丨 or 呢丨 broadcloth.

洋丨 foreign velvet.

打丨圓 to work chain embroidery or the mandarin stitch.

細丨 narrow native flannel.

哆囉丨 heavy woolen cloth.

丨花樹 one of the names of the *Acacia julibrissin*, or silk tree.

香丨花 a species of *Centaurea*.

俄 *ˏzhung* One of the six tribes of the Si-jung 西戎 living on the west of China, which are described as having three horns, — a feature probably derived from their head-dress.

狨 *ˏzhung* From *dog* and *weapon*; but others say from *dog* and *floss* contracted, from its soft fur; occurs used for 戎 warlike.

A species of large and very agile ape, also called *ˏyiu* 猱, found in Sz'ch'uen and towards Annam; it has long yellowish-red hair, suitable for making cushions and other uses; it is probably the entellus gibbon (*Hylobates entelloides*), or an allied species; the fur was worn in the Sung dynasty as one of the insignia of high rank; *met.* violent, fierce.

駥 *ˏzhung* A horse described as eight *chih* in height; martial like a war-horse; valiant.

絕有力丨 truly he had great prowess.

Read *ˏsung*. Fine fur.

茙 *ˏzhung* A malvaceous plant resembling the Hibiscus; also a sort of pulse, called 丨菽, that tastes like millet.

丨丨 thick, abundant.

搣 *ˏzhung* From *hand* and *weapon*; like its primitive, and interchanged with *ˏjăng* 仍 as.

To aid; to help and countenance; to oppose; to push away.

毧 *ˏzhung* Similar to the next.

Fine, soft fur; the downy or short hair next to the skin; felt, felted; things woven of camel's hair.

丨鞋 felt shoes.

丨毯 felt rugs; hair rugs.

氄 *ˏzhung* The fine down on birds, or the close hair on animals; downy; full of feathers.

鶴丨 the down of storks, used to stanch blood.

丨鷄 a chicken just hatched.

丨羽 down; pin feathers.

子丨 or 丨毛 the fine, soft hair below the coarse.

丨毛不自煖張翼强相呼 my own feathers don't keep me warm; but though I clap my wings, what good will it do? *met.* your skill or knowledge cannot serve me.

茸 From 艸 plants and 聰 intelligent contracted.
ᶜzhung The luxuriant growth of plants; collected thick together; to push; a deer's horns; soft, plushy, downy, like young antlers.
草 丨 丨 thick rank grass.
闒 丨 degenerate, base: not fit to hold an office.
新蒲含紫 丨 the new sweet-flag shows its rosy shoots.
鹿 丨 草 a rocky herb, like the *Utricularia*, with quadrifoliate petioles.
龍 丨 crowded thickly, as plants.
狐裘蒙 丨 the fox-skin robe is disordered or rumpled.
紫 丨 裘 a purplish fur robe.
鹿 丨 the young antlers of deer.
丨 膠 hartshorn jelly or glue.
丨 片 horn shavings;—are more valuable than the 丨 墊 base of the horn.
麋 丨 a roe's horns.

鬆 Disheveled, unkempt hair; in Canton, the people apply
ᶜzhung it to the lank, slovenly hair of Manila men.

穠 Fragrant, the aroma of rice; others say, the tops of grain.
ᶜzhung 丨 芽樹 a tree resembling the locust, (*Sophora*,) found in north of Honan, having leaves like the *Ligustrum*; it bears small white flowers, and a green fruit; people scald and eat the leaves.

慵 From *heart* and *ordinary*; it is often read ᶜyung.
ᶜzhung Indolent, easy-going, careless.
疎 丨 heedless and lazy.
丨 懶 lazy, good for nothing, self-indulgent.
丨 而陋 a sordid, slovenly country-woman.
丨 懦自安 seeking one's ease; idle, and without energy.
丨 妝髻 a disheveled and frowzy head-dress; slatternly hair.

襛 From *clothes* and to *cultivate*; also read ᶜnung.
ᶜzhung Thick, wadded clothes; well clothed.
丨 厚 well-dressed, richly clad.
何彼 丨 矣 how comes that fellow to be so finely dressed?

冗 宂 From *cover* or *residence* and *man* underneath; *q. d.* as when a farmer has nothing to do in his fields; the first is commonly used.
ᶜzhung Scattered; gone home, as officers off duty; furlough allowances; a calling and its duties; affairs, duties, occupation; mixed up; hurried, perplexed by calls; without fixed abode, gypsy-like, squatters.
丨 食 a sinecure.
貴 丨 your official duties.
丨 從 a great retinue.
公 丨 public matters.
丨 官 or 丨 吏 officers who are off duty, those who are shelved or retired; the first term also denotes a supernumerary.
爲俗 丨 所纏 or 俗事繁 丨 I am hampered by my business; my private affairs are troublesome, — and take all my time.
流 丨 道路 houseless wanderers; tramps, vagabonds.
撥 丨 前來 I laid aside my work, and have come to see you.
丨 費不可不省 I must reduce these extra expenses.

搑 To push; to beat, to pound, as in a mortar; to stuff, to
ᶜzhung fill; to receive.

軵 Also read ᶜfu; and sometimes written 軵 with the same sense.
ᶜzhung To push a cart back and
ᶜfu tip up the body, so as to occupy less room; to push, to thrust, to crowd.
丨 車奉饟 to take a tumbril and carry refreshments to a friend before he alights.

JWA.

Old sound, na. *In Canton*, ya; — *in Amoy*, ju; — *in Shanghai*, sûé.

矮 From *grain* and *deputed*; it is like the next, and is also read ᶜjui.
ᶜzhwa Four handfuls of grain; in Shensi, to push, to crowd on one. In *Pekingese*. Rumpled, wrinkled, full of folds.
紙張都 丨 了 this paper is everywhere creased and rumpled.

稜 Like the preceding; it is also interchanged with ᶜlo 稞 which last also means grain heaped up.
ᶜsui In Hunan, a name for four handfuls of grain.

JWAN.

Old sounds, nwan *and* nioan. *In Canton*, ün-*and* ü ; — *in Swatow*, nŭng ; — *in Amoy*, jian, joan, *and* jèng ; — *in Fuhchau*, niong ; — *in Shanghai*, niüⁿ ; — *in Chifu*, yung.

撋 ꜀zhwan To rumple a thing; to rub between the hands, as in washing; to push back.

Read ꜀no, and used with 挼 To rub.

丨抄 to rub the palms.

䌾 ꜀zhwan The seam of a garment; the selvedge or binding on the border of a skirt; coarse cloth; to plait or braid.

Read ꜀nwan. Short drawers or skirts.

堧 壖 𤱿 ꜀zhwan From *earth* or *field* and *increasing;* the first is most common.

Land near a river's bank; the vacant space inside the wall of a city; an interval between a high inclosing wall, and next to an inner fence or lower wall; the space between a temple and its inclosing wall.

丨垣 the spare ground between walls at the side entrance of a temple.

耎 ꜀zhwan From *whisker* and *large;* its meanings appear in several of its compounds.

To increase from small beginnings, as growing hair; soft, weak; to withdraw and then increase.

以丨脆之體 it is owing to my weak decrepid body; said by Sz'ma Ts'ien.

腝 ꜂zhwan A palsied leg, a diseased foot; upper bone of the arm or the humerus.

Read ꜀nun. Meat pickled with the bones.

愞 ꜂zhwan Timidly; fearful, cowardly.

畏丨 timorous, apprehensive.

丨弱 disheartened and weak.

丨懦 hesitating; nervously timid; having no energy.

軟 輭 ꜂zhwan From *cart* and *to owe* or *soft;* the first is mostly used.

Muffled wheels, such as are hung to go easily; soft, delicate, weak, tender; ductile, the opposite of 硬 stiff; pliable, yielding; limber, lithe; no fixed principles, infirm of purpose; to limber, to stretch.

丨脚 a soft leg; *i. e.* a ninny, a rich simpleton.

丨牙 teeth set on edge.

柔丨 flexible, pliant; kind-hearted; no grit, no energy.

丨弱 infirm, debilitated, feeble.

浸丨 or 泡丨 soak it soft.

欺丨怕硬 he imposes on the weak, but fears the strong or violent.

和丨 conciliatory, ready to accommodate.

細丨 delicate and soft.

丨丨勢 one without much influence; gentle in manner.

丨飽 light refreshment, as congee; soup, gruel.

丨片子 a silk robe.

耳丨心活 mind perplexed at the different stories one has heard.

丨身 lissome, supple, as an acrobat; having a jointed body, like a puppet or doll.

遍身丨 richly dressed.

伸丨腰免困 to stretch one's self, and get out the cramps, as after a ride.

㮕 ꜂zhwan A species of the date plum or *Ziziphus*, called 黑棗 or black date; it is small and dried for use.

Read ꜀'rh. A synonym of 栭 the boletus or fungus on trees.

蝡 ꜂zhwan A synonym of ꜂jun 蠕 to squirm.

The crawling or wriggling of worms.

丨動 just able to move, as a worm; squirming, wriggling.

丨丨 name of a horde of Huns, given them in contempt.

碝 瑌 瓀 ꜂zhwan A variety of opaque, whitish quartz like massive chalcedony, with pieces of cornelian interspersed in it, which can be worked into ornaments; for which the second form is used.

士佩丨珉而青組綬 the literati wore crystal at their girdles on silken cords.

琢丨爲瓶 carve the quartz into a cup.

鍒 zhwan꜄ Soft, ductile silver.

丨色九成 bullion with ten percentage of alloy in it.

KAI.

Old sounds, kai, kak, kap, *and* kat. *In Canton*, koi, hoi *and* k'oi; — *in Swatow*, kai, k'ai, *and* koi; — *in Amoy*, kai *and* k'ai; — *in Fuhchau*, kai *and* k'ai; — *in Shanghai*, ké *and* yé; — *in Chifu*, kai.

該 ˓kai From *words* and a *horary* character; it is interchanged with 胲 and the next.

Rules established in the army, a military code; an engagement made at enlistment; to connect, to belong to, — and thus is used as a euphuism for to owe money; to prepare; fit, just; what ought to be, or is right; deserving; necessary, permissable, or convenient; proper, that which it has to do; what was spoken of, the aforesaid, the beforementioned, that thing, the one; behooving; deserving; all; the whole; abundant.

丨備 prepared, ready.

丨銀若干 how much should he pay?

丨管 it belongs to his functions; he has the control of it.

本丨 it belongs to me; it is incumbent on me (or him.)

應丨 it ought to be; it is proper, it behooves.

總丨 it must be; doubtless; really should be.

丨死 he ought to die; he is to die; an exclamation, alas! dreadful!

丨死的 an epithet, like You scape-gallows!

丨欠 or 丨賬 a debt; to owe.

悔不丨 I am sorry for what I did.

不丨當 it is not proper; like 唔丨 at Canton used for I beg pardon; I ought not to have done so.

丨人 the said man, that person, — used of inferiors; 丨大臣 the said magnate, would be used by the Emperor.

萬物兼丨 everything was ready.

不丨如此 it should not be so.

丨衰 unlucky, blundering.

丨部 the proper Board, the one to take cognizance of this case.

丨合死 you ran a narrow chance; what a rare death you would have had!

晐 ˓kai From *sun* and a *horary* term; it is also regarded as an unusual form of the last.

The bright light overspreading the world; all, the whole, prepared.

丨諗 to thoroughly meditate on.

兼丨 all is well done; all prepared.

祴 ˓kai Like the next, when denoting the name of an ancient tune, played as a warning to guests in olden times, lest they drank too much; it seems also to have marked the time and step of the guests.

陔 ˓kai A step, a terrace; a gradation or succession, as in steps; a kind of music used in the Hia dynasty, to denote that the feast was over.

一壇三丨 an altar of three terraces.

九丨之上 above the nine ascents; *i. e.* in the highest heaven, even above the 九丨 or imperial palace grounds or domain.

南丨 name of an ancient ode, setting forth the duties of filial obedience.

垓 ˓kai Also read ˓*kiai*; it is interchanged with the last.

A boundary, a circuit; a step, a terrace; to strengthen the limits or frontier; a cardinal number denoting a hundred millions.

丨級 a degree; a step or ledge.

兼丨 all the limits; *i. e.* the wide world.

丨限 a limit, a frontier.

丨下 a place in the present Péi-hien 沛縣, just north of the Yellow River in Kiangsu, where Liu Pang obtained the victory.

峐 ˓kai A hill without grass or trees.

可洛丨 ancient name of a place among the Huns in ancient times.

荄 ˓kai Roots of plants.

根丨 the roots of grass.

邪丨 perverse roots; *i. e.* evil principles or doctrines.

浮丨 floating plants, like the *Hippuris*.

胲 ˓kai The great toe; the hair on it; the articulation of the jaw; the jowl; occurs used for 該 to prepare; an enlisting contract.

頰丨 the cheeks.

奇丨 a book of tactics; a military code.

骸 ˓kai From *bone* and a *horary* term; it is also written 骸 and read *hieh*˯.

The shin-bone or tibia; the bones of the body.

四肢百丨 the four limbs and all parts of the body.

六丨 the head, trunk, and four limbs.

屍丨 a corpse.

乞丨骨 to beg the bodies, as of the victors after a battle; but alone, 丨骨 means a skeleton.

忘形丨 forgetful of self, devoted friendship, self-abnegation.

賅 / **侅** ˓kai From *pearl* or *man* and a *horary* term; the first is most used.

To give, to present; unusual, rare, uncommon.

奇丨 extraordinary.

丨物 a rarity, a curiosity.

丨事 an unusual affair.

丨載 it is also written in.

丨括 it involves several meanings or references.

建業之丨 he laid the basis of this great prosperity.

剴 ˏ*k'ai* From *knife* and *how*.

To rub or sharpen a knife carefully; a bill-hook; assiduously, diligently, fully; to influence, to move.

丨切曉諭 let all you people clearly understand this; — a phrase common in edicts.

丨重民心 to move the people.

改 ˎ*kai* From 己 *self* and 攴 to *strike*; *q. d.* to knock off one's errors.

To change, to alter; to reform, to amend; to correct, as a composition; to exchange; to make as new; it sometimes has the force of a disjuctive conjunction, as

茲丨 but then, on the other hand.

丨日領教 I will call on you another day

丨過 to mend one's errors.

丨換 to change, to put another in place of; to exchange.

丨換門閭 to change the door; — *i. e.* to prosper, to rise in rank.

丨造 to rebuild; to make over new, as old garments by dyeing; to amend and add to.

丨造衙門 to carry a case up to another court.

其容不丨 their deportment always proper.

丨變 to do better; to alter.

地方丨變 the locality has been entirely changed.

丨風水 to improve one's luck, as by changing the family sepulcher, or the front door.

痛丨前非 you must reform from your old errors.

丨歲 next year.

丨嫁 to marry another husband, or a second betrothed.

請丨正丨正 will you please revise my composition.

丐 匄 *kai'* The first form is now most used; and must not be confounded with ˏ*mien* 丏 a wall; the second is composed of 勹 to *wrap* and 亡 *lost*, intimating that the man is utterly destitute; and is very similar to ˏ*hiung* 匈 the breast.

To ask alms, to beg; to request; to give; a mendicant.

丨子 or 丨者 a beggar, a suppliant.

吹簫丨食 to play the flute and beg for food; as was done by Wu Tsz'-sü 伍子胥 of the Cheu, after whom one of the gates of Su-chau is named.

丨施貧民 distributed some to the poor people.

乞丨 a mendicant.

丨頭 the chief of the beggars, one who is held somewhat responsible for them; each ward of a town has one.

槪 槩 *kai'* From *wood* and *finished*; occurs used for *k'ai'* 慨 generous; the two forms are the same.

A striker to level off grain; to even, to adjust; affected by; a summing up, a resumé; a sacrificial wine-cup, for which the first alone is used.

斗丨 a striker, usually called 斗刮 a bushel-scraper.

一丨 every sort, the whole, altogether.

丨行豁免 all are forgiven and set free, — as by the emperor.

大丨 on the whole, generally speaking, most probably.

丨同 all are alike.

丨乎不論 or 一丨而論 all are included in it; we speak of the whole.

湀丨 profound, dark, as a place.

丨免 all is settled.

百折不回之丨 he will not reform (or change) for any alternative.

風丨 a courteous manner, an easy way of doing things.

丨無虛意 thoroughly ingenuous.

氣丨 pompous; resolute; for which 志丨 is nearly synonymous.

丨不准行 it will no longer be allowed, as the sale of poor salt without paying the excise.

統丨百人 the whole were about a hundred men.

漑 摡 *kai'* From *water* or *hand* and *done*; it occurs used for its primitive.

Name of a river in Liao-tung; to lead on water for irrigation; to roll on like a torrent; swashing, inundating, flooding; to rub clean; to scour utensils, to wash bright.

沆丨 gently flowing.

灌丨 to lead on water; to irrigate, to water.

滌丨 to scour and scrub.

蓋 盖 葢 *kai'* From *plants* and to *cover*; the second and third forms are common; it must be distinguished from *hoh*, 盍 to cover, for which it is sometimes used.

A kind of coarse grass used for thatching; a covering; a roof, a canopy, a vaulted covering; a cover; to roof, to overtop, to overshadow; to build, to put a roof on; to include, to embrace; to be, is; to screen; to conceal, both literally and figuratively; an initial *particle*, for, since, for that, now then.

上丨 a house, or whatever is erected on the land.

丨上丨子 put the cover over it.

起丨房屋 to build houses.

屋丨 the roof of a house.

碟丨 a dish-cover.

丨碗 or 丨盅 a covered-tea-cup.

丨被窩 pull the coverlet over.

丨住面 to veil the face; to hide one's feelings.

丨瓦 to lay tiles.

天如圓丨 the sky is like a round canopy.

遮丨 to shade, to screen.

丨寶塔頂 [please] cover this pagoda [with a] top; —*i. e.* help me out with a last subscription.

愆尤難丨 his faults cannot be screened or hushed up.

丨不了羞恥 the shame can no longer be concealed.

我行既集丨云歸哉 our expedition being accomplished, we then said, we go home!

苫 丨 a thatch of grass.
丨 因 because that.
丨 來 since you are here; having come.
丨 曰 now it is said.
謂天丨高 if you speak of heaven, it is high.

掩 丨 to screen, to hide from.
丨 時 at that time, then it was.
地 丨 edible toadstools, agarics.
功名丨世 his merit overtops that of all others.
膊稜丨兒 the knee-pan, from its movable nature.

丨 聞 now I have heard.
翠 丨 the emerald cover, — a name for the lotus leaf.
丨 有之矣 it is on this account.

襤 *kai'* Outer garments like dusters, which may be used to protect the dress.

K'AI.

Old sounds, k'ai, k'ak, *and* k'at. *In Canton*, hoi *and* k'oi; — *in Swatow*, k'ai *and* k'ui; — *in Amoy*, k'ai; — *in Fuhchau*, k'ai *and* kw'i; — *in Shanghai*, k'é; — *in Chifu*, k'ai.

開 *'k'ai* From 門 *door* and 幵 *level*.
To open, to unfold; to explain; to reveal, to disclose; to enact, as rites; to institute; to begin, to start, to initiate; to clear, as land; to dig out; to write out, to particularize, as items; to separate, to unloose, to liberate; to favor; in *rhetoric*, to digress; a digression; to heat up; boiling, hot.
丨 張 to open a shop.
丨 價 the asking price; to state a price.
丨 船 or 丨 身 to weigh anchor.
丨 折舊賬 to compound old debts.
丨 光 or 丨 眼 to vivify an idol by marking the black pupils, the last act before it is worshiped.
丨 年 or 丨 歲 newyear's day.
丨 心 to amuse one's self, to divert one's grief.
丨 心見誠 perfect sincerity; I am strictly honest.
丨 路 to make a new road; to clear the way for the ghost.
丨 解 to open out the meaning; to console one.
丨 通 to open intercourse with; clearly explained.
丨 釋 to enlarge upon; to resolve the difficulties, as in a text; to free.
丨 闢天地 to spread out the heavens and earth; creation.
不如丨交 that matter cannot well be brought about.
走 丨 get out of the way! — as to a crowd stopping the road.
走不丨 I have no time to get away.
丨 而勿達 explained indeed, but not fully comprehended.
丨 士 an appellation for a priest; who 丨示 explains and enforces the tenets of Budha.
丨 口不如緘口穩 it is safer to keep silence than to speak.
丨 名 to state the items; and 丨發 to pay them; — said of accounts.
丨 水 bubbling, boiling hot water.
鍋丨了 the pan is ready heated, as for the rice.
丨 陽 to open out, to free from; name of the star ζ Mizar in the Great Bear.
丨 科 to open the tripos for *küjin* degrees; to begin to assess taxes.
推 丨 to digress and explain a point, to adduce an illustration.
撥 丨 to assort, to place each kind by itself.
丨 導人 one who instructs others in morality.
打丨看 open and let me see it.
丨 啓 to instruct.
丨 封府 the capital of Honan province; it was the metropolis of China in A.D. 907; and again in the Sung dynasty, A.D. 1000 to about 1120.

鍇 *'k'ai* Many; numerous.

鎧 *'k'ai* Armor; mailed armor, as a cuirass, a hauberk; a defense.
首丨 or 盔丨 a helmet.
丨 甲 armor, plaited mail.
袈裟爲忍辱丨 the priest's surplice is a defense against insult and wrong.

愷 *'k'ai* From *heart* and *how*; it is interchanged with the next.
Joyful, contented; gentle, balmy; good, kind.
丨 澤 benevolent, kind towards one; happy.
丨 悌君子 a kind and urbane official.
八元八丨 the eight ministers and eight secretaries of Shun.

凱 *'k'ai* From *stand* and *how*; it is interchanged with the last and next.
A victory; the triumphant return of an army; the joy of peace; gentle, soothing; excellent; balmy, as the wind.
奏 丨 to celebrate a victory.
丨 旋 to return in triumph.
鞭敲金鐙響人唱丨歌還 the rapping of the whips on the golden stirrups was heard with the people's pæans of victory, as they returned.

𩗴 *'k'ai* Used for the last in the phrase 丨 風 the genial balmy south wind.

闓 *'k'ai* To open; to set open, to unloose; to desire; an archer's thumb-ring.
丨 澤 滂 流 he benefits others greatly; — said of a god or a man.
豁 丨 予 心 I now fully understand the matter.

磑 *'k'ai* From *stone* and *how*; also read *wéi'* and *'hwui*.
An instrument for breaking stones or other things to pieces; a mill; to triturate or break; to accumulate; solid.
刀 利 丨 丨 a sharp sword breaks them easily.

塏 *'k'ai* A high and cheerful spot; a knoll good for a residence.
爽 丨 a pleasant location.
廿 泉 之 爽 丨 a residence near a spring of good water.

慨 *'k'ai* From *heart* and *done*.
Generous, noble-minded; honorable; loving integrity; loyal, hearty in a cause.
慷 丨 disinterested, above all meanness; generous; magnanimous.
忼 丨 loyally supporting a just but failing cause.
英 雄 丨 悴 a man of talents who is kept in private life.
丨 歎 how sad! what a pity!
感 丨 fervent, as in a good cause; devoted to.
丨 然 impulsive, warm-hearted.
悲 丨 pained at a wrong act.

嘅 *k'ai'* To sigh after; unavailing regret.
丨 然 mournfully.
無 不 丨 矣 everybody regrets it.
丨 其 嘆 矣 sighed out his unavailing regrets.
In *Cantonese*. The sign of the possessive case, equivalent to 之 or 的; a personal pronoun, mine, yours, its; for, instead, to use for; at the end of a sentence has the force of a possessive adjective.
我 丨 書 my book.
要 肥 丨 要 瘦 丨 do you wish the fat or the lean?
拂 蚊 丨 for killing musquitoes.

顗 *k'ai'* The top of the skull.
天 靈 丨 the fontanelle.

KAN.

Old sounds, kan *and* kam. *In Canton*, kon, kín, hon, *and* kòm; — *in Swatow*, kan, kam, kⁿa, *and* han; — *in Amoy*, kan, kam, han, k'am, *and* kong; — *in Fuhchau*, kang, kòng, *and* hang; — *in Shanghai*, köⁿ, kíⁿ, küⁿ, kéⁿ, *and* héⁿ; — *in Chifu*, kan.

干 *'kan* The original form is composed of 入 to *enter* reversed, and 一 *one* drawn across it; it is the 51st radical of a few unassorted characters, many of them primitives; it is interchanged with the next two, and must be distinguished from 于 in, and 千 a thousand.

To oppose, to offend against; to provoke, to draw on one; to try to obtain; to seek; exposed to; a shield, a buckler; *met.* those who carry them, soldiers; arms, defensive armor; whatever fends off or protects, as the bank of a stream; a boundary; a rivulet; offense, crime; occurs used as a *preposition*, for, concerning; the consequences of; resulting; stems of small trees; few, one or two persons.
天 丨 or 十 丨 the ten celestial cyclic characters, with their dual combinations, and the elements and planets they are supposed to act on, are given in this table.

NAMES AND AFFINITIES OF THE TEN CELESTIAL STEMS.

TEN STEMS.		ASTROLOGICAL NAMES.	DUAL COMBINATION.	CORRESPONDING ELEMENTS.	BINARY EXHIBITION.	PLANETS.
Kiah	甲	閼逢	甲 乙	木 Wood.	Fir, as the *yang*,	木 星 Jupiter.
Yüeh	乙	旃蒙			Bamboo, as the *yin*.	
Ping	丙	柔兆	丙 丁	火 Fire.	Burning wood, as the *yang*,	火 星 Mars.
Ting	丁	彊圉			Lamp flame, as the *yin*.	
Wu	戊	著雍	戊 已	土 Earth.	Hill, as the *yang*,	土 星 Saturn.
Ki	己	屠維			Plain, as the *yin*.	
Kăng	庚	上章	庚 辛	金 Metal.	Weapons, as the *yang*,	金 星 Venus.
Sin	辛	重光			Kettle, as the *yin*.	
Jăn	壬	玄默	壬 癸	水 Water.	Waves, as the *yang*,	水 星 Mercury.
Kwéi	癸	昭陽			Brooks, as the *yin*.	

The ten sterms are used in geometry to denote angles, sides, and figures; and enter into many geomantic and astrological calculations.

丨戈 arms, munitions; troops.

動丨戈 to take up arms, to go to war; strife, hostilities.

丨犯 to break the laws intentionally, to sin boldly.

丨證人 a witness.

不相丨 of no serious moment, no matter to either of us.

丨係 of consequence.

丨礙 or 丨連 involved in; compromised by bad results.

我不丨涉 I have no concern in that affair.

拿話丨他 talk to and dissuade him; to convince one it must not be.

若丨 how many? so much.

寘之河之丨兮 he puts it on the river's bank.

何敢自丨重戾 how can you attribute such a crime to me?

不丨己事少當頭, if you would only look after your own business, you would have less trouble.

丨祿豈弟 in seeking dignity how self-possessed!

丨諛富貴 to wheedle rich grandees.

丨祿 to seek for emolument.

舞丨 a fencer's staff, an acrobat's pole.

非丨我事 it was not my doing; it does not affect me.

丨己大 it is a serious matter to me.

那丨人 those few persons; or 一丨人 a crowd, a group of people, a party.

他們又是一丨人 they are quite another sort of folks.

欄丨條子 a narrow strip of flowered edging sewed on a hem.

善罷丨休 to be able to arrange (or quiet) a dispute.

In *Shanghai.* A child; a thing.

幾丨 how many children?

小丨 ..i.tle child.

孛相丨 a play-thing.

丨把 more than one.

竿 桿 ˓kan — From *bamboo* and *stem*; the second form is unusual.

The culm of the bamboo; a slender stick, as a staff, cane, rod, shaft, or pole; a handle; a clothes-horse.

一丨竹 one bamboo cane.

箭丨 shaft of an arrow.

秤丨 beam of a steelyards.

釣丨 a fishing-rod.

插丨 to stick in or set up a pole.

筆丨 handle of a pencil.

日三丨 the sun is three rods high; — *i.e.* it is nine o'clock.

杆 ˓kan — From *wood* and *stem*; interchanged with the last, and ˓*kan* 秆 a stem; it resembles ˓*yü* 杅 a tub.

A valuable tree, good for making the shafts of spears, or to ward off attack; a club, a staff; a high post; a classifier of guns, pencils, pipes, &c.; to drive together, as sheep into a flock.

桅丨 a ship's mast.

旗丨 a flag-staff.

一丨鎗 one spear; one matchlock.

便丨 a walking-stick.

一丨子 one man alone, by himself. (*Shanghai.*)

玕 ˓kan — An inferior gem, which resembles a pearl.

琅丨 a sort of corol, or the ornaments made of a branching corol like the genus *Isis.*

琅丨樹 a fine tree in the Kwăn-lun Mts. or fairy land.

忓 ˓kan — From *heart* and *stem*; it is sometimes wrongly used for *han*˒ 悍 ardent.

Much disturbed by; concerned with; good, worthy.

與我無丨 it gives me no anxiety.

無丨時事 I cannot well venture to interfere in this present affair.

肝 ˓kan — From *flesh* and *stem*, because the liver is the viscera of wood, and therefore rules the system.

The liver, which is described as having three lobes on the left and four on the right, and to 藏魄 contain the feelings; an umber or liver color; intimate; *met.* passionate, irritable.

丨氣疼 a pain in the liver.

丨火盛 plenty of liver-fire; *i. e.* apt to get angry.

比當˒心丨 he is as my heart and liver; — as myself.

丨腸寸斷 my liver and bowels are cut into inches; — I am greatly afflicted.

他心丨不好 he has a bad disposition.

丨腦碎裂 his entire energies were exhausted — in the service of his country.

丨氣有餘多怒 a fullness of liver produces anger.

猪丨色 a dark brown color, like pig's liver.

作事有丨胆 he is very audacious and brave.

丨木剋脾土 the woody liver neutralizes the earthy stomach, — therefore I have no appetite.

鳱 ˓kan — From *bird* and *stem*; it is sometimes used for *yen*˒ 鴈 the wild goose.

A name for the magpie is 丨鵲; it is reputed to know what is coming, and its cry indicates that a stranger has come.

甘 ˓kan — From 口 *mouth* and 一 *one* inside; *q. d.* the mouth has one taste; it forms the 99th radical of a few characters relating to sweetness.

Sweet; sweetness, one of the five tastes; grateful, relishing; pleasant; agreeable to the taste or feelings; to esteem to be sweet; happy, delightsome; winsome; voluntary; refreshing, as sleep; name of a place in Hu hien 鄠縣 in Si-ngan fu in Shensi, where the great battle of K'i with the prince of Hu took place B. C. 2194.

丨味 luscious, sweet.

丨丨的 rather sweet.

丨霖 a timely rain.

丨棠遺愛 like a sweet pear was the remembrance of his love; — said of a kind ruler.

丨苦 sweet and bitter, prosperity and adversity.

丨言 a kind answer, soft words.

食不丨味 he does not relish his food.

丨結 a willing bond, a voluntary agreement.

丨心 pleased, contented, resigned; also used ironically.

丨旨 savory food, such as is given to aged parents.

丨草 liquorice; also written like the next.

丨者 a smooth-tongued fellow.

死也丨心 now death will be sweet, — for I have obtained my desire.

丨厭 to stamp, as when delighted or half drunk.

自丨貧賤 I am contented with poverty and reproach.

丨肅 the province of Kansuh, so named from Kan-chau fu 丨州府 in its northern part; and Suh cheu 肅州; in A. D. 540, this prefecture and a large region south of it was named Kan chau 丨州, and afterwards used for part of the name of the province.

丨羅十二爲宰相 Kan Lo [of Ts'in, B. C. 220,] was made premier at 12 years of age, — and died at 15.

In *Cantonese*, read *kòm'*, and usually written 咁, which is properly read *ˏhan*, meaning to carry food in the mouth, as a monkey does. An adverb of quantity, so; such; an exclamation.

丨多 such a quantity!

丨早 so early!

相象丨臭 such an ugly face!

苷 ˏ*kan* Liquorice; called 丨草 or the sweet plant; Chinese herbalists say "it cures all complaints of the breast and bladder, and corrects the bad influence of other plants;" the Păn Ts'ao puts it at the head of all plants.

柑 ˏ*kan* From *tree* and *sweet;* it is also interchanged with ˏ*k'ien* 鉗 a bit.

The loose jacket (*Citrus margarita*), called also the coolie-mandarin orange, is 丨子 or 黃丨; at the North, this name denotes the bitter orange, and in some places is even applied to the Budha's hand.

丨皮 orange peel.

鬥丨票 to bet on orange seeds, by guessing their number.

分丨同味 to have one taste after dividing an orange, — *i. e.* to share a pleasure or delicacy with another.

泔 ˏ*kan* Water in which rice has been scoured, called 米丨水, and used for washing sores; to boil thick, as gruel.

丨淡 watery; full.

疳 ˏ*kan* A disease of children, arising from bad treatment or indigested food; atrophy.

丨瘡 venereal ulcers.

牙丨 a gum-boil; canker-sores; infants have the 走馬牙丨 galloping canker, or *cancrum oris.*

丨積 an infantile marasmus; pot-bellied; it is applied to several forms of disease.

餌 ˏ*kan* A bait; others say, a sweet cake or dumpling.

雸 ˏ*kan* Hoar-frost, or as the character indicates, *sweet rain;* it is also used for dew in the petition 澤沛丨霖 may we be favored with copious showers and dews.

乾 ˏ*kan* From 乙 the *power of nature* and 倝 *sunlight;* the form 幹 is mostly used for these senses.

Dry, exhausted; to dry; clean; all gone; entirely; dried, cured by drying; adopted by a sworn contract, as is often done by persons having children to get company for them.

丨淨 clean, limpid.

賣丨淨 all are sold; cleaned out.

杏丨 dried apricots.

丨爽 clean, airy, dry.

照丨一盃 to drain the glass, to see the bottom of it.

丨工 a sinecure.

炕丨 to dry at a fire.

丨沒 a defalcation, use of another's goods; peculation, underhand gain.

丨回報 to report falsely, to make up a story.

來了就丨丨兒的 I got no refreshment at all when I reached his house.

送丨禮 I sent him a present of dried fruits, cakes, &c.

暵其丨矣 the heat has dried it up.

丨燥 feverish, heated, dry, parched.

丨弟兄 persons who have bound themselves fraternally, as Jonathan and David.

丨兒子 an adopted child, but one who cannot succeed to the inheritance, and does not change his name.

丨娘 so the child calls its adopted mother.

Read ˏ*k'ien.* Heaven, the power or agency of heaven; the first of the eight diagrams, meaning that which goes without ceasing; a sovereign; a father; firm, stable, enduring; untiring, diligent; superior; on the compass-card, denotes northwest.

丨元 heaven.

丨坤 heaven and earth; the cosmos; *met.* male and female.

終日丨丨 diligent all day long.
朝丨夕惕 continually showing prudence and care, — lest he went wrong.
體丨 to embody heavenly principles, as a good prince does.
丨書行禮隨換坤書 when the boy's betrothal card and presents have gone, the girl's card is immediately returned.
丨陀羅國 Gandhara, an old kingdom in India.

In *Cantonese.* To lift off, as a cover; to take off, to turn over, as a leaf; to pull up, as a coverlet.

敢 ʻkan The original character is composed of 受 to *hold on* from above and below, and 古 *old* altered in combination.

To walk up to boldly, to dare, to venture on; presuming, bold, intrepid, rash; saucy, offensive to good manners; how can, ought I, — in polite language, I cannot, I may not.

不丨 or 不丨當 I do not presume; I ought not — to receive such a compliment.
豈丨 how can I do it! *i. e.* I am unworthy — of your regards.
膽丨 or 膽做 bold, daring, impudent; how brave!
丨作丨爲 afraid of no difficulties.
丨則是 decidedly so, no doubt.
果丨 valiant, decided.
誰不丨讓 will any one dare to resist?
丨自 or 丨竟 really, certainly it is.
丨死士 a fearless, daring soldier.
邀駕至丨 I venture to ask you, Sir, to come.
用丨直陳 I have used boldness in plainly stating my case; — a phrase in complaints to a ruler.

In *Cantonese.* An adverb of manner, so, thus; in this manner; an interjection of surprise.

就丨 stop, well!
丨話 if you say so; if so.
丨做得 this will do; enough.

橄 ʻkan The Chinese olive or 丨欖 the fruit of a species of *Canarium*, a fine tree of the Terebinth family, which is common in the southern provinces; there is a white and a black sort; it is also called 青菓 from its green color; and 忠菓 the loyal fruit, or 諫菓 the remonstrant fruit, because like expostulation, its taste at first is harsh; another name is 回味 returning flavor, referring to the after relish.

丨欖泥 a condiment made from salted olives.

澉 ʻkan Insipid, no flavor; to wash, to clean.

澹丨手足 to wash the hands and feet.
丨浦 Kanpu, the old Canfu, the port of Hangchau in Chehkiang, during the Sung dynasty and earlier.

衦 ʻkan To unfold or spread out garments; to smooth clothes by the hand.

感 ʻkan From *heart* and *all.*

To move the feelings, to excite; affected by, acted on; influenced either physically or mentally; indignant, moved; to touch.

丨恩 grateful, filled with a sense of kindness.
丨激之至 exceedingly grateful.
丨嘆 sorry, mournful.
無丨我帨兮 do not take my kerchief.
丨格 moved by another's earnestness; the response of the gods to a prayer of faith.
丨化人心 to move the heart; to reform; to convert; regenerated.
丨動 to move, to influence; the emotions acted on.
丨冒風寒 affected by the weather.
交丨 reciprocal influences, as of the dual powers; conception.
丨孕而生 supernatural conception.
丨謝你 obliged for; I thank you; the word *cumshaw* is derived from the Amoy pronunciation of this phrase.
銘丨五內 it is graven on my heart; lasting thanks for.
丨應 an appropriate recompense.
丨德深 I am deeply thankful for your goodness.

鱤 ʻkan From *fish* and *daring*, alluding to its ferocity and gluttony.

A fish three feet long found in the Yangtsz' River, having a large mouth and yellowish gills, greenish on the back; no other fish can live peaceably in the same stream with it, whence it is called 鰥魚 or bachelor fish; it seems to be a sort of pike or pickerel.

鰔 ʻkan From *fish* and *all;* said to be a contracted form of the last.

A kind of mud-fish.

丨魚 or 花丨 a silure of a dusky green color, with serrated spines, the *Pimelodus guttatus*, common at Canton in the spring months.

稈 秆 ʻkan From *grain* and *dry* or *staff;* the first form is commonest; it is interchanged with *kan* 杆 a staff, and the next.

The culm of grain; straw; stubble; used as a classifier of spears, guns, &c., but not properly.

丨人 an effigy, a figure made of straw.
丨帚 a rice broom.
禾丨 paddy straw.
丨頭 roots of grain, stubble.
一秉丨 a sheaf of straw.

桿 ʻkan In the dictionary read *han*ʾ, but usually used as a synonym of ʻ*kan* 杆 a pole; and sometimes of the last.

A staff, a handle, as of a spear; a lever; a classifier of spears, guns, steelyards.

一丨鎗 one spear; one musket.
一丨秤 one steelyard or dotchin.

‘赶 ‘趕 ‘kan From to *go* and a *stick*, as the phonetic.
To cock the tail and run; to chase; to pursue; to hasten to a place; to hurry, to do quickly; to drive, as sheep; to expel; to strive for, to emulate; urged by, in a hurry, busy, punctual; hastened, stimulated.
丨路 to hurry on; to go faster.
丨快 in a hurry.
丨出 to drive out; to expel; to dismiss, to turn away.
丨緊做 do it as quick as you can.
丨逐 to expel, to eject.
丨脚的 a donkey-boy, one who runs after the carriage or horse; a betto, a syce.
我丨到你 I'll catch up with you.
丨順水 avail one's self of the tide.
丨工生活 to hurry through a job, — and slight it.
丨站 to hurry on to the post-house, as when traveling.
丨市 to display goods at a fair.
丨到無路 driven to a corner; no shift, no resource.
丨不上 I cannot catch up to him.
丨赴 to repair to a post immediately.
丨早起來 you must get up early.
穖丨得上 we shall get there in time.
丨着拿出來 be spry and take them out, — to dry in the sun.
丨到那時候 try to be there at the time; be punctual.

‘擀 ‘kan To stretch out anything with the hand; to open out, as a scroll.

‘簳 ‘kan A slender variety of bamboo, fit for arrows.
箭丨 the shaft of an arrow.
丨珠 a kind of pearl-barley.
北丨山 a mountain in Tsing-pu hien, about 80 miles from Shanghai.

‘匱 ‘kan A cheap box or trunk woven of bamboo splints, called 丨箱, and much used in traveling; a lid; to cover with a lid.
Read ˏkung. A cup.
蓋丨收藏 shut down the lid, and keep it securely.

幹 kan’ From 干 a *shield* and 倝 *sunlight*; this is sometimes incorrectly used for ‘kan 乾 dry, and is interchanged with the next.
The trunk of a tree; the material of, the original substance of; skillful, capable; to give money for, to intrigue for a post; to attend to business; affairs, business; to follow a calling; a well-curb.
公丨 public affairs.
丨父之蠱 to follow a father's occupation.
丨事 or 丨事情 to do business; to manage affairs.
可以丨任大事 capable of doing great things.
能丨 or 才丨 ability, talent.
打丨 to bespeak aid in order to obtain a situation.
丨頭人 to seek to be made a headman.
有何貴丨 what is your business with me?
丨員 an able officer.
不扎丨 nothing can be done; no resources; no one helps me.
丨局 a clever player; a man of ability.
骨丨 the style of a man, his size or strength.
你不丨我丨 if you cannot (or will not) do it, I can.
鑽丨營謀 collect together in pursuit of trade.
取其丨材 I must select the best timber — or talent.
丨無天大事 wicked deeds done without a thought of Heaven; reckless villainy.

黚 kan’ Black spots or streaks on the face, as from age and half-starved fare with exposure.

榦 kan’ The root of a tree; a handle; a well-curb; an old name for the sugar-cane; boards used in making adobie walls.
丨不庭方以佐戎辟 strengthen [me against those] princes who absent themselves, and thus assist your sovereign.
井丨之上 on the well-curb.
枝丨 branches and trunk; also a ridge of hills and its spurs.
枝不得大於丨 the branches cannot grow larger than the stem.
强丨弱枝 a stiff trunk and weak branches; a wise father and foolish sons.

倝 kan’ From 㫃 a *banner* contracted and 彐 a *head*; it is used only as a primitive.
The dawn, the red blush of morning.
日光丨丨 the sun illumines the day.

旰 kan’ From *sun* and *shield* as the phonetic; not the same as *han*’ 旱 dry.
Sunset, dusk.
日丨不照 the evening sun does not shine.
皓皓丨丨 abundant, luxurious.
日丨天子忘食 the emperor forgot his meal at evening.
宵丨之勞 daily labors, the toil from dawn to eve.

紺 kan’ A violet or purple color, called 丨紫, which it is said the good man does not wear, as it is appropriate to women's apparel.

詌 kan’ To shut one's mouth; to bridle one's speech, to restrain one's anger.

淦 kan’ Water leaking into a boat; mud; to sink; a superlative, very; name of a small stream in Sin-kan hien 新丨縣 a district in the central part of Kiang-si on the River Han, just south of Lin-kiang fu; also used as another form of the next.

灨 滇 *kan'* } Interchanged with the next, and sometimes contracted like the last; the second form is also a common contraction.

The name of the central river of Kiangsi, the River Kan 丨江 which flows from the Mei-ling range north into the Poyang Lake, and with its branches drains the province; it is navigable for boats to Nan-ngan fu, about 300 miles from the lake.

贛 *kan'* Formed of 章 and 貢 combined, the first being part of Yü-chang 豫章 the old name for Kiangsi, and the other denoting *kung'* 滇 a name for the river Kan; it is used with the last.

A region south of Poyang Lake, called Chang-kung 章貢 in the Han dynasty, and altered to Kan cheu 丨州 in the Sung dynasty.

丨州府 a large prefecture in the south of Kiangsi, and sometimes used to denote the whole province.

Read *kung'*. To present, to offer tribute.

Read *hung'*. Foolish; stupid.

骭 *kan'* The tibia or shin bone; the sides of the body on the ribs; any bone in the body.

丨瘍 boils on the leg.

K'AN.

Old sounds, k'an *and* k'am. *In Canton*, hon *and* hòm; — *in Swatow*, k'an, k'am, han, tⁿ'oi, *and* k'ang; — *in Amoy*, k'am *and* k'an; — *in Fuhchau*, k'ang *and* hang; — *in Shanghai*, k'üⁿ, kéⁿ, héⁿ, tsièⁿ, *and* köⁿ; — *in Chifu*, k'an.

刊 刋 *ˎk'an* } From *sword* and *obstinate*; the second form is now synonymous, though it was once read *tsien'*.

To cut, to carve; to engrave blocks for printing; to erase or cut out from blocks; used with the next, to hew, to chop.

丨板 to cut blocks.

丨刻文字 to prepare blocks and carve characters.

不丨之書 an original unmutilated (or unaltered) edition.

丨碑立石 to carve and set up stone tablets.

不丨之論 his talk is insipid and senseless; — *i. e.* it is not worth carving.

栞 *ˎk'an* Used with the preceding.

To blaze the trees in order to know the road in a forest; to notch trees.

隨山丨木 to go over the hills marking or blazing the trees.

堪 *ˎk'an* From *earth* and *very*; occurs used with the next.

To sustain, to bear; able, adequate to; worthy of, fit for; a projection over a hollow; a covering let down to protect or overshadow; the canopy of heaven.

不丨 unfit for; intolerable, cannot be borne.

丨用 useful, serviceable.

丨任 fit for a post; able to sustain.

丨輿 heaven and earth, one covering the other; *scil.* the chariot which bears man and his fates.

丨輿先生 a geomancer, one who chooses graves.

丨議 satisfactory, suitable.

情何以丨 how can I ever repay your kindness?

受苦難丨 how can I bear this suffering?

丨勝重任 he is fit for any responsibility or station.

下賤不丨 a vile wretch; I can't bear him!

未丨家多難 I am unequal to the many troubles in the state.

戡 *ˎk'an* To pierce, to stab; to conquer; to kill; fully to sustain; equal to, in which it is like the last, and seldom used.

丨亂 to suppress a riot, to put down an insurrection.

丨敗 to win and lose; victory and defeat.

丨己 self-mortification.

丨定厥功 fully estimated (or settled) their achievements.

坩 *ˎk'an* An earthen vessel; a sort of crucible which holds five *ˎshing* 升 or pints.

嵁 *ˎk'an* A rocky bank, precipitous ledges; irregular.

山丨 a cliff, a steep ledge.

丨崿 mountain ridges.

丨巖 uneven, as a mountain defile; a rugged summit.

龕 *ˎk'an* From a *dragon* and to *join*.

To receive or contain; to inclose; to take; a niche, a shrine to hold images or ancestral tablets, sometimes movable; it is made in imitation of the room under pagodas where the god sits; a receptacle or jar for the ashes of priests; it has a high cover, and in Kiangsu, a dying priest is placed in it, and the cover closed on him; in this condition he is called 坐丨和尚 a priest waiting for death, and is buried in it; to overcome; a sound.

丨受 to contain, as a shrine does.

香丨 an incense-box.

禪丨 a priest's tomb.

聖人丨 a binnacle in a junk; it usually holds an idol.

凵 'k'an — The original was intended to represent a receptacle, the bottom line denoting the level earth; it is the 17th radical of a few characters, some of them analogous to it, but it is never used by itself.

A vessel to put things in, and still unfilled.

扣 'k'an — To take things by the hand; to bring or take.

In *Fuhchau.* To carry by a bale, or as a bundle by its string; the bale of a bucket.

侃 'k'an — Composed of 信 or 仙 *truth* and 川 flowing *streams*.

Plain, unvarnished speech; faithful, upright, plain-spoken, as Confucius is said to have been.

子路丨丨如也 Tsz'lu (a famous disciple of the sage) was very brusque and stern.

丨丨而談 converse with sincerity and directness.

坎 埳 'k'an — From *earth* and to *owe* or a *pit.*

A pit, a hole; a cavity; a dangerous place, a precipice; to dig a pit; to fall into a snare or danger; a hazard; a critical time, as of life; noise made in striking, a rap, a smack, a crack; a wrench; the bridge on a lute to support the strings; a small vase; the second of the eight diagrams, and refers to water.

丨穴 or 掘丨 to dig a pit.

心丨 the pit of the stomach.

丨丨伐檀 chop! chop! the ax sounds, as the teak comes down.

丨丨鼓我 rub-a-dub go my drums.

丨其擊缶 rapping so on your earthen jar.

丨坷 uneven; irksome to do; difficulties in life.

丨陷 to set a pit, as for beasts; to involve a person maliciously.

是個丨兒 there is a difficulty in getting on that road; it is a critical time — with the disease.

In *Cantonese.* A classifier of the trunks of trees, or clumps of stunted trees.

一丨芋頭 one head of taro.

In *Pekingese.* An innuendo, an enigma, a double-entendre; often used for 'hien 檻 a threshold.

調丨兒 he was making a pun.

砍 'k'an — From *stone* and to *owe;* occurs interchanged with the last.

To cut, to chop, to fell; to cut off; to stone, to throw stones at; a mortar or small vase.

刀丨 cut it in two.

丨傷 to wound by a stone.

丨開 to split open.

灰丨 a mortar for mixing lime.

丨腦袋 cut off his head.

丨伐 to fell trees.

丨下來 it is cut down.

丨肩兒 a waistcoat, a vest.

丨得動 I can cut it.

舂丨 a large mortar, like those used for hulling rice.

扻 撖 'k'an — From *hand* and to *owe;* the second and unauthorized form is used at Canton.

To strike, to knock; to run against, to throw down; to stone one.

丨磪 to make a notch in.

磁不丨瓦 porcelain may not batter pottery; — I'll not contend with him.

丨爛 or 丨破 to smash; to throw down and break.

拿石頭丨狗 throw a stone at the dog.

Read *'tsz'.* To comb, to dress the hair.

欿 'k'an — From to *owe* and a *pit*, it is also read *'t'an,* to covet.

Discontented with one's self; dissatisfied because of imperfection; humble, but energetic; a sour look, sorrowful; to strive for.

自視丨然 he felt that he was imperfect.

歁 'k'an — To eat and not be satisfied; not enough to eat; dissatisfied.

轗 壈 'k'an — From *carriage* or *earth* and *moved* by; the second is unusual.

Impeded; hard to get on; no luck; always losing.

丨軻 going slowly, experiencing difficulties, no opportunity; unfortunate, unsuccessful in life.

矙 瞰 k'an' — Like the next, and not so much used.

To spy, to watch, to try to find out; to look down at.

魚丨 open-eyed, like a fish.

丨臨城中 [a thousand carts] came into the city.

丨孔子之亡也 he watched when Confucius was away from home.

闞 k'an' — From *door* and to *presume*, referring to the spying.

To peep through; to look down or towards with expectation; to come to; name of an ancient city in Lu; a pavilion.

鬼丨丨室 a devil is spying his house; — said when one thinks he can do an ill deed unknown to any body.

Read *'han* Angry, irate; a tiger's scream.

丨如虓虎 growling like a savage tiger.

勘 k'an' — From *strength* and *very.*

To compare evidence; to investigate a case; to personally examine, as an officer the place where a crime was done; to collate; diligent, able, adequate.

驗丨 to go and investigate, as on an inquest.

查丨 or 丨問 to examine, to cross-question.

丨斷 to take evidence and decide.

覆無丨異 a revision of the case showed no error.

磨 ｜ to criticise closely; to ferret out the facts.

踹 ｜ 田畴 to walk over and examine the boundaries of fields, as in a litigation.

｜ 對 or 校 ｜ to compare, as papers or texts.

In *Cantonese*. To straighten out; to replace.

｜ 床 to put up a bedstead.

｜ 好 put it back properly.

墈 磡 *k'an'* From *earth* or *stone* and *adequate*; it is often wrongly written like *'chăn* 碪 a block, or *ˏkan* 堪 worthy.

A dangerous bank; a precipitous ledge on a river's shore; a cliff; the shelter under a high bank; a diked bank.

砌石 ｜ to build a stone bund or sea-wall.

｜ 邊 the edge of the cliff.

山 ｜ 將崩 that cliff will soon fall.

井 ｜ edge or brink of a well.

門 ｜ the door-sill, of which some are movable and others fixed; the 石 ｜ 子 is the upper stone step near it.

In *Cantonese*. A short breakwater running out into the stream or sea, as a ledge of rocks.

衎 *k'an'* From *to go* and *obstinate*.

Pleased; contented; to go joyfully, to be happy; sincere, truthful.

｜ 定 settled, at ease.

式燕以 ｜ to feel happy after a feast.

｜ 然而坐 he sat down contentedly.

鶣 *k'an'* Name of a bird, the ｜ 鴠 which is probably akin to the robin; it is said to resemble a fowl, and to sing night and day.

鑒 *ch'ien'* A small covered tub for holding ice, in order to preserve sacrificial meats from becoming tainted during the hot weather.

看 翰 *k'an' ˏk'an* From 目 *eye* under 手 a *hand*; the second antique form has gone out of use; this character somewhat resembles *choh* 着 to cause.

To look at, to see; to desire to see; to examine, to regard carefully; to practice; a grammatical term, having the sense of taken for, similarly; likeness; equivalent; aspect, manner; what is for show, a dummy; after some verbs of sensation, it denotes present time.

好 ｜ or 受 ｜ it is good looking; attractive

｜ 不見 I don't see it; I cannot see it — clearly.

｜ 不上眼 I don't want to see it; the sight is repulsive.

｜ 相 to practice physiognomy.

｜ 書 to read silently; to skim over a book.

｜ 破 seen through it; the trick has been found out.

｜ 機會 to watch for a good opportunity.

｜ 不出 I cannot perceive it, illegible; not recognizable.

聞聞 ｜ smell it; 試試 ｜ try to do it. (*Shanghai*.)

｜ 在友人面上 I see my friend in your face, — and will say nothing.

｜ 見 look at it.

難 ｜ ugly looking, repulsive.

｜ 透世界 acquainted with life; worldly wise.

｜ 得出 I saw it; I knew it.

｜ 輕 to regard with contempt.

念起來 ｜ read it and let me hear.

｜ 其情景 consider all the circumstances.

問一問他可 ｜ ask him once, and see (or find out).

作人字 ｜ it has the meaning of the character 人 man.

一樣 ｜ 法 have the same look; identical in object.

｜ 着辦 I must see how he is doing that business.

｜ 茶來 bring in the tea.

探 ｜ to make a visit.

｜ 病的先生要 ｜ 脈 a doctor must first feel the pulse.

善ˏ｜ 馬應 ｜' 馬 a skillful groom ought to know how to tell a horse.

Read *ˏk'an*. To watch, to look after, to see to; to examine; to take a careful view of; to keep an eye on, as a guard over a suspicious fellow.

相 ｜ a mutual look or watch.

｜ 牛 to watch cattle.

｜ 待 to behave to one; manner towards a person.

｜ 門人 a doorkeeper, a porter.

讓我 ｜'ˏ｜ ｜' please let me have a look at it.

｜ 更 a night watch.

獨 ｜ to look at alone, as an emperor does from his seclusion.

｜ 財奴 an avaricious fellow; an old niggard.

眼 ｜ 人盡醉 I see that everybody is drunk.

KĂN.

Old sound, ken. *In Canton*, kăn ; —*in Swatow*, kùn ; — *in Amoy*, kún ; — *in Fuhchau*, kòng *and* kūng ; — *in Shanghai*, kăng ; — *in Chifu*, kăn.

根 ꜀*kăn* From *wood* and *obstinate* as the phonetic.

The roots of plants; origin, root, beginning, cause, foundation; a base, as the lower part or substruction of a wall; thoroughly, fundamental; a classifier of trees, sticks, and pieces of wood, such things as are long and stiff, and even of ropes and hawsers; among the Budhists, an organ or faculty of the mind, and also of the body.

一條丨 one root, often denotes that a man has only one son.

丨本 evidence; cause; radical; parentage.

無丨本 baseless; no proof of, or power to do; singular, unreasonable.

丨底 bottom of a thing; the cause; origin of a thing.

地丨 beginning; first influences.

好丨底 of a good family or stock.

說話無丨 a baseless rumor.

丨末 the root and spray; altogether, throughout.

歸丨 at last, finally; to return to its first condition.

丨由 mode of origin, circumstances of its beginning, details of the affair from the first

尋丨究底 to make a thorough investigation and sift it to the bottom

無丨之草 [he is no better than] grass without a root; — unreliable.

丨深蒂固 the root is deep and the branch tough; — it is a difficult affair.

除丨 to eradicate; to do away with utterly.

有丨基 he has much vigor, said of a child.

絕了丨兒了 pull it up entirely; his family is extinct.

雲丨 and 倉琅丨 are poetical names for the bamboo.

五丨 among Budhists, the five organs (*indrya*) or powers of the mind, which produce 發生 sound moral life, as 信丨 the faculty of faith, &c.

六丨清凈 his faculties are all in perfect quiet (or comatose); — *i. e.* he is near his absorption.

跟 ꜀*kăn* From *foot* and *obstinate* as the phonetic.

The heel; to follow at one's heels; a servant, an attendant; to follow up, as an inquiry; to imitate; according to, following.

脚後丨 or 脚丨 the heel.

丨班 a lackey, a footman, a servant, a valet.

丨人做 do it as he does.

丨前兒 before you; one in the presence; to be with, as a friend.

丨壞品 to follow bad examples.

丨隨 or 丨我來 he came with me; come on.

丨着又是雨 following this, there was also some rain.

丨踪 to follow the clue: to trace it up.

別丨來 don't tag after me.

丨話尾 an assenting word.

他是我丨前的 he is my own child.

栽丨斗 to slip and fall down.

丨誰學的 under what teacher did you study?

緊丨着 very near, familiar with; to be next to one.

丨轎 a runner to a sedan.

詪 ꜂*kăn* To speak with difficulty; to wrangle, to act perversely.

Read ꜂*hăn*. Disobedient; unwilling to listen.

艮 *kăn*꜄ This character was originally formed of 目 *eye* and 匕 to *compare*; *q. d.* disobedient ones will not meet your eye; it is the 138th radical of only five characters; it resembles ꜁*liang* 良 good, and is much used as a contraction of ꜁*yin* 銀 silver.

The third of the eight diagrams, corresponds to mountains; a limit or bound; to stop; hard, perverse, obstinate.

丨磑 a kind of hard stone; stony, hard like stone.

丨覆碗 the diagram ☶ resembles an inverted cup.

茛 *kăn*꜄ From *plant* and *perverse*, alluding to its virulence.

A wild plant, the 毛丨 a sort of butter-cup or crowfoot, the *Ranunculus auricornis*, which is regarded as poisonous.

K'ĂN.

Old sound, k'en *In Canton*, hăn *and* ngăn ; — *in Swatow*, k'ùn ; — *in Amoy*, kún *and* gún ; — *in Fuhchau*, k'òng, ngūng, *and* kaung ; — *in Shanghai*, k'ăng ; — *in Chifu*, k'ăn.

懇 'k'ăn From *heart* and to *root*; the primitive is interchanged with it.

To beg, to ask earnestly; importunate, truly, earnestly.

丨切 very urgent.

丨惻 to feel for deeply.

丨求 to supplicate, to intreat of.

丨給 to beg; to ask for.

丨恩 to beg a favor.

丨爲過信 I beg you to believe me.

肫肫丨丨 once again I beg of you — to help me.

墾 'k'ăn From *earth* and to *root*.

To open new land; to plough new soil; to commence tillage; to work energetically so as to injure; to break up, as a plough does.

開丨田地 to clear land, to prepare virgin soil.

耕丨 to plough new land.

丨種 to plough and sow.

丨地稅 duties on newly cleared land.

盡力丨傷 broke it with all his strength.

丨佔騎葬 he encroached on the [limits of the] grave by tillage.

豤 'k'ăn From *beast* and *obstinate*; interchanged with the last two.

To root up ground, as hogs do; to bite at, to gnaw.

齦 'k'ăn From 齒 *teeth* and 根 *root* contracted.

To gnaw, to bite on; to bark, as a tree; the crunching noise made in eating.

丨聲 a gnashing sound.

丨杏核 to clean an apricot seed.

丨骨 to pick a bone clean.

Read *yin'* The gums.

硍 k'ăn' From *stone* and *obstinate*; this character is often wrongly used for 銀 in 銀硃 vermilion.

A stone with a crack, flaw, or seam in it; the rumbling noise of stones; loud noise of bells.

丨晶 rock crystal. *Cantonese.*

丨雷之聲 the rumbling of rolling stones or grinding.

琨 k'ăn' A stone or gem marked with veins.

丨疵 the stone has a flaw.

Read ˏ*yin.* A stone much like jade, probably resembling serpentine.

裉 k'ăn' An unauthorized character.

A seam like a garment.

縩丨 or 絲丨 to sew a seam.

丨小 a small seam.

KANG.

Old sounds, kong *and* kung. *In Canton*, kong ; — *in Swatow*, kang, kăng, *and* kung ; — *in Amoy*, kong ; — *in Fuhchau*, kòng *and* kaung ; — *in Shanghai*, kong ; — *in Chifu*, kang.

岡 ˏkang From 山 a *hill* within 网 a *net*; it is easily confounded with ˏ*wang* 罔 a net.

The backbone of hills; a water-shed; a peak, a stony hill; a range; a summit, the culminating point; a hillock, a heap.

砂丨 a dirt heap.

血丨 the bloody wales left after a whipping.

山丨子 peaks and summits among the hills.

如丨如陵 [his goodness is enduring] as the hills and ridges.

高丨兒 a steep pass or road over the mountains.

臥龍丨 Wo-lung Mountian in Sz'ch'uen where 諸葛亮 was born.

丨背風 a side wind.

剛 ˏkang From *knife* and *hill*.

Hard, solid, unyeilding; rigorous, firm; in *music*, a sharp tone; constant, enduring, intrepid; an *adverb* of time, recently, now, just, momently.

丨纔去 he has just gone.

丨到 or 丨丨兒到 they have just arrived.

丨一來 he has just been here.

丨勇 courageous, valiant.

丨志 resolute, firm in purpose.

丨烈 irascible; overbearing and willful.

丨柔 hard and soft; energetic and easy; positive and negative in electricity.

丨日 and 柔日 the odd and even days in the moon.

丨性 or 丨惡 vicious, pigheaded; stiff-set.

丨正 upright, firm in principle.

丨毅 resolute in a purpose; noble.

丨健中正 constant in rectitude

四大金丨 the four guardians of the gate in Budhist temples, for which the next is more correct.

罡 ˛kang A large star; the god who lives in it; the Budhists reckon thirty-six 天丨 in the large stars, but the four stars which form the bowl of the Dipper are specially called the 天丨, and the four guardians put in the gateways of Budhist temples, called 四大金丨, are the gods who reside in them; they have red, green, white, and black faces.

堈 鋼 缸 ˛kang From *earth* or *jar* and a *peak*; the third form is most common. A jar; a glazed earthen vessel to contain water, lotus flowers, fish, or manure; they are large and coarse, have bulging sides and wide mouths.

丨瓦 earthen-ware vessels.

甕丨 or 水丨 water jars; the squat shaped ones are called 金剛腿丨, referring to the thighs of the temple guardians.

一口金魚丨 one gold-fish jar.

糞丨 or 坑丨 a public retiring shed.

七石丨 a seven picul jar, a very large sized one, big enough for a cistern.

茳 ˛kang A trailing plant, the 丨草 or *Vitis ficifolia*, which bears white flowers and small grapes that are said to remove stupidity.

丨芋 said to be a variety of squash.

犅 ˛kang A red bull.

騂丨 a bullock which was used by a king of Lu in sacrifice.

杠 ˛kang A cross piece, as on the legs of a bed; the thills of a sedan; poles of a bier; yards on a mast; beam of a flag as the Chinese fly it; a ridge or line in cloth; a foot-bridge; a cross-bar.

牀丨 a bedstead.

徒丨成 the foot-bridge is finished.

扛 㧏 摃 ˛kang From *hand* and *work* or *hard*; the second and third are unusual forms. To carry a burden between two on a pole; this is the meaning in Canton, but in Peking, it means for one to carry a burden on the back or shoulders; to lift; to hold up; to manage; several men lifting a thing.

丨轎 to carry a sedan.

丨抬 to carry with or on poles.

筆力獨丨 to vigorously throw off an essay or sketch.

這事我丨起來 I can manage or bring about that affair.

力能丨鼎 he is able to lift a tripod in his hands.

肛 ˛kang The large intestine or colon.

丨門 the rectum.

脝丨 fat, bloated.

脫丨 a protruded intestine; blind piles.

釭 ˛kang From *metal* and *work*; also read ˛kung in some of its meanings. The iron band on the nave of a wheel, through which the spokes pass; ornaments on the beam which ran around the hall, and resembled golden hub-rings; the barb of an arrow; a lamp-jar, a sconce.

排丨 to trim the lamp.

金丨 an ornamental ring carried on the girdle, which jingled.

銀丨 or 金魚丨 a globular jar in which lamps are suspended; used also for gold fish; the Cantonese make large ones.

鋼 ˛kang From 金 *metal* and 剛 *hard* contracted. Iron hardened by the fire, *i. e.* steel; hard, as steel; strong, able; to sharpen.

鐵丨 steel; and 純丨 pure steel.

丨刀 to strop a razor; also, a well tempered sword, which can 切玉如切泥焉 cut a gem just as it can cut clay.

丨刀雖快不斬無罪之人 an innocent person has no cause to fear the sharpest knife.

丨勁 vigorous, lusty.

男兒無志鈍鐵無丨 a spiritless boy is like dull iron that has no steel in it.

豇 ˛kang A large kind of bean, the 丨豆 shaped like a kidney, and used in renal complaints; it has red and white flowers, and the pod is two feet long, round, and contains many seeds, with a red hilum or eye.

綱 ˛kang The large rope which binds the meshes of a net; a restraining bond or institution of society, a great principle, to which human affairs are responsible; control; a controler.

統丨 the chief bond.

三丨 the "three net-ropes," are the personal and relative duties of a prince, father, and husband; the bands of human society.

丨常 constant obligations of morality.

提丨 to deduce a principle; to sum up the matter.

丨目 a general outline; the subject and predicate of a sentence.

丨維默運 to have the entire control.

豈弟君子四方為丨 O happy prince, whom the four quarters [of the realm] take for their regulator.

丨鑑 a chronological view of history, a narrative; annals.

丨紀 principles, as of government; fundamental; to control; to spread.

丨開一面 let open the net [of the law] a little.

丨領 the leading points, the scope, the argument.

焵 kang˒ A hard, well tempered blade; to harden iron by passing it through the fire.

K'ANG.

Old sounds, k'ang *and* k'ung. *In Canton*, k'ong *and* hong ; — *in Swatow*, k'ang *and* kăng ; — *in Amoy*, k'ong ; — *in Fuhchau*, k'ŏng *and* k'aung ; — *in Shanghai*, k'ong ; — *in Chifu*, k'ang.

康 ꜀k'ang This character seems to be derived from 庚 the *year* and 米 *rice* combined, in allusion to the harvest.

Joy, peace, ease, repose; the feeling of vigor, a healthy body and quiet mind; delightful, excellent; broad, as an avenue; to quiet, to secure the repose of; stability, repose; a name for Sogdiana.

丨寧 health and peace, the third of the five happinesses.

丨健 or 丨强 robust, hale, strong.

丨莊大路 a great highway.

丨居 living quietly.

身其丨强 your person will be in perfect tranquillity.

丨熙 the reign K'anghi (A. D. 1662—1723; the copper cash then coined are now selected as gifts for children.

穅 糠 ꜀k'ang From *grain* or *rice* and *peace* as the phonetic; occurs used for the last.

Chaff or skin of grain; blasted grain; poor, chaffy, despicable; troublesome; in epitaphs, denotes being remiss in duties.

粃丨 petty, insignificant; what is hardly worth doing.

鋸丨 or 木丨 saw-dust.

麥丨 wheat bran.

糟丨之妻不下堂 my bran wife cannot come into the parlor; — alluding to a man who rose to office from great poverty.

丨豆不贍 he has not even bran to give; — famishing.

丨古老 a northern name for the heads of fungous millet (*Setaria*), used as a diuretic.

In *Pekingese*. To become soft and spongy, as pears and turnips do in the spring, after the winter's storage.

梨丨了心 this pear is unsound.

㡾 ꜀k'ang Empty, unoccupied, vacant.

丨㝩 a vacant house.

躿 ꜀k'ang Tall, above the usual stature.

躴丨 tall in person; it is also applied to garments which are too long, or which do not fit the person.

慷 ꜂k'ang From *heart* and *peace*.

Firm, decided in a good cause; generous, magnanimous, public-spirited.

這人丨慨得很 what a noblehearted man he is!

忼 k'ang꜄ From *heart* and a *neck*; it is similar to the last.

Excited by disappointment, grieved at; roused, disquieted.

丨爽 in high spirits.

丨然嘆息 highly annoyed as he sighs out his regrets.

亢 k'ang꜄ The original form is composed of 大 *great* contracted, and two lines denoting the large veins in the neck; it is interchanged with some of its compounds, to which it gives a portion of its meaning.

Overbearing, unbending; strong; to shelter; to oppose, to attack; an error, mistake; very, excessive, applied to dry weather; the second of the 28 constellations nearly answering to the stars ι κ λ μ ρ in Virgo, also called 丨金龍 from an idea that they cause drought.

丨氣 domineering, violent in temper.

不卑不丨 he is neither obsequious nor arrogant; well done; discreet.

丨池 four small stars near Arcturus.

Read ꜀k'ang The neck or throat of a man.

炕 k'ang꜄ From *fire* and *neck*, as the phonetic; used with the next.

To dry; to toast; to bake; to roast on a spit; dry; a drought; to spread out to dry before a fire; a brick bed or divan.

火丨 to dry at the fire; a fire of coals; embers.

丨陽 or 丨旱 very dry weather; a hot sun.

一鋪丨 the brick bed used in Northern China to warm rooms.

丨爐子 the flue of the *k'ang*; also the baking furnaces of traveling cake-peddlers.

㷗丨 a warm *k'ang*; to light the fire under a *k'ang*.

丨洞 the flue for the smoke under the tiles.

In *Cantonese*. To run a boat ashore.

丨沙 to ground on the sand.

匟 k'ang꜄ Like the last; but properly denoting the divan or wide couch, placed at the head of the parlor, and wide enough for a low table in the middle, on each side of which the host and guest are seated; tea and cakes are served on the 丨几 or 丨桌子 the divan table.

丨攏 to hide away, to conceal an article. (*Shanghai*.)

伉 k'ang꜄ From *man* and *neck*; interchanged with the next two.

To compare; to match, to pair; a married pair; to compete with, to oppose; to dislike; to store; straight, blunt, sincere.

和諧丨儷 the pairs are well matched and harmonious, — as a husband and wife.

丨禮 the courtesies of equals.

丨敵 to pit against, to compete.

抗 *k'ang'* To raise with the hand; to oppose, to resist, to rebel against; to screen, to protect; to rescue; to set up; steep cliffs on the east and west of a hill.

丨旨 to disobey the Emperor.

丨官 to oppose the government.

丨性 stiff-necked; seditious.

大侯既丨 the great target was set up.

丨拒 to stand in opposition.

丨舉 to enliven one's spirits, as by music.

丨頸之人 an obstinate, stiff-necked fellow.

丨粮 to refuse to pay the land tax.

丨斷不依 to resist strongly.

違丨 to rebel, to resist lawful rule.

分庭丨禮 to settle precedence — without strife.

丨口袋 a barrow-man, a coolie. (*Pekingese.*)

丨價 to keep up the market-price.

閌 *k'ang'* From *gate* and *net*; occurs used with 伉 to match.

A high gate is 丨閬, like that at the entrance of a palace.

砊 *k'ang'* The sound of stones striking against each other.

淩驚雷之丨礚 the thundering sound which struck a chill of terror.

犺 *k'ang'* A fierce strong dog; a hedgehog; in Siam is found the 丨狼, a short and small animal living on trees, resembling a gibbon, of a fierce disposition, with round yellow eyes; it is said that people there train it to catch the hornbill, get elephants' tusks and rhinoceros' horns for them, and reward its success by giving it fish and arrack.

KĂNG.

Old sounds, kang. *In Cantòn*, kăng *and* kang; — *in Swatow*, kⁿó *and* kwang; — *in Amoy*, keng; — *in Fuhchau*, kéng, kaing, *and* kang; — *in Shanghai*, kăng *and* kang; — *in Chifu*, kăng.

庚 *ˏkăng* The original form represents two *hands* receiving a thing, as at autumn when all things are full.

The seventh of the ten stems, answers to metal in the form of swords, and to north-east on the compass; to change, to alter; the reason or cause of; age, years; to restore; to bestow or reward; a path or course, as of the stars.

同丨 of the same age.

丨柬 or 丨帖 a card containing the horoscope of two persons betrothed.

年丨八字 the eight cyclic characters of a horoscope, two each for the year, month, day, and hour.

貴丨多少 or 今年尊丨 what is your respected age? — said to persons in the vigor of life or under fifty.

長丨 Venus or Hesperus, the evening star; old, aged.

呼丨癸 to beg for aid, as in extremity; *lit.* to bawl north and west.

鶊 *ˏkăng* One name for the mango-bird or oriole, is 鶬丨; it refers probably to its yellow plumage and black stripes; it is also known as 黃鶯 and 黃鸝 by southern people; it is also written without the radical.

賡 *ˏkăng* To carry on a song; to encore; to connect in parts, to join the harmony.

乃丨載歌 he then took up the song.

丨揚功績德著淩烟 [the emperor] proclaimed his merits to the land, and inscribed his name in the Hall of Worthies.

更 / 叓 *ˏkăng ˏching kăng'* Composed of 丙 a *horary* character and 攴 a *beat*, in allusion to the watch; the second is not an uncommon form.

To change, to alter, to renew; to substitute, to repair; to act for; emendation; a night watch, of which there are five from 7 o'clock P.M. to 5 o'clock A.M., or twilight to dawn, each of them two hours in duration, and divided into five *ch'ang'* 唱 or beats.

丨夫 or 丨練 a watchman.

丨鼓 a watchman's drum or bamboo.

落丨 or 起丨 to set the watch.

看丨 or 守丨 to keep watch.

丨點 one-fifth of a watch, or 24 minutes.

轉丨 to relieve the watch.

丨衣 to change the dress.

丨迭 to alternate.

丨變 entirely different; all are changed.

丨番 many times, repeatedly.

説話不丨移 my words do not change.

五丨侍漏 a courtier, one who stands in waiting at dawn.

丨改 to change, to make proper.

丨換 to replace by a better one.

少'不丨事 this youth cannot act in the affair, — or attend to it.

Read *kăng'* An adjective of comparison; more, better, still; moreover, again.

丨好 better; that is preferable.

丨是 still more proper.

丨甚丨妙 still more so and more remarkable.

丨有一件 there remains one more thing or point.

粳 秔 稉 From *rice* or *grain* and to *alter* the first is the common form.
kăng *ching*

Rice which is not glutinous; the kernel is white and long; it is known as 丨米 and 丨秈; one variety called 香丨米 is somewhat fragrant when boiled.

旱稻丨米 upland rice, thus distinguished from the 水稻丨米 or water grown rice.

羹 Composed of 羔 a *lamb* and 美 *beautiful* contracted; another origin is from 羔 a *lamb* and 鬻 *gruel* altered.
kăng

A thick broth, soup; a savory porridge with flesh; a spoon; a small ladle.

送丨飯 dainties offered to hungry ghosts.

魚丨 fish-chowder.

和丨 a delicious soup; *met.* harmony between states.

亦有和丨既戒既平 there are also well-seasoned soups, already mixed in due proportion.

梅丨 broth made of plums boiled with sugar.

一碗丨湯 a bowl of good soup.

茶丨 a tea-spoon.

調丨, or 挑丨, or 丨匙 spoons; often made of porcelain.

塵丨土飯 [nothing better than] dust-soup and mud-rations; — said of a pretentious appearance; a plagiarist.

若作和丨爾惟鹽梅 as if I was making a well-seasoned soup, be you to me as the salt and prunes.

耕 畊 From *plow* or *field* and a *well.*
kăng *ching*

To cultivate, to till; to plow; a plowing, the time for plowing; to be diligent, to follow up fully; to labor at.

丨夫 or 丨田人 a farmer, a plowman.

舌丨 a teacher; to teach for a living.

亦服爾丨 attend too to your plowing.

目丨 to read much.

筆丨 to write or copy for a living.

青丨 the green grain just sprouting after plowing.

開丨 to begin plowing.

丨種 agricultural pursuits.

丨道得道 if you seek after virtue, you will be virtuous; a Budhist phrase.

埂 A sluice or channel to lead water on the fields; a shallow tank for irrigating.
'kăng

梗 From *word* and to *alter.*
'kăng

A spinous tree likened to an elm, and fit only for fuel; some say it is a species of *Erythrina;* thorny; to prick as a thorn; straight, strong, willful; sickness, distress; to ward off sickness; to obstruct; a resumé; a stem, a petiole; the midrib of a leaf.

丨概 on the whole, generally speaking.

粗陳丨概 it is a succint view of the matter.

丨直 upright, honest, unsophisticated.

頑丨 obstinate, perverse.

强丨 fierce, violent, imperious.

土丨 apparent, counterfeit.

脖丨子 the neck; *i. e.* the stem of the shoulder.

丨性子 of an obstinate, cruel nature.

誰生厲階至今爲丨 and who reared these evil stair-steps which have led to the present distress?

In *Cantonese.* Fixed, finished; certainly so; made of one piece, the whole of.

丨板 it is too late now; it cannot be changed.

頭丨丨 a stiff neck.

生成丨者 it was so made; irremediable.

㾘 Disease; a sickness.
'kăng

In *Cantonese.* To stick out, to press into or on; to emboss, to inchase.

生石丨 to get a stone bruise.

丨花 to emboss, as silver-ware.

丨心 disturbed, as by bad news.

哽 A stoppage in the throat; a rising gorge; rage or grief causing an impediment in talking.
'kăng

丨塞 unable to talk.

丨咽 or 丨丨咽咽 sobbing and stammering, as from weeping.

綆 A well-rope.
'kăng

丨短不可汲深 if the rope be short, it cannot draw the deep water.

汲古得修丨 to understand the ancients you must have a well trimmed rope, — *i. e.* a critical mind.

挭 To stir up by a stick when feeling for something in the water.
'kăng

拿竹丨過 bring a bamboo and feel for it.

In *Cantonese.* To reel, to wind off thread; to wade.

丨繭 to reel cocoons.

丨水過河 to wade the streams and cross the rivers.

骾 鯁 Fish-bones; bones or other things sticking in the throat; unyielding as a bone; stiff, brusque, blunt, plain spoken.
'kăng

骨丨之臣 officers who speak their mind; incorruptible.

丨不落頸 the bone won't go down; — *i. e.* you can't impose on me.

直丨 finical, critical, blunt, misanthropic, querulous.

耿 ˊkăng From 耳 *ear* and 炯 *bright* contracted; another says it is composed of *fire* and 火 *holy* 聖 contracted.

The ears reaching to the jaw, which is thought to be indicative of nobility or long life; bright; constant, sincere, ingenuous; something that saddens the mind, restless, melancholy.

丨介 upright, high-minded.

丨丨不寐 so disquieted that I could not sleep.

丨光 dazzling bright; to illumine.

以覲文王之丨光 and thereby display the bright glory of Wăn Wang.

忠心丨丨 an upright character; a loyal and incorruptible man.

丨直 in a good sense, firm, correct; also, misanthropic, — for which the last character is most proper.

菮 ˊkăng The stalks of the taro or *Caladium* and *Euryale;* one defines it the culm of grain.

蔿丨 the young stalks of the *Euryale ferox.*

亙 kăng' From 二 *two* with 舟 *a boat* or 月 *moon* inside, referring to the crescent shape of the moon at her quarterings; it must not be confounded either with hu' 互 or ˏsüen 亘 revolving.

A border, a limit; the extreme point; to fill, to reach everywhere, universally; — for which ˏhăng 恒 is also used; relics; the crescent moon.

丨古一人 the man who fills antiquity, — Confucius.

丨古至今 from of old till now.

綿丨數千里 many thousand miles away from here.

堩 kăng' The path leading up to a sepulcher; it is often lined with stone statues and tablets in honor and to guard the dead.

搄 kăng' To thrum the threads of a lyre rapidly, so as to endanger breaking them.

K'ĂNG.

Old sounds, k'ang, k'eng, *and* k'ung. *In Canton,* hăng *and* kang; — *in Swatow,* kⁿé and kéng; — *in Amoy,* keng *and* k'eng; — *in Fuhchau,* k'éng and k'ang; — *in Shanghai,* k'ăng; — *in Chifu,* k'ăn *and* k'ăng.

坑 ˏk'ăng From *earth* and *a neck.*

A ditch, trench, pit, excavation, or hollow, either natural or artificial; a gorge, a gulch; a quarry; a pit to entrap animals; to throw into a pit; to involve, as in a snare; to injure, to wrong.

丨坎 a pit, a hole, a trench.

丨渠 a sewer, a drain.

煤丨 a coal-pit.

水丨子 a puddle, into which one steps in the road.

山丨 a deep ravine.

丨害 to endanger, to injure grievously, so as to hazard life.

跳火丨 to fall into a fire-pit, — to meet great calamity, to be in very sad case.

砂丨 manure cakes.

丨人 to damage another.

丨儒 [Tsin Chi Hwangti] buried the literati in a pit.

丨降卒 he killed the soldiers who had submitted.

丨騙 to overreach, to defraud.

塡丨不用好土 any kind of dirt will do to fill a pit, — *i.e.* do not be finical in your diet.

In *Cantonese.* A row of tiles on a roof.

闊廿二丨 [the house] is twenty-two rows broad.

阬 ˏk'ăng A synonym of the preceding.

A valley, a pool; a tumulus; an opening; to beguile in order to destroy.

丨谷 a valley.

丨其民 ruined his people.

東丨 a name for the eastern sea.

脛 ˊk'ăng The shank bone of an ox's leg.

宋丨 a certain scholar, Sung K'ăng, in the days of Mencius.

硜 硻 ˏk'ăng From *stone* and *path* or *firm.*

The tinkling of stones; stones dashing against each other.

丨丨然小人哉 what a mean, tinkle-tinkle, worthless sort of a fellow he is!

掔 ˏk'ăng From *hand* and *firm;* also read ˏk'ien, and used for 掔 to drag.

To thump the head; to knock on, to rap; to butt against.

鏗 ˏk'ăng From *metal* and *firm.*

The ringing of metals; a metallic sound; a hacking sound, as in coughing; to knock on.

丨鏘頓銼 the jingle of bangles and gongs, thumping and filing; — all kinds of noises, a din.

鼓瑟希丨爾 pausing while his harpsichord was a twanging.

丨丨聲 the ding-dong sound of a bell.

丨鐘 to strike a bell.

肯 ʻk'ăn The original form is made of 肉 *flesh* surrounded by 冂 a *covering.*

The flesh joined to the bone; the attachment of the muscle to the bone; to assent: to permit; willing, acquiescing; voluntary.

不我丨穀 [these people] refuse to treat me civilly.

允丨 to allow, to consent.

首丨者再 he bowed the head twice; — entire assent.

你丨不丨 are you willing or not?

惠然丨來 you are very kind to consent to come.

丨指天日盟心 he voluntarily pointed to the heavens and swore.

中ʼ丨 all is agreeable to my mind.

丨幹 willing to exert one's self or spend money.

丨構丨堂 a son following out his father's plans; — a reference to 厥子乃弗丨堂矧丨構 if the son be unwilling to raise the hall, how much less will be willing to roof it!

揹 ʻk'ăn From *hand* and *willing.*

To oppress, to extort from; to vex; to detain or take by force; to obstruct; overbearing, arbitrary, with a sense of illegality.

丨勒 to levy black mail; to extort.

丨手 to catch the hand, as when rubbing a thing.

强丨 to force from.

丨口說話 vile, abusive talk.

丨贖 to interfere and prevent the redemption, as of a property mortgaged.

儘自丨着 to take all the shares to one's self, as in dividing an estate.

啃 ʻsoh Read *sheh*, in the dictionaries, but now generally read ʻk'ăng.

To bite one, as a dog; to gnaw; to wear away.

只有靴子丨襪子沒有襪子丨靴子 the boot can wear out the sock, but the sock can never gnaw the boot; — I cannot contend with him at all.

KAO.

Old sounds, ko *and* kok. *In Canton,* kò; — *in Swatow,* kao *and* ko; — *in Amoy,* kò; — *in Fuhchau,* ko; — *in Shanghai,* ko; — *in Chifu,* kao.

高 ꜀kao The original form is thought to represent one looking from a high terrace; it forms the 189th radical of a few miscellaneous characters.

High, lofty; elevated, as a place or condition; height, elevation; loud; eminent, exalted; excellent, noble, a high degree of; old, advanced; high priced, good quality; answers to the personal pronoun *your* in direct address.

丨姓呀 what is your surname?

丨見 your opinion.

丨大 lofty, high, as a house; in good proportion.

不分丨低 cannot nicely distinguish between them; there is not much difference.

丨興ʼ pleased, elated; a show, a festival.

志氣丨 aspiring, ambitious; has lofty views.

價丨 high-priced.

味丨食部 its taste is the most delicious of viands.

丨矮不等兒 the big and little don't sort well together.

才丨學廣 learned and talented.

眼角丨 supercilious, disdainful.

登丨必自卑 you must begin at the bottom when rising.

丨手 forgiving; skilled; able.

清丨 ambitious; setting one's self a high aim.

年丨 aged; and 丨壽 what is your age? are said of and to people over fifty years old.

丨名 a great name; also, your name.

巴丨枝兒 trying for the high branch, ambitious.

丨祖 a great-great-grandfather.

幾丈丨 how many poles high is it?

丨風 a great reputation and influence.

丨登 to be promoted.

丨昌國 a state of the Ouigurs, perhaps Khoten.

丨麗國 Corea; this name first denoted the northern part of the peninsula.

篙 ꜀kao A *tall bamboo,* or pole with which to push boats along.

撐丨 to push off a boat; to pole boats.

船丨 poles for poling a boat.

膏 ꜀kao From *flesh* and *high* as the phonetic.

Fat, grease; ointment; preparations which look like grease, as gambier; fat expressed from meat; blubber; rich food; greasy; fertilizing, rich; genial; anointed; to anoint; to enrich, to lubricate, to grease.

陰雨丨之 the genial rains have fattened it.

猪丨 or 丨油 clarified fat or lard.
丨藥 a plaster; but 藥丨 is prepared opium.
丨糧 rich fare, sumptuous living.
綠丨 green dye wafers prepared in Chehkiang.
丨火 fat and fire, a term for a scholar's stipend.
丨露 fertilizing dew.
丨澤 sleek, fat.
恩丨 rich favors.
丨肥 fat; fatty, greasy.
丨以脂 grease it with fat.
丨粱子弟 a rich man's son, a useless spendthrift.

皋 皐 ꜀kao From 白 *white* and 本 *ten men*; the second form is now more common than the original.

To stand on a high place and praise or bless; to announce, to harangue; to whine, to drawl out; high, eminent; a marshy bank.
江丨 a river's bank.
丨門 a palace gate.
丨月 a term for the fifth moon.
丨丨 disorderly, stupid; insolent; plain diet.
丨比 a tiger's skin.

槔 橰 ꜀kao From *tree* and *eminent* or *fault*; the second form is unusual, and also used as a synonym of *kiu'* 桕 the tallow-tree, in both cases apparently, from a confusion of the phonetics.

Name of a tree.
桔丨 a well-sweep; they are each used in irrigating lands near rivers in the northern provinces; also a water-wheel worked by the feet.

櫜 ꜀kao From *bag* and 咎 *error* as the phonetic; it resembles *t'oh* 橐 in form and meaning.

A case or sack for arrows, or for armor, attached to a chariot, similar to the drawings found at Nineveh; a wrapper for a bow; to put up a bow.
丨鞬 cases for bow and arrows.
垂丨而入 he put down his quiver and came in.
載丨弓矢 he has returned the bows and arrows to their cases.

羔 ꜀kao From 羊 a *sheep* and 照 to *show* contracted.

A lamb.
丨子 or 羊丨 a kid.
胎丨皮 unyeaned lambskins.
珍珠丨 curly-haired lambskin or astrakhan.
黑丨皮 black lambskin.
羊丨美酒 a stewed lamb and delicate wine; — a feast.

糕 ꜀kao From *rice* and *lamb* as the phonetic; often written like the next.

Cakes, pastry; a dumpling made of rice or wheat flour and raised very light; it is cooked by steaming or baking, according to the kind of flour.
百菓丨 fruit dumplings.
鬆丨 leavened cakes of rice flour.
年丨 dumplings of glutinous rice made for new-year.
蛋丨 sponge cake.
丨點 cakes; a dessert.
丨餅 a cake, a bolo.
神丨 large cakes offered in worship by the emperor on the sun's festival on the 2d day of the 2d moon, and presented to officers whom he honors.

餻 ꜀kao Interchanged and nearly synonymous with the last.

Steamed cakes; a bit, a bait, a nice morsel.
丨粉 rice flour.

鼛 ꜀kao From *drum* and *fault*.

A large drum, twelve feet long; it was in olden times put on a cart, and struck to arouse workmen to resume their labor.
丨鼓弗勝 the roll of the great drum did not drown — the hum of their labors.

稾 稿 ʿkao From *grain* and *high*; the second form is commonest.

The culm of grain, straw; a first draft of a paper, a sketch, a minute; the original copy; a proof, as of a printer.
禾丨 rice straw.
起丨 to prepare a statement, to make a draft.
腹丨 to have the whole subject in one's mind.
草丨 a first draft; the rough copy.
打丨 to take a proof, as from a block.
丨公 or 丨案 the head clerk, who keeps the record of cases.
窓丨 a theme, as for a composition.
文丨 a draft of a paper.
丨案留在丨房 let the documents in the case remain in the record office.
留丨同正 keep both the draft and the fair copy.
丨荐 a mattress or bed made of rice straw rolled in wisps.
肚皮裏打丨子 to think over a composition before writing it out.

槁 ʿkao Dry, rotten, as wood; withered, as grain; a tree resembling the chestnut, though others describe it like the tallow tree; desire gone; no resource; to accumulate.
丨魚 dried fish; stockfish.
形容枯丨 attenuated, thin; forlorn-looking.
丨木朽癈 a dry and useless stick; *met.* a shiftless fellow.
丨本 a plant like water-hemlock or cowbane (*Cicuta*), whose seeds are used as medicine.

藁 ʿkao From *plant* and *decayed*; it is interchanged with the last two.

Straw good for thatching; decayed wood; a draft, a first copy.
丨席 a straw mat; a bed of straw.
丨卷 the original documents.
空丨 blasted straw.

‘㾸 ‘kao A scabby itching disease.

丨疙 the itch.

關門賣丨疙藥 he sells itch ointment with closed doors; *met.* he (the clerk) trades in a private way.

‘杲 ‘kao From *tree* and *sun* over it, as the sun appears in sight.

The rising sun shining over the trees; clear, high as the sun.

丨丨出日 the rising sun shines brightly.

丨乎如登乎天 it rises glorious in the heavens.

‘暠 ‘皜 ‘kao From *sun* or *white* and *high*; the second form is most common, and is synonymous with *hao’* 皓 luminous; there are other forms.

Clear; pure, white; hoary, as hair.

丨身赤足 naked and barefooted.

丨然白首 truly a venerable white head.

‘縞 ‘kao A kind of thin lustrous silk; plain white or undyed silk; simple, unornamented; to boil silk.

丨衣綦巾 white thin silk garments and gray kerchiefs.

丨冠 white caps, worn in old times.

丨素 plain white silks.

‘夰 ‘kao From 大 *great* and 八 *eight* altered in combination.

To let go; to part; the sky.

泰丨入于淵 the skyey vapors enter the abyss.

告’ kao’ From *mouth* and an *ox*.

To gore, to butt with the horns; to announce to a superior, to inform by petition or prayer; to impeach, to indict; to tell of, to advise of; to ask, to request, as in courtesy; to proclaim, to order, to decree.

丨訟 to accuse before a court; to bring charges against.

丨狀 an indictment.

丨賬 to sue for a debt.

原丨 the plaintiff; 被丨 the defendant; 兩丨 the parties in the case.

丨訴 to tell another, to inform, to speak to; also, the accusation and defense.

丨示 to proclaim to all; an official proclamation.

丨白 a notification, a placard, an authoritative declaration.

上丨 or 控丨 to appeal to the higher court.

丨下你來 I have entered an accusation against you.

抱丨 a deputy or pleader who appears as proxy in a case; women and old people are required to have one.

稟丨 to inform a superior or any official.

丨貸無門 I have no resource to help myself.

日月丨凶 the sun and moon forebode evil.

無丨 no one to appeal to;— the helpless and weak.

丨祖 to inform one's ancestors — by prayer.

丨竣 or 丨成 to announce that a thing is finished.

君子作歌維以丨哀 I, an officer have made this song to let my complaint be known.

丨假 to get leave of absence.

丨辭 I am about to take my leave, said by a visitor.

丨身 to give an officer his seals.

丨休 to renounce office.

丨終養 to resign and go home to wait on one's parents.

Read *kuh*, To tell one's parents.

必丨父母 he must inform his parents.

誥’ kao’ From *words* and to *announce*.

To enjoin upon, to order those under one, and thus it is the opposite of the preceding; to signify one's wishes; a patent or seals; a decoration.

丨命 credentials, a commission.

丨命夫人 a patent ennobling an officer's mother.

丨封三代 he ennobled three generations of his ancestors.

金花丨 the patent given to an officer's wife.

丨書 a scroll from the Emperor.

丨誓 orders given to combatants.

皇清丨贈 his Majesty of the Ts‘ing dynasty conferred these honors;— a phrase in epitaphs.

郜’ kao’ An appanage conferred on Wăn Wang's son, now comprising most of the department of T‘ung-ch‘ang fu 同昌府 in the western part of Shantung.

K'AO.

Old sounds, k'o, k'ok, *and* k'ot. *In Canton*, hao, k'ao, *and* kò; — *in Swatow*, k'ao *and* kò; — *in Amoy*, k'ò; — *in Fuhchau*, k'o; — *in Shanghai*, k'o; — *in Chifu*, k'ao.

尻 ⿰骨尻 *k'ao* — From *body* and *nine*, or with *bone* added.
The end bone of the spine, the *os coxendicis*; the sacral extremity; the rump of an animal.
黑 丨 the black rump, — a term for the heron.

考 攷 *k'ao* — From 老 *old* and 丂 *ingenious* contracted; the second ancient form is pedantic.
Aged; longevity; ancestors, especially a deceased father; completed, as his life; to complete; to have long life; finished; to examine, with reference to office or enlisting; to question, as candidates at a competitive examination; to strike on.
丨 驗 a triennial examination of officials.
丨 試 to examine for degrees.
丨 例 or 歲 丨 triennial examination for *siuts'ai*, to see if they maintain their scholarship.
小 丨 or 府 丨 the annual prefectural examination for *siuts'ai*.
大 丨 the triennial examination for *küjin*.
丨 案 首 the first on the list of *siuts'ai*.
丨 中 了 passed his examination.
丨 察 or 丨 究 to search into officially; to ferret out a matter.
丨 成 to finish a work.
擔 丨 成 I will see that the matter is accomplished.
無 可 稽 丨 there is no good evidence for it.
出 丨 語 to give an opinion as to one's fitness for a place.
丨 鼓 to beat a drum.
丨 卜 to search out by divination.
先 丨 my deceased father.
壽 丨 very aged; a wish that one may reach old age.

拷 *k'ao* — From *hand* and to *question*, referring to the torture; occurs used with the last.
To put to the question; to extort a confession; to snatch, to grab.
丨 訊 to examine by torture.
丨 脚 眼 to beat one's ankles.
私 刑 丨 打 to bamboo or torture one without a warrant.
丨 打 to bamboo and force a confession; to torture for robbery.
丨 脚 骨 to rob like a footpad. (*Cantonese.*)
三 丨 書 供 after the third confession, endorse the evidence.

栲 *k'ao* — A tree producing a kind of varnish sap; it seems to refer to the *Ailantus glandulosa* by the synonyms, but may also denote a kind of Rhus, (*Rhus cotinus?*) whose sap is useful in making wood paints, for which the Ailantus is not employed.
丨 皮 mangrove bark (*Rhizophora*), used to dye canvas and cotton a brown color; it comes from Siam.
丨 紬 pongee dyed umber, — with this bark.
丨 栳 a well-bucket made of osier, rattan, or other twigs.

烤 *k'ao* — From *fire* and to *test*; it is an unauthorized character.
To toast, to dry at the fire; to fry, to grill; to char, as a beam.
丨 饅 頭 make some toast.
丨 木 to bend a stick by heat.
丨 手 to warm the hands.
丨 焦 burned in roasting.
丨 餅 to bake a cake.
丨 一 丨 warm it a little.
伏 天 丨 日 頭 in dog-days we are all roasted by the sun.

熇 燺 *k'ao* — From *fire* and *dried* or *high*; apparently the original forms of the last, which has supplanted them; the first is also read *hao* and *hiao*, fiery; and *hoh*, hot.
To dry at the fire; to grill; to toast; hot, stifling; radiation of heat; burning.
多 將 丨 丨 the heat is oppressive, — and there is no way of relief.
丨 肉 to roast meat.
微 火 兒 丨 着 dry (or warm) it over a gentle fire.

焅 *k'ao* — Interchanged with the last.
Hot air; a dry, burning atmosphere.

犒 *k'ao* — From *ox* and *high*, perhaps referring to the entertainment.
To feast victorious soldiers on their return; bounty money; to reward workmen with a treat.
丨 賞 to confer bounties; batta money.
丨 工 to entertain the workmen, as on a building.
丨 農 official largesses to farmers.
大 丨 三 軍 a great largess to the army.
吃 丨 勞 to give a feast to laborers.

靠 *k'ao* — From *not* and to *inform*; *i. e.* stating that we will not agree.
To mutually oppose; to lean against; to rely on; to depend on for support, connected with; occurs wrongly used for *kuh*, 梏 fetters.
倚 丨 or 丨 着 to lean against, literally and figuratively; to depend on, to trust to.
丨 枕 to rest on a pillow.
丨 火 warmed; looking to the fire.
丨 背 椅 a high-backed armchair.

丨山吃山丨水吃水 a mountaineer must depend on the hills for his living, and a waterman on his fish; — *i. e.* every man must look to his own calling for a living.

丨此生意 dependent on this for a living.

終身之丨 a continual reliance, as a widow on her son, a wife on her husband.

丨賴 to confide in, to rely on.

丨不住 unreliable; not to be depended on.

丨山 abutting on a hill, as a grave or a fort; *met.* a dernier resort, a resource.

妥丨 trustworthy; reliable.

KEU.

Old sounds, ku, kot, *and* kop. *In Canton*, kau; — *in Swatow*, kau *and* kò; — *in Amoy*, ko, ho, *and* kau; — *in Fuhchau*, kau, kéu, *and* kaiu; — *in Shanghai*, kù; — *in Chifu*, kò.

勾 ˛keu Originally a contracted form of *kü'* 句 a sentence; and sometimes used for the next two.

To mark off and reject, as items in a list; to divide off a composition into sentences, to entice, to invite; to enveigle; to hook on, to connect; a hook; in *geometry*, the short sides of a triangle.

丨决 to mark off the names of criminals to be executed.

一筆丨銷 to cancel an account.

丨除 to reject, to mark out.

丨引 to entice, to lead astray.

丨當' a scheme; a job; underhand doings; illicit connection.

誰知你的幹丨當' who can tell what job you are hatching now?

丨脂紛 toying with women; lewd dalliance.

丨生意 fishing for custom.

丨通 to join in a plot; privy to; drawn into a scheme, in league with; secretly connected.

丨股 a hook to indicate a paragraph; the two short legs of a triangle; *met.* trigonometry.

丨上我的心事來 you have anticipated my idea.

兩人丨搭丨上了 the two are engaged in an illicit intrigue.

丨芒神 to invite the Blade God, *i.e.* to worship an agricultural deity, whose image is broken to pieces about new-year's day with the clay ox.

拘 ˛keu Another form of ˛*kü* 拘 to seize, but this is usually read ˛*keu*, and used with the next and last.

To collect, to get; to join together, to clasp; to grasp; to restrain.

丨連 to unite, like a chain; to rabbet together.

丨賬 to check an account as balanced.

丨拿 to nab; to seize; to lug along.

In *Pekingese.* To point bricks.

丨抹牆縫子 point the bricks in the wall.

鈎 鉤 ˛keu From *metal* and *hook* or *sentence;* used with the last.

A hook, a barb, a claw, a fluke; a sickle, a bill-hook; a crooked sword; a hasp, a clasp; a catch on a sword hilt; in *penmanship*, a hook to the right; to hook; to make crooked or hooked; to detain, to influence; to tempt, to entice; to search into; to consider.

釣魚丨 a fish-hook.

丨出來 hook it up or out.

帳丨 a bed-curtain hook.

丨格 a hook for hanging things on.

丨住了 hooked or linked together; detained, as if by force.

丨誘致詣我所 beguile him to come here by some means.

丨止 or 丨留 to detain, to keep; unable to get on, as for want of money.

丨索義理 to search out the principles of a thing.

丨深致遠 to consider the abstruse and search the remote results, as in philosophy.

倒丨鬚 I was caught on the barb, I've been taken in.

撓丨 to hook up by feeling for.

內丨外連 to have coädjutors inside; to be leagued with people outside.

丨帶 to fasten the girdle.

刎 ˛keu A sickle or bill-hook.

鐮丨 a crooked blade used by grass and faggot-cutters.

畇 ˛keu The bank of a field raised above the level, on which vegetables are grown.

緱 ˛keu From *silk* and *prince.*

Cord used to wrap the hilt of a sword in order to grasp it better.

蒯丨 a hilt wrapped with grass.

溝 ˛keu From *water* and *connected* as the phonetic.

A water-course in a field; a drain, a ditch; an aqueduct; to surround, as with a moat; a current in the ocean; used by Budhists for ten billions, for which the primitive alone is also written.

田 〡 field drains.
臭 〡 路 a filthy sewer.
陽 〡 裏 鴨 子 [like] a duck in a gutter, — the cook eats a little of everything.
一條 〡 or 一溜 〡 兒 a sewer, a gutter.
旱 〡 the dry ditch, a name for the hollow in a horse's back.
開 〡 渠 to open sewers and drains.
死 于 〡 壑 [the people] died in the ditches.
瓦 〡 gutters between the tiles.
黑 水 〡 or 黑 〡 the black current or sewer, a name for the *kuro-siwo*, or gulf-stream along the Chinese and Japanese coasts.

篝 ˓keu A bamboo frame or hamper for drying clothes over a fire; a *chauffe-lit;* a sort of basket.
燈 〡 a lamp shade or screen.
〡 籠 a bamboo drying frame, used by washermen.

褠 ˓keu Single garments with narrow straight sleeves; plaits in a dress.
臂 〡 a sort of gauntlet or cuff drawn over the sleeve.

韝 鞲 ˓keu A kind of leathern vambrace or vantbrace, called 射 〡, used by archers to strengthen the arm.

苟 ˓keu From *plant* and a *hook.*
Plants, herbage; wayward, to the right or left; impromptu, inconsiderate, offhand; illicit, adulterous; as an *adverb*, carelessly, improperly; as a *conjunction*, if, if so; but, nevertheless.
〡 合 illicit intercourse, fornication.
〡 得 to get unfairly.
〡 且 了 事 careless in doing; to finish off a matter anyhow; to huddle up.

作 事 不 〡 to manage a business properly.
〡 不 然 if it be not so.
〡 能 如 此 yet if it can be done in this way.
〡 犯 to offend inconsiderately.
臨 難 無 〡 免 do not desert a cause when it is danger.
〡 磯 a ledge of rocks in a stream; a stumbling-block.
卑 汙 〡 賤 個 人 a hireling, a baseborn mercenary, who will commit crimes for money.

岣 ˓keu A hill known as 〡 嶁 山, situated in Hăng-yang hien 衡 陽 縣 in Hunan, where the tablet in honor of Yü was placed.

笱 ˓keu From *bamboo* and *hook.*
A conical or cylindrical trap made of bamboo for catching shrimps and minnows; it is dragged along the bottom.
無 鬚 蝦 〡 a weel without barbs; *met.* a heedless, inattentive man.
蝦 〡 艇 a kind of boat at Canton used by travelers and fishermen.
毋 發 我 〡 don't disturb my fish-traps.

枸 ˓keu A high tree found in Sz'ch'uen, resembling an aspen; the long sweetish seeds are prepared for preserves; the Japanese apply the name to the *Hovenia dulcis;* crooked.
〡 棘 a spinous species of barberry (*Berberis chinensis*).
〡 杞 seeds of the *Berberis lycium*, and of the last, used as a febrifuge and collyrium.
〡 橘 (or 〡 菓 at *Canton*) a small orange (*Citrus bigaradia*), full of small seeds; its spinous branches make the shrub suitable for hedges.

狗 ˓keu From 犬 *dog* and 句 *hook*, a contraction of 苟 *loose;* but others say it is used for *k'eu'* 叩 to call, as a dog guards by his bark.
A dog; petty, contemptible; a term applied in contempt to infants and children, a puppy, a brat; it is used in the names of many living things, insects, fish, &c.
〡 子 or 一 隻 〡, one dog.
〡 偷 a petty theft, done by a 〡 賊 pilferer.
〡 吗 or 〡 吠 the dog barks.
〡 蚤 or 〡 虱 a flea.
大 〡 a term for gentlemen's servants or waiters in offices.
獅子 〡 or 巴 兒 〡 Peking lap-dogs, the pug-nosed sort.
山 〡 rustics who cut grass or watch graves. (*Cantonese.*)
〡 腿 子 dog's legs, a nickname for police-runners, from their greediness for money.
海 〡 another name for a species of seal; used for the fur.
看 門 〡 or 掌 門 〡 a doorkeeper, a porter.
癲 〡 [you are like a] mad dog; — an abusive term.
木 〡 a climbing animal resembling the racoon; its fur is used for garments; also a term for manacles.
〡 星 the stars ψ and χ in Sagittarius; and 〡 國 are the stars ω a b c in that sign.
天 〡 a star in Argo.

耇 ˓keu From 老 *old* and 句 a *hook*, which is regarded as really used for the next.
A face looking as if grimed with dirt from very age; senile, very old, decrepid.
〡 老 infirm, superannuated, in second childhood.
胡 〡 or 黃 〡 very infirm; extreme age.
〡 造 德 benefits of age and experience.
你 〡 長 過 我 you are older than I am.
以 祈 黃 〡 黃 〡 台 背 he prays for the very aged, those with hoary heads and bended backs.

垢 ˋkeuˊ From *earth* and *queen*.

Dirty, filthy; scurf, dandruff, the dirt grimed in; sordid, disgraceful; immorality; a stain, a reproach.

泥丨 or 丨穢 dirt on the body or clothes; filthy, unwashed.

刮丨 scrape off the dirt.

塵丨 slovenly, dirty; *met.* infamous or disgraceful conduct.

洗丨 to wash away filth; to reform.

蒙丨 to get dirtied, covered with dust; disgraced, lost his good name.

無丨 stainless, a Budhist term (*mani*) applied to one of the *sapta ratna*, a fabulous brilliant pearl, used as a symbol of Budha and his doctrines.

雊 keuˊ The crowing of a pheasant.

丨瞀縣 old name of a district in the present Süenhwa fu in the north of Chihli.

雉丨鷄乳 the pheasant crows and the hen broods.

越有丨雉 now there was a crowing pheasant.

軥 ˏchü The ends of the yoke which press on the sides of the animal's neck.

Read ˏ*keu.* The projecting end of an axle; the hub.

丨牛 a small ox.

丨車 the chariot used by the empress in the Hia dynasty, having bent axle-ends.

詬 **訽** keuˊ A sense of shame; to reproach, to rail at, to shame one; to taunt; outrageous, unprincipled.

丨詈 or 丨罵 to vilify, to curse.

相丨 to abuse each other.

丨病 ashamed, a feeling of mortification.

丨怒 to speak angrily at one.

丨感之情 sentiments of shame and thankfulness.

余不忍其丨 I will not bear his mortifying me.

閉門而丨之 he barred the door and railed at him.

姤 keuˊ To pair, to copulate; to meet, to encounter; name of the 44th diagram, referring to union.

交丨 union of the dual powers; coition, sexual intercourse.

丨好如初 make it as good as at first.

媾 keuˊ From *woman* and *to connect*; it resembles the last.

A second marriage, as of a widow; to wed a kinswoman; fondness, affection, love; conjugal embraces.

婚丨 a second marriage.

不遂其丨 she did not reciprocate his love.

媒丨 a go-between.

購 keuˊ Occurs used with the next.

To buy; to hire; to procure for one's self, to induce, to bring on one.

丨買 to purchase.

丨辦 to manage purchases.

丨線 to start one on the trail of another.

自丨寃仇 to bring down deep hatred on one's self.

搆 keuˊ From *hand* and *to connect*; occurs used with the next.

To pull, to drag; to plot, to stir up, to implicate; to reach up to; to put a thing high up.

結丨不解 they formed a very close connection, as an undying enmity or friendship.

丨怨 to contract a dislike.

丨兵 at war; moving troops.

丨思 to think upon.

丨禍 to bring evil on one's self.

丨不着 I can't reach up to it.

樹上一個筐子你丨丨看 see if you can get that basket down from the tree.

構 keuˊ From *wood* and *to connect*, as interlacing beams; used with the preceding.

To roof over with beams; the truss of a roof; to construct; to unite; to copulate; to burst forth, as fire; completed, finished.

丨火 to take fire.

事已丨 the matter is now done with.

勿用傍人解丨之言 there is no need of invidious remarks from by-standers.

丨精 the procreative principle; sexual intercourse.

丨膠 to mix glue, as in a paint.

如其宿丨 it is like what I once did.

遘 keuˊ To met with, to happen; to come upon one suddenly; accidentally, unexpectedly.

丨遇 a chance affair.

丨逢 to fall in with.

無有丨自疾 no sickness has befallen me.

覯 keuˊ Interchanged with the last.

To see or meet one suddenly; to occur; to finish; accidentally, unforeseen.

丨見 to encounter one, as in the street.

鮮我丨爾 seldom do I see one who matches you.

無曰不顯莫予云丨 do not say, No one sees me here, it is not an open place.

丨成其事 finished this business.

罕丨 rarely met with.

易丨 readily infected with, as malaria; occurs easily.

冓 keuˊ The original form is thought to represent the timbers in the frame-work of a house, as they interlock and cross each other; many of the compounds show traces of this meaning.

A high number, ten billions, for which 溝 is also used; a room.

中丨之言 words spoken in the closet or hareem.

彀 *keu'* From *bow* and a shell or *husk*; used with next.

To draw a bow to its full stretch; bowmen, archers; full; enough, adequate, for which the next is more common.

射者能丨 archers can draw the arrow to its head.

不丨 not enough, inadequate, unable.

學者必志於丨 scholars should exert their faculties to the utmost.

入丨 the string is on the thumb; *i. e.* the thing is all right; it suits, it matches.

你能丨做嗎 are you able to do that?

夠 *keu'* From *much* and a *hook*; it has almost superseded the last.

Enough, sufficient; adequate; satisfied; filled up, to the brim; thoroughly.

丨得很 too much by far.

不丨本 not the original cost; *i.e.* I shall lose on it.

巴不能丨 it is my wish; I shall be sorry if I don't get it.

不丨用 or 沒丨 not enough, insufficient.

丨算 that will do; we'll stop now.

丨奇 singular, unusual.

丨不丨呢 is there enough?

丨纏的 impracticable; one can make nothing of him.

K'EU.

Old sounds, k'u, k'up, *and* k'ut. *In Canton*, k'au *and* hau; — *in Swatow*, k'ao, k'u, k'a, kò *and* k'ò; — *in Amoy*, k'o *and* ko; — *in Fuhchau*, k'au, k'éu, *and* k'aiu; — *in Shanghai*, k'ü *and* hio; — *in Chifu*, k'ò.

摳 *ₒk'eu* From *hand* and a *store-room*.

To raise, as the skirt; to feel for with the hand; to lay away, to store.

丨衣升堂 lifted up his dress and ascended to the hall.

丨不出來 you can't get it back — or out again; as money that has been spent.

丨搶 the return, as of harvest.

Read *ₒngeu*. To strike.

In *Cantonese*. To dilute; to mix; to adulterate.

丨匀 mixed thoroughly or evenly.

丨砂 adulterated with sand.

對丨 mixed in equal parts.

丨亂 mixed without order, or not in proper proportions.

剾 *ₒk'eu* To pick out with a knife.

丨剜 to cut out or dig out through a hole, as a fruit without cutting it up.

瞘 瞜 *ₒk'eu* A deep sunken eye, such as the southern Chinese often have.

深丨 sunken eyes.

猴兒眼丨瞜着 monkeys' eyes are very deep set.

彄 *ₒk'eu* The notch or catch at the end of a bow, to which the bow-string is fastened.

丨環 the thumb-ring used by archers.

藏丨之戲 an old game common in Hupeh, of hiding the ring about newyear's time.

芤 *ₒk'eu* From *plant* and *hollow*.

A species of onion; its hollow culm.

丨脈 a medical term for an irregular pulse, which is thought to be hollow like an onion stalk.

口 *ᶜk'eu* The character is designed to represent the mouth; it forms the 30th radical of a natural group of characters relating to speaking; and is often added to a character to show that it is to be read phonetically.

The mouth, defined to be "that from which words proceed, and at which food enters;" an entrance, an opening; a hole; a rip or tear; a gorge, a pass, a gap or notch in mountains; end of a street; a port for trade; a gate in the Great Wall; to mouth, to reiterate; speech, utterance; a classifier of swords, persons, cannon balls, bags, hatches, screws, boxes, a fill of a pipe or a draught of water, &c.; verbally; by word; pronunciation.

利丨 talkative; specious.

人丨 persons, individuals.

好丨才 a good utterance, fluent.

以就丨食 when he was able to feed himself.

戶丨 the population; a family.

無丨齒 untrustworthy.

子丨 the rim on a box which receives the cover.

吃兩丨烟 smoke two pipes.

一丨藥 a dose of physic.

丨皮 sheep-skins or lamb-skins from Mongolia.

兩丨子 denote husband and wife.

張丨 or 開丨 open your mouth.

丨外 outside of the Great Wall, meaning Mongolia and beyond; extra-provincial China, and even in foreign regions.

海丨 an estuary, a firth.

誇海丨 a great brag; to vapor and boast greatly.

港丨 or 丨岸 a port for trade.

八丨之家 a family of eight persons.

害 丨 a vicious appetite, a pregnant woman's longing.

丨是心非 his heart is wrong though he speaks well.

禦人以丨給 to confute another for his loquacity.

收了丨兒了 the sore has healed up.

丨占 to dictate to a writer.

丨技 a mimic, a ventriloquist.

丨號 a vocal signal; a cry as a signal.

撕個丨子 ripped open a hole.

數丨 several persons.

丨實 that which fills the mouth, matter for remark.

丨角 a phraseology; a dispute.

丨糧 rations, allowances.

丨腹之奉 living to gratify his palate and belly.

半邊丨 an old horse or mule, alluding to the difference in the teeth.

犳 狗 *k'eu'* The first form is most common. A domesticated animal, especially equine ones; an ox with its head awry, for which the second is used.

牲 丨 an animal fit for work or sacrifice, as the camel, mule, ass, horse, dog, &c.; they are also called 六畜 or the six animals which are reared.

扣 敂 *k'eu'* From *hand* and *mouth*; the second form is rarely used. To strike, to knock against, to rap on, — in which senses only the second form is used; to deduct, to discount; to hook on, to link in; to buckle; to rein up a horse; a skein; a deduction, a discount.

丨門 to rap on a door.

丨折 to take off, to deduct.

丨數 to reduce an account.

丨鈕 to button.

丨帶 to buckle the girdle.

九五丨 to reduce to ninety-five, to take off five per cent.

九九五丨 to take off one-fifth per cent.

丨除 to subtract; to strike off, as a name from a list.

丨回 to deduct from wages till the advance is all paid up.

丨頭 or 丨水 the discount.

丨留 to hinder.

活丨兒 a slip-knot.

線一丨 one skein of silk.

一丨摺子 one opening or two folds of a document.

丨馬而諫 he stopped his horse to expostulate with him.

丨關 to knock on the gate; *met.* to enter a country.

丨布 a narrow kind of cotton; it is eight *ts'un* wide.

釦 *k'eu'* From *metal* and *mouth*; used with the last. A gold or silver rim on a cup, enchased on the edge; to engrave; to enchase; chased or filagree-work; a round or chased button; a button, a clasp; to button; to make a din.

丨口 a button hole.

鈕丨 round buttons.

銅丨 brass clasps or links.

譁丨 a great clamor or noise, as when beating gongs, &c.

絈 *k'eu'* An unauthorized character, probably formed to indicate the different material. A button, differing from the last in that it is made of thread or cord, wound like a ball; to fasten, as the hasp on a door by a nail; to loop, to tie up and fasten.

丨上鈕子 loop on the button.

寇 *k'eu'* From 完 to *finish* and 攴 to *beat*. Tyrannical, cruel; riotous; to rob, to plunder; to act as a robber; to do mischief; banditti, thieves, highwaymen; an enemy; a local term for a flock.

丨盜 or 丨賊 insurgents, outlaws in armed bands.

式遏丨虐 to put down robbers and oppressors.

海丨 pirates, dacoits.

仇丨 an enemy, a mortal foe.

民之未戾職盜爲丨 the people are unsettled because of the robbers who plunder them.

草丨 an open robber, a Robin Hood.

司丨 in ancient days, the Minister of Crimes, a criminal judge.

丨盛 an abundance, said of birds.

簆 *k'eu'* The reed or slaie of a loom, made of bamboo.

機丨 the slaie through which the warp runs.

紮丨 to make a slaie of bamboo splints.

蔻 *k'eu'* A term for the seeds of cardamoms and similar spicy fruits.

荳丨花 the mace or flower of nutmeg.

荳丨 and 肉荳丨 the nutmeg.

白荳丨 the whole cardamoms (*Amomum cardamomum*), or the cluster cardamoms, growing in Kwangtung.

草荳丨 the round cardamoms (*Amomum globosum*), found in Kwangtung.

荳丨含葩 the cardamom bud; *met.* a blooming girl.

鷇 *k'eu'* From *bird* and *shell*, referring to the recent exit of the chick. Fledgelings which must be fed by the parent bird, like the young of sparrows or swallows.

丨音 chirp of a newly hatched bird.

風胎雨丨 they are wombed among the winds and fed under the showers; *viz.* the birds of the air.

怐 *k'eu'* Silly and inefficient, but good-natured.

丨愗 dull, doltish, stupid-looking.

叩 ˀ k'eu From *mouth* and *seal;* it is said to have been originally written 訌 from *words* and *mouth*, and this last is explained by a reference to a man who distinctly states his object when he asks for a wife.

To ask; to tap, to strike lightly; to knock the head on the ground, as in worship; to raise the hand to the forehead and bow low; prostrate, humbly, respectfully; to exhibit; a kotow or prostration.

丨問 to earnestly ask for.

丨首 the ceremony of kneeling and putting the forehead on the ground.

三跪九丨 thrice kneeling and nine times knocking the head; the highest act of reverence; it is paid to the Emperor, to Confucius, and to ancestors.

以杖丨其脛 [Confucius] hit him on the shins with his staff.

丨稟 to humbly petition.

十丨柴扉九不開 [out of] ten raps on a country gate, nine of them did not open it; — persevere if you wish to attain an object.

丨見 to visit a superior.

我丨其兩端而竭焉 I made known the cause and effect of this in the fullest manner.

小丨則小鳴 a slight rap produces only a slight ring; — be earnest in asking.

KI.

Old sounds, ki, kit, gi, git, k'i, *and* kői. *In Canton*, ki, kei, ké, *and* kwei; — *in Swatow*, ki, koi, *and* kúi; — *in Amoy*, ki, ké, k'i, k'ai, kòé, *and* kúi; — *in Fuhchau*, ki, kie, kwoi, k'ai, hi, *and* ké; — *in Shanghai*, ki *and* dji; — *in Chifu*, ki.

幾 ˏchi ˋchi Composed of 幺幺 *minute* and 戍 a *guard* of soldiers on the frontier; *q. d.* provided against the first approaches; it is interchanged with the next, and others of its compounds.

Subtle, hidden, like the unseen springs of motion; the interior or recondite parts of a thing or subject; moderately; a few; as an *adverb*, nearly, about, rather, somewhat; the time for, the chance; having stated periods; to approximate to; a sign of; to examine into; to expect.

庶丨 if, yet, for all that; probably, it is likely.

式食庶丨 we will try the viands, and see if they satisfy.

卜爾百福如丨式丨 they allot you all blessings, each one as expected, and sure as law.

丨乎 or 丨丨乎 at the point of, not far from.

事父母丨諫 one should mildly remonstrate with his parents.

月丨望 the moon is nearly full.

日理萬丨 [the emperor] daily attends to every kind of affair.

不可丨及 no one can equal him; he is unsurpassible.

丨微 subtle, incipient, atomic.

Read ˋki. An interrogation, implying quantity; how much? little; nearly, a part, several.

丨多 how many?

丨時來了 when did he come?

第丨 which number? which one?

丨希 almost; only a portion; not many.

遠來丨許 how much farther is it?

人生丨何 how long is a man's life?

來日無丨 the days to come are not many; — I am old.

丨萬 several myriads.

所ˏ差無丨 almost the same.

爾居徒丨何 but who and what are your followers?

無丨相見 you will not see each other long.

機 机 ˏchi From *wood* and *subtle;* it is interchanged with the last; the contracted form is very common.

Changes, motions; the origin or spring of, the moving power, as in a machine; a principle, a natural cause of; a catch, a contrivance; a loom; a machine with complicated parts; a secret, a stratagem; secret, occult.

丨會 an occasion, an opportunity, a chance.

丨關 designs; the intentions of; the power or spring in a machine.

一架丨 or 織布丨 a loom.

丨房 a weaver's shop; a cloth manufactory.

見丨而作 do it at the right moment; mind and improve your chance.

神丨 skilled in judging.

失丨 lost the right moment; defeated, thrown off.

天丨 the natural bent of a mind; fate, destiny, decrees.

丨謀 an artifice, a clever dodge.

丨密 undivulged, secret; occult causes.

丨械 an ingenious contrivance or machine.

丨械變詐 crafty and full of dodges; a slippery device.

丨巧伶俐 an unscrupulous, clever fellow; shrewd at guessing; a neat machine.

丨務 councils of state.

軍丨處 the General Council of State.

丨星 a name for the star Vega.

用盡心丨 using every power of the mind to accomplish it.

鐖 ˓chi Occurs used for the last.
A barb on a hook, a fluke.
丨發 or 進丨 a catch, a spring, as in machinery; the motive power.
丨器局 a machine shop.
無丨之鈎 a hook without a barb — catches no fish.

禨 ˓chi An auspicious prognostic; also an omen of evil; felicitous, opportune.
Read *ki*ˀ To bathe, and then drink as a precaution.
進丨 to take the bath cup.

磯 ˓chi Stones or ledges in a stream producing a ripple; a pier or jetty to protect a bank, which is a good place for fishing; shallows; an eddy; an obstacle, an obstruction; to rub; to impede, to grate.
是不可丨 it will not do to oppose them.
丨頭 a breakwater, a jetty, a mole; a headland jutting into the ocean.

璣 ˓chi A pearl not quite globular; a large mirror.
滿腹珠丨 his belly is full of pearls; — his knowledge is extensive and useful.
天丨 the star γ Phad in Ursa Major.

畿 ˓chi The demesne which in ancient times pertained to the Emperor; it measured a thousand *li* on each side, the court being in the center; the court; a limit or border; a high threshold, shielding the inside of the door.
皇丨 the imperial domains; the court.
九丨 the nine tenures of appanages lying beyond the demesnes.
丨輔重地 the capital, the region near the palace.
不遠伊邇薄送我丨 only a little way did he go with me from the doorway.

嘰 ˓chi A sound.
丨嘵怪症 an obscure disease, which baffles the doctor's skill.

譏 ˓chi To slander, to speak of, to ridicule, to mock, to joke; to blame, to reprove; to examine into, to test; satire, contumely; machinations.
丨諷大臣 to satirize officials.
丨笑 to ridicule, to laugh at one.
丨刺 pasquinades, gibes; to insinuate, to jeer at, to caricature.
丨誚 to scoff at, to deride.
丨察 to inspect; an inspector, whose duty is to mark traitors and spies going into court.

魕 ˓chi Among the southern tribes a ghost or demon which bewilders men; devilish; in Canton, 撞亞丨 to meet a brownie, means to see a foreigner, because they have usually shrill voices as these elves are supposed to have.

饑 **飢** ˓chi From to *eat* and *moderately*; a distinction is often made between these forms, the latter being confined to bodily hunger.
Dearth, scarcity; failure of the harvest; famine; hungry, famished; necessitous; to starve.
丨荒 a time of dearth.
打丨荒 in distress; wanting supplies; borrowing money; also to pretend to be in want; to act as if starving.
丨色 a starved, cadaverous look.
丨成不遂 famine has done its work, but he goes on — to nothing good.
丨死 starved to death.
丨渴之際 in the midst of sore need, at the last extremity.
肚丨 or 丨餓 hungry, famishing.
丨饉 a dearth of crops, a bad harvest.
賙道路之丨寒 aid the naked and starving along the roads.

肌 ˓chi From *flesh* and *seat*.
The flesh or firm muscles under the skin; the meat on the bones.
丨膚壯 robust, muscular, firm-fleshed, brawny.
丨體 the body.
丨巴 the virile member.
裏丨 the tender loin.
氷丨玉骨 or 玉丨 clear complexion and fine limbs; said of a girl.
米丨 a viscid preparation among the Miao-tsz', made by chewing rice and spitting it into a vessel, where it ferments before it is drank.

羈 ˓chi The bit on a bridle; to restrain or check a horse.
是猶以丨而御騂突 it was like a man trying to rein in a horse which shied and run.

鷄 **雞** ˓chi From *bird* and *why*; both forms are authorized, but the first is most used.
The bird which knows place and time; the cock; gallinaceous birds generally; a symbol of the hour 酉, from 5 to 7 o'clock P. M.
丨公 or 公丨 a cock, a rooster.
母丨 or 丨乸 a hen.
丨子 or 一隻丨 a fowl.
山丨 a pheasant. (*Phasianus.*)
犗丨 a capon.
雛丨 or 丨仔 chickens, pullets.
丨鳴 or 丨啼 cock-crowing; early dawn.
鬭丨 or 丨鬭 cock-fighting.
風丨 dead fowls preserved in winter with their feathers.
錦丨 the golden pheasant (*Thaumalea* [*Phasianus*] *pictus*); it is embroidered on civilian's robes of the second rank.
氷丨 or 田丨 the frog.
竹丨 a species of partridge. (*Bambusicola.*)

火 丨 Pallas' eared pheasant, the *Callipogon Pekinense;* also the Canton name of the turkey; and given too to the moor-hen (*Gallinula chloropus*).

沙 丨 the sand-grouse of Chihli (*Tetrao* [*Syrrhaptus*] *paradoxus*), a bird like the dotterel.

吐綬 丨 the medallion pheasant. (*Lophophorus Impeyanus.*)

金錢 丨 the peacock pheasant or *Phasianus torquatus.*

松 丨 a francolin pheasant in Chihli.

烏骨 丨 or 絲毛 丨 the silken cock with black bones.

畫 丨 Formosan silver pheasant (*Euplocomus* [*Phasianus*] *Swinhoii.*)

海 丨 母 the albatross (*Diomedia nigripes*), found near Formosa.

暴暴 丨 the goura or crowned pigeon (*Lophyrus*) of Amboyna or Papua, as the name tries to indicate.

蓑衣 丨 the Nicobar ground pigeon. (*Columba Nicobarica.*)

銀 丨 a boatswain's whistle.

樹 丨 mushrooms.

生 丨 眼 to have corns on the feet.

彰 丨 the whimbrel or curlew (*Numenius*), common in Chihli.

丨 冠花 the cockscomb flower or *Celosia.*

丨 冠油 a cook's name for the omentum of a sheep.

鉄 丨 公 a northern name for a skin-flint, a stingy fellow, from whom nothing is to be got.

牝 丨 司晨 the hen governs the hour; — *i. e.* the wife bears rule.

引魂 丨 the cock which leads the manes; — a white cock which is carried on a coffin to its distant tomb, under the belief that this bird alone can guide the ghost to its destination.

叫天 丨 只餘一張嘴 the meadow lark has nothing but its long bill, and no meat on its body; so is a talkative fool who can do nothing.

卟 ˓chi

From a *lot* and *mouth;* analogous to ˓*chen* 占 to divine.

To ask the spirits to decide doubts by some token; to divine by lots.

乩 ˓chi

From 乙 *primal* and 占 *to cast lots;* similar to the preceding.

To divine; to seek counsel or aid of spirits by a stylus; a willow twig or peach stick, used to write charms in the dust; there are several modes of placing it.

請 丨 to ask the spirits.

降 丨 the spirits have come to the table.

扶 丨 to write a charm on a table covered with dust or ashes by allowing the hand to move itself.

丨 仙 to consult the fairy, which is done on the 丨 壇 or divining altar; the one consulted is usually Lü Shun-yang 呂純陽 one of the eight genii.

剞 ˓chi

A crooked burin or chisel, called 丨 劂, used to gouge out the deeper parts of the block.

丨 劂氏 the guild or calling of block-cutters.

稽 ˓chi

From 禾 *grain* and 尤 *more,* combined with 旨 the *will.*

To examine into by comparing documents, facts, or circumstances; to hunt up, as a quotation; to study out; to investigate, to deliberate and arrange; to agree with; to detain, to embarrass; to reach to; to cultivate.

丨 遲 to hinder greatly; to defer.

丨 查 to search, as custom-house officers do; to investigate.

無 丨 之談 unfounded talk; idle assertions.

反脣相 丨 mutual bickerings and envies.

滑 丨 crafty, specious; one who can gloss or lie.

有 丨 時日 to procrastinate.

丨 留 to detain; to make one wait.

無 丨 之言勿聽 do not receive doctrines for which there is no proof.

Read ˊk'i. To bow down on the ground.

丨 首 or 丨 顙 to prostrate one's self, as in worship.

拜手 丨 首旅王若公 folding my hands and bowing my head, I present these before the King and your Grace.

枅 ˓chi

From *wood* and *level.*

A tie-beam connecting two posts or supporting the roof; it is a short piece of wood morticed on the post, and into the beam or ridge-pole to strengthen the truss; the ends usually project beyond the post.

笄 筓 ˓chi

From *bamboo* and *level;* often contracted to the second form.

A broad hair-pin laid across the back of the head, so as to bind on and support the coiffure; marriageable; a girl at the age of fifteen or sixteen; to do up the hair.

丨 禮 the ceremony of putting up the hair; the presents sent by relatives on the occasion.

年及 丨 she is now marriageable.

副 丨 六珈 a complete head-dress and ornament — for an empress.

十五而 丨 [girls] can be married at fifteen.

羈 ˓chi

Composed of 网 a *net* over 馬 to *tie* contracted, and 革 *hide* showing the material; used for the next.

A halter; to restrain, to pull the bit; to bridle or hold in; to detain in durance; to arrest; to economize; tufts of hair or floss on the heads of horses; a coiffure, a girl's tuft of hair.

丨 所 or 外 丨 a lockup attached to a yamun.

丨留 to stop, to seize, to take in custody; detained, as at an inn.

賤務丨身 I was detained by my business.

無所丨 unoccupied, leisurely.

丨縻 to restrain; to keep quiet, as a garrison does the frontier.

丨絆 to tie a horse; hampered, fettered, as by business.

男角女丨 [in ancient times,] the men's hair was done up like a horn, and women's like a halter.

羈 ˏchi An inn, a hospice, a caravansary, a tavern; to lodge.

丨旅 a wayfarer, a sojourner, one who is not a native.

丨客 a guest at an inn.

丨愁 the discommodities of travel.

畸 ˏchi From *field* and *odd;* used with its primitive.

Land left after marking out a square; poor land; odds and ends, an overplus.

左丨 a picket or advance guard of an army.

丨零 bits, refuse, fragments.

丨籍 a list of wandering people, such as the tanka people at Canton.

丨於人 one who depends on cultivating the corners for his living.

攲 椅 掎 ˏchi From to *tap* and *odd*, and *wood* or *hand* and to *send;* all the forms are rather unusual, but the last is commonest, and also read *kwéi;* it also means to carry on the head.

To take up anything with chopsticks or pincers; inclined, uneven, not upright, a sense confined to the first.

䩭丨 irregular and distorted.

丨得來吃 take up some of it and eat it.

姬 ˏchi From *woman* and the *neck.*

The name of Hwangti's family, derived from the 丨水 or River Ki where he lived; it was the surname of the emperors of the Cheu dynasty.

Read ˏi. A handsome girl or woman, a Hebe, a houri; a queen; an imperial concubine.

丨妾 a beautiful concubine.

彼美淑丨可與晤歌 that beautiful and chaste lady can respond to you in a song.

基 ˏchi From *earth* and *it* as the phonetic.

The foundation of a wall; a dyke or bank; a basis; a point-d'appui; a beginning, a starting-point, that on which a thing depends; fundamental; a patrimony, a possession; founding; to found, to establish; farming utensils; a waiting-place inside the door, an ante-room.

創丨 to lay the foundation, as of a family.

立丨 to fix the rules for, or basis of action.

開丨 or 肇丨 to commence an undertaking.

登丨 to ascend the throne, sometimes termed 丕丨 or the great patrimony.

丨址 foundation of a wall.

丨圍 a dyke, an embankment.

丨業 a family possession; inherited honors.

新丨 new land, as that gained from a river.

壽丨 a burial-place, which one prepares for himself.

丨地 a basis, material of; the quality of a thing. (*Cantonese.*)

厝丨 to prepare a little house over the coffin, in which it is raised from the ground, and filled in solid up to the roof.

朞 稘 ˏchi This character is to be distinguished from ˏk'i 期, and is used in mourning papers; the second and unusual form indicates its etymology, meaning the *return* of *harvest.*

A full year of twelve or thirteen moons; an anniversary.

丨之喪 a year of mourning.

丨服 one year's mourning.

丨月 a return of the same month.

我見其不逮再丨 I shall not see him again at the return of the year.

箕 ˏchi From *bamboo*, a *basket*, and a *stand* underneath; it is regarded as the original form of its primitive.

A corn-fan or winnowing basket; a sieve; a refuse-basket; to spread out like a fan; a tough wood used for quivers; the seventh zodiacal constellation of the stars γ and δ in Sagittarius; *met.* rain, because it forebodes rain; the striæ on the fingers' ends, which are fancied to resemble a corn-fan; an old name of Liao cheu 遼州 in the east of Shansi.

簸丨 a corn-fan; a winnower.

奉丨箒 I who have received the basket and broom; — *i. e.* the wife or concubine.

丨裘世業 to continue the family calling or profession.

驗明丨斗 look carefully at the lines on his fingers, — whether round or square, to guess his luck.

坐無丨 when seated don't spread out your legs like a fan.

丨伯 Eolus, the god of Wind.

丨子 the Viscount of Ki, who was made prince of the region east of Yen towards Corea by Wu Wang, after his conquest of the Shang dynasty.

成是南丨 [those twinkling points] may be made out to be the Sieve.

萁 ˏchi The stalks of pulse; the tendrils of vines.

丨草 a kind of aquatic grass, which is woven into quivers and other things.

丨蕨 a species of edible fern; perhaps a variety of *Pteris.*

錤 ˏchi An iron implement of husbandry, called 鎡丨, which resembles a large hoe, with a long blade.

己 ʻchi — This character is connected with the center of a thing, as it is considered to be altered from 中, and because it is the sixth of the ten stems, and with 戊 belongs to earth, and to central, and to the belly; it forms the 49th radical of a few incongruous characters, and is to be distinguished from *sz'* 巳 and *ʻi* 已 by its open mouth.

A personal pronoun, one's self; I, my myself; it is placed before the verb when it is the subject, and after when it is the complement; self, added to pronouns; selfish, private, personal; special; used for the next, to record.

我自丨 (or 丨ʻ名兒 in Peking) I myself; in Fuhkien, 家丨 is used in the same sense.

你我知丨 you and I know each other.

彼丨 or 人丨 he and I; that man or thing and I.

私丨 selfish; to appropriate to one's self.

守丨 self-respect; personal welfare.

安分守丨 to mind one's own special duties.

捨丨從人 to yield one's wishes for another's good, or to his judgment.

先人而後丨 to prefer others to one's self.

克丨後利 to deny or conquer self and return to rectitude.

人之有技若丨有之 if others have talents, they can serve him as if he had them himself.

不由丨 I am not the one to decide; I am not my own master.

紀 ʻchi, chi' — From *silk* and *self* as the phonetic.

To sort threads; to arrange, to separate; to narrate; to ascertain, to write down; to rule; to exhaust a subject; a history, annals, chronicle; a year; a period or score of twelve years, and a longer one of 1440 years, or twenty *ʻp'u* 蔀 of 72 years; a skein of forty threads; a decimal series of numbers; space between the peaks of mountains; name of a small feudal state, in the present I-shui hien 沂水縣 in the south of Shantung.

年丨 a person's age; as 尊丨 is to ask how old he is.

五丨 the five divisions of time, *viz.*, hours, days, months, years, and æons or ages.

丨錄 honorably recorded — by the Board of Civil Office.

丨功 recorded for merit.

丨事 to make a note of.

南國之丨 regulators of the southern states; — said of rivers which define their limits.

旣歷三丨 I have already been in this post three years.

增壽一丨 added twelve more years to his life.

丨事本末 to write a narrative from first to last.

經丨學問 to be well acquainted with trade and its affairs; also a broker's calling.

有丨有堂 there are adits and plateaux — among the hills.

丨綱法度 outlines and arguments, as of an essay.

几 ʻchi — The character represents a stand to lean on; it forms the 16th radical of a few characters relating to stands.

A bench or low table, which could be placed on a divan to lean on, or when sitting on the floor, as the Japanese do; a side-table.

茶丨 a tea-poy, a stand; a small table.

文丨 a study table; *met.* a student.

丨丨 tranquil and self-composed.

丨案 a large long table with the legs framed in.

匟丨 a low table on a divan.

安丨 quietness; composed.

隱丨而臥 he leaned on the table and slept.

或授之丨 for some of them stools are provided.

机 ʻchi — Used for the preceding, but more frequently as a contracted form of *ˏki* 機 a loom.

A tree likened to an elm; its ashes make a good manure.

麂 ⿸鹿旨 ʻchi — From *deer* and a *stand*, referring to its cry of *ki-ki*; the second form refers to its *ˏchi* 脂 or delicious fat.

A large species of deer found in Kwéicheu and westerly, having long tusks and fond of fighting; its feet are said to resemble the dog's; this animal is probably a kind of musk-deer, and under the name of 銀丨 or silver deer, perhaps describes the ***Moschus leucogaster***, or white bellied musk-deer; in Kiangnan, the name is applied to a small deer resembling a fallow-deer, with a white belly and large spots, the antlers having four prongs.

丨肉 a term for venison in **Fuhkien**.

庋 庪 ʻchi — From 广 a *shelter* and 技 *clever*, the contracted form being most used; it is also read *ˏkw'éi*, and then regarded as a synonym of ⿰礻支 to worship the five mountains.

A pantry; a cupboard or repository for keeping valuables; to put aside carefully; the second also means to bury things on mountains when worshiping the gods.

丨食物 lay away the eatables.

丨閣 a press or safe for storing precious things; a depository for records, applied to the imperial books and writings.

蟣 ʻchi — A nit, a louse; a small insect, such as an *Aphis* or *Ptinus*; the Budhists use it for *liksha*, an infinitesmal distance, the hundred-millionth part of a *yodjana*.

丨蝨 lice, nits.

Read *ˏk'i*. A synonym of 蜞 a leech.

觭 ʻchi — To treat well, and wait for, as two friends at a meeting.

計 chi' — From *words* and *ten*, explained as showing that ten persons make a complete number or party, and gives opportunity for full deliberation.

To plan, to consider and devise; to reckon, to calculate, to compute; in formal documents means to inclose, to append or annex, referring to accompanying schedules; a scheme, a stratagem, a plot; an assembly whereat merit can be discussed; a comrade, one who is joined in the same plans.

丨數 to count the number.
心丨 to reckon mentally.
丨上心來 to think about a plan, to conceive a scheme.
共丨一百兩正 it all amounts to just a hundred taels.
生丨 to get a living.
多丨 fertile in expedients, shrewd and rather unscrupulous.
丨賬 or 丨簿 a book of estimates or accounts; a balance-book; an account opens with 丨開 the reckoning begins thus:—
丨謀 to scheme, to contrive.
家丨 means of livelihood, domestic outlay.
丨策 a plan, a stratagem, as in military movements.
丨到遠 to forecast contingencies.
有何丨較 what plan have you to propose to meet this?
丨辦不出 it cannot be effected; you can't raise the loan.
中'丨 to fall into a snare.
妙丨不遂 the fine or cute scheme did not succeed.
暗丨 a dark plot, an underhand practice.
丨口而耕 he cultivated as much land as he had mouths to provide for.
百丨的營謀 a hundred ways to get a living; many schemes to press a business.
詭丨多端 he is full of underhand schemes.
除巳往之不丨 let the past go, let bygones be bygones.
丨相 an ancient officer like a lord of the treasury.
塡大丨 noted at the great reckoning, which is made triennially of the standing of all officials.

薊 chi' — From *plants* and *to cut open*.

A general name for thistles, as the *Cnicus*, *Carduus*, and other large kinds.

馬丨 a high great thistle.
丨州 a small department in the northeast of Chihli, the ancient capital of the state of Yen.

繼 chi' — From *silk* and *continuous*.

To connect, as with threads; a line of succession in kindred; to continue on, as one taking the duties or place of another; to adopt an heir; to follow after; succeeding to, successively; hereditary.

丨母 a step-mother or adopted mother, one who is 丨室 brought afterwards into the house.
丨襲 hereditary rank.
承丨子 to adopt a son.
丨志 to carry out a father's plans.
過丨 to pass over a son to a brother or clansman.
糧食不丨 inadequate supplies.
丨續 to continue; following on.
相丨而來 they came one after the other.
始而丨而 from the first and ever after; at the beginning and so on.
丨善會 a benevolent association.

檵 chi' — A tree or shrub found in Kiangsi, which produces white flowers like the honey-suckle in form and growth; the leaf is ovate and hispid, and when chewed serves as a styptic.

㥛 chi' — Violent, crafty, overbearing.

丨忮 proud, like a truculent, villainous officer.

髻 䰏 chi' — From *hair* and *lucky*; the second and unauthorized form is common at the south.

The tuft or coiffure of a Chinese woman's hair; it has many names and fashions among females of different places and ranks in the country; that at Tientsin, for instance, is called 美人丨 the beauty's head-dress; but it is often named from the town.

梳丨 to do up the hair.
丫角丨 a term for children under five years old, when their hair is trimmed like two horns.
山如螺丨 these hills look like a spiral head of hair.
竹笋丨 the bamboo-sprout tuft; — a nickname in Canton for a procuress.
丨押 or 丨壓 a back hair-pin.
光丨 the first time of shaving a boy's head, when a month old.
肉丨 the fleshy tuft, — a protuberance on the cranium (*ushnisha*), a distinguishing mark of a Budha.

冀 chi' — From 北 *north* and 異 *another*.

To hope, to desire; eager for, desirous; to expect; one of the nine divisions of Yü in ancient China, comprising the present Shansi and the part of Chihli north of the River Wéi, reaching east to the River Yaloh near Niuchwang; the capital of Yao and Shun was in it, at or near Ta-yuen fu the present capital of Shansi.

丨州 a town and inferior department in the southeast of Chihli.
丨望 or 希丨 to wish for.
丨幸 to wish one good luck, to hope that he will succeed.

驥 chi' — From *horse* and *to hope*.

A steed of noble blood, great speed and good points, perfect in all respects.

赤丨 the bay Bucephalus, one of Muh-wang's eight famous steeds.

白 丨 the white steed, a name for the carp in Shantung.

蠅 附 丨 尾 to follow like a fly at a steed's tail; *i. e.* to tag to a great man's train to get on; to beg to accompany one.

丨 不 稱 力 a fine steed is not reckoned by his strength alone.

洎 *chí'* From *water* and *self;* it resembles *léi'* 泪 tears.

The broth of boiled meats; thick soup of meats; fertile; to reach to; name of a river.

寄 *chí'* From a *covering* and *odd.*

To lodge, to remain awhile in a house; to confide to, to hand over or to deliver in charge; to put under another heading or list, to transfer; a responsibility; a message; the east.

丨 居 to visit, to lodge at; a name for the hermit crab.

丨 信 to send a letter.

丨 來 to receive from.

丨 生 an epiphyte, a parasitic growth.

丨 賣 to send for sale, to put on commission.

丨 語 or 丨 口 信 to send a verbal message.

丨 寓 a rented or temporary residence.

丨 情 to convey one's feelings, as by a metaphor or present.

丨 客 a visitor, a sojourner.

丨 附 to confide a thing to another.

重 丨 a great charge, as an office.

丨 託 to lay on one, as a duty or obligation.

丨 放 to leave with another.

我 身 如 丨 I am like a wanderer.

丨 箱 to send on [paper] trunks —to the dead, by burning them.

彐 *chí'* Supposed to represent a hog's snout turned upward as he snuffs or looks; it is the 58th radical of a few characters, mostly relating to swine.

A hog turning up his snout.

垍 *chí'* Hard soil, or the clay which is used in making pottery.

覬 *chí'* From to *see* and *how.*

To covet; to long for inordinately; lucky.

丨 覦 to wish for ardently.

丨 幸 to hope for a stroke of luck.

旡 *chí'* Composed of 反 to *revert* and 气 *breath,* thus altered and contracted in combination; it is not the same as *wu* 无 not.

A rising in the stomach, resulting from indigestion; a hiccup; eructation, belching.

既 *chí'* From 旡 *indigestion* and 食 to *eat* contracted; as a primitive, it imparts an idea of completeness to many of its compounds.

To finish a meal; to exhaust, to finish; to lose; an *adverb* of time, when, since, already; a sign of the past tense, and nearly synonymous with *i'* 已, but is placed before the verb; all, entirely.

丨 見 I saw it; seen.

丨 往 passed away; gone, ended.

丨 是 這 樣 or 丨 然 如 此 being so, since it is so, whereas.

丨 月 the end of the month.

丨 雨 丨 處 seeing that the rain then had past.

予 丨 烹 而 食 之 I had cooked and eaten it.

文 王 丨 勤 止 Wăn Wang has labored earnestly.

國 丨 卒 斬 the state is even now approaching destruction.

亦 丨 見 止 亦 丨 覯 止 let me have seen him and have met him.

日 有 蝕 之 丨 a total eclipse of the sun.

沾 恩 無 丨 I shall be infinitely obliged to you.

穊 *chí'* To plough deep for sowing; plants set out close; rice or grain thickset; ancient name of a place near Nanking.

暨 *chí'* From 旦 *morning* and 既 *already.*

The sun peeping out; the end of; to reach; an extreme degree of; to give; as a *conjunction,* and, also, further; together with, and often followed by 咸 all; exactly; just.

丨 今 up to this time, just now.

丨 候 to send respects to one.

汝 不 盡 丨 the whole (or rest) cannot be told; — this phrase and the last occur in letters.

丨 丨 strenuously; daring.

靡 丨 without end.

如 羲 丨 和 do you Hi and Hwo.

丨 及 together with, and.

尙 胥 丨 顧 do you consult one with another.

丨 鳥 獸 魚 鼈 咸 若 birds, beasts, fishes and turtles, all and each where so happy.

墍 *chí'* From *earth* and *already* as the phonetic.

To plaster and color a wall; to stop cracks in a wall; to gather, to collect; a rest, a breathing spell; displeased.

一 丨 之 安 a short resting time.

頃 筐 丨 之 in this shallow basket gather them.

不 念 昔 者 伊 余 來 丨 you forget the olden times, and are now angry with me.

塗 丨 to plaster, as a wall; to fill in the holes with mud.

民 之 攸 丨 the people found their rest — in him.

蔇 *chí'* Grass growing thickly; to reach, to arrive at; name of an ancient place in Shantung, where a compact was made.

猶 懼 不 丨 it is to be feared that he will not come at all.

季 *chí'* Composed of 子 *child* and 稚 a *young* thing contracted.

Tender, little, the young and immature; the least or last of a series; the youngest of brothers; inferiors, subordinate; a season or quarter of the year; the end of a time or close of a period; in the southern provinces it is used for a crop, or half of the year, when speaking of rents.

四 丨 the four seasons.

下 丨 or 晚 丨 the second crop; the last half of the year.

丨 春月 the third moon of spring.

孟仲 丨 a series of three, applied to the three months of a season, three brothers, three qualities of goods, &c.

丨 世 the last generation; a waning age or dynasty.

丨 指 the little finger.

幾昆 丨 how many brothers are there of you?

丨 細 small, junior.

丨 父 an elder-born uncle.

丨 女斯飢 this young lady is suffering from hunger.

母曰嗟予 丨 行役 my mother says, Alas! my child is now away on public duty.

一 丨 子的東西 a thing used during only a part of the year, as a fur pelisse or a straw hat.

悸 *chi'* From *heart* and *young*.

Uneasy, perturbed; a sudden start; shaking, like the loose ends of the girdle.

驚 丨 a great fright.

垂帶 丨 兮 his girdle ends hanging so jauntily!

痵 *chi'* Like the preceding.

Frightened, nervous, uneasy; starting, as in sleep.

鯚 *chi'* Regarded by some as the same fish as the *kw'ei'* 鱖.

A delicate fish, common in the Yangtsz' R., about a foot long, with a pointed nose and small scales, beautifully marbled like the garoupa; it is called 丨 婆婆 at Nanking, and 花 丨 魚 at Shanghai; it resembles a perch, and is probably allied to a *Sciæna*.

安 丨 a small kind of silure about a foot long with formidable jagged dorsal and pectoral spines, with which it is believed to make a noise; the back is dark marbled, and the belly yellow.

罽 *chi'* From *net* and a slight *wound*; occurs used for the next.

A kind of fishing-net or seine made of hair.

氂 丨 a small felt rug made of hair, probably from the yak.

䍁 *chi'* Similar to the last.

A coarse carpet or felt rug made of camel's hair; it is like shag, and comes from the Si Hu 西胡 or Western Tartars, probably the Turfan tribes.

記 *chi'* From *words* and *self*; it is also used with 紀 a record.

To remember, to recollect; to record, to register, to note down; a record, a history, a memorial of; a style or name; a mark, sign, or signal, which is to be borne in mind, and thus becomes a classifier of strokes laid on a culprit; it is used after names or signs, intimating that they are to be remembered; the Budhists employ it in the sense of prophecy, or an account of the future fate of saints.

有 丨 性 a remembrance of.

好 丨 性 a good memory.

你 丨 得不 丨 得呢 do you remember it?

忘 丨 forgetful; to forget.

丨 牢住 don't forget it. (*Shanghai*.)

丨 號 a mark, a sign; the name or style of a shop.

登 丨 簿 make a note or memorandum of it.

打印 丨 to stamp a mark on; but 打了三十 丨 means he got thirty blows.

丨 載 placed on the record.

丨 賬 charge it in account.

丨 憶 to remember fondly.

丨 念 to keep in mind; to recall to mind.

丨 不清楚 I do not distinctly remember it.

丨 謹 remember it carefully; keep it in mind.

强 丨 to rack one's memory, as in trying to recall a thing.

丨 室 a record office.

史 丨 annals of a state, archives of a government.

一時 丨 不起 I cannot recall it at this time.

忌 *chi'* From *heart* and *self*.

To fear, to shun, to avoid; to be cautious of, to keep at a distance; to dislike; jealous, for which the next is used; a superstitious dread of; to keep aloof from; to dislike trouble, to shirk; distasteful; antipathy, a dislike or shrinking from; a final particle.

丨 日 or 丨 辰 the dreaded day when a friend died or an emperor; the days when each of the Manchu emperors and their empresses died, in all 29 days, are still observed at court.

燒 丨 or 拜 丨 to keep the anniversary of a death.

叔馬慢 丨 叔發罕 丨 Shuh's horses are slow, and he shoots seldom.

畏 丨 or 敬 丨 respectfully avoid the use of, — as the emperor's personal name.

百無禁 丨 nobody forbids you; just as you please.

丨 其才能 to dread another's ability.

丨 避 to evade, to keep shy of.

多 丨 諱 he has many dislikes, he is very unlucky or crotchety.

戒 丨 to avoid doing what will mar joy or impede luck.

丨 恨 to hate with a 丨 心 or loathing feeling.

肆無 丨 憚 he has no respect for anybody; reckless and irreverent.

娸 chi' From *woman* and to *avoid*; used with the last.

To envy; angry with; the rage of a woman, because of the conduct of her husband.

丨 妬 jealousy; envious of.

跽 chi' To kneel a long time, to bow on all fours, a more reverential act than *kwéi'* 跪; to feel dread; awe-struck, trembling in the knees, discomposed.

敬 丨 a respectful dread of.

擎 丨 拳 曲 人 臣 之 禮 to kneel and brace the arms on the floor is the obeisance of ministers.

伎 chi' From *man* and a *branch*; it is similar to *'k'i* 技 clover.

Talent, ability; cleverness.

丨 巧 ingenious, skilled, as a mechanic.

丨 倆 astute, cunning.

無 他 丨 能 he has no other capacity, he is fitt for nothing else.

鹿 斯 之 奔 維 足 丨 丨 the buck is fleeing, but his steps are steady and quick, — as if waiting for his fellows.

Read *ˏk'i*. Agile; also an extra finger or toe.

芰 chi' A variety of the water-caltrops (*Trapa incisa*), having three or four prongs on the fruit; it is not so much cultivated as the *ˏling* 菱 or common sort, but the two characters are applied to both plants.

丨 荷 caltrops and lotuses.

妓 chi' From *woman* and a *branch*.

A courtesan, a singing girl, one who earns her living by singing and vice; Han Wu-ti is said to have begun the practice by getting women into his camps to beguile the soldiers while away from their families.

丨 館 a brothel, a bagnio.

丨 女 a prostitute; also another name for the day-lily.

目 中 有 丨 心 中 無 丨 the whores were indeed in my sight but not in my heart; said by a virtuous sage.

惎 chi' Injurious, fatal, poisonous; to teach, to instruct; to institute.

瘈 chi' From *disease* and *contracted*; it is also read *ch'i'*.

Wild, incoherent; agitated, nervous; mad, as a dog.

丨 狗 a rabid dog, or one which has fits.

丨 瘲 convulsions; fits of young children.

K'I.

Old sounds, k'i, gi, k'úi, gúi, géi, k'it, git, *and* kúit. *In Canton*, k'i, k'ei, *and* hi; — *in Swatow*, k'i, ki, k'a, hi, *and* k'oi; — *in Amoy*, k'i, ki, k'é, *and* kia; — *in Fuhchau*, k'i, ki, k'a, k'ié, *and* k'é; — *in Shanghai*, ch'i *and* dji; — *in Chifu*, k'i.

溪 ˏch'i From *water* and *why* as the phonetic.

A rivulet running into a river, the headwaters of a stream; a mountain streamlet; it is much used in Fuhkien and Chehkiang; a creek, a side runlet; *met.* what has been handed down.

清 丨 a clear brook.

釣 丨 to fish in rivulets.

尤 丨 縣 a district in Yenping fu in the north of Fuhkien.

丨 鬼 虫 a large beetle found in rivulets; it resembles the stag-beetle, and is probably a *Dytiscus*.

善 丨 無 擾 the clear stream [of truth] will not be roiled.

屯 丨 the stream in Tai-ping hien in the east of Nganhwui, where Twankay tea grows.

丨 船 boats made to run on shallow rivulets.

丨 水 freshet waters, the rising of the hill-streams.

谿 嵠 ˏch'i Interchanged with the last.

A valley with a stream in it; a gorge and the rivulet that runs through it.

深 丨 a deep cañon or gulf.

丨 子 國 an ancient region in Yunnan.

山 丨 之 險 the risks of traveling among mountain passes.

鸂 ˏch'i From *bird* and *rivulet*; *i.e.* the bird which frequents streams.

A bird with variegated plumage, found in marshes, whose high tail is likened to a rudder; it is called 丨 鶒 鳥 because it goes in regular file, and 溪 中 之 鶒 order in the stream; other names are, the red mandarin duck 紫 鴛 鴦, the 丨 鶒 and 谿 鶒; it is common in eastern China, and its description assimilates it closely to the pied duck; it is embroidered on the official robes of ladies of the 7th rank; this bird has sometimes been referred to the leaf-walker or jacana, but probably not correctly.

欺 ꜀ch'i From to *owe* and *this*.

To cheat, to impose upon; to deceive one's self or others intentionally; to insult, to upbraid, to abuse, when in power; to ridicule, to befool; to fail in one's duty, to disappoint another; deceived; hardened from self-deception.

丨負 to oppress, to insult.

丨淩 to rail at, to blackguard.

丨侮 to ridicule, to mock.

毋自丨 allow no self-deception.

丨弄 to make fun of, to jeer.

丨笑 to laugh at, to banter.

丨人 an impudent rascal.

丨人太過 to cheat others without the least scruple.

丨君 to deceive a ruler, to fail in duty to him.

丨住 to overpower, as the sun does a taper.

丨心 to harden one's heart.

丨壓 to grind the weak; to overpower and put down, as the poor.

攲 ꜀ch'i From *branch* and *odd*; not the same as ꜀ki 攲 to nip up.

Not standing even on its base, tipped up, inclined.

丨器易覆 leaning vessels easily upset.

徛 ꜀ch'i A stone bridge; stones laid to step across the water; to step out and stride, as when crossing water; to stand up.

崎 ꜀ch'i From *hill* and *odd* as the phonetic.

A steep rough path along and over mountains; precipitous, abrupt, sheer; a cape, a projecting headland.

丨嶇 a dangerous hill-path; a rise and fall; knolls and holes, such as are left after an inundation; irregular, as a stony road; *met.* disquieted and anxious.

In *Fuhchau*. Steep, inclined, sloping.

踦 ꜀ch'i From *foot* and *odd* as the phonetic.

Having only one good leg; crippled, halt; an incomplete thing, a defect; single, alone, as the thread on which a spider lets itself down; the shin-bone.

丨跜 lame, halting.

丨閭 a gate ajar, and a person within talking with one outside.

蟜 ꜀ch'i An insect, 長丨 the long legged spider which runs over the house, a *Myrmecia*? a kind of cicada.

丨蛭 a variety of the leech.

觭 ꜀ch'i From *horn* and *odd*; it occurs used with its primitive.

One horn, as of an ox, elevated, and the other depressed; single, without a match; to obtain.

丨角 an inner or reëntering corner.

丨夢 a dream which comes to pass.

丨偶 single and paired; unequal and equal.

丨輪無反者 not a single car returned; — an utter defeat.

㩻 ꜀ch'i A stiff bow, too stiff to bend easily.

丨弓勁矢 a stiff bow and springy arrow.

竒 ꜀ch'i Uneven, like the leaves of the bamboo, which the character is intended to represent.

榿 ꜀ch'i From 木 *tree* and 愷 *pleased* contracted.

A tree whose habitat is near the streams, and flourishes in damp grounds; it grows up in three years, and people find it a useful tree around their villages; it may be a species of the willow.

僛 ꜀ch'i From *man* and *to cheat*.

To act as when tipsy and boisterous; to walk unsteadily, to reel like a sot.

屢舞丨丨 reeling and gambolling without stopping.

魌 ꜀ch'i A demon of an ugly shape, the 丨頭, which has two heads and four eyes; in olden time it was personated by men to drive off pestilence.

其 ꜀ch'i This is considered to be a contraction of ꜀ki 箕 a *fan*, its original form.

A relative and personal pronoun referring to the person, place or thing spoken of; he, she, it; his they, their's; the, that, the one, the thing; wherever, whoever; an *adverb* of place, there, the spot; a final or auxiliary expletive; it is sometimes put between a noun and a verb to emphasize the former, as 天丨運乎 the heavens, do they revolve? also a sign of the vocative and imperative, as 王丨毋忘 O Prince! never forget; as a *conjunction*, if, premising; then, therefore; stands for ꜀chi 之 as a relative or sign of the genitive, — a use common in Fuhchau and northerly towards Ningpo; it sometimes has a future sense, as 予丨太賚汝 I will thus greatly reward you; — or a hortatory sense, as 帝曰我丨試哉 the emperor said, I will then try him; let me try him.

丨人丨言均不足信 this man and these words are alike unworthy of credence.

丨餘 the rest, what is over; furthermore.

是丨否 is it he? 是丨也 it is.

是丨個否 is this thing his? 是丨個也 yes, it is.

丨次 the next.

丨如 as if.

丨然 if it be so; supposing that to be the case.

丨中 in the center; the center; therein; among them.

灼灼丨華 how exuberant are these flowers!

只知丨一不知丨二 I only know one of them, but not the other.

夜如何丨 how is it by night?
未丨有若汝封之心 nobody has a heart at all like your's, Fung!
君丨待之 Prince! wait for that.
我丨敢求位 I! how dare I demand the throne?

幱 *ch'i* A napkin; a bandage.

棋 碁 綦 *ch'i* From *wood* or *stone*, and *this* as the phonetic; occurs used for *ki* 基 a base.

The game of chess, called 象丨, played with thirty-two men, of which Wu Wang is said to have been the inventor, B. C. 1120; anotherg ame, called 圍丨, played with 360 black and white pieces, to represent a year of day and nights, on a board of 361 squares, is ascribed to Yao; fox-and-geese, checkers or draughts, and other similar foreign games; checker-wise, in squares, starred.
一着丨 a move in the game.
丨盤 or 丨枰 a chess-board.
一套丨子 a set of chess-men.
着丨, or 奕丨, or 捉丨, or 下丨, to play chess.
世事紛紛一局丨 the affairs of life are as changing as a game of chess, — bringing mankind into many relations.
敲丨 to take a man.
一盤丨 or 一局丨 a game of chess or draughts.
丨子塊 triangular pieces, as of wood, meat, &c.
打丨局 to try to solve a chess problem.
一步丨 a move on a board.
根丨 a good foundation.
丨布 very thick together, as villages; a kind of wafer cakes.
丨布星羅 the squads are scattered over the plain.
丨譜 a book of chess problems.

淇 *ch'i* A tributary of the River Wéi 衛河 in the north-east of Honan; near their junction lies the old town of K'i hien 丨縣 in the department of Wéi-hwui fu; name of an affluent of the River Han in Siang-yang fu in Hupeh.
丨墺 the island of Kee-ow off Kumsing-moon, north of Macao.
瞻彼丨奥 look at those little coves along the K'i.

綦 *ch'i* From *silk* and *this*; occurs interchanged with its primitive.

A dark gray color, the natural hue of some silks, worn only by women; variegated; shoe latchets or ties; strict; an *adverb* of comparison, very, the highest, the utmost of.
丨嚴 very strict.
丨大而王，丨小而亡 so the great reigned and the small died, — in the contest.

藄 *ch'i* A variety of edible fern, the 蕨丨 or 紫丨 which grows in Kiangsi; the drawing resembles that of an *Osmunda*, where the seeds are arranged in a spike.

祺 *ch'i* Fortunate, lucky; felicitous, composed, tranquil.
近丨不一 may your prosperity soon be more than usual.
安丨 happy contentment.
陞丨 increasing prosperity and peace; may you soon be promoted.
壽考維丨 may your old age be very happy.

琪 *ch'i* Used with the next.

A valuable stone of a white color.
丨玗 an inferior gem; it is also applied to a kind of coralline tree in fairy land.
瑤草丨花 perennial grass and unfading flowers—in fairy land.

璂 *ch'i* Gems set in the leathern caps or coronets of rulers and nobles as ornaments, so as to resemble stars by their luster and color.
弁丨 cap gems; they were probably made of jade.
星丨 star-like ornaments.

蜞 *ch'i* Often used for the next, and both seem to be correct; this is the commonest.

A small land crab, the 蟚丨 found in rice fields.
水丨 a white slimy grub dug out of the ooze for food; it is perhaps the larva of a *Dytiscus*.
馬丨 or 牛丨 the blood-sucker.
雷丨 a worm like the gally-worm (*Julus*), or perhaps a *Nereis*.
流丨 an edible worm of a greenish color found in fresh water.

蚑 *ch'i* Considered to be another and unusual form the last.

To crawl along is 丨丨, spoken of rows of insects, ants or caterpillars.
長丨 or 長蛴 the long legged spider common in houses.
如丨行喘息 they stop to take breath, like a row of traveling insects; said of women.

騏 *ch'i* A dappled horse, marked like a chess-board; a fine looking horse, of a deep black color; spotted like the skin of the axis.
我馬維丨 my horses are piebald.
其弁伊丨 his cap is of that spotted skin.
乘其四丨 in his chariot drawn by four dappled horses.

萁 *ch'i* The stalks of beans; the stems of pulse; camels are fed on them.

踑 *ch'i* The tracks of a horse; a footstep; to cross the legs.
丨踞 to sit cross-legged.

期 ꜀ch'i From *moon* and *this*; it is not exactly the same as ꜀*ki* 朞 a year

A set time, a fixed period, a day agreed on; then, at that time; times, seasons; to meet; to expect, to wait for; hoping that; to engage to do; to aim at; a hundred years old; reached his time, full of years; used for 其 as a final particle.

日〡 the set day.

滿〡 the time is up, the set period has come.

到〡 or 屆〡 the day has come.

上〡 in advance of the date.

過〡 beyond the time.

無定〡 uncertain, no fixed time.

不〡而會 an unexpected interview, to meet without previous arrangement.

實維何〡 really, who are those people?

〡許 highly probable; I may venture to promise.

總〡 during the whole period, till the completion.

約〡 to make an engagement.

於〡 at the time.

限〡 to limit the time.

其〡必往 I think he will go.

〡當 to aim at what is suitable.

昌〡 flourishing times.

帝鄉不可〡 I dare not look up to the Court.

刑〡于無刑 to punish in order that there may be no [need of] punishments.

即〡票 a promissory note, payable at sight.

近〡銀子 a note of hand, payable in two or three days.

粸 ꜀ch'i A thin and sweet kind of cake.

鵙 ꜀ch'i A kind of small wild goose; or more probably a bird like a sheldrake; the name is also applied, strange to say, to the horned owl.

旗 旂 ꜀ch'i From *banner* and *this* as the phonetic; the second form is a common contraction, and is also defined as a pennon with bells or jingles hung to it.

A flag, a standard; a banner with devices or tiles on it, a tribe or corps under one banner.

八〡 the Eight Banners, under which the Manchus are marshaled; they are distinguished by four plain banners, 正〡, the yellow, red, white, and blue; and by the 鑲〡 or bordered banners, which are the same colors with a margin of another color.

〡下 or 〡人 Bannermen, either Manchus, Mongols, or registered Chinese.

〡號 a signal-flag, a marker, a telegraphing flag.

銷除〡檔 to cashier a man from his flag — for misconduct.

〡杆 a flagstaff; the 〡杆斗 is the frame near the top.

〡幟 a flag bearing an inscription.

各率〡〡 each of them led his company or division.

掛〡 or 升〡 hoist the flag.

下〡 furl the colors; lower the flag.

清道〡 a banner carried to clear the way in processions.

花〡國 a common name for the United States along the coast, derived from the spangled appearance of the flag.

打着人家的〡號 to fight under a man's flag; to take another's banners, to fight under false colors.

麒 ꜀ch'i A fabulous, auspicious animal, which appears when sages are born; the male of the Chinese unicorn; it is drawn like a piebald, scaly horse, with one horn and a cow's tail, and may have had a living original in some extinct equine animal.

〡麟過山龍滾水 the unicorn passes over the hills [scattering fire], and the dragon churns the water, — to put it out

娸 ꜀ch'i Ugly, ill-looking; to criticise sarcastically; to chaff one.

詆〡其文 he ridiculed the composition or expression.

竒 奇 ꜀ch'i From *great* and *able*; the second form is common, but somewhat pedantic.

Extraordinary, rare; surprising, monstrous, remarkable, out of the common way, unnatural; new, strange, unexpected.

〡怪 wonderful, startling.

出〡 unusual; it excites surprise.

〡才 remarkably clever.

〡逢 an unusual good chance.

〡横 perverse, crotchety, mulish.

三〡 or three essentials, are the 精 semen, 氣 vital energy, and the 神 animal spirits.

〡特 unequaled, unique.

〡緣 a pleasant meeting; unusual fortune.

〡功 distinguished merit.

〡像 a strange or unpromising countenance.

〡書 rare books, or fine editions.

〡兵 a reserve; liers in wait.

〡異 extraordinary, as a lusus naturæ; amazing, bizarre.

〡男子 a smart lad, a clever boy.

〡門 rare skill or art, as of a geomancer.

Read ꜀*ki*. Odd, a single one; a surplus, a remainder.

三十有〡 there are over thirty of them.

〡數 or 零〡 odd numbers.

〡幾毫 an odd, few tenths.

〡日 the odd days in a month.

琦 ꜀ch'i From *gem* and *remarkable* as the phonetic.

A valuable stone; a curiosity, a rarity, a plaything; large.

〡瑋 valuable, as a stone.

〡賂 or 〡貨 a valuable or unusual article.

玩〡 a toy, an article of vertu.

騎 ꜀ch'i To stride a horse; to ride on; to sit astride; cavalry, horsemen; a rider; an animal to ride.

丨馬 to ride a horse.

飛丨 light-horse; horsemen for scouting, or a body-guard.

丨軍 or 丨兵 cavalry; horsemen; lancers.

丨射 mounted archers.

善丨 a good horseman.

丨虎難下之勢 he who rides a tiger has need of great skill to dismount.

一丨上長安 with this beast I shall get to Chang-ngan (*i. e.* Peking, or the metropolis), referring to the capital in the T'ang dynasty.

岐 ꜀ch'i From *hill* and *branch*; interchanged with the next.

The state or appanage where the ancestors of the Cheu dynasty lived, in the present Fung-tsiang fu 鳳翔府 in the southwest of Shensi, not far from the River Wei, and so called after 丨山 or 天柱 Heaven's Pillar in K'i-shan hien 丨山縣; an independent state existed here B. C. 904-924; a hill with two peaks; a fork in a road; a headland; high, as a peak; to diverge; ambiguous, double dealing.

兩丨 two modes of action, two views of; whence 兩丨語 a double entendre.

克丨克嶷 the hill is both prominent and rich in foliage.

通丨黃 he is a good physician; *i. e.* he understands the 丨黃篇 a vade-mecum of repute.

歧 ꜀ch'i From to *stop* and *branch*; similar to the last.

Forked, bicuspidate; a spike with two heads, as wheat sometimes has; diverging; schismatic, different; unlike; a discrepancy.

丨丨 rapid running, of a man.

丨路 a fork in a road; a diverging path; erroneous conduct.

心無他丨 the mind fixed on one object.

原無丨 there should be no divergence, — as of opinion.

這話兩丨了 those differing views are both exaggerated; that expression has two meanings.

爲他丨所惑 I have been deceived by his vacillation.

跂 ꜀ch'i From *foot* and *branch*.

A foot with six toes; the crawling of insects, the progress of an animal.

Read ˋk'i and used for 企. To stand on tiptoe; to sit with the legs hanging down.

丨踵而望 I stand on tiptoe waiting for you.

丨行 to crawl; to walk.

丨而及之 to follow and overtake.

忯 ꜀ch'i Also read ˋti and ꜀shi.

To respect; to esteem.

丨丨 to love one; to meet one in a cordial, friendly manner.

祇 ꜀ch'i From *worship* and *name*; it was originally the same as ꜀chi 祗, but is now written without the dot.

Rest, repose; great; the god or spirit which animates the earth.

地丨 Terra, the earth as a divinity; the productive energy, in which it is used like Cybele or Hecate among the Greeks.

壹者之來俾我丨也 if you would come here once, it would make me at rest.

無丨悔 no great regret.

天曰神地曰丨 heaven is God, earth is Goddess.

神丨 a term for the gods of the land.

丨樹園 or 丨桓 a monastery; any place where Budha stopped; the term is derived from *Jeta-vana*, his residence at Sewet.

祁 ꜀ch'i From to *worship* and *city*, referring to the old city of ꜀K'i hien 丨縣 in the south of Shansi.

Full, abundant; very; large; numerous; at ease; leisurely, gracefully; in the language of epitaphs, constant; multitudes.

諸姊從之丨丨如雲 the crowd of virgins followed her like a [beautiful] cloud.

采蘩丨丨 the crowds collect the celery.

丨州 a district south of Pao-ting fu in Chihli.

冬丨寒 the coldest time in winter.

興雨丨丨 the rain falls very gently.

蝌 ꜀ch'i The name 蛜丨 is an old term for the scorpion; also called 主簿虫 the clerk's bug, from an old story about its having been brought to Kiang-nan from the north by an enthusiastic man.

祈 ꜀ch'i From *worship* and *hatchet*, but some regard the primitive as a contraction of the next.

To offer a sacrifice and supplicate the gods for happiness; to state one's case to a god; to pray, to invoke aid; to recompense; in polite language, to request, to beg, to trouble, to intreat; multitudes.

丨雨 to pray for rain.

來假丨丨 they come in crowds.

以丨爾爵 I pray you drink that cup.

丨望 I beg [the gods, and] hope — for your happiness.

千丨 I urgently beg of you.

丨求 to beseech.

丨天永命 to ask for eternal life.

丨文 a printed form of prayer; the suppliant writes his name, date, and object of desire, &c., and kneeling burns the form before the shrine.

丨禱天主 to pray to the Lord of Heaven.

蘄 ˏch'i To seek for, to beg, to try; a bridle.

丨至其人 to endeavor to come up to another, to try to equal him.

丨州 a district in the north-east of Hupeh on the Yangtsz' River, below Hankow; it produces a yellow venomous snake, called the 丨蛇, which has short horns.

丨艾 a species of *Artemisia* found in K'i cheu, from which the Chinese moxa, used in cautery, is obtained; it is also applied to cure ulcers, and used as a tonic.

丨棍 a low succulent weed in Kiangsi, whose thick, fleshy leaves are covered with white hairs like flour, which the people apply to boils.

蚚 ˏch'i A fierce fly which is constantly rubbing its head; perhaps a *Tabanus*, though one name given is applied to the rice-weevil.

丨父 a species of mantis.

蝬丨 a green grasshopper or *Truxalis*.

頎 ˏch'i From *head* and *hatchet*.

Tall; personable, elegant; erect.

丨長 tall, as a tall man.

丨丨然 how tall and graceful!

Read *kăn'*. Extreme; to feel kind to another; hard; a few of; small.

丨典 enduring; hardened and set to bear suffering.

圻 ˏch'i From *earth* and *hatchet;* it was regarded as another form of ˏyin 垠 a *dyke*, and is now interchanged with ˏki 畿 a *domain*.

A border, a limit; confines; the frontier; imperial lands.

無丨 illimitable, boundless.

丨父 a term in the Cheu dynasty for a master of the household troops, the minister of war.

芪 ˏch'i This character seems to be confounded with ˏchi 栀 and ˏshi 蓍 in some names.

A medicinal plant, a kind of lungwort, of which three or four sorts are spoken of.

黃丨 a yellowish root, with a thick rind and pith inside, used in asthma, supposed to be derived from the *Ptarmica Sibirica;* the flexible roots of the *Sophora tomentosa* are referred to under the same name; they resemble liquorice.

鬐 ˏch'i From *hair* and *old man*.

A horse's foretop or mane; the dorsal fin of a fish.

鰭 ˏch'i Like the last.

The spines in the dorsal fin of a fish; a spinous dorsal fish; a species of sea-blubber which furnishes a condiment.

振丨奮鱗 it bristled its dorsal and fled with glancing scales; said of a passionate man.

耆 ˏch'i From 老 *old* and 旨 divine *will* contracted.

A man of sixty, one who should advise others; old, aged, superior; strong, to bring about, to direct, to adjust; to promote; a scar.

紳丨 the gentry and elders.

丨老 old people; the elders, the seniors.

丨艾 an instructor or professor.

丨定爾功 when you become old in the service, your merit will be rewarded.

瘢丨 scar on a horse's back.

脪 ˏch'i The wooden platter on which the tongue and heart of the sacrificed ox or sheep was placed; to reverence.

佐食升丨俎 to present the sacrificial tray with all the accompaniments for the feast.

丨之爲敬也 the sense of ˏk'i is to reverence.

碕 ˏch'i A craggy shore; winding and stony banks; a stone bridge or jetty.

丨嶺 an uneven ridge or precipice.

軝 ˏch'i From *chariot* and *name;* it is not the same as ˊti 軧 rear of a cart.

The long axle end which projects from the hub; in Peking it is eight inches long, and called 軸頭兒 hub head.

約丨錯衡 the leather-bound axles and ornamented yokes.

豈 ˏch'i From 豆 a *dish* and 微 *fine* contracted.

An interrogative particle, how? what? — implying a mere negative, but usually with a stronger meaning than 不 or 非; can it be? how can?

丨敢 how dare I! — a polite expression for I cannot, I beg you not to say so.

丨若 it is better, it is preferable.

丨賢於子乎 how can he be more worthy than you?

吾丨匏瓜也哉 am I only a bitter gourd?

丨非 it is so, it is nothing else.

丨非乎 is it not? *i. e.* it surely is.

丨可如此 how can it be this way?

丨其然乎 will it be so? — No.

丨若是乎 how can it be so?

丨不相同 why are they not the same? *i. e.* they are identical.

丨能獨樂 how can he alone rejoice!

丨有此理 whence such a rule? *i. e.* there's no such principle.

丨徒教讓而且與仁 [the rulers] not only taught [the people] courtesy, but further they promoted humanity.

Read ˊk'ai, and used for 凱 and 愷 to rejoice. Delighted; joyous; to sing songs of victory; to advance, to ascend.

孔燕丨弟 easy and joyful we have our grand feast.

起 From to *walk* and *self* as the phonetic.
'ch'i To rise, to stand up; to begin, to originate; to raise up; to take the first step; to undertake; to build; to produce; to give occasion to; to open the meaning of; to aid; the beginning, origin; in *rhetoric*, an exordium, a proposition; in colloquial, it shows the beginning of an action or the present tense; after a verb, it is an auxiliary, like going or being, denoting that the action is going on; a classifier of cases in court, a number of people, vessels, carts, animals, &c.

丨身 to rise, as from bed; to start, as on a journey.

丨馬 let us start; to get up the horses.

丨立 stand up; standing.

丨手 to put hand to a work.

幾時丨轎 when does the bride start?

丨火 to catch fire; this in Hangchau denotes a rocket, which in Peking is termed 丨花 to raise a flower.

丨來 to rise; it expresses an action going on, as 怒丨來 he became angry.

笑丨來 he burst out laughing.

題丨來 I just remembered it.

陡丨風波 to suddenly raise the wind and waves; — to make an excitement by false rumors.

丨初 or 丨頭 the commencement, first; to begin.

丨心 to long for; covetous.

丨意 the idea of, the notion.

丨居 rising and sitting, *i. e.* under all circumstances.

一丨的人 a company, a crowd; a party of not less than three.

一丨兒來看 come in all at once and see it.

丨見 thus set agoing, begun on this account; a motive, the mental view of.

丨釁 cause of strife.

丨予者商也 he who can bring out my meaning is Shang.

丨倒 from beginning to end; the rise and fall or finish of.

丨興 prospering, starting well.

元首丨哉 let the prince be zealous in his duties.

丨兵 to raise troops.

我是當不丨的 I am quite unfit or unworthy of it; inadequate to.

想丨 to remember.

丨發 to prosper, to get rich; to send off, as goods.

丨坐不安 to behave strangely or uneasily.

丨貨單 a permit to clear cargo.

In *Cantonese*. A sign of the past tense, equivalent to 了 ended.

寫丨 written; 做丨 done.

邔 An old name for I-ch'ing
'ch'i hien 宜城縣 on the River Han in the northern part of Hupeh near K'i hien 丨縣 over which there was a prince of K'i.

杞 An acid fruit, the 枸丨 or
'ch'i seeds of the barberry (*Berberis lycium*), used in diseases of the eyes; a tree which the Chinese liken to the willow, but is more probably an alder.

丨柳 a tree out of whose wood bowls can be cut; it is perhaps a large alder or birch.

丨國 a small feudal state, now K'i hien 丨縣 in Honan, lying southeast of K'aifung, of whose people it was said 丨人憂天 the men of K'i grieved lest the sky should fall on them.

無折我樹丨 do not break and trample down my osiers.

玘 A stone ornament, intended
'ch'i to be hung at the girdle, as a chatelaine.

芑 A plant with a bitter taste,
'ch'i good to cure gunshot wounds and cuts.

屺 A hill without trees or grass;
'ch'i a bare, bleak mountain, such as a hermit chooses.

登丨岵而增悲 he ascended the hills K'i and Hu (in Shantung), increasing his regrets; *i. e.* his sorrow at not seeing his parents was added to the toil of travel.

技 From *hand* and *branch*; also read *ki'* and used with 伎' agile.
ch'i' Skilled; ingenious at making or contriving; art, dexterity; talent, ability.

丨藝 mechanical arts.

丨異 very clever; wonderful.

丨巧 ingenious, quick; having a gift for mechanics.

口丨 apt at imitating sounds, a good singer or mimic.

丨勇 military talent.

手丨 sleight of hand; dexterous.

芑 A variety of succory (*Cichorium*), the 丨菜 whose leaves
'ch'i are milky and can be eaten; also a kind of white millet or panic seed; grass; a kind of prickly tree.

啟 啓 From 启 to *open* and 攴 to *strike*; the first is correct, but both forms are common.
'ch'i To explain, to make clear; to open, as a door; to tell another, to report to, to make known; to state, to inform; to reveal; to instruct; to publish, as a book; to divide, to separate or distinguish; to uncover; the van or left wing of an army; a clear sky after a rain; to begin, as the spring.

敬丨者 or 逕丨者 I beg to state; — an opening phrase in a letter; the first is most respectful.

丨蒙 to teach the ignorant or young.

丨服 a horse with a white forefoot.

不遑丨處 I've not time even to take a rest.

不好丨口 (or 丨齒) it is not easy to speak of it, I am embarrassed about mentioning it.
天丨示人 Heaven revealed it to men.
子曰不憤不丨 Confucius said, I do not explain to one who is not eager for knowledge.
安丨 may you open it in peace; — a superscription on letters.
丨顔 to look pleasantly, to smile.
丨閉 to open and to shut.
丨口告人難 it is hard to awaken the sympathy of people.
附丨 an inclosure in a letter.
丨迪後人 to undeceive or to point out to others the true way, to disseminate truth.
丨明星 the morning star, Lucifer, the harbinger of brightness.
丨奏 to memorialize the Throne.
丨封 to remove the seals.
書丨先生 a centurion's clerk, who writes his letter, &c.

棨 *ʿch'i* A signal flag or board like a semaphore or marine signals.
丨戟 an embroidered streamer on a lance, sent by way of credence or borne in state.

綮 *ʿch'i* A scolloped or embroidered banner borne by an aid or escort; cover of a lance-head; to fold silk.
丨幟遙臨 see the banners coming in the distance.

Read *ʿk'ing*. The articulation of the tendons and bones.
肯丨 the place where flesh and bones unite.

綺 *ʿch'i* From *silk* and *odd* as the phonetic.
An open worked, variegated kind of silk, with criss-cross figures, called 丨羅, used for summer dresses; its wear was once regulated by sumptuary laws.
綠丨 a lute, from its silk cover.
丨縠 fine silk garments; *met.* elegant apparel.

气 *ch'iʾ* The original form of the next, supposed to represent curling vapors rising; it is used for the 84th radical of a dozen characters, mostly relating to vapors, and 乞 to beg, because prayers ascend to the gods.
Cloudy vapor, aura, effluence.

氣 *ch'iʾ* From *vapor* and *rice*.
Fume or vapor ascending from heat acting on moisture; steam, exhalation; ether, the aerial fluid; breath, air; a halo or cloudy vapor; the vital force or fluid, the primordial aura, nervous matter or the stamina of a being; spirit, courage, temper, or feelings of men or animals; aspect, air, influence, attraction; a convenient and mobile term in Chinese philosophy for explaining and denoting whatever is supposed to be the source or primary agent in producing and modifying motion, as if it was animated air; it is more material than *ʿli* 理 and *taoʾ* 道, more external than *ˏsin* 心, and is restrained by the *ˏhing* 形 which confines it, so that it is said 丨有限 the vital fluid has limits; *chih,* 質 is opposed to it, as ςῶη or spirit is to the body it animates; to smell; to irritate; an apparition; a semi-lunar period; after some nouns it has the force of like, or makes the noun adverbial.
莫生丨 don't get angry.
好丨血 plump, healthy, fresh.
好丨色 a pleasant countenance.
丨象 air, bearing, carriage.
天丨 weather, temperature.
二丨 the dual powers, or *yin* and *yang*.
五丨 the five agencies or vapor a *ʿyü* 雨 rain, *ˏyang* 暘 sunshine, *yuh,* 燠 heat, *ˏhan* 寒 cold, and *ˏfung* 風 wind; these proceed from the five elements.
六丨 the dual powers, wind and rain, light and darkness.
風丨 or 土丨 climate, miasma, air.
丨節 spirited; high toned; sensitive.

有丨度 veracious, honest.
濕丨 a damp, musty smell.
志丨 energy, nerve, vigor.
望丨者 a fortune-teller.
丨死人 to vex one, to exasperate.
受丨 or 丨着了 to be scolded; I have been blamed.
舒丨 to ease off one's bad feelings.
出丨 to vent one's spite.
丨絕 exhausted, no recuperative power left; dead.
下個丨兒 abate your anger, don't you get excited.
丨候 or 節丨 times, seasons; the twenty-four terms.
丨盡 annihilation; total absorption into another form.
地有丨脈 the vitalizing fluids in the earth, which the Chinese say produce minerals and waters, cause vegetation, and act on health.
伏丨 to hold the breath.
鍊丨 to imbibe energy, as by gulping morning air according to the Taoists.
占雲丨 to divine by the clouds.
勿丨 don't smell things rudely; don't snuff at it, don't get cross.
浩丨 elevation of mind.
你好運丨 you are in good luck.
正丨滿乾坤 his (Kwanti's) rectitude filled the universe.
冤丨 a revengeful spirit, as a sense of injustice seeking redress.
倒抽噎丨 to impede the respiration.
賜紫茸雲丨帳 present him with a soft purplish curtain, light as a cloud.
一鼻孔出丨 [the brothers] are all of the same sentiment.
元丨 original or inherited constitution.
一股丨兒作了 let us make one vigorous effort and finish it.
揚丨 to vapor about, to dress fine, to put on airs.
習丨 to imitate another, to ape his dress or gait.

炁 *ch'i'* Another form of the last; used by the Taoists in writing charms, to denote the powers of nature.

煞 ┃ and 吉 ┃ noxious and fortunate influences.

一 ┃ 化 三 淸 at one afflatus he transformed the Three Pure Ones; — done by the Taoist creator.

傶 *ch'i'* To unloosen the collar of a coat.

佳 ┃ to march or stride with regular steps.

┃ 襟 敞 領 an open bosom and rolling collar.

棄 *ch'i'* The original form is composed of 艸 *plants* and 華 *flowers* modified in combination, meaning to pluck and throw away flowers.

To push aside, to reject; to break or throw off; to relinquish, to renounce; to forget, to abandon, to discard.

┃ 世 to leave the world, to die.

厭 ┃ to disdain, to dislike much.

┃ 業 to waste a patrimony.

┃ 之 cast it aside.

自 ┃ to abandon good, to throw one's self away.

遺 ┃ to forsake, as a friend.

見 ┃ 於 人 to feel despised by men.

拋 ┃ or 丟 ┃ to throw a thing away; to fling off, as a good name.

不 我 遐 ┃ do not discard me because I am far away.

┃ 儒 就 賈 to leave a literary course and become a trader.

┃ 邪 歸 正 to leave the heretical and embrace the orthodox; to reform, to mend one's ways.

┃ 市 to abandon business, to retire to one's home.

器 噐 *ch'i'* Formed of four *mouths* of vessels and a *dog* guarding them; the second form is common but unsanctioned.

A vessel, a dish; a tool, an implement, a utensil; a thing formed by molding or cutting for use; a finished thing; an officer; to use a man where his talents are applicable; ability; useful, meritorious; body or substance as opposed to *hing* 形 form or quality; in which sense *kü'* 具 is also put in contrast.

┃ 皿 a dish or utensil of stone, earthen, glass, or metal; those of wood are called ┃ 具 in common usage.

┃ 械 or 兵 ┃ military weapons.

大 ┃ a man of talent.

小 ┃ an impatient, little minded man.

不 成 ┃ 的 東 西 an inefficient man, one unfit for a place.

┃ 局 不 大 方 he is not well versed in public matters, or fitted to manage them.

君 子 不 ┃ the capable man is not confined to one thing.

┃ 重 他 regard him with great respect.

┃ 用 utensils, implements; also useful, capable, available.

大 ┃ 晚 成 a great vessel is slowly made, — a talented man slowly matures.

量 才 ┃ 使 try and see what he is fit for.

企 *ch'i'* From *man* and *to stop*.

To rise on the heels and look for; to stand erect, to stand and look at; erect, perpendicular; steep, precipitous.

┃ 不 穩 it does not stand firm.

┃ 高 to stand higher.

高 ┃ high and steep, as a hill.

┃ 望 to expect eagerly, to look for anxiously.

行 ┃ 不 斷 uncertain in all his ways.

┃ 候 回 音 I shall look for a reply.

┃ 及 尊 府 I have been to your house, — but did not see your face.

┃ 倦 tired from standing.

┃ 仰 to look up to.

┃ 立 to stand erect; stand up!

㓞 *ch'i'* From *knife* and *elegant*, referring to the fine work of the carver when making records on bamboo or wood; it is now used only as a primitive, the next two having superseded it.

To cut a notch in a stick.

契 *ch'i'* From *great* and a notched *stick*.

A covenant, an agreement or bond intended to be enduring; quipos were anciently used until superseded by writings; to compare the parts of a contract or check; to join; mournful, distressed; scared; adopted, devoted to a god or person; a spit used in scorching land tortoise-shells for divination.

┃ 約 a written contract, of which the 紅 ┃ has an official seal, and the 白 ┃ has only the signatures; the former pay the 稅 ┃ official fee, and are more binding and legal.

書 ┃ documents, deeds, contracts.

田 ┃ or 房 ┃ deed of a lot or house; a bill of sale; a register.

┃ 合 bound together, united, sworn.

┃ 神 devoted to a particular god.

拜 ┃ to exchange cards and become sworn friends.

┃ 父 one who is served as a father; he answers somewhat to a godfather.

立 ┃ 據 to draw up a bond in evidence.

┃ ┃ 寤 歎 I watch mournfully.

┃ 刀 coins of the Han dynasty, B. C. 190, shaped like a sword.

賢 ┃ a pupil or adherent of a great scholar; also my worthy friend, used in direct address.

┃ 女 an adopted daughter.

┃ 子 an adopted or devoted child, especially so consecrated by parents when sick; the Buddhist priesthood is chiefly recruited by such children.

┃ 樹 to ask the protection of the [*yung* 榕 banian] tree, a common custom in Canton, from its long life.

爰丨我龜 there he began to singe our tortoise-shells.

丨丹國 Kitans who ruled northern China, A. D. 1118 to 1235, under the name of the *Kin Ch'ao* 金朝 or Golden Dynasty; the name is supposed to have been given them from their tattooing; it is the original of the Persian word *Cathay* applied to China.

Read *kieh,* To sunder; separated; unlike; uneven.

生死丨闊 as far apart as life and death.

Read *sieh,* One of the five celebrated statesmen of Shun, the progenitor of Ch'ing T'ang 成唐, the founder of the Shang dynasty; he was the minister of instruction, and ruler of Shang 徜 as his own state.

契 *ch'i'* To carve; to cut, especially characters.

Read *k'ieh,* To cut off.

丨丨 grieved, afflicted; cut up.

罄 *ch'i'* A vessel entirely emptied of its contents.

瓶中酒丨 the wine is all gone from the bottle.

KIA.

Old sounds, ka, kap, *and* kat. *In Canton,* ka; — *in Swatow,* ké *and* kia; — *in Amoy,* ka, ko, *and* kak; — *in Fuhchau,* ka *and* kià; — *in Shanghai,* ka *and* kia; — *in Chifu,* kia.

加 *chia* From *strength* and *mouth;* explained by the continual addition of words when conversing.

To add to, to place upon, to superadd; to confer upon; to advance, to promote; to increase; to inflict; to charge, as interest; accelerated; that which hastens motion; impulse; addition; over and above, extra.

丨增 to add to; to superimpose.

丨刑 to punish, to inflict punishment.

丨冠 to put on the cap, *i. e.* to come of age, — like wearing the *toga virilis*; marriageable.

丨封 to doubly envelop a letter.

丨意 beyond expectation.

丨官 to rise in office.

丨恩 to confer favor; increased kindness.

弋言丨之 when your arrows and line get — the birds.

于我又何丨焉 what more should I have to do with him?

有丨無已 there is no limit to the increase.

丨一抽 to take out a tenth; to charge ten per cent. a month.

丨息六厘 six per cent. interest per mensem.

丨減 to add and subtract; to increase and diminish.

丨法 the rules of addition.

無以復丨 there will be no such [good luck] again.

丨銜 a nominal rank, a titular dignity.

較去年價錢丨倍 the price is double what it was last year.

枷 *chia* From *wood* and to *add;* it is not the same as *kia'* 架 a stand.

One stick added to another, as a flail; a cangue or a wooden collar, in which minor criminals are pilloried, called in irony 木風領 the wooden neck-tie; there are several shapes and sizes; to wear the cangue.

丨號 the sentence written on the cangue; to wear it, called 擔丨 and 扛丨 in some places.

披丨帶鎖 to carry the cangue and be manacled.

丨責 to sentence to the pillory.

那見死鬼帶丨 who knows what punishments the devils put on the dead?

手丨 small board stocks for fastening both hands.

木匠做丨自丨自 the carpenter made a cangue and wore it; *met.* his violent dealing came down on his own pate.

耞 *chia* A flail, in which it is used with the last.

連丨 a flail; the fly is usually a bamboo stick.

珈 *chia* Ornaments attached anciently to the hair-pin, or hanging loosely on the head; a kind of fillet or head-band, worn by women.

丨飾 a marriage head-dress.

笳 *chia* A small whistle made of reed, without holes for the fingers, used among the nomads; some descriptions make it more like a flageolet.

鳴丨協節 blow the whistle to aid in singing the stanzas.

胡丨十八拍 the Mongol whistle has eighteen sounds.

袈 *chia* A coarse description of sleasy camlet.

丨裟 (in Sanscrit *kashaya, i. e.* a colored garment), the clerical dress, a gray, black, or leaden colored stole or surplice worn by Budhist priests when officiating, called 貧衲 or poor jacket by themselves, and 壞色衣 or spoiled color garment by others; it is made of thin cotton.

丨裟布 muslins.

痂 ꜀chia The scab or skin which grows over a sore.
結丨 to form a scab; to heal over.

𨍭 ꜀chia To plow.
雨後有人丨綠野 two men turned up the green field after the April rain, — the term from April 20 to May 5.
丨田 to plow fields.

跏 ꜀chia To sit with the feet under one; to sit cross-legged.
結丨而坐 to double the legs under one and sit down, — the proper posture when meditating on Budha.
丨趺 to sit in state; now used by the Budhists for a solemn sitting.

Read hiai'. A synonym of 邂 in the phrase 丨逅 to meet accidentally.

迦 ꜀chia A word used for Sanscrit ka or kia, as karanda 丨蘭陀 the cuckoo.
釋丨牟尼佛 Sakhya-Muni, the founder of Budhism; it is defined as meaning the solitary one (le moine μόνος the lone) of Sakya, the family name of Sud-dhodana his father, the king of *Kapila-vastu* 丨毘羅, his birth-place near the present Gorukpoor in Northern India; this name is defined by 妙德城 city of wonderful virtue.
丨葉摩縢 the name of Kaçyamatanga, who brought Budhism into China, A. D. 64.

嘉 ꜀chia From 加 to *add* and a *band* of music standing; a character much used in names.
Good, excellent; fine, delicious; what is happy, especially a marriage; to commend, to eulogize, to praise; pleased; to please; to rejoice in; to bring about what is admirable, to take a wife.
丨意 an excellent idea, a good object or suggestion; your proper remark.
可丨 commendable, praiseworthy.
丨禮 good manners; fine presents; a term for a wedding.
褒丨 to commend, as a historian does.
丨偶 a happy union.
丨樂君子 to gratify one's sovereign.
丨獎 to encourage and praise.
丨乃丕績 admirable are your great achievements.
深堪丨尚 worthy of all praise, very estimable.
丨峪關 the pass at the extreme west of the Great Wall, leading to Barkoul.
丨魚 a species of barbel (*Barbus deauratus*), which makes nests in the banks; it is named from its use as presents.
丨魚縣 lies in Wu-chang fu above Hankow, on the Yang-ts'z River.
丨州 an old name for the present 丨興府 in the north of Cheh-kiang.
丨平月 the twelfth moon, so called from the term given to the winter sacrifice in the Shang dynasty.
文王丨止大邦有子 when King Wăn would take a wife, in the large kingdom was found the lady.

脘 ꜀tsa From *flesh* and *child*.
The nipple; a teat; a pap; an old name for it in Hu-kwang.
刁鲞丨兒 [the infant] sucks the breast.

佳 ꜀chia From 人 *man* and 圭 a court *baton*; it is often confounded with ꜀chui 隹, which it much resembles both alone and in combination.
Beautiful and good of its kind; superior, nice, excellent; beauty; goodness, excellence.
丨人 a pretty woman.
丨音 good news, as by letter.
丨作 a fine composition; elegant, as a sonnet or essay.
甚丨 first rate, exceeding good.
不甚丨雅 not very elegant, common, not in good taste; dowdy.
丨筆 elegant penmanship.
不見丨 I don't like it; it is not very attractive.
漸入丨境 I gradually see the beauties of this region; *met.* to learn the delights of a study or art.
丨期 a good time; *met.* a wedding day; an assignation, as 會丨期 the time for the meeting.

葭 ꜀chia From *plant* and to *borrow*; occurs used for ꜀k'ié 茄 *brinjal.*
A bulrush or reed like a *Phragmites* or *Arundo*, before it has flowered; a musical pipe can be made of it; old name of a stream in the south of Chihli.
丨笛 a simple reed or pipe, used by herdmen in leading flocks.
丨葦 water grasses, rushes.
丨月 the seventh moon, when this plant is in seed.
鳴丨 the shrill pipe.
丨灰飛 or 丨管飛灰 the ashy reed down is flying about; *met.* winter has come.
丨州 a district on the Yellow River in the extreme north of Shensi.

Read ꜀hia. Wrongly used for 蕸 the nelumbium leaf.

豭 ꜀chia A boar.
寄丨 to debauch another's wife.
艾丨 a black young boar, an old term used in Corea and Chihli.

家 ꜀chia At first this was formed of 宀 a *shelter* and three 人 *persons* under it; now the primitive is changed to 豕 a *pig*, which one says is a contraction of the preceding, and imparts the sound.
What is within the doors, a household, a family, a dwelling;

home; a house, a building, and in some parts involves the idea of a village; domestic; domesticated; title of a husband and of some dignitaries; the country or government; to dwell; to live in; one of the viscera or regions of the body; a sect, a profession or class; a suffix to nouns to denote persons, as 兒 ㅣ children; or sometimes as an expletive.
一 ㅣ 人 all are connected, only one family.
ㅣ 人 a domestic; retainers, hangers-on; the 37th diagram.
ㅣ 身子 a slave, one bought with money.
自 ㅣ I myself.
兩 ㅣ or 兩 ㅣ 頭 both of us.
冤 ㅣ an opponent, an enemy.
肺 ㅣ the lungs.
五 ㅣ 生火 I am all out of sorts; feverish and sick.
五大 ㅣ the five great families denote five animals, the fox, the rat, the 黃鼠狼 or pole-cat, the snake and the 刺猬 or hedge hog, which are impish.
本 ㅣ one of the same clan or *sing*.
ㅣ 長 our clan elder or chief; the master of the house.
富 ㅣ rich people.
ㅣ 室 husband and wife.
安 ㅣ an allotment or advance to support the family.
ㅣ 父 my father; paterfamilias.
合 ㅣ or 闔 ㅣ the entire family.
ㅣ 用 for family use, usually denotes a better quality of goods.
八嘸 ㅣ eight persons having no home;—nothing to eat, destitute.
回老 ㅣ gathered to his fathers; to return to the old homestead when old, to come back from a long sojourn.
成 ㅣ to take a wife.
有 ㅣ 裏 I have a family.
ㅣ 臣 courtiers; persons who follow the fortunes of an officer; clan aids.

大 ㅣ the whole, all of us (or you) together; 大 ㅣ 行運 may you all be prosperous.
大 ㅣ 小戶 rich, and poor together, as the houses in a village.
二十多 ㅣ more than twenty dwellings.
在 ㅣ at home, in the house.
天 ㅣ or 國 ㅣ the emperor; our sovereign.
世 ㅣ an ancient and honorable family.
削髮出 ㅣ to become a priest.
老 ㅣ 兒 or 管 ㅣ your retainers, your household; the clerks.
視天下爲一 ㅣ regard all mankind as one family.
因 ㅣ 焉 because I wish (or am) dwelling here.
其人諸子百 ㅣ this man understands everything; he is a universal genius.

傢 *ˏchia* An unauthorized character, formed from the last; *q. d.* what the *man* supports his *family* with.

Tools, furniture, family things.
一副 ㅣ 生 a complete set of tools. (*Shanghai.*)
ㅣ 伙 or ㅣ 具 household gear, fixtures, furniture; all things belonging to a craft.

麚 麔 *ˏchia* A buck, a male deer, which sheds his horns in summer. 特 ㅣ 昏髟 [in winter] the stag's hair becomes bushy

嘏 *ˊchia* From *old* and to *borrow*; it is also read *ˊku*.

Great felicity or prosperity; propitious; distant; large and strong; stable, to bless; he who blesses.
祝 ㅣ to implore blessings.
降 ㅣ the blessings of heaven.
純 ㅣ unalloyed happiness.

瘕 *ˊchia* From *disease* and to *borrow* as the phonetic

A disease of the bowels, arising from cancer, worms, or concretions; a disease of the lungs, difficulty of breathing; croupy; a flaw, a defect.
ㅣ 喘 to breathe hard; asthmatic.
蟯 ㅣ short worms in the bowels.
ㅣ 嗽 to cough distressingly.

Read *ˏhia* A female complaint.

假 *ˊchia* From *man* and to *borrow*; occurs used for *ˏkia* 嘉 fine.

False, fictitious; illusory; feigned, hypocritical; unreal; a pretext; to pretend; to avail of, to borrow, to get an accommodation; to dress in costume; as a *conjunction*, supposing, if, because; for instance, to suppose; great; equitable.
不知眞 ㅣ I don't know if it be true or not.
ㅣ 若, or ㅣ 如, or ㅣ 使, or ㅣ 此間 granting that; if; supposing.
ㅣ 然 for instance.
ㅣ 手於人 to put into another's hand; to transfer to.
花 ㅣ simulated, not genuine.
ㅣ 名 an alias, a feigned name.
ㅣ 冒官 a counterfeit officer.
ㅣ 局 it's all humbug.
攙 ㅣ to falsify, as goods; to mix inferior sorts.
ㅣ 借 to borrow, to ask of; to use as a substitute; a metaphor.
ㅣ 扮官差 to dress up like policemen.
天 ㅣ 其便 heaven gave him the chance; he ran a great risk, he had a narrow escape.
ㅣ 穴 a false hole, a name for an unlucky grave.
狐 ㅣ 虎威 the fox borrowed the tiger's roar.
ㅣ 哉天命 how sublime are the decrees of Heaven!
ㅣ 以溢我 how does he (or by what (show his kindness to us?
ㅣ 僞 spurious, hypocritical.
自 ㅣ self-elated.
ㅣ 情 an affected regard for; pretended love.

Read *kia'*. Leave of absence, usually for a brief period; a furlough.

告 丨 to apply for leave.

放 丨 to give a vacation.

寬 丨 to extend a leave.

滿 丨 his furlough has expired.

休 丨 a leisure time, a vacation

斝 斚 'chia — From 斗 a *measure* placed under 吅 to *call* out as when invoking, with 冂 *border* between to represent the object.

A small gem or metallic cup or tripod with ears, of a graceful shape, used in the Yin dynasty to receive libations before the gods, and drink out of; it contained six 升 or gills, and was ornamented with carved stalks of grain.

洗爵奠 丨 he washed his cup, and [the guests] put theirs down.

盥 丨 候敘 I have washed the goblet and await your coming; — a phrase on an invitation card.

檟 榎 'chia — A *tree* of *price*; a small evergreen shrub like a *Gardenia* in size and appearance, whose leaves furnished a bitter infusion, and without much doubt denoted the tea shrub; the second character, is by some taken to be another name for the ,*ts'iu* 楸 or *Catalpa Bungei* of the north, but the trees are doubtless different, and the second is the proper form for it: the second gathering of the tea leaves.

舍其丨梧養其樲棘 he discards the tea and oil trees, and cultivates the thistle and thorn; — *i. e.* he consorts with the vile and neglects the good.

價 chia' — From *man* and *price* as the phonetic.

The value of a thing; the price.

市 丨 or 時 丨 the current rate, the market price.

丨錢很貴 (or 昂) the price is exorbitant.

索 丨, or 講 丨, or 要 丨, or 開 丨 the asking rate, the nominal price.

報 丨 單 a prices-current.

無 丨 no sale; no price.

無 丨 寶 priceless, inestimable.

待 丨 而沽 sell when you can get a good price; — *i. e.* wait till your merits are appreciated.

減 丨 or 落 丨 or 跌 丨 a falling market, a lower rate.

丨廉 or 丨錢便宜 a reasonable, moderate price.

實 丨 or 不飾 丨 the real price, not a false or (put on) value.

春宵一刻千金 丨 an hour of spring is worth a thousand taels.

聲 丨 高 a high responsible office; also an honorable spirit.

言不二 丨 we mention no two prices; — a shop sign.

㝢 chia' — To build a house; to rear a dwelling; a house.

駕 chia' — From *horse* and to *add* as the phonetic.

A horse in the harness; to prepare the carriage; to harness a horse; to yoke; to drive or sit in a carriage; a chariot; he who sits in it; to ride; to mount; to ascend, as on a cloud; to go in, as a ship; to embrace, to avail of; a title of respect, you, Sir.

丨子大 pompous, lofty, arrogant, assuming.

丨上 or 台 丨 or 尊 丨 are terms of address, as Sir, Your Honor, Respected Sir, — as if speaking to one in a chariot.

御 丨 the emperor's chariot; his Majesty.

聖 丨 his Majesty, his Holiness, his Godship, applied to the emperor and to gods when speaking of them.

戎車既 丨 the general's carriage is harnessed.

丨言行狩 we yoked up and went to the hunt.

法 丨 the emperor's car; now used as a polite term for priest.

騰雲 丨 霧 to mount the clouds and ride the mist, — to become one of the genii.

丨 船 to be or sail in a ship.

返 丨 to return home, to get back.

丨 船的 the hands or sailors, the crew of a ship.

屈 丨 you have done me great honor; *lit.* bent to honor me.

別 丨 an aid or deputy to an officer.

乘輿已 丨 矣 get into the carriage, it is ready.

行 丨 or 騰 丨 to start on a journey.

隨 丨 followers in an idol procession; the household guards.

擋 丨 to stop the car — *i. e.* to excuse one's self to a visitor.

丨 訟 to present a joint complaint to a magistrate.

In *Fuhchau*. Divining blocks.

三聖 丨 three lucky throws.

架 稼 chia' — Not the same as ,*kia* 枷 the cangue; the second form is unusual, and confined to the noun.

An open frame on which to place things; a stand, a waiter, a rack, an étagière, a case; a frame-work, staging, or scaffolding; to lay on a frame, to put up; to support, to uphold; to ward, to fend off; to avail of; a classifier of screens, pictures, clocks, ladders, pier-glasses, and other framed articles, bedsteads, balustrades, &c.

打 丨 to fisticuff; to come to blows, as with sticks.

招 丨 to resist, to head off, to oppose an attack.

丨 物 to support a thing.

十字 丨 a letter 十 ten frame, a cross, a crucifix.

丨 生 to ingraft.

書 丨 a book-rack, a book-case without doors.

一 丨 畫 one framed picture.

擺 丨 子 a foppish fellow, one who puts on airs; proud.

丨 橋他過 lay a bridge for him to pass, help him out of his trouble.

丨 之高閣 place it on the high loft.

金鐘 丨 or 舉 丨 the truss which supports the roof.

丨 詞揑控 to heap up calumnious charges.

支虛 丨 子 a cleaned-out case, a family with more show than substance; a pretentious, unreal man.

支 丨 子 he has nothing but a frame, said of a miserable, paltry shop-keeper.

丨 着他 to make a cat's paw of another.

拿 丨 子 a frame-wearer — a swaggering ignoramus, one on his high horse.

人命 丨 子 a row involving life.

丨 起 to prop up, as a box on trestles; or a beam on forks.

嫁 chia' From *woman* and *household; q.d.* the woman goes to her family.

To marry a husband, to send a bride to her husband's house; to impute to, to implicate.

送 丨 to escort the bride.

丨 夫 or 出 丨 to wed a husband.

丨 女 to give one's daughter in marriage.

丨 奩 or 丨 妝 a dower, a dot.

女大當 丨 when a girl is of age, she should be wedded.

改 丨 or 反頭 丨 to take a second husband.

丨 禍於人 to bring evil on another maliciously.

丨 怨 to feel a grudge.

隨 丨 了頭 a waiting-maid given at marriage; also called 從 丨 bride's follower.

丨 鷄隨鷄 if you marry a cock follow a cock; — a woman must follow her husband's lot and position.

任來 丨 于周 Jin came to be married to the prince of Chen.

爲人作 丨 to prepare a bridal outfit; to do others' work.

稼 chia' From *grain* and *household; q.d.* sowing is the business of a household; it is like marrying a daughter, something will come of it.

To sow grain; farming; wild, self-sown; grain, cereals; the spike of grain; a sheaf.

禾 丨 the full grown grain.

丨 禾 to sow corn or wheat; done by dibbling.

學 丨 to learn husbandry.

不知 丨 穡艱難 you don't know the hardships of sowing and reaping, — *i. e.* of getting a living; said to a spendthrift son.

莊 丨 growing grain; the crops, harvested by 莊 丨 漢 stalwart harvest-men.

我 丨 旣同 our harvest is all in.

十月納禾 丨 in November the sheaves are all gathered.

榎 chia' A tree, whose fruit resembles a shaddock, with a very thick skin, and furnishes a wood useful in cabinet-work; a lever; manacles or gyves.

爲 丨 舁物 to raise a thing with a pry.

K'IA.

Old sounds, k'a *and* k'ap. *In Canton,* fa *and* ya; — *in Swatow,* gé; — *in Amoy,* k'ia; — *in Shanghai,* k'a; — *in Chifu,* k'ia.

呿 ch'ia From *mouth* and *to go.*

To gape; to open the mouth, as if in stupid wonder.

㛙 ch'ia Pretty.

㛙 丨 the mincing motions of a girl who thinks herself to be beautiful.

㛙 丨 處 or (㛙假局 in Cantonese) simulated, pretending.

㤉 ch'ia To prostrate one's self; to fear.

惡 丨 hiding one's face from view, as a bashful child.

跒 'ch'ai To walk, to step.

跁 丨 the motion of walking, but making no progress, as when drilling soldiers; it is also used to intimate reluctance to act.

愘 ch'ia' From *heart* and *guest.*

Covertly hiding.

丨 㤉 hiding away, as children in playing hide-and-go seek; bashful and keeping out of sight.

髂 ch'ia' The pelvis bone; the haunch bone.

KIAH.

Old sound, kap, gap, *and* kat. *In Canton,* kap, kíp, kít, *and* at ; — *in Swatow,* hiap, ka, k'iat, *and* k'ak ; — *in Amoy,* ka, kiap, k'iat, k'ai *and* siat ; — *in Fuhchau,* kak, kĕk, hiék kiék, *and* ngak ; — *in Shanghai,* kăh *and* yăh ; — *in Chifu,* kia.

甲 'chia — The original character is described as composed of 木 *wood* with a *cap* over it, representing the first motions of the sprout in spring; others say it is a man's head which ought to have a cover on it.

The plumule or scaly covering of a growing seed just bursting; cover of a sprout, a bud; the first of the ten stems, belonging to wood, — hence, the first, the head, the best; number one, from its common use in ordinal numbers; to begin, to excel, to get the start of; armor, a cuirass, a corselet; a soldier; military, and hence at Peking, in the main city, it denotes a ward or beat, which the troops guard and keep watch in; hard coverings, as the carapace of turtles, elytra of beetles, scaly plates on crocodiles, gurnards, &c.; the finger nails.

保 丨 a tithing, a hamlet; its elder.

丨 頭 the chief of a ward or street.

丨 乙 are used hypothetically for persons, as the one, the other; as John Doe, Richard Roe; as A. B. in geometry; 1st, 2d, &c.

科 丨 literary men; graduates who have passed, and not bought their step.

丨 '長 head-constable of a ward, a village elder.

響 丨 jingling scales, such as actors wear or peddlers use.

爪 丨 or 指 丨 claws, the finger-nails.

正白旗第三 丨 the third ward of the plain white Bannermen.

富 丨 天下 the richest man in the world, a Crœsus.

三鼎 丨 the highest three on the list of *hanlin* or *tsinsz'* graduates.

丨 卒 veteran soldiers.

丨· 帳 the general's markee.

丨 庫 an armory, a dépôt of military stores.

丨 坼 a sprout, a bud.

兵 丨 military equipments; 丨 兵 *met*, armor and weapons.

丨 香 or 丨 煎 a medical name for the operculum of snails.

丨 蟲 the class of scaly animals, as snakes, reptiles, turtles.

丨 魚 tortoises (*Triouyx*), also called 鼈 a name for marsh tortoises.

能不我 丨 does his ability exceed mine? — he is not my superior.

名登黃 丨 he has attained to high literary rank; — the names of *küjin* and *tsinsz'* graduates are written on yellow paper.

鎖子 丨 a kind of chain armor.

六 丨 the gravid uterus.

六十花 丨 the sexagenary cycle.

TABLE OF THE SEXAGENARY CYCLE.

甲子	己巳	甲戌	己卯	甲申	己丑	甲午	己亥	甲辰	己酉	甲寅	己未
1804	1809	1814	1819	1824	1829	1834	1839	1844	1849	1854	1859
1864	1869	1874	1879	1884	1889	1894	1899	1904	1909	1914	1919
乙丑	庚午	乙亥	庚辰	乙酉	庚寅	乙未	庚子	乙巳	庚戌	乙卯	庚申
1805	1810	1815	1820	1825	1830	1835	1840	1845	1850	1855	1860
1865	1870	1875	1880	1885	1890	1895	1900	1905	1910	1915	1920
丙寅	辛未	丙子	辛巳	丙戌	辛卯	丙申	辛丑	丙午	辛亥	丙辰	辛酉
1806	1811	1816	1821	1826	1831	1836	1841	1846	1851	1856	1861
1866	1871	1876	1881	1886	1891	1896	1901	1906	1911	1916	1921
丁卯	壬申	丁丑	壬午	丁亥	壬辰	丁酉	壬寅	丁未	壬子	丁巳	壬戌
1807	1812	1817	1822	1827	1832	1837	1842	1847	1852	1857	1862
1867	1872	1878	1832	1887	1892	1897	1902	1907	1912	1917	1922
戊辰	癸酉	戊寅	癸未	戊子	癸巳	戊戌	癸卯	戊申	癸丑	戊午	癸亥
1808	1813	1818	1823	1828	1833	1838	1843	1848	1853	1858	1863
1868	1873	1878	1883	1888	1893	1898	1903	1908	1913	1918	1923

This is the only mode of reckoning years employed by the Chinese. Their records state that Nao the Great 大撓 was commanded by his sovereign Hwangti, in the 61st year of his reign, to examine the relations of the five elements, and form a cycle to name the years; he did so by taking *kiah*, the first of the ten stems, and joining it to *tsz'*, the first of the twelve branches, to denote the first year of the cycle; the second characters of each series were then joined to form *yueh-cheu*, and so on, going through the ten stems six times, and the twelve branches five times, as shown in this table. This is supposed to have been in the year B. C. 2637, which according to Hales was 518 years after the deluge. The Chinese have never kept up a serial numbering of the cycles, but the 75th ended in 1863 with the 4500th year of their annals; there were 44 before the birth of Christ, ending A. D. 3; and there have been 31 cycles since that date, up to A. D. 1864. This mode of naming the years is followed by the Coreans, Japanese, and Lewchewans, and has done much to simplify and preserve their chronology.

岬, ˏchia The side of a hill; a steep place between hills.

車駕丨嶇 carriages and horses following on in a line.

胛, ˏchia From *flesh* and *scale*.

The part under and between the shoulder-blades.

夾, ˏchia From 大 *great* supported by two 人 *men;* others consider it to be formed of two *men* holding up one by the *elbows;* it much resembles ˓*shen* 夾, and is interchanged with its next three compounds, as also with *kiah*, 袷 lined, and *chah*, 鍘 shears.

To take or press under the arms; to carry secretly; to succor; to squeeze; to take up, as with pincers; to press between two; to aid; to take to one's bosom; to insert between; to keep near to; doubled, lined, as a dress; assistants; near, connected, as a side-chamber or recess; boards for pressing; shears with the hinge at the end of the blade.

丨其皇澗 [the people] occupied the Hwang Valley.

丨帶 to carry or secrete in the girdle.

丨帶私貨 to smuggle with one's baggage.

丨板 boards for pressing or supporting the sides of a thing, as the chocks of a mast.

丨板船 foreign rigged sailing vessels; the term seems to be derived from the word *captain*.

丨雜 mixed in, ill assorted; foisted in.

是單是丨 is it a single or double—jacket?

鉗丨 nip it up; to delude by false statements.

丨輔 councilors; aides-de-camp.

丨攻 to attack on both sides.

丨緊 or 丨住 press it tightly.

針線丨 a needle-case, a housewife or hussy.

書丨 boards to retain Chinese books in order.

衣丨 a portmanteau, a carpet-bag.

用丨剪丨開 use the sycee shears to cut it open.

丨着 put it inside; take it under your arm.

挾, ˏchia ˏh'ié From *hand* and to *press;* it is also a synonym of *hieh*, 脅 to assist, and the last.

To clasp under the arm, or between the legs; to pinch; to hide away, to put in the bosom; to appropriate; to help, to support; to cherish, to protect; to assume, to presume upon; to extort, to squeeze; to bring together; to store up.

丨佐 to assist, to protect.

丨貴 to presume on one's rank.

丨持甚大 great ability to manage affairs.

丨日 an interval of ten days or so.

丨嫌 or 丨恨 or 丨仇 to cherish hatred, to hold a grudge against.

既丨我矢 our arrows are on the string.

丨制 to oppress, as by preventing an appeal; to shut out from; to force to a course by threats of consequences.

丨太山 [you might as well try] to tuck Mt. T'ai (in Santung) —under your arm.

俠, ˏchia ˏh'ie From *man* and to *press;* it is also read *hieh*, and sometimes used for the last two.

Generous, noble-minded, public-spirited; bold, zealous for the right; ready to maintain another's cause.

丨氣 disinterested, magnanimous.

丨烈 ardent and brave; resolute to maintain her chastity.

丨客 or 劍丨 a friend in need; a supernatural aid or advocate.

任丨有名 he has a name for equity and energy in a cause.

豪丨 a man of moral courage and power, a hero.

遊丨 to roam and wander, as a fairy does over the world.

梜, ˏchia A kind of nippers or chopsticks; the irregular veins of wood.

丨棍 a machine to torture the ankles.

莢, ˏchia From *plants* and to *squeeze*.

Pods of leguminous plants; legumes generally; seeds; the sheath on the leaf stalk of grasses; a clasping petiole.

榆丨 elm seeds.

丨錢 small light coins used in the Han dynasty.

蓂丨 a felicitous plant found in Yao's courtyard; also called 歷丨 from its curious growth.

郟, ˏchia A district in Jü cheu 汝州 in the center of Honan on a branch of the River Hwai.

丨鄏 an ancient place in the north of Hupeh, where Ch'ing Wang 成王 established the Cheu dynasty, about B. C. 1100.

丨室 a lodge over the city gate.

頰, ˏchia From *head* and to *press;* *q.d.* the jaws receive and press the food.

The jaws, the sides of the face; the cheeks; utterance, articulation; a side.

腮丨 the chops, the jowl.

桃丨 peach-bloom or rosy cheeks.

丨車 or 丨骨 the jaw-bone.

丨巴頦兒 a Peking term for the chin.

旁丨 to guard, to be at the side of.

緩丨往說 to use metaphors, to bring far-fetched insinuations.

赤丨 the red jowl,—a poetical name for the stork.

鋏, ˏchia A pair of pincers or prongs to hold a crucible over the fire; to take up with tongs; a double-edged sword.

火丨 a pair of tongs.

彈丨而歌 [Fung Hwang] went about thrumming on his sword and singing.

袷, ꜀chia From *clothes* and *joined;* occurs interchanged with *kiah*, 夾 to assist.

A lined dress without wadding; lined, doubled.

丨 衫 a lined dress.

單 丨 衣 服 single and double garments.

Read *kieh*꜀ A kind of collar; a lappel.

視不上于丨不下于帶 do not look at people above the collar, nor below the girdle.

丨 輅 the second chariot.

䀫, ꜀chia From *eye* and *united.* Eyes dim and tired; eyes blinking and dull; sleepy.

丨 眼 倦 nodding, sleepy. (*Cantonese.*)

韐, ꜀chia A close cuirass or breast-plate of hide; an under-shirt made firm and hard so as to ward off blows, and often plated with metal.

丨 革 a leather cuirass or jerkin; it was doubled over the breast.

韐, ꜀chia A knee-pad of leather; a white narrow sash or girdle, worn by mourners.

餄, ꜀chia A kind of cake or bait.

稭, 秸, ꜀chié From *grain* and *altogether* or *happy;* it is also read ꜀*k'iai*, and occurs interchanged with the next.

The straw or stalks of corn or hemp; grain still in the straw, but with the outer sheaths removed; clean; to weave into hassocks to worship heaven; usual, customary.

三 百 里 納 丨 服 he paid the usual taxes on 300 *li*.

棉 花 丨 cotton stalks used for fuel.

戛, ꜀chia ꜀ka Said to be composed of 百 *hundred* and 戈 *spears.*

A lance, a long spear; to spear; uneven, jagged; usual, as rules or ceremonies.

丨 擊 鳴 球 his spear struck the sounding ball.

丨 禮 usual rites, accepted usages.

不 率 大 丨 the intractable must come under (or be judged by) the great laws.

丨 丨 乎 how he hesitates in saying it!

嘎, chia' ꜀ka From *mouth* and *lance;* it occurs in many proper names of foreign origin for the sound ꜀*ka.*

The chirping or singing of birds is 丨 丨; apparently an attempt to imitate the chatter of a magpie.

In *Pekingese.* Loud laughing.

丨 丨 的 笑 a jolly, ringing laugh.

㓤, ꜀chié To scrape off the rust and dirt; to brush and clean.

劼, ꜀chié From *knife* and *lucky.*

To brand or tattoo the face as a punishment; to flay the skin from the face.

恝, ꜀chié Also read *kiai*'

An indifferent heartless manner, shown when others are sad; want of sympathy.

丨 然 light-hearted, flippant, thoughtless, careless.

K'IAH.

Old sounds, k'ap *and* gip. *In Canton,* hap *and* k'ap; — *in Swatow,* k'ap *and* kip; — *in Amoy,* k'ap *and* kip; — *in Fuhchau,* k'ak; — *in Shanghai,* häh *and* kah; — *in Chifu,* kia.

恰, ch'ia' From *heart* and *joined.*

Seasonably, in good time, luckily, opportunely, fitly; to the purpose; just, exactly; to apply the mind to.

丨 遇 happily met.

丨 好 or 丨 當 just the thing, fitting, all right, fortunately.

丨 似 or 丨 如 just so, much alike, nearly.

野 航 丨 受 兩 三 人 the rude boat would just hold two or three persons.

丨 可 very suitable.

剛 丨 巧 it is just in the nick of time, not too early or too late.

丨 丨 鶯 啼 the parrots are crying *k'iah k'iah.*

㓣, ch'ia' A synonymous form of *k'oh*, 割 to cut.

To pierce, to stab; to cut.

欱, ꜀ch'ia From to *breathe* and *guest.*

To emit vapor; to send forth breath.

帢, ch'ia' A scholar's cap, used about A.D. 300, like a military cap without corners, to distinguish the literati of Wei.

跲, ch'ia' To stumble; to fall or jump back; to stammer in speaking.

丨 後 to stumble or slip down backwards.

言 前 定 則 不 丨 consider well what you are to say, and you will not hesitate.

Read *k'ieh*꜀ For, instead of.

招, *ch'ia* From *hand* and *pitfall*. To dig the nails into; to lacerate, to claw; to grab, to pinch, to twist; to tear up.

丨鼻炙眉頭 clawed his nose and burned his eyebrows and head.

丨指算來 reckon them up on the fingers.

丨草帽 to twist braid for straw hats.

促丨見識 a mischievous disposition, liking to play jokes.

丨出血 to force the blood out.

丨驚風 to pinch the skin to remove spasms, — in children.

牙齒丨入肉 to bite [the lips] till the blood comes; — irritated, indignant, mad at.

丨不齊 unequal, uneven.

手丨訣 to twist the fingers, so that the middle one stands upright; the Budhists do it when praying.

丨嗓子眼兒 to grab one by the throat.

㓣, *ch'ia* Occurs used for the last. To dig the nails into; to pinch; to enter, to go into.

丨花兒 to pluck a flower; to tear into strips, as the edges of paper; to pull to bits.

菰, 葜, *ch'ia* A felicitous plant, the 菝丨, which appears to denote a fern resembling the common brake, but not yet fully expanded.

KIAI.

Old sounds, ka, ha, ga, kak, *and* kap. *In Canton,* kai; — *in Swatow,* kai *and* koi; — *in Amoy,* kai *and* ké; — *in Fuhchau,* kai *and* ka; — *in Shanghai,* ka *and* kia; — *in Chifu,* kiai.

皆 *chié* From *white* and *to compare*. All alike, things of the same sort; an adjective of number denoting people; used after two nouns or a series of items, for the whole all, altogether; but often simply a sign of the plural; all at once; manifold.

丨知 everybody knows it.

丨不及 no one came up to him; unequaled.

老少丨在 old and young are all here.

所作丨然 all he does is in the same style.

丨同一體 we are all of the same rank.

丨是 all are so; all correct.

具丨一樣 all are alike.

丨大歡喜 all are alike happy — when in presence of Budha.

偕 *h'ié* From *man* and *all;* it is similar to the preceding. To accompany, to take along with one, as a parent his son; jointly; all at once, together, with; a joint, vigorous effort; robust.

丨男 with my son; — a phrase used on cards and tablets.

百年丨老 the couple have grown old together.

魚水和丨 [as amicable as] the fish and the water.

丨丨士子 an able vigorous officer.

與子丨行 I will go with you.

夙夜必丨 morning and night he must consort with them.

清濁不丨 purity and impurity cannot coëxist.

徣 *chié* To act badly is 徘丨; — the manner and reason for it to be determined by the context.

喈 *chié* From *mouth* and *all*. The harmony of birds; distant music or melody, as the sound of bells or drums; the soughing of the wind.

鳥鳴丨丨 their sweet concert was heard afar.

北風其丨 the whistling of the northern wind.

湝 *chié* The rippling sound of water; incessant rain and wind.

淮水丨丨 the murmuring waters of the River Hwai.

階 堦 *chié* From *place* or *earth* and *all;* there is a trifling distinction between these two characters, the second being restricted to literal steps.

Steps, especially those leading up to the gate; the ascent to a hall; a grade, a degree, a rank; to emulate, to rise; a source, as of an evil; that which helps to rise, as an elementary treatise, a gradus, an easy lesson.

丨級石 the outer stone steps.

丨梯 four or five steps, which lead up a landing.

丨砌 a parapet or balustrade on the sides of steps, to put flowers.

丨級 an official grade.

遊金丨 to walk the golden steps — or palace, the privilege of the three highest Hanlin graduates; also called 玉丨 and 天丨 the gemmed or heavenly steps.

台丨 your house or mansion.

丨上 at the top of the steps, high in office.

文丨 literary office or degree.

孔步亦步以聖爲丨 Confucius reached the summit of excellence only step by step.

言語以爲丨 there should be progressive steps in a discourse.
亂丨 steps of disorder, bad government, corruption.
升丨 to rise in office.
丨州 an inferior department in Kansuh on the River Kia-ting.
興廢之丨 the successive progress of advancement or decay.

藒 ˏchié From *plant* and *dark*. The stalks of the northern or Abutilon hemp (*Sida tiliæfolia*), which are dressed for ropes and cordage; straw stripped of its leaf sheaths.

痎 ˏchié An intermittent or tertian ague, the 丨瘧, which comes on every other day.

䳚 ˏchié A cock quail that proves to be cowardly, is 丨鶉, and is soon sent to the cook.

街 ˏchié From 行 to *go* and 圭 a *baton*. A thoroughfare, a broad street, an avenue; a place which leads to the four points; a place where markets are held; out of doors, abroad, in the street.
出丨 to walk abroad; gone out.
丨閘 a street gate.
一道丨 or 一條丨 one street.
鬧市丨 a noisy thoroughfare, a bustling street.
丨坊 the street, a neighborhood; the neighbors; also used sometimes as a compellation, as 丨坊阿 Neighbor! — in Canton, the householders of three or four streets, forming a kind of ward.
花丨 an ornamented or illuminated street; a street of playhouses or courtesans.
查丨 to patrol the streets, as the 看丨的 watchmen or policemen do.
丨衢洞達 went through all the streets, as a procession.
氣丨 the pulse of the femoral artery; a medical term.
巷議丨談 street rumor, gossip.
天丨 the stars *κ ν* in Taurus; the phrase is also used for the Milky Way in 天丨夜色涼如水 [in the seventh moon] the Galaxy at night is clear as water, — so that the Herdboy and Weaver can be seen.

In *Cantonese*. The town; a row of houses.
落丨 to go into town, as from the country; to go abroad.
上丨 or 埋丨 to go ashore.

繲 ˋkié Old garments.
挫針治丨 sharpen the needle to mend the old clothes.
浣丨 to cleanse old soiled clothes.

解 鮮 ˋchié From *horn*, *knife*, and *ox*; *q. d.* cutting open a horn; the second form is common; it is interchanged with some of its compounds.
To open, to take off or apart; to extricate; to disjoint, to sever; to dissipate, to scatter; to dispel, as sorrow; to explain, to understand, to make clear; to stop; to do away with the effects of; to release, as from bonds; an explanation, a commentary; a trace of.
丨帶 to unloosen the girdle.
丨除 to neutralize, as the effects of a poison; to propitiate or exorcise noxious influences.
丨說 to make clear.
註丨 an explanation, a comment.
講丨 to preach on, to expound.
無丨救 there's no way of escape from it.
丨錯 the explanation is wrong.
丨悶 to alleviate sorrow, to dispel grief.
丨手 to urinate.
丨圍 to raise a seige; to settle a quarrel.
丨罪 let me explain my error; I beg your pardon.
丨暑湯 to allay heat, as by cooling drinks.
丨渴 to quench thirst.
丨任 to retire from office.
唱丨心 to sing a cheerful ballad.
丨難ˋ to succor, as in extremity; to relieve one in straits.
丨構 to set at variance; annoying interference.
丨散 to explain away, as a difficulty; scattered, as a crowd.
分丨 to discriminate.
殊不可丨 I really can't understand what it means.
丨息, or 丨和, or 排難丨紛 to make up a quarrel, to settle amicably; to explain the difficulty and become friends.
丨屨 to take off the shoes.
尸丨 magic arts of the Taoists, who pretend to vivify a corpse.
丨脫 to let go; to free, as a grasp; to let off; to escape, as from punishment.
丨脫處 or 丨脫 a Budhist term for self-liberation, or the state of liberation (*vimoksha*), of which 八丨脫 eight enfranchisements (*ashtau vimokshas*) are enumerated, being as many intellectual states through which their writers say every *arhan* passes on his road to *nirvana*.

Read *kiaiˀ* To transmit, to forward, to hand over or up to; to conduct; to transfer an officer to another post; to exclude.
丨犯 to deliver over a prisoner.
丨送 to forward, as a culprit.
丨發 to forward on, as boxes.
丨餉 to send on the duties — to Peking.
押丨 or 丨差 the escort or guard of a prisoner.
丨案 to remit a case to a higher court.
丨報 to forward with a report.
丨元 the first of the *küjin* graduates at a tripos.

Read *hiaiˀ* in the sense of 懈. Idle, remiss.
不丨ˀ于位 not carelessly occupying his post.

廨 From *shelter* and to *forward* as the phonetic.
chié

An apartment adjoining or in a *yamun* where persons can stay, or visitors be received; a sort of hospice; a lodging for subordinate officers.

公丨 or 公丨地方 a public office, away from the chief *yamun;* a magistrate's lodging, or where he temporarily holds his court.

戒 From 戈 a *spear* and 廾 to *hold up* with both hands, as if to alarm an intruder; occurs used for 界 a *boundary,* and the next.
chié

To warn, to caution; to guard, to watch against; to beware of, to refrain from, as wine; to observe a regimen; to inhibit; to wean from the use of; to inform; to prepare for; cautions, injunctions, precepts, inhibitions; a limit; a region.

丨口 to be careful of one's diet; to fast, to live sparingly.

切丨 most carefully guard against.

丨烟方 a prescription for curing opium smokers.

丨斷癮 quite cured of the habit.

丨殺 avoid killing animals

丨條 rules to be observed.

旣種旣丨 having the seed and also seen after the utensils.

豈不日丨 ought we not to warn each other daily?

勸丨 or 告丨 to urge to break off, as a vice.

丨酒 to abstain from wine or spirits.

以丨將來 in order to deter others after them.

河丨 the river's limit.

警丨不虞 sedulously guard against all hazards.

受丨 to take orders, as a priest or nun; it is done by burning moxa on the head in many places.

丨愼恐懼 carefully observant of and fearing to offend, as a disciple.

丨之丨之 guard against it! beware of it! — similar to 丨哉 take care!

不丨于火 did not guard against the fire; — an accidental conflagration.

丨尺 a ferule; a foot ruler.

丨指 a finger-ring, explained by some as worn by or presented to people, to hint the necessity of restraining anger.

誡 From *words* and *warning;* it is often used with the last, and is sometimes mistaken for ˏch'ing 誠 truly.
chié

A rule of conduct; a precept, an injunction; a warning; to deter, as by a penalty; to dehort; to prohibit.

禁丨 to forbid; prohibitions.

十丨 the Ten Commandments

規丨 rules of conduct, things to be avoided.

敎丨 to teach and warn.

有丨 to lie under a prohibition.

大丨 an injunction of importance.

懲一丨百 to rebuke one warns a hundred — from transgressing.

悈 To enjoin on, to urge one to obey; to charge.
chié

Read *kih,* Hasty, urgent.

Read *keh,* Headstrong; alarmed, fearful of.

介 The old form resembles 爪 *scales,* but is composed of 人 *man* over 八 *eight,* for every man has his limit; interchanged with the next two.
chié

An assistant, an attendant, one who announces visitors; to assist, to wait on; to border on, to enlarge; a limit, conterminous; firm, immovable; armor of mail, a cuirass; the carapace of tortoises, crabs, &c.; a privy; because, for; small, petty, trifling; alone, one single person or animal, and used as a classifier for a person; icicles on trees; good; great; to be or make great; resolute; to act or represent.

一丨不以取諸人 he would not take a straw from anybody.

丨人之寵 because of human affection.

我一丨武夫 I am only a soldier.

丨爾景福 may he enlarge your high happiness.

鱗丨類 the scaly and shelly tribes, — in zoölogy.

纖丨 petty, unimportant.

小丨 a valet, a waiting-boy.

節丨 well principled; firm.

丨於兩可 it can appertain to (or border on) either side.

木丨 or 樹丨 trees covered with ice, — like mail.

保丨 an agricultural assistant.

以丨眉壽 to comfort and cherish your great age.

耿丨 or 丨丨 earnest, upright.

不丨意他 I do not bear any grudge against him.

不丨其意 it is of no consequence, it is immaterial.

价 From *man* and *petty;* used with the last.
chié

One who assists, a waiter; good; great.

佋丨 avant-couriers.

貴丨 or 令丨 your servant.

丨人惟藩 only a good man can be a protector or fence.

芥 From *plant* and *petty.*
chié

The mustard plant, including also other pungent *crucifera;* unimportant, trifling, petty; a mote, an atom.

丨菜 mustard greens. (*Sinapis.*)

丨蘭菜 a coarse vegetable common at Canton, like a cabbage or *Brassica.*

大丨菜 a long white turnip, grown in the northern provinces.

丨末 or 丨花麪 pulverized or ground mustard

荆丨 a hirsute species of sage (*Salvia plebeia*), used in medical preparations.

水丨菜 kinds of cress, like the *Sisymbrium iria*, *Eruca*, and similar plants.

蘿蔔生兒丨有孫 the turnip has a son while the mustard has a grandson;—it grows so fast.

丨草 a bit of grass, a sliver, a mote; a contemptible person.

丨蔕 unimportant, like a fish-bone in one's throat; of no note, a matter that need cause no alarm; hence 丨子 a mustard seed, is used by the Budhists for a measure (*sarshapa*) the ten-millionth part of a *yodjana*.

尬 chié' To walk irregularly; to walk awry.

尷丨事體 to go on doing things at hap-hazard and making little progress.

玠 chié' A small tablet, the 丨圭, made of jade; it was over a foot long, and held by officials in olden times when in court as an index of their rank.

疥 chié' From *disease* and *petty*.

A scratch, a little sore; an itching place; the itch; to scratch.

瘡丨 an itch sore.

甲丨 a variety of lepra or scab.

丨癩之疾 a mere scratch, a trifling sore.

'長丨的 to have the itch.

癬丨之患 [no more serious] than a ringworm or an itch.

丨膿 pus, matter in a sore.

界 chié' From *field* and *petty*; the radical is sometimes written at the side; occurs used with its primitive.

A division between fields to mark different owners; a limit; a boundary, a border, a terminus, a frontier; to limit, to draw a line; to sunder; to sow strife; in *Budhism*, a world, a sphere, a division, a condition.

山丨 confines of a grave (*Cantonese.*).

丨石 a boundary stone.

交丨 a frontier; to border on; adjoining.

境丨 the boundary, the frontier.

丨限 or 丨至 restricted; a limit in time or place.

丨址 the edge, as of a lot.

以禮爲丨 decorum must mark the limit.

意丨 the world of thought; a Budhist term (*manodgatu*) for the mental faculties.

世丨 this world, the age, the times; society, people, men, hence, 下丨 the lower regions; and 上中下三丨 the three worlds heaven, earth and hell.

丨尺 a rule with which to measure.

三丨 the upper, middle, and lower worlds,—heaven, man, and earth, over which gods are placed; the Budhists call them the world of desire, form, and void or formless (*tri-lokya*).

蚧 chié' A red spotted lizard, the 蛤丨 six inches long, with small scales and a long tail, common in damp places; it is considered to be transformed from a swallow, and is employed as a tonic or aphrodisiac; this name is usually applied to the gecko, but the description answers rather better to a species of chameleon or *Anolis*.

衸 chié' Facings on clothes, or the stripes on a uniform; long robes.

Read *hiai'*. Coverings for the knees.

衩丨 broad knee-bands, made like wide garters.

魪 chié' The sole fish or plaice; the flounder; it is called 達沙魚 and 左口 in Canton; 鞋底魚 in Amoy; 龍鄉魚 or 龍舌丨 in Peking; and 比目魚 in other places.

砎 chié' Hard, like stone; rocky; firm, immovable.

丨如金石 firm as iron and stone,—as an obstinate man.

屆 届 chié' From 尸 *corpse* and an old form of *kw'ai'* 塊 *clod* contracted; *q.d.* the body returned to a clod of earth, or placed on clods, and got to its end; the second form is most used.

To reach to, to arrive at in time or place; a limit; the set time; termination, summit.

丨期 punctual; at the time.

天丨 the horizon.

靡丨靡究 without limit or end;—said of curses.

節丨夏至 it is now the summer solstice.

無遠弗丨 there was no place [the virtue of Yü,] did not reach to.

罔識所丨 nobody knows where they reach to;—said of mountain wilds.

犗 chié' From *ox* and *to injure*.

A gelded bull; a strong animal, as castrated ones usually are.

丨刑 the punishment of castration.

丯 chié' Plants growing up in a confused manner, which the character is supposed to delineate; it is not the same as *fung* 丰 easy.

K'IAI.

Old sounds, ka. *In Canton*, k'ai *and* hai; — *in Swatow*, k'ai; — *in Amoy*, k'ai; — *in Fuhchau*, k'ai; — *in Shanghai*, k'a; — *in Chifu*, k'iai.

揩 ˏch'ié From *hand* and *altogether*.

To rub, to wipe with the hand; to brush, to clean; a kind of long drum or sounding-board.

丨乾淨 wipe [the shoes] clean.

丨磨 to deface by rubbing; to rub and chafe; to scour off.

丨埋牆 rub it against the wall; (*Cantonese*.)

行過丨親人 to brush by one.

丨面 to wipe the face.

丨排 to rush against one, as in the streets; to elbow one's way.

楷 ˋch'ié Name of a straight, graceful, and durable tree which grows on the grave of Confucius; a model, a pattern, an example.

模丨 a mold; a precedent; a rule; an exemplar.

丨書 the square, elegant style of Chinese characters, mostly used in printing fine books.

筆甚端丨 your penmanship is very regular.

强丨 a precise and firm disposition.

鍇 ˏch'ié A local name in Kiangsi for pure white iron; strong firm.

KIANG.

Old sounds, kong *and* kiung. *In Canton* kong *and* keung; — *in Swatow*, kang, kiàng, *and* kian; — *in Amoy*, kang, kiòng, *and* kòng; — *in Fuhchau*, kiòng, kòng, kaung, hòng, kăng, *and* hung; — *in Shanghai*, kong, kièng, k'ièng, *and* kong; — *in Chifu*, kiang.

江 ˏchiang From *water* and *work*; it is etymologically explained by 共 and 貢, a river being the place where *all* waters flow, and on which *revenue* goes.

A river; par excellence, the Chang kiang 長丨 or Long River, also known as Ta kiang 大丨 or Great River, and in Kiangsu as the Yang-tsz' kiang 揚子丨, the river in the province of Yang, one of the nine provinces of Yü; *met.* a country; a province.

兩丨 formerly denoted Kiangnan and Kiangsi, and now includes the three provinces of Kiangsu, Nganhwui, and Kiangsi.

丨山 or 丨河 the empire, the country, the land.

各丨貨物 goods from every province.

過丨兄弟 brothers in affliction.

丨米 a name for glutinous rice.

大丨不擇細流 the Great River does not reject the little stream; — liberal-minded.

丨山如畫 the prospect is like a picture.

行丨湖 peddlers, sellers, of nostrums, jugglers, tramps.

九丨 nine affluents of the Yangtsz'.

丨湖客 itinerant traders or professional men; hence 老丨湖 is a man who knows a ruse, a tricky fellow, one who has seen a thing or two; a traveler, a well-informed man.

丨豬 or 丨豚 a porpoise found in the Yangtsz'.

丨右 and 丨左 the south and north sides, or right and left banks of the Yangtsz' River.

外丨人 a northerner, one from beyond the river. (*Cantonese*.)

丨裏來水裏去 the water came and went by the river; — *i. e.* he wastes money as fast as he gets it.

丨星 a star near the Milky Way, which helps people across the water.

姜 ˏchiang From *woman* and *sheep*; *q. d.* a shepherdess; it must be distinguished from ˏk'iang 羌 a tribe.

The surname of Shin-nung 神農, derived from 丨水 the river of this name.

丨太公 or 丨子牙 a famous general, B. C. 1122; — when his name is used as a charm, the phrase 在此 He is here, is added.

不丨 a river, supposed to be one of the headwaters of the River Yang-tsz'.

舡 ˏchiang To lift up, in which sense it is a synonym of ˏkang 扛 to carry on a pole.

僵 ˏchiang From *man* and *boundary*; it is nearly the same as the next.

To lie down; stretched out; stiffened, prostrate; to push over.

丨仆 to fall; fallen, prostrate.

倔丨 to get vexed with, to oppose; to be willful.

手凍丨了 hands stiff and benumbed with cold.

丨臥 to recline, as if asleep; stretched at full length.

硬白丨 willful, immovable, set in his way.

殭 From *death* and a *boundary*; used with the last and the next.

c'hiang Withered, stiff; dead, but not corrupted; lying as if dead, senseless; no feeling, as the face in a freezing wind; stolid, unmoved; rigid; scirrhus, as the skin or a gland.

丨尸 a corpse; a body in a trance.

丨性 immovable, no feeling.

直丨丨 stretched out stiff, as when in a fit; also actually dead.

丨臉子 one who never changes countenance, impassive, imperturbable.

丨蠶 silkworms stiffened, which they do just before weaving the cocoons.

僵 Silkworms turning white and dying from weather or bad

c'hiang food are called 丨白; they are used medicinally.

疆 畺 From 土 *eath* and 彊 *strong*; the second form is the primitive, and intended to show the partitions which divide two fields.

c'hiang A limit, a boundary, a border; to draw a limit; to bound or define a frontier.

丨界 a limit, a border; the frontier.

丨域 the marches of a country; the limits of a prefecture.

無丨 ilimitable, boundless.

出丨 to go to another province; to emigrate.

新丨 or 丨土 the new frontier, denotes Turkestan, conquered by K'anghi and Kienlung.

戰丨塲 the field of battle.

封丨大臣 the high officer in charge of the frontier.

韁 繮 From *silk* or *leather* and to *limit*; the bridle keeps a horse in bounds.

c'hiang A bridle; but particularly, the reins of a bridle, made of silk or leather.

丨皮 bridle and reins.

放丨 or 鬆丨 and 收丨 to loosen and draw in the reins; to slack off and restrain.

野馬無丨 a wild, unbridled horse; a runagate, a demirep.

馬丨 a bridle, a headstall.

賞用黃丨 [the Emperor] allowed him to use a yellow bridle.

橿 The handle or helve of a hoe; another term for the

c'hiang 萬年木 *i. e.* the everlasting wood, used for bars and parts of carriages, especially pins and wedges.

丨丨 vigorous, brawny.

薑 蘁 姜 From *plant* and a *limit*; the second and full form is now mostly disused, but the third is common, though not correct.

c'hiang Ginger; applied also to other plants of the same family as the *Alpinia*, *Amomum*, *Curcuma*, and those in which the aromatic taste is perceptible.

生丨 fresh ginger.

糖丨 preserved ginger.

丨黃 a yellow dye, turmeric.

黃丨粉 or 黃丨材料 curry-powder.

請飲丨酒 to invite one to drink ginger wine — after a birth; hence in Canton, where the custom prevails, 開丨 denotes having a child.

子丨 or 紫丨 or 丨芽兒 tender ginger; the small ginger roots; their color is reddish.

艮丨 or 高艮丨 galangal root (*Alpinia galanga*); it comes from Kao-cheu fu in the southwest of Kwangtung; its fruit, known as galanga cardamoms, is used in medicine.

丨通神明 ginger exhilirates and clears the system.

醬丨 salted ginger relish, a condiment.

煨丨 to toast ginger by throwing it on the fire wrapped in wet paper.

礓 Gravel, small stones.

c'hiang 丨點淺波 the pebbles in the shallow brooks.

茳 A leguminous plant, (*Cassia tora*,) whose seeds called 丨

c'hiang 芒英明 are used in eye diseases; they are small, bean-like seeds, black and shining.

豇 豨 From *pulse* and *work*; the second and unusual form is also defined a Mongol bean.

c'hiang A beautiful variety of small kidney bean, common in northern China, a species of *Dolichos* with very long pods; the beans are called 白丨荳 and 青丨荳, both green and white, representing two species; the pods are eaten as 菜丨 or string beans.

丨荳辮子 a cue like a bean-pod.

矼 From *stone* and *work*; it is used with *˛kang* 杠 a *spar*.

c'hiang A bridge of stepping stones; a stone foot-bridge; reliable.

徒丨 a way-side or foot-bridge.

德厚信丨 his virtue was great and his words sincere.

跨石丨 to stride across the stones.

講 From *words* and crossing *beams*; *i. e.* speech blended harmoniously.

'chiang To converse, to speak, to narrate, to explain; to unfold; to discourse, to preach upon; to investigate; to plan, to discuss; to confer together; discourse, explanation; speech, conversation.

沒丨究 disagreeable; not well tasted; inelegant.

丨求 or 丨究 to inquire into the truth of; to analyze, to search out, for the purpose of teaching.

丨究得很 exceedingly fine, as a dress; splendid, fine, first rate; delicious; a term of praise.

丨古 to tell the old stories, to talk of old times; to preach the Gospel is sometimes so termed.

丨和 to propose peace, to talk about a settlement.

丨習 to practice, to get accustomed to.

丨解文藝 to lecture on literature.

不再丨 no need of speaking more, I know all about it.

丨心 honest talk, a real opinion.

丨面子 on good terms with; to say pleasant things.

丨東丨西 to carp at this and that.

丨妥了 all is agreed upon; finally arranged.

丨經 a smooth-tongued salesman.

丨事 to attend to business; to speak or request about a matter.

丨話 to speak; set discourse; talk, speech.

這且不丨 we will not speak of that now.

丨章兒 a great talker, a chatter-box.

耩 ʻchiang To plow, to cultivate the soil.

雨下透了該丨地 when the rain has moistened the ground, then plow it up.

膙 ʻchiang An unauthorized character. *Skin* that has become *hard* on the hand and foot; callous skin; a corn.

修去丨子 to remove bunions.

蔃 ʻchiang From *plant* and to *force*. Small roots; the branches of roots.

樹丨 roots of trees, those which are near the surface.

無根丨之人 an untrustworthy man.

竹丨 bamboo canes; whangees.

丨朮 a white day lily, a species of *Hemerocallis*.

襁 **繦** ʻchiang A swathing-cloth to carry infants pick-a-pack, or which serves as a cradle for them.

丨褓 the cloth which confines a child; it is sometimes a wadded sack, others make it square with corner cords.

丨負 to strap infants on the back, to carry pick-a-pack, like a papoose.

鏹 ʻch'iang Money, coin; the cord which runs through a number of cash; a string of a thousand cash; to thread cash on a cord.

冥丨 paper ingots burned to the dead.

白丨 silver in bullion.

藏丨巨萬 he had myriads of money in store.

港 ʻchiang From *water* and a *lane* as the phonetic. Streams diverging as one ascends a river; a rivulet entering the sea; the entrance of a river; a port; a reach, the channel in a stream; a firth, an estuary, a ford, an arm of the sea.

收丨 to run in for shelter, as boats.

丨口 a port, a mart.

領丨船 pilot boats; tug-boats.

本丨船 native junks, those which ply only on the river.

各丨貨 products of every clime.

船丨 an anchorage.

荻丨漁燈 the reedy creeks where the fishermen's lamps—sparkle as they fish.

丨脚 the embouchure; a port.

丨脚船 an old name at Canton for ships from India.

說得入丨 he talks very reasonably.

Read *hung*ʼ Vacant.

丨洞 empty caves; those which open into each other.

傋 chiangʼ Unsubmissive.

傋 unsubdued, as rebels; contumacious.

洚 chiangʼ From *water* and to *descend; used* for ˛*hung* 洪 a flood, and also read ˛*hiang*.

Water overflowing; a stream not keeping to its banks, and running over the country; an inundation; name of a tributary of the old Yellow River, flowing easterly from Shansi across through Kwangping fu to the River Wéi.

丨水儆余 the inundation frightened me.

丨洞之世 a reckless, dissolute age,—*scil.* like a shoreless sea.

絳 chiangʼ A deep, red color like the petals of the shoe-flower or *Hibiscus rosa-sinensis*; rosy, crimson.

丨工 the dyer's art.

丨紫 a purplish or deep rose color.

丨州 a small inferior department, and 丨縣 a district, both in the southwest of Shansi on the Yellow River.

設丨帳以受徒 to display a red curtain and get scholars,—refers to a noted scholar in the Taʻng dynasty, and has become a term for starting a school.

蜂 chiangʼ An unauthorized character used in the North for ˛*hung* 虹 the rainbow; it has been composed to represent its common sound, and offers an instance of the use of a phonetic in the formation of new characters.

降 **夅** chiangʼ From a *place* and to *descend;* the second ancient form is now only used as a primitive.

To descend from a higher level; to come from the sky; to fall, as rain; to come into the world, as Christ did; to send down, as from the gods or the sovereign; to confer, to inflict on; to come to, said to another in politeness; to degrade, to reduce in rank, as an officer, or as a prefecture to a district; to subject, to reduce to submission; to spare, to deal leniently.

丨落 to descend, as a bird or snow.

丨生 to be born into, to become incarnate.

丨世 to come in the world, as a supernatural being.

丨福 to bless, to send happiness.

丨階相迎 to go down the steps to meet a guest.

丨級留任 to degrade in rank but retain in office, — in order to give the officer a chance to do better.

你幾時光丨 when will you give me the light of your presence? — a fulsome phrase.

何勞下丨 how much trouble you have taken to visit me.

明升暗丨 apparent promotion but a real descent—from power, as when one is shelved to a high nominal post.

丨調 to reduce and transfer to another post.

誕丨奇才 Heaven has sent us a great genius.

丨香 or 宿丨 a resinous wood like cedar, burned by the Taoists at worship.

流星丨下來 a meteor fell.

丨火 to reduce a fever.

Read ˏ*hiang*. To submit; to return to loyalty and allegiance, to throw down arms and give in; to reduce to terms.

投丨 to give up rebellion.

歸丨 to return to lawful rule.

丨兵 troops coming in to their duty.

丨魔 to exorcise or bind the demons or efreets; one furious-looking temple guardian brandishes a 丨魔杵 or restraining-demon club.

丨龍伏虎 he reduces the dragon and humbles the tiger; — said of Yoh Wang or the Chinese Esculapius.

丨婁 a star in Aries, which brings fair weather, when it is on the meridian in the fifth moon.

丨服 to surrender to rightful authority.

In *Cantonese*. A perpendicular line.

打丨 to erase or mark out a passage; also to fire at a picture of Shwang-kiang shǎn 霜丨神 in October.

糨 糡 *chiang*ˀ Starch; to starch.

丨子 or 丨糊 or 漿丨 starch; congee used fo. starching.

打丨子 to starch.

丨稠麻子 a face marked with the small-pox.

稀的丨的 starch it slightly.

強 *chiang*ˀ To hate, to dislike.

決丨 willful, unaccommodating.

傲丨 disobedient; to resist parental authority.

K'IANG.

Old sounds, k'ong *and* k'iung. *In Canton*, k'éung, kéung, *and* hong; — *in Swatow*, kⁿió, kiang, *and* k'ông; — *in Amoy*, k'iông *and* kông; — *in Fuhchau*, k'iông *and* kiông; — *in Shanghai*, ts'ièng, k'ièng, *and* jièng; — *in Chifu*, k'iang.

羗 羌 ˏ*ch'iang* From 羊 a *sheep* and 人 a *man; q. d.* a shepherd, the distinctive features of the savage western tribes being to rear sheep; the first is the common form, and sometimes wrongly used for ˏ*kiang* 姜 a surname; the second is used for ˏ*kiang* 薑 ginger.

An ancient tribe in Tangut, shepherd nomads living from early times west of Sz'ch'uen and Kansuh; they are commonly known as 戎丨 and 丨胡, but the name cannot yet be identified with Indian or Scythian tirbes; some think it denotes the Kurus of Hindu legends; contrary, strong, obstinate; educated, elegant; an interjection; to return.

丨戎 or 丨人 tribes on the west of China.

自彼氐丨莫敢不來享 even from those Ti-k'iang tribes they dared not but come with their offerings.

丨內恕己 Ah! he excused himself,—in order to employ others.

Read ˏ*kiang*. In want.

丨量 famished and helpless, — said of fledgelings.

蜣 ˏ*ch'iang* A term for such coleopterous insects as the *Ateuchus* or *Scarabeus*, which lay their eggs in dung.

蛣丨 a small species of Scarabeus, to which an apothecary is sometimes likened; it is also called 推丸 the pill-roller, a word like *pilularia* in its application.

丨蜋之志在于轉丸 the skill of the tumble-dung is seen best in rolling its ball.

啌 ˏ*ch'iang* The sobbing of infants, the unceasing wail of children.

腔 䐁 ˏ*ch'iang* From *flesh* and *empty*; the second form is unusual, and confined to tunes, but is interchanged with the other in certain senses.

Hollow, vacant, puffed; a hollow bone; a horse's flank; the breast or throat, when the head is gone; a tune, the air of a ballad; the patois or brogue of a place; vain, pretentious, puffed up.

丨子大 pretending, ostentatious.
丨調 a tune, a singing tone; clear enunciation, distinctly spoken.
裝丨 unreal, specious, assuming; affecting to speak in falsetto.
京丨 a northern style of speaking.
你改過丨來 you must alter your tune — or conduct.
裝面丨 to do eye-service, to slight things.
二簧丨 and 梆子丨 terms for a drawling and for a high key in singing on the boards.
滿丨怨氣 her breast was filled with bitter griefs.
人丨子 a headless neck.
按丨合拍的 you must make the tune and instrument harmonize; — *met.* to work in accord, to get along well.
高丨 treble notes, high but not falsetto.
昆丨戲 play-actors from Suchau
捧丨兒 you are fooling me; I think you are a humbug.
丨口好 an excellent tone or diction, in singing or reading.
起丨 to rise in one's demands, to strike for higher wages.

羫 Interchanged with the last.
ch'iang The ribs or skeleton of a sheep; a sheep's tendons; a classifier of sheep, after they have been butchered.
一丨羊 one butchered sheep's carcase. (*Pekingese.*)

Read *k'ung'*. Dried mutton.

啌 An impediment in the throat, as phlegm or a swelling; the
ch'iang sound of coughing.

瘗 A disease of the throat like quinsy, or as if something
ch'iang was sticking in it; empty, as a valley.

腔 The *bone* that is *empty* or useless, *viz.* the end bone of the
ch'iang spine, the 髗丨 or *os coccygis*.

椌 From *wood* and *empty*.
ch'iang' A kind of hollow wooden image, or sounding-board, smaller and similar to the *chuh*, 柷 and used to mark music by running a stick across the ridged back.

強 彊 From 弓 a *bow* and 畺 a *border*; the first form is the most common, and considered by some to be not altogether synonymous with the other.
ch'iang' A black bug or weevil in rice; a strong bow; violent, headstrong, determined, firm; the violent; violence; boisterous, surly, overbearing; relying on force, or regardless of right; sturdy, brawny, full grown; *met.* laborers; in *arithmetic*, a remainder, an excess; a term of comparison, better for.
丨水 acids, as 硝丨水 nitric acid; — a foreign term.
丨乞 to beg with threats.
丨壯 or 丨士 vigorous, hale, in the prime of life, forty years old; *met.* sturdy troops.
他比我丨 he is cleverer than I.
丨弱 strong and weak, robust and puny.
爭丨弱 to wrangle; try who is the strongest.
丨暴 or 丨横 truculent, peevish.
丨盜 a robber, a highwayman, a bandit.
丨些兒 a little improved, stronger, better, brighter.
五軍兵丨 the five divisions of an army.
丨賣 to compel one to sell; a forcible sale.
舌丨 double-tongued.
自丨 enduring, persevering, firm.
持丨 violent; boastful.
鵲之丨丨 how decided and valorous are the magpies!
算是丨了 or 以爲丨 I think that will be better; that will be more agreeable.
賞賜百千丨 he gave him more than a hundred thousand.
丨哉矯 how firm in his energy!
必丨命不丨 his will is strong, but his fate is against him.
雖柔必丨 though weak, he will get stronger.
剛丨 strong and willful.
少飲丨如醉 to drink little is better than to be drunk.

In *Shanghai*, a synonym of *tsien'* 賤 for which only the first form is employed. Cheap, low-priced, to think cheap.
價錢太丨 the price is too cheap,
男兒當自丨 a young man ought to control himself.
頂丨 very cheap.

Read *'k'iang*, but confined to the first form. To compel, to force; to invigorate, to strengthen; to try; to prevail on against the inclination.
勉丨 constrained to do; to force one's self to do.
丨求不得 you can't obtain it; you can't get it out of him, as wisdom from a fool.
丨說 a forced confession.
丨而後可 at first he was unwilling, but afterwards he did it.
屈丨 forced to bear; springing back; resilient; elasticity.
丨忍 nerved himself to bear it.
丨性 set in his way; answering back.
富貴莫丨求 rich and honorable men should not seek it by underhand ways.
丨派着 to set one to do a thing for which he is unfitted.
丨行 forced to do.
木丨 stiff as a stick, mulish; can't be forced.
雖丨記猶不清 though I try, I do not recall it clearly to mind.

勥 To urge on, to exert one's
ch'iang' strength; to pursue after, to resist forcibly.

弶 A trap or gin set in the path to catch animals; a net for
ch'iang' birds.

KIAO.

Old sounds, kio, kok, kot, gio, *and* gok. *In Canton*, kao *and* kiu;—*in Swatow*, kao, kiǒ, kié, kⁿa, *and* kué;—*in Amoy*, kao, kiao, *and* hiao;—*in Fuhchau*, kau, kieu, hieu, kéu, ka, kao, *and* kiǒ:—*in Shanghai*, kio, ko, *and* jio;—*in Chifu*, kiao.

交 ˏ*chiao* Said to be changed from 大 *great* to represent the appearance of a man's legs when crossed, or the crossing of lines in writing.

To blend, to unite, to join; to deliver up or hand over to, to communicate with; to pay to, to exchange; to copulate; trade, barter, dealings with; contiguous, conterminous; intercourse of society, friendship; intimately; the part of a garment that folds over the breast; placed before a horary character shows that the hour has just begun; prefixed to other verbs denotes a present action, as 丨寄 transmiting it; 丨託 requesting him to do it.

丨盤 to deliver over,—as a shop to another.

丨代清楚 to hand everything over, to get free of the job.

丨手 to hand to one; a trading constituent; also hand to hand fighting.

丨齒 to dovetail; to interlock.

丨錯 interlocking, like the crooked frontier of two countries; to pass around, as a wine cup.

丨合 sexual commerce.

心丨 a cordial friendship.

丨涉 or 丨參 intimate with, connected, on good terms.

其丨也以道 his friendships were likewise reasonable.

丨鋒 to join battle.

丨脚 to cross the legs.

丨接 to receive and entertain—a visitor.

丨遊甚廣 his friends are scattered far and wide.

雨雪丨加 rain and snow mingled.

淡丨 a slight acquaintance.

丨加 to pile on each other.

絕丨 to dissolve friendship.

丨不準你 I cannot come up to your standard.

丨情 pleasant intercourse.

丨易 trade between two; to barter; to swap.

丨椅 an arm chair.

喝丨杯 to drink the wedding cup.

難打丨道 one who is hard to get along with, a dangerous comrade.

丨申時 just three o'clock P.M.

丨白露後 after the term White Dew begins.

四五月之丨 last of the fourth and first of the fifth moon.

丨丨黃鳥 the yellow orioles flit about.

蛟 ˏ*chiao* The dragon of thickets and morasses, which has scales, but no horn; the description, size, and figure are intended to denote the crocodile, which has been nearly driven into Siam from southern China, and is now regarded as mythical, the gavial family; the popular idea contained in the name 螞蟻丨 or ant-dragon, that it is gradually produced in the earth by myriads of ants, is curiously like the snakes that are found in ants' nests near Bahia in Brazil.

騰丨起鳳 [he will become] a rising dragon and soaring phœnix,—*i. e.* a great scholar.

丨龍豈是池中物 how can a crocodile be reared in a fishtank?—*met.* how can a Cæsar be kept in a village?

茭 ˏ*chiao* Dried grass, fodder ready for storing; a kind of jointed marsh grass cultivated for its celery-like stems called 丨笋 at Canton, 丨白 at Shanghai, and 丨瓜 at Peking; the roots or rhizomes remain in the soft ground, and the young shoots when boiled are white and tender like the early bamboo shoots; the leaves are broad like Job's tears (Coix), and the seeds blackish.

丨耳菜 a water greens obtained from the stalks of a small wild grass similar to this.

丨牧 to cut grass for fodder.

峙乃芻丨 prepare the forage.

丨塘司 the township in which Whampoa lies.

郊 ˏ*chiao* From *region* and *adjoining*.

Waste or forest land near the frontier; an open common beyond the city, a suburb; a place proper to have a sacrifice; a suburb; an altar; the worship of heaven and earth at the solstices, anciently offered to the 五帝 Five Rulers, but since the Ming dynasty (A.D. 1369), confined to Shangti.

丨外 remote wilds, savage lands, not yet reached by civilization.

丨廟 temple to heaven.

丨天 imperial sacrifice to Heaven.

農丨 farmsteads, villages.

丨社之禮所以事上帝也 the ceremonies at the solstices to the heavens and land were in worship of Shangti.

鵁 ˏ*chiao* A long legged bird, the 丨鶄, described as having a mallard's body, long legs, and a reddish feathery crest; the color is dun yellowish; it nestles on high trees, and makes its nest in their hollows; the young bite hold of its wings, and are thus carried down to get their food of fish; another name is 魚丨 fish ibis; it is probably the egret, or a bird akin to the ibis.

丨鵁 also called 魚丨 and 頭丨 is another sea-bird, more like the cormorant or smew.

鮫 *chiao* A large shark, so called from the blending of its stripes, (a *Scyllium?*) whose skin affords good shagreen; the description resembles that of the viviparous shark.

丨鮒 a skate or sting-ray of immense size; a kraken.

丨人 a mermaid, said to weep pearls.

馬丨郎 the mango fish (*Polynemus xanthonemus*) common at Macao, from which some have erroneously derived the foreign name of the town.

嬌 *chiao* From *woman* and *curved*; it is much used for famale names.

Beautiful, delicate, comely, graceful; dear, lovely; an elegant, affected manner; a stylish figure; to pet, to bring up delicately; indulged, petted; to cry for.

丨貴 dainty, delicate; a high-born lady.

丨養 to spoil by over fondness, as to wink at a child's vices.

丨客 the distinguished guest, *i.e.* one newly married into a family, a son-in-law.

詐丨 teasing, crying for, as spoiled children do.

丨聲 a kind, winning voice; a high, querulous tone, like a woman's voice.

丨妻 my dear wife, my dear.

丨兒 my pet, my darling daughter.

黃丨 the yellow beauty, *i.e.* wine, spirits.

丨態 lady-like, genteel.

丨媚 fresh, beautiful, a Hebe.

丨羞 bashful, retiring, modest.

若得阿丨當以金屋貯之 if I can get Akiao for my wife, I'll keep her in a golden house; *met.* doting love.

丨姿 sprightly, winsome.

妖丨 delicate, as a tint.

丨嬈 seductive, fascinating, siren like.

丨艷 vivid, lustrous, bright; gay, as flowers.

喚丨娘 calls the handsome girls, the name of the racket used by artificial flower peddlers.

驕 *chiao* A horse six cubits high; a wild, restive horse; proud, haughty, presuming on; ungovernable; disdainful, self-confident; to glory in, to be proud of.

丨傲 overbearing, haughty, proud.

丨矜 or 丨誇 presumptuous.

丨奢淫佚 pride, extravagance, lewdness, and idleness.

丨縱 willfully conceited.

僨丨 impetuous, testy.

丨泰 great self-assurance.

憍 *chiao* From *heart* and *curved*; resembles the last.

A low-minded man flushed with success; bragging; self-indulgent; kind, compassionate towards the sad.

鷮 *chiao* From *bird* and *curved*.

A species of long tailed pheasant, probably allied to the barred tailed or Reeves' pheasant (*Syrmaticus*), named 丨 from its cluck.

丨雉 the long tailed or Tartar pheasant.

儌 *chiao* To do, to act; intent on.

丨倖 lucky; beyond one's deserts or expectations; prosperous; this phrase is written 僥倖 in some books.

憿 *chiao* From *heart* and *gliding*; like the last.

Lucky; prosperous.

丨憭 to honestly.

Read *kih*, Hasty; a quick temper.

漻 *chiao* Name of a river; a vast prospect.

丨滈浩汗 illimitable; vast and dreary, as the ocean or a barren pampas.

澆 *chiao* From *water* and *eminent*.

To sprinkle, as by hand; to irrigate, to moisten; to dip; illiberal; perfidious.

丨花 to water flowers.

丨燭 to dip candles.

丨灌之功 diligent in dressing a garden.

丨風 an infamous custom, bad reputation of a country.

丨薄 unfaithful, ungrateful contrary to.

Read *liao*. An eddy, a place where the water whirls.

嘐 *chiao* The screaming of a cock, as when he is caught; boasting, bragging, bombast; alarmed.

鷄鳴丨丨 the fowls are crowing and cackling.

Read *kiao*. Talkative, garrulous.

丨啁 verbose.

丨丨然其志也 he boasted and talked about all his plans.

膠 *chiao* From *flesh* and *flying high*; occurs used with the next.

Glue; gum, such as exudes from peach trees; glutinous jelly; to glue, to cohere; to deceive by sticking to one in apparent friendship; viscid, cohering, as potter's clay; sticky, joined or sticking together; obstinate, pertinacious, stupid, set; intimate, compacted, bound by a pledge.

牛皮丨 cow's glue.

黃明丨 clarified glue.

魚丨 isinglass, fish-glue.

麪筋丨 wheat-flour and lime mixed for joiner's work.

丨鍊 well-boiled glue.

丨粘 to glue.

東丨 an old name for a kind of prefectural college.

丨丨擾擾乎 what utter confusion and turmoil!

既見君子德音孔丨 when I see the princely man, his virtuous fame draws him close to me.

丨固力 the power of cohesion.
丨連 banded for one purpose, either good or bad.
丨漆相投 united as glue and varnish, very intimate.
如丨之愛 unalterable love.
美人丨 bandoline used by women in dressing the hair.
三仙丨 a medicine of tortoise-shell, deer's antlers, and tiger's bones boiled together.
阿丨 a medical glue named from Tung-o hien 東阿縣 in Shantung, where the Glue Well 丨井 furnishes water possessing peculiar properties in which ass-skin is boiled seven days; it is taken as a tonic.
丨州 a maritime district on the southwest side of Shantung promontory.
丨葛 unsteady, irregular; to offset and confuse, as in rendering accounts; used with the next.

轇 ˏchiao Something indistinctly seen in the distance; confused.
丨輵不清 the accounts are confused; the mode of managing the affair is perplexing; the reference is to a row of spears on a chariot glancing in the eye; it is applied to offsetting debts, or transferring from one account to the other, so as to juggle and confuse them.

艽 芁 ˏchiao The second form is disused, though deemed to be most proper for the name of the plant.
A medicinal plant, the 秦丨 found in Shansi; it is one of the Acanthaceæ, and supposed to be allied to the Indian *Gendarussa;* it has leaves like lettuce, which grow as a tuft from the top of the short stem; thread can be made from the root, which is also used in rheumatism and jaundice.

Read ˏk'iu. A remote wild; the lair or form of a wild beast.
丨野 a waste wilderness, a barren.
丨背 burrows of marmots, said to be arranged in regular rows; these cannot well be wild hogs, as the native dictionary describes them, but may be like the Syrian coney, the *Hyrax* or daman.

晈 皎 ˊchiao From *white* and *crossing;* the second and ancient form is similar to the next.
The bright, white face of the moon; an immaculate, pure white; effulgent, splendid, as the sun.
丨潔 clean and pure.
丨日 clear daylight, sunshine.
丨丨 spotless, unsullied white, as a thing, a reputation, or a colt.
月色丨兮滿畫堂 the bright moonlight filled the gay hall.

皦 ˊchiao Similar to the last.
White and brilliant, like a fine gem, as the opal.
丨丨 the sparkling stars.
則有如丨日在上以監我矣 [if you doubt me,] there is [one] above like the bright sun watching me.

絞 ˊchiao From *silk* and to *cross* as the phonetic.
To bind around, to wrap; to strangle; to twist; to turn, as a crank or windlass; unceremonious, blunt.
丨纜 to twist ropes.
丨緊些 bind it rather tighter.
丨頭布 a turban, such as the Fuhkien sailors wear.
丨紗 to spin thread.
三丨繩 a threefold cord.
丨縊 to strangle one's self.
丨椿 the windlass used to hoist boats up the sluices in the Grand Canal; the stake at which criminals are strangled.
問丨 to condemn to be strangled.
丨死 or 丨犯 to strangle a criminal.
直丨 blunt and severe, as a Cato.
丨刺人非 to pick at and expose people's faults.

Read ˏhiao. Silk of a bluish yellow color; a sash, a bandage.

狡 ˊchiao From *dog* and to *cross.*
Crafty, black poodles with large mouths, such as are reared in the northern provinces, though other descriptions assimilate the animal designated nearer to the genet; wily, crafty, as the doublings of a fox; wild, maddened; cruel; specious, cunning.
丨徒 a wily chap, a sharper.
丨猾 or 丨獪 tricky, fraudulent.
丨計 a wily plan.
丨詐 cunning, deceitful.
丨戾 raging, ungovernable, perverse.
丨童 a young rascal, a street Arab; a clever lad.
丨賴 to force a creditor to take less than his due.
丨棍 a fraudulent villain.
丨犬 a black Peking dog.
丨兎三窟 [he is like] the clever rabbit with his three burrows; *met.* don't trust him.

姣 ˊchiao 㚣 Frequently used for the last, but referring rather to females; the second form is unusual, and also read ˏhiao.
Handsome, pretty; clever, intriguing, flattering; artful.
丨生慣養 a petted, indulged youth with an overbearing, willful disposition.
丨美 beautiful, winsome; captivating.
丨態 attractive, desirous to please, coquettish.
丨童 a pretty and petted lad.
寵而旃丨 he loves [his concubine,] who makes a fool of him.

Read ˏhiao. Lewd, dissolute; amorous, in love.
丨仔 a youth in love.
發丨 in love, passionately attached to (*Cantonese*).

ʿ僬 ʿchiao Like the last.
Handsome, beautiful.
丨好 fair, as a 丨人 or beauty.
丨人僚兮 how fair and graceful — is that lady!

ʿ筊 ʿchiao A rope made of bamboo splinths; a rude musical instrument, called 丨丨, with sixteen tubes, made on the principle of the pandæan pipes.
丨張 atap or coarse matting woven of bamboo splinths and lined with leaves, used in the South for awnings and roofs.

ʿ袨 ʿchiao Long leathern drawers, 丨衧 worn by fishermen when wading through the fens and rivers in their calling, to protect them from wounds and cold; they are often made to reach to the arms.

ʿ幧 ʿchiao Wrappers to strengthen the legs, and prevent varicose veins; used by porters, sedan-bearers, and travelers.

ʿ鐓 ʿchiao A metal handle or ear of a vessel; to cut cloth with shears.
丨開 cut it in two.
丨剪絲羅 cut the silk in two with scissors.

ʿ繳 ʿchiao From *silk* and *gliding* as the phonetic.
Leg wrappers; to reel; to wind around, to bind; to deliver up, to hand over; to surrender, as to an officer; to pay a mulct; to act violently.
丨線 to wind thread.
丨卷 to hand in an essay.
丨呈 to hand over to, to transfer.
丨贓 to deliver up stolen goods.
完丨 everything has been handed over; paid, settled.
丨還 to pay back.
紛丨爭言 to wrangle and browbeat another.

Read *choh*, A thread tied to an arrow to draw it back after shooting.

Read *keh*, Tape bound on the hem of a garment.

ʿ譑 ʿchiao Wordy, verbose; to make known.
糾丨人罪 to divulge the faults of others; to tell on; to complain against.

ʿ觽 ʿchiao Uneven or distorted horns; to raise one horn higher than the other; crooked.
角丨 a horny covering on a scabbard.
郭其目丨其角 he glared at him and raised his horns, as a bull.

ʿ蟜 ʿchiao A species of ant; to wriggle; to stretch out; the writhing of a snake is 夭丨, applied also to its stretching the neck out and drawing it into the hole.

ʿ矯 ʿchiao From *dart* and *curved*; it occurs interchanged with the next.
An arrow issuing from the bow; straight; to bend to; to straighten, to rectify, to correct what is wrong; to falsify, to simulate; to usurp, to exercise undue authority; martial, strong, obstinate; a dissembler; deceitful.
丨命 to feign orders.
丨强 to force the unwilling; exorbitant, unreasonable, unconscionable.
丨健 vigorous, brave.
丨誣上天 falsely assuming the sanction of high Heaven.
丨丨虎臣 his bold, martial leaders.
丨首 to lift up the head.
丨揉造作 to do hard and soft, *i. e.* to act for one's interest, to put on as exigencies suggest.
丨情 one who pretends what he does not feel.
丨託 to make pretense to, as knowledge or acquaintances.

ʿ撟 ʿchiao From *hand* and *curved*; it is interchanged with the last.
To lift up the hand; to grasp; firm, unyielding; feigning, false; to straighten; to twist; to bend, as by fire.
丨然剛折 he will break before he will bend.

Read *kiao*ʾ To take a little, to select; to pry open, to raise with a lever; to stick in; to obstruct.
丨針 to pin together.
丨田杠 a spendthrift; one who can carry off (or spend) a field.
丨眼睛 an eyesore, one who sticks in my eye.
丨住馬脚 to prevent the horse's legs, to hinder, to interfere; to argue against.
丨折 to break in prying.
丨起來 pry it up.
舌丨然而不下 his tongue was stiff and immovable.

In *Cantonese*. To rub; to wipe.
丨嘴 to wipe the mouth.
丨手 the arms akimbo.

ʿ鱎 ʿchiao From *fish* and *curved*, referring to its head and tail, which both turn up.
A fish *Culter* and *Pseudo-culter* found in fresh, clear water, and perhaps allied to the pike, otherwise called 白魚 and 河白魚 white fish; one, it is said, leaped into Wu Wang's boat when he was on his way to destroy Shang; its belly is thin and white, the back blackish; the lower jaw projects and turns upwards; it is sometimes four feet long.

ʿ灚 ʿchiao A small boiler or kettle; to stir up water and make it muddy; to roil.
把糖丨一丨 stir up the sugar a little.
丨蔴醬 to leach ground sesamum seeds with hot water to separate the oil.
丨和勻了 it is mixed very equally

攪 ʻchiao — From *hand* and to *rouse*. To stir up or about; to confuse, to disorder; to beguile into doing evil; to annoy, to incommode; to excite, to make discontented.

丨亂 to make a disturbance, to raise a row; to throw into disorder, as banditti.

打丨你 I have incommoded you, said by a visitor.

丨是丨非 to dispute warmly.

祗丨我心 designing only to perturb my mind.

日丨夜丨 constantly doing evil, as thieves and gamblers.

混丨 impudent interference.

丨匀 mixed evenly.

丨唆 to annoy and provoke.

丨星 a blackleg, a baleful star.

丨擾 to embroil, to stir up, as sedition; to stand out against others, as the single juryman.

敿 ʻchiao — To roll up many things, or tie them fast; to tie round and round.

丨乃干 tie the spears fast.

連丨 or 數丨 tied up tightly, as with cords.

㽱 ʻchiao — A colic with gripes.

丨腸痧 the Asiatic cholera.

丨肚 griping pains in the bowels.

轎 chiao' — From *carriage* and *curved*. A small covered chair, such as can cross a mountain; a palanquin.

丨子, or 一頂丨, or 一乘丨, or 一座丨 one sedan, one chair.

竹丨 a bamboo sedan, the cheapest kind.

丨杠 sedan poles or thills.

花丨 or 喜丨 a bridal sedan.

坐丨 to ride in a sedan.

坐丨子 one who is plucked at cards by his fellows.

丨担 the short pole used to support the chair.

丨夫 or 擡丨的 chair-bearers.

遷丨 or 起丨 or 裝丨 tip the chair, so as to receive the sitter.

八座丨 a sedan with eight bearers, as a governor's, but the governor-general's 八丨八撮 has eight bearers and eight outriders.

騾馱丨 a mule litter.

輿丨 a light chair, otherwise called 過山丨 a mountain chair.

燒丨馬 burn his sedan and horse—*i. e.* he is dead, these paper things being fired the instant the breath has gone.

嶠 chiao' — The ridge or watershed of a high peak, where the water cannot stay; a hill-path.

員丨 a lofty hill in Punglai in Santung, one of five where the genii dwell.

𡰖 chiao' — Uneven; rough, as a path; uneasy, mind not quiet.

我亦行踏丨𡰖 I also went along the level road, stumbling and toddling as I stepped.

叫 呌 訆 chiao' — From *mouth* or *words* and *twining* or a *peck*; the second form is now the most in use, and the third is obsolete.

To call to or upon; to cry out; the cries or voices of animals and birds; to send for; to name; to command, to tell to do, to persuade; to sing, as an insect; to induce, to cause, in which sense it is often only a sign of the passive voice; by, with; named, called, termed.

丨魂 to invoke the spirits of persons who have fainted, or are in a fit.

丨風吹了 the wind blew them about.

明月丨人行 the bright moon leads people to go abroad.

不相丨 not on speaking terms.

一丨就到 he comes when he is called.

丨賊賊 to cry Thieves!

丨救命 to cry out for help, to cry Murder!

丨他來 (or 丨伊來 in Shanghai, or 丨佢嚟 in Canton,) call him here.

丨喊 to bawl out, to yell to, to call loud.

色丨 only the name of; nominal, like a sinecure.

丨破口嗓 to bawl one's self hoarse.

丨甚麼名字 what is it called? what's the name of this?

大語丨丨 the hum of much talking.

噭 chiao' — Similar to the preceding. To wail; to call after; to roar; a classifier of horses from their neighing.

丨哭 crying and sobbing.

毋丨應 don't bawl out in reply.

丨丨 a deep tone.

丨噑 to call out.

馬二千丨 two thousand horses.

徼 chiao' — From a *step* and *gliding*. To go around, to take a turn, either to ward off or to obtain; to assume; a sort of defensive palisades across streams to prevent savages landing; a narrow road; frontiers; end of.

丨妙 mysterious, hard to understand.

丨外 beyond the limits.

丨遊禁盜 to go on circuit and put down or prevent robberies.

Read *kiao*, and interchanged with 僥. To desire; to pry into; to seek; lucky, fortunate; to follow, to imitate.

惡丨以爲知者 I dislike those who make their wisdom to consist in prying.

丨福 to seek for happiness.

丨倖 succeeding; happily, as in answer to prayer

Read ˏyao. To conceal or suppress, as when one is quite exhausted, and will not own it.

瓞 ˋ*chiao*ˀ A long white crook-necked squash, having green stripes running lengthwise, the 丨瓜, which is hashed raw with mutton, and made into a dumpling, called 餃子餶 at Peking.

窖 **窌** *chiao*ˀ From *cave* and *to announce* or a *horary* character; the second form is unusual.

A bin or room in the ground for storing grain and other things; a pit; a vault.

氷丨 an ice house.

丨氷 to cut out store ice.

地丨 a cellar, a souterrain, an underground store-room.

丨藏 stored up, laid in the cellar.

丨密 profound, deep, as in the heart.

白菜上丨 put the winter cabbages into the pit.

瓦丨似的房子 handsome as a new tiled house.

鹽滷丨 salt pits, like those near Chapu in Chehkiang.

潑水挖丨 pour on water and [see if we can] dig up the treasure.

滘 *chiao*ˀ In *Cantonese*. An unauthorized character, side creeks which cross the country; canals or small water channels serviceable at high tides; the mouth of creeks; it occurs in the names of many places.

船過丨 the boat can go up the creek.

大黃丨 a creek at the 車馯砲臺 or Tee-totum Fort near Canton.

教 *chiao*ˀ ˏ*chiao* Originally described as composed of 攴 to *beat*, 子 a *child*, and 爻 to *imitate*; but the common form is now made of 攴 to *beat* and 孝 *filial duty*.

To instruct, to teach; to show how; to order, to command; precept, doctrine; opinions, tenets; the people who hold them, a religious or political sect, for the Government prescribes the opinions and ritual of its subjects; a school, those who hold similar opinions; a party, a class.

打丨 to be strict in teaching.

好丨法 good method of instruction.

丨館 a school-house.

丨學 to teach a school.

出丨 to excommunicate; to turn one out of the priesthood; to leave it.

丨授 the superintendent of education in a department.

丨諭 the overseer of schools in a district.

五丨 the five constant virtues.

匪用爲丨 you would not regard me as your teacher.

丨化 to influence by teaching; to civilize; to change the heart.

來領丨 I have come to receive instruction, *i. e.* to make a call, to visit you.

未請丨 I have not yet asked your name.

丨誨 to instruct, to indoctrinate.

丨師 or 丨習 a professor, a teacher, one who imparts his knowledge, as in archery, medicine, pugilism, &c.

三丨 the three sects in China, 儒丨 Confucianists (who call themselves the 大丨), 佛丨 or 釋丨 Budhists, and 道丨 Taoists.

丨門 disciples, adherents; but it usually denotes 回丨 or Moslems.

丨友 a Christian disciple, a convert, one who 奉丨 has received the doctrine.

傳丨 to teach religion, to propagate tenets, as a 丨師 missionary does.

主丨 a bishop in the Roman Catholic church.

天主丨 the Roman and Greek churches.

耶穌丨 the Protestant church.

Read ˏkiao. To cause, to induce, to make, to enable.

丨你好 this [medicine] will make you well.

免丨留落野人家 avoid all excuse for the vagabonds staying in the country.

酵 *chiao*ˀ From *spirits* and *filial duty*.

Leaven, the residuum left after distilling arrack.

糟丨 yeast cakes.

發丨 to raise, as dough; to ferment.

麪丨 levened barm, or yeast, which is usually the 酒丨 or cakes made from the mash of spirits.

餃 ˋ*chiao* From to *eat* and *adjoining* as the phonetic.

A meat dumpling.

丨餌 or 丨子 kneaded flour paste boiled in water, and made in a triangular shape, containing a bit of meat; they are also called 扁食 from their shape.

鉸 ˏ*chiao* Pivots on which a door turns; a hinge, a joint; a clamp, a hasp; to inlay metals; in some places used as a verb, to clip, to shear; to cut, as hair.

一把丨剪 a pair of shears.

丨釘 the pin of a hinge.

鎖丨 bolt of a Chinese lock.

丨紙花 to cut out artificial flowers.

Read ˋkiao. A slender knife, the 丨刀子, with which barbers cut the hair in the ear and nose.

較 *chiao*ˀ From *carriage* and *adjoining*; used with the next.

To compare; to measure strength; to try the accuracy or worth of; dissimilar; rather, somewhat more; in general.

丨臺ˀ to see which can drink the most; but 丨ˏ量 is to compare measures.

比丨 to compare; to argue.

丨重 compare their weights; also, the heavier.

丨射 trials of archery.

丨準 like to measure or guage.

丨早 sooner, earlier, quicker.

丨之 compare them.

大丨 generally, on the average.

丨然 glittering, bright.

丨繁 perplexing discussions; entanglements.

Read *kioh*, A sort of curved iron brace on a carriage, like a horn or ear; the boot of a carriage; to butt with the horns; to contend.

校 *'chiao h'iao'* Used with the preceding and next.

To compare; to collate, to revise books; to recompense; to examine, to judge of; a pen for beasts; stocks for the feet; a lockup; to oppose, as when sparring; to join battle.

丨對無訛 I have compared them and found no error.

犯而不丨 though wronged he did not seek revenge.

丨訂 to revise, as for publication.

丨正 to correct, as a proof; to make accurate.

考丨 to adjust, to carefully compare, to scrutinize.

計丨 to compare accounts, to audit.

Read *hiao'* A building for a school in the Hia dynasty; a high-school or gymnasium in the small towns; an inclosure for horses, a corral.

丨尉 an officer over city gates.

學丨 a school-house, a seminary.

丨人 a man who keeps a pond, but the term seems to have been applied too to purveyors and bailiffs of the ménage.

丨者敎也 the *hiao'* indicate (or are for) teaching.

挍 *chiao'* Like the last two, but less used.

To compare; to criticise, to discuss; to measure with; to choose; to oppose a superior; confused; disturbed by; irritated against.

丨講是非 to criticise others' doings.

君父之命不丨 do not oppose the will of prince or father.

珓 *chiao'* A pair of stones of a hemispherical shape, which are thrown on the ground by worshipers to divine the answer to their prayers; they are called 丨杯 and 丨卦, and are now made of wood, scollop shells, or bamboo roots; if both convex sides turn up when thrown, it is 陽丨 negative; if both plane faces it is 陰丨 indifferent; if one of each, it is 勝丨 or 勝卦, and the most propitious.

K'IAO.

Old sounds, k'io, k'ok, gio, *and* gok. *In Canton*, k'iu, hao, hiu, *and* kéuk; — *in Swatow*, k'a, kiò, kⁿa, k'iò, *and* kió; — *in Amoy*, kiao, k'iao *and* k'ao; — *in Fuhchau*, k'ieu *and* ngieu; — *in Shanghai*, ts'o *and* djo; — *in Chifu*, k'iao.

蹻 蹺 *'ch'iao* From *foot* and *curved* or *eminent*; it is also read *kioh*,

To raise the feet, as when sitting; to lift them high, as when climbing; to march; prancing, caracoling; tickled, pleased; to collude with.

搭丨 to play into another's hands, as sharpers do.

屐丨 straw sandals or spiked shoes in which to ascend hills.

丨足待也 to put up the feet (as on a stool) and wait patiently; — *i. e.* I am in no hurry.

丨丨 martial, noble, as a charger; puffed up, as with pride.

你踹我的丨 you have been riding my footsteps, you have been playing me false.

丨然不固 floating, unsettled.

丨脚 to cross the legs; the stroke to the right in writing, like that in 弋 or 戈; the surname 成 is thus called 丨脚成 or cross-legged Ch'ing.

In *Fuhchau*. To take advantage of another's ignorance or necessity; to speak in irony, saying one thing and meaning another.

橇 轎 *'ch'iao* From *wood* and *down*; the second form is unusual.

A sledge or support for the feet, shaped somewhat like a winnowing-fan, on which to be drawn or slip over the mud; a mud shoe.

磽 墝 *'ch'iao* From *stone* or *earth* and *eminent*; the first is erroneously, but commonly used for *'nao* 硇 soda.

Stony or arid soil; poor, gravelly land; upland; dry fields.

丨瘠 thin soil.

地有肥丨 there are both fertile and barren lands.

敲 *'ch'iao* From to *beat* and *high*; it resembles *'kiao* 敿 to roll.

A short club, a baton, a beater; to pound hard; to strike sideways; to tap, to rap on; to rattle on; to take, as a man in chess; to mark time.

丨詩 to mark or tone the rhythm of poetry.

丨碗丨筷窮死萬代 if you rattle your chopsticks on your basin, you'll starve for aye.

丨門 to knock on the gate.

丨經念佛 to chant prayers to Budha, while 丨木魚 rapping on the wooden fish.

丨鼓 to drum.

丨碎 to smash, to break in pieces.

給他丨死 I would like to see him struck dead.

風雨丨窓 the driving rain patters on the window.

砧杵丨殘深巷月 the racket of the pestles and washingboards obscures the moon in the alley; —a conceit of Li Tai-peh.

喬 *ᶜch'iao* Composed of 夭 *weird* and 高 *high* contracted; it is interchanged with some of its compounds.

High, stately, lofty; curving and open, like the highest branches of a tree; rising, as spears in serried array; crooked, curved; idle; discontented; proud.

丨木類 stately trees, a class in Chinese botany.

丨矛 a hook on a spear.

丨而野 proud and very rude.

丨志 insolent.

丨遷之喜 congratulations on moving into a stately (*i.e.* new) residence.

賢丨梓 your father and his family.

橋 *ᶜch'iao* From *wood* and *curved*; occurs used with the last.

Planks laid across a stream; a bridge; a cross-beam to support a frame; a stand with arms, anciently used at weddings to hold the bride's basket of dates and millet; the cross-piece of a well-sweep; a saddle-tree; a viaduct; perverse, disrespectful; a stately tree, whose branches all point up, as a cypress or poplar; to warp; to bend up, to curl.

一度丨 or 一道丨 one bridge.

丨梁冲壞了 the bridge has been swept away.

門丨 the lintel of a door.

五洞丨 or 五眼丨 a five arched bridge.

虹丨 the rainbow.

板丨 or 草丨 a footbridge.

紅丨 a suspension bridge; a rope by which to pull a ferry-boat across a stream.

丨砧 or 丨甃 buttresses or piers of a bridge.

過丨收丨 (or 撤跳) to take in the plank (or split it) after crossing over; —*i.e.* to leave one in the lurch.

屈丨 to bend a bridge; *met.* gigantic strength.

過鐵丨 to pass the iron bridge—into paradise.

給我窟窿丨走嗎 are you going to get me to cross on a bridge with a hole in it?—are you hoaxing me?

丨木高而仰梓木低而俯以喻父子 the lofty pine looks up, but the Rottlera bows its head, and thus they are likened to father and son.

風雨吹晒丨了 it has become warped in the sun and weather.

僑 *ᶜch'iao* An inn, a lodging-place; to lodge, to sojourn; temporary, transitory; stately.

丨居却是家 the inn will serve him for his home.

丨木與天參 this lofty tree interlaces with the sky.

蹻 *ᶜch'iao* Agile at climbing; robust, vigorous; to lift the feet.

輕丨 nimble; light and skillful in clambering.

丨丨 walking fast and stepping firmly.

蕎 *ᶜch'iao* From *flower* and *curved*; often interchanged with the next.

Buckwheat is 丨麥, called 三角米 or three-cornered rice in Canton; it is probably indigenous in China.

丨麥麪 buckwheat flour.

丨麥糝子 buckwheat grits or coarse meal.

荍 *ᶜch'iao* Much used as a contracted form of the last.

A thorny kind of mallows; it has greenish red flowers, which are edible and slightly bitter; one drawing resembles the hollyhock.

視爾如丨 I think you are as [handsome as] an Althæa.

丨葵向日 the sunflower turns toward the sun.

翹 *ᶜch'iao* From *wings* and *eminent*.

Long tail-feathers, which turn up; to elevate; to raise the head, to look up; high, elevated; a kind of alarm flag; excelling; dangerous, suspended; distant.

丨首 to raise the head

丨望 to look for hopefully.

丨丨 stately, as trees; hazardous, as a falling ledge.

春丨 spring bursting forth.

丨發其意 elevated his thoughts.

尾丨 to cock up the tail.

翠丨 a feather coiffure.

連丨 a medicine, the oval carpels of a species of *Anchusa*.

高丨 stilts; often written 高脚 high legs; the 高丨會 or stilt holiday lasts in the North for three days in the third moon.

翹 *ᶜch'iao* To fly downwards.

丨翬 to soar and sail round and round, as a falcon.

丂 *ᶜch'iao* From 一 *one* representing an obstacle, and *air* as it undulates; the original form of the next.

Air striving to free itself.

巧 *ᶜch'iao* From *work* and *air* stopped; the last was the old form.

Handy, skillful, dexterous; ingenious, clever at; adroit, talented; wily, crafty, intriguing; subtle, shrewd, witty, acute, apt; opportune, equal for an emergency; pleasing; ingenuity, mechanical aptness, genius.

丨妙 fine work, well done.

丨樣 an ingenious mode or pattern

丨匠 or 丨手 a skilled workman, a cunning hand.

丨言令色'鮮矣仁 fine words and a smooth bearing seldom indicate virtue.

丨笑 artful smiles; ogling; affable.

丨笑倩兮 what dimples, as she artfully smiled!

湊丨 a fortunate opportunity.

淫丨 specious, tricky; assumed.

丨捷 good at repartee, witty.

丨言如簧 his speech is alluring as a flute.

大丨若拙 this great genius acts like a simpleton.

投丨 ingenious, complex, as a machine.

丨妻常伴拙夫眠 a clever wife is usually mated to a dunce.

丨計 a fine plan, a shrewd device.

丨月 the seventh moon, — when women 乞丨 pray for skill in needlework.

遇丨 or 恰丨 just then, it just happened at the time.

丨言勿如直道 specious words are not equal to correct principles.

'鷮 'ch'iau — The *clever bird*, as the parts of the character indicate; the tailor-bird, (*Sylvia sutoria*,) known as the 丨婦鳥 or clever housewife.

鼽' ch'iao' — Of the three modes of writing this character, this is the common one.

A turned-up nose, a nose retroussé.

丨頭鞋 the retroussé shoe, having the end much turned up.

竅 ch'iao' — From *cave* and *gliding*.

A hole, an orifice; a pore or aperture; an interstice; a cavity, a hollow; the mind; the heart as the physical organ of thought; the accent or rhythm of a language.

九丨 the nine passages of the body.

一丨不通 he is thoroughly stupid, not a hole is open.

合丨 of the same mind.

七丨 the seven openings — in a sage's heart.

懂丨 I see how it is.

靈丨 clever; sprightly, acute.

百丨 all the pores, as in the skin.

地秉丨于山川 the springs in the hills are the adits or pores of the earth.

殊未中'丨 you are very wide of the mark.

通丨藥 sudorifics and sternutatory medicines.

不得訣丨 he has not a good accent; he does not see it.

心丨 the intellect, power of comprehension.

撽' ch'iao' — To whip, as a horse; to screen; to lay hold of.

撬' ch'iao' — From *hand* and *down*; it is interchanged with '撟 in some senses.

To pry up or open; to raise by a lever or crow-bar.

把釘子丨起來 pry out the nail.

丨門 to pry up a door; *met.* a thief.

丨棍 a crow-bar; a handspike.

丨不動 it will not move; it can't be raised or pried open.

丨孔 to make an opening with a spike, to pry open a hole.

丨破了 broke it in raising it up.

In *Cantonese* wrongly used for 繳. To coil around, to wind.

丨辮 to coil the cue on the head.

翹' ch'iao' — Composed of *eminent* repeated.

High, elevated, turned up at the ends; raised or curled above the level.

弓兩頭丨起來 both ends of the bow curl up.

踹丨 tipped it up by stepping on it.

丨頭白 a fish of the dace family, with a recurved mouth.

丨辮子 the cue is turned up; he is dead. (*Nanking.*)

K'IE.

Old sound, k'a. *In Canton*, k'é; — *in Swatow*, kié; — *in Amoy*, ka; — *in Fuhchau*, kià; — *in Shanghai*, ka; — *in Chifu*, k'ié.

瘸 ˛ch'üé — From *flesh* and a *scab*; used with the next.

A disease of the hands and feet, which curls and cripples them, preventing their full use; to limp, to halt.

腿丨了 a lame leg.

丨子 a lame man.

胎裏丨 congenital lameness.

˛髍 ˛ch'üé — Analogous to the last and interchanged with it; both are also pronounced ˛chui.

A malformation of the joints causing a contraction or stiffness of the limb; a congenital halt, a limping leg.

胑丨 a deficiency of the limb, or a stiffened muscle, that prevents its free use.

˛伽 ˛chié — A work adopted by the Budhists for the sounds *ga* and *ka*, for which ˛*kia* 迦 is also used.

丨藍 or 僧丨藍 a monastery or nunnery, from the Sanscrit *sangharama*.

丨藍佛 a Chinese name for Budha, and sometimes also applied to Kwanti.

樂丨山 a hill where Kwanyin dwells.

丨邪 Gayah, an ancient city in India, where Budha lived seven years; it has a famous monastery, which is still visited.

丨那 an elephant, perhaps derived from the Sanscrit word *karnoth*, a tusk.

丨藍子兒素珠 plain beads made of fragant wood like lignaloes.

茄 *ch'ié* From *plant* and *to add*.

The stem of the lotus, as distinguished from the stalk and leaves; a general term for the tomato, egg-plant, mandrake, nightshade, and some kinds of squashes.

丨子 or 牛心丨 the egg-plant or brinjal (*Solanum melongena*), also called in Shanghai 落蘇, an older term.

毛丨 okra or gumbo (*Cantonese*).

顛丨 mad-apple, dwale, or belladonna, the *Solanum insanum*, and similar species.

丨苞兒 unripe egg-plants, used to make sweetmeats.

番丨 the tomato, a southern term.

荷包丨 the bottle squash.

五丨 a medicine, probably made from the 苦丨 bittersweet or *Solanum dulcamara*.

倒丨 to grow upside down, (*Cantonese*).

KIEH.

Old sounds, kít, kíp, *and* gít. *In Canton*, kít, kíp, kät, *and* k'ít; — *In Swatow*, kat, kiat, k'íat, *and* kiap; — *in Amoy*, kiat, kiap, k'iat, kiat, *and* keh; — *in Fuhchau*, kiek *and* kak; — *in Shanghai*, kih, djih, *and* tsi; — *in Chifu*, kié.

結 *chié* From *silk* and *happy*.

A knot; a skein, a hank, a knob; a knotted button; to tie, to fasten; to work or weave in knots; to crochet; to braid, to knit; to make a contract, to bind by an agreement; an engagement, contract, or bond; united, banded together; fixed, engaged; hampered: curved; important; to induce, as ill-will; to stiffen, as cooling lava; to decide, as a case; to set, as fruit; to form, as a friendship or partnership; sometimes a suffix to a verb to show that the action is finished.

丨繩 or 打丨 to tie a knot.

一丨絲線 a skein of silk thread.

丨網 to knit or crochet a net.

菓丨了 the fruit has set.

凝丨 to coagulate, to congeal, to freeze, to stiffen.

丨舌 tongue-tied, unable to speak.

丨賬 to pay up or on an account.

丨淸 settled, made up, as a quarrel; paid all.

丨親 to contract a marriage.

日後歸丨 I will pay it to you by and by; he will receive retribution some day.

丨拜 to pledge or form a connection, like sworn friends.

丨局 the affair is finished; ended; results, event, out-turn.

草草了丨 to finish up a case anyhow. to decide needlessly.

出丨 to give security, to endorse for one, to give bonds.

丨訟 to enter a plea, to present the evidence on both sides.

丨案 to decide a cause.

完丨 finished, as a case at law, a contract or affair.

同鄉官印丨 a fellow-townsman who certifies to an officer's standing.

交丨 friendly intimacy; to hold communication with.

丨實 firm, durable; lasting, fast.

丨締 to tie together; a close union.

丨言 the last words.

丨穴 a good spot for a grave.

丨月 the twelfth or finishing moon.

收丨 to wind up, as a discourse.

丨果性命 I'd finish your life at a stroke; — used in angry talk.

巴巴丨丨的 troublesome, hard to do; grievous, a labor.

心之憂矣如或丨之 my heart in its sorrow is as if hampered and bound.

巴丨生意 he is diligent in his business.

丨繩而治 he made quipos and ruled the state, as in early Chinese history; to strike a line and plan work, as a carpenter.

拮 *chié* From *hand* and *happy*, but the etymologists explain it by 手口共有所作也 hand and mouth both busy.

Occupied, laboring hard; to seize a plant firmly to pull it up; to press after, to pursue.

丨据 embarrassed, as a trader for funds; hampered, perplexed.

桔 *chié* From *wood* and *happy*; it is used in the south as a contracted form of *küh*₂ 橘 an orange.

A water-wheel or bucket worked by a pully; a small orange.

車丨橰 to work the water-wheel, either by a winch or by the feet on treddles.

丨梗 a common medicine for coughs, the root of the *Platycodon grandifolium*.

丨仔 the small orange called loose jacket at Canton.

劫, 刼, ꜀chié } From *strength* or *sword* and to *take away*.
To take by violence, to plunder; to rob openly; to snatch; hurried pestered; a Hindoo kalpa, an æon or cycle, an era; suffering.

丨 奪 or 打 丨 to plunder, as highwaymen; to rob.

丨 盜 robbers, guerillas, banditti.

丨 掠 一 空 made a clean sweep, plundered everything.

丨 色 to ravish women.

丨 灰 long gone to oblivion, unknow, turned to ashes.

浩 丨 the palace steps.

避 丨 to avoid hell; to flee unavoidable ruin.

丨 數 a fatal calamity, one not to be escaped; ordained fate.

丨 丨 importunate, eager.

丨 皇 貢 to intercept revenue.

萬 丨 莫 贖 a myriad ages [of suffering] cannot atone for it.

受 丨 the unavoidable ills of life.

丨 波 a *kalpa* or Budhist age of millions of years, of which there are 大 丨 and 小 丨 great and small *kalpas*, having periods of increase and decrease, or perfection, continuance, and destruction; the *maha kalpa* lasts 1344 millions of years.

丨 貝 cotton in the boll, (from Sanscrit *karpasa*,) when it is ripe for picking.

In *Cantonese*. Astringent; to pucker the mouth, like alum; bitter; sleepy.

茶 十 分 丨 the tea is very bitter.

眼 丨 sleepy, dozing.

蛣, 蜐, ꜀chié } The first is also read ꜀k'ü, meaning a toad.
A sea animal, called 紫 丨 and 石 丨, likened to a tortoise's foot; or, as one says, a tortoise-shaped thing; it is the sea-anemone, which is described as producing flowers, and spreading itself out like a crab's claws.

鉣, ꜀chié An iron hook or strap fastened to the girdle.

孑, ꜀chié The character is supposed to represent a man who has lost his right arm, being reduced from *tsz'* 子 a *son*.

Alone, one only, orphan-like; a remnant; short; one who comes behind or last.

句 丨 a halberd.

丨 影 孤 單 left alone, no one to help, friendless and solitary.

丨 然 一 身 left quite alone.

靡 有 丨 遺 not a solitary man (not half a man) will be left; said of the effects of a drought.

丨 丨 the larvæ of musquitoes; preëminent, as a flagstaff.

潔, 絜, ꜀chié } From *water* and a *marking-line*; occurs used with the next; the second and less used form is also the old name of a river in the south of Shensi.
Clear, limpid, pure; free from sin or defilement, ceremonially clean; neat, trim, tidy; untainted, above bribes, pure-handed; to purify, to correct.

清 丨 pure-minded; clean, limpid.

丨 心 ingenuous, pure in heart, single-minded, unsullied.

丨 己 奉 公 upright in attending to public duties.

氷 清 玉 丨 [like the] icy crystal and pure gem; irreproachable, undefaced.

處 身 高 丨 to preserve one's integrity and purity.

丨 盃 候 敍 I have cleaned my cups and await your coming [to dinner] to have a chat.

絜, ꜀chié Formerly used with the preceding.
A marking-line; the end of a hempen thread; pure, as a sacrifice; to rule, to measure; to test by law; to repress, to reduce to order; to bring within bounds, as waters.

丨 度 to adjust, to limit.

丨 爾 牛 羊 our oxen and sheep are all pure.

丨 靜 tranquil.

丨 矩 之 道 the rules of just restraint.

丨 齊 to regulate exactly,

丨 粢 to prepare a plentiful repast.

榤, ꜀chié A hen-roost; a stick or perch for fowls to rest on.

桀, ꜀chié From *wood* and *perverse*; see the last and next.
A hen-roost; cruel, savage; harsh, truculent; high-spirited, courageous, one of a thousand, — for which the next is now used; to lift, to carry on the shoulder; name of the last monarch of the Hia dynasty, B. C. 1818, detested for his cruelty.

丨 丨 luxuriant, as growing weeds.

鷄 丨 a hen-roost.

桔 丨 a form, aspect of.

丨 驁 proud and domineering.

惟 受 罪 浮 于 丨 but the crimes of Sheu exceed those of Kieh.

傑, ꜀chié A hero, one eminent for virtue and prowess; heroic; proud, self-willed; a tender blade of grain; to raise up.

英 丨 a hero or heroine; a valiant man, a Chevalier Bayard.

有 厭 其 丨 the thrifty blades are growing long.

豪 丨 a famous leader, as Cæsar.

丨 作 like a hero, well done; finely written, as a composition.

俊 丨 a superior, leading man; said of scholars.

杰, ꜀chié From *wood* over *fire*; sometimes used with the last.

魏 丨 a famous statesman and general of the After Cheu dynasty, A. D. 956.

搩, 挈, ꜀chié } From *hand* and *roost* or *perverse*; the first is also used as a synonym of the next.
To measure with the thumb and forefinger, to span; to measure an ell; to uncover.

揭, ˛chié From *hand* and *why*.

To lift up or off, as a cover; to erect; to raise, as the skirt; to lift up, to bear, to carry off; to bring to mind; to borrow; to make known, to state to superiors; to drive rapidly; uprooted, as a tree by force.

丨丨 rank growing, as sedges.

顛沛之丨 when a tree falls utterly.

丨借 to borrow money.

丨單 or 丨字 a promissory note, a certificate of indebtedness.

丨項 or 丨數 borrowed capital; the debts of a firm.

唇丨齒寒 when the lips are opened the teeth get cold; — if you go away, I shall be lonely.

丨帖 a pasquinade, an anonymous charge, a placard.

丨封 to take the seals from a door; *met.* to drink, because jars of spirits are always sealed.

丨揚 to publish abroad, as an accusation; to post one.

丨榜 or 丨曉 to publish the list of successful graduates.

淺則丨 in shallow water raise — your skirt to the knees.

丨欒 or 短丨 to make known others' defects, to find fault.

丨蓋紅巾 to lift the red veil, — a wedding ceremony.

楬, ˛chié A board put up where a person has died, and been buried on the highway, stating his name and other particulars; a wooden instrument to mark time.

丨豆 a sacrificial platter.

禿丨 baldheaded.

丨櫫 a ticket or slip nailed on a door of a house which has been sealed up or confiscated.

羯, ˛chié From *sheep* and *why*.

To castrate a ram; a deer's skin.

丨室 ancient name of a place near Wu-hiang hien 武鄉縣 in the southeast of Shansi, which derived its name of Wether House from the Huns who settled there about the fourth century.

丨羊 a gelded goat; a wether; there is a discrepancy in this use, however, for in Chihli 丨子羊 is a ram, and 騸羊 is a wether.

柘丨 a Scythian word for warrior.

擊丨鼓以催花 to beat the deer-skin drum to hasten the blossoming of the flowers.

碣, ˛chié A round or flat stone pillar or tablet; a high, isolated peak; an aiguelle or sharp high rock like the Skillig Rock near Ireland; the 丨石 in Lin-yü hien on the coast of Chihli is a noted one; the fluttering of birds.

碑丨 the square and round monumental pillars.

指路丨 a stone guide post.

偈, ˛chié chi˒ From *man* and *why*; it is sometimes used for the next.

Martial, brave; to exert one's strength; vehement, hasty, as chariots racing.

丨丨爲義 diligent in the practice of right.

匪車丨兮 not for the swift chariot.

Read *ki*˒ An enigma or apothegm of the Budhists; motions which the priests make with their hands; sign language, like a token or grip; a conundrum; a charade; to rest; to idle away the time.

知丨 to recognize the allusion; to take the cue; to understand the sign.

閒談講丨 to tell riddles and talk gossip.

講丨語 or 講佛丨 to explain the Budhist stanzas, *i. e.* the Sanscrit *gatha* 伽他 or 丨締 a verse or stanzas.

In *Cantonese*. A hinge; a catch in a door; a spring; a joint of the finger.

竭, ˛chié From to *stand* and *why*; it is sometimes interchanged with the last, and is not the same as the next.

To exhaust, to carry to the utmost; to sink away; wanting, exhausted; used up; gone, finished, as the power of one of the elements, to be succeeded by another, — or as a revolution, that then recommences; defeated, weakened.

泉之丨矣不云自中 a spring drying up is only because [no water] rises in it.

力丨 exhausted; to give out, as a laborer.

丨力 to do one's best, to exert all the strength.

旣丨吾才 I have put forth all my abilities.

三鼓而丨 at the third drum-roll they will be quite disheartened.

丨盡 energy quite gone; with full purpose of heart.

丨憊 wearied out.

丨蹶以赴 exerted his utmost strength to reach.

丨誠來見 I have come to see you in full sincerity.

朅, ˛chié From *to go* and *why*.

To go and then return, as a carriage; to turn about; a brave martial appearance.

庶士有丨 all the escort officers bore themselves finely.

愒, ˋchié From *heart* and *why*; it is also read *ki*˒

To rest a while, to stop; to hold up; urgent, in a hurry.

棲丨 to lodge, to sojourn a while.

少丨半晌 stop an hour or so and rest.

汔可小丨 perhaps they can get a brief repose.

Read *hoh*, To desire, to long for.

丨生 to love life.

不侜丨焉 who would not like to get — under it?

Read *koh*, A mutual fear of one another.

愒, ˏchié This form is more antique than the last; it is also read *ki*ʾ.

To rest, to take breath; to repose, to lay a thing down.

丨息 to rest; a stop.

暫丨 to hold up a little; to breathe and rest.

遊丨 to take a rest and walk; to ramble or take a walk.

藒, 藒, ˏchié The first form is regarded as the most correct.

A very fragrant plant found in Sü-cheu fu in the northwest of Kiangsu, the 丨車 or 丨耳香, it is cultivated, and grows among the young rice.

訐, ˏchié From *word* and *shield*; occurs used with 揭 to lift off, and much resembles ˏhü 訏 to boast.

To charge one with a fault; to bring another's misdoings to light; to reveal, to discover secrets, to tell tales; to divulge.

面丨 to accuse one to his face, or before his master.

丨揚人過 or 丨人短處 to blazon people's faults.

控丨 or 告丨 to bring charges; to denounce, as the people do bad rulers to the higher officers or the sovereign.

惡ʾ丨以爲直者 I hate those who denounce others to raise their own reputation.

蛺, ˏchié From *insect* and *to compress*; referring to their wings; others say that the allusion is to the way some species sun their wings.

A butterfly; the 丨蝶 a small species, like the cabbage or sulphur butterfly; the name, however, seems to be of general application.

魝, ˏchié From *fish* and *knife* referring to the fishwife's art.

To split and prepare fish for drying; to open; to cut apart; to dissect, as the faults of people.

极, ˏchié A pack-saddle frame-work or slings, on which loads are bound when prepared for mules or camels to carry.

In *Cantonese*. A camp-stool is 馬丨; a folding chair.

丨側瞓 to sleep on the side.

袺, ˏchié From *dress* and *fortunate*.

To pull out or hold up the skirt, as if carrying something in it.

丨衣上衽 from the skirt up to the breast or lapel.

薄言丨之 now we will put [the seeds] in our skirts.

KʻIEH.

Old sounds, kʻít, kʻíp, kʻiep, *and* kʻam. *In Canton*, híp *and* hap;—*in Swatow*, kʻiak, *and* kiap;—*in Amoy*, kiap, kiap, *and* kʻiat;—*in Fuhchau*, kiek *and* kʻiek;—*in Shanghai*, ch'ih *and* chiah;—*in Chifu*, kié.

怯, chʻiéʾ From *heart* and *to go*.

Timorous, fearful, cowardly, dreading, careful against.

丨恥 bashful, blushing; trepidation.

畏丨 or 心丨 fluttering, weak-hearted, timid.

丨陣 afraid to go into battle.

丨風 careful of the draught, as an invalid.

丨志 weak of purpose; vacillating.

見大不丨 do not be abashed when you see great men.

瘦丨丨 lean and strengthless, one of no account for anything.

痃, chʻiéʾ Weakness, strength all gone; lassitude, languor, debility; infirm.

呿, chʻiéʾ From *mouth* and *to rob*.

A sound, like 丨丨 one resembling creaking; a rustling or whispering noise.

挈, chʻiéʾ From *hand* and *to carve*; it sometimes occurs used for 契 a bond.

To raise from the earth; to suspend; to hold; to assist, to help another; to put in order, to adjust; to singe, as a shell.

提丨 to raise and carry; to recommend.

丨出凡塵 raised him above the vulgar world.

Read *kʻi*ʾ Exhausted, failing; wanting; to record on a board the offenses of criminals.

鍥, chʻiéʾ A sickle, a bill-hook; used with *choh*, 斮 to cut off, to amputate; to carve; to exterminate.

丨朝涉之脛 [Cheu-sin] cut off the leg-bones of those who were crossing the ford.

丨薄 to oppress, to maltreat.

刻丨 to engrave, to carve.

音信丨斷 all letters and news have ceased to come.

猰, ˏchʻié Harsh, malevolent is 丨犺, referring to a vicious dog.

Read *haih*ʾ A mongrel dog, 丨貐, a nondescript beast resembling a tiger, which leaps suddenly on its prey.

㚗 ˏch'ié To lean or loll the head, as one does when wearied out.

慊 ˏch'ié From *heart* and *together*.

Happy, contented, as when one's wishes are gratified.

自 丨 I am much pleased.

丨 足 fully satisfied.

丨 快 great alacrity.

無 丨 於 鼻 nothing pleasant to his nostrils; he is always snuffing at things, always dissatisfied.

Read ˋk'ien. Enraged, angry; to gnash the teeth with vexation; to dislike, to cherish ill-will against.

匧, **篋** ˏch'ié From a *receptacle* and to *press*; the second form is most common, showing the material

A trunk to contain books and writings; a porte-feuille; a chest, a dresser or pannier; a carpet-bag, a satchel, a reticule; to put away in a box.

鼓 丨 to strike on the chest when entering school; — an old custom.

丨 笥 a scholar's satchel.

行 丨 a traveling-trunk or box.

丨 子 a case for holding papers or sewing materials.

書 丨 a case for books.

箱 丨 a bamboo hamper; a clasping clothes-box.

囊 丨 蕭 然 the money-bag is all cleared out.

愜 ˏch'ia The mind pleased; cheerful, satisfied; ready, prompt.

爽 丨 joyful, in good spirits.

意 丨 or 丨 心 a contented mind.

諸 事 丨 洽 everything was arranged satisfactorily.

不 丨 其 意 the principles are not the same; I do not agree with this notion.

丨 志 convinced, satisfied.

KIEN.

Old sounds, kin, gin, kim, kien, gieu, kiem, giem, *and* kan. *In Canton*, kin, kan, kam, nam, *and* kim; — *in Swatow*, kian, k'ian, kⁿoi, kan, kam, *and* kiam; — *in Amoy*, kiau, kiam, k'iam, giam, han, kan, *and* kam; — *in Fuhchau*, kieng, k'ieng, kang, hang, keng, kiòng, *and* kiek; — *in Shanghai*, kiⁿ, kèn, *and* djiⁿ; — *in Chifu*, kien.

堅 ˏchien From 土 *earth* and 賢 *virtuous* contracted.

Stable, immovable, firm, hard, strong; durable, wears well, lasting; stout, hale, in good liking; well-made, sound; constant, determined; resolute, unwavering; to establish, to strengthen; to confirm; to harden, to concrete; in epitaphs denotes one who screens his faults.

丨 固 immovable, firm; durable; substantial, as a family or a mercantile house.

丨 實 solid, strong.

心 丨 or 丨 志 resolute, a fixed purpose; persevering.

丨 執 obstinate, pig-headed.

丨 忍 firm endurance.

丨 信 to establish in faith; the rite of Confirmation.

丨 凝 congealed; hardened, as lava; solidified, as metal; curt, as a style.

以 丨 其 信 德 it confirmed his belief.

丨 信 之 禮 the rite of confirmation; — a foreign term.

丨 壯 hale, robust, said of old men.

中 丨 the main or center of an army.

丨 不 吐 眞 really his confession was not true.

鑽 之 彌 丨 the more [Confucius'] doctrines are tried the more convincing are they found to be.

好 丨 硬 的 性 having fixed principles.

丨 强 不 屈 firm and unyielding; unbending in a good sense.

執 銳 披 丨 he grasped his spear with the firmest resolve.

鰹 ˏchien A fish described as like the *t'ung* 鮦 but larger, and belonging to the same family; it is perhaps the bonito, which is common in Chinese waters, and much consumed by the Japanese fresh and preserved; but the Chinese description assimilates it rather to one of the mullet family.

肩 ˏchien From *flesh* and inner *door*; but the original form is thought to resemble the shoulder.

The top of the shoulder; the scapula; to take upon, to sustain; competent to; firm, solid; a beast when three years old.

丨 頭 or 丨 膊 the shoulder; 丨 膊 闊 broad shouldered; influential from having friends.

丨 髈 the fleshy part of the arm.

比 丨 compared shoulders, *i. e.* equal in merit or rank.

並 丨 而 行 to walk abreast, to be an equal or friend.

披 丨 an official cape laid over the robe and made of silk; worn by graduates.

坎 丨 a vest or waistcoat.

雲 丨 a kind of mantilla or victorine worn by brides.

息 丨 to withdraw from, to desist.

口 水 丨 a bib for a child.

丨 挑 背 負 hard, toilsome labor, peeling the shoulders; hard-worked.

仔 丨 to take charge of; adequate to, as a duty; its burden.

一 丨 擔戴 to take the whole charge of; to carry a business through.

丨 負重任 to carry on important and responsible duties.

朕不 丨 好’貨 We will not employ those who love bribes.

扛 丨 兒的 a bearer of burdens, a coolie.

丨 挑生理 a huckster's occupation.

作事有 丨 勝的 I have got a capable man for the business.

姦 ˓chien From *woman* thrice repeated; it is interchanged with the next.

Amours and intrigues among and with women; illicit intercourse, as adultery, incest, rape, fornication, for the word does not distinguish; to debauch, to ravish; wild, horrid, brutal, ogre-like; applied to genii and spirits, villainous, wicked.

丨 淫 or 丨 汚 to defile; fornication.

强 丨 to force a woman; a rape.

情 丨 or 和 丨 consenting to adultery.

通 丨 criminal conversation.

丨 夫 an adulterer.

丨 宄 villains and traitors; to act like a traitor.

丨 拐 to seduce and carry off, to kidnap.

丨 生 an illegitimate birth.

奸 ˓chien From *woman* and to *offend*; used with and for the last.

Inordinate, unregulated desire; to violate decorum; to offend against propriety; crafty, plotting, unprincipled; traitorous; malicious; selfish; clandestine; corrupt, adulterous.

丨 詐 false, fraudulent; to cheat.

丨 臣 a traitorous official or vassal.

丨 雄 a sanctimonious traitor.

漢 丨 a disaffected Chinese; one who has intercourse with foreigners is often so stigmatized

丨 賊 a villain; you traitor!

丨 佞 or 丨 巧 double-faced, designing, specious.

丨 壞 or 丨 猾 artful, deceptive; said of cunning children, who love to make mischief.

丨 細 a spy, an eaves-dropper.

丨 黨 a traitorous cabal.

盤 丨 緝盜 lookout for the smugglers and seize thieves; — a notice on custom-houses.

丨 絕我好’ you craftily deprive me of what I love.

丨 仔 a slippery fellow. (*Cantonese*.)

間 ˓chien From *door* and the *sun* shining through; the authorized form is 閒, but usage now confines that to the oblique tone *kien*’

A crevice; a space, an interval; between, during, while, in the midst of, among; to make room for; to set apart; a classifier of houses, buildings, rooms, gardens, &c.; at the North, a division of a large room made by the framework of the house; but in the South, where a different mode of construction prevails, it denotes the room or apartment.

一年 丨 a whole year, within the twelve months.

正在訊 丨 while I was examining him.

忽然 丨 suddenly, just now.

陽 丨 in this world; during life.

終食之 丨 a little while; during the time of a meal.

其 丨 that affair; this time, this business.

兩 丨 heaven and earth.

一座三 丨 three rooms in one house.

第幾 丨 which house is it?

房 丨 a house; houses, buildings.

中 丨 人 a midsman.

天地之 丨 無此法 there is no such law in the world.

Read *kien*’ To sunder, to put a space between; to divide, to interrupt; to intrigue, to part friends, to slander; to interfere in; to alternate, to intermit; vacant, unoccupied, as a road; far removed; to bear with; a tale-bearer; mixed, as colors.

丨 隔 to set apart; a partition; to intermit.

所 丨 人 one who separates people, as a busybody.

丨 或有之 supposing it to be so; what if there be?

反 丨 to make counter stratagems; to deceive an enemy.

丨 別許久 separated for a long time.

丨 踈的 put them rather wider apart.

新不 丨 舊 the new will not supersede (or estrange) the old.

離 丨 骨肉 to sow discord among relatives.

聲音相 丨 the sounds alternated with each other.

丨 遠 far removed.

丨 隙 a crack; an offense, a grudge; to set at variance.

丨 壁隣舍 or 丨 壁的 next door neighbors; those in the same yard.

是 丨 壁兒的院子 it is in the adjoining yard or garden.

兩夾 丨 兒 in the space between the two.

居 丨 而排難 to try to reconcile differences between people.

棡 ˓chien An unauthorized character used for the preceding in the southern provinces.

A room, an apartment; a classifier of houses, and used mostly in deeds or leases.

用木板隔 丨 divide off the apartment by a board partition.

蕑 ˓chien A climbing plant bearing a fruit of a pear shape, red as a cock's comb, with a scaly pit, and fit to be eaten raw.

丨 草 a well-known fragrant plant, reckoned among the orchids in consequence of its perfume; it grows in 武岡州 in Honan, where it is found in marshy places and called 澤蘭 or marsh orchid, and 都梁香 or the perfume from Tu-liang district; the plant, from the Chinese drawing and description, is probably the *Valeriana dioica* or an allied species; the roots are called 地笋 earth shoots; the leaves were gathered in spring to ward off miasma, and preserve clothes from insects.

士與女方秉丨夯 the gentlemen and ladies then carried bouquets of valerian.

艱 ˛chien From 艮 *perverse* and 堇 *sticky earth* altered, referring to the difficulties of turning over the ground.

Land that is hard to till; whatever is difficult or toilsome; to inflict hardships; distressing, sorrowful; origin of.

丨辛 miserable, wretched.

丨險 difficult and dangerous.

丨煩 thanks for your trouble.

丨難 in unhappy circumstances; hardships; to realize the hardships of.

天方丨難 Heaven is now inflicting calamities.

生意丨難 trade is dull, business goes hard.

丨食 the food of toil,— as from agriculture.

居丨守制 he is at home observing the mourning — for his father.

丨阻 seriously obstructed.

莫或不丨 do not undervalue the difficulties.

丨苦備嘗 I have been through all kinds of griefs; I've tasted sorrow.

其心孔丨 his mind is full of dangerous devices.

鋄 ˛chien Also read ˛wan.

To plate, to overlay with silver; to inlay silver in other metals, or in leather, as is done on housings or saddles.

丨銀什件 to plate with silver.

金丨玉鑲 plated with gold and inlaid with gems.

菅 ˛chien From *plant* and *officer*.

The stalks of a coarse grass resembling an *Imperata*. whose fibres, after rotting, become white, and are fit for making coarse cloth; they serve too for thatch or mats; name of a place in the state of Sung.

白丨爲席 mats are made of the white flowered rush.

犍 ˛chien From *ox* and to *establish* as the phonetic.

A gelded bull, an ox; a strong ox; a fabulous monster, half leopard, half man.

丨爲縣 a district in Kia-ting fu in the center of Sz'ch'uen on the River Min; during the Han dynasty, it was a prefecture near Chingtu.

鞬 ˛chien A case for bows used by cavalry.

丨櫜 a horseman's quiver to hold his bow and arrows.

兼 ˛chien From 又 a *hand* grasping 二禾 *two stalks* of grain, as ˊping 秉 represents it holding one.

To comprehend in, to embrace with; to absorb; as a *conjunction*, moreover, and, along with, and also; together with, in addition to; additional; equally; to join several together; to attend to many things; connected.

更丨 or 丨有 still there are more; there is another matter.

丨合 to unite various ingredients.

彩色相丨 many colors contrasted.

丨幷 to coalesce, to bring into one.

丨全 both (or all) complete; full efficiency.

丨人之量ˋ a trencher-man, one who can drink double what another can.

丨理 or 丨攝 to manage several duties, as a pluralist.

本末丨該 applies to both cause and effect.

丨愛 to love all equally.

丨且我不得閒 moreover, I have no leisure.

丨雜 to adulterate or mix in, as goods.

丨旬 both or two decades.

二者不可得丨 you cannot, however, have them both.

In *Cantonese*. To squeeze through, as a crevice; to force one's way through, as a crowd.

丨入去 push through and get in.

蒹 ˛chien A marshy plant, which appears to be a tall kind of sedge, the 丨葭, perhaps the *Phragmites*, on which cattle thrive when it is in seed; people in the north of Kiangsu make door-screens of it.

丨葭蒼蒼 the reedy grasses are now a dark green.

丨葭倚玉樹 [like] the rush leaning against the precious tree, — so I have confidence in your power or friendship.

縑 ˛chien From *silk* and *united* as the phonetic.

A kind of thick levantine, woven with double threads and close so as to shed rain; it is like the *küen*ˋ 絹 or taffeta.

丨緗 a variegated silk; *met.* fine writing.

細緻染丨 fine and beautiful colored silks.

丨袋運水 the lutestring bags transported the water, alluding to a story of Ts'ao Ts'ao, who filled bags of it with water, which when frozen enabled him to defend his camp.

鶼 ˛chien Described in Chinese books as a strange bird like a duck, the 比翼鳥 or paired-wings bird, with one eye and one wing, affiliated to the plaice in its structure, and so made that two must unite for either of them to fly; the spoonbill (*Platalea major*) found on the coasts of Formosa, and regarded by the natives as an anomaly among birds.

鰜 ˏchien — From *fish* and *united*.

The plaice or sole fish, also called 比目魚 or paired-eyes fish, said by the Chinese to swim in pairs, clasped to each other, as each has only one eye.

尲, 尷 ˏchien — To walk lame or in a stumbling manner.

丨尬 walking in an irregular limping manner, like a staggering horse; at a loss what to do when affairs go wrong; nonplussed.

搛 ˏchien — To grasp a morsel with the chopsticks.

Read *lien*ʾ To strike a drum.

慳 ˏchien — From *heart* and *solid* as the phonetic.

Sparing, parsimonious, stingy niggardly, avaricious; saving, to use very carefully; to reduce, to economize; to spare.

丨儉 close-fisted, grudging.
丨吝 unwilling to spend.
丨節 to diminish expenses, to reduce the outlay.
丨囊 to shut up the purse strings.
丨力 saving of strength.
丨煩 saved the trouble, spared the outlay.
丨省 closefisted, sparing, frugal.

Read *hien.* The experience of an old man.

豜 ˏchien — A pig three years old, a full grown, strong hog.

獻丨于公 [the farmers] offered a hog to their ancestors — at the ingathering.

鳽 ˏchien — Also read *ngeh*.

Another name for the 鵁鶄 or egret, a species found along the coast of Chehkiang; also called the 茭鷄 or grass hen.

虔刂 ˏchien — From *knife* and *firm* as the phonetic.

To cut off; to castrate an ox.

緘 ˏchien — From *silk* and *all;* sometimes wongly written as the next.

Cords used to bind a coffin or hamper; to tie up, to sew up, to bind; to close, to seal; to fill up cracks; a letter sealed.

丨封 to seal, as a letter.
丨口無言 to keep one's mouth shut.
丨密 firmly sealed.
書丨 a letter envelope.
吉丨 a letter, as from a son.
丨默 to keep silence.
接到玉丨 your esteemed favor has been received.
機丨 a confidential letter inclosed.

椷 ˏchien — From *wood* and *all;* it is sometimes erroneously used for the last.

A casket, a box; a cup, a wooden bowl; to allow.

丨粧 a dressing-box.

減, 减 ˏchien — From *water* or *ice* and *altogether;* the second form is the most common.

To diminish, to decrease; the opposite of ˏ*tsăng* 增 and ˏ*kia* 加; to take away a part; to contract, to abbreviate; to lighten; to retrench; to make less do; name of a river in Chihli.

丨半 to take off half.
丨價 or 丨色 to cheapen, to lower the price; cheaper.
丨筆寫 to abbreviate a character, to write short-hand, or with many contractions.
淸丨 wearied out, overworked, poorly.
丨省 laconic, plain; nothing superfluous, as 丨省得過 less will do, it does not need so much.
有得丨 you can sell it cheaper.
丨少 too few, deficient.
丨刻 to keep back, as rations or wages.
丨損 to prejudice or disallow the rights of others.
丨等議處 to abate somewhat from the legal punishment.
蒙丨 I thank you for the abatement.
輕丨 to alleviate, to make easier, to lighten.
風味不丨桃子 its taste does not yield to that of the peach.

繭 ˏchien — From 糸 *silk* 虫 *worm*, and 蔽 to *cover* contracted, to denote its purpose.

The cocoon of the silkworm, which is like a canopy to the larvæ; the silky pupæ of other moths.

蠶丨 a silkworm's aurelia.
丨綢 an undyed, coarse, durable pongee.
程鄉丨 pongee from Kia-ying cheu in the east of Kwangtung.
丨丨 a low mournful tone.
結丨 to weave the cocoon.
丨虫 the cocoon worm; a fur moth.
窖丨 cocoons which are buried to delay their hatching.

襺 ˏchien — From *clothes* and *cocoon*.

Silk wadded cotton clothes, especially those lined with fresh cotton.

重丨衣裘 [put on] double wadded garments and then a fur robe, — to protect you.

揀 ˏchien — From *hand* and *to abridge*.

To select, to chose; to discriminate; selected, chosen; elected, picked out.

丨擇 to select, as from a lot of good; to choose, as a day.
丨選 to choose, as proper persons for a duty.
丨貨 to garble goods.
丨剩 what is 'eft after garbling.
丨淨 sorted clean, as tea or fruit.
丨練揣摩 to select and practice upon, so as to imitate and relish, as compositions or models.
丨起來 picked it out; he has selected it.
丨採名山 to select and purchase [teas] from the best localities.

ˊ柬 ˊchien Composed of 束 to *bind* and 八 to *divide;* it is an old form of, and is often interchanged with the next; it resembles ˏ*tung* 東 east, when written badly.

To select, to condense, to abridge; a visiting-card; a classifier of slips of paper.

丨帖 or 紅丨 a common red card.

全丨 a five-leaved card, used at weddings.

禮丨 a note and card sent with presents.

庚丨 a horoscope card exchanged with the proposals for marriage.

丨理精神 to husband one's strength.

傳書寄丨 to send letters, as by a postman.

ˊ簡 ˊchien From *bamboo* and an *interval;* used with the last.

A slip of bamboo used for making notes on; an official writing; documents; to abridge, to condense; to choose; to examine, to mark; to treat negligently or rudely; unruffled, not excited; laconic, terse; discriminating; great; sincere; hasty, curt, impetuous; a classifier of folios or sheets of paper; sound of drums.

丨略 to abridge; a synopsis, a resumé.

丨慢 or 丨褻 to treat impolitely; I fear you will deem me rude; — a polite phrase.

牙丨 an ivory tablet.

政丨刑清 to show some leniency in punishments.

狂丨 wild and rude, not yet tutored; said of a lad.

奏鼓丨丨 the loud resounding drums.

畏此丨書 we feared those wooden missives.

夏迪丨在王庭 in the days of Hia, [officers] were chosen and promoted to the royal court.

丨直的 concisely, in short; direct, the nearest road; plain spoken.

丨缺 of less importance, said of certain districts or offices.

丨札 or 丨策 an official document.

特丨 specially selected — for this post.

丨丨决决 glibly, readily.

丨丨 an easy manner; abundant, as blessings; loud and sweet, as music.

丨捷 shortly, expeditiously; laconic.

毋乃太丨乎 are you not quite too brief?

丨閱 to examine, as essays; to review, as troops.

丨旨 specially commissioned — by his Majesty.

丨牒 a slip, a memorandum, a billet.

五刑不丨 the five punishments do not meet the case.

丨牘 a register, a record-book.

請旨丨放 to request orders to select a man to send to the post.

丨用總鎮 a brevet major-general.

ˊ襇 ˊchien The embroidered plaits in front of a lady's skirt, a plait; a furbelow on an officer's robe, attached to the back; it was common in the Ming dynasty.

裙丨 flounces on the skirt.

腰丨 a plait on a robe.

摺丨 to plait a trimming or flounce.

ˊ蹇 ˊchien From 足 a *foot* and 寒 *cold* contracted; occurs interchanged with the next two.

Lame, halt, weak in the legs; feeble, inadequate to; hesitating; difficult, unfortunate; afflicted; crooked; lofty, proud; to pull up; name of the 61st diagram, denoting ill-luck or danger ahead.

命丨時乖 the times and fates are against me.

中歲偃丨 found himself thrown out or stranded, in the middle of his days; a dead-heat.

丨産 twining and curling around.

丨跛 crippled, unfittedf or work.

俾作丨脩 that he may become a Kien-siu, the upright minister of Fuh-hi; — a good wish.

王臣丨丨 the prince and his officers anticipate great trouble.

ˊ僊 ˊchien From *man* and *lame.*

Used for the last in 偃丨 proud, haughty.

ˊ謇 ˊchien From *words* and *cold* contracted.

To stutter, to speak with difficulty; to talk cut boldly; straightforward, correct words; to beg, to intreat.

丨諤 faithful; truth-telling, as a statesman.

廣納丨丨 to hear many honest truths, as from subjects.

丨丨直言 plain, honest words; warning words.

丨而無憯 to intreat one with much embarrassment.

ˊ寋 ˊchien The men whose duty is to strike the cymbals or stones; name of a woman.

ˊ蹇 ˊchien From *horse* and *lame.*

A lame mule or ass.

覓個丨驢跨 [he wished] to find a lame mule to straddle, — as it would not throw him.

ˊ囝 ˊchien From to *inclose* and *child;* the character dates from the T'ang dynasty.

A child of one's own; in Amoy, used mostly for a boy; but at Shanghai 女丨 is a girl, and 男丨 a boy or son.

丨子 a varlet, a menial, a boy in waiting

小丨 the children in a family.

ˊ梘 ˊchien A bamboo tube or flume to carry water; to run through a sluice; a wooden peg or pin; a covering for a coffin.

筧 ʻchien From *bamboo* and *to see;* used with the last.
A bamboo spout or flume to bring water on fields.

趼 ʻchien Callous hard skin on the foot or hand, a blood-blister; a sore on the foot.
重 丨 thick hard skin.
胝 丨 a corn; hard skin on the foot caused by work.

Read *yen*ʼ The cloven hoof of an animal, which is well adapted for going up hill.
蹄 丨 the horn or nail of the hoof.

鹼 **鹻** ʻchien From *saltish* and *altogether;* the first is most used.
The impure carbonate of soda or natron, which is collected from the saline lakes in Mongolia by lixiviation, and extensively used for soap; a nitrous efflorescence on the earth, such as is common in Chili and Bengal, and that called *tequesquite* in Mexico; barilla made from sea plants; saltish incrustation.
丨 沙 soda in powder.
鹵 丨 soda made from the natron lands.
丨 店 shops where salt provisions are sold.
石 丨 hard soda; or crude soap.
丨 水 lye lixiviated from soil.

梘 **䤾** ʻchien The first is an unauthorized character used at Canton, for which apparently the second is the correct form, though it is defined *saltish* in the lexicon.
Soap; barilla; soft soap.
香 丨 scented soap.
番 丨 foreign soap.
丨 沙 the sediment in lye.
丨 水 lye; any liquid from ashes, nitrous soil, or sea-sand.

檢 ʻchien From *wood* and *all;* it is interchanged with the next.
An envelope; a case; a title or label on a book; a rule, a model, a pattern; to sort, to arrange, to collate; to compose, as a book; to examine; to pick up, to come across as a purse in the street.
丨 式 an example.
巡 丨 the magistrate of a *sz*ʼ or township, who is subordinate to a *chi-hien.*
丨 封 to label, to mark on a name or contents.
丨 驗 to examine, as a corner; to hold an inquest.
都 丨 點 to keep all things in order, to take an account of; to dispose orderly.
金泥玉 丨 the gilded precious note, the name of the billet of a Hanlin informing his family of his success.
搜 丨 王大臣 a prince-examiner of the candidates coming to the imperial and last examination.
丨 了 來 he was taken up.
丨 點 丨 點 look over and count them carefully.
上山 丨 柴 to gather faggots on the hills.
踰 丨 踰閑 to carelessly disregard rules and limits.

撿 ʻchien From *hand* and *all;* used with the last.
To coerce, to repress; to gather; to revise, to collate and sort; to hold up in both hands; to examine.
丨 束 to restrain, to keep in check.
丨 校 an officer who arranges and collates the books; also, the secretary of a prefect.
丨 書 to criticise or revise a book.
失于 丨 點 I was very bungling; to be disorderly or careless.

見 chienʼ Composed of 目 *eye* above 儿 a *man;* it forms the 147th radical of a natural group of characters relating to sight.
To see; to notice and know what it is, which 看 does not always involve; to observe, to perceive by the senses; to visit; to feel, as snow the sun's heat; feeling seeing, observing, impressed by; appearance of; an opinion, a mental view; before another verb, it sometimes forms the passive voice, and in other cases the past tense.
丨 過 I saw it; I have seen it.
丨 不着 I did not see it.
聽 丨 I heard and understood it.
相 丨 an interview; to see one.
願 丨 無由 I wished to call on you, but had no way.
丨 面勝比聞名 a personal interview is more agreeable than to hear his fame.
丨 的透 I've looked it through; I know him well; I've seen all.
丨 天到 he comes every day.
請 丨 教 please let me know it.
丨 新 as good as new, looks as if it were new.
丨 笑 it is laughable, you will smile at it;—a polite phrase.
丨 他有病 seeing that he was sick.
何以知其將 丨 殺 how do you know that he will be killed?
丨 肚滯 I feel very full in my stomach.
有何高 丨 what is your opinion?
何以 丨 得 how can it be ascertained?
丨 識廣 extensive experience or knowledge.
意 丨 相符 their views entirely agree.
試可 丨 好歹 its quality then can be seen.
丨 利 profitable; beneficial.
丨 機而做 to improve a good opening; sagacious to see his interest.
陛 丨 or 引 丨 to be admitted to an audience.
丨 禮 rules of politeness, etiquette; the ceremonies of a bridal pair before ancestors and relatives.
不 丨 佳 I do not think it is first rate.
丨 疑 suspicious; doubtful.
自尋短 丨 he seeks his own destruction; shortsighted policy.
丨 証 a witness, a surety.
丨 棄 rejected, as a present; dissatisfied.

Read *hien'*, but for which 現' is now mostly used. To manifest, to come out; to see one, to appear before, as a prince to his people; to introduce to; the morning sun.

頁心發丨 his conscience pricks him, his better mind is returning.

丨龍在田 the dragon has appeared in the fields;—*i. e.* the harvest is ripe.

從者丨之 [Confucius'] disciples introduced him.

莫丨乎隱莫顯乎微 there is nothing clearer than what is hidden (*i. e.* the conscience); and nothing more manifest than what is intangible (*i. e.* its promptings).

In *Cantonese*. To temper.

丨水 to harden iron; to temper, as tools.

再丨火 it must be tempered again.

件' *chien'* From *man* and *ox*, because an ox is big and can be shared.

To divide, to partake; to distinguish; a classifier of very wide application, used to denote a particular article, subject, or affair, and applied to dress, food, occurrences, law cases, &c., like item or thing; often corresponds to an, one.

一丨事 one affair.

人命案丨 a case involving life.

丨丨俱全 we have everything; all things are ready.

分開一丨丨 arrange each one by itself.

一丨衣裳 one garment.

條丨 an index, a list, a schedule.

許多物丨 a great many things.

丨丨都能 expert at all sorts of trades, adequate to anything.

宗宗丨丨俱全 every article is here, all are complete.

大八丨兒點心 a complete collation, a fine tiffin.

內二丨 two inclosures are in—this dispatch.

建' *chien'* From 廴 to *journey* and 律 a *standard* contracted.

To establish; to set up, to erect, to constitute; to confirm, as laws or institutions; to build; occurs in names of many places; the length of a moon as fixed by the imperial calender.

丨立 to establish.

丨功 to act bravely, to deserve well of one's country.

丨都 to found a capital.

丨造房屋 to build houses.

屢丨奇謀 he frequently formed admirable plans.

丨星 the stars $\nu\,\xi\,o\,\pi\,\rho$ in Sagittarius' head.

丨州 a name of Fuhchau fu and its vicinity in the T'ang dynasty.

本月大丨小丨否 is this moon a long or a short one?

健' **徤'** *chien'* From *man* or *step* and to *establish*; the second is an unauthorized, but not uncommon form.

Strong, robust, vigorous, hearty; persistent, indefatigable; unwearied, as the heavenly bodies in their courses; difficult; to raise, to strengthen, to invigorate.

筆力丨 a bold handwriting.

硬丨 strong, firm, as a muscular arm.

强丨 in the prime of life; sturdy, able-bodied.

精丨 feeling well.

天行丨 the stars are regular in their courses,—so should the princely man be in his practice of virtue.

很康丨阿 have you been in good health?—a polite inquiry.

丨卒 able-bodied soldiers, who should be 壯丨 hale and brave.

丨的過 strong to endure, as a hardship.

實屬丨訟爲能 he is one who thinks persistency in litigation to be a mark of talent.

踺' *chien'* From *foot* and to *establish*.

To walk; walking; one says 踢丨 is to kick, as when children play shuttlecock.

毽' *chien'* A thing to kick, as a shuttlecock or foot-ball.

楊柳而死踢丨子 when the aspen and willow are dead (or leafless), then kick the shuttlecock.

鍵' *chien'* From *metal* and to *establish*.

The bolt of a Chinese lock, called 鎖鬚 or beard of the lock; a door-bolt; a nave or hub.

丨閉 the two parts of a Chinese lock.

管丨 the spring or catch of the bolt.

一部書的大關丨 the leading or important doctrines of the work; also applied to a case in law.

天丨星 the star ν in Scorpio.

楗' *chien'* Like the last.

The bolt or bar to fasten a gate, usually the outer and greater gate.

關丨 to push in the bar; to stop a water-course or sluice with mud.

Read *küen'* A horse going slowly.

諫' *chien'* From *word* and a *slip*.

To point out the right of a thing, to remonstrate, to plead with a sovereign;—it shows his superiority if he listen to it; to urge to reform, to advise, to reprove, to awaken to duty; to testify against; a remonstrance, advice, an exhortation.

丨官 or 丨臣 advisers, counselors; a censor, a historiographer.

諷丨 satirical reproof, as by an innuendo.

規丨 good counsel, fortified by sound arguments.

苦丨 unpalatable reproof.

是用大丨 on this account I use strong remonstrance.

丨止 to dehort, to urge a change in one's conduct.

丨菓 the olive, so called because its first bitter taste afterwards becomes pleasant.

丨勸 to urge one to mend his evil courses.

事父母三丨 to remonstrate thrice with one's parents,—and weep if they still persist.

直丨 plain, personal remonstrance,—the fifth and final reproof; if it is ineffectual, an officer should resign

澗 *chien'* From *water* and *interval*.

A rivulet or torrent at the bottom of a gorge; *met.* a valley; name of a small stream mentioned in the Shu King, which rises in 澠池縣 and runs south and east, joining the River Loh, west of Honan fu; a Budhist term for a hundred billions.

山丨 mountain streams.

溪丨 brooks, runlets, rivulets.

于丨之中 up through the valleys.

覸 *chien'* From to *see* and *interval* as the phonetic.

To spy, to look carefully into; to mix up, as millet and other grains in spirits at offerings.

鐧 *chien'* From *metal* and *interval*.

The iron inside the hub to prevent the axle fretting it; a kind of triangular truncheon or heavy rapier.

使兩把雙丨 to brandish a pair of truncheons, as actors do.

監 *chien'* *'chien* Composed of 臥 to *sleep* or 臨 to *come to* contracted, and 血 *blood*, or 皿 a *dish* to hold the blood, explained as referring to the ancient mode of taking an oath by mingling the blood of the parties when the gods witnessed it; interchanged with the next; the present distinction of tone in this character is modern.

To examine carefully; to revise another's acts; and office, a bureau; to control by inspection.

丨守自盜 he purloined what he was set to guard.

丨督 to oversee, to take an oversight, as a collector of customs; in foreign use, a bishop.

丨察 to examine, to investigate, to inspect, as an official.

丨寐 to lie awake; to pretend to sleep.

丨生 or 才丨 a literary degree between the first and second grades, usually purchased.

入丨 to enter the Academy.

丨寺 or 太丨 an eunuch.

丨觀四方 [Shangti] looked down over the kingdom.

欽天丨 the Board of Astronomy.

國子丨祭酒 the augur of the National Academy, the one who pours the libations to Confucius; he is the first Hanlin graduate.

Read *꜀kien*. To look down upon or into, as a god or sovereign; to look upon and study; to visit subjects; to oversee; to take charge of, to superintend; to compel, to force; a jail, a prison; a halo; to imprison.

司獄丨 a turnkey.

丨獄 or 丨牢 a prison, a place for condemned criminals.

丨裏 or 坐丨 in prison.

收丨 to put in prison.

丨工 an overseer of workmen; a boss, a head-contractor.

丨臨 to superintend examinations.

走丨犯 an escaped prisoner.

丨押 to keep in custody.

不可强丨 you cannot force him to do it.

丨你做 I will make you do it.

丨國 a resident in a subdued state, appointed to watch it.

丨造 to oversee work.

丨視行刑 to superintend an execution.

鑑 **鑒** *chien'* From *metal* and to *look down on*; interchanged with the last.

A large dish in which the moon is reflected; a still, glossy surface which reflects the light; a mirror, a speculum; an example, a precedent; historic events; whatever can serve as a warning or rule; a precept, an admonition; to revise, to audit, to examine for approval; to survey widely; to reflect light.

聖丨 the sacred glance,—his Majesty's approval or revision.

明丨 prespicacious, to examine clearly; a clear apprehension.

台丨 or 雅丨 for you, Sir, to see;—an epistolary phrase.

丨前矩 to heed previous examples.

察如氷丨 to examine a matter with the greatest clearness.

光可以丨 it was so bright that you could see yourself in it.

盍丨于人無丨于水 why can't you see into men as clearly as into the water?

髮光可丨 her hair was so lustrous you could see your face in it;—said of a beautiful woman in the Tsin dynasty.

前車之丨 there is the example of the head carriage; *met.* you can see what you will come to.

通丨 or 綱丨 a general mirror, historical annals.

丨空衡平 [Heaven] oversees the universe with power and equity.

永思民瘼弗忘丨寐 in my constant thought of my people's sufferings I even forget to sleep.

儉 *'chien* From *man* and *all*.

Moderate, temperate, frugal; economical, the opposite of *꜀ché* 奢 lavish; close, saving stingy, thrifty.

太丨 overfrugal parsimonious.

丨薄 to treat one meanly; to grudge another.

丨用 or 節丨 or 省丨 careful and thrifty.

恭丨有禮 a decorous and plain style is good taste — or manners.

不丨之害 the evils of a want of carefulness.

約丨 parsimonious.

凶年不丨 do not be stingy in years of dearth.

丨要得其所 just enough is all we want.

丨德 self-restraint.

與其奢也甯丨 economy is better than such waste as that.

劍 chien' A two-edged sword, a rapier, a straight sword, a claymore; a blade, a trusty weapon.

一把丨 a straight sword, a poniard.

丨殼 or 丨鞘 a scabbard.

舞丨 to fence, to brandish a sword.

丨術 the art of fencing, the sword exercise.

用仁義作丨鋒 [let an officer's] sword-point be humanity and equity.

舌丨唇鎗 a tongue like a sword and lips like spears; biting, sarcastic.

書丨 a student's rapier.

撫丨疾視 he grasped his sword and glared at him.

七星丨 the seven starred sword, was Kung Ming's blade; the Taoists exorcise with one like it.

丨仙 a fairy stiletto, — which would kill when ordered to.

鴛鴦丨 a mandarin-duck sword; —it has two blades in one sheath.

匕首丨 an assassin's dagger; the handle and blade are at an angle.

歉 chien' From to *owe* and *all*; it is often read *k'ien*.

To eat without being satiated; scanty, deficient; to covet, to desire; dissatisfied with or at; discontented, bashful.

丨歲 a year of dearth.

丨收 a bad harvest.

甚丨 much displeased, very grouty

抱丨 I feel my deficiencies.

丨餘 a deficiency and an overplus.

丨事 timid, irresolute, afraid of not succeeding.

丨仄 regretting, as when unable to keep an engagement.

豐年玉丨年穀 in plenteous years gems [are dear], but grain in years of dearth; — a metaphor for able men.

K'IEN.

Old sounds, k'ín, k'ien, gien, k'iem, *and* giem. *In Canton*, k'ín, k'ím, hín *and* hím; — *in Swatow*, k'ien, k'an, *and* k'iam; — *in Amoy*, k'ian, gian, kiam, k'iam, k'am *and* ham; — *in Fuhchau*, k'éng, k'ieng, kieng, *and* kang; — *in Shanghai*, chíⁿ, djíⁿ, *and* k'èⁿ; — *in Chifu*, k'ien.

牽 ˏch'ien Supposed to represent an *ox* and a *halter* attached to it.

To pull, to haul along, as an animal by a rope; to pull, as a cart; to guide, to induce; to connect with, to deduce; to influence; dragged into; in suspense.

丨纜 to track a boat.

丨連 to implicate, to compromise; connected with, as one subject with another.

意惹情丨 their feelings only provoke them wider apart.

丨掛 held in suspense, undecided.

丨挽 to pull one along by the hand.

混丨 lugged in, as an irrelevant topic; incongruous, as a metaphor.

丨絲 to stretch the silk — when twisting thread; to pull the floss, as a spider its web.

丨涉 dragged into an affair; criminated, implicated.

拘文丨議 confused and illogical arguments.

學者丨于所聞 scholars should attend to all they hear.

丨牛 to lead an ox; 丨牛織女遙相望 the Herdboy and Weaver see each other from afar — across the milky Way.

掔 ˏch'ien Nearly the same as the last but not much used, and also interchanged with ˏk'ăng 控 to thump.

To ravel up, to wind around; to strike, to grasp; thick, firm.

縴 ˏch'ien From *silk* and to *drag*; also, read *k'ien'*

To unravel silk; silk which has been spoiled; a towrope; the cord which works puppets; one who connects an affair, or brings parties together in a bargain, is a 丨手, but his position differs from a broker.

拉丨 to act as interlocutor

丨板 the tracking-yoke.

背丨 boat-trackers.

丨繩 a tow-rope, a tracking-line.

皮條丨 the string in a show-box.

汧 ˏch'ien Name of branch of the River Wéi in the west of Shensi in Lung cheu near K'ien-yang hien 丨陽縣; water forming a pool, a lake having no outlet.

岍 ˏch'ien A noted hill in the northwest of Shansi in Fung-tsiang hien 鳳翔縣 also called 吳嶽 where the preceding river rises, and which is also used for this mountain, on which there are two or three summits.

芊 *ch'ien* A medicinal plant, the 秦 ｜; it may be allied to the *Scutellaria*.

愆 *ch'ien* From *heart* and *much.*

A fault, an error; a mistake, a peccadillo; failure; a noxious disease; to go beyond, to be in error, to overpass; to chastise.

｜ 期 passed the appointed time.

｜ 尤 a crime.

｜ 爽 a venial offense.

罪 ｜ a transgression.

繩 ｜ to draw a line so as to show shortcomings; to repress one's errors.

不 ｜ 不忘 I am not in fault, nor have I forgotten it.

騫 *ch'ien* A belly-band, a surcingle, a girth; a horse diseased in the belly; to fail, as in business; to be disgraced; nimble; failing; injured.

不 ｜ 不崩 neither failure nor ruin; never waning or falling, said of the moon and hills.

高 ｜ 了 you've risen quickly.

｜ 污 disgraced, as in reputation.

沓沓 ｜ ｜ rude and supercilious, as when entering a room.

搴 *ch'ien* From *hand* and *cold* contracted.

To pluck up, to snatch or take out; to extirpate; to take hold of.

｜ 旗 to capture a flag—in battle.

褰 攓 *ch'ien* From *garment* and *cold* contracted; the second form seldom occurs.

Inner garments, as petticoats, trowsers, or drawers; to plait; to tuck up.

｜ 裳涉溱 raise the skirt when crossing the brook.

蚈 *ch'ien* A fire-fly, the 螢 ｜, which is thought to be transformed from rotten grass.

幵 开 *ch'ien* Composed of two 干 *shields* of the same height placed side by side; the second form is a common contraction for it when used as a primitive.

Even, level; to raise in both hands.

罕 ｜ were two families or clans of the Kiang 羌 tribes in Sz'ch'uen.

歒 鵮 *ch'ien* To peck at a thing, as a bird does when getting its food.

｜ 破 了 [the sparrows] have pecked it through,—as the paper-window.

相 雞 ｜ 的 [my foot feels as if] a fowl was pecking at it;—said by women.

｜ 碎 米 [the fowls] pick up the broken rice.

歉 *ch'ien* Generally regarded as a synonym of the last; also to suit; to desire; things that match.

嗛 *ch'ien* From *mouth* and *all*; like the last two, and used with the next and for *hien* 銜 to *cherish.*

The pouch of a monkey or marmot; to peck as a bird; not filled, as a measure; deficient; to hold in the pouch or chops.

｜ 然而終日不言 so disturbed that he said not a word the whole day.

｜ ｜ 之德 deficient in virtue.

鳥 ｜ 草 the birds peck the grass.

謙 *ch'ien* From *words* and *altogether*; occurs used for the last, and *hien* 嫌 to *dislike.*

Respectful, retiring, unobtrusive, unassuming; yielding; modest, lowly, complaisant; to think little of one's self; to revere, to be respectful to others; name of the 15th diagram, referring to lowliness.

｜ 讓 to cede, to yield kindly, to give way.

｜ 遜 humble, lowly.

｜ 恭 or ｜ 厚 modest and sincere.

｜ 退 retiring, keeping in the back-ground.

｜ 敬 respectful, reserved.

何 用 太 ｜ why are you so very retiring and modest?

｜ 己 下 問 [Confucius] condescended to ask advice of common people.

太 ｜ or 過 ｜ quite too bashful or unassuming.

｜ ｜ 君子 an unassuming scholar.

｜ 口 polite, courteous language.

嵌 *ch'ien'* From *hill* and *perhaps.*

A deep vale among hills; a grotto in the side of a hill; to fall into.

｜ 巖 dangerous cliffs.

Read *k'ien'* To inchase, to inlay; to infix.

｜ 鑲 to set, as a jewel.

｜ 銀 匠 a jeweler, a silversmith.

拑 *ch'ien* From *hand* and *sweet*; used with the next two.

To pinch, to nip; to grasp, as with forceps.

｜ 住 to seize firmly.

｜ 口 to hold one's tongue, to keep silence.

｜ 客 an agent for selling things.

箝 *ch'ien* From *bamboo* and *to nip*; similar to the last and next.

Tweezers, nippers; to gag; to lock, to fasten or clasp; to forbid, to put on the screws.

｜ 語 to interdict free opinion, to stop people's mouths.

馬 ｜ the bit of a bridle.

鉗 *ch'ien* From *metal* and *sweet*; interchanged with the last two.

A pair of tweezers, pinchers, nippers, tongs; a barber's twirl; a ring on children's necks; a sort of collar put on prisoners; to clasp, to pinch, to gripe; to injure, to hate; in Hunan, to rail at, a term of abuse.

夾 丨 carpenter's circular pinchers.

丨 口 to gag by a cross-stick.

鐵 丨 iron forceps.

螃蟹 丨 a crab's claws.

火 丨 fire-tongs.

手 丨 manacles, gyves.

頸 丨 a variety of neck-ring or torque worn by children.

好口 丨 a good enunciation. (*Cantonese.*)

丨 惡 griping, grasping, like a Shylock.

丨 徒 convicts, prisoners.

鈐 ꜀ch'ien From *metal* and *now*; occurs used for the last.

A large wooden plough; a kind of door-lock or latch; axle of a wheel; to use a seal; an official stamp; a spear handle or haft.

丨 記 a wooden seal, used by inferior magistrates, as an inspector of boats.

丨 鎖 a door-lock.

丨 鏵 a large plough, or more properly the share.

鈎 丨 two stars ω in Scorpio, used by astrologers; the are connected with obedience, filial duty, and brotherly love.

黔 ꜀ch'ien From *black* and *now*; occurs used with the last.

Black, as the hair; the province of Kwéi-cheu; to hold fast, as a bird its prey by the beak.

丨 黎 blackhaired people.

丨 首 black heads; a name given to the Chinese in Ts'in Chi Hwangti's time, because they wore black caps or kerchiefs.

丨 中 an ancient name for the region west and northwest of the River Siang in Hunan, because of the black tribes who lived there.

丨 雷 or 丨 羸 a god of the Taoists, one who is said to create or transform all things.

石着 丨 衣 the stones have grown mossy.

虔 ꜀ch'ien From *tiger* and *letters*; it is often written so as to resemble ch'u' 處 a place.

The firm step of a tiger; attentive, correct; pious, devout; inflexible, determined; ingenuous, sincere; to respect, to venerate; to seize, as prey; to take by force, to kill; to cleave, to hew; trifling, of no moment.

丨 潔 clean, pure, guileless, spotless; unsullied integrity.

丨 心 attentively devout.

丨 告 or 丨 禱 to respectfully inform by prayer.

方斲是 丨 we reverently hewed them square.

丨 誠 truly sincere, unaffectedly devout.

丨 劉我邊陲 he has forcibly ravaged our frontiers.

髯 ꜀ch'ien To remove a criminal's hair and make a wig of it; a dull purplish or dun color, which may have been given to artificially dressed hair.

慽 ꜀ch'ien Uneasy.

丨 悴 or 丨 丨 discontented, anxious.

揵 ꜀ch'ien From *hand* and *firm*.

To lift up, to carry, as on the shoulder; to raise; firm, stable; to settle or mark off a border by stones; to run a boundary; to bar, to close, as the course of a sluice.

丨 鰭 to raise the fins; to frisk, as a fish.

墘 ꜀ch'ien An unauthorized character from *earth* and *heaven*, alluding perhaps to the horizon.

In *Fuhchau*. An edge, a border, a shore; a bank, a margin; eaves.

口 丨 the verge, the border.

水 丨 the water's edge.

腱 ꜀ch'ien The insertion of a muscle or the tendon; a large muscle; to twang a dried tendon.

遣 ꜂ch'ien From *to go* and a *fragment*; it resembles ꜀i 遺 to leave, in its general form.

To commission, to depute, as a government agent; to send; to let go, to send off, as into exile; to send away; to chase.

差 丨 to dispatch, as an envoy on state affairs.

丨 逐 to drive off, to expel, as disorderly people.

丨 使 a messenger, an envoy, an emissary.

丨 人問候 he sent a man to salute him.

丨 車 to send one's carriage to accompany a funeral; this custom has now given place to sending a servant with a card and a small douceur to defray expenses.

丨 罪 to exile for crime.

丨 發 to send on a message.

消 丨 世慮 to throw off the cares and toils of life, as at a watering place.

桃花莫 丨 隨流水 don't let the flowing waters carry away the peach blossoms,—lest people find out that we are here.

戻 ꜂ch'ien From *door* and *wood*; it is also regarded as one form of 戶 a door.

A little door inside of the house; one says, the high board laid across the threshold in gateways.

膁 肷 ꜂ch'ien From *flesh* and *all*; it is often contracted to the second form from the similarity of the phonetics, but that is correctly read *hiüh*, and is an obsolete word for beef, though usage has made it a synonym of the first.

The flank or hollow part of the rump or loins of an animal; the meat in a dumpling.

丨 窩 the flanks, or the hollow of the thigh in an animal.

丨 皮 a term used by furriers for the fur on the breast and flanks.

小 丨 the part above the hip bone.

金銀 丨 the yellowish and whitish fur of the fox.

慊 ʿch'ien To eat insufficiently; unsatisfied.

Read ʿlien. A dessert, a lunch; something brought on after the meal; the meat in a dumpling.

鼸 ʿch'ien A hamster, or pouched lemming with large cheek pouches, in which it retains its food.

丨車 a person who stuffs his mouth in a rude manner when eating, like the hamster.

傔 ch'ien' From *man* and *ali*.

To wait on, to accompany.

丨人 an aid, an attendant.

傽 ch'ien' From *man* and *devout* as the phonetic.

To follow on, as going by the track on an Indian trail.

傗丨 a crowd or row of people going along.

梌 ch'ien' A board which lies crosswise; name of a tree.

繾 ch'ien' Joined inseparably; attached to, as warm friends, or as bad men in a ring or cabal.

丨綣 parasites, unscrupulous retainers; a camarilla.

丨綣難忘 I can never forget our close friendship; the allusion is to a case securely corded and sealed.

掔 ch'ien' A stubborn ox which cannot be led; obstinate, pig-headed.

譴 ch'ien' From *words* and to *send*.

To reprimand, to find fault with; displeased at, to scold, to blame angrily; to sternly question.

丨怒 a get angry at.

丨罪 to charge with a fault.

丨喘 to quiet down, as one out of breath.

不加嚴丨 I will not condemn him too severely.

丨責 to reprimand, to blame, as for dereliction.

干天丨 he had provoked the displeasure of Heaven — by his crimes.

韆 ch'ien' A leathern girdle, a belt.

欠 ch'ien' The original form is intended to represent 气 the *breath* above 儿 *man*, denoting gaping, breathing; it forms the 76th radical of characters mostly relating to motions of the mouth.

To yawn and stretch when weary; deficient in strength or spirits; insufficient, wanting; to we money; to be short of.

丨爽 or 丨安 out of sorts, ailing, indisposed; — always said of or to others.

打丨 or 打呵丨 to yawn.

丨身 or 丨伸 to stretch.

丨債 a debt owed by a 丨戶 debtor.

丨單 a list of debts.

丨負 or 拖丨 a bad debt.

抵丨 to give pledge for a debt, to give collateral security.

丨錢大王 a very prince at owing money; *i. e.* one deeply in debt.

丨項 the sums owing, liabilities.

丨撿點 unmethodical, no care of.

丨莊整 slovenly, untidy in dress.

丨缺 deficient in.

丨解 unintelligible not perspicuous.

丨至誠 not reliable, untrustworthy.

芡 ch'ien' A water plant allied to the water lily, the *Euryale ferox* called also 鷄頭 or cock's head; it has round spotted leaves, and is cultivated for its 丨實 seeds, stems, and roots, which contain much starch; there is a red and white sort which must be boiled before eating; a decoction of the leaves is given when the after-birth is retarded, and the meal of the seeds is made into a coarse biscuit; as a verb, to stir in, as flour in porridge.

勾丨粉 stir in some flour to stiffen them, as meat cakes.

KIH.

Old sounds, kít, kík, kíp, gík, gíp, *and* gak. *In Canton*, kăt, kăp, kik, *and* kek; — *in Swatow*, kít, kek, k'ek, kíp, k'íp, *and* kia; — *in Amoy*, kiat, kek, kip, k'íp, *and* kiòk; — *in Fuhchau*, kék, kík, ngék, *and* k'iòk; — *in Shanghai*, kíh, chíh, kiăk, yih, *and* kiĕk; — *in Chifu*, ki.

吉 ˏchi From *mouth* and *scholar*; *q. d.* a scholar should speak what is suitable.

Fortunate, lucky, felicitous; gainful, advantageous, prosperous; happy, auspicious; good, as promoting or indicating success; fine, elegant.

丨日 a lucky day, auspicious to begin an undertaking on.

近來納丨 I hope you've been well lately.

丨祥 fortunate, a happy omen.

卜丨 to divine for a lucky day.

丨人 a prosperous man.

大丨利市 a good chance for a speculation.

丨便 at your convenience, when opportunity offers.

萬年丨地 the imperial tombs.

丨信 or 丨函 a family letter; a private and not an official letter.

王多丨士 many admirable courtiers you have, O King.
開張大丨 let great prosperity attend the opening — of the shop at new-year; a phrase seen on shop-doors.
丨星共照 may prosperous stars shine on you.
初丨 the first day of a moon.
丨莫 the heavy tramping of leather soled shoes on a floor.
丨蠲爲饎 with happy auguries and purifications the offerings were presented.
丨貝 or 刼貝 an Indian name for cotton or some of its tissues; in Sanscrit *karpasa* or *kapas*.

佶, ꜀chi Robust, strong; exact, correct.
四牡旣丨旣丨且閑 the four war-steeds seem strong, strong and trained for the fray,

姞, ꜀chih A wife or chief concubine of Hwangti.
燕丨 a woman of the state Ching (B.C. 670), who dreamed that a spirit gave her an orchid flower, telling her he was Poh-yiu, her ancestor; an officer explained the dream to foreshow that she would rise like her ancient namesake to high position.

狤, ꜀chih An animal described as a monkey with a short tail, a black stripe down the back, and yellowish with a black face; it is very lively by night, and sleeps in the day; it is the 丨狐 or 風狸 wind fox, an animal like a lemur, and allied to the *Loris tardigradus* of India.

劼, ꜀chi Earnestly, with determined purpose.
In *Shanghai*. To get the seeds out of a pod.
丨棉花 to gin cotton.

皵, ꜀chi Black spots on the skin; the blackness of the skin.

訖, chiˀ From 言 *word* and 气 *air* contracted; it is interchanged with *ngeh*, 迄 to *reach*.
To close or desist; to stop, because the end has been reached; to finish, as a speech; to extinguish; to clear off, as an account; up to the time, till; entirely, all; ended, finished, wound up, terminated.
驗丨 the examination or inquest is finished.
淸丨 [the accounts] are all settled.
丨今 till now, even to the present.
丨不告 to the last he did not tell him.
何丨至此 how has it come at last to this?
咨覆去丨 after the letter in reply had gone.
已丨 already done.
兩丨 the account is cleared off.
付丨 stamped, settled, as a bill.
盖印丨 it having been stamped.
無丨糴 do not engross all the sale of grain, — or hinder the traffic in it.

鬾, ꜂chi The mustache, called 丨髭 because it is divided into two parts like a halberd's head.

戟, ꜂chi From 戈 *spear* and 榦 a *staff* contracted.
A lance with two points, a kind of halberd or partisan, with a crescent-shaped blade on the side; wooden ones are now carried in processions.
劍丨 swords and spears.
持丨 to grasp the spear, to take up arms.
執丨郎 a halberdier of the imperial guard, — in old times.
矛丨 a lance; lances and spears.
射丨牙與袁劉和好 if I hit the halberd's point, then Yuen and Liu must make peace; sc said Lü Pu.

蕺, ꜂chi Interchanged with the last, and used to distinguish the plant.
A medicinal plant, the 大丨 a species of *Euphorbia*; an infusion of the tender leaves is said to be drunk, at first the taste is bitter, then pleasant; the rootstocks are a purgative.

棘, ꜀chi From 朿 a *thorn* repeated; it is not the same as ꜂tsao 棗 a date.
Small species of the genera *Rhamnus* and *Zizyphus*, useful for hedges; the jujube tree; thorny bushes, brambles, spinous thickets; troublesome, like thorns; earnest, prompt; to be urgent; perilous, thorny; swift.
棗丨爲薪羹棗何攻之太急 to roast dates with a rhamnus bush, what an extremity of enmity! — like a brother destroying his brother.
匪丨其欲 not that he wished to have his desire.
如矢斯丨 like the rapid whirr of an arrow.
叢丨之中 among the brambles; *met.* in prison.
九丨 the outer halls of a palace.
丨匕 spoons of jujube wood.
觸處皆丨 wherever [my eye] strikes, it is all thorny; — *i. e.* I know few of the characters.
枳丨棲鸞 [like] the phœnix resting on a bramble; — a great mind in obscurity.

襋, ꜀chi The collar of a coat; the part which envelops the neck.
要之丨之 she makes a waist band and fits the collar.

屐, **屐**, chiˀ From 履 a *shoe* contracted and 支 to *give*.
A patten; a wooden shoe or sabot, used in rainy weather.
紅皮丨 red-top pattens.
木丨 a wooden shoe.
套丨 an open-heeled galoche.
丨齒印蒼苔 the patten's points leave their dents on the yellow moss.

亟, ˏchi Composed originally of 二 *two* lines representing heaven and earth, and 人 *man* in the middle, with 口 *mouth* and 又 *hand*, denoting that the farmer should promptly act with mouth and hand to avail himself of the times which heaven gives, and of the good things which the earth yields; it is sometimes wrongly used for the next, and wrongly written like ˏhan 函 a letter.

Haste, speed; prompt, ready; irascible; to hurry on, to urge, to hasten; troublesome, hurried; often.

丨餽鼎肉 he often sent him many delicacies.

經始勿丨 no need at first of so much haste.

丨應 it is now necessary—to do it.

丨速 urgent; quick as possible.

旣丨只且 the need is urgent.

合丨傳知 it is very important to inform you.

極, ˏchi From *tree* and *prompt*; occurs written like the last.

The ridge-pole of a house; the utmost point; an apex, a verge; a degree or place; an intensive *adverb*, very, extremely; the utmost of; to search to the end of; to serve as a model or law; to urge to it; the end; to reach the end, to exhaust; weary, languid; to let go, as a bow; to take; applied to the moon when in 癸 or the north.

丨多 plenty; rather too many.

妙丨 admirable; how excellent.

阻碍之丨 a real annoyance, a great obstacle.

是丨 truly; it is so; just right.

忙得丨 overwhelmed with work.

四丨 the four quarters; of which the 南丨 is the south pole or axis of the earth, and the 北丨 the north pole and north star.

六丨 the four quarters, with the zenith and nadir; also six calamities that happen to man, *viz.*, early death, incurable disease or crippling, grief, poverty, hatred, and utter weakness.

三丨 heaven, earth and man, the Chinese trinity.

群星拱丨 all the stars bend towards the Pole;—applied to officers at court.

五丨 the five virtues.

八丨 the four points of compass and their halves.

皇丨 the principles of the sages, moral axioms, real perfection.

丨地 or 丨是 completely; done his best.

曷其有丨 when will it come to an end?

丨其數 he completed his designs.

丨品 the best sort, the highest post.

莫非爾丨 you went everywhere.

丨力奉承 extremely polite, obsequious. (*Shanghai.*)

辛苦的丨 the acme of misery.

丨樂世界 the abode of perfect bliss,—in the Budhist heaven.

渺無丨 an illimitable vista, as on the ocean; unknown, as the future.

義理之丨 the highest rationale of rectitude and reason.

太丨 the primum mobile, the ultimate immaterial principle of Chu Hi and other Chinese philosophers; it is sometimes described as synonymous with Shangti, an animated Heaven from which emanates the 兩儀 or dual powers, that produce all things; it is the 理 or fate that acts by laws, but differs from the 無丨 which pervades the universe, and approaches to the idea of a universal mind or spirit.

殛, ˏchi From *evil* and *prompt*.

To put to death or punish by perpetual imprisonment; to leave to perish; to kill, to destroy.

我乃其大罰丨之 I will go further in severe punishment, and kill you.

鯀則丨死 Kwun was kept a prisoner for life.

急, ˏchi From 心 *heart* and 及 *reaching above it*; *q. d.* the point where opposing causes meet.

Hasty, impatient, anxious; hurried, uneasy, solicitous, urgent, hard up, needy, wretched, at extremity; to urge, to straiten; to be zealous for; to hurry.

你莫心丨 don't be in such a hurrry.

氣丨 out of breath, breathing hard; choking from anger.

事丨 the matter is urgent; no time to lose.

濟丨 to relieve one's necessities.

氣性甚丨 hasty, quick-tempered, irascible.

着丨 anxious about, pressed by.

丨丨 impatient, in a hurry;—the word *chop-chop* for be quick, is derived from *kăp-kăp*, the Cantonese sound of this phrase.

丨死 or 丨殺 nonplussed, at his wit's ends; hurried to death.

丨機 quick-witted, of ready invention, fertile in expedients.

丨公 zealous for the public welfare.

緊丨做 be prompt, do it now.

流不丨 it don't flow off fast enough.

丨迫 urged, forced, impelled.

告丨 to report to a superior the danger or necessity one is in.

何苦事此不丨務 why are you so anxious about this matter, which can easily wait?

丨症 a virulent disease.

請丨 to request [leave on account of] urgent affairs.

丨用 or 丨需 I want it very much.

給, ‘chi ‘ké From *silk* and to *join*.

To receive, to be the recipient of; to allow one the opportunity; to afford; to give out.

丨事中 a class of under-secretaries in the Censorate, divided into six Bureaus 科, one for each Board.

賞丨 to confer upon, as a rank or a present.

日 丨 daily needs.
口 丨 eloquent, ready at talking, but not at doing; of a ready wit, prompt to reply.

Read ‘*ké*. To give, to supply, to provide what is necessary; to issue, to put forth, as an edict; to affix, as a seal; as a *preposition*, for, instead of; towards, to; a sign of the passive.
我 丨 你 寫 let me write it for you.
丨 我 說 他 speak to him for me.
我 丨 你 磕 頭 I'll knock head to you.
丨 我 罷 give it to me.
丨 足 give him enough.
丨 不 丨 都 一 樣 it is all the same whether you give it or not.
供 丨 to supply, to furnish food.
丨 誰 家 作 活 呢 at whose house do you work?
無 暇 于 丨 I've no time to attend to it for him.

Read *k'ieh*, Loquacious; earnest words.
㨗 丨 a ready, glib tongue.

及, ˏchi chi' Derived from 又 *hand* or having, and 人 a *man*; *q. d.* to follow a man till he is taken.
To effect, to reach to; to extend towards or stretch on to, to influence at a distance; to communicate; to connect; to implicate; effected, done, and thus becomes a sign of the past tense; as a *copulative*, and, with, also; at, to; about, concerning; used with a negative, denotes unavailing, impracticable, unequal to, deficient, not up to.
說 丨 we have spoken of that.
來 得 丨 I can do it; or 來 勿 丨 I can't do it. (*Shanghai.*)
丨 時 seasonable, suitable.
累 丨 involving other persons.
連 丨 also reached that, as one house caught fire from another.
追 莫 丨 I could not catch him.

丨 此 concerning this.
立 丨 ready at; tact; repartee.
以 此 丨 彼 to get to this by that, one step leading to another.
丨 冠 or 丨 笄 come of age; a boy at 18, a girl at 16 years.
論 丨 何 事 what are you discussing?
後 悔 不 丨 there will then be no place for repentance.
六 師 丨 之 the six hosts followed close on.
丨 第 the highest steps, denotes the three first scholarships in the empire.
丨 今 如 何 how is it getting on?
將 丨 到 he is nearly here, or he will soon come.
比 不 丨 it is not so good.
彼 此 不 相 丨 this does not equal the other.
丨 門 at the door; a disciple.
馬 不 丨 a horse could'nt catch him.

伋, ˏchi Empty, unsatisfying.
丨 丨 unreal, unsatisfactory.
孔 丨 the grandson of Confucius, whose style was Tsz'-sz' 子 思; he wrote the Due Medium.

岌, ˏchi A sharp, lofty peak, which soars far above the rest of the range; hazardous, imminent; unsteady.
丨 丨 乎 殆 哉 how dreadfully hazardous it is!

汲, ˏchi From *water* and *reaching* to.
To draw water from a well; to draw forth, to lead; to drag; to imbibe, as doctrine or example.
丨 氷 or 丨 井 to draw water in a bucket.
不 丨 丨 于 富 貴 don't be too eager for riches and honors.
丨 引 高 風 to imitate or emulate his high example.
丨 縣 the prefect district of Wéi-hwui fu in Honan north of the Yellow River.

笈, ˏchi A box or satchel.
負 丨 從 師 to take the satchel and follow one's teacher, as Su Tsin did, who afterwards became a minister.

級, ˏchi Threads arranged in order; a series, a gradation, a degree or gradus in office, or honor, or merit; a step in a ladder or stairs; a storey in a pagoda; classed, sorted; a classifier of decapitated heads; in *music*, a scale of the notes.
板 丨 a step in a stairway.
品 丨 a grade in official rank.
等 丨 a sort, a class, as of officials.
升 一 丨 advanced one step or grade.
一 層 丨 子 an octave in music.
一 丨 丨 上 he rose gradually to high office.
加 十 丨 promoted ten steps, refers to honorary mention recorded in the Board of Civil Office.
首 丨 one head — of a criminal.
拾 丨 聚 足 he rested as he went up stairs.
七 丨 浮 圖 a dagoba of seven storeys.
登 幾 丨 坡 how many steps are there to the top?

阪, ˏchi Used with the last to denote steps or stages.
梯 丨 頻 登 go up the ladder slowly.

衱, ˏchi The hinder skirt of a robe, a train; a coat-tail; the part which lies under the collar; a lapel.

芨, ˏchi The name of a plant, the 白 丨 or 白 及, which is an orchideous plant like the *Cymbidium*, with pink flowers; its roots are mucilaginous, and are employed to rub on the ink-stone with vermilion to fit it for writing.
紙 丨 a plant growing in Yesso, from whose bark paper can be made.

敫, *chi* From 白 *white* and 放 to *loosen;* it is used as a primitive, and imparts its meaning to a few compounds.

To respect; to beat.

Read *yoh*, A bright, pleasing sight, as a fine landscape.

激, *chi* From *water* and to *beat.* Water impeded in its course by rocks; a breakwater; a dike to turn the current; to impede, to lead aside; to set back, as water; to rouse the feelings, to excite, to vex; to beat on; stirred up; excited, either to gratitude or anger.

感 丨 不 忘 I can never forget your kindness.

丨 烈 vehement, exasperated, roused, as on hearing of injustice.

丨 反 to excite to rebellion.

丨 病 worried to illness.

丨 怒 angered irritated.

丨 流 a noisy, fretted current.

為 世 奮 丨 misused and persecuted by the world.

丨 滚 exasperated, boiling over.

丨 筒 a hose pipe; also the fire engine itself.

毄, *chi* From to *attack* and *mouth;* others say from *spear* and *chariot.*

To jostle and hit, as carts do when rushing by each other; to rub or brush.

丨 拂 to clean by beating, as a cushion; to rub.

丨 兵 a spear, twelve or more feet long.

轚, *chi'* An old form of the last, denoting jostling *chariots* and *spears* now; used only in combination.

To attack.

Read *ki'* and used for 繫. To belong to, to connect; to nourish or rear animals or stock.

墼, *chi* From *earth* and to *attack.* Unburnt bricks.

炭 丨 a small hand-stove or brazier.

擊, *chi* From *hand* and to *knock* against. To tap, to beat on, to knock; to rouse to action, to attack, to rush on; to run against or contray to; to impinge, as parts of a machine.

雷 丨 killed by lightning.

丨 殺 to kill; to attack furiously.

丨 發 蒙 童 to arouse stupid scholars, as by punishment.

丨 鼓 to drum.

衝 丨 to rush against, to make an onset.

目 丨 to see myself.

攻 丨 to charge on a foe.

丨 破 to break by striking; to defeat, to break the ranks.

丨 打 to strike, to beat.

劇, *chi'* To increase, to add to; unhappy, and; an adverb of comparison, more; very, a great degree of; troublesome, annoying; to trifle, to sport; a comedy, a play; a trifle.

玩 丨 to skip and play; to divert one's self.

戲 丨 plays on the stage.

地 丨 清 閒 a quiet, agreeable place.

一 生 苦 丨 miserable all his life long.

病 丨 a distressing malady.

汝 癡 丨 我 you were more foolish than I.

理 繁 治 丨 difficult and troublesome to manage, as affairs in a yamun.

K'IH.

Old sounds, k'ít, k'íp, and k'iak. *In Canton,* hăt, yăp, kwik, *and* k'éuk; — *in Swatow,* k'ít, k'íp, kŭt, k'ia, *and* k'iak; — *in Amoy,* k'ít, gút, giat, k'iat, k'íp, k'iok, *and* k'ek; — *in Fuhchau,* k'ek, k'éük, *and* k'ík; — *in Shanghai,* chih, chăk, chiek, hih, *and* kih; — *in Chifu,* k'i.

乞, *ch'i'* This is said to be a contraction of 气 *air.*

To beg, to ask alms; to intreat; to pray to humbly.

伏 丨 to humbly beg.

丨 恩 to ask for mercy, to implore favor.

丨 企 to earnestly expect.

丨 食 to beg food, as a priestly mendicant; it is a sign of an *arhat*, that he chooses a monastic life and renounces the world.

丨 士 a mendicant priest, of which the 內 丨 and 外 丨 are two classes.

丨 子 or 丨 兒 or 丨 丐 a beggar.

求 丨 to supplicate.

丨 為 示 知 please inform me.

丨 身 or 丨 假 to ask for leave.

丨 巧 to beg [the Weaver Goddess] for skill in needlework.

Read *k'i'* To give.

丨 我 give it to me.

吃, *ch'ih* From *mouth* and to *beg;* occurs used for *kih*, 給 to give, and for the last, but oftener for the next.

To stutter, slow of speech; a difficulty in talking; a sign of the passive; to let, to allow, to permit.

口 丨 to stammer.

丨 奔 to hurry, making haste, as on a journey; in straits, as when one cannot meet expenses.

丨 舌 an impediment in speech.

丨 不 起 I cannot afford it.

丨丨 the sound of giggling and merriment.

丨丨叱叱 a suppressed girlish giggle.

口丨不言 not fluent, hesitating in speech.

難丨不過 this is not very fresh or savory; I can't eat it—as a nauseous dose; I can't pay that price.

丨力 very arduous; laborious.

喫, From *mouth* and a *deed;* it is interchanged with the last.

ˌch'ih To eat, to drink, to swallow; to suffer, to bear, and thus forms the passive voice.

丨酒 to drink wine.

丨飯 to eat, to take a meal.

丨不得 uneatable; can't take it, as a chessman.

丨食 eatables, fare, victuals.

丨緊事 an urgent matter; instantly.

丨苦 suffering; lost money on it.

丨壞 or 丨傷 injurious if eaten; injured by improper food.

丨虧 suffered the loss; injured; losing.

丨了一驚不小 I was alarmed in no small degree.

犵, *ˌch'i* A tribe of Miaotsz', the 丨狫, which name seems to be a foreign word; they still exist in Kwéichau, and have many strange customs; one is to knock out the two front teeth of brides on their marriage day, under the belief that this will prolong their husband's lives; another tribe cut their hair short like the Siamese.

丨猩兒 a ground squirrel found in northern China.

芞, *ch'i'* A fragrant plant or grass, the 丨輿, also called 藒車, which is said to be common in Yunnan under the name of 野草香 wild sweet grass, and much used for offerings in autumnal festivals; the drawing resembles valerian or mint.

泣, From *water* and to *stand.*

ch'i' To weep silently, as for a parent's death; grieved, heart-broken; lamenting.

丨思 to think of with grief.

丨血稽顙 to weep bitterly and prostrate one's self to the ground;—a phrase written on funeral cards.

丨數行下 tears coursed down her cheeks.

丨訴 to narrate with tears.

佇立而丨 long I stood weeping.

丨露蛬 a poetical name for a large species of *Gryllus.*

Read *lih,* Impetuous.

淼丨 rapid, swift.

湆, *ch'i'* Damp; juicy, as meat; dark.

浥丨 dark and dank.

In *Cantonese.* Sticky or oily; muddy, slushy; to stick things together; slow; tough, sinewy; indisposed, ailing.

丨糯 dilatory; stuck in the mud.

濕丨丨 very muddy.

丨丨的 ailing, out of sorts.

丨幾日 indisposed for a few days.

㡿, 隙, *ch'i'* From 小 *small* repeated, and the 日 *sun* coming through a crevice; the second form with *place* is the one in use.

A fissure in a wall, a crack, a chink, a cleft; a gap; an interval, leisure time; a pretext, an occasion or cause of dislike; discord, suspicion; a quarrel, a grudge.

有丨 cracked; at variance, resentful; he has a bone to pick.

開丨 to commence strife, the beginning of a quarrel.

與他有閑丨 I have a quarrel with him.

人生如白駒過丨 man's life is like a white colt passing a crack.

尋丨 to seek occasion against, to raise points of difference.

乘丨而入 he seized that pretext and entered—or began the row.

郤, 郄, *ch'i'* From 邑 *town* and 谷 *valley;* both forms are used for the last, and the first is a surname.

Name of a city belonging to Tsin; to look up to; the intimacies of relatives, illustrated by the junction of bones and flesh.

丨地 interjacent countries.

虩, From *tiger* and *crevice;* it is also read *ts'ih,*

ch'i' To terrify, to scare; frightened, as when treading on a tiger's tail; a species of leaping spider which catches flies.

震來丨丨 to be terrified at thunder claps.

噝, *ch'i'* Laughter; to laugh boisterously and incessantly.

僁, *ch'i'* Labor, toil; exertion in a meritorious cause.

徼丨 to be ill-used; wronged; languor, weariness.

綌, From *silk* and *valley.*

ch'i' A coarse fabric made of threads of the *Dolichos* formerly used for towels and handkerchiefs.

絺丨 fine and coarse hempen cloth.

詰, From *word* and *fortunate* as the phonetic.

ˌch'ié To demand, to ask with authority, to investigate; to judge, to blame, to inquire about faults, to set to rights, to keep in order; to restrain, to prohibit; to reduce the seditious to order, to punish.

丨邦國 to reduce refractory states or vassals.

丨口供 to take depositions.

丨屈 intractable; cacophonous or harsh, as sounds.

丨誅暴慢 to judge and punish the rebellious and intractable.

丨罪 to examine culprits.

盤 丨 to judge a thing, as an official; a severe trial.

以 丨 四 方 in order to restrain [the people of] all regions.

丨 朝 or 丨 旦 to-morrow morning; — *q. d.* I will ask in the morning.

蛣 ˎch'i Beetles of the families of *Copridæ* and *Scarabei*, including some dorr-beetles.

丨 蜣 the dung-beetle or *Geotrupes*, including also other allied genera.

蝎 丨 a tree grub.

蟆 丨 parasites found on crabs, an inch or more long, which eat the crab's eggs.

梅 雨 生 丨 the summer rains bring the paddy-worm, — a caterpillar which eats the kernel of the grain.

KIN.

Old sounds, kín, kím, *and* gím. *In Canton*, kăn *and* kăm; — *in Swatow*, kùn, kím, *and* kín; — *in Amoy*, kún, kím, k'ím, *and* gím; — *in Fuhchau*, king, k'ing, küng, kéüng *and* kéng; — *in Shanghai*, kiăng, djăng, *and* niăng; — *in Chifu*, kin.

巾 ˎchin Said to be composed of 冂 a *border* and 丨 *depending* from, in imitation of a cloth hanging from the girdle; it forms the 50th radical of a large group of characters giving the sorts and uses of cloth.

A napkin, a kerchief, a neckcloth; a bonnet which the common people anciently put on when of age, as a token of carefulness; a cap or turban folded square; a cover of cloth; a curtain.

手 丨 or 汗 丨 a kerchief, a handkerchief; a towel.

頭 丨 a turban; a cloth coiled on the head.

佩 丨 a girdle napkin.

儒 丨 the literati.

公 子 丨 a cap formerly worn by young noblemen.

丨 車 an ornamented carriage; a kind of royal equerry.

丨 飾 an ornamented tiara or cap.

長 丨 a scarf.

搭 膊 丨 or 膊 肩 丨 anything to protect the shoulders, as a shawl, a mantilla, a cape.

斤 觔 ˎchin The original form is designed to represent an ax with a splinter under; it forms the 69th radical of characters mostly relating to cutting; the second, composed of *horn* and *strength*, refers to a vigorous horse, and is now common in accounts for the weight.

To chop, to fell timber; an ax, a hatchet; a test or machine for weighing; the Chinese pound or catty, which was at first, perhaps, confined to dealing out medicines; it should properly contain sixteen taels, but differs in various localities according to the nature of the article, from 3 to 21 taels, the highest being the weight by which coal is sold in Honan, the lowest the catty of tea in Peking, — discrepancies which arise from an effort to equalize an apparent price at the expense of the quantity given; by treaty a catty is fixed at $1\frac{1}{3}$ *lb. av.* or 604.53 grammes.

Read *kin'* To examine into.

幾 多 丨 兩 what is its weight?

虛 丨 a short catty; and 足 丨 a full catty.

量 丨 斗 measure its weight by pecks.

斧 丨 axes and hatchets.

鹽 丨 千 包 the number of bags of salt was one thousand.

打 丨 斗 to turn somersaults, an acrobat's performances.

千 丨 重 担 he can raise a thousand catties; — a man of ability.

丨 ' 丨 ' 其 明 critical and clear was their intelligence; the phrase 丨 丨 also means humane.

釿 ˎchin From *metal* and *ax*; also read ˊyin, and occurs as a synonym of the last.

To smooth; to chip, as with an adz; to carefully remove the marks of the ax, as with a shave or draw-knife; the point of a tool.

丨 鋸 制 焉 smooth and saw the wood to fit it for use.

丨 木 to hew timber.

Read ˎkí. An adz.

斧 丨 axes, adzes, and such like tools.

筋 ˎchin From *bamboo*, *flesh* and *strength*, because of the strength of bamboo splints and cuticle.

The tendons, the sinews; applied also to the veins and nerves; sinewy, stong; related to by blood.

好 丨 力 brawny, muscular.

三 條 丨 a very lean person.

有 丨 骨 sagacious, prudent; can be depended on; he is of my bone and flesh.

皮 鞋 丨 cobbler's ends of threads.

血 丨 the veins, blood-vessels.

麪 丨 tough or rolled out dough.

丨 竹 篦 a fine toothed bamboo comb.

丨 綻 綻 的 [as close and griping] as if his tendons were pulled out.

篁 ˎchin A fine large variety of bamboo with a white skin, from Kwéicheu, having the joints near each other; the culms are used to pole boats, the twigs furnish pipes, and the tabasheer and roots supply medicine.

今 ˓chin Formed of 亼 a *triangle*, or 人 *man* and 一 *one* indicating union, and an old form of 及 *up to*, intimating that all past durations have centred in the present.

An *adverb* of time, now, at this time, presently.

如丨 or 目丨 now; right off.

丨日 or 丨天 to-day.

至丨 till this time.

丨朝 this morning.

丨後 or 自丨而後 henceforth, from this time.

迄丨 up to this time, hitherto.

丨世 this world, the present existence.

當丨皇上 the reigning emperor.

丨昔不同 times are not now what they were then.

丨翼日 the next day; *lit.* the day winged on to-day.

庭燎夜明追古傷丨 while watching the night lamp in this moonlit hall, we think of old times and sorrow at the present.

丨我不樂 why should we not make merry now?

紟 ˓chin From *silk* and *now* as the phonetic.

A sash; a tape or string to fasten the dress; a kind of silk.

丨者 old men and gentry.

襟 衿 ˓chin From *dress* and to *forbid* or *now*; the second form is most used, and is not the same as ˓*k'in* 衾 a coverlet; both are like the last.

A garment of a single thickness; the lapel or fold of a coat, which used to distinguish the gentry as the gowned class; a collar; to tie with strings; the bosom, the feelings.

對面丨 a coat opening in the middle.

絞丨 an ancient court dress of fine and coarse cloth.

丨兄弟 a brother-in-law; the husbands of two sisters call each other 連丨 or connected lapels.

大丨 a large lapel.

丨頭表 a lady's watch.

丨懷 the feelings.

胸丨闊 easy, forgiving, liberal.

單丨 a single covering.

霑丨 [tears] bedewed his garment.

青丨 a term for *siuts'ai* graduates, who wore a blue-black gown.

持丨 relying on their lapeled gowns, — they oppress others; said of the literati.

丨山帶河 the winding hills and girdling streams.

In *Cantonese*. Firm, lasting; able to endure; well placed, settled in a stable manner.

丨使 durable; it will last long.

丨不住 irritable, testy.

丨得鬧 good-tempered, patient.

金 ˓chin The original form is said to be composed of 土 *earth* under 今 *now*, as metal comes from the ground; it is the 167th radical of a natural group of characters describing metals and their uses.

Gold, the metal par excellence; metal, one of the five elements and belongs to the West; mounted or ornamented with metal; gilded; a weapon, arms; yellow, golden; metallic; firm, hard; a coin or piece of gold; money; during the Han dynasty, a catty of gold; musical instruments of percussion; to make as precious as gold; precious, true; imperial, royal; perfect, noble, honorable, as applied by the Budhists to their gods.

白丨 silver; 赤丨 copper.

百丨 a hundred pieces of coin; anciently they weighed as many catties.

黃丨 gold; whence 黃丨地 is applied to a temple as the abode of the gods; also to a good stand for shop, a desirable spot which is worth gold.

千丨 your daughter.

衽丨革 to make clothes of sword and shield, *i.e.* to lie under arms.

玉堂丨馬 [reach the] gemmed hall and gold horse; — high literary rank.

丨戈 arms, warlike instruments.

五丨 all metals; the five are gold, silver, copper, iron, and tin.

丨葉 gold-sheets, thicker than the 丨箔 gold-leaf, and used as bullion.

足丨 pure gold.

屑丨 spangled gold, a poetical name for the stars.

飛丨 bits of gold-leaf on cakes.

丨針菜 yellow needle greens, the dried blossoms of a *Lilium* and *Hemerocallis*, used to give a relish to fish and flesh.

執丨 to take up and reïnter the ashes of the dead. (*Cantonese*.)

丨星 or 罰丨 the planet Venus.

丨星石 iron and copper pyrites.

丨花 brass-leaf ornaments made like flowers, used in offerings.

丨花娘娘 a goddess answering somewhat to Juno Lucina, worshiped at Canton.

丨安 your good health, said to superiors.

丨玉之言 your precious words, — are honest as jade is real.

丨烏 the golden crow; — the sun.

丨樞 the golden pivot; — the moon.

毋丨玉爾音 do not make news [from you as rare as] gold and gems.

丨陵 the golden burial-ground, a name for Nanking, derived from King Wéi of Tsu, who, it is said, buried gold there.

大賂南丨 great revenues of the southern metals, — of gold, silver, and copper.

丨諾 a sure promise.

丨色 a yellow color; golden.

丨臺 the golden terrace, a name for Peking.

煉丨丹 a pill of great virtue conferring immortality.

丨剛力士 the diamond warrior, or 手執丨剛杵 he who grasps the diamond club (*vadjra*), a Budhistic name for Indra (*vadjra-pani*), as the defender of the faith.

丨翅兒 the goldwing (*Chlorospiga sivica*) so called at Peking.

丨馬門 a term for the Hanlin College, from a bronze horse placed there by Han Wu-ti.

裝丨 the gold dressed, a term for an idol.

丨朝 the Golden dynasty of the Jü-chi, which ruled the north of China, chiefly at K'ai-fung fu, from A. D. 1115 to 1235; it was established by Agutha 阿骨打, and endured 120 years under nine princes; the people were the ancestors of the Manchus.

錦 'chin From *gold* and *silk* goods, intimating that much labor has been bestowed on it.

A kind of thin brocade peculiar to China, like tapestry, and used in ornamental work; embroidered, worked in colors; elegant, figurative writing; flowery, diversified.

衣丨 dressing in embroidered robes; *i.e.* noble ladies or gentry.

丨綢 figured pongee.

丨繡 elegantly colored, adorned; figurative, as style.

美丨 beautiful embroidery.

什丨碗碟 painted chinaware.

丨文 fine writing, a flowery style.

花如丨 these flowers are like tapestry.

雲丨 roseate clouds.

衣丨夜行 to wear brocade by night; — *i.e.* to be in high renown away from one's native place.

無煩丨念 don't feel so anxious about me.

丨衾爛兮 what a splendid embroidered coverlet!

果然奪得丨標歸 I shall certainly get the tapestry flag and come back here; — *i.e.* I shall rise to be *chwang-yuen*.

巹 巹 'chin From 己 *self* under 丞 to *receive*; or from 豆 a *platter* under 蒸 *steaming*; the first is commonest.

The nuptial wine cup, in which the pair pledge each other; it was made of half a cocoanut or gourd, and even of silver or pewter, but a porcelain cup is now used.

交丨 or 合丨 to pledge the wedding goblet.

謹 'chin From *words* and tenacious *clay*.

Diligent, careful, vigilant; serious, attentive, respectful; to venerate; to sedulously watch against, to heed; to make others take care; to give the whole mind to; to prohibit.

丨愼 circumspect, watchful.

丨記 careful to remember.

無縱詭隨以丨醜厲 give no licence to the wily and obsequious, that the evil crowd may learn to take heed.

丨具 to send presents to one.

舉大事不細丨 do not be too finical when you have a great object before you.

丨盜賊 carefully look out against thieves.

敬丨 to respect carefully.

恪丨天命 carefully observe the warnings or will of Providence.

丨遵 to carefully obey.

以丨無良 to watch against wicked men.

緊 'chin From 糸 *silk* and 賢 *worthy* contracted, explained as referring to winding silk close.

To bind fast, to press tight; a cord; urgent, prompt, pressing, on the point of, instant, diligent; confined, strait; swift, as the flow of water; tight, as a pair of shoes.

丨要 urgent, necessary, will not bear delay.

無關丨要 not so very important.

等丨 waiting for, needed now.

丨急 trouble, hardships, in extremity.

趕丨做 do it carefully.

手丨 in present need, hard up.

綁丨 tie it tightly.

水丨 the water runs swiftly.

丨丨閉着 it is very securely shut.

軍情甚丨 military affairs are very imperious and urgent.

眼丨 a good memory of persons one has seen.

槿 'chin A tree like the rose mallows, which blossoms and fades in one day; *met.* human glory, transient beauty, fleeting prosperity; it has several names, and is cultivated for hedges; a handle.

黃丨 the *Hibiscus hamabo*

木丨 the *Hibiscus syriacus*.

堇 'chin Composed of 土 *earth*, 人 *man*, and 黃 *yellow* combined and altered; others derive it from 土 *earth* and 革 *hide*; it is now superseded by its derivatives.

Tenacious, adhesive clay such as is deposited by streams; yellow loam or loess, which covers large portions of Northern China, said to be sometimes eaten; to daub; a time, a season; few.

赤丨山 a hill in Fung-hwa hien, near Ningpo, which once produced tin.

墐 'chin From *earth* and *clay*; used for the last.

To daub, to plaster; to stop up, to lute with mud, as the solitary wasp does its nidus; a path over a drain; to cover up a corpse, to bury.

塞向丨戶 stop the holes of the windows — towards the north.

行有死人尙或丨之 on the path lies a dead corpse, somebody will bury it.

殣 'chin Interchanged with the last.

To die of starvation on the roadside; to cover a corpse by the road.

僅 chin' From *man* and *clay* as the phonetic.

Exactly, nothing over, hardly enough; scarcely, almost, a little short; just missed, as a fall; only, nothing more.

丨可 nothing to spare.

丨丨敷用 barely sufficient for what is wanted.

丨丨用得 I can make it do; a little scrimped.

丨到 he has just come.

支用丨够 hardly enough for the outlay.

丨足日給 just able to meet expenses.

丨以不驗 barely examined it, only just looked into it.

丨有 just had a little.

丨幸得免 I luckily just escaped unharmed, — as from robbers.

丨彀足矣 I have had enough of his trouble; I am quite supplied.

廑 **㢙** From *shelter* and *clay*; the two are regarded as different by some, but their definitions are too similar; used with the last.

'chin A small house, a hut, a hovel; a lodge of one or two rooms, just big enough for a shelter; just enough; diligent, careful; a surplus.

茅丨 a rustic cabin.

丨念 or 丨系 thoughtful of; anxiously.

丨能勿失 with care you will be able to avoid error.

丨窄 rather narrow, cabined.

堇 From *plant* and *earth*; it is easily confounded with its primitive, and some say it is another form.

'chin A plant like monk's bane, also called 烏頭 or crow's head, and is poisonous, it seems to be the field violet (*Viola*) common in northern China, though the water-hemlock may be meant.

丨丨菜 a wild flower in Kiangsi, whose seeds fructify like the nightshade.

紫丨 a Japanese name for the *Corydalis incisa*, and a *Dielytra*.

丨荼如飴 its violets and sow-thistles [were sweet] as dumplings.

饉 A dearth of vegetables; three years without a crop.

'chin 飢丨 famine and dearth, no crops.

瑾 The brilliancy of gems, which is intended to set forth their luster, hardness, and fine texture; it is much used in names of men.

'chin

丨瑜之美有瑕匿焉 even in the most brilliant gems, defects are still found.

丨發奇光 the gem will emit its rays; — genius will show itself.

懷丨握瑜 he is a man of great clearness and sagacity.

覲 From to *see* and *clay* as the phonetic.

'chin To have an audience with the Emperor, especially in autumn; to look towards the North, or his throne; to see a superior; to grant an audience.

朝丨 or 入丨于王 to see his Majesty.

乃日丨四岳羣牧 he daily gave audience to [the rulers] of the Four Mountains and the crowd of officers.

靳 From *hide* and an *ox* as the phonetic.

chin' A sort of martingale; a kind of ornamental plume under a horse's neck; firm, strong; parsimonious; to restrain; to take; to ridicule, to put to shame.

丨制其行 the martingale impedes his progress.

禁 From to *proclaim* and a *forest*.

chin' To prohibit, to warn against, to forbid; to stop the completion of, to regulate; to restrain, to keep off; to impose restrictions; forbidden; imperial, governmental; a cup or tray for wine; an instrument of music.

丨條 or 丨戒 prohibitions, laws, restrictions.

丨貨 contraband goods.

開丨 to annul or remove restrictions; to abrogate laws.

丨城 or 丨中 his Majesty's residence, usually called 紫丨城 the Vermilion Closed citadel.

丨地 secluded, forbidden places, such as belong to the emperor.

丨卒 or 丨子 a turnkey, the lowest grade of jailer.

違丨 to disregard the prohibitions.

喜不丨 irrepressible joy.

不能丨遏 he was powerless to prevent it.

丨禦風寒 to keep off the wind and cold.

百無丨忌 there is nothing at all to be afraid of, there are no unlucky things.

丨忌無犯 have a care, don't intrude — into an infected room.

Read 'kin. To bear, to endure, to withstand.

苦楚難丨 my sufferings are intolerable.

不丨頑笑 he won't stand any fun, he can't bear joking with.

矜 Considered to be another form of the next.

chin' A disease in a cow's tongue; to be silent.

直辭一以薦巧舌千皆丨 one honest direct introduction for him will put to silence a thousand crafty words.

噤 From *mouth* and to *forbid* as the phonetic.

chin' Unable to speak from lockjaw, mumps, or other disease; to refrain from speaking; silent, as from utter grief.

丨口痢 dysentery and difficulty of swallowing.

In *Cantonese*, read *t'am'* To deceive, to play a trick on; an imposition; to try.

丨丨吓 try it once.

不聽你丨 I'll not be imposed on by you.

襟 *chin'* From *heart* and *to forbid;* also read *˛kin*.
Determined, resolute.
心一丨 my decision is made.

凚 *chin'* Cold, chilled; affected by cold.
打冷丨 to have a cold shiver.

僸 *chin'* A kind of musical instrument; to look up and follow another up-hill.
後丨丨而方馳 the rest came following after with their heads up.

顲 *chin'* To gnash the teeth in rage; debilitated, exhausted, all energy gone.
丨顩 to gnash the teeth in rage at one.

妗 *chin'* From *woman* and *now* as the phonetic.
A wife's sisters; a sister-in law on the wife's side.
丨娘 a sister-in-law.
大丨 women who help and direct the bride during the three days of wedding.
連丨 or 丨兄弟 the husband of a wife's sister.
丨毋 a maternal aunt.
Read ˛*chin.* Laughing; the joyous merriment of girls.

近 *chin'* From *to walk* and *ax* as the phonetic.
Near in time or place; recently, lately, soon; to bring near, to approach, to close upon, to draw close to; to touch; to like; familiar; according to, like, consonant; adjoining, conterminous, next to; in official papers, denotes that an officer is stationed as near his parents as the law permits; in *Budhism*, those who are near or in attendance; assisting, as a priest.
丨日 or 丨時 these few days, lately, these times.
將丨 about to be, presently.
丨海 maritime, coastwise.
丨來如何 how have you been recently? how do you get on?
路丨 the distance is not very far.
丨道 or 丨理 reasonable, not far from right.
丨視眼 near-sighted.
以丨有德 to associate with the virtuous.
附丨 near one; neighboring.
貼丨 go near to him, join him.
可丨 it can be approached.
不敢丨前 he did not venture to come close to him.
少親丨 [I have failed] in visiting you so seldom.
親丨 intimate, to be familiar, near one.
丨取諸身 [reason] should be taken to one's self, or assimilated by the mind.
切丨 made familiar to the mind.
丨好不一 [I hope you are] every way happy these days.
性之所丨 the natural bent will soon manifest itself.
丨善男 and 丨善女 male and female attendant devotees (*upasaka, upasika*), denote the lay members of the Budhists.
往丨王舅南土是保 go, my royal Uncle, and protect the south country.
挨丨 adjoining, as a house.

劤 *chin'* Great strength brawny.
不吃丨 nothing to rest on, no leverage.
使丨拍門 I pounded the door with all my might.
學得渾身有了丨兒 he felt his whole body reïnvigorated and refreshed for action.
費我一股子丨 I have spent all my strength for you.

K'IN.

Old sounds, gim, gin, *and* k'ím. *In Canton,* k'ăm, k'ăn, *and* yăm; — *in Swatow,* k'ím *and* k'ŭn; — *in Amoy,* k'ím, k'ún, *and* gím; — *in Fuhchau,* k'íng *and* k'ŭng; — *in Shanghai,* chăng *and* djiăng; — *in Chifu,* k'in.

欽 ˛*ch'in* From *breathing* and *gold* as the phonetic.
One stretching and yawning; to respect; that which commands respect or ought to be revered; specially that which comes from the emperor; to regard as by or from the emperor; imperial, governmental; majestic.
丨賜 a gift from the Throne; by royal grant.
丨差 one sent to represent the emperor; an imperial commissioner.
丨召進京 called to the capital by the Emperor.
丨奉 respectfully received, as a mandate.
丨定 when prefixed to names of books, shows that they are printed by or with the order of government.
丨此 or 丨遵 respect this, imperialize this; — *i. e.* let this be reverently regarded as from the Emperor.
丨丨 longed for sadly; the measured tone of bells and drums.
丨敬 every one joins in reverencing him, as a loyal statesman.
丨點翰林 to mark off the selected academicians.
丨命 by imperial command.

嶔 From *hill* and to *respect* as the phonetic.
ch'in
High peaks shooting up aloft.
嶇〡 steep peaks.
〡〡 gaping, yawning, opening the mouth wide.

瘽 A severe chill or ague; a great shivering.
ch'in

衾 From *clothes* and *now*; interchanged with *k'in* 捦 as the verb.
ch'in
A coverlet, a large quilt; to cover a thing, as a dish; to pull the coverlet over one; two coverings of white and red cloth laid over the corpse in its coffin.
被〡 a bed-quilt.
抱〡與裯 wrapped in the quilt and clothes; — *i. e.* married.
〡影無慚 no shame under the quilt's shadow; — conscious innocence
翡翠〡 the emperor's bed-quilt.
枕冷〡寒 a cold pillow and chily coverlet; — no bedfellow.

禽 From 禸 a *paw's* trace joined with 今 *now* as the phonetic; used for the next.
ch'in
Birds; the entire class *Aves*; flying and feathered creatures; unimpregnated birds.
家〡 chanticleer, a cock.
委〡 to make and send the betrothal presents.
絲〡 an egret, also called 雪客 snow guest in Chihli.
仙〡 or 胎〡 a poetical name for the crane, which is regarded as 〡之宗 the chief of birds.
〡獸 birds and beasts; animals.
〡圖 civilians, because their insignia are mostly birds.

擒 **捦** From *hand* and *bird* or *gold*; occurs written as the last.
ch'in
To seize, as a hawk does; to clutch; to grasp, as by the collar; in *rhetoric*, to hold by the literal sense; a rigorous adhesion to terms.
生〡 to take alive.
〡拿 or 〡獲 or 〡捉 to seize; to arrest, as a thief.
〡賊須〡王 in order to put down rebels, their leaders must be caught.
〡虎 to grasp a tiger, as a filial boy did to save his father.
猩猩啼而〡之 the orang-outang weeps and then seizes— its prey when near.
〡王封王 seize a king and get him to make you king — 'twill condone the violence.
七〡孟獲 Măng Hwoh, a chief who was arrested seven times.

檎 A species of *Pyrus*, called 林〡 common in northern China, which bears a small red apple, rather insipid, known as 沙果 or sand fruit, and 花紅 flower-red; the blossom is white, the unripe fruit is boiled in green tea as a cooling drink.
ch'in

蠄 A spider, the 〡蟧, having very long legs, probably a species of *Phalangium*; the name is usually applied to spiders without webs.
ch'in

噙 An unauthorized character.
ch'in
To hold in the mouth, as a bird does a twig.
龍〡一顆珠 the dragon holds a pearl in its mouth.

懄 Brave, intrepid; deep compassion for; careful for.
ch'in
〡然後得免 with care you can avoid trouble in future.

勤 From *strength* and tenacious *clay* as the phonetic.
ch'in
Laborious, diligent in one's post; to toil in or for; sedulous, attentive to, kind; to stir up, to assist, or excite to exertion; laboriously.
〡儉人家 a diligent and frugal man.
恩斯〡斯 lovingly, toilingly.
〡愼 diligent and careful in attending to business.
〡工 diligent workmen; to work well.
〡力 or 〡勞 laborious, faithful in work, industrious.
〡家立業 exerting one's self to look after the household.
〡王 zealous in serving one's prince.
大富由〡 rich people have need to be careful.
殷〡 very attentive to.
周公咸〡 Duke Cheu exhorted all to be diligent.
憂〡惕厲之心 a sympathizing, earnest, unwearied heart, — such as a ruler should have.

懃 From *heart* and *diligent*.
ch'in
Zealous, earnest.
慇〡 anxious about one's duties, persevering under opposition; no rest; bowed down.

琴 Formed of two *pearls* and *now*, but the original form was intended to represent the shape.
chin
The Chinese lute, or harpsichord, having seven strings, which are drawn tense by nuts; lute strings; to control one's feelings; to restrain, because its notes quell the passions; foreign musical instruments; a singer on a kite.
〡音亂 the lute is out of tune; *met.* disconcerted, unexpected.
〡心 a motive, an intention.
〡堂 your bar, your court — said of a district magistrate.
抚〡 or 彈〡 or 鼓〡 to thrum the lute.
風〡 an organ (also called 筒〡); a melodion; a seraphine, an accordion; also applied to the jingling stones hung in the wind.
提〡 a theorbo or virginal.
月〡 a four-stringed guitar with a round belly.
洋〡 a lute, consisting of thirty copper strings running across two bridges, struck with hammers.
〡瑟之絃 lyre and lute strings, *met.* matrimony.

八音丨or小洋丨a music-box.
妻子好合如鼓瑟丨 loving union with wife and children is like the harmony of lutes.
對牛彈丨 to thrum the lute to a buffalo; — to cast pearls before swine.

芹 ˏch'in From *plants* and *ax*.
Celery or parsley; applied also to similar plants, as cress, pimpernel, honewort, and water-hemlock.
水丨菜 water-cress.
採丨 to pluck cress, to become a *siuts'ai;* alluding to the lines 思樂泮水薄採其丨 pleasant is the college pool where we plucked the green cress.
旱丨菜 celery.

丨筵 or 丨酌 a festival cup given to graduated bachelors.
野人獻丨 [it will be polite, if] the villagers offer some parsley.

㝻 ˏch'in A general of cavalry in Lu, named 費丨父 about B. C. 720, spoken of in the Tso Chw'en.

芩 ˏch'in From *plant* and *now*.
A salt marsh plant with lanceolate leaves like a bamboo, and creeping roots, whose seeds are eaten by deer and cattle; it is probably a panic grass or a *Cyperus*.
黃丨 a yellowish colored medicinal root, common in western China, the *Scutellaria viscidula* or skull-cap, used as a tonic.

坽 ʻch'in A pit.
甸人築丨坎 the foresters dug and built up a well.

捦 ch'inʼ To press down, to settle or adjust with the hand; to put the hand on; to lean on.
丨壓 press it down.
丨桌 to lean on the table.
丨地泅水 hold on to the ground when you swim; — *met.* have something to depend on.
搓圓丨扁 roll it and flatten it; *met.* an easy disposition.

In *Cantonese*. To cover; to pull over one.
丨被 draw the quilt over you.
丨住 cover it, as a dish.
丨水車 to work a fire-engine.

KING.

Old sounds, king, kăng, *and* ging. *In Canton,* king *and* keng; — *in Swatow,* keng, kⁿia, kⁿé, *and* am; — *in Amoy,* kéng *and* géng; — *in Fuhchau,* kíng, k'íng, kèng, *and* kéng; — *in Shanghai,* kiăng *and* djiăng; — *in Chifu,* king.

驚 ˏching From *horse* and *to reverence* as the phonetic.
A shy horse; to terrify, to scare; to fear; to make confusion; afraid, apprehensive, alarmed, perturbed, astonished; to apprehend.
丨動 to excite, to arouse; used as a polite phrase for troubling one.
丨駭 afraid, much startled.
丨怕 to fear; much alarmed.
壓丨 to suppress as alarm; to remove sudden frights.
震丨 frightened, as by thunder.
丨死人 frightened to death.
徒御不丨 neither footmen nor drivers created any alarm.
丨風 afraid of the wind or a draught; convulsed; fits, such as children have.
腰細丨風 her waist was small, as if a breath of wind would snap it.
膽戰心丨 quivering and shaking with fright.
丨異 marvelous; strange, frightful.

丨衆 or 丨墉 afraid of the public gaze; bashful.
馬丨了 the horse shied or bolted.
丨得呆了 frightened out of his senses.
巧語丨人 strange words that astonish people.

荊 ˏching From *plant* and *to punish*, because this thorn was once used to beat people.
A bush found in Hunan, slender, lithe, and thorny; spinous, prickly; brambles, furze.
拙丨 or 丨妻 the dull thorn; *i. e.* my wife.
初得識丨 I have only just made your acquaintance; — *i. e.* just learned that you are like a jadestone from 丨山 where a pure piece was found.
手生丨棘 this affair proves to be very vexatious.
素未班丨 I have not before seen you.

丨蒿花 the *Vitex incisa;* its stems 丨條 are woven into baskets like those of the osier.
蔓丨花 another species of *Vitex*.
丨州 one of the nine divisions of Yü; it comprised all Hunan and most of Hupeh, with part of Kwéicheu; it constituted the kingdom of Tsu, sometimes called 丨楚 during feudal times;
丨州府 King-cheu fu on the Yangtsz' River was its capital.
紫丨 the *Cercis siliquastrum* and *Chinensis*, two varieties of the Judas tree.
丨釵布裙 she has a boxwood hair-pin and cotton skirt; *i. e.* poor and well-behaved.
丨棘 thorny; useless, annoying.

京 ˏching The original form is composed of 高 *high* and 丨 a line indicating *height*.
Great, exalted; the highest point which men can reach; a high peak; a mound; a capital or metropolis, where the sovereign

resides; fine, excellent, from the capital; in *arithmetic*, the eighth place in decimals, denoting ten millions.

莫之與 丨 he has no equal.

如坻如 丨 like islets and mounds; said of descendants.

乃覯于 丨 丨 師之野 he then beheld the grand elevation, a plateau with room for many.

憂心 丨 丨 the grief of my heart is intense.

上 丨 to go to Peking.

丨 報 the Peking Gazette.

南 丨 Nanking, the southern capital, the metropolis of all China during two reigns (A. D. 1368-1403).

北 丨 or 丨 都 Peking, the northern capital.

The following list exhibits the principal capitals of the Chinese rulers from early times, with the approximate dates of occupation; some of the shorter dynasties are not given.

DYNASTY.		CAPITAL.	PRESENT NAME.
夏	B.C. 2180	陽夏	now 太康縣 in Honan.
商	1766	亳	now 歸得府 in Honan.
周	1122	鎬	near the capital of Shensi.
	781	洛邑	in Honan fu.
秦	249	咸陽	near 西安府
漢	200	長安	in Shensi.
東漢	A.D. 25	洛陽	near 河南府 in Honan.
後漢	221	成都	now capital of Sz'ch'uen.
晉	280	洛陽	in Honan.
東晉	317	建業	now Nanking.
隋	582	長安	in Shensi.
唐	904	洛陽	in Honan.
宋	960	汴梁	now 開封府 in Honan.
	1129	臨安	now 杭州府 in Chehkiang.
元	1280	燕京	now 順天府 in Chihli.
明	1368	南京	now 江甯府 in Kiangsu.
	1403	北京	to the present time.

丨 師 a capital, the metropolis

丨 式 Peking fashions.

丨 水 a good kind of pencil.

丨 畿道 the capital of Corea; also a metropolitan board of magistrates.

Read *kiang*. Sorrowful.

憂心 丨 丨 my sorrow grows intense.

麖 *ching* From *deer* and *great*; rarely occurs with 畺 as the primitive.

A large deer, described as having one horn and a cow's tail, perhaps referring to the nylghau of India; in Canton, the 黃 丨 denotes a small deer, a species of muntjac (*Cervulus*) and the delicate chevrotain (*Moschus*) or mouse-deer.

丨 皮袋 a leather fob.

經 *ching* From *silk* and a *path* as the phonetic.

The warp of a web in the loom; what runs lengthwise, as the great or straight veins or arteries; the meridians of longitude; lines; to pass through or by, to cross; what has passed, and thus often becomes merely a sign of the past tense; as an *adverb*, already, then, at that time; to manage, to plan, to regulate; the person who manages a business; what is regular, orderly, or standard; laws, canons, religious manuals, classical works; the *sutras* of the Budhists, and 論 denotes their *shastras*; in *silk* trade denotes organzine or thrown silk.

丨 緯 warp and woof; lengthwise and crosswise.

丨 緯萬端 to attend to everything methodically.

丨 營 to speculate, to trade, to plan for a livelihood; to map out.

丨 紀 a broker, an agent.

丨 承 the head clerk in a custom house.

丨 廳 chief secretary in a prefect's office.

丨 歷 a clerk who ascertains the statistics of a prefecture; to examine thoroughly.

一 丨 他洗就回來 as soon as he is washed he will return.

不 丨 手 it did not go through my hands.

旅力方剛 丨 營四方 while my back retains its strength, I must everywhere plan and labor.

毋失 丨 紀 they never fail in their regular courses, as the stars.

丨 手作 I did it with my own hand.

曾 丨 見過 I have already seen it.

丨 目 it passed before his eyes.

丨 過 passed, over, gone through.

念 丨 or 誦 丨 to repeat prayers, to read the liturgy; to con the Classics.

丨 絡 blood vessels of all kinds, divided into main or straight, and lateral or small.

不 丨 事之人 an inexperienced hand; 不 丨 also means unclassical, heretical, or non-conformist, in the minds of Confucianists.

丨 水 or 月 丨 the menses.

聖 丨 canonical books, the classics or Budhistic; also applied to the Bible and Koran.

丨 費 current outlay.

不 丨 管 it is out of my jurisdiction.

丨 常 what is regular and necessary in morals, the basis of society.

幾度 丨 I've tried it several times; I have often been there.

事非 丨 過不知難 you don't know its difficulties till you've tried it.

丨 濟救民 men of deep learning can save the people.

丨 綸 the highest principles of nature, the rules of morals.

法 丨 the Budhist canons; Budha's own words are termed 契 丨 or documents.

正法華 丨 a sutra, the Lotus of the true Law (*Saddharma-pundarika sutra*), the standard classic of the Lotus school.

Read *king'* To kill one's self.

自 丨 于溝瀆 to commit suicide in a ditch;—a disgraceful end.

涇 ˏ*ching* Name of a large river which rises in Kansuh, and drains its eastern part, joining the River Wéi in Shensi, near Sz'-ngan fu; it has very clear water, and gives its name to several places near it; also a river near Wu-hu, and one in Annam; to run through or straight across; a creek which joins places; a fountain.

丨 涎 to flow straight through.

淠彼丨舟 quickly go those boats on the King.

巠 ˏ*ching* From 巛 *streams* under 一 *one*, representing the earth, and 壬 contracted to 工 *work*.

Streams running under the ground; a quiet flow of water without waves; name of a stream and of a place, for which the next in now used.

郅 ˏ*ching* A village in Kao-mih hien 高密縣 lying in the east of Shantung in Lai-cheu fu.

兢 ˏ*ching* Formed of 兄 *brother* and 丰 *vigorous*, both repeated, referring to the pleasant sight of brethren agreeing; it is similar to 競 in appearance and sound.

To fear, to forbear from, to refrain; cautious, solicitous lest a thing miscary.

丨丨 wary, respectful; strong, as sheep.

戰丨 or 戰戰丨丨 tremblingly alive to; wary, very anxious for.

丨懼 dreading, apprehensive of consequences.

丨丨業業 feeling the peril and afraid.

矜 ˏ*ching* From a *spear* and *now*.

The handle of a spear; a rod; to compassionate, to pity, to feel for; the pitiable; concerned for, regretting; to attend to earnestly; careful, sparing; boastful, elated, conceited; to rule one's self; to respect, to value.

丨憐 to commisserate.

可丨 worthy of compassion.

居以凶丨 I then should be in pitiable misery.

丨誇 bragging; to vapor, to talk.

有所丨式 to respect, as a model.

丨而不爭 firm but not quarrelsome.

自丨己善 a good opinion of one's self.

丨孤恤寡 to feel for and help widows and orphans.

不丨細行 to disregard small affairs.

魚丨鱗而拼凌 the fish close their scales and huddle under the ice.

丨丨 vigorous looking, said of a flock of sheep.

何人不丨 which of them was not wifeless, — and to be pitied?

景 ˎ*ching* From *sun* and *eminent*; occurs used for ˎ*ying* 影 a shadow.

Bright sunlight; brilliant, illuminated; illumined by the sun; a fine view, a good situation or prospect; figure, aspect; circumstances of a place or thing; a rarity, a lion, a curiosity, a sight; a resemblance, fancy, imagining, form; a style, as of dress; to regard kindly, longing for; large; a shadow.

丨緻 a vista, a prospect; a view.

光丨 circumstances, prospects; character of; peculiarities; a landscape, appearances of nature.

擺丨 to display rare things.

無丨 disreputable, it has a bad look.

淸丨 neat and well arranged.

以介丨福 by this we try to increase our great happiness.

佳丨 or 美丨 fine scenery, a good site; easy circumstances.

好晚丨 a good sky at sunset; it all ended well, as the honorable end of a toilsome life.

順丨 pleasantly situated.

見丨生情 cautious and discreet, able to judge men and things.

丨像 a statue; a portrait.

年丨 the prospects of the year.

丨行' 行止 to set a mark and strive to reach it, to act up to principle.

丨色 the look of the country, a landscape.

時丨 signs of the times.

丨山 Prospect Hill in Peking.

丨敎 the luminous doctrine; — so Christianity is called on the Nestorian tablet.

八丨 the eight sights, the lions, the remarkable objects of a place.

西洋丨 stereoscopic views.

丨泰藍 cloisonné, enameled ware.

老丨 an old person, an old resident, but yet able to work.

汎汎其丨 their shadows went dancing on the stream.

警 儆 ˎ*ching* From *man* or *words*, and to *respect* as the phonetic.

To warn against, to caution, to threaten with a penalty; to arouse, to urge to reform; to set judgment before the mind, to alarm the heedless.

丨世 to arouse or warn the age.

丨戒下次 to caution against doing it again.

丨悟 to startle and put one on his guard.

丨衆 to caution the people.

殺一丨百 executing one man deters a hundred.

懲丨 made a warning example of.

丨勵 to stimulate to exertion.

境 ˎ*ching* From *earth* and *end* as the phonetic.

A limit, a boundary; the marches; a place where one lives, abode; a region, place, neighborhood, district; state, condition of life, position.

丨界 frontier, boundary, limit.

貴丨 your place of residence.

蓬萊仙丨 Taoist fairy land.

邊丨 on the border.

入丨問禁 when you cross the border, inquire what are the prohibitions.

隣｜vicinity; the neighborhood.
處逆｜難 it is hard to be in straitened circumstances.
｜遇 condition in life.
｜社 the neighborhood temple.
｜份 fees or tax levied for this temple.
苦樂｜alleviating circumstances, some compensatory things.
越｜to go around (not through) a lot or country; to get beyond.

'剄 'ching To cut one's throat; to cut off the neck.

'頸 'ching 'kăng From 頁 *head* and 巠 a *stem* contracted.

The neck, especially the front part of it; the throat; a narrow part of a thing; an isthmus; *met.* the temper.
火｜irascible, testy.
｜項 or ｜子 the neck.
｜帶 or ｜巾 a neck-ribbon, a neck cloth, a neck-tie.
刎｜交情 intimate friendship.
生｜癧 lumps growing in the neck, ganglionic swellings.

'璥 'ching A gem, a fine stone used in jewelry.

敬' ching' From 攴 to *tap* and 苟 *careful*, diligent, but this is regarded as different from 苟 *careless*; their original forms are unlike, and this is derived from *sheep*, to *wrap*, and *mouth*, with to *tap*.

Reverent, sedate, attentive, respectful; that feeling of the heart which springs from self-respect and a due regard to all positions; to honor, to show respect to; to worship, to venerate, to stand in awe of; to watch one's self; self-poised; reverently; that which honors one, as a present; a douceur.
｜神 to venerate the gods.
｜身 self-training; to be studiously careful of one's conduct.
｜酒 to present a glass of wine.
失｜I have offended, I beg your pardon.
可｜可｜admirable! surprising!
｜惜字紙 respect written paper; when added to handbills, means "Do not deface or tear this down."
｜達者 or ｜啓者 I who respectfully inform you; the first sentence in a letter.
足以有｜也 fitted to secure respect.
不成｜意 this is an incomplete respect to you;—said by a host to excuse his feast.
聊以爲｜take it as a mark of respect.
｜信 devout faith; reverence and belief.
｜干事 attentive to business.
禮主於｜all decorum consists chiefly in respect.
節｜a present to a teacher, or to the examiner at the three great tripos; it is also termed 炭｜the charcoal supply, and 別｜a parting present, and other names.
｜重' to hold in esteem.
豐｜a generous present.
肅｜grave and reverently.
修己以｜respect tends to make one virtuous.
親｜一盃 let me give you one glass.

竟' ching' From 音 *sound* and 儿 a *man*; *q. d.* a tune or song carried through.

To exhaust, to finish, to go through a matter to the end; at the close, the end, the utmost, the termination; endless; as an *adverb*, and usually succeeded by a negative, at last, finally, then; only, nothing but.
｜無一言 he never said a word.
｜然不至乎 won't he come at all then?
｜自去了 still you went.
｜不曉得 after all he did not comprehend it.
｜甯 endless repose.
畢｜to the last, after all.
無｜illimitable, vast expanse.
｜然如此 ah! is it so?
｜送一個空箱 only sent one empty box after all.
究｜thoroughly examined, sifted to the bottom.
巴究｜the name of the last of the eighteen heavens of the Budhists (*akanishta*), that which is the limit of the world of desire.

獍' ching' A feline animal which is charged with eating its dam as soon as born, and is hence called 梟｜owl-cat.
破｜or ｜虎 the muntjak tiger (*Felis brachyurus*) of Manchuria.

鏡' ching' From *metal* and the *end* as the phonetic.

A metallic mirror; a looking-glass: any reflecting surface, as the sea or moon; often applied to books which reflect knowledge; to brighten; to illustrate; bright; lustrous.
面｜or 玻璃｜a looking-glass.
千里｜a telescope, a spy-glass.
顯微｜a microscope.
取火｜a sun-glass.
｜粧 a toilet, a dressing-case.
照身｜or 穿衣｜a pier-glass, a large mirror.
｜架 picture frames.
百花｜a sconce, a reflector; a kaleidoscope.
明｜高懸 it is clearly reflected in your view; said of an astute officer.
明｜聖法 he clearly illustrated the holy law.
護心｜a sort of cuirass or breastplate.
近視眼｜near-sighted or concave spectacles.
花｜convex glasses or lenses.
心｜用書磨 the mind's glass must be rubbed up with books,—to be intelligent.
｜花水月 [vain and empty] as the reflection of a flower in a mirror, or the moon in a pool.

徑 **逕** ching' } From *man* or *step* and *streamlet* as the phonetic.

A bye-way, a foot-path; a short cut; a narrow track, a diameter; a radius; a bridle track or goat-path; direct, straight; prompt, quick; to pass by.

丨路 a nearer way, the shortest path; 曲丨 is a circuitous way.

斜丨 smart, tricky; the opposite of 丨情 straightforward.

行不由丨 don't go in the bye-ways.

丨到 to go directly to it.

環軸半丨 in *mechanics*, the radius of gyration.

捷丨 a quick way, an easy mode.

逕 ching' Interchanged with the last.

To pass by, to approach; to flow by, as a river near a town; to go up to; a short path; directly; across.

大相丨庭 they are very unlike, or far apart.

丨啓者 I would at once mention, I beg to inform you now; — an opening phrase in a letter; in some cases this phrase is employed where 敬啓者 would be more polite.

勁 ching' chin' Strong, robust; stiff, hard; unyielding, overbearing, prejudiced; muscular, as a pugilist.

丨弓 a stiff bow.

風丨 a stiff breeze, a chilly gust.

丨敵 well matched foes.

對丨的朋友 a congenial friend, one with whom you can easily get on.

桱 ching' A kind of timber resembling pine, but harder, perhaps a sort of larch or spruce; a roller used by silk dyers to straighten the silk.

競 **誩** ching' } Originally formed of 言 *words* above 儿 a *man* repeated, to denote the bickering of people; it is sometimes reduced to the second form, and bears a resemblance to 兢 *wary*.

Strong, violent; emulous, envious, pragmatic, bickering, testy, diotrephian; great; abundant; to emulate; to do vigorously; to struggle for, to contend, to force; to be quarrelsome; to rival in zeal for.

開丨 to begin a fray.

爭丨 to wrangle, to contest; excitable, captious.

出人頭丨 to excel, a head above others; distinguished.

灰心無丨 inanimate, unambitious.

不丨不絿 neither quarrelsome nor remiss; *fertina lante*.

丨節 plain-spoken; honest and earnest.

大丨 great strength; herculean.

K'ING.

Old sounds, k'ing *and* k'iang. *In Canton*, hing, k'ing, *and* heng; — *in Swatow*, k'eng, keng, k'ín, *and* kw'ang; — *in Amoy*, k'éng *and* kéng; — *in Fuhchau*, k'ing *and* k'éng; — *in Shanghai*, chăng *and* djiăng; — *in Chifu*, k'ing.

卿 ch'ing' From *credentials* 卯 given to an officer and 皀 an *object* which all look towards; it is very easily mistaken for hiang 鄉 a *village*.

A noble, a lord, a high officer, one to whom men look; a term of respect applied to courtiers by the prince, and by gentlemen to each other; intelligent.

丨相 a grandee; a cabinet minister.

公丨大夫 noblemen, courtiers, officers.

丨家 our ministry.

丨子 a young lord, an officer's son.

丨雲 (for 慶雲) propitious clouds.

丨士 noble officials, high civilians.

先丨 my deceased wife.

愛丨 my loving concubine, my dear girl.

六丨 the six Officers in the Cheu dynasty were similar to the 六部 six Boards of the present day, and were named after heaven, earth, and the four seasons; before this time, they donoted six imperial generals.

正丨 and 少丨 are the presidents and vice-presidents of four lower courts, *viz.*, the Ta-li Sz', the Tai-chang Sz', Tai-puh Sz', and Kwang-luh Sz'; they wear blue buttons.

輕 ch'ing From *carriage* and *stream* as the phonetic.

Light, not heavy, as an empty car; to think lightly of, to disesteem, to disregard; to slight; levity; dissipated, frivolous, paltry; gently, lightly.

丨重 light and heavy; unimportant and serious; to despise and to esteem.

無所丨重 of no great account; mediocre, common.

丨薄 light and thin; disrespectful, impudent; a prostitute.

丨狂 dissipated, light; harum-scarum.

丨言亂語 light, incoherent words, half witted talk.

丨挑浮躁 unstable and volatile.
非丨容易' it is not at all an easy matter.
口丨 or 丨許 heedless of his word or promise.
丨載 lightly laden, as a cart; drawing little water.
丨丨君子重重小人 you may be uncivil to a noble man, but you must be polite to a mean man.
年丨 young, under twenty.
丨之 he disregarded it.
丨可 or 丨巧 portable, light.
丨丨巧巧 nimbly, agile, cleverly.
丨生 to risk life without cause; audacious, venturesome.
丨身 himself alone; to lay aside dignity and condescend to the lowly.
關係匪丨 the results are really serious.
丨粉 calomel, so called from its delicate appearance.
丨騎 light horsemen, cavalry.

Read *k'ing'* Quick, fast.

傾 *꜀ch'ing* From *man* and an *instant*.
The head leaning one side; aslant, inclined, falling; entirely, the whole of; to overturn, to subvert, to waste; to squander; to assay, to test, to smelt; to debate, to compete, to wrangle; to pour out, as tea from a spout.
丨耳聽 inclined his ear to hear.
丨側 inclined; leans on the side.
丨跌 fallen over.
丨倒 subverted, prostrated, tumbled down, upset.
丨頹 utter imbecility, as of a ruined country.
丨家 to impoverish the family.
丨溢 to run over, to overpass.
丨才學 to compete on a trial of abilities.
丨銀爐 a crucible to assay silver.
丨囊相贈 he gave him all his purse.
丨盃 to drain the glass, so as to turn it up.
丨酒量 to try which can drink the most.
丨敗 defeated, dispersed, beaten.
丨心悅伏 to submit cordially, to repent unreservedly.
一顧丨城再顧丨國 one of her glances would subvert the city, and another would overturn the empire; said by Madame Li 李夫人 the concubine of Han Wu-ti, for which she was degraded.

擎 *꜀ch'ing* From *hand* and *respectful*.
To raise on high with the hands, to elevate; to lift.
丨拳 to elevate the folded hands, as in making a salutation *a là Chinoise*.
持丨 to raise on high.
丨起 to lift up, to raise.
丨天柱 a pillar which bears the sky;—*met.* a statesman who upholds the country.
丨受 to receive respectfully.

In *Cantonese*. To settle, as turbid water by alum; to freeze, to curdle, to coagulate.
等丨清 let it settle clear.
丨乾 to stand till dry.

檠 **檠** *꜀ch'ing* A stand for a lamp or wall-light; a frame to set a bow in when stringing or adjusting it; a stand for dishes.
燈丨 a wall-lamp.
丨子 a bracket or stand.

勍 *꜀ch'ing* From *strength* and *great*.
Strong, violent.
丨敵 a powerful foe.

鯨 *꜀ch'ing* From *fish* and *great* as the phonetic, alluding to the fish.
The whale, the largest of sea monsters, fabled to be a thousand *li* long; enormous, vast, overwhelming.
丨吞 to gulp or swallow all; to swindle completely out of.
騎丨上天 to ride a whale to heaven, as they say Li Tai-peh did.
丨波未靖 the surging billows have not yet settled down;—said of a rebelion.

黥 **剠** *꜀ch'ing* From *black* or *knife* and *great*; the second form is also read *lioh*, when used as a synonym for 掠 to rob.
To mark the faces of criminals with black spots.
丨面 to brand the face.
墨丨 to tattoo the face with ink or pigment.
椓丨 to cut marks on the face.

檾 *'ch'ing* From 林 *hemp* and 熒 a *taper* contracted.
A grassy plant, five or six feet high, of whose fibers cloth can be made.
丨麻 the abutilon hemp (*Sida tiliæfolia*), cultivated in the northern provinces for ropes and cordage.

謦 *ch'ing'* From 言 *word* and 聲 *tone* contracted.
To cough, to hawk in the throat; a slight irritation or hacking in the throat; to speak pleasantly; the sound of a swinging bell; a man's name.
丨欬 clearing the throat, deemed to be indecorous before a ruler.
丨談密語 to converse pleasantly and in a whisper.

熒 *ch'ing'* From *fire* and *tone* contracted.
Heat withering up things; hot, feverish.
頭丨 head hot, as with fever.

In *Cantonese*. To toast, to dry at the fire, to roast.
被火丨佳佢 dry it thoroughly before the fire.

罄 *ch'ing'* From *jar* and *tone* contracted for the phonetic.
Exhausted, as an empty vessel; to empty, to drain, to exhaust; entirely; stable, strict.
囊丨 an empty purse.
丨矣夫 [this jar] is wholly empty.
不能丨述 I cannot now detail the whole.

室如懸 | my house is like an empty jar hung up; — *i. e.* I am very poor.

| 吐平生 let me tell you everything about my life.

| 然 stern and self-possessed.

用的 | 盡 quite used up; it is all gone.

漀 *ch'ing'* A stream flowing from the side of a hill; to pour out wine or any fluid.

磬 *ch'ing'* From *stone* and *tone*, or as another explains it from 石 *stone* and 擊 to *strike* contracted.

Sonorous stones or plates which are suspended like a bell on a frame and struck by hammers; they were of different materials, and are now made of bell metal resembling a triangle or a carpenter's square; the tinkling of these stones; to hang up; to give the reins to, to gallop; a sort of dulcimer made of glass or stone; pictures of this instrument are seen carved on the ends of the antefixæ or beams under the eaves or on lintels, as an emblem of the next character, which has the same tone.

擊 | to strike the musical stones these two characters are sometimes turned into 吉慶 to denote a wish.

| 折 to stoop very low, alluding to the shape of these stones.

抑 | 控忌 now he gives loose rein, now he pulls in; this is also applied to the rapid or slow playing on the dulcimer.

| 於甸人 hung him like a forester.

銅 | a thin copper, kettle-shaped bowl used in temples in chanting, and accompanied by the 引 | a small hemispherical bell, struck by the priest when at worship.

| 口盃 tumblers or cups which do not flare.

掉 | to clash; to exasperate one.

慶 *ch'ing'* Composed of 心 *heart*, 夂 *following* one, and 鹿 a *deer* contracted, to denote the practice of presenting a deer's skin on festive occasions; it is symbolized by the last.

Good, excellent; to congratulate, to console; to bless; to present, as on a birthday with good wishes and gifts; happy, joyous; joy, felicity; the path of righteousness; an *interjection*, happily, lucky.

| 賀 to congratulate, to wish joy.

吉 | lucky and blessed.

| 喜 to rejoice with.

餘 | extra happiness, an overplus of luck, such as virtuous families have.

| 賜 to confer on.

| 鬧 jolly, lively, a great festivity.

| 興 joyful, merry.

| 中秋 to enjoy the mid-autumn moonlight — on the 15th of the 8th moon.

KIOH.

Old sounds, kak *and* kiah. *In Canton*, kok *and* kéuk; — *in Swatow*, kak, kiȯk, *and* k'a; — *in Amoy*, kak, k'iȯk, *and* k'ak; — *in Fuhchau*, kauk *and* kéuk; — *in Shanghai*, koh, kièk, chièk, *and* kiah; — *in Chifu*, kiȯa.

角 *chüe* *chiao* This character is described as formed of 力 *strength* and 肉 *flesh*, and supposed to resemble a horn; it is the 148th radical of characters mostly relating to the uses and forms of horns.

A horn; a corner, a point, an angle; a headland, a cape; a protuberance; horny; adorned with horns; horned; a wing or skirmishing party; the tuft on a young child's head; a pod; hard; a quarter, and now in use for a dime, or the tenth of a dollar; to gore, to butt; to dispute, to test one's strength with another; a wine-cup; a constellation; third note of the ancient gamut.

天涯海 | remote lands, the corners of the seas.

| 勝 to drive, as cattle do.

| 鬪 to spar; to wrestle.

轉灣八 | to go through (or box) the compass.

屋 | 晴 the sign of fair weather, when spiders spin their webs.

| 嘴 to wrangle, to dispute.

| 星 the first of the Chinese constellations, comprising the stars α (Spica) and ζ in Virgo.

| 田 an angular field.

八 | star-anise, a spice, the *Illicium anisatum.*

| 音 the tones of some musical instruments.

眼 | 傳情 to ogle, to glance at.

號 | a cornet or trumpet.

口 | 有嫌 bickering is odious.

總 | 之宴 when I was a happy girl; *i.e.* had tufted horns.

開 | to borrow money. (*Cantonese*.)

皂 | black horns, the pods of the *Gleditschia sinensis*, used to wash with; another kind is a dye.

三 | 四分 thirty-four cents.

| 箱 a quarter chest — of tea.

一 | 文書 one official dispatch.

眞 | a right angle; 銳 | an acute angle; 鈍 | or 參 | an obtuse angle; 原 | angle of incidence; and 回 | angle of reflection.

犄 | a projecting point; wing of an army; this and 拐 | also both mean the corner inside of an angle.

捔, Used with the last.
꜀chüé To seize by the horns; to stab; to lay hold of an animal to stab it.
攙 〡 to stab, to bayonet.
掎 〡 to seize by the horns and feet, as a deer.

In *Pekingese*. A corner.
站在犄 〡 'stand there in the corner.

埆, Rough land, hilly and rocky; barrens; a heath.
꜀chüé 墝 〡 a rugged country.

桷, From *wood* and *horn* as the phonetic.
꜀chüé A rafter, the strips on which the tiling rests; the ends of the 榱, the ante fixes or projecting beams supporting the eaves; a mallet; a handle.
〡 板 lathing for a roof; shingles.
松 〡 有舄 our pine beams were large.

脚, 腳, From *flesh* and to *throw* aside; referring to the leg hanging back when sitting; the first form is commonest.
꜀chüé ꜀chio ꜂chiao The leg, the shank, the foot, but is usually applied to the last two; base of a hill; stable, firm; a profession, a calling; cleverness, skill; workmen, laborers.
〡 眼 the ankles.
〡 閘 stocks for the feet, things to torture the ankles.
停住 〡 to rest, to stop walking.
〡 肚 or 〡 囊 the calf of the leg.
〡 跡 traces, footsteps; evidences of an act.
〡 夫 a coolie; one to whom 〡 價 or 〡 錢 porterage is paid.
留 〡 to detain one.
軟 〡 spiritless, placable.
好地 〡 trustworthy; well established, as a firm.
扦 〡 or 修 〡 的 a cheiropodist.
〡 底下幾位兄弟 how many brothers younger than you?
〡 程 journey on foot.
〡 色 profession, occupation, life; antecedents of a person, rank.
上好的 〡 色 an excellent man in his way or line.
〡 力大 influential, of high repute.
〡 貨 poor goods, inferior sorts.
畫鬼 〡 to write a devil's foot, — is to decide by drawing a lot.
抱佛 〡 to clasp Budha's feet — when in distress and danger.
大手大 〡 的人 an extravagant, wasteful man.
好手 〡 clever, sprightly, lucky.
弄手 〡 to do tricks of legerdemain.
陽春有 〡 the beauties of spring have feet, — and soon flee.
擔 〡 peddlers; retailers.
粧 〡 actors disguised as women, who wear the small shoes.
黐 〡 a sticky foot, a hanger-on, a sorner.
露出馬 〡 來 the secret is out, the trick is known.
攪 〡 to seduce to evil courses.
雨 〡 the rain coming down in separate showers, as seen from a distance.
赤 〡 or 光 〡 barefooted.
有 〡 路 he has a powerful protector.
多少水 〡 what is the freight on it?
先打好墻 〡 first make minute inquiries as to the chances.
拾淸蓬 〡 索 see well which rope you got hold of; — lookout what you say.

噱, Loud laughing; the lolling and panting of animals after running.
꜀chüé 談笑大 〡 immoderate laughing and talking.
大 〡 醉 throughly drunk, maudlin.
張 〡 吐舌 opening the mouth and lolling, as a dog.
嘔 〡 boisterous laughter.

覺, 𧢲, From 見 to *see* and 學 to *learn* contracted; the second form is rather pedantic and unusual.
chiao' ꜀chio To understand, to perceive; to notice, to advert to; to feel; to bring to light, to manifest; straightforward; correct; grand, exalted; intelligent; wide awake, aroused; conscious; in *Budhism*, innate intelligence.
發 〡 divulged, brought to light.
失 〡 inattentive, oblivious.
〡 痛 it hurts; I feel pain.
有 〡 其楹 lofty are its pillars.
先 〡 後 〡 the first foreseeing and the others understanding, as a sage and his disciples.
有 〡 德行'四國順之 people in all quarters render homage to upright virtuous conduct.
〡 悟 aroused to a sense of.
昏迷不 〡 stupid from grief, heavy from amazement.
知 〡 to perceive; perception.
夫子 〡 者 you, Sir, are intelligent.
〡 世 to manifest to the world.
〡 有些倦意 I feel rather languid.
不知不 〡 到了 I have got here quicker than I thought I should.
淨 〡 Budhist name for a dagoba.
〡 王 a term for Budha, denoting his innate intelligence.
七 〡 分 or 七 〡 支 are seven sections of degrees of intelligence (*Bodhyanga*), belonging to every Budha.
獨 〡 alone intelligent, or 圓 〡 wholly intelligent, terms referring to persons who become Budhas in hermit life (*pratyeka Budha*), and who cross *sansara* without attaining perfection.
〡 羅 a Manchu word, *Ghioro* or Golden, the surname of the reigning Manchu family, probably derived from the Kin 金 dynasty, A.D. 1115 to 1235.

Read *kiao'* To awaken from a dream; to wake.
睡 〡 asleep; to sleep.
倘寐無 〡 I would sleep and never wake more.

In *Cantonese*. To hush.
〡 〡 a lullaby for babies.

榷 ꜀chüé A slight drawbridge in olden times where the government levied toll on spirits brought over; a foot-bridge, a plank over a stream; a fruit like the pumelo.
〡 酤 toll on liquor.
渡 〡 a toll bridge, established to levy duties on produce.

傕 ꜀chüé Name of a celebrated general, 李 〡 mentioned in the San Kwoh Chi, who helped Tsao Ts'ao, and was killed by him.

屩 ꜂chiao ꜀chüé Wooden soled shoes or clogs made of twisted hempen cords; a kind of patten.

臄 chü' The raphe or line on the upper lip; the meat on the cheeks and lips, as of hogs; sausages made of kidneys and tripe; dried or frozen birds.
嘉殽脾 〡 delicious and fat sausages of tripe and meat.

珏 ꜀chio Two gems laid side by side; this character occurs used for names.

玃 ꜀chüé From 犬 *dog* and 矍 *to catch*, from its readiness to seize people.
A species of large ape or *hoo-luck*, found in Western China, and said to be six feet high; it is figured as an old combination of ape and deer, and many strange things are said of it; the color is brown, and it can walk like a man; it probably denotes the great gibbon (*Hylobates*), or one of that genus.
〡 取 pounced down on it, as an owl on a mouse.

K'IOH.

Old sounds, kak *and* k'iak. *In Canton*, k'éuk, hok, *and* hòk; — *in Swatow*, k'iak *and* k'ak; — *in Amoy*, k'ak, k'iòk, *and* hak; — *in Fuhchau*, k'iòk *and* k'auk; — *in Shanghai*, chièk, k'ok, kièk, *and* djü; — *in Chifu*, k'iòa.

却, 卻 chüé' ch'io' From 卩 a *knot* and 谷 the *roof of the mouth*, which has become reduced to 去 to *go*, as given in the common form.
To curb the desires, to decline doing or accepting; to refuse, to deny; to retire; to look up; as an initial *adverb*, adds force to the assertion, like really, truly, certainly, — and often needs no translation; then, thereupon; as an *interjection*, oh! behold!
〡 是 or 〡 係 evidently, the fact is.
〡 有 來 eh! have you come again? — behold, again!
忘 〡 I really forgot it.
〡 是 為 何 but why so, pray?
了 〡 to reject, to finish off; to disdain.
推 〡 to decline, to put off with excuses.
幸 勿 見 〡 I shall be glad if you will not decline.
〡 之 為 不 恭 to decline it will be disrespectful.
〡 行 to walk backwards, to go away; but 〡 不 行 is an adversative phrase, by no means; no, not at all.
〡 說 turn we now to say; truly it is said.
〡 意 to disappoint another.
〡 是 一 件 美 事 ah! this is a fine affair.
遠 〡 繁 華 to flee luxury and vanity.

愨 ch'üé' From the *heart* as seen through a *shell*; it is much the same as the next.
Guileless, upright, ingenuous; conduct that is thoroughly honest.

確 ch'üé' From *stone* and *high*.
A rock rising prominently; hard, firm, solid; as an *adverb*, really, certainly, indeed, in truth; resolute, fixed.
的 〡 even so, in fact.
〡 然 surely; certainly so.
〡 實 or 〡 〡 實 實 verily; there is no mistake.
〡 鑿 substantially; trustworthy reliable, as evidence.
〡 據 proved to be so; evidence is certain.
〡 乎 能 其 事 he really is able to manage the thing.
〡 否 I am not sure about it; is it so really?

搉 ch'üé' From *hand* and *high*; it much resembles *ts'ui* 推 to trace out.
To knock on; to beat, to cudgel; to peck; to ridicule; single, as a garment without lining.
〡 眼 to pick or gouge out the eyes.
揚 〡 古 今 書 cite the ancient and modern books.
商 〡 to ridicule, to bestow epithets on.
〡 腫 swollen up, as from a blow.
〡 瓜 子 to eat dried melon seeds.

㱿 ꜀k'ö An egg-shell from which the chick has emerged.
鷄 出 蛋 〡 the chick has come out of its shell.

殼, 壳, 殸, *k'ŏ* *ch'io'* From to *strike* down on and *screen-like*, as given in the third form; the other two have now superseded it.

The husk, skin, or covering of fruits; the shell of eggs; the exuviæ of snakes, insects, chrysalides, &c.; the shell of mollusks; a hard outer covering; bark, crust; a ladle or dipper; among weavers, a skein or knot of raw silk; an old hollow tree.

湯 丨 a soup ladle.

水 丨 a dipper, especially of gourd or cocoa-nut.

帽 丨 a hat without a fringe.

笑面 丨 a mask.

龜 丨 a tortoise or terapin's shell, used by diviners.

空 丨 an empty husk; a charlatan, a pretender, a humbug.

丨 灰 lime burned from shells.

梡, *k'ŏh* A common bitter medicine, called 枳 丨, which are probably the dried skins of a spiny kind of *Citrus*, likened to the pumelo but smaller.

敲, *ch'üé'* To strike the head; to pass crosswise; to throw a thing across.

燩, *ch'üé'* To dry anything at the fire, or in the sun; dried thoroughly.

醵, *ch'üé'* From *spirits* and a fleet *animal*.

To contribute to a feast; to club together for a picnic or great dinner.

無以祭祀進 丨 飲食 having nothing to sacrifice with, they joined their funds for a good feast.

半 丨 醉 half the contributors to a picnic get drunk.

礐, 硞, *ch'üé'* A hill covered with large boulders; crash of stones rushing against each other, or of water dashing over the rocks.

硈, *chiéh* Firm, solid; abruptly; heavy.

丨 然不動 it is far too heavy to move.

丨 然而來 he arrived very suddenly.

谻, *ch'io'* Weary, tired, as from walking.

精神忽 丨 I am all at once utterly fagged out.

㩴, *ch'üé'* To take trouble about.

Read *kih*, Exhausted, wearied.

悃 丨 tired out, needing rest.

KIU.

Old sounds, ku, gu, kúk, *and* gút. *In Canton*, kau; — *in Swatow*, kiu, k'iu, kao, *and* ku; — *in Amoy*, kiu, k'iu, *and* ki; — *in Fuhchau*, kau, k'au, kiu, kò, k'éu, kéu, *and* k'éüng; — *in Shanghai*, kiù *and* djù; — *in Chifu*, kio.

鳩, 勼, *chiu* From *bird* or to *envelope* and *nine*; the second form is limited to the verb in its meanings.

The turtle dove; a pigeon; it is regarded as a stupid bird, because it makes no proper nest; from the references, the cuckoo, or a bird with similar habits, seems to be sometimes intended by the name; to assemble, to call together, to live quietly, to rest, to sojourn; to collect in, as a subscription.

斑 丨 a grey black pigeon; the name alludes to the iridescent neck, and is widely applied.

火 丨 the fire dove of Formosa. (*Turtier humilis.*)

白 丨 the Pescadore dove.

蒙 丨 a name for the grass warbler.

鷄 丨 the sand grouse of Mongolia (*Syrrhaptes.*)

鳲 丨 the cuckoo, also known as 喀咕 in imitation of its note.

金 丨 golden dove of Formosa. (*Chalcophaps formosanus.*)

惟 丨 居之 the cuckoo came and lived in [the magpie's] nest; said of people who expel or supplant others.

丨 聚 to flock together, to assemble.

于嗟 丨 兮無食桑葚 ah! you foolish dove, do not surfeit on the mulberries.

丨 杖 an old man's staff, refers to an old custom of giving a staff to an octoginarian on which a pigeon was cut.

丨 丨 聲 the noise of wrangling.

丨 居 to live with or on one; to reside, as a bride in her new house.

丨 其民 he pacified his subjects.

䳕 丨 a book name for the black dronge.

丨 口 the pubes, a medical term.

丨 工 to collect or invite workmen.

丨 茲邑 an ancient name of Wuhu on the Yangtsz' River.

丨 錢修路 to collect money to repair a road.

鬮, 鬮, *chiu* From to *contest* and a *tortoise* because the carapace of tortoises is used in sortilege; it is wrongly read *kwéi* by some.

A lot; a ticket or ballot, made of paper or wood; to draw, as lots.

拈 丨 to draw lots or tickets.

丨 分 to divide by drawing lots.

疝, *chiu* A disease; a sharp pain.

瘵 丨 成痌 it will prove fatal at last.

樛 ˛*chiu* — From *wood* and *to fly high.*

Twisted or distorted branches; pendulous, crooked twigs; to twist; crisscross.

丨流 to roam about aimlessly.

南有丨木 in the south are drooping trees, perhaps referring to trees like the weeping cypress.

摎 ˛*chiu* — From *hand* and *to fly high.*

To strangle, to put to death by hanging; to inquire into.

丨天道其焉知 who by searching can find out Heaven's doctrine?

Read ˛*liu.* to bind, to tie tight.

Read ˛*kiao.* To curl up; to tie up.

天雨芻而葉相丨 when the rain fell on the plants, all their leaves curled into each other.

Read ˋ*nao.* Confused, mixed up.

生死相丨萬物乃纒 life and death are indissolubly linked, all creation being bound up therein.

丩 ˋ*chiu* — The character is intended to represent creeping plants twining over the wall; now superseded by 糾, and this is used only in combination as a primitive.

To catch hold and join things, as creepers do; connecting.

九 ˋ*chiu* — The character is intended to represent the winding, transforming mutations of the *yang* principle, as exhibited in the courses of rivers.

The numeral nine; to collect together; many; the best or the highest, from nine being a square number; deep, to the end of; the highest; perfect.

丨丨 or 丨歸 arithmetic, the rules of reckoning the abacus.

丨丨合數 a multiplication table reaching to 81.

丨泉之下 down to the nine fountains, to the lowest depths; in hades, in the grave.

丨州鑄鐵 [as hopeless as to try] to melt all the iron in the land.

丨曜 nine lustres; — the sun, moon, and 7 stars of the Dipper.

丨丨圖 cabalistic tables.

丨子母 the mother of many sons.

丨錫 nine gifts of investiture bestowed upon high officials.

丨使 the fox elf, a god adored at Fuhchau; an attendant of Ten-to-wang.

丨宮 the emperor's palace; this refers to the 丨重 or nine ascents to heaven.

丨十 ninety; 十丨 nineteen.

丨成丨有 it is ninety-nine to a hundred; — *i. e.* it is most likely that it is so.

丨五之尊 Ourself; I the Emperor.

丨合諸侯 to call the princes and noblemen together.

三丨 three novenaries of days following the winter solstice; the belief is 丨盡花開 that when nine of them have passed, flowers open, — about the 10th of March.

重丨 ninth day of the 9th moon.

丨州 the nine divisions of China in ancient times; *met.* China. They were:—

I. — 冀州 included Shansi south through Honan to the Yellow River, and north to the Desert, and east to the River Liao.

II. — 兗州 included the north of Shantung and middle of Chihli.

III. — 青州 included Shantung Promontory, over to Liao-tung and Corea.

IV. — 徐州 included the south of Shantung, Kiangsu down to the Yangtsz' River, and part of Nganhwui.

V. — 揚州 included the rest of Kiangsu, all Chehkiang, and to the mountains on the west, probably most of Kiangsi.

VI. — 荆州 included Hunan, most of Hupeh, and much of Kwéicheu.

VII. — 豫州 included Honan, and a small part of Hupeh, and borderd on all the other divisions except Ts'ing Cheu.

VIII. — 梁州 included all of Sz'-ch'uen north of the Yangtsz' River, and the south of Shensi.

IX. — 雍州 included the rest of Shensi and Kansuh to the Desert, and west indefinitely.

玖 ˋ*chiu* — From *gem* and *long;* it is used as the complex form of the last in accounts.

A valuable stone of a black color, but not regarded as precious; it is probably smoky quartz or cairngorm stone.

報之以瓊丨 I returned a fine ornament of smoky quartz for it.

久 ˋ*chiu* — Some say it is a contracted form of the next character, while others describe it as something following a man's legs.

Enduring, lasting; to make or continue a long time.

長丨之事 a long, protracted affair.

丨丨來坐 come in often and sit awhile.

好丨 a good while.

色不耐丨 the color is not lasting.

年丨 or 日丨 for some years; a long time.

長長丨丨 for ever.

丨別 or 丨違 we have long been separated, said by friends on meeting.

丨慕丨仰 I have long looked up to and thought of you.

丨而敬之 I have long known and still respect him.

丨病知醫 when one has long been sick, he knows all about the disease.

灸 ˋ*chiu* — From *fire* and *long* as the phonetic; it resembles *chih,* 炙 to scorch.

To cauterize; to raise blisters by burning moxa, or the dried tinder of the *Artemisia,* on the skin.

用火 丨 the actual cautery; moxa is always burned.

艾絨 丨 to apply the moxa.

丨瘡 to make a sore by burning, as a counter-irritant; it is done mostly on the scalp.

定然是神針法 丨 [his advice] was just like a skillful needle and a healthy cautery.

ʻ韭 ʻ韮 ʻchiu } Formed of 一 *one* denoting the earth with 非 *not* above it, intended to represent the appearance of the growing leaves of garlic; it forms the 179th radical of a few incongruous characters, but is now superseded by the second form.

A plant which grows a long time from one root, perhaps denoting especially the *Allium setaceum* or *uliginosum*; scallions or chives; a salad onion, with fistular, ligulate leaves and minute bulbs.

冒雨剪 丨 cutting the scallions out in the rain.

腸腸 丨 丨 entrails and chives; they are sent to a mother by her parents on the birth of a child, symbolic of their wishes for its long life.

烏 丨 black chives, a name for the 石髮 stone hair, a species of split moss (*Andreæ*) found under trees.

丨有百補最損兩目 scallions are in many ways nourishing, but they greatly injure the eyes.

禹 丨 Yü's chives,—is a synonym of the 麥門冬, a species of *Allium* like the bulb-bearing tree onion, which produces bulbs on the stems.

ʻ赳 ʻchiu From to *walk* and *twining* as the phonetic.

To carry the head high; to act with martial vigor.

丨 丨武夫 a martial and gallant soldier.

果 丨 energetic, wise and firm in action.

丨蝮 a dragon stretching its neck on high, and moving it menacingly.

ʻ糾 ʻ糺 ʻchiu } From *silk* and *twining*; it is sometimes wrongly written ʻt'eu 糾; the second form is unusual.

A threefold cord; to twist or wind up; to collect, to bring together; to cabal, to combine for unlawful purposes; to head a sedition; to place in order, to station, said of rebel posts or pickets; to examine, to bring to light, to inform; to raise, to prohibit.

丨察 to examine.

丨殛 mutual destruction, as among clansmen.

丨萬民 to announce to the world.

丨合匪盜 to join hands with robbers.

丨衆 to head the populace.

丨纏爲禍 misfortune will result from connecting and leaguing these together.

丨纏 involved, tangled, perplexed.

丨謬 to exhibit evil courses,—and thus to reform one.

丨 丨葛屨 their open worked grass-cloth shoes.

丨打不開 two fellows twisting each other's cues, as in a quarrel.

舅ʼ chiuʼ From 臼 *mortar* as the phonetic, and 男 a *male*.

A mother's elder brother is 丨父, and her younger brother is 母 丨 or 娘 丨, maternal uncles.

妻 丨 a wife's brothers.

丨姑 formerly a phrase for a husband's parents.

小 丨 or 細 丨 or 亞 丨 a wife's younger brother.

丨 丨理 an overbearing assertion or reason.

甥 丨 relatives of one's wife and mother, those of another surname; 元 丨 great uncles.

外 丨 old term for a wife's father.

大 丨 a wife's elder brother.

以速諸 丨 in order to hasten the arrival of my uncles, *i. e.* the princes of another surname.

臼ʼ chiuʼ The character is intended to depict a *morter;* which was anciently dug in the ground; it is the 134th radical, and is often confounded with 臼 *küh*, to cross hands or interlock the fingers.

A mortar, either of earth, stone, or wood; applied to bowls and deep or broad dishes; to work in a mortar.

井 丨 drawing water and pounding in the mortar;—women's work; the name of a wooden hitch put in a jar's mouth to let it down into the well.

瓦 丨 stone seltzer water bottles (*Cantonese.*)

門 丨 a socket for the door-pivot.

杵 丨之利 the proceeds of the pestle and mortar—help the people.

桕ʼ chiuʼ From *wood* and *mortar;* in Canton it is sometimes written 桕 as the name of the tree.

The tallow tree (*Excœcaria* [*Stilingia*] *sebifera*); also called 烏 丨樹 or 丨子樹, because its leaves are used to dye black.

丨油作臘燭 candles are made of vegetable tallow,—from the 皮 丨 which is the external covering; the oil expressed from the seeds by pressure is 青油, used in lamps and cooking.

鴉 丨 the tallow tree, because crows like the seeds.

舊ʼ 旧ʼ chiuʼ } From *mortar* and a sort of *owl;* the contracted form is in common use.

Old, worn out; formerly, anciently, as of yore; passed away, defunct; long before; venerable, venerated; the old ways; long kept, long standing; curdled or spoiled; turned, as milk; soured, as paste.

丨時 or 丨日 in former days, the olden times.

丨交 an old customer or friend.

故 丨 bygone, olden, ancient.

不念 丨惡 do not remember old wrongs.

丨年 last year.
丨人 an old servant.
仍丨做 doing the same as before; make it like the old one.
丨家風 relics of former prosperity and fame.
丨物 or 丨貨 old things or goods.
故丨知 an old intimate friend.
丨恨 an old grudge.
無傷丨好 don't injure the old friendship.
玉堂話丨 to talk over old times at your house.
山水依丨 the scenery has not changed.
原丨 still the same; as before.
依丨 the same thing over again.

救 *chiu'* From to *tap* and to *ask* as the phonetic.

To stop, to cause to cease; to assist, to rescue; to save from evil, to liberate; what a thing seeks naturally, as the habitat of an animal; to protect, to defend; to prevent from going wrong, to prohibit; salvation; relief, rescue; that which saves; a tassel.
丨火 or 丨息火 to put out a fire.
丨難 to help out of distress.
丨命 to save life.
丨命王到了 the rescuing lord has come.
丨世 to deliver the world; whence comes 丨世主 the Savior of the world.
望主搭丨 to look to the Lord for salvation.
打丨 to haste to the rescue.
丨援 to raise a siege, to relieve the hemmed-in force.
丨濟 to succor and relieve.
丨護 to deliver and protect.
拯丨 to save, to get out of misery.
丨駕 to rescue the emperor.
丨急回生 it quickly restores to life — or strength, as a pill.
丨飢 to appease hunger.
見死不丨 not to rescue those in mortal danger — is criminal.
丨荒 it affects the wilds, as a plant found growing on the hills.
不可丨藥 they are beyond help or remedy.
丨生局 a society for rescuing drowning people; a life-boat company.

咎 *chiu'* Composed of 各 *each* and 人 *man*, misfortune and man being opposed to each other.

A fault, a defect, an error; a misdemeanor; wicked acts; evil, criminal; unfavorable; a judgment, a providential calamity; to blame, to criminate.
改丨 to reform.
丨由有歸 the fault is charged to the proper one.
天降之丨 a heaven sent calamity.
問休丨 to consult fortune-tellers about — one's luck.
災丨 calamities; unavoidable misfortune.
既往不丨 let past faults go.
引丨不道 she did not bring up their faults.
誰敢執其丨 who will venture to take the responsibility on himself?
爾卜爾筮體無丨言 you had divined and cast the lots, and the response was not unfavorable.

麔 *chiu'* The male of the 麇 or elk.
丨麔短脰 elks and stags have short necks.

究 *chiu'* From *cave* and *nine* as the phonetic.

To examine into judicially, to inform one's self about, to search out, to push or examine to the utmost; to lay bare; to scheme; to hate; an examination; deep, profound; as an *adverb*, after all, finally, at last; in the end.
追丨 to follow up the investigation, as into a crime.
深丨 thoroughly investigated, profoundly versed in.
丨治 to examine, as a criminal.
嚴丨 to strictly inquire into.
丨辦 to prosecute and punish.
考丨 to inquire into a matter; to hunt up, as a topic.
丨度 to look into a plan; to examine the schemes.
丨竟 even then, after all, at last.
其丨安宅 at last we rested at home.
疾不及丨 it is not to be found out so quickly.
自我人丨丨 you act towards us very unkindly.
窮丨根源 to examine exhaustively, to the very bottom.
靡届靡丨 without limit, without end.

廄 / **廐** *chiu'* From *shelter* and to *finish* a meal; the first is most used.

A stable; a stall where horses are housed.
丨圈 the stalls in a stable.
丨號 a large stable, such as officers have, or an army.

柩 *chiu'* From 木 *wood*, 匚 *a case*, and 久 *a long* time, referring to the coffin.

A corpse laid in a coffin; a coffin with the body in it.
送丨 to accompany a funeral; to carry a body to its ancestral tomb.
運丨 to take a body home; to carry torches with it.
靈丨 a coffin with the corpse.
旅丨 coffins of people who die from home.
停丨 a coffin still unburied.
丨車 a hearse.
出丨 to carry out the coffin.

咎 *chiu'* To destroy; to demolish; a personal *pronoun*, I, me.

In *Cantonese*. A lump, a clod; a piece, as of dirt; a loaf.
一丨石 one stone.
攣埋一丨 cuddled up, from cold.
打風丨 a high gale.

疚 *chiu'* From *disease* and *long* as the phonetic; interchanged with the next.

A chronic disease; ailing, disheartened; to distress; misery.

丨惡 wicked, incorrigible.

災丨 an epidemic.

憂心孔丨 an incurable sorrow distresses us.

在丨 he is still sick.

故君子內省不丨無惡於志 the wise man therefore examines himself that there be nothing wrong in his will.

宄 *chiu'* Like the preceding.

Poor and diseased; to live long in a place.

慦 *chiu'* From *heart* and *to save* as the phonetic.

To be pleased; diligent, attentive.

K'IU.

Old sounds, k'u, gu, *and* guk. *In Canton*, k'au *and* yau; — *in Swatow*, k'iu; — *in Amoy*, kiu, k'iu, *and* hiu; — *in Fuhchau*, kiu *and* k'iu; — *in Shanghai*, chù, djù, *and* h'iu; — *in Chifu*, k'io.

ˏ丘 ˏ坵 *ˏch'iu* The original form is intended to represent a mound; it is formed of 一 *one* which represents the earth; and 北 *north* above it; the first is not used commonly; it is interchanged with the next, and looks a little like *ping* ˏ兵 a soldier.

A natural hillock; a hill with a hollowed or level top for worshipers, a high place; to collect, to heap up; great, empty; a classifier of parcels of land. The first is read *meu'* and used for 某 out of respect, to avoid saying the book name of Confucius, for which it stands.

營丨 the tumulus over a grave.

旄丨 a sloping mound.

一丨地 a plat of land; a lot.

圓丨方丨 round and square eminences for worshiping heaven and earth.

三丨 hills where the fairies dwell in the eastern seas.

丨里 a small village.

九丨 the nine divisions of Yü.

丨起棺材 to heap earth over the coffin, as when making the barrow.

丨子 a brick vault for a coffin above ground, in which it is kept till it can be carried home.

邱 *ˏch'iu* Nearly the same as the preceding.

A place; a tumulus; *met.* to affect, to appear to have.

歸丨園 [to give up office,] and return to one's home.

丨壠 a high mound; *met.* a wasteful or useless toil, like raising a high mound of earth.

以丨壠勞費天下 to make useless trouble in the country.

丨縣 a district in Lin-tsing cheu in Shantung.

一丨一壑 a small place, a pretty spot, a hill and a pool.

不須丨壑他 it is not necessary to try to please him.

蚯 *ˏch'iu* From *insect* and *hillock*.

The common earthworm, the *Lumbricus*.

丨蚓 (or 曲蟺 the curling eel) the common worm; it is poetically called 歌女 the singing girl, from the belief that it sings under ground at night.

求 *ˏch'iu* The next was the original of this character.

To ask, to implore; to beg, to supplicate; to search for, to seek, to aim at, to wish for; to invite, to call out; covetous, earnest for; very desirous of; to class, to sort; an object; information; name of a disciple of Confucius.

哀丨 or 懇丨 to implore with tears; to intreat.

苛丨 to importune, to demand peremptorily.

丨則得之 he asked and got it.

祈丨 to pray for.

有丨必應 ask and you will receive.

丨財 to aim after gain, to seek advantage.

丨勝 to aim to surpass.

稟丨 to petition a superior..

丨借 to request the loan of.

力丨 to be compelled to ask.

丨謀 to suggest a plan.

丨名 to strive for reputation.

務丨無過 it must be got without blame.

夫子之丨之與 the Master's way of getting information, or what he seeks.

裘 *ˏch'iu* From *clothes* and *to seek*; it is regarded as the original form of the last, and represents the hairs of fur lying on each other, the radical *clothes* being afterwards added to restrict its application.

Fur garments; furs made up; to wear furs; to maintain a family reputation, alluding to handing down fur robes as heirloomes.

輕丨 fine fur dresses.

征丨 to collect peltry — for tribute.

千金丨 a name for sable furs.

夏葛而冬丨 [wear] linen in summer and furs in winter.

狐丨 fox-skin garments.

羔丨如濡 his lamb's skin is glossy.

兢兢業業勉紹箕丨 to exert himself carefully to maintain the reputation of the family; as to carry on his father's calling.

⿸尸求 ꜀ch'iu — The virile member; a medical term.

璆 ꜀ch'iu — Used with the next.
A hard jaspery kind of stone hung up to tinkle in the wind; the ringing of jade ornaments.
環珮玉聲 | 然 the gentle tinkling of the gems that hung at the girdle.

球 ꜀ch'iu — From *gem* and *to seek*.
A sonorous kind of jade; a round gem, once used as a token of rank; a ball, a sphere; a cluster, as of grapes.
地 | the earth, the globe; a terrestrial globe.
天 | a celestial globe.
受小 | 大 | he received the small and great signet balls.

毬 ꜀ch'iu — Used with the preceding.
A ball, such as children play with; globular; a festoon, a knob; a balloon; a bladder blown up; the scrotum.
蹴 | or 打 | to play with balls; to play billiards.
踢 | to tick balls,—a game with iron or leaden balls.
花 | a bouquet of flowers.
線 | a corded cap-knob.
拋繡 | to throw the embroidered ball,—*i. e.* to choose a husband.
| 塲 a racket-court, a fives-court, a bowling-alley.
燈 | a chandelier, a candelabra.
雪 | 花 the snow-ball or *Viburnum*.
洋繡 | 花 the Hydrangea.
糖 | the sugar plum, a name for the *shan-cha* or haw. (*Cratægus*.)

觩 ꜀ch'iu — Crooked, like a buffalo's horn; strong and crooked, like a bow of horn.
角弓其 | they pull their horny bows to the utmost.
兕觵其 | the carved tripod goblet of rhinoceros' horn.

莍 ꜀ch'iu — The seeds of the 茱萸 or *Boymia*, one of the Xanthoxylons or wild pepper-trees, which grow in clusters.

銶 ꜀ch'iu — A single headed pick or ax; a description of stone chisel.
有缺我 | we splintered our chisels.

賕 ꜀ch'iu — From *precious* and *to seek* as the phonetic.
To pervert the right, to swerve from rectitude; to seek in an underhand way; to solicit; to bribe, to suborn; a consideration; corrupted, bribed.
| 賄 to bribe, to influence by presents.
受 | 枉法 to take bribes and turn aside justice.
| 謝 to beg favors by gifts.

蛷 ꜀ch'iu — A sore; an old name for the spider-millipede (*Cermatia*,) is | 螋, now better known as 蜒蚰, or the 錢串蟲 cash threading insect; it is also called 蓑衣蟲 or the rain-cloke bug.

梂 ꜀ch'iu — The cupule or cup of an acorn; a raft; the cap or shield of a chisel.
櫟 | the acorn's cup, a botanical name.
羊 | 子 old name for the haw.

俅 ꜀ch'iu — A cap ornamented or embroided in any way; to wear a cap.
| 冠 to wear the manly cap.
載弁 | | wearing his cap so respectfully and grave.

逑 ꜀ch'iu — From *to go* and *to seek*; used with the next; it is also written 仇 when used as a surname, but that is usually read ꜀ch'eu, an enemy, and ꜀kü, to decant.
To collect; to gather at; to pair, to match; to seek an alliance; to join two in marriage; wedlock, a union; pressing, urgent.
| 合 persons pairing.
君子好 | our prince desires her for a partner.
| 偶 to match; betrothed.
以為民 | make [the place] a gathering-spot for the people.
賓載手 ꜀| the guest draws off the liquor.

絿 ꜀ch'iu — Interchanged with the last.
Particular about; to ask, to seek for; testy, petulant, gruff; pressing.
東 | an asylum for old statesmen in the Cheu dynasty.

鼽 ꜀ch'iu — Formed of *nose* and *nine* *i. e.* long.
The nose stopped up as when one has a cold; a cold in the head; snuffles; a catarrh.
| 嚏 catching a cold, as shown by sneezing; the phrase seems to imitate the sound of sneezing.

虬 虯 ꜀ch'iu — A young dragon without a horn, though others say with one; to writhe, to wriggle, to squirm; a quick, wriggling motion.
| 髯 curly whiskers, like Kwanti's.
百尺 | a name for the shell-bark pine of the North.

朹 ꜀ch'iu — From *tree* and *nine*; occurs used for ꜀仇 an enemy, and ꜀簋 a dish.
A tree resembling the bullace, whose fruit is like the haw.

朻 ꜀ch'iu — A tree is called | 木 when its branches droop or grow downward like the willow, or the locust (*Sophora*) when trained to droop.

⿱九厶 ⿱九口 ꜀ch'iu — A spear whose head has three edges like the beech-nut; vapor rising high, the breath going out.
| 猶 old name of a district in Suh-tsien hien 宿遷縣 in Sü-cheu fu, near the Hung-tsih Lake.

粠 ʿch'iu From rice and stinking. Roasted or parched rice or wheat; rice grits, or grain broken coarsely.

丨粠 cured dry grain.

丨餡 a sort of rice cooky.

丨餌 cakes of parched rice, furnished to troops.

餱 ʿch'iu Food broken and spoiled, which consequently is offensive.

訄 ʿch'iu From words and nine or long. To laugh at to urge on by raillery; to play or chaff with.

鼽 ch'iuʾ A turned up nose, retroussé and short, like the nose of a Peking dog.

KIÜN.

Old sounds, kún, gún, *and* giun. *In Canton,* kwăn *and* kw'ăn; —*in Swatow,* kún, k'ún, *and* kùn; —*in Amoy,* kún, k'ún, *and* ún; —*in Fuhchau,* kung, k'üng, king, *and* kòng; —*in Shanghai,* kün *and* k'ün; —*in Chifu,* kiün.

君 ʿchün From 口 *mouth* and 尹 a *director* giving out his orders. One who is honored as a prince or chief ruler; a sovereign; honorable, in high station; presiding, taking the lead; exalted, superior, one who influences others; a term of respect, and when used in letters and direct address after the name, answers to gentleman; to rule; to fulfill the duties of a ruler; to honor as a ruler.

丨子 the princely man, the perfect gentleman, the wise man; the beau ideal of goodness; the artsman; in direct address, good people, noble Sirs; 丨子女 noble dames, high-born ladies.

國丨 the sovereign.

丨國 to rule a state.

丨嗣 the son of a monarch.

寡小丨 I, the-empress or queen.

府丨 and 太丨 in epitaphs, denote a father and mother.

先丨 my deceased father.

夫丨 my husband.

尊丨 your father.

少丨 or 頁丨 your son.

丨知否 do you, Sir, know or not?

嚴丨 the head of the house.

細丨 my wife.

丨使 to commission one to go as a 使丨 or envoy.

老丨 or 道丨 Laotsz', the founder of the Taoist sect.

天丨 the mind, the intellect.

皂丨 the black prince, a poetical name for the heron.

中書丨 a term for a pencil.

昏丨 the blinded emperor, a term of reproach to him; also, an unkind husband; *i. e.* you are as bad as Cheu-sin, the vile prince, who was so styled.

丨丨臣臣 let the prince act as a prince, and his ministers fulfill their duties.

莙 ʿchün A lacustrine plant, growing in the deep waters of canals, having the leaves in whorls; the Chinese class it with the *Confervæ*, but it is a *Hippuris* or mare's tail, and one name is 牛尾蘊 or cow's-tail bundle; it is used to nourish gold fish.

丨蓬菜 a coarse kind of cabbage at Canton.

袀 ʿchün A soldier's dress or uniform; it was put on of plain black when the Ts'in dynasty was destroyed, about B. C. 206; plain as a dress; common soldiers.

紺丨服 reddish plain dresses, worn in the Han dynasty.

均 ʿchün From *earth* and *equal; q. d.* to level off the ground; occurs used for the next and the last A lathe for molding pottery or tiles; equal, just; in similar parts; even, level; what balances or makes level; a collective adjective following a number of items all, altogether, all these; to hit, as an arrow; to equalize; to adjust, to harmonize; adjusted, well in hand; an earthen musical instrument by which time was marked.

丨平 impartial, equal.

丨齊方正 all is regular and proper throughout.

五丨八音 the five tones and eight sounds; *i. e.* music and musical instruments.

苦樂丨沾 grief and joy are equally allotted.

大家丨分 each had an equal portion.

一丨 altogether, in mass.

丨服 martial dresses or armor.

丨勻 uniform,—in thickness.

丨輸 in *mathematics*, a term for allegation.

各商丨有益 all merchants will then be benefited.

大夫不丨我從事獨賢 the great officers are unfair, and I attend to affairs as if I alone was meet.

不患寡而患不丨 they are not anxious lest [their people] be few, but lest they become discontented.

鈞 鉤 ʿchün Similar to the last; the second form is uncommon. To equalize; to classify, to methodize; important, just, and used politely for what comes from another person; an equal; a weight of thirty catties; a quarter of a 石 or stone; a potter's lathe.

丨座 your seat; you, Sir.
丨諭 your orders, your wishes.
丨函 your letter, your report.
丨同其聲 he harmonized all their voices.
大丨or 洪丨 the Great Framer or Potter, the wheel of events; heaven, Providence, nature.
力足以舉百丨 he is able to lift a hundred stone.

軍 From 車 war *chariot* and 包 to *envelop* contracted.
ˏchiün An army, troops; a legion of 12,500 men; the emperor could have six, great princes three, and smaller tributaries two and one; the headquarters; an inclosure, *scil.* that restrains men; military, warlike; awe inspiring, martial; what pertains to an army.
丨營 a camp; an intrenched camp.
五丨 the main body and the five supporting divisions of an army.
行丨調將 to move troops and appoint generals.
丨民府 a military sub-prefect, placed at important points with civil jurisdiction; there is one near Macao.
勇冠三丨 the bravest of the brave, the first in the army.
投丨 to enlist troops.
丨功 military merit.
問丨 banishment to a garrison.
兩丨對壘 the two armies threw up defenses.
丨命 discipline of the army.
丨田 lands set off for soldiers or exiles.
屯丨 to intrench the forces.
丨禮 the etiquette of force, the *ultima ratio*.
本丨門 I, the general or admiral; — used by the chief of an army or squadron.
招丨 to call the troops; a term for a trumpet.
丨裝局 dépôt of military articles, ammunition, arms, &c.

皸 The skin chapped and wrinkled, as from cold, disease, or neglect.
ˏchiün
手足丨裂 their hands and feet were chapped and sore.

麕 麇 From *deer* and a *pen* or *grain*; the second form is not very common.
ˏchiün A general name for small and hornless deer; the muntjak (*Cervulus Reevesii*), which the Chinese confound with musk; it is figured like a large musk deer, and is said to fly from its own reflected image; also the river deer (*Hydropotes*); and sometimes given to the roebuck, to bind, to seize; to collect in crowds.
丨集 banded, leagued together, said of seditious people.
賊匪丨聚 the banditti herded together.
水中丨影猜疑輙奔 as the muntjak saw her form in the water, and fled suspecting evil.
丨脯 dried venison.
野有死丨 there is a dead deer in the woods.

窘 From *cave* and a *prince* as the phonetic.
ˋchiüng Afflicted, enfeebled; in urgent want of, straitened; no way out of; to harass, to distress; to persecute; still, as before.
丨迫 to molest, to egg on and provoke.
丨窮 miserably poor.
丨急 in the utmost need.
丨口無言 said nothing — owing to conscious guilt.
視人之災丨 to look on men's miseries — with pleasure.
有丨陰雨 to be embarrassed by a soaking rain.
計丨 our plans are all null.

捃 To pick up, to put to rights; to complete.
ˋchiün
丨摭 to sort and collate; to pick out.

郡 From *region* and a *prince* as the phonetic.
chiün' A place of resort, as a capital; an old political division, whose extent has varied at different times, from a province or principality down to a district; in the T'ang dynasty, it corresponded to a province; a princedom.
府丨 a department, indicating the territory as distinct from the prefectural city.
丨王 a regulus or prince of the second rank, the grandson of an emperor.
丨馬 a king's brother-in-law.
丨主 and 丨君 the daughters of a first rank prince and a *peile*.
丨會之區 chief city of the region.
首丨 first prefecture in a province.
清河丨張子房 the region of Ts'ing-ho [was the primitive seat] of Chang Tsz'fang, — the head of the clan Chang.

菌 The mushroom; mold on bread or paste.
chiün'
發丨 to grow moldy.
地丨 the toadstool; mushrooms of all kinds.
耳丨 watery tumors in the ear.
丨桂 a sort of fine quilled cassia.
朝丨 fugacious plants, such as come and go in a morning like a mushroom.
丨蕈 fragrant, toothsome plants.
鷄爪丨 branching mushrooms, an edible species of *Clavaria*, like the *C. corniculata*.
天花丨 an edible fungus found on willow trees, like the *Agaricus* [Pleurotus] *ostreatus*.

呁 啒 To vomit; to feel sick at the stomach.
chiün' In *Cantonese*, the second is read *ˏlun* To gnaw; to lie uneven; rumpled, not lying flat and smooth.
丨骨頭 gnawing a bone.
說話ˏ丨哼 to hesitate; to stammer in talking.

K'IÜN.

Old sounds, k'ún *and* gún. *In Canton,* kw'ăn; — *in Swatow,* k'ún *and* kún; — *in Amoy,* k'ún *and* kún; — *in Fuhchau,* kung *and* k'üng; — *in Shanghai,* k'ün *and* k'üin; — *in Chifu,* k'iün.

群 羣 ꜀ch'iün From *sheep* and *prince;* the forms are identical.

A flock of sheep, as few as three; a herd; a concourse, a company, a multitude; all men of the same kind; friends, equals, companions; a form of the plural; the whole of, entire; to sort with, to agree with; to move in unison.

一 丨 羊 a flock of sheep.

俴 駟 孔 丨 his mailed team kept step.

丨 生 all mankind.

丨 后 all the princes or feudal states.

丨 黨 clans, cliques; a mess; parties, various clubs.

狐 丨 狗 黨 a rascally, oppressive set of fellows.

一 丨 兒 a party of children.

丨 臣 a crowd of courtiers.

同 丨 of the same sort.

丨 材 men of talent.

失 丨 lost from the company; strayed away.

慍 于 丨 小 I am disliked by all the petty underlings.

丨 迷 the irreligious, besotted world.

離 丨 索 居 to leave one's associates (or line), and live alone.

超 丨 excelling, surpassing others.

所 有 丨 房 以 及 丨 牆 all the houses with the walls.

丨 陣 a flock which goes in regular order, as geese, or fishes.

裙 帬 ꜀ch'ün From *dress* or *napkin* and *prince;* the second form is obsolete.

The plaited skirt of a lady's dress, which is sometimes embroidered; rim of a terrapin or tortoise's shell; part of a priest's attire (*antara vasaka*), a sort of under-waistcoat.

帷 丨 or 圍 丨 an apron, a bib; a plaited skirt.

朝 丨 an embroidered silk apron worn by officers.

丨 脚 妹 waiting-maid who comes with the bride.

中 丨 or 內 丨 a petticoat.

紅 丨 a damsel, a young lady.

丨 帶 之 親 near relatives of different surnames.

響 丨 a skirt with jingles.

百 摺 丨 a plaited skirt.

丨 下 雙 鈎 a pair of hooks (small feet) peeped from under the skirt.

着 木 丨 he wears the wooden apron, or counter; — a shopman.

丨 拖 a fringe or things hanging from the girdle, which are over the skirt.

囷 ꜀ch'iün From to *surround* and *grain.*

A granary of a round shape; a pen, a bin; spiral, screw-like.

輪 丨 contorted like roots; spiral; growing in an involuted manner.

天 丨 a group of stars in Cetus.

In *Fuhchau.* A stack, a pile; a heap, as of stones or earth; to pile, to heap up.

丨 一 堆 to pile a heap.

箘 ꜀ch'iün A fine sort of black bamboo used for arrows; bamboo shoots; in *chess,* to cry Check!

K'IÜNG.

Several of these are read K'UNG. *Old sounds,* k'iong, king, giong, *and* ging. *In Canton,* k'ung, k'ing, hung, *and* kwing; — *in Swatow,* k'iòng, kw'ang, kwang, *and* kéng; — *in Amoy,* k'iòng, kiòng, k'eng, keng, *and* heng; — *in Fuhchau,* k'üng, küng, king, k'ing, *and* héng; — *in Shanghai,* djiüng, kiüng, *and* chüng; — *in Chifu,* k'iüng.

穹 ꜀ch'iüng From *cavern* and a *bow.*

Lofty; high and vast as the sky; empty, spacious; eminent; to stop the entrance of; a chink which needs to be covered or closed.

丨 蒼 the azure canopy, the empyrean, the abode of the higher Powers.

丨 窒 熏 鼠 to smoke out rats by stopping their holes.

丨 窿 eminent, lofty, as a peak.

窮 竆 ꜀ch'iüng From a *cavern* and *body;* the second form is the oldest, but has been mostly superseded, though the dictionaries adhere to it.

Brought to the last degree; all exhausted, at one's wits end; impoverished, abandoned; the poor; to render helpless or poor; to exhaust; to search out, to investigate thoroughly, to probe; poverty, termination of, the end; old name of a region south of the Yellow River.

丨 困 utterly straitened, no strength or resource; the distressed.

貧 丨 poor, reduced, in needy circumstances.

丨 極 at the end of, as one's resources.

其味無 丨 its relish is inexhaustible or perpetual.

水盡山 丨 no way open, the road shut up, headed off on all sides.

無 丨 盡 exhaustless.

丨 日子 I must go without food to-day; supplies gone.

丨 究 to thoroughly examine.

丨 追 pursue everywhere.

丨 學者 a poor scholar.

丨 途 the road is closed; I am left penniless.

壽夭 丨 通 longevity and premature death, poverty and success — are all opposites; 丨 and 通 also denote lucky and unlucky in a horoscope.

詞 丨 unable longer to answer (or argue) the matter.

丨 國 a small fief in the Hia dynasty lying near Tsi-nan fu in Shantung, in the present Teh cheu 德州, whose ruler Prince I, 后羿 opposed T'ai-kang, B. C. 2180.

藭 ˛ch'iūng A reddish root, called 芎 丨 brought from Sz'ch'uen, which is furnished by an umbelliferous plant allied to the *Levisticum* or *Angelica*; it is used for liver complaints and headaches.

丨 菜 a plant cultivated in Kiangsi, also called 茢芹; it seems to be allied to fennel; the stalks are eaten.

茾 ˛ch'iūng The seeds of the 蓂莢, a bulbous plant, considered in ancient times to be highly felicitous.

堯階生 丨 the day-lily grew on Yao's steps.

桊 ˛ch'iūng To reap grain when ripe; grain fully ripe and ready to cut.

椰 ˛ch'iūng A tree allied to the coir palm (*Chamærops*) according to one author, and to a willow by another; at Canton, it usually denotes the tallow-tree.

邛 ˛chiūng Name of a river; infirm, ailing, poorly, weary; troublesome; in distress; a mound.

維王之 丨 such are only a trouble to the king.

丨 有旨苕 on the mound are beautiful plants.

丨 州 name of an inferior department, formerly called 臨 丨 situated southwest from the capital of Sz'ch'uen.

筇 ˛chiūng A variety of bamboo with many large knots, fit for making a staff for an old man to 扶 丨 lean on.

丨 杖 a bamboo walking stick.

蛩 蛩 ˛chiūng One name for the cricket which sings in walls; a species of locust; the exuviæ of a cicada.

丨 鳴砌畔 the chirping cricket sings in the steps.

丨 丨 a monstrous animal resembling the griffon, which is connected with the 蹷 or jerboa in its habitat, and dwells in the Desert; also to be hungry.

志 丨 丨 而懷顧兮 his heart is weighed down, and he regards them all so kindly.

飛 丨 滿野 the flying locusts fill the wilds.

山 丨 虫 one name for the *Cermatia* or spider-millipede, or perhaps a large *Julus*.

丨 吟 the crickets are chirruping.

蛬 ˛chiūng From *insect* and *all*; it seems to be intended for the last.

A cricket, which keeps in its hole by night; it is very testy, and when it sees another, attacks it.

銎 ˛chiūng The eye of an ax or hammer; the lower blade of a halberd

方 丨 a square hole.

斧 丨 the hole in the head of an ax.

瓊 ˛chiūng A carnation or red stone, considered to be valuable, and is probably a sort of red veined marble; excellent, pretty, beautiful; brilliant, as a gem.

丨 花 a kind of Hortensia, a rare flower with which the emperor Yangti of Sui (A. D. 605) was charmed.

丨 瑤 beautiful, lustrous, as a gem or precious stone.

丨 漿 a poetic name for good wine.

丨 枝 the red branch, — a name for precious coral, alluding to a beautiful and gigantic stone tree in fairy land.

丨 臺 a magnificent terrace.

尚之以 丨 英乎而 and the beautiful crystals hung from — his girdle.

丨 州府 the prefecture of Kiūngcheu or Hainan I., so named from its red breccia marble.

煢 ˛ch'iūng From 營 *labor* contracted and 凡 *all*.

To fly back or return quickly; alone, desolate, unprotected, as a lone orphan, or one who is helpless.

丨 獨 forsaken, friendless, childless.

丨 丨 無告 I have no friend to whom I can open my heart.

丨 丨 在疚 left desolate in his sickness.

瞏 睘 ˛ch'iūng From 目 *eye* and 袁 *a robe*; it is interchanged with the preceding, and in composition abbreviated to the second form, in which it is alone used.

Gazing at in great fright, as Belshazzar did at the writing; alone, without help or resource.

丨 丨 sorrowful from loneliness; nobody to help; uncared for.

惸 Like the last two.

ˏch'iüng Alone, helpless, without relatives.

憂心｜｜mournful and sick at heart

哀此｜獨 alas, for these helpless and solitary people!

頃 From 頭 *head* and 匕 or 比 to *compare*.

ˋch'ing The head inclined or awry; to incline; the largest of Chinese land measures, equal to a hundred *meu*, 15.13 square acres, or 6.11 French hectares; shallow, as a basket; an instant, a moment; just now, presently; a glance; in epitaphs, denotes respectful, trembling; and at other times, to horrify.

俄｜a short time, presently, in a moment.

｜閱 a brief glance, a cursory reading.

｜聞 I have just heard.

｜刻不離 they were not separated for an instant.

｜耳而聽 put your ears down to hear.

少｜等吓 wait an instant.

｜畝多少 how many acres are there?

萬｜波濤 an unlimited expanse of waving water.

不盈｜筐 my shallow basket was not filled.

｜心料理 pay attention strictly to what you are doing.

䔛 苘 A plant from whose fibers cloth is made; the Abutilon hemp ｜蔴 (*Sida tiliæfolia*) is sometimes so written, but another plant was probably originally intended.

ˋch'ing

跫 The noise of men marching along; the sound of many stamping.

ˏch'iüng

聞人足音｜然而喜矣 I heard the tread of people tramping on, and I was glad

恐 志 From *heart* and *sick* of; the second form is common but unauthorized.

ˋk'ung Apprehensive, anxious, agitated, alarmed; suspicious of; to doubt, to suppose, to imagine or reckon upon; perhaps, supposing, if it should be; thinking, believing.

莫｜don't think so.

｜懼 tremor, fear of.

｜怕 or ｜其 fearful lest, supposing; I am afraid it will be so.

—｜惶 frightened, alarmed; with great respect to you.

｜怕他不來 I think he will not come.

絅 褧 A single garment, one of a plain color without lining; a cloak, a mantle; to drag one along quickly; a jerk.

ˋchiüng

衣錦｜衣 over my embroidered silk pelisse, I have put a single garment.

迥 From to *go* and a *void* as the phonetic; it resembles ˏkung 㓊 in meaning.

ˋchiüng

Remote; waste, desert; void, as a wild; bright, lustrous, splendid; a superlative.

｜隔地方 places wide asunder.

風光｜不同 the look of things is so entirely different, — as an old man returning to his early home.

｜異前時 very unlike the former days; — *i. e.* better.

｜別 very dissimilar.

殊｜鄉景 everything there was totally different from my own town.

冂 同 坰 The first is intended to represent a void waste, and is the 13th radical, but the characters under it mostly relate to caps; the second is an old form of the third and common form, and also of the preceding.

ˋchiüng

A wild, remote from towns; the edge of a forest, a desert, a border prairie, the remotest bounds of civilization.

畝｜a prairie, a steppe, a pampas.

在｜之野 out in forest wilds, far remote.

火燒到｜the fire has burned itself quite out.

炯 烱 Hot; bright, clear; severe, like fire.

ˋchiüng

以昭｜戒 in order to illustrate the rigor of law.

｜｜clear, lucid, as an able examination.

兩眼｜｜如寒星 both eyes sparkle like stars in winter.

日光｜｜the brightness of the [gods'] eyes shines everywhere.

囧 冏 The second is the common form, altered from the other, and defined as a synonym of the preceding; the first is supposed to resemble, and was intended to depict a window, with the light shining through it.

ˋch'iüng

A small window or lattice to let the light in.

月吐窗｜｜the moon shines out brightly through the window.

命｜the title of the 26th chapter in the Shu King, called the Charge to K'iüng, *i. e.* 伯｜, a statesman who flourished under King Muh, about B.C. 1000.

伷 Small, diminutive, dwarfish; to bend, to crouch to, as when supplicating; to live in a mean place.

ˋch'iüng

｜居陋處 cuddled up and crowded into a miserable hole.

謥 To question, to ask; prolix, wordy.

ch'iüng'

In *Fuhchau*. To drawl in singing; voice, tone; utterance.

長｜a drawling tone.

好｜a fine voice, sweet singing.

擤 To press down with the hand, so as to steady a thing.

ch'iüng'

KO.

Old sounds, ka *and* kat. *In Canton*, ko, *and* o; — *in Swatow*, ko, k'o, *and* kai; — *in Amoy*, ko, *and* k'ŏ; — *in Fuhchau*, ko; — *in Shanghai*, ku, *and* kăk; — *in Chifu*, kwŏa, *and* ku.

歌 **謌** ˛ko } From *breath* or *words* and *elder brother* as the phonetic; the second form is not common.

To sing in a recitative or chanting style, the common mode among the Chinese; to sing verses, to carol; to sing to music; to make a song; a song, a ballad; a rhapsody, in which the lines differ much in length, and the rhymes recur at intervals.

既作爾 丨 I have made this song about you.

丨聲 the sound of 唱 丨 or singing.

丨本 a song book, a music book.

丨聲嘹喨 the clear sounds of sweet music.

丨謠 to sing when playing; to lampoon in verse; a kind of second-sight ditty, intimating coming events.

詩言志丨永言 poetry expresses thought, and singing prolongs its utterance.

丨舞 to sing and beat time or step to it, as mummers do.

秧 丨 the merry song of those who transplant rice.

謳 丨 local ditties.

秋 丨 a ballad sung by people on stilts in the North.

副 丨 a chorus; a fugue.

朝 丨 an old name of Wéi-hwui fu in Honan

哥 ˛ko The original form of the last, composed of 可 *can* repeated, in imitation, and to denote the prolonged sound of singing.

An elder brother; a term of respect, and sometimes of sneering.

阿 丨 the Emperor's sons, as 三阿 丨 the third prince imperial; it is of Manchu origin.

丨丨 or 大 丨 or 丨子 my elder brother.

老 丨 venerable Sir.

丨兒們 the brothers; the friends; all the company.

表 丨 an older cousin on the mother's side.

關靈 丨 a spiritualist medium, one who calls up souls.

八 丨 a singing bird (*Acridotheres cristatellus*), known at Canton.

白鼻 丨 a white nosed fellow,— a rascal, alluding to the custom of actors whitening their noses.

鴚 ˛ko A wild or tamed goose, probably a local change in sound from ˛*ngo* 鵝; a parrot.

柯 ˛kŏ From *wood* and *can* as the phonetic.

A helve, an ax-handle; a stalk; a large branch fit for a handle; an agent or cause, a means; a go-between.

執 丨 伐 丨 to seize one handle to cut down a second; to use another's agency.

代人執 丨 to act as a matchmaker.

一 丨 菜 one head of greens; one root, as of celery.

斧 丨 an ax-helve; an agent.

舸 ˛kŏ Sometimes written like the last.

A painter to tie a boat; an extensive region in the Han dynasty, named after the 牂丨江, which flowed through its southern part.

滒 ˛kŏ From *water* and *oppressive*; it is often wrongly written 菏, which is the name of a sort of turnip, and a duplicate form of 荷 the lotus.

Name of an ancient lake or marsh which was drained by Yü, now preserved in Ko-tseh hien 丨澤縣 a district near Ts'ao-chen fu in the southwest of Shantung.

又東至于 丨 eastward it (the River Tsi) flowed further to lake Ko.

哿 ˛kŏ ˊkŏ From *can* and *to add*.

Excellent; to be well off; to commend; may.

丨矣富人哀此惸獨 well off are the rich, but alas for the poor and unassisted.

丨矣能言 well enough it is if we can speak such words.

舸 ˊkŏ A large galley or transport; a barge; a lighter.

丨艦 a large traveling boat.

笴 ˊkŏ The shaft of an arrow; the name of a place.

妢胡之丨 the slender culms [for pencils] from Fán.

箇 **個** **个** kŏ' } From *bamboo* or *man* and *firm*; the first is not common, and the contracted form, which is supposed to represent the three last leaves on a twig of bamboo, is much used.

The culm of the bamboo, for which the first character alone is used; a classifier of very wide application, and used for thing, piece, or article; it is applied to human beings and animals, to coins, schemes, periods of time, furniture, globular or compact things, as boxes, fruit, &c.; an individual or thing, as 那 丨 that one, 這 丨 this one; to multiply; multiplied into; a demonstrative *pronoun*, this, this one—but not always susceptible of, or needing translation.

那 丨 都有 or 丨丨都有 each one of them has some

第二 丨 the second, the next.

幾 丨 箱 several boxes.

你是丨中人 you are one of the craft;—*i. e.* you can appreciate the case.

丨換丨 you can change one for the other.

一丨都去了 every one has gone.

十丨八八十 ten multiplied into eight makes eighty.

每丨 each one.

丨件 or 丨的 that one, that thing.

一丨一丨的走 they went one after another.

In *Cantonese*. After a negative, often used to denote a transitive sense upon the individual spoken of or to.

莫丨去 don't go.

無丨不怒 who is not angry at such things?

In *Shanghai*. A sign of the genitive.

人丨面孔 the human face.

伊丨 that person, his; 第丨 this; 伊粒丨 it is his; 要丨 yes, I wish it; 儂丨 yours.

K'O.

Old sounds, k'a, *and* k'ap. *In Canton*, fo, o, *and* ho; — *in Swatow*, k'o, k'o, k'úó, *and* lo; — *in Amoy*, k'ò; — *in Fuhchau*, k'o, wo, *and* kw'o; — *in Shanghai*, k'u, *and* kò; — *in Chifu*, kw'òa.

科 'k'ö From 禾 *grain* and a 斗 *peck*, because the latter measures grain.

A class, order, or series; a rank, a gradation; a rule, a line; to class, to estimate; a hollow in the trunk of a tree; practice, as in medicine; the examination for the two highest degrees; a classifier of herbs.

開丨 to begin the examination of *küjin* graduates.

丨房 or 房丨 are six departments or bureaux in provincial *yamuns* which attend to the current business.

六丨 six bureaux in the Imperial city which manage its internal affairs.

丨目出身 to get office by merit, — not by purchase.

正丨年 the alternate third years when examinations take place.

恩丨 extra examinations.

內丨 and 外丨 clinical and surgical practice.

丨收 an extra tax levied in an emergency.

丨派 to levy the proportion each one is to pay.

丨頭 bareheaded, unhelmeted.

丨第 grade of scholars; a literary degree.

力不同丨 their abilities are not the same.

丨籃 a hamper carried by students into the examination, holding dishes, writing materials, &c.

二罪相等同一丨斷 two crimes of the same sort deserve the same punishment.

盈丨而後進 when well taught then you can take the precedence.

如何丨罪 how the crime should be estimated or punished.

丨場 the examination, the arena for the tripos.

丨道 two classes of secretaries in the Censorate, the former oversee the Six Boards, the latter the provinces.

祝由丨 to give away or transfer a sore or an ulcer, as by writing a charm which is then burned, and the sore spot rubbed as if thrown at an animal.

尊駕是丨甲出身嗎 did you, Sir, pass the examination when you got your degree?

珂 'k'ö A quartzose gem of inferior value like white chalcedony, or flocculent quartz-crystal; a sea-shell (*Conus*) of different colors.

誄丨 a red legged bird with striped plumage, that is said to consort with foxes.

丨金 pure gold, or some kind of fine alloy.

馬丨騾 cone shells or cowries once used in ornamenting bridles and horse-trappings.

蝌 'k'ö From *insect* and a *grade*.

The tadpole is 丨蚪蟲, but in Canton it is also called 雷公魚 or thunder-fish.

軻 'k'ö Wheels on their axles; wheels connected with each other.

轗丨 carriages dragging along; impeded, disappointed.

孟丨 the infantile name of Mencius.

薖 'k'ö From *plants* and to *pass*; also read 'kw'o in some places.

Plants, herbage; a hungry look; large.

碩人之丨 that large man with such a nonchalant air.

窠 'k'ö From *cave* and *real*.

A hole; a nest made in a cliff or underground; a burrow; the roost of a pheasant; hollow.

鼠鳥同丨 mice and birds in the same nest; *i. e.* they are all villains alike.

蜂丨 a wasp's nest.

蛇蠍一丨深知可畏 when the serpent and scorpion are in the same burrow, they are really dreadful.

In *Cantonese*, wrongly used for 綱 crape. Crumpled, wrinkled, creased, corrugated; shriveled, as withered fruit.

髁 *k'ö* The pelvis or hip bones; the acetabulum.

丨髏盖 the knee-pan or patella.

Read *kwa'* Uneven in stepping.

諜丨無任 to walk awkwardly, like one whose legs are unequal.

顆 *'k'ö* From *head* and *real*.

A little kernel or clod; a classifier of beads, bullets, pearls, cherries or similar fruit, and small round things.

一丨珠 one pearl.

萬丨明珠 myriads of lustrous pearls.

幾多丨 how many of them are there?

丨粒不收 not a kernel have we harvested — this season.

可 *'k'o* From 口 *mouth* and 丂 a sign of *breathing*, alluding to a consent given without words.

To be willing, to permit; free or able to do; to tolerate; tolerant to; sign of the potential mood, can, may; convenient, proper, worthy, competent; used as an interrogative, and to soften the sense; at the beginning of a sentence it is like a hypothetical particle, then, if so; in regimen with a negative, it becomes like a relative pronoun, as 無行丨悔 he did nothing that he had need to regret; it also forms verbal adjectives or gerunds, as 丨恕 excusable.

丨惡' despicable, disgusting.

丨憐 to compassionate; pitiable; sad enough!

丨以做得 it is allowable, it can be done.

不我丨 he has nothing to do with me.

丨以 yes, it can be allowed.

非同小丨 by no means a little thing, it is of importance.

有丨不丨 why not, what forbids?

你丨冷 are you cold?

丨不悲歎 is it not most lamentable!

無丨無不丨 as you deem it to be convenient.

丨口 palatable, toothsome.

丨也 it will just do.

丨就晚了 it is now too late.

丨行 it should be done.

丨丨慌了 it will only scare him.

少丨 a very little.

丨否 will it do or not?

丨人 capable man.

丨不是麼 to be sure it is; can it be?

丨以不必 not absolutely necessary.

坷 *'k'ö* Uneven, rough land; unfortunate, not getting on.

坎丨 rugged paths; *met.* disappointed, always in trouble, ne'er-do-well.

岢 *'k'ö* A range of hills in the north of Shansi, called 丨嵐; they have given name to K'o-lan chen 丨嵐州 in the northwest of Tai-yuen fu near the Yellow River; it is said to produce very good horses.

課 *k'ö'* From *words* and *real* as the phonetic.

An example, an exercise, a lesson, a task; what comes in order; a series, an order; to essay, to try; to reckon, to see what the issue will be; literary pursuits; to counsel, to exhort; to examine, to levy taxes on salt.

會丨 to compete in writing essays.

丨文 to criticise compositions.

丨議 to settle the rate of taxes.

橐丨錢 an allowance to students.

差丨 clerks or overseers in the salt department.

工丨 a day's job, a set task.

丨業 the literary profession.

月丨 a monthly trial for composing essays.

日丨 a daily lesson or task.

鹽丨 or 丨稅 the salt tax.

訓丨 to explain and teach.

丨期 the set time for writing themes.

起丨的 a diviner, one who calculates matches.

六壬丨 the book or rules for deducing good or ill luck.

騍 *k'o'* A mare is commonly called 丨馬, and 丨騾 is a she-mule.

稞 *k'o'* Grain deprived of its husk; the grain itself; a name for wheat in Shantung.

青丨 a name for oats.

堁 *k'o'* Clouds of dust filling the air; a lump or clod of dirt.

揚丨而弭塵 [the wind] raised clouds of dust, filling people's ears and eyes.

敤 *k'o'* To thump; to beat or pummel slightly.

丨打臭蟲 to knock the bedbugs out of it.

丨打烟灰 to knock the ashes from the pipe.

丨丨乾凈了 knock it till it is quite clean, as a box.

丨籃賣了 sold them all in a lump.

砢 *k'o'* From *sand* and *can*; it is usually written *koh*, 擱 and is now obsolete.

To ground; to run a vessel on the shallows, to put her ashore.

丨淺 struck on the bank.

丨在樁上 she ran on a snag.

齣 *k'o'* To crack with the teeth, as a dog does.

丨齸 arranged like teeth, as the seeds are in a slice of muskmelon.

KOH.

Old sounds, kak, kat, kap, kít, hít, *and* ngít. *In Canton*, kok, kak, kot, hòp, *and* yik; — *in Swatow*, ko, kak, hok, k'òp, kek, kat, *and* kwa; — *in Amoy*, kap, k'ap, kòk, kek, kat, *and* gút; — *in Fuhchau*, koh, k'o, kah, kaik, *and* kak; — *in Shanghai*, kòk, kăk, kak, keh, *and* köh; — *in Chifu*, kwòa.

閤 ˎhö ˎkö From *door* and to *join*; it is often used with the next, and is also read *hoh*,

A door by the side of the great gate, or a small door leading through a side passage into the court-yard.

入 丨 to see the Emperor in his cabinet.

闈 丨 the door leading into the harem.

丨 閭 a sort of forecastle in state barges.

丨 邑 a name for the region of Tăng-cheu fu in Shantung.

閣 ˎkö From *door* and *each*; occasionally written like the preceding, and used for the next.

A door screen which prevents passers-by looking in; the posts supporting a gate; a balcony; a belvedere over a gateway; a porch, an ante-room where guests can wait; a vestibule, a corridor; female apartments; a council-chamber; the officers assembled in it; the court; a book-closet; a cupboard, a safe for eatables; to lay by or on.

內 丨 the Inner Council.

丨 老 a courtier, a cabinet minister; — the old word *Colao* is derived from this term.

丨 下 your honor; you, Sir; your Excellency.

入 丨 to become a cabinet minister.

坐 丨 waiting in the hall, denotes the seclusion of a girl three or four days before marriage.

在 丨 上 he is upstairs.

水 丨 樓臺 a summer-house over the water.

約之 丨 丨 the frames [for the adobe walls] were one on top of the other.

丨 道 the stars δεθνξοπ in Cassiopeia.

煖 丨 乃大龕 a warm hall is the great shrine, — such as is built up to receive the chief god, as Kwanti.

擱 ˎkö An unauthorized character, for which the last was once used; occurs interchanged with *k'o*, 㪙 to grow.

To lay on, to put down, to place carefully; to hinder, to obstruct; to strike, as a vessel on a bank.

丨 在那裏 where shall I put it?

躭 丨 or 丨 住 to delay, to be impeded, to put difficulties in the way.

躭 丨 多時 to stop a long time at a place.

延 丨 to procrastinate an affair.

置之高 丨 placed it on a high shelf; *i.e.* paid no more attention to the matter.

丨 筆費思量 to lay down the pencil and think over the matter carefully.

船 丨 沙 the vessel went on the spit.

丨 不住 unable to leave off.

各 ˎkö From *mouth* and *to follow*; *q.d.* following and calling after one who hears not; it is often carelessly written to resemble ˏ*ming* 名 a name.

A distributive *adjective*, each, every; all; wherever; various, separate, apart.

丨 人 each man.

丨 有所長 each one has his own gift.

丨 色貨 all sorts of goods.

天 丨 一方 each one has his sky; — we are world wide apart.

丨 人 丨 見 each one to his taste.

丨 有一說 each has his own story.

丨 一人 to each [post] one man.

他自 丨 兒坐 he sat alone by himself.

丨 處 everywhere.

In *Fuhchau*. Strange, unusual; odd.

格 ˎkö From *wood* and *each* as the phonetic; occurs used for 䓊 an onion.

The spreading and rising of the branches of a high tree; to reach, to arrive at the end; to make to reach to; to examine, to sift thoroughly; to influence; to affect; to attack; to change, to correct; reformed, corrected, to grow old; a line, rule, a mark by which one writes; a limit or pattern, a statute; a frame; intelligent; excellent; unusual; obstinate, stiff; all years which have the branch 寅 in their cycle name; a wild onion.

丨 外 beyond the usage or law; extra, as kindness; unusual; very great.

間 丨 to draw lines.

印字 丨 a copy-slip.

神保是 丨 報以介福 the gods quietly come and reward with their great blessings.

丨 物 to inquire into the nature of things, to philosophize.

丨 式 a muster, a pattern.

神之 丨 思不可度思 the influences of spirits cannot be reckoned upon — or calculated when they will come.

丨 局 presence; carriage.

品 丨 temperament, habits, character.

感 丨 moved upon, as by the Holy Ghost.

丨者不赦 the recusant will not be pardoned.

丨殺 manslaughter, homicide.

看他骨 丨 look even to his bones, narrowly watch him.

丨濼 come here, you Shun!

地 丨 方圓 a broad chin, a heavy jowl.

丨于皇天 to influence Heaven itself.

資 丨 regular gradation of officers.

不拘一丨 not rising by regular grade — in office.

丨其非心 to correct his vicious heart.

一點兒 丨 磴都沒有 there is no difficulty about it; I can go through it perfectly.

庶有 丨 命 may the people have a lengthening of life.

上 丨 蒼穹 [the mind of man] can ascend and speculate on things in the heavens.

挌, *ˏkö* To strike, to attack; to box; to fend off, to ward off a blow; to fight with beasts.

揺 丨 to break a blow.

丨鬥 a brawling row; fisticuffs.

丨拳頭 to practice boxing.

丨武藝 the science of pugilism.

蛒, *ˏkö* A species of beetle.

蛭 丨 one of the names of the millipede (*Julus*).

杜 丨 an unusual term for the mole-cricket or *Gryllotalpa*.

虼, *ˏkö* An unauthorized character, which has superseded the last.

丨蚤 a flea, for which the last was perhaps at first the correct form.

觡, *ˏkö* A horn with branches, and no flesh inside.

鹿 丨 a hook to suspend things on, as a deer's antlers; a kind of tree.

茖, *ˏkö* A species of wild onion, having a small stem and large ligulate leaf; it is known as the 丨葱 and Budhist priests are forbidden to eat it.

袼, *ˏkö* Short sleeves covering the armpits, are 丨褙, used in warm weather.

Read *loh*ˎ A bib for children.

骼, *ˏkö* From *bone* and *each*; used with the next.

The skeleton of a man or beast; dried bones lying on the ground; the tibia or shank bones of quadrupeds; lean.

掩 丨 薶胔 cover up the bones and carcasses.

丨膊 the arm from the shoulder to the wrist.

胳, 肐, 骯, *ˏkö* From *flesh* and *each* or *breath*; the third is unauthorized, and the second is wrongly used, as it is properly read *hih*,

The armpit; the side.

丨肢窩 or 丨肋底 the armpit, the part of the body covered by the arm.

丨膀 the arm, the upper arm.

丨臊人 a rank smelling man.

丨膊折在袖兒裏 the arm is hid in the sleeve; — the fees are included in the price.

In *Pekingese*. A stain, a flaw, a blemish.

有 丨 星 there is a dirty spot on it.

疙, *ˏkö* Also read *ki*ˀ

A pimple, a boil, a sore.

ˋ長 丨 瘩 a sore has come out.

脾氣 丨 瘩 an irritable disposition, fretful.

瘋 丨 瘩 a rash has broken out all over the body, as the washerman's rash.

Read *yih*ˎ Bewildered, foolish, out of one's head.

趷, *ˏkö* An unauthorized character, for which 硌 is wrongly used.

To jolt; to come down with a thud; an impediment, a hindrance.

走路 丨 蹬 to go jolting and thumping along.

忔, *ˏkö* Discontented, not liking; to like, to rejoice.

丨憎 uneasy and angry at; not relishing.

隔, *ˏkö* From *place* and earthen *vase*; it is also frequently contracted to its primitive in cheap books.

A partition, a bulk-head, something that divides off; apart; a shelf; a bar in music; to obstruct, to interpose, to separate off; to strain or filter; next to, separated, neighboring.

丨開 to intervene, to put asunder.

丨一條水 a stream divides the places.

一水之 丨 wide waters roll between them.

丨夜 left over night, as a dish of meat; to spend the night.

丨別多年 I have not seen him for many years.

三 丨 架 a case with three shelves.

丨日來 come on alternate days.

丨渣盤 a filtering dish.

阻 丨 to embarrass, to interpose.

丨絕 to suspend; to cut off, as intercourse.

窩風 丨 a movable portico to screen from the wind.

丨壁居住 to live next door.

丨斷 a partition, a bulkhead; to block up, as the way.

門 丨 a door or window frame.

丨得遠 very far apart.

丨牆搔癢 [it's like] scratching a sore through the partition; — useless indignation.

天淵相 丨 as unlike as elysium and tophet.

丨扇 a folding screen.

準 丨 a bar in music; 準 alone denotes the measure or strain.

槅, From *wood* and *partition*; occasionally wrongly used for the last.
ˏkö The yoke of a wain or cart; interstices of a lattice window or net; a kernel.
紗 丨 a muslin or gauze screen.

膈, From 肉 *flesh* and 隔 *partition* contracted.
ˏkö The diaphragm; any thin membrane in bodies, or pellicle in plants, which separates parts; the breast, the mind; inability to eat, want of appetite; a bell-frame.
丨 膜 the midriff, separating the thorax and stomach; something which hides or screens a thing.
不下 丨 or 丨 食 food disagreeing with one
無留胸 丨 don't keep thinking of it all the time.
打丨饐 or 打 丨 兒 to hiccough.

嗝, The cackle of a jungle-fowl or pheasant; to vomit; to gag.
ˏkö
丨 泛 to vomit; colic and vomiting.
丨 噎 unable to swallow.

革, The original character is thought to represent the look of a raw skin as it is stretched out, and when the hair has been scraped off; it forms the 177th radical of a natural group of characters relating to hides and their uses.
ˏkö
To change, to renew, to molt; to skin; to degrade from office; musical instruments made of skin, as drums; a skin; a hide; defensive armor, leathern; human skin; a wing; reins of a bridle.
丨 名 strike off his name from the roll.
丨 役 or 丨 退 to dismiss a man from a yamun.
丨 職 or 丨 頂 to degrade from office; to cashier.
丨 俸 to mulct the salary.
兵 丨 military armor.
天地 丨 而四時成 the heavens and earth change, and thus the four seasons are completed.
丨 故更新 to leave off old habits and reform.
改 丨 to alter, to mend and change.
丨 車 a war chariot.
此俗遂 丨 this usage then died out, or was superseded.
條 丨 沖沖 the ends of the reins dangling.
丨 條 notice of dismissal put up on an office-door.
丨 酒 to break off from drink, to keep sober.
丨 面洗心 to skin the face and wash the heart; *met.* a thorough reform; to turn over a new leaf.

鴿, From *bird* and to *join*, referring to its constant pairing.
ˏkö A general term for doves; domestic pigeons; its young are called 鵓 丨, and the old ones 飛奴 or flying slaves.
丨 子 or 白 丨 house doves.
放白 丨 to let fly the white dove; *i. e.* to lose one's loan by knavery.
丨 傳信 the carrier pigeon takes letters.
野 丨 a wild pigeon.
蒲 丨 a fancy name for the cantelope melon.
白 丨 眼 one who scowls at the poor; to look down on one.

蛤, A frog; a lizard; bivalve shells, thin and marked, are called 蚌 丨, a general name for those like a *Unio*, *Tellina*, or *Donax*; a mussel a clam.
ˏkö
ˏha
文 丨 ribbed shells, like a *Cardium* or *Arca*.
山 丨 a large kind of yellow reptile found in rocks, which lives on air and drinks the dew; it probably denotes the tree-frog.
田 丨 and 丨 魚 names of the frog.
丨 蚧 a red spotted lizard; but the 丨 蚧 is applied to the gecko in the Archipelago, though the two names are interchanged.
丨 蜊 a species of clam (*Venus*) with a thick shell.
丨 蜊板 boards halved at the edges for rabbeting.

佮, To bring together, as a company of one's comrades; to take.
ˏkö

割, From *knife* and to *injure*.
ˏkö To cut, to gash, to wound; to divide, to cut in two; to deduct, to take off; to injure; to cede, as territory; to turn, as a debt over to a creditor; afflictions, calamities.
丨 斷 to cut apart.
丨 情 to sever friendship, to break off intercourse.
丨 開 to slice off, to divide.
丨 數 to deduct part of an account, to force to take less.
丨 價 to reduce the price, because the goods are inferior.
丨 禾 to reap grain, usually means rice.
丨 工錢 to cut the wages, to deduct from them.
丨 紋 a flaw in a gem or wood.
洪水方 丨 the flood injured it much.
難以 丨 愛 I won't part with the loved — thing.
丨 鷄焉用牛刀 why use a cleaver to kill a chicken?
丨 地 to cede territory.
捨 丨 obliged to part with.

葛, From *plant* and *why*.
ˏkö A creeping, edible bean, a species of Dolichos (probably *D. trilobus*), of whose fibers cloth is made; the culms are sometimes eaten; a creeper; relatives, posterity, alluding to the long vines.
粉 丨 the mealy taro *Pachyrhizus trilobus*), a long shuttle-shaped tuber used for food.
丨 布 a sleazy, coarse, yellowish summer cloth, made of this fiber.
丨 之覃兮 how the dolichos vines stretch themselves out!

有何瓜丨 is there any relationship between us?

毫無膠丨 I have not the least alliance (affinity or friendship) with him,

丨藟 vines, creepers; *met.* a numerous progeny.

丨籐 a hanger-on; a needy, troublesome fellow.

野谿丨 very fine grass-cloth.

擖, ꜀kö The noise of scraping or filing; the rubbing or grating of wood; to manage.

輵, 轕, ꜀kö The appearance of spears and chariots drawn up in martial array.

轇丨 a line of glancing spears or bayonets; mixed up, confused, precipitate; in a hubbub and muddle.

KʻOH

Old sounds, kʻak, kʻat, *and* kʻap. *In Canton,* hak, hăk, kʻăt, hòp, hot, kak, *and* kwak; — *in Swatow,* ké, kek, kʻek, hai, kat, kwa, kút, *and* kʻap; — *in Amoy,* kʻak, kʻap, kʻat, *and* kʻek; — *in Fuhchau,* kʻah, *and* kʻaik; — *in Shanghai,* kʻak, keh, kʻăh, kăk, *and* chièk; — *in Chifu,* kwʻòa.

恪, kʻö˒ Reverent and attentive to the duties of an office, as a sacristan should be; to respect, to feel awe for; reverently, vigilant.

執事有丨 those who serve [in temples] should be reverent.

丨恭己職 he sedulously attends to his official duties.

謹丨 very respectful.

丨守規範 to carefully maintain the rules, to hold to the old ways.

客, kʻö˒ From *shelter* and *each*; *q. d.* a person sheltered in an inn.

A guest, a visitor, an acquaintance; a dealer, a customer; a stranger; a squatter, an alien; transitory, visiting, as an officer; foreign, from afar; to lodge.

丨人 or 人丨 a visitor, a gentleman, a stranger.

丨房 a guest-chamber.

丨歲 last year.

好丨情 a cordial reception.

茶丨 teamen who come in from the country.

丨貨 inferior goods; foreign products.

堂丨 a lady, a gentlewoman.

主丨 host and guest; shopman and customer.

賓丨 a guest.

丨地 a trading place.

暴丨 footpads, highwaymen.

丨兵 foreign or subsidized troops.

丨妻 or 淸丨 a kept mistress; the second term also denotes a factotum, an under companion.

嘉丨 a respected guest.

食丨羅列 retainers or parasites in large crowds.

說丨 a peacemaker.

丨套 respect or ceremony paid a visitor.

丨居 to make a visit.

丨店 an inn, a hotel.

拜丨 to make a visit; to call.

丨棧 warehouse for taking goods on storage; a lodging-house.

丨家人 the *Hakka* people (*i. e.* squatters) from Kia-ying cheu 嘉應州 in the north-east of Kwangtung, who emigrate to other parts of that province.

喀, kʻö˒ ꜀chʻia From *mouth* and *guest*; it is now superseded by the next.

The noise of coughing; to cough, to retch

In *Pekingese* read ꜀chʻia. To gag and strain to get something out of the throat.

丨着嗓子 cough it up.

In *Cantonese* read *lak*, A final particle denoting past time, and intimating that a thing is done without recall.

去丨 he's gone.

咳, 欬, kʻö˒ From *mouth* and *breath* and a *horary* character; it is properly read *kʻai*˒ but is now substituted for the last, as that is much used in Mongolian and Turkish names; the second form is little used.

To cough; to retch, but without vomiting; to hack, from irritation in the throat; to cry out, to bawl, to eructate, to hiccough.

丨嗽 to cough and expectorate.

風丨 a dry cough.

驚怕丨嗽 to hem when fearful.

丨頃 the time of a cough, a moment.

丨痰 to throw up phlegm.

嗆丨 to gag, as from food entering the larynx.

丨吐 to cough and spit.

Read *kʻai*˒ or *hai*˒ The laughing smile of a child; a cry of those who bear burdens; an interjection of pity.

謦丨爲洪鐘響 they bawled and shouted like the clanging of bells

髂, ꜀kʻö Excessive exertion, which is like a bloody sweat; to vomit blood.

鄭人擊我吾伏弢丨血 the man of Chʻing had the better of me, but I skulked under the bow-cases in the most desperate resistance; — and the drums never ceased.

搕, k'ö, chiu — To lay hold of forcibly, as if to detain or take away.
丨出去 drag him away, as a thief.

渴, k'ö — From *water* and *why*.
Thirsty, dry; to thirst for, desirous of, longing; to pant after; sudden; to dry up.
口丨 thirsty.
解丨 to quench the thirst.
話梅止丨 he mentioned plums, and their thirst ceased.
丨葬 suddenly buried him.
丨想 to long for; ardently panting for, as an absent friend.
丨念 to dote on, to cherish fondly.
氷丨 the water has dried up.
嗜義如丨 to relish righteousness as a thirsty man does water.
丨慕 I greatly long to see you.
匪飢匪丨 I was neither hungry nor thirsty.
丨者甘飲 the thirsty man fancies all waters sweet.

刻, k'ö — From *knife* and a *horary* character.
To carve, to chisel; to sculpture; to cut out; insulting; griping, oppressive; the eighth part of a Chinese hour or fifteen minutes; a little while.
雕丨 to engrave, as wood-cuts.
丨字 or 刋丨 to cut characters, as on blocks.
丨骨銘心 [your kindness is] graven on my bones and inscribed on my heart.
時丨 incessantly.
限丨 the set time.
丨下光景 the present state of affairs, this view of the matter.
少丨 a little space.
減丨 to reduce by arbitrary order, as rations.
一丨的工夫 a little while.
丨薄 to oppress, to insult and harass.
丨漏 a clepsydra.
重丨 a second edition.

剋, **尅**, k'ö — From *knife* or *inch* and to *sustain*; it occurs used with the last and next.
To subdue, to overcome; to exorcise, to repress; to deny one's self, or to yield one's rights for others; to save or limit; the chemical action of acids and re-agents; urgent; a set time; to insist on.
丨煞凶神 to drive off malicious demons.
丨制 to lord it over; to dominate, as one acid will another in elective affinity; to restrain; to prevail against.
相生相丨 reciprocally producing and destroying each other, as the five elements.
丨期而至 he came at the appointed time.
硬命丨妻 his tenacious fate will be too much for his wife.
刑丨 to exercise a secret or baleful influence over another.
肝旺丨脾 the liver is too active and injures the spleen.
In *Fuhchau*. To crowd, to press; incommoded, as in a crowd.
丨熱 heated by the jam.

克, k'ö — The original form is said to represent the carved beams which sustain the roof and contains an allusion to the help given to a man by his shoulder to sustain things; used with the last.
To sustain; adequate to; to attain to, able for; to subdue, to prevail over; to repress; crossing; subduing; as an auxiliary *verb*, can, able; and often used merely to give efficacy to the next verb.
攻丨 to break through an opposing or besieging force.
丨己 to govern one's self.
丨當 fit for, adequate to.
弗丨勝任 he is not fit for the post.
丨復 to recover, as a captured city.
不忌不丨 don't be envious or overbearing.
丨滅俗情 to mortify earthly affections.
丨私 to curb the appetites.
惟予弗丨于德 I do not excel in virtue.
掊丨 extortionate tax-gatherers.
丨勤丨儉 very diligent and stingy too.

瞌, k'ö — Sleepy from fatigue.
丨睡 dozing; asleep from sheer weariness.
丨眼 the eyes sleepy.
打丨揰 nodding, sleepy. (*Shanghai.*)

溘, k'ö — To get to suddenly, as a boat striking the bank; to ground; to lean against; to reach.

殰, k'ö — From *bad* and to *cover*; used with the last.
To comply with; to die.
丨逝 to yield and depart — on the long journey; used when speaking of the death of statesmen.

磕, k'ö — A cave or grot in a hillside; to store away.

搕, k'ö — To strike; to take or gather; to pat or beat with the hand.
丨碎 to smash to pieces.
丨扁 to flatten.
Read *ngoh*, To cover; also a dung-barrow.

榼, k'ö — A wooden cup or bowl to hold spirits; a creeper.
執丨承飲 he lifted the mug and took a drink.

磕, k'ö — The sound of stones striking together; to hit against, to run against.
丨頭 the ceremony of the *kotow*, to knock the head on the ground when saluting the emperor.
路有丨絆 there are hindrances or obstacles in the road; difficulties in the way of success.
丨烟灰 to knock out the ashes, as from a pipe.

繂, ‚k'ö To seam; to form the woof for a piece in the loom.
〡絲 tapestry which has the figures woven in with the woof.

In *Cantonese.* A loop, a bight of a rope; to loop up; to stroll, to go about.
打一個〡 make a noose.
〡住佢 noose him, lasso him.

峇, ‚k'ö A cave or hole in a hill; in the Indian Archipelago, 〡〡 is a term for country-born Chinese, whose fathers were immigrants.

KU.

Old sounds, ku, kút, *and* kúp. *In Canton,* ku; — *in Swatow,* kò, ku, *and* k'u; — *in Amoy,* ko, *and* k'o; — *in Fuhchau,* ku, k'u, *and* kò; — *in Shanghai,* ku; — *in Chifu,* ku.

孤 ‚ku From *son* and a *melon.*
A young son whose father is dead; fatherless; alone, orphan-like, solitary, no protector; applied by the emperor to himself as peerless, unrequaled; ungrateful, not cherishing a sense of kindness.
〡寒 alone and neglected.
〡家 I, the emperor.
勢〡 diminished and reduced, as a chieftain; friendless, in a strange land.
〡魂 a neglected, orbate spirit.
〡獨 alone, no brothers or sisters, or relatives.
伴〡燈 living alone; *lit.* no partner at the lamp.
〡子歸宗 an orphan rejoining his own family shrine; this is done after a prosperous life, by officers who may have been adopted by others.
〡哀子 the afflicted orphan; — a phrase on mourning cards.
〡單 orphaned, solitary.
〡望 to disappoint hopes.
〡零屋宇 detached buildings, houses far separated.
〡陋寡聞 an unpolished scholar of limited opportunities.
撫〡 to comfort and help the destitute.
托〡 to confide an orphan to the care of a friend.

胍 ‚ku This resembles *meh,* 脈 the pulse.
Corpulent, large bellied.
〡肫大腹 obese, very fat.

蛄 蛌 ‚ku From *insect* and *old;* the second character is unauthorized, and is usually applied only to the cicada.
The mole cricket is called 螻〡 and 蟪〡, but the last name also denotes a grasshopper or cicada, small and short lived, called in Peking 喇喇〡 in imitation of its note.

觚 ‚ku From *horn* and *melon.*
A wine-vase or goblet used in village feasts, holding two or three pints; angular, cornered; an angle, a corner; a law, a rule; a plan, a kind of writing-board.
〡法 tactics; *lit* the rules for cornering.
〡不〡 the wine tankard has no corners now; *i. e.* things change.
劍〡 a sword hilt.
譎〡之人 a cunning man of strategy.
操〡 to grasp the table; *i. e.* to begin school.

柧 ‚ku A corner; angular, triangular, or octangular; sea-going triangular sticks which hold up a cornice.

罛 ‚ku A large fishing-net, such as is dragged between two smacks off the southern coasts.
一〡刮 a clean haul; we took them all.
施〡濊濊 splash went the net into the water!

箍 箛 ‚ku From *bamboo* and *to bind* or *melon;* the second form is not much used.
A hoop; a circlet, a fillet; to hoop; to draw tight, as a belt; to surround, as by a wall.
打〡 to hoop a bucket.
〡子 or 篋〡 a hoop.
造屋錯請了〡桶匠 [if you think of] building, don't call a cooper to do it;—the means should suit the end.
金鋼〡 a gold headband or fillet worn by Tao priests.
一〡柴 a faggot of firewood.
你可以〡鑊乎 are you smart enough to hoop an iron boiler?
花〡 a garland of flowers, a wreath.
蛇〡腿 the snake coiled around his leg.
〡嘴 a muzzle put on animals to prevent them eating.
〡綻 the hoop has broken.
催〡 to batter the hoop down to its place.

菰 ‚ku From *plant* and *orphan.*
The core or tender stalks of a water grass with broad, lanceolate leaves, cultivated in ponds throughout the central provinces; they are eaten like celery, under the name of 茭白, both raw and cooked; the reddish seeds, called 胡米 are shaped like oats, and furnish a poor flour used in pastry.

菇 From *plant* and *damsel*; frequently used with the last.
ˏku A kind of tuber.
茈 丨 a water vegetable, the *Caladium* or *Sagittaria*, cultivated for its tubers.
蘑 丨 and 土 丨 edible varieties of the mushroom allied to the *Morellia*.
灰 丨 or 牛屎 丨 the puff-ball or *Lycoperdon*.
草 丨 or 冬 丨 edible mushrooms.
山茨 丨 or 山慈姑 a tulip; *lit.* the kind damsel of the wilds; also a species of *Amaryllis*.

苽 From *plant* and *melon*; probably another form of the last.
ˏku The ancient name of an aquatic grain whose seeds resemble rice, having stiff stalks; the seeds ripened in autumn, and a spirit was distilled from them.
丨 蔣 a water plant producing rhizomes in autumn like a child's arms, which are cleaned and eaten with fish.

箛 An ancient trumpet, or a kind of musical instrument blown at the end; a whistle in a whip; a bamboo good for switches.
ˏku

姑 From *woman* and *old* as the phonetic.
ˏku A polite term for females, especially young and unmarried; a wife calls her mother-in-law 翁 丨, while 大 丨 and 小 丨 are names she gives to her husband's sisters; to tolerate; lenient, yielding; for the time; just, merely.
亚 丨 or 阿娘, a lassie, a girl.
丨 娘 a young lady, a damsel; a belle; an old term for a paternal aunt.
丨 毋 and 丨 婆 a father's and grandfather's sisters.
村 丨 village girls.
丨 爺 a son-in-law, so called by remoter relatives.
丨 嫂 sisters-in-law.
三 丨 六婆 disreputable women, thieves, and procuresses.
丨 息 indulgent, easy with.
丨 且 慢 慢 gently; let it rest awhile; take it easy.
决不 丨 寬 certainly no indulgence will be shown.
丨 念 indulgent towards, feeling kindly for.
丨 恕 to forbear with.

沽 Name of a river in Ts'üen-cheu fu in Fuhkien; in Chihli it is applied to branches of large rivers, especially to those of the Pei ho and Peh-tang ho; to trade in, to buy and sell; to abridge, to lessen; unworthy, trashy, coarse.
ˏku
丨 酒 to deal in spirits.
零 丨 to sell by retail.
丨 之哉 sell it at once!
丨 名 to fish for praise, to vaunt one's self.
丨 物 poor articles.
大 丨 Takoo at the mouth of the Pei ho, one of five towns near the embouchure, all of them trading places.

酤 From *spirits* and *old*; used with the last.
ˏku To deal in spirits; liquor just made and kept over night; a wine shop.
禁民 丨 釀 [Han Wu-ti] forbade the people dealng in [free] spirits.
屠 丨 之肆 an inn or eating shop.
有酒湑我無酒 丨 我 when I have spirits I strain them; when I have none, I buy them.

鴣 A partridge, 鷓 丨 (*perdix cinerea*), common in central China, and supposed to have affinity with the pigeons; one name is 懷南 from its turning southward when is rises on the wing; and in Kiangsi it is called 逐影 chasing its shadow; it is described as having white spots on the breast, and many markings; the birds call to each other, and their cry is 鉤輈格磔 *heu-cheu-koh-tseh*, when they stop.
ˏku

軲 A wheel, 丨 轆 applied to the heavy wooden ones found in northern China.
ˏku
依 丨 name of a hill.

辜 From *bitter* and *old* as the phonetic.
ˏku A fault, a crime, a failure of duty, a dereliction; sin, guilt; to hold to be guilty; to hinder others so as to monopolize; to engross an article; to dissect or examine a sacrificial victim; necessary, must.
無 丨 受 累 to compromise the guiltless.
夜殺不 丨 it is no crime to kill [a robber] by night.
丨 潔 they will be clean, said of the rains in May.
丨 月 a classical name for the eleventh moon.
以救無 丨 伐有罪 the guilty are punished in order to save the innocent.
丨 負你的恩 disregarding your kindness.
丨 恩市義 ungrateful, thankless.
惟予汝 丨 I shall hold you only to be guilty.
丨 較 to monopolize an article; generally speaking.
王曰於乎何 丨 今之人 the king said, Alas! what crime is now chargeable on us?
亦罔非酒惟 丨 [the ruin of states] can always be traced to their crime in using spirits.

鈷 A short javelin, called 鏷 丨 anciently made light to use as a spear.
ˏku

古 From *mouth* and *ten*; *q. d.* that which has passed through ten generations, and may be regarded as a tradition.
ˋku Ancient, old, antique; former, of old; to grow old, practiced in, old, accustomed to; antiquity; olden, hoar.

丨今 ancient and modern.
丨丨的 old-fashioned, ancient.
講丨怪 to tell a strange story.
終丨 permanent.
丨人 or 先丨 the ancients; one's ançestors.
丨木昏鴉 the crows resort to the old trees at sunset.
丨跡 relics; sacred places; heritages received from old times.
丨文 ancient writings; the classic style.
自丨以來 from of old.
歸丨 gathered to the ancients; *i. e.* dead.
人心不丨 man's heart does not grow old; men are not now the same as of old.
丨訓是式 the lessons of antiquity are his pattern.
博丨通今 versed in the writings of all ages.
丨董玩器 antiques, curiosities, old articles.
三丨 the three periods of antiquity, *viz.*, of Fuhhi, B. C. 2850; of Wăn Wang, B. C. 1120; and of Confucius, B. C. 550.

估 ʻku ku' To estimate, to reckon, to guess; to think; to set a price on; value, worth, price.
再不丨 very unexpected.
丨量 to suppose, to give an opinion.
你丨中' you have guessed aright.
丨計 to reckon the number.
不同你丨堆 I am not going to lump these articles to sell them.
招丨 to force up the price.
丨衣 old, second-hand clothes.
時值丨價 the market price for an article.

罟 ʻku From *net* and *old*; it is the same kind as the ꜀*ku* 罛 *drag-net*.
A net for birds; a drag-net; involved, as in a net; a net full.
畏此罪丨 I fear I shall be implicated in the crime.

一丨撓 altogether. at one haul; lump the things.
拋丨船 fishing smacks.
網丨 fishing nets.
掌丨田獸 to take the net and hunt the game.

股 胋 ʻku From *flesh* and to *kill* or *old*; the second form is not regarded as quite correct.
The upper part of the thigh, the haunches, the rump; a strand in a rope; a slice; a share in a concern; a division a detachment, a squad; in *geography*, a portion of a country, a bay or a peninsula; a proportion, a quota; in *mathematics*, the long side of a right-angled triangle; a chapter, the head of a sermon; a period, a proportion; part of a wagon-box; stable, firm.
分丨貲 pay each one his douceur.
大丨分' the head partner.
這丨 this portion or share.
分丨 share the assets.
一丨生意 one share in the business.
丨戰而慄 knees shaking from fear.
一丨熱氣 a puff of hot air, a spurt of steam.
八丨 eight heads,—as of an essay.
股之丨肱 Our highest officers; *lit.* the emperor's legs and arms.
三丨繩 a threefold cord.
一丨氣力 one strong pull.
赤芾在丨 the red knee-covers were on their legs.

牯 ʻku A bull; the male of quadrupeds, especially of domesticated; it is also defined a heifer; a cow.
水丨 a buffalo of a black color.
牛丨 a bull; in some places it is used for a steer.
對丨牛彈琴 [like] playing the lute to a bull;—he does not appreciate it.

羖 羖 ʻku An old name for a ram or ewe, as used at different times; a sheep of black and white color; the sheep in Chihli generally have black heads and white bodies.
羊丨 a ram.
五丨大夫 the lord of the five sheep-skins, refers to a story of Peh Li-hi 百里傒 B. C. 660, who asked his sovereign to ransom people with them.
俾出童丨 to make you produce a (hornless or) young ram,—which is an impossibility.

盬 ʻku A coarse, earthen utensil made in the north of Chihli, called 丨子 or 砂丨子, for boiling meat and vegetables; it is the cheapest kind of pottery, and like the kedjeree-pots of India; in other places it is made of copper.
銅丨 a copper tea-kettle.

盬 ʻku From 鹽 *salt* contracted and 古 *old*.
A salt pond situated in or near I-shi hien 猗氏縣 in the southwest of Shansi, near which there is a deposit of rock salt; temporary, not lasting or durable, for the time; slackly, carelessly.
王事靡丨 the king's affairs must not be done carelessly.

鹽 ʻku Nearly the same as the last.
The sluice or ditch through which salt water is led on the vats, or where it is evaporated.

臌 ʻku From *flesh* and *drum*; an unauthorized character; it is nearly a synonym of *chang'* 脹 dropsy.
Dropsical, swollen; tumid pudgy, puffy, bloated.
氣丨 flatulent; the bowels distended from wind.
丨脹 a swollen belly.
水丨 abdominal dropsy.
丨膨膨 he is much bloated.

ʻ蠱 ʻku From *worms* and a *dish*.

Worms in the belly, which are thought to be the cause of dropsy; a venomous worm used to poison people; a slow poison; to disquiet, to stir up; to harass one with doubts, to pervert the mind; an unquiet ghost; the 18th diagram, referring to occupation.

丨脹 or 丨腹 the dropsy.

丨毒 poisonous, noxious.

丨疑 deluded by superstitious qualms, to cozen, to bewitch.

受丨 poisoned; possessed, infatuated, bewitched.

放丨 to poison, said to be done by women in Kwangsi.

飛丨 flies from worms in rotten grain.

幹父之丨 to hide a father's faults.

被妖丨惑 possessed by a goblin, elf-shot.

ʻ鼓 ʻ鼔 ʻ皷 ʻku From 壴 a *band* of musicians, and 支 to *stretch out*, or 攴 to *strike*, or 皮 *skin*; the second is regarded as the correct form for the verb, but all are used; it forms the 207th radical of characters relating to kinds and noises of drums.

A drum; musical instruments made of skin; earthenware drum-shaped seats; drum-shaped or sounding like a drum; bulging, like a barrel; an old name for a 斛 or measure of five pecks; to drum; to excite, to arouse, to encourage; to urge, as a fire by a blower; to dilate, to bulge, to swell, to protrude; to warp; the round spot on a bell where it is struck; a watch of the night; to play on the lute, bell, or other instrument of percussion.

擂丨 to drum very fast.

一副丨樂 a band of musicians.

吹丨手 pipers and drummers.

丨樂 instrumental music.

丨板一副 drums, gongs, castanets, &c., usually eight kinds.

丨掌 to clap the hands.

太平丨 or 扁丨 tambourines.

銅丨 a knobbed gong.

幫丨 a side drum.

以鉄作于口横丨之 with a piece of iron placed across the orifice, it makes the quivering sound,—speaking of the reed in an organ.

打更丨 to strike the watches.

丨噪 a great uproar, a hubbub.

石丨 earthenware seats shaped like drums.

丨火 to urge a fire.

丨鑄 to melt metals.

坐在丨裏 you sit in a drum; *i.e.* you have not heard the news.

丨勵 to stimulate to effort.

丨腹 big-bellied, fat; having enough to eat, as the people in Yao's time.

自扒船自打丨 I can myself paddle and drum,—I am independent.

漁丨 a kind of tabor used by Taoists, made of bamboo two or three feet long.

丨舞 diligent, earnest, to exert one's self.

丨盪 to excite, as the growth of things.

丨蟲 an insect like the water tick or *Hydrachna*.

河丨 the stars $\alpha\,\beta\,\gamma$ in Aquila.

丨起來 filled out, as a hose by the water driven through it.

In *Fuhchau*. To roil by stirring; to stir, as a boiling kettle by a ladle.

ʻ瞽 ʻku From *eye* and *drum*, alluding to the skin over the cornea.

An eye without a pupil, or closed pupils, or those having a film over them, as in *pterygium;* blind; a musician; those in charge of the court music, a band-master.

丨目人 a blind man.

丨目院 an asylum for the blind.

御丨 imperial musicians.

未見顏色而言謂之丨 to talk of its color before seeing a thing may be called blindness.

丨瞍 the name of Shun's blind father, given to him late in life.

兩丨相扶 one blind man leading another.

ʻ賈 ʻku From *precious* and a *canopy* above.

A shopman, a resident or settled trader, as distinguished from 商 a traveling one; to sell, to traffic.

丨市 a bazaar, a market.

商丨 merchants, traders, dealers in general.

大丨 a wholesale dealer.

坐丨科 a local tax levied on shops, usually exacted to defray a special exigency.

丨買 to purchase.

如丨三倍君子是識 as if the princely man would have any knowledge of a trader's 300 per cent.

Read *ʻkia*. The price of a thing, for which *kia*ʼ 價 is now substituted, and this character is used as a surname.

ʻ詁 ʻku To explain the *words* of the *ancients*, as its composition intimates; to comment.

丨傳 ancient tradition.

章句丨訓 to illustrate and teach each sentence.

詳訓丨 to adduce proofs and illustrations.

故ʼ kuʼ From to *strike* and *old*; occurs used with its phonetic.

The cause or reason of a thing, that which affects a result; what is purposed; the occasion, the pretext; an illative particle, because, for, therefore, on that account; on purpose; that which was of old, long in possession; the ancients, forefathers; formerly, forgotten, old; to die; death; an affair.

日日如丨 daily the same as before.
丨鄉 my native village.
丨事 an old affair, a legend; old ways, antiquated.
丨犯 a presumptuous sin, a willful act.
大丨 the death of parents.
身丨 or 物丨 deceased, departed.
丨人 or 丨交 an old friend; a deceased friend.
何丨 what's the reason? why?
丨此 therefore, on this account.
丨意 purposely, intentionally.
丨舊 old, long used, out of date, unfashionable.
無丨 causeless, unreasonable.
些須細丨 a trifling matter.
詐丨 crafty acts, guileful.
是丨知幽明之丨 from this we can infer the recondite and the intelligible.
丨舊無大故則不棄也 old tried servants should not be dismissed for trifling errors.
亦惟汝丨 moreover it is only on your account.
變丨 a sudden change of views; an important change, as one caused by a death.
天然緣丨結絲羅 it was certainly Heaven's ordination which tied up this silken net — of marriage.

In Shanghai. A demonstrative pronoun.
丨個物事 that thing.
丨頭 or 丨塊 there, in that spot.
丨搭 that place.

固 ku'
From an *inclosure* and *old* as the phonetic; used with the next.

Shut in on all sides, shut up; strengthened, fortified, impervious, firm, constant, pertinacious, fixed; chronic, as disease; assuredly, firmly; vulgar, rustic, rude; to make firm, to defend; to render stable.
丨然 surely, without reserve.
丨執不通 immovable, deaf to reason, perverse.
丨耳如此 it certainly is so; these are the reasons.
堅丨 or 主丨 lasting, well-made; masterly, *i. e.* the master would do it.
丨城 it secures the city.
丨宜 assuredly so.
丨陋無文 rustic and unlettered.
君子丨窮 the princely man retains his dignity in poverty.
閉丨 to conceal from, to shut up closely.
丨守 will defended; to carefully guard.
天保定爾亦孔之丨 Heaven has protected and settled you in the greatest security.
皇圖鞏丨 the imperial realm is well guarded.
愼丨封守以康四海 carefully strengthen the outposts, and the security of the whole country will be assured.

痼 痁 ku'
From *disease* and *firm* or *old*; used with the last.

A chronic, incurable complaint, as leprosy, gout, palsy, &c.
丨疾 a long standing or chronic complaint.

錮 ku'
To run metal into cracks; to close or stop securely; to interfere and prevent.
禁丨 to stop up a way, to restrain; to prevent, as good men getting office; to keep, as one in banishment.

鯝 ku'
The maw and entrails of fish; a freshwater fish, about a foot long and an inch wide; the scales are small and the belly white; it is so fat that it furnishes a yellow oil used in lamps, whence its name of 黃丨魚, often erroneously written 黃骨魚 or yellow boned fish; it is ascertained to be the *Culter exiguus*, a kind of leuciscus or roach and is much used for sauces; another name is 黃花條子.

凅 ku'
Bound up with frost, as the composition of the character indicates; to freeze hard.

雇 僱 ku'
From *bird* and *door* or with *man* added; the second is the common form, but it is unauthorized, and is interchanged with the next.

To hire for a price; to engage one's services, but its use is rather confined to things; to call or procure for a temporary use, to borrow on time.
丨工 to hire laborers; hired workmen.
丨車 to hire a cart.
丨脚夫 hire or call some coolies.
丨賃 to rent, on a lease.
受丨傭工 to be engaged as a laborer.

Read *hu'* A synonym of 鳸 a hawfinch.

顧 頋 ku'
From *head* and to *hire*; it is interchanged with the last, and the contraction is well known

To turn the head and look after; to attend to, to care for, to regard; to reflect on, to consider; corresponding, consonant to; to assist by counsel or custom; to consult; to patronize; as an initial *conjunction*, but, on the contrary, on the other hand; a petty state mentioned in the Shi King.
反丨 on the contrary.
丨念 to remember, to consider.
不丨 inattentive; to care little for; overlooked it.
丨後 to reflect on the consequences; to lay up, as money.
首尾相丨 the beginning and end correspond.
丨本 careful of one's capital.
自丨不暇 I have not even any leisure for myself.
丨臉 careful of his reputation.
蒙光丨 I am obliged for your custom.
不丨門戶 to disregard the credit of the house or family.

照 丨 or 主 丨 to give custom — to a shop; to patronize.

丨 客 a customer, a steady purchaser.

丨 我無酒 just remember that I have no wine.

丨 如是乎 is it then so, indeed?

言行相 丨 his words and works agree.

首丨居下 his head, on the other hand, hung down.

丨 諟天之明命 he seriously studied the lucid decrees of heaven.

四 丨 青山 the green hills on every side.

丨 乃德 examine into your virtue.

開厥 丨 天 [Heaven tried] to stir up that man who would look towards it; — *i. e.* be worthy.

K'U.

Old sounds, k'u. *In Canton*, fu *and* k'u; — *in Swatow*, k'ò, *and* k'u; — *in Amoy*, k'o; — *in Fuhchau*, k'u, ku, *and* k'ò; — *in Shanghai*, k'u; — *in Chifu*, k'u.

枯 *k'u* From *wood* and *old*.
Rotten or dry wood; decayed, putrid, rotten; arid, withered, sapless; dried up bogs.

丨 槁 decayed, attenuated, cadaverous.

丨 骨 old dried bones; soft bones.

漸漸乾 丨 it has gradually dried up and withered away.

如摧 丨 朽 [I can beat them as easily] as I can push over a rotten stump.

骷 *k'u* The bones of the body, as of the skeleton; the lower end of a thigh-bone; the shoulder-blade.

丨 骨 the knee-bone, under the patella.

丨 顱頭 a skull, old and withered.

嘆 丨 髏 to compassionate and quiet the ghosts — by masses.

跍 *k'u* To crouch down, to cuddle up; said by the people of Hunan of living at large, or roaming about as a tramp.

刳 *k'u* From *knife* and *boastful*.
To cut open, to cut in two; to rip open, to rive; to cut down.

丨 皮 slice off the skin.

丨 木作臼 to scoop out a block of wood for a mortar.

丨 剔孕婦 to rip up pregnant women.

丨 心 to make a clean breast.

苦 *'k'u* From *plants* and *old* as the phonetic.
Name of a marshy plant which becomes sweet when frozen; bitter, one of the five tastes; unpleasant, troublesome; painful; painstaking; urgent, pressing; afflictions; to dislike; to mortify; to feel grieved for; mortifying; used ironically for joyful, contented; the sow-thistle.

辛 丨 or 勞 丨 laborious, distressing.

何 丨 why so much trouble?

何 丨 認眞 why take it up so seriously? why be so particular?

丨 難 distress, trouble, calamity.

丨 辣 a bitter and acrid taste.

丨 命 a hard lot.

丨 口 faithful but unpleasant advice.

丨 口利於病 the medicine is bitter, but good for the ailment.

丨 楚 extreme grief, bitter sorrow.

丨 志 to mortify the desires; resolved, firm in endurance.

丨 丨 哀求 I urgently implore you to help me.

丨 盡甘來 after the bitter comes the sweet.

艱 丨 備嘗 I have been through all these troubles.

丨 急 urgent; I cannot wait.

不耐 丨 he can't bear any trouble.

丨 膽 the gall-bladder. 太 丨 死 to die of sorrow.

丨 船 or 丨 坐於船 I dislike going to sea, or sailing in boats.

丨 勸 to urge pressingly.

秋無 丨 雨 there are no unseasonable rains in autumn.

丨 樂不均 the trouble and reward are disproportionate.

丨 邑 the ancient name of the birthplace of Laotsz' (born B. C. 604), now part of Luh-yih hien 鹿邑縣 in Kwéi-teh fu, in the southeast of Honan.

其毒太 丨 the poison [of my lot] is too bitter.

丨 雨凄風 bitterly cold winds and rains; — the discommodities of travel.

筈 *k'u'* A variety of bamboo; a basket or net for catching fish.

庫 *k'u'* From *shelter* with a *cart* under it, referring to its uses.
A storehouse for carriages; an armory, an arsenal; a storehouse, a shop; a dépôt; *met.* a lexicon, a thesaurus; a magazine; a treasury, or belonging to one.

國 丨 the national exchequer.

銀 丨 a treasury.

丨 廳 the sub-treasurers in the *pu-ching sz'* department.

丨 房 a counting-room in a yamun or monastery.

關 丨 the customs' revenue.

倉 丨 a government granary.

土 丨 a go-down, the basement story of a house.

燒丨 to burn a grass or paper house full of paper ingots to the dead.

丨項 stores in the treasury.

武丨 an arsenal.

丨大使 a treasury auditor.

蕗 *k'u'* The stalk and flower of the onion or garlic as it rises and blossoms in the spring.

蒜苗丨兒 the onion flower.

褲 袴 絝 *k'u'* From *garments* and a *storehouse*, or from 跨 to *stride* contracted, referring to their use; the first and common form is unauthorized, and the last is rather unusual.

Covering for the legs; trowsers, pantaloons, breeches.

套丨 overalls, leggings.

一條丨 or 丨子 a pair of trowsers.

一幅丨襠 one pair of pantaloons.

丨褶 short riding breeches.

內丨 drawers, the garment next to the legs.

牛頭丨 short breeches, worn by laborers.

藏于丨中 concealed it in his trowsers.

短衣大丨 short jackets and wide trowsers.

丨子合着 they wear the same trowsers; — they are very intimate friends.

KÜ.

Old sounds, ko, kot, kút, kòp, kuk, kiu, gu, gút, *and* guk. *In Canton*, kü; — *in Swatow*, kù, ku, *and* ki; — *in Amoy*, ku, k'u *and* u; — *in Fuhchau*, kü, kèü, *and* kwo; — *in Shanghai*, k'ü; — *in Chifu*, kü.

居 尻 屋 *chü* From *body* and *old* or *seat*, which as one explains it, denotes to study the ancients; the second form has gone out of use, but the third is not uncommon.

To dwell, to live in a place, to reside; to remain stationary; to fill an office, to fulfill a condition; the virtue or capacity fit for it; dwellings, families; residence; the settled parts of a country; to sit down; to hoard, to collect; to engross, as a market; merely, only; tranquilly; retired from public life; to desist; to consist in; to be, or acting, in which sense it makes a present participle of the next verb, as 丨喪 in mourning;

丨艱難中 in jeopardy.

閒丨 to live in retired ease.

丨住 to live at a place.

歇丨 to stay for a time; to lodge.

丨民 those who live in a locality, the denizens.

茶丨 a tea-shop.

蝸丨 my snail-shell of a house.

民丨 the people's dwellings.

善丨室 he well knew the management (or economy) of a household.

丨處 a residence.

温丨 a house-warming.

丨奇 goods kept back to raise the price, or make a corner.

丨敬 being respectful.

起丨 acting and resting; condition of; qualities, circumstances.

問候起丨 to inquire after one's circumstances.

丨身 personal habits, disposition.

丨官 in office; he holds a post.

丨士 a retired scholar; out of office.

丨孀 widowed; still a widow.

自丨 self-possessed.

丨然 unsociable, reserved; presuming on; contrary to expectation; easily.

丨公段直 he is really honest and fair, and speaks truthfully.

丨仁 to be benevolent.

丨心散蕩 his heart is bent on dissipation.

匪丨匪康 he would neither rest nor take his ease.

豈敢定丨 dare we stay settled, *i. e.* remain inactive?

其意何丨 what can be the meaning of it?

何丨 wherefore? what's the case?

成丨多不成丨少 the chances are great that it will be done.

謀人之保丨 planning how to protect and domicile the people.

丨月 in childbed.

丨生子 she easily brought forth her son.

官丨極品 he has reached the highest rank.

職思其丨 he knows and well considers their relations.

丨之不疑 it seemed most certainly to be so.

日丨月諸 behold the sun and moon!

丨中中 middling, medium; in the middle. (*Fuhchau*).

据 *chü* From *hand* and to *dwell*; used with the last.

A spear handle; a disabled hand; a position or place; embarrassed, restricted; hurried; in need of money.

丨以驕傲 he prides himself on his hauteur.

丨法 accordant to the laws; legal.

予手拮丨 with my claws I tore and placed — the grass for my nest.

丨難開口 unable to express one's self from trepidation.

In *Cantonese*. The grip of the hand between the thumb and fingers.

椐 ˏchü A tree, the 丨橨, full of protuberant knots; the sticks are used for staffs by old men, and for whip handles.

丨木 a timber tree like the elm, growing in Kiangsu, used for furniture, carts, &c.; probably the hornbeam (*Carpinus*).

啓之辟其檉其丨 the tamarix and stave trees were thinned and cleared out.

琚 ˏchü Ornamental girdle gems.

瓊丨 bijoux, precious ornaments worn on the person.

丨佩 girdle trappings.

報之以瓊丨 I returned for it a fine girdle clasp.

裾 ˏchü From *dress* and *dwelling*; used for *kü*ˀ 倨 proud.

The tail of a coat, the skirt; a robe; a lapel.

長丨 a long train.

爲人廉丨 he is a man of little pretension.

腒 ˏchü The dried flesh of pheasants and poultry; long duration.

夏用丨 use dried poultry in summer, — as it does not become offensive.

鶋 ˏchü A beautiful, elegant sea-bird, the 鶢丨 which has a white breast; these birds go in flocks, and are probably akin to the sandpiper.

鵯丨 is the eastern jackdaw (*Lycos dauricus*) also called 小寒鴉兒 at Peking.

賰 寠 ˏchü To *store property*, as the composition of the character intimates; to lay by property in a guarded room.

丨賣 to keep on hand for sale.

崌 ˏchü Name of a high, snow-topped peak in the northwest of Sz'ch'uen; this and 崍山 are situated near the source of the River Min.

丨州 the old name for Sung-pan ting 松潘廳 the district in Sz'ch'uen where these peaks lie.

俱 ˏchü From *man* and *prepared*.

A collective adjective of number, denoting things or people; all, the whole; altogether, at once, and placed after the noun; both, together with; fully supplied; all right.

丨在 both [parents are] still living.

丨全 all are complete, as a set of tools.

丨備 all is ready, as an outfit; all kinds are kept on hand.

丨是一樣 all are alike.

丨存乎一心 all then resolves itself to one end or purpose.

所爲丨善 whatever he does is good.

丨是隱瞞 they were only deceiving him all the while.

拘 ˏchü From *hand* and a *sentence*; it is also read ˏ*keu*, and is then a synonym of 枸 to join.

To grasp so as to detain; to stop; to grapple with; to restrain, to moderate, to repress; to adhere to; attached to, bigoted; bent, hooked; to hook; to take, to receive; to collect.

不丨往來 there is no limit to your proceedings; come and go as you please.

丨禮 very formal; too precise.

丨拿 to seize, to arrest.

丨執 or 丨泥 obstinate; fixed in one's views.

丨束 to restrain, as one's subordinates.

不用丨 don't be formal; don't put yourself to much trouble.

丨泥不通 obscure, involved, as a style; slow to understand the relations of things.

不丨 immaterial; no restraint; not to insist on.

丨押 or 丨管 to hold in custody.

盡丨以歸于周予其殺 arrest the whole of them and send them to me to Cheu, where I will put them to death.

給他丨住了 I was [so to speak] forced to stay.

跔 踞 ˏchü The feet useless or benumbed by cold; stiffened, chilled.

丨跓 to lean or skip about on one foot, as when it is asleep; the hands and feet benumbed.

攣丨 the feet curled up.

痀 ˏchü A crooked back, a curved spine; a hunchback.

丨僂 a humpbacked dwarf.

丨長 an old man bent with age.

駒 ˏchü A colt under two years; a fine colt; strong, spirited; a small horse, like a Shetland pony.

頁丨 a fine horse.

千里丨 a swift pony; a term for a sprightly lad.

丨光易逝 the bright racer quickly disappears; — *met.* time gone cannot be recalled.

我馬維丨 my horses are smart as colts.

老馬反爲丨 an old horse still thinks he is a colt.

株丨 a rotten stump.

斛 ˏchü From a *peck* and a man's *name*; it is regarded as a synonym of ˏ*k'iu* 仇, when that is read ˏ*kü* to decant.

To remove from one vessel to another; to lade.

挹丨 to decant liquids.

捄 ˏchü From *hand* and to *beg*.

To fill a hod or basket with earth, as in building adobe walls.

丨之陾陾 the hod-carriers came on one after the other.

Read ˏ*k'iu*. Long and curved; to lengthen, like a horn; to protect or defend; to stop.

有丨其角 it has crooked horns.

有丨天畢 long and curved [like a rabbit-net] is the constellation Hyades.

ʿ舉 ʿ牵 Composed of 與 *with* and 手 a *hand* contracted, denoting two men raising a thing; the contracted form is common in cheap books.

ʿchü To raise with the hands or between two men; to elevate to raise in public opinion, to recommend, to introduce to; to rise or fly up; to rise in one's esteem, to venerate; to praise, to speak of; to promote; to begin; to set about; to strike up, as music; to confiscate; a proposition, an affair proposed for deliberation; all, the whole, said of persons; it sometimes indicates the present action of the succeeding verb, as 丨 飲 drinking; an ancient weight of three taels.

丨 鄉貴 to nominate (or promote) a village worthy.

公 丨 put forward by the public.

丨 世不忘 I will not forget you through life.

丨 薦 to recommend, to give one a good character.

不中擡 丨 he is not worth bringing forward.

丨 手 to raise the hand.

丨 止大方 a good deportment.

丨 其貨 confiscated his goods.

丨 爲民上 he was promoted over all the people.

丨 善 to promote the good.

丨 不信 I don't believe a word of it.

丨 動 gestures, actions.

一 丨 成名 passed to his degree of *kü jin*.

義 丨 a just act; a public spirited proposal.

客不先 丨 the visitor should not begin the conversation.

自行檢 丨 to reform one's own conduct.

丨 人 or 丨 子 a promoted man, a graduate of the second degree; each of the first eighteen *kü jin* on the tripos is allowed to put up a tablet over his door with 鄉魁 or village leader on it; others write 文元 or literary senior.

所當爲之 丨 any undertaking which is deemed to be proper.

丨 目無親 I raise my eyes and see no relatives. — as a stranger in a strange land.

ʿ櫸 ʿchü A small tree with pinnatifid leaves, the leaflets like a chestnut, and flexible willow-like branches; the intervals on the stem are slightly winged like the orange; the flowers are reddish.

丨 柳 a species of willow whose wood serves for boxes; it grows in the central provinces; the people call it 胖柳 or the fat willow.

ʿ柜 ʿchü From *wood* and *great*; a synonym of the last, but now also used as a contraction of *kwéi'* 櫃 a case.

A large leaved tree likened to the willow, of whose bark a tea can be made; a vessel for catching drippings; an old town in Shantung.

ʿ莒 ʿchü An old name in Tsi for the arum or something like it, of which cordage could be made.

丨 國 a petty, short-lived state, now Kü cheu 丨 州 in the southeast of Shantung on the 沭河 River Shuh; seven rulers are mentioned between B. C. 600 and 518; it was absorbed by Tsu in 431.

子夏爲 丨 父宰 Tsz'hia was governor of Kü-fu, — a town in the eastern part of Lu.

ʿ筥 ʿchü A round osier basket holding about half a peck; a bamboo basket; to put things into a basket.

禾 丨 four handfuls of grain or a small sheaf.

米 丨 a hamper for rice.

筐之 丨 之 put them into the various kinds of baskets.

ʿ蒟 ʿchü The betel pepper, for which ˏ*lin* 蔞 is the correct form, but this has taken its place and sound, and is no longer read ʿ*kü*.

丨 蒻 a kind of wild arum.

ʿ矩 ʿchü From *arrow* and *great*; others describe it from 工 *work* in a 方 *square*, and an 矢 *arrow* that hits it.

A carpenter's square; a rule, a usage, a law, a custom; a pattern; strict, exact, constant, as a law; to adjust, to square; an angle.

不踰 丨 [Confucius] did not overstep propriety.

循規蹈 丨 carefully conform to the rules.

是以君子有絜 丨 之道 thus the prince has a principle by which he can square his conduct.

規 丨 之繩 like a carpenter's marking-line, a rule of guidance.

ʿ秬 ʿchü A variety of the panicled millet, (or perhaps of the sorghum, for no species of *Milium* now cultivated has black seeds as this is said to have), from which was distilled a fragrant spirit anciently used in sacrifice.

有稻有 丨 there were rice and black millet.

ʿ狗 ʿchü Plumes which have become crooked; a horse whose hind feet are white; the feather on an arrow.

ʿ踽 ʿ偊 From *foot* or *men* and *loose*; the second is also read ʿ*yü*.

ʿchü To walk alone, unsociable; a stately, undaunted gait; morose, sulky.

獨行 丨 丨 walking alone; I am going unbefriended; to act independently.

丨 丨 涼涼 a self-reliant manner.

ʿ棋 ʿchü The edible fruit of the *Hovenia dulcis*, whose taste is likened to that of a plum; it is also called 金鈎李 gold hook plum 萬字菓 the Vitruvian scroll fruit, 拐棗 crooked date, 鷄爪子 cock's claws, and other names; the fleshy peduncles are steeped in spirits to flavor the liquor; fancy dishes are sometimes made in imitation of them.

具 chü' Derived from 貝 *precious* above 廾 to *present* to; it is interchanged with 俱 in some senses.

Prepared, well arranged; all, all at once, throughout; to be all present; placed together in order; written out properly; to present, to furnish; to amass; an utensil, implement; common, unimportant.

謹 丨 carefully arranged, as a present.

備 丨 all is ready.

知名不 丨 as you know the name, I omit it.

名內 丨 my name is written inside.

丨 奉過你 I give them to you.

刑 丨 implements of punishment.

丨 曰予聖 they all cry, We are wise folks.

老 丨 an old man's staff; an ironical term for a coffin.

爾牲則 丨 your victims have abundant provision.

文 丨 a set of small drawers for holding nice articles, stationery, &c.

丨 文 an official paper.

視爲 丨 文 regard it as a mere form, as a public duty; look upon it as unreal; merely talk.

丨 神之靈者 one into whom the spirit of the god had entered.

丨 辦 to make all fit and ready.

全 丨 entirely prepared.

丨 呈 to send in a plea.

兄弟旣 丨 和樂且孺 when your brothers are all present, then be joyful and harmonious as children.

埧 chü' From *earth* and *prepared*; it resembles *pa'* 垻 in both form and meaning.

An embankment to restrain water from overflowing a town; a shore.

堤 丨 a bank to restrain the water.

築 丨 to build a dike.

抵通 丨 [the boats] reached the shore or jetties at Tung cheu, —near Peking.

颶 chü' A furious cyclone, a whirlwind; a tyfoon, common along the southern coasts of China.

丨 母 or 丨 風蓋 prognostics of a tyfoon.

打風 丨 to meet a tyfoon.

句 chü' From 口 *mouth* and 丩 to *spread*; it is often synonymous with 勾 when it is read *keu*, but the two are now carefully distinguished.

A step in reading; a full period, a complete sentence; an expression, a phrase; a line in verse; a classifier of phrases; to write or compose.

分 丨 讀 mark it off into sentences and clauses.

點 丨 勾股 punctuate and divide it into paragraphs.

丨 就鬼神驚 when he had written the sentence, the gods started with affright.

不成 丨 the sentence is incomplete; it makes no sense.

一 丨 話一 丨 詩 one sentence, one stanza.

並無半 丨 虛言 he has no half sentences or unmeaning words; —he is truthful.

琢 丨 to polish a composition.

佳 丨 a fine sentence.

丨 丨 中圈 each sentence hits the circle; —*i.e.* your remarks are quite correct.

題 丨 to write a line, as for a tablet or album.

兩扇 丨 a period composed of two evenly balanced parts.

四六 丨 an unequal sentence, not considered to be elegant.

丨 容縣 a district 90 *li* south of Nanking city, famous for furnishing barbers; the name dates from about B. C. 200.

Read *keu*, and formerly much used with 勾 a hook. Full, as a bow; crooked; a corner; to embarrass.

敦弓旣 丨 their bows were drawn to the car.

懼 惧 愳 chü' From *heart* and the timid *look* of a bird; the first is the common form,

To fear, to stand in awe of; to regard with reverent awe, apprehensive, fearful; trembling from awe, as when before a superior.

赧 丨 mortified, chagrined.

戰 丨 trembling from fright.

恐 丨 or 怯 丨 afraid of, cowardly.

畏 丨 王法 to stand in awe of the laws, as good subjects do.

毫無 丨 怕 reckless, he is afraid of nothing.

恐 丨 修省 to scrutinize one's conduct carefully.

丨 內 to be afraid of one's wife.

巨 chü' The old form is composed of 工 *work* and 手 a *hand* grasping it; it looks somewhat like *ch'än* 臣 a statesman, and occurs used with some of its compounds.

The chief, the great one; great, vast, mighty; large; very; how?

丨 萬 myriads, innumerable.

丨 擘 the thumb; *met.* the leading one.

丨 工 a fine performance, said of an essay.

丨 盜 powerful insurgent.

張開 丨 口 stretched his mouth wide; he told a big story.

詎 chü' From *words* and *great*.

An adversative *conjunction*, how, in what manner, implying the opposite of what is said; as however, but then, to my surprise; startling unexpectedly; to reach to; ignorant of.

丨 意 who would have thought it? unexpected, unforeseen.

丨 于此乎 has it come to this?

丨 料 surprised at.

丨 否 or 丨 非 is it so! how not?

粔 chü' Cakes or krullers of rice flour, made in the shape of rings, and steamed.

丨 敉細點 cakes and pastry of the finest kind.

鉅 *chü'* Great; hard, as iron; fierce, implacable; obdurate.

丨公 the Emperor; a title of high respect.

犯伊之威怒如丨鐵 if you offend his dignity, his wrath will be obdurate as iron.

怇 *chü'* From *heart* and *great*; some regard this as a corruption of *k'w'ang* 恇 which it resembles.

Disrespectful, haughty towards one; to fear; apprehensive of.

拒 *chü'* Used with the next.

To ward off with the hand; to obstruct, to withstand, to stop; to reject, to oppose a plan; to stand out against; to prepare for resistance.

抗丨 to resist by force.

力丨 strenuous opposition.

丨絕 to repel utterly; to break off intercourse with.

丨傷官兵 he opposed and wounded the troops.

丨住 to stop one; to defend one's self.

相丨 to resist; to stand out against.

丨捕 to resist an arrest.

距 *chü'* From *foot* and *great*; it is interchanged with the last.

A spur, the dew-claw or hallux on birds; the warts on a horse's legs; to go to, to reach; to stand over against; border on; opposite, conterminous; the distance between, distant from; to skip over, to oppose; to stab from behind.

鷄丨 a cock's spur.

超丨 to leap over.

閉丨 to obstruct, as a passage.

不丨朕行 do not resist Our proceedings.

東西相丨 the distance from east to west.

丨乎西海 I have gone over all the country.

違丨 to resist.

佔丨城池 [the rebels have] established themselves in the city.

敢丨大邦 they dare to oppose this great realm.

岠 *chü'* Like the last.

To reach, to go to; a high hill or peak.

炬 *chü'* A torch of reeds, a link made of old bamboo withs cut up; to burn, to light.

寶丨 a painted candle.

火丨 a torch, otherwise called 丨枝 or fire-twig.

付之一丨 he threw it into the flames.

臘丨成灰淚始乾 when the candle has burned to ashes, its tears are then dried up;—violent grief soon dies out.

苣 *chü'* From *plants* and *great*; used for the last.

A small rush; a vegetable; succulent plants allied to the chicory, lettuce, endive, sow thistle, and similar species.

丨藤 a name for the sesamum.

束丨 to bind rushes for links.

白丨 lettuce; a hairy sort.

山萵丨 or wild lettuce, the lion's foot. (*Prenanthes.*)

苦丨 or 丨藚菜 chicory and endive (*Cichorium intybus* and *C. endivia*), and probably the sow thistle.

家丨藚 cultivated in Kiangsi, and resembles a coarse sort of *Lactuca*.

駏 *chü'* Offspring of a stallion and she-mule, according to the dictionaries.

丨驉 a wild equine animal like a mule, which loves the grass, and carries off the jerboa on its back whenever it sees the hunters, as that will show it where pasture is, and the jerboa too escapes thus on the onager's back.

倨 *chü'* From *man* and *dwelling* in; occurs used for the next.

To stand or sit carelessly; a free and easy way, nonchalant, haughty; a bold, assuming gait; strong.

丨牙 tusks, strong teeth.

丨傲 haughty.

驕丨 imperious, domineering.

踞 *chü'* To crouch, to squat; to sit impolitely, with the feet out.

丨處 to give no attention.

箕丨而坐 to sit on the haunches, like a seive.

丨坐 to squat one's self down, as in the best seat.

盤丨 to sit impertinently.

虎丨江東 I shall forcibly occupy all east of the Yangtsz' River.

鋸 *chü'* A saw: to saw; to divide, as by a saw; to mend crockery by joining the edges of the pieces with copper clamps; to reduce; serrated, toothed, like a saw.

丨齒 the teeth of a saw.

葉有丨齒 the leaves are serrated.

丨頸 he cut his throat.

刀丨不加 it cannot be divided; *met.* he is not to be executed.

丨價 or 丨減價 cheapen the price a little.

丨木 or 拉丨 to saw wood.

丨糠 or 丨屑 saw-dust.

丨不結實 it is not clamped securely.

補丨碗 to mend dishes.

窶 **寠** *'chü* From *cave* or *shelter* and to *lasso*.

Unceremonious, rustic; sordid, miserable; in want; to intrude.

丨人子 an indigent man.

終丨且貧 poor and withal in great straits.

丨數 a straw pad for the head when carrying burdens.

Read *'leu.* A narrow gore of land.

屨 'chü' From 履 a *shoe* contracted and 婁 a *lasso*.

Sandals; poor shoes woven of the dolichos fiber; shoes.

葛 〡 cheap cloth shoes.

穿 〡 to put on shoes.

瓜田不納 〡 don't tie your shoes in a melon-patch; — avoid the appearance of evil.

戶外之 〡 滿矣 shoes fill up his doorway,—he is so popular; it was the old custom to enter barefooted.

懅 chü' Ashamed and bashful; much alarmed.

慚 〡 chagrined and humbled.

豦 chü' From *boar* and *tiger*, because these two beasts are hard to separate when fighting.

A wild boar; name of a doubtful animal resembling a yellow and black baboon, which butts with its head, and is very rapid in its motions; it is said to be found in Kienping mountain 建平山 in Nganhwui; fighting, tussling, wrestling.

臄 chü' The part of the face of an animal above the mouth, the upper lip.

嘉殽脾 〡 the delicate tidbits were tripe and lips.

據 chü' To lay the hand on; to fend off, to maintain; to occupy a place; to lean on; to have form or substance; tangible, evident; testimony, evidence, warranty; as a *preposition*, according to, conformably to; it appears that; and is often a sign of past time.

茲 〡 覆稱 he has now replied, saying, ...

〡 鋪拖租 to withhold the rent when in possession of the shop.

佔 〡 to encroach on, to appropriate by fraud.

霸 〡 to usurp by force.

〡 守 to guard vigilantly.

〡 說 from what he says.

有何證 〡 what proof is there?

實 〡 reliable proofs.

〡 於德 let your confidence be in virtue.

〡 事論事 each subject must be taken up by itself.

立此爲 〡 this agreement is made as evidence.

神必 〡 我 the gods will surely comfort me.

亦有兄弟不可以 〡 though I have brothers, I cannot depend on them.

〡 稟已悉 I have fully examined the petition.

〡 來函云 according to what your letter says.

遽 chü' From to *go* and *scuffling* as the phonetic.

Hurried, rapid; agitated, trembling; suddenly, instantly; swift, urged on; to dispatch, to forward; to send on, as a post; an express, a courier.

急 〡 hurried, urgent.

〡 見 I hastily saw it, I glanced at it.

傳 〡 之役 a government courier.

卒 〡 or 〡 爾 or 〡 行 suddenly; without notice, no intimation of, unknown to.

〡 然加之 all at once he struck him.

驚 〡 flurried, frightened.

慌 〡 而手足亂 he is so fluttered (or nervous) that he gets confused.

鐻 chü' A padded stick to beat a bell or drum.

Read ˛k'ü. An ancient table utensil of silver or gold; a description of ear-jewel or ring.

䀠 chü' Composed of two *eyes*; it is another form of k'ü' 瞿 to look.

To look to the right and left; to look, as if seeking a trail.

彥 〡 a statesman of the Sung dynasty.

K'Ü.

Old sounds, k'o, k'op, gio, gop, *and* giot. *In Canton*, k'ü *and* hü; — *in Swatow*, k'u, k'ù, *and* kù; — *in Amoy*, k'u, ku, *and* hu; — *in Fuhchau*, k'ü, kü, hü, k'o, *and* k'ëü; — *in Shanghai*, k'ü, kü, *and* chi; — *in Chifu*, k'ü.

區 ˛chü From 匚 to *conceal* and 品 many *sorts* inside; occurs used with the next.

A place for storing or concealing; a dwelling, a hamlet; a petty locality; a small store-room; to dwell; to sort; to assign to its own place or rank; a line, as of division or boundary; a measure of four cups.

〡 別 to discriminate properly, as between two similar articles or statements.

〡 〡 之心 my private feelings or regards.

就是 〡 〡 it is only I myself.

〡 〡 之地 my petty region; a small state.

〡 處不安 living in small quarters at great discomfort.

勿以我爲 〡 don't regard me as the standard.

〡 域 an outlying region, a far off spot.

省會之 〡 a place of great concourse.

自有 〡 '處 I have a good plan for it.

大丨 heaven and earth.
丨藏 to hide away.
不可一理丨 they cannot all be classed alike.

嶇 墟 ꜀ch'ü A rugged, steep mountain; a difficult ascent up a peak.
崎丨 a rough road.

軀 ꜀ch'ü The body, the person; a body or substance.
為國捐丨 to offer one's self for his country.
肉丨 or 丨體 or 全丨 the body, the physical man.
佛像一丨 an effigy of Budha, like those cut in rocks.
全丨保妻子之臣 an official who cares only for himself, his wife and family.

驅 駈 敺 ꜀ch'ü From *horse* and a *place* or *to go*; the last two forms are obsolete, though the second is employed for a horse's speed.

To turn animals out of a field; to drive them into an inclosure for a battue; to drive on, to lash, to whip up; to urge, to animate, to exhort; to order people into their proper places; fleet, racing; the length of the road, the journey or course.
先丨 the vanguard.
後丨 the rear, the reserve.
丨逐 to expel, to drive off; to turn out, as loafers.
馳丨奔走 to whip up and gallop fast.
丨邪 to expel noxious influences.
丨使 to urge by force.
丨兵前進 to urge troops forward, to drive them into the fight.

墟 ꜀h'ü From *earth* and *empty*; it is frequently contracted to ꜀syü 圩 a dike, but the two are distinct.

A mount; old mausolea or burial wastes; a deep gorge; a neglected spot, an old fortress; a wild; a fair, a market; an open area where fairs are held.
郊丨 the open country, the fields and woods, places to ramble in.
歸丨 gone to the tomb; buried.
丨墓之間 among the old tombs.
幾時丨期 when is the fair to be held?
赴丨 or 趁丨 to go to market.
丨塲 the place for the fair.
丨咁嘈 as noisy as a market-place. (*Cantonese.*)

袪 ꜀ch'ü The sleeve, the cuff; a wrist-band, an ornamented cuff or edging, such as ladies wear on sleeves.
摻執子之丨兮 I hold you, Sir, by the cuff.
以車丨丨 stout, lusty, carriage horses.

阹 ꜀ch'ü To inclose a pen or yard for keeping the cattle and fowls, especially one near the hills.
江河為丨 let the streams make the boundary of the inclosure.
周丨環瀆 the whole circuit of the corral was surrounded by a ditch.

祛 ꜀ch'ü From *worship* and *to depart*; as the phonetic.

To dissipate or expel noxious influences or malaria; to avert; to disperse.
丨風去濕 to expel wind and bad humors.
丨散 to disperse; to alleviate, as pain.
丨丨 strongly built, as a carriage

魼 ꜀ch'ü The flounder, whiff, or sole-fish; it is said to resemble a cow's tripe, and has minute scales; an animal described as resembling an ox with a snake's tail, and wings on its sides, which perhaps denotes a seal or dugong.
禺禺丨鰨 the serried schools of plaice and flounders.

抾 ꜀ch'ü From *hand* and *to go* as the phonetic; it is also read *k'ieh*.

To feel for a thing, to take away; to hand up to; to lade out; to lift; to grasp; to carry off in both hands.

胠 ꜀ch'ü The side over the ribs; the flank, as of an animal; an opening in the side; to open as a carpet bag; to throw down; to discard, to reject.
陽鮢丨於沙 the minnows are stranded on the sands.
右丨 the right flank of an army.

朐 ꜀ch'ü Strips of meat cut from the flanks and dried in the wind; to offer dried meat in sacrifice.
丨肉 cutlets.
丨脯 jerked slices or collops of pork.
臨丨縣 a district in Tsing-cheu fu in the north of Shantung.

劬 ꜀ch'ü From *labor* and a *sentence* as the phonetic.

Anxious solicitude, labor, distress; toil of a severe kind, in obedience to duty.
丨勞 grievous toil, as the pangs of childbirth or the care of parents for their children.
身丨莫擬獄苦 corporeal toil is not to be compared to the sufferings of a prison.
丨勞于野 we toiled grievously in the wilds.

絇 ꜀ch'ü Thread or cord used to ornament shoes; a band once used to fasten on shoes; the blunt figured toes of shoes, which are likened to a head and robe.
丨屨 the blunt toes of shoes.

鴝 鸜 ꜀ch'ü A species of thrush, reared as a song bird, the *mainah* (*Acridotheres cristatellus*) called 丨鵒 or 八哥 the eight brothers; its plumage is black, with a crest and a white spot on the secondaries.
丨鵒眼 greasy-white spots seen in argillite inkstones.

渠 ꜀ch'ü From 水 *water* and an old form of 矩 a *rule;* occurs used for the next.

A place for water to run into, a cess-pool; a drain, a gutter, an aqueduct; the felly or rim of a wheel; a canal; great, ample, wide; the chief one; gradual; a personal pronoun, now superseded by the next.

於我乎夏屋丨丨 he assigned us a wide and spacious mansion.

捦其丨帥 he seized their chief and leader.

車丨 the scallop shell (*Pecten*), regarded by the Budhists as among precious things; it is also called 海扇 sea-fan, in allusion to its shape; others think the mother-o'-pearl shell is intended.

丨縣 a district in Shun-king fu near the River Pa in Sz'ch'uen.

倮 佢 ꜀ch'ü From *man* and *canal;* the first is an alteration of the last, but the second and contracted form is alone used.

That person or thing.

In Cantonese read ꜂k'ü The third personal pronoun, he, she, it, they.

꜂丨嘅 his, her's their's.

問꜂丨 ask him.

就係꜂丨 it is he; that is it.

共꜂丨講 we told him about it.

蕖 ꜀ch'ü The water-lily, the *ditch flower* as the name indicates, called 芙丨 after the blossom has opened.

灼若芙丨 splendid as the full-blown lotus.

石丨 a mineral like pumice, found floating on water.

磲 ꜀ch'ü A veined stone resembling pyrophillite, the 硨丨, used for the opaque with buttons of officers of the sixth rank.

鸈 ꜀ch'ü A water bird, the 鶌丨, whose description allies it to the ibis or egret; it has many synonyms.

瞿 ꜀ch'ü From two *eyes* and a *bird; q. d.* the restless, eager glance of a hawk pecking its prey, a sense found in several of its compounds.

The timid look of a bird; to examine hurriedly, to glance at; to stare at wildly; heedless; sparing, economical.

良士丨丨 the upright man is anxiously thoughtful.

狂夫丨丨 these rattle-brained fellows are awed.

丨視 to look frightened.

丨然 alarmed, drawing back.

丨丨 startled, disconcerted.

丨曇 a term to imitate the name Gaudama, the priestly name of Sakya-muni.

丨耶尼 or 丨陀尼 Go-dhan-ya, one of the four continents of a universe, whose inhabitants, according to the Budhists, have circular faces.

臞 癯 ꜀ch'ü From *flesh* or *disease* and *timid;* the second refers rather to disease, causing loss of flesh.

Thin, emaciated; cadaverous, ghost-like; ghastly, lean.

形容甚丨 his aspect is very emaciated.

心戰而丨 fear makes one become lean.

欋 ꜀ch'ü A rake with four teeth; the twisted and contorted roots of great trees like the banian.

衢 ꜀ch'ü From *to go* and *timid* as the phonetic.

A road where many ways meet; a highway, a main street, a thoroughfare; an avenue.

通丨 a public broadway.

天丨 the equator; though others say it is the Milky Way.

步入天丨 to get on to the equator; — *i. e.* to see the emperor.

雲丨 a high literary degree.

丨州府 a prefecture in the southwest of Chehkiang.

氍 ꜀ch'ü A square mat, called 丨毹, made of hair, which was anciently spread for the emperor to sit on when worshiping Shangti; a variegated carpet.

籧 ꜀ch'ü A kind of coarse, strong bamboo matting, used for fish weirs and palings.

丨筐 trays for silkworms.

丨篨 decrepit, bloated, dropsical and ugly, a term derived from the appearance of a roll of this matting.

燕婉之求丨篨不鮮 a genial pleasant mate was sought, and lo! this vicious, decrepit fellow.

蘧 ꜀ch'ü A vegetable resembling the sweet basil (*Lophanthus*); also a synonym for a plant akin to the chicory, otherwise called 苦葵 or bitter mallows, which is probably a *Scorzonera* or skirret.

蘧 ꜀ch'ü A species of *Triticum* which resembles wheat, but has no eatable kernel.

丨蔬 mushroom or agaric, of a dark gray color, which grows on rotton plants, and is eaten fresh; several spring from the same root.

丨丨然 encouraged, as from a favorable dream.

璩 ꜀ch'ü A synonym of 鐻 an earring; as a surname, used with the last.

應丨 a celebrated general and statesman of the Wéi state.

洵 ꜀ch'ü The west branch of the Peh-tang River in the east of Chihli; it rises beyond the Wall, and runs near San-ho hien 三河縣 for which 臨丨 was an old name.

Read ꜀keu. The murmuring noise of water.

齲 'ch'ü Defective, rotten teeth; the Chinese ascribe them to worms, which cause the toothache; the toothache; a flaring set of teeth.

丨朽 carious, as teeth.

割唇治丨 to cut away the lips in order to cure toothache, — is very great folly

虡 'ch'ü A mythical celestial animal, the 飛丨 which has a deer's head on a dragon's body; it was carved on the supports of bells.

丨業維樅 on the bell-posts was the toothed front-board.

簴 'ch'ü Posts carved with dragons, forming part of a bell-frame in olden time, so called because they supported (舉) the bell, drum, or cymbal.

去 'ch'ü ch'ü' Formed of 厶 *perverse* and 大 *great;* others derive it from 大 *great* and 凵 a *receptacle*, all modified in combination.

To leave, to depart from; to quit; to lay off; to dismiss, to conceal, to hoard; to remove.

不得已而丨之 he could not do otherwise than dismiss him.

丨留 to dismiss or to retain, as an official.

欲丨告朔之餼羊 he also wished to send away the ram he was to sacrifice to the new moon.

丨惡 to expel the badness; *i. e.* to reform the conduct.

Read *k'ü'* To depart, to separate; to go, to proceed; to pass on in a regular course; to go out from or through; past, gone; former, following; to discard, to repudiate; following a verb, it implies its action or completion; departing, prolonging, as a sound.

丨罷 go away! be off!

拿丨 take it away; carried off.

丨來 a finished act.

進丨 to enter; go in.

丨不得 I can't go; it is impossible to go there.

一丨不回 once gone, never returns.

丨年 or 丨歲 last year.

丨世 dead, gone.

丨聲 the departing tone.

賣不丨 I cannot sell it.

過得丨 you can go that way; passable, as a road.

過意不丨 I cannot sufficiently thank you.

來丨 everywhere; universally; continued; again and again.

過丨之事 past affairs.

你丨那裏 where are you going;

丨拜客來 I am going out to pay a visit.

丨來未定 it is uncertain whether he goes or comes.

我想出丨 I intend going out — of the house.

罷不得丨見他 I was obliged to go and see.

相丨不遠 they are not very unlike, or far apart.

說來說丨 talking this and that, tautology.

丨官 to retire from office.

出處丨就 to go or remain at home; to leave or take office.

丨文 the dispatch forwarded.

丨修行 to turn priest.

說不丨 it should not be said; better not said; improper.

丨就不苟 do not think it indifferent whose service (or which side) you take.

天所丨 Heaven repudiated him.

鳥鼠攸丨 the birds and rats would soon depart, — because they found no nest.

看花丨來 I have been to see the flowers.

KÜEH.

Old sounds, kít, ket, gít, *and* ket. *In Canton,* küt, *and* kwăt; — *in Swatow,* k'iat, kué, kiòk, kwat, *and* kút; — *in Amoy,* kwat, kw'at, k'òeh, wat, *and* kút; — *in Fuhchau,* kw'òk, kwoi, kiòk, *and* kuk; — *in Shanghai,* küih, *and* djüih; — *in Chifu,* küeh.

欮 ˏchüé From 欠 to *breathe,* and 逆 *adverse* contracted; its compound 瘚 and other derivatives have now superseded it.

To hiccough; in Hunan there is a tree whose sap cures hiccough by causing sneezing, to dig out; to expand; to put on.

肝丨病 a fit with fixed eyes, and frothing at the mouth.

[illegible], [illegible], chüeh' An old form of the next, but now disused; the second form only is employed.

Short, as a dress; a garment reaching only to the hips; docked, curtailed; a man's name.

短丨丨 very short — and rather unseemly, as a dress; stumpy, as a queue; lopped, as a horn; short, as a broom.

厥 ˏchüé From a *cliff* and to *hiccough;* occurs used for the next.

A machine for throwing stones like a balista; a particle directing attention; a personal pronoun, he, she, it, its, sometimes used for the second person, and a synonym of 之 when used for the accusative or genitive; that one, that man; these; short; to bow the head.

丨疾不瘳 this malady is incurable.
無愧丨職 he is not ashamed of the office.
丨等 they, those persons.
此時丨後立王 the kings who arose after them.
此丨不聽 if you will not hearken to this.
播丨百穀 sowing all our sorts of grain.

瘚, ꜀chüé The hiccough; a disagreement in the humors of the system, called 寒丨 and 熱丨, which is thought to cause paralysis.
氣丨 convulsions, fits.
痰丨 foaming at the mouth, as in epileptic spasms.

劂, ꜀chüé A gouge, a graver, a small chisel.
剞丨刀 a burin, such as carvers and block-cutters use.

蹶, ꜀chüé From *foot* and to *hiccough* as the phonetic.
To stumble and nearly fall; to slip, to leap; to push down; to miss one's footing; to kick up the heels; to move, to incite; a hoof.
蹻丨 subverted, turned upside down; dispirited.
今夫丨者趨者是氣也 now when a man stumbles or runs, it is from his determination.
崩丨 it came crashing down.
丨子踢傷 wounded by a kick — of the horse.
文王丨厥生 Wăn Wang stimulated their natural virtues.

Read *kwéi*ʾ To go quickly; spry, alert, quick; diligent, careful; to play with the feet.
良士丨丨 the conscientious man is sedulously careful.
丨然 suddenly, sprightly.
丨丨從事 to stir up one to his duty.
足毋丨 do not kick your feet about.

橛, ꜀chüé A large platter anciently used in sacrifices, whose single leg had a cross-piece; the wife of the Great Yü used it.
Read *kwéi*ʾ A hill suddenly rising up.

橜, ꜀chüé A post, joist; a stanchion; a pile; a post in the middle of a gateway; a stake to tether an ox; an axle; the bit of a bridle; a button to pull open a door; a peg to hang things on; a lever; a drumstick.
丨杙 a stake, a post.
丨子 a peg; a bit.
銜丨之變 [like the] sudden turn of the bit, — which causes loss or mishap.

In *Cantonese*. A block; a moiety, the half of a thing; a large piece of it.
減一丨 cut off one half — of the height.
鋸一丨 saw off a piece.

劂, **憠**, ꜀chüé } Energetic; to urge; to use pressure to get others to do; to stimulate, to push on; to compel.
丨折了 to break off.

獗, ꜀chüé From *dog* and to *hiccough* as the phonetic.
Insolent; on the rampage.
猖丨 unruly, ferocious; disobedient, seditious; fierce, as banditti.

蕨, ꜀chüé A fern whose tender sprouts can be used for food; the root is likened to a tortoise, and the farina 丨粉 is used as a starch; the name includes probably several species of ferns like the *Pteris esculenta* and *Nephrodium esculentum*, whose tuberous roots furnish it.
陟彼南山言采其丨 I went up that southern hill and gathered the turtle-foot fern.

蟨, ꜀chüé An animal found in Shansi, likened to the rabbit for size; it has short fore legs, and the natives say that one must help to carry another, whence its descriptive name of 比肩獸 mutual-shouldering beast; it is the mongolian jerboa or helamys (*Dipus annulatus*), and its common name is 跳兎 or jumping hare.
丨蟲 a worm found in wells, the legless larvæ of a kind of fly, or perhaps a species of leech.

䠇, ꜀chüé The end of the backbone; the bones of the tail.

趉, ꜀chüé To skip, to jump; a horse stumbling in his paces.

鐝, ꜀chüé From *metal* and *hiccough*; it is unauthorized in this form, but in Kanghi's Dictionary has the radical at the bottom, and defined to grind.
A pickax, a pick; a hoe; to turn up the ground.
丨頭掘地 the pick is for digging the earth.

噘, ꜀chüé An unauthorized character.
To pout.
丨着嘴擘着臉子 to pout and look glum.

豥, ꜀chüé A hog rooting the ground; a pig turning over the sod, and seeking his food, commonly called 猪蹟地 the pig lifting the earth.

譎, **憰**, ꜀chü } From *words* or *heart* and to *pry* a hole in.
Wily, timeserving; feigning in word, or agreeing with, in order to gain an end; to impose on; hypocritical, false; counterfeiting.
丨而不正 agreeing with but still disingenuous.
詐丨 deceiving, guileful.
欺丨 to delude, to gull.
詭丨 treacherous, untrustworthy.

潏, ꜀chü Land filled up or regained from a river; islets raised in the stream; to bubble, to gush out; water flowing rapidly; name of a small branch of the River Wei on the west of Singan fu in Shensi.

獝, chüh' Fluttering, terrified as birds; to scamper, to stampede.
鳳以爲畜故鳥不丨 if you can domesticate the phoenix, you may then be sure that other birds will not run away from you.

鐍, 觼, ꜀chü The tongue of a ring or a buckle; the clasp or latch which fastens a trunk; a ring with a tongue to secure a strap; a buckle.
鎖丨 hasp of a padlock.
丨軜 a ring on a carriage for tying the reins to.
自固扃丨 fasten the clasp securely.

抉, ꜀chüé From *hand* and *to stretch*.
To dig, to rake; to pluck out, to snatch; to twang a bowstring; to castrate, said of boars.
丨眼 to gouge out an eye.
丨弦 to stretch a bow.

⿰弓夬, ꜀chüé An archer's ring worn on the right thumb to aid in shooting.

玦, ꜀chüé A broken or half a ring, once used to indicate disrupted friendship, or that an officer was cashiered; a semicircle; an archer's thimble; personal ornaments.
烏玉丨 a fine quality of ink.
指丨 a bowman's thumb-ring.
佩丨 girdle-rings or chatelaine.

亅, ꜀chüé The character represents a catch or *nick* to mark a thing; it forms the 6th radical of a few primitives, and is superseded by the next.

To mark off; a mark on the left of a column to denote a new paragraph; a barb, as of a fish-hook; in *penmanship*, it is read ꜀keu as if it was 鉤 a hook, from its form.
勾丨 to mark criminals' names for execution, as is done by the emperor at the autumnal assizes.

決, 决, ꜀chüé From *water* or *ice* and *to stretch*; occurs used with the next and last.
Streams diverging; to lead streams in channels; to disperse; name of a small affluent of the River Kan in Kiangsi; to decide, to settle; to cut off; to pass sentence; an *adverb*, doubtless, decidedly, certainly, finally; an archer's ring.
丨然 it is positively so.
丨定 quite certain.
丨丨乎 certainly, positively.
丨不食言 I certainly will not retract my words.
丨絕 to utterly renounce.
丨要 I must have it; indispensable.
丨意不往 I am determined not to go.
丨斷 to decide finally, as a judge.
꜀處丨 to sentence to death.
非禮不丨 do not decide against the rules.
丨獄 to take out of prison.
熱丨 to execute a criminal immediately.
大丨 the annual execution of state criminals at Peking, ten days before the winter solstice.
以理丨之必無是事 it stands to reason that there has been nothing of the kind.
丨諸東方則東流 if you lead it easterly then it flows east.
銳喙丨吻 [the crane's] sharp bill snaps up things quickly.
河丨 the Yellow River has burst its banks.
石丨明 the ear-shell or *Haliotis*.

芵, ꜀chüé Occurs mostly written like the last.
A medicinal plant like senna, the 丨明 (*Cassia tora*), whose seeds are used in diseases of the eye; there are two sorts, one of which is called 馬蹄丨明 or horse-hoof cassia, whose leaves are edible.
丨明子 seeds of the *Cassia tora* and *C. absus*, and probably of other species.

訣, ꜀chüé From 言 *words* and 决 *to decide* contracted; it is interchanged with its primitive.
Parting or dying words; a farewell; to take leave; an art, a rule; a mystery, as of the pulse; esoteric, occult doctrines, as the precepts of Budha; a trick, as in legerdemain; hidden, occult, abstruse.
長生之丨 rules for attaining immortality.
丨法 a transmitted rule; the secrets of the craft.
丨別 to part from a friend.
丨疑 to remove doubts.
甚丨竅 what is the mystery of the thing?—as of the telegraph.
留丨 last dying words.
秘丨 inviolate secret, as in a trade.
言無丨斷 there's no end of his talk or his promises, as a maundering, undecided man.
口丨 gibberish, mumbling.
妙丨 recondite instructions, hidden meanings.
丨詞 farewell advice.
永丨 or 長丨 an eternal farewell.
與其母丨 parted from his mother

觖, ꜀chüé From *horn* and *to dispart*; occurs interchanged with the preceding.
Grievously disappointed in one's expectations, and therefore angry; to expect impatiently

dissatisfied; deficient, wanting; to criticise and tell another's faults.
摘 丨 to disclose.
丨 望 to impatiently hope for.
自視 丨 如 I am not at all satisfied in my wishes.

In *Cantonese*, sometimes written *yueh*, 玥, but this form is better. To make one end higher; to sit upright, to perk up; to cackle; to order off.
丨 高頭 to stand on tiptoe.
丨 高 to curl up, as a dog's tail.
丨 丨 脚 to limp in walking.

鴃, *ˏchüé* A shrike (*Lanius*). for which 博勞 is another name.
南蠻 丨 舌之人 his talk is like the chattering of the southern savages.

倔, *ˏchüé* From *man* and *to stoop*.
Obstinate, set in one's way, grouty, perverse, opinionated; hard to please.
丨 强猶昔 he is just as sulky and intractable as ever.
老發 丨 a crabbed or particular fellow; an exacting man.

In *Cantonese*. A dull edge, a broken or blunt point, abrupt, inelegant, as a style or expression; stopped, as a highway; a cul-de-sac or blind alley.
說話 丨 rude, abrupt speech.
刀仔好 丨 this penknife is very dull.

崛, *ˏchüé* Rising abruptly like a lofty peak; eminent.
洪臺 丨 出 a vast terrace rising up by itself.
丨 起 distinguished, as a single brother who gains the honors; exalted above his fellows.
丨 起於田間 he attained to these high positions from being a mere farmer.

掘, *ˏchüé* From *hand* and *to stoop*; occurs used for the last and for 堀 a hole.
To dig into the ground, to scoop, to excavate, to hollow out; eminent, extreme.
丨 井 to dig a well.
丨 坑 to open a pit or drain.
丨 塚 to prepare a tomb.
丨 城池 to dig a fosse.
蜉蝣 丨 閱 the dung-chaffer works its way out of its hole.
丨 墓頭一款 he opened the grave and [learned the] first cause — of his death; refers to a device of Han Lin 韓信 to be avenged after his death.

趹, *ˏchüé* The quick pace of a horse; swift, speedy; to gallop; to paw, as if anxious to go.
突前 丨 後 [the racer] throws out his fore feet, and kicks up the dust with his hind feet.
要 丨 追蹤 we must gallop on fast in their tracks.

鴂, *ˏchüé* A bird which sings at the equinoxes, and thus marks the seasons, called 工雀 the working sparrow; it is the tailor bird, though the Chinese class it among the owls; other names for it are 女匠 the female artisan, and the 巧婦鳥 the cunning-wife bird. 鶗 丨 (also called 子規 or the rule-child) is a synonym for the goatsucker

K'ÜEH.

Old sounds, k'ít *and* k'et. *In Canton,* küt *and* hüt; — *in Swatow,* kué, k'úi, *and* kiat; — *in Amoy,* kw'at; — *in Fuhchau,* kw'ok; — *in Shanghai,* djüeh; — *in Chifu,* k'üeh.

闕, *ˏch'üé* From *door* and *to hiccough*; used with the next.
A passage through the great gate; the gateway, or the lookout tower above it; the gate or city of imperial power; a fault; a blank; a deficiency; defective, lost; to erase, to expunge; to dig; to miss, to err; disrespectful, wanting in; to exercise reserve; to blame one's self.
丨 門 or 丨 廷 his Majesty's palace.
金 丨 the golden gate — of paradise.
月 丨 the waning moon.
鳳 丨 the capital or Peking.
書 丨 一篇 the book lacks one leaf.
丨 文 a deficiency or hiatus in the text, a lacuna.
在城 丨 兮 at the lookout tower on the wall.
毫無少 丨 not the least part or bit is wanting.
望 丨 行禮 I look towards the palace [from a distant province], and make my obeisance.
盈 丨 waxing and waning; full, then decreasing.
丨 地及泉 he dug down to the water.
義 丨 the meaning [of this word] is lost.
袞職有 丨 維仲山甫補之 the sovereign's shortcomings only Chung Shan-fu can supply.

缺, *ˏch'üé* From 缶 *a dish* and 決 *to dispart* contracted.
A broken or defective vessel; short, deficient; defects; nothing said upon the point; to vacate, as a post; the duties of an office, of which three classes are made, as 簡 丨 an easy post, 中 丨 an ordinary post, and 繁 丨 a troublesome post, and their salaries are proportionate.

補 ǀ to supply a vacancy.
開 ǀ or 出 ǀ to resign, to take leave, to make a vacancy.
好 ǀ a good office, a lucrative situation.
ǀ 乏 or ǀ 少 or 虧 ǀ wanting, incomplete, not the full tale.
ǀ 本 to affect or reduce the principal.
崩 ǀ to give way, or break down, as a dike or canal bank.
ǀ 憾 a grievance; a grudge at.
破 ǀ cracked; a bit chipped out.
欠 ǀ deficient, as a set of things.
ǀ 角 [one] corner is knocked off.
既破我斧又 ǀ 我錡 we have broken our axes and splintered our chisels.
問心無 ǀ I am conscious of doing no wrong.
明月圓 ǀ the moon is a little beyond her full.
列 ǀ 天閃 the lightning flashed across the sky.
ǀ 陷 deficient; imperfect; disappointed in, as in the quality of goods ordered.
ǀ 疑 nothing said upon the point, either from ignorance or no data.

闋 ˎch'üe From *door* and a *horary* character.
To shut the door, to close the office, as when a case is judged or quashed; to stop, to rest; done; terminated; to prohibit; rested, pacified.

ǀ 鬈 a curly-maned horse.
服 ǀ to lay aside mourning,
歌數 ǀ to sing several tunes.
樂 ǀ the music ends; the band has stopped.
不 ǀ 時月 not resting for times or moons; unceasing vigilance.
君子如屆俾民心 ǀ if good men will take it, the people's hearts will be pacified.

䍍 ˎch'üeh From *feathers* and *bent* over.
Birds with short feathers, which come out just after molting.
毨 ǀ 了 [this bird has] its pin feathers just growing.
ǀ 䍨了 curled feathers.

KÜEN.

The characters under this and the next syllable are frequently heard KIÜEN and K'IÜEN. *Old sounds*, kien, gien, k'ín, *and* gín. *In Canton*, kün, *and* ün; — *in Swatow*, kien, käng, *and* kwan; — *in Amoy*, kwan; — *in Fuhchau*, kiòng *and* kwòng; — *in Shanghai*, küⁿ; — *in Chifu*, küen.

娟 ˏchüen From *woman* and *round*.
Beautiful, comely, elegant; pleasing, sprightly, graceful; subdued, calm; somber.
ǀ ǀ flitting easily, as a butterfly; swaying gracefully to and fro.
嬋 ǀ lady-like and pretty.
聯 ǀ arched, crescent-shaped.
便 ǀ light, sylph-like in one's movements; buoyant.
ǀ ǀ 明月 the clear, calm moonlight.

蜎 ˏchüen From *insect* and *round*; occurs used for the last, and is also read ˏyuen.
Little red worms like musketoes' larvæ, found in puddles; to disturb; to agitate, to stir about; sprightly.
ǀ ǀ 者蠋 the caterpillars were creeping about.
蔭脩竹之蟬 ǀ the pretty lively cicadas in the shady bamboo copse.

捐 ˏchüen From *hand* and *round*; it resembles ˊsun 損 to *injure*, and is also read ˏyuen.
To reject, to throw away; to renounce, to leave; to part, as at death; to offer up; to disdain; to subscribe; to contribute at a call from government; to buy title or office; a benevolence levied for a state exigency.
開 ǀ to open a subscription.
ǀ 題 to subscribe, to give for state use.
ǀ 銀 to subscribe and pay a call.
ǀ 納 to pay in to government.
ǀ 銜 or ǀ 職 to purchase a title.
ǀ 官 to buy an office; an officer who buys his post.
ǀ 棄 to hazard; to cast away; to die.
ǀ 軀赴義 he preferred death to disgrace.
房市 ǀ a tax levied on shops and markets.
軍柴 ǀ a tax to supply the fuel for troops.
ǀ 命 throw away life.
In *Cantonese*. To examine carefully; to pry; to stoop; to make a hole; to guess right.
ǀ 過去 to wriggle through or in.
ǀ 竅 to squeeze through a hole.

絹 **琄** ˏchüen The traces of a harness; a scabbard; a crupper; long-looking; the reins, for which alone the second form is used.
ǀ ǀ 佩璲 like long dangling gems hanging at the girdle,—so is one who takes the salary and does no work.

睊 ˏchüen From *eye* and *round*.
To look at with displeasure; to look at askance; with dislike; reciprocal dislike.
ǀ ǀ 胥讒 they all began to glare at him and grumble.

涓 ˏch'üen A murmuring brook; a small rill which swells as it flows; name of a river in Shantung; pure, clear; to cleanse; to select; to exclude.

丨吉 to choose a lucky day.

丨惡 to expel miasmatic evils.

泉丨丨而始流 the spring bubbled and began to flow off.

丨澴 water flowing around.

雨洗山丨丨 the rain has washed the hills so bright.

鵑 ˏch'üen The goatsucker (*Caprimulgus stictomus*) whose song indicates the time for sowing; it lays its eggs in other birds' nests; it is called 杜丨 and 子規; another name 催歸 alludes to the mournful cry which it is fabled to sing all night till blood comes into its eyes, singing for its mate to hasten home.

杜丨花 the Azalea flower; perhaps so named from its blossoming when the goat-sucker is heard.

稍 ˏch'üen The stalks of rice or wheat; wheat straw.

蠲 ˏch'üen From 虫 *insect*, 目 *eye*, 益 *advantage*, and to 勹 *cover*, showing its worm shape.

A species of glow-worm or phosphorescent grub, produced in rotten vegetables; bright, pure, shining; lustrous, as glazed paper; to clean, to maintain purity; to regard as innocent; manifest; to exclude, to excuse, to let off; haste.

除其不丨 exclude whatever is impure.

丨免 to remit, as taxes.

丨賬 to excuse from paying an account.

丨潔 to clean up.

吉丨爲饎 with happy auspices and washings, the sacrifices are offered.

上帝不丨降咎于苗 Shangti could not hold them guiltless, and visited Miao with calamities.

埢 ˋch'üen Earth or wall inclosing a grave; a limit.

丨垣 a round wall.

錈 ˋch'üen From *metal* and to *roll*.

To bend iron; pliable.

柔則丨剛則折 if it be soft, it can be bent; but if hard, it will snap.

菤 ˋch'üen From *plant* and a *roll*; altered from its primitive.

A common wayside plant, the 丨耳, which, if the synonyms do not mislead, is the burweed (*Xanthium strumarium*), and is common in northern China; its leaves and seeds are sticky.

采采丨耳 we gathered the mouse-ear.

捲 ˋch'üen From *hand* and a *roll* as the phonetic; occurs used for the next, and for ˏk'üen 拳 the fist.

To roll up, as a scroll; to seize, to gather; to pack up; to whirl about; spiral, crisped; rolled up; to exert strength; vigorous.

丨髮 curly hair.

風丨雨 the wind swirls the rain.

丨起來 roll it up, as a curtain; whirls it aloft, as dust.

席丨山川 he seized on the whole region.

丨丨乎 what great strength!

舒 and 丨 are opposites, — to open out and roll up.

席丨而回 [the robbers] made a clean sweep and went off.

風丨殘雲 [passed away] as the wind rolls away the clouds.

卷 ch'üenˋ ˋch'üen From 卩 a *seal* and 𢍏 to *hand up a dish* of food; it is interchanged with the two last, and with ˏk'üen 拳 the fist.

To cut around or crookedly; a roll, a scroll; a book; a section or division of a work; ruled paper for writing essays on; to roll up; elegant; indented; having recesses or adits; curved, curled, as hair; elegant; a classifier of books, rolls, maps, and such things as roll up.

開丨 to open the roll, to begin to read.

丨袋 a satchel, a bag for papers hung on the neck.

初開丨 he has begun his studies.

落丨 rejected essays.

污丨 a spotted or dirty essay, which is thrown out.

硃丨 or 墨丨 accepted essays of the candidates for *küjin*.

書丨 books, manuscripts, &c.

一ˏ丨石之多 [the mountain far off looks] only like a stone for size.

手丨 a long picture on a scroll; a map of a country.

案丨 the papers concerning a case in court; the records; archives.

丨髮如蠆 their chignons curled like a scorpion's tail.

丨舌 the star *ν* in Perseus.

有丨者阿飄風自南 into the recesses of the mound came the whirling breeze from the south.

倦 ch'üenˋ From *man* and *roll* as the phonetic.

Tired, fatigued; to desist from labor.

身丨 tired out, exhausted.

困丨 fagged, knocked up.

不知厭丨 he is indefatigable.

居之無丨 the mind fixed on its purpose.

丨極 tired enough.

疲丨不堪 wearied out; I can bear no more.

精神怠丨 listless, tired of a work; it is distasteful to me.

眷 ch'üenˋ From the *eye* and to *roll* as the phonetic; used with the next.

To love, to care for, to regard kindly; those whom one loves, kindred, family; related to; gracious, fondly lovingly; fine, as goods for family consumption.

寶丨 your family; your wife.

丨姻弟 your wife's relatives.

丨屬 or 家丨 a family; one's household.

無家丨 unmarried.

丨顧 to regard affectionately; to see to carefully.

天丨世人 Heaven's gracious regard for men.

丨米 family or best rice; that given to soldiers.

內丨 the women are within; — a notice put on the door of inner apartments.

丨丨不忘 unalterable affection for.

丨注 to set the heart on.

丨念 the emperor's regard; his kindness to others, or friendly thoughts.

乃丨西顧此維與宅 [Shangti] turned his kind regrads to the west, and gave this abode — to King T'ai.

皇天丨佑 high Heaven graciously protected him.

睠 chüen' Almost the same as the last.

To turn the eyes back upon fondly; to remember kindly.

還顧丨丨 looked back after him with longing eyes.

丨丨不捨 unremitted care, not taking one's eyes off.

帣 chüen' A bag holding three 斗 or pecks, with the bottom made of board; to slap or turn down the cuffs.

丨鞲鞠跽 to roll down the sleeves and bow reverently.

餋 chüen' Wafers, thin cakes in which meat is rolled.

蛋丨 thin dry wafers rolled.

春丨 meat hash rolled in wafers or flapjacks, and slightly fried.

鄄 chüen' An ancient place in the kingdom of Wéi, in the present 亳州 in the north of Nganhwui, near the River Wéi.

絹 chüen' From *silk* and *round*.

A thin, sleazy, cheap silk like lustring or taffeta, woven for linings, of which there are many sorts used for fans, toys, lanterns, pictures, &c.; applied to some kinds of pongee; a bird-net; a target.

丨布 cotton-like lutestring.

紗丨 gauzy lustring.

黃丨 yellow silk; *met.* an imperial order.

丨子 a silk handkerchief.

畫丨 glazed lustring for paintings.

罥 羂 chüen' From *net* and *round* or *taffeta*; these two are not altogether identical.

To suspend; to hang up, to bind with a cord; for which the first is proper; to entrap by a noose; to entangle in a gin, to catch in a net; a bird-net.

丨結 caught in a net.

埍 chüen' A lodge for policemen or followers; a prison for women; a sort of arbor or pavilion.

悁 懁 chüen Also read *küen*.

Angry, irritated; distressed; impetuous, anxious.

中心丨丨 my very heart is torn with grief

忿丨 angry, excited to wrath.

搔首立丨丨 stood scratching his head in his anguish.

狷 獧 chüen' Hasty, prompt; light-minded; frisky, as a dog; timid; a modest man of probity, who is not talented, and must be guided.

丨者有所不爲也 the cautious man will keep himself out of wrong.

丨介不敢行也 the modest and careful man will never venture on doing anything.

桊 棬 弮 ˏchüen From *ring* and *cow* or *wood* or *uphold*; the first form is commonest, and the third is deemed to be erroneous.

The ring thrust through an ox or camel's nose by which it is led.

丨牛 to ring buffaloes.

Read ˏk'üen. A wooden bowl or dish.

K'ÜEN.

Old sounds, k'in, k'ien, gien, *and* gin. *In Canton,* k'ün, *and* hün; — *in Swatow,* k'ien, kw'an, *and* käng; — *in Amoy,* kwan, kw'an, *and* k'ian; — *in Fuhchau,* kung, kw'ŏng, kwŏng, *and* k'éng; — *in Shanghai,* chöⁿ; — *in Chifu,* k'üen.

圈 ˏch'üen ch'üen' From *inclosure* and a *roll*.

A small circle; a full stop or period in grammar; to punctuate; to encircle, to surround; roundish, curved.

打丨 to draw a circle.

跳不出丨子裏 do not overpass the ring; to bring into order.

丨聲 to mark the tones of characters at their corners.

可丨可點 this should be ringed, and pointed, — *i. e.* italicized or marked for its importance.

出丨 to publish the names of the successful *siuts'ai;* they are written in a ring or round robin.

丨脫 to cancel; to erase, by drawing a ring around.

上'他的丨套 I was caught by his ring, I fell into his snare.

打個紅丨 draw a red ring around it, as is done by officers on parts of a proclamation.

丨椅 a rocking-chair.

Read *küen'* A coop or pen for animals; an inclosure, a prison; a snare; a cup of wood, for which the next is better.

馬丨 a horse-shed or paddock.

棬 ˏch'üen Small wooden bowls or cups made in a lathe; they are much used by Mongols.

桮丨 a wooden cup or porringer.

Read *küen'*, and used for 桊 The ring or stick which is run through a cow's nose.

弮 ˏch'üen From *bow* and to *roll* contracted.

A part of a crossbow; two rattan rings suspended so as to permit the archer to put his arms in them as he begins to learn to draw the bow.

吊丨習射 hang up the rings and practice your archery.

惓 ˏch'üen Careful; to stop, to desist; mournfully.

丨丨 attentive, earnest; applying one's mind; intent on.

拳 ˏch'üen From *hand* and to *roll* up.

The fist; to double up the hand; to grasp in the hand; boxing, fisticuffs; athletic, vigorous.

丨頭 the fist.

丨教師 a teacher of boxing or gymnastics.

打丨法 to learn boxing, so as to 耍丨 box and spar.

空丨 empty-handed, as when beginning life.

猜丨 or 嘩丨 to play the game of morra.

雙丨難敵四手 two fists are no match for four hands;—don't quarrel with your superiors.

不勝丨丨 [I received it] with the utmost respect and care.

丨丨服膺 to carefully clasp in the arms.

磨丨擦掌 itching to have a fight, to strip and go to blows.

殷丨 very thoughtful and attentive.

無丨無勇 without energy or courage.

蜷 ˏch'üen From *insect* and to *roll.*

The squirming of a snake when trodden on or not progressing; the convolutions of a snake coiled on itself.

踡 ˏch'üen The legs contracted or doubled up; to pull the legs under one.

丨跼 contracted and stooping, as persons exposed to the cold; cuddled up.

丨着腿子 legs drawn up, as when asleep.

鬈 ˏch'üen A fine head of hair; frizzled or curly hair.

其人美且丨 [their master] is personable and has fine hair, referring to the whiskers or beard.

權 ˏch'üen From *wood* and a *water-fowl* for the phonetic.

The weight or balance on the steelyards; a weight; direction, authority, power, intimating that the man acts by rules of expediency, or as the position he is in demands; influential; circumstances, position; to balance, to equalize; to plan; meanwhile, temporary; contracted; a kind of yellow veined wood.

丨且 under the circumstances; the exigency demands.

從丨 comply with the position of things, to act as the exigency requires; deviating from strict rules.

丨輕重 weigh it well, estimate the *pros* and *cons*.

丨便 to adapt one's self to the times.

丨臣 a poweful officer.

天丨 the star δ Megrez in Ursa Major.

丨勢 awe inspiring, as one having authority.

兵丨 military power.

丨柄 influence, power, force.

丨詐 intriguing, to trim one's course.

丨謀 to plan on the instant, quickwitted, having tact.

平丨 to equalize.

丨衡 to weigh justly, to deliberate equitably.

丨宜 temporarily obliged to do.

丨子母 to get interest on money.

丨任 a substitute, a deputy in office.

ˎ于嗟乎不成丨輿 unhappily he did not go on as he began.

通丨達變 to act as occasion requires.

掌丨的夥計 the leading director, the head manager.

丨木 is given as another name of the 木槿 or ***Hibiscus syriacus;*** its bark is used to cure the tetter, and the white flowers are sometimes eaten.

顴 ˏch'üen The cheek-bones.

丨骨高聳 one who has high cheek-bones — is cruel.

兩丨高殺夫刀 [a wife] with high cheek-bones is a husband-killing knife.

犬 ˎch'üen The original character is thought to bear a rude resemblance to a dog; it is the 94th radical of a natural group of characters relating to wild beasts, and is sometimes prefixed to words denoting an enemy, or one of another nation to show contempt or spite.

A dog, especially a large one; it is a metaphor for wickedness and treason.

丨子 my son, a depreciatory term.

丨才 a whelp's ability; my poor services.

効丨馬之勞以報 I will requite [your kindness] with the zeal of a dog or a horse.

狠心丨肺 he has a villainous, wolfish heart.

丨牙相錯 it winds in and out like dog's teeth;—*i.e.* has many defiles and passes.

丨 窩 a dog's kennel.
丨 守夜 the dog watches at night.
虎落平陽被丨欺 the tiger has got down on the plains, and is laughed at by the dogs.
村中無丨狗爲王 if there's no mastiff in the village, any cur may be king.
虎女焉配丨子 how can a young tigress mate a puppy? — keep to your own class.

畎 甽 'ch'üen } From *field* and *dog* or *stream*; the first form is most used.

A small drain between fields a cubit deep and wide; a rill running in a drain; to flow, as a current; to be diffused, as good instruction.
丨 畝 furrows or drains in the fields; lands, farms.
丨 田 to divide fields by ditches.
丨 流大道 let the great principles of reason be everywhere diffused.
丨 澮 sluices and ditches, such as drain off fields.

綣 ch'üen' Bound with silken cords; confederate; connected, as by friendship, or as parasites.
困丨 bound up, strapped.
以譴繾丨 in order to caution the parasites.
丨 領 a leathern strap or gorget for the neck.

券 ch'üen, From *knife* and *roll*; *q. d.* a roll cut with a knife.

A bond, deed, or contract, anciently made on wood, of which each party retained a serrated or notched half; a section; written evidence as such papers are.
丨 約 a bond; the contract.
酒 丨 a sort of ticket for a feast.
契 丨 an agreement; a deed, as of a house.
地 丨 written tiles placed in graves as proof of possession; a custom of the Ming dynasty.
操丨而得 hold on to the deeds and you are sure of the land.
搬丨頭 to bring up old scores, to rake up former evil deeds.
執左丨 he took the left half of the bond.

寶 丨 precious bond; — is the bank bill of the Kin.
案 丨 legal documents in a case.
書 丨 volumes, papers, documents.
丨 據 a certificate, as of payment.

勸 劝 ch'üen' } From *strength* and a *water fowl* as the phonetic; the contracted form is common.

To exhort, to advise, to admonish; to encourage, to praise; to assent willingly, to acquiesce; to take advice; to be stimulated; influenced, as by arguments.
丨 諫 to remonstrate with — as a superior.
丨 厲 to encourage to diligence.
丨 勉 to inspirit, to incite.
丨 化 to urge to reform; to change.
丨 解 or 丨 和 or 丨 息 to exhort to peace; to urge people to make up their quarrels.
丨 世文 writings to reform mankind; moral tracts.
相 丨 to admonish and inspirit each other.
丨 捐 to exhort people to subscribe to the government.

KUH.

Old sounds, kok *and* kot. *In Canton,* kòk, *and* kwăt; — *in Swatow,* kòk, kút, *and* k'òk; — *in Amoy,* kòk, kút, k'òk, *and* gòk; — *in Fuhchau,* kòk, kiak, *and* kauk; — *in Shanghai,* kòk *and* kweh; — *in Chifu,* ku.

谷 ,ku 'ku Composed originally of 水 *water* issuing from a 口 *mouth* or opening in hills; it forms the 150th radical of a small group of characters relating to gullies and ravines; and is sometimes wrongly used for the next.

A ravine, a gully; a gulf, a gulch, a gorge or channel between hills; a wady; the bed of a torrent; an empty space; to nourish, to sustain; impracticable; difficulty, embarrassment; a bamboo sprout; a gap or low place in hills.
暘 丨 and 昧 丨 the places of sunrise and sunset.
山 丨 a valley; ravines, gulches.
丨 神不死 to nurture the soul, so as not to have it dissipated or exhausted.
進退維 丨 it is equally hard to advance or to draw back.
被困窮丨 completely exhausted and hemmed in.
出于幽丨遷于喬木 getting out of the dim gorges up on a lofty tree; — rising in the world, his prospects are improving.
丨 風 the east wind.
丨 穴 the hollow space behind the ankle.
窰 丨 a house dug out of a hill side, as in Shantung.
嘯聲丨應 an echoing valley.

穀 穀 ,ku 'ku } From *rice* or *grain* and a *hollow*; the first is the common form.

Grain, cereals, corn; the seeds of cereals; real, substantial, well-off; to be happy; good, virtuous; lucky; goodness; a succession; to continue, to connect; emoluments, income, salary, living; to live, while alive; to bless with plenty, to nourish; to be deemed worthy of having a salary; in *medicine*, fecal matter.
五 丨 all kinds of grain.
丨 倉 a granary; a bin.
丨 精草 a species of *Eleocharis*, a grass used in eye diseases.

丨子 the spiked millet (*Setaria*) when growing; its grain is called 小米 or small rice.

君子有丨詒孫子 may the prince keep his goodness and transmit it to his heirs.

百丨 grain; vegetables and fruits generally; the crops.

收丨 to lay up provision.

丨道 the fecal passage.

錢丨先生 the clerk in a prefect's office who manages the revenue and assessor's department.

丨槍 the awn of grain.

不丨 the unworthy one; *i.e.* I your servant; sometimes used even by an Emperor.

丨育 to bring up, to nourish.

握粟出卜自何能丨 I take a handful of grain and go out to divine how I may be good

丨旦 a lucky day.

丨祿 a salary, which was once reckoned in rice, as it still is in Japan.

穀, ʻku From *wood* and a *hollow*; not the same as the last, but easily confounded with it.

A variety of the ʻch'u 楮 or paper mulberry (*Broussonetia*), especially a sort with white bark.

迷丨 name of a fabulous tree; when used as a charm, it helped people to keep the right road.

其下維丨 beneath them were paper mulberries.

亳有祥桑丨共生於朝 in Poh are fortunate mulberries, but all the paper trees grow here in the palace, — and are like useless courtiers.

轂, ʻku The nave or hub of a wheel; a carriage, a wheel.

輪丨 or 丨轆 a wheel.

推丨 to push on the hub, *i.e.* to recommend one.

笠丨 followers carrying screens over a general in his chariot; such as are seen in Assyrian sculptures.

輦丨之下 at or near the court.

散, ˏku The top of the foot; hind feet of cattle; plain, not particolored.

骨, ʻku From 肉 *flesh* and 冎 a cavity, referring to the hollowness of bones: it forms the 188th radical of characters all relating to bones.

A bone; anything hard inclosed in or connected with something soft, as a seam, a kernel, rib of a leaf or umbrella, seed in cotton, &c.; the figure, the person; when contrasted with flesh 肉, it often means hard, resisting, difficult.

丨格大 a large, gaunt man.

一副丨格 a whole skeleton.

白丨 dry bones.

銅皮鉄丨 he has a skin of copper and bones of iron; — a very Samson.

樹丨 heart wood.

無腰丨 he is regardless of his promise, he has no backbone.

鬆丨 to crack the joints.

字有丨力 the characters are vigorously written.

賤丨頭 you baseborn runt!

丨子 finical; particular, one who is hard to please.

貴丨 a fine figure.

丨瘦如柴 lean and bony as a stick.

山露丨 the rocks show on the hills.

執丨 to reïnter bones after disintegration, for good luck or other reasons.

反丨 to turn against one.

恨入丨髓 his hatred goes to his marrow.

弄(or 鬪)丨牌 to play dominoes.

丨醉 drunk so as almost to kill himself.

龍丨 fossil bones; asbestos when it resembles a bone.

縎, ˏkü A sort of silk like sarsnet; tied up, raveled, knotted.

必殊結丨 the mind much disturbed and straitened.

榾, ˏku A fine-grained wood, white as bone, which is good for making arrows or handles.

愲, ʻku The mind perturbed, all in a snarl.

必結丨兮 how distressed and desolate is my heart!

汨, ʻku From 水 *water* and 冥 *dark* contracted; the primitive is often wrongly written 白 *white*.

The noise of waves; to confound, to mix, to let flow; to unstop; to float, to rise; pervious, confused.

丨陳是非 to confuse right and wrong.

丨沒 to rise and to sink.

丨陳其五行 he confused the order of the five elements.

丨沒一朝伸 my distress and anxiety were all at once removed.

滔滔丨丨 unceasing discussion and talk.

Read *mih*, Name of a river, the 丨羅江 which flows into Tungting Lake on the southeast, in which Kuh Yuen 屈原 drowned himself about B. C. 314.

梏, ku' From *wood* and *to announce*.

Manacles, handcuffs; a wooden collar like a bow; fettered, restricted.

桎丨 fetters, gyves.

陷于丨亡 he was involved in disloyalty and revolution.

Read *kioh*, Self-restrained; actuated by good principles.

牿, ku' A shed, stable, or pen for cattle and horses; the animals inclosed in such a place.

丨牢 a pen or corral.

今惟淫舍丨牛馬 we must now let out the cattle and horses from their folds.

嚳, ku' The cluck of a Tartar pheasant; the cry of the pheasant.

鵠 ku' From *bird* and to *tell*, in imitation of its note *kuh kuh*.

A target made of concentric rings of leather, the inner one of which falls when hit; name of a large web-footed bird, which is called 天鵝 or aerial goose, from its high flight; it is described as white and the plumage soft; it is perhaps the snow goose (*Anser-hyperboreus*); there are the yellow and reddish sorts; hoary, venerable like an old man; an end, a design.

射丨仔 to hit the target.

丨立 to stand on the lookout like a wild goose; said of sentinels, or in letters when expecting an answer.

禾丨 small species of crane, the paddy bird, at Canton (*Munia minima*); and given too to the ortolan (*Euspiza aureola.*)

丨面菜色 pale and sallow and lean as a goose.

丨髮童顏 a grayhaired man with a fresh countenance.

仙人乘黃丨 the genii ride on wild geese to heaven.

刻丨成鶩 [he tried to] carve a swan, but only made a duck;—a vain attempt.

燕雀安知鴻丨之志 what can swallows and sparrows know of the feelings (or designs) of wild geese and swans?

扢 'ku hö' To rub, to clean.

丨嘉壇 brush and clean up the fine altar.

Read *heh*, Sprightly, antic.

丨然 capering about; active, as from a happy heart.

K'UH.

Old sounds, k'ok, *and* k'ot. *In Canton*, hòk, füt, *and* kòk;—*in Swatow*, k'ok *and* k'út;—*in Amoy*, k'út, gút, *and* k'òk;—*in Fuhchau*, k'òk, k'ok, *and* k'uk;—*in Shanghai*, k'ok, kw'eh, and djüih;—*in Chifu*, k'u.

哭 k'u Composed of 吅 to *bawl* and 獄 a *prison* contracted.

The noise of grief or pain; to wail, to cry, to scream and groan; to weep bitterly; to cry to, to bemoan.

丨泣 or 涕丨 crying, sobbing.

僞丨 crocodile's tears.

痛丨 crying bitterly.

哀丨 lamentation, deep sorrow.

丨喪 wailing for the dead, as is done by mourning women.

鬼丨神嚎 [now only is heard] the wailings of demons and moans of ghosts,—in the waste places.

子丨之慟 the sage bitterly mourned for him.

丨也無益 it is no use to cry about it.

丨黃天 the wailing mournful music around a corpse.

窟 k'u From *cave* and to *bend*; used with the next.

An underground chamber, a cellar; holes in the ground, or side of hills fitted for dwellings, such as are common in Shansi and Honan; a hut.

闖出了虎丨龍潭 I only rushed out of the tiger's den to get into the dragon's pool.

鼠丨 a rat-hole.

狡兎三丨 the cunning hare has three holes.

丨竉 a hole, an opening.

營丨 to make earth dwellings, these 丨室 are mostly in hill sides.

窮士之丨 the hovel of a poor scholar.

蟾丨 or 月丨 the full disk of the moon.

挖丨小賊 a pilferer, one who digs holes in walls.

經行禪丨 a corridor or promenade in a monastery (*changkramana*), where the priests perform peripatetic contemplation.

堀 k'u From *earth* and to *bend*; like the last.

A cave used for a dwelling; the hole of an insect or small animal.

丨穴 abodes dug out of the hillsides.

伏甲于丨室 the soldiers were hid in the cave houses.

猦 chü The term 猪丨 seems like a local word imitated, and from the description to denote an animal akin to the loris; it gets its name of 風母 from the trick it has of feigning death when hit, and of reviving by gasping for breath; it is found in Kwangsi, and is not difficult to tame; other accounts refer it to Tibet, and describe it as nearly hairless, except a black stripe of bristles along the back, but this probably refers to another animal.

朏 膈 k'u From *flesh* and *projecting* or to *bend*; the second form is most common.

The seat.

丨臀 or 髀丨 the buttocks, the nates.

崛 k'u Hilly; a rounded low summit near a high hill.

丨屼 a line of hills, a range of low mountains.

淈 k'u Deep water, as in a pool.

無溶丨而泉出 there was no flow and no deep pool, still the spring flowed out.

圣, *ck'u* From *earth* and *hand*; this is most commonly used as a contraction of *shing'* 聖 holy.

In *Honan*, 丨 丨 is to toil in farming, to hoe and dig with the utmost strength.

嚳, 俈, *k'u'* From 告 to *inform* and 學 to *learn* contracted; the second form is seldom used.

To inform quickly; an urgent communinication.

帝 丨 the Emperor K'uh, the father of Yao, who reigned seventy years, and died about B. C. 2366, or 790 years after the deluge.

酷, *ck'u* Superior, mellow spirit; ripe, as grain; hard-hearted, inhuman, tyrannical, said of officials; an adjective denoting the extreme of; the bitter feeling arising from having suffered wrong.

丨 法 cruel, unjust laws.

貪官 丨 吏 avaricious rulers and cruel policemen.

丨 虐 fierce, oppressive.

丨 熱 exceedingly hot.

慘 丨 cruelly severe, callous.

遭火蕩盡銜 丨 茹恨 owing to the fire having destroyed his all, he cherished the most bitter hatred for the cruelty received.

丨 氣蒸人 the hot air stifles one; the bad smell is very offensive.

矻, *ck'u* Fatigued; to fag at; hard and strong.

丨 丨 窮年 the livelong year I am toiling hard.

窋, *k'u'* From *cave* and to *issue*; it is also read *ch'uh*,

Something just appearing in a hole, as a mouse peeping out; a hole.

鼠 丨 而未竄 the rat peeped out but did not rush by.

不 丨 the son of Shin-nung or Heu-tsih.

K'ÜH.

Old sounds, giok, giot, *and* kiok. *In Canton*, kòk, kwät, *and* küt; — *in Swatow*, kek, kiòk, *and* kít; — *in Amoy*, kiòk, kiat, *and* kwat; — *in Fuhchau*, kwòh, kéük, hwoh, *and* k'ek; — *in Shanghai*, djòk *and* küih; — *in Chifu*, kü.

局, *cchü* From 口 a *mouth* or square inside of 尺 a *cubit*, referring to the squares on a chessboard.

A game of draughts or chess; an order, a rank; the body confined or cooped up; coiled, contracted, bent; curly, as hair; narrow; mean; debased; aspect, appearance; an affair, an undertaking, an enterprise; a committee to oversee it; a company, a club; an association of a legal nature; the place where their proceedings are carried on; a depôt, a wholesale store; a place where things are manufactured or guarded, as a mint, a foundery, a manufactory; a gaming-shop; to delude, to put out a bait for, to enveigle; complete, as the squares in a chessboard.

丨 外之人 a looker-on, one not concerned in the plan.

當 丨 者迷 the dullest are those who are playing the game.

不成 丨 an unfinished game or affair; a flash in the pan.

平 丨 一式 a fair, even transaction; both sides satisfied.

不能了 丨 you can't bring that about.

美人 丨 a lure into a house of ill fame; a stool-pigeon.

設 丨 or 擺 丨 to take in one nicely, to play one's card well.

格 丨 appearance, physiognomy, bearing.

丨 量褊小 a mean-spirited fellow; an old fogy.

藥 丨 a dispensary.

錢 丨 a mint; bank owned by government.

印書 丨 a printing office.

賑濟 丨 a sort of soup-house for the poor.

騙 丨 to trick one.

收 丨 to be taken in; cheated.

不入 丨 it is not suitable for him, he is not up to that style.

丨 勢已成 the matter is all arranged.

丨 勢 the position of a game; the situation, as of two armies.

是串 丨 it was a great imposition on their part.

世事如棋 丨 life is like a game of chess.

大 丨 the best interests or plans of.

作 丨 to play cleverly; a trick.

不敢不 丨 I cannot but stoop.

省會總 丨 a provincial committee of supervision.

予髮曲 丨 my hair is in a wisp.

In *Cantonese*. To bake, to heat under cover; to make tea.

丨 得水 to sponge cloth.

丨 盅 a covered tea-cup in which to 丨 茶 decoct tea.

丨 爐 an oven, a baking-dish.

侷, *cchü* Small, narrow; pursed up, as a tone or sound.

丨 促 cramped, no room to expand or act; cribbed.

跼, *cchü* From *foot* and *cramped*.

To bow the head, to bend down, to humble one's self; crooked, bent; contracted for want of room.

丨 躅 to hobble, to limp, as a fettered horse.

丨 蹐 legs uneven or bent, cramped.

鋦, *ꞔchü* To bind or hoop a thing with iron.

挶, *ꞔchü* The part of a spear where it is held; a barrow or cart for carrying dirt.

梮, *ꞔchü* To drive iron spikes in the shoes, to prevent slipping when ascending a hill or ice, as was done by Yü when draining the country in old times; a kind of canteen put in carriages.

蓳, *ꞔchü* A great cart for carrying dirt, offal, or manure.

匊, 掬, *ꞔchü* From 勹 to *envelop* and 米 *rice*, as one does in taking up a double handful; *hand* has since been added, and the second form is now common.

To hold or grasp in both hands; a handful; the two hands filled; the cavity made by both hands.

不盈一丨 not enough for a handful.

丨氣包腮 to swell out the cheeks in anger.

笑容可丨 very much pleased with.

丨水擎天 [he is able] to take a handful of water and raise it to the sky;—*i. e.* to manage the affairs of the country.

In *Cantonese*. To urge on, to encourage to extra effort.

丨起力 to incite to effort.

In *Fuhchau*. Coagulated; curdled; excited, angered.

菊, *ꞔchü* Syngenesious flowers like the *Aster*, *Pyrethrum* marygold, daisy, &c., with a broad disk.

萬壽丨 the marygold.

丨花酒 spirits with petals of the China-aster steeped in them.

賞丨 to enjoy the beauty of a bed of Chrysanthemums.

丨月 a name for the ninth moon.

丨放蟹初肥 crabs begin to be fat when the asters bloom.

毱, *ꞔchü* A leathern ball filled with hair or chaff; or blown full, and used to play with; it is like the next.

踘, *ꞔchü* From *foot* and a *handful*; like the last and next.

A stuffed football made of leather, or a bladder.

蹋丨 to kick a football.

鞠, *ꞔchü* From *hide* and a *handful*; like the last, and occurs used for the next.

A ball; a large chaff or bran ball; an awl; to nourish; to bear, to bring up; to rule; being, life; a child; to bore into, to investigate to the utmost; to exhaust, to push to an extreme; to inform; to address, full, much.

丨育 to rear, to nurture.

丨丸 a ball to play with.

丨子 a stripling.

丨躬 to bend the body.

丨躬盡瘁 he gave himself entirely to the public.

陳師丨旅 he drew out his men and addressed them.

昔育恐育丨 beforetime it was to be feared the means of living would be exhausted.

母兮丨我 my mother, she bore and cherished me!

爾惟自丨自苦 you must yourself just fairly look at your own troubles.

鞫, 諊, *ꞔchü* From *leather* or *words* and *noise*; the first is sometimes erroneously written for the last, and even occurs used for it.

To investigate a case judicially; to question a criminal to get out the truth; to oppress; reduced to extremity; the further bank of a river.

訊丨 or 丨審 to examine and judge a case.

丨哉庶正 all exhausted are the chiefs of the people.

丨窮 reduced to the very last; in extremity; searched into thoroughly.

鶪, *ꞔchü* A bird, the 詰丨 or larkheel cuckoo (*Centropus affinis*), a name probably given in imitation of its note, *ki-ku*, *ku-ku*, or *kăt-kuk*; it is supposed by this note to say 吉穀 happy grain, and thus announce the time of sowing grain; another name 布穀 alludes to this.

鵙, *ꞔchüé* A shrike (*Lanius schah*), also called 伯勞 uncle Trouble; colloquially called 虎伯勞 *hu-pa-la* at Peking; when it sings in the summer, its note indicates the time for spinning; it has the reputation of eating its dam.

丨鳥 or 山伯勞 the butcher bird; *met.* an undutiful child.

七月鳴丨 the shrike is heard in the autumn.

鴉丨 crow shrike is the black drongo (*Dicrurus cathoecus*).

痀, *ꞔchü* A crooked spine arising from disease; a bent back.

泦, *ꞔchü* The ripples made on water by the wind; the bank of a stream.

怚, *ꞔchü* Extravagant and imperious in one's acts; angry; stupid looking.

丨怒 very angry; irate.

丨狂 furious and unreasonable.

橘, *ꞔchü* From *wood* and to *bore* into; it is contracted to *kih*, 桔 in the southern provinces, but without any authority, to distinguish the sorts.

An orange; it comes nearer the generic term than any other word.

丨子 a large bitterish orange or bigarade, common in the north.

廣丨 at the North denotes the *Citrus amantium*.

丨白 or 丨絡 the dried fibers of the orange; orange-zest.

丨瓣 the carpels or sections of an orange.

弔門丨 an orange or its peel hung on the lintel.

金 ｜ the kumquot orange. (*Citrus madurensis* and *C. Japonica.*)

金 ｜ 子弟 a dear little fellow, a darling. (*Cantonese.*)

硃砂 ｜ (or 桔) the mandarin orange. (*Citrus nobilis.*)

四季 ｜ (or 桔) a nutmeg orange.

金錢 ｜ a gold nutmeg orange.

｜ 餅 a comfit of oranges.

｜ (or 桔) 仔 the loose skinned orange at Canton.

紅 ｜ or 福 ｜ Fuhchau orange.

｜ 紅 dried orange skin brought from Hwacheu 化州 in Kwangtung for coughs.

蹻, *chü'* Lame in the feet; to run about wildly.

K'ÜH.

Old sounds, k'iok, *and* k'iot. *In Canton,* hòk, k'òk, wăt, *and* kwik;—*in Swatow,* kak, kiòk, k'iòk, *and* k'út;—*in Amoy,* k'iòk, kút, k'ek, *and* lut;—*in Fuhchau,* k'ùük, kw'oh, *and* k'òk;—*in Shanghai,* djòk, chöh, *and* hüeh;—*in Chifu,* k'ü.

曲, *ch'ü* The original form represents a cavity as a dish, and the upright strokes a 玉 *gem* lying in it; others describe it as depicting a silkworm curled up; as a primitive it seldom influences the meaning of its compounds.

Crooked, bent; a bend; scheming, false, tortuous; to oppress, to wrong; bent; forced, obliged to do; wronged; songs, lyrics, ditties, ballads, or popular verses; they are of different metres, and now often include dramatic compositions; a carpenter's square.

分解 ｜ 直 to discriminate the merits of, to set things straight.

｜ 直 crooked and straight, wrong and right.

理 ｜ distorted, perverted, as evidence.

私 ｜ tricky, underhand.

｜ ｜ 行 crooked paths; to act in a mean underhand manner; double-dealing.

受委 ｜ I have been deceived; greatly wronged; imposed on.

心 ｜ or 衷 ｜ the corners of the heart; *i. e.* thoughts, ideas.

唱 ｜ to sing ballads accompanied by instruments.

人情多 ｜ 折 man has many crafty devices,—*i. e.* "crooks and bends," excitements, or tricks.

委 ｜ 求全 to seek to make up a difficulty.

灣 ｜ meandering, not straight.

七灣八 ｜ a crooked roundabout road.

｜ 心的 thoroughly deceitful.

｜ 體眠 to sleep cuddled up.

鄉 ｜ village patois or brogue.

笛, *ch'ü'* A bamboo frame called 蠶簿 having its surface made of thin splints doubled in bows, to furnish silkworms more surface on which to spin their cocoons.

苖, *ch'ü'* A coarse tray made of rushes on which silkworms feed and wind their cocoons; it is used in Kiangsu, and is doubtless similar to the preceding, made of a different material.

蛐, *ch'ü* The common earthworm, called ｜ 蟮, which the Chinese affirm can sing, mistaking it for the mole cricket.

In *Pekingese*. The cricket.

鬪 ｜ ｜ to fight crickets.

麯, **麴**, *ch'ü* Leaven, barm; the mother or slime which collects on vinegar or liquors.

｜ 丸 balls of leaven.

｜ 蘖 cakes of yeast used in fermenting liquors.

酒 ｜ distiller's grains or yeast.

神 ｜ 茶 a decoction of a common medicine for colds brought from Chinchew near Amoy.

紅 ｜ or ｜ 米 a kind of upland rice which reddens the dishes in which it is cooked.

屈, *ch'ü* From 尾 a *tail* contracted and 出 to *issue*, intimating a tailless thing.

Bent down or awry; to stoop, to crouch, to kneel, to bend over; to submit, to give in; to subject; to make in accord; to adapt to circumstances; to invite; grievance, wrong; afflictions, evil fate.

能 ｜ 能伸 he can either stoop or stand.

指不成 ｜ the fingers cannot count them; very numerous.

｜ 駕 I invite you, Sir;—*i. e.* you will bend or demean yourself by coming to my house.

｜ 此群醜 subduing to himself all these vulgar people.

冤 ｜ oppression, wrong; helpless against outrage.

受 ｜ outraged, oppressed wrongfully,

｜ 膝易, ｜ 心難 it is easier to bend the knee than the will.

｜ 節 to crouch before, mean-spirited.

｜ 曲 to bend by force; crooked, devious.

忠勇不 ｜ the loyal and brave will not basely yield.

｜ 殺 to kill wrongfully, to kill an innocent man, whose death too was a blunder.

｜ 身 to bend down; to submit, to yield to, as suffering.

｜ 指一算 reckoning by the fingers.

｜ 枉 oppressed, ill-treated.

詘, *chü* Like the preceding.

Forced to act against one's will; to conceal; to stammer; to rumple; a fold, a wrinkle; stuttering, any impediment in the speech; to stop, as music; to exhaust; to remove from office.

詞 丨 to hesitate.

道不可丨身丨何傷 if you do not pervert the truth, what harm is it to bend your body?

丨然 stopped, cut off.

不充丨于富貴 do not violate propriety, when before the noble and rich.

陳衣不丨 to smooth the folds in garments.

習其俯仰丨伸 practiced in looking down and up, in concealing and expressing; — *i. e.* understanding all the duties and customs of a place.

蝠, *ch'ü* From *insect* and to *bend;* used sometimes incorrectly for *choh,* 蚰 a spider.

Grub of the carpenter bee; worms which eat plants.

蛣丨 a large grub which bores into trees; the locust (*Sophora*) is infected and destroyed by it.

齣, *ch'ü* An unauthorized character.

In *Pekingese.* A stanza, a *tooth sentence,* as the character denotes, one which is short; a verse of four lines; a classifier of verses and plays.

小曲一丨 one short ditty, one nursery rhyme.

一丨戲 an act of a play.

一丨詞 a single psalm; a verse.

臭, *ch'üh* From *dog* and *eye,* referring to a dog watching, and barking when he sees a man.

A species of ape, with thick lips, said to be of a greenish hue; hawks opening their wings.

丨丨然搖動 he shook his wings and then flew away.

鶪, *ch'üh'* Said to be another form of *küh,* 鵙 the shrike; but one author describes it as resembling a pigeon of black plumage; a legend says that when a wife is badgered to death by her mother-in-law, she is changed into this bird, which then cries *k'u-k'u* 苦苦 to denote its grief; it is probably the cuckoo.

闃, *ch'ü'* *k'i'* To live alone; unoccupied; still, quiet.

丨寂 silent, alone, solitary;

窺其戶丨其無人 he spied over the empty house, and saw that nobody was in.

KUNG.

Several of these are also read KIÜNG. *Old sounds,* kong, kíong, gong, king, *and* ging. *In Canton,* kung kwăng, kwing, kwong, *and* kăng; — *in Swatow,* kòng, kang, kw'ang, keng, *and* kiòng; — *in Amoy,* kong, kiong, k'eng, eng, *and* kwan; — *in Fuhchau,* kung, kong, kăng, küng, kèüng, *and* kwòng; — *in Shanghai,* kung, kòng, kwong, kiung, *and* kiăng; — *in Chifu,* kung.

公 *kung* From 八 *eight,* here defined to turn the back on, and 厶 *selfish* or private.

Public, common; open, equal to all, general; just, equitable; a merit, a service; a term of respect and dignity added to names; the first of the five ranks of nobility, a duke; in olden time, the prince of a fief; a lord, a master; the male of animals; a husband.

丨所 a town-house; a public hall.

丨會 a public company.

丨爵 a duke; 丨爺 my lord duke.

丨子 at first the son of a feudal prince; then officers, gentlemen; now a young gentleman; 令丨子 your son.

大相丨 a term for addressing a head servant or the first brother.

相丨 a young man; play-actors; in the South it is a term of respect, as honorable Sir; but in the North it has a vile meaning.

丨主 the emperor's daughter, a royal princess; the original term seems to have been 宮主 the ruler of the rear palace.

丨家 the imperial family.

家丨 or 丨丨 a husband's father; the second term and 外丨 also denote a maternal grandfather.

太丨 my grandfather; an old man.

某丨 a certain gentleman.

羅丨 Mr. Lo; — only used when speaking of him.

諸丨 all you gentlemen.

丨祖大人 a title often given to a prefect.

明丨 your honor, Sir.

王丨伊濯 his kingly merit was luminous.

兩丨婆 the pair, the man and wife; — spoken of them.

三丨 three honorary guardians of the heir-apparent; also three stars between $\upsilon\ \delta\ \eta$ in Virgo.

丨項 public funds or articles.

丨心 public spirited.

不丨 mean, unjust.

丨道 or 丨平 fair, equitable.

當丨務 for the general use.

事頭丨 the head of the shop. (*Cantonese*).

丨餘之暇 leisure from public duties.

丨門 a public office; a teacher or sage's school.

丨堂 a court, a hall; the room for meetings.

是非丨論 to get the public sentiment as to the merits of a question.

丨私 public and private; governmental and personal; fair and mean.

一秉至丨 the utmost equity in managing the affair.

丨烟 the best opium, a term derived from 丨司 the old E. I. Co., at Canton, an appellation there given also to other goods.

In Cantonese. A toy.

丨仔 a puppet, a doll; a picture, a plaything.

蚣 ˌkung An insect; used in many descriptive terms of things.

蜈丨 the centipede, commonly called 百足 or the hundred legs.

Read ˌ*sung*. A grasshopper.

丨蝑 an unusual name for the *Truxalis* or green grasshopper.

魟 鮣 ˌkung A name for two or three large species of skate, but those having slender spinous tails (*Myliobates*) seem to be more particularly referred to; the back is reddish or black, and tail as long as the body; a common name is 鍋盖魚 or kettle cover; another sort has a shovel-nose snout, with three spines on the tail; a stingray.

厷 肱 ˌkung The original form is thought to represent the arm; it has been superseded by the second since *flesh* was added, and is now only used as a primitive.

The upper part of the arm, the humerus; the arm; *met.* an officer, a support to the ruler.

丨臂 the arm.

麾之以丨畢來既升 he waved his arm and the whole flock came and went up — into the fold.

嗣爾股丨純其藝黍稷 employ your limbs in constantly cultivating your millet and sorghum.

作股丨心膂 be as my limbs, my heart, and my spine.

疘 ˌkung From 疒 *disease* and 肛 *colon* contracted.

The prolapsus of the rectum.

脫丨 bloody piles; prolapsus ani.

工 ˌkung The original form is supposed to represent a compass and rule; it is the 48th radical of a few heterogeneous characters.

Ingenuity, work, skill; a laborer, a workman; an officer, as of agriculture; an artisan; service, duty; a job, a piece of work; labor; art, an ornament requiring skill; able, skilled; a work.

丨人 laborers; a hired workman.

丨匠 artisans, mechanics.

丨銀 or 丨錢 or 人丨 wages.

動丨 or 開丨 to begin work.

收丨 to stop work as at night.

竣丨 or 完丨 finished the job.

丨作 skill, quality of work.

苗頑弗即丨 the Miao are contumacious, and refuse their duty.

費丨 troublesome work.

整河丨 to mend the river's banks.

打丨 at work; to work for an employer.

一個丨 a day's work.

人巧奪天丨 works of art may even surpass nature.

散丨 or 短丨 or 碎丨 job-work.

粗丨 or 拙丨 poor, slipshod work.

巧丨 or 精丨 fine, skillful work.

丨夫多大 much work, varied calls on one; at the North applied to low manual labor rather than occupation, as in the South.

丨課 literary or superior employments; — not manual work.

不大的丨夫 wait a little, presently, before long; 枉廢丨夫 to fail in an undertaking; the affair miscarried.

沒有丨夫 I have no time; in *Cantonese*, I have nothing to do.

替一個丨 to work in my place one day.

長丨 constant occupation.

包丨 to engage to do a job.

論丨 reckoned by the job.

花丨 a florist; one who makes flowers; — but 花丨不少 may mean, the fine labor on this thing is great.

化丨育物 the Maker and Preserver of things — *i. e.* Heaven and Earth.

太大丨程 too expensive or troublesome.

丨字不出頭 the character 工 has no head; — *i. e.* a workman cannot become a 主 boss.

他懂百丨 he understands all sorts of work.

宗丨 heads of clans, the honored officers; as 百丨 is a classical term for all officials.

丨祝致告 the skillful [priest] announces it.

亮天丨 the ministers and officers of the empire.

丨者巧于所能 the workman is seen in his cunning work.

動河丨 he set to work repairing the banks of the river.

功 ˌkung From *strength* and *work* as the phonetic; its resemblance in form and sound sometimes makes this to be confounded with the next.

Actions that deserve praise, honor or reward; work done, achievements; meritorious; worthy, virtuous; a good service or affair which will bring reward; the virtue of a medicine.

丨力 merits; efficacy, as of a medicine

用丨 or 勤丨 study diligently; to work hard.

記丨 to record merit.

丨勞 merit; earnest, meritorious labor and devotion.

成丨 a finished work.

丨積大 a great stock of merit.

誇丨 boastful of one's doings.

有丨 meritorious; reported of.

丨德已滿 [the priest's] good works are all now completed.

無丨 undeserving; no merit.

大丨 nine months' mourning, as for an uncle; it is made of coarse cotton.

小丨 five months' mourning, as for cousins or a great uncle.

謀道不計丨 do not reckon too much of the toil in trying to do right.

明試以丨 this was clearly proved by their works.

勞而無丨 to toil at but to get no advantage.

丨名 honor, merit, rank.

邀丨 eye-service, work done in view of reward.

將丨贖罪 to expiate faults by [after] good service.

丨難報過 no merit can wipe out his crimes.

丨同再造 your goodness has [as it were] made me new.

藥力丨效 the virtue of this remedy is very great.

自以爲丨 he made it his own work or affair.

攻 ꜀*kung* — From *work* and to *strike*; its form somewhat resembles the last.

To attack, to assault, to fight with; to put in order; to set to work at, to apply to, to take work in hand; to rouse by reproving; to stimulate the vital or mental powers; to be made strong; the urgency of desire, temptation; strong, enduring.

丨打 or 丨擊 to fight, to engage in battle, to set to.

丨書 to study hard.

他山之石可以丨玉 the stones of that hill may be used to polish gems.

一心丨之者衆 a crowd of lusts attack the heart.

丨人之過 to reprove the man's faults.

毋丨人之惡, don't bruit out other people's faults.

丨拔 to take; to capture, as a city.

以藥丨瘡 remove the boil by medicine.

我車既丨 our carriages were equipped and strong.

丨城爲下丨心爲上 it is a higher point to draw off the regard [of his followers], than to take the citadel.

丨匪 to repress banditti.

庶民丨之不日成之 the people heartily undertook the work and soon completed it.

愛丨人者非君子 one who likes to scold people is not a princely man.

丨心者上畧 that is the superior mind which can see through another's craft.

弓 ꜀*kung* — Intended to represent a bow; it forms the 57th radical of a natural group of characters.

A bow; a catapult; archery; bow-shaped, arched, crescent; a cover of a carriage; a measure of five or six cubits, of which fifty make a bowshot, and 300 a *li*; the Budhists used it for *dhanu*, or the 4000th part of a *yodjana*; to measure; to pull the bow.

丨箭 bows and arrows.

拉滿丨 to draw the bow to the head.

虎丨 a spring noose to catch a tiger.

丨杈 a rest for an archer's arm.

開硬丨 he draws a stiff bow, he can manage people.

丨丈 or 丨步 a wooden square for marking off land.

丨手 an archer; a tidewaiter who measures vessels; an underling who measure's land.

丨足 or 丨脚 a woman's feet.

彈丨 a bow with a circle in the string for a clay ball.

彈棉丨 a bow for flocking cotton.

虛拽丨弦 he vainly drew the bowstring; — *i.e.* a failure, a flash in the pan.

響丨 a singer on a kite.

開丨不放箭 to stretch the bow without shooting the arrow; — empty threats.

芎 ꜀*h'iung* — A medicinal plant, the 丨藭 whose decoction is used to purify the blood; the root is like tormentilla or strong orris root, and it is probably a species of *Levisticum*, allied to the Angelica root in its effects.

茯丨 is one sort, but the 川丨 from Sz'ch'uen is the best; it is probable that two or three plants furnish this drug, one of which is an *Angelica*.

躳 躬 ꜀*kung* — From *body* and *spinal* vertebræ, but the second has now become the common form through the power of the phonetic.

The body; one's person or body; personally.

聖丨 the sacred person.

曲丨 the bended body.

朕丨 I the Emperor; Ourself.

丨親其事 to work at or do a thing personally.

王丨是係 you must protect the royal person.

打丨 to make a bow with the hands joined, and then raised over the head.

反丨自問 then just ask yourself — what is right.

丨身下拜 personally worshiped it.

扃 ꜀*chiung* — A bar or latch outside of a door; to bar a door; a board or frame in front of a chariot, to hold weapons or to lean on; a dashboard; an ear or handle

丨門 to bolt the gate.

丨試 to close the examination.

叩玉丨 to knock at the gates of paradise.

終年丨閉 the doors are constantly closed.

Read ꜂*kăng*. To inquire into.

꜂丨꜂丨 a full investigation.

駉 ꜀*chiung* — A large horse in good condition; a paddock for horses.

丨丨牡馬 fat and stout are the stallions.

洞 Analogous to 逈 and also pronounced like it.

ˏch'iung Vast, as water; distant, extensive.

丨野 a wild pasturage land in the state of Lu.

丨遠 distant, waste and stretching far away.

恭 From *heart* and *all* as the phonetic; it somewhat resembles ˏch'a 茶 when badly printed.

ˏkung The exhibition of respectful feeling towards one; to treat with a sedate courteous air, to venerate; to revere; collected, complaisant; affable, decorous, polite; devout-minded, reverent; respectfulness; as an *adverb*, very, highly.

丨喜 I respectfully wish you joy, as at the newyear.

丨丨敬敬 reverently; great awe in doing, as worship.

丨順 very submissive.

鞠丨如禮 very polite, according to etiquette.

丨賀 congratulatory words or presents; congratulations.

丨行 to carefully execute orders.

丨候命下 I await your orders.

自古丨敬不如從命 obedience has always been held to be better than courtesy.

丨人 wives of officers of the fourth rank.

温温其丨 harmonious and reverent, said of guests.

丨錄飭知 I have respectfully copied [the rescript], and now send it for your information.

供 From *dragon* and *all* as the phonetic; it occurs used for its primitive.

ˏkung To place before, to lay out, to offer to; to supply, to provide with; to succor, to give; to confess; to give in evidence, to declare before judges; grain for troops or revenue in kind.

我丨出他 I accuse him, I testify against him.

口丨 verbal testimony.

畫丨 to sign one's deposition.

用丨王能祈天永命 I present [these gifts] to the King to aid in his prayers to Heaven for its long abiding decree.

丨稱 he deponed, saying. . . .

丨認 to confess on trial.

反丨 to retract one's testimony.

傳丨人 interpreters for witnesses, who are necessary in all courts, owing to differences in dialects.

取具親丨 to extract evidence from his own letters.

丨職 to assume an office, or resume its duties after a temporary absence on a special service.

丨會 to pay in one's share to the Company.

丨黨 to tell of one's accomplices, to turn state's evidence.

丨奉 to offer up, as to one's ancestors or the gods.

應丨 to provide for superiors; to pay the dues of office.

敢不丨給 how can I hesitate to furnish you?

天庾正丨 the usual revenue sent to the imperial granaries.

丨口不上 there is not half enough to eat.

Read *kung'* To nourish, to support; offerings, presents.

丨養 to sustain, as one's parents.

上丨 or 丨筵 to offer in worship.

設丨 to arrange the presents.

In *Cantonese*. To eat to excess, satiated.

食調丨 I've had plenty, eaten quite enough.

打調丨 to have a fight, to try a bout.

龔 From *man* and *all* as the phonetic; it is interchanged with the last two.

ˏkung To give, to present to; docorous, reverential; an old name for the southeast part of Kwangsi, now known as Sin-cheu fu 潯州府 lying south of the West River.

宮 From 宀 a *shelter* with 躬 *body* contracted underneath it.

ˏkung A mansion, a building, now confined to imperial private residences; the palace; an ancestral temple; a district college; the circuit of; to surround; to geld; the ancient name for the first note in the gamut, but now the sixth, for which 工 is also used.

丨殿 palaces, halls, state edifices.

丨寢 or 丨禁 the seraglio.

正丨 the empress; her Majesty.

丨妃 or 丨娥 imperial concubines, of whom the odalique is called 東丨 or east palace, and the one next to her is called 西丨 or west palace.

丨刑 castration; *lit.* the punishment of the palace; hence 老丨 denotes a eunuch.

月丨 the moon palace; the bright moon.

學丨 a college in a prefecture or district.

行丨 an imperial lodging house.

皇上孝奉兩丨 your Majesty dutifully receives the orders of the two Empresses, *i. e.* the 東丨 or Empress Dowager, and the 西丨 or Empress Mother.

東丨 the heir-apparent of a feudal prince.

守丨 the warden of the palace, a poetical name for a lizard.

冷丨 the cold palace where discarded concubines were formerly sent; also applied to a neglected wife.

子丨 emperor's ancestral tablet; in medical books, the vagina.

中丨 the thorax; a medical term.

丨報 a title by which a Guardian of the Heir-apparent is addressed; it resembles the old French term of *maire-du-palais*.

若天丨 like the court of heaven, said of a fine house.

拲 To fasten a prisoner's hands in a board, like putting them in the stocks.

ˊkung

ʿ廾 ʿkung Formed of 手 *hand* repeated, or of 屮 a *sprout* and 又 a *hand* on the right; it is the 55th radical of a few unassorted characters, and used only in combination; it much resembles *ya* 廿 twenty.

The two hands joined and held up, as when presenting a thing.

ʿ巩 ʿ𢪛 ʿkung The first is composed of 工 *labor* and 丮 *lifting* a thing; the second has taken its place, and it is used only as a primitive.

To embrace, to fold in the arms as when carrying a thing; to push from one; to press upon, to scrouge.

ʿ鞏 ʿkung To bind with thongs; to strengthen, to bind securely; a thong; firm, strong, rigid; stiffened; well-secured, well-guarded against attack.

丨乾 to shrink or dry at the fire.

昊天無不克丨 high Heaven is able to strengthen everything.

丨縣 a district in Ho-nan fu near the entrance of the River Loh into the Yellow River; it was a small feudality in the Cheu dynasty.

丨昌府 a prefecture in the southeast of Kansuh, famed for its musk and other deer, where the Kung tribes once lived.

丨固 well guarded, as a city.

闕丨之甲 [like the] strong mailed men-at-arms of Küeh-kung state; *met.* well equipped soldiers.

ʿ蛬 ʿkung An unauthorized character.

To squirm as a worm or maggot; to wriggle in or out, as a weasel through a crack; to bend, as when squeezing into a hole; to work at in order to get into, as a thief through a wall.

丨孔 to go into a hole, as a snake.

猪丨地 the hog roots up the ground.

丨來丨去 dodging in and out, as people through a crowd.

ʿ穬 ʿkung The awn on barley, wheat, or other grains or grasses; unripe rice or paddy.

丨麥 a variety of wheat with a long awn.

ʿ獷 ʿkung Fierce like an untamed dog; furious, desperate; rude, uncivilized.

丨丨難近 he is very difficult to approach.

政移丨俗 the government has altered those savage customs.

ʿ鑛 ʿ礦 ʿkung From *metal* or *stone* and *broad;* it occurs incorrectly written 壙; the second form is used mostly for the mine.

The ore of iron, lead, gold, or other metals; the lode of metals; a cangue or matrix of gems or fine jade; a mine whence ore or coal is taken; the bed or vein in it.

鐵丨 iron ore.

丨朴 metallic ores.

挖丨 to work a mine, to get out ore or coal.

開丨 to open a mine.

丨丁 a miner, a collier.

丨井 a pit of coal, a mine; the shaft.

紫丨 the Budhist name for the red kino made from the sap of the *Butea frondosa* in India.

ʿ拱 ʿkung To place the hands before the breast so that the thumbs come together, as when making a bow; to reverently hold or take with both hands; arched, bowing; an arch; to encircle.

丨手 to bow with the hands raised even with the head.

丨別 to bow and take leave.

丨候 to respectfully await one's coming.

丨瓦 semi-cylindrical tiles.

垂丨 to drop [the raiment] and hold the hands.

丨衛 to guard; to uphold, as a wall does the gateway.

丨立 to stand in a reverent posture.

丨頂 a dome, a cupola.

丨篷 a matted porch or entrance, sometimes arched.

福星丨照 may happy stars shine all around you.

丨門 a round or arched doorway.

北丨宸樞 [looking towards] the north, I reverently bow to the Imperial Court.

五十三丨橋 a bridge in Su-chau fu, with fifty-three arches.

ʿ栱 ʿkung A post, a prop, a pillar; a king-post over a girder or tie-beam in a roof.

丨斗 or 斗丨 the capital or head of a pillar; a kind of frame on top of a post to support the rafters.

ʿ珙 ʿkung A stone scepter or official badge; a precious stone.

玉丨 a statesman in the T'ang dynasty.

丨縣 a district in Sü-cheu fu in the southwest in Sz'ch'uen, south of the Yangtsz' River.

丨璧 a very large piece.

ʿ供 ʿkung To fear and tremble, as at calamity.

心丨而不安 my heart is so alarmed that it cannot be quieted.

ʿ憬 ʿching To be roused and appreciate a thing; to be excited upon; to understand; distant; to appear far off.

丨覺 to perceive, to appreciate.

丨彼淮夷來獻其琛 it will arouse those aborigines on the River Hwai, and they will come offering us their gems.

ʿ熲 ʿkung From 火 *fire* and 頃 *suddenly;* it is interchanged with 耿 cloudy.

The brightness of fire; brilliant; imperfect views.

無思百憂不出于丨 do not brood over your many griefs or you will never get out from your gloomy views.

璟 ˓*ching* The luster of a gem; brilliant; often used in personal names.

貢 *kung*˒ From *precious* and *work* as the phonetic.

To offer to a leige lord things for service; contributions from fiefs to their proper rulers; taxes in kind levied in early days, now applied mostly to the gems, peltry, provisions, &c., sent to Court from Mongol tribes; presents from foreign nations given in homage; fit for presents or tribute, the best sort, superior; to announce; to go forward, an offer of service, and hence merits, worthy actions.

進丨 or 朝丨 to offer presents, to send things to Court.

丨品 articles of tribute.

丨使 the tribute-bearer.

無以釗冒丨于非幾 do not you let Chao proceed to do things from wrong motives.

丨院 the provincial examination hall, in which the graduates are supposed to *offer* their talents for the country's service.

納丨 to pay taxes; as of silks.

作丨 to assess land taxes, done by the *chi-hien*.

丨船 a tribute-bearing ship.

丨禮 presents sent to Court.

拔丨 the *siuts'ai* graduates selected to send to Peking; there are five ranks of them designated from the circumstances of their appointment 恩丨 or extra-favor examination students.

副丨 those *siuts'ai* who nearly succeeded as *küjin*, and were placed at the head of the second list.

歲丨 those *siuts'ai* who have tried ten years to get the next degree.

優丨 selected or best graduates.

丨生 presented *siuts'ai*, includes the four preceding grades.

𥎦 *kung*˒ To fly to a place; to reach, to arrive at.

丨天門兮 See! it soars away to the gate of heaven.

共 *kung*˒ From 廿 *twenty* and 廾 *to raise* up; *q.d.* all taking it together.

Generally; all, altogether, in all, collectively; in fine, in short, to sum up; and, with, together; the same, alike; to include in, to live with; to discharge one's duties; an ancient name of Hwui hien 輝縣 in Wéi-hwui fu in the north of Honan.

合丨 altogether, taking the whole, in all

丨總 the whole, altogether.

丨計 reckoning the whole.

不丨一室 we cannot live in the same house.

不丨戴天 one must not live under the same sky — with his parent's murderer.

我丨你飲 let us take a drink together.

同心丨意 being of the same mind.

孰與丨之 who will befriend him?

未丨事 have no dealings with him.

Read ˓*kung*, and interchanged both with ˓供 to give, and ˓拱 to bow. To superintend a work; to protect, to hold fast; to encircle; to turn towards; to give; offerings; old name of a place in Kiang cheu in the south of Shansi.

克丨明刑 so as to hold fast to the wise laws — of the former kings.

匪其止˓丨 they do not fulfill their duties.

念彼丨人 I reflect on those people at the court.

居其所而衆星丨之 [like the pole-star,] which keeps its place, and all other stars turn towards it.

K'UNG.

Some of these are also pronounced K'IUNG. *Old sound,* k'ong. *In Canton,* hung, *and* hong; — *in Swatow,* k'ang, k'ong, *and* k'ông; — *in Amoy,* k'ông; — *in Fuhchau,* k'ung, k'üng, *and* k'ông; — *in Shanghai,* k'ung; — *in Chifu,* k'ung.

空 ˓*k'ung* From *eave* and *work* as the phonetic; occurs interchanged with 孔 a hole.

An opening or crevice, showing an empty place; a hole, a tunnel, an opening; void, vacant, empty; time, leisure; unemployed, standing still, as a loom; the expanse above, the firmament; poor, broken; unprejudiced, able to appreciate; abstraction, ecstasy, emptiness, torpor of the faculties, as understood by the Budhists; they also use it for *sunya*, the unreality of all phenomena, comparing them to dreams, shadows, lightning, dew, bubbles, &c.

丨屋 an empty house.

丨手 empty-handed.

丨肚 an empty stomach.

丨地 a vacant spot.

丨丨如也 entirely empty.

囊丨 moneyless, poor.

搶家財一丨 they plundered the house of all its contents.

一場丨 all gone, everything lost.

丨閒 unoccupied, no employment.

搬丨呢箇箱 empty this box.

丨孔 a hollow, a hole, a cave.

丨中 or 太丨 sky, heaven; also a Peking name for a hummingtop.

丨勞無益 I have lost all my pains.

丨口講 to speak without evidence.

丨首拜伏 bowed himself to the ground.

丨想 a vapid wish for.

買丨賣丨 to speculate on the rise and fall of prices or in stocks.

乃召司丨 he called in the superintendent of works.

丨門 the abstracted class, *i. e.* the Budhists; 入丨門 to become a priest or devotee.

視一丨切 to regard everything as nothingness.

歸到丨丨 to revert to nothingness; annihilated, as ice apparently is on melting.

一心直丨 all the faculties reaching a state of entire inanition and indifference.

丨心 disinterested, loyal, humble; nothing sinister.

平丨播弄 all is without any proof.

乘丨 to come while he was absent; took advantage of their unpreparedness.

Read *k'ung'* To separate, to leave a space between; to empty, to depauperate, to exhaust; a deficiency; a deficit, a defalcation; to make room for.

丨乏 wanting a thing; impoverished; empty; no funds.

丨開寫 write it after the space.

預印丨白 previously stamped in blank; — a note put on official papers before the newyear.

沒有丨兒 I have no time, I am busy.

是甚麼丨兒 when was it?

抽丨 to take time for.

不宜丨我師 it is not right for us to be so reduced and impoverished.

箜 *k'ung* A description of wide lute, the 丨篌, used in ancient times when worshiping; it was pressed against the breast when played, and thrummed like a guitar.

崆 *k'ung* A famous mountain in P'ing-liang fu in the eastern part of Kansuh, 丨峒, in which the River King rises; another peak of the same name lies west of it in Kung-chang fu; a mountain of this name is supposed to uphold the Dipper or North Pole.

硿 *k'ung* A mineral, called 丨青, which is brought from Chehkiang, and seems to be an ore of copper, or perhaps copperas; it is used as a medicine; the sound of stones falling.

悾 *k'ung* From *heart* and *empty* as the phonetic; like the next.

Ignorant, rustic-looking; dissatisfied, as from ill-luck or incompetence; sincere, guileless.

丨誠 truly sincere.

丨丨而不信 simple-minded and yet not confiding.

倥 *k'ung'* Interchanged with the last in some senses.

Rude, clownish; careworn, pressed.

丨侗 ignorant, raw; doltish.

賤務丨傯 my private affairs have been urgent and many.

孔 *'k'ung* From *child* and *bird;* the combination alludes to the time of pairing.

A hole, an orifice, a cave, an opening; hollow; an adverb of praise, excellent, great, superior; very, highly; through.

丨雀 the peacock, particularly the Malayan peacock. (*Pavo muticus.*)

丨竅 openings, pores; the inlets of knowledge into the heart.

丨道 a thoroughfare, a way.

丨脩 great perfection.

丨昭 widely known, as a doctrine.

毛丨 pores of the skin.

丨方 the holed square; — *i. e.* a copper cash.

丨般 urgent, much needed, busy.

戎車丨博 the war chariots are very large.

威儀丨時 his serious demeanor was just what the occasion required.

丨子 or 丨夫子 the sage K'ung, or K'ung futsz', *i. e.* Confucius; his birthday is kept on the 27th day of the 8th moon, when all the butchers are forbidden to slaughter animals.

丨子不語怪 Confucius would not speak of the weird.

控 *k'ung'* From *hand* and *empty.*

To pull as a bow; to rein in, to check; to accuse, to inform the rulers; to impeach; to maintain, to hold up; to claim, as indemnity; to eject, to suppress; to beat.

丨告 to accuse; to bring charges.

揑丨 to accuse falsely, a trumped-up charge.

上丨 to carry up an accusation; to take it to a higher court.

越丨 to petition the high officers directly.

丨于大邦 complained of it to the leading state.

丨馬而問 he reined in the horse to ask.

丨弦四十萬騎 he held his legions of cavalry well in hand.

鞚 *k'ung'* A bridle, or the reins to hold a horse.

抽韁緊丨 he grasped the bridle and stopped him.

KWA.

Old sounds, kwa, kap, *and* kat. *In Canton*, kwa, wo, *and* wa; — *in Swatow*, kúé, wa, o, kwa, *and* kw'a; — *in Amoy*, kwa, kwaⁿ, *and* wa; — *in Fuhchau*, kwa, *and* wò; — *in Shanghai*, kwò *and* wò; — *in Chifu*, kwa.

瓜 ꜀*kwa* The original form is designed to represent the weak tendrils of melons; it is the 97th radical of a natural group of characters relating to the parts and sorts of gourds, &c.

A generic term for cucurbitaceous plants, as cucumber, melon, gourd, squash, including also the brinjal and egg-plant; the follicles of milkweed (*Asclepias*) and similar seed vessels.

西丨 the water-melon.

及丨 the time of melons.

絲丨 is applied to two or three fruits, the *Cucumis longa*, and a hairy kind of egg-plant.

黃丨 or 王丨 the common cucumber; the second is an ancient name.

冬丨 a large coarse squash. (*Benincasa cerifera.*)

冬丨臉 a long oval face, ugly-shaped; not like the 丨子臉 or melon seed shaped face.

木丨 the quince; in *Canton*, the papaya.

節丨 a hairy kind of brinjal.

陰丨 a sort of orange-gourd, with a thick rind.

番丨 a small yellow squash; another name for the papaya.

苦丨 the bitter gourd, a cucurbitaceous plant, (*Momordica balsamina* or *charantia*,) whose oblong, shuttle-shaped fruit is covered with warts; it is much cultivated in southern China.

香丨 a muskmelon, a cantelope.

丨期以待 wait till the melons come again, — *i. e.* next year; for which 丨代 has also become a common expression.

有丨葛 there is some relationship; I have an understanding, or business relations, with him.

地若丨分 the country is divided like the slices of a melon.

醬丨 a pickle made of 白丨 or young cucumbers.

綿綿丨瓞 [like] long lines grow the gourds; — applied to numerous descendants.

倭丨 at *Peking*, the crook-necked squash, thought to have been brought from Japan.

守丨 the cucumber guard, *i. e.* the plant lice which eat its leaves.

金丨 a wooden gilt bludgeon with a head like a melon.

抓 ꜀*kwa* From *hand* and *melon*, and also read ꜀*wa*; it is now confounded with ꜀*chao* 抓 to grab, and read ꜀*chwa*; this having generally superseded the right character.

To lead, to drag; to strike; to clutch, to grab; to take up.

丨一把 take up a handful.

好像丨素菜 [he is fingering things,] like a cook of green vegetables.

丨周 to pick out of the whole, — as is done by a child a year old at his birthday.

一不着 he could not grab it.

媧 ꜀*wa* The Chinese Pandora called 女丨 (also read *yü-wa*,) who is said to have 煉五色石補天 melted fine stones to repair the heavens, and invented the organ; some think the name alludes to Eve, the Chinese say she was Fuh-hi's sister, had the body of a serpent, and a human head, with the virtues of a sage; others deny that she was a woman at all.

騧 ꜀*kwa* A yellowish, cream-colored horse with a black mouth.

季丨 name of a scholar in the reign of Wăn Wang.

刮 ꜀*kwa* From *knife* and *melon*; it is now used as a synonym of ꜀*k'u* 刳 to slice.

丨心丨肝 [my grief is like] cutting out my heart and liver.

蝸 ꜀*kwa* A garden slug; a snail; small, low and poor huts; hovels.

丨牛 the land snail (*Helix*), so called in allusion to its horns or pedicillate eyes.

丨舍 my snail-shell of a house.

丨角虛名 [like the] empty reputation of a conch's sound.

咼 ꜀*kwa* This primitive is thought to represent a distorted mouth when crying; it is now used as a synonym of the next.

A wry mouth, whether born so or diseased.

剮 ꜀*kwa* To cut a criminal in pieces, as is done at the disgraceful execution, by slicing off his lips, ears, eyelids, and limbs.

問丨之罪 the punishment of cutting to pieces.

丨爛面皮做事 if you cut my face and spoil my skin, I'll do it; — regardless of ridicule.

千刀萬丨 all cut into small pieces; — the extremity of torture.

色是丨骨刀 lewdness is a knife which will cut the bones.

另 ꜀*kwa* From *mouth* and *knife*, and regarded as an ancient form of the last two; now used as a primitive, and sometimes written like *ling*' 另 another.

To cut the flesh from the bones.

篙 ꜀*kwa* A shallow splint tray common at Canton; a spool for winding silk; it is placed on a stand (called 四墊) with sticks on the four corners, and the spool in the center.

丨籃 shallow basket trays for drying tea leaves.

擺到一丨丨 spread out the trays singly.

'寡 'kwa From 宀 a *covering* and 頒 to *give* largesses, each one receiving a little.

Few, little, moderate; easily satisfied; seldom, rarely, unusual; solitary, friendless; alone, deficient, short, and hence comes to mean unworthy; the regal We, Ourself.

多丨 much or few; how many?

丨不敵衆 a few can't stand them all; I am no match for so many.

丨聞 little experience.

丨言 taciturn; of few words.

丨兄 I, your unworthy brother.

孀丨 or 丨婦 a widow.

丨情薄行 having little feeling and slow to act; callous.

丨人有弟 I the king have a younger brother.

刑于丨妻 his example was a pattern to his unequaled wife.

丨君 I, the ruler; — *i. e.* the prince who is alone or unequaled.

詿 kwa' From *words* and a *baton;* occurs used with the next.

To impose on, to deceive; to make another miscarry; to fail in one's promise; to disturb.

丨誤 to mislead.

丨亂 to distract and confuse.

罣 kwa' An impediment, an obstacle; to fall into a snare, to hinder; not at ease, as a bird in a net; to think of.

丨礙 to hinder, as a snag stops the sailing boat, and impales it.

丨念 to think of much.

觸丨 to rush against the obstacle, to fall into the net.

懸丨 much afraid lest some ill has happened.

絓 kwa' The coarse silk obtained from refuse cocoons; a knotted cord to fasten a horse; to stop, to impede, as by a net.

心結丨而不解 I am so anxious that nothing can enliven me.

驂丨而止 he fastened the horse and stopped.

掛 } 挂 } kwa' To suspend, to hang up; to dwell on or prolong; in suspense, anxious; to distinguish; to remember, to note, to make a minute of; to divine by straws; to lay by out of use; colloquially used as a classifier of things usually hung up, as necklaces, bridles, &c.

丨號 to keep a list of names, as a tax-payer; to enter names in a record.

丨齒 hanging on people's lips.

丨望 to anxiously hope for.

丨心 or 丨慮 anxious about.

丨上 to hang up; put it on a nail.

丨名 to call by; only a name.

丨意 undecided; in suspense.

丨麪 strips of dough made by stretching them on two sticks.

丨官 to leave office.

丨欠 to record one's debts.

丨隊 to suspend work, to knock off, as a gang from rain or want of material.

簪花丨紅 to put gilt flowers in the cap and hang on the red scarf; — a joyful occasion.

轡子二丨 two bridles.

丨起飯鑊 you may hang up your griddle; — out of business.

唱丨枝 to sing ballads.

丨帳子 to hang curtains.

倒丨 a parrot, from its turning over and over.

丨單 to put up for one — night, as begging priests do at temples.

丨紫衣 he who hangs up the crimson dress, — the abbot.

卦 kwa' From 卜 to *divine* and 圭 a *baton*, or the last contracted.

Divining marks; to divine, to cast future events; a sign.

丨命先生 an astrologer.

占丨 or 卜丨 or 打丨 to divine, to cast lots; to draw.

牙齒打丨 teeth chattering with the cold.

丨頭準 his cast was just, he guessed right.

變丨 the luck has changed against you.

八丨 the divining lines or diagrams said to have been invented by Fuh-hi in remote times to serve as a kind of abacus to philosophize with, and indicate by their combinations the mutations and aspects of nature; the first eight diagrams were defined to represent the interchanges of elemental forces and their results, as follows:—

1	2	3	4	5	6	7	8
☰	☱	☲	☳	☴	☵	☶	☷
乾	兊	離	震	巽	坎	艮	坤
N.W.	W.	S.	E.	S.E.	N.	N.E.	S.W.
Heaven, Yang, the celestial producer; ether; humidity.	Water, vapor ascending; fountains, pools; lightness.	Fire; light; life, beauty, giving heat, actuating power; warmth.	Thunder, igneous exhalations, mover of things; stiffness.	Wind; vapors, energy of expanse; flexibility.	Water, liquid elements; rigidity, cold.	Mountains, solids, what sustains motion; quiet; gravity.	Earth, Yin, the terrestrial recipient of corruption; drought.

These were subsequently multiplied to sixty-four double ones, and on them are based the speculations of the *Yih King* or Book of Changes, composed by Wăn Wang about B.C. 1109, which amount to nothing better than a mechancial play of idle abstractions.

丨衍河圖 in the diagrams were seen the map of the rivers; an ancient legend.

In *Cantonese*, also written 啩 A final sound indicating a doubt; or probability of a thing.

或者係丨 I rather think it is so.

怕唔係丨 I am really afraid it is not so.

褂' From *dress* and to *divine*; an unauthorized character.

kwa' An outer jacket or robe; when it has no lapel, it opens in the middle.

袍丨 ceremonial robes, either long or short.

軍機丨 a coat which opens at the side.

號丨 a soldier's uniform.

馬丨 a riding jacket reaching to the loins; a description of dress overcoat, of which the 黃馬丨子, like the caftans given by Persian kings, is conferred only on high officers.

得勝馬丨 has long sleeves; the last often has very short ones.

丨子 or 大丨 a pelisse, a robe reaching below the knee.

KW'A.

Old sounds, kw'a, *and* k'at. *In Canton*, kw'a; — *in Swatow*, kw'a; — *in Amoy*, kw'a; — *in Fuhchau*, kw'a, *and* k'iè; — *in Shanghai*, kw'ò; — *in Chifu*, kw'a.

夸 From 大 *great* and 于 *in*; now superseded by the next.

꜀kw'a Prodigious; magniloquent; bragging, conceited talk.

丨奢自大 boasting and vaunting one's self.

無爲丨毗 do not boast of yourself nor flatter others.

誇 To boast, to brag of one's performances; to exaggerate; laudatory; conceited, grandiloquent; arrogant; wide, fine, ample, said of a dress.

꜀kw'a

丨口 or 丨嘴 vaunting, boastful.

自丨 or 丨誇 self-laudation.

丨讚 to overpraise.

丨能 boasting of one's ability.

大而不丨 great, but not vain; modest, self-poised.

丨丨 earnest, really.

丨布 ample; spreading out wide, as a robe.

恗 To think highly of one's self; self-complacent; dissatisfied with, captious.

꜀kw'a

心中自丨 to feel satisfied with one's doings.

Read *꜀hu*. Afraid, timorous.

侉 Like the two last.

꜀kw'a Presumptuous, disdainful, ostentatious.

姱 Vain, conceited, as of one's looks; pretty, neat, good; a mincing, ogling, manner.

꜀kw'a

丨修 elegant, stylish deportment; decorous manner.

丨節 careful of one's appearance, fastidious.

Read *hu'* Finical, particular.

姣丨 dissolute, loose, wanton.

骻 The bones of the pelvis, and used nearly like the next.

'kw'a

胯' From *flesh* and *bragging*; occurs used for the next.

kw'a' The thighs; the crotch or space between the legs; a fat appearance.

丨夫 a term of contempt for one who is cowed or yields cravenly.

手丨 the forearm. (*Cantonese*.)

受丨下之辱 to be disgraced by crawling between one's legs.

大丨子 large fat thighs.

跨' To straddle, to bestride; to step across, to pass over, to surpass, to excel; to border on two countries, as a chain of mountains; the thighs; a stride, the stretch of the legs.

kw'a'

丨越 to excel; to pass over; to supersede.

不丨其國 do not incroach on his territory.

丨馬 to bestride a horse.

丨開對手 to stretch out the arms.

丨海內制諸侯之術 a scheme for engrossing the empire and curbing the princes.

開丨箭衣 a riding robe or archer's dress, which opens in front.

丨祖 to incroach on the grave of one's ancestor, by burying behind his tomb.

丨坐 to sit in a straddling manner.

丨竈 he bestrides the fire-place; *met.* he excels his father.

丨子 a long and narrow traveling boat, used on the upper part of the Yangtsz' River.

丨所兒 a side-room in large houses, one set off with its own court.

In *Fuchau*. Overbearing, insolent, riding over one.

丨的倒 I've gotten the victory over him.

絝' A riding dress; overalls to protect the trowsers from chafing.

kw'a'

丨衿 an under-shirt or small vest.

KWAH.

Old sound, kwat. *In Canton*, kút, *and* kwat; — *in Swatow*, kwak, *and* kwat; — *in Amoy*, kwat; — *in Fuhchau*, kwak, *and* kwah; — *in Shanghai*, kwĕh; — *in Chifu*, kwa.

刮, ˎkwa From *knife* and *tongue*, but the primitive was first written *hwoh*, 舌 to stop the mouth.

To pare, to scrape off, to abrade; to plane, to shave; to rub, to burnish; to brush away, as leaves are by the wind; to even off, as a bushel of grain; to extort; to raze; to run against, to scrape by, as two carriages passing.

丨 削 to scrape, to trim; *met.* to oppress.

丨 漿 to stiffen cloth by starch.

丨 斗 a striker, used by millers.

丨 平地方 to level the ground; to raze a place.

丨 目相看 to rub one's eyes and treat respectfully; to regard one highly.

東 丨 西 丨 borrowing right and left; sponging on people.

丨 木 to plane boards.

兩個耳丨子 to box one's ears.

丨 字 to erase a writing.

丨 面光 he cut off the light of his face; — *i. e.* lost his good name.

丨 削價錢 to pare down or deduct from the price.

丨 衣裳 to sprinkle and brush clothes.

丨 着 [lookout, or we] shall hit! — said by cartmen.

丨 腿 to run against, as two horsemen.

In *Cantonese*. A quarter of a dollar or a pound, in imitation of the English word *quarter*.

括, kwa' kw'o' To inclose in a bundle, to envelop; to tie up; to embrace, to include; to comprehend; to meet; to arrive at; to place an arrow on the string; to brush.

丨 髮 to coil the hair in a knot.

囊 丨 四海 his bag holds the four seas; — he knows everything.

機 丨 ingenious mechanism.

德音來 丨 [I wish that one of such] virtuous fame would come to me.

丨 水 to bale out, as from a boat.

日之夕矣牛羊下 丨 at eventide the cows and goats come home from the hills.

包 丨 to bundle up, to contain; to have an understanding of.

聒, kwa' From *ear* and *tongue*; it looks like the next.

A clamor, a din; very importunate; bothering, distracting; to stun one; to injure an affair by talking.

多言 丨 耳 to din or croak in one's ears.

丨 擾 clamorous.

丨 丨 inapt, ignorant; others say, a continual din.

蛙 丨 通夜 the frogs kept up their croaking the whole night.

聒, kwa' To look at angrily; dim eyesight.

丨 視於人 to glare at a man.

栝, **桰**, ˎkwa A kind of frame or measure, called 檃 丨 used by masons in marking chords and angles when building.

Read *kwai'*. A tree allied to the yew or juniper.

丨 樓 the roots of the bryony (*Tricosanthes*) are so called by the medical faculty, perhaps from a fancied resemblance to the 蛞 蝼 or mole-cricket.

Read *tien'* for the first character. A pipe to blow up the fire in a cooking-range.

苦, **菰**, ˎkwa Interchanged with the last; and probably more correct.

A bitter plant, the 丨 簍, otherwise called 瓜 蔞, whose fruit is used by the Chinese in coughs; it is nearly round and has a soft rind.

蛞, kwa' The spawn of frogs.

丨 蝓 the garden slug or *Limax*, called at Nanking 連連蟲 the insect that follows, and 鼻涕蟲 or snivel worm at Canton.

丨 螻 the mole cricket.

适, kwa' Fleet, hasty; to hurry one.

丨 疾 to drive on; to hasten one to act quicker.

髺, kwa' The hair unpinned and disheveled, as when in mourning.

主人 丨 髮袒 the chief mourner, should have his hair undressed, and wear a single garment.

鴰, ˎkwa A species of wader, allied to the crane.

鶬 丨 the black crane, so called from its plumage, and 丨 鹿 from its cry; it has red cheeks, and is described as having nine tails from the manner in which the tail feathers turn up; the same name is given to a strange bird with nine heads, perhaps denoting a crested variety like the Balearic crane.

老 丨 a crow, in imitation of its croak; in Peking, it is the Japanese raven.

劀, ˎkwa To cut away the proud flesh from an ulcer; to remove the pus and blood.

筈, ˎkwa The butt or notch of the arrow where it is placed on the string.

颳 ˏkwa From *wind* and *tongue*.

A gust, a flurry which whirls about the dust; to drive on or sweep up, as a whirlwind does; to blow fitfully and strong.

丨着跑了 the gusts drive them rapidly, as clouds.

丨起風來 a rushing blast arose.

丨得一句在耳朶 I have only heard a slight inkling of it.

你是甚麼風丨來的 what lucky wind blew you here?

丨得滿天飛 [the dust] was all blown sky high.

丨不開得 it could not blow away — the clouds.

KWAI.

Old sounds, kwai, kai, *and* kat. *In Canton,* kwai; — *in Swatow,* kwai; — *in Amoy,* kwai; — *in Fuhchau,* kwai; — *in Shanghai,* kwa *and* kwé; — *in Chifu,* kwai.

乖 ˏkwai The original form is described as made up of a ram's head and horns, which the middle part depicts, and the two side portions are from 剮 to *scrape* modified; another etymologist says it depicts the backbone and ribs.

To turn the back on; perverse, cross-grained; strange, sulky; cunning, crafty; unlucky; to contradict; at cross purposes, untoward.

丨巧 wily, tricksy; knavish; full of deceits.

丨異 old in his way, intractable, eccentric.

丨口 glib-tongued, plausible.

丨紊 to pervert all reason.

精丨伶俐 ingenious, clever at devices.

倫使丨 to trick one out of, to get a sharper's advantage.

丨張 or 丨戾 mulish, intractable, bad tempered.

運途丨蹇 what an unlucky catastrophe I have met with!

丨兒子 a pert, mischievous child.

In *Fuhchau.* Good, amiable, pleasing; a lullaby.

拐 ˋkwai From *hand* and to *scrape* off the flesh.

To deceive, to swindle; to seduce, to decoy; to entrap persons, to delude in order to carry them off; to twist, to turn, as in following a road.

丨子 a kidnapper, a man-stealer.

丨騙人妾 to elope with a man's concubine.

丨去 to decoy and carry off.

丨跌了他 pushed him down with his elbow.

丨賣猪仔 to entrap and sell a man as a coolie (*Cantonese*).

我口腔不能丨彎 I cannot change the note in my mouth, — as in whistling; *i. e.* I cannot whistle a tune.

順牆丨丨過去 go along by the wall and turn the corner.

枴 ˋkwai A staff for old men, usually made to resemble a crutch, with a crooked top.

丨杖 an old man's staff.

丨子棍 a truncheon or quarter-staff used in fencing and fighting.

怪 恠 kwaiˋ From *heart* and to *till* the ground or *in;* the second form is not very common.

Strange, marvelous; bizarre, portentous, monstrous; supernatural, weird; curious; to dislike, to bear a grudge against; to blame, to find fault with; to deem strange; surprised at; sometimes it has the force of an *adverb,* very, unusually.

奇丨 surprising, unusual.

丨物 an apparition, a monster.

鬼丨 ugly, horrid.

不要見丨 don't feel angry; don't get annoyed at it.

丨責 to reprimand, to berate.

反丨你 he blames you without cause.

丨哉此言 what strange talk!

莫丨 no wonder! (*Cantonese*).

丨澀的 harsh-tasted.

丨不得 it is not surprising.

見了丨閉不得眼 it is useless to shut your eyes when you've seen the spook; — you must meet the crisis, face the music.

令人見丨 to bring blame on one's self.

丨誕之事 unfounded tales.

恕丨 don't be displeased, ease your wrath.

聽着丨害怕 I was much frightened at hearing it.

受人丨頭 blamed by people.

丨燙的 scalding hot.

素隱行丨 to delight in secretly doing odd things.

陸離光丨 rare and new things.

夬 ˋkwai From 又 the *hand* and a thing passing through it; it is easily mistaken for ˏ*yang* 央 midst.

Parted, as streams; differing; to pull or flow different ways; certain, absolute; name of the 54th diagram, denoting what is decided, stern, or settled.

Read *küeh,* and interchanged with 訣 an art. To place the middle finger pointing upward within the knuckles of the others; people often do it when alone to frighten away the bogies.

靈官丨 a guardian image often seen in the door of Budhist temples, having a knotted club in one hand, and the middle finger of the other sticking up.

KWʻAI.

Old sounds, kwʻai, kwʻat, *and* kwʻak. *In Canton,* fai, kúi, *and* kwai; — *in Swatow,* kwʻai, ko, *and* kúi; — *in Amoy,* kwʻai *and* kwaì; — *in Fuhchau,* kwʻai; — *in Shanghai,* kwʻé *and* kwa; — *in Chifu,* kwʻa.

擓 ꜀kwʻai From *hand* and an *eddy;* also read ꜀*kwai.*

To rub, to smooth; to scratch; to carry with one.

丨癢 to scratch an itching place.

丨水 to absorb or wipe up water.

丨筐子 to sling a basket on the arm.

丨破臉 to cut one's acquaintances.

丨了五條痕 her nails left five scratches.

蒯 ꜀kwʻai A kind of rush of which door mats can be woven; sandals and wisps are also made of it.

丨索 straw ropes.

丨履 straw sandals, such as are worn by mourners.

丨金緱 cord wound around the hilt of a sword.

丨蓆 coarse rush mats.

快 kwʻai꜄ From *heart* and *disparting.*

A flow of spirits; glad, cheerful; pleasure, cheerfulness; alacrity, promptness; quick, hasty, rapid, speedy; used for 就 just on the point of, almost, about to be; sharp, keen, as a blade.

丨些 a little quicker, hurry on.

丨樂 happy, in good spirits.

丨活 delight, joy; pleasure; 丨活的人 a cheerful happy man.

丨馬拿來 bring it quickly *i. e.* — like a courier with a letter.

丨馬 a courier, a fleet post.

丨丨 quick, smart; instantly.

丨人 a keen, efficient man.

縣裏馬丨 the thief detectors in a magistrate's office.

丨來了 he will soon be here.

丨的回來 come back quickly.

丨利 sharp, keen; smart.

風雲丨慢 the wind is swifter than the clouds.

丨子 "nimble lads," *i. e.* chopsticks; for this meaning the radical 竹 is often added, making the correct form, and showing that the literal rendering of the common name was not the original idea.

丨子插 or 丨籠子 a fob for the chopsticks.

不爽丨 indisposed, out of sorts.

丨班 policemen, thief-catchers.

一時之丨 something which demands instant attention.

大丨于懷 you rejoice my heart greatly.

丨艇 a fast-boat, — at Canton.

丨冷 it is getting cold.

丨完 it will soon be done.

磨丨 or 磨的鋒丨 grind it sharp.

駃 kwʻai꜄ Used for the last; it is also read *küeh,*

A sprightly colt that in a week can beat its dam at running; swift as the wind.

丨馬 a racer, a fleet horse.

丨流如竹箭 its waters are swift as an arrow.

噲 kwʻai꜄ From *mouth* and *united.*

To swallow, to drink with avidity; voracious; an impediment in swallowing; meager; clamor.

顏色臞丨 her beauty has gone.

丨丨其正 cheerful and pleasant are the front rooms.

襘 kwʻai꜄ The place where the girdle is joined, or the collar fastened; a loose sash, or the girdle put on loosely.

塊 kwʻai꜄ From *earth* and *demon,* which has been altered from 土 *earth* inside of 凵 a *pit.*

A clod, a lump; a fraction, a piece of; doltish; used for I in a demeaning manner; a classifier of things thin or flat, or in pieces, a, boards, panes, slices, lumps, coins &c., rather shapeless and squarish

一丨肉 a slice of meat.

一丨地 a piece or lot of land; a clod.

一丨兒 altogether, all at once, lumping the whole; used to indicate a union or joining of people or things in one spot.

破丨 to break the clods.

與之丨 [the peasant] offered him a clod of earth, — *i. e.* to Chung-'rh, the son of the Prince of Tsin, when passing as a beggar through Wéi in great distress (B. C. 539); he afterwards got his throne.

胸如壘丨 my heart is like a pile of clods; — *i. e.* in great distress.

大丨 creation, the globe; nature.

丨然無知 doltish and ignorant.

丨然一物 he is a blockhead, just like a clodhopper.

KWAN.

Old sounds, kon, *and* kwan. *In Canton,* kwan, *and* kún; — *in Swatow,* kwan, *and* kw^{n}a; — *in Amoy,* kwan, kw^{n}a, *and* wan; — *in Fuhchau,* kwang; — *in Shanghai,* kwé^{n}, wó^{n}, *and* wèh; — *in Chifu,* kwan.

官 ‹*kwan* From 宀 a *covering* and 𠂤 *many*, which etymologists also regard as a contracted form of 師 an *officer;* this character is often dissected as meaning two *mouths* under a *roof*, alluding to the mendacity of officials; it looks like *hwan*' 宦 official.

An officer of government; the magistrates, the authorities; rulers; an officer; the government; official, public; a public court of law; a business; a title of respect or adulation, placed after the name; first rate, the best of.

做丨 in office.

丨府 or 丨員 or 丨吏 or 丨曹 officials, magistrates.

丨燕 the best kind of birds-nest.

清丨 an honest officer, a pure handed magistrate.

入丨 or 歸丨 to confiscate.

丨天下 a public sway, a republican or democratic rule.

丨路 a highway, a public road.

打丨事 to carry a case before the authorities.

丨體 or 丨樣 official dignity; stately, awe-inspiring.

丨場中人 one of the rulers.

文武學丨 dignitaries in the civil, military, and literary departments.

六丨 the six Boards in ancient times, called 天丨, 地丨, 春丨, 夏丨, 秋丨, and 冬丨, answering respectively to the present boards of Civil Office, Revenue, Rites, War, Punishment, and Works.

正印丨 five officers of the regular grade, *i.e.* not being deputies or of particular appointment; — they are the district magistrate, the prefect, judge, governor, and governor-general.

幾品丨 of what rank are you?

丨板 officer's boards; *i.e.* money, coin, cash.

丨星顯 his star appears, he will soon be in office.

糊塗丨府 an untrustworthy official, a muddle-headed fellow.

大丨丨 a pet name for a lad.

丨人 one in office; a term of respect for a husband; an epithet for prostitutes.

藉丨勢 trusting to official power.

五丨 the five senses are the ears, eyes, mouth, nose, and heart, which rule the body.

丨媒 old women who are appointed by the local magistrates to redeem repentant magdalens, to stamp the papers for sale of girls, or aid in punishing female prisoners at Canton, women who are sentenced to be sold for their crimes.

亞丨仔 or 小丨 an appellation for a young man.

丨話 court or mandarin dialect.

蘇丨 Mr. Su, or Su-qua as it is called, adopting the Amoy pronunciation *kw^{n}a*, which sound the people at Canton often write 呱, not knowing its origin.

天丨賜福 may Heaven's Ruler bless you; this refers to the god who rules the 吏部 in the skies.

大老丨 a man who swaggers along; at Suchau, a term for one's eldest brother.

倉丨兒 the granary-keeper, is a local name for the dwarf hamster (*Cricetulus griseus*), from the grain it stores away.

倌 ‹*kwan* The emperor's charioteer or master of his chariots; an assistant in an office.

命彼丨人 he would then order his groom.

啗 ‹*kwan* Two birds singing in response; to coo to each other, as doves do; or answering, as two orioles.

棺 ‹*kwan* From *wood* and *ruler; q. d.* that which secures the corpse.

A coffin, that which closes up all affairs; the inner of two coffins; to encoffin, to close up.

丨材 a coffin.

運丨 to take a parent's coffin home.

施丨 or 捨丨 to give coffins; — a religious act.

磁器丨材 a crockery coffin; *met.* a hard hearted man.

丨罩 a great pall or catafalque carried at funerals.

丨材餡 said of one dangerously sick or very old.

丨材鑿 a coffin-chisel, an epitnet of a petty rascal; — you body-snatcher!

丨材伸出手 his hand comes out of his coffin; — *i. e.* he is grasping to the last.

金丨 a golden coffin; at Peking, it is only used for a prince.

𢇇 ‹*kwan* From 幺 *fine* threads repeated over the *shuttle*, through which they pass in weaving; it is the primitive of the next, and now used only in combination.

To run the threads through the web.

關 ‹
闗 ‹*kwan* From *door* and to *pass* threads through a web; the second form is commonest.

To stop a gate, to bar the door, to shut up a doorway; to fasten, to stop a thing or road for a while; to guard, to place a post at; the cross-bar of a gate; a gateway to a market; a frontier-pass; a ford; a post-house, douane, custom, or excise house; governmental; a limit, a boundary; a crisis, a Rubicon, an important point in one's life; to bear upon, to effect, to belong to or concern; to allude to; involving, having a relation to; consequences, results; to pass by or through; to penetrate, to pierce.

丨門 bar the gate; shut in for the night; shut the door!

海丨 a marine custom-house.

丨部 administrator of customs, who writes of himself as 本丨部 I, the collector.

丨口 a pass, a place where customs are paid.

丨汎 a post or station of guard.

丨脈 the middle pulse in the wrist, connected with the liver.

你不丨心 you did not pay attention.

放丨 to pass free of duty.

丨帝 the Chinese God of War, named Lord Kwan 丨公 a noted hero of the Three States, A. D. 219; also called 丨聖 the holy Kwan, and 丨老爺 or 丨夫子 the martial Sage Kwan, and other names.

不丨我事 it is none of my business.

不丨涉 independent of, disconnected.

生死的丨頭 a matter of life and death.

丨煞開通 may the crisis of his danger be gotten through safely; — written on children's caps to ward off ills.

王慾之丨 the line between reason and passion.

丨係 or 丨繫 consequences, results; what comes of an act.

丨守 to defend bravely — the pass.

丨中 a term for Shensi and the adjacent regions lying west of 函谷丨 in Honan.

丨東 Manchuria, the region lying east of the 山海丨 at the end of the Great Wall.

丨節 covert assistance of; the circumstances of.

打丨節 to give funds for underhand aid.

丨心照料 look after it carefully.

承蒙丨注 I shall be obliged if you will look after this thing.

開丨散 a sneezing powder.

丨書 a proposal for engaging a teacher or secretary; and 簽丨 is the money sent with such an application.

爲學有三丨 three means pertain to study, — *i. e.* seeing, hearing, and talking.

丨防 the official seal.

丨防衙門 an office of the *Néi-wu-fu* which oversees the marriages, funerals, and allowances of the Imperial Clan.

閉丨 to stop the passes; to shut up the douanes.

丨弓而射 to pull the bow and shoot.

識透機丨 I see now the real motive.

國課攸丨 this pertains to the country's revenue.

丨丨 the scream of the osprey.

坐丨 sitting in the pass, *i. e.* inside of a laticed box lined with spikes; Budhist priests do so to excite compassion, and get people to buy out the nails.

鰥 ꜀kwan A huge fish, found in the Yellow River, and reported to be large enough to fill a cart; the story is that it cannot close its eyes and never sleeps, whence the name is applied to a widower, or an old man who has never married, because they cannot sleep soundly without a bedfellow; alone, unattended.

丨夫 a widower.

丨居 to live alone.

目丨丨而不寐 restless and unable to sleep.

憐丨 to befriend the lonely.

哀此丨寡 also pity the widowers and defenseless.

丨身漢子 a lonesome fellow, having no kith or kin.

有丨在下曰虞舜 there is a bachelor among the people whose name is Yu Shun.

瘝 ꜀kwan Diseased, infirm, incompetent to fulfill the duties of; incapable; to distress, to make void or useless.

丨官 an inefficient, idle official.

恫丨在抱 to have great solicitude and anxiety for.

智㵟丨在 the wise are in obscurity and the incapable in office.

若時丨厥官 [if you thus act,] the offices will in time be all made of no effect.

莞 ꜀kwan The district of Tung-kwan 東丨縣 in Kwang-cheu fu, lying along the eastern side of the Pearl River above the Bocca Tigris; also an old name of Ishui hien 沂水縣 in the south of Shantung.

Read ʿ*kwan*. Marshy plants like the cat-tail reed or sedge; of which mats can be made; the *Juncus effusus* is one sort; a coarse grass mat; to smile.

丨爾而笑 [the sage] then smiled and laughed out.

合丨 a native medicine; perhaps the seeds of the *Euonymus*.

冠 ꜀kwan From 冖 to *cover*, 元 the *chief* or head, and 寸 a *rule*.

A conical cap or bonnet, — applied now to the Taoist cap; caps with red silk; any proper covering for the head; the crest or comb of birds.

平天丨 the ancient flat topped crowns of the Chinese.

加丨 to cap a young man when he has 入丨 come of age; formerly done at twenty.

丨鳧 the sheldrake.

請升丨 please remove your hats; — said to guests.

免衣丨 no need of wearing your hats and robes; — in undress.

丨纓盡落 deprived of every office and rank.

堂皇丨冕 with strict etiquette and decorum.

怒髮衝丨 he was so angry that his hair lifted his cap.

道士丨 a priest's cap; a small squarish hut of one or two rooms.
下丨 wattles on birds.
丨縣 a district in Tung-chang fu in Shantung, lying west of the Grand Canal.

Read *kwan'* To cap a youth at his marriage, an old usage, equivalent to putting on the *togo virilis;* to promote in office to the highest post; the chief or head; able, superior.
勇丨三軍 the bravest [of the brave] in three legions.
丨塲 excelling all competitors.
未丨 a bachelor, unmarried.
弱丨 immature, not yet reached full strength.
職丨秋曹 he was raised to be the head of the Board of Punishments.

觀 覌 *ˎkwan* From to *see* and a *water-fowl;* the contraction is very common. To look at carefully; to contemplate; to observe, to travel and see; to manifest, to display; an evidence of, proof; observed, manifested, the appearances of; a spectacle, sights; many.
丨望 to idle about; to look on; as 幸勿丨望 well for you not simply to look at it—but buy it.
丨光 one's first entrance into the examinations.
丨風 to test the literary spirit of a place.
丨音兵 a lady's man.
美丨 a fine view; a good action.
丨一丨氣色何如 look carefully at his features to see what they indicate.
壯丨 a fine front; beautiful facade.
大丨 a great performance; something seen from afar.
大失丨瞻 to lose the regard of others by undignified manners.
閒丨 to stroll about sight-seeing.
無有可丨 nothing worth seeing there.
丨察 or 丨察使 the style of an address to the intendant of circuit.
奇丨 a rare event.
容丨 the deportment; the style.
鑑丨四方 looking down upon this lower world.
丨天文 astrology, star-gazing.
越王丨潮 Yueh-wang looks after the bore — at Hangchen.
奄丨銍艾 very soon we shall see the sickles at the grain.
丨星臺 the Observatory at Peking, where the 丨星的 or astronomers worked.
薄言丨之 while they looked.
丨相 to judge physiognomy.
丨音菩薩 Kwanyin, usually called Goddess of Mercy, a Budhist deity; the name is a translation of the Sanscrit *avalôkitêswara* or Hearer of Cries; other names are 丨世音自在 the sovereign who regards the prayers of the world; 丨世自在 the ruler who regards the world; and 光世音 illuminating the sounds of the world; she is also termed the 大慈大悲 the Merciful and Compassionate; the sex has changed in course of time, and it seems to have been at first a Chinese native god, on which the Indian deity was afterwards foisted.

Read *kwan'* A temple of the Rationalists; a hermitage, a secure retreat; a gallery; the 20th diagram, meaning to make known.
丨樓 a gallery, a belvidere.
仙丨 Taoist temples.
寺丨 monasteries and temples.

筦 *ˋkwan* Similar to the next, and used for it. The rope by which bells and drums are suspended; to direct; a pipe; a key; a shuttle.
磬丨將將 the dulcimers and flutes sound their harmonies.
丨諸會計事 he managed every department and recorded events.

管 菅 *ˋkwan* From *bamboo* and a *ruler;* the contracted form is common in cheap books. A tube; a reed, a short pipe or flageolet, having six holes, and sometimes in former days two tubes to one mouth-piece, like the shepherd's pipe of the Arabs; a classifier of fifes, flutes, pipes, guns, quills, and other tubular things; in *anatomy,* a duct or passage, for which the next is more suitable; to rule, to control; to have the government of, to sway, to dominate, to influence primarily.
丨家 or 丨事 a butler, a steward.
丨事房 a pantry, a buttery.
丨下 to rule over.
丨店 a shop-boy or a coolie, at Canton; elsewhere, the salesman, the head of the shop.
丨窺 the tube through which to see things.
丨理 to manage, to govern.
畧陳丨見 I think so on the whole, it is my imperfect opinion.
丨數 or 丨賬 the book-keeper, the money-keeper.
受他丨轄 governed by; I am under his rule.
丨不住 or 不丨他 he is beyond my control.
只丨講 let him talk; talk on.
只丨做 it must be done.
總丨 to superintend; a head-ruler; an overseer.
筆丨 tube of a pencil; barrel of a quill
五丨 the ducts of the five viscera.
丨城子 a poetical name for a pencil.
弦丨 stringed and wind instruments.
一丨手鎗 one pistol, a revolver.
嘒嘒丨聲 how shrill the pipes sound!
聖也者道之丨也 the idea of perfect virtue is being guided by reason.
靡聖丨丨 as there seem to be no sages, you have no guiding men.

‘⿰月官 ‘脘 From *flesh* and *ruler* or *finished;* the preceding is commonly used for it; the second also means flesh, marrow.

‘*kwan* The œsophagus, though anatomists define it as the part of the bowels near the pylorus, which they divide into three parts; also the larynx, the ureter, or other ducts; the core of a boil.

血丨 arteries, blood-vessels.

漏丨 a running ulcer.

水丨 the urethra.

肺丨 the larynx, the windpipe.

胃丨 the pylorus or the cardiac orifice, both being included under the same term.

脫丨丸 a pill which will extract the core of a boil.

‘琯 ‘*kwan* A tube of stone made into a flute; a sight tube attached to an azimuth or theodolite; a beautiful pebble: to burnish metals.

翎丨 the tube which holds the peacock's feather on an official cap.

西王母來獻其白丨` [after Shun began to reign] the Mother of the Fairies came offering him a white jade.

‘悹 ‘悺 From *heart* and *officer* as the phonetic.

‘*kwan* Sorrowing and sad.

丨丨 friendless, having no one to rely on.

有丨丨之凄涼 utterly abandoned, totally friendless.

丨’念 sad thoughts.

‘痯 ‘*kwan* Exhausted, worn out, weak; sick from grief or disheartened by failure.

四牡丨丨 the four horses were worn out.

丨楚甚篤 dangerously sick.

捾 From *hand* and *ruler;* it is often read *wah,*

‘*kwan* To take up, to lift; to take out of; to rescue.

丨取 to take away.

‘館 ‘舘 From to *eat* or a *cottage* and *officer;* the second and common form is unauthorized, and has probably arisen from the similarity of the radicals.

‘*kwan* An inn, a caravansary; the hotel of a feudal prince; a lodging-place or club-house erected in a town by the people from another town or region; a council-room, an assembly-hall; a hall, a room for public use; an exchange, an office or counting-room; a saloon, a restaurant; a school-room; to lodge, to stay for a short period; to build temporary lodgings or booths.

公丨 a government hall, a public room.

書丨 or 學丨 a college, a school.

會丨 mercantile or literary club-rooms erected for public purposes, generally by the people of one place or ward.

適子之丨兮 we will go up to your city house.

客丨 a hotel, a tavern.

丨舍 a hired hall; hired lodgings.

賭丨 a gambling place, a hell.

酒丨 or 高樓丨 or 茶丨 an eating-house, a restaurant.

稅丨 a custom-house.

醫丨 a hospital, a dispensary.

丨所 a public hall.

丨地 a post in an office; an opening for employment.

班丨 a kind of lock-up in a yamun.

開丨 and 解丨 to open a school and close it, — as at the terms.

賊丨 thieves' nests, the places or houses seized or occupied by rebels or banditti.

丨接天下賢豪 to collect all the good and brave in the country.

楚丨 brothels, bagnios.

翰林留丨 Hanlin graduates placed on the list for promotion.

‘輨 ‘*kwan* The iron band placed on the hub of a wheel to prevent it from splitting.

‘斡 From a *measure* and *sunrising;* it is also read *wah,* or *woh,*

‘*kwan* A handle, a wheel by which to turn a machine; a striker to even off grain; to revolve, to turn around; to circulate, as commodities; that which causes a turning; to superintend; in *rhetoric,* to explain, to open out a text or topic.

旋丨 to revolve, as the seasons.

各國之貨皆如輪丨 the products of all countries circulate as a wheel rolls over.

貫’ From *pearl* or *property* and to *string.*

kwan’ A string of a thousand cash; to run a thread through, to string on; strengthen, as a piece of board by an iron band; to connect, to traverse; to implicate, to involve; to penetrate, to go through; to bear with; pervading, associated with, linked to.

一丨錢 a string of cash.

籍丨 the origin or parentage of a man, an account of which is required of candidates at the examinations.

丨徹其事 I see through this plan.

如雷丨耳 [your fame] has pierced my ear like thunder.

丨穿 to get on or bore through; to run on a string.

語不丨串 this expression is irrelevant, the idea is not continuous.

丨通 passes through, as water in a tube, or ideas through the mind.

精忠丨日 his loyalty can bear the sunlight; — *i. e.* he is unimpeachable.

三歲丨‘女 for three years you have been through — our grain; — said of rats, *i. e.* officials.

萬丨家財 a very rich man.

丨跤 to wrestle, as an athlete.

射則丨兮 when he shoots, his arrow goes right through.

習丨成自然 the practiced expert finishes his work up soon.

慣 kwan' From *heart* and to *go through*; *q. d.* the heart gets accustomed to the thoughts passing through it; used with the next.

Habitual, experienced, accustomed to; addicted to, practiced in; inured to; the customary way.

丨熟 used to, expert in, habitual.

去丨 I often have been there

不丨 unused to, unskilled.

做丨 well practiced in, capable.

賭丨 addicted to gambling.

丨戰 a veteran in the wars.

不可縱丨 don't be too lenient — to the boys.

丨壞了 he is quite spoiled, — as a petted child.

不要丨了脾氣 don't get wedded to bad habits.

習丨 accustomed, skilled in.

摜 kwan' Like the last two.

To be familiar with; to take, to lift; to let drop; to push over.

丨珓盃 to throw down the divining-blocks.

丨瀆鬼神 to treat the gods irreverently.

丨在地下 pushed him down.

In *Cantonese*. To stumble, to slip.

丨倒一交 slipped down once.

反丨 playful.

祼 kwan' From *worship* and *real*; occurs interchanged with the next.

To pour out libations before the dead; to pour out and drink wine.

丨酒 to offer a libation of spirits.

丨奠 to pour out a libation.

灌 kwan' To run or flow together; to discharge, to disembogue into; collected, assembled; to water, as flowers; to give one drink, to force one to drink; luxuriant, bushy, as trees; much; used for the last, to pour out a libation; to pour into holes to fill them; to run full, as a mold.

丨木 trees with dense foliage; a class in Chinese botany comprising the *Althea* and *Morus*.

丨花 to water flowers.

丨醉 they made him drunk.

丨頂 a Budhist term for a kind of baptism or holy unction by sprinkling, which conferred goodness.

丨注 to flow into, as rivers into a lake.

丨漿 to pour liquid mortar into the holes in a pavement, or between the bricks in a wall.

老夫丨丨 the old man is truly honest.

丨水 to blow water — into pork.

丨藥 to force one to take physic.

盥 kwan' Composed of a *dish* under *water* in a *mortar*.

To wash the hands before worship; to wash in a basin.

丨洗 to wash clean.

丨櫛 to wash and comb, to make one's toilet.

丨誦 having washed, I read — your note; intimating the respect paid to it.

罐 礶 kwan' A jar, a gallipot, a crock; a mug, a cruse; a pitcher or jar having no spout, to contain water or oil.

水丨 a pitcher.

茶丨 a tea-canister.

蜜丨 little pewter jars for carrying honey.

瓦丨不離井上破 the earthen jar will get broken at last at the well, — so a soldier will go to battle once too often.

鑵 kwan' Like the last.

A water jar, a bucket to hold fluids.

柳丨 a bucket made of osiers or willow-twigs.

瓘 kwan' The name of a valuable stone, a variety of jade, which was used in making the 圭 or ancient official batons.

懽 kwan' From *heart* and *heron* as the phonetic; it is usually interchanged with 歡 *hwan*.

Joyful, pleased.

丨心 an approving mind, hearty congratulations.

丨忻未已 my pleasure or gratification is extreme.

Read ˏ*kwan*. Grieved, desolate.

丨丨愮愮 cast down, like one who has no bosom friend to complain to.

爟 kwan' Read ˏ*hwan*, and interchanged with 歡 to rejoice, glad, happy.

To set fire to a thing with the sun's heat, as Sui-jăn-shi did; to light a fire or beacon; hot, bright.

司丨 an ancient officer who brought fire in this manner.

祭丨 to worship the discoverer of fire.

鸛 kwan' A general name for herons of which there are many sorts; in north China it denotes the stork.

丨鳴于垤 the heron screams on the knoll.

白丨 the lesser white heron or egret (*Egretta alba*), which nestles on trees; it is in Chihli, the common stork, as 黑丨 is the black stork.

烏丨 the common heron (*Ardea cinere*), having an ashy plumage and a black tail.

雚 kwan' Another and older form of the last; a small mug or cup.

丨芄 a creeping plant which exudes a white juice.

丱 kwan' The two tufts made in dressing an infant's hair, called 亞角髻 at Canton; the character is intended to resemble them.

總角丨兮 bind up the two horn-like tufts.

KW'AN.

Old sound, kw'an. *In Canton*, fún; — *in Swatow*, kw'an; — *in Amoy*, kw'an; — *in Fuhchau*, kw'ang; — *in Shanghai*, kw'ê^{n}; — *in Chifu*, kw'an.

寬 ˎkw'an From 宀 a *covering* and 萈 a small-horned *large goat*.

Large, spacious, ample; gentle with, forgiving, easy, benignant to, clement, indulgent; slow, lax; gentleness; to make gentle; to extenuate; to widen, to enlarge, to relax; to forbear.

丨闊 wide, broad; ample for the purpose.

費用丨闊 more than enough for the occasion; profuse outlay.

丨大 or 丨量 liberal, indulgent.

丨容 a pleasing face; gracious to.

丨餘 an abundance, an overplus.

丨房大屋 large, roomy apartments; a spacious house.

丨猛並濟 gentleness was well tempered with severity.

丨恕 to forgive, to remit.

撫民以丨 to soothe the people by clemency.

丨宥 to let pass, to overlook.

丨縱 to connive at, too easy with; heedless of one's duties.

事丨 the affair is not urgent.

丨則得衆 kindness will win the hearts of the people.

丨懷 to alleviate one's grief.

在丨 be gentle, act forbearingly.

丨免 to forgive, to pass by.

丨緊帶 an elastic belt.

作丨一點 make it a little wider.

丨一尺 one foot wide.

眼界丨 a pleasing view, a charming prospect.

丨兮綽兮 how magnanimous and gentle!

丨必耐守 to be forbearing, to be considerate and patient.

丨限 or 丨緩 to extend the limit of time.

丨恩 courteous, condescending.

丨慰 to cheer up; sympathizing.

丨懷 to take things easy.

髖 ˎkw'an The hind quarters of an ox.

丨髀 the first bone of the leg, the femur; the thigh.

梡 ˋkw'an From *wood* and *end*; it is sometimes wrongly used for ˋ*wan* 碗 a bowl.

A small four-legged copper stand used in sacrifices; fuel cut up in faggots; name of a tree likened to the oak, whose fruit is edible; and of another like the *Terminalia*; a branch.

款 欵 ˋkw'an From to *breathe* or long for, and that which *satisfies* the longing; the second is the common form.

Something desired but unattainable; sincere, true, single-hearted; to venerate, to respect, to treat well; to knock at, to reach; to repay; to enumerate; a memorandum of; inscriptions, such as are on jars showing the date of manufacture; a proof stamp; a kind, a sort, an instance; a paragraph, an affair; an article, as of a treaty; a circumstance; a style or fashion.

丨待 to treat courteously.

闊丨 pompous, haughty.

一丨事 one affair or incident.

題丨 an autograph.

單丨 and 雙丨 the inscriptions on an autograph, with or without the name of the one for whom it was written.

近來丨段淒淸 affairs have latterly all gone against me.

各丨 or 丨丨 every sort, all sorts.

丨式 a sort, an article; a style, a manner; habit, as of a plant.

丨曲 according to the exigency.

歸丨 to repay a loan.

必須籌丨 we must consult on the ways and means.

丨段如何 what is his condition? how is he getting on?

丨丨然 longing for what is impracticable.

丨頭大 haughty, difficult of access.

缾有丨識 the jar has a record of its maker.

大明瓷丨 the inscription on the jar is the Ming dynasty.

丨丨飛 flying and flitting where it likes, as a dragon-fly.

丨丨中誠 wholly loyal and sincere.

丨留 to detain a visitor.

丨冬 a small root used as a tonic; but 丨冬花 designates the dried flowers of the loquat (*Eriobotrya*); the tea is used in coughs.

窾 ˎkw'an Hollow, like an empty vessel or decayed tree; dried up; inexperienced, ignorant; an empty pate.

丨啓 an uninformed mind.

丨竅 an empty hole.

丨空 a vacuum.

中心丨櫃 my heart is like an empty casket; — *i. e.* I am totally indifferent.

鍁 kw'anˀ A branding-iron; a kind of gridiron; to solder.

丨刻 to brand or burn in.

丨縫 to seal the seam, as a letter with wax.

KWANG.

Old sounds, kw'ang, *and* kung. *In Canton*, kwong *and* kwăng; — *in Swatow*, kwăng *and* kw'ang; — *in Amoy*, kong; — *in Fuhchau*, kwòng; — *in Shanghai*, kwong *and* hwong; — *in Chifu*, kwong.

光 ꜀*kwang* The original form was composed of 儿 a *man* with 火 *fire* above it intimating the brightness of mind.

Light, luster; brilliant, illustrious, bright; honor, glory, éclat; the presence of a distinguished person; naked, smooth, bare, bald; as an *adverb*, only, barely, solely; about, simply, to illuminate, to adorn; to reflect credit on; the lenses in spectacles.

日 | daylight.

| 鮮 smooth and new, as a dress.

| 頭 bald; bareheaded.

夜 | a pearl.

主 | the lord of light, said of the sun and of the gods.

| 彩 splendid, brilliant; said too of one who is just shaved clean.

| 射 a sunbeam, a gleam of light.

放 | brilliant, sparkling, as a gem.

| 景 state of affairs, aspect of things, circumstances, exigencies; a landscape.

十個人 | 景 just about ten men were there.

分外 | too bright.

豪 | a coruscation like an aurora; the aureola on divine personages.

圓 | the copper nimbus on an image of Budha.

放 | 蟲 a glow-worm.

候 | I await the light — of your presence.

借 | to borrow another's clothes or finery; to ask one to yield the path; by your leave.

| 宗耀祖 to make one's ancestors illustrious.

| 身來 I came alone, without any baggage.

食精 | it is all eaten up, a bare cupboard.

| 陰似箭 the day goes like an arrow.

| 額 he increased the set number.

| 天化日 in open day, before all the world.

水 | 接天 the bright horizon at sea.

| 你一個人 only you are left, you alone.

沒有沾一點 | I have not made a cent, I have taken nothing.

耗得精 | it is clean gone, nothing at all left.

天 | 早 at early dawn.

賞 | give me the pleasure of your company.

叨 | be kind now; oblige me, — and give me better coin.

回 | flickering of a lamp.

放毫 | to sparkle, as a star.

胱 ꜀*kwang* The bladder, called 膀 |; the second character refers to its breadth.

洸 ꜀*kwang* Also read *hwang*꜄

Water glistening and sparkling in the sun as it bubbles and foams; a small river in Shantung near Yen-cheu fu, a feeder of the Grand Canal; wide; distant, angry.

武夫 | | how martial the warriors looked!

有 | 有潰 you are cold and angry — towards me.

觥 ꜀*kwang* Ardent, valorous.

| | 將軍 a courageous leader; a general with military ardor.

觵 / 觥 ꜀*kwang* A cup made of rhinoceros' horns holding five gills; anything crooked resembling such a cup.

| | obstinate, determined.

| 羊 a great ram.

我姑酌彼兕 | I will just fill up that wine-cup — for a drink.

廣 ꜂*kwang* From a *shelter* and *yellow*.

Broad, extensive, wide, spacious; large, ample; stout; the breadth of, as of a room; to make broad, to enlarge, to extend; to diffuse; enlarged; a squad of fifteen chariots; occurs in many names of places, but when used alone refers to Canton city or Kwangtung province.

| 行 everywhere made known; to propagate, as to teach doctrine.

| 大 large as a vast place; profound, as deep learning.

| 布天下 circulate it through the empire.

| 揚 to diffuse far and wide.

量 | able to drink much; kind and lenient to others' faults.

| 交 an extensive acquaintance.

見識不 | his experience is very limited.

| 量多少 what is the breadth?

| 運 the area of a region, its dimensions; the superficies.

| 貨 goods from Canton.

| 東人 or | 東仔 Cantonese.

桄 *kwang*꜄ From *wood* and *bright* as the phonetic.

A cut-water; a kind of palm, the | 榔 belonging to the genus *Caryota*; its wood is highly prized at Canton for sedan thills.

機 | the beam of a loom.

絖 / 纊 *kwang*꜄ Fine floss not yet sorted; silky cotton not spun.

| 絮 unsorted cotton.

絲 | refuse silk left after spooling.

厥篚纖 | their baskets contained fine silks and soft floss.

三軍挾 | the soldiers had quilted garments.

屬 | 之際 near death, dying; floss is used to test the breathing.

In *Cantonese*, A loop; to latch; to fasten two doors with a string; to brush against, to run over one in the street.

丨門 fasten the door.

丨狗 tie up the dog.

睇丨 look out, [lest I] run over you! — a chairman's cry.

誑 From *words* and *wild*.
kw'ang Incoherent, wild talk; to delude by it; to deceive, to mislead.

丨言 wild talk.

欺丨 to impose on, to make a fool of.

不要丨我 don't mislead me.

幼子常視無丨 children never delude anybody.

遞相欺丨 they mutually fooled each other.

丨騙不下 you can't hoax me, that dodge wont go down.

丨于彼 I was taken in by him.

KW'ANG.

Old sounds, k'ung, *and* gung. *In Canton*, kwong, kw'ong, kwang, hong, *and* fong; — *in Swatow*, kw'ang, k'eng, *and* kang; — *in Amoy*, k'ong *and* kong; — *in Fuhchau*, kw'ang *and* kw'ong; — *in Shanghai*, kw'ong *and* hwong; — *in Chifu*, kw'ong.

匡 From a *receptacle* and *king*; occurs used with the next; as a primitive, it often imparts some
kw'ang of its meaning to the compounds.

A square box to hold cooked rice or millet; regular, square; correct; to rectify, to direct; to assist, to deliver; deflected, not upright.

丨救 to rescue.

丨正 to reform, to put in order.

丨方 regular, placed properly.

跂丨大 very lame.

旣丨旣敕 you have been correct and sedulous.

以丨不逮 do not spend all your income.

丨輔 to sustain, as an aid does.

以丨王國 in order to rescue the royal kingdom.

一丨天下 he united and rectified the country.

丨州 an old name for Yun-nan fu in Yunnan; and also for Ta-ming fu 大明府 in Chihli.

丨人其如予何 what can the people of Kw'ang do to me? — some say that this was a town near the present K'a-fung fu, others put it in the state of Lu.

筐 A basket of a square shape without a cover or bail; a
kw'ang general name for open baskets; the bottom of a bed; to put into baskets.

丨筥 open baskets, such as presents are sent in.

丨牀 a basket bed, a basinet.

一丨線 one hank of thread.

籮丨 large baskets or bins.

燈籠丨 the lantern, as distinguished from the candle in it.

框 The end or head of a coffin where it can be opened; a
kw'ang' bordering, like that which holds a pane of glass; the frame of a thing, which defines or defends it; the skeleton or frame of a lamp.

丨檔 a sash, as of a window; a frame, as of a door.

閶 From *door* and *square*; interchanged with the last.
kw'ang The frame of a door or window which is set into the wall.

門丨 a door-frame.

牆丨 a wall which incloses, or frames the opening; a surrounding wall.

苑丨 the wall around a yard.

洭 One of the headwaters of the River Siang in the south of
kw'ang Hunan near the mountains, in Kwei-yang hien 桂陽縣 called Kwei shui 桂水 or Cassia Water.

恇 From *heart* and *squared*.
kw'ang To fear; apprehensive lest one will not act aright; timid.

嗟丨丨兮誰留 oh, how I am scared! who can stay here?

衆不丨懼 none of them had the least fear about it.

狂 From 犬 *dog* and 㞷 *sprouting* contracted to 王 *king*.
kw'ang Mad, raving, wild, incoherent, insane, crazed; unable to judge of things; cruel, irascible; eccentric, enthusiastic, mad on; rash, excitable, impudent; a term of disparagement, as, he is daft on, has a mania for; a mad fellow.

丨犬 a mad dog; an epithet for a conceited person.

丨妄 vicious, extravagant, raging.

酒丨 silly from drink.

發丨 out of his head.

書丨 pedantic; a bibliomaniac; one who loves to scribble.

丨士 or 丨儒 a conceited fellow, a pedant.

丨躁 light minded, eccentric.

丨性 headstrong.

癲丨 delirious, wandering.

丨蕩 stolid, dumpish, lethargic.

猖丨 outrageous, violent, loud-talking.

丨言 lying talk; nonsense.

丨者進取 an ardent man has entered on the course of study.

丨風大作 a furious gust came rushing down.

丨吠 [only] a mad dog's bark; — *i. e.* a sudden passion.

丨童之丨也且 oh, you fool of all foolish fellows!

許人尤之衆穉且丨 the people of Hü blame me, but they are all like hasty, captious children.

乃見丨且 but I see this madcap.

誆ʼ Wild, lying talk intended to
ˎkw'ang mislead; to lie to, to deceive; to cheat.

丨騙 to swindle, to jockey.

眶ʼ The *frame* of the *eye*, the
*kw'ang*ʼ eye-socket; the corner or canthus of the eye.

高丨 sunken eyes.

眼丨大 proud, supercilious.

淚滿丨 tears filled his eyes.

大眼丨 a careless look; one who thinks little of the price of a thing.

勯ʼ Zealous, prompt; an appella-
ˎkw'ang tion of the first rank of the Beile 貝勒 princes among the Manchus.

丨勷 quick, in haste; an emergency.

逛ʼ From to *go* and *wildly*.
*kw'ang*ʼ To ramble, to wander about; to visit and see a place; to go to and fro, to roam without a particular object.

去丨 to take a walk.

丨一丨 to go out for an airing.

遊丨 to go on a pleasure excursion; to go sight-seeing.

丨街 to stroll through the streets.

丨廟 to visit the temples.

丨的腿酸 I've walked till my legs ache.

俇ʼ From *man* and *wild*.
*kw'ang*ʼ Abrupt, quick, sudden; to go far off.

魂丨丨而南征 his soul has gone far down to the southern regions.

壙ʼ From *earth* and *broad* as the
*kw'ang*ʼ phonetic; it is sometimes erroneously used for *ˋkung* 礦 a mine.

The vault or pit under a tomb, in which the bodies are laid; it is sometimes entered by an underground brick passage at the side; a grave, a sepulcher; a tumulus or mound grave; a solitude, a desert.

丨野 a wilderness, a sepulchral wilderness.

丨埌 a wild region; the concave vault of heaven.

出丨 to be buried outside of the great tomb.

進丨 to make a tumulus over a coffin; to put it in a vault; — both modes are common.

曠ʼ From *day* and *broad*; used with the last.
*kw'ang*ʼ Vacant, empty, waste; spacious, extensive, far distant; leisurely; relaxation; of long duration, olden; to leave empty.

丨遠 or 丨隔 far sundered.

無丨庶官 no useless placemen in the offices.

丨日 to waste the day; otium, laziness.

外無丨夫 there were no unmarried men abroad.

空丨 a vacant waste.

開丨 to occupy wastes and wilds.

丨功 to neglect one's duties.

丨安宅 to abandon the quiet dwelling.

頒丨典 unusual favors conferred by the emperor.

懭ʼ To hate, as with impotent
*kw'ang*ʼ malice.

丨恨 to abhor, to bear deep dislike to.

Read *kung.*ʼ Violent, impracticable.

丨悍 scornful, haughty.

KWÉI.

Old sounds, kwei, kei, kúi, kek, ket, *and* kút. *In Canton*, kwei, kúi, *and* fúi; — *in Swatow*, kúi, ku, *and* kwai; — *in Amoy*, kúi, k'úi, húi, *and* kòé; — *in Fuhchau*, kwi, kié, *and* koi; — *in Shanghai*, kwé *and* kü; — *in Chifu*, kwéi.

歸ʼ **归**ʼ *ˎkwéi* } From 止 to *stop* with 婦 a *wife* contracted and 𠂤 as a phonetic; *q. d.* the wife stops at home after marriage; the contracted form is very common in cheap books.

To return, to go or send back; to revert to the original place or state; to become loyal; to restore, to betake one's self to, as for help or shelter; to end, to terminate; to depart from; to belong to; to go home; to return, as a divorced wife; to marry out; gathered to one's husband; to send a present; to promise; to unite, to assemble; a terminus *ad quem*; a home, a country, a refuge; in *mathematics*, to divide by one figure.

丨入 makes part of, belongs to, inserted in.

葉落丨根 the leaves fall back to their root, — so one returns to his home.

丨服 or 丨降 to submit; to yield, as rebels.

丨咎 to bring the fault on the right one.

催丨 hurry home! a name given to the cuckoo.

丨還你 I send it back to you.

無所 丨 without a home, no resting-place, no refuge; — said of wandering ghosts as well as houseless mortals.

丨古 or 丨世 dead, departed.

丨寧 a bride's visit to her parents.

丨佳城 or 丨于土 returned to dust, to be buried.

丨田 to resign and go home.

丨老 to resign on account of age.

士如丨妻 the gentleman is to bring home his bride.

丨除法 rules of arithmetic.

大九丨 and 小九丨 division and addition, — on the abacus.

天下丨心 the country looks to me.

誰將西丨 who will go west and give in their allegiance!

丨無 to be annihilated.

丨結 the end of a career, the winding-up of an affair; upshot; a composition to creditors.

分丨本行 to analyze and bring out the original constituents.

翻去丨 gone home; 使佢去丨 send him home (*Cantonese*).

丨之烏有 where is it to come from? — as money to pay you.

物丨原主 the thing must revert it is first owner.

丨與丨與 let us go home, go home!

丨孔子豚 he gave Confucius a pig.

當丨 roots of the false sarsaparilla or spikenard, (*Aralia edulis*), much used as a tonic by women.

百歲之後丨于其居 on the lapse of a century, I shall go to my husband's abode.

皈 *kwéi* From *white* and to *return*; used alone by the Budhists in the sense of the preceding.

To conform to law, to comply with.

丨依佛法 to attend to and follow the laws of Budha.

三丨 to follow Budha, the law, and the priesthood.

巋 *kwéi* A group of small hills, which look as if they had been brought together.

丨崋穹崇 high and grand-looking, as a pile of buildings.

Read *wéi* Solitary.

丨然 alone, by itself.

龜 龟 *kwéi* The character is intended to represent the general appearance of a tortoise, the top depicting its snake-like *head*, below which are drawn the *shell*, *feet* and *tail*; it is the 213th radical of characters relating to *chelonia*; the contracted form is usual.

The tortoise and terrapin, regarded as the chief of mailed animals, and employed as an emblem, of longevity; the shell; applied to some kinds of beetles; ornamented; to advance.

丨背 arched over like a tortoise's back; a kind of hexagonal ornament.

丨殼 a tortoise's carapace.

丨板 the breast-plate or plastron.

金丨 a small species of *Emys*, whose shell has 28 plates on its edges, and therefore much used in divination.

丨脚 a sea anemone.

水丨 a sea-turtle.

秦丨 the land tortoise, so called from its occurring in Shensi.

綠毛丨 the green-haired terrapin from Sz'ch'uen, on which a species of conferva grows.

丨齡 long life.

丨貨 a coin, from an old use of shells or cowries.

見乎蓍丨 [fates] may be discovered by the straws and shell.

螭看丨趺 [made with a] dragon's top and tortoise crouching, — referring to the official tablets before tombs supported on tortoises.

丨鶴同春 [may your] days be long like the tortoise and crane's.

靈丨 the penis, referring to a tortoise's head.

丨爪 or 丨頭 a procurer.

In *Cantonese*. A pie, from its resemblance in shape.

邽 *kwéi* An ancient district lying on the River Wéi in the present Ts'in cheu 秦州 in the south-east part of Kansuh; there was a 上丨縣 and a 下丨縣 in which some noted battles were anciently fought.

圭 珪 *kwéi* From *earth* repeated; the addition of *gem* was to show its material.

A small stone scepter or baton, anciently given to nobles as a sign of rank, and held in both hands at levees; it was a tablet with a rounded top and square base, and made 9, 7, or 5 inches long, according to its bearer's rank; one sort was also carried before the king like a mace; a nominal measure equal to a pinch, or six grains of millet, though others say 64 grains, or what three fingers can grasp.

執丨 to hold the baton; having political rank.

白丨之詩 the ode of the White Scepter, — a reminder to be attentive, referring to the 白丨之玷 flaw in the pure jade baton.

袿 *kwéi* From *dress* and a *baton*; it is unlike 褂 a robe.

The upper gown or robe of women, which was thought to have some resemblance to a baton; a sleeve; a lapel.

簪珥光彩丨裳鮮明 her head-dress was magnificent, and her robes bright and new.

閨 *kwéi* From *door* and *baton*; the shape of the door resembled the baton, and it stood alone.

The door which separates the public rooms of a house from the private; the women's apartments; unmarried girls; still at home; female, ladylike, feminine.

丨女 a virgin, a young lady.

丨門 or 丨閤 the door to the inner apartments; the females; shrinking from view, modest.

深｜ a lady's chamber.

金｜籍 an official register of scholars in the Han dynasty.

｜秀 an educated girl; girls.

蘭｜ the flowery boudoir, a courtesan.

老｜女 an old maid.

寂寂春｜ a retiring young lady.

鮭 ˎkwéi One name for the fresh-water white porpoise; its liver is reckoned to be unhealthy, and the Cantonese avoid eating it.

｜菜 an old term for flesh and vegetable diet in Chehkiang.

Read ˎwa. The ｜蠪 is a Taoist god, represented as a child two feet high holding a sword.

雉 ˎkwéi A small species of blackcap, with white on its shoulders, called 子｜; it is common at Peking, and resembles a miniature magpie.

嬀 ˎkwéi The name of a river, the ｜汭 in the east of Shansi, and of a place near it where Shun obtained his two wives from Yao; crafty, artful.

｜州 an old name in the T'ang of Yen-k'ing cheu 延慶州 in the north of Chihli, near Süenhwa fu.

頍 ˎkwéi To raise the head; a strap of silk which retains the cap on the head; it is put under the chin, or hangs down behind.

有｜者弁 these with their leathern caps bound on,—who are they?

規 ˎkwéi From 見 to *see* and 夫 a *man*; some say that 矢 an *arrow* was the original form, but this arose probably from 矩 being under that radical.

A pair of compasses; a law, a regulation, a bye-law; custom, usage; a fee, a douceur, a vail; a rate for taking a farm; to rule men by law; to line out, to draw a line; to regulate, to plan; the disk of the sun or moon.

｜例 a regulation, a law.

｜矩 or ｜模 usage, regulations.

月半｜ the moon at her quartering.

收月｜ received the monthly fee.

節｜ official perquisites paid thrice a year to superiors.

定｜ to settle upon a rate, to close a bargain.

額｜ a fixed fee.

行｜ bye-laws of a hong or guild.

｜正 to admonish others.

相｜ mutual remonstrances.

私收陋｜ to receive illegal fees, intimating that it is disgraceful to take them.

｜避 to pervert or evade the laws.

｜諫 to remonstrate with a superior.

｜畫 to draw diagrams or lines.

不逾｜ do not overpass the law.

摫 ˎkwéi To cut out cloth for garments; to divide by a pattern.

嫢 娊 ˎkwéi From *woman* and *rule* or *seeing;* also read ˋtsui, while *hien*ˋ is another sound of the second form.

A graceful, elegant woman, especially one with a small waist, was anciently so called in Shansi; the fashion of tight lacing was once common in northern China.

鱴 ˎkwéi A fish shaped like a tadpole; it seems to refer to a species of sun-fish (*Orthagoriscus*), or perhaps a *Tetraodon;* it is called the 河豚 or river pig, and "can inflate its belly and float; it has no gills or gall-bladder, and when it hits against anything, it makes a noise."

｜魚 a local name for the Yangtsz' porpoise.

槻 ˎkwéi A tree whose wood makes good bows, called 樊｜; a kind of indelible ink is made by steeping the bark in water.

瑰 kwéiˋ A perfect pearl of a reddish tint; rare, extraordinary, admirable.

瓊｜ a variety of pearl; a kind of red breccia marble.

｜意琦行 your just ideas and admirable actions.

玫｜茶平肝 a tea of red roses soothes the liver; — quiets the temper.

玫｜紫 a purplish red, or reddish brown color.

鬼 ˋkwéi Formed of a demon's *head* on a man's *legs*, with 厶 *crafty* added to denote its guile; it forms the 194th radical of characters relating to devils.

The spirit of a dead man before it is enshrined in the hall; a manes, that which the soul turns to at death; a ghost, a goblin, an apparition, a specter; a devil; a horrid repulsive object, a sordid wretch; foreigners are so stigmatized, because (so the Cantonese say,) their blue eyes suggested the malice, and their shrill voices resembled the plaintive cry, of ghosts; foreign, as a lock, or any other thing made abroad.

你見｜嗎 have you seen a ghost? what are you afraid of?

｜頭風 a whirlwind, an eddy of wind.

鴉片｜ a besotted opium smoker.

｜鼠 a suspicious person.

說｜話 empty words, false commendation; to whisper, to lisp, to speak with aside.

｜神 the gods, both good and evil; supernatural beings.

犯｜ under demoniac influences, possessed.

打｜ to exorcise a place, to drive off evil spirits; it is annually done about new-year's time by the Board of Rites.

丨 鳥 a name for the ringed crow (*corvus torquatus.*)
丨 迷 你 you are possessed.
番 丨, or 丨 子, or 洋 丨 子, an opprobrious term for foreigners.
丨 宿 the 23d constellation, answering to the stars γ δ η ϑ in Cancer.
冤 丨 the unavenged spirit of a murdered man.
入 丨 門 關 he has entered the door of the demons; — dead.
丨 商 量 consulting together privately, so as not to be understood. (*Shanghai.*)
攝 精 丨 acted on by an ogre; bewitched.
丨 打 算 two villains joining to swindle a person.
小 丨 頭 a penurious man. (*Shanghai.*)
冒 失 丨 a heedless booby.
丨 火 will-o'-wisp.
食 人 丨 demons who devour men; the Budhist 羅 刹 *rakshasa*, the original cannibal islanders of Ceylon; also a class of demons of both sexes invoked by sorcerers.
丨 車 a goatsucker (*Caprimulgus stictomus.*)
丨 頭 丨 腦 to hide and seek; to peep about.
丨 拿 丨 a rogue catching a rogue.
覃 及 丨 方 [the indignation against you] extends even to the demon's regions.
門 丨 the catch in a door bar.
講 丨 or 丨 唧 唧 to whisper to one aside, to speak mutteringly.
家 丨 害 家 神 the family imp has injured the family god; — the junior has deceived the elder.

癸 ʻkwéi The original form is like two sticks laid across to represent water flowing into the ground in all directions.

The last of the ten stems, which belongs to the north and to water; to consider; to belong to.
呼 庚 丨 to call out the watchword.
天 丨 至 arrived at puberty, said of a girl.

垝 ʻkwéi To destroy or demolish a wall; dilapidated; a ruinous wall.

佹 ʻkwéi To duplicate, to add on; resembling, near; short posts, small stanchions; used for the next, to deceive; simulating.
爭 爲 丨 辯 they urged each other to pretend to be for him.

詭 ʻkwéi From *words* and *dangerous*.
To deceive, to cheat, to defraud; to vilify, to defame; to oppose good things; to blame, to reprimand; malicious, perverse; odd, unusual.
丨 譎 crafty, fraudulent, cunning.
莫 從 丨 嘴 don't hearken to cunning tales.
丨 詐 lying; treacherous.
丨 天 to oppose Heaven.
丨 計 多 端 full of schemes and tricks.
爲ʾ 之 丨 遇 一 朝 而 獲 十 [I drove] for him so as to cunningly meet them, and in one morning he got ten — birds.
丨 異 uncommon and doubtful, strange, wonderful.
無 縱 丨 隨 don't give way to wily and obsequious people.
丨 話 的 it's all put on, or make believe, as a boy's sobbing.

恑 ʻkwéi To change, to alter, to repent; standing alone.
丨 變 to alter and trim, in order to entangle another.
丨 異 to adapt one's self to exigencies; to lay snares for.

祪 ʻkwéi This is regarded as a synonym of 庋 and 禔 though seldom used.
To worship the five mountains by sacrificing upon them.
丨 縣 to worship the protecting mountain outside of the court.

厬 ʻkwéi Water dried up, as in a fountain or well; water exhausted.
泉 丨 the spring is dried up.

宄 ʻkwéi From *covering* and *nine;* it is like *kiuʾ* 究 to examine in its form.
Traitors; schemers, villains; an officer who plans sedition when pretending to be loyal; to rob.
姦 丨 traitors and enemies, in and out of the court.
結 爲 內 丨 he was in league with the traitors inside.

軌 ʻkwéi From *carriage* and *nine;* it occurs used for the last.
A rut, a trace; an orbit, a path; a vestige; a law, a rule; to imitate; to hatch treason; the hub of a wheel.
不 丨 unconformable, aberrant, irregular; seditious, lawless.
丨 道 a constant path, an orbit; to follow rules.
城 門 之 丨 兩 馬 之 力 與 are the ruts at the gate of a city made by a single two-horse carriage alone?
丨 法 or 丨 範 a rule; a mode like a rut, which is not easy to follow, or to get out of.
濟 盈 不 濡 丨 the full ford will not wet the axle of my carriage.

氿 ʻkwéi A spring issuing from the side of a hill.
有 冽 丨 泉 these cold waters flowing from the spring — let them not soak my faggots.

匭 ʻkwéi A box for papers, a casket bound with metal and fit to hold seals; to box up; to bind around with cords.
包 丨 菁 茅 [they brought] the caskets wrapped in sedge and rushes.

簋 ʻkwéi From 竹 *bamboo*, 皿 *dish*, and 艮 *good* between them.
A round shaped basket or vessel, woven of fine splints, used for holding grain at sacrifices, made square within, and reckoned to hold twelve 升 or pints.
丨 碗 a large dish or platter.
九 大 丨 nine platters; — an entertainment, a complete set-out.

木 丨 wooden dishes to contain the grain offered at the semi-annual worship of Confucius.
於我乎每食四 丨 he then gave us four dishes at each meal.
食土 丨 [Yao and Shun] ate from earthen platters.

晷 ʻkwéi From *day* and *fault*, because the gnomon notes the variations in the sun's course.
A gnomon or the shadow which it makes; a dial; day-time; the day.
日 丨 a sun-dial.
日影光 丨 the sun's shadow goes over the bright dial.
焚膏繼 丨 he burned the candles to eke out the day, or lengthen the shadow, as Han Wăn.
飛 丨 the flying shadow; time flies.

貴 kwéiˀ Formed of 貝 *precious* and 臾 a *basket*, which was an old form of 蕢 a *grass*; *q.d.* pearls in a basket.
Not mean or cheap; honorable, noble, exalted, illustrious; dignified, good, — and hence in direct address used as an appellative, you, your; dear, high-priced; precious, valuable; honor; to give dignity to, to esteem, to honor, to desire; to value.
丨 賤 dear — cheap; noble — base; patricians — plebeians; your — my.
尊 丨 有德 specially honor and respect the virtuous.
丨 相 a noble, ingenuous face.
丨 丨 to honor the noble.
丨 大人 or 丨 大臣 your Excellency; honored Sir.
丨 姓 what is your surname?
金 丨 precious; priceless, as a medicine.
丨 妃 and 丨 人 terms for two grades of imperial concubines.
不 丨 乎此 it cannot exceed this; not to value this.
嬌 丨 a darling, a little pet.
有何 丨 幹 what is your business with me?
甚麼 丨 業 what is your calling?
丨 得很 or 甚 丨 very dear, exorbitant.
提高 丨 手 lift up your hand; please let me off.
丨 細 elegant manners; delicate.
丨 器 precious things said of children.
丨 合於秦 he wished to form a league with Tsʻin.
事 丨 原心 their original intentions in the affair; their real desire.
丨 重物件 a rare article.
不 丨 異物 do not unduly value strange curiosities.
正 丨 有恒 in government, be consitent and constant.

憒 kwéiˀ Troubled, anxious; harassed and perturbed.
丨 丨 vexed, confused.
丨 亂 all in a maze of doubts.
昏 丨 stupefied, dazed, as when suddenly scared.

桂 kwéiˀ From *tree* and *baton* as the phonetic.
The tree which produces cinnamon and cassia, the *Laurus cassia, Cinnamomum aromaticum*, and other sorts; the Chinese *Olea fragrans*, a fragrant plant, used as a metaphor for literary honors; it is often difficult to distinguish which of these two plants is intended; spotted, figured.
丨 皮 cassia bark.
丨 子 cassia buds.
丨 皮油 cassia oil.
肉 丨 thick cinnamon bark.
月 丨 子 immature flowers of cinnamon, dried as a drug.
丨 林府 the capital of Kwangsi on the 丨 江 or Cassia River.
丨 花 the *Olea fragrans*.
手攀丹 丨 his hand has plucked the red olive; — *met.* he has become a Hanlin.
丨 子蘭孫 his posterity is famed for literary honors.
蟾宮折 丨 or 折 丨 葉 to break the olive twig in the moon, — the picture is thought to be most distinct in autumn; *met.* to become a *küjin*.
米珠薪 丨 rice was like pearls and fuel as cinnamon, — in the famine.
丨 花布 figured calicoes.
丨 圓 dried longan fruits.

In *Fuhchau*. A classifier of things strung, as beads or keys.

愧 媿 kwéiˀ Ashamed, abashed, disconcerted; bashful, shrinking from notice; to feel ashamed when detected; remorseful, conscience-stricken.
羞 丨 shamefaced, modest.
負 丨 conscious of guilt.
丨 我無才 I am mortified at my stupidity.
不 丨 不怍 neither ashamed nor discouraged.
問心有 丨 ask yourself if you have any regrets.
不 丨 于人 he is not ashamed before men.
無所 丨 I am perfectly innocent.
丨 死 excessively chagrined.

跪 kwéiˀ From *feet* and *dangerous*.
To kneel, to bow down when reverencing another; a crab's legs, because they are bent.
丨 下 kneel down.
拜 丨 bow and kneel as in worship.
丨 鍊 to kneel on chains.
丨 膝 knee-pads, or garter-fronts.
丨 送 he knelt as he bade him good-bye.
丨 丨 四大四小 four of the legs are large and four small, as the claws and legs of the hermit-crab.
丨 香 kneeling and holding incense — in worship, or as a truant scholar.

鱖 *kwéi'* *ˌchüé* From *fish* and *stiff*, because this fish cannot easily turn; also read *ki'* and *küeh*,

A general name in books for variegated perches, also called 鯚魚 and 石柱魚 a rock bass; one kind has a broad belly, large mouth, small scales, thick skin, flesh firm and sweet; the body is striped with black bands and the fins are spinous; abundant in Chehkiang, and resembles the garoupa (*Serranus*) of Canton, but is nearer a *Sciæna;* the natives say it buries itself in the mud in winter.

桃花水丨魚肥 when the peach-blossoms fall on the water, the marbled perch is in prime order.

撅 *kwéi'* To hold up the dress when crossing a ford.

Read *küeh,* To hold a thing in the hand; to throw down, to strike.

劌 *ˈkwéi'* To wound, to cut open; to injure.

不丨於義 do not violate justice.

丨痛之後尙忌操刀 after you feel the hurt, then you begin to think it is best not to handle the knife.

君子比德于玉廉而不丨 the wise man regards virtue as a gem, and will on no account wound his principles.

劊 *kwéi'* To cut off, to amputate; to decollate; to cut in two.

丨子 or 丨子手 an executioner.

儈 *kwéi'* From *man* and to *assemble;* it much resembles *ˌsăng* 僧 a priest.

One who acts as broker to keep up, or settle the price of goods; to give the wink to.

市丨 or 牙丨 one who studies the markets, and acts as agent in sales; a bull or a bear in the stock market.

丨心 to communicate by a nod, to tell by a sign.

廥 *kwéi'* An out-house for grass or fodder.

天丨 and 丨積 names of two groups of stars; the last is near the Pleiades.

癐 *kwéi'* Very sick; a grievous disease.

Read *ˌwéi.* To halloo.

丨丨 to bawl after; used in Kiangsu.

In *Cantonese.* Very tired, worn out, exhausted, weak, weary; like the next.

够丨 no strength left.

脚丨 weary from walking.

攰 *kwéi'* Strength all given out; wearied, exhausted, as from a war.

彫丨之民 the people are entirely exhausted and weakned.

途長而足丨 my limbs are wearied from the long travel.

檜 *kwéi'* A tree like the juniper or cypress, whose durable timber is prized for coffins, boats and oars; in Japan, the stately Japanese cypress (*Retinispora obtusa*) is so called; a sort of catapult.

丨柏 the Chinese cypress.

輸丨 ornaments on a coffin.

丨楫松舟 oars of cypress and boats of pine.

鄶 *kwai'* From *place* and to *assemble;* it was also once written like the last from the cedars which grew there.

Name of a small ancient principality, and of a city, now Yung-yang hien 榮陽縣 in K'ai-fung fu in Honan; its limits varied much at different periods.

澮 *kwéi'* From *water* and to *assemble.*

Streams flowing together; a gutter or drain in a field; a great tank for irrigating a thousand fields; a reservior, like those in India.

溝丨 a sluice, a ditch.

涓丨 a brook, a rivulet.

丨河 the northern branch of the River Hwai, which rises near Kwéi-teh fu in Honan, and joins it at Wu-ho hien 五河縣 near its mouth.

丨州 an old name of Yih-ch'ing hien 翼城縣 in the south-west of Shansi, derived from the 丨河 a tributary of the River Făn which flows by it.

獪 *kwai'* Crafty, cunning; one who stirs up strife.

狡丨 deceitful, a seditious plotter.

旝 *kwéi'* A flag or banner with which to signalize; a machine like a catapult, made of sticks so placed as to throw stones when sprung.

丨動而鼓 when the flags moved the drums were sounded.

膾 **鱠** *ˈkwai'* From *flesh* or *fish* and to *assemble.*

Flesh or fish hashed fine; living fish are often thus treated; a meat salad; to mince fine; to hash up.

丨炙 hash up meat and bake it.

魚丨 a fish salad.

炰鼈丨鯉 they have roast terrapin and minced carp.

丨殘魚 or 吳王魚 the Chinese white-bait (*Leucosoma argentea*), the 白飯魚 of Canton 麪長魚 of Shanghai, or 銀魚 silver fish, so called from a legend that it was transformed from some hash which the king of Wu threw overboard when sailing on the Yangtsz' River.

下鍋再丨 put it into the pan and mix it up again.

禬 *kwéi'* From *worship* and to *assemble*, referring to the grouping of all blessings.

To pray that the shades of a man may not harass one, but be cut off from the house; to call on the gods; to pray alone.

櫃匱鐀柜 *kwéi'* From *honorable* as the phonetic, added to *wood*, *case* or *metal*, denoting that valuables are stored away; the fourth contracted form is common, and also read *kü'*

A case with drawers or a door; a press, a closet, a locker, a chest; a drawer; a treasury; to store away; the second form (read *kw'éi'*) also means exhausted, wearied; to fail in.

書 丨 a bookcase.

衣裳 丨 a wardrobe, a bureau, an almirah; a cabinet.

押 丨 a deposit given when renting a house.

寄 丨 a clerk who aids the manager; a junior partner.

水 丨 covered water jars, a street precaution against fires.

本 丨 貨物 the goods of the firm; our stock.

打羅 丨 a machine for bolting flour.

廚 丨 子 a case for storing books, food, or other things; a pantry.

丨 圍 or 丨 檯 a counter in a shop.

金縢 丨 chronicles; archives of state.

日給不 丨 the daily allowance was not deficient.

丨 桶 a drawer; an open chest or box.

孝子不 丨 永錫爾類 on such an unceasingly filial son, honors will ever be conferred.

膭䏿 *kwéi'* A sudden pain in the loins, a stitch in the back; a shooting pain across the back.

丨 腰 my back pains me much.

筀 *kwéi'* A fine kind of bamboo growing in Kwangtung and Chehkiang; its sprouts are not eaten; and a wound from it is dangerous; the joints are two feet long, which makes them much in demand for opium pipes; and the fine long splints are prized for weaving; the leaves are small.

丨 籢篋 a fine covered basket used for sending things.

丨 竹鎗 bamboo opium pipes.

KW'ÉI.

Old sounds, kw'ei, gwei, k'ui, k'et, k'ek, k'ít, *and* gít. *In Canton*, kw'ei, *and* fúi; — *in Swatow*, k'úi *and* kⁿúi; — *in Amoy*, k'úi, kúi, hòé, *and* k'òé; — *in Fuhchau*, kw'i, hwi, k'ié, kié, ki, *and* koi; — *in Shanghai*, kw'è, hwé, *and* kü; — *in Chifu*, kw'ói.

虧 *kw'éi* From a kind of *bird* and *breath* issuing.

Shortness of breath; to pant; a failure; broken, lacking; a deficiency, a defect; diminution; waning, as the moon; to injure; a grievance, an affront; wanting, not enough; to trouble one; owing to, in consequence of.

丨 了你 I thank you much.

丨 人 to annoy, to trouble another.

丨 心之人 an ingrate, one lost to all honor.

吃 丨 or 受 丨 made a mistake; forced to stomach the loss; ill used; I lost on the venture.

丨 負 deficient in, as in recompensing for mercies received; ungrateful.

丨 得伊 timely aid. (*Shanghai.*)

丨 我言語 owing to what I said.

月滿則 丨 the moon waxes and then wanes.

丨 短 not up to the tale.

不 丨 不崩 [may your country] never wane or fall.

問心無 丨 I am conscious that I am not culpable.

丨 欠 in arrears; debts.

丨 空 a defalcation, a deficit.

無 丨 心自安 if you lack in no duty, your mind will be composed.

丨 損 deficient, short; it has lost in weight, as camphor by evaporation.

幸 丨 a lucky hit, a fortunate chance, a pleasant contingency.

丨 本 loss of capital, drawing on the principal.

血 丨 his blood has lost its strength; debilitated, weakened.

魁 *kw'éi* From *demon* and a *peck*, defined as the demon who bears aloft the peck, referring to the Dipper or Charles' Wain.

The head, the chief, the highest; first of a class; best of a sort; monstrous.

丨 首 he who bears the palm, first of the *küjin* graduates.

元 丨 the first on the list; the head of, as a band.

五 丨 the five who head the list.

文 丨 the literary chief; — borne on a tablet placed over the door of a *küjin*.

亞 丨 one who missed getting his degree of *küjin;* also those graduates numbering from six to twelve on the list.

文昌 丨 the best composition.

烟 丨 the best tobacco; and by a figure of speech intimating that its seller is the corypheus of his class.

丨 梧 or 丨 偉 of great stature; gigantic, a Goliath.

邪教 丨 an arch-heretic, the ringleader of a sect.

殲厥渠 丨 he killed [only] their chief leaders.

丨 手 he is the best hand.

占春 丨 the plum flower.

斗丨 the Dipper, which is regarded as the 文昌宮 palace of the God of Literature; he is supposed to have once been a mortal, whose spirit was deified by Yen-yoh of the Yuen dynasty, A. D. 1314, and is now worshiped by students; the picture of this god represents him as standing on one leg holding a pencil, and is called 丨星踢斗 Dubhe kicking the Dipper.

詼 ꜀kw'ei From *words* and *ashes*; interchanged with ʿli 悝 to jest.

To play with, to laugh at, to ridicule; to jest, to dally.

丨笑 to make game of.

丨劇 to gambol with, to sport.

丨啁 to rally, to retort on; a repartee.

丨諧 to jibe and jeer with; to quip.

恢 ꜀kw'ei Great; liberal; to enlarge; to esteem great, to magnify.

志量丨宏 liberal-minded and great.

丨復城池 he recovered the city — from the rebels.

盔 ꜀kw'ei From *dish* and *ashes*.

A helmet, a casque, a morion; a defense for the head; a basin, a porringer; a block on which caps are ironed.

頭丨 a plated helmet.

丨甲 mail armor, both helmet and cuirass.

闚 ꜀kw'ei From *door* and *rule*; interchanged with the next.

To peep from behind a door; to observe, to glance at, to view stealthily.

丨視 to spy at; to secretly mark.

竊往丨之 to steal a look at one, to slyly peep at.

上丨青天 he looked up to the azure heavens, — and reflected.

丨覩 to peep, as at a door.

窺 ꜀kw'ei From a *cavern* and *rule*; like the last, and used with ʿ跬 to step out.

To peep through a crack or hole; to spy, to keek, to look furtively at; to observe on the sly; to put the left foot forward.

管丨蠡測 he looks [at the sky] through a tube, and measures [the sea] with a clam-shell; *met.* a slight examination of, a narrow view of things.

丨探 to spy, to pry; to go about looking into.

丨同 to see what each other is doing.

丨事 to wait for and see how a thing will turn out.

暌 ꜀kw'ei In opposition, as the sun and moon at apogee; distant from; separated, absent.

丨違日久 our stars have been in opposition many days; *i. e.* we have long been separated.

丨別一月 separated a whole month.

丨隔 sundered; far removed.

奎 ꜀ / **奞** ꜀ ꜁kw'éi From *great* and a *baton* or *excellent*; the second form is unusual.

The stride made by a man.

丨宿 the 15th constellation, answering to β Mirac δ ε ζ η μ ν π in Andromeda and part of Pisces; it has sixteen stars imagined to resemble a person striding, and is called 狼 the Wolf by the Chinese; it is regarded as auspicious to students; in A. D. 967, the five planets met in it.

丨光閣 a hall for worshiping the God of Literature.

丨踽 to hop along on one foot.

睽 ꜀kw'éi A cast in the eye; a dull, lifeless eye; to look at angrily; to stare; placed outside of; unusual, strange.

丨孤 an outcast.

萬目丨丨 all eyes were gazing at it.

刲 ꜀kw'éi To cut open and clean, as a fish; to butcher victims for sacrifice; to stab, to put a knife into.

聧 ꜀kw'éi Very deaf, unable to hear when the ear is close to one; formerly used in Shansi, and westward.

耳丨 deaf, hard of hearing.

騤 ꜀kw'éi A majestic horse; the stately gait of a thorough-bred; strong, untiring.

四牡丨丨 the four stallions.

葵 ꜁kw'éi From *plants* and a *horary* character; occurs used with the next.

The sunflower; a term for some malvaceous plants, as the Malva, Althea, and Hibiscus, it also includes other large leaved plants; to measure, to estimate.

丨花 the *Althea rosea*.

黃蜀丨 the *Hibiscus manihot* and *esculentis*; 丨黃 is the color of the latter or okra flower.

冬丨子 seeds from the *Hibiscus abelmoschus*.

向日丨 or 照日丨 the sunflower (*Helianthus*), whose seeds are called in Shanghai, 香瓜子 fragrant melon seeds.

倍切丨傾 I bow my head most respectfully, — *i. e.* like a sunflower; a phrase in letters.

丨扇 palm-leaf fans; made of the broad leaves of the 蒲丨 or *Livistona*, cultivated in Kwangtung.

丨蓬 thatch, attap, awning; thatch made of palm or bamboo-leaves.

丨表 a letter, because the talipot palm leaf was used for paper.

丨猶能衞其足 the sunflower acts as if it wished to shield its root.

七月烹丨及菽 in the seventh moon they cook okras and pluse.

丨菜 an esculent mallows.

天子丨之 the emperor scans [their merits].

揆 ˏkw'éi To consider, to guess, to calculate; to surmise, to weigh in the mind; to examine and conclude.

百丨 a high statesman, a general supervisor; an ancient office.

丨度,事理 to estimate the bearings of this principle or motive.

丨 — to reason in the same manner, — as the sages have done.

丨之以日 he determined [its location] by the sun.

戣 ˏkw'éi A halberd, with a waved point like a Malayan kris.

一人冕執丨 one man with a coronet held a lance.

孔丨 a noted descendant of Confucius in the 38th generation, who lived in the T'ang dynasty.

逵 ˏkw'éi A place where four roads and other bye-ways meet; a thoroughfare.

丨泉 a name of a place in the Lu state.

鴻漸于雲丨 the wild geese enter the cloudy roads, — *i. e.* fly very high.

馗 ˏkw'éi From *head* and *nine*; *q. d.* the center of nine roads; it resembles the last, and is used for the next.

The cheek bones; side of the face; high; a center of travel.

鍾丨 a hero of the T'ang dynasty, now deified as a protector against demons, drawn standing on one foot and brandishing a sword.

大門口掛鍾丨 [you had better] hang up Chung-kw'ei at your door, — for no one will come to this cheating shop.

中丨 a species of mushroom.

夔 ˏkw'éi The component parts are 夂 to *pursue* under two 角 *horns*, 面 a *face*, and two 又 *hands* much modified, to represent the dragon.

A one-legged monster, resembling a dragon, an ox and a man combined; name of an officer whom Shun made 典樂 Director of Music.

丨丨齊慄 he looked grave and awe-struck; — said of Shun.

丨州府 a prefecture north of the Yangtsz' River in the easternmost part of Sz'ch'uen; during the Cheu, it was a small fief.

傀 ˋkw'éi Great, gigantic, part man part devil; monstrous, as a meteor or an eruption.

人丨 a hermaphrodite.

大丨異災 a great and amazing convulsion, as an earthquake.

丨然獨立 he was altogether without an equal.

丨儡 puppets, called 鬼仔戲 at Canton; Punch and Judy.

我不給你作丨儡 I'll not be your puppet or servant, — and work for nothing.

跬 ˋkw'éi To advance the foot, to step out the left foot; a stride, half a 步 or pace, reckoned to be three cubits.

丨步不能行 I am not able to take a step, — I am so busy.

Read *sich*, Weary from great effort; great exertion.

敝丨 utterly wearied out.

喟 kw'éiˋ To breathe heavily, to lament and groan.

丨然而嘆 he sighed deeply and moaned.

憒 kw'éiˋ Agitation of mind.

丨丨 concerned and anxious.

簣 簣 kw'éiˋ A basket, a wicker hod for carrying earth; bamboo arrows.

爲山九仞功虧一丨 he has made a mound nine fathoms high, and still it lacks one basketfull; — *i. e.* complete a work before praising it; do not reject it for a trifling flaw.

饋 kw'éiˋ From to *eat* and *honorable* as the phonetic; similar to the next.

Provisions, food, viands; a present of food; to prepare food and present it; to attend to the kitchen.

丨人 a king's butler.

丨食 to offer food.

陳丨八簋 I arranged my viands and the eight baskets.

Read *tui*. A sort of cake made of broken rice and honey steamed.

餽 kw'éiˋ Nearly the same as the last.

To offer in sacrifice; a present of food; to offer it to one.

丨餞 meats and wine, presented to one leaving on a journey.

王丨金而不受 the king offered him gold but he declined it.

厚丨有加 the valuable presents were duplicated.

蕢 kwéiˋ A basket or straw hamper to carry earth in; a vegetable like the blite or strawberry-spinach (*Blitum*), having a red stem, and resembling the goose-foot in its habit; name of a hill.

有荷丨而過孔氏之門者 one carrying a straw basket one day passed Confucius' gate.

襀 kwéiˋ The loop with which garments are fastened; loop and button; colored, embroidered.

繢 kw'éiˋ From *silk* and *honorable*; occurs interchanged with *hwui*, 繪 to draw.

Thrums left from weaving; red threads used in adorning hats; to color, to sketch, to limn; to embroider.

丨畫文采 to draw and paint beautiful flowers.

鬢 kwéiˋ The fillet or ribbon for securing the hair in a knot; curly hair.

丨帶 a band for the hair.

樻 kwéiˋ A small tree full of knots, the 椐丨 which produces good walking-sticks; another species, known as the 靈壽木 vigorous longevity tree, is classed with the oil-bearing *Elæococca* or *Jatropha*.

KWO.

Old sound, ka, kwo, *and* kai. *In Canton*, kwo; — *in Swatow*, k'o, túé, *and* lo; — *in Amoy*, kò; — *in Fuhchau*, kwo *and* kwi; — *in Shanghai*, ku; — *in Chifu*, kwòa.

戈 ‹kö From 弋 an *arrow* and 一 *one*, to denote the cross-bar on a halberd, which it rudely represents; it forms the 62d radical of words relating to spears and arms.

A kind of lance with a hook; a javelin, a spear; weapons; war.

干丨四起 shields and spears everywhere arose; *i.e.* civil war ensued.

枕丨待旦 slept on their arms till morning.

倒丨相向 he turned his force against his master.

戢戢干丨 he has recalled the shield and spear; — a time of peace.

堝 ‹kwo A clay crucible used by goldsmiths.

銀丨 a crucible for melting silver.

Read *t'o*. A bit; a little spot.

一丨之地 just a small patch of ground; an inch or so.

噕 ‹kwo The prattle of children.

丨唆 the questions and answers of children.

鍋 ‹kwo A skillet or iron pot used in cooking; a boiler like a deep pan, the upper part being made of earthenware; a vessel to hold fat; the iron ring inside of the nave to protect it from the axle.

㸌丨 a copper heater to warm spirits.

鐵火丨 an iron pan, a saucepan.

丨頭 a small boiler, a frying dish.

果 'kwo From 木 a *tree* and a *knob* on top to represent the fruit; it is interchanged with the next in some sense, and in Mencius is once used for 婐 to wait on; it resembles ‹tung 東 east.

The fruit of trees; seeds; with a covering and pulp; really, truly, indeed; results, effects; to overcome; to surpass; to conclude, to see the end of; reliable, or to do as one promises; determined, courageous, hardy; perfection among the Budhists; a classifier of plants, trees, stalks, &c., in which cases the radical 木 is sometimes erroneously added, but for which ‹ko 柯 is more proper.

百丨 all kinds of fruit.

丨木 fruit trees and other kinds.

結丨其命 I have finished his life-fruit; — said of one killed.

丨然 certainly, really.

丨斷 to decide finally.

丨敢 courageous, daring.

陰丨 retribution or reward, as for one's secret deeds.

因丨 cause and effect; conduct in a previous life producing its results in this.

正丨 reformatory actions in this life earning a title to happiness; perfection.

歸正丨 to reform one's conduct, to enter on the path to perfection.

如丨 or 若丨 if, should, suppose.

如丨這樣 if it be really so.

其事不丨 the thing failed; his plan did not mature.

不丨來 he did not come according to agreement.

美丨 the beautiful fruit, a Budhist name for the *madahka* or *Bassa latifolia*.

青丨 the pickled Chinese olive (*Canarium*), from its color.

二女'丨 two women waited on him, — on Shun.

菓 'kwo From *plant* and *real*; used with the preceding.

Edible fruit, and thus distinguished from the last; fruits with a nut or kernel, especially edible fleshy fruits.

丨品 kinds of fruit, such as are set before idols.

丨子 fruits, berries, nuts, &c.

生丨 to bear fruit.

樣丨 imitation fruit, used in worship.

結丨 the fruit has set.

時丨 the fruits now in season.

糖丨 sweetmeats, preserved fruits.

丨蓏 fruits on trees, like plums; and on vines, like melons.

五丨 the five fruits, are the peach, apricot, plum, chestnut and date.

京丨 sugar-plums, with flour inside.

倮 'kwo From *man* and *really*; occurs used for ‹lo 裸 naked.

Narrow-minded; petty.

貒丨 low-lived, mean.

輠 / 楇 'kwo The second form is antiquated; the first is also read *hwo*' and ‹*hwa*.

A pot hung at the axle to grease the wheels; the spot which is greased.

炙丨雕龍 he can grease an axle and carve a dragon; — *i.e.* he is very persuasive and eloquent in speech.

錁 kö' From *metal* and *real*; also read 'kw'a, and used with the last.

A grease-pot for carts; an ornamental appendage to a girdle; bullion; paper money.

銀一丨 an ingot of silver, from one to five taels weight.

送丨子 or 燒丨錠 to burn paper ingots for the dead, or to the gods.

帶丨 an ornament for the girdle.

元絲丨 a small ingot with a coil on its top.

惈 'kwo Used with its primitive.

Courageous, brave.

丨毅先身 he courageously put himself forward.

丨決 or 丨敢 daring, regardless of danger.

猓 ˏkwo The proboscis monkey, the 丨猓 or kahau (*Semnopithecus larvatus*), found in Annam; the name is given because its cry seems to say 果然 Yes, really, — when it hears its fellows coming; the Chinese say the tail is bifurcated, and used to stop up the projecting nostrils when it rains; the hair is soft and long, and used for ornament; the Miautsz' are contemptuously called 丨玀 by the Chinese, especially those tribes living within Ta-ting fu in Kwéicheu.

蜾 ˏkwo The solitary wasp or *Sphex*, including the genus *Pelopœus* or dirt-daubers.

丨蠃 the wasp or dauber which imprisons caterpillars in its cell to feed its young.

螟蛉有子丨蠃負之 when the caterpillar has young the sphex carries them off, — and as the Chinese believe, turns them into wasps.

綶 ˏkwo To bandage the foot.

丨脚 to bind up the feet of girls.

裹 ˏkwo From *garment* and *real*; this and ˏli 裏 inside must be carefully distinguished.

To wrap, to wind around; to bundle up, to envelop; a bundle; fettered; the receptacle of a blossom, the place where the fruit sets, as a paccit.

丨來的鴿子 a decoy pigeon, a stool-pigeon.

包丨 to wrap up, as a parcel.

丨肚 a stomacher, a wrapper; a band for the belly.

裝丨 to wrap up, as a corpse for burial.

丨上的姻緣 an engagement made personally without a go-between.

丨餱糧 bundle up [their rations] of jerked meat and rice.

丨而又纏 rolled it up and then strapped it tight.

粿 ˏkwo To cleanse rice; rice diet; rice cakes boiled in oil, or steamed, and then laid upon each other.

九重丨 rice cakes in layers.

糖丨 steamed cakes with sugar.

Read ˏkwa The best of grain, which has been hulled.

餜 䊹 ˏkwo Cakes made of wheat flour; confectionary, biscuits.

茶丨店 a tea-house, an eating-shop; a restaurant.

抓丨 an olio of cakes and fruits.

喜丨 presents of cakes, &c., sent after betrothal.

過 过 kwoˋ From to *go* and a wry *mouth*; also read ˏkwo; the second form is common in cheap books.

To pass by, to go beyond or up to; to exceed, to overpass; to spend, as time; to transgress, to violate propriety; an imprudence, an error, a fault, a transgression; a sin of ignorance; beyond, further; a sign of the past time or the pluperfect tense; an adverb of comparison, than, more, too, the rather; excessive; to approach; to send to.

丨去 passed, gone; to go by or over to; the past Budha is so named.

不丨三個 only three of them.

丨不去 impassable; you can't go that way; I can't manage it; I don't see how it is to be done.

大丨 too much.

丨多 excessive, overmuch.

太丨 a great blunder.

再去丨 he has gone again

去丨來 I've been there.

好丨那個 this is better than that.

沒見丨 I have never seen it.

無丨於是 this mode will be the best.

自以爲丨 he thought he had excelled him.

經丨 passed by; done; over.

丨日 to pass the day.

丨身 or 丨世 deceased, dead.

丨意不去 I was quite mistaken.

知丨必改 reform when you see your errors.

試丨 I have tried it.

丨期 passed the time; too late.

丨載 to change the lading into another boat.

丨不來 I can't stomach [that dish]; this place disagrees with me.

丨造 the season is past, as fruit; dead.

丨信一二 give me a little credit.

丨夜 to pass the night.

難丨 hard to get by or over.

丨藥 to remove the bad taste of a medicine.

丨不得眼 intolerable; I can't suffer it.

丨失 a peccadillo, an offense.

丨犯 a crime, a misdemeanor.

無所丨責 do not punish excessively.

有丨 faulty, delinquent.

丨光 to gloss over, to make a vain show.

丨於秘密 he kept much too close or private.

丨頭 it goes over the head; very much; at Canton, used for a common superlative; as 大丨頭 it is much too large.

大丨 or 小丨 are the 28th and 62d diagrams.

不我丨 she would not come near us.

雨丨山青 after the rain is over the hills look green.

In *Cantonese*. A particle like then; in that case.

問丨佢 then ask him; also, I have asked him.

In *Fuhchau*. To do over, to repeat a process; the turn or crisis in a disease.

丨鼎 to heat over in the pan.

KWOH.

Old sounds, kwok, *and* kwak. *In Canton*, kwok, kwik, kwak, *and* fòk; —*in Swatow*, kwak, kúé, *and* kòk; —*in Amoy*, kòk, k'òk, hék, *and* kéh; —*in Fuhchau*, k'iòk, *and* kwòk; —*in Shanghai*, kwok, hwok, *and* kòk; —*in Chifu*, kwòa.

國, 囯, *kwo* From 口 to *encircle* and 或 a *border*; the contracted form is met with in cheap books.

A state, a country, a kingdom, an empire; a region; a nation, a people; a dynasty; national, governmental; the rulers or government; to maintain the dignity or independence of a state.

萬 丨 all nations; the kingdoms of the world.

丨 母 the empress-dowager.

丨 家 the reigning family, the sovereign; the state; our country, our ruler.

丨 王 or 丨 主 a ruler, a sovereign; a dependent prince.

外 丨 and 外 丨 人 foreign lands and foreigners.

丨 子 監 the academy at Peking for educating youth for office.

天 丨 the kingdom of heaven; —a foreign term.

相 丨 a minister of state.

丨 帑 the national treasury.

列 丨 戰 丨 the contending states in feudal times; the separate feudal states from B. C. 460 to 220.

Their number varied at different periods of the Cheu dynasty, and as many as fifty-five are enumerated as existing altogether; but there are only twenty named during the period embraced in the *Ch'un Tsiu*, extending from B. C. 722 to 481, and this number diminished after this date, till all were conquered by Tsin Chi Hwangti before B. C. 222.

1. Lu 魯 the most famous of all, occupied the south of Shantung; the capital lay near the present Kiuh-feu hien 曲阜縣 east of the Grand Ganal.
2. Tsai 蔡 in the southeast of Honan; its capital was at Sin-tsai hien 新蔡縣 southeast from Jü-ning fu.
3. Tsao 曹 in the southwest of Shantung on the Yellow River; its capital was Ting-teu hien 定陶縣 in Tsao-cheu fu.
4. Wéi 衛 in the north of Honan on the Yellow River; its capital was Ki hien 淇縣 just north of Wéi-hwui fu.
5. Tăng 滕 a very small state not much larger then its old capital, the present Tăng hien 滕縣 in Yen-cheu fu, in Shantung.
6. Tsin 晉 a powerful state in the south of Shansi; its capital was Yih-ch'ing hien 翼城縣 in Ping-yang fu on the River Făn.
7. Ching 鄭 an important state near the mouth of the River Wei in the southeast of Shensi; its capital was Hwa cheu 華州 south of Tung-cheu fu.
8. Wu 吳 a large kingdom in the south of Kiangsu; the capitals were Wu-sih hien 無錫縣 and the present Su-cheu fu.
9. Tsi 齊 a large and important state in the north of Shantung; its capital was Lin-tsz' hien 臨淄縣 north of Tsing-cheu fu.
10. Tsin 秦 the largest, and final conqueror of the others, lay in the south of Kansuh; its capital was Tsing-shui hien 清水縣 north of the River Wéi in Tsin Cheu.
11. Yen 燕 a wide state in the north of Chihli; its capital was Ta-hing hien 大興縣 now a part of Peking.
12. Tsu 楚 a powerful state on both banks of the Yang-tsz' River; its capital was Kiang-ling hien 江陵縣 now the prefect city of K'ing-cheu fu in Hupeh.
13. Sung 宋 was in the east of Honan, south of the Yellow River; its captial was Shang-kiu hien 商邱縣 now the prefect city of Kwéi-teh fu.
14. Ki 杞 a very small state southwest of the preceding; its capital was Ki hien 杞縣 in K'ai-fung fu.
15. Chin 陳 a small state south of the two last; its capital was Chin-cheu fu 陳州府 in the east of Honan.
16. Sieh 薛 was the smallest of the twenty states; its capital was Sieh ching 薛城 near the town of Tăng hien in Shantung on the Grand Canal.
17. Chu 邾 a small state north of the last, occupying most of Tsao hien 鄒縣 south of Yen-cheu fu in Shantung.
18. Kü 莒 a small state along the seacoast in the present Kü cheu 莒州 in the southeast of Shantung.
19. Siao Chu 小邾 a small short-lived state in Shantung; its capital is supposed to have been within the limits of Yen-cheu fu, south of the prefect city.
20. Hü 許 a small state in Honan, supposed to have comprised the present Hü cheu 許州 south of K'ai-fung fu.

Beside these, may be mentioned five others among the most powerful subsequent States.

Han 韓 which occupied the south of Shensi and western part of Honan.

Liang 梁 whose capital was at Nanking.

Yueh 越 in Chehkiang, south of Wu (No 8.), and reaching to the sea.

Chiao 趙 in the north of Shansi and west of Chihli; the capital was Chao-ch'ing hien on the River Făn.

三丨 the three State which divided China from A. D. 222 to 265. The leading one was Shuh 蜀, which had its capital at Ch'ing-tu, and comprised all the region west of K'ing-cheu fu; — the next was Wéi 魏, whose king Ts'ao Pi 曹丕 ruled at Loh-yang, and swayed most of the region north of the Yangtsz' River; — the third was Wu 吳, whose king Sun Küen 孫權 was invested by the preceding at Nanking, and ruled all the eastern provinces.

本丨 my country; this kingdom.

丨都 the realm, the state.

開丨 to found a state.

君子正是丨人 the princely man rectifies the people.

故丨 fatherland, the old country; said by emigrants.

丨事 national affairs.

山丨 and 土丨 a hilly and a level region; — geographical terms.

何以爲丨 how can the majesty of the state be upheld?

大失丨體 the credit of the kingdom will suffer greatly.

嘓, *kwo* Troublesome loquacity.

嘮丨丨 her tongue goes clack! clack!

幗, *kwo* A hempen cap or kerchief worn by women in mourning; a woman's headdress which conceals the hair; females.

巾丨之辱 the disgrace of kerchiefs and caps; — *i.e.* a poltroon.

丨匪 insurgents who wore red turbans.

摑, **搋**, *kwo* The second form is unusual.

To slap the mouth or face; to strike with the fist; to box.

丨一把 a slap, a cuff.

丨醒你 you need to be awakened with a box.

膕, *kwo* The popliteal space under the knee; the calf of the leg.

脚䐢丨 the calf of the leg.

蟈, *kwo* A small frog, of a green color, having long thighs, the 螻丨; it is applied also to a brown toad found among rocks; in the North, this name is applied to the mole cricket.

丨丨 in Chihli a large kind of cicada called scissor-grinder from its sound, having short greenish-black wings, and a short flight.

郭, *kwo* From 邑 *a city* and 回 *to surround* repeated and contracted.

A place where people intend to dwell; the second wall inclosing the gate of a large city to defend it, and make an enciente that is often protected by a temple to Kwanti; it is called 甕城 and 甕圈, whether within or without the main line of wall.

丨外 wastes outside the city.

城丨 the defenses of the city.

輪丨 the rim of a cash, the raised edge of a coin; a felly.

依山築丨 let the hill serve as the city wall.

槨, **椁**, *kwo'* The outer coffin, the casket or case which incloses the coffin; to estimate, to measure.

石丨 a stone sarcophagus.

丨周于棺 the casket incloses the coffin.

崞, *kwo'* A celebrated hill in the north of Shansi, near the Great Wall, from which Kwoh hien 丨縣, a district west of Wu-tai hien on the River Hu-to, derives its name.

彍, *kwo'* To *broaden* a *bow*, to pull it to the full stretch; quick, agile.

丨騎 cavalry bowmen in the T'ang dynasty, famed like Parthian archers for shooting as they fled.

駕塵丨風與電爭光 if I could ride the dust and pull the wind, then I should be as quick as the lightning's flash.

聙, *kwo'* The rim of the ear, the outer part of the lobe.

矍, *chioh* From two *eyes* of a *bird* in the *hand*; *q. d.* a frightened bird struggling to escape from the hand; also read *tsioh*,

To look right and left in alarm; to glance the eyes about in trepidation.

丨丨 to look scared and seek escape.

丨踢 to run and look here and there, as in a fright.

丨鑠哉是翁也 what a smart robust old man you are, Sir!

丨覛 to look hastily at.

攫, *kwo'* To seize with the claws, as a cat or an eagle does its prey.

丨取 to seize by force.

鷹丨兎 the falcon seizes the hare.

钁, *chioh* A large hoe or pick used by farmers; a sort of bill-hook or partisan used by soldiers to clear away abattis or thickets; to cut down.

負丨臿 shouldered his pick and spade.

躩, *chioh* A short quick step, deemed to be a respectful gait in the presence of superiors; to leap; to bend as if ready to kneel.

丨走 to walk with a long and quick stride.

丨跳 to leap, jump across.

足丨如也 [Confucius'] limbs seemed to bend, — as he received guests.

鳧浴蝦丨 when the mallard bathes, the prawns jump out of the way.

蹇裳丨步 lift the dress so that you can step quicker.

虢, *kwo'* From a *tiger* and to *pinch* a finger-full.
The marks made by a tiger when seizing his prey; name of an ancient feudal state, afterwards combined with Shen 陜, and now Yung-yang hien 榮陽縣 in the center of Honan, south of the Yellow River.

馘, **聝**, *kwo'* To cut off the heads of the slain and of stubborn prisoners taken in battle; and then to take their left ears as evidence of victory.
斬丨甚多 he cut off the heads of many rebels.
載獻丨 he then brought in and offered him the ears.
攸丨安安 their left ears were leisurely cut off.
以訊丨告 to cut off the ears of the living as proof — of capture.

昏, *'kwo* From *mouth* and *surname*; as a primitive it is often contracted to *sheh*, 舌 the tongue.
To stop up the mouth.

KW'OH.

Old sounds, kw'at *and* kw'ak. *In Canton*, kwok, fok, *and* fút; — *in Swatow*, kwat, kw'a, *and* kw'ak; — *in Amoy*, k'òk, kòk, *and* kòng; — *in Fuhchau*, kw'ak *and* kwoh; — *in Shanghai*, kw'eh; — *in Chifu*, kw'ò.

闊, **濶**, *kw'oh'* From *door* and *living*; the second form is a common but unauthorized alteration.
Broad, open, wide, ample; sundered, distant; long parted; liberal, lavish; able to afford rich things; to widen, to enlarge; diligent; a separation; perverse.
丨大 capacious, ample; liberal.
疏丨 long separated, as friends; 丨遠 far apart, as places; open, as interstices.
寬丨 to enlarge, to make wide; indulgent; spacious.
迂丨 anyhow; vague, wide of the mark.
閒丨 while long separated, as friends.
死生契丨與子成說 living or dying, however separated, to our wives we pledged our word.
那人很丨 that man is rich, or elegantly dressed.
高談丨論 to talk about things in general.
胸襟丨 a generous minded, noble person.
横丨 the breadth of a thing; 丨丨布 wide sheetings; a shop term.
乖丨 reckless, disobedient.

廓, *kw'oh'* Wide and empty; open, as a region; to enlarge; to make more spacious; great, as a state; vacant; to augment; to pare with a sword.
開丨 to enlarge; to develop.
丨然大公 an open field and no favoritism.
丨然獨居 he stood, as it were, unequaled.
憎其式丨 he disliked all those great — states.
性度恢丨 his desires are unbounded.

鞹, **鞟**, *kw'oh'* Skin from which the hair has been taken; soft, well curried leather; bound with leather; chamois-leather; 朱丨 red leather, once used in covering carriages.
虎豹之丨 the hides of tigers and leopards.

廓, *kw'oh'* Occurs wrongly used for the next.
A ravine or gorge, 嵾丨 referring to the indistinctness of things in it.

霩, *kw'oh'* From *rain* and a *wall*; the last is sometimes wrongly written for this.
The clouds breaking away and the rain ceasing; the snow melting.
雨止雲丨 the rain has stopped and the clouds dispersed.
道始于虛丨虛丨生宇宙 energy (Reason) began in chaos, and chaos begot the visible universe.

擴, *kw'oh'* From *hand* and *broad*; in such combinations as this, the radical seems to have been added as a means of distinguishing the verb
To stretch a thing till it becomes large; to expand, as the mind.
丨而充之 if raised higher, he will fill the post; — extend your views to higher aims; develop and complete it, as a plan.
推丨其理 apply this principle further.

廓刂, *kw'oh'* To cut off; to trim, as a sapling of its branches; to make a post; to unfold, to lay open.

KWUN.

Old sound, kun. *In Canton,* kwăn *and* kw'ăn; — *in Swatow,* k'un *and* kún; — *in Amoy,* k'ún, hún, *and* kun; — *in Fuhchau,* k'ung, kung, *and* kòng; — *in Shanghai,* kw'ăng *and* kwăng; — *in Chifu,* kwăn.

昆 *kw'un* From 日 *day* and 比 to *compare;* q. d. all days are alike; used with the next.

Alike, comparable; of the same time or race; together, subsequent, afterwards; futurity; brothers, descendants; many, a multitude; fine, superior.

丨弟 or 丨仲 brothers.

後丨 descendants.

你幾位丨季(or 丨仲,or 賢丨玉) how many brothers have you?

蜫 蚰 *kw'un* From *insect* and *many;* the second form is not usual.

Insects generally, but the term 丨蟲 or 昆蟲 includes also crabs, lizards, newts, and other small animals, as well as insects properly so called.

崑 *kw'un* A peak beyond comparison; a high mountain, the 丨崙山 in Tibet, said to contain the sources of the Yellow River; it is now usually applied to the almost unknown range of the Koulkun Mts., lying about lat. 35 deg. N. between the Desert of Gobi and Tibet; it is, like Caucasus among the Arabs, the fairy land of Chinese writers, one of whom says its peaks are so high that when sunlight is on one side moonlight is on the other.

玉出丨崗 gems are found in the Kw'un-kang peak.

眞如丨山片玉 it is like a gem from the Kw'un-lun; as a fine essay.

丨崙州 Pulo Condore I. in the China Sea, in imitation of the Anamitic name Conon or Kohnoong.

琨 *kw'un* A stone resembling a pearl, perhaps the cat's eye or mother-o'-pearl.

瑤丨 a fine stone.

鯤 *kw'un* The young of fishes just hatched; a sea-monster, like a kraken or sea-serpent.

魚禁丨鮞 when fishing don't take the minnows.

丨化爲鵬 the leviathan was changed into the rokh.

兒丨 little minnows; small fry.

鵾 *kw'un* A kind of gallinaceous bird, larger than the cock, whose cry is plantive; it is perhaps the heath-cock, or a bird like the capercailzie, jungle fowl, or a kindred species.

錕 *kw'un* A kind of red steel, called 丨鋙 from a mountain where the ore was found; the swords made of it could cleave gems; a ring on a wheel.

褌 *kwun* From *clothes* and *army.*

Drawers or loose trowsers.

丨襠 breeches, which do not open behind.

犢鼻丨 waist breeches, such as laborers wear.

丨貫 shirt and trowsers in one.

丨 *kw'un* The 2d radical; it is used only in combination.

A line which joins things perpendicularly, diverging from the middle up and down.

鯀 *kwun* From *fish* and *band.*

A great fish; the name of Yü's father, in ancient times.

於丨哉 what, that man Kwun!

蓘 *kwun* To heap earth around the roots of plants when set out; to mulch plants; to blanch by earthing the stalks.

是穮是丨 both weed and hoe them all.

袞 衮 *kwun* From 衣 *garment* and 公 *public,* often altered as in the second form.

Robes used by the emperor when honoring his ancestors, and by high princes; they were embroidered with dragons and in different styles; royal; court robes; coiled, convoluted, as a serpent.

丨冕 a robe and crown; a royal suit.

丨龍袍 an imperial robe.

丨職有闕 defects in the royal duties.

丨衣繡裳 embroidered robes and royal apparel.

丨邊 a black border or edging on a dress.

滾 *kwun* Water flowing in a rapid bubbling manner; boiling; welling up; to boil anything till it bubbles; to stir up; to roll about or over.

丨水 boiling water.

財源丨丨 my capital must be circulating; — a shopkeeper's phrase.

丨來 to come rolling along.

丨濁 to muddy the water, as by rolling in it.

丨丨東流 like the surging floods rolling eastwards, — so go our days.

丨亂 to disarrange; to throw topsy-turvy.

打一丨 to roll over, to turn a somerset, as when fencing, or as a mule rolls in the dust.

丨罷 or 丨旦罷 be off! begone, the whole of you!

丨木 to whirl the club, to resort to force.

珠淚丨丨 the pearly tears coursed down.

丨油煎心 my heart is just a hot whirl of troubles.

緄 'kwun An embroidered or woven sash; to sew; to stitch; a cord; a ribbon.

丨帶 a pretty flowered sash, such as a child wears.

竹閉丨縢 bound fast to the bamboo frame, as a bow.

輥 kwun' To roll, as a cylinder; the rapid turning of the spokes of a wheel; a rolling, rotatory motion.

丨轉之速 quick as the turning of the spokes.

丨子 a lemon-shaped stone roller dragged after a drill to roll in the seed.

亂丨動 rolling, unsteady, as a vessel; reeling, vibratory.

丨動 a rotatory motion.

惃 kwun' Confused, disturbed.

丨亂心事 you disturb my thoughts; you put me out.

棍 kwun' From *wood* and *alike* as the phonetic.

A fencing-stick, a quarter-staff, a club; to bind up reeds or sticks, as when making a hurdle or wattled fence; a sharper, a knave.

習染丨成 practices makes a thing natural.

舞丨 a fencer's wand, a balancing pole, a single stick.

光丨 or 丨匪 a bare-stick, a blackleg, a rascal.

光丨兒 a bachelor; a man who lives alone, a single resident.

訟丨 a pettifogger, a shyster.

丨徒 a pestilent fellow, a villain.

丨脚 a dangerous fellow.

丨騙 to wheedle out of.

丨棒 a shillelah, a club.

打花丨 to fence, to play broadsword exercise.

地丨 rowdies of the place, roughs.

折頭丨 a kind of flail used in fighting.

五花丨 a banded stick used to smash the clay ox.

㨰 kwun' To muddy one; to spatter.

丨污衣服 to dirty or spatter the dress.

謴 kwun' To take in one, to run a rig on; to sport, to play a trick on one.

KW'UN.

Old sound, k'un. *In Canton*, kw'ăn; — *in Swatow*, k'ún; — *in Amoy*, k un; — *in Fuhchau*, k'ŏng, k'ung *and* k'aung; — *in Shanghai*, kw'ăng; — *in Chifu*, kw'ăn.

坤 堃 kw'un kun From *earth* and to *stretch* out; the second form is pedantic, and used chiefly for names.

What is inferior and should be obedient; said especially of the earth to heaven, and applied to the moon, to a wife, and to statesmen, who owe a correlative obedience; the second or eighth diagram, denoting this kind of compliant accord; favorable, compliant; on the compass card, southwest.

有何乾丨 what remarkable talents have you?

壽極乾丨 may your life be coëval with the duration of the world.

丨道 dames, ladies; a lady.

丨造 a girl's horoscope.

髡 kw'un To shave the head, a punishment anciently substituted in the palace for castration; a pollarded or leafless tree; a man's name.

壼 'k'un From 口 an *inclosure* with walks and walls within it, which the lower part rudely depicts; it resembles *hu'* 壺 a pot.

Paths and corridors between and among the palace buildings and grounds, which intersected each other.

閨丨 a virtuous damsel.

室家之丨君子萬年永錫祚胤 through all the paths of his palace, the prince shall always move; while dignity and posterity shall for ever be granted to him.

門丨 a path leading to the door.

悃 'kw'un From *heart* and *confined* as the phonetic.

Single-minded, sincere; real feelings, genuine sentiments; unadorned, clear, as a style.

丨丨款款朴以忠乎 in everything I sincerely undertake, am I not wholly loyal?

丨愊 earnest and sincere, as in a purpose.

謹抒忱丨 I most respectfully express my views.

容申謝丨 I cannot sufficiently thank your kindness; — epistolary phrases.

丨實 unaffected, single, guileless.

稇 'kw'un To bind, as a sheaf or bundle of sticks; full, well provided with.

丨載而歸 they returned home well laden — with sheaves; *met.* successful in business.

梱 'kw'un To plait finely, to bind evenly, as a whip handle is corded; to work at and make fine by beating; to pound firm, to join securely, — in which it is like the next.

丨緻 to make fine and thorough.

丨屨 to bind shoes.

綑 ʻkwʻun From *silk* and *confined;* used with the preceding.
To bind, to cord up; to tie on; to plait, to braid; a border or trimming on the edge of a garment; to hem; to put on a band; a coil, a roll; a bundle, as of straw, rattan, faggots, &c.
丨領 to bind the collar of a garment.
丨綁 to cord, to tie tightly.
丨作一塊 tie them all up together; also 丨一丨 often has the same sense.
丨籐 to bind with rattans, as a box.
一丨繩 a coil of rope, a ball of twine.
鑲丨 to put on a band or edging, as a trimming.
丨在身 to bind or strap on one.

裍 ʻkwʻun From *clothes* and *inclosed;* like the last.
A border or band on the edge of a dress; to finish up quickly.

梱 ʻkwʻun The movable sill of a gateway, which can be taken up when a carriage passes; arranged in order.
丨丨 to approach the end of a thing.
丨外之事 affairs outside of the camp; frontier duties.

閫 ʻkwʻun From *gate* and *confined;* used with the last.
A threshold; the door-posts; a gateway or a small door inserted in a large gate; the door leading to the hareem; females, feminine; inner apartments.
丨範 [she was a] pattern of female decorum.
勿談閨丨 don't gossip about women's affairs.
丨內 and 丨外 place for females and males; within and without the palace, the court, or the country, &c.
天丨 the gate of heaven.

困 kwʻun' From an *inclosure* and a *tree;* q. d. a plant fading for want of room.
An old ruinous tenement; confined, cribbed; exhausted, disheartened, weary, jaded; needy, insufficient, wanting, beggared; diseased; to weary; to distress; to cripple, to render subject to; to impoverish; victimized by, enslaved to, oppressed with, distressed about; sorry for, afflicted; to put forth toil; flustered with drink; the 47th diagram, meaning dried up as a pool, or unable to attain.
不爲酒丨 don't let drink get the better of you.
行李丨乏 neither baggage nor funds, as a traveler.
病丨 extremely ill, laid up.
丨而學之 to study it earnestly.
丨住 to restrain, to disable; hemmed in, hampered, surrounded.
丨急 imperiled; in extremity.
丨獸猶鬬 pent-up beasts will fight, — so will people living too clossely.
丨于心衡于慮而後作 when men are chafed in mind and thwarted in their ways, then they will surely act.
丨守 poor, without resources; helpless, as an environed force.
丨極 beggared; at extremity.
圍丨 to hem in, as a band of rebels in a city.
被丨 inclosed, surrounded, shut in.
英雄多丨于酒色 wine and women have entangled many brave heroes.
不廢丨窮 do not neglect the poor and oppressed.
公無丨哉 O Duke! do not put me into this dilemma.
丨愁城 a heart cast down with grief.
丨倦 wearied out, exhausted.

睏 kwʻăn' An unauthorized character formed from the last; q. d. wearied eyes.
In *Pekingese.* To nod, as a watchman on his post; to take a nap, to sleep.
一半丨着了 he is half asleep.
稍丨一會 take a short nap.

LA.

Old sound, la. *In Canton,* la; — *in Swatow,* lúi; — *in Amoy,* lui; — *in Fuhchau,* lwi; — *in Shanghai,* nièh; — *in Chifu,* la.

磊 ʻla From *plant* and a *heap* of stones.
Uneven, rocky, — alluding to the way stones are piled up.
丨蓬 heedless; careless about appearances.
丨苴 clay not well worked; dirty.
丨漾分蘋 the roughened waves scatter the pond-weed, — as it is drifted on the rocks.

LAH.

Old sounds, lap *and* lat. *In Canton,* lap, lat, *and* lai; — *in Swatow,* la; — *in Amoy,* liap, la, *and* lat; — *in Fuhchau,* lak *and* la; — *in Shanghai,* lèh; — *in Chifu,* lah.

拉, ꜀la From *hand* and to *stand; q. d.* one stops when tugging at a thing; the books read this character as *lah*, but it is oftener pronounced in the first tone.

To pull, to drag along or up to one; to bend, as a bow; to tug, to break; to lead; to seize with the talons or fingers; to force; to borrow, to buy on credit; to get out in any way, where effort is implied, as coal from a mine; to appropriate, to embezzle; the sound of the wind.

丨住 or 丨緊 to hold fast, to detain.

拖丨手 to take one's hand in walking.

丨鋸 to saw, as a log with a double-handed saw.

丨纜 to haul or track a boat.

丨得貨 to get goods on credit.

丨穿丨敗 no one will trust me.

丨個平過 the account is now even; the matter is settled.

丨脅 to break the ribs.

丨殺 completely defeated.

丨不出 I can't pull it out.

丨他來 pull it along, as a horse by a halter.

帮丨 to help him.

丨扯 to pull; to be put about; to work into each other's hands.

丨倒 finally, after all is done; no more need be said; to quash, to hush up; that's the end of the matter.

丨煤 to get out coal, to work a coal mine.

In *Shanghai.* A sign of the past tense; a preposition, at, in, to; used alone or with 勒 as a dissyllable.

勿丨上海 he is not in Shanghai.

好丨否 are you well?

勿勒丨 not in; they are not at home.

撥丨伊丨者 I have given it to him.

送禮物丨儂 I present you with gifts.

話丨者 I've said it.

䶐, lah꜄ Dissatisfied.

丨𪗇 unsatisfied, as when one has not eaten enough; to eat greedily.

磖, ꜀la The cracking sound of things breaking is 丨磼; applied also to a stony appearance, as a field covered with boulders.

臘, 臈, 腊, la꜄ From *flesh* and a *bristle* or the *Dolichos;* the second character is also read *koh,* and the contracted form is properly *sih,*

To sacrifice to the gods three days after the winter solstice; to dry flesh in the north wind; dried meats.

丨味 cured meats.

丨乾肉 to jerk meat.

丨月 a name for the twelfth moon.

丨鴨 dried ducks, common at Canton.

天丨 and 地丨 two of five Taoist sacrifices, made on the newyear and the fifth day of the fifth moon.

眞丨國 Cambodia or Tsiampa.

蠟, 蜡, la꜄ From *insect* and *bristle;* the contracted, form, also read *cha*꜄, is in general use, and sometimes incorrectly used for the last.

Wax, especially of bees; waxy, glazed, varnished; a candle.

丨丸 pills coated with wax.

丨紙 glazed or marbled paper.

白丨 insect wax, deposited by the *Coccus pe-la* on the 丨樹 *Fraxinus chinensis.*

丨石 yellow or greasy quartz.

丨夾子 a pair of snuffers.

點丨 or 點丨燭 light the candle.

白丨桿子 ashen sticks used for spears.

丨箋 fine waxed paper used for scrolls.

黃丨 or 蜂丨 beeswax.

丨餅 tapers curled in a flat coil.

蜜丨 fossil copal, or a mineral resembling it.

湯油丨 swealing or guttering of a candle.

丨嘴禾鵠 the hawfinch or *Coccothraustes melanura* of Canton.

丨嘴 a large, gray, blackheaded waxbill from Kiangsu.

丨梅花 Japan allspice or the *Chimonanthes fragrans.*

邋, la꜄ To exceed, to pass by; to go ahead.

丨雜 mixed up, unassorted; confused; sweepings, rubbish.

丨遢 or 丨裡丨遢的 slovenly, filthy; neglected, dirty; walking along.

攋, 擸, la꜄ From *hand* and *bristle;* the unauthorized contraction is used at Canton.

To hold and manage; to lump, to take together; to draw up, as hair off the face; to take up a number of things in the arms; to pull at, as a thread.

丨起髮 brush aside your curls.

丨丨 noise of branches breaking in the wind.

丨撬 mixed; odds and ends.

丨㩸灣 the bend of Pootung at Shanghai.

Read *lieh,* To smooth, to straighten out, to arrange orderly.

丨鬚 to stroke the beard.

丨纓 to smooth a cap fringe.

襰, 𧞤, la' } Mean apparel; that which is put on awry, or does not fit.

丨𧞤 poor, dilapidated garments.

鑞, la' Tin; the old name 白丨, is applied to white copper and pewter.

皶, la' Chapped skin, very common in northern China.

手上很有丨皶 my hands are badly chapped.

揧, ˏla To rub to powder; to grind, as paints.

剌, la' From 刀 *knife* and 束 to *bind*; it is often written wrongly like *ts'z* 刺 a thorn.

Inhuman, harsh; perverse, intractable, wicked; to cut in two; to mangle, to hack.

丨屍 to mangle a corpse.

乖丨 cross-grained, intractable.

丨下 cut it off.

丨戾 unkind, wicked.

丨開 cut it in twain.

撥丨 to stretch, as a bow; the twang of a bowstring.

In *Cantonese.* A row of things; a lot of articles.

種開一丨丨 plant them in open rows.

交齒丨 a dovetail in carpentry.

喇, ˏla ˋla To talk fast; a final particle indicating certainty, or having finished; the permission of an act.

喝丨 rapid utterance.

罷丨 get away! Begone!

丨丨不休 chattering, loquacious.

丨叭 a long pipe or trumpet.

歪嘴吹丨叭 [like] a wry mouth [trying] to blow a trumpet; — a barefaced demand or scheme.

你纔曉得丨叭是銅鑄的 you've just found out that a trumpet is made of brass, eh? — *i. e.* you now know that I was in earnest.

丨嘛 a lama, the yellow priests.

瞯, ˏla The eye distorted from any cause; a cast in the eye.

揦, 攋, ˏla } The second is the proper, but the first is the most common form.

To grab at, to clutch; to turn over or pull about; to slip or shove; to carry off in the mouth; to tear or spoil; to rob or scrape with the hand.

丨過來 pull it here.

丨去 to pull off, as a finger-ring.

丨子 a wine bottle. (*Pekingese.*)

撥丨 to move a thing by pulling or turning it; to sift over, as dirt for nails, &c.

辣, la' From *bitter* and to *bind.*

One of the five tastes; a biting, pungent, acrid, or hot taste, as pepper or turmeric; severe, grievous, as punishment; injurious; ungrateful.

味丨 poignant, sharp.

苦家丨子 a desperate rascal.

羊丨子 a poisonous caterpillar.

下丨手 to come down with a heavy hand, to punish severely.

禁條丨 the strict prohibitions.

苦丨備嘗 I have been through many troubles.

冷的丨實 bitterly cold.

丨嘴子 a species of gray finch which eats Cayenne pepper.

瘌, lah' Severe, grievous, as pain.

痛丨 an old term for dangerous drugs; wounds; injuries.

丨痢 bald; smooth-headed.

丨痢跟着月亮走沾光沾光 when the scald-head goes by moonlight, he gets double light; — good luck.

In *Cantonese* read *ts'ik*, because the primitive is there usually written 刺. A fullness of the stomach; twinges of pain, rheumatic pains.

頭丨 nervous headache, neuralgia.

笑到肚丨 he laughed till his sides ached.

心丨 sorry for; deeply grieved.

𩃎, lah' The sound of rain.

雨聲丨丨 the pattering of rain.

LAI.

Old sounds, lai, lat, *and* lak. *In Canton,* loi *and* lui; — *in Swatow,* lai *and* nai; — *in Amoy,* lai *and* nai; — *in Fuhchau,* lai, li, *and* lòi; — *in Shanghai,* lé *and* la; — *in Chifu,* lai,

𡥵, ˏlai From *child* and *finished,* denoting the final.

In *Cantonese.* The last child; the son born to an old man.

丨尾 the last one of a lot.

丨子 the youngest, the Benjamin.

丨瓜 the small or late melons.

最樂生個老丨子 how happy he is to have a son in his old age.

丨且孿 not only a son but a pair of twins, — cheered his age.

來, 来, ˏlai The ancient form is derived from 束 to *bind* a sheaf, and 芒 *awns* of wheat in it, to intimate that the grain comes from heaven; interchanged with the two next; the contracted form is common.

To come, to reach; to bring,

to get; to effect, to bring about; to obtain, to induce; coming, and thus makes a form of the future; joined with 去 it denotes coming and going, here and there, repeatedly; after 去, it is a form of the pluperfect; after other verbs, it often indicates their present action; if a negative comes between, the inability of the first verb is implied, as 帶丨 bring it here, 帶不丨 I cannot bring it; after 起 and 出, it shows the commencement of the action indicated in a previous verb, as 想不起丨 I cannot recall it; used for the substantive verb, or for euphony; to make a personal application; the coming times, posterity; wheat, which *came* down from heaven.

我行不丨 I don't know how to do it; I shall not come back.

福祿丨成 their happiness and dignity are complete.

公尸丨燕丨處 the personators of the [deceased] noble, feast and enjoy themselves.

生出病丨 you will become sick.

做不丨 it is impossible.

怎樣做得丨 how can it be done?

丨往 going and coming; wayfarers; intercourse with.

丨日 to-morrow; by and by.

丨文 the dispatch now here, or under reply.

丨手 the bearer, one who brings a thing.

丨頭 a source of.

原丨 the original condition of a thing.

原丨無此理 but there never was this mode, or principle.

丨因 cause, reason of.

問其丨由 he asked the reason.

有丨歷 there is proof of the antecedents; an origin or history; prestige, position.

他丨了 he has arrived; he is here.

他幾時回丨 when will he return?

二丨丨 common, second rate.

一丨二丨 firstly, secondly; now because — therefore.

說不出丨 he don't express himself, as from fear.

從丨不面 I could never get a sight of him.

禮尚往丨 courtesy requires to be reciprocated.

歸去丨兮 this going and coming!

丨孫 a grandson's grandson.

Read *lih*, and *lih*⁵ and used for 勑. To receive one, to meet one coming; to encourage.

東人之子職勞不丨 the men of the east are summoned to toil without encouragement.

勞之丨之 console and encourage him.

棶 ꜀*lai* A tree found in Kiangsi, sometimes written like the last; it is regarded as the same as the 椋, and bears a plum-shaped fruit called 冬青菓 winter-green fruit; the timber is used by wheelwrights; the bark is prickly, and the leaves resemble those of the persimmon.

淶 ꜀*lai* A river in the southwest of Shantung, a tributary of the Yellow River; also a small branch of the Pei-ho in the west of Chihli, which gives its name to Lai-shui hien 丨水縣 in I cheu.

田卒汙丨 our fields are all left as a marsh or a wild.

蒿丨迷徑 weeds and brush cover the pathways.

萊 ꜀*lai* A thistle; wild herbs like the sow-thistle or the *Tribulus*; waste untilled land; to clear up jungle.

田丨 a fallow-geld.

丨野 to clear off underbrush.

丨菔 a vegetable found in Yunnan, like the turnip, from which the people obtain a red dye.

丨草 a sow-thistle (*Sonchus*.)

丨州府 a prefecture in the northern part of Shantung Promontory, said to be named from the aborigines 丨夷 who anciently lived there.

䅘 ꜀*lai* A local and ancient term in Shantung for wheat, said to denote the *grain* that *came* down to man; some suppose that the grain here referred to is rye, but that seems not now to be cultivated in China.

騋 ꜀*lai* A mare seven cubits high; a powerful draught horse, fit for the farmer's use.

丨牝三千 his three thousand tall mares.

宛丨 great horses brought from Bactria in the T'ang dynasty.

崍 ꜀*lai* A peak in Sz'ch'uen in the range of the Min mountains, near the confines of Shensi.

郲 ꜀*lai* An ancient city in the country of Ch'ing 鄭 in Yung-yang hien, now a part of K'ai-fung fu south of the Yellow River.

邛丨山 a peak in Sz'ch'uen.

鯠 ꜀*lai* A fish belonging to the eel family, probably akin to the conger eel.

箂 ꜀*lui* A variety of bamboo.

In *Fuhchau*. A kind of hamper or open basket without a bale, having cords, and used by coolies.

䐯 *lai*' Obese, gross; excessively fat.

丨臞 ill-looking; gross, as an unwieldy hog.

Read '*lui*. A pimple, a small blister.

鑗 ꜀'*li* To tie a cord to a hook to fish with; to angle for.

唻 ꜀*lai* A sound in singing; one says, a large mouth drawn awry.

囉丨 the tune or melody of a song.

徠˺ 倈˺ 勑˺ (*˛lai*) The first is read *˛lai*, the name of a hill in Lu; the third is also read *ch'ih*, as another form of 勅 an order.

To induce one to come; to meet one, to encourage; to treat strangers kindly; to warn.

丨 獃 臭 to get laughed at for a bumpkin; one whose dress is ridiculous and bizarre.

招 丨 百 姓 to encourage people, as to settle on vacant lands.

睞˺ (*lai˺*) To squint; the pupil of the eye distorted; to glance at.

眄 丨 to look at sideways; a glittering eye.

多 蒙 盼 丨 I thank you to help me a little.

明 眸 善 丨 to glance about with a sharp look.

賚˺ (*lai˺*) To confer on; to bestow on an inferior; a largess; to promise, as for a service received.

勞 丨 to reward for services.

丨 我 思 成 the realization of our hopes is given to us.

夢 帝 丨 予 良 弼 I dreamed that the High Ruler gave me an honest assistant.

我 尚 丨 汝 I will reward you.

丨 至 京 都 I will thank you to send (or take this letter) to Peking.

賴˺ 頼 (*lai˺*) From 貝 *precious* and 剌 *harsh;* the second form is common but unauthorized.

To depend on, to lean on; to rely, to confide in; to assume; to act on a false basis, to trump up; to profit, to get advantage; to calumniate, to accuse an innocent man; to deny, to ignore, not to recognize.

無 丨 之 徒 or 丨 詞 a loafer, a suspicious chap, a lazy fellow.

丨 錯 人 or 丨 別 人 to accuse wrongly, to implicate another.

仰 丨 or 倚 丨 to repose trust in.

放 丨 to cry for, as a spoiled child.

丨 有 此 耳 I have this to depend on.

你 贓 丨 人 you are a malicious accuser.

恃 强 丨 債 trusted to his impudence and denied the debt.

無 聊 無 丨 a hap-hazard life; no dependence on; unprofitable.

丨 債 不 如 丨 人 情 to evade one's debts is not so risky as to fail in one's respects to a man.

丨 厚 朋 友 an intimate friend.

丨 屋 to stick to a house, as a tenant who cannot be evicted.

In *Cantonese*. To leave behind; to forget; to omit, to pass over; tired, indisposed to.

腰 丨 骨 脊 my back aches.

丨 落 to forget; I left it.

丨 一 個 字 he omitted a character.

癩˺ 㾢˺ (*lai˺*) From *disease* and *depending;* the second form is rarely used.

A virulent chronic blotch or eruption, like scabies or leprosy, anciently regarded as a reason for divorcing a wife; its application differs in places, and it is now used in the southern provinces for itch, impetigo, and other chronic skin diseases; pustular, rough, as the skin.

生 丨 to have the itch.

濕 丨 or 丨 瘡 running ulcers, impetigo; scrofulous sores.

乾 丨 the itch.

麻 丨 丨 rough-skinned, said of the lichi.

丨 仙 a fellow covered with the itch.

丨 大 蠱 or 丨 團 the big leprous belly, a name for the toad.

過 丨 to infect another, or pass a complaint over to him.

瀨˺ (*lai˺*) Water flowing over the sand; a shallow reach; rippling over stones; a branch of the Cassia River 桂江 in Kwangsi, near P'ing-loh fu.

亘 丨 a stream in Shantung.

籟˺ (*lai˺*) A musical pipe with three reeds; the tubes of an instrument; an ingenious arrangement of musical tubes like an organ; a whizzing, creaking, or moaning sound.

天 丨 自 鳴 Heaven's pipes (or music) sings of its own accord.

竹 丨 the creaking of bamboos swayed by the wind.

萬 丨 無 聲 all pipes are still, no sound of any kind.

襰˺ (*lai˺*) Remiss in sacrificing; to destroy; to fall into, or involve in ruin.

祩 丨 to curse.

藾˺ (*lai˺*) A species of fragrant labiate plant allied to the hoarhound, which was burned in worship; to shade, to cover.

蔭 丨 shady, umbrageous.

丨 蕭 a fragrant leaved plant having whitish leaves, and many branches.

三 丨 or 三 奈 capoor cutchery, (or *kafoor-kutchri* in Bengali,) the aromatic roots of the ***Hedychium spicatum*** brought from India; a tuber from Fuhkien powdered to use in plasters.

鯠˺ (*lai˺*) A small kind of goby, common about Macao, called 紅 丨 from its red body, which looks like raw meat; it is the *Trypauchen vagina*, and lives in the salt ooze where it burrows.

蠇˺ (*lai˺*) Insects with stings, like the wasp, sphex, bee, or scorpion.

酹˺ (*lai˺*) From *spirits* and to *take* up with the finger; also read *lüeh*,

To pour out a libation on the earth; to sprinkle.

沃 丨 to pour out spirits.

丨 花 to sprinkle flowers.

丨 奠 to make a libation.

淋 丨 a sprinkling, an aspersion.

LAN.

Old sounds, lan *and* lam. *In Canton,* lan, lam, *and* lăm; — *in Swatow,* lam, lan, nam, *and* nan; — *in Amoy,* lan *and* lam; — *in Fuhchau,* lang; — *in Shanghai,* lè^n; — *in Chifu,* lan.

闌 ꜁lan From 門 *door* and 柬 to *choose*; interchanged with the next two.

A door-screen; to shut in or off; to seclude; to separate; late, evening; failing, ruined; exhausted; rare, few, in limited quantities; moderate; a wristlet.

｜入 to go in abruptly, to enter without a pass.

歲｜ late in the year.

更深夜｜ very late at night, nearly dawn.

酒｜ to drink moderately; the feast is about over.

遮｜ a porch or screen; an obstruction; to screen from view.

｜門 in *anatomy*, the *caput coli*.

欄 ꜁lan From *wood* and a *screen*; used for the preceding.

A railing; a balustrade for support or defense; a row of posts; a den or pen for animals; to rail in, to cage, to shut in.

｜架 a wooden chevaux-de-frise placed before a yamun.

｜杆 a railing; a baluster; the eye-socket; oblique; crosswise; also applied to flounces.

馬｜ a corral, a horse-pen.

牛｜ a cattle yard.

下｜錢 cash given to servants and porters.

昆｜樹 a tree found in Japan (*Trochodendron aralioides*), akin to the magnolia, so called from the whorls of leaves growing like a balustrade.

畫個圈｜ draw a circle around it.

In *Cantonese*. A bazaar or row for the sale of an article; a market.

落｜去 gone to market.

菓｜ a fruit market.

攔 ꜁lan To stop with the hand, to hinder, to embarrass; to obstruct, to divide, to separate, to screen off.

｜阻 to stop, to interfere with.

｜輿 to stop an officer's cart or sedan, to give him a petition.

｜路搶劫 to block the road in order to rob.

無關｜ nothing to prevent it, no impediment.

｜截 to hinder; to cut off one's way, as by banditti.

｜開 to interfere, to part.

瀾 ꜁lan Swelling waters rolling on in continuous surges; billows, waves; dirty water in which rice has been washed.

波｜ great billows.

｜漫 successive showers; driving rain; scattered.

普慶安｜ to quiet [the people] everywhere by restraining the overflowing waters.

必觀其｜ you ought to look [at the water] when surging high.

襴 幱 ꜁lan From *dress* or *napkin* and a *screen*, as the phonetic.

An ancient kind of literary dress called ｜衫, a sort of doctor's robe; a suit of inner and outer garments.

囒 ꜁lan Unintelligible talk, gabble.

｜哰㑩拏 gibberish, confused talk.

蘭 ꜁lan A general name for orchideous plants, like the *Malaxis, Epidendrum, Vanda,* &c.; and extended to other gay and fragrant flowers growing on single peduncles, or alternately in a spikelet; adopted, sworn; pleasant, joyous, delightful; excellent.

｜孫 many grandchildren.

結拜金｜ to adopt one for a brother or sister.

｜兄 an adopted brother.

｜姐 an adopted sister.

｜閨 a maiden's boudoir.

｜也王者之香 the fragrance of the orchid is royal.

｜形棘心 beautiful in form but a villain at heart.

芝｜氣味 the fragrance of an orchid; *met.* a dear friend

萑｜ to shed tears.

二月｜ the spring beauty, the *Orycophragmus sonchifolius* at Peking.

馬｜ a small iris. (*Iris pumila.*)

珠｜ the *Chloranthus inconspicuus*, used to scent tea; a name for certain kinds of tea, chulan hyson and scented caper.

吊｜ or 風｜ air plants.

三葉｜ the *Aglaia odorata.*

玉｜ the *Magnolia yulan.*

｜州府 the capital of Kansuh.

斕 ꜁lan A mixture of colors, like the stripes on animals.

斒｜ striped, brindled; ornamented with bands.

籣 ꜁lan A wooden quiver for carrying a cross-bow on the back.

抱弩負｜ grasp your bow and strap on your quiver.

屋｜縣 an old name during the Han for Chang-yeh hien in Kansuh, towards the western end of the Great Wall.

讕 ꜁lan To defame, to calumniate; to charge a thing falsely on another.

｜誣 to accuse falsely.

｜辭曰四等畏死見誣耳 to accuse is said of criminals who, fearing death to themselves, charge others with crime.

躝 ˬlan To overpass, to step over; to creep, to twine around.

丨踰 to pass over.

丨籐 to climb over, as a vine on a frame.

丨地 to run, as a melon vine.

藍 ˬlan From *plant* and to *survey*; occurs used for the next.

A plant used to dye blue; blue, indigo blue; indigo.

丨色 a blue color.

洋丨 foreign blue; foreign indigo.

老丨 a blue-black color.

二丨 a deep blue; navy blue.

丨田 a famous place near Si-ngan fu the old capital of China, now Lan-tien hien 丨田縣 in Shensi, noted for its jade.

終朝采丨 all the morning I gather the indigo flower.

青出于丨 the light blue comes from dark blue; — *met.* doctors had to learn their alphabet.

槐丨 the greenish blue produced by locust (*Sophora*) flowers.

大丨 the indigo plant. (*Indigofera tinctoria.*)

丨菜 or 廿丨 the woad or *Isatis tinctoria.*

丨澱 seems to be a species of *Ruellia.*

蓼丨 a species of smart-weed. (*Polygonum tinctorium.*)

丨本 essays written on thin paper for lazy students.

僧伽丨 the abode of Budha and his priests, (Sanscrit *sangarama*) the house of reunion; — *i. e.* a temple and its shrine.

襤 ˬlan A single coverlet; ragged, mean garments, without a lining, a collar; trimmings.

丨褸 tattered, dirty clothes; shabby.

䃹 ˬlan Thin, a mere surface; boulders, rocks.

慾壑丨䆾 the lusts and desires [are never satisfied; they are like] a deep cave.

籃 ˬlan Baskets of bamboo or rattan or straw, made with a bale, and often with cover.

丨筐 baskets of all sorts.

花丨 wire baskets made of flowers.

食隔丨 a partition-basket made with trays.

場丨 a long shallow basket carried into the examination hall.

鬛 ˬlan Long and abundant hair.

丨鬖 disheveled hair; heedless, slovenly; this phrase is written several ways.

婪 ˬlan From *female* and *forest*, explained as referring to the tricks of gamblers.

Covetous, greedy of money; to desire; scheming for gain.

貪丨 close-fisted; avaricious.

賍丨 hoards got by extortion.

丨索 to oppress and harry people.

啉 ˬlan Greedy for gratifying the appetite; to have a drink all around, and finish the bottle.

惏 ˬlan Like the last two.

貪丨 gluttonous; covetous; this use is found in Shansi.

Read ˬlin. Cold.

丨慄 frigid, chilly.

霖 ˬlan From *rain* and *soaking.*

A long continued rain.

雨水丨漓 the rain poured incessantly.

嵐 ˬlan From *hill* and *wind*, but the primitive is a contraction of ˬlan 葻 wind moving the grass.

Vapor or mist on a hill top; smoky vapor.

山丨 mountain mist.

夕曛丨氣陰 as the evening mist covers the earth.

烟丨 smoky vapor on a hill top.

丨縣 a district named from the Lan-ki peak 丨奇山 within its borders; it lies northeast of T'ai-yuen fu in Shansi, and west of the River Făn; the region is famed for its horses.

躝 ˬlan To go quickly; to stride over, to step across; to omit, as in reading.

丨過去 step over it, as a ditch. (*Cantonese.*)

燣 ˋlan To toast or roast a cake before the fire till it becomes browned.

丨一丨 toast it for a while.

丨黃 to brown, to toast slightly.

丨焦芋頭 to roast taro in the ashes.

丨脆 to toast crisp, as cakes.

ˋ覽 ˋ覧 ˋlan From to *see* and to *survey*; the second is the complete form but the first is most used, and looks like ˬhien 賢 worthy.

To take a view of, to inspect; to behold from a distance; to understand, to perceive.

台丨 for you, Sir, to see.

週丨 to look around, to inspect.

一丨盡知 understood the whole affair at one look.

丨視 to examine, as an inspector.

丨觀今古 an extensively read man.

恭呈御丨 I respectfully send this up for your Majesty's inspection.

丨悉 I have learned the whole matter.

批丨 to make known judicial decisions.

博丨 a general scholar.

攬 ˋ擥 ˋlan From *hand* and to *inspect* as the phonetic.

To grasp, to carry with a firm hand or in the arms; to interfere with; to engross; to monopolize; to hold the market, to make a corner; to hug up close; grasping; engrossing; an armful; to clutch, as in reaping.

丨取 to seize all; to take up.

寫承丨 to write a contract to take goods.

丨得過 able to get one's arms around it.

丨頭 the head of, as a guild.
柴一丨 an armful of wood.
他全兜丨 he will try to manage it all; he assumes the direction.
丨榜 the last on the list of *küjin* graduates.
丨貨 to engross an article.
小船丨風 the gust brings the boat up in the wind.
包丨厘金 to become surety for, or to manage the duty.
着力丨 reap the grain faster.

欖 ʻlan The Chinese olive, 橄丨 or 丨子 has two varieties, the 白丨 or largest sort (*Canarium album*), and the 烏丨 or sweetest kind (*Canarium pimela*); the first is better known at the North as 青菓 the green fruit.
鹹丨 salted olives.
丨糖 a resinous exudation from the Canarium tree like *elaine*.
喉丨 the Adam's apple.
雕丨核 carved olive seeds.
含木丨 to suck a wooden olive; — to keep still about a thing. (*Cantonese.*)

漤 ʻlan From *water* and *greedy*.
To pickle fruits in brine; to divine by dropping water through a tortoise-shell.

爁 燣 ʻlan Fire burning furiously; a hot raging fire carried on by the wind, and not to be quenched; to scorch, to heat, to singe.
給火丨熱了 heat it over a fire, as a basin of milk.
丨去茸毛 singe off the pin feathers.

壈 ʻlan Disappointed, repulsed.
坎丨 lost one's aim, unable to attain one's object.

罱 ʻlan A two leaved clasping net, which springs together as it incloses the fish, and holds them from escaping.

懶 ʻlan From *heart* and to *lean* to.
Lazy, listless, sluttish; remiss; sleepy, heavy; averse, disinclined to.
躲丨 to shirk work.
丨惰 lazy, unwilling to work.
大食丨 a lazy glutton.
慵丨 lazy, inefficient.
伸丨 to gape and stretch.
一身丨骨 incurably lazy.
花叢丨回顧 I don't care about going back to see the flowers.
丨省 to slur over, to slight work.
丨怠動彈 too lazy to lift a ball — or a finger.

濫 lanʼ From *water* and to *view*.
A freshet, a rising of water; incroaching, overflowing; intruding on; to float; to soak; profuse, excessive; lawless; irregular; time-serving; addicted to, beyond bounds; unsettled; wet, oozy, like land recently overflowed.
水丨 or 丨溢 it overflows.
丨出來 the water runs over.
丨刑 illegal punishments.
丨寫 to write without regard to facts or order; to scribble.
丨費 to waste; too profuse.
急流泛丨 [the dike] has suddenly overflowed.
無丨 no excess; about enough.
丨開數目 to make out an account loosely; to salt a bill.
丨保 to go as security carelessly; to recommend without full knowledge.
丨交 to associate with low people.
不僭不丨 [the king] showed neither favoritism nor excessive punishment.
叨丨 insatiable of your kindness; — a polite phrase.
以免枉丨 to avoid needless trouble and tumult.
丨奏 to needlessly memorialize the Throne.
兜丨 an officious busy-body.
冒丨軍功 to assume great bravery to one's self in the war.

纜 lanʼ A rope, a hawser, a twisted cable; a painter; to drag with a rope.
拉丨 to drag the rope.
打丨 to twist hawsers.
船丨 or 牽丨 to track a boat.
大丨 a cable, such as the 篾丨 or bamboo cables.
鉄丨 twisted wire rope for rigging.
解丨 to weigh anchor, to start on a voyage.
丨路 a tracking-path.
In *Cantonese*. To bind on with a cord, to tie on.
丨頭白 tie on a mourning cap.

惏 lanʼ Greedy of good eating, covetous; longing for; strong, hale.
貪丨 to desire good things to eat.

糷 lanʼ Rice gruel made thick and glutinous.

鑭 lanʼ The luster of burnished metal, especially of gold.
光丨 brilliant.

瓓 lanʼ The luster or chatoyency of a gem; its quality of reflecting light.

爛 lanʼ From *fire* and to *shut* in as the phonetic.
To cook thoroughly, bright, splendid; brilliant; tattered, torn; dilapidated, dirty; worn out; rotten, corrupted, over-ripe; running, as a sore; old, ruined; very, exceedingly.
丨眼邊 blear eyed.
煮丨 boiled to shreds.
明星有丨 the bright stars are glittering.
魚丨 phosphorescence of fishes.
破丨 broken down; ragged, worn out; smashed to pieces.
糜丨其民 he oppressed his people; *lit.* made a pulp of them.
以丨爲丨 to carry to the bitter end, to dare the worst.

路上｜來不堪 the road is insufferably muddy.

｜醉 dead drunk.

打｜ to break, to smash.

｜賒惡討 to loosely give credit and then sue one for the pay.

｜多 very many.

｜其盈門 filling the gate with a gorgeous crowd

｜命 a hard lot; suffering.

｜瞓｜食 he does nothing but eat and sleep. (*Cantonese.*)

｜仔 a rascal, a loafer. (*Cantonese.*)

蛀｜ worm-eaten.

｜嘴 or ｜口 a blackguard.

講話｜老 he talks like an old hand. (*Cantonese.*)

LANG.

Old sound, lung. *In Canton,* long; — *in Swatow,* lang; — *in Amoy,* long; — *in Fuhchau,* long *and* laung; — *in Shanghai,* long; — *in Chifu,* lang.

郎 ꜀lang From 邑 *place,* and 㒸 *expert* to give the sound; as a primitive it often drops the radical.

A place or summer-house situated in Lu; a term of respect for officers and other persons; a man; a gentleman; in Fuhkien, a common word for a person.

令｜ your son.

新｜ a bridegroom.

｜君 or 才｜ my husband, said of him; your husband.

花｜ a beggar, from his tatters.

男｜ a gentleman.

無如此｜者 [I have seen] no one equal to this man.

內閣｜中 a clerk in the Inner Council.

白頭｜ the white headed lad, a bird. (*Pycnonotus occipitalis.*)

In *Pekingese.* Used after some nouns to denote a quality.

明｜ brightness.

硬｜ hardness.

廊 ꜀lang From a *shelter* and a *gentleman.*

A verandah; a porch or passage on the side of a house, like a corridor or gallery; chambers adjoining a hall.

遊｜ a covered way connecting buildings.

暗｜ the piazza built in as a part of the main room in houses, while 明｜ is an open piazza or verandah.

屋｜ porches.

｜廡 a side gallery or piazza.

巡｜ a watchman's lodge or portico.

｜廟材 distinguished talents or position, as a statesman.

榔 ꜀lang A term applied to several trees in Honan, having serrated leaves like the elm, and producing great numbers of flies from galls; the 𤬪｜ and 蚊｜樹 are two kinds.

檳｜ the betel-nut.

檳｜膏 pale catechu or gambier, because so generally eaten with the nut.

桹 ꜀lang Used with the last, but not correctly.

A species of palm likened to the *Areca,* from whose pith sago flour can be made.

枸｜ a species of *Prunus* found in Kwangtung.

鳴｜ a kind of rattle used to drive fish into nets.

桑｜ an old name for the dragon-fly.

螂 蜋 ꜀lang An insect, the common mantis; an ineffectual effort is likened to 螳｜擋車 the mantis trying to stop a carriage.

蜣｜ the common tumble-dung, a species of *Ateuchus* or *Geotrupes.*

鬪｜點水 the dragon-fly (an *Agrion*) dips up the water.

琅 瑯 ꜀lang A whitish stone, prized as an ornament.

｜璫 a kind of necklace.

｜玕 white coral of a firm texture, branched like a *Gorgonia,* but not susceptible of polish.

｜函 your jewel of a letter, *i. e.* your valued favor, alluding to the rarity of this kind of coral.

琳｜ tinkling of gems or stones.

｜琊郡 an ancient name for the eastern part of Shantung, including Tsing-cheu fu; during the Tsin 晉 dynasty, A. D. 350, ｜琊王 was a title of the heir-apparent.

鋃 ꜀lang Interchanged with the last.

A kind of locket or clasp.

金｜鐺 a gold chain for the neck; — *met.* something grievous to bear, but which cannot be avoided.

硠 ꜀lang The sound of stones or waves.

磅｜ sound of a drum.

｜｜ hard, strong, as a rock.

｜｜磕磕 stones and rocks crashing and rumbling against each other.

㝗 ꜀lang An empty deserted house.

寂靜㝗｜ the place was utterly silent and deserted, as if banditti had robbed it.

狼 ꜀lang From *dog* and *expert*, because it is said to be clever at divining where it should go.

A beast whose howl scares other animals; "it has a den, and its hind legs are the shortest;" the wolf; cruel, wolfish, furious, oppressive; very, greatly; to injure; to deceive and harm; occurs applied to snakes on account of their venom.

丨心 unmerciful, cruel.

丨毒 savage, truculent, merciless.

粒米丨戾 the grain is very plentiful.

丨籍 more than enough, scattered about.

黃鼠丨 the weasel, so called from its yellow belly.

過樹丨 a venemous snake found in Kwangtung.

天丨 the star Sirius.

丨跋其胡 the wolf springs forward on his dewlap; — said of a very aged one.

稂 ꜀lang A useless grass growing in rice fields, much resembling the grain, but which one native author describes as a species of *Digitaria*, a common sort of panic grass in northern China, and not improbably intended.

丨莠 darnel, tares.

不丨不莠 he is neither grass nor tares; — *met.* he is good for nothing.

浸彼苞丨 the water overflows that tussock of grass.

躴 ꜀lang Tall; as the component parts of the character, *body* and *fine* were perhaps intended to intimate.

丨躿 a very tall person.

崀 ꜀lang Name of a hill, the 峻丨 behind which the sun goes down at the winter solstice.

筤 ꜀lang Young bamboos; a basket; a screen for carriages.

蒼丨竹 tender green bamboo.

筲丨山 a range of peaks in the west of Sz'chʻuen, north of the Ta-tu River.

莨 ꜀lang Also read ꜀*liang*.

A species of reed or marsh grass; a kind of dye-stuff.

丨菪 a plant resembling scammony, which produces delirium and giddiness.

薯丨 a dye-stuff like gambier, made from the juice of a plant, and used at Canton to dye silks umber brown.

薯丨噉頭 he is as ugly as a lump of dye-stuff. (*Cantonese.*)

朗 ꜂lang From *moon* and *expert*.

Clear, as moonlight; bright; luster; clearness; a distinct utterance.

光丨 bright, as a lamp.

淸丨 limpid, pure, transparent.

丨照 to receive or ask aid of; blessed of.

月丨 bright moonlight, moonshine.

丨丨誦經 to recite the liturgy in a distinct voice.

老爺丨鑒 you, Sir, understand this thing very clearly.

In *Cantonese.* To rinse the mouth; to stir or rinse in water in order to cleanse, as a plate.

烺 ꜂lang Fire; the bright blaze of a fire.

塱 ꜂lang From *earth* and *bright*; an unauthorized character.

In *Cantonese.* A bank raised around a field; a terrace or raised plateau, walled up from a natural slope.

浪 lang꜄ Waves, billows, surges; profligate, dissipated; wasteful, extravagant; rude, impertinent, lawless, as a wave seems to be; the mind not settled, undecided; a drum.

波丨 or 風丨 billows; waves, as they rush on shore.

丨子 a spendthrift.

麥丨 the wind undulating the growing grain.

丨用 a prodigal use of.

忙丨 unmannerly; indecent haste.

孟丨 or 猛丨 rude, unpolished.

丨語花言 foolish; lewd talk.

嘔丨 seasick, squeamish.

謔丨 audacious ridicule of.

丨蕩 inconstant, fluctuating; vagabondish

眼 lang꜄ To expose to the air to dry; bright, clear.

誏 lang꜄ To speak distinctly; idle, ridiculous talk; a double entendre.

埌 lang꜄ A desert; a tomb, usually in lone places.

墳丨 a burial-place.

壙丨 a wild dreary waste, a steppe.

閬 lang꜄ A high door; vacant, unoccupied; wide, as a desert.

高丨 a lofty gateway.

丨苑 fairy land.

土丨 a wild place.

丨丨 extensive and waste, like the pampas.

丨苑奇才 a man of remarkable talents.

丨中縣 chief district in Paoning fu, on the river Kia-ling in Sz'chʻuen; it was formerly called 丨州, and comprised a large region in this valley.

LĂNG.

Old sounds, leng, ling, *and* lang. *In Canton*, ling, lăng, *and* lang; — *in Swatow* leng *and* né; — *in Amoy*, leng; — *in Fuhchau*, ling *and* léng; — *in Shanghai*, lăng *and* lang; — *in Chifu*, lăng.

稜 ꜀lăng Interchanged with the next. A corner, an angle; a classifier of fields; the awe or influence of a god.

烏 丨 a kind of rice.

威 丨 the majesty of a god.

幾 丨' 田 how many fields are there?

丨 角 a right angle; a square corner.

三 丨 草 a kind of triquetrous sedge (*Cyperus*), fit for making rain-cloaks.

棱 ꜀lăng From *wood* and *high* as a tumulus; used with the last and next. Squared or hewn timber, such as is used in buildings; a beam in a roof or piazza which projects beyond the post; a sleeper on which a board rests; to mortise things together; a corner; four-cornered; to raise up on trestles, to support on a frame or on sleepers.

瓴 丨 the turned up corners of a roof; the peak of the roof.

模 丨 手 one who never decides; a trimmer; a time-server.

作事模 丨 to waver in one's views, to act hesitatingly.

剛 丨 domineering, intractable.

楞 ꜀lăng Anciently the same as the last, but now used by the Budhists for the Lenga Sutra, one of their celebrated classics, the 丨 伽經 containing the tenets of Bodhi-Dharma, a teacher and successor of Sakyamuni, A. D. 526.

丨 伽 Ceylon in Budhist books.

崚 ꜀lăng Hilly, uneven country.

丨 嶒 the undulating appearance of a hilly region, as the eminences succeed and rise in the distance.

崒 丨 a lofty peak, which excels others.

睖 lăng' To look ahead.

丨 瞪 or 丨 睜 to stare, to look directly at without moving the eyes.

丨着眼睛 to fix one's eyes on angrily.

薐 lăng' The old name for spinach, 菠 丨 菜, the seeds of which were brought from Ni-po-wéi or Nipaul, by a priest in the T'ang dynasty.

冷 ꜂lăng From *ice* and an *order*. Cold, chilly, icy; aguish; indifferent, frigid; cool, miffed; still, clear; lonesome; unusual; to cool, to chill.

丨 淸 or 丨 落 quiet, comfortless, lonely.

丨 淡 distant, cool, as friends; insipid, as a book; dull, as trade; to quiet down, to let a few days pass and cool off, as parties in a brawl.

發 丨 to have a chill.

人情 丨 暖 people's feelings are changeable.

丨 氷 氷 cold as ice.

丨 傷 風 snuffling from the cold.

丨 眼 瞧 他 to look at coolly; to regard with doubt.

丨 子 sleet, fine icy rain

丨 熱 鍼 one name for the thermometer, now called 寒暑表 more frequently.

丨 瘡 chilblains.

丨 笑 a cold heartless laugh, a sardonic grin.

丨 字 an unusual character, one seldom met with.

抽 丨 子 an unlooked for event; a sudden mishap.

丨 不 防 he does not know who is watching him.

丨 化 器 a condensing engine or reservoir; — a foreign term.

丨 河 the cold river (*sita*) or the headwaters of the Yellow River, which the Budhist fable says runs underground all the way from Sir-i-kol in Pamer to Lake Lop, and thence to the 星宿海 Sea of Stars.

丨 丨 淸 淸 quiet, as a street at night; very still.

丨 宮 the still palace — where his discarded women are kept by the emperor.

丨 言 丨 語 mocking words; suspicious allusions or innuendoes.

丨 孤丁的 alone, no companion, as when the crowd has gone.

殑 lăng' Deathlike; ghostly; similar to the next.

丨 殑 exhausted by sickness; comatose; dying.

倰 lăng' To go as if tired out.

丨 僜 completely wearied out; strength all gone.

LAO.

Old sounds, lo, lot, *and* lok. *In Canton,* lò, lao, *and* liu ; — *in Swatow,* lao ; — *in Amoy,* lò *and* liao ; — *in Fuhchau,* lo *and* lau ; — *in Shanghai,* lo ; — *in Chifu,* lao.

勞 劳 ꜀lao From 力 *strength* and 熒 *brilliant* contracted, explained as alluding to the energy of fire in burning itself to exhaustion ; the contracted form is common.

To toil, to labor, to fag at ; to exert one's self for another ; to trouble one, as with a commission ; to distress ; in distress ; careworn, distressed, burdened ; services to the state ; toil, exertion ; meritorious deeds, worthy actions.

丨神 to weary one's self ; wearied of, tired.

勤丨 to be diligent.

民亦丨止 the people are indeed greatly burdened.

丨苦 toilsome labor ; distress.

丨丨碌碌 wearied and distracted.

莫大功丨 unparalleled merit and effort.

丨駕 excuse me, Sir, for the trouble I give you ; — *scil.* I beg pardon.

有丨你心 obliged for your kind thoughts.

徒丨 unrequited labor.

丨瘁不辭 I cannot tell how careworn and weary I am.

丨力者食人丨心者食於人 the employed live on their employers, and these are anxious how do feed them.

劬丨于野 painfully toiling in the open wilds.

丨金 or 酧丨 a douceur, a reward for services ; the person who gets it, a day-laborer, a coolie.

聰得手皮丨 I've only had my trouble for my pains.

丨人草草 the troubled are in gerat sorrow.

丨動人 or 多丨你們 I wish to engage your aid.

憂丨 anxious for.

Read lao' To reward labor, to recompense services ; to console ; to aid.

賞丨 to animate by bounties.

丨兵 to reward soldiers.

君丨則拜 he made obeisance at the king's commendation.

蟧 ꜀lao A kind of univalve shell-fish, perhaps the hermit crab, as it is said to occupy many sorts of shells.

蝭丨 a small whitish cicada, common in Chihli.

蟾丨 a spotted spider.

撈 ꜀lao From *hand* and *toil* as the phonetic.

To drag for ; to scoop up, to grapple from a deep place ; to dredge for, to hook out of the water ; to mix and stir up.

丨起 to haul up ; to grapple for.

丨屍 to search or drag for a dead body.

水底丨月 clutching the moon in the water, as Li Tai-peh did ; — *met.* ineffectual effort.

海底丨針 dredge for a needle in the sea ; — *met.* useless pains.

心癢難丨 it is not always easy to gratify one's desires.

丨摸 to feel for things in the water.

丨魚 to scoop out fish, as by a dredging net.

丨糖 stir in some sugar.

丨蠔殼 to dredge for oyster-shells.

In *Cantonese.* To mix up, to put in disorder ; to hash, to chop up ; to bother.

丨脚 to sorn on.

丨亂 to confuse ; to cause disturbance.

丨家仔 a clever, shrewd chap ; a blackleg.

嘮 ꜀lao From *mouth* and *ringing.*

A great noise.

丨嘈 a hubbub, a din ; to make a bother.

牢 ꜀lao From *ox* and a *shelter,* which is regarded as a contraction of 冬 the *winter,* which the cattle are to pass in the pen.

A corral or stable for cattle, especially sacrificial animals ; an aviary ; a granary ; a jail, a prison ; domestic animals ; firm, strong ; to know or do certainly ; securely.

太丨 an ox ; because it is offered to Confucius.

少丨 a sheep.

丨靠之至 [the two braces] firmly rest on each other ; *met.* it is wholly trustworthy.

執豕于丨 he took a pig from the pen.

丨籠計 a scheme to catch one.

丨固 secure ; strong.

丨丨謹記 to have a distinct remembrance of.

獄丨 a prison.

天丨 the emperor's prison, a special room in the Board of Punishment for officials.

坐丨 imprisoned ; in jail.

丨不可破 the prison can't be broken ; — *i. e.* the thing is certain ; unalterable custom.

哰 ꜀lao To talk without meaning or coherency.

丨叨 loquacious, gabbling.

嘲丨嗹嘍 unintelligible talk, like that of foreigners.

燕丨丨 the swallows twittering — as they fly in and out.

醪 ꜀lao Spirits mixed with sediment.

浮丨 muddy spirits, lees stirred up.

醇丨 generous wine.

香丨 sweet, pleasant spirits.

'老 *'lao* Composed originally of 人 *man*, 毛 *hair* and 匕 to *compare*, because at seventy a man's hair changes to white; it forms the 125th radical of a few characters mostly relating to age.

Aged, venerable; a term of respect and honor used before names, and resembling Sire; his honor, Señor; prefixed to names of relationship; an officer; to treat respectfully, as an old man should be; old, out of date, used a long time; old at, skillful; to grow old; tough, as meat; stringy, as vegetables; inert, not zealous; backing out; as an *adverb*, really, decidedly, very; sect of the Rationalists.

丨頭子 an old man; a husband, my husband.

丨公 and 丨婆 a husband and wife (*Cantonese.*)

丨同 one of the same age.

丨王 Mr. Wang.

父丨 the old people, our seniors.

丨人家 this old gentleman; you, Sir; this man; my parents.

丨先生 and 丨大人 titles of respect given to the aged.

丨少 the old and young.

丨早的 very early; too soon.

丨實 honest, trustworthy; real; gentle, tractable; an euphemism for witless, simple, gullible.

丨是不要 I really don't want it.

丨練 or 丨成 well learned in.

丨拙 [I am] old and stupid.

丨行長' an old customer.

丨見不着 you will not live to see it.

丨君 the old prince, or 丨子 the old boy, the name of Lao-tsz', founder of the 丨氏之教 or Rationalists, whence 老 alone sometimes denotes the sect.

丨子 your father, or our father; — used in a family like *the old man.*

丨沒看見 I have not seen you for a good while.

丨弱 the old and weak.

國丨 a nobleman who has served three sovereigns; a poetical name for liquorice.

丨吾丨 my old folks I treat with respect.

不憖遺一丨 he could not bear to leave one minister.

丨夫灌灌 I, an old man [speak] with entire sincerity.

永錫難丨 may he have the rare felicity of a green old age.

丨忌多思 the aged should avoid many cares.

丨江湖 an old traveler.

他丨不聽 he won't hear me any way.

'咾 *'lao* A tone, a noise, a final sound.

In *Shanghai.* A word placed after nouns to distinguish the members of a sentence; and, also; a final particle completing the sense.

米丨肉禿有 there is rice and meat too.

已經話拉丨 I've already said it.

'恅 *'lao* Confused.

慞丨 perturbed; very much disturbed.

'栳 } **'䇭** } *'lao* A basket or hamper made of osiers or bamboo splints, which turns up and forms a kind of box with trays.

栲丨 a bucket; also a hanaper or basket in stories.

'⿸疒老 *'lao* The *old disease*, the itch.

生瘑丨 to have the itch.

'狫 *'lao* An ancient name for the Laos, or some tribe of Miao-tsz', the 犵丨 part of whom are still found in Kwéichau, and divided into many tribes; some are very brutish, live in holes roofed over like sheep-cots with logs and thatch, or poor hovels; others, as the 木丨 in Kwéi-ting hien, more resemble Chinese in their habits.

'荖 *'lao* Also read ˌ*péi.*

The 丨葉 or siri leaf used with betel-nut; a term common in Fuhkien instead of 蔞葉 the correct form.

'橑 *'lao* The short rafters which support the eaves of houses over the piazza, and are sometimes curved; a sort of bow over a cart.

丨椽 small rafters in a verandah.

雕丨以爨 to carve rafters to cook with.

'潦 *'lao lao'* From *water* and a *blaze*; also read ˌ*liao.*

A great rain; or the overflow which it produces; a puddle left by rain; to macerate, to soak; careless, neglectful; name of a river.

水丨 the puddles made by rain, or left after a freshet.

丨死 drowned.

丨丨 tangled, complicated.

丨漫 overflowing; brimming.

旱丨 [either] a drought or freshet.

泂酌彼行丨 bring from afar the water left in the pools.

丨倒 unmannerly; not trained, assuming.

丨草了事 to slight work; to lump for mere appearance.

湖面丨闊 the lake is too wide to see across.

澇' *lao'* Like the preceding, and interchanged with it.

A torrent; name of a river, and of a rapid; great waves; to macerate; floods, an overflow.

飛丨相磢 the flying waves scrape on each other.

⿱艹勞' *lao'* *Toil* among *plants*; to weed the ground.

丨荳 a species of wild bean.

憦' *lao'* To be sorry for, as when one has made a mistake.

懊丨 to regret, to repent of.

癆 ˀ ˬlao From *disease* and *toil* as the phonetic.

Wasting away from toil or anxiety; atrophy of the viscera, like a consumption of the bowels, marasmus; poisonous drugs; to produce atrophy or wasting.

公鴨〡 a wheezing sound, resulting from a thickening of the glands of the throat.

〡病 pining away, phthisis; emaciated and consumptive.

〡辣 the pain of a sting.

牛筋〡 a chronic cough and leanness; applied to people who manage to live above beggary.

〡人之物 a thing which poisons people, as arsenic.

〡傷 sprained, injured, as by an immoderate lift.

嫪 ˀ lao' From *woman* and to *fly high*.

To dote on, to hanker after; lustful, lecherous, given up to whoring; to be jealous; envious.

〡戀 lovesick, enamored with.

〡毒 a lover of Tsin Chi Hwang-ti's mother, a term for a libertine, as Sir Francis Chartres.

姻〡 a paramour.

LEH.

Characters under this syllable are often sounded like LÜEH. *Old sound,* lek. *In Canton,* lăk, lut *and* lik; — *in Swatow,* lek; — *in Amoy,* lék, lek, *and* lút; — *in Fuhchau,* lek; — *in Shanghai,* lăk; — *in Chifu,* lù.

仂 ˀ lieh' From *man* and *strength* for the phonetic; occurs used with the next.

A fraction, an overplus; the tenth of a thing, but others say it is a third.

喪用三年之〡 mourning occupies parts of three years.

阞 ˀ lieh' From *mound* and *strength* as the phonetic.

A sewer obstructed, and its waters forcing a passage; the quality or strata of the earth as affected by the springs and channels in it; geomantic veins; the diameter of a circle; a fraction of; a third.

地〡不行 the channels of water cannot flow.

散〡 to wear out or injure the good luck of a place, as by these veins drying up.

扐 ˀ lieh' From *hand* and *strength;* occurs used with the next two.

A word used in Shansi, to bind; to divine with fifty straws placed between the fingers; they are first reduced to 49, and sorted at hazard into two parcels; from one lot a straw is taken and put by the little finger, and four others are put with it, and the rest distributed between the other two fingers; the other parcel is then divided in the same manner in the other hand, and the lengths of the two compared with the 64 diagrams to find the luck, or to tell when an intercalary moon will occur in the next five years.

〡縣 an old name for P'ing-yuen hien 平原縣 in Shantung.

艻 ˀ lé' From *plant* and *strength*, the primitive being substituted for 棘 thorns.

Spines on plants; prickly; very hispid; a species of spinous tree found near Annam, good for palisades and very durable.

對面〡 the *Gardenia spinosa.*

蘿〡 a rough-leaved fragrant plant allied to the sweet basil, found in Honan.

老鼠〡 a prickly grass at Canton (*Spinifex squarrosus*), used to stuff rat-holes; applied also to the *Argemone mexicana.*

勒 ˀ lö' ˬlé From *strength* and *hide; q. d.* hide is strong to curb a horse.

A bridle, the reins, a head-stall; whatever binds the head by which to lead the animal; to rein in, to restrain; to force, to require of, to oblige to do; to exact unjustly; to vex; to tie up, to bind; to strangle; to cut in stone; in *penmanship,* a horizontal stroke.

馬〡 the bit of a bridle.

〡兵 to environ a force so that it cannot escape.

捎〡 restrain from doing.

〡令 to insist on; to force compliance.

〡索 to extort money, to compel assent.

〡死 to strangle.

苦〡 or 〡逼 to ill-use, to disturb.

〡名碑上 he carved his name on the tablet.

〡休 to force an officer to vacate his post.

臨崖〡馬 hold in the horse when you come to a dangerous place.

女〡 a woman's fillet or head-band.

紅〡 to score out parts of a paper by the magistrate running a red line through it.

肋 ˀ lé' From *flesh* and *strength.*

The ribs; the side of the body.

〡條骨 a spare rib; one rib.

〡傍 or 〡門 the side.

脅〡 the ribs; 短〡 the false ribs.

Read ˏkin, and used with 筋. A tendon, a sinew.

鶏 丨 [only] a fowl's tendon; — *met.* a useless thing or fellow.

泐ˎ *lŏ* From *water* and *veins*; it is also read *lih*ˎ

To split rocks; the cleavage or veins of rocks; to split open; to clarify or settle, as sugar-syrup with eggs; to write.

石 丨 the cleavage of a rock.

名另 丨 my name is written elsewhere; — *i. e.* my card is inclosed; — a phrase used instead of signing the name.

素感大恩銘 丨 無似 your constant kindness and great favors are indelibly engraven on my heart.

石有時而 丨 rocks often split asunder.

王陽敬 丨 I, Wang Yang respectfully write — this letter.

嘞ˎ *lieh'* A sound, such as is made by an instrument; the note or tone.

In *Cantonese.* Morose, cross; disposed to annoy; troublesome; to talk out of proper place or order.

丨 黐 disarranged; confused, as a style; involved and obscure.

丨 起官話 to attempt to talk mandarin.

啉 丨 sullen, hard to suit.

LÉI.

The characters under this syllable are often read LUI. *Old sounds,* lui, lat, *and* lút. *In Canton,* lui; — *in Swatow,* lûi; — *in Amoy,* lui *and* lé; — *in Fuhchau,* lòi, lai, *and* lwi; — *in Shanghai,* lé; — *in Chifu,* léi.

雷 ˏ*léi* From *rain* and *field*, but the primitive is regarded as a contraction of 回 *repeatedly*, referring to the reverberations.

Thunder, which is produced by 陰陽以回薄而成 丨 "the *yin* and *yang* coming into mutual collision;" a deafening, thundering noise; to imitate, to do like, to echo.

一聲 丨 a clap of thunder.

行 丨 or 打 丨 to thunder.

丨 公 or 丨 神 the god of Thunder.

丨 鞭 the Thunderers's whip, *i. e.* a streak of lightning.

丨 同 to reiterate, to hit upon another's performance; to steal his thunder.

平地一聲 丨 a sudden surprise, a clap out of a clear sky.

丨 公轟 a peal of thunder.

丨 鼓 to beat a drum.

丨 醮火醮 be spry; hurry fast, as if the fire had caught.

滾木 丨 石 spiked logs and hollow stink-pots, used in defending city walls.

請息 丨 霆之怒 pray abate your great wrath.

疾 丨 不及掩耳 the clap came before one could cover his ears; — *scil.* sudden as lightning.

犯 丨 or 丨 厄 struck by lightning.

丨 公魚 a tadpole. (*Cantonese.*)

天 丨 打死你 may Heaven strike you dead with its bolt!

丨 火 the marks of lightning.

丨 丸 the thunder-pill, a species of truffle, the *Mylitta lapidescens* found in western China.

水 丨 a torpedo to blow up ships.

擂 ˏ*léi* To rub fine, to triturate, which makes a rumbling sound; to treat harshly; to drum; to precipitate.

丨 顏料 to grind paints.

丨 鎚 a pestle for triturating.

丨 漿 to rub flour for starching.

丨 鼓三通 three raps on the drum, as in a yamun.

蠕 ˏ*léi* An edible, salt water clam, common near the Bocca Tigris and in Lintin Bay.

罍 櫑 ˏ*léi* A carved wine-jar made of wood, bronze, or porcelain, with looped ears, having clouds painted on it to show its inexhaustibility; a sacrificial bathing-vessel.

缾之罄矣維 丨 之恥 when the pitcher is dry the jar feels the mortification.

縲 ˏ*léi* From *silk* and *to bind*; used with the next.

To bind with ropes; to secure, as a criminal; a black rope.

丨 絏之中 in bonds, bound; a prisoner; in custody.

纍 ˏ*léi* From *silk* and *fields* as the phonetic; its origin is similar to ˊ累 to bind, and it is interchanged with the preceding.

To join in a series, to concentrate; to place on, to add to; to die or be condemned when innocent; to involve; to creep, to wind about; to bind; to arrest; the hooks or ties in armor; an ancient weight used in reckoning weights of coins, equal to about four-fifths of a drachm, for which the next perhaps has been substituted.

甘瓠 丨 之 the sweet gourds cling to them.

葛藟 丨 之 the tendrils of the *Dolichos* cling to it.

串珠 丨 丨 connected, like a string of beads.

丨 縶 bound, as with a cord; intricate, entwined.

丨 絲首飾 a fine filagree worked bridal crown.

丨 丨 forsaken, lost; discontented.

鐳 ˏléi A pot or jar; in the Indian Archipelago, denotes the small copper coins in circulation, as doit, pice, fanams.
丨柚 a pumelo or shaddock.
漢丨 a bronze jar of the Han dynasty.

虆 ˏléi A trailing raspberry.
丨梩 a basket hod in which to carry dirt.
盈丨 full baskets

羸 ˏléi From *sheep* and a *monstrous* animal.
Lean, meager, emaciated, fallen away; feeble, infirm, debilitated; entangled; turned over.
丨瘦 very thin and lean.
丨其角 caught by his horns.
老丨 old and cadaverous.
丨其瓶 turned the jar bottom up.

畾 ˏléi From three *fields* parted or laid out; as a phonetic it is often contracted to one *field*.
Fields parted off by dikes; the space occupied by a field or plat.

儡 ˊléi To injure each other; to mutually destroy, as in fighting.
敗丨 to rout, to discomfit.
自丨其身 he only injured himself.
傀丨棚 a Punch and Judy show-box.
兩軍對丨 the two armies are in conflict.

壘 ˊléi From *earth* and *piled* up; used with ˊ累 reiterated.
A military wall, a rampart; to pile up, to lay on each other; a pile, a heap; reiterated; a row of graves; robust, strong.
軍丨 an intrenched camp.
丨卵之危 in such imminent danger as a pile of eggs — is of being broken.
深塹高丨 a deep fosse and a high fortification.
丨壁陣 a starry region including parts of Capricornus, Aquarius, and Pisces.
魁丨之士 a vigorous, brave soldier.
荒坆丨丨 the multitude of graves out in the wilds.
一丨石 a heap of stones.

磊 ˊléi A heap of stones; to throw stones into a heap.
丨落不群 a man superior to the common run.
丨丨落落 one of great abilities; having clear perception of.

藟 / 虆 ˊléi From *plant* and *piled up*, because its involved growth forms a thickset bush.
A creeper like a melon or a pea.
千歲丨 a kind of vine or running bramble like a raspberry, said to prevent the hair turning gray.
蓫丨 the *Rubus Thunbergii*, a kind of trailing berry found in Honan.

蕾 ˊléi A flower-bud; flowers partly opened.
花丨 a flower-bud.
蓓丨 many buds and opening flowers.

瘰 ˊléi Small pimples or blisters, which smart much.
痱丨 prickly heat; nettle rash.

鸓 / 貙 / 猓 ˊléi From *bird* or *dog*, and *reiterated*; the last two forms are old.
The flying squirrel, (*Pteromys*) called 丨鼠; it is considered to be medicinal, and the Chinese regard it as allied to the bat in its habits and structure.

腽 ˊléi To swell; to bulge or project as a barrel; a bulge, a boss.
背有丨腽[the sea-turtle's] back has protuberances on its shell.

誄 ˊléi From *words* and a *plow* as the phonetic.
To eulogize the dead; to write epitaphs, or confer the temple title; an obituary; a eulogy; praises of the dead, prayers.
丨述 to narrate one's virtues, to write a biography.
丨文 eulogistic prayers for the dead, which are usually burned for them.
賤不丨貴 the ignoble must not make eulogies on the honored.
丨功 to narrate one's great deeds.
丨曰禱爾于上下神祇 in the litanies it says, you should pray to the gods of the heaven and earth.

樏 ˊléi A tray or box with partitions in it, used for fruits, comfits, &c.; a fleshy fruit; iron spiked shoes for going up hills

絫 ˊléi Considered to be a contraction of ˏ纍 and of the next.
Now used chiefly as a weight equal to ten millet seeds, or one tenth of a ˏshu 銖 or the 88th part of a drachm avoirdupois; to add to.
脅肩丨足 to shrug the shoulders and cross the feet.

累 ˊléi léiˀ From 糸 *silk* and 畾 *fields* contracted; it is interchanged with ˊlü 屢 repeatedly.
To bind; to tie together; to repeat, to accumulate, to heap on; often, repeatedly.
繫丨 to tie or unite persons.
丨月經年 month by month the years pass on.
丨次 often, again and again.

Read *léi*ˀ. To involve, to compromise, to implicate, to put an affair on another which gives him trouble or responsibility; dependent on; perplexed with many affairs; embarrassed.

帶丨 or 拖丨 or 連丨 to involve another.
無掛丨 I am not anxious about it.
丨及人 he is implicated in it.
家計丨 he is troubled how to support the family.
丨墮 embarrassed with, as a child trying to carry three big apples.
受丨 involved in.
丨事 an embarrassing affair.
丨贅 verbose, much repetition; wordy; tiresome.
賠丨 to suffer or make amends for another.

儽 *léi'* Lazy, shirking work; tired out, worn down.
丨得很 or 丨得慌 quite fagged out and sick.
丨的發喘 he was wearied even to panting.
丨了一生 I have wearied out my whole life.

攂 *léi'* Interchanged with ʽ擂 to rub.
To beat a drum, to call the tattoo; to roll stones.
丨鼓 to drum.
丨研 to rub ink on the stone.
ʽ丨拳頭 to play morra; — *lit.* to rub the knuckles.
散丨砲 to beat the réveillé and fire the gun, — when calling off the watch.

礧 *léi'* To roll stones down hill; a rocky rough appearance.
丨石相擊 the rolling rocks struck each other.
生磈丨相連 [the oysters] grow irregularly one upon another, like stones piled up.
丨磙 falling with a heavy thud.

櫑 *léi'* From *wood* and *thunder* as the phonetic; interchanged with the last.
Name of a tree; to roll down stones on an enemy approaching a city wall.
備丨石以禦敵 prepare the stones so as to resist the enemy.

耒 *'léi* Combined of 木 *wood* and 丰 *easy*, to represent the crooked handle of a plow; it is the 127th radical of characters pertaining to tillage; the character ˏlai 來 to come is often thus contracted.
To plow; the handle and beam of a plow; a plow, of which Shinnung is the reputed inventor; its description shows that it has since undergone very little modification; old name of a river in the south of Hunan, one of the headwaters of the River Siang.
丨耜 a plow; — *met.* agriculture.

類 類 *léi'* Composed of 頪 *quick* and 犬 a *dog*, which is altered to 女 a *woman* in most cases.
Good, unselfish, excellent; a blessing; a species, a sort, a kind, rather less than a 部, and more than a 種, like class, genus, species; to assimilate; to class with; to become equal with; to discriminate between things; an ancient sacrifice to Heaven, not at the winter solstice.
同丨 of the same sort.
威儀不丨 your bearing and presence does not comport with your station.
丨似 similar in kind.
不相丨 unsorted, unlike; cannot be classed together.
善丨 the good; moral people.
畜丨 domestic animals; a term of abuse, You brute!
等丨 others similar to it.
人參狀丨人形 ginseng root resembles a man's figure.
不可比丨 they cannot be classified or compared.
各從其丨 each one after its own sort.
貪人敗丨 a covetous man tries to injure his equals.
丨見 to appear at court on succeeding to a father's estate or title, — in feudal times.
其形丨鷺 [the curlew's] form assimilates it to the egret.
丨書 collectanea, miscellanies.
肆丨于上帝 to sacrifice to Shangti, which was done by the sovereign.
丨我 be like me, make one of us, — as the solitary wasp is thought to tell the caterpillar it kills for its young.

Read *li'* An animal resembling a fox in shape, and marked like a leopard, formerly found in Hunan; it is a kind of civet, and those who eat its flesh will, it is said, be cured of jealousy.

纇 *léi'* Knots in silk thread; a defect, a flaw; incomplete, as the moon in its various phases; perverse, harsh; out of sorts.
忿丨 morose, crabbed.
疵丨 defective; it has flaws.
無丨 no incompleteness, perfect.
鉏丨除荒 to root out what is imperfect, and remove what is uncouth.

淚 泪 *léi'* From *water* or *ungovernable* and *eye*; the second form is least used, though the most consonant to the meaning.
Tears; to weep; to cry; a dropping like tears.
珠丨 pearly tears.
丨痕 traces of weeping.
雨丨 to rain tears; to weep much.
流眼丨 or 泣丨 or 下丨 to cry.
揮丨而別 they brushed away their tears and parted.
拂丨 or 抆丨 to wipe away tears.
丨沾襟 tears bedewed his coat.
含丨 tears standing in the eyes.
悲丨 mourning and weeping.
丨盈頤 tears wet his cheeks.
玉燭滴乾風裏丨 drops fall from the wax candle guttered by the wind

Read *li.'* Water flowing rapidly.
淒丨 a cold, comfortless look.

LEU.

Old sounds, lu *and* lút. *In Canton*, lau; — *in Swatow*, lao *and* lò; — *in Amoy*, lo; — *in Fuhchau*, lèu, lao, *and* laiu; — *in Shanghai*, lù; — *in Chifu*, lò.

樓 ꜀leu A loft; a staging; a tower; the upper floor or story of a house; the framework or space of a door; in stories, storied; an upper room; a chamber; a large fine shop, as an incense shop; a porch or raised portal; a layer; to assemble.

大丨 the chief hall in a house.

丨上 up-stairs.

丨下 ground-floor; down-stairs.

上高丨 to go to an eating-room, which at Canton, is usually up-stairs.

二層丨 two storied.

丨上丨 story above story, or more stories; a gambler, if he wins, says 丨上丨 I shall pile story on story; but if he losses, says 愁上愁 I shall pile grief upon grief.

秦丨 or 青丨 brothels; the first term is from a woman's name.

城丨 a tower over the city gate.

鐘丨 a bell tower; a belfry.

玉丨 a poetical name for the shoulders.

丨陣 the sleepers on a floor.

更丨 a watchman's loft.

走馬丨 a corridor; a verandah which goes around the house.

譙丨 a sentinel's watch on a wall.

望丨 a lookout, a high terrace, an upper porch.

岑丨 the highest peak or house.

丨車 a kind of movable watch-tower.

丨臺 a staging for performances.

望月丨 a belvedere on top of a mosque.

丨井 a skylight.

牌丨連絡道旁立 honorary portals stand by the wayside all along the road.

In *Fuhchau*. Cheap, low-priced.

婁 ꜀leu The original form was combined of 女 *woman*, 毋 *mother*, and 中 *within*, intended to denote empty; as a primitive, its use is chiefly phonetic.

To trail along, as a dress; to tie or lasso, as an ox; troublesome from repetition, annoying, frequent; simple, stupid; a tumulus.

丨宿 the sixteenth zodiacal constellation in the head of Aries.

離丨 a man mentioned by Mencius, who had good eyesight.

丨縣 a district in Sung-kiang fu, southwest of Shanghai.

牛馬維丨 the cows and horses are all tethered.

式居丨驕 they thus become more troublesome and overbearing.

子有衣裳弗曳弗丨 you have dresses and robes, but you will not wear them.

嘍 謱 ꜀leu From *mouth* and *words* and *annoying*; the second is not common, and restricted in its meaning.

Loquacious; troublesome and talkative; a tone in singing.

丨來丨去 to talk much.

嗹丨 the prattle of an infant beginning to talk; gabble.

嗹丨萬種 a thousand impertinences.

丨囉卒 guerilla troops; banditti; the men under an enemy.

丨哌 the chattering of birds.

摟 ꜀leu ꜂leu To drag or pull; to bring together; to embrace, to hug; to carry off, to drag away.

丨住 to hold by the arms.

丨抱 to fall on one's neck.

丨挽 to detain one, as by locking his arms.

丨處女 to elope with a girl; to carry off virgins.

丨人出街 dunning him to go out, — and take a stroll.

丨人賣 urging him to buy.

In *Cantonese*. To throw or wear over the shoulders; to hang down, as a shawl.

口水丨 a child's bib.

丨膊巾 to wear a shawl.

耬 ꜀leu A small dibbling cart, the 丨車 or 丨斗, which makes a furrow and drops the seed as it is dragged over the fields; one common name is 種斗 or seed hod.

甊 ꜀leu A small long-necked jar, shaped like a bottle, called 瓿丨; it is usually made of earthen-ware.

髏 ꜀leu A skull without skin or flesh. 髑丨 or 枯丨骨 a skull; the upper bones of the head.

螻 ꜀leu The mole-cricket (*Gryllotalpa*), which is thought to help devils and spirits in some way, and is killed by those who meet it by night; it is called 丨蛄 and 土狗 or earth-dog.

天丨 a kind of bat.

土丨 a four-horned fabulous goat.

丨蟻尚且貪生 even the mole-cricket and ant also desire to live.

䝏 ꜀leu A sow in heat.

既定爾丨豬 it is plain that you are little less than an old sow; — said to a lewd woman.

慺 ꜀leu Diligent, respectful; contented, joyous.

丨丨之心 sedulous and attentive to orders.

遱 ꜀leu Continuous.

連丨不斷 unceasing flow; never intermitting, like the passing of people in a street.

艛 ꜀leu A vessel with high poop galleries; high tops where marksmen were placed.

丨船 a war junk with a great and high stern.

䮫 ꜀leu A large horse; some define it an ass, and make it a synonym of ꜀lü 驢 the ass.

𣂼 ꜀leu To plunder.

𣂼丨 to plunder and forage on people, as soldiers and guerilla bands do.

塿 ꜀leu A small tumulus or mound is 培丨, often raised over graves in the northern provinces.

嶁 ꜀leu A peak, the 岣丨峰 in the Hăng range in the east of Hunan province, whereon it is said that the Great Yü set up a tablet.

簍 ꜂leu A hamper or basket for carrying coarse articles; an oil-basket woven of withes, and covered with layers of paper pasted inside and out.

一丨炭 a crate of coal.

油丨 an oil hamper; some of them will hold 150 catties.

薰丨 open baskets for drying or scenting teas or other things.

笆丨 an osier basket for carrying provisions.

鏤 ꜀leu leu꜄ From *metal* and *troublesome*; like the next.

Hard, pure iron; a graver to cut iron with; to engrave, to cut characters; to inlay; a frying-pan, a boiler.

丨空的花兒 open carved work, as on a frame.

器不雕丨 a plain article, no carving on it.

雕丨 or 丨刻 to engrave nicely.

刻骨丨心 [your love is] cut on my bones and graven on my heart.

虎韔丨膺 a tiger-skin bow-case adorned with inlaid work.

𠠐 leu꜄ To bore into and carve; to cut out flowers; to hollow out; a graving tool.

雕丨 to carve flowers in relief on wood-work, common in ornamented dwellings.

丨橘傳書 he dug out an orange to convey his letter, — refers to an incident in the life of Yoh Féi of the Sung dynasty.

瘻 **瘺** leu꜄ A swelling with a hard core in it; a purulent tumor, a running ulcer.

痔丨 the bleeding piles; an anal tumor.

丨瘡 ulcers breeding worms.

瘰丨 glandular scrofulous swellings on the neck.

烟丨 ulcers which result from opium smoking.

漏 leu꜄ From *water* and to *leak*; but the phonetic, by its composition of *house* and *rain*, shows the idea.

A clepsydra; to drip, to leak, to sipe, to ooze out; to drop on; to lose; to disclose, to blab; to forget, to lose sight of, to let slip; to let in, as a light; to moisten; a crack, a leak, an aperture.

補丨 to mend a crack.

接丨 to catch the dripping water.

失丨 to forget; to leave behind.

滲丨 it leaks; a dripping.

丨數 I omitted to put it in the account.

無個滴丨 no such lucky thing has leaked down. (*Cantonese.*)

更丨 a clepsydra to mark time.

丨網 to escape the net; — *i. e.* to evade punishment, or the consequences of a crime.

不愧於屋丨 do not be ashamed before the light which comes into your house; — *met.* act honestly even in private.

盛水不丨的人 a frugal, careful man.

丨規 hush-money; exactions.

洩丨 to let out a secret.

謹疎丨 be careful how you overlook things in your work.

洩丨天機 to disclose heaven's purposes, — usually refers to calamities.

船到江中補丨遲 it is rather late to stop the leak when the boat is in mid-channel; — be foreseeing and prudent.

㔷 leu꜄ From a *hiding* place and one of the ten *stems*; it is only used as a primitive.

To retire into obscurity; to go away from the world's gaze; a kind of sieve or fan.

陋 leu꜄ From a *tumulus* and to hide away.

A narrow dirty residence; a vile place; a strait; low, rude, rustic, vulgar; ill-favored, sordid, griping; uninformed; ignorant.

丨劣 vile looking, detestable.

在丨巷 in my mean lane; — an affected phrase referring to the place where Yen Hwui dwelt.

孤丨 alone and ignorant.

丨室 a country abode.

醜丨 horrid-looking; deformed.

狃于丨習 to follow vulgar usages.

明明揚側丨 recommend one among the intelligent, or point out one among the obscure and lowly.

LI.

Old sounds, li, lei, lai, lak, lap, *and* lat. *In Canton*, li, lei, *and* tei ; — *in Swatow*, li, loi, *and* lai ; — *in Amoy*, li, lè, ni, *and* lò ; — *in Fuhchau*, li, lè lé, *and* lie ; — *in Shanghai*, li ; — *in Chifu*, li.

黎 ꜀li From 黍 *millet* and 利 *profit* contracted ; as a primitive, its use is chiefly phonetic, and it occurs interchanged with the next two.

To prepare ground for rice; glutinous rice; a black or dark brown color; many, numerous.

丨明 early dawn, still dark.

丨民 or 群丨 or 丨衆 the multitude, the people; the black-haired people, *i. e.* the Chinese.

丨人 or 丨母 certain tribes of aborigines in Hainan I., resembling the Miaotsz'; the name seems to be retained in Li-ping fu 丨平府 in the southeast of Kweicheu, because of its relation to the same races.

丨城縣 a district in the southeast of Shansi, the place of an ancient small state on the upper waters of the River Chang.

民靡有丨 there are no black-haired (*i. e.* able-bodied) men among the people.

丨豆 a small black bean, found on a trailing vine in Kiangnan, a decoction of which is drunk to remove night sweats; the crickets begin to chirrup when it flowers.

In *Cantonese* read ꜀lei, and usually written 嚟. To come; to begin; used after verbs like 來, to denote the present tense; able.

有丨有去 coming and going.

返丨 come back.

丨紙牌 to play cards.

丨未曾呢 has he come yet?

黧 ꜀li From *black* and *profit* ; interchanged with the last and ꜀犂 a plow.

A blackish yellow color; a dark dun color, as of many oxen.

丨庶 the Chinese.

丨黑 a sallow yellow, as of a face.

丨黃 a poetical name for the oriole, from its black and yellow plumage.

瓈 璃 ꜀li A vitreous, translucent substance like strass, the 琉丨 which resembles glass and porcelain, but is different.

玻丨 glass.

琉丨榻 a bedstead with glass at the sides.

藜 ꜀li From *plant* and *numerous*.

A kind of herb whose young leaves are edible, and the mature stalks fit for canes.

丨蘆 the white hellebore. (*Veratrum.*)

丨杖 a staff used by old men.

配丨四施 a confused multitude around.

梁有懸丨 the jaspers jingled from the beams.

剺 ꜀li To rive or split through from one end to the other, as a log.

犂 ꜀li From 牛 *ox* and 黎 *black* contracted ; occurs used for its primitive.

A plow; to plow, to prepare ground for sowing; dark, obscure; a piebald ox; applied to the Huns.

丨刀 a plowshare guard of iron.

一把丨 or 一張丨 one plow.

扶丨 or 丨田 to plow fields.

負丨人 a ploughman.

丨色 swarthy, tawny, sun-burned.

丨牛之子 calf of a brindled cow; — *met.* a good son of a vile father.

一丨春雨 at the first plowing look for the spring rains.

播棄丨老 he has rejected and discarded the sires, — time-worn and useful men ; the reference is to an old plowman.

梨 ꜀li From *tree* and *profitable* as the phonetic.

A pear, called also 快菓 the jolly fruit; the term includes several species of *Pyrus*.

鴨兒丨 or 雪丨 a russet pear.

白丨 the white juicy pear of Peking; it resembles a billiard ball in size and shape.

秋白丨 a soft juicy yellowish pear.

你是屬秋白丨的 you are just like an autumn pear, — which is rotten at core; an untrustworthy man.

廣丨 the strawberry pear of Chihli, so called from its taste; the 棱丨 resembles it, but is coarser.

沙丨 an insipid pear common in Shantung.

凍丨 a frost pear; — *met.* an old man's face.

丨膏片 sugared pear jam dried in cakes.

黃丨 the pine apple. (*Fuhchau.*)

丨園子弟 play-actors, so called from a pear garden where they were taught by an Emperor of the T'ang dynasty.

花丨木 rosewood. (*Cantonese.*)

胡丨 a small species of dragonfly.

棠丨 a small coarse pear; also the seeds of the mountain-ash or rowan, and of the *Grewia elastica*.

金鈎丨 the fruit of the *Hovenia dulcis* in Chehkiang.

蜊 ꜀li From *insect* and *profitable* for the phonetic.

A kind of clam or *Mactra*, the 蛤丨 found on the coast of Fuhkien and pickled for food; the shell is smooth and white, with reddish edges.

莉 ꜀li li꜄ A much esteemed flower, the 茉|花 or white jasmine (*Jasminum sambac*), cultivated for its fragrance and for scenting tea; the blossoms are woven on wire baskets called 茉|花籃 to place in rooms; the name of a well-known song.

茉|針 a kind of hair-pin, with a head shaped like an unopened jasmine, common at Shanghai.

茈| twigs fit for making baskets

𠩺 ꜀li From 厂 a contraction of 厓 a *cliff* and 攴 a *stroke*, with 未 *not*; it is used only as a primitive.

To split, as a ripe fruit does its skin; to rive; to chap.

𨤲 厘 ⿸厂兀 ꜀li From 里 a *village* and the preceding; or 厂 a *cliff* as its contraction; the second form is also read ꜀ch'en, and defined a market place, but it is now mostly used for the decimal, of which the third form is a common contraction.

To subject, to cause to submit; to regulate, in which sense it is used with 理; domestic joy; in *arithmetic*, the third term in fractions, a hundredth; the thousandth part of a tael, nominally equal to the copper mill, or native coin called a cash by foreigners, from *caixa*, the Moorish name for the tin coin found at Malacca in early days, coined in Malabar before A. D. 1500; in long measure, half a 寸 or inch, the smallest division of the ꜂li; a very little, a grain, a hair-breadth; an extra tax of a cash on a quantity of goods or the property in a place, according to an assessment; a pair, twins; to give, to bestow.

允|百工庶績咸熙 directing the various officers according to this, all the [year's] works will be well done.

命畢公保|東郊 he ordered the duke of Pih to protect and govern the eastern frontier.

|爾女士 a heroic wife is given to you.

王|爾成 the king has given you perfect rules.

無|用 not the least use.

淸| paid it to the last cash.

毫|不錯 just; exactly, to a hair's breadth.

|捐 a *pro-rata* extra assessment.

抽|金 to levy the *li-kin* tax, a levy on goods for defending the region; there is also a 房| or house tax, and |斤 or extra assessment on tare and tret of certain articles.

地| a lucky spot.

|孳 twins.

|分之間 very minute, can't be reckoned, — *i. e.* between a cash and a candareen.

漦 ꜀li From *water* and *to split*; also read *shi*꜄ and ꜀*lai*, and interchanged with the last.

To float with the stream; name of a river; water all run out; drying up.

龍| the mucus on a fish or eel's body; — applied to good liquor.

氂 ꜀li From *hair* and *to split*; used with the next.

A horse's tail; a chowrie; stiff hair; long, mixed hair for felting; small, minute.

牛| or 毛| a cow's tail, especially of the yak; a fly-whisk.

|牛其大若垂天之雲 the magnitude of this hairy ox was like a cloud which covered the sky.

犛 ꜀li Also read ꜀*mao*.

The Tibetan yak, sarlyk, or grunting-ox (*Poëphagus grunniens*), of whose tail chowries are made.

嫠 ꜀li A widow.

|婦 a woman who has been left desolate.

恤| to relieve the widowed.

夫爲義死|也何害 if you my husband, are martyred for your patriotism, what harm in my being a widow?

罹 ꜀li From 网 a *net* and 惟 *but*; it resembles 羅 a net.

Sorrow, grief; to encounter, to happen to; to incur.

|其凶害 I suffered his deadly malice.

逢此百| we are meeting with all these griefs.

滅無| my miseries have all passed away.

自|重咎 to incur grave punishment.

無父母詒| [daughters] are to cause no sorrow to their parents.

我獨于| I only am miserable.

⿰礻离 ꜀li Favorable, lucky prognostics.

福| or |祥 good omens, happy signs.

漓 ꜀li Water dropping and soaking into the ground; the pattering of rain or hail; to instil by drops; thin.

淋| dripping rain.

筆勢淋| the letters fell rapidly from his pencil; — rapid composition.

謧 ꜀li Sportive talk; jokes; to banter, to chaff; deceitful talk.

|詍 to make fun of; to ridicule; exaggeration.

縭 褵 ꜀li From *silk* or *dress* and a *bogie*; the first form is most used.

An ornamented girdle which was put on a bride by her mother; a perfume or scent-bag; to sew shoes.

親結其| the mother herself tied her sash.

紼|維之 tied on with cords.

Read ꜀*ch'i*. Sharp, cutting, like the cold wind.

樆 ꜀li Wild pears, or those which grow in neglected places, and gradually become harsh, are distinguished by this term from the 梨 cultivated pears; probably a kind of service-tree or sorb is intended, and not a true pear.

醨 ꜀li — Thin, poor spirits; weak liquor or the dregs of the still.

啜丨 to sip the lees.

丨酪 dregs, feculence.

摛 ꜀li — Also read ꜀*ch'i*.

To stretch; to spread, as wings; to exhibit, to display.

丨筆 to take a pen in hand.

丨藻如春華 his composition is as full of beauties as the spring is of flowers.

离 ꜀li — Altered from 禽 a *bird*, but the etymologists disagree about its construction; it is now mostly superseded by the next.

A weird beast, a bogie; bright; elegant; to scatter; to oppose.

形神支丨 his appearance is very much altered; — *i. e.* old or sickly.

離 ꜀li — From *bird* and *weird;* it is interchanged with the primitive.

A yellow bird of brilliant plumage; a fairy, an elf; to retire, to disperse; to dismiss, to go from, to part, parted, absent; to cut in two; to arrange or divide off; scattered; vis-à-vis, paired; to meet, to get into; to be in; to pass through; the 30th of the 64 diagrams, or 5th of the eight diagrams, referring to elegant things and brightness; in *rhetoric*, a digression caused by a similar idea, or a verbal allusion carried out; drooping.

不丨 employed on, engaged in; attached to.

丨開 parted; to put apart.

丨孫 a sister's grandchild.

丨散 to disperse; scattered.

丨別 to part from, to bid adieu.

不丨飛鳥 [the parrot is yet] nothing but a bird.

用丨間計 to sow dissensions.

丨坐丨立 to sit or stand in pairs.

流丨失所 no certain dwelling-places.

丨得幾遠 how far off is it?

丨心 to wean people from you.

陳丨 to dispose in order.

馬不丨鞍 the horse is always saddled; — *met.* I am always busy.

出丨輪廻 to escape the law of transmigrations in consequence of great austerity.

丨書 a bill of divorce; it is usually sealed by an impression of four finger ends.

魚網之設鴻則丨之 the net was set for the fish, but a wild goose got into it.

不丨于裏 did I not remain in [my mother's] womb?

彼黍丨丨 [see] those full millet heads drooping over.

載丨寒暑 I have passed through cold and heat.

Read *li*꜄ To leave, to withdraw from, to retire; retired, withdrawn; distant, as an interval.

丨家 to leave home.

丨開一尺 they are one foot apart.

遠丨 keep far from, as bad men.

丨群 to leave the company.

丨席 or 丨檯 to get up from the table.

籬 ꜀li — From *bamboo* and to *pass off;* occurs used with the next, but not quite correctly.

A fence or wattle of bamboo; to fence, to inclose; a small basket; a skimmer; a tray.

竹丨 a bamboo fence; also a kind of tray.

荳丨 a trellis for peas.

村墟丨落 villages and farmsteads.

籓丨 fences and hedges; the first is made of posts, the second of interlaced splints.

沒有不透風的丨笆 where's the hedge that will keep out the wind?

東丨佳色 a poetical name for the China aster, a bed of which a poet once made into a fence.

篱 ꜀li — A skimmer used by cooks; it is shaped like a scoop.

笊丨 an open worked skimmer made of osiers, wire, or bamboo; in some places the blinder, and also the muzzle, on a mule is so called.

麫丨 a bamboo skimmer to lade out from soups.

蘺 ꜀li — From *plants* and to *separate;* used with the last.

A kind of darnel grass, or perhaps a *Carex*, which injures the growing rice.

江丨 water grass, sedge.

䍦 / **䍦** ꜀li — From a *covering* or *net* and to *separate;* the two are nearly identical.

A kind of white straw hat, the 接丨 which was adorned with egret's plumes and feathers, and hence called 白鷺纕 the white egret girdle; it was formerly worn by the people of Kiangnan.

纚 ꜀li ʿsi — A rope to fasten a boat; a painter.

紼丨維之 tie it with the painter.

索胡繩之丨丨 braid a pretty cord of the long leaves of the sweet vernal grass.

Read ʿ*si.* A well-woven gauze with square checks, used for kerchiefs.

髮丨 a small skull-cap made of gauze.

丨紗 a head scarf of gauze.

丨乎淫淫 people going on, or traveling in a crowd.

Read ʿ*shi.* Long.

堸丨 dangling and flapping, as a sleeve which is much too long.

鱺 ꜀li — A fresh water eel, the 鰻丨, of which there are several sorts; it is thought to be very pugnacious, and the Chinese say its dried body preserves grain and other things from insects.

鸝 ˏli A beautiful yellow songster, the 黃 丨 or oriole (*Oriolus Chinensis*), common in central China, and known at the North as 丨 子; it is sometimes called the mango bird, but that is the *Oriolus kundoo* of India.

驪 ˏli From *horse* and *elegant* as the phonetic.

A fleet horse; a charger; a black horse; to drive a span of horses.

丨 駕 a carriage and pair.

鐵 丨 an iron gray horse.

盜 丨 a fleet racer, like Eclipse, which ran a thousand *li* in a day; one of Muh Wang's eight famous steeds.

比物四 丨 well matched were the four black steeds.

丨 城 old name of Fu-ning fu 撫寧府 in the northeast of Chihli.

孋 ˏli A beautiful woman of Hunnish origin, named 丨 姬, mentioned in the history of Tsʻin, B. C. 670, who was captured from the 丨 戎 a tribe of Scythians then living in the present Shensi; pretty.

穲 ˏli Grain growing in rows, as when it is in the blade.

綠野嘉禾排 丨 丨 beautiful grain on the green prairies spreads out in many rows.

狸 貍 ˏli From wild *beast* or *dog* and *village*, because it lurks about villages and hamlets.

A name for the fox, and including also other small animals like the wild cat, racoon, loris, souslik, &c.

野 丨 an animal resembling the wild cat.

家 丨 the house fox, — *i. e.* a cat.

海 丨 a seal, found off Manchuria.

菓子 丨 an animal whose habits are like the ratel; it is good for food.

香 丨 or 靈 丨 a civet.

丨 子 a spotted wild cat found in Kiangsi.

玄 丨 the silver fox.

風 丨 an animal found in Kwangsi, whose description assimilates it to a loris.

被狐 丨 精纏着 a fox brownie (or vampyre) possesses him.

矖 ˏli To stare at, to look at angrily.

眼 丨 丨 to gaze at fixedly.

長 丨 a long fixed gaze.

酈 liˋ A place in Lu now the south of Shantung, where a battle was fought B. C. 659; a region in the present Nan-yang fu 南陽府 in the southwest of Honan, near Tăng cheu 鄧州, along the River Han.

梩 ˏli A basket or hod for removing earth; a spade or narrow mattock for shoveling in earth; also the name of a tree.

里 ʿli Originally composed of 田 *field* and 土 *earth* combined; it forms the 166th radical of a few incongruous characters, and occurs used for the next.

A place of residence; a neighborhood; a village of 25 or 50 families; a lane in a town, a close or wynd, where there is a gate at each end, and the residents exercise a supervision over it; a short street; a place; mournful; the Chinese mile, reckoned to be 360 paces; — it has been of various lengths, from 1158 to 1894 feet, but now usually measures 1800 *chih* or 1894.12 *ft.* English, making $27\frac{4}{5}$ *li* equal to ten miles; the geographical *li* is 1458.53 feet, of which 250 make a degree, and ten a French league.

鄰 丨 a neighborhood.

一 丨 路 one *li* distant.

鄉 丨 or 梓 丨 the country; one's native place; the first phrase can be used in addressing one, like 鄉 丨 啊 neighbor!

悠悠我 丨 far away is my native village.

歸故 丨 to return home, — *i. e.* to resign office.

千 丨 馬 a courier or post-boy.

丨 人 one of this place.

云如何 丨 I ask, why am I so sorrowful?

戚 丨 relatives by marriage.

丨 居 residence, a place of abode.

丨 長 the oldest man in the village.

悝 ʿli To pity; pitiable; afflicted, sad; infirm, invalided.

Read ˏkwéi, and interchanged with ˏ詼 to laugh at. To talk much; to jest with.

哩 ʿli An adverbial particle, denoting excessively, unreasonably.

說起來話長 丨 they talked a very long time.

In *Cantonese* read ˏlé. A final particle indicating certainty, doubtless, surely; so, the manner of doing; pronounced ʿli, it sometimes indicates a question.

係 丨 it is so; yes, it is really.

天不早 丨 it is not at all early in the day.

來 丨 come here.

去 丨 gone; let us go.

過頭 丨 too much by far; it certainly is so.

In *Shanghai*. A final to an indicative proposition.

未 丨 not yet, for some time.

勿 丨 not yet, wait.

好用個 丨 it can be used.

未時未拉 丨 not yet for a long time.

娌 ʿli From *woman* and *village*.

Brother's wives; sisters-in-law.

妯 丨 the wives of several brothers, also called 嬸母 in some places.

俚 ‘li From *man* and *village*.

Unpolished, low-bred; vulgar; gross, ribald; a villager, a rustic, country-people; to protect, to support; sociable, talkative; a trust, a resource.

鄙丨 vulgar; the canaille, country rowdies, roughs.

丨言 low expressions, coarse talk.

無所丨賴 I have nothing to look to for help.

丨歌 rustic songs and ditties.

丨醫 a village doctor.

⿰巾里 ‘li From *napkin* and *village*; an unauthorized character used mostly about Canton.

A mat sail; any small sail.

頭丨 top or studding-sails.

丨纜 the halliards.

扯丨 hoist sail.

減丨 take in sail.

丨頭 the foot of the sail.

駛盡丨 go off under full sail; *met.* exert all your power.

理 ‘li From *gem* and *village* as the phonetic.

To work a gem like an agate, according to its veining; to polish, to burnish, as gems; veins, striæ; to govern, to manage, to look after; to regulate; the governing principle, that which is felt to be right or suitable (自然之則也 as the Chinese express it), and depends not on force; reason, right doctrine; rule of action; among Chinese philosophers, the principle of organization by which matter is preserved, or the Power that inheres to direct it, otherwise defined as god 神, or animated air 氣; to rectify, to adjust according to principle; to depend on; to think of, to regard; to meddle with; a go-between; following some verbs, it shows that they are or should be well-done, as 修丨 to repair.

生丨 to live by lawful calling, to do business.

天丨 Heaven's reason, *i. e.* a retributive, overruling Providence.

看地丨 a geomancer: one who chooses sites.

辦丨 to manage well.

調丨 the rules of healing.

空丨 pure reason; — a Budhistic term.

丨不到 I have no time to see to it.

丨論 to debate, to reason upon.

大不丨於口 I am far from depending upon the mouths — of men.

丨事 to attend to an affair.

丨會 to comprehend, to regard kindly.

必丨會這一句 you must attend to that expression.

丨髮 to dress the hair.

丨直氣壯 I am right and my purpose is firm; I am conscious of having a good cause.

丨數 the recondite reason of; to settle or wind up accounts.

不丨料 I have nothing to do with it.

合丨 reasonable; as it should be.

你丨偏 or 你丨虧 you are in the wrong.

紋丨 veins or streaks, as in wood.

丨當 it is all right, I am as I would be, don't urge me; — a polite expression, declining an invitation or courtesy, or answering the inquiry if one has dined.

丨所當爲 what ought to be done; in good taste or time.

强辭奪丨 to distort the right and talk speciously.

上京講丨 we are going to Peking to talk of our rights, — a banner of the Taipings in 1853.

裏 / 裡 ‘li From *clothes* and *village*; the first form nearly resembles ‘*kwo* 裹 to wrap.

A lining; the inner face of a garment; inner, inside; within; to the left, as in passing a cart.

丨面 or 丨頭 within, in; inside.

在家丨 at home, in the house.

丨布 coarse cotton lining.

表丨精粗無不到 I understand all about it, the inside and out, the fine and coarse too.

丨外受敵 enemies on all sides, within and without.

肚丨 in the stomach.

頭丨 formerly, a while ago, once on a time.

丨走 turn or go to the left; — a cartman's cry.

忙丨偷閒 to steal a little breathing-spell in my hurry.

不在心丨却在意丨 I have not forgotten it, but I dislike to do it.

鯉 ‘li From 魚 *fish* and 理 *veinings* contracted, said to be from the resemblance on the scales to the figure 十 *ten*.

The carp, which includes other kinds of *Cyprinidæ*, as the bream, sucker, &c.; it is regarded as the king of fish, and is fabled to turn into a dragon.

孔丨 the name of Confucius' son.

金丨 the yellow carp.

火丨 fire or red carp. (*Cyprinus flammans.*)

綠丨 green carp (*Cyprinus viridi-violaceus.*)

塘丨 the pond carp. (*Cyprinus rubro-fuscus.*)

屐丨 the clog carp. (*Cyprinus sculponeatus.*)

黑丨 the black carp. (*Cyprinus atrovirens.*)

雙丨 a letter, so called from the shape it was folded, while others say that anciently a pair of fish was sent with a letter, a trace of which custom is still kept up in Japan.

丨化龍 or 丨魚跳龍門 the carp has become a dragon, or has leaped the dragon's gate; — rapid promotion in getting degrees.

木丨 a log struck for meals in Budhist refectories.

李 *'li* From *wood* and *son*; it much resembles *ki'* 季 a season.

A prune or gage; a plum of a red or yellow color; to get ready for a journey.

丨子 a plum.

南華丨 a yellow gage at Canton, perhaps the same as the 夫人丨 of Fuhchau.

鹹丨 salted prunes.

桃丨爭春 the peach and plum emulate each other in spring, — which shall blossom first.

薦士如桃丨 to recommend a scholar is like a peach and plum — flowering and fruiting, for one can not tell how he will turn out.

行丨 luggage, baggage; this term is explained as referring to the things that are proper 理 on a journey, making it like a pun on that word.

履 *'li* From *body* and to *step again*.

That on which the foot rests; a leather shoe; to put on a shoe; to walk; to act; acts; action, conduct; the body, the man; a living, a salary, a subsistence; the personal name of T'ang the Successful.

鞋丨 shoes, covering for the feet.

丨底 the sole of the shoe.

踐丨 to tread in another's footsteps; to step on.

步丨維艱 it is hard for me to walk; an idler's excuse.

丨行 the conduct; to walk.

丨歷 a record of conduct; statement of one's antecedents.

丨仁 to do humane acts.

如丨薄氷 [be as cautious] as if treading on thin ice.

珠丨三千客 three thousand guests with pearly shoes; — a compliment to rich friends.

可以丨霜 one can walk on the hoar frost in them.

丨我發兮 she treads in my steps, and then she's away!

福丨綏之 the salary will comfort him.

豊 *'li* A contracted form of *,fung* 豐 abundant, composed of a *dish* and *plenty*, the next is now used, and this occurs only as a primitive.

A vessel used in sacrificing.

禮 礼 *'li* From *worship* and a sacrificial *vase*: the character *'t'i* 體 body resembles it; the contracted form is common.

A step, an act, particularly acts of worship 事神, which will bring happiness; propriety, etiquette, ceremony, rites; the decent and the decorous in worship and social life; decorum, manners; official obeisance, worship; courtesy; offerings, gifts required by usage, vails.

丨法 or 丨數 rules of society, usages, politeness, ceremonies.

丨貌 good manners; courtesy.

丨體 gentlemanly conduct.

丨儀 a present; a courtesy; while 還丨 denotes the gifts or obeisance made in return for it.

丨儀卒度 every form is according to rule.

丨金 or 聘丨 money paid at a betrothal.

丨多 very formal, too obsequious.

常丨 the usual etiquette; customary.

送丨 to send a present.

百丨既至有壬有林 when all the rites have been fully and grandly performed.

謝丨 and 丨物 money or other presents sent on festive or funeral occasions.

越丨 unreasonable, harsh.

丨之用和爲貴 good feeling is the most desirable thing in etiquette.

丨賢下士 [a prince should be] courteous to the worthy, and condescending to the learned.

讚丨生 a master of ceremonies in a temple, as when adoring Confucius.

丨縣 a district in the southeast of Kansuh on the Kia-ling River.

丨部 the Board of Rites.

丨方 the office in a yamun which attends to the ceremonies.

行大丨 to make the great prostration — at court.

合丨 and 無丨 polite and impolite; courteous and rude.

非丨勿言 don't talk if you can't say what is right.

丨拜 obeisance, reverence, thus used by Moslems for religious service, and now applied to all foreign worship.

丨拜完了 worship is over.

丨拜堂 a church, a chapel.

丨拜寺 a mosque.

七日一個丨拜 seven days make a week.

後進于丨樂君子也 in these later days, men are accomplished in rites and music.

In *Cantonese*. To turn, as the head; stiff, as the neck; to accuse falsely.

丨手送 gave it to him behind his back.

丨手倒背 he'll take less if pressed.

醴 *'li* Sweet or newly distilled spirits; must, new wine; sweet, as a fountain.

饗丨 an imperial feast.

甘丨 good wine, luscious beverage.

丨泉 pure fountain water; a term for rich liquor, derived probably from the district of 丨泉縣 in the south of Shensi.

酒丨 spirits of all kinds, used for libations.

以御賓客且以酌丨 [the spoil] will be offered to the guests with the goblet of sweet must.

澧 *'li* One of the large affluents of the Tung-ting Lake, the 丨水 which drains the northwest portion of Hunan, and comprises a basin of about eight thousand square miles.

丨州 a prefecture lying near the mouth of this river.

邐 ˓*li* To walk on the side, as of a road.

迤丨於道 the passengers come and go along the sides of the road.

鱧 ˓*li* A fish of the mullet family, also called 七星魚 in Canton, which has seven spots on its body, thought in their arrangement to resemble the Dipper, to which the fish makes its obeisance; the liver is sweet, but priests do not eat it; this fish most probably denotes the *Ophicephalus*, as well as a kind of mullet, for one synonym of it is 黑魚 or black fish, by which the former is commonly known at the North, and supposed to be transformed from a snake; other synonyms evidently refer to the eel, by which it is defined in Japan, and the two are externally somewhat alike.

魚麗于罶魴丨 the fish pass into the weirs, bream and mullet.

蠡 ˓*li* Insects in wood; a wood-borer like the carpenter-beetle; a variety of ring-worm; used also for the last in 丨魚 one name of the *Ophicephalus*.

彭丨湖 the northern end of Po-yang Lake, which in early times was said to be 彭丨旣豬 confined to its proper limits, and probably denoted the whole lake; the name was perhaps derived from the clams found in it.

Read ˓*li*. A calabash.

以丨測海 to measure the ocean with a gourd.

丨丨 to go in regular rows, like platoons of infantry; placed in lines.

Read ˓*lo* A volute shell.

丨蚌閉戶 the periwinkle and clam both shut up their doors, —so the wise man will retire within himself.

Read *li*˒ To partition.

參丨 to cut off, as a portion of territory.

利 *li*˒ From 刀 a *sword* and 和 *harmony* contracted, because gain is the result of mutual harmony.

The edge or point of a knife; sharp, acute; advantageous, useful; happy, fortunate, beneficial; gains, profit; cleverness, shrewdness; greedy for gain, covetous; smart, slippery; interest on money; to benefit, to oblige; to nourish.

磨丨 to grind sharp, to sharpen.

丨市 prosperous trade, a good market.

爲民不丨 it worked to the disadvantage of the people.

丨器 edged tools, arms; cutlery.

丨息 or 丨錢 interest on money.

納丨 or 開丨錢 to pay interest.

不丨 unlucky, unsuccessful.

丨口 fluent of speech.

丨毒 gluttonous; mean.

丨便 convenient, at hand.

每月加一丨 to pay ten per cent. a month.

快丨 keen-edged, sharp.

丨見大人 happy if your Honor notices me.

名丨兩途 the two pursuits of letters and trade.

無不順丨 he is always prosperous, all goes as he wishes.

丨嘴花牙 talkative and specious.

順順丨丨 agreeable and accommodating.

戰不丨 an unsuccessful attack.

小人以身殉丨 the mean man will sacrifice himself for gain.

丨濟往來 [this boat] is for the convenience of those crossing the ferry.

丨害 severe, injurious, painful; used as a superlative, 似得丨害 [the photograph] is exceedingly like him.

丨路 prosperous.

丨益 gain, advantage.

其丨斷金 its sharpness will cut metal.

水丨 a marine tax-collector; he is under the district magistrate.

唎 *li*˒ Sound, noise; a final word used in Budhist books, indicating the end of a thing; talkative.

一張丨口 talking about this and that; gossiping.

In *Cantonese*. A final particle implying an order, or the finishing of an act; the tongue, so called by contraries, because the sound of 舌 in that dialect also means to lose; when read ˓*lé*, it means careless.

伸條丨 put out your tongue.

丨衣 a furred tongue.

丨音 a final particle.

去丨 they have gone.

做事˓丨唎 he does his work slovenly.

痢 *li*˒ A dysentery; a flux; a diarrhea.

白丨 severe diarrhea.

紅丨 or 血丨 bloody flux, dysentery.

瀉丨 a rumbling flatulent diarrhea.

休息丨 a chronic diarrhea.

禁口丨 a cholera and loss of appetite.

俐 *li*˒ From *man* and *advantage* as the phonetic.

Clever, talented; trim, neat; showing skill and accuracy.

伶丨乖巧 ingenious, clever; quick, active.

畫的伶丨 it is drawn very neatly.

例 *li*˒ From *man* and to *compare* as the phonetic; it looks like the last.

To classify, to adjust, to arrange; to compare; to make a precedent of; laws which are less stringent than the 律 or statutes; rules, regulations, bye-laws, directions; custom, usage; the order or disposition of things.

違丨 to transgress the laws.

開丨 to make a rule.

成丨 it has become a custom.

額 丨 or 定 丨 a settled usage, as a fixed number or style.

照 丨 legal; customary.

音不偕 丨 the sounds are unharmonious.

丨不符 not according to usage.

不合事 丨 that is not the way to do it

丨禁 the rules forbid it.

下不爲 丨 don't make this a precedent; don't come again.

則 丨 rules of the Boards, as a tariff or a ritual.

不得援以爲 丨 or 不可以彼 丨 此 it is not to be taken as a precedent

丨耗 ordinary outlay, constant expenses.

吏 *li*ʾ From 史 a *recorder* and 一 *one*, implying unity of purpose in the mind of rulers; it needs to be distinguished from its primitive.

An officer; magistrates; executive, as a subordinate, a deputy, or a secretary in offices; to rule.

丨部 the Board of Civil Office at Peking; its branch department in each province is called 丨房, and 丨科 in the districts, and each of them superintends the appointment, salaries, and movements of officials.

滿 丨 completed his clerkship

書 丨 the government clerks and copyists.

長 丨 or 典 丨 head-writers

丨目 the deputy or under-secretary in a prefecture.

丨員 official attendants, subalterns.

官塲 丨 治 rules for magistrates.

清 丨 司 a department or bureau in a Board; there are four or five of them.

污 丨 a dirty-handed, covetous official.

循 丨 an active magistrate

天子之 丨 the emperor's ministers.

光棍難逃滑 丨 手 the blacklegs will hardly escape the sharp policemen.

詈 *li*ʾ From *words* and to entangle in a *net*.

To scold about, to grumble at; to blame one, to rail at

丨辱 to disgrace one by scolding him.

怒不至 丨 though angry he did not rail.

丨謗 to slander and backbite.

丨罵 to vituperate, to swear at

君子絕交不出 丨 言 a princely man breaks off a friendship, but he never descends to abusing others

覆背善 丨 but turning their backs, they show their skill in reviling — the good.

小人怨汝 丨 汝 the lower classes murmur against and revile you.

㗚 *li*ʾ Irritating, useless talk; unceasing fault-finding.

丨㤙 useless reproach.

莅 涖 蒞 *li*ʾ From *plant* or *water* and a *seat*; the third form is unusual

The sound of running water; water grass or rushes; to descend towards, to arrive at; to overlook, to see about; to enter upon, as an office; the seat of office, an officer's chair, the bench

丨任 to exercise an office.

丨民 to govern the people

丨事 to attend to official duties.

不學牆面 丨 事惟煩 without study you face a wall, and your management of affairs will be full of trouble.

丨位 the place of judgment

臨 丨 百事 in the midst of official duties.

丨治 to rule, to govern.

丨斯土 I [the *chi-hien*] rule this region.

方叔 丨 止其車三千 when Fang Shuh took command, his chariots were three thousand.

丨 丨 下瀨 the noisy waters rush down the rapids.

荔 𦷹 *li*ʾ From *plants* and *strength* tripled; the original character somewhat resembles a bunch of berries.

A fruit found in southern China, the lichi or laichi (*Nephelium lichi*); a species of celery.

丨枝菓 the lichi, of which there are eight varieties common at Canton, the 香 丨 丨 枝 from Hiangshan, with a small seed is a good kind, but the 糯米枝 with a withered seed, is considered the most delicious.

丨枝核色 a light umber, or deep purplish brown, the color of lichi pits.

假 丨 枝 the *Stauntonia*, whose berries are eaten.

番 丨 枝 the custard-apple.

壁 丨 a trailing climbing plant like ivy.

厲 *li*ʾ From 厂 a sheltering *cliff* and 蠆 a *sting* contracted, though others say 勵 *endeavor*; it is interchanged with its next four compounds.

A whetstone; to sharpen, to grind; to discipline, to inspirit; to oppress; to chide; to commence; severe, harsh, stern; majestic; furious, excessive; evil; disorder, ugly, cruel; dangerous, as a disease; conscious of peril; to wade with the clothes on; a deep ford.

嚴 丨 severely strict, awfully stern

丨民 to oppress the people

秣馬 丨 兵 to groom the horses and drill the troops.

丨鬼 a discontented orbate ghost

垂帶而 丨 excessively long were their hanging girdles.

深則 丨 if the water be deep, I will cross in my clothes

予罔殺 丨 I will not harshly put men to death.

今茲之正胡然 丨 矣 the government nowadays is oppressive beyond measure.

降此大 丨 these great calamities are inflicted on us.

丨聲而言 to talk very boisterously.

濿 砅 li' From *water* and to *oppress*, or *stone*; the second form is unusual, and both are like the last.

To cross a stream on stepping-stones, or when fording it, as the composition of the second character shows.

礪 li' A coarse kind of sandstone; gritstone; large untrimmed stones good for pavements; whetstones.

磨丨 to polish, to sharpen.

丨石 coarse sandstone, graywacke.

互相砥丨 mutual oversight and reproof, such as friends should give.

周丨石爲墻 the whole outside wall was built of rough stones; — *i. e.* in cyclopean style.

爲海水礱丨 the waves rub and grind the shells to pieces.

勵 li' To animate, to encourage; to incite.

勉丨 to rouse to effort.

鼓丨 to urge to exertion.

用丨相國 to stimulate others to help the country.

丨志 to stimulate one's self, to resolutely bend one's mind on.

癘 li' A pestilential malaria; a plague sore; virulent; foul ulcers; swellings and sores caused by fresh lacker; to encourage; to kill, as birds.

疥丨 ulcers on the skin.

疫丨 a plague; epidemic.

不丨雛鷇 do not kill fledgelings.

糲 li' From *rice* and to *oppress*; it is also heard pronounced ˏ*la*.

Coarse, as grain; husks and grain mixed; unhulled or uncleaned rice.

丨食 coarse food.

粗丨 poor quality; rough, as the harsh taste of unripe Indian corn.

精丨 fine and coarse.

蠣 li' Rock oysters, as distinguished from the agglomerated kind, are called 牡丨 because they are all regarded as males, thus showing that the hermaphrodite nature of this mollusk has been observed by the Chinese.

丨乾 dried oysters.

丨房 oysters in the shell; also the shell, regarded as medicinal.

蛤丨 oysters and clams; — an old term.

㦒 li' Vicious; bad; to fear; timid.

惡丨 wicked, depraved; a cruel disposition.

唳 li' The cry of a heron.

嘹丨 or 鴈丨 the scream of a wild goose.

戾 li' From *door* under which a *dog* crouches to get out; occurs used with the next.

To stoop, to bend, to crouch; to offend, to reach, to come to; at; determined; to stop, to quiet, to settle; set; crooked, distorted; perverse, rebellious, ungovernable; guilty, impenitent; calamities, tribulations.

罪丨 wicked, hard-hearted.

暴丨 outrageously vicious.

乖丨 perverse, restrained by no law.

丨愆 error, crimes, sins.

民之未丨 the people are not yet settled; they do not acquiesce.

重丨 a grave crime.

未知獲丨于上下 I am not sure but that I have offended [the Powers] above and below.

其飛丨天 it soars to the heavens.

靡所止丨 there is no way of stopping or remedying [these troubles].

哲人之愚亦維斯丨 the stupidity of the clever man is because he does violence — to his right nature.

盭 li' Composed of 盩 to *lead* and 弦 a *chord*, both contracted, referring to tying a person's limbs till the blood starts; like the preceding, and used for the next.

Incurable; violent, as a disease; extravagant; truculent, perverse; to oppose; a green color; a thick skin.

丨夫 an unreasonable man.

賊丨 an audacious villain.

丨草 a labiate plant which furnishes a green dye, said to grow in Shantung.

綟 li' A dark dull green, made by using a dye derived from the 帛丨草 which grows it is said in Shantung; during the Han dynasty, seal ribbons were made of this color.

䓞 li' A stiff grass resembling a *Sesleria;* the awns are stiff, and the spike of a brick red color when ripe; the leaves are suitable for weaving into sandals; another kind is called by this name, whose leaves are used to dye a dull green color.

蜧 li' A black dragon-snake, which can bring rain or clouds, called 黑丨 and 陰丨, and goes into the deep at a jump; this description probably alludes to the water-spout.

悷 li' Sad from fright.

懔丨 looking very sorrowful.

捩 棙 li' From *hand* or *wood* and *perverse;* the first is also read *lieh* to twist or tie; to bend.

Coverings put on the nails to protect them when thrumming the guitar; to twitch the strings, to thrum; to snap asunder; to guide, as a helm; to twirl, as to whirl a spoon.

拗丨 obstinate, willful.

丨柁 to steer, as a boat.

丨三弦 to play the cithern.

隸ʾ *li*ʾ From to *reach* and a *bullace;* others derive it from 體 *body* altered.

Attached to; belonging or joined to; underlings, official attendants; menial, ignoble, abject; vile.

僕丨 slaves, retainers.

丨書 the square plain style of writing Chinese characters.

丨人 a vagabond, a menial retainer; such cannot compete at the examinations.

皂丨 lictors who precede an officer's retinue.

不丨管轄 he is not under his control.

配丨 attached to, as a fief to a prince.

直丨廳 an inferior department whose magistrate is directly responsible to the provincial governor, and not to the *chifu* or prefect.

麗ʾ *li*ʾ From 鹿 *deer* and an old phonetic form; a deer runs to its pasture-grounds on seeing them; it is interchanged with a few of its compounds.

Elegant, graceful, as the step of a stately stag; fair, beautiful, ornamented; glorious; fond of display; luxurious, extravagant; flowery; bright; to pass into, as a net; to couple; a pair, for which the next is used; a number; attached to, as clothes to the body; to depend on; relying, what belongs to a matter, the particulars; to hit, as a mark; to tie; a beam; a boat.

不克開于民之丨 he would not promote the resources of the people.

華丨 magnifical, adorned.

美丨 beautiful, in good taste.

相附丨 proportional; correspondent, as guilt and punishment.

丨乎衣食 lavish in his dress and living.

丨辭 a well-expressed sentence.

秀丨 elegant, as a fine composition.

艷丨 dressy, bedizened.

其丨不億 their numbers did not stop at lakhs.

壯丨 grand, as a building

丨春 enlivening, refreshing, as the opening spring.

匪察于獄之丨 they would not examine into the details of the criminal cases.

丨江府 a large department in the northwest of Yunnan, through which the Yangtsz' River flows.

儷ʾ *li*ʾ A pair, a couple; a companion, a mate, a fellow; conjugal union.

伉丨 conjugal fidelity.

束帛丨皮 a pair of dressed skins and a roll of silks; — ancient betrothal presents.

LIANG.

Old sound, liang. *In Canton*, lüng; — *in Swatow*, liang *and* niõ; — *in Amoy*, liong; — *in Fuhchau*, liòng; — *in Shanghai*, liang; — *in Chifu*, liang.

良 ˛*liang* The original form is described as altered from 畐 *filled* with and 亡 *lost* combined; as a primitive, it needs to be distinguished from *kăn*ʾ 艮 perverse.

Good, gentle, considerate, mild, benignant; excellent of its kind, valuable; natural, instinctive; a term of praise; freeborn, in distinction from 賤 mean or slaves; loyal, obedient; skillful; not vicious, as a horse; very; a high degree.

丨人 my goodman; my goodwife.

丨善 virtuous, good, pure.

丨心 concientious, desirous of doing right, devout.

無丨心 heartless, ungrateful, hardhearted.

蓄意不丨 to harbor suspicions of another.

丨久 a good while.

丨夜 late at night; a wedding-night.

丨田 a fertile field.

丨民 loyal people, as tax-payers.

丨多 or 丨深 very, exceedingly.

丨辰吉日 a lucky hour; now's the time for it.

天丨發現 his better heart has asserted itself, he is reforming.

丨法 an equitable law.

弗丨及 unable to effect.

丨能 natural instinct or skill.

丨馬 a gentle horse.

丨知 innate knowledge or genius; born to it.

陡起不丨 he has suddenly turned ungrateful.

丨有以也 it is chiefly on that account.

丨以 or 丨由 it is just for that reason.

踉 ˛*liang* From *foot* and *good*; it resembles ˛*kăn* 跟 to follow.

To jump.

跳丨 to hop and skip about.

Read *lang*ʾ Ready for a start.

丨蹡 urgent to go, but unable.

丨丨蹌蹌 to hurry, as when escaping a shower; to press on rapidly, as when belated.

粮 糧 ˛*liang* From *rice* and *good* or *measure;* the second form is the most used.

Rations, soldiers' pay; food, provisions; taxes in grain or kind.

丨臺 an army paymaster.

食丨的 to be a soldier.

錢丨 pay; salary or rations from government.

納錢丨 to pay taxes or their commutation.

錢丨子 buckshot, small shot. (*Pekingese.*)

乾丨 provision for a journey.

關丨 or 發丨 to pay out rations.

丨草 rations, fodder; eatables.

劫丨 to forage, to make a raid.

口丨 victuals, stores.

打丨食 to house the harvest.

白丨 rice, as it forms the greatest part of the grain tax.

丨道 the commissioner who collects the revenue of a province.

丨儲豐足 an abundant supply on hand.

凉 涼 ˏ*liang* From *ice* or *water* and a *capital;* the first is most used.

Cool, fresh; refreshing; cooling, as refrigerant medicines; distant, cool towards; hypocritical; in need, straitened; sparing of, a little; to trust in, to assist.

丨風 a cool breeze.

着丨 to get a cold and sweat; to get a rheumatic cold.

丨德 having small virtue.

招丨 or 納丨 or 乘丨 to enjoy the air; take an airing.

丨爽 or 丨快 cool, refreshing.

丨薄看待 to treat one coldly.

秋丨 cool autumnal days.

民之罔極職丨善背 the vast disorders of the people are owing to those hypocrites who so skillfuly prevaricate.

世態炎丨 the deportment of mankind is now fervid and then chilly.

丨藥苦口利于病 if this good physic embitters the mouth, it benefits the ailment; — so does good advice.

丨國 the names of several small short-lived states in northwestern China, which existed from A. D. 400 to 420.

丨州府 a large prefecture in the western part of Inner Kansuh.

荒丨 devastated, pillaged, as a region by robbers.

丨彼武王 he assisted Wu Wang.

䬤 ˏ*liang* Used with the last.

A cold north wind.

丨䬲颼 the draught blows very chilly.

椋 ˏ*liang* A small tree with a rough bark, the 丨子木 found in Kiangsi; the wood serves for axles and hubs; the fruit is pictured growing from the trunk on short stems; it is black when ripe, has a sweetish, astringent taste, and goes by the name of 冬青菓 or winter-green.

惊 ˏ*liang* Compassionate; pitiful.

悽丨景况 melancholy and sad thoughts.

何事傷丨 what are you so grieved about?

綡 ˏ*liang* The strings of an official cap; the throat-clasp.

輬 ˏ*liang* A kind of sleeping-car.

輼丨 a hearse; one description had closed sides, the other was open; a hearse for the sovereign.

粱 ˏ*liang* From *rice* and the next contracted, which some say was given to it from the region near Sz'ch'uen, where it was early grown.

The common spiked millet or canary-seed (*Setaria italica*); the only difference between it and the *suh*, 粟 is its size and the awns on the spikes, this having the largest grain and longest awn; this distinction is not now maintained, and the application is disused.

高丨 sorgo (*Sorghum vulgare*), the Barbadoes millet, Guinea corn, or dana, of which there are several varieties.

童丨 a grass which resembles the sorghum, but useless; tares.

丨米 or 高丨子 sorghum seed, used chiefly to make 高丨酒 strong spirits.

膏丨之體 [just] a body of fat and grain; — said of a rich gormand.

梁 ˏ*liang* From 木 *wood*, 水 *water* and 刅 *wound;* it somewhat resembles 染 to dye, and the last.

A bridge to cross a brook, a foot-bridge; a ridge-pole or plate in a roof; a beam, a sleeper; a lintel; a dam, flood-gates to hinder a current; a support or seam in a cap; curved end of a carriage-pole; self-reliant; aggressive; the principal; the chief reliance.

橋丨 bridges; the timbers or ties of a bridge.

澤丨 a pond banked in a ravine in order to make a 魚丨 or fish pond.

强丨 overbearing, atrocious.

造舟爲丨 he made a bridge of the boats.

雕丨 a frieze in the ceilings of Chinese rooms, often highly carved.

鼻丨 the bridge of the nose.

鞋丨 the double seam on top of Chinese shoes.

駕丨 to ride the beam; *i.e.* to involve another by false accusations.

丨州 one of the nine ancient divisions of China, lying south of River Wéi in Shansi, and thence down to the Yangtsz' River and west of the River Han, including Sz'ch'uen and Hupeh.

小醜跳丨 the rascals can [only] jump bridges, — and need not be feared.

頭懸丨 [Li Mih] fastened his head to the beam, — lest he should fall asleep when studying.

丨朝 the Liang dynasty, which existed from A. D. 502 to 556, under six princes; its capital was Nanking.

樑 ˏ*liang* Used with the last.

The mast of a boat; *met.* a statesman.

屋丨 a ridge-pole.

杠丨 a girder, a beam.

上丨大吉 let good luck come on raising the ridge-pole; — a phrase written by house-builders.

棟丨之材 great talents and influence; the one who is the country's dependence.

架海金丨 a great man, one who is the stay of his country.

丨上君子 a thief, a burglar.

緉 ʻliang A pair of shoes; a string for tying shoes.

魎 ʻliang A naiad, called 魍丨 which inhabits fountains; it is described as a purple child three years old.

兩 两 両 ʻliang Originally composed of 㒳 *two* entering 冂 a *cave*, denoting equal division, to which 一 *one* was added when it was applied to a weight; the third form is used only for money; occurs interchanged with the next.

Two; a pair, usually intimating some likeness or relationship; doubled; both; twice, again; dual; a classifier of chariots; a weight, originally 24 銖 grains, now the highest one used in Chinese money transactions, and by the Portuguese first called a tael from the Indian *tola*, apparently because both these weights were the highest money terms known in Bombay and Canton; the *tola* weighs 180 *grs.* troy, and the standard *liang* 579.84 *grs.* or about 1⅓ *oz.*; its weight varies little in comparison to the catty, but there are trifling discrepancies all over the empire to the extent of even forty grains; it is worth from $1.38 to $1.47 according to its purity, and is usually reckoned at 6*s.* 8*d.* sterling.

丨個人 two persons.

是丨個也 yes, there were two.

丨分ʼ分 divide it equally.

有丨個拉 there were three or four. (*Shanghai.*)

丨大 heaven and earth.

人居丨間之中 man dwells between heaven and earth.

丨親 one's parents.

丨不相照 we just missed seeing each other.

丨可之間 I am in a dilemma.

丨江 the two Riverine provinces, *i. e.* Kiangnan and Kiangsi.

十丨銀子 ten taels of silver.

第丨個人是肯個獨是伊丨個勿肯 one set was willing enough, but the other side would not consent. (*Shanghai.*)

丨傍 both sides.

Read *liang*ʼ A chariot.

百丨將之 a hundred chariots escorted her.

輛 liangʼ A *pair* of *wheels*; a chariot; a classifier of carriages, carts, wheelbarrows, and wheel carriages.

車三丨 three carts.

倆 ʻliang ʻlia From *man* and *two*; *q.d.* as if no other could match him.

Clever at, skilled.

有何伎丨 what are you skilled in?

In *Pekingese* often abbreviated to ʻ*lia.* Two, as persons; it is occasionally applied to money.

咱們丨人 we two.

丨三個人 two or three persons.

量 liangʼ ˛liang From 重 *heavy* and 𣄼 *suddenly*, both contracted; others derive it from 日 the *sun* above the earth 一 里 *one li.*

To estimate, to measure, to judge; to keep an account of; a measure, a limit; cubic or solid contents; a determinate point or quantity; appetite, ability to drink; longing for a particular kind of food; an enlarged liberal mind; good feeling, an opinion; capacity, powers, calibre.

酒丨淺 my ability to drink is small.

器丨淺 a poor capacity, mediocre talents.

限丨多少 what is the limit?

局丨大方 a good presence and high abilities.

不自丨 an over estimate of one's self.

月以爲丨 a month was the limit.

打丨 to guess, to reckon.

惟酒無丨 he laid down no limit for his drinking.

同律度丨衡 he made uniform the standard tubes, the measures of length and capacity, and the steelyards.

多見其不知丨也 it is all the plainer then, that he does not know his own capacity.

Read ˛*liang.* To measure the quantity or size of; to deliberate, to take counsel upon, to think over.

丨度, to measure; to consider how much.

丈丨 to measure the area of.

丨米 to measure out rice.

頗有商丨 it will be best to consult carefully.

亮 liangʼ Composed of 京 a *capital* and 无 *not*, intimating something bad or untoward in an officer; occurs used for the next.

Clear, brilliant; bright, as the moon; lustrous; tidy, neat; transparent, illumined; to display, to illustrate; to aid; to believe in, sonorous, as a voice.

丨紗 transparent or shining gauze.

天丨 daylight.

好月丨 bright moonlight.

丨轎 an open sedan or chair.

響丨 musical notes, clear and sweet.

清丨 neat, clean, as a room or dress.

光丨 light up, as a room.

丨晃晃 a glimmer of light; bright, as the reflection on the water.

弼丨四世 you have helped to make four reigns illustrious.

君子不丨惡乎執 if the superior man has no faith, he will refuse to take hold — of principles.

諒 liang' Sincere words, faithful; to accredit, to believe; credulous; to suppose, to guess; to aid; to know certainly; to oversee.

佐 丨 to assist, to support.

見 丨 to excuse, to hope for the best.

不能見 丨 he is inexcusable; he must be kept to his work.

丨不我怪 if you will not think strange of me.

丨必如此 I am pretty certain of it.

各宜自 丨 each must reckon his own resources.

原 丨 or 體 丨 to be considerate of others, to estimate their difficulties; put yourself in his place.

友 丨 friendship with the sincere.

君子貞而不 丨 the princely man is firm from principle and not from opinion.

母也天只不 丨 人只 O my mother! O Heaven! can you not understand me?

倞 liang' Distant; to search into thoroughly.

Read *kiang'* and used for 競. Wrangling, harsh, violent.

秉心無 丨 they follow a good end without rivalry.

哴 liang' 㖡 liang' The incessant crying of infants; to weep without making a noise.

咣 丨 children wailing.

晾 liang' From *sun* and a *capital* as the phonetic.

To dry in the air; to hang out to dry, but not in the sunshine; to hang, as clothes on a line.

丨一丨 air it awhile.

丨開 to spread out to air.

丨乾 drying in the air.

陰 丨 drying in the shade.

花梢蝶 丨 衣 the butterflies sun their wings on the flowery spray.

晒 丨 to dry in the sunshine.

In *Cantonese*. To place a thing on trestles; to raise it from the ground; to put on a frame; to shore up; to dash against.

丨高的 raise it a little higher.

LIAO.

Old sounds, lio *and* lot. *In Canton*, liu; — *in Swatow*, liò; — *in Amoy*, liao; — *in Fuhchau*, lieu *and* lao; — *in Shanghai*, lio; — *in Chifu*, liao.

遼 ˏliao From to *go* and kindled *wood* as the phonetic.

Distant, far off.

丨望 to see afar off.

遠 丨 丨 [that hill] is really a great way off.

丨闊 a broad expanse, as a prairie.

道途 丨 遠 the road is a very long one.

丨葉 the leaves of the broad bamboo used in weaving mats, hats, &c.

丨東 the region east of the River Liao 丨水 which empties into the north of the Gulf of Chihli, now known as Shingking.

丨國 the designation of the Kitans between A.D. 937 and 980; it was revived again by a small tribe in A.D. 1066, during the decadence of the Sung dynasty, and continued with various fortunes and changes until extinguished by the Mongols in A.D. 1201.

僚 ˏliao From *man* and kindled *wood* as the phonetic.

A companion, a colleague, an official associate; one of the same class or rank; to labor or hold office together; a kind, a class.

同 丨 officials, compeers; those of about the same rank and time.

官 丨 fellow-officers.

百 丨 the magistracy; the rulers.

一 丨 人 one profession of men.

Read ʿ*liao*, and used with 嫽 pretty. A courteous manner; a gentle, leisurely, affable manner.

佼人 丨 兮 how lovely is that beautiful woman.

寮 ˏliao Interchanged with the last.

A fellow-student or officer; to study in the same room; a small window.

丨房 a room in an office like a tea-room, where officials meet.

In *Cantonese*. A stall; a cabin, a board or attap hut, a shanty; dwellings of the poor, like old boats shored up and roofed in.

水 丨 aquatic peddler's boats.

娼 丨 brothels.

柴 丨 a wooden hut.

蛋家 丨 thatched hovels used by boat-people.

嘹 ˏliao A clear note, as of a bird at night; the wailing cry of pain.

丨喨 a shrill wail or scream.

丨嚦 a cry, as of a wild swan on high.

撩 ˏliao From *hand* and kindled *wood*; used with the next, and when meaning to baste, it is sometimes written 繚 but that character is unauthorized.

To take hold of, to pull about; to manage a thing, to regulate; to play with; to provoke, to pick a quarrel with; to incite to evil, to seduce into sin;

to assist, as in walking; to tickle; to brush away, or jerk off, as an insect; to stir up, as mud in a stream, or to take up from the bottom; to baste, to sew together.

丨弄 to contrive how to reach an aim; intriguing.

好丨人 to play jokes on; loving to interfere.

丨醒他 tickle him to wake him.

丨動肝火 to excite one's wrath

花柳丨情 the flowers and willows excite the feelings.

丨戰 to challenge to a battle

丨人打鬧 to dare one to a fight.

丨火 to stir up the fire.

丨禍 a mischief-loving boy, who likes to play and break things

丨耳 to tickle or brush the ears

丨人 to pull and haul, as in play

丨邊 a basted edge.

丨縫 to sew a seam, to hem.

嫽 ˓liao Similar to the preceding, and used with ˓僚 good looking

To trifle; to dally; to play with; pretty, good looking, winsome

丨戲 to sport with.

丨刁 boisterous; annoying.

Read ˓lao at the North.

丨丨 a maternal grandmother.

屪 ˓liao The virile member; a term used in Shantung

簝 ˓liao A bamboo trencher, the 竹丨 on which the beef was placed by the sacrificial officer, and the blood in another dish, during the state worship in the Cheu dynasty.

互與共盆丨 get ready the dishes for the blood and flesh.

蟟 ˓liao The cicada; it is often interchanged with ˓lao 蟧 to denote the 蝭丨 a small whitish kind found in Chihli

蛁丨 a variety of the mole-cricket.

鷯 ˓liao Small birds like the wren, pipit, tarin, or tomtit; a grass-warbler.

鷦丨 the little tailor-bird of southern China, but also applied to other small birds as the sedge-wren or blue-bird.

白丨 a butcher bird or shrike.

鷦丨巢于蚊睫 [like a] nit's nest in a musquito's eyebrow; — i. e. excessively small.

膫 膋 ˓liao The fat or tallow covering the intestines; the omentum.

取其血丨 take out the blood and caul

脂丨 hard tallow.

獠 䝤 ˓liao From *dog* or *beast* and kindled *wood*, these characters are also used for 狫 the name of the Laos tribes.

To hunt at night by torches, as in deer-stalking

丨田 a night hunt.

䜍 ˓liao Artful words.

嘮丨丨 incessant altercation and gabble

丨謱 deceitful talk.

鐐 ˓liao Silver of the purest kind; a furnace with a flue to it; a fetter; to fetter, to secure

丨子 a cook; an old term

手丨 manacles for securing prisoners

聊 ˓liao From *ear* and a *horary* character; occurs used with the next, and is also read ˓liu.

A ringing in the ears; to wish, to depend on; to guess; to consider; a support; an initial particle, implying a diminution of; careless of, anyhow; perhaps, then

丨丨無幾 not much, not many

丨且 off-hand; readily; perhaps

丨與之謀 then let us consult about it.

無以丨生 nothing upon which to live; no employment, as a farmer during a drought

丨浪 a waste; heedless; rash

丨以行國 I think I had better travel over the state

丨與子同歸兮 I am half inclined to go and live with her!

椒丨之實 Ah, those pepper seeds!

丨城縣 the district in the city of Tung-chang fu on the Grand Canal in the west of Shantung

憀 ˓liao Used for the last.

To trust; to depend on, as true and real; care, anxiety for; impatient.

無所丨賴 nothing to look to, no resources.

Read ˓liu. To pity, to commiserate.

翏 ˓liao From *wings* above streaming *hair*, representing the look of a bird as it darts on high.

The continuous blast of a gale is 丨丨, applied also to a steady breeze

Read liu' The darting of a lark, as it soars on high

漻 ˓liao Deep and clear like the deep sea

清丨 limpid; still depths, as in a lake.

寥 ˓liao From a *covering* and to *fly* high.

Empty, void, silent; vacant, solitary; vast; unoccupied, leisurely.

丨落 deserted; unoccupied, idle

丨廓 boundless, vast, like the heavens.

甚屬丨丨 reduced to a very few; there are indeed not many as the neglected and poor.

軍民逃出丨丨 a few of the troops and people got out, and escaped — the crash

蹘 ˓liao To run, to get away, to escape a danger; to cross the legs

丨唎 begone! clear out!

丨好久 he has been away a good while

In *Cantonese* read ˏmau, and sometimes written 卯 To sit on the heels; to perch, to roost; to thump.

丨底 squat down.

丨頭殼 to rap his head.

丨到處 squat you down there!

廖 ˏliao To point out; to select; to sew, and put in complete order.

善丨乃甲冑 repair and carefully look after your mail and helmets.

佬 ˏlao From *man* and *old* as the phonetic.

Large, great.

丨丨 of huge proportions, gigantic.

In *Cantonese*. A man, answering to 的 in the court dialect; a person, a fellow, rather a demeaning term; one of a class, and not unfrequently added to the name of his calling, as 剃頭丨 a barber.

大丨 an elder brother.

細丨 a younger brother

鄉下丨 or 鄉巴丨 a villager, a clown

老大丨 old fellow.

個丨 that stranger; that man.

外江丨 a Northerner.

蓼 ʿliao From *plant* and *to fly* high.

An acrid herb, the seeds of which fly about; usually applied to the knot-wort, persicary, or smart weed (*Polygonum*); *met* troubles, griefs.

紅丨 the prince's feather (*Polygonum orientale*)

水丨 or 小丨 the water pepper. (*Polygonum perfoliatum*)

予又集于丨 I am brought among the smart-weed; — *i e* into bitter trials

馬丨 or 辣丨 a small species in Kiangsi, with bright red flowers, and the lanceolate leaves marked with many black spots; the roots are used to boil with persimmon seeds.

天丨 the water persicary. (*Polygonum amphibium.*)

毛丨 the hairy smart weed (*Polygonum barbatum*), or an allied species with thick hirsute leaves, also called 白馬鞭 the white horsewhip

Read *luh*, Luxuriant growth.

丨丨者莪 how finely grows the Artemisia.

鄝 ʿliao The proper name of the small state, for which the last is often written; it lay in the present Ku-chi hien 固始縣 in the south-east corner of Honan, on a branch of the River Hwai.

繚 ʿliao To bind or wind around; to wrap; gyves; fetters; to manage; the leechlines of a sail; anciently, a sacrifice to the emperor's ancestors.

丨鈕 to wind or tie in a ball.

丨遶 to saunter; to go about and look, as at a fair.

丨繞 to wind or wrap around, as when bandaging a limb.

丨絲 leechlines along the edge of a sail.

鬆丨 slack off the sheet.

眼花丨亂 the eyes wearied with looking; amazed at what I have seen.

丨起辮 to wind the cue around the head.

一丨髮 the hair coiled in a tuft.

In *Cantonese*. To lead a horse about to cool, for which 𨂾 is more common and correct.

燎 ʿliao From *fire* and kindled *wood;* it is nearly syncnymous with its primitive.

To burn; to set on fire; a blaze; to illuminate; torches placed on stands; a link, a signal light; fuel; to enlighten; brilliant, as fire

門丨 a door-light, a hall-lamp

丨如指掌 plain as pointing to the palm.

丨郊原 a fire in the woods; a burning jungle

寫完丨 it is all written out.

丨之方揚寧或滅之 a blazing faggot may perhaps be easily put out

丨薪 blazing faggots.

庭丨之光 the torches are blazing in the court yard.

民所丨之 which the people burn for fuel.

瞭 ʿliao Bright.

山丨水秀 the clear hills and picturesque waters.

丨然而明 bright and splendid

瞭 ʿliao A clear, bright eye; far-sighted; distinct vision.

眸子丨焉 the eye clear and honest; an eye of conscious integrity.

一目丨然 I can see it all at a glance.

蹽 ʿliao Tall.

丨蹻 or 丨䠷 a tall lank man; one who walks unsteadily, or on his toes

憭 ʿliao Intelligent; cheerful, lively, discerning; empty; to sympathize with, to think on; empty

丨慄起寒襟 I am greatly grieved at their sufferings from cold and nakedness.

了 ʿliao The etymologists describe this character as 子無臂 child without arms, referring to the horizontal stroke on the character 子 *son*, it somewhat resembles ˏya 丫 a fork

Fixed, concluded; intelligent; knowing how to carry a thing through; to bring to an end; finished, done; after a verb, it forms past time, before a verb, very, fully, wholly; preceding the negative 不 it forms the superlative; between two verbs, it has the force of one action; as 笑丨笑 he laughed once.

燒丨房屋 burned all the houses.

事不能丨 this matter cannot be done.

洗丨 washed.

一目丨然 one can fully understand it at a glance.

丨不得 exceedingly, matchless; — either good or bad; no help for it; how sad!

丨局 that's the end; now it is finished; he's dead.

丨件事 the job is done.

丨不丨 it cannot be done or brought about.

化得不見丨 melts till it is invisible, as ice or a mist.

丨然明白 to understand fully.

見丨 I saw it, I've seen it.

都買丨來 all will then have been bought.

丨得 a consequence; in irony, can you! how so! estimable.

還丨得 an exclamation of surprise or pity; how dreadful!

丨然 clearly, fully.

非可稍丨 not so easy of completion.

罷丨 enough; that will do; let be.

天發丨白丨 the sky is brightening.

丨丨也未 finished? is it not yet done?

丨丨丨只是有一些怕 done! so it is, but I've some fear of it.

你去丨好丨 you had scarcely then gone.

也不關你事丨 it is just none of your business.

小而丨丨大未必奇 when a child is very precocious, he is not so certain to be remarkable when old.

海南丨哥 the wattled grackle from Hainan. (*Eulabes indicus.*)

丨哥 a species of blue grackle.

丨哥翠 a singing grackle. (*Eurystomus orientalis*).

衦 ‘liao A short leggings, such as are worn by fishermen.

校丨 leggings made of cowhide to protect the legs and feet when fishing or wading.

料 liao’ From a *peck* and *grain*, — one is measured by the other; it looks a little like *k‘o* 科 a rank.

To estimate, to measure, to judge of; to take a census; to reckon; to dispose properly, to give out orderly; to reflect; to rub, to smooth the hair; materials, stuff; provender, grain, and in the North, especially denotes pulse for animals; strass, a vitreous substance imitating stone, used for making rings and cups; colored glass; an employé, one who is of service, a useful man; his ability, skill, cleverness; a peddler's drum with two rattles, because it emits a distinct sound; to pull; to set a saw.

照丨 to oversee and direct.

丨理 to manage.

難丨得中’ it is hard to say exactly.

丨事如見 I think you will find it to be so.

自丨不能 I think that I cannot do it.

難以逆丨 it cannot be foreseen.

誰丨 who would have thought it?

不丨 or 初不丨 unexpectedly; unforeseen.

丨事不到 a contingency I had not thought of.

不出所丨 it is what I rather expected.

朝廷器丨 a statesman; a worthy loyal government officer.

廢丨 a careless wasteful workman; a ne'er-do-well.

馬丨 a provender of pulse.

丨器 strass, in imitation of stone; the 京丨 is the best.

丨片 window glass.

猪丨 paste or priming made of pig's blood.

丨物 materials, stuff; the raw product.

作丨 materials to make a thing of, as spices, sugar, &c., for the cook.

揭算工丨 reckon what the work and materials will come to.

田丨 manure, fertilizers.

一丨藥共二斤 all the ingredients of the medicine weigh two catties.

丨鋸 to set a saw with a 鋸丨 or vice, so as to widen the kerf.

墩 liao A surrounding wall.

丨以周垣 surround it with a wall.

療 liao To heal, to resist the progress of disease by proper remedies.

丨法 practice of medicine.

丨病 to cure sickness.

丨飢 to appease hunger.

榆錢不丨貧 elms seeds cure no poor folks.

殯 liao’ Destroyed, defeated, ruined; in Kiangsu, used for badness; badly, wickedly.

話丨 to slander.

學丨 learning bad habits.

雖不殊而必丨 though he is not dead he is still badly defeated.

廖 liao’ A small ancient town or state, probably derived from 伯丨 a son of Wăn Wang, who had an appanage in Tsi or Shantung.

尞 liao’ Derived from 火 *fire* and an ancient form of 愼 *sincere* both contracted, intimating that in sacrificing to heaven, faith is the most important point; it is now used only as a primitive.

Fuel used in sacrifices.

尥 liao’ To cross the hind legs in walking, as a donkey does, and sometimes as an ox; weak in the legs, as an old man or a spavined horse; to turn back the hoof, as when kicking.

丨掉 to toddle along; to crawl or drag the legs, as when weak or palsied.

丨蹶子 a kick by a horse.

LIEH.

Old sounds, let, lep, lit, *and* lip. *In Canton,* lit, lat, *and* lip ; — *in Swatow,* liet, lip, li, *and* la ; — *in Amoy,* liat *and* liap ; — *in Fuhchau,* liek *and* lak ; — *in Shanghai,* lih ; — *in Chifu,* lieh, *and* lié.

列, *lieh'* From a *sword* and a contracted form of the next or *flowing* water.

To separate, to distinguish; to arrange or state in order; to place according to rank or rule; each, severally; regularly, seriatim, methodically; a rank, a series; a file, as of soldiers; a class, as of officials.

開丨明白 write out the particulars clearly, as in a bill.

丨陣 or 行丨 troops in rank; drawn up in array, as for battle.

排丨 to set out in order.

不鼓不成丨 if the drums do not sound, the ranks cannot be formed.

丨位 or 丨公 or 丨位兄台 you, Sirs; Friends; all you Gentlemen; — used in direct address.

丨坐其次 each one sitting in his place or rank.

𡿪, *nié'* From 巛 *streams* and 歹 *evil,* the last being a contracted form of the preceding, and often further contracted to 夕 *evening*; it is only used as a primitive.

The motions and looks of rippling water.

烈, *lieh'* From *fire* and *to arrange* as the phonetic; occurs used with the next.

Burning, ardent, hot; violent as a wind; impetuous, energetic, enthusiastic; daring in a good cause; fierce, cruel; meritorious, high principled; eminent in any way; chaste; merit; energy; fame; brightness, vigor; majestic, imposing, dignified; cold, bleak; to broil; to set fire to.

火丨 a fierce fire.

性丨 irritable and violent.

節丨 inflexibly loyal; rigorously chaste, as a widow.

丨祖 an eminent ancestor.

前丨 and 先丨 our meritorious predecessors.

栗栗丨丨 shivering, shaking from cold.

丨女 a woman who prefers to die rather than to marry again.

丨丨 majestic; mournful; blazing, raging; ardent.

載燔載丨 we have roasted flesh and broiled to offer you.

休有丨光 admirable was their majesty and elegance.

丨士 a patriot, a noble statesman.

益丨山澤而焚之 Yih set fire [to the plants] on the hills and marshes and burned them.

冽, *lieh'* A cold air; harsh, raw, chilly, as the weather.

風丨 a freezing wind.

井丨泉寒 cold wells and cool fountains.

有丨氿泉 the cold rivulets gliding from the spring.

洌, *lieh'* Used for the last, but not quite correctly.

Pure, clear.

酒丨 limpid, clear wine.

Read *li'* To dash water about.

丨泉 a bubbling rivulet

茢, *lieh'* Sedge; rushes, useful to make brooms.

桃丨 a peach wood used by necromancers to expel demons.

紫丨 a plant used in dyeing.

栵, *lieh'* From *tree* and *arranged;* it is also read *li'*

Trees in rows; a tree like a chestnut, with a hard grained tough wood; the serrated leaf resembles the elm, and the nuts are coarse; it is called 丨栭, and the wood is used for carriage shafts.

其灌其丨 water each tree in the rows.

咧, *lieh'* The chatter of birds; a final particle expressing certainty; occurs as a synonym of 罷 for the imperative, as 吃丨 eat it.

丨丨 birds quarreling and chirping.

醉丨 he is quite drunk.

定規丨 it is just fixed in that.

鴷, *lieh'* The woodpecker, of which five species are mentioned, a large, a small, a variegated, and a gray sort; another kind is greenish black with a red crest, and called 火老鴉 or red crow; a sort found in Nganhwui is fond of wallowing in the dust.

趔, *lieh'* Not progressing.

打丨趄 to stumble, to stub one's foot, but not to fall; to slip.

裂, *lieh'* From *garments* and *separated.*

Cuttings, leavings, remnants, cabbage; to crack open, to split; to tear; to slit; a crack, a fissure; a flaw, as in glass; cracked, seamed, creased.

自己丨 it split open.

破丨 broken, fractured, as a jar.

一條丨紋 one crack.

逼丨藏梅 angular and irregular carvings with flowers.

丨衣 to tear or rip the clothes.

丨開 riven, split, fissured.

滅丨 heedless; blundering and malingering, as officials do; to subvert, as a custom.

打丨 to break, to crack; cracked.

劃丨 or 綻丨 ripped, riven; torn, as clothes.

颲, *lieh'* A violent gust of wind is 丨風, referring to its suddenness and fury.

儠 *lieh'* Robust; having a long beard, not common among the Chinese.

｜｜ tall and strong.

長｜者相之 the old and vigorous helped him.

巤 **鬣** *lieh'* From 巛 *streams* and 囟 the *fontanelle*, referring to a horse's mane, and its bristly appearance like a 鼠 *rat's* legs; the second form is the commonest.

Stiff hair on the head; a mane; bristles on a hog; dorsal fins, especially those with long flexible spines; bristly, stiff hair.

剛｜ the stiff-bristled,—a poetical name for a boar.

長｜ a long beard.

馬｜ the tumulus of a grave, which at first was made like a ridge resembling a horse's neck.

奮｜昂然 he shakes his mane and raises his head,—as a war-horse.

綠藻翻朱｜ the red bristles are sporting amidst the green grass;—said of gold fish in a tank.

獵 *lieh'* From *dog* and *bristles* as the phonetic.

To hunt wild animals; the chase; field sports; hawking, gunning; to pursue earnestly, to get with difficulty; to hunt up; as a quotation, or select phrases; to strike with dread

打｜ or 田｜ to hunt; to go shooting.

｜狗 a pointer, a hunting-dog.

放｜ to unleash the dog.

｜戶 huntsmen, foresters.

｜其菁華 he searched out their elegant extracts.

躐 *lieh'* To stride over, to leap over; to overstep; to go out of the way; to tread.

涉｜世務 he had had experience of worldly affairs.

｜席 to sit rudely or out of one's order; to occupy a wrong seat at table.

學不｜等 do not overstep the regular order when learning

鱲 *lieh'* From *fish* and *bristly*, alluding probably to the spinous dorsals.

A general name at Canton for fish with spinous fins like the perch, wrasse, gilt-head, &c

軟唇｜ the soft-lipped perch (*Pristipoma grammopœcilum*)

金絲｜ the gold-thread wrasse (*Chrysophrys cardinalis.*)

上海｜ sea-going carp (*Cyprinus acuminatus*)

尖嘴｜ the sharp-nosed sun-fish (*Chætodon modestus.*)

黑石｜ the black perch. (*Hoplegnathus fasciatus*)

大眼｜ the big-eyed perch (*Priacanthus tayenus*)

紅｜ red perch (*Pagrus unicolor*)

LIEN.

Old sounds, lien *and* liem. *In Canton*, lín *and* lim; — *in Swatow*, liam, niam, lien, *and* noi, — *in Amoy*, lian, liam, *and* kiam; — *in Fuhchau*, lieng *and* léng; — *in Shanghai*, li^n *and* ni^n, — *in Chifu*, lien.

連 *ˏlien* From to *go* and a *cart*, referring to the continuous track made by wheels.

To connect, to continue; to join; to unite, as in marriage; to compromise; to stick to; contiguous, annexed, reaching to; a succession of, a junction; a lumping; connected, following, attached; at the beginning of a sentence, it forms an adversative *conjunction*, even, still; elsewhere it is a copulative, and, also, with, together; applied to drugs obtained from the roots of several plants of the genus *Justicia*, each of which has its specific name.

通｜ joined, as by a thoroughfare.

結｜ banded together, as a ring of people.

相｜ close, next, adjoining, conterminous.

｜累 or 牽｜ to implicate, to involve; compromised.

｜姻 allied by marriage.

｜｜ unceasingly, again and again

｜｜不斷閃 incessant lightning.

五子｜登 his five sons became *küjin* one after the other.

｜日 successive days.

水｜天 the water meets the sky, — as at sea.

接｜喜歡 he is continually in good spirits.

｜上數 with the other accounts.

｜臉也不洗 he does not even wash his face

｜綿不斷 it never stopped, as the rain

｜環計 a plan that effects two objects

黃｜ or 黃蓮 a common medicine furnished by species of *Leontice* and *Justicia*.

｜理枝 plants whose roots connect.

｜環保 mutually responsible for, and leagued together.

苦似黃｜ my griefs are bitter as wormwood.

工錢五千｜飯在內 the wages are 5,000 cash, which includes the cost of his food.

｜州 an inferior department in the northeastern part of Kwangtung.

｜架 a flail.

漣 ˏlien The wind raising ripples on the water; unceasing
丨水 bathing water
涕泣丨丨 her tears flowed unceasingly
丨江 a river in the south of Hunan, in Kwei-yang hien
河水清且丨猗 the river flows clear and rippling.

蠊 ˏlien A species of snake or red lizard, the 火赤丨, found in Chehkiang, which is attracted by a light; it eats sparrows and mice, and is regarded as dangerous
捲丨 a serpent coiled up

蓮 ˏlien The lotus (*Nelumbium speciosum*), the flower consecrated to Budha; much used in names of people and places
丨花 the lotus flower or water lily, of which there are numerous varieties.
丨米 or 丨子 lotus nuts
丨蓬 or 丨房 the seed-case or torus of the lotus
荷葉丨 the nasturtium.
丨駕 or 丨座 the lotus seat, a name of Kwanyin.
採丨船 a pleasure-boat.
百子丨 the *Agapanthus*, a showy liliaceous flower
丨青色 a pinkish purple color
木丨 a species of fig (*Ficus pumila.*)
獨脚丨 a plant like the arum (*Caladium xanthorizum.*)
青丨 a damsel; a nun
金丨 golden lilies, a term for women's small feet
丨步 a lady-like step, a fine gait
丨花樂 name of a common song

槤 ˏlien From *wood* and *connected*, interchanged with 璉 a vase.
A side apartment or closet adjoining a large hall; a kind of latch or crossbar on a door
丨子 the loose skinned orange (*Citrus margarita*)

褳 ˏlien From *dress* and *connected*; an unauthorized character.
A pouch, a waist-bag
褡丨 a purse or pouch attached to the girdle; it is like a bag slit in the side, and is chiefly worn at the North.

鏈 ˏlien Unrefined lead or tin ore; a chain
鎖丨 a lock and chain.
跪丨 to kneel on chains; a mode of torture
上丨 wind it up, as a watch
丨完了 the chain (or watch) has run down or out.

鰱 ˏlien From *fish* and *successive*, because it goes in shoals.
Two species of bream, the *Abramis bramula* and *terminalis*, called 扁魚 or flat fish at Canton; it is applied also to a plated fish like a gurnard; but at Nanking the 丨魚 is a silure.
丨子 a species of tench of a whitish color, about two feet long, much reared in Kiangsu; it is one of the gifts to a bride by her parents as a wish for children.

麪 ˏlien Baked cakes made from fresh oats, called 麯丨, a coarse kind of food

穛 ˏlien A term for white rice and green grain; rice which is not glutinous and does not stick.

聯 ˏlien Derived from 耳 *ear* and 絲 *silk* altered to indicate the connection of the ear to the cheek
Connected, joined; associated, united; a term for ten householders acting as a neighborhood; to combine with; to make alliance with; to assemble. to join in a regular order
對丨 parallel sentences or distiches: they are written on scrolls. or inclosed in 丨匡 frames, to hang upon walls.
柱丨 scrolls fitted for hanging on pillars and doors
素丨 or 挽丨 funeral distiches hung up during mourning; the letters are white on a blue ground
丨黨 to form cabals
丨居 to dwell together as in a row or terrace, where the houses are built in connection
丨甲 a union of ten families.
丨手 united strength.
丨群 to crowd together; a flock
丨心合作 to do with united purpose
丨名 to subscribe names, as to a petition
丨保 mutual security
丨志 united public opinion, as on a grievance
丨邦國 a federation of states. like the United States or the German bund
丨絡一片 to combine parts into one whole, as in composition
丨宗 adopted brothers of the same surname

In *Cantonese*. To baste; to stitch together
丨衣服 to baste clothes.

奩 ˏlien From *great* and *dark corner*
A lady's dressing-case; a perfume or toilet-box
丨儀 money given to a bride
鏡丨 a dressing-case with a glass
謹請觀丨 we respectfully request you to come and see the bridal outfit, — an invitation to a wedding

帘 ˏlien From *napkin* and *cave*.
A flag or sign of any kind, showing where wine is sold; in Shantung it is a blue flag about two feet long
酒丨 a grog-shop, a tavern, a spirit dealer's stall
門丨 cloth screens hung outside of doors.

獜 ˌlien The quick jumping run of some animals is 丨㺜 said of a monkey running up a tree, the leaping of a hare, or a dog scampering in his play.

憐 ˌlien From *heart* and *ignis fatuus* as the phonetic.

To commiserate, to have charity for; to sympathize with

丨卹 to pity and help.
愛丨之心 a loving heart.
不堪丨 unworthy of pity.
同病相丨 afflicted people feel pity for each other.
萬望見丨 I earnestly look for your pity
可丨我一個大 pity me just one cash. (*Pekingese.*)

廉 ˌlien From 广 a *shelter* and 兼 *together.*

A corner, an angle; by the side; moderate, economical, sparing, frugal; pure, disinterested; to discriminate, to examine candidly; discrimination.

有丨耻 modest, shamefaced, humble minded, reputable
慳丨 avaricious, too close
養丨銀 an anti-extortion allowance, — a legal addition to the salary of officials; it is about a thousand taels to a *chi-hien*
丨明 to examine and judge equitably.
清丨 incorruptible, honest
丨隅 a corner; particular, strict, as a corner is immovable
矯丨 affected moderation in refusing money.
丨節 sparing, frugal.
價丨而味高 delicate-flavored and cheap.
簡而丨 easy with, but sagacious; one of the nine virtues.
六丨 six virtues belonging to the wise officer, his purity in 善 goodness, 能 ability, 正 rectitude, 敬 reverence, 法 regard for law, and 辨 equity in decision

簾 㡘 ˌlien From *bamboo* or *napkin* and *frugal;* the second form is often restricted to cloth screens.

A door screen of cloth, matting, or bamboo splints; window-screens; curtains.

竹丨 or 珠丨 bamboo blinds.
布丨 a cloth curtain
木板丨 venetian blinds
捲丨子 roll up the blinds.
蘆丨 a grass woven screen.
丨內 at home, private, secluded
內丨官 deputies appointed by the chancellor to read the essays
垂丨聽政 to let fall the screen and hear politics; said of an empress-regent or dowager
丨幙 a curtain screen, as between rooms
水晶丨 the crystal screen; — *i e* a waterfall under which one sees the sun.
花影一丨 [the sun] brightens the flowers on the screen

濂 ˌlien A rivulet falling in a sheet of water from a cliff; thin; poor

蒲澗丨泉 a pretty cascade near Canton
丨溪 a stream in Tao cheu 道州 in the south of Hunan
丨水 a term used by the Chinese in Manila for Christian baptism.

溓 ˌlien Interchanged with the last.

To stick; to adhere to, as mud to wheels; thin ice; cold, icy; water lying still in a pool and just ready to freeze; unsavory.

水丨丨而微凝 water in a pool and skimmed over with ice
深泥弗丨 deep mire does not stick

凁 ˌlien Used with the last.

A thin sheeting of ice.

水面初丨 the water is just skimmed over with ice.
見日消丨 the thin ice melts in the sun

蠊 ˌlien An insect thought to smell like ginger, the 蜚丨, found in the grass during summer; it is also known as 香娘 or fragrant damsel, and probably belongs to the *Cimex* family, though one of its synonyms, 滑虫 or smooth bug, is now applied to the cockroach.

臁 ˌlien The calf of the leg; the spleen in animals

外丨骨 the shin bone.
脛丨 the leg
猪丨貼 a hog's spleen or milt.

鐮 鎌 ˌlien A sickle; a reaping or bill-hook

禾丨 or 鋸丨 a sickle.
鈎丨 a pruning-hook.
丨把兒 handle of a sickle
新月似丨刀 the new moon is like a sickle
火丨包 or 火刀丨子 a tinder-case with steel and flint

磏 ˌlien A coarse kind of red sandstone, not fine enough for polishing; hypocritical, spurious; reddish.

丨仁 feigned benevolence or kindness

鰜 ˌlien An unauthorized character

A species of silure or mud-fish (*Arius falcarius*), common at Canton, of a dull green color, stout jagged spines, and large mouth with six cirri, other sorts have four cirri

斂 ˊlien From 攴 to *rap* and 僉 *all;* this is often wrongly written like ˌhan 歛 to beg, and interchanged with *lien*ˀ 殮 to enshroud.

To collect, to gather in, as a harvest, to amass, to hoard up, to husband; to concentrate; to desire; to give; to enshroud; in *medicine,* to neutralize, to repress; an ingathering

入丨 to put into a coffin.

收丨 to harvest, to gather in crops.

丨時五福 [the ruler] concenters in himself the five happinesses.

聚丨 to hoard, to lay by; to get by griping.

丨脚 or 丨跡 to stay at home; to refuse to go, as to a place or on a visit.

丨手 to sleeve the hands, to decline.

丨怨以為德 to get people's hatred you deem to be a virtue.

丨事 be patient with; don't meddle with the thing.

丨存 to lay up little odds and small sums.

味酸性丨 acids are neutralizing; they repress heat.

Read *lien'* Exactions; the act of gathering.

用又讐丨 the government uses hateful exactions.

In *Cantonese.* To lick, as a dog.

襝 *'lien* Used for the last.

To withdraw the hands into the sleeves; an apron.

丨衽拜 I sleeve my hands at my lapel, and pay my respects; — a phrase on a lady's card; the hands are put one above the other.

臉 *'lien* From *flesh* and the *whole.*

The cheek; the face; reputation, honor; countenance, character.

丨旦兒 the face, the cheeks; the countenance.

無丨 shameless, brazen-faced.

做鬼丨 a face that shows disgust and displeasure.

丢丨 to disgrace one's self or another.

傷丨 dishonorable; bad-faced.

惹怪丨 an ill-tempered sullen face.

失丨 or 沒有丨的 disgraceful, reproachful.

杏丨 ruddy cheeks.

做丨 to give moral support, to keep in countenance; creditable, praiseworthy.

賞丨 to commend, to countenance; to visit at [my] house.

背着丨就不同 it makes all the difference whether it is my back or my face, — how you do your work.

笑丨相迎 to meet one with a smile.

哭喪丨 cast down, out of humor.

丨熱 to interfere to make up a quarrel, to urge to peace.

有不上前又不露丨 you neither go ahead about your work, nor do you let your face appear; — you are neither useful nor respectable.

丨上抹不開 really mortified, much ashamed.

銀盆丨 a silver-dish face, — *i. e.* a clever friend, capable and kind.

Read *ˏts'ien.* A dish made of fish and vegetables spiced, given to the poor.

蘞 蘝 *'lien* The second form is unusual.

A medicinal plant, the 豨丨草 or *Siegesbeckia orientalis,* a syngenesious plant of a milky nature; also a species of scallions or *Allium.*

五丨莓 the berries of a species of wild vine.

白丨 the white berry or grape (*Ampelopsis serianæfolia*), found in Chihli, and used in medicine.

輦 *'nien* From 車 *carriage* and two 夫 *men* to draw it along.

A barrow or hand-carriage, shaped like an easy-chair and pushed by men; the Emperor's chariot; the court; the sovereign; to transport; to take up.

丨下 at court, at the capital.

駐劄丨轂之下 appointed to reside near the imperial government.

我任我丨 we took up our loads, we trundled our barrows.

丨道 paths within the palace grounds.

京丨 the metropolis.

以車丨母 he took his mother in a carriage.

丨郎 household or body-guards.

玉丨 or 象丨 the emperor's chariot.

鳳丨 her Majesty's carriage; the car of a goddess.

璉 *'lien* A vase or plate used to hold the rice of a sacrifice in the imperial ancestral temple.

瑚丨 ornamented vases employed for this purpose in the Hia dynasty and later.

羷 *'chien* A ram or deer with three curls in its horns, is called 三匝丨 *i. e.* a thrice rolled horn.

摙 *'lien* To transport, to remove, to take a thing in a barrow; to change places, to move about; to pick up and arrange.

丨來丨去 to take back and forth.

丨起 to take out of.

丨過人 take it to the man.

丨開曬 take them out and sun them.

丨負之勞 a coolie's toil.

蜾蠃丨泥作房 the sphex-wasp brings mud to make its nest.

殮 *lien'* From *evil* and *all;* sometimes written 斂 but this form is right.

To shroud a corpse; to lay out a body in its best clothes for coffining; the shroud or bandages.

收丨 to put in a coffin.

大丨 and 小丨 a pompous funeral and a plain one.

丨具 bandages or scarfs to wrap the body in.

瀲 *lien'* Water overflowing; crests of waves.

丨灩 to overwhelm; to roll and tumble, as billows.

楝 *lien'* A tree bearing lilac flowers, the *Melia azederach* or pride of India; the seeds shake in the pod like a bell, whence one name is 金鈴子; the phœnix likes it, but the dragon abhors it, say the geomancers; white ants keep away from it.

黃丨樹 a small leaved sort found in Honan; a bitter medicine is prepared from the leaves.

練 *lien'* From *silk* and to *separate*; occurs used with the next.

To boil raw silk to soften it; to experiment upon; to practice, to drill in; to select; a bright white color; a piece of silk.

丨習 to practice at a thing.

丨熟絲 dressed silk, that which has been prepared for weaving.

丨時日 to select a day.

水丨 water police.

拖白丨 a species of magpie with a very long tail.

操丨 to drill and exercise troops.

丨鵲 the long tailed blue jay (*Urocissa cerulea*), also called 長尾三娘 long tailed damsel.

湅 *lien'* To boil raw silk when preparing it for weaving.

丨白坊 a shop for whitening raw silk.

煉 *lien'* From *fire* and to *separate*; interchanged with the next.

To separate dross by fire; to test character, to discipline the mind.

丨丹 to refine the pill, — and become immortal, as the Taoists pretend.

久丨成鋼 [iron] by long purifying becomes steel, — so a man improves by affliction.

鍊 *lien'* From *metal* and to *separate*; interchanged with 鏈 *ore* and the last.

To smelt ores, to refine, to forge; wrought, as iron; to work over thoroughly; to discipline; to mortify one's desires; to act and react on, as the five elements mutually do; expert, matured, experienced, practiced; a chain.

百丨 thoroughly refined.

修丨 becoming religious, as a recluse or an ascetic.

丨仙 to become a 丨師 or virtuous doctor of the Rationalists by austerities and meditation.

精丨 to chasten the passions.

丨土生木 it is the nature of earth to produce wood.

丨熟 well worked, as a metal; matured in.

結丨 solid in texture, durable.

鎚丨 well hammered, as iron.

詞語精丨 well chosen and lucid sentences.

一丨串七粒 run seven seeds on one string.

帶丨 to put a chain on a prisoner's neck.

脫丨 or 解丨 to unchain.

敹 *lien'* To pound a thing with a hammer; to beat a thing firm.

丨金爲箔 to hammer out gold leaf.

僆 *lien'* From *man* and to *connect*.

A pullet or young cock.

丨子 twins.

丨鷄 chickens.

LIH.

Old sound, lik. *In Canton*, lik, lek, lăk, lăp, năp, *and* lut; — *in Swatow*, lip, liap, lek, lé, *and* lat; — *in Amoy*, lek, lip, liap, *and* chek; — *in Fuhchau*, lik *and* lék; — *in Shanghai*, lih; — *in Chifu*, li.

力 *li'* The original form represents the *tendons*, for these direct the exertion of strength; it is the 19th radical of a natural group of characters relating to effort of any kind.

Muscular prowess, brawn, force, strength; mental energy, spirit; nerve, the actuating power; divine succor; full use of an organ; assiduous, smart; the properties or strength of a thing, as the stiffness of a bow, vigor of a style, severity of disease, or tenacity of a wire; to labor at; among *Budhists*, the energy of a faculty of the mind, an emotion, a power.

用丨 or 出丨 exert yourself, be spry, work harder.

佛丨 the help of Budha.

丨爭 a trial of strength.

筆丨 a forcible style; a heavy hand in penmanship.

好牙丨 talkative; ordering people about.

財丨 influential from his wealth.

助一臂之丨 lend a helping hand, afford us assistance.

丨田 to work at farming.

眼丨 sharpsighted, good eyesight.

此弓幾個丨 how much does this bow's strength measure?

丨量 vigor, ability, aptitude.

量丨而行 act according to your powers or skill.

學丨 assiduous in study.

分丨 resolution of forces; distribution of powers; as 幷丨 is the composition of forces in mechanics.

方能得丨 the place can thus be made effective.

五丨 the five *balas* or negative moral powers among the Budhists; — *i. e.* faith, energy, memory, meditation, and wisdom; which prevent the growth of evil.

丨行 to practice earnestly.

竻, 簕, *li'*

From *bamboo* and *strength* or to *cut*; the second form is common at Canton but not authorized.

A scrubby variety of bamboo, full of spines, and therefore good for hedges; bamboo roots; spines or thorns on plants

丨林 a thicket of thorns, like the Rhamnus; a bramble, a quick set bush

丨竹 spinous bamboos.

秝, *li'*

From growing *grain* 禾 repeated.

Rare, seldom met with.

曆, *li'*

This has been superseded by the next, from its having been the personal name of Kienlung

The heavenly bodies, chiefly the sun and moon, which are appointed to divide and note times and seasons; the course and changes of the spheres; to calculate, as an eclipse

丨書 an almanac.

皇丨 the imperial calendar.

丨法 laws of astronomy

丨數 astrological fates or calculations; Heaven's will; the calculations of the calendar.

丨象 the aspect of the heavens.

丨家 astronomers

歷, *li'*

Now used for the last.

To pass over, by, or to; passing away, as generations; to experience, to pass through; to transgress; arrayed in order, orderly; next, successive; wide apart, as the teeth; separated; disordered, confused; to say all that is needed; to exhaust; silent, seclusive.

丨朝 successive dynasties.

丨來 from the first, hitherto; continuously.

來丨 antecedents of, notices of; annals, historic events.

曾經丨 passed, gone, as times.

丨年 yearly, for a series of years; year after year.

丨丨可考 every particular can be proven.

丨久 long since, years ago.

丨丨可數 I can count all to this time.

丨位 to go out of one's seat or place

丨日 successive days.

丨山 a hill lying thirty *li* south of Pu cheu 蒲州 in Ping yang fu in Shansi, where Shun plowed.

丨刼 to undergo kulpas of suffering.

船桅丨亂 a confused appearance of masts

丨盡悽涼境 I have passed through all trials.

丨告爾百姓于朕志 I have fully declared to you, my people, all my views.

丨人 those who pass (or harbor) criminals

閱丨 to pass through, as trials; to experience.

⿰歷刂, *li'*

To cut up or open, as an animal.

丨開 to cut apart.

嚦, *li'*

A noise of splitting

丨丨 a crackling, crashing sound, like ice breaking up; the scream of wild geese

鳥聲丨亂 the birds make a great din

瀝, *li'*

From *water* and *successive*.

A drop, a little left in a cup; to drip, to trickle; to drain out; to filter, to strain

竹丨 bamboo sap, regarded as a febrifuge

飲盡餘丨 drank it to the last drop

丨血 to shed one's blood; blood dripping.

丨情稟求 I humbly petition with the most earnest feeling

丨青 pitch or gum which exudes from trees, as the cherry.

丨陳申 to urgently represent, as to an officer.

In *Cantonese* A row, a line of things

開一丨 open a furrow.

一丨菜 one row of vegetables.

癧, *li'*

From *disease* and *successive*, as if alluding to its hereditary character

Large, scrofulous swellings on the neck; struma; humors on the ganglions of the neck.

蚊咬生瘰丨 the mosquito bites have raised pimples

筋丨 hard tendinous swelling.

生頸丨 scrofulous humors and swellings on the neck.

靂, *li'*

A clap of thunder

霹丨響 the splitting sound of thunder; the god of Thunder

⿰羊歷, *li'*

A black goat is 羖丨; its skin is used for garments

轣, *li'*

From *carriage* and *successive* as the phonetic.

The path worn by carriages; to crush under a wheel.

丨轆 a carriage rut

藶, *li'*

A plant like the cress, 葶丨 said to intoxicate or kill fish; it is perhaps a species of *Lepidium*, like the *L. piscidium*, which has this property; the reddish mucilaginous seeds are used to relieve asthma and hoarseness; the same name is given to the *Sisymbrium atrovirens*, a cruciferous plant whose seeds are laxative

櫪, *li'*

The *enduring tree*, a species of oak, which may be the same or nearly akin to the next; it bears edible acorns; a stable

丨㯕 sticks or frames to torture the fingers by squeezing.

蠶丨 frames on which silkworms spin their cocoons.

馬丨 a stable, a horse pen.

老馬冀伏丨 the old courser is tethered in the pen.

櫟, *li'* From *wood* and *pleasure*; also read *loh*,

A species of scrubby oak, (*Quercus serrata?*) the wood of which is so hard and tough as to be deemed unfit even for fuel, and hence employed as a depreciatory term by officials for their unworthiness; any useless unserviceable material; a black striped bird with a red crest.

山有苞丨 on the mountains are the bushy scrub oaks.

瓅, 皪, *li'* From *gem* or *white* and *pleasure*.

The luster of a pearl.

玓丨 brightness of a pearl; a bright, shining form.

礫, *li'* Small stones, gravel, shingle; coarse pebbly sand.

丹丨 an ore of quicksilver like cinnabar.

瓦丨 potsherds, broken pottery and tiling.

擽, *li'* To strike; to choose; to allow; to exclude; the utmost degree of.

轢, *li'* Like the last.

The trace or rut of a wheel; the creaking of a cart; to crush under wheels.

狂車踐丨 the furious chariots ran over the course.

轔丨 the creaking wheels.

陵丨邊吏 an attendant on a carriage, an outrider or runner.

躒, *li'* A step, a pace; to move, to go; to step on.

一丨 one step or jump.

騏驥一丨不能千步 the finest steed even cannot get over a thousand paces at a jump; — every ceremony must be duly observed.

Read *loh*, To exceed; remarkable.

英才卓丨 unusual ability, extraordinary talents.

岦, *li'* From *hill* and *strength* as the phonetic.

A high range or hill.

崱丨 a cordilleras.

立, *li'* The original form represents 大 *great* used for 人 *man*, over 一 *one* denoting earth, to show that he is fixed; it forms the 117th radical of characters mostly relating to position and posture.

To stand erect; poised, set, established, fixed, upright; to rear, to found, to set up, to institute, to establish; to be settled in principles; to succeed to, or to seat one's self on the throne in place of the legitimate heir; to appoint, to agree on; to settle terms, as when drawing up a contract; to fix; reached, arrived, as the seasons; to place in order, to arrange; as an *adverb*, just, now, soon, presently, while one is standing; at the time of.

起丨 stand up; to erect.

丨刻 quickly, instantly, now.

丨然 in a twinkling; very soon.

丨心 or 丨意 resolved on, determined.

丨功 to establish one's fame.

我沒丨水毛不能出去 I cannot go out, for I have no rain-crest, — alluding to the feathery crest on the egret.

丨妾 to take a concubine.

丨品 or 丨人品 reformed his habits, sown his wild oats.

丨室 to take a wife; to rear buildings.

丨定脚 his foot is fixed; *i. e.* he has agreed to stay, as a workman.

丨鹽茶課 the regular excise on tea and salt.

丨見 you will see it now.

不學禮無以丨 if you do not learn etiquette, you will not know how to act.

三十而丨 at thirty I was set in my principles.

丨水 raining; to rain.

赤丨 to be in great want, naked and poor.

丨嗣 to adopt an heir.

理慾不並丨 principle and passion cannot both rule.

孤丨無助 to stand alone or uncountenanced; no backer.

成丨 established in life; married and in business.

丨打丨死 died of the blows; died during the beating.

丨我蒸民 who maintained our people with grain, — said of Heu-tsih.

丨規條 to establish rules and regulations.

笠, *li'* A rain hat of bamboo leaves or splints; a conical hat of straw; a hamper, an open crate or basket; a cover.

一頂丨 or 一頂斗丨 one wide rain hat.

炭一丨丨 each basket of coal or charcoal.

何蓑何丨 wearing rain cloaks and umbrella-hats.

臺丨 a flat straw hat.

秧丨 a basket to carry rice shoots when transplanting.

丨屐赴詩盟 he put on his hat and pattens and went to the tryst to make verses.

其丨伊糾 their splint hats worn so neatly.

In *Cantonese*. To cheat, to hoodwink; to pull wool over one's eyes; an imposition, a cheat.

丨倒 humbugged, imposed on.

丨騙佢 deceived, taken in.

一對手丨 a pair of gloves, in imitation of the English word.

丨住手 put on your gloves.

苙, *li'* Like the preceding.

A pen, a yard for pigs; an open basket for carrying pigs or game.

猪丨 a pig hamper.

既入其丨 it is already in the pen.

白丨 orris root.

岦, *li'* From *hill* and *standing*.

Hilly.

丨岌 mountainous; lofty ridges of hills.

粒, *li'* From *rice* and to *stand*; *q. d.* rice supports people.

A kernel, a grain of wheat or rice; a classifier of small things, like grain, beads, pellets, buttons, pearls, &c.; food, eatables.

一丨米 a grain of rice

不丨食 not a morsel to eat.

一丨荳 one bean.

顆丨不收 no kernels or seeds are gathered; — it is a year of dearth.

烝民乃丨 all the people had grain to eat.

鴗, *li'* A small species of green kingfisher, called 水狗 and 丨虎 water dog or tiger, which burrows a nest in the banks a foot or more deep; it has a red bill and white breast, and is about eight inches long.

砬, *li'* A mineral used as an antidote to poisons; the sound of ringing stones.

蚸, *li'* A species of green winged locust, the 螇丨, which has a long flight; the name is thought to resemble its note

栗, *li'* From 木 *wood* and 卣 fruit *hanging down*, contracted to 西 *west*; it resembles *suh*, 粟 millet, and occurs used with the next two.

The chestnut, including also some kinds of oak; the wood is deemed to be suitable for ancestral tablets; firm, durable; full, as ripe grain; strict; to overpass, to exceed; to respect; cold.

丨子 or 風丨 a chestnut; the second name refers to the mode of drying it in the wind.

砂炒丨 to roast chestnuts in sand.

茅丨 or 栵栭 a variety of chestnut, smaller than the last, common in Kiangsu; the wood is used for making carrying-beams and cart thills.

石丨 nuts of the *Aleurites*.

寬而丨 affable and yet dignified

水丨 fruit of the water caltrops.

地丨 the water-chestnut.

行丨 a tree which serves as a guide-post.

積之丨丨 the sheaves were massively piled up.

烝在丨薪 [the gourds] hang from the chestnut branches

錐丨 an evergreen species of oak in Hunan, with many acorns on a stem; the leaves are small, yellowish underneath, hispid, and thick; the cupules bristly, and acorns sharp pointed.

凓, *li'* Cold, as a north wind

丨冽 chilled by a cold wind; shivering

北風慘丨 the north wind pierces me through

乍炎乍丨 now hot and then shivering.

慄, *li'* Afraid; pale and trembling; majestic and dignified.

戰丨 quaking with fear.

悚丨 trembling at.

丨丨危懼 all in a tremor of dread, like one afraid of falling

憭丨 awestruck and fearful, as at a horrid sight.

傈, *li'* Ancestral tablets made of chestnut wood on account of its durability; they are not now made of it.

溧, *li'* A small stream in the south of Kiangsu, giving name to two districts, Li-shui hien 丨水縣 and Li-yang hien 丨陽縣 lying south of Nanking.

丨洲 an island in the Yangtsz' River near Wuhu

篥, *li'* Bamboos used for spears or to pole boats; a musical instrument like a long flageolet, mournful in sound, and used to call horses together.

搮, *li'* To rub in the hand, to pull through the hand in order to smooth

丨紗線 to smooth a skein of thread.

鬲, *li'* The original form is thought to resemble the mouth, belly, and crooked legs of a three footed caldron or kettle, the upper line being the cover, it forms the 193d radical of a few characters relating to boilers and food cooked in them.

An incense caldron of iron having hollow feet, holding six pecks, used in temples; a handful.

Read *keh*, and used as a contracted form of 隔 to sunder. An earthen pot; to close; to grasp.

重丨 a large earthenware jar with upright divisions.

膠丨 an ancient statesman called to power from being a seller of salt-fish.

沥, *li'* Water dripping down, and the streams uniting as they flow, as when a roof leaks, or rills run down a hill-side.

颲, *li'* Wind and rain driving on furiously

丨丨 a driving blast.

LIN.

Old sounds, lim *and* lin. *In Canton*, lám *and* lun ; — *in Swatow*, lim, ním, lin, *and* lien ; — *in Amoy*, lim *and* lin ; — *in Fuhchau*, ling *and* lăng ; — *in Shanghai*, ling ; — *in Chifu*, lin.

林 ˏ*lin* From *tree* repeated to indicate many trees together.

A forest, a wood; a grove, a clump of trees; luxuriant, abundant; one's village or native groves; home; fully attended to; a group, a company; a place where men assemble, or a special commodity is sold; a collection of, as words or extracts.

樹丨 a forest; groves, copses.

丨下財主 an opulent retired officer.

文丨 the literary body.

瓊丨 the highest or ripest scholars.

御丨軍 the imperial guard.

僻處陰丨 living in a retired spot.

綠丨山 a famous mountain in the southwest of Hupeh, an old resort of banditti, whence 綠丨客 denotes robbers.

退歸丨下 to leave office and return home.

士者之丨 scholars, educated men.

疎丨晚照 the evening sun gleams through the grove.

禪丨 a Budhist temple.

紫竹丨 the red bamboo copse, name of the foreign settlement at Tientsin.

烟丨 a tobacco-shop.

羽丨軍 the stars $\delta\ \tau\ \upsilon\ \chi\ \psi\ \omega$ &c. in Aquarius.

百禮既至有壬有丨 when every rite has been fully and minutely performed.

獨木不成丨 one tree does not make a forest; you alone cannot do all.

In *Cantonese*. An unopened bud; to cover; to bend down; to slope.

整丨的 slope it somewhat.

丨丨雀 a hooting owl.

亞丨仔 a girl of the streets.

淋 ˏ*lin* Dropping, as water from the roof; water running off; to moisten, to soak; to souse; to cause to drop drops.

丨花 to sprinkle flowers.

山水丨丨 the torrents rolled down from the hills.

丨濕 wet through by the rain.

蜜丨噞 honeyed drippings; — a kind of sweet wine.

照頭丨 water pouring down on one, as in a shower bath.

丨一丨 I got well drenched.

可丨以爲飲 if [the flower be] squeezed the drops are drinkable, or will make a wine.

霖 ˏ*lin* Interchanged with the last.

A continuous rain of three days; the rainy season.

愁丨 a mildewing rain, one which deluges the land.

甘丨 an opportune rain.

用汝作丨雨 employ you to bring a plentiful rain; — *met.* to diffuse great benefits.

丨以救旱 rain is the remedy for a drought.

凡雨自三日以往爲丨 a rain which lasts for three days is called ˏ*lin*.

琳 ˏ*lin* A valuable stone mentioned among the articles of tribute with the 球 in the Shu King; it was brought from the west, and was probably a variety of veined jade.

丨國 a country lying near the Caspian Sea which produced topazes.

痳 ˏ*lin* A disease of the bladder or ureter; gravel, stone; strangury or dysury.

砂丨 gravel in the bladder.

血丨 bloody urine.

石丨 calculi; the stone.

五丨 five sorts of urinary ailments.

急丨 strangury.

白丨 stringy or ropy urine.

箖 ˏ*lin* A variety of slender bamboo, the 丨箊 whose young shoots are very sweet; the leaves are long and thin, and the poles are fit for flag supporters.

菻 ˏ*lin* A plant resembling the *Artemisia* in fragrance and habit, but which is probably a species of *Vitex*.

拂丨大食諸胡七十二國降附 seventy-two states of the Turks and nomads submitted to the Arabs of Constantinople.

臨 ˏ*lin* Composed of 臥 *sleeping* and 品 a *sort*, which gives sound.

To behold with care and concern, to look down on sympathizingly; a superior regarding or visiting an inferior; to bless or curse by coming to; commencing, at the point of, about; during, whilst, time of meeting, and it thus often makes the present participle; like, to imitate; the 19th diagram, meaning great; an ancient engine used in sieges, probably a kind of movable turret.

丨終 or 丨死 when dying, near death.

丨民 to rule the people.

丨世 or 丨凡 to come into the world, as Jesus did.

親丨見 I went and saw it myself.

丨去 I am just going.

丨財毋苟得 when getting rich do not become unscrupulous.

丨夜 at nightfall, eventide.

丨帖 to imitate a copy-slip.

丨症 to examine a disease.

丨水八家 neighbors living near the same pool or tank.

丨時悞事 when the time came, he hindered the affair, as by delay.

如丨深淵 as if standing on the brink of an abyss.

丨急 or 丨忙 hurrying one's self.

光丨茅舍 you honor my hamlet, — by coming to see me.

丨朝 to hold a levee.

丨陣退縮 to skulk when going into battle, to skedaddle.

丨大節 at a great emergency.

粦 燐 ⿱炎舛 ˏlin — From 炎 a *flame* altered to 米 *rice* and 舛 *unlucky*; the second is the common form.

An ignis fatuus, called 鬼火 which is seen hovering on old battle fields, and supposed to proceed from the blood of men and horses.

鬼火丨丨 will-o'-wisps flitting here and there; 丨丨 is also applied to fire-flies.

⿰粦刂 ˏlin — To pare off the skin of a fruit.

璘 ˏlin — A veined appearance, like the striæ in agate or marble.

丨彬 beautifully marked and inlaid.

磊落金盤爛丨丨 the golden chargers and plates looked brilliantly as they were piled up.

磷 ˏlin — Water flowing over stones; to grind or abrade stones; thin; shingle.

磨而不丨 you cannot rub that stone thin.

瘦骨丨丨 his poor bones stick out.

Read ˏling. Lofty; eminent.

粼 ˏlin — Pure water, such as flows from hills.

揚之水白石丨丨 amidst the fretted waters the white pebbles are plainly seen.

車聲丨丨 the carriages went rolling and rattling along.

潾 ˏlin — Like the last two.

Name of a river; clear water rippling down rocky ravines.

金丨 a place in Annam.

丨混澣灦 a vast expanse of pure water.

鄰 隣 ˏlin — From *place* and *ignis fatuus*; the second form is considered to be rather incorrect.

Near, contiguous; connected with; supporting, assisting, as a minister his prince; neighboring; a neighborhood, a group of five families; to make affinity with.

丨里 the neighborhood.

丨舍 or 隔丨 or 丨壁 the next house; a near neighbor.

近丨 near by; the next hamlet.

丨國 conterminous states.

睦乃四丨 keep on good terms with your neighbors.

不幸與君子爲丨 it was a sad day when I became your neighbor; — said by a wife.

洽比其丨 they call in their neighbors.

德不孤必有丨 don't keep its virtues to yourself, — let your neighbors share them.

轔 ˏlin — From *carriage* and *ignis fatuus* as the phonetic; occurs interchanged with the last.

The rumbling of wheels; a threshold; abundant.

有車丨丨 the chariots come rumbling and rolling.

戶丨 a doorway; used in Hukwang.

疄 ˏlin — A path crossing a field, and raised above the level in order to retain the soil, as at the base of hills.

獜 ˏlin — Strong, fierce, enduring; a name for the scaly manis or pangolin, and perhaps this character imitates the last syllable of its Javanese name *pangiling*; used for 令 in the phrase 盧丨丨 the dog Lu yelped and barked.

嶙 ˏlin — Precipitous; lofty peaks of mountains.

山勢丨峋 this abrupt cliff is the beauty of the hill.

驎 ˏlin — A piebald horse; a horse with black lips.

驒丨 a whitish horse marked with spots like scales.

鱗 ˏlin — The scales of fish, defined as smaller and softer than the 甲 or plates; repeated, overlapping, like scales.

魚丨 fish scales.

丨物 all scaly animals, as snakes and fishes.

丨部 fishes, the finny tribes.

風細水丨丨 the gentle breeze raises the scaly ripples.

丨次 in orderly rows, like trained bands.

巨口細丨 big mouth and fine scales; a delicious species of *Labrax* found along the coast.

金丨甲 a species of perch (*Holocentrum albo-rubrum*), having five spines on the gill covers.

青丨 or green scale, a kind of herring with a small mouth. (*Clupea tsinglecna.*)

長腰丨 a green herring with a small mouth. (*Clupea nymphæa.*)

魚丨丨兮媵予 what a number of fishes he has sent me!

麟 麐 ˏlin — From *deer* and *ignis fatuus*; the second form is not much used.

The female of the Chinese unicorn, which is drawn with a scaly body; it is considered to have some influence in aiding parturition; the first form seems to have also been intended for a large elk.

麒丨在此 the unicorn is here.

丨趾呈祥 may the unicorn's hoof bring you good luck; — may your sons be many.

獲丨絕筆 when the unicorn was caught, [Confucius] threw aside his pencil.

‛[亻臨] ‛lin — To stoop in walking is 丨伶, applied to round-shouldered people.

‛稟 ‛ling — From *grain* and *storehouse* or *bin*; similar to the next, and not to be confounded with ‛pin 禀 a petition.

To give grain to the poor and to students; to provide food or pay; to nourish, to provide for.

既 丨 稱 事 these stipendiaries attend to public business.

丨俸 salary, stipend.

‛廩 ‛ling ‛lin — From *shelter* and *granary*.

A government granary; a dépôt for rice or food used in sacrifices; a grange; to give grain to students.

倉 丨 a state or public granary.

丨 祿 a stipend formerly given to 丨生 or those selected *siuts'ai* who were not yet *küjin*.

丨 保 one of this degree who introduces a student to the lowest examination.

補 丨 to be placed on the list of stipendiaries.

‛僯 ‛lin — Ashamed, abashed; shameful.

‛懍 ‛lin — From *heart* and to *provide*; used with the next.

Fear; respect for one, because he is dangerous; to heed with profound care.

慘 丨 aching with the cold.

心一丨 I was quite startled.

百 姓 丨 丨 his people are awestruck; they stand reverential and obedient.

丨 之 愼 之 tremble at this! attend to this! *i. e.* carefully beware of these commands; — a closing phrase in edicts and warrants.

‛凜 ‛ling — Shivering with cold; an awe-inspiring manner; trembling, as in the presence of rulers, which the latter try to compel.

丨 遵 a trembling respect for; scrupulously obedient.

丨 冽 piercingly cold, cutting one's face.

威 風 丨 丨 a stern awful manner, with a degree of menace.

‛檁 ‛标 ‛lin — From *wood* and *granary*; the second contracted form is common at Peking.

The beam or plate which rests on the wall and joists, and connects with the girders to support the rafters.

丨 子 a plate or purlin.

橉ʾ linʾ — A tree found in Kiangnan, the ashes of which are steeped in spirits to use in bowel complaints, and the bark as a dye; the name 丨 木 is applied to the *Prunus spinulosa*; a door-sill was once so called in Hunan, and men said demons would step on the heads of whoever slept on it.

吝ʾ 恡ʾ 悋ʾ linʾ — From *mouth* and *letters*; the other forms are seldom met with; it somewhat resembles ‚t'un 呑 to swallow.

Stingy, covetous, sordid; sparing of, close; to dislike to part with, parsimonious; ashamed, regretting; sorry for.

丨 惜 to hold on to, close-fisted.

丨 嗇 niggardly, screwing others.

不 丨 open-handed, liberal, generous.

君 子 不 丨 財 the princely man does not grudge his wealth.

貪 丨 stingy and avaricious.

丨 步 afraid of one's steps.

悔 丨 to regret, to repent of.

羞 丨 ashamed of, mortified.

幸 勿 丨 玉 I hope you will not regret your steps; — a phrase used in an invitation.

[虫粦]ʾ linʾ — From *insect* and *will-o'-wisp* as the phonetic.

A fire-fly.

螢 丨 a fire-fly, a lightning bug.

遴ʾ linʾ — To go or do with difficulty, to choose, to select, to designate; grasping, covetous.

丨 選 to carefully choose.

丨 才 to choose talented men.

不 可 以 丨 do not make it dificult.

丨 員 任 理 appoint a man fit to attend to the affair.

藺ʾ linʾ — A rush, the leaves of which can be used for making mats.

馬 丨 花 a species of *Iris* or fleur-de-lis.

丨 石 stones placed to throw down on besiegers from a wall.

[足藺]ʾ linʾ — The rut of a wheel; to run over one with a cart, to drive against one.

蹂 丨 to trample down, as a field by hunters.

[扌林]ʾ linʾ — To kill, to beat.

In *Cantonese*. To pile up, to lay things on each other; a group, to go in a crowd; to soothe; to soften what is harsh.

丨 起 pile them up.

丨 茶 箱 to pile up tea-chests.

丨 齊 lay them even.

丨 磚 to lay bricks.

丨 髻 to smooth the hair-knot or coiffure.

丨 尖 條 尾 rub down his tail, smooth his harsh expressions.

走 埋 入 丨 to hide in a crowd of people.

LING.

Old sounds, ling *and* leng. *In Canton*, ling *and* leng; — *in Swatow*, leng *and* nia; — *in Amoy*, leng *and* lin; — *in Fuhchau*, lăng, léng, liăng, *and* ling; — *in Shanghai*, ling *and* lăng; — *in Chifu*, ling.

靈 灵 ˏling — Composed of *rain-drops* and 巫 an *enchanter*, though 玉 was the original form, because *gems* are offered to the gods; the contracted form is common in cheap books.

The spirit or energy of a being; that which acts on others to produce effects; its *anima* or soul as exhibited in any way, the 魂 being the substance; spiritual, etherial, intelligent; that which is efficacious, as the virtue of a remedy; the majesty of a god; felicitous; effective, powerful; mysterious; unseen, obscure; a disembodied agency; divine, supernatural aid; whatever can hold converse with the unseen; a coffin, as it contains the departed spirit; the highest type of a class, as man is of created beings; lucky, opportune; subtile, ingenious; marvelous, showing genius; astute.

丨機 a curious effective contrivance.

丨神 an efficacious god; one who answers his worshipers.

丨應 a divine response, an effectual answer.

四丨 or 四丨物 the four types of all hairy, feathered, scaly, and shelly beings, *viz.*, the unicorn, phœnix, dragon, and tortoise.

先丨 one's ancestors.

陰丨 ghosts; the dead.

丨魂 the human soul; the departed spirit.

丨臺 the mind, the reasoning powers.

精丨 smart, apt, clever (*Cantonese*).

澀神定丨 he purified his soul and quieted his spirit, — by turning recluse.

素著丨異 continually manifested his supernatural wonders.

無丨變 he has no versatility

明丨 smart, intelligent, quick of apprehension.

丨便之至 very quick at perceiving; very important, as the pith of a machine.

威丨 [the god's] awful efficacy.

丨雨 a much needed shower.

丨位 the ante-burial tablet, which is 回丨 brought back to the house from the grave, and 燒丨 burned at the expiration of mourning.

丨牌 the ancestral wooden tablet.

扶丨 to go with the coffin to the grave.

恭尊丨 to reverence and pour out a libation on the right of the coffin.

三丨 the sun, moon and stars.

一丨萬感 at once he can act on many, — as a god who hears many worshipers at once.

不丨 inefficacious, as a pill or a charm; no response, as from a god; stolid, dull of apprehension.

巨丨 the great Spirit, a Taoist term for what comes very near to the idea of a Creator or original Cause, but is commonly applied to the god of Mt. Hwa near Si-ngan fu in Shensi.

聖丨 the Holy Spirit, a foreign term.

以赫厥丨 which thus showed his marvelous power.

生丨 all animated beings.

水不在深有龍則丨 it does not matter how deep the water is to make its dragon efficacious.

霝 ˏling — From *rain* and scattering *voices*, which last indicates the drops of rain; it is another form of 零 scattering, and occurs used for the last.

Drops of rain; to fall in drops; to fall down.

⿰氵靈 ˏling — A winding reach in a river; the 東丨 a reach or rapid in the Yangtsz' River east of the Ma-kan gorge, is celebrated for its bold scenery.

醽 ˏling — A rich kind of liquor, called 丨醁, which was made in Hăng-yang hien 衡陽縣 in Hunan.

酃 ˏling — A district in the southeastern part of Hunan on the Mien River, 沔水 a branch of the River Siang.

凌 ˏling — From *ice* and *tumulus*, interchanged with the next.

Ice; an ice-house; to insult; to shame, to treat vilely; injurious; shameful; aspiring; to advance; to exalt.

丨謔 to oppress, to maltreat.

丨辱 to put to shame; to deflower, to humble.

丨雲 trying to reach the clouds; ambitious; high in rank.

丨室 or 丨陰 an ice-house or pit.

丨霄 peering above others; preeminent.

丨遲 the ignominious slow punishment of quartering a criminal.

陵 ˏling — A mound; a tumulus over a grave; a hillock, now confined to the mausolea of emperors, as if they were their citadels; to aspire, to aim high; to usurp; to desecrate; to insult.

皇丨 or 寢丨 or 丨塚 imperial tombs.

塡丨 a raised mound, a Budhist term for a tope or *stupa*, where the relics of priests are buried.

武丨 the warrior's tomb, — an old name of Hangcheu.

丘 〡 a barrow, a hill.

侵 〡 to invade; to usurp.

十三 〡 the tombs of the Ming emperors near Chʻang-pʻing cheu 昌平州 north of Peking; each one has its own name, as follows:—

Yung-loh who died	A.D.	1424 is	長 〡	
Hung-hi	„	„	1425 is	獻 〡
Süen-teh	„	„	1435 is	景 〡
Ching-tʻung	„	„	1449 is	裕 〡
Chʻing-hwa	„	„	1487 is	茂 〡
Hung-chi	„	„	1505 is	泰 〡
Ching-teh	„	„	1521 is	康 〡
Kia-tsʻing	„	„	1566 is	永 〡
Lung-kʻing	„	„	1572 is	昭 〡
Wan-lih	„	„	1619 is	定 〡
Tʻai-chang	„	„	1621 is	慶 〡
Tʻien-kʻi	„	„	1627 is	德 〡
Tsung-ching	„	„	1644 is	思 〡

輘 ꜀*ling*
Occurs written like the last.
A trace of; to run over; to accompany.
〡 輷 a rumbling carriage.
〡 轢 a chariot rut; an outrider or escort was called 〡 轢邊吏 one who went by the rut.

祾 ꜀*ling*
A sacrifice at the royal tombs; the blessing of the gods or the ancestral manes.

菱 ꜀*ling*
An aquatic vegetable, the 〡 角 or buffalo-horn, the water caltrops (*Trapa bicornis*), whose fruit is eaten.
水紅 〡 the best sort of caltrops.
〡 粉 flour or arrow-root made by grinding the dried fruits.
〡 華 a poetical term for a metallic mirror.

綾 ꜀*ling*
Damask; thin silk with one glossy surface, like satin.
羽 〡 lastings.
花 〡 damask, figured sarcenet.
板 〡 thick glossy damask, like satin.
裱 〡 邊 paste on an edging of sarcenet.

掕 ꜀*ling*
To curb in a horse; to rein him in tightly.

淩 ꜀*ling*
Interchanged with the last.
Old name of a river in the south of Shantung; to pass over quickly, as a horse galloping, or a swift vessel; to travel across.
汎海 〡 山 to roam over the seas and cross the mountains.
〡 懅 to tremble; apprehensive; afraid.

鯪 ꜀*ling*
A fresh water fish, the dace or tench.
土 〡 魚 a broad species (*Leuciscus molitorella*), reared in ponds.
黃尾 〡 the yellow tail dace. (*Leuciscus xanthurus.*)
〡 鯉 the pangolin, or 穿山甲 which the Chinese regard as a carp made to go on dry land.

泠 ꜀*ling*
A small affluent of the Yangtsz' River in the district of Tan-yang hien in Kiangsu; also the name of three other streams.
〡 〡 the noise of running water, or of the rising tide, or of the wind.
〡 風 a pleasant breeze.
〡 水 a stream in the south of Hunan.
〡 濕 to wet by sprinkling.

櫺 ꜀*ling*
Cross-pieces of wood in windows and lattices; lintel of a door.
窻 〡 a window-sill.
櫓 〡 the plate under the eaves.
〡 星 gate of a temple to Confucius, or of a college.

伶 ꜀*ling*
From *man* and an *order*.
Alone; to employ, to be employed; a droll, a mime or mummer, a posture-maker; to play, to perform antics; clever, sprightly.
〡 官 master of the musicians.
〡 使 a servant, an attendant.
〡 仃 lonely, going away by one's self; disconsolate.
〡 便 lithe, active, as children.
〡 人 a mummer, a musician.
〡 俐 shrewd, cunning; quick to observe and imitate; this phrase is written in various ways.

玲 ꜀*ling*
The gentle tinkling of sonorous gems.
〡 瓏 finely carved or cut like grottoes; bright; witty, smart; ornate, as style.

囹 ꜀*ling*
From an *inclosure* and an *order*.
A prison, an inclosure for confining men.
仲春省 〡 in mid-spring examine the jails.

瓴 ꜀*ling*
A long necked jar or amphora; concave tiles for roofing.
〡 甋 a water jar with ears to put a cord through.

拎 ꜀*ling*
From *hand* and an *order* as the phonetic; probably the same colloquial sound at Shanghai which is written ꜀*ning* 擰 in Cantonese.
To dangle a thing; to hold a thing up to look at or play with; to carry in one hand, as a bucket; to lift, to take.
〡 起來一桶水 bring in a bucket of water.
〡 得起個 I can take it.
〡 勿起 I can't lift it. (*Shanghai.*)
〡 着頭皮子幹 it is a job as bad as raising my scalp, — he is so particular.
〡 他一把 I shall give him a helping hand.

柃 ꜀*ling*
An evergreen tree, the *Eurya japonica*; the ashes from its leaves are used as a mordant in dyeing; the wood is prettily veined.

笭 ꜀*ling*
A kind of bamboo tray carried in carts.
〡 箵 a small basket or creel used by fishermen.

舲 ꜀ling A boat with windows; a boat fitted up to receive visitors. 孖丨艇 a small covered boat at Canton propelled by two rowers standing with their faces to the bow.

羚 麢 ꜀ling From *sheep* or *deer* and *spirit*, so named because it is said that being afraid of man it hangs itself on a tree to sleep.
A deer like a sheep, having small horns, which are prized as a medicine; the drawings of it very much resemble the *Antilope crispa*.
丨羊角 stag's horns, used as a stimulant like hartshorn.

聆 ꜀ling From *ear* and *order* as the phonetic.
To hear, to try sounds; to pay attention to; to listen; to obey.
耳聽丨丨 acute hearing.
得丨清誨 or 得丨雅教 I shall be happy to receive your instruction; — a polite phrase.
耳丨心悅 the ear and mind are both charmed, as with music.

苓 ꜀ling A tuber or underground fungus.
雲丨 the Yunnan root.
猪丨 a tuberous fungus found growing on liquidambar roots above ground.
丨耳 a sort of truffle or fungus used for food.

蛉 ꜀ling An insect with two wings; it is a kind of mosquito, and seems to be akin to the *Ceratopogon*.
白丨 a venemous fly in Chihli usually called a *sandfly* (a *Simulium?*); it has round white wings and feathery antennæ.
蜻丨 a dragon-fly (*Libellulidæ*); the species have many names.
蜻丨國 kingdom of the dragon-fly; — a poetical name given to Japan, the islands Kiusiu and Sikok being supposed to represent the wings, and Nippon the body.

翎 ꜀ling A plume or pendent tail feather, like those on the peacock, argus-pheasant, or bird-of-paradise; pheasant's tail-feathers were anciently worn by warriors; a single feather; feathers worn as ornaments; the feather on an arrow.
花丨 peacock's plumes, used as an official badge only since the present dynasty.
戴花丨 to wear a feather.
藍丨 a plain plume from the raven.
三眼花丨 a three-eyed feather, worn by high nobles.
雙眼花丨 a two-eyed feather.
拔丨 to take away the feather; often done to mark official disapprobation.
箭丨 the feather on an arrow.
丨管 the tube to hold the feather.
雁丨刀 a dress-sword.

鈴 ꜀ling A round hollow ball like a sleigh-bell, hung on horses or flags to announce approach; a bell with a clapper.
銅丨 a brass bell.
馬丨 horse-jingles or bells.
響丨 tinkling bells hung under eaves to jingle by the wind.
丨鐺似的 in drops; globular, like grapes.
說丨 tinkling novels, light literature unworthy of credit.
馬兜丨 capsules of the bladder-tree (*Kolreuteria*), used as a medicine.
丨兒草 a blue harebell, common in Chihli.
丨釘 a pike or halberd.
In *Cantonese*. A tinkling sound; the clap of a bell.
丨丨聲 the ring of coin.

零 ꜀ling The last drops of a shower; small rain; what exceeds a round number; a fraction, a residue, a remainder; in *numeration*, a cypher showing that one denomination is not used.
丨碎銀 broken bits of silver.
三兩丨二分 three taels, no mace, and two candareens.
丨星 or 丨星東西 miscellaneous, fractions, odd ends.
一百丨一 a hundred and one.
無丨 no remainder, nothing over.
丨落 stripped of leaves, standing alone; scattered or rid of, as a population.
丨丁 an individual by himself, solitary.
丨賣 sold by retail; retailed.
丨多少 or 丨幾多 how much (or many) are there over?
丨剪 sold by the yard or cut.
十點丨 after ten o'clock.
丨餘 a superfluity, what is over.
丨露漙兮 the sparkling dew so bright.

鴒 ꜀ling A general name for birds of the wagtail (*Motacilla*) and lark (*Alauda*) families.
百丨 the thick-billed lark (*Menalocorypha mongolica*), a singing bird highly prized by the Chinese.
角丨 a laverock, the sky-lark, a crested lark (*Alauda cœlivox*), also called 半天飛 mid-heaven flyer.

齡 ꜀ling From *teeth* and an *order* as the phonetic.
The front teeth; the age of a person; years.
丨苗 infantile, very young.
壽丨 sixty years old.
遐丨 grayhaired, very old.
妙丨 in the flower of her age, sixteen or eighteen years old.
少丨 young, over ten years.
冲丨 a minor.

領 ˈling From *head* contracted and an *order* as the phonetic.
The throat; the collar of a garment, a tie or neck wrapper; a bib, a vandyke; a classifier of upper garments; to manage, to put in order, to oversee; to receive from, to take; to

be charged with, usually indicating government acts; to record; to clear goods at a custom-house.

丨子 or 丨緣 or 風丨 a throat-band, a choker; a close collar or neckerchief.

一丨馬掛 one pelisse.

收丨 or 承丨 to receive.

丨謝 received with thanks, — as a present.

深丨 I am much obliged.

丨教 to be instructed; to wait on one; it is as you say.

丨命 to receive orders; to assent to a request.

足丨 I've taken enough, as wine.

心丨 deeply indebted for.

不敢丨 I cannot think of taking it, as a present.

丨袖 collar and sleeve; — *met.* a headman, a leader.

丨出來 to go and receive.

左丨 a captain of 150 Bannermen; a deputy resident holding office in the colonies.

一杯丨落 to assent to everything, a promise given in one's cups.

帶丨引見 to introduce oneat court.

丨事官 an officer who manages affairs, — now applied to a foreign consul, and 總丨事官 is a consul-general.

首丨 a head officer of any kind.

丨洗禮 to be baptized.

總丨 a superintendent.

丨惡 to restrain the wicked.

統丨 a commander-in-chief.

不丨人情 no sense of gratitude.

丨善黜惡 to assent to goodness and discourage evil.

赴關請丨 go to the office and clear the goods.

借丨 to lend to; a receipt or certificate of the loan.

嶺 ʿling From *hill* and *collar*; *q. d.* a girdle of hills.

A break or pass in a mountain, a road over a peak; a ridge or sierra; a mountain range.

丨頭 or 丨表 a high, or the highest peak.

山丨 mountain ranges.

行到絕龍丨 driven to the jumping-off place; — no way of retreat.

梅丨 the Méi-ling or Plum Pass in the northeast of Kwangtung.

丨南 [the region] south of this pass, denotes Kwangtung and Kwangsi provinces.

葱丨 the Onion Mts. or Kara-korum Range between Ladak and Tibet.

袊 ʿ Inner garment.

繞丨 a bride's apparel.

令 ling' Composed of 亼 or 會 to *assemble* and 卩 a *seal* of authority.

A law, a rule, an order; to enjoin upon, to command, to warn; one who orders, an officer; to oblige to do; to occasion, to cause; a cause; a period of time, or that which marks it; good, worthy of regard; to make or reach good, and thus forms the optative; in direct address, used for your; your honored; insinuating, fawning.

丨尊 your father.

丨堂 or 丨慈 your mother.

丨愛 or 丨千金 your daughter.

敕丨 an imperial order.

時丨 divisions of time; times and seasons.

縣丨 the district magistrate; it is used too when speaking of them, as 李丨 the magistrate Li.

嚴丨 a stringent law; to govern strictly.

三丨四申 repeated orders and injunctions.

酒丨 a forfeit in drinking.

丨德壽豈 may their virtue shine to old age.

莫不丨儀 every one worthy and courteous.

丨他來 bring or get him here.

丨名 a good name.

號丨 a written order.

丨人生氣 it will make people angry.

丨箭 a triangular headed flag on a dart; it is put in a bag to be taken to the execution ground, or at times given to messengers by the governor to show his urgency.

丨聞丨望 I have heard your fame and wished to see you.

巧言丨色 guileful words and insinuating looks.

另 ling' From *mouth* and *strength*.

Dwelling or living apart; separate, by itself, distinct; another, besides, furthermore; to divide in two.

丨自 by itself, isolated, apart.

丨外 still, again; in addition to.

他丨自去 he went off alone.

丨來 he came alone.

丨日 another day.

丨有多少 how many more are there?

丨眼相看 to regard with particular attention.

各丨去做 let each do his own work.

名丨具 my name is written elsewhere; — a phrase at the end of a note.

丨有一家 he can do still better; there is another better way, or another dodge.

LIOH.

Old sound, liak. *In Canton,* léuk ; — *in Swatow,* liak, lòk, *and* lia ; — *in Amoy,* liok ; — *in Fuhchau,* liok ; — *in Shanghai,* liék ; — *in Chifu,* liŏa.

略 **畧** *liao'* *lüéh'* From *field* and *each ;* it occurs used for the two next.

To mark off fields ; a boundary between them ; to share with others ; to plan, to counsel ; astute, shrewd ; to diminish, to abridge ; a resumé, a sketch, a digest of ; a little, in general, rather, slightly ; to disesteem, to slight ; a path, a rule ; to offend ; to go on a circuit ; to sharpen ; to take, to kill.

要丨 the radical or important parts of.

丨有 only a few.

謀丨 foreseeing, clever at devising.

經丨天下 to [politically] divide the empire.

丨多的 rather too many.

好' 丨賣人 very apt to seize and sell people.

丨知一二 I understand it a little.

大丨 for the most part.

丨丨曉 I comprehend it somewhat.

丨記 an account of ; a sketch.

丨同 much alike ; very similar.

丨可 it will perhaps do.

三丨 three degrees of cleverness.

丨道 principles.

其言丨 his words were important.

丨地 to visit a place, as an official.

有丨其耜 having sharpened their plowshares.

丨利 advantageous.

砉 *lüéh'* To sharpen, to grind.

劍鈍其丨諸 if the sword be dull, sharpen it.

掠 *lüéh'* From 手 *hand* and 諒 to *plan* contracted.

To rob, to plunder, to take openly and by force ; to invade, to make a raid ; to punish with a stick ; in *penmanship,* the sweep stroke to the left, more frequently called — 撇 a dash.

爪丨 to snatch.

抄丨 to seize and confiscate.

侵丨 to make a foray.

丨食 to seize food ; to forage.

丨治 to bastinado.

謍 *lüéh'* To commend ; to exclaim in admiration of a thing.

汝丨 name of a noted man of the Sung dynasty.

擥 *liao'* *lüéh'* To take by force or strength.

In *Pekingese.* To cast aside ; to throw off, as an insect from the hand.

丨開手 to cast out of the hand.

丨下 lay it down, put it aside.

睔 *lüéh'* Also read *loh,*

To look aside at ; to glance at ; to ogle.

LIU.

Old sounds, liu, lút, *and* lok. *In Canton,* lau ; — *in Swatow,* liu *and* lau ; — *in Amoy,* liu ; — *in Fuhchau,* liu *and* lau ; — *in Shanghai,* liù ; — *in Chifu,* liu.

畱 **留** *꜀liu* From 田 a *field* and an old form of 酉 the hour of *sunset ;* the second form is the commonest.

To detain, to stop a guest ; to keep back, to hold on to ; to lay up, as a record ; to delay ; remaining ; dilatory, slow ; a long time ; leisurely ; to engage or get the refusal of an article.

丨別 a parting gift, a keepsake.

丨落 or 丨下 handed down, as from one's ancestors ; relinquished ; to leave behind.

不丨心 inattentive.

丨他不住 I could not detain him.

丨起 to keep for future use.

挽丨 to stop, by holding one's arm.

丨任 to retain in office, but usually under disfavor, and that the man may retrieve his character.

請丨步 don't trouble yourself to come out ; — said by a visitor.

無丨匪 no brigands remain.

不停丨 not to stop ; unceasingly.

丨餘地 leave him some ground ; don't press him too hard.

丨飯 to detain to dinner.

丨戀 he is doubtful whether to go or stay.

不丨獄 do not procrastinate the decision of cases.

丨城 to leave the gates open.

不丨情 unselfish, guileless.

丨心辦事 mind what you are about.

丨在這裏 leave it here.

榴 *꜀liu* The pomegranate, introduced from the west of Asia, and said to have been so called from its resemblance to a goiter ; *met.* a crimson color.

火石丨 the flowering pomegranate; the Camellia is also called 石丨茶 from its hard nuts.

番石丨 the guava (*Psidium.*)

石丨開笑口 the pomegranate displays its smiling mouth.

反轉石丨皮 a pockmarked face.

丨丨 a variety of the fox.

丨月 a poetical name for the fifth moon.

騮 ˏ*liu* This and the next are often interchanged.

A bay horse with a black mane and tail

紫丨馬 a sorrel horse having a black mane.

⿰犭留 ˏ*liu* Described as a kind of rodent that feeds on bamboo sprouts; the 海丨 is the sea otter, and their skins come to Peking from Tibet or Kokonoor (?); the same name is given to the beaver skins from Russia.

In *Cantonese.* A monkey; a pert fellow.

獁丨仔 a monkey's cub; a nickname for children; you little monkey!

瘤 ˏ*liu* A tumor, a wen; an excrescence or swelling

肉丨 a fleshy tumor.

血丨 a vascular tumor

氣丨 swollen muscles in the neck arising from anger.

捶起個丨 a swelling caused by a blow

鶹 ˏ*liu* A species of owl, called 鵂丨 the large horned owl, noted for its ugliness and ominous hootings

⿰鼠卯 ⿰鼠留 ˏ*liu* A pretty animal as large as a rabbit, called 竹丨 and 竹鼠 frequent in the central provinces, the *Rhyzomys sinensis;* it feeds on the bamboo sprouts, near which it burrows; its flesh is likened in taste to that of a duck.

琉 瑠 ˏ*liu* A pearl, or something very precious.

丨璃 a vitreous, strass-like composition, used for cups, bangles, and colored glaze; from the Sanskrit *vaidurya,* or lapis-lazuli, as this enters into the finest blue kinds; a smooth, glazed surface; applied also to a quick tact at seeing things.

丨璃瓦 glazed yellow or blue tiles; encaustic tiles

點丨璃 light the water lamp; it is a cup holding oil on water.

丨球物 frail, fragile, not very durable

丨球國 Lewchew Is.; the inhabitants are said to have black hands, remove their beards, and keep the skulls of the dead in their houses.

飀 ˏ*liu* The sighing of the wind

丨丨 the motion of the air, as when waving a fan.

遛 ˏ*liu* From to *go* and *stopping;* this is interchanged with 溜 in some cases.

Lingering, delaying; to lead; to saunter.

逗丨 lurking, loitering, hanging about when ordered off

丨馬 to lead a horse up and down to cool.

丨打丨打 to ramble, to take a stroll

劉 ˏ*liu* A sort of halberd used in old times; to kill; to arrange, to set out in order; to wish another's death; leaves falling in autumn.

丨兵驚敵 to dispose troops so as to alarm the enemy.

重我民無盡丨 he showed compassion to our people and would not have them all die.

金風飄而木葉丨 the bleak winds blow, and the trees are bared of their leaves.

捋采其丨 [the tree] will be stripped till it dies.

瀏 ˏ*liu* Clear, limpid, deep water; the wind blowing in gusts; the soughing of wind.

丨亮 a clear air.

丨莅 the fitful autumnal gusts

丨陽江 an affluent of the River Siang in Hunan, on which Chang-sha fu stands

丨其清矣 [the Wei] shows its deep clear stream

蟉 ˏ*liu* Also read ˊ*liu* and ˏ*kiu.*

The tortuous curling motion of a snake is 蚴丨 alluding to its writhing as it moves.

Read *liao'* A cicada, and used for 蟟, but not rightly.

鏐 ˏ*liu* Pure gold; the bridge of a crossbow.

美丨百鎰寧堪饑饉之餐 what will even a hundred bars of pure gold do to assuage your hunger?

丨珌 gold mountings on a scabbard

鷚 ˏ*liu* A species of lark, which soars early to meet the sun, singing and flying as it rises into the clouds; it is called 告天鳥 and 叫天子, the bird which calls on heaven, as well as the 天丨; its voice is like a fife, shrill and sweet.

鎏 ˏ*liu* From *gold* and to *flow;* used for the next.

Pure gold; pendent gems on a crown.

丨金 pure gold.

旒 旈 ˏ*liu* From 㫃 *flag* and 流 to *flow* contracted; the second is a common contraction.

The strings of pearls which anciently hung before and behind crowns; their length and number indicated the wearer's rank; pennants on a flag

旗丨 streamers, called also 旗帶 attached to a banner

冕丨 crown gems; they are now seen only on images of idols.

㐬 ꜀*liu* The original form of the next, and now used only as a primitive in combination; the lower part represents the pendents, and the upper the cap, but others dispute this.

流 ꜀*liu* From *water* and a *pendent* as the phonetic.

The flowing of water; to pass, to go from place to place; to circulate, as news; to diffuse itself, to spread, to make known; to look askance; to become reckless, to cast off restraint; to contract bad habits; to abscond; to transport criminals; to shed, flowing out; fluid; to select; to beg, to intreat; a class, a set; a fluid; roving, vagrant, shifting; an old term for eight taels of silver.

丨下 and 丨上 tide ebbing or rising.

丨血 to bleed.

願丨其血 [Jesus] willingly shed his blood.

丨眼淚 to shed tears.

丨民 vagrants, gypsies.

一丨無病 I have never been sick before.

長丨 everflowing, as a current.

丨質丨力 the impulse of fluids.

丨離失所 without a home, vagabonds.

丨支 rivulets; headwaters; the branches of a stream.

一丨人 a class of men; a calling.

九丨 all kinds of employment.

女丨 womankind.

中丨砥柱 [firm as] a rock in mid-current; — said of a high statesman.

丨風 or 丨言 a hearsay; a report.

丨罪 a crime punished by transportation 3000 *li*.

丨落 prodigals who cannot return; squatters.

下丨 the vulgar.

丨毒生民 it will vitiate the people's habits.

丨沙 shifting sands.

不丨 unceasingly; no stop to it, as a practice. (*Cantonese.*)

丨通 a free flow, as of water; in general use.

細水長丨 small streams [should flow softly] to flow long; — be economical.

硫 ꜀*liu* Sulphur is 丨磺粉; brimstone is 丨磺; and 丨磺强水 is sulphuric acid.

熮 ꜀*liu* To scorch; to put in the blaze; burning; heating.

丨毛子 to burn hair.

吹燈丨鬍鬚 to singe the beard when blowing out a lamp, as a near-sighted man does.

丨手臭 to singe woolens or furs, as when drying them.

幸而不丨 [the dose] is bitter but not heating.

瀏 ꜀*liu* Benumbed with cold.

丨涑 hands and feet frost-bitten.

𤎼 ʻ*liu* To burn over the stubble and grass on a field is 丨田, as when preparing the ground for planting.

柳 ʻ*liu* The willow, which is much cultivated for making charcoal; a groove; striped; brindled; arched, crescent-like, alluding to the shape of the leaf; slender, wasp-like; pleasure, dissipation, because these trees are planted about houses of gaiety; the 24th zodiacal constellation, or the stars δ ε ζ η θ ρ σ ω in Hydra.

垂絲丨 a delicate long-leaved willow.

觀音丨 the tamarix; a broth of the leaves is given in small-pox.

丨絮 willow catkins.

丨眉 an arched eyebrow.

丨條身 a sylph-like figure.

丨條布 striped cottons.

開丨 make a groove. (*Cantonese.*)

丨谷 the valley or place where the sun sets.

花丨地方 places of dissipation.

桃紅丨綠 the peach's bloom and willow's green; — *met.* licentious pleasures.

丨州府 a prefecture in Kwangsi on the River Liu 丨江, a branch of the Pearl River.

輀 ʻ*liu* A hearse; a large car used to carry the coffin.

抑 ʻ*liu* To cover, as a drum; to rub, to feel with the hand; to touch, to lay the hand on.

罶 ʻ*liu* A line of stakes across a stream to entrap fish; a weir; an oval coop trap for taking crabs.

魚麗于丨 the fish rush into the weirs.

三星在丨 three stars [are seen] in the weirs, — but no fish.

綹 ʻ*liu* From *silk* and *crime*.

A skein of silk containing ten or twenty threads; a knot of a hundred lengths in tens; a fob or pocket.

提防剪丨 lookout for the cut-purses!

In *Fuhchau*. A classifier of a beard or wig, and a lapel.

懰 ʻ*liu* To dislike, to have a grudge; to be grieved by ingratitude.

月出皓兮佼人丨兮 the moon is shining in its beauty, and this fine lady is as beautiful too.

Read ꜀*liu*. Sorrowful looking; 丨慄 sad, mournful.

廇 *liu*ʼ The beam in the eaves of a roof; the middle hall of a house.

餾 *liu*ʼ Rice well steamed; the steam of boiling rice or other dishes.

涼了再丨一丨 if it has cooled, then steam it again.

溜 Interchanged with 流 to flow, it is also read ˏliu, and interchanged with 遛 to idle.
ˏliu
liuˀ

A river in Kwangsi; a current; to issue forth, as a fountain; edge of the eaves; gliding about, scouting, prowling; smooth, glossy; to float.

飛 ∣ a cascade.

出門 ∣ 打 gone out on a walk or ramble.

滑 ∣ slippery, glairy; cunning, tricky.

氷上 ∣ 着 gliding over the ice, as in skating.

船順 ∣ 行走 the vessels were drifting down together.

∣ ∣ 食 to take a constitutional after dining.

滴 ∣ dripping eaves.

∣ 氷 to skate.

∣ 黑的 a fellow prowling about in the gloaming to steal or mark things.

一 ∣ 烟兒去了 they were off in a cloud of dust, as race horses.

引 ∣ 通渠 the water flows up into the sluices.

塯 A beggar's clapdish to receive the food given him.
liuˀ

土 ∣ an earthen clapdish.

飂 A steady monsoon wind; a breeze; name of an ancient state.
liuˀ

∣ ∣ 的風 an equable stiff breeze.

∣ 戾 a boisterous wind, a gale.

霤 From *rain* and to *remain*.
liuˀ

Water dripping from the eaves; the eaves of a house.

頤如屋 ∣ he slobbered like the dropping eaves.

承 ∣ catch rain from the eaves.

中 ∣ 神 an ancient god of the earth; his shrine was placed in the inner court, but as often in a skylight in the hall; it answers nearly to the ancient Roman penates.

搯 Properly read ˏch'au, and regarded as an old form of 抽 to select.
liuˀ

In *Cantonese* To toss in the arms, as a baby; to toy with, to fuss over.

∣ 火爐 to make a fire.

∣ 匀佢 shake them up thoroughly.

LO.

Old sounds, la, lat, *and* lap. *In Canton*, lo, — *in Swatow*, lo *and* lúa; — *in Amoy*, lò; — *in Fuhchau*, lo, liò, *and* lwò; — *in Shanghai*, lu; — *in Chifu*, lòa.

羅 Composed of *net*, *silk*, and *bird*, to indicate its purpose, it is used in Budhist words for *l* and *r*, and interchanged with some of its compounds.
ˏlo

A spring-net for birds; a kind of fabric woven like a net or grenadine in knots, with interstices like gauze; openworked, lace like; to spread out, to arrange orderly; a sieve; to bolt, as flour; occurs in many proper names.

一疋 ∣ one piece of *law*, as this kind of silk is sometimes called.

∣ 布 netted woven hempen cloth, used for curtains.

賜紅 ∣ to bestow a red sash; *met.* to order a man to strangle himself.

∣ 帷孤冷 alone and cold in the curtained bed, as a deserted wife.

∣ 網 a bird-net; nets for fish or birds.

∣ 列星宿 the constellations all follow or are placed in order.

∣ 漢柏 the arbor-vitæ (*Thujopsis.*)

∣ 漢頂 the Romish tonsure; some Budhists wear it.

趁早去張 ∣ 罷 you should right away try to raise some money; but 張 ∣ also means to attend to other duties, as 有客來該張 ∣ you must look after the guests when they come.

大 ∣ the great net, *i e* the sky.

∣ 盤 or ∣ 經 the compass.

∣ 國 a small ancient state near Tungting Lake, in the present Ping-kiang hien, 平江縣 in the northeast of Hunan.

∣ 刹 or rakshas, the demons in Budhist mythology.

十八 ∣ 漢 or 阿 ∣ 漢 the 18 *arhans*, *arhats*, or *rahans*, the personal disciples or worthies of Budha; the term is defined by 應供 deserving worship, and 殺賊 destroyer of the enemy, *i. e.* passion.

∣ 吼 ∣ Rahula or Lagula, the son of Sakya-muni, who founded a school.

排 ∣ 漢 to arrange people in rows around a room.

∣ ∣ the Lolos or Laos tribes now living in the north of Siam 暹 ∣, the last syllable of which name probably refers to these people, once possessors of much of Yunnan and Kwéichau; in writing this appellation the radical *dog* is sometimes added, as 玀玀 to show contempt for them.

門 ∣ 吐鳳之才 this family has produced men of great talent.

搜 ∣ 書籍 to collate and compare records.

∣ 星 the star *v* in Capricorn.

秋雲似 ∣ the autumnal sky resembles figured netting.

∣ 櫃 a frame for bolting flour.

∣ 鍋 humpbacked.

儸 ꜀lo — Clever, sharp.
傱 丨 resorting to force.
僂 丨 the braves among banditti; rebel troops.

囉 ꜀lo — A note or refrain in singing; the prattle of children; annoying, vexing.
丨 唆 troublesome, fretful, disappointing.

In *Cantonese*. A final, probably altered from *loh*, 咯, to express the end of a sentence.
係 丨 yes; it is so.

欏 ꜀lo — The horse chestnut or buckeye, the 桫 丨 found in the western regions.
草 丨 a tree in Hunan whose wood is easy to ignite.
丨 落 a stake fence.

灑 ꜀lo — A river named 汨 丨 江 flowing into Tung-ting Lake on the southeast; it is a small stream, and joins the River Siang near its mouth.

籮 ꜀lo — From *bamboo* and *net*.
Deep and open baskets without covers or handles, sometimes made with holes to run cords through; they are chiefly used to hold grain, or by the peddlers; a sieve.
擔 丨 頭 a peddler.
丨 仔 small baskets. (*Cantonese*)
茶 仔 丨 peddling baskets.
坐 丨 a basket-sitter, — denotes a criminal taken out to execution. (*Cantonese*)
穀 丨 a corn-basket.
磕 丨 賣 了 the whole lot is sold off.

蔂 ꜀lo — Used with the last.
A basket, especially one like a hod for carrying dirt; it is interchanged with 虆 to pile up earth.
劓 鼻 盈 丨 the basket was filled with the noses which had been cut off.

蘿 ꜀lo — From *plant* and *net*, referring to the habit of growth.
Parasitic plants like the *Epidendrum*, or those which twine around trees like the *Wisteria*, are called 女 丨; those like dodder are called 兎 絲; whence the phrase 共 結 絲 丨 the vines and tendrils have interlaced, to denote a marriage alliance.
丨 蔔 a turnip, or roots like it.
丨 蔔 仔 or 水 丨 蔔 a radish.
紅 丨 蔔 and 黃 丨 蔔 names given to the carrot or beet.
似 丨 蔔 的 心 heart as big as a turnip; — *i. e.* generous.
剪 邊 丨 the pink. (*Dianthus*)
丨 纒 to entwine around.

鑼 ꜀lo — A gong; a brass drum used to announce approach or give the alarm; soldiers use them for wash-basins.
打 丨 to beat the gong.
丨 鼓 喧 天 the gongs and drums resounded to the sky.
打 頭 丨 sound the head gongs, as when an officer comes.
鳴 丨 會 衆 collect the people by the gong.

騾 / 羸 ꜀lo — From *horse* and *to involve*; the second is the original form but is now seldom met.
A mule, the offspring of an ass and a mare.
丨 馬 or 丨 子 a mule.
海 丨 皮 seal skin.
丨 馱 子 the load of mule.
丨 馬 以 報 [I hope to] requite you as with the service of a mule or horse.

饠 ꜀lo — A baked wheaten cake, called 食 丨 having fruit inside.

螺 ꜀lo — From *insect* and *to involve*.
A term for spiral univalves like the *Lymnœa*, *Voluta*, *Murex*, &c.; spiral, screw-like; a conch.
嚮 丨 conches used for sounding, when summoning people to resist.
田 丨 fresh water snails.
丨 絲 釘 or 丨 旋 a screw.
丨 髻 a spiral headdress.
丨 殼 univalve shells in general.
丨 靨 the operculum of snails.
丨 魚 a flying-fish.
吹 海 丨 blow the sea-conch.
右 旋 白 丨 the white conch with whorls turning to the right, is a large rare shell kept at Peking and lent to envoys going to Lewchew to insure them a safe voyage; it is probably a Buccinum.

腡 ꜀lo — The fine marks and lines in the palm, by which one's fortune is determined.
你 手 沒 有 丨 your fingers have no striæ; — you let everything slip.

In *Cantonese*. To waste or misapply a thing; to apply it uselessly; to throw away, as pearls before swine; rotten, as eggs.
鬱 丨 wasted, as energy.
丨 妥 to spoil an affair.

覶 / 觀 ꜀lo — To look about.
丨 縷 carefully, repeatedly; in a particular and detailed manner; tautology; a periphrase.
丨 次 the order of words in a sentence.

氌 ꜂lu — A sleazy woven narrow cloth, resembling bunting or coarse worsted, made in Tibet from yak's hair.

裸 / 躶 ꜂lo — From *clothes* or *body* and *real*.
Naked, unclothed, barebacked; the naked; to strip, to unclothe.
衣 丨 clothe the naked.
丨 裎 the upper part of the body naked.
丨 蟲 the naked animal, *i. e.* man.
丨 體 罵 賊 he threw off his dress and railed at the rascal.
丨 身 nude; having no clothes.

ˋ𧕮 Like the preceding.
ˊlo Unclothed; fruits with hard shells.
丨行 going about naked.
丨物 name of a beast like the caracal.
果丨 a long roundish gourd, the fruit of the *Tricosanthes anguina* and *palmata*, which are generally known as snake gourds.

ˋ𦉼 A contracted form of the last, and now used only in combination as a primitive.
ˊlo Naked-like animals having very short hair, like the elephant, tiger, or leopard; a fabulous monster like the tapir.

ˋ蠃 Interchanged with 螺 a shell.
ˊlo The solitary wasp.
蜾丨 the sphex, or dauber wasp, supposed to be transformed from caterpillars.

ˋ鸁 The grebe 鸊鷉 is called the 須丨 in old books; the
ˊlo 果丨 is an old name for the tailor bird, but perhaps also alludes to the preceding.

ˋ蓏 From *grass* and *melons*.
ˊlo Fruit which ripens on the
ˊkwo ground as melons, tomatoes, ground-nuts, pine-apples, &c.; those having no kernel.
菓丨 fruits of all kinds.

ˏ摞 To manage; to arrange, as a dress.
lo' 丨頭 to comb and dress the hair and arrange the bands and fillets, as the ancients did.
Read *lo'*. To take, to get, in which senses it is used with the next; to put one thing on another; to lay nicely in a pile; a lot of things, a parcel, a load.
把書丨起 pile up these books.
丨兩塊 two lie on each other.

攞 To split, to rend; to select, to pick out.
lo' In *Pekingese*. To rub off, to wipe.
丨汗 wipe off the sweat.
In *Cantonese*. To get, to buy, to procure for one; to vex; to injure.
你來丨銀 you come and get the money.
丨命 to vex one's life out; bewitched.
丨債仔 a child that dies early, before he can recompense his parents.
丨魚 to fish; to go a fishing.
丨回信 bring the answer back.

砢 Stones piled up.
lo' 磊丨 a pile of pebbles or gravel; — *met.* prominent talent, distinguished parts.
坑衡閜丨 all the interlacing branches supported each other.

ˋ瘰 The king's evil; strumous enlargements.
ˊlo 丨癧 scrofulous swellings; the first are small, the second large, and the two follow each other like beads; the swellings from musquito or flea bites are sometimes so called.

躍 Embarrassed; to miss one's footing.
ˏlo 丨跬 to walk slowly; not to advance, either from weakness or inability.

邏 To cruise about, to patrol; to make a circuit; to spy; to
ˏlo inspect, as a guard does; to screen, as hills do a glen.
巡丨 to go around examining.
丨丨轉 playing about, in and out.
設卡丨守 to set a guard to watch the place.
春山丨繞 the green hills shelter the spot.
偵丨 to spy out; a scout.
丨娑 the capital city in Tangut or Turfan.

嚲 Also read ˏto and ˋtan
lo' To droop, to hang down; extensive; generous, thick.
柳丨鶯嬌花復般 the oriole's sweet note is heard amid the drooping willows, and the flowers come out in their beauty.

LOH.

Old sound, lak. *In Canton*, lok; — *in Swatow*, lòk, lak, *and* lo; — *in Amoy*, lok; — *in Fuhchau*, lòk; — *in Shanghai*, lok; — *in Chifu*, lòa.

洛 From *water* and *each*.
lo' A famous tributary of the Yellow River, rising in the S.E. of Shensi, flows easterly about 250 miles, and enters it west of Kai-fung fu in Honan; another river in Shensi, about 350 miles long, draining the northern third of the province, which flows in near T'ung-cheu fu; the glare on water.
丨陽 capital of China in B. C. 770, and often afterwards, till razed by the Kin, A. D. 1126; it lay west of Loh-yang hien in Honan.
丨陽景 a comfit made from the loose-skin orange.
丨陽花 a flower like the *Caryophyllus* or myrtle.

洛 From *ice* and *each*; also read *hoh*,
lo' 丨澤 frozen, bleak; icy, like a glacier or frozen lake.

剳 To trim off the knots on the
lo' bark of wood.
丨淸污吏 he removed all the grasping officials.

咯, *lo'* From *mouth* and *each.* Wrangling, disputatious; to contend; a final particle, denoting indeed, certainly; so; used for 了 done, finished.

就是丨 that will answer.

是丨我知道了 it is so, I know it.

完丨 done; all over; ended.

係丨 yes, indeed. (*Cantonese.*)

Read *koh*, The cackling of a fowl; to cough and spit, to clear the throat; to hawk.

烙, *lao' lo'* To burn in, to brand; to toast, to spit or roast in cooking; to bake; a branding-iron; red hot.

打丨印 to brand in a mark.

丨鐵 a branding-iron; a sort of flat-iron for smoothing cloth.

丨到焦 it is roasted brown.

丨餅 a fried wheaten cake, a description of flapjack like shortcake.

丨衣裳 to iron clothes.

珞, *lo'* Ornaments for the neck.

瓔丨 brooches, necklaces, and other ornaments for the neck.

絡, *lao' lo'* Silk or hemp not yet reeled or rotted; the fibre or staple of cotton; joined, continuous; to bind, to tie up; to encompass; a net for carrying boxes, rope slings; blood vessels which diverge from the great veins or arteries.

脈丨 the pulse.

丨馬頭 to halter a horse.

橘丨 the dried strings or *chalaza* in the orange.

丨緯娘 a name for the cricket, alluding to the hum of a spindle.

心包丨 the pericardium, as it is supposed to be a fatty kind of strap inclosing the heart.

一對籐丨 a pair of rattan slings.

線丨 net or rope slings.

丨綢 a kind of sarcenet.

受人籠丨 duped, taken in.

聯丨 tied together, like a line of camels; to assist each other.

麻丨 unspun hemp.

丨繹不絕 an unbroken line, closely linked.

扇丨子 a fan-case, hung on the girdle.

酪, *lo'* Cream; dried milk; racky from mare's milk; fat, unctuous.

丨餅 cheese.

杏丨 an emulsion of apricot seeds or almonds.

丨漿 butter, thick whey; the fat of meat expressed.

乳丨 a kind of milk porridge.

丨凍裏加糖 add some sugar to the cream.

鵅, *loh'* A water bird, a species of kingfisher (?) having a short neck, reddish plumage with white spots, and greenish on the back.

Read *koh*, A synonym of the white owl is 鉤丨 so called from its screeching voice.

雒, *lö'* From *bird* and *each*; occurs used for 洛 in names of places, and also for the next.

A kind of bird.

丨丨然 afraid.

丨縣 an old name of Han cheu 漢州 in Sz'ch'uen.

駱, *lö'* A white or cream-colored horse with a black mane.

丨駝 a camel.

丨田 a place near Annam.

我馬維丨 my white horses have their black manes.

落, *lao' lo'* The fall of the leaf or of rain; to scatter; to fall; to tumble in or off; to let fall; to descend, to come down to; to gather at a place to make a settlement; to lay a thing down; to enter, as in an account; the place to which one falls or goes, one's gathering place or abode; fixed, settled, arranged; a *preposition*, at, in; in colloquial, often merely adds to the force of the verb.

丨來 come down.

村丨 or 邨丨 a village; hamlets.

丨價 the price or rate has fallen.

上丨平安 may you suffer no harm going up or down stairs.

丨薄 reduced in property, decayed, poor.

丨成 the job is done.

日丨西山 or 太陽丨 the sun is setting.

丨力 be smart, stir about!

丨魄 no energy, spiritless.

丨定 to pay earnest money.

丨筆 to put pen to paper, to begin a work.

丨髮 to become a priest or nun.

丨沙 to mix in sand.

丨船 to go aboard a vessel.

丨貨 export cargo.

跌丨地 he fell down.

你住那兒丨地 in what spot do you live?

有着丨 it is all settled, everything is arranged; 着丨 also sometimes means married, settled in life.

無下丨 I have no certain knowledge of, I don't know about it.

丨丨大方 perspicuous, forcibly stated.

丨卷 or 丨孫山 rejected essays.

丨丨難合 our views are quite different.

丨在何方 where has it gone? where has it been put?

拖人丨水 to pull one into the water, to impose on one.

座丨何方 where is your dwelling, where's your house?

丨丨脚 let us rest our legs.

In *Fuhchau.* A suite of rooms; a building, usually with front and rear courts.

硌, lo' Large boulders on hills; an inferior stone.

磊丨層峯 peaks rising over peaks.

丨丨 hard, gritty, as amygdaloid, or the kinds of rock not easily worked.

樂, lö' yüe' yao' yoh' The original form resembles the ornamented *frame* on which a bell or drum is hung, the *drums* on the sides and the *bell* in the middle.

Pleasure, quiet, ease; to rejoice in, to take delight in, to esteem a pleasure; a joy; dissipation; good, as a year.

丨心 contented.

丨天之命 to accord with heaven's decrees.

行丨圖 a portrait.

作丨 to make merry.

何丨如之 where shall I be better pleased?

你何丨於此 what pleasure can you find in this?

丨何如也 where will you be happier than here?

何丨之有 Ah! what pleasure is there here!

以善為丨 to take pleasure in virtue.

丨人之丨 to rejoice with those who rejoice.

丨得的 or 丨得乎 how lucky! just the thing; hit it exactly.

喜丨 joy and merriment.

丨奏元霄 to hail the in-coming year with joyful music.

Read *yoh*, Music, one of the 六藝 or six liberal arts; instruments of music; *met.* the refinements and elegancies of life; musicians.

大丨 great music, a term by which ancient writers seem sometimes to have obscurely intended to express the working and harmony of creation, music of the spheres.

丨器 musical instruments.

丨表 the staff in musical notation.

作丨 or 奏丨 to play on instruments.

移風易俗莫善于丨 there is nothing so good as music to reform the manners and change the customs.

丨部 the Board of Music, a bureau in the Board of Rites.

丨具入奏 the musicans all go in to perform.

Read *yao'* To take delight in; to choose and use or enjoy.

各有所丨 each one has his own hobby or pleasure.

丨丨 pleasurable, delightsome.

智者丨水 clever people are charmed with water scenery.

丨道人之善 to rejoice in, and speak of others' goodness.

Read ꜀*lao*. A man's name in olden times, Earl Lao 伯丨, famed for his knowledge of horses.

濼, lo' A river near the city of Tsi-nan in the north of Shantung; a bank; an estuary.

犖, lo' From 牛 an *ox* and 勞 *toil* contracted.

A brindled or speckled ox; manifest, open, patent.

卓丨 to excel; preeminent.

駁丨 a particolored ox.

丨确 hard and level, as a road.

丨丨 clearly understood.

LU.

Old sounds, lu, lut, *and* lok. *In Canton*, lu *and* lò; — *in Swatow*, lò, lu, *and* lù; — *in Amoy*, lò; — *in Fuhchau*, lu, hò, lò, *and* tiò; — *in Shanghai*, lu, — *in Chifu*, lu.

꜀盧 ꜀lu From 皿 *dish* with 虍 a *pan* above; it is often contracted to 戶 in combination, and its compounds have nearly superseded its use.

A vessel for containing rice; a pan to hold fire; a grog-shop; black; a wild tribe that occupied anciently some parts of Hupeh; a kind of hound.

胡丨大笑 a boisterous laugh.

丨弓 a black bow.

丨꜀令꜀令其人美且仁 the hounds tinkle their collars; their master is handsome and kind.

當丨 a dram-shop.

꜀嚧 ꜀lu One calling to his pigs, cries 丨丨, but the phrase is written several ways.

呼丨 to laugh.

꜀攎 ꜀lu To take hold of; to spread out; to lead; to select.

捗丨 to gather, as a harvest.

꜀壚 ꜀lu Black, stiff clods, not fertile, and not yet broken by the harrow; a shop.

酒丨 a wine-shop.

草丨 my cottage.

黃丨 yellow clods, the grave, hades.

꜀鑪 ꜀lu Used with the last and next.

A vessel to warm spirits; a censer; a copper brazier; a furnace.

當丨 a grocery, a spirit shop

手丨 a hand-stove.

一副香丨 one set of incense censers, of three or five.

丹丨 a crucible.

提丨 hand censers, carried in processions, and before the governor-general.

丨鼎 a tripod in temples.

擁丨而坐 he called them to sit around the brazier.

爐 炉 ꜂lu From *fire* and *black*; the contracted form is in common use.
A stove, fireplace, grate, furnace, chafing-dish, or other place for holding a fire.
傾銀 丨 a refining furnace.
吊 丨 a swinging oven.
風 丨 a portable furnace, often called *fo-gong*, a word corrupted from 火方 or fire-place.
丨 房 a mint; governmental assay shops.
茶 丨 子 a stall to sell boiling water.
明 丨 an uncovered fireplace.
局 丨 an oven; a bake-pan of any kind. (*Cantonese.*)
丨 瓶 a set of censer and vases, usually of metal.
丨 坑 the draft and coal-hole in a *k'ang*, where it is warmed.

獹 ꜂lu A variety of dog, the 韓 丨 which seems to be a large shepherd's dog.

櫨 ꜂lu A short post over a girder; a king-post, which upholds the roof, as a peduncle does the flower.
丨 橘 the Canton name for the loquat (*Eriobotrya japonica*), the 枇杷 or Chinese medlar.
楊 丨 a species of *Diervilla* or *Wiegela* found in Japan; also applied to a fine timber.

瀘 ꜂lu A river in the northeast of Kiangsi in Lu-ki hien 丨 溪 縣 which borders on Cheh-kiang.
丨 州 a prefecture in the south of Sz'ch'uen along the Yangtsz' River, where the 丨 水 flows into it, and sometimes gives its name to the main stream; the region is said to be malarious.

瓐 ꜂lu A gourd.
瓠 丨 the bottle gourd or *Lagenaria*.
壺 丨 a jar shaped like this gourd.

瓐 ꜂lu A valuable gem, called 碧 丨 whose description allies it to the topaz.

罏 ꜂lu From *jar* and *black*; it is sometimes used for 鑪 a brazier.
A wine jar, short and wide mouthed, made of bronze or porcelain.
携 丨 覓 沽 to take the jug to get grog.

瘻 ꜂lu A kind of ulcer.
食 丨 pot-bellied, as children from bad food.

玈 ꜂lu Black, painted, or varnished.
丨 弓 black bows such as were given to princes in olden time.

纑 ꜂lu Hempen threads; to hatchel and dress flax or hemp, and prepare them for weaving.
妻 辟 丨 his wives dressed the thread.

臚 ꜂lu From *flesh* and *black* as the phonetic.
The skin; the belly; to arrange in order, to spread out; to state; to convey orders, to intimate to, to transmit.
丨 列 to state seriatim, to set out orderly.
丨 陳 to make out a list.
丨 歡 萬 姓 to speak of the good qualities [of an official] among the people.
鴻 丨 寺 the Court of Ceremonies.
傳 丨 the fourth in rank of the Hanlin.

艫 ꜂lu A stout, square built boat, fit for transport; stem of a boat where the trackers work, but others say the stern.

籚 ꜂lu A small rush like an *Arundo*, from which baskets can be made; a large basket with a handle or bale; shaft of a spear.
丨 籃 baskets of different sizes.

蘆 ꜂lu Water rushes; applied to various sorts of hollow stemmed grasses, as *Phragmites* and *Arundo*, used for mats and awnings, or to repair dikes.
丨 柴 faggots of rushes.
丨 葦 rushes.
黃 丨 遶 宅 the yellow rushes environ the house; — a rural abode.
丨 薈 膠 juice of hellebore, used to rub on the hair; the name is also applied to an impure catechu or terra japonica.
木 葫 丨 wooden floats tied on boat-children at Canton.
丨 課 taxes on reed lands along the banks of rivers.
漏 丨 a variety of the cactus.
丨 粟 the sweet sorghum (*S. saccharatum*), grown over central China.

轤 ꜂lu A windlass; a pulley; a snatch-block.
轆 丨 a sheave on which a rope runs to raise things.

鸕 ꜂lu From *bird* and *black*.
The 丨 鷀 or fishing cormorant (*Phalacrocorax carbo*), also poetically called 烏 鬼 the black devil.
山 伯 丨 a name given at Canton, to a species of thrush (*Garrulax perspicillatus*), reared for its vivacity.

鱸 ꜂lu From *fish* and *black*, from the spots.
A Canton name for perches of the *Labrax* family; it includes the gilt head
班 丨 the spotted wrasse. (*Labrax japonicus.*)
白 丨 the white perch. (*Pristipoma pihloo.*)
頭 丨 red headed labrax. (*Pristipoma kaakan.*)
花 點 丨 the spotted perch (*Pristipoma nageb*) is the best sort; it is made into 丨 膾 or fish salad.

矑 ꜀lu The pupil of the eye; to see.
清丨 a clear bright eye.

顱 髗 ꜀lu The skull of a man; the forehead; bones of the head.
頭丨 the skull of a man.
枯丨頭 a decapitated head, a dried skull, often left on the execution-ground.

鹵 ʿlu The character is thought to represent a spotted nitrous efflorescence; it forms the 197th radical of a few characters pertaining to salt.

Rock salt; salt licks; land from which salt or nitre is obtained; barren, saltish land; rude, uncivil; violent, insolent.
丨味 meat corned with spirits.
丨鹹 saltish; nitrous.
丨餅 a steamed wheaten biscuit at Peking, with or without fruit.
淳丨 barren salt lands.
丨簿 order of the emperor's traveling equipage.
丨莽 flippant; rash or heedless, in speech or act; abrupt.
丨草 careless, as when writing.

滷 ʿlu Very similar to the last.

Salt land, such as occurs on the coasts where salt is evaporated; earth from which salt can be leeched; a salt preparation, pickle, brine.
丨水 a pickle used in bean curd.
丨香 spice for a pickle.
丨煑肉 beef or mutton boiled with salt and soy.
鹽丨 the leechings of salt earth.

磠 ʿlu From *stone* and *saltish*.

Gravel, shingle; fine stones on a beach.

擄 ʿlu Violent, ready to resort to force; movable, swaying.

In *Pekingese* read ꜀lu, and used with *lo'* 攞. To strip off; to wipe away; to rub down, as a groom his horse.
丨汗 to wipe off the sweat.
一丨到底 stripped of all — his honors, as an officer degraded to private life.
丨樹皮 to peel off the bark.

魯 ʿlu From *fish sauce* and *white*, both contracted.

Stupid, slow of speech; blunt, not intelligent; untaught.
丨鈍 dull of understanding.
粗丨 rustic, coarse.
丨惘 dull and heedless, a little pig-headed.
樸丨 unassuming, plain, honest.
丨國 an ancient state.

This state has been rendered famous by the sages Confucius and Mencius, and their disciples. It was granted to Cheu Kung Tan 周公旦 or Tan, the Duke of Cheu, about B. C. 1122; but his eldest son Peh-kin 伯禽 first made his capital at Kiuh-feu 曹阜 about the year 1115, and was called Duke of Lu 魯公. A successor Duke Yiu 幽公 was killed in 1038, by his brother Duke Wéi 魏公, who has the infamy in Chinese history of being the first regicide. In 838, Duke Wu 武公 made a feudal visit to the court of Süen Wang 宣王 to render him homage for his fief. The Annals of Lu, called *Chʻun-tsʻiu Chʻwen* 春秋傳 or Spring and Autumn Records, by Confucius, commence with the reign of Duke Yin 隱公 the son of Duke Hwui 惠公 in the 49th year of Pʻing Wang 平王 B. C. 722, and end with the accession of Duke Tao 悼公 in the 39th year of King Wang 敬王, B. C. 481, two years before their author's death. Their names and reigns, as here given, are constantly referred to in Kang-hi's Dictionary in quotations from the Annals.

STYLE OF REIGN.	PERSONAL NAME.	ACCESSION AND LENGTH OF REIGN.		GENEALOGY.	COTEMPORANEOUS EVENTS.
Duke Yin 隱公	姑息	722	11	Killed by his brother.	722 Shalmanezer takes Samaria.
Duke Hwan 桓公	軌	710	18	Brother of the last.	716 Romulus murdered.
Duke Chwang 莊公	同	692	32	Son of the last.	696 Manasseh, king of Judah.
Duke Wăn 閔公	啓方	660	2	Son of the last	672 Tullus Hostilius of Rome.
Duke Hi 僖公	申	659	33	Brother of the last.	641 Amon, king of Judah.
Duke Wăn 文公	興	626	18	Son of the last.	621 Josiah dies at Megiddo.
Duke Süen 宣公	接	608	18	Son of the last.	601 Daniel at Babylon.
Duke Chʻing 成公	黑肱	590	18	Son of the last.	594 Solon at Athens.
Duke Siang 襄公	午	572	31	Son of the last.	588 Jerusalem destroyed.
Duke Chao 昭公	稠	541	32	Son of the last.	536 Cyrus restores the Jews.
Duke Ting 定公	宋	509	15	Brother of the last.	508 Darius conquers India.
Duke Ngai 哀公	蔣	494	27	Son of the last.	481 Xerxes invades Greece.
Duke Tao 悼公	寧	467		Son of the last.	460 Pericles rules Athens.
Duke Muh 穆公	Probably the grandson of Duke Tao.				445 Nehemiah builds Jerusalem.

Not much is known of the state after this period. In the year 255, the king of Tsu removed its prince to Kü, and in 249 he abolished its separate existence, after a duration of 873 years from the investiture of Duke Cheu. During this long period, its limits changed but little, and included the southern and eastern parts of the present province of Shantung.

‛櫓 ‛艣 ‛樐 ‛[木虜] ‛lu

From *wood* or *boat* and a phonetic; the first is most used.

A turret of wood used on walls; a movable wooden tower for archers; the propelling scull on Chinese boats worked on a pivot on the taffrail.

丨棒 the scull-pivot.

扳 丨 port the helm!

推 丨 push the scull, is starboard the helm.

搖 丨 to scull.

城 丨 a lookout on a fortification.

‛[口虜] ‛lu

The noise made in calling pigs is 丨 丨; it is the sound usually heard in the North.

‛虜 ‛擄 ‛lu

From a *tiger*, to run on a *string*, and *strength*; the second is the form in common use.

To capture prisoners, to seize men in battle; prisoners, slaves taken in war; devoted, addicted to, enslaved by.

丨 掠 to take alive.

守錢 丨 a slave to money, a miser.

丨人勒贖 to hold captives to ransom.

丨 人 a kidnapper; to catch men.

路 lu'

From *foot* and *each*; *q. d.* in a road each one goes his own way, and leaves his own traces.

A road, a path, a way where people go and make it plain; in the Mongol dynasty and before, it denoted a 道 circuit, and it is still used occasionally for political divisions; in *mechanics*, a space, an extension; a way of duty or action, an opportunity; grand; loud; fallen; to travel, to journey; used for the next.

三岔 丨 joining of two roads.

十字 丨 cross-roads.

丨不通行 no thoroughfare, a cul-de-sac.

行私 丨 to go in bye-paths, to act improperly.

問 丨 to ask the way.

陸 丨 a land journey.

水 丨 to go by boat; water communication.

無門 丨 nothing to do; out of work.

丨 上 on a journey; on the road.

一 丨 風霜 the discommodities of a journey, the weather and travel.

丨 滑 the road is slippery.

無 丨 可 走 no alternative, no resource or work; penniless.

買 丨 錢 to pay black mail.

開 丨 to make a road; to clear the way, as for the lares.

青雲得 丨 to become a *küjin*.

趕 丨 to hurry on, to hasten one's steps.

橫 丨 a shorter way; a cut-off.

車 丨 a carriage road; in *mechanics*, the plane in which a machine or part of it works.

彼 丨 斯 何 君 子 之 車 what chariot is that? it is our leader's.

熟識 丨 道 I know the way (or places) well.

走小 丨 to go by a side path.

In *Cantonese*. To pour out, to decant.

丨一埕油 to pour oil from a standard jar, — in order to save weighing it.

輅 lu'

A chariot, a state carriage; the traces of a cart.

玉 丨 the imperial carriage.

丨 馬 a large cart to sleep in.

賂 lu'

From *property* and *each*.

To give a present, to bribe, to corrupt; to aid the state; a vessel used in ancestral worship.

賄 丨 to bribe, especially an official.

財 丨 to send presents to officials.

大 丨 南 金 heavy contributions of southern metals.

簵 lu'

A slender, lithe sort of bamboo, fit for darts or arrows; it anciently grew in Yangcheu.

璐 lu'

A beautiful gem, hung as an ornament from the girdle.

逵似連 丨 the [frost on] the roads [glistens] like strings of gems.

潞 lu'

A river in Lu-ngan fu 丨 安府 in the southeast part of Shensi, flowing into the Yellow River; also a river in Yunnan; and a branch of the Pei-ho flowing near T'ung cheu.

露 lu'

From *rain* and *road*.

The dew; mist that forms in drops of rain; to bedew, to bless; to disclose, to manifest; to expose, to show through; to exhibit; disclosed, apparent, naked.

丨 天 open to the sky.

丨 水 dew.

丨 水珠 the drops of dew.

敗 丨 ruined by betrayal.

丨 出 馬 脚 the horse's hoof shows; the thing is divulged.

丨 齒 exposed teeth.

不 丨 面 not to see a visitor.

丨 形 to see the real shape.

丨 宿 風 餐 sleeps in the dew and dines on the wind; — miserably poor.

花 丨 水 cologne water.

藏頭 丨 尾 the cat is let out of the bag.

丨 骨 his bones show, emaciated; the evil deed is known.

丨 布 to publish abroad, as general orders.

覆 丨 萬民 to relieve and soothe the people.

不 丨 風 don't tell of it.

屍骸暴 丨 the corpses and bones were left uninterred.

甘 丨 下 降 the sweet dew descends from heaven; the 甘 丨 is regarded as the ambrosia of the gods, and priests sprinkle it for ghosts to sip.

富貴花間 丨 riches and honors [fade] like the dew on flowers.

鷺 lu' From 鳥 *bird* and 露 *dew*, because when it comes the dew falls, and it is warm weather.

A wader common throughout China.

白丨or 白丨鷥 the white egret heron (*Egretta* [Herodias] *garzetta*); it is embroidered on the court robes of officers of the sixth grade.

朱丨a russet headed small white heron or paddy-bird. (*Bubulcus russata.*)

丨序 arranged in order of precedence.

丨伏 a stealthy step like a heron's.

丨門 or 丨島 a poetical name for Amoy from the sea-birds in its vicinity.

鏴 lu' To plug or stop up, as the holes in an iron boiler.

錮丨鍋 to mend a boiler by soldering a piece in.

LÜ.

Old sounds, lu, lio, lút, *and* lot. *In Canton*, lü *and* lau; — *in Swatow*, lù, lu, *and* li; — *in Amoy*, lu *and* lò; — *in Fuhchau*, lü *and* lëu; — *in Shanghai*, lü; — *in Chifu*, lü.

廬 ꜀lü A thatched hovel, a hut; a cottage; a choultry by the roadside; a laborer's lodge in the field; to erect a booth; a term for one's own house; to lodge, to pass the night.

敝丨my house.

丨舍 a cot; my lodgings.

茅丨an attap hut; a thatched mud hut.

淸丨a pure cottage; — a Budhist term for a monastery.

于時丨旅 here then booths for people might be built.

田丨a cabin in the fields.

藘 ꜀lü A plant called 茹丨, like madder in that its roots dye a red color; it is a species of *Rubia*, and is now mostly superseded by sapan-wood.

茹丨在阪 the madder grows on the slope.

驢 駈 ꜀lü From 馬 *horse* and 臚 the *belly*, because its strength is thought to be in the belly.

An ass; its skin furnishes a highly prized glue.

丨子 a donkey.

野丨a wild ass.

叫丨a jack, from his braying.

蹇丨a slow or limping ass.

丨駒子 an ass's foal.

騸丨a castrated ass.

騲丨a jenny, a she-ass.

小丨a species of squirrel.

丨唇不對馬嘴 the donkey's lips don't match the horse's mouth; — the two statements do not at all agree.

丨皮 obstinate, mulish, said of children.

閭 ꜀lü From *gate* and the *spine*.

The gate of a village; a hamlet of twenty-five houses; a habitation.

門丨a dwelling.

依丨leaning against the gate, — as a mother who longs to see the loved child return.

仙丨fairy land.

丨巷 a side lane or alley containing a few houses.

藺 ꜀lü From *plant* and *gateway*; it is often written like the last.

A plant whose stalks, when old are used to thatch temples, and called 菴丨 in consequence; the name is applied to the *Siphonostegia chinensis*, but must also denote another plant.

丨茹 a species of euphorbia (*Esula latifolia?*); the milk thistle.

櫚 ꜀lü A palm (the *tree* of the *village-gate*, as its composition denotes,) common in the central provinces; the round leaves are fringed with deep fissured points.

椶丨the coir-palm. (*Chamærops*), from whose fibers ropes, mats, and trunks are made.

花丨木 or 花棃木 a fine-grained, reddish cabinet wood brought to Canton from Annam; rose-wood?

駼 ꜀lü From 馬 *horse* and 旅 to *travel* contracted.

A post-house keeper.

丨站 post-house.

使丨the courier who carries letters for government.

由丨寄函 the letter was sent on by the post-house.

蔞 蒟 ꜀lü Also read ꜀*leu*; from *plant* and *lasso*; the two are not exactly identical.

A plant used to flavor cooked fish; it resembles parsley.

丨蒿 a kind of celery.

女丨菜 bachelor's button.

丨室 the room where pregnant women awaited parturition after the seventh moon.

丨葉 betel leaf, for which the second and aberrant form is now used with 荖 at the South.

青丨fresh betel leaf; the best comes from Hai-fung hien 海豐縣 near Swatow.

丨皮 the skin of a species of bryony, used as a purgative.

栝〡仁 seeds from the *Tricosanthes* 瓜〡 used as an expectorant.

ʿ侶 ʿlü A companion, a mate, a fellow-traveler; to associate with, to keep one company; to mate together.

行〡 a traveling comrade.

結〡 to agree to travel together.

伴〡 a comrade, a chum.

麟不〡行 the unicorn never herds with other animals.

儕〡 our whole company.

燕〡 one who lives among his own people.

其如知音之寡〡何 what shall I do? I want a companion who understands music.

ʿ梠 ʿlü A supporting beam, called 連簷 in Peking, running under the short rafters at the eaves, outside of the plate.

桊〡 the turned-up corners of a Chinese roof.

ʿ儢 ʿlü From *man* and *anxious*.

Indisposed to act; no energy; heedless, indifferent.

〡〡然 careless about, easy-going.

〡〡其事 he cares nothing for this affair.

ʿ呂 ʿlü From two *mouths* joined to represent the spinal vertebræ, for which the next is now also used.

The back-bone; tones in music; a kind of sword.

六〡 six flat or 陰 notes.

忠〡之臣 a loyal, devoted minister.

律〡 keyed tones, not a natural note.

〡宋國 Spain; so called from 小〡宋 Luzon, or the island of Luçonia.

〡宋菓 St. Ignatius bean; the *Strychnos ignatia*.

〡后 the empress Wu Tseh-tʻien of the Tʻang dynasty.

擊之以輕〡 struck him with his dirk.

ʿ膂 ʿlü From *fleet* and *guest*; occurs interchanged with the next.

The backbone, the basis of one's strength.

〡力過人 he excels others in strength.

作股肱心〡 he exerts all the energies of body and mind.

ʿ旅 ʿlü From 㫃 a *banner* and 从 *men* who belong to it; occurs used for the last.

A regiment of 500 men; forces, troops; a visitor, a guest, a sojourner; immigrants; many, a company; the multitudes; brothers; to travel, as to other provinces; to sojourn at; to be arranged; the imperial sacrifice 大〡, offered to Shangti on the round hillock in time of calamity; a path; to arrange in order; to display; self-sown grain; the 56th diagram relating to trade.

行〡 a traveler.

〡客 or 商〡 traveling merchants.

勁〡 victorious soldiers.

〡次 set in order; by ranks.

〡店 a lodging-house.

〡夜書懷 while in the inn I indite my sorrows.

軍〡之事 military affairs.

羈〡臣 officers sent to the provinces.

侯亞侯〡 the younger sons of princes and their children.

羞與〡等伍 I am ashamed of my comrades.

〡力方剛 while my backbone is still strong.

ʿ祣 ʿlü Used with the preceding.

The emperor's sacrifice to Heaven and the hills.

〡上帝 he worshiped Shangti.

ʿ梠 ʿlü A tough kind of wood suitable for arrows.

〡松 a name for the *Abies firma*, or Japan larch, which probably furnishes this wood.

ʿ僂 ʿlü Also read ˏleu.

Hunchback; stooping; curved, distorted in the limbs; *met.* crouching to, humbled before one.

背〡 a crooked back.

〡指而算 to bend the fingers and reckon up.

〡佝 or 〡傴 an ill-made, distorted person; ill-fitting clothes.

ʿ漊 ʿlü A drizzling, incessant rain; in Honan, ability to drink much without becoming intoxicated.

雨〡〡也 the rain continues incessantly.

Read ʿleu. A sewer or conduit.

〡河 a branch of the River Li on the northwest of Tungting Lake.

ʿ縷 ʿlü Hempen or silken threads not yet spun; a hank or knot; a forfeit of cloth; to arrange facts in a statement.

布〡 coarse cotton; but 〡布 is to state in detail.

一〡絲 one knot of floss.

不能〡述 unable to tell the whole, too many to detail.

〡伸妥了 the threads are all straightened out.

不敢〡褻 I do not venture to annoy you with unnecessary details.

條分〡晰 to bring up each point in order.

〡肉 the tender-loin. (*Cantonese*.)

ʿ褸 ʿlü Used with the last.

The lapel of a coat; spoiled, sordid clothes.

衣衫襤〡 dirty and torn garments; ragged in dress.

屢 lüʾ From 尸 *body* and 數 a *number* contracted; the radical was added to distinguish it.

A number; frequent, often' reiterated; successively, constantly, continually; prompt; to do over and over, to keep up.

丨次 many times.

丨年 for a series of years.

丨番 very many times.

丨經 he has often experienced it.

丨蒙過愛 I have repeatedly enjoyed your great kindness.

丨顧爾僕 if you constantly look after your driver, — you will not upset.

丨丨 again and again.

丨豐年 successive good harvests.

丨試丨效 as often as you try it, you will find it serviceable.

慮 *lü'* From 思 to *think* and 虍 *tiger* which gives sound.

To care for, to feel sad, to think upon anxiously; to devise, to cogitate, to turn over in one's mind; to plan; concerned for, suspicious, doubtful about, anxious; thoughtful for.

思丨 serious thoughts of.

丨後 to take thought for the morrow.

丨到 forecasting, precautionary plans.

念丨 anxiously thinking on.

亡丨 a general plan; without particularizing.

一致而百丨 to plan the whole in detail.

旻天疾威弗丨弗圖 merciful Heaven, quick with terrors, how can you have no forethought, no plan?

勴 *lü'* From *strength* and *sad*.

To give one good advice; to help.

丨助 to aid heartily.

相丨辦公 to attend to the affairs of state with united energy.

濾 *lü'* To filter; to strain liquids through a cloth; to wash, to purify.

丨水羅 or 丨布 a straining cloth.

丨去渣 strain off the sediment.

鑢 鐧 *lü'* The second is an unusual form.

A file, a rasp; a polishing tool; to burnish, to give luster to; to refrain, to restrain one's self.

磨丨 to polish.

躬自丨 to keep one's body under.

丨成槽 it has worn a groove.

讗 *lü'* Deceitful; to deceive.

不丨 a man in the Sung dynasty, who is perhaps the origin of the god Wu-hien 武顯 who is worshiped at Nanking to heal children.

LÜEH.

Many persons pronounce these characters LIÜEH. *Old sound*, liet. *In Canton*, lüt; — in *Swatow*, liat; — *in Amoy*, loat; — *in Fuhchau*, liök *and* lwök; — *in Shanghai*, lih *and* löh; — *in Chifu*, lüeh.

劣 *lieh'* From *strength* and *few*.

Infirm, feeble, inadequate; humble, poor, insignificant, used in speaking of one's self; barely, scarcely; unpolished, rustic; vile, degraded.

丨才 my inferior abilities.

丨衿 the oppressive gentry, who tyrannize over the villagers.

惡丨 exceedingly bad.

丨等 those poor fellows, as *siuts'ai* who cannot pass examination.

丨馬 a vicious horse.

丨德 little ability; perverse.

丨腹無文 empty-headed, very ignorant.

優丨 best and worst, talented and stupid; — terms of comparison.

丨跡 a bad reputation, as from former crimes; old follies.

鄙丨 truculent, unreasonable

埒 *lieh'* From *earth* and a *pinch*.

A low dike dividing fields; to mark the limits of fields; banks of a pool or lakelet; a sort; alike.

才相等丨 their talents are much alike.

馬丨 a corral for horses.

寽 *lieh'* From 又 a *hand* altered and 爪 *claws*.

As much as can be grasped with the five fingers, especially of ears of grain.

捋 *lieh'* *lö'* From *hand* and a *pinch*.

To clutch in the fingers; to rub or draw through the hand; to stroke; to brighten; to scrape off or thin; to bare; to pull off.

丨鬚 to stroke the beard.

手丨 to peel off, as leaves from a twig.

磨拳丨掌 to rub the fists, as if eager for a scrimmage.

丨鑊 to scrape the crust from a boiler or pan.

丨奶 to milk, as a cow.

丨乾淸 to clean up, as rubbish with a shovel.

丨取 to take by force or fraud; petty extortions.

予所丨荼 the rushes which I got in my claws.

丨一堆 to pile together, to amass.

丨膏 to scrape or pick off the fat.

厚者丨薄 peel the fat till it is lean; — *met.* fleece the rich fellow till he is poor.

薄言丨之 now we rub out its seeds

嘞 *leh'* A sound; a note on a musical instrument.

In *Cantonese.* Morose, cross; disposed to annoy, troublesome; to talk; out of proper order.

啉 丨 sullen; hard to suit.

丨 黜 disarranged; confused, involved, as a style.

丨 起官話 to talk the court dialect.

鋝 *leh'* An ancient weight, now differently estimated; some say it was 20 taels, and that a spear's head should balance three of them, and a heavy sword six; many authors assert that it was 6⅔ taels, or 48,000 grains of millet; but a few maintain that it was six taels, though the same as the 鍰 a ring weight.

LÜEN.

Many persons pronounce these characters LIÜEN *or* LWAN. *Old sound,* lon. *In Canton,* lün, — *in Swatow,* lúan; — *in Amoy,* lwan; — *in Fuhchau,* lwang *and* liòng; — *in Shanghai,* lö^{n} *and* li^{n}; — *in Chifu,* lan.

䜌 *ˏlwan* From *words* and *silk,* some regard it as another form of 鑾 a tinkling bell.

To tie or bind together; to rule, to manage; confused; to put in disorder; interminable, as talk.

南 丨 former name of a district now Kü-luh hien in the southwest of Chihli.

丨 祕 the chief ruler of one of the principalities in the time of Han.

攣 *ˏlwan* From *hand* and *to connect* properly; occurs used for 㦣 and the next.

To bind or tie in any way; bent or contracted, as the fingers by palsy; crooked, winding; to crook; to drag along, to take hold of; to dote on, to think of lovingly.

丨 曲 crooked, curved; winding, devious.

丨 腰 or 丨 躬 bent over, as a hunchback; a curved spine.

丨 毛 curly hair.

屈 丨 to bend; warped.

膝 丨 bandy-legged.

丨 拘 cramped, as a burnt tendon.

丨 其手足 forced his limbs into distorted positions.

指頭拘 丨 了 fingers stiffened, as with cold.

癵 *ˏlwan* A contraction of the hands and feet, as when palsied; thin, emaciated.

拘 丨 bent, doubled, as the fingers when paralized.

臠 *ˏlwan* Flesh cut into slices or minced; to jerk meat.

一 丨 肉 a slice of meat.

丨 魚 a piece of fish; a fish's stomach cut into strips.

視爲鱗 丨 [the chief] looked upon us as merely fish and flesh, — only to be eaten.

孌 *ˏlwan* Handsome, beautiful, as a woman; to follow, to obey; to long after, to love.

婉兮 丨 兮 how bewitching, how charming.

思 丨 季女逝兮 I thought of the young beauty far away.

丨 童 unmanly, effeminate, aping women.

戀 恋 *lien'* *lwan'* From *heart* and *to connect;* the second form is a common contraction.

Ardently loving; to long after; to dote on, to lust after; to hanker for.

丨 色 lecherous; a lecher.

眷 丨 affectionate.

丨 慕 strongly attached to.

丨 酒 hankering after drink.

丨 丨 不忘 in constant tender recollection.

丨 職 ambitious for office.

蝶 丨 花 name of a popular tune.

相 丨 mutual love, as brothers.

丨 土難移 I do not want to leave my native soil.

䊵 *lien'* To cook congee very thick into a kind of porridge.

粥 丨 湯 thick congee or rice soup.

LUH.

Old sound, lok. *In Canton*, lòk, lut, *and* lăt; —*in Swatow*, lek, lòk, lak, *and* tek; —*in Amoy*, liok *and* lok; —*in Fuhchau*, lük, lok, lăk, liòh, *and* lúk; —*in Shanghai*, lòk *and* lih; —*in Chifu*, liu *and* lu.

六, 陸, liu^5 Composed of 八 *eight* and 入 to *enter* over it; the second is the complex form used on bills.

Six; it belongs to the eighth diagram of earth.

丨丨 thirty-six.

第丨 the sixth, number six.

丨合 the four points, zenith and nadir; all over, everywhere; also the 十二支 when paired off.

丨師乃之 the six divisions (the whole army) followed on.

丨處 the six places or abodes of sensation (*bahya ayatana*);—*i.e.* the organs of sense.

雙丨 double-sixes — on the dice.

丨國 the six states which combined to resist Tsin, B.C. 240, were Sung, Tsi, Liang, Chăn, Wei, and Tsin.

擲丨紅 to throw the six reds.

丨安州 in the west of Nganhwui, noted for its good tea.

丨丁丨甲可以搬山倒海 the gods Luhting and Luhkiah can move mountains and empty the sea.

陸, luh' From *place* and a *clod*.

High dry land, terra firma; land, in distinction from water.

行丨 to go by land.

丨路兵 land troops.

考槃在丨 he rears his hut on the high plat.

丨地行舟 [he is strong enough] to sail a boat overland.

丨離 rugged, mixed, uneven.

丨續來 they arrived successively.

北丨 and 西丨 the stars β Aquarius and Pleiades, because they are central stars in the northern and western regions of the sky.

水丨並進 the land and sea forces pressed on — to the fight.

丨月丨看穀秀 on the sixth of the sixth moon see if the rice or millet are in flower.

坴, luh' From 土 *earth* repeated; it is the original form of the preceding, and only used in combination.

A clod of earth; dry land.

蛙, luh' A small marine bivalve, called 魁丨 with smooth shells, marked with reddish lines; it may be a species of *Tellina* or *Mactra*.

漋, luh' Frozen rain, sleet; cold.

稑, luh' Grain sown late, which yet ripens early in the season.

黍稷重丨 the panicled millet ripened early, and the sorghum late.

鹿, lu' The original form bears a rude resemblance to the horns and legs of a stag; it forms the 198th radical of a few characters relating to cervine animals; in pictures used as a symbol for 祿 *emolument*, by a pun upon the sound of the latter.

A deer, especially the males; stags which have horns, and yet are timorous.

丨茸 and 丨筋, deer's antlers and tendons, two aphrodisiacs.

金錢丨 or 梅花丨 the spotted deer or axis.

丨鳥 the cassowary, so called in the Archipelago.

家丨 the house deer; — a poetical name for the rat.

指丨爲馬 to call a deer a horse, — impudent; this phrase refers to an anecdote of Tsʻao Tsʻao, who asked his attendants whether the stag was a horse or not, in order to ascertain who of them would be subservient to him.

丨王 the deer-king, a title of Shakyamuni (*mrigala*), because he had been a deer in a former life.

摝, lu' To move; to roll as a ball, to rock; to rattle, to shake.

丨球 to roll a ball.

丨落地 rolled over and fell down.

丨坭 to roll the ground smooth.

丨一世丨到滑 he has been well polished for a long time;—you'll not deceive him.

丨來丨去 rocking (or rolling) to and fro.

丨墨 to roll ink, as in printing.

丨鼓 a rattle drum, used by peddlers.

轆, 槺, lu' The rut of a wheel; a roller, a pulley, a wheel; the second character is also the name of a nut-bearing tree.

線丨 a spinning-wheel.

丨轤 a windlass; a caster.

車丨 a wheel, and 丨車 a wagon or hand-cart. (*Cantonese.*)

罭, lu' A small lifting net made fine to inclose minnows and young fish.

簏, lu' A box for cosmetics, a dressing-box.

筐丨 a high pannier hamper for carrying fowls.

書丨 a book-basket; — a term for a pedant.

漉, 淥, lu' Name of an affluent of the River Siang in the northeast of Hunan; to ooze out, to leak; water drained off; dregs; to cleanse water.

丨汁灑地 the drippings sprinkled the ground.

丨浚 deep, pellucid, as a pool.

盝 *lu'* From *dish* and *carving*; occurs used for the last.

To let a thing drip; to exhaust, to empty; to strain-off; a casket for holding a seal.

帽 丨 a hat-case.

納寶小 丨 put the seal in the small box.

麓 *lu'* From *deer* and *forest*; it somewhat resembles *li'* 麗 beautiful.

The declivity or base of a hill; a copse at the bottom of a hill; places from which the water soon runs off.

丨 守 the royal forester or overseer of the woods.

納于大丨烈風雷雨弗迷 when sent to the great slopes, he (Shun) never went wrong amid violent wind, thunder and rain.

螰 *lu'* A species of cicada that has many appellations, of which 蟟 丨 is one.

甪 *lu'* Contracted from 角 a *horn*, as if an antler had fallen.

Some define it, a wild animal; others, a surname.

In *Cantonese*. To let go, to loosen, to take off the grasp; to sneak off; come off, parted, slipped, severed, fell apart.

丨 手 let go your hand; to separate, as friends.

丨 底 the bottom fell out; ruined.

除 丨 去 take it down.

精 丨 辮 he is smart enough to take off your cue.

打 丨 broken off.

丨 臼 slipped from the mortar; *i. e.* divulged, come out.

娽 *lu'* To follow, as in a train.

丨 妃 a concubine of the monarch Chwen-hüh 顓頊, B. C. 2500; one defines it, "that which cannot be clearly established."

祿 *lu'* From a *sacrifice* and *carving*; it is often symbolized by 鹿 a *deer*, from the identity of their sounds.

The happiness conferred by the emperor; official emoluments, salary, rations, pay; prosperity, enjoyment of a thing or income; dignity; to salary; a sacrificial feast.

長生丨位 the imperial tablet set up in temples.

俸 丨 salary from government.

受天百 丨 you receive every heavenly favor.

念我無 丨 I think of my unprovided condition.

食 丨 to live on a salary.

無 丨 食 I have no salary.

不 丨 one who died before entering office.

光 丨 寺 the Banqueting Office.

衣 丨 不足 food and raiment are insufficient.

丨享千金 he enjoyed an income of a thousand ingots.

慘遭回 丨 he unluckily was burnt out.

後 丨 the second or after feast at an ancient worship.

干丨豈弟 how self-possessed was he in seeking dignity!

丨 位 salary and dignity.

綠 *lu'* *lu'* From *silk* and *carving*, and not to be confounded with ꜀*yuen* 緣 a reason.

A green color, the hue of leaves; things which produce green; a kind of pretty grass.

青 丨 color of fresh grass.

蠓 丨 dark green.

石 丨 or 丨 青 malachite.

丨 礬 green vitriol.

呂宋 丨 a turquoise color; a kind of green dye.

丨 衣郎 a promising student.

丨 轎 green covered sedans, in which statesmen ride.

丨 野 a prairie, a steppe.

碧丨的 very green, bright green.

丨 膏 the dye-stuff called sap-green, made chiefly from the bark of the *Rhamnus infectorius*.

墨 丨 invisible green.

碌 *lu'* A green colored stone, green jasper; rough, stony ground; toilsome, laborious; small; a chunk of wood.

丨 丨 rough; unimportant.

丨 丨 風塵 trudging after through wind and dust; wearying effort abroad to get a living.

勞 丨 unwearying, painstaking; *met.* the result of toil, tired, wearied.

一 丨 樹 a log of a tree.

庸 丨 or 丨 丨 庸人 an inefficient drudge, a useless fellow.

皴 *lu'* The skin shriveled.

丨 瘯 the skin and flesh dried and looking badly, as in leprosy.

菉 *lü'* *lu'* A kind of lentiles or pottage.

丨 荳芽 bean sprouts.

丨 蓐 an herb of which cloth can be made.

丨 穀 maize; so called in Ningpo.

醁 *lu'* A pleasant kind of spirit, known as 醽 丨 made with water from Lake Ling in Hăng-cheu fu in the south-east of Hunan.

踛 *lu'* To move, walking about; to go up or down, as stairs; respectful.

丨 起來 get up.

丨 下去 go down.

丨 到塔頂 go up to the top of the pagoda.

打一個谷 丨 to turn a somersault. (*Shanghai.*)

逯 *lu'* To go carefully.

行則丨丨 to go with a crowd.

丨 然而往 to go off without a definite aim.

彔 *lu'* The original form is supposed to resemble an engraver's stippling on wood; it is now written like the next.

To cut on wood, to carve.

錄 lu' From *metal* and to *carve*.

A metallic luster or color; striæ on shells, veins in stone; to copy, to transcribe; to record, to make a note of; records, annals; lectures, summary of doctrine; an index, a series, an order.

抄丨 to copy off.

丨供 to take down evidence.

丨出來 to jot down, to write out.

目丨 an index; table of contents.

言行丨 record of one's acts, a biography.

實丨 the authentic records of an Emperor's reign.

取丨 to be selected as worthy of a degree.

丨事 to detail an affair, a narrator.

一長足丨 something worth recording.

記丨十次 recorded ten times, as worthy officers are in the books of the Board of Civil Office at Peking.

試丨 the list of successful *küjin*.

丨籍 a family register, one's lineage.

大計丨 the triennial report on officers.

總丨 a resumé; a summary.

丨丨 ordinary, like the generality.

揀選丨用 to select and record men for employment.

丨囚徒 to release prisoners.

語丨 and 別丨 are classes of Budhist books, like lectures or synopses of doctrines, and treatises on particular subjects.

騄 lu' A famous steed named 丨耳 one of eight belonging to the emperor Muh-wang about B.C. 1000.

籙 lu' From *bamboo* and a *record;* occurs used for 簏, a pannier.

A map, a chart; a nota-bene, as of events, recipes, &c.

丨璽 a signet, a seal.

圖丨 a chart of a country.

符丨 a talisman on wood, a magic writing.

題名丨 list of successful *küjin*.

戮 lu' From a *spear* and to *fly high;* occurs used for the next.

To kill in war, to massacre; to slaughter; to be put to death; in danger of death; to mangle and insult; to act foolishly; to ruin; to exert.

殺丨 to put many to the sword.

丨囚 to kill prisoners.

丨尸梟示 to mangle a corpse and expose the head.

引頸就丨 he bared his neck to the sword; — he met his death bravely.

刑丨 to execute capitally.

伐丨敵兵 utterly destroy the rebel soldiers.

屠丨 ruthless slaughter.

In *Cantonese.* To scald, as a fowl for plucking; to steep in boiling water.

丨魚粥 a fish soup or chowder.

丨酸手 scalded his hand badly.

勠 lu' Used with the preceding.

United strength.

丨力相攻 joined our forces and made a combined attack.

僇 lu' To disgrace, to bring contempt on; to act foolishly.

為天下笑丨 to get the derision of everybody.

羞丨 feeling ashamed and foolish.

碌 lu' A stone roller, 丨碡 used for smoothing gravel walks and paths.

硉 lu' Gravel.

丨矹 sand and rubble washed down by floods in a dangerous way.

踛 lu' Impeded, as when carrying a burden.

丨踈 making little progress; embarrassed, as when leading a child in a crowd, or when in a hurry.

LÜH.

Old sound, lot. *In Canton,* lut; — *in Swatow,* lút; — *in Amoy,* lút *and* tsút; — *in Fuhchau,* lúk; — *in Shanghai,* lih; — *in Chifu,* lü.

律 lüh' From a *step* and *pencil;* occurs used with the next.

To divide, to distinguish between, to govern, to regulate by law; a statute, a fixed law, an ordinance; to be a law to; a military regulation; used by the Budhists for discipline, ascetic rules; and for the *vinaya* or works relating to them; a stanza or distich; the rules of versification; to state or put on record; to adjust, to weigh the merits of; to trim the hair; standard tubes used as pitch pipes in ancient music; steep, as a peak.

法丨 a code.

丨誡 commandments, prohibitions.

丨例 the statutes and rescripts; the former are regarded more fundamental than the latter.

丨書 or 丨條 law books; the laws.

以丨己者丨人 he applied the same rules to himself that he did to others.

一丨 a uniform mode, entirely.

好音｜ in good tune, a good rhyme.

一首七｜詩 a heptameter verse of four couplets.

六｜ are the sharped 陽 musical notes.

不｜ an old term for a pencil.

依｜ according to law.

上｜天時 to determine the seasons or times.

｜師 ascetic Budhists, those who follow the strict rules of Budha.

嵂, *lüh'* A sharp, high peak.

南山｜｜ the steep cliffs of the southern hills.

隆崇｜崒 magnificent and lofty summits.

⿰扌律, *lüh'* From *hand* and to *distinguish*.

To separate the dregs of a liquid.

繂, *lüh'* From *silk* and *cord;* occurs wrongly used for *luh*, 轆 a roller.

A bamboo rope or hawser for tracking boats; lines for pulling up ores from a mine.

｜繞 to lower a coffin into its grave.

｜轤 a pulley or windlass.

｜｜不墜 let it down without upsetting.

⿱艹率, *lüh'* Seeds beginning to germinate, the plumule showing above ground.

膟, *lüh'* Bloody flesh offered to the gods.

｜膋 the fat on the inwards of a sacrifice, anciently burned or roasted in worship.

驈, *lüh'* A black horse with white hind quarters.

有｜有皇 there were black horses and cream-colored.

葎, *lüh'* From *plant* and *rule*, because the hispid stem restrains trespassers.

The wild hop, ｜草 of which the *Humulus japonicus* is the most common, and found over the northern provinces; one common name is 拉拉藤 the pulling vine.

LUN.

Old sound, lon. *In Canton*, lun ; — *in Swatow*, lun ; — *in Amoy*, lun ; — *in Fuhchau*, lung ; — *in Shanghai*, lăng ; — *in Chifu*, lăn.

侖, *lun* Composed of 亼 or 會 to *collect* and 冊 *archives;* it is chiefly used in combination as a phonetic.

To think, to arrange; to unify.

昆｜ the canopy of the sky, spherical and concave.

倫, *lun* From *man* and to *think*.

Constant, regular, that which is acknowledged by men as proper; natural relationships, affinity of things by classes and orders; a species, class, sex; to choose.

五｜ or 人｜ the five human relationships, — of husband and wife, father and son, brothers, prince and officer, and friends.

｜次 a series.

天｜之樂 the happiness of a family gathering.

逆｜ it violates human obligations, atrocious, unnatural.

絕｜ surpassing others; unsurpassed.

莫比其｜ no one who can compare with him.

圇, *lun* Finished; 囫｜ complete; entire in all its parts, as a dress.

不可囫｜讀過 do not study without carefully understanding it; — *i. e.* do not slight your studies, as one bolts his food.

崙, *lun* The long range of the Koulkoun Mountains, lying on the north of Tibet; also called the Ancuta Mts.

｜崓巍峨 peaks of different heights; Alps o'er Alps.

掄, **⿺辶侖**, *lun* From *hand* and *thinking* as the phonetic; the second form is common but unauthorized; occurs used for 輪 to wheel.

To choose fit persons, as for office; to select, to pick out; to come in turn, to take by turns; the second form also means parsimonious; to walk with difficulty.

｜選 to select fit persons.

｜才 to select talented men.

｜材 to pick out timber.

｜元手段 choose this as the very best.

｜拳就打 he lifted his fist and gave him a blow.

淪, *lun* A ripple, or "white caps," which the Chinese liken to wheels or circles; an eddy, a whirl in the water; turbulent, chaotic, as waters; engulphed, submerged; lost in perdition, ruined, damned.

沉｜ lost for ever.

｜沒｜喪 ruined; lost, as a dynasty; extinct.

｜｜ curling ripples following each other.

｜落 sinking down, as in vicious courses.

｜迴 an eddy, undertow, chow-chow water.

混｜ turbid, roiled up; chaos.

In *Pekingese*. To dash on, as the rain driving against a window; to wet and spatter.

綸 ˏlun Silken threads; to twist silk fit for weaving; to wind silk; to compare, to distinguish, to classify; to adjust; to know; to bind or cord.

經丨天下 to oversee the affairs of the country.

絲丨 sorted silk; *met.* fine or royal plans.

收拾絲丨 to leave literary pursuits.

其出如丨 his words are [smooth] as silk; — said of the sovereign.

丨音 silken sounds; *i. e.* his Majesty's words.

丨扉 the palace or court.

滿腹經丨 full of just thoughts, eloquent.

丨之繩 I adjusted his fishing-line.

彌丨 a pervading doctrine or principle; natural principles.

釣丨 a fish-line.

Read ˏ*kwan* A cap called 丨巾, worn by K'ung Ming 孔明 a hero of the San Kwoh Chi.

蜦 ˏlun To squirm; a large snake like the 蜧, that can bring rain and clouds, is called 蝹丨; applied to the crawling of worms or snakes; a frog big as a shoe, otherwise called 田父 or field father, which eats snakes, because they devour the small frogs.

艙 ˏlun The bow of a vessel, or the timbers forming the bow.

丨艅 a kind of boat.

輪 ˏlun From *cart* and to *think* as the phonetic.

A wheel with spokes; a wheel, a disk; a round face; a revolution, a circuit, a turn; to rotate, to take in turn; to roll around; a symbol of Budhist doctrine; great.

丨轉 to revolve, to turn round and round; the revolutions and changes of the ages.

丨門 to go from door to door.

放一丨砲 to fire a salvo of artillery.

耳丨 the rim of the ear.

丨流看守 to stand watch in rotation.

今天丨到他 it is his turn to-day.

舉車丨 to lift the [stone] wheel; — a trial of strength.

丨廻 the return of the wheel, *i. e.* transmigration; this Budhist term answers to the Sanscrit *sansara*, the 生死大海 or great sea of life and death, human existence which must be crossed to reach *nirvana*.

廣丨 the breadth and circuit, — *i. e.* the area of a country; the latitude and longitude.

丨軸 wheel and axle.

月丨 the moon's disk.

丨囷 to curl around and up.

貨如丨轉 may our goods circulate like a wheel; — a shop inscription.

丨班 the reliefs appointed to act in rotation.

丨王 the king of the wheel, or 轉丨聖王 the holy king with the revolving wheel, a Budha who hurls the *chakra* or spike wheel against his enemies, and becomes a great conqueror (*chakravartti raja*.)

轉法丨 to turn the wheel of the law (*darma chakra*), to preach Budhism.

碖 ˏlun Rocks standing in a dangerous position.

稐 ˏlun To bind grain in sheaves; a sheaf; to plough.

惀 ˊlun From *heart* and an *egg* as the phonetic.

To act heedlessly.

暶丨 to act regardless of strict rules, to be grossly negligent; one says, to compare and rate goods.

論 lun' From *words* and to *think* as the phonetic; also read ˏ*lun*.

To discourse upon, to consider, to discuss; to criticize, to find fault with; to reason, to think over; discourse, counsel; a train of reasoning upon a subject, a full account of a matter; a *preposition*, by, according to, speaking of; used by the Budhists for a *shastra* or theological treatise, and for works on metaphysics, called *abidharma* in Sanscrit; unison, as of instruments.

丨斤賣 sold by the catty.

談丨 to converse.

丨來丨去 to talk on, prolonged discussion.

丨人 to talk about people.

於丨鼓鐘 how accordant were the drums and bells!

議丨生風 he talks upon a matter intelligently.

丨語 discourses and dialogues; table-talk; name of the Confucian Analects.

不丨多少 no matter how many.

各有對丨 each one maintains his own view.

作脉丨 to write a treatise on diseases.

若丨 supposing, if we admit.

無丨 it is immaterial; no matter.

辯丨 to argue, to contradict.

無用追丨 it is needless to bring that affair up again.

丨起 to talk about.

丨及 to speak on a matter.

詳丨 to speak upon critically.

語丨無次 to discourse without method.

丨功丨過 to estimate the merits and demerits of officials.

丨千者來 thousands have come.

丨換一雙鞋子 you must certainly change this pair of shoes.

作罷丨 to fail in convincing a man.

推丨 to infer, to deduce from.

LUNG.

Old sounds, long *and* liong. *In Canton*, lung; — *in Swatow*, lòng, leng, *and* lang; — *in Amoy*, liong, long, *and* kong; — *in Fuhchau*, lung, léng, lăng, léung, liòng, *and* lwòng; — *in Shanghai*, lung; — *in Chifu*, lung.

龍 ˓lung — Composed of 童 a *lad* contracted for the phonetic, 肉 *flesh*, and 飛 to *fly* altered to represent flying in a gyratory motion; it forms the 212th radical of a few unused characters referring to dragons; occurs used for ˊch'ung 寵 favor, and the next.

A dragon, the chief of scaly beings, and invested with supernatural power to change its shape; used as an emblem of imperial power and awe; the emperor's person; imperial, dragon-like; by Budhists, used for *nagas* or snake gods; to pervade; to bud; in matters relating to betrothals, it is often used for a man; gracious, kind; much used by geomancers to embody those terrestrial and occult influences and positions which act on and determine human prosperity; figured with dragons.

丨類 the class of lizards, dragons, serpents, &c.

斑丨 a poetical name for a deer, the axis, because it plays with dragons.

丨船 a dragon boat, so named from the carved figure-head.

丨香 the ancestral effigy at weddings. (*Cantonese.*)

丨位 the throne.

丨飛 the reigning emperor.

丨體 the emperor's person.

旣見君子爲丨爲光 now that I see these noblemen, I understand their favor and brightness.

白丨 or 烏丨 poetical names for the dog.

丨眼菓 the longan fruit. (*Nephelium longan.*)

丨顏大悅 his majesty was greatly pleased.

丨牌 the imperial tablet, reverenced by officers.

丨殿 the ornamented shed for the 打醮 at Canton.

丨馬精神 he has the vigor of a dragon or a horse.

海丨王 Sea-dragon king or the Neptune of the Chinese; he is *Sagara*, a *naga* or dragon-king, whose glorious palace is at the bottom of the ocean, north of Mount Meru.

丨脈 the dragon's pulse, the subtle geomantic tokens and influence of a locality.

尋丨點穴 to seek the dragon and point out his den; — *i.e.* to fix on a lucky spot.

乘丨 to get married.

丨鳳帖 betrothal cards.

丨鍾之年 decrepid, old.

地丨 an earthworm.

扒丨 scrambling dragons, *i.e.* boats. at Canton that paddle very fast.

擒丨捉虎 to sieze a dragon and hold a tiger; — *met.* very clever and brave.

鯉跳丨門 the carp has leaped over the dragon's gate; — *met.* rapid promotion.

丨神 the gods of waters and springs; a general term for the ruling powers of nature, and their worship.

丨涎香 ambergris; though it seems to be also applied to the paint called dragon's blood.

丨鬚菜 asparagus.

大丨風 a typhoon, a cyclone.

丨腦香 Baroos camphor.

合丨 the dragon is pleased; *i. e.* the waters are quiet, the stream runs in its bed.

竜 ˓lung — Regarded as an old contracted form of the preceding.

Also to rise, to issue forth.

起丨 in heat, said of dogs; pairing, as birds.

佴革丨 a place in Yunnan where are nine steep mountains.

蘢 ˓lung — A species of water weed (*Polygonum amphibium*), otherwise called 葒草, and often written like the last.

隰有游丨 in the marshes grows the spreading smart-weed.

蒙丨 overgrown with weeds, concealed, obscured by something.

Read ˊlung. To collect.

丨蓯 or 丨茸 brought together, to collect in one.

隆 ˓lung — From 降 to *descend* and 生 to *bear*, denoting that what is born will be high and great.

Grand, eminent, surpassing; high, like a peak; exalted; abundant, fertile, opulent, overfilling; glorious; to glorify, to exalt; to magnify; the irritation of great heat.

興丨 prosperous.

丨薄 generous — mean.

尊丨 highly honored.

丨盛 affluent; wealthy.

深領丨情 to receive many favors.

貌豐丨 fat and hearty looking.

丨冬時候 winter; cold weather.

丨丨 a thundering noise.

丨儀 your valuable present.

父者家之丨 a father is the eminent one of the house.

窿 ˓lung — The vault of heaven is 穹丨 referring to its arched expanse; a cavity, an orifice.

窟丨 a hole.

掘丨而居 to dig out a cave for a dwelling.

癃 ˓lung — Infirm; weak in the back from age.

丨病 old and useless, bent over.

丨閉 costive, torpor of bowels.

瀧 *ˏlung* A stream in Lo-ting cheu 羅定州 in the west of Kwangtung, called 三丨; a river or town in Kansuh.

儱 *ˏlung* Rude and incomplete.
丨侗 unpolished, like a rude rustic; long and straight.

嚨 *ˏlung* The throat, the œsophagus.
喉丨 the gullet.
好喉丨 a very loud voice.

蠪 *ˏlung* An insect found on the olive in Kwangtung, the 丨蜂 probably a species of walking-leaf. (*Mantis.*)
丨蛭 a fabulous monster.
鮭丨 a goblin like a child two feet long found in the sea.
蛈丨 a crab which gets into pearl oysters.

曨 *ˏlung* The rising sun obscured.
曈丨 break of day, the sun not clearly seen.

朧 *ˏlung* The rising moon.
朦丨 dim, obscure, as the beclouded moon or a dirty glass; the mumblings of one half asleep.

櫳 龒 *ˏlung* Often used for the next.
A pen for animals, like a corral or stockade; the bars or slats of a window, a jalousie.
囚丨 a cage for prisoners.
房丨 a blind over a window.
月透疎丨 the moon shines through the open lattice.
門丨子 the bars across a doorway.
簾丨 to screen off by a blind.

籠 *ˏlung* A cage; an open basket for carrying birds or animals; a quiver; used with ʻ壟 to monopolize or engross the market; to cover, to rest on.
打丨 to entrap birds.
焙丨 a frame to hang clothes on to dry over a fire.
雀丨 a bird-cage.
猪丨花 the *Nepenthes* or pitcher plant.
猪丨 a pig-basket.
丨罩 an open basket to cover fish; to include all.
丨括 the key to an essay; its scope given in a sentence.
虛丨全題 to refer to by allusions, to make an indirect appeal.
丨絡 a snare, the noose of a trap; to insnare, to inveigle and control.
丨貨物 to buy up goods.
受人牢丨 taken in by others.
烟丨柳 the smoke rests on the willows.
丨住那馬 catch hold of that horse.
立丨 to stand in the cage; a cruel mode of execution.

瓏 *ˏlung* A gem cut in the form of a dragon, and placed on the altar when praying for rain.
玲丨 tinkling of gems; the sighing of wind; bright.

𤮱 礱 *ˏlung* Earth built up on which to grind grain; a wooden mill; to sharpen; to grind to flour.
丨穀 to hull grain.
磨丨 to grind down; to fag at study.
穀丨 a wooden hand-mortar.
丨利 to sharpen, to rub bright.

穠 *ˏlung* To reap grain and scatter the handfuls to dry; smut in grain.

聾 *ˏlung* Deaf, hard of hearing; unperceived or hidden, like a thing covered up.
亞丨 a deaf person.
粧丨詐啞 to feign to be deaf and dumb.
不癡不丨難作阿家翁 if you are not silly and deaf, 'twill be hard for you to be an old boss.
倒底丨 totally deaf.

襱 *ˏlung* The leggings or overalls worn by the Chinese in winter.

𩏙 龓 *ˏlung* From *leather* and *dragon*, or rather a *cage*, referring to the shape; the second form is unusual, and is also interchanged with the next, to buy up.
A halter.
馬丨頭 a headstall, a halter.

壟 *ʻlung* A barrow, a grave or mound over it; a pile of earth; to monopolize goods.
丘丨 a tumulus over a grave.
丨斷 undulating, as a road or country; to speculate; to buy up goods.
瓦丨子 a scollop; shells like the *Arca* or *Pecten*.

隴 *ʻlung* Used with the last.
A dike to prevent water breaking in; a classifier of rows of tiles and growing grain.
一丨瓦 a row of tiles on a roof; one gutter.
滿丨黃雲 the yellow clouds [of waving grain] fill the fields.
丨畝之間 among dikes and fields; — busy at farming.
丨西 an old name for the west of Shensi, now comprising part of the eastern side of Kansuh; probably derived from the mountain sources of the River Wei.
得丨望蜀 having got Shensi he wanted Sz'ch'uen too; — *met.* unsatisfied ambition.

徿 *ʻlung* To walk awkwardly.
丨侗 to walk straight ahead.

攏 *ʻlung* To grasp, to seize privately; to drag; to attack; to assemble or collect; to exert one's self; to work on, to operate; to act with; to push out or through; to visit, to call at; to bring near, to draw close to.

丨埋手 to put the hands in the sleeves. (*Cantonese.*)

丨在袖裡 to conceal in the sleeve.

聚丨來 gathered together.

做得丨 can you finish this?

丨衙門 to call in at the yamun.

丨總來了 they have all come; everything is here.

丨近 to bring near: to near, as a boat.

丨掠 to plunder, as a highwayman.

把刀丨他 he covertly stabbed him with a knife.

丨敵 to charge at the enemy.

丨岸 to lie along shore.

丨髻 to bind the hair.

拉丨 to drag up to one.

丨前解勸 they all came forward and urged them to cease, — or to part.

窿 ʻ*lung* A hole, an aperture; a wide cleft; a cave; empty, hollow.

開丨 make a hole.

老鼠丨 a rat hole.

入黃泥丨 he has entered the clay hole; — *met.* he is buried.

孔丨 a hole.

穿丨 holes are in it; bored.

空丨 empty, contents all run out.

丨罅 a cleft, a crack or crevice.

棺材丨 an empty grave, an old tomb.

他的窟丨太多 his schemes for taking people in are very many.

你給我窟丨橋走嗎 are you trying to deceive me? — *i. e.* are you trying to get me to fall through the hole in the bridge?

槓 *kang*ʼ An unauthorized character, said to be altered from 籠 a cage.

A trunk, a box; a basket shaped like a jar; a valise; any traveling case to carry clothes.

皮丨 a leathern trunk.

椶丨 a coir trunk or valise.

伙食丨 a case for eatables.

衣服丨 a clothes' trunk.

In *Pekingese* read *kang*ʼ. A Corean ream of 100 quires of 20 sheets each; the frame on which coffins are carried.

抬丨絆嘴 to get into an altercation; to bandy loud words, as coffin bearers are apt to do.

丨房 an undertaker's shop.

In *Fuhchau*, partly used for 杠 a pole. A carrying-beam; thills of a sedan; a classifier of loads borne by two; a set of boxes for presents.

先丨 and 後丨 the fore and rear thills; *met.* the chair-bearers.

弄 *lung*ʼ *nung*ʼ From 廾 *hands* folded and 玉 a *gem*, denoting to play with things.

To trifle and toy with; to use badinage, to treat with undue liberty; to do; to handle, as a tool; to make, to feel, in which senses it sometimes merely indicates the action of the next verb; to plan, to try to get by scheming.

戲丨 to sport with, to dally.

丨璋 and 丨瓦 to bear a son or daughter.

侮丨 treat with indignity.

丨飯 to cook food.

丨假成眞 to fulfill what was promised in joke.

丨壞 to spoil, to put out of order.

賣丨手段 to show off one's expertness.

丨慣了 thoroughly practiced in.

不要丨翻了 don't tip it over, don't spill it out.

丨神丨鬼 to make much ado about the gods.

丨權 to abuse power.

忽倘丨兵 he suddenly moved up his forces.

不懂得丨 I do not know how to do that.

丨巧反拙 the pretended expert turned out to be a fool; he thought he would do a smart thing and got into trouble.

丨出事來 to have a squabble, to get into a dispute.

丨神儂 I have given you a great deal of trouble; I thank you. (*Shanghai.*)

丨成 or 丨神 to deceive another, to cheat.

㛞 **𢙂** *lung*ʼ The first of these is regarded as the correct form.

Stupid, foolish; unable to understand readily; to make a fool of.

蠱丨我上當 he took me in completely.

丨愚人 to impose on a simpleton.

㑝 *lung*ʼ Stupid, foolish; unable to understand readily.

哢 *lung*ʼ The note or song of a bird.

喨丨 to chirp.

鳥丨春光 the birds' music greets the spring.

吟丨 a hum of many voices, as in a school-room.

躘 *lung*ʼ Walking.

丨踵 the imperfect attempts of a child to walk; a child stepping.

扯丨來 to draw another toward one.

LWAN.

Some of these characters are often pronounced LÜEN. *Old sound,* lon. *In Canton,* lün ; — *in Swatow,* lúan ; — *in Amoy,* lwan ; — *in Fuhchau,* lwang ; — *in Shanghai* ; lö^{n} ; — *in Chifu,* lan.

欒 ꜀lwan — A small malvaceous tree, called 丨華, having yellow flowers ; a slender tree with yellow wood and reddish branches which produces the 丨荆 a medicine ; some say the 丨木 is the bladder tree (*Kœlreuteria paniculata*), but this is erroneous according to the Păn Tsʻao ; the two corners of a bell.

丨城縣 in the southwest of Chihli near the Hu-tʻo River.

棘人丨丨兮 the earnest mourner has worn himself thin.

檀丨 well trimmed bamboos.

朱丨 a Japanese name for the shaddock.

巒 ꜀lwan — The peaks of a hill ; a line of pointed summits winding along.

層丨疊翠 the successive peaks and multiplied [fields of] emerald grass.

圝 ꜀lwan — Spherical ; round.

團丨 globular ; round, as the moon or a tambourine.

𢄔 ꜀lwan — A cord of silk.

絲丨 braided cord used for waistbands.

鑾 ꜀lwan — From *metal* and *connected.*

Little bells formerly hung from the phœnix that marked the royal cars ; imperial, royal ; a term of respect.

恭迓丨輿 I shall await your arrival ; — a phrase used on a lady's invitation card.

玉丨 the royal chariot.

金丨殿 the palace, or strictly the hall of audience ; the court.

金丨坡 an old name for the Hanlin college.

啓丨 and 回丨 his Majesty's departure and return ; also applied to the movements of a god.

丨儀衛 the imperial guard ; it is the office at Peking which manages the escort of the Emperor.

丨駕 the emperor's carriage or sedan ; also, his godship.

丨鈴 tinkling bells.

丨座 an idol's shrine to carry in a procession.

鸞 ꜀lwan — A fabulous bird, described as 神靈之精 the essence or seminal power of divine influence, and regarded as the embodiment of every grace and beauty ; the 丨鷄 or argus pheasant seems to have furnished the type ; this is the cock, the hen is 和 ; hence the phrase 丨鳳和鳴 the phœnixes sing harmoniously, to denote a marriage ; small bells hung on bridles.

丨聲將將 the sound of their tinkling bells draws near.

丨箋鳳柬 the marriage papers of a bride and bridegroom.

五彩珠丨 elegantly adorned.

丨刀 [he holds the] knife with the jingling bells.

羉 ꜀lwan — A net for catching pigs and other small ground animals.

丨開而彘突 when the pig sees the net laid he runs away.

灤 ꜀lwan — To flow drop by drop.

丨河 a large river in the northeast of Chihli flowing into the Gulf of Liaotung, near whose mouth is 丨州 a small town.

孿 ꜀lwan, shwan’ — To bear twins ; to suckle two children at once.

丨子 or 丨伴兒 twins.

丨生 to have twins, two at a birth.

卵 ʻlwan — The character is designed to represent two eggs.

An egg ; the roe of fish ; testicles of animals.

鷄丨 hen's eggs.

丨生 oviparous.

壘丨之危 like the danger of a pile of eggs breaking.

丨子 the testes.

丨翼 to brood, to cherish.

勢如覆丨 my power is like a bird setting on her eggs.

亂, **乱** lwan’ — From 乙 *one* and a phonetic meaning to govern ; the second form is in common use.

To bring into good order ; a state of order ; to confuse, to throw into disorder ; to mislay ; discord, confusion ; insurrection, anarchy ; out of place, disarranged ; tumultuous ; raveled ; to ferry over ; the end of a song.

作丨 to rebel.

丨而敬 having tact at ruling and yet reverent.

涉渭爲丨 he crossed the River Wéi by boats.

叛丨 to raise a revolt.

丨臣十人 [Wăn Wang had] ten ruling statesmen.

丨世 seditious officers.

大丨 great commotion in a state.

心丨 disturbed in mind.

丨嚷 great clamor, a hubbub.

丨坐 to sit without respect to rank.

天降喪’丨 Heaven has visited us with death and anarchy.

丨言 to talk wildly or without any order.

丨線 raveled thread.

弄丨 to disarrange, as papers.

丨日甚 anarchy daily increases.

丨跑 to play truant.

澳门基金会
※
北京外国语大学
中国海外汉学研究中心
※
大象出版社

合作项目

卫三畏文集
Selected Works of Samuel Wells Williams

汉英韵府
（卷下）

Syllabic Dictionary of the Chinese Language

［美］
卫三畏　编著
Samuel Wells Williams

中原出版传媒集团
大地传媒
大象出版社
·郑州·

MA.

Old sounds, ma *and* mak. *In Canton*, ma ; — *in Swatow*, ma, mo, múa, *and* bé ; — *in Amoy*, ma, ba, *and* bé ; — *in Fuhchau*, ma *and* mwai ; — *in Shanghai*, mò ; — *in Chifu*, ma.

麻 ˻ma Composed of 林 *flowers* and 广 a *shelter*, referring to the labor bestowed on the fibers; it forms the 200th radical of a small incongruous group.

Hemp, particularly the female (*Cannabis*) plant; a plant furnishing textile fibers, as the *Cannabis*, *Bœhmeria*, *Linum*, *Hibiscus*, and *Sida*, which all bear this name; the linen of the Chinese; hempen; sackcloth or mourning apparel; pock-marked; a kind of drum; in colloquial, used for ˊ馬 sprightly, lively, quick.

野 丨 the *Hibiscus cannabinus* or an allied malvaceous plant that furnishes fibers.

丨 布 hempen fabrics, grasscloth.

丨 栗 樹 板 planks of a heavy wood like teak.

丨 線 linen thread.

丨 布 粗 衣 clad in coarse hempen; — very frugal.

心 亂 如 丨 my mind is troubled like tangled hemp.

丨 俐 or 丨 丨 俐 俐 quick-witted, clever, ready; expert.

丨 籃 a hamper for holding 績 丨 or hatcheled hemp.

黃 丨 the *Sida* or abutilon hemp.

白 丨 and 黃 丨 old terms for imperial rescripts or gazettes.

山 西 胡 丨 flax, grown in Chihli.

胡 丨 油 linseed oil.

王 丨 子 pockmarks, from a man named Wang who first had them.

In *Cantonese*. Occasionally; unimportant.

丨 丨 的 of little moment, let it pass.

丨 嗏 obscure, dim, badly lighted.

In *Fuhchau*. Mean, defrauding; troublesome, indistinct, incomplete; obstinate; lively; scarred, disfigured.

蔴 ˻ma A common but unauthorized form of the last.

Sesamum; the hemp plant.

芝 丨 油 sesamum oil.

丨 醬 ground sesamum seeds used by cooks.

大 丨 油 castor oil.

丨 骨 拐 杖 [like] a staff of hemp; — useless dependance.

漚 丨 to rot hemp.

波 羅 丨 布 coarse gray or unbleached grasscloth.

痲 ˻ma A disease of children, the measles or chicken-pox; numbness; paralysis; the torpor of the tongue after tasting hot things.

丨 子 the pits or scars left after small-pox or chicken-pox.

出 丨 to have the measles.

脚 丨 my foot is asleep.

丨 瘋 leprosy. (*Cantonese.*)

丨 痹 numb, no feeling.

味 道 丨 a hot peppery taste.

發 丨 to feel benumbed; to have no taste of things.

䁶 ˻ma To look at long; eyes weary and blurred with looking.

眼 丨 了 indistinct vision.

𩔗 ˻ma An obstruction in speech.

丨 頣 to speak with hesitation; stammering from malformation of the organs.

蟇 ˻ma A frog.

蝦 丨 a striped frog, used for food.

Read *moh*˼ A species of gnat.

䳈 ˻ma A bird akin to a wild goose.

丨 雀 (oftener written 麻雀) a sparrow.

山 丨 雀 a small species of lark.

犘 ˻ma The yak is called 丨 牛 in the 'Rh Ya, but the name has now become obsolete.

穈 ˻ma From *millet* and *hemp*.

A kind of grain allied to the panicled millet; a spikelet of the head of this millet; a part of a panicle.

馬 ˊma The original form represents the *head*, *mane*, and *legs* of a horse; it forms the 187th radical of characters relating to colors and qualities of equine beasts.

A horse; warlike, spirited; cavalry; the white knight in chess; quick, as a horse; emblem of 午 noon, the seventh of the twelve stems, and of heaven.

頁 丨 a gentle horse.

兒 丨 or 公 丨 a stallion.

丨 上 要 I want it immediately.

千 里 丨 a racer; a swift courier.

野 丨 a wild horse; a column of dust flying over the desert.

聽 不 出 金 丨 騾 駒 子 my golden horse has not brought forth a mule's colt; — I've made nothing on this venture.

丨 頭 or 碼 頭 a landing-place, a ferry, a jetty for boats.

阻 住 丨 頭 to stop a horse's head,—so as to give a petition; to hinder another.

丨 夫 a groom, a syce; it strictly denotes one belonging to an official or grandee; he is also called 丨 王 at the south.

頂 丨 an attendant who rides ahead.

丨 錢 doctor's fees.

丨 撒 歡 兒 the horse is capering and curveting about.

丨 扱 a camp-chair.

背 丨 to saddle a horse.

初 下 丨 I have just arrived.

慣騎丨慣跌跤 the best riders know best what falls are.

下丨酒 a dinner given to a new arrival.

丨桶 a close-chair; it is changed perhaps from 丨通 horse-dung.

快丨來 come very quickly, as a racer.

丨房 or 丨號 a stable.

丨蹄 a horse's hoof; also the water chestnut. (*Eleocharis.*)

海丨 a seal, probably the *Phoca equestris*; the Hippocampus.

司丨 inspector of cavalry.

勉出一丨 I'll serve as a horse and go on foot.

戎丨 a war horse.

一匹丨 one horse.

丨到成功 it will be arranged in a moment; — *i. e.* as if done by a fast horse.

In *Cantonese* used for 榪' To clamp; a stretcher; to plant the right foot firmly forward.

丨住 to clamp, as a broken dish.

好丨步 a firm standing.

丨緊佢鷄頂 seize him by his coiled-up cue.

媽 ʿma ˏma From *woman* and *horse* as the phonetic.

A mare; an old woman, a dame; a mother; a waiting woman, a duenna.

婆丨 a grandma. (*Cantonese.*)

乾丨 a maid-servant, a nurse.

老丨 or 阿丨 a nurse; an old dame; the Manchus so call a mother.

丨丨 mother! — so children cry.

碼 ʿma Interchanged with the next.

Weights for money or goods; in Canton, an English yard (imitating the word) or a French metre.

法丨 or 丨子 money weights.

司丨枰 sixteen taels to a catty.

足司丨 full weights.

籌丨 counters used in games.

石丨 a water dam of stones across a stream.

In *Batavia.* The farm of taxes.

酒丨仔 or 酒丨子 the arrack farm.

瑪 ʿma The agate; veined stones.

丨瑙 a name given to quartzose minerals having laminæ or colored markings like the cornelian, chalcedony, opal, jasper, or agate.

丨瑙文 angular lines like those in fortification agate.

苴草丨瑙 moss agate.

燈草丨瑙 lamp-wick agate, a beautiful variety with white spiculæ.

膽青丨瑙 bloodstone.

螞 ʿma A leech; a locust.

丨蟥 a bloodsucker.

丨蟻搬泰山 the large ant would carry off Taishan; — an impossibility.

鰢 ʿma Prawns.

蝦丨 a small prawn; it is also called 水馬; the last is also the name of a species of water spider.

罵 **傌** ma' From *net* or *man* and *horse*; the second form is obsolete, or is only used in chess as the name of the black knight.

To rail at, to scold; to abuse with vile language.

呪丨 to curse; malisons.

丨不絕口 his mouth was full of railing.

辱丨 to vilify, to scold harshly.

笑丨 to ridicule and scold.

不受丨 he won't bear a scolding.

不要丨他 do not scold him.

嗎 ma' Used for the last.

To berate; to scold.

Read ˏma. An interrogative requiring an affirmative answer; when there is an alternative, it ends the first clause.

這筆是你的丨還是他的 is that pencil yours or his?

酒丨 to gabble over one's wine.

這樣丨 is it not so?

他來了丨 has he come?

這不是張姓的丨 does not that belong to Mr Chang?

禡 ma' A sacrifice offered to the god of War or Mars, when reaching the borders of the enemy's country, in order to propitiate a victory; it was offered on horseback; worship to the *dii viæ* when traveling.

是類是丨 they worshiped Shang-ti and Mars.

佛丨 a paper painted effigy or substitute for other gods, which is worshiped in houses at Shanghai, and then burned.

In *Cantonese.* The day after the full and new moons.

頭ˎ丨 the 2d day of the 1st moon.

做ˎ丨 to observe these days.

榪 ma' A head-board, that stretches from the bed-posts to secure them; to stretch a thin board between two things; to clamp, to join by clamping; a stretcher; some say that 馬桶 a close chair, is more correctly written 丨桶 than the common way.

上両個丨子 nail on a couple of slats, — as on a pile of logs to prevent thefts.

獁 ma' A southern name for a monkey.

丨猫洲 Monkey Island off Macao; in Shantung, 丨子 denotes a wolf.

隲 ma' Also read ʿma.

Advantageous, useful; profitable, clever, skilled; to pile up, to lay in regular piles, as bales or books.

丨上磚 pile up the bricks.

擠似丨帮猪 as thick here as piled-up hogs.

MAH.

Old sound, mít. *In Canton*, mat *and* mút; — *in Amoy*, biet; — *in Fuhchau*, mak *and* mwak; — *in Shanghai*, mak.

𢱢 *ma'* From *hand* and *secret*.
To strike.

𠋫 *ma'* From *man* and *secret*.
Brawny.
丨 俗 stout, strong, able to carry much.

帓, 袜 *mo', méi'* From *napkin* or *clothes* and the *end*; also read *moh*.
Low socks or other covering for the feet, made of cloth.
丨 靿 a garter, often prettily embroidered.

Read *méi'* A napkin, a handkerchief; a girdle or stomacher worn over the breast like a corset; to bind on.
丨 額 a fillet worn by women.
丨 巾 而 裘 [the northern people] wear turbans and dress in skins.
丨 肚 to bind or strap the waist.
丨 額 鳳 a bridal phœnix headband, often seen on the stage.

MAI.

Old sounds, mai, ma, *and* mat. *In Canton*, mai; — *in Swatow*, mai *and* boi; — *in Amoy*, bai, mai, *and* mai^n; — *in Fuhchau*, mai *and* mè; — *in Shanghai*, ma; — *in Chifu*, mai.

埋 *ˏmai* From *earth* and *village*.
To secrete, to cover, to conceal; to lay by, to hoard; to harbor; to bury, to cover over without regard to the rites.
丨 葬 to inter, to put into the grave.
丨 藏 to hoard, to lay up in secret.
丨 沒 to conceal; to take another name; *sub rosa*.
丨 伏 兵 馬 to dispose the forces in ambush.
丨 怨 to bear a grudge against.
收 丨 to lay by safely.
贓 丨 to falsely accuse.
丨 身 隴 畝 to retire [from office] and hide in the country.
隱 姓 丨 名 to take an alias and secrete one's self.
丨 沒 人 心 to disappoint one and not carry out his plans.

In *Cantonese*. To connect with, to annex; to crouch; to congeal, to set, to curdle; to harden; following other verbs it denotes up, in, with, at, to, or merely a form of the past tense.
丨 岸 or 丨 街 to go ashore.
做 丨 done, finished, all over.
丨 來 come near to me.
丟 丨 to throw aside.
打 得 丨 agreeable, fit.
出 丨 to furnish means.
丨 手 to begin a job.
行 丨 一 邊 step aside a little.
撮 丨 to abridge, to make small.
無 開 丨 nothing at all to give.
天 熡 不 丨 it will not harden in warm weather.

薶 *ˏmai* Regarded as another form of the last.
To bury; to store away.
瘞 丨 the place where sacrifices are offered at graves.

Read *ˏli*. To stop up.
窒 丨 to close, to stuff.

Read *ˏwéi*. Filthy; to make dirty, to defile.
鑒 明 者 塵 垢 弗 能 丨 dust will not dirty a mirror; — conscious integrity cannot be defiled.

霾 *ˏmai* From *rain* and a *fox*.
Sand or dust storms, common in northern China; a misty, foggy sky, arising from dust or fog.
風 雨 丨 晦 the storm obscures everything.
終 風 且 丨 the wind brings up a dust-storm.
撥 丨 見 天 he brushed away the mists to see the sky; — said of a clear writer.

買 *ˊmai* From *property* and a *net*, which the etymologists explain by Mencius' phrase 网 市 利 to net the market gains.
To buy, to purchase; to obtain.
做 丨 賣 a trader.
丨 受 to buy real estate.
丨 入 to purchase.
丨 水 to buy water at a parent's death; — a southern usage.
零 碎 丨 to buy by retail.
丨 辦 a comprador or butler; a purveyor.
丨 服 民 心 to win people's hearts.
收 丨 古 玩 curiosities bought in here; — a shop sign.
丨 囑 to suborn villains to inform against; to bribe one to obey orders.
丨 怕 to buy fear; — to give hush money.

潤 *ˊmai* One of the headwaters of the Mih-lo River 汨 羅 江 which rises in Kiangsi, and flows westerly into the Tungting Lake.

‘嘪 ‘mai The bleating of sheep.

‘蕒 ‘mai From *plant* and to *buy*.

A name for several milky plants, of which the 丨菜 or 苦丨菜 is the chicory (*Cichorium*), and the dandelion (*Leontodon*); and also a species of sow-thistle (*Sonchus*).

水苦丨 a small annual growing in damp places; applied to a *Veronica* and an *Icteris*.

苣丨 a wild kind of greens like lettuce, probably a chicory.

‘勱 ‘mai To give *all* one's *strength* to a thing; to exert it.

丨相國家 to aid the state energetically.

丨種德 to sedulously cultivate virtue.

賣’ mai’ From 買 to *buy* and 出 *going out* contracted.

To sell, to vend; to betray, to inveigle; to make game of, to mock; to vaunt, to show off.

丨貨手 a salesman.

丨了 or 丨出 or 丨去 sold.

丨得貴 it is held at a high rate.

出丨 for sale.

丨俏 to prink one's self out; to show off, as a woman.

丨嘴乖 to gabble, to talk glibly.

丨瘋 to give another the leprosy.

丨弄丰情 to set off one's charms, meretricious adorning.

丨國 to betray one's country, to serve the enemy.

丨力 to do jobs, to hire out.

丨面光 to keep up appearances; eye-service.

丨放 to let prisoners get away.

丨主求榮 to betray the king in order to get high station.

丨人情 to try to curry favor; to act officiously.

丨猪仔 sold as a pig [in a basket]—into foreign servitude; a Canton phrase for coolies.

丨武 to act for people's amusement.

丨人口 to sell people, as girls for brothels.

邁’ mai’ From to *go* and a *myriad*.

To pass away, to wax old; to surpass, to exceed, to go beyond; energetically; to depart; to travel far; to make a royal progress; senile, old.

年丨 aged.

老丨 over sixty years.

如彼行丨 like any one going astray.

丨大步行 he then marched himself off.

日月旣丨 the days and months fly away.

丨種超羣 he surpassed them all, a *facile princeps*.

不能丨步 he could not move a step.

視我丨丨 he thinks of me without regard.

時丨其邦 he was then visiting his dependencies.

譪’ mai’ To brag, to *talk ten thousand* things; to speak angrily.

丨不自覺 he does not know he brags.

MAN.

Old sound, man. *In Canton*, man *and* múan; — *in Swatow*, man, mún, *and* mûa; — *in Amoy*, ban *and* bòan; — *in Fuhchau*, mang *and* mwang; — *in Shanghai*, méⁿ *and* mèⁿ; — *in Chifu*, man.

蠻 ˏman From *insect* and to *connect*.

A large snake found in the south; ancient name for barbarous tribes in the south of China, unreformed by Chinese civilization; the southern regions; external, barbarous people; fierce, brutish, trusting to strength alone; unreasonable, beyond reproof.

南丨 an old term for people south of the Méi-ling and in Formosa.

丨夷 savages, wild tribes; southerners are still termed 丨子 by the northern Chinese, as they were in Marco Polo's time.

丨性 ungovernable.

打丨講 you talk like a savage.

丨力 herculean strength.

丨石 rubble stone.

刁丨 passionate, willful.

以先祖受命因時百丨 as his ancestor had received a charge to regulate all the wild southerners.

丨邦 or 丨繈 uncivilized regions.

丨悍 valiant.

In *Shanghai*. An *adjective*, obstinate, unreasonable; an *adverb* of comparison, very, highly, exceedingly.

丨囝 an obstinate child.

丨好 very good, first rate.

丨會話 he speaks fluently.

丨清爽 clear and distinct.

話丨話 unreasonable opposition.

攣 Meaning and sound both lost.

In *Cantonese* used for ˏpan 扳 To pull or take down; to push, to turn over; to work a scull; to bring down as pride.

丨開門 pull open the door.

丨個件落 get down that article.

丨倍 to contest with one.

禮 ꜀man — Large coarse garments such as the nomades wear; trowsers made close are 丨 褡褳, referring especially to the seat not being split.

鬘 ꜀man — Beautiful hair; garments; head-gear; wreaths or frontlets; fringe on caps, like that on official hats.

貫雹爲華 丨 he could string hailstones to make a beautiful wreath; — said of Budha.

指 丨 a Budhist term for a rosary of finger bones.

眞金 丨 [she who wears] a pure gold coiffure, — was Kanchanamala, wife of Kunala, noted for her conjugal fidelity.

縵 ꜀man — Thin, plain sarcenet; unadorned, simple.

操 丨 to play in tune.

丨 田 an unploughed field.

卿雲爛兮糺 丨 丨 兮 the rosy clouds roll up in lofty piles.

謾 ꜀man — From *words* and *long*; interchanged with 慢ˀ *slow*.

To deceive or insult a superior; unfaithful to a trust.

丨 言 exaggerated talk

大 丨 great disrespect.

詐 丨 cunning.

誕 丨 to draw a long bow.

饅 ꜀man — Steamed bread or wheaten cakes; bread of any kind.

丨 頭 a loaf of bread.

丨 頭餅 a bun or dumpling.

丨 頭蘿 or 木 丨 頭 the dried fruit of the *Ficus stipulata*.

鰻 ꜀man — A salt water eel, the 丨 鱺; there are black and yellow sorts, with large pectoral fins.

海 丨 鱺 a large species of conger eel.

海 丨 a brown eel common at Shanghai, three feet long, allied to the *Ophisurus*.

丨 鱔 eels of all kinds.

槾 ꜀man — To covet; a ploughshare, name of a thorny tree.

丨 丨 to smooth, as mortar.

鞔 ꜀man — An empty shoe; a bridle thong; occurs used for ʻmin 憫 to pity; troubled.

In *Pekingese*. To cover with skin, as a drum or tambourine.

丨 鼓皮 to stretch a drum-skin.

瞞 ꜀man — From *eye* and *even*.

A flat eye, one whose canthi or corners are nearly level with the face; dull, half-closed eyes, as if drunk; to deceive, to impose on one, to conceal the truth.

隱 丨 to hide from.

包 丨 deceived, gulled, tricked.

欺 丨 to deceive, to pull wool over his eyes.

實不相 丨 I will keep nothing from you.

丨 目 to shut or wink the eyes.

丨 騙 to cheat, to palm on.

老 丨 a bridesmaid. (*Pekingese.*)

蹣 ꜀man — To jump, as over a wall.

丨 牆 to leap a wall.

Read ꜀pʻan. To limp.

丨 跚 to reel, to walk awry or lame.

顢 ꜀man — A large, full, round face.

這麼 丨 頇 why are you so set to do it?

墁 ꜀man — Used for 墁ˀ to cover over.

To overlay with earth; one says, iron rust.

丨 堦磚 to lay or pave with square tiles.

滿 ʻman — From *water* and *even*.

Full, replete, surfeited; bulging, stuffed; complete, entire; fullness, pride; to complete, to fill, to suffice, to abound; to finish a set time; the Manchu people; Brahminic writings (*puranas*), so called on account of their completeness.

丨 身 the whole body.

丨 載 full, as of cargo laden in.

乘 丨 or 放 丨 packed full.

做 丨 一任 complete a term of office.

丨 月 the month of a confinement; a honey-moon; to pull a full bow.

丨 意 quite to my liking.

志自 丨 九族乃離 when he is full of his own sufficiency, his kindred all desert him.

丨 到處 everywhere, here and there, all over.

丨 期發賣 the time having passed, the goods were sold.

丨 洲人 the Manchus.

丨 口春風 fluent and eloquent.

丨 招損 the presumptuous bring on their own calamities.

充 丨 the whole, the entire circuit.

丨 載而歸 may you return home fully satisfied.

丨 腹經綸 profoundly learned and clever.

丨 下巴 a very full beard.

丨 慈子 the son of complete compassion, a name of *Purna-maitreyani-puttra* 彌多羅尼子 a budhisatwa, once a disciple of Sakya-muni.

曼 manˀ — From 冒 to *feign* altered and 又 a *hand*; it is also read ꜀man.

Long, extended, like a vine; prolonged; marked with fine lines.

丨 衍 infinite, endless.

丨 倩偷桃 [may the old fairy] Man-tsien get a peach for you; — a wish on an old man's birthday.

路 丨 丨 a long tedious road.

Read wanˀ Fine, personable; good, well taken care of, as the body; without, not having; also.

孔 丨 且碩 tall and fat, a fine figure.

平脅 丨 膚 an even waist and plump limbs.

丨 辭以自解 with a fine apology he exonerated himself.

幔 man'
A curtain, a screen; tapestry or brocade hangings.
轎丨 sedan curtains.
幛丨 to screen off.
錦丨 embroidered screens.

嫚 man'
From *woman* and *long;* interchanged with the next.
To despise, to affront; to reproach.
汚丨 to vilify.
褻丨 to show contempt to.
僭丨鬼神 to despise the gods.
侮丨 to slight.

僈 man'
Interchanged with the next.
Negligent, remiss.
丨些 stop a little.
君子寬而不丨 the wise man acts leisurely but is not lazy.

慢 man'
From *heart* and *long;* interchanged with the last two, and the next.
Indifferent, negligent, remiss; rude, disobliging, supercilious, proud; to treat haughtily; late; slow, easy, sluggish; dilatory, taking a long time for.
丨丨走 or 丨丨跑 go slower.
怠丨 to insult.
不快不丨 moderate, easy.
做事無急丨 he'll take his own time for it.
丨丨 or 丨且 slowly, easy; stop a little while.
輕丨 to disesteem, to slight.
丨手 a slow hand.
丨道如此 be careful how you speak thus.
寫太丨 you write very slowly.
丨說 do not speak so; better be silent.
花開得丨 the flowers are late in blossoming.
且丨 stop a minute! wait a bit! — a call to one passing by.
丨不驚心 to throw off the care.

In *Cantonese.* Light weight; as ꜀鮮 is over weight.
丨不㲉 the steel-yard falls.

漫 湯 man'
From *water* and *long;* also read ꜀man, and occasionally used for the last; the second form is rare.
An expanse of water; an overflow of water, spreading and ruining as it runs; breaking bounds, like a torrent; diffused, spreading; boundless; to set loose, to let go; vague, diffuse, as writing; expanding, as clouds; wild, reckless.
爛丨 all dispersed, widely diffused.
丨丨 long and far, like a road; level, even.
水丨河堤 the water overflows the dikes.
丨種 to sow broadcast.
指東西之丨丨 a view as wide as the east from the west.
汗丨 illimitable, like the ocean.
瀰丨天恩 the continual blessings of heaven.
丨酸 sour eructations.
澶丨爲樂 to give loose to one's evil desires.
肆口丨駡 to vociferate and talk wildly; to rail and swear at.
꜀丨꜀丨大霧 the fog is very dense.

墁 man'
To cover, as a wall with plaster; to paint or ornament walls; to pave; a trowel.
丨牆 to plaster walls.
丨地板 to lay a board floor.
毀瓦畫丨 he broke the tiles, and disfigured the plastering.

鏝 man'
Interchanged with the last.
A trowel.
泥丨 or 丨刀 a trowel.
錢丨兒 the obverse of a coin (*Pekingese.*)

MĂN.

Old sound, mún. *In Canton,* mún; — *in Swatow,* măng *and* bún; — *in Amoy,* bòan, muiⁿ, *and* bún; — *in Fuhchau,* mwòng *and* mòng; — *in Shanghai,* măng; — *in Chifu,* măn.

門 ꜀măn
The original has two 戶 *leaves* of a door face to face; it forms the 169th radical of a natural group of characters relating to entrances.
A gate, a gateway; an outer door; a house; the family in it; an entrance, an opening; a harbor; a sect, a profession, a class; an occupation; in *anatomy,* a short duct or passage; a classifier of cannon and affairs.
丨閂 the bar or bolt of a gate.
一扇丨 a one-leaved door.
橫丨 a side or private door.
月丨 a circular entrance.
丨口 in the door; a gateway.
大丨 the great or outer gate.
衡丨之下可以棲遲 beneath my door of scantling I can rest at my leisure.
丨丁 or 看丨的 a doorkeeper; but 公丨 is the style for the porter of a palace or grandee's house.
不入丨 he'll never learn his trade.
聽丨 to wait for one at the gate, as at night.
敲丨 to rap, to pound on the gate.
丨神 the god who guards official gateways.
丨籠子 posts to bar and secure the shop-shutters.
丨牌 the door-tablet, which contains the names of the family.
醫丨 the medical profession.
冷丨 obsolete, old fashioned, as an old fogey practitioner.

十｜砲 ten cannon.

｜｜曉得 he knows a little of all kinds of trades.

｜外漢 one not in the trade.

專｜生意 a specialty, a single branch, as an oculist.

｜風 the reputation of a family; usages of a household.

開｜七件事樣樣罷不得 seven things are absolutely necessary in housekeeping, — fuel rice, oil, salt, soy, tea, and vinegar.

出｜ entered an office; married a husband; gone abroad, not at home.

｜鎖上了 the door is locked.

耳｜ a small side door.

｜上 or ｜子 a gentleman's butler or major-domo; attendants at a court.

大｜口 a noble rich family.

｜生 or ｜人 or ｜徒 a pupil, a disciple.

｜戶不對 the families are not matched, an unsuitable alliance.

｜路 occupation; an opening.

朱｜ or 高｜ a distinguished family.

忠節一｜ a loyal and virtuous household.

拜｜下 to acknowledge one as a teacher or patron.

｜包 or ｜規 or ｜敬 fee to the porter; his perquisites.

金星｜ the harbor of Kum-sing Moon north of Macao.

道義之｜ the path of truth and right.

｜斗 attendants on a district school-inspector.

幽｜ and 賁｜ the pylorus and cardiac orifice of the stomach.

闌｜ the obstructed passage, — is the ilio-cœcal valve.

們 ꜀*măn* From *man* and *door* as the phonetic.

The sign of the plural of persons.

你｜ you; often used for one person

我｜ we, who are together; us.

爺｜ gentlemen, elders, uncles, official attendants; an honorable appellation for a husband.

爺兒｜ you, Sirs, spoken to the last if they are older; but if equal in rank or age, 哥兒｜ is a more polite term.

他｜ they, those people.

弟兄｜ the brothers.

Read *măn'* Plump, full-looking.

｜渾 fat and hearty, as a horse.

捫 ꜀*măn* From *hand* and *door* as the phonetic.

To feel, to lay the hand on; to touch, to examine, to search for, to hold; to cover; to draw a cover over.

｜心 lay the hand on the heart; self-examination.

｜虱 to crack lice.

｜足 to stamp the feet in anger.

無曰苟矣莫｜朕舌 do not say, It is of no moment, and no one can prevent my speaking.

｜鼓 to cover a drum.

｜緊 pull it on tight, as a cover.

｜黑路 a dark, unlighted road.

｜紗 to put gauze over.

｜書皮 to cover a book.

穈 ꜀*măn* Also read *mé*.

A variety of millet with reddish culms; now applied in Chihli to the glutinous grain of the ꜀*shu* 黍 or panicled millet (*Milium*), called ｜子米, and used in distilling spirits; congee.

維｜維芑 there is the red millet and the white.

｜蔗 the red sugar-cane of Fuhkien.

璊 ꜀*măn* A jaspery stone of a reddish color, probably a cornelian.

毳衣如｜ his robes of state shine like a cornelian; — perhaps in allusion to the feathers on them.

樠 ꜀*măn* A species of fir; the heart wood of the fir; a globule or drop of gum oozing from the fir.

｜溪 or ｜木 in Hunan, a large kind of fir allied to the *Podocarpus*, and like the 杄 of Shansi with which it is said to be identical; the tree is also called ꜀*liang* 椺 probably from a mistake in confounding the primitives.

津液暗出｜｜ the gum [of the fir] silently exudes in separate drops.

悗 ꜂*măn* From *heart* and *without*; it is also read ꜀*man*.

Afraid, amazed; out of his mind; suspicious; only one, unmatched, without a mate.

｜乎忘其言 he was so dismayed he forgot what he had said.

｜密蠢愚 reserved and dull of apprehension.

悶 ⿰忄門 懣 *măn'* From *heart* and *door* or *full*; the three are nearly synonymous, though the last refers rather to cares, while the former alludes to afflictions.

Sad, unhappy; melancholy, chagrined; heavy at heart.

消｜ to dissipate sorrows.

憂｜ distressed, grieved.

煩｜ bothered and anxious; impertinent to.

｜得很 very much cast down.

散｜ to dissipate care, to amuse one's self.

愁｜不解 his grief is not alleviated.

心不納｜ he became sorry at; melancholy.

｜得慌 perplexed, harassed; dull, *ennuyé*.

作｜ to turn sick from faintness or heat; a sickness at the stomach.

⿰米㒼 *măn'* Gruel or congee stiffened and cold.

MANG.

Old sound, mung. *In Canton*, mong *and* p'ong ; — *in Swatow*, mang *and* buang ; — *in Amoy*, bang *and* bong ; — *in Fuhchau*, mang, mâng, *and* mòng ; — *in Shanghai*, bong *and* mong ; — *in Chifu*, mang.

狵 尨 ꜀mang From *beast*, *dog*, and *pelage*, modified in combination ; the second form is preferred.
A shaggy haired dog, perhaps referring to the large Tibetan mastiff ; mixed, blended, variegated, like different furs.

丨服 particolored garments.

丨茸 confused, as the colors of furs ; a jargon.

無使丨也吠 do not make the dogs bark at you.

厖 庬 ꜀mang Like the last and the next ; the first only means a rock.
A large rock ; bulky, great ; abundant, numerous, mixed ; generously provided for.

民生敦丨the people multiplied greatly.

爲下國駿丨 acted towards the inferior states as a strong horse — bears its burden

湛恩丨洪 I have received many liberal favors.

駹 ꜀mang From *horse* and *mixed* ; interchanged with the last.
A horse with a white face ; horses with white and black hair mixed, such as the Huns once rode ; mixed, as a dog's color ; name of a savage tribe.

哤 ꜀mang From *mouth* and *dog*.
A jargon of dialects and sounds, such as is spoken where people from many regions live together.

鄉音丨雜 each speaks his own patois ; a babel of sounds.

言丨 a confused jargon.

浝 ꜀mang Water.
丨河 a small affluent of the Yellow River in Hwai-k'ing fu in the north of Honan.

牻 ꜀mang A brindled ox, having black and white stripes.

丨牛 a bull.

丨牛兒苗 a species of geranium gathered for eating when young ; it is also called 敁巴巴 or the woodepcker's bill, from the shape of the seeds.

忙 ꜀mang From *heart* and *dead* ; it is not the same as ꜀wang 忘 to forget.
Busy, hurried, occupied, distracted with care, fluttered ; no leisure ; precipitation, undue haste.

不要丨 don't be in a hurry.

丨丨然歸 he went home in a great hurry.

着丨 flurried, as by a sudden arrival.

急丨 urgently pressed.

丨速 bustle, confusion and haste.

悤丨 or 冲丨 hurried overmuch, too much to do.

丨甚麽 what are you so hurried about ?

丨丨碌碌 to bustle about ; fluttering and distracted.

連丨 very much hurried at once.

帮丨 help one in his hurry ; to lend one a hand in trouble.

慌丨抖亂 I am overwhelmed with work.

雲歸月丨 the moon drives past the clouds.

恾 ꜀mang Like the last.
Hurried and alarmed, as by a sudden danger.

丨然無以應 he was so flurried, he did not know how to act as he ought.

汒 ꜀mang From *water* and *dead* ; an old form of the next.
Sudden, startling ; wide, like the ocean ; name of a valley near the capital.

茫 ꜀mang Vast and vague, like the expanse of the ocean ; dazzling and immense.

丨然 on a sudden, surprising.

滄丨 dreary, obscure and vast.

苦海丨丨 the world and its care, — like a bitter shoreless sea, as the Budhists say.

丨丨堪輿 illimitable and vast, as creation.

丨丨大海 the boundless ocean.

芒 ꜀mang From *grass* and *extinct* ; used with the last.
The awn or beard of grain ; applied to grasses like the *Erianthus*, *Eulalia*, or *Imperata* ; a sharp point ; a ray of light ; tail of a comet.

光丨 a flash of light ; a shooting star ; twinkling rays.

鋒丨 an acute point.

丨丨其稼 to sow wide a crop.

針尖遇見麥丨 to meet a wheat awn between needles' points ; — *i. e.* two individuals equally obstinate and sharp.

丨丨 great, crowded ; to become great, as posterity.

絲丨 the ground pine (*Lycopodium*), from its sharp leaves.

洪水丨丨禹敷下土 when the boundless deluge covered the country, Yü arranged and divided the lands.

敖丨 the clay man, who bears a stick as if to strike the clay ox.

宋 ꜀mang The ridge-pole beam in a roof.

丨棟 heavy beams in the framework of a roof.

甿 ꜀mang Farmers ; field-laborers who have little education, and are rude in speech, as if they were 懵懵 dunderheads.

以田里安丨 he satisfied the peasants with fields and villages.

鋩 ꜀mang — The edge of a sword; a smooth, easy style.
微丨 very sharp.
筆丨勁捷 a trenchant, animated style.

邙 ꜀mang — Name of a hill, the 地丨山 near Loh-yang in Hunan, where a great battle occurred A. D. 761 in the Tʻang dynasty.

蘉 ꜀mang — To exert one's self; to encourage, to stimulate.
汝乃是不丨乃時惟不永哉 if you do not bestir yourself, you cannot be of long continuance.

硭 ꜀mang — A mineral soil or shale which furnishes, when leeched, the 丨硝 an impure saltpeter, sometimes mixed with nitrate of soda and alumina.

砬 ꜀mang — Sometimes written 芒, but it is nearly identical with the last.
A crude saltpeter.
丨硝 a form of saltpeter, so called from its acicular crystals.
丨碭山 a noted hill, bare and stony, situated in Tang-shan hien 碭山縣 in the northwest corner of Kiangsu, famous for a battle.

杧 ꜀mang — Blasted grain; grain turned black as if with ergot or rust.

莽 ꜂mang — From 艸 *grass* repeated with 犬 *dog* between, denoting a hound pursuing a hare in the thickets.
Thick grass, jungle, underbrush; matted; confused, indistinct; rude, rustic, regardless of etiquette; heedless.
草木丨丨 tangled, thick, like a hedge; boscage.
草丨之臣 a countrified officer.
丨草 a plant which stupefies fish, perhaps the *Illicium religiosum* whose leaves are poisonous.
粗丨 brusque and arbitrary.
丨撞 intrusive, disorderly.
丨漢 an inconsiderate fellow, a happy-go-lucky.

暽 ꜂mang — The sun obscured.
丨曭 or 丨昧 the sun not visible, cloudy.

㟌 ꜂mang — Perturbed, disquieted, and therefore unable to attend to business.
鹵丨 heedless, careless; inattentive and untrustworthy.

蟒 ꜂mang — From *worm* and *thicket* as the phonetic.
A large serpent, the 王丨 or 丨蛇 a python with yellow scales found in Yunnan and Annam, twenty or more feet long.
丨袍 ceremonial robes embroidered or woven with dragons having four claws.
丨蟲 a species of snake said to eat leaves
丨龍 a horrible dragon.
巨丨千尋 [a weapon like] a great boa, a thousand feet long.
丨神 a class of demons, called *mahoraga* by Hindu Budhists, shaped like anacondas.

漭 mang꜄ — Level and waste as a desert; vast, like the ocean.
丨浪 desert-like; a howling waste.
晨光泱丨 the morning light is still dim.

MǍNG.

***These characters and those under* MUNG *are often sounded alike. Old sounds,* mong *and* măng. *In Canton,* măng *and* mang; — *in Swatow,* mó *and* meng; — *in Amoy,* beng; — *in Fuhchau,* maing *and* meng; — *in Shanghai,* măng *and* mang; — *in Chifu,* măng.**

萌 ꜀măng — From *plant* and *bright* as the phonetic.
The budding of plants; sprouting of seeds; to germinate, to shoot forth; a sprout; fixed; incipient, first risings of; the reviving of evil habits; to plow.
丨芽 to sprout, to put forth roots.
早丨于心 he early cherished these designs.
故志復丨 his old desires then revived.
丨動 risings of discontent.
意念未丨 even before he had any idea of it.

盟 ꜀măng — From *dish* and *bright*; but originally composed of 囧 *window* and 皿 *blood*, referring to the mode of taking an oath by turning towards the north when calling upon heaven, after which bullock's blood was smeared.
A solemn declaration before the gods, when blood was sipped or smeared on the body, to ratify the treaties made among the princes in feudal times; an alliance, a contract, a compact; to swear, to bind one's self before the gods; to make a treaty of peace; among the Mongols, a *chulkan* or tribe.
約丨 a marriage alliance.
丨誓 to swear and bind it by blood.
丨書 the form of oath; the papers signed by the parties.
丨心 guileless, consciously innocent.
丨府 a record or treaty office.
海誓山丨 a contract wide as the sea and firm as the hills; — marriage.
丨兄弟 sworn brothers, as the members of a lodge; persons banded for evil purposes.
丨國 allied states.

蜢 ʿmăng A small grasshopper or locust, the 草〡 or 蚱〡, often caught by children to hear it chirp.

胡〡 a species of small frog.

〡虫 a small fly or gnat found near kitchens.

艋 ʿmăng A small boat; a pinnace, a long boat.

舴〡 a gig, a junk's dingey, which can go like a grasshopper.

頭〡 large junks with a square open framework on the bows, secured by transverse rails, known at Canton as the West-coast junks.

掹 măngʾ From *hand* and *eminent* as the phonetic; an unauthorized character.

In *Cantonese.* To pull, to stretch; to pull to and fro, or up; to tug at; to cover, to draw over for shade; coarse; a strap.

〡꜀長 stretch it out; pull taut.

〡風扇 pull the punka.

〡疎 to thin out, as grain.

櫓〡 a scull-tie.

〡甪 pulled it off.

〡麥 to gather wheat, by pulling it up.

脚〡 gaiters used by women.

緊〡〡 keep it tight, as a hawser; also, hard pressed for money.

粗〡 very ordinary and coarse.

孟 măngʾ From *son* and a *dish* to give the sound.

Great, eminent; large; senior, eldest; the first month of a season or quarter; an old name for a woman's brothers; to use effort; to begin; a beginning.

〡仲季 a trio; the first, second, third of a trine series.

〡侯 an heir-apparent when he is eighteen years.

〡浪 exaggeration; to boast and vapor about.

〡夫子 the sage Mencius.

〡母三遷 the mother of Mencius thrice changed her abode.

〡晉 to exert one's self to become learned.

MAO.

Old sounds, mo *and* mok. *In Canton,* mò, mao, nao, *and* miu; — *in Swatow,* mao, bo, mo, ngiò, *and* bau; — *in Amoy,* bò, bau, *and* mò; — *in Fuhchau,* mo *and* mau; — *in Shanghai,* mo; — *in Chifu,* mao.

毛 ꜀mao The original form is thought to bear a rude resemblance to the *eyebrows;* it forms the 82d radical of characters relating to the uses and appearances of hair and feathers; at Canton, it is used as a contraction of ꜀*hao* 毫 for a dime.

The covering of animals or birds, as hair, fur, pelage, feathers, or down; mold; herbage, the covering of the earth; the nap of felt; tare of goods; to deprive of hair, as by scalding.

圓〡 the round haired, and 扁〡 the flat haired;—*i. e.* quadrupeds and birds.

命若鴻〡 our life [is light] as stork's down.

柔〡 the soft wooled; — *i. e.* a sheep or goat.

二〡 two sorts of hair — *i. e.* turning gray, grayhaired.

〡病 a flaw, a defect in an article; a failing, a queer way, an idiosyncrasy.

〡重 weight of a case, the tare.

〡管 the barrel of a quill.

〡手〡脚 a busybody; a tricky, lively, pestering boy; a tease.

發〡 to grow moldy.

不〡 a victim of mixed color; also, barren land.

深入不〡 he penetrated even to the deserts or wilds.

一〡不拔 [he's too stingy] to pull out a hair for you.

食〡踐土 [you, my people, who] eat the produce and live on the soil.

羽〡 a feather, a quill.

不屬於〡 am I not connected with the hair — or life, of my father?

〡血 fowls and flesh, — offered in worship.

雁過拔〡 he pulls a feather from every goose which passes; — he exacts a fee from each.

鷄〡報 an urgent notice or warning; — a white cock's feather is fastened to it.

In *Shanghai.* Rough, not smooth; nearly, said of a number.

旄 ꜀mao From *flag* and *hair,* referring to its material.

A chowry or tail of the yak, fastened to the end of a high staff, to give signals on certain occasions, for which leopard's tails are now used; an old man.

〡牛 the yak or grunting-ox.

杆〡 a yak's tail on a staff, — the insignia of a high grandee.

〡頭騎 to ride, as an acrobat, wildly but skillfully.

反其〡倪 he returned the old men and children who were captured.

〡頭 a name for the Pleiades.

髦 ꜀mao The hair on the head or forehead; tufts on an infant's head, trimmed up on each temple, called 孝順〡 or filial tufts; eminent, excelling in force; applied to long hairs which excel the rest.

〡士 eminent, picked men.

乘〡馬 to mount a long-maned horse.

酕 ꜀mao Drunk.
丨 醄 exceedingly drunk.

牦 ꜀mao The *hairy ox*, as the character itself imports.
丨 牛 a wild yak; it is described as found in Kansuh and further west, and to be caught and tamed by the people.

髦 ꜀mao A kind of feather screen or flabellum on a carriage, anciently used to protect riders from the wind and dust; a horse with long hair.

茅 ꜀mao From *plants* and a *lance*.
High rank grass like an *Arundo*, good for thatching houses; also applied to a white striped grass; a species of low palm resembling a *Thrinax*, or perhaps a kind of scrub pine; thatched; poor, lowly.
丨 舍 a cottage; my humble dwelling.
丨 棚 or 丨 寮 a lodge in a field.
草 丨 下 士 [I am as] the least of grass and stubble scholars; — said on receiving an honor.
丨 屋 a hut, a thatched house.
丨 草 quickset grass, thatch.
白 丨 根 roots of couch grass; — a febrifuge.
上 丨 the best grass, among Budhists denotes the *kuja* or fragrant *Poa cynosuroides*.
求開丨塞 pray to enlighten my dull mind.
舞 丨 山 the incantations of the Tao priests to relieve evils.
丨 厠 a privy, a jakes.
英英白雲露彼菅丨 the light and brilliant clouds bedew the rushes and grass.
黃 丨 a tough, tall grass used for thatching.
丨 廬 a poor country dwelling.
丨 州 an old name for Kü-yung hien 句容縣 near Nanking.

蟊 蝥 ꜀mao From *insects* and *spear*, alluding to their mischief.
A grub which attacks the roots of grain; any insect which eats grain.
斑 丨 a coleopterous fly (*Mylabris*), used in the native pharmacy for its blistering qualities.
丨 賊 丨 疾 [these evil men are like] grubs and flies in grain.
丨 弧 old name for a large banner which led the van.

貓 猫 ꜀mao, ꜁mao From *beast* and *sprout*, explained as intended to denote that cats eat mice, the destroyers of young grain.
A cat; the mewing of cats.
淨 丨 a castrated cat.
丨 子 or 丨 兒 puss.
丨 兒 眼 石 the cat's eye.
山 丨 the hill cat, (*Felis viverrinus*,) a species of tiger cat.
丨 狸 a striped fox.
野 丨 the wild cat; and poetically used for a fox; in Peking, it denotes the hare.
丨 鼠 同 眠 the cat and the rat are asleep together; — *i. e.* officers and thieves are in league.
丨 兒 眼 a common species of spurge. (*Euphorbia.*)
懶 骨 丨 a lazy cat; — *met.* an idle lazy-bones.
斑 丨 (or more correctly 蟹 蝥) the cantharides or a similar fly.
躲 丨 丨 blindman's buff; — *lit.* hiding from the cats.
氣 死 丨 a store-room, a cupboard, a safe to store in. (*Pekingese.*)
靈 丨 the civet of the Indian Archipelago, regarded as hermaphrodite; its scent bag, called 香丨卵, is brought from Yunnan.
丨 兒 嘴 a fellow who is eating constantly.

錨 ꜀mao An anchor; a grappling-iron.
抛 丨 to cast anchor.
起 丨 or 絞 丨 to weigh anchor.
丨 泡 or 丨 桴 an anchor-buoy.
丨 纜 a hawser or cable.
船 丨 an anchor.
事 已 落 丨 the anchor is down, — the thing is settled.

卯 夘 ꜂mao The old form is like an open door, said to be analogous to the springing up of vegetation in March; it is defined by 冒 a cover, as the earth is then covered; the second form is rather incorrect.
The fourth of the twelve branches; belongs to wood, and is designated by the hare; it stands for the hour from 5 to 7 A.M.; and for east; morning; a time, a day; a term, an instalment; flourishing.
交 丨 5 o'clock in the morning.
正 丨 6 o'clock.
丨 月 the second moon.
丨 鐘 the matin bell in a monastery.
丨 期 the third and eighth days of a moon; *i. e.* the 3d, 13th, and 23d, with the 8th, 18th, and 28th.
比 丨 to bamboo remiss policemen or recreant debtors.
開 丨 to make the first payment, as of duties; to begin to bamboo recreant policemen.
點 丨 to call the roll of clerks and employés, so called because once the names were marked at that hour, and the phrase 丨 期 now denotes the periodical days on which the roster is called.
晝 丨 to appear and answer to a summons.
悞 丨 to fail at roll-call.
過 丨 to pass by, to overdo.
應 丨 to answer by a substitute.
替 丨 substitutes who sell themselves to be bambooed.
死 丨 time of death.

In *Cantonese.* The buttocks, — perhaps wrongly used for 蹘 to squat.
揸 丨 to be taken in; to fail in a promise.

昴 ʻmao The eighteenth of the zodiacal constellations, answering to the Pleiades; it is one of the four that always marks a Sunday in the calendar, and is the center of the seven western constellations.

泖 ʻmao A river in the southeast of Kiangsu, in Sung-kiang fu; watery; stagnant water.

茆 ʻmao An aquatic vegetable, otherwise called 鳧葵 duck mallows, resembling the *Nymphæa* or pond lily; the raw leaves are edible.

丨菜 the water chestnut (*Eleocharis*), so called in Hunan.

薄菜其丨 we will gather the mallows out of it.

貌 **皃** mao' From 白 *white* over 儿 *man*, to denote the expression or countenance; the radical was added later, as a contraction of 豹 a leopard; the contracted form like ˏ'rh 兒 is often used.

The outward mien; gait, style, manner, form, appearance, habit; the visage, the face; in definitions, denotes the abstract quality of things, or the act of doing something; like, similar to; to draw a likeness.

容丨 the aspect of; one's manner.

面丨 the countenance.

美丨 pretty, engaging.

丨醜 ugly, homely.

形丨 the outline; figure.

好品丨 elegant; noble in conduct.

花容月丨 fair as a flower and beautiful as the moon.

丨善防心毒 be careful of smooth-faced fellows.

用力丨 exerting his strength.

命工丨妃 he bade the artist paint his concubine.

憂懼丨 the feeling of sedulous dread of offending.

芼 mao' From *grass* and *hair*, alluding to the appearance.

To pull out, as the roots of tangled plants; overgrown with grass; vegetables; to cook or prepare for eating.

丨羹 soup of meat and greens.

沼丨 water cresses or other water greens.

左右丨之 on the right and left we made soup — of duckweed.

耄 mao' From *old* and *hair*.

An old man over seventy up to eighty or ninety; senile, decrepit, in second childhood.

丨耋 a very old man.

年期垂丨 he is becoming very infirm.

丨期 a centenarian.

眊 mao' A small pupil; dim-sighted, dull; old; boozy, bewildered.

憒丨 beside one's self; irate and confused, muddled.

胸中不正則眸子丨焉 if the heart be perverse, the eye will be unsteady.

丨矂 unsuccessful and turning to drink.

冒 mao' From a 冃 *covering* and 目 *eye* underneath; occurs used for the next two.

A covering for the head; to go on rashly, to rush on heedless; to assume, to feign, to presume; to overspread; to venture on, to brave out; blind to, rash, reckless; to falsify, to counterfeit, to affirm a falsity.

丨名 to assume a name; an *alias*.

丨犯 to willfully (or heedlessly) offend.

假丨官差 to pretend to be a policemen.

丨雨 indifferent to the rain.

假丨字號 to counterfeit a label.

丨昧 ignorant and rash, headstrong.

這麼丨失 such utter rudeness and frowardness.

丨險 to brave danger.

躬丨矢石 he exposed himself in the battle.

下土是丨 [the sun] overshadows this lower world.

丨出來 emitted spontaneously.

感丨風寒 to take a slight cold.

貪丨 not wishing to know the truth; desperate, set in evil.

丨瀆 to willfully insult another.

湄 mao' This is often written like the last.

To rise and overflow; to leak, as a chimney; to spurt out.

水丨出來 the water runs over.

丨漿 the sap or gum oozes out.

丨熱氣 the steam comes up.

丨烟 the smoke comes out.

丨出來水 the water is leaking through.

媢 mao' Envious dislike at the excellence or prosperity of another; ill-will and jealousy.

丨嫉以惡之 she hated her with jealous dislike.

帽 mao' A cap or head covering of any kind; *met.* an imposition, as a price above the real.

丨店 a hat-shop.

涼丨 a summer hat.

丨子 a hat, cap, turban, or bonnet.

紅纓丨 a cap with a red fringe.

煖丨 a winter cap.

烏紗丨 official cap of the Ming dynasty.

雪丨 a cloth hood.

好ʼ戴個高丨子 he loves to wear the high hat; — *i. e.* he loves praise.

筆丨 a pencil cap.

射皮丨子 a leather hat-shaped target, three feet high, shot at by horsemen.

悁 mao' Inordinate desire for, covetous.

MÉ.

Old sound, mi. *In Canton*, mé *and* măt; — *in Swatow*, mé *and* mi; — *in Amoy*, bé *and* miⁿ; — *in Fuhchau*, mah, miè, *and* mieh; — *in Shanghai*, mi *and* mé; — *in Chifu*, mé.

孭 ˓ An unauthorized character, probably derived from 貝 *precious* or 背 *back*, and 子 *child*.

In *Cantonese*. To carry a child pickapack, like a papoose; to back or shoulder anything; an interrogative word.

丨子 to carry a baby on the back.
丨帶 a pack-wrapper.
丨上身 to take the responsibility of a thing.
係丨 is it so?

哶, **咩** ˓*mié* From *mouth* and *sheep*; the first form is antique.

The bleating of sheep.
羊丨 a sheep, kid or lamb.
丨羊 the cry of sheep.

乜 *mié*˒ The eyes crossing; squint-eyed; in the Western Hia, 厮丨 was a local term for necromancers.

In *Cantonese* read *măt*. An interrogative pronoun, who, what; how? before a negative, why, wherefore; a diminutive quantity; a person.

叫丨名 what is its name?
無丨人 not many persons.
亞丨 a term for servant boys.
老丨 Mr. Such-an-one.
係丨呢 what is it?
生丨倒要來 you must come in anywise.
爲丨事不做 why don't you do it?

MEH.

Old sound, mak. *In Canton*, măk; — *in Swatow*, bé, mé, *and* mek; — *in Amoy*, bek; — *in Fuhchau*, mah, mek, *and* paik; — *in Shanghai*, mak; — *in Chifu*, măh.

麥˒ *mai*˒ *mo*˒ Composed of 來 *coming* and 夂 a *sprout*, because it is sown in autumn; it is the 199th radical of characters relating to wheat.

Wheat, or the grain with an awn, of which there are several sorts; it belongs to metal.

粗丨 or 大丨 barley.
莜丨 or 油丨 麫 oatmeal.
三角丨 or 烏丨 buckwheat.
丨秋 wheat harvest.
丨芽 wheat sprouts, used in soups.
宿丨 winter wheat.
丨麩子 or 丨糠 bran.
拔丨 or 割丨 to reap wheat.
丨餘子 wheat chaff.

貊˒ *mo*˒ From *beast* and *hundred*; occurs wrongly used for the next.

A tribe of ancient aborigines on the north, in the valley of the River Hwai, and after in the Ortous country; quiet, settled like a firm and just government; silently.

雖蠻丨之邦行矣 although the barbarians of the south and north may act so.

蠻丨不矢之邦 [like the] ignorant savages, who do not know the rules of a state; — said of inexperienced people.

丨其德音 the fame of his virtue silently grew.

貘˒, **貉**˒, **獏**˒ *mo*˒ Sometimes written like the last.

The Malacca tapir (*Tapirus malayanus*), which the Chinese say was found in Sz'ch'uen, and is still found in Yunnan; they describe it as like a bear, with a black and white body, able to eat iron and copper, and having teeth that fire cannot burn; it has the nose of an elephant, eye of a rhinoceros, head of a lion, hair of a wolf, and feet of a tiger; a distorted figure of it was anciently drawn on screens as a charm.

陌˒ *mo*˒ A raised path going east and west which divides fields; a street going through a market-place; a road.

丨上 on the street.
街丨 a market-street.
丨路人 a rude fellow, a stranger; one who treats you coldly.
丨生人 a complete stranger.

駬˒ *mo*˒ The 駝丨 is described to be the offspring of an ass and a cow; probably a misprint.

驀˒ *mo*˒ To get on a horse; to leap on a horse's back.

丨越 to spring over; to pass, like a flash.
烟底丨波乘一葉 under the fleecy clouds see that leaf [of a shallop] skipping over the waves.

霢˒ *mo*˒ Small rain; misty dew that soaks everything.

丨霂 drizzling rain; applied to imperial favors.

脈, 脉, 衇, *mo'* From *flesh* and dispersing *streams*; the other forms are less common.
The pulse, the blood running in the veins; streaks or veins in wood; water courses in the ground; argument of thought, the idea running through; a line of succession; descent, parentage.
診丨or 看丨or 搭丨to feel the pulse.
丨理 philosophy of the pulse.
何處發丨where did your family come from?
丨絡相連 the veins run into each other; — *met.* the streets all lead into one another.
點丨to hit a pulse; the Chinese think an enemy can destroy health in this way.
地丨signs and streaks in the earth, marked by geomancers, indicative of internal water courses, which harmonize with the crops and health of a place.
一丨而來 an unbroken descent.
入丨to enter upon the argument, to assume the point.
丨門 the pulse in the wrist.

脈, *mo'* To look around one, to take a survey of; to look at each other, to ogle.
丨丨不得語 they looked at each other, but could not converse.

溗, *mo'* Shallow water; shallows, strands.
溪丨鄰鄰 the mountain streams ripple over the stones.

礣, *mieh'* Pebbly; hard, solid.
丨砎 small stones; shingle.

MÉI.

Old soundss, méi, mi, mai, mík, mít, *and* met. *In Canton*, múi *and* mi; — *in Swatow*, bai, bué, múi, múe, mi, *and* man; — *in Amoy*, múi^{n}, bi, bún, mò^{n}, *and* mai^{n}; — *in Fuhchau*, múi, mi, mwi, mwoi, mé, ngwoi, *and* meng; — *in Shanghai*, mé; — *in Chifu*, méi.

梅 *˛méi* From *tree* and *each* as the phonetic.
A general name for plums, prunes, and the the bullace; the flowering almond.
酸丨sour plums; pickled plums.
楊丨the tree strawberry or arbutus. (*Myrica sapida.*)
楊丨釘 a bubo, from the resemblance to the fruit.
丨酌 the plum bumper, name of a cup drank after weddings.
丨嶺 the Plum Range lying between Kiangsi and Kwangtung.
丨月 a poetical name for the tenth moon.
標丨marriageable.
丨丨downhearted, mourning.
丨占百花魁 the plum stands as the first of flowers.
丨雨 summer rain.
丨花骨瘦 lean as a prune flower, refers to a girl coming of age.
丨桃 the *Prunus tomentosa.*

脢 *˛méi* The meat on the breast, between the mouth and heart.
猪丨肉 or 夾心肉 a brisket of pork.

粬, 酶, *˛méi* The cakes of leaven, called 酒母 wine mother, used in fermenting the grain before distilling; they are also called 媒蘗 or the intermediate barm, because they produce the result of fermentation or leavening.

莓 *˛méi* A general name for berries, as blackberry, potentilla, raspberry, or other edible kinds.
丨苔 moss or lichens covering damp walls.
蛇丨one name for the strawberry.
蔺渚丨丨the green herbage by the streams.
藨丨a kind of red sour raspberry.
木丨a berry like the raspberry at Fuhchau.

霉 *˛méi* Summer rains, humid weather; damp, moldy, mildewed; to mildew.
送丨雨 the rains of July.
丨爛 spoiled by damp and mold.
丨壞 ruined from damp.
發丨turned moldy.

玫, 玟, *˛méi* From *gem* and *veined.*
The 丨瑰 is a bright red sparkling gem, perhaps precious garnet, from whence the red rose has its name.
丨瑰油 attar of roses.
Read *˛wăn* or *˛min*, but only written like the second. The strize in an agate or jade; an orange colored jasper, called 瑌丨which was once worn on the girdle by scholars..

枚 *˛méi* A small tree, a shrub; the stalk of a shrub; a cane, a switch or stick; a gag; a classifier of rings, coins, seeds, fruit, nails; one of, each.
銜丨a gag held inside the mouth.
猜丨to guess by throwing the fingers, the game of morra.
幾丨how many? — as plums.
一丨釘 one nail.
丨卜功臣 to cast lots among the worthy officers.
丨丨close and fine work, said of temples.

沬 From *water* and *not*; it is also used for 妹, and read *wi*ʾ
ˎmèi Name of a stream; and of a town in the state of Wéi 衛, now K'i hien 淇縣 in the north of Honan; indistinct; dark; a small star near the Dipper.

爰采麥矣丨之北矣 I go to gather wheat in the north of Méi.

Also read *hwui*ʾ To wash the face.

眉 The old form represents the *eye* and the *hairs* above it.
ˎmèi The eyebrows; old, aged; edge of a well.

眼丨 or 丨毛 the eyebrows.

蛾丨 arched eyebrows.

丨清目秀 beautiful eyes.

愁丨不展 contracted eyebrows, scowling, rueful.

丨州 a prefecture on the River Min above Kia-ting fu in Sz'-ch'uen.

老君丨 Lao-tsz' eyebrows, — a kind of fine black tea.

蛾丨月 the crescent, or young moon.

燃丨之急 in as much danger as if my eyebrows were singeing.

丨壽 eyebrows which indicate long life, being bushy and long.

以介丨壽 that he might get long life.

丨麗 beautiful eyes and brow.

揚丨吐氣 in high spirits, jolly.

丨間白毫 white hairs between the eyes denotes the *urna*, a mark of every Budha, out of which light radiates through every universe.

楣 From *wood* and *eyebrow*.
ˎmèi The lintel of a door or window.

橫丨 a timber in the eaves.

生女作門丨 to bear a daughter is like a lintel, — as it allows exit and entrance into other families when she marries.

嵋 A famous peak, the 峨丨山 in Kiating fu in the center of
ˎmèi Sz'ch'uen near the Ta-tu River, in a district of the same name.

溦 Like the next; also read ˎwéi.
ˎmèi Fine and drizzling, as rain; the bank of a stream.

丨絲雨 a slow drizzling rain.

丨水 the edge of the water.

湄 From *water* and *eyebrow*.
ˎmèi The brink of a stream; plants growing thick and tangled along the edge of a pool or river.

丨湖 a lake in Hunan.

丨潭縣 a district in the center of Kwéicheu.

所謂伊人在水之丨 the man of whom I speak is on the river's margin.

郿 A district town in Fung-tsiang fu in the southwest of
ˎmèi Shensi, lying on the River Wéi; name of an old town in Lu.

媒 From 女 *woman* and 謀 to *consult* contracted; occurs used for
ˎmèi 昧 obscure.

A go-between, an arranger of marriages; to covet; a person or cause which produces an effect.

丨婆 an old woman who settles matches.

謝丨 to remunerate go-betweens.

丨人 or 作丨 a matchmaker.

誘丨 an attraction, an inducement.

自丨 to interfere, to thrust one's self forward.

見譽而喜者佞之丨也 he who is praised and loved gives occasion for sycophants to act.

腜 The first movement of the fœtus.
ˎmèi 丨胎 to quicken; a quickened womb.

丨丨 fat and strong, lusty; good looking.

煤 Soot; coal, charcoal, embers; fossil coal.
ˎmèi 火丨 soot.

火丨絨 tinder, punk.

硬丨 or 石丨 anthracite coal.

丨精 brimstone.

烟丨 or 油丨 soft or bituminous coal.

丨廠 a coal-dépôt.

烟丨 lampblack, collected to make india-ink.

丨球 coal balls; made of coal-dust and clay.

紙丨 a paper match to hold fire.

丨炭 charcoal; it is burned from chestnut and willow.

掘丨 or 拉丨 to dig coal.

丨根石 jet; fossil lignite.

禖 A sacrifice or special worship held by the emperor in the
ˎmèi spring to supplicate heaven for a son.

劘 Also read ˎmo.
ˎmèi To cut, to pare off, to slice or divide up; to cut open, to dissect.

丨告諄諄 I now most particularly admonish you.

鋂 A door-ring having two locks bolting the door in it; a
ˎmèi dog-chain.

盧重丨 the double ring on a shepherd's dog.

門丨 a door-ring; a lock with rings on the bolt.

黴 From *black* and *small* as the phonetic.
ˎmèi Moldy or black spots appearing on things soaked in the rain; dirty, grimed spots on the face; spoiled; to dot with ink.

老于農則丨黧也 old farmers are usually sunburnt and have grimy faces.

丨黑 swarthy.

媺 Similar to the next.
ˎméi A small delicate woman; elegant, handsome.

美 ʿméi From 羊 *sheep* and 大 *great* beneath it, the largest animal being the best.

Toothsome, delicious, savory; beautiful, as a woman; excellent; good-looking; well; happy; to delight in, to esteem; to commend.

丨女 a pretty girl; a belle.
丨味 well-flavored.
丨地 fertile lands.
丨食 a delicate dish, sumptuous.
丨色 handsome, winning.
華丨 elegant, ornate.
讚丨 to praise, to extol.
丨中不足 his happiness is incomplete.
一塲丨意 a good intention, a kind thought.
予丨亡此 my admired man is no longer here.
丨樂不可勝言 inexpressibly happy.
丨國 or 大丨國 America; contracted from 大亞丨理駕合衆國 the United States of America.

每 ʿméi The original form represents the *grass* springing in a tangled way.

A distributive particle, each, every, each one, any one; constantly, always; although; to desire.

丨時 each time.
丨丨如此 it is usually so, it is ever thus.
丨一件事 each affair, or item.
原田丨丨 each field is alike fertile.
丨受人欺 he is always imposed upon.
我丨 all of us — who are here.
丨個三文 each one [sells for] three cash.
丨人 each man; every person.

浼 浼 ʿméi From *ice* or *water* and *do not*; the second form is most used.

To defile, to foul, as with dirty water; in polite language, to annoy, to request, to ask a favor of.

拜丨 to intreat of.
丨托 to be obliged for, to ask a kindness of.
焉能丨我哉 how can you defile me?

The second is also read ʿmien. Flowing water.

河水丨丨 the river current flows smoothly by.

妹 méi' From *woman* and *not yet*.

A younger sister; a sister; an old name of the capital of Cheu-sin, now K'i in Wéi-hwui fu in the north of Honan, still retained in the village of 丨鄉 near Shansi.

小丨 or 丨丨 one's sister.
外丨 half sister on a father's side.
兄丨 brothers and sisters.
歸丨 a woman's marriage arrangements; the last diagram, meaning finished, ended.
令丨 your sister.
表丨 female cousins of different surname.
丨夫 or 丨丈 or 丨婿 my or a younger sister's husband.

In *Cantonese*. A girl; a woman.

丨仔 a girl, usually one bought.
使丨 a servant-girl.
盲丨 a blind songstress.
蛋家丨 the tanka boat-women.

昧 méi' From *day* and *not yet*.

No sun; dark, obscure, difficult to distinguish things; perfidious; the mind not clear about a thing.

明丨 clear and bright; transparent.
丨爽 and 丨谷 dawn and dusk.
丨頁 or 丨心 to go against conscience, to deceive one's heart.
三丨眞火 denotes mental energy, eliciting the real fire, and thus repressing disease or pain; — a trick of the Rationalists.
丨丨我思之 I have deeply pondered on it.

魅 méi' An ogre or demon brute of the woods; a brownie, with a man's face and four legs.

髟 méi' From *demon* and *hair;* similar to the last.

The manes of a thing; a gnome which beguiles people into danger.

瑁 méi' Tortoise-shell.

玳丨 or 瑇丨 the precious tortoise or turtle shell; marbled, clouded, like shell.

玳丨石斑魚 the marbled garoupa. (*Serranus megachir.*)

Read mao' A kind of cover for a scepter or signet, used in ancient times by the monarch in some way to test the batons of the princes.

韎 méi' A kind of leather buskin of soldiers; a plant used to dye purple.

媚 méi' From *woman* and *eyebrow*.

Smirking, ogling, smiling, attractive; to speak soft words; to adulate; to flatter; sycophantic; dalliance, blandishment; passionate glances; to think of lovingly.

狐丨 seductive, alluring.
諂丨 to toady, to flatter.
公之丨子從公于狩 the ruler's favorites go with him to the chase.
嬌丨 fascinating, exciting love.
側丨 to stick to one for base ends.
思丨其婦 they think fondly of their wives.
丨態 the mincing gait of a pretty woman.

In *Cantonese*. To close; to purse up the mouth; to keep still.

袂 méi' From *clothes* and *to divide*.

A sleeve, along whose edges ladies display embroidery; to draw back the sleeve; to open out.

分 丨 to take leave of one.
把 丨 to seize the sleeve, as at meeting a friend to detain him.
短右丨所以便作事 [Confucius] made his right sleeve short, that he might easily attend to business.
攘 丨 to roll up the sleeve.

寐 *méi*' From an old form of 夢 to *dream* and 未 *not yet*.
To rest from labor and doze; to sleep; to lose one's ideas.
寤而不丨 uneasy, disturbed sleep.
夙興夜丨 rising early and late to bed.
丨水舂牆 to dive under water and lay a wall; — *met.* hard labor. (*Cantonese.*)
夢丨 to dream

假丨 to nod, to pretend to sleep.
假丨永歎 I lie down undressed, and am sighing constantly.

穤 *méi*' From *grain* and *black*.
Grain injured and mildewed by the rain; smutty grain, covered with black spots.

抹 *méi*' To feel with the hand.

痗 *méi*' Anxiety causing illness; disease induced by care; fading, as color of a dress.
願言思伯使我心丨 as I longingly think of my lord, it makes my heart ache.
痰丨 sick from vexation and multiplied cares.

塺 *méi*' Dust; dusty.
丨丨 the air full of dust.
氛霧其如丨 the misty fog is thick as dust.

眛 *méi*' Color blind; unable clearly to distinguish the various colors.
盲丨 dimness of vision preventing one discriminating colors.

眑 *méi*' Interchanged with *huh*, 曶, and more in use, but the two are somewhat unlike.
The eyes growing long sighted through age; to see dimly; long in time; vanishing, passing off, as an indistinct sight; to eye askance.
丨昕 the morning light, when one looks up and thinks.

MEU.

Old sounds, mu *and* mút. *In Canton,* mau; — *in Swatow,* mau, mong, mỏ, mⁿò, *and* bò; — *in Amoy,* bo *and* bau; — *in Fukchau,* mau, móu, mu, *and* maiu; — *in Shanghai,* mù, 'm, *and* mo; — *in Chifu,* mu.

謀 *ₛmeu* From *words* and *certain*.
A stratagem, a device, an artifice; to plot, to make plans; to obtain; to ponder, to deliberate, to consult with; to contrive.
丨害 to plot against.
奇丨 a cunning scheme.
營丨 or 丨生 to plan how to get a living.
丨反 or 丨叛 to cabal; traitorous plots.
丨略 a plan, a stratagem.
丨事在人成事在天 the planning is with man, but the completion is with Heaven.
丨慮 to meditate carefully on.
丨面 to be acquainted with, to see or mark one's features.
丨財 to lay schemes to get people's wealth.
丨殺 to contrive or compass a murder.

爲人丨 to consult with others.
圖丨 to contrive, to plan.
主丨 the contriver of a plot.
丨士 a clever adviser, like Ahithopel.

蟱 *ₛmeu* A species of spider the 蚰丨, an *Epeira*, otherwise called 草蜘蛛 or grass spider, which weaves its nest on plants; its web is regarded as noxious.

矛 *ₛmeu* *ₛmao* The character is thought to represent a three clawed halberd, such as were stuck in chariots; it forms the 110th radical of characters denoting spears.
A lance with a narrow head; a spear.
自相丨盾 the spear and shield oppose each other; — *i. e.* it is a self-contradiction, a solecism.
天丨 star β in Boötes.
丨鎗 spears and javelins.

牟 *ₛmeu* From 牛 *ox* and 口 *mouth* above to represent breath; interchanged with the next two.
To low, to bellow; to usurp, to incroach on; to surpass; to like; to double; a vessel in temples to hold grain; barley; a weevil; the pupil of the eye.
丨利 to get gain.
丨賊 a fly which eats the blade of grain; *met.* thieves, blacklegs.
丨鳴 to low; the lowing of kine.
侵丨 to usurp.
中丨縣 in K'ai-fung fu is the old 丨州, a small feudal state in Honan.
貽我來丨 conferring on us the wheat and barley.

麰 *ₛmeu* Barley; also called 大麥, or great wheat.
丨麥 barley; it can either be cooked for food, or vinegar can be made of it, or sweetmeats.

眸 ˏmeu The pupil of the eye; the eye.
明丨 a bright eye.
丨子 the apple of the eye.
丨子不用僞 the eye cannot play the hypocrite.
堯舜參丨子 Yao and Shun both had a double iris.
凝丨 a fixed eye, as when watching narrowly.
存乎人者莫良于丨子 of all parts of the body, there is none more excellent than the pupil.

菽 ˏmeu Small bushy plants.
丨蕿根 a liliaceous plant found in damp places, with ensiform leaves and red flowers; the roots are warm like sweet flag, and are made into a powder.

侔 ˏmeu Equal, of the same sort or class; to accord with.
丨莫 to exert great effort.
逈不相丨 they are utterly dissimilar.
造物不丨 all things are not made alike.
畸於人而丨於天 the unequal pertains to man, but Heaven has things in harmony.

蛑 ˏmeu An enormous crab, called 蝤丨, so big that it can nip a tiger; perhaps a gigantic cuttle-fish is alluded to.

髳 ˏmeu An old name for Ting-yuen hien in the northern part of Yunnan was 丨州; it lay on a small tributary of the Yangtsz' River; this was one of the wild tribes which helped Wu Wang against the Shang dynasty, and perhaps the name has been retained in its old location.

鍪 ˏmeu An iron pan or boiler; a hin case or plating inside of a cap to protect the head.
兜丨 a kind of helmet with a flaring rim.

某 厶 ʿmeu ʿmu From *wood* and *sweet*, an old form of 梅 the sour plum; the contracted form is like *sz'* 厶 private.
Sour fruit; a certain person or thing, used when its name is unknown, or respect or caution forbids the use; and also for I; used as a blank, by writing one or more of the contracted form instead of the characters which are to be filled in.
丨月丨日 such a month and day.
丨做的 I did it; who did it?
丨人 a certain person, that party.
打丨 to emphasize a passage by adding 一連丨 a row on the side of the column, equivalent to capitalizing it.
丨在斯 I am here.
丨何爲哉 what does such an one do?
丨人來 nobody has come. (*Cantonese.*)
子善于丨乎 which [dish] do you, Sir, like best?

畝 畞 ʿmeu ʿmu From 田 *field* and 每 *each* altered.
A Chinese acre, which has varied at different ages, and now varies in different provinces; it measures 240 square 步, which makes 733⅓ square yards, or 6.6 ʿ*meu* equal to an English acre; but in fact, it takes 4.766 at Amoy, 6 at Shanghai, and 6.61 further north; the average is 6 to 6.1 ʿ*meu* to an English acre; fields, arable land; in the fields; to mark out fields.
一丨地 an acre of ground.
稅丨 taxable fields.
丨丘 a cultivated terrace.
實丨實籍 laying out the fields and collecting the revenue.
不服田丨 not to cultivate the fields.
半丨方塘 just a small half-acre fish-pond.
延桑數十丨 the mulberries stretch on for acres.

牡 ʿmeu ʿmu From *ox* and *earth.*
The male of quadrupeds and of a few plants, — seldom of birds; a bull; a stallion; a screw or bolt; part of a Chinese lock which slides in; a piston.
牝丨 female and male.
於薦廣丨 while I present this noble bull.
丨丹茶 a large variety of the camellia, so named from a likeness to the Chinese peony 丨丹花 *Pœonia mowtan.*
雉鳴求其丨 the hen pheasant cries to her mate.
門丨 bolt of a door.
四丨有驕 the four steeds were strong.

拇 蹈 ʿmeu From *hand* or *foot* and *mother.*
The thumb; the great toe.
駢丨 an odd or sixth thumb or toe.
大丨指 the thumb.

瞀 meuʾ To look at closely; to go with the head low, as near-sighted people do; to look down; dim, indistinct vision; disheveled, as hair; dull, ignorant.
是非丨亂 to confound right and wrong.
丨視 sight confused and wearied.
丨丨然 timid, bashful, afraid to look in the face.
淚目矇丨 eyes obscured with tears.

Read *muh*, Hard to see at night.
雀丨 night blindness.

袤 meuʾ The part of a dress above the girdle, a waist; long; a stretch from north to south.
着丨服者 he wears a long gown.
廣丨 the entire extent of a region, the four points of the compass.
延丨數十里 [the mountain] stretched along from north to south scores of miles.

楙 *meu'*

From *forest* and *dart*.

Luxuriant, as a forest; an old name for the 木瓜 which probably refers to the quince rather than the papaya.

懋 *meu'*

From *luxuriant* and *heart*; occurs interchanged with the last and the next.

To exert one's mind; force of purpose; to be or make great; high principled; energetic; to labor strenuously; luxuriant.

予丨乃德 I am convinced how great is your virtue.

丨修 earnest efforts to correct what is wrong.

功丨丨賞 to persons of great merit, he gave great rewards.

茂 *meu'* *mao'*

From *plant* and *flourishing*.

Exuberant, thrifty foliage; flourishing, highly developed, a high rank or quality of; elegant, fine, a term of praise often used in names; to exert, to endeavor after; healthy, vigorous, strong; a group of five persons; used for grain when ripe.

丨盛 luxuriant, exuberant.

丨繁 or 丨衍 numerous, as progeny.

丨才 fine, varied talents.

方丨爾惡 now your wickedness is rampant.

秀丨 beautiful verdure or foliage.

丨正其德 he sedulously cultivated his virtue.

子之丨兮 how skillful you are?

丨州 a large prefecture in the northwest of Sz'chʻuen on the River Min.

貿 *meu'* *mao'*

To barter, to exchange, to deal; to do business, to carry on commerce.

互丨 commercial dealings.

丨易 trade, interchange of articles.

丨丨 obscure vision; unenlightened and callous.

鄮 *meu'*

Name of a city and region in the Han dynasty, now occupied by Ningpo prefecture, especially the districts of Fung-hwa and Tsz'-yü.

MI.

Old sounds, mai, mei, *and* mi. *In Canton*, mei, mi, *and* ni; — *in Swatow*, mi, bi, *and* ni; — *in Amoy*, bi, bé, *and* ji; *in Fuhchau*, mi, pʻi, mé, *and* né; — *in Shanghai*, mi; — *in Chifu*, mi.

迷 *ˏmi*

From to *go* and *rice*; it can easily be confounded with *shuh*, 述 to narrate.

To deceive, to delude; to bewitch, to fascinate; confused, perturbed; stupefied, beclouded; blinded, as by vice; mad after, infatuated; besotted by.

丨惑 deceived by, seduced.

丨魂陣 infatuated by, fooled, out of one's mind, bewildered.

昏丨不醒 dead to all remonstrance.

丨拐人口 to bewitch and carry off or kidnap people, — as by cozening and charms.

威儀卒丨 to depart utterly from all proper demeanor.

丨失物件 to carelessly mislay a thing.

鬼丨 crazed, possessed.

丨丨濛濛 a thick shade; overcast, cloudy.

丨路 out of the right road.

執丨不悟 stolidly and willfully dull.

財丨 mad after riches.

烈風雷雨弗丨 [Shun] was never discomposed in the most terrible thunder storm.

彌 *ˏmi*

From 弓 *bow* and 璽 a *seal* contracted.

A bow discharged; to shoot an arrow; to reach everywhere, to pervade; to prevent, to close up, to stop; to complete; full, universal; an *adjective* of comparison like 愈 more, still; long; distant, prolonged.

丨多 very many.

丨遠 still further.

丨月 a month old.

丨縫 to patch up, to disguise, to screen from.

丨縫不過 the patch is too small.

丨災 to use charms or take precautions against evil.

仰之丨高 this doctrine constantly grows more exalted to my mind.

俾爾丨爾性 may you [O king,] complete all your years!

丨丨 in a small degree.

丨勒佛 Maitreya, the expected Budha, who already controls the Budhist faith, and is believed by some to have been incarnate in Djetar; his name is explained by 慈氏 the compassionate name.

蘼 *ˏmi*

A plant called 莢丨 whose leaves resemble elm seeds, growing in pairs; it may be allied to the *Bauhinia*; another description says the seeds are red and edible, and that a pleasant soup can be made by boiling the twigs and adding rice to the broth; the bark can be made into cordage.

瀰 *ˏmi*

A vast expanse of waters.

河水丨丨 wide and full is the River.

渺丨 an ocean-like waste of waters.

有丨盈濟 the ford is full to overflowing.

獼 ꜀mi A she monkey.

丨猴 a monkey of any sort.

丨猴桃 the monkey peach, a drupaceous fruit common in Nganhwui, resembling the peach in shape and seed, firm flesh, and rather harsh; the leaf is like the persimmon; in Honan it is called 胡自賴 what is it like?

麛 ꜀mi A fawn; it is also applied to the new-born young of other quadrupeds.

丨裘 skins or furs of unyeaned fawns or lambs.

不取丨卵 [in hunting,] do not take the young or the eggs.

麋 ꜀mi From *deer* and *rice* or 迷 to *deceive* contracted.

A large species of deer with a short neck, that frequents marshy woods in herds; the description likens it to the elk; a grassy place on the banks of a river; the plain brown deer (*Rusa Swinhoii*) of Formosa.

沈牛麈丨 the cattle, elks, and stags hid themselves — in the wood.

丨茸 elk's horns, deemed inferior to deer's horns in efficacy.

丨鹿 a stag.

犨丨 an ugly awkward person.

居河之丨 like those who live on the river's bank.

蘼 ꜀mi A kind of rose called 薔丨 resembling the cinnamon rose.

秋蘭兮丨蕪 what an ornament to autumn is the Angelica flower.

糜 ꜀mi Rice gruel, thin congee; macerated, dissolved by the action of fire or water; scum; entirely.

丨粥 rice boiled to congee.

丨爛 boiled to a pulpy mass; *met.* harassed, as by destructive wars; oppressed, harried to death.

丨費 extravagant waste.

國家丨敝 the state is utterly ruined.

煲起層丨 a scum floats on the top after boiling. (*Cantonese.*)

無不滅 an utter destruction.

縻 ꜀mi Used for the last.

Boiled to pieces; entirely macerated; consumed, destroyed, as a people by oppression.

縻 ꜀mi A halter for an ox; to tie up; to ally, to bind to one.

羈丨不絕 bound by a strong alliance.

醾 ꜀mi A kind of liquor, called 酴丨 made from grain by distillation, and drank without straining; it resembles double-brewed malt; the name is derived from a small yellow rose.

罙 ꜀mi From 网 a *net* contracted, and 米 *rice*, intimating the way a net covers things.

Universal, around; to enter and go all about; deep; rash, venturesome.

扜丨 a state in the Han dynasty lying near the present Kokand.

丨增兢惶 in the deepest fear and distress.

米 ꜂mi The character represents four *grains* on the figure 十 *ten*; it forms the 119th radical of characters relating to rice, its growth and uses.

Rice after it is hulled; small grains of other plants, even including millet, maize, and grass; a seed, a kernel; food; small things like rice, as 槐丨 Sophora flowers, or 蝦丨 dried prawns.

小丨 or 辛丨 canary seed, the grain of yellow millet. (*Setaria.*)

丨粉 rice flour.

爆丨花 popped rice.

丨眼 white sores growing on the side of the nail.

西丨 or 砂穀丨 sago.

紅穀丨 red rice.

食失丨 he's not worth his rice.

不知丨價 he does not even know the price of rice; — inexperienced.

丨牛 the *Curculio* or weevil.

舂丨牛 a nickname for one who hulls rice.

一稃二丨 two kernels in one glume.

粒丨如珍 [in famine] a grain of rice is like a pearl.

倒丨壽星 the affair is all spoiled.

丨色 a straw color.

巧媳婦作不出沒丨粥 a clever wife even cannot make congee without rice; the last three words also mean gabble, blarney.

丨飯 allowance for table expenses.

呀蘭丨 cochineal.

一個丨 one allowance of rice, *i. e.* to graduates of the first degree. (*Pekingese.*)

In *Cantonese*, used for 莫 Do not; not.

丨個做 don't do that yet.

丨反 don't idle.

丨來自 wait a little, stop a moment.

敉 侎 ꜂mi From to *tap* and *man* or *rice*.

To soothe, to pacify, to like; to settle, to establish.

丨寧武圖功 to restore peace and perpetuate the plans — of my father.

丨栽兵 to quiet the seditious troops.

眯 ꜂mi Sand or dust in the eye, obscuring the vision; the nightmare.

丨眼 an irritable tender eye; granulations in it.

丨了眼睛 it blinds the eyes.

播糠丨目 to winnow chaff blinds the eyes.

處蒙塵而欲不丨 if you get to that dusty place, you cannot avoid getting your eyes blinded.

靡 ꜀mi ꜂mi From *not* and *hemp*.
Laid out, spread abroad, dispersed; soldiers fleeing and defeated; to divide; overturned; poured out; not, without, not having; to implicate in crime; profuse, showy, extravagant; small, petty, selfish.
丨丨 slowly.
無丨費 no waste of it.
丨日不思 to reflect on it each day.
天命丨常 the decrees of Heaven are not fixed.
丨然從風 to go with the fashion of the multitude.
吾與爾丨之 I will divide it with you.
丨麗紛華 showy and elegant.
侈丨 prodigal.
丨封丨于爾邦 do not bring your country into peril.

䭧 ꜀mi ꜂mi To feed an infant by hand, to give it congee.

穈 ꜀méi ꜂méi From *millet* and *hemp*.
A name for a variety of 黍 or small glutinous millet (*Milium*) of which spirit is made; it is now used chiefly in Chihli for 丨子米 the seed of the millet, and is not so frequently applied to the growing grain.

洣 ꜂mi An important affluent of the River Siang in Hunan, flowing into it from the east near Hăng-shan hien; it drains a well watered region.

鮇 ꜀mi ꜂mi From *fish* and *rice*; referring to its granular appearance.
Fish-spawn, called 丨鯢 in some places, but more commonly 魚子 or fish-young.

芈 ꜀mi ꜂mi From *sheep* and *breath* issuing forth.
The bleating of a sheep, now usually written 咩; a famous man in the state of Tsu.

弭 ꜀mi ꜂mi From *bow* and *ear*.
A bow without ornaments; at ease, resting; unbent, as a bow; to desist, to stop; to forget; to destroy, to put down.
丨盜安良 to keep down the seditious and quiet the loyal.
消丨時災 to remove the present calamities.
丨暈 a halo around the moon.
象丨魚服 the ivory-tipped bow and shagreen quiver.
心之憂矣不可丨忘 the sorrows of my heart cannot be repressed or forgotten.
丨耳 pendulous ears.

謎 mi꜄ From *words* and to *mislead*.
A riddle, a conundrum, an enigma; to puzzle, to quiz.
丨語 a hint, a double entendre.
打燈丨 puzzling writing put on lanterns.
啞丨 or 隱丨 enigmatical sentences.

MIAO.

Old sounds, mio *and* mok. *In Canton*, miu; — *in Swatow*, miô, ngiô, biê, *and* biô; — *in Amoy*, biao; — *in Fuhchau*, miéu; — *in Shanghai*, mio; — *in Chifu*, miao.

苗 ꜁miao ꜁miao From *plant* and a *field*.
The tender blade of herbs and grass, especially of grain; sprouts; suckers; descendants, progeny; the issues of, the outgoings; an index, as the tongue of the health; the emperor's summer hunt; in Yunnan, 16 cowries made one *miao*.
丨裔 posterity.
銅丨 the pipe at the end of a hose to direct the jet.
禾丨 paddy shoots.
丨子 the Miaotsz' aborigines in Kwéichau; they were anciently described as men having wings on their thighs, and ignorant of all propriety.
生丨 are the savage, and 熟丨 the subdued, aborigines.
之子于丨 those officers who went to the hunt.
魚丨 minnows, small fry.
功臣丨緒 a worthy statesman succeeded by his son.
愛花丨 to love finery and display.
態度丨條 her style and figure are both elegant.
黎丨 many; prolific, like shoots.
蘿蔔丨 radish sprouts, used as greens.
舌乃心之丨也 the tongue is the exponent of the heart.
勿心丨 unhappy, troubled, grieved. (*Shanghai.*)

In *Pekingese*. The flame, as of a lamp; a blaze.
火丨太高 the lamp is too high.

緢 ꜁miao ꜁miao To wind off silk; the fringe attached to a flag.

媌 ꜁miao ꜁miao Light and beautiful, sylph-like, bright eyed; in Amoy, 娼丨 means a strumpet, but in Kiangsi the word has a good meaning.

𧊅 ꜁miao ꜁miao Silkworms just emerging from their eggs.
蠶丨 or 蠶苗 the worms hatched out.

描 ꜁miao ꜁miao From *hand* and *blade*; it is wrongly used at Canton for the next.
To trace, to limn, to draw; to design, to sketch, to outline; to copy paintings; to strike; to throw away.

丨畫 to paint or sketch.
丨金 to gild; to make pictures in gold, as on lackered-ware.
淡丨 blue flowered, as porcelain.
丨摹一様 take an exact copy.
丨眉 to paint the eyebrows, alludes to conjugal love.
心丨萬里江山 the mind can delineate distant scenes.
丨寫 or 丨情事 to describe well; word painting.

眇 ˋmiao From *eye* and *few*; occurs used for 妙ˋ small.
One eye small or contracted and deep sunk; to look at with one eye, or eyes drawn up; to glance at; to take aim; small, the fag end; subtle; all, nothing more or better.
丨能視 a one-eyed man can still see.
丨身 my unworthy self.
丨一目 one-eyed; a cyclops.
幼丨 minute, very fine, delicate.
丨然有身 most minute is this single person, — amid the vast creation.
丨靶 to aim at the target.
丨中ˋ紅心 aim at the red eye.
微丨 fine, as the lines on a sector.
丨丨予末小子 I am insignificant, only a mere child.

緲 ˋmiao Occurs interchanged with the last.
Minute, indistinct; dissipating; vanishing.
丨微 a nothing, an atom.
香烟縹丨 the incense diffuses itself little by little.

渺 ˋmiao From *water* and *to glance at.*
The vast, dazzling, and indistinct appearance of the ocean; vague, boundless.
丨茫 confounding, misty; hardly the subject of proof, doubtful and vague.
丨丨乎 how boundless!
丨丨兮余懷 how inexplicable are my thoughts!

淼 ˋmiao Formed of *water* thrice repeated.
The vastness of the sea; synonymous with the last in the phrase 丨茫 vast.
海闊丨難卽 the wide sea is not easily crossed

杪 ˋmiao From *wood* and *few*.
The tapering end of a tree or post; a small branch; the limit of, the end of a year or season.
歲丨 end of the year.
林丨 edge of the forest.
枝丨 end of a branch.
丨末 the little end, as of a post.

秒 ˋmiao The beard of grain; minute; a second in a degree; in *decimals*, a ten-thousandth, next to *hwuh*, 忽 a floss.
造計丨忽 he counts the least mite; — avaricious.

仯 ˋmiao Small.
僬丨 delicate, tender.
Read ˏch'ao. Alarmed.
驚丨 frightened, as when suddenly surprised.

藐 ˋmiao From *plant* and *aspect* of.
A plant yielding a purple dye; petty, contemptible, small; far off; to slight, to treat haughtily, to look down on; supercilious.
丨視 to disdain; to look coldly.
輕丨 to disregard, as a law.
欺丨 to insult, to show contempt.
丨人 to despise others.
丨丨㣲 dull, thick-headed; also, beautiful.
見大人則丨之 before a magnate, one must rather slight him, *i. e.* not lose one's self-possession.

妙ˋ 玅 miaoˋ From *woman* or *somber* and *small*; the second is used by Taoists to denote the profundity of their doctrines.
An adjective of admiration; perfect, excellent, capital; wonderful; subtle, mysterious, difficult to fathom; spiritual, supernatural; to beautify; to penetrate, as a spirit does what it is supposed to influence.
丨事 a fine affair.
丨計 a capital scheme.
丨品 a fine thing, a rarity.
丨手 a skilled artist or physician.
丨年 a youth, a minor.
丨藥 a wonderful remedy, an excellent medicine.
精丨 admirable, ingenious.
丨化 subtle or divine influence.
奇丨 surprisingly clever.

廟ˋ 庙ˋ miaoˋ From *covering* and *to have an audience*; the second is a common contraction.
To honor the gods; a temple containing ancestors or gods, a fane; front hall of a palace; the Budhists use it for the Sanscrit *chaitya*, and include tombs, topes, and other objects of religious worship.
家丨 or 祖丨 an ancestral temple.
奕奕寢丨君子作之 very grand is the ancestral hall, which our prince made.
太丨 the imperial ancestral temple.
神丨 an idol temple.
廊丨之器 a vessel for a palace; — *met.* a likely, rising man.
丨堂之上 the government.
丨見 a bride's worship of her husband's ancestors.
丨祝 a sexton, a temple curator.
香火丨 a popular temple, one much frequented.
丨號 the emperor's temple name.
宮室宗丨 the emperor's palaces and temples.
逛丨 to visit temples.
丨宇 temples of every kind.

In *Pekingese*. A fair, because they are often held in temples.
明天有丨 a fair will be held to-morrow.
趕丨 to attend a fair.

MIEH.

Old sounds, mit *and* met. *In Canton*, mít; — *in Swatow*, mít *and* bi; — *in Amoy*, biat; — *in Fuhchau*, miek; — *in Shanghai*, mih; — *in Chifu*, mié.

蔑, *mieh'* Composed of 苜 *heavy eyes* and 戍 the *evening* hour, to intimate the sleepy feeling of a tired laborer; used with the next.

Not, without; minute, worthless; to throw away, to discard; to pare, to scrape thin.

丨禮 without manners.

不丨民功 do not overlook merit among the people.

丨有 none at all.

人勞則丨然 wearied with toil.

丨然無言 he never uttered a word.

丨星 minute stars, star-dust.

人烟寂丨 the inhabitants are all extinct.

滅, 威, *mieh'* From *water* and to *destroy*; the original form, now disused except as a primitive, is composed of 火 *fire* under the horary character *süh*, 戌, denoting combustion going out at evening.

Destroyed by fire; fire gone out; to exterminate, to cut off; to finish by destroying; to put out, as a fire.

丨燈 put out the lamp.

燈丨 the lamp has gone out.

打丨 or 撲丨 beat out the fire.

勦丨 to exterminate utterly; to raze, to root out.

丨跡 destroyed all the evidence.

自取丨亡 he brought on his own ruin.

盡丨其類 he extinguished the whole race.

過涉丨頂 the water was over my head when I crossed the ferry.

淡丨丨 very insipid. (*Cantonese.*)

丨掉 destroyed them utterly, as banditti.

搣, *mieh'* To pluck up; to pull off; to peel; to rub, to work with; to pinch.

丨耳 to pull the ears.

丨紙 peel off the paper.

丨面珠 to pinch the cheeks.

揃丨 to pluck out, as stray hairs from the eyebrows.

蠛, *mieh'* Sand flies or ephemera, called 丨蠓 generated in damp places, and seen flying about stagnant pools; the sun destroys them.

篾, *mieh'* Bamboos or reeds split into strips; splints for baskets; hoop slats, splinters, lath-like rods; skin of the bamboo; slim, as the end of a twig.

一條箍丨 a hoop.

竹丨 or 丨青 bamboo splints.

紙丨 young bamboos when fit for making paper.

丨蓆 coarse mats woven of bamboo.

丨車 a basket carriage.

丨片的客 a man who sorns, a hanger-on, a lackey.

衊, *mieh'* Blood or gore; the nose-bleed; to defile, as by smearing; polluted, desecrated.

誣丨 to calumniate, to asperse and blacken.

污丨宗室 he vilely defamed his ancestors, — or their hall.

血丨 to stain with blood.

櫗, *mieh'* To beat.

丨楔 irregular in any way, as in morals, bearing, or position; badly done; awry, not square.

MIEN.

Old sounds, mien *and* min. *In Canton*, mín; — *in Swatow*, mien, mi, *and* mín; — *in Amoy*, bian; — *in Fuhchau*, mieng; — *in Shanghai*, mi^n; — *in Chifu*, mien.

綿, 緜, *mien* From *silk* and *pure silk*; this and the next are interchanged.

Soft, cottony, like fine floss or raw silk; a floculence in an otherwise limpid substance; drawn out, prolonged, extended, as a thread or fibre; lasting, uninterrupted, enduring; soft, ripening, as fruit; weak; thick; close.

丨絮 floss, soft fibres.

丨丨不絕 continuous, unbroken, as a genealogy; said of creepers, an army marching, or any other continuous succession.

言語纏丨 interminable talk; garrulous.

絲丨 refuse silk.

丨柔 delicate, soft.

丨蠻黃鳥 the warbling little oriole.

軟如丨 delicate, weak as floss.

丨裏針 [a hard spot] like a needle in cotton.

連丨 continued succession, as a drizzling rain or of passers-by.

丨州 an inferior prefecture in the north of Sz'ch'uen, in the valley of the River Feu.

丨力 not strong.

丨子 silk wadding or quilt.

福壽丨長 may your happines and life be lastingly prolonged.

棉 ˏmien From *wood* and *silky*; used with the last.

The cotton plant, probably so called from the resemblance of its fibres to those of the native 木丨 cotton tree (*Bombax ceiba*); it was called 古貝 or 吉貝 by those who described it about A. D. 670, a name probably altered from the Sanscrit *karpasi*.

丨花 raw cotton.

丨襖 a wadded jacket.

丨胎 a cotton quilt.

坐丨花包 like sitting on a cotton bale; — secure, stable.

眠 ˏmien From *eye* and *people* as the phonetic; its resemblance to ʻyen 眼 the eye, often confuses.

To sleep; to close the eyes; to hang down the head; the sleep of animals; dim vision; bewildered; the molting of silkworms, when they sleep.

丨牀 a settee, a couch, a sofa.

柳丨 the drooping or pendent willow.

丨牛[illegible] a sleeping cow's form, is regarded as a lucky spot for a grave.

長丨 the long sleep — death; particularly applied to the death of a monarch.

丨得幾闊 you use just so much room to sleep in; — *i. e.* enough is all that is necessary.

竟夕不丨 I did not sleep at all during the night.

蠶丨 the sleep of silkworms.

丨娗 to play together.

宀 ˏmien The dot represents a cover over a *shelter*, such as savages make; it is the 40th radical of characters relating mostly to dwellings.

A shelter, more rude than a cave 穴 or a hole in a hill-side; or a mere leafy thatch, used before houses were built.

愐 ʻmien To reflect, to consider maturely; to recall to mind.

丨愌 ingenuous; bashful.

免 ʻmien A contraction of 兔 a *hare*.

To get off, to evade; to put away, to free from, to dispense with; to forego, to excuse, to spare; to avoid; to dodge; escaped from; to remove, as from office; a negative, do not, no need of.

丨冠 to take off the hat.

丨罪 to forgive an offense.

丨見 he need not come in, said to a visitor.

丨不了寫字 you cannot well avoid writing.

丨例 to elude the law.

丨勞 don't trouble yourself, do not put yourself out of the way.

丨戰 to decline battle.

丨來 he need not come.

丨粮 to remit the taxes.

丨致他來 saved his coming here.

未丨費身 he spares no labor or pains.

幾乎不丨 just barely escaped.

臨難無苟丨 you cannot evade the hour of trouble by force.

脫丨 to escape from.

Read *wan'* and like the next. To bear a son; anything new and fresh.

喪丨 disheveled hair, as a mourner's.

陳丨 stale, not fresh.

挽 ʻmien To bear a son.

分丨 or 分娩 parturition; to be brought to bed.

勉 ʻmien From *strength* and to *evade* as the phonetic.

To force one's self; unpleasant to the feelings; constrained, urged by circumstances; to animate, to urge, to persuade; to put forth effort.

丨强 unwilling to do, by constraint.

丨力 diligent, strenuous.

奮丨 urgent effort; to stir one up.

勸丨 to animate by words.

丨丨我王 ever active is our king.

俛 ʻmien To put down the head.

丨首 to hang down the head.

丨啄 to stoop and peck.

鮸 ʻmien A yellow fish called in Peking 石首魚 from two small white bones in its head; it is brought from the sea and Corean isles; the sound is fit for making glue; it is probably akin to the sea bass.

冕 ʻmien A crown, a coronet; the diadem of the Cheu emperors was shaped like a trencher; most of them had rows of pendents before and behind, whose number indicated the wearer's rank; each sort ha[s] its own name; its form resembled a Cantab's cap.

堂皇冠丨 an imperial, noble bearing.

做得冠丨 it was finely and royally done.

麻丨 a kind of linen mitre.

端丨 a crown properly worn.

露丨馳驅 your coronet has been seen in many campaigns; said of a vigorous ruler.

丏 ʻmien The character is supposed to represent a wall to screen one; not the same as *kai'* 丐 to beg.

An embrasure or curtain to ward off arrows; screened, hid, out of view.

沔 ʻmien Overflowing banks; a flood bursting through barriers; a mighty stream; a name of the River Han near its junction with the Yangtsz' River, but more accurately of a reach or lake west of the junction, which gives its name to the two districts of 丨陽州 and 丨縣 situated near it.

丨彼流水朝宗于海 Lo! this mighty current goes to its audience with the ocean.

'眄 *'mien* To half shut the eye, to look at askance; to ogle, to cast glances.

眳藐流丨一顧傾城 she cast her ogling glances on him, and at once the city was lost.

按劍相丨 they grasped their swords and surveyed each other.

'緬 *'mien* Fine silk thread; to think of the absent; to reflect; to imagine; light.

丨然 longing for one.

丨思 or 丨想 to remember the absent.

丨甸國 the kingdom of Burmah; it is intended as an imitation of the first syllable of Myanma; Marco Polo speaks of Amien or Mien as the chief city of the country, called Ta-kung in Chinese for Ta-goung, which seems to refer to the town of Paghan, whose ruins still attest the power of their builders; it lies near the Irrawadi River in lat. 23° 25′ N.

'湎 *'mien* Sunk in excess; flushed with liquor; drunk, intoxicated; addicted to.

天不丨爾於酒 Heaven does not flush your face with drink.

流丨忘本 so given to drink that he had lost all character.

丨丨紛紛 grand and general.

'勔 *'mien* To stimulate, to urge on, to excite.

劭丨 to endeavor after, to encourage one's self.

面 *mien'* The original form bears a rude resemblance to the face, having the eyes in the center of a profile and the forehead above; it forms the 176th radical of a small natural group of characters.

The visage, the countenance; the front, the top, the surface; a plane, the surface in which a machine works; a side; the forward part, the side towards one; face to face, in one's presence; the south; honor, character, reputation; the look of a thing; to front, to face; to show the face, to see one; personally; a classifier of drums, mirrors, and gongs; following words meaning portions of water, it refers to their surface or extent.

丨貌 the expression.

丨目 the visage, the looks.

雍也可使南丨 Yung has virtue equal to ruling a kingdom

丨稽天若 he looked up and examined the mind of Heaven to follow it.

一丨之辭 a one-sided, ex-parte statement.

丨珠 the cheek or cheek-bone.

八丨 the four points of compass and their halves.

丨交 to give to personally.

丨向上 let the top be this side up.

丟丨 to lose face or reputation.

裏丨 inside, the inner surface.

當丨 to his face; facing, to face.

對丨 face to face, opposite.

一丨鏡 one looking-glass.

丨色 the complexion.

丨前 in sight, before one.

背丨 back to back; to his back.

丨奏 to state to the emperor.

半丨之識 I scarcely recognized him.

出必告返必丨 when you go out, tell your parents; when you return, let them see you.

一丨做 go and do it without referring to me.

丨皮厚 thickskinned, barefaced.

反丨 displeased with, turned against.

切丨 the surface of contact, as in mechanics.

你只管丨杳 then go and look for yourself.

一丨追緊一丨放鬆 one while he pursues them closely, and then again he is very slack.

丨丨相覷 they all stood gaping at each other, — not knowing what to do.

打照丨 I made him a visit.

數日不丨 I have not seen you for several days.

丨交之友 a face friend, a casual acquaintance.

丨東 facing the east.

白丨人 a good-looking man, one who has a fair face.

洋丨捕盜不力 they made no effort to seize the pirates in those seas.

偭 *mien'* To look towards; to accompany, to go with; to turn the back on.

麵 麪 *mien'* From *wheat* and *face* or *hid*; the the first is the commonest form.

Flour made from wheat, buckwheat, or oats; vermicelli.

上白丨 best white flour.

丨粉 or 麥丨 wheat flour.

丨食 pastry, puddings, the dessert of a dinner.

丨包 or 丨頭 a loaf of bread.

重羅白丨 twice-bolted white flour, the very best.

丨條 or 丨片 dough in strips or slices.

發丨 to raise bread.

黑丨 shorts and middlings.

丨灰 slaked lime for plastering.

揑丨人 to make little figures of flour or putty.

㴐 *mien'* A vast expanse of water is 滇丨, probably referring to Lake Tien in Yunnan.

滇丨淼漫 like the vast and open sea, a waste of waters.

MIH.

Old sounds, mít *and* mík. *In Canton*, măt, mik, *and* mat ; — *in Swatow*, mít *and* bat ; — *in Amoy*, bít *and* bek ; — *in Fuhchau*, mik ; — *in Shanghai*, mih ; — *in Chifu*, mi.

密, **峹**, *mi* } From *still* and *hill*; the second form is merely a common alteration of 必 in writing.

Hills forming an amphitheater, and surrounding a place; thick, close together; tight, as a wedge; fine, small; hidden, occult, mysterious; intimate, friendly; still, retired; secret, confidential, as an order; to hush; to stop or rest; to repeat; to ply; at Amoy used in native almanacs for every seventh day, which coincides with the still day or Christian sabbath; the word is probably derived from a western language.

｜交 intimate friendship.

親｜ constantly with one, nearly related.

秘｜ hidden; undivulged.

機｜ a moving cause; the real power, as in a state.

｜眼 close, fine interstices.

｜口 keep silent; hush!

｜言 a secret; private talk.

｜｜的 be quiet about it.

｜室 the inner or rear house.

｜縣 a district near K'ái-fung fu in Honan, an ancient principality.

細｜布疋 very finely woven cloth; close texture.

功夫嚴｜ to keep diligently at a work.

基命宥｜ to meditate in quietness on the decrees — of heaven.

｜湏 an ancient state in Kansuh, in the present P'ing-liang fu, on a branch of the River Wêi.

宓, *mi* From a *shelter* and *certainly*.

Still, silent; rest; to stop; quietly.

秦｜ a sage mentioned in the San Kwoh Chi.

｜汨 the disease has all gone.

樒, **榓**, *mi* } From *tree* and *hidden*.

A tree said to resemble the *Sophora* in form, found in Cambodia; when it is cut down, and the outer wood has rotted, the solid heart wood is taken out for its fragrance, and called 沉香 because it sinks in water; the lighter sort is called chicken bones 鷄骨, and the poorest common fragrance 棧香; it is the eagle-wood (*Aquilaria* or *Aloexylon*) of Eastern India.

蔤, *mi* The small rootlets of the Nelumbium, which grow from the joints of the rhizome.

蜜, *mi* Honey, nectar; sweet, sugary; honeyed, flattering.

蜂｜ or ｜糖 honey.

｜蠟 beeswax.

波羅｜ the jack-fruit.

飴｜ confectionary.

口有｜而腹有劍 his words were as honey, but his heart was like a sword.

｜餞砒礵 sweetmeats made with arsenic; — delusive words.

｜王 the queen bee.

幦, **幭**, *mi* } A leather screen or canopy for a cart, made of tiger's skin, and allowed only to grandees; the second also denotes a coverlet or overall.

簚, *mi* Similar to the preceding.

A covering for the front of a carriage, of which the 素｜ was made of white dog fur.

塓, *mi* To plaster a wall; to whitewash it.

圬人以時｜館宮室 the mason fits up the walls of the shops, halls, and houses at the proper times.

幎, *mi* From *kerchief* and *obscure*.

A veil to cover the face of the dead; a curtain; to veil.

｜目用緇 the covering for the eyes should be black.

謐, *mi* To speak quietly in a low tone, to whisper; quiet, still, careful, attentive.

寂｜ solitary and still.

｜然清靜 how peaceful and still!

寧｜如常 times are as quiet as usual; peace has returned.

覓, **覔**, *mi* } From to *see* and *not* or *claws*, indicating a search for; another says it was composed of 日 *sun* with 否 *not* above it.

To seek, to go about searching for; to hunt up, as a quotation.

｜句 to seek an apt phrase.

｜路 to seek the right road.

｜得 found it.

｜飲食 on the lookout for a meal.

｜索 to demand, as a bonus.

鑽頭｜縫 to watch for a good opportunity.

糸, *mi* The ancient form is intended to represent a skein of floss; it forms the 120th radical of silken fabrics, and is called 絞絲邊 or winding silk at the side.

Fine floss; the threads from five worms are reckoned to make half a 忽; anything small, delicate; connected.

冖, **冪**, **幂**, **鼏**, *mi* } The first is the 14th radical of a few characters meaning to cover, to overspread; the second and third a napkin to cover food; to veil, to cover with a cloth; the fourth a covering thrown over a dish containing sacrifices to protect them from dirt.

｜女 a waiting maid.

MIN.

Old sound, min. *In Canton*, măn ; — *in Swatow*, mín, mien, *and* man ; — *in Amoy*, bín, bún, ban, *and* sín ; — *in Fuhchau*, míng ; — *in Shanghai*, ming *and* măng ; — *in Chifu*, min.

民 ꜀min

Said to be a synonym of 萌 *sprouts*, because the people know no more than so many sprouts or young plants.

The people; the uninstructed mass, who grow up as plants without education; the common multitude, the unofficial part of mankind, of whom the prince is the mind, they are the body.

四 丨 the four classes of society.

下 丨 mankind; the vulgar.

化外頑 丨 the canaille, the degraded.

萬 丨 or 羣 丨 all our subjects; the masses, mankind.

子 丨 you my people; — said by the ruler.

軍 丨 人等 men of all classes, soldiers and common people.

良 丨 loyal people.

丨 風 popular customs.

丨 部 name of the Board of Revenue in the Sui dynasty.

丨 父母 a district magistrate.

勞 丨 傷財 he oppressed the poor and beggared the rich.

丨 籍 a census record, one's registration.

丨 壯 or 丨 丁 militia, volunteers.

丨 人 in Peking a Chinese, not a bannerman or a Manchu.

人 丨 mankind in general.

哀哉爲猶匪先 丨 是程 unhappily our leaders will not take the ancients for their pattern.

In *Cantonese*. The limit of a thing, the brink; the last moment, just in time; to go near the edge.

企得太 丨' he stands too near the edge.

丨' 尾 the last of.

行 丨' 過頭 you go too near the edge.

割好 丨' it is trimmed or cut very close, as a book.

緍 ꜀min

A net to catch pheasants or hares; to angle.

緡 ꜀min

A fish-line; a cord; to string cash on a cord; to bind on; to use garments as bedding; abundant; an ancient town in the southwest of Shansi, now Kao-p'ing hien 高平縣.

釣 丨 a fish-line.

丨 被 to throw one's clothes over the bed.

腰纏一 丨 he tied a string of cash around his waist.

罠 ꜀min

Somewhat similar to the last.

To entrap, to hook; a net to catch the hares, and wild hogs, and does.

岷 ꜀min

A range of mountains in the north of Sz'ch'uen; a spur of the range divides the valleys of the Yellow and Yangtsz' Rivers; it was the scene of Yü's labors.

丨 州 a small prefecture in the south of Kansuh.

丨 江 an affluent of the Yangtsz' River in the northwest of Sz'ch'uen.

珉 砇 碈 ꜀min

From *stone* and *mark*; *q.d.* the viened stone; the last form is also often met with.

A fine kind of stone, clouded alabaster; the last is also defined an inferior stone, a pebble.

白 丨 pure white alabaster.

丨 石 common alabaster.

丨 玉雜淆 stones and gems all mixed together, as among scholars of various talents.

忞 ꜀min

To force one's self to exertion, to practice self discipline; desires unattained.

丨 丨 distracted by cares.

旻 ꜀min

From *day* and a *mark*.

The autumnal sky as if it regretted the fall of the leaf; sad feelings; to feel melancholy.

丨 天疾威 compassionate Heaven arrayed in terrors.

苠 ꜀min

The skin of bamboo; a multitude, the people.

人 丨 丨 而處乎中 see what a mass of people, and they are all under the canopy.

閩 ꜀min

From *door* and *insects*, alluding to an old fable that the aborigines south of the Méi-ling were sired by a serpent.

A sort of snake; the ancient name of Fuhkien, and also applied to its principal river.

七 丨 the old tribes of Fuh-kien.

丨 浙總督 the governor-general of Fuhkien and Chehkiang provinces.

丨 隸 the royal aviary keeper or poulterer.

閔 ꜂min

From *door* and *writing*, referring to the obituary notices put up at front doors.

To feel for, to mourn with; indisposed, ailing; heartsick, grieved; to urge on, to encourage.

痛 丨 sick from sorrow.

丨 勉從事 to animate one to do his duty.

憫 愍 𢡆 ꜂min

From *heart* and *feeling*; or *thinking* and *people*; the second form usually refers to grief for the state, and the third is unusual; used with the last.

To mourn for, to commiserate the suffering of others; lamentable, as a calamity; concerned for.

丨 恤 to befriend one.

不足 丨 惜 not worth one's pity.

丨 不畏法 grieved that they disregard the laws.

潣 ʻmin Water flowing gently; a watery expanse.

敏 勄 ʻmin From *branch* or *strong* and *each;* the second form is unusual.

Active, clever, prompt; serious, respectful; witty, ready, fluent of speech; ingenious, skilled in; to be active in, to be in earnest; used for *shang* 商 the second of the five notes.

丨捷 quick-witted; celerity in doing.

聰丨 or 穎丨 quick at catching the idea or expressing it.

丨力 energetic, quick.

丨求 to earnestly beg.

丨辯 ready at answering; an able disputant.

心靈手丨 a lively mind and quick hand.

丨愼 clever and careful.

丨而好學 he is very bright and loves to study.

農夫克丨 the farmers are encouraged to diligence.

湣 ʻmin Used in epitaphs for 閔 to mourn, and interchanged with the next.

Turbid, foul, chaotic; died early.

Read ˏhwun, and used for 溷 which it resembles. Disturbed; in suspense.

置之滑丨 I am undecided what course to decide on.

泯 ʻmin From *water* and *people*; used with the last.

A vast sheet of water; to flow off; exhausted, drained; destroyed, put an end to; distant, obscure, confused.

丨亂 anarchy; utter misrule.

靡國不丨 every state is going to ruin.

丨沒 dead and forgotten.

丨滅 no record or trace of.

丨丨棼棼 all in confusion; dark and disorderly.

春流丨丨 the spring torrents roll on grandly.

刡 ʻmin From *knife* and *people*; interchanged with ʻwăn 抆 to wipe.

To scrape off, to pare; to brush off; to seam; to turn in, as a frayed edge.

油丨 or 丨子 a narrow spatula of horn used by women to put up their hair or oil it; a species of grass, allied to the *Eriochloa* is called 丨子草 from its resemblance to this thing.

捪 抿 ʻmin Interchanged with ʻwăn 抆 to wipe.

To feel and smooth down; to stroke with the hand.

丨摹 to handle gently.

In *Cantonese*, used as a synonym of 拔. To pull up, as weeds; to pull out, as a hair; to let down, to lower as a cord; to pull down, as the dress; to drag, to haul along.

笢 ʻmin The outer skin of bamboo; a brush for smoothing the hair.

丨子 a narrow hair brush, used to dress the tresses or soften the scalp.

丨笏抑隱 to move the fingers in playing the fife.

鰵 ʻmin A perch-like fish (*Corvina catalea*), of a spotted dark brown color, two feet long and coarse flesh; it is common at Macao.

暋 敃 ʻmin The second form is rarely used.

Strong, robust, able to perform things.

丨不畏死 the brave man does not dread death.

Read ˏmin. Sorry, mournful; troubled, anxious.

僶 ʻmin Used with the next.

To act under constraint; to exert, to use effort.

丨勉 great effort, under urgent necessity to do.

黽 ʻmin The character is supposed to represent a toad with its big belly; it is the 205th radical of a few obsolete characters relating to the *Rana*.

To be constrained to do; to exert one's self, to strive to reach.

丨勉從事 I have exerted myself to do my duty.

Read ʻmung. A toad, called 土鴨 and 蛙丨; it is a dark striped species.

MING.

Old sounds, măng *and* ming. *In Canton*, ming *and* meng; — *in Swatow*, meng *and* mia; — *in Amoy*, beng; — *in Fuhchau*, ming; — *in Shanghai*, ming; — *in Chifu*, ming.

鳴 ˏming From *bird* and *mouth*; it is very similar to ˏwu 鳴 to lament.

The cry of a bird or animal, as its song, buzz, hum, yell, &c.; a sonorous note, as of a gong or drum; to sound, to cause to yield a sound; to resound, as one's fame over the country; birds calling to each other.

大叩則大丨 a heavy blow will make [the gong] sound loud.

丨鼓 to beat the drum.

孤掌難丨 you can't clap with one hand.

丨寃 to cry out for redress, as to officials.

自丨得意 to sing from feeling happy.

不過狗吠雞丨之徒 he is just a fellow who can only bark or crow; — a boaster.

洺 ꜁ming A small stream near Kwang, ping fu in the south of Chihli, one of the headwaters of the Hü-to River.

銘 ꜁ming From *metal* and *name* as the phonetic.

To carve, to engrave on metal or stone in order to be remembered; to record for the purpose of preserving; to inscribe on the memory; a book of precepts, a guide for the conduct.

丨心 engraven on the heart.

丨感五內 I shall hold you in grateful remembrance.

丨旌 an imperial inscription given to worthy people.

丨鼎相傳 carved on tripods to be handed down.

碑丨 an engraved epitaph.

明 朙 ꜁ming From *sun* and *moon*; others derive the second and obsolete form from 月 the *moon* and 囧 a *window*.

Bright, clear; the dawn; plain, evident, open; ostensibly, apparently; brilliance, splendor; perspicacious, intelligent; to be illustrious, as in virtue; to illustrate, to shed light on, to explain; to distinguish clearly.

丨白 clear, apparent; plain.

丨白了 I understand it clearly.

正大光丨 upright and pure-minded.

丨日 or 丨兒 or 丨天 to-morrow; *lit.* the brightening day.

丨兒個見 I will see you to-morrow.

精丨人 a trustworthy man.

聰丨伶利 very intelligent and clever.

分丨其類 to discriminate its various classes.

鮮丨 new and showy.

丨知故犯 a crime done willfully.

高丨鑒察 let your clear mind examine the matter.

丨丨是你 it was you without a doubt.

丨丨上天 the bright and high Heaven.

丨丨在下赫赫在上 [the gods have] full knowledge of things among mankind, but above is majesty and power.

丨買丨賣 a fair, lawful business.

東方旣丨 it is already daylight.

丨發 the dawn is coming.

難丨 hard to comprehend.

丨往唔懶 he says he wants to go, but really he is too lazy.

丨火的是自己作死 one who robs will bring retribution upon himself.

丨倫堂 a hall for discourses and public deliberations adjoining the Confucian temple.

丨朝 or 大丨 the Ming dynasty. Its founder Chu Yuen-chang 朱元章 was a native of Fung-yang fu 鳳陽府 in Nganhwui, and holds a high place among Chinese monarchs. The first column of this table contains the *Nien Hao*, or style of the Reign by which the ruler is called in life; and the second gives the *Miao Hao*, or style of the Temple, the name by which he is worshiped in the hall of his ancestors; for instance, the reign of Chu Ti 朱棣 the third monarch, was known as Yung-loh 永樂 or Perpetual Joy while on the throne; but when he died, he was enshrined as Chʻing-tsu Wăn Hwangti 成祖文皇帝 our Perfected Ancestor, the Emperor Accomplished, and is referred to in history by this name.

EMPERORS OF THE MING DYNASTY.

STYLE OF REIGN.		TEMPLE NAME.	PERSONAL NAME.	ACCESSION A.D.	REIGNED YEARS.	GENEALOGY.
Hung-wu	洪武	太祖高皇帝	元璋	1368	31	Founded the dynasty.
Kien-wăn	建文	恭閔惠皇帝	允炆	1399	4	Grandson of the last.
Yung-loh	永樂	成祖文皇帝	棣	1403	22	Uncle of the last.
Hung-hi	洪熙	仁宗昭皇帝	高熾	1425	1	Son of the last.
Süen-teh	宣德	宣宗章皇帝	瞻基	1426	10	Son of the last.
Ching-tʻung	正統	英宗睿皇帝	祁鎮	1436	14	Son of the last.
King-tʻai	景泰	景皇帝	祁鈺	1450	8	Brother of the last.
Tʻien-shun	天順	英宗復位		1458	8	Restored from his captivity.
Chʻing-hwa	成化	憲宗純皇帝	見深	1465	23	Son of the last.
Hung-chi	宏治	孝宗敬皇帝	祐樘	1488	18	Son of the last.
Ching-teh	正德	武宗毅皇帝	厚照	1506	16	Son of the last.
Kia-tsing	嘉靖	世宗肅皇帝	厚熜	1522	45	Grandson of Chʻing-hwa.
Lung-kʻing	隆慶	穆宗莊皇帝	載垕	1567	6	Son of the last.
Wan-lih	萬歷	神宗顯皇帝	翊鈞	1573	48	Son of the last.
Tʻai-chʻang	泰昌	光宗貞皇帝	常洛	1620	1	Son of the last.
Tʻien-ki	天啓	熹宗悊皇帝	由校	1621	7	Son of the last.
Chung-ching	崇禎	莊烈愍皇帝	由檢	1628	17	Brother of the last.

名 ꜀ming From *mouth* and *evening*, because at dusk it is necessary to speak to be known.

A name, that which designates a person or thing; the given name of people, as distinguished from the clan name 姓, or the style or appellation 號; a person; fame, honor, reputation; a title; credit, merit; famous, celebrated, renowned, well-known; nominal, under pretence of; to name, to designate; the frontal sinus; an order in which the name is given; a character.

丨聲 reputation, fame.

丨目 the name of a thing.

買丨 or 沽丨 to fish for merit or notoriety.

丨號 or 丨字 the name or style by which a shop, person, or thing is known.

借丨 to pretend to; to assume another's name, as at the examination.

御丨 the Emperor's name.

乳丨 and 書丨 and 官丨 are the infantile, school, and official designations of people.

求丨 to seek reputation.

點丨 to call over the names.

花丨 or 混丨 a nickname.

冒丨 to forge a name; to simulate another's name.

匿丨 to conceal the name; anonymous, an alias.

實在丨工 it is really beautifully done.

丨山 celebrated mountains.

丨敎綱常 correct instruction in established principles of action.

有丨無實 it is merely nominal.

幾丨 several persons.

久聞大丨 I have long heard of your fame.

丨爲漢相 he was called a minister of Han.

不顧丨 regardless of one's reputation, reckless.

職丨 an officer's card, a visiting card.

動無丨火 to stir up the nameless fire; *i. e.* to get angry, to be petulant;—a Budhist expression.

冥 ꜀ming From 冖 to *cover*, 日 *day*, and 六 *six* for sixteen, for on the 16th day the moon begins to be obscured.

Dark, obscure, doleful; dim, cavernous recesses; to render obscure; night-like, dismal; mind uninformed and immature, like a child's; the unseen world, hades.

靑丨 heaven.

丨府 or 丨間 hades, sheol; the underworld.

幽丨難測 it is hard to fathom the mysterious and obscure.

無將大車維塵丨丨 do not push on a carriage, for its dust will only blind you.

丨福 the joys of elysium.

丨頑不靈 stupid, doltish, unreformable, heedless.

開丨路 to open the dark road,—to ring bells and pray for the departed.

丨吏 an agent or messenger from hades.

溟 ꜀ming Used with the last; also read *mih*.

The wide boundless sea, the deep; a sea whose waters are black and sluggish; drizzling rain; a fine fog, mist on hills.

小雨丨丨 a fine soaking rain.

北丨 the arctic sea.

丨海 the unknown and dark sea.

丨沐 a still drizzling rain.

滄丨 the illimitable ocean; this name and 東丨 have been applied to the black ditch 黑溝 or *kuro-siwo*, the hot stream which flows along the east coasts of Japan and Formosa.

瞑 ꜀ming ꜀min From *eye* and *dark*; it is nearly synonymous with ꜀mien 眠 to sleep.

To close the eyes, as in death; dull, indistinct vision.

甘心丨目 to cheerfully shut the eyes upon this world.

丨臣 the blind statesman, an appellation of Sz' Kwang 師曠 of Tsin, B. C. 540.

魚目不丨 fishes' eyes never close.

丨丨 dull sight; to see and not to perceive.

色中丨丨 people in love are blinded.

藥不丨眩 the medicine is not efficacious.

嫇 ming' A young wife of sixteen; clear and pure.

丨丨 small, undersized.

丨奵 to control one's self; to keep one's countenance.

蓂 ꜀ming A lucky plant, called 丨莢 which grew in Yao's palace, a leaf grew every day till full moon, and then one fell off daily; it was perhaps a bulbous plant, whose leaves alternately sprouted and died.

丨月 a poetical name for the first moon.

螟 ꜀ming An insect which eats young grain, probably akin to the hessian fly. (*Cecidomya.*)

丨蛉之子 an adopted son.

丨蛉 a caterpillar which the sphex is said to adopt for its own.

去'其丨螣 drive off the caterpillars and young locusts.

覭 ꜀ming From *to see* and *obscure*, refering to the difficulty of understanding minute things.

To take a look at, as something in a dark place, to examine what is minute.

丨丨 to examine things in a dark place.

Read *mih*, Plants growing in bushy clumps.

榠 ꜀ming The heart-wood or pith of a tree; the name of a tree.

鵬 ꜀ming A bird from the Indian Archipelago, called 鷦丨 denoting its 焦明 or scorched brightness, and considered to be allied to the phœnix; it is beautifully marked, and is one of the pheasant tribe, whose plumes are used by actors.

茗 ʻming From *plant* and *famous* as the phonetic.

The tender leaves or leaf buds of tea.

治丨 to prepare tea.

香丨 fragrant tea.

眞香丨 a kind of white rose. (Macartney's ?)

丨邈 lofty, as a flowering tree.

酩 ʻming A strong kind of whisky called 醴丨, made of rice and barley.

丨酊 drunk, very intoxicated.

皿 ʻmin The ancient form resembled a low fruit dish ; it forms the 108th radical of characters mostly relating to dishes.

Utensils and vessels used in eating; bowls, plates.

各欵器丨 all sorts of dishes.

慏 ʻming The thoughts kept back is 丨悜, either from unwillingness or inability to express them.

Read *mih*, Extensive.

暝 ʻming The sun obscured ; night, dark.

晦丨 obscure.

詺 ming' From to *speak* and a *name*.

To distinguish things by their names; to name, to discuss the names of things.

命 ming' From 口 *mouth* and 令 *order* as the phonetic.

To orde..—to command; to charge; to request authority; to consult, as a god; an ordinance, a charge; a rescript, a decree; behests, directions, requirements, orders; a symbol of power; in polite usage, a request, a wish; heaven, fate, weird, destiny, luck; an appointment from a superior power, one's appointed lot; the natural habits of; limit of the life of beings; animated, living creatures.

好丨 a happy lot; pleasant lines.

苦丨 unfortunate, luckless.

天丨 fate, heaven's decree.

性丨 life, existence.

算丨 to calculate fortunes.

大丨近止 my end draws near.

長丨 a long life; — over sixty years.

生丨 the horoscope; being, life.

丨運 a horoscope; a ruling influence over one's life, and its correlative of a ruling character over every five years.

丨所招 the natural bias.

奉丨 to receive orders.

丨門 the gate of life, a medical name for the right kidney, or a supposed passage between the rectum and bladder for the semen; in a woman, it is applied to the womb

丨案 a case involving life.

王丨 the death-warrant; it is held by every governor-general.

償丨 to give life for life.

孤獨丨 alone in the world.

一一如丨 everything has been done as required.

丨也如何 how will his inclination then be?

三演十二丨 the three systems and twelve precepts of Budha.

丨薄如紙 my luck is as thin as paper.

MIU.

Old sounds, miu *and* mok. *In Canton*, mau ; — *in Swatow*, niu *and* mok ; — *in Amoy*, biu ; — *in Fuhchau*, miu ; — *in Shanghai*, míu ; — *in Chifu*, niu.

謬 miu' niu' From *words* and to *fly* high.

The extravagant words of a madman; falsity, error; to deceive, to err; to mislead; fallacious, misleading.

大丨 a great mistake.

毫無差丨 not the least error.

丨悞 an error, a blunder.

虛丨 fabulous, incredible.

口切心丨 to promise with no intention of doing.

丨傳 it is all a false report.

狂丨 wild stories; a canard.

繆 miu' From *silk* and to *fly* giving the sound ; used for the last.

Ten hempen strings with which things can be corded; wrong; to mislead; in error; to oppose.

綢丨束芻 the faggots of grass are bound round and round.

聖人達綢丨 good men take pains to teach their deep thoughts.

紕丨 apparently in error.

未雨而綢丨 [like one who] fears it will rain, and hesitates to go wrong.

Read *ˏkiu*. Mourning worn loosely; to wind around, to tighten.

衣衰而丨経 the mourning hung loose, and his hempen cap was unbound.

Read *liao'* and used for 繚. Going around; in league with.

丨繞王綏 he carried the royal banner around — the place.

丨丨 silky, soft.

Read *muh*, and used for 穆. The order of precedence in the ancestral hall.

MO.

Old sounds, ma *and* mat. *In Canton*, mo ; — *in Swatow*, mo, bo *and* búa ; — *in Amoy*, mò, bò, *and* moh ; — *in Fuhchau*, mo *and* mwo ; — *in Shanghai*, mu ; — *in Chifu*, mù.

磨 礳 ꜀mo — From *stone* and *hemp*; it is sometimes interchanged with the next; the second and ancient form is now disused.

To rub, to polish, to reduce to powder; to sharpen, to grind; the rumbling sound of grinding; distressed, brought down by affliction; trials; to examine, as by torture.

丨利 or 丨快 to grind sharp.

丨顏色 to grind colors.

打丨 to polish.

丨鍊 to pass through, as affliction; to fag at, as study.

受災丨 or 折丨 tried by misfortunes; harsh treatment.

照丨 custodian of an official seal.

丨勘 to scan in order to criminate the writer of a document.

丨勵以需 wait till encouraged to act.

Read *mo*ʾ A quern; a mill for grinding grain.

推丨 to turn the quern.

丨心 pivot of the upper stone.

水丨 water-mill, used for pounding bamboo or hulling rice.

如蟻旋丨 like an ant [trying to] turn a mill.

In *Pekingese*. A classifier of actions, deeds, &c., similar to 會 or 次; a time; the end.

丨過來 to turn a cart around.

我去過兩丨兒 I have gone there twice.

一天作工歇幾丨兒 rest several times in a day's work.

下丨兒 the next time.

摩 ꜀mo — To feel, to rub with the hand; to handle, to feel the texture of; to rub together; to polish; to destroy; to act upon, as an acid does.

拊丨 to pat gently.

丨挲 to toy with, to rub.

鼠丨 to pilfer, to steal like a rat.

鬼丨你咩 has the devil got into you!

丨盪 operations of nature.

陰陽相丨 the elements act on each other.

丨伽陀 or 丨揭佗 the kingdom of Magadha now Bahar or Berar in India.

丨耶夫人 Maha Maya or Lady Maya, was Sakyamuni's mother, called also 大淸淨 Great Purity.

丨那婆 or 那羅丨那 a young Brahmin, a descendant of Manu.

In *Cantonese*. Slow.

你行丨丨 you walk very slowly.

餍 饝 ꜀mo — The second form is unusual; similar to both ꜀mi 糜 and ʿmi 饝.

To feed an infant by hand; to eat; congee.

丨丨 in Honan, steamed bread loaves.

丨丨粥 feed it with congee.

盧 ꜀mo — A cup for water; a drinking vessel, a basin.

魔 ꜀mo — From *demon* and *hemp*.

A malignant spirit, a devil, a demon.

丨鬼 the evil spirit.

妖丨 a mischievous efrit, a spook.

酒丨 delirium tremens.

詩丨 a poetic afflatus or frenzy.

降服諸丨 he subdued all the demons.

邪丨病 delirious, raving.

瘋丨了 he is out of his head.

丨羅 or Mara, the Budhist god of lust, sin, and death, called 慾界主 the lord of the world of lust, and 破壞善 the destroyer of good; his attendants are called 丨民 people of Mara, or 丨子丨女 sons and daughters (*Mara-kayikas*) of Mara.

蘑 ꜀mo — A sweet mushroom, the 丨菰 common in northern China.

蘿丨 a creeping parasite allied to the milkweed. (*Metaplexis chinensis.*)

嫫 嬤 ꜀mo — The second form is seldom seen, and has got into use from the resemblance of the phonetic; it alone means mother.

A woman named 丨母, who was Hwangti's fourth concubine and very ugly; a mother.

In *Pekingese*. A wet nurse is 丨丨, but one in the palace is known as 丨母, from the ancient dame.

麼 広 ʿmo ꜀ma — From *hemp* and *small*; the contracted form is very common.

Small, delicate; an interrogative particle; also used ironically; a sort, referring to something seen.

這丨 this kind.

甚丨 or 什丨 what?

哼好丨 eh! do you call *that* good?

你來了丨 ah! have you come?

他來丨 has he come?

你那丨說 what do you say?

這丨着 that will do; so, this is the way.

丨丨小兒 contemptible brats!

幺丨 trifling, insignificant; an affair beneath notice.

那丨爲甚丨給我送了來 why then have you brought it to me?

示 ʿmo — Another form of the last.

Small, delicate and minute; commonly used in Fuhkien.

MOH.

Old sounds, mak *and* mat. *In Canton*, mok, măk, mút, *and* mat; — *in Swatow*, mok, búé, mòng, múé, mo, múat, bak, *and* mek; — *in Amoy*, bok, bò, bòat, bek, *and* moh; — *in Fuhchau*, mòk, moh, mwak *and* măk; — *in Shanghai*, mòk, meh, măh, *and* mio; — *in Chifu*, mù.

莫 mo' mu' The original form has 艸 *plants* above and below 日 the *sun*, indicating that it shines through intervening trees.

A negative forbidding an act; do not, no need of; a particle exciting a doubt, if, unless; perhaps; preceding an adjective, it forms the superlative, nothing like, incomparable; an adjective of comparison; to plan; ample, great; tardy, late in maturing.

丨來 you need not come.

丨非 makes a strong postulate, as 丨非寫錯 unless you have written it wrong.

丨非他 it can be nobody else.

丨若 or 丨如 nothing like it, not so good as, the best way is, better than; the properest.

丨不是 it cannot but be so; is it not so?

丨大於天 nothing greater than heaven.

丨說 don't say it, wonder not if; — a phrase implying comparison.

丨須有 it certainly must be brought about.

丨定 it is quite uncertain.

丨過於 nothing more than.

丨爲 or 丨作 don't do it.

丨自 stop, stop! (*Cantonese*.)

丨往丨來 there is no intercourse between us.

求民之丨 seek the welfare of the people.

子曰文丨吾猶人 Confucius said, In literary ability, I am probably equal to other men.

丨道無神却有神 say not there are no gods, for there are gods.

Read *mu'* Quiet; dull, shady, evening; a species of sorrel, the *Rumex acetosa*, which can be eaten.

丨夜有戎 in the dusk move the troops.

君婦丨丨 the married pair were very quiet.

幕, **幙** mu' The two are nearly identical.

A curtain hanging down, a screen; a tent, a large marquee; defenses for the legs like greaves; a military secretary, a confidential clerk or aid.

丨府 an encampment.

丨友 or 丨賓 a private secretary, the official adviser of an officer.

作丨 to act as clerk.

六丨 the six curtains; *i. e.* the universe.

遊丨 a clerk out of employment.

長丨寂寥 during the silence of night.

漠 mo' Moving sands, a sandy plain; dry; a careless manner; indifferent to, as pleasure.

淡丨 simple desires.

沙丨 the desert of Shamo or Gobi.

丨丨然 vast and sandy, like a pampas.

丨不相關 of no consequence to me.

雲丨丨 the spreading clouds.

寞 mo' Still, silent, as at night; alone.

寂丨 no noise; quiet, as a sedate woman's apartments.

寂丨冷落 desolate and alone, like a hermit, or a man whose family has gone.

塻 mo' Dust.

塵丨 fine dust, atoms.

摸 ˛mo To feel for or after; to feel and grasp; to cover with the hands.

丨東丨西 feeling about for.

丨不着 I do not feel it; I don't know what to do, I can't say.

難以捉丨 it is impossible to decide.

丨一丨 rub or feel it once.

丨着黑走 groping one's way in the dark.

估丨 to suppose, to reckon, to think that such was the case.

瘼 mo' Sickness; distress; to cause disease by hard usage.

丨此下民 to distress the people very much.

亂離丨矣 scattered abroad and made sick, as a people by banditti.

暯 mo' From *sun* and *do not*.

Dark, obscure; one says, empty and still.

瞙 mo' The eyesight obscured, as by a pterygium, or a thickening of the cornea.

膜 mo' The filmy skin between the flesh and epidermis; the thin peel inside of eggs; any thin membrane or pellicle in plants or animals, as the mesentery or cornea; to soothe, to accord with, to submit.

眼丨 the sclerotica.

一層丨 one thickness of skin.

膏丨 the mesentery.

下碁眼有丨 when he plays chess, his eyes are skinned over.

Read ˛*mo*. To raise the hands to the head in making obeisance.

丨拜而受 he kneeled on both knees to receive it.

鏌, mo' A marvelous two-edged sword, like King Arthur's Excalibar, called 丨鋣 mentioned in the Lieh Kwoh.

邈, mo' From to *go* and *style*; when read 'miao, a synonym of 藐 to slight.

To look at from afar off; to disregard; remote, high.

丨丨 sorrowful.

丨然不可復求 irrecoverably gone, too far to be regained.

遙丨 far distant.

神道元丨 divine principles are deep and abstruse.

末, mo' From *wood* and *one*, referring to the end of a bough; it closely resembles wéi' 未 *not yet*.

The end of a branch, the outmost twigs; the end, the last, no more of; finally; ever, always; the least or meanest part of; actors who personify servants, lictors, &c.; the opposite of the origin or root of a matter; small, weak, insignificant; the remnants or last of, as leavings, powder, dust, or refuse; the limbs; traders, who are the last of the four classes of society; a negative; after other words often has the force of after all, then, well then, what then; after a verb, frequently forms a question.

本丨 the origin and end, the fundamental and the accessory.

丨世 or 丨日 end of the world.

檀香丨 sandalwood dust.

丨丨了兒 at the last, finally, the last one or time.

終丨 the very last.

微丨 subtle atoms.

研細丨 grind it very fine.

丨將' I, the military officer.

得在其丨 obtained the lowest or last place.

雖欲從之丨由也巳 even if I wish to follow or do this, I don't know how; or I have no means of doing so.

丨之也巳 I would not go there.

丨脚 the last, the end. (*Shanghai.*)

In *Shanghai.* An illative particle between the parts of a sentence, then.

做來好丨撥儂銅錢 if you do it well, I will pay you money.

抹, 'mo From *hand* and *refuse*.

To wipe clean, to rub out, to obliterate, to blot out; to dust; to daub, to rub on, to besmear; to color.

丨去 to rub out; wipe it off.

洗丨 to wash and rub.

丨頸 (or 丨脖子 in *Pekingese*) to cut one's throat.

丨檯 to rub a table.

丨數 to wipe out an account.

塗脂丨粉 to use cosmetics and rouge.

一手丨過 refused to pay a cash.

丨了頁心 obliterated all moral sense.

In *Pekingese.* To change the bills of one bank for those of another, and not for coin.

茉, mo' The word 丨莉花 for the jasmine, is thought to be derived from the Sanskrit *metati*, introduced by the Budhists.

紫丨莉 red jasmine, a name at Peking for the four-o'clock. (*Mirabilis jalapa.*)

韎, mo' A name for red socks.

丨鞨 a tribe of nomads who wore them, or from whom they were named, living in Koko-nor.

沫, mo' The old name of a branch of the Yangtsz' River in Sz'-ch'uen, which formed a boundary line; froth at the mouth; to drool in sleep; foam, bubbles on water; to perspire; to finish.

吐丨 to sputter or spit out.

浮丨 spume on water.

口丨 or 涎丨 expectoration.

流丨 for 流沫 bathed in perspiration.

至今猶未丨 it is not even now finished.

紅丨 a preparation like mosaic gold.

妺, mo' From *woman* and *last*; it closely resembles méi' 妹 a sister.

丨嬉 the name of the infamous wife of Kieh-kwei 桀癸 of the Shang dynasty.

丨學 sleight of hand or useless tricks or arts.

炢, mo' The last of a fire; a dull fire, *i. e.* the *fire's end*, as its component parts indicate.

灼火不丨 a little fire will not blaze brightly.

秣, mo, From *grain* and *refuse.*

To feed a horse with straw; fodder, rations, provender.

丨其馬 he fed his horse.

征車丨馬 he prepared his carriage and horses — for the journey.

芻丨 grass and corn for cattle.

丨陵 an old name for Nanking, now a large town south of it.

麩, mo' Grain, as rice or wheat, broken small; grits.

丨糠 bran and broken grain mixed.

䁼, mo' From 見 *to see* and 冒 *to dare.*

To rush out or into the presence of one suddenly.

墨, mo' From *earth* and *black.*

Ink, said to have been invented in the Wéi dynasty, A. D. 220, before which time paint or varnish was used for writing; dark, obscure, black; style, letters, writings; to brand with ink; a measure of five cubits; a mournful countenance.

一方丨 one cake of ink.

丨水 liquid ink; shoe-blacking.

有繩丨 it is all lined and marked; it is quite correct and proper.

彈 丨 線 to strike a line, as carpenters do.
文 丨 之 人 a student.
御 丨 the emperor's autograph.
落 丨 to put pen to paper.
未落 丨 做 the thing is not yet begun.
講筆 丨 to talk like a book.
闈 丨 文章 the successful *küjin* essays, which are published.
面甚 丨 lugubrious, mournful; chopfallen.
貪 丨 greedy of presents.
丨 魚 the cuttle-fish, from its bag.
丨 丈之間 about ten feet long, more or less.
石 丨 a kind of bitumen from Nan-hiung cheu in Kwangtung.
潑 丨 to write large characters.
丨 壺 an inkstand.
丨 綠 a blue-black color.

默, **嘿**, *mo'* From *black* and *dog* or *mouth*, denoting a dog driving off a man; the second form is little used.

Dark, cloudy, night; still, retired; secret, internal; meditation, quiet retirement; not at ease.
丨 念 to reflect on.
丨 丨 無言 not speaking a word.
丨 示 a silent or spiritual revelation or impression, something like an inspiration or afflatus.
丨 寫 to write from memory.
丨 丨 不安 sulky and silent, moody, out of temper.
丨 而識之 think it over and you will understand it.
丨 會 to intuitively understand.
幽 丨 in retirement.
丨 祐 secret protection, as of God.

嗼, *mo'* From *mouth* and *do not*; similar to the last.

Silent, still; quiet, settled.
呶 丨 quiet and undisturbed.
愁懷 丨 丨 grieved and keeping one's self quiet, as when upbraided.
丨 然 not saying anything.

纆, *mo'* A cord of two or three strands; a string of hemp.
福與禍何異糾 丨 happiness and misery are closely involved.

嚜, *mo'* To speak erroneously.
丨 尿 an artful child, a term used in Hunan.

In *Cantonese*, used in imitation of the word *mark*. A direction; a mark by which a thing is known.
打個字 丨 mark it.

MU.

Old sounds, mu, mot, *and* mok. *In Canton*, mò; — *in Swatow*, mo *and* bo; — *in Amoy*, bò; — *in Fuhchau*, mwò; — *in Shanghai*, mu *and* 'm; — *in Chifu*, mu.

模, *ˏmu* From *wood* and *without*.

A tree that grew on Duke Cheu's grave, which seems to have been a tree like the beech; a mold; a pattern, a model; a form or guide to go by; the rule; the figure.
丨 子 a model.
規 丨 the usage; the rules to follow.
形 丨 or 丨 樣 a pattern; manner, fashion, style.
打指 丨 to make a sign-manual by pressing the inked finger on a document.
丨 糊 blurred, indistinct.
丨 棱其說 he talks very ambiguously.

摹, *ˏmu* Similar to the last, but not the same as *moh*, 摸 to feel.

To follow a pattern, to go according to the rule; a pattern, a muster.
描 丨 to copy a thing by laying the paper on it.
丨 寫 to write by lining the letters.
丨 古 to pattern after the ancients, to copy an old style.
丨 倣 to follow the sample, to copy it.
丨 造樓臺 to make a plan of a house.

謨, *ˏmu*, *ˏmo* From to *speak* and *do not*; this character is said by Kanghi to be used south of the Méiling as a negative for 無, but it is not improbable that the colloquial word 'mò 冇 used from Canton to Fuhchau, meaning none, nothing, hollow, is intended, as this well-known character derives its meaning from leaving out the two inner strokes of 有 to have.

Consultation, matured plans; instructions; a well settled course of action; to imitate; false, unreal.
謀 丨 to devise plans.
嘉 丨 a fine plan.
僞 丨 counterfeit, a forged thing.
丨 先聖之大猷 to practice the maxims of ancient sages.

母, *ʿmu* The old form is thought to resemble the female breasts; it is distinguished from *ˏwu* 毋 not, by the two dots.

A mother, a dam; she, or that which produces; earth; the ten stems; *met.* a local ruler; the source of; inferior, small.
丨 親 a mother; one's mother.
乳 丨 a wet nurse, a foster-mother.
主 丨 the principal wife.
外 丨 or 岳 丨 a wife's mother.
繼 丨 or 後 丨 a step-mother.
國 丨 the empress-dowager.
大父 丨 heaven and earth.
公 and 丨 cock and hen; the male and female of animals.

子丨錢 interest and principal; 子丨 is applied to sorts, inferior and superior, small and great, the produced and producer.

字丨 initial characters; alphabetical letters.

民之父丨 [good officers are] the parents of the people.

姆 ʻmu
姥 ʻlao

The second is also read ʻlao.

An elderly widow, who teaches female duties; a schoolmistress; a brother's wife is so called by her 嬸 or younger sisters-in-law.

大丨 my sister-in-law.

丨師 a governess, a matron.

使丨 or 丨丨 a monthly nurse; a midwife.

斗丨 a Taoist goddess supposed to reside in the Dipper, who is probably the Hindu *Chundi* or goddess of Light.

䳇 ʻwu

From *bird* and *mother*; a synonym of 鵡 derived no doubt from dialectical variations.

The parrot, regarded as still a bird even if it can talk; many varieties are described.

慕 mu'

From *heart* and *do not*.

To think upon with affection, to recall fondly; fond of, to long for, to hanker for; aspiring, ambitious.

丨父母 affection for one's parents.

愛丨 to love ardently.

仰丨 to esteem, to respect.

丨名利 longing for fame and fortune.

心手丨之 sighing and longing for him.

暮 mu'

From *sun* and *do not*.

The evening, sunset; the decline of life; end of a period of time.

日丨 sunset.

昏丨 dark; the glooming.

朝丨 or 旦丨 morning and evening.

丨年 aged.

丨春 the last part of spring.

丨景 a sunset sky.

朝往丨返 go in the morning and return at even.

慔 mu'

To exert one's self.

讀書丨丨 to study most diligently.

墓 mu'

The *ground* which the filial heart loves to *think* of; a burial spot, a grave; a tomb, a sepulcher.

丨碑 a tombstone.

修丨 to repair a tomb.

開丨 to open a grave.

丨道 the hole when open.

丨厲 the limits or wall of the tomb—are seven 尺 feet beyond the grave.

丨誌 the epitaph.

掃丨 or 省丨 to sweep the tombs, — at the spring worship.

募 mu'

To call upon the people to do; to invite; to enlist, to give a bounty to; to circulate a general call for aid; a public invitation.

招丨壯丁 to enlist volunteers.

丨應 to respond to a levy.

丨兵 to raise troops.

丨化重修 to circulate a subscription paper to repair — a temple.

丨緣 to ask subscriptions to get up an idolatrous festival.

MUH.

Old sounds, mot *and* mok. *In Canton,* mòk *and* mút; *— in Swatow,* mút, mak, m^{n}o, *and* bo; *— in Amoy,* bok *and* bút; *— in Fuhchau,* múk; *— in Shanghai,* mòk *and* meh; *— in Chifu,* mu *and* măh.

沒 ˏmé mo'

From *water* and *to go under* it.

To sink in the water, to perish, to die; to finish one's own prospects; dead, gone; to enrich one's self by another's loss; to exceed; a negative, implying none of, not the least, utterly, without.

丨有 none, not yet, there is nothing; after an assertion, it has the force of a question as 你有兄弟丨有 have you a brother?

丨有好味 quite insipid; senseless, as a book.

丨有甚麼 nothing; unimportant.

丨藥 myrrh, — the product of the *Balsamodendron myrrha* of Arabia, a name imitated from the Hindustani *murr*.

埋丨 to secrete or keep back another's things.

丨極 at extremity, not knowing what more to do.

乾 and 丨 are opposites, — profit and loss, benefit and distress.

丨奈何 compelled to do, no alternative.

丨禮犯分 to neglect courtesy and come short of one's duty.

丨用 useless.

出丨靡常 appearing and disappearing without any regularity, as clouds.

感恩不丨 I can never forget your kindness.

歿 mo'

Used with the last in some senses.

To end, to die; the dead.

丨於陣 died in battle.

丨世不忘 I won't forget you in death.

丨存均感 the dead and living will both thank you; — said to friends who aid at a funeral.

坶 *moh'* Regarded as a synonym of the last, and also used for 埋 to bury.

To inter the dead.

偷合取容以致｜身 to contract underhand liaisons in order to let affairs go as they list, will just bury you in their ruins.

叟 *mo'* From *hand* below *water*; it resembles ˛*shu* 殳 to *kill*, but is only used as a primitive.

To dive for anything under water.

目 *mu'* The old form represented the pupil within an oval; it forms the 105th radical of characters relating to the eye and vision.

The eye; a director, a principal man, a leader; an index, a list or summary; squares on a chess-board; meshes of a net; the mind, the perception; a look; to eye; to designate, to name, to particularize.

｜下 before the eyes, now.

反｜ unfriendly; to cut one.

數｜ numbers, the account of.

幾化數｜ how many are there? (*Shanghai*).

條｜ a list of the articles.

題｜ a theme for an essay; a topic.

科｜出身 he rose to office by merit, not purchase; 科｜ denotes the three highest literary degrees.

｜中無人 supercilious, very haughty.

前｜而後凡 first particulars and then generalities.

耳｜長 long ears and eyes, a good detective, not easily gulled.

請問其｜ please tell me the general points.

｜無法紀 he does not regard the laws.

｜諸物 I have named everything.

怒｜ angry, looking displeased.

夷｜ the barbarian eye, a name formerly given to the English chief at Canton.

｜伊爲小人 characterized him as a mean fellow.

統｜之爲外國人 regarded them all alike as foreigners.

苜 *mu'* From *plants* and *eye*; it is not the same as *tieh*˒ 苜 squinting.

A cultivated plant, a small leaf clover, or trefoil (*Medicago sativa*), the ｜蓿 on which horses are fed and the young leaves cooked for greens; when used as a manure it is called 草頭, and plowed in; some have supposed this name indicates a similarity to the old Greek name *madixa*, *i. e.* brought from Media.

木 *mu'* The old form represents a tree striking its roots down and sending branches up; it forms the 75th radical of a large group of characters relating to trees and wooden things.

Wood; a tree; what grows on a tree; wooden; one of the five elements; *met.* the East, which wood affects; honest, unpretending, plain; in musical books used as a contraction of *moh*, 抹 to strike the string when playing the lute.

多少樹｜ how many trees are there?

｜匠 a carpenter.

｜料 timber, lumber, stuff.

一塊｜ a billet, a block.

｜香 putchuck brought from India; the 青｜香 is a species of *Aristolochia*; at Ningpo a species of *Clematis*.

｜訥 inflexible, honest.

｜部 the class of trees in botany.

四方｜ a square block; *met.* a stupid block of a fellow.

｜偶人 a fellow like an idol, a dunce.

｜星 or 危｜ the planet Jupiter.

撞｜鐘 to strike the wooden bell, *i. e.* to pretend to have influence with rulers, and take bribes to bring about an end.

伐｜ to fell trees.

投我以｜李 he presented me with a pear.

囫圇｜頭 a stupid dolt of a fellow, just a log of wood.

沐 *mu'* To wash the hair; to cleanse, to bathe; to enrich by kindness, to receive favors, to rule kindly; favored, blessed; to regulate; a branch of the River Han in the east of Sz'ch'uen.

｜浴 or 洗｜ to wash the body.

｜恩弟子 I, the disciple who have received favors — from this god; said by devotees.

｜手謹序 I washed and then carefully wrote this.

霂 *mu'* Fine rain.

霢｜ a gentle shower.

望｜滋生 to hope for the soft rains to cause the herbage to grow.

楘 *mu'* Certain leathern bands put around the front of a car to strengthen and ornament it.

鶩 *mu'* Mallards or wild ducks, but others say domesticated ducks; the former application is the usual one.

刻鵠不成尙能類｜ if you cannot carve a snow goose, you still may be able to produce a duck; — try your best.

庶人執｜ the common people presented a duck.

牧 *mu'* From a *cow* and to *strike*; it must not be confounded with ˛*sheu* 收 to receive.

To tend cattle, to pasture, to put out to grass; a shepherd, a cowherd; to superintend, to have oversight or watch of; to get one's living by pasturage; pasture-grounds; one in charge, as a ruler or teacher.

天｜ the shepherd of Heaven; an ancient term for a governor.

｜童 a shepherd boy; and hence ｜童詩 for pastoral ballads or bucolics.

丨牛 to tend cattle; a cowherd.

乃爲民丨 he is a shepherd of the people.

井丨 a head husbandman.

丨司 an old term for overseer.

丨師 a Christian minister or pastor.

遊丨 nomads, as of the Desert of Gobi.

丨人掌丨六畜 the herdmen oversee all the domestic animals.

卑以自丨 not presumptuous; a humble demeanor; to be mild.

丨野 the pasture wilds, name of the battle ground in K'i hien 淇縣 in the north of Honan, where Wu Wang defeated Sheu.

萊夷作丨 the wild tribes of Lai (now Shantung) practiced pasturage.

穆, *mu'* From *grain* and *striped*. The waving, graceful appearance of grain; pleasing, beautiful; majestic, inspiring awe and admiration, like a divine or imperial power; cordial regard; to revere; to gratify.

丨丨 royal, admirable; exciting wonder; to be profound; with deep reverence.

丨罕默德 Mohammed; whence the Moslems call themselves 丨民, and say 丨迦 for Mecca.

丨君之色 to admire the prince's mien.

鞠恭丨丨 profoundly respectful and reverent, as in worship.

丨如淸風 [let my song] gratify him like a gentle breeze.

睦, *mu'* A benignant, loving eye; harmonious, affable; concord among relatives, neighbors, or nations; to cultivate amicable relations; to make or keep peace with.

親丨 united, neighborly.

和丨鄉鄰 to keep peace in the villages and neighborhoods.

毣, *mu'* A gust of wind is 丨丨, as it rushes by; also the attitude of thinking; the hair wet through.

殁, *mu'* To die early; to come to the end of life.

楚王其不丨乎 is not the Prince of Tso near his end when young?

MUNG.

Old sound, mong. *In Canton*, mung *and* mang; — *in Swatow*, mong, mín, mang, *and* meng; — *in Amoy*, bong, bín, *and* eng; — *in Fuhchau*, mung, mang, mòng, *and* méung; — *in Shanghai*, mung, măng, *and* mong; — *in Chifu*, măng.

蒙 *₍măng* From *plants* and *covered over*, as a *pig* under a *covert*.

A trailing plant, also called 女蘿, the cypress-vine (*Ipomea quamoclit*); beclouded, dull, obscure perception of; ignorant, immature, rash; a child, a pupil; to deceive, to conceal; to cover; to pull over one; to behave rather rudely, and from this implied sense, it has become an affected term for thankful, obliged to, grateful for favors; to gammon; the 45th diagram, denoting reciprocal; name of an ancient city in Honan, and of a tribe of aborigines, now preserved in Mung-hwa ting 丨化廳 in western Yunnan.

丨古人 the Mongols, said to be an imitation of *moengel* or celestial.

啟丨 to direct the first studies.

丨士 or 丨稚 an untaught man.

多丨你 many thanks for, I will be obliged to you for, I beg the favor.

訓丨 to teach boys.

丨取 or 丨光顧 obliged for your taking [the goods,] or your custom; — a shopman's phrase.

丨恩 thankful for the favor.

丨教 kindly tell me; I am obliged to you for the information.

丨首冠 a cap that envelopes the head.

狐裘丨戎 (or 茸) our fox furs are frayed and shabby.

欺丨人的話 beguiling, deceptive talk; chaff, jokes, quips.

丨昧 rash, to act heedlessly, willful; uninstructed.

丨混 dull, cloudy in mind, confused.

丨養作聖 to gradually bring him on till he becomes a sage.

丨死 to expose one's self to death.

深丨過愛 greatly obliged for your undeserved kindness.

丨劄 I was honored by receiving your orders; — said by an inferior to a superior officer.

濛 ₍ 霿 ₍ *₍măng* The first of these is often used with the preceding; and the second is also defined thunder.

Small, drizzling rain; foggy; names of several rivers, one of which is in the southwest of Kwéicheu.

丨淞雨 a misty rain.

丨鴻 chaotic, vapors; nebulous.

丨丨小雨 a tedious, drizzling mist.

₍丨₍丨痛 a slight pain. (*Fuhchau.*)

丨丨天 gloomy weather.

幪 *₍măng* A covering; to screen off or shelter; to protect, as against the bleak rain; to cover the head.

帲丨 a screen; to cover, to roof.

麻麥丨丨 luxuriant and beautiful as hemp and wheat.

曚 *₍măng* From *sun* and *obscured*. The sun below the horizon.

天丨矓 before sunrise, early dawn.

朦 ꜀măng — From *moon* and *obscured;* like the last and interchanged with its primitive; not the same as the next

The moon about to set; to deceive or cajole, to humbug.

月色丨朧 the moon is clouded over.

丨亮兒 the first blush of dawn, earliest dawn.

丨混 a misunderstanding; not clear, as a law; to mislead, to gammon.

䑃 ꜀măng — From *flesh* and *obscured.*

Corpulent, large; fat.

丨面 full faced.

豐丨 abundant.

[illegible] ꜀măng — Silk thread all in confusion, raveled and tangled.

亂丨 raveled.

丨茸 thick, like a tussock of grass.

細丨 fine and coarse together, said of floss or thread.

矇 ꜀măng — Dimsighted, weak eyes; unable to see from age; blind from disease of the nerve, as in amaurosis or gutta serena, commonly called 發青光; unlearned, untaught, ignorant of one's self.

眼丨 bad sight.

發丨 to enlighten another's ignorance.

丨瞍奏公 the blind musicians played their parts.

艨 ꜀măng — A fast sailing war-junk, called 丨艟 long and narrow, used in the revenue service, and now known at Canton as a 爬龍 or scrambling dragon.

丨艟魚貫 the galleys followed each other like a school of fishes.

檬 ꜀măng — A tree like the locust (*Sophora*), with yellowish leaves.

丨菓 the mango, is sometimes so written but 檬菓 is also met with.

礞 ꜀măng — A shaly bole, called 青丨石, which seems to be a kind of micaceous schist of a fine quality, prescribed in cases of derangement or fits; there are also varieties called gold and silver 丨石, according as the mica is mixed with other minerals.

饛 ꜀măng — A dish filled with food; a plentiful table.

有丨簋餐 there was a most abundant meal.

[illegible] ꜀măng — A long flowing mane of a horse; the hairs falling along the neck.

罞 ꜀măng — A large lasso or net for catching deer by throwing it over their horns.

甍 ꜀măng — The poles or rafters which uphold the tiles; the ridge-pole.

氓 ꜀măng / 甿 ꜀măng — From *people* or *field* and *lost;* a synonym of ꜀min 民 people.

Fugitives who cannot be brought together, those who have become vassals from other countries; the ignorant, imprudent country people.

丨之蚩蚩 a simple looking man of the people.

流丨 vagabonds, gypsies; houseless wanderers.

編丨 lists or census of the people.

盲 ꜀măng — From *eye* and *lost.*

Blind from any cause; an eye without an intelligent pupil; blinded in heart, deceived, easily deluded.

丨眼 blind, as from amaurosis.

丨年 a blind year is one which has no 立春 term in it.

發鷄丨 to have night blindness.

丨風 a variable gusty wind.

視己則丨 self-love makes people blind.

丨於心 blindness of mind.

瞢 ꜀măng — Similar to the last.

Dimness of vision; dark, obscure; to feel ashamed, mournful.

日月丨丨 the sun and moon are darkened.

丨容 looking mortified.

莔 ꜀măng — Occurs used for the next.

A liliaceous plant, also called 貝母, cowrie-mother, whose roots are small; the corms, round like cowries, and ranging from a pea to a marble in size, are used in fevers; it has white flowers and hastate leaves like buckwheat; it is perhaps a species of *Uvularia,* or the *Fritillaria thunbergia* according to Japanese books.

蝱 ꜀măng / 虻 ꜀măng — From *insect* and *lost,* but the primitive is a contraction of 吂 and imitates the buzz.

A stinging fly that infests animals; a pretty plant, for which the last is now used.

蜚丨 a breeze or gadfly; the fly that bites cattle.

丨虫 or 蚊丨 gadflies and musquitoes.

牛丨 a horsefly.

飛丨 a kind of barbed dart fired like a rocket.

黃丨 a fly that infests cattle.

木丨 a kind of fly like a bee, found in grass and on trees.

言采其丨 I will gather the fritillarias.

鄳 ꜀măng — An old name in the Han dynasty, for part of Lo-shan hien 羅山縣 in the southeast of Honan, south of the River Hwai, at that time a part of Shăn cheu 申州 prefecture.

鸏 ꜀măng — Fledglings of water birds.

丨鷾 a bird from Annam, large as a peacock, having a long beak, of which dishes are made; it is the rhinoceros hornbill (*Buceros*), and is also called 鶴頂 crane's head.

蠓 ʻmăng Ephemera or sandflies; small flies over ordure or water.
丨蚋 dung-flies, midges.
丨螉 wasps.

猛 ʻmăng From *dog* and *first*.
A fierce, violent dog; strong, determined, resolute, brave; inhuman, severe, cruel; hot, as fire; biting, as the wind; violent, excessive in any way; to rouse, to inspirit.
火丨 a rousing fire; too hot.
勇丨 valorous.
丨烈 rigid, firm and stern.
威丨 awful, majestic.
丨性 a violent temper.
來勢甚丨 their meeting was terrible, as two armies.
丨然間 suddenly, startling.
丨陵 an old name for Pʻing-nan hien 平南縣, in the east of Kwangsi.
威而不丨 dignified but not violent.

懵 懞 ʻmăng From *heart* and *blind*.
Dull, senile, not intelligent; vexed, perturbed; grieved, ashamed; to cover, to blind.
丨懂 forgetful, doubtful of.
老丨懂 an old dotard; a forgetful lout.
丨丨蔽 foolish-like, dull of comprehension.
丨丨無知 ignorant and dull.
丨蔽眼 to close or cover the eyes.

夢 㝱 梦 瞢 măngʼ From 夕 *evening* and 瞢 *dimness* contracted, the last form often occurs in its compounds.
To dream, to see visions; a dream, of which diviners make six classes; a vanity, a phantasm; obscure.
丨見 dreamed about it.
丨不到 my dream did not come to pass.
丨魘 the nightmare.
丨洩 nocturnal emissions.
丨想 empty hopes, day-dreams.
丨兆 a prophetic dream, one that comes to pass.
一塲大丨 one long dream; *met.* this life, the world.
丨寐之事 a visionary affair; what was dreamed about.
你發丨嗎 are you dreaming?
浮生若丨 life is passed like a dream.
託丨 communicated in a dream.
視天丨丨 [the people] looking to Heaven, all is dark.
丨話三千 all of it is false, lying words; — the reference is to a character in fiction like Munchausen.
甘與子同丨 it would be pleasant to lie by you and dream.

瞢 ˏmăng Just awaked from sleep, is 丨瞢, intimating that the mind is not quite collected; it is the name of a mountain in Wu-tai hien 五臺縣 in Shansi.

NA.

Old sounds, na *and* nap. *In Canton,* na; — *in Swatow,* na; — *in Amoy,* na *and* lò; — *in Fuhchau,* na; — *in Shanghai,* nò, na, ha, *and* ʼm; — *in Chifu,* na.

拿 拏 挐 ˏna From *hand* and a *slave* or *joining*; the second form is unauthorized but it is most common, and the third is unusual.
To lay hold of, to seize; to apprehend, to take; to bring; to get an idea of, to appreciate; a form of the accusative like 把 or 將, placed before the noun.
丨衣食養活他 to feed and clothe him.
丨來 bring it here.
丨緊住意 it is firmly resolved upon.
捉丨 to arrest one.
丨不穩 I am unable to get firm hold; — I hardly understand the matter.
一把死丨 certainly, no mistake about it; a death clutch of a case.
丨事人 a clerk who receives applications, a factotum.
無揸丨 nothing to hold on by, or get a clue of; also a nickname for a Budhist priest.
丨出來 taken out; abstracted.
丨大價 to overcharge; to raise the price of.
丨不着 I cannot seize (or get) it.
丨手做得 I will see that it is done.
丨他的錯 availed himself of his mistake.

袈 ˏna Tattered clothes; garments which have been torn in some way.

那 ʻna From *city* and *weak* giving the sound.
To point to a place or thing; an interrogative particle, which, where; the unauthorized character 㑚 used in Kiangsu for you in the plural number, seems to have been designed to denote *that man*, or those men.
丨裡去 where are you going?
丨年丨月 which year and month?
丨裡知道他必來 how could I know that he would come?
丨堪如是 how can I bear such treatment?
丨裏一個 which one of them?
丨一個人 which man?
丨兒來的 where is it from?

Read *na'* A vocative, Oh! a final particle drawing attention, and implying certainty; see, here it is! lo! a demonstrative particle donoting the farthest of two things, the opposite of 這; that, there, then.

丨裏丨 it surely is there.

你丨 Oh, you! you, Sir; a respectful form of address, also written 您呀 or 你納 and otherwise.

丨處 or 丨兒 or 丨邊兒 there.

丨個 that, as a man or thing.

丨些人 those few persons.

誰能丨 who then is able?

丨一塊兒 there, that spot.

丨麽樣 thus, that way.

丨樣不妥 that kind will not do.

Read *˛no.* An ancient state in the present P'ing-liang fu 平涼府 in Kansuh, called Ch'ao-no 朝丨; to point; to transfer, in which sense 挪 has taken its place; to rest, to terminate; peaceful; much.

王在在鎬有丨其居 the king is here, even in Hao, dwelling in peace.

受福不丨 to enjoy endless happiness.

哪ˀ *na'* A colloquial, final particle used in replies, denoting certainty; an interjection of pain or surprise; an interrogative word.

沒丨 there is nothing; there are no more.

何其難丨 where's the difficulty in it?

是在這兒丨還是在那兒呢 is he here or there?

Read *toh*, or *to'*. The cry of 丨丨 made by people who exorcise demons.

Read *˛no.* The name of a mythological character.

丨吒 a phantom man; one story makes him to have been foster brother of the third son of Wăn Wang, and to have destroyed Ta-ki's spirit when she returned to heaven.

媽ˀ *na'* Read *'tso*, *the last mother*; an old form of 姐 sister.

In *Cantonese.* A dam; the female of animals.

猪丨 a sow.

亞丨 granny, old dame.

丨形 a girlish boy, effeminate.

蛤丨 a frog.

兩仔丨 mother and child.

瘵ˀ *na'* Disease; ill.

In *Cantonese.* A scab.

瘡丨 a scab of a sore.

結丨 to form a scab.

痘丨 the small-pox scab.

In *Cantonese* read *˛na.* With, together with; even, alike; for; to join in, to take part with; to stick to, as glue.

我丨你去 I'll go with you.

丨埋擔去 carry them all at one load.

丨粘 sticky, unctuous.

我丨佢剃頭 I've shaved him often.

NAH.

Old sounds, nap, not, *and* nat. *In Canton,* nap *and* nat; — *in Swatow,* nap; — *in Amoy,* lat *and* lap; — *in Fuhchau,* nak; — *in Shanghai,* nah *and* neh; — *in Chifu,* na.

捺ˀ *nah'* From *hand* and a *plum.*

To press the hand down heavily; in *penmanship,* it is the sweep to the right.

一撇一丨 one stroke to the left and one to the right.

瑣丨 a copper clarionet. (*Canton.*)

丨底 to pull waxed-ends.

納ˀ *na'* From *silk* and *inside*; used for the next, and also contracted to its primitive.

Silken threads shrinking; to enter, to collect, to receive; to insert; to enter on possession; to be appointed; silk put in soak; to hand up, to pay or present to government; within.

丨貢 to pay taxes in kind.

丨稅 to pay taxes in money.

丨女 to present a daughter to the Emperor.

受丨 to receive, to take in.

丨福 are you well? may you be happy!

丨涼 to get the cool breeze.

容丨 to contain or take in; liberal, generous.

望祈笑丨 I hope you will favorably take — my gift.

其言不丨 I cannot assent to his words.

丨悶 in sorrow; melancholy.

丨職 to purchase office.

丨妾 or 丨寵 to take a concubine.

置丨 to place carefully.

出丨朕命 make known abroad our orders and receive all petitions.

丨幣 to send betrothal presents.

寅餞丨日 respectfully escort the setting sun.

丨采 a Manchu word for ceremonies of marriage.

抐ˀ *na'* From *hand* and *within.*

To put a thing in or under the water, to immerse or dip; to stain.

揾丨 to put in soak.

衲, *na'* From *clothes* and *within*.
To patch; to line; to overlay; padded or quilted; priestly garments; *met.* a Budhist priest.
夾丨 a lined coat.
棉丨 a quilted lining
皮丨 a fur lining.
貧丨 or 丨子 I, a priest.
着木丨 to dress in a wooden lining, *i. e.* to be put in a coffin. (*Cantonese.*)

妠, *na'* To take a wife; to get; to go in.
婠丨 a fat little child, a handsome chubby child.

笝, *‗na'* A rope or hawser made of bamboo withs to tow boats; to mend a hedge.
篾丨 a bamboo tow-rope.
拔丨 to track a boat.
溪丨 links or torches made of old bamboo hawsers. (*Fuhchau.*)

貀, 豽, *na'* A kind of striped seal probably from Corea, described in the Pǎn Ts'ao under the name of 海狗 sea dog, as having no fore feet; its face resembles that of a dog, its skin a leopard's, but dark; it has horns and short fur; it is now unknown in that region, and was brought to court in the T'ang dynasty. One account places it in Koko-nor, or among the Turks, so that it may refer to seals in some of the Tibetan lakes; the testes are brought as medicine under the name of 膃肭 from the west.

魶, *na'* A synonym of the 鯢 seal or dugong, which is considered to be a turtle without a shell; it is said to have its mouth in its belly, and to ascend trees in times of drought; the Chinese descriptions of it are so contradictory, that it is plain they have seldom seen the animal.

軜, *na'* The inner ornamental reins of a team of four horses, used in olden time; they were tied to the carriage front.

鈉, *na'* To sharpen wood, as for a helve; to hammer iron to a point.

In *Cantonese.* To iron out, as clothes; to sear, to smooth; to lay over, to press on; to touch off, as a cannon.
煎骨丨肉 my bones and flesh are scarred and blistered;—pressed out of measure.
丨砲 to fire a cannon.
丨眼 to press on the eye to cool it, as with an agate.

蒳, *nah'* Name of a fragrant plant.
丨子 the seed of a species of palm, resembling the areca nut; the leaves resemble the fan palm, but are smaller and aromatic when dry.

NAI.

Old sounds, nai *and* nat. *In Canton,* nai *and* noi; — *in Swatow,* nai; — *in Amoy,* nai^{n}; — *in Fuhchau,* nai *and* nè; — *in Shanghai,* né^{n}, na, *and* né; — *in Chifu,* nai.

㾍 *‹nai* Similar to 疓 weary.
Weary, sick; sordid, ill-looking, exhausted, seedy.

乃, 迺, 廼, *‹nai* The character is intended to represent air curling and issuing, which cannot be recovered; the other two forms are frequently used.
An adversative particle, but, it may be; doubtless, forsooth; also, moreover; before a negative, if; also used for the substantive verb to round the rhythm, or as a connective particle, to wit, then, thereupon, till then, if, &c., and often needs no rendering; it occasionally stands for pronouns, as your, your's; that, those; such a one.
丨者 at this time, at this period.
丨如 or 丨若 but as to.
死而丨葬 he is dead and buried too.
此丨周之父 this is Cheu's father.
丨可 will then do.
無丨不去 if not, then I will not go.
何丨府形同木偶 how is the prefect like a wooden statue?
丨祖丨父 the grandfather with the father.
無丨不可乎 is it then quite impossible?
時丨天道 that was heaven's rule.
時丨功 it was your work.
丨聖丨神丨武丨文 he was altogether wise and divine, brave and accomplished.
汝猷黜丨心 you must constantly check that heart of your's.
丨有不吉不迪 those who are destitute of virtue and principle.
惟丨之休 only by your virtue.

艿 *‹nai* From *plants* and the next contracted; it is read *‹jăng* in the dictionaries, but with a different primitive and meaning.
The small tubers which grow around the taro called 芋丨 and 毛芋丨 in Shanghai; they are not unlike teats in shape.

嬭 妳 奶 ˊnai — From *woman* and *you* or *is*; the first two are not much used, and the third is unauthorized. The breasts of a woman the udder, the dugs; nipples, teats; applied to the Malaga grape; to suckle; milk; a nurse; a pet word for mother; a married woman; a lady.

丨頭 the nipple; a teat.

牛丨 cow's milk.

丨媽 a wet nurse.

食丨 to nurse; nursing.

丨皮 cream.

丨頭腐 dried milk cake; cheese made by the Mongols.

丨丨 a grandmother; an old lady.

師丨 or 丨丨 madam; a lady. (*Cantonese.*)

大丨丨 and 小丨丨 the wife and concubines; as 丨丨們 denotes all the married woman in the house, the hareem.

少丨丨 a bride; the appellation of the daughter-in-law in the house.

老丨丨們 you ladies! especially those older than the speaker.

大丨, and 二丨, and 三丨 are the compellations for the wives of three brothers, or the three wives of one man.

黃丨 a siesta; an ancient term.

丨丨兒 my wife; wife!

亞丨 nurse! ma! (*Cantonese.*)

小孩毀丨 the child is weaned.

疓 ˊnai — Sick, tired, weary, worn out. 見丨 I feel very weak and exhausted.

In *Cantonese.* To tie up, to fasten on; to hang on or depend on one, as a family; to belong to.

丨船尾 fasten it astern.

丨烟貨 he pays for the fireworks.

拖手丨脚 to tag after one.

鼐 naiˋ — An iron tripod of large size to burn incense in temples; it has two ears.

調和鼎丨 to keep the country in order, as a premier does.

柰 奈 naiˋ — From *tree* or *great* and *to exhibit*; the second is the commonest form. A kind of bullace or large yellow plum, sour yet edible, three sorts are described; the Budhists use it for the globular berries of the fragrant musk-like *Nyctanthes*, in Sanscrit *mallika*; a remedy, a resource; to meet, to occur; an interrogative or adversative particle, how? what way? but.

丨何天 you must be resigned to Heaven.

丨何丨何 what shall be done now? what next?

出於丨何 I must make up my mind to it.

無可丨何 or 無丨何 I could not help it; there is no help for it.

心欲食丨肚飽 I would like to eat, but I am full.

丨甚麽何 what can you do to help yourself?

丨隔一水 but the stream lies between us.

丨不過 or 丨不住 you must (do or) bear it.

愁無丨 no alleviation of grief.

怎丨他不依我 I must needs depend on him, but he would not agree with me.

過丨河橋 [this road is as bad] as the bridge over the Styx.

丨河 the Budhist river Styx, so called because the soul cannot help crossing it; paper boats are burned sixty days after death to aid in the passage, otherwise it may be drowned.

耐 耏 naiˋ — The original or second form is made of 而 *whiskers* and 彡 *pelage*, and is defined to punish by shaving the whisker; the first is now used instead. To bear with, to endure; to suffer, to forbear; patient.

丨冷 it bears the cold.

誰丨得 who can stand it? who can endure — such treatment?

丨慣 I am well used to it.

丨守時候 bear the present times patiently.

不能丨煩 I can't be so bothered; I have no time for it.

丨性 a patient kind temper.

癀丨性子 a placid temper.

難丨虛度青春 it is hard for [the girl] to pass her spring-time of life so vainly.

有能丨 great ability.

Read ˏnăng. To be able, a synonym of 能 power.

故聖人丨以天下爲一家 therefore the sages were able to regard mankind as making one family.

In *Cantonese.* A time, a while, a period of endurance.

好丨 a long time.

冇幾丨 not a great while.

等丨的 wait a little.

丨丨來吓 come in a little while.

褦 naiˋ — Stupid, raw.

丨襶 ignorant of affairs, unacquainted with the world.

NAN.

Old sounds, nam *and* nan. *In Canton*, nam *and* nan; — *in Swatow*, lam, nam, lan *and* nan; — *in Amoy*, lam *and* lan; — *in Fuhchau*, nang; — *in Shanghai*, nóⁿ *and* naⁿ; — *in Chifu*, nan.

䗴 ˓*nan*ʾ Name of an insect.

In *Cantonese*. The bites of gnats or fleas; a sore, a pimple; to stitch together; a cleat on a box, to cleat or join together.

一身丨 the body is covered with eruptions.

丨衣服 to baste clothes.

難 难 ˓*nan* *nan*ʾ From 鳥 or 隹 a *bird* and 堇 *clay*; this character suggests whether its initial and final may not have been joined, *n*-iao and k-*in*, to make the sound *nin* or *nan*; the second is a common abbreviation; occurs used for ˓*no* 儺 soft.

A species of bird; hard, difficult, grievous, not easy or pleasant; seldom attained, as happy old age; irksome, fatiguing; to distress, to harass, to force another to do; full-leaved; to be careful.

丨做 hard to do.

丨成 hard to bring about.

丨道 hard to say, it cannot be; also used as an interrogative as 丨道他不來 can you think he won't come?

丨道你忘了 can you have forgotten it?

丨道還想我 will he still think of me?

丨得 hard to get.

丨爲之 to vex him; to injure one.

丨看 repulsive, obscene; hard to see; not familiar with.

丨乎免於今之世矣 it is very hard to escape the dislike of men in this world.

丨以測度, hard to comprehend.

其葉有丨 the leaves are abundant.

Read *nan*ʾ. Adversity, calamity, trouble, difficulty; to reprove, to reprimand.

災丨 natural calamities.

天之方丨 Heaven is now sending its calamities.

受丨 fell into trouble.

未堪家多丨 I am unequal to the many cares of state.

人笨世間丨 a dolt always thinks the world goes hard with him.

大丨ʾ˓丨逃 it is impossible to escape this affliction.

月丨 the sufferings of childbirth.

於禽獸何丨 how can you reprove the birds and beasts?

互相反丨 mutually obnoxious.

死丨之節 he died honorably for his country.

In *Shanghai*. Now, at this time.

丨朝後 from this time forward.

丨末 then.

男 ˓*nan* From *field* and *strength*, because strong men are required in tillage.

The male of the human species; a man; a son; a baron, the lowest of the five ranks of nobility; a part of the domains of the Cheu dynasty.

丨人 a husband, a man.

生丨 to bear a son.

丨子漢 a high spirited man.

孝丨 a filial son; — said after a parent's death.

偕丨 [I came] with my son.

丨爵 a baron.

丨家 pertaining to the husband.

丨女 men and women.

南 ˓*nan* The original form represents plants vigorously bursting forth, and leaning towards the south.

The south; it belongs to fire and the diagram 離, and is the region of heat and vegetation, where things get nourishment; to face or go south; southern, austral; summer.

丨方 the southern regions; southerners.

可使丨面 he can face towards the south; — he can reign.

向丨 southward.

丨枝先 first shows the south; — said of the plum tree indicating spring by its early blossoms.

回丨 changed to a south and moist wind. (*Cantonese.*)

坐丨 a northern exposure.

和丨 to clasp the hands in prayer.

丨無 from the Sanscrit *nama* adoration, explained as 皈依 humbly trusting; to recite prayers; a formula like the *avè* of the Roman Catholics.

丨無佛 (or in full 丨無阿彌陀佛 *namah amitabha*) to call over Budha's name.

丨無師 or 丨無先生 at Canton denote Tao priests who use formulas and spells; elsewhere Budhist priests are also intended.

地北天丨 he is there and I am here; — we are far separated.

丨貨鋪 at Peking, a shop which sells Canton goods.

周丨召丨 the odes of Cheu and Chao.

雙丨 gold; an old poetic name.

丨海 the south regions, as Canton, or the Indian Archipelago, according to the speaker's position.

丨海縣 Canton city.

終丨 a famous hill near Si-ngan fu in Shensi.

楠 枏 ˓*nan* An even grained, yellowish, fine wood, called 梗丨 much used for furniture; it grows in Kiangsi.

伽丨 a fragrant wood now brought from Annam, and used for beads.

丨柴 a fine grained hard wood.

喃 ˏnan Incessant talking; gabble.
呢 〡 chattering; twittering, as swallows.
三日不〡口生荆棘 if you stop study for three days, thistles will grow in your mouth; — continual study is necessary to attain rank.
〡〡菓 a name given in the Archipelago to the fruit of the *Cynometra cauliflora*, the Malay *puki-andjing*.

諵 ˏnan Like the last.
The noise of general conversation; to sing out, to call over; to mutter, to perform incantations.
〡〡 incessant talking.
〡誏 to grumble at another.
〡過他聽 call them over in his hearing.

蝻 ˏnan An unauthorized character, composed of *insect* and *south*.
The immature locusts, whose wings have not fully grown, are so called in Kwangtung.
〡子 or 蝗〡 unfledged locusts.

腩 ˋnan To boil meat; dried meat.
In *Cantonese*. The flesh on the belly of an animal; a fat abdomen.
肚〡大 a big belly.

揇 ˋnan To grasp with the hand.
In *Cantonese*. To measure by spanning the fingers; a span, a finger's length; to thwack, to beat.
兩〡一尺 two spans make a foot.
〡倒 to push down.
一篙竹〡一船人 to lamm a whole crew with one stick; — to rail at a class for the fault of one.

In *Fuhchau*. To push out or away, as by the hand or foot.
〡開 to push open; to push off, as a boat.

赧 ˋnan From 赤 *red* and 艮 *flexible*.
To blush, to turn red, but not with any desire to reform; a blush.
〡顏 blushing.
驚〡 to redden when detected.
心〡面赤 mortified at heart and blushing.
能無〡然愧哉 [can you see this,] and not blush for very shame?
鹹〡〡 too salt. (*Cantonese.*)

戁 ˋnan To venerate, to respect; to be in awe of; reverence.
不〡不悚 neither terrified nor discomposed.

NANG.

Old sound, nung. *In Canton*, nong; — *in Swatow*, lang; — *in Amoy*, long; — *in Fuhchau*, nòng; — *in Shanghai*, nong; — *in Chifu*, nang.

囊 ˏnang From 橐 a *satchel* and 襄 to *praise*, both contracted.
A bag, a sack; a purse; perquisites, salary, property; to put in a bag.
行〡 baggage; a havresack.
空〡 the bag is empty; *met.* poor.
皮〡 a leather sack.
解〡 to open one's purse, to pay money.
官〡 official income.
酒〡飯袋 only a wine-bottle and rice-bag; — you lazy lout!
〡螢映雪 they bagged the fireflies and reflected the snow — in order to study.

臭皮〡 a vulgar term for a corpse.
探〡取物 [easy as] feeling for a thing in a bag.

曩 ˋnang In former times, days gone by; previously; passed by.
〡昔 anciently, formerly.
〡日 on that former day, lately, recently.
不念〡者 forgetful of former times.
彩〡 the crowned cock. (*Gallicrex cristatus.*)

灢 nangˀ Muddy; water dammed up or thick, so that it will not run.
泱〡 muddy water.

攮 ˋnang, **擃** ˋnang To fend off; to push from one with violence; to stab.
推〡 to force one's way, as through a crowd.
戳針〡線 to stick in the needle and brandish the thread.

齉 nangˀ An unauthorized character.
In *Pekingese*. To speak through the nose; an indistinct, nasal enunciation.
〡鼻子 a nose stuffed like a bag, as one who has a cold.

壤 nangˀ Dust, dirt; a cave.

NĂNG.

Old sound, neng. *In Canton*, năng *and* ning; — *in Swatow*, neng; — *in Amoy*, leng; — *in Fuhchau*, neng *and* ning; — *in Shanghai*, năng; — *in Chifu*, năng *and* ning.

能 ꜀năng A strong animal resembling the 熊 bear, with deer's hoofs and solid bones, — perhaps a moose; power, ability, skill; apt, capable, skillful; competent, talented; duty, function; capability, as of a machine; serves as an auxiliary, may, can; to be able.

他有丨幹 (or 丨耐) he has ability; he is clever at business.

丨否 can it be done?

才丨 talents, power.

丨人所不丨 he can do what others cannot.

折脚的丨彀行走 the lame are able to walk.

丨一不丨二 you cannot do that over again.

爾焉丨浼我哉 how can you presume to defame me so?

無所不丨 or 全丨 almighty, powerful, omnipotent.

無丨 incapable; powerless, uninfluential.

丨率 the action or function of a machine.

In *Cantonese*. Unlucky, ill-omened; to walk on the heels; to tie up, to connect with, attached to; to accompany.

初日꜀丨꜀丨 to meet a bad sign at the new moon.

꜁丨꜁丨吓 limping along.

丨꜄住佢 tie it up, as a boat.

In *Shanghai*. An adverbial termination like *ly*, following verbs; just, nothing more, in which cases it is an expletive.

險險丨 dangerously.

稀稀丨 very rarely.

那丨 that way, how? *q.d.* what-ly?

如同皇帝丨 just like the emperor.

檸 ꜀ning A tree, from whose bark a medicinal tincture is made.

丨檬水 lemon syrup.

丨頭 a tenon.

𩟗 ꜀ning To stuff the inside; to eat to repletion.

獰 ꜀ning Long hair of dogs; fierce; repulsive, like the guardian images in temples.

噪丨 clamor, loud contention, like the baying of dogs.

鬡 ꜀ning Hair in confusion is 鬡丨; the same phrase is applied to thickets, brambles, and any tangled growth.

儜 ꜀ning Distressed, weak, wearied.

苦於拘丨 embarrassed and sad on account of inability — to do things or fill one's post.

NAO.

Old sound, nio, mio, mò, nok, *and* not. *In Canton*, nao, nò, *and* nau; — *in Swatow*, ngio, nau, lo, *and* lau; — *in Amoy*, lau; — *in Fuhchau*, nao *and* no; — *in Shanghai*, no *and* nung; — *in Chifu*, nao.

鐃 ꜀nao Small hand-bells, which were used in the army to stop the music of drums; a bullet was hung inside as a tongue; hand cymbals; the clang of brazen instruments.

一對丨 a pair of cymbals.

丨鈎 a watchman's hook to grapple thieves.

譊 ꜀nao Noisy wrangling; contentious disputations, as among sectaries.

諠丨 noisy disputes.

丨丨者天下皆訟也 the whole country was annoyed by their disputations.

呶 ꜀nao From *mouth* and *slave*; used with the last, and also read ꜀na.

Clamorous vociferation.

嘮丨 the noisy bickering of people.

丨丨數千言 babbling out many thousand words.

丨讓于道 a street brawl.

載號載丨 they bawl, they clamor; said of drunken guests.

怓 ꜀nao Perturbation or confusion of intellect, beclouded; boastful.

殉慾致丨 vicious desires becloud the mind.

以謹惛丨 in order to check those who brag and disturb.

猱 ꜀nao From *dog* and *flexible*, alluding to its long soft hair.

A species of monkey, also called 金線狨 or gold-thread entellus, having long yellowish hair, larger than the common monkey, and described as clever in scratching the tiger; it is probably the entellus.

毋教丨升木 you need not teach a monkey to climb trees.

峱 ꜀nao A mountain near the capital of Tsi, not far from the present northern boundary of Shantung, famous in ancient history.

子之茂兮遭我乎丨 how skillful you are! you met me going to Mt. Nao.

獶 ˛nao Also read ˛nung.

A large and fierce watch-dog, with long, shaggy hair, like the Mongolian shepherd dogs.

丨匪 banditti in Yunnan and Sz'ch'uen, who do not shave their heads.

旄丨 long haired, as dogs.

丨苗 a tribe of aborigints still existing in Sz'-ch'ing fu in the northwest of Kwangsi.

憹 ˛nao From *heart* and *husbandry*.

Disquieted and vexed.

懊丨 annoyed or disturbed, as by untoward events; to deeply regret.

Read ˛nung. Pleased, glad.

硇 ˛nao A mineral, 丨砂, found in the salt lakes in Tibet; it is impure sal-ammoniac, with traces of sulphur.

腦 堖 ʻnao Composed of 肉 *flesh* or 匕 *spoon*, 巛 which represents the *hair*, and 囟 the *medulla*; the second form is unusual.

The brain; glossy, smooth, like marrow; gum camphor.

丨漿 the brain.

丨袋 the head; *met.* the mind or capacity; the wits.

丨蓋 the skull or brain-pan.

丨後見腮 to see the jaws from behind, — is a bad phrenological sign.

無頭丨 no head for the matter; heedless, stupid, imprudent.

潮丨 gum camphor; a northern name, showing that it is from Ch'ao-cheu fu in Kwangtung.

剌丨 to scratch the head, as when cogitating.

惱 ʻnao From *heart* and *brain*.

Something that vexes the brain; indignant, annoyed; hating, revengeful.

發丨 to get angry.

丨恨 irritated at; hating.

煩丨 or 懊丨 disturbed, troublesome.

一股丨氣 a fit of anger.

丨你 vexatious; it disappoints you.

瑙 碯 ʻnao From *gem* or *stone* and *brain*, alluding to the striæ.

The general name for stones like opal, cornelian, agate, onyx, jasper, &c., is 瑪丨; they are distinguished from similar quartzose minerals called 玉 by their veinings and colors.

撓 挠 ʻnao From *hand* and *eminent*; similar to *jao'* 橈 and also read *jao'* to bind up; the second is a vulgar form, and used only in the sense of scratching.

To disturb, to vex; to disarrange; to twist; to pervert, to distort; to scratch.

丨心 to annoy the mind.

丨亂是非 to pervert right and wrong, as by malicious talebearing.

丨屈 to keep up one's pluck.

不膚丨 not to show fear; give no sign of faint-heartedness.

癢癢丨 a back-scratcher.

丨癢 to scratch an itching spot.

丨頭 at a loss what to do; not easy to effect.

大丨 an ancient statesman who is said to have established the sexagenary cycle in B. C. 2637, and whose name, some writers have suggested, may be intended for Noah.

鬧 閙 nao' From *quarrel* and *market*, contracted to *door* and *market*.

The noisy wrangling and confusion of a market; a bustle, hum, tumult; obstreperous; to scold, to rail; to make a disturbance, to embroil.

太熱丨 a great noise, a great stir and parade, as at a review.

丨玩 to play, to romp.

丨人 to scold one.

丨事 to make trouble.

丨酒 a carouse; a drunken rout.

大丨一塲 a great tumult.

直慣丨 always in some mischief.

丨稟帖 to bother with petitions.

高興丨熱 an enthusiastic reception.

相丨 to berate; to talk harshly.

大丨花燈 a great display of lanterns, as on the 15th of the first moon.

丨駕子 a proud impracticable fellow.

丨裝 great parade and glitter.

丨掃 a head-dress shaped like a broom.

In *Pekingese*. To occur suddenly, to meet anything untoward; troubled by, particular about.

丨了一身的水點 unluckily I got well spattered.

愛丨連陰天 there will be several lowering days.

丨穿衣 finical about his dress.

淖 nao' From *water* and *excelling*.

Mud, slush, mire; thoroughly wet; a certain stream.

丨泥 miry; deep mud, as after a long rain.

肥肉丨人 fat meat disgusts one.

Read *chao'*. Harmony, as seen in a well ruled state.

Read *choh*ˎ Gentle; delicate, as a girl.

丨約 easy, graceful.

臑 nao' The ulna or outer bone of the arm; others say the humerus

臂丨 the fore quarter, as of a bullock.

Read ˛'rh. Hot and broken, as overdone meat.

搙 nao' Also read *noh*ˎ

To handle, to play with; to prop up.

捻丨 to fumble over, to play.

別丨壞了 don't spoil that by handling it. (*Pekingese.*)

NÉI.

Old sound, nui. *In Canton*, noi *and* nui ; — *in Swatow*, lai *and* nui ; — *in Amoy*, lōe ; — *in Fuhchau*, noi *and* nòi ; — *in Shanghai*, néi ; — *in Chifu*, néi.

餧 餒 ˋnéi — From to *eat* and *stable* or to *depute*; the second of these is least used, though most proper, and is also read *wéi*ˀ to feed.

Hungry, half famished; to expose to starvation; putrid fish.

魚丨而肉敗不食 do not eat putrid fish or tainted meat.

丨爛 rotten, spoiled.

凍丨其妻子 he exposed his wife and children to cold and starvation.

鮾 ˋnéi — Like the last.

Putrid fish.

魚丨 stinking fish.

內 néiˀ — From 入 to *enter* and 冂 a *border* from out of it.

Within, inner, inside; internal, in distinction from external; interior; in the court or palace; in; that which is inclosed or within; near to, personal; among, in the midst of; the internal organs, the viscera; the inner rooms of a house.

丨地 the Inner Land, China, the secluded land; into the country.

丨人 or 賤丨 my wife.

尊丨 your wife.

丨眷止步 stop at the female apartments.

庭丨 or 大丨 the seraglio.

丨姪 my own nephew.

感刻五丨 deeply engraved on my bowels; *i. e.* affectionately remembered.

有丨才 he has book learning; — a mere theorist.

丨中有幾個 there are some among them.

不在丨 it is not included.

作丨吉 an internal operation will succeed.

丨 and 外 are widely applied in contrast, outer and inner; internal and external; native and foreign; home and abroad; inclusive and exclusive, &c.

丨云 in which it is said, the abovementioned.

丨務府 Office of the Imperial Household.

分丨 it belongs to my post.

丨傷 an internal injury.

有諸丨必形諸外 if it be in the heart, it will appear in the face.

Read *nah*, as a synonym of 納. To insert in.

以柄丨孔 to put a handle in the hole.

NEU.

Old sounds, nu, net, *and* nok. *In Canton*, nau ; — *in Swatow*, no ; — *in Amoy*, lò ; — *in Fuhchau*, niu ; — *in Shanghai*, nú ; — *in Chifu*, no.

䨲 ˏneu — A rabbit or hare was once thus called in Kiangnan.

Read *wan*ˀ. The name of an official 丨杰 in the Liang state during feudal times, about B.C. 300.

㲋 ˋneu — Also read *k'au*ˀ Milk; to give milk to, to suckle, as was once done by a tigress in the state of Tso.

丨於菟 suckled by a tigress, as was a child named Teu 鬥 when cast out in his infancy.

耨 鎒 槈 neuˀ — From *plow-handle* or *metal* and *disgrace*; the third form is obsolete.

A hoe for weeding; to weed, to clear grounds of grass; to study.

丨草 to root out weeds.

鋤丨 to hoe and weed.

耒丨之利以敎天下 to teach the people the advantages of plowing and weeding.

筆耕舌丨 to plow with the pencil and hoe with the tongue; — to be a pedagogue.

獳 neuˀ — A snarling dog, a snappish cur.

侯丨 a servant of Earl Tsao mentioned in history about B.C. 630.

Read ˏ*jü*. A marine animal, the 朱丨, having fins and a fox's shape; probably a seal.

檽 neuˀ — A kind of pine growing in Kiangnan, the 丨梓, whose wood is suitable for coffins.

構丨 a kind of bark used in dyeing pink.

NGAI.

See also under AI *for similar sounds. Old sounds,* ai, ngai, at, ngat, *and* ngak. *In Canton,* oi, ngei, *and* ngoi; — *in Swatow,* ngai, ai, *and* gai; — *in Amoy,* ai, gai, *and* ngaiⁿ; — *in Fuhchau,* ai *and* hai; — *in Shanghai,* é, ngé, *and* téⁿ; — *in Chifu,* ai.

哀 ꜀ai — From *mouth* and *clothes.* To grieve for, to compassionate, to feel for; to sympathize; sorrow; grieving; lamentable, distressing, sad, woful; mournful, minor, as music; pity, grief, commisseration; urgently, heartily; a lament, as for a dear friend; alas, alas!

丨憐 to feel for other's woes.

丨哉 alas, how sad!

丨懇 I urgently beseech you.

可丨 lamentable!

丨丨痛哭 bitter sorrow and weeping.

悲丨 to sorrow; grief; pity for.

丨丨上告 with bitter grief is this presented; a phrase in petitions.

丨衣 mourning clothes.

丨丨父母 alas! my parents.

丨子 an orphan.

今此下民亦孔之丨 henceforth the common people will be in a sad plight.

其音丨其節寡 its tones are sad and its stops are few.

丨而不傷 mournful but not distressing; said of music.

丨求 a sorrowful supplication — for aid.

唉 欸 ꜀ai — A signing, mournful tone; an interjection of disgust or regret; a tone or word of reply, yes, so; a belching sound.

訊丨 to ask in alarm.

丨可憐 oh, how sad!

丨丨 hushaby! used by nurses.

埃 ꜀ai — From *earth* and a *particle.* Fine dust, the particles floating in the air; in some places used for dead as dirt, *i. e.* stiff, stark, dust that no longer moves.

丨的 dead; also dusty.

丨字 a grammatical term for a noun.

塵丨封了 the dust has settled on it; 塵丨 is used by the Buddhists for the defilements of the world.

丨丨滾滾 the dust fills the air.

獃 呆 ꜀ai, ꜀tai — From *dog* and *how;* it is also read ꜀*tai;* the second and common form is regarded as erroneous; some say it is a contraction of ʿ*pao* 保 to protect; others, a sort of plum.

A puppy not yet able to take care of itself; foolish, silly; acting without an end, having no aim or energy.

丨人 a silly, unready man.

詐丨 to feign or act like a fool.

癡丨 stupid, doltish.

丨住 to linger about, to loaf in the streets.

丨進不丨出 he looks stupid, but he has wit enough.

丨笑 a silly laugh.

賣賣丨 to gaze in the doorway, to idle away time in looking at the passers by.

皚 ꜀ai — Whiteness, as of snow.

霜雪丨丨兮 how white is the glistening snow and hoar-frost!

敳 ꜀ai — Able to regulate, or order and arrange; to reform.

隤丨 the second of eight brothers of the clan Kaoyang 高陽 B. C. 620, all of whom were statesmen.

毐 ʿai — From *mother* and *scholar;* it resembles *tuh,* 毒 noxious.

One who has no principle; given up to lust.

丨人 a rake, a vile fellow.

愛 ai˒ — Originally composed of 旡 or 旣 above 心, and contracted to the present form; the radical 夊 was afterwards added to denote their action; it is also read *wéi*˒ in poetry.

The exhibition of humanity 仁 in the actions; the utterance of benevolent feeling; to love, to take delight in; to think on affectionately; attached to, fond of; to like, to desire, to wish; love, kindness, regard; the object of affection, a beloved; sparing of, to grudge; forbearing of, tender towards, — a sense found in epitaphs.

親丨 friendship; mutual love, as of relatives.

丨莫助之 I love him but am unable to help him.

令丨 your daughter; in Fuhkien, this sense is sometimes expressed by adding 女 to this word.

可丨 lovely, amiable; desirable.

蒙你過丨 many thanks for your great kindness.

丨己須丨人 you should love others as yourself.

丨借日子 sparing of time.

溺丨 excessive and blind love for, as a girl or a child.

丨情 amorous.

丨酒 fond of drink.

靡丨斯牲 I have not grudged one of my [sacrificial] cattle.

你丨得多 you want too much.

丨學好 you should imitate the good.

In *Cantonese.* Imminent, near to.

丨死 dangerously sick, near death.

僾 ai˒ — Like, similar; appearing as if; hard to see; to pant, out of breath.

丨然如見 it looks like it, it is very natural.

如彼遡風亦孔之丨 like going against the wind, which puts one quite out of breath.

噯 *ai`* To belch; warm, genial air; to grunt in a disapproving tone.

丨呀 or 哎呀 an exclamation of surprise, heiya!

曖 *ai`* The sun hidden by clouds; obscured, clouded.

丨丨 moon behind clouds.

丨昧 obscure; careless, untidy; underhand.

暧 *ai`* Like the last.

Dull, hidden.

丨曃 dim, as the clouded moon; not fully acquainted with.

薆 *ai`* Plants growing very luxuriantly; hidden, as by the thick growth.

丨障 hidden, shaded.

晻丨 fragrant.

玉丨 a fig common in Formosa and the south, which grows on a vine. (*Ficus stipulata.*)

草木丨蔚 the grass and trees are very thick.

丨丨 hard to be seen.

艾 *ngai`* From *plants* and to *reap*.

Mugwort, artemisia, or any plant from which moxa, or rather the punk is obtained; a general term for labiate plants like mint or catnip; old, fifty, from the hair turning gray, like moxa; to take relaxation, to quiet; to finish, to carry out; to stop; to nourish; prospered; finished.

丨絨 moxa punk; it is also used with castor-oil to make red-ink paste for stamping.

丨符 an artemisia charm hung over the door on the 5th of the 5th moon.

丨把 mugwort, steamed to dispel pain.

保丨爾後 I will protect and care for your posterity.

夜未丨 the night is not yet over.

少丨 a beautiful woman.

老丨 an old man

天下丨安 the country is now quieted.

丨旗招福 the mugwort standard brings luck;—a phrase used at the dragon-boat festival.

礙 碍 *ngai`* From *stone* and to *hesitate*; the second form is mostly used.

To hinder, as a rock in the road; to embarrass, to oppose; to impede, to limit, to stop progress; to restrain, to let, as one's conscience does; to be an offense to, to irritate; an objection, a restraint, a hindrance.

不丨 no objection, that will make no difference, no harm in it.

有丨於人 to offend one.

丨口 to hesitate in telling.

丨石 a stumbling stone.

丨着 injured by, stopped.

總不丨着 does not at all interfere with or impugn.

妨丨 a hindrance; there may be serious consequences.

丨諸以禮樂 [sages] restrained the people by etiquette and music.

不丨此只丨於彼 it is no obstacle to this, but it vitiates that.

四無丨智 a Budhist phrase denoting four kinds of limitless knowledge (*pratisamvid*) that belongs to every *arhat*, who knows every meaning, every law, every argument, and every pleasant discourse.

閡 *ngai`* Analogous to the last.

To shut a door to keep others out; shut off by a wall; stopped by, headed off.

阻丨 prevented.

傷丨 hindered by an injury.

止丨 deterred, restrained.

進則丨山 if we go on, we shall be stopped by the hills.

鳷 *ngai`* The hen of the 桃蟲鷦 or tailor bird.

餀 *ai`* From to *eat* and *mugwort*, referring to the odor.

Food which has become tainted.

暑物丨壞 in hot weather things spoil.

NGAN.

Old sounds, an, ngan, am, *and* ngam. *In Canton*, an, on, òm, ăm, ngon, *and* ngam;—*in Swatow*, an, am, *and* ngai;—*in Amoy*, an, am, gan, *and* jen;—*in Fuhchau*, ngang, ang, *and* eng;—*in Shanghai*, ö^n, ó^n, a^n, *and* ngö^n;—*in Chifu*, an.

安 *˛an* From *shelter* and a *woman* under it, denoting peace; it is much used in proper names.

Still, quiet; rest, tranquillity; peaceful, calm; at ease, not fearful; to settle, to tranquillize, to make easy; to place, to lay down, as a cup; to substitute, to put for; to put to rights, to mend; contented; an interrogative, how? how can? where? as a *preposition*, in, during.

丨樂 joy, content.

丨樂公 a mere man of pleasure; a term derived from the son of Liu Pi, who took it easy when he lost his crown.

你丨心 make yourself easy.

老者丨之 he quieted the aged.

丨享太平 to enjoy the pleasures of quiet.

偷丨 to steal leisure, — *i. e.* lazy.

竟得丨然 after all he does as he pleases.

丨分 contented with one's lot.

如今丨在 where is he now?

丨是丨非 which is right, which is wrong?

丨慰 to console, to soothe.

丨息香 gum benjamin or benzoin; by some referred to 丨息國 or Parthia, whence it was brought; others suppose it was so called because it was burned in worship; it also includes storax, obtained from the *Liquidambar orientalis,* and brought to China.

丨息日 the Sabbath; a foreign term.

丨置 prepare all things in readiness.

問丨 to inquire after one's health.

丨好 to wish health to.

朕丨 Ourself is well; a reply by the Emperor.

丨神 to set up a god in its shrine.

身體欠丨 indisposed; I feel out of sorts.

丨家 an allotment out of one's wages.

丨閒 a leisure time.

丨南國 Cochinchina, Annam.

丨丨 naturally, without constraint or effort.

托你丨好了 I beg that you will fix this, as a blade into its handle.

丨拉那裏 where have you put it? (*Shanghai.*)

丨不上這句話 do not say such a thing; do not talk so.

生丨白造 it is made out of whole cloth; a concocted story.

丨作乜字 what character will you put for it? (*Cantonese.*)

丨放好 or 丨埋 put it away carefully, lay it aside safely. (*Cantonese.*)

鞍 ꜀ngan — From *leather* and *ease* as the phonetic.

A saddle.

卸丨子 take off the saddle.

馬丨橋 an arched bridge.

丨前馬後 [I would fain be one] to run by your horse.

據丨上馬 saddle and mount quickly.

堷 ꜀an — A burying place on a moor, such as is granted to the poor for free interment.

媶 ꜀an — An impure minded woman; an adulteress; dirty.

丨䁆 filthy; occurs written thus, and like the next.

腤 ꜀an — To boil flesh; to make soup.

In *Pekingese.* Dirty.

丨䐶 another form of the last.

諳 ꜀an, an꜄ — From *words* and *sound.*

Versed in, accustomed to, skilled in; to know about, fully acquainted with; to memorize; to recite or chant.

丨練 skilled in any craft or art.

不丨世事 ignorant of the world.

丨識書理 he knows all about books.

深丨兵法 deeply skilled in strategy.

盦 ꜀an — From *dish* and *wine* in it; also read *hoh,*

A cover of a dish or tripod; to put on a cover.

交虬丨 a cover with dragons carved on it.

鵪 ꜀an — From *bird* and to *conceal;* this and 鶕 are regarded as synonyms, but their descriptions vary.

The quail is 丨鶉, but the term is applied to two or three species of *Coturnix,* of which the *Coturnix dactylisonans* is one.

鬪丨鶉 to fight quails; the beaten birds, called 籠丨 are eaten.

庵 菴 ꜀ngan — From *shelter* and to *cover;* the second form has gradually come most into use, but it originally denoted a plant for thatching.

A round hut or thatched cottage; a shelter for a guard; a religious house; a reception hall, or small temple.

入丨 to become a nun.

丨堂 a convent, a monastery.

尼姑丨 a nunnery.

山丨 a summer retreat.

丨廬 soldiers' huts.

丨羅菓 a fruit first brought from India; the *amra* or mango. (*Mangifera indica.*)

Read *ngoh,* The bottom or low part; a pig-sty.

儑 [言㬎] ꜀ngan — This is sometimes read *yeh,*

Devoid of intelligence; not at ease; foolish gibes, jokes, raillery.

唵 ꜂an — To feed one's self with the hand, after the manner of the Hindoos; to hold in the mouth; used by the Mongol Budhists as the first word in their incantation 丨嘛呢叭彌吽 *Om Mani Padmi Hom.*

俺 ꜂an — A personal pronoun, common among uneducated people in the north; I, myself; it is also used in singing.

丨的 mine.

揞 ꜂an — From *hand* and *sound;* it is interchanged with ꜂yen 掩 to close.

To cover with the hand; to lean on the hand; to hide, to screen with something; to put the finger on; to suppress, to extinguish; to finger, as a flute.

被手丨住 cover your hand over it.

丨滅 to put out, as a fire; to quash.

丨脈 to feel the pulse.

丨以試之 to cover a thing and make one guess.

丨風琴 to play a melodion.

丨密鑼鼓 muffle the gong and drum; — keep it quiet.

暗 *an'* The sun obscured by clouds; dimly lighted, obscure, somber; gloomy, not shining; in the dark; clandestine; stealthily, secretly, unobservedly; unintelligent; private, mental.

黑丨 dark, as a room.

天色丨 a dark day.

丨想 to cogitate, to think it over.

丨輪 a hidden wheel, as in a propeller.

打丨號 to give a hint, to signal.

丨中做事 to do things in the dark; underhand doings.

丨害 to secretly injure.

丨間 in the dark.

燈丨 a dull, glimmering lamp.

丨洞裏 in the dark.

丨昧 dull, obscure; stupid.

丨訪民情 to secretly learn what the people think.

丨室 or 丨地 a secret place.

明鎗易當丨箭難防 an open gun is easily withstood, but the unseen arrow is hard to guard against.

丨丨裏 without thought and unpremeditated, privately done. (*Shanghai.*)

暗 *an'* Like the last.

Obscure, dark.

丨然 how gloomy and dim!

闇 *an'* To shut the door and withdraw from society; retired, dark, like a recess, badly lighted; undiscernible; evening; dark; eclipsed.

丨門謝客 to refuse one's self to one's friends.

丨然而日彰 dark indeed, but daily becoming brighter, — as a good man's mind.

丨昏時 night, in the dark.

丨弱 ignorant and irresolute.

案 *an'* From *wood* and *rest;* occasionally used for the next.

A table on which to lean; a table, bench, or bar before a judge; that which lies on it, a case in law, an action; an occurrence, event, affair, spoken of judicially; a sentence, a decision; to try, to decide a case; a limit or frontier; in order, a series; a cup, a goblet.

丨卷 or 丨文 official records, law papers.

丨情 the circumstances of a case.

一件丨 a case in court.

丨由 the merits of a case.

丨查 it appears from the records.

審丨 to try a case.

定丨 to decide a case.

命丨 a case of murder or one that involves life.

傳丨 to summon the parties, witnesses and all, to court.

在丨 on record, is in court.

丨房 the room for records; the writers of dispatches, &c.

丨前 at the bar.

翻丨 or 反丨 to rehear or revise a case.

舊丨 an old or decided case.

舉丨齊眉 to lift the goblet and compare the eyebrows; — a wedded pair.

刑名丨件 the punishment meets the crime.

一副香丨 a set of incense furniture placed on altars.

無頭公丨 a case without evidence; unaccounted for.

調丨 to appeal a case.

丨首 first on the list of graduates in a district or prefecture.

拍丨 to slap the table.

按 *an'* From *hand* and *rest.*

To put down, to lower; to stop, to desist; to prevent moving; to put the hand, to hold, to grasp; to pull in; to rub, to chafe; go about and to examine, to try; a *preposition*, as, according to, by, in conformity to.

丨月支銀 to pay wages by the month.

丨劍而立 he grasped his blade and stood ready.

丨法 according to law.

丨摩 to shampoo.

丨當 to give security, to pledge.

手丨心頭 to lay the hand on the heart, as in self-examination.

丨兵 to halt the troops.

丨據 according to the evidence.

丨止 stop it.

丨扳眼 to play on the keys — as when testing the pitch.

丨察司 the criminal judge in a province.

丨轡 to rein in a horse.

以手丨物 to press the hand on a thing.

Read *ngoh,* To repress, to press, to press down.

爰整其旅以丨徂旅 he then marshaled his troops to stop these invaders.

岸 *ngan'* *an'* From 屵 a steep *bank* and 干 a *shield.*

A shore, bank, or beach; the edge or brink of a stream; a high cliff; end of a journey, the goal, the object of effort; steps of a palace; a high forehead; a valorous or eminent person; a prison in the country.

丨上 on the bank.

上丨 to go ashore; to disembark.

無涯無丨 boundless and shoreless.

回頭是丨 the shore is just behind you; you can mend your ways.

魁丨 a fine-looking person.

攏丨 tie [the boat] to the bank.

兩面駁丨 both banks are walled up.

道丨 the end of a doctrine.

隔丨 separated from that shore, beyond the bank.

上丨思財 when he has been dragged ashore, he'll think of gain, — as a man rescued.

宜 丨 宜 獄 some are put in one jail and some in another.

到 彼 丨 to reach that shore, — by crossing the Sansara, the equivalent of *param* or *paramita*, which is the 六 渡 or six means of passing over, of which the last is *pradjna* or wisdom, and alone fits the soul for *nirvana*.

嫸 *ngan'* A well dressed, elegant woman.

黯 *an'* Turned black, as ripe mulberries or spoiled olives; sudden, quick.

丨 然 而 雷 擊 之 how suddenly the lightning struck him!

嬸 *ngan'* To restrain one's anger; hard to know; large cheeks; a bad temper; a woman who is partial to one.

颱 *an'* A gust; a hurricane.

丨 颱 縈 海 若 霹 靂 a blast swept over the sea like a clap of thunder.

NGĂN.

Old sound, en. *In Canton*, yăn; — *in Swatow*, ùn; — *in Amoy*, ún; — *in Fuhchau*, òng; — *in Shanghai*, ăng; — *in Chifu*, ăn.

恩 *ₒăn* From *heart* and *because*, intimating that the heart has reason for its love.

Favor, grace, mercy, kindness; benefits, obligations; imperial favor; charitable, compassionate; to oblige, to enrich, to show favor to; private, heartfelt, partial to.

皇 丨 or 天 丨 imperial favor.

天 丨 divine, heavenly grace.

開 丨 to show favor, lenient to.

忘 丨 負 義 ungrateful and reprobate.

丨 德 於 百 姓 his kindness reaches to the people; — said of a magistrate.

丨 情 loving affection, as among relatives.

丨 將 仇 報 to requite evil for good.

受 丨 benefited; received mercy.

感 丨 feeling grateful.

大 丨 人 怎 做 敵 頭 how can my benefactor turn to be my foe?

報 丨 單 a placard of the cure effected by an idol; they are like votive tablets, and the thankful devotee often vows to post hundreds of them in the streets.

丨 斯 勤 斯 鬻 子 with love and with toil I nourished my young.

丨 賞 gracious rewards.

NGAO.

Old sounds, ngo, nga, *and* ngap. *In Canton*, ao, au, ò, *and* ngò; — *in Swatow*, ngao, ao, t'ap, kao, *and* ka; — *in Amoy*, ao, ngò, ò, *and* kao; — *in Fuhchau*, ngo, ngao, *and* o; — *in Shanghai*, o, *and* ngo; — *in Chifu*, ao.

鏖 *ₛao* From *metal* and *deer*.

To slaughter, to exterminate; to fight and give no quarter; a copper pan.

丨 兵 destroyed all the troops.

丨 塲 大 戰 a bloody field of battle.

丨 騙 to deceive, to impose on.

爊 *ₒao* From *fire* and *antelope*.

To warm or bake in a close vessel; in Canton, it means to boil or stew meats; to warm in water.

丨 齋 to stew vegetables.

丨 夜 to watch, to sit up nights.

丨 熟 stewed thoroughly.

坳 *ₒao* A hollow in the ground, a cavity, a depression; undulating, rolling, as land.

山 丨 depression in the hill.

丨 堂 a little hollow.

In *Cantonese*. A turn, a corner; poor, destitute.

轉 丨' turn the corner.

ₒ丨 屭 in great want.

凹 *ₛao* *ₛwa* Like the last, but the character is designed to depict its meaning; it is read *ₛwa* in the north of China.

An indentation, a hollow, a hole; a cavity; the undulations in a ridge.

丨 字 charaters cut in bas-relief.

窪 丨 a hollow, where rain collects.

丨 減 的 lost a little. (*Cantonese.*)

敖 *ₛngao* Composed of 放 to *open* and 出 *out* contracted; it is used for 傲' and the next three.

To saunter, to ramble; proud; tall; pleased; a stage for pantomimes and mummers; old name of a region near K'aifung fu, in which there was a noted hill.

微 我 無 酒 以 丨 以 遊 it is not because I have no wine, and might neither ramble nor travel, — that I grieve.

高 丨 丨 a very tall man.

彼 交 匪 丨 in their intercourse they were not proud.

遨 ˓ao To ramble, to divert one's-self; to travel for pleasure.
四海丨遊 to roam over the world.
丨戲 to go and see shows.
笑丨風月 to divert one's self in the breezy moonlight.

驁 ˓ao A vicious, spirited horse; stubborn, plucky; indomitable and willful.
桀丨 resolute; proud and overbearing.
丨然不顧 stubborn and careless of consequences.

謷 ˓ao Occurs used for 慠 proud.
A degenerate unworthy fellow; needless, harsh words used by an officer; to dislike advice; high.
丨丨乎大哉 how exalted he is! — as Laotsz'.
丨丨然 the cry of weeping and sobbing.

熬 ˓ngao It is often wrongly used for the next from confusion of radicals.
To boil, to cook by boiling; to parch grain, to kiln-dry; to distil; to simmer; to brew or decoct; to hanker for; to disturb.
丨糕 to boil cakes.
丨藥 to decoct medicine.
丨夜 to watch all night.
衆庶丨丨 the people were all perplexed.
丨不過 to long for; unable to resist, as a drunkard his cups.
丨膏 to seethe, as opium; to simmer to a paste.
In *Shanghai*. Offensive; repellant.
丨勿得 disgusting, nauseous.
丨勿過 I can't endure it.

獒 ˓ao A large dog, described as four feet high, fierce but tractable; it is probably the powerful mastiff of Tibetan shepherds.
神丨 a powerful massive dog.

勢 ˓ao Strong, brave.
丨力 great prowess, fearless.

嗷 ˓ao A loud wailing; a mournful clamor, as of hungry beggars; noise of many voices.
嘈丨 incessant noise.
衆口丨丨 all are clamoring at once, every one teases me.
家口丨 children crying for food.
哀鳴丨丨 doleful is the screaming — of the wild geese.

撽 ˓ao To shake, to joggle, to rattle, to twirl.
丨鐘子 to ring a bell.
丨骰子 to throw dice.
丨簽 to shake the lots, as when divining.
丨檯 to joggle the table (*Canton.*)
丨椿 to shake the post.

璈 ˓ao Musical instruments in general.
彈八琅之丨 to play on the eight (or all) instruments.
奏雲丨 the distant band is playing.

磝 ˓ngao A stony surface, covered with pebbles.
山丨丨而相軌 see the stony hills as if following one another in a line.

聱 ˓ao From *ear* and *pleased*.
Refusing to hear another.
丨牙 disinclined to listen, inattentive to wily words.
丨耴 noisy cries of a multitude.

鼇 ˓ao A sea-monster allied to the turtle, which bears up the earth; a kraken which carried off the Pung-lai mountains 蓬萊 where the genii lived, into the eastern sea; its legs were used by 女媧氏 for the four poles 極 of the earth; this fable may refer to the ark.
金丨奠海 [like as] the golden kraken rests quietly in the sea; said of Lewchew.

鰲 ˓ao Like the last.
A huge sea fish.
丨頭 a gargoyle like a fish.
莫名丨戴 I cannot express the obligation I shall feel.
獨占丨頭 perched alone on the whale's head; *i. e.* to become the *chwang-yuen* or first Hanlin.
丨魚 a species of scorpæna (*Pterois*); and the 石丨魚 an orange colored species (*Sebastes platycephalus*), are both found at Canton.

螯 ˓ao The nippers or large claws of the crab, called also 蟹鉗.
車丨 a shell like the *Spondylus;* an immense bivalve, which probably denotes the great *Chama*, under which fishermen are fabled to build a fire to open the shell and obtain its flesh.

廒 ˓ao The buildings of a granary; a room or bin for storing grain within a dépôt.
倉丨 the various buildings in a granary.

艔 ˓ao The stem or cut-water of a vessel; also the keel and false keel.

鷔 ˓ao An infelicitous bird, probably a species of owl, with a white body and red mouth, whose presence indicates ruin to the state.

翺 ˓ao To fly like a hawk, to skim.
丨翔 to soar to and fro, to wheel around in the air.

襖 ˓ao From *dress* and *hidden*.
A robe; an outer garment to keep off the cold; its cuffs are not made like a horse's hoof, and it does not open in front like the 袍; a coat, a jacket
綿丨 a wadded coat.
長夾丨 a lined coat.
皮丨 a fur lined robe.

懊 ᶜao Vexed, angry; to regret; avaricious.
丨恨 to hate.
丨惱 irritated, impatient; harassed.
氣怒丨鬱 to brood angrily over an act, to cherish hatred.
丨悔 self-reproach, to blame one's self, to regret a thing.

鰲 ao' A large and coarse kind of perch (*Sciæna*), brought to Macao in winter, weighing sometimes a hundred pounds; the name is also given to a species of eel.

傲 慠 ngao' From *man* and *trifling*. Proud, arrogant, uncivil, assuming; pride, rudeness; to treat rudely, to brave.
怠丨 lazy and selfish.
高丨 arrogant, supercilious.
丨慢 to scorn, to treat contemptuously.

鏊 ao' A round, iron cooking utensil, flat and shallow; a griddle.
餅丨 a griddle.
丨燒 to fry, as greens or cakes.

奧 ao' From *great* and a *bin*, but the etymologists derive it from 宀 a *shelter* and a dark *corner* where two *hands* are putting away things.

The southwest corner of a hall where the lares used to be placed, and one can be quiet; retired, deep; mysterious, obscure; within, further than one has penetrated; an office; collected; blended; genial, warm.
丨妙 abstruse, mysterious, wonderful.
深丨 difficult, esoteric, hard to understand.
祭丨 to worship the lares.
昔我往矣日月方丨 formerly, when I started, the sun and moon were warm.

澳 ao' yü' From *water* and *hidden*. A bank or high shore; a bay, inlet, cove, or bight, which can shelter ships; a dock for repairing ships.
船入丨 the ship came into the harbor.
丨門 Macao.
崎丨 Keeow Island north of it.
南丨 Namoh Island below Amoy.

墺 隩 ao' Interchanged with the last; it is also read *yuh*,

A piece of ground for building a house; an even, flat, and open plat, like a terrace; to retire into winter quarters; the inner apartments; in the water.
丨隈 the bays and headlands along a coast.
厥民丨 the people are hybernating;— they keep in their houses.
四丨，旣宅 the four shores have been built on,—referring to the deluge of Yü.

奡 ao' Assuming, haughty, lofty; name of a man in the Shang dynasty, son of Han-tsuh 寒浞 B. C. 2145 who was so strong that he could 盪舟 pull a boat on the land.

擙 ao' To grind.
In *Cantonese*. To reach up (or out) to with the hand.
丨遠的 reach out a little further.
唔丨得到 I can't reach it.

NGEU.

Old sounds, o, wu, ngu, ngot, op, *and* ok. *In Canton*, au *and* ngau;—*in Swatow*, ao *and* ngò;—*in Amoy*, ao, ò *and* ngò;—*in Fuhchau*, éu *and* ngéu;—*in Shanghai*, ù *and* ngù;—*in Chifu*, ò.

慪 ᶜeu Respectful, careful, attentive.
In *Pekingese*, read *ngeu'*.
To excite, to irritate.
不免丨氣了 he could not avoid exasperating him.

Read ᶜ*keu*. Stingy, mean.
丨得狠 excessively close and saving.

甌 ᶜeu A bowl, a deep cup.
瓦丨 an earthen bowl.
木丨 a wooden bowl.
烟丨 a tobacco-box.
半丨 half a glass, as of drink.

瞘 ᶜeu Deep sunken eyes, as of one wasted with illness.
丨斜 a cast in the eye.
額丨凸 a projecting forehead.
丨眼睛 a hollow, cavernous eye.

鷗 ᶜeu From 鳥 *bird* and 漚 *bubbles*, because it floats over the sea, and rides on the waves like the white caps.

A gull (*Larus*), including also the tern and other similar marine birds.
白丨 or 閒丨 a brownish gull common near Macao.
沙丨點點 the white gulls spot the sands.

謳 ᶜeu To sing local ballads in recitative; a song or ditty in the local patois.
粵丨 Canton songs.
丨歌 ditties; ballads, songs.
丨吟 or 丨咏 to sing songs.

歐 ᶜeu From to *breathe* and *conceal*; used for the next, and liable to be confounded with the next to that; it was anciently synonymous with the last.

To vomit, to retch; the noise of retching.

꜀嘔 ꜀eu To vomit; the sound of retching; to spit out; to disgorge, to give back unwillingly; a child's prattle; to quiet.

丨血 to spit blood, to bleed at the lungs.

作丨 a disposition to vomit.

丨吐 to puke; to cascade.

丨絲 to spin cocoons.

哾丨之 the child prattled to her.

丨回出來 to pay back money.

Read ꜀hü Loving words; to be kind to.

言語丨丨 kind and consoling talk.

꜀毆 ꜀毆 ꜀eu The second form is common in cheap books. To fight with sticks or fists; to slap; a cudgel; to bully, to wrangle; to switch up, to drive on.

丨打 to maul as in a riot.

丨傷 to wound by beating.

丨辱斯文 to disgrace a scholar by a blow.

丨斃 to beat to death, to kill in a brawl.

꜀偶 ꜀ngeu From *man* and *satyr*. An image, an idol, a statue; a pair, a match; an even number; a corresponding thing or quantity; double, paired; a companion, a mate; to pair, to marry; to accord with; to fit; as an *adverb*, abruptly, suddenly, unpremeditatedly; for the instant, for once, accidentally.

匹丨 a married couple, a pair.

佳丨 a happy, and 怨丨 an unhappy pair; a good and bad match.

丨人 a wooden man, a dolt.

丨遇 happened to meet him.

丨然 or 丨爾 by chance, suddenly, unforeseen, casual.

失丨 he has lost his mate.

丨書 to write off-hand.

拜丨像 to worship idols.

如同木丨 he is no better than a wooden image.

丨合 to unite, to pair; union.

꜀耦 ꜀ngeu Similar to the last. A pair, an even number; two persons plowing together; a fellow, a mate; to match; to pervade all nature, thorough.

配丨 to pair, to match.

千丨其耘 in thousands of pairs they weed — their fields.

丨而耕 they (長沮 and 桀溺 in Confucius' time) were plowing together, — and refused office.

對影爲丨 make a mate of your shadow.

꜀藕 ꜀ngeu The large rootstock of the *Nelumbium*, used for food.

蓮丨 the water-lily root.

糖丨 comfits of this root.

丨粉 arrow-root made of it.

丨斷絲連 snap the lily root, and the threads still join; this is applied to people singing in parts, and to the faults which geomancers guess to exist in the underground water veins.

擦丨 to rasp the roots, — and dry the water for the flour.

丨芽 tapering fingers of a lady.

꜀熰 ꜀eu The time of great heat and drought, when a sacrifice and prayers were offered.

漚꜄ ngeu꜄ To soak, to steep, to macerate; to rot or soften by soaking, as hemp.

丨霉 moldy and spoiled.

丨爛 dampened and spoiled; rotted by water.

丨到臭 soaked till it smells.

芬芳丨鬱 delicious fragrance.

Read ꜀ngeu. Bubbles on water.

泡丨 frothy spume.

驁꜄ ꜀ao To gallop wildly.

In *Cantonese*. Stupid.

丨逗 dull, heavy; no aptness or spirits for.

丨仔 a dunce.

NGO.

Old sounds, nga *and* ngap. *In Canton*, ngo; — *in Swatow*, ngo, go, *and* ho; — *in Amoy*, ngò, bé, múi, *and* húi; — *in Fuhchau*, ngo, ngwò, *and* ngwai; — *in Shanghai*, ngu; — *in Chifu*, wòä.

꜁訛 ꜁譌 ꜁ngö From *words* and *to change* or *do*; the second is least used, and often wrongly read ꜁wéi. To lie, to deceive, to change speech; to transform; to rouse, to move; to promulge error; to move about; unauthorized, as a character; false, erroneous; a fabulous sphynx that could speak and lie; an ignis fatuus.

丨言 or 丨語 false stories.

以丨傳丨 to propagate idle rumors or fables.

式丨爾心以畜萬邦 if you would reform your hearts and change all the states.

隻字無丨 not a single error in the characters.

丨詐人錢 to extort money by false pretences.

心丨丨如懸旌 my mind flutters like a dangling banner.

平秩南丨 to arrange the transformations of summer.

虛丨 superficial, erroneous.

꜁鈋 ꜁ngö To pare away the corners of a thing and make it round; a ring.

丨方爲圓 round off this square piece.

吪 ˏngö Like the last.
To move; to influence; to civilize.
尙寐無 丨 O that I might sleep on and never stir!
周公東征四國是 丨 Duke Cheu marched eastward to reduce and thus reform the four states.

娥 ˏngo Good, beautiful, its meaning in the Tsin 秦 state.
宮 丨 imperial concubines.
丨 皇 the wife of Shun.
嬌 丨 lady-like, genteel.
嫦 丨 the concubine of Prince I 羿 in early days, who stole and drank the liquor of immortality, and was translated to the moon; she represents the Diana of the Chinese.

俄 ˏngö Suddenly; a moment, momentarily; falling, imminent.
丨 然 or 丨 爾 suddenly.
丨 頃 a short time.
側弁之丨 their caps awry and like to fall.
丨 倫 袋 a kind of spencer or overcoat which buttons on the side, while a *ma-kwa* properly buttons in front.
丨 國 or 丨 羅斯國 Russia.

哦 **誐** ˏngö To chant, to rehearse in recitative; to hum over to one's self.
丨 詩 to intone or hum verses, — a common practice with literary men.
吟 丨 to sing verses.

峩 **峨** ˏngö High, like a lofty peak; a commanding manner.
丨 眉山 a snowy peak in Sz'chʻuen near the junction of the Ta-tu and Min rivers, which gives its name to the district of Ngo-mêi.
容儀丨丨 of a commanding presence.
奉璋丨丨 they bore their libation cups with gravity.

硪 ˏngö A rocky cliff.
山勢丨丨 the aspect of that cliff is grand; a tremendous high peak.

蛾 ˏngö The silkworm moth; a general name for nocturnal moths, millers, and sphinges.
蠶 丨 the silkworm moth.
丨 眉 月 the crescent moon, likened to the silkworm moth's antennæ.
燈 丨 a candle miller.
In *Pekingese*. A disease of the throat, like diphtheria.
白丨瘋 a white ulcer in the throat.
ʻ長單丨 his throat has a swelling.

鵝 ˏngö From *bird* and *I*, because it carries its head high and proudly.
The domestic goose, which has a bulb on the upper mandible; applied to large water birds of similar habits; also to a disposition of vessels in a triangle for a battle.
草 丨 the common goose.
塘 丨 the pelican.
企 丨 a penguin.
丨 毛 片 large flakes of snow.
天 丨 a crane, from its soaring.
水 鸂 丨 a kind of teal.
丨 毛 筆 a quill-pen.
獃 丨 頭 a stupid goose-head sort of fellow.
丨 眼 small cash, counterfeit cash, big as a goose's eye.
丨 酒 禮 the present of a goose and jar of wine, — at a wedding.
身先丨鸛 I myself led the squadron of ships.
布袋丨 or 海丨 a white albatross (*Diomedea brachyura*); the webbed feet are made into bags.

莪 ˏngö A small species of artemisia, or mugwort, the 丨 蒿 whose tender stalks are edible when boiled; it is also called 抱娘蒿 and the drawing resembles the tansy-leaved wormwood.

我 ʻwo ʻngö Formed of 戈 a *spear* and 手 *hand* combined, denoting the grasp on a spear; it resembles ʻ*chao* 找 to exchange.
The first personal pronoun I; mine, my, me; our; we, us.
丨 周 公 our Lord Chau.
丨 朝 Our dynasty.
丨 們 or 丨 等 or 丨 曹 we all.
在 丨 belongs or appertains to me.
丨 自 己 I myself.
丨 同 你 去 I will go with you. (*Cantonese.*)
未生丨誰是丨 who was I before I was born?
丨 的 mine, my.
無人無丨 without others or myself; — a Budhist phrase to denote abstraction and repose.
無分爾丨 no distinction between us, I'll treat you as myself.
丨 顧 丨 I look out for myself.

餓 ngöʾ öʾ Starved, hungry, faint for want of sustenance; to fast; death, famine.
丨 死 starving to death.
肚 丨 famishing.
丨 蚊子見了血 the hungry gnat has seen the blood; — said of one who snatches dainties.
丨 了一日 fasted all day.
丨 眼 a hollow, sunken eye.
丨 倒 fallen down from hunger.
丨 殍 bodies of the starved.
窮思丨想 the poor think only of appeasing their hunger.
丨 鬼 hungry ghosts, the manes of desolate families who are propitiated on the 15th of the 7th moon in a general festival; such beings are divided by the priests into 36 classes, and are represented as titans in size with mouths like needles' eyes; this condition is one of the six paths of transmigration or *gati*, and the demons, or *pretas*, are thus appeased; they act as jailers in hell; also a term of abuse to self-invited guests.

NGOH.

Old sounds, ngak, ak, *and* ngek. *In Canton*, ngok, ok, ak, ăk, ngăk, *and* ngak; — *in Swatow*, ngak, ngiak, ek, ć, at, *and* hia; — *in Amoy*, gok, ok, gek, lek, at, *and* ek; — *in Fuhchau*, ngauk, ngòk, lòk, ngao, ngiăh, aik, *and* ak; — *in Shanghai*, ăk, ngok, ok, hok, ngĕk, *and* ùh; — *in Chifu*, ùh *and* wòa.

鄂, *ngö*, ꜀ö. Used with the next two. An ancient principality lying on the Yangtsz' River in the present Hupeh, and often applied to that province; an old name for Wu-chang fu; a boundary.

丨王 Prince Ngoh of the Sung dynasty; his tomb is at Hangcheu.

愕, **㦍**, *ngö*, ö. From *heart* and *responsive*; the second form is seldom used. To shudder; startled; to wonder at; to oppose; to loathe, as food; to hinder; a hindrance.

丨然 frightened, startling.

錯丨不能對 he was so thunderstruck that he could not answer.

諤, **讍**, *ngö*, ö. Honest, blunt words; sincere sentiments of the mind.

謇丨 abrupt remarks.

直丨 to speak plainly.

千人之諾諾不如一士之丨丨 the sycophantic assent of a thousand persons is not equal to the unbiassed opinion of one scholar.

咢, *ngö*, ö. Intended to represent two persons singing in alternate strains; occurs used for the last two. To strike the drum in interludes of singing; to startle.

或歌或丨 some of them were singing and some of them drumming.

In *Cantonese*. To lift up, or stretch out the neck.

丨高頭 to perk up the head.

萼, *ngö*, ö. The receptacle of a flower, including also its persistent calyx; called also 花托 or the flower's support.

崿, *ngö*, ö. A cliff, a precipice.

崖丨 a steep ledge.

垠丨 a beach or slope at the foot of a cliff.

碍, *ngö*, ö. Stones piled up in a dangerous way.

丨嘉縣 lies on the headwaters of the Meikon River, south of Tsu-hiung fu in Yunnan.

鍔, *ngö*, ö. The sharp point of a spear, edge of a sword.

劍丨 the point of a sword.

丨丨列列 the peaks and aiguelles, — as of mountains.

鶚, *ngö*, ö. From 鳥 *bird* and 愕 *scared*, *q. d.* because of the terror it causes. The osprey or fish-eagle; also called 鵰鷄 harpy hen and 魚鷹 fish eagle; the term is applicable to all birds of the genus *Haliœtus*.

丨立 to patiently wait, as this bird does for its prey.

秋闈丨薦 in the autumnal examination he became a *küjin*.

丨展鵬程 the osprey has spread his wings and the rokh begun his journey; — *met.* a successful graduate.

腭, **齶**, *ngö*, ö. The roof of the mouth, more usually called 口嚨頂; those of swine are esteemed a delicacy.

內丨 the mouth.

上丨 the roof of the mouth.

斷丨 the gums.

堊, *ngö*, ö. White or washed clay used for porcelain; colored earths; whitewash, plaster; to plaster; a wall which has not been plastered.

噩, ö, *ngö*. From *mouth* repeated and *king*; no etymology is given; occurs used for 愕, startled. A grave and serious manner; startling, awe-struck.

丨夢 a dreadful dream.

作丨 a term for the five years in the cycle with 酉 in them.

詻, *öh*. From *words* and *each*; occurs incorrectly used for the last. Harsh, scolding words; severe orders, stern injunctions.

言容丨丨 his manners and conversation were repulsive and harsh.

鱷, **鰐**, *ngö*, ö. From *fish* and *alarming*, as the phonetic. The crocodile and the Gangetic gavial; the former is said to have formerly existed in the R. Han near Swatow, whence they were exorcised in the T'ang dynasty; *met.* rapacious, cruel.

丨紳劣吏朋比爲奸 the rapacious gentry and unscrupulous underlings make a worthy union of rascals.

丨魚 an alligator, cayman, or crocodile; it seems to be sometimes wrongly applied to fresh water dolphins.

額, **頟**, ꜀*ngö*, ꜀ö. From *head* and *guest*, or *each*; the two are not altogether identical, the second being the adverb. The forehead; the front or what is before; a fixed or regular number or quantity; what ought to be or is settled by law; incessant.

丨丨 the creaking of a cart; unceasing.

丨頭 the forehead.

丨 角 the temples.
丨 外 over and above the fixed amount; low military officials.
丨 數 the legal or settled number.
匾 丨 a tablet, such as are placed over doors by graduates.
丨 然 suddenly.
無缺 丨 there is no vacancy in the number.
寬 丨 a liberal allowance.
罔晝夜 丨 丨 day and night he unceasingly acted thus.
以手加 丨 he pats his forehead, — delighted at the good news.

頞, *ngŏ'* The root of the nose, the frontal sinus; a saddle.
幽 丨 an animal resembling the lemur.
疾首蹙 丨 to droop the head and knit the brows, as when in pain.

厄, **戹**, *ŏ'* From 厂 *cliff* and 卩 a *seal*, or a *door* and *one*; the first also specially means a knot in a tree, and the second a small inner door; both are like the next.
Impeded, cramped; in difficulty, distressed, ill-used; that which is fated to harm one; a ring fastened to reins near their ends.
困 丨 miserably off.
危 丨 in danger.
丨 窮而不憫 poor but light-hearted.
命逢水 丨 his fate will be to experience jeopardy by water.

呃, *ŏ'* From *mouth* and *impeded*; also written *ai'* 呝 to crow.
The cry of birds.
丨 喔 the cackling of a hen.
丨 丨 the note of birds.

軛, *ŏ'* From *carriage* and *hampered*.
A yoke; a collar on a horse; a restraint, a conscientious principle.
加之以衡 丨 put a yoke on him.
丨 制 to restrain another in his actions.

阨, **阸**, *ŏ'* From *place* and *impeded*, as an army by a defile; it is also read *ai'* and used with 隘' a pass.
A dangerous obstruction; a defile or pass; a limit, a hindrance; to distress, to impede; hazardous, urgent. calamity, utter want.
艱 丨 calamity, utter want.
窮 丨 brought to great distress, at extremity.
丨 狹 a defile, a gorge.
據 丨 to guard the passes.
凶 丨 in great straits.
In *Cantonese*. To deceive, to impose upon.

鈪, *ŏ'* From *metal* and *impeded*; an unauthorized character.
A bracelet or bangle.
丨 金 gold wristlets.
脚 丨 an anklet. (*Cantonese*.)
鑲 丨 a plated or inlaid ring.

餩, *ŏ'* Straitened for food; famished; one says, it is used with 呃' to hiccough or belch.

胺, *ngŏ'* Putrid meat; flesh that has corrupted by hanging too long.

堨, *ŏ'* *ngŏ'* A crack in a wall.
壅 丨 to stop a crevice with clay.
Read *kieh*, Blue clay.
石 丨 a levee near the ancient capital Chang-ngan in Shensi.

遏, *ŏ'* *ngŏ'* From to *go* and *why*.
To stop or bring to a standstill; to reach; to cut off, to terminate; an unforeseen obstacle.
毋 丨 糴 by no means stop the sale of rice.
丨 慾難 it is hard to curb one's lusts.
丨 惡揚善 to repress the wicked and encourage the good.
阻 丨 to embarrass.
心豈 丨 然 how then can I feel depressed?

丨 絕 to cut off, as a way.
丨 佚前人光 to neutralize (or eclipse) the fame of the ancients, — by not emulating them.

閼, *ŏ'* *ngŏ'* From *door* and *in*; used with the last; it is also read *yiu'*
To shut, to stop; to obstruct; to prevent superiors knowing; to hoodwink; at ease.
遮 丨 to hide from, to keep snug.
壅 丨 to stop the flow of water; to prevent a thing coming to another's ears.
丨 逢 the years of the cycle which have 甲 in them.
丨 與 an old name of Ho-shun hien 和順縣 in the west of Shansi.
Read *yen*. 丨 氏 the Hiung-nu term for a princess, used in the History of the Han dynasty.

匎, *ŏ'* An ornament in a headdress worn over the braid.
翠爲 丨 葉 the head ornaments are made of feather work.

遻, *ŏ'* *ngŏ'* To encounter, to meet another when it is undesirable; an unwelcome meeting.
重華不可 丨 兮 Ah! the honors of life I never can meet again; — said by K'üh Yuen in his Ode.

搤, *ŏ'* *ngŏ'* To seize, to hold fast, to grasp; to keep down or cover with the hand; to drag.
丨 持 to get the control of.

扼, **捉**, *ŏ'* *ngŏ'* From *hand* and *impeded*; they are nearly the same as the last.
To gripe, to clutch; a grasp; to have the hand over.
滿 丨 to grasp a handful.
丨 捥久之 held him by the wrist a long time.
力能 丨 虎 he throttled a tiger by main strength.

NI.

Old sounds, ni *and* nít. *In Canton*, ni *and* nei ; — *in Swatow*, ni *and* jù ; — *in Amoy*, ni, bi, *and* ji ; — *in Fuhchau*, ni, nè, *and* nó ; — *in Shanghai*, ni ; — *in Chifu*, ni.

꜀**閮** To hide away.

In *Cantonese.* To keep quiet in a place, to keep secret; perdue; to secrete.

丨埋 or 丨身 hidden away.

丨到密密 keep yourself closely hid.

尼 ꜂ni From *body* and a *spoon*, explained as a person following; the two next are sometimes used for it.

To follow another; to accord with, to agree; near; a nun.

丨姑 or 丨僧 a nun; some of the former do not shave their heads.

仲丨 the infantile name of Confucius, taken from Mount Ni 丨丘 to which his mother prayed, and which her son's cranium was said to resemble.

Read *nih*, Near.

丨遠咸安 all is quiet, both at home and abroad.

屔 ꜂ni The name of the hill, 丨丘 in Lu, where the mother of Confucius prayed; the preceding form is now generally used.

呢 ꜂ni A twittering sound; a murmuring, humming sound; to speak low.

耳語丨喃 to whisper in the ears.

Read ꜀*ni.* An interrogative particle; a particle implying doubt, and used in the protasis of a conditional sentence; an affirmative particle; a common sound in Budhist books.

哆囉丨 woolen cloth; usually contracted to the last word, as in 大丨 broadcloth, and 小丨 kerseymere.

他有什麽病丨 what is his ailment?

唔丨 is it not so? (*Cantonese.*)

他是往西去丨還是往東去丨 is he going east or west?

怎麽是孝丨 what then is filial piety?

他不是死乃是睡覺丨 she is not dead but asleep.

若好了丨就上舖子 if he is well, let him go to the shop.

In *Cantonese.* A relative pronoun; this, the nearer of two.

丨個 this one, this thing.

丨的 this; 丨處 here, this place.

妮 ꜂ni A slave girl.

小丨子 a maid of work.

怩 ꜂ni To blush, to color.

忸丨 a feeling and look of shame.

狀有丨色 he looks ashamed.

臡 ꜂ni From *flesh* and *difficult.*

Meat pickled with the bones.

麋丨 a sauce made of liver and brains.

苨 ꜂ni Used for the next in the phrase 零露丨丨 heavy dew; also plants extruding their roots above the ground.

泥 埿 涅 ꜂ni From *water* or *earth* and *near* as the phonetic; the first is generally applied to mire, and the third is pedantic.

Mire, slush, mud; dirt, clods, earth, soil; to daub with mud; miry, dirty; adhesive.

一塊丨 a lump of dirt.

丨土 earth; soil.

丨金色 a pinchbeck color.

丨磚 adobie, mud-bricks used in walls.

拖丨帶水 [as if] dragged through mud and water; — said of a bad style.

丨墻 adobie walls.

紅錦丨窓 to paste brocade over the window.

丨首 to put one's head in the mire; — said by courtiers.

丨封 to seal or paste a letter.

丨丨 grass wet with dew; soft and glossy, as leaves.

Read *ni*꜄ Bigoted, opinionated, attached to; doating on.

丨於風水 a firm belief in geomancy.

丨人 one lost to reproof.

拘丨不通 he is set in his opinion and beyond argument.

住丨 stuck in the mud, mulish, obstinate.

黏 ꜂ni To adhere, to stick; adhesive, gluey; sticky, as undried paste, or oiled hair.

丨封 to seal or paste a letter.

丨緊 to harden, as dirt; to stick tight.

秜 ꜂ni Rice which was self-sown, and this year has grown up.

你 伱 ꜂ni From 人 *man* and 爾 *thou* contracted.

The second personal pronoun, thou, you; your's.

丨的 your.

丨們 you; used for one or more persons.

丨貴姓 what is your surname?

丨老人家 my good Sir; old gentleman! used in direct address.

與丨不相干 it is no business of your's.

伲 ꜂ni This form of the preceding is used in Kiangsu for the first person plural, we, us; as 丨個 ours.

丨自家 ourselves.

苨 ˓ni From *plant* and to *follow*; interchanged with ˓泥 mud.

A wild medicinal plant once called 丨蔗丨, but now known as 薺丨, a species of Primulaceæ (*Apochoris*), the hairbell found in Chihli.

愚與直相像若薺丨之亂人參 I am so very much like you, as a hairbell's root can be mistaken for ginseng.

丨丨 luxuriant; glossy, as leaves.

馜 ˓ni Very fragrant.

馦丨 an agreeable smell. (*Cantonese.*)

旎 ˓ni The fluttering of flags in the wind.

柅 ˓ni A chock for a wheel; a tree whose wood is hard and like the pear; to inquire into, to search; a distaff-handle.

捷丨姦冐 to inquire carefully into his evil and treacherous conduct.

禰 ˓ni A father when enshrined in the ancestral temple; an ancestral shrine; a place near Lohyang, the old capital of Wéi, in the north of Honan.

公丨 to carry a tablet home to its own hall.

瀰 ˓ni Many, abundance of; rising, overflow.

垂轡丨丨 what an array of reins hanging down!

丨迤平原 the floods rise over the banks along the whole length.

Read ˓mi, and similar to 瀰. A wide expanse of waters.

膩 ni˃ From *flesh* and *two*.

Greasy, fat, oily, unctuous, smooth, glossy; a mixture of oil and brick-dust used as priming by painters.

丨滯 indigestion, uneasiness in the stomach.

油丨 greasy; oily, as rich gravy.

肥丨 very rich, as food.

細丨之見 notional, finical, scrupulous.

NIANG.

Old sound, niung. *In Canton*, néung; — *in Swatow*, nié, niang, *and* jiàng; — *in Amoy*, léong *and* jiong; — *in Fuhchau*, niòng *and* nòng; — *in Shanghai*, niang; — *in Chifu*, niang.

娘 ˓niang From *woman* and *good*.

A girl, a miss; a young lady; a female; a goddess; often applied to insects and flowers, to indicate their beauty.

丨親 a mother.

二姑丨 the younger sister.

姨丨 maid servants.

爹丨 father and mother.

丨行 a mother and her friends.

新丨 a bride, the newly-made lady.

師丨 a schoolmistress.

大丨 the madam, used by concubines.

丨丨 the empress is usually so addressed; a goddess, and used like Our Lady; as 天花丨丨 Our Lady of the Small-pox.

伴丨 a bridesmaid.

乾丨 you, my good woman; — said to workwomen.

丨媽 the goddess T'ien-heu, the Amphitrite of the Chinese.

雪衣丨 a poetical term for the cockatoo, from its plumage.

丨子軍 a female general, like Joan of Arc.

送丨 at *Ningpo*, a term for a go-between; they also act as paranymphs.

丨家 my wife's family.

孃 ˓niang Used with the last.

Troubled, overpressed with cares; fat, corpulent.

不聞爺丨哭子聲 don't you hear the cry of fathers and mothers mourning for their children?

釀 niang˃ To make liquor from boiled glutinous rice with yeast cakes; to brew; to stuff, as a sausage; to mix condiments; to foment, as sedition; to breed disturbance.

丨酒 to ferment spirits.

酒丨 a sweetish kind of rice beer.

丨黃瓜 a cucumber stuffed with mince-meat.

蜂丨蜜 the bee works its honey.

丨成大患 to bring down a great calamity, as on a state.

丨疑起衅 to excite suspicion and create strife.

穰 niang˃ Mixed, blended.

丨雜之粮 various sorts of grain mixed together.

NIAO.

Old sounds, uio, tio, not, *and* nok. *In Canton*, niu *and* nau ; — *in Swatow*, niò, ch'iò, *and* jió ; — *in Amoy*, liau, niau, *and* jiau ; — *in Fuhchau*, néu, chéu, no, niè, *and* niu ; — *in Shanghai*, nio ; — *in Chifu*, niao *and* miao.

鳥 ʿniao — The original form has a resemblance to a bird ; it forms the 186th radical of a natural group of characters relating to birds ; it must not be confounded with ʿwu 烏 black.

The feathered tribes ; a bird.

飛丨 a bird of the air.

丨鎗 a fowling-piece.

丨巢 or 丨檻 nests ; an aviary.

過山丨 a culverin or jingal.

玄丨 a swallow.

鬼丨 seems to denote a night-hawk or goat-sucker ; it is supposed to receive the souls of the dying.

丨道 a winding way.

丨媒 a decoy, a stool-pigeon.

丨革飛翬 beautifully adorned, grand and spacious ; — said of a great mansion.

白丨 musquitoes.

褭 裊 ʿniao — From *garment* and *horse* or *bird* contracted.

To tie a horse with a silken halter.

騕丨 a fine horse.

蔦 ʿniao — A climbing plant, the cypress-vine ; an epiphyte like the misletoe, was also once denoted.

丨蘿之親 connected like the cypress-vine and the Wisteria ; — said of parties related by marriage.

嫋 嬝 ʿniao — From *woman* and *weak* ; the second form is rare.

Delicate, girlish ; slender, lissome, flexible ; a hum, a variable, gentle sound.

丨丨 curling, like smoke or waves ; waving, as reeds.

丨娜 a mincing gait ; wriggling, squirming ; graceful.

㒟 ʿniao — Small-waisted ; agile.

㛹丨 tumblers, acrobats.

丨丨而舞 squirming and climbing, as a mountebank.

㜵 ʿniao — A long, flexible piece of wood.

In *Cantonese.* Small, delicate, pretty ; tapering ; natty.

手骨ʿ丨 delicate hands.

長ʿ丨ʿ丨 ridiculously long.

丨ʾ小 attenuated, becoming small.

嬲 ʿniao — From a *female* between two *males*.

To play with women, to dally with ; to bother and vex ; lewd sports.

In *Cantonese.* Angry, annoyed ; to scold, to be angry at.

發丨 an angry fit ; grouty.

丨親 he scolded him.

丨怒 angry, displeased at.

嬈 niaoʾ — From two *females* beside a *male* ; the character seems to be merely a variation of the last.

To dally with women.

In *Cantonese* read *nătˌ* Joyous, frolicsome, sportive ; irritating, as smoke to the eyes.

我丨ˌ佢 I rather like him.

火烟丨嬲 the smoke hurts.

尿 niaoʾ — From *body* and *water* ; it is also read ˏ*sui*, and is otherwise written 溺, in this sense.

Urine ; to urinate.

丨壺 a urinal.

撒丨 or 屙丨 to make water.

流丨 incontinence of urine.

遺丨 to wet the bed.

NIEH.

Old sounds, niep, nit, *and* nap. *In Canton*, níp *and* ním ; — *in Swatow*, niap *and* liam ; — *in Amoy*, liap ; — *in Fuhchau*, niek ; — *in Shanghai*, nih *and* nich ; *in Chifu*, nie.

聶 niehʾ — Composed of three *ears*, showing one ear coming close to two ears ; occurs used for *sheh*, 攝 to take.

To whisper, as when putting the mouth to another's ear ; to mix ; to lisp ; to take up, as one's garments.

囁 讘 niehʾ — To vilify another ; the unbridled grumbling of a discontented, lawless person.

丨嚅 wordy, garrulous.

詀丨 loquacious.

曡 爆 niehʾ — A little warm ; a genial, agreeable temperature, as from the sun or a fire.

貂狐茸丨 sable and fox furs are very warm.

躡 niehʾ — To tread or step on ; to ascend ; urgent, hasty.

丨登 to go up.

丨足行伍之間 in active service with the army.

丨足不前 not to move a step.

丨踪 to track, to pursue a trail.

丨草履 to wear straw sandals.

鑷 niehʾ — Forceps, pincers, tweezers ; to pull out, to nip up ; a kind of hair-pin ; a fish-snare.

丨子 a pair of nippers.

丨毛 to pull out hairs.

籋 niehʾ — Used with the two last.

A small basket ; nippers.

丨浮雲 to tread on the flying clouds.

驫, nieh'

A horse with a quick trot or amble.

丨驄 a fleet horse.

捻, 捏, nieh' 'nien

From *hand* and to *remember*; it is synonymous with and is often read 拈 ꜀nien; 搌 is also incorrectly written for both; the second form is rarely used, and is also read *tieh*,

To pinch up, to take a pinch; to take up with tongs or nippers; to filch; a pinch.

丨一丨 take a pinch.

一丨紅 a poetical name for the mowtan flower.

丨手 to snap the fingers; a fillip.

手丨 a handkerchief.

丨綿 to spin thread on a distaff.

丨絲 to shake out skeins of silk.

丨匪 or 丨逆 bands of filchers; marauding banditti.

燃點油丨 the lighted wick draws up the oil.

揑, 捏, ꜀nié

From *hand* and to *fill up*.

To collect with the fingers; to work or knead with the fingers, as in clay; to fabricate, to trump up, to find a pretext for accusing another.

丨控 or 丨稱 to inform against falsely.

誣丨 or 丨陷 to involve others by groundless accusations.

丨肚 to knead the bowels.

丨造 to insinuate against.

泥丨的 a worker in clay, a molder, one who 丨像 makes models of people in costume.

啰, ꜀nié

Wrathful, abusive; to rail at.

丨着喉嚨說 to mimic people's tones of voice.

㘸, ꜀nié

Composed of 土 *earth* sometimes altered to 工 *work*, and 臼 *mortar* contracted to 日 *day*, probably referring to lime-pits.

Same as the next, and now used only in combination as a primitive.

埕, ꜀nié

To fill up, as a hole; to put or go down.

涅, ꜀nié

Black mud at the bottom of pools; to defile, to blacken, to muddy; a river in the south of Honan; an old name for Yü-shé hien 榆社縣 in the east of Shansi.

丨而不緇 though muddy, I am not black; — *i. e.* my integrity is unstained.

丨盤 the defiled vessel, *i. e.* the world; also the Sanscrit *nirvana* or *nighban*, the Budhist state of beatitude in deity, explained by 離生滅 separated from (unaffected by) both life and annihilation; indifferent to all joy or sorrow.

隉, ꜀nié

From 阜 a *place* and 毀 to *damage* contracted.

Dangerous, unsettled; whatever causes dread.

邦之阢丨 the distracted, disturbed state of the realm.

惗, ꜀nié

To love; to recite in a low tone, as when humming a lesson.

敜, ꜀nié

To fill up a hole; to level up, as a hole where wild beasts were trapped; to put the hand over, as a hole.

丨乃穽 fill up that pitfall — to preserve the cattle from falling in.

諗, ꜀nié

To stop a sound; cessation of a note or strain.

苶, ꜀niéh

Worn out, debilitated from age; weary, as after work.

衰丨 lost his energy; said of an officer,

甈, niéh'

Also read *k'i'*

An empty and large earthen jar; to burn in the fire, as pottery is; cracked, having flaws.

甄陶天下者在和剛則丨柔則坏 he who directs the empire should always act in accord with circumstances; for if too harsh he will break things, if too soft they will crumble away; — *i. e.* the people will rebel if tyrannized over, or will excite sedition if not kept in order.

囡, 囝, ꜀nié

From *inclosure*, and to *have* or *woman*.

To take anything and hide it away secretly; to steal.

丨取 to carry off.

In *Shanghai*. The second form is used to denote a girl, a lassie.

篞, ꜀nié

A short, coarse bamboo wisp, used to scrub saucepans and boilers of the food sticking on them.

喦, ꜀nié

From 品 a *sort*, each *mouth* united to the others, to denote loquacity; to be distinguished from 嵒 or 巖 a cliff.

To talk much, to quarrel.

曳丨 to have an altercation.

纅, nieh'

To overstitch a seam.

丨縛 to tie up with a cord, as the hair.

紉丨 to bind a seam.

NIEN.

Old sounds, nien, miem, *and* nin. *In Canton*, nín, ním, nǎm, *and* chin ; — *in Swatow*, nieⁿ, niam, ni, *and* jien ; — *in Amoy*, lian, liam, *and* tian ; — *in Fuhchau*, nieng *and* tieng ; — *in Shanghai*, niⁿ *and* nèⁿ ; — *in Chifu*, nien.

年 ˓nien Composed of 禾 *grain* above 千 *thousand*, modified in combination.

A year, a revolution of the seasons ; the years one has reached, but not used like ˓*sui* 歲 for the years of one's age.

現 ｜ 二 十 四 歲 this year his age is twenty-four.

少 ｜ young ; a minor.

老 ｜ old, grayhaired.

｜ 紀 長 aged, growing old.

來 ｜ or 明 ｜ next year.

去 ｜ or 舊 ｜ or 頭 ｜ last year.

｜ ｜ yearly ; year by year.

｜ 底 or ｜ 尾 close of the year.

｜ 頭 first of the year.

拜 ｜ new-year's congratulations.

過 ｜ or 做 ｜ to perform new-year's rites.

隔 ｜ 同 about the same age.

同 ｜ [illegible] graduates of the same year.

好 時 ｜ a prosperous year.

多 曆 ｜ 所 through many years' duration.

不 盡 天 ｜ a premature death.

萬 ｜ for ever, perpetually.

｜ 等 者 of the same age.

｜ 華 虛 度 I have vainly spent the best of my days.

舞 象 之 ｜ the age of gymnastics, *i.e.* 15 years old.

拈 ˓nien From *hand* and *to divine*.

To take up in the fingers, to pick out ; to pick up ; to handle ; to carry.

｜ 鬮 to draw lots.

｜ 香 to offer incense ; to worship.

｜ 鼻 to catch by the nose ; — a vain grasp.

｜ 起 來 pick it up.

｜ 筆 to write, to take pen in hand.

多 ｜ to take much or more.

詩 ｜ 一 韻 select me a proper rhyme for my ode.

懶 ｜ 針 線 lazy in plying the needle.

｜ 書 to look over a book.

粘 ˓nien From *rice* and *to divine*.

Paste ; glutinous, viscid ; to paste or attach to, to stick up ; attached to a person

｜ 貼 告 示 to paste up an edict.

｜ 補 to cut out a word and paste in clean paper on which to write a correct character.

此 後 不 ｜ 手 I will have nothing more to do with it.

｜ 信 口 or ｜ 封 to paste an envelop.

草 色 ｜ 天 the grassy green [of the hills] reached to the sky.

｜ 抄 一 紙 one inclosure or supplement, such as are attached to a document.

｜ 虫 caterpillars that eat millet.

淌 ｜ 涎 to drool, to drivel.

｜ 杆 子 to put birdlime on a rod.

In *Pekingese*. To fade, to wilt ; to wither, as flowers.

黏 ˓nien Used for the last, and regarded as the most correct of the two.

Glutinous, viscid ; rice.

｜ 得 狠 very sticky.

｜ 米 the common table rice, of which there are many varieties.

鮎 ˓nien From *fish* and *to handle* contracted for the sound.

A general name for the mud fish ; a bull-head, whose pectoral fins are very stout, a *Pimelodus* common at Peking, of a dark greenish tint, with four cirri, and about a foot long.

｜ 魚 鬚 a trailing plant found in Honan, with long tendrils at the axils, and the flowers in a head like clover.

攆 ˓nien From *hand* and *imperial car* ; an unauthorized character, for which the next is suitable.

To expel a man ; to turn him out ; to dismiss a man summarily.

｜ 逐 to drive him away.

｜ 走 了 they have all been driven away.

｜ 他 出 去 turn him out of doors.

撚 ˓nien From *hand* and *truly*.

To work over in the fingers, to fumble over ; to toy or play with ; to make by fingering ; to tread.

｜ 鬚 to fondle the beard.

｜ 乾 手 巾 to wring a napkin dry.

｜ 毛 to felt wool.

｜ 緯 to twist red silk for a hat-fringe.

｜ 一 個 紙 ｜ 兒 roll up a slip of paper, as for a string or an allumette.

｜ 指 間 while you can turn your finger,— in a moment, instantly.

碾 ˓nien A stone roller turned on an axle by a lever to clean husk from grain, or the seed from cotton, or to make flour ; to roll, to triturate.

｜ 船 an iron trough and wheel, in which medicine is pulverized.

｜ 碎 to pulverize, as paints.

｜ 房 a mill-room.

｜ 盤 the nether large scored stone, and ｜ 柁 the fluted roller.

｜ 輥 子 the roller on a mill.

跈 蹨 ˓nien From *foot* and *pearls* or *truly* ; the second is most used.

To tread to powder, to stamp on ; to cast out ; to connect ; to grasp ; tight ; urgent ; to tread in another's steps.

趍 Read ˏkien in the dictionary.
ˋnien To pursue, to run after in order to overtake or seize; to stoop the head and run.
快丨 to hurry on after.
丨不上他 you cannot catch him.

淰 ˋnien Muddy, splashy; turbid; to dig out or dredge mud; smooth, flowing water.

In *Cantonese*. Sound, as sleep; to reiterate, as a throw of dice; slow moving, deliberate; soaked through.
墨水丨 the ink spreads.
丨三 to successively take threes at gambling.
點丨筆 soak the pencil full of ink.

涊 ˋnien Muddy water.
淟丨 dirty and drunk.
丨然 dirty, as from perspiring profusely.

Read ˋjăn. A branch of the R. Wéi in the southeast of Shansi.

念 nien˒ From *heart* and *now*.
To reflect on, to ponder over; to remember and consider; to regard; to meditate; thoughts; thoughtful; to repeat memoriter, to learn by heart; to chant or drone; thoughts, reflections; in Budhism, the power of memory (*smriti-bala*), of which the 丨根 (*smriten-drya*) is its organ, and 四丨處 are four objects on which it should dwell.
思丨 to think of.
懷丨 or 服丨 to reflect on, to bear in mind.
丨所當丨 to bend the mind to.
丨丨不忘 in constant remembrance.
丨着父母 to remember one's parents.
丨書 to learn or commit books.
丨佛 to repeat Budha's name.
除雜丨 put away wandering thoughts.

丨頭 first notion of the thing.
丨及諸姑 thinking of my relatives.
丨茲在茲 fix your attention on what you are doing.
丨口供 to give testimony, to bear witness.
一丨之誠可動天地 one sincere desire can move heaven and earth.

In *Shanghai*. Used for 廿 twenty, as 丨一 the 21st of the month.

艌, 綜 nien˒ The painter of a boat, a tow-line or tracking-rope; some say, to calk seams
丨索 a boat-hawser.
丨舟 to pull a boat along.

鯰 nien˒ A small hair-pin; a nail with a small head.
雜華丨之葳蕤 her many colored flowers and pins make a fine effect.

NIH.

Old sounds, nik, niak, ngiak, niek, *and* nít. *In Canton*, nik, yik *and* ngăk; — *in Swatow*, nék, nió, ngek, *and* chit; — *in Amoy*, lek; — *in Fuhchau*,ník *and* ngík; — *in Shanghai*, niăk; — *in Chifu*, ni *and* i.

匿 ni˒ From to *conceal* and *if*.
A big wine jar; to hide, to secrete; to abscond, to elude search; to gloss over; hidden, clandestine.
丨名 anonymous, to give an alias.
藏丨 to hide away; to keep out of sight, as from creditors.
丨喪 to conceal a parent's death and not put on mourning; — a crime in officials.
丨避 or 逃丨 to hide or run away.
自丨 to keep out of sight.
丨怨而友其人 he cherished a grudge, and yet appeared friendly to the man.

䁥 ni˒ To blink the eyes; to half shut the eyes.

慝 ni˒ Ashamed at what one has done.
內丨 mortified.
羞丨 chagrined and abashed.

榽 ni˒ A fabulous tree, said to be a thousand feet high; it flowers once in a millenium, and perfects its fruit in nine more.

暱, 昵 ni˒ The sun drawing near, time near at hand; familiar, daily intercourse with; favorites, familiars.
丨比罪人 to be familiar with rascals.
親丨 to be hand and glove with.
私丨 a familiar, a constant attendant.
丨就寡人 come near to Us.

Read ˋni. The shrine or hall where the ancestral tablet is placed; *met.* the tablet.

溺, 氼 ni˒ From *water* and *weak*; the first is also read *niao*˒ and the second and unusual form is meant to depict a man under the water.
To sink, to drown; to be drowned, to put under the water; to suffocate; sunk in any excess, reprobate; greedy; fond of, doating on.
丨愛 lovesick, blindly doating on.
丨酒 inebriate, given to drink.
丨於名利 ambitious of fame and wealth.
丨水 submerged, drowned.
丨女 female infanticide
陷丨其民 he ruined his people.

蟨 *ni*ˋ From *worm* and *hid*.
The disease of worms in the intestines.

蟚 *ni*ˋ From *insect* and *two;* it is properly read *teh*, a synonym of 蟦, but it is read like the last, probably from the primitive.
Plant lice; small insects on leaves.
丨虫 aphides.

齯 *nih*ˋ Carious teeth; the toothache
In *Cantonese*. To mouth one's words; to speak thick or indistinctly; to make a note of.
丨牙 to speak with the teeth shut.
丨丨的 a little sour or turned; raw, not well boiled.

搦 *ni*ˋ To grasp; to catch hold.
丨戰 to provoke to battle.
捉丨 to seize, as a bird.
In *Cantonese*. To carry in the hand.
丨高的 carry it higher.
丨來 bring it here.

惄 *ni*ˋ Mournful; anxious and care-worn from want of food; to long for.
丨思 to think of fondly.
丨如調飢 sad as if he had nothing to eat.
丨焉如擣 I sorrow and sigh till I feel as one pounded — in a mortar.
恚丨悠悠 to feel great solicitude for.

暱, 𪏆 *ni*ˋ Putty, glue, or an adhesive which causes things to stick; a kind of papier-maché stuff of hemp-tow, lime, and oil, used to cover pillars.
上丨子 put on some glue.
不義不丨 do not associate with unjust men.

疒 *ni*ˋ Formed from 爿 a *bed* and 人 *man*, representing a sick person on a couch; it is the 104th radical of a very natural group of characters relating to diseases.
Sickness; to recline, as a sick man.

逆 *ni*ˋ From to *go* and to *rise against;* the next is the original form, it is also read *yih*.
Rebellious, seditious, illegal; contumacious, refractory; contrary as the tide; to resist, to oppose; to encounter; to go to meet; to receive, as an order; to reckon on, to calculate on or know beforehand; to comply; in the Cheu dynasty, to hand in a memorial; among *physicians*, fatal, not likely to recover, as a patient with small-pox.
忤丨 willful, stubborn, froward.
丨子 a disobedient child.
反丨 or 叛丨 to rebel; to rise, as insurgents do.
丨水 a head tide.
丨知 or 丨了 I knew it beforehand or already.
丨行 perverse; to go backwards, as a mule.
橫丨 outrageous, rude, violent.
不丨詐 he did not think of any treachery.
丨風開船 [he will] start in a head wind; — he is headstrong.
敬丨天命 [his majesty] respectfully complied with the orders of Heaven.
忠言丨耳 to reject wholesome advice.
大丨不道 thoroughly turbulent and unprincipled.
丨黨 a band of rebels.

屰 *ni*ˋ From 干 a *spear* and 凵 *cavity*, intended to represent a forked spear.
Disobedient, for which the last is now used.

NIN.

Old sound, nîm. *In Canton*, yǎm *and* ngǎn; — *in Swatow*, jîm; — *in Amoy*, jîm; — *in Fuhchau*, éng *and* îng: — *in Shanghai*, niǎng; — *in Chifu*, min *and* nin.

紉 ˏ*zhǎn* To thread a needle; to twist a thread; a cord.
丨針補綴 she threaded her needle to mend the garment.
丨秋蘭以爲佩 I will braid a fillet of orchid flowers to keep as a remembrance; — *met.* I cannot forget your kind acts.

拰 ˊ*lin* To move.
丨搦 to try the strength of a bow.

您 ˏ*nin* From *heart* and *you;* an unauthorized character.
The second person singular used in addressing superiors; and spoken to any one for special respect.
丨呀 (also written 你納,) your Honor; you, Sir.
丨們 you, Sirs, is also used, but not so frequently.
向丨說 let me tell all of you about it.

賃 *lin*ˋ From *precious* and to *use*.
To rent, to lease; to hire, as a house; to charter, as a vessel.
出丨 to lease to another.
租丨 to take on lease.
招丨 to invite lessees; to let.
永丨 a perpetual lease.
傭丨於人 I am engaged to work for them.

NING.

Old sound, **ning.** *In Canton*, ning *and* ying; — *in Swatow*, leng *and* ngeng; — *in Amoy*, leng, lin, *and* geng; — *in Fuhchau*, ning, nging, néng, *and* ngik; — *in Shanghai*, nŭng; — *in Chifu*, ning.

凝 ˏning From *ice* and to *suspect*; its authorized sound of ˏ*ying* has been retained in the south.

To freeze, to congeal; to coagulate; to turn, to curdle; frozen, stiffened; fixed, finished, settled; abundant, vigorous, collected; accomplished, brought to a close.

丨結 or 丨住 to freeze; to turn sour; curdled.

丨喜 great happiness.

丨神遠視 to look afar with fixed gaze.

丨祥 much felicity.

丨聚 gathering, as clouds in a storm.

丨寒 very cold, freezing weather.

丨據 stern, set, rigorous; adhering to old usage, as a martinet; unaccommodating.

丨芳 flourishing, vigorous, as plants.

庶績其丨 thus all their duties will be well done.

丨固 very precise.

丨命 to accomplish the decree — of Heaven in one's favor, as a righteous prince does.

寍 寧 寕 ˏning Composed of 宀 a *shelter*, and 心 *heart* above 皿 a *dish*, intimating the gratification that food gives the heart; the second form, having *breath* 丂 underneath, is the common one, but since the reign Taokwang, it has been contracted to the third form.

Rest, repose, quiet, tranquillity, serenity of mind; to salute; to wish peace to, to bring repose to; to soothe; a bride's visit to greet her parents; to prefer, as lief; how, why; followed by a negative, it becomes a term of comparison, rather, better, then, more desirable; enters into the names of many places.

丨願 I had rather, I prefer.

安丨 quiet repose.

丨死不辱 I prefer death to disgrace.

丨可濕衣不可亂步 he had rather wet his robes than quicken his steps — to get out of the rain; said of a formal official.

丨靜 tranquil times, as after a rebellion.

其丨惟永 its repose will be lasting.

丨死不去 I had rather die than go.

無丨謙 nothing like being humble; but 無丨 is sometimes better rendered certainly, really.

丨可信其有不可信其無 it is better to believe that it exists, than it that does not.

耗斁下土丨丁我躬 this wasting and exhaustion of the land, would that it fell on my own person.

予丨 the three years' official retirement, when mourning for one's parents.

丨不我顧 would he then not regard me?

不用命者丨入我網 those who disregard the orders will certainly involve themselves in my net — of penalties.

胡丨忍予 how can they bear to have me thus?

嚀 ˏning To direct.

叮丨囑咐 to charge straitly, to enjoin upon, to reiterate orders.

薴 ˏning Plants growing thick and like a jungle is 薴丨, applied to wild plants and shrubs.

薺丨 a marshy labiate plant of the habit of hoarhound. (*Marrubium.*)

擰 ˏning To pull and haul about, to throw into confusion; to pinch, as a cheek.

搶丨 to make a turmoil.

In *Cantonese*. To take in the hand; to bring, to carry.

丨開 take it off.

丨反轉頭 turn it end for end.

顊 ˋning The top of the head.

頂丨 the crown.

聹 ˋning Ear-wax.

挖出耵丨 pick out the secretion from the ear.

甯 ningˋ Regarded as identical with 寧, but written in this form out of respect.

A surname.

丨波府 Ningpo city or prefecture, is often so written.

濘 ningˋ Miry.

泥丨 the slippery mud which is made by a rain.

汀丨 very shallow water.

佞 ningˋ From 人 *man*, 信 *belief* contracted, and 女 *woman*, because her confidence is easily won.

Eloquent, persuasive, insinuating; artful, specious, flattering; tart, ready in reply.

奸丨 treacherous; subtle.

我不丨 I am unready of speech.

焉用丨 why argue with him?

丨婦 an artful woman.

In *Cantonese*. To twirl, to turn with the fingers; to whirl.

螺絲丨 a screw-driver.

丨轉頭 turn your head around.

隨風丨 a weather-cock, a trimmer.

丨頭 to shake the head when refusing a thing.

NIOH.

Old sound, nok. *In Canton*, yéuk; — *in Swatow*, ngiak; — *in Amoy*, giòk; — *in Fuhchau*, ngiòk; — *in Shanghai*, niök *and* nok; — *in Chifu*, yòa.

虐 *nio'* From 虎 *tiger* and 爪 *claws* reversed; it is also read *yoh*, and *nih*,

Unfeeling, harsh; cruel, tyrannical; barbarities, outrages; to maltreat, to harry; troublesome, rude, rudeness; oppressors; natural calamities.

爲丨 to act savagely.

丨民 to maltreat the people.

殘丨 to ravage; to misuse inhumanly.

天降大丨 heaven sent great calamities.

惟作五丨之刑曰法 they just made the five punishments means of oppression under the name of laws.

敢行暴丨 he has dared to become a cruel oppressor.

瘧 *nio'* From *disease* and *harsh;* also read *yoh*,

Fever, especially a remittent fever; febrile complaints, influenza, ague.

鬼丨 an irregular fever.

丨疾 an intermittent or remittent fever; the cold fits are 寒丨 or 牝丨; and the hot fits are 牡丨 *lit.* male fevers.

NIU.

Old sounds, nu, ngu, *and* nuk. *In Canton*, nau *and* ngau; — *in Swatow*, niu *and* gu; — *in Amoy*, liu, jiu, *and* giu; — *in Fuhchau*, niu *and* ngiu; — *in Shanghai*, nù; — *in Chifu*, niu.

㖻 *˛niu* The cry of a child.

丨呢 the imperfect speech of an infant.

牛 *˛niu* The original form represents a *head* and two *horns* with a *tail* behind; it is the 93d radical of characters relating to bovine animals, and is sometimes read *˛yiu*.

An ox, a cow; a bull; kine, cattle; to lead oxen; applied to some kinds of deer.

丨公 or 牡丨 a bull.

牝丨 or 母丨 a cow.

丨肉 beef.

水丨 a buffalo.

黃丨 common cattle; a bullock.

丨奶餅 cheese.

丨油 butter.

我車我丨 we drove our wagons, and led our cattle.

丨皮燈籠 a leather lantern; *met.* a stupid fellow.

丨宿 the ninth zodiacal constellation, — in Capricorn.

自羊徂丨 he goes from the sheep to the oxen.

丨百葉窓 venetian blinds, so named from their resemblance to tripe.

笨丨 a dolt.

當丨使 I am used like an ox.

土丨 the clay ox, — made in the spring to propitiate crops.

丨黃 cow-bezoar.

丨郎 or 牽丨 the constellation of the Herdboy, the stars $\alpha\ \beta\ \gamma$ in Aquila.

天丨 an insect with long antennæ, yellow and white spots; probably a kind of Cerambyx beetle.

割雞焉用丨刀 why use an ox cleaver to kill a chicken? — you should proportion the means to the end.

臥丨 earth piled at the foot of walls to protect them from injury.

大丨音 the lowing of a big ox, a Budhist measure of distance, a *krosa*, or eighth of a *yodjana*, a distance of five *li*.

妞 *˛niu* An unauthorized character much used by the Manchus, probably a corruption of 女, for which it was formed.

A lass.

小丨兒 a girl under twelve.

芉 *˛niu* A medicinal plant, called 丨膝 or cow's knees; it is three feet high, with spoon-shaped, obovate leaves in pairs opposite; the nodes resemble a cow's knee, and the spikes grow above them in the axils; the root is light yellow, and when eaten salivates one; the plant is probably an *Achyranthes* or *Amarantus*, and allied to the cockscomb family.

土丨膝 a species of *Achyranthes* with oval leaves, exhibited in coughs.

鈕 *ʻniu* From *metal* and a *horary* character.

A knob on the top of a Chinese seal; a button, a knob; a hilt or handle; a process by or on which one thing turns, or connects with another; the point of attachment in a bivalve.

一粒丨 or 丨子 a button.

丨扣 or 丨絆 a button-loop.

結丨 a corded or knotted button.

花丨 ornamental buttons.

樞丨 seals and other official insignia; a pivot; *met.* the Dipper.

瓜丨 melons just set.

紐 ʻniu The knot; to braid into a knob; to tie; a fastening, a slipping-noose; a point of junction, as the tie of a girdle.

丨結 to fasten, so as to easily untie; a bow-knot.

丨別 very unwilling to do, distasteful. (*Pekingese.*)

杻 ʻniu A thick bushy tree found in marshes, which blossoms in April; its leaves resemble the apricot, the bark is reddish, and the branches are very crooked, but their wood is good for bows; another name is 檍 and 萬歲枝 everlasting branches; this plant resembles a *Prunus* or wild cherry, but its affinities are doubtful.

Read ʻchʻeu. Manacles, handcuffs.

扭 ʻniu To twist, or turn with the hand; to wring or wrench; to sprain; to collar, to seize by the cue; to wriggle; griped; cramped, as one's muscles; to reflect on.

丨轉 to turn over; to flirt, as with a fan; to throw the arms about.

丨計精 a lad clever at any mischief.

丨頸 perverse, testy.

丨鎖 a door-knob; turn the key.

脚丨 a club-foot.

丨稟 to seize a man, and report it to an officer.

丨乾 to wring dry.

丨紋木 wood with a crooked grain; *met.* a cross-grained fellow.

他心素多情性丨 his affections are very inconstant.

丨肚 colicky pains.

丨轉心腸 to reform one's ways.

揪丨 to grab hold, as in a tussle; to clutch, as a thief.

狃 ʻniu A dog which is sulky and needs coaxing; a fox's footsteps; proud, inclined to evil; to escort or guard; familiar with; doing repeatedly; accustomed to.

丨習 used to, versed in.

丨於姦宄 practiced in guileful tricks.

忸 ʻniu Like the preceding.

Accustomed to; annoyed.

丨惡 set in doing evil.

慦丨 unwilling to do.

Read *noh*, when used for 恧 To be ashamed.

丨怩 to blush.

NO.

Old sound, na. *In Canton*, no; — *in Swatow*, no *and* chut; — *in Amoy*, lō, na, *and* noⁿ; — *in Fuhchau*, no; — *in Shanghai*, nò *and* no; — *in Chifu*, nòa *and* lòa.

挪 ˏno From *hand* and *to transfer*; it was at first written ˏ挪, but that form is now disused.

To move; to change the place or purpose of; to misapply to another use.

丨移 to move a thing aside.

丨借 to borrow of, to embezzle, to appropriate wrongfully.

丨開的 move it a little.

丨轉 to lend [a deposit] to another; to hypothecate a security.

挼 捼 ˏno To rub between the hands, as pill-makers do; to rub or burnish; to rub on paint; to play the sycophant.

丨油 to rub on paint.

丨手 to rub the hands.

丨財主老 to cajole rich people.

丨沙 to clean the hands with sand.

儺 戁 ˏno From *man* and *affliction*; the second form is unusual.

To exorcise the demons which cause pestilence, to perform a lustration; to walk with a genteel step.

巧笑之瑳佩玉之丨 how her white teeth show in smiling, and the chatelaine tinkles on her girdle!

猗丨 pliable, as twigs; to look delicate.

丨神 the gods of the pestilence.

𠆳 ˏno A sound in Budhist books, probably employed for the letter *n* in transcribing names.

In *Shanghai* read ˏna. A pronoun, the second person you.

跡 ˏno To slip down, as on ice.

娜 ʻno The elegant carriage of a lady; affable, courteous, winning; leisurely.

婀丨 graceful, handsome.

花腰呈嫋丨 her graceful gait appeared most attractive and charming.

糯 稬 no' From *grain* and *soft*; it is said to be the term for rice in 沛國 Bahar?

The grain of the glutinous rice (*Oryza glutinosa*), also called old man's rice; it is now used chiefly in pastry, and occasionally for distilling; sticky; persistent in.

丨米酒 a sweetish kind of spirit.

丨米臀 epithet for a lazy man who never stirs from his seat.

懦 no' From *heart* and *soft*.
Timid, infirm of purpose; sluggish, imbecile; soft.
百巧者必有一丨 in any hundred fellows, there is always one skulk.
丨夫有立志 the sluggard has determined to do something.

哛 no' A final particle, used in the same senses as ˓na 哪, of which it seems to be an unusual variant.

NOH.

Old sound, nok. *In Canton*, nok, nut, *and* nuk; — *in Swatow*, nut, nap, *and* niu; — *in Amoy*, lok *and* lut; — *in Fuhchau*, nok *and* néük; — *in Shanghai*, no *and* neh; — *in Chifu*, nòa.

諾 noh' From *words* and *if*.
A reply in answer to a call or order; an assent of approval; a nod; to promise.
應丨 to answer a call.
輕丨 a rash promise.
一丨千金 his single promise is worth a thousand taels.
許丨 to make a promise.
無宿丨 do not let the night pass without fulfilling your promise.
不敢不丨 no one will dare to refuse his call.
承蒙金丨 I am under great obligations for your sure promise.
唯而不丨 answer [a father] promptly, and not with promises.

踳 no' To step firmly, to tread down
Read ˊjé. To step.
踨丨之子 a child just learning to walk; a toddling infant.

In *Cantonese*. To work or tread with the feet; to mix up, to press with the feet.
丨出腸 trampled out his bowels.
丨衣服 to tread out clothes, as a washerman.

衄 no' niu' To bleed at the nose, supposed to arise from fright; a defeat, a rout; to be discomfited.
驚丨 dreadfully frightened.
祝丨祝丨 a ballad prayer that an enemy may flee.

訥, 吶 no' To speak cautiously; not to promise or speak hastily; slow of speech, sparing of words; to stammer.
口丨丨 to stutter.
欲丨于言 he wishes to restrain his words.
丨舌 an impediment in the speech.
呱丨 the wailing of infants.

The second is also read *nah*, To raise the voice, to blurt out.
丨一聲喊都走了 he burst out in a loud voice, when they all ran away.
丨嘴 to pout the lips.

恧 no' Interchanged with ˓niu 忸 used to.
Ashamed, mortified.
慙丨 chagrined
莫吾知而不丨 I am not ashamed because nobody appreciates me.

肭 na' From *flesh* or *moon* and *inside*; the meanings show the uses of two radicals, and the character is duplicated in the dictionary, but 朒 is given as a synonym of the one under *moon*.
The new moon seen in the east is 縮丨, to be taken as an equivoque denoting great haste.
膃丨 very fat, or the shaking of fat flesh; applied to the testicles of seals.

NU.

Old sound, no. *In Canton*, nò; — *in Swatow*, nò *and* no; — *in Amoy*, lò; — *in Fuhchau*, nu; — *in Shanghai*, nu; — *in Chifu*, nu.

奴 ˓nu From *woman* and *hand*, because slaves lay their hands to things.
Formerly a person bought with money, chiefly now those sentenced to slavery; an abject; a term of contempt; in Fuhchau, often used for I.
丨才 your slave; used by only Manchus when addressing the emperor.
丨僕 a bond-servant.
看財丨 a stingy fellow.
當丨 serving as a slave.
狸丨 an otter; a domestic cat.
竹丨 a bamboo pillow.
念丨 a courtesan.
飛丨 a carrier pigeon.
燭丨 a candlestick.
錫丨 a hot water foot-warmer.

詉 ˓nu From *words* and *slave*; also read ˓ná and ˓nao.
Unintelligible gibberish, as of a drunkard; a wrangling, a pother.
譇丨 an inexplicable jargon.
醉到丨呢 fuddled with drink.
諠丨聒耳 their brawling disturbs my ears.
加責丨 to brawl at angrily.

伮 ˏnu Great strength; violent.

丨力爭强 to strive with one's utmost effort.

孥 ˏnu From *child* and *slave;* it is sometimes written 帑, but that form is now usually read ˊt'ang.

A child; my children; anything weak and tender, which needs to be soothed.

妻丨 wife and children.

丨丨 weakly, as a woman

予則丨戮汝 I will immolate you with your children.

駑 ˏnu A weak old horse, a broken down steed.

丨駘竭力 I am like a jaded horse, but will still exert all my strength; — said by old officers to the emperor.

弩 ˊnu A crossbow, called 諸葛丨 from its inventor, Chu-k'oh Liang; a ballista; it is sometimes made to shoot several darts, and is set as a trap for animals.

方丨 to shoot a crossbow.

萬丨齊發 all the bows were discharged at once.

强丨之末 [it was like the] strength of a spent bow; — *met.* a great cry and little wool.

砮 ˊnu A kind of flint which is chipped for arrow-heads; they are said to come from the Amoor River.

努 ˊnu To exert the utmost strength; to agonize for, to strive for, to put forth the last effort; a desperate, deadly struggle; in *penmanship*, a perpendicular stroke.

丨力行善 to do good with all one's energies.

胬 ˊnu From *flesh* and *slave* as the phonetic; an unauthorized character.

Granulations, as in the eyelids; the healthy granulations on a sore; salt-rheum, pustules, roughened skin; psora.

專去丨肉不用刀針 a special skill in curing granulated (or proud flesh), without using the knife or needle.

怒 nuˋ From *heart* and *slave;* this combination has been aptly likened to the latin *patior* or *passio* in its etymology.

Anger, fury, ire, passion; vigor, spirit, mettle; impatient; to get into a passion, incensed.

丨色 flushed with rage.

丨氣傷肝 anger hurts the liver, — and by sympathy the eyes.

發丨 angry; to express anger.

不遷丨 do not get angry with those not implicated.

丨冲冲 in a great rage.

忿丨 and 慍丨 are opposites, denoting outrageous noisy anger and repressed indignation.

丨氣衝冠 his rage even lifted his cap.

丨目相視 they eyed each other angrily.

敬恭明神宜無悔丨 I deeply reverence the gods, and they ought not thus to be angry with me.

請息雷霆之丨 pray abate your thundering rage.

威丨 sternly angry.

NÜ.

Old sounds, no *and* nu. *In Canton,* nü; — *in Swatow,* năng *and* ni; — *in Amoy,* lu; — *in Fuhchau,* nü; — *in Shanghai,* nü; — *in Chifu,* nü.

女 ˊnü The original form is said to have resembled a *female*, but it is now lost; it forms the 38th radical of characters mostly relating to women and vicious conduct.

Women, females; a girl, an unmarried woman; a lady; a bride, a wife; feminine, female; young.

丨人 a woman; females.

丨弟 my younger sister.

丨兒 a girl, about ten years old.

童丨 a girl, a marriageable virgin.

丨流 females, women, the sex.

婦丨 women generally.

仙丨 a fairy, a sylph, an elf.

乃生丨子 a daughter shall be born to him.

丨中丈夫 a masculine woman.

丨夷 the goddess of flowers.

天丨 a Budhist term for the *apsaras*, or wives of genii, from which probably arose its poetical use to denote a swallow.

丨宿 the tenth constellation, the stars ε μ &c. in Aquarius.

丨媧氏 or 丨希氏 a goddess whom some think denotes Eve.

織丨 the constellation of the Weaver, the three stars α ε ζ in Lyra, worshiped by women on the 7th of the 7th moon, when this and the constellation Aquila are nearly equidistant from the zenith at midnight.

丨冠 a Taoist nun.

丨僧長 a lady superior.

致丨 a custom of feudal princes sending to salute their daughters.

Read nüˋ To give a daughter in marriage.

丨ˋ于鄰國 he married her to the neighboring king.

Read ˊjü, and used with 汝. The personal pronoun you, thou.

丨何人 who are you?

丨則異于彼 are you, then, so different from them?

將恐將懼維予與丨 when fear and dread prevailed, you and I were all in all.

NÜN.

Old sound, nun. *In Canton*, nün, — *in Swatow*, lun ; — *in Amoy*, lwan ; — *in Fuhchau*, naung ; — *in Shanghai*, năng ; — *in Chifu*, lăn.

嫩 嫩 *nun'* Delicate, small, young, immature; weak, slender; soft, fine; supple; tender.
年紀丨 tender years.
肉丨 flabby, tender flesh.
一隻丨雞 a tender fowl.
丨藍 a light blue. (*Cantonese.*)
字丨 lean-faced characters
細丨 fine and delicate, like sprouts.
你長得丨 you are very young and fresh looking.
嬌丨 fresh complexion; delicate said of women and colors.
老 and 丨 are opposites, old and tender as a fowl; dark and light, as colors.
丨了枝 tender twigs; shoots on a tree.
臉丨 timid, no self-confidence.
有點老丨 though old he is as bashful as a young man. (*Shanghai.*)
煑的太丨 [this egg] is not cooked enough.

NUNG.

Old sound, nong. *In Canton*, nung *and* yung ; — *in Swatow*, lòng ; — *in Amoy*, long ; — *in Fuhchau*, nung *and* nüng ; — *in Shanghai*, niung *and* nung ; — *in Chifu*, nung.

濃 *ˏnung* From *water* and to *cultivate*.
Thick, as liquids; heavy, as dew; strong, as a decoction; rich, seasoned, spiced; lowering, as clouds; nervous, terse, as style; kind, hearty.
丨 and 淡 are opposites, as light and shade; rich and thin; strong and weak.
丨密 close, tangled, as bushes.
丨睡 deep sleep.
香丨 a highly flavored aroma.
丨看 thick eyebrows.
丨厚 nervous, as style.
茶丨到㓞 the tea is so strong as to be bitter. (*Cantonese.*)
丨陰 a dense shade.
領你丨情 I am indebted for your great kindness.
相思苦更丨 the bitterness of my longing is still greater.
丨粧 a rich attire, as of a bride
零露丨丨 the thick falling dew.

醲 *ˏnung* Like the last.
Thick, generous, rich, as spirits; liberal.
丨酒 high flavored wine.
酣丨 sweet or oily wine.
香丨 aromatic liqueurs.
丨于用賞 be liberal in your rewards.

饋 *ˏnung* To gorge.
饋丨 to force one to eat against his inclination.

噥 *ˏnung* Full of talk but not to the purpose; irrelevant.
丨丨 unintelligible muttering; in *Shanghai* used for so so; it will do; let it pass
唧丨 indistinct talk.
竟日徒丨 vainly bawling all day long.
丨丨末者 passable; I will do it; — an unwilling assent.

穠 *ˏnung* Thick, close set, like grain.
丨密 luxuriant, dense, as trees or corn.
何彼丨矣 what great luxuriance! — as a peach tree in full flower.

農 莀 *ˏnung* Composed of 辰 *times*, and 曲, which was originally written 臼 a *mortar* or 林 a *grove* alone, or with 凶 *unlucky* in the middle, all denoting the season for planting; the second and ancient form composed of *plant* and *time*, refers to the same thing.

To cultivate the ground, to delve and dig; to break up the soil; to carry on farming; agriculture; cultivated, tilled; earnestly; widely.
丨夫 or 丨人 a husbandman.
不違丨時 do not pass over the season for sowing.
丨城 an old name for Wu-cheu fu in the east of Kwangsi.
丨家 agriculturists.
三丨 tillage on plains, hills, and marshes.
神丨 or 先丨 the ancient monarch who reigned B.C. 2737 to 2697; he is now worshiped as the god of Agriculture and Medicine.
寓兵于丨 soldiers are obtained from among farmers.
玆予其明丨 hereafter I will learn about husbandry.
丨殖嘉穀 he widely cultivated the best kinds of grain.

儂 *ˏnung* From *man* and *husbandry*; it once meant a man.
The first person I, in which sense it was used in the T'ang dynasty, and is still employed in Nanking and Fuhchau; it is explained as denoting that when one is called, it is as if he answered *ˏnăng* 能 I can; in Kiangsu, it means you, thou, as
丨自家 you yourself.
阿丨 I, myself.
渠丨 he; they.
叫丨就來 I told you to come at once.

齈 ˬnung. A heavy dew; and used with ˬ濃 in this sense.

In *Pekingese* read *năng*'. Soft, miry ground, where water has settled.

地下丨得很 the ground there is very miry; — unsafe.

膿 ˬnung. Pus, matter; to slough away; to rot, as stubble or compost.

丨水 pus.

丨血 bloody sloughing.

灌丨 ripe for opening, as a boil.

揑丨出 or 放丨 to open a boil.

嘔丨 to spue pus; — to revile.

齈 nung'. From *nose* and the last character contracted.

A running at the nose, from cold.

丨鼻不辨花香 a stuffed-up nose cannot distinguish fragrant flowers.

丨涕 snivel.

NWAN.

Old sound, non. *In Canton*, nün; — *in Swatow*, núan; — *in Amoy*, lwan; — *in Fuhchau*, nwang *and* nòng; — *in Shanghai*, nöⁿ; — *in Chifu*, nan.

暖 暝 ʻnwan. From *sun* and *at*; the first is most in use, and like the next.

The pleasant warmth of the sun, as on a spring day; warm, warmed; bland, mild.

風丨 a genial breeze.

呵丨手 to warm the hands with the breath.

不關冷丨 it has nothing to do with cold or heat; it must be done.

今天丨的長 it is warmer to-day.

煖 ʻnwan. Like the last.

To warm, to put near the fire; warmed; friendly, kind.

丨氣 warm vapor.

春丨 spring time; balmy.

飽丨 filled and warmed, well provided for.

人情冷丨 people's feelings are changeable.

餪 ʻnwan. From *to eat* and *at*.

To send a present of food to make a feast.

丨房 a house-warming.

丨酌 a bridal feast.

丨女 or 丨席 a feast given three days after a wedding.

渜 nwan'. Warm water; the water left after bathing; old name of a river in Chihli.

丨濯 hot bathing water.

偄 nwan'. Also read *lwan*'.

Weak, unable to work from illness.

O.

Old sounds, a, ha, *and* ya. *In Canton*, a *and* o; — *in Swatow*, a *and* o; — *in Amoy*, o; — *in Fuhchau*, o, a, *and* i; — *in Shanghai*, u, ku, *and* hu; — *in Chifu*, a.

阿 ˬŏ. From a *mound* and *can* to give the sound.

A high ridge, the bank of a stream; one side or end higher than the other; distorted, prejudiced; near, leaning against; a beam; to cringe, to flatter, to assent; an answer to an order denoting assent, as aye, aye, Sir; beautiful, as trees; who? what? an exclamation, alas! O! this character and 亞 are used as sounds before proper names in the south of China; also in the phrase 丨哥 the emperor's sons.

唯之與丨相去幾何 to reply Sir! or Ah! — where is the great difference?

丨媚奉承 to servilely agree with one.

丨丘 a slope or hillside.

丨斗 the son of Liu Pi, A. D. 260, a confirmed sot; *met.* a blockhead and shiftless fellow.

丨魏 asafœtida.

家中有丨誰 who is that in the house?

丨比 following another's lead, servile.

丨姐 elder sister.

汙不至丨其所好' though humble, they would not flatter their favorites.

丨迷州 a district in the southeast of Yunnan.

丨娘 mother!

丨香 a fairy who helps Léi-kung 雷公 the god of Thunder, to roll his chariot.

丨恕迦 or 丨育 Asoka, the great king who favored Budhism, B. C. 319.

In *Cantonese*. A final interrogative particle, implying doubt.

等我送你丨 shall I send it to you?

婀 㛮 ˬŏ. Undecided, unstable.

婃丨 not having a mind of one's own.

丨娜 flexible, lithe, graceful; delicate, like a girl.

啊 This is interchanged with ˛ho 呵 to breathe.
˛ö An interjection of pleasure or disgust; an interrogative particle, implying no doubt.
你好 丨 are you well?
丨 喲很痛 Haiya! it hurts me badly.

喝茶 丨 will you take some tea?
丨 口氣 to breathe as when warming one's hands.
你用心聽 丨 you must hear.

屙 To ease nature, chiefly used in the South.
˛ö 丨 血 to pass blood.
丨 尿 to urinate.

疴 痾 Sickness; pain.
˛ö 丨 病 a sickness; convulsions in children.
口 丨 sores about the mouth.
微 丨 a slight ailment.
病染沈 丨 his sickness is likely to result fatally.
丨 癢相關 he itches and then I scratch; — a close friendship.

PA.

Old sounds, pa, pak, *and* pat. *In Canton*, pa; — *in Swatow*, pa *and* pó; — *in Amoy*, pa; — *in Fuhchau*, pa; — *in Shanghai*, pò; — *in Chifu*, pa.

巴 The original form is fancied to represent the serpentine windings of the chief rivers which are in the south part of, and gave name to Sz'ch'uen, or the squirming of a snake itself.
˛pa An ancient feudal state in Sz'ch'uen; a classifier of slaps with the hand; a clap; to gather or collect; to adhere; a clamp, such as is used to mend dishes; the butt or head of a bolt to prevent it slipping out; a sign of the optative.
掌嘴 丨 slap his mouth! — said by a magistrate.
丨 結 to attach one's self to a rich or powerful man for one's advantage.
丨 結到手 to hang on (or flatter) one in hopes of a reward.
鍋 丨 the crust in a boiler.
丨 不得有一兩 would that I had just one tael!
丨 圖魯 a title of Manchu origin, meaning a brave chevalier, and nearly equivalent to knight or baronet.
丨 蜀 two ancient states, now used to denote Sz'ch'uen.
丨 蛇 a python, fabled to swallow elephants; its bones made the hills in 丨 陵縣 in the north of Hunan.
丨 豆 the croton-oil fruit.
In *Shanghai*. About, nearly.
里 丨 about a mile.
半夜 丨 it is nearly midnight.

吧 Large mouthed.
˛pa 呀 丨 the crying and wrangling of infants; dumb.
啞 丨 子 a dumb man.
唊 丨 子 a stammerer, one who stutters.
莫 丨 蔽 don't make such a hubbub — or *bobbery*, as this phrase has been imitated. (*Cantonese.*)
丨 國 or 丨 Java, a contraction of 噶喇 丨 Kalapa or Batavia.

豝 羓 A sow; a two year old or large hog; dried or jerked meat.
˛pa 羊尾 丨 dried or cured sheep's tails.

疤 Disease of the joints; a scar.
˛pa 丨 痕 or 丨 瘌 a cicatrix, the mark of a wound; a large scar, a *nævus materna*, or birth-mark; the latter is the vulgar phrase.
丨 眼兒 a distorted or scarred eyelid.
好了瘡 丨 忘記疼 when the scab is healed one forgets the pain.

芭 A fragrant plant.
˛pa 丨 蕉 a banana.
丨 蕉緋 a cylindrical jar, of a plantain shape.
丨 蕉扇 a palm-leaf fan, — so called in Nanking.

笆 A species of bamboo with spines or abortive branches, used for hedges; a fence.
˛pa 籬 丨 a bamboo wattle.
丨 斗 a conical basket to take up rice in.
丨 城 an inclosure hedged with the bamboo.

蚆 A species of *Cypræa* or cowry marked with lines, broad in the middle and tapering at both ends, called 海 丨, and used for money by islanders.
˛pa

把 From *hand* and to *adhere* as the phonetic.
ˊpa To take hold of, to grasp, to seize; to hold for the purpose of using; a classifier of things held in the hand, as a fan; a faggot, a bundle, or what is bound together; a particle denoting the cause, manner, or instrument, and forming either the accusative of the noun following it, as 丨 門關緊 he bolted the door fast; or the object of the verb following, as 丨 我爲何人 whom do you take me to be? a *preposition*, with, the means by which a thing is done; to regard as, to take a thing to be, to consider as, having, for.
火 丨 a link, a match.
丨 爲無用 I regarded him as useless.

要丨柄 we must have some evidence; something to lay hold of.
丨持 to hold on to, to control, to take care.
一丨扇 one fan.
一丨嘴 one lip, a great talker.
丨衙人 bailiffs or serjeants in a court.
丨關 a high officer guarding the customs and passes.
丨手撥開 push it aside with your hand.
有幾丨手 there were several fellows, as in a scuffle.
丨家人 the housekeeper.
拜 (or 打) 丨子 adopted or sworn brothers.
拱丨 the grasp of both hands; all the things.
丨總 an ensign in an army.
禾丨 a handful of grain.
莫丨工夫 悮 do not waste your hours of work.
丨袂之時 our times of friendly intercourse.
做 (or 弄) 丨戲 or 打丨式 to play tricks of legerdemain; to perform feats, as acrobats or monkeys; the allusion was probably originally to Pa 巴 or South Sz'ch'uen, to which the radical 手 was in time added.
丨他怎麽樣 what will you do with him?

In *Cantonese*. Over, upwards, an excess.
百丨銀錢 more than a hundred dollars.
千丨 more than a thousand.
(*Shanghai.*)
個丨月 a month and more.

耙 **鈀** *pa'* *ₛp'a* A drag, a harrow; the second is also a war chariot, or the guard in front of it; a clamp used in mending crockery.
犂丨 a harrow.
駕牛丨田 ride the ox to harrow the field.
舞三丨 to flourish the trident; — a kind of gymnastics.

弝 *pa'* The part of a bow which is grasped when shooting.
丨瑪油 dammar, a sort of pitch brought from Borneo.

欛 **㰈** *pa'* The handle of a knife or hilt of a sword made of horn or wood; authority.
丨柄 a handle, either actually or figuratively.
無丨欛 I have no authority; no power to act.

靶 *pa'* The part of the reins or bridle held in the hand; the dash-board; a target.
丨子 a bull's eye.
射中丨 to hit the mark.

霸 *pa'* From *rain*, *hide* and *moon*; the two first form the phonetic, but the whole indicates that the moon appears on the third day; anciently contracted to *poh*, 伯 an earl.

To be chief among feudatories; to reign by force rather than by law or virtue; to make a high prince; to incroach on; to hold one in check through fear; a feudal prince in ancient times, now rather a tyrant or usurper, like Dionysius of Syracuse; one who defies legal control.
以力假人者丨 he who by force makes a pretense to benevolence is a chief of the princes.
丨王 a valiant ruler, but one who is not legitimate or restrained by law.
侯丨 a sort of prince palatine in the Cheu dynasty; there were 五丨 in the days of Confucius.
丨佔 to infringe on another's right.
土丨 a village tyrant or head of robbers.
丨氣 audacious, fearless.
行丨道 to act vigorously, as a physician in practice; to intimidate, as a sturdy beggar.
各丨一方 each one lorded it over a district.

丨州 a district south of Peking.

Read *p'oh*, The moon just appearing, for which 魄 is now used instead; 死丨 and 生丨 denote new and full moon.

壩 **垻** *pa'* The second form is most commonly used; the other seems to have been formed in consequence of the change of sound requiring a primitive of the same tone; not the same as *kü'* 埧 shore.

An embankment or dike to narrow and restrain the waters; a breakwater; it is given to many towns on the Yellow River from their position near the levees; in Sz'ch'uen, it is applied to low banks just awash formed by silt; a slope where boats pass up and down, as in the Canal.
東丨 a series of dikes in Lihyang hien 溧陽縣 which protect the country from the overflow of the Yangtsz' River.
拖丨 to drag a boat up the slope or lock.
倒丨 the levee or dike has given way.
築丨 to raise a levee.
丨頭 a mart, a port, a factory.
打丨 to build a dam.
半丨 a hamlet beyond Kalgan, so called because it is halfway up the ascent of the plateau.

灞 *pa'* A small affluent of the River Wéi, called 丨水 near Singan fu in Shensi.

罷 *pa'* From *net* and *able*, implying that the good are able to speak and deliver from false charges.

To suffice, to cease from, to leave off; to discontinue, to finish, to quash; to strike work; to turn out; at the end of a sentence, enough, no more; a final particle indicating the imperative mood; or an interrogative implying great probability.
丨了 very well, stop now.
丨手 to close a shop.

歇手丨 to stop work.
作丨論 let us have done talking.
丨工 to strike for wages.
丨試 to foreclose an examination by the candidates refusing to attend.
丨官 to dismiss from office.
去丨 or 走丨 be off!
丨不了 it cannot be helped or resisted.
寫就丨 just write it, that's all.
欲丨不能 he could not stop though he wished to do so.
這樣丨那樣丨 will you have it this way or that?
客人出門去了丨 has not the visitor gone out?
如何丨休 why is the affair stopped?

Read ˬp'i for 疲. Wearied.
丨勞 great fatigue and exhaustion.

Read ˬpai. To escape from evil consequences.
郎丨 a term for father in Fuhkien.

爸 pa˒ A father; Mohammedans address their mollahs by this term, as 張丨 mollah Chang.
阿丨 or 丨丨 papa.
老丨丨 a term for an old Mohammedan.
阿丨賺錢子享福 the daddy lays up pelf, and his boy enjoys himself with it. (*Cantonese.*)

叭 ˬpa ˒ Also read *páh*˒
Sound; the mouth open.
喇丨 a long narrow necked trumpet, made of brass, used in camps or theaters, and at funerals.
喇丨花 the white stramony (*Datura*); also the fox-glove (*Rehmannia*), and other trumpet-shaped blossoms.

P'A.

Old sounds, p'a, p'at, p'ak, ba, *and* bat. *In Canton,* p'a; — *in Swatow,* pé, p'é, *and* p'a; — *in Amoy,* pa *and* p'a; — *in Fuhchau,* p'a *and* pa; — *in Shanghai,* p'ò *and* pò; — *in Chifu,* p'a.

葩 ˬp'a From *plant* and *white.*
The corolla or inflorescence of a plant.
含丨 a flower bud; elegant, said of verse.
詩正而丨 the verses are correct and beautiful.
蝶探奇丨 the butterfly comes seeking the rare flower; — said of young people.

舥 ˬp'a A floating bridge, usually made of boats, but sometimes of spars.

筢 ˬp'a A bamboo rake with five teeth or more, used to get grass out of the mire, called 丨子 or 九齒竹丨; it is easily wielded in one hand.

杷 ˬpa Interchanged with 耙˒ a harrow.
A kind of beetle to break clods in a field; a rake; to gather straw.
枇丨梗 loquat stems; — a kind of sweetmeat.

妑 ˬpa A woman's name.
丨頭 the headdress of a female done up double.

琶 ˬpa From 琴 a *lute* contracted, and 巴 to collect as the phonetic.
A guitar with four strings, the 琵丨; it is pear-shaped, and resembles the harp of Pythagoras; to draw the hand in when thrumming it.
腿彈琵丨 shivering with cold.

爬 ˬp'a Interchanged with 耙˒ a rake and with 扒 to paddle.
To scratch; to crawl, to creep; to claw, to rake up; to climb, to clamber, to scale; a gridiron; a pick.
丨飯 to eat with chop-sticks.
丨行 to crawl, as a tortoise.
丨上 to climb up.
手丨丨 to climb and scratch.
牛肉丨 a beefsteak, so named from the gridiron.
搔丨 to scratch.
釘丨 an iron rake, used like a hoe.
郡女丨柴 the village women rake up the chips.
丨山虎 a chain of hills; the ivy; a grape (*Ampelopsis*) that climbs like the ivy. (*Pekingese.*)
丨起來 to creep up or out.

趴 ˬp'a An unauthorized character often used for the preceding.
To fall on; to fall along, as on the ground; to burrow.
兩手丨在地下 he fell on his hands to the ground.
丨山覓藥 to roam over the hills gathering simples.

舥 ˬp'a The horns of an ox spreading wide; horns stretching out.

跁 ˋp'a To walk without advancing is 丨跒; to squat, to crouch down; to grovel; dwarfish.
丨行 to crawl on all fours.

帊 p'a˒ Used for the next.
A bundle of clothes or roll of silk; a kerchief, a coif.
錦丨 a brocade napkin.

帕 p'a˒ A kerchief, a veil for protecting the head; a stomacher for children.
手丨 a handkerchief.
遮羞丨 a foreign lady's veil.
頭丨 a red veil, worn by brides.

Read *mih*˒ A turban or fillet worn by soldiers.

袙ˀ Interchanged with the last; also read *mih*ˀ

*p'a*ˀ A turban to cover the head, which the Fuhkien sailors still use; a napkin; turbans of different colors were used after the Han dynasty to distinguish ranks.

首 丨 a turban.

怕ˀ From *heart* and *white*; occurs used for 霸 the dark orb of the moon, and 魄 the manes of a person.

*p'a*ˀ To fear, to dread; to apprehend, to suppose; lest, perhaps; to think or fear that something may happen.

恐 丨 跌 lest it fall.

丨 死 afraid of death.

丨 臭 I am afraid of the ridicule.

丨 他 來 I daresay he will come.

嚇 丨 to frighten one.

不 丨 黒 don't fear the dark.

駭 丨 to intimidate.

PAH.

Old sounds, pat *and* bat. *In Canton*, pat, păt, *and* p'a; — *in Swatow*, poi; — *in Amoy*, pat *and* pwat; — *in Fuhchau*, pak, *and* paik; — *in Shanghai*, pĕh; — *in Chifu*, pa.

八ˀ 捌ˀ } The original form represents two things back to back; it forms the 12th radical of a few incongruous characters; the second form is used in checks for security.

ˏ*pa* Eight; to divide; opening out, flaring.

丨 字 形 flaring, slanting, not straight sides.

第 丨 the eighth; number eight.

丨 丨 sixty-four.

丨 十 eighty.

二 丨 sixteen.

忘 丨 or 王 丨 頭 a cuckold, one who forgets all virtue.

丨 刀 to divide, alluding to the composition of 分 to divide.

丨 角 油 aniseed oil.

丨 音 instrumental music; a band.

丨 字 好 a good horoscope; these are the cyclic characters for the year, month, day, and hour of a person to be betrothed.

七 手 丨 臂 seven hands and eight arms; — agile, clever.

丨 寶 the eight precious things, which the eight genii 丨 仙 carry in their hands.

丨 仙 桌 子 an octagonal table.

丨 拜 之 交 intimate, friendly.

丨 字 兒 沒 見 一 撇 兒 not the first stroke of the eight is to be seen yet; — nothing at all has been done.

丨 行 書 Chinese note-paper.

叭ˀ The cry of a bird; the noise of a cockatoo, or some kind

ˏ*pa* of a parrot.

水 丨 哥 兒 a kind of pie or blackbird found in Kiangnan.

胈ˀ Hair on the thigh; the short hair on the flesh.

ˏ*pa* 腓 無 丨 his calves had no hair, — from his severe toil.

拔ˀ From *hand* and *to drag*; also read *poh*ˀ and *péi*.

ˏ*pa* To pull up, to eradicate; to root up, to extirpate; to take by storm, to assault; to pull the skin when ill, done as a counter-irritant; to elevate, to promote; to excel; quickly; conspicuous; the barb of an arrow; to exclude.

提 丨 to raise to a higher post.

丨 沙 to irritate the skin to relieve a colic or cholera.

丨 劍 to draw a sword.

一 毛 不 丨 he won't pull a hair; closefisted, he'll give nothing.

丨 草 to pull up grass.

丨 力 to exert one's strength.

出 類 丨 萃 eminent above all his fellows.

丨 城 to capture a city.

連 根 丨 pull up the roots too.

丨 貢 生 a selected *siuts'ai*, one who excels the common rank, and can be employed.

魃ˀ The demon of drought, represented as a naked or tat-

ˏ*pa* tered pigmy, having one eye and fleet as the wind; others represent it like a bird with eyes on its hands and head, and a red sash on the shoulders; perhaps this fable is derived from the summer-colt.

旱 丨 為 虐 the drought is very severe.

朳ˀ An agricultural instrument to level beds after the seed

ˏ*pa* is sown; it is like a rake without teeth.

In *Cantonese* used with *pai*ˀ 扒. A paddle; to paddle.

丨 燈 心 to trim the lamp-wick.

丨 三 板 to paddle a dingey.

菝ˀ From *plant* and *to pull up*.

ˏ*pa* The 丨 葜 is a species of *Smilax*, the trailing stem of which is hard and stiff, and the root edible; the same term is applied to the unexpanded leaves of brake.

軷ˀ A sacrifice offered to the gods of the road at starting

ˏ*pa* on a journey, where the roads cross.

取 羝 以 丨 take a ram and perform the sacrifice to the road guardians.

PAI.

Old sounds, pa, pat, ba, *and* bat. *In Canton*, pai *and* pa, — *in Swatow*, pai, pⁿoi, *and* pi; — *in Amoy*, pai, pòe, *and* pút; — *in Fuhchau*, pai *and* pè; — *in Shanghai*, pa, pò, *and* ba; — *in Chifu*, paĭ.

擺 ʻpai From *hand* and to *stop*.

To spread out, to expose, to arrange, to set in order; to move, to strike; to strut; to get rid of; to work, as the scull of a boat; an axis or balance in machinery; the tongue, as of a bell; to sway to and fro.

丨開什物 to display articles.

丨布 or 丨設 to place, to exhibit in order.

丨布他 to order him, to do him, to injure him.

丨隊伍 to parade troops.

丨架子 to make a display, to put on airs, as a rich or learned man. (*Shanghai.*)

搖搖丨丨 to strut, to act the swell.

丨執事 to arrange a procession.

丨左 and 丨右 side off to the left — or right; — said by the front chair-bearer to his fellow.

丨手 to warn off by the hand.

丨花街 to dress out a street.

丨空架子 a needy man vaporing about his means.

丨渡 or 丨過去 to ferry across a stream. (*Pekingese.*)

丨唆 to induce, to flatter, to coax.

丨針 the pivot of scales, the balance in machinery; the axis in a watch.

丨龍門陣 to draw a long bow, to gossip, to talk.

風丨旗 the wind shakes the flag.

拜 pai' From two 手 *hands* down on the ground; others derive it from 手 *hand* and 首 *head* to the earth.

To honor, to reverence; to kneel to, to make an act of worship or obeisance; to visit, to salute, to pay one's respects to; to appoint to an office; a salute, an obeisance, a visit.

禹丨昌言 Yü did homage to his excellent words.

丨神 to worship the gods.

丨墳 to worship at the graves.

丨託 to request, as a favor of another.

回丨 to return a visit.

丨見 to go and see a friend.

丨相 a minister of state.

丨本 to memorialize the emperor.

甘丨下風 I willingly take your lead, or learn of you.

長揖不丨 made him a low bow, but did not kneel.

丨手 to salute with folded hands.

丨匣 a card-case or envelope.

丨服 I acknowledge your superiority; you do it better than I.

官丨何職 to what office has he been appointed?

勿剪勿丨 don't clip or bark — the tree.

唄 pai' Imitated from a Sanskrit word, to praise or chant, as is done in Budhist temples.

敗, **退** pai' From 攴 to *strike* or 辵 to *go* and 貝 *wealth*, denoting that robbers 賊 run away with, or destroy property; the second form is unusual.

To subvert, to destroy; to nullify; to ruin; to violate; defeated, discomfited; broken, ruined, as an affair; those who destroy; ruin; a defeat, a rout.

破丨 broken, defaced, ruined.

丨家子 a disgrace to the family.

打丨仗 defeated in battle.

丨壞 rendered worthless; spoiled.

一丨塗地 a complete loss, an entire smash.

丨殘軍馬 a total defeat of the army.

事丨了 the affair is ruined.

丨門風 to disgrace the good name of the family, as an erring daughter.

丨風俗 to corrupt public morals.

肉丨 tainted meat.

損丨 ruined.

稗 pai' From *grain* and *small*.

Tares, cockle, cheat, chess; weeds found among grain; a kind of panic grass cultivated in Chihli; dissemblers, hypocrites.

丨草 darnel; false grain.

丨說 vicious books, fables.

丨販 a huckster.

丨官 a low or supernumerary official.

丨官野吏 contemptible underlings.

丨子 and 光豆丨子 are two kinds of *Panicum* grown in damp places for their seeds, which are eaten; the latter is the *Panicum crus-corvi*, and also called 水丨 water darnel.

䅭 pai' Used with the last; denoting only the grain.

丨子麵 flour of panic-rye.

韛 pai' A leather tube used to blow and urge a fire, such as is appended to a bellows.

憊 pai' From *heart* and *prepared*.

Exhausted, debilitated, no strength.

倍形困丨 he is altogether knocked up; he appears quite wearied out.

丨倦 tired.

丨累得很 utterly exhausted.

忒丨懶 very rude, unmannerly and rustic.

扒 pai' To eradicate; to reverence. Read *pah*, To break; to injure; to lean against; to divide, to cut in two.

In *Cantonese* used with 扒. A paddle; to paddle; to grab, to pull a lot of things towards one.

一枝丨 a paddle.

丨攤 to quadrate the cash in gambling.

In *Pekingese* used for 爬. To crawl; to fall on the ground; to lie on or down; to strike; to put the mouth to one's ear.

丨在炕 lying on the *k'ang*.

丨手 a rower; a man in douanes who measures rafts for duty.

棑 pai' A raft or float; a shield; the taffrail of a vessel, or the timber at the stern; sometimes wrongly used for 'fěi 榧 the hazel-nut.

粺 pai' Good white rice, or millet, well washed and hulled, which is usually reckoned to be three-fourths of the paddy, but of millet equal only to three-fifths.

彼疏斯丨 those were [like] coarse, these [like] fine — rice.

P'AI.

Old sounds, ba, bat, p'a, *and* p'at. *In Canton*, p'ai; — *in Swatow*, pai *and* p'ai; — *in Amoy*, pai *and* p'ai; — *in Fuhchau*, pai, pw'ai *and* pè; — *in Shanghai*, p'a *and* pa; — *in Chifu*, p'ai.

排 ꜀p'ai From *hand* and *not*; often interchanged with 擺 to arrange.

To place properly; to make a show; to shove, to push open, as a door; a row, a set out, a line; the rank or place of a person in his family.

丨列兩行 arranged in two rows.

平丨 uniformly arranged, as the entrances of a house.

丨丨坐 seat them in rows.

丨難解紛 to make up a difficulty and explain a misunderstanding.

羊丨骨 mutton chops.

我丨二 I am the second in age, as a brother or sister in comparison with their seniors.

大丨丨兒 a swaggerer, a fop, one ignorant of good society.

安丨 to order about, to put in their places.

丨闥而入 he pushed open the door and went in.

平丨禮 of equal rank or station.

着得好丨塲 to dress with great bravery.

丨字 to distribute types.

丨卦 to cast out the lots

In *Cantonese*. A time, a chance, a while.

呢丨症多 much sickness prevails at present.

先個丨 on that occasion.

俳 ꜀p'ai From *man* and *not*; it is sometimes wrongly used for 徘 ꜀pêi to walk.

Dissipation.

丨優 theatrical shows; musicians or actors.

捭 ꜀p'ai Interchanged with 擺 to set in order.

To strike with both hands; to throw aside; to cut off and roast meat on hot stones.

牌 ꜀p'ai From a *slip* and *mean*.

A shield, a buckler; a signboard; a notification of government; a tablet, a memorandum; a warrant, a credential, a writ, a token; an official permit of any kind; dominoes, cards; a flat piece of iron struck for meals in temples

火丨 an express.

籐丨 rattan shields.

丨位 the ancestral tablet; a board with the names of gods on it.

丨票 a warrant to arrest one.

丨照 a commission, a warrant.

一副紙丨 a pack of cards.

紅丨 a port-clearance, often called the *grand chop*; the large vermilion stamps give it a red look.

丨坊 or 丨樓 honorary gateway.

腰丨 a waist warrant, as of a policeman.

耳丨 flat ear-rings.

賞銀丨 silver medals given to soldiers.

虎頭丨 the tiger-head tablets at a yamun on which edicts are put.

打丨 or 鬪丨 to gamble, to bet.

行丨該屬 he gave orders to his subordinates.

牙丨神數 to divine the fates by dominoes.

請丨 to request an official permit.

簰 ꜀p'ai From *bamboo* and a *board*; 排 is often used instead in Canton.

A raft of wood or bamboo; name of a river near Tan-yang hien in Kiangsu.

竹丨 a raft of bamboo.

木丨頭 a market-place in Canton.

擘 ꜂p'ai From *hand* and to *move*; it is also read *wai'* and sometimes written 掰, made of two *hands dividing*, an unauthorized form.

To pierce; to open out a thing, to separate its parts; to snap in two.

丨鋸 to set a saw.

丨開 to break open or apart, as a cake.

丨了一塊 broke off a piece.

哌 ꜂p'ai The noise of spitting or clearing the throat, or of vomiting; another says, the noise of snoring.

辰 *p'ái'* The original form represents the headwaters of a stream joining the main trunk; others say it is altered from 一 *one* and 水 *water*, or from 反 *back* and 水 *water* combined.

To branch off; occurs only as a primitive in combination.

派 *p'ai'* From *water* and *dividing*.

To branch, as a stream; to ramify, as a family; a branch, a rill; to appoint to a post; to distribute to each person; a tribe; a classifier for all, a lot, the whole quantity.

支丨 a tribe or clan; to branch out.

字丨 the name given to brothers to distinguish them or their generation from others of the same sept or surname.

丨名 the marriage name; the part of the given name common to several brothers.

丨書 to distribute books.

同丨 of the same generation in a family.

一丨都是白的 they are alike white.

好一丨地方 what a fine spot!

丨他前去 send him on ahead.

嫡丨子孫 my entire posterity.

正丨 honest, upright.

一丨浮言 the whole is a made up story.

分丨 to appoint each to his place.

湃 *p'ai'* The sound of dashing waves; the noise of breakers.

澎丨 roaring billows.

PAN.

Old sounds, pan *and* ban. *In Canton,* pan; — *in Swatow,* pan, pw^{n}a, pwan, p^{n}oi, pien *and* peng; — *in Amoy,* pan, p'an, pwan, *and* p'eng; — *in Fuhchau,* pang, pwang, pw'ang, paing, *and* pieng; — *in Shanghai,* pè^{n}, bè^{n}, *and* pé^{n}; — *in Chifu,* pan.

班 *pan* From two 玉 *gems* and 刀 *knife*; to divide a gem and give one to each prince; used with the next.

To confer rewards and places on soldiers; to make known, to extend everywhere; to place in a series; a rank, order, grade, or class of persons; a set; a troop; a turn; a classifier of groups of men and of plays; a manager.

一丨人 a class of men.

門丨 door-keepers at a yamun.

輪丨 a turn; to take one's turn.

改丨 it comes my turn.

上丨 to take one's turn, and 下丨 to retire from it.

皂丨 torturers, the "black set."

快丨 official messengers.

長丨 a servant in constant use.

退丨 dismiss the court; to give way to the next set.

同丨輩 of the same rank or class.

分丨列坐 to seat each one in his place.

站丨 each one standing in his place.

丨門弄斧 to wield an ax before Lu-pan 魯丨 the god of Carpenters; — *met.* to be conceited.

打丨杖 a children's game of striking a taw; it resembles marbles.

丨師 to return with the troops after victory.

大丨 a supercargo; a manager; the head of a firm. (*Cantonese.*)

排丨 to arrange in order, to give each his duty.

丨子 a company of actors.

頒行天下 to publish to the empire.

令鴉丨登桅望 sent a sailor up the mast to lookout.

斑 *pan* Variegated, striped, streaked, mottled; applied to mildewed and spotted things.

面丨 pock-marked.

丨竹 a mottled black kind of bamboo.

丨絹 mixed lustring.

丨色 variegated.

丨衣 theatrical costumes.

汗丨 pustules, pimples, white spots.

丨文 mottled, spotted.

媥 *pan* Like the last.

Veined, like agate; marbled.

丨爛 ring-streaked.

癍 *pan* An unauthorized character.

A blotch; discolored spots, such as come before small-pox breaks out; purple spots.

出丨 petecchiæ have come out.

挑丨 to probe the spots.

般 *pan* From 舟 *boat* and 殳 *turning*, here equivalent to 旋; it is used for 班 and for some of its compounds.

To drive back water, as a boat in turning; to transport; a sort; way, manner of; an affair.

多丨 many ways.

十八丨武藝 the eighteen kinds of military drill and fencing.

這丨 that sort, such, these, so.

一丨兒 same, alike, as.

吾進丨泥洹後 after I have entered *pari nirvana.*

千丨or丨丨or萬丨 all kinds of things; every variety.

搬 *pan* To remove from one place to another; to transport; to bandy, to discuss.

丨屋 or 丨家 to move one's residence.

丨貨下船 take the goods on board.

丨來丨去 to carry things here and there.

丨運粮餉 to transport stores for the army.

喜丨是非 he likes to move right and wrong, — to compass his ends; said of an unscrupulous man.

In *Cantonese*. To cleave.

丨細的 split it smaller.

盤 ˬpan A striped, poisonous fly.

丨蝥 or 斑蝥 Chinese cantharides or blistering fly (*Mylabris*); it is like a lady-bug, and feeds on the Dolichos bean.

頒 ˬpan From *head* and to *divide*, referring to fish with large heads; used for 班 and the next.

To confer by the emperor, to donate; to divide among, to distribute, as a king does; to publish abroad.

丨白者 a gray, grisly head.

丨賜 or 丨給 to confer on, by the sovereign.

有丨其首 [the fish] show their big heads.

丨下 to promulge.

丨指 an archer's thumb-ring.

丨詔 imperial proclamations.

丨發 to make known.

Read ˬ*fän*. Numerous.

魚首丨然 a great school of big-headed fishes.

肦 ˬpan Like the last.

To confer; many.

不丨賦 they would not pay tribute or taxes.

Read ˬ*fän*. Big-headed.

丨顋頭 a projecting forehead, one which bulges.

板 ˊpan From *wood* and to *return*.

A board, plank, or slab; a shingle; a slip of ivory or stone; a block for a book; a page; the palm or sole; an instrument of flagellation, or a stroke of it; things made of planks; the skin of a fur; a winnowing fan; set, fixed, as a board; obstinate, doltish; unbending, solemn; the board on which names were written, a register.

一塊丨 one board.

打丨子 to bamboo.

藏丨 to keep the blocks of a book; to print or publish a work.

翻丨 blocks which have been re-cut for a second edition; blocks retouched that have been worn.

打手丨 to ferule the hands.

响丨 castanets.

過橋抽丨 to pull up the planks after crossing the bridge;— *i. e.* to act like a dog in the manger.

三丨 a ship's gig, a row-boat.

古丨人 an old fashioned man, one not up to the age.

夾丨 boards to inclose or secure a thing, as Chinese books, when lettering them.

夾丨公文 a flying dispatch from court; it is put between boards.

丨滯 stiff, not apt to take a hint.

丨執不通 impenetrably dull.

望丨 boards which support the tiling.

負丨 grieved, orphaned.

上帝丨丨 Shangti has reversed all his ways.

老丨 manager of a company of actors; the head of a shop.

船老丨 captain of a junk.

丨眼 or 丨路 a rest in music.

太丨 unbending, firm, precise; too solemn, very grave, rather gloomy.

夫妻兩個丨 the husband with the wife.

丨數 it is certainly so.

丨要 it must be so.

唔係丨定 it is not certain; not fixed, variable. (*Cantonese.*)

版 ˊpan Synonym of the last.

A schedule, a register; an insignia; to divide; planks for building adobe walls.

築丨牆 to make mud walls.

縮丨以載 they bound the planks firmly in tiers.

丨圖 or 丨籍 a census or register of the people.

投丨棄官 he threw down his baton and resigned the office.

玉丨 tinkling stones hung in the wind to jingle.

丨法 laws of planetary motions.

瓪 ˊpan The lower or under tile made flat for forming channels for the rain.

昄 ˊpan Great.

爾土宇丨章 your country is beautiful and extended.

半 panˋ From 八 to *divide* and 牛 an *ox*, (the latter standing for 物 a thing,) which is large and can be halved.

To divide in two; a half; a large piece of; the greater part of.

對丨 to divide equally.

多丨 or 大丨 the larger part, the greatest half.

丨夜 midnight.

大你一丨 as old again as you are.

年將丨百 about fifty years old.

丨世人 a middle aged man.

丨信丨疑 in great doubt.

丨刻 a very little while.

丨子 a son-in-law.

丨人丨鬼 half dead with fright.

一丨氷 a piece of ice.

丨路棄妻 to divorce a wife after having her half one's life.

折丨 to halve.

丨途而廢 to stop halfway, to fail to complete a thing.

丨遍面 a profile as of the side face.

丨不道兒 not half-way there.

丨有丨無 now it appears, and then it is gone, as smoke or thin vapory clouds.

姅 panˋ A woman who is ceremonially unclean; anciently she marked her face red.

伴 pan' From *man* and his *half* as the phonetic.

A comrade, a fellow, an associate; to follow, to attend on.

同 丨 an equal, one in the same position.

丨 奐 爾 游 矣 you are very happy in your rambles.

丨 靈 to keep the manes company, by sleeping near the coffin while it is in the house.

陪 丨 to accompany one.

丨 郎 a boy who waits on a bridal pair.

丨 娘 a bridesmaid.

優 游 丨 奐 to ramble and enjoy one's leisure.

老 丨 an old comrade; — a pleasant term for one's wife, a Joan.

畔 pan' From *field* and *half*; interchanged with the next.

A path dividing fields, a landmark; a side or bank; to resist. — as sumptuary laws respecting dress.

耕 者 讓 丨 the farmers yielded the landmark.

傍 丨 a bank.

河 丨 a quay or bund.

丨 援 to reject insidious, seductive leadings.

丨 道 side of the road.

叛 p'an' From to *turn* and *half*.

To rebel, to revolt; to resist and escape from the authorities of a country; brilliant.

丨 逆 to rise in rebellion.

背 丨 to conspire against, to desert from.

離 丨 to throw off allegiance.

丨 賊 a rebel.

謀 丨 to plot rebellion.

丨 赫 輝 煌 beautiful and glittering, as the stars around the north pole.

絆 pan' A lasso to catch horses; to lasso, to trip up a horse's legs; to stumble, to stub; to restrict, to hamper, to entangle; to trip; a restraint, an obligation.

丨 馬 索 to fetter a horse, as when training him to amble.

爲 道 所 羈 丨 restrained by reason.

丨 住 detained, as by business.

磕 磕 丨 丨 的 hindered in one's progress, prevented in any way.

鈕 丨 a button loop, — is often so written.

丨 脚 to stub the toes.

In *Fuhchau*. To brush away; to strike, as with a rope.

丨 風 蚊 to brush away musquitoes.

靽 pan' Like the preceding.

Ropes or traces to restrain oxen drawing a cart.

辦 pan' From *criminals* scolding each other and *strength*; it resembles *pien'* 辨 to distinguish.

To exert one's self, to manage, to attend to; to prepare, to provide; to go on with; to transact business, to act as a factor; after other verbs often shows an official act, as 查 丨 to enqire into.

備 丨 to prepare for, to make ready against.

丨 罪 to inflict punishment.

丨 貨 to contract for goods.

丨 酒 to prepare an entertainment.

丨 差 an officer's confidential deputy who manages for him.

丨 案 to depute one to attend to a case.

丨 得 好 well manged.

丨 不 來 it cannot be obtained; cannot be brought about; impracticable.

丨 妥 當 all is well arranged.

丨 事 to manage an affair.

大 丨 the lingering punishment. (*Cantonese.*)

In *Cantonese*. A sample, a muster.

茶 丨 a sample of tea.

對 丨 to compare musters.

瓣 pan' The carpels or division of an orange; a slice, as of a melon; a slip.

花 丨 the petals of a flower.

蒜 丨 the scales of an onion.

兩 丨 兒 two slips only, as a tract or issue of a single play.

扮 pan' From *hand* and to *divide*.

To dress up, to beautify; to apparel, to disguise, to rig out, as in a costume; to counterfeit; dress, ornament.

打 丨 or 裝 丨 dressed out, a gay show; to dress gaily.

丨 色 gay processions.

假 丨 官 差 to simulate policemen.

丨 故 事 to dress up in the old style, as in processions.

丨 檯 閣 to carry children on high frames in processions.

丨 戲 to dress as an actor.

丨 民 核 訪 to dress as a commoner and inquire into affairs.

涼 丨 iced fruits or preserves.

Read *făn'* To seize with the hand; to move.

丨 動 to shake.

In *Cantonese*. To beat.

棍 丨 佢 take a stick to him.

搫 pan' Synonym of 絆' a noose.

To tie up, to tie fast; a band, a tether, a loop.

帽 丨 a hat-band.

槳 丨 an oar-tie.

湴 pan' From *water* and *together*.

Deep mud made in the streets, the mire of the roads; to get mired, to overflow.

一 身 丨 I am muddied all over.

泥 丨 slush, mud.

爛 丨 防 有 刺 beware lest there are thorns in the mud; — *met.* take heed how you injure the feeble.

溝 渠 丨 sewage.

丨 河 an unlucky star.

P'AN.

Old sounds, p'an *and* ban. *In Canton*, p'an ; — *in Swatow*, pw'an, p'an, pan, *and* pw'ⁿa ; — *in Amoy*, pan, p'an, pw'an, *and* p'ian ; — *in Fuhchau*, p'ang *and* pw'ang ; — *in Shanghai*, p'èⁿ, pèⁿ, *and* pé ; — *in Chifu*, p'an.

攀 扳 ꜀p'an — To grasp, to drag; to pull down or towards one; to raise the hand; to clamber, to mount, as a tree; to implicate.

丨索 to heave one a rope.
丨扯 to implicate.
丨不到 I can't pull it down.
拱丨 to inform against an accomplice.
丨扶 to hold on for support.
不敢高丨 I cannot venture to equal you.
敢丨台駕 I presume to drag you [to my house]; — a form of invitation.
手丨丹桂 he has grasped the red olive flower; — *i. e.* has obtained his doctorate.
丨留 to civilly detain.
丨下來 pull it down.

拚 ꜀p'an — From *hand* and *cap* ; easily mistaken for 拌 to halve.

To brush clean; to lay the hand on; to fly; to risk; to disregard.

既丨以俟 I have made all ready and wait for you.
丨命 to risk one's life.
丨去 or 丨棄 to reject.
丨飛維鳥 but it flew off as if it had been a bird.
跟他丨了 to follow him at every hazard.
丨財 to speculate rashly.
丨爛 to act recklessly; to venture any way.

潘 ꜀p'an — An affluent of the River Han in Yun-yang hien in the northwest of Honan; dirty rice-washings used to scrub the face.

丨州 an old name of Meu-ming hien 茂名縣 in the southwest of Kwangtung.

眅 ꜀p'an — From *eye* and *turning*.

An eye which shows much white, turned up or awry.

丨睛 a cataract.

磻 ꜀p'an — Name of a tributary of the River Wei, the 丨溪 in the west of Shensi, where Taikung 太公 fished; a kind of flint fit for arrowheads.

蟠 ꜀p'an — From *insect* and a *track* : like the next.

To curl up, to crouch under, to coil around; writhing, squirming; curling around, wreathing; to commit to.

龍丨棍 a cane with dragons carved around it.
龍丨於泥 the serpent lay coiled in the dirt.
丨繞 to encircle spirally.
丨踞 to occupy, as squatters do.
上極下丨 it reaches from the zenith down to the ground; said in exaggeration of the height of a tree, peak, or house.
雲丨大地 the clouds enveloped the land.
丨桃核 the seeds of the flat peach.
丨桃會 the meeting of the gods and genii to honor 王母 at the tree of life; her birthday festival, on the 3d of the 3d moon, is much observed.

Read ꜀*fan*. Sow-bugs and similar insects which are found under vessels left long in damp places.

嶓 ꜀p'an — To hinder and irritate others by abusive talk.

瘢 ꜀p'an — A cicatrix; marks, pits, or other scars on the skin.

瘡丨 scar of a wound.
花底丨 pock-marks.

蹩 蹳 ꜀p'an — From *feet* and *sort* ; occurs interchanged with the next; the second is also another form of ꜀*man* 蹣 to jump.

To bend the feet under one; to jump.

丨膝而坐 to sit with the feet bent under one.

盤 ꜀p'an — Occurs used synonymously with ꜀*păn* 盆 a bowl.

A platter, a basin, a tub; a deep dish or vessel to contain liquids or grain; a press, frame, or machine; a containing thing, like the pelvis; a market; a game; an affair; curved, coiled, winding; to coil, to wind, as rope.

交丨 to transfer the business to another.
收丨 to wind up an affair.
洗身丨 or 洗澡丨 a bathing-tub.
丨香 a coil of insense stick.
開丨 to open the market.
丨纏 or 丨費 traveling expenses, disbursements.
丨古氏 Panku, reputed to be the first man.
丨查 to examine judicially.
成丨 to finish a transaction.
丨旋竹林路 to go around by way of the bamboo grove.
丨桓數日 to take a few days' relaxation.
一丨棋 one game of chess.
丨屈 coiled up.
水晶丨正托金山寺 the crystal bowl (*i. e.* the water of the Yangtsz') truly upholds the Golden Island temple.
丨問 to interrogate.
不定丨 no fixed rate, no test by which to try it; the allusion is to the sale of grain by the measure.
和丨托出 all the leading facts of the case are presented.

屈燒猪丨 bound up like a roasting pig; — said of persons punished by lynch law.
丨踞 or 丨膝 to sit like a tailor.
In *Fuhchau*. To buy goods for retailing; to retail.
丨去賣 I bought them for retailing.

槃 ˓p'an Used for the last.
A tray, a waiter; a hut; to rejoice; to turn around.
考丨在陸 he is happy in his hut on the plateau.
托丨 a waiter to carry things.
丨停 to turn without going on.

鬆 ˓p'an Grisly hair, that which is turning gray.
丨頭髻 the hair curled roughly for sleeping.
髮未丨 his hair is still black.

磐 ˓p'an A large rock, a foundation stone; a conspicuous rock, like the Tarpeian; firm, stable, immovable.
丨石之安 peace like a great rock.
盜賊丨牙 the banditti are leagued together.
奠山河於丨石 his throne and dominion are firm as a rock.
丨礴 imposing, as a gateway.

鞶 ˓p'an A wide sash of leather made hollow to hold things; a purse.
絲丨 a lady's silken girdle.
丨鑑 a mirror appended to the girdle.
錫之丨帶 his majesty gave him a fine girdle.

胖 ˓p'an From *slice* and *half*.
A division, a half; to join.
夫婦丨 the husband and wife are now united in one grave.

㿻 ˓p'an In Canton, the placenta; also called 胎盤; in Peking, it means a falling womb.

媻 ˓p'an Extravagant; an old woman.
丨丨 going to and fro; back and forth.
丨藪天 a Budhist name for the Hindu Vishnu.
丨跚 to crawl towards, as when showing great reverence.

判 p'an˒ From *knife* and *half*.
To divide in twain; to halve; to decide, to judge; a decision, a verdict; to join two halves to see if they match; to marry.
丨斷 to give sentence.
批丨 an official decision, a verdict.
丨合 to join in wedlock.
丨官 the Decider of Life in hades; he has a book in which people's fates are written; the Chinese Atropos.
通丨 a syndic in an inferior department, under a sub-prefect.
丨書 a check or seal divided to serve for proof when compared.

拌 p'an˒ From *hand* and *half*; often used for ˓拚 to risk.
To separate; to mix; to divide; to throw away.
丨石 to throw a stone.
丨嘴 bickerings.
丨上草料 to mix the fodder.
丨財 to speculate rashly.
丨匀 to mix properly.

泮 p'an˒ Occurs used for 畔˒ and for the next three; it is sometimes written like the third.
The semicircular pool before the provincial colleges; to melt, to scatter; a shore; an affluent of the Grand Canal near T'aingan fu in Shantung; used for 判 to divide, to direct.
遊丨池 to pass [on the bridge] to the college-pool; — *i. e.* to become a *siuts'ai*.
丨宮 the college of a prefecture; in olden time the state college.
剖丨 to divide or spread abroad, as the heavens and earth.
入丨 to enter the public schools for becoming graduates.
濕則有丨 the marsh too has its shores.

冸 p'an˒ Used with the last.
To melt as ice.
冰丨 the ice has thawed.
迨冰未丨 before the ice melted.

頖 p'an˒ Used for 泮 a pool.
To manage.
丨宮 an old title for prince or an aulic councillor, those who shared in the administration of the empire.

沜 p'an˒ The banks of a stream; water flowing.

襻 p'an˒ A loop; a sash; a belt or band; a chin-strap; to loop.
鈕丨 a button-loop or tie.
丨帶 a girdle.
帽丨 a hat-band

盼 p'an˒ Not the same as hi˒ 盻 stern.
A clear, piercing eye; a beautiful, bright eye; languishing eye of a female; to glance at.
丨望 to hope for anxiously.
丨雨 looking for rain.
深蒙憐丨 I am deeply thankful for your kind regard.
顧丨 to look watchfully.
仰丨復音 I shall earnestly expect your reply.
巧笑倩兮美目丨兮 how artful her smiling dimples, how bright her beautiful eyes!

袢 p'an˒ Clothes suitable for summer wear.
紲丨 a long light gown worn in summer.
Read ˓fan. Plain, undyed cloth, suitable for under-clothes in summer, like coarse grasscloth.

PǍN.

Old sounds, pen *and* ben. *In Canton*, pǎn; — *in Swatow*, pún; — *in Amoy*, pún *and* p'ún; — *in Fuhchau*, pwǒng; — *in Shanghai*, pǎng; — *in Chifu*, pǎn.

奔 犇 ˏpǎn From *three oxen* in a fright, or from the same contracted under 天 an *apparition*.

Cattle scattering from fright; to flee, to run away; to hasten on, as a messenger; to run about in confusion; to be busy with, to fag at; to flee to and submit; hurry, bustle; urgent; to marry without observing the rites, to elope.

丨走 to scamper, to flee; to hurry about.

丨馳 to hasten, like a courier.

丨喪 to return home to bury a parent.

淫丨 a clandestine marriage.

丨天涯 to go over the world, — as a trader.

丨來丨去 running about, busy.

丨逐 to drive out.

丨波 disquieted, uneasy as the billows.

丨告 an urgent report or notice.

丨波勞苦 toiling and moiling in the anxieties of life.

駿丨走 to walk in a dignified way, as in performing rites.

鶉之丨丨 the hurry-scurry of a covey of quails.

驞 驛 ˏpǎn These are both regarded as synonyms of the preceding, applied chiefly to horses.

To run, to hurry off.

駟馬丨馳 the two spans galloped off rapidly.

錛 ˏpǎn An adze; the helve is in the middle like a pick.

捹 ˏpǎn To fumble things over, and throw them into confusion.

In *Cantonese*. To braid; to swing; to dangle; to sprinkle; to fling off.

丨辮 to plait the queue.

本 ˋpǎn From 木 a *tree* and a 一 *line* across the bottom to denote the *earth*.

The origin, the root; source, cause; the fundamental part of; radical, essential, what must be first attended to; rooted in; the beginning; and when used before a verb, sometimes merely strengthens it, as 丨期 we originally expected, *i. e.* we *did* hope; native; one's ancestors; the direct line in a family; capital, principal; proper, appropriate to; used by people, but more by officials before their titles, for I, me, mine, our; this; a classifier of books, documents, &c.

丨 and 末 are opposites, as 物有丨末 things must have a root and apex, an essence and qualities.

丨國 my native land.

丨錢 capital in trade.

折丨 or 侵丨 to incroach on one's capital.

上ˋ丨 to petition the Throne.

好丨事 able, clever, capable.

丨院 I, the governor.

丨身 I, myself.

忘丨 to forget one's parents.

一丨書 one volume.

丨來面目 the original expression, the natural form.

無丨 no capital.

丨應 what is proper, requisite.

丨地人 natives of a place; the aborigines, those who live in it.

丨息對淸 to square all accounts, as at a banker's.

虧丨 or 賠丨 to sell under cost, to lose in trade.

手丨 a visiting-card of an official sent to his superior.

抄丨子 a plagiarist.

木丨水源 my root and fountain, — *i. e.* those who brought me up or patronized me.

丨屬可惡ˋ it is truly worthy of detestation.

守丨分 I'll attend to my own duty.

丨心 my first intention.

歌丨 a book of songs.

丨屬 really is or belongs to.

君子務丨丨立而道生 the princely man attends to what is radical; and when that is established, practice comes natural.

人生丨 Brahma as the creator. (*narayana.*)

畚 ˋpǎn From 甾 *waste* land and 弁 an *officer*, contracted in their combination.

A basket or hod for containing earth, manure, or grass, used by bricklayers and farmers.

荷丨 a dirt hod.

丨臿之勞 the toil of a farmer.

笨 体 pǎnˋ From *bamboo* or *heart* and *root* as the phonetic; the first is most used, and also means a ship's deck.

Stupid, doltish, dull of apprehension, slow but honest; sluggish, as a ship; dull, not sharp; the inner scurf of the bamboo.

愚丨 thickheaded.

大丨象 a dunderhead.

刀丨 a dull or useless knife.

粗丨 rude and untaught.

丨工 an unskilled workman.

丨上 on deck.

逩 pǎnˋ To walk or run quick.

丨命似的 running as if for dear life.

投丨 to go to meet or seek one, in order to get aid.

P'ĂN.

Old sounds, ben *and* p'en. *In Canton,* p'ăn ; — *in Swatow,* p'ún ; — *in Amoy,* p'ún ; — *in Fuhchau,* pwòng *and* p'òng ; — *in Shanghai,* p'ăng *and* păng ; — *in Chifu,* p'ăn.

盆 ꜀p'ăn From *dish* and to *divide ;* it is interchanged with ꜀p'an 盤 dish.

A bowl; a tub; a basin, a cup; an ancient measure for grain; a jar on which persons beat time.

面丨 or 洗臉丨 a wash-basin.

浴丨 or 洗澡丨 a bathing-tub.

臨丨 parturition; it is done near a vessel of warm water.

鼓丨而歌 he drummed on the jar and hummed a tune.

缺丨 the collar-bone.

骰子丨 a chinaware dice-bowl.

一丨花 a pot of flowers.

葐 ꜀p'ăn Used with the last in 覆丨子 a species of wild raspberry (*Rubus idæus*), growing in Hupeh.

Read ꜀făn, and used for 䩭. Fragrant, as flowers.

湓 ꜀p'ăn A stream flowing into the Yangtsz' River west of Kiukiang; water bubbling and roaring, as in a swift current; to soak.

丨湓 overflowing.

丨城 an old name for Kiukiang.

噴 歕 呠 p'ăn꜄ Also read ꜀făn ; the first form is mostly used.

To spurt, to expel the breath forcibly; to snort, to hoot; struck, as by an effluvia; a puff, as of steam.

打丨嚏 to sneeze.

丨壺 a watering-pot.

丨氣 to snort violently; an aspirate or strong breathing.

花叢丨鼻香 this parterre of flowers greets one with its sweetness.

丨花筒 to let off a rocket.

丨布 to spurt water over clothes, as a tailor or washerman.

令人丨飯 it will make him spurt out his food, — as by laughing; it is also used as intimating that the person will despise the gift.

信口丨 he blurts anything he lists.

丨水 to spurt water, as over clothes.

丨符水 to spurt holy water, as Rationalists do in exorcising.

含血丨人先污其口 he first dirties his own mouth who spits blood on his neighbor.

疾言丨丨 to talk fast and thick.

体 p'ăn꜄ From *man* and *root;* it is chiefly now used as a contraction for ꜂t'i 體 body and is used with 笨 stupid.

Rude, coarse, rustic, like a carter or grave-digger.

PANG.

Old sounds, pong *and* bong. *In Canton,* pong ; — *in Swatow,* pang *and* pong ; — *in Amoy,* pang *and* pong ; — *in Fuhchau,* pang, pòng, paung, *and* p'aung ; — *in Shanghai,* hong *and* bong ; — *in Chifu,* pang.

邦 ꜀pang From *city* and *flourishing ;* this character formed part of the name of Liu Pang 劉邦 the founder of the Han dynasty, and respect for him led to its disuse, and the prevalent adoption of 國 as a synonym, and this has gradually led to a modification of its use in modern books.

A region contiguous to the emperor's territory; one which has been conferred on a person by patent for his merits, and still forming part of the 朝 or demesne; a fief, a region, a country; a region beyond the frontier; to confer the rule of a region.

丨家之光 the glory of our empire; the nation's fame.

丨國 states and kingdoms; nations generally.

修好鄰丨 reëstablish amity with the contiguous states.

丨有道則見 a state prospers by observing righteousness.

友丨 nations in amity with one.

丨畿 the imperial domain.

有丨 a subordinate state.

保其家丨 to protect his clans and states.

鉫 ꜀pang An unauthorized character.

In *Cantonese.* A broad hoe or mattock.

丨田 to hoe the fields.

一張丨 a hoe.

梆 ꜀pang Name of a tree; a wooden cylinder used in a yamun or temples to attract notice, or by watchmen to strike the watch.

丨鼓 a kettle-drum.

更丨 a watchman.

丨子二簧調 denote a staccato and a slow movement.

傳丨鳴鑼 strike the rattle and sound the gong; give the signal of alarm.

挷 ꜀pang A thing like a child's palm, that came out of the ground in Nganhwui; it had no fingers, and gave great strength when eaten.

鞤 *ˏpang* The lining of a shoe; the vamp or upper part of a shoe or boot; like the next.

韸 *ˏpang* The leather heel-band of a shoe sewed in to strengthen the back when putting it on.

帮 幫 幇 *ˏpang* From *napkin* and *to confer* or *country*; the third and most common form is unauthorized.

To bind the edge of a shoe; a binder, a support; to shore up a thing; to help, to succor, to defend; to replace, as a new strip for the old; a classifier of fleets, of pickings of tea, or lots of goods; and in some places, of guilds or classes of people.

生意丨 the mercantile class.

丨助 to assist.

丨丨忙 help him in his great hurry.

丨滯官 a lieutenant-colonel.

丨補 to try to eke out a deficiency, as in one's expenses.

丨差 a substituted policeman.

丨口 one who speaks for another.

丨皷 a subsidiary drum.

丨襯 or 丨顧 to patronize, to give custom to, to employ.

一丨船 a fleet, a squadron.

頭丨茶 the first gathering of tea.

押丨 to guard a lot of goods; the agent who goes with them.

In *Cantonese*. A huge haul, a vast lot.

發大丨財 made a grand speculation.

大丨銀 a heap of money.

㨍 *ˏpang* Like the preceding.

To oppose, to withstand; to protect by surrounding.

搒 挷 *ˏpang* To screen, to hide; to propel a boat; to wrest from; to beat.

丨人 a boatman.

丨笞數千 to beat a man thousands of strokes.

棍丨 a club, a shillelah.

榜 *ˋpang* From *wood* and *side*; occurs used for the last.

A support put on a bow; to propel a boat; to beat; a splinter or slip; to bamboo; the rule for choosing graduates; a list of successful candidates; to praise.

黎明放丨 (or 開丨) to placard the names of the *tsinsz'* or *küjin* graduates at the break of day.

金丨 the official list of these men.

同丨中 fellow-graduates.

丨上無名 his name is not in the list.

丨眼 the "eye of the list," a term for the second scholar in the land; the idea is that he is second in order, as the eye is under the forehead.

丨掠 to rob with violence.

兩丨出身 a *tsinsz'* entering office.

明心丨 a list of subscribers, as for repairing a temple.

標丨 to praise, to countenance; to commend for one's own ends, to celebrate.

好丨頭 a firm standing when drawing the bow.

作個丨樣 make a model or drawing of that.

丨名 what is your name? — said to a literary man, whose name is supposed to have been once published.

丨女 a boatwoman.

牓 *ˋpang* Similar to the last.

Tablets or books on which registers are inscribed to be kept, as archives or records; a model for a shoe sole.

粉丨 a board to inscribe the debts at an eating-shop.

髈 *ˋpang* From *bone* and *side*; this and ˏ膀 are often interchanged, and this is also read ˋp'ang.

Anciently the pelvis, the hip-bone; now used for the arm bone, the humerus.

肩丨 the shoulder bone.

胈丨肘兒 the elbow.

縍 *ˋpang* To bind the edge of a shoe.

丨履 to hem and bind shoes.

綁 *ˋpang* From *silk* and *country*.

To tie, to bind, to bandage; a bandage.

鬆丨 loosed the thongs.

丨緊 tie it tight.

丨腿 leggings or gaiters.

背身丨住 his hands are tied behind.

丨赴市曹 bind and take [the criminal] to the market-place, — and execute him.

謗 *pangˀ* From *word* and *side*.

To vilify, to injure another's good name; to detract.

誹丨 to slander.

丨是非 to talk of other's faults, to defame.

丨書 a scurrilous book.

侮丨 to vilify, to defame.

訕丨正事 to reproach that which is good.

艕 *pangˀ* A double boat made by laying two alongside and fastening them together; this is done when drifting with the current; to swim or float.

丨人 a boatman, a waterman.

蚌 *pangˀ* Thin nacreous, fresh water mussels (*Unionidæ*), long and thin shelled; large and thick marine mollusks, as the *Mya* and *Ostrea*.

丨蛤 a clam or mussel.

丨精 the naiad in the oyster.

老丨生珠 the old clam has a pearl; — an old man has a child.

鷸丨相持漁人得利 when the snipe and oyster nip each other, the fisherman is the gainer; — said of going to law.

棒 *pangˀ* A club, staff, cudgel; a stick to beat with, as a drum-stick; to strike, to cudgel; used to imitate the report of a gun; — bang!

熱火丨 a hot poker — cannot be grasped at both ends; *met.* an unmanageable affair.

教習拳丨 to teach boxing and fencing.

當頭一丨 got a rap on the noddle; — taken by surprise.

丨他出 drive him out, take a stick to him.

幾丨弓 several shots of a bow.

水上一丨 [useless] as slapping the water.

丨子 indian corn or maize in the ear, from its resemblance to a drumstick. (*Pekingese.*)

丨子麵 indian meal.

In *Pekingese.* A wing.

雞膀子 a fowl's wing.

一對翅丨 a pair of wings.

胖 ˎp'ang From *flesh* and *flourishing.*

Fat, obese; large limbed; slices of meat.

肥丨 corpulent.

丨肛 swelled up, as a boil.

丨脹 puffed, swollen, dropsical.

怦 ˏpang Harsh, unable to please.

丨慃 perverse, cross; bad tempered and morose.

P'ANG.

Old sounds, p'ong, bong, *and* p'an. *In Canton,* p'ong; — *in Swatow,* p'ang; — *in Amoy,* pong, pang, *and* pw'an; — *in Fuhchau,* p'aung, pòng, p'òng, *and* pwang; — *in Shanghai,* p'ong; — *in Chifu,* p'ang.

滂 ˏp'ang Great rain; the noise of a heavy rain, roar of running waters; soaked with the rain.

丨沱大雨 a heavy shower.

丨洋 extensive, ocean like.

丨沛 copious rains.

霶 雱 ˏp'ang Like the last.

An abundant fall of snow or sleet; the noise of a driving storm.

雨雪其丨 thick falls the driving snow.

飄忽淜丨 the blast then drove furiously on.

Read ˏ*fang.* Sleet.

雱丨雪亂飄 the whirling snow drives by in gusts.

磅 ˏp'ang The noise of stones crashing down.

丨唐 to occupy great space.

In *Cantonese.* A pound avoirdupois, or a pound sterling, in imitation of the word; to weigh in pounds.

十二兩爲一丨 twelve taels make one pound.

丨茶 to weigh tea.

砧丨 large weighing scales.

鎊 ˏp'ang To scrape off, to level; one says a water-level.

傍 ˏp'ang, p'ang˞ From *man* and *side;* occurs interchanged with its primitive.

Near; the side; to depend on, to lean.

丨晚 dusk, early candlelight.

依丨 to lean against; a rest, a support, one to lean on.

丨人門戶 to depend on others for living.

近丨 approximating in quality.

王事丨丨 the king's business is urgent.

左右兩丨 both the right and left sides.

耳丨風 a mere ear rumor.

道丨立 stood waiting, as for the procession to pass.

旁 㫄 ˏp'ang Composed of 二 *two* referring to doors, and 方 *square* underneath; the second antique form shows something of the original.

Great, extensive; the side; everywhere; lateral, sideways; by the side of, near; following.

丨邊 the side.

丨人 a by-stander.

根蕵丨出 sprouts or suckers springing up near the root.

丨門 a side-door.

莫信丨言 don't heed people's talk.

丨觀者淸 the looker-on sees clearly, as in a game.

海丨 the seaside.

丨若無人 as if nobody was near by him; — proud.

丨招俊乂 everywhere to seek able men — to put in office.

觸類丨通 pursuing one subject, you will be able to appreciate another.

袖手丨觀 to sleeve the hands and look idly on.

駟馬丨丨 the four horses went on without resting.

丨午 in confusion, from a variety of affairs; crosswise; transverse.

丨近 adjoining; approaching.

徬 ˏp'ang To walk by the side of a cart, as the driver does; used like the next in 丨徨 timid, fearful, in a fright.

㥬 ˏp'ang Fearing; eariness.

丨惶 scared, intimidated.

蒡 ˏp'ang A medicine, called 牛丨子 whose seeds resemble sunflower seeds in shape.

膀 ˏp'ang From *flesh* and *side;* it is interchanged with ˊ髈 the shoulder.

The region of the groin and false ribs.

丨脇 the lower ribs.

丨胱熱 inflammation of the bladder.

丨子 the arm or shoulder.

艂 ꜀p'ang — A kind of scow used in the central provinces, called 丨舡 and 丨艭 two of which could be lashed together stern to stern, and sailed very slowly; it differs from 艕' or boats lashed alongside; — hence applied to dull, stupid things.

胮 ꜀p'ang — To swell, as with the dropsy or a tumor.

丨肛 swelling; to tumefy.

水泡丨了 [the body] has swollen in the water.

In *Fuhchau*. Dull, stupid; fatty; to cover close; to line, as the bowels with fat.

螃 ꜀p'ang — A crab, a sea-crab; *met.* a harpy.

丨蟹 the swimming crab. (*Portunus.*)

蹗 ꜀p'ang — To go on hastily and wildly.

踉丨 rushing on; urgent to get forward.

龐 ꜀p'ang — From *dragon* and a *shelter*.

A high palatial house; filled, crammed; confused.

蒙丨洪之恩 I am greatly obliged for your kindness.

丨丨 fat, lusty, said of oxen.

風俗敦丨 the customs there are orderly and moral.

胖 p'ang' — Also read *p'an'*.

Fat, hearty; jolly, as if one had nothing to disturb him; the half of a carcase; a slice, collops on the ribs.

心廣體丨 his mind is enlarged and his body at ease.

一身的丨肉 he is all fat.

丨子 a fat fellow.

PĂNG.

Old sounds, păng, peng, beng, *and* bang. *In Canton,* păng *and* pung; — *in Swatow,* peng; — *in Amoy,* peng, p'eng, *and* hong; — *in Fuhchau,* péng, p'éng, pung, p'ung, *and* ping; — *in Shanghai,* păng, ping, *and* fung; — *in Chifu,* păng.

崩 ꜀păng — From *hill* 山 and a *friend* 朋 as the phonetic; occurs used for the next.

The fall of a mountain; to fall from a high position into disgrace; to fall in ruins; to let fall or loosen; an emperor's death; infected, as sheep.

山丨 the mountain rushes to its fall; the state is ruined.

驚丨聖駕 I fear that the emperor is dead.

血丨 or 血山丨 flooding at childbirth or from disease.

大丨敗 a great ruin; what a fall!

丨墜 to fall in ruins.

爾羊來思不騫不丨 your flocks come, none injured, none diseased.

被砲丨着 knocked down by the cannon.

丨角 to knock horns; a euphuism for the *kotow*.

若丨厥角 as if their horns were falling off.

In *Cantonese*. A fracture, a flaw, a breach; to nip out,

豇丨吹笛 if a harelip plays a fife, — he only loses his breath.

丨口 a harelip.

丨基圍 it breached the embankment; the rush made a crevasse.

漰 ꜀păng — An issue of blood, dysmenorrhœa.

產血丨 a miscarriage.

Read ꜀p'ang. A puffy or dropsical swelling of the flesh.

堋 ꜀păng — To inter, to cover a thing with earth; the crashing noise of a falling wall; to lead water on the fields; an archer's target.

丨土埋葬 to fill up the grave with earth.

弸 ꜀păng — A stiff bow; full, complete, furnished.

丨中彪外 a man of real talent and fine person.

丨弓 a strong bow; *met.* stout archers.

丨彊 the recoil sound of a bow.

祊 ꜀păng — From *worship* and *square*; it is often read ꜀fang.

The space within at the side of the ancestral temple gate, where in early days the gods or lares were worshiped; a sacrifice to the manes in this spot; old name of a town near T'ai-shan in Shantung.

繃 **綳** ꜀păng — A cloth to carry an infant on the back; to bind, to tie; to strap up.

小兒丨 a child strapped pickapack.

In *Cantonese*, sometimes used for 㧜 or 掹 to stretch or pull, from the confusion of the initial consonants.

In *Shanghai* read *mang*, and used as a synonym of 密. Close, crowded, jammed.

伻 ꜀păng — From *man* and *equal*.

To send, as a messenger; to make to do; a convoy, a messenger; to conduce, to cause; following, according to, quick.

相丨爲伴 they accordingly became comrades.

丨來 to send a messenger.

丨嚮卽有僚 make them work with their associates.

抨 Used with the last.
ˎpăng To cause; to grasp with power; to follow after.

In *Cantonese*. To set things to rights; to arrange; to compare.

丨皮草 to sew a fur in style.

丨埋鴨蛋 to hatch ducks' eggs artificially.

丨好 to put in order.

不怕折丨骨 don't fear breaking your ribs.

丨砝子 to guage weights.

丨論人品 to weigh people's merits or qualifications.

浜 From *water* and *soldier*.
ˎpăng *ˎping* A wet dock for calking; a side-creek or canal where boats can go; a wide creek in which boats can find shelter.

洋涇丨 a creek at Shanghai.

跳丨 to leap a ditch, as in racing.

骿 To pull a crossbow to its full stretch.
ˎpăng

丨斷了 pulled it till the string snapped.

絣 Plain, cheap fabric like sarcenet or cotton; to unite, to join, to follow after; to snap a marking-line; to pull the bow-string.
ˎpăng

將丨萬嗣 may a numerous progeny succeed you.

丨衣服 to baste clothes together previous to sewing them (*Pekingese*.)

帲 A screen or awning; a shelter.
ˎpăng

丨幪之下無限瞻依 under your protection I shall be perfectly satisfied.

袢 Urgent, impetuous; the noise of striking boards.
ˊpăng

急丨丨的 very hasty; to urge too much; vehement, in a good sense.

琫 Ornaments of gold or gems on the hilt or scabbard of a sword; an emperor had gems, a prince had gold.
ˊpăng

鞞丨有珌 his scabbard ornaments gleam brightly.

菶 Luxuriant, full of leaves or fruit.
ˊpăng

梧桐丨丨草卉萋萋 the thrifty oil-trees and the flourishing plants.

唪 A loud laugh; boisterous merriment; a big mouth.
ˊpăng

迸 To be scattered; to expel, to drive off; to idle, to wander about; to open, to crack; to issue.
păngˋ

丨散 to dissipate.

丨逐 to drive away.

四民逃丨 the people all run.

丨諸四夷 send him off to the four wild tribes.

石榴丨開 the pomegranate has split open.

綠楊市岸蒲芽丨 when the willows along the bank have green sprays, the sprouts of the cat-tail show themselves.

丨水 to spatter.

蠯 **鲂** A kind of bivalve, which furnishes a long narrow shell, used in Kiangsu as a ladle or scoop in shops; it was apparently used in ancient worship, and is probably a species of *Unionidæ*.
păngˋ

丨蛙 a long freshwater clam.

蹦 An unauthorized character.
păngˋ

In *Pekingese*. To jump, said of an animal; to rebound, as a ball; to fly back.

丨起過頭 bounded up over his head.

丨跳 to jump, as a frog.

P'ĂNG.

Some of these characters are also read P'UNG. *Old sounds*, p'eng, p'ăng, băng, *and* băm. *In Canton*, p'ăng, p'ung *and* p'ang; — *in Swatow*, p'eng; — *in Amoy*, p'eng, peng, hong, *and* ping; — *in Fuhchau*, p'éng, péng, păng, p'ang, pang, *and* p'ung; — *in Shanghai*, p'ăng, păng, pung, *and* bong; — *in Chifu*, p'ăng.

亯 From *fire* and *odor* of *sacrifice*; the upper part alone was the ancient form.
ˎp'ăng

To boil; to decoct for food; it once meant to eat, as beasts eat their prey.

丨茶 to make tea.

丨調 to mix ingredients, as when boiling medicine.

自丨其身 he burnt his own fingers.

丨煉 to seethe, as glue; to decoct, as medicines.

大丨 a feast.

治國若丨小鮮 to rule the country is as easy as to boil a little fish.

澎 Like the next.
ˎp'ăng

The noise of billows is 丨渤

丨口 ancient name of a place in the south of Shensi.

澎 From *water* and a *drumming* sound.
ˎp'ăng

The noise of dashing waters.

丨湖廳 the Pescadore Islands off Formosa.

砰 The crashing roar of a falling rock is 丨磅, probably in imitation of the sound.
ˎp'ăng

丨然如雷 a sudden thundering noise.

丨隱 abundant, numerous.

怦 p'ăng Hasty; warmhearted, earnest and impulsive; ardent for the right.

忠 〡 faithful.

忿 〡 〡 而欲動 I am so indignant that I want to do something — to remedy it.

急 〡 vehement, as for reform.

淜 p'ăng The noise of water.

〡 滂 the banging of anything by the wind or waves.

硼 p'ăng A mineral.

〡 砂 the sub-borate of soda or natural borax, brought from Tibet.

搬 p'ăng The noise of striking boards together.

姘 p'ăng Illicit intercourse with maidservants; a fine of four taels was anciently imposed for this offense during a fast.

莽 p'ăng A coarse plant of which brooms can be made, the 蓍 〡, probably like a coarse kind of yarrow or *Achillea*; to cause, to make; to have oversight.

民有肅心 〡 云不逮 some of the people desire to advance, but they are led to say it is of no use.

莫予 〡 蜂 I will not meddle with a wasp.

蓬 p'ăng From *plant* and *to meet*.

A species of *Rubus* or raspberry growing sporadically among hemp; others describe it as a weed that the wind roots up and drives across the wastes; overgrown, tangled, as jungle; waving as grass; disheveled, as hair.

〡 萊仙境 fairy land, an elysium far from man's abode, whence 〡 萊縣 a district in Tăng-cheu fu in Shantung derives its name; some regard it as denoting Kiusiu in Japan.

〡 〡 luxuriant foliage, as of oaks.

〡 星 a baleful star.

〡 累 to wander at will.

鬔 p'ăng Disheveled, uncombed hair is 〡 鬆; it is also applied to the unbound hair of girls.

〡 頭垢面 unkempt hair and a dirty face.

篷 艂 p'ăng The first is constantly interchanged with 棚, and the second is used only for mat-sails.

Mats made at the South by interlacing bamboo leaves within splints to serve as a roof or covering for boats, stagings, &c.; attap; at the North, rushes and millet stalks are used; the sail of a vessel; an awning; a ceiling.

〡 寮 mat huts or shanties.

搭 〡 to put up an awning.

蓮 〡 the torus of the lotus.

半 〡 月色 to enjoy the moonlight under easy sail.

轉 〡 to go on the other tack.

駛勾 〡 to beat in sailing.

〡 褲 the housing of a sail.

〡 過腳 to gibe the sail.

車 〡 子 matting or awning on a cart.

〡 腳索 ropes to pull an awning.

糊 〡 to paper the ceiling.

扛 〡 an arched ceiling or covering; a domed roofing.

帳 〡 huts for soldiers.

一 〡 傘 one state umbrella.

飄 〡 unfixed, no settled abode.

韸 p'ăng The noise of drums.

芃 p'ăng From *plants* and *all*; it resembles *hwan* 芄 an orchid.

Grassy, luxuriant; bushy, like a fox's tail; name of a plant.

〡 尾 a long bushy tail.

我行其野 〡 〡 其麥 I am going through the country, through this wheat so flourishing.

埄 塳 p'ăng Dust raised by the wind; to whirl the dust about.

〡 起塵土 it carries about the dust in clouds.

In *Cantonese*. To fill the eyes with dust or smoke; a classifier of walls.

一 〡 煙隨 an offensive smoke, like burning hair.

一 〡 牆 one stretch of wall.

烟 〡 〡 the smoke is very smarting to the eyes; a smudge.

朋 p'ăng Now composed of two 月 *moons*, but at first it was two 鳳 *phœnixes*, a bird said to draw all others after it.

A friend, a companion, a peer, an equal; one of the same views or school; a couple or a set; to consort with; to join in; to form selfish associations; a pair of two; a set of fine cowries of different sizes.

〡 友 an associate.

彼其之子碩大無 〡 that hero is large and peerless.

〡 黨 to form a junto or cabal, a clique.

〡 比爲奸 to club together to plot treason.

良 〡 a good friend.

賓 〡 滿座 his guests fill the house.

好 〡 情 very friendly or polite to.

〡 酒斯饗 entertained them with two kinds of wine.

群居而 〡 飛 they fly in flocks, and crowds of them live together.

鵬 p'ăng A monstrous bird, like the *rukh* or roc of Arabian story, and the *simurg* of the Persians; the Chinese fable that it was transformed from the leviathan, and some think the extinct *Æpyornis* of Madagascar may have been heard of and exaggerated.

大丨展翅 the roc has flapped his wings; — said of a smart man.

丨程萬里 the roc has got a myriad miles at one jump; — said of those who early attain office.

棚 ₍p'ăng A scaffold or staging for weddings, plays, &c.; a framework; a shed or banksal of attap, for which it is interchanged with 篷 a sail; a booth; a mess of ten men among soldiers.

涼丨 an awning.

捲丨 roll up the awning.

戲丨 a temporary theater.

曬丨 a drying shed.

拆丨做過 take it down and do it over again.

頭丨丨頭 the corporal of the head mess.

丨民 people who live under booths, like woodcutters and lumbermen.

天丨 an open staging.

丨匠 an awning-maker.

更丨 a watchman's lodge.

捨茶丨 to open a free tea-booth it is done when a new shop is opened, as a means of attractin custom, and by devout people near noted shrines for the refreshment of worshipers.

捲丨一座 arch the awning.

丨廠 a shed for storing things.

過街丨 a shop awning, a street screen.

倗 ₍p'ăng To associate with; to assist, to help; to recommend or bespeak.

彭 ₍p'ăng Formed of 鼓 a *drum* and 形 *form* contracted in combination.

To go, to travel; a way; abundant; near, on one side; powerful; to fix the spears in a war-chariot; name of a stream in Sin-ch'ang hien 新昌縣 in Kiangsi; an ancient city in P'ing-liang fu in the east of Kansuh.

丨亨 full of one's self.

匪其丨 do not stay by his side.

竊比於我老丨 [Confucius said,] I venture to compare myself with our old Păng; — supposed to have been a worthy officer of the Shang dynasty; he is now called 丨祖 and 丨公, and the Cantonese say that his wife weeps whenever a sudden shower comes up.

丨縣 a district near the capital of Sz'ch'uen, named after an ancient tribe.

丨丨 the exciting beating of drums; numerous; a crashing noise; handsome, strong; grand, as an array.

丨城 an old name for the city of Sü-cheu 徐州府 in Kiangsu.

以車丨丨 [the horses] pranced grandly in their cars.

膨 ₍p'ăng Very fat; bloated, like a sow.

丨脝 obese; puffed out, swollen.

肚丨脹 flatulent; the belly distended, as from overeating.

蟛 ₍p'ăng A land crab, common in the rice-fields, or on seaside beaches.

丨蜞子 crab's eggs.

無爪丨蜞 a clawless crab; — an inefficient, lazy lout.

髶 ₍p'ăng Loose hair is 丨髻 when it hangs down the back.

丨鬢 the hair dressed in puffs on the temples, and worn over the ear; a style common in Canton.

抨 'p'ăng Same as 捧 which has now superseded it.

To receive in both hands; to beat; to scoop up in both hands; an open handful; to hold a dish by the rim.

丨水飲 to drink out of the hands.

丨了一丨 took up a handful.

唪 'p'ăng Fragrant.

香丨丨 a sweet smell.

搒 **碰** **磞** p'ăng' From *hand* or *stone* and *together*; the second form is most common.

To run upon or against; to bump; to try, to see how a thing is; to meet unexpectedly; a thump; experimentally, on trial.

丨着 hit against him.

丨見 to meet, as in the streets.

丨機會 to make a trial.

丨撞 to thump against.

丨運氣 it depends on my luck.

丨鼻轉灣 when you get to the cross street, then turn.

丨釘子 to meet disappointment; a vexatious nonplus; got into trouble.

丨頭聚飲 to divide the cost of a meal equally among the eaters.

兩家相丨 they ran against each other.

丨壺 to play cards.

船丨船 the vessels have collided.

丨不着 I have not come across one, — as a book.

甏 p'ang' A large bellied jar or amphora, containing a barrel or more, used to hold spirits; or it is sometimes sunk in the earth, and fruit sealed up inside till winter; a pitcher; a small jar.

PAO.

Old sounds, po, p'o, pok, bo, bok, *and* p'ot. *In Canton*, pò *and* pao; — *in Swatow*, pau, p'au, p'ak, po, *and* p'o; — *in Amoy*, pau, p'au, pò, pa, *and* p'ok; — *in Fuhchau*, pau, po, *and* pàk; — *in Shanghai*, po *and* bo; — *in Chifu*, pao.

包 勹 pao — From 勹 to *infold* and 己 *self*, representing the fœtus inwrapped in the womb; the second and original form is now used as the 20th radical of a few incongruous characters, mostly relating to wrapping and inclosing.

To wrap up, to envelop; to contain, to hold, to be included in; to be patient; to undertake, to manage an affair; to assume; to engage, to warrant; to insure; a bundle, a bale; a wrapper; plated, as with gold; occurs used for the next, and in musical books for *keu* 勾 to hook the string of the lute.

丨工料 to take a job and find the materials.

丨辦館 a shop that provides entertainments.

丨換 I will change it if it is not good.

丨支丨結 I am sure that it will be accurate.

打丨 to wrap in a mat, as a box; to mat.

能丨容 patient, forbearing.

沒丨含 he has no self-restraint; impatient.

丨頭 a fillet, a headband.

丨在裏面 it is included or reckoned in.

丨庇 to screen, to countenance; to harbor, as a criminal.

管丨你無事 I assure you there's nothing to fear.

丨攬訟詞 to conduct a lawsuit.

丨袱皮 a wrapper, such as is wound around bedding.

丨裹 a bundle; to wrap up.

丨起來 bundle it up.

銅丨口 to strengthen a joint with copper.

開丨 open the bundle; to take a contract.

所丨甚廣 what it includes is very wide, as a proposition.

丨涵 to comprehend, to involve.

三丨 three bales, as cotton.

丨完錢粮 to farm or contract for paying the taxes.

腰丨 a double purse or fob.

丨種茶 powchong tea.

丨子 a meat patty or steamed dumpling.

苞 pao — The husk of grain; a sort of rush fit for making sandals or mats; rank, luxuriant; food wrapped in mulberry leaves for presents.

丨桑永固 enduring for ever.

竹丨松茂 luxuriant bamboos and thrifty firs.

爾貢丨茅不入 you have not brought your tribute of fine mats.

開丨 to blossom.

丨苴 presents of food, which used to be wrapped in mats.

胞 pao — From *flesh* and *to wrap* as the phonetic.

The placenta; brotherly; uterine; a fish's bladder; the crop of birds; a vesicle, a blister; to swell up.

丨衣 the after-birth.

同丨兄弟 uterine brothers.

尿丨 the bladder.

丨姪 own brother's sons.

民若同丨 [Confucius] regarded the people as brothers.

善藏我兒丨 it will be well to keep my child's secundines.

炰 pao — From *fire* and *protection*; an unauthorized character.

To heat, to boil; to cook with water; an earthen-pot; a saucepan; a grenade.

丨水 to heat water.

砂丨 or 瓦丨 a coarse earthenware pot; a kedgeree pot.

丟火藥丨 to throw stink-pots.

一丨水 a kettle of water.

穿丨 to let the secret out. (*Cantonese.*)

盡呢丨 try your last chance; one more throw.

銅丨 a copper skillet.

鼠摩試砂丨 try a pot through the rat-hole first; — a thief's phrase for using a decoy.

襃 褒 pao — Long robes, such as the sovereign gives; to set off the beauties of, to admire; to laud, to praise; in titles, commendable, illustrious, serene.

丨貶 praise and blame.

丨獎 or 丨美 to extol, to magnify.

丨拜 to salute again, in order to show double respect.

一字之丨榮於華袞 one word of [Confucius'] commendation was more honorable than an embroidered robe.

寶 宝 寚 pao — From *shelter* with a *gem*, *pearl*, *and vase* underneath; the second contracted form is common.

Precious, valuable, as a jewel; a gem; a coin; value, worth; a term of compliment, as honorable, noble, respected; your; to regard as fine, happy, precious, or good; an imperial seal; to esteem, to value; a symbol of rank; biliary calculi.

狗丨 the dog's bezoar, a medicine.

你丨號 what is your shop name?

丨貝 or 奇丨 costly, rare, precious; my jewel, my delight; a pet, the baby; to esteem.

爲善爲丨 goodness makes a thing precious.

丨貝來死 my little pet, my darling, my jewel.

三丨 or 三丨佛 Budha, law, and priesthood (*tri-ratna*); these theological abstractions personified are worshiped as three gods.

珍 丨 jewels; valuables.
無價 丨 priceless, invaluable.
賣通 丨 to guess the reign on cash; a mode of gambling.
開 丨 to gamble by guessing the number. (*Shanghai.*)
文房四 丨 writing materials.
丨 善 to esteem the good, to appreciate goodness.
你識 丨 you are a judge of the value — of these articles.
國 丨 worthy men of a country; the precious metals; specie
紅 丨 石 a ruby.
丨 砂 emery.
藍 丨 石 a sapphire.
丨 藏興焉 the treasury is filling up.
登大 丨 to mount the throne.
丨 座 the throne; any seat which is specially set apart for the Emperor.
丨 相花 a stock rose, red and white; the bush is about four feet high.
丨 光 an unusual brightness.
錫爾介圭以作爾 丨 I confer a great baton on you as a symbol of your rank.
別 丨 to distinguish or detect gems, as when in the rough.
丨 瓶 the Budhist name for the *amalaka*, or fruit of the *Myrobalanus emblica.*

ᶜ鴇 ᶜ*pao* From *bird* and *tithing-man*, because this bird flies in files.

A bird allied by the Chinese to the goose, but probably a bustard with spotted plumage; it has no hallux, and is said to fly in crowds against its enemies; a bird that has no mate; a white spotted horse; a cuckold.
肅肅 丨 羽 the bustards fly slowly aloft.
老 丨 子 a procuress, from the promiscuous habits of the bustard, whose hens are said in the Păn Ts'ao to breed with all other birds.

ᶜ𠂤 ᶜ*pao* From 比 to *compare* contracted to 匕 a *spoon* and 十 *ten*, because ten tithing men go in succession.

Ten families made a *pao* or tithing in the Cheu dynasty; the next character is now used instead.

ᶜ保 ᶜ*pao* From *man* and *stupid*, but some say that the primitive is altered from 孚 to *trust* to; occurs used for the next.

To protect, to defend, to guard; to feed, to nourish; to be surety for, to warrant; to secure, to keep safe; a protector, a guardian; bail; an advocate; happily, tranquilly.
丨 祐 to bless as God does.
丨 養 to nurse tenderly.
更 丨 a watchman.
丨 重身體 to take care of one's health.
明哲 丨 身 to regard one's own safety.
中 丨 人 a middleman.
神 丨 是饗 their spirits tranquilly enjoy their offerings.
甲 丨 a village elder or constable.
丨 ᶜ長 a constable, a headman.
永 丨 無虞 to preserve it from future injury.
聯 丨 to get a neighborhood to be bail for one.
丨 全 to preserve entire, to place in easy circumstances.
丨 舉 to promote, to electioneer for.
丨 領 an endorser.
丨 險 to insure against, as fire.
丨 船 to secure ships, as the 丨 商 or hong-merchants formerly did.
丨 家 a surety.
丨 不住 it is left unsettled or insecure.
太子太 丨 chief guardian of the heir-apparent.
具 丨 狀 to give written bail for.
若 丨 赤子 as one protects her infant.
酒 丨 a vintner.
師 丨 a family tutor.

ᶜ堡 ᶜ*pao* ᶜ*p'u* From *earth* and to *protect* as the phonetic.

A low wall for defense; a small earthwork or fortified town; a citadel or refuge against robbers; a post-house or guard-station along the banks of a river where dikes are to be kept in order; a hamlet that has grown up near a citadel; a division of a *sz'* 司 or township, larger than a *kiah*, 甲 or tithing, ruled by elected headmen; a ward or parish in some cities, derived probably from citadels formerly erected in them.
丨 障 a defense, a wall.
丨 內升平 peace be within thy walls.

ᶜ褓 ᶜ緥 ᶜ*pao* A swaddling-cloth, a froth; it is made so as to strap the child on the back, and is chiefly used in the southern provinces.
襁 丨 嬰孩 swathe the child in its bands.
始免襁 丨 he has just thrown off his swaddling-clothes.

ᶜ葆 ᶜ*pao* From *plants* and to *protect*; it is used with the four last.

Luxuriant; thick herbage that makes a cover; sprouts of a pollarded mulberry; even; to store up; to cover.
頭如蓬 丨 his head is touseled as a bramble-bush.
大 丨 to magnify.
丨 其天眞 expand his natural gifts.

ᶜ飽 ᶜ*pao* From to *eat* and to *wrap*, as the phonetic.

To eat enough; satiated, satisfied, gratified; flattered, happy.
丨 學之人 a very learned man.
食 丨 or 吃 丨 I have dined.
丨 滿 eaten too much.
丨 暖 fed and warmed.
饑 丨 由人 hunger and fullness are much as people please.

飫丨以德 virtue was his ruling principle.

丨看一回 I always wish to see it, as the theater.

見你就丨 the sight of you is enough.

鮑 pao' Dried oysters; pickled fish; putrid or salted fish; frozen fish.

丨魚 *awabe* or dried fish from Japan, chiefly shell-fish.

與惡人之居如入丨魚之肆 living with the vile is like going into a fishmonger's; — you soon forget the bad odor.

抱 pao' From *hand* and to *wrap* as the phonetic; occurs used for the next.

To infold, to contain, to hold in; to carry in the arms; to grasp, to compress; to feel, to have in the heart; to adhere to; the bosom, the lap; an arm's length; vapor rising towards the sun; to hatch.

懷丨 to think of, to care for.

丨住 to lullaby, to carry a babe.

丨病 still sick.

懷才丨德 to cherish and maintain one's virtue.

丨恨終身 I shall feel angry as long as I live; I never can forget it.

雲丨日 the clouds encircle the sun.

幼子在丨 a tender child in the lap.

丨膝長吟 to hold the knees and sing away; — literary leisure.

丨告人 one who pleads for the plaintiff.

丨屈含寃 to keep one's wrongs to himself; I can get no redress.

挾丨 to hold tight, as under the arms.

丨義 to maintain the right.

丨愧 ashamed.

丨負不凡 a rarely-clever man, one not of the common sort.

丨怨 found fault with, to bear a grudge against.

丨不平 willing for a quarrel, ready for a scrimmage.

菢 勽 毦 pao' The second and unusual form, composed of *enveloping* and *man*, refers to the meaning; interchanged with the last.

To incubate, to sit on eggs, as a bird; to hatch.

雞丨竇 the hen is sitting.

鷄丨鵝 [like] a hen trying to hatch goose eggs; — he cannot manage the affair.

鉋 刨 pao' A plane; to plane off, to smooth; to level off; to deduct from; to grub up.

丨子 a carpenter's plane.

馬丨 a curry-comb.

丨花 or 丨柴 shavings.

丨木 to smooth boards.

丨削 to correct, as a style; to polish; to arrange properly.

丨槽地 to dig a trench.

丨煙丨 a box-plane for shaving tobacco.

齙 pao' The teeth exposed; protuberant, projecting.

丨眼 projecting eyes, which physiognomists say indicates a harsh temper.

西瓜丨 a water-melon row of teeth, at Canton denotes a man whose projecting incisors enable him to scrape a melon easily.

豹 pao' From *brute* and a *pinch.*

A name for spotted felinæ, as the leopard, panther, jaguar, cheetah, or ounce; the leopard is the insignia of military officers of the fourth rank; spotted, marbled; as big or like a leopard's spots.

金錢丨 or 丨子 the leopard. (*Leopardus japonicus.*)

艾葉丨 the tiger-cat of Formosa. (*Leopardus brachyurus.*)

君子丨變 the princely man comes out beautiful as the leopard's skin.

丨飾 edged or ornamented with leopard's skin, as sleeves.

赤丨黃羆 red panthers and mottled bears.

管中窺丨 you have been gazing at the sky through a little tube; — *met.* you talk big.

丨眼圓睜 staring fiercely with open eyes.

儤 pao' Also written like the last.

A censor who used to remain on guard five days in the office, called 丨直, because he crouched in his post like a cheetah.

報 pao' Composed of 㚔 *sins* and 𠬝 to *submit* contracted; occurs used for *hoh*, 合 to join.

To recompense, to requite; to revenge; a retribution, a reward; to state, to inform, to tell, to report; a messenger; a report; a gazette, a reporter; to debauch a superior; to unite.

有恩丨恩 he who receives favors must requite them.

惡丨 a retribution for evil deeds.

丨仇 to revenge one's self on an enemy.

眼現丨 the retribution has come quickly.

陰丨陽丨 a secret reward, as by the gods; an open reward, as from men.

回丨 an answer.

通丨 for general information; a public notice.

日丨 the daily Court circular.

丨條 a notice put up at doors to announce an honor received.

紅旗丨捷 to send a courier to the capital with good news.

丨子 a messenger; a hand-bill, a placard.

泥金帖捷丨 may the gold sprinkled card speedily announce — that you have become a high graduate.

丨信者 one who reports a thing; a newsmonger.

丨老 to plead age for retiring.

丨答 to recompense.

丨馬 a courier.

丨稅 to pay duties on moving goods.

圖丨 I hope to reward your kindness; I shall try to requite you.

遭天丨 met a divine retribution, as when struck by lightning.

丨本追源 to requite one's ancestors by sacrifices.

何以丨我 how can you repay me?

接到家丨 I received my family letters.

速丨司 the Speedy Recompenser, a deity in municipal temples before whom oaths are taken with great solemnity.

暴 虣 *pao'* Originally composed of 日 *sun*, 出 *emitting*, 廾 *to receive*, 米 *rice* (or 本 *source*), intimating the effect of the sun in ripening grain; now contracted to 日 *sun* and 恭 *respect*; the second and antique form is composed of *tiger* and *martial*, a lexigraph hinting at its meaning.

A very dry or scorching heat; stormy, tempestuous; cruel, violent, oppressive, fierce; to strike; to waste; an intensive particle; to bring to light, to discover; a plat six *li* square.

丨虐 to harry the people.

丨風 a fierce wind.

丨虎 to throttle the tiger, as Fung Fu did; a fearless daredevil; brave to excess.

丨羅 a demon who kills one of the successful graduates of the *tsinsz'* list soon after they are gazetted.

强丨之徒 an unscrupulous wretch.

丨怒 very angry.

丨然 or 丨丨 suddenly.

兇丨衆著 his savage conduct was exhibited to all.

狂丨 outrageous.

酷丨 very cruel.

丨病 dangerously sick.

自丨自棄 to act violently and throw one's self away.

除丨安良 to punish the cruel and quiet the peaceful.

Read *puh*, To dry in the sun; to discover, to exhibit, to proclaim.

一日丨之 to put it in the sun one day.

丨之于民 to show to the people.

曝 *pao'* Also read *puh*, and used for the last.

To sun, to air.

丨晒 to dry in the sun.

丨書 to dry books.

野人負丨 laborers must bear the sun.

爆 *pao'* To burn, to scorch; to snap, to pop; to crackle; to blast rocks; to chap, to burst or shrink from dryness; hot; sputtering, crackling; to dry by the fire.

丨火 a crackling fire.

丨竹 or 串丨 a string of fire-crackers.

丨煤 coal that snaps.

丨穀 parched rice.

桶箍丨了 the hoops have burst.

烟花丨像 all kinds of fire-works.

丨裂 chapped, cracked.

放花丨 to let off fire-works.

謈 *pao'* Passionate.

丨譟如雷 he flies off in a passion, like a clap of thunder.

P'AO.

Old sounds, p'o, p'ot, p'ok, bo, bot, *and* bok. *In Canton*, p'ao *and* p'ò; — *in Swatow*, p'au; — *in Amoy*, pau, p'au, *and* pauh; — *in Fuhchau*, p'au, p'a, *and* po; — *in Shanghai*, p'o *and* bo; — *in Chifu*, p'ao.

拋 *,p'ao* To fling, or throw down; to cast off, to reject; to toss up; to cut, to deduct; in *mechanics*, to project.

丨錨 to cast anchor.

丨棄 to abandon, to reject.

丨別 to abscond.

丨梭 to throw the shuttle.

丨除多少 how much do you take off?

丨頭露面 to appear in public; said of women.

丨毬 to play or throw ball.

丨撇父母 to leave one's parents, to go from home.

丨磚引玉 to spend a brick to get a gem.

丨費 to spend recklessly; extravagant.

脬 *,p'ao* Used for *,pao* 胞 a pustule.

A bladder.

氣丨 an air-bladder.

尿丨 the bladder.

卵丨子 the pellicle enveloping the white of an egg.

庖 *,p'ao* A place for killing and dressing food; a cook-room.

丨人 or 丨丁 a cook.

丨廚 a kitchen.

暫行代丨以重館務 we must get a substitute for the cook in order to carry on the household.

咆 *,p'ao* To roar, as a lion or bear; to bluster; furious, raging.

丨勃 to put on bravado.

丨哮公堂 the angry bluster of officials in the yamun.

炰 *,p'ao* Used for the last, but more often for the next.

To roast; to fry, as a hash; to exhibit violent passions.

毛丨胾羹 roast-pig, hash, and soups.

女丨烋于中國 you show your fierce will in the center of the state.

炮 From *fire* and to *envelop*; it is erroneously used for 砲 a cannon.
ₛp'ao To bake or roast in the ashes; to wrap up in clay and roast.

丨之燔之 roast it and toast it.

丨製 to mix; to temper, as condiments.

丨祭 to char wood for sacrifices.

丨燥 to get angry, is thus written for 譟 譟 the correct form.

丨烙之刑 the punishment of climbing hot pillars — in hell.

匏 From 包 to *envelop* and 瓠 a *gourd* contracted.
ₛp'ao A calabash or bitter squash, anciently used for drinking, or making musical instruments; a gurglet shaped vessel.

丨瓜 a hard shell gourd.

丨羹 a soup of young gourd leaves.

苦丨不材 the bitter squash is only worth picking — for a float.

瓟 Used with the last.
ₛp'ao A gourd; drinking utensils are made of the dried shell.

丨瓠爲飲 a calabash for drinking.

鞄 To work over hides or skins, and make them soft, like
ₛp'ao wash-leather.

袍 From *dress* and to *envelop*.
ₛp'ao A robe longer than a 褂; a long inner garment which covers the skirts; a quilted or plaited gown; the front skirts.

皮丨 a fur mantle.

誼切同丨 they are so friendly as to have but one mantle between them; *i. e.* they are of the same calling, have gone through the same hardships, as soldiers.

割丨斷義 to disrupt a dear friendship.

道丨 a Taoist's robe.

穿藍丨子 the blue-mantled one, *i. e.* Heaven.

戰丨 defensive armor.

黃丨加身 they threw the yellow robe over me; — said by the founder of the Sung dynasty.

麃 A small deer with spots like
ₛp'ao the axis; it is a native of northern China, and affords fine venison; this animal is also described as like the ₛ*piao* 麃, and as having one horn and a cow's tail, which may refer to the nylghau.

跑 To run, to gallop; to paw
'p'ao the earth; to prance; to ride like Jehu; to hasten, to travel; to go or walk, a meaning common at Shanghai.

丨馬 to canter; to race horses.

丨走 to run off; to run hard.

丨風 a strong, fair wind.

逃丨 to abscond.

快丨 go faster; to hurry on.

丨路 to journey.

丨文書 a postman.

丨堂 a waiter at an inn or restaurant.

捊 To take in hand, as a hus-
ₛp'ao bandman does his tools; used for 否 whether.

丨鋤 to till the land.

譻 From *words* and *violent*.
ₛp'ao To cry out when in pain is 阿丨; overcome by pain; to bawl.

奅 Occurs used for the next.
p'ao' To harvest; to brag over others; to swell up, like a fish.

礮 砲 From *stone* and a *griffon*; the second is commonly used, and often wrongly written ₛ*p'ao* 炮 to roast.
p'ao' A ballista, with which the Chinese used to throw great stones; a cannon, great guns; an explosion, as of a gun; fireworks; the cannonier in chess, whose powers are like those of a castle.

一門丨 or 一口丨 a cannon.

丨眼 the touch-hole.

一架丨 a gun and its carriage.

放丨 or 開丨 to fire the gun.

丨臺 a fort.

放排丨 a salvo of musquetry.

燒花丨 to burn the flowery gun, as when worshiping Ceres.

丨手 a gunner.

放丨迎接 to receive with a salute.

二丨候 hour for two guns, fired at noon in a governor's office.

號丨 to fire a signal-gun.

馬後丨 one who fires after the horse has fled; — an after-wit.

田雞丨 the frog-gun, *i. e.* a mortar.

丨隊 a company of artillery men.

丨車 a ballista; a gun-carriage.

泡 From *water* and *envelop* as the phonetic; used with the next.
p'ao' A bubble; froth, spume;
ₛp'ao water rushing on; a murmuring, bubbling noise; to soak, to rinse, to dip; to steep and soften; a river in Shantung; in *medicine*, hot infusions as distinguished from 漬 or cold infusions.

水丨 a water blister; a bubble.

丨製 to decoct, as medicines.

丨濕 to wet, to dip; wetted.

身如丨沫 a Budhistic term for the unreality of all phenomena, like the body changing as the bubble on the water.

丨茶 to soak in tea, as a biscuit.

熱湯丨死 scalded to death.

下雨冒丨 when it rains, bubbles are made — on the water.

渾渾丨丨 as a foaming torrent.

如夢幻丨影 [life is] like a dream, a glittering bubble.

水裏丨着 let it soak long.

丨氣去了 the froth has all gone.

沒有丨氣 there's no bubble; *met.* my outlay (or trouble) is quite in vain.

瘻疬丨兒 to break a pimple.

In *Pekingese.* Light, as a thing; floatable.

丨炭 light willow charcoal.

疱 炮 *p'ao'* From *disease* or *skin* and *envelop.*

A pustule on the face; a blister coming out suddenly, like chicken-pox; a blister, as from a burn.

燙了一個丨 I have made a blister.

走起兩脚丨 I have raised blisters on my feet.

㨰 *p'ao'* To strike, to chastise; the sound of beating, a clattering noise.

丨去衣塵 knock the dust off your clothes.

PÉI.

This sound and PI *often run into each other. Old sounds,* péi, pai, pít, pat, *and* bat. *In Canton,* pi, púi, *and* p'úi; — *in Swatow,* púi, púe, pi, *and* pwat; — *in Amoy,* pi, p'i, pòe, *and* p'ai; — *in Fuhchau,* pi, p'i, *and* pwoi; — *in Shanghai,* pé, p'e, bé, *and* bé^n; — *in Chifu,* péi.

悲 *ˎpéi* From *heart* and *negative* or bad, *i.e.* what the mind thinks is bad.

To commisserate that which is bad or distressing; grief for another's woe; to be sad; to feel for, sympathy; tragic, as a play.

丨夫 how melancholy; pitiable!

丨哉 alas! how sad.

丨嘆 to sigh sadly.

慈丨忽發 he all at once shows much pity.

丨秋 to lament the fall of the leaf; *met.* regret at passing the flower of life.

離合丨歡 parting and meeting, tragic and comic; as plays.

丨痛之懷 to suffer with others' in their griefs.

丨切 acutely grieved.

我心傷丨 my heart is wounded with sadness.

桮 杯 盃 *ˎpéi* From *wood* or *dish* and *not*; the first form is least common.

A cup, a vessel for drinking from; a tumbler, a glass; divining-blocks used before the gods, for which the second form is used.

一隻丨or丨子 one tumbler or cup.

敬酒三丨 offered him three cups of wine.

拿一丨水來 bring a glass of water.

一丨祈准 his prayer was heard at the first fall of the blocks.

丨中蛇影 he sees a snake's shadow in the cup; — said of a very suspicious man.

貪丨 a wine-bibber.

請照勝一丨 let us take a full bumper together.

丨盤 a salver; a waiter.

丨茗候叙 my entertainment is waiting ready for you to come.

換丨 to change cups.

In *Cantonese.* To coax, to flatter.

丨打之言 irony, jokes, double entendre.

你丨奬我 you are only wheedling me.

卑 𤰞 *ˎpéi* Formed of 左 *left* contracted and 甲 *first* above; it is the opposite of *chung'* 重 weighty.

Base, low, vulgar; plebeian; mean, inferior, contemptible; a term for one's self; yielding, respectful, humble.

丨陋 vulgar, low-lived.

丨賤 mean and cheap; *met.* the lower classes.

丨職 I, the magistrate.

丨丨不足道 not worth mentioning, too unimportant.

丨污苟賤 a vile and worthless — fellow.

登高必自丨 to attain eminence one must start from lowly life.

天尊地丨 heaven is exalted, earth is lowly.

丨以自牧 the inferior must watch themselves.

萆 蓖 *ˎpéi* A medicinal plant.

丨蔴草 the castor-oil plant. (*Ricinus.*)

丨蔴油 oil used in making vermilion ink for seals; the second form is chiefly used in this sense.

丨薢 applied to several plants, one of which, the 湛紅丨薢 is a vine like the *Smilax,* with cymes of purple flowers.

Read *pih,* A rain cloak.

椑 *ˎpéi* Handle of an ax; a kind of wine-cup; a fruit, the 丨柹 *Diospyros glutinifera,* or yellow skinned persimmon; also called the green persimmon.

碑 *ˎpéi* From *stone* and *lowly.*

A stela; stone tablets, such as are set up in temples or public places; a grave-stone; a pillar to which victims were anciently tied.

石丨 a stone tablet of any kind.

丨文 an epitaph.

路上行人口似丨 traveler's words last like tablets.

丨記 the inscription on a tablet.
丨墓 a tombstone.
丨銘 carved on stone.
丨帖 fac-similes printed from tablets.
口丨 the public opinion of a man or affair.

簞 ˏpéi A basket or creel for fishing; a bamboo float; a basket to inclose fish to drag astern; thin.

俾 ˋpéi ˋpi From *man* and *trifling* as the phonetic.
To cause, to enable; to let, to allow; to give; to benefit; to accord; to employ; an instrumental *conjunction*, that, so that if, to the end that; a form of the *accusative*, by, with.
丨石擊人 he struck the man with a stone.
丨予從欲 let me follow my desires.
不丨人行 don't let the people go.
送丨佢 give it to him (*Cantonese*.
丨爾職守 to enable you to fulfill your official duties.
罔不率丨 they consented and followed him without exception; — everybody submitted.
丨得安焉 that he may be quieted.

庳 ˋpéi Low, unpretending, as a cottage; humble, mean; short; insufficient; used for 鼻 the nose; a hen quail.
有丨 a small fief which the brother of Shun governed, lying in the southwest of Hunan in Tao-cheu 道州 on the River Siang.
宮室卑丨 the halls and buildings are common and low.
其民豐肉而丨 those people were fat and well fed, but low in stature

背 péiˀ ˏpéi From *flesh* and *north*, intimating that the face properly turns to the south.
The back; the opposite of front or face; behind, rear, the back side; under side of a book; the north of a hall or house; rays of the sun; top of a bow; a steep convex bluff near a stream, from a fancied resemblance to a back; to turn the back on; to carry on the back; to be proved false; to feign; to oppose; to prevaricate.
手丨 back of the hand.
丨脊 the back; the backbone.
丨心 a vest; a sleeveless jacket.
時無丨無側 you have therefore no one at your back or side — to advise you.
寒丨 cuddled up with the cold.
佗丨 humpbacked.
向丨 front and rear, as of a house.
違丨 to resist; contumacious.
丨後 behind it.
丨信 or 丨教 to apostatize.
丨約 to discard treaty obligations.
丨口言 to talk of one behind his back.
發丨 or 搭丨 to have a carbuncle on the back.
相丨 back to back; opposition.
丨負 to carry on the back.
丨書 or 丨出來 to repeat a lesson; to say memoriter.
丨陰 a shady spot not reached by the sun.
丨地裏 aside, a retired spot.
丨兒 the obverse of a coin.
丨諱爺娘 to disregard one's parents.
丨井 to leave one's home, as to get a living.
丨着手 to walk with the hands behind the back.
丨面 the back side, the rear.
丨刼前言 to violate one's word.
噂沓丨憎 many [fair] words, but hatred behind one's back.
丨地 clandestine, underhand.

In *Cantonese*. Unusual, rare; secret.
十分丨 exceedingly rare, as a character.
講丨語 to make signs to one.
耳丨 hard of hearing.

In *Pekingese*. Unlucky; to miss a chance.
你眞丨了 you are truly unlucky.

偝 péiˀ From *man* and *back*.
To reject, to discard; to stand awry.
莫丨立 do not stand improperly.
民不丨上 the people do not dislike their superiors.

褙 **緋** péiˀ Fine silk of many colors; to paste paper hangings.

被 péiˀ From *clothes* and *skin*.
The covering of a bed; to cover; to put on or dress one with; to reach to; to protect; to provide or prepare; to suffer, and thus becomes a sign of the passive voice, showing that what follows was suffered or done; a *preposition*, by, from.
綿丨 or 丨竇 a quilted coverlet.
丨水災 suffered by a flood.
丨及天恩 heaven's blessings came to him.
馬汗丨 a saddle-cloth.
丨人欺負 misused by others.
丨具 all is ready.
光丨四表 his glory reached to all places.
丨單 sheets, as for a bed.
丨害 injured, misused.
佗羅經丨 a pall with Budhist prayers on it.
丨胎 or 丨綿 a cotton wool quilt without a cover.
丨風吹着 the wind blew on him.
鋪丨 to condole with friends.

In *Cantonese*. A *conjunction*, or, one of two; a particle expressing certainty.
公丨乸 is it a male or female?
係丨 yes, it is.
丨點樣 then what? how will it turn out?

倍 *péi'* From 人 *man* and 否 *not* altered.

To rebel, to oppose authority; low, vulgar; to withdraw; to increase; a fold; a hundred times.

水勢丨湧 the water rushes faster.

鄙丨 unseemly, vulgar, lowbred.

加一丨 double it.

十丨 tenfold.

丨世離俗 to leave the world and its vulgarities.

丨增惆悵 overburdened and perplexed, as with varied affairs.

丨文 very learned, good memory.

丨加整肅 extra care in putting it in order.

如'賈三丨 suppose a trader gets 300 per cent.

焙 *péi'* To dry by or over a fire, as tea is cured; to hatch eggs artificially.

火丨 kiln-dried.

丨乾 to dry; to cure by drying.

丨茶 to fire tea.

丨鴨苗 to hatch ducklings.

炕丨 to make fretted work, as with metals.

丨火 to dry before the fire.

丨的脆 roasted till it is crisp.

貝 *péi'* The upper part represents the body of a cowrie, the inner strokes the teeth, and the lower its feelers; it is the 154th radical of characters relating to values and trade; used with the next three.

A cowrie shell or *Cypræa*, used for money in China in early feudal times; its name 丨齒 referred to the denticules; a conch; precious, valuable; money, riches, property; adorned with shells; shell-like.

丨錦 rich brocade.

丨勒 and 丨子 are Manchu titles of nobility, *beile* and *peisse*, somewhat like baron and baronet.

紫丨 or 文丨 mottled or colored cypræas.

丨冑 a helmet ornamented with shells, used in old times.

丨多 the *peito* or palmyra palm; it is also incorrectly applied to the pepul or Indian fig.

棋 *péi'* A lofty tree in India and Burmah, the *Borassus* or palmyra palm, of whose leaves books are made; called 丨多樹 in Sanscrit *patra*, and also 思惟樹 or the tree of reflection.

琪 *péi'* Ornaments of tortoise-shell; ornaments inlaid.

丨飾 the round flat stone or carving on a string of beads, which hangs to it like a cross on a rosary.

茛 *péi'* A bitterish expectorant medicine, a kind of mealy bulb called 丨母 or 貝母 found in Sz'ch'uen and Chehkiang; it is the root of a liliaceous plant (*Uvularia*), and used in fevers and ointments.

狽 *péi'* An animal allied to a wolf, called 狼丨 with short fore or hind legs, or wanting one, so that in order to get along, one must ride the other; it probably alludes to the jerboa.

狼丨爲奸 they are banded together in their traitorous schemes.

狼丨折札之命 my fate is as bad as a fettered *lang-péi*; — I am quite helpless.

犻 犋 *péi'* A two year old heifer; the first is also defined an ox with a long body and long legs.

輩 輩 *péi'* From *chariot* and *not*; the second and irregular form is common.

A hundred chariots made a squadron; a long line of chariots; a company; a class, a sort, a generation; things, kinds; a sign of the plural; to compare or class with.

我丨 our kind.

視爲一丨 he regarded them all alike.

同丨 comrades; alike, same sort.

丨兒大 they are his seniors; a rank above this.

尊丨 you all — *i. e.* those older than the speaker.

卑丨 we all; — *i. e.* your juniors.

無丨 incomparable.

過丨 to leave one's place.

營利之丨 traders, merchants.

前丨 seniors; those who have the pas.

班丨 a colleague.

一丨子 throughout his whole life, during life.

類丨 different sorts.

老前丨 one of the old sort, *i. e.* an old [Hanlin] scholar, an instructor.

佩 *p'éi'* From *man*, *all*, and *napkin*.

Things worn on the girdle, as pendents; to wear about one, to hang on the gridle; to keep by one, as a souvenir; to gird on to carry, to remember.

丨劍 to wear a sword.

丨服不忘 I will ever bear it in my memory.

感丨深恩 I shall ever remember your great kindness.

曷勝欽丨 I greatly rejoice to remember you.

丨身 to wear or have on the person.

其餘不丨服 I will yield to nobody else, I cannot give in [my opinion] to the others.

去'喪無所不丨 when mourning is laid aside, wear all your ornaments.

知子之來之雜丨以贈之 when I know those whom you wish to have come, I will give them of my girdle ornaments.

珮 *p'éi'* Gems worn by women, girdle ornaments; tinkling things hung in the wind.

環丨鏘鏘 the girdle appendages tinkled as he went.

旆 旆 *péi* From *flag* and *market*; the contracted form is most common.

A pennon or swallow-tailed streamer attached to the staff over the flag; to fasten on a pennon; to journey, to take a trip.

白 丨 央 央 their white streamers fluttered brightly.

丨 丨 streaming out and fluttering, like a banner; or the long tendrils of the bean.

旌 丨 飛 揚 the fluttering flags.

旗 丨 a flag.

返 丨 to return from a long travel.

行 丨 to go on a journey.

悖 *péi* It is interchanged with *puh*, 詩 to mislead.

To rebel; to set one's self against nature or usage; perverse; contumacious, unreasonable.

丨 禮 uncivil; crabbed, as when rude to friends, and civil to strangers.

丨 逆 rebellious.

丨 理 opposed to propriety.

貨 丨 而 入 亦 丨 而 出 unjust gains may come to one, but they will as certainly leave him.

邶 *péi* A feudal city, or small region in the Shang dynasty, mentioned in the Book of Odes, lying north of the Yellow River in the present Ki cheu 冀 州 in the southwest of Chihli.

P'ÉI.

This sound and P'I *often run into each other. Old sounds*, p'éi, béi, p'ai, p'it, bit, *and* păt. *In Canton*, p'úi, p'i, *and* pi; — *in Swatow*, p'i, pi, púi, púe, *and* hui; — *in Amoy*, p'i, pòe, p'ai, *and* pi; — *in Fuhchau*, p'i, pw'ò, púi, pié, *and* pai; — *in Shanghai*, p'é *and* bé; — *in Chifu*, p'éi.

醅 *p'éi* From *spirits* and *whether*.

Liquor not yet strained; must; eaten and drunken to satiety; surfeited.

丕 *p'éi* *p'i* From *one* and *not*; occurs interchanged with 不 and 否 as an adverb.

Unequaled; first, distinguished; to receive with respect, as orders; an expletive or intensive particle, adding elegance to the style.

丨 子 the eldest son of a king.

丨 著 聲 名 an unsurpassed reputation.

嘉 乃 丨 績 he lauded his great merit.

丨 顯 考 your great and illustrious ancestors.

呸 *p'éi* The noise made in spitting or hooting; to snort at.

秠 *p'i* A kind of black millet, the variety which has two seeds within one glume, used in making the spirits offered in olden time in the ancestral worship of princes, it being regarded as an unusual thing.

伾 *p'éi* Sturdy, stout; valiant, robust; many.

大 丨 山 is near the Yellow River in Wéi-hwui fu, in the northeast of Honan.

以 車 丨 丨 all are strong steeds fit for the chariot.

坯 坏 *p'éi* *p'i* A mound; unburnt or sun-dried tiles or pottery; to stop a crack in a wall; a back wall; the model of a thing, by which it is to be molded; crude material.

泥 丨 unburnt earthenware.

取 石 丨 to get out a rough block, as for a statue.

丨 模 a model, a rough cast.

多 器 丨 士 they had many sundried utensils.

一 丨 黃 土 盖 英 雄 now only a clod covers the hero.

磚 丨 bricks not yet burnt.

烟 丨 子 rough stones for pipe mouths.

怌 *p'éi* Idle; frightened, alarmed.

柔 則 丨 the weak will be much alarmed.

芣 *p'ieh* The luxuriant gay look of plants in flower.

丨 蘭 a species of green skinned turnip, of a sweet taste like the rutabaga, grown about Peking.

痞 *p'éi* A disease not yet developed; one says, the pain of dyspepsia.

胚 肧 *p'éi* From *flesh* and *not*.

An embryo, a fœtus one month old; an unformed, unfinished thing; misty, uncondensed vapor.

丨 胎 pregnant.

身 丨 fat, in good liking. (*Canton*.)

拔 八 丨 子 a marplot, a dolt.

衃 *fu* From *blood* and *not*; it occurs used for the last.

Coagulated blood, of a dark red color.

赤 如 丨 血 者 死 if his face is of the color of clotted blood, he will die.

Read *feu*. Another name for oats is 蚍 丨, not now used.

邳 ˏp'éi A place in the state of Lu. 丨州 a district, formerly called 下丨 in the north of Kiangsu, near the Grand Canal.

髤 ˏp'éi Going out with the hair disheveled.
丨鬛 a bushy beard.
Read *fu'* The hair on the head.

豾 狉 ˏp'éi The second form is most used.
A cub, especially the 丨貍 or fox's cubs.
草木榛榛鹿豕丨丨 the trees were strange and tangled, the deers and swine savage and wild, — as at the creation; the last two words are also spoken of wild tribes of men.

駓 ˏp'éi A white and yellow speckled horse.
丨丨 running along; hurrying on.

裴 ˏp'éi From *clothes* and *not* as the phonetic; occurs used for the next.
Dressed in long and beautiful robes; an old name for Hoh-fi hien 合肥縣 in the center of Nganhwui.
丨回 to go to and fro; some apply it to wild people in Hainan Island.

徘 ˏp'éi From *step* and *not*; it is sometimes wrongly written ˏp'ai 俳 an actor.
To walk.
丨徊 flying and wheeling about, like swallows; walking to and fro; irresolute.
丨徊花 a variety of rose. (*Rosa rugosa.*)

培 ˏp'éi From 土 *earth* and 否 *not* altered.
To add or heap up dirt; to hoe, as maize; to cultivate; to assist, to add energy to; to dam up, as a sluice.
丨養 or 丨補身體 to invigorate the body.
丨磚 to lay up bricks.
栽丨 to heap earth around a sapling; *met.* to patronize, to make a protegé of one.
丨土 heap up the earth; hence 丨植起來 means that what one was early accustomed to, he does naturally, as the earth develops the sapling.
丨高的 raise it higher, as a roof. (*Cantonese.*)

陪 ˏp'éi From *place* and *not*; used with the last and 倍 to double.
To add earth to plants; attached to, subordinate; to assist; to accompany, to fellowship; to double; to match; to fill.
丨你出門 I'll go out with you.
丨客坐 to entertain a visitor.
丨送 to see a guest out, to escort.
丨伴 a companion.
丨賓 to associate with.
加丨 to multiply, to add to.
丨助 to assist, to take a part in.
丨臣 a subsidiary officer; a term used by feudal princes.
招丨 I beg your pardon.
欠丨 excuse my leaving you; — a polite phrase.
丨嫁了環 a servant-maid like Zilpah, who accompanies a married daughter.
秉德丨仁 to match humanity by virtue.
丨襯 a kind of double entendre; to praise or blame by allusions; to bring up an illustration.

賠 ˏp'éi To make up a loss, to indemnify; to supply a deficit; to offset; to confess; to cover, as in gambling.
丨還 or 丨償 to repay; to make good a loss; to compensate.
丨錢貨 goods sold at a loss.
丨塡 to pay, as a surety; to make up, as an officer the losses of government.
丨禮 to return a call.
丨不是 I own that I am in the wrong.
丨罪 to acknowledge a fault.
丨反定銀 to restore earnest money.
有失無丨 no repayment for losses.
丨了本兒 to lose one's outlay.
照丨 to pay the value.
丨送 to give out without a return.

毰 ˏp'éi The feathers of the wing spread out.
丨毸 a phœnix fluttering and gamboling.

棓 ˏp'éi A flail; to strike; an elevated plank or stand for gazing.
五丨子 or 五倍子 the gall-nut; they are produced on a species of sumach, the 鹽麩子 or *Rhus semi-alatus*, and are better than the 沒石子 or oak galls.

蓓 'p'éi A flower bud is 丨蕾, the opening blossom.
黃丨 a kind of flower.
瑞香丨蕾百花愁 when the *Daphne odora* is blossoming, all other flowers are ashamed.

琲 'p'éi A string of five hundred pearls.
編個丨子 string on those pearls.

配 p'éi' From 酉 *spirits* and 妃 *princess* contracted.
The color of liquor; a mate, a marrow, an equal; a companion, as a wife; to pair, to mate; to put on the same grade; to accompany; to compare to; equal, comparable; conjointly; to copulate, said of animals.
丨偶 a married pair.
合丨 to match, to fit; suitable.
不丨 unworthy of, incongruous, not fit for, ill-assorted.
他不丨活着的 he is not fit to live, — or be spared alive.
丨色 to match colors.
相丨 equaled, coupled.
許丨 to consent to a match.
問丨 to banish.

丨 馬 to saddle or harness a horse.
丨 婚 to consummate a marriage.
丨 祖考 to put in the same rank with one's ancestors.
丨 享千秋 let him enjoy perpetual felicity — in hades.
德丨天地 his virtue equaled heaven and earth.
丨 不上 it makes no match to that, it does not fit, unsuitable.
他也丨 that will match.

轡 p'éi' From 車 *cart*, 絲 *silk*, and 口 *mouth*.
The reins of a bridle, vulgarly called 扯手 or hand-pullers.
執丨 hold the reins.
六丨 six reins [in hand]; — a clever man.
一丨頭跑了多遠 how far can you gallop without drawing rein?

沛 p'éi' A river in Liaotung, and one in Kiangsu; copious; humid; moving or enlarging in any way; prostrate, as a tree pulled up; to run or flow; to irrigate, or to dam up water for irrigation; aquatic plants.
丨澤 kind, beneficent; fertilizing; blessing.
丨縣 a district in the northeast of Kiangsu.
丨然下雨 it rained copiously.
顛丨流離 sudden confusion, in a sudden emergency, imminent.
丨然自大 vain-glorious.
丨艾 graceful, blooming.
顛丨必於是 in seasons of danger, [the wise man] retains — his virtue.

霈 p'éi' Copious rain.
滂丨 sloppy, rainy; drenching showers.
丨丨 raining and blowing.

帔 p'éi' A cape; a mantle.
裙丨 a woman's robe.
鳳冠霞丨 [to wear] the phœnix crown and cloudy mantle; a woman's marriage.

P'EU.

Old sounds, pu, p'u, bu, pút, p'út, *and* bút. *In Canton*, fau, pau, *and* p'au; — *in Swatow*, pi *and* p'ò; — *in Amoy*, p'ò; — *in Fuhchau*, p'éu *and* p'aiu; — *in Shanghai*, pù *and* p'ù; — *in Chifu*, pò.

抔 ˓peu To take up in both hands, as when drinking water from them.
一丨土 a handful of earth.
飲水一丨 drink a handful of water.
丨錢濟貧 to give generously.

裒 ˓p'eu From *clothes* and *mortar*; it bears a resemblance to ˓*shwai* 衰 decayed.
To collect, to bring together; to diminish; many.
丨聚 to add to.
丨減 to take from.
丨荆之旅 he brought the multitudes of King together.
丨多益寡 decrease the surplus to supply the deficit.
丨時之對 an answer fitting to the time.
原隰丨矣 when collected on the heights and lowlands.

掊 ˓peu Like the preceding.
To grasp, to appropriate; to take from; to get salt from sea-water.
丨坑得鹽 he took the pits to get the salt.
丨克 to rigorously exact, as duties.
丨擊于世俗 I reject and drive off worldly affairs.

呸 ˓peu To draw in the breath.
吸丨 to suck through, as a draught through a doorway.
In *Cantonese*. Swollen, tumid, puffed; empty, deceptive; spotted and flaking off, as the plaster from a damp wall.
鬆丨嘅 flabby, no solidity.
丨腮 glum, gruff; cheeky.
溜丨 not firm; soft, like flesh.
一團一丨 a sinking and a swelling.

剖 ˓p'eu, ˓p'eu To split in two with a knife; to cut out; to halve; to judge, to decide; to lay open, to disclose.
丨開 to rip open, to rive.
丨判 to give judgment.
丨明 to decide intelligently.
丨訴前因 it clearly sets forth the previous circumstances.
丨腹明心 to bring out the real feelings.
丨符 to halve a cheque or evidence.
丨析曉諭 a proclamation explaining the minutest details.
蚌因珠而致丨 oysters are cut open because of their pearls, — so for a chance of gain much is lost.
丨瓜 to cut up a melon.

瓿 ˓p'eu A kind of earthenware jar or gallipot, to hold food.
瓦丨 a jar.
銅丨 a copper pickle-pot.

PI.

Some of these characters are often read PÉI. *Old sounds,* pi, pai, péi, bai, pit, pat, *and* bat. *In Canton,* pi, pé, *and* pei; — *in Swatow,* pi, pⁿi, pʻi, pⁿoi, *and* púi; — *in Amoy,* pi, pʻi, pó, *and* pit; — *in Fuhchau,* pi, pé, pie, *and* pik; — *in Shanghai,* pi, bó, *and* pih; — *in Chifu,* pi.

鎞 釓 ˓pi — Used with 篦 a comb; the second form is not common.
The colter of a plow; barb of an arrow; a probe used by surgeons; a skewer used in a head-dress; a lever.
鉄 丨 a crowbar.

比 ˋpi — Altered from *two men* following each other; it forms the 81st radical of a few unusual words, and much resembles *poh,* 北 north.
To compare, to put in a class, to sort; to effect a union; to equal, to correspond; an illustration; to bring into harmony; to select; near to one; a sign of the comparative; each, every.
丨較 to compare with.
丨對 to pair, to match.
丨照 over against.
丨一丨 making a comparison.
丨方 for instance, suppose; to measure.
丨戶慶賀 every household visits and congratulates — at newyear.
克順克丨 rendering a cordial submission, and making a cordial union.
無人丨得上 no one can compare with him.
丨並 to class and compare.
丨歲 these years, recently.
丨差 to punish policemen for a dereliction of duty.
一陣丨一陣大 each gust blew harder than the last.
丨體 a metaphor, an allegory.
五家為丨 five houses make a neighborhood.
丨語 a simile, an illustration.
他丨我強 he is more violent than I.
丨丨然也 everybody is just so.

Read *pi'* To harmonize; to sympathize; according with, equal, regular; to assemble; to be near to; to join; intimate; to wait for; an account of; matched.
不丨 peerless, not comparable to.
丨丘 or 丨邱 (Sanscrit *bhikshu,*) a mendicant priest, though it has now somewhat lost its first meaning.
丨丘尼 a female religious, still retained in the Japanese word *bikuni,* a nun.
阿丨 partial, mean, party-spirited.
洽丨其鄰 they assemble their neighbors.
丨及三年 through three years' service.
丨于 as to, respecting; in regard.
丨年 the triennial examination of officials.
義之與丨 it is consonant with justice.
丨其反也 when he had returned; wait for his return.
願丨死者一洒之 I wish, because of him who is dead, to altogether wash out this affront.

妣 ˋpi — A deceased mother.
祖丨 a deceased grandmother.
顯丨 my departed mother.
為酒為醴烝畀祖丨 to make spirits and must for offering to our male and female ancestors.

匕 ˋpi — The character delineates a *spoon;* it is the 21st radical.
A ladle; in poorly printed books used as a sign of repetition as 日丨 for 日日 daily.
丨首 a spoon; a stiletto.
有捄棘丨 long and curved, thorn-like spoons
丨箸 chopsticks.

粃 秕 ˋpi — Blasted, withered or unformed grain; grain that has not grown to its full size.
丨糠 chaff, refuse, husks; annoying, trifling.
塵垢丨糠 a dirty and troublesome business.

鄙 ˋpi — From *city* and *granary;* the primitive is composed of *mouth* and a *receiver, i. e.* that which takes in the grain.
A frontier or country town; a border; a place of five hundred houses, and five such were at first reckoned to be a *hien* district; low, country-like, rustic; the lower classes; to despise; to disesteem.
丨吝 parsimonious, niggardly.
丨夫 a scamp, a mean wretch.
丨劣 brazenfaced.
可丨 despicable.
丨薄 to vilify.
丨意 my poor notion; in my humble opinion.
丨我 he despises me.
丨俚之詞 a vulgar expression.
無丨小費 don't hesitate at a little outlay — to attain a great object.
邊丨之邑 a town on the frontiers.
肉食者丨 people who live in luxury are often mean.

柀 ˋpi — The 榧子 or nuts of the *Torreya nucifera,* an evergreen; an old name for the pine.

彼 ˋpi — From a *step* and *skin.*
A distributive *pronoun,* that, those, there, the further of two; the other party; to exclude, to leave out; following a verb or adjective, often adds force to its meaning.
丨哉 him, indeed! don't speak of that fellow!

丨此 are correlatives, as that, this; there, here; then, now; you, I; the two, both parties.
丨處 there, in that spot.
有丨君子 that great man.
在丨中河 there in the middle of the rivers.
丨有旨酒 they have their good wines.

髀 ʻpi The pelvic bones of the thigh; the rump.
丨下 the buttocks.
剖其右丨 he cut off the right leg.
徙丨丸 a tonic pill to restore appetite.
周丨 "Cheu's thigh-bone" is the name of a mathematical treatise.
丨肉復生 he is fleshing up again.

𩨼 ʻpi A shelving bank is 丨豸, with a marshy place at the bottom; a sloping bank or hill-side.

篦 **笓** pi˒ The second form is regarded as a contraction of the first.
A fine toothed comb; to comb; a net or crawl for catching crabs; to lead.
丨髮 to comb the hair.
丨子 a fine-tooth comb.
鉄丨子 a gridiron; the basket in a grate to hold the coals.

贔 pi˒ Strong, robust, like a tortoise which can bear great weights.
丨負 great exertion.
好丨屭 in sorrow, borne down by affliction; unlucky; sad; the allusion is to the tortoise bearing its great burden. (*Cantonese.*)

糒 pi˒ Dried rations such as are taken on a march; dried food.
棗丨以待賓客 to prepare dates and cakes to present to guests.

嬖 pi˒ A mean-minded but prosperous person; partial to, blinded to; a favorite, a parasite; lecherous, depraved.
丨妾 a favorite concubine.
丨童 or 丨倖 a catamite, euphuistically known as 相公 in some circles.
便丨 a great favorite.
愛丨 a loved companion.
丨子配嫡 for the sons of the concubines to be reckoned legitimate, — is the beginning of ruin to the state.

避 pi˒ From *to go* and *a ruler* as the phonetic.
To flee from, to escape, to avoid, to shun; to dodge; to shirk; to retire, to stand aside; to abscond, to hide away.
丨債 to avoid one's creditors.
廻丨 to stand aside, — as when a procession passes.
躲丨不著 to abstain from going out, — as when dunned for debts.
丨暑 to avoid hot weather, — as by going into the country.
丨世 to seclude one's self.
丨過一次險 he escaped the danger this time.
丨嫌疑 avoid the appearance of evil.
丨重就輕 to shirk the hard work and take the easy.
丨諱 to avoid the use of the Emperor's personal name.
引身丨匿 to keep in complete privacy.
丨難 to shun difficulties.

薜 pi˒ An herb, 丨荔 resembling celery or smallage; it is also one of the names of the *Ficus pumila* in Formosa.
丨蔴 wild hemp.

Read *pʻoh*, Cracked, as a jar.

畀 pi˒ From 田 a *field* or 由 *from* and 丌 a form of 其 *this*; in combination it is often written like 㽮 low, and occurs interchanged with 俾 to give.
To give, to confer on; to distribute amongst.
賦丨 to grant, as heaven does.
田祖有神秉丨炎火 let the god the Father of Tillage gather them (the worms) for the blazing fire.

婢 pi˒ pé˒ From *woman* and *base* as the phonetic.
A maid-servant; an unmarried female slave.
丨女 a maid; the maids.
丨子 a term used by women when speaking of themselves; a girl; a slave.
官丨 women condemned to be sold.
奴丨 male and female slaves.

痺 pi˒ From *disease* and *to give* as the phonetic.
Rheumatism; weakness or paralysis, arising from dampness; enlargement of an organ; numbness of a limb.
脚丨 my foot is asleep.
口丨 croup, or some difficulty in swallowing.
着丨 aches from damp weather.
痿丨不仁 so aching and weak as to be unfit for work.

睥 pi˒ To look askance; the eyes glancing about; to spy out a chance.
丨睨到我 your scolding reflects on me too.
丨睨人 a fault-finder, a prying fellow.

淠 pi˒ The motion of a vessel; the ripple of water; name of a branch of the River Hwai in Nganhwui, which joins it near Hoh-kiu kien.
丨丨 flourishing, abundant, as reeds.
其旂丨丨 the waving flags.

敝 pi˒ From 攴 to *strike* and 㡀 *broken*; occurs used for 蔽 closed.
Bad, unfit for use; poor, unworthy; vile, abject; defeated, ruined; tattered; to stop, to close; a demeaning, respectful term for my, mine, our.

丨鄉 my poor village.
自丨 self-ruined.
丨俗 our native customs.
丨壞 ruined; lost.
丨端太多 many delinquencies, great errors and incompetence.
甕丨漏 the jar leaks badly.
丨東 my master.

弊 **獘** *pi'* From *vile* and folded *hands* or *great*; the second form is unauthorized; occurs interchanged with its primitive.
Defeated; distressed, reduced to extremities; corrupt, vicious, tricky; troubles, mischiefs; deteriorated, as coin; worn out; my, mine.
作丨 to impose on, to hoodwink.
丨傢伙 what a bad business! or
丨咯 that's bad! (*Cantonese.*)
疲丨 worn out with fatigue.
舞丨 to deceive, to alter underhand.
揭丨 to point out deficiencies.
丨丨然 to go about, as a trader.
流丨太多 a continuous series of great troubles.

幣 *pi'* A single piece of silk; things sent as presents; wealth, riches, — of which fine gems, gold, and copper were formerly regarded as the three chief kinds; jade counters or tokens issued for coin by the Mongols.
丨鏟 an ancient token or coin shaped like a spade; it was issued by private persons.
丨帛 presents, usually of silk.
皮丨 fine furs.

斃 *pi'* From *death* and *spoiled.*
A violent death; to fall prostrate or be struck dead; to kill; quite dead.
淹丨 drowned.
倒丨 he fell dead.
因傷丨命 to lose one's life from a wound.
立丨杖下 thereupon died from the beating.

獘 *pi'* Very similar to the last.
To fall down suddenly, as if dead or fainting; to tumble down.
與犬犬丨 give it (the poison) to the dog, and he will fall dead.

貱 *pi'* To transfer, to pass on to another.
丨益 to augment; to benefit.
貤丨而來 to bring on in order.
丨移 to change or hand over to another.

韠 *pi'* A frame for keeping a bow in its right tension; a catch or bridge at the ends of the bow to retain the string, so that it cannot fly off.

祕 **秘** *pi'* From *divine* or *grain* and *must*; the second form is most used.
Divine, supernatural; secret, private; reticent, reserved; inspired, possessed; unaccountable; abstruse; scientific, above the common.
丨傳 privately handed down, as a recipe; secretly made known
丨密 undivulged, close.
丨書 secret archives; a mysterious or private book.
丨文 written in cypher; abstruse style.
隱丨 kept secret, not made known.
丨受神方 I privately received this infallible recipe.
妙丨 a great secret.
丨色 porcelain.

閟 *pi'* Like the last.
A closed door; to shut; to skulk, to hide; hidden, close, secret; spiritual.
深丨 occult, very close.
事丨 a secret affair.
丨匿 to abscond or keep out of the way.
丨愼無洩 be very careful to keep it quiet.
丨靈 to decline further visits of condolence, to shut the coffin.

毖 *pi'* Laborious, fatigued; to warn; admonitions; to distress, to be distressed; to guard against, to foresee; careful, heedful.
丨彼泉水 how the water bubbles out there!
無丨于恤 do not grieve with so much sorrow.
丨其後患 to prevent future trouble.
劼丨 diligent.

搠 *pi* To strike; to push away with the hand.

閉 *pi'* From *door* and the *hand* used to shut it.
To close a door; to exclude, to bar out; to screen, to shade; to store, to lay up; to stop, as a hole; obstructed, closed; the case of a Chinese lock.
丨經 obstruction of menses.
丨塞 stopped up.
幽丨數年 he has been secluded for many years.
禁丨 to prohibit.
丨門思過 stay at home and reflect on your misdeeds, as guilty officers are ordered to do.
丨目 to close the eyes.
瞞丨 to deceive; to throw dust in one's eyes.
丨月羞花之貌 her grace causes the moon to hide and the flowers to blush.
丨藏 stored up or laid by, as nature is in winter.
丨丨 full, plenty.
啓丨 spring and autumn or winter.
掩丨 to close, to hide; to screen.
丨關不通 to prevent communication by closing the pass.
丨門造車出門合轍 if you stay at home and make a carriage, when you go out you should follow its ruts; — be consistent at home and abroad.
予不敢丨于天降威用 I dare not restrain Heaven's majesty as seen in its inflictions.

蔽 *pi*ˋ From *plant* and *ruined*; it is interchanged with the last and its primitive.

Small plants, brushwood; delicate, small; to keep out of view, to repress; to decide firmly; decided; to shade, to screen; to include; to cut off, to prevent advance; obscured, dull.

雲丨月 clouds hide the moon.

蒙丨 to conceal from, as superiors.

一言以丨之 one account explained it all.

足以丨辜 it expiates his crime; to atone for guilt.

利慾昏丨 covetousness and lust beclouded his mind.

丨賢 to prevent the promotion of good men.

庇 *pi*ˋ From a *shelter* and to *compare* as the phonetic.

To shelter, to cover; to protect, as the gods do; to lodge; affording shade.

丨祐 divine aid; to countenance.

永丨 continual protection.

保丨 to give protection to.

托丨平安 to wish one full peace.

護丨 to defend against enemies.

藉丨康寧 may I live happily under your protection.

鼻 ˏ*pi* Composed of 自 *self* and 畀 to *grant*; it is the 209th radical of a few characters, all relating to the nose.

The nose, which the Chinese think is the part of an animal that is first formed; to bore the nose; nasal; the first, original.

丨孔 or 丨竅 the nostrils.

丨樑 the bridge of the nose.

丨準 the end of the nose.

丨涕 mucus from the nose.

丨界 the cartilage of the nose.

丨烟 snuff.

丨祖 the first ancestor of a family.

勾丨 or 鸚鵡丨 a Roman or crooked nose, *i. e.* a parrot's.

丨牛 to bore an ox's nose.

丨塞 the snuffles.

白丨子 a slippery fellow, a swindler.

坒 *pi*ˋ From 土 *earth* and 比 *even*, defined as being the leveling of the ground in making steps or ascents; now used as a primitive, the next having taken its place.

To compare or match; even shoulders, *i. e.* to go together as equals.

陛 *pi*ˋ From *place* and *step* as the phonetic.

To ascend high places; the steps to the throne; or the platform on which it stands; ascent to a palace or court.

丨下 under the steps, where officers stand to hear and report to the monarch, and hence to speak to those ministers came to mean your Majesty, in directly addressing him, *i. e.* we who are before the throne.

丨見 to have an audience.

丨殿 the audience-hall.

楓丨 the palace; the Emperor; your Majesty.

丨丨 regular and numerous, as a progeny.

人君如堂羣臣如丨 the prince is the hall, his ministers are the steps to it.

梐 *pi*ˋ A wooden palisade or stockade around a camp, somethink like a Maori *pah*.

周丨 a pen for prisoners.

蜌 *pi*ˋ An old name for long and narrow shell-fish like the razor-fish (*Solen*); a mussel found on the coast of Fuhkien dried and eaten; the large kind is also called 馬刀 or horse-knife, but several kinds of shells having similar shape, as the *Tellina*, *Mytilus*, *Anodonta*, &c., are included under this name; one sort, found in the Yangtsz', is six inches long.

海丨 dried mussels.

賁 *pi*ˋ *péi*ˋ From 貝 *precious* and 卉 *flowers*.

To adorn; variegated, as a parterre of flowers; elegant, brilliantly; the 22d diagram, which belongs to fire.

丨若草木 beautiful as trees and plants.

Read ˏ*păn*. Energetic, strenuous effort, as when serving the state at the head of troops.

Read ˏ*făn*. Great; a three-footed tortoise.

用宏玆丨 we shall thus enlarge our great inheritance.

備 俻 *pi*ˋ From 人 *man* and 葡 a *thing* in use; the contracted form is very common.

To prepare, to make ready; to provide for; to provide against; to retain; to fill, as an office; ready, prepared; sufficient; complete; entirely, all, wholly; sometimes it makes a form of the past tense.

準丨 to be ready for.

凡事齊丨了 every preparation has been made.

足丨 enough is done.

有丨無患 forethought prevents calamity.

丨悉纖微 he knows it all minutely.

丨考 to lay aside for investigation.

預丨急需 prepare what is most necessary.

君子不求全責丨 the princely man does not look for perfection.

丨歷安危 he knows both prosperity and misfortune.

泌 *pi*ˋ To gush forth, as a fountain; a rapid flow, like a torrent; a river in the southwest of Honan near Pi-yang hien 丨陽縣 which joins the River Han.

丨之洋洋 a rushing roaring torrent.

詖 *pi'* From *words* and *skin* as the phonetic.

To adulate, to flatter; to dispute; to beguile with telling only half the truth.

險丨私謁之心 a heart that tries to implicate another by secret insinuations.

丨辭知其所蔽 when one's words are partial, I know how [his ideas] are clouded.

丨辯 to argue for the wrong.

臂 *p'i'* *p'é'* From *flesh* and *ruler*.

The fore-arm, the cubit; also includes the whole limb; the shoulder or leg of an animal when butchered; the strength of the arm; to stretch out the arm with power.

手丨 the whole arm.

羊丨 a leg of mutton.

巨靈丨華 the great Spirit stretched out the Hwa mountains.

幫一丨之力 lend us a hand.

把丨而談 to seize one by the arm to talk with him; a button-holder.

攘丨 to bare the arms.

長丨 long arms; the Chinese speak of a country of such people, probably confounding them with the gibbon of Borneo.

In *Cantonese.* To decant.

丨到清 pour it off clear.

箄 *pi'* Not the same as ˏ箄 a creel.

A round withe or ring on which to place a boiler to keep it upright, called 鍋圈 the boiler ring.

輪丨 a wheel which cannot revolve.

鞴 **絥** *pi'* The first is a synonym of the second in its meaning of to harness a horse, to make him ready to carry his load; but the latter is also read *fuh*, denoting a rest in front of a carriage, which was anciently placed so as to allow the rider to lean forward.

丨韍 a partition box to contain arrows.

丨馬 to harness a horse.

丨驢 to saddle a donkey.

眡 *pi'* Also read *mih*.

To look straight ahead; looking angrily; humbled or feeling ashamed.

倦眼逾丨 if your eyes are tired you must look more earnestly.

奰 *pi'* Originally from 大 *great* under three 目 *eyes*.

Great and robust; to be elated, but not by drink; angry at.

內丨于中國 [the people are] angry at you in the Middle Kingdom, — and it reaches even to the demons' regions.

P'I.

Old sounds, p'i, p'ai, p'ei, p'it, p'ik, bit, *and* bat. *In Canton,* p'i *and* p'ei; — *in Swatow,* p'i, pi, p'úe, *and* pai; — *in Amoy,* p'i *and* pi; — *in Fuhchau,* p'i, pi, p't, *and* p'ie; — *in Shanghai,* p'i, bi, *and* pé; — *in Chifu,* p'i.

披 ˏ*p'i* ˏ*p'é* From *hand* and *skin* as the phonetic; like the next.

To open, to spread out; to unroll, as a scroll; to break, as clouds; to uncover; to rive; to throw on, as a cloak; to oppose; sleazy; disheveled.

丨簑 to throw on a rain-cloak.

丨髮 hair is disarranged, *i. e.* not braided.

丨開 to open, as by splitting.

丨甲 a cuirassier; the cavalry.

椅丨 a chair-cover; a tidy.

丨書 to look at a book; to make running comments.

丨星戴月 to cloak one's self with the stars, and wear the moon; — to travel by night.

丨展 to open out, as a map or letter.

丨拂 to wave, as a flag.

軍皆丨靡 the army was thoroughly demoralized.

丨肝瀝胆 I will open my liver and let the gall ooze out, — to prove my sincerity.

全副丨挂 a complete suit or outfit of clothes.

丨肩 a graduate's wide cape.

翍 ˏ*p'i* Used with the last.

To spread out, to expand, as wings; outspread wings.

皮刂 **剫** ˏ*p'i* From *knife* and *skin;* the second form is uncommon.

To peel, to pare off the skin; to trim with an ax; to divide into parts.

丨橙 to peel an orange.

丨手甲 to trim the nails.

丨削 to scrape or shave off.

丨篾 to split up splints.

噪丨 cracked open by the wind.

唔 **哇** ˏ*p'i* Both of these are unauthorized characters.

Dissatisfaction and contempt; begone, get out!

丨一發胡説 be off! you talk too vilely!

鈹 ˏ*p'i* A large needle or bodkin; a knife like a poniard or bowie-knife.

丨針 a sail needle.

長丨都尉 guards who wear swords.

旇 ˏ*p'i* The fluttering of banners in the wind is 旌旗丨靡 alluding to the difficulty of reading their inscriptions.

批 撓 p'i — From *hand* and to *compare*, or *clear;* the second form is the oldest and least used.
To cuff with the back of the hand; to push from one; to pare, to peel; to revise, to criticise; to assist; to reply officially to an inferior; to give a decision or order to subordinates; to post a judgment, as is done at the door of the office; notice or report of a case; to lease; a charter-party, a lease; a gloss, a criticism.
丨准 to assent to a petition.
丨回 an official reply, as to a petition.
丨示 to publish a case.
硃丨 notes in red ink.
丨斷 to finally decide a case.
丨頭 a lease fee of a month's rent in advance. (*Cantonese.*)
丨單 a lease of a house.
我丨中你 I can guess what you've been at.
領丨 to take a lease of.
丨明 to comment on.
立丨 to make a contract.
丨評 criticisms; to censure.
手丨其頰 slapped him on the cheeks.
旁丨 side notes; apostills.
丨駁 to reverse the decision of a lower court.

紕 p'i — Silk tassels or fringes put on flags; a scolloped border; sleazy silk; silk that is spoiled or rotted.
丨繆 faulty; deficient, as a character.

秛 p'i — The rent on land paid in kind by dividing the crop with the landlord; an income from fields; one says, the culms of grain.

砒 磇 p'i — An ore of arsenic.
丨礵 realgar or the red sulphuret of arsenic; it is applied to ulcers.
丨信 arsenic.

諀 p'i — Wrong, mistaken; erroneous.

屄 p'i — From *body* and *cavity.*
The vagina.
婦丨 the vulva or female organs.

枇 p'i — From *wood* and *equal;* occurs interchanged with 篦 a fine comb.
A fruit, the *pibo* or *biwa* 丨杷 the Chinese medlar (*Eriobotrya japonica*), called loquat 蘆橘 at Canton; a prong or fork to lift sacrificial victims out of the boiler.
丨杷桶 a barrel, which a little resembles this fruit. (*Cantonese.*)

琵 p'i — A musical instrument, the 丨琶 Chinese guitar or viol; its shape often serves for an illustration.
丨琶精 a louse, from its shape.
丨琶魦 a species of ray. (*Rhina ancylostoma.*)
丨琶 (used for 批把) to push and pull, as when thrumming the guitar.
丨琶別抱 [she now plays] her viol on the other arm; — said of a widow married again.

毘 毗 毘 p'i — From 囟 the *fontanelle* and 比 *like*, and meant originally the navel; the second forms are altered from it, and in common use.
Contiguous, as fields; kind, liberal; substantial; grieved; to assist; manifest.
丨連 conterminous.
犀丨 a girdle of rhinoceros hide.
夸丨 flattering, cringing; supple, pliant, as in making obeisances.
丨陵 an old name of Chang-cheu fu in the the south of Kiangsu.
丨舍闍 a Budhist term for *pisacha*, a class of vampire demons.
丨沙門 (*i. e.* Wesamuna or Vaisramana,) a king of demons, who has a yellow color, and guards the north; he is worshiped as the god of wealth in many parts of China.

麰 p'i — Broken wheat boiled and dried is 丨黎; it is used for provisions on a journey.

芘 p'i — Interchanged with the next.
A thorny kind of malvaceous plant, the 丨芣 or 莜 which may be allied to the *Sida;* to shade, to protect.

蚍 p'i — The moth in furs.
丨蜉 a sort of large black ant; a reddish flower like the *Hibiscus*, for which the last is better.

螕 p'i — Sometimes used for the last.
A tick or louse, called 牛丨 which infests cattle; the seeds of the castor-oil plant are likened to it.
蝦丨 shrimp's eggs or young.

皮 p'i — Derived from 又 the *hand* and 尸 *body* contracted above it; it is the 107th radical of a natural group of characters denoting the colors and uses of skins.
The skin on the body, or when undressed; leather; furs; a surface; bark, peel; a cover, a wrapper; the case around goods, the tare; a quartering in gambling; coated; reputation, character; to cover, as skin does.
丨膚 the skin.
丨貨 or 丨草 furs.
丨板 the skin of a fur.
不顧面丨 regardless of one's good name.
醃丨店 a tanner's shop.
好丨色 a clear complexion.
剝丨 to flay; to unwrap a case.
除丨 not including the case.
莊丨信 wily, seductive; pandering to another's whims.
丨統 a fur garment without a lining.
頑丨 regardless of reproof.
射不主丨 he did not hit the target.
丨油 tallow from the tallow tree.
丨蛋 eggs coated with lime.

邊丨之地 the extreme end, the frontier.

脫去丨囊 he has shuffled off this skin bag — or mortal coil.

重丨 a blunt disposition.

大丨臉 a great reputation.

丨室 region of the heart.

丨相 the external air, dress, or style.

死丨賴臉 a dead-skin face; *i. e.* brazen-faced effrontery.

疲 ˬp'i From *sickness* and *skin* as the phonetic.

Lassitude, fatigue; loss of strength.

丨倦 tired out.

丨難缺 wearisome and difficult duties, said of an official post.

縱愧丨弊 although we are ashamed at our weakness.

丨馬 a jaded horse.

丨民 an exhausted population.

丨玩 remiss, obstinate; lazy and reckless, as in discharging official duties.

脾 ˬp'i The spleen, which lying near the stomach, assists to digest the food, and is supposed to open into the heart; it belongs to earth; the digestion; the temper; the whimsies of a character; to stop.

丨胃 the stomach.

丨虛 languid, feeble.

蜜丨 cells of a bee's comb.

丨氣 the ruling desire; the temper, disposition.

淸丨理胃 to clear the stomach, as by an emetic.

膍 ˬp'i Used for the last.

The manyplus or stomach of a ruminant animal; the navel in man, which is supposed to communicate through the mammæ; substantial, important.

丨析 tripe.

丨胵 entrails of birds; the latter character refers to the gizzard particularly.

貔 ˬp'i A savage feline beast or 丨貅 resembling a leopard, referred to Liaotung; it is sometimes pictured on flags; the ground color is nearly white, and therefore others describe it as like the next.

如虎如丨 like tigers and leopards.

獻其丨皮 presenting his leopard skins.

帳擁丨貅百萬兵 gather the legions of your fierce soldiers.

羆 ˬp'i From 罷 *fixed* contracted and 熊 *a bear*.

A species of bear spotted white and black, found in olden times in northern China, and now driven into the mountain ranges of Sz'ch'uen and Koko-nor; it is described as having a long head, is high on its legs, and so strong as to pull up trees; there are the yellow spotted and red spotted kinds with white lines; it is fiercer than the bear. This animal is probably the *Ailuropus melanoleucus* of David, an animal akin to an *Ursus*, recently found in the mountains of Sz'ch'uen; it has black head and feet, and the body is spotted white and black.

維熊維丨男子之祥 [dreams of] brown and spotted bears are auspicious of sons.

舟人之子熊丨是裘 the sons of boatmen wear robes of the mottled bear.

崥 ˬp'i Hilly.

丨嵃 a rough country.

峽丨 the base of a hill, or its foundation; — a simile for security.

裨 ˬp'i, péi˒ Small, said of caps or mitres; inferior; beneficial; to assist, to supply; to reinforce, to be useful; to give over to; to permit, to enable.

大有丨益 of great advantage.

丨輔 to second, to support.

丨將 an assistant or brigadier-general.

丨附 to grant to.

丨冕 a little crown.

有丨政治者 what aids in the government.

陴 ˬp'i A parapet with embrasures; to add a breastwork, or build a wall higher.

城丨 the battlements.

登丨 to mount the walls.

守丨 one who guards the walls.

埤 ˬp'i Like the last.

A low wall; a plat of a hundred *meu;* liberal, generous in feeling; to add to, to augment; to be attached to.

丨垷 a parapet.

丨海環之 shallow seas surround — the island.

政事一丨益我 in managing the affairs of the state, all adds to my advantage.

掖垣竹丨梧十尋 near the low wall was a bamboo hedge and gigantic *wu-tung* trees.

Read *péi*˒ A low, damp place.

栢不生丨 firs do not grow in low marshy lands.

鼙 ˬp'i A drum used on horseback, and beaten in battle near the general; to drum.

丨舞 drum used by mummers.

征丨動地 the rolling drums made the earth itself move.

媲 p'i˒ To pair, to match; equal, paired, matched.

丨美 the two are alike pretty.

郫 ˬp'i An old town, 丨邵 in the Tsin 晋 state, somewhere in the southwest of Shansi.

丨縣 a district in Sz'ch'uen lying north of the capital.

丨筒酒 spirits from this district which are put up in bamboos.

骳 骴 ₍p'i Pliant, limber; having no vigor.
丨 弱 weak.
身 體 丨 my body has no strength.

In *Cantonese*. To lean against; to crowd, to press upon.
丨² 丨² 吓 it is rather crowding upon one.
丨² 落 地 pushed it to the ground.

ʿ骳 p'i Distorted and twisted; said of a limb.
其 文 訛 丨 his style is obscure and involved.

ʿ仳 p'i To take leave of; ugly.
有 女 丨 離 a woman made to leave her husband.
丨 倠 plain, as a woman.

ʿ㧗 p'i A crack in wood; to split, as wood does in dry weather.
竹 子 丨 了 the bamboo has split.

ʿ痞 p'i A stoppage or constipation; a stitch in the side, palpitation or sudden fainting.
丨 滿 indigestion.
丨 積 marasmus, general debility.
丨 塊 a swelling from obstructed bowels.
丨 匪 rebels or marauders who interfere with the communication; obstructives, disturbers.
害 錢 丨 one who thinks only of gain; a miser.

ʿ庀 p'i To regulate; to prepare for presentation or for use; to hand up.

ʿ圮 p'i From *earth* and *self*; it looks very similar to ₍i 圯 a bridge.
A bank broken in; destroyed, subverted, as from some internal cause; prostrated, as a wall.
傾 丨 overthrown; tumbled down, as a ruined wall.
丨 毀 spent lavishly; ruined.
方 命 丨 族 he resisted my orders in opposition to the feelings of the people.

ʿ狴 p'i Used with the next.
A fierce animal, the 丨 犴 allied probably to the tapir; it is applied to a prison, and its savage looking head is drawn over the doors of prisons.

ʿ陛 p'i Superseded by the last.
A place for confining prisoners; a lockup.

ʿ嚭 p'i Great; name of a high officer in the Wu 吳 state, mentioned in history.

譬 p'iʾ From *words* and *chief*.
To compare, to illustrate; to make a thing understood; a simile, a comparison, a parable; if, suppose.
丨 喻 or 丨 如 for instance.
取 丨 不 遠 the comparison is not far-fetched.
丨 若 if; like as.
丨 誠 善 言 my warnings are good.
丨 彼 舟 流 I am like a boat adrift.
丨 不 得 incomparable.
未 丨 I do not fully understand it.

屁 䊻 p'iʾ The second and obsolete form indicates the meaning more than the first.
To break wind.
放 丨 to fart.
放 丨 胡 說 what stuff he talks; said in contempt.
丨 股 the buttocks.

PIAO.

Old sounds, pio *and* pot. *In Canton*, piu; — *in Swatow*, piò *and* p'iò; — *in Amoy*, piao *and* p'iao; — *in Fuhchau*, piu; — *in Shanghai*, pio; — *in Chifu*, piao.

標 ₍piao From *wood* and *soaring*; it is interchanged with its primitive.
The topmost branch, the opposite of the root; a signal, a flag or banner, used as a marking-flag; the troops under one banner, a corps; a spear; a signboard, ticket, or card; a warrant; to make a signal; to put up a notice; to write, to inscribe in; to appear, to exhibit; to rise; best, fine, beautiful.
以 爲 丨 準 to serve as an aim or example.
丨 旗 to exhibit, or raise a flag.
插 丨 to put out a signal.
丨 起 張 字 to put up a notice.
丨 麵 the finest flour.
丨 緻 very pretty, attractive.
龍 榜 丨 名 to have one's name in the list of graduates.
互 相 丨 榜 to help each other; log-rolling.
袖 丨 a stiletto, a dagger.
發 丨 to swagger, to bully, to act the swashbuckler.
打 丨 to sell the tickets.
奪 丨 to get the highest prize.
開 丨 to draw the lottery.
撫 丨 the governor's flag; his body-guard, his troops.
丨 紀 to record.

髟 ₍piao From 長 *long* and 彡 *pelage*; it forms the 190th radical of characters relating to human hair.
Locks hanging down; bushy hair.
垂 丨 flowing locks; — *met.* a damsel.
斑 鬢 丨 丨 long and grisly locks.

麃 ˏpiao From 鹿 *deer* and 火 *fire*, or sparks flying about.

Described as a species of one horned deer or unicorn, but is probably the ˏp'ao 麅 or spotted deer; to hoe up weeds; feathers changing color, as in winter.

駟介丨丨 the mailed war-horses looked so martial.

緜緜其丨 pulling up the many weeds.

穮 ˏpiao Used with the last in the sense of weeding.

To hoe fields, to clear them of weeds.

Read ˏpao. Empty grain, unfilled seeds.

儦 ˏpiao People passing and repassing; a group, a company.

行人丨丨 the people are going and coming in crowds.

猋 ˏpiao *Three dogs* scampering here and there; spiral, whirling.

丨風暴雨 a violent storm of wind and rain.

飈 颮 ˏpiao More correct forms of the last.

A strong whirlwind.

金丨忽起 a violent norther suddenly arose.

冬丨撼壁 the wintry gust shook the wall.

Read p'oh, A crowd of things.

丨丨紛紛 said of a thick flight of arrows, as at a battue.

丨丨 fluttering, falling down, as a wounded bird.

臕 ˏpiao Fat, gross; very corpulent.

肥丨 obese.

厚丨 thick fat, layers of fat.

長丨 a long strip of fat; to gain flesh.

脂丨 very plump; in good case.

掉丨 and 上丨 to fall off in flesh, and to flesh up.

幖 ˏpiao A streamer of silk tied to the top of the staff; a pennant above a flag.

鑣 ˏpiao An ornamented bit; the trappings on a bridle.

欲扣丨 he reined in his bridle.

駟馳之丨丨 a team of fat horses.

瀌 ˏpiao Sleet and rain falling fast.

雨雪丨丨見晛曰消 the snow falls abundantly, but when it feels the sun it will melt.

滮 ˏpiao Water flowing.

丨池北流 the rippling pond ran to the north.

丨池 a noted pool in Shensi.

表 ˋpiao From 衣 *dress* and 毛 *hair* contracted, because skins are worn with the hair outside; occurs used for ˏ標 a signal.

The upper garments; exterior, outer; the borders; the carriage of a person; an external manifestation; to make known; a guide, a signal; statement presented to emperor; a permit or manifest.

丨親 relatives of a different surname from one's own.

一丨人才 altogether he looks the clever man.

丨裏 coat and lining; outside and inside.

丨裏如一 his heart and hand are the same; wholly sincere.

丨兄弟 maternal cousins.

丨台 or 老丨 a term of address, stranger! Sir.

時辰丨 a watch.

丨出 or 丨彰 to make known; to show through, — as at a hole.

旌丨建坊 let an honorary gateway be erected to show his merit.

丨明白 represented it plainly.

丨丨者 noted people; renowned personages.

丨章 a memorial; a prayer burned before an idol.

丨奏朝廷 to send a minute or memorial to the throne.

丨異 remarkable beyond others.

華丨形 a high peak; — a geomantic term.

聽我丨一丨 permit me to make a statement of it.

必丨而出之 it will surely come to light at last.

畧丨寸心 I now disclose my earnest feelings.

不丨 not to speak of it any further, as in a narrative.

婊 ˋpiao A prostitute.

丨子 or 老丨 a public woman.

丨子養的 you son of a whore!

嶠 ˋpiao A peak rising high above others on the ridge.

稍雲冠其丨 the light cloud capped the high peak.

覞 ˋpiao To see carefully, to examine.

丨了一眼 I have taken a look at it.

俵 ˋpiao To distribute.

丨散 dispersed, scattered.

丨給 to give and send away, as to beggars.

褾 ˋpiao A neckcloth, a kind of comforter or wrapper; to mount maps or scrolls; to paste on; to line, as a picture.

丨畫舖 a picture-framer's shop.

丨褙 to paste paper together.

丨糊匠 one who papers rooms.

藨 ˋpiao A kind of sedge grass, of which mats for awnings and sandals can be made; it is perhaps allied to a *Scirpus*.

P'IAO.

Old sounds, p'io, p'ot, bio, *and* bot. *In Canton*, p'iu ; — *in Swatow*, p'iò, p'ie, *and* pie ; — *in Amoy*, p'iao *and* piao ; — *in Fuhchau*, p'iu *and* p'éu ; — *in Shanghai*, p'io ; — *in Chifu*, p'iao.

飄 ˓p'iao From *wind* and *soaring*; interchanged with the next.

A spiral gust of wind; noise of the wind; swayed, whirled or rocked by the wind; a whirlwind; graceful, easy manner, like a fairy; projecting, as eaves.

丨蕩 to rock, as a boat; rolling, unfixed.

其爲丨風 he is like a violent wind.

丨零 leaves fallen from the trees; deserted, roaming, as a stranger.

丨風弗弗 the wind is very blustering.

丨僻地方 a deserted spot.

風丨 blown about by the wind.

輕丨 of no great weight; light, as a gauze dress.

丨落 blown down.

丨丨若仙 her motion is flowing as a fairy's.

丨丨乎有凌雲之氣 his spirit rose like a floating cloud.

丨動 moved; fluttering, as a flag.

丨潑大雨 it rained excessively.

漂 ˓p'iao Similar to and used with the last.

To float; to drift; to be moved, as by the waves; cold, bleak.

丨泊江湖 to travel over all the country.

丨海 or 丨洋 to voyage; to come over the seas.

丨洋布 white shirtings.

風雨所丨搖 tossed about in the wind and rain, as a nest.

丨流浪子 a floating wave; — *i. e.* a dissipated vagabond.

丨丨 soaring high.

Read *p'iao*˒ To bleach.

丨白夏布 to whiten grass-cloth.

丨晒 to bleach in the sun.

丨去顏色 to take out the color.

丨得亮 bleached very white.

鷅 ˓p'iao A bird molting.

白丨 a sea-bird resembling the tern, which follows the ebb and flow of the tide.

鷗丨 a bird skimming over the water.

魒 ˓p'iao Name of a god who dwells in one of the stars of Ursa Major.

嘌 ˓p'iao A carriage rushing wildly along; lawless, irregular.

丨唱 to sing songs.

匪車丨兮 not the lawless rushing of a car.

鏢 ˓p'iao From *metal* and *to soar*; it is sometimes wrongly used for ˓表 a watch.

The ornamented mouth of a scabbard, covered with copper; the point of a sword.

丨鎗 an iron-pointed spear.

嫖 ˓p'iao Light, trifling; flirting with, wanton; lewd; a man given to lewdness, to follow women.

丨客 a fornicator.

好˒丨 lecherous.

丨舍 a bagnio.

丨窰子 a whoremonger.

瓢 ˓p'iao A calabash; or a drinking vessel made from it; a gourd ladle.

椰丨 a cocoa-nut dipper.

一丨飲 I have only a gourdful to drink.

捧丨的命 [you will be reduced] to the fate of holding a dipper, — if you are so idle.

螵 ˓p'iao A chrysalis.

桑丨蛸 a chrysalis having a woolly envelop, like that of the mantis.

海丨蛸 a cuttle-fish bone.

薸 ˓p'iao From *plants* and *floating* as the phonetic.

Small water-plants, like the *Lemna* or *Pistia*, floating on fish-ponds.

浮丨 duckweed.

丨萍 water moss.

瞟 ˓p'iao To look askance or crosseyed; one eye diseased or gone; small eyes.

丨眇 to see indistinctly.

膘 ˓p'iao The flanks of a bullock or other quadruped.

丨肥 fat sides.

摽 ˓p'iao Interchanged with ˓piao 標 to *signalize*.

To lay the hand on the heart; to strike, to knock down; to fall, to throw down; to heave away, to push off; the point of a sword.

丨旗 to signalize with a flag.

丨出門外 show him out of the door.

丨落底下 throw it down.

丨有梅 the plums have fallen.

寤辟有丨 awaking I beat my breast with pain.

Read ˓*piao*. Defined by some to issue a public notice; to record.

縹 ˓p'iao Blue or greenish silk; an azure or cerulean color; a limpid tint; a semi-transparent hue.

丨丨 buoyant; rising and sailing away like a phœnix.

碧丨 clear topaz color.

翠丨 a pure leek green.

丨白 a clear white.

丨渺 floating away, like a balloon; vague and doubtful.

虛無丨渺間 soared away into the vast empyrean.

醥 ˛p'iao Clear limpid spirits.

殍 莩 'p'iao From *bad* or *grass* and to *hatch*.
To die of hunger; trees or shrubs shriveled and dying
野有餓丨 the famished dead lay in the wilderness.

皫 'p'iao Used with ˛漂 when meaning to bleach.
To molt; to change color, as feathers do when the bird molts; to whiten.
鳥丨色 when the birds are molting, — don't eat them.

票 p'iao' From 示 to *manifest* and 西 *west*, but originally composed of 火 *fire* below a character meaning to *remove*; interchanged with ˛標 a signal.

To rise swiftly like fire; to make a signal with fire; scintillating, light, waving; a mittimus, a warrant; a bill; a ticket; a certificate; an evidence of authority; occurs in the sense of a job or transaction.
出丨 to issue an official summons, as a 傳丨 or subpœna, a 差丨 policeman's warrant, or other kind of orders.
當丨 pawn-tickets.
錢丨 or 丨子 a bank-bill.
投丨 to give in tenders.
丨摺 a wallet, a pocket-book.
丨金 a bribe to policemen.
轉丨 to renew a pawn-ticket.
船牌丨 a ship's clearance.
火丨 a dispatch sent in great haste.
鈔丨局 an exchange bank.
發丨 to issue bills; to send a warrant.
串丨 to exchange bank-bills for other bills, and not for cash.
路丨 a passport; a pass to cross the lines.
匯丨 a draft for money.
會丨 to transact banking business.

剽 p'iao' A small bell which emits an acute sound; to strike, to pierce, to stab; to puncture; to rob; to cut off; swift, alert.
丨鎗 a spear.
丨掠 to rob and kill.
輕丨 or 丨疾 nimble, like soldiers.

勡 p'iao' Like the last.
To seize by violence, to rob; to plunder or take forcibly.

影 p'iao' To paint, to adorn, to ornament.
丨丨 having tassels, ornaments.

僄 p'iao' Light, airy; volatile, giddy; careless of propriety.
丨狡 guileful, rude, artful.
怠慢丨桀 impertinent and proud.
烟丨而上升 the smoke floats away into the sky.

瞟 p'iao' To dry things in the sun.
丨曝 to dry crisp.

驃 p'iao' A fleet and brave horse; a white tailed horse or cream-colored.
丨騎 a cavalry officer.
丨勇 a valiant horseman.
一丨軍殺出 a body of horse suddenly rushed out.
丨國 a name given in the T'ang dynasty to the eastern part of Burmah.

鰾 p'iao' The air-bladder of fishes; the part from which glue is made.
丨膠 fish-glue.
魚丨 the slime on eels and other fishes.

PIEH.

Old sounds, pit *and* bit. *In Canton*, pit; — *in Swatow*, pit, piét, *and* pi; — *in Amoy*, piat *and* p'iat; — *in Fuhchau*, pék; — *in Shanghai*, pih *and* bih; — *in Chifu*, pié.

別 ˛pieh From 刀 *knife* and 另 *besides*, but the last is here a contraction of ‹*kwa* 冎 to scrape bones clean.
To separate, to divide; to part, to distinguish; to leave, to go off, to recede from; different, another; unlike; a separation, a parting; besides, moreover.
分丨是非 to discriminate the merits of the case.
告丨 to announce one's leaving.
丨後 after we parted.
送丨 to see one to his chair.
丨的 another; different.
丨人 another man.
丨話 said something else.
辯丨 to discuss the points of a question.
男女有丨 the sexes are separated by proprieties.
小丨 a short absence.
隔丨日久 we have long been separated.
丨下毒手 in some other way he will do great injury.
無區丨 no great difference.
丨業 to leave office or literary pursuits.
識丨字先生 a superficial scholar, one who only knows a character to be some other one. (*Shanghai.*)
丨有天地 here is quite another sort of life.
丨向 to alter one's views.
丨而稱之 to speak of them separately.

形具雖同情性各 丨 though they all look much alike, their qualities (or dispositions) are much unlike.

丨 丨 的 but few such, unique.

In *Pekingese*. A negative, not, do not; equivalent to a contraction of 不要; as 你 丨 管我 don't interfere with me.

狠 丨 致 very rare; there are few of this kind.

丨 生氣 don't get angry.

丨 晒着 don't stand in the sun.

丨 跟來 don't follow me.

諳 *pieh* From *words* and to *divide* as the phonetic.

To discriminate cause and effect; to analyze a thing to seek its origin; to search out the hidden.

丨 地理陰陽 to scan the luck of a place, and learn its open and secret things.

儆 *pié* Ordinary, as 丨 偞, denoting that one's garments are neither very fine, nor yet despicable or shabby.

澂 *pié* Name of a great mart which formerly lay north of Mienyang cheu 沔陽州 in the south of Hupeh, not far from the Yangtsz' River; Hankow has since superseded it.

憋 **憋** *pié* A hasty temper; vicious, irascible; sad, mournful.

丨 性 nervous, hasty.

惡 丨 wicked.

丨 腸狗態 an irritable temper and snappish manner.

丨 忸 vexed, annoyed; unwilling to do.

丨 悶 melancholy, mournful.

瘷 *pié* An ulcer or tumor which has begun to suppurate.

溺 丨 子 a urinal.

丨 着一肚子委曲 to cherish one's griefs in silence. (*Pekingese*.)

拯 *pi* To strike or knock down, as in play; to brush away.

跡 *pi* To kick at as in playing football, or in the game of kicking iron balls.

丨 蹴 to kick, as at a ball.

珌 *pi* A glittering gem on a sword of state; an ornament on the end of the sheath.

瑒琫瑒 丨 a baton and its base; seen in the hands of idols.

鼈 **鱉** *pié* From *toad* or *fish* and 敝 to *hobble* contracted, alluding to its gait on land.

A turtle, which the Chinese suppose hears with its eyes; also called 團魚 the lump-fish; a term for all marine Cheloniæ, but seems particularly to denote those with smooth shells like the *Emys*.

馬 丨 a bloodsucker.

土 丨 a brown, six-legged insect, about an inch long, resembling the sow-bug.

大沙 丨 a sea turtle.

丨 人 fishermen.

丨 星 constel. of Corona Australis.

將鰕釣 丨 use a shrimp to hook a turtle; give him a present to get his good-will.

酒 丨 a wine-bottle, flat and shaped like a palmer's flask.

蕨 丨 the unopened fronds of brake.

丨 甲 shell of an *Emys*.

納 丨 a turtle without feet and unable to retract its head; perhaps the diodon is really meant.

木 丨 子 seeds of a sort of squash (*Muricia cochinchinensis*), used medicinally.

鷩 *pi* A species of pheasant called 丨 雉, which is a variety of the golden pheasant, but smaller in size; it is said to like to see itself in the water; other names are 錦鷄 variegated fowl, 金鷄 golden fowl, and 采鷄 the adorned fowl.

丨 冕 a kind of ancient crown with these birds drawn on it, because they were plucky.

癟 *pi* *pieh* Feeble and unable to fly; shriveled, blasted, as grain; empty, limp, as a dry hose; dried up, for which the next is better.

一層 丨 皮 nothing but a skin.

乾 丨 dried and withered.

屄 丨 distorted, not straight.

丨 下去 emptied, as a bag.

丨 嘴子 one who has no teeth, and his cheeks have fallen in.

晡 *pieh* To dry in the sun; applied to fruits and vegetables.

乾 丨 葡萄 dried grapes, raisins.

白菜晒乾 丨 了 the cabbages are dried enough.

縪 *pi* The seams or fringe on a man's cap; a pad for the knees; to stop; a badge or ribbon tied to the 圭 or jade batons of office carried by princes.

P'IEH.

Old sound pit. *In Canton*, p'it; — *in Swatow*, bún *and* púa; — *in Amoy*, p'iat; — *in Fuhchau*, p'iek; — *in Shanghai*, p'ih; — *in Chifu*, p'ie.

擎, 撇, p'ieh } To tap, to strike; to brush off, to wipe; to skim off; to divide; to lead; gently, somewhat; a down-stroke or dash to the left in writing; in *rhetoric*, the figure of preterition, or pretending to pass over; a classifier of mustaches.
兩丨鬍子 mustache with points.
丨雨入來 a dash of rain drove in, as at the window.
丨開 to set aside, to push away, to end a matter.
做事丨脫 do things promptly.
丨回馬頭 to turn the horse's head.
丨淸 to leave off, as smoking.
一丨一捺 one dash to the left, one to the right.

丿, p'ieh The original form of the last, exhibiting a stroke to the left in penmanship; it is employed as the 4th radical of a few common characters.

Read *i'* To reach down to the ground.

嫳, p'ieh To pare off; to cut.
一刀丨斷 cleave them apart at one blow of the sword; *met.* settle the thing at once.

瞥, p'ieh To look at slightly, to glance at; a nictitating membrane.
丨見 just had a sight of it.
丨觀 a momentary view of.
丨眼 a hasty look at.
一丨之時 a moment of time.

潎, p'ieh To sport in the water; billowy; pure; to beat silk in the water.
丨洌 light and brisk, like dancing ripples.

蹩, p'ieh Lame, halt, hobbling; to lean or walk on one foot; club-footed.
丨躠 to limp, as in walking; others say to go round and round.

蟞, p'ieh A species of large ant, the 丨蛶 of a reddish black hue.
珠丨 a newt or similar small amphibia.
丨蚨 a small species of butterfly.

嫳, p'ieh To be soon angry; light, testy.
丨怒 irritated.
丨輕 foolish, light-headed.

甓, p'ieh An unauthorized character.
In *Pekingese*. A kind of bottle, with a large belly and long neck, used to hold spirits; it is sometimes made of paper, but usually of pewter or porcelain.

PIEN.

Old sounds, pien, bien, pin, *and* bin. *In Canton*, pin; — *in Swatow*, pien, pⁿi, *and* p'ien; — *in Amoy*, pian *and* p'ian; — *in Fuhchau*, pieng; — *in Shanghai*, piⁿ *and* biⁿ; — *in Chifu*, pien.

邊, 边, pien } From to *go* and obscurely *seen*; the contracted form is common.
A bank between fields; an edge, a margin; on the border or side; a place; a boundary.
丨疆 the frontier.
丨外 beyond the frontier.
丨戍 at a frontier post.
丨側 or 旁丨 on the side.
丨坐 to sit at the side.
丨欄 a raised edge; a rim.
花丨 an embroidered or worked border.
花丨銀 a milled dollar.
天丨 the horizon.
那丨兒 that side, there.
北丨 on the north side.
鑲丨 an inlaid or veneered border.
身丨 at one's side; hence 身丨人 a companion, a concubine.
刮响丨 to scrape reeds to make hummers for a kite.
半丨面 a profile face.
裏丨 inside; the inner face of.
丨套 the side mule in a cart.

In *Cantonese*. A distributive particle; where? which.
丨得至好 which is the best?
丨一處 in what place?
丨得來 where did you get this?
無去丨處 don't go away; I have not been anywhere.
丨省 which province?

籩, pien A flat basket of fine splints made like a dish with a rim, to contain fruits offered in worship.
丨人 the eunuch who brings in this basket of fruit.
丨豆有踐 the baskets and trenchers stand in rows.

㣐, pien The body bent; squirming or awry in any way.
丨僊而舞 whirling and making antics, as mummers do.

編 From *silk* and *flat* as the phonetic.
ˏpien To connect with a cord; a ligature; a line to join bamboo tablets together; to arrange, as when preparing a book; to compose; to twist, to plait; records, books.

簡 丨 to edit a book.

丨 年 annals, year-books, annual registers.

丨 入 to be enrolled; to enlist.

丨 修 a reviser of books; — the lowest rank of the Hanlin.

丨 列 字 號 to arrange marks or letters in order.

丨 髮 to braid the hair.

丨 次 to dispose things in a series.

丨 愁 to brood over one's griefs.

丨 連 to continue, to piece on.

韋 丨 三 絕 three of the skin tablets were worn out.

In *Pekingese*, apparently substituted for 騙ˀ by change of tone. To deceive.

瞎 丨 just a blind's man's story; it is all false.

丨 造 謠 言 to trump up a story.

蝙 From *insect* and *flat*.
ˏpien The bat 丨 蝠, also called 仙 鼠 the fairy rat, 飛 鼠 flying mouse, 天 鼠 sky mouse, and many other names.

鞭 / 夋 From a *hide* and *convenient*; the old form, composed of 入 to *enter* and 支 a *stroke*, is more ideographic.
ˏpien A whip; a lash; a cut or stroke of a whip; to flog; an iron cudgel; penis of a horse.

執 丨 之 事 it belongs to the whip; — *i. e.* an inferior business.

丨 撻 or 丨 笞 or 丨 背 to chastise, to whip with a rattan.

丨 杆 a walking-stick; a whipstalk.

籐 丨 a rattan scourge.

鐵 丨 an iron bludgeon.

執 丨 從 事 to drive a thing through, to obey summarily.

一 丨 殘 照 whip up, the light is failing.

馬 丨 or 丨 子 a horsewhip.

丨 長 莫 及 that lash won't reach him, though it is long.

恐 着 先 丨 I am afraid he will get ahead of me.

箯 A bamboo sledge or car for
ˏpien conveying earth.

鯿 The bream (*Abramis bramula*), of which one or two
ˏpien species are much reared at Canton; the name includes all broad fishes of the carp family.

思 不 出 手 鮒 丨 I never expected to get a fine bream; a fish by this name is found in the River Han, which sometimes weighs 20 catties.

壁 丨 燈 a bream-shaped lantern.

砭 A stone probe, used to puncture sores.
ˏpien 針 丨 acupuncture needles; to probe.

丨 灸 to puncture and cauterize.

胼 The hard skin on a laboring man's hands or feet; loose
ˏpien skin over a callosity; callous, hard.

丨 手 胝 足 horny hands and tough feet.

扁 From 戶 *door* and 冊 *slips*.
ˋpien A tablet hung over doors by graduates, to denote their rank; flat, thin; to flatten, to crush flat; low.

上 丨 to put up a tablet.

挑 丨 擔 shoulder the flat stick, to turn huckster and peddle.

有 丨 斯 石 how thin is this slab of stone.

蹍 丨 了 to press flat under foot.

壓 丨 to flatten, as a dried fig.

Read ˏpʻien, and used for 艑 A skiff.

駕 一 葉 之 丨 舟 to sail away in a yawl no bigger than a leaf.

匾 Like the last.
ˋpien Flat, like a plate; a slice; a board with an inscription.

掛 一 塊 丨 to put up a tablet — over a door.

丨 額 or 牌 丨 a votive tablet.

惼 From *heart* and *flat*; interchanged with the next.
ˋpien Narrow-minded; hasty, petulant.

丨 急 impertinent, irascible.

褊 From *dress* and *flat*; used with the last.
ˋpien Cramped, contracted, narrow; small, petty; straitened, as a territory.

局 量 丨 窄 his mind is crabbed and ignorant.

丨 小 mean, scrimped.

丨 心 a craven, timid mind.

丨 陋 low-lived and contracted.

丨 淺 limited, petty, as views.

丨 僻 之 室 a little side house or room.

碥 To step on a horse-block when getting into a carriage.
ˋpien 燕 子 丨 a dangerous rapid in the Han River near King-mǎn.

糄 To parch paddy in order to
ˋpien get out the kernel.

萹 An herb found in Chihli, the 丨 蓄 or 丨 竹, having
ˋpien leaves like the oleander, with small white flowers in the axils of the leaves; it runs over the ground, and the young leaves are boiled as greens; it is the *Polygonum hydropiper*, or an allied species, and known as 竹 葉 菜 bamboo-leaf greens.

藊 / 稨 A trailing bean (*Phaseolus lablab*), also written 扁 荳; the seeds are like Lima
ˋpien beans in shape, and considered as one of the best kinds; the second form is seldom used.

ˎ貶 From *precious* and *wanting*.
ˎpien To censure, to detract, to disparage; to diminish, to abate; to dismiss, to cashier.

丨下 or 丨謫 to degrade, to humble, as an officer.
丨損 to disparage, to injure by blaming.
丨減 to diminish.
我位孔丨 we are liable to lose our posts.
一字之丨嚴于斧鉞 one word of his censure was sharper than an axe.
丨黜 to deprive of dignities.
這貨有褒丨 these goods are not in the best condition; or they are injured.

ˎ緶 Used with ˏ編 to plait.
ˎpien To sew clothes, to make a seam; to lift up the dress.

ˎ骿 The flank; it is also applied to the back of a chair.
ˎpien 丨脅 the ribs and flesh on the side, taken together.

便ˀ From *man* and *change*; *q. d.* to alter one's inconvenient position.
pienˀ To put at ease, to accord with; convenient, expedient, opportune, advantageous; handy, readily; at hand; accustomed to, ready at; as an *adverb*, then, so, forthwith; just as; thus; that is.

順丨 to avail one's self of a good chance; to be convenient.
利丨 serviceable.
丨宜 suitable, fitting; cheap, reasonable.
公丨 just and suitable.
何等丨宜 how easy and convenient.
未有丨 not yet ready.
茶丨 tea is ready.
隨丨 as you please, suit yourself, when you like.
方丨 that will be handy; beneficial; practical.
不丨 unhandy, unattainable, inconvenient, undesirable.
丨是 is just so, that is it.
丨安 at leisure, *otium*.
丨中就說 he said it unadvisedly, blurted it out.
就丨 I will be ready presently.
錢銀丨換 money readily exchanged here; — a shop sign.
丨當 all right; in its place; convenient.
丨着 it will do.
幾時丨了 when will it be ready?
遇丨則爲 do it when occasion serves you.
小丨 to pass water.
大丨下血 the bloody piles.
丨至 at last, then it is thus.
丨門 a side door.
丨衣 to lay aside one's robe.
丨飯 food at all hours.
買丨買不買丨罷 buy it if you like; if not, then let it alone.

Read ˏp'ien. To discuss, to argue; to describe.

丨丨言 to talk of minutely, as Confucius did.
丨辟 to curry favor by great respect to one.
貪丨易ˀ one who seeks his own ease or promotion.

卞ˀ From 卜 to *divine*, but no etymology is given; it resembles *tsah*, 卡 a pass.
pienˀ Hurried; to do a thing smartly; a law or rule of action.

大丨 a great system of laws.
丨邑 an old name of Sz'-shui hien 泗水縣 in the south of Shantung.
丨急 neat and alert.

抃ˀ To pat; to clap the hands, or beat, when keeping time with music.
pienˀ 丨頌 to rejoice at.

丨以爲節 to mark the stops by clapping.
丨舞 to encore and applaud the players.

忭ˀ 昪ˀ The second form is unusual, and also means the bright light of the sun; used with the last.
pienˀ Delighted, joyous, pleased.

曷勝欣丨 happy in the highest degree.
丨頌頁般 you have my sincerest wishes for your happiness.

汴ˀ A branch of the River Han in Hupeh.
pienˀ 丨梁 an old name for K'aifung, the capital of Honan.

辨ˀ From 辛 *acrid* repeated, with 刀 *knife* between, to show the bitterness of wrangling.
pienˀ To cut asunder; to divide or distinguish things or qualities; to dispute and discuss, so as to learn the value of; to inquire into; supporting framework of a bedstead; an ancient land measure, one-ninth of a 井 or village lot.

丨色 to distinguish colors.
丨清 to discriminate clearly.
分丨是非 to separate the true from the false.
不丨眞假 he cannot tell the true and counterfeit.
丨別高低 to discriminate the good from the cheap, the best from the poor.
丨味 to try the taste of.

辡ˀ From *bitter* repeated, to denote the acrimony of a dispute; it is an old form of the next, and is now only used as a primitive.
pienˀ Two criminals accusing each other; the passionate recriminations of angered men.

辯ˀ From *acrid* recriminations and *words*; it is analogous to the last.
pienˀ To dispute, to quarrel about, to argue opinions; to criticise; to wrangle for a notion; to dispute a proposition; to insinuate; artful, specious, sophisticated; logomachy.

丨駁 to contradict.
爭丨 to bicker.

丨論 to debate.
高談雄丨 to talk loud and browbeat.
强丨 to force a construction; an *ex-parte* argument.
善於丨詞 good at arguing on either side.
丨轉 to cajole into a view of.
丨明白 to show a matter clearly.
丨正方位 to place a house in its true position.

辮 *pien'* To plait, to braid; to intertwine; a cue.
梳丨 or 打丨 to braid and comb the cue.
留丨 leave [some hair] for a cue.
大鬆丨 a loosely plaited cue.
丨頂 the hair left on the head.
丨攄子 or 丨牌 a false cue.
盤起丨子 to curl the cue around the head.
珍珠丨 fine silk braid, with knots on it.

膈 *pien'* The muscle or flesh attached to a tendon.

變 变 *pien'* From 䜌 to *bind* and 攴 a *stroke*; the contraction is much used.
To transform, to metamorphose; to change; a mutation from one state of being to another, or to the original condition; a turn in affairs, a revolution; a calamity or judgement.
改丨 to reform; an alteration in affairs.
丨通 accommodating, as a trimmer.
丨心 to alter one's views.
丨化 to change, to alter the substance of; to transmute.
逼丨 to excite to revolt by oppression.
天丨 celestial phenomena.
災丨 a providential calamity.
權丨 a change from expediency or constraint.
丨臉 to change countenance.
丨戲法 rules of legerdemain.
丨換 to change, as money.
至死不丨 I'll never change my views; constant till death.
丨了卦了 to retract one's word, to deny a promise.
丨亂 revolution in the state.

遍 徧 *pien'* From to *go* or *step* and *flat*.
Everywhere; the whole; entire; to go around, to make a circuit; to pervade; a visit or walk.
丨身 the whole body.
一丨 one visit.
丨爲爾德 universally practice your virtue.
丨國終 to travel to the ends of the country.
念一丨書 recited the whole book once.
丨告 to inform everybody.
丨地發青 the whole land looks green, as in spring.
丨于羣神 to visit all the temples.

弁 *pien'* A conical cap or bonnet of deer skin or linen, worn in the Cheu dynasty; it was close fitting, and resembled the Parsee turban, or a low miter; a kind of casque; military officers of a low grade; quick; alarmed, hurried; to wear a cap; to clap the hands.
文員武丨 low civilians and army officers.
皮丨 or 革丨 the military cap; it is now disused.
視如丨髦 regard [honors] as no better than a hair cap.
衆皆股丨 the whole multitude clapped their hands—in their excitement.
丨行 to go fast.

窆 *pien'* From *cave* and *wanting*.
To put a coffin into the grave.
丨器 the things connected with an interment.
及丨執斧 when the box was lowered, he grasped the ax.

釆 *pien'* The original form rudely depicts the five *claws* of a cat spread out as if to seize prey; it forms the 165th radical of only a dozen characters.
To discriminate, to part, to sort out.

P'IEN.

Old sounds, p'in *and* bin. *In Canton*, p'in *and* p'ing; — *in Swatow*, p'ien, pien, pin, *and* pⁿia; — *in Amoy*, pian *and* p'ian; — *in Fuhchau*, p'ieng, p'eng, *and* pieng; — *in Shanghai*, p'iⁿ *and* biⁿ; — *in Chifu*, p'ien.

偏 *pien* Inclined to one side; at or by the side; deflected; excessive; a side; in polite language, by your help, as if the speaker was at the other's side like a companion; partial, addicted to, selfish; hybrid; bent on, longing for; before verbs has the force of must, will; twenty-five chariots; fifty men; one half.
丨側生心 to have partialities; favoring or disliking.
丨私 selfish private ends.
丨愛 undue partiality.
丨曲 willful, set in one's way.
丨房 a concubine.
無丨無黨 perfectly candid, no favoritism.
一丨之見 a prejudiced opinion.
丨過了 or 有丨 I have already had my own; — a reply when asked if one has eaten, and equivalent to "I am well, thank you."
丨坐 I have sat and eaten by your side at table; — a polite phrase.
丨倚 to lean on.
不丨不倚 no bias, no selfish end.

僻丨門生理 illicit; to follow a despicable business.

丨勞 I'll thank you to do this; please oblige me.

丨丨不依你 I certainly cannot agree with you.

丨在一旁 it leans to one side.

丨墜 a swollen testicle.

丨要這樣 it must be this way.

地方丨北 the place is very far to the north.

丨廈 a library, a side office.

丨拗 opinionated, stubborn.

丨生要 or 丨要 I must have it.

丨僻 out of the right way, depraved; rough, unused, as a path.

丨氣 a hybrid conception, as in rearing mules of any kind.

瘺 ꜀p'ien The body half paralyzed.

丨病 a kind of spotted fever with eruptions.

篇 ꜀p'ien From *bamboo* and a *splint*.

A slip of bamboo, such as was anciently used to carve writings on, and denoting a page or section; one leaf of a book; books, publications; a bamboo for punishing; a red skinned bamboo which produces delicately tasted shoots.

一丨 one leaf.

翻丨 turn over the leaf.

說出一丨云云 he went on talking very long.

長丨大論 a long and minute description.

一丨書看到老 he has looked at one book till he is old;—partially informed.

丨章 pages and chapters.

丨什所載 it is found in poetical books.

七丨出身 he rose to office through the tripos.

翩 ꜀p'ien To fly about; to run to and fro; fluttering; bustle, running here and there.

蝶舞丨丨 the butterfly is hovering about.

丨丨 fluttering, like birds or a row of banners; or people babbling and gadding.

丨丨巍巍 imposing and stately, as a gateway or façade.

楄 ꜀p'ien From *tree* and *flat*.

A flat piece of wood, called 丨部 or 丨柎 anciently placed under the corpse in the coffin.

禁丨 a short purline on a roof near the eaves.

丨木 a species of soap-berry tree. (*Sapindus.*)

犏 ꜀p'ien A zebu or Brahminee bull; but the description seems to denote the cross between it and the yak; the character means the *hybrid cow*.

蹁 ꜀p'ien To walk lamely, as from weak ankles; to drag the feet, as a lame horse; the knee-pan; to walk about.

丨躚而起舞 going round and round making his antics, as an acrobat.

艑 ꜀p'ien Occurs used for its primitive.

A flat-bottomed large boat; a lighter; a shallop.

丨艖 a punt or scow.

西瓜丨 a chop-boat at Canton to take cargo to ships.

軿 ꜀p'ien Also read ꜀p'ing.

A light carriage with screens for women to ride in.

丨輷 the rumbling of carts.

輜丨 carriages of all kinds.

后乘丨車 the queen rode in her curtained car.

駢 ꜀p'ien From *horse* and *equal*; it is also read ꜀p'ing.

A span of horses; to associate; to arrive simultaneously; to join or clan together; anything redundant.

百福丨臻 may all blessings come to you.

丨拇 a double thumb.

丨邑 an old name for Lin-k'ü hien 臨朐縣 in the north of Shantung.

丨字 dissyllabic phrases; characters made by divisible type.

黨丨 to clan or go together.

楩 ꜀p'ien A valuable kind of timber tree that furnishes wood for cabinet ware; it grows in Kiangnan, and resembles the cedar in color.

企抱丨楠 I had hoped to retain [his counsels, which I valued] like cedar and sandal-wood.

蝙 ꜀p'ien The red sand tick or 沙虱 is also called 丨蜣 from its gyratory mode of working itself under the skin; its venomous bite makes it much dreaded.

諞 p'ien꜄ Also read ꜀pien.

To pare, as a fruit of its skin; to slice off, to cut thin.

丨鷄 to cut a fowl into slices.

丨白肉 just take off a slice of plain (unseasoned) meat.

諞 p'ien꜄ Artful and deceitful words; a plausible account of a thing

丨人的話 a made-up story.

丨佞 smooth-faced and eloquent.

惟截截善丨言 it is nothing but a fine-spun, skillful story to take you in.

鶣 ꜀p'ien A hunting falcon of a reddish plumage, two years old.

青丨 a bird shaped like the raven, of a dark color, also called 白丨 when its plumage turns whitish; it may be allied to the jays.

片 p'ien꜄ Intended to represent a piece of wood cut; it forms the 91st radical of characters denoting slips.

Anything thin and small, as a leaf, flake, strip, bit, chip, or slip; a classifier of plats of land, space of time, a piece of paper, or petals of flowers; a half, a section of; to slice, to divide; a statement, a paper.

一 丨 假 or 一 丨 浮 言 it is all false, a mere rumor.
一 丨 紙 a slip of paper.
丨 函 a note, a chit, a billet.
丨 時 a little while.
丨 言 half of the story, a word.
名 丨 or 丨 子 a card.
丨 奏 a short memorial, an explanatory minute.
夾 丨 or 附 丨 a supplement or inclosure in a larger document.
氷 丨 baroos camphor; so called from the glittering of the hard gum as it is taken from the tree.

飲 丨 shavings of roots.
一 丨 奏 摺 a long memorial.
瓦 丨 broken potsherds.
切 丨 to slice, to shave off.
丨 影 毫 無 there is not the least trace or evidence of it.
落 花 丨 丨 the flowers are all falling.
薄 脆 丨 crispy cakes.
一 丨 嘴 she is all gabble.
丨 言 折 獄 one word from him would clear the man from prison.
一 丨 青 一 丨 白 here it is green, there it is white.

騙 騗 p'ien' From *horse* and *side;* the second is rather restricted in its use to leaping on a horse.

To take an advantage of, to cheat, to deceive, to delude; to lie to; to mount a horse; to vault into the saddle.
哄 丨 or 誆 丨 to defraud one; to impose upon.
受 丨 deceived, cheated.
丨 局 a plan for cheating.
誰 丨 你 who took you in?
丨 賴 to impose on one, to swindle out of.
丨 了 去 swindled out of.

PIH.

Old sounds, pít, pík, bít, *and* bík. *In Canton*, pik, păt, *and* pít; — *in Swatow*, pít, pia, *and* pek; — *in Amoy*, p'ék, pék, *and* pít; — *in Fuhchau*, pék, p'ék, piêh, pík, péuk, *and* paik; — *in Shanghai*, pih; — *in Chifu*, pi.

壁 pi' From *earth* and *ruler*.

A partition wall; the wall of a house; a screen; an obstruction or defense; a ridge; a dividing cliff or water-shed.
墻 丨 a wall.
照 丨 a curtain-wall before a temple or yamun; an opposite wall.
影 丨 wall to screen a door from the street, or a partition to separate houses; they are often adorned.
丨 喜 a species of flat spider.
巉 巖 削 丨 a sheer, steep cliff.
隔 丨 a partition-wall.
間 丨 的 next door neighbors.
面 丨 facing the wall; — *i. e.* abstraction, hard study,
丨 立 千 仞 the ridge rises in lofty peaks.
丨 宿 the 14th zodiacal constellation of γ in Pegasus and α in Andromeda.
丨 州 an old name for T'ung-kiang hien 通 江 縣 in the north of Sz'ch'uen on the River Pa.
家 徒 四 丨 a family reduced to four walls; — *met.* very poor.
丨 疊 一 新 new ridges rise beyond these.

躄 pi' Lame.
跛 丨 lame of both feet, unable to walk.

Read *p'ih*, Upset, overturned.

鐴 pi' The handle of a plow.
丨 刀 to sharpen a knife.

縪 pi' From *silk* and *chief;* occurs written like *pih*, 辮 to dress hemp.

A net for catching fish, having a frame, which shuts down and incloses them.

襞 pi' Clothes folded and laid in a pile; a seam in leather; a long garment.
裙 丨 the gathers in a skirt.
丨 積 the folds or plaits in a lady's skirt.
丨 衣 中 有 刀 斧 手 some armed headsmen were concealed among the robed attendants.

璧 pi' A *princely gem*, an ancient jade badge of office, made round with a hole in it, and held in the hands at court; this and the 圭 were a sort of letters-patent; to decline.

返 丨 or 丨 回 去 to send back.
丨 謝 to return [a present] with thanks; — written on the card.
原 丨 歸 趙 the original gem will be returned; — the debt will be repaid.
連 城 之 丨 a priceless article; one which money cannot get.
日 月 合 丨 the stars are propitious; — *i. e.* the sun and moon rise together; the phrase 合 丨 refers to the junction of two parts to make a whole, as a marriage, a check compared with its block, an interlinear translation, or a seal and its impression.

碧 pi' From *stone*, *gem*, and *white*, denoting its value and clearness.

Green jade stone; some kinds are blueish, and others greenish like the deep sea; it is like jadeite, and highly prized.
黃 丨 璽 the precious topaz.
丨 玉 fine serpentine.
丨 雲 azure clouds.
丨 樹 a coralline tree fabled to grow in the Kwănlun Mts.
丨 落 the cerulean.

畢 pi

Some say, it is combined of 由 a *demon* and 弗 *not* underneath; others derive it from 田 a *field* and minute particles.

To finish, to bring to a full end; over, terminated; the last or end of; all, entirely; a trestle used in sacrifices; old name of a small dukedom near Si-ngan fu in Shensi; a bird-net with a long handle like a scoop; a document; the fifth gate of the palace in old times.

丨竟 after all; at last; finally.
丨至 they have all come.
事未丨 the job is not yet done.
公事丨 after the public business is over.
丨宿 the 19th zodiacal constellation beginning at ε Tauri and including the Hyades.
收丨 all are received.

滭 pi

A cold wind.

韠 pi

A knee-pad made of leather, worn when making prostrations; a kind of fringed apron, wide at the bottom.
丨膝 coverings for the knees.

蓽 pi

Interchanged with the next.

A variety of pulse.
丨菝子 the seeds of the *Chavica Roxburghii*, or long pepper; this name seems to be an imitation of the Hindu word *pippali*.
丨澄茄 cubebs, including probably the seeds of the *Cubeba* and *Daphnidium*.
丨苣 dock or common sorrel.

篳 pi

A wicker hedge; an inclosure hedged in by bamboo.
丨篘 a dray or cart to haul fuel.
蓬門丨戶 a country cottage with a wicker gate; — a poor hovel.
丨篥 an instrument like a flageolet.

熚 pi

Fiery; the roar or noise of a great fire.

蹕 pi

To warn persons off the road, and thus make way for the sovereign; an imperial journeying.
警丨 to order people to retire.
丨臨 to reach the imperial stage.
塡丨 a great guard.

饆 pi

A delicate wheaten dumpling with meat inside, called 丨饠 because two persons called 畢 and 羅 were fond of them.

愊 pi

From *heart* and *full*.

An earnest resolute feeling; oppressed, borne down with.
心丨 sincere.
丨意紛紜 distracted and oppressed with grief.

楅 pi

From *wood* and *full*; also read *fuh*.

A strip of wood, called 丨衡 fastened across the horns of oxen to prevent them goring; a frame for supporting darts; a place for drying fish.

逼 pi **偪** pi

From to *go* and *full*; the second is also used for *fuh*, 幅 a buskin or light gaiter.

To crowd, to press upon, to approach too near; to constrain; to arbitrarily urge; to ill-use, to harass, to reduce to straits; to distend or fill; urgent; imperious.
丨死 to ill-use so as cause death.
丨近 bordering; to draw near, to crowd on.
丨勒 to constrain another to do.
丨壓 to browbeat, to put down.
人丨擠擁 a great press, a jam.
丨令改嫁 to force a wife to marry another man.
丨屧 a bandage bound around the legs by coolies.
邪丨 overalls or leggings.
丨民爲盜 to egg the people on to robbery.
丨于無奈 I am obliged to do it; no help for it.
丨迫 to compel, to urge on, urgent.

必 pi

Formed of 八 to *divide* and 弋 an *arrow*, and explained as marking off the four cardinal points.

Minutely divided; a strong affirmative, certainly, must; determined on.
何丨 why? what necessity is there?
丨需要用 we cannot do without it.
丨然 or 丨定 certainly.
不可丨 uncertain, doubtful.
可不丨走 it is not necessary for me to go.
丨得 doubtless so.
不丨要 you may not want it.
未丨 perhaps not; not certainly so.
丨竟 after all it must be so.
丨也使無訟乎 if you have the essential thing, why not dissuade him from appealing?
毋意毋丨 there is no idea that it must be so.
勢丨 most surely, undoubtedly.

咇 pi

Interchanged with the next two.

To smell sweetly; a pleasant taste; to talk.
丨節多言 very smooth-tongued, talkative.
鳴丨丨 twittering of birds.

嗶 pi

Same as the last.

丨嘰 long-ells, a kind of woolen cloth.

苾 pi

Fragrant; a sort of pot-herb.
丨芬 odoriferous; grateful to the smell like food, for which see the next.
丨薺 a kind of *Scirpus* or sedge with an edible root; probably a variety of the water-chestnut.
丨芻 or 比丘 (Sanscrit, *bhikshu*) a priest; and 丨芻尼 (Sanscrit, *bikshuni*) a nun.
丨芬孝祀 fragrant has been your filial sacrifice.

餕, *pi'* The fragrance of food just cooked, which the spirits will smell and accept.
有 丨 其香 the savory odor of the cooked rice.

愎, *pi'* Perverse, self-willed, disobedient; resisting reproof.
剛 丨 自是 set in his way.

筆, **笔**, *'pi* From *bamboo* and a *stylus* or *hair*; the first is most common.
A Chinese pencil or small brush; a pen; to write, to compose; style, composition; drawing, penmanship; a stroke in a character.
一管 丨 or 一枝 丨 one pencil.
鵝毛 丨 a quill pen.
丨 竿 the shaft, 丨 鋒 the tip, and 丨 筒 the cover, of a pencil.
工 丨 a labored writing, and 易' 丨 a free hand-writing.
大 丨 your penmanship; in good large characters.
紙 丨 相向 pen and paper opposed to each other; — a great litigation.
親 丨 丨 之 I wrote it with my own pencil.
鐵 丨 批准 my iron pen will assure you of its certainty.
落 丨 or 下 丨 to begin to write.
記上一 丨 write out a note of the particulars.
丨 氣壯勁 to read a piece straight through.
手 丨 or 的 丨 an autograph.
文 丨 塔 towers or pagodas of three storeys, dedicated to the god of Literature; they are shaped like a pencil.
木 丨 the reddish variety of the *Magnolia purpurea*, referring to the pencil-like tuft of stamens, which are used in making a kind of perfumery.
丨 之于書 write it in a book.
丨 底生花 his pencil bears flowers.
丨 走龍蛇 his pen runs off dragons and snakes; — a beautiful, firm hand.
丨 資 fees to a writer.
開了 丨 to begin to learn composition.
頓 丨 and 折 丨 rhetorical terms for the foundation argument, and the opposing argument in a discourse.
番 丨 a species of wagtail. (*Motacilla boarala.*)

In *Cantonese*. Straight, direct; lengthwise.
一 丨 上去 it went straight up.
鬆 丨 丨 loose, like cotton-wool.

滗, *pi'* To strain off the water or gravy from a dish, as of rice; to squeeze out the juice.
把米湯 丨 乾 drain all the water from the rice.
不要 丨 乾了茶滷 do not pour all the drainings from the tea-leaves.
丨 掉白醭 strain off the mother — from the vinegar.
丨 藥 drain off the decoction.

榫, *pi'* A light-yellow, even-grained wood, brought to Canton from Kiangsi; it is very light, and used for carving statuettes.

觱, *pi'* *'pieh* A musical horn, 丨 栗, used by Tartars to frighten horses; the boys in Peking make them from reeds like a whistle; the whistling sound of a north wind; a whistle or other small musical toy.
吹 丨 兒 to blow a flageolet.
丨 沸檻泉 the lively bubbling fountain gushing forth.
水 丨 a syringe.
一之日 丨 發 during this first month (November), the wind blows cold.

In *Cantonese*. Tender, as a shoot.
丨 出來 an oozing out; it falls in drops.

滭, *pi'* Similar to the last.
The bubbling of water in a fountain; a deficiency.

弼, *pi'* From 弜 a strong *bow* with 百 a *hundred* between, which is changed from an old form of 舌 the *tongue*, intimating that advisers of a prince should be neither obstinate nor supple; 佛 is used with it in this sense.
A splice on a bow to prevent its breaking; to aid, to guide, as a statesman; to shelter, as hills do a site; perverse; high.
良 丨 an able minister.
輔 丨 assistants, near the throne.
船頭 丨 a ship's bowsprit.
明刑 丨 教 distinct penalties assist the instructor.
垣局輔 丨 this recess or position [in the hills] is well protected.

邲, *pi'* A place in the state of 鄭 Ching, near the present Tsing-loh hien in the south of Shansi. Read *pi'* Good.

鮅, *pi'* A species of trout with pink eyes, otherwise called 鱒魚; another sort, the 石 丨 魚 has a reddish body an inch or two long, used in making a sauce; perhaps a kind of pilchard.

怭, **佖**, *pi'* Dignified, grave; to treat others rudely when flustered with drink; full, filled with.
既醉止威儀 丨 丨 when they are drunk, their dignity and courtesy are all gone.

駜, *pi'* A strong and well fed horse, fat and sleek.
丨 彼乘黃 fat and strong is the chestnut team.

湢, *pi'* A bathing-house.
丨 然 terrified; stern but agitated.
丨 浴 a public bathing establishment.

煏, *pi'* To dry by the fire.
In *Cantonese*. To boil flesh till the water is gone.
丨 捻牛肉 beef is boiled to rags.
燒 丨 了 burned (or boiled) dry.

P'IH.

Old sounds, p'ik, p'it, bik, *and* bit. *In Canton*, păt, p'ik, *and* p'ek; — *in Swatow*, p'it, p'ek, *and* pia; — *in Amoy*, p'ek, p'it, *and* pit; — *in Fuhchau*, p'ék *and* p'iah; — *in Shanghai*, p'ih; — *in Chifu*, p'ié.

辟 p'i' Composed of 辛 *acrid* and 卩 for 節 a *rule*, intimating that it is hard to observe laws, and 口 *mouth*, denoting their delivery to the people; it is interchanged with the next, four, with 譬, and others of its compounds.

A prince or sovereign; a term for heaven, and for a deceased husband; to rend or split open; grave and pretentious; quiet, secluded; law, example; to repress, to punish; a crowd frightened away; to perceive fully; clear; as; to beat the breast; perverse; to open.

丨若 as, like as, similar.
大丨 the severe punishment, death.
丨名 nominal; false, a pretense.
丨除 to exorcise.
皇丨 my imperial lord, — so a widow calls her late husband.
后丨 a queen, an empress.
丨雝 the emperor's hall for examining the Hanlin graduates; it is one of the most artistic buildings in Peking.
丨以止丨 to punish in order to prevent further punishment.
如何昊天丨言不信 how is it, high Heaven, that he will not listen to just words.
便丨 subtle.

僻 p'i' Mean, low-live; base, licentious, depraved; partial, prejudiced; cramped, straitened, incommodious; private, bye or secluded.

丨陋 rustic, untaught.
荒丨之地 a desert, neglected spot.
邪丨 heretical, flagitious, as doctrines; depraved and insubordinate.
丨見 prejudiced; a partial view.
丨巷 a side lane; a private alley.
放蕩偏丨 abandoned and reprobate in character.
幽丨 a covert or dark glen.

擗 p'i' To cleave, to open, to rive; to beat the breast; to drive away; to bend.

丨開 to break open.
丨踊哭泣 to beat the breast, wail and stamp, as for a parent's death, or from vexation.
摘丨爲禮 bend the knee and bow is the etiquette.

闢 p'i', 'p'i To burst forth, to disclose; to develop, as nature does; to open up; to set in order; to retire; to shun.

開丨八寨 he newly constituted eight cantonments.
一闔一丨 a shutting and an opening, a decline and a culmination.
丨處海濱 retired to the sea-side.
丨戶 the germinations of nature, production.
透丨 to unravel a sophism, to see through a fallacy.

澼 p'i' To wash clean, to whiten; to brighten, as knowledge does the mind.

世世以洴丨絖爲業 their occupation during many generations was to bleach cocoon-silk.

緶 'p'i To work fibres of hemp or grass-nettle into thread for weaving.

丨縷 to roll or dress fibres between the fingers.

鵯 ˏp'i A small gregarious bird of the crow kind, called 丨鶋 having a white breast; the 丨烏 is another name in Nganhwui; it is probably allied to the blackbird.

霹 ˏpi A clap; a sudden, loud noise.

丨靂車 the rumbling crashing noise of chariots; a kind of war-chariot.

劈 'p'i, ˏp'i To cut open; to rive, to split, to rend; to tear asunder; a wedge; wedge-shaped.

丨破 to break open.
丨臉的人 a harsh man.
丨行 the voussoir course in bridges.
丨水 the split-water, or the long bow-scull on big boats.

In *Cantonese*. To meet one suddenly.

丨面撞見 I met him so abruptly, — as when turning a corner.
初丨歷 the first crash, the first word.

癖 'p'i Indigestion; costiveness; any derangement of the circulation of the humors or blood, giving rise to boils, cancers, &c.; a morbid appetite; a craving for food, an inordinate fancy for things; partial to.

食丨 a vicious appetite.
人皆有一丨 everybody has one craving, — is mad on something.
性丨 a propensity, a hobby.
丨疾 dyspeptic, hysteric.
書丨 doting on books.
嗜丨太過 he has a mania for it.
痰丨 expectoration of phlegm from drinking.

甓 p'i' A prettily veined or glazed tile made to resemble tortoise-shell, and used in paving paths and facing walls.

瓴丨 fine or encaustic tiles.
習勤軍丨 he made them move tiles in order to learn to be industrious.
中唐有丨 the middle aisle was paved with tiles.

廦 p'i' Oblique, leaning, deflected; poor, mean.

丨瓜之廬 the poorest mud hovels.

匹, ʻpʻi. From 匸 to *conceal* and 八 *eight*, because a piece of silk of four 丈 was folded eight times.

A piece of silk, for which the next is now used; a pair; a fellow, a mate; one of two who are, or have been united; responsive; to match, to pair; a compeer, one who is to be matched; classifier of horses, because they are so often spanned.

一 丨 配 a married pair.

丨 配 之 際 the time of marriage.

丨 夫 a husband, a man.

丨 夫 丨 婦 a common man and woman.

作 豐 伊 丨 he ruled in Fung according to the pattern — of his ancestors.

世 無 其 丨 the world has not his equal.

馬 丨 horses of all kinds.

丨 鳥 the mandarin-duck, which is noted for its fidelity.

疋, ʻpʻi. The original form is made of 止 to *stop* with *bowels* above, or more like 足 *enough*; others make it from 𠂊 and 正 a *right cover*; it is the 103d radical.

A classifier of pieces of cloth.

一 丨 布 a piece of cotton.

丨 頭 鋪 a dry-goods' shop.

成 丨 a whole piece of goods.

Read ꜀*su*. Sufficient; to record.

Read ʻ*ya* for 雅. Correct, elegant, exact; cultivated.

大 丨 and 小 丨 are two parts of the Book of Odes.

肶, ʻpʻi. To blow water into meat to increase its weight; gross, fat, as blubber.

鴄, ʻpʻi. A wild duck; the mallard; also called 末 匹 by some authors.

庶 人 摯 丨 a countryman takes a duck — as a gift.

鷿, ʻpʻi. A bird called 丨 鷉 the description of which answers nearly to the brown grebe (*Podiceps*), which is common in Southern China; it is also called 油 鴨 the oily duck, 刁 丨, the small duck, and other names.

PIN.

Old sounds, pin *and* bin. *In Canton* p'ao; — *in Swatow*, pin; — *in Amoy*, pin; — *in Fuhchau*, ping; — *in Shanghai*, ping; — *in Chifu*, pin.

賔 賓, ꜀pin. From 貝 *precious* and *obscure*.

One who receives attention, a stranger, a visitor who comes willingly to pay his respects, as 客 is rather a customer; the entertainment of a guest; to entertain, to act the host; to submit, to acknowledge; to come under civilizing influences.

丨 客 a visitor.

丨 朋 a friend; guests and friends.

西 丨 a domestic tutor.

序 丨 以 賢 the guests are arranged according to their skill — in archery.

丨 主 guest and host; servant and employer; lord and fief; secondary and principal proposition in rhetoric; — according to the context.

四 海 丨 服 all China submitted willingly.

丨 服 to regard, to respect, to help, to care for.

龍 丨 a fairy who helps students.

出 門 如 見 大 丨 when you go abroad, let it be as sedately as if you met a distingushed visitor.

濵 瀕, ꜀pin. The bank of a stream; a brink, a shore, a beach; near, adjoining; to border on, outlying.

丨 死 nearly dead.

丨 臨 大 海 I had nearly reached the ocean.

問 諸 水 丨 ask it of the water-side; refers to K'üh Yuen.

三 面 丨 海 three sides [of Corea] border on the sea.

丨 州 a superior district in Wuting fu near the mouth of the Tsing ho in Shantung.

泗 丨 浮 磬 the sounding stones found near the River Sz'.

率 土 之 丨 莫 非 王 臣 within the sea-bounds all are the king's servants.

鑌, ꜀pin. A fine steel which makes very sharp swords, called 丨 鐵; it is mentioned as one article of trade from Persia, and is not improbably damasked steel of Arabian make.

檳 梹, ꜀pin, ꜀ping. From *wood* and *guest*; the contracted form is unauthorized.

The areca-nut, called 丨 榔 in imitation of the Malay word *penang*.

丨 資 betel-nut money; *i. e.* postage.

丨 蒟 the nut and leaf prepared for chewing; the husk is called 大 腹 皮 the big-belly skin.

棗 丨 a hard astringent seed used for the areca.

丨 崩 子 the fruit of a species of fig (*Ficus stipulata*), used in poultices.

獱, ꜀pin. A small species of otter; others say, a large kind.

丨 獺 a kind of otter, described as having a head like a horse; but the two words probably denote different sexes or ages of the otter.

繽 ˛pin Colored silks mixed; a confused blending of colors; mixed, crowded.

丨亂 confused, disordered.

錦繡丨紛 the varied embroidery confuses the eye.

丨丨 a mélange of colors.

其說丨紜 his words are not perspicuous.

蠙 ˛pin From *insect* and a *guest*.

The oyster from which pearls are taken, now found in the Gulf of Tungking; the pearl is supposed to be the concreted semen of the sparrow when transformed into the oyster.

丨珠 a pearl oyster.

淮夷丨珠曁魚 the tribes on the River Hwai brought pearl-oysters and fish.

得水土之際則爲蛙丨之衣 when you get where land and water meet, you are at the dressing-place of the frogs and oysters.

彬 斌 ˛pin From *pelage* and *forest*, or *civil* and *military*, denoting a due mixture; the second form is chiefly used as a surname.

Ornament and plainness properly mixed.

丨丨 neat but not gairish; the parts well contrasted.

文質丨丨 simplicity and elegance are in harmony; a well balanced mind.

邠 豳 豳 ˛pin The second form is the name of a *hill* where many wild *hogs* were found, as its composition indicates.

Name of a small principality in the south of Shensi ruled over by 大王 of the family of Cheu, before they got the throne, B. C. 1134.

丨州 an inferior department in the southwest of Shensi.

瑸 ˛pin Ornamented with a mosaic of agate and ivory, or other things inlaid, is 璘丨; the phrase is differently written.

霦 ˛pin Interchanged with the preceding.

The brilliancy of a gem is 璘丨, especially of the most precious; often used in names.

攽 ˛pin To divide, in order to reduce; to part, to make a partition.

稟 ˋping The original form 禀 was composed of *grain* and *granary* contracted, because food was distributed on request; that is now written ˊlin 廩 and this has taken its place.

To make known one's case to a superior; to announce; to petition; to ask of, and is employed in courtesy to friends, and by servants to their master; a petition, a statement, a report; to receive from heaven; endowment, disposition.

丨受 endowed with; to receive by permission.

回丨 or 丨覆 to reply, as to a superior or a friend.

丨告 to petition the magistrates.

申丨 to inform a superior.

丨帖 or 丨詞 an official statement, a petition.

丨辭 to decline the request; to announce one's departure.

丨命 to ask for leave to do; to report on orders received.

具丨 a prepared statement.

當面丨白 to complain against in person, to accuse before officials.

丨性 or 氣丨 the temper, one's talents.

丨神 to pray to the gods.

丨安 to pay one's respects.

丨明 to state clearly.

臏 髕 pinˋ The knee-pan, vulgarly called 波羅 (or 稜) 蓋 from its cup-like shape; to cut off the knee.

丨脚 to cut off the patella.

爲仇所丨 he cut off the legs of his enemies.

鑽丨 to cut off the knee-pan; a punishment employed in the Ming dynasty and previously.

殯 pinˋ From *body* and *guest*.

To encoffin a corpse; to carry out to burial; to make a funeral.

送丨 to accompany to burial.

出丨 to carry to the grave.

丨殮 to put into the coffin.

祓丨 funeral rites at the burial.

丨葬 to inter, to lay in the tomb.

儐 pinˋ From *man* and *guest*; interchanged with the next and its primitive.

To receive and entertain a guest ceremoniously; to honor, to do reverence to; to arrange orderly; to advance.

山川所以丨鬼神也 the hills and streams are available as a media to honor the gods.

丨爾籩豆 display your dishes and trenchers.

丨接 to receive guests; to respect, as the gods.

丨相 a court master of ceremonies.

丨其宗器 to set out the ancestral vessels.

擯 pinˋ Used for the last.

To expel, to put out forcibly; to find fault with; to receive.

丨棄 to reject.

丨逐出境 drove him out of the country.

丨斥 to find fault with and reject, as an account or a workman.

丨斥端異 to expel heresy.

使丨 an officer sent to the frontiers to receive an envoy.

鬢 鬂 pinˋ The hair on the temples, or side of the cheeks; tresses, curls; whiskers.

雲丨 hair on the forehead puffed out; fine hair.

兩丨 the tresses; curls.

白丨 an old man.

綠丨朱顏 dark hair and red cheeks; — pretty.

一事無成兩丨絲 I have done nothing, though my hair is gray; — a regret of old age.

P'IN.

Old sounds, bin *and* p'im. *In Canton*, p'ăn ; — *in Swatow*, p'in *and* pin ; — *in Amoy*, p'in *and* pin ; — *in Fuhchau*, p'ing *and* ping ; — *in Shanghai*, bing *and* ping ; — *in Chifu*, p'in.

貧 ꜀p'in From *wealth* and to *share*, intimating that the share is very little.

Poor, having a small part; poverty; destitute, impoverished.

丨窮 pennyless, no resources.

丨陋 ignoble and poor; base.

一丨如洗 all cleaned out, destitute as if I had been washed.

丨乏 destitute; not enough.

丨賤之交不可忘 do not forget those who were your friends in poverty.

怪丨的 no wonder he is poor.

君子安丨 the princely man is contented even in poverty.

丨而樂 he is poor yet happy.

頻 ꜀p'in Composed of 頁 *leaf* and 步 *step*, but the last is rather a contraction of 涉 to *ford*, and this is sometimes used for 瀕 a brink.

Urgent, pressing, like one waiting at a ford; hurried, precipitate; incessant, continually; imminent; a brink, a shore.

丨依 a covering, a shelter, as a house.

丨丨的 unceasingly.

丨來丨往 coming and going repeatedly.

丨催 incessantly urging.

認憑你所為 I agree to anything you may do.

丨數 uninterruptedly.

仁丨 an old name for the areca-nut.

國步斯丨 the doom of the state draws nigh.

丨速 urgently to hasten.

櫇 ꜀p'in A fragrant fruit, the 丨婆 (*Sterculia balanghas*), used as a substitute for chestnuts.

丨菓 the apple or 平菓 is correctly thus written.

蘋 ꜀p'in From *grass* and to *urge*; occurs used with the last.

A water plant common in Kiangnan; the four leaves at the end of the stalks are about as large as a cash, and are divided equally so as to resemble the character 田; they are covered underneath with a gelatinous secretion; the white flowers appear in June, whence its name of 白丨; it is probably a species of water shield (*Hydropeltis* or *Cabomba*), and the leaves are fed to animals.

苹之以丨藻 stuff it (the fish) with water-shield and duckweed; these two plants were once used in marriage rites.

登白丨兮騁望 when the water-shields bloom, I'll hurry there to see.

于以采丨 she gathers the water-shields.

嚬 顰 ꜀p'in To knit the brows; to grin, as when one fords a stream; to smile; to simper.

丨笑不苟 don't smirk with everybody.

東施效丨 [it is like the miserable attempt of] Tungshi imitating [Si-shi] in knitting her brows, — which only made her the more ugly.

丨眉 to frown and look provoked.

丨蹙 to knit the brows.

嬪 ꜀p'in From *woman* and *guest*; *i. e.* the accommodating woman.

A handsome lady; a regal concubine of the first rank, who waits in the presence, as a maid of honor; a deceased wife; a fairy; to be a wife to.

妃丨 ladies of the palace hareem.

九丨 the emperor's secondary wives.

丨婦 his late wife.

來嫁于周曰丨于京 [Jin] came to wed the prince of Cheu, and became his wife at the capital.

丨然成行 the women made many rows.

牝 ꜂p'in From *cow* and a *ladle*.

The female of beasts, and sometimes of birds; rarely applied to plants.

丨鷄司晨 the hen rules the morning; *i. e.* the wife wears the breeches.

谿丨 a valley.

丨戶 the vulva of animals.

澡丨 to wash the body.

與他魚丨牡 [the eel] copulates with other kinds of fish.

品 ꜂p'in From *three mouths*, intimating that when *two* people wrangle, *one* can preside over them.

A kind, series, rank, order; a sort out of a variety; a rule or guide to go by; actions, conduct; a thing, an article; a delicacy; to classify, to rank; in *music*, a part.

丨貌 countenance; the expression.

丨性 temper, feelings.

丨格 carriage, air, or talents, of a person.

無丨 no character; abandoned.

低丨 a low class.

他是劣丨 he is a reckless scamp.

何丨級 what rank is he?

極丨 the highest rank.

丨物 articles; various things.

上上丨 the very best sort.

佳丨 a good kind.

一家丨 singular, eccentric, one by himself.

丨之最上者 it is reckoned to be of the very best sort.

丨行 actions, conduct.
一桌丨盌 a set of dishes.
丨平 to classify; to arrange in its proper place.
敦丨 a trustworthy man.
丨題 different kinds of themes.

修德立丨 to act virtuously and establish a character.
正丨 in *music*, the air, soprano; 下丨 the bass; and 副丨 the alto; foreign terms.
丨味 delicacies; rare viands.

丨級臺 a terrace ascended by steps, as in the Temple of Heaven.
九丨 the nine official grades; they are divided into 正 and 從, principal and secondary.

INSIGNIA OF CIVIL AND MILITARY OFFICERS.

The distinguishing badges of civilians are all birds; they are worn on the breast and back of their official robes in a square patch of embroidery, as follows.

1. 仙鶴 Manchurian crane (*Grus montignesia.*)
2. 錦鷄 golden pheasant (*Thaumalea picta.*)
3. 孔雀 peacock (*Pavo muticus.*)
4. 雲鴈 wild goose (*Anser ferus.*)
5. 白鷳 silver pheasant (*Euplocamus nycthemerus.*)
6. 鷺鷥 lesser egret (*Egretta garzetta.*)
7. 鸂鶒 mandarin duck (*Anas galericulata.*)
8. 鵪鶉 quail (*Coturnix dactylisonans.*)
9. 練雀 long-tailed jay (*Urocisso sinensis*); or magpie.
10. 黃鸝 oriole (*Oriolus chinensis.*)

The insignia of military officials are all animals, but they are not so strictly distinguished as the civilians; they are worn in the following order.

1. 麒麟 the unicorn of Chinese fable.
2. 獅子 the lion of India (*Felis leo.*)
3. 豹 the leopard (*Leopardus japonicus.*)
4. 虎 the tiger (*Felis tigris.*) of Manchuria.
5. 熊 black bear (*Helarctos tibetanus.*)
6. 彪 tiger cat (*Leopardus macroceloides*); the 6th also
7. wear the mottled bear 羆 (*Ailuropus melanoleucus.*)
8. 海馬 the seal (*Phoca equestris.*)
9. 犀牛 the rhinoceros (*Rhinoceros sondaicus.*)

The oriole is worn by the lowest grade of underlings. The *chwang-yuen*, or senior Hanlin, wears the egret. The wives of officials wear the same embroidery as their husbands, but no knobs.

The ranks in both services have been further distinguished in the present dynasty by different colored knobs on their caps. The first two wear red coral; the third, clear blue; the fourth, lapis lazuli; the fifth, quartz crystal; the sixth, opaque white stone or adularia; and the last three, gilded yellow.

PING.

Old sounds, pang, ping, *and* bang. *In Canton*, ping, peng, *and* pǎng; — *in Swatow*, peng, pⁿia, *and* pⁿé; — *in Amoy*, péng *and* pin; — *in Fuhchau*, píng, pièng, *and* péng; — *in Shanghai*, ping, bing, *and* pang; — *in Chifu*, ping.

冰 氷 冫 ˛ping From *ice* and *water*, contracted to *water* and a *dot*; the third is the form of the 15th radical, under which are grouped characters referring to cold, freezing, and ice.

Ice; clear, pure; icy, frozen; crystallized; to freeze.
丨凍 frozen hard.
丨水 ice-water.
伐丨 to cut out ice for storing.
丨雪 ice and snow.
丨得慌 icy cold, exceedingly cold.
丨室 or 丨窖 an ice-house.
丨冷 cold as ice.
賊丨 a glairy spot on the ice.
丨錐 or 丨凌 an icicle.
丨益壯 the ice is thicker.
丨糖 crystallized sugar-candy.
滴時更結紅丨 [as her tears] fell they congealed into bloody ice.

丨桶 a refrigerator.
丨脂 the hard fat of animals.
丨淸玉潔人 a pure-minded man.
久置丨擱 the matter has long been in suspense; it has long been unsettled.
丨人 or 代丨人 a go-between.
丨霜之操 chaste, unsullied.
未追丨 she is not yet married.
一片丨心 chaste, irreproachable, guileless.
丨山不可靠 don't trust to an ice-hill; — high station has its dangers.
落丨塊 a hail-storm.
丨了一下 cool it off with ice.
丨魚 frozen fish.
綁丨鞋 strap on your skates.
丨解 or 丨消 or 丨化 the ice is melting.

兵 ˛ping From *eight* and a *hillock*; but the original form is derived from 廾 two *hands* with an 斤 *ax* between them, or from 人 *man*, 廾 *hands*, and 干 *spear*.

A soldier; troops; a force; an army; a weapon, arms; military, warlike; to kill, as with troops; to fight, to use arms; the black pawn in Chinese chess.
丨丁 or 丨卒 soldiers, marines.
起丨 to call out or marshal troops, as from a garrison.
勾丨 or 調丨 to bring a force to the rescue; to reinforce one in danger.
修爾車馬弓矢戎丨 see after your chariots and horses, your bows and arrows, and all the weapons of war.
丨器 weapons, guns, artillery.
胸中有甲丨 he is firmly resolved to conquer.

左右欲丨之 those about him tried to kill him.
大丨 the main body of an army.
丨戈 spears, muskets, arms.
短丨 swords, knives, &c.
出丨 to go out on a campaign.
一枝丨 one corps of the force.
伏丨 an ambush.
馬丨 cavalry; the horse.
步丨 infantry; the foot; the line.
操丨 to exercise or drill troops.
救丨 a force sent to succor.
點丨 to call the roll; mustering.
官丨 government troops.
招丨 to enlist troops.
丨反賊亂 the troops have revolted and the rebels are rampageous.
閱丨 to review troops.
用丨如神 he fights like a god.
丨頭 a commander, an officer; the governor of Hongkong or Macao is commonly so called.

栟 ꜀ping Another name for the *Livistona* or 椶櫚, from whose leaf sheaths coir ropes are made, and fans and attap from its leaves, is 丨櫚; it is cultivated in the southern provinces.

掤 ꜀ping A quiver; to put the hand on the quiver, so as not to let the arrows drop out.

丙 ꜂ping Composed of 一 *one* 入 *to enter* and 冂 a *receptacle* or door; 一 represents the 陽 principle.

The third of the ten stems, which with 丁 belongs to fire, and refers to the south; therefore they denote bright; a fish's tail, from a fanciful resemblance in the seal character.
文丨 or 青丨 heaven; a clear sky.
丨丁火 the heat of the sun.
壬丨坐向 facing north and south, — as a house or grave.

In *Cantonese*. To burn.
房屋被丨 the houses were consumed.
閱後付丨 burn this after you have read it.

炳 ꜂ping Like the last and the next.

Bright, light, like fire; luminous, perspicuous.
丨如日星 clear as noonday.

昺 ꜂ping Bright and glorious, like the sun.
帝丨 the last emperor of the Sung dynasty, A. D. 1278.

蛃 ꜂ping One name for the *Lepisma* or clothes moth is 丨魚, so called from its forked tail resembling the character 丙; another name is 白魚 white fish.

邴 ꜂ping A city in the ancient principality of Sung 宋, now Sücheu fu in the northwest of Kiangsu; also another in the state Ch'ing 鄭 near K'aifung fu.

怲 ꜂ping Sad, mournful.
未見君子憂心丨丨 when they do not see their prince, mournful sorrow fills their hearts.

餅 ꜂ping From to *eat* and *joined* together.

A cake; a biscuit which has been baked; pastry made into small pieces; fritters, dumplings.
麪丨 wheaten cakes.
丨乾 dry biscuit or crackers.
丨食 pastry, cakes.
中秋丨 or 月丨 cakes made at the full of the 8th moon, and used in worshiping it.
丨餡 the stuffing of a cake.
畫丨充饑 [to try] to satisfy hunger with a painted cake; a Barmecide feast.
牛奶丨 cheese.
丨金 presents of cake money.

鉼 ꜂ping Thin plates of gold or silver, shaped somewhat like the old Japanese obangs, employed in offerings to the Five Emperors; a certain badge of office; an iron boiler.
傾銀一丨 to cast a plate of sycee; they are sometimes so cast instead of the shoe ingots.

秉 ꜂ping Composed of 禾 *grain* and 又 a *hand* grasping it.

A handful of grain; an ancient dry measure containing two stone 石, or 160 pecks 斗; to seize, to grasp in the hand; to have power, as Heaven grants it; to uphold, to maintain, as principles; decided; maintained.
禾丨 a sheaf of grain.
丨燭待旦 to hold a candle and wait for the dawn, as Kwanti did.
丨德明恤 be just and yet compassionate.
一丨至公 he acted most justly; the whole is very fair.
遺丨 to drop a handful.
與粟五丨 gave him 800 pecks of millet.
把丨 to direct, to oversee.
非我有周丨德不康寧 it is not that we of the House of Cheu regard it best to make you unhappy and harassed.
權丨朝綱 to sway the scepter.
丨持 to grasp.
誰丨國鈞 who really holds the power in the state?
丨性愚蒙 his natural disposition was incorrigibly stupid.

鞞 ꜂ping A scabbard.
丨琫有珌 the sheath of his sword glittered with its gems.

箳 ꜂ping A bamboo mat or covering behind a carriage to keep off the dust.
丨篁 a cloth screen at the back of a cart.

幷 竝 并 並 ping' — From 幵 *even* with two 人 *men* above; or from 二 人 立 *two* men *standing* together on the same level; the last two forms are in common use.

Two standing or going together, a dual arrangement; a copulative particle, altogether, both with, and, also; moreover; even with, unitedly, at once; used before a negative, it enforces it, really; to compare.

丨非 by no means.

丨坐 to sit together.

你丨過 do you compare them together.

丨力 mutual assistance.

丨重 equally heavy or important.

一丨 all, the whole.

丨不是 not so at all.

民之無辜丨其臣僕 the unoffending people will all be reduced to servitude.

丨呑六國 he absorbed the six states.

丨蒂蓮 two lotuses on one stalk.

丨合 united.

兼丨 to bring all into one.

丨州 an ancient name of Chingting fu 正定府 in the southwest of Chihli.

丨且 moreover.

葉兒丨在一塊兒 the leaves have closed (or curled up), as the sensitive plant.

併 傡 ping' — Used for the last, and for p'ing 屏 to reject.

On a line with, even, equal; to reduce to a uniformity, to equalize; to expose, to endanger.

丨倨 to oppose.

丨命 careless of one's life, as in battle.

丨起 to rise up together.

丨八部爲一部 he reduced the eight books to one.

丨絕己私 renounced his own private views.

病 ping' — From *disease* and *fiery*.

Sickness, illness; longing for; an ailment or pain; vicious, vice; a defect; sad, sorrow, affliction; to damage, to render worse; to vitiate; to distress; to dislike; distress, misery.

疾丨 maladies and ailments.

患丨 or 染丨 or 有丨 sick.

丨復發 a relapse.

丨愈了 or 丨痊 convalescent.

報丨 to plead sickness, to get a furlough.

丨得狠重 dangerously sick.

治丨 to cure ailments.

酷虐丨民 to tyrannically harass the people.

丨容 he looks ill.

臥丨 sick in bed.

丨國 to injure the state.

丨於天亢 distressed by the drought.

丨黃眼 you have jaundiced eyes. (*Cantonese.*)

相爲訴丨 they injured each other.

修己以安百姓堯舜其猶丨諸 to reform themselves in order to quiet the people, is what even Yao and Shun were defective in.

丨世之學 a principle that injures the country; a radical, revolutionary idea.

暴丨 a sudden attack.

人丨不求耳 the evil with men is that they will not seek — the truth.

丨故 died from sickness.

寎 ping' — Somewhat like the last.

To start in the sleep; drowsy; an old classic name for the third moon.

柄 棅 ping' — The second form is seldom used.

A handle, a haft; a crank; a source; having control of; authority, power.

把丨 to take by the handle.

無話丨 nothing to make the story plausible; nothing to talk about.

有把丨 powerful; something to rely on; a basis of action; an excuse or occasion for proceeding against.

一丨尺 a foot-rule.

掌權丨 to have the control of.

二丨 the two powers, *i.e.* punishment and instruction in ruling.

國丨倒持 the power of the emperor has passed out of his hands.

執民丨 to seize the authority.

斗丨 handle of the constellation called the Dipper.

沒丨的流星 the handless meteor, — are two wooden balls tied together; applied to an unsteady, unsafe man.

曲丨折了 the crank is broken.

凭 ping' — From 几 *bench* and 任 to *depend* on.

To lean on or against; to confide in, to trust to; proof, evidence.

依丨 to rest on; to look to; a support, a reliance.

丨欄 to lean on the railing.

丨几托腮 resting his head as he leaned on the table.

乾柴丨火 [like a] dry stick near the fire, — so is going into temptation.

丨月起相思 thinking of you while leaning over and looking at the moon.

挨丨 to rest on or lean, as a wall against a house.

拼 摒 ping' — To drive off, to expel; open, cracked; to make a bad joint in cabinet-ware.

碎丨的木器 a patched-up article, one made of pieces.

丨湊 to subscribe to make up a deficiency.

In *Cantonese.* A crashing noise 丨澎, as of smashing crockery, or the din of an orchestra.

P'ING.

Old sounds, p'ing, p'ang, bing, *and* bang. *In Canton*, p'ing, p'eng, *and* p'ăng; — *in Swatow*, p'eng, pan, *and* pⁿé; — *in Amoy*, p'eng, peng, *and* pin; — *in Fuhchau*, ping, pang, *and* p'eng; — *in Shanghai*, p'ing *and* bing; — *in Chifu*, p'ing.

娉 ꜀p'ing From *woman* and *impulsive*; used with ꜀聘 marriage presents. Elegant, as a lady; to inquire.

丨婷 graceful, lady-like; gentle and beautiful; sometimes applied to speech or tone of voice.

砯 ꜀p'ing From *rock* and *ice*. The rushing sound of the billows against a cliff.

丨崖鼓作 the roaring noise of the surf rushing under a hollow cliff.

砰 ꜀p'ing The crash of stones.

丨磅 a smash, a breaking sound, as of glass or crockery.

丨磕的 a deep rumbling noise, like thunder.

休嘉丨隱 to give thanks with great noise.

閛 ꜀p'ing The noise of shutting or opening a door; a creaking sound, as when a door turns in its socket.

平 ꜀p'ing From 丂 or 亍 *in* and 八 *eight*. Even, equal, level; just, equitable; common, ordinary, usual; uniform, equable; peaceful, undisturbed, tranquil; to tranquillize; to restore quiet, to subdue; to adjust, as weights; to harmonize, to pacify, to conciliate; to regulate; regulated; blended; plenty; a plain.

公丨 just, fair; equally sorted.

丨和 at peace; it is all settled.

天丨 a pair of balances.

丨丨的 smooth, tranquil, even.

太丨 a state of peace; the name taken by the Nanking insurgents in 1853 for their dynasty.

丨地 smooth ground; to level.

地丨 a plain; a level place.

丨日 daily; commonly.

丨常 or 丨時 common, ordinary; usually, constantly.

丨素 heretofore.

丨明 the dawn; very early.

丨班 or 丨品 of equal rank.

丨民百姓 the untitled and common people.

丨服 to subjugate, to reduce to order.

丨安 well, contented, prosperous.

均丨一式 all are of the same kind.

丨地起風波 to raise a needless disturbance.

丨分 equally divided.

好'報不丨 to desire to take the part of the injured.

丨速行 uniform motion; and 丨加速 uniform accelerated motion; terms in mechanics.

丨聲 the *p'ing shing* or even tone, the first of the four.

丨陽大路 an open, level highway.

丨空 no ground for, trumped up.

生丨 habitually; the temperament.

心不丨 unreconciled, uneasy.

丨心而論 to discuss candidly.

嘉丨月 the twelfth moon.

丨丨無奇 very ordinary, nothing remarkable.

王道丨丨 the royal road is level and easy.

丨天下 to tranquillize the empire.

In *Cantonese*. Cheap, reasonable in price.

丨的做得 a little cheaper will do.

好丨 very cheap.

In *Pekingese*. To weigh in scales.

丨準 weigh it exactly.

坪 ꜀p'ing A flat, level place; a plateau; an area where people collect

枰 ꜀p'ing To make a board plane and smooth, fit for playing chess; a wood suitable for tables and footstools; a chess-board; a game of chess.

丨板 a smooth, plane board.

丨盤 or 棋丨 a game of chess.

評 ꜀p'ing From *words* and *equal*. To discuss the merits of; to settle the order of; to arrange; to criticize a writing, to revise and edit; to deliberate and weigh.

批丨 to review a book, to make notes on a manuscript; to moralize on.

丨註 comments, criticisms.

丨閱詩文 to review and correct essays and poems.

賞丨 to commend a composition.

品丨 to estimate the merits of.

丨論 to discuss, to argue on.

丨事 to judge the merits of an affair.

譏丨 to censure, to detract from.

泙 ꜀p'ing From *water* and *even*; like ꜀砯 a rushing wave. A ravine, a wady, a gully.

澎丨 a roaring, as of the surf rolling into caves along the shore; also a dashing torrent.

洴 ꜀p'ing Also used for the last. The noise of water; to wash and whiten cocoons or silk.

丨澼絖者 people who cleanse silk.

萍 p'ing From *plant* and *gully*. Duckweed, such as covers pools and fish-ponds, called 浮丨 and 水丨, including species of *Lemna* and *Riccia*; wandering, floating about; traveling.

丨水相逢 unexpectedly meeting abroad, like drift-wood on the waters.

丨蹤無定 it is uncertain where he is now

苹 Sometimes interchanged with the last.

꜀p'ing A species of succulent cress, the 丨蕭 of whose sprouts deer are very fond; the stem is straight and slender, and the leaves greenish white.

芳草丨丨 the fragrant grassy herbage.

食野之丨 [the deer] are eating the tender cress.

Read ꜀p'ien. A protection.

丨車 a kind of war chariot with a screen or shield.

屏 From *body* and *together*.

꜀p'ing A screen wall, built before a door-way; a defense; ornamental tablets; to cover, to screen, to hide or keep out of view; to act defensively; to serve as a defense.

丨風 a movable door-screen.

帷丨 a dividing curtain; a veil.

圍丨 a folding-screen.

鏡丨 a pier-glass in a frame.

丨帳 a hanging curtain.

椅丨 back of a chair.

丨立 a guard or servant, *i. e.* one who stands like a screen.

丨藩之臣 an officer on guard on the frontier.

腰丨 a waist-cloth; a fig-leaf.

壽丨 a scroll given to old people.

桌丨 or 插丨 table ornaments of small stone screens.

Read ꜂ping. To expel; to scatter; to reject, to put aside, to keep outside; to spoil, as robbers; to remove.

丨除 to cease from, as smoking.

丨退左右 to keep back the attendants.

丨斥其非 blamed him for his faults.

丨逐 to drive out.

丨人耳目 to make people to retire, — in order to be alone.

丨氣 to hold the breath, as when before a superior.

作之丨之其菑其翳 he raised up and took off the dead trunks and fallen boles.

瓶 缾 A water-pitcher, an earthen jug; a vase; a bottle; a gurglet; a vessel with a tubular neck, and usually without a handle or nozzle.

꜀p'ing

花丨 a jar for flowers.

膽丨 a big bellied vase.

酒丨 a wine jar.

守口如丨 keep the guard over your mouth as [when pouring from] a bottle.

水丨 a pitcher, an ewer, a jug.

憑 凴 凭 凗 From *heart* or *bench* and a *horse running*; it is similar to ping' 凭; the third contracted form is not uncommon.

꜀p'ing A stand for a stone; to lean upon, to trust to; confiding in; according to, as; proof, evidence; that which can be proved.

丨中 midsman, surety, a broker.

有丨 there is proof.

無丨據 unfounded; no evidence.

口說無丨 words [alone] will not serve for proof.

以物爲丨 this thing will be the proof.

有所丨依 whatever you put your trust in.

王后丨玉几 the great lord leaned on the gemmed bench.

文丨 an officer's commission.

人丨神力 men trust to the power of the gods.

丨你說 it is as you say.

丨帖 a card sent as sign of having received a thing.

丨單 a receipt; a draft.

任丨怎麼樣 do it whichever way is agreeable to you.

丨仗 a staff.

丨票取規銀 current money will be paid on presenting this bill.

郱 An ancient place in the present Lin-k'ü hien 臨朐縣 in the central part of Shantung; this and 駢 seem to be the same place.

꜀p'ing

聘 From *ear* and *impulsive*; interchanged with ꜀娉 pretty.

ping꜄ To ask, to inquire; to send messengers to an equal to make inquiries; to invite with a present, as an officer by a prince; to negotiate with a present; to espouse, to betroth; the betrothal presents; a gift, a portion.

丨金 money paid at betrothal.

丨請 to engage a teacher.

丨賢下士 to engage a worthy man to fill a certain post.

下丨 or 過丨禮 to send betrothal presents.

厚丨 a generous dower.

行小丨 to send the first betrothal presents.

丨則爲妻 a wife is espoused by presents.

三丨 thrice invited, as the ancient I Yin 伊尹 was by his prince.

丨君 to answer the prince's call.

却丨 to decline the presents.

徵丨 to request scholars to serve the state.

丨姑娘 to betroth a virgin.

待丨 to a wait the presents; to tarry till sought for.

靡使歸丨 we cannot send any one home to inquire about our families.

俜 To repose confidence in, and employ on messages; to send.

p'ing꜄ 丨俠操權 reckless and dangerous in using power.

靐 From *thunder* thrice repeated.

꜀p'ing The sound of thunder; a thundering racket, like a salute or cannonading.

PIU.

Old sound, bio. *In Canton*, piu ;— *in Swatow*, piu ; — *in Amoy*, piu ; — *in Fuhchau*, piu ; — *in Shanghai*, pio ; — *in Chifu*, piu.

彪 *piao* From *pelage* and *tiger*.
The markings on a tiger ; a small beast, striped like a tiger, probably denoting one of the tiger-cats, but doubtless an animal common in China ; some refer it to the Himalayan leopard (*Leopardus macroceloides* of Hodgson), a much larger animal ; streaks, veins ; ornate.

文丨 or 丨炳 elegant composition ; perspicuous in style.

一丨軍馬 one company of horse and foot.

丨外 external accomplishments.

PO.

Old sounds, pa *and* pat. *In Canton*, po ; — *in Swatow*, po, p'o, *and* pua ; — *in Amoy*, pò, p'ò, *and* pw'an ; — *in Fuhchau*, po, p'o, *and* pwai ; — *in Shanghai*, pu ; — *in Chifu*, pù.

波 *po* From *water* and *skin*.
A wave, a ripple ; moved, ruffled, as water by the wind ; a glance of the eye ; shining bright, as the glare from water ; glossy ; vast, wave-like ; to communicate, to flow along ; rushing waters ; a stream ; a river in Shansi ; wrinkled, venerable, as 丨祖 my aged grandparents ; this phrase is also a name for father among the Miaotsz'.

丨平浪靜 quiet smooth water.

恩丨恬於江海 [your excellency's] kindness spreads over the region as a wave.

秋丨 bright glances of the eye.

微丨 a tender glance.

烝涉丨矣 [the pigs] are wading in the streams.

金丨 moonlight, alluding to its reflection on the water.

丨及 the coming wave, the evil will reach him ; to compromise.

水丨紋 ripples ; purling, rippling, as a current.

餘丨不了 the rest of the account will come by and by ; the remainder is not written.

奔丨勞碌 hurrying here and busy there, — in the cares of life.

丨羅文國 the kingdom of the Brahmans, — or India.

文有丨瀾 the essay is very discursive or figurative.

心中無丨浪 I have no griefs or enmities.

丨斯國 Persia ; but the name seems to have also been applied to a part of Sumatra, in the ignorance of Chinese geographers.

丨羅蜜 the jack-fruit.

丨羅菓 the pine-apple ;— *i. e.* the Borneo fruit.

丨州 an old name for Ngan-ping cheu 安平州 in Kwangsi.

In *Cantonese*. Used in imitation of the word *ball*.

打丨 to play billiards.

打地丨 to roll nine-pins.

菠 *po* From *plant* and *wave*.
A general name for spinach and other similar greens, like the *Convolvulus reptans*.

丨菜 spinach (*Spinacia*), a common article of food ; it is an exotic, and also called 丨薐菜 or the Persian greens, from whence a priest brought the seed.

嶓 *po* A hill or peak, called 丨冢 from its resemblance to a tumulus ; it is in Liang cheu in Hanchung fu in the southwest of Shensi, at the source of the River Han.

蚾 *'po* An unusual name for the toad 蚵丨, described as like a huge wood-louse or sowbug (*Oniscus*).

跛 *'po* To walk awry, as when one foot is lame, or weak, or longer than the other ; favoritism, unfair leaning to ; partial.

丨能履 the lame can get on or walk.

丨向不明 an unreasoning partiality.

Read *'pi*. Halt, lame, crippled ; to stand on one foot, considered to be rather indecorous.

丨脚 or 丨腿 lame.

亞丨 one who limps ; and 丨手 lame in the hand. (*Cantonese*.)

丨倚 inclined ; not upright.

恭立無丨 stand respectfully and do not loll.

播 *'po* To sow seed ; to strew, to scatter abroad ; to promulgate, to publish ; to disperse ; to reject, to throw aside ; to be separated ; to shake, as grain ; to encourage ; to flee.

丨種 to scatter seed broadcast.

遠丨 to make known afar.

丨揚 to winnow, as in a fan ; to promulge.

丨弄 to act as runner or spy for another ; to cozen ; to curry favor.

丨棄 to reject carelessly, to throw off.

威丨九州 the dread of him is felt through the land.

傳 ┃ to disseminate, as a doctrine.

是 ┃ 其 惡 于 衆 也 he published his wickedness to the people.

In *Cantonese*. A final particle expressing an intention, but oftener indicating a certainty.

不可亂信人 ┃ it is not well to believe everybody.

想學唐話 ┃ I really think of studying Chinese.

譒 po' Like the last; it is also wrongly used for ˓fan 繙 to translate.

To spread or proclaim abroad; to tell foolish rumors; reports, stories.

周 ┃ an officer of the Empress Wu in the T'ang dynasty.

簸 po' ˋpo A winnowing-fan; to winnow or shake grain.

拿 ┃ 箕 ˋ ┃ 米 take the fan and separate the chaff.

┃ 穀 to winnow grain.

┃ 籮 an open basket for grain.

船 顛 ┃ the ship rolled and pitched.

┃ 颺 to clean grain in the wind.

P'O.

Old sounds, p'a, ba, *and* p'at. *In Canton*, p'o; — *in Swatow*, p'o, po, *and* p'úa; — *in Amoy*, p'ò, p'i, *and* pw'an; — *in Fuhchau*, p'o *and* po; — *in Shanghai*, p'u *and* bu; — *in Chifu*, p'ù.

坡 ˏp'o A declivity, a slope; the side of a hill, a brow, a brae; a mound, a heap of rubbish, a hill; hills which contain gems.

山 ┃ a terrace or ascent of a hill.

平 ┃ a gentle slope.

青 ┃ green hills.

下 ┃ 子 溜 the ground at the foot of the hill was slippery.

上 ┃ 路 to go uphill.

陂 ˏp'o From *place* and *skin*; it is interchanged with ˓fan 阪 a brink, which it resembles, and with the last and next.

Uneven; inclined, tipped over; a declivity; falling down, dilapidated.

Read ˏpéi. A bank, a side; a rising shore; an embankment, a dam; banked up; to inclose by dikes; a pool.

┃ 池 an artificial pond.

路 ┃ the roadside.

彼 澤 之 ┃ by the shores of that marsh.

┃ 塘 a dike to inclose water.

世 運 平 ┃ 之 故 because of the ups and downs of life.

岥 ˏp'o Like the last, of which some regard it as another form.

Uneven, as a road; the side of a road.

┃ 陀 uneven, as a rugged slope.

玻 ˏp'o A vitreous transparent glaze.

┃ 璃 or ┃ 瓈 glass (perhaps in imitation of the Portuguese *vidro*); also called 水玉 because it is 瑩 如 水 堅 如 玉 clear as water and hard as gem; said to have been brought from the west by 三 保 a eunuch in the Ming dynasty.

洋 ┃ 璃 foreign glassware.

┃ 碎 broken glass, an article of trade.

┃ 璃 片 window-glass.

婆 ˏp'o From *woman* and *wave*, but the original form is made of *woman* 女 and 般 a *sort*.

An old woman, a mother; at the South, a dame, a crone, a gammer, a granny; in the North, it is rather like hag, virago; motherly, matronly; used by Budhists to express immortality.

┃ 迦 ┃ (in Sanscrit *bhagavat*) a term applied to every Budha, denoting one who possesses the highest virtue.

公 ┃ husband and wife, Darby and Joan.

老 ┃ my wife; the goodwoman.

┃ 娘 or 老 ┃ ┃ an old lady.

紡 紗 ┃ a humming, green cicada, with broad wings.

媒 ┃ a matchmaker.

接 生 ┃ a midwife.

漁 ┃ fishwomen, fishwives.

繙 頭 ┃ a stepmother.

蛋 家 ┃ the boatwomen at Canton.

大 ┃ the legal wife.

一 片 ┃ 心 a motherly feeling.

湯 ┃ a bed-warmer, a kind of hot water pan.

仙 ┃ a witch; a spiritual medium.

寡 婦 ┃ a widow.

孟 ┃ a god of the wind, once known in K'ai-fung fu.

闍 ┃ 國 Ava, whose king once received investiture from the Mongols.

┃ 羅 吸 摩 or Brahma, regarded by the Budhists as inferior to every Budha.

皤 ˏp'o White, plain; gray, like old men; hair turning silvery; the white on the belly; abundant.

┃ ┃ 國 老 a venerable statesman.

┃ 腹 big bellied.

短 鬢 ┃ ┃ 雪 your temples are beginning to turn white a little.

鄱 ˏp'o A district in the north of Kiangsi, Poyang hien ┃ 陽 縣 contiguous to the Poyang Lake, from which it is named.

礬 ˏp'o From *stone* and *wave* for the phonetic.

Stones like flint or obsidian, which can be used for spear or arrow-heads.

頗 ˓p'o ˓p'o The head inclined one side; leaning, uneven; somewhat, a degree, a little; an excess; rather doubtful; perverse, one-sided.

丨可 it will answer very well.

丨多 rather too much, a good deal.

丨有 rather too much of it.

丨知一二 I know a thing or two.

丨久 rather too long a time.

丨合 can be used.

人用側丨僻民用僭忒 when officers pervert equity and have favorites, the people will overpass their place.

丨丨曉得 I understand it very well.

偏˓丨 partial, prejudiced.

叵 ˓ 𠀋 ˓ ˓p'o From 可 *can* reversed; it needs to be distinguished from *kü*ˀ 巨 *great*: the second form is employed for the latter senses.

An *adverb*, do not, may or can not, ought not; then, forthwith; insufferable.

丨信 unworthy of belief.

丨耐心煩 I can't bear so much inconvenience.

丨欲討之 he thereupon wished to reduce him.

人心丨測 man's heart is inscrutable.

笸 ˓p'o An unauthorized but common character.

A basket tray, about four inches deep, 丨籮 used to carry grain in a cart.

破 p'oˀ From *stone* and *skin*.

To rend, to break; to ruin, to defeat; to take by storm; to detect, to lay bare; to solve; to explain; split, tattered, broken, injured; detected; ruined, as a family; understood, seen through, as a plot; to guess, as a riddle; resolved, as a doubt; a hard blow.

丨壞 destroyed, useless.

丨碎 smashed; broken to shivers.

丨裂 cracked; torn; split.

驚丨膽 fear has split his gall-bladder; — *i. e.* lost all courage.

丨開 split it open.

打丨 break it; knock it to pieces.

丨敗 defeated, ruined.

看丨了 detected, all found out; seen to be vanity, as the world.

丨財 to lose property, as by theft.

舍矢如丨 the arrows went like blows to the mark.

丨解詳細 he explained the sense most carefully.

丨費 to waste, to spend recklessly.

丨一塊洋錢買花 I spent a dollar for flowers.

丨家子弟 he is the ruin of the family.

丨落戶 a decayed family.

丨案 the case has been found out.

丨鏡重圓 the mirror was broken and he has made it round again; — said of a second marriage.

丨地獄 to open hell; *i. e.* to get souls out of purgatory.

丨謎 to guess a riddle.

丨計 to detect a scheme.

丨法 to match and neutralize a plot or scheme.

丨腹 to lay bare one's heart.

攻丨池城 carried the city by storm.

小莫能丨 nothing is too small to be discovered or reached, as by the microscope.

請主人丨丨 I beg you, Sir, to guess — my riddle.

婆 ˓p'o From *plant* and a *matron*.

Luxuriant vegetation.

丨娑 or 丨丨娑娑 flourishing, exuberant; bewitching, as the way of an actress.

POH.

Some of these are often read PEH. *Old sounds*, pak, pat, bak, *and* bat. *In Canton*, pak, pok, păk, pút, *and* mak; — *in Swatow*, pak, pòk, pó, bwa, hwat, pék, *and* po; — *in Amoy*, pok, p'ok, pek, p'ek, pít, pwat, p'aoh, *and* p'iau; — *in Fuhchau*, pòk, poh, pauk, p'auk, paik, p'aik, pah, pek, p'ek, péik, pwòh, pwak, păk, *and* pwòk; — *in Shanghai*, bŏk, bok, pak, p'ăk, bo, beh, bah, păh, *and* p'ih; — *in Chifu*, pù.

薄 ˓pao poˀ From *plants* and *extended*; it resembles *pu*ˀ 簿 a book.

Plants extended; trees appearing singly, no brushwood, grassy; thin; attenuated; subtle; a thin leaf or plate, a pellicle; poor, unfortunate; economical; light, few; to diminish; to slight, to treat coldly; suspicious of; to approach; an initial particle, ah, so; to reach or extend over; careless, inattentive to, anyhow; trifling; a curtain or screen.

丨罪 a slight offense.

厚 and 丨 thick and thin; liberal and stingy; intimate and distant.

丨命 unfortunate in life.

輕丨 contemptuous, regardless of.

丨言采之丨言有之 thus we pick them; now we have them.

丨行人 a heartless man.

丨荷油 essence of peppermint.

今且丨暮 it is now twilight; in the gloaming.

日丨食 the sun is partly eclipsed.

丨禮 shabby presents.

直丨城下 he came directly up to the city walls.

丨情 no sense of gratitude.

人丁單丨 a few descendants.

外丨四海咸建五長 in the regions lying beyond out to the seas, I established five presidents.
無所倚丨 no refuge, no reliance.
地皮丨 a sterile spot; a poverty stricken place; a spiritless race.
臉皮丨 timid, retiring, bashful, thin-skinned, craven.
林丨 woody thickets.
淡丨 to stint; frugal; dull, as trade.
丨言往訴 every time that I go and say a little, — he gets so angry.
丨待 to care little for.
丨集 to gather, to crowd to; to form a squad.
帷丨不修 the curtain was not cared for; — *i. e.* the women were too public.
雷風相丨 the thunder and wind struggled with each other.
戦驅丨丨 the cries and din of the jostling carriages.

箔, *po'* Used with the last and the next.
A door-screen, made of splints.
蠶丨 a frame on which worms spin cocoons.
魚丨 small fishing-stakes; a weir.
葦丨 a screen made of rushes.

鉑, *poh'* A thin sheet of metal; mock-metal.
金丨 gold leaf.
銅丨 brass leaf, tinsel.
錫丨 tin foil.
銀丨 silver leaf.

搏, *poh'* To spring upon, to seize; to wrest from, to strike; to clutch, to grasp; to play, as a lute; to lay the hand on.
丨擊 to strike.
丨取 to seize.
以手丨虎 he pommeled the tiger with his fist.

簙, *poh'* A simple ancient game played with six sticks in twelve squares; it resembled the game of fox-and-geese.

膊, *poh'* From *flesh* and *thin* contracted; it is often wrongly used for *‚pang* 髈 one of its synonyms.

A slice of meat for drying, a collop; the humerus, the upper arm in some places, but in the southern provinces denotes the shoulder; to slice, to shred; to strip and mangle, as a carcase; the clinking of stones.
搭丨巾 a shawl, a scarf, or kerchief, worn loose over the 丨頭 or shoulders. (*Cantonese.*)
赳丨 to shoulder.
殺而丨諸城上 they slew and then gashed the bodies on the walls.
轉丨 to change shoulders.
大肐丨根兒 great brawny arms, — able to box.
腷丨戰聲喧 [the cocks] spread out their wings and set to with a scream.

博, **愽,** *poh'* From 十 *ten* or complete, and 尃 *extended;* the second form is erroneous.

Ample, spacious, extended; universal, general; intelligent, versed in, learned; to cause, to make; to barter; to game, to play for money.
丨學 or 丨聞 extensively read, well informed.
戎車孔丨 their war-chariots are very large.
丨雅 learned and accomplished.
丨物院 a museum.
六丨 or 丨六 to play dice.
丨局 a gaming-house.
丨古 relics of olden time, antiques.
丨我以文 he taught me letters.
以丨一笑 it will amuse you a little.
以貨丨貨 to barter goods.
丨士 a professor in a college.
丨州 an old name for Liaoch'ing hien 聊城縣 in the west of Shantung.
丨濟于民 universal kindness to the people.

爆, *poh'* Used with *pao'* 爆 to burn.
To crackle, to burst from heat; the crackling noise of a fire.

鎛, *poh'* A large bell; others say a small one, which responded; similar to the next.
丨鎒 a light hoe used for dibbling and weeding.
丨鱗獸 ornaments carved on bell frames.

鑮, *poh'* A large bell used to mark stops in music, or at the end of the twelve Chinese hours; an implement of husbandry, a kind of hoe.

礴, *poh'* Opened out; to repress; to cram; stuffed.
旁丨 filled; vast, as the atmosphere.
槃丨 to sit cross-legged.

欂, *poh'* A pillar in the wall; the tie-beam that connects the inner and outer pillars of a portico.

白, *po'* *‚pai* Said to be formed of 合 and 二 contracted in combination, because *white* is the color of the even numbers; it forms the 106th radical of characters relating to white.

White, a color now regarded as rather an unlucky hue; clear, immaculate; bright, as moonlight; plain, easy to comprehend; low, without rank; freely, without price; disinterested, pure; unstamped; explicit, manifested; mournful; obvious, auricular, as in writing; to state to; to manifest, to make clear; easily understood; to redress, to vindicate; in Canton, the reverse of a coin; the white part, as of the eye or an egg.
丨色 a white color.
丨撞 a loafer; a sharper who looks about while he pretends to seek a friend.
丨抄 a pasquinade, a libel.
丨丨給你 I now freely give it to you.

丨得了 I got it for nothing.

丨長了 I have grown old uselessly; I have done nothing in life.

道丨 the spoken parts of a play, those not sung.

寫丨字 words written by the sound, as 金 for 今.

曉丨話 or 曉土丨 he understands the local patois.

眼丨丨 he could only see it with his eyes; — *i. e.* he could (or would) do nothing.

丨人 or 丨衣人 or 丨丁 a commoner, a man who has no rank, or has been degraded from office.

丨文 the simple text.

丨手成家 to rise in life by one's efforts, self-made.

丨食 a free meal; a plain dish.

丨瞧 I had a look for nothing.

丨色人 or 丨屑 an albino, known as 天老兒 in Peking.

丨日 or 丨晝 in open day; daylight.

紅丨事 lucky and unlucky affairs, pleasant and sad events; referring especially to marriages and funerals.

丨屋出公卿 a plain family has produced a high statesman.

搶丨一頓 I got the better of him in that argument.

月丨 bright moonlight.

胡說丨道 gasconade, bragging.

太丨 the planet Venus; this name was given to the poet, Li T'ai-poh, by his mother, who dreamed that she conceived him under the influence of this star.

三丨 snow in the first moon.

年經九丨 it is already nine years — meaning snows.

剖心自丨 to open one's heart, to clear one's reputation.

丨降 a medicine, corrosive sublimate.

飛丨 to miss a leaf in turning over, — which spoils the essay.

穿丨掛孝 to wear white for filial mourning.

豈含冤莫丨乎 shall I not redress those who have been wronged?

丨下 a name of Nanking in the T'ang dynasty.

百 'pai poh' From 白 *white* or clear, and 一 *one*; *q. d.* one round sun.

A hundred; the whole of a class or sort; many, numerous; all, everybody.

丨中無一 not one in a hundred.

丨工 all mechanics; craftsmen.

丨千萬 thousands of thousands; — a vast number.

丨發丨中' a hundred shots and a hundred hits; — he's always lucky.

丨子高升 the rocket rose very high.

丨足 the centipede.

丨官 all officials; the rulers.

丨盤 all kinds, as of speculations.

丨合花 lily flowers, alluding to the layers on the bulb.

丨計叢生 all the various occupations of life.

丨厭之極 everybody hates him heartily.

丨年之後 after death, a euphuism.

丨家姓 the surnames or clan names of the Chinese.

丨會 the brain.

丨里侯 a district magistrate, alluding to the extent of his jurisdiction.

佰 poh' A hundred men, the leader of a band, a centurion; a string of a hundred cash; it is used for the last in writing numbers for security.

壹丨兩 100 taels of silver.

伯 poh' From *man* and *white*; the word *beg* or *bey* 伯克 is derived from this; occurs used for *pa* 霸 a tyrant.

A father's elder brother; the eldest of brothers; a title of respect; a senior, a superior; an earl, the third rank of nobility; anciently, also a constable of princes, heads of departments, leaders, nobles, and chiefs; to control; term by which a husband or elder brother is addressed.

將丨助予 O Sir, come to my help!

丨父 or 大父 my paternal elder uncle, called 大爺 in familiar address; an old gentleman.

丨公 a great uncle.

丨叔 paternal uncles; used for uncles on both sides.

丨氏 an uncle, an elder, a senior.

丨母 an aunt, an uncle's wife.

宗丨 an ancient rank, like a high-priest.

丨勞 the shrike.

丨仲叔季 a mode of calling four brothers, answering to first, second, third, and fourth.

帛 poh' From *kerchief* and *white*.

Plain white silk, taffety; a present of silk; wealth, property.

布丨 fabrics generally.

寶丨 paper money burned at worship.

掛丨 to place long strips of paper on graves, as at Ts'ing-ming.

財丨 riches; estates.

束丨 a small present, a single roll.

三丨 three sorts of colored silks used for presents.

財丨星君 the Chinese Plutus, or god of Wealth.

泊 poh' From *water* and *white*; used with 薄 thin.

The glare on the water; a ripple; to stop; to fasten or moor a boat; to anchor; anchored, at leisure; a marshy lake.

灣丨 or 丨船 to anchor a vessel.

澹丨自如 frugal, contented, with little.

漂丨 unsettled, roving, as a gypsy; a vagabond.

河丨所 the *ho-po*, *i. e.* the hoppo or boat-master at Canton; as 河丨司 is a harbor-master.

迫, 廹, *poh'* From to *go* and *white*; the second and common form is unauthorized.

To urge, to insist upon; to vex, to harass, to provoke to extremity; embarrassed and driven on, as by an enemy.

惶丨失措 flurried and driven so as to make mistakes.

急丨 hurried; pressed, as by work.

窮丨 not a cash left, penniless.

窘丨 straitened; in distress, as by poverty; overburdened, as with cares.

爲勢所丨 driven by circumstances.

丨于嚴命 bound by a strict command.

柏, 栢, *poh'* *'pai* From *wood* and *white*, referring to its durability, emblematic of purity; the first form is correct.

The cypress; the cedar; large; to impel, to crowd on, to urge.

扁丨 the juniper; the arborvitæ. (*Thuja orientalis.*)

丨府 a governor's palace.

黃丨 bark of the *Pterocarpus flavus*, used to dye silks yellow.

丨香樹 the swamp cedar, used for incense.

丨子油 oil from juniper seeds, used in the red ink for stamps.

丨操 chaste, refusing to wed again.

丨地之席 the guests crowded each other on the ground.

舶, *poh'* A great junk fit to cross the ocean; a sea-going vessel.

海丨 a ship.

丨艚船 a junk from Tientsin or Siam. (*Cantonese.*)

襮, *poh'* An embroidered collar or cape, anciently worn over the dress at court or state sacrifices; it was of red or differently made to indicate rank.

領丨 an outside cape.

表丨 to show outside, to indicate by some symbol.

皺, *pao'* To swell up suddenly, as a pustule; the skin breaking, as from chilblains.

涷瘃丨皮 the skin chapping in winter from the cold.

剝, *poh'* From *knife* and *to engrave*.

To flay, to peel, to skin; to split; to uncover; *met.* to degrade, as by depriving of robes; to wane; to extort, to fleece, to demand by force; to slaughter an animal; the 23d diagram, meaning to change from soft to hard.

丨皮 to skin, to flay, — it was an ancient punishment; to fleece, to extort.

抽丨 to exact sharply, as in custom duties; to levy on.

復丨之秋 good times have returned, the worst has passed.

丨殼 to peel the husk.

或丨或亨 kill and then cook it.

狠丨 to take without mercy.

丨下來 take off your coat.

Read *puh*, To strike, to knock down.

八月丨棗 in October, they pick (or thrash down) the dates.

駁, 駮, *poh'* From *horse* and *to blend* or *join*; the first form is correct.

A piebald or particolored horse; a fabulous tiger; mixed, diverse; to dispute, to argue against, to criticise; contradictory, impracticable; to graft; to tranship; to thrust in, to insert; to splice, to scarp on, to piece out; to continue, to take up where one left off; suddenly.

丨罪 to find fault with.

丨價 to cavil at the price.

丨色 particolored, variegated.

丨樹 to graft trees.

丨船 a boat which makes a connection with another.

丨貨 to tranship goods.

丨通句話 to correct the expressions.

批丨不准 to reverse the decision of a lower court.

丨然大怒 he suddenly waxed angry.

丨回 to reject a petition.

丨渡 to take from a cart to the boat, to transport.

丨詰 to browbeat, to cross-question.

丨斥 to expose an error.

接丨 to receive from another, as goods.

拆丨 a prolepsis; to answer objections beforehand.

雹, *ˏpao* *poh'* From *rain* and *to wrap*.

Hail; sometimes called 硬頭雨 hard-headed rain.

丨子 a hailstone.

下丨 or 落丨 to hail.

傷丨 hurt by hailstones.

趵, *ˏpao* The tramping noise made in walking over stones.

踣丨 noise made by a horse striking his hoofs together.

癶, *poh'* The original form is intended to represent a man's legs stretched out; it was composed of two 止 placed back to back, and gradually contracted to the present form; it is the 105th radical of a few characters.

Two persons standing back to back; to progress.

撥, *ˏpo'i* From *hand* and *to issue*; originally like the last.

To spread or distribute in their proper places; to appropriate or set aside for; to rule, to dispose; to detach, as troops; to expel, to root out; to abrogate; uprooted; to get rid of, to exclude; to scatter, as the wind does clouds; fluttering, as a dress; to flirt, as a fan; to thrum, as a lute; to cut grass; to separate; ropes for a hearse.

丨弓 to draw the bow.

丨蚊 to drive off musketoes.

玄王桓丨 the dark king ruled with vigor.

丨闢烟 to dissipate the smoke.
丨着火 to fan the flame.
丨紗 to reel thread.
分丨兵丁 to detach troops to a post.
搬丨 to allot each one his duties.
丨擷 a great worker.
丨擷開 move aside the things, make a way.
丨馬尾 a lick-spittle.
丨亂反治之才 a vigorous ruler who can reform abuses, or put down rebels to restore order.
本實先丨 it must first be uprooted.
丨轉 altered, as for the better.
丨歸一邊 to put one side, partial.
丨雲見日 when the clouds disperse you can see the sun; *met.* to dissipate error.
丨浪 a door-latch or knob. (*Pekingese.*)
丨動絲絃入臥房 the thrummer on his guitar has come into the bedroom; — *i.e.* a musketo is buzzing.
丨冗前來 I beg of you to let nothing prevent your coming.
請丨正 please straighten it; amend or revise it.

In *Shanghai.* An instrumental verb; using, with, by; to give, to hand.
丨勒爺娘責備 he was reproved by his parents.
丨拉我 give it to me.

襏, *poh'* A rain garment, made of leaves or coarse gunny cloth, called 丨襫, worn by laborers; a short jacket.

鱍, *poh'* From *fish* and to *exhibit.*
A fish wagging its tail, when swimming.

北, *poh'* *'pé* Designed to represent two *men* inimical to each other, and standing back to back.
The north; northern; to the north; northwards; the capital; conquered and fleeing.
丨方 the northern regions.
恭辭丨上 to bid farewell to a graduate going to Peking.
敗丨 defeated, demoralized.
丨極 the north pole.
丨口外 beyond the Wall.
攻于後以丨血流漂杵 they attacked those behind, who fled, and the blood flowed till it would float a pestle.
追丨 to pursue the defeated.
丨面而朝 to have an audience with the Emperor, alluding to his position as always facing the south.
丨京 Peking, or the northern capital; it has been chiefly current since the Ming dynasty began.

Read *péi'* To separate; to oppose.
違丨 to turn the back on.
分丨 parted, placed in divisions.

跋, *poh'* To walk through the grass; to trudge, to draggle; to travel off; to presume to do of one's self; to stumble, to slip; the end of a candle.
狼丨其胡 the old wolf steps on his dewlap.
大夫丨涉 a high officer has gone over the prairies and streams.
足丨 the heel.
丨本 the root; the base.
題丨 an addenda to a book; another preface to a new edition.
丨涉勞苦 the discommodities of traveling.
丨陀 or 丨達 (Sanscrit, *bhadra*) virtuous or sage, a title applied to every Budha.
丨倒 to stumble and fall.
丨提河 the River Gunduck in Nipal, called *Hiranya vati* by Budhists.
丨扈 to tread down legal rights, to threaten reprisals.

盋, *poh'* Similar to the next.
A large dish for eating from.

鉢, *˛poh* An open earthen-ware basin to cook in, common at Canton; a globular, narrow-mouthed dish used by priests for their alms-bowl, contracted from 丨多羅 or the Sanscrit *patra*, a beggar's clap-dish; a stone-ware patera to grind colors on.
丨盂 a priest's dish, shaped like a flat globe.
傳衣丨 to hand down the [priest's] robe and clap-dish — to a disciple.
銅鑼丨 a large platter dish. (*Cantonese.*)
托丨空門 the Budhist profession.
漏丨 a tunnel.

茇, *poh'* The roots of grass; stubble; a thatched cottage.
丨舍 a hovel or mat house.
根丨 sprouting grass.
蔽芾甘棠召伯所丨 under this shady sweet crab-tree the chief of Shao lodged.

鈸, *˛poh* A small bell, like a sleigh-bell, used by Budhists in chanting, or in music to respond; sometimes written 鈢 and used in Siam for a tical.
鐃丨 small cymbals.

骲, **膊**, *poh'* The shoulder-blade; the scapula; commonly called 膊甲 or shoulder-scale.

鼥, *poh'* The beaver, known as 鼧丨 and also 土撥鼠; it is found in Koko-nor in watery places, and burrows; some eat it, and the name denotes its fatness.

餑, *˛po* A baked cake made of flour confectionary; comfits.
硬麪丨丨 hard biscuit.
炕丨丨 to cook cakes.
香丨丨似的 like sweet cakes.

妭, *poh'* A name for a wife among the northern tribes; a pretty woman; another form of *pah*, 魃 the demon of drought.

馞, *poh'* Fragrant.
香 ｜ ｜ an exceedingly good smell.

蘗, 檗, *poh'* } A small tree found in Hunan, producing a yellow wood called 黃 ｜; the root wood is reddish; the bark is bitter and dyes yellow; it is like the pomegranate in habit.

擘, *poh'* From *hand* and a *chief*; it is not identical with *p'ih*, 擗 to bend.
To break asunder, to break in two; to open, to split, to pull asunder; to disgrace.
你 ｜ 開 口 open your mouth.
｜ 父 兄 面 to make one's father and brother blush.
巨 ｜ the thumb.
｜ 餅 to break bread.
｜ 紙 to tear paper.
｜ 了 交 情 to disrupt friendly feelings.
塗 皆 乾 ｜ 之 the plastering has dried and cracked off.

In *Cantonese*. To throw a thing on the ground; to fling it away.

亳, *po'* Resembles *ˏhao* 毫 down.
Name of ｜ 州 in Ying-cheu fu in the north of Nganhwui; a term for the northern part of that province; an early capital of China, B. C. 1760, lying in the present Shang-k'iu 商 邱 in the east of Honan; there was another in Yen-sz' in Honan fu in the west of that province; and a third near the first.
朕 哉 自 ｜ I began my operations at Poh; said by Chingtang.

P'OH.

Old sounds, p'at, p'ak, *and* bak. *In Canton*, p'ok, p'út, p'ak, pak, *and* pòk; — *in Swatow*, p'òk, p'ó, p'úa, p'a, pek, *and* p'ek; — *in Amoy*, pw'at, p'ek, *and* p'ok; — *in Fuhchau*, pw'ak, p'iák, pwok, p'éuk, p'auk, *and* puk; — *in Shanghai*, p'eh, p'ak, p'òk, and bòk; — *in Chifu*, p'ù.

潑, *ˏp'oh* From *water* and to *issue*.
To throw water down, to bespatter; to drip, to ooze out; dissipated; a dash of water; to waste; bold, vigorous.
一 ｜ 雨 a smart shower.
活 ｜ ｜ 的 cheerful, in good spirits; unselfish; to enhearten.
散 ｜ to use things recklessly.
｜ 墨 a bold handwriting.
刁 ｜ perverse; incurably evil.
｜ 失 生 意 to lose custom, as by rudeness.
｜ 水 難 收 water thrown out cannot be gathered up; — one must abide the results of his own acts.

In *Cantonese*. Slender, acute.
十 指 纖 ｜ ｜ all her fingers taper prettily.

𠞊, 鏺, *ˏp'o* } A sickle or hooked knife, sharp on both edges, to cut grass; a small scythe or grass-knife.

醱, *ˏp'o* Grape-juice, not yet settled or strained is ｜ 醅; must, newly made spirits.

珀, *p'oh'* From *gem* and *white*.
Amber is 琥 ｜, supposed to be of resinous origin; when 拭 熱 能 吸 芥 rubbed hot it will attract straws.
蜜 蠟 ｜ a yellowish red-amber; also false amber.
血 ｜ red amber.
明 ｜ clear, light colored amber.

𢷎, *ˏp'u* The thud of an arrow; the noise it makes when striking, as if it was a hailstone.

葧, *p'oh'* *ˏpi* An edible tuber, the ｜ 薺 called at Canton 馬 蹄 or horse's hoof, the *Eleocharis tuberosus* or water-chestnut.
馬 ｜ or horse's tuber, one name for the puff-ball (*Lycoperdon*), some of which are said to be as large as a pint measure.

撲, *ˏp'u* *p'oh'* From *hand* and a *case* for rods; contracted like the next.
To lean or recline against; to flog, to strike; to tap; a blow; to impinge, to strike against; to flit, as a bat; to flap.
花 ｜ 鼻 the flowers excite the nose.
｜ 翼 to clap the wings.
｜ 滅 火 to tread or slap out a fire.
｜ 了 來 they came rushing on.
一 ｜ 納 心 a fixed design, a settled resolution.
蛾 ｜ 燈 花 the moth flits about the lamp.
｜ 過 來 to rush on one; to close in upon, as a robber.
｜ 三 斗 塵 to brush away three pecks of dust; — *met.* to render perspicuous, to clear up.

扑, *ˏp'u* Interchanged with the last.
To use a club or cudgel; to beat, to pound; a tap.
｜ 馬 to whip a horse.
｜ 作 教 刑 the rod is the punishment in teaching.
顛 ｜ to push one over.
｜ 倒 to fall down, as in a fit.

樸, *ˏp'u* From *wood* and a *case* for bamboo reeds.
Hard, fine-grained wood; rough, scrubby timber; the body, as of an unfinished vessel; sincere, plain; the substance, material; a body without appendage or ornament.

丨實 simple-minded, honest, rustic, sincere.

丨素家風 a family of unpretentious, plain habits.

簡丨 scrimping, parsimonious.

丨儉 frugal; just what is necessary.

歸眞返丨 to reform one's habits and expenses.

朴, p'oh' Used as a contraction of the last, and of *fu'* 訃 to announce.

The bark of two kinds of *Magnolia*; the 赤丨 is the *M. rubra*; the other is the *Magnolia hypoleuca*, called 厚丨 a tonic of a bitterish pungent, aromatic taste.

丨樹 the dwarf nettle tree, the *Celtis orientalis*.

聞丨 the note to inform friends of a parent's decease.

米丨 paddy, unhulled rice.

璞, p'oh' The crust or gangue of a gem; an unpolished gem.

丨玉 a gem in the rough.

卞和獻丨兩刖其足 Pien Ho offered a rough gem [to King Li of Tsu], who cut off both his legs, — for his impudence.

墣, p'oh' A clod of earth.

丨塊 a lump of dirt.

骲, p'oh' An arrow-head of bone is 骨丨; and 丨頭箭 are arrows tipped with blunt bone, so as not to wound.

撲, p'o' To take out of, to pluck up; to turn, is found in the Shanghai phrase 丨轉 to turn over or turn around.

瞨, p'oh' The eyesight somewhat indistinct, as from near-sightedness.

眹丨 protuberant eyeballs.

僰, p'oh' From *man* and *thorn*; *q. d.* a bushman.

To banish, to exile or drive men to live among the western savages; to drive into the desert; certain aborigines who lived in Kien-wéi hien 犍爲縣 in Sz'ch'uen in the Han dynasty, and are still found in Pu-ngan cheu 普安州 in the southwest of Kwéichau.

匐, fuh' From to *wrap* and *wide*; also read *fuh*,

To fall prostrate, to crawl on the hands and knees; to exert one's self to relieve another.

匍丨扶柩 he fell on and clasped the coffin.

匍丨救之 I even crawled on my knees to save them.

蔔, p'oh' A fragrant, white flower called 薝丨; a general name for spindle-shaped roots is 蘿丨, as radishes, beets, turnips, &c.

生蘿丨 raw carrots; to have chilblains. (*Cantonese.*)

拍, p'o' ,p'ai From 手 *hand* and 百 *hundred* contracted, intimating many hands.

To pat, to caress; to slap, as a table; to beat, as cymbals; in Peking, the projecting cornice over a shop or house, which serves as an ornament, or a protection to the entrance.

丨手 to clap the hands, as when calling a servant.

丨案大怒 he slapped the table in great anger.

丨和 to act as a peacemaker.

丨掌而笑 clapped their hands and laughed.

雪浪丨長空 the foaming billows beat against the sky, — as in a tyfoon.

丨張 to play ball.

音調合丨 the notes accord.

丨肩 to pat on the shoulder.

丨賣貨物 to buy by bidding, as at an auction.

丨胸 to strike the breast, as when vexed.

席丨子 a cornice made of matting.

粕, p'oh' The grains of liquor.

糟丨 that which floats on the vat.

魄, p'oh' From *demon* and *white* for the phonetic.

The animal soul, inferior to the 魂, and partaking of the 陰 principle; it goes earthward on death, and forms the ghost; the faculties, especially the senses; the animal spirits or nervous perception, as distinguished from the reason; figure, form; the dark disk of the moon, that which cannot be seen.

死丨 and 旁死丨 the first and second days of the new moon, when no disk can be seen.

始生丨 the sixteenth day of the moon.

三魂七丨 the three souls and seven spirits of a man, the last being the action of the five senses and limbs, which some persons omit as not being really a spirit.

丨附陰之靈 the *p'oh* is the energy belonging to the body.

精丨 bodily vigor.

形丨 body, form.

三月哉生丨 when the moon began to wane in the third month.

月丨生光 the moon begins to brighten.

Read *t'oh*, and also written 托. Desolate.

落丨 disheartened, spiritless.

家貧落丨 a wretchedly poor family.

PU.

Old sounds, po, bo, pok, bok, pot, *and* bot. *In Canton*, pò *and* fau; — *in Swatow*, pu, pò, *and* p'ò; — *in Amoy*, pò, p'ò, *and* hu; — *in Fuhchau*, pu, pwò, *and* pw'ò; — *in Shanghai*, pu *and* bu; — *in Chifu*, pu.

逋 ˏp'u From to *go* and *first*.
To flee, to abscond; to hang in suspense; to owe government; a defaulter, a peculator.
丨欠 obligations to government
丨負 a debt.
丨逃 to abscond, to escape from arrest.
丨竄 to skulk and secrete, as a fellow fleeing from the police.
丨臣 vagabond, disloyal officials.

晡 ˏpu The period from 3 to 5 o'clock P. M., same as 申時 the afternoon hour.
下丨 sunsetting.
日將丨 the sun is nearly down
日已丨兮 ah! the sun is now declining.
日丨潮熱 the fever increases as the day wears away

庯 ˏpu A flat roof; the roof made flat so as to be used.
丨長 the headman of the roof, — a name given to the local headmen of Chinese emigrants in Siam and elsewhere.

餔 ˏpu From to *eat* and *first*; interchanged with 哺ˋ to feed, and erroneously used for 舖ˋ a shop.
To eat; an afternoon lunch; a cake; gruel.
晚丨 an evening or late meal.
徒丨啜也 good at nothing but to eat and drink.
豆丨 bean cakes; food of pulse.

圃 ˋpu A vegetable garden, an orchard; a place for recreation; to cultivate a garden; mat sheds erected by squatters.
老丨 a gardener.
九月築場丨 in the ninth moon, they beat smooth the stacking-floors in their gardens.
農丨 farmers and gardeners.
園丨 gardens of all kinds.
玄丨 an elysium in the Kwănlun Mts. 崑崙山 where the Heavenly Ruler 天帝 resides.

補 ˋpu From *clothes* and *first*; occurs used for the next.
To repair, to mend; to close up, as a breach; to patch; to supply, to substitute, to make up; to aid, to assist; to recruit, to strengthen, as the body; the insignia of rank sewed on the robe; a supplement or addenda; in *arithmetic*, a thousand millions or a billion.
丨身 to strengthen the powers.
丨藥 tonics, restoratives.
丨衣服 to patch clothes.
丨血氣 to recruit the vital energies.
丨服 the embroidered official robe on which the 丨子 or insignia is sewed.
丨銀水 (or 色) to supply (or make up) the discount.
丨平頭 to make up for light weight of money.
丨諫君王 to reprove a prince, that he may amend his faults.
不無小丨 there is doubtless some small advantage.
賠丨 to supply a new one.
丨還 to make it up to one, as a breakage.
丨些罅漏 fill up this little crack; — *met.* make this affair work better.
功不丨過 no merit can atone for this fault.
剜肉丨瘡 to cut off the flesh to patch an ulcer, — is utter folly.
丨髒 a patch.
正進丨進 a primus and secundus; an appointer and his alternative.

譜 ˋpu From *words* and *pervading*; interchanged with the last.
A list, a record; a chronicle; a treatise on an art, or a history of its productions; an escutcheon; a genealogical list; a census list; a biographical work; to insert in a register; to put in a proper place; belonging to, as a clan or rank.
家丨 or 丨系 a family genealogy.
族丨 a clan register.
修丨 to revise the family records.
棋丨 book of games of chess.
畫丨 a treatise on drawing.
歷丨 historical annals.
丨錄 scientific repertories, notices of antiques, and similar works.
同年丨 about the same age.
蘭丨 a certificate of sworn brotherhood.
說話無丨 his talk is unreliable; extravagant speeches.
鄉丨 a village census or annals.
都有丨 everything has its rules or usages; there's a right way for doing everything.

In *Cantonese*. Reasonable; evidence for.
有的丨 rather near.
話個丨來 set an upset price; give me some idea of its value.

埔 ˋpu An unauthorized character, probably changed from ˏ浦 a reach.
An open level place, an arena; a port or anchorage.
平丨 plain at the base of hills; a level region.
黃丨 Whampoa Reach near Canton.
丨頭 a mart, a place of trade on the sea.
遠丨歸帆 the distant sails can be seen coming to the anchorage.

In *Pekingese.* A measure of length of five *li*, where a rest-house is erected; the house is called 丨房 and contains a guard; also a neighborhood or part of a street in the outer city, placed under the direction of a 總甲 or policeman.

埠 *pu'* From 土 *earth* and 阜 *a hillock;* it is used with the last.

A port; a landing where trade is carried on; a mart; an unwalled seaside town.

丨頭 a port; a marine landing-place; a mart, as for sale of salt.

穀丨 a grain warehouse.

鹽丨 a salt dépôt.

過丨 to trade along at the ports.

盛丨 your port.

大丨 a great mart, like Shanghai.

新丨 the new port usually denotes Singapore.

步 *pu'* From 止 *to stop* and 少 *a little,* denoting the rest between steps.

To step, to walk, to march; a stride, a step; a pace in land measure is reckoned to be five 尺 3.055 square yards or 30.3234 feet; in long measure five 尺 is nearly a fathom; in geography, a length of 4.05 feet, 360 of which make one 里; in Japan, a square *pu'* is 36 square yards; footmen, infantry; a way, a course, manner; a jetty, an anchorage for ferry-boats; a god that injures men and animals; to go leisurely, as by paces; what comes on surely, as a doom, a fate; to ride in a barrow; to train a horse; a classifier of situations.

丨跑 or 丨行 to go afoot.

丨頭 a landing-place.

這丨田地 such a position as this.

丨金 or 謝丨 a doctor's or geomancer's fees.

行千丨 to travel much.

天丨艱難 the ways or steps of Heaven are difficult to understand.

丨從 an idol's attendants.

丨弓 a measure of five feet.

丨道 a footpath, a bridle-path.

得丨進丨 give him a step and he'll take a step; *i. e.* yield him an inch and he will take an ell.

見丨 not very dark, I can see my way.

未到丨 he had not reached the place.

一丨一丨 step by step, gradually.

留有餘地丨 don't push matters; treat him so that you can make it up; leave some room for grace.

國丨 fortunes of a state.

丨兵 foot-soldiers, infantry.

試着丨兒來 practice comes gradually on one; this way is attained step by step.

丨丨高陞 he gradually rose to eminence.

有勞貴丨 may I trouble you to step in, — or do something.

玉丨 your steps; a polite phrase.

止丨 or 留丨 don't come out, as at parting.

分丨 a pair of compasses or dividers.

改丨 to ascend a throne.

丨師 to move the army.

遜丨而行 please go first.

進丨之階 the true way to rise to eminence.

丨履之間 while taking a few steps, a little while.

踏穩脚丨 look well to your steps, be careful how you behave.

丨輦兒來的嗎 did you come afoot?

丨軍統領 the general-in-chief over the gendarmery of Peking.

布 *pu'* Composed of 巾 *a kerchief* and 父 *father* contracted.

Cotton, linen, or hempen fabrics, as nankeen, grasscloth, longcloths, or calico; to spread out, to arrange; to publish, to make known; to display, to diffuse; to infer; a source, a spring; to scatter; oblong, flat coins of Wang Mang, used as tokens for a thousand cash.

丨衣 cotton clothed, *i. e.* common people.

丨國 Prussia.

丨穀 the crow-pheasant (*Centropus*) of southern China; at the North this name is given to the hoopoe or 山和尚 hill-priest.

丨置得宜 well arranged, all done properly.

丨施 charitable gifts.

丨政司 the treasurer of a province.

丨告天下 to publish in all the provinces.

瀑丨飛泉 a high and foaming cascade.

丨列左右 arrange everything (or body) in its place.

丨匹 piece-goods.

白丨 longcloths.

斜紋丨 drillings.

夏丨 summer cloth, grasscloth.

紫花丨 nankeens.

竹丨 foreign linen.

油丨 oiled or painted cloth.

羽丨 bunting.

蠟花丨 glazed chintz.

印花丨 prints.

緞丨 damasked, figured cottons.

毛丨 ginghams.

柳條丨 dimities or quiltings.

大丨 and 二丨 large and small needles. (*Fuhchau.*)

原色丨 domestics.

昆丨 a thick leaved seaweed or tangle, (*Laminaria*) dried and cut into long strips, and used for food.

佈 *pu'* Used for the last and the next.

To extend, to diffuse; reaching, spreading everywhere.

敷丨 extending all over.

特此丨聞 I write this for your information.

丨覆 an answer in return.

拸 *pu'* To open out; to disperse, to scatter.

丨散 scattered about, as dust.

擺丨 to direct, to give orders.

怖 *pu'* From *heart* and to *spread.*

Afraid, surprised; to frighten; alarmed, as from fear of punishment.

詐丨愚民 to scare silly people.

驚丨 frightened.

簿 *pu'* From *bamboo* and *pervading;* this and *poh,* 薄 thin, are liable to be mistaken for each other.

A register, a tablet; a memorandum book; ivory tablets anciently used at audiences; a blank book; an account book; to record.

丨籍 books and records.

主丨 keeper of records and accounts in a district; he is like an under-treasurer.

數丨 or 賬丨 account-books.

會丨 the records of a club.

登丨 or 上丨 to charge in account.

日記丨 a journal, a diary.

流水丨 the blotter.

收支丨 the cash-book.

門丨 a door-register.

花丨 an embroiderer's pattern book.

丨書錢穀 to keep an account of the specie and grain revenue.

緣丨 a subscription-book for the relief of Budhist priests, or for repairs, &c.

Read *poh,* A door-curtain; a tray for silkworms to lay their cocoons; to urge.

部 *pu'* From 邑 a *town* and 否 *whether* altered; it is sometimes used for the last.

The sum, the totality or entire amount of; to take a general control of; a tribe, a sort; a class or division in a serial arrangement, as a family in natural history, the radicals or keys in the Chinese language, the zodiacal constellations, a region of the body in anatomy, &c.; a tribunal, a board, a department; a public court; the officer in a board, or the one who holds the office; a division of a treatise larger than a 卷; a classifier of books; a Mongol clan, a horde; a colony, or separate authority; to divide; to spread abroad; among the Budhists, a school or sect; a part of a canon.

六丨 the six Boards in the government, are the 吏丨 Board of Civil Office; 禮丨 of Rites, 戶丨 of Revenue, 兵丨 of War, 刑丨 of Punishments, and 工丨 of Works.

歸丨候選 attached to a Board waiting for orders.

丨堂 the governor-general and 丨院 the governor of a province.

五丨 the five elements.

丨下 under such an officer.

貴關丨 you, the collector.

丨屬 the personnel of a Board.

各有丨位 each has his own jurisdiction.

丨將 a commander-in-chief.

字丨 the radical or key of a character.

丨落 belonging to or within a jurisdiction, as part of a state.

丨照 a commission of titular rank issued by the Board of Office.

上丨 and 下丨 in *medicine,* above and below the navel.

名聲丨發 his fame was widely spread.

一丨書 a whole work; sometimes, a single volume of it.

逐我丨曲 follow on after my brigade in your place.

交丨議處 [let him be] delivered to the [proper] Board for trial and punishment.

哺 *'pu* To feed an infant with a spoon, to mumble for a child; to give to eat, as a bird does; to chew; a mouthful.

丨乳 to suckle, to feed with pap.

吐丨 to disgorge and feed one's young.

張口受丨 [the fledglings] open their bills to take the food.

烏鴉反丨 crows disgorge to feed their young.

捕 *'pu* To pursue and capture; to seize; to search for and arrest; to hunt, to fowl.

丨魚 to angle; to catch fish.

丨盜 to arrest thieves.

緝丨 on the lookout, as for a thief.

丨廳 a police-office; a superintendent of police in a sub-district magistrate's office; a sort of justice of the peace.

丨差 or 丨役 or 丨快 constables.

丨風捉影 to chase the wind and grasp shadows; — to follow visionary objects.

丨務 business of a policeman.

賻 *pu'* To give thanks for a gift; to give douceurs to people for services.

丨償其勞 give him something for his trouble.

P'U.

Old sounds, p'o, 'o, pok, bok, *and* bot. *In Canton*, p'ò; — *in Swatow*, p'u *and* p'ò; — *in Amoy*, pò, p'ò, *and* hu; — *in Fuhchau*, pw'ò *and* pwò; — *in Shanghai*, p'u *and* bu; — *in Chifu*, p'ù.

鋪 ˏp'u From *metal* and *first*; it is improperly used for 舖 a shop.
A door-knocker, made like a tortoise or tiger's head, called 金丨; to spread out, to arrange; to lay in order; to make known, to pervade; to marshal, as forces; universal; tired, worn out; to sleep with; bedding.
丨檯 to spread a table.
丨席 to make a feast.
丨排 to put things in their places.
打地丨 make up a bed on the floor.
丨設 or 丨陳 to lay in order, arranging.
打丨蓋 put up the bedding.
同丨 a bedfellow.
淮夷來丨 we were marshaled against the tribes on the River Hwai.
丨墊 to spread a cushion; — *met.* to defray the expenses of officers or guests.
一丨榻 one settee or sofa.
丨張揚厲 to extol and commend one.
細草丨毡 the verdure spreads like a carpet.

誧 ˏp'u Great; to reprove; to consult; people helping one another; to boast, to talk big.

踊 ˏp'u The print of a horse's foot; the mark of a hoof.

痡 ˏp'u Sickness, weakness; atrophy, wasting; internal obstruction.
毒丨四海 he grievously afflicted (poisoned and sickened) the whole empire.
我僕丨矣 my servants are disabled.
Read *fu'*. To make ill.

鯆 ˏp'u Broad species of the stingray or skate, of the order *Raiæ.*
黃點丨 yellow spotted ray, with spines arranged like a T. (*Platyrhina sinensis.*)
氷紗丨 a purple bellied ray, spinous tail.
木勺丨 the wooden ladle ray. (*Narcine lingula.*)
白玉丨 the white fleshed ray. (*Trygon carnea.*)
飛翀丨 the flying shoulder ray. (*Pteroplatea micrura.*)
丨鱸 a green colored ray, body semicircular.

莆 ˏp'u Used for the next.
A lucky plant known in ancient times.
丨田縣 a district in Hinghwa fu, in the south-east of Fuhkien.

蒲 ˏp'u From *plant* and *rivulet* as the phonetic.
The cat-tail rush or *Typha*, of whose leaves mats are woven; the calamus or sweet-flag; huts made of grass.
香丨 and 丨黃 are two species of the cat-tail, though the last is also applied to the pollen of the plant when used as a drug.
丨劍 sweet-flag leaves, hung over doors as a charm on the 丨節 flag festival, or the dragon-boat festival.
丨公英 or 丨公草 the dandelion; it has many local names, one of which is 黃花郎 the yellow gentleman.
丨草鞋 grass sandals.
丨包 coarse baskets woven of the bulrush to contain fruits, &c.
丨鞭示辱 a cat-tail whip will make him ashamed.
丨柳之姿 the beauty of the flag and willow, — is transient.
坐丨團 sitting on a rush mat, as a priest when at worship.
揚之水不流束丨 the curling waters will not even float a bundle of bulrushes.
丨扇 fans woven of rush leaves.
丨芹 a Nanking name for parsley.

蒱 ˏp'u Used for the last, when meaning sedge grass.
樗丨 an old name for playing-cards; they are described as much used by swineherds and slaves.

脯 ˏp'u The breast, especially of a fowl or game-bird, is 胸丨; a cook's term.

匍 ˏp'u To crawl, as an infant; to lie prostrate; to strive for.
丨匐哀求 to fall prostrate and sorrowfully beg.

葡 ˏp'u The vine.
丨萄紫 a purple color.
丨萄一都魯 or 一球丨萄 a cluster of grapes.
丨萄酒 or 丨萄汁 juice or wine of grapes.
丨萄果 a sort of rose-apple, which the Cantonese steep in spirits.
癩丨萄 or leprous grape, from the warts on its skin, is a rather unusual term for the *Momordica balsaminea* 苦瓜 or bitter squash.

酺 ˏp'u To drink largely; jolly, in high spirits, as from drink.
大丨 to quaff.
丨五日 they drank for five days.
天下大丨 the country is greatly exhilirated or joyous.

莩 ˏp'u Fodder for horses and cows; dry grass chopped up.
丨蘆 tangled grass or hay.

菩 ꜀p'u A tree, the 丨提樹 brought from Magadha, the sacred *bo* or pipul tree (*Ficus religiosa*) of the Budhists.

丨提 (Sanscrit, *bodhi* or *puti*) intelligence or Budha.

丨提薩埵 an inferior Budha, (Sanscrit, *Budhisatwa*,) contracted to 丨薩 and used commonly for an idol; a god; *Deva Budhisatwa*, a reformer and deified hero of the Budhists, who was born in Benares, and died B. C. 274.

丨薩出遊 an idol's procession.

生丨薩 a living Budha; it means a skillful physician at Canton.

七丨提分 are seven sections or degrees of intelligence towards perfecting a Budha.

諸天丨薩 all the Budhas, all the demigods.

丨提子 raisins; and 白丨提 sultana raisins. (*Cantonese.*)

丨提紗 macerated and varnished grape or other leaves used for painting the 丨提畫 leaf pictures; the same name is also applied to a linden (*Tilia argentea*), or an allied plant, growing in Kwangtung.

Read ꜀p'éi. Grass, herbage; matting; thatch for a hovel.

溥 ꜀p'u Sometimes used for the next.

Large, extensive; pervading; to smear, to daub or rub on.

丨漠 vast, as the sea.

恩澤丨徧 [God's] gracious goodness pervades all.

我受命丨將 We have received the appointment in its widest scope.

丨斯害矣 great is the injury to all.

丨仁 universal benevolence.

普 ꜀p'u From 日 *day* and 並 *equal*, explained to mean that when the sun is unseen, all things are alike obscure; used with the last.

The sun undistinguished in the sky; a uniform light; great, large; all, throughout, everywhere; universal; pervading, like light.

丨天下 the whole world, under the heavens.

丨濟院 a hospital, a poor-house, an asylum or retreat for invalids.

丨救衆生 she saves all living beings; said of Kwanyin.

丨施 to disburse to all.

丨耳府 a prefecture in the south of Yunnan.

丨遍 generally diffused, as air.

丨照 early morning.

丨度 to get souls out of torment.

丨揚 to promulge widely.

丨陀山 or Priest's Island in the Chusan Archipelago, where Kwanyin is said to have lived nine years; the name is a contraction of *putala* 丨陀洛迦, the ancient seat of Sakyamuni's ancestors near the mouth of the Indus, called *Pattala* by the Greeks, now *Tattah*; it is also applied to the mountain near Hlassa where the *dalai lama* lives, and to similar great temples.

丨州 ancient name of Chung-king fu in the S. E. of Sz'ch'uen.

氆 ꜀p'u An open woven, thick woolen cloth, about a foot wide, with a nap on one side; it is called 丨氌 and resembles coarse long ells; it comes from Tibet, where it is called *p'ruh* and *p'uru*; the Mongols call it *chengmé* and *chalma*, and use it for saddle-cloths and riding-cloaks.

浦 ꜀p'u A bank; margin of a lake; a branch of a river; a broad reach, joining a larger stream, where vessels can lie a small outlet to a lake.

清江丨 a town near the banks of the old Yellow River at the outlet of Hung-tsih Lake.

率彼淮丨省此徐土 along the banks of the Hwai we can examine the land of Sü.

黃丨 the river at Shanghai.

合丨縣 a district in Lien-cheu fu in the southwest of Kwangtung, which produces pearls.

荒丨 a deserted region.

盙 ꜀p'u From *dish* and a *bank* as the phonetic; it is a synonym of ꜀餔 to feed.

The afternoon meal or dinner.

蔀 ꜀p'u A luxuriant growing plant, eaten by fish; an awning, a screen; a small mat; a cycle of 72 years, twenty of which make one 紀, like a Julian period.

丨首 the excess of days caused by the intercalated moons.

丨屋 a mat house or hut.

白丨 a medicine to kill lice.

舖 p'u꜄ From *cottage* and *first* as the phonetic; it is a common but unauthorized form of ꜀鋪, and is also written 舗 but incorrectly.

A shop; a store or workshop; a league of ten or seven *li*; a ward in a town; in some parts, a small town or market-place.

老丨 the old stand.

正丨 the office or retail shop, as distinguished from the warehouse.

丨子 or 丨頭 a shop.

丨分 a row of shops.

丨家 shopkeepers, tradesmen.

丨底 fixtures in a shop; the goodwill of a stand.

丨客 landlord of a shop.

收丨 to wind up a business.

踞丨拖租 to stay in a shop and refuse to pay rent.

丨東 the moneyed partner.

丨夥 the working partners.

寶丨在那兒 where is your shop?

雜貨丨 a general or variety shop.

窩丨 a watchman's lodge or station; a post for a guard.

PUH.

This sound and POH *run into each other. Old sounds,* pot, pet, bot, bok, *and* bet. *In Canton,* pòk, pát, *and* pút; — *in Swatow,* p'ok, pòk, pút, *and* pwat; — *in Amoy,* pút, pok, *and* p'ok; — *in Fuhchau,* pòk *and* pùk; — *in Shanghai,* peh, bok, pok, *and* p'ok; — *in Chifu,* pu.

不 ˏ*pu* The upper stroke originally represented *heaven*, and the lower part a swallow or other *bird* darting down.

An *adverb*, no, not, and is placed before the verb, as 丨能 cannot; 丨可 do not; — before adjectives it answers to *un, dis, in,* &c., in combination, as 丨便 inconvenient; 丨同 unlike; 丨肖 disobedient; — when repeated with 得, or following another negative, makes an affirmation, as 丨得丨去 I cannot but go; — when placed between two verbs, it forms a question, as 來丨來 will he come? — but when repeated before succeeding verbs, answers to neither – nor, as 丨加丨減 it neither increases nor diminishes; — before 若 or 如 it is like 莫 and makes a comparison, as 丨若去 it will be best to go, I had rather go.

應當丨 is a contracted alternative, where it has the force of 否; ought it, or ought it not to be so?

丨如坐 nothing like sitting.

莫丨明矣 you cannot fail of being understood.

好丨 is a strong affirmation, as 好丨嬌嬈 she is incomparably handsome.

好丨歡喜 can we do anything but rejoice?

丨一 not a few; unlike.

丨一定 uncertain; unsettled.

丨日 erelong, not many days.

丨然 not at all; on the contrary.

丨是 not so; by no means.

丨是麽 is not that it?

豈丨是 how can it not be so? it surely is so.

兩人有丨是處 both of them were wrong.

丨甚好 only tolerable.

丨必 need not; there is no necessity for it.

丨消題 don't speak of him; let that pass.

丨亦樂乎 will not that be pleasant?

難道就打我丨成 ought I to be beaten for that?

丨一而足 a few more and there will be enough.

丨無辛苦 he took no small trouble; 'twas rather difficult.

丨卽丨離 neither instantly nor remotely; *i. e.* reasonably, moderately, a middle course.

丨足道 inadequate for, incompetent, not up to the mark.

敢道個丨字兒 does he presume to disagree with me? *i. e.* I venture to say *no* to that.

丨必生氣 you need not get angry.

一丨作二丨休 well, I'm in for it, and I'll go through.

是這樣丨足 is it so or not?

丨三丨四 unsteady, neither one thing nor the other.

有周丨顯帝命丨時 was not our House of Cheu illustrious, and did not the Ruler's decree come at the time?

丨夜 ancient name of Wăn-tăng hien 文登縣 in the east of Shantung.

Read ˏ*pei*, and used with 丕. An adverbial particle, adding elegance or energy to the sense.

我生丨有命在天 there was nothing less than a decree from Heaven at the time of my birth; *i. e.* to assure me the rule of the empire.

徒御丨驚大庖丨盈 didn't the coachmen make a noise? were not the kitchens full — of game?

卜 ˏ*pu* Supposed to represent the *veins* in a tortoise-shell as the heat develops them; it forms the 25th radical of a few miscellaneous characters.

To divine by looking at, or rattling coins inside of a tortoise or terrapin's shell; to guess; to bestow on; sortilege, divination.

丨魚 a wooden block like a skull, used by priests to beat time when chanting.

杯丨 to divine by blocks or a toss-penny.

未丨其期 I have not yet thought when it will come to pass.

丨筮偕止 by the shell and the straws have I divined.

問丨 to inquire of the fates.

未丨先知 to know beforehand without casting lots.

君曰丨爾萬壽無疆 the prince says, We give to thee myriads of years without end.

僕 *p'u'* *p'o'* From 人 *man* and 業 an *estate* altered.

A vassal, a retainer; a servant or menial, one who aids in laborious duties; a charioteer; palace officers, chamberlains; a junior, a term used by one's self, as "your servant;" to follow, to serve; to belong, to appertain; attached to, as an order of merit; to hide.

家丨 domestics; my retainers.

丨臣 a vassal, a fief.

主丨 master and servant.

ʻ處丨區 I, your humble servant.

丨婢 men and maid-servants.

丨丨風塵 impertinent, troublesome.

景命有丨 the bright order is upon your person.

太丨寺 the office of the Emperor's stud.

丨隷 criers or lictors in a yamun.
徒丨 disciples, adherents.
丨射 or 車丨 the driver of a war-chariot.

In *Cantonese.* To kneel or fall down on the ground before one.

鏷, poh' Sometimes written like the last.
A kind of light dart.
丨鉄 raw or unwrought iron.

濮, ꜀p'uh A river in the southwest of Shantung; an ancient tribe in Hupeh, which assisted Wu-wang against Sheu, and perhaps extended into Sz'ch'uen; an ancient district in Shin cheu 深州 in the south of Chihli.
丨州 an inferior department in the southwest of Shantung.

瀑, pao' A cascade; a waterfall; water rushing down a hill.
丨水 or 飛丨 a waterfall.
丨布 a cataract; a mountain torrent.
丨泉 a tank or reservoir fed by a cascade or torrent.

Read *pao'*. Bubbles, froth; a heavy rain.

醭, ꜀puh The mother on vinegar; a mold or efflorescence, as on leather or walls; scum on spirits.
起了白丨兒了 skim off the white mother.

幞, 襆, poh' A kind of cowl or hood worn by soldiers; a kerchief for the head; the skirt trimmed or braided.
丨帕 a kind of square cap or turban anciently worn.
頭丨 a jib on a junk's foremast.

轐, pu' p'oh' The sticks under a cart that clasp the axle to prevent it moving; they are likened to a crouching rabbit; the common name is 鈎銜 or hook-clasp.

孛, poh' From *child* and *sprouting*; also read *péi'* and interchanged with the next; it resembles 字 word.
Plants suddenly shooting up; disobedient, intractable; a change of countenance.
丨星 a comet, in allusion to its sudden appearance and supposed malign influences.

勃, poh' Suddenly, hastily; flurried, disconcerted, as when caught doing wrong; to change color, confused.
丨然大怒 all at once he flew into a great rage.
色丨如也 his face suddenly changed color.
丨起不頁 he thought how he could injure him.

浡, poh' p'éi' Occurs interchanged with the last.
Full; bursting, like a plant; copious, like a fountain; sudden; excited at.
丨潏 bubbling, gurgling.
英氣丨丨 very valorous, boastful, Falstaff-like.
滂丨 perturbed; dispersed, as clouds; convulsed.
丨里 name of a country, by some thought to be Borneo.

渤, poh' An arm of the sea; mist.
渤丨 a noise of water.
丨海郡 an ancient region in the Han dynasty lying along the 丨海 or Gulf of Chihli, between two rivers, the Pei ho in Chihli and Ta-ts'ing ho in Shantung; used for Shantung people, and persons of the surname ꜀Sü 徐.

哱, poh' A large trumpet or trombone, a 丨囉, sounded to bring the troops into line when going into battle; the sound of blowing a fire.

埻, poh' Dust, a cloud of dust.

鵓, poh' A wood pigeon with white spots on its neck, called 丨鴣 from its note.

桲, poh' A kind of flail, a stick to beat out grain; a small acid fruit, a variety of the quince or *Cydonia*, shaped somewhat like a medlar

誖, poh' Interchanged with *péi'* 悖 perverse.
To mislead by fair speeches, to stir up rebellion by seducing talk; obstinate, disorderly; perverse.
丨亂 revolutionary; sedition.
惛丨 rude, giddy.
四達而不丨 he knows all kinds of matters, and yet he is nowise obstinate.
或丨其心 it may perturb him.
乖丨 wayward, cross-grained.
丨謬 conspiring against.

脖, ꜀poh The neck, especially the back of it; the navel.
丨梗子 the neck.
癭袋丨 the goitre.
丨臍 the umbilical cord; a medical term.
打丨子拐 to slap one on the neck.
肓之原出於丨胦 the stamina of life comes through the navel.
縮着丨子 to draw in the head, as a tortoise.

粰, poh' The grits and bran of rice after it has been hulled.

蹼, poh' From *foot* and *sticks*.
The web feet of water fowl; web-footed.

In *Cantonese.* To lie down, like a beast; to lean on or over, as on a table; to turn upside down.
丨到地來 he fell prone on the ground.
丨轉 turn it bottom upward.

攴, ꜀pu Composed of 又 *hand* and 卜 to *divine*; it forms the 66th radical of characters relating to motions and strokes.
A slight stroke, a tap; to rap.

P'UH.

Old sound, p'ok. *In Canton*, p'út; — *in Swatow*, pút; — *in Amoy*, ch'uh; — *in Shanghai*, p'eh; — *in Chifu*, p'u.

昢 p'uh' From *sun* and *issuing*. The sun not fully showing itself; the moon just rising. 時丨丨兮日旦 see, the sun is just showing himself! he is just peeping out.

Read *p'ei'* The sky beginning to clear up.

餢 p'o' To eat much. 丨餪 eaten to satiety.

霈 p'uh' From *rain* and to *go out*. Cloudy, but breaking away. 秋雲丨然而卷舒 the autumn clouds are scattering and rolling themselves away.

'RH.

Old sounds, ni *and* n'ip. *In Canton*, i *and* ngi; — *in Swatow*, jù, hⁿi, ji, *and* no; — *in Amoy*, ji *and* jiⁿ; — *in Fuhchau*, i, ngi, *and* né; — *in Shanghai*, 'rh *and* ni; — *in Chifu*, 'rh.

而 ꜀'rh The original form is supposed to represent the *hair* on the sides of the face, now written as the next; it forms the 126th radical of a few incongruous characters.

The whiskers; the bones of the jaws; a copula often used between verbs, and, together, and yet, and then, also; but more commonly a *disjunctive* conjunction, still, yet, as if, contrariwise; an initial particle indicating a progress or causation, if, as, in consequence of; when in regimen with 雖, it precedes the main proposition; when with 不, it has an adversative sense; a final particle confirming the assertion or winding it off; used for you, your.

丨今丨後 now and henceforth.

丨益 still more, still again.

丨后 after that, then.

丨况 with still stronger reason.

丨且 moreover, furthermore.

不思丨得 even without any thought he got it.

丨已 a phrase following and enforcing the subject; that is all, nothing more, all has been done that can be; as 有仁義丨已矣 humanity and justice, they are all.

拖帶丨來 it had been towed; the phrase 丨來 being a form of the pluperfect.

九人丨已 nine men in all.

于此丨已矣 this and nothing more.

其鱗之丨 the jaw bone (or maxillary bones) of fishes.

瓜時丨往瓜及丨代 when the melons are ripe you can go; and at their next season, some one will relieve — your post.

日出丨作日入丨息 when day appears then work; when it is sunset, then rest.

善人雖多丨不厭 many as the good may be, they will not be disliked.

俟我于箸乎丨 can you wait for me there, eh?

學丨時習之 learn and then constantly practice it.

不嚴丨治 he governs without severity.

用晦丨明 to regard darkness as if it were light.

丨月斯征 your months go on.

圜廛二十丨一 he taxed one in twenty of all the gardens and shops; *i. e.* five per cent.

髵 ꜀'rh A recent form of the last, denoting the whiskers; hairy. 髿丨 an animal bristling up its hair or mane in anger.

胹 ꜀lan Boiled too much, overdone. 丨熊蹯不熟 he could not boil the bear's paw tender, or quite through.

咡 ꜀'rh The sides of the mouth; to put the lips to.

In *Cantonese*. To shut, to close; the last; small, minute; to sip.

꜀丨的酒 taste a little wine.

落雨꜀丨 a fine still rain.

手指꜀丨 the little finger.

洏 ꜀'rh Water flowing in diverging streams; warm water. 涕流連丨 the tears flowed abundantly.

栭 ꜀'rh A queen-post resting on the top of a beam, to support the roof; a small variety of chestnut, the 丨栗 or 栵丨 found in Kiangnan; a fungus, the *Peziza* or *Boletus*, which grows on decayed wood, and known as 木耳 tree's ears; some are used medicinally.

荋 ꜀'rh A species of agaric or *Boletus* the 芝丨 which grows from the ground and not upon trees, though the distinction is not always made.

鮞 ꜀'rh The roe or caviare of fishes; a beautiful salt-water fish, perhaps the parrot fish or *Scarus*. 魚禁鯤丨 the fishermen are forbidden to take fish with their eggs.

輀 ˏ'rh A car for carrying a coffin, a hearse or funeral carriage.

陑 ˏ'rh A place south of the elbow of the Yellow River, where 伊尹 aided to overthrow the Hia dynasty, B. C. 1760.

兒 ˏ'rh From 儿 *man* and 囟 the *fontanel* altered, to show that it has not closed up, it is often written so as to be mistaken for *mao* 皃 form.

An infant, especially a boy; a child; infantile, feeble; a suffix in speaking to denote that a word is a noun; a final particle indicating that the sentence is complete.

小丨 or 小丨子 my boy; I, your son.

丨女 girls and boys.

寶貝丨 my pet, my precious.

丨孫 posterity; children and grandchildren.

丨童 a small lad.

不負男丨志 he was not recreant to his high resolve.

莫視爲丨戲 don't look on this affair as child's play.

黃髮丨齒 the old man has had a new set of teeth.

一點丨不錯 wholly correct.

今丨 to-day, 明丨 to-morrow, and 前丨 day before yesterday.

沒有風丨 there's no wind.

這邊丨 that side, there.

丨茶 catechu or cutch, the terra Japonica, also described as 烏爹泥 or black *teni*, from the Hindu name.

騀 ˏ'rh From *horse* and *child*.

A small horse.

丨馬 (or 兒馬) a stallion, so called in northern China.

餌 ᶜ'rh ˏni To eat; cakes or dumplings made with meat and boiled.

餅丨 a flour cake.

糖丨朶 a common kind of sugar cake.

Read *ni*ˀ Bait for fish; a temptation, an allurement.

食丨 or 呑丨 to take the bait; to be cajoled.

水寒魚不丨 the fish won't bite when the water is cold.

誘丨 to lay a bait for, as a gambler does.

耳 ᶜ'rh Intended to represent the shape of the ear; it forms the 128th radical of a natural group relating to hearing; in composition it is often written like 目 the eye.

The ear, the organ of hearing; a handle, an ear; a side; a final particle, used to intensify what precedes, but more frequently a euphonic sound to close the sense; used as a relative pronoun like 者 in some cases.

丨朶 the ear.

挖丨 or 掏丨 or 取丨 or 看丨 to pick the ears, as barbers do with an 丨挖 ear-pick.

丨朶帽 ear-tippets; ear-tabs.

丨邊風 [like a] wind passing the ears; — unheeded.

丨目之官不思 the organs of hearing and seeing do not think.

賴有此丨 depend on me for this thing only.

充丨目之官 officers who act as eyes and ears to the ruler.

充丨琇實 ear-plugs of bluish jade; an ancient ornament.

順風丨 an attendant of Hwakwang 華光 the god of Fire at Canton, who hears quick.

丨孫 a great-grandson's grandson, a descendant who can only hear of his ancestor.

丨房 a side-room, a small room added to a large one.

掩丨盜鈴 to cover one's ears and steal the bell; — to think that others will not perceive one's craft.

丨朶軟 soft ears, open to all reports.

丨食 credulous; paying no attention to what is said.

汝得人焉丨乎 have you any one's protection?

丨丨 soft, pliable, said of reins; complying.

門丨 a door-knocker.

珥 ᶜ'rh Ear ornaments of any kind; a reflection or ring near the sun, like a parhelion or mock-sun; belonging to.

簪丨 hair-pins and ear trinkets.

洱 ᶜ'rh A small affluent of the Yellow River in the northwest part of Honan in Shen cheu; name of a lake in the south of Yunnan in Pu-'rh fu.

駬 ᶜ'rh A famous steed, called 騄丨 one of eight belonging to Muh Wang of the Cheu dynasty, B. C. 1000.

尒 **尓** ᶜ'rh From 小 *small* and 入 to *enter*, but said to be formed of 入 to *enter*, 丨 to *descend* and 八 to *separate*, alluding to the dispersion of vapor; it is a common contraction of the next.

An emphatic particle, implying a certainty.

爾 ᶜ'rh From 爻 to *imitate* repeated and 冂 *inclosure*, denoting the involvement of lines or influences.

The second personal pronoun, thou, you; a particle of affirmation, so, just so; often makes an adverb of the word before it; to remove; abundant.

丨曹 or 丨等 you all.

丨衆士 all you scholars.

絜丨牛羊 pure indeed are the oxen and sheep.

丨丨 plentiful.

乃丨 just that way, it is thus.

聊復丨耳 and then it will be the same thing over again.

故丨如是 it therefore happened in that way.

云丨 just so; and so forth.

式丨 purposely.

適丨 accidentally.

邇 'rh Near, at hand; close, as relationship; proximate.

遠｜ remote and near by.

｜來 hitherto; recently.

密｜ conterminous.

歲暮在｜ the year draws to an end.

咡 'rh From *mouth* and *ear*.

The sides of the mouth, the space between the mouth and ears; to turn the head towards one when speaking to him.

辟｜而對 turn your face when answering.

In *Cantonese*. To purse up the mouth and hold one's tongue.

｜｜口 to pucker the lips.

毦 'rh From *hair* and *ear* as the phonetic; it resembles *mao'* 旄 dim vision, and is also read *ˏni*.

An elaborate kind of woven feather and hair work, once made into ornaments, and used on mantles; a chowry or feather-duster; the hair of the yak woven into a tassel for bridles; colored hair used on flags.

納妃有白｜拂二枚 he gave the princess two white chowries.

刵 'rh The punishment of cutting off the ears.

無或劓｜人 you may not of yourself cut off the nose and ears of a man.

衈 'rh The blood of a fowl offered in sacrifice; to cut off or pull out the hairs of a victim's ears before killing it, intimating that the officers wished the gods to hear them; to smear.

耳｜ blood of the ears.

佴 'rh Like the next.

A second; an assistant.

僕又｜之蠶室 your servant again [reports that he] is made an assistant in the silkworm house; — *i.e.* made a eunuch.

二 貳 弍 'rh Formed from 一 *one* or heaven, multiplied into itself, thus making *two* or earth; it is the 7th radical of a few primitives; the other forms are employed for security in accounts.

Two; the second; to divide in twain; to duplicate.

第｜ the second.

｜十 twenty.

｜則 in the second place, next.

｜次 twice; the second time.

無｜心 faithful, not double-minded.

於斯｜者 in these two things.

｜天之戴 [I am as it were] restored to life.

明發不寐有懷｜人 when at dawn I lie awake, I think of my parents.

｜來來 or ｜來謂 a woman who has her second husband.

德｜三動罔不凶 when the zeal is wavering, the actions all are unfortunate.

不｜其心 do not distract the heart from its purpose; be not vacillating.

｜吾猶不足 even if you double it, I shall not be satisfied.

貳 'rh Used for the last.

A substitute, a second; to reiterate, to suspect; to oppose; to divide or share.

雖｜不辭 he did not decline, though [the dish] was twice offered.

任賢勿｜ don't suspect good men when you employ them in office.

上帝臨汝無｜爾心 Shangti is with (or among) you, banish all doubt from your hearts.

樲 'rh An acid variety of jujube plum (*Rhamnus*), found on a wild and very thorny plant; the 酸棗仁 a kind of medicine, is not from this tree.

SAH.

Old sound, sap. *In Canton*, sat, sap, chap, *and* sa; — *in Swatow*, sat, sap, *and* san; — *in Amoy*, sap, sat, k'ip, *and* ch'ap; — *in Fuhchau*, sak *and* chak; — *in Shanghai*, sèh; — *in Chifu*, sah.

薩 ˏsa A Sanscrit syllable introduced by the Budhists.

菩｜ or *Bodhi-satwa*, (*i. e.* he whose essence has become intelligence,) the third class of saints; such a one has only to pass through a human existence once more before he reaches Budhaship.

卅 ˏsa A contraction of 三十 or thirty.

In *Pekingese*, used for 三. Things occurring by threes.

買｜ I bought three.

撒 ˏsa From *hand* and to *separate*.

To scatter; to throw one side and the other; to set loose.

｜穀種 to sow grain.

｜手 to throw back the hand, to pay no more regard to an affair.

｜災 to scatter calamity, to send down trouble, as pestilence or drought; thought to be done by the gods.

｜開 spread them out, scatter them; to arrange amicably, as a lawsuit.

｜潑 to waste, to spend recklessly.

｜手不理 to shake one's hand of a thing.

｜米 to feed hungry spirits; also to throw rice on a bridal chair.

｜賴 to implicate another for a trifle; to trump up a charge.

｜謊 to tell a lie.

｜放 to let loose, as a bird.

｜手不及 very unexpectedly.

｜野 to make much ado about nothing, to act impudently, to bluster and demand of.

撒, ꜀sah From *hand* and to *kill* as the phonetic.

To give a backhanded blow; to slap one; to disperse.

抹 丨 to extirpate; to wipe out, as a sum or statement.

粱, ꜀sah From *rice* and to *kill*; occurs as a synonym of *ts'ai* 蔡 in this sense.

To send off prisoners or criminals, as one scatters rice, to their exile.

𥈫, ꜀sa From *eye* and to *scatter*; an unauthorized character.

In *Pekingese*. To glance at.

丨 了 一 眼 I just had one quick look at it.

丨 一 丨 take a look at it.

㗇, ꜀sa The voice changed from too much or too violent use; a hoarse or gruff voice.

喝 丨 to yell out, to scream.

喊 丨 了 聲 to bawl in a hoarse or shrill voice.

口 嚨 丨 my throat is hoarse.

鈒, ꜀sa From *metal* and *at*.

A spear or javelin; to engrave; to inlay, to enchase on metal; to sprinkle, to scatter.

丨 鏤 to inlay with silver thread; to enchase on.

In *Cantonese* used for *chah*, 鍘 Money shears, having one cutting blade working on a bar to cut the metal; to slice, to cut open.

梹 榔 丨 betel-nut shears.

丨 碎 slice it fine.

丨 剪 or 丨 刀 sycee shears.

丨 開 cut it open.

馺, ꜀sa Horses going irregularly, without any order; swift.

丨 娑 capricious, unequal; name of an ancient palace.

丨 遺 風 to overtake the wind; very fleet.

趿, ꜀sa From *foot* and *at*; occurs used for the next.

To step forward and take a thing; to tread on.

丨 脚 鞋 open-heeled slippers.

丨 拉 着 鞋 to wear the shoes slipshod.

靸, ꜀sa Children's shoes; a shoe with a high instep, a half boot.

鷹 嘴 丨 a low shoe, ornamented like scales.

颯, ꜀sa The sound of the wind; a gust, a sudden blast; suddenly, for a moment.

風 丨 丨 the wind comes fitfully.

衰 丨 declining, going down, growing old.

丨 沓 a multitude, as of horsemen.

丨 然 來 了 he came suddenly.

飄 丨 自 如 it blows fitfully as it lists.

𠇆, ꜀sa From *chives* and *heaven*; used only as a primitive; altered sometimes to 叄 but not correctly.

Bad, wicked,— for which the next is the proper form.

㑲, ꜀sa Inattentive; bad, wicked.

傷 丨 heedless, incautious, disrespectful, unobservant.

攃, ꜀sa The sound of breaking things; to hold a thing tight.

拂 攃 丨 brush up and carry off the refuse.

攃 丨 捐 money paid for removing sweepings or dirt.

𧝓, ꜀sa Tattered, as raiment.

袪 丨 disordered, as one's dress; old, worn; not fitting, as a garment.

SAI.

Old sounds, sai *and* sak. *In Canton*, soi; — *in Swatow*, sai *and* sù; — *in Amoy*, su *and* sai; — *in Fuhchau*, sai *and* swoi; — *in Shanghai*, sé; — *in Chifu*, sai.

顋 腮, ꜀sai From *head* or *flesh* and to *think*; used with the next.

The lower part of the face, the jowl, the chops, that which moves when eating; the gills of fish.

丨 頰 the jaws.

手 托 香 丨 she leaned her head on her hand.

腦 後 見 丨 to see the cheeks from behind, — is a bad feature.

淚 滿 丨 the tears coursed down her cheeks.

滿 丨 eaten to repletion.

脹 起 丨 to puff out the cheeks.

痄 丨 scrofulous sores on the cheeks.

肥 丨 鼓 腹 fat cheeks and a big belly; also a term for sand banks in a stream, and those mud banks that narrow the channel from deposits on each side.

鰓, ꜀sai The gills of a fish, or the bones supporting them.

丨 丨 alarmed.

四 丨 魚 a delicate species of perch or wrasse, spotted white and black, found in Kiangsu.

鰓, ꜀sai The fleshy column or marrow in some horns; the bur at the base of an antler, or its velvety covering.

丨 角 a hollow horn like an ox.

愢, ꜀sai From *heart* and to *think*.

The mind not fixed in its own conclusions; to say one thing and do another; hesitating.

揌, ꜀sai To move or shake; to choose.

擡 丨 to agitate; to shake.

𢹿 ˓sai An unauthorized character used for *seh* 塞ʾ to stop.

In *Pekingese*. To fill or stuff a hole, to stop up.

丨子 a cork, a stopple.

丨子拔 a corkscrew.

鬛 ˓si Little hair on the head.

鬇丨 a bushy, heavy beard.

賽 saiʾ From 貝 *pearl* and 塞 to *stop up* contracted.

To announce a thank offering, or report after presenting it; to emulate, to contend for, to strive for; to rival; to thank, to recompense; contesting, matching; to try who can make the best show.

丨色 to show colored or fancy figures, to make a great display, as in processions; first quality.

丨神 or 報丨 to render thanks; to get up processions to thank the gods for the crops, or to worship Ceres; it is an ancient rite.

丨馬 to race horses.

丨燈 to show off lanterns, the feast of Lanterns, at the middle of the first moon.

亞丨 a match for a thing.

賭丨 to wager, to bet.

丨雪 its color rivals the snow.

兩人對丨 they are well matched.

丨眞兒的珠子 it is almost as good as the real pearl.

簺 saiʾ Used for *seh*, 塞 to confine in bounds.

To beat in the large game of chess of 360 pieces by confining an opponent within four squares; a fish-weir made of interlaced bamboos.

SAN.

Old sounds, san *and* sam. *In Canton*, sam *and* san; — *in Swatow*, san, $s^{n}a$, *and* $sw^{n}a$; — *in Amoy*, san *and* sam; — *in Fuhchau*, sang; — *in Shanghai*, $s\grave{e}^{n}$; — in *Chifu*, san.

三 **叁** ˓san Supposed to represent the three powers, heaven, earth, and man, which proceed from 一 or *heaven*; the second complex form is used on bills.

Three; thrice; several, several times.

丨十 thirty.

第丨 number three; third.

再丨 again and again.

丨回 or 丨次 three times.

二丨子 you two or three scholars; my children, my people.

丨兩日 in two or three days, shortly.

丨元及第 the three highest graduates of each degree.

丨羣二隊 knots and groups of people.

丨摩提 (in Sanscrit, *samadhi*,) defined by 定 fixed, *i. e.* 等持 self-possession, or by 正定 correct tranquillity, and by 寂靜 listless stillness; the highest mortal state of extatic meditation, when the devotee's mental and physical faculties are in a state of complete torpor, and he soon departs or consumes by the fire of *samadhi*.

丨生有幸 I should be happy to be with you for ever.

丨子不全 you cannot have all the three *tszʾ*,— *viz.* 兒子 sons, 銀子 wealth, and 鬍子 a beard. (*Pekingese*.)

丨仕丨已 he thrice held office and thrice retired; — an inconstant trimmer.

事不過丨 this affair must be done within three days.

丨尺法 an instrument for torturing the ankles.

丨隻手 a pickpocket; a shoplifter, from the arm being drawn out of the sleeve when stealing.

汝無面從二丨其德 let your virtue be fixed on one thing, and do not vacillate in your loyalty.

人丨成衆 three people make a company.

丨姑六婆 three maids and six beldames; *i. e.* strolling women who wander about.

丨陽開泰 in the 1st moon all nature develops itself.

Read *sanʾ*. To reiterate, to do thrice.

丨復 to con over again and again.

丨思而行 think thrice before you do it; — take good advice and then act.

鬖 ˓san The hair in confusion.

丨髿 disheveled, unkempt hair.

毵 ˓san Long feathers, especially the long crests like those on the head of the egret or demoiselle crane, which are 丨丨然 long and elegant.

衫 ˓shan Ragged clothes.

襤丨 tattered and torn; all at loose ends.

饊 **糤** ˋsan Flour cakes fried crisp.

丨子 or 油丨 wheat cakes.

丨麪 fine wheaten flour.

酹神丨 to requite the gods with cakes.

丨飯 well boiled rice.

糝 **糂** ˋsan The second form is disused.

Rice mixed in meat soup, and boiled to a porridge; applied also to buckwheat flour; a hash of minced meat and rice fried in balls; mixed, blended.

丨食 food of thick soup.
飯丨 or 米丨 a rice ragout.
楊花丨逕 the willow catkins spread their grains on the path.
熬丨 to boil congee.
丨子粥 congee of rice grits.
丨粒 in separate grains, as rice looks when properly boiled or steamed.

ʻ傘 ʻ繖 ˊsan } Composed of *men* under a *cover* which is held up by a *handle;* the second is a modern form.

A shelter, a cover from the sun or rain; a parasol.
雨丨 an umbrella.
羅丨 a round canopy or state umbrella carried in processions.
日照丨 a sun-shade.
開丨 open the parasol.
萬民丨 a testimonial umbrella presented to a popular officer, or others by appreciative friends; sometimes got up to his memory.
荷葉魚兒丨 lotus leaves are the fishes' umbrellas.
丨扇騎從 a retinue of umbrella and flabellum bearers and horsemen.

ʻ散 ʻsan From 攴 to *strike* and 昔 *formerly*, and this is itself said to be changed from ˏpa 林 *small*.

A wine vessel or amphora; a medicinal powder; name of a song; a musical instrument like a lute; slatternly, untidy; tangled, in confusion; sporadic; miscellaneous, odds and ends.
丨工 day-laborers; odd jobs.
打丨錢 break a string of cash.
懶丨 heedless, indolent.
丨褲爪 to have the trowsers loose at the ankles.
閒丨 leisure, taking things easy.
磨丨 to grind to powder.
一副清涼丨 [it is like] one dose of good medicine; *met.* it is all cleared up, I understand the matter now.
分丨人馬 sent out men and horsemen, as in a search; or posted them in places.
弄丨了 not to finish a thing, no perseverance.
失丨 missing, as papers; scattered, as soldiers.
丨人丨木 useless people and timber.

Read *san'*. To scatter, to dissipate; to fall all apart; to separate; to disperse, to break up; to apportion; — the leading idea being that no external force is used.
丨場 to separate, as an audience.
丨班 to break up, as a company or set.
丨步 to refresh one's self by a walk.
丨襲 to distribute (*i. e.* burn) clothes for departed spirits.
發丨 to dissipate, as a cold.
家丨人亡 the family is scattered or dead.
事情丨了 the affair is spoiled.
花丨 to spend recklessly.
布丨流言 to spread rumors, to circulate hearsay.
丨開 dispersed, as clouds.
丨花仙子 a certain fairy who scatters flowers; *met.* a spendthrift.
聚丨無常 they collect or scatter as they list, there is no order in their movements; said of banditti.
丨了麽 have they all gone? is the meeting dismissed?

SANG.

Old sound, sung. *In Canton*, song; — *in Swatow*, sang, săng, *and* súang; — *in Amoy*, song; — *in Fuhchau*, sòng; — *in Shanghai*, song; — *in Chifu*, sang.

ˏ桑 ˏsang From *wooa* and a tree like the mulberry, which grows where the sun rises.

The mulberry tree; to cultivate silkworms; mulberry leaves; peaceful retirement.
丨子 or 丨黮 or 丨棗 mulberries.
丨梓之情 village quiet and rural occupation.
丨榆暮景 peaceful end of days under the mulberry and elm; *i. e.* in one's own village.
猗彼女丨 they strip those trees which are tender, — or having no fruit.
丨中之約 illicit intercourse.
丨白皮 bark of mulberry roots, a diuretic.
滄海變丨田 the sea has become a mulberry field; *i. e.* great changes have taken place.
指丨罵槐 to revile the locust tree while pointing to the mulberry; — to scold one person over another's back.
丨者閑閑 the pickers of mulberry leaves are idling about.
丨州 an ancient district in the east of Sz'chʻuen, now part of Kwéi-chau fu.
丨門 the Shamans, (in Sanscrit *sramani,*) an ascetic, a recluse, one who 息心 quiets his heart.

ʻ嗓 ʻsang The throat; the larynx; the glanders.
好丨子 a good singer.
喉丨 or 丨子眼 the uvula.
丨子啞 a hoarse voice.
大丨子喊道 cried out with a loud and bitter cry.
丨食 the glottis.
潤潤丨子 wet your whistle, take a cup of tea.
氣丨 the larynx.

In *Cantonese*. A dialect, a local brogue, a patois.
京丨 the Peking colloquial.
講廣丨 he talks the Canton dialect.

癳 ʿsang Used with the last.
The glanders in horses; also known as 馬癀 the horse jaundice.

顙 ʿsang The forehead, the part which strikes the ground in bowing.
廣丨 a broad forehead.
稽丨 to knock the head on the ground.
其丨有泚 his brow was wet with perspiration, — at seeing his father's corpse.

搡 ʿsang To push off or over with the hand; to oppose, to stop one.
丨在地下 he tipped it on the ground.
用手一丨 pushed him back with his hand.
推推丨丨 pushing and struggling, as in a crowd.

磉 ʿsang The stone foundation or plinth of a pillar.
榪丨 the underground brickwork on which the plinth rests.
丨柯 the stone base to uphold the pillar.

喪 sang' ˏsang Formed of 哭 to *weep* and 亡 *dead*, altered in combination.
To mourn, to lament for one's parents; a funeral; apparel or time for mourning.
丨事 funeral affairs.
丨服 mourning clothes.
國丨 mourning for the emperor.
出丨 to carry forth to burial.
送丨 to attend a funeral.
居丨 to mourn for a parent three years.
嚎丨 to wail for the dead.
守丨 to watch with a corpse.
哭丨棒 staff used by the eldest son at funerals.
報丨 to officially report a parent's death.
弔丨 to bewail the dead.
丨家 the bereaved family.
居丨讀禮 during mourning study the Book of Rites; hence 讀禮 denotes one in retirement on account of mourning.

Read *sang'* To lose, to fail of getting, the opposite of 得 to obtain; bereaved of; to pass into obscurity, forgotten, out of mind; to let be lost, to destroy; to die; ruin.
丨明 blind; losing his sight.
丨國 he lost his kingdom.
丨良心 he has lost all conscience.
丨失家業 ruined his family.
丨心病 he is out of his mind.
丨氣 melancholic, looking downcast.
丨與其易'也寧戚 in mourning, deep sorrow is worth more than minute observances.
何患於丨 why are you so depressed at this ill-luck?
天之未丨斯文也 while heaven does not let this doctrine perish, — what can the men of Kwʻang do to me? — said by Confucius.

SǍNG.

Old sound, seng. *In Canton*, săng; — *in Swatow*, cheng; — *in Amoy*, cheng; — *in Fuhchau*, cheng; — *in Shanghai*, săng; — *in Chifu*, săng.

僧 ˏsăng From *man* and *already*, imitating the Sanscrit *sanga*.
A Budhist priest, one who eats vegetables; a lama; the third in the Budhist trinity.
丨人 a bonze; he is often addressed as 上人 the exalted man.
丨家 the Budhist priesthood.
貧丨 I, a poor priest.
山丨 hermits, recluses.
丨俗 the clergy and laity.
老丨打坐 an old priest meditating.
流丨 a luxurious, worldly priest.
法丨 a scrupulous priest.
丨道無緣 I'll have nothing to do with Budhists or Rationalists; — a placard on doors.
蜜佗丨 litharge.
請到一衆丨 [do you think that] I have asked you [to sit here like] a priest? — *i. e.* to idle and talk instead of work.
喇嘛丨 a lama, or Mongol priest.
丨伽 (in Sanscrit *sanga* or *samgha*,) the assembly of priests.
丨伽婆羅 or *Sanga Pala*, name of a Burmese priest, who introduced into China the first alphabet (A. D. 506) for writing Sanscrit words.
丨房 a dwelling of priests, a monastery, a *sanga-rama* 丨伽藍 or park and buildings with it.
丨伽胝 the *sanghati*, or double robe of a priest, reaching from the shoulders to the knees, and tied at the waist; it is defined 重雜衣 doubled mixed dress.
丨錄司 or 丨綱司 a high official who governs his fellow priests; there is one in each district, to whom the criminals among the priesthood are sent.

鬙 ˏsăng Short hair.
鬅丨 the hair in much disorder; tangled locks.

SAO.

Old sounds, so, sok *and* sop. *In Canton*, sò *and* ts'ò ;— *in Swatow*, sau, sao, *and* ch'au ;— *in Amoy*, sò ;— *in Fuhchau*, so ; — *in Shanghai*, so *and* sù ; — *in Chifu*, sao.

騷 ˛sao From *horse* and a *flea* as the phonetic.

To rub down a horse; to disquiet; perturbed, mournful, sad; eccentric, moody; clever; sorrows, griefs; to sweep.

勞 丨 grieved, miserable.

離 丨 the Dissipation of Sorrows; a celebrated monody by K'üh Yuen of Tsu, B. C. 280.

丨 丨 hurried; in unseemly haste.

丰 丨 bewitching, attractive.

丨 殺 fluttering in the wind.

丨 人墨客 a renowned bard.

丨 擾 to annoy, to harass.

丨 屑出穴風 the cold, sharp winds are coming from Æolus' cave.

風 丨 elegant; clever, poetic talent.

`丨 動 to stir up.

徐方繹 丨 the land of Sü was disturbed in all its stages or posts.

搔 ˛sao From *hand* and *flea* as the phonetic.

To scratch; to rub gently; to titillate; to irritate, to annoy; the nails.

丨 爬 to scratch.

丨 首問青天 to complain to Heaven in a great dilemma.

丨 首踟躕 he scratches his head in great perplexity.

丨 破臉 to set people at variance.

隔靴 丨 癢 [as well try to] scratch yourself through your boot; — *i. e.* a useless attempt.

慅 ˛sao Similar to the last.

Moved, excited; troubled, distressed.

勞 丨 morose; painstaking.

念子 丨 丨 I have constantly had you in my mind.

艘 ˛sao A general name for boats and junks.

鹽 丨 子 a salt junk.

欲淩洪波而遐濟必因 丨 楫之器 if you wish to get over those billows, and cross to the other shore, you cannot do it without using boats and oars.

颾 ˛sao The sound of the wind.

丨 風雨 a driving storm.

被風 丨 爛了 broken in by the wind.

心不偷涼 丨 丨 my heart is quite easy that I did not commit the theft.

溞 ˛sao The sound of washing rice in an earthern dish.

淅之 丨 丨 a rinsing and scouring sound, as when cleaning rice.

鰠 ˛sao A large fish found in the River Wéi, in Shensi.

丨 魚 a species of bream or tench. (*Leuciscus.*)

繅 ˛sao, ch'ao From *silk* and *nest*.

To reel off silk from the cocoons; a piece of worked silk for placing a gem on.

丨 繭 to wind off cocoons.

丨 絲 to reel off silk.

臊 膰 ˛sao From *flesh* and birds *singing*, or a *flea*; the second form is unusual.

Rank, rancid; strong, as goats; reeking, fetid.

膏 丨 rank pork fat.

腥 丨 noisome, offensive.

身 丨 redolent of perspiration.

丨 丨 rank smelling, like newly-killed meat.

丨 仔 a newly born infant. (*Cantonese.*)

丨 鼠 at Canton, denotes a shrew-mouse; in the North, perhaps the polecat.

嘴 丨 bad breath.

In *Pekingese*, used for 燥. Bashful, mortified.

羞 丨 ashamed.

不害 丨 brazen-faced, impudent.

嫂 嫂 ˊsao From *woman* and an *old* person.

An elder brother's wife; a sister-in-law; a woman; a matron.

姑 丨 sisters-in-law, one's own sisters and sisters-in-law.

家 丨 I, the goodwife.

亞 丨 the goody; goodwoman! a term of address.

大 丨 or 丨 丨 Madam; lady.

大 丨 or 兄 丨 my sister-in-law.

某 丨 a certain man's wife.

表 丨 a cousin's wife.

薅 ˛sao Wrongly written like the last.

A small plant like the chick-weed (*Stellaria*), also called 鷄腸草 chicken's gut.

菽 丨 根 the fragrant root of a liliaceous plant.

掃 ˊsao From *hand* and *besom*; as a noun also read ˊsao.

To sweep, to brush; to clean up; to clear off, to rid; to dampen, as one's ardor; a broom, a besom; to search in order to seize.

一把 丨 one broom.

丨 乾淨 sweep clean.

鷄毛 丨 a feather-duster.

打 丨 to sweep.

丨 艙 sweepings of the hold, — is the last lighter of a cargo.

丨 把星 a star-sweeper; — *met.* a slovenly, wasteful man.

丨 靖海氛 to sweep off the sea-mist; — *i. e.* to destroy pirates.

丨 興 to disappoint one's hopes, to take down one's hilarity.

丨 邊 關 to clear the frontiers.

丨 除 奸 黨 to rid [the government] of the traitors.

丨 楊 以 待 I shall make ready for your coming

一 丨 兒 光 all swept away.

拜 丨 to sweep and worship the tombs.

丨 數 to clear off an account.

埽 sao' Same as the last in its literal meaning of a broom; to sweep; a bank constructed in with earth like an abattis of bamboos filled.

竹 丨 a bamboo broom.

於粲洒 丨 how brightly I have sprinkled and swept—the yard.

銅 丨 a copper brush to polish buttons.

掌 丨 門 庭 to keep the doorway and hall constantly swept.

隄 丨 a dike.

喿 噪 譟 sao' From *three* mouths originally 吅 and *tree* or *mouth* and *besom*; the second form is most used.

The chirping and singing of many birds; the hum of men.

歸 鴉 丨 晩 林 [when] the crows come cawing home to their roost in the evening, — we'll go.

蟬 丨 the chirping of cicadas.

鵲 丨 晴 magpies chattering for fair weather.

索 餉 鼓 丨 in getting their stipends, [the soldiers] stirred each other up to great clamor.

譟 sao' Like the last.

The noise of a crowd; a clamor, a disturbance.

鼓 丨 而 起 they roused them up with a great clamor.

譁 丨 a hubbub, vociferation.

丨 擾 to rouse up and disturb.

丨 讓 altercation; a row.

鐰 sao' Hardened iron or good steel; broken steel; the scoria of iron or other ores; used with *ts'iao* 鍫 meaning a spade.

瘙 sao' A sore, a pustule; an itching; to itch.

皮 膚 丨 痒 the skin itches continually.

燥 sao' Dry, scorched; chapped, parched; to dry by the fire; used for *tsao'* 懆 violent.

乾 丨 dried up; drought.

風 高 丨 物 the [north] wind dries and warps things.

口 丨 a parched mouth.

秋 丨 autumnal heats.

丨 烈 fierce, raging, as with passion.

丨 濕 之 劑 a remedy against weakness and dropsical habits.

髞 sao' High, prominent, as a hill; imposing, lofty, as a house.

亮 丨 light and spacious.

SEH.

These characters and those under SHEH *are often pronounced alike. Old sounds,* shik, shet, *and* ship. *In Canton,* shik, shăt, săk, *and* săt; — *in Swatow,* sek, sat, *and* siap; — *in Amoy,* sek, sat, *and* sip; — *in Fuhchau,* saik; — *in Shanghai,* sák *and* seh; — *in Chifu,* sö *and* seh.

色 seh' Composed of 人 *man* and 卪 a *seal*, and defined "the effluence from the countenance," referring to the change of color in the face; it forms the 139th radical of a few congruous characters.

Air, manner; form; color, hue; complexion, expression of the face; the deportment; to look blandly; mode, sort, quality, kind; glory, beauty; lust, venery; a show of well dressed women; in *Budhism*, one of the six outward perceptions, that of (*rupa*) form.

丨 水 a color, the tint of a thing.

彩 丨 particolored, variegated.

出 丨 人 員 an officer above the common run.

丨 相 form and substance; aspect and reality.

國 丨 famous beauties; noted courtesans.

作 丨 to bridle up; angry.

五 丨 are 青 green or blue, 黃 yellow, 赤 carnation, 白 white, and 黑 black.

成 丨 the touch or quality of specie.

不 大 聲 以 丨 [your virtue] is not loudly flaunted abroad.

戴 丨 戴 笑 blandly he looks and smiles.

丨 水 低 alloyed; an inferior color, said chiefly of sycee.

足 丨 pure, as gold or silver.

喜 丨 laughing, pleased.

扮 丨 to dress up, as girls who are carried in processions.

雜 丨 various kinds, as of goods.

丨 膽 如 天 heaven-daring in his lewdness.

丨 身 a Budhist term for the organic body.

丨 丨 俱 全 every sort is kept on hand.

正 丨 sedate, composed.

聲 丨 貨 利 music, lewdness, property, and gain, are four snares to mankind.

女 丨 venery; licentious.

留 心 物 丨 I'll remember to find one for you.

重 丨 不 重 友 he thinks more of women than of friends.

丨 中 餓 鬼 a miserable whoremonger.

好' 丨 or 丨 慾 libidinous, salacious.

擲丨子 to throw dice.

丨卽是空空卽丨 this world is all emptiness, and emptiness is life.

日有起丨 the color daily rises; *met.* increasing prosperity or improvement.

名丨 a Budhistic term for *nama rupa*, one of the twelve *nidanas*, or causes of existence, which shows the unreality of thought and material phenomena.

懎, *seh'*

To hate, to abhor, though with regret.

嗇, *seh'*

Composed of 㐭 a *granary* and 來 *to come* both contracted; *q. d.* crops come into the storehouses.

The harvest, which should not be wasted; to amass, to accumulate; to begrudge; avaricious, sparing, mean; frugal, stingy.

丨夫 an officer who oversaw the harvesting.

丨言 sparing of words.

他是丨刻子 he is a closefisted fellow.

丨賬 it is hard to get an account settled with him.

丨刻 stingy, mean, griping.

穡, *seh'*

Used for the last and the next.

To gather in the harvest; husbandry, culture; grain ready for the sickle.

歛丨 to get in crops.

稼丨卒痒 the crops are all in an evil case.

后稷之丨有相'之道 Heutsih's culture was on the principle of helping — nature

丨事 harvesting, reaping.

省丨 to be economical.

先丨 a name for Shinnung.

儙, *seh'*

Used for the last two.

A surname; a harvest; to gather grain.

丨夫 a farmer.

澀, **澁**, *seh'*

Rough, harsh, not smooth; corrugated, as skin; astringent, as a taste; uneven; rippled, like water running over stones; difficult of performance.

味兒發丨 this taste is very astringent.

言語艱丨 his speech is imperfect and rude.

摸着丨手 it rasps the hand to rub it.

丨滯 stopped, obstructed.

歰, *seh'*

Considered to be an obsolete form of the last, and composed of 止 to *stop* repeated four times to show how rough a thing is.

Rough; an impediment in speech; too shallow for a boat to float; hard to turn around.

㒊, *seh'*

Unattainable, what cannot be reached or accomplished.

Read *sah*, To talk very fast, to gabble much.

㴔, *seh'*

Frugal, sparing; stingy.

羞丨 ashamed, mortified.

瑟, *seh'*

From *gems* and *must*; but the upper half is a contraction of a musical instrument.

An instrument like a large lute, differing from the 琴 in the cords crossing bridges to tighten them; it had 50, 25, 15, or 5 silken strings, according to the size; elegant and dignified; pure, stern, harsh; massive; to be grave.

琴丨調和 the lutes and lyres harmonize; — conjugal union.

丨兮僩兮 grave and dignified.

丨丨 a bleak soughing of the wind.

蕭丨 chilly, autumnal winds.

丨彼玉瓚 massive is the libation goblet.

In *Cantonese*. To walk carefully.

丨丨吓 be careful how you go; said to a child.

摵, *shuh*

Used for the last.

The rustling fall of the leaf is 丨丨; some say it is from the sad strains of the lute; applied also to autumnal flowers withering.

Read *siao*. To brush away.

Read *suh*. To reach.

璱, *seh'*

Originally like its primitive.

The pure, bright look of a lustrous gem.

近而視之丨若也 come near and see how bright it is.

虱, **蝨**, *shuh*

From 虫 *insect* and 迅 *quick*, from its motions; the second form is rarely used.

A louse; a parasitic insect; small bugs or insects, like fleas, aphides, *Cimex*, *Acarus*, and other wingless sorts.

丨子 or 人丨 a louse.

跳丨 or 狗丨 a flea; the last is also the dog-tick.

木丨 a bedbug.

釘丨 or 破丨 or 招丨 to crack lice.

沙丨 sand-bugs, sand-fleas.

捉字丨 to take occasion from a little flaw — to accuse or reject.

塞, *sai'*, *sö*

From *earth* and *habitation*.

To stop or fill up, to close; to obstruct, to hinder, to prevent by obstacles; to spike, as a gun; an important pass or position in a country; when speaking of strategetic obstacles of an enemy's approach, 啓 refers to a gate or bridge, and this to a dike or wall; unintelligent, dull, hard to apprehend; sincere, honest.

丨了鼻子 nose stopped, as in a cold.

閉丨 closed, obstructed, impeded.

其心丨淵 her heart felt deeply.

丨住 stop it up.

丨口 to stop a hole; to gag or bribe, so as to quiet one; to put him down by argument.

堵 丨 to block up, as approaches.
頓開茅 丨 all at once his dullness of perception was removed.
搪 丨 to pass [a bore] on to another person; to give the cold shoulder to.
充丨天地 to pervade and fill the world; — as the Gospel will.
聊以 丨 責 to slur over (or trump up) so as to prevent censure.
丨 丨 agitated, disconcerted.

Read *sai'* A boundary, a frontier; a limit.
丨 外 beyond the borders.
邊 丨 the frontiers.
出 丨 to pass beyond the borders, as a princess did to marry a Hun.

In *Pekingese*, used for *tseh*, 摺. To fold under; to double in, to tuck in; also, to stop up.
把桌幃 丨 進去 fold this tablecloth under.

痓 *seh'* An ague.
瘆 丨 chills and fever; to catch cold.
丨 寒暮作 this chill comes on at evening.

翜 *seh'* To fly swiftly; to clasp.
丨 飛而投長林 the swift flying birds are hastening to the deep forest.

Read *shah*, Feathers used to adorn a coffin.

SEU.

See also under SHEU. *Old sounds*, su, sok, *and* sot. *In Canton*, sau; — *in Swatow*, sò; — *in Amoy*, sò *and* sòh; — *in Fuhchau*, sóu *and* sau; — *in Shanghai*, sù; — *in Chifu*, sò.

鎪 *seu* To engrave on metal; ornaments on a horse's ears.
彫 丨 to inlay; to carve or inchase.
丨 竹根 to carve bamboo roots.

叟 変 傁 *seu* Composed of 又 a *hand* or 寸 *inch* under 臼 a *mortar;* the third form is used more than the others.
An appellation for an old person; Sir.
老 丨 venerable Sir.
田 丨 this old farmer.
丨 丨 the sound of washing rice in scored pans.
黃童白 丨 boys and old men.

瞍 瞍 *seu* Occurs used for the last.
Blind from having no pupil, as in amaurosis; an old man whose sight is poor and step feeble.
矇 丨 blind, but having eye balls; a term often used for blind musicians.

嗾 *seu* Also read *so'*
To spur on a dog to attack; to incite, to stir up.
丨 狗 to set on a dog; to wind the hounds.

擻 *seu* From *hand* and *number*.
To shake, to arouse; to refresh.
抖 丨 精神 to excite or stir up one's self or one's spirits.

籔 *seu* A basket or bamboo vessel to wash rice; a flat basket; an old measure of sixteen 斗 pecks, ten of which made a 秉 or tierce; it is now disused.

藪 *seu* Used for the last.
A marshy preserve in which game is kept and fish are reared; fat, gainful, rich, because such places produce much food; a place where people gather.
麓 丨 the edge of a hill.
澤 丨 marshy edges of a hill.
利 丨 a market; an exchange.
郊 丨 a wilderness, a waste.
丨 盜 a retreat for robbers.
蜂 丨 the bees are swarming.
逋逃 丨 a refuge for people (or criminals) to flee to.

嗽 瘶 *seu'* *su'* The first is also read *shuh*, to draw in the breath.
To clear the throat; to cough; to expectorate; to hack; a cough.
乾 丨 a dry cough.
痰 丨 to raise phlegm.
唶號咳 丨 to give the signal by a slight cough.

謏 *seu'* From *words* and to *scour*.
Angry or reproving words.
Read *ˏsiao*. To allure, to induce to act right.
丨 善 to urge to goodness.
丨 說 a novel, a story to commend virtue.
足以 丨 聞 this is fame enough.

SHA.

Old sounds, sha, shak, *and* shat. *In Canton,* sha ; — *in Swatow,* súa, sa, săng, *and* sé ; — *in Amoy,* sa *and* swa ; — *in Fuhchau,* sa, sai, swa, *and* sò ; — *in Shanghai,* sò *and* sa ; — *in Chifu,* sa *and* swa.

沙 *sha* From *water* and a *few* ; *q. d.* when the water is little the sand appears ; like the next.

Sand, gravel; pebbles, shingle; reefs, banks; granulated, as sugar; gritty; broken fine; friable and mealy, as fruit; frequenting sandbanks and beaches; a sandy, brown, or gray color.

丨糖 common or brown sugar.

丨尾 or 丨角 a sandy spit, a spot where the still water allows silt to settle.

丨虫 larvæ of musketoes.

丨漏 a water filter of sand.

丨面 shallow sand-banks; at Canton, boats remain on them.

丨白 the sand clam, a species of *Mactra.*

丨塵大 clouds of dust.

小丨彌 a Budhist novice.

丨門 (or 桑門 from the Sanscrit *sramana* and Pali *samana,*) quieting of the passions, as ascetics strive to do; it now denotes the Mongol Shamanism, though at first it referred to all priests, Budhists and Brahmins.

丨猛 a file-fish. (*Aluteres berardi.*)

丨甲 the dragonet fish. (*Platycephalus guttatus.*)

丨錐 a sandpiper or snipe; also a species of loche. (*Cobitis psammismus.*)

流丨 quicksands; moving sands, a name given in the Book of Records to the Gobi Desert.

丨漠 the desert of Shamo.

東丨 the Pratas shoal.

打丨袋 to learn boxing.

鱗丨 a fish like the sardine.

In *Fuhchau,* Skillful at, ready.

砂 *sha* Used with the last.

Pebbles, coarse sand; gravel; gritty, like sand.

寶丨 emery.

硃丨紅 a bright red.

解玉丨 or 金鋼丨 corundum; diamond dust.

拜丨 to winnow hulled rice. (*Cantonese.*)

辰丨 the best kind of cinnabar from Shin-cheu fu in Hunan.

出丨子 the pilferings of servants or cooks. (*Pekingese.*)

丨仁 or 西丨仁 grains of paradise, obtained from the *Amomum xanthioides* and the *Elettaria;* the 陽春丨 from Yang-chun district in Kwangtung, are from the *Amomum villosum.*

丨皮 cowhide; *met.* stubborn, indocile.

靈丨 æthiops mineral, a sulphide of mercury.

𤛓 *sha* The largest sized buffalo is called 水丨牛 in the central provinces, and usually denotes the cow.

痧 *sha* From *disease* and *sand* as the phonetic ; an unauthorized character.

The cholera.

絞腸丨 Asiatic cholera.

刮丨 to scarify for cholera.

丨氣丸 cholera pills.

塘棲丨藥 a good remedy for cholera from Su-chau.

粆 *sha* The first and coarse kind of sugar, 丨糖 (otherwise 沙糖) like brown muscovado.

桬 *sha* A valuable timber tree, 丨棠 brought from Tibet, whose soft, berry-shaped fruit tastes like a plum.

丨梨 a russet pear.

丨木 a species of pine from Nganhwui, which furnishes a valuable light wood, highly prized for coffins.

紗 *sha* Gauze, thin silk; reticulated, gauzy, lace-like, transparent; a fiber, an untwisted thread.

縐丨 crape.

白丨 white gauze.

脫丨帽 to lose the 烏丨帽 or black gauze hat, is to be turned out of office, — this having been the official hat during the Ming dynasty.

綿丨 mull, fine muslin, lawn.

經丨 to lay the warp.

羽丨 English camlets.

月照丨窗 the moon shines through the latticed window.

裟 毴 *sha* } A surplice or outer robe of a Budhist priest; the second character is used for a shaggy woolen surplice, woven from coarse sheep's wool.

袈丨布 cambric or muslin.

魦 鯊 *sha* } From *fish* and *sand,* referring to the gritty skin.

The shark family, including some rays and skates.

丨綠色 a bright slate blue.

丨魚皮 shagreen.

公子帽丨 hammer-headed shark. (*Sphyrna zygæna.*)

鋸丨 the saw fish (*Pristis*), which is said to be able to strike at and injure vessels.

琵琶丨 the spotted ray. (*Rhina ancylostoma.*)

貓兒丨 spinous shark. (*Cestracion zebra.*)

犂頭丨 the shovel-nosed shark. (*Rhinobatus hynnicephalus.*)

丨魚 a fresh water fish, six inches long, round body and big head which buries itself in the ooze and spurts sand; it may be a kind of bull-head, as its dorsal spines are dangerous.

髿 *ˏsha* Long fine hair.
鬖 丨 the hair hanging in tresses; disheveled or loose hair.

洒 灑 *ˊsha* *ˊsa* From *water* and *west* or *elegant;* also read *shaiˋ* and *ˊsa;* it is also used for 洗 to wash; the first form is easily confounded with *ˊtsiu* 酒 spirits.

To sprinkle with a liquid; to scatter, as the wind does the leaves; to divide; deep and steep water; respectful; swift; snow; to cast, as a fisherman the net.
丨 水 sprinkle it.
丨 濕 衣 my clothes were wet by the rain.
丨 釣 to cast a hook.
丨 灰 水 to whitewash.
丨 泪 to weep much.
霏 霏 丨 丨 a continual small rain.
丨 然 alarmed.
丨 綉 衣 silk robes with speckled embroidery.
那 些 水 丨 了 this water spilled over, as when carrying a bucket-full.

Read *ˊtsˊui.* Lofty and new.
新 臺 有 丨 high and fine is the new terrace.

Read *sinˋ* Shivering.
丨 丨 時 寒 shaking from the cold.

In *Cantonese.* A shed; to stretch out.
鷄 丨 the hen stretches her wings.
一 頁 丨 an open shed.
丨 丨 晾 to hang out to dry.

傻 *ˊsha* Foolish, thoughtless.
丨 子 a simpleton, a careless fellow.
獃 丨 doltish, silly.
丨 得 很 how stupid that is!
丨 俅 不 仁 palsied.

In *Pekingese.* Rather, an adjective of comparison.
丨 好 的 pretty good, it will do.
丨 俏 rather fine.

耍 *ˊshwa* From *whisker* and *woman;* it resembles *yaoˋ* 要 to wish.

To sport, to play with; to trifle with, as fire-arms; to fence; play, jollity; games.
丨 棍 to fence with shillelahs.
丨 刀 牌 to play with foils and shields.
丨 戲 to sport and dance; to waste one's time.
丨 戲 的 話 joking talk, banter, badinage.
丨 錢 to gamble; to pitch coppers.
不 是 丨 的 I am quite serious.
悞 了 人 性 命 不 是 丨 it is no trifling matter to cost another man his life.
丨 脾 氣 to create disturbance, to provoke needlessly.
丨 花 鎗 to bandy words and angry talk, as a man and wife.
尖 丨 expert, clever.
丨 獃 子 to chaff a bumpkin.
丨 拳 脚 to act gymnastics, to play the acrobat.
丨 貨 舖 a toy-shop.
作 丨 playing, making sport.

In *Cantonese.* To waive off.
丨 手 to shake the hand to intimate that a thing is not to be done; to motion away.

歃 嗄 *shaˋ* The changing of the voice; the voice becoming hoarse through bawling.
丨 喉 a hoarse throat.
丨 聲 a hoarse, gruff voice

刎 *shaˋ* To make an eyelet hole.
眼 丨 small holes in a thing; cavities, as in porous iron.
割 丨 治 瘡 to cut and probe ulcers.

SHAH.

Old sounds, shat *and* shap. *In Canton,* shat, shap, *and* sap; — *in Swatow,* sat, súa, *and* siap; — *in Amoy,* sat, siap, chʻap, *and* chʻiap; — *in Fuhchau,* sak *and* sai; — *in Shanghai,* sèh; — *in Chifu,* sah.

殺 *ˏsha* Some derive this from 殳 to *kill,* 木 a *club,* and 又 *hand;* but its etymology is doubtful.

To slay, to put to death; to murder; to kill, of which crime Chinese law recognizes five grades; to die by famine or frost; penalty of death; death; to hunt and kill game; to mow grass; to seize or get; to gather up; a form of the superlative, furiously, murderously.
丨 頭 to decapitate.
丨 蟲 to drive off worms; to kill bugs.
丨 手 a headsman.
丨 數 to finish an account.
丨 生 to butcher animals.
威 風 丨 氣 an awful, dreadful look.
丨 入 陣 he fought his way into their ranks.
嚇 丨 了 scared to death.
急 丨 in great haste, in a killing hurry.
丨 緊 繩 子 the cord is tied too tight.
笑 丨 人 a comedian, a droll.
氣 丨 人 in a towering passion.
兩 家 頭 好 丨 they are inseparable, as two friends.
丨 尾 the very last.
故 丨 willful murder.
格 丨 accidental manslaughter.

好 ˀ 丨了是他人壞丨了是自己 if you love the child greatly, yet he is another's; if you feel that he is a ruined child, still he is my own.

誤丨 homicide, manslaughter.

氣丨他 to overawe; to enrage another; to force to comply.

弗蠲乃事時同于丨 as you do not cleanse your way, you shall consequently be classed with those who are to be put to death.

天丨的挑的禍 a heaven-condemned fellow who brings down evil on people.

Read *shai*ˀ To pare off, to reduce; to clip or shear; to bend down in order to effect; to make a seam or sew together; part of a shroud.

其聲噍丨 his voice was broken and confused.

親親之丨 act like a relative to all your kindred.

煞 *sha*ˀ *ˏsha* Another form of the last, but now usually confined to malign and noxious influences.

To strike dead, as by the sun; to murder; baleful, detrimental; to injure by malaria; to end; a twinkling; an *adverb* of intensity, often heard in Kiangsu.

丨氣 sickly vapors, malaria; the active spirit of death, baleful influences which destroy luck.

丨星 a malignant star.

凶丨 deleterious, as a location.

命帶刧丨 my fate carries evil to all my family.

當丨 it wards off evil, as the 八卦 eight diagrams, or the inscription 石敢當 of the Stone Warden.

關丨 crises in life, which occur triennially from three to sixteen, modified by the signs one is born in.

坐丨 and 向丨 back and front noxiousness, geomantic terms connected with the position of graves.

說不丨角 never-ending talk, garrulous.

强盜多丨 the robbers are very numerous.

近丨 very near.

䙾 *ˏsha* The edges of a seam left over which are to be felled; to sew up the seam; clothes folded up.

鎩 *ˏsha* A spear with a guard; to clip the wings of birds.

長丨 a long halberd.

武將虎戟而交丨 the bristling lances of the troops were crossed and blended — as they marched.

歃 *sha*ˀ From to *owe* and to *pierce*.

To smear the sides of the mouth with blood when taking an oath; it was done in ancient times.

丨血 to sip the blood of a sacrifice.

丨而忘 he quite forgot his oath.

箑 *sha*ˀ An old and formal term for a fan, which Wu Wang is said to have invented.

佳丨 a beautiful fan.

丨書 to write in a rapid running hand.

丨脯 thin, fan-like collops of meat dried for winter use.

霎 *sha*ˀ A slight shower; a passing rain; an instant, the moment of action.

一丨時 a little while.

丨時 momentarily.

丨然間 for a moment, on a sudden.

光丨眼 the gleams dazzle the eyes.

微風丨雨 a gentle breeze and slight shower.

丨丨雨聲 pattering of rain.

翣 *sha*ˀ Feathers used to adorn coffins; a great flabellum of thin wood, ornamented with clouds and figures, carried with the coffins of dignitaries, and set at each corner of the grave.

置丨 to set up the flabelli.

大丨 a great fan.

唼 *sha*ˀ To speak much; loquacious, talkative.

SHAI.

Old sounds, shai *and* shak. *In Canton,* shai *and* shei; — *in Swatow,* sù *and* sai; — *in Amoy,* su; — *in Fuhchau,* sai, sü, *and* t'ai; — *in Shanghai,* sa *and* sò; — *in Chifu,* sai.

篩 簁 簛 *ˏshai* The first form is commonly used.

An immense reed, a hundred feet long and 25 feet in diameter, said to grow in the south, and used for skiffs; a sieve of wire, bamboo, or thread; to sift, to strain.

丨子 or 丨箕 a sieve.

粉丨 a flour sieve.

竹丨月影 the bamboos intercept the moonbeams.

丨錢板 a board with grooves for cash to drop in, so that the coins can be shaken in and counted quickly.

丨粉雨 a mizzling rain.

丨糠狀 shaking with ague.

丨風毯月 the sifting breeze carpets the earth with moonlight.

攦 *ˏshai* To disperse and get lost; to strike.

丨鑼擂鼓 to beat the gongs and tap the drums.

曬 晒 *shai*' The second form is unauthorized, but in common use.

To dry in the sun; the reflection of the sun; to air and sun; to cure in the sunshine, as fruit.

丨乾 dry it in the sun.

生丨 to dry fresh fruit.

丨衣服 to sun garments.

丨棚 a drying-terrace or frame.

不要丨黑 don't get sunburnt.

小心丨迷糊了 take care that you don't get a sunstroke.

丨不透 the sun does not get through, as a curtain.

鳧雛丨陽 the ducklings are sunning themselves.

SHAN.

Old sounds, shan *and* sham. *In Canton*, shan *and* sham; — *in Swatow*, $sw^{n}a$, sam, *and* san; — *in Amoy*, san, sam, sian, *and* ch'am; — *in Fuhchau*, sang; — *in Shanghai*, sè'n; — *in Chifu*, san.

山 *shan* The original form resembles three peaks; it forms the 46th radical of characters relating to the names and forms of hills.

A mountain; hills, heights; a mound; a range; uncultivated; wild, not domesticated or subdued; strong, loud, as a tone of voice; the gable end of a wall; a hill site.

丨呼萬歲 he cried out aloud, Your majesty!

丨峯 separate peaks.

名丨 celebrated mountains; it is also the name of Mount Hwa.

靠丨 posted against a hill, as an army.

丨貨 wood and bamboo-ware, baskets, tubs, &c.

丨人 wild tribes; a mountaineer, a hermit.

錫丨土田 I confer on you hills, plains, and fields; — *i. e.* the territory.

隱丨 to retire into obscurity.

丨禽 wild fowl.

屋丨一垛 the end wall of the house.

左右臨丨 both of the gable ends open on vacant ground.

丨水 spring water.

丨珍海錯 pearls and delicacies from the hills and seas; — nice dishes of every kind.

錦繡江丨 the tapestried hills and embroidered rivers; — *i. e.* our sovereign's empire.

好家丨風水 a prosperous family.

童丨 a bare peak.

丨水相逢 the hill and water will yet meet; — you will see him again.

丨東 or 丨左 the province of Shantung; as 丨西 or 丨右 denotes Shansi.

妙高丨 the wonderful high mountain, is Mount Meru, or *Su-meru* 須彌 of the Budhists, the axis of the universe.

In *Cantonese*. A grave, which in the south are on hill-sides; the country.

拜丨 to worship at the graves.

拜龍丨 to worship a dragon (or lucky) grave.

丨狗 grave-diggers; grass-cutters.

壅丨 to bury, to inter.

姍 *shan* Good, beautiful; to ridicule, to laugh at, to gibe.

丨笑 to make sport of.

Read *sien*. To go.

丨丨 a slow gait, a stately manner.

Read *soh*, The trailing skirt of a lady.

跚 *shan* Used for the last and the next.

To hobble or limp.

蹣丨 to walk lamely, or as if unable to go forward.

珊 *shan* Precious coral, 丨瑚 the fine red kind, which is highly prized.

丨瑚頂 a red coral button, the highest in rank.

闌丨 spread abroad; scattered about, as fallen flowers.

雜佩丨丨 his girdle chatelaine made a jingling.

删 *shan* From *knife* and a *register*.

To pare; to amend, to correct and expunge; to edit and settle a text; to reject, as an account.

丨改 to alter and erase

丨去 or 丨除 to expunge.

漆丨 a stiff brush used by painters.

丨詩定禮 [Confucius] edited the Odes and settled the Ritual

丨減 to abridge.

杉 *sha* *shan* A species of deal used for boards.

丨竿子 a joist; pine piles.

丨木 deal; pine boards.

丨板 is sometimes written for 三板 a ship's boat.

丨樹 the coarse pine (*Cunninghamia lanceolata*) of Southern China; it also includes the *Cryptomeria*.

丨木靈牌 a pine ancestral tablet, — is a worthless thing.

衫 *shan* From *clothes* and *pelage*.

A garment for the body, as a coat, shirt, or jacket; it usually refers to those without a lining.

衣丨 garments; body clothes.

汗丨 an under-shirt.

長丨 a robe, a summer-gown.

脫 丨 to take off a garment.

藍 丨 a *siuts'ai*, because he goes tc salute his friends in a blue robe.

雺 A slight rain.
꜀shan
丨 雨 a fine drizzling rain.

彡 Intended to represent *feathers* or long hair; it forms the 59th radical of characters alluding to stripes.
꜀shan
To adorn with feathers or colored hair.

摻 A delicate hand, one with tapering fingers; tapering, small; to pull along, to take hold of.
꜀shan
丨 丨 女 手 a lady's beautiful hand.

丨 執 子 之 手 兮 I'll hold you by the hand.

Read *꜀ts'an*. To mix together, to mix in; to introduce surreptitiously; to feel or rub.

丨 雜 to mix up.

丨 和 to put together, as ingredients in a dish.

丨 假 to adulterate by mixing in other things.

穇 From *grain* and *tapering*, alluding to the four slender spikelets, which are likened to dragon's claws.
꜀shan
A marshy grass resembling a *Panicum*, cultivated in Yunnan; it has large clasping leaves like rice, a three-sided stem, and thick spikelets, bearing a reddish grain like canary-seed; it is probably allied to an *Eleusine;* the flour is glutinous.

芟 / 刬 From *plant* or *knife* and to *kill*.
꜀shan
To mow; to cut grass or herbs; to root out; a large bill-hook, a sort of scythe.

丨 草 除 根 to mow the grass and root it up.

載 丨 載 柞 he cleared away the grass and the bushes.

潸 To weep, to cry piteously.
꜀shan
丨 然 出 涕 the tears flowed freely.

兩 泪 丨 丨 both her eyes were streaming with tears.

摌 To move or manipulate with dexterity, to make signals.
꜀shan
揀 丨 to pick over and sort rapidly and well, as tea is prepared.

汕 Fish jumping on the surface; to snare fish in a wicker net; name of a river in Corea; a spit or point of a beach.
shan'
丨 頭 the port of Swatow.

嘉 魚 烝 然 丨 丨 the barbel are caught in great numbers.

疝 Rupture of the bowels, or hernia; pain from hernia; a mode of the pulse; swelling of the testes.
shan'
心 丨 angina pectoris.

丨 氣 hernia; also a stricture or retention of urine.

水 丨 or 牡 丨 hydrocele.

訕 To vilify, to slander; to murmur at.
shan'
丨 謗 to backbite.

丨 上 to revile superiors.

諫 而 無 丨 reprove without railing at one.

丨 其 良 人 she slandered her husband.

丨 言 grumbling slanders.

釤 A large bill-hook or sickle.
shan'

SHĂN.

Part of these characters are sometimes read SHIN. *Old sounds*, shím, shín, zhím, *and* shem. ***In Canton***, shăn, shăm, ch'ăn, *and* ch'ăm; — *in Swatow*, sín, siam, sien, *and* sím; — *in Amoy*, sím, sín, *and* ch'ím; — *in Fuhchau*, seng, sing, *and* leng; — *in Shanghai*, săng, zăng, *and* sing; — *in Chifu*, săn *and* shin.

森 From *three trees* to indicate their number.
꜀săn
An abundance of trees, close together; overgrown with wood; somber, as a forest; severe, as laws; to plant trees.

丨 嚴 rigorous, majestic, severe.

丨 木 Chinese mahogany, the timber of the 丨 樹 pride of India. (*Melia azederach.*)

綠 丨 丨 的 thick and shady, as a green forest.

蕭 丨 蓊 茂 thickly wooded and grassy.

衆 山 丨 列 the hills rise in numerous peaks.

戈 戟 丨 丨 the serried spears are closely seen.

莘 From *plant* and *bitter*.
꜀shăn
꜀sin
Name of an ancient place or state in Shensi, not far from the present Hoh-yang hien 郃 陽 縣 on the Yellow R.

丨 縣 a district in the west of Shantung.

丨 丨 翼 翼 numerous, said of camp-followers.

有 丨 其 尾 showing their long tails; — said of fishes in a pond.

有 丨 之 野 a marshy waste place.

Read *꜀sin*, and used with its primitive. A marshy plant with yellowish green, thick oval leaves, like those of the birthwort (*Asarum*), whose root is acrid, and when dried used in rheumatism; it is called 細 丨, and is perhaps a species of *Heterotropa*.

痒 *shăn* A shivering *bitter ailment*, such as the ague induces.

籼 *shăn* The oil made from hemp or *Sida* seed; it was used to light the old year out by firing fir sticks in a 丨盆 till the morning came; the refuse of flour; the settlings of gruel.

麻丨 linseed cake which is left after the 葫麻油 or linseed oil is expressed.

駪 **侁** *shăn* *sin* Men and horses in company; a large crowd of people.

丨丨征夫 many guests and customers.

丨丨往來 many coming and going.

詵 *sin* From *words* and *first.*

To begin a conversation, to inquire of; public opinion; many talking about a thing; numerous, as a swarm.

子孫丨丨 a numerous progeny.

螽斯羽丨丨兮 those locusts, winging their way, what happy swarms of them.

葠 **參** *shăn* The second form is now mostly used; it is also read *ts'an.*

The ginseng plant (*Panax schinseng*), a name altered from 人丨, and so called from the resemblance of its forked roots to a man; it is also called 神草 the divine plant, and 地精 earth's essence; this term is also applied to many roots of a mucilaginous nature used by the natives in medicine, and deemed to partake of the virtues of ginseng.

關東人丨 Manchurian ginseng, deemed to be superior to the 高麗人丨 or Corean ginseng.

洋丨 foreign ginseng; of which the 白玉人丨 or 洋丨鬚 is the crude, and 紅玉人丨 is the clarified sort.

荷蘭丨 saffron, *i. e.* Dutch ginseng.

海丨 biche-de-mer. (*Holothuria.*)

元丨 a weak sort of ginseng.

苦丨 the bitter ginseng. (*Robinia amara.*)

丨商 ginseng traders.

丨局 ginseng shops.

黨丨 a species of *Convolvulus.*

丹丨 the red ginseng, a species of sage or *Salvia.*

蔘 *shăn* Branches wide apart; a medicinal plant; pendent branches.

丨綏 large and wide; a local phrase.

身 *shăn* The original form bears a rude resemblance to the body walking; it is the 158th radical of characters relating to the shapes of the body.

The trunk; the body; the main part of a thing; the hull; one's self; I myself, and when used in a letter, a petition, or official document, it is often written smaller than the rest; personal, the presence; one's character or duty; pregnant; the conduct.

本丨 my body; I, myself.

赤丨 naked, bared, stark.

丨體 or 丨材 the person; the body.

下丨 the privates.

出丨 to enter on office; the origin or early life of a person.

酣丨 given to drink.

倭仁丨爲大臣 Wo-jin is himself a high official.

托丨何地 where can he now go to hide his disgrace?

設丨處地 suppose you were in that position.

終丨 whole life; the end of life.

終丨結局 to reap life's results — after death.

老丨 [I,] an old woman, — or old man.

忘其丨 careless of himself, as a brave soldier.

衣不稱丨 his dress does not fit him, or is unsuitable.

前丨 a former existence.

出丨理事 one who manages the business.

丨長 rather tall, above usual size.

過丨 dead, passed from the body.

如可贖兮人百其丨 could he have been ransomed, we would have given a hundred lives.

有丨 pregnant.

有丨家 he has some property.

分丨不暇 I have no time to attend to that.

賣丨 to go out to work; to mortgage one's person, as a coolie; peonage; to sell one's self.

開丨 to weigh anchor.

動丨 to start, to go.

渾丨亂顫 whole body shivering with cold.

破丨 the first sexual act.

丨後事宜如何料理之處 in what manner the obsequies were attended to after his death.

伊親丨老朽無能 he saw that I was old and weak.

把這丨筋骨活動 keep the muscles of the body in full exercise.

丨子 the body; the separate beads in a string of court beads. (*Pekingese.*)

丨分高 high in rank; a noble spirit; integrity.

放在我丨上不成 is he not trying to get me involved in the scrape?

罔有擇言在丨 they had no need to choose words [to defend] their conduct.

色丨 and 法丨 are Budhist terms for material and spiritual bodies, the latter being regarded as an embodiment of the law.

三丨 is also used for the triune body of every Budha (*trikaya*) consisting of 性 essence, 相 reflex, and 用 use, which is evolved to his perfection in the divinity, law, and priesthood.

丨毒國 Sindhu, an old name denoting India; or perhaps only that part now known as Scinde.

如意 〡 a magic body (*riddhi*) which can instantly transport itself anywhere, and assume any shape.

꜀深 ꜀*shăn* From *water* out of a *cavern*.

Name of a river in the south-east of Hunan; deep; profound, abstruse; intimate; ardent, as affection; well read, learned; strong, as spectacles; retired, inner, as an apartment; late at night; many, as days; intense, as dislike; deep-tinted; as an *adverb*, very, extremely, carefully, well; to secrete; a coat and trowsers joined in one; to measure the depth.

有幾〡水 how deep is the water here?

不知〡淺 I don't know the depth; I am not very familiar — with that subject.

〡厚 on very good terms with.

〡恩 great kindness.

〡揖 a profound bow.

〡沉 crafty, silent and scheming.

〡銘五內 [your favors are] deeply engraved on my heart.

更〡夜靜 from midnight till daybreak.

〡究 deep research.

〡以爲然 it is very true.

自有〡心 he indeed has his own deep purposes.

此字很〡 this character is very complex.

〡州 an inferior prefecture in the south of Chihli.

〡藍 a deep blue.

穆然〡遠 of a reserved and awful manner.

何其憂之〡也 what a depth of sorrow is his!

꜀申 ꜀*shăn* Formed of 臼 a *mortar* and 〡 to *join*; others say the character is intended to represent the *backbone*; used with the next.

To extend, to stretch; to reiterate; to prolong, to increase; to state to a superior, or enjoin on an inferior, for which senses the next is also erroneously used.

〡時 the ninth of the 12 stems, the hour from 3 to 5 P.M., over which the monkey has sway.

〡月 the seventh moon.

〡命 [Heaven] has given [the emperor] injunctions.

〡文 a report to a superior.

〡詳 to send up a statement.

〡飭 to reprimand; to enjoin an official to behave better.

〡〡如也 easy, composed, self-possessed.

〡明 to explain clearly.

〡國 a small, feudal principality in the Cheu dynasty where Nan-yang fu now lies in the south of Honan, on the head-waters of the River Han.

〡江 Shanghai district, a name supposed to be derived from the preceding state by mistake, as if it once belonged to it; but others more probably derive it from 春〡君 a prince over the region in those days, who is still worshiped by sailors at his temple in the city.

〡示 to promulge, as an order.

꜀伸 ꜀*shăn* Used for the preceding, and often erroneously.

To stretch and yawn; to dilate, to straighten; to explain; to report to; to right, to redress, to clear up a cause; vindicated; worth, valued, equal to, as in pricing things.

〡直手 to stretch out the hand.

〡寃屈 to redress a grievance.

〡陳 a statement to a superior.

欠〡 to stretch when tired.

〡直脚 dead, laid out for burial.

足〡雅懷 these fine sentiments can be expressed.

〡銀多少 how much is it worth?

〡懶 to stretch and yawn.

〡縮 to stretch or dilate and retract or shrink.

〡出來 push it out.

꜀呻 ꜀*shăn* To groan, to lament; to read in a chanting way.

〡吟 to recite or hum, as books.

長〡短嘆 whining and complaining.

〡其佔畢 he sings the books he reads — without understanding them.

In *Cantonese*. To complain, to whine about.

莫來〡' 〡' don't come about here whining.

꜀柛 ꜀*shăn* Trees that die of themselves; trees that wither away.

柳未全〡 this willow is not quite dead.

꜀紳 ꜀*shăn* From *silk* and to *extend*.

A large sash or girdle with ornamental ends; to gird; those who are privileged to wear sashes, the literati, graduates, officials, the gentry.

〡耆 or 鄉〡 or 〡董 or 〡衿 the gentry, official people in and out of office.

〡商 gentlemen and merchants, the higher classes.

書諸〡 write it on the girdle.

劣〡 an oppressive man among the gentry.

〡士 elders and headmen.

꜀訷 ꜀*shăn* To make known.

言不失〡 his words are reliable.

〡說 to state truly.

꜀娠 ꜀娠 ꜀*shăn* From *woman* and to *move* or *body*; the first is sometimes wrongly used instead of 孕 and then read *yin*꜄, their meanings being the same.

Pregnant, quick with child.

胎〡 the gravid uterus.

〡動 taken in labor.

〡喜 conceived, pregnant.

落〡 an abortion; a miscarriage.

꜀㑗 ꜀*shăn* Similar to the above, and defined as 神存乎身也 a spirit confined within the body; name of a god.

甡 ˏshăng ˏsin A multitude of living things moving together.

丨衆 numerous, herd-like.

瞻彼中林丨丨其鹿 look into that forest at the herds of deer roaming there.

棯 ˏshăn Also read ˏtsăn.

A species of cinnamon tree found in Yunnan, the bark of which is called 肉桂; it is an evergreen; the *Cinnamomum Loureiri* has the same name; the name 木丨 is also applied to a species of *Andromeda*, both being evergreens.

神 ˏshăn From *divine* and to *extend* as the phonetic.

That power or cause which operates by its own energies, diffused, formless, and inscrutable, yet making things develop; the 陽 powers above, as opposed to the 鬼 or 陰 powers below; the gods, the divinities, a god, in the usage of pagans; used by many for the true God; a spirit; a supernatural good being; the human spirit, the directing power of the body; the animal spirits, in which senses the Taoists use it much; divine, spiritual, as being higher than man; supernatural, godlike, wonderful, superhuman; as an *adverb*, very, exceedingly, mysteriously; to deify; in the language of epitaphs, nameless.

丨明 the gods.

丨鬼仙佛 gods, demons, genii, and Budhas, — are the four orders of beings above man.

事丨 to serve the gods, as an acolyte who presents offerings.

拜丨 to worship God; to adore the gods.

安丨 to set up gods to be worshiped; to quiet the manes of the dead; to cheer one's spirits; to relieve one's ailments.

丨像 images of the gods.

家丨 the lares or deified spirits of ancestors.

丨魂 the soul, the vital principle, before or after death.

丨效 wonderfully efficacious.

丨妙 supernaturally clever, as a physician.

谷丨 immaterial spirits, of Taoists.

養丨 to refresh one's spirits, as by a show.

丨銜 the name of a god.

心動丨知 the heart moves and the gods know it.

好用丨 keep your wits about you.

丨之聽之 the gods will then listen to him.

丨人 a shrewd guesser, a prophet.

丨保是格報以介福 [their ancestral] spirits quietly come and reward them with great blessings.

予念我先丨后之勞爾先 I think of the toils of my predecessors, those divine sovereigns for your ancestors.

丨心 devout, religiously inclined.

沒有精丨 out of spirits, low-spirited.

心丨不定 his health is not very certain.

留丨假票 be on the lookout for counterfeit bills.

關帝丨靈默佑 Kwanti's divine influences secretly protected him.

和丨當春 one's agreeable feelings [at this landscape] are like those when spring comes.

丨散解 mind not composed.

舉頭三尺有丨明 only three feet above you is a god.

丨其說 regard his words as divine; to deify him.

眼丨 a bright eye; the eye flashing.

兇丨附體 an evil spirit has got hold of you.

不可測度之謂丨 ˏshăn is that which cannot be fathomed or estimated.

跳丨的 a witch, one who calls up spirits; an exorcist.

出丨兒 absent-minded.

丨速 unusually quick.

開路丨 a sort of scarecrow that is carried before funerals as a pursuivant of the dead.

天丨 angels in the Roman Catholic usage.

原丨 the form or being a man had before birth; his prototype or protoplasm.

諶 **訦** ˏshăn From *words* and *very* or *more*.

Sincere, faithful; true, trustworthy; to speak honestly.

丨實 fidelity.

天難丨命靡常 I cannot be certain that heaven will always decree the throne to me.

丨離國 a small state in the Han dynasty.

忱 **忎** ˏshăn ˏch'ăn Both these are like the last, but the second form is rare.

Sincerity, especially its expression in the face; a good man; honest; devoted to.

丹丨 guileless.

忠悃之丨 an open and candid bearing.

天難丨斯 heaven will not uphold him at any any event.

愖 ˏshăn Similar to the last two.

To believe; sincere.

斟丨 to retard; dilatory; slow to believe.

Read ˏhin. Crafty.

丨丨 guileful, untrustworthy.

煁 ˏshăn A brazier or portable furnace, such as are used to warm rooms; some have three corners.

烘于丨 to warm one's self at the furnace.

葚 **椹** ˏshăn zhăn` The second form is also read ˏchăn, but is most usually regarded as a synonym.

The berries of the mulberry, called 桑丨, which Chinese authors fable will improve the harsh voice of owls and kestrels.

黮 ‘shăn’ Used for and with the preceding, because of the deep black of ripe mulberries.

Read ‘t‘an. Black clouds bringing rain.

雲黮丨而將雨 the lowering clouds will soon bring rain.

丨闇 void of intelligence, vacant-minded.

審 ‘shăn From 宀 a *covering* and 番 a *time*, which last is defined as if from 釆 to *distinguish*, *i. e.* to get things together, and carefully separate them.

To investigate, to inform one's self, as a judge; to discern between, to discriminate; to restrain; to weigh evidence; the mind settled on a point; a bundle of ten plumes.

丨判 to judge to; examine and decide.

丨問 a judicial inquiry.

調丨 or 提丨 to carry up a case.

對丨 to confront witnesses.

丨實 a final judgment.

丨卦 to inquire by sortilege.

開堂丨 to open court for a trial.

承丨官 an officer specially sent to try a cause.

丨的確 it has been fully and honestly examined.

丨音 to discriminate musical tones.

嚴丨 a severe investigation.

丨察其源 trace it up to its origin, find out the cause.

丨時度世 observe the times and judge the occasion.

候丨 to stand a trial, to await examination.

嬸 ‘shăn A father's younger brother's wife is 叔丨; a brother's wife is 丨母, including any sister-in-law.

亞丨 or 丨婆 or 丨丨 a respectable, middle aged woman; a nurse, a woman of all work.

瀋 ‘shăn Gravy; sap; to pour water into a vessel.

漉丨 to leak out, to dribble away.

哂 ‘shăn 吲 ‘shăn From *mouth* and *west* or to *lead on*.

To smile with a slight contempt; a sneering smile; to look pleased.

丨笑 to smile.

祈爲丨納 I beg that you will receive [this present] favorably.

見丨 to smile on seeing — the gift.

諗 ‘shăn From *words* and to *read*.

To consult carefully with; to make known one's views to a superior; to reprove, to expostulate; to hide away, as fish in a covert.

將毋來丨 shall I not think of my mother?

丨念 to reflect on.

丨諫百端 admonish him by every argument.

丨告 to conjure, to urge upon.

矧 ‘shăn 訠 ‘shăn From *dart* and to *lead*, because it shows the purport of a sentence, as a dart the way.

A particle that prolongs the thought to another point; still more, how much more; still less; to laugh in a boisterous way.

丨如是乎 how much more then so!

丨伊人矣不求友生 and shall man not seek much more to have friends?

丨曰 more still to say.

伈 ‘shăn Timorous; cowardly.

丨丨俔俔爲民吏羞 he was so fearfully craven-hearted that the officers of the people were ashamed.

發丨 scared, afraid.

㑗 shăn’ Also read *ts‘in’*

Bent, stooping.

偏丨 to bend the head forward; to stoop.

甚 shăn’ From 甘 *sweet* and 匹 to *pair*, denoting an increase of joy.

Social delights; an adverb denoting the superlative, very, extremely, — and usually placed before its subject.

丨好 excessively good.

丨大 too big, huge.

太丨 excessive in any way.

一之已丨 once is quite too much.

丨不相宜 altogether unsuitable.

凌辱已丨 the disgrace is already at its utmost pitch.

丨矣 too many; too far.

不爲已丨 do not go to excess.

丨是 very right, just the thing.

丨事 or 丨麼事 what thing? what affair?

干你丨事 what is that to you?

慎 shăn’ From *heart* and *true*.

To act carefully and seriously; cautious, attentive; still, quiet, sincere; considerate.

謹丨 heedful.

不丨 heedless.

丨言 careful of what he says, guarded in speech.

丨重 circumspect.

不可不丨也 the utmost care is necessary.

丨勿怠荒 take heed and be not idle.

君子丨獨 the princely man is careful what he does when he is alone.

腎 shăn’ From 肉 *flesh* and 賢 *worth*, contracted, for which it is occasionally mistaken.

The kidneys, which the Chinese connect with water, and make to preside over wisdom and force; they call one of the kidneys 內丨 and the other 命門, because it is thought to secrete the semen, and pass it to the 外丨 or testes; a gizzard; to lead; to harden.

丨囊 the scrotum.

鴨丨 a duck's gizzard.

丨水虧 incontinence of urine.

心腹丨腸 the heart and belly, reins and bowels, — *i. e.* the whole mind.

蜃 ʻch'ăn zhăn' From *insect* and *time* as the phonetic.

A huge clam, said to be transformed from a fowl, and perhaps referring to the great *Chama*; a marine monster which can change its shape, or appears in the rain.

丨氣 or 丨市 the mirage; some discriptions assimilate it rather to a water-spout.

丨車 a road along which a coffin goes.

丨炭 ashes or coals of the clam put in coffins.

海市丨樓 exaggerated reports, wild stories; refers to a legend about sea-fairies.

丨疆 the mirage land; a native name for Lewchew.

滲 shăn' To leak; to run to waste, to flow along noisily; to soak through.

丨漏 to leak.

淋丨 newly fledged.

丨井 a hole for water to run into the sewer.

丨灕 running off or flowing.

丨水出來 the water is leaking out.

飲則丨入膀胱 whatever is drank filters into the bladder.

In *Cantonese.* To sprinkle over, as with salt or ashes, not with water; bad, inelegant, worthless.

ʻ丨的鹽來 sprinkle or spread some salt on it.

罧 shan' From *net* and *forest.*

A trap for fishes, made at Canton by digging a hole in a tidal creek, covering it with sticks, and collecting the fish at low water.

乾個丨 clean out the trap.

槮 shan' Used for the last.

Leafless trees, as bare and tall ones in winter; stakes for catching fish.

攕丨可哀 how sad to see the bare trees.

圍丨 a fishing-weir.

魚寒入丨 the fishes seek the cool pit-weir.

Read ˏshăn, and used for 摻. To take, to grasp, to hold on.

SHANG.

The sounds SHANG *and* HIANG *are easily confounded. Old sounds,* shung *and* zhung. *In Canton,* shéung; — *in Swatow,* siang *and* siⁿé; — *in Amoy,* siong; — *in Fuhchau,* siŏng; — *in Shanghai,* song, dzong, zang, dzang, *and* long; — *in Chifu,* ch'ang.

商 賣 ˏshang Composed of 冏 to *stutter* and 章 *sentences* contracted, denoting that by words one's inner thought, are known; not to be confounded with *tih,* 啇 enemy.

To consult, to devise, to deliberate, to arrange; to adjust by consultation; to trade; a merchant, a traveling dealer; the second of the ancient five musical notes; an hour or so before sunrise and sunset.

洋行丨 the old hong-merchants of Canton.

客丨 or 丨買 a traveling merchant.

丨旅 a merchant from another province.

丨朝 the Shang dynasty, founded by 成湯 T'ang the Successful, B. C. 1766, and destroyed by Wu Wang, B. C. 1122.

丨國 an ancient state now in Kwéi-teh fu in the east of Honan.

當丨 a pawnbroker.

鹽丨 a salt-merchant.

丨功 in *mathematics,* solid mensuration.

丨量 or 丨酌 to consult on.

宮丨迭奏 the music sounded again and again.

各國通丨 general trade with other countries.

謫 ˏshang Interchanged with the last.

To consult, to deliberate.

丨德而定位 to estimate his virtue and fix his standing.

丨議行規 to consult and settle the rules of business, as a Chamber of Commerce.

萬丨雲集 merchants collect there from all quarters.

蔏 ˏshang A kind of medical plant, whose root, called 常山 is a remedy for the ague.

丨蔞 a labiate plant, like the *Vitex* or chaste tree.

傷 ˏshang From 人 *man* and 煬 *to wound* to give the sound.

To injure, to hurt; to wound to grieve, to distress; to mourn; to cause sorrow; to waste, to lavish, as the strength; sad at heart, chagrined, mortified; harm, objection.

丨害 to injure; to take revenge.

丨風 to catch cold.

內丨病 an internal disease, such as spitting blood.

我心丨悲 my heart was sad and wounded.

無丨 no harm is done; it makes no difference, it will be no obstacle.

丨弓之鳥 crippled like a bird wounded by the dart.

維以不永丨 to the end that I may not long sorrow.

何丨 what objection is there?

嘯歌丨懷 I hum and sing with a wounded heart.

重丨 a mortal wound.
丨財 to waste money.
丨心 grieved at heart.
受三丨 wounded three times.
丨口 lips of a wound.
丨和氣 to violate confidence.
悲丨 filial grief at a parent's death.
有丨風化 it will injure public morals.
損丨 to damage; to wound
無丨舊好 do not destroy old friendships.
謂暴無丨 he says tyranny is no injury, of no moment.
丨及父母 to cause grief to parents.
丨心事 a bad business. a grief to one.

殤 ˏshang ˏch'ang An untimely death, under nineteen years of age; to die before puberty; to die.
夭丨 or 短丨 died young.
嫁丨 to wed the effigy of a betrothed husband.
國丨 manes of soldiers who have died for their country.
無服之丨 unmourned youths, those who die before seven years.
丨丁口 it will involve the death of one's children, as an unlucky spot.
痘丨 the child died of small-pox.

觴 ˏshang ˏch'ang From *horn* and to *wound*.
A cup, a goblet; a bumper; a feast, a banquet; to give to drink.
酒丨 a wine-cup.
潔丨 or 治丨 to prepare a feast.
舉丨 to take wine with a guest.
傳丨 to exchange glasses.
曲水流丨 crooked streams flowing into goblets; — *met.* fine scenery.
稱丨 to drink to one's health.
濫丨 to exceed bounds, to overrun.
杯丨交錯 to change cups and drink fast.
春丨 a newyear's feast.

常 ˏch'ang From 巾 *napkin* and 尙 *manifest*, referring to the meaning of the next, of which this was a synonym.
Constant, ordinary, always, ever, frequent, usual; habitual, long continued, in usage; unchanging; to keep, to maintain, as a law; to possess always; a rule; a stint; constancy; a regular principle or way; a long spear put in war chariots.
丨時 ever, always.
平丨 usual, ordinary.
非丨 unusual; few such; extra.
無丨 it happens rarely, not often seen.
丨有 I keep it always, as an article in a shop.
照丨 customarily, according to the routine.
純嘏爾丨矣 may pure happiness be your constant lot.
丨日 the whole day.
丨人 an ordinary man.
家丨飯 a common meal.
五丨 the five cardinal virtues, *viz.* 仁 humanity, 義 rectitude, 禮 courtesy, 智 knowledge, and 信 faith.
丨丨掛念 constantly bear it in mind.
往丨 formerly.
無丨心 variable; no perseverance.
如丨 as customary.
太丨寺 the Sacrificial Court.
可暫不可丨 it can be done for this time, but not allowed as a regular thing.
無丨鬼 the god who cuts the thread of life, the Chinese Atropos.

裳 ˏch'ang ˏshang From *garment* and to *manifest*.
The lower garments which conceal the person; the skirt, the petticoats; clothes; curtains of a carriage.
衣丨 apparel, dress, clothes.
雲丨 fleecy clouds.
衣丨竹 rods to hang clothes on.

丨丨者華芸其黃矣 how splendid are the flowers in their deep yellow.

嫦 ˏch'ang Name of a goddess.
月裏丨娥 the goddess in the moon; she is also 天妃 heaven's consort.

徜 ˏchang Irresolute.
丨徉 going to and fro; volatile, playful, unsteady.

鱨 ˏchang From *fish* and to *taste*, alluding to its delicacy.
A large fish, described as having a yellow body with horns, and able to fly; it is also called 黃丨魚 and seems to be a kind of flying gurnard, having orbital spines and large maxillary bones; but the synonyms rather denote a species of goby or *Tænia*, a fish which can jump.

賞 ˊshang From *wealth* and to *manifest*.
To give to an inferior; to bestow, to confer; to grant, as heaven does; rewards; to make largesses; to celebrate, as a day; to congratulate, to rejoice, to take pleasure in; to exhort.
丨月 to celebrate the harvest-moon; to enjoy the moonlight.
丨心 to delight one's self in.
丨花 to enjoy the flowers.
丨給 to bestow a reward.
丨銀牌 to distribute silver medals.
嘆丨 to express admiration.
丨臉 to treat well.
丨格 a scale of rewards.
丨帖 a placard offering a reward.
丨謝花紅 to pay the reward offered.
丨以酒肉 presented him with wine and meats.
獎丨 to commend and reward, as a scholar.
丨封 to give a present to children or servants.
恩丨 imperial bounty.

扃 ʻshang The ring placed upon doors to use as a knocker.

饟 ʻshang The meal at noontide, and that when the sun is setting. 備丨饍以待子歸 she prepared a repast, and waited for her husband's return.

晌 ʻshang From *sun* and *towards*.
Noontide, meridian; used for the Manchu word *del'he*, a piece of arable land measuring six *meu*, or about 1½ acre, set apart for the support of the Gendarmery of Peking, and for which each man pays a land tax.

丨午 or 丨半天 midday.

下半丨 afternoon.

半丨無言 he was quite silent for half the day.

晚半丨 towards sundown.

早半丨 forenoon; but 小丨午 is rather just before midday, 11½ o'clock.

上 ʻshang Formed of two parts signifying that an affair or thing is above the level.
To go up; to go to court; to write in; to esteem, to exalt; to go in, as into a net; to place on; to mount; to send or hand up; upwards; the ascending or second tone; the upper series of tones.

丨京 to go to Peking.

丨船 to go aboard, and 丨岸 to go ashore.

丨本 to send a report to court.

丨學 to enter school.

紹庭丨下ʼ continuing [his example] as I go up and down in the court, — and reign.

丨人當 to be swindled or taken in.

你不丨心 you didn't bear it in mind.

丨表鏈 to wind a watch.

丨前去 to go on; go ahead.

丨貴 to honor superiors.

不丨一月 not a full month.

丨那兒去 where are you going?

丨平聲 the upper even tone.

丨不來 he cannot come up.

丨落平安 be careful in going up and down stairs.

丨平 or 丨兌 to weigh, as money.

Read *shang*ʼ Top; above, on, upon; facing; high; ancient, early times; before, previously; that which is above or high; superior, excellent; superiors; honorable, exalted; Heaven; supreme; imperial; ascending, rising; in *rhetoric*, what goes before, antecedent; as a *preposition*, by, on, near.

繳丨 to sum up, to conclude from what goes before.

主丨 or 皇丨 the Emperor.

丨下 above and below; up and down; about, more or less; on the one hand and on the other; heaven and earth; emperor and people;—according to the scope.

天丨 in heaven.

丨天 the sky overhead.

丨日 the other day; the first day.

丨怒 the Emperor was angry.

丨諭 an imperial decree.

丨好 very good, superior.

丨丨 or 頂丨 the best quality.

街丨 in the street.

丨愼旃哉 may he still be careful.

河丨乎逍遙 they saunter about by the River.

丨古 in remote antiquity.

身丨 it is on me; in my hand.

早丨 early in the day.

尊無二丨 honorable beyond comparison.

丨頭 up there; the head or chief.

以丨 what is before.

丨房 the best room, a parlor.

丨次 the previous occasion.

丨午 forenoon.

丨人 upper classes; it is used in addressing a priest, or speaking of one's employer or parents.

書丨說 it is said in the book.

丨位 a chief seat; a magnate.

丨 and 中 and 下 are three terms used for qualities or degrees.

尙 shangʼ Composed of 向 *towards* with 入 to *go in* above it; occurs used for the last.
To add to; desirous of; to honor, to esteem, to adorn; to reckon good; to like, to approve; to have the care of, to control, in which sense it occurs in official titles; to ascend; to marry a princess; noble, high; as a *conjunction*, still, but, furthermore, and notwithstanding, yet, perhaps; a form of the *optative*, would that, may it be that, pray.

丨白 to esteem a white color.

丨且 still, however.

丨有 there are still some.

丨公主 to wed a princess.

不自丨 do not praise yourself.

六部丨書 the presidents or controlers of the Six Boards.

好ʼ丨 to prefer.

高丨其志 ambitious and pure in spirit.

行有死人丨或墐之 a dead man lies in the road, and somebody will perhaps bury him.

無以丨之 nothing can be superior to it.

雖老丨能馳馬 though I am old I can still ride to battle.

俗丨繁華 the world likes dash and folly.

丨德 to respect the virtuous.

丨享 at the end of a prayer, Mayest thou enjoy or receive this! Let this be accepted!

SHĂNG.

Old sound, shing. *In Canton*, shăng *and* shang ; — *in Swatow*, seng *and* sʳó ; — *in Amoy*, seng ; — *in Fuhchau*, sang, seng, ch'ang, *and* sing ; — *in Shanghai*, sang ; — *in Chifu*, săng.

生 *shăng* The lower half represents the 土 *earth* from which 屮 *sprouts* arise above it to denote growth ; it forms the 100th radical.

To bear, to produce ; to arise, as an event ; to grow ; to beget ; to bring about the birth of, causing to grow, to excite ; to live ; to come forth ; life, vitality ; the living ; birth ; means of living ; unripe, raw ; unsubdued ; unpolished, inelegant, as a bad style or uncouth phraseology ; unacquainted ; the natural conscience.

平 ㅣ the whole life.

ㅣ 平 之 力 the entire strength.

學 ㅣ or 門 ㅣ or 晚 ㅣ a young man, a pupil.

先 ㅣ a teacher ; a doctor ; a blind fortune-teller ; an appellative like Mr. or Sir, as 李 先 ㅣ Mr. Li.

監 ㅣ and ㅣ 員 grades of the *siuts'ai* graduates, who designate themselves as 生 juniors in official papers.

優 貢 ㅣ the first *siuts'ai* graduate on the list of the district.

副 貢 ㅣ a degree intermediate between a *siuts'ai* and *küjin*.

書 ㅣ literary men.

ㅣ 意 or ㅣ 理 occupation, business.

ㅣ 臉 人 or ㅣ 面 a stranger.

ㅣ 疎 not familiar with ; not to see one for a long time.

ㅣ 民 保 厥 居 the people will preserve their possessions.

旣 ㅣ 旣 育 比 予 于 毒 now, your means being abundant, you liken me to poison.

ㅣ 息 to get interest ; to make a profit, as by increase of herds

ㅣ 菓 unripe fruit.

魚 ㅣ a preparation of raw fish.

放 ㅣ to set free living things, considered to be a meritorious act.

ㅣ ㅣ 不 已 age after age, unceasing succession.

ㅣ ㅣ 自 庸 foster the life of the people as your best work.

亂 之 初 ㅣ disorder then arises.

利 用 厚 ㅣ to secure abundant means of support.

ㅣ 得 天 然 made so by heaven, a natural production.

ㅣ 來 的 or ㅣ 出 的 spontaneous ; natural ; it grew so.

ㅣ 殺 之 權 the power of life and death.

ㅣ 日 a birthday.

今 ㅣ and 來 世 this life and the next.

畜 ㅣ animals, more especially the six domesticated kinds.

ㅣ 揭 to borrow money on interest.

四 ㅣ four modes of production, *viz.* viviparous, 胎 ㅣ ; oviparous, 卵 ㅣ ; by moistness 濕 ㅣ ; and transformed 化 ㅣ ; the last is applied to the miraculous birth of incarnated Budhas (*anupa padaka*).

托 ㅣ doctrine of rewards and punishments by a second life.

偷 ㅣ to save one's life, as by treachery to a prince.

輕 ㅣ to set light by one's life ; reckless of danger.

ㅣ 氣 to get angry.

ㅣ 瘡 an ulcer has come.

ㅣ 敗 子 he bore a profligate son.

ㅣ 而 知 之 knew it when he was born ; intuitive knowledge.

ㅣ 靈 living things, the people.

ㅣ 辰 八 字 the eight horoscope characters.

好 ㅣ 不 然 it certainly is not so.

無 以 爲 ㅣ nothing to live by, ready to perish.

ㅣ 沒 遷 徙 births, deaths, and removals.

ㅣ 旦 凈 末 丑 five classes of actors, *viz.*, scholars, girls, old men and women, and fools ; of each class there are various ranks, of which 武 ㅣ are military characters ; 正 ㅣ princes ; 總 ㅣ old statesmen ; 小 ㅣ youths ; &c.

甥 *shăng* From *to bear* and *a mate*.

Relatives of other surnames ; the sons of a sister, and the nephews and cousins by aunts and sisters, are 外 ㅣ, who are all of a different surname.

外 ㅣ 婿 a sister's daughter's husband.

姨 ㅣ children of a wife's sister.

舅 ㅣ maternal uncles and cousins.

汾 王 之 ㅣ a niece of king Făn.

牲 *shăng* From *ox* and *living*.

Sacrificial animals, of which there are six ; victims.

犧 ㅣ a victim.

ㅣ 口 usually denotes draught animals, or cattle ; but also includes fowls and sheep.

三 ㅣ poultry, pork, and fish (or mutton).

六 ㅣ the six victims, — horse, ox, lamb, cock, dog, and hog.

爾 ㅣ 則 具 your victims are all provided for.

笙 *shăng* An instrument of the organ kind, a Pandean pipe, composed of 13 dissimilar reeds inserted in a gourd bulb, with a bent blow-tube ; the music is made by inhaling the air through the reeds ; small ; slender.

ㅣ 歌 to play and sing ; *met.* peace and plenty.

鼓 瑟 吹 ㅣ thrum the lutes and blow the organ.

ㅣ 簧 寫 心 music relieves the heart.

鼪 ˏshăng An animal of the weasel family, and given by some as the weasel itself; it is grayish black, and called 鼠狼 from its destructiveness to mice; pencils are made of its tail-hairs; it is probably the polecat, but others describe it like a *Pteromys* or flying squirrel.

賸 shăngʾ Wealth; rich, opulent.

眚 ʿshăng Used for the next.

To lessen, to circumscribe; meager, emaciated; a disease of the eye, like a staphyloma or film, that obscures the vision; a crime, a fault, an inadvertent offense.

丨病 disease caused by demons, a sort of black vomit or plague.

丨災肆赦 inadvertencies and crimes from calamities might be forgiven.

丨語 a mistake, a fault.

丨沴 calamity, pestilence.

霪丨禾苗 the excessive rains have injured the grain.

省 ʿshăng From *eye* and *few*, but really formed of 眉 *eyebrows* and 屮 *sprout* both contracted, intimating a close inspection of a subject.

A spot guarded for officers; a province of the empire; to diminish, to abridge; in topographical works, to erase, to incorporate with or abolish, as a district; to use sparingly; to lay by; to avoid, to spare; frugal; saved, avoided.

各丨 every part of the country.

丨事 to avoid the trouble of, to prevent doing over again.

丨得我去 it saved my going there.

丨費 to saved the outlay.

丨費心 save one's self trouble.

丨刑罰 reduce the punishment.

丨約 to abridge.

丨文 terse, an abridged expression.

丨減 reduce it, lighten it; be moderate.

分發丨分ʾ sent him to a provincial post.

丨城 or 丨會 a provincial capital.

十八丨 the eighteen provinces or China Proper.

丨銅錢 to lay by money.

撐一頂傘丨之雨淋濕 take an umbrella to save yourself a wetting.

In *Cantonese;* also written 㗂. To scour, to rub bright.

丨光 rubbed bright.

丨胃 to whet the appetite.

丨口 to clean the mouth.

Read *singʾ*. To examine, to inquire carefully into, to inspect; to discern; to regard as good; a fault; watchful; to awaken.

丨心 to examine one's heart.

丨自己過 self-examination.

丨察 to investigate.

吾日三丨吾身 I daily examine myself on three points.

丨安 to keep the country quiet.

丨丨 uneasy.

丨于其君免于大難 to act faithfully toward the ruler, and thus avoid great trouble.

丨覺 to be aware of.

丨悟 to arouse to a sense of one's danger.

丨親 a wife visiting her parents.

NAMES, etc., OF THE EIGHTEEN PROVINCES.

PROVINCES.		AREA SQUARE MILES.	POP. BY CENSUS OF 1812.	DEPARTMENTS.	DISTRICTS.	CAPITAL.	HIGHEST OFFICERS.
Chihli,	直隸	58,949	27,990,871	17	144	保定府	A Governor-general.
Shantung,	山東	65,104	28,958,764	12	105	濟南府	A Governor.
Shansi,	山西	55,268	14,004,210	19	94	太原府	A Governor.
Honan,	河南	65,104	23,037,171	13	103	開封府	A Governor.
Kiangsu,	江蘇	44,500	37,843,501	12	67	江寧府	A Governor-general 兩江 at Nanking, and Governors at the three capitals.
Nganhwui,	安徽	48,461	34,168,059	13	54	安慶府	
Kiangsi,	江西	72,176	23,046,999	14	78	南昌府	
Chehkiang,	浙江	39,150	26,256,784	11	78	杭州府	A Governor-general 閩浙 and two Governors.
Fuhkien,	福建	53,480	14,777,410	12	65	福州府	
Hupeh,	湖北	70,450	27,370,098	11	67	武昌府	A Governor-general 兩湖 and two Governors.
Hunan,	湖南	74,320	18,652,507	16	67	長沙府	
Kwangtung,	廣東	79,456	19,174,030	15	89	廣州府	A Governor-general 兩廣 and two Governors.
Kwangsi,	廣西	78,250	7,313,895	12	66	桂林府	
Yunnan,	雲南	107,969	5,561,320	21	71	雲南府	A Governor-general 雲貴 and two Governors.
Kwèicheu,	貴州	64,554	5,288,219	16	52	貴陽府	
Sz'chʻuen,	四川	166,800	21,435,678	26	125	城都府	A Governor-general.
Shensi,	陝西	67,400	10,207,256	12	83	西安府	A Governor-general 陝甘 and two Governors.
Kansuh,	甘肅	86,608	15,193,125	15	65	蘭州府	
		1,297,999	360,279,897	267	573		

DIVISIONS, &c., OF MANCHURIA.

PROVINCES.	CAPITALS.	DISTRICTS.	GOVERNMENT.
SHINGKING, 盛京	Mukten, 奉天府 Kincheu fu 錦州府	11 dists. and 13 posts. 4 districts.	Ruled by a *tsiang-kiun*, who controls all Manchuria, aided by six Boards, filled mostly by Manchus.
KIRIN, 吉林	Kirin, 吉林廳 Pedné, 伯都訥廳 Changchun 長春廳	8 garrisons, answering to districts.	Under a *tsiang-kiun* at Kirin, aided by five *fu-tutung* at Kirin, Ninguta, Pedné, Sansing, and Altchuku.
HEH-LUNG KIANG, 黑龍江	Tsitsihar 齊齊哈爾	6 commanderies.	One *tsiang-kun* at Tsitsihar, aided by three generals at Merguen, Tsitsihar, and Heh-lung Kiang.

DIVISIONS, &c., OF MONGOLIA.

PROVINCES.	KHANATES	GOVERNMENT.
INNER MONGOLIA, 內蒙古		6 corps 盟, divided into 24 tribes and 49 standards, each *aimak* or tribe being under its own chieftain.
OUTER MONGOLIA, 外蒙古 has four khanates,	Tuchétu, 土謝圖汗 Sain-noin, 三音諾顏汗 Tsetsen, 車臣汗 Dzassaktu, 札薩古圖汗	Overseen by a Governor-general at Urga or Kurun 庫倫 in the Tuchétu khanate, under whose superintendance each prince rules his own tribe.
TSING-HAI 青海	Si-ning fu, 西寧府	Divided into 29 standards, under a resident at Sining fu.
ULIASUTAI, 烏理雅蘇台	Cobdo, 科布多城	Divided into 11 tribes and 31 standards.
	Urianghai, 烏艮海	Tribes are under 21 *tso-ling*, and an amban at Uliasutai in Sain-noin khanate.

DIVISIONS, &c., OF ILI OR CHINESE TURKESTAN.

PROVINCES.	CITIES AND DISTRICTS.	GOVERNMENT.
SONGARIA, the Northern Circuit 天山北路 or Ili 伊犂.	Nine garrisons, 城 or districts.	Under a military governor, two councillors, and 34 residents in cities.
	Kur-kara-usu, 庫雨喀喇烏蘇 Tarbagatai, 塔爾巴哈台	Subordinate to the *tsiang-kiun* at Kuldja or Ili, under local residents.
EASTERN TURKESTAN, the Southern Circuit 天山南路, occupying the valley of the Tarim River, having ten garrisoned cities 十回城 each the post of local rulers under Chinese sway.	Harashar, 喀喇沙拉 Kuchay, 庫者	Under a resident and native begs.
	Ushi, 烏什 Sairim, 賽哩木 Bai, 拜 Oksu, 阿克蘇	The officer at Ushi rules over the three next; it is also called Yung-ning-ch'ing.
	Khoten 和闐	
	Yarkand, 葉爾羌 Cashgar, 喀什噶爾 Yengishar, 英吉沙爾	The *tsiang-kiun* resides at Yarkand, with general supervision over the ten garrisoned cities.

TIBET 西藏 is regarded by the Chinese as one of their dependencies, and a resident constantly lives at Hlassa; the eastern part, called Anterior Tibet 前藏, or Yuiba 衛, is divided into eight cantons; the western part called Ulterior Tibet 後藏 or Kambu 康, is divided into six cantons, one of which, Ari 阿里 occupies most of its western half. A portion of the eastern part of Turkestan 新疆 is politically included within the province of Kansuh, which extends across the Desert to Urumchi and Barkoul; but since the year 1865, the Chinese sway over the whole region has been reduced to appointing nominal officers over its various districts; and the Southern Circuit has been completely lost to them since the Mohammedan insurrection in Kansuh and Shensi; these divisions are therefore likely to be superseded by others under a different rule.

SHAO.

Old sounds, sho, zho, shok, *and* zhok. *In Canton*, shiu *and* shao; — *in Swatow*, sié, siò, *and* sao; — *in Amoy*, siao, sao, *and* ch'iao; — *in Fuhchau*, siu, séu, *and* sau; — *in Shanghai*, so *and* dzo; — *in Chifu*, shao.

燒 *˛shao* From *fire* and *eminent*.
To burn, to ignite, to light; to burn pottery; to roast at the fire; roasted, fired; hot, feverish; to burn over; to offer incense; inflammable.

野 丨 a fire on the moors.

丨 酒 ardent spirits, such as will burn, sometimes called 三 丨 or thrice fired, whence comes the word *samshoo* through the Cantonese dialect.

高 梁 丨 strong whiskey made from sorghum.

丨 着 on fire; to set on fire.

丨 化 burnt up, consumed.

丨 鵝 a roasted goose.

丨 山 to burn the grass on hills, to manure them with the ashes.

內 外 發 丨 he has fever in and on him.

內 丨 大 作 the fever is very high.

丨 紙 to worship at the tombs, when paper is burned.

丨 烟 火 (or 花) to let off fireworks.

插 丨 仔 a concubine's child. (*Cantonese.*)

丨 路 頭 to worship Plutus; — at Shanghai also means to feast with one.

丨 猪 a hog roasted whole.

打 丨 紙 a mode of torture among prisoners to extort money.

丨 窰 a kiln.

丨 火 light the fire; put on fuel.

開 一 座 丨 鍋 to put up an oven to roast at.

丨 拜 香 to supplicate the gods for a parent's recovery.

颾 *˛shao* A drying wind; sound of the wind.

用 風 丨 乾 let the dry wind blow on it.

丨 落 葉 it blows the leaves down.

莦 *˛shao* Coarse jungle grass in which wild animals burrow, and form a den; the roots of grass.

芃 丨 槎 櫛 the holes of the marmots run through the jungle.

娋 *˛shao* The eldest of a number of sisters.

Read *sioh*, To despise, to disesteem; to regard slightingly.

捎 *˛shao* To select; to reject the bad; to catch; to pluck or brush away; to move, to take along, to carry.

丨 掠 to seize.

撟 丨 or 丨 着 手 to fold the arms.

丨 在 背 後 to put the arms behind the back.

門 丨 a door-bolt; a latch or catch. (*Pekingese.*)

丨 帶 貨 物 to carry goods, as in a ship.

丨 信 to send a letter.

旓 *˛shao* Scallops or small tags on the edge of a banner called 燕 尾 丨 swallow-tail scallops, the number of which once indicated official rank.

旌 旂 丨 the tags on a flag's border.

丨 帶 飄 搖 the wind flutters the streamers finely.

蕱 *˛shao* The small rootlets of the Nelumbium, different from the 藕 or large rhizomes which are edible.

弰 *˛shao* The ends of a bow; a bow discharging the arrow; the arrow leaving the bow.

䙚 *˛shao* The lapel of a coat; the waist-band of a pair of trowsers.

梢 *˛shao* From *wood* and *resembling*; used with the next.
The end of a branch, a twig; a tapering leafless branch; a staff used by mummers; small sticks for fuel; a rudder; a sailor; to knock off, as a thing that sticks; a sort of harrow.

丨 公 a steersman.

篙 丨 those who pole boats.

商 丨 a ship's crew.

丨 子 boatmen.

丨 末 small end of a thing.

丨 丨 small.

鞭 丨 a riding switch.

扳 丨 下 屬 to screen one's subordinates.

丨 長 大 漢 tall and portly. (*Fuhchau.*)

艄 *˛shao* Like the preceding.
Stern of a vessel; a swift and small boat used in coastguard duty.

丨 工 a captain or master.

綃 *˛shao* A painter for fastening a boat.

髾 *˛shao* End of the hair; tuft on end of a tail; a comet's tail; long hair appended to banners.

頭 髮 丨 long hanging hair.

筲 *˛shao* *ts'iao'* A basket or hamper, 丨 箕 larger than a peck, and used to hold cooked rice.

水 丨 a wicker or osier bucket.

斗 丨 之 人 an ordinary person, "a peck-measure man," *i. e.* one who knows chiefly about eating.

揱 **籍** *˛shao* Similar to the preceding.
A small basket used in cooking, which holds the rice to steam it; used for ˛梢 a rudder or tiller.

韶 From *sound* and *to call*.
꜀shao An ancient musical instrument; the music of Shun; captivating harmony; to continue, as Shun did the virtues of Yao; voices in harmony; excellent.

聞丨不知肉味 [Confucius] heard Shun's music, and forgot the taste of meat.

丨華 splendid but fading.

虛度丨光 I have vainly passed the prime of my life.

丨州府 a department in the north of Kwangtung.

少 From 小 *small*, and 丿 a contraction of 夭 *impish*.
꜂shao Little, not much; few; briefly, a little while; seldom; in a slight degree; limited; to owe; wanting, deprived of; to disparage, to detract.

丨不免 unavoidable, very necessary.

丨不得 or 不可丨 it is indispensable, can't do without it.

短丨 inadequate, limited supply.

不知多丨 I don't know how much.

不丨 not a few, many, enough.

丨可 it is but seldom.

丨欠 to be indebted to.

丨廣 in *mathematics*, evolution.

丨候 I have failed in calling on you; — a polite phrase.

丨刻 or 丨焉 in a little while.

以多報丨 to report few when there are many.

丨之 to underrate.

丨不了也有件把事兒 there will doubtless be some l tle affairs.

丨些 a little less, fewer.

丨錢 to owe; to deduct from a sum.

太丨 altogether too few.

鄰國之民不加丨 the population of the adjoining states does not decrease.

丨算 to cheapen, to reckon less.

Read *shao*꜄ Young, juvenile; tender; a youth; to assist, to second; a secondary or junior.

丨年 young in years.

老丨 old and young.

丨子 the youngest son.

丨爺 a young gentleman; your son.

立丨妾 to get a young concubine.

丨艾 a young girl or wife, in the flower of her age.

人丨則慕父母 a young boy cleaves to his parents.

丨我 he treats me as a child.

稍 From *grain* and *small*.
꜀shao Grain gradually expanding; gradually, slowly; slightly, partially, for the most part; even, small.

丨食 a ration of grain doled out by government to pensioners.

丨小 rather small.

丨能 or 丨可 tolerable, it will perhaps do; has some ability.

丨有不合 it is not exactly the thing, it does not quite match.

丨乾 somewhat dried.

丨丨做得 we'll make it do, let it pass.

丨事 an unimportant matter.

丨微不利 rather unlucky.

紹 侶 From *silk* or *man* and *to call*; the second form is rarely met with.
shao꜄ To connect, to join, to tie together; to hand down, as a trade; in co-relation with; to act in relation with another; to imitate a predecessor; massed or supporting, as an army.

丨介 one who serves as a medium or aid between two principals.

弗念厥丨罔敷求先王 you never think of your connection with the past, or carefully study the former kings.

丨復 to reëstablish or maintain, as an inheritance.

丨位 to succeed to a dignity.

繼丨 to perpetuate, as the virtues of a predecessor.

丨酒 spirits from Shao-hing fu 丨興府 in Chehkiang, considered to be of the best sort.

會丨乃辟 continuing [the links] to your chief.

家聲克丨 he will keep up the credit of the family.

丨天明 to be put in relation with the intelligence of Heaven.

袑 The crutch of a pair of
shao꜄ trowsers; a lapel of a coat.

袴丨 the seat of trowsers.

劭 From *strength* and *to call*; also read ꜀k'iao.
shao꜄ Effort, exertion; to stimulate; to take courage, to exert one's self; beauty, excellence.

丨農 to encourage husbandmen.

才丨 fine talents.

雋聲清丨 a distinguished and unsullied name.

卲 From *seal* and *to call*; it is often confounded with the last, and looks like the next.
shao꜄ High, as in virtue.

年高德丨 aged and greatly honored for virtue.

邵 From *city* and *to call*; different from the last.
shao꜄ A city in the state of Tsin 晉 now Shansi.

丨陵 a noted city in history, now Pao-king fu in central Hunan.

丨武府 a prefecture in the north of Fuhkien.

丨子神數 Shao knew the auguries of the gods.

潲 From *water* and *gradually*.
shao꜄ Water driven by the wind and dashing against things; wet by the rain; to sprinkle.

風丨雨 the wind dashes the rain against it.

雨丨濕了 soaked by the driving rain.

哨 shao' From *mouth* and *similar*; it is also read *ts'iao'* in the senses of loquacious; a wry mouth.

A small or crooked mouth, like that of a jug; loquacious, gabbling; cry of guards or lictors; a guard-station, which is connected with a garrison or encampment where a military officer is placed to preserve the peace; there are four around Peking; to patrol, to walk about; to act the scout; to sing, as a bird; the mouth-piece of a horn.

巡丨 or 丨遊 to go about as a patrol; to cruise on guard.

丨下 stationed on guard.

充當營丨各官 all officers in charge of garrisons and stations.

丨長 a local officer in the western provinces, who is a native of the place.

丨人 a sentry.

左丨 and 右丨 a guard of honor.

打丨子 to whistle.

帶丨子 to put a whistle on a dove's tail, as in Peking.

丨探 to spy, to scout around.

吹丨子 one who blows a conch or horn.

丨口 a wry mouth.

丨堡 an intrenchment.

In *Cantonese*. To smear; to ramble; teeth sticking out.

丨油 to grease, as boats in breaming.

丨牙 projecting teeth.

丨一條氣 I've been there once, I've seen the elephant.

丨船 to smear boats.

In *Pekingese*. The rate or value of a lot, estimated in respect of its rent.

上丨的鋪子 a very eligible stand.

SHÉ.

Old sounds, sha, zha, shat, zhap, *and* zhak. *In Canton*, shé; — *in Swatow*, sia, sé, ch'ia, ché, *and* chúa; — *in Amoy*, sia *and* ch'ia; — *in Fuhchau*, siè; — *in Shanghai*, sò *and* zò; — in *Chifu*, shié *and* sié.

賒 ˏshö From *property* and a *surname* for the phonetic.

To buy or sell on credit; to borrow; slow, remiss; distant; to defer, to put off, to shirk.

丨買 to buy on credit.

丨錢 to get a loan.

丨貨 to get credit for goods.

丨賬 credit.

寧現不丨 better to sell for cash than give credit.

舊歲全丨丨乾凈一副本錢浮似水 last year I trusted everybody till I was cleaned out dry, and all my capital has run off like water.

暫丨 trust me a little time.

丨數簿 a day-book.

酒不丨 wine must be paid for.

一概不丨 no credit given for anything.

奢 ˏshö From *great* and a *person*.

To spread out; wasteful, extravagant; profuse, affluent.

丨望 wild, unfounded hopes.

丨華 showy.

驕丨 proud and prodigal.

阿丨 a widower who has married a widow.

蛇 ˏshö The primitive was the original form, representing a snake on its tail, and gradually changed to ˏt'o 它 to carry.

A serpent, including some lizards; serpentine, crooked; malicious, treacherous, subtle; the constellation Hydra.

一條丨 one snake.

毒丨 a venemous snake.

筆如龍丨 his pen makes dragons and snakes; — *i. e.* beautiful writing.

長丨陣 the long serpent evolution, — in military strategy.

兩頭丨 the two-headed snake, an *Amphisbœna* or *Cecilia.*

丨頭鼠眼 a snake's head and rat's eyes; — wily.

佛口丨心 good words but a wicked heart.

維虺維丨女子之祥 to dream of cobras and snakes is the token of a daughter.

畫丨添足 to paint a snake and add legs, — is useless.

扒草尋丨 to beat the grass for a snake; *met.* to stir up strife.

丨行而進 came by a winding path.

丨皮身子 a disease of the skin like lepra.

倒拔丨 I've got the snake by its tail; — a bad bargain, a sell, a swindle; I've been cheated.

丨菓 or 丨枕頭 a strawberry, from its resemblance to a snake's head.

雷公丨 a gecko.

丨吞象 the snake [would] swallow an elephant; — inordinately greedy.

Read ˏi. Easy, self-possessed.

委丨 a swaggering, self-satisfied gait; sauntering at ease.

丨丨碩言 easy, magniloquent talk.

佘 ˏshö From *man* and *to exhibit.*

This is not now regarded the same as ˏyü 余 I, and is only used as a surname; some say it is a contraction of 沙家, that is 余家, which was a phrase in the Sung dynasty for I, myself.

闍 ꜀shö Adopted for the sound of a Sanscrit word, meaning a recluse.

丨維 to burn a priest.

丨黎 a title of honor (*acharya*), given to those who have finished their novitiate.

海丨黎 a Budhist priest.

Read ꜀tu. A tower or lookout turret over a city gate.

闉丨 the upper gateway over a city gate.

捨 ˊshö From *hand* and *house*; used for the next.

To let go, to relinquish, to part with; to leave, to abandon; to renounce; to spend, as one's energies; to give alms; to impugn or reject, as the authority of.

有丨心 charitable.

丨得去 left behind, as one's friends.

丨板 to give a coffin, or the boards for one; a meritorious act.

難丨 hard to part with it.

丨不得 I cannot part with it.

丨富 to abjure riches.

丨身入寺 to leave one's family and become a priest.

求丨點 I beg you to part with one cash.

丨其命救世 [Jesus] gave his life to save the world.

丨得切割 to part under strong self-denial, to give up to.

丨勿得 to regret my pains for him; I am sorry I did it. (*Shanghai.*)

In *Cantonese*. Very; immediately.

丨好 very best.

舍 ˊshö shö˒ Composed of *tongue* and *man*, originally from 亼 three *men* over 屮 a *sprout* to represent a dwelling, and 口 to represent a *wall*; it is used both for the next and the preceding; it resembles ꜀han 含 to contain.

To lodge, as at a fair; a stall in a market; to halt, to rest in; to stop; to dwell; a breathing-spell; a cottage; a hospice; a shed, a booth; a stage of 35 *li*; lodgings; as a *pronoun*, my, when speaking of one's junior relatives; to put away, to set aside; to neglect; to let go, as a bird.

丨居 to lodge.

丨彼有罪 let those criminals go.

築丨 to build a house.

屋丨 tenements, houses.

丨弟 my brother.

丨親 my relatives.

丨下 or 寒丨 my residence; — a polite term.

丨息 to rest awhile.

少丨 take a short rest.

出丨於郊 he went and dwelt in a cottage on the border.

一丨 one of the 28 zodiacal constellations; a cottage.

避君三丨 we were distant three marches from you.

客丨 a wayside inn.

丨矢 to shoot an arrow.

施丨 to be benevolent.

赦丨 to remit, as punishment.

丨己從人 to yield one's opinion for another's.

依依不丨 to hold to and not let go.

丨匿 to conceal from.

丨利子 (in Sanscrit *sarira*, defined as 骨分 bone particles) sacred relics, especially of saints or Budha, over which 丨利塔 topes and dagobas are erected.

號丨 or 籍丨 cells in the examination-hall; they are numbered by the characters of the Millenary Classic.

ˊ丨生 to give up one's life.

福丨 a Budhist term for almshouses, dispensaries, and asylums.

丨軍 to halt an army.

不ˊ丨晝夜 they cease not day or night.

In *Shanghai*. An interrogative pronoun, and usually written 啥; who; what?

丨物事 what is the matter?

丨所去 where are you going?

丨人 who is that?

丨戶蕩 or 丨所頭 what place; where?

赦 shö˒ From *carnation* and to *strike*.

To remit punishment; to forgive, to pardon, to excuse; to set aside; to pass over, to reprieve; amnesty, pardon.

丨罪 to forgive sins.

丨過一次 I will pass it over this time.

大丨天下 a general amnesty or release.

天丨 three days in the year when heaven forgives sins.

丨免 to pass by, to overlook.

常刑不丨 no pardon for relapsed criminals.

寬丨 act leniently towards one.

法無可丨 the law cannot remit punishment.

社 shö˒ From *worship* and *earth*.

The god who rules over a particular spot; the tutelary gods or *lares rustici*; sacrifices to them; the altars to gods of the land, usually without roofs; a village, a hamlet, — and in Formosa, the clan or tribe living in a place or collection of hamlets; a society or company of persons.

丨稷 gods of the land and grain (also called 后土) worshiped by officials; the tutelary gods of the state.

立丨壇 to set up an altar to the gods of the land.

宗丨化爲幽墟 the gods of the empire have gone to oblivion.

私丨 private lares, once forbidden to individuals, but now seen in almost every street and village in Kwangtung.

郊丨之禮 the sacrifice to the state gods.

田 丨 a hamlet of 10 to 25 houses; a field altar; and hence 赶出 丨 is to be ejected from one's home or village.

丨 日 two festivals like the Roman *compitalia*, for honoring the lares; the 春 丨 is about the 16th of March, and the 秋 丨 the 18th of September.

丨 會 a society or brotherhood.

天 丨 the star η in Argo.

弓箭 丨 a band of archers.

射 shö' ˏsh' From 寸 *inch* changed from 矢 *dart* or 手 *hand* and 身 *body*, intimating that arrows proceed from the bow near the body; an older form resembles a *bow* with an *arrow* across it.

To project from the body; to shoot out; to spurt, to squirt; to issue forth, as a ray or evil influence; to glance at; to scheme for; a ray, as of light.

日 丨 光入來 the sun shines in here.

丨 影 to project a shadow, or reflection, as the sun in the water.

丨 箭 to shoot arrows.

影 丨 to counterfeit, to palm off.

丨 中靶 to hit the bull's eye.

丨 言 to joke, to try with words; to pun.

丨 利 to counterfeit another's trade-mark.

善 丨 a skillful archer.

丨 來 丨 去 darting here and there.

丨 御不違 his archery and charioteering are faultless.

冲 丨 opposed to or overlooking, like the gable or chimney of another's house, which is unlucky.

丨 夫既同 the archers acted together.

丨 父 a poetical name for the musk deer.

鳴 丨 a whirring arrow.

Read *shih*, To point at and hit.

弋不 丨 宿 in shooting do not hit the sleeping game.

Read *yé'* A lord's servant.

僕 丨 his principal and secondary servants, as valet and fan-bearer.

Read *yih*, To abhor, to dislike, to loathe.

好爾無 丨 I love you, and will never weary of you.

矧可 丨 思 but the more let them not be slighted; to be treated slightingly.

In *Cantonese*. A time, a payment; an issue, as of dividends.

分開幾多 丨 how many times (or places) do you divide it into?

麝 shö' From *deer* and to *shoot*, because the fragrance is so penetrating.

The musk deer (*Moschus moschiferus*), found in Sz'ch'uen and other western provinces.

丨 香 musk.

假 丨 香 adulterated musk.

丨 臍 musk bags.

榭 shö' The genius called 宜 丨 who presides over pleasant dreams; given in the Taoist books.

騇 shö' A mare; the term has now become obsolete.

SHEH.

The sounds of these characters and those under SEH *run into each other. Old sounds*, shet, zhep, ship, *and* shak. *In Canton*, shit, ch'it, *and* ship; — *in Swatow*, chih, siot, siap, *and* niap; — *in Amoy*, siat *and* siap; — *in Fuhchau*, siek, niek, *and* tiek; — *in Shanghai*, seh *and* zeh; — *in Chifu*, sö *and* sheh.

舌 ˏshö Composed of 口 *mouth* under 干 to *try*, because the tongue tries whatever enters the mouth; it forms the 135th radical of a few characters relating to the uses of the tongue.

The tongue, — in Canton called 利 to profit, because the next word of the same tone means to lose in trade, which would be unlucky; a tongue or clapper of a bell; a valve in a pump hook of a clasp; to speak; talkative, wordy.

丨 頭 the tongue.

官非口 丨 to discuss politics and tell scandal.

丨 耕 tongue plowing, *i. e.* to teach.

滑 丨 smooth-tongued.

丨 短 thick of speech.

丨 苔 a foul or furred tongue.

丨 尖 tip of the tongue.

學口學 丨 to mimic and mock.

長 丨 婦 a virago.

茶香留 丨 本 the aroma of the tea remains in the mouth.

劍 丨 a witty fellow sharp at repartee.

丨 戰 to argue; bickering.

捫 丨 to keep silent.

吐 丨 or 伸 丨 to put out the tongue; to loll it.

揷 丨 to intrude one's remarks.

莫捫朕 丨 nobody can hold my tongue for me.

賒 An unauthorized character, for which the last and 餂 are also used.

In *Cantonese*. To lose in trade; to be imposed on; quick, soon.

丨 本 lost by the trade.

丨 了虧 to be swindled.

忕 shö' To be well acquainted with; 忸 丨 弓矢 well skilled in archery.

豢 丨 to plot against one's ruler treacherously.

設, *shŏ'* From 言 *words* and 殳 to *kill*, here defined to *impel people*.

To institute, to establish; to spread, as a net; to arrange, to set up; to set in order; to suppose; as a *preposition*, if, supposing, for instance; a squad of men or their guardhouse; large, said of a sword.

丨立 to establish, to open.

丨宴 to make a feast.

丨法 to devise means.

其丨心 he settled it in his mind.

丨或 or 丨使 suppose that, if.

布丨 to prepare, to set in order.

丨帳 or 丨教 to open a school.

一丨 one band, one picket.

丨身處地將若之何 if you were in my place, what would you do?

丨有不測 it appears as if the scheme could not be fathomed.

額丨 to estimate the number.

In *Cantonese*. A very little, not nearly enough; a bit.

蔎, *shŏ'* A fragrant plant, from which tea or an infusion is made, though it is not the proper tea plant.

丨丨 fragrance, sweet.

揲, 揲, *shŏ'* From *hand* and to *divine* or *plate*; the second is most usually read *t'ieh*, to fold.

To take hold of, to count; to sort off; to grasp.

丨蓍 to divine by straws.

占丨 sortilege.

丨荒 to feel the symptoms of disease.

攝, *shŏ'* From *hand* and *whispering*.

To collect, to gather; to control, to inspect; to take; to put in order; capable of directing; skilled; to act for; to pursue and seize; to substitute; to record; the hiss of a snake, used in imitation of the sound.

丨位 to succeed to the throne.

丨政 to be associated in the government.

丨石 the loadstone.

丨去魂 to take away another's wits, done by the Taoists.

朋友攸丨丨以威儀 your friends who assist in the service, have done so reverently and properly.

丨持 to take up, as a thing to carry.

兼丨 he also manages it; to fill several offices, as a pluralist

管丨 to administer, to oversee.

丨事 to attend to the affair.

丨衣升堂 [Confucius] raised his clothes when he went up to the hall.

Read *nieh*, To pacify; peaceful; used for 捻 to take up, as from the ground.

天下丨然 when the empire is pacified.

丨取物 to take up a thing.

丨精鬼 a brownie or ghoul, supposed by the Cantonese to wander invisible among men, and injure its enemy's life or goods.

涉, *shŏ'* From *water* and to *step*.

To ford; to wade; to pass through, as the world; to spend, as time; to investigate, to pore over, as books; to implicate, to concern; to cross a stream in a boat; to tread; acquainted with; having a tendency to; to attract, for which *shih*, 拾 is sometimes used.

丨水 to wade across.

舟丨 ferried over.

丨世人 a man acquainted with the world; liberal, generous.

丨事 to intermeddle in a matter.

毫無干丨 I had nothing at all to do with it.

丨于春冰 [trembling as if] I was crossing on spring ice.

丨及非禮 it tends to indecency.

丨獵書籍 to wade and hunt through books; to read much; conversant with affairs.

丨縣 a district in the northern part of Honan.

跋丨勿動 I am too tired to stir.

丨訟 to plead in a case, as a lawyer; to interfere in it.

經丨 already attended to.

歙, *ˏshŏ* To draw in the breath to snuff up, in disgust.

丨縣 the prefect city of Hwui-cheu fu in Nganhwui.

灄, *shŏ'* A river in Han-yang fu in Hupeh.

Read *nieh*, Watery.

溼丨 misty, foggy, rainy.

韘, 韘, *shŏ'* Often pronounced *tieh*, from the primitive.

An archer's thumb-ring, usually called 搬指; a thimble for archers.

童子佩丨 the lad carried his thimble on the girdle.

澨, *shŏ'* Also read *shi'*

Name of a river in the center of Hupeh near King-shan hien; a bank deposited near the shore by silt, on which people can land.

泛舟遊于海丨 hoist sail and let us pass along these banks.

三丨 were three ancient levees on the River Han near the present Siang-yang fu.

SHEN.

Old sounds, shen, zhen, shem, *and* zhem. *In Canton*, shin *and* shim ; — *in Swatow*, sien, sⁿi, *and* siam ; — *in Amoy*, sien *and* siam ; — *in Fuhchau*, sieng ; — *in Shanghai*, séⁿ, zéⁿ, *and* tséⁿ ; — *in Chifu*, shen.

羶 羴 ˓shan From *sheep* and *plenty* or three *sheep* ; the second form is unusual.
The rank odor of sheep or goats ; frowzy.
臭 丨 or 腥 丨 fetid, rank.
丨 氣 musty, goatish.

煽 ˓shan From *fire* and *fan* ; used with 謆˒ to beguile.
To make a blaze ; a blaze ; to excite people, to seduce to sedition, to fan discontent, to make a ferment.
丨 惑 人 心 to agitate and incite people's minds.
艷 妻 丨 方 處 the beautiful wife blazes, now in possession of her place.

搧 ˓shan To brush off ; to fan ; to strike, as with a fan ; to agitate.
丨 打 to flog.
丨 風 to move the air.
丨˒ 你 浸 皮 I'll skin you, I'll take your hide off. (*Cantonese*.)
丨 扇 to flirt a fan.

挻 ˓shan Not the same as ˓*t'ing* 挺 to root up.
To lead on, to draw out ; long ; to prolong, to delay ; to slap ; to turn, as a key.
相 丨 爲 亂 to countenance each other in rebellion ; to egg on.

蟾 ˓shan ˓ch'an A striped toad, 丨 蜍 or 丨 諸, which is thought to be longlived ; this reptile is fabled to be in the moon, and to swallow it in eclipses ; *met.* the moon.
丨 光 moonlight.
幾 歷 丨 圓 the moon has fulled many times — since we parted.
丨 宮 Diana's hall, the lunar palace.
丨 酥 a kind of venereal medicine.

梣 ˓shan A tree found in Kiangsu, producing a small, pear-shaped fruit of an acid taste, which ripens late in the season.

苫 ˓chan To cover with grass, to thatch ; a mat of straw.
被 丨 to make a thatched cover ; to put on a rain cloak.
寢 丨 枕 塊 to lie on straw or matting, or to make a clod one's pillow ; — as in grief, or when watching a grave.

禪 ˓shan ˓ch'an From *worship* and *alone*, this word changed its tone when it was adopted by the Budhists to imitate the Sanscrit *jaina*, now an Indian sect.
To sit abstractedly in contemplation, as required by *dhyana* or abstraction, whence this word has become a term for Budhist priests ; contemplation, meditation ; the Budhists.
丨 廟 or 丨 林 a Budhist temple.
丨 師 the priests, who are supposed to contemplate and pray.
四 丨 the four states of meditation.
丨 法 Budhism.
坐 丨 to sit and meditate ; and 丨 定 in fixed contemplation, are Budhist performances.
丨 機 Budhistic spells.
丨 堂 reception hall of an abbot.
丨 延 the fabled palace of Indra on Mt. Meru.
參 丨 to become a priest and enter on a life of meditation.

Read *shen*˒ To level an area for an altar, to sacrifice to the hills and fountains ; to resign the throne to another family, as Yao and Trajan did.
封 丨 to make a hill sacred and worship on it.
丨 位 to resign the throne.

嬋 嬗 ˓ch'an The second character is likewise used for the preceding ; and is also read ˓*tan*, slow, negligent.
Beautiful and graceful, as women or grasses.
丨 連 relatives.
丨 娟 waving, like the bamboo ; easy in motion, as bamboos ; attractive, as flowers ; transitory, as falling snow.

譂 ˓shan To falsify, to distort the truth of a thing.

蟬 ˓ch'an From 虫 *insect* and 禪 to *contemplate* contracted.
The cicada or broad locust ; it is common over China, and has many names, as 秋 丨, or 紗 丨, and 秋 涼 兒 the autumn cooler.
丨 脫 the exuviæ of the cicada, used as a febrifuge.
丨 聯 a pair of sentences.
丨 吟 or 丨 噪 the chirp of the cicada.
丨 鬢 hair on the temples dressed in puffs, thought to resemble the cicada's eyes.
丨 花 or 冠 丨 a horned or capped cicada, a variety found in Sz'ch'uen ; perhaps it is really a species of *Fulgora*.
金 丨 脫 殼 之 計 this plan is just like the last, as the exuviæ is like the cicada's body.
丨 嫣 to connect or join.
丨 不 知 雪 a katydid knows nothing of the snow ; — *i. e.* he is a booby.

澶 ˓shan Still water.
丨 淵 the name of a river, a branch of the River Hwai, in the east of Honan, in the ancient state of Sung.
Read *tan*˒. Lazy, self-indulgent.
丨 漫 vast and great, as an expanse of water.

儃 ˓shan Manner, air, figure.
丨丨 easy, sans-souci.
丨佪 irresolute, unable to get on.

閃 ʿshan From *door* and a *man* in it.
To put one's head out of doors; one crossing a doorway; to shun, to evade; to slip aside, to dodge; to wriggle; glittering, flashing; transient; chatoyant, iridescent; adulatory.
打丨 to lighten; to shimmer.
丨電一丨 a flash of lightning.
丨射 to flash; on to throw a reflection, as from a mirror.
丨在一邊 to slip aside, to avoid one.
豪光丨丨 glorious, dazzling, as an angel.
丨開些罷 get one side; move out of the way a little.
丨眼 it dazzles or glares the eyes.
丨緞 changeable satin.
丨丨縮縮 dodging in and out, as if afraid to be seen.
丨見 I saw it for an instant.
東扯西丨 squirming and writhing.
丨喻 to adulate, to cajole.
言詞丨爍 to jump from one topic to another, to talk wildly; incoherent and untrustworthy.

⿰氵閃 ʿshan Water rippling and glinting as it flows rapidly; name of a place.

睒 ʿshan From *eye* and a *blaze*.
To glance at; to peep; to dart, to flash.
丨目 to take a look at.
丨丨 lustrous, glittering like a quartz crystal.
目微丨 the glance of an eye.

陝 ʿshan To be distinguished from *hiah*, 陜 narrow.
The region west of the Yellow River, now the province of Shensi.
丨州 in the west of Honan gave its name to the region, which is regarded as the cradle of the Chinese; Tsin Chi-hwangti called it 關中 because it was easily defended.

善 shan' Originally composed of 羊 a *sheep* placed between 言 repeated denoting *wrangling;* it resembles ʿ*hi* 喜 in form.
Good from principle, virtuous; merit from good works, as the Budhists teach; goodness; eminent, wise; meek, docile; fitted for; clever, skillful, expert, handy, *au fait;* to take to naturally; in a high degree; to do a thing well; to expedite; to admire, to praise, to approve.
丨惡 good — evil; meritorious and evil works.
丨事 a good act.
行丨 to do right or benevolently; and then the 丨行' or good deeds are known.
相丨 well acquainted with.
丨法 or 丨策 a clever scheme, a feasible plan.
丨死 or 丨終 a peaceful end.
丨馬 a gentle horse, not tricky.
丨有丨報 good acts will be well rewarded.
女子丨懷 women are apt to be anxious.
丨會交友 he likes to mix with his friends.
氣色不丨 an ill-favored face, a bad expression.
丨德 morality.
不敢以丨漁利 I dare not make virtue a bait for getting gain.
守死丨道 sincerely attached to virtue; a martyr to the right.
丨丨類而惡' 惡徒 he takes to the good and dislikes villains.
丨丨靜靜 fair and serene, as the sky.
丨哭 apt at weeping; he cries easily.
僞丨者 hypocrites.
丨會作這個 he is skillful at doing that.
面丨 I know him by sight.
丨後 to make good or complete what comes after, as bye-laws attached to previous rules.
辦理丨後事宜 to arrange well the supplementary negotiations.
丨于文藝 well versed in literature and elegant accomplishments.
丨行之于己公之于人 practice goodness yourself, and exhibit it towards others.
人之初性本丨 the nature of man is originally good.
丨搖 to wave elegantly, as trees.

膳 shan' / **饍** shan' From *flesh* or *eating* and *good*.
Provisions dressed for the table; viands; savory food, delicacies; the richest fare; a meal.
早丨 breakfast.
晚丨 evening meal; supper.
供丨 supplies furnished to a tutor.
珍丨 savory food, rare viands.
丨夫 a king's butler; the chief cook.
御丨房 a royal dining hall.
牲丨 the flesh of sacrifices.
用丨未 have you dined?

繕 shan' To mend; to put in order; to brighten up; to prepare; to copy, to write out; to state correctly; a scrivener.
丨寫 to write out.
丨正 to correct and copy.
丨錄 to transcribe.
丨單 a list of things wanted.
修丨 to put in repair.
丨摺子 an official paper.
征丨 to put to rights.

僐 shan' An elegant person, a refined manner.
丨態 graceful, lady-like.

蟮 蟺 *shan'* From *insect* and *good*; much used for the next; the second form is little used.
The earthworm or 蛩丨, called in Canton 黃犬 the yellow dog.
曲丨 the squirming worm.
曲丨唱歌有雨勿多 when the earthworm sings, it will soon be fair weather.

鱔 鱓 䱇 *shan'* Interchanged with the last; the last form is also read *tan'*
The eel, especially the small freshwater sorts; the Chinese suppose that eels, as well as snakes, are transformed from the roots of plants and hair.
丨羹 a soup of stewed eels.
黃丨 a small yellow mud eel.
捉白丨 to snare white eels.
鶴丨 hawk-bill eel. (*Congrus tricuspidatus.*)
黃腮丨 yellow jawed eel. (*Ophicardia xanthognatha.*)
烏耳丨 the brown eel (*Anguilla avisotis*), also called 籐丨 the rattan eel.
非蛇即丨 if he is not a villain, he's a slippery eel.

墡 *shan'* White fine clay used to plaster walls.

墠 *shan'* A level place at the base of an altar, a smooth hard spot leveled off for sacrifices; a small terrace; to level the ground; a wild or common.

扇 *shan'* From 戶 an inner *door* and 翄 *fins* contracted.
A folded fan; a round fan or fire-screen; the leaf of a door; and hence applied as a classifier to other things, as a shutter, a screen, &c.; to fan; to wave, for which 搧 is also used; to move to and fro.
打丨 or 撥丨 to fan.
風丨 a punka or table fan.
羽丨 a feather fan.
自丨 it fans itself,—as a butterfly.
單丨門 a single leaved door.
丨子 or 一把丨 a fan.
風起丨無功 when the breeze comes the fan is discarded.
秋後丨 [useless as] a fan after autumn.
掌丨 a state flabellum.
丨袋 or 丨墜兒 a fan-case.
小芭蕉丨 [he is like] a leaf fan, — and stirs up strife.
摺丨 and 圓丨 or 團丨 folding fans, and round or fire screens.
一丨屛風 the screen before an entrance.

謆 *shan'* From *words* and to *fan*.
To seduce people by fair speeches; to wheedle others into following one's plans.
布丨謠言 to stir up ill-will with false rumors.

擅 *shan'* From *hand* and *plateau*.
To act as one pleases; to take the responsibility of doing without orders; willful; illegally, arbitrarily; to assume, to usurp; despotic.
丨權 to act hastily, to usurp powers.
丨自爲 to act out one's own will.
丨專 to act unauthorizedly.
丨用 a despotic use of.
胆敢丨行 he acted boldly and without orders.
丨呼聖諱 he had the impudence to use the forbidden name.

禪 *shan'* To sacrifice to or worship Heaven; to yield, to abdicate in favor of.
讓丨 to give up the throne.
舜禹受丨 Shun gave the government to Yü, who received it.

騸 *shan'* To geld a horse or ass.
丨牯 a steer.
丨馬 a gelding.
丨樹 to graft.

劗 *shan'* To work on, to trim, to cut out; to geld; to manage or arrange well.

燀 *shan'* To blow a fire and make it burn brighter; to incite; to blaze up; bright, clear.
丨火 to make the fire burn.
丨之以薪 make it burn with some faggots.
夏不炎丨 we do not need a fire in summer.

贍 *shan'* From *wealth* and *excellent*.
To give, to supply; to aid; abundant; liberal.
丨補 to supply deficiencies.
丨助 to help the poor.
恐不丨 I fear there's not enough.
家丨人足 abundance of means and men.

䢾 *shan'* To walk quickly.
尾踵之逾丨 I chased him as fast as I could run.

磰 *shan'* To polish a gem; to calender cloth; to slip, as when walking.
丨布石 a calendering stone.
丨倒 I slipped down.
丨滑 to make cloth glossy.

磰 *shan'* White porcelain clay; clay good for the potter's use is 白丨土, but it is of an inferior quality.

傓 *shan'* From *man* and *fan*; it is like 煽 in some of its uses.
To excite, to inflame; exasperation; a blaze, a flame.
勃怒方丨 his fury then blazed up.

SHEU.

Old sounds, shu, shut, zhu, *and* shuk. *In Canton*, shau *and* sau; — *in Swatow*, siu, siò, chʻiu, *and* sò; — *in Amoy*, siu *and* sò; — *in Fuhchau*, siu, séu, chʻiu, *and* saiu; — *in Shanghai*, sù *and* zù; — *in Chifu*, shu.

收 抖 収 ˏsheu } From to *tap* or *hand* and to *wrap up;* the third is a common contraction; the first resembles *meh*, 牧 a shepherd, and the second is little used.

To receive, as when one goes for it, or it is his due; nearly synonymous with 受; to gather; to harvest; to insnare, to involve; to quit, as work; to bind, to restrain; to conclude, to bring to an end; to remove; to close or wind up, as a shop; annoyed or moved by, in which sense it sometimes merely gives a passive form to another verb; a back board in a carriage; a hat worn in the Hia dynasty which received the hair-knot like the Corean hat.

丨入 or 丨拆 to receive and open, as a letter.

丨規 to collect the fees.

丨買人心 to win people's hearts — by largesses.

丨割 to reap the harvest.

不丨雷 it still thunders. (*Cantonese.*)

丨工 to quit work.

丨鋪 to shut up shop.

丨單 a receipt for money.

丨賬 to collect accounts; on which 丨訖 received in full, is then marked.

丨拾 to make things ready; bear a hand! sharp at it! also, to restrain, to overrule.

丨拾你 I'll fix you off! I'll pay you back; — as by a trick.

丨拾三軍回朝 to gather up the army and return.

丫頭丨房 the maid has been taken as a concubine.

丨成 to get in the crop or rent of land.

丨心世務 to withdraw the thoughts from worldly affairs.

丨兵 to recall troops.

丨贖 to redeem, to get out of pawn, to raise a mortgage.

丨藏 or 丨埋 to put by, to lay in store.

丨買玩器 curiosities bought here; — a sign-board.

夜不丨 one who spies the conduct of others.

手 ˋsheu Said to represent the *fist*; others say the three lines depict the hand, fore-arm, and arm; it is the 64th radical of characters relating to its uses.

The arm; the hand; the fist; the fingers; handy, quick; to handle with the hand; the power of the hand; a person, a hand; to grasp, to hold in the hand; to cuff; to act; an autograph; actions; skill; a quire or fold of paper; a handful, a lot.

一把丨 one hand.

魁丨 a first rate workman.

丨下 under orders.

下丨 or 開丨 to begin a work.

閒丨 unoccupied, no employment.

丨笠 or 丨套 a glove; a mitten.

丨掌 or 丨心 the palm.

丨紋 lines on the palm.

丨本 or 丨帖 visiting-cards of different sizes.

丨足 brothers.

丨作 an art, a handicraft.

熟丨 or 老丨 expert at doing a thing; an old hand.

十丨所指其嚴乎 [what many eyes see] and many hands point to, is worthy of respect.

打丨 hired athletes or men who practice with bludgeons.

好作丨 elegant composition.

過丨 to give over, to transfer.

丨拗 the inner side of the elbow.

揸丨 to shake hands.

白丨做 to do a thing off-hand.

丨模 or 丨印 the impression of the thumb or hand for a signature.

國丨 a great doctor or surgeon; also a champion chess-player.

丨指罅疎 open fingers — will never hold money; this refers to the fingers lying close together.

遊丨 a lazy fellow, an idler.

㑳丨 a hard-worker, a drudge, a toiler and moiler; also, I have given you some trouble. (*Pekingese.*)

丨生 raw, inexperienced, new at.

佛丨 Budha's hand, the fingered citron. (*Citrus sarcodactylus.*)

束丨無策 folded his hands and knew not what to do.

甚爲棘丨 very difficult to do; hurried and perplexed.

丨緊 penniless; stingy.

順丨 or 帶丨 convenient, by the way.

先丨放鎗 I fired the first shot.

小丨 or 三隻丨 a thief, a shop-lifter.

莫失丨勢 don't disappoint me now.

請搶丨 to hire aid in passing the examinations.

丨談 to talk with the fingers.

丨執劍而立 he seized his sword and stood.

丨容恭 the hands exhibit respect.

一丨貨 a lot of goods.

一丨骰 one throw of dice.

一丨蛋 a handful, *i. e.* five eggs.

丨乏 out of funds, short of money.

措不丨及 I could not attend to them all.

丨之舞之 the hands then begin to move.

予丨拮据 with my claws I seized it, — as an owl.

叟 ₍seu The sound of driving away birds or fowls.

蒐 ₍seu From *grass* and *devil*, because this herb is supposed to strengthen the blood; interchanged with ₍si 茜 madder and the next.

A plant whose root is allied to madder, and used in dyeing red; it is a species of *Rubia* found in Honan, perhaps the *Rubia munjista* or munjith of India; the vernal hunt, when 丨取不孕 pregnant animals were not to be taken; to assemble, as for a hunt; to provision cavalry for a war, to order troops; to screen or hide; to search, to come across.

丨羅 to search out or read up, as a subject; to meet with accidentally, as a rare book, alluding to one snaring birds in a hunt.

春丨 the spring hunt.

搜 摉 sheu' ₍seu From *hand* and a *senior* or to *scour*.

To search a house, as police do; to throw things about when searching; to inform one's self, to search out; to inquire into the meaning of, for which the last is also used; literary researches; the ideas of a multitude, popular opinion; to assemble; rapid, swift, arrowy.

丨尋 to seek for, as secreted things.

丨緝 to search for and seize.

丨檢 or 丨身 to search the person of a candidate when going in.

鷄丨毛 a cock pecking its feathers.

未及旁丨 without investigating the attendant circumstances.

窮丨 to pursue a subject to its source.

丨匿 to search for hidden things.

丨然 quick.

東矢其丨 how their swift arrows whiz!

丨票 a search-warrant.

廋 ₍seu Used with the preceding.

To secrete, to conceal; to search for hidden things; crafty; hidden; to examine into, as a hidden meaning.

丨求 to search for, as in a suspected house.

丨人 a kind of rector in the Cheu dynasty who superintended education.

人焉丨哉 how can the man conceal his character?

問丨緣由 to search out the causes of.

颼 飕 ₍seu These two forms are sometimes regarded as different.

The chilling sound of wind; noise of rain and wind.

丨丨 the whirring of an arrow; rustling made by the wind.

風丨得慌 the wind makes me shiver.

丨飀 a cold blast.

丨瑟 the chilling sound of a driving rain.

餿 ₍seu Rice heated by dampness and spoiled; meat or vegetables spoiled from heat.

飯丨了 the rice is cooked too much.

汗丨 the smell of perspiration.

膄 ₍seu To slice up, to make mince meat, and mix it with rice flour and steam it.

丨丨 dried fish, stockfish.

膴胖骨丨 slices of meat with the bones in them.

螋 ₍sheu An old name for the *Cermatia*, or spider-millipede, is 蛷丨; it is better known as 錢龍 a harmless, agile insect; two or three kinds of insects seem to be included under its synonyms; this is described as having six legs near its head, a forked tail like an earwig's, and two long antennæ, which all point out a species of *Julus*.

鄋 ʻseu The 丨瞞 was the name of a tribe of northern people dwelling towards Liaotung, which invaded the state Tsi in the Hia dynasty.

守 ʻsheu From a *cover* and an *inch*, defined to represent 官 *official* and 法 *rules*.

To keep; to hold in order to guard; to have in custody; to ward off, to protect; to keep vigils; to supervise; to attend to, to maintain; to go on a round of inspection; a charge, a post; steadfast; a prefect.

丨得緊 keep close watch over it.

丨備 a major.

丨制 in mourning for a parent; the phrase is put up on the outer gate.

丨節 to remain unmarried after a betrothed or husband is dead.

官丨 to exercise an office.

丨本分 to keep to one's own business; self-collected.

丨更望夙 to watch and wait for the dawn.

丨業難 it's not easy to keep an estate.

丨土 the local authorities.

有丨 men who maintain probity.

丨己 self-control.

丨風 waiting for the wind.

太丨' a prefect or prince in the times of the Han; now applied to a prefect, and sometimes used alone as 張丨 the prefect Chang.

城丨 a garrison; the commandant.

丨者曰 the warden said.

犬丨夜 dogs watch by night.

把丨 to stop, as a gate.

失丨 lost the rule of, as a territory to rebels.

丨寡 to remain a widow.

艏 ʻsheu The bow of a vessel, called 艌丨 on which a huge bird was sometimes carved.

溲 ˓seu From *water* and a *senior*.

To soak meal in water; to steep in water; to macerate.

丨丨 sound of washing rice.

丨酒 to make spirits.

Read ˓sheu. To urinate.

丨溺 to make water.

前後丨 natural evacuations.

首 ˓sheu Said to represent the *hair*, *forehead*, and *eyes*; it forms the 185th radical of a few characters referring to the head.

The head; a chief, a leader; the heads of a matter; foremost; the beginning, the origin; to manifest, to display; sorts, kinds; a classifier of flags, stanzas, and corpses.

稽丨 or 頓丨拜 to bow the head in respect; — written on cards.

元丨 the head of all, the Emperor.

為丨 acts as a leader.

有兔斯丨炮之燔之 there is only one rabbit, bake it or roast it.

丨名 the first or leading name.

丨領 the leading man.

丨先 the first, most important.

案丨 first on the list of *siuts'ai*.

丨善 the very best, the head of goodness; applied to the metropolis.

泥丨宮門 to dirty the head at the palace door; — to make the kotow.

丨尾相顧 look after both ends; we must examine everything.

告汝言丨 I will tell you the important points.

到門丨 came to the street door.

魁丨 superior to all, one who excels.

丨事 one who takes charge of or leads.

丨縣 the leading district at the prefect city.

不分丨從˒ no difference between leaders and accomplices.

一日上一丨生書 every day get a little out of the Books.

Read sheu˒ To acknowledge, to take upon one's self; to confess guilt; to go first, to put at the head.

丨罪 to confess a crime.

降丨 to submit.

出丨 to denounce, to turn state's evidence.

投丨 to give up, as a rebel.

東丨 to sleep towards the east.

狩 sheu˒ From *dog* and *to guard*.

A hunting dog; a hunt in winter on grounds burned over.

冬丨 the winter hunt.

巡丨 an imperial inspecting tour on the frontier.

獸 sheu˒ From 犬 *dog* and an old form of 畜 *domestic animals*.

A wild animal, a beast, a hairy brute; a gamekeeper, a forester; brutal, violent.

走丨 quadrupeds.

人面丨心 a human face with a beast's heart; — cruel.

百丨 all kinds of animals.

六丨 six beasts, — are the musk deer, deer, bear, moose, wild boar, and hare.

猛丨 fierce beasts, as a tiger.

售 sheu˒ From 口 *mouth* and a 雙 *brace* contracted.

To sell, to dispose of; to trade; to restore, to pay back, to recompense.

出丨 or 賣丨 to sell.

丨價 price of an article.

丨主 the purchaser.

消丨 consumption of goods; sold off.

丨時之器 merchantable goods; *met.* one who rules the times.

綬 sheu˒ The cord or ribbon on a seal to carry it; a tent or curtain cord; ties for a knee-pad.

印丨 ribbon of a seal.

組丨 silk bands and cords, such as denote official rank.

受 sheu˒ From 𠬪 to *fall* as ripe fruit and 舟 a *boat* contracted, for the primitive.

To receive; to acquiesce in; to contain; to inherit, to succeed to; to endure, to bear, — and thus becomes a form of the passive; susceptible of, affected by; a charge, a thing to be kept; one of the seven senses of the Budhists, answering to sensation or mental conception.

不敢丨 how can I receive it? — a polite phrase.

補藥丨不起 I cannot bear this tonic.

買丨 to buy; bought.

典丨 to offset the use of money for the rental of a piece of property.

丨罪 suffering for a crime or an accusation.

丨刑 he has been punished.

丨授不清 the receipts and payments are muddled.

忍丨 very patient.

丨教 docile, teachable.

丨賤 poor; willing to be poor.

熱得難丨 or 熱丨不得 this heat is hard to bear.

丨業門生 a pupil under your instruction.

丨高帽 or 丨獎 to get the high cap, to be fond of praise.

丨難財主 a miserly wretch, who stints himself.

承丨 to inherit; to accept; to come into one's hands.

丨福無疆 may you be blessed in every way.

有所丨之 it had been received from a proper source.

容丨 to take in, as a guest; to give in; to refrain from, as revenge.

丨氣 to be scolded.

丨人之託 requested by another to do a thing.

小人不可大丨 the small man cannot be intrusted with onerous responsibilities.

授 *sheu'* From *hand* and to *receive* as the phonetic.

To give; to communicate; to grant, to confer.

傳 丨 to impart, as a recipe; to make known to another.

秘 丨 to make known a secret to.

男女丨受不淸 men and women should not touch each other when giving and taking things.

口丨心法 to orally deliver rules of life.

天丨人與 heaven and man both conferred it, — *i.e.* the throne.

壽 *sheu'* Composed of 老 *old*, 曰 to *speak* and 句 *word*, altered in combination; it is varied to an unlimited extent for ornamental purposes, and is also symbolized by a diagram resembling rhombs interlaced endwise.

Age, years; longevity, the first of the five happinesses; long life; a long reign; a birthday; the dead; to endure; to grant long life to; aged; for ever.

丨物 or 丨禮 birthday presents; the first commonly refers to those from the Emperor.

上丨 and 中丨 and 下丨 are respectively 120, 100, and 80 years of age; others place them at 100, 80, and 60 years.

拜丨 or 賀丨 to congratulate one on his birthday.

尊駕高丨 what is your age?

丨誕 an old man's birthday.

丨衣 a burial dress, given by a son when his father is over sixty.

丨錢 coin given by old people to children for amulets.

長丨 old, aged.

爾萬丨無疆 [they say,] We divine for you myriads of endless years.

丨木 or 丨板 a coffin.

萬丨 the Emperor's birthday.

丨星公 or 老丨星 or 丨星公公 or 丨星老兒 the god of longevity; the star Canopus or 南極 is regarded as his star.

罔或耆丨 there are probably no men of age and experience.

仁者丨 the benevolent (or placid) become old.

丨二百年 [shields of rhinoceros, hide] will last 200 years.

丨酒 a birthday entertainment.

瘦 *sheu'* From *disease* and a *senior*.

Lean, poor, thin; meager from disease.

丨影 lean as a ghost.

面丨 hatchet-faced, peaked.

骨丨如柴 his bones stick out like sticks.

花容丨減 her fine face grew thin.

丨田 poor land.

丨雪梅花 the bright prune flowers.

丨貨 goods on which no profit is to be made.

丨肉 lean meat.

漱 *seu'* From *water* and to *suck* in.

To rinse the mouth, to scour; to wash out a thing; to purify; to gnaw.

丨口 to cleanse the mouth.

丨石枕流 the water wears the rocks which impede its flow.

丨浣 to scour and purify one's self.

SHI OR SH'

Old sounds, shei, shai, shi, zhi, shik, shit, shap, shet, zhit, *and* zhik. *In Canton*, shi, shei, ch'i, *and* sz'; — *in Swatow*, si *and* sai; — *in Amoy*, si, su, ch'i, *and* k'i; — *in Fuhchau*, si, sü, sie, sé, séü, ch'i, ch'é, *and* sai; — *in Shanghai*, sz'; — *in Chifu*, shi.

尸 *sh'* The original form is designed to represent a corpse laid out for burial; it forms the 44th radical of characters relating to parts and positions of bodies.

A corpse, for which the next is now mostly used; an image or effigy of an ancestor; living persons were anciently dressed to personate them, and then worshiped; inefficient, corpse-like; useless, like a statue; to personate; to fill in a sham way, to make a sinecure of; to arrange; to superintend; to lay in order.

丨位素餐 to neglect the duties but take the pay of an office.

氣得三丨躁跳 he danced and hopped about from the excess of his rage.

寢不丨 do not sleep lying like a corpse.

坐如丨 sitting stiff and motionless.

誰其丨之 who arranged these so?

設丨 to parade idols; also, to fill a post uselessly.

丨謖君與卿四人餕 when the impersonator had got up, the prince and his officers, four in all, enjoyed the sacrifice.

公丨 effigy of an ancestor.

屍 *sh'* From *body* and *dead*; it is like the preceding.

A carcase; but more especially a body that has been mutilated.

死丨 or 丨身 a dead body.

丨首 or 丨骸 a corpse.

驗丨 to hold an inquest.

以丨跳害 to involve one by putting a body — at his door, or otherwise.

某丨親 the friends of a dead person.

借丨還魂 he has borrowed a corpse and revived — from a trance.

鳲 *sh'* The turtle dove or wood-pigeon; called 布穀 or 桑鳩 from its note and roost.

丨鳩在桑 the wood pigeon roosts on the mulberry

師 *sh'* Composed of 帀 the *whole*, and a contracted form of 堆 a *heap*, denoting coming together from all parts.

The people; multitudes; a legion or brigade of 2500 men; part of an army; troops; to marshal a force; a *place* where people meet, as a metropolis; or a *person* who leads them; a leader, a general, one who orders men; a model, to take as a model; a master, a professor; a patron; a sage, a pattern to the world; to teach; to imitate.

先丨 ancient wise men.

丨表 patterns for men.

丨傅 one skilled in an art, an expert, a clever workman.

見老丨 to visit a learned scholar or one's teacher.

丨兄 a teacher's son; a chum.

丨爺 official secretaries in a yamun, who transact the routine of daily business; there are seven classes of them.

出丨 to march out the troops.

班丨 to recall the army from foreign service.

水丨 marines, men-of-war's men.

大丨(or 老丨太 when addressed) a priest; also known as 法丨 and 禪丨 denoting their position as leading teachers.

教丨 a teacher of fencing and boxing.

軍丨 a strategist who advises the general; *met.* a guide, adviser, or conductor.

太丨 and 少丨 are high nominal offices of the prince's instructors.

卿士丨丨非度 the nobles and rulers imitate each other in breaking the laws.

房丨 and 座丨 terms for the 18 under-examiners, and 4 head-examiners at the tripos in Peking for *tsintsz'*.

溮 *sh'* A short tributary of the River Hwai in the southeast of Honan near Lo-shan hien.

蒒 *sh'* A floating marine plant which furnishes small seeds tasting like barley, and which ripen in the seventh moon; they are called 自然穀 spontaneous grain, and 禹餘糧 Yü's extra rations; it is probably a kind of *Zostera* or sea-wrack.

獅 *sh'* From *beast* and a *leader*.

The lion, which has long been extinct in China; a slut that has two pups.

丨子 a lion.

丨子狗 Peking dogs.

石丨 stone lions before a yamun.

錢丨 a paper lion stuck over with cash; at Canton it is made for a bridal present.

衝親丨鼻 you've just tweaked the lion's nose; *i. e.* you've made him cross enough.

丨子吼 the lion's roar, a Budhist term (*singhanada*) for preaching.

丨子之座 a throne supported by carved lions, an insignia of a king.

丨子國 the land of lions, Singala or Ceylon.

舞丨 to play masked lions.

螄 *sh'* A *Murex*, *Turritella*, or similar spiral shells are termed 螺丨; a crenulated shell.

丨蚶 an *Arca*, *Pecten*, or other scallop ribbed shells.

蓍 *sh'* From *plant* and *old man*.

A sort of syngenesious plant resembling the *Anthemis* or mayweed, the *Ptarmica sibirica*, called 丨草 which grows around Confucius' grave in Küh-feu, and as was done in ancient times, is still sold there in parcels of 64 stalks for divination; the stems were once used for hair-pins.

黃丨 a dwarf species of *Sophora*? thought to resemble the preceding in its habit.

施 *sh'* From 㫃 a *flag* contracted and 也 *also*, for the primitive.

The appearance of a banner; expanded, exhibited; developed; granted; to give, to bestow, to relieve, to aid; to diffuse, to distribute; to do, and often merely aids the meaning of the next verb; to concede, to permit; to add to, to use; to set, as a net; to move leisurely; to arrange, to set out.

載丨之行 they only occupy their places.

丨恩 to be kind to.

丨行 grant that it be so, allow it, let it be thus; — a phrase in courtesy or petitions.

丨于中林 [the net is] set in the forest.

丨主 a benefactor, especially to temples.

丨捨 to bestow in charity.

丨濟 to give a donation to the poor.

丨食 to feed the poor.

丨張 to expand, to do one's best.

將其來丨丨 he will come along most pleased, or daintily.

丨攞 to boast, to vaunt one's self.

丨爲 let it be done so.

丨諸己而不願亦勿丨于人 what you dislike others to do to you, don't do that to them; this sentiment is also expressed by 己所不欲勿丨於人 what you do not yourself wish, do not give or do to others.

Read *shi'* To distribute.

雲行雨丨 the clouds give down their rain.

Read *ch'i'* and used for 弛. To leave to; to remove; to spread out; to let go, as a string.

丨從良人之所之 she furtively followed her husband's steps.

Read *i'* To change; to climb, as a vine; to transfer to; extend, to stretch to.

釃 *ˏsh'* *ˏshai* To decant and strain liquors; to pour out a libation; to divide, as streams.

丨酒 to pour off spirits.

禹丨五湖而定東海 Yü marked out the five lakes and put bounds to the eastern sea.

筮 *shi'* From *bamboo* and *straws*.

To divine with stems of the millfoil or mayweed.

丨人 a fortune-teller.

卜丨偕止 by shell and by wands have I made the lots.

見乎丨龜 let us try what the lot will show.

噬 *shi'* From *mouth* and to *divine*.

To eat, to gnaw; great grief; reaching to; snapping at, as a dog for a morsel; an initial particle.

牙丨丨 to grate the teeth.

丨臍何及 how can you bite your navel? — an impossibility.

丨嗑 the 21st diagram, denoting desire.

丨肯來遊 if he would come and ramble.

反丨 to bite back, to revenge on.

齝 呞 齥 *ˏc'h'* From *teeth* or *mouth* and *officer*; it is also read *ˏch'i*.

To chew the cud; to ruminate; at Canton, it is called 牛倒草 ox turning the grass; and at Peking, 倒嚼 turning the cud.

邿 *ˏsh'* A small fief in the state of Tsi, now Tsi-yang hien 齊陽縣 on the Ta-ts'ing River in Shantung.

丨山 a hill not far from this region.

詩 *ˏsh'* From *words* and *temple*.

To express the feelings in set rhythm; poetry, verse; odes, hymns; a poem; to receive or take in the arms.

吟丨 to hum over or sing songs.

作丨 to write verses.

丨翁 or 丨人 a bard, a poet.

公乃爲丨以貽王 the duke then wrote a poem which he gave the king.

一首丨 a verse, a stanza.

丨韻 the rhyme of the verse.

丨以言志 poetry expresses one's feelings.

丨詞歌賦 verses, ditties, odes, and songs, — the four sorts of poetry.

和丨 to match rhymes with another person.

題丨 to improvize a stanza.

廻文丨 verses that can be read both backwards and forwards.

絁 *ˏsh'* Coarse thread for weaving; a sort of sleazy sarsnet made of poor silk.

時 旹 *ˏsh'* From *sun* and *temple*; the second, from *sun* and *sprout* above the *earth*, is an unusual form.

Time; a season, an hour, a period; a Chinese hour; a quarter of a year; an occasion, an opportunity; now, timeous, convenient; recent, in season; to time rightly, to take a fit time for; to be; after a verb, when, while, during, as, — or as a copula; at the beginning of a sentence, when, then, at that time; sometimes.

十二丨辰 the Chinese hours, named after twelve animals.

四丨 the four seasons.

一丨 inadvertently, hastily, rashly; on the spur of the moment.

一丨就要 I want it at once.

丨興 or 丨尙 fashionable, in demand.

即丨 instantly, forthwith.

當丨 then, at that date.

幾丨 or 何丨 when?

丨習之 constantly practice it.

隨丨 at a good time, when convenient.

天丨 weather; a favorable juncture.

不丨 incessantly.

丨丨 always, continually.

先丨 before, previously.

丨令不好 unpleasant weather; a disagreeable day.

丨其亡也 [Confucius] marked when he was not at home.

丨日 the date, the time of.

丨常 constantly.

丨勢 times, condition of things, circumstances.

得丨失丨 a lucky and unlucky hour; a proper or unfortunate moment.

不合丨 not in fashion; unsuitable to the season.

不達丨務 unacquainted with the world.

不丨不食 [the sage] would eat only at the set time.

因丨制宜 wait a good time, then do it.

丨萬丨億 in myriads and lakhs.

丨刻 every moment.

此一丨彼一丨 times are different now, things are altered.

不一丨 a little while, not an hour's time.

於變丨雍 everybody has now become prosperous.

日止日丨 it will, he said, do to build or stop there.

一丨不及起錨 he could not instantly weigh anchor.

那丨節 just at that time.

溡 *ˏsh'* A small stream in Shantung, an affluent of the R. Shing 澠河, which is a tributary of the Ta-tsing River.

糘 *ˏsh'* From *rice* and *season*; an unauthorized character.

In *Fuhchau*. Cakes of the glutinous rice eaten at the winter solstice.

丨粑 dry cakes of this grain.

塒 *ˏsh'* An open hen-roost made in a wall, with perches placed across it for the fowls.

雞棲于丨 the fowls roost in their holes.

蒔 ˎsh' From *plant* and *time*.

To plant; to set out shrubs or trees as a memorial of an event or victory; to set up a pole.

丨槙 to transplant a tree.

丨羅子 coriander or fennel seed.

丨田 to put up poles or trees in a field.

榯 ˎsh' Like the preceding.

Erect, lofty, as a high tree.

丨立 to set up, as a flag-staff.

若松丨 like a lofty erect fir.

落丨 to put a door in its socket.

鰣 ˎsh' The shad, (*lit.* the *time-fish*) or *Alosa reevesii*, enters the rivers in May, and returns to the ocean in September; it is known at Canton as 三犂 three plow-shares; the name also includes other kinds of the herring family.

糟丨魚 salted or pickled shad.

匙 ˎsh' ˎch' From a *ladle* and *to be*.

A spoon; a key, which in China resembles a spoon.

茶丨 a tea-spoon.

鎖丨 or 鑰丨 a key.

羹丨 a soup-spoon.

扭丨 turn the key.

丨子 a spoon.

門丨 a door-key.

鍉 ˎsh' Regarded by some as the correct form of the last, denoting the hook or catch on the end of a Chinese key.

Read ˎt'i. Point of a spear; a vessel used in smearing blood when taking an oath.

箷 ˎsh' A kind of bamboo; a clothes-rack.

竿丨 bamboos for hanging clothes on.

Read *t'i*, A spittoon.

茬 ˎsh' A grassy appearance, like a lawn.

丨平縣 in Shantung, the capital of T'ung-chang fu.

Read ˎch'a. To cut down trees; the sprouts growing on a stump; suckers.

史 ˊsh' Composed of 又 *hand* grasping the 中 *middle* of a subject; *q. d.* the historian should be unlike a partisan, and display his sense of the right; it resembles *li'* 吏 an officer.

A narrator of events, an impartial annalist; a history, especially one published by authority; a register; chronicles, annals, acts.

國丨 records of the state.

丨官 or 御丨 a historiographer.

丨記 a history.

二十一丨 histories of the various Chinese dynasties.

丨書 historical books; name of a compilation written about B. C. 800.

女丨 an ancient governess in the palace; now applied to any literary woman.

左丨 and 右丨 the court annalists.

太丨第 a Hanlin graduate.

名垂青丨 your name will descend through the evergreen annals.

駛 駃 ˊsh' From *horse* and *official*; both forms are authorized, but the second is most used; in Fuhchau it is interchanged with 使 to use.

A horse running swiftly to sail a vessel; to hasten; strong, as a wind; prompt, speedy.

丨船 to sail a boat or ship.

丨往何處 where are you sailing?

丨法 rules of navigation.

丨勾風 to beat with a head wind.

丨馬 to turn the horse quickly.

丨錯港口 to miss reaching one's port.

豕 ˊsh' An animal akin to a badger or ratel, called 丨犺; it is likened to a dog, a fox, and a monkey, and has a resemblance to them all.

豕 ˊsh' The character is designed to represent the *legs*, *bristles*, and *tail* of a hog; it is the 152d radical of characters mostly referring to swine; it is sometimes written 豸 in combination.

A hog, a pig; it represents the 12th stem, and the hour from 11 to 1 at night; it appertains to the second diagram 坎, and relates to water.

牧丨 a swineherd.

畜丨 domestic animals.

丨苓 a root resembling China-root.

矢 ˊsh' Composed of 入 and 矛 contracted to resemble the *barb* and *feather* of an arrow; it is the 111th radical of a few similar characters relating to darts.

A javelin; in *mathematics*, the versed sine; swift as an arrow; direct, openly; to arrange; to marshal; marshaled; to resolve, to form a purpose; to swear; used for the next; a game of pitch rod.

一丨之地 a bowshot, a little distance.

發一丨 shot one arrow.

丨直 straight as an arrow's flight.

丨誓 to take an oath.

丨其文德 he displayed his virtue and accomplishments.

丨志不移 he will not violate his word.

馬丨 horse-dung.

屎 ˊsh' From *body* and *rice*; but the original form is composed of 艸 *plants* and 胃 *stomach* contracted.

Filth, ordure; secretions; small stars near Columba.

丨坑 a public necessary.

丨桶 a close chair.

丨棋 a poor chess-player.

眼丨 secretion of the eyes.

Read ˛*hi*, and used with the next. A low moaning sound.

民之方殿丨 the people now sigh and groan.

呞 ˛*sh'* An obsolete form of the last.

Read ˛*hi*. To groan; to mutter.

丨咿 to grumble, as when dissatisfied.

舐 䑛 舓 ʿ*sh'* From *tongue* and *person*; the other two forms are rarely used.

To lick, as a cow; to lap; to take up with the proboscis.

老牛丨犢 the old cow will lick her calf; — *met.* parental love.

丨痔 to lick the piles; *met.* an abject sycophant.

丨糖箬 he licks sugared leaves; —he flourishes on other people's money or patronage.

弛 ʿ*sh'* From *bow* and *also*.

To ease off the bowstring, to unstring a bow; to cast off, to relax; to annul, to abrogate; dissolute, unconcerned; spoiled, injured.

廢丨 careless; failing, growing old or useless; obsolete.

解丨 to unloose, to throw off restraint.

丨力 slack, remiss.

丨放 to allay, to weaken.

規模日丨 the regulations daily become weaker.

丨禁 to rescind a law; to abrogate.

始 ʿ*sh'* From *woman* and *noble*.

The beginning; an opening, a start; to begin; the earliest; to be first; as an initial, then, at that time, was.

丨初 or 起丨 the beginning; the commencement; first.

丨終 or 丨末 first and last; the circumstances; human life, the whole period.

萬物資丨 the outburst of nature in spring.

丨創 invented, first made.

丨准賣 it will then be right to sell it.

丨知大道 he then understood the true philosophy.

未丨 there is nothing of the sort.

丨祖 the founder of a family.

元丨 creation; when the thing began.

諟 ʿ*sh'* From *words* and *is*; formerly used with its primitive.

Right principles; right, proper; to examine whether a thing is proper; to discern.

審丨 to lay or compare things together.

丨日 this day, now.

顧丨天之明命 to inquire into the lucid decrees of heaven.

使 ʿ*sh'* From *man* and *office*; in Cantonese read ʿ*shai*, because ʿ*sz'* has the same sound as 死 death.

To order, to command; to send, to employ, to commission; to cause, to effect; to occasion; to permit, to serve one's self of; expense, use, service.

丨喚 to call, as a servant; to be at one's call.

丨不挾四方 he was not permitted to possess the realm.

丨不得 unserviceable; useless.

是信是丨 he both trusts and employs them.

可以丨得 it will answer; it can do.

白丨口 idle talk; he has only to talk; — he does nothing.

丨人進京 send a man into Peking.

丨用 an outlay; the necessary expenses.

丨民以時 employ the people when they have leisure.

假丨 supposing, if so.

丨脾氣 sulky, cross.

丨費大 it will be expensive.

丨勁兒 to exert strength.

指丨 to direct; to allot to their places or duties.

公丨 a public officer, an envoy.

Read *sh'*ˀ A messenger; a servant sent to inquire; an agent.

丨臣 an envoy, a legate.

丨者 one who is sent.

丨出 a deputy.

天丨 an angel.

一個來丨 one messenger.

侍 *sh'*ˀ From *man* and *court* as the phonetic.

Near to, waiting on; following, as an attendant; to receive, as orders; to accompany.

丨衛 imperial guards; their office is the 丨衛處 within the Forbidden City in Peking.

群僕丨御之臣 all the [Emperor's] personal attendants and officers.

丨郎 a gentleman in waiting; a vice-president of a Board.

服丨 to wait on, to serve.

常丨 a eunuch.

垂手丨立 to stand respectfully waiting.

丨以仁義 he maintains his humanity and rectitude.

丨從ˀ followers.

丨奉 persons in waiting.

恃 *sh'*ˀ From *heart* and *court* as the phonetic.

To lean on, to trust to; looking up to for protection or support; *met.* a mother; to presume on; dull, unintelligent.

失丨 to lose a mother.

無母何丨 who shall I lean on, now my mother is dead?

倚丨 to depend on.

丨勢 to presume on one's power or station.

丨有手足 he relies on his adherents or brothers.

丨寵 to presume on being a favorite, and oppress others.

不足丨 untrustworthy.

丨財 to confide in riches.

丨刁 impudent, audacious.

自丨 self-confident.

怙丨 one's parents.

士 *sh'*) From 十 *ten* and 一 *one*, because a scholar is acquainted from one to ten, or with all things; it resembles *t'u* 土 *earth*, and is the 33d radical of a few incongruous characters.

In early times an officer, a minister; a warrior; then a learned or upright man, a scholar; a gentleman; an able-bodied man; a husband; in some cases, Sir, you; soldiers, statesmen; one who manages a department, and hence the duties of his post; one of the aids to the white king in chess.

紳 丨 the gentry.

丨 大 夫 gentry, officials, and graduates.

大 學 丨 title of first rank of cabinet ministers.

丨 卒 a soldier.

有 依 其 丨 you have the strong to depend on.

釐 爾 丨 女 there is given you a heroic wife.

庶 吉 丨 a Hanlin doctor out of office.

騎 丨 a stout horseman.

居 丨 or 處 丨 a private scholar, a country gentleman.

天 文 丨 an astronomer.

勇 丨 or 壯 丨 a valiant or strong man.

惟 其 丨 女 篚 厥 玄 黃 its men and women brought their baskets of azure and yellow silks.

文 丨 a student.

丨 農 工 商 the literary or official, agricultural, mechanical, and mercantile classes; — an ancient division of Chinese society.

女 修 丨 sisters of charity; female teachers; — a foreign term.

仕 *sh'*) From *man* and *scholar* as the phonetic.

To fill an office; to learn; to serve, to occupy a station or post; a public officer; one of the aids to the black king in chess.

出 丨 to enter on office.

致 丨 or 卸 丨 to resign a post.

丨 宦 之 家 an honorable family.

不 爲 祿 丨 to hold office not for salary and name, — but for the good of the people.

弗 問 弗 丨 he neither inquires [about people], nor puts them in office.

丨 途 official affairs.

丨 版 a merit register of officials.

閧 *sh'*) From *door* and *court*; it was once synonymous with its primitive.

A eunuch; a chamberlain, an officer in waiting; a court or official hall.

丨 人 a eunuch.

是 *sh'*) From 日 the *sun* and 正 *exact* altered to 𤴓, denoting the sun on the meridian.

The substantive *verb* is, to be, am; it is so, it is proper, denoting a quality of truth rather than of mere existence; right, correct, that which the mind approves; when repeated, it has the force of a contrast, and may be rendered whether — or, whatever; after an assertion 丨 也 is used to enforce it, like verily, no mistake; a *pronoun* this, these, that which, — in which case it follows the subject; before a clause, it has often a passive meaning, and throws it into the past tense; such, thus.

不 丨 no, not so.

若 丨 乎 is it so? perhaps.

丨 必 certainly.

丨 的 or 丨 也 truly so, yes; just so.

丨 日 on that day, at the time spoken of.

丨 以 therefore, by this means.

有 不 丨 partly wrong, in error.

百 祿 丨 荷 a hundred perquisites were what he received; — he enjoyed all kinds of emoluments.

你 丨 他 打 傷 麽 丨 的 was you injured by his blow? Yes, I was.

丨 伊 踹 死 了 it was trodden to death by him.

豈 丨 水 之 性 哉 how can that be the property of water?

丨 假 丨 眞 is it false or true?

丨 故 on this account; this is the reason.

丨 則 言 丨 if it be so, say so.

丨 否 or 丨 不 丨 is it so or not?

丨 否 有 當 if it be deemed proper or right.

第 個 丨 儂 個 呢 勿 丨 is this your's or not? (*Shanghai.*)

曾 丨 在 位 [sad it is] that he would have them in office.

一 塲 丨 非 a great debate about the rights of it.

丨 實 in very truth.

擔 不 丨 or 擔 待 人 的 不 丨 to take another's faults; to bear with people's errors.

丨 凡 丨 聖 三 教 原 歸 一 理 whether among laic or clerical, the three religions all have one principle.

禔 *sh'*) From *dress* and *correct*; also read *t'i*, and to be distinguished from 禔 ease.

Fully and handsomely dressed.

衣 厚 丨 丨 elegantly and richly apparelled.

市 *sh'*) Said to be composed of 冂 a *wild* and 及 to *reach* within it, because things reach a market.

A square or open place for bartering; a market; a crowd, as of market-people; crowded, vulgar; saleable, marketable; to trade, to bid or offer a price; to encourage, as talent.

丨 價 the market price.

丨 井 or 丨 頭 or 丨 口 兒 a market; *met.* the air or manner of the market, vulgar.

罷 丨 to refuse to trade, to withdraw from the market; it is often done to resist exactions.

鎮 丨 a great market.

墟 丨 a country-fair.

發 丨 or 開 丨 to commence selling.

起 丨 saleable; said too of one who thinks too much of himself.

行丨 the exchange or bourse; current rate.

初上丨 just come into market, — as the first shad.

丨恩 to get people's goodwill.

丨平 (or 秤) market scales.

丨俗 vulgar, unpolished.

丨語 billingsgate, low slang.

丨井之流 a lowlived skinflint.

都丨 the fair of a township.

行丨機靈 the market price is rather going up.

柹 *sh'*) From *tree* and *market* as the phonetic.

The persimmon or China fig (*Diospyrus*), of which there are several varieties.

丨餅 or 乾丨 dried persimmons (called figs), prepared for export.

牛心丨 the ox-heart persimmon; a small yellowish sort.

鷄心丨 a small red kind.

水浸丨 a yellow persimmon that is soaked to remove the astringency.

丁香丨 the small cherry persimmon, from Nganhwui.

丨霜 sugar obtained from the persimmon.

西紅丨 the tomato. (*Pekingese.*)

氏 *sh'*) Supposed to be altered from 𠩺 or 岸 a *cliff;* as the original form delineates a beetling crag ready to fall; it is the 83d radical of a few incongruous characters.

A family; one of a clan or gens; after a name, once denoted the head of the clan, but now also that the person is a woman; an ancient title of honor; after a principality, denoted its ruler; an officer; a person.

羅丨 the clan or family of Lo.

黃門李丨 Mrs. Hwang née Li.

該丨 the said female.

釋丨 the Budhists.

張丨宗祠 the ancestral hall of the Chang family.

王謂尹丨 the king said to the chief of the Yin gens.

視 眎 眡 *sh'*) The last two characters are rarely met with.

To see, to inspect, to observe; to see and imitate, to take knowledge of; to behave to; to compare and regard; to have a regard to; to cause to be seen, to view as; to display.

近丨眼 near-sighted.

不丨其饋 he disregarded his offering.

丨而不見 I looked but did not pay attention to it.

丨乃厥祖 he imitated his ancestor.

丨死如歸 I look upon dying as going home.

藐丨我 he is supercilious towards me.

斜丨 to glance at sideways.

丨聽言動 to see, to hear, to talk, and to act — properly, are four duties.

丨法故人 to imitate the ancients.

丨履考祥 observe their conduct and act like the good.

丕丨功載 widely display the record of their meritorious services.

丨人猶己 to view others as one's self.

丨事 to examine a case.

明丨 the hare in the moon.

丨此有加 it seems to be bigger than this.

莫丨爲具文 do not regard it as a trifling matter.

昔與絲伍今乃芥丨 it was formerly classed with silk, but is now regarded as more like mustard; — said of a kind of hempen plant.

示 礻 *sh'*) Composed of 上 or 二 *above* and three lines below it to represent the *light* of sun, moon, and stars coming down to earth; it forms the 113th radical of characters relating to religious matters, and is often contracted to the second form in composition, when it is easily mistaken for the contracted form of ˏ衣 garments.

To show, to make known the will of heaven to mankind; to proclaim, to signify to the people; to show to the sight; an edict, or notice from an official; a manifestation or revelation; a prognostic or sign; in polite phrase, another's wishes; a letter; to see into, to compare, and occurs interchanged with the last.

出丨曉諭 to issue an edict for general information.

來丨 your answer.

訓丨 will you give directions to me? — said by inferior officers.

丨下 to let me know, an epistolary phrase.

手丨 your letter.

丨衆 to admonish the people, as by an execution.

祈爲丨知 I beg you will acquaint me.

指丨 to indicate.

Read ˏk'i, when used for 祇. The god which animates the earth.

世 *shi'*) From 一 *one* under 卅 or three 十 *tens*, to denote the prolongation of days to thirty years.

An age, a generation; the world, mankind; times, life, seasons; experience of life; hereditary; successively; to enfeoff; during the times of; from age to age; perpetual; in divination refer's to the diagrams which denote ones self.

一丨 one generation.

丨代 generations.

丨丨 during the ages; for ever.

出丨 to be born.

過丨 or 辭丨 or 去'丨 to die.

今丨 or 當丨 the present time, this age.

刑罰丨輕丨重 punishments and fines should be light in one age, and severe in another.

永丨克孝 all your life you was filial.

丨上人 or 丨間人 people now-a-days.

創丨界 made his own way in the world.
丨界不好 bad times, unlucky in life, not getting on.
不近丨情 he does not know the world.
丨業 a calling, an occupation.
丨兄 a friend's brother.
丨姪 an old friend's son; used by one's self.
丨交 friends of many generations.
幾丨傳 how many generations has it been handed down?
丨襲男爵 a hereditary baron.
來丨 a future life; the next transmigration, which contains the 西方極樂丨界 or paradise of the West, the elysium of common people.
無丨情 in no business, retired.
丨界如輪轉 the ups and downs of life; vicissitudes.
沒丨而名稱 your reputation will be known after you are gone.
終丨 the whole life.
論其丨也 he considers their history and times.
不丨之功 unequaled heroism.
丨尊 one honored by the world, (Sanscrit, *lokadjyeshta*,) an epithet of every Budha.
丨家 an old and honorable family.
濟丨之才 able to rescue the country.
必丨而後仁 one generation must pass before his humanity will be appreciated.
應丨作丨 to act one's part in the world.
丨態炎涼 the feelings of people alter much; *lit.* are cold and hot.
丨守無失 in perpetuity, as land kept in a family, or held in fee simple.

貰ˀ *shi'* From *wealth* and *world;* also read *shé*.

To get credit for, to buy on credit; to borrow; to show lenity.
丨赦 to pardon.
出丨器皿 to let out furniture.
丨酒 to get drink on the score.
丨貸 to borrow.

逝ˀ *shi'* From to *go* and to *break*.

To pass away, to depart; to go to, approaching; lost to life, to die; gone; an initial and affirmative particle.
丨者如斯 such are the dead,—as flowing water.
長丨 or 溘丨 gone the long journey, passed away for ever.
知音已丨 my bosom friend has gone.
言不可丨矣 words are not to be cast away.
丨不古處 he certainly cannot stay here as before.

謚ˀ **諡**ˀ *sh'ʾ* From 言 *words* and 益 *basin*; the second form is an erroneous alteration.

The results of virtuous conduct seen after death; a laudatory name conferred by the Emperor after death, as 封 denotes one given in life; the custom began in the Cheu dynasty; the posthumous title; to confer such titles, as Commissioner Lin 林則徐 was called 林文忠 by the Emperor; a memoir or eulogy; peace, as of the grave.
丨法 rules for honorary titles for the dead.
死丨 or 丨名 or 丨號 the epitaph name

豉ˀ *sh'ʾ* *ˎch'* From *pulse* and to *exhibit;* to be distinguished from *ˎku* 鼓 drum.

Salted oysters, beans, olives, or other fruits, dried and used as condiments; the taste of salt fish.
荳丨 salted beans.
麪丨 salted beans and flour.
丨油 soy, an English word probably derived from this name.
欖丨 olives salted without the stone.
丨蟲 a species of water beetle.

事ˀ *sh'ʾ* Composed of 史 and 之 *write it*, contracted in combination, to denote a record of events.

An affair, a matter; business, traffic; an occupation, a service; its course or conduct; duties, functions; to go at, to take in hand; that which is done, an act; a case in court; a subject, a theme; to serve, to obey; to have business to do; an officer; to manage a business..
公丨 public business.
緊丨 important business.
丨禮 rules or courtesies of a profession.
好心丨 good natured, friendly.
好丨 to give to beggars or to charitable objects.
有丨 busy; something going on.
丨頭 and 丨仔 master and servant; boss and clerks or men. (*Cantonese.*)
你做甚麼丨 what are you doing?
丨父母 to help one's parents.
丨丨周到 everything is done.
不丨丨 he does not attend properly to anything.
一件丨 a single affair.
主丨 secretaries in the Boards; a graduate lower than a *tsinsz'*.
多丨 troublesome.
丨情 or 丨務 business, affairs; the first also means employment, a place, a post; — the second its duties.
丨丨如意 may everything be as you wish.
理丨官 a senator, — in Macao.
丨有不實 this is erroneous.
不曉丨 ignorant of life; stupid, malaprop.
老世丨 or 歷練世丨 well versed in worldly affairs, an old stager.
奉差丨 sent on special business.
不丨遷延 not use (or allow) any further delay.
隄防丨中生丨 have a care lest some trouble grow out of this.

戺 扆 sh'' } From *door* and a *horary* character; the second is most used. The pivot in a door which rests in sockets above and below, and turns in them; the projecting edge of a raised platform near the ascent, where a sentry stood; a wall on sides of a stairway.

人夾兩階丨 four men stood on each side of the steps on the platform.

澨 溡 sh'' } A small islet in the midst of a stream; a hummock in a river; water rising still higher, and standing at that point.

嗜 sh'' From *mouth* and an *old man*. To relish, as good living; to take delight in; to have an appetite for, to indulge in, greedy; sensual, lecherous.

丨于飲食 fond of the table.

不丨酒 not given to wine.

丨慾無窮 unrestrained licentiousness.

如蚊之丨 as greedy as a musketo for blood.

丨好' to love, as a dish.

不丨善言 to disrelish good advice.

試 sh'' From *words* and a *pattern*. To try, to experiment; to use, to serve of; to compare and find out; to tempt, to test; to experiment; to examine, as the literary graduates; a trial, an examination; disciplined, tried.

丨一丨 or 丨丨看 try once; see how it goes.

嘗丨 to taste, to make a trial of.

立丨 to institute a trial.

丨手勢 to try one's skill or prowess.

丨驗 to verify; see if it turn out so.

丨演 to practice, to drill, to test.

會丨 the examination for *tsinsz'*.

鄉丨 the examination for *küjin*; and 殿丨 is that for Hanlin.

丨想 think it well over once.

私人之子百僚是丨 the sons of the poor are the officers in the public service.

丨看 or 但丨 try if it will do; take a look.

丨用 let him have a trial, as an expectant officer.

刑不丨而民咸服 if punishments are not reckless, the people generally obey — their rulers.

探丨口供 let us see what he will say.

丨而言之 first try and then speak about it.

弒 sh'' From 式 *pattern* and 殺 to *kill* contracted. To murder a superior.

丨君 a regicide.

丨父 a parricide.

丨其主 he killed his master.

啻 ch'' t'i' Composed of 口 *mouth* and 帝 *ruler*; not to be confounded with 啼 to crow; 翅 is used for it. Only; to stop at; an overplus.

不丨 not only, more than.

何丨萬千 can it stop at thousands and myriads?

不丨不有爾土 you will not only not have your lands.

不丨如自己口出 it was not merely his own assertion.

感之不丨父母 more grateful to him than to his parents.

奚丨 why stop?

扡 sh'' To drag along; to trail after.

析薪丨矣 he cut up the faggots and hauled them along.

丨徙桑梓 to move one's residence.

Read *'t'o*. To lead, as water.

Read *'i*. To add to; to separate from, to leave.

誓 shi' From *words* and to *break*. To take an oath, to swear; to bind one's self or another; an oath; a vow or binding promise; it is performd by breaking an arrow, killing a cock, burning a writing, and otherwise; none are required by native magistrates; to caution, to order; to receive orders; to contract with; solemnly; private espousals, regarded as improper.

發丨 or 矢丨 to swear.

盟丨 to take an oath, involving a penalty or sanction.

丨愿 to adjure.

燒丨章 to burn a written oath, as testimony sent to the next world.

發假丨 to swear falsely.

丨約 a private contract of marriage.

丨不爲此 I swear it is not this one.

山盟海丨 [an unalterable oath of marriage,] stable as the hills and seas.

丨師 to get the loyalty of troops.

丨不兩立 I swear that both of us cannot stand.

當天明丨 I swear it before Heaven.

勢 shi' From *strength* and *skill*. Power, authority; influence; pomp, dignity, grandeur; strength, or that wherein it lies; resources; virility of males; air, exterior, figure; condition, state of.

丨力 strength, prowess, ability.

威丨大 having great authority.

好丨頭 a good omen.

嚇丨 to scare, to pretend to browbeat.

丨利之人 fawns on the rich.

在丨 in authority.

割丨 to castrate, usually refers to man.

來丨甚兇 very savage looking.

大丨 the empire.

丨所必然 I am compelled to have it so, it must be so.

丨兇 fierce, irascible, desperate; in excess.

形丨 aspect, position; mostly said of places or buildings.

丨子 figure, bearing, attitude; also, the male organ.

乘丨 improve the occasion.

打把丨 to show one's strength or skill in boxing or gymnastics.

打手丨 to do tricks.

騎虎之丨 [in for it,] as when one rides a tiger; — there's no backing down.

忘丨 indifferent to the powerful.

倣虎丨 to use a tiger's power; *met.* inexorable, severe.

SHIH.

Old sounds, ship, snek, shap, zhit, zhik, *and* zhak. *In Canton*, shăp, shik, shek, shat, shit, ch'ik, *and* ship; — *in Swatow*, sit, sip, sek, chió, *and* chap; — *in Amoy*, sip, sit, siet, *and* sek; — *in Fuhchau*, sik, sek, siòh, sóü, *and* sièh; — *in Shanghai*, sak, säk, zäk seh, *and* zeh; — *in Chifu*, shi.

石, *₍shih* Said to be formed of 厂 a *cliff* over 口 *mouth*, to represent rocks; it is the 112th radical of a natural group of characters relating to rocks.

A stone; rocks, called the bones of hills; ledges; stony, as land; made of stone; petrified; hard; sonorous musical stones; firm, decided; barren, as the womb; a stone or weight of a picul, varying from 100 to 180 and more catties, in different places and for various articles; a liquid measure; an ærolite; a stone used to test strength in lifting; a classifier of coarse cloth and hides; in common usage, it is sometimes written for 擔 a picul, and pronounced *₍tan*.

丨頭 a stone; stones, rocks.

粉丨 soft stone, figure-stone or agalmatolite, used for seals.

他山之丨可以攻玉 we work gems by using stones from other hills; — each thing has its use.

丨膏 gypsum.

浮丨 pumice.

青丨 common granite at Canton.

硯丨 or 老坑丨 argillite or shale, good for inkstones.

磵丨 or 紅丨 freestone, red sandstone.

臘丨 greasy, yellowish quartz.

打丨 to cut stone.

玄精丨 blue limestone.

戥猪丨 one who is brought to a wedding uninvited, as a makeweight to the groom. (*Cantonese.*)

風起丨燕飛 [the fable is,] when the wind blows, the stone pectens fly away.

丨街 a paved street.

丨花 or 丨衣 lichens or fungi.

青苔丨 a mossy stone; knaves are likened to it.

丨敢當 it can resist the noxious influences like a rock; — a phrase cut on tablets to ward off bad luck.

玉丨俱焚 the good and bad were alike consumed.

一拳丨之多 as much as a fistfull of stone; — a little.

米丨 the amount or piculs of rice; rice in bulk.

飲酒一丨 he can drink a jug of spirits.

頑丨點頭 the playful stones nodded their heads — to Budha.

頭號丨 the heaviest stone tried by military candidates; it weighs 300 catties.

In *Cantonese.* To calender cloth with the stone.

丨加 twice calendered.

碩, *shi˒* *shwoh˒* Also read *shoh*,

Great, corpulent; full, ripe; eminent, highminded; to fill.

丨彥 eminent, talented.

丨學高才 of solid learning and great talents.

丨大無朋 of unequaled ability.

苗丨 filled shoots, *i. e.* ripe grain.

丨輔 a high statesman, one near the throne

食, *₍shi* Formed of 亼 to *collect* and 皀 *white*, referring to a *white kernel* of rice; it is the 184th radical of characters relating to food.

To nourish the body by eating and drinking; to take food; to live on; to devour; a meal; viands; to take back, to retract; to smoke; to be in the receipt of, to enjoy; to impose on, to fool; to take, as in chess; a support; food; emoluments; revenues; used for the next, an eclipse.

丨物 food.

伙丨 daily allowance, wages, supplies.

丨自己 to find one's self.

丨祿 drawing pay, on a salary.

今也每丨無餘 now nothing is left at any meal.

耳丨不化 to hear and not attend to or understand.

終丨之間 during a meal, a little while, a half-hour.

大丨 a name given to the Arabs in the T'ang dynasty, and denoting the Tajiks and Bagdad caliphs.

丨二尺 [this boat] draws two feet.

小丨 a lunch.

丨人餘唾 a plagiarist, one who pilfers his compositions.

目丨 ornamental dishes; to look at wistfully.

决不丨言 don't promise and not perform.

丨開來 to injure as it spreads, as oil on paper.

隔丨 my food does not set well.

好丨 well-tasted, delicious.
獵丨者 one who forages around, a bummer, a sorner.
丨肉 to eat flesh; to feast on a sacrifice.
餴丨 fruit and wild animals, food eaten without dressing.
丨貨 food and goods; it sometimes answers nearly to political economy.
對丨 husband and wife.
血丨 a sacrifice.
丨量 to be a soldier.
吞丨肥己 to eat one's self fat, to grow rich out of others.
飯丨錢 allowance to servants for food.
白丨 a white patch in the skin.

Read *sz'* and used with 飼. To feed, to set food before; to rear, to bring up; food, provision.
牛羊人所丨 men rear sheep and oxen.
飲之丨之 give them food and drink.
治人者丨於人 governors of men are supported by men;—rulers are fed by their people.

蝕, *shih* From *insect* and *to eat*.
To injure gradually, to eat away, as a worm does; to incroach on.
日丨 and 月丨 solar and lunar eclipses, so called because the disks appear as if gradually eaten away.
侵丨家產 to gradually incroach on and use up the patrimony.
丨損 damage; to fritter away, as an estate.
丨本 to lose money in trade.
丨子 to take, as in chess.

祏, *sh'* From *worship* and a *stone*.
A stone shrine placed in the family temple to keep the ancestral tablet safe in case of fire.
典守石丨 I enjoin on you to guard well the stone shrine.

飾, **餙**, *shih* From 食 *to eat* for the phonetic, and 人 with 巾 denoting *personal things;* the second form is little used.
To adorn, to paint, to ornament; to set off; to gloss over, to pretend, to patch up; to excuse; to make believe; to wipe, to brighten; concord in music; to dress a victim for sacrifice; a facing or binding; an ornament; weapons.
首丨 female head ornaments.
裝丨 bedizened, tricked out; to impose on, specious.
粉丨彌縫 the facts were glossed over and colored; it was all whitewashed.
修丨 to adorn, to brighten up; to polish, as style.
掩丨不來 his pretense did not do.
矯丨外貌 to put on an appearance — of sternness.
厲丨 a martial look; said of the Emperor.
文過丨非 he slurred over and excused his crimes.

釋, *shih'* From to *distinguish* and to *keep* at, referring to selecting and separating.
To unloose; to free; to liberate, to put from one; to explain, to open out the meaning; to relax; to slight or let alone; to leave; to melt or dissipate; to soften by soaking.
丨門 Budhist priests.
丨回 to liberate, as from exile or the sway of evil passions.
丨放 to let out from confinement.
丨恨 to hate no longer.
丨手 to unhand, to part from.
冰丨瓦解 the ice has melted and the tiles loosened; *met.* to remove or explain misstatements, to allay fears; to dissipate rumors.
註丨 to unfold the meaning.
如丨重負 [glad] as one relieved of a heavy burden.

丨難攻易 to avoid the difficult, to attempt the easy.
丨迦提婆 (Sanscrit, *sakra deva*) Indra, known as 能天主 the valiant Lord of devas, and regarded as inferior to Budha.
丨家 or 丨氏 the Budhists, derived from 丨迦牟尼 Sakya-muni, the solitary, the monk of the Sakyas, who died B. C. 543; defined by 能仁寂默 one who is mighty in humanity, and dwells in seclusion and silence; also called Budha, the most celebrated of the titles applied to him, because it is the name of the religion he founded, and denotes "the learned or awakened one;" it is a simple attribute added to the name by which the prince of Kapilavastu is known in the world; he is also called 帝丨 and 天帝丨 even by the Confucianists.

式, *shih'* From 弋 *dart* and 工 *work*.
A form, a fashion; an example; a rule, a law for a pattern; to make or do like a copy; to imitate; to respect, to look up to; reverently; to measure; to use, to serve; to cause; thereby, thereon; a cross-bar in a carriage, for which the next is also correct; to bow to it; and; an initial particle having the force of a copula, or an illative particle.
丨微丨微胡不歸 all reduced and poor, why do we not go back home?
丨樣 a pattern.
中'丨 or 合丨 like the sample, or to meet the standard; as 中'丨進士 the *tsinsz'* graduates who passed the examination.
丨號丨呼 amid clamor and bawling.
丨序在位 he regulates the position of the princes.
字丨 a copy-slip.
惟公是丨 taking your honor as my example.
格丨 a model.

欵 〡 form of address; style, air; sort, kind.

各 〡 all kinds — of goods.

〡 爾 purposely.

筆帖 〡 a copyist in the Boards.

軾, *shi'* A stretcher before a carriage or in a sedan, to lean on when bowing to others, called 扶手板 or leaning-board.

拭, **栻**, *shih'* From *hand* and *pattern*.

To wipe, to rub and dust with a duster; to brush away; to cleanse, as sheep.

〡 桌 wipe the table.

拂 〡 to wipe and dust.

〡 涕 or 〡 淚 to brush away tears.

〡 淨 to wash and rub clean.

適, *shi'* From to *go* and *origin*.

To go to, to reach; to pass over a long distance; a bride going to a husband's house; to marry out; to happen, to occur; to satisfy; to follow, to accord, to suit, to chime in with; an *adverb*, suddenly, presently just now, just then; usual; pleased, contented; a good degree, accomplished; to supply deficiencies.

〡 然 or 〡 爾 suddenly; accidentally.

〡 嫁 to marry a husband.

〡 意 very well, in good health; agreeable, charming, as a location.

〡 因 just because, then.

〡 從何來 where did you then come from?

無所 〡 從 no one to take the direction of the affair.

〡 間 just at that time, not long ago.

〡 值 happened just right, opportune.

妥 〡 properly done.

室人 〡 我 all the family blame me.

〡 我願 it meets my wishes.

〡 有客來 a visitor has come.

Read *tih*, and used for 嫡. To direct, to take the lead; superior; principal; to be bent on; to oppose; the legitimate heir; an enemy.

無 〡 I am not set on doing it.

誰 〡 與謀 who will devise the plans?

〡 士 a fine scholar.

無 〡 也 no settled purpose, no grit

胸中無 〡 莫之見 I have no fixed opinion upon the point.

Read *tseh*, and used for 讁. To blame, to take to task.

勿予禍 〡 do not punish nor reprove us.

邿, *ₛshi* Frequently written like the next.

A small fief, 〡 邡 in the present Sz'ch'uen, conferred on a general in the Han dynasty.

十, *ₛshi* "East and west is 一 *one*, north and south is 丨 *descending*, joined they make 十 *ten*, and complete a circuit;" it forms the 24th radical of a few miscellaneous characters; the next is its complex form.

Ten, "the end of reckoning."

第 〡 the tenth.

〡 一 eleven.

〡 分之一 one tenth.

〡 幾個 ten and more.

〡 來個 there are nearly ten.

〡 足 complete; pure, as gold.

〡 分 ten parts, all; very, first-rare, perfect; a common superlative.

〡 字路 cross-roads.

〡 全 entire, as a recovery.

〡 賒不如九現 better sell nine things for ready money than ten for credit.

〡 死一生 ten to one he'll die.

〡 成得八 I got eight parts out of ten.

〡 不全 all are incomplete.

聞一知 〡 he perceives all on hearing a little.

〡 分稱讚 to lavish praise indiscriminately.

拾, *ₛshi* From *hand* and to *unite*; occurs for *sheh*, 涉 to wade, and much used for the last as a complex form.

To collect, to gather up, to pick up; to clear away, as dishes; to bring together, to arrange; an archer's armlet; to take turns in shooting a bow; to ford a stream; inclining to, gradual approach to.

〡 起來 to pick up.

收 〡 絲綸 I am going to take my fishing-tackle — somewhere else; *i. e.* try a new business.

〡 下去 take them away.

執 〡 東西 to properly arrange things.

路不 〡 遺 they did not pick up what was dropped in the way.

〡 級而登 to lift up the dress and ascend.

〡 地芥 [easy] as picking up a straw.

〡 翠踏青 to clean up the green [grass], and tread the verdure, as when worshiping the tombs.

什, *ₛshi* From *man* and *ten*; used for 甚 very.

A file of ten soldiers or two files of five each; sundries; a tithe.

〡 物 things, household gear.

〡 錦小菜 condiments, seasoning.

其實皆 〡 一也 the real [proportion paid] was a tithe.

〡 麼 what? this dissyllable has a wide signification, and is much used after a negative like not at all, none of, not so; as 不是 〡 麼正經話 not at all the correct thing in talking.

收買 〡 物 we buy up any odds and ends.

算 〡 麼東西 who is that fellow? what can that thing do?

篇 〡 verses of ten lines; books, writings.

炒 〡 件 to roast fowl giblets.

不犯了 〡 麼罪 I have done no wrong.

〡 長 the corporal over a decury, a decurion.

失ˎ ˏshi Composed of 手 *hand* and 乙 *curved* combined.

Without control; to lose, to mislay; to omit, to neglect, to disregard, to fail; to err, to miss, to jeopardize; to leave behind; to slip; to fail in; to lose favor; failure, an omission, a fault; accidental.

丨物 to lose a thing.

過丨 an error, delinquencies.

丨覺 to overlook, to forget; absent-minded.

丨信 to forfeit one's word.

丨手 to let slip, to drop.

丨脚 or 丨足 to slip up, to lose one's foothold.

丨風 foundered; upset.

丨了 lost, as a thing, a dog; but 丨之 used after an assertion indicates that it is erroneous.

丨禮 disrespectful, rude to; or 丨敬 wanting in regard; — are polite phrases for, You do me honor; Thank you.

丨時 behind time; to miss the hour.

丨本 lost the principal.

萬無一丨 not the least deficiency or mistake in it.

丨察 to neglect to inquire into, to be careless in overseeing.

丨記 I forgot it.

不丨其馳 no error was seen in driving — the carriage.

丨口 speechless, dying; mistaken, spoke wrong.

丨身 she has lost her virtue.

丨體面 disgraced, unbecoming, reproachful.

丨位 or 丨國 lost his crown.

丨民心 forfeited the people's affections.

丨魂 stupid, inattentive, witless; — a term of abuse.

丨神 absent-minded; abstracted.

患得患丨 distressed till he gets it, and then distressed lest he loses it, — as an office.

不丨爲好人 yet he may be regarded as good.

丨火 it caught fire, as a house.

丨落 lost by mislaying; dropped and lost it.

丨所 driven from their homes.

丨於敎訓 lost the proper time for instruction.

不丨言不丨人 [the wise man] does not mistime his words, nor use the wrong man for his purpose.

丨傳 lost the record of or use of.

打前丨 to stumble, as a horse.

實ˎ **寔**ˎ ˏshih From a *covering* over a *string of pearls* or *is;* the first form is commonest.

Real, solid; full, compact; true, honest, sincere; fixed, as a price; hard, as a knot; the reality, the results; effects, fruits, or facts of a thing; fruit of plants, harder and smaller than 菓 fleshy fruit; verily, in fact; to fill, to cram; to put inside, though not implying filled; to be really; positively, exactly; is; the worked factor in a sum, as the multiplicand or dividend; in *rhetoric*, a thesis, an argument.

丨在 or 丨首 really, verily, in fact.

丨情的 it is certainly so.

丨丨落落 securely, safely, honestly.

丨丨 solid-looking.

老丨話 I speak the truth.

結丨 or 成丨 the fruit has set; —*met.* the affair is done; too late.

老丨人 an honest plain man.

丨價 the fixed, actual price.

丨事 an actual thing or event.

事丨 the facts of a matter.

徙富民丨北京 [Yung-loh] moved the rich people to Peking to fill it.

丨命不同 our lots are not alike.

丨堅丨好 [the grain] became strong and good.

丨心相交 a real sincere friend.

軍丨 military stores.

着丨 in earnest, to set about vigorously.

丨數 the full tale or complement.

丨不瞞你 I really do not deceive you.

以昭核丨 is according to the real facts.

予恐來世以台爲口丨 I am afraid future ages will fill their mouths about me.

丨授任署 the real incumbent of the office.

丨銀 the real amount.

不肯丨吐 he refused to confess or disclose the matter.

名者丨之賓 reputation is the guest of real merit.

湜ˎ shi' Limpid clear water, like the River King in Shensi.

正丨 a sincere mind.

涇以渭濁丨丨其沚 the King is muddied by the Wei, but its bottom may be seen near the islets.

奭ˎ c'h'' From *great* and *two hundred.*

To flourish, to abound; to color up, to flush; a carnation color.

召公丨 Shih, the duke of Chau, B. C. 1110; he was also called 君丨 Prince Shih, and was Grand Protector to King Ching.

路車有丨 red shone the state carriage.

螫ˎ shi' ˏchŏ From *insect* and to *forgive.*

To poison, to sting; venemous; the poison of a sting; a sting; troublesome, malignant.

丨虫 the poisonous insect, applied to the scorpion.

辛丨 a virulent poison, malignant.

丨着 stung, bitten.

蠍子丨了 the scorpion stung me.

毒丨 poisonous; oppressive, as bad laws.

襫ˎ c'h' A rain cloak, called 襏丨 made of leaves.

禮義以爲襏丨 propriety and right should be [as close to one] as his garments.

識, From *words* and *marl* or sticky clay as the primitive.

ˎshi *chih'* To know by learning; to recognize, to distinguish; knowledge; a mental power or emotion, in which sense Budhists use it for consciousness; to be aware of, acquainted with; versed in, expert; an acquaintance.

不丨不知 I neither understand nor know — the reason of the thing.

認丨 to recognize.

見丨過人 he is more clever than most men.

丨貨 a connoisseur of things.

丨透機關 I am fully aware of his plans.

舊相丨 an old acquaintance.

目不丨丁 he does not know [a character as easy as] 丁 *ˎting*.

熟丨 intimate with.

禮丨 polite, easy in his manners.

不丨有諸 I do not know whether it is so or not.

迷丨 knowing evil.

六丨 a Budhist term for the six *vidjnanas* or mental functions, of which 意 thought (*manas*) is the last.

多聞丨 of varied and great information.

似曾相丨叉歸來 it seems as if I recognized him, like a swallow which has returned in the spring.

Read *chi'* and used with 誌 To remember; to keep in mind.

三爵不丨 at the third cup you lose your recollection.

埴, *shih'* Adhesive clay.

搏丨 to mold in clay.

擿丨 to feel one's way with a stick.

鞋, *shi'* A leather sheath for a sword.

刀丨 a scabbard for a knife.

室, From *shelter* and *at; q. d.* he has reached the place where he stops.

shih' A place of rest, a house, a dwelling, an abiding place; a mansion, as for a king; a room or inner apartment; a wife; kindred, family; a household; the royal family; to marry; a nest; a grave, a last resting place; a case for a thing.

正丨 or 配丨, and 側丨 terms for a wife and concubine.

三十有丨 at thirty marry.

受丨 to take a wife.

世丨 an ancestral hall.

家丨 a family; house; a household; a state.

丨家 houses; house, holds, people; betrothal ceremonies; a palace.

宮丨 the palace; noblemen's mansions.

箭丨 a quiver.

氷丨 an ice-house.

宗丨 of the Imperial clan.

乃有丨競競 when his House was in its prime.

升堂未入丨 you have reached the hall but not the chamber; — you have yet something to learn.

歸于其丨 he was gathered to his abode; *i. e.* buried.

丨人 my late wife; also attendants; females in a house.

丨星 the 13th zodiacal constellation of the stars Markab α and Sheat β in Pegasus; it is also the name of Raivata, a celebrated Budhist leader.

濕, 溼, From *water stagnant* and covered with earth; the second form is irregular.

shi' *ˎshi* Name of a river; wet, humid, moist, damp; lowlying grounds; disappointed, dejected.

丨水貨 damaged goods.

風丨 rheumatism.

漢其丨矣 scorched are the moist places.

丨氣 humid exhalations which cause disease.

丨生 animals produced in water, as fish, reptiles, mollusks.

鹹丨 saline efflorescence; damp; *met.* vulgar talk; dirty, frowzy, as clothes. (*Cantonese.*)

發丨 it has gathered dampness.

送丨禮 sent him a present of food, — not money.

印丨 stamp struck off and wet it.

水過地皮丨的事 a small matter, it only wet the ground.

丨丨 glossy, polished.

陰丨 dampened under cover, or from not being aired.

冷露丨桂花 the chill dew wets the olea.

搘, *ˊch'* To lean on a staff.

Read *ch'i'* To throw into; to hold, to grasp.

甚, From *ten* and *very*.

shih' Full, abundant, said of silkworms; to collect, or assemble.

鼫, From 鼠 *mouse* and 碩 *great* contracted; *q. d.* the great rat

shi' A grayish yellow animal found in hilly places, which burrows, and is destructive to the grain; it has a bushy tail which furnishes hair for pencils; it occurs in the northern and western provinces, and from the description seems to be the long tailed marmot, akin to the loir of Italy.

榊, Also read *ts'z'*.

shi' A hard, coarse-grained wood, fit for axles and naves.

丨楂子 a species of hawthorn or *Cratægus*, found in the midland provinces.

SHING.

Old sounds, shing *and* zhing. *In Canton*, shing *and* sheng ; — *in Swatow*, seng *and* sⁿia ; — *in Amoy*, seng *and* sìn ; — *in Fuhchau*, sing *and* séng ; — *in Shanghai*, săng *and* sang ; — *in Chifu*, shing.

升 ˏ*shăng* The original form is like that of 斗 a *peck*, both representing two things in a measure; interchanged with the next.

A Chinese measure of ten 合 and nearly equal to the English pint, or to 1.031 litre; it is the most common retail measure, and was once made to hold a catty of rice; to complete or bring about; a skien of 80 threads; the 46th diagram, denoting advancement; to advance, as by its own power; to rise, as in office; to accumulate.

一丨米 a pint of rice.
丨沈巳定 the good or bad luck of it is already fixed.
丨階 to go up the steps.
丨遐 to ascend to the distant place, — *i. e.* heaven.
丨堂 to enter court, to sit on the bench; in the outer hall.
筆丨 a pencil-cup.
男女無辨則亂丨 if the sexes are not kept apart, incests will arise.

In *Cantonese*. The thill of a sedan; a bamboo carrying-pole; to slap with the hand.
丨幾把掌 slapped him several times.
竹丨 a bamboo pole.

陞 ˏ*shăng* From *mound* and to *ascend*; used with the last.

To ascend, as stairs; to advance, to go up to; to rise, as in office.
丨官 promoted in rank.
丨啓 open it in your hall; — written on a letter.
指日高丨 may you soon be promoted to a high post.
丨炮 to fire a salute. (*Cantonese.*)
丨轎 to get into a sedan.
丨降 promotion and degradation.

昇 ˏ*shăng* To ascend, as the sun does; the sun in the zenith; tranquil, peaceful.
紅日東丨 the ruddy sun rises in the east.
丨平盛世 a tranquil and plenteous age.

勝 ˏ*shăng* *shăng*ˋ From *strength* and a *phonetic*.

Adequate to; to bear, to sustain, and usually preceded by a negative; worthy of; to elevate, to raise.
不丨 the highest degree of.
不可丨言 it cannot all be told, it is beyond description.
不丨任 inadequate to the post.
苦不丨言 words cannot describe my sorrows.
曷丨詑異 what inexpressibly strange talk!

Read *shăng*ˋ. To conquer, to get the victory; to excel, superior; best, excellent; to add.
花丨日 the seventh day of the first moon, or 人日 man-day, when a flowery head-dress used to be worn.
打丨仗 to win a battle.
好ˋ丨 to love to be first, Diotrephian.
得丨 victorious, conquering.
丨意 your fine thoughts; — a polite phrase.
不分丨負 neither had the victory.
丨過人 superior to others.
同心方丨兒 it is very well if we are of one mind.

聲 声 ˏ*shăng* From 耳 *ear* and 罄 tinkling *stones* contracted; the second is a common contraction.

A sound; a voice or tone; a note in music; music, harmony; the tones or inflections of words in speaking, of which from four to eight are indicated in various parts of China; a cry, a wail; language; verbally; reputation, celebrity; to speak; to utter sounds; to make known, to declare; to praise; in epitaphs, to exhibit, to be an example.
丨音 a sound, a noise.
丨勢大 powerful, influential.
平丨 and 仄丨 are the even tones and the deflected tones of words.
高丨 and 低丨 a high key and low key, as in singing.
丨尾 final sounds in talking or chanting; drawling tones.
聞丨 to hear a noise or rumor; to listen to your words.
丨聞 to report to a superior, to tell him what took place; in Budhism, a name (*sravaka*) for the personal disciples of Sakyamuni, who listened to his utterances; now applied to the lowest degree of saintship.
丨價 honored, in repute.
丨稱 to state verbally.
丨明此案 report clearly about this case.
丨名狼藉 a reputation for avarice.
先丨奪人 his name is enough to appal them.
發丨喊 call out loud to him.
響丨兒 a loud report.
此秋丨也 this then is the sound of autumn coming on!
丨敎不行 [the people] will not regard his admonitions.
有丨氣嗎 is there an answer? (*Cantonese.*)

In *Cantonese*. Careful; steady, as when lifting or carrying things.
好丨 be very cautious, take good care.

繩 From *silk* and a *frog*.
˛*shăng* A cord, string, or line, especially a builder's line; a line stretched taut; to adjust, to make right; to mark by a line; to enforce conformity to rule; to warn and restrain; to continue in succession; to praise.

丨子 or 一條丨 a string.

準丨 a line to go by; up to the mark.

搾成丨兒 or 打丨 to spin or twist cord.

繫赤丨 to tie the red cord; — to betroth.

子孫丨丨 a continuous line of descendants.

丨墨 a marking-line.

丨其祖武 to continue (or imitate) an ancestor's valor.

丨愆 to mark faults or shortcomings.

憴 Used with the preceding.
˛*shăng* To carefully guard against, is 丨丨 referring to infraction of laws or rules; beware of.

澠 A river in the state Tsi, a branch of the Ta-tsing River in Shantung.
˛*shăng*

Read ʿ*mien*. A town in the northwest of Honan, 丨池縣 a district on part of the River Loh.

乘 From 入 to *enter* over 桀 *excelling*, here referring to military rules; it resembles ʿ*ping* 秉 a sheaf.
˛*shăng*, *shăng*ˀ, ˛*ch'ăng*

To ride, as in a chariot; to mount; to avail one's self of, to take advantage of, to seize the right time; to put in order; to drive; in *arithmetic*, to sum up, to multiply; to direct; to calculate.

丨隙而入 [the wind] gets in at the crack.

丨時 to improve the moment.

丨機會 or 丨其無備 to seize the opportunity; to catch him unprepared.

丨風縱火 light the fire when the wind is fair.

丨龍 to take a wife.

丨法 rules for multiplication.

丨雲上天 to ride on a cloud to heaven.

歲月丨除 years and months come and go; time runs on.

不如丨勢 nothing like using your advantage.

Read *shing*ˀ. A span; a team of four horses; a classifier of vehicles or sedans, and also of machines having wheels, as a loom, a railroad car, a mill; a Budhist term for the different means of salvation, or getting across *sansara* to *nirvana*.

一丨ˀ車 one cart.

發丨ˀ矢 to shoot four arrows.

家丨ˀ a family carriage.

臻上丨ˀ he has attained the highest position.

大丨 the third degree of saintship (*maha-yana*), that of Budhisatwa; such a one, like a great conveyance, can transport himself and all mankind to *nirvana*.

剩ˀ 賸ˀ From *knife* and to *multiply*; the second form is unusual.
*shăng*ˀ An overplus, a residue; fragments, leavings; what is left, as a tailor's cabbage; to retain, to keep back a part; to lengthen; not only.

有丨 there is something over.

丨有限 only a little is left.

下丨多少 how much is left?

丨一半 one half remains.

丨家產業 the family property left to me.

丨貨 remnants of goods, driblets.

丨出 to put aside out of.

殘茶丨飯 what is left after a meal.

寧丨莫缺 better to have an overplus than to want; — waste not, want not.

晟ˀ From 冒 a *cover* contracted and 成 *complete*; also read *ch'ing*ˀ.
*shăng*ˀ A dish for holding rice or other cooked food.

騬ˀ Also read ˛*tsăng*.
*ch'ăng*ˀ To geld a stallion.

攻特謂丨之 to operate on the stallion is called to geld him.

嵊ˀ A district in Shao-hing fu in Chehkiang, lying south-
*ch'ăng*ˀ west of Ningpo; a noted hill in the same region.

藤ˀ A plant.
*shăng*ˀ 苣丨 another name for the sesamum.

長春丨 a wall creeper, an evergreen species of ivy or wild grape.

盛ˀ From *vessel* and *complete*; *q.d.* a dish full of grain ready.
*shăng*ˀ, ˛*ch'ăng* Full, abundant, plenteous; heaped up, exuberant; in perfect condition, flourishing, prosperous; a term of praise, superlative, excellent, fine.

丨處 your dwelling-place.

丨惠 your great favor.

丨世 a prosperous time.

丨事 a generous action, a fine affair.

丨京 the affluent capital, *i. e.* Mukten in Manchuria; applied also to the province.

越說越丨 the more they talk the more they have to say.

生氣方丨 just in the bloom of life.

丨德 stanch virtue.

丨 and 衰 are opposites, thriving, declining; — robust, failing.

丨名難副 it is hard to match his fame.

丨大 very great.

氣丨言宜 he has a strong voice and speaks rightly.

衆丨 very numerous, prolific.

Read ˛*ch'ing*. A cup, a vase for millet, once used in worship; a vessel full; to receive, as into a vessel; to deposit; to contain; contained in; heaped, as grain; to be complete; arrayed, in full costume.

丨不起來 it will not hold all.

丨不住話 he cannot keep a secret; he tells all he hears.
丨酒 to fill with spirits.
丨飯 bring on the rice, as at the end of a feast.
杏花丨開 the apricots are in full bloom.
丨高 raise it higher.
丨服 dressed in full robes.
丨箱 to pack or put in a box.
德丨不狎侮 complete virtue is never rude or familiar.
卬丨于豆 we load the stands with the offerings.
犧牲粢丨 the victims and vessels of millet.

晟 *shăng'* From *sun* and *complete*; not the same as 晟 a dish.
The brightness of the sun; light, splendor; glorious sunlight.
曉日丨明 a bright and fair day.
月映澄波丨 the moonlight glitters on the placid water.

聖 圣 *shăng'* From 耳 *ear* and 呈 to *inform*; the common, contracted form is also read *k'uh*, to hoe.
One who, on hearing a sound knows the whole case; the highest degree of moral and intellectual powers; intuitively wise and good, and possessing universal knowledge; wisdom; to be wise; holy, sacred, and unattainable by common mortals; perfect; sage, wise; the emperor; imperial; the sage, *i. e.* Confucius; a tree of knowledge; in epitaphs, a condescending and liberal prince.
丨人 and 至丨 the holy man and the most holy, are profane titles of Confucius.
丨門 his disciples, the literati.
丨主 or 丨天子 or 丨上 the Emperor.
丨諭 his Majesty's commands.
丨廟 a temple to Confucius.
三丨 the three holy ones, are Yü, Duke Cheu, and Confucius.
亞丨 the second sage, or Mencius.
丨王 Yao and Shun.
丨像 [Kwanti's] sacred effigy.
以達丨聰 this is for the information of your Majesty's intelligence.
丨神天從 the holy and divine [Confucius] came from heaven.
大而化之之謂丨 he is holy who can make the greatest things accommodate themselves to him.
丨靈 and 丨日 foreign terms, used by some for the Holy Ghost and the Sabbath.
惟狂克念作丨 the foolish by thinking become wise.

塍 塖 *shăng'* The raised paths between different patches of grain in a large field, available for walking.
香稻一丨 a patch of red rice.

SHOH.

See also SOH. *Old sounds,* shak *and* shot. *In Canton,* shok, shak, sok, sut, chéuk, lok, *and* yéuk;—*in Swatow,* chiak, chút, súak, sòk, *and* yiak;—*in Amoy,* chiok, liok, sek, *and* sut;—*in Fuhchau,* ch'iòk *and* sauk;—*in Shanghai,* sak, zak, sok, ts'òk, *and* süih;—*in Chifu,* shŏa.

芍 *ˌsho ˌshao* From *flower* and *ladle*; occurs written without the radical.
The peony (*Pæonia albiflora*), whose roots 丨藥 are used as a tonic.
白丨 and 赤丨 are two varieties of the dahlia.
贈之以丨藥 presenting each other with white pæonies.

爍 *ˌsho* Interchanged with the next.
Bright, splendid, brilliant; to glisten, to shine; to embellish.
閃丨 to reflect light.
灼丨 glorious.
霜木葉暴丨 the bright falling leaves of the autumnal woods.
Read *loh*. Dead branches of trees, withered twigs.

鑠 *ˌsho* Like the last, and also read *yoh*.
To melt a metal; to fuse it for founding; to urge; impelled, as by another's influence; lustrous, shining, burnished.
丨金 to polish metals or gold.
非由外丨 [genius does] not come from outward polish.
丨目 brilliant eyes.

朔 *soh' shwoh'* From *moon* and *perverse*.
The first day of the moon, the new moon; to begin; north.
正丨 new-year's day.
告丨 to announce the new moon, when of old a sheep was offered.
丨風凜凜 the biting north wind.
城彼丨方 to build a wall in those northern regions.
賀丨 congratulations at the new moon.

槊 鎙 *soh'* A great spear, eighteen feet, such as Chang Fi wielded.
握丨 to play chess.
手使長丨 he brandished his great spear.

矟 *soh'* Like the last.
A kind of fizgig or harpoon.
刀丨 a pencil.

濼 *soh'* From *water* and *a cup*.
The gentle murmuring of a brook over the stones is 濺丨, and also the sportive leaps of fish; waves dashing against each other.

揱 soh' To smear, to daub.
提鎗便丨 to thrust right and left with a spear.

鷟 tsu' A bird likened to a mallard, with fine plumage and red eyes; it is regarded as a felicitous bird.
鸑丨 the young chicks of this phœnix mallard are so called by some, but it may denote a beautiful species of teal. (*Anas.*)

摗 soh' From *hand* and *cord;* it was also written 索, but that being read *soh*, the radical *hand* was added.

To feel for with the hand; to pull out, to select, to take; to experiment upon; to seek out or solve.
摸丨 to turn over and look at, as goods; to finger.
丨隱行怪 to search into mysteries and do occult things.
丨數 to solve a problem.

In *Cantonese.* The natural divisions of an orange, pumelo, mangosten, or other fruit; a quarter, as of a bird; a place; a part of.
解三丨 cut it into three parts.

鎍 ˊso Iron thread; iron wire; small chains.
跪丨子 to kneel on chains.
鐵丨 iron wire or thread.

嗦 shoh' To sip; to take a taste of a thing; to put up the lips and taste.

蟀 soh' A cricket, especially the house-cricket.
蟋丨居壁 the cricket lives in the wall.
鬪蟋丨 to fight crickets.

梀 shoh' Name of a tree.
In *Cantonese.* A catch, a fastening, a snick, a button; to button or fasten, to latch.
門丨 a movable post which is run into holes in the lintel and sill, and holds the leaves of the door.
丨住寔 fasten it tight, as a window-blind.

掔 soh' ˏsiao Long and beautiful arms; small and tapering.
輻丨而纖 the fellies are long and slender.

SHU.

Old sounds, sho, zho, shiu, shot, shiut, *and* zhot. *In Canton*, shü *and* sho; — *in Swatow*, su, chù, ch'ù, súe, *and* so; — *in Amoy*, su, sò, tsu, ch'u, *and* ju; — *in Fuhchau*, sü, chü, ch'ü, su, sùü, sò, sauk, saú, siò, *and* t'ü; — *in Shanghai*, su, sü, tsü, *and* tsz'; — *in Chifu*, shü.

書 ˏshu From 曰 to *speak* and 聿 a *stylus*, but the former is regarded as a contraction of 者 for 著 to *manifest*, *scil.* with the pencil.

A book or volume, which should properly have a soft or limp cover, though it is applied to all kinds of books; a record; a letter; documents, dispatches; to write, to compose; the form of characters; characters as the delineation of ideas; a clerk or writer.
一本丨 one book, one volume.
一套丨 or 一部丨 one set.
丨稟 to write a petition.
丨房 a library, an office.
丨衣 a book-cover of cloth.
關丨 an engagement for a tutor.
離丨 or 休丨 a bill of divorce.
丨金 money for school-books.
丨館 a school-house.
丨鋪 or 丨林 a book-store.
丨生之見 a scholastic, pedantic mind
丨信 a letter.
文丨 dispatches on service.
丨生 a scholar.
丨香之家 a literary family.
中丨君 a writing-pencil.
四丨 the Four Books.
丨班 clerk in a yamun who writes petitions, copies edicts, &c.
丨童 a boy who dusts a library.
手丨 written with my own hand.
丨迂兒 a pedantic scholar.
清丨 custom-house clerks.
草丨 the running hand.
八分丨 the square characters.
攻丨 to learn books.
中丨 clerks in the Boards.
腹有詩丨氣自華 his mind is full of classic lore, and his manners show his parts.
致丨 to inform by letter.
丨啟先生 the clerk in a prefect's office who prepares documents.

瑹 ˏshu Also read ˏ*tu.*
A fine gem; an ancient tablet, the 笏 of after times, held by feudal princes at audiences; it was made of ivory.

舒 ˏshu From *house* and to *give.*
To unroll, to open out; to expand; to disburden the mind; exhilirated; tranquil, at ease; lax, easy, leisurely; comfortable; to be remiss; an old tribe on the River Hwai, retained in the district of 丨城縣 near Lu-cheu fu in Nganhwui.
丨展 to spread out, as a roll; large, spacious, as a house; free and easy.
丨服 easy, in good health, happy; to give in to.
不丨究之 [our lord] does not leisurely examine it.
丨丨徐徐 to do anything leisurely and orderly; well done.
丨用 roomy, enough and to spare.
丨暢 in good spirits, cheerful.

丨遲 pleasant spoken, in good humor.

卷丨自如 I shall act as I please about it.

未免太丨服 really much too comfortable.

丨緒 a clue.

丨伸一個懶 be stretched out once at full length.

安丨 wholly at ease.

丨國 a small state in the present Liu-ch'ing hien 柳城縣 in the north of Kwangsi.

丨鳧 a wild duck, one that goes where it likes.

紓 *shu* Interchanged with the last.

Slow, remiss; insensibly, little by little; to relax; to free from.

丨緩 procrastinating.

以丨民困 to remit the burdens on the people.

彼交匪丨 there is no remissness in their intercourse.

丨革非心 to change one's wicked conduct.

丨禍 to free from calamity.

輸 *shu* From *carriage* and *to assent*; presents were sent up in a cart.

To rotate; to send in, as revenue; to bring what is due; to submit one's self; an offering; to lose, to be beaten; to exhaust; to overturn; ruined, decayed.

交丨 skirt or flap of a garment in ancient times.

丨帳 to help one in sickness or in need.

丨納 to pay taxes.

丨敗 discomfited, defeated.

丨錢 to lose money.

打丨 to get a thrashing.

丨他一着 I lost one game to him.

捐丨 to subscribe to government.

丨打贏要 if he loses he will thrash you, and want the wager if he wins.

丨賭 to bet; what will you bet?

委丨 to send in the tribute; officers who superintend its reception.

丨服 to confess willingly, as a prisoner without torturing.

丨盡 to exhaust.

毹 *shu* A kind of rug or mattress for sleeping, or kneeling in worship; woven of horse and other hair.

鄃 *shu* An old name for Hia-tsin hien 夏津縣 in Lin-tsing cheu in the northwestern part of Shantung; it reached then into Chihli.

疏 疎 *shu* *su* From 疋 *piece* and 㐬 *streams* or 束 *a sheaf*; sometimes used for the next two.

Open, wide apart, coarse; distant in space, time, or relationship; sundered, widened; sleazy; remiss, free, lax, careless; to make passable; pervious; to divide, to partition off; to part with; to cut or carve open work; to discard; to spread or enlarge; to manage; a correlative of 親 distant and near, as relatives.

丨通舊河 to clear out an old river.

丨懈 heedless, *laissez faire*.

丟丨 not tried for a long time, quite out of practice.

丨財大義 to give generously and equitably.

丨遠 more distantly related.

丨窓 an open lattice, a jalousie.

丨眼 a crevice; open-worked.

丨闊 not met for a long time.

丨忽 just slipped my mind.

丨失 just lost (or mislaid) it.

稀丨 coarse in texture.

丨於防範 remiss about the rules, heedless of the stipulations.

丨林 trees in autumn when half stripped of foliage.

丨虞 evils arising from remissness.

丨丨 full dressed, spreading robes.

Read *shu'* To state to a superior; to discuss, to lay before; a statement.

奏丨 a memorial.

竈君丨 annual statement to the god of the Furnace.

丨文 a clear report.

抗丨直諫 an urgent memorial and direct remonstrance.

蔬 *su* A general term for edible greens and vegetables is 丨菜 including pulse.

嘉丨 table rice.

丨食' the coarsest kinds of herbs.

鼠壤有餘丨 the mole's nest has some greens left;—don't eat all up.

丨油 a cheap oil obtained from the seeds of a kind of comfrey or *Boragineæ*.

丨水即屬家常 water and herbs are [the student's] daily fare.

落丨 the black egg-plant; so called at Suchau.

老丨菜 may you die soon—like greens; a curse.

吃丨菜 he eats herbs; *i. e.* he is a priest.

梳 *shu* From 木 *wood* and 疏 *open* contracted.

A coarse-toothed and single comb; to comb.

丨頭 or 丨髮 to dress the hair.

一隻丨 or 丨子 a comb.

丨齒 teeth of the comb.

丨粧 to dress up, said of women.

丨粧盤 a trunk containing a paper toilette to burn for the dead.

分丨 to send a comb to put in the coffin of a deceased fiancée. (*Cantonese.*)

丨粧檯 a toilette table furnished for a bride.

綀 *shu* A coarse kind of grasscloth or linen formerly made, mixed with hempen threads; a variety of sackcloth.

殳 殺 ˎshu — Formed of 又 the *hand* and 几 a *bench*; not the same as *moh*, 殳; it is the 79th radical of a few characters, mostly relating to striking.

A pole or spear twelve cubits long, projecting before a war-chariot; handle of a spear; to kill with a spear.

丨書 a variety of running hand.

攝丨 a flail.

藷 薯 ˋshu — From *plants* and *all* or *court*; the second is the usual form; the first is also read ˏchu.

A term for plants with tubers; a tuber, a bulbous root; the Chinese yam 山藥 (*Dioscorea batatus*), cultivated in central China.

丨萸 a whitish tuber, probably the common yam.

丨仔 or 荷蘭丨 Irish potatoes.

紅丨 or 白丨 or 番丨 sweet potatoes.

大丨 or 坭洞丨 the yam. (*Dioscorea sativa*.)

丨粉 sweet-potato flour.

殊 ˏshu — From *dead* and *red*.

To kill, to cut off, to exterminate, to slaughter; to wound; to distinguish; to mark off; differing, unlike; to exceed; a sign of the superlative, really, very; it is often followed by a negative.

丨戰 to kill in battle.

萬丨一本 all these different things have the same principle.

丨無本事 not the least ability.

年丨七十 rather over seventy.

丨方 various regions.

丨属可憐 it is truly lamentable.

丨色 different colors.

丨不可解 I really cannot understand — your intention.

丨堪詫異 it is still more strange.

丨庭 palace of the genii.

丨不然 certainly not so.

丨不得知 who would have thought it! Is it possible?

銖 ˏshu — A small ancient silver coin; an old weight like a scruple, equal to 100 grains of millet (some authors rate it at 105) and the 24th part of a tael; blunt, dull; farthings, coppers; trifles.

錙丨計較 to reckon to the uttermost farthing.

五丨錢 a cash of Wang-mang of the Han dynasty.

抒 ˋshu — To strain or decant liquids, to pour out; to take out; to exclude; to state freely, to lay open one's mind.

揄丨 a rice mortar.

丨箭袋 to pull arrows from the quiver.

丨恨 to allay anger, to pacify.

暑 ˋshu — From *sun* and *this*; not the same as 署 an office.

Summer's heat; hot weather; heat of the sun.

丨天 dog-days.

天時丨熱 sultry weather.

深林避丨 to go into the dense groves to escape the heat.

中丨 or 受丨 sun-struck, affected by the heat.

寒來丨往 cold and heat succeed each other.

我心憚丨 my heart is affrighted by the heat.

鼠 ˋshu — The original form is intended to represent the *head*, *teeth*, *tail*, and *legs* of a rat; it is the 208th radical of characters relating to the *Rodentia*; used for the next.

A rat, including the mouse, weasel, squirrel, &c.; timorous; thieving; skulking, lurking; mean, rascally; brooding over, mournful.

老丨 a rat, the black rat; a southern term.

竹丨 the bamboo rat. (*Rhizomys sinensis*.)

石丨 field or meadow mouse.

松丨 or 灰丨 a squirrel.

銀丨 an ermine.

田丨 a mole.

飛丨 a bat; the flying squirrel.

黃丨狼 a weasel.

丨思泣血 my thoughts pain me even to weeping blood.

鼷丨 a shrew mouse; in the North, the 騷丨 is a polecat, or perhaps a muskrat.

渠丨 a water rat.

詭丨 a skulking thief.

丨眼 timorous; villainous.

丨竊狗偷 pilfering and thieving, like rats and dogs.

首丨兩端 irresolute, undecided; looking two ways, as a rat peeping from its hole.

老丨跌落天平 the rat fell into the scales — to weigh himself; self-praise.

投丨忌器 look out for the vase when you throw at the rat in front of it; — don't run too great a risk to attain an object.

癙 ˋshu — Sick from grief; moping, a settled melancholy, a disorder of the mind; fearful, as a mouse in his hole.

丨憂以痒 my pent up sorrow makes me ill.

黍 ˋshu — Composed of 禾 *grain* and 雨 *rain* contracted, as it is sown when the rains come; it is the 202d radical of characters relating to millet and pasting.

The panicled millet (*Milium nigricans* or *Panicum miliaceum*) when growing; the grain is called 小麋 little wheat and 黃米 yellow rice; some varieties are glutinous; this word in ancient times probably denoted the sorghum.

角丨 a preparation of millet also called ˋtsung 粽, made from the variety called 黏黃米 on the 5th day of the 5th moon.

糜丨 spoiled millet.

啄我丨 don't peck my sorghum.

蜀丨 Sz'chʻuen millet, a variety of sorghum with a clumpy head; the grain is used for spirits; but the 玉蜀丨 is Indian corn or maize.

螋 ʻshu The sow-bug or slater, the 螋丨 (*Oniscus* and *Porcellio*), known as 地虱 ground louse, and 地鷄 ground chicken.

數 ʻshu soh' From 攴 a *tap* and 婁 *frequent*.
To enumerate; to count; to deal out; to find out the number; to blame; to recapitulate, to discriminate; an art, as of numbers.
丨幾多 how many do you reckon?
丨錯 you have reckoned wrong.
再丨一丨 reckon it up again.
歷歷可丨 I can enumerate the whole number.
丨丨看 look over and count it carefully.
使吏丨之 to order the officers to reprimand him.
丨不着你 he is not to be reckoned with you.
奕之爲丨小丨也 chess-playing is an art, it may be a small art.
算丨末者 it will do; you may do it; I agree.
難丨 they cannot be counted up.
往來言行心焉丨之 even the words of wayfarers can be discriminated by the mind.

Read *shu'*. An account, a bill; a number; a list; several, a few; a lot, destiny, fate; a classifier.
不丨年 not many years.
丨日 some days.
丨次 several times.
丨尾 final balance of an account
分丨 a dividend, a share.
對丨 to compare accounts.
記丨 or 上丨 put it to my account.
計丨 to count.
打丨 or 算丨 to reckon accounts.
無丨 innumerable; the Budhists use it for countless (*asamkyea*), representing it by 1 with 17 cyphers after it.
收丨 to collect accounts.
清丨 to clear off an account.
丨目糊塗 the accounts are confused.
天丨 or 曆丨 destiny.
在丨難逃 you cannot easily escape your fate.
有定丨 it is determined beforehand; it is a destined thing.
十丨個 ten and over.
充丨兒 one only fit to fill up, a poor stick of a fellow.

Read *shoh*, Worried, as by many cares; in a flurry or dilemma.
丨丨 hurried, irreverent.
煩丨 distracted with cares; too often, reiterated, it tires me.
朋友丨 to weary a friend with expostulations.

Read *tsuh*, Close; as 丨罟 a fine net.

嗾 shu' To egg on a dog; to set a dog on one; the noise made in doing so.

樹 shu' From *wood* and to *stand* erect.
A tree; erect woody plants; plants in general; to set out, to plant; to produce, as by the trees planted; to insert in rows; to screen; to erect, to set up, to establish, for which the next is better; tall, stately, like a tree.
丨木 trees, vegetables.
一柯丨 or 丨條丨 one tree.
丨頭 or 丨樁 a stump.
丨脂 resin or gum of trees.
丨林 a grove or forest.
枯丨 dwarfed trees.
接丨 or 駁丨 to graft trees.
丨塞門 to build a screen wall before the door.
丨屏 to put up a screen.
丨大招風 high trees invite the wind; rich people attract friends.
丨掛 rime, frozen hoar-frost.
丨德 to establish one's virtue, to make a reputation.
丨其丨以蔭行人 to set out trees to shade wayfarers.
丨成 the tree is made, *i. e.* the scheme is effected or brought to a head.
丨子 the confirmed heir-apparent of a feudatory.
樂彼之園爰有丨檀 pleasant is that garden where are the laurel trees.

豎 竪 shu' From 豆 *vessel* or 立 to *stand* and 賢 *virtuous* contracted; the second form is most in use, and resembles ꜀kien 堅 stable.
A vessel on its base; to erect, to set up; to stand upright; to establish, to render sure; upright, well-principled; chaste; perpendicular, lengthwise; a page, an attendant, a low officer; short jerkins worn by servants.
丨旗竿 to plant a flag-staff.
丨立 to stand up; to raise; to establish, as a name.
丨婢 a slave girl.
丨子 a servant, a waiting-lad.
丨儒 a mean fellow.
牧丨 a herdboy.
自拔倒丨 he pulled up and overthrew the tree.
橫丨是這樣 either way will do; it comes to the same thing.

墅 shu' From *land* and *wilderness*.
A shed or lodge in a field; a cottage, a house in the country; a house and a garden plat.
家廬別丨 another lodge away from the family house.

戍 shu' From 戈 *spear* and 人 *man*; not to be confounded with *süh*, 戌.
To guard the frontiers; exiled to a frontier post.
丨卒 soldiers on guard there.
遣丨 sent to the frontier.
丨邊關 a frontier customs' post.
丨所 a garrison.
邊丨 the frontier.

恕 shu' From *heart* and *according* to; it is somewhat like nu' 怒 anger.

Benevolent, benignant; excusing others; tender, considerate of; reciprocal duties; reciprocity; merciful, sympathizing; treating others as one wishes to be treated; to pardon, to excuse; to bear patiently.

丨罪 indulgent to others' faults.

丨我不陪 excuse me for not longer waiting on you.

丨怪 don't think it strange, don't be angry.

寬丨 not strict; indulgent.

忠丨 loyal and humane.

丨己丨人 excuse others as you do yourself.

丨報不週 excuse me for not going around — to my friends; a notice written at the outer door by a mourner.

這還可丨 that however can be passed over.

曉丨 to pass by.

忠丨違道不遠 [if one practices] his sincere convictions and reciprocal duties, he is not far out of the true path.

曙 ˓shu Bright; the light of the rising sun; dawn; clear, manifest.

丨色 luminous, dawning.

丨日 in the morning.

庶 shu' From 广 *shelter* over 光 *effulgent* altered, denoting all the people in a house.

A multitude, the whole, all, a great number; various; the people, the mass, the herd; as an *adverb*, if but, would that; near, nearly about, so, in this wise, it may be, probably; an *adjective* of number, placed before the noun; fat and sleek; a concubine.

丨幾 or 丨乎 or 丨幾乎 not far from, almost, probably.

丨子 a concubine's son; who says 丨母 for his mother.

丨室 a concubine.

丨無錯 most probably it is correct.

丨物 all things, every kind.

命般丨丨般丕作 [when the] people of Yin had received their orders, they vigorously did them.

丨民 or 黎丨 the masses, the people.

吉士 a Hanlin graduate.

丨多 very many.

丨人 a commoner; ordinary people; several classes.

In *Cantonese*, also written 嗻. A place, a spot; there, at; — and usually used after nouns.

草丨坐 he sat on the grass.

個丨 there; 尼丨 here.

喺丨 he is here.

署 shu' From *net* and *that; q. d.* all in a net; to be distinguished from 暑 heat.

A public court, an office, a tribunal; to place, to appoint to an office; acting, in the place of; temporary, as an officer.

公丨 or 衙丨 a court or yamun; a consulate.

丨任 an acting officer.

丨理 to manage, to oversee.

寓丨前 I live near the yamun.

部丨豪傑 the most capable men of all were selected.

內丨 in court.

木天丨 the office of the Hanlin Academy.

丨欽差 the acting minister; a chargé d'affaires.

裋 shu' Garments made of camel or yak's hair, coarse and thin; worn by peasants.

丨褐不完 their coarse clothes were far from being whole.

侸 shu' To stand; to be erect, like a tree.

佔丨之行' to act boyishly, to behave heedlessly.

Read ˏteu. Fatigued, tired out.

僂丨下垂 hanging the head and nodding, as from fatigue.

SHUH.

Old sounds, shok, zhok, shot, zhot, *and* dok. *In Canton*, shòk *and* shut; — *in Swatow*, sút, sòk, chek, *and* chwak; — *in Amoy*, sút, tsút, siok, *and* siap; — *in Fuhchau*, súk, sòk, séük, chéük, t'éük, *and* sauk; — *in Shanghai*, sòk, zeh, zăk, *and* sok; — *in Chifu*, shū.

術 shu' From 行 to *go* and 朮 a *sprout*.

A path in a town or field; the way of doing a thing or effecting an end; an art, a plan, a trick, a hocus-pocus, a device; a precept, a mystery, and usually something magical or demoniacal; the black-art; a craft or occupation; to narrate.

法丨 or 妖丨 magical rules.

丨士 a conjurer.

心丨 a design, plan; notions.

同丨 similar doctrine, same craft.

四丨 the four elegant accomplishments, *viz.*, poetry, composition, ceremony, and music.

丨家 a trickster; people who practice sleight of hand.

邑丨 an ancient division of a thousand families.

技丨 legerdemain.

經濟學丨 to diffuse abroad good principles.

劍丨 sword magic.

Read sui' and used for 遂. An old name for a circuit of villages, containing 12,500 families.

茂 ꜀shu'

Also written like the next in the name of a plant, the 蓬莪 丨, growing in Cheh-kiang, which produces pendulous tubers; some refer it to an *Amomum*, others regard it as allied to the turmeric or *Curcuma*.

朮 shu'

Similar to the next; the form is intended to represent growing grain.

A glutinous grain; a medicinal, bitter vegetable like an artichoke, the *Atractylodes lancea*, *rubra*, and other species; in the 白 丨 the root is fragrant; the 蒼 丨 is a bitter medicine, and the stalk is used; both of them resemble putchuck in smell.

秫 shu'

A sort of millet (*Milium*), whose glutinous seeds serve to make spirits; in former times this term denoted a variety of the glutinous rice which was used by distillers.

丹 丨 dark red millet.

丨 楷 sorghum or doora stalks, used for fuel and many other purposes.

玉 丨 子 兒 near the Great Wall, is a term for maize after it is shelled.

沭 shu'

A river in the southern part of Shantung.

丨 陽 縣 an old district near the mouth of the Yellow River.

述 shu'

From to *go* and *a sprout*.

To follow another's steps; to practice what another has invented; to narrate, to tell the particulars; to put into another idiom or publish; to compile a book; a memoir, an essay.

丨 職 to place princes in their rank at an audience.

據 丨 其 畧 this is the gist of what he said.

丨 古 詞 to tell old legends.

丨 而 不 作 he made it known, but he did not invent it.

修 丨 to revise a work.

丨 人 之 言 relate another's words.

著 丨 to make known abroad.

丨 說 to tell what one has heard, as news.

不 丨 contrary, as to reason.

束 shu' soh'

From 木 *wood* and 口 *mouth*, meaning to inclose; it closely resembles *ts'z'* 朿 a thorn.

To bind many things together; to tie in a bundle, as faggots; to restrain, to coerce; a sheaf, a bundle; a classifier of such things as are bound.

一 丨 once denoted 5 pieces of cloth, 50 darts, or 10 strips of meat.

白 華 菅 兮 白 茅 丨 兮 the fibers of the white rush are bound with the white grass.

丨 脩 a teacher's wages.

管 丨 to restrain those under one's hand.

丨 手 待 斃 with tied hands waiting for death; — *i. e.* no resource, nothing further can be done.

丨 縛 to cord up.

一 丨 柴 a faggot of firewood.

嚴 加 約 丨 to closely restrain, as by explicit directions.

不 自 檢 丨 never let down your self-respect.

丨 裝 回 南 to pack up and return south (or home.)

嗽 軟 嗍 shu'

The second of these characters is sometimes read *seu'* to cough; the third is unusual.

To suck in; to smoke; to draw in the breath, to hem; to inhale; to absorb.

丨 鼻 to snivel, to sniff.

丨 氣 to whimper.

丨 濕 it imbibes the moisture.

丨 口 to hold water in the mouth.

孩 子 丨 奶 the babe sucks the breast.

酒 醪 傾 共 丨 he poured out a generous cup, and they all drank around.

叔 ꜀shu

From *hand* added to an older form of it.

To collect, to hoard; a father's younger brother, an uncle of the same surname; a respectful term for older persons or strangers; a squire.

丨 丨 or 亞 丨 an uncle.

大 丨 the senior of the younger uncles.

丨 公 a father's uncle; also, a husband's uncle.

小 丨 a husband's younger brother.

丨 父 my uncle; used in letters.

丨 姪 uncles and nephews; — a father's relatives.

老 丨 父 my father's old friend.

丨 季 之 世 a time of general decadence; times of decay.

家 丨 my uncle, speaking of him.

丨 台 a family friend.

丨 兮 伯 兮 O Sir, O Sir!

俶 shu'

From *man* and *uncle*; it is also used as a synonym of *t'ih* 倜 free.

To begin, to do, to act; good, fine; to repair.

丨 載 to commence, as agricultural labors.

丨 望 終 虛 my great hopes are after all quite frustrated.

淑 shu'

From *water* and *uncle* as the phonetic.

Clear, limpid; virtuous, uncorrupted, correct, mostly applied to females; skilled in; fine, said of a banner.

丨 人 or 丨 女 an accomplished lady; the first is the title of wives of the third rank of officials.

丨 德 female virtue.

丨 氣 genial, balmy, mild.

丨 慎 heedful, careful, honorable.

頁 丨 charming, gentle.

丨 問 如 皋 he was as skilled at questioning as Kao-yao.

丨 旂 綏 章 [the king gave] a fine flag with its feathery pennons.

菽, ʻshu Originally denoted probably, the soy bean, but has been extended till it includes edible pulse of any kind.

丨水承歡 with pulse and water [the poor] gratify their parents.

不辨丨麥 he does not know the difference between pulse and wheat;—*i. e.* he is ignorant of farming.

孰, ˏshu The original complex form denoted eating well dressed viands, and was first used for the next.

A *pronoun*, who? which? what? a large crop, a plentiful harvest; to exercise in.

丨輕丨重 which is the lightest?

未知丨是 I do not know which (or who) is right.

丨不知禮 who does not know manners? *i. e.* you and I know each other well.

丨不可忍也 what then could he not bear?

丨爲來哉 why then has he come?

丨若另籌一法 the best thing will be to devise another way.

熟, ˏshu ˏsheu From *fire* and *who* as the phonetic; it closely resembles *jeh*, 熱 hot.

Ripe, mellow, mature; well cooked; acquainted with, perfect at; skilled, experienced, apt at; intimate, very friendly; soft, pliable, as silk; smoothed off, cleaned; sound, as sleep; to succeed in; a crop; the wife of the eldest son.

丨成 or 成丨 mellow, as fruit.

一年一丨 one crop yearly.

丨識 well acquainted with, profound in it.

睡丨了 sleeping sweetly.

丨人 or 丨手 handy, skillful.

樹上丨 it ripened on the tree.

丨習 practiced till he was perfect in it.

丨米 to hull rice in a mortar.

爛丨 well cooked.

思之丨矣 to think a matter over fully.

丨路歸來 I shall return the way I came.

相丨 intimate with each other.

書早已讀丨 a finished scholar.

丨視無睹 looked at it a long time but could not make it out.

書勿丨 your lesson is not well learned; a teacher's rĕprimănd.

何愁不丨 what fear have you of not succeeding (or learning?)

塾, ˏshu An ante-room or vestibule, such as officials going into court used to meet in for consultation; study rooms let at the examinations; a domestic or village school-room.

家丨 a family school.

丨師 a private tutor.

丨門 an ancient porch room.

縮, ˏso From *silk* and to *lodge*.

To confuse, to disorder; to retract, to draw in, the opposite of ˏ*shăn* 伸; to pull in; to collect again; to coil up, as a snake; to bind fast; to draw back from, to back out; to shrink, to pucker up, to shorten; to strain, as spirits; to condense, as steam; retractile; fearful, tangled, snarled; straight, upright.

退丨 to retreat, as an army; to draw back, as a snail's eyes.

丨手 to pull in the hand; to decline to aid in an affair.

丨成一團 to cuddle up in a heap; to keep close.

丨短 to shrink up.

丨酒 to strain spirits.

丨縫 [the ancient cap had] a straight seam in front

尖嘴丨腮 a peaked mouth and shrunk cheeks; lean.

嘗丨地以論心 I would shorten the distance so as to express to you my affections.

丨版以載 the wall-boards were bound tight to hold the earth,—as in beating a wall.

局丨 confined, in close or narrow quarters.

自反而丨 I examine my own heart and find it upright.

蹜, ˏso To shuffle along, to walk with short steps; to walk carefully, as in a narrow way.

足丨丨 to walk and see where one steps.

蜀, ˏshu From 虫 *insect* under 目 *eye*.

A worm, for which the nextl is now used; a sacrificia utensil or tripod; a tribe anciently living along the River Min, near the present capital of Sz'chʻuen.

鹿丨 a striped horse, and probably refers to the zebra, of which one may have been seen.

丨國 the western of the Three States, in A.D. 221, all west of Tung-ting Lake; it was first established by the king of Tsin.

巴丨 the province of Sz'chʻuen.

丨葵 the Sz'chʻuen hibiscus.

蠋, ˏshu The caterpellar of the sphynx moth, green, and large as the finger; it feeds on the mallows, and another kind on the filbert. (*Torreya.*)

蠶丨 a worm found on the mulberry; the chrysalis is collected for medicine.

屬, **属**, **屌**, ˏshu ʻchuh From 尾 the *tail* and 蜀 an *insect*; the contracted forms are both common; used with *chuh*, 囑 to order.

Attached to, as an animal's tail is to its body; belonging to, connected with; depending on, pertaining; allied, related to; kinship; subject to, under orders, as a deputy; used for the substantive verb, and indirectly also has the sense of appears to be, I think it is; actual, existing; a sort, a rank, a grade; nearly of the same kind; to enjoin on, to direct; to be joined to, in accordance; near to.

耳丨于垣 ears may be behind the wall — to overhear.

親丨 or 家丨 relatives of every grade.

丨下 inferiors at one's order, underlings.

丨在相好 intimate, as friends.

事丨兩難 to act either way is difficult.

草木之丨 it is a sort of plant.

縣丨 it belongs to the district.

丨員 a subaltern, a lower officer.

丨國 feudatories, dependent countries; colonies.

丨誰管 who orders you?

久丨騎射 he has long practiced riding and archery.

事丨當行者皆丨于我 I have the direction of everything which should be done.

丨正 to dictate and write.

丨陰 it is hidden, as a disease.

尙丨公允 it also seems both just and legal.

十二丨相 the twelve animals that denote the twelve branches.

自丨 or 實丨 really is, truly so.

丨甚麽的 what [animal] do you belong to? — referring to the animal which sways the year of birth.

丨客 guests, visitors.

贖 *ˏshu* From *property* and to *sell*.

To give security, to give a pledge for; a pledge; to ransom, to redeem; to commute punishment for a fine; to atone for delinquency or failure by subsequent merit.

丨回 or 取丨 redeemed out of pawn.

將功丨罪 atoned for his guilt by good actions.

收丨 to redeem the pledge.

丨罪 to commute a punishment, to give satisfaction for a crime; to redeem from sin.

百身莫丨 a hundred persons would not ransom him.

丨身 to ransom one's self.

儵 *k'iuh'* A dark ground with blue spots on it, mottled or striped.

倏, 條 *k'iuh'* From 攸 *which* and 犬 *dog* or 火 *fire*; the first is correct, the second most common.

Hastily, quickly, as a dog running off; a change.

丨忽 suddenly.

丨爾不見 suddenly disappeared.

襡, 襩 *ˏshu* From *dress* and *alone* or to *sell*; also read *ˏteu*.

A tunic or frock reaching to the knees called 襦丨, such as loose women anciently wore; also, short clothes.

Read *tuh*, To put up a bow in its case.

斂箠而丨 to pack the baskets and put up the bows.

鸀 *ˏshu* Also read *chuh*, and *tuh*,

A red billed bird, resembling a crow or chough; also another bird of this class with a yellow body and red legs.

丨鳿 or 鸑鷟 a water bird, whose description allies it to a rail, or the stilt-plover.

SHUI.

Old sounds, zhui, shìp, zhíp, *and* shut. *In Canton*, shui *and* sui; — *in Swatow*, sui, chui, *and* súe; — *in Amoy*, sui *and* sòe; — *in Fuhchau*, sui, sòi, swòi, *and* chwi; — *in Shanghai*, süé, tsüé, *and* sz'; — *in Chifu*, swéi.

誰 *ˏshui* From *words* and *bird*.

A relative *pronoun*, who? whose? whom? in writing, it often precedes the verb it rules, when the other nominative is expressed; an initial particle.

是丨 who is that?

是丨的 whose is that?

丨敢 who dares?

丨能彀 who is able to do it?

王丨怒 who is the sovereign angry with?

丨昔然矣 long indeed has it been thus with him.

奈得丨何 what matters it? who is then to act? — *i. e.* do your worst.

不知丨之子 I don't know whose son he is.

丨想的到 who would have thought it?

丨不知 who does n't know it?

丨不做 any body can do it.

丨阿 who is there?

當今之世舍我其丨 if the [prince of Tsi] does not employ me in this time, who is there he will call to serve him?

脽 *ˏshui* The buttocks, or their bone the *os sacrum*; an ancient mound at 汾陰 in the southwest of Shansi, in the present Yung-ho hien 永和縣 near the Yellow River, where was erected a temple to Heu-tsih or Ceres, on an enormous tumulus, whose shape was likened to the nates, and so called.

水 *ˋshui* The original form represents three *ripples* or currents flowing; it is the 85th radical of characters relating to uses of water and names of streams.

Water, the first of the five elements; a fluid; clear, limpid; aquatic; a stream; a tide; a passage, a trip from one place to another; an inundation; dangers by flood; trivial, common, as water; unstable, gentle, easy; among geomancers, all low land, because water rules such places, as the dragon does all high places; discount on coin or bullion; to wet, to soak.

一滴丨 or 一點丨 a drop of water.

丨漲 or 丨大 the tide is flood.

丨退 or 丨乾 ebb tide.

順丨 fair tide, and 逆丨 head tide or current.

丨夫 a water-carrier.

投丨 to throw or jump overboard.

丨脚 freight or passage money.

丨手 or 丨手人 a sailor.

失丨 lost at sea; drowned.

打平丨 to make equal; to divide fairly, neither party losing.

丨波紋 ripples.

銀子扣丨 to take off a discount.

不服丨土 the climate does not agree with me.

十日丨路 a ten days' passage.

推人下丨 pushed a man into the water; — to involve another in ruin.

丨車 an irrigating water-wheel; a water cart; a fire-engine.

開丨 to boil water. (*Pekingese.*) To weaken tea by adding water. (*Cantonese.*)

丨紅 a light red.

丨長船高 as the water increases the boat rises; — good prices bring good profits.

丨火無情 water and fire have no sympathy.

丨性楊花 a water disposition and aspen flower; — unstable and specious.

一丨兒 they are all alike; 頭丨 and 二丨 first and second rate, the best kind and inferior.

送丨禮 to send a present of eatables.

丨嘴愛放丨 gabbling lips will always let out secrets.

丨族 aquatic tribes, as fish, sea-weed, or mollusks.

丨菜 vegetables that need watering, as greens, melons, &c.

丨星 or 伐丨 the planet Mercury.

丨落石出 when the water falls the stones appear; — murder will out.

逝丨 [gone like] the passing water.

你會丨麼 do you know how to swim?

守丨 [the boat was] detained by the [high or low] water.

一身丨 I am wet through and through.

橫丨 cross-wise waters, — one name for rivers and canals which intersect the country.

瑞 *zhui'* From *gem* and *source* of.

A flat stone signet or baton a foot long, which was given to princes on their investiture as a sign of authority and rank; a favor, a keepsake; a happy omen; felicitous, auspicious.

祥丨 a lucky sign.

丨氣 auspicious influences — of the emperor.

班丨于羣后 to distribute the signets to all the princes.

丨國 Sweden.

睡 *shui'* From *eye* and *hanging down.*

To nod or doze in one's chair; to sleep.

丨覺 he is asleep.

打磕丨 to nod in sleep.

丨入眼 he is going to sleep.

丨椅 a lounging chair.

想丨 or 丨眼朦朧 very sleepy.

丨不着 I can't get asleep.

丨着了死一樣 he sleeps like a log.

丨醒 to awaken.

說丨語 to talk in sleep.

丨的很香甜 his sleep was sweet unto him.

深丨 or 熟丨 deep sound sleep.

丨菜 the marsh trefoil (*Menyanthes trifoliata*), used as a sedative to bring on sleep.

稅 *shui'* From *grain* and to *weigh out.*

The rent for houses or land; taxes in kind; duties on goods; to bequeath, to leave by will; to put up at; to halt, as at a post.

納丨 to pay taxes or excise.

收丨 to receive taxes.

漏丨 to lose revenue by smuggling.

丨館 or 丨局子 a custom-house.

丨額 the stated or legal revenue of a place.

丨口子 a point or station where duties are levied.

丨駕 to put up the carriage, as at an inn.

丨務 the custom-house business, under a 丨務司 or collector of customs.

薄丨斂 to get a diminished revenue.

Read *tui'* To dress in mourning on hearing the death of a brother at a distance; to change the dress.

Read *chwen'* Black, as clothes.

帨 *shui'* A napkin hung at the girdle; a handkerchief.

巾丨 a napkin.

無感我丨兮 do not interfere with my handkerchief.

生女則設丨于門右 when a girl was born a napkin was put on the right side of the gate; hence 設丨 is a woman's birthday, as 懸弧 is a man's.

SHUN.

Old sounds, zhon, shon, don, zhun, *and* dun. *In Canton*, shun *and* yun ; — *in Swatow*, sún, sín, *and* tun ; — *in Amoy*, sûn, tun, *and* ch'un ; — *in Fuhchau*, sung *and* sòng ; — *in Shanghai*, zăng, săng, *and* tsăng ; — *in Chifu*, tswun *and* swun.

脣 唇 ꜀ch'un — From *mouth* or *flesh* and *hour* ; the first, though most common, is least correct, and is defined to be afraid.

The lips.

朱 〡 ruby lips.

口 〡 the lips.

費 〡 舌 to spend lips and tongue ; — loquacious.

齃 〡 protruding, open lips.

〡 亡 齒 寒 if the lips are lost, the teeth will feel cold ; — if the outlying states are taken, I am in danger.

〡 齒 之 邦 states that mutually depend on each other.

劃 〡 子 or 崩 口 〡 a hare-lip.

點 〡 to rouge the lips.

漘 ꜀shun — From *water* and *lip*.

The margin of a stream, a steep bank ; a brink, the slope of a bank.

海 〡 a sea-beach.

淳 湻 ꜀shun ꜀ch'un — From *water* and to *enjoy* ; this character, being the personal name of the present Emperor, has been altered to the second form, which alone the people use.

Pure, limpid ; unmixed ; genuine, honest ; to cleanse, to wash ; to sprinkle ; saltish land ; a double banked war-chariot.

〡 〡 rippling, flowing on.

風 〡 俗 美 the manners and customs are courteous and pure.

鹹 〡 saltish barren earth.

〡 樸 之 鄉 honest and frugal villagers.

〡 淸 pellucid.

〡 沃 rich, fertile, as land.

〡 州 an old name of Nan-ning fu in the south of Kwangsi.

秉 性 貞 〡 a pure and chaste heart.

醇 醕 ꜀ch'un — From *spirits* and to *enjoy* ; interchanged with the last and next ; the second form is rarely used.

Generous, rich, as wine ; thick, as syrup ; singleminded ; unmixed, as a color ; liberal, generous in feeling ; clear, healthy, as a complexion ; subtle, essential, seminal.

〡 謹 careful, observant of the thing in hand.

〡 厚 kind and placable.

〡 酒 good wine.

精 〡 rich wine.

惟 厥 攸 居 政 事 惟 〡 let your mind rest in proper objects, and the affairs of government will be pure.

純 ꜀ch'un — Pure silk ; unspotted, unmixed ; fine, best ; simple, guileless, whole, sincere, — as the context indicates ; to be decided ; determinedly ; an old measure of 15 cubits, like a rod.

〡 乎 是 這 樣 it certainly is that way.

〡 一 不 雜 uniform in color ; a single purpose in view, earnest-minded.

〡 淨 gentle, tractable, as a dog.

〡 品 人 a first rate man.

土 性 〡 沙 the nature of the ground was pure sand.

〡 全 without any failing, said of character.

〡 樸 simple, honest.

〡 色 unspotted, as a sacrificial victim.

學 問 深 〡 thoroughly learned.

〡 銅 pure or solid copper ; it is all brass, not an outside plate.

〡 忠 perfectly loyal.

Read ˊchun. The selvedge or edge of a dress or mat, made of a different color.

焞 ꜀shun — From *fire* and *enjoyable*.

Bright, fiery, blazing ; the color or glory of fire.

火 〡 the blaze of a roaring fire.

Read ꜀t'un. To scorch a tortoise-shell for divination ; obscure.

天 策 〡 〡 the stars in Argo show dimly.

Read ꜀t'ui. A succession of ; full, abundant.

戎 車 〡 〡 the war chariots rolled on their thundering way.

鶉 ꜀ch'un — From 鳥 *bird* and 醇 *undivided* from its persistency in its habitat.

A quail, thought to be transformed from the frog.

〡 衣 百 結 poor clothes with many patches, — referring to the quail's shabby tail.

懸 〡 quails hanging up dead.

〡 之 奔 奔 quails are faithful to their mates.

〡 陰 縣 an old district in the north of Shensi.

蓴 蒓 ꜀shun — The first form is most in use.

A water vegetable of the gentian family, the 〡 菜, whose slippery and tender stalks are eaten in Kiangnan in the summer ; it is a marsh-flower (*Limnanthemum*), and is also called 水 葵 water mallows, and 金 絲 荷 葉 gold thread lily-leaf ; another plant, of which 馬 蹄 草 horse-hoof grass is a synonym, seems to be a species of edible sedge or *Scirpus*.

犉 ꜀ch'un — From *ox* and an old word for *who* ; also read ꜀jun.

An ox, seven ancient cubits high, yellow, and having black lips.

九 十 其 〡 ninety great oxen.

楯 ˏshun From *wood* and *shield;* also read *jun'* and ˏt'un, and used with the primitive.

The beam of a railing, which supports the bars; a baluster; a parapet, a defense; a light shield used by mummers; to develop.

欄 丨 a railing.

引 丨 萬 物 羣 美 萌 生 [this principle] animates and draws out all things into beautiful forms and groups.

揗 shun' To feel, to rub.

撫 丨 to soothe, to tranquilize.

順 shun' From *head* and *streams* flowing from it.

To accord with, to follow, to agree to; to obey, to comply with, to yield; to let a thing pass and not hinder; to be in sympathy with; docile, retiring, compliant, unresisting, agreeable, filial; convenient; fair, as a wind, or as with the grain of wood; flowing, rhythmical, as style; easy, graceful, as penmanship; among *physicians,* favorable, a mild form, as of small-pox.

丨 利 prosperous; free, no trouble with; easy, as a ready market.

丨 從 favorable, condescending.

丨 丨 harmoniously; working together, submissive.

借 丨 吓 a little one side; said by sedan bearers at Canton.

百 丨 to agree to everything.

丨 德 人 a mild person.

丨 水 fair tide.

掛 丨 風 旗 the flag follows the wind; *met.* docile.

丨 路 by the way, doing it if convenient.

丨 and 逆 are opposites, direct and inverse; fair and foul; mild and perverse.

丨 筆 寫 to write off for another.

丨 其 自 然 let it go, such is the luck, I can't help it.

丨 口 or 丨 着 嘴 兒 說 to speak heedlessly, to babble; to let out.

文 理 不 丨 a harsh style.

滑 丨 enticing, winning.

歸 丨 to return to obedience.

丨 事 a nice thing, it happens at a good time.

于 理 不 丨 not accordant with reason.

丨 河 下 all has gone to the bottom, all is lost, an entire ruin.

In *Pekingese.* A sort, said of people.

一 丨 子 they are just alike.

舜 shun' Composed of 舛 *obstinate* with, tangled *grass* above it.

Thick, tangled brushwood; in epitaphs, benevolent, wise; ephemeral.

帝 丨 and 虞 丨 the ancient monarch Shun, who reigned B. C. 2255 to 2205, or nearly coeval with Terah.

堯 天 丨 日 like the halcyon days of Yao and Shun.

顏 如 丨 華 her face is like the gay althea.

蕣 橓 shun' Used with the last.

Name of a transient blooming reddish flower, the 丨 英 *Hibiscus syriacus,* a type of transitory things; it is also called 木 槿 tree mallows.

瞬 眴 瞤 瞋 shun' From *eye* and the *transitory* flower, or a *decade;* but the second form is not used, and the last two very seldom.

To wink; to flash, to roll the eyes, to glance at; sparkling eyes, as a child's at seeing a dainty.

丨 息 an instant.

一 丨 之 間 in a twinkling.

轉 丨 工 夫 in a moment.

目 丨 如 電 eyes glancing everyway like the lightning.

爾 先 學 不 丨 而 後 可 言 射 if you learn it slowly, you will be able by and by to hit the target.

Read ˏhüen for the second only. Dizzy; a fit accompanied by indistinct vision; brilliant.

丨 煥 粲 爛 brilliant and elegant, said of a headdress.

裖 脤 shun' Flesh offered to the gods of the land by the emperor, and afterwards divided among his family; sacrificial flesh offered in a sea-shell in the ancestral hall; raw flesh.

貍 丨 name of a region.

石 尙 來 歸 丨 Shih Shang came [to Lu] with a sacrificial offering of flesh.

SHUNG.

Old sound, shong. *In Canton,* chung; — *in Swatow,* cheng; — *in Amoy,* chiong; — *in Fuhchau,* chüng; — *in Shanghai,* sung; — *in Chifu,* tsung.

摏 ˏch'ung From *hand* and to *pound;* interchanged with its primitive.

To pound, to ram down; to rush on; to run against; to batter on.

丨 其 喉 以 戈 he rushed on and put the spear through his throat.

丨 脫 之 牙 齒 丨 還 個 牙 齒 to take a tooth for a tooth.

丨 門 甚 迫 to pound on the gate violently.

丨 跌 倒 knocked over, as by being run upon.

丨 盌 盞 to smash the dishes.

SHWAH.

Old sound, shwat. *In Canton*, shat; — *in Swatow*, súe; — *in Amoy*, swat; — *in Fuhchau*, sauk; — *in Shanghai*, seh; — *in Chifu*, swa.

刷 ꜀shwa 㕞 From *knife* or *hand* and to *wipe*, the second form is unusual.

A brush, a scraper; to brush, to cleanse, to scrub; to wipe out; a card for dressing cotton; to rub ink blocks for printing.

刊丨 to cut and print books.

丨丨好 brush it well; brushed clean.

叨糊丨 to bite a paste-brush, *i. e.* to have a big mustache.

丨洗 to brush and clean.

掃丨 to sweep up a room.

丨恥改行 to wipe away disgrace by reformation.

根丨 to investigate thoroughly.

丨馬 to groom a horse.

丨貨 to garble goods.

河漫成口丨開三丈 the river overflowed making a crevasse, and washing away [the bank] for three perches.

丨招帖 to post bills.

一丨聲 a whizzing sound.

一把丨子 a brush.

剔丨弊端 to pick and brush off other's secrets, — and tell them.

唰 ꜀shwa From *mouth* and *brush*.

To preen feathers; a bird preening and arranging its plumage; a slight taste of.

鳥丨翎 the bird is preening itself.

SHWAI.

Old sounds, shwai *and* shat. *In Canton*, shui *and* sut; — *in Swatow*, swai, súe, lut, *and* chut; — *in Amoy*, sōe; — *in Fuhchau*, sòi, sauk, *and* séuk; — *in Shanghai*, sé *and* süih; — *in Chifu*, swai.

衰 ꜀shwai From *clothes* and *weak*; it resembles ꜀pau 裒 to collect.

Wearing away like a garment; diminished, cut off; small, fading, growing old, — and contrasted with 興 and 盛 flourishing; declining, decaying, unprosperous; to lessen, to deteriorate; adversity, misfortune.

丨敗 falling away, losing vigor.

丨微 dwindled away very much.

丨殘之兆 a sign of weakness and poverty.

丨世 a vicious, declining age.

三丨六旺 ups and downs of life, more good than bad luck.

丨老 or 丨了 old and feeble.

丨頹 failing, decayed, as a state.

丨邁 all vigor gone, debilitated.

丨草寒烟 the fading trees and chilly mists — of autumn.

丨分 in *mathematics*, a rule like fellowship.

In *Cantonese* read ꜀sui. To ravel, to fray an edge.

丨口 a raveled border.

好丨嘅 an unlucky chap.

摔 ꜀shwai To pull over a thing.

丨破了 pushed it over and broke it.

摔 ꜀shwai From *hand* and to *catch*; it is read tsuh in the Dictionary, but has now supplanted the preceding.

To wrestle; to push off or down; to shake, to quiver; to shy, as a horse.

丨打傢伙 shoved the thing off, threw it down.

丨袖子 one who flirts his sleeve, — a generous, profuse man.

丨交 to wrestle.

風丨破了門 the wind broke the door by slamming it.

馬丨下人來 the horse threw him off.

丨膝子 one who retracts his promise.

抓泥丨身上 he grabbed up dirt and threw it over him.

丨死了 to dash to pieces, as holding a cat by its tail and killing it.

丨鷄蛋 to poach eggs; to make an omelet.

甩 ꜀shwai An unauthorized character, used for ꜀tiu 丟 to discard.

To throw away, as worthless; to discard, to reject.

丨脫 throw it away.

丨拉外頭 throw it outside.

事丨不開 I cannot leave this work.

丨磚打人 to throw a brick at a man.

丨瓦 to toss tiles up.

帥 shwai꜄ From 巾 a *napkin* and an old form of 以 *using*, the kerchief being put in the girdle; it much resembles ꜀shi 師 an official.

A leader, a commander-in-chief; the black king in chess.

元丨 or 將丨 a generalissimo.

掛丨 the seal of this officer.

Read *soh*, To lead on, to conduct, to be chief; to follow, to be led.

丨天下以仁 to control the country by humane acts.

丨師征伐 to lead an army to battle.

領丨 to command.

率 shwai' shoh' lü' The original form is supposed to represent a *silken net* on a *handle*, such as birds are snared with; it is also read *shoh*, and *soh*.

A bird-net; to follow, to conform to; to act in accordance to; to lead, to command; to cause to follow; to observe, to direct; to give free course to; to receive under one's orders; a leader, a captain; a mark, a guide; the most or first; universally, for the most part, a resumé; active, spry; suddenly, hastily; from; along, about.

帝名丨育 Shangti ordered them (wheat and barley) for general nourishment of man.

大丨如此 for the most part they are like this.

丨由舊章 observing carefully the old statutes.

丨塲啄粟 pecking the millet about the thrashing-floors.

丨衆來侵 to bring a band of men to take possession.

表丨 an example, a leader.

草丨 carelessly; inexact.

丨領 to take the lead.

丨性 to adhere to one's opinion; to follow one's fancies.

丨兵 to lead troops.

莫不丨從 every one follows him.

丨規矩 to follow the usage.

統丨 to have general command.

丨眞 to speak the truth; the portrait is accurate.

不丨教 he won't hear advice.

丨然 or 丨爾 suddenly, hastily; the first is used in tactics, to bring up forces in a battle to succor.

輕丨 superficial, doing things on the spur.

以此爲丨 make this the rule.

丨屬有方 chiefs and subordinates, each have their places.

三口爲丨 three persons is the maximum or highest number.

Read *luh*, In *mathematics*, a term in a series.

Read *léi'* To reckon, to perform arithmetical calculations.

丨更 an officer who attended to the clepsydra.

SHWAN.

Old sound, shon. *In Canton*, shan *and* ts'ün; — *in Swatow*, chw'an *and* chw'ⁿa; — *in Amoy*, chw'an, swan, *and* wan; — *in Fuhchau*, sòng, swang, ch'aung *and* chw'ang; — *in Shanghai*, séⁿ *and* liⁿ; — *in Chifu*, swan.

拴 ˏshwan From *hand* and *all*; also read *ts'üeh*; at Canton, it is used for the next.

To select, to pick out from among a large quantity; to bind, to strap up; to buy; to entangle; to fasten, as a horse.

丨繩 to fasten with a cord.

丨車 to purchase a cart.

丨不住心 he can't keep his mind fixed on it.

丨扣兒 to make a noose or knot.

給人家丨對兒 to stir up strife between others.

丨娃娃 to bind a clay image to a string around the neck, which is thought to intercede for progeny.

丨住 to strap on, as skates.

閂 檂 㩾 ˏshwan From *door* and a *line*; or *wood* and *bar*; the last form is obsolete.

The bolt or beam which is used to bar doors; a cross-pin or key-bar; to bolt a door.

丨門 bar the door.

丨鋪 to shut up the shop.

丨柵 to shut the street gates.

竪丨 the upright post which fastens a gate.

暗丨 a secret bolt.

背面挿丨 to influence adversely and secretly.

栓 ˏshwan A wooden peg; a pin for suspending things; a cup or small bowl.

涮 shwan' Also read *shwah*.

To scour and wash out; name of a stream.

丨蔴 to soak and rot hemp.

拿水丨一丨 bring some water and rinse it clean.

丨金作 to wash with gold, to gild metals.

丨丨大雨 it rains heavily.

雨丨空堦 the rain washes the outer steps.

灥 shwan' To wash; to rinse; used with the last.

丨馬 to scrub a horse.

簨 shwan' To repair the axles and hubs of carriages.

SHWANG.

Old sound, shung. *In Canton,* sèung *and* shong ; — *in Swatow,* súang *and* sǎng ; — *in Amoy,* song ; — *in Fuhchau,* sòng *and* sǎng ; — *in Shanghai,* song ; — *in Chifu,* swang.

霜 ˛*shwang* From *rain* and *mutual.* Frozen dew, hoar-frost ; the goddess of hoar-frost is 青女 the green woman, who causes it and snow to descend ; rime, congealed vapor ; applied to powders resembling it, as quinine or soot ; and to efflorescence, as the exudation on the *Benincasa* gourd ; crystallized ; stern, severe, frigid.

丨雪 frost and snow.

挂一層丨 the hoar-frost is on the trees.

落丨 frosty, freezing.

草上丨 a furrier's name for unyeaned lamb-skin.

鬢邊丨 hoary temples ; *met.* growing old.

令肅秋丨 his orders and his severity [are decisive as] the autumn frost.

丨降 the 20th term from Oct. 24 to Nov. 8 ; whence 丨桑葉 is a name for falling mulberry leaves

丨威 majestic, awe-inspiring.

履丨之懼 as careful as stepping on the frost.

柿丨 a candied persimmon.

氷丨之操 a rigid adherence to one's principles.

粉丨 acetate of lead.

地丨 nitrous efflorescence seen on the ground in Chihli and elsewhere ; it is impure potash.

Read *shwang*ˀ To kill plants by frost ; the radical 水 is sometimes added to denote this meaning.

礵 ˛*shwang* An unauthorized character, used instead of the preceding in the name 砒丨 for arsenic shale.

孀 ˛*shwang* From *woman* and *frost.* A widow.

丨婦 a widow.

孤丨 a lone widow.

居丨 to live alone, as a widow.

驦 ˛*shwang* A famous Bucephalus called 驌丨 belonging by 郭璞 Kwoh Poh of the Tsin dynasty about A. D. 280.

鷞 鸘 ˛*shwang* A bird whose flight indicates the time of hoar-frost ; it is the turquoise kingfisher, of a green and blue color (*Halcyon smyrnensis*) ; its plumage is used in feather work.

丨鳩 a synonym for a hawk with a crest.

艭 ˛*shwang* A kind of river boat, called 艅丨 which is used in the central provinces.

雙 双 ˛*shwang* From two *birds* in one *hand* ; the contracted form is common.

A pair, a brace, a couple ; a match of anything ; an equal, a mate ; to go with, as a mate ; to be doubled or matched ; anciently, a plat of four or five *meu.*

丨料 thick, firm ; said of cups or glassware.

蓋世無丨 he is unequaled, he has no compeer in the world.

丨親 one's parents.

丨層兒的 doubled, in folds.

丨刀 two swords in one sheath.

丨六 double sixes, *i. e.* dice.

丨生兒 twins.

不論丨單月 it need not wait till an odd or even month.

成丨作對 when two come you'll have a match ; — it takes two to make a quarrel.

寡二少丨 it is rare to find the duplicate of this.

丨丨携手 they went along by twos hand in hand.

丨首白髮 an old hoary headed couple.

爽 ˊ*shwang* From *sleazy* cloth and *great.* To admit the light and make cheerful ; light-hearted, cheering ; sunny, delightsome ; grateful ; healthy, vigorous, comfortable, happy ; impetuous, noble ; crisp, tender ; to miss, to be in error ; to change ; a defect.

丨快 in good spirits.

乾丨 dried up, not sloppy.

口丨 ready to promise ; quick.

丨約 to fail in an engagement.

丨神 in good health.

一些不丨 not perfectly right.

光丨 bright, refulgent.

丨然若失 too great haste begets errors ; — the more haste the worse speed.

丨德 distinguished virtue.

丨甜 crisp and sweet.

秋丨 bright autumnal weather.

丨目悅心 it pleases the eye, and gladdens the heart.

丨當 lightly dressed, — and ready for work.

丨手的事 it is something he can easily do.

縔 ˊ*shwang* The strap which ties the shoe on across the instep, fastened from the heel.

SHWOH.

Old sound, shot. *In Canton*, shüt, üt, *and* shui; — *in Swatow*, súe *and* súat; — *in Amoy*, swat; — *in Fuhchau*, siòk, yok, *and* swòi; — *in Shanghai*, söh *and* sih; — *in Chifu*, shüé *and* sòa.

說 *shwo'* *shui'* From *words* and to *exchange*. To talk, to speak; to stir up one by conversing with him; to say, to narrate; to set forth, to discourse upon; a promise; words, speech; sayings, doctrines; to speak for, to excuse.

丨話 to converse; language, speech.

解丨 to explain words; a comment, an explanation.

丨神丨鬼 to talk of gods and demons; to propound mysteries.

丨破 to blab, to divulge.

丨文 to explain characters, to tell their component parts.

丨夢話 to tell dreams; big stories.

談天丨地 to talk about everything, vague talk.

丨不得他 I cannot speak to him (or about it).

丨知 to state verbally.

沒有得丨 there is nothing to say.

丨不得 can say no more; cannot be described.

有成丨 it is all settled, the die is cast.

丨白淸唱 to sing and tell stories.

丨不了 I could not (or did not) tell it all; could not finish the account.

好丨 well said, thank you; often used like — You are too kind; I beg pardon.

小丨 novels; story books.

再丨 we'll talk of that by and by; no matter about it now.

丨反了 to retract a promise.

難丨 hard to say; I am not sure about it.

不容分丨 I won't hear any more.

于子成丨 to them (our wives) we pledged our word.

Read *shui'* To urge one, to influence and persuade; to halt.

遊丨列國 he went around and persuaded all the states—to join.

丨客 intriguing men, persuasive politicians.

召伯所丨 Chao Peh rested a while — under this tree.

丨于株野 I will tarry in the country near Chu.

Read *yueh*, and used with 悅. Pleased; to delight in; numbers or fate.

民丨無疆 the people were delighted beyond measure.

亦既覯止我心則丨 let me but meet him, and my heart will then be happy.

Read *t'oh*, and used with 脫. To take off.

丨驂而賻 he loosened the outer horses and gave them to him.

SI.

Old sounds, si, sei, sai, sit, *and* sat. *In Canton*, sei *and* sai; — *in Swatow*, sai, soi, si, súa, jù, *and* sù; — *in Amoy*, sé, si, su, *and* ch'é; — *in Fuhchau*, sè, ch'è, *and* sai; — *in Shanghai*, si; — *in Chifu*, shi.

西 *si* The original form represents a *bird* on its *nest*; a synonym of the next, for when the sun is in the west, birds go to roost.

The west; in divination, the region belonging to metal; among Budhists, refers to heaven, and occasionally to India; western, at the west, westward; foreign, European; to place in the west.

病老歸丨 he is dead and gone.

丨賓 or 丨席 a private tutor, because the west side of the hall was the place for guests.

丨天 or 丨方極樂世界 the paradise of Budha (Sanscrit, *sukhavati*), the *nirvana* of the common people.

丨人 or 丨國的人 Occidentals, men from the west.

丨洋人 Europeans; but in the open ports, it means only the Portuguese.

不是東丨 he is nothing; *i. e.* what use is he? *met.* a useless man.

老丨兒 a man from Shansi. (*Pekingese.*)

日平丨 the sun declines to the west.

丨南之丨 west-southwesterly.

丨北 northwest.

東一嘴丨一句 here a mouth there a word; — everybody must talk.

棲 栖 *si* *ch'i* From *wood* and *wife* or *west*; the first is most used; used for *ts'i* 萋 staid.

To roost, to perch; to sojourn, to stay at; to settle down after wandering, to rest; to desist; at peace; a perch or roost; a sleeping-place.

鷄丨 a hen-roost.

丨遲 slow going; at leisure.

暫時丨住 live here for awhile.

丨身無定 no fixed dwelling-place.

丨丨皇皇 anxious and hurried.

借此以爲丨身之所 to get this place to rest myself in.

六月丨丨戎車既飭 all was bustle in the sixth month, for war-chariots were preparing.

丨屑 stopping here and there, as when traveling.

栖 ˓si Troubled and angry; used for the last.

丨惶 vexed, grieved.

何爲丨丨若是歟 why do you wander about so much?

粞 ˋsz' The broken rice left in the mortar after hulling is 米丨; but the common name is 米沙 or 碎米 broken rice.

犀 ˓si From 牛 ox and 尾 tail.

The rhinoceros still found in Chin-India; one kind is described as having the horn on the nose, while the other has it on the head; hard, good metal, as a sword; a section or slice of a melon.

丨角 a rhinoceros' horn, thought by the Chinese to detect poison, and often carved into cups.

丨牛 the rhinoceros.

心有靈丨一點通 a mind acute as a rhinoceros; *i. e.* he understands a point at once.

丨利 sharp and acute, as a rapier.

毛丨 a poetic name for the yak.

齒如瓠丨 her teeth were like the seeds in a slice of melon.

樨 ˓si From *wood* and a *rhinoceros*; an unauthorized character.

A diminutive variety of the *Olea fragrans*, with reddish flowers, is the 木丨; it is regarded as more fragrant than the white.

嘶 ˓si The neighing of a horse; a hoarse, crashing, slashing, or clattering noise.

丨殺 the din of battle; a furious onslaught.

丨丨聲 a cricket's chirp. (*Cantonese.*)

馬丨芳草地 the horse neighs over his pasture.

凘 ˓si Afraid.

惿丨 alarmed.

蠡 ˓si Also read *li*.

A wingless insect allied to the centipede, the 蝭丨 or millipede.

洗 ˓si ˋsien From *water* and *first*; it is also written 洒, but that form is more usually read ˋ*sha* or ˋ*shai*.

To wash the feet; to wash, to bathe; to purify; to reform; to wash out, to exterminate; to rinse; a bathing-vessel.

丨臉 or 丨面 to wash the face.

丨浴 or 丨澡 or 丨身 to bathe.

丨心 to cleanse or reform the heart.

領丨禮 or 收丨禮 to receive baptism.

丨城 washed out the whole city.

丨三 wash [the child] on the third day; the midwife bathes it in water having artemisia and other herbs in it, and places a slice of ginger on the fontanelle.

丨冤 avenged his wrong.

自此丨手 hereafter I'll do so no more.

丨耳恭聽 to hear with reverent attention.

筆丨子 a water-cup for ink.

丨刷 washed and brushed; a grammatical term for repetition of expressions.

Read ˋ*sien*. To wash, especially the feet; to clarify spirit.

丨馬 a reviser of books attached to the Hanlin.

姑丨 the name of a tune or pipe which was anciently played in the ninth moon.

自丨腆致用酒 to make spirit clear and potent and use it.

徙 ˓si Originally composed of 辵 to *go* and 止 to *stop*, altered to its present form; it resembles both ˏ*tu* 徒 a disciple, and ˏ*ts'ung* 從 to follow.

To move one's abode, to shift one's things; to exceed or overpass, to evade.

移丨 to move one's abode.

遷丨 to change about or move elsewhere.

丨居 to live elsewhere.

丨任 moved to another post.

丨善 to change for the better.

丨月 to incroach on another month.

丨陽 name in the Tang dynasty for Ya-cheu fu 雅州府 in the west of Sz'ch'uen.

孟母三丨 Mencius' mother thrice moved her dwelling.

In *Cantonese* read ˏ*sai*, and often written 嘥. To waste; to throw away; wasted, used up.

Also read *sai*,' and used for 了 All, the whole; complete, entire.

白白丨 uselessly wasted.

丨父兄面 disgraced his family.

丨得重 he uses more than is necessary.

去丨' all are gone.

見過丨' I've seen everything.

無丨' none at all.

鬆丨' let go all, as a rope.

寫唔丨' I have not written it all.

屣 蹝 躧 ˓si From *body* or *foot* and to *move*; the third form is very little used.

Straw sandals or slippers, worn by mummers and singers; shoes that have no heel-backs, like a patten or slip-shoe.

脫丨 to throw off a slipper.

猶棄敝丨 [Shun renounced the empire] like throwing away an old sandal.

倒丨迎賓 went out to meet his friend with his sandals turned end for end; —*met.* in a hurry.

蓰 ˓si Name of a plant; to increase fivefold.

或相倍丨 I think there may be five times as many.

縰 ʻsi A fillet to confine the hair under the cap, when the hair is worn like the Lewchewans.

櫛丨笄總 he prepares the comb, fillet, and hair-pin — for the toilet.

丨丨莘莘 coming on as people do,—numerously and one after the other.

葸 ʻsi From *plant* and to *think.*

Afraid, shirking, looking terrified; bashful, excessively timid; thrown off one's guard, showing the white feather.

畏丨 abashed, powerless to act.

色丨 looking afraid.

愼而無禮則丨 the cautious who are not used in courtier's ways are terrified.

璽 壐 ʻsi Originally composed of 土 *earth* and 爾 *thou*, denoting the ruler's seal, the radical now changed to 玉 *gem.*

The royal signet, the great seal, now called 寶; the impression of the seal.

國丨 the state seal.

符丨 the halves of the seal agree with each other.

枲 ʻsi From *wood* and raised; it is sometimes written with *grass* added.

The male nettle-hemp plant whose fibers called 麻 are used for making cloth; others say it is the female plant; and a third, that the plant is 麻 and this denotes the fibers.

丨耳 (or 卷耳 as given in the Book of Odes,) the burr-weed (*Xanthium strumare*), common in the northern provinces.

丨布 linen.

細 si' From *silk* and *field*, but the primitive was originally 囟 the *fontanelle.*

Fine, small; the particulars of a thing; delicate, finely made; soft, as a texture; trifling, petty; vexatious; subtile; carefully, thoroughly.

丨粗 fine and coarse.

丨心 be careful.

子丨 or 仔丨 heedful, attentive.

不矜丨行 don't be too careful about little things.

丨事 a small matter.

丨談 conversation; to speak minutely or carefully about.

丨察 to thoroughly examine.

丨緻 fine-looking, beautiful.

丨丨兒的 very particularly.

丨作 a spy; to sift to the bottom

丨微 minute atoms, subtle; the finest parts.

丨絲銀 sycee silver; — the foreign word is derived from this term.

丨切 to mince, to cut up.

丨小 small; petty.

丨君 a concubine.

婿 壻 si' From *woman* or *scholar* and to *help.*

A son-in-law.

夫丨 a husband, so spoken of by his wife.

女丨 my son-in-law.

賢丨 a worthy son-in-law.

翁丨 father-in-law and son-in-law.

東床佳丨 an excellent man for a son-in-law.

亞丨 two brothers-in-law so call themselves.

In *Shanghai*, used for 想 Fancy; thoughts.

白丨丨 to amuse one's self; having no cares.

有心丨 diligently, cheerfully.

SIANG.

Old sounds, siung, ziung, *and* niung. *In Canton*, séung *and* tséung; — *in Swatow*, sⁿié, sièng, *and* chⁿié; — *in Amoy*, siong; — *in Fuhchau*, siòng *and* ch'iòng; — *in Shanghai*, siang *and* djiang; — *in Chifu*, shang.

相 ˎsiang From *eye* and *wood;* for, according to the Yih King, there is nothing more agreeable to the eye than trees.

Looking among trees; to examine, to inspect; to blend with; mutually, reciprocally, by turns, from one to another; together; often merely a reflective form of the verb, and also answers to the Greek prefix ϛυν with; the substance or essence, as distinguished from the accidents.

丨與 acquainted with; friendly to.

丨與一塲 associated with for a while.

丨近 near to, not very distant; not on very good terms with.

丨左 at variance, differing in views.

丨似 much alike, a great resemblance.

不丨干 no matter about it; no difference which.

丨煩你 I will trouble you.

丨見恨晚 I am sorry to be so late in seeing you; — a polite phrase.

丨隔天淵 separated as wide as the heaven is from the abyss.

丨思病 lovesick, deeply attached to.

金玉其丨 [he is like] the strength of gold and the beauty of a gem.

丨思豆 a red bean, the *Abrus precatorius.*

丨承 to agree with, not to dispute about.

Read *siang*' To assist, to help; to select; to direct, to encourage and lead on; to watch the times, as a trader does; to look at; to receive an envoy; a minister of state; the black elephant in chess, it moves diagonally like the bishop through two squares; physiognomy;

the art of palmistry; small stars near Megrez δ in Ursa Major.

丨法 rules of physiognomy.

看丨 to tell the destiny by the countenance.

照丨 to take a photograph.

丞丨 or 宰丨 a prime or high minister.

丨時而動 act when it is a favorable time.

本丨兒 original temper.

內丨 disposition; real qualities of a person; an old name for a privy councillor.

色丨 the realities of life;—a Buddhist phrase.

丨維辟公 the princes and lords assist.

君火 and 丨火 fire-prince and fire-minister, — medical terms for causes of sickness.

丨彼泉水 look at the waters of that spring.

大丨公 young or respected Sir.

眞人不可貌丨 the sincere man must not be lightly contemned.

丨月 a classical name for the seventh moon.

丨者 the leader of a blind man.

廂 ꜀siang From *shelter* and *assisting*; occurs used for ꜀鑲 to inlay, and interchanged with the next.

The side rooms or building, called 丨房 situated on the east or west sides of the court, and subordinate to the large buildings.

關丨子 the houses over a city gate; the suburbs near the gates.

城內丨外 inside and outside of the city.

丨黃旗 the bordered Yellow Banner, one of the Manchu army corps.

箱 ꜀siang A box, coffer, trunk, or casket; boot of a carriage; *met.* a cart; a closet or storeroom; a granary; a room, a side apartment.

一箇丨 or 一隻丨 one box.

裝丨 to pack a trunk.

火食丨 a partition-box or tray for carrying eatables in processions.

當面落丨 I told him to his face to go away. (*Cantonese.*)

關丨子的 a peddler of tapes and needles. (*Shanghai.*)

皮包丨 a pure leather trunk.

棺丨 or 紙杠丨 a paper trunk for burning at funerals, with paper clothes in it.

頂丨 the upper small part of a wardrobe.

衣丨行李 trunks and baggage.

車丨兒 the body of a cart, where the passenger sits.

千倉萬丨 thousands of storehouses and myriads of granaries.

湘 ꜀siang A large tributary of the Yangtsz' River flowing north through the eastern half of Hunan into Tungting Lake, and giving its name to the 三丨 three Siang and other towns near it; its basin measures about 39,000 square miles; a lake in Chehkiang; to boil and cook.

丨妃竹 the bamboo of Shun's wife, which became speckled from his tears for her death.

于以丨之維錡及釜 hereupon she boiled it in her tripods and kettles.

緗 ꜀siang A light yellow color.

丨色 likened to the budding leaves of the mulberry.

縹丨 a bluish yellow, as of silks.

葙 ꜀siang A medicinal plant, the *Celosia argentea*, whose black smooth seeds, called 靑丨子, resemble those of the cockscomb; an oil is extracted from them.

襄 ꜀siang Composed of *clothes* and an old word for *confused*; it is interchanged with some of its derivatives.

To disrobe in order to plough, to remove, to put away; to overtop; to overflow, as a flood; to effect, to do; to exalt as superior, to praise; to complete; perfection; to assist; to bring about; meritorious valor; to yoke up; to saddle a horse.

上丨 the best riding — horse.

贊丨 to encourage by praise.

丨陽府 a prefecture in the north of Hupeh on the River Han.

不克丨事 the affair could not be brought about.

不可丨也 it cannot be excluded.

鑲 ꜀siang To inlay, to inchase, to let in; to insert or set, as a jewel; to veneer; to coat or plate; to rivet, to clamp on; bordered, as one color on another, for which 廂 is also used.

丨玻璃 to glaze a window.

丨快子 inlaid chopsticks.

丨杯丨盞 the inlaid cup and saucer — of cocoanut, used at a wedding.

丨牙 false teeth.

丨嵌 to let in, to emboss.

欀 ꜀siang A tree in Annam, which contains within its bark white grains like rice, that can be cleaned and pounded for food; it may be a species of sago palm, as it is also called *sha-muh.*

驤 ꜀siang A spirited horse shaking his head, caracoling and cantering; a horse with a white hind leg; to hold the head proudly; remote.

龍丨虎步 [his step is like] a dragon's gambols and a tiger's paces.

騰丨 capering and prancing.

纕 ꜀siang A cord to hold up the sleeves; to pull by the arm; to carry in the girdle; a surcingle or belly-band.

瓖 ꜀siang Like the last.

Ornaments on a horse; enchased hair-pins and head ornaments; a girth.

丨珠子的扁簪 flat hair-pins embossed with pearls.

𦢊 ˓siang — Also read ʿjang.

The fat of hogs is 丨脂油 when taken from the animal.

儴 ˓siang — To stroll about, to ramble.

丨徉 to go on an excursion, to saunter idly.

丨丨 to walk fast.

祥 ˓siang — From to *make known* and *sheep*; it is often symbolized by 吉羊 the lucky sheep, 示 and 吉 being sounded alike in the North, thus making a sort of anagram.

Happiness; felicity or good luck indicated in some way; an omen or harbinger of prosperity granted by superior powers.

丨瑞 lucky signs.

吉丨 a good prognostic.

不丨之兆 an unpropitious omen.

小丨 and 大丨 are the sacrifices to a parent at the end of one and two years, when the mourning costume is changed.

不弔不丨 regardless of the bad omens.

背人之惠不丨 it is not meet to forget the kindness showed to you.

詳 ˓siang — From *words* and *sheep*; it occurs used for the last.

To examine into and report upon; to learn fully; to discourse or reason upon; to watch over, to pay attention to; to minutely narrate; an official minute or report; the detail, the particulars, the arguments; minutely; fully; good, skillful; to feign.

丨審 to judge carefully.

丨細講 told every particular.

丨問 ask the real facts.

丨文 an official report to a superior.

丨悉 a clear, intelligible account.

推丨 to infer the consequences.

不丨其故 I have not inquired into the reason.

申丨 to report on.

會丨 a joint inquiry.

丨知 to minutely inform.

願聞其丨 I wish to hear all about it.

言不可丨 words cannot fully describe it.

丨乃視聽 be careful what you see and hear.

翔 ˓siang — To soar, to hover over; to look back on; to roam.

丨丨 dignified, severe.

高丨 risen to be a graduate.

室中不丨 in the house do not bow so grandly, — *i. e.* with spreading arms.

回丨 to look back on — one's native village.

齊子翱丨 the lady of Tsi moves on at ease.

庠 ˓siang — From *shelter* and *sheep*.

An asylum for old people; a gymnasium or college in the Cheu dynasty for poor students; to teach.

邑丨 the graduates of a district.

入丨 to become a 丨生 *siutsʻai.*

身列膠丨 his name is well known in the Academy.

想 ʿsiang — From *heart* and to *aid*.

To think on; to meditate, to reflect on; to plan; to hope, to expect; to anticipate; an idea, a conception.

沒有丨頭 no hope of getting it; it is impossible.

你丨頭太大 your notions are too grand; how extravagant you are!

渴丨 earnestly desiring or thinking of.

丨不來 or 丨不出 I don't comprehend it; I can't remember or think upon it.

思丨 to consider, to reflect on.

丨起 to recollect, to recall to mind; to imagine.

丨不到 or 沒丨到 I shouldn't have thought it; no one would have supposed that.

丨念 to think on.

丨必是 I think it will surely be so.

妄丨巴高 he has wild hopes of becoming great.

心裏丨 I will think of it.

丨壞肺 I fear it will hurt your lungs.

痴心妄丨 undecided, unreliable, chimerical.

丨一丨 let me think a little of it.

鮝 鯗 ʿsiang — From 魚 *fish* and 美 *fine*; which some regard as a contraction of 養 to *nourish*; the second form is most used.

Dried salt fish; in Peking, the 丨魚 is applied usually to the salted *Trichiurus* and perch; but in the Pǎn Tsʻao only the 石首魚 or sea bass, is so called; in Kiangsu, the 白丨 is one of the herring family, with very small fins.

象 siang˒ — The original character represents its four *legs*, *ears*, *trunk*, and *tusks*; used with the next.

The elephant; ivory; a figure, form, image, because in ancient days the bones of a dead elephant were found and put together to look like the living animal; the white elephant in Chinese chess, it moves two squares diagonally; the shape things take; emblematic auguries or fancies; to resemble; to delineate; pictured; a resemblance, a likeness; a law or ordinance of nature, applied to the change of the 八卦 diagrams; to imitate; acting, playing.

丨牙 ivory.

丨闕 the ivory gate, the palace.

丨皮 elephant's skin, used as a medicine; india rubber.

笨丨 stupid, dull.

丨州 a large district in the north of Kwangsi, where elephants were found in the Han dynasty.

各物丨數 each thing called by its own name.

丨教 the Budhist tenets.

丨奴 a mahout.

豐年有丨 there are signs of a plentiful year.

有子丨賢 a son should imitate the virtuous.

天丨 or 乾丨 celestial signs or luminaries.

包函萬丨 it comprehends all nature.

乃審厥丨 he then minutely delineated his form.

體無形丨 immaterial, no form.

丨服是宜 her pictured robes well became her.

丨鼻眼 looped holes to hang things by.

像 *siang'* From *man* and *elephant*; used with the last.

Like, such, so, similar; a figure, image, likeness; an idol, a statue; to symbolize; to resemble.

形丨 or 丨貌 figure, form.

畫丨 to paint portraits.

神丨 or 偶丨 an idol.

想丨 a conception, an idea.

丨生 life-like, as a statue.

丨似 similar to.

不丨樣 ill-looking, no comeliness.

作的不丨 not made like the pattern.

丨模丨樣兒的 elegant and stylish; well arranged, as a house.

橡 *siang'* The chestnut-oak (*Quercus sinensis*), called 丨椀樹 which grows near Peking.

丨粉 the meal of acorns.

丨椀子 the cupules of the acorns; they are used to dye black.

鱌 *siang'* The *elephant bird*, (as the character imports,) is the *Buceros* or hornbill of Siam the 丨鵰, of whose hard beak the people make vessels and carved ornaments.

SIAO.

Old sounds, sio, siok, *and* sok. *In Canton*, siu; — *in Swatow*, siò, ch'ié, *and* chiò; — *in Amoy*, siau, ch'iau, *and* sau; — *in Fuhchau*, siu *and* ch'iu; — *in Shanghai*, sio; — *in Chifu*, shao.

消 *˓siao* From *water* and *likeness*; occurs interchanged with the next two.

To melt, to liquefy, to thaw; to lessen by using, to do away with; to annul; to need and consume, as stores; hence *participially*, needed, required, exigeant; to allay, as thirst; to digest; to exhaust; to eliminate; diminished, dispersed; sold out, saleable; transpiring; an ancient city north of the Yellow River, near Wéi-hwui fu.

丨化 digestible.

丨渴病 intolerable thirst.

丨滅 destroyed utterly, lost all, as by fire.

花丨不管 not including the fees to the porters.

丨熱 to allay the fever.

下棊丨閒 play a game of chess to pass the time.

丨息 to transpire, as news; a report, a rumor.

丨釋 melted away.

丨悶 cheer up, dissipate your grief.

丨災降福 to remove judgments and induce blessings.

令我丨魂 it has taken away all my spirits; said of extreme joy or grief.

等他丨丨氣兒再說 wait till his temper has cooled, and then talk about it.

丨耗 wasteful.

無福丨受 he has no enjoyment of it at all.

丨河 a branch of the Yellow R. near Tsing-yuen in Kansuh.

丨夜 to carouse through the night.

只丨 only that, just needed only that.

丨停 leisurely, quietly; to become composed.

銷 *˓siao* From *metal* and *to resemble*; similar to the last.

To fuse metals; to dissolve, to finish; to spend, as time; deficient, as in politeness; to make void; to cancel, as a check; to exhaust; to spade up.

除丨 to clear off, as an account.

丨案 to decide a case in court.

丨號 to cancel a certificate, to give back a permit.

丨金 to wash with gold.

丨鎔 to melt, as ores.

丨差 to carry an order or message into effect, — and report.

丨毀 to destroy what is no longer of use; to ruin; to dissolve.

此恨難丨 such hatred is hard to appease.

一筆勾丨 the affair is quite settled.

坐丨歲月 to spend the years in leisure.

開丨 to render an account of government expenditures by a 奏丨 or memorial of outlays.

撤丨勇號 to deprive of an honorary title for cowardice.

有丨塲 in great demand; a large stock, as goods.

硝 *˓siao* Niter, or similar looking salts; saline efflorescence, whether having a soda or potash base; to use salts; to tan.

丨廠 a saltpeter dépôt.

朴丨 crude glauber's salts, or sulphate of soda; it is called 玄明粉 when purified.

丨皮 to tan leather.

丨子石 a chalky stone used for marking.

洋丨 foreign saltpeter.

皮走丨 the leather creaks, as after a wetting and drying.

丨鹽 carbonate of soda from the natron lakes in Mongolia.

苦丨 a saline substance left when lixiviating salt.

馬牙丨 crystals of niter, copperas, or other salts.

丨强水 nitric acid.

宵 ˛siao Night, in the night; dark; traveling by night; small, few.

丨行 or 丨燭 the glowworm.

通丨 or 終丨 throughout the night.

元丨 the full moon of the first month.

丨衣'旰食 I dress before the dawn and eat at noon; said by the emperor from his cares of state.

三朝連丨 for three days and nights.

深丨 in the silent night.

綃 ˛siao Raw silk; plain stuffs like lustring; the woof of silk.

玄丨衣以爲褐 blackish silks are made into vests.

鮫丨 a kind of byssus or silk brought up by divers.

Read ˛shao, and used with 梢. To comb the hair; a spar; a yard to support a sail or a flag.

鞘 鞘 ˛siao tsiao' From *leather* and *likeness;* the first form is common, and is also read ˛shao, a whip, a cudgel.

A sheath; the scabbard of a sword; a case for a knife or other thing.

劍丨子 a scabbard.

刀出丨 the blade left its case.

餉丨 cases for revenue treasure; they are made of small logs iron-bound and hollowed out.

蛸 ˛siao The chrysalis or egg-cocoon of the mantis.

蜱丨 the aurelia of the mantis.

Read ˛shao. A long-legged spider, the shepherd spider.

鮹 ˛siao From 魚 *fish* and 鞘 a *sheath* contracted.

A fish found in the lakes and the Yangtsz' River, and along the coasts, with a body like a whip and having a forked tail; it is probably the *Fistularia*, known at Canton as the 馬鞭; though it may be the gar-pike (*Belone*), also common in the southern seas.

痟 ˛siao Excessive thirst.

酸丨 a headache said to come on in the spring.

逍 ˛siao To ramble and saunter; applied to the easy diversions of immortals.

河上丨遙 to wander along the banks of the river.

丨遙自在 quite at leisure enjoying a ramble.

霄 ˛siao From *rain* and *likeness.*

Misty snow or sleet, also called 濕雪 which melts as soon as it drops; vapory haze, fleecy clouds; the empyrean, heaven, the highest region of the air; a halo or parhelion.

雲丨 fleecy clouds.

騰淸丨 to ascend to the pure vapors, to rise to heaven.

冲丨之忿 outrageous, heaven-daring anger.

淩丨花 the trumpet-flower or *Bignonia.*

魈 ˛siao A 山丨 is a brownie with one leg sticking out behind, found in thickets, especially in Ting-chau fu 汀州府 in Fuhkien; it tries to injure people, but desists on calling its name; the Miaotsz' in Kwéichau worship it at the new-year by a procession; other descriptions suggest that by this name is meant the demon which produces malaria, or ague.

橚 ˛siao Abundant foliage; the leaves falling in autumn; slender trees; used by some as a synonym for the catalpa.

簫 箾 ˛siao An instrument of music like the pandean pipes with 23 or 16 short, unequal tubes inserted in a frame; the ends of a bow.

洞丨 a bamboo flageolet.

品丨 to tune the pipes.

吹丨 to play on the orphic pipe.

丨韶 the ancient pandean pipes.

籟丨 the wind singing, as through a crack; æolian music.

丨管備舉 the pan-pipe and double-pipe begin together.

蠨 ˛siao A long-legged spider, called 丨蛸 akin to the *Phalangium;* the name seems to be applied to other long-legged insects, as the *Tipula* or crane-fly.

丨蛸在戶 the harvest spiders are in our doors.

蕭 ˛siao From *plant* and *to venerate.*

A plant, also called 香蒿 and 牛尾蒿, a very fragrant and common species of artemisia, about four feet high, numerous whorls of leaves, and a square stalk; a small principality near the Yellow River, now Siao hien 丨縣 in Sü-cheu fu in the northwest of Kiangsu.

丨斧 a bill-hook good for cutting plants.

丨條 lonely, desolate, poverty-stricken, in extremis.

丨丨馬鳴 quietly neighed the horses on their return.

丨牆之禍 in imminent danger.

丨然煩費 pestered, troubled.

風樹丨颯 the wind soughs fitfully through the trees.

蓼彼丨斯 how high is that artemisia!

瀟 ˓siao Name of a river in Yunnan, an upper tributary of the West or Pearl River.

丨水 a branch of the River Siang, entering it at Yung-cheu fu in the south of Hunan.

丨丨 a driving wind and rain.

丨洒風塵 the delights and troubles of the world.

彇 ˓siao The ends of a bow, which often turn backwards in Chinese bows.

翛 ˓siao Also read ˓yiu and shuh˒ The rapid flight of birds; injury to a bird's plumage; quick flighty.

予尾丨丨 I am [like a bird whose] tail is plucked; *i. e.* in a sad plight.

丨然而往 he suddenly went away.

小 ˋsiao Formed of 八 to *divide* and 亅 *appearing*, *i. e.* a thing just big enough to divide; it forms the 42d radical of a few miscellaneous characters.

Small, little; trifling, petty, mean; contracted, narrow; a depreciating term for what belongs to me, my; before proper names often means junior; inferior in rank or quality; young; uneducated, vile; a concubine; subtle, minute; to disesteem, to regard as trifling; to be particular, to become small.

丨人 a mean unprincipled man, also, the common people; a man naturally base and selfish; used sometimes by a poor man for I.

丨的 I, as used by a menial, seems to be an affected change for 丨弟, and is said by his betters in the same sense.

丨子 my servant; my pupil; young men; my children; I; you, my son.

羣丨 many concubines; they are also called 丨星, and 做丨 means to become a concubine.

妻丨 wife and children.

丨店 my shop.

丨姐 a miss, a young lady.

丨心 be careful; sedulously.

無大丨 it will suit, neither large nor small, as a sock.

丨意思 it was a mere trifle; said by one's self.

丨器 a small vessel, a person of contracted, mediocre ability.

房裏有個丨 I have one concubine.

慍于羣丨 I am hated by all the mean people.

狹丨 contracted and small.

丨家數 a petty finical person; a trifling way of acting.

自用則丨 he who lives within himself becomes selfish.

丨道兒貨 stolen things offered for sale.

丨心丨膽 petty and cowardly, frightened at little things.

丨寓 my house.

丨貨 to cheat in little things to pilfer, to overreach in trifles. (*Shanghai.*)

筱 ˋsiao From *bamboo* and *branch*; it is a synonym of ˓簫 a pipe.

A dwarf variety of the bamboo, useful for arrows and organ tubes, which grows in Shantung and the islands lying near; the culm of one kind is said to be nearly solid.

丨簜既敷 the fine and coarse bamboos were presented.

笑 咲 siao˒ From *bamboo* and *weird*; but as this gives a forced meaning, others think it denotes that bamboo instruments make people laugh by their joyous sounds; the second form is in common use.

To laugh, to smile; to be pleased; to laugh at, to ridicule, glad, smiling, smirking, giggling; jolly; a smile.

可丨 laughable.

佛見丨 a pure white rose.

喜丨顏開 to laugh outright with joy.

見丨大方 laughed at by all respectable people.

發丨 to laugh.

惹人丨 to act ridiculously.

丨死丨 to laugh immoderately.

丨話人 to jeer at one.

丨嘻嘻 giggling and smirking.

偷丨 to smile at secretly.

冷丨 a forced smile, to grin a ghastly smile.

可發一丨 a thing to be laughed at.

破涕爲丨 to dry up one's tears and smile.

丨面虎 a deceitful smile.

陪丨兒 to smile because another does.

先號啕而後丨 to grieve and cry, and afterwards rejoice with one; — the pleasures of success after a toilsome struggle.

肖 siao˒ From *flesh* and *small.*

To be like, to assimilate; a likeness or relationship between parent and child, said to be proveable by mixing their blood; like; small; dwindling, deteriorated; scattered and lost.

不丨 not equal to or like it; degenerate, used by a son when writing to his father.

丨似 resembling.

丨子 a filial son.

微丨 a little like it.

象形惟丨 their look and form are alike; — a chip of the old block.

嘯 歗 siao˒ From *mouth* or *breathing* and to *venerate*; the first is most used.

A whistling, hissing sound, like letting off steam; to scream; to whistle; to sigh, to groan.

虎丨 a tiger's scream.

善丨 good at whistling.

其丨也歌 he whistled and then sung, — to divert his mind.

吟丨成羣 to sing in chorus.

條其丨矣 long drawn are her moans!

SIÉ.

Old sounds, si, zi, sit, *and* sip. *In Canton*, sé, tsé, *and* ts'é ; — *in Swatow*, sia *and* sé ; — *in Amoy*, sia, ch'ia, *and* sòe ; — *in Fuhchau*, siò *and* sie ; — *in Shanghai*, zia, sia, *and* si ; — *in Chifu*, shié.

些 ˏ*sié* From 二 *two* and 此 *this* ; *q. d.* pointing to this and then to that.

A little ; a sign of the plural ; an adjective of comparison, analogous to the termination *er*, when following another adjective or adverb ; shortly, partly, rather, somewhat ; small in number ; short, as time.

一丨 a little.

沒有一丨 I have none at all.

這丨 and 那丨 these, those.

有丨不是 it is not very proper.

這丨小物 these trifling matters ; an unimportant affair.

快丨 quicker.

略略好丨 it is a little better.

爛了好丨 he broke a good many.

丨須 trifling, a little of, a little while.

沒丨意思 unintelligible.

似乎多丨 it seems as if there were more.

稍丨有位 I have only a little of it left.

少丨 too little ; fewer.

無丨味 disagreeable, disgusting.

作丨甚麽 what are you doing ?

丨微的不同 a very little different.

有那麽丨個菓子 there are so many kinds of fruits.

Read *so*'. A final particle expressing regret.

何爲四方丨 why alas ! does the manes thus wander about, — and not return to its home ?

蒳 ˏ*sié* A plant, the 丨蒿, which is probably allied to the *Vitex*, a species whose leaves are transversely veined.

Read *yé*. To accumulate.

Read ˏ*fu*. An ear of grain.

斜 ˏ*sié* From a *peck* and *I*.

Slanting, inclined ; oblique, diagonal, criss-cross ; aslant, not by the line ; distorted ; irregular, scattered ; not level, as a rising road.

丨視 to look askance.

丨風 an unsteady or side wind.

丨眼 cross-eyed.

丨陽 oblique beams of the sun.

歪丨 awry, slanting ; perverse.

丨街 an oblique street.

丨丨兒的 it is somewhat crooked.

西丨熱 the afternoon sun is hot. (*Cantonese.*)

放丨 lay one end of it higher.

丨坡 a slope, a hill-side.

邪 ˏ*sié* From *city* and *tooth* ; it has superseded the next character, once used with this meaning.

Deflected, inclined, swerving from the right line, — the opposite of 正 ; depraved, vicious, deluding ; illegal, heterodox, heretical ; corrupting, radical ; specious ; unsanctioned by law or custom, or whatever leads away from the writer's standard.

丨道 erroneous doctrines.

丨法 sorcery, unlawful tricks.

丨神 illegal gods, false deities, whose worship is unacknowledged, or whose ritual is subversive of morality.

丨偪在下 their buskins were on below — the knee.

丨術 charms ; philters ; black art.

心丨 impure ; plotting evil.

丨淫 obscene, depraved.

奸丨 illicit ; seditious ; malicious, underhand.

改丨歸正 forsake heresy and return to the right way.

思無丨 his thoughts are upright.

丨氣 possessed, mad, haunted by ; malaria.

Read ˏ*yé*, and used for 琊 and 耶. Name of an ancient place, 琅丨 lying in the east of Shantung ; a final particle.

莫丨 name of a sword or rapier, so called from its maker.

Read ˏ*yü*. An excess, as of days.

Read ˏ*sü*, and used for 徐. To delay.

其虛其丨既亟只且 we can no longer delay, it is a very urgent moment.

衺 ˏ*sié* From *clothes* and *tooth* ; used with the last two.

A garment like a buskin that wraps around the leg ; awry ; out of fashion or not becoming ; vicious, lewd.

奇丨 slanderous, lewd, uncouth, said of common people ; a depreciating term.

寫 **冩** 'sié From a *shelter* and a *wooden clog* ; occurs used for the next ; the second form is vulgar.

To write, to draw ; to compose, to write on a subject ; to design or sketch ; to put a thing in its place ; to make out, as an account ; to remove, to put aside ; to quiet, to calm, as one's passion ; to ease one's mind ; to disburthen ; to dissipate ; to found, to mold, as an image ; to leak.

丨字 to write.

丨信 to write a letter.

丨字人 a clerk.

丨得好 written finely.

丨捐簿 a subscription book.

太丨意 very heedless ; careless how he does it.

丨正官板 write the characters out in full.

再丨過 rewrite it.
丨生 to draw living objects.
丨字端楷 he writes evenly and carefully.
為之丨照 described it like a picture; word-painting.
洩丨 to disburden, to let out one's mind.
摹丨傳神 the figure is drawn to the life.
我心丨兮 my mind is quite satisfied.
丨不得字 I am unable to write, as from a sore.
駕言出遊以丨我憂 I tell him that I wish to go on an excursion to relieve my low spirits.

蕮 ‘sié A medicinal plant.
澤丨 or 澤瀉 an umbelliferous plant found in damp places in Fu-cheu in Kiang-si, the dried tubers of which are used for their diuretic properties.

灺 ‘sie The ashes of a lamp or pastile; an expiring wick.
香丨燈光奈爾何 the torch has burned out its light, alas, how quickly!
餘丨猶明 the end of the candle flashes up.

謝 sié’ From *words* and to *shoot arrows* as the phonetic.
To decline, to withdraw from, to refuse; to thank, to express gratitude, and rather intimates that one intends to do so with money or something substantial; to acknowledge, to confess; to excuse one's self; to diminish, as strength; to resign, to throw up; to stop intercourse with; thanks.
多丨 or 丨丨 many thanks for.
丨過 to own one's faults.
燭丨淚 the candle drips.
丨帖 a card of thanks; a notice of reward offered.
領丨 received with thanks.
花丨 fading flowers.
丨酒 to call on one after a feast; an after-dinner call.
丨絕 to break off intercourse.
丨步 to return a call.
丨儀 a return present; a doctor's fees.
丨客 to decline a visitor.
丨世 to die.
感丨 to feel grateful for.
拱手稱丨 I thank you with my folded hands.

榭 sié’ An ancient terrace or arbor with trees around it; a kind of roofed altar whereon to place sacrificial implements; a gymnasium; a fencing room.
臺丨 a wooded mound with a lookout or belvidere on it.
武丨 a military practicing room, like a shooting-gallery.

卸 sié’ From 卩 a *seal*, 止 to *stop*, and 午 *noon*, referring to the time when animals are unharnessed from the cart.
To lay aside, to relinquish, to leave; to put off, as clothes; to vacate; to deliver over to; to take off, as a load; to unroll.
丨事 to throw up an affair; to vacate an office.
丨任 or 丨仕 to resign.
形丨神短 he looks exhausted and worn out.
丨貨 to deliver cargo.
拆丨 to pull down, as a house; to take away, as an awning.
花丨瓣 the flowers are falling off.
丨煤 to deliver coal.
丨甲而走 to throw off armor and flee.
丨離禍 to avoid evil, to escape danger.
投行交丨 to send to a hong to deliver goods.
脫丨 to undress; also, to abridge, to take the précis of a paper.
丨媒 to dismiss the go-between.
丨擔 to let down a burden
丨車 to unharness a cart.
丨載 to unload.

瀉 sié’ To let water flow off, to drain land; to leak, to ooze; to purge; to eliminate; diarrhea; slippery, as from the rain.
肚丨 a bowel complaint.
丨藥 a purgative.
丨火 to reduce a feverish feeling by purging.
水丨 a watery stool.
丨水 to open a sluice or way for water to flow.
丨底事 it has no foundation to rest on, hollow.
打丨茶 spilled the tea, — to lose a betrothed before the nuptials.
丨土 barren, herbless land.
傾談如丨瀑 he sputters his words out, as if he had a flux.
丨二次 purged twice.
抽筋腹丨 spasms and gripes with a diarrhea.
路上滑丨一交 the road was so wet that he slipped down once.
駁岸崩丨 the water swashes up and crumbles away the bank.
文佳如水銀丨地 a polished composition covers the whole subject as quicksilver flows over the ground.

瀉 sié’ Occasionally used for the last.
A diarrhea, a purging ailment; to itch.
肚丨 a flux.

SIEH.

sit and sip. In Canton, sit, ship, sip, *and* tip ; — *in Swatow,* siak, siat, *and* si ; — *in Amoy,* siat *and* sek ; — *in Fuhchau,* siek ; — *in Shanghai,* sih ; — *in Chifu,* shié.

薛 ‘*h'üé* A plant resembling the 莎 a large marsh grass like a *Carex* or *Cyperus ;* it is found in Nganhwui and Shantung.
丨國 ancient name of a very small state, lying east of Tăng hien 滕縣 in Yen-cheu fu in the south of Shantung ; three rulers are mentioned before B. C. 484.

躠 ‘*h'üé* To walk awry, as a club-footed man, or one who is lame.
蹩丨爲仁 it came hard for him to be kind.

僁 ‘*h'üé* A whisper.
丨丨 to speak in a low whisper ; — a phrase whose sound imitates its meaning.

屑 *h'üé*’ *h'ioh*’ From *body* and *likeness.*
A fragment, a crumb, a bit ; to powder, to break in pieces ; to regard ; to take pains for ; to regard as pure ; upright ; respectful, diligent ; minute, troublesome ; lightly, triflingly.
往來丨丨不憚煩 coming and going constantly, and caring nothing for the trouble.
瑣丨 trifling, vexatious.
丨有辭 making trifling excuses for his conduct.
不丨 unworthy of thought, to disregard ; to keep aloof from.
不丨去 no need of going.
輕丨 to depreciate.
丨播天命 to lightly set aside the decrees of Heaven.
丨丨不已 the annoying part is not yet over.
不我丨以 he thinks I am not fit to be with him.

搹 *h'üé*’ To push or pull out a stopper ; to unstop a hole.

糏, 粞 *h'üé*’ *h'ioh*’ The grits of rice or corn which remain after hulling or pounding.
丨末 rice grits.
粉丨 flour and grits.

徆 *h'üé*’ *h'ioh*’ To wave.
徹丨 to flutter as the skirts of a garment in the wind.

洩 *sié*’ From *water* and *to drag ;* sometimes read *i*’ as a synonym of 泄.
A stream in Chehkiang ; to leak, to drop, to ooze ; to drip and soak through ; to burst forth ; to divulge ; to tell a secret ; to desist from ; to reduce, to diminish.
惱未丨 he is still angry.
丨氣 lost all its smell or virtue.
丨漏 divulged ; it has got abroad.
發丨 it leaks ; to exude, as perspiration ; to come out, as flowers.
事丨 or 丨底 the affair has leaked out ; the thing is known.
不丨其過 he did not lessen his fault.
莫丨了風聲 do not lisp a breath of it.
丨了底 the copy has got abroad.

痖 *sié*’ A dysentery.
丨痢 a bloody flux.

媟 *sié*’ From *woman* and *leaf ;* also used with the next.
To treat disrespectfully or to insult females ; to lust after ; to outrage.
丨狎 indecent trifling.
汚丨 lewd conduct.

偞 *sié*’ Extravagant.
丨華放蕩 to spend in a reckless manner.

褻 *sié*’ From 衣 *dress* and 埶 *apt* contracted.
Undress, dishabille ; common, ragged, dirty garments, fit for working in ; tattered ; impure ; to revile, to treat irreverently ; to dishonor.
丨瀆 to profane ; to blaspheme, as the gods ; to make ashamed.
丨慢 to treat disrespectfully, wanting in attention.
丨服 in undress.
丨穢 indecent, filthy, as a dress.

暬 *sié*’ From *sun* and *apt* contracted ; nearly synonymous with the last.
To treat disrespectfully ; dark, obscure ; attendants, chamberlains, familiars.
丨御之臣 imperial eunuchs.
曾我丨御 only a groom of the chamber as I am.

屧 *sié*’ From *body* and *lamina.*
The lining or stuffing of the soles of shoes ; a sandal or wooden shoe ; to fill up level.
步丨尋幽 put on your clogs and let us seek a shady place.

楔 ˏ*sié* The side-posts or heavy pillars which uphold a gate ; a tree resembling the cherry ; a thorny juniper ; to fill a crack with a wedge or reglet.
加一個木丨子 stop it up with a wooden slip.

揳 *sié*’ From *hand* and a *deed.*
To rub, to wipe off ; to measure ; to play with in the hand, to fumble ; to stop ; queer, angular.
攕丨 irregular, not a rectangle ; angular.
拭丨 to clean or brush so as to injure.
揣長丨大 guess its length and measure its size.

In *Pekingese.* To strike.
丨打丨打 pound it in, as a tenon.

絏 *sié'* To tie up, to secure; to fetter; tied; fetters, bonds.
縲 丨 bound with cords.
囹圄中攣丨所驅 in prison bound hand and foot so that he cannot stir.
羇 丨 a bridle; that which restrains.
憂于縶丨 my grief fetters me like bonds.

紲 緤 *sié'* The first is most used, but both are nearly synonymous with the preceding.
A halter to secure an animal; to fasten with cords; a bow-rack; to remove.
是丨袢也 she removed the warm dresses.
弓 丨 a frame to retain a bow in proper shape.

躞 *sié'* To walk.
蹀 丨 to advance rapidly, to walk fast, to get on.

燮 *sié'* From 炎 *fiery,* 言 *words,* and 又 a *hand.*
To blend, to harmonize; to adjust properly, to keep in due relations; to mature.
丨理陰陽 to adjust the dual powers properly.
丨和 to arrange equably.
調 丨 to harmonize forces.
丨伐大商 he in accordance [with the decrees] destroyed the great Shang dynasty.

SIEN.

Old sounds, sin, sim, sen, *and* zien. *In Canton,* sín *and* ts'ím; — *in Swatow,* sién, sⁿnoi, ch'ⁿi, sⁿúa, yièn, sèn, *and* siam; — *in Amoy,* sian, siam, sím, ch'iam, san, *and* swan; — *in Fuhchau,* sieng, sing, ch'ieng, *and* chieng; — *in Shanghai,* siⁿ *and* ziⁿ; — *in Chifu,* shien.

先 *,sien* From 儿 a *man* and 之 *to go above* it; *i. e.* he who goes on, or precedes others.
First, before; formerly, past; to go ahead; to regard as first, to put first; a cause; to begin; firstly; previous; deceased, late, gone before; early, soon; the ancients.
丨後 before and after, in time or place; first and last; various times; several things.
丨漫 light — heavy, as in weighing, when the beam goes up or down.
丨君 or 丨父 my late father.
丨天足 a good constitution, in full vigor.
當 丨 in front; formerly, at that date.
丨時 before; previously, last time.
你丨走一步 do you step ahead a little.
丨人 my ancestors; forefathers.
爭 丨 to strive to be first or get ahead.
丨馬 a forerunner, an avant-courier, a harbinger.
為我丨容 he acts as my spokesman or messenger.
丨事豫防 to be prepared beforehand.
丨見之明 the ken of a prophet, sagacious.
桌上丨生 the teacher on the table; — a euphuism for a dictionary.

Read *sien'* To assume the precedence, to take the lead; to put first; to be beforehand.
倘或丨之 perhaps some one will be ahead of you — and save it.
疾行丨長者謂之不弟 to press on ahead of one's seniors may be termed very disrespectful.

硃 *,sien* A fine pebble, inferior to a gem, such as red jasper or rose quartz.

秈 籼 *,sien* Common rice when growing is called 丨米 in Kiangnan by the people, to distinguish it from glutinous rice; another name is 粳丨 applied to the grain,

仙 *,sien* From *man* and *hill*; *i. e.* those who dwell in wilds.
An immortal; human souls endued with divine powers; beings of benign nature inferior to gods, and having the power of becoming invisible, like the Arab jinnee; fairies, called 神丨 and 丨人; the Budhists use it for sanctified personages or immortal *rishis,* of whom they make five classes, heavenly, spiritual, human, earthly, and devilish; an angelic or disembodied man; an old recluse, who changes into another form but does not die; to become immortal, deathless; anything puzzling or curious; graceful.
臣是酒中丨 I am the genius of the wine bottle.
天 丨 angels, so called by the Mohammedans.
丨遊 or 登丨 to die; *lit.* to ramble with or go to the genii.
丨境 elysium, fairy land.
丨姑 a fairy, an elf.
丨馭升遐 [the emperor] mounted the fairy car, and ascended to the far country.
修 丨 to strive to become an immortal.
丨藥 the liquor of immortality.
丨骨 lithe, slender, lissome, graceful, fairy-like.
鳳丨花 the touch-me-not flower. (*Impatiens*)

飄飄欲 | sprightly as a fairy.

| 家妙術 mystic arts of the Rationalists; used for the sect, from their constant reference to these beings.

八 | the eight genii; they are deified mortals and regarded now as the patrons of arts; they are of Taoist origin, and are named as follows:—

1. 呂洞賓 who carries a 劍 sword, and assists in fencing; he is worshiped by the sick.
2. 漢鍾離 carries a 扇 fan, with which some say he fans and revives the souls of the dead.
3. 藍采荷 carries a 花籃 basket of flowers and a spade, and aids florists.
4. 鐵枴李 carries a 葫蘆 gourd and crutch, and helps magicians.
5. 曹國舅 wears an official cap and carries 版 castanets; the patron of mummers and actors.
6. 張果老 has a bamboo pencil-cup, and guides writers and scholars to a good style.
7. 韓湘子 a youth playing the 笛 flute, who helps musicians.
8. 何仙姑 a female standing on a floating petal carries a 荷花 lotus flower, chowrie and basket, and helps in housewifery.

僊 *ₒsien* From *man* and *to mount high*; it is used for the last.

To caper and perform antics.

屢舞 | | they hopped and capered, — the drunken fellows.

䙴 *ₒsien* The original form is composed of 舁 to *rise* and 大 *great*, contracted in combination; it is only used as a primitive.

To rise high, as a bird; to climb a height.

躚 蹮 *ₒsien* To walk round and round; to amble or pace, as in a pantomime.

蹁 | to whirl, as dervishes; to wriggle and turn in a ring.

褼 *ₒsien* Dressed.

褊 | the clothes shaking when walking; the dress fluttering in moving.

韱 *ₒt'ien* From *leek* and a *pick* or *hoe*; it is chiefly used as a primitive, and altered in combination; also read *ₒtsien*.

Wild onions or leeks, with which the shallot 薤 is sometimes confounded from their similarity.

襳 *chié'* Small under-clothes; a girdle; clothes of hair or feathers; waving, as a flag.

蜚 | 垂髾 her waving girdle and flowing skirts, were like fluttering pennons.

纖 *ₒsien* From *silk* and a *slip*; used with the next.

Small, fine, like silken fibers; silk woven with black woof and white warp; ornaments hung on the lapel; tapering, delicate; mean, niggardly; to prick, as in tattooing; in silken work, denotes ten fibers of silk or other minute threads; atom-like, a millionth part.

| 細 fine, delicate; all the minute details.

巨細宏 | very great and very small.

| 巧 skillful work.

| 指 slender fingers.

不沾 | 塵 it did not get dusty in the least.

| 毫 a very little; too small to reckon.

孅 *ₒsien* From *woman* and a *slip*, as of a garlic leaf.

Similar to the last; slender and sharp pointed; delicate, slender, like a girl.

| 悉 to perceive fully; he knows it all

| 弱 weak and delicate.

| 介之事 a bagatelle, a trifling affair.

| 趨 artful, cunning.

銛 *ₒsien* From *metal* and *tongue*.

A kind of hoe; sharp; acute, fine pointed; a fish barb.

| 利 sharp-edged.

| 筆 [he has a clever] sharp pen.

| 于詩學 skilled at writing poetry.

Read *'t'ien*. To take a thing; to cut, as with an ax.

暹 *ₒsien* From *day* and *to enter*.

The increasing light of the sun; rising higher and higher, to advance.

| 羅國 the kingdom of Siam; the first word is an imitation of the native word *Sayam*, which Pallegoix says means a brown reddish-ochery color, alluding to the hue of the people; the other word perhaps refers to the Laos or Lolos people.

憸 *ₒsien* From *heart* and *all*.

Disputation, skilled in argument; sharp-mouthed, litigious; insidious; flattering.

| 人 a smooth-tongued man.

相 | 時民 look at these poor people; *i. e.* those who must defend their own case.

撏 *'sien* To take, to select, to feel after.

燖 *'sien* It is also read *ₒts'ien*.

To scald; to boil in water, as for soup; warm, comfortable.

| 毛 to scald the hair off, as from pigs.

鮮 鱻 *ₒsien* From *fish* and *sheep*, but the primitive is a contraction of 羊 repeated thrice, and a synonym of 羶 meaning *frowzy*; the second form is obsolete.

The strong smell of fresh fish; good, caller, fresh; just killed, as meat; bright, new, clean, in good order.

| 魚 a fish just caught.

海 | marine delicacies, a dainty fresh from the sea.

五色俱丨 everything was bright and new.

丨明貨物 bran new goods.

丨衣 new clothes.

丨雞 a fine, fat fowl.

唯君用丨 but the prince may eat fresh game.

丨花 new flowers.

淸淸丨丨 fresh, nice, as game, fruit, or fish.

丨甜 fresh tasted, pure.

鮮 尟 尠 ʻsien The second form, composed of 是 *is* and 少 *few*, is rarely used; 是 is explained by 正 *upright*, of whom there are few; the third form of *few* and *very* is occasionally met.

Few, rare, seldom; rarely; used up, exhausted; standing isolated, like lofty peaks.

民丨 the people are few.

丨乏 impoverished, not enough.

丨少 very few.

丨覯 seldom seen.

丨矣仁 humane people how few!

愛我頁多慢我不丨 those who love me are numerous, and my enemies are not few.

關係實非淺丨 the consequences will be neither trifling nor usual.

丨卑 a race of Tungusic origin, which came down upon northern China in early times; they afterwards founded the Liao 遼 dynasty, and were called Kitan 契旦 in later years.

蘚 ʻsien Mosses on damp walls and ground; low, mossy vegetation growing in patches.

苔丨 moss and lichens on trees and banks.

瓦丨 the green mossy covering on walls.

丨痕 a moss scar; *i. e.* a vestige.

癬 ʻsien From *disease* and *new*.

Tetter, ringworm; scaldhead; scrofulous or leprous sores; scabby eruptions.

生丨 he has a ringworm.

牛皮丨 a kind of lepra.

金錢丨 a leprous patch.

白面丨 the white face.

環丨 incurable morphew or scurf; *met.* an intractable disposition.

廯 ʻsien From *shelter* and *new* as the phonetic.

A small storehouse for grain, a place where it can be kept clean and fresh.

廩丨 granaries of different sorts, the former being the smaller.

筅 ʻsien A small bamboo broom, 丨帚 used by cooks to clean the rice boiler.

狼丨 a stout stockade or abattis of halberds to resist an enemy.

挄 ʻsien To take up in the fingers.

撫丨 to hold a thing by the fingers.

銑 ʻsien A small chissel; burnished, bright, as metal; ends of the rim of a rhomboidal bell; a metal ornament at the end of a bow; chilly, raw, as weather.

物飾其丨 it is gilded and prettily adorned.

毨 ʻsien From *hair* and *first* as the phonetic.

To molt, to renew the hair or feathers; glossy, sleek, as newly molted birds.

鳥獸毛丨 the birds and beasts shed their coats.

跣 ʻsien From *foot* and *first*; it occurs interchanged with 躧 and 蹝 to tread.

Barefooted; to walk without shoes; to put the naked feet on the ground.

若丨弗視地 if you walk barefooted do not look down on the ground.

披髮丨足 disheveled hair and bare feet.

燹 ʻsien From *fire* and herd of *swine*.

A fire lighted on the moor or wilds, to drive out the game; a fire; fiery.

兵丨之餘 left from the ravages and burnings of troops.

地經兵丨 the soldiers have clean swept the region.

獮 ʻsien From 犬 *dog* and 璽 *signet* contracted.

The autumnal hunt taken by the ancient emperors; it was also the time of a yearly progress and assize; to kill.

丨田 a hunt.

鐵 剈 sienʼ From *metal* and to *scatter*; the second and unauthorized form is now only used.

To castrate a fowl; the first is also read *san*ʼ and defined the trigger of a cross-bow; a cross-bow.

丨雞 a capon.

線 綫 sienʼ From *silk* and *fountain*, or *small*; the primitive in the least used form gives the sound.

Thread of any kind; fine cord or lines; a clue, a trace; needlework; a way for, a chance for, a hope; a remnant or relic, like an orphan to continue a family.

絲丨 silk thread.

縫丨 to sew a rip or seam.

一子丨 a skein of silk.

紡丨 to spin thread.

針丨活計 she gets her living by sewing.

引丨 a fancy name for a needle.

丨步疎 the stitches are coarse.

作丨 to act the spy.

一丨之路 a slight chance for.

一丨之光 a gleam of light.

買眼丨 to hire a spy.

日長添丨 do a little more as the days lengthen.

通丨 to get a clue of.

火藥丨 a slow match; a fuse.

察其丨 inspect her needlework.

一架丨 a spool or stick of thread.

丨蔴 a kind of hemp.

羨 *sien'* From 羊 contracted from 羑 to *lead*, and 次 *saliva*.

To desire, to covet; to long for morbidly; an overplus, a remainder; to laud, to estimate highly; this character, or with the radical 木 added, is used in Java to denote the mango fruit.

稱丨 to praise very highly.

丨餘 or 奇丨 too much; a surplus; a profit.

欽丨其德 he highly extolled his virtue.

無然歆丨 do not be ruled by your likings and whims.

欣丨 to delight in.

以丨補不足 supply the deficiency with what is over.

丨門 name of a genie in the days of Tsin Chi-hwangti.

四方有丨 all around there is ease and plenty.

丨慕 to long for affectionately.

Read *ˏyen.* The path leading under ground to a tomb by which fortunate influences reach it.

霰, 霓 *sien'* From *rain* and *powdered* or to *see*; the second form is unusual.

Sleet; snow and sleet falling, poetically called 米星雪 rice star snow; freezing rain.

丨雪 sleet.

如彼雨'雪先集維丨 when the snow begins to fall, there is first a little sleet.

丨尼 a schismatic from the Budhist sect, a schism among the Budhists; — an Indian word.

望空捉丨 [it will be like] looking up to catch the sleet; — a vain hope.

SIH.

Old sounds, sik, zik, zit, *and* zip. *In Canton*, sik, sek, *and* tsik; — *in Swatow*, sek, sia, cha, sip, *and* ch'ek; — *in Amoy*, sek, sip, *and* ch'ek; — *in Fuhchau*, sek, sik, *and* ch'ek; — *in Shanghai*, sih *and* zih; — *in Chifu*, shi.

昔ˎ *ˏsi* Composed of 日 *sun* and a contracted form of 肉 *flesh* cut up for jerking.

Dried meats; old, a long time ago, anciently; former; the previous; the time of a night.

丨時 olden, in former days.

丨日 on a previous day.

丨者 formerly, whilom; the previous case or person.

古丨 of old.

曩丨 yesterday and long before.

今丨不同 it is not now as it used to be.

爲一丨之期 it was the space of one night.

自古在丨先民有作 from of old in the ancient days, the former men gave the practice or example.

腊ˎ *ˏsi* From *meat* and *old*; like the last; it is also often read *lah*, for 臘 a candle, and used for 措 to lay by.

Dried meat, or slices prepared for a journey; a long time; extreme, very; to lay aside, to put down.

丨酒 old, ripe wine.

丨人 an officer who jerked game.

六三噬丨肉 [the Book of Changes says] the sixth and third diagrams require dried meat.

惜ˎ *ˏsi* From *heart* and *formerly* as the phonetic.

To compassionate, to regard, to feel for; to regret, to scrimp, to be sparing of; close, parsimonious.

可丨 lamentable; how sad!

吝丨 stingy.

不丨工本 reckless of labor or money.

丨光陰 careful of one's time.

禹丨寸陰吾人當丨分陰 if the Great Yü cared for every inch of time, we should regret every line.

不丨勞苦 do not dread a little trouble.

丨物 careful of, not wasteful.

丨身 careful of one's self, not exposing one's body or health.

不丨小費 don't mind a little expense.

痛丨 pained for.

晰ˎ, 晳ˎ, 皙ˎ *ˏsi* From *day* and to *divide*; it is also occasionally written like the third form.

Clear, bright; to distinguish, to discriminate; a pale or white face.

明丨 perspicuous, clear.

詳丨 to judge carefully, to narrate clearly.

問ˊ難丨疑 to inquire into what is difficult and have one's doubts resolved.

丨眸丨齒 a clear eye and white teeth.

揚且之丨也 her high forehead, so white.

白丨丨 white; fair and beautiful, as a complexion.

析ˎ *ˏsi* From *wood* and *ax*; it resembles *chih*, 折 to break, and *toh*, 柝 a rattle.

To split wood; to distinguish, to discriminate; to set off or constitute, as a new district from a large one.

丨薪 to cut up wood for fuel.

同居丨爨 to live together but have separate messes.

分丨 to divide.

丨 翳 a poetical name for the rainbow.

丨 產 to divide the patrimony.

丨 津 an old name for the region where Peking lies.

菥, *ₑsi* The shepherd's purse 丨 蓂 (*Capsella* or *Thlaspi*), eaten as greens.

葴 丨 a kind of panic grass.

淅, *ₑsi* From *water* and to *split*; it resembles *cheh*, 浙 in Chehkiang.

An affluent of the River Han in the southwest of Honan flowing by Sih-ch'uen hien 丨 川 縣 in Nan-yang fu; to wash or scour rice; the water in which it has been cleaned.

丨 瀝 the pattering of a driving rain.

接 丨 而 行 he took up the washed rice and went off.

丨 米 to clean rice.

蜥, *ₑsi* A species of lizard like the *Lacerta muralis*, common in central China, the 丨 蜴 *i. e.* the easy changing, from the various hues it takes; its skin is thin, smooth, and livid, and the head large; it does not stir when one approaches near, and is called 石龍子 from its living among the stones; also 猪 婆 蛇 the sow's snake, and in Canton is known as 狗 𧊅 蛇 the slut's snake; these names probably include two or three species.

惁, *ₑsi* Sorrowful is 丨 丨; it is also defined to venerate.

舄, *ₑsi* The character is thought to represent a magpie hopping, as people wearing clogs often hop from one spot to another; used for *ts'ioh*, 鵲 and the next three.

A wooden shoe open behind, to keep one out of the mire, or an over shoe into which the other could be slipped; they were anciently worn, and seem to have been highly ornamented; large, said of beams; great reputation.

赤 丨 几 几 [the duke] was easy in his red pattens.

丨 奕 乎 千 載 how glorious and enduring!

蕮, *ₑsi* A plant.

馬 丨 an unusual name for the purslane (*Portulacca*), because its leaves resemble the sole of a shoe.

潟, *ₑsi* Land which has been overflowed by the tide and thus become salt; saltish.

鹹 丨 saltish, as lands that are overflowed.

磶, *ₑsi* The stone on which a pillar rests.

礎 丨 the base of a column; in Chinese houses it is solidly laid in brick work, and intended to support the structure; when of marble it is called 玉 丨 and usually projects several inches.

澙, *ₑsih* A wave, the rolling of waves.

丨 淢 the power and motion of waves as they rush on.

水 波 丨 淢 the roaring waves, likened to a dragon's scales.

錫, *ₑsi* From *metal* and *change*; occurs interchanged with and used for *tsz'*, 賜 to give.

Tin; pewter; an alloy harder than pewter, like white copper, whose constituents vary much according to its uses; a gift; to grant, to confer; a fine kind of asbestos cloth.

丨 器 pewter articles.

粉 丨 white lead.

斗 丨 and 花 丨 are Straits' tin and Banca tin.

蠟 丨 bright pewter, a fine sort.

王 三 丨 命 the monarch thrice gave him his order.

丨 縣 an old name for Yun-yang fu in the northwest of Hupeh.

連 丨 tin ore.

永 丨 無 疆 unending and illimitable — happiness.

掛 丨 or 邊 丨 or 包 丨 to tin a copper dish; to guard or bind with pewter edging.

裼, *ₑsi* From *dress* and to *change*.

To expose the breast through a single garment.

袒 丨 to bare the bosom in bravado, to strip for a trial of strength.

丨 衣 a thin jacket, which discloses the body or the under garment.

丨 裘 a sort of duster worn over a fur garment.

Read *t'i'* A night-gown; a swaddling cloth or wrapper.

載 衣 之 丨 [the girl] will be clothed with wrappers.

息, *ₑsi* From *heart* and *self*.

A full breath, a gasp, a respiration; to breathe, to respire, to sigh; to rest, to desist and repose; to produce; offspring; interest on money; to suspend, to put a stop to; repose, quiet; a rest, a breathing-spell; a moment, a short time.

氣 丨 an unusual smell.

一 丨 間 for a moment.

丨 肩 rest awhile, to intermit.

歇 丨 to rest, to hold up.

長太 丨 to draw a long deep sigh.

喘 丨 不 停 I can't stop panting.

有 出 丨 兒 they are very useful and profitable, — as children or servants; 出 丨 also means little perquisites, as shavings or scraps.

子 丨 children, posterity.

生 丨 to bear interest.

丨 心 to have no more thought or anxiety about.

姑 丨 to over-indulge a child.

丨 怒 pacified, appeased.

丨 兵 to suspend military operations.

抽 丨 to catch the breath, to sob.
止 丨 to stop the breath; used by Budhists for *samadhi*, the highest degree of extatic contemplation.

熄, ˛si From *fire* and to *stop* as the phonetic.

To cover a fire in the ashes; to put out a fire; to quash.
丨 燈 put out the lamps.
打 丨 to knock out the fire, as of a link.
烽烟未 丨 the rebellion is not yet put down.
滅 丨 to quench; to put down.
救 丨 不曾 is the fire yet put out?
王者之跡 丨 the relics of the [ancient] kings are obliterated.

瘜, ˛si A polypus.
丨 肉 or 鼻 丨 a nasal polypus or tumor in the nose, so called because it interrupts the breathing.

郋, ˛si A place in the south of Tsi state taken from it by Lu; another town was called 新 丨 in consequence, lying north of the River Hwai in the southeast of the present Jüning fu.

媳, ˛si The wife of a son, grandson, or nephew, is 丨 婦 or 子 丨; in the northern provinces, it is used for the wife of any person, from the custom of regarding her as a daughter-in-law.
婆 丨 mother-in-law and daughter-in-law.
新 丨 婦 a bride.
娶 丨 婦 to get married.

饄, ˛si To draw the breath; an ancient term used in Shantung; to eat.

夕, ˛si Intended to represent the half 月 *moon*; it forms the 36th radical of a few heterogeneous characters.

Evening of the day, dusk; late; the last day of a month or year; aslant, out of the perpendicular.
旦 丨 morning and evening.
除 丨 last day of the year.
丨 室 a house out of line.
七 丨 the 7th night of the 7th moon, when women worship the Weaver.
朝不保 丨 the morning cannot secure the evening; — who can know what a day will bring forth.
今 丨 何 丨 見此良人 why is this the evening [of my joy], that I see again my goodman?

汐, ˛si The evening tide, night tide; name of a stream.
潮 丨 逐波浪 the ebb and flood beat off the waves.

窀, ˛si From *cave* and *eve*.

The long dark night of death; the gloomy tomb.
窀 丨 之事 burial rites.

席, ˛si From 巾 a *napkin* and 庶 *people* contracted, referring to the courtesies paid to guests; interchanged with the next.

A mat to sleep or eat on before tables were used; a table; an entertainment; a repast; to cover with mats; to spread out, to depend on; a chair of a teacher; rest, quiet.
酒 丨 a banquet.
西 丨 an instructor.
設 丨 to spread a feast.
赴 丨 or 坐 丨 to sit at table.
丨 地而坐 to mat the ground and sit down.
同 丨 a fellow-guest.
丨 上爆 fire-crackers let off at a feast.
割 丨 to break with, to cut one who was a friend.
一 丨 話 a single remark.
丨 卷天下 he rolled up (conquered) the empire like a mat.
丨 珍待聘 arranging his rarities while waiting for official employment.
丨 寵惟舊 relied on their long enjoyed favors.

蓆, ˛si From *grass* and *mat*; now used for the last.

A mat of any kind; ample, flowing, wide, as garments; laid up for use; overgrown with jungle.
草 丨 grass mat; matting.
籐 丨 a rattan mat.
織 丨 to braid or weave mats.
丨 包 mat bags, as of sugar.
蘆 丨 coarse rush mats.
緇衣之 丨 兮 this black robe fits you well!
一包 丨 a roll of matting.

悉, ˛si From 心 *heart* and 釆 to *distinguish*.

To investigate throughout, to comprehend in all particulars; fully, altogether, minutely, entirely; every way; both, unitedly.
知 丨 to acquaint one's self with; inform yourselves about it.
熟 丨 I know all about it.
聆 丨 I fully understand it.
諗 丨 一切 knows all the details.
丨 自教工 yourself in everything train the officers.

蟋, ˛si From *insect* and *thoroughly*.

The cricket.
打 丨 蟀 or 鬭 丨 蟀 to fight crickets.

膝, ˛si From *flesh* and *varnish*, but the older radical was 卩 joint or *seal*.

The knee; to gather around the knee, as children do.
鶴 丨 a kind of shield; an enlarged knee-joint.
屈 丨 to bend the knee.
抱 丨 長吟 to hold the knee and sing away; quite at leisure.
丨 頭 or 磕 丨 the knee.
丨 下 or 丨 下兒女 one's children.
丨 行 to creep.
打半 丨 to bend one knee.
促 丨 而談 holding their knees and talking.

丨下丨下行 to go carefully, as one in the dark. (*Cantonese.*)

丨蓋骨 or 丨頭骨 or 丨饅頭 the knee pan.

膝, ˬsi An amaranthaceous plant, the 牛丨 (or rather more commonly 牛膝 or cow's knees,) a cooling medicine used in dropsy; it is the bitter stalks of the *Pupalia geniculata* or *Achyranthes aspera*, both allied to the amaranths.

習, ˬsi From *wings* and *white*. A continued flight; to repeat the same act, to practice; skilled, used to, ready at; custom, use, habit; repeatedly, familiarized to; mellow.

學丨 to learn about; apprenticed to.

丨熟 habituated to, versed in.

丨口音 to practice speaking.

丨慣成自然 practice will make it natural.

丨俗使然 I have learned all their usages.

丨尙 I learned to esteem him.

温丨書史 to thoroughly con the classics and histories.

丨丨谷風以陰以雨 gently blows the east wind, and clouds and rain come.

丨染 corrupted by evil example.

丨而不察 superficial learning; to learn and not practice.

庶丨逸德之人 men who counted idleness a virtue.

一丨吉 [the omens] were all favorable.

相丨成風 usages arise from everybody practicing them.

嶍, ˬsi A noted mountain in Sihngo hien 丨峨縣 in the south of Yunnan in Lingan fu.

槢, ˬsi A hard wood; a weapon having this hard wood in it.

丨木 in Canton denotes any hard wood besides pine or fir, as olive, rose-wood, pride-of-india, &c.

嘒, ˬsi The noise made by one shivering with cold.

丨丨 the cry of one chilled through.

隰, ˬsi From *place* and *wet*. Low, marshy land; a morass or wet grounds, whence streams take their rise; what grows in swampy spots.

丨州 a department in the west of Shansi, near the Yellow River which includes the 汾丨 marshes near River Făn.

丨田 marshy fields.

度其丨原 he measured the marshes and low lands.

丨桑有阿 in the marshes the mulberries are beautiful.

緆, ˬsi From *silk* and to *change*; used with 裼, a shirt. Fine cloth of hemp, fit for under-clothing.

賉, ˬsi hü' From a *property* and *blood*. To distribute largesses to destitute people.

賑丨 to give aid to the poor.

丨孤 to help the friendless, — old or young.

襲, ˬsi From *garment* and *dragon*. The lining of garments; a court dress; a robe fastened on the left side; to line or attach to garments; collected; to invade, to make a foray, to steal into; to inherit; hereditary, descending in a family; repeated; because; united or drawn together; inherent; attached.

服丨 a lining.

一丨衣 one suit of clothes.

丨蔭 hereditary protection and pension — for the merit of my ancestors.

世丨罔替 a hereditary rank having no alterations; — it is a special favor.

世丨子爵 a hereditary baron.

承丨 to come into the dignity.

追丨 to pursue or surprise an enemy.

丨國 to make a raid.

丨彼後路 to come around upon the enemy from behind.

風丨袂 the air blows up the sleeve.

不相丨 they do not correspond or refer to each other.

丨以爲利 this is regarded as advantageous.

抄丨成文 to write another essay on the same subject.

卜不丨吉 to divine because it was not lucky.

丨于休祥 the auspicious omen has been repeated.

嗜鴉片者氣丨于人 the odor of the opium clings to him.

冷丨骨 chilled to the bone.

庶繼承丨 to adopt a nephew as my heir.

袈裟一丨 one priestly surplice.

乘隙丨取 I availed myself of the chance and got the advantage; to seize on for a slight offense.

霫, ˬsi From *rain* and *practiced*. A great and continuous rain.

霊丨 a heavy rain.

奚丨 a tribe of people living on the headwaters of the River Yaluh in Manchuria towards Corea, spoken of during the T'ang dynasty.

SIN.

Old sounds, sin, sim, zim, *and* súm. *In Canton*, sun, săn, săm, *and* ts'ăm; — *in Swatow*, sín, sím, *and* ch'im; — *in Amoy*, sin *and* chím; — *in Fuhchau*, síng *and* seng; — *in Shanghai*, sing *and* zing; — *in Chifu*, shin.

辛 ꜀sin From 一 *one* and 辛 *error*, explained as depicting the arms of a man holding up a thing, and referring to the sorrow one feels at winter coming; it is the 160th radical of a few characters relating to bitternesses; occurs used for the next and 莘 birthwort.

The eighth of the ten stems, which corresponds to metal and the west; a slightly bitter, sharp, pungent, or acrid taste; whence, by *met.* (because a peppery taste makes the tears run,) toilsome, suffering, grievous, sad; the melancholy feeling in autumn when vegetation turns sere.

丨金 or 丨俸 workmen's wages, a soldier's stipend, or courier's allowance.

五丨盤 five varieties of alliaceous vegetables.

莫自求丨螫 I will not seek for myself its painful sting.

丨辣 biting, peppery.

高丨氏 name of Ti-k'uh, B. C. 2435.

丨味 acrid.

丨夷 the *Magnolia yulan*.

丨痛 sad and painful.

新 ꜀sin From *ax* and *wood standing*.

To cut wood; to renew, to improve or restore; to add, to increase; to grow better; new, fresh, the latest; just made, the best; recent, late; a field tilled two years.

丨人 and 丨郎 a bride and bridegroom.

起水丨鮮 these river fish are fresh.

丨聞紙 a newspaper.

丨樣 new-fashioned.

丨喜 or 丨春 the new year.

德化日丨 his virtuous example daily increases — its influence.

丨民 to improve the people.

試試丨 try a new one.

從丨再作 make it all over new.

丨近 lately, recently.

改過自丨 to reform and become better.

薪 ꜀sin From *plants* and *new*.

Fuel; wood cut for the fire; brambles.

柴丨 firewood.

丨草 grass for fuel.

樵彼桑丨 cut down that mulberry for firewood.

負丨 to carry faggots.

月給丨水 give him his living every month.

丨之槱之 cut it down and burn it.

心 忄 㣺 ꜀sin The original form represents the two lobes of the heart; the second form is used in combination underneath as in 恭, and the third on the side; it is the 61st radical of characters relating to the feelings.

The physical heart, considered as the lord 主 of the body, and regarded by the Chinese as one of the five senses and ruled by fire; the center, the middle, as a wick or the heart-wood; the mind or understanding; the will, intention, motive; affections, desire; origin, source; the fifth of the zodiacal constellations, answering to *α* Antares and *ς* and *τ* in Scorpio.

有人丨的 he has human feelings; *i. e.* not like a brute.

丨清 or 丨水清 not alarmed, imperturbable.

有丨機 clear-headed, attentive.

在丨坎上 in the mind; to bear on the heart.

丨定 certain of, not mistaken.

丨腹人 a trustworthy man.

丨田 or 丨地 design, intention.

丨丨相印 our views tally exactly.

丨不在肝 absent-minded.

天理良丨 charitable, good, grateful.

丨多 capricious, suspicious.

本丨 my view, my notion.

天丨 meridian, the zenith.

用丨作 be careful in doing it, pay attention to it.

丨花開 in hopes of, one's expectations blossoming.

有丨 willful, designedly; also I have a heart, thank you, I am obliged.

回丨 to reform, to recover one's senses.

空丨 or 通丨 hollow, tubular.

留丨 or 在點兒丨 be very careful to remember it.

小丨 or 當丨 be careful.

丨眼兒 the real intention.

你沒有丨眼 you are very dull of perception.

放丨 be easy about it.

丨領 my heart receives it; — a form of declining an invitation or present.

丨不死 my intention is not given up.

他人有丨予忖度之 what those men have in their thoughts I can measure.

耳軟丨活 a credulous disposition.

丨丨懷念 or 丨丨念念 continual thought of, set on doing; persevering, energetic.

言乃丨之聲 words are the hearts's voice.

丨跳 fearful and trembling.

丨印 the heart's seal, a term for the *swasta* 卐 when drawn on an image of Budha.

他丨 another's heart, a Budhist term for *parachitta djnana*, the knowledge of another's thoughts.

隨丨草兒 it is as you have a mind for it.

軐 ꜀sin The axle of a wheel, as the composition of the character indicates.

姺 ꜀sin Name of a small state, the 丨邲 existing in the Shang dynasty; its location is uncertain.

尋 ꜀sin ꜀sün From 工 *work* and 口 *mouth*, denoting *confusion*, with 又 a *hand* above and 寸 *inch* below, to indicate *measuring*.

To put things to rights; to search for, on the track of; to investigate, to seek; to use or employ; to continue; soon after, presently; commonly, usually; temporarily, unexpectedly; a measure in the Cheu dynasty like that of the outstretched arms, about a fathom, called eight *ch'ih*.

丨不着 or 丨不見 I can't find it.

丨味 to wish more of, as a good story; to inquire further into.

丨常 usual, ordinary, common; said of expressions and articles.

丨求 to hunt after.

丨歿 died suddenly.

丨找 to seek for.

千丨之高 a thousand fathoms high; — very lofty, up in the clouds.

丨根究底 to investigate thoroughly.

丨繹 to study into the reasons of.

丨一條計 I have thought of a plan.

丨物 yesterday. (*Cantonese.*)

丨死 to try to kill one's self.

遍丨 to search widely for.

丨事 to meddle with.

潯 ꜀sün From *water* and to *seek*.

A steep bank where the water is deep.

丨州府 a prefecture in the south-east of Kwangsi.

丨陽琵琶 the guitar of Sin-yang, a small stream near Kiukiang on the Yangtsz' River.

鐔 ꜀sün The knob at the end of the guard of a sword, called its nose; the edge of a sword; a sort of dirk.

懸丨臥所 he hung a sword over his bed.

丨州 an ancient name of Yen-ping fu in Fuhkien.

鄩 ꜀sün A place called 斟丨 in early times, now Wéi hien 濰縣 in the east of Shantung; another town anciently called 丨中 in the time of Cheu, is now known as Kung hien 鞏縣 in the west of Honan on the R. Loh.

鱏 ꜀sün Also read ꜀yin.

A large fish, with a long nose, found in the Yangtsz' River, otherwise called 鮪 or the snouted sturgeon.

丨鰉魚 the sturgeon brought to Peking from the Songari River.

鱘 ꜀sün From *fish* and a *fathom*, from its length.

The sturgeon; it is often written like the last, but the fish are unlike; in Peking, this character is also erroneously written 鰊 from the similarity of sound

丨龍魚 the sturgeon at Canton, where it is sometimes reared.

蟳 ꜀sün A marine swimming crab (*Pilumnus*), called 青丨 or greenish crab, from the color of its shell, which is rough and hairy; it is common about Lewchew and Formosa.

鬵 ꜀sün An iron boiler which supports a wooden tub like a barrel in shape, with short feet; the cover was one third of its size, and the shapes were probably different; some of them were all iron; quick, speedy.

誰能烹魚漑之釜丨 who cooks the fish? I'll wash his caldrons and boilers for him.

灊 ꜀sün An affluent on the north of the Yangtsz' River in Sz'ch'uen; interchanged with 潛 in the name of Tsien-shan hien 丨山縣, a district near the capital of Nganhwui.

信 sin' From *man* and *words*; *q. d.* "a man's words are true; if they cannot be believed, they are not man's words;" occurs used for ꜀*shăn* 伸 to declare.

Sincerity, truthfulness, integrity, faith; one of the 五常 or five virtues; a man of his word; to believe in, to confide in, to trust; to accord with, to follow; a seal, a stamp, which gives ground for trust; a letter or note; a messenger; two nights' lodging; to express or declare.

丨筒 the envelop of 一封丨 a letter.

實丨 authentic, worthy of belief.

未丨得眞 I cannot altogether believe it.

不我丨兮 we cannot declare or make good — our promise.

輕易丨 credulous.

不丨 incredible; faithless, doubting.

失丨 to falsify one's word, to retract a promise.

丨步行 to follow one's nose, to gad about.

丨口胡言 to talk at random.

音丨 news, rumor.

丨德 faith, belief.

丨筆 a ready penman.

吉丨 or 安丨 a pleasant letter

固丨 a firm trust in.

丨行君子 a man of probity.

花丨風 a genial air that opens the flowers.

丨女 a believing woman — in Budha.

實丨子 stopped up, obstructed, as a pipe.

丨石 arsenic in powder.

有客丨丨 to entertain a man four days.

丨使 a faithful agent.

似屬可丨 it seems worthy of belief.

火藥丨子 a gunpowder match.

汛 h'ün' From *water* and *rapid flight*; it differs but little from *fan'* 汎 to float.

To sprinkle; watery, wet; quick, as a courier; a guard-house or post-house, placed about ten *li* apart on the high roads.

丨掃 to sprinkle and sweep.

水丨 a station along water-courses or canals.

丨地 a station for guards.

一塘丨 a stage of a league between the stations. (*Cantonese.*)

各岸房丨 each guard at the various banks.

營丨 a guard-house.

迅 h'ün' Quick, swift, hasty; to hurry like a wolf to its prey.

丨速 fleeting.

丨雷 quick as thunder.

奮丨 vigorous and quick, zealous.

丨雷不及掩耳 as a clap of thunder which gives one no time to stop the ears; — a word and a blow.

丨步追踪 hurry your pace after him.

訊 h'ün' From *words* and *quick*.

To inquire into judicially, to investigate; to examine; to wrangle, to speak sharply to, to scold; to accuse; to direct; to move; to cure; to announce to; to admonish; bickerings, squabbles.

丨問 to interrogate judicially.

審丨 to try in court, to examine a prisoner at the bar.

執丨 to seize and take to trial; a bearer of a warrant; to wrest people's words; captives to be questioned.

丨其所親 asked about his dealing and intercourse with him.

莫肯用丨 none are willing to tell — the truth to the king.

堂丨 a trial in open court.

丨供 oral testimony at a trial.

打問丨 to salute after the manner of a Budhist priest, with closed palms.

刑丨 to interrogate by the question.

丨斷 to try and sentence.

蕈 sin' A mushroom or agaric, those with a slender stalk to distinguish them from the thick stemmed kinds or monceron; they are dried, and form an article of trade under the name of 丨菜 or 香信, the last term being an equivoque.

地丨 ground mushrooms.

囟 顖 顣 sin' sing' The first character is intended to represent the temporal suture before it grows up; it is now seldom used.

The sinciput; the calvaria.

丨門 the fontanel in a babe.

生埋膥丨 his fontanel has grown up — you can't hoax him now. (*Cantonese.*)

丨帽 the common skull-cap, worn in China.

SING.

Old sound, sing. *In Canton*, sing; — *in Swatow*, seng, s^n^é, *and* ch'^n^é; — *in Amoy*, seng, sin, *and* t'im; — *in Fuhchau*, sing *and* seng; — *in Shanghai*, sing *and* zing; — *in Chifu*, shing.

星 sing From 日 *sun*, which is a contraction of 晶 *crystal*, and 生 to *bear*; explained that "the seminal influence of nature ascends and arranges itself into stars."

A star, a planet, a meteor; a spark; a dot, a point; spotted, dotted over; miscellaneous; quick; shooting; the 25th of the zodiacal constellations, answering to Alphard *a* Hydra and others near it; a classifier of lights, and applied to islets or whatever studs a surface.

一粒丨 or 一顆丨 one star.

流丨 or 丨過度 a shooting-star.

一丨之火 a single light, as of incense sticks.

丨隕 an ærolite.

丨象 the groups of stars.

丨散 scattered like stars; sprinkled over, as gold-leaf on lacker-ware.

丨丨點點 a few only, sparse.

丨宿海 the sea of Stars, regarded as the source of the Yellow River.

行丨 are the 五丨 five planets, *viz.* 金丨 Venus, 水丨 Mercury, 火丨 Mars, 木丨 Jupiter, and 土丨 Saturn.

經丨 fixed stars.

丨丨 the stars; stars; starry, spotted, numerous; white hair; hence a 數丨丨的手 one who can count the stars, denotes a careful accountant, a skillful and particular reckoner.

丨士 an astrologer, a fortune-teller.

火丨 sparks.

丨次 the positions of the stars.

打破頭丨 the affair is quite spoiled.

八敗丨 beggared, as from a lazy wife.

救丨 a timely aid, a helper in distress; as 一位救丨 an unexpected deliverer.

丨河 the milky way.

秤丨 marks on a steel-yard.

丨處 the starry dwelling, a Budhist term for Magadha in India.

丨馳 a fleet courier who goes by night.

定盤丨 zero on a steelyard.
賊丨 a robber.
丨期 the day set for a wedding.
丨君 the zodiacal star that rules the year.
眉金丨 to see stars, as when one is hit on the eyes.
丨眨眼 the stars twinkle.
小丨 my little concubine.
記罣本命丨 my thoughts are all on my business.
丨夜犇馳 to travel by night.
耍流丨 to brandish a fire-arrow.
丨言夙駕 he yoked his carriage by star-light.
他是個丨丨兒 he is a cantankerous fellow.
丨速修埶 to fill up and mend the gap with star-light haste; *i. e.* as quickly as possible.
三丨在戶 Orion's belt is seen in the door; some think three stars in Scorpio are meant.

煋 *ˏsing*

A raging, hot fire.

惺 惾 *ˏsing*

From *heart* and *star* or *to examine*; the second form is least used.

Intelligent; to consider, to comprehend; awed; tranquil, still, passionless, imperturbable.
丨悟 to recall to mind.
丨憁 astute, shrewd.
假丨丨 false, as a deceptive face.
丨丨惜丨丨好漢愛好漢 a clever man feels for another, as a brave man loves a hero.

腥 *ˏsing*

From *flesh* and *star* as the phonetic; similar to the next.

Small, ganglionic protuberances growing in the flesh, pustules like rice; measly flesh; rank, noisome, strong, frowzy.
丨羶 a goatish smell.
丨臭 stinking, rancid.
丨聞 a bad reputation.
丨氣 smell of newly killed meat.
魚丨 odor of newly caught fish.
肉丨 a smell of meat; new flesh.

鯹 *ˏsing*

Putrid, bad fish.
又吃魚又嫌丨 when you eat fish, lookout for the bad ones; — when you take a chance, don't mind the hazards.

篂 *ˏsing*

The curtain of a cart is 箳丨 whether of cloth or not; the phrase is also written 屏星, meaning to screen from stars, and exhibits the tendency of the Chinese language to multiply synonyms.

鍟 鉎 *ˏsing*

From *metal* and *born*; the first form gets the phonetic.

The rust of iron, called 鐵衣 or dress of iron; some apply it also to verdigris.
鉄丨氣 a musty or rusty taste or smell.

猩 *ˏsing*

A singular colored ape, the 丨丨 a name derived from 惺惺 on account of its intelligence; probably the newly discovered *Rhinopithecus roxellana* of David, found in Sz'chʻuen; it is described as having yellow hair, sharp ears, and a human-like face; strange stories are told of its ability to speak, wear shoes, drink wine, and go in companies.
丨丨菓 a wild kind of Rhamnus or jujube plum.
丨紅氈 small red hair rugs.

騂 *ˏsing*

A red or chestnut color; a brown, loam color; lusty, fat, strong.
從以丨牡 following with a red bull — in the offerings.
丨丨角弓 how nicely adjusted is the horn bow.
丨且角 strong with wide horns.

觲 *ˏsing*

Used with the last.

Lithe and strong, like a horn bow.

餳 餹 *ˏsing* *ˏtsing*

These two forms are considered identical, but are sounded differently; the second is *ˏtʻang*.

A preparation of sugar molded into forms; cakes with sugar in them.
丨餅 sugar cakes.
飴丨 sweet pastry.
簫聲吹暖賣丨天 when the notes of the pandean pipe are heard, we'll then buy the soft bonbons in the warm days; this usually refers to the worship at the tombs in April.

醒 *ˋsing*

From *wine* and *star*; but the primitive is said to have been 呈醒 making it the same as *ˏchʻing* tipsy.

To awake from intoxication, to become sober; to rouse up; to wake one; to incite, to startle, to stir up one; awakening, arousing, as an appeal.
打丨 or 推丨 or 叫丨 to wake one; wake him up.
醉丨 to get over a debauch.
丨目 to attract one's notice, to catch the eye.
丨世之言 words to startle people, and excite them to thought.
丨覺 to give attention to.
喚迷不丨 calling to besotted errorists who will not listen.
別吵丨他 don't make a noise to waken him.
衆皆醉而我獨丨 all are besotted except me, who alone am awake, — *i. e.* virtuous.
晨鐘驚丨夢迷人 to arouse the dreaming age as does the matin bell.

性 *singˋ*

From *heart* and *to bear*.

Natural disposition, temper, spirit; a quality, property, faculty; naturally, unconstrainedly; to enjoy from or by nature the limit given by nature.
丨情 the disposition.
硬丨 obstinate, mulish.
無定丨 flighty, unsteady; no perseverance.

好記丨 a good memory.
有血丨 tender-hearted; earnest in doing things.
丨拙 dull, as a stupid pupil.
天丨 natural gifts.
丨命 life, existence.
丨子如何 what kind of a temper has he?
丨急 hasty, irascible.
藥丨寒涼 the medicine is cooling.
索丨 willfully, determined.
俾爾彌爾丨 O that you may fulfill your life.
修眞養丨 to cultivate and develop the true spirit, as the Rationalists do.
丨理 mental philosophy, metaphysics.
小丨兒 testy, peevish, a quick temper.

姓 *sing'* A surname of a family or clan; a clan; to bear a son; a man, one of that clan.
丨氏 the surname.
同丨 of the same surname.
貴丨 or 高丨 what is your family name?
敝丨 or 賤丨 my poor or humble name is Wang.
百丨 the people, whose leading clan names are contained in the 百家丨 or Hundred Clan Names; in the Shu King it occurs for famous officers.
萬丨 people, mankind.
同丨不宗 of the same surname but not relatives.
隱丨 or 匿丨 to conceal the name.
賣闈丨 to buy or bet on the names of the successful candidates; — a form of gambling.
丨甚名誰 what is his surname name and style?
崔林二丨 the two men Tsui and Lin.
出丨 changed his surname.
個丨衛 that man Wéi.
雙丨 a double surname, as 司馬 Sz'ma; in writing the 姓 and 名 of the Chinese, the two should properly be distinguished by capital letters, as 王有意 Wang Yiu-i, or 聞人義德 Wănjin Iteh, not Wangyiui or Wăn-jin-i-teh; in some cases the surname and name are separated by the title of an officer, as 張遊擊焜 Colonel Chang Hwăn; the Manchus do not use their clan names, and consequently their given names should be written together, as 穆彰阿 Muhchango or Muh-chang-o.

SIOH.

Old sound, siak. *In Canton*, séuk; — *in Swatow*, siak; — *in Amoy*, siat; — *in Fuhchau*, siòk *and* swòh; — *in Shanghai*, sièk; — *in Chifu*, shòa.

削 *sio'* *siao* *'h'üé* From *knife* and a *likeness*. To cut or pare off, to shave, to scrape off; to erase; to extort from; to despoil, to seize territory; to deprive of title or rank; impoverished; debility; a graver with which to erase characters.
批丨 to trim, to mend, as a pen.
改丨 to correct and polish.
丨職 to dismiss from office.
丨到薄 scraped very thin.
丨地 to seize territory.
其丨也滋甚 his [state] is already greatly impoverished and reduced in size.
針尖上丨鐵 petty gains.
丨骨難填 I could not make it up if I scraped my bones.
丨髮 to shave the whole head.
稀丨 sleazy, as cloth.
斧丨 to trim down; to revise and correct, as a composition.
丨面光 to lose the respect of others.
丨跡 no traces are left.

SIU.

Old sounds, siu, ziu, sok, *and* zok. *In Canton*, sau, yau, tsau, *and* ts'au; — *in Swatow*, siu *and* ch'iu; — *in Amoy*, siu; — *in Fuhchau*, siu, séu, *and* wòng; — *in Shanghai*, siu *and* ziu; — *in Chifu*, shiu.

羞 *ˎsiu* From 羊 *sheep* and 丑 one of the twelve branches, meaning to *enter*, *i. e.* brought in as an offering.

Viands, delicacies, savory food, for which the next is also used; to present, to send in or offer up; to feel ashamed, to blush; ashamed, bashful, confused; chagrin; to nourish; to bring forward, to employ; conscious of demerit or guilt, unworthy of.
知丨 to know shame, to have a sense of honor.
丨辱 insulted, disgraced; feeling guilty.
丨愧 or 丨慚 abashed, shamefaced, blushing.
珍丨百味 all sorts of delicacies.
不害丨 no feeling, callous to, brazen-faced.
惟口起丨 he felt abashed after he had spoken.
含丨 to redden, to blush.

饈 膳 脩 ˓siu — Used with the last; the first is most common.

To present savory food to another; to feed or nourish; delicacies.

丨 膳 a present of food.

八 丨 豈 所 敢 望 how can I look for these eight kinds of dainties?

進 丨 to send a toothsome gift.

脩 ˓siu — From 肉 *flesh* and 攸 *that*; it is constantly interchanged with the next.

Dried meat; meat prepared with spices; to prepare; to enlarge; to play on; an *adverb* intimating difficulty in reaching, as a place or time.

丨 治 to set to rights, to govern.

丨 金 a teacher's wages.

丨 遠 very far.

丨 久 a very long time.

丨 長 to make longer.

丨 敬 to show respect by sending one a present.

山 川 丨 阻 hills and streams intervene between us; — far sundered.

修 ˓siu — From 攸 *that* and 彡 *pelage*; used with the preceding.

To adorn, to clean up or renovate; to repair, to mend; to adjust, to regulate; to cultivate, to practise, to study how to do, — and often precedes other verbs as an auxiliary; to chasten, to examine and school; to increase; long.

丨 飾 to dress elaborately; to beautify.

丨 葺 to rebuild or repair, as a house.

丨 補 to repair, to fit up.

丨 理 to regulate.

丨 身 to act correctly.

丨 書 to write a letter.

丨 陰 功 to do good privately.

丨 得 到 his virtue has availed — to bring bliss.

百 官 丨 輔 the officers carefully assisted — their sovereign.

德 之 不 丨 he failed in acting rightly.

四 牡 丨 廣 the four steeds were long and stout.

代 作 蹇 丨 to act as the go-between.

前 丨 the former worthies.

丨 好 nourish the good — that is in you, as the beggars cry out.

囚 ˓siu ˓ch'iu — From *inclosure* and *man*, indicating the purpose.

To imprison, to confine; to handcuff; imprisonment; a prisoner; a place of detention; the accusation, the plea.

丨 籠 cage to carry prisoners.

丨 犯 a felon.

掌 丨 a jailer; to oversee prisoners

監 丨 a jail.

幽 丨 日 久 imprisoned for a long time.

要 丨 服 念 五 六 日 examine the evidence in criminal cases, and reflect on it five or six days.

泅 ˓siu ˓ch'iu — From *water* and *prisoner*; it is also read often ˓yiu.

To swim; to float.

勇 於 丨 bold in swimming.

丨 水 to swim.

丨 過 海 to swim across the river. (*Cantonese.*)

茵 ˓ch'iu — A kind of gynandrous plant, the 丨 芝 which is regarded as felicitous because it flowers three times in a year.

鮂 ˓tsiu — Another name for the 白 鯈 魚 a long thin fish of the pike family like the *Thryssa*, which delights to gambol on the water; its flesh makes an excellent condiment.

Also read ˓tsiu. A kind of fish with spines on its head, which are supposed to prove that it was transformed from a crested bird.

緧 ˓siu — To put a crupper on a horse; a crupper; another says, to shackle a horse's fore legs.

滫 ˓siu — Water in which rice has been boiled or rinsed.

丨 瀡 以 滑 之 make it slippery with rice gruel.

秀 siu˒ — From 禾 *grain* depicted with its ripe *head* hanging down.

Grain in seed, which then bends in an easy, graceful way; to flourish, to grow beautiful; adorned, fair, comely; accomplished, cultivated, elegant; first, best; to fill the ear; to seed.

丨 才 cultivated talents, *i. e.* a graduate of the lowest grade, a bachelor of arts.

丨 士 an accomplished scholar.

得 天 地 之 丨 [man is] the best thing in nature.

丨 氣 delicate lineaments, fine manners.

丨 茂 green and charming, as a fine garden.

頗 丨 麗 unusually fine looking.

丨 色 可 餐 [it is, or she is] beautiful enough to feast on.

丨 水 縣 the beautiful waters, a district in Kia-hing fu in Cheh-kiang.

丨 眼 embroidered eyebrows, a tiny yellowish-green warbler (a *Sylvia*), with a white ring around each eye.

銹 鏽 鏥 siu˒ — The rust of iron, steel, tin, or other metals, called its 衣 dress; an oxide.

生 了 丨 or 長 丨 rusty, rusted.

那 個 人 是 錢 丨 that fellow is very stingy.

銅 丨 verdigris.

繡 綉 siu˒ — The second form is read ˓teu in the Dictionary, and defined a strip of cotton batting; but it is more frequently used as an abbreviation of the first character.

To embroider; to adorn with needle-work of various colors; embroidery; ornamented, embellished; variegated, figured, beautified; to illustrate a book with prints.

丨花 or 刺 丨 to embroider.
丨房 a young lady's chamber.
洋 丨 毬 the Hydrangea flower.
玉 丨 毬 the *Hoya carnosa.*
丨巾 a worked handkerchief.
錦 丨 worked in gold or colors.
描龍 丨 鳳 [handsome as] pictured dragons and embroidered phœnixes.
袞衣 丨 裳 [Duke Cheu's] tapestried coat and worked frock.
剳花捺 丨 to stitch and embroider.
丨面 to tattoo or mark the face.
錦心 丨 口 a finished and eloquent scholar.

袖 siu' From *clothes* and *by* or *through.* The sleeve; to draw up the hands; to put a thing into the sleeve; to receive in the hand, to pocket.
丨口 the cuff.
抱 丨 a woman's embroidered sleeve.
丨手 to hide the hands in the sleeves.
丨頭 or 馬蹄 丨 an official sleeve or cuff like a horse's hoof; it is a Manchu style of dress.
駕 丨 to sleeve; to take a thing with particular care, as a letter.
領 丨 a chief, a head, a chairman.

城中好大 丨 the whole city will make a good sized sleeve, *i. e.* store-room.

岫 siu' A cavernous cliff under a hill; a ravine or gorge.
窻中列遠 丨 to see the far off glens and cliffs through the windows.
巖 丨 a sheer cliff.

琇 siu' Also read ʿ*yiu.* A coarse jade or jasper called 丨陽石, used in making pipe mouths.
丨瑩 a variety of a whitish color, used for ear-drops or ear-plugs.

SIÜN.

Old sounds, sin, zin, *and* dzin. *In Canton,* sun, sün, *and* ts'un; — *in Swatow,* sún; — *in Amoy,* sún *and* tsún; — *in Fuhchau,* sung *and* chòng; — *in Shanghai,* sing, dzing, tsing, *and* sung; — *in Chifu,* shiün.

旬 ꜀sün From 日 *day* and 勹 to *inclose,* which is regarded as a contraction of 匀 a *time.*
A decade of days or years; a complete or finished time; all, entirely; in mourning, it is a period of seven days; a stated time for reviewing lessons; wide-spreading.
丨日 ten days.
七 丨 the seven weeks of deep mourning.
六 丨 sixty years of age.
三 丨 one month, divided into 上 丨 and 中 丨 and 下 丨 or first, middle, and last decade.
三 丨 客 the guests sat down at the tables in three sets.
丨歲 a full year.
來 丨 來 宣 when [the princes] have all come, then make it known to them.
背到第幾 丨 how many times have you reviewed them?
朞三百有六 丨 a year has 300 days and 6 decades more.

荀 ꜀sün A herbaceous plant, 丨草 having a yellow flower and red fruit, which fattens those who eat it; used for the next.

郇 ꜀sün A small and shortlived feudal state in the Cheu dynasty, under the Tsin state, now Pu-cheu fu 蒲州府 in the southwest of Shansi.

洵 ꜀sün From *water* and *decade;* it resembles 殉' in form, and the next in sense.
A branch of the River Han in the south of Shensi, on which Siün-yang hien 丨陽縣 stands near its junction; to weep silently; justly, really; distant; even, equal.
丨涕 to shed tears.
不如叔也 丨 美且仁 they are not like Shuh, who is really admirable and humane.
丨堪 really suitable.
吁嗟 丨 兮 alas, for our stipulation!

恂 ꜀sün Interchanged with the last.
Sincere; respectful, stern; pleasing, kind; to cherish veneration for; attractive, as virtue.
德行 丨 丨 his virtues were conspicuous.
丨實 sincerely honest.
丨慄 tremblingly attentive.

徇 ꜀sün From to *go* and *all;* it is often wrongly written 狥' from the similarity of their radicals; and occurs interchanged with it and 殉' to comply.
All around, pervading everywhere; a camp; to follow, to accord; to cause; to employ; quick, in haste; generally, somewhat.
丨疾 quick, witty, bright.
丨義 to follow rectitude.
丨齊 to fully and quickly understand.
丨通 to comprehend fully.
丨庇 to uphold another, to stand up for the undeserving.

珣 ꜀sün A species of gem anciently brought by the tribes from the eastward, called 丨玗琪 which seems to have been branching coral; it is used as a proper name.

詢 ꜀sün From to *speak* and *all* as the phonetic.
To inquire about, to inform one's self thoroughly; to deliberate or consult.
丨訪 to investigate fully, as an officer.

丨問 to ask particulars.

丨事考言 to consult with and hear what is said.

丨及人 to ask about one.

丨爾仇方 take measures against the lands of your foes.

咨丨 to plan with, to deliberate together.

峋 ˏsün Hills stretching beyond hills; abrupt, up and down, as hills appear.

嶙丨不群 a grotesque and singular hill.

巡 廵 ˏsün From *streams* and to *go;* the first is regarded as the correct form.

To go about from place to place in order to examine what is doing; to go on a circuit; to cruize, to patrol; a course at a feast, to fill up the glasses all around.

丨撫 the governor of a province.

丨檢司 (sz') a supervisor or judge in a township.

丨捕 special aids to the chief provincial authorities.

丨更 on his beat, as a watchman, or a 丨緝 patroling police.

丨視 to go on a visit of inspection.

丨船 revenue cruisers.

出丨 to reconnoitre; to start on a cruise.

丨風 to secretly learn rumors.

梳丨 to patrol the streets like 丨丁 tide-waiters or policemen.

循 ˏsün From to *go* and a *shield.*

To follow a leader, to revolve, go around with; to comply with, to accord; to go about and examine, to perambulate; to soothe or console; easy, docile.

丨丨 orderly, leisurely.

丨規蹈矩 to accord with the custom or law.

丨丨善誘 to comply with good influences.

丨法 to observe the laws.

因丨誤事 lazily hindering an affair, dilatory and obstructive.

有所持丨 something that can be depended on.

丨良 docile, conscientious.

天理丨環 the disposals of Heaven go on in their circuits.

丨牆而走 he ran along close by the wall and got away.

紃 ˏsiun Fine silken cords for bindings; tassels, ornaments; a pattern or law.

丨以五采 bound it with many colored silks.

鐵丨 spindle of a spinning-wheel. (*Cantonese*)

組丨 silk bands and cords.

以道爲丨 make reason its rule.

馴 ˏsiun From *horse* and *streams.*

A tame, docile, well-bred horse; yielding, mild, amiable, mellow; to tame; to attain to gradually.

良丨 tractable, well-trained.

雅丨 elegant, polished.

丨至 to reach gradually to.

丨畜 tame trained animals.

揗 ˏsün To pat, to stroke; to encourage, to take a sympathizing interest in.

拊丨 to condole with, to pacify by caressing.

笋 筍 ˋsun From *bamboo* and a *decade* or to *rule;* the first form is commonest.

The tender shoots of bamboo; a sprout, a shoot, as of asparagus; a tenon, a dovetail; conical, pointed; projecting.

竹丨 or 丨芽 bamboo shoots; the 玉班丨 from Chehkiang are the best.

火丨 or 丨乾 split shoots dried for export.

合丨符式 to join every part nicely according to rule.

青丨 salted sprouts.

茭丨 cone-shoots, the tender stalks of the *Hydropyrum latifolium.*

丨峰 a peaked hill; an aiguelle.

丨字樣 conical, pyramidical.

作丨 to circumcise; a Mohammedan term.

Read ˏyun. A variety of fine bamboo whose flexible splints make fine mats.

隼 鵻 ˋshun From *bird* and *ten;* the first form is used in the classics.

A falcon, kestrel, or harrier; a common bird of prey, which is said to 丨憫胎 spare pregnant birds; it flies swiftly, and is fabled to be transformed from the pie.

丨發必中' the falcon always hits its quarry.

鴥彼飛丨 rapid is that flying falcon.

栒 簨 筍 ˋsün The cross-beam of the frame on which bells or drums are hung in temples; a species of tree; the first was an ancient district in Fu-fung hien 扶風縣 in the west of Shensi on the River Wéi.

峻 chün' Dangerous; lofty, steep, as mountains; severe, stern, impetuous.

高丨 exceedingly high.

險丨 precipitous, dangerous.

克明丨德 lofty ideas and commanding virtue.

丨嶺深坑 precipitous ridges and deep defiles.

晙 chün' Early in the morning; bright, clear.

浚 濬 chün' Deep, as an abyss of water, to deepen, to dig a channel; to regulate; serious, profound, as regard; abstruse, well read; to take out from, to use part; an ancient town in Poh cheu 濮州, in the west of Shantung.

丨縣 a district in Wéi-hwui fu in the northeast of Honan on the River Wéi.

莫丨匪泉 nothing is deeper than a spring.

丨井 to deepen a well.

深丨 very deep.

禀丨 to venerate.

丨我以生 he took of mine to live on himself.

丨哲文明 [Shun] was both profound and clear-headed.

丨明有家 to guide and enlighten the family.

鵕 *sün'* A fabulous bird resembling a golden pheasant, a phœnix which lives in the sun, and illumines the heavens when it flies.

丨鸃冠 ancient caps with birds resting on them.

殉 狥 侚 *sün'* From *bad* or *dog* or *man* and a *decade;* the second is often interchanged with ˎ徇 everywhere. To follow the dead to their graves and be buried with them; to comply with, to follow after; to pursue an object zealously or inordinately, given up to, engrossed in, greedy for; to exhibit.

丨葬 to bury the living with the dead.

丨於貨色 addicted to gain and pleasure.

貪夫丨財烈士丨名 the covetous fellow desires gain, but the hero seeks for glory.

丨難之民 the people committed suicide to escape their miseries.

丨情 or 丨私 favoritism, obsequious to other's wishes.

丨國 to lose one's life for one's country.

丨縱 subservient for selfish ends.

丨求 to seek after.

以身丨道 to be a martyr for the truth.

斬羊以丨 he killed a sheep as a sign — what would be done to them if disobedient.

烈女丨節 an honorable woman most esteems purity, — and prefers death to its loss.

迿 *sün'* To go ahead, to begin a quarrel; a railing expression.

朋友不相丨 friends should not strive to use the first harsh word.

SO.

Old sounds, sa, sak, sat, *and* sap. *In Canton,* so *and* ts'o; — *in Swatow,* so, sui, swai, *and* sa; — *in Amoy,* soé, sa, sò, *and* ch'ò; — *in Fuhchau,* so *and* soi; — *in Shanghai,* su; — *in Chifu,* sòa.

蓑 *ˏso* From *grass* and *fading.* A cloak made of bamboo or palm leaves, or of grass, woven in strips and laid on like a thatch; to cover, to screen from the rain; hanging loose, like a ruff, or a goat's long hair; in Siam, the mango fruit.

丨衣 rain garments.

丨衣鶴 a white crane with pendent neck feathers.

丨笠 a leaf coat and hat.

負丨救火 put on a grass cloak and then help put out a fire; — to run foolishly into danger.

荷丨荷笠 to dress up in rain clothes, — as a watchman.

Read ˏ*sui.* Pendent, as flowers.

丨丨 hanging down.

挱 挲 *ˏso* To rub in the hand.

摩丨 to finger, to toy with; to rub on.

Read ˏ*sha.* To open.

手挓丨 to open the hand.

莎 *ˏso* From *plant* and *sand;* used for the last and next.

A triquetrous grass, the 侯丨 or 丨草 a species of sedge, or *Cyperus;* to rub in the hand.

丨雞 a species of grasshopper or young locust; by some applied to the cricket.

丨羅樹 the saul or *sala* tree (*Shorea robusta*), under which Budha was born and died.

桫 *ˏso* A tree, the 丨欏 the buckeye or horse-chestnut (*Æsculus chinensis*), prized by the Budhists, because they think it to be the *saul;* its nuts furnish a kind of arrow-root.

娑 *ˏso* To dance, to frisk, to skip and trip about; to play with the dress; to lounge, to sit at ease; sound of the lute.

婆丨世界 an idle careless world; some say, unending ages, long continued.

婆丨 to go sauntering along, to gambol; to display the dress; idle and dissolute; among the Budhists, to bear with patiently, as Kwanyin does.

丨訶 a phrase (*swaha*) like Amen, used by Budhists and Brahmins.

駁丨 the galloping horse; — name of a palace of the Han.

丨羅王 a title (*salu-raja*) given to every Budha, meaning 最勝 most victorious over vice and passion; the name refers to the stately saul tree.

蓌 *ˏso* Abundant vegetation.

丨蓌 exuberant growth; also roots of plants.

梭 *ˏso* From *wood* and *to walk slowly.* A shuttle; to and fro, like a shuttle; darting here and there; swift.

龍丨 a long narrow punt.

抛丨 or 穿丨 to throw the shuttle.

日月如丨 the days and months fly like a shuttle.

魚丨 a fish darting through the water.

鷹穿丨 the falcon soars about.

Read ˛*siun*. Name of a tree.

娑 ˛so A woman's name, implying maidenly; it is given to highborn virgins, who are virtuous and retiring.

唆 ˛so The prattle of children; to incite, to set at variance; to importune, to dun.

丨訟 to stir up litigation.

調丨 or 挑丨 to intrigue; to sow discord.

使丨 or 丨使 to instigate to evil.

丨慫 to enrage, to provoke by sarcasm or dunning.

喝丨 the talk of children; to irritate by implicating another; to involve.

傞 ˛so A drunkard's reeling.

屢舞丨丨 they gamboled and danced without stopping.

惢 ˋso The *heart thrice* agitated; suspicious, doubtful.

Read ˋ*jui*. A sacrifice after the grain had ripened, called 大丨, performed by ancient kings; used for ˋ蕊 the stamens of flowers.

麨 ˋso Coarse wheat grits; unbolted and coarse flour is 丨麴, also applied to other grains.

鎖 ˋso From *metal* and *jingling shells*. A lock, a clasp; to lock; to fetter; to frown, to contract the brow; to detain; to envelop; rings or chains for locking.

一把丨 one lock.

丨匙 or 丨鑰 a key.

丨子甲 chain-armor.

封丨 to seal and lock, as an office at the newyear.

扭丨 or 捽丨 to turn the key.

丨鑰之勳 the merit of keeping well the key of the country; — said of a high officer.

丨拿 to secure, as a prisoner.

丨不住心猿意馬 I cannot be restrained, for my heart is agile as an ape, and my thoughts swift as a horse.

丨鬚 or 丨簧 the inner toothed part of a Chinese lock.

丨眉 to knit the brows.

雲丨陽臺 the clouds cover the bright terrace.

烟丨柳 the haze hides the willows.

荷包丨 a padlock.

瑣 ˋso Fragments; the tinkling of stones; fine, minute; petty, troublesome, annoying; connected, chain-like.

丨碎 trifling, impertinent.

丨兮尾兮流離之子 people drifted about, like fag-ends and remnants.

丨丨 broken fine; fidgetty, petty; contemptible.

連丨 connected; following, like beads in a chain.

丨聞 rumors, tittle-tattle, on dits.

繁丨 troubled by petty cares.

青丨 a poetical name for the palace.

SOH.

Old sound, sak. *In Canton*, sok *and* sòk; — *in Swatow*, sòk; — *in Amoy*, sòk *and* sek; — *in Fuhchau*, sauk *and* soh; — *in Shanghai*, sok; — *in Chifu*, soa.

索 ˏ **繛** ˏ **㮦** ˏ ˛soh From 糸 *silk* and 木 *wood* or 朩 *exuberant* growth above it; the second and third forms are unusual; occurs used for *su*ˀ 素 pureness.

Stalks or leaves of plants whose fibers furnish strings; in Yunnan, eighty cowries was once so called; a cord, twine; reins; to cord, to tie up, — and hence applied to some plants that furnish cordage; to get, to obtain; to ask, to demand; a rule, an obligation, that which binds the mind; to search into, to inquire; scattered, parted; loosening, ruin, as of authority; disquietude, apprehension.

一根丨 a bit of cord.

㹇丨 sails and cordage. (*Cantonese.*)

丨取 to get a thing forcibly.

玩丨 to delight to study a subject.

丨詐 to extort.

逼丨 to get by threats.

丨思 to comprehend, to think out.

丨居 to live apart.

丨命 to involve one's life.

玄胡丨 the tubers of a kind of fumitory. (*Corydalis ambigua.*)

丨欠 and 丨賬 to sue or press for a debt.

宵爾丨綯 in the evening you should braid grass ropes.

丨力 tension, as of a rope or strip.

惟家之丨 indicates the dissolution of the family.

人家消丨 the family cord is used up; money all gone, poor.

大丨天下 to seek for over the whole empire.

丨性作完了再歇罷 let us stretch a point and finish it up now, and then we can rest.

丨然無味 it is insipid by itself.

Read *sih*, To seek, to ask.

摍 ˛soh To select or pick a thing out by the hand.

Read *sung*ˀ To respect; to act on or move.

Read *shuh*, To bind tight.

SU.

Old sounds, so *and* sok. *In Canton*, su, sho, *and* sò ; — *in Swatow*, sò, su, *and* so ; — *in Amoy*, sò ; — *in Fuhchau*, sü *and* sò ; — *in Shanghai*, su *and* sû ; — *in Chifu*, su.

穌 甦 ˓su From *grain* and *fish*, or *life* and to *change*; the second form is not usual; used for the next.

To collect, as a sheaf of grain; to rest or enjoy ease, to cease from; to resuscitate, to revive, as when wilted or from apparent death; to breathe again; to rise from the dead.

耶丨西國言救世生也 Jesus is said by western countries to save the world of living — men.

丨軟 out of sorts, tired, apathetic, no strength for.

復丨 to revive; [as if] restored to life, as when eased of pain.

丨醒 to revive, as from a fit or debauch.

蘇 ˓su From *plant* and to *revive*; used for the preceding.

A species of thyme, whose fragrant, cinnamon smell refreshes and revives the weary spirits; to cheer up; happy; to take.

后來其丨 we shall revive when our prince comes.

以丨民困 to relieve the people from their distresses.

震丨丨 trembling and panting.

丨子 a species of *Lophanthus*, (a *Perilla* or *Ocymum*?) cultivated in Chihli for its 丨油 oil, which is burned in lamps; the seeds are fed to canary birds, and the leaves are eaten.

紫丨 sweet basil. (*Ocymum.*)

丨合油 or 丨合香 rose-maloes, a kind of liquid storax obtained from the liquidambar tree and the *Altingia excelsa.*

亞丨 or 丨仔 a new-born babe. (*Cantonese.*)

落丨 a local name in Kiangnan for the egg-plant. (*Solanum melonongena.*)

丨州 Suchau city; also known as 姑丨 from its riches.

丨相' features of the Kiangsu people, regarded as the comeliest in China.

丨木 sapan or brazil-wood; for which the next form is also used.

櫯 ˓su The 丨枋 is sapan wood, a word in imitation of its Malay name *sapang*.

擜 ˓su To rub or feel with the hand; same as ˓so 挲 in 摸丨 to fumble, to rub over.

廝 ˓su A convent.

庵丨 a nunnery.

蘇 ˓su Sickness; a caries or softening of the bones.

酥 ˓su From *spirits* and *grain.*

A preparation of curd like butter, which melts in the mouth; it is made by the Mongols, who call it *wuta*; flaky, crisp; short.

油丨 butter.

福壽丨 crisp sugar-cakes.

牛奶丨 cheese.

丨餅 short cakes.

丨脆花生 crisply baked groundnuts.

丨酪 kumiss.

素 su' From *silk* and *hanging down* contracted.

Pure white silk; unornamented; in the original color or state; white and coarse, like mourning; empty, clean gone; simple, plain in dress or manners; contented in; formerly, usually, as at first, heretofore.

食丨 a diet of vegetables.

丨手 empty handed.

葷丨 common food and lenten food.

樸丨 plain dressed and honest; sincerely spoken.

丨啟 for the mourner to open; address on a letter.

穿丨 to wear mourning.

縞丨衣裳 white or blue-tinted garments.

丨裝 simply dressed.

丨手無憑 empty-handed and nothing to act on.

丨貧 always poor.

丨不安分 he does not attend to his own business.

丨性 a uniform character; one always the same, whether good or bad.

丨王 the moral king or Confucius, so called because he exercises sway over men without being actually a sovereign.

彼君子兮不丨餐兮 that princely man! he would not eat the bread of idleness!

寒丨家風 a frugal and plain family.

丨富貴行乎富貴 when you are rich act according to your station.

平丨 or 丨日 commonly, usually.

丨不相識 we have not known each other much.

丨來 or 丨本 the first state of; it was so originally; heretofore.

Read *soh*, and used for 索. To search into, to seek.

丨隱行怪 to search into hidden and strange things.

傃 su' Towards, facing, inclined; to attend to one's proper duties.

南丨 looking to the south, as a house.

嗉 膆 su' The crop or gizzard of a bird; a fat, full crop; in furs, the skin on the throat of an animal.

倒丨子 to retract a sale, to get the thing back.

愫 su' From *heart* and *simple.* Guileless, sincere; one's honest purpose, real intentions.

託短章聊伸情丨 let me in a brief note inform you fully of my real wishes.

塑 塐 su' From *earth* and *new moon* or *simple.* To model things in clay, to mold into shape; to make a statue; modeled.

丨像 to make an idol.

繪丨 to draw and color.

泥丨 a clay image; *met.* a dolt, a stupid fellow.

丨一尊佛 to make an image of Budha. (*Shanghai.*)

謖 su' To understand, to thoroughly comprehend; a man's name.

餗 su' From to *eat* and *simple.* To fast, *i. e.* to eat vegetables.

丨菜 plain greens.

食丨 to dine on vegetables.

有葷有丨 there are meats and onions, and also simple greens.

訴 愬 su' The second form is unusual, and the derivation of the first doubtful; it must be distinguished from *hin* 訢 joyful. To tell, to inform, to make known; to expose; to reply in one's defense; to state; calumny, detraction.

赴丨 to go and accuse in court.

丨稟 or 丨呈 or 丨帋 a plea in reply, a counter statement.

丨狀子 the defendant in a case.

丨寃 or 丨苦 to state one's grievance or wrong.

丨訟 to accuse another.

心如丨也 he has made known all his heart.

越丨 to pass by the lower officer and irregularly complain to his superior.

丨情 or 丨辭 to expose the facts.

丨譭 to defame.

遡 泝 su' Originally formed of 逆 *contrary* and 水 *water*, now changed to *go* and *new moon;* the first is most common; like the next. To go against the stream, or with it; to go from; to meet one; to push up, as to a source; to revert to, to carry one's thoughts back; formerly, long ago.

丨風 a head wind.

丨洄 to go against the stream.

丨遊 to go with it.

遙丨從前 in generations past, long ago.

追丨 on reverting to that time or occurrence.

丨流而行 to go against the current.

丨自 since then.

丨斗 a pail for bailing a boat.

溯 泝 su Nearly synonymous with the last. To trace up to a source, to go against a stream; water.

丨湜 clear, pellucid water.

追丨從前 to trace up previous things to their origin.

丨洄 to drive a current back.

丨查 to inquire into the reasons or circumstances which originated a thing.

丨自五月 it appears (or it has been ascertained) that since the fifth moon.

所 su' so' From *door* and *ax;* the primitive is said to represent the sound of chopping wood. To fell timber; the place it falls on; a place, a spot where houses are grouped, a compound; a building; a town, a military post; a classifier of houses and plats of ground; at the beginning of a sentence often has the force of if, supposing, in reference to, as to; a copula or relative pronoun, that which, the things which, who, what; it follows the subject and precedes the verb it rules; in regimen with 者 or as 丨以, it is usually separated by the subject of the verb; a cause by which; a lot or situation in life; to direct the mind to an act; a final expletive.

丨有 whatever there is.

人丨愛 what men like.

人人丨同 men are everywhere alike.

丨爲何事來 why then has he come?

丨在 wherever; where one lives; the place in.

爰得我丨 then shall we find our places.

處丨 or 房丨 a place, a locality.

屋一丨 or 房子一丨 a single building.

幾丨 how many houses?

你有丨不知 you are ignorant of some things.

無丨事事 nothing to do, no occupation.

丨以 wherefore, therefore.

丨以然 for this cause; the reason why.

丨自 whence it comes, the cause or origin of a thing.

丨當 the right thing.

供給丨 place where the government receive or lodge students.

得其丨哉 Ah! he has at last obtained his wishes.

各得其丨 each is now in its place.

無丨不能 omnipotent.

在丨不無 it cannot but be; no one can do without it.

必有丨思 there is still another view.

早爲之丨 it should be thought of beforehand, must be taken in time.

視其丨以觀其丨由 see what it serves and mark whence it proceeds.

伐木丨丨 the sound of the woodman's ax.

丨關係處 it is a very serious matter. (*Cantonese.*)

丨謂不孝者 those who are called undutiful.

好' 臣其丨敎 [princes] prefer officers whom they can teach or influence.

國之丨存者幸也 it is happy if the state can, in this case, be preserved.

多歷年丨 it extended over many years, that it did.

此行屋子有三丨 this long street has three sets of shops; *i. e.* three well distinguished by a different style or size.

SÜ.

Old sounds, su, zu, sok, sot, zut, *and* nu. *In Canton*, sü, ts'ü, *and* tsü; — *in Swatow*, su, ch'iu, *and* ch'u; — *in Amoy*, su *and* u; — *in Fuhchau*, sü *and* süü; — *in Shanghai*, sü, zü, su, *and* dzi; — *in Chifu*, shü.

需 ˓sü From *rain* and *still*; *q. d.* to stop for the rain; it is interchanged with the next.

Stopped by the rain; compelled to stop; to doubt, to hesitate; fixed, obstinately bent on; what is required, needful, legal, usual, or forced; necessary; the fifth of the 64 diagrams, appertaining to water.

軍丨 supplies of rations and pay for the troops.

些丨 a little of.

急丨 it is wanted soon, urgent.

丨索 obstinately bent on, to get anyhow; to extort; to levy.

以待子不時之丨 he will wait till such times as you want him.

須 湏 ˓sü From *head* and *hair*; used with the last; the second form with *water* is common but erroneous, and is rightly read ˓*hwui*, another form of 潿 still water; both resemble *shun*˒ 順 compliant.

The hair on the chin, for which the next is now used; to wait for, to expect; to get what is asked or required; ought, must, should be; necessary, requisite; good for use, serviceable; slow, dilatory.

丨臾 momentarily, for a little while.

丨用 necessary, needed for use.

必丨 or 丨要 must be had, absolutely necessary.

丨待時 you must wait awhile.

丨要小心 you need to be very careful.

丨如此 it must be (or let it be) this way.

少丨 rather slow.

丨女 a waiting maid; a star in Aquarius.

終丨 it will be wanted.

卬丨我友 I am waiting for my friend.

丨彌山 Su-Meru Mt., one of the Budhist peaks.

丨至照會者 let this dispatch come before him — whose name is.....

還丨若是 we had better follow the old way.

斯丨之間 a short time.

鬚 ˓sü From *hair* and *necessary.*

The beard on the chin; cirri of fishes; whiskers of animals; long awns of grasses; silk of maize; the rootlets of a rhizome; bearded, hairy.

花丨 stamens of flowers.

剃丨 to shave the beard.

留丨 to wear the beard.

撚丨 to twirl the mustaches or beard.

吹丨 puffing and blowing, as an actor.

髭丨 a stiff, flowing beard.

五綹長丨 five long tufts of beard, as Kwanti.

丨眉凜然 a commanding, imposing man.

帽丨 the tassel of a cap.

繻 ˓sü A coarse white hempen kerchief, 頭丨, which women wore at funerals in the Sung dynasty; end of a piece of silk.

繻 ˓sü Close-woven variegated silk like balzarine; the selvedge of silk; the edge; loose fringed or raveled edges, frayed out, which when brought together would afford proof of the identity of the piece.

鑐 ˓sü The toothed-edge bolt which runs into a Chinese lock to hold it; also called 鎖簧 and 鎖鬚 or the beard of the lock.

胥 ˓sü From *flesh* and a *piece.*

Salted, mince crabs; to wait or expect; to help; mutually; all, altogether; to store up, to have ready on hand; a final particle denoting all who have been spoken of; a writer or clerk in an office, employés.

丨皆 all, every one.

儲丨 to accumulate.

丨吏 clerks who attend to the cases or write papers, and serve in a yamun; they do not go on arrests.

于丨斯原 he had looked at the region — he lived in.

君子樂丨萬邦之屏 those princes are to be congratulated, they are screens to all the states.

糈 ˎsü From *rice* and *to help*.
Rations; fine rice used in offerings to the gods; income, official salary.
原 丨 large perquisites.
懷椒 丨而要之 carrying pepper and rice, we approach towards — the gods.

徐 ˏsü From *to go* and *I*.
A composed, dignified step; to walk carefully and daintily; serious, grave; slow, tardy; an ancient region along the Yellow River, now the prefecture of Sü cheu 丨州 in the northwest of Kiangsu; it was one of the nine divisions of Yü, extending along the Yellow Sea, from Tai shan in Shantung to the Yangtsz' River and westward to Poyang Lake, occupying large parts of Kiangnan and Shantung.
很舒丨 quite at leisure, easy.
清風丨來 a pleasant cooling breeze blows.
姑待丨丨 wait quietly for him a while.
丨行後長者 go slowly behind your superiors or seniors.
稟性安丨 nature has given him a prudent mind.

醑 ˊsü Used with the next.
To strain spirits; fine, pure liquor.
丨酒 excellent wine.

湑 ˊsü
To put herbs or grass in a basket or vat for spirits to drip through, and thus become clear; abundant; pure, limpid; in drops like dew.
零露丨兮 how limpid the scattered dew-drops!
有酒丨我 furnished me with the best of wine.

諝 ˊsü
Knowledge, discrimination; possessing learning and ability; sage, prudent.
才丨 clever.
智丨 a good judgment.
詐丨 deceiving; untrustworthy.
謀無遺丨舉不失策 if nothing is forgotten in the planning, it will not fail in the execution.

嶼 ˊsü From *hill* and *to give*.
An islet which has level arable land at the foot of its hills; applied to many islands on the coast of Fuhkien.
鼓浪丨 Ku-lang su (*lit.* the Drum-wave I.,) opposite Amoy.
孤丨媚中川 the solitary islet looks prettily in the stream.

序 sü' From *a shelter* and *to give*.
The east and west walls of a room; short walls to screen the private rooms in the palace; seated on the east and west sides, or right and left, as host and guest; a college or school in ancient times; order, precedence, as in ages; a series; a preface or argument to a book, in which its subjects are stated in order; to follow in order.
次丨 in regular sequence, seriatim.
作一篇丨 to write a preface.
丨齒 to go by ages.
長幼有丨 seniors and juniors have their regular order.
東丨 and 西丨 in the Hia dynasty, were retreats for aged scholars within the palace.
丨事妥當 to arrange everything properly.

敘 敍 sü' From 攴 *to tap*, or 又 *hand* and 余 *I*; it is similar to, and used with the preceding.
To arrange in order, to put things in proper places; arranged; arrangements; to converse; to discourse or argue upon; to employ according to worth; a series; order, rank.
丨談 or 相丨 to talk together.
丨論 to discuss in order.
議丨 to deliberate upon the best way.
丨述 to quote from.
暢丨 to talk with great zest, as with a dear friend.
天丨 the five social relations.
丨舊 to talk over old times.
鋪丨 to detail minutely.

漵 sü'
A stream in Shin-cheu fu in the west of Hunan, the 丨水 a small branch of the Yuen River; it flows near 丨浦縣 Sü-pu hien.

緒 sü' From *silk* and *that*.
The clue or end of a ball of thread or cocoon; a thread, a clue, a hint; the beginning; a guide or rule for what follows; course of events; what is handed down in a family, a calling, a patrimony; to succeed, as to an office; to search out; to perfect what others began.
頭丨 the beginning or cause; the clue to, that which is necessary in order to understand what is to be done, or what follows.
接丨 to connect with what has gone before or been done.
丨餘 a remnant, an addenda; something unimportant to the main thing.
心丨不寧 I cannot fix my mind on it.
無情無丨 disappointed; nonplussed, no means of effecting the object.
事已就丨 the affair is likely to be effected, the clue will be found.
基丨 the royal power or realm.
尋事丨 to find the thread of the business.

絮 sü' From *silk* and *as*.
Coarse, refuse silk or cotton, left after the best is reeled; woolly, silky; to stir up; compounded; to reiterate, to repeat; verbose; to pad or quilt.
柳丨 catkins of the willow.
丨丨叨叨 jabbering, loquacious clack.

朔風捲丨 the north wind brings the curled wool, — *i. e.* snow.

毋丨羹 do not stir up the soup.

丨煩 or 丨聒 talkative, tautological.

丨棉花 to line with cotton.

晴雲如擘丨 the fleecy clouds are like the bowed cotton.

破丨 old or refuse cotton.

芧 sü' A species of sedge (*Carex*); used by some as a synonym of 'ch'u 苧 the coarse nettle hemp, good for cordage.

丨粟 a kind of edible corn.

埾 sü' From *earth* and to *take*.

To pile up earth, to make a wall of earth; a pile of dirt.

丨土爲垣 to pound earth to make a wall.

鱮 sü' From *fish* and *together*, from its companionable ways, but others say from *fish* and the next contracted, because of its fine taste.

A kind of tench; a large coarse species of carp found in the Yellow River and its southern tributaries.

其魚魴丨 the fishes in it are the bream and tench.

藇 **醑** sü' From *plant* or *wine* and to *give*; the second form has become common.

Agreeable; pleasant, as good liquor, which has been well strained.

醴酒有丨 I have strained my wine till it is clear.

Read ˏyü. A fragrant plant; a tuber like the potato; tangled, weedy growth.

序 sü' The walls of an inclosure which lie on its east and west sides.

SÜEH.

Old sound, sit. *In Canton,* süt; — *in Swatow,* so *and* sòk; — *in Amoy,* swat; — *in Fuhchau,* siŏk; — *in Shanghai,* sih; — *in Chifu,* shüé *and* shié.

雪 ˋsüeh From 雨 *rain* and 彐 contracted from 彗 a *broom*.

Snow, *i. e.* congealed rain; at Canton, ice is so called; to whiten, to blanch, to make like snow; to wash clean; to clear one's self; to wipe out, as an injury; to avenge, to be revenged; white, snowy, frosted.

丨花 flakes of snow, falling snow.

丨恥 to avenge the disgrace of an insult.

紛紛大丨 a fine fall of snow.

陷丨死 frozen to death.

米心丨 round sleet like rice.

丨白 snowy white.

抓一把丨 to make a swow-ball.

丨冤 to prove a person to be innocent.

丨山 snow capped mountains; *i. e.* white in winter.

消讎丨恨 to wash out one's injury by revenging it.

丨青 a purple color.

下丨 or 落丨 it snows.

丨蛆 or 丨蠶 the ice worm, a kind of insect found in the glaciers of the Ngo-méi Mt. in Sz'ch'uen.

𠜂 ˏsüeh A synonym of *sioh*, 削 to pare; to scrape or shave off.

擤 ˏsüeh To sweep away; to rub to pieces, to brush off or destroy by the hand.

SÜEN.

See also under HÜEN. *Old sounds,* sien *and* zien. *In Canton,* sün *and* sun; — *in Swatow,* súan; — *in Amoy,* swan *and* ch'wan; — *in Fuhchau,* sòng *and* siòng; — *in Shanghai,* sín, dzín, *and* tsín; — *in Chifu,* shüen.

宣 ˏsüen From a *shelter* and to *revolve*; *q. d.* a place where the winds evolve the energies of nature.

To extend throughout; to pervade, to expand; to publish, to proclaim to the people for their observance; to summon, as a ruler; to circulate, as the wind; extended, manifested; diffusive, pervading; comprehensive; slow; perspicacious, to fully understand; a bald crown.

丨召 to summon, as to court.

丨示 or 丨揚 to publish.

必照不丨 I think there is no need to say more; — a phrase in letters.

丨讀上諭 to read out the emperor's order.

口丨 to proclaim by the voice.

丨誥 an imperial proclamation.

丨化 to make known the principles of good order; whence Confucius is sometimes called 丨聖 the Holy One who diffuses transforming doctrines.

丨福音 to preach the gospel.

秘而不丨 it is a secret (or abstruse), and cannot be made known.

丨室 the palace.

丨洩積水 to drain off collections of stagnant waters.

亘 ˎsüen From two strokes representing *heaven* and *earth* and 回 between them to show the *revolving* of the air and wind; it is not the same as *kăng'* 亙 a limit, and is now superseded by the last.

To revolve and return whence it came.

揎 ˎsüen From *hand* and to *make known*.

To raise the dress or bare the arm, in order to work easier.

裸袖丨拳 to roll up the sleeves and bare the hand.

瑄 ˎsüen A stone insignia or medal made of jasper, resembling the 璧; it was six inches around, and held by courtiers in the Han dynasty, when attending at the imperial sacrifices to Heaven, and formed part of the offerings.

朘 ˎsüen Shriveled, diminished; to take from.

丨削民膏 to extort from the people, to exact unjustly.

民日削月丨 the people daily diminish in numbers.

Read ˎ*tsui*. The privates of an infant; to move the mouth.

剶 ˎsüen ˎtswan To prune a tree.

丨樹 to lop off the branches of a tree.

旋 ˎsüen From 㫃 a *banner* and 疋 a *foot*; *q.d.* the feet of soldiers go round after their signals.

To wave a flag so as to signalize soldiers; to skip, as stones over the water; to revolve, to move in an orbit, to come back to the same point; to do a thing in turn, as an officer who reports in course, or replies to a dispatch; then, next, forthwith; readily, quick; curling, rippling; a whorl; a spire, as in a whelk.

丨轉 to go round and round, as a clock's machinery.

丨輪 to revolve.

回丨 to wheel round and round.

丨里 or 鄉丨 to return home, to go back to one's village; to retire from office.

錦丨 a graduate returning home with honors.

左丨右抽 the left-side man wheels [the chariot], and the other pulls out — his spear.

盤丨 to see one after another.

周丨 to greet or entertain several friends; to bring things about.

丨即 forthwith.

何時丨至 when will it come round again? when will his turn come?

丨紋 curling, as ripples.

丨得丨失 he lost it as soon as he got it.

Read *süen'* and used for 颴. Revolving; to revolve, as on a lathe.

丨風 a whirlwind.

丨暈 giddy, or as when sick at the stomach.

漩 ˎsüen An eddying fountain; a circling eddy.

丨窩 a little whirlpool.

流丨 the undertow of a wave.

璇璿 ˎsüen A *revolving gem*, a valuable stone, called 丨瑰, worn as an ornament by ancient monarchs.

丨璣 a kind of armillary sphere or planetarium, furnished with a 玉衡 or tube, through which ancient astronomers noted eclipses, the culmination and motions of the stars.

天丨 star Merach β Ursa Major.

蜁 ˎsüen The 丨蝸 seems to denote a species of land snail, or perhaps a kind of *Bulimus*.

丨螺 a spiral univalve with whorls, like a *Lymnea*.

選 ˋsüen From to *go* and *compliant*.

To select, to choose out or elect; what is chosen, choice, fine; to appoint good men to office; to dance in a ring; an instant, a moment; an old word for a myriad, applied to paces in measuring land; apprehensive, timorous.

丨擇 or 丨下 to pick out.

丨派 to choose and appoint, as to an office.

白丨 a coin of the Han dynasty with a dragon on it.

少丨 or 丨間 a little while, a space.

中'丨 chosen.

青錢萬丨 a good cash out of myriads, one of ten thousand.

舞則丨兮 his dancing so choice!

世丨爾勞 generations have approved your labors.

Read *süen'* To number, to reckon; to reckon with or take to task; selected for office.

候丨 expectant officers.

即丨 presently to be appointed, — said of expectant officers.

丨補 appointed to fill the vacancy.

儘先丨用 take the first on the list for the post.

弗去懼丨 do not go, lest he take you to task.

文丨司 under-clerks who select the names for appointments.

丨懦 cowardly, timorous.

颴 süen' A revolving wind, as the composition of the character intimates.

颰丨風 a whirlwind which carries the dust on high; the people say the gods use such for ascending and descending.

縼 süen' A long rope with which horses and cattle are tethered.

罥 süen' A snare used by hunters for entangling the feet of birds or beasts.

鏇, *süen'* A metallic heater for keeping spirits warm; a copper or pewter tray; a pully or windlass; to cut things round in a lathe.

丨牀子 the chissel on a lathe.

砍的沒有丨的圓 you cannot make it perfectly round by hewing it.

小手丨兒 a small wash-basin.

匴, *süen'* An osier basket for washing rice in; to bind the edges of sieves and baskets with cord.

丨簸箕 to strengthen the basket-tray or fan.

SUH.

Old sounds, sok *and* zok. *In Canton*, sòk, tsòk, *and* ts'òk; — *in Swatow*, sòk, súa, *and* ch'ek; — *in Amoy*, siok, *and* sok; — *in Fuhchau*, séuk, sòk, *and* sük; — *in Shanghai*, sòk *and* zòk; — *in Chifu*, su.

肅, *suh'* From 聿 a bamboo *tube* over an 㘣 *abyss*.

Respectful, reverential, as when one is desirous to do his duty fully; fear, caution, dread; religious veneration; cold; to advance, to get on; to render severe or majestic; to inspire awe; to receive one courteously; in epitaphs, a resolute will; used at the beginning of letters as an introduction, and thus comes to mean to write a letter; as 合丨 I now write this letter.

丨丨 decorous, stern and distant; quick; severe, as an officer; adjusted, as nets; regular, as flying geese.

嚴丨 commanding, imperious.

一律丨清 at once make it quiet, as a disturbed province.

丨客而入 he bowed in his guest and then entered.

丨霜 [nature is] bound up by the frost.

其音清丨 its notes are clear and sweet.

端丨斂袵 in a lady-like, modest, and respectful manner.

丨州 a city in the northwest of Kansuh on the confines of the Desert.

丨愼 an old name for the 女直 Jüchih tribes.

翿, *suh'* The sound of many birds flying.

丨丨其羽 the rushing sound of wings, as of a flock of geese going by.

驌, *suh'* A famous horse belonging to 唐成公, of the Cheu dynasty; it is now applied to a thoroughbred horse.

鷫, *su'* The 丨鷞 described as a matchless bird from the west, whose feathers are used to adorn or cover dresses; it is the turquoise kingfisher, whose skins are brought from Burmah for plumagery.

𢺋, *su'* To strike, to pound.

飛罕丨箾 with rapid strokes they beat [the men] with bamboo poles.

夙, *su'* From 夕 *evening* and 丮 to *grasp*.

Early in the morning; dawn; early and careful attention to business; among the Taoists, belonging to or in a former life; to live retired.

丨夜 morning and evening; early and late.

丨夜在公 at earliest dawn she was in the hall.

丨仇 they were enemies in a former life; said by the Budhists to explain casualties, as when a mad dog bites one.

丨緣 they were former friends, *i. e.* in a previous life; or were betrothed by fate in a previous existence.

祈年孔丨 in praying for a good year, I was in good time.

丨聞聲 I heard of your fame long since.

溲, *su'* The noise of rain and wind.

風雨丨丨 how furiously the wind and rain drive by!

窣, *su'* From *cave* and *abrupt*.

To rush out of a den.

勃丨 to crawl on all fours.

丨堵坡 a tope, (Sanscrit, *sthopu*,) a tomb erected over the remains of a priest.

窸丨有聲 there is a rustling, as of the wind moving things; a whispering sound.

俗, *,su suh'* From *man* and *valley*.

What the common people desire or delight in; inelegant, uneducated; common; vulgar; the low and groveling business of life; the laity; the world.

丨話 common talk, brogue, argot, a conventional dialect different from the book language.

世丨 manners of the times.

丨字眼 a vulgar phrase.

還丨 to leave the priesthood; a priest then resumes his 丨家姓名 laic surname and name.

塵丨 the busy world.

丨人 a vulgar person.

雅丨共賞 both the educated and common people are able to profit by it.

鄙丨 a base custom; unbred, vulgar manners.

習丨移人 constant habit changes one's ideas.

丨物不娛目 base or inelegant things do not please the eye.

粟, *su'* From *rice* and *west*, but the primitive is a contraction of a character meaning pendent; it resembles *lih*, 栗 chestnut.

Rice in the husk, paddy,—and much used in Fuhchau; it was a general name for grains, and is still applied to the spiked millet (*Setaria*), and maize (*Zea*); the seed of panic grasses; small sand; rent in kind, tithes.

丨米 Indian corn or maize. (*Cantonese.*)

丨布 in *mathematics*, a term like rule-of-three.

金丨 seeds of the *Olea fragraus.*

屋丨 the rent or tax of a house.

輸丨 to pay grain as tax.

一包丨 an ear of Indian corn.

六丨爲一圭 six grains of millet make a *kwéi.*

藏世界於一丨 I can hide the world in one grain of millet; — a Budhist comparison.

納職丨 to buy a titular office.

㓘, *su'* To mince, to cut into fine pieces.

速, *su'*, *su* From to *go* and a *sheaf*; used for the next.

Hasty, hurried; fleet, as a deer; quick, speedily; to call, to invite; to urge to do a thing; lowlive.

丨丨的 in haste, urgent.

火丨 or 即丨 quick as possible.

丨去 or 走得丨 go quickly.

不丨之客 an uninvited guest.

丨玉 hurry your steps; written to an invited guest.

不要忙丨 you need not be in such a hurry.

躬丨丨而不吾親 I am by myself, and he has no connection with me.

何以丨我獄 why then did you urge on this trial to me?

欲丨不達 if you are too urgent it cannot be effected; — the more haste the worse speed.

蔌, *su'* A general name for vegetables, legumes, and kitchen herbs.

肴丨 food; any provision.

其丨維何 what viands had he to eat?

丨丨風威 the cold whistling wind.

丨丨方有穀 abjects as they are, they will have their emoluments.

倲, *su'* To shake the head, as when doubting or hesitating.

觫, *su'* To start; to tremble, as an ox at the sight of a lion.

觳丨 frightened beyond measure, as a beast at the look of a lion.

吾不忍其觳丨 I can't bear to see him so frightened.

涑, *su'* A river in the southwest of Shansi flowing into the Yellow River through Kiang cheu.

Read *seu'*. To wash clothes; spoiled by water.

丨口 to rinse the mouth.

樕, *su'* A low tree, a sapling, a stock.

樸丨 scrubby oaks, trees suitable for posts in wet grounds; the plant is called 槲丨 and is probably a species of oak with smooth acorns, like the *Quercus serrata.*

餗, *su'* The contents of a boiler or kettle; boiled rice, pot-luck.

鼎折足覆公丨 if the kettle's feet be broken, my lord's food will be poured out.

續, *suh'*, *sü'* From *silk* and to *sell*; this and 賡 were once used as synonyms.

To succeed to, to continue, to join on; to keep up, to carry on what another began; attached to, tied together; following, continuous; a ring or coupling which makes a connection.

丨嗣 an adopted heir.

丨絃 to join the guitar string, to marry a second wife.

陸丨有來 coming one after another.

丨祀 he continued the ancestral worship.

在後頭接丨做 did the rest of it afterwards.

丨假數日 extended his leave of absence several days.

丨麻 to splice the rope.

接丨 to carry on another's work; to succeed to.

謖, *su'* To arise, to get up; to draw up, as the garments.

丨然 to draw one's dress around one.

丨丨 decided, erect; stern, like the wind blowing through the pines.

馬丨 a noted general of Wéi, in the days of the Three States.

佩, *suh'* From *man* and *early* as the phonetic; it resembles *péi'* 佩 to carry.

To be kept in a constrained posture, unable to stretch.

慄, *su'* Hypocritical, sycophantic; one who watches the countenance and humors of a great man.

藚, *su'* A marsh plant, whose leaves resemble purslane; one synonym is 澤瀉, and the drawing resembles an *Angelica* in its inflorescence and habit; another name is 牛脣 or ox-lips.

丨斷 or 續斷 a medicinal plant which resembles a cardoon. (*Cynara.*)

彼汾一曲言采其丨 along those bends of the River Fǎn they gather ox-lips.

宿, *su'*, *siu* From a *covering* for a *hundred men*; occurs used for 夙 dawn.

A halting-place or choultry at the posts, anciently three leagues apart, designed as a small guard-station and sometimes defended by a picket of soldiers;

a stage where one rests for the night; a lodging-place; a night's rest; to allow to remain, to keep; to pass the night; to lodge, to sojourn, to stay at; early; to delay; of old, former, long standing; damaged, old, kept over; musty, turned; to advance with the cup when sacrificing.

留丨 to detain one to spend the night.

丨鳥歸巢 the birds are going to their nests.

一丨兩餐 a bed once and two meals,— is a rule of hospitality for travelers at temples.

求丨 to ask for a night's lodging.

丨恨未除 the old enmity is not appeased.

丨昔 formerly.

隔丨小菜 stale or moldy food.

有客丨丨 the guest who tarries over two nights.

住丨 or 歇丨 to lodge over night, as at an inn.

宮廬丨衛 to guard the palace by night at the posts.

丨饅頭 stale or old bread.

丨肉 spoiled meat.

丨儒 an old scholar.

隔夜飯係丨 rice left over night sours.

無丨諾 do not delay to fulfill your promises.

丨貨 damaged goods, shelf-worn articles.

丨國 an ancient state, now part of Fung-yang fu in Nganhwui.

丨丨的 rather musty.

Read *siu'*. A constellation; a night; during the night.

整丨的睡覺 I slept the whole night through.

丨王戲 the sports of the star king, a Budhistic term (*nakshatra raja vikrimata*) for a high state of extatic meditation.

星丨 or 二十八丨 the twenty-eight zodiacal 宮 or houses; the names are given in the table, with their corresponding animals and elements, the longitude of their determinant stars in A. D. 1800, and their approximate constellations; half of them are lucky, and half are unlucky; 角斗, 奎 and 井, stand for Thursday in a weekly series, which is continued through the years.

THE TWENTY-EIGHT CHINESE ZODIACAL CONSTELLATIONS.

SIGNS.	ANIMAL.	LONGITUDE.	CONSTELLATION.	SIGNS.	ANIMAL.	LONGITUDE.	CONSTELLATION.
1 角 *kioh*	木蛟 dragon	201° 3′ 0″	Spica, ζ Virgo.	8 斗 *teu*	木獬 griffon	277° 23′ 6″	ξ λ Sagittarius.
2 亢 *k'ang*	金龍 dragon	211 42 1	ι κ λ μ Virgo.	9 牛 *niu*	金牛 ox	301 15 11	a β Sagittarius.
3 氐 *ti*	土貉 badger	222 17 35	a β γ δ Libra.	10 女 *nü*	土蝠 bat	308 55 54	ε μ γ Aquarius.
4 房 *fang*	日兎 hare	240 8 48	β δ Scorpio.	11 虛 *hü*	日鼠 rat	320 36 16	β Aquarius.
5 心 *sin*	月狐 fox	245 0 25	Antares, Scorpio.	12 危 *wéi*	月燕 swallow	330 33 45	a Aquarius and ε Pegasus.
6 尾 *wéi*	火虎 tiger	253 27 15	ε μ Scorpio.	13 室 *shih*	火猪 boar	350 41 59	Markab, a Pegasus.
7 箕 *ki*	水豹 leopard	268 28 15	γ δ Sagittarius.	14 壁 *pih*	水貐 porcupine	6 22 9	Algenib, γ Pegasus.
15 奎 *kwéi*	木狼 wolf	17 48 12	Mirac, β Andromeda.	22 井 *tsing*	木犴 tapir	92 30 21	Gemini.
16 婁 *leu*	金狗 dog	31 10 39	a β Aries.	23 鬼 *kwéi*	金羊 sheep	122 56 24	γ δ θ Cancer.
17 胃 *wéi*	土雉 pheasant	44 8 47	Musca.	24 柳 *liu*	土獐 muntjak	127 31 4	δ ε ζ Hydra.
18 昴 *mao*	日雞 cock	57 12 1	Pleiades.	25 星 *sing*	日馬 horse	144 29 44	Alphard a Hydra.
19 畢 *pih*	月烏 raven	65 39 58	Hyades.	26 張 *chang*	月鹿 deer	152 54 37	κ λ μ Hydra.
20 觜 *tsui*	火猴 monkey	80 54 47	λ Orion.	27 翼 *yih*	火蛇 snake	170 56 9	a Crater Alkes.
21 參 *tsan*	水猿 apo	79 34 6	Rigel, Orion.	28 軫 *chăn*	水蚓 worm	187 56 52	γ ε Corvus.

蓿, *su'* A clover grown in the central provinces for fodder, manure, and greens.
苜 ┃ the *Medicago sativa* or lucerne.
野苜 ┃ is of two sorts, and uncultivated; one is a species of lupine, the other a succulent trailing plant.

遬, *su'* To step quickly into one's place on seeing a superior; attentive, alert; to hurry.
疾 ┃ nimble.
輕利剽 ┃ light and active in all his movements.

簌, *su'* A fine sieve; to sift; close, thickset, as leaves on a tree.
風動落花紅 ┃ ┃ the breeze makes the flowers sift down like a red shower.

梀, *su'* A tree considered to be allied to the 樕, having a red and thick bark, of whose gnarled, tough wood felloes can be made; a birch?
白 ┃ a kind with small bifurcate leaves.

SÜH.

See also under Hü *and* HUH. *Old sounds,* sit *and* hok. *In Canton,* hök *and* sut; — *in Swatow,* hak, hiök, *and* sút; — *in Amoy,* hek, hiok, *and* sút; — *in Fuhchau,* hek, héük, éük, *and* sök; — *in Shanghai,* hiök, hüih, *and* sih; — *in Chifu,* shü.

洫, *sü'* From *water* and *blood;* occurs used for *yuh,* 淢 swift flowing.
A ditch or gutter to drain a field, eight feet broad and deep; the moat of a city; a gate to regulate water flowing; to empty; overflowing, flooded.
盡力乎溝 ┃ let them exert themselves to open gutters and sluices.
┃ 水 ancient name of a branch of the Pei-ho in Chihli.

旭, *sü'* From 日 *sun* and 九 *nine,* but the primitive is defined as being equivalent to the next, for nature is moved at the dawn.
The dawn, the rising sun.
┃ 日之旦 at the day dawn; very early.
┃ ┃ puerile joy at having got one's wishes.

勖, **勗**, *sü'* From 力 *strength* and 冒 a *cap,* arranged in two ways; the first form is unusual.
To excite, to stimulate, to urge to exertion.
┃ 哉夫子 exert yourselves, O men!
先君之思以 ┃ 寡人 in thinking of our deceased lord, she stimulated worthless me.

㖅, *h'ü'* To whistle; to blow with the mouth; to call a dog.

頊, *h'ü* From 頁 *head* and 玉 a *gem.*
Confiding; to walk carefully and erect; the vexed air of one who has failed in his object.
有 ┃ ┃ 而不自得之心 his mind is perturbed and off its balance.
顓 ┃ a star in Aquarius, named after the ancient ruler Chwen-süh.

戌, *h'ü* From 戊 a *horary* character and 一 *one* inside of it, denoting fullness, for things start in 戊 and get ripe in 戌, when the sun's heat declines; it must not be mistaken for *shu'* 戍 to guard.
The eleventh of the twelve branches; it relates to earth, and is denoted by the dog; nature fading, as it does in ┃ 月 the ninth moon.
┃ 時 the 11th hour of the day, answering to 7-9 o'clock P. M.

訹, *h'ü'* To induce; to allure, to beguile by false rumors.
誘 ┃ to lead astray.
引 ┃ an introduction.
惟賦詩酌酒相 ┃ 曩日之懷 but let us make verses and take a cup, and thus we will forget our former troubles.
糧乏 ┃ 飛 the rumors of insufficient rations spread abroad.

侐, *h'ü'* Still, quiet; silent, as the interior of a palace or a temple.
秘宮有 ┃ pure and still are the dim fanes.

恤, **卹**, *h'ü'* From *heart* or *seal* and *blood.*
The heart's blood affected; to feel for, to commisserate; to love; to be anxious about; pity, sympathy, sorrow for; anxiety; compassionate.
相 ┃ mutual regard for.
憐孤 ┃ 寡 to relieve the orphans and widows.
賑 ┃ to give alms to the poor.
┃ 政 help given to the poor by government.
體 ┃ to help and pity, to give body to one's compassion.
議 ┃ to consult what is the proper reward to be given, as by the Board of Rites.
撫 ┃ 局 a dépôt for relieving the poor.
毫無 ┃ 念 a hard hearted man.
┃ 典 regulations for honoring the dead.
┃ 宅 the house or room where the emperor mourns.

珬, *h'ü* Another name for the 珂 or cone shell (*Conus*), which the Chinese fancy to be a metamorphosis of the eagle.

SUI.

Old sounds, sui, zui, sap, sot, zot, *and* zap. *In Canton*, sui *and* ts'ui ; — *in Swatow*, sui, sué, ch'ué, ch'ui, *and* hui ; — *in Amoy*, sui, tsui, soé, ch'ui, su, *and* húi ; — *in Fuhchau*, sui, sòi, chwi, swòi, ch'oi, *and* ch'òi ; — *in Shanghai*, sé, si, süé, *and* züé ; — *in Chifu*, sói.

雖 ꜀sui From 虫 *insect* and 唯 *only*.

A species of ground lizard; an old name for the 果然 or proboscis monkey ; a *conjunction*, although, if, supposing, even if; to repel, to turn away.

丨然 albeit.

丨則係 even if it be so.

丨請退可也 you can still decline, even if he does invite you.

丨非目擊然巳耳聞 even if your eye can't perceive it, you still can hear it.

丨有這個不如那個 though you have this, it is not equal to that.

吾丨留之不能去之不忍 I cannot send him off, nor can I bear to have him go.

睢 ꜀sui From *eye* and a *bird*; it is easily confounded with ꜀*tsü* 雎 a pigeon.

To look upwards; to gaze at; a large stream flowing into Hungtsih Lake.

恣丨 a supercilious manner; to look at angrily or disdainfully.

丨州 a district in the northeast of Honan, in Kwéi-teh fu.

萬衆丨丨驚怪連日 all the people stared about for many days in great terror.

奞 ꜀sui From *great* and *bird*; also read *sin*ʾ; used as a primitive.

To spread the wings ready to fly off; to mantle the wings, as an eagle does.

荽 ꜀sui The coriander (*Coriandrum sativum*) is 芫丨 or 胡丨 which last name is also given to caraway (*Carum*); they are also known as 香菜 the fragrant herb; both names are occasionally given to 芹菜 parsley. (*Petroselinum*.)

綏 ꜀sui From *silk* and *stable*; occurs used for its primitive and for 縗; also read ꜂*hwui* and ꜂*t'o*.

The traces to a harness; reins; a strap or stick to hold on by in a carriage; to tranquillize, to give repose to; steady, quiet; to retreat or decline a battle; settled, peaceful, firm; a fringe.

丨軍 to draw off troops.

死丨 and 交丨 military terms for maintaining one's ground firmly, and for a drawn battle.

執丨 to hold the reins.

撫丨 to tranquillize, to treat kindly.

永丨吉兆 a happy omen of lasting peace.

鼎履多丨 [I hope that] you have been every way prospered; — a phrase in letters.

有狐丨丨 that lonely fox goes about suspiciously.

丨丨兮 how tranquil and placid.

丨定 to establish peacefully.

丨萬邦 how peaceful is all the empire.

Read ꜀*jui*. Feathery ornaments on a flagstaff-top.

浽 ꜀sui A drizzling fine rain is 丨溦 like a Scotch mist; also the name of a river; muddy.

痿 ꜀sui From *disease* and *failing*.

Weak; feeble, as from long sickness.

痿丨不振 he is so weak as to be incapable of acting in his office.

夊 ꜀sui ts'ui The original form delineates a man dragging his legs; it is the 35th radical of a score of unusual characters; also read ꜀*ch'iu*.

To walk leisurely, as if wearied out, or following another person.

毸 ꜀sui To spread out the wings; gamboling and fluttering; said of the phœnix.

隋 ꜀sui The name of a short but famous dynasty from A. D 581-618, which reduced the empire under one sway, and made a map of its divisions; its founder Yang Kien 揚堅 altered the next character to that form to denote his dynasty, but it ended with his grandson.

贊丨 worship of the ancestral effigy.

Read *t'o*ʾ and used for 惰. Flesh torn to pieces; idle; to fall; cylindrical; conical; a hollow place.

隕丨 to fall down or off.

隨 ꜀sui From 辵 to *go* and 墮 to *fall* contracted.

To accord, to follow, to comply with; to let, to permit; the way or usage of; like, as, according to; wherever, forthwith, presently; obsequious.

丨國 a small feudal state under the western Wéi 魏 state, A.D. 250, lying on the River Hwai, of which Sui cheu 丨州 in the north of Hupeh once formed a part.

丨時作 do it as you have time.

丨便 or 丨意 as you please; very well; if you like.

丨我來 do you come after me.

丨下丨凍 it freezes as it falls.

丨得他 let him do as he likes.

丨處說 everywhere talking about it.

丨即 immediately.

丨少來 bring a little as you can get it.

無縱詭丨 do not yield to the crafty and obsequious.

丨禮 vails paid to official attendants, about one tael in ten.

長 丨 a retinue, personal attendants.

丨 常 common, not remarkable.

丨 行偶坐 he goes with him everywhere, and stands by him as he sits.

各 丨 所好' each one follows his inclination.

跟 丨 to follow after one, to tag.

丨 和 supple, lithe in limb.

距 丨 to stand in a dressed line, as soldiers.

丨 身帶 carry it on the girdle, as a fan or a fob.

丨 心所出 just as one's fancy suggests, as in ornaments.

丨 寓而安 to feel at ease wherever one lives or stays.

In *Cantonese*. A smell, a stench; bad breath.

有的 丨 息 the air is foul here, there is a stink.

髓 ʻsui The marrow in a bone.

牛骨 丨 beef-suet.

恨入骨 丨 revenge has penetrated his very bones.

啜其 丨 to suck his marrow.

鳳 丨 龍肝 like a phœnix' marrow or dragon's liver, — *i. e.* a rare delicacy.

淪肌浹 丨 [your kindness] has watered my midriff and wet my marrow.

猪脊 丨 hog's marrow.

瀡 ʻsui Slippery, smooth, a term used in Tsi; something which will make slippery.

滫 丨 rice soup or congee.

饈 ʻsui Cakes made of broken pulse mixed with sugar.

嶲 ʻsui Originally written 巂, but afterwards changed to this form to denote this place.

Name of a prefecture 越 丨 erected by the Sui dynasty in the northwest of Yunnan, now Likiang fu 麗江府 on the Kinsha or Yangtsz' River.

歲 嵗 亗 岁 sui' From 步 to *pace* and 戌 *fullness*, which is explained that the year has paced through the 5 planets, the 28 signs, and the 12 moons; the contracted forms are common.

A year of one's age; to pass over a limit; the revolution of the seasons; a harvest, the year's produce; age, years; yearly; by the year.

你幾 丨 or 幾多 丨 how old are you?

千 丨 a term for the heir-apparent, or a prince 王 under the Ming dynasty; anciently a feudal prince.

萬 丨 the Emperor, used in direct address, and changed to 萬 丨 爺 in his titles.

丨 次 the order of the year, according to the cyclic characters.

新 丨 next year.

去 丨 last year.

守 丨 to watch the old year out.

壓 丨 the year's settler, a present of money to children.

丨 星 the planet Jupiter, twelve of whose courses through the zodiac make the 太 丨 great year.

太 丨 a return of the same branch character in the cycle, or twelve siderial years; the image of a boy to represent the Chinese Cybele, carried in procession to meet the spring.

丨 登大有 may you have a prosperous year.

壯 丨 robust, vigorous.

丨 數 a man's age.

丨 月如流 the months and years run by like a stream.

辭 丨 to wish the old year farewell.

丨 成 acts or duties of the year.

繐 sui' From *silk* and to *be kind to*; also read *kwui'*

Fine cloth brought from the West, open and loose in texture; perhaps a sort of Dacca muslin, worn by mourners or for coolness.

采 sui' From *grain* and *claws*; *q. d.* the grain which men seize; it is an unusual form of the next.

Grain in its fullness and beauty, when it hangs down in its ripeness; a term properly applied to rice and panicled millet.

穗 sui' An ear of corn or spike of wheat; the head of a grass; a spikelet, a tufted ear; elegant, graceful.

花 丨 a panicle or thyrse.

丨 城 the New City at Canton.

一禾九 丨 nine heads on one stalk; *met.* an abundant year.

秀 丨 兒 grain filling out.

嘉 丨 rank grain.

麥 丨 兩歧 each stalk of wheat has two ears.

彼有遺秉此有滯 丨 there handfuls are left, and here ears untouched, — for the widows.

穟 sui' Similar to the last.

The fine appearance of flowering and ripening grain.

秀 丨 fine looking grain.

禾役 丨 丨 the rows of rice grow beautifully.

碎 sui' From *stone* and *dead*.

To break to pieces, to smash or pound fine; bits, fragments, pieces, endings; petty, troublesome; broken in spirit.

砸 丨 or 打 丨 to break in bits, to shiver.

丨 貨 retail goods, driblets.

什 丨 or 零零 丨 丨 odds and ends, remnants, cabbage, leavings; miscellaneous things.

丨 銀 broken silver.

心驚膽 丨 disheartened and chopfallen.

散 丨 銀兩 to lavish money carelessly.

丨 嘴子 a chatterbox.

丨 磁 cracknel-ware.

丨 工 odd jobs of work.

丨 景 small views of scenery.

粹 ts'ui' Sometimes used for the last.

Pure, unmixed grain; alike, mere, all of the same sort.

精丨 unmixed.

純丨 containing no mixture, unadulterated; perspicuous, as a clear style.

丨而能容雜 he is so guileless that he will not be injured.

啐 ts'ui' To scare; to sip, to taste, to take a smack; to chew; the noise of tasting; to spit out.

丨唾沫 to spit phlegm.

丨人一口 to spit at one.

丨醴 to smack good wine.

嘈丨 babble, uproar, hubbub.

晬 sui' The revolution of a complete year in the age of a person.

誶 sui' To vilify, to scold, to rail at; to impeach, to accuse; angry.

凌丨 to disgrace.

丨駡 to vilify and abuse.

詬丨 to abuse; opprobrious language.

恣丨不恭 he raved and scolded most disrespectfully.

睟 tsui' A clear, bright, pure eye; to look straight at; the angles or canthi of the eye.

丨天 the fifth of the nine heavens.

丨然見於面 his honesty of heart appeared in his face.

遂 sui' From to *go* and *according to one's wishes.*

To accord with, to follow, not to oppose or hinder; to give loose to; an *adverb*, then, next, after that, presently, thereon, and so, forthwith, finally; to go through with, to do as one wishes; to speak of; to complete; a moor.

不丨 to resist, not to comply.

丨意 or 丨心 as one likes, agreeable to one's desire.

順丨 condescending, no hindrance.

丨至如此 if it then be thus.

訛詐不丨 forced to disregard his wishes.

百事乃丨 everything has gone right.

丨有今日 therefore, to-day it is agreeable.

容兮丨兮 what a mien! what complaisance!

隧 sui' A sluice or ditch between fields to drain them.

燧 sui' From *fire* and to *follow* as the phonetic.

To get fire from the sun by a speculum mirror; to get fire by friction of wood is 木丨 or 鑽丨取火 boring for fire.

丨人氏 the Chinese Prometheus.

烽丨夜舉警寇 beacons are lighted by night to give the alarm of banditti.

鐆 sui' Like the last.

A speculum or burning mirror.

陽丨 a sun-glass or lens for drawing the sun's heat.

邃 sui' A deep apartment far in the rear; quite in the rear, as the banners of a rear guard.

深丨 deep, far in; abstruse, recondite.

閨中旣丨遠兮 truth it is, the women's apartments are very far back.

璲 sui' Gems hung at the girdle made of a certain shape for good luck; a chatelaine.

鞙鞙佩丨 beautiful array of girdle jewels.

襚 sui' From *clothes* and to *follow* as the phonetic.

A shroud; to present graveclothes to a family where one has died; money is now sent instead.

丨衣 grave-clothes.

繸 sui' A string to hang things to the girdle; a fringe, a tassel, an edge of loose threads.

帽丨 a tassel on a cap.

燈丨 lantern tassels.

一縷丨 a tassel.

珠丨 a knotted fringe.

辮丨 a tassel on the cue.

隧 / 墜 sui' A path leading down to a tomb, an underground passage to the vault; a side path leading to a tomb; a bye-path; a tunnel, a mine; to revolve; to return.

墓丨 the road to a tomb.

出入不當門丨 do not use the main path when going in and out.

大風有丨 high winds have a path, *i.e.* come from the valleys.

丨道 a way, a road.

彗 hwui' sao' From ⺕ or 又 a *hand* grasping two 竹 *bamboos*, altered in combination.

A besom of bamboo switches, for which the next is used.

丨星 a comet, the besom star, commonly called 掃帚星 or broom star.

日中不丨是謂失時 "not to have a comet at noontide," is to say, he has lost his opportunity.

篲 hwui' Altered from the last to denote a bamboo besom, one with which to sweep fields of their stubble.

擁丨 to sweep.

繀 sui' A spinning-wheel or 丨車 on which spools of thread are reeled of a certain size.

祟 sui' Foom 示 *omen* and 出 to *exhibit;* not to be confounded with *ch'ung* 崇 honorable.

Calamities sent from heaven, which men cannot prevent, as 禍 refers to those which men bring on themselves; an evil spirit, a ghost, a wraith.

怪 丨 a monstrous apparition.
送 丨 or 驅 丨 to exorcise or send off a sprite by rites.
作 丨 to act wildly, as if possessed.
河爲 丨 the rivers have ouphes.
鬼鬼 丨 丨 perverse, cross, demented.
邪魔鬼 丨 haunted by a demon; possessed by a goblin of another family.

槥 suiʾ A small coffin, called 丨 櫝, made of wood and used to send home the bodies of soldiers killed in battle.

檖 suiʾ A whitish fruit like the pear, but small and sourish, which has different names; the tree resembles the aspen, its wood is fine grained and striped; compliant.
隰有樹 丨 the wild pear is found along the bottoms.

SUN.

Old sound, son. *In Canton*, sun *and* sün; — *in Swatow*, sún *and* chun; — *in Amoy*, sún; — *in Fuhchau*, sung, saung, *and* chung; — *in Shanghai*, săng; — *in Chifu*, sán.

孫 ꜀sun From 子 *son* and 系 a connecting *link;* it occurs used for 遜ʾ compliant.

A grandson; a grandchild; whatever is reproduced or grows by suckers; courteous.
丨 子 a grandson.
子 丨 sons and grandsons, posterity.
曾 丨 or 重 丨 a great-grandson.
玄 丨 or 來 丨 a great-great-grandson.
外 丨 a daughter's son.
丨 女 a granddaughter.
灰 丨 a remote descendant.
子 丨 娘娘 a goddess worshiped for children.
稻 丨 a second shoot of rice.
子 丨 物兒 a legacy, an heirloom.

蓀 ꜀sun A fragrant and very pretty purple orchid, the 溪 丨 also called 石菖蒲 or rock sweet-flag, which is cultivated; the drawing is like a *Cymbidium;* the fresh roots are steeped in spirits as a tonic.

猻 ꜀sun Also written 孫 in some places.

A monkey.
猴 丨 a small species of monkey (*Semnopithecus?*) found in the central provinces; it is also called 王 丨 and 胡 丨 in poetry.

搎 ꜂sun To feel or rub with the hand.

飧 ꜀sun From to 食 *eat* and 夕 *evening*, but the primitive is constantly written 歹 bad; it is also used for ꜀ts'an 餐 to eat.

An evening meal, tea, supper; to dine, to eat; the food in the dishes; cooked millet; to soak or separate rice in cold water.
饔 丨 難繼 it is hard to keep up breakfast and supper;—poverty-stricken.
君未覆手不敢 丨 till the prince has withdrawn his hand, we (his courtiers) do not presume to eat.
捫 丨 to pat or feel, to rub or make sleek.

損 ꜂sun From *hand* and *official;* it resembles ꜀kuen 捐 to reject.

To diminish; to wound, to spoil; to lose; to blame, to criticise; detrimental, injurious; ill luck, damage; the 44th diagram denoting to spoil and lessen.
有益無 丨 it is altogether advantageous.
丨 傷 or 丨 壞 to injure; to wound; it is spoiling.
丨 破 broken, ragged.
滿招 丨 a display of riches invites misfortunes.
減 丨 軍粮 to peculate in the rations of the troops.
打 丨 to damage.
治一經 丨 一經 while it cures this part, it hurts that.
丨 德 to outrage morality.

膞 ꜂sun From *flesh* and to *select*.

To cut up cooked meat with the bloody gravy; to make a hash of cold meat for recooking; to mix rice with meat.

榫 㮼 ꜂sun From *wood* and *falcon;* the second form is not uucommon in badly printed books.

To fit a piece of wood into a hole; a tenon.
丨 子 or 丨 頭 a tenon, a dovetail; a wooden pin.
丨 牙 a dovetailed edge.
丨 卯 tenon and mortice; a catch on a carrying-pole.
円 丨 to mortioe in, to dovetail.
說話不對 丨 卯 your talk is contradictory.
做 丨 or 作 筭 a Mohammedan term for circumcision; they imitate a foreign word by the characters 交奮咿嘛呢 to express the same thing.

遜 愻 ꜂sun sünʾ From to *go* or *heart* and *grandson;* the second form is unusual.

Complaisant, conciliatory; humble, modest, docile; retiring, respectful; obsequious; to accord; to observe docilely; to give in, to yield to another; to get out of the way of; to be lying hid; to deteriorate.
丨 志 an obedient mind.
吾家耄 丨 于荒 the old people in our households have withdrawn to the wilds.

梅須丨雪 the plum of course yields in whiteness to the snow.

丨讓 to cede, to yield gracefully, to defer to.

退丨 to give up, as one's seat to another.

恭丨 respectful, reverent.

惟學丨志務時敏 a learner should have a humble will, and strive to maintain his zeal.

五品不丨 all the relations of life were utterly disregarded.

巽 *sun'* *sün'* From a *stand* having *things* arranged on it; used for the last.

A stand; the 5th of the 8 diagrams, and the 57th of the 64 diagrams, denoting the wind; and on the compass card stands for north-east; mild, bland, insinuating; to select; to grasp firmly.

丨言 peaceful words.

出言不丨 to talk harshly; overbearing words.

丨入 to insinuate; to ingratiate.

丨者亦無所不容 *sun'* means what agrees with everything.

噀 潠 *sun'* To spurt out of the mouth.

丨符水 to squirt water in which a charm has been washed, over a place, to drive off evil.

含酒三丨 he drank the wine and thrice spurted it out.

SUNG.

Old sound, song. *In Canton*, sung, tsung, *and* ts'ung; — *in Swatow*, sòng, seng, *and* sang; — *in Amoy*, song, siong, jong, ch'iong, *and* ch'ong; — *in Fuhchau*, sung, süng, séung, sòng, *and* sùüng; — *in Shanghai*, sung *and* dzung; — *in Chifu*, shung *and* sung.

松 *sung* From *wood* and *duke*, it being the chief of trees.

The pine tree; it is made to include firs and yews, but the word is not very accurately used; its sap is said to turn into amber after a thousand years, and hence it is an emblem of longevity.

丨香 or 丨樹膠 rosin, pitch; also applied to a sort of mastich.

丨針 and 丨子 and 丨塔 or 丨球 pine leaves, seeds, and cones.

水丨藴 corky roots of cedar used to line the soles of over-shoes.

丨樹 the *Pinus sinensis*, common in southern China.

丨毛 a fascicle of pine leaves.

白菓丨 the white pine (*Pinus Bungei*), of northern China.

羅漢丨 the yew. (*Podocarpus thuya.*)

丨竹梅 pine, bamboo and plum, — are like three friends, because they keep green in cold weather.

丨花江 the Songari River.

丨江府 the department in which Shanghai lies.

甘丨香 spikenard, the perfume obtained from the *Nardostachys jatamansi*, called *kumtsi* 苦彌哆 by the Budhists.

丨兒石 or 綠丨石 turquoise.

淞 *sung* From *water* and *pine*.

The river which runs near Sung-kiang fu, and has given name to the town of 吳丨 Wusung; the preceding is now used instead.

菘 *sung* From *plant* and *pine* as the phonetic.

A general term for cabbage, as the 丨菜 which keeps green all winter; it is regarded as the same as the 白菜 or *Brassica*.

紫花丨 the turnip, so called from its flower and the hardy nature of the root.

鬆 *sung* From *hair* and *pine* as the phonetic.

Disheveled hair; shaggy hair; confused, disordered; to relax, to let go, to cast off; slack, easy, loose; flaky, flabby; not urgent, unimportant; not careworn; spongy, soft.

雲鬢鬖丨 her tresses were all in confusion.

法令丨 the civil and military officers are too remiss.

心丨 easy about it, contented.

丨爽 elated, pleased, hilarious.

丨丨肩兒 hold up a little, rest a while.

丨脆 crisp and soft.

太放丨 lawless, reckless.

丨的手 do it quickly.

丨開的 or 丨點兒 ease it off, loosen it a little, slack it; not too tight.

稀丨 too loose.

丨動 no haste or urgency; in funds, in easy circumstances.

丨綁 let go his bundle; yielded up all; set him free; untied it.

稍丨 not very urgent, give him a little time.

丨些 a little less tight.

嵩 崧 *sung* From *hill* and *high* or a *pine*; the first common form indicates the idea, the second has the phonetic; used with *ch'ung* 崇 high.

The highest and central peak of the 五嶽 or five sacred mountains, on which the ancient emperors worshiped Shangti; it lies in Ho-nan fu in Honan province, on the watershed between the Yellow and the Han Rivers; eminent, lofty, as a great statesman.

丨呼萬歲 his Majesty is exalted as the lofty Sung Mt.

丨高維嶽 how majestic and grand are the lofty peaks!

鬆 ˏsung From 髟 *hair* and 絨 *floss* contracted.

Fine hair of the head.

丨髭 velvety cloth, plush, cloth woven with a long nap.

娀 ˏsung Name of 丨氏 the second concubine of Ti K'uh 帝嚳 B. C. 2430, whose son 契 was made prince of Shang, and was the ancestor of T'ang the Successful, founder of the Shang dynasty.

有丨 an ancient state mentioned in the Book of Odes.

鵝 鵞 ˏsung The second form comes from mistaking the primitive, but it is now most in use at Peking.

A brown sparrow-hawk, the 丨兒 reared in northern China to catch sparrows and small birds; it closely resembles the *Accipiter nisus*; the best come from Mongolia.

憽 ˏsung Intelligent.

惺丨子 an educated and clever man.

竦 ˋsung From *standing* and a *sheaf*.

To stand as if bound, stiff and precise; to bring forward, as good people for office; respect, fear; to shudder; the flesh creeping from awe or terror; moved, horrified.

丨善 to incite to goodness.

丨立 to stand trembling.

丨動 excited, aroused.

毛髮丨然 his hair stood on end.

丨翅而上也 to clap (or start) the wings and soar on high.

丨敬 to greatly respect.

摗 ˋsung To fear; to hold, to grip; to push forward; like the last.

丨身 to stretch one's-self to a full height.

悚 慫 ˋsung Sometimes wrongly read *ch'uh*, the second form is rarely used.

Fearful; agitated by hopes and fears; terrified.

丨惕 tremblingly fearful.

丨然 timorous, alert.

唆丨人家 to slander people, to make strife.

宋 sungˋ From a *covering* and *timber; q.d.* timber made up into a dwelling.

To dwell; a habitation; a feudal state.

丨朝 Sung dynasty of Liu Yü 劉裕 as it is sometimes called from its founder, existed from A. D. 420 to 480 under eight princes.

南北丨朝 the northern and southern Sung dynasty, founded by Chao Kwang-yun 趙匡胤 and existed 320 years, under the following princes:—

EMPERORS OF THE SUNG DYNASTY.

TEMPLE NAMES.		NIEN HAO OR STYLES OF REIGN.	ACCESSION A. D.	REIGNED YEARS.	GENEALOGY.
		PEH SUNG, WHOSE CAPITAL WAS K'AIFUNG			
太祖神德皇帝	T'ai-tsu	建隆 3; 乾德 5; 開寶 9	960	17	Founder of dynasty.
太宗皇帝	T'ai-tsung	太平興國 8; 雍熙 4; 端拱 2; 淳化 5; 至道 3	976	22	Brother of the last.
眞宗皇帝	Chăn-tsung	咸平 6; 景德 4; 大中祥符 9; 天禧 5; 乾興 1	998	25	Son of the last.
仁宗皇帝	Jăn-tsung	天聖 9; 明道 2; 景祐 4; 寶元 2; 康定 1; 慶歷 8; 皇祐 5; 至和 2; 嘉祐 8	1023	41	Son of the last.
英宗皇帝	Ying-tsung	治平	1064	4	Nephew of the last.
神宗皇帝	Shăn-tsung	熙寧 10; 元豐 8	1068	18	Son of the last.
哲宗皇帝	Cheh-tsung	元祐 8; 紹聖 4; 元符 3	1086	15	Son of the last.
徽宗皇帝	Hwui-tsung	建中靖國 1; 崇寧 5; 大觀 4; 政和 7; 重和 1; 宣和 7	1101	25	Brother of the last.
欽宗皇帝	K'in-tsung	靖康	1126	2	Son of the last.
		NAN SUNG, WHOSE CAPITAL WAS HANGCHEU			
高宗皇帝	Kao-tsung	建炎 4; 紹興 32	1127	36	Brother of the last.
孝宗皇帝	Hiao-tsung	隆興 2; 乾道 9; 淳熙 16	1163	27	Nephew of the last.
光宗皇帝	Kwang-tsung	紹熙	1190	5	Son of the last.
寧宗皇帝	Ning-tsung	慶元 6; 嘉泰 4; 開禧 3; 嘉定 17	1195	30	Son of the last.
理宗皇帝	Li-tsung	寶慶 3; 紹定 6; 端平 3; 嘉熙 4; 淳祐 12; 寶祐 6; 開慶 1; 景定 5	1225	40	Collateral branch of T'ai-tsu.
度宗皇帝	Tu-tsung	咸淳	1265	10	Nephew of the last.
恭宗皇帝	Kung-tsung	德祐	1275	2	Son of the last.
端宗皇帝	Twan-tsung	景炎	1276	3	Brother of the last.
帝昺	Ti Ping	祥興	1278	2	Brother of the last.

丨國 a feudal state of renown, dating from Wéi-tsz' Ki 微子啓, a brother of the vile Cheu-sin of the Shang dynasty, B. C. 1113; the names of eighteen princes are given down to B. C. 285, when it was conquered by Tsi; it occupied the lower part of the valley of the Hwai River, and its capital was first in Kwéi-teh fu, and latterly in Suh cheu 宿州 in Nganhwui; it gave its name to the preceding dynasties.

聳 ʻsung From the *ear* and *buzzing sound* represented by the phonetic; it is interchanged with the last two.

Deaf, born deaf; to urge, to excite, to astonish; to incite, to egg on; high, elevated, ambitious; to rise, as leavened dough; to respect; to alarm.

高丨 lofty, high.

高丨丨 immeasurably high.

丨人耳目 to arrest one's attention.

丨肩 high shoulders, chuckle-headed.

巧言丨聽 his brilliant words make one's ears tingle.

丨起 to spurt out; to emit; to rise out of suddenly.

送 sung' From 辵 to *go* and 倂 to *escort a bride* contracted; it can be easily mistaken for *tieh*, 迭 change.

To accompany, to wait on, especially a bride; to see a guest out; to send a present; to give; a gift.

丨行 to go with; to see one off, to escort.

拜丨 to bow one out to the gate.

丨了命 to shorten one's life.

恕不丨 excuse me from going out.

丨親 to see a bride to her house.

順風相丨 may you have a fair wind.

丨下程 to give a man something for his journey.

丨一程 to go with one a short distance.

丨禮 to send presents; the presents.

丨三 the ceremonies on the third day after death by the family and priests, when the manes is invited back, and the tablet first worshiped.

目丨 to follow with the eye.

迎丨 to meet [a guest] and after see him out.

丨貨 to send the goods to the buyer.

丨十蠟 to send [presents to a bride] ten days after marriage.

丨官 to hand up a prisoner.

丨給你 I give this to you.

一丨 a ride in a cart one way. (*Pekingese*.)

丨肉上砧 to go with the meat on the chopping-block;—to run into danger.

In *Cantonese*. The vegetables or viands which are eaten with the rice; all on a table besides the rice.

去買丨 he has gone marketing.

丨菜大把 a great variety of dishes.

誦 sung' To hum, to read in a murmuring tone; to chant or sing; to croon over; a recitative, droning way of reading; to relate or repeat to; to dispute.

背丨 to recite memoriter.

丨經 to chant the liturgy.

丨讀 to read aloud, to hum the words.

丨習 to get by heart.

默丨 to repeat in the mind.

訟 sung' From *words* and *public*.

To contend before rulers about property; to demand justice; litigation; pleadings or wrangling before the courts; law cases; *met.* confusion in the state; the sixth of the 64 diagrams, denoting disagreement.

丨詞 an indictment.

拿丨 or 扭丨 to grapple one and carry a dispute into court.

息丨 to quash a case, to settle it.

丨庭 the court-room.

涉丨 to go to law, litigation.

官丨 legal cases.

自丨 self-reproach.

丨棍 pettifoggers, lawmongers, shysters.

健丨 skilled in law cases.

頌 sung' To praise publicly, to eulogize, to extol the virtues of; to laud; eulogy, panegyric; a song of homage; ballads to explain moral teachings.

丨讚 to commend.

調丨 and 重丨 hymns and chant refrains (*geya* and *gatha* of Hindu canons) of the Budhists.

順丨升祺 I avail myself of the occasion to wish you high advancement; used in official notes.

丨德 to commend virtuous acts.

丨揚載道 every body lauded his great merits.

丨祝三多 may you be pleased in every way.

Read ˏ*yung*, and used for 容. The countenance, the face; free, easy.

從丨 at leisure; in no haste.

凇 sung' Frozen dew-drops or rain on the branches of trees.

霧丨 frozen rime; icicles on twigs, like pearls.

SWAN.

Old sound, son. *In Canton*, sün *and* tsun; — *in Swatow*, săng; — *in Amoy*, swan *and* chw'an; — *in Fuhchau*, sòng *and* saung; — *in Shanghai*, sö^n *and* tsing; — *in Chifu*, san.

酸 ‹*swan* — From *spirits* and *slowly* drawn off; occurs interchanged with the next.

One of the five tastes, sour, acid; it belongs to wood, and is said to nourish the bones; the tart, sharp taste of vinegar or unripe fruit; prickling, harsh to the skin; irritating, distressing; grieved, afflicted; debilitated, loitering from weakness; acrid, fretful, irritable.

丨醋 vinegar.

嘔丨 sour eructations.

丨菜 pickles.

丨鼻 cold, shivering, snuffling; afflicted, sorrowful for.

賣酒不說酒丨 the grocer never says his liquor is sour.

心丨 to commisserate, sympathizing.

丨漿氣 a sour smell; a frowzy odor.

寒丨 bitter sorrow and suffering.

丨棗 acid dates; an ancient name of the present Yen-tsin hien 延津縣 in the northeast of Honan.

醎丨 begrimed, sordid, loathsome.

痠 ‹*swan* — Aching, painful.

骨丨 rheumatic pains.

丨疼 very painful.

走得腿丨 my legs are tired with the walk.

丨輭 a prickling, aching feeling; uncomfortable, as the hand after writing a long time.

⿱雨酸 ‘*swan* — A slight shower.

狻 **⿰豸夋** *swan'* — A young lion, called 丨猊; it comes from Tibet, and is said to eat tigers; others describe it as a fleet wild horse.

算 **筭** *swan'* — From *bamboo* and to *play* with; both forms are common.

The Chinese abacus or counting-board; to cypher; to estimate, to regard; a plan, a calculation, a scheme; slips of wood like counters to reckon with; a myriad.

丨卦 to divine the luck.

打丨 to reckon on it, to calculate.

丨法 arithmetic.

丨命 to tell fortunes, to cast destinies.

合丨 to estimate rightly.

丨計 a calculation.

妙丨 a fine plan.

丨計人 to counterplot, to scheme against one.

無丨 innumerable.

丨度 to calculate and estimate, as the cost.

丨盤密 or 丨盤利害 very sharp; close-fisted and cunning.

丨我怕 I'll give in, I won't do it.

好打丨 a good speculation; to guess right.

丨來丨去 full of schemes, contriving this and that.

不出我所丨 it turned out much as I supposed it would.

不由人丨 it could not be expected.

丨得是 is regarded as, taken as

丨計着 while one was reckoning; one would have assumed.

打小丨盤 he uses a little abacus; penurious, narrow-minded.

丨我差 do you think I am wrong? — *i. e.* I reckon I am not.

限訾十丨 limited the sum to ten myriads.

不上丨 it does not pay.

丨盤珠 the abacus balls, to which a stupid fellow is likened, as he goes no farther than he is pushed.

蒜 *swan'* — From *plants* and an old form of the last as the phonetic.

Alliaceous plants with ligulate leaves, called 葷菜 or rank herbs by priestly people.

青丨 fresh garlic.

丨頭 or 卵丨 garlic bulbs.

丨瓣 the flakes of the bulb.

小丨 a native kind of garlic or chives.

老鴉丨 a plant like an asphodel in its habit, with sweetish tubers and yellowish flowers.

回回丨 a kind of butter-cup. (*Ranunculus ternatus.*)

銀丨條 hooks for a door-screen.

匴 *swan'* — A bamboo case or box for holding the hats of officers, square and covered; a basket, a creel, such as rice is washed in.

冠丨 a hat-box.

淦米丨 a rice-basket.

SZ'.

This sound and SHI *or* SH' *closely approximate. Old sounds,* si, sei, sai, zi, sit, zít, zhít, dít, *and* sat. *In Canton,* sz', tsz' *and* ts'z';—*in Swatow,* sù *and* si;—*in Amoy,* su *and* si;—*in Fuhchau,* si, sé, sùö, *and* sü;—*in Shanghai,* sz' *and* si;—*in Chifu,* sz'.

思 ꜀sz' From 心 *heart* and 田 *field*, the primitive being altered from *sin'* 囟 the brain; it is to be distinguished from ꜀*ngān* 恩 kindness.

To think, to reflect, to consider; the desire or thought of the heart; to wish; thinking; to commisserate; a final or an initial particle rounding off a sentence, and used occasionally as a mere auxiliary.

丨想 to reflect on, to think about.

丨念 thoughts; to consider.

好心丨 a good design.

丨索 to deeply meditate on and trace out.

丨家 to think of one's family.

丨前 to recall former days.

豈不爾丨室是遠而 do you think I forget you? but you live far away.

兩地相丨 to think of each other when far apart.

不可泳丨 you cannot dive over.

丨皇多士 that emperor has many brave men.

無丨不服 there were none who did not submit.

Read *sz'*'. Thoughts, ideas; pure-minded.

秋丨 melancholy thoughts.

不好意丨 indecent, disreputable, vile, impolite.

詩丨 a poetical idea.

偲 ꜀sz' From *man* and *to think*.

To reprove; to admonish or urge, as a friend does.

切切丨丨 faithful and earnest with a friend.

Read ꜀*sai*. A heavy beard.

其人美且丨 this man is clever and has a fine beard; others render this,—he is fine looking and talented.

禠 ꜀sz' Also read ꜀*shi* and ꜀*i*.

Happiness.

祈丨禳災 pray for blessings and deprecate calamity.

罳 ꜀sz' A movable screen placed in the passages and gateways of a house

罘丨然 think what you are to say, as an officer about to see his ruler.

緦 ꜀sz' A coarse kind of cotton cloth, reckoned to have 1200 threads in a piece; silken; fine threaded.

丨麻服 mourning worn at the funeral and three months after, by relatives at a fourth remove.

四世而丨服之窮也 the three months' mourning of the fourth generation is the limit for wearing mourning.

颸 ꜀sz' From *wind* and *thought*.

The first cool breeze of autumn; others say, a southwest wind.

習丨 a high wind.

涼丨 a cool breeze.

榲 ꜀sz' A tree whose timber is hard.

相丨荳 or 相思子 the red-spot seeds of the *Abrus precatorius*, used for beads.

斯 ꜀sz' From *ax* and *this*.

To rive, to split with an ax; to lop off; white; low, as an office; as a *pronoun*, this, that, these, those; any, such; an *adverb*, forthwith, presently, then; a particle thrown in to suspend the sense, like an interjection, or at the end to prolong a line; it also serves as a copula of preceding nouns; formerly appended to names of animals, as 兒 or 子 are at present.

丨時 this time.

丨事 this affair.

丨文 or 丨丨文文 elegant, courteous, scholarly, polished.

丨文掃地 he has disgraced his reputation.

朝丨夕丨 the morning and evening at — his study.

如鳥丨革 like a bird molting.

彼何人丨 what sort of a man is that?

丨須之間 in a twinkling.

斧以丨之 split it with the hatchet.

何丨違丨 why then does he oppose it?

大約如丨 it is for the most part so.

職丨祿薄 his rank is low and salary small.

弓矢丨張 the bows and darts are ready for shooting.

丨焉取丨 where did this man get such learning?

如響丨應 he answers or comes like an echo; said of a servant.

鹿丨之奔 the stag is running off

廝 厮 儩 ꜀sz' From *shelter* or *man* and *this*.

A menial, a servant, an attendant; to divide; a forager or woodcutter; to feed or take care of; to serve.

丨殺 or 丨打 a melée, a scrimmage; broken, hacked, split open.

小丨 my servant boy.

丨徒 servants who get the forage.

丨養卒 a camp-follower.

女丨 a waiting-woman.

你這丨 you mean fellow.

澌 ꜀sz' Often written like the next.

To thaw, to melt and flow off.

泮丨 to thaw the ice.

澌 ₍sz'
Often used for ₍si 嘶 to neigh, and the last.
To exhaust, to run dry; the crash of ice breaking up.
丨澌 to put out a fire; also to lose by throwing or dropping in the water.

殲 ₍sz'
To die, to be no more; said of enemies.
丨殲殆盡 utterly destroyed and rooted out, as rebels.

撕 ₍sz'
From *hand* and to *split* as the phonetic.
To rend, to rive; to tear apart.
丨開 to tear in two.
提丨 to direct, as a tutor does; to nudge, to recall, to direct attention to.
丨破 to tear and spoil.
丨臉 to tear the face, as in a brawl.
丨攞 to tear, to rip.
風丨 torn or frayed by the wind.

燍 ₍sz'
The smell of anything burning; scorched, as food when cooking.

覗 ₍sz' **眮** ₍sz'
To peep, to steal a glance at, to pry and see; to get ready and wait for.
窺丨 to furtively look at.

司 ₍sz'
From 后 *prince* reversed, to indicate that an officer serves his prince out of the palace.
To control, to manage, to preside over; the officer who presides; to attend to, to give orders upon; a commissioner, a superintendent, an officer; a court or office; a subdivision of a district like a township, over which a 巡檢 presides.
大丨務 a capable man, one who can do and direct.
打官丨 to go to law.
三丨 at Canton denote the commissioners of 藩丨 revenue, 臬丨 justice, and 鹽運丨 salt.
各有所丨 each one has his own duties.
丨獄 a jailer.
丨命神 the god of the kitchen.
所丨何事 what department does he superintend?
丨員 writers in the Boards.
吃官丨 involved in a lawsuit.
公丨 a public company, like the old East India Co.; a mercantile firm; a managing committee of officers; a revenue let out by government, as 鴉片公丨 the opium farm in Singapore.
彼其之子邦之丨直 that officer in the state will hold to the right.
耳丨聽 the ear tries sounds.

絲 ₍sz'
From 系 a *fiber* of floss repeated.
Silk as it comes from the cocoons; silk in general; the fibers of nettle hemp (*Bœhmeria*) and other plants; fine, silky, flossy; small, minute; to reel off cocoons; to sew with silk; a cord, a line, a fiber; wire; veins in wood; in *decimals*, a hundred thousandth, or the hundredth part of a cash; stringed instruments of music.
丨髮 silk goods.
湖丨 raw silk from Chehkiang.
紐丨 to coil fine wire.
土丨 Canton raw silk.
丨綿 silk batting, used for linings or in shrouds.
微丨細雨 a fine drizzling rain.
游丨 or 飛丨 wandering or flying silk, are streaks seen in the sky, gossamer webs.
打烏丨 to draw an ink line.
肉丨 fine strips of meat, as in a fricassee.
抽丨 or 紡丨 to reel cocoons.
丨忽之間 the least bit of, as silver.
銅丨 copper wire.
丨衣 the gentry, well to do people; in old days, a sacrificial dress.
丨音 stringed instruments.

蕬 ₍sz'
A medicinal plant, 菟丨 the dodder (*Cuscuta*), whose seeds are used as a mild tonic; that found on pines is deemed to be the best.

鷥 ₍sz'
The *silken bird*, the white egret heron, 鷺丨 so called from its fine crest of silken feathers; it is common in the southern provinces.

虒 ₍sz'
From *tiger* under a *cliff*.
A wild beast, called 委丨 resembling a tiger, having one horn and able to go in the water; perhaps an animal akin to a sea-lion.
綿丨 an old name for Wăn-chʻuen hien 文川縣 in Szʻchʻuen.
Read *chai'* Uneven.
茈丨 rough, uneven, as the ground.

私 ₍sz'
From 禾 *grain* and 厶 *private*, because the proprietor of a field of grain was once called 丨主人 its private lord.
Private, personal; selfish, illiberal; to favor, to act selfishly; secret, partial; underhand, treasonable, nefarious; illicit, contraband; to take for one's own use; plebeian or below the throne; confined to a few; members of the family; a brother-in-law.
走丨 to smuggle.
丨下貨 smuggled goods.
丨客 a smuggler. (*Cantonese.*)
丨心 partial, unfair.
先公後丨 public before private interests.
丨衷 my private opinion.
丨家 personal effects, private gear.
丨情苟合 illicit intercourse.
賤丨 an old term employed by officers, and by sisters for each others' husbands.
丨阿 favoritism, to screen a friend.
丨家 to be selfish, prejudiced.
日月無丨照 the sun and moon shine on all alike.

丨地無出片言 not a word escaped him privately.

丨鹽越禁越好賣 the higher the salt tax the more the people will smuggle.

丨官 female officers in the palace during the Han dynasty.

厶 'sz' Original form of the preceding, but is now used as a contraction of 某 certain; it is the 28th radical of a few incongruous characters.

Private; selfish; used as a sign of a blank to be filled in.

死 'sz' From 歹 *evil* and 人 *man; i. e.* the evil which parts men.

"The running out of the vital energies, the emptying of the breath;" death; to die; said of young persons, while old people 終 come to an end; dissolution; pale, ghastly; dangerous, mortally; fearless, to the death; a superlative after a verb, and in Shanghai after an adjective; urgent, intense; to die for, a martyr for; firm, fixed, not loose; not open, closed, as a passage.

不知丨 reckless, regardless of consequences.

心丨 indifferent to.

丨心踏地 having no other purpose; single-minded and earnest in the work.

丨白 a livid, pale face.

丨性不改 even death won't make him change.

丨路 a dangerous road; an impassable or closed way; *met.* deadly habits.

丨巷 a cul-de-sac, a close.

忘丨之士 one fearless of death, as a brigand or a hero.

氣丨人 insolent, one who despises another's anger.

丨工夫 a work to which one is devoted.

丨水 stagnant water.

病丨 died of sickness.

丨於非命 died by a casualty, a premature death.

嚇丨 scared to death.

丨有餘辜 your crimes deserve more than death.

厭惡丨我了 he disgusted me excessively.

打丨 killed outright.

打丨結 tied in a hard knot.

丨不明 [the cause of] death does not appear; a legal phrase, when foul play is suspected.

作丨 you'll kill yourself, as by smoking opium.

釘丨的 nailed fast, it can't be moved.

長生不丨 immortal.

善丨 a peaceful death.

丨守 defend it to the last, as a fort.

枉丨城 the abode in hades of those who have been killed for revenge.

丨心眼兒 wedded to his own way.

丨樣 stupid, doltish.

丨去活來 he revived when nearly dead.

好丨了不過如此 I'll have it this way if I die for it; he'll stick to his notion to the very last.

有用來丨 absolutely necessary; I must have it. (*Shanghai.*)

四 肆 sz' From 口 *four-square* with 八 to *divide* inside, *i. e.* to separate it into parts; the second is the complex form.

Four; all around, everywhere; it is the even number, and answers to earth.

第丨 the fourth.

初丨 the fourth of the month.

丨方 or 丨處 or 丨下裏 everywhere, all over.

丨角 or 丨方 rectangular, cubical, square.

丨圍 [the length of] the four sides.

這人很丨海 that man is hale-fellow with everybody, he is an agreeable man.

丨路無門 no resource whichever way I go.

丨不象 unlike everybody; a self-wise man, so erratic he never does anything well; a name of the *Elephurus davidii.*

丨方木 [he is like] a block of wood, — and goes no farther than he is pushed; a dolt; but 丨方個兒的人 is a square-built, stout man.

不三不丨 neither one thing nor another; he is of no use.

丨眼人 a pregnant woman.

往丨下裡看 went everywhere looking around the place.

很丨至的 very neat and precise.

丨平八穩 very firm; well done; no fear of a disappointment.

丨通八達 opens out on all sides, as a passage.

丨大天王 or 丨天王 four demon kings (Sanscrit, *loka palas* and *chatur maha-raja*) whose images are placed at the doors of monasteries; they guard the four quarters of the world from *asuras*, and were renowned kings in their day.

泗 sz' Mucus; a short river near Tsi-ning cheu in Shantung, and a feeder of the Grand Canal.

洙丨 a place where Confucius opened a school; hence him or his teachings.

丨涕橫流 from her eyes and nose streams ran down.

丨州 a district in Fung-yang fu in the northeast of Nganhwui.

丨水縣 a district in the south of Shantung; it was one capital of Lu in early times.

駟 sz' A team of four horses.

丨馬車 a chariot and four, a stage-coach.

丨乘 a war chariot.

一言既出丨馬難追 when a word has been spoken, four horses cannot overtake it.

天丨 four stars $\beta\ \delta\ \pi\ \rho$ in Scorpio.

丨鐵孔阜 the team of rust grays is in fine condition.

肆 **肆** sz'' From a *pencil* and *long*; the second form is seldom used, and the first resembles i' 肄 to practice, and is used for 四' four.

To expand or exert to the utmost; set forth, as a sacrifice; greatly; excessive, to the verge; reckless, ruinous, dissolute, unrestrained; to be at ease, to take heart; a market-place, a shop in a bazaar; to display, as virtue; to expose, to arrange; to exhibit, as an executed carcase; an initial particle, now, although; therefore, formerly; abruptly; to refuse.

放丨 profligate, disorderly.

丨行無忌 he cares for nobody in what he does.

丨筵設席 to make a great feast.

丨類於上帝 to sacrifice to Shangti.

市丨 a market-place.

酒丨 a wine-shop.

丨諸市朝 to expose bodies of criminals in the market.

涼彼武王丨伐大商 assisting Wu Wang, he at one charge smote the Great Shang.

大丨猖獗 the brigands ravaged the region.

侈丨 profuse in spending.

丨掠 to rob by violence.

丨力 to exert one's strength.

丨陳 to dispose in order, as goods.

丨口大罵 he abused him outrageously.

丨舍 or 四舍 the four divisions of the 28 constellations.

似 sz'' From *man* and *by*.

Like, similar; as, as if, as it were, appearing, resembling; to have the aspect of; to continue, as by inheritance.

好丨 very like.

相丨 alike; resembling.

丨不丨 is it like him or no?

不很丨 not much like him.

丨續妣祖 he took the inheritance of his ancestors.

教誨爾子式穀丨之 teach and train your sons, and they will become as good as you are.

丨是而非 like the reality, but not it; apparently so.

丨乎有理 it looks somewhat reasonable.

無丨 incomparable, unlimited.

有勝丨我的 there are others who can excel me.

淸丨水 clear as water.

丨不能走 as if he could not walk.

丨這等看來 I have seen like that before.

反丨多了 he almost regretted that he had so many.

姒 sz'' An elder brother's wife; an elderly woman.

丨娣 sisters-in-law.

太丨 name of Wăn Wang's virtuous concubine.

赫赫宗周褒丨滅之 the majestic capital of our honored Cheu is going to ruin by Sz' of Pao, — the abandoned concubine of 幽王 B. C. 781, who caused the ruin of the Western Cheu dynasty.

兕 **舄** sz'' Intended originally to represent the rhinoceros, which the ancient form shows more perfectly, the legs and horn appearing.

The Malayan rhinoceros, the 丨牛 described as having a horn three cubits long; its body is black, and weighs a thousand catties; its skin is fit for making armor.

丨觥 a cup of rhinoceros' horn.

匪丨匪虎 we are not rhinoceroses or tigers, — to be kept in the wilds.

寺 sz'' From 寸 an *inch* and 之 to *issue forth*.

A hall or court from whence laws are promulged; there are four at Peking; a council chamber, a bureau; an official residence, public chambers; a monastery of the Budhists; Budhists; a mosque; a eunuch.

丨丞 a clerk in the 大理丨 or Court of Appeals.

府丨 a public office.

丨門 Budhists.

遊丨 to visit the temples.

入丨 to become a priest.

報恩丨 the Porcelain Tower, once at Nanking.

官丨 a eunuch.

丨院 temples, fanes, mosques, &c.

耜 sz'' The 耒丨 a kind of ancient ditching spade with a foot-rest, shaped like a plowshare or the Irish fac.

肂 **殔** sz'' Also read i'.

To dig a grave in a void place; a grave opened to receive the coffin.

三日而丨三月而葬 dig the grave on the third day, and have the funeral in the third month.

俟 **竢** sz'' From *man* or to *stand* and *so*; the second resembles *tsiun'* 竣 to stop.

To wait upon; to expect, to look; to await; to prepare for; until.

丨候 or 等丨 waiting for.

一丨 a little while.

丨死 to prepare for death.

立丨回音 wait for an answer.

丨下月 wait till next moon.

不丨駕而行 don't wait to prepare your carriage, but go — when the prince calls for you.

儦儦丨丨 some rushing about, some waiting together; — said of herds of animals.

伺 sz'' From *man* and *office*; *q. d.* a man sent from the office.

To wait upon; to spy, to reconnoitre, to carefully examine.

叫丨候 call the attendants.

窺丨 to privily spy out.

伏丨不來 the servants refuse to work.

嗣 ˀ sz'' From 口 *mouth*, 冊 *records* and 司 *office; q. d.* to read the family records in the ancestral hall.

To connect, as a family; to adopt; to inherit, to succeed to in a regular, lawful manner; to continue; the expectant heir; children, heirs, posterity; to learn fully, to employ or labor with; to practice; hereafter, till; then; the following.

後 丨 male descendants.

無子丨 he has no son to succeed.

絕 丨 their posterity is cut off.

無 丨 壇 an orbate temple, where tablets of extinct families are worshiped; common at Canton.

丨 位 to succeed to the throne.

丨 子 an adopted son.

丨 王 the king who has succeeded, the new king.

丨 音 to follow a father's profession.

因 丨 別 故 from other causes following it.

綿 延 其 丨 his posterity goes through many generations.

以 興 丨 歲 in order to usher in the coming year.

丨 後 hereafter.

枱 ˀ **鈶** ˀ sz'' The first is used at Canton for a contraction of ꜀*t'ai* 檯 table.

The handle of a bill-hook or sickle; the first is also read ꜀*i*, the share or iron-bound end of a plow; the second also means a sort of spear.

笥 ˀ sz'' A hamper; a square basket or trunk.

腹 丨 learned, well read.

箱 丨 a clothes-trunk.

書 丨 a portable book-case.

惟 衣 裳 在 丨 let the robes and apparel be in their chests.

丨 匱 囊 空 their trunks were empty and the larder bare.

飼 ˀ **飤** ˀ sz'' From to *eat* and *man* or *office*; the radical is also used alone with this tone and meaning.

To feed, to nourish; to set food before; provisions, food; provender.

酒 丨 wine and meat.

牛 羊 人 所 丨 men rear oxen and sheep.

丨 鷹 犬 to breed falcons and setters.

丨 於 人 to set food before one, to sustain.

寄 丨 to live on another.

丨 虎 傷 身 rear a tiger and he will hurt you.

賜 ˀ sz'' tsz'' From *property* and to *change*.

To confer, to bestow on an inferior, the opposite of 貢 and usually denotes from an emperor or a god; imperial grants or favors; a benefit; used by suppliants when asking favors.

賞 丨 to reward.

欽 丨 imperial favors.

受 丨 to be rewarded.

丨 公 死 he allowed the duke to kill himself.

拜 丨 to return thanks for favors.

蒙 丨 顧 obliged for your patronage; — a phrase on bills.

恩 丨 his Majesty's kindness.

丨 帛 to send a scarf—for an officer to strangle himself.

丨 頂 戴 permit him to wear a button; to reward without giving an office.

乞 丨 回 音 I beg of you a reply.

丨 命 to give orders.

僿 ˀ sz'' Particular, scrupulous, petty; thoroughly deceitful.

救 丨 莫 若 以 忠 there is no better remedy or offset against deception and villainy than true loyalty.

巳 ˀ sz'' The original form represents a serpent, the emblem of this branch; it is unlike ꜂*ki* 己 in the closed back.

The sixth of the 12 branches, and belongs to fire; a horary character for the hour of 9-11 A. M.; and for the fourth moon, when all nature is in full vigor.

上 丨 the 3d day of the 3d moon.

丨 飯 時 the breakfast hour.

祀 ˀ sz'' From *worship* and *hour*.

To sacrifice to the departed; for one says, in explaining the word, that it means if, like, and is like meeting with those who have gone before; to offer sacrifices to gods or devils; a sacrifice, sacrificial; to set up and worship a god; in the Shang dynasty, a year; like, as if.

丨 神 make offerings to the gods.

丨 祖 to worship ancestors.

元 丨 the first year of the reign.

惟 十 有 三 丨 訪 于 箕 子 in the thirteenth year the king inquired of Viscount Ki.

春 秋 享 丨 in the spring and autumn [Confucius] enjoys the offerings; — each district magistrate makes them.

無 丨 孤 魂 nobody worships the orphan ghost.

涘 ˀ sz'' The banks of a river; the embouchure of a stream.

水 丨 the bank, the shore.

河 丨 banks of the Yellow River.

汜 ˀ sz'' A stream leaving the main branch, and afterwards flowing into it; stagnant water.

丨 水 a small river in Honan, west of Kai-fung fu, having the town 丨 水 縣 of the same name on it.

TA.

Old sounds, da, dap, *and* tăng. *In Canton*, ta *and* tai; — *in Swatow*, p'a, tai, *and* tóa; — *in Amoy*, tai *and* taⁿ; — *in Fuhchau*, ta, twai, *and* tai; — *in Shanghai*, tang *and* ta; — *in Chifu*, ta.

打 'ta From *hand* and *man*; it was once read *'ting* in the phrase 捶丨 to cudgel each other.

To strike, to pound, to beat, to maul; to fight; to pummel and take blows; to excite or do; to add; to play on or with; a blow, a stroke; punishment by bambooing; to buy spirits, oil, or flesh; to act on, to operate on; to do, to perform, and always used in an intransitive sense; an auxiliary verb denoting action, or the present time, not the future tense; a *preposition*, by, in, at, through, from.

丨水 to draw water.

丨這兒走 go by this path.

丨那裏來 by which road did he come?

丨架 to squabble; a brawl.

丨不到 [the shot] will not reach.

有蟲丨 the worms have eaten it.

丨鐵的 a blacksmith.

鐵丨的 made of iron.

丨把式 or 丨秋風 to raise the wind.

好丨扮 elegantly dressed.

丨石頭 to cut stones; to throw stones at.

丨箇轉兒 take a turn, make him go a little way.

丨他一頓 gave him a beating; I punished him once.

丨雷 it thunders.

雷丨 killed by lightning.

丨眼 to perforate, to make holes.

丨了中火 they had eaten dinner.

丨門前經來 I was passing before the door.

丨下你的驢頭來 I'll cut off your donkey head for you!

丨聽軍情 informing himself about military affairs.

不丨緊 not very important.

丨礬水 the alum settles the water.

丨香油 to buy lamp oil.

丨魚 to fish.

大 ta' The original form was intended to represent a *man* or *king*, the greatest of earthly things; it forms the 37th radical of many common and very miscellaneous characters.

Great, big; noble; chief, distinguished; plump; prominent, important; as an adverb before other adjectives, forms the superlative, entirely, highly, very; superior, best, as the quality of goods; the extreme or farthest; to enlarge; to exceed, to surpass; to grow large.

不丨 is often used in the sense of 不多 not much, as 不丨高 not too high.

不丨老 not very old.

未丨痊 not fully recovered.

不丨對 not just the thing, not analagous.

丨不同 very unlike.

丨同小異 for the most part alike, not very different.

丨開門做的 do it with open gates, let everybody know it.

好丨臉 you think yourself rather an important person.

丨千世界 the great thousand of the world; — *i. e.* its people and cares.

丨限 the great limit; — *i. e.* death.

丨畧 in general.

兩丨小 wife and concubine.

丨想頭 a grand plan.

丨丨的福氣 the highest happiness; extreme bliss.

丨着胆子 he enlarged his liver, *i. e.* began to brag of his courage.

丨有所益 he has made a great gain, it will be very advantageous.

丨不可 totally impossible.

其丨無外 [his doctrine] cannot be surpassed.

丨叫 or 丨呼 great howling, is the name for one of the eight hot hells or *maha raurava*, surrounded by mountains of fire.

丨年 year of triennial examinations.

丨老爺 the official address of a prefect and lower officers; also applied to gentlemen in common talk.

丨人 a term for those higher in rank, but also used in letters and in direct address, like your Honor; a full grown man.

行丨事 to strike a good blow, to make a decided impression.

至丨 or 儘丨 or 丨極 the biggest.

丨抵 for the most part, perhaps.

丨衆 or 丨家 or 丨夥 we all, the whole, people, men generally, all of us.

丨棉 and 二棉 first quality of cotton, and second sort or inferior cotton.

不丨穿 it is not much worn; not many wear it.

老丨 an elder brother; a compellation for any respectable elderly man. (*Cantonese.*)

Read *ˏt'o*. Excessive; as a temper; very; grand, enormous.

Read *t'ai'* An epithet of a distinguished person, for which 太 is now more common; the chief of, great, high.

丨夫 a physician.

丨原府 a prefecture in the north of Shansi.

In *Pekingese* read ʻ*chwa*, and probably derived from ʻ爪 a claw. The claws of a cat; the talons of a hawk; toes.

老虎丨 tiger's claws; a species of fern.

猪丨尖 pig's feet; pettitoes.

Read *ta'* A large cash, in which sense it is a contracted expression for 一個丨錢, referring to the 當十 ten-cash coin.

In *Shanghai*, used for 多. Several, many; also a classifier of rows; a line, as of trees.

丨回 several times.

丨日勿來 you have not been here for many days.

一丨兵 a platoon of soldiers.

T'A.

Old sounds, tă *and* t'ap. *In Canton,* t'a; — *in Swatow,* t'a; — *in Amoy,* t'aⁿ; — *in Fuhchau,* t'a *and* to; — *in Shanghai,* t'a; — *in Chifu,* t'a.

他 ꜀t'a From *man* and *also*.

A personal pronoun, he, she, it; that, the other; another.

丨人 that man.

丨們 they, them.

丨的 his, her's.

誰管丨 who oversees him.

不必理丨 don't interfere with him.

遠處丨方 to live in another distant place.

是丨的事情 that's his affair.

至死靡丨 even to the end of life, she should not have another.

由丨去罷 let him go; don't have anything more to do with him.

TAH.

Old sounds, tat, tap, dat, *and* dap. *In Canton,* tap, tat, *and* t'at; — *in Swatow,* tap, tat, t'at, *and* ta; — *in Amoy,* tat, tap, t'ap, t'at, *and* t'an; — *in Fuhchau,* tak, t'ak, *and* tan; — *in Shanghai,* tah *and* dah; — *in Chifu,* ta.

笪 ꜀ta From *bamboo* and *morning*.

A coarse mat, used on beds; it is woven of rushes, or as at Canton, of coarse bamboo; a coarse basket; a stroke; a star seen in the daytime.

輭丨 flexible mats.

竹丨 heavy mats used for fences or sheds.

鞭丨一百 gave him a hundred lashes.

In *Cantonese.* A patch, a daub; a classifier of patches, spots, areas, lots, &c.

箇丨地方 that spot, that plat.

爛得大丨 tore out a large piece.

怛 ta' Also read ʻ*tan*.

Moved, grieved, distressed; alarmed, shocked, afraid; urged by oppression; to pity, to commisserate.

惻丨 to feel for.

勞心丨丨 anxious, heart-broken.

何必驚丨 why are you so shocked and afraid?

靼 ꜀ta Soft leather; well dressed leather.

丨革爲靴 make boots of soft skin.

妲 ꜁ta An infamous woman, 丨己 the concubine of King Sheu 紂王 who caused the ruin of the Shang dynasty, B. C. 1150.

羍 ꜀ta From *sheep* and *great*; it is another form of the primitive of the next character.

A lambkin recently born; to have an easy parturition, like Shinnung's mother.

先生如丨 she had then a birth as easy as a ewe when lambing.

達 ꜁ta From to *go* and a small *sheep*; ewes are said to bear their young without pain.

Open, permeable; to reach all around; to permeate, to pervade; to see through, to perceive; to inform, to make known to; to give or transfer to; to promote, to bring forward or advance; suitable; all, every, every where; intelligent; intelligible; penetrable; successful in life; a small sheep.

丨人 a shrewd fellow.

通丨事理 well versed in the matter.

丨部 to inform the Board.

丨知 let him know.

發丨 or 上'丨 advancing in office, rising as in degree or fame.

丨不離道 in his elevation [the good man] does not depart from right.

丨于河 [the water] flows in the river.

未丨一間' not yet learned anything, not a line.

事極相丨 the business is very proper.

丨縣 a district in the northeast of Sz'chu'en, in Sui-ting fu.

丨子 the Tartars.

ʻ上丨天聽 to make known to His Majesty.

生丨 producing, growing up.

丨磨法 (Sanscrit, *dharma*) the law or the Budhistic canon; also perception of character, and the god who personifies the first person in the Budhist trinity.

丨摩難提 the Hindu priest Dharma-nandi, who came to China about A.D. 383, fabled to have come across the waters on a reed; he is reverenced in Japan as the discoverer of tea.

薘 ˏta An edible plant, the 紅莙丨菜 a root like beet or mangel-wurzel; the root and leaves are both eaten.

莆丨 the brinjal or egg-plant?

縫 ˏta An unauthorized character.

A knot.

絖丨子 a knot in thread.

係打的絖丨 tie a silken knot, for a button.

韃 ˏta The 丨靼 was a nomadic tribe dwelling on the north-west in the days of the Kitan, in the ninth century.

丨子 or 臭丨子 a term of contempt for the Mongols.

荅 ˏta From *bamboo* and *joined;* often contracted to the next alone, and as a primitive.

A bamboo hawser for dragging boats; an answer, that which follows a question; to respond, to echo; to recompense, to feel an obligation; suitable, congenial; thick, coarse.

丨問 question and answer.

報丨君恩 to requite the emperor's favors.

回丨他說 to reply to his remarks.

丨應 to answer.

總不丨 I would make no reply.

聽言則丨 answer when you hear the words.

豁丨如流 he rattles on like a babbling brook.

不必對丨 there is no need for an answer.

布丨 a kind of coarse cloth.

丨謝 to return thanks; to send a return present.

荅 ˏta Often used for the preceding.

A species of pulse; small grain; to sustain, to take upon one.

奉丨天命 to appreciate and carry out heaven's orders.

布渠丨 to lay iron spikes to serve as a chevaux-de-frise.

鮓丨 a concretion like the cow bezoar.

瘩 ˏta An unauthorized character.

A sore, a boil.

疙丨破了 the ulcer has burst.

疙丨事體 a difficult and mysterious affair.

踏 ˏta To jump or stride in walking, as when crossing a muddy or wet place; to lay hold of anything to jump by.

褡 ˏta From *clothes* and to *reply.*

A wrapper to wrap one's-self.

丨被 a wrap for one person.

丨包 the band which holds the purse.

洋丨褳 foreign drills.

丨縛難以遮其全體 it is hard to cover the whole body with only a tippet.

搭 ˏta From *hand* and to *answer;* it is interchanged with *t'ah*, 搨 and the two are nearly identical.

To place on, to pile up; to strike; to join; to engage a place or take a passage; to add to, to suffix; to suspend; to carry, as on the shoulder; to lean against; laid on or made higher.

丨船 to take passage in a boat.

丨客 passengers.

丨住 to stay at, as a guest; to sojourn on for a room.

丨架 to make a scaffolding.

丨單 additions to a manifest.

丨桴橋 to put up a foot-bridge.

丨在繩子上 hang it on the line.

丨些碎銀 add a few bits of silver to it.

手丨香腮 to rub cosmetic on the cheeks.

丨夥計 people connected with the same house or business.

In *Shanghai.* A spot, a place; a *copula,* with; and.

日頭丨之月 the sun and moon.

第丨 or 此地丨 here; this place.

故丨去住 go and live there.

伊拉丨儂 they will go with you.

瞎七丨八 in confusion, blindly placing things at sevens and eights.

勿丨講 I do not make them my friends.

䵬 ˏta The skin loosely hanging on the body.

耷 ˏta Great ears, those which hang over like a hog's or spaniel's.

丨拉着 dragging, going heavily; slovenly; applied to a sentence that is not well arranged.

鼛 ˏta From *drum* and *together.*

The sound of little drums or tambourines.

丨丨 a great drumming in concert, as in an orchestra.

沓 ˏta Piled on each other.

磊丨沓而相㢘 the rocks and shingle piled up and crashed over each otheor.

丨丨 piled on each other.

剳 ˏta The character *chah*ˀ 劄 is often wrongly contracted to this form.

A hook; hooked, curled; a quire.

毛丨 curly hair.

丨鉤 a long hook.

一丨子紙 a quire of paper of 50 sheets.

沓 ta' From 水 water and 曰 to speak; q. d. the murmuring of water is like babbling words.

Rippling water, the bubbling of a stream; jabbering, prattling; to join, as the sky does the earth; to pile on; sluggish, remiss; greedy, avaricious; to backbite; foolhardy; blindfold.

丨丨 a murmuring sound; gabble, loud talking; dilatory.

出入日月與天地丨 the sun and moon when rising and setting, look as if they rested on the sky and earth.

丨水 a river in Liaotung.

In *Cantonese*. A division or separate house in a long row or hong; to lay on; to pile up.

一丨屋 one house in a hong.

一座丨 one division of it.

一丨紙 a pile of paper.

丨起 pile them up.

搨 t'a' The noise made when a body falls to the ground, a thud; to pile up earth or dirt.

榙 t'a' The chapiter of a pillar, the capital of a column.

錔 ta' To cover a thing with iron to protect it; to shield the heel with an iron plate.

丨距 iron-bound for defense.

幍 ta' A covering to protect a tent or carriage, and keep out the rain; a large screen or tester.

丨幔 an outer tester to a large bed.

鞜 ta' Shoes made of leather.

革丨不穿 hide shoes do not quickly wear through

儋 ta' To idle.

傝丨 to neglect business, and idle away the time.

髻 ta' The hair on an infant's head when born, otherwise called 胎毛 or womb hair.

踏 t'a' To put the foot on the ground, to tread; to walk and beat time when singing.

踐丨 to trample or step on.

丨青 to step on the green, *i. e.* to worship at the tombs.

一脚丨兩船 a foot on each boat; *met.* two strings to his bow; or he has two wives.

丨破 broken by stepping on it.

丨實地步 feel a firm tread; — *i. e.* look before you leap; he is trustworthy, you may rely on him.

丨雪尋梅 to go over the snow looking for plum flowers.

足丨王土 all you tread on is still his Majesty's land; *i. e.* China is a vast region.

丨勘 to carefully investigate, as the place and manner of a murder by an official.

蹋 蹹 t'a Interchanged with the last, though they are not identical; the second form is little used.

To tread heavily; to stamp; to make a noise in walking.

丨踘 to kick a football.

丨倒 to slip down.

芒鞋丨破楚山青 his grass sandles have trodden down the green hills of Tso; — a great traveler.

丨伏 to steal along the ground in a manner not to be discovered, when coming on the enemy.

䂿 嚃 t'a These two are nearly identical.

To eat fast, as a hog; to slobber when eating; to gulp with a noise.

毋丨羹 do not eat soup with a noise.

丨丨 the slobbering noise made by pigs.

䶀 t'a A coat of skin or fur, a sheepskin made into a coat.

丨丨 sweltering, hot, as from wearing many garments.

䶀 t'a A clash.

丨鉤 the noise of knocking and pounding with sticks.

毾 t'a A kind of coarse woolen serge, first called 丨㲪 but now 氆氇 and brought from India and Tibet; the dictionary regards it as similar to the 多羅絨 plush or broadcloth brought to Canton.

䈳 t'a A window; one sash or window frame; it is also called 客扉 the guest's door.

丨篩日影 the latticed light shines in here.

遝 t'a' Repeated; abundant.

雜丨 mixed.

衆靈雜丨 all the spirits came trooping on together.

遝丨 following on, as people in a crowd.

溻 t'a To dampen, to soak through; soaked.

溼丨丨的地方 a very boggy, wet spot.

汗丨溼了衣裳 the perspiration has soaked through my dress.

搨 韜 ta From *hand* or *leather* and to *pile on*; some use it as a synonym of 搨 to rub.

A thimble used in sewing; a skin cover for the fingers when playing a guitar.

指丨 a thimble.

丨碑揭帖 to take a rubbing from a stone tablet.

躤 t'a To walk proudly; to step off, as when one straddles.

丨跎 (also written 蹉丨) tired, as from walking or travel. (*Shanghai.*)

T'AH.

Old sounds, t'at, t'ap, *and* dap. *In Canton*, t'ap *and* t'at; — *in Swatow*, t'ap, t'a, t'òa, *and* t'at; — *in Amoy*, t'at *and* t'ap; — *in Fuhchau*, t'ak *and* t'iak; — *in Shanghai*, t'ah; — *in Chifu*, t'a.

塌, *'t'a* To fall in ruins, as when the foundation sinks in; to crumble down; to slide, as the earth on a hillside; a first ploughing; underground.

房屋倒丨 the house fell down.

垂頭丨翼 hung its head and folded its wings.

死心丨地 all hope is lost, in despair.

那個人丨鼻子 that man has no bridge to his nose.

天丨地陷 [as if] the heaven had fallen and the earth caved in.

遭丨 to knock about; to waste uselessly; to vex people.

都坍丨了 it is in ruins; all fallen down; also applied to utter exhaustion and weariness.

傝, *'t'a* Disquieted in mind; a low-minded brutal man.

丨茸 a stupid brutish man; sordid, mean; plebeian.

榻, *t'a'* From *wood* and a rushing *flight* of birds.

A long bed; a couch, a settle to sleep on; a sort of cotton cloth.

榻妃丨 a sofa, a long couch.

半丨清風 lolling in the soft breeze; — at leisure.

一張丨 a couch.

上丨 to go to bed.

下丨 to lodge at, to sojourn.

籐丨 a rattan-bottomed couch.

磍, 碣, *t'a'* The first means a mortar for pounding and hulling rice in; to beat; the second is unauthorized, but both are used at Canton for large, brown, unglazed jars to warm or hold things.

埕丨 earthenware jars and jugs.

闒, *'t'a* A door in an upper storey opening on a terrace; a window in a loft.

樓丨 a lookout loft.

遢, *t'a'* To walk carefully; hurried, careless.

邋丨的很 very slovenly in his work.

屋裡邋丨 the house is greatly neglected.

丨穩地步 to walk with careful steps.

邋丨從事 he attends to his duties negligently.

丨靸鞋 or 丨拉鞋 shoes down at the heels.

㒓, *'t'a* Depressed, lost to all hope, in despair.

死心丨地 my soul is utterly cast down; I've no longer any hope.

情性㒓丨 a nerveless, insipid character.

鰨, *t'a'* Also read *nah*.

A synonym of the 鯢 or dugong, an animal of the seal kind, also called 魼丨, and strangely confounded with the sole-fish.

丨沙魚 the plaice or sole-fish. (*Cantonese.*)

㒶, *'t'a* From *wings* and to *speak*; used only as a primitive.

The rushing sound of wings, as of a flock of scared wild fowl suddenly rising.

漯, *t'a'* Ancient name of a stream in north of Shantung, perhaps a branch of the Ta-tsing River, or one of the streams north of it, as 丨陽縣 was an old name of Tsing-ch'ing hien in that region.

澾丨 rushing waters.

嗒, *t'a'* To be absent-minded; in a flurry, to lose self-possession; to lose a half of; to lick or lap, to sip up.

丨然 bewildered, stupefied, as at the loss of a partner or husband.

塔, 墖, *'t'a* From *earth* and *answer*; the second and ancient form is now disused.

The sound of dirt or earth falling down; a pile of dirt; used as a contraction for the Sanscrit *sthoupa*, a tumulus, to denote a pagoda or tower, for what the English call a pagoda, the French more correctly call a *tour* or tower; a dagoba or pile erected over a relic of Budha, or tope raised over a Budhist priest; applied to a tower, a lighthouse, monument, or pillar; pagoda-like, as the cone of a pine.

一座丨 one pagoda.

文丨 a three-storied pagoda, dedicated to the God of Literature; it resembles a writing-pencil.

寶丨 a dagoba or pagoda, regarded as precious.

普同丨 a cemetery of Budhist priests; a receptacle of infants.

鴈丨題名 he has written his name in the wild goose tower, — he is a *tsin-sz'*, alluding to a building at Chang-an 長安 the capital in the T'ang dynasty, where successful scholars wrote their names.

丨肚 a fearless man (*Cantonese.*)

搨, *ta'* Used with 搭, to *strike*, in this sense alone.

To rub over, to take an impression of a writing on stone; a fac-simile, an impression; to echo; to sheathe, to cover.

宋丨 impression [of inscriptions] in the Sung dynasty.

丨摸 to rub.

元丨 an original copy.

丨地錢 to levy a duty on produce; the present made to the gate keepers or servants.

舊丨 ancient fac-similes.

丨冐 stupid, easily imposed upon.

鞳 t'a' hö' A leather cuirass; it occurs written 鞈; the clamor of drums and tambourines.

㒓 t'a' To run away, to abscond, to desert.

佻㒓丨㒓 how impertinent! rude and mulish in disposition.

撻 t'a' 'ta To punish, to chastise, as a parent does; to reduce; to beat, to strike, as a warning; a slap, a blow; quick; the spot where the arrow rests.

鞭丨 to horsewhip.

丨以記之 whipped him that he might remember it.

丨子 the Tartars or Mongols.

楚丨 to ferule.

若丨于市朝 as if bambooed in the market or court.

In *Cantonese.* A dead loss, entirely gone; to throw at; the residue; to press down; a flat.

丨乾淨 lost the whole, cleaned out.

丨埋墙 throw it against the wall.

丨賬目 a bad account.

丨身家 to injure one's self, to waste one's patrimony.

丨沙魚 the sole fish.

澾 t'a' Slippery and miry.

甚是滑丨 it is very muddy walking.

闥 t'a' An inner door, a small door in a palace; a screen.

閨丨 the door of the women's rooms.

排丨直入 open the inner door and go straight in.

黃丨 door of the hareem.

臥丨 a niche or recess where the bed stands; the recesses or nooks of a country.

躂 t'a' The feet slipping; to stamp on.

丨倒 he slipped down.

丨足 to slip, to slide.

蹧丨 to revile, to slander, to defame.

丨脖鞋 slipshod shoes. (*Cantonese.*)

獺 t'a' An otter.

山丨 a fresh-water otter; applied also to the beaver.

海丨 a seal; the sea otter.

臧丨 a species of otter from Tibet; the fur is short and a bright brick red.

丨皮領 otter skin collars or tippets.

水丨帽沿 otter skin trimming on a winter cap.

丨仔 a boat-woman at Canton.

TAI.

Old sounds, ta, da, tat, dat, tak, *and* dak. *In Canton*, toi *and* tai; — *in Swatow*, tai, t'ai, t'oi, to, *and* tòa; — *in Amoy*, tai *and* t'ai; — *in Fuhchau*, tai; — *in Shanghai*, dé, t'é, ta, *and* t'éⁿ; — *in Chifu*, tai.

懛 ˳tai From *heart* and a *terrace*; it is also interchanged with ˳ngai 獃 a common character, which has taken the same sound and sense.

Alarmed, frightened; silly, acting like a fool.

丨獃 a silly, needless terror.

書丨子 a pedantic booby.

賴丨 careless, dress out of order, inappropriate.

歹 歺 'tai The original form delineates *cutting* up *bones*; it is the 78th radical of characters denoting misfortunes, deaths, corpses, &c.

Bad, vicious; evil, perverse, in some places it was once used for the pronoun I, my.

不知好丨 he does not know good from bad.

丨人 a bad man.

心懷丨意 he cherishes evil thoughts.

這人丨毒 that fellow is a villain.

爲非作丨 to make confusion and evil.

戴 tai' From 𢦏 to *injure* and 異 *different*; *i.e.* to divide things and pile them on each other.

To carry or wear on the head or face; crested, as some birds; to bear, to sustain, to uphold; to cover, as the sky does; to respect, to honor; to occur, to happen; to meet; in epitaphs, to love the people.

丨帽 to put on a cap.

丨眼鏡 to wear spectacles.

愛丨 to love and respect.

感丨深恩 to be deeply sensible and grateful for.

丨月披星 to wear the moon and wrap in the stars; — *i.e.* to travel and peddle.

擔丨 to undertake for.

頂丨 [allowed] to wear the knob or button.

賞丨花翎 allowed to wear a one-eyed peacock feather.

不共丨天 I will not live with him under the same sky.

丨高履厚 high as the sky and thick as the earth; said of favors.

丨日 place where the sun's rays reach in the solstice.

丨州 an old name of Ch'ing-wu-hien 城武縣 in the extreme south-west of Shantung.

丨德 imbued with virtue.

穢 *tai'* Unskilled, inexperienced. 䆿丨子 a raw hand; an unpracticed stupid fellow.

待 *tai'* From *to go* and a *court*. To wait for or on, to await, to expect; to treat, to behave to; provided against.
丨時而動 wait till the right time and then act.
丨價 to watch the price or rate.
寬丨 to treat liberally.
慢丨 to treat rudely.
接丨賓客 to wait on guests as they enter.
以丨來年 you must wait till next year.
相丨 to behave towards.
丨人厚道 to treat very kindly.
無丨商辦 there is no occasion for discussing and arranging the matter.

瑇玳 *tai'* From 玉 *gem* and 毒 *poisonous*, afterwards altered to 代 *instead*, probably for the phonetic.
Tortoise-shell is 丨瑁殼, especially the precious sort from the hawk's bill tortoise. (*Chelonia imbricata.*)
假丨瑁 imitation shell made from horns.

代 *tai'* From 人 *man* and 弋 *javelin*, which is a contraction of *t'eh*, 忒 to *change*.
To alter, to supersede; to substitute; to change; for, instead, in place of; delegated, vicarious; a generation; a reign, a dynasty.
年丨 or 世丨 a generation.
丨丨 age after age.
五丨同堂 five generations alive at once.
殘唐五丨 the Five Dynasties (A. D. 907–959) trode down the T'ang dynasty.
三丨 usually denotes the Hia, Shang, and Chen dynasties; but sometimes the first three monarchs, Fuhhi, Shinnung, and Hwangti.
後丨 posterity; after ages.
歷丨 successive reigns or ages.
丨辦 to manage for one.
丨你往 I'll go for you.
以旦丨某之身 let me Tan, be a substitute for his person.
力民丨食 their work as common people supersedes their living on their salaries.
丨月光明 a fancy name for a lantern.
丨書 an attorney; a copyist.
丨署 a deputy.
丨印 holding a seal for another officer.
丨勞 to labor for another.

祋 *tai'* A short spear or halberd; a defense or screen of sheep's hide let down suddenly from the walls to scare cattle or horses coming into the town.
彼候人兮何戈與丨 those escorting officers have their lancers and halberdiers.

岱 *tai'* From *hill* and *reign* as the phonetic.
The high peak in T'ai-ngan fu in Shantung, the 東嶽 or eastern and most famous of the five mountains; it was once known as 丨宗 but now is called 泰山 and is a place of great resort by devotees who crawl to its top and visit its temples.
至于丨宗柴 [Shun] came to Tai-tsung, where he made a burnt-offering.

帒袋 *tai'* From *napkin* or *dress* and a *reign* as the phonetic.
A bag, a sack, a case; a pocket, a purse; a covering to inclose or protect things.
風丨 wind sail.
衣丨 or 衫丨 a coat pocket.
搭丨 a fob inside the girdle.
火藥丨 a cartridge-box.
酒囊飯丨 a wine sack and rice-bag; — *met.* a glutton.
書丨 a book-sack or satchel; *met.* a pedant.
打砂子口丨 to play with sand-bags, as in a game of boxing.
卷丨 a satchel carried by candidates.
撒丨 a quiver.
襯丨 embroidered fobs hanging to the girdle.
昭文丨 ancient name of a satchel used in court by officials.
In *Cantonese*. A pipe.
食丨烟 to smoke one pipe.
水烟丨 a bubble-bubble, or water pipe.

黛 *tai'* To blacken the eyebrows, or paint a black mark instead; umber, black; an invisible green.
青丨 a dark color, as the hue of distant hills.
環螺丨 the dark circling hills, as around a temple.
眉丨 black eyebrows.
粉白丨黑 to whiten the face and blacken the eyebrows.

貸 *tai'* To lend on interest; a loan; to intrust to another; to confer, to give; to release.
借丨 to loan money.
乞丨 to ask a loan.
責罰不丨 he will punish and not pardon.
决不寬丨 I will not let him off.
Read *t'eh*, and used for 貣. To borrow.

怠 *tai'* From *heart* and *raised*.
To treat harshly; rude, careless, impertinent; supercilious; to be idle; remiss, lazy; discourteous, inattentive, self-indulgent; idly; to grow weary.
丨惰 indolent, heedless of.
丨慢 disrespectful.
得時無丨 don't hesitate when the right moment comes.
丨倦 irked and tired of a work.
丨緩 remiss, negligent, slow.

殆' *tai'* Dangerous; imminent; perilous; to endanger, to hazard, to run risks; beginning, approaching, and thus like the next, at, about, at the limit, nearly; occurs used for the last.
行' 丨 to run into danger.
危 丨 hazardous.
民今方 丨 the people are now amid their perils.
無小人 丨 do not approach vulgar people.
丨 及 nearly to, drawing near.
丨 至一載 nearly a whole year.
天下 丨 哉 the empire is in great danger.

迨' 逮' *tai'* An adverb of time, till, to, even until; when, and when; to reach, to come up with.
丨 今 till now.
丨 後 till afterwards.
丨 至其時 up to that period or date.
水火相 丨 [uncongenial, as] when water and fire come in contact.
皇恩下 丨 the emperor's kindness reaches to all.
求我庶士 丨 其吉兮 for those gentlemen who seek me, this is their lucky time!
丨 天之未陰雨 wait till the rains cease.
追 丨 to come up to, as a pursuer.
不 丨 it cannot be effected; also deficiencies; to be deficient.

Read *ti'* Harmonious; affable.
威儀 丨 丨 his air and presence were very agreeable.

隶' *tai'* Original form of the last, now used as the 171st radical of half a dozen characters; it is made from 又 *hand* or 及 *reaching* and 尾 *tail* all combined.

To reach to, to overtake; a surplus.

埭' *tai'* A dam; a noted water-race in Shih-tai hien 石 丨 縣 in the southeast of Nganhwui, where the rocks inclose the stream; an inclined plane on a canal, where boats can be passed up or down by a windlass; to make a lock or dam on a canal.
丨 格 the scale of charges at a lock.
花 丨 an old name of the Flower gardens 花地 near Canton.

靆' *tai'* From *clouds* and *reaching* to.

Cloudy.
天雲靉 丨 the sky is cloudy and dull.

帶' 帶' *tai'* From *kerchief* and a diagram of *clothes bound*, intended to represent a girdle; the second form is only used as a noun; interchanged with the next.

A sash, a girdle, a belt; men's were of leather, women's of silk; a compress, a bandage; a tape, ribbon, or scarf; a region; a zone in geography; places connected with each other, as a neighborhood; a classifier of regions of country; to take along with one, as if in the girdle; to lead, to conduct; to remind; connected with, implicated in, related; rather, somewhat, slightly; to latch, to close.
褲 丨 or 腰 丨 or 大 丨 a girdle.
襪 丨 garters; knee-pads.
絲 丨 舖 a tape and thread shop.
峨冠博 丨 a high cap and a broad sash.
連本 丨 息 principal and interest altogether.
黃 丨 子 and 紅 丨 子 a son of the yellow and red girdle, denotes one of the imperial family, and one allied to it.
丨 手 to do by the way.
飄 丨 streamers or bands appended to a scroll or flag.
山環水 丨 the circle of the hills and line of the river.
拐 丨 人口 to entrap and carry off people, — usually children.
冠 丨 起來 to dress in good clothes.
丨 累 involved in, implicated with.
一 丨 地方 a region of country; a plateau, an expanse.
暎 丨 in *rhetoric*, associated ideas, a continuous idea.
丨 水艇 a pilot-boat.
引 丨 to introduce one, to guide.
出入 丨 門 latch the door when you go out or in.
無掛 丨 no cares on my mind.
所屬一 丨 whatever places are under his jurisdiction.
管 丨 幫 丨 the officer in charge of a force or fleet, and his deputy.
海 丨 sea-weed, especially the long *Laminaria* used for food.
丨 點愁意 he shows his sorrow.
順 丨 a kind of lady's fob; to take along with one.
丨 封信 to take a letter.
面色 丨 黃 his complexion is rather sallow.
忠孝 丨 the court girdle worn by all who see the Emperor.

In *Cantonese* used for 太. Overmuch, rather.
丨 熱的 it is rather too hot.

癤' *tai'* From *disease* and *girdle*; the last form is most usually written.

A disease of women.
丨 症 or 白 丨 fluor albus, whites, or leucorrhea.
赤 丨 a bloody discharge from the womb, not menstrual.

Read *chi'* A dysentery or bloody flux; a diarrhea of great violence; the head half covered with sores.

懘' *tai'* Ill at ease.
丨 忦 disturbed in mind, distressed.

蔕' *tai'* Interchanged with *ti'* 蒂 a peduncle; and used for the last.

The rootlets of herbs or grasses; unimportant.
細故 丨 芥何足以疑 what is the use of being suspicious about such a trifling affair?

嗁' *tai'* To talk fast and continuously.

T'AI.

Old sounds, da, dat, t'ai, *and* t'ap. *In Canton*, t'oi *and* t'ai ; — *in Swatow*, t'ai *and* t'o ; — *in Amoy*, t'ai ; — *in Fuhchau*, t'ai *and* tai ; — *in Shanghai*, t'é, dé, téⁿ *and* ta ; — *in Chifu*, t'ai.

台 ˏt'ai From 口 *mouth* and 厶 (contracted from 以) *by;* occurs used for ˏ臺 and the next.

Eminent, exalted; used in direct address, your honor; venerable, old; wrinkled, infirm.

老丨 great Sir.

老兄丨 exalted Sir.

老父丨 our district magistrate.

丨駕 your honor.

丨甫 your honored style; written in letters before the 字 name.

丨照 for your honor's inspection.

三丨 three stars ι κ λ in the feet of the Great Bear; also applied with 三鼎 to the three highest dignitaries of the empire.

丨州府 a maritime department in the southeast of Chehkiang.

Read ˏi, and used for 怡. Pleased, gratified; to rejoice; in classical use I, me, when said by rulers.

非丨小子敢行稱亂 it is not me alone an obscure person, who dares to act so as to call it a rebellion.

夏罪其如丨 what are the crimes of Hia to us?

鮐 ˏt'ai A globular fish, the *Tetraodon* or 鯸丨 which can inflate itself; it has a white belly and greenish back, wrinkled and sallow, whence 丨背 (or 台背) comes to mean wrinkled and growing old, like the tetraodon's back.

黃耇丨背 with hoary face and wrinkled back.

胎 ˏt'ai From *flesh* and *raised.*

The pregnant womb; to commence; congenital; a receptacle; a condition of; having a womb; to run away.

懷丨 or 有丨 with young.

丨衣 the placenta.

石丨 or 不做丨 barren.

墮丨 or 落丨 an abortion.

丨生 viviparous.

安丨 to compose or quiet the womb, — and prevent miscarriage.

脫丨 parturition, to be born.

投丨 to quicken.

鹿丨 unborn fawns, used as a medicine.

帽丨 an official cap without any fringe or button.

殺不及丨 do not kill pregnant — animals.

丨瞽 born blind.

化丨 to make an abortion.

丨禽 the crane, from a notion that it is viviparous.

頭一丨 the first born.

邰 ˏt'ai A small ancient feudal state, made by Wăn Wang, situated in the modern Kien cheu 乾州 in Shensi, north of the River Wéi.

髻 ˏt'ai A woman's headdress of false hair; it is sometimes fancifully arranged.

臺 ˏt'ai From 至 *extreme*, 之 to *go* and 高 *high* altered in combination; it is often contracted to ˏ台 and used with the next three.

A square and high open terrace built up for a lookout; a turret; a staging; an observatory; a fort; a watchman's post over a gate; a stand, a frame; a title of respect to officers; an underling, a servant; a kind of marsh grass.

晒丨 a terrace to dry things.

作一丨戲 to perform one play.

幾時開丨 when will the play begin?

築一座高丨 to build a high terrace.

戲丨 the stage, the boards.

南山有丨 the sedge grows on the southern hills.

燈丨 a lamp-stand.

靈丨 a marvelous tower; among Taoists, the physical heart.

氷丨 punk, tinder.

門丨 a guard-place over a gate.

平丨 a flat roofed house without tiling. (*Pekingese.*)

丨前 in your presence.

丨翁 your worship.

制丨, the 撫丨, the 臬丨, the 藩丨 and the 道丨 denote the five highest provincial officers.

憲丨 a censor; the magistrates.

容丨 the Board of Rites.

提丨 a captain-general.

丨榭 a pic-nic arbor in a garden.

檯 ˏt'ai **枱** ˏt'ai From *wood* and *terrace;* the second form is properly read sz' but at Canton is the common contraction of the first.

Name of a tree; a table; a theater; a stage, and then interchanged with the last.

一張丨 one table.

寫字丨 a desk, a writingtable.

日字丨 a sofa table.

開丨 or 擺丨 to set a table.

一丨送 a table full of viands.

大丨人 and 二丨人 a partner and his clerk.

儓 ˏt'ai A servant or major-domo,

陪丨 in an officer's house.

田丨 a farmer's help, a field laborer.

輿丨 a charioteer.

薹 ˏt'ai A triquetrous grass (*Scirpus maritimus*) growing in boggy spots, of which hats and cloaks are made; the flower stalk of a vegetable, as of cabbage or turnip.

丨菜 a culinary vegetable also called 油菜 the *Brassica chinensis,* or oil cabbage, grown in Chehkiang, and eaten like spinach.

丨乾 dried slips of lettuce.

中心丨謂之菰首 the fleshy center of its stalk [the *Hydropyrum*] is called *ku sheu.*

擡 抬 ꜀t'ai From *hand* and *elevated;* the contracted form is also used as a synonym of ꜀ch'i 笞 to bamboo.

To carry between two or more on a pole; to move; to raise, to lift; to elevate; put above the rest; to praise.

八人丨 eight bearers to carry his chair.

丨頭字 characters raised above the line.

扛丨 to carry on a beam.

高丨市價 to raise the current price.

丨貴手 to own one's error and beg pardon.

丨不動 we cannot carry it.

丨舉 to advance, to recommend.

丨回去 or 丨返來 carry it back.

苔 ꜀t'ai Moss; also small plants like liverworts, growing on rocks, confervæ and crystal-worts on water, and scale-mosses (*Jungermannia*) in damp places; moss-grown, mossy.

丨菜 a species of algæ used for food.

青丨 fucus on water; green mold along the shore; mossy growth on stones.

蒼丨 green moss.

丨痕上堦綠 the mossy marks covered the green steps.

丨錢 patches of moss — won't feed beggars.

青丨石 a moss-covered stone; *met.* a swindler, a slippery chap.

駘 ꜀t'ai A wearied or worn-out hack of a horse freed of his bits; jaded; useless.

馬丨其銜 the horse has dropped his bits.

丨蕩 unrestrained, vast; the joyous free appearance of spring.

丨鈍 free of restraint, doltish.

炱 ꜀t'ai The soot or cinders from a fire; smoky soot.

炭丨 ashes and soot.

丨煤 cinders.

口鼻丨黑 the mouth and nose blackened with the soot.

嚺 ꜀t'ai To speak erroneously or pettishly; to mock.

丨嗂 to talk without cessation.

檯 ꜀t'ai To sharpen or smooth wood against the grain; small sticks used by children to play a game like quoits.

紿 ꜀t'ai Silk thread raveled; tangled; dilatory; to doubt, to jeer at.

惡公子之丨 to hate the young prince's ridicule.

泰 t'ai꜄ Composed of 水 *water* inside of 廾 *both hands* and 大 *great* combined; it is often contracted to the next.

Slippery, smooth; exalted, honorable; large, extensive, liberal; superior in station or excellence; extreme, extravagant; pervading; the 11th diagram denoting vigor.

天地交丨 heaven and earth vigorous and productive.

丨而不驕 exalted without being proud.

國丨民安 may the state be prosperous and the people peaceful.

丨山 in the west of Shantung, the 東嶽 which gives fame to Tai-ngan fu.

丨山 and 丨水 terms used in speaking of another's wife's parents.

否 and 丨 are opposites, disorder — peace; misfortune — prosperity, referring to their diagrams.

丨運 a prosperous reign.

太 t'ai꜄ Contracted from the preceding, but the two are not used alike.

An intensive *adverb* implying an extreme; too, very; excessive; a term of high respect.

丨丨 or 老丨丨 an officer's lady, Madam, her ladyship.

亞丨 a lady. (*Cantonese.*)

丨夫人 your mother.

丨子 the heir-apparent.

丨子丨保 senior guardian of the crown prince.

丨過 or 丨多 too much by far; intrusive, froward.

丨早 too early.

丨不及 it is quite insufficient, will not do at all.

丨上老君 an honorable name for Laotsz'.

何丨無禮 why such great discourtesy?

丨平洋 the Pacific Ocean.

丨好 better than I wish.

丨小 much too small.

丨冷靜些 a little too cold or haughty.

題目丨出容易 the theme is very easy.

丨古 in very early times.

說也丨說重了 you said it with too much severity.

不要丨謙 do not be too modest.

汰 t'ai꜄ Slippery; excessive, overpassing; waters swashing over; to wash and rinse, to clean; to correct, as style.

沙丨 to scour with sand.

淘丨 to purify by scrubbing or rinsing.

忲 㥭 t'ai꜄ The first form is also written 忕 and read *shi*꜄, and defined to practice.

Extravagant, careless.

侈丨 or 奢丨 wasteful, profuse; dissolute.

黙 t'ai꜄ From *black* and *exceedingly.*

Very black.

黑丨 excessively black.

艜 *t'ai* A long narrow vessel having two masts; some of them can be armed; they resemble the revenue cutters at Canton.

In *Cantonese*. A rudder.

丨 檣 a tiller.

揸 丨 to steer.

鬆 丨 to crane up the rudder; to let it go.

推 丨 to ease off the helm.

態 *t'ai* From *heart* and *able*; *q. d.* when the mind feels its ability to act, the body takes the impress; it resembles *hiung* 熊 a bear.

Figure, form; the gait, air, habit, or attitude of a man; the expression of an idea; configuration; circumstances.

不忍爲此 丨 I can't endure such an air; it is insufferable.

驕 丨 a haughty bearing.

丨 度 behavior.

夭冶之 丨 a seductive, ogling way.

小人 丨 the manner of a rascal.

情 丨 exhibition of the feelings, amorous; the circumstances.

世 丨 炎凉 the cordiality or coldness of people.

故 丨 復作 he has gone back to his old way of acting.

僞 丨 affected, pretending, put on.

TAN.

Old sounds, tan, dan, *and* tam. *In Canton*, tan, t'an, *and* tam; — *in Swatow*, tan, tam, tⁿa, *and* tⁿòa; — *in Amoy*, tan, tam, *and* t'an; — *in Fuhchau*, tang; — *in Shanghai*, téⁿ, tèⁿ *and* dèⁿ; — *in Chifu*, tan.

丹 *tan* The *point* is supposed to represent the red stone, and the other part a 井 *pit*, whence it (the cinnabar) is brought; this character forms the radical of a dozen characters relating to vermilion, which might have well been grouped under it.

A carnation or cinnabar color; loyal, sincere, trustworthy; medicines decocted or distilled; before a metal answers to an oxide of it; a pill coated with cinnabar; a remedy, a prescription; to color or paint red.

靈 丨 an efficacious remedy.

煉 丨 to distil medicines.

丨 方 an excellent prescription.

仙 丨 the liquor of immortality of the Rationalists; there were two schools of them divided upon this subject, called the 外 丨 and 內 丨, one holding for the external application, the other that the reformation of the heart was itself immortality.

丨 沙 cinnabar.

紅 丨 red lead, minium.

一片 丨 心 entirely devoted to one.

丨 色 light red.

丨 家 or 丨 爐家 a chemist, an alchemist.

用盡 丨 田之力 used all the strength he possessed.

丨 田 in *anatomy*, the pubic region; the base or power of the breath.

丨 娘 or 丨 鳥 a fire-fly.

丨 灶 the pomegranate flower.

顏如渥 丨 ruddy cheeked, florid.

散 丨 花 a red lily (*Lilium tenuifoluim*) common near Peking.

丨 青 a painting, because red and blue enter into every painting.

㐤 *tan* To loll the tongue, as a dog when heated.

玄熊 丨 談 the black bear lolled his tongue.

聃 *tan* Ears without a rim on the lobe; an ancient term for teacher.

老 丨 a name of Laotsz'.

眈 躭 *tan* From *eye* or *body* and *hesitating*.

To look at a thing and yet be thinking of something distant; to obstruct, to prevent.

丨 丨 a majestic look.

虎視 丨 丨 the tiger glares fiercely on his prey.

丨 擱我們的工 he retards our work.

丨 延 to procrastinate.

丨 悞 careless and neglectful.

耽 *tan* Often confounded with the last.

Pendent ears, reaching to the shoulders, considered to be a sign of longevity; lustful, addicted to pleasure.

目 丨 丨 視之 gloating over it with his eyes.

和樂且 丨 excessive delight in sensual pleasures.

女之 丨 兮不可說也 when a lady goes astray, nothing can be said for her.

丨 羅 Quelpaert I. near Corea.

酖 *tan* Also read *chăn'* when used for 鴆 a poison.

Given to drink; fond of wine.

丨 嗜 gluttonous.

荒 丨 酒色以伐體膚 to be excessively fond of wine and women destroys the body.

單 单 *tan* Single, alone, isolated, by itself; a single garment; odd, as odd numbers; an orphan, an individual; thin, poor; debilitated, exhausted; one side of; greatly; sincere, credible, that which is the surety of belief, — and hence a check, a bill, a receipt; to complete; to surround or wrap; an *adverb*, only, but, nothing but.

丨 是 or 丨 係 merely, only that, just.

歲暮衣裳 丨 one's wardrobe gets scant at the end of the year.

丨 兵守孤城 a single company [trying to] hold the solitary post.

其軍三 丨 his army was in three corps.

丨 獨 only one.

開一張丨子 make out a bill.
收丨 a receipt.
匯丨 a draft, a bill of exchange.
丨薄 thin, not durable; poor; deficient; weak.
貨丨 an invoice.
支丨 an order to pay money.
丨身 one alone; as 丨住 to live by one's-self, and not with the parents.
丨身漢 a bachelor; one who lives or trades alone.
丨日作 do it on the odd days.
丨寒 thinly dressed; poverty-stricken.
自己丨走 I went alone.
乃丨文祖德 to carry out the virtue of your grandfather Wăn.
丨丨淸 only one, one kind, unique.

Read ˛*shen*. A famous chief of the Huns, 丨于 about B. C. 25, and used afterwards as a title like *khan* or *rajah*; vast like the deserts these tribes lived in.
丨閼 the years of the cycle which have 卯 in them.

Read *shen*ʾ. A district, 丨縣 in Tsao-cheu fu in the west of Shantung.

匰 ˏ*tan* From *receptacle* and *alone*.

A shrine where the effigies or tablets are kept in the ancestral hall.
木丨主 the ancestral shrine of the defunct.

殫 ˏ*tan* From *dead* and *alone* as the phonetic.

The extreme, last stage of; the utmost; entirely; to exhaust.
丨力 with the whole energy.
歲既丨矣 the year has quite departed.
丨究 to thoroughly investigate.
丨厥心 devoted his whole mind to it.
丨思極慮 deeply meditated on it.

襌 ˏ*tan* From *dress* and *single*; it closely resembles ˛*shen* 禪 meditation.

A garment without lining; single, as a thickness.
被丨 a sheet for a bed.
丨襦 an under-shirt.
汗丨 a shirt, a chemise, a shift.

癉 ˏ*tan* Also read ʿ*t'an*, and interchanged with 疸 and 疸 though the last is rather a contraction than a synonym.

Disease arising from over-work; worn out, wearied with; ulcerated, vitiated, as the blood; discontented, angry.
彰善丨惡 to praise the good and punish the wicked, — in order to encourage the people.
火丨 a bloody discharge to which children are subject; strangury, arising from debility.
下民卒丨 the common people are full of distress.
黃丨 jaundice; sallow-looking.
喉丨 an ulcerated throat, diphtheria.

鄲 ˏ*tan* An old region in the south of Chihli and Shantung, and Luh-yih hien 鹿邑縣 in the east of Honan.
邯丨夢 a dream in Hantan is one like Mohammed's, in which a life's work is passed through in a moment to show the vanity of life.

Read ˏ*to*. A region in the valley of the River Han, of which 周隱 was made prince A. D. 149.

簞 ˏ*tan* A small round open basket of different sizes, for holding rice when steamed, or after it is cooked; a round hat-box; fine bamboo splints; to put rice into a basket
丨瓢屢空 the panniers and calabashes were repeatedly empty, — in the famine.
一丨食 only one dish to eat; — poor.
挂丨和尙 a begging priest with a basket.
竹丨 a bamboo basket.

驔 ˏ*tan* A blackish horse with yellow or white flanks and forelegs.
有丨有魚 there were white legged horses and those with fish-like eyes.

儋 ˏ*tan* Interchanged with the next.

A load of two peculs of grain; a long necked vessel for holding fire.
丨州 a large town in the north-west of Hainan Island.

擔 ˏ*tan* *tan*ʾ From *hand* and *talkative*; also contracted to the *dawn*, as in the next character.

To carry on a pole across the shoulders after the manner of peddlers; to bear, to undertake, to sustain; to be responsible for, to go as security; to grab at; to reduce on account of defects.
丨這個箱 carry this box.
你丨得起嗎 can you lift it?
丨保 to go as bail for; to insure; to be responsible for.
丨上來 take it up stairs.
丨頭 one's bail or security. (*Cantonese.*)
丨勿起 it's too heavy to lift. (*Shanghai.*)
丨上身 I'll take the responsibility.
丨任 adequate to the post.
丨贏 to stake one's credit on the luck.
丨當不起 he is incompetent for the situation.
不敢丨承 I am not able to undertake it.
狗丨糭 the dog grabbed the pudding; — he did not take the hint.
丨心害怕 to be terribly alarmed.
你格外丨戴我 you have often borne with my faults.

Read *tan*ʾ A burden, a load; a pecul of a hundred catties.
好重ʾ丨 a very heavy load.
丨干 or 扁丨 a colstaff, a carrying-beam.

一 丨 重 it weighs a pecul.

丨 頭 a peculage levied by tide-waiters.

家有丨石未足爲貧 we have a pecul of rice in the house, and so are not yet beggared.

一 丨 ʻ ˏ 丨 take it at one load.

担 ʻtan Much used for the last as a noun; and also for *tʻan*ʼ 擹 a duster.

Properly to brush off; to exact, to raise; a duster.

丨 灰 塵 to brush off the dust.

丨 丨 衣 服 to dust clothes.

布 丨 子 a duster of tape or strips of cloth.

意 恣 睢 以 丨 撟 his ideas are comprehensive, so that he will surely raise himself to fame.

礑 ʻtan A mineral from Sz'chʻuen, described as having a liquid or juice like gall; it is now used with the last for 丨 礬 or 石 丨 blue vitriol or sulphate of copper.

膽 胆 ʻtan The gall; the gall-bladder; courage, bravery, because it is supposed to be connected with this organ; fortitude, endurance.

丨 水 the bile.

黃 丨 the gall.

丨 量 小 or 丨 細 timid, fearful.

嚇 破 丨 子 scared almost to death.

丨 生 毛 his gall has got hairs; — dauntless, audacious.

丨 大 and 丨 虛 are opposites, courageous and craven; brave and white-livered.

肝 丨 liver and gall; intimate, mutually dependent.

丨 丨 大 大 indomitable courage.

喪 丨 downhearted.

瀝 丨 披 肝 [he has a] a dropping gall and rent liver; brave.

丨 志 moral courage.

丨 識 intelligent and determined.

丨 作 丨 爲 we are not afraid to do as we plan.

炭 丨 fine lignite or jet. (*Pekingese.*)

龍 丨 草 a bitter plant used in rheumatism; perhaps the *Gentiana asclepiadea.*

薝 ʻtan A white and very fragrant flower from India, the 丨 蔔 which is called 冠 諸 香 the cap of all fragrances; this is probably the champaca (*Michelia champaca*), also written 旃 簸 迦 in Budhist books; and called 白 玉 蘭 from its purity.

丨 棘 a timber tree, perhaps the *Michelia Rheedii.*

紞 ʻtan A silken fringe worn on the sides of a crown, or on a coronet in ancient times, to cover the ears; the sound or roll of a drum.

衡 丨 side fringes on a crown.

芜 ʻtʻan The drawing resembles an *Iris;* the plant has many names, of which 知 母 is the most common; the root is whitish and slightly mucilaginous.

丨 藩 the dried water orris root.

菡 ʻtan An opening flower, especially those of the lotus and *Hibiscus mutabilis.*

白 菡 丨 香 初 過 雨 the white lily gives out its scent just after a rain.

刞 ʻtan To cut; others say, to trim or sharpen a little, to scrape off somewhat.

亶 ʻtan From 㐭 *granary* contracted and 旦 *morning.*

Plenty of grain; to trust, sincerity; really; to render sincere; the name of Wăn Wang's grandfather.

丨 其 然 乎 will you not find it really so?

誕 告 用 丨 veracity should be in every proclamation.

不 實 于 丨 your sincerity is not real.

古公丨父來朝走馬 the old Duke Tʻan-fu came in the morning on the fast horses.

丨 洲 probably an island lying southwest of Hainan.

蛋 蜑 tanʼ A tribe of aborigines, the 丨 蠻 who once lived south of the Méi-ling in Fuhkien and westward; it was a term of abuse, and derived from a colloquial name for egg, for which the first form only is now used; an animal's testicles.

雞 丨 a hen's egg.

鴨 丨 a duck's egg.

皮 丨 or 卞 丨 eggs preserved in salt for exportation.

丨 家 the boat-people at Canton, who are supposed to be allied to the Miaotsz' in the north of the province.

丨 戶 boat-people.

丨 家 婆 a boat-woman.

旦 tanʼ From *sun* above a *line, i. e.* the horizon; it is often written carelessly like ʻtsʻié 且 moreover.

The morning, the dawn; light, clear; daylight; to be clear seeing; occurs wrongly used for 神 a god; actors who take the parts of females.

元 丨 newyear's day.

自 夜 達 丨 to watch through the night for the dawn.

坐 以 待 丨 to sit and wait for daylight.

一 丨 in a morning, instantly.

花 丨 those who act the parts of women.

打 武 丨 to personify female warriors.

生 丨 戲 a play of a love affair.

明 丨 而 行 we will go in the morning.

昊 天 曰 丨 乃 爾 游 衍 great Heaven is clear as the rising sun, and is near you in all your roaming and dissipation.

信 誓 丨 丨 we were clearly pledged to good faith.

但 tan' A disjunctive *conjunction*, but, but very; an *adverb*, only, simply; whenever, as soon as,—and usually begins a sentence to add force, or serve as an introduction; unrestrained, set at liberty.

丨不知 but I don't know.

丨係 but so it is.

丨凡 but, however, whosoever.

丨願如此 I simply wish it so.

丨見人山人海 he sees the men like hills or waves;—a vast multitude.

丨特無匹 only one, no mate.

丨坐不妨 you may sit down.

不丨如此 it is not only this way.

丨說不怕 come, speak out boldly.

豈丨 how only? not so.

詐丨 to deceive.

丨託空言 it was only empty words; it all came to nothing.

丨只恨年過四十却無子 he was much vexed that at forty he still had no son.

呾 tan' Also read *tah*, and *toh*,

To call to each other; to recriminate; others say, to hum, to sing low.

丨丨 or 丨嗟 to stammer, to pronounce badly,

疸 tan' From *sickness* and *morn*; similar to '癉, but not to be confounded with ,tsü 疽 an ulcer.

A disease which turns the eyes yellow and the urine red, and makes one hungry and sleepy.

黃丨 the jaundice.

鴠 tan' A species of nightingale or thrush, the 鶡丨 which 求旦 waits for dawn with its song; this name is also written 渴旦 thirsting for the sunrise; other names are 城旦 guarding the dawn, and 獨春 first or alone in spring.

彈 tan' ,t'an From *bow* and *alone*.

A cross-bow to shoot bullets; a bullet, a ball, a shot; a pill.

丨子 a pellet.

丨丸 a bolus, a pill; *met.* a small piece of ground, a little country.

打丨弓 to shoot clay balls.

鉛丨 leaden bullets.

炮像丨襯 the fire-crackers snap against one.

Read ,t'an. To fillip, to thrum on stringed instruments; to snap, to throw at; to mark, as with a line; to decry, to depreciate; to accuse, to find fault with, as a censor.

丨棉花 to bow cotton.

丨琴 to thrum a lute.

丨墨線 to strike a mark with a line.

丨染 to dye by sprinkling.

丨唱 to play and sing for hire.

丨指須臾 [like] a snap of the finger, a brief moment.

丨糾 to bring charges against, to suspect and accuse.

丨壓 to suppress; to put down.

奏丨 to report against one.

丨章 an accusation against an officer.

丨腦鑿子 thump your noddle and get out the character.

丨冠出仕 to snap the cap and go to take the office.

丨瘡者痛 to open a sore is painful.

撣 tan' To seize with the hand; to grasp; to butt; used for the last, to thrum, to play on; to hold with a slight grasp; name of a country in the Han dynasty on the eastern frontiers of the present Burmah, along the Irrawady River.

動丨 to take exercise, to stretch the limbs; to move.

Read ,chen. To pull along.

丨援 to drag or lead, as an animal.

僤 tan' Quick, impetuous; the whole heart in a thing; urgent; to annoy, to move.

逢天丨怒 to meet the dire anger of Heaven.

憚 tan' From *heart* and *alone* as the phonetic.

To dread difficulty or pain; to shirk; fearful; worn out with.

肆無忌丨 reckless, fearing nobody or nothing.

不丨煩 don't be afraid of duty; don't fear a little trouble.

丨勞 disliking trouble.

過則勿丨改 don't hesitate to reform when you've done wrong.

延 tan' Great; large.

誕 誕 tan' From *words* and *protracted*; in the south only the second form is commonly used for a birthday.

To boast, to talk wildly, to brag; to be disorderly; foolish or unfounded, incoherent; great, wide; to magnify, to make great; to enlarge; greatly; to bear children; to bring up; to be widely separated; an initial particle.

放丨 he is careless how he talks.

怪丨 strange talk.

口銳者多丨而寡信 people with sharp tongues brag much, but do not heed the truth.

丨告萬方 he proclaimed it abroad to all regions.

何丨之節兮 how wide apart are the joints—of the dolichos!

妄丨 a fabulous story; to talk wildly.

丨子 to have a son.

丨彌厥月 to complete the first moon after birth.

聖丨 or 寶丨 the birthday of a god.

賀丨 to congratulate the emperor on his birthday.

丨日 or 丨時 or 丨辰 a birthday.

朕丨膺天命 Ourself has been magnified by receiving Heaven's decree.

丨日 a birthday, the day in which the person is magnified, and therefore applied only to gods, saints, and the emperor, whose natal day is called 降丨 in allusion to his appellation as the son of heaven

甔 tan' A large earthenware jar, capable of holding a pecul.

憺 tan' Interchanged with the next.

Tranquil, easy; contented; sense, judgment.

丨然寡欲 he is satisfied, having few desires.

遊子丨忘歸 the wanderer is so contented, that he has forgotten his home.

淡 tan' From *water* and *hot*; *q. d.* fire thins or carries off the water.

Insipid, flat, tasteless; fresh; weak, insipid, watery; heartless, volatile; cold or distant, as an offended friend; light, as color; dull, as trade; indifferent to.

心丨 no liking for.

人丨如菊 he is remarkable as the aster flower, — which can resist the frost.

清丨 poor, flat.

生理冷丨 business is dull.

平丨 ordinary and inferior.

輕雲丨月 the clouds are light and the moon glimmering.

丨食粗衣 simple food and coarse clothes.

丨定 dispassionate, unbiassed.

丨菜 dried mussels or clams.

丨丨薄薄 insipid; profitless.

啖 **啗** **噉** tan' Used for the last; the third form which is rarely met, is read ʿkòm at Canton, for which see 敢 to dare.

To eat, to chew, to masticate; to entice, to hold out lures; a bite, a morsel; a bait; a swallow; wild, unfounded.

丨棗 to bite dates.

一丨飯 a mouthful of rice.

丨丨 to gulp or take all at once.

味丨 insipid, not salt enough.

丨以利乎 can he entice him with the hope of gain?

施捨丨飯 give [a poor beggar] a bite of food.

食丨 a poor table.

醈 tan' Having no salt, tasteless, flat, insipid.

T'AN.

Old sounds, t'an, t'am, dan, *and* dam. *In Canton*, t'an *and* t'am; — *in Swatow*, t'am, t'an, *and* tⁿòa; — *in Amoy*, t'an, t'am, *and* tam; — *in Fuhchau*, t'ang *and* tang; — *in Shanghai*, té̤ⁿ, tèⁿ *and* dèⁿ; — *in Chifu*, t'an.

貪 ˏt'an From *wealth* and *now*.

To covet; to worry for, to desire inordinately; ambitious, bent on; avaricious of; a fabulous beast, drawn like a scaly unicorn with cloven feet and a large horn, which is painted on the screen or wall opposite yamuns to warn officers against covetousness.

丨心不足 the covetous man is never satisfied.

丨婪 avaricious.

丨前 eager to get on.

丨頭 the object of desire.

丨酒 fond of drink.

丨人敗類 the covetous man injures his fellows.

丨得無厭 not at all particular what he gets, wishing everything.

丨天之功爲己功 he covets the merits of Heaven as his own.

探 ˏt'an t'an' From *hand* and *issuing* from a cavern.

To feel for with the hand; to feel and search; to speculate on, to explore, to sound; to try, to bring on one, to experience.

見不善如丨湯 to find that a man is evil is like being scalded.

丨天之威 to dare (or bring on) Heaven's wrath.

丨囊取物 to feel for things in the bag.

丨賾索隱 to investigate what is confused and deduce its hidden order.

Read *t'an'*. To go in search of, to visit; to examine, to spy; to essay.

丨聽 to try to hear about.

丨友 to ask after a friend.

丨馬 or 丨子 a spy.

打丨 to inquire about.

丨討 to explore, to search for.

丨一丨 inquire a little.

丨試 to essay; to experiment on.

丨一個確信 try to get some authentic news.

丨花 the third of the Hanlin academicians; the name has reference to the metaphor of plucking the sprig of *Olea fragrans*.

丨涉水 to find soundings.

坍 ˏt'an From *earth* and *carnation* as th phonetic.

A bank or wall thrown down, as by water dashing against it.

丨塌倒壞 the wall has all tumbled down.

丨了半截 one face of the wall has fallen; — a common occurrence during a rain from the bricks being laid in mere mud.

水沖丨了堤 the water has burst the dike.
樓丨倒 the tower has fallen in ruins.
以防續丨 to guard against another breach — in the bank.
崩丨 a crevasse.

灘 灘 From *water* and *difficulty* or *alone*; the second form is unusual.
Rapids made by a stream rushing through a pass, or over a rocky descent; the obstruction arising from rocks or sandbanks.
‚t'an
沙丨 rapids and shoals.
丨師 a pilot through rapids.
丨頭小調 boatmen's songs, bacchanalian songs.
足踏白石丨 he stepped across on the white stones.

In *Cantonese* read *'tan*. Beach covered at high tide; a flat shore; reclaimed land lying along river banks.
丨田 reclaimed rice fields.
一幅丨 a strand.
坭丨 a mud flat.
黄浦丨 the river banks at Shanghai.
駛上丨 run the boat ashore.

癱 *‚t'an* A numbness, paralysis, or stiffness of the tendons, thought to arise from damp and cold.
丨子 a palsied cripple.
瘋丨 or 丨瘓 paralysis, palsy; rigid muscles, as from rheumatism.
丨手 a crippled hand.

攤 *‚t'an* From *hand* and *difficulty*.
To open and spread out, as for sale; to spread out thin; to rate, to apportion, to share, to divide amongst; to pay instalments; to defer to another time, to adjourn; a stall or mat on which goods are displayed in the street; a dividend, a share; slow, easy going.
菓丨 fruit stalls.
丨手丨脚 to gesticulate much.
丨開丨薄 to spread out thin, as a plaster.
丨派 to assess, to proportion rateably.
擺丨 to display on a stall.
丨涷 wait for it to get cold.
算命丨 a fortune-teller's stand.
丨錢 an allotment, a share.
壓丨 or 賣丨 to bet on and put down the stakes.
番丨館 or 丨局 a gambling-house, where cash are 扒丨 or divided by four. (*Cantonese.*)
搖丨 to shake dice.
丨賠 to make up a loss by assessments.
丨分 to pay a share.

摊 *‚t'an* To hold a thing up, or carry it in both hands.

嘽 *‚t'an* To breathe fast, to pant; horses snorting.
丨丨駱馬 the black-maned creams snorted and panted.
丨丨 joyful, hilarious, as of many people; vigorous; numerous, said of chariots in full array.

Read *‚chen*. Slowly.
丨咺 leisurely, at ease.

瘆 *‚t'an* Also read *‚to*.
Jaded, ill, worn out, as a horse.

Read *'shi*. Reckless, vicious, like a libertine.

壇 坛 *‚t'an* From *earth* and *sincere*; the contracted form is occasionally used.
An open altar on which to offer sacrifices; an altar before a shrine; a high terrace for worship; an arena for a concourse and trial, like the literary competitions.
文丨 a hall for literary trials; as the 文丨老將 or hero of the hall is a *facile princeps* among scholars.
臨丨 the spirit is here.
開丨 to begin the ceremonies of the lemuria.
築丨 to erect an altar.
設丨 to begin religious services; to set up the implements of worship, as the Taoists do.
仙丨 fairy land.
祭丨 an altar for sacrifices.

檀 *‚t'an* From *wood* and *sincere* as the phonetic.
A hard tough wood resembling the rosewood, suitable for axles; the term is not confined to one plant, as the *Cæsalpinia* is sometimes so called.
紫丨木 a fine-grained, hard wood like mahogany, used for carvings and furniture; it is probably a species of *Laurus*.
赤丨 the *Pterocarpus santolinus* which furnishes a kind of gum kino and a dye-wood.
丨香木 common sandal-wood.
苦丨 a heavy wood like beech, good for handles.
丨 or 丨那 (in Sanscrit *dana*,) are 丨越 the benefactors 施主 of a convent, the offerers of gifts, who thereby traverse 越 the sea of poverty, *dana* being the virtue of religious charity and self-denial.

繵 *‚t'an* A rattan cord or string for binding; a bandage or inner girdle.

Read *‚ch'en*. A single garment, othewise called 涼衣 the cool dress; to bind, to wrap.
丨縧 a ligature or membrane which Chinese physicians suppose encircles the stomach, probly meaning the mesentery.

蕁 *‚t'an* Used as a synonym for 菀 *'tan*.
A wild plant whose leaves resemble an onion or chives; a kind of marine algæ or delicate seaweed likened to hair.
丨麻 a variety of the nettle (*Urtica bulbifera*), whose fibers can be used.

覃 ₍t'an

From 襾 to *cover*, contracted from 鹵 *salt*, and 早 *early*.

An enduring taste; reaching to, extending to; great; vast, spreading out wide; long, prolonged.

䆱 ₍t'an

Spread out thin, like gold leaf or a large sheet of paper.

窰 丨 a deep cave; flat and thin.

In *Fuhchau.* Large rocks; bowlders.

粉 丨 a soft sandstone used in making crockery.

潭 ₍t'an

The name of a river near Tungting Lake; deep, unfathomable; deep pools in a river; an expanse of water, a vast pond.

黑龍丨 a noted pool near Peking.

萬丈深丨 very deep waters; *met.* no end to the affair or subject.

丨恩下逮 his vast kindness reaches to the lowest.

閤丨均吉 my best wishes to all your family.

乾白鵝丨 as well dry up the Macao Passage [near Canton]; *i. e.* you talk wildly.

丨州 an old name of Chang-sha fu in Hunan.

醰 ₍t'an

Sour spirits which have lost their flavor; a rich taste, sweet; generous, like good wine; fine, as music.

宅心丨粹 his whole heart is pure and like generous wine.

亘丨丨而有味 most delightful was the music, and its relish still remains.

譚 ₍t'an

From *words* and *big*; occurs interchanged with the next, but not as a surname.

To talk big, to boast; contented; extended; extravagant; a small feudal appanage lying east of the present Tsi-nan fu in Shantung.

參丨不絕 continuing on without cessation.

修業居久而丨 they boast of him because he has long been diligent in his post.

丨公維私 the lord of T'an was her brother-in-law.

談 ₍t'an

From *words* and *hot* as the phonetic.

To converse familiarly, to discuss; to talk about, to cavil; a patois, a local speech; conversation, chitchat.

丨論得當 to discuss a thing sensibly.

閒丨 easy conversation.

土丨 the local pronunciation.

高丨 loud talk.

抵掌而丨 to gesticulate while talking.

手丨 to play chess.

笑丨 to talk playfully; repartee.

共你丨丨 let us chat awhile.

今夕只丨風月 let us give this pleasant evening to chitchat.

丨兵 to discuss the war.

倓 ₍t'an

To pacify, to quiet; at peace.

丨然無懼 I am quite at rest about the matter.

丨靜 loving quiet and ease, keeping at home.

郯 ₍t'an

A small ancient principality occupying the present T'an-ch'ing hien 丨城縣 in the south of Shantung, which was conferred on the son of Shao-hao 少皞 B. C. 2560.

痰 ₍t'an

Phlegm, mucus from the lungs.

丨涎 slimy spittle.

化丨 an expectorant.

吐丨 to cough up phlegm; to hawk and spit.

中'丨 suffocated by phlegm; to fall dead.

丨盂 or 丨罐 a spittoon, a cuspidor.

丨喘症候 his disease is expectorating and shortness of breath.

丨傷頸 or 丨壅 in the death rattle.

丨堵住喉子了 he cannot raise the phlegm.

餤 ₍t'an

To serve up food; to enter; to eat; cakes done up with meat inside, a sort of sandwich or croquet; to allure, to bait.

亂是用丨 the disturbances will soon reach this.

餅丨 a meat cake.

丨餌 a bait, a temptation.

䞡 ₍t'an

To hurry and run, as people do to see a show.

趁丨 to run together, to crowd up.

罈 壜 墰 ₍t'an

From *earthenware* or *earth* and *cloudy.*

Earthenware jars or jugs for spirits, oil, or other liquids, holding four gallons or less; they are inclosed in netting with handles.

破丨子 a cracked jar.

耍丨子 to throw up jars and catch them; — a play.

酒丨子 a great wine sot.

曇 ₍t'an

From *sun* and *cloud.*

Clouds spreading themselves over the sky.

丨丨 lowering, black clouds; overcast.

丨繞白雲飛 the white scud flies beneath the dark cloud.

澹 ₍t'an

Name of a river; tranquil, placid, like flowing water; to move.

丨心 to disturb the mind.

平丨 smooth and undisturbed.

丨淡 rippled water.

丨欲 satisfied desires.

橝 ₍t'an

The end of the rafters supporting the eaves, also called a silkworm beater; ashes of the wood of a kind of *Prunus* used in dyeing.

燂 ₍t'an Also read tsan'.
To dry at the fire; to scorch; to put in the blaze; to singe; to warm or boil.
丨船 to bream a boat's bottom.
丨水 to heat water.
丨啖茶 warm a cup of tea.
火丨鑊底就知窮 when the fire scorches the boiler, you will know what poverty is.
五日則丨湯請浴 every five days she must heat water and ask [her mother-in-law] to bathe.

毯 ₍t'an From wool and hot; at Canton tah, 笪 is occasionally used for this.
Rugs, carpeting, or drugget, made of wool or hair yarn; serge, ratteen.
椶丨 coir matting.
鋪一條丨子 spread down a carpet.
五彩線丨 a beautiful carpet.
栽羢丨子 yarn carpets with colors inserted; used on beds.
床丨 a bed-wrapper.

惔 ₍t'an From heart and fiery.
The mind much distressed, as though fired up; to burn.
憂心如丨 my heart is burned with grief.
如丨如焚 like scattering flames and fire, said of a drought.

菼 ₍t'an A species of marsh grass or rush (*Imperata?*) useful for making brooms.
葭丨揭揭 the rushes and sedges grow rank.

緂 ₍t'an The same as the preceding in the Book of Odes, but others apply it to the tender sprouts of a plant, used to dye a brown salmon color or grayish yellow.

憛 ₍t'an From heart and seeking; like the next.
Disquieted, anxious.
丨忒 not at ease, afraid.

忐 ₍t'an From heart and to rise.
Disquiet of the mind, inconstant, no fixed will.
丨忑 timorous; the composition of the phrase seems to allude to a palpitation of the heart, or a fluttering as when startled.

禫 **襌** ₍t'an A sacrifice offered at the end of the twenty-seven months, or the three years' mourning for a parent, when the garments are put off.
丨服 to lay aside mourning.

袒 **襢** ₍t'an From garment and early; the second form is rather pedantic.
To bare the arm to do work or otherwise; to strip, to take off the upper garments; to disclose; bared, naked.
羞丨 an undershirt.
丨而示之背 he stripped and showed him his back.
上司丨庇屬員 superior officers screening their underlings.
左丨 to help one when in the wrong, or underhandedly.
勞毋丨 it is improper to disrobe, even when suffering from heat.

膻 ₍t'an Used for the last; also for ₍shen 羶 frowzy.
The sternal region or center of the thorax, between the mammæ, is called 丨中 in anatomy, and Chinese physicians say it is the seat of the breath; they probably intend to describe the mediastinum, or membrane that divides the lungs.

坦 ₍t'an A plain, level place; tranquil, composed, quiet; a son-in-law.
令丨 your son-in-law.
履道丨丨 to go in a fine even path.
丨然不疑 a guileless, unsuspecting heart.
丨腹東床 a son-in-law.
寬丨 liberal-minded.

心裏舒丨 happy and contented, quiet and unconcerned.
丨平的路 a level good road.

癉 ₍t'an Often interchanged with 㿇 weariness.
Disease; to vex, to punish; a ringworm; an epidemic.
下民卒丨 the common people at last got sick, — from the evil deeds of their rulers.

窞 ₍t'an From cave and a pit for beasts.
A small pit or recess in the bottom or the end of a large cave, entered from the side.
入于坎丨 it then goes into a deeper pit, — said of cosmical and other influences of the *yin* and *yang*.

醓 **監** ₍t'an Salted mutton or pork deviled; the meat is fried anh then minced and mixed witd salted soy; the condiment is used with bread and soy.
丨醢以薦 sauces and pickles are furnished — to the guests.

噴 ₍t'an The noise of many people eating with haste; the slobbering and munching of a full table.
有丨其饁 [the field hands] gobbled down their broth.

髧 ₍t'an From hair and moving.
Tresses or curls on children; a fringe of hair on the crown left by the barber; the hair falling on the forehead.
丨彼兩髦 with his two locks over his forehead, — he was my only one.
萋₍丨 falling curls. (*Cantonese.*)
In *Cantonese*. A fringe, a valance; ornamental carvings under eaves; a fathom.
蚊帳₍丨 curtain around a tester.
幾多₍丨水 how many fathoms deep is it?
丨口 the eaves.

炭ˋ *t'an'* From 火 *fire* and 岸 *bank* contracted.

Charcoal, charred wood; embers; black.

柴丨 or 木丨 charcoal.
燔丨 burning coals.
白丨 charcoal with the bark of the wood.
生靈塗丨 everything, men and beasts, were involved in the calamities.
搥丨基 to make charcoal cakes.
石丨 or 煤丨 mineral coal.
麩丨 charcoal balls.
愛戴丨簍子 you seem to like to wear a coal basket for a hat; — said of vain persons or conceited fellows, who swallow ridicule as praise.
丨渣兒 charcoal fragments.
水火丨 coke made from bituminous coal.

歎ˋ 嘆ˋ *t'an'* From to *breathe* or *mouth* and a kind of *bird*.

The voice accordant with the feelings; to sigh, to moan; to praise, to applaud; some say, the first alone has the first of these senses, the other the latter and more unfrequent meaning, but the two characters are used as synonyms; a drawl, a final tone in singing.

長丨 a long groan.
丨息 to regret.
丨一口氣 to heave a deep sigh.
可丨 how sad!
不勝浩丨 he ceased not to bemoan and cry.
有心一丨千古知音 if the heart grieves once, after ages will hear the moan.
開丨情 to bewail with companions before marriage, as girls in Canton often do.
長吁短丨 sighing and crying.
丨美 to admire and praise.

In *Cantonese*. Given up to vicious courses, as to gambling or drink.

丨鴉片 victimized by opium.
好ˋ丨 lustful, licentious.

撢ˋ *t'an'* ˊ*tan* To feel for with the hand, to take out with the hand; to seek out; a swab, a duster.

丨帚 or 丨子 a feather-duster.

儃ˋ *t'an'* Out of one's head, foolish.

丨倈 silly, acting nonsensically; having a foolish, fuddled look and manner.

賧ˋ *t'an'* From *wealth* and *burning*.

To ransom criminals from punishment by paying fines, as is done in barbarous countries.

TANG.

Old sounds, tong *and* dong. *In Canton,* tong; — *in Swatow,* tang *and* tăng; — *in Amoy,* tong; — *in Fuhchau,* tòng *and* taung; — *in Shanghai,* tong *and* dong; — *in Chifu,* tang.

當 ˏ*tang* From *field* and honor or *value* set upon it; as a primitive its use is chiefly phonetic.

What is suitable, opportune, convenient, or just; adequate to, competent; to bear, to take the responsibility; to act as, to be; equal to, to match, to make, to stand in contrast; to meet or occur; at the time of, when, — in which sense it is often a form of the present participle; used as a particle, as, then, or throwing the sentence into the future tense; to decide, to manage, to mete out; to withstand, to bear against; to screen.

我擔丨 I'll assume the responsibility, I'll bear the cost.
不敢丨 I cannot presume; *i. e.* you are too kind.
丨家 to be head of, as an abbot; to take charge of, to oversee.
丨國 to rule a state.
丨兵 to be a soldier.
丨不起 inadequate to.
丨時 at that time.
丨下 or 丨今 or 丨卽 just now, presently, immediately.
丨街 in the streets, abroad.
丨天 out of doors; open; under the sky.
丨中人 to act as the midsman.
禮所丨然 etiquette requires it.
相丨 convenient, suitable.
丨差使 an officer of government, one who manages or fills the commission.
莫能丨之 nothing could withstand it.
不丨 it ought not to be; *i. e.* I ask pardon; excuse me.
難丨 insupportable, irksome.
勾丨 to usurp another's place, a job, an intrigue; underhand.
丨罪 he then was punished for it.
一夫丨關萬夫莫開 when a real captain holds a pass, a myriad men cannot force it.

Read *tang'* To pawn, to pledge; to consider as, reputed or looked upon as; to serve an end, instead of, as, for; to suit with; suitable, favorable; safely, properly; to deceive, to swindle; basis, foundation.

丨舖 a legalized pawnbroker's shop, over which this character is the sign.
妾不丨妻 the concubine cannot equal the wife.
去丨 or 丨丨 to pawn.
費銀丨水 to spend money like water.
我ˋ上他的丨 I've been taken in by him.
丨得多人 equal to many persons

贖 丨 to get out of pawn.
餉 丨 a licensed pawnshop.
丨 票 a pawn-ticket.
穩 丨 settled firmly, secure.
他丨我呆 he thinks I am a fool.
丨作 to use one thing for another.
有錢只丨沒錢 he has money, but pretends that he has none.
丨十 worth ten [cash], — a debased coin used in Peking.
丨日 to-day; that day, then.
的 丨 all right, proper.
丨 爲無事 he thinks I've nothing to do; he regards it as a mere trifle.
決事不 丨 to decide a matter unfairly.
只 丨 耳旁 風 only a passing rumor; a wind by the ear; in at one ear and out at the other.

璫 ˎtang Ear-pendents made in short links of pearls or plates of jade; jewel like a chatelaine, worn on the girdle or head.
耳丨 an ear jewel in three strings.
金琅 丨 jingles swinging in the wind; in Canton, a silk-peddler's gong; also a kind of locket.

聸 ˎtang An ear whose lobe reaches to the neck is called 耳 丨; such are seen on images of gods and *arhans*, and regarded as a mark of intelligence.

簹 ˎtang A species of bamboo, with long internodes, the 筫 丨 in whose joints is the likeness of a man; it is said to be found in Fuhkien in Kien-ngan hien.

襠 ˎtang From *garment* and *suitable*.
Breeches, trowsers; coverings for the legs; the crutch of a pair of trowsers.
肥褲 丨 wide trowsers.
繡 丨 embroidered pantaloons.
這 褲子兜 丨 these trowsers are too strait or small.
開褲 丨 children's trowsers.

轕 ˋtang The tail of a cart.
後 丨 車 a cart whose body reaches to the end, used only by grandees.
四六丨車 a common cart. (*Pekingese*.)

鐺 ˎtang A lock or clasp; a tripod for warming wine; a small gong struck by peddlers; the twang or tang of the instrument.
喚頭丨的一聲 the twang of a barber's call; it is like long tweezers.
丨 丨 a hand gong like a cymbal.

党 ˋtang A name of one of the sons of Ta Yü of the Hia dynasty, upon whom the office of general was conferred.

In *Fuhchau*. A classifier of packages, as several quires of paper or rolls of incense-sticks.

黨 ˋtang From *black* and *high*; it is often contracted like the preceding.
Not a few, not rare; a village of 500 houses, or the elder of such a village: to aid in concealing or doing evil; to club together, to fraternize, to form a cabal or union, — the idea always partaking of opposition to government; a faction, an association, a league, a junto or seditious company; associates, fellow-villagers; to intrigue, to side with; to compare; to bring to mind; a place, a time; a sort or class; kindred; to expect; to implicate.
鄉 丨 自好者 the best man in the village.
丨 正 a head-man or elder.
君子不 丨 the good man will not join secret doings.
無偏無 丨 neither taking sides nor cabaling.
同 丨 of the same faction.
母 丨 a mother's kindred.
吾 丨 my company; our class.
賊 丨 a band of robbers.
匪 丨 a company of thieves.
各於其 丨 each one holding to his calling.
丨 羽 adherents, partisans.
結 丨 to form cabals.
不朋 丨 do not join factions; not to follow the fashion — in evil.
往 丨 past times.
丨 州 an old name for part of K'ing-yang fu in the northeast of Kansuh.

攩 擋 挡 ˋtang Sometimes interchanged with the last; the second is also read tangˀ and the third is unauthorized.
To strike; to impede, to obstruct; to push; to screen, to cover, to stand in the way of.
阻 丨 to obstruct.
丨 住 to prevent, to stop effectually.
丨 頭 陣 the vanguard of a battle.
用手丨住 brace it with your arm.
錢來 丨 丨 it is easy enough if you'll spend the money.
抵丨不住 you cannot withstand them.
丨 網 a scoop to take fish out of a net.
兵來了將 丨 if the enemy's troops come, I will resist them.
攔 丨 to embarrass and resist.
推 丨 to put off or aside; to defer, as a request.
丨 駕 to detain the carriage; *i. e.* to receive the card and let the visitor go, in order to save him time.

曭 ˋtang Obscure, as the sun when hidden by clouds.
丨 莽 dull, cloudy.

讜 ˋtang Right words, proper advice, persuasive speech.
忠 丨 faithful remonstrance.
善 丨 good counsels.
正言丨論 right advice, and faithful talk.

欓 檔 tang' } A wooden bench or settle; purlines on a roof; a tub; a cross-piece, as a rung of a ladder; small sticks to connect, as the slips in trellis or lattice work; name of a tree whose fruit is peppery.
椅子〡 round of a chair.

In *Cantonese* wrongly used for 趟 A heat on a course.

闣 'tang Wrongly used for the last.
To run across a doorway; the sound of a drum; full.

蕩 tang' From *plant* and *hot water*; the next and abbreviated form is constantly used for it.
Large, vast, magnificent; unsettled, vagrant, dissipated; to overturn, to subvert; to squander, to waste; agitated, unsettled; ready to spill over or upset; in *rhetoric*, an exclamation of the nature of a comparison; level, as a road.
倒〡花消 to waste riotously.
〡產 to spend an estate.
〡失 lost his way or reckoning; mislaid, not to be found.
〡〡 vague, vast; incomprehensible; said of the greatness of Shangti.
王道〡〡 the royal road is broad and long.
以〡陵德 they become loose and injure all virtue.
諸生〡 all nature is bursting forth.
流離浪〡 gadding about, no fixed employment.
閒游浪〡 idle, loafing, doing nothing.
掃〡 or 〡平 make a clean sweep of it; destroyed utterly.
放〡不拘禮貌 heedless, rude, no regard for decorum.
〡檢踰閑 to violate laws and overstep all bounds.
〡然 all spent, wasted.
把這欵懸〡着 let those items remain unsettled; we will not now take up that affair or point.

宕 tang' From 宀 a *shelter* and the next character contracted; it is mostly used as another form of the preceding.
A covered way or gateway; a passage through a house.
文筆跌〡 the style is very parabolical; to make an allusion whereby to imply the real meaning.
佚〡 easy, mild, leisurely.
〡渠 the covered sewer, an old name for places in Shun-k'ing fu in the southeast of Sz'ch'uen.

碭 tang' From *stone* and *expanding*.
A beautiful stone of brilliant colors, with striæ or veins running through it; to overrun, to exceed; old name of a region now occupied partly by 〡山縣 in Sü-cheu fu in Kiangsu, derived from 芒〡 a hill in Péi hien.
〡溢 to overflow.

莨 tang' An herb that is reputed to stop the flow of milk, and produce hysteria and delirium; its seed-vessels are shaped like the *Thlaspi*.
水莨〡 or water scammony, an acrid and dangerous kind; it has round, glabrous leaves.

愓 t'ang' From *heart* and *expanding*; it resembles t'ih, 惕 grieved.
Reckless, dissipated, profligate.
〡悍 wild and wasteful, as a profligate.

Read ˛shang. To go ahead without turning to the right or left.
〡〡 one intent on a purpose, like a fleet courier.

婸 tang' From *woman* and *expanding*; it resembles sih, 媳 a woman's name.
Dissolute; wanton in conduct; ogling.
阿〡 an old term for one's self in some parts of Sz'ch'uen.

垱 tang' From *earthen* and *elevated*; it occurs wrongly used for 'tang 党 a surname.
A large basin or bowl of earthenware; the lining or wall inside of a well.

璗 t'ang' Gold of the purest kind; yellow and beautiful, as a gem.

簜 tang' A large species of reed or bamboo whose joints, some say, are six or ten feet apart; it was found in Yang cheu in the days of Yü.

盪 tang' From *dish* and *hot water*.
A tub for bathing; large, great; moved, disturbed; to shove a boat over the mud; to propel a boat by oars.
震〡 to startle.
滌〡 to swash about, to cleanse, to agitate much.
動〡血脈 to stir up one's feelings and spirits, as by music.
跳〡 to draw off in a retreat, to fall back in disorder.
推〡 the reciprocal influences of the elements.
〡意平心 compose your mind and thoughts.
〡風冒雪 take a dram to withstand the snow storm.
雙槳〡中流 two oars men can stem and cross the current.

In *Cantonese*. To smear; to rub over.
〡黑面 to blacken one's face, as for passing bad money.
〡灰 to plaster.

T'ANG.

Old sounds, t'ong *and* dong. *In Canton*, t'ong ; — *in Swatow*, t'ang *and* t'ăng ; — *in Amoy*, t'ong *and* tong ; — *in Fuhchau*, t'ong, tong, t'aung, *and* taung ; — *in Shanghai*, t'ong *and* dong ; — *in Chifu*, t'ang.

湯 ˌt'ang From *water* and to *expand*. Name of a river in the southwest of Chihli ; warm water ; broth, soup ; gravy ; warm, as a spring, and is found in many proper names in this sense ; clouds passing in showers ; a scald ; to bathe in warm water ; to remove grievances ; repelling injustice ; awesome, grand ; the founder of the Shang dynasty, B. C. 1766, commonly called 成丨 T'ang the Successful.

丨兜 a soup-tureen.

丨水 gravy, broth of meat.

豬肉丨 a pork soup.

煤丨 or 熬丨 to boil a soup.

丨麪 vermicelli soup.

茶丨 a sort of flour porridge.

赴丨蹈火 [not afraid] to get scalded or burned.

熱丨 boiling water.

見不善如探丨 regard an evil action like putting your hand in boiling water.

哈丨泥 slush, mire. (*Pekingese*.)

鞏固丨池 the everlasting and awe-inspiring moats and walls — of the imperial palace.

Read ˌ*shang*. Waves in motion.

丨丨洪水方割 see the roaring billows of the flood, how injurious they are !

江漢丨丨 the impetuous waves of the Yangtsz' and Han Rivers.

劏 ˌt'ang An unauthorized character used in Canton. To butcher, to kill and dress meat ; to dissect ; to dismember.

丨牛 to slaughter an ox.

丨開 rip it open.

生丨 to cut up alive.

丨死牛 a foot-pad.

摥 ˌt'ang From *hand* and *warm water* ; interchanged both with ˌ當 and ˊ擋 to oppose. To stop or brace up a thing with the hand ; to oppose, to stand against.

誰敢丨他 who dares resist him ?

你只管丨丨試一試 try if you alone can oppose it, or can do it.

趟 ˌt'ang To step in the mire ; to get wet or mired ; to go ahead.

水過不去只好丨罷 you can't get over the water, you'll have to wade through it.

丨一脚的泥 I got one foot covered with mud.

丨濕了 wet and muddy.

鼞 ˌt'ang Noise of a drum.

把鼓打的丨丨的響 make a great clamor with the drums.

鏜 ˌt'ang Like the preceding. Noise of gongs and drums ; to bore through.

擊鼓其丨踴躍用兵 when the instruments make a great noise, the troops are inspirited.

螗 ˌt'ang A species of field spider, named 王蚨丨 which resembles the burrowing spider (*Mygale* or *Actinopus*) in the form of its nest.

堂 ˌt'ang From 土 *earth* and 尙 *honorable*. A dignified, honorable mansion ; a hall, a place to which steps lead up ; a court, an official room ; a public establishment ; the principal room in a house ; a hospital, a church, a chapel, and often applied to large shops ; the officer who presides in a court ; the persons assembled in a hall ; to control, as with authority ; honorable, venerable ; to complete or build a hall ; designation of relatives of the same clan ; a household or family, because the 丨名 sept name is set up in the ancestral hall ; a plateau or glade among hills ; in Budhist temples, the assembly-hall and confessional ; a classifier of trials and graves.

一間丨 or 一座丨 one mansion, one hall.

穿丨 a hall-door or room.

ˌ朝丨 hall of audience.

法丨 the Board of Punishments.

佛丨 a shrine or oratory of Budha.

玉丨 the Hanlin Academy.

公丨 the court-room.

琴丨 a district magistrate.

黃丨 the prefect's office ; *met.* the prefect himself.

正丨 and 左丨 and 右丨 a district magistrate and his two deputies ; used also for other officers and their aids.

當丨分開 divided it in the open hall, *i. e.* fairly.

審過一丨 I have examined the case once.

一丨墳墓 one grave.

高丨 my parents.

令丨 your mother.

拜丨 a bride's worship in her husband's house.

客丨 the guest-room or parlor ; a visitor's room in a temple.

丨兄弟 cousins and second cousins.

禮拜丨 a church ; rarely applied to mosques.

丨客 a lady, a madam.

相貌丨丨 a stern, forbidding expression.

中丨 style for cabinet ministers, members of the Nêi Koh.

本閣部〡 I, the cabinet-minister and governor-general; used in edicts and proclamations.

〡〡 justly, honorably.

〡號 the particular style or branch of a family.

祠〡 an ancestral hall.

洗澡〡 a bathing-house, upon which 浴〡 or this character alone, is often painted.

哄〡 a general laugh.

棠 ˻t'ang A species of sorbus or crab of the genera *Pyrus* and *Cratægus;* certain boards or bars on a cart's side to stop its way.

海〡花 the *Cydonia Japonica* and *Pyrus spectabilis* or *baccifera.*

海〡樹 the crab-apple, cultivated for its fruit and flowers.

春海〡 the *Begonia discolor.*

〡棣之依 a brother (or friend) to rely on; the tree here referred to is probably the *Corchorus pyriformis.*

甘〡之蔭 the shade of the sweet crab-tree; *met.* powerful protection.

蜜餞海〡 sugared crabs, made by dipping the fresh fruit into melted sugar.

膛 ˻t'ang From *flesh* and *hall.* Fat, plump, corpulent; the swell or bellying of a jar; the capacity of a vessel.

胷〡 the bosom; the breast.

上〡 roof of the mouth.

〡子大 it has a great bulge; it holds a great deal.

開〡 open the crop.

淚〡 the space under the eye.

唐 ˻t'ang From 口 *mouth* and 庚 to *alter.* Boasting talk, gasconade, exaggeration; a trailing plant, the dodder (*Cuscuta*) now called 兔絲 or rabbit's silk; a path up to an oratory or ancestral hall; the name of Yao's principality, the P'ing-yang fu in the south of Shensi.

爰采〡矣 I am going to gather the dodder.

〡朝 a famous dynasty which ruled China from A. D. 618 to 913, founded by Li Yuen 李淵 its capital was at Chang-an in Shensi, and during the sway of its twenty princes, the empire probably was more powerful in comparison with other nations than at any other period.

〡山 and 〡人 are used in the southern provinces for China and Chinese.

那個實在荒〡 that man is really talking wildly.

〡虞之世 the halcyon times of Yao and Shun.

〡國 a small state occupying the southwest of Chihli; the present T'ang hien 〡縣 near the 〡河 was its chief town.

傏 搪 ˻t'ang The second form is most used. Wayward; to stretch.

〡突 brusque, froward, presuming, lacking in humility.

〡塞 or 〡抵 to evade, to turn one off, to decline politely, to put a makeshift, to make promises in order to avoid importunity; to make up for one thing by another.

〡不得風 he is too stupid to do anything.

煻 ˻t'ang To warm, to toast.

〡煨 to put before the fire.

〡煨池 a fire-well or inflammable spring in the north of Liaotung, which gives light in the night.

塘 ˻t'ang A pool, a pond, a tank; a stagnant or artificial reservoir; a bund, a dike to resist the waters; a post-station about a league apart.

魚〡 or 池〡 a fish-pond.

三〡汛遠 it is three posts' distant.

蓮〡 a lotus pond.

乾〡 to drain a pond.

春草池〡處處蛙 lo, the frogs in every pool announce the spring.

提〡官 the provincial officer over the postal department.

海〡 a sea-wall of stone.

磄 ˻t'ang A stone on the bank; a strange, supernatural stone.

螗 ˻t'ang A kind of cicada, the 蜩〡 which is common in the North, and called 髻鳥兒 the crested bird; by others written 蝭蟧 but referring probably to another species.

糖 餹 ˻t'ang Sugar; honey; candy; sugared, prepared in or with sugar; sweet.

沙〡 granulated sugar.

〡水 molasses, syrup.

冰〡 sugar-candy.

〡霜 or 冰〡粉 powdered candy or pingfa sugar.

片〡 brown sugar in cakes.

冰〡子 sugar-plums; bonbons.

〡菓 preserved fruit.

揸〡 or 砑〡 to press the cane.

吹〡人兒 to blow sugar images.

刀尖上舔〡 the sweetmeat is on the sword's point; — *met.* the risk is too great.

糯米〡 barley sugar.

螳 ˻t'ang A mantis.

〡蜋 the *Mantis precatorius.*

〡臂擋車 [like a] mantis' shanks [trying to] stop a carriage; refers to an old story of prince 莊公 of Tsi, mentioned in early history.

儻 ˊt'ang Interchanged with the next. An unforeseen thing; accidental.

〡來之物 fortuitously; a thing which unexpectedly came to hand.

倜〡 extraordinary, unusual.

倘 'tang From *man* and *superior*.
If, perhaps, supposing, may, should; unexpectedly.
丨若 if; premising.
丨然不行 then it will not do.
丨或可得 it can probably then be done.
丨其不願 if he be unwilling.
心丨丨 an intelligent, liberal mind.
丨能彀作 if he will (or is able), then it can be managed.

帑 'tang From *cloth* and *slave*.
A store of gold or precious things, such as are offered to or given as presents, by the emperor; a treasury, a jewel-house.
國丨 or 府丨 a national store-house; the treasury.
耗費丨銀 to squander the wealth of the country.
丨藏 a store-house.
Read 'nu, and used with 孥. The children of the legal wife.
樂爾妻丨 rejoice in your wife and child.
鳥丨 a bird's tail, which must be looked after as if it was its child.

潒 'tang From *water* and *elephant*; similar to *tang*' 蕩 vast.
Water roaring and rushing along.
浩浩丨丨 a rapid, surging torrent.

躺 'tang An unauthorized character.
To lie stretched out, to lie down, to sprawl, unable to get up.
丨着沒睡 I was lying down but not sleeping.
丨丨歇歇 lie down and rest a while.
丨板 an ambulance chair; a kind of lounging sedan.
丨下 fallen flat; he is down.

踼 'tang From *foot* and *wide*; not the same as *t'ih*, 踢 to kick.
To slip down; to fall on the face; to fall along; to lie down.
栽丨下了 fell down flat.
丨了好半天 to lie down half the day.
趺丨 to walk stumbling and reeling.
丨倒了 stumbled and fell.

逿 tang' Like the preceding and next, but different from *tih*, 逷 far off.
To pass by or miss; to fall, to miss a step and fall; a classifier of times, rows of characters, acts; a heat on a course; the narrow road in which horses race at the military trials.
醉丨地 he was drunk and fell down.
心丨 heart palpitating.
In *Cantonese* also written 橕' A way; a course.
一丨街 one street.

輖 t'ang' The iron covering of an axle; used like 次 a time; a classifier of a journey or trip; a row; a ruled line.
一丨瓦 a row of tiles.
丨軸 an axle of a cart.
只走一丨 I went there but once.
掃地一丨 swept the ground once.

摥 t'ang' To separate, to sunder.
排丨 to part, as people who are quarreling; to settle a dispute.

燙 t'ang' From *fire* and *hot water*; i re sembles its primitive.
To wash; to smooth or iron, to rub smooth; to scald with boiling water; to boil, as water; blistering hot, as iron which will burn the hand.
丨衣服 to iron clothes.
丨斗 a chafing-dish, a flat-iron.
把水丨一丨 boil some water for it.
熱水丨手 scalded his hand with the water.
丨了泡兒 a scald blister.

鐋 t'ang' From *iron* and *hot water* as the phonetic.
A carpenter's plane; to smooth.
磋以鑢丨 to smooth (or take out creases) with a plane.
摩丨 to rub smooth, as a slab of stone.

TĂNG.

Old sounds, teng *and* deng. *In Canton*, tăng; — *in Swatow*, teng *and* seng; — *in Amoy*, teng; — *in Fuhchau*, teng, ting, *and* tsing; — *in Shanghai*, tăng *and* dăng; — *in Chifu*, tăng.

豋 tăng Composed of 豆 a *vase* with *flesh* 肉 in it, raised up by 又 the *hand*; to be distinguished from the next.
Coarse sacrificial platters which hold the soup or gravy of offerings.
設三丨 lay out three dishes of sacrifices.
于豆于丨 the stands of wood and earthen — for the offerings.

登 tăng From 癶 to *stride* and 豆 a *dish* that is stepped on; unlike the preceding.
To ascend, to step up; to advance, to go higher; to attain; to commence, to start; to ripen, to complete; to record, to note; an *adverb*, as soon as, specially, at the time.
丨時 presently, immediately.
丨簿 charge it in the account.
丨科 to succeed at the examina tion.
丨程 to start on a journey.

五穀豐丨 the products of the earth are abundant.

丨對 suitably matched.

丨高 to ascend heights, a custom on the 9th day of the 9th moon, when people fly kites; to go on a walk over hills.

丨時變相' he incontinently changed countenance.

丨極 or 丨位 to begin to reign; the first is restricted to the emperor of China.

丨記 to record, to make a note of.

共丨青雲梯 they together mounted the azure cloud ladder; *i. e.* became high graduates.

築之丨丨 [the men] pounded the wall in concert.

丨州府 a department on the north of Shantung promontory; the city is about fifty miles west of Chifu.

In *Cantonese*. To push off with the foot.

燈 灯 ꜀tăng — From *fire* and *to elevate*; the contracted form is common, and is also read ꜀*ting*, a flame.

A lamp; a lantern; laws or precepts of Budha; moral lights.

一盞丨 one lamp.

丨籠 a lantern.

天丨 or 月爲丨 the moon; a midstreet lantern.

走馬丨 horse-racing lanterns.

點丨 light the lamp; but 長丨的時候 means early candle-light or early in the evening.

洋取丨 matches.

吹丨 or 滅丨 put out the lamp.

烏丨 a lamp not lighted.

丨謎 or 丨虎 a riddle, a conundrum.

在丨節雪打丨 [once] on the Feast of Lanterns, the snow put out the lights.

丨心草 the *Scirpus capsularis*, a grass whose pith furnishes lamp-wicks.

玻璃丨 a glass lantern; a name for a crystal button of the fifth grade.

紗風丨 a gauze safe for food.

傳丨 to teach the laws of Budha.

海丨 a lamp burning before a god.

蕟 ꜀tăng — A plant, the 金丨 allied to a *Hypericum* or tutsan, alluding to the shape of the flowers.

簦 ꜀tăng — A long handled bamboo umbrella; a bamboo mat shade or screen, like those used by hucksters to shade their stalls.

擔丨就道 to raise an umbrella and go on the road or journey.

等 ꜂tăng — From *bamboo* and a *court*.

A comparison; to compare, an order, class, sort, or quality; equal, like, same; a grade or rank; a sign of the plural for inferiors, for things, &c.; others, such like; it often renders the preceding verb a noun, as 該逆丨 these seditious persons; to wait, to permit, to let; to graduate; to class.

丨緊用 it is instantly wanted.

丨一丨 wait a little.

丨候 waiting for one; I am now waiting.

丨得許久 I've waited long for him.

丨我作 let me do it.

丨水過河 when there is water, we will cross the river.

爾丨各守本分 let each of you attend to his own business.

同丨 of the same sort, without distinction.

晝夜丨 day and night equal.

不丨 not to be compared; unlike; a variety.

下丨 inferior, the second-rate, said of things or people.

丨閒不出 ordinarily she did not go out.

丨因 or 丨由 or 丨語 such and such circumstances or words; so and so; often winds up a quotation.

丨百世之王 to arrange the kings of all ages by merit.

戥 ꜂tăng — From *spear* and *star*, alluding to its shape and notching; it is unauthorized.

A small steelyard used for weighing money or jewels.

丨子 a money steelyard.

丨星 the marks on its beam.

較丨盤 to test its accuracy.

鐙鳥 tăng' — A bird resembling a hen, called 丨鷄, having long legs and a red crest; the male is brown, the female mottled, and has a loud voice; it is regarded as a variety of the 秧鷄, both of them being probably marsh birds allied to the ibex.

鄧 tăng' — A small feudal state, now mostly occupied by Tăng-cheu 丨州, a district in Nan-yang fu in the south of Honan, on a branch of the River Han; the capital of the principality was near Siang-yang fu further south.

凳 櫈 tăng' — From 几 a *bench* and 登 to *ascend*; the second character is used in Canton, and resembles ꜀*ch'ăng* 橙 an orange.

A form, a long bench; a stool; a settle.

丨子 a seat without a back.

方丨 or 斗丨 a square stool.

板丨 or 長丨 a long bench.

脚丨 or 脚踏丨 a footstool, a cricket.

梯丨 a step-ladder.

三隻丨 a three-legged stool, which will let one fall; a cheat.

In *Cantonese*. A stem, a petiole.

柿丨 the stem of the persimmon.

僜 tăng' — Exhausted; to walk lame and wearily.

倰丨 exhausted; unfit for work, incapable of exertion.

殀 tăng' — Like the last.

Ready to perish.

殑丨 sick, moribund.

殘丨 exceedingly sick.

磴 嶝 tăng' A ledge on a precipice; stone steps; projecting rocks leading up hills.
懸 ㄧ a suspension bridge.
趴石 ㄧ climb up by the ledges.
石 ㄧ 縈紆 the path winds up the hill-side.
ㄧ 道穿雲 the winding path cleaves the clouds.

墱 tăng' Like the last; also read tun'
Stairs leading to a loft or belvidere; a slight or gentle ascent; to go up such an ascent; streamlets, as they flow down.
ㄧ ㄧ the thumping sounds of workmen pounding down a wall, for which the primitive alone is oftener used.
ㄧ 流 diverging rivulets.

蹬 tăng' From *foot* and to *ascend*.
To hurry but not get on, to lose one's strength; doubtful; to step, to tread.
蹭 ㄧ wearied; at one's wits' ends; not to attain the end.
功名蹭 ㄧ disappointed in reaching his honors.
In *Cantonese*. To pity
ㄧ 你鼠屭 I am sorry for your misfortunes.

鐙 tăng' A stirrup; occurs used for ˏ燈 a candlestick.
馬 ㄧ or 鞍 ㄧ a stirrup.
願隨鞭 ㄧ I am willing to hold your whip and stirrup; — to be your servant.

饍 tăng' Food offered to the gods or ancestors; to hiccup.
打嗝 ㄧ to hiccup (*Nanking*.)

瞢 tăng' From 瞢 to *dream* contracted, and 登 to *ascend*.
To wake from sleep; just opening one's eyes, or half awake.

瞪 tăng' From *eye* and to *ascend*; it is also pronounced ʿch'ang or ˏch'ing.
To stare at, to fix the eyes on; to look one through.
ㄧ 眼望 gazing at fixedly; to look angrily.
眼 ㄧ 的銅鈴那麼大 his eyes stuck out like sleigh-bells.
ㄧ 神 in a fixed gaze.

撜 tăng' From *hand* and a *sack*; also read tun'
To carry on the shoulders, to bear away; the straw matting which covers a baggage cart.

T'ĂNG.

Old sounds, t'eng *and* deng. *In Canton*, t'áng; — *in Swatow*, t'eng *and* tin; — *in Amoy*, teng, t'eng, *and* t'ong; — *in Fuhchau*, teng; — *in Shanghai*, dăng; — *in Chifu*, t'áng.

鼟 ˏt'ăng The sound of drums is ㄧ ㄧ, an imitative phrase like rub-a dub.

滕 ˏt'ăng Water spurting out or bursting up; to open the mouth wide when talking; empty.
ㄧ 國 name of an ancient state near the present Sü-cheu fu in Kiangsu, and now given to Tăng hien ㄧ 縣 in the southeast of Shantung near the Grand Canal.
ㄧ 口說也 to talk loud and fast.

籐 藤 ˏt'ăng A general name for *lianas*, vines, creepers, and trailing plants, especially the rattan; the word is perhaps an imitation of the Malay *rotang*.
ㄧ 黃 gamboge.
沙 ㄧ rattans, as they are known in commerce.
ㄧ 縣 a district in the east of Kwangsi on the West River.
ㄧ 條 or ㄧ 肉 split rattans.
ㄧ 絲 rattan shavings.
打 ㄧ to bind with rattan.
青 ㄧ rattan cordage.
ㄧ 柄 a braided whip.
無葉 ㄧ dodder. (*Cantonese*.)
好花空被老 ㄧ 纏 the old creeper (or man) has entwined itself around the fair flower.
紫 ㄧ the *Wistaria* or glycine.
他們上葛 ㄧ they have fastened their tendrils on him, — as pestering duns.
鉤 ㄧ the hooked vine, *i. e.* the gambier plant. (*Nauclea*.)

螣 ˏt'ăng A serpent or dragon, the ㄧ 蛇 which, though wingless, is fabled to fly above the clouds and fogs; it is regarded as a demon who interferes in good luck coming to one.
Read *teh*, An insect which eats young grain; a kind of locust, probably when it is wingless.

騰 駦 ˏt'ăng From 馬 *horse* and 滕 to *spout* contracted; the second and old form is now only found in combination as a primitive; used with the next.
To leap on, to mount, to ascend; to gallop, to run; to communicate, to inform.
議論沸 ㄧ a wordy discussion.
ㄧ 馬 to cover mares; an old term.
百川沸 ㄧ the streams everywhere bubble and overflow.
飛 ㄧ to soar aloft.
ㄧ 躍 to prance, to rear.
升 ㄧ 有日 you will erelong get on prosperously.

In *Pekingese*. To move and give place to another.
ㄧ 房 to move out of a house for another to take it.
ㄧ 挪 to move away from, as a seat.
ㄧ 出伙傢 turn out the furniture and things.

黲 ꜀t'ăng Dark.
黑〡〡的 dark, pitch dark.
天欲雨而先〡 it grows very dark before a shower.

謄 ꜀t'ăng From 言 *words* and 朕 *I*.
To copy, to transcribe; to trace a copy by superposition.
〡錄生 a copyist.
〡出底稿 make a copy from the original.
〡眞 or 〡淸 to copy exactly, to make a fac-simile.
〡抄 or 〡寫 to copy off.
尋風捕影難〡口舌 to write from his flippant tongue, is like seeking a breeze or seizing a shadow.
〡黃 a manifesto or address issued by the emperor himself in times of trouble.
〡羅兩日 our work must be deferred two days.

縢 ꜀t'ăng To bind; to fasten, as with ropes; to cord, to secure; bands for confining a thing to prevent it warping; cords.
行〡 a sort of galligaskins or buskins, used by pedestrians.
金〡 the banded coffer or record chest, a chapter in the Shu King; *met.* statutes, fundamental laws.
甲不組〡 mail-armor cannot be tied together.
緘〡 to secure the cords; *i. e.* to guard the contents.

儯 ꜀t'ăng Tall; idle, heedless; sullen.
倰〡 long, stretching up; spindling, said of very tall, slender people.

疼 ꜀t'ăng From *sickness* and *winter* as the phonetic.
Pain, ache; affection for, great regard; to love, to have a fondness for.
〡痛 a dolorous pain.
〡愛 ardent love.
怪〡 acute pain.
心〡 I greatly regret it, as something lost.
〡腫 a painful swelling.
不見〡 it does not hurt.
好了瘡疤忘了〡 when the scab is well, then he forgets the pain; — a rich man forgets the miseries of his poverty.
叫人〡 he gets the love of others.

螣 ꜀t'ăng A kind of mailed fish, a gurnard or *Scorpæna*, having a greenish body and red tail; also a fish resembling a crab, with red marks.

滕 ꜀t'ăng Fine eyes.

霯 t'ăng꜆ A heavy rain.

瀊 t'ăng꜆ From *water* and *ledge*.
Little streamlets or drippings running into a brook; carried away, as by a flood; soaked, saturated; to settle, as sediment.
〡落海 swept out to sea.
〡倒 overflowed and swept away.
〡得淸 it has settled clear.
In *Pekingese* used for *luh*, 漉. To drain off.
〡米湯 or 〡飯 to drain the water from rice.
〡出來 strain off the liquor, — and leave the sediment.
〡漿盆 earthen-ware made of drained mud; it is a cheap black kind of pottery.

TAO.

Old sounds, to, do, tot, *and* dok. *In Canton*, tò; — *in Swatow*, to *and* tau; — *in Amoy*, tò *and* tiau; — *in Fuhchau*, to *and* t'o; — *in Shanghai*, to *and* do; — *in Chifu*, tao.

刀 ꜀tao The old form represents a weapon's *blade* and *handle*; it is contracted to 刂 in combination as the 18th radical of characters relating to cutting, &c.
A sword or cimetar; a knife; a punt, a canoe, for which the next is preferable; a quire of paper, containing from 20 to 100 sheets; a knife-shaped coin, first made by Wang Mang of the Han dynasty.
一把〡 one sword.
小〡子 or 〡仔 a pocket-knife.
〡口鈍 the edge is dull.
〡背 back of the blade.
切菜〡 a cleaver, a chopper.
腰〡 a rapier; a short sword.
兩面〡 a two-edged cleaver, such as is used by bean-curd sellers; *met.* a double-faced sycophant.
馬前〡 a guard of swordsmen.
舞〡花 to fence; broadsword exercise.
二把〡 a scullion or cook's-mate. (*Pekingese.*)
關〡 a claymore, such as Kwanti used.
弄〡筆吏 writers of petitions or law papers.
〡子匠 sword-wracks or banditti.
快〡 or 利〡 a sharp knife.
〡斧手 a headsman.
誰謂河廣曾不容〡 who says the river is wide? it will hardly admit a canoe.
〡嘴 or 〡鋒 the point of a knife.

舠 ꜀tao A long narrow canoe or barge; a load of 300 斛 bushels or 1500 斗 pecks, probably because this sort of boat would carry so much.
征〡 a passage-boat.

忉 ˛tao — From *knife* in the *heart*; it was once written like ˛*jăn* 忍 patience.

Overwhelmed with care; grieved or cut to the heart.

無思遠人勞心丨丨 do not think to win people far away, for your aching heart will grieve.

絮絮丨丨 tiresome verbiage; garrulous.

魛 ˛tao — From *fish* and *knife*, alluding to the row of spines on the belly.

A fish of the herring family, the *Thryssa mystax* or an allied species, common off the Yangtsz' River; it is about a foot long, and has a prolongation of the slender maxillary bones an inch beyond the mouth like a knife blade; the pectoral fins consist of six separate rays six inches long; the anal fin reaches to the tail.

丨稍魚 a kind of sucker about eight inches long, common in the Pei-ho.

島 ˋtao — From 山 *hill* and 鳥 *bird* contracted.

An island out at sea; *i. e.* a hill on which birds can alight in crossing seas.

海丨 islets; this term is chiefly given to isles in northern China.

蓬萊仙丨 the isles of the genii.

壔 ˋtao — Like the last, but not in the sea.

A tumulus; a solitary hill rising in a plain; a butte.

擣 **搗** ˋtao — From *hand* and *age* or *islet*.

To beat with a mallet; to pound or grind fine, as in a mortar; to ram down, to make solid, as adobie walls; to lean on; to collect; to misuse, as a woman.

丨出汁 to squeeze out the juice.

丨爛 to beat to pieces or fine.

惄焉如丨 I sorrow till I feel as if I had been pommeled.

丨衣聲 the clatter of [washermen] beating clothes.

丨實 to beat down solidly.

丨米 to hull rice, in a mortar.

懤 ˋtao — Also read *cheu*ˋ.

Grieved to excess, injured by grief and sorrow.

丨恨不釋 my grief and rage have no vent.

吾心丨丨 I am really heart-sick.

禱 **禂** ˋtao — From *worship* and *age* or *around*; the second form is rare.

To give utterance to prayer, to make supplication or announce one's desires to the gods; to request, in the language of courtesy.

丨告 to make known to the gods.

是丨 thus I intreat; — used at the end of letters.

默丨 secret or inaudible prayer.

獲罪於天無所丨也 if you sin against Heaven, there is none [higher] to pray to.

丘之丨久矣 I, Confucius have long since prayed.

既伯既丨 we sacrificed to the Father [of horses], and prayed — for success in hunting.

倒 ˋtao, taoˋ — From *man* and *reaching* to; it is similar to the next.

To fall over, to prostrate; to sink; to throw one's self down; to pass over or transfer; a disjunctive particle, but, why, after all, well then; still, then, indeed, on the contrary; when followed by 也 its force is increased, or it indicates the end of the matter.

打丨 knocked him over.

打不丨 did not knock him down.

他丨大意 he went contrary to his best interests.

丨床 to take to one's bed.

死丨地 fell dead to the ground.

辯丨 convinced him, argued him down.

丨運 unlucky; a misadventure.

我丨不言語你丨說長說短 I have said nothing, but you prate as you like.

絕丨 very laughable, excessive laughter.

丨行 the bankruptcy of a firm.

丨地葫蘆 [just a sot rolling] on the ground like a gourd.

丨運 unfortunate, unlucky.

丨不如大雨 there's nothing like a heavy rain after all.

把舖子丨出去 gave up the shop to him; sold its good-will.

丨像 why, it is like, &c.

今日無酒丨莫如喝點茶 as we have no wine to-day, we shall have to drink tea.

別隨風丨 don't follow after the wind; *i. e.* don't steer by another's compass.

索性拉丨不賣罷 then that's the end of it, and I'll not sell it.

跌丨 he fell down.

推丨 pushed it over.

本來笨的丨說聰明 he was stupid, but he now speaks very cleverly.

我唱你丨不彈 though I sing, yet you won't play.

傾丨是非 to confound right and wrong.

你是那裏人丨會說話 where are you from, for you speak very well?

丨頓 trowsers to pull over others.

Read *tao*ˋ To subvert; to turn over or upside down; to pour out.

丨茶來 pour out the tea.

丨像厭惡ˋ人 it looks as if you had taken offense at him.

丨背着手 to put the hands behind the back.

丨也罷了 well, let it pass.

丨掛鳥 the bird which turns upside down, the love-bird of Formosa. (*Loricula.*)

丨草 or 丨嚼 to chew the cud.

是非丨置 to confuse truth and error.

猶解丨懸 as if the people had been given up to every kind of disorder and evil, or were between two fires.

In *Cantonese*, used for the next. A sign of the past tense.

捉丨佢 seized him.

到 tao' From a *knife* and to *reach*; used with the last.

To arrive at, to attain, to reach; to go or come to; often merely a sign of the past tense, finished, completed; as a *preposition*, to, at, up to; from, of; a disjunctive particle still, but, yet, on the contrary; when followed by 也 its force is elegantly increased.

丨處一樣 it is everywhere the same.

來丨 he has come.

丨那裏去 where is he going?

丨如今 even till now.

丨底 to the bottom; after all, finally, however, at last.

無所不丨 it reaches everywhere, omnipresent.

借丨紋銀一百兩 borrowed from him a hundred taels.

收丨 received; it has come.

丨過了 I have been there.

丨了沒有 has he come?

想得丨 I have thought of it.

事丨頭來 the matter is even now pressing.

這丨也說得是 this is said with truth.

週丨 complete; all around.

不丨處 not quite perfect; still some defect.

作不丨 it cannot be effected.

事丨其間 the affair has reached its limit, it must be given up.

快丨 he will soon be here.

道 tao' From *to go* and the *head*; *q. d.* being at the head; occurs used with the next and last.

A road, path, or way; in *geography*, a zone or belt; in *medicine*, anal and urinal passages; a circuit; the officer who oversees a circuit or region; a principle, a doctrine, that which the mind approves; and used in the classics in the sense of the right path in which one ought to go, either in ruling or observing rules; rectitude or right reason; in early times up to A. D. 500, the Budhists called themselves 丨人 men [seeking for] reason or intelligent men, denoting thereby their aspirations after *pu-ti* (Sanscrit, *boddhi*) intelligence; the Reason or Logos of the Rationalists, denoting an emanation, the unknown factor or principle of nature, the way it acts in matter and mind; to lead; to direct, to follow out; to go in a designated path; to speak, to talk, to converse; as a *preposition*, by, from; the way or cause a thing comes; a classifier of courses at a feast, edicts and dispatches, gateways, walls, rivers, bridges, &c.; a coating, a layer.

不知丨 *q. d.* 知不到 I don't know; *lit.* I am not yet up to that, or not acquainted with it.

丨理 reason, propriety, what is right evidently.

不合丨 unreasonable, unconscionable.

丨德 virtue, virtuous.

這八字是坤丨的嗎 is this horoscope for a lady?

國有丨其言足以興 if the state be well governed, he is sure to rise by his words.

丨心惟微 the principle of right in the heart is small.

正丨 right reason.

丨家 Taoists or Rationalists.

丨綱司 or 丨錄 the civil head of the Taoists in a prefecture.

丨士 a Taoist; he calls himself 小丨 or 丨末 the little Taoist.

王丨 the royal road, the perfect way of the ancient kings; public spirit or regard for the general welfare.

赤丨 the equator.

穀丨 the rectum.

丨路 or 丨途 a way; a road.

找一條丨路 I try to find something to do; some livelihood.

不丨 not to say.

丨聽途說 everybody is talking about it.

說丨 to converse.

自古丨 as saith the proverb.

內墻六丨 the six inner walls.

丨隆丨污 a doctrine or faith in favor and in disrepute, — as when accepted or despised by people.

丨臺 an intendant of circuit or *taotai*; — he speaks of himself to his superiors as 職丨 the officer of the circuit.

一丨公文 one public dispatch.

志以丨寧言以丨接 aims should rest in their right, and words be accepted if right.

當丨 now in the road; *i. e.* at present exercising the power.

外丨師 heretical teachers (*tirthaka*) — who do not believe in Budha.

得丨 to become perfect and enter *nirvana*; used by Budhists.

丨也者不可須臾離也 a reasonable man will not for a moment abandon his principles.

繞丨 a roundabout way.

耨草三丨 weed it three times.

上頭丨菜 bring on the first course.

抹灰二丨 put on two coats of plaster.

衜 tao' From to *walk* and a *head*; interchanged with the preceding.

A street; a highway.

街丨 the streets and avenues of a town.

導 tao' From an *inch* and *road*.

To lead, to conduct; to point out the way, to induce to do right; to lay down the way or plan; to exhort, to urge to follow.

引丨 to direct in right courses.

鄉丨 a village guide.

開丨 to undeceive, to show the right way.

先丨 a messenger, an avant-courier.

訓丨 to teach easy doctrines, to lead where people wish to go; a district instructor.

悼 From *heart* and *excelling*.
tao' Wounded in mind, afflicted; to grieve for; to bear with, as an offender who is a minor; to dread; to die early.

七年日丨 when seven years old he is called pitiable.

丨哭 to bewail and cry.

悲丨 to compassionate.

丨嘆 to sigh for.

丨亡詩 a monody, a mournful poem on the death of a friend.

稻 From *grain* and to *lade* out.
tao' Rice when growing in the field, paddy; rice.

撒丨 to sow rice.

早丨 early rice.

陸丨 or 旱丨米 upland rice.

氷丨米 family rice.

打丨子 to thrash rice on the 丨塲 or thrashing-floor.

蹈 From *foot* and to *lade* out.
tao' To tread on, to put down the foot; to violate, to disregard; to tread in another's steps.

自丨法網 to willfully violate the laws.

足之丨之手之舞之 the feet dance and the hands gesticulate, — as in extreme joy.

高丨 to travel far.

赴湯丨火 to get scalded and run into the fire; — heedless.

踐丨 to walk on or along.

幬 From *napkin* and *age*; also read *ˌch'eu*.
tao' The everlasting canopy, *i. e.* the sky; a curtain, a veil; to canopy over; a carriage screen or partition.

無不覆丨 there's nothing which is not covered — by the sky.

素丨 a plain curtain.

燾 Like the preceding.
tao' To cover over, to overspread, as the sunlight; to envelop, as a mist or smoke.

盜 盗 From 皿 a *vessel* and 次 an old form of 涎 *spittle*; the primitive is constantly contracted to 次 a time.
tao' A robber, a footpad, a highwayman, a pirate; one who robs openly; to covet and take by fraud or force; to feather one's nest, to peculate; to rob, to plunder; to appropriate another's goods or country.

强丨 a bandit.

洋丨 or 海丨 pirates.

丨賊 or 大丨 a highway robber.

小丨 a pilferer, a footpad.

丨言孔甘 the scoundrel's words are very plausible.

掩耳丨鈴 to cover the ears and take the bell; — to steal and think nobody will know it.

丨名 to rob another's reputation or name, as in counterfeiting trade-marks.

丨神像 to take out an idol.

丨汗 night-sweats.

慢藏誨丨 to be careless of things tempts to thievery.

遇丨 waylaid and robbed.

導 From *rice* and *way*.
tao' To choose; to remove the husk from grain and make it ready for food; rice with six spikelets.

丨去粃糠使成精鑿 take off the chaff that the clean grain may be ready for use.

T'AO.

Old sounds, t'o, t'op, t'ok, do, dot, *and* dok. *In Canton*, t'ò; — *in Swatow*, t'au, t'o, *and* to; — *in Amoy*, t'ò, tò, *and* tiau; — *in Fuhchau*, t'o *and* to; — *in Shanghai*, t'o *and* do; — *in Chifu*, t'ao.

叨 From *mouth* and *knife*; it is unlike *chao'* 召 to call.
ˌt'ao To desire food; to love honor or gratification; to long for; addicted to; inordinately; in polite phrase, to feel deeply grateful for, sensible of, ashamed of having had a strong desire for.

丨蒙 deeply thankful for.

丨光 earnestly desirous of your favor; ashamed of asking you.

幸丨天眷 all enjoyed the care of Heaven.

貪丨凶淫 addicted to cruelty and lust.

丨教 desirous of seeing you.

丨忝 ashamed of so many favors.

貓丨着 just in the cat's mouth.

Read *ˌtao*. To talk or gabble; muddled, hard to unravel.

他的事情眸丨極了 his affairs are very much involved.

饕 From *eat* and to *cry out*; its use is like the preceding.
ˌt'ao Gluttonous, gormandizing; rapacious, covetous.

丨腹 to make a god of the belly.

丨餮性成 he is a confirmed gormand.

何能滿其貪丨 who can satisfy his greed?

謟 To doubt, to suspect.
ˌt'ao 天道不丨 heaven's doctrines are not to be suspected.

絛 縚 From 糸 *silk* and 攸 *string* contracted, or 舀 to *lade*; it is used with the next, and the second form is unusual.
ˌt'ao A plaited sash; a band or cord; a fringe of threads; silk gimp or edging.

絲丨 a silk cord or girdle.

丨子辮子 silk braided in the cue.

打丨子 to twist cord.

狗牙丨子 a notched or scolloped edging.

韜 韔 ˏt'ao } A bow-case; a scabbard; a flag-bag; a vantbrace; to sheathe; just, liberal.
將帥須知丨畧 a general must know all about military strategy.
丨弓 put the bow in its case.
六丨 ancient books containing rules of war, written by the Great Duke Kiang 姜太公 for Wăn Wang.

慆 ˏt'ao From *heart* and *to lade out.*
To rejoice; indulgent, excessive; reckless; to store, to lay up; to treat badly; to doubt; slow, lazy.
丨丨 a long time.
丨心 reckless, careless.
丨閒 not hurried; leisurely.
天命不丨 Heaven's decrees are certain.
以樂丨憂 to conceal sorrow by a joyful air.
無即丨淫 let there be no insolent dissoluteness.

搯 掏 ˏt'ao } To pull out by the hand; to tug at; to fumble for; to draw, as a sword; to knock on; to lay hold of.
丨虱子 to crack a louse.
丨錢 to take out some cash.
丨耳躲 to clean the ears.
丨家雀兒 catch the sparrow.
左旋右丨 he presented his shield and drew his blade.
小洞丨不出大螃蠏 I shan't find a big sea-crab in this little hole; — your paltry shop has nothing fit to buy.

槄 ˏt'ao A tree resembling a *Sophora*, but by others classed with the 楸 or *Catalpa;* it is not now certainly known.

滔 ˏt'ao From *water* and *to lade out.*
The rapid continuous waters of a stream; to overpass bounds; name of an upper branch of the River Han in Shensi.
丨濫 to overflow and inundate.
丨丨不斷古今流 it has never ceased to flow in this same great current.
白浪丨天 the waves touch the sky, — at the horizon.
汶水丨丨 the never-ceasing River Wăn.
丨風 the east wind.
丨丨者天下皆是也 the whole empire is in the same disturbed state.

洮 ˏt'ao From *water* and an *omen;* interchanged with ˏ淘 to rinse.
Name of a large affluent of the Yellow R., west of Lan-cheu fu in Kansuh, flowing near the town of 丨州 lying southeast of Kokonor; an ancient region in Shantung; to wash.
丨湖 a lake in I-hing hien 宜興縣 in Kiangsu, a part of Ta-hu.
汰 to rinse; to cleanse.
臨丨 a former name of Min cheu in the north of Sz'ch'uen, where is produced the 丨羊 a great goat, nearly as large as a donkey.

夲 ˏt'ao From *great* and *ten; i.e.* ten men together; easily confounded with ˊ*păn* 本 root.
To enter, to go in gladly; going and coming, in and out.

陶 匋 ˏt'ao } From 缶 a *dish* and 阜 a *place;* the primitive was once used for it, but has now become obsolete, and is also sometimes regarded as a synonym of ˏ*yao* 窰 a mine.
A furnace for burning pottery or earthenware; a hill like a kiln; to make like a kiln; name of the domain of Tao in Ping-yang, now Ta-yuen fu in Shensi, whence he is called 丨唐氏 Lord T'ang of Tao; mournful thoughts; to please, to give vent to the feelings; correct, straight; used for the next.
丨人 a potter.
甄丨 a kiln.
丨冶 to burn pottery.
駟介丨丨 the mailed team prances proudly.
丨正 an ancient term for a district superintendent of schools.
丨鎔 to melt; to transform and reform.
丨然 jolly, exhilirated.
丨暢 to relieve one's feelings, to enjoy, to give rein to.
丨丨自得 very well pleased with himself and others.
君子丨丨 my husband looks delighted.
亶父丨復丨穴 Tan-fu made them kraals and cave-houses.

Read ˏ*yao.* The upright judge of Shun, named Kao Yao 皐丨 B. C. 2200.

萄 ˏt'ao The cultivated vine is 葡丨; the name is supposed to be of western origin, as the grape was brought from the Caspian Sea in the Han dynasty.
葡丨蔓子 a grape-vine.
牛奶葡丨 white malaga grapes.

鋾 ˏt'ao Dull, as a knife.
In *Cantonese.* A saw, with a dull edge to cut metal.
鋸丨 saws; a saw.

祹 ˏt'ao Happiness; divine, spiritual, pertaining to the gods.

綯 ˏt'ao To bind up; to braid cord, to twist; a cord, a strand.
丨住 to tie up, as a dog.
宵爾索丨 in the evening braid the grass ropes.
結丨 to secure fast.

裪 ˏt'ao The sleeve of a robe; a term used in olden time.

醄 ˏt'ao From *spirits* and a *dish.*
Drunken, tipsy.
惜花連日醉酕丨 while lamenting the transient flowers, he got tipsy and went reeling about day after day.

淘 ꜀t'ao From *water* and *kiln* as the phonetic.

To scour, to wash out, as rice; to sift, to stir about; to search for, as gold dust; to clean out, as a well; to excite; to play; to fidget.

丨米 to scour rice.

丨乾净 to sift clean.

丨沙 to wash sand or rubbish, as to find things.

丨井 to clean out a well.

丨氣 playful, tricky, mischief-loving; sprightly.

流水丨丨 rippling waters.

In *Shanghai*. An adverb of quantity; altogether.

一丨 one wash; *i. e.* at once.

擺拉一丨 put them altogether.

替我一丨去 go with me.

啕 ꜀t'ao Used with the last, but not correctly.

Loquacious, verbose; the prattle of a child.

號丨 to cry, to bewail, to weep.

咷 ꜀t'ao From *mouth* and *omen*; the preceding is often wrongly used for this.

The wailing of infants; to cry and weep.

號丨痛哭 the noise of bitter wailing and agony.

噭丨 bawling and squalling, as children.

桃 ꜀t'ao A peach, a nectarine, considered as 五木之精 the best of all trees; it is used as a metaphor for females and nuptials; a flower-bud, alluding to its plumpness.

鶏嘴丨 the beaked peach.

扁丨 or 剛兒丨 or 合丨 or 蟠丨 the flat peach.

丨子 a peach.

合密丨 the honey peach from Khamil.

丨仁 peach-meats.

碧丨花 the white double peach.

丨紅 peach bloom.

核丨 a walnut; but 核丨骨 is a term for the ankle.

洋丨 the sweet carambola (*Averrhoa*); but in Kiangsi, this name is applied to the 獼猴丨 a fruit like the *Actinidia* or *Dillenia*.

含丨 a cherry.

董斯目丨 a kind of white peach at Peking.

丨氏爲刃 the cutler made swords.

仙丨 a poetical name for a fig.

丨葉丨根 peach leaf and root; *i. e.* a wife and concubine.

丨乳 or 丨膠 peach gum.

丨虫 the peach bug; *i. e.* a wren.

香丨 a lemon. (*Pekingese.*)

丨花水 spring freshes.

丨符 the peach charm, hung over the lintel about newyear.

綿花丨 flower bud of cotton.

丨園結義 they (Liu Pi and others) made their compact in the peach-garden.

丨月 a poetical name for the third moon.

佛丨 Budha's peach, a fragrant variety of orange which does not become fingered.

鞉 鼗 ꜀t'ao A hand-drum or tambour, furnished with buttons tied to strings on each side, and twirled by peddlers as a cry; it is called 播楞鼓 and 玲琳鼓 by many.

逃 迯 ꜀t'ao From *to go* and *omen*; the second form is common but rather vulgar.

To abscond, to elude search, to desert; to flee, to escape; to hide; escaped, skulking; a vagabond, a wanderer; fugitives.

丨跑 or 丨走 to run away.

丨學 to play truant.

拐丨 to abduct, to carry off children.

丨人 a fugitive, a deserter.

天下逋丨主 this chief of the vagabonds in the land.

丨避 to shirk, to hide, to skulk; to flee, as from the police.

丨奴 a runaway slave.

丨籠鳥 a well trained bird.

丨荒 fugitives, wandering outcasts.

丨不出去 cannot get away, as from the besiegers.

丨旗 he deserted his flag, said of a Bannerman.

丨軍 to escape, as a banished man.

脫丨 to sneak away, to skulk off.

駣 ꜀t'ao A horse four years old, according to the Păn Ts'ao; though some say a three year colt.

檮 ꜀t'ao From *wood* and *age*.

A block of wood; a useless stick; to stab.

丨杌 an inauspicious animal; name of a noted bandit spoken of in the Ch'un Ts'iu; an ignorant dolt, who cannot be trusted or taught; a history of the Tsu state.

丨昧 ignorant of, stupid.

Read ꜀ch'eu. Unworthy of a mate, one whom nobody will consort with; a coffin.

翿 ꜀t'ao A sort of flabellum used by mummers; a banner ornamented with feathers, used by actors, similar to the 翳 a feather insignia.

旗丨 standards which distinguish officers.

右執丨 in his right hand he holds his feather panache.

濤 ꜀t'ao Great waves; billows dashing on the shore; a river in Sz'ch'uen.

波丨 billows following each other, and dashing ashore.

松丨 the wind sighing through the pines.

海丨翻滾 seething, foaming billows.

討 'ťao. From *words* and an *inch*; *q. d.* a ruler's words should be guided by reason.

To manage, to govern; to make war on, to punish the refractory, to curb the seditious; to put to death; to put away, to put down; to investigate, to search, to ask for, to seek; to bring upon one's self; mixed.

丨賊 to extirpate robbers; to attack the foe.

丨債 or 丨賬 to dun.

丨伐 to reduce to subjection.

丨保 to guaranty; answerable for

丨厭 or 丨嫌 to get people's ill-will, to incur dislike.

丨飯 to ask alms or food.

丨情 to intercede for a criminal.

丨不着好 I won't have it so; don't put it that way.

丨好 to toady, to cater to.

丨個公道 I only wish to get a fair price.

檢丨 a Hanlin reviser of low rank.

丨取 to exact, to demand and take.

自丨 he brought it on himself.

套 ťao'. From *great* over *long* altered.

Large, wide; what envelopes another thing; to enwrap; to add or superadd; to include in the whole; of general observance; to run one thing into another; to make a circuit; to be tedious, to talk prosily; a snare, a trap; a noose or lasso; a shell, a wrapper, a case, an envelop; a classifier of a set of books, a suit of clothes, and plays.

不落丨 I did not fall into the trap.

一丨書 one copy of a book.

丨書 encase the books.

丨褲 overalls, leggings.

一丨衣服 one suit of clothes.

通丨的 or 丨用的 generally in use, commonly known.

圈丨 a noose, a snare.

客丨話 polite greetings.

丨住 cover it; noose it; keep him.

脫丨 he escaped that snare; also, not to conform to the fashion or current opinion; peculiar, puritanical.

手丨 a pair of gloves or mittens.

一件外丨 an overcoat or outer robe

丨言不敘 no need of many compliments.

丨板 blocks for two colors.

一丨戲法 a conjurer's trick.

河丨冬洇 the bend or cut-off in the river dries in winter.

俗丨 vulgar or common.

一丨全傢伙 a complete set of tools.

In *Pekingese*. To put on; communicating by.

丨車 to harness the cart.

二房丨間 the two rooms open into each other, as by a door.

TEH.

Old sounds, tek *and* dek. *In Canton*, tăk; — *in Swatow*, tek *and* tít; — *in Amoy*, tek; — *in Fuhchau*, taik; — *in Shanghai*, tăk *and* dăk; — *in Chifu*, tö.

德 悳 ,töh. From 彳 to *go* and 直 *straight* and 心 *heart;* the combined primitive is the ancient form of the character; as a proper name, it is often written without the radical, and like the second form.

Moral excellence or virtue, goodness; benefit, favor; energy, virtue; quality, power, whether good or bad; to show kindness; accomplishments; to flourish, as the seasons; good example; sensible of a favor; grateful; good instruction; to improve, to increase in; to benefit others; happy; in epitaphs, mild and yet just, humble when reproved.

有丨 he is worthy.

祖宗之丨行所致 [his success] is owing to the virtuous acts of his fathers.

仁丨 humanity, beneficence.

惡丨 vicious qualities; the quality of badness, wickedness; a bad efficacy.

地丨 the energy of earth, as a god manifesting itself in producing things.

神丨 divine power, spiritual virtue.

改於其丨 correct their [bad] qualities.

作功丨 to perform meritorious acts, as a devotee.

喪丨 or 損丨 reckless, to violate right.

大丨敦化 great virtue converts many.

女有四丨 females have four accomplishments; *viz.*, 丨 chastity, 言 words, 容 manners, and 工 skill.

丨色 appearance of good.

丨己 to take merit to one's self.

丨之不忘 ever grateful for it.

六丨 six virtues, *viz.*, 知 knowledge, 仁 humanity, 聖 innate goodness, 義 rectitude, 中 integrity, and 和 conciliation.

修丨 to give in charity.

丨潤身 virtue adorns the person.

丨禽 a cock, chanticleer.

大丨 used for *bhadanta* a title like Reverend given to Budhist priests.

三丨 three virtues, *viz.*; 正眞 even justice, 剛克 stern rule, and 柔克 mild rule; these are the essence of the 九丨 nine virtues of mankind in all relations.

得, ˓*töh* From 彳 to *go* and 㝵 an *obstacle; q. d.* going on till the object be attained.

To attain, to get the object of one's wishes; to wish, to desire covetously; special; between two adjectives it is an *adverb*, very; an auxiliary *verb*, can, may, able to be done; after another verb, expresses the potential mood, or a form of the past tense; to do; to become, to gain; gain, a possession; covetousness.

不丨 unattainable, very difficult; when it follows a negative, it indicates inability; when it precedes it, unwillingness; as 來不丨 he will not come; 不丨來 he cannot come; 不丨了 there is no end; after 巴 or 很 it indicates desire, or the optative; as 我巴不丨要來 I greatly desired to come; after adjectives the highest degree of; as 少不丨 infallibly, certainly enough.

不大丨意 I am rather disappointed; mortified.

丨錢賣放 to take bribes to let a thief escape.

沒有丨說 there is nothing to say.

丨乎天 got it from heaven; came naturally.

丨着 or 丨了 it is got; I've got it.

今日丨見 I had a sight of him to-day.

走丨多 I walked too much.

是用不丨于道 and therefore we did not advance on our road.

省丨路上泥 you will thus avoid the mire.

丨丨來 I came here on purpose.

不丨已 cannot but, necessary, not able to stop.

看丨見 I can see it; it is visible.

焉丨知 how can he obtain wisdom?

凡民自丨罪 all people who commit [these] crimes.

等不丨 I cannot wait.

使丨 or 做丨 very well, it will do.

丨一失一 got one and lost one.

戒之在丨 restrain your covetousness.

丨手夥計 fellow-workmen.

必丨 you will get it.

丨意丨狠 exceedingly well satisfied, just what I wanted.

極甚相丨 they agree together (or fit) very well.

丨其所哉 what a fortunate man I am!

那丨不爾 how can it but be so?

In *Pekingese* read *té*. Ought, should; required of.

丨用多少 how much is needed?

丨甚麼時候去 at what hour must we start?

淂, ˓*töh* Often erroneously written for the last.

Water, watery; the appearance of water.

搨, ˓*töh* To strike with the fist, to thump; to crowd close up to each other, to scrouge.

貣, *tö*˒ From *precious* and *dart*; it is interchanged with *tai*˒ 貸 to lend.

To ask a loan, particularly of the crop for future needs.

假丨 to borrow.

有積穀者丨得十分之三 he borrowed one third of the crop of the corn-dealers.

T'EH.

Old sound, t'ek. *In Canton*, t'ăk *and* t'ik; — *in Swatow*, t'ek; — *in Amoy*, t'ek *and* lek; — *in Fuhchau*, t'aik; — *in Shanghai*, t'ăk; — *in Chifu*, t'ö.

特, *t'ö*˒ From *ox* and a *court*.

A bull, a male beast; a three year old beast; a bullock fit for sacrificing, three years old; a stallion, three mares were allowed to one; alone, single, separately; prominent; special, purposely; to stand forth; to isolate; a mate; a man eminent among others; grain shooting up.

不丨 not alone, not only; and followed by 即, as 不丨愚民即士大夫亦信 not only did the common people believe it, but the scholars also.

丨意 or 丨地 single, specially; a special design.

丨要 I specially wish it.

丨牲 a sacrificial bullock; to pair, to wed.

丨來 I came on purpose.

不思舊姻求爾新丨 you do not care for our old affinity, and seek to please your new mate.

丨白 to announce particularly.

丨旨 or 丨諭 a special edict; an order given for this single purpose.

丨立 to stand up for bravely.

丨字通知 I write this to inform you.

丨示 a special notification.

犆, *t'ö*˒ Almost the same as the last.

One, a single one; special, single.

不丨弔 not alone to condole; *i. e.* one who is a near friend does not make a formality of the condolence.

丨言同時也 specially spoke of it at the same time.

Read *chih*, The margin or selvedge of the dress.

忒, *t'ö*˒ From *heart* and *dart*.

An excess, an error; to alter, to change; to err; to doubt; as an *adverb*, a synonym of 太 highly, too, very.

丨兇猛 very furious.
疑丨 to suspect.
丨小 too small.
年紀丨輕 too young.
四時不丨 there is no deviation in the seasons.
昊天不丨 high Heaven never errs.
下手丨很了 you hit him quite too hard.
丨晚 very late.
孰無差丨哉 who is there who has never erred?
丨精細了 too refined and delicate.

In *Shanghai*. Instead of, for; with, along with.
丨我去買 go and buy it for me.
丨伊一淘去 go along with him.
丨煞要緊 in too great haste.

⿰亻忒ʾ *t'ö'* Foolish.
儓丨 silly.

忑ʾ *t'ö'* From *heart* below *under*.
Downhearted; timorous.
素固忐丨 he is always just so cowardly.

慝ʾ *t'ö'* From *heart* and to *hide* from; it differs from *nih*, ⿰忄匿 mortified.

Secret vice and a depraved heart; dissolute, lewd; filthy; noxious; to gloss over vice, to act hypocritically, to do evil.
隱丨 to hide one's vile conduct.
姦丨 profligate, licentious.
修丨 to put away evil habits.
方丨 local balderdash or ribaldry —should be avoided.
邪丨 vicious, depraved.
無俾作丨 do not let them act out their evil.
匿丨而言善 he conceals his vice by talking good.
丨於惡雜 abandoned to vile practices.
仄丨 the moon seen after sunrise.
旌別淑丨 to discriminate between the pure and impure.
負罪引丨 taking punishment to himself and bearing all evil; — said of Shun.

蟘ʾ *t'öh* Insects which eat leaves; plant-lice or aphides, called 蜮虫 in Peking, and 花虱 in Canton.
去其蟊丨 [that thou mayest] remove the grubs and lice — from the grain and vegetables; part o. a prayer to the gods of the land

TEU.

Old sounds, tu, du, tút, dút, *and* dúk. *In Canton*, tau; — *in Swatow*, tau *and* tò; — *in Amoy*, tau *and* tò; — *in Fuhchau*, tau, téu, *and* taiu; — *in Shanghai*, tù *and* dù; — *in Chifu*, tò.

꜀兜 *꜀teu* From 皃 *form* and an old form of 瞽 *blind*, which incloses it.

A kind of helmet or morion; helmet shaped; to carry in a napkin, to make a loose parcel; to retain; to get by crooked ways; to reach.
丨鍪 an iron casque.
丨肚 or 肚丨 a stomacher; a support to the breast like a corset.
丨了好些東西 he tied up many things in his kerchief.
放驩丨于崇山 [Shun] sent Hwan Teu (a villainous officer) into confinement on Mt. Chung.
下吧丨 an old man's chin.
丨貌 repulsive, ill-looking.
丨轉來 I came by a roundabout way.
丨頭 to dodge and run ahead.
風丨 a hood or cowl to keep the head warm.
丨收 to keep wrongfully.
丨到 I have got it.

In *Fuhchau*. At, by; near in time or place.

꜀⿰扌兜 *꜀teu* To lift up, to raise in the hand; to correct, to criticise; to retain, to control; to get hold of; to seize; to meddle with; to fit; to bring near to.
丨領 to get commissions.
丨攬 to engross, to grasp after.
丨紙 a percentage taken by a house-broker from the nominal price.
丨開 to lift aside, to raise and put elsewhere.
丨得水 to take up water in the hands.
跟丨 to fit tightly, as a shoe.
丨緊 take it up carefully.
丨起轎 to tilt or lift the sedan-poles, and thus causing the sitter to go under them.

In *Fuhchau*. To befriend, to care for; to fold under, to tuck in.

꜀篼 *꜀teu* A horse-trough or bucket to give the animal drink; a basket to muzzle it; a classifier of trees.
一丨樹 one solitary tree.
驢丨 the muzzle on an ass.
山丨 or 丨子 a mountain chair; a basket to carry things.

꜀⿰口殳 *꜀teu* From 口 *mouth* and 投 to *throw* down contracted.

Talkative; trifling discourse.
讘丨 very loquacious.
⿰口反丨 garrulous.

꜀䁱 *꜀teu* From *eye* and *wine vessel*; it is often read *꜀leu*.

Sunken or hollow eyes; deep-set eyes, arising from high eyebrows; unwashed eyes.
瞘丨眼兒 beetle-browed eyes; hollow-eyed.
骷髏丨子 the sockets in a skull.

斗 ʿteu The lower part is intended to represent the *handle* of a grain measure; it is the 68th radical of a small group relating chiefly to measures.

A dry measure of ten 升 or pints; one size, called 市丨 or 十斤丨 holds ten catties of rice, and measures 1.63 gallon; a more common kind, the 倉丨 holds 6½ catties, and measures 309.57148 *cubic ins.* or 1.13 *gall.;* the 雙丨 or double peck holds 13 *catts.;* the 秭關丨 is larger and holds about 14 *catts.;* the size used in the Tʻang dynasty held 18.15 pints or 1.13 peck; a vessel which can hold things like a peck; a simile of size, small, contracted, or large; the cupule of an acorn; a wine-vessel; a top on a mast; the eighth constellation, composed of the stars $\zeta\ \lambda\ \mu\ \sigma\ \tau$ and ϑ in Sagittarius; another of ω in Hercules.

丨室 a little house.

丨底房 a little room.

盜丨子 a body-snatcher, who opens coffins to pilfer them.

丨膽 great courage.

水丨 a dipper.

灰丨 or 丨子 a hod; it is often only a rag with corner strings.

車載丨量不可勝數 I have many of the common people with me, more than can be counted.

才儲八丨 a man of great talents.

墨丨兒 a carpenter's marking-cup and line.

指丨文 the striæ or the finger-tips.

朝丨 or 拜丨 to worship the Dipper — for long life.

北丨 the part of Ursa Major containing the four stars $\alpha\ \beta\ \gamma\ \delta$ in the Dipper, which is regarded as the chariot of Ti, and to revolve in the center of the sky.

滿天星丨 the sky is full of constellations.

丨方兒 composite characters, where several parts are written together so as to look like one.

抖 ʿteu To shake; to shudder, to shiver; to throw off; to arouse.

丨了去 shake it off, as dust.

精神丨擻 excited, ready for any effort, in prime spirits.

丨丨身上的雪 shook off the snow from himself.

渾身發丨 he trembled all over.

軆丨丨的 it moves up and down; quivering, as a twig in the wind.

In *Cantonese.* To touch, to handle; to work in wood.

莫丨 let that alone.

枓 ʿteu The capital of a pillar.

丨栱 the square block on its top.

Read ʿ*chu.* A long-handled ladle likened to the Dipper.

沃水用丨 use a ladle to dip the hot water.

蚪 ʿteu From *insect* and *dipper*, alluding to the shape.

A tadpole, a porwiggle.

科丨文 tadpole characters, fanciful forms of characters in imitation of them and fishes, birds, or other things.

枓 ʿteu The sleeve of a dress.

陡 阧 ʿteu The slope of a hill; a sluice or drain for irrigation; to stand; suddenly.

丨然富貴 all at once he became rich and great.

天雲丨起 the sky was quickly overcast.

丨發 suddenly burst out or occurred.

大計丨參 at the triennial survey, he was abruptly dismissed.

山丨而不能上 the hill is too steep to be ascended.

丨門 the openings of sluices for irrigating rice-fields.

其心丨險 he is perfectly fearless; a dare-devil.

鬥 鬭 鬪 閗 teuʾ The first form rudely represents two 士 *braves* fighting and supported by their respective armies in the rear; it is the 191st radical of a few characters relating to contests, and is often written like ˓*măn* 門 a door; the third form is the most common, and read ʿ*teu* when used as a surname, but the second is the correct one.

To wrangle, to contest, to fight; to set by the ears, to make others fight; to contend for, to strive to excel; to play at; to set, as types; to discuss sharply.

丨氣 pugnacious, belligerent.

爭丨 a brawl; to fall to and fight.

丨毆 to fight; to have a shindy.

丨訟事 to debate about.

丨份 to squabble about the divisions of a thing.

丨不過你 I can't compete with you; I'll knuckle under.

丨跑馬 to race horses.

丨趣 to make merry with games or trials of skill, as at a feast.

丨三板 a regatta.

丨駁 to dispute fiercely.

坐山睇虎丨 sit on the hill and see their tigers fight; — *met.* let people settle their own quarrels.

好勇丨狠 he likes to show his pluck; he will not yield.

丨紙牌 to play cards.

In *Cantonese.* To make things or furniture; to touch, to play with.

丨木佬 a carpenter.

丨亂 to throw into disorder.

咪丨 don't touch it.

不丨湊 I cannot bring it about; it won't do or match.

豆 teuʾ The character represents a *dish*, the cover, opening, and legs making its parts; it forms the 151st radical of characters relating to vessels, but also to pulse, as it is now chiefly used for the next.

A wooden trencher, a charger; a sacrificial dish; pulse, legumes; an ancient weight equal to 16 grains of millet, or the 144th part of a tael; to measure out; a peck.

籩 | 之 事 matters relating to sacrifices and worship.

木 | a wooden platter.

君 婦 莫 莫 爲 | 孔 庶 the presiding women are still and reverent, and prepare the numerous trays.

In *Cantonese.* A father is 老 |, a phrase said to come from a mispronunciation of the northern term 老 頭 or 老 頭 子 used like "the governor."

豆 *teu'* A recent character constantly used for the last.

Legumes of every kind; peas, beans.

| 角 or | 甲 string-beans; peas in the pod.

青 | green peas.

地 | or 土 | ground-nuts.

| 腐 腦 (or 花) bean-curd jelly.

紅 | lentiles; also, the bean of *Abrus precatorius.*

| 石 and | 餅 bean cakes.

胡 | a Budhist name for lentiles.

豇 | kidney beans.

蠶 | common bean (*Faba sativa*), from the fancied similarity of the hirsute pods to silkworms.

水 | 兒 a lacustrine plant with thread-like leaves, which produces small edible tubers like peas.

豋 *teu'* Interchanged with its primitive.

A sacrificial vessel, that which holds the meat.

梪 *teu'* Like the last.

A wooden trencher to hold meat; an old measure of four 升 pints, less than half a peck.

獨 | a high tree, whose fruit resembles colored bags, and the leaves bright mirrors; perhaps the bladder tree or *Kœlruteria paniculata.*

痘 *teu'* From *disease* and *pea.*

The small-pox.

| 疹 the pustules.

| 漿 vaccine virus.

染 | caught the small-pox.

出 | or 出 | 子 the smallpox has appeared.

種 | or 種 牛 | to vaccinate.

天行 | took it naturally.

| 皮 pock-marked.

| 疤 the scabs.

| 毒 a broken pustule.

| 母 or | 神 娘 娘 goddess of the small-pox.

逗 *teu'* To delay, to loiter, to remain without permission; to stop, to detain; to avoid, as an enemy; to peer and peep, to skulk around in order to escape detection.

在 路 | 遛 不 能 直 赴 任 所 he loitered by the way and could not go right to his post.

引 | to beguile and lead astray.

| 住 to delay, to dawdle.

脰 *teu'* The neck, the throat.

絕 | to break off the neck; as in hanging.

| 頸 the neck.

鼃 以 | 鳴 frogs croak through (or in) their neck.

餖 *teu'* To set out food.

| 飣 the part of a feast which remains, and is spread for the servants.

酘 *teu'* To distil again.

猶 一 | 之 it must be distilled once more.

竇 *teu'* From 穴 *cave* and 瀆 *disgraceful* contracted.

A hole, a burrow; a duct, an aqueduct, a drain; a waste-weir; an error by which some one is disappointed; loss, waste, damage; to dig a hole or channel through a bank or wall.

水 | a water sluice or drain.

狗 | a kennel.

弊 | 百 出 from a trifling error (or damage) many bad results follow.

| 路 a narrow road, as in a gorge.

保 無 疑 | we can assure them that there will be no remissness.

塞 | to let down the sluice-gate.

In *Cantonese.* A rendezvous for thieves and their plunder; a *guet-apens.*

圍 | 口 to beset or watch a lurking-place.

T'EU.

Old sounds, t'o, du, t'ot, *and* dút. *In Canton,* t'au; — *in Swatow,* t'au *and* tau; — *in Amoy,* t'ò, tò, *and* tau; — *in Fuhchau,* t'au, tau, *and* t'aiu; — *in Shanghai,* t'ù *and* dù; — *in Chifu,* t'ò.

偷 *t'eu* From *man* and *to answer;* it was originally written like *yü* 媮 to deceive.

Remiss; careless, so as to incur loss; stealthily, underhand; secretly; disrespectfully; to pilfer, to steal, to obtain unfairly; to undervalue, to despise.

| 安 to take one's ease, when he ought to work; to let things slide.

忙 裏 | 閒 to shirk work even when very busy.

| 生 to shamefully save one's life.

| 拈 to pilfer, to purloin.

| 走 to go silently, as a thief.

| 盜 to steal and rob; a brigand.

狗 | a petty thief, a shop-lifter.

| 得 浮 生 半 日 閒 I have escaped the frothy bustle of life, and am going to take a half holiday.

| | 去 to steal away, to slink off.

丨巧 to save human labor.
丨薄 remiss, negligent.
丨看 to steal a look at.
丨工減料 to deceive in work and stock; dishonest work and scant materials; to peculate in a job.

鍮 ˓t'eu An ore called 丨石 resembling pure copper, which comes from Persia; it attracts and forms an amalgam with quicksilver, and is probably a rich ore of gold and copper.

頭 ˓t'eu From *leaf* and *platter*.
The head, which is highest on the body; the front, the top; the chief, the first, the best; the end, as of a beam; the beginning of, the entrance of a matter; a classifier of affairs or acts, and occasionally of cattle and horses; it is added to many names of things because they are roundish like a head, or to make a distinctive noun.
丨殼 the head, the skull.
丨瘟 vertigo, dizziness.
包丨 a fillet or headband.
回丨 to turn the head.
出丨 to take one's part, to undertake for, to interfere; distinguished, rising.
一丨親事 this marriage affair.
走那丨 go by that way.
上丨 and 下丨 upper and lower people, as master and servants, the boss and his men.
下丨 down-stairs. (*Cantonese*).
丨貨 carriage animals.
丨腦 a headman, the guiding hand; a clue, a way.
無丨公案 no cause for an action, it is a doubtful case.
作事有丨無尾 he begins a thing but never finishes it.
丨一個 the leading man, the first or most famous.
他丨一天 the day before that.
丨等丨兒 the very best of.
無想丨 no other way, no help for it.
走丨無路 no opening anywhere; I can find no occupation.
丨丨是道 he can easily find employment.
出人丨地 he excels most men.
點丨 to nod assent; to bow.
丨丨個時 that first time.
凡事丨難 the first time of doing anything is hard.
In *Shanghai*. An *adverb*, about.
丨二百里 about 200 *li*.

亠 ˓t'eu Read like the last, and used only as the 8th radical of a few miscellaneous characters.
It has no meaning.

投 ˓t'eu From *head* and *weapon*.
To throw at, into, or down; to take or go to, to deliver; to cast off, to reject; to give one's self up to; to present to; to receive; to have recourse to; to engage another to do; to intrust; to act with; to join, to consort with; to suit, to agree on; to raffle, to bid for; to conceal; towards or inclining to.
丨宿 or 丨店 to seek a lodging.
不丨緣 not pleased with.
出丨貨物 to sell by auction.
丨明 to bid for viva-voce or publicly; not 丨墨 to write a bid.
丨票 to give in bids at a raffle.
丨文書 to hand in dispatches.
丨井 to drown one's self in well.
丨其所好' to agree to whatever another likes, sycophantic.
說話丨機 to agree with in opinion, to coincide with, to bear the same testimony.
丨遞 to take to, to give over to.
自丨羅網 he fell into his own snare.
丨西 going westwards.
丨桃報李 to send a peach and get a pear in exchange.
丨誠 or 丨降 to submit and return to allegiance.
丨軍 to enlist, to enter the army.
自行丨首 he went and owned his misdeeds.
話不丨機半句多 half a sentence is too much to say to one whom we dislike.

骰 ˓t'eu ˋshai From *bone* and *weapon*; it is sometimes used for ˋku 股 a part.
Dice are called 丨子 from their being made of bone
耍丨子 or 打丨子 or 擲丨子 to throw dice.

豆 ˋt'eu The character is designed for a rude delineation of a *wine cup*; and is now reduced to 斗 a measure.
An ancient sort of beaker or flagon.

浢 ˋt'eu Said to be used for the last, and defined to wash.
A small affluent of the Yellow River in the southwest corner of Shansi in Jui-ch'ing hien, where once was 丨津 a mart.

欨 ˓t'eu From to *breathe* and *pulse*; used in Cantonese, and incorrectly written ˋ抖 to shudder.
To pant, to take breath, to breathe hard and sigh; to rest, to hold up.
小兒歟丨 the child is very passionate.
丨一日 to rest for a day.
丨涼 to take an airing.
丨吓手 hold up for a while.
嘆丨 to moan and sigh.
丨一丨 rest a little while.
丨氣 to puff the breath; to pant.

尌 ˋt'eu To loot; to carry off things.
丨尌 to plunder, as lawless soldiers do.

黈 ˋt'eu From *yellow* and *lord*.
Yellow, a dark yellow; the 丨纊 were yellow cotton flaps or tabs which hung from the crown over the ears, intimating that the king must not listen to rumors.

糾 ˊt'u From *silk* and *peck;* it is used with the preceding, and is not the same ˊ*kiu* 糾 a cord.

Yellow ear-covers; to inform.

透 t'eu' From *to go* and *beautiful.*

To pass or leap over; to go from this to that; to pass through, as light does through glass; to comprehend, to discern; throughout, thoroughly; an alarmed or doubtful look.

丨情講 or 丨地說 to tell one's feelings, to make a clean breast.

丨心涼 to chill one through, as when drinking iced-water.

丨徹 or 通丨 to understand fully.

丨光 an opening for light, a kind of skylight.

丨光者 a transparent thing.

丨家子 a shrewd, artful, clever fellow.

好丨 perfectly well, just right.

測不丨 I do not comprehend the subject; it is hard to fathom.

丨化人心 to convert the heart.

看丨他的機關 I see through his scheme.

密不丨風 do not let a lisp of it be spoken.

勿曾熟丨 not ripe, underdone, not ready. (*Shanghai.*)

濕丨了 wet quite through.

In *Cantonese.* To offer, as a price; to light, as a fire.

丨着炭 the coal has lighted.

丨底撈 to price a thing dirt cheap.

丨火爐 light a fire in the grate

訃 t'eu' To deceive.

引丨 to lead into evil ways, to vitiate.

杏 音 t'eu' From 否 *not* and 丶 *lord,* denoting one woh hening something bad, spits it out and rejects it; the second form is now only used as a primitive.i

To spit out.

TI.

Old sounds, té, dé, da, tét, dét, *and* dék. *In Canton,* tei *and* ti; — *in Swatow,* ti *and* toi: — *in Amoy,* ti, té, t'é *and* tòe; — *in Fuhchau,* ti, t'i, té, tie, tè, *and* t'é; — *in Shanghai,* ti *and* di; — *in Chifu,* ti.

隄 ˏti From *place* and *right;* similar to the next.

To dike, to bank; to prepare against, to guard, to oppose a barrier; to stop, or fill a levee; a defense; a causeway, a bank.

丨防小人 be careful of evil people.

水漫了丨 the water has overflowed the dike.

堤 ˏti From *earth* and *right;* used with the last.

A dike, a bund; a ridge, a barrier; to divide by dikes; to fix a thing on its base.

築丨 to build a causeway.

丨岸 a bank of earth.

丨邊 near the bank.

鞮 ˏti Skin shoes; plain shoes; a single thickness without ornament.

丨屨 buskins.

絡丨 leathern greaves or shin plates.

狄丨 an old name for a region near Koko-nor.

低 仾 ˏti From *man* and *low* or *mutual;* the second form is pedantic.

To bend or hang down, to droop; to incline; to sink, as money; in a low place; below, down; base, humble, low; under the standard; ordinary, vulgar, common; the lower classes.

高 and 丨 with 丨 and 昂 are opposites, high — low; honorable — base.

丨頭 to hang the head.

價丨 cheap, low-priced.

出身丨 low born, a humble origin.

水向丨流 water runs downward; — the heart turns to evil

愁壓眉丨 to knit the brows when sorrowful.

丨丨說道 he spoke in a low tone.

薩菩丨眉 the gentle look of Budhist gods.

丨一格 put the line one character or place lower.

丨徊欲絕 to revolve in the mind when in sheer despair and ready to kill one's self.

丨音 or 丨聲 in a low voice.

丨僞 counterfeit; low, mean, as a disreputable business.

不丨三下四 I am not going to submit to do everything.

磾 ˏti A mineral 丨石 used in dyeing silk black; it may be a sort of iron-alum or massive alum shale; it occurs in the southeast of Shantung.

羝 ˏti Used with the next.

A ram or buck; a he-goat; a ram three years old.

丨羊觸藩 the ram butts against the fence.

牴 觝 ˊti From *ox* or *horn,* and *reaching* to as the phonetic.

To gore, to butt; to push with the horns; to strive against; to push, as off a shore.

丨觸 to push and drive with the horns.

角丨戲 pushing and pulling, an ancient sort of wrestling.

丨排異端 to resist heretical or strange doctrines.

骶 ʿti The sacral extremity, or the end of the spinal marrow, by which it communicates with the brain; the *os coccygis*.

氐 ʿti From 氏 *reaching* and 一 *one* denoting the earth; *q. d.* one tumbling down; used for the next, and for ˏ低 to hang down.

The third zodiacal constellation, consisting of $\alpha\,\beta\,\nu\,\delta\,\varepsilon\,\zeta\,\iota\,\mu\,\upsilon\,\xi\,o$ in Libra; to revert to; a foundation; fundamental, radical; to lodge a night; the bottom of.

大 丨 on the whole, generally.

丨 羌 a tribe in the Shang dynasty which occupied a region on the upper waters of the River Wêi in Kansuh.

Read ˏti. To reach; to hang down; cheap.

其價丨賤 the price is low.

邸 ʿti From a *town* and to *reach;* it is interchanged with the next and last.

A hotel where feudatories lodged at the capital; a royal residence, where courtiers repair; a lodging-house; the basis, the support of a thing; fundamental, going to the bottom of; a stand for a tablet; a screen; to arrive at.

丨 舍 a lodging-place.

根 丨 堅 固 a firm foundation.

旅 丨 a tavern, one's hotel.

丨 抄 the Peking gazette, so called because it is supposed to be copied out at the royal hotel.

丨 京 to reach the capital.

抵 ʿti To oppose, to ward off; to rush against, to butt; to hit together; to substitute; to forfeit a pledge; to atone for; to sustain, to bear; to get what one deserves; to offend; to reach, to arrive at; up to, reaching to; a pledge, a security, a lien.

丨 擔 關 係 to bear the consequences.

丨 住 hold it up; stop it, as from falling.

丨 得 住 it will sustain it; it will not give way.

丨 換 to barter, to swap.

丨 罪 to atone for crime, to bear the blame.

丨 賬 to settle a debt; to compound for a money payment by other property.

丨 兌 to give an equivalent for.

丨 銷 to make compensation; to pay a mulct, to settle an affair with money.

丨 命 or 丨 償 to forfeit one's life; to atoné by life.

丨 水 tide or current against one.

丨 掌 to gesticulate, to flourish the arms.

丨 几 to slap the table, as when talking.

相 丨 to give in return as good as he gave; to revenge upon.

大 丨 in general, for the most part.

Read ʿchi. To clap.

丨 掌 而 談 he clapped his hands and said.

In *Cantonese* used for ˏ低. To value; worth, valued at; cheap, at a bargain.

不 丨 錢 not worth much.

丨 手 clever, skillful.

眞 正 唔 丨 I was not up to him, I was taken in.

丨 得 咯 well worth it.

眞 係 丨 嘅 it was very cheap.

疧 ʿti Also read ʿki and ʿchi; the primitive is also written shiˀ 氏.

Disease; sickness caused by constipation; afflicted, sorrowing.

祇 自 丨 兮 you will just make yourself ill, — by brooding over these troubles.

厎 ʿti From *cliff* and *bottom;* it is not the same as the next, but is constantly used for it; and for ʿchi 砥 a hone.

A soft stone, like steatite; to come to; to cause to approach; to fix, to settle; to produce; to execute; to reach; a whetstone.

既 丨 法 had decided on the plan.

周 道 如 丨 the highway is level as a whetstone.

三 邦 丨 貢 厥 名 the three regions contributed their best sorts.

我 祖 丨 遂 陳 于 上 our ancestor rendered his deeds manifest in former days.

底 ʿti From *shelter* and *bottom;* to be distinguished from the last.

At the base of, under the shadow of; the bottom of; below, underneath; below the level of; low, menial; a servant; to the end, lasting; to reach the bottom; to impede; to settle, as sediment; a copy, a rough draft; natural vigor, constitution; a *conjunction*, but, only; in the Sung dynasty and before, used for 的 as a sign of the possessive.

丨 面 the under surface.

不 到 丨 it don't reach the bottom.

到 丨 怎 麼 樣 how will it turn out at last?

下 丨 down stairs, below.

丨 下 under, underneath.

小 丨 servant boys.

打 丨 put it last, goes last; to lay on priming in painting.

你 先 打 丨 do you first broach the matter.

好 丨 子 vigorous, hearty; of good ancestry, respectable parentage.

什 麽 丨 子 出 身 what was his start in life?

眼 丨 無 人 he cares for nobody; supercilious, upstart.

伊 于 胡 丨 what do you think will be the end of it?

地 丨 underground; hades, in the abyss; the underworld.

家 丨 family possessions.

後 丨 behind, rear, last, after all.

細 丨 carefully, in detail.

靡 所 丨 止 so that there is no end or final rest.

知 丨 you know it to the bottom; that's very wise, you see the whole thing clearly.

丨 稿 a draft, a first copy.

弤 ˓ti The famous bow of the emperor Shun, which was red and ornamented with carvings.

詆 ˓ti To vilify, to slander, to defame; to accuse wrongfully; to blame.

丨毀 to calumniate.

醜丨 vile slanders.

誣丨是非 to pervert the right or call it wrong.

丨陷人於罪 to implicate one in a crime unjustly.

Read *tih*, Artful, crafty.

聜 ˓ti From *ear* and *cavity*; also read *chih*, and *toh*,

Hard of hearing from disease; a disease in the ear.

地 ti˒ From *ground* and *also*.

The earth, "the heavy gross particles which sank at the time of separating the primeval ether;" the second of the three prime powers, worshiped as 后丨 Queen Earth; a spot, a place; a territory; grounds; a space; terrestrial, earthy; in the ground; the bottom, the support of; only, but, merely.

丨下 on the ground.

大丨 the whole world, the empire.

丨面 or 丨方 a place, the locality, the region; a spot referred to.

丨脚堅固 the ground is firm; his friends are influential; the firm is sound.

丨保 or 丨防 or 丨方 constables, police-men, headmen.

丨主 a landlord; god of a spot, his shrine is usually in the hall.

丨租 ground rent.

他有丨 he is a man of substance.

心丨 the disposition.

丨皮兒是太緊 the times are very hard, the market is tight.

本丨人 a native of a place or country.

落丨 to fall to the ground.

丨利 productions, produce.

金丨 a gilt ground in lackerware.

餘丨 vacant ground; a resource; a character or principle.

丨瓜 or 丨蛋 sweet potatoes.

暗丨 a dark room or spot; in secret, *sub rosâ*.

人丨相宜 the man and the spot agree, he is familiar with the place.

好丨位 a good locality or situation.

未到他的丨步 I have not attained his skill (or standing.)

心懸兩丨 his thoughts wander, his mind is not on the subject.

丨理 geography.

In *Cantonese* often written 哋. A sign of the plural of persons; used for 的 as a sign of the possessive; also read ˏti an adjective denoting a little of, rather, a diminutive.

我丨 mine; ours.

中中丨 ordinary, poor quality.

佢丨錢 his money.

好得ˏ丨 a little better.

送ˏ丨點 give me a little more.

快ˏ丨行 go quicker, hurry!

柢 ti˒ The root of a tree or the part of the trunk near the ground; the bole; root, origin, foundation.

深根固丨 a firm and deep set root.

棣 ti˒ A white crab or small apple, larger than a cherry, but there is much discrepancy in the descriptions of the plant; the 唐丨 is evidently a sort of plum, and is known as 丨李; it is common in Shensi; there is also another sort described like a wild cherry.

丨棠花 a yellow flower like the *Spiræa* in form; probably a *Kerria* or *Corchorus*.

Read *tai*.˒ Mannerly, polished, elegant.

威儀丨丨 a grave and highly decorous deportment.

泜 ti˒ Name of a stream in Linch'ing hien 臨城縣 in the southwest of Chihli.

弟 ti˒ The ancient form represents a strap rising by degrees as it is wound around a stick; used with the next, and as a primitive interchanged with ˏi 夷 ample.

A younger brother; to act as becomes a younger brother; cousins; relatives; a junior, a friend; easy.

内兄丨 my wife's brothers.

外兄丨 sons of a mother's brother.

你丨兄幾個 how many brothers have you?

令丨 your younger brother.

舍丨 my younger brother.

丨子 a pupil.

愚丨 or 小丨 your unworthy friend, your humble servant.

亚丨 a boy, a lad; my boy!

出則丨 when in active life, fail not to act the part of a younger brother.

不丨 disrespectful to superiors.

異母丨 half blood relatives.

作兄丨 to act like a brother.

齊子豈丨 the daughter of Tsi is happy and unconcerned.

悌 t'i˒ From *heart* and *brother*, to indicate the feeling; used with the preceding.

To act as a younger brother; respectful brotherly; indifferent to.

慈祥愷丨身之德也 courtesy and respect are virtues honorable to all.

第 ti˒ From *bamboo* and a *strap* screwing around and ascending; it is often contracted to ˏt'i 苐 a grass.

A series, an order, a class, a gradation; to grade; a consecutive rank or place; to make or arrange in a series; placed before figures it forms the ordinal numbers; a literary degree; a mansion, a house; a *conjunction*, but, yet, also an *adverb*, merely, however.

丨一 number one, the first
次丨 a regular order.
丨一好 the best.
丨幾號 which number is it?
丨二處 or 丨處 another place.
宅丨 an officer's house; a fine mansion.
得丨 he has got a higher grade.
不丨 not graduated higher.
及丨 attained to the degree, as of
甲丨 a Hanlin doctor.
賜丨 to confer a house on a deserving officer.
落丨 failed in getting the degree.
潭丨凝庥 a fine spacious establishment.
詩書門丨 the literary profession.
不丨如此 not merely this way.

In *Shanghai*. A demonstrative *pronoun*, this, that.
丨個 this.
丨頭好跑 is it good walking here.
丨塊 this place.
丨邊 this side.

遰 *ti'* To go off, to migrate; to leave; a knife-case.
鴻鴈丨 the wild geese have gone south.

鬀 鬄 *ti'* From *hair* and *also* or to *change*.
Hair falling over the shoulders, disheveled or unbound; women's false hair; to shave.
不屑丨也 do not desire false hair; — you have enough.
斂髮毋丨 bind up the locks and do not let them fall negligently.

螮 蝃 *ti'* From *insect* and *girdle* or to *connect*; the first read *t'ai'* means also a snake; and the second read *choh*, also means a spider.
The rainbow, supposed to be formed of small ephemeræ generated in the ether, which
天地淫氣之所致 heaven and earth's noxious vapors produce.
丨蝀在東莫之敢指 when the rainbow is in the east, nobody ventures to point the finger to it, — lest a boil grow.

嚏 𪖐 *t'i'* A sneeze; a running at the nose.
鼻丨 snivel.
一連打了好幾個丨噴必定有人說我 somebody is talking of me, for I have been sneezing many times.

軑 軚 軟 *ti'* From *cart* and *great* or *dog*; the first form only is authorized, but the other two are met with.
The linch-pin in an axle; to put in the pin; in Tso, a wheel was once so called.
齊王丨而並馳也 the king of Tsi put in his linch-pin, and the chariots raced off together.

Read *tai'* A district in the Han dynasty near the present Wu-chang in Hupeh; the marquis of Tai 丨侯 was the title of the king's son.

杕 *ti'* From *wood* and *great*; occurs used for *to'* 舵 a scull.
Standing alone, like a fine tree; distinguished, eminent; flourishing.
有丨之杜生于道左 there was a single spindle-tree growing on the left of the road.

釱 *ti'* Fetters of iron; to fetter.
煑鹽者丨左趾 those who [illegally] made salt were fettered on the left leg.

娣 *ti'* From *woman* and *brother*.
A younger sister; a bridesmaid.
丨婦 a younger brother's wife.
丨仔 or 亞丨 a waiting boy; a lad. (*Cantonese*.)
丨姒 brothers' wives, both older and younger.
家生丨 a slave-girl born in the house.
諸丨從之 all the maidens followed her; — *i. e.* the bride.

珶 *ti'* A piece of whitish jade, once worn on the girdle as a symbol of sincerity.

睇 䏲 *ti'* From *eye* and *brother* or *is*; the second form is seldom used.
To gaze at, to stare, to look at boldly and disrespectfully.
不敢丨視 do not presume to stare at him.
丨而弗識 to look at without recognizing, to cut.
旣含丨兮又宜笑 Ah! how furtively she glanced, and then smiled!

In *Cantonese* read *ʿtei*. To keep watch of, to lookout for; to suppose, to deem, to see, to look.
我丨得有 I think there are some; I guess it is so.
丨更 to watch, as a watchman.
丨慣 used to it; I've seen such things before.
俾人丨笑 you'll make people laugh at you.
丨銀 to shroff money.
丨過 I've seen it.
丨仔細 look carefully after it.
丨頭丨尾 I've seen that all is right.
眼丨丨 not taking his eyes off, staring at.

帝 *ti'* Said to be formed of 丄 (an old form of 上) *above* and 朿 to *pierce*; but its composition is obscure.
To judge, for which the next is now used; one who rules by his own power, a god, a divine being; one writer, says 丨者生物之主 *ti'* is a lord of living things; an audacious designation of him who rules the world, *i. e.* China; of one whose virtue, being like that of heaven and earth, is made their vicegerent among men; — *ergo*, a sovereign, a potentate or autocrat, an emperor, of whom the world can properly only have one; Heaven; the Taoists apply it to heroes and genii; a deity supreme in one department or endowed with a peculiar attribute; as 關丨 or 武丨 the god of War; 文昌丨 the god of Letters; and 炎丨 or 華丨 the god of Fire.

上丨 the Supreme Ruler, the highest being in the heavenly pantheon, and now worshiped by the emperor alone, as the source of his vicegerent power; he is known by other names, as 皇皇上丨 the highest august Shangti; 天丨 the heavenly Ruler; 天皇上丨 heavenly august Shangti; and 昊天上丨 bright heavenly Shangti; the Rationalists have degraded the term by making many Shangti, among whom 玉皇上丨 the perfect august Shangti, whose throne is supposed to be in the Dipper; 玄天上丨 the somber heavens Shangti, and 協天上丨 helping heaven Shangti (Kwanti), are much worshiped; these have almost wholly taken the place of the ancient divinity in the minds of the common people in China.*

上丨天也 Shangti is Heaven.

* There are strong reasons for the inference that the early sovereigns of the Chinese worshiped the spirits of their deified ancestors under this term, to whom they looked for help; one 上丨 was sufficient for the guardian of the empire, and continued on from one dynasty to another, whatever family was deputed to hold the throne, and unlimited dignity and powers were ascribed to him while the monarch holding the seat would include in his devotions and sacrifices all his predecessors whose spiritual favor he desired. The idea therefore involves many monarchs who have been deified, and as the guardians of the throne they once occupied, they have been and are still all supplicated for their spiritual aid by its actual incumbent down to this day.

To understand many passages in the Books of Odes and Records, they need to be read with this understanding, and no other so well explains them. See especially the Odes called 文王 and 皇矣 in the Shi King, and the Chapter 湯誥 in the Shu King. It is doubtless true that the radical idea of 帝 is a ruler of the highest kind, but there is not that proof that the designation 上丨 ever denoted the true God, which is required to enable one to use it for Jehovah in teaching Christian truth to the Chinese without great risk of serious error.

丨王 the sovereign and 丨后 his queen.

皇丨 the emperor.

五丨 the five elected rulers before Yü the Great, B.C. 2597–2255; also five gods of the Rationalists which rule the four quarters and the zenith.

丨星 the star β in Ursa Minor.

胡然而丨也 how strikingly beautiful she is!

丨子 a class of beings like angels or created spirits; genii.

諦 ti' From *words* and *autocrat* as the phonetic.

To judge, to examine into; to fix the mind on; to decide between.

審丨 to inquire into a case.

微丨 careful attention.

四丨 the four truths (*arya satyani*) which must be mastered by all converts to Budhism.

丨毫末者不見天地之大 though he can investigate small subjects, he has not a wide reach of mind.

禘 ti' From *worship* and *autocrat* as the phonetic.

The religious ceremonies observed by the sovereign twice a year in honor of his ancestors and predecessors, both remote and near.

大丨 a great Imperial sacrifice offered once in five years; it was mixed with that of 上帝, and indicates that both were directed to the same objects, and partook of the ancestral worship.

丨始帝舜 the royal sacrifice originated with Shun.

渧 ti' To run by drops; a drop of water.

丨哭 crying and weeping.

丨下水來 to run drop by drop.

一毛一丨一沙一塵 a hair, a drop, a sand, an atom of dust, — Budhist metaphors for minute objects.

締 ti' An indissoluble knot; bound so as not to be loosed; closely joined.

丨結 betrothed, engaged.

丨交 closely allied, as friends; bound closely.

氣繚轉而自丨 the smoke curled upwards wreathing itself into knots.

蒂 ti' From *plant* and *autocrat*; it is also interchanged with tai' 蔕 in this sense, and the dictionaries uphold the latter, but this has supplanted it.

The peduncle or footstalk of a flower or fruit; the persistent calyx, as of brinjal or persimmon; stem of a melon; a root, a stem; baseless, unfounded.

花丨 a flower-stalk; the leafy calyx.

並丨蓮 a lotus where two stems have united.

丨盤 the receptacle of the flower and calyx; it usually includes the green calyx.

上無所丨 nothing to support above.

瓜熟則丨落 when the melon is ripe the calyx falls; applied to a birth.

蔕 ti' High, exalted; the highest or best of; tired out, weary of.

高丨 lofty.

極丨 the extreme of.

Read *chai'* A stout thorn 丨芥; whence the simile 曾不丨芥 I have not offended a hair's breadth.

遞 逓 ti' From *to go* and a screaming *tiger*, contracted to the second form; it is also read *tai'* to encompass around.

To transmit, to send on, to convey from hand to hand; to hand in, as reports are given to a superior; to exchange, to alternate; a *preposition*, for, instead of.

傳丨 to send, as by post; to transmit intelligence; traditional, handed down.

丨稟 to petition for another.

丨年 next year.
煩你丨傳 may I trouble you to send this for me.
迢丨難追 it will not be easy to catch him so far off.
丨起脚 to change the legs over.
丨代 substituted for, instead of; takes the place of.
丨迭 to exchange.
長丨 gone a long way, — and not returned.
丨到 or 丨至 send; has been sent.
丨相往還 alternating, changing about.
丨更 to change, as the seasons; to pass from one to another.
丨給我 hand it to me; bring it here.

T'I.

Old sounds, t'ai, dai, t'at, *and* dat. *In Canton*, t'ei; — *in Swatow*, t'i, ti, *and* t'ui; — *in Amoy*, t'é, té, t'i, *and* i; — *in Fuhchau*, t'i, tè, t'è, t'é, *and* t'ai; — *in Shanghai*, t'i *and* di; — *in Chifu*, t'i.

梯 ꜀t'i From *wood* and *brother* as the phonetic.

A ladder; movable steps; stairs; the steps of a stair; a means to reach an end; to recline against; to scale, to mount.
一都樓丨 a flight of stairs.
樓丨房 a closet under the stairs.
樓丨口 the opening of the stairs.
丨子 a ladder.
板丨 or 香丨 a step-ladder.
輭丨 a rope-ladder, scaling-ladder.
天丨 a ladder leading to the roof.
丨橃 or 丨子檔 the rungs or boards of the ladder.
上雲丨 to ascend the cloudy ladder; — to become a Hanlin.
蜈蚣丨子 a ladder of one rope with rundles.
毋虐民以爲亂丨 don't oppress the people and give them cause for revolt.
上屋徹丨 to leave one in the lurch.
丨几深思 he leaned on the stand in deep thought.
丨城爬入 they scaled the walls and scrambled into the town.

膊 ꜀t'i A bent bone; a wry nose.
連丨 the spleen of a hog.
膈丨 a crooked nose.

鷉 ꜀t'i A species of grebe called 鷿丨; it has a whitish, streaked plumage, very fat, and rather smaller than the common wild duck; its legs are placed so far behind that it walks with difficulty.

苐 ꜀t'i From *plant* and to *wreath* around; it is often used as a contraction of ꜀ti 第 a series.

Name of a grassy plant.

稊 / **稗** ꜀t'i Tares found among rice or wheat; it is a species of panic grass, not at all like darnel; weeds, cockles, tares.
丨米在田亂生混目 when the tares are in the field and growing together, it bewilders the eyes to distinguish them.
丨稗 a panic grass cultivated in Chihli for its grain.

荑 ꜀t'i Interchanged with the last.

Sprouts or suckers; tares; leaves opening out; plants starting; a whitish grass resembling panicled millet.
手如柔丨 her hands were like the soft white grass.

Read ꜀i. To cut down grass; to root up weeds.
芟丨 to cut up grass and weeds.

綈 ꜀t'i Greenish, thick plain pongee, suitable for robes or skirts, and given as presents.
丨袍 a silk robe.
身衣弋丨 he was clad in dark silk.

罤 ꜀t'i A net for entrapping rabbits, which was made by a bow that sprung and caught them by the leg.
丨中之兎不復獮猭兮 alas for the hare in the trap, it will jump no more!

鵜 / **鶘** ꜀t'i The pelican found along the Chinese coast.
丨鶘候魚無獵食騷人共目信天翁 the pelican waits for the fish, never hunting for his food, whence bards have called him the old man who trusts in Heaven.

Read ꜀i, for the second. A pheasant.
丨鶘 an unusual name for the flying squirrel.

提 ꜀t'i From *hand* and *is*; occurs used with the next.

To lift or take in one hand; to hold, to raise, to carry; to bring into notice, to suggest, to bring to mind, to bring forward; to attend to; to bring before a magistrate; a kettle drum used on horseback; a Budhist syllable, as in 丨婆 for *deva*, the gods of the Brahmins; unconcerned.
丨及 to speak of, to refer to.
丨起 to bring to notice or mind; to suggest.
丨拔 to raise up, to promote.
丨升 to advance.
丨携 to take up in the arms, to carry; to nourish, to help on.
丨攝精神 to rouse to action, to reinvigorate the energies.
丨水 to carry [a pitcher] of water.
丨防 to watch against.
丨塘 a courier of the government.
丨醒 to bring to mind.
丨牢廳 keeper in the Board of Punishments.

好人丨丨 this wealthy person moves about at ease.

丨刑 a provincial judge.

丨督 a major-general, marshal, or captain-general; the highest military grade.

丨調 a proctor or manager of colleges; the overseer of candidates at examinations; he also has the general care of the chancellor's yamun, and marks off the names.

丨撕警覺 to bring forcibly to notice.

面命耳丨 to give orders personally with authority.

丨鞋 to pull up the heel of the shoe.

招丨 the location of a dagoba.

Read ˏshi. To collect, to flock together.

歸飛丨丨 [the crows] come flocking back.

題 ˏt'i The forehead, the front or head; conspicuous; the title or argument of a book; a subject for writing upon, a theme, a proposition; an inscription; to compose, to write; used for the last, to notice, to discuss, to bring forward; to praise; to subscribe; to do or attempt; to look at.

丨詩 to compose verses.

丨額 or 丨匾 the inscription on a tablet.

大丨目 an important matter, an urgent order from high officers to attend to a thing.

破丨 the exordium or argument of an essay; it must be only two sentences, and is followed by the 承丨 or enforcement; there are other terms of this kind in rhetoric, as 出丨 to repeat the theme; 長丨 a long text; and 文不對丨 it contradicts the theme.

小丨大作 to make too much of a little matter.

丨醒我 he has aroused me.

書丨 the name or purport of a book; a text or theme.

不消丨 or 不丨出口 be silent, don't say anything about it; don't let a word drop.

丨簽 the title printed on a book.

難丨目 an undertaking hard to do, a difficult job.

一經品丨便作佳士 they then discussed his merits, showing him to be an excellent person.

休丨起 say no more, let the matter drop.

你先丨個頭 do you broach the matter, or speak of it.

丨頭 to prompt, as one repeating a lesson.

雕丨交趾 the tattooed-forehead Annamese, who anciently marked their brows with colors.

蝭 ˏt'i An insect.

丨蟧 or 丨蟟 a light colored, small cicada, common in the north of China.

Read ˏshi. A bird, the 丨蛙 or night jar.

禔 ˏt'i From *worship* and *is*; also read ˏshi, and used for ˏchi 祗 but.

Rest, repose; at peace, in accord with; happiness.

丨福 great happiness.

丨躬 in full health and prosperity.

丨取辱 I got nothing but disgrace.

醍 ˏt'i From *spirits* and *is*.

Reddish, but pure clear liquor; the essential oil of milk or elaine, a liquid refined from butter.

粢丨在堂 the rich wine is on the buffet.

丨醐 an unctuous rich liquor skimmed from boiled butter or ghee; *met.* the beneficent mildness of Budha.

媞 ˏt'i At ease; name of a *woman*.

丨丨 beautiful, winning as Si Shi 西施 the beauty of Wu in olden time.

Read ˏchi. An old term for mother in Nganhwui.

騠 ˏt'i A frisking, fine horse.

駃丨 a swift-footed palfrey.

丨茲 an ancient place in the Han dynasty, situated in the east of Shantung.

鶗 ˏt'i Also read ˏshi.

A bird of the accipitrine order, which is thought in spring to turn into a dove.

啼 嗁 ˏt'i From *mouth* and *sovereign* or *tiger*; it is also written other ways, but differs from shi' 啻 only.

To howl and bewail; to lament, to cry; to crow; to caw; to coo and call; to scream, as an ape or parrot.

丨哭 to weep and moan.

鷄丨 a cock's crow.

鷄初丨 the third watch.

日夜悲丨 constantly wailing and mourning.

月落烏丨霜滿天 when the moon sets [near dawn] and the crows caw, the hoar-frost fills the air.

丨叫 the cries and calls of birds.

踶 ˏt'i From *foot* and *is*; occurs interchanged with the next.

To tread on; to step; to kick.

分背相丨 [angry horses] turn back to back and kick each other.

丨跂爲義 exhort him to be just; to urge one to practice uprightness.

奔丨 to gallop.

蹄 蹏 ˏt'i A hoof, solid or cleft, either of horses or oxen; a horse; a trap to catch hares; to kick; a leg of pork or mutton.

丨角 hoofs and horns, *i. e.* horses and cattle.

猪丨 pig's feet or pettitoes.

牛丨子八瓣子 the four hoofs of an ox have eight phalanges—but they are so matched they cannot unite; *i. e.* we seem to be unable to agree upon this matter.

得意春風快馬丨 in the joyous spring weather one likes to gallop his horse.

大沙丨 elephantiasis. (*Cantonese.*)

赫丨 a variety of red paper very thin and strong

七星丨 a seven spotted [pig's] leg; — women often eat it to increase their milk.

獸丨鳥跡之道交於中國 the paths made by the tracks of animals and steps of birds crossed one another over the whole land.

羊丨草 the dock (*Rumex*), used as a vermifuge.

鴨捺丨 a sprawling duck's foot; *i. e.* a poor man who never wears shoes. (*Cantonese.*)

馬二百丨 horses two hundred hoofs; — *i. e.* fifty horse.

鯑 ꜀t'i A newt or water lizard; an eft; the name is applied to a large carp in some books.

鏣 ꜀t'i A vessel used in making spirits; a sort of boiler.

霋 ꜀t'i The clouds breaking and the rain ceasing; fair weather.

鮧 鯷 ꜀t'i These two characters are synonyms in the Pǎn Ts'ao, but they are badly described; a common name for the mudfish or silure, of which many species exist, and probably this denotes the broadheaded bull-heads (*Bagrus*, *Silurus* and *Pimelodus*); caps are said to be made from their skins, which perhaps led to the Chusan islanders being called 東丨人 in the Han dynasty.

體 ꜁t'i From *bone* and sacrificial *vessel;* it is constantly contracted to 体 so that the proper sound *p'ăn*꜄ of that form is almost lost.

The body; a frame consisting of many parts; the whole person; a solid, a cube or other solid body; a class, a body of officers; the important, real parts of, the essentials; the substance, the capacity, which is shown by 用 use or emanation; becoming, respectable, decorous, influential; to embody, to realize, to represent in action the views and orders of a superior; to partition; fully formed, said of plants; a response to a sortilege; completeness; attracted, related to, joined; to receive courteously; a style for writing Chinese characters, of which there are six.

大丨面 having a great reputation; honored and dignified.

一丨 the whole, all concerned; in accord.

禮丨 courtesy, politeness.

四丨 the four limbs.

全丨 or 百丨 the entire organization; the body complete.

識大丨 to understand the highest principles of propriety.

失丨 impolite, rude.

好丨裁 elegant, fine-limbed.

丨恤 to befriend.

夫婦一丨 husband and wife are one flesh.

文武二丨 two classes of civil and military officers.

丨局 the general look, the effect.

不合丨式 inelegant, as a bad style; unusual or outré, as the dress of a clown.

貴丨違和 I fear your good self is indisposed.

形丨 the frame, the aspect and body of.

身丨平安 enjoying bodily health.

聖丨 the Emperor's person; also used by some for the Eucharist.

一篇之丨要 a resumé of the whole work.

就賢丨遠 assimilate to the virtuous, and you will have a love for those who are distant.

丨國經野 to apportion out the state and mark off the territory — to feudal princes.

丨貼人心 willing to help another; sympathizing.

丨統 decorous, befitting.

替 t'i꜄ From 竝 or 並 *together* contracted, and 白 *white* altered.

To abolish, to reject, to set aside; to substitute, to change for; to supersede; to wait, to stop; to intermit; for, instead of, in place of; a sign of the dative.

我丨你去 I will go for you.

丨身 a substitute.

丨工 one who takes another's work.

丨他說 speak to him.

世襲罔丨 hereditary titles are not abrogated.

丨死鬼 a criminal's substitute.

無丨 without change, no abrogation.

丨換 to change or rotate.

屜 屧 t'i꜄ Anything that intervenes or fends off; a buffer.

鞍丨子 a saddle-cloth.

抽丨 the drawer of a table.

紗丨 gauze over a window.

籠丨 a bamboo steaming-frame on which cakes are laid to cook.

駱駝丨 a rug of camel's hair.

涕 洟 鼻弟 t'i꜄ From *water* and *brother;* the other two forms are unusual.

Tears; the water from the eyes; to weep; the second is also read ꜀i, and more properly means snivel, mucus; but the two are much interchanged.

泣丨如雨 to weep bitterly.

鼻丨 running from the nose.

丨零 sorrowful tears.

剃 鬀 t'i꜄ From *knife* or *hair* and *brother;* the second form is seldom used.

To shave.

丨頭 to shave the head.

丨得乾淨 shaved smooth

丨頭的 or 丨頭佬 a barber. (*Cantonese.*)

丨鬚 or 丨髯 to shave the beard.

丨髮修行 to shave and turn priest.

丨眉 to trim or dress the eyebrows.

薙 t'í — Considered to be wrongly used for the last.

To shave a child's head; to root up grass, to weed out completely.

燒 丨 burn [the underbrush] and eradicate the grass, — before planting.

芟 丨 to clear off the weeds.

楴 t'í — An old name for a long, round hair-pin, which women used to coil their hair on, and to scratch the head when dressing it; it may have been like that still used by the women of Lewchew.

佩其象 丨 she hung her ivory hair-pin on her girdle.

揥 t'í — Used for the last; also read *ch'í* and *t'ih*,

To go away, to leave; to put away; a comb-pin; to play, to point at.

意徘徊而不 丨 he thought of walking about, and not at all of leaving; — he did not wish to leave the service.

TIAO.

Old sounds, tio, dio, tau, tok, tot, *and* dok. *In Canton*, tiu; — *in Swatow*, tiò, t'iò, tⁿié, *and* chau; — *in Amoy*, tiau, t'iau, *and* tsau; — *in Fuhchau*, tiu, t'iu, *and* chau; — *in Shanghai*, tio *and* dio; — *in Chifu*, tiao.

琱 ꜀tiao — Like the next, and interchanged with it.

To engrave gems, to work jade and other stones; to ornament and carve; a sort of fine, gem-like stone.

雕 㓮 彫 ꜀tiao — From *knife*, *bird*, or *pelage*, and *around*; the first is also a synonym of 鵰 and the others are interchanged with the next.

To engrave, to cut figures on, to carve and adorn; to polish, as when finishing off a composition; to tattoo; ornamented, engraved.

丨 花 to carve figures or pictures.

丨 刻 to engrave, as blocks.

峻宇 丨 牆 the wall of the great hall was adorned with carvings.

丨 工 carvers.

必使玉人 丨 琢之 you must employ a carver to work the gem.

凋 ꜀tiao — From *ice* and *all around*; it is interchanged with the last.

To be exhausted; injured and lost its vitality; fading; falling, as the old leaves.

丨 卸 or 丨 落 fallen, as blossoms; withered, as the leaves in autumn.

枝葉不 丨 the foliage does not wither; evergreen.

爲 丨 爲 瘵 he is debilitated and enervated.

丨 零 the leaves are scattered.

早 丨 to fade early.

鵰 ꜀tiao — From *bird* and *all around*.

The great sea-eagle, a large and fierce bird of prey, called 皂 丨 plumage yellowish, and whose plumes seen on the ground are enough to make other birds cast their feathers; the name is also applied to the Mongolian *barkut* or bearcoot, the *Aquila albicella*.

丨 翎 eagle plumes; — a name for an arrow.

丨 扇 a fan of eagle's feathers.

一矢貫雙 丨 with one arrow he pierced two eagles.

丨 盼青雲倦眼開 the eagle gazes at the clear clouds and his weary eyes are refreshed.

碉 ꜀tiao — A stone house, usually called 石室, common in the western and northern provinces; they are rude structures.

丨 寨民房並倒 the stone houses, forts, and common dwellings all fell down, — from the earthquake.

貂 ꜀tiao — From a *reptile* and *to call*.

The Siberian sable (*Mustela zibelina*), of which several varieties are known; the finest are called 梭倫 丨 from the region of the Songari; the 芝麻 丨 is not so dark, and the tips of the long hairs are whitish; but not so white as the 白針 丨 which are longer, and give the fur a speckled hue.

紫 丨 undyed or reddish sable.

丨 尾 sables' tails, worn by military men.

狗尾續 丨 a dog's tail tacked on a sable; — incongruous, unfit.

丨 帽沿 a winter hat trimmed with sable.

太平 丨 a kind of thick, short, fine fur, like sea-otter skin.

刁 ꜀tiao — Said to be originally the same as 刀 *sword*, afterwards altered in the writing.

Perverse, recusant, seditious; cabaling, restless; unscrupulous and aggressive.

丨 風 depraved manners, truculent.

丨 筆 rabid writings.

丨 惡之至 outrageous and bad beyond endurance.

丨 斗 a soldier's cooking basin; it is sometimes used for beating the watches at night.

丨 蠻 barbarous and violent.

放 丨 dogged, unrepentant.

丨 乖 a knave, a perverse rascal.

丨 丨 gusty; wind coming in blasts.

逞 丨 dictatorial, overbearing.

丨 頑 spiteful but trifling.

叼 ꜀tiao — An unauthorized character, used for ꜀han 含 and probably altered from ꜀t'ao 叨 greedy.

To hold in the mouth; to suck, to seize.

狗 丨 一條骨 the dog bites a bone.

鷹 丨 肉 the hawk snaps the meat.

鳭 ꜀tiao The 丨鷯 seems to be allied to the 鷦鷯 or wren, but a larger bird, which gets the name of 剖葦 or reed splitter, from its cutting open reeds to get the insects; also 葦串 the rush winder, from its rapid motion from one stalk to another; it has a brown plumage, and the cock two or more black feathers rising from the eyes; it is perhaps akin to the ortolan or *Euspiza aureola*.

弴 ꜀tiao Also read ꜀tun.
An ornamented bow.
天子丨弓 the emperor's painted bow.

嬥 ꜀tiao Upright, trustworthy.
丨丨 going to and fro.
丨歌 local, barbarous ditties.
丨嬈 vicious, inhuman, ruthless.

Read ꜂t'iao. Slender waisted; handsome.

船
舠 ꜀tiao A boat.
客丨 a passage-boat, used on small rivers; it is shaped like a scow, blunt and wide, and carries 15 tons, or half a dozen men.
吳丨 boats of Kiangnan.

屌 ꜂tiao From *body* and *pendulous*.
The penis.

弔
吊 tiao꜄ Composed of 弓 a *bow* grasped by a 人 *man*, because the watchers of the dead shot at the birds which pecked them; only the second form is now usually applied to a string of cash.
To condole with mourners, to ask respecting the dead; to wail or otherwise assist at a burial; condolence; to compassionate others, to pity; to suspend, to hang; to lift up, as by a cord; to demand, to ask for; a thousand cash.
弗丨 not to mourn with others.
丨案 to order a rehearing; to revise a case.
丨生丨死 to feel for the living and lament the dead.
開丨 to perform the funeral rites before the burial; usually the previous day.
丨紙 to assist at a funeral; the friends often write 丨文 or monodies, which are burned.
丨起來 hang it up.
丨客 the ghost of a suicide.
丨頸 to hang by the neck.
丨桶 a well-bucket.
一丨錢 a string of cash, nominally a thousand; also a bank-bill representing the money.
丨驗 or 丨覈 to ask and verify, as a passport; to request an inquiry into, as records.
丨民 to lead on the people.
吉丨 a half fabulous, amphibious animal in southern China, having the body of a tortoise and a snake's head; it may denote a kind of mailed triton.

Read *tih*꜀ To reach to; to move; to get to the extreme; in good order.
神之丨矣 the gods have come! — speaking of the fumes of incense.
無敢不丨 be careful that none are not in order.

挒 tiao꜄ From *hand* and *suspended*; an unauthorized character, apparently altered from the last.
To take; to carry.
提心丨膽的 he took up his heart and carried away his gall; said of one in excessive fear.

佻 tiao꜄ Uncommon.
丨儻 unusual, not uniform or regular.

絩 tiao꜄ To hang up or suspend; to tie up any one with cords.
丨賊私刑 to tie up a thief and beat him one's self.

怮 tiao꜄ From *heart* and *ladle*.
Sorrowing, cast down.
憂丨 mournful.

釣 tiao꜄ From *metal* and *ladle*.
A hook, a fish-hook; to fish; to bait, to set a trap for; to use something as a means; to fish for, as praise; to seek.
其丨維何 what are used in angling?
丨魚 to angle.
沽名丨譽 to buy a reputation and fish for praise.
丨竿 a fish pole.
丨撻沙 to hook a sole-fish; *met.* to steal shoes. (*Cantonese.*)
他不上你丨 he don't take your hook; he'll not be gulled.
子丨而不綱 Confucius angled and did not use a net.
香餌丨金鰲 to hook a golden grampus with fragrant bait; — *met.* to swindle one, to inveigle.

杓 tiao꜄ The full, ripe ear of grain hanging down; to hang up.

䏚 tiao꜄ The boards of a bed; the bars which support them.
丨凳 benches for upholding bed-boards.

窕 t'ao꜄ From *cave* and a *prognostic*.
Secluded, reserved, elegant, refined.
輕丨 delicate.
窈丨 admirable, attractive; said of beautiful women, pleasing landscapes, or spacious mansions.

誂 tiao꜄ From *word* and an *omen*; occurs interchanged with 調꜄ tone.
To speak alluringly; to excite by dallying words, to tamper with in sport; to woo, to court; to seduce; suddenly.
丨弄 to lewdly play with.
丨戲 to entice to lewdness.
丨姦 fornication.
聲音噭丨 the chords harmonize; clear, accordant sounds.
雖丨合刃于天下 if the two armies suddenly join battle in the empire, — who will dare to lead them?

窵 From *cave* and *bird;* alluding to their mode of concealing nests.

tiao' Deep; to go far into a recess.

丨窅 dark and deep, cavernous.

離城丨遠者 one who lives very remote from the city, — and is inconvenient to reach.

丨角 a secluded spot, out of the way and hard to find.

丨窕 far off; to penetrate far into.

谷丨不可測 the cavernous recess cannot be explored.

In *Shanghai*, altered in sound from 鳥. A bird.

丨窠 a bird's nest.

丨籠 a bird's cage.

裑 Short clothes.

tiao' 丨衣待戰 short garments are the best for fighting in.

掉 From *hand* and to *exceed;* occurs incorrectly used for *chao'* 棹 to row and 調' to change.

tiao' To move, to shake; to clash or strike against; to change, to interchange; correctly placed; to adjust; to row; to change; occurs used as an auxiliary verb following another, as 殺丨 to kill; 滅丨 to exterminate.

心裏有點丨動 I have thought of a wise step or a nice plan.

丨磬 to strike stones together; *met.* people's opinions clashing.

丨脾 obstinate, perverse. (*Shanghai.*)

丨舌 to speak thick or with an impediment.

丨臂 to brace the arms, to stand defiantly.

反丨 an indirect argument; to prove by indirect means.

丨尾 to wag the tail.

Read *'t'iao.* To joggle.

丨動 to shake, as a table.

In *Pekingese.* To fall into or down; fell down, slipped off and fell; to shake off; to come off, to part.

丨在地下拾起來 it has fallen on the ground, pick it up.

天上丨下來的 it fell down from the sky.

心中丨不下 I certainly shall not forget it.

丨過胎 cast her young.

去丨身上的泥 shake the dirt off from yourself.

丨猴 a slippery fellow, one who will play a trick on you.

銚 An unauthorized character.

tiao' Black-glazed earthen jars, made at Canton; they are usually without ears.

水丨 a water-jar.

T'IAO.

Old sounds, t'io, dio, t'au, t'ok, *and* dok. *In Canton,* t'iu *and* tiu; — *in Swatow,* t'iò, tiò, t'ié, *and* siò; — *in Amoy,* t'iau, tiau, *and* siau; — *in Fuhchau,* t'iu, tiu, téu, *and* siu; — *in Shanghai,* t'io *and* dio; — *in Chifu,* t'iao.

挑 From *hand* and *omen;* it is interchanged with 調' to change.

ˏt'iao To lift, to carry on the shoulder, or sometimes by a beam; to mix, to stir about; a load, or what one can carry on the shoulder; sprightly, lightly, quickly.

担丨 to carry a burden as a porter 丨夫 does, slung on a pole across his shoulder.

丨唆 to make mischief, to set at variance.

丨開 to open, as a boil; to clear out, as a channel; to put aside, to scatter.

丨兮達兮 how volatile, how unsteady!

一丨子菜 the whole load of vegetables.

肩丨貿易 to peddle, to hawk; a huckster.

丨不起 too heavy to carry.

丨燈 raise up the wick.

丨引 to lead into evil.

丨攀線 scratch-cradle.

丨水的 a water-carrier.

丨剔 to cavil at, to find fault without cause.

Read *ˏt'iao.* To provoke, to irritate; to jeer or play with, to act triflingly; to take away; to pick up, as a dress floating off; to pick out; to select, to choose.

丨秀女 to select Manchu girls for the hareem.

大丨一等 the great decennial selection of graduates for district magistrates.

丨選 or 丨揀 to pick out.

不丨換 in changing this bill, there can be no choice of particular banks; — a notice on bank bills in Peking.

丨動 to disturb; to excite suspicion; to sow strife.

丨事 to embroil.

丨不起 there is not one fit to select.

丨戰 to challenge to battle, to provoke a fight.

丨好的 pick a good one.

沒人丨撥我 nobody has shown me how to do it.

In *Cantonese.* To baste, to sew in an edge.

丨衫骨 to sew clothes.

丨花 to embroider.

剕 To cut open; to cut.

ˏt'iao 丨破了癤子 to open a boil.

丨足筋 to hamstring; it is sometimes illegally done to criminals.

佻 ꜀t'iao Weakly, young; going unsteadily, as if wary of the path; envious; impatient of labor.

丨僥成風 their manners and usages are loose and impudent.
丨天之功 to assume the merit of Heaven.
丨丨公子行彼周行 the elegant gentlemen travel that road to Cheu.

Read tiao' To provoke; to regard lightly, to disregard.
惡'其丨巧 I dislike his contemptuous way of depreciating others.

Read ꜁yao, and used for 徭 a vassal. Slow, dilatory.

祧 ꜀t'iao From *worship* and *omen*. To move or replace the family tablets; the earliest ancestral shrine, the founders of the race.

宗丨 an ancestral hall; *met.* an estate, a patrimony.
遠廟爲丨 the far off shrines [of the chief] are our founders.
守丨 to guard the lares; name of an ancient office.
一子雙丨 a son who inherits two estates.

朓 ꜀t'iao From *flesh* and *omen*. To offer flesh at a sacrifice; the flesh thus offered.

Read ꜁yao. Good.

銚 ꜀t'iao From *metal* and *omen*; also read ꜁yao and ꜁ts'iao. To burn, as in a kiln; a pan with a handle and spout; a warming ladle; a bill-hook or scythe; a mattock; a spear.

長丨利兵 long spears and sharp military weapons.
丨銳 a ladle; a warming griddle.

恌 ꜀t'iao Mournful; to despise, to be mean to; to have little kindness for.

視民不丨 do not look down upon the people with contempt.

庣 ꜀t'iao A place that is not full; a sinus, a cavity.

調 ꜁t'iao tiao' From *words* and *all around*. To harmonize, to blend; to restore the peace, to adjust; to mix or compound; to tame; to temper, to regulate, to moderate; to intrigue, to induce; to tune; to try a note on an instrument; to find the tone of a character; to spell; to combine initials and finals according to tone, as the Chinese manner is.

丨音 to harmonize, to put in good tune.
丨味 to spice, to season nicely.
丨羹 a spoon; to season soups.
丨理 or 丨養 to nurse one's health.
丨笑 to laugh at.
丨處 to revise and rearrange an affair.
勿入丨 inharmonious; a troublesome, peevish person. (*Shanghai.*)
丨字聲 to find the right note or tone.
丨濟 to assist, to speak in favor of.
丨絃 to tune the strings.
琴瑟不丨 the lute and lyre do not chord; *met.* domestic discord.
丨戲 to insult a female; lewd dalliance.
丨諧音丨' to harmonize the musical chords.
丨伏 to moderate and subdue the passions; — a Budhist term for *vinaya*, or the division of Budhist dogma referring to the discipline and organization of the sect.

Read tiao' A tune, a song; a ballad; to move, to transfer, to station; used for ꜁挑 to seek; to select.
一枝丨 a tune.
曲子腔丨 a ballad in a certain tune.
丨換 to transpose, to exchange.
丨轉 to change about; to put end for end.
丨兵 to station troops.
丨用 to remove an officer to another post.
多丨度 many alterations and changes, never satisfied.
丨上丨下 put this higher and bring that down.
才丨 clever, capable.
降丨 to appoint to a lower office.
唱小丨 to sing street songs.

In *Cantonese*. A classifier of a meal and a beating.
打丨佢 he gave him a thrashing.
食丨工 I had a good meal.

蜩 ꜁t'iao A cicada or katydid, that chirps in July; another name 秋涼兒 refers to its din in autumn.

丨甲 the exuvia of the cicada.
丨螻偃蹇 to roll the head from side to side, as when suffering pain.
鳴丨嘒嘒 the chirping cicadas cry *wi wi*.
如丨如螗 [country all in confusion] like the din of cicadas and grasshoppers.
五月鳴丨 the broad locusts are heard in July.

條 ꜁t'iao From 木 *wood* and 攸 *hanging*. A branch, a twig; an old name for the pumelo tree; anything long and slender; to prolong; a classifier of long slender things, as a river, a chain, a string, a towel, a snake, a worm, a rainbow, a feather; also of a bill, an item, an article, a section or a law; a manner; to strip a twig of leaves.

髮丨 the hair-spring or main-spring of a watch.
一丨手巾 a handkerchief.
丨桑 to strip the mulberry of its leaves.
丨丨有理 every sort of thing, or every section, has its rules.
規丨 bye-laws, or the several rules of a thing.
上丨陳 sent up a lucid statement — to the Throne.
隔幾丨街 only a few streets off.

一丨題目 one thesis; a topic.

天丨 moral principles; natural, reasonable rules.

丨風 the northeast wind.

丨丨 thrown into disorder, no regularity.

丨例 rules for procedure.

不丨達 this item (or these portions) is not well explained.

In *Pekingese*. A rectangle; oblong.

一丨兒紙 a strip of paper.

鰷 鯈 ˏt'iao From *fish* and *slender*; the second is also read ˏyiu, explained by one author to mean a dark color.

Small white fish, like dace; long narrow fish such as the *Trichiurus* or *Thryssa*, called 白丨魚; many sorts are common along the coast of China.

丨魚出游 the white minnows sport on the water.

鞗 ˏt'iao From 革 *leather* and 條 *a strip* contracted.

The reins of a bridle.

丨革沖沖 the reins are amply long.

鯛 ˏt'iao A general name for hard spinous fishes like the perch; also applied to the sturgeon's nose, with its india-rubber like flesh.

苕 芀 ˏt'iao Clover, or a small leguminous plant (*Lathyrus?*) like a pea.

陵丨 a marshy plant, called 鼠尾 or rat's tail, whose leaves furnish a black dye, and when boiled will blacken the hair; it is perhaps a *Bignonia*.

饒丨 a kind of leguminous plant.

丨丨 high, tall, like a spindling reed.

邛有旨丨 along the bank grows the pretty pea.

丨之華芸其黃矣 the *Bignonia* flowers are deep yellow.

笤 ˏt'iao Like the last.

A broom made of reeds; divining-blocks made of bamboo roots.

丨帚 a broom made of the sorghum top; a coarse besom.

扨丨 or 打丨 or 擲丨 to throw the divining-blocks, as is done in the temples.

岧 ˏt'iao A lofty peak.

丨嶤之山亭亭獨立 how grand and lonely the lofty peak stands out!

迢 ˏt'iao From to *go* and to *call*.

Far off, remote; cut off from constant intercourse.

丨遙 remote.

路途丨遠 the journey is very long.

千里丨丨 a thousand miles off.

髫 ˏt'iao The tuft of hair on children's heads; ringlets.

丨齡 or 丨年 young, under six or seven years.

丨髮厲志 precocious in his energy and wisdom.

齠 ˏt'iao To shed the teeth; young, childish.

未逾丨齔 before I had shed my teeth.

尚在丨年乳猶臭 you still have your first teeth, and the smell of milk is in your mouth; — *i. e.* what do you know?

卣 ˏt'iao It is fancifully drawn to represent hanging fruit.

A tree laden with fruit.

一樹朱櫻垂丨丨 see the red cherries hanging from this tree!

䠷 ˋt'iao From *body* and *omen*.

A tall man.

細高丨兒 a tall, slender person.

朓 ˋt'iao From *moon* and *omen*.

The moon appearing in the morning before sun-rise.

跳 趒 t'iao' ˏt'iao To leap, to skip, to jump; to dance, to hop about; to palpitate, to beat; to shoot upwards, as sprouts; to intrude on; a board to pass over; a plank to reach a boat.

丨下來 jump down.

丨過來 jump over it.

耍丨 skipping about.

丨粉墻 to leap a whitewashed wall; — *i. e.* to have an assignation.

搭上丨板 step on the plank.

嚇了一丨 gave me a great fright.

丨槽 he bolts his manger; — *i. e.* leaves the employ recklessly.

龍丨天門 the dragon has jumped the heavenly gate; — a rapid rise in degrees.

心丨 my heart beats.

丨神 to exorcise or invoke spirits, witches do.

丨躍 to leap and skip, as a kitten.

Read ˏt'iao. To raise both the feet, or leap up on them.

丨然復出 they all at once reappeared.

眺 t'iao' To look aslant, to glance or peep at.

丨望 to gaze at from afar, to look at.

凝眸而丨 to gaze fixedly.

頫 t'iao' ˋfu From *head* and *omen*; it is also read ˋfu, to stoop; like the next.

High officers sent to court from feudal princes; to have an audience.

享丨有璋 when they enjoyed the banquet of audience, the gems or rarities were displayed.

覜 t'iao' From to *see* and *omen*.

To see; to have an audience once in three years, as feudal princes, who sent presents by their ministers; to see afar.

丨聘 to bring presents to the emperor.

蓧 莜 t'iao' A bamboo basket or 丨草 in which laborers carry muck or produce.

以杖荷丨 carrying his basket across his staff.

丨子 a local name for chives in Kiangnan.

Read ˏyiu, for the second character only. Oats, a name mostly confined to the north of China.

丨麥 growing oats.

丨麪 oat-meal.

糶 t'iao' From 米 *rice*, 出 to *go out* and 翟 a *jungle fowl;* but 糴 by itself means *ripe rice.*

To sell grain, to dispose of breadstuffs.

出丨 to sell grain.

丨糧 to sell rice.

窱 t'iao' Deep, profound as a cave; distant.

杳丨 gloomy and lonely, as a glen or shaded gorge.

望窱丨以徑廷 I see the distant paths winding along the silent glades.

藋 t'iao' A weed resembling the hellebore (*Veratrum*); also a kind of violet.

丨粱 a variety of sorghum which grows very tall.

Read t'ih, A kind of amaranth.

灰丨 the pigweed (*Chenopodium album*) with mealy leaves.

TIÉ.

Old sounds, tia *and* tap. *In Canton,* tè ; — *in Swatow,* tia ; — *in Amoy,* tia ; — *in Fuhchau,* tiè ; — *in Shanghai,* tia ; — *in Chifu,* tié.

爹 ˏtié From *father* and *many ;* it is also read ˏto.

An appellation for a father.

阿丨 or 丨丨 papa; daddy!

丨娘 or 丨媽 my parents.

老丨 venerable Sir! addressed to old men.

乾丨 an adopted father.

In *Cantonese.* Remiss, inattentive to duties.

丨丨吊 very heedless and untrustworthy.

TIEH.

Old sounds, dít, díp, *and* típ. *In Canton,* típ, tít, *and* tăt ; — *in Swatow,* tiat, tiap, t'a, *and* chui ; — *in Amoy,* tiat, tiap, *and* tút ; — *in Fuhchau,* tiek *and* tòk ; — *in Shanghai,* dih, deh, *and* tih ; — *in Chifu,* tié.

耋 ˏtiéh From 老 *old* and 至 *extreme,* indicating hoar years.

Age of seventy or eighty, an octogenarian; aged, infirm; dun featured and colored like iron, whence this and 鐵 are read alike.

今者不樂逝者其丨 if we are not joyful now, the days will glide on till we are eighty.

絰 ˏtié From *silk* and *extreme.*

Badges of coarse white hempen cloth, worn by the nearest mourners on the head and waist at funerals.

首丨 a mourning cap; it is like a skull-cap without a crown.

喪丨 mourning apparel.

蹀 ˏtié To step, to put the foot down.

丨足 to stamp, to take firm steps; a step.

垤 ˏtié A high hillock.

泰山之於丘丨 the lofty Tai-shan [in Shantung] is one in looks with this hillock.

Read chih, An ant-hill, because in piling it, the ant though so tiny, exerts itself to the utmost.

鸛鳴于丨 the cranes were screaming on the ant-hill.

蝶 蜨 ˏtié t'ié From *insect* and a *slip* or *quick ;* the second was once read sieh,

A butterfly, the *Papilio.*

夢爲蝴丨 he dreamed that he was a butterfly.

穿花蛺丨深深見 see the butterflies flitting in and out among the flowers.

瘦丨 a late butterfly, one seen in November.

鳳丨 a purple *Vanissa.*

褶 ˏtié ˏchö Regarded by many as another form of *cheh,* 襵 to plait, and often thus used; also read *sih,*

A double garment, but not wadded; used to protect from the dust.

黑袴丨 black overalls; a riding jacket or spencer.

丨衣 double robes, lined with thin cloth.

丨褲 a sort of buskin worn by ladies around their ankles.

堞 ˏtié From *earth* and a *slip.*

A battlement on a wall, having embrasures 垛口 like a parapet; to surround with a parapet or breastwork.

雉丨 or 城丨 a parapet.

丨其宮而守之 make a breastwork around the palace, and guard it.

渫, *ˏtié* Waves surging along; clever, smart.
長波浹丨 the long billows roll in over each other.
瞶眊不丨 stupid and unintelligent.

Read *sieh*, and very similar to 洩. To ooze; to desist; dirty, unsettled, muddy.
井丨不食 don't drink from a turbid well.
爲歡未丨 he could not stop for joy.

諜, *ˏtié* Interchanged with the next two in some senses.
To tamper with soldiers; to sound the minds of others; to inform the enemy, to spy; a minute, a paper.
往來間丨 (or 丨賊) a secret agent of another party, a spy.
丨丨利口 an eloquent, constant talker.
伺丨 a spy.

喋, *ˏtié* To chatter; loquacious, fluent; to taste or smear blood, as when taking an oath; flowing blood.
丨丨 wordy.
唼丨平蕪 [the ducks] are noisily feeding in the duckweed.

牒, *ˏtié* From *board* and a *slip.*
Tablets for writing on; a diploma; a warrant; records of families; official instructions, dispatches; archives.
玉丨 royal genealogies.
文丨 official dispatches; an indictment.
譜丨 family records.
戒丨 a priest's certificate, entitling him to three days' lodging.
簡丨 boards on which orders used to be written.

苜, *ˏtié* From *eye* and *sheep's horns;* it is often read *muh*, but not correctly.
The eyes squinting or distorted.

牒, *ˏtié* Used for *yeh*, 楪 in some of its senses.
The boards of a bed; also the mat on it.
牀丨 the boards on which one sleeps.
詢事呈丨 to investigate an affair and send in a report on it.

碟, *ˏtié* From *stone* and a *slip.*
A plate, a dish; a platter, flat and broad.
漆丨 lackered plates.
盌丨 bowls and plates, table-furniture.
賞丨 a douceur to a waiter, a vail.
醬油丨 or 豉油丨 side plates for condiments.
四丨一盌 put four plates to one bowl.

Read *sheh*, To cure or tan leather.
丨里國 a country in the Indian Archipelago.

鰈, *ˏtié* From *fish* and a *slip;* it is also read *t'ah*,
A flounder, a plaice, whose peculiar conformation leads to the belief that two fish are required to clasp each other in order to swim; other names are 丨沙魚 and 鞋底魚 or sole fish.
丨國 an old name for Lewchew.

昳, *ˏtié* The sun beginning to decline towards the west; the hour from two to three o'clock P.M.

眣, *ˏtié* The eye-ball very protuberant, like some varieties of gold fish.
丨䁢 bulging eyeballs.

Read *chih*, The eyes unsteady, resulting from imperfect vision or nearsightedness.

詄, *ˏtié* To forget; to be mistaken.
天門開丨蕩蕩 the gate of heaven opens (*i. e.* the clouds part), and discloses the clear firmament.

瓞, *ˏtié* From *melon* and *lost.*
Melons or cucumbers just set on the vines; gherkins; *met.* posterity.
綿綿瓜丨 in long lines grow gourds, — so do our people.
大瓜小丨 the large are melons and the small are gherkins.

迭, *ˏtié* From *to go* and *to lose;* used for *yih*, 軼 to risk, and for *yih*, 佚 ease; it resembles *sung'* 送 to escort.
To alternate, to change; to exchange, as places; reciprocal; suddenly; alternate, now this now that; rotation; for, instead of; easy, lazy.
丨用柔剛 alternately employed kindness and severity.
更丨 to change places.
丨爲賓主 they treated each other as host and guest.
丨興丨廢 now rising and then declining.
丨次 again and again, repeatedly.
逃命不丨 unsuccessfully ran for his life.
丨不的去逛 I have no time to ramble.

跌, *ˏtié* From *foot* and *to lose.*
To slip and fall; to fall over or down; to make a false step; to walk quickly, to stride unceremoniously; to pass or jump over; to fall, as in price.
打丨 or 丨倒 fell down.
丨着 fallen; he is down.
丨打損傷 hurt badly by a fall.
丨破 or 丨爛 broken by a fall.
丨價 the price has declined.
丨足 to stamp the feet when vexed or nonplussed.
丨跟頭 a fall.
丨一跤 I had a tumble.
丨蕩放言 unfounded and wild talk.
東西丨倒不扶 when a thing falls he never picks it up, — the lazy fellow.
魚丨子 the fish jumps.

跕, *tie'* Like the last.

To fall, as a bird from the sky; to dart down into the water.

飛鳶｜｜ the swift hawk darts — on its quarry.

Read *t'ieh*, To keep time with the foot in singing and playing.

彈絃｜屣 she thrummed the strings as she tapped with her slipper.

Read *'tien.* Lame; to walk limping; to stand on tiptoe.

｜脚兒 his leg is lamed.

｜着脚在架上拿書 stood on tiptoe to reach down the book from the shelf.

凸, *tieh'* *₍töh* The character is intended to depict its meaning; the original idea is derived from 垤, an ant-hill; it is also read *tuh,*

Protuberant, jutting, anything above the surface, as a wen, a boss, a mole-hill; convex; that which causes a convexity; elastic, springy; a tenon.

｜眼 protruding eyes.

｜字 letters cut in alto relief.

｜嘴凹鼻 pouting lips and flattened nose; — sullen, cross.

挺胸｜肚 a high breast and capacious belly.

｜出 extruding.

｜然出水 see it rise out of the water! — as a whale.

｜路 a rounded or raised road.

｜力 and 無｜力 elastic and inelastic; both are foreign terms.

In *Cantonese.* An overplus; too much.

有｜ more than enough.

嘔｜ to disgorge more than was received, as a swindler is made to do.

疊, 叠, *tieh'* *₍tieh* Formed first of 日 *day* repeated thrice as 晶, which were afterwards changed to 田 with 宜 *correct* under it, referring to successive official investigations to get at the *right* of an accusation; the contracted form is common; it is interchanged with the two next.

To redouble, to reiterate; to complicate; to fold; to fear; a doubling.

重重｜｜ tiresome reiteration: to pile on.

｜次 several times.

遠山｜翠 the distant green hills rise one above another.

莫不震｜ everybody was trembling with fear.

擅, *₍tieh* To pile on; to fold over and over; to gather up; to suspend.

摺｜ to fold together.

｜起行李 pile up the luggage.

整｜ pile them in the form of a square; fold it even.

鋪牀｜被 make the bed and fold up the bedding.

｜埋 to pile up; to put in order, to close up a business transaction. (*Cantonese.*)

｜埋心水 don't give yourself anxiety on that point. (*Cantonese.*)

氎, *tieh'* From *hair* and *doubled.*

Very soft, whitish cloth of a firm texture, called 白｜ like silk in appearance, which is woven from a cocoon-like fruit, and was brought from Kao-chang 高昌 the Uigur country; the Tangut people have 霞｜ embroidered goat's hair cloth, which seems to be something like Cashmere shawls, but the old 白｜ brought from thence is now called 紅氆氌 or red pilot-cloth.

蹀, *tieh'* A short step; a small pace.

｜足 to stamp the feet, as when vexed.

鐷, *tieh'* A fine seive or fan called ｜簸 which farmers use to winnow grain.

艓, *tieh'* A punt, a shallop.

｜子 a canoe, a dingey, such as poor people use.

棹花裝小｜ put the lotus flowers in the shallop.

渫, *tieh'* From *ice* and a *slice.*

Frozen hard.

泆｜ frozen together or into, as water in a pitcher.

㮥, *tieh'* The ceiling of a room, which is often divided into panels and painted.

｜板 the boards below the tiling.

揲, *tieh'* To hoard, to lay up, to engross.

｜財役貧 [when merchants] engross the stocks, it produces poverty — among dealers.

Read *ti'* Lofty, elevated; to intercept, to hide from.

霓旌｜翳 the starry banners dazzled the view, — alluding to their number and beauty.

惵, *tieh'* Afraid, timid; fearful of trespassing.

憂心｜｜ with great care and apprehension.

戜, *tieh'* From 戈 *dart* and 呈 to *inform;* it is now used only as a primitive, and is altered to 戴 when in combination.

To scrape, to pick; sharp; advantageous.

T'IEH.

Old sounds, t'it *and* t'ip. *In Canton*, t'ip *and* t'it; — *in Swatow*, t'iap, t'i, *and* t'iat; — *in Amoy*, t'iat *and* t'iap; — *in Fuhchau*, t'iek *and* t'aik; — *in Shanghai*, t'ih; — *in Chifu*, t'ié.

帖 t'ié — From *napkin* and *to divine*. Written scrolls; writings; documents, manuscripts; a billet; a visiting-card, which has many sorts; a placard; settled, decided.
名丨 a visiting-card.
紅單丨 a blank card.
單丨 a single card; and 全丨 one of five folds, a more formal sort.
法丨 black paper copyslips; rubbings of inscriptions on stones.
出白丨 to issue anonymous bills.
招丨 proposals for a contract.
行丨 or 投丨 to send a card.
訪丨 to send out invitations.
賞丨 notice of reward offered.
丨套 a card-case or envelop.
事不妥丨 the matter is not quite settled or decided.
錢丨 a bank bill.
執丨 a doorkeeper, one who takes in cards.
試丨 themes for verses in pentameters.

怗 t'ié — Quiet, peaceable; convinced; resigned.
安心丨服 quietly submissive to, as to God's will.
丨靜 appeased.
Read *chen*. Discord.
丨滯之音 the tones do not harmonize.

呫 t'ié — From *mouth* and *to divine*. To taste, to sip.
丨血爲盟 to lick blood when swearing.
Read *ch'eh*. To whisper in the ear; loquacious.

貼 t'ié — To leave in pledge; to throw over one, as a cloak; to supply, to make up; to lean on; attached to; adjacent; to paste up.
丨在牆上 paste it on the wall.
丨近 attached to; contiguous.
丨身 next to the body; attached to, as a servant or one's children.
丨心 intimate, fellow-feeling.
丨寫 under-writers; copyists in a yamun.
體丨 to accommodate, to yield to; to patronize; to take up another's cause; on another's behalf.
丨邊 a wide hem or facing.
丨補 to make up what is wanting; to meet an exigency, by a donation; to help, as by giving alms.
丨妥 well adjusted, properly arranged. (*Shanghai.*)
丨準 at that time; just then.

揲 t'ié — From *hand* and *a slip*; it is used with 摺, to fold, and also read *sheh*. To fold, to pile up; to grasp divining straws in the hand.
丨蓍 to cast lots.
摺丨 to fold, as paper.

鐵 鉄 銕 t'ié — From *metal* and *great*, *lost*, or *good*; the second form is very common. Iron, called 黑金 or black metal; made of iron; firm, decided, iron like; without doubt, really.
丨器 iron tools.
打丨 to work in iron.
生丨 cast iron, raw iron.
丨線 or 丨絲 iron wire.
丨條 rod iron.
馬口丨 or 洋丨 or 白丨 tin-plates.
黃丨 brass.
丨砂 iron filings.
丨匠 a blacksmith.
丨石人 a man of fixed will, a mulish man.
丨筆不開 an unalterable writing, like a verdict.
丨主意 an iron will; a fixed resolve.
丨公鷄 or 丨沙梨 an iron cock or iron pear, denotes a mean and stingy prig.
丨面無私 a man of integrity and firmness.
丨華粉 a preparation for cyanizing iron with vinegar.

驖 t'ié — From *horse* and *iron* contracted. An iron-gray horse.
駟丨孔阜 the team of four iron-grays is in fine condition.

餮 t'ié — From *to eat* and *exhausted*. Gluttonous.
饕丨 an ogre-like monster engraved on ancient vases, a head without a body, or merely a belly on a basin, to represent the vice of gluttony.

僣 t'ié — From *man* and *instead of*. Artful, cunning.
丨侻 villainous, crafty, cruel.

蛈 t'ieh — A kind of burrowing spider, called 丨毋 and 丨蝪; it resembles the *Mygale* in the manner of making its nest.

TIEN.

Old sounds, tin, tim, *and* dien. *In Canton*, tin *and* tim ; — *in Swatow*, tiam, tian, *and* tʰoi ; — *in Amoy*, tian, tiam, chiam, *and* liam ; — *in Fuhchau*, tieng *and* taing ; — *in Shanghai*, tiⁿ *and* diⁿ ; — *in Chifu*, tien.

顛 ˛tien From *head* and *true* ; it is interchanged with the next three.

The top, the apex, the summit ; the forehead ; the beginning of ; to upset, to fall over ; to overthrow, to subvert ; to die, to be ruined.

丨頂 the vertex, the crown.

丨倒 turned upside down.

事有丨末 everything has a beginning and ending ; — there is a right way of doing it.

丨而不扶 he has fallen and nobody will help him ; his fate is remediless.

丨沛 calamities ; distracted with troubles ; to fall utterly.

書丨 devoted to, as to a particular branch of art or science.

乃爾丨覆 they will come with you to utter ruin.

丨連 trouble from anarchy and rebels ; embroiled, as an affair ; at sixes and sevens.

癲 瘨 ˛tien From *disease* and *inverted*.

Crazed, deranged, the mind overthrown ; mad after ; infatuated ; silly, giggling, wild ; in convulsions, fits ; afflicted with.

發丨 insane ; delirious ; also used as an objurgation, are you mad ?

丨狂 raving mad.

丨氣 hot-headed, rash.

多喜爲丨 too great joy causes madness.

丨狗 a mad dog.

想銀丨 mad after money.

傎 ˛tien Interchanged with its primitive.

To turn over or upside down.

丨倒衣裳 clothes put on wrong ; *met.* people in their wrong places, things topsy-turvy.

丨之倒之 turn it end for end, or top for bottom.

巔 ˛tien A word indicating a high degree of distance or height.

丨遠 very far off.

丨高 extremely high.

槇 ˛tien The topmost or outer boughs of a tree ; a fallen tree.

狗丨 a species of yew or larch.

Read ˛*chăn.* Trees growing too closely, and their roots interfering with each other.

齻 ˛tien To get one's wisdom teeth ; the large double teeth.

丨牙 to get the last molars, which in man the Chinese place at 24, and in women at 21 years of age.

巓 ˛tien The peak or apex of a hill.

山丨 the highest peak of a number of mountains.

滇 ˛tien A lake south of Yunnan fu, the 丨池, about forty miles in length ; it is connected with the Yangtsz' River by the Pu-to River 普渡河 flowing northerly about a hundred miles.

丨國 a wide region near it, formerly occupied by Lolos and other tribes ; and 丨省 or 古丨 are still used for Yunnan province.

Read ˛*tʻien.* Vast, full.

丨汚 a wide expanse of water.

趲 ˛tien To go unequally ; to trot, as a horse or donkey ; to jolt in trotting.

馬丨的慌 this horse jolts one unmercifully.

搷 ˛tien To beat, to knock a thing to pieces, as when throwing it away ; to lead ; to spread out.

丨鳴鼓些 to beat a rub-a-dub on the drums.

蹎 ˛tien To stumble, to trip.

丨仆 to fall down, as from weakness or fatigue.

驔 ˛tien A horse with a white spot in his forehead.

掂 敁 ˛tien To weight a thing in the hand ; to jolt or bob up and down, as a nurse does a baby.

丨操 to estimate the weight of anything in the hand.

丨搭 to shake in the hand.

丨丨有多少重 heft it and guess the weight.

In *Cantonese.* To lay up and down, to lay straight ; directly ahead, straight on.

計唔丨ʼ cannot be numbered.

丨ʼ路 a direct road.

丨ʼ頭呑 to bolt the food.

打丨ʼ放 to lay along.

唔得丨ʼ I can do nothing, I am headed off.

丨ʼ線 straight, a bee-line.

刮 ˊtien From *knife* and *to divine* ; used with 玷ʼ a flaw.

A nick in a blade ; broken off or having a flaw.

白圭之丨 an official baton with a spot ; *i. e.* not a pure color.

典 ˊtien Originally written with 儿 a *stand* now contracted to 八 *eight*, with 冊 *records* on it, denoting the books of the 五帝 placed high out of respect.

A canon, a standard or ritual ; a statute or code ; written, authentic documents, records ; law, rule ; ordinances ; statutory ; constant ; to put in charge of another ; to mortgage ; to consider ; to rule or manage ; to take oversight of ; to be directed to, bent on.

丨田 to mortgage land, as a 出丨 mortgager does to a 丨主 mortgagee.
老丨 or 永丨 to mortgage for ever.
丨守 to keep in charge.
尙有丨刑 still you have the statutes and laws.
丨籍 books, records.
古丨 ancient records, like the Domesday Book.
恩丨 or 大丨 [your] great favor, or bounty.
丨史 a writer of the court, or a clerk who has no grade; an inferior justice under a *chi-hien.*
五丨 the five social relations.
䘏丨 a grant to deceased soldiers of merit.
自作不丨 doing what is illegal.
出經入丨 [such a style] comes from the classics and savors of the canons.

䩄 ʻtien From 老 *old* and 點 *spot* contracted.
The grimy spots on the face of an old person, — defined by 老人面上如點 something like spots on an old man's face.

蒧 ʻtien Occasionally used as another form of the next.
The name of a grass.
曾丨 the father of the commentator Tsăngtsz' 曾子 a disciple of the Sage.

點 **点** ʻtien From *black* and *to divine;* the contracted form is common in cheap books.
A black spot, a speck; a dot, a little, a mite; a comma; the stroke of a clock; an old name for the fifth part of a night watch, or about 13 minutes; in *mechanics,* a point, the spot where the weight or power acts or touches; a particle; speckled, starred, dotted; to punctuate, to italicise with dots; to nod, to bow slightly; to blot out, to mark for correction; to point out; to prick off; to soil or spot; to light, as a lamp; to nod in assent; in *penmanship,* a slanting dot, a 丶 which is also read ʻ*chu.*
指丨 to point out; to show which or how.
丨眼 to give one the wink.
打丨 to sort or arrange, to put in order.
幾丨鐘 what time is it?
擺丨心 to spread out a luncheon.
欽丨 designated to be a *hanlin.*
一丨一畫 a point and a line; to write.
丨過數 made out the list.
一丨氣頭 a little vexed.
一丨好心 a goodhearted man.
一星半丨 or 半丨子 a very little.
多一丨兒 a very little more.
長一丨 rather long.
自丨 to bring ridicule on one's self.
丨景 to describe and illustrate, as in describing a region.
丨染甚都 it is beautifully adorned.

In *Cantonese.* An *interrogative,* how, in what manner? what?
丨呢 how is it then?
丨樣 how, in what way?
丨心事 what does he intend to do?
丨做得呢 how shall it be done?
丨知 how do you know?
丨算好 which is the best way?

In *Pekingese.* The iron plate or 鐵丨 on which watchmen strike when about to shut the city gate.

店 tienʼ From *shelter* and *to divine.*
A place to put goods; in Canton, it usually denotes a shop, a stand; but at the North rather an inn or tavern, because of the abundance of animals and teams there.
老丨 the old stand.
一座丨 one inn; one shop.
客丨 a rest-house, an inn, an eating-house.
管丨 or 出丨 a coolie, a porter in a shop. (*Cantonese.*)
丨客 travelers, guests, lodgers.
收丨 to shut up shop.
丨主 or 丨家 an innkeeper; the latter term also includes servants.
野丨 a rest-house.
住丨 or 歇丨 or 下丨 to stop at the inn.
酒丨 a wine-shop, a grocery; a restaurant.

坫 tienʼ An earthen table or ledge, used as a sort of earthen buffet or stand, and indicating rank; it was placed between two pillars at state interviews among feudal princes.
土丨 a tray or side-board made of earth.
反丨 to put back the cups on the stand.

扂 tienʼ To bar a gate with beams of wood or iron inserted in the wall.
丨楔 to bar the gate by inserting the beam into the side-posts.

玷 tienʼ ʻtien A flaw or stain in a gem; a defect, a spot; to disgrace, to injure; to split; chipped; disgraced.
丨汚 to deflower; to defile.
丨辱 to be disgraced; debauched.
丨缺 a defect; deficient, imperfect.

In *Cantonese.* To run against, to hit unintentionally.
睇丨 lookout for yourself! — a street cry of porters.
丨頭殼 to bump the head.
是丨是着 it is a good hit for you.

痁 tienʼ The fever and ague; intermittent fever.
單丨 tertian ague; a fever that comes on odd days.
雙丨 one that recurs on the second or fourth day.

墊 From a *tile* and *table*.
tien' To steady a thing by putting bricks or other things under it; to shore up; to prop or raise in any way.

丨穩 to steady by a prop.
丨平 even it off, as the ground; make them of the same level.
丨棹脚 wedge the table's legs.
丨高 raise it higher.

惦 An unauthorized character.
tien' To remember, to think of, as of the absent.

丨念 to ponder, to reflect on.
丨記 to bear in mind; to recall.

殿 A high and grand hall; a palace; the hall of audience;
tien' a main building in a temple; the rear of an army, as distinct from the van 啓, or when it flees in battle; small military merit; fixed; to preserve, to establish; to protect; to sigh.

一座宮丨 a royal palace; also called 金丨 the golden hall.
光明丨 the Resplendent Hall at Peking, in which audiences are held.
丨下 your Highness; said only to the crown prince.
飛行丨 an old name for the imperial chariot.
大雄寶丨 the grand hall of idols in Budhist temples.
便丨 the side halls in a temple.
丨定 to establish firmly.
丨最 inferior merit, as when bringing up the rear in a defeat.
奔而丨 the rear fled defeated.
丨天子之邦 to defend the royal domain.
丨陛恩濃 your Majesty's bounty is vast.

佃 From *man* and *field*; occurs used for ₛt'ien 畋 hunting.
tien' To till the ground; to dress fields; to hunt; to catch wild animals.

丨戶 farmers; field hands.
丨丁 or 丨夫 a husbandman.
以丨以漁 by hunting and fishing.
官丨 government lands.
坟丨 graveyards, cemeteries.

甸 From *field* and *to envelop*; occurs used with the last.
tien' Anciently, a royal domain around the capital, extending 500*li* each way; government lands, measuring 64 square roods, which furnished one war chariot, three men-at-arms, and 72 footmen; a squad of this size; to rule; to cultivate; to extend; to stretch out; to hunt; frontier lands; the imperial domain of Yü.

禹丨 the empire.
丨人 foresters.

蜔 From *insect* and *domain*; it is also often written 鈿 ₛt'ien.
tien' Inlaid shell-work, made by laying scales or powder of thin nacre in wood, and filling it up with lacker-paste.

螺丨 lackered ware with shells in figures inlaid.

電 From 雨 *rain* and 申 *to emit*, referring to the collision of the dual powers which produce it.
tien'

Lightning; a flash of lightning; electricity; to glance at, to regard with attention, as a superior is asked to do; to telegraph; electric.

丨線 the telegraph wires.
丨報 a telegram.
丨光 glare of lightning.
閃丨 a flash of lightning.
丨氣表 an electrical machine.
丨照 [please to] give this a careful look.
丨母 the goddess of Lightning.
目光如丨 you will see it all at one glance.
暗室欺心神目如丨 when deeds are done with scoffing hearts, the eyes of the gods notice them instantly.

奠 From 大 *great*, altered from 丌 a *stand*, with 酋 a form of 酒 *spirits* above it for worship.
tien'

Fixed and settled, as the hills and streams; to set up or enshrine, as a god; to offer libations; to lay or put down; to discriminate the qualities of.

丨酒 to pour out a libation.
丨土 to put up the mound for the terminalia.
祭丨 offerings and libations.
丨定 the country is now quiet.
丨雁 to pour out a libation to the geese at a marriage; it indicates a promise of conjugal fidelity during their lives, and the geese are often supported for life at a temple.
丨敬 or 丨儀 an offering in money sent to mourners.
丨之而後取 lay it down and then she will take it up, — it being a rule for men and women not to touch hands.
丨鼎 to consolidate an empire.

墊 From *earth* and *to grasp*; occurs used with the last.
tien' To sink into, overwhelmed in; flooded; to place on, to lay down; engrossed with; to advance money, to pay for another; to place under, to wedge so as to stand firmly; to buttress, to shore; a spring, as of a carriage; a cushion.

椅丨 a chair cushion.
籐丨 rattan mats, used on dinner tables.
炕丨 a cushion laid on the divan.
丨不出 I cannot assist you.
丨債 to pay another's debt.
鋼丨 a steel rest or support; the spring of a carriage.
丨賬 to settle another's bill.
丨鋪 a cushion shop.
椶丨 or 楊丨 a coir-mat frame on which a bed lies.
沒錢丨 I've no money to advance.
丨本 to advance money, as to one opening a shop.

香 丨 overwhelmed by the flood.
代 丨 to pay for another.
賠 丨 to make up for a loss.

Read *tieh*, Ancient name of a river and district in Chung cheu 忠州 in the south of Sz'ch'uen.

捻 *tien'* A synonym of the last.

To descend, to sink down.

Read *nieh*, Advantage; to benefit; to involve, to fall into.

Read *nien'* and used with 𡒄. A bank, a dike, and especially a levee to protect the land.

隄 丨 a causeway to restrain an overflow.

簟 *tien'* A fine bamboo mat, woven from small slips or threads, and often worked with figures; a tall beautiful bamboo; the reed mouth-piece of a pipe.

丨席 fine variegated mats; good ones come from Nganhwui.

布之丨丨然 he spread it out very smoothly.

下莞上丨乃安斯寢 with a coarse mat under and a fine one above, he can repose quietly.

靛 *tien'* From *azure* and to *fix*.

Indigo, or any of the blue dyes found in China; an indigo color.

洋 丨 prussian blue.

藍 丨 the blue dye made from the *Isatis*.

丨缸裏扯不出白布來 you can't get a white napkin out of a bluing jar; — *i. e.* a good fellow will not be found among thieves.

漚 丨 to rot the indigo leaves.

京 丨 best indigo.

丨花 the indigo as it floats on the liquor.

唸 *tien'* From *mouth* and to *read*.

To sigh for; others say clear, bright.

丨吚 Oh! alas! to mourn over.

淀 *tien'* Shallow water.

西 丨 a lake in Chihli near Pao-ting fu.

海 丨 a small pond north of Peking, near which is a great Manchu Cantonment.

墊 *tien'* The roof of a house fallen in from decay, caused by the damp earth and heavy tiles upon it; this often happens to neglected buildings which admit the rain.

有 An unauthorized character.

In *Fuhchau*. Firm, solid, durable; hard, not soft; obtuse, stupid.

丨道 firm, strongly made.

丨心 a hard kernel or center; dull.

T'IEN.

Old sounds, t'in, t'im, din, *and* dim. *In Canton*, t'in *and* t'im; — *in Swatow*, t'ian, tian, t'iam, *and* chan; — *in Amoy*, t'ian, tian, t'iam, *and* chin; — *in Fuhchau*, t'ieng *and* tieng; — *in Shanghai*, t'i^n *and* di^n; — *in Chifu*, t'ien.

天 **靝** *t'ien* From 大 *great* with 一 *one* above it, denoting that it is incomparably the greatest; it is much used in anatomical terms and names of places; it resembles *yao* 夭 weird, and the second form, denoting the *blue ether*, was introduced by the Rationalists.

The highest of things, heaven both physically and divinely; it is defined, "the condensation of the original ether; it appears blue and vaulted, having a shape but no substance; it envelops the earth on all sides, and beyond it the sun, moon and stars are attached to it; it nourishes all creation, going through the four seasons; it revolves on the north and south poles as on an axis, once each entire day in its regular course without change;" the sky, the air, the firmament, the heavens; a day, a season; weather; ages of the world; celestial; the Power above, Nature, Providence, Heaven, — and though without definite personality is employed more than any other term to indicate God; the emperor, who is Heaven's vicegerent; to regard or honor as heaven; among the Budhists, used for *deva* or gods, and explained by 丨神 gods of heaven, and by 梵丨人 or inhabitants of the Brahma-lokas.

丨地人 heaven, earth, and man, the three ruling powers in creation.

丨下一家 all mankind are one family.

丨眼近 Heaven's eye is near; the gods know it.

丨大過神 Heaven is greater than the gods.

丨下 or 通丨下 the empire, the world, that which the 丨子 son of Heaven rules over.

丨顏 the emperor's face.

蓋丨 and 渾丨 the concave sky and the chaotic sky, are two ancient terms for different modes of drawing the stars.

丨然 naturally, of itself.

丨老爺 the ruler of the sky.

非丨 a Budhist term for strange beings like titans, who are not *devas*.

丨堂 paradise, Heaven; the term is of Budhistic origin, as 丨宮 is used for *deva-loka*, or celestial worlds above the earth; they also speak of 33 heavens (*traiya strimsas*), in which the city of Belle-vue 善見城 the abode of Indra, is in the center.

丨分'高 he has noble endowments.
滿丨神佛 gods and budhas enough to fill Heaven.
丨開眼 Heaven has observed it.
丨生丨養 Heaven produced and brought it up.
飛丨本事 extraordinary talents.
好丨 fine weather.
好半丨 full half a day, a good while, an hour or more.
夏丨 summer times.
丨氣 vapors, air, climate.
丨丨 or 每丨 every day.
隔一丨 every other day.
丨然圖畫 Heaven itself draws pictures or landscapes.
響晴的丨 a clear bright day.
丨元 a term for a system of mathematical symbols like algebra; 丨 and 地 are also used like *x* and *y* for unknown quantities.
六丨水路 a passage of six days.
今丨 to-day.
家丨下 and 公丨下 a hereditary monarchy, and one where the ruler chooses a successor.
民乃王所丨 the king regards the people as heaven.
丨朝 the celestial dynasty, *i. e.* the reign of the son of Heaven.
丨涯 or 丨邊 the horizon.
丨爵 nature's nobleman; nature's gifts, as humanity, justice.
鈞丨 heaven's music.
丨師 the head of the Tao sect who lives in Lung-hu shan 龍虎山 near Nan-chang fu in Kiangsi; he is known as 張丨師 from his family name, and is invested with power to appoint spirits to rule in all municipal temples.

添 ˛t'ien From *water* and *disgrace*.
To add, to increase; to put in more, to throw in; extra, additional, more than the limit.
丨多 put in more.
丨價 raise the price.
丨丁 to have an increase in one's family; also expressed by 丨八進口 to add in another mouth.
丨補 add something to make it enough.
丨差使 to add to a clerk's official duties.

In *Cantonese*. An adverb indicating certainty; really, too, exactly.
無解丨 it has no meaning either.
有雨丨 it is coming on to rain too.

田 ˛t'ien The character delineates the divisions of a field; it forms the 102d radical of characters relating mostly to fields and land; as a verb read *tien'*, and used with the next.

A field, a spot laid out in plats; to arrange for planting; cultivated fields; lands; a plantation of; to hunt; to plant, to cultivate.
井丨 lands anciently held in fief which surrounded the royal domain.
屯丨 lands assigned to military.
水丨 fields overflowed, tidal lands.
丨租 ground-rent.
書丨 fields whose rental is given to scholars.
籍丨 the field plowed by the emperor.
十畝丨 a field of ten [Chinese] acres.
竹丨 a bamboo plantation.
丨賦 the crown tax.
丨祖 the god of Agriculture.
有幾多丨畝 how many acres are there in all?
丨庄 a farmhouse.
丨家 farmers, agriculturists.
丨丨然 orderly arranged, like beds and fields.
滄海桑丨 the blue sea has become woods and fields; — *met.* times have much changed.
搬丨 or 刮丨 to hoe up the earth.
叔于丨 Shuh has gone hunting.
解組歸丨 to unloose the girdle and go home; — to resign office.
無丨'甫丨 do not try to cultivate fields too large.
公丨 imperial domains.
硯丨 literary pursuits or wages.
心丨福地 the ground of virtue and happiness.
蓮葉何丨丨 the lotus leaves spread out like plats.

畋 ˛t'ien From *field* and *to strike*.
To prepare a field for cultivation; to hunt for a living.
丨獵 to pursue game.
丨食 to live by agriculture.
爾尚丨爾田 you still cultivate your fields.
盤于游丨 his occupation is to roam and hunt.

鈿 ˛t'ien Metallic flowered or inlaid work made into headdresses.
釵丨 two broad enameled hair-pins or clasps, worn on the sides of the head.
金丨 golden enameled gear.
鳳丨 the empress' headdress, with feather work and jewels.

Read *tien'* and used for 蜔. Inlaid shell-work.
丨子 a head ornament used by Manchu ladies covering the hair, made with enamel, nacre, or feathers.

䡘 ˛t'ien To caper or hop about from joy is 丨丨 expressing both hilarity and health.

湉 ˛t'ien From *water* and *peaceful*.
The gentle flow of water; a tranquil noiseless stream.

塡 寘 ˛t'ien From *earth* or *cave* and *true*.
To fill up, to fill in; to level the earth by filling in a hole; to stuff; to supply a deficiency; to complete; noted for, characteristic of; compliant with; flowing; a rumbling sound, like that of many drums; a long time; to pay a debt; to add to; a designation of the planet Saturn.

丨還費空' to pay back the waste or outlay.

丨補 to supply enough.

丨房 to take a new wife.

丨大計 [this officer is] noted as superannuated.

再丨滿 fill it up again.

丨命 to give one's life for another.

丨殼 cancelled, paid up in full.

讀書爲益心非爲丨心 study should strengthen the mind, and not stuff it pedantically.

丨履歷 to note the age, residence, &c., of officials in the register.

丨鴨 to stuff and fatten ducks.

倒丨年月 to ante date a document.

丨塞 to stuff up, or fill in, as a pillow with hair.

丨格 the details and report of the coroner at an inquest.

闐 ꜀t'ien From *door* and *true*; used for the last.

To fill up, to stuff; the noise of drums; full, ample.

轟轟丨丨 the noise and tramp of a vast army or procession.

振旅丨丨 he led out a great troop.

賓客丨門 guests and friends filled his doors.

Read *tien'* The name of a country.

于丨 now called 和丨 or Khoten, a region north of the Koulkun Mts., of which Ilchi is the capital.

鷏 ꜀t'ien A wader, probably akin to the gallinule or water hen, found in the southern provinces, of a black color with yellow stripes and a large bill; it frequents marshes and feeds on fish; its note is said to resemble a dove's, or a man vomiting; one name is 蚊母鳥 from the flies or musquitoes which infest it, and which it is supposed to vomit.

[illegible] t'ien' The sound of drums is 丨丨, probably imitating the sharp rapid sound of a *réveillé*.

甜 ꜀t'ien From *sweet* and *tongue*; *q.d.* the tongue distinguishes sweetness.

Whatever is sweet or pleasant to the taste; one of the five tastes; savory, agreeable, well-tasted; to like.

丨醇 oily, smooth, as old wine.

丨言蜜語 smooth and honeyed words.

丨睡 sweet sleep.

得點丨頭 had small winnings at first, pleased with a little success.

丨思思 very sweet.

黑丨香 sound asleep.

丨水 spring or sweet water.

磌 ꜀t'ien The noise of stones falling with a crash; the plinth or base of a pillar.

霣石聞其丨然 he heard the whiz of the falling ærolite.

恬 ꜀t'ien From *heart* and *sweet* contracted.

Peaceful, contented; to pass life tranquilly.

丨靜 tranquil, as after a storm; undisturbed.

波丨海內 the waves are now everywhere quiet; the rebellion is quelled.

以丨養志 strengthen the resolution by cultivating placidity.

引養引丨 to lead [the people] to enjoy plenty and peace.

菾 ꜀t'ien An herb with leaves like a cabbage, having a slightly sweetish taste, used as a remedy in fevers; it grows in Yunnan; flourishing, as a stately tree; luxuriant, as herbage.

忝 ꜂t'ien From *heart* and *heaven*; *q. d.* the heart implores heaven with a feeling of self-reproach and intention of reforming.

Ashamed, humiliated, stricken with grief; unworthy of being or doing; to disgrace, to incur infamy; out of favor.

丨在相好 to be intimate with; — a polite phrase.

丨辱 feeling disgraced.

丨備 unworthy of being used to serve — as a guard.

丨不知羞 brazen-faced.

無爾丨所生 don't disgrace those who bore you.

否德丨帝位 a want of probity dishonors the diadem.

毋丨厥職 do not reproach the office.

丨蒙敎誨 I am ashamed that I have given you so much trouble to teach me.

丙 ꜂t'ien Regarded as representing the *tongue protruding*; it resembles ꜂ping 丙 and is now superseded by the next.

To lick.

丨嘴唇 to lick the chops.

丨菜碟 to lick the platter clean.

舔 **餂** ꜂t'ien From *tongue* and *reproach* or to *eat*; the second is also a synonym of ꜀甜 sweet.

To lick, as animals do; to taste; to hook, to catch, as by tripping one's speech; to try with the tongue.

丨一丨 taste it a little.

丨破了窓紙 [the thief] licked and thus broke open the lattice paper — to look in.

是以言丨之也 by his words catching some one, and thus seeking an end of his own.

丨乾淨 licked clean.

腆 ꜂t'ien From *flesh* and *rule*.

Abundance, plenty; enough of; rich, good, as food; to be prosperous; to go to excess; to forget; a long time; skilled at; to strengthen spirits.

不丨 unworthy of receiving; deficient, indifferent.

辭無不丨 his words are all well chosen.

設腆丨丨 to spread out a rich and bountiful repast.

丨忘 I've forgotten it entirely.

丨着臉 thick-skinned, shameless.

'淟 't'ien Dirty; muddied; to sink in water.

丨涊 filthy, sordid

丨染 defiled.

'怏 't'ien Ashamed, bashful; to feel disgraced or cowed; to blush. 先丨而後語 she first blushed and then spoke out.

苟無丨可乎 if you have nothing to be ashamed of, can't you do it?

'靦 '䩄 't'ien From *face* and to *see* or *rule*; like the last.

To show one's face; to feel ashamed; mortified because of one's plain features.

余雖丨然而人面哉 if I am ugly, still I have a man's face.

有丨面目 to blush up to the eyes.

大有丨色 she colored deeply.

還丨着臉不知恥 he acts in the highest degree brazen-faced.

未見人先面丨 she blushed lest she should see a man.

沴 't'ien In confusion, disordered, out of harmony.

陰陽之氣有丨 the elements (or the weather) are all in confusion.

丨戾 opposed, counteracting each other; said of the forces of nature.

Read *li'* Stagnant or still water; malarious, injurious.

丨氣 a bad air.

丨崖 a deep hole in a stream near a steep bank.

'殄 't'ien From *body* and *spots*.

To terminate, to prevent, to make to cease, to finish; to root out, to exterminate; to cast off; to waste, to use up; good.

丨絕 to destroy utterly.

丨滅 to extirpate, as rebels.

餘風未丨 some of the [bad] customs are not yet eradicated.

暴丨天物 to recklessly destroy Heaven's gifts.

丨草 to injure the herbage.

朕聖讒說丨行' [the emperor Shun said,] I dislike slanderous speakers, and those who destroy right ways.

邦國丨瘁 the countries are all disabled and exhausted.

丨戮 to inflict death, to destroy many.

'跈 't'ien To stand in a respectful attitude, waiting for one.

'琠 瑱 t'ien' Name of a gem; ancient ear-ornaments attached to the headdress or cap, which hung down and covered or stopped the ear, as if to prevent its hearing what was improper.

耳丨 ear-covers or plugs.

栝 桰 t'ien' A poker made of wood, and armed with an iron point for stirring the fire; a club or staff. The second character is a synonym of the 檜 or larch, prized for its durable wood; it is also read *kwah*, and used for 苦 in the name 丨樓 the bitter gourd or *Tricosanthes*.

掭 t'ien' From *hand* and *disgraced*; an unauthorized character.

To raise, as a wick. 丨

丨鎖 to pick a lock.

丨燈 push the wick out of the oil.

丨筆 to rub the pencil on the stone.

諔 t'ien' To hesitate; one says, to put in a word, to interfere in another's talk.

丨讖 undecided talk.

舚 t'ien' To loll out the tongue.

丨舌 to put out the tongue.

TIH.

Old sounds, tik *and* dik. *In Canton*, tik *and* tek; — *in Swatow*, tek *and* tia; — *in Amoy*, tek'; — *in Fuhchau*, tek, tík, *and* tiah; — *in Shanghai*, tih *and* dih; — *in Chifu*, ti.

的 ,tih From 白 *white* and 勺 a *ladle*, but the original radical was 日 *sun*, intimating brightness.

Clear, evident, as the sun; bright, clear; real; an important circumstance; a spot which shows distinctly, as a bull's eye in a target; a red spot on a woman's face; much used in speaking for 底 *below*, which was formerly employed by the scholars of the Sung dynasty as a possessive; after nouns and pronouns, or between two nouns, it is a synonym of 之 and denotes the genitive; as 我丨書 my book, 中國丨人 a Chinese; after verbs it makes a participle; a relative pronoun, who, what, the one who, — and answers to 者 making the phrase a noun; as 寫字丨 he who writes words, *i. e.* the writer; after adjectives, it becomes a sign of comparison and qualification.

貴丨 dearer.

白丨 whitish.

小丨 the smaller; I, your junior; — used by servants and inferiors to denote themselves.

是丨 really so; just that.

有丨 there is some.

丨確 evidently true; certainly, really, honestly.

對他說話丨是誰 who is that who spoke to him in reply?

丨當 careful; properly.

打鉄 丨 a blacksmith.
打 丨 鉄 wrought iron.
愛 丨 loved, loving; what is loved.
吃不丨 he will not (or cannot) eat.
丨然而日亡 certainly the [vile man] will day by day go to ruin.
射箭中ʾ丨 to hit the bull's eye in archery.
端 丨 the original cause, the root of the matter.

In *Cantonese.* A small quantity; a diminutive.
爭 丨 音 the tones differ slightly.
一 丨 very little.
無點 丨 you don't take any care.
近 丨 come nearer.
丨咁耐 a little while.

靮, ꜀ti Reins; a bridle.
執羈丨而從 he took the reins and followed after.

罗, ꜀ti From *net* and *ladle.*
To string fish.
貫鰓丨尾 to tie fish by the tail and gills, as on a twig.

駒, ꜀ti A bay horse with a white spot in his forehead is 丨顙, regarded as an unlucky sign.
丨盧 the name of Liu Pi's steed.

扚, ꜀ti To lead with the hand; to strike quick.
Read *yoh,* To point out with the fingers.

玓, ꜀ti The color of a bright pearl is 丨 瓅 to which the reflection of the moon in the water is likened.

菂, ꜀ti Also read ᶜ*hiao.*
The white seeds of the water lily, after the spongy testa have been removed.
綠房紫丨 the green capsule (*torus*) and reddish seeds of the lotus.

狄, ꜀ti From 犬 *dog* and 火 *fire,* but this is said to be a contraction of 赤 *red;* occurs used for *tʻih,* 逖 distant.

Name of an ancient Scythian tribe, the 北 丨 who were savage and fiery, the composition of the character indicating their licentious and lawless character; the district of 丨道州 in Kansuh preserves a remembrance of them; a stag or elk; inferior offices; menials about the court in old times, probably men of these tribes; to drive off, as invaders.
夷丨之人尚有廉恥之節 even savages also regard modesty as a virtue.

荻, ꜀ti Water grasses with solid or hard stems, like the sugarcane or sorghum.
蘆 丨 water rushes generally; coarse mats are woven from some of them, but they are mostly gathered for fuel, or to make dikes.
蕭 丨 or 丨 蒿 a variety of *Artemisia,* which in autumn gathers a woolly foliage.
丨 蔗 the sweet sorghum from which sugar is made, grown on Tsungming I.

啇, ꜀ti Originally written like *shiʾ* 啻 but, and afterwards altered; it resembles ꜀*shang* 商 to consult, and is used chiefly in combination.

The part on which others rest, as a stalk or stem, a foot or hoof, a root, &c; the basis or origin of.
不求根丨而欲茂盛 he does not care for the root, and yet thinks to get leaves and fruit.

樀, ꜀ti The short rafters that support the projecting eaves, the 檐 丨 or 椽子 which are painted; a spool on which silk is wound.

鏑, ꜀ti The barb of an arrow; the head of a javelin.
鳴 丨 a whizzing arrow.
鋒 丨 the sharp arrow-head.

蹢, 蹄, ꜀ti From *foot* and *basis;* the second form specially denotes petitoes.
The hoof of a pig or horse; to travel; to have recourse to, to join.
有豕白丨 there was a white footed pig.
丨于彼者 I am going to that place.
Read *chih,* as another form of 躑. To stop walking.
丨躅 embarrassed, stopping and going on, not settled what to do.

嫡, ꜀ti From *woman* and *basis;* 適 also occurs used for it.
The consort of a man, the proper wife, called 正室 or the one in the main house.
丨室 and 丨子 the wife and her children.
丨母 the mother of the house, said by a man's children or the domestics, when speaking of his wife.
丨堂兄弟 cousins german of the same surname.
丨親 blood relatives.

滴, ꜀ti From *water* and *basis.*
A drop of water; a very little; to drip, to ooze.
丨血 to drop blood — into water; if the drops from two people coalesce, it is thought to prove their relationship.
丨水成氷 the drops make ice as they fall.
點點丨丨 drizzling and dropping as the rain.
丨瀝 dripping slowly.
一丨何曾到九泉 [get drunk here], for how can a drop of wine get into hades?
丨多一點 drop one drop more.
丨丨金 a local name of the 旋覆花 or 覆盜庚 the elecampane or *Inula sinensis,* with a head of yellow flowers, clasping leaves, and milky sap; an infusion of it relieves coughs.
俾丨油 put in a drop or two of oil. (*Cantonese.*)
挑一丨 take a little in a spoon.

敵, ˏti From to *strike* and *basis.*

An opponent, an antagonist; a match, a competitor; an enemy, a foe; an equal; to withstand, to fight; to match; to compete, to strive for mastery, to be resisted; to control, to supervise, as an outlay.

對丨or 相丨 inimical, opposed.

匹丨 well matched, equal in force.

丨國 the enemy's country.

丨得住 well able to match him.

不丨 unequal, not matched.

丨手 a competitor, as in a game of chess.

大恩人怎做丨頭 how can one who has received great kindness turn to be such an ingrate?

仁者無丨 the humane man has no enemy.

丨體同尊 equally honorable; — said of a married pair.

丨兵 the enemy's troops; it is never applied to insurgent forces.

寡不丨衆 the few can't withstand the many.

甋, ˏti A jar, like a fish-jar, called 瓴丨 having small ears.

翟, ˏti From *feathers* and *fowl;* it occurs used for 狄, a tribe of Scythians, and when denoting a bird, sometimes is written like the next.

The Tartar pheasant, whose plumage furnishes feathers for flabellums and other articles; its feathers; a panache held by worshipers; dresses ornamented with feather-work worn by royal ladies at pageants; a feudal state near Gobi, now Yen-ngan fu 延安府 in the north of Shensi.

右手秉丨 their right hands held the plumes.

丨羽飾車 a carriage ornamented with feathers, used by court ladies.

丨者 underlings about court who taught the use of these plumes.

夏丨 and 青丨 the wild pheasant.

鸐, ˏti Same as the last, applied only to the bird.

The Tartar pheasant, called 丨雄 and 丨鷄, reared for its long tail feathers, which are used in many ways.

青丨 a fabulous and felicitous bird in the days of Yao, which was probably based on this bird.

糴, ˏti From 糶 *grain* and 入 *coming in.*

To lay in rice, to buy grain; hurrying.

丨米 to purchase rice.

無遏丨 do not prohibit people from buying grain.

檄丨 quickly.

籊, ˏti Long tapering bamboos suitable for fishing-poles.

丨丨竹竿以釣于淇 with slender bamboo rods fishing in the River Ki.

笛, **篴,** ˏti From 竹 *bamboo* and 由 *from,* alluding to the material; the second form is obsolete.

A fife or flute; it had seven holes, and now has ten, one of which has a skin over it; the Tartars are said to have invented it.

吹丨子 a flute player.

玉丨 a flute inlaid with jade.

短丨無腔 you cannot play tunes on a whistle.

長丨一聲人倚樓 the trill of a flute came from a man leaning on the balcony.

廸, **迪,** ˏti From to *go* and *from* or *by;* the first is most used.

To follow, to tread where others have been; to advance in knowledge; to bring forward; to direct in right paths; to lead forward, to develop; to go to a place; to intimate to; the right way.

啟丨後人 to set a good example to one's descendants or others.

惠丨吉 he will be blessed who follows the right path.

由丨 to admonish each other.

允丨厥德 he fully followed his virtuous example.

不丨 unprincipled men; also not to follow, not to treat properly.

覿, ˏti From to *see* and to *buy.*

To see a person face to face; to be admitted to an audience.

私丨 to see the prince alone; a private audience.

三歲不丨 he came not to court for three years.

丨用幣 at audiences they gave gifts.

丨面相失 they did not recognize each other at the interview.

滌, ˏti From *water* and a *slip;* occurs used with the next.

To wash, to scour, to cleanse vessels; to clear, to purify; to reform; to dilute; a stable or pen for keeping cattle when fattening; arid, parched.

丨去 to wash away.

丨塵 to wash off the dust.

蕩垢丨瑕 to rub off the grime and wash away the flaws; — *met.* to reform.

丨硯 to scrub the inkstone, — and be ready for study.

洗心丨慮 to purify the heart from sordid cares.

蔋, ˏti Arid; hot air, a scorching air; used with the last.

旱旣大甚丨丨山川 the drought is distressing, parched are the hills, and the streams are dried up.

Read ˏtsiao. Hills on which the grass is dried up.

踧, ˏti From *foot* and *uncle;* it is also read *tsuh,* and used with 蹙 embarrassed.

To travel along a smooth road.

丨丨周道鞠爲茂草 the road to Cheu is level and easy, yet it is overgrown with weeds.

T'IH.

Old sound, t'ik. *In Canton*, t'ik *and* tek ; — *in Swatow*, t'ek *and* tek ; — *in Amoy*, tek *and* t'ek ; — *in Fuhchau*, t'ek, tiah, *and* chaik ; — *in Shanghai*, t'ih ; — *in Chifu*, t'i.

剔 ˏt'i From *knife* and to *change*.
To cut the flesh from the bones, to scrape away; to hew off; to pick or dig out; to reject.

挑 丨 to sort out and reject; to cut, as with a graver.

丨 齒 or 丨 牙 to pick the teeth.

丨 燈 棍 a wire to push up the wick in Chinese open lamps.

攘之 丨 之 he hewed and thinned out — the trees.

丨 骨 肉 meat without bone in it; — pork is usually sold with the bone, beef and mutton without.

揚 ˏt'i Like the last, and not the same as ˏyang 揚 to spread.
To select and expunge.

In *Cantonese*. To lift up, to bring with both hands; to animate one's spirits; to excite; to lay down or on; to put aside.

一力 丨 lift with all your strength, — for it is heavy.

丨 起 去 hurry off with it.

丨 埋 to lay by.

丨 落 個 處 put it down there.

丨 起 心 肝 to rouse one's spirits.

惕, **愁** ˏt'i From *heart* and to *change*; the second, from *savage* combined with *heart*, is a form less used.
Respect, regard and fear for; to stand in awe; surprised in, alarmed; careful of giving offense, and diligent to fulfill duties.

怵 丨 sadly cautious; to be alarmed.

朝 乾 夕 丨 in the morning respectful, and vigilant at evening.

心 焉 丨 丨 the heart afraid of offending.

卒 無 怵 丨 at the last he lost all his respectful conduct.

倜 ˏt'i From *man* and *all*; occurs used with *shuh*, 俶 to begin.
Not restrained; no embarrassment; a law to one's self; worthy of promotion.

丨 儻 noble and kind, courteous.

丨 然 recommended, as one fit for high employment.

踢 ˏt'i From *foot* and *change*.
To kick; to kick up.

丨 毬 to play foot-ball.

一 丨 脚 at one kick; *i. e.* lumping the lot. (*Cantonese*.)

丨 毽 子 or 丨 燕 to kick the shuttlecock.

丨 死 人 to kill by a kick.

丨 球 to roll iron or stone balls with the foot; — a common game.

Read *shoh*, Excited, greatly moved and fearful.

逷, **逖** ˏti From to *go* and to *change* or a *horde*; the first is mostly used, and occurs used for the last.
To remove far away, to send off; far, remote.

離 丨 爾 土 get far away from your country.

移 爾 遐 丨 move yourself off far away, as an exile.

悼 來 者 之 丨 丨 Alack! what hard-fisted fellows these are that have come here!

丨 矣 難 追 he is too far, it will be hard to overtake him.

擿 ˏt'i From 手 *hand* and 適 to *meet*; it is often written like *chih*, 擲 to fling.
To select; to break up; to agitate, as by close examination.

發 奸 丨 伏 如 神 he discovered traitors, and detected intriguers with the sagacity of a god.

丨 巢 探 卵 [he forbid] disturbing nests and seeking eggs — in the spring.

TING.

Old sounds, ting, teng, ding, *and* deng. *In Canton*, ting ; — *in Swatow*, teng *and* t'ia ; — *in Amoy*, teng ; — *in Fuhchau*, teng, ting, *and* tieng ; — *in Shanghai*, ting *and* ding ; — *in Chifu*, ting.

丁 ˏting Originally written with 人 *man* above and 亅 *below* it, standing for 心 the *heart*; but others with more probability say it represents a bee's sting; occurs used with the next four.
The fourth of the ten stems, connected with fire, and denoting that things are perfected; a sting; a nail, for which 釘 is now used; to lose a parent; robust; a full grown person, a yeoman, a workman, an individual; a brave; to sustain, to bear; to order.

丨 憂 or 丨 艱 an officer mourning three years.

抽 丨 a levy, a conscription; to call for soldiers.

人 丨 a man; used when individualizing people, or speaking of population.

成 丨 he is now full age or 16; and not 小 丨 a minor.

丨 字 街 or 丨 字 路 口 a cross street, or a corner where a cross street ends in another street.

目 不 識 丨 he does not know a single word; *i. e.* not even so simple a character as 丁.

六 丨 a god of the Taoists who sways the demons.

丨香花 the lilac, because its flowers resemble 丨香 cloves.

發丨 to have posterity; fortunate, as a grave.

砂丨 a workman who digs sand; a miner.

丨年 a young man of 16 or 18.

寧丨我躬 rather would I myself bear it.

丨東 jingling stones hung in the wind.

丨子 a tadpole.

地丨錢粮 the land revenue as estimated in money.

Read ˏchăng. The sound of chopping.

伐木丨丨 merrily sound the woodmen's axes.

仃 ˏting Alone, no protector or support.

伶丨洋 the bay of Lintin northeast of Macao, so called from the islet of this name in it.

孤丨丨 quite alone by itself.

叮 ˏting To enjoin on one.

丨嚀告戒 repeatedly bade him to take heed.

丨囑 to order strictly; friendly council from a superior.

In *Shanghai.* Bitten or stung by insects.

丨之一個塊 bitten in one spot.

丨一口 I was stung once.

疔 ˏting From *disease* and *nail.*

Boils with a nail-like head; a venereal ulcer, a bubo; syphilitic sores.

生丨 to have pox sores.

火丨瘡 a pimple, a burning sore.

指丨 a felon or whitlow.

口丨 fever boils on the mouth.

玎 ˏting The jingling noise of stones hung in the wind; a clattering noise.

丨丨 a jingling noise.

丨玲 sound of jingling stones.

月丨 a blind fortune-teller's gong.

丨鐺 a hand gong hung in a hoop with two buttons to strike it when twirled; sometimes called 喚嬌娘 the beauty's call.

虰 ˏting A synonym of 蜓 the dragon-fly, alluding to its nail-like form.

丨蛵 or 蜻丨 a dragon-fly.

Read ˏch'ing. The razor sheath the 蟶 or *Solen.*

Read ˏch'ăng. A kind of ant.

釘 ˏting A nail, a spike, a bolt; to work metal into bolts.

鐵丨 iron nails.

螺絲丨 a screw.

以丨丨' 物 to nail things together.

丨靴 nailed boots for wet weather.

可中' 丨 hits the nail; *i.e.* admirable.

拔去眼中丨 take out that nail (or eyesore) from my eye.

Read ting' To nail together; to bind, as books.

丨牢 or 丨死 to nail securely.

丨封 a very important dispatch to provincial officers from their superiors.

丨書 or 丨裝 to bind books.

靪 ˏting To mend shoes; to patch, to put on a patch.

丨底 to patch up soles.

打補丨 to put a patch on a rent or hole.

鼎 ˏ**鼑** ˊting The lower part and sides represent the legs and body of a tripod in which metals are fusing, the contents being depicted in the contained *eye*; it forms the 206th radical of a few characters.

A caldron with three feet and two ears, a tripod kettle; then; firm, settled; to secure, to establish; the 50th diagram, denoting new; the state.

定丨 or 立丨 to establish a new dynasty.

革丨 abrogate the old dynasty.

丨足之勢 three of equal power.

扛丨 to lift a caldron; *i. e.* great strength.

三丨甲 the three highest of the new Hanlin, referring probably, to the three legs of a tripod.

喪事丨丨爾 attend to the funeral rites with deliberation and gravity.

望祈丨力 I humbly intreat your powerful influence.

丨臣 a high minister of state.

天子春秋丨盛 the emperor's years were then many.

鐘鳴丨食 when the bell sounds the food comes from the kettle; *met.* rich and honored; — the expression refers to an ancient patriarchal custom.

八聲丨沸 the clamors of the people bubbled up, as a seething caldron.

頂 ˏ**頂** ˊting From *leaf* or *head* and *nail.*

The top, peak, or summit; the crown; a knob or button adopted by the Manchus, and worn on official caps to indicate rank; a classifier of hats, caps, sedans, and state umbrellas; to carry on the head or apex; to point the head at; very, superior, a form of the superlative; to substitute, to put instead; food rising on the stomach; opposing; ahead; contradictory.

丨頭風 a head wind.

一個丨子 or 一粒丨 an official button.

紅丨 a red or coral button; the insignia of the highest rank.

革丨 or 摘去丨戴 to degrade an officer.

把頭丨着 carried it on his head.

丨脫 baldheaded.

招丨 or 召丨 to invite offers for a shop; to sell the stock or the goodwill.

丨換 or 丨包 to slily put worse in, as shopmen do at times.

丨天立地 one whose crown reaches to heaven; — very talented.

丨中意 I like it best.

丨銀 adulterated sycee.

丨好 the very best.

氣丨心 my food does not set well.

冒名丨替 to enter the examination under a false name; a crime.

丨不住 unable to manage, inadequate for.

謝丨 to become bald.

絕丨聰明 of the very highest talent.

灌丨 to sprinkle or wash the crown, a kind of Budhist baptism (*murddha-bishikta*) administered to children, idols, &c.

自丨至踵 from the crown to the sole.

丨爛市 to spoil the market by underselling. (*Cantonese.*)

戴雀丨 to wear the bird crest, *i. e.* to be a *siuts'ai*, alluding to a peculiar shaped button.

濎 *'ting* A rivulet or brook.

丨濘 the appearance of a watery expanse.

薡 *'ting* A lacustrine plant like a bulrush, called 丨董 whose leaves can be woven into sandals or withes; it is probably a species of *Scirpus* or *Juncus*.

酊 *'ting* From *spirits* and a *nail*.

Drunk; stupefied with drink.

酩丨無所知 too drunk to know anything.

耵 *'ting* The secretion in the ear.

丨聹 ear-wax or the dry scurf formed in the ear.

訂 *ting'* From *word* and *nail* as the phonetic.

To arrange satisfactorily, to settle terms; to criticise, to compare; to edit, to collate; to adjust, to equalize, as taxes; to fix on; to loiter; a meeting, a consultation.

丨明 to settle clearly.

丨盟 to make peace, to promise.

較丨 or 丨正 to revise, to edit, to prepare for publication.

丨期 to set a time.

拜丨 to invite to a consultation.

飣 *ting'* To set out a table handsomely; plates arranged for show, like the six offered to ancestors.

丨坐 ornamental dishes for show.

餖丨之文 fancy, high-sounding expressions, and not very sensible.

丨盤松徑下 spread the handsome dishes by the path under the pines.

定 *ting'* From 宀 a *covering* and 正 *correct* (others say 乏 *wanting*) changed to 疋 a *foot*.

Tranquil, secure, fixed, steady; used after an expression to enforce it; really, certainly, absolutely; brought to a proper state; at rest, set; in a trance-like state; to fix, to settle on; to curdle or set by means of an acid, as when using rennet to curdle milk; to decide, to adjust finally; to stop; the forehead; contracted, settled, determined; the star α Markab in Pegasus, so called because it is a good time to fix on a work when it culminates; in Budhism, a state of fixed contemplation.

一丨 positively, surely.

必丨 it must be, certainly.

丨親 to betroth.

丨貨 to contract for goods, when a 丨單 bill of particulars is drawn, and 丨銀 the bargain money is 下丨 paid.

未丨 or 不丨 uncertain, not yet settled.

無丨准 nothing decided finally.

丨局 it is fixed.

丨歸 settled on; all is arranged.

保不丨 I can assure you it is not fixed.

入丨 lost in abstraction, or mesmerized, as Budhists pretend to be; a state called 丨覺 the wisdom of tranquillity or quietism; it has a particular organ (*indrya*) by which it is perfected, called 丨根 *samadhi-indrya;* a previous state to this is termed 欲入丨 wishing to enter perfection (*sama-patti*).

丨做的 made to order.

丨而后能靜 fix the mind on it without distraction, and then you will quietly receive it.

晨昏丨省 at morn and eve salute your parents.

丨論 to speak to the purpose and settle the argument.

因功丨爵 to promote according to merit.

丨之方中 Markab was then in the zenith.

In *Cantonese.* A spot, a place.

有丨無呢 is there a place for it?

個笪丨 that spot.

唔知丨 I don't know the spot.

矴 碇 *ting'* From *stone* and *nail* or to *fix*; occurs used with the next.

Ballast to steady a boat; a stone which serves to anchor a boat; a grapnel.

下丨 or 抛丨 drop the anchor.

丨住海面 anchored in the roadstead or offing.

錠 *ting'* A platter or trencher with feet, used in sacrifices; an alloy of tin or spelter; an ingot or shoe of bullion; often used for 錨 an anchor, and because anchors are often made of wood, it is wrongly written with that radical; a medical preparation made into hard round sticks; the needle of a spinning wheel.

十兩一丨 ten taels in one ingot; in Canton, this phrase often means, the affair is certain, from the usual weight of ingots.

元寶丨 or 南銀丨 paper ingots burned in worship.

一丨銀子 an ingot of bullion.
一丨墨 a cake of ink.
粉丨兒 cosmetic of white lead.
燭丨 a candlestick of tutenague.
紫金丨 a medical pastile used to rub on sores.
寄丨 to anchor.
筆丨式 a button on a door or box.
馬蹄丨 a hoof-shaped ingot.
糊丨 to paste hollow wooden ingots with silvered paper.
硃丨 a cake of vermilion.

掟 ting' From *hand* and *to fix*; also read ˋchăng.
To throw away or abroad; thrown down, as hail from the sky; to throw at; to smash.
丨破頭 to get one's head cracked in a fray.
丨茶盃誓願 to smash a teacup when taking an oath.
無銀丨口 no silver has been put into his mouth; *i. e.* you cannot believe his word, alluding to the custom of putting silver in a corpse's mouth. (*Cantonese.*)

丨佢 throw it at him. (*Cantonese.*)
丨栗包 to thump a boy's head with the knuckles.

梃 ting' Grain, as rice or wheat, standing upright and full eared; the culm of grain.
麥丨兒 the stalk of wheat.
In *Cantonese.* The stem of a fruit.
口嚨丨 the adam's apple.
甪丨碌柚 a pumelo with a broken stem; — a worthless fellow.

T'ING.

Old sounds, t'ing *and* ding. *In Canton,* t'ing *and* t'eng; — *in Swatow,* t'eng *and* t'ⁿia; — *in Amoy,* teng *and* t'eng; — *in Fuhchau,* t'eng, t'ièng, t'ing, *and* ting; — *in Shanghai,* t'ing *and* ding; — *in Chifu,* t'ing.

聽 听 ˌt'ing From 耳 *ear* and 悳 *correct* with 壬 as a phonetic; the contracted form is very common, and is also read ˏyin, to smile; smiling.
To hear, to listen; to understand; hearing; quiet, still.
丨而不聞 to hear and pay no attention.
丨聞 I heard about it.
丨得見 I can hear; I have heard.
丨得出 I understand it all.
丨不明白 I do not quite understand; I did not hear well.
丨事 one who waits, an attendant.
高乃丨 think highly of what you have heard.
好丨話 docile, obliging.
Read *t'ing'* To receive, to comply with; to hearken to; to accord; to hear and decide judicially; to be listened to; to acknowledge; to wait for, to tarry, — and in this sense often answers to according to, as, let.
打丨 or 探丨 to learn the news; to inquire of.
丨從 to comply, to agree with.
丨訟 to determine a cause.
丨審 to abide the examination, to stand a trial.
丨他頁心 as his kindness prompts, — let him act.
重丨 hard of hearing.
丨天由命 just as Heaven decrees.
丨他來 wait till he comes.
丨任 to allow.
丨其自然 let it be as it likes, let it go.
道丨途說 to hear on the road and talk of in the way; *i. e.* heedless of what he hears.
丨罪 to own one's offense.
In *Cantonese.* To-morrow.
丨日 next day.
丨朝 to-morrow morning.

廳 ˌt'ing From *shelter* and *to hear* as the phonetic.
A hall, a parlor, a saloon; a court, a place where cases are heard; the officer in his court.
大丨 a drawing-room.
客丨 or 花丨 a reception-room; a parlor.
門丨 the porter's lodge.
官丨 a police-station.
神丨 the room for the oracle or shrine in a house.

經丨 deputy in a prefect's court.
戎丨 the military office of the captain in a district.
河丨 a superintendent of boats at Canton.
司務丨 a clerk of records in the six Boards.
丨兒 a policeman. (*Pekingese.*)

汀 ˌt'ing A low spit or tongue of land; an isthmus; a low, level bank along a stream.
沙丨 a sandy beach.
丨州府 prefecture in the southwest of Fuhkien.
丨瀅 a small beach left by deposit.

朾 ˌt'ing Also read ˌchăng and ˏch'ăng.
The sound of chopping timber; to strike.
楔丨 the door-posts; the sockets of a door with their entering tenons.
虚丨 an ancient place in the state of Sung 宋, now the northern part of Kiangsu.

桯 ˌt'ing A stand near a bed; a headboard of a bedstead, or the board which binds it firmly together.

鞓 *'t'ing* The straps of hide, the 箱丨 which fasten and strengthen the top of the trunk after it is locked.

骾 *'t'ing* The thigh bone or femur is 腿丨骨, but it is also applied to other long bones.

廷 *'t'ing* From 廴 to *go* and 壬 *good*; it much resembles *'yen* 延 to extend, and is used with the next.

The place where audiences are held; the court of the palace; a court-yard; courtly; correct, regular; erect.

朝丨 the hall where audiences are held; the Emperor.

丨臣 privy councillors.

子有丨內 you have court-yards and private rooms.

丨杖 to bastinado a courtier, as was done in the Ming dynasty.

丨檄 a dispatch sent by express direct from the palace to the provinces.

丨尉 a palace officer, head of the guard; an ancient title.

庭 *'t'ing* From *shelter* and a *hall*.

The family rooms, a boudoir, the rooms used by children for study or work; parental; domestic; to grow straight; the court of a palace, the hall of audience; to appear at court.

丨訓 parental instruction.

家丨 home, one's own residence, a family seat; one's relatives.

家丨樂 domestic enjoyment.

丹丨 or 彤丨 or 天丨 or 禁丨 all denote the imperial palace, especially the private apartments.

門丨如市 his door-way is like a fair, speaking of an officer besieged by applicants.

天丨飽滿 a high spacious forehead; a term in physiognomy.

逕丨 very unlike; greatly mistaken.

四征弗丨 he punished all those chiefs who would not appear at court.

椿丨 a father.

蜓 *'t'ing* A dragon-fly.

蜻丨 a name for all *Libellulidæ*; the common names are 老流利 the water courser, 螳尾 the mantis' tail; 赤卒 the red soldier, 螞螂 and others.

Read *'t'ien*. A kind of livid striped lizard, called 蝘丨 found about damp walls.

霆 *'t'ing* Thunder; the first clap; the noise of many animals.

雷丨 rumbling thunder.

電丨 a flash of lightning.

雷丨之怒 thundering mad, very angry.

疾丨不及掩耳 a clap of thunder, so sudden that one has no time to cover the ears.

如丨如雷 like a clap and a crash of thunder, — was the onset.

莛 *'t'ing* The culm of grasses; the peduncle of flowers; small beams in a roof.

以丨撞鐘 to hit a bell with a blade of grass; *i. e.* to use very inadequate means.

舉丨與楹 he raised the purlines with the pillars.

麥丨 wheat straw.

花丨 a flower stalk.

亭 *'t'ing* From 高 *high* contracted and 丁 a *nail*, as the phonetic.

A portico; an open roof or dome supported on pillars; an arbor, a pavilion; a shed for travelers to stop at or lodge; straight, even, level.

不丨 irregular, awry.

茶丨 a tea-booth.

涼丨 or 花丨 a summer-house.

丨長 or 地保 an old name for policemen; they wore black clothes and a red cap.

八角丨 an octagonal pavilion.

碑丨 a porch for a stone tablet; they are often built very solidly with ornamented roofs.

坐龍丨 he who sits in the dragon pavilion; — *met.* the Emperor.

丨丨聳立 exalted and lofty, like an isolated peak.

申明丨 a sort of porch or hall, where the names of bad people are hung up for exposure and general information.

香丨 an open, sedan-like stand, to exhibit things in a procession.

停 *'t'ing* From *man* at a *shed*.

To rest, to stop; to hold up, as when there is enough; well-arranged; suitable, fitting, honest, trusty; to delay; after another verb, denotes the cessation of the act.

丨工 or 丨手 to rest from work.

丨止 to cease.

丨一會子 rested once.

丨當 all arranged rightly, everything in its place.

打扮丨當 well dressed; painted up; to put on a gay dress.

調丨 to part, as quarrelsome people; to set to rights, to arrange; to coöperate in attaining an end.

十丨已折其七 about seventenths were defeated.

丨車道左 stopped the carriage at the roadside.

臂膶三丨 the three joints of the arm were brawny and proportioned.

丨驂 to put up a horse, as for the night.

丨勻 even, uniform; well proportioned, or corresponding, as the parts of a thing.

淵丨 the water course has stopped running.

丨屍首 to lay out a corpse.

痛得丨 it has stopped aching.

哭不丨 she continues to weep.

渟 *'t'ing* From *water* and *arbor*; used with 汀 and the last.

Water stagnating; water running back and making a still deep pool in a stream.

决丨水致之海 to let the stagnant water flow out to sea.

聤 ˏt'ing A fluid and fetid secretion from the ear.

丨耳 a running ear.

婷 ˏt'ing Lady-like and beautiful.

當年不嫁惜娉丨 Alas, she did not marry that year, the luckless beauty!

葶 ˏt'ing A peduncle springing from the axil, and bearing many flowers.

丨藶 a plant found in Honan, said to kill fish like a *Lepidium.*

丨藶 a medicinal plant, allied to the shepherd's purse (*Thlaspi*) by the Chinese; the drawing shows that it is akin to the mustard, the flowers are yellow, the leaves broad lanceolate and obtusely serrate, and the siliques long; other descriptions confuse it with other cruciferous plants.

圢 ˋt'ing Used with the next.

A raised path through fields, such as are seen in rice grounds; a smooth place.

田丨有人行 people are walking through the fields on the paths.

町 ˋt'ing From *field* and a *nail.*

A raised path or dike through or between fields for passengers; a piece of waste land, a neglected corner; a lane, an alley; a parcel of land.

田丨 field-paths, fields.

丨畦 a bit of a garden.

句丨 an old name of Lin-ngan fu in Yunnan.

Read ˋ*tien.* A paddock, a park.

丨疃鹿場 our paddocks will be like deer-parks; — uncultivated.

挺 ˋt'ing From *hand* and *erect;* used for the next, and easily mistaken for ˏ*shen* 挻 to lead on.

To pull up or out; to strain, as at stool; to lead out; to rush or stand forward; to push out; to relax a little, as with prisoners; straight, to straighten; to carry one's self stiffly; decided, resolute in principle.

丨身 to stretch one's self up straight.

丨出 to project or grow out.

丨胸 to stretch and expand the chest.

丨節冰心 to firmly adhere to chastity.

直丨丨的 very stiff and upright.

丨刑 to bear a punishment without flinching or confessing.

丨不住 not to give in, good pluck.

以丨與刃 to use the stick as a sword; — *i. e.* to punish offenses too severely.

丨立 to stand stiff, as a grenadier.

In *Pekingese.* Very, greatly.

丨粗丨奘的 very coarse and bulging, as a water-jar.

丨梆子硬 a hard bit, as a nut to eat, or a piece of tough beef.

梃 ˋt'ing A club, a stick; a single branch or stalk.

甘蔗百丨 a hundred stalks of sugar-cane.

可使制丨 I can manage [the enemy] with even a shillelah; — a boast of a general.

奪丨相逐 he grasped the staff and drove him out.

丨榦之人 an efficient and clever man.

珽 ˋt'ing From *gem* and *erect.*

The name of a gem; a flat baton or scepter made of stone, held by the emperor in ancient times as a sign of authority; some were three feet long, others six inches.

天子搢丨方正於天下 the emperor took the scepter, and straightway the realm was regulated.

脡 ˋt'ing Meat which has been dried in the sun and out in strips; straight, stiff.

十丨爲束 ten strips of jerked meat form a bundle.

丨祭 a carp used in offerings.

與四丨脯 gave him four slices of dried meat.

艇 ˋt'ing A punt, a canoe, a dug-out; long and small boats, such as people live in at Canton, of which there are many sorts; inland boats, small craft.

小丨 or 丨仔 a small boat.

快丨 a fast-boat.

書信丨 express or post-boats.

花丨 flower-boats, used for parties.

丨家 boat-people.

二水丨 a sort of lighter.

採菱丨 punts to gather caltrops.

鋌 ˋt'ing A bolt or rod of iron or copper; the hollow barb or bolt of an arrow; finished, exhausted; to hasten.

丨而走險 to run away from danger.

頲 ˋt'ing A narrow head or forehead; straight.

丨庭 a direct path.

娗 ˋt'ing From *woman* and a *court.*

A woman who has recovered from disease.

眡丨 to disguise one's feelings; stolid, imperturbable.

眡丨人家 to rail at another.

Read ˏ*ting.* Handsome.

丨丨 fair and graceful.

壬 ˋt'ing From 土 *earth* and 人 a *man* but it is not the same as ˏ*jăn* 壬 as this usually has the lower stroke longest; it is thought to resemble sprouts coming out of the ground.

Good; complete; full; to verify; whatever is the business of life.

TIU.

Old sounds, tiu *and* tŭp. *In Canton*, tiu ; — *in Swatow*, tiu ; — *in Amoy*, tiu *and* piu ; — *in Fuhchau*, tiu *and* liu ; — *in Shanghai*, tiù ; — *in Chifu*, tiu.

丟 ꜀tiu From 一 *one* and 去 *gone*, not to return.

To cast away; to rid, relieved of; to cast off, to throw aside; to throw at, to pitch; to leave, as a family when going from home.

丨開 to put away; to throw aside; not to mention.

丨下去 left it behind.

丨下 lay it aside, as for a future occasion.

丨下水 thrown into the water.

丨着就走 he threw it down and then ran off.

丨臉 or 丨人 blasted his own reputation.

丨了一匹馬 lost one horse; — strayed.

丨棄 to reject, to discard finally.

丨開手 don't do it; let it alone; leave off.

丨不下 I cannot get it off my hands; cannot avoid the question.

丨眼色 to ogle.

丨不準 you did not hit — the hub.

丨空 to miss every other row.

丨冷 to utter a bon-mot.

颩 ꜀tiu From *wind* and *pelage*; read ꜀piu in the dictionary.

To fan; to move with the wind, as the trees.

丨了僧伽 the breeze fanned the priest.

TO.

Old sounds, ta, da, tap, *and* dap. *In Canton*, to *and* tù ; — *in Swatow*, to *and* tòa ; — *in Amoy*, tò *and* tui ; — *in Fuhchau*, to, tiò, t'iò, *and* twò ; — *in Shanghai*, tu *and* du ; — *in Chifu*, tòa.

多 ꜀to From 夕 *evening* repeated ; *q. d.* evening after evening.

An *adjective* of number, numerous, many, often, and is usually placed before the noun; not a few, more; much; mostly; how many? a *superlative*, very, excessive, too; to crave for more; to add; to become many; to praise; after a noun, it has in some places the force of a distributive adjective, as 年丨 every year.

丨事 officious; interfering.

幾丨 how many?

丨少 or 丨寡 how much?

丨得你 much obliged to you.

丨蒙你 I thank you much.

重得丨 this is the heaviest.

太丨 or 許丨 too much.

丨言 or 丨嘴 loquacious.

差不丨 nearly the same.

丨見 or 丨聞 well informed.

期逝不至而丨爲恤 the set time has passed, and he is not here, to the increase of my sorrows.

丨手 a meddlesome fellow.

丨大年記 how old are you?

替我丨丨問候 make my best respects to him.

丨之 to admire him; to make much of him.

不丨 not overmuch; these will do.

祝三丨 to pray for the three manies, — *i. e.* sons, wealth, and years.

阿丨 a Mongol or Ouigur word for papa.

丨羅呢 a charm-word (Sanscrit *dharani*) used by Budhists.

丨喈來 when will he come?

丨丨益善 the more [troops] the better.

既丨受祉 he enjoys great happiness.

丨重皮 what is the tare?

今夫地一撮土之丨 the earth as now before us, is a mere handful of soil.

袳 ꜀to A long sleeve, 裲丨 such as were worn in olden times.

朶 **朵** ꜂to From 木 *wood* and 乃 or 几 to represent *pendent* things above it.

Branches hanging, with flowers in bunches; a cluster, as of dates or lichis; a head of flowers; pendent things; to move; to lead, as a child; a classifier of clouds, flowers, and flames.

繡丨 to embroider.

耳丨 the lobe of the ear; for which sense the radical 耳 is often added, but the compound is not authorized.

丨丨香 an orchid like a *Cymbidium* with yellow flowers.

白雲丨丨 the snowy clouds are piled upon each other.

一丨花 a sprig of flowers.

觀我丨頤 are you looking at my chin moving — as I eat?

花丨 flowers; many blossoms.

一丨火 a flame.

丨丨 all sorts of flowers.

丨殿 the side buildings in a palace court.

放長耳丨聽聽 keep your ears open and hear all that is said.

垛 ˊto A round target made of straw hung near a race-course, to be shot at by archers going at full speed.

射丨 or 箭丨 a straw target.

城丨口 openings in the crenulated battlement of a wall.

城丨子 buttresses to the wall.

丨頭 side rooms or galleries in which to practice archery; so called in Kiangnan.

躲 ˊto The body; to conceal one's self, to hide away, to skulk, to secrete, to slip away; to escape.

丨懶 to shirk work.

丨學 to play truant, to idle at books.

丨藏 to secrete one's self.

丨匿 or 丨避 to lie perdu, to be out of the way; to escape from, as 收口丨避 to seek shelter from a storm in port.

丨債 to take leg bail, to evade one's creditors.

丨閃 to dodge out of one's sight.

丨不開 you cannot shun him.

丨一會子 he dodged him once

跺 ˊto To walk.

丨脚 to stamp the foot in anger.

揣 ˊto To guess the weight of, to heft a thing; to drop a sail.

丨忖其理 carefully estimate its qualities or value.

埵 ˊto From *earth* and *falling*.

Hard compact clods; firm ground.

土丨 a mound; a hillock raised for any purpose.

哆 ˊto ˏt'o To fall down, to come to pieces; to tumble down or be carried away.

石盤欲丨 the great bowlder threatens to fall.

鬌 ˊto Hair which has been cut from the head; the hair left on children's heads when they are first shaven.

剁 toˋ To chop fine, to hash with a chopping-knife, to mince; to carve.

丨排骨 to cut up chops.

一丨兩段 cut it in twain at one stroke.

丨碎了 hacked or minced it fine.

丨成肉醬 hashed it into fine mince meat; used as a threat.

稞 toˋ From *grain* and *bunch*.

A heap or stack of grain.

柴火丨 a pile of fuel.

堆成一丨 heap it up into a stack.

糞草丨 a dung-heap; a pile of compost

花稭丨 a stack of wheat straw.

舵 toˋ ˏt'o Also read ˏt'o, and written ˏ柁 but not accurately.

A rudder.

丨公 a helmsman

把丨 to steer.

耆丨 a captain or manager of the crew.

丨尾 the part of the rudder in the water.

推丨 or 裡丨 to port the helm.

無丨隨飄 rudderless, at the mercy of the winds.

外丨 starboard the helm.

船到江心拿穩丨 be careful how you steer when in the Yangtsz';— be steady in danger.

跢 toˋ The unsteady walk of a young child; to lead a child.

Read *tai*ˋ To overthrow; upside down.

Read ˏ*chi*, and used for 踟. Unsteady; undecided.

丨跦 embarrassed and vacillating.

惰 toˋ From 心 *heart* and 墮 to *fall* contracted.

The mind nerveless, flagging and heedless; indolent, remiss; rude, indifferent.

怠丨 careless, never completing a thing.

語之而不丨者 tell him that he must not be lazy.

股肱丨哉萬事墮哉 the members (or officers) are idle, and all affairs will go to ruin.

臨祭不丨 do not be negligent at worship.

懦丨已極 a stupid, useless dolt.

丨遊 to loaf about.

丨耕作 they are careless of plowing; — *i. e.* they do not attend much to agriculture.

墮 toˋ From 土 *earth* and 隋 to *fall*, or an old form 隓 which represents it; used for the preceding.

To fall in ruins; to fall over; to hang down, to sag; to fall, as tears; setting, as the moon sets; fallen, dilapidated, ruined; decayed, poor; disused, effete.

推丨 push it over

丨馬 fell off the horse.

門戶丨落 a decayed family

丨胎 a miscarriage.

團丨 to beg food, and throw the morsels into a clap-dish 鉢, as Budhists do on begging excursions.

丨落後 to fall behind.

褙 toˋ A jacket without sleeves; a kind of long gown like a cassock.

隋 toˋ An obeliscal aiguelle or peak; some say, the undulating line of a range of hills.

丨山喬嶽 the slender mountains and magnificent peaks.

Tʻo.

Old sounds, tʻa, tʻap, da, *and* dap. *In Canton*, tʻo *and* tui ; — *in Swatow*, tʻo *and* tʻòa ; — *in Amoy*, tʻò *and* tò ; — *in Fuhchau*, to, tʻo, twʻa, tʻie, *and* swoi ; — *in Shanghai*, du *and* tʻu ; — *in Chifu*, tʻòa.

拕 拖 ꜀tʻo — From *hand* and to *bear;* the first form is most used.

To pull, to drag along ; to draggle ; to lead, to take by the hand ; to implicate, to drag into ; to protract.

丨帶 to track, to drag.

丨累 involved, as in loss or danger.

丨一條棍 to trail a stick after one.

丨花翎 to wear a peacock's feather.

丨紳 ends of the girdle hanging low ; an official girdle.

丨泥帶水 I was draggled through the mud ; *met.* turbid, verbose, as a style.

丨罟船 a fishing-smack which drags the net after it.

大丨 a large smack.

丨延 to put off, to procrastinate.

杝 椸 ꜀tʻo — The second is also used as another form of 柁 ; also read ꜀li, ꜀i, and chai꜄

To split wood with the grain ; to break sticks ; to fall or come down ; a kind of tree whose wood is used for coffins, on account of its durability.

丨棖 an inner coffin.

析薪丨矣 when cleaving faggots, follow the grain.

麰 麧 ꜀tʻo — From *wheat* and to *carry* ; the two are nearly synonymous.

Cakes made of bean-flour ; the 粉丨子 are boiled with soy in little tin cups.

粘糕丨子 cakes of glutinous rice mixed with flour.

丨羅 a fancy wheaten cake in three round stories, common at Nanking, used in the worship of ancestors at newyear.

黃米丨 a cake made of bean-flour and millet meal.

泥丨子 the clod of earth wrapped around plants when transplanting them.

陀 陁 ꜀tʻo — The second is also used for ꜀chʻi 阤 a slide.

Steep and rugged paths ; dangerous acclivities.

丨羅尼 a *dharani*, a 呪 or magic formula.

沙丨 sandy steppes and wilds.

趨下陂丨 he hastened down the steep declivity.

跎 ꜀tʻo — To slip ; to miss ; to stumble, to misstep, as a horse.

命運蹉丨 an unlucky fate ; missed the chance.

驥垂兩耳兮中坂蹉丨 this old horse, whose ears lop down, has stumbled with me half way on the journey ; — referring to missing an opportunity, or a superannuated officer.

佗 它 ꜀tʻo — From *man* and *that ;* it was once written 他 ; the second is a synonym of the next, and an old form of 蛇 a snake.

That, another ; to charge.

丨背 humpbacked.

委委丨丨 elegant and easy in manners, as a virtuous dame.

君子正而不丨 the princely man regards [their doctrine as] true, and seeks for no other.

丨髮 to adjust the hair.

Read *tʻo*꜄ To add to ; to impute.

舍彼有罪予之丨矣 he remits that man's crime, that I may have the more.

馱 駄 ꜀tʻo, *to*꜄ — From 馬 *horse* and 大 *great ;* but the second is the common form.

An animal that carries burdens ; to lade on, to back a load.

背丨 to carry on the back.

牲口丨着 let the animals carry it.

負丨 to carry, as a pack ; to load on.

丨不動 it is too heavy to carry.

丨上山去 carry it up the hill.

In *Cantonese.* To suspend, as from the neck or girdle ; to hang upon.

丨肚 with child.

丨在襟頭 hang it on the lapel.

駝 ꜀tʻo — Used for the last.

A camel.

丨子 a burden.

帶丨 to a carry on camel's back.

少所見多所怪見駱丨以爲馬背腫 he who has seen little, and exaggerates in describing it, is like the man who saw a camel, and said it was a horse with a swollen back.

鴕 ꜀tʻo — A large gallinaceous bird, the 丨鳥 which probably refers to the ostrich, or to the cassowary of the Indian Archipelago ; it is also called 大馬爵 the large horse prince ; and 丨蹄鷄 or 駝鳥 camel fowl, from its large feet ; it is said to be 8 or 9 feet high, and the wings spreading ten feet.

鼧 ꜀tʻo — A name for the beaver, 丨鼥 which is said to be found in western countries, and among the Mongols ; it resembles the otter, and makes its nest in the ground.

驒 ꜀tʻo — A sort of wild horse ; a horse of a dark color with marks causing the whole to resemble fish's scales.

有丨有駱 there were many sorts of dappled and spotted horses.

柁 ꜀t'o Often used for 舵 a rudder.

A tie-beam or girder in the framework of a house which connects the large pillars; under it is the 二 丨 or supporting girder; firm wood; leaves falling.

一 對 丨 a pair of girders; a room with such a pair is regarded as having 三 間 three partitions.

丨 頭 彩 畫 painted beam-heads or corbels which project outside; the Chinese often carve characters on them.

凌 波 縱 丨 in a strong tide-way, humor the helm.

駝 ꜀t'o From 它 to *bear* and 束 *sheaf.*

Panniers, saddle-bags; slings used in securing the burdens with which animals are laden; to carry on the back.

𤵸 ꜀t'o Humpbacked; having a diseased and crooked spine.

丨 子 a hunchback.

丨 背 crook-backed.

鮀 ꜀t'o The *snake-fish,* as its name imports; a species of bullhead which burrows in the sand, and spurts it out; it is also called 鯊 魚 or sand fish, a name oftener given to the shark.

鼉 ꜀t'o From 黽 a *frog* and 單 *alone* contracted; it is apparently confounded with the last by some authors.

A large triton, gavial, or water lizard, found to the south of China, ten feet long, of whose hard skin drum-heads are made; its gruff voice is heard at night and indicates rain, whence the phrase 丨 鼓 逢 逢 the bass roar of the drums; the animal digs a deep hole in the bank; its eggs are numerous and eaten by itself; the flesh is prized, and served up at weddings.

伐 蛟 取 丨 to kill the dragon and catch the gavial.

丨 更 to strike the watches.

酡 ꜀t'o Face flushed with drink; rubicund.

顏 丨 red in the face.

醉 丨 half drunk.

朱 顏 丨 些 her rosy face was quite flushed.

沱 沲 ꜀t'o Water diverging into streamlets; a name anciently applied to small branches of the Yangtsz' River in part of its course, especially to one west of King-cheu fu in Hupeh; an affluent; a heavy rain; falling tears; forms part of the names of many streams, of which the 滹 丨 河 an affluent of the Pei-ho, is one.

出 涕 丨 若 the tears fell like rain.

潭 丨 waves surging and foaming.

丨 江 a branch of the Yangtsz' in the southeast of Sz'ch'uen, near Lu-cheu 瀘 州.

紽 ꜀t'o A skein or hank of silk or floss; braiding to ornament furs.

素 絲 五 丨 five braidings [adorned] their plain silk dresses.

砣 碃 鉈 ꜀t'o The third is applied to iron weights; it is also read ꜀shé, a short spear.

A stone roller; a game called 飛 磚 or flying bricks, swinging heavy stones from hand to hand; a weight or ball on the end of cords; the weight on a steelyard; a pilot's lead.

打 飛 丨 to swing weights.

秤 丨 a steelyard weight.

掅 ꜀t'o Like the last.

To sling stones, or heavy weights from one to another, practiced by athletes and military men.

砲 丨 to throw at.

In *Pekingese.* To pile up, as in steps.

𦍧 ꜀t'o A fabulous animal like a ram, having nine tails and four ears.

丨 羅 呢 broadcloth; and 丨 羅 絨 velvet; *to-lo* being an imitation of an Indian word, and written in different ways.

詑 ꜀t'o To deceive; to lie to, to impose on.

Read ꜀i. Self-possessed.

丨 丨 satisfied.

庹 ꜀t'o ꜂t'o From to *measure* and a *foot.*

To measure anything by stretching the arms out.

丨 不 過 you cannot span it, as a big tree.

量 一 丨 it measures one fathom.

妥 ꜂t'o From 安 *quiet* contracted to 女 *woman* and 爪 *claws; q.d.* what the claws have safely.

Secure, safe, stable, firm; to seat well; at ease, settled, quiet; ready, prepared,—and often merely a sign of the past tense.

丨 咯 an exclamation at the end of a sentence indicating the end, that's right; so; well now!

丨 當 or 穩 丨 everything right; properly done, secured.

作 不 丨 貼 he did not do it satisfactorily.

有 的 不 丨 there is something unsafe; there's a screw loose.

極 丨 or 丨 極 very well, that's just right.

設 祠 以 先 丨 靈 erect a hall to quiet the ancestral manes.

講 丨 well said.

周 丨 all correct, as well and safe as it can be.

欲 丨 協 則 不 能 迅 速 if the thing is to be done safely, it must not be hurried.

楕 ꜂t'o Anything round, long, and slender, like a pipe, pencil, or rod; a mathematical term for cylindrical; a tube for holding salt.

丨 圓 long, slim and round.

擶 ˓t'o To clip the four corners of a thing that is too long; to lessen by clipping; to throw aside; to cover, to feel over.

䄍 ˓t'o Full and ample, as a dress where the skirts spread out.
垂肩丨袖 drooping shoulders and ample sleeves; said of a beauty.

婧 ˓t'o Fascinating, engaging, seductive; not correct, heedless of propriety; idle, careless.
妾不敢以燕丨見帝 I dare not see his Majesty in the least dishabille.

唾 涶 t'o˒ tu˒ From *mouth* and *to drop*; the second also means a port, a place to land at.
To spit; saliva; to do a thing easily.
丨面 to spit in one's face.
丨涕 to blow the nose.
丨沫盒 a small spit-box.
丨生花 to compose off-hand.
讓食不丨 do not spit when giving one a dish of food.
不顧而丨 to heedlessly hack up phlegm — is ill manners, because one can't well hear.
丨口水 to spit.
丨罵 to spit on and revile.

蛻 t'ö˒ From *insect* and *to weigh*; it is also read *tui*˒ and *shui*˒.
The exuviæ or cast-off skins of cicadas, snakes, or crabs; to slough off the skin.
蛇丨 a snake's skin.
丨殼 cast-off shells or skin.
一朝忽虛丨 one morning he suddenly became an empty skin; — his spirit left the body.
蟬丨龍變棄俗登仙 when the katydid molts and the dragon transforms itself, it is like my discarding the world and going among the immortals; a Taoist sneer at life.

TOH.

Old sounds, tat, dat, *and* dak. *In Canton*, tok, tüt, *and* chüt; — *in Swatow*, tȯk, tat, *and* tak; — *in Amoy*, tȯat, tok, *and* tȯ; — *in Fuhchau*, twak, chwȯk, tȯk, *and* t'ȯk; — *in Shanghai*, töh, döh, *and* dok; — *in Chifu*, tȯa.

掇 to˒ From *hand* and to *join*.
To collect, to arrange, to gather up; to take up with both hands.
丨採 to gather.
拾丨 to put in order, to furbish up, to make as new; to put to rights.
薄言丨之 now we pluck the ears — of the plaintains.

剟 to˒ Used with the last; also read *choh*˒
To cut, to prick; to cut blocks, to engrave; to cut open and rob.
丨訂 to print and publish books.

敠 to˒ To estimate the weight of anything by lifting it; to eat slowly.
战丨准不准 can you guess its weight exactly?
丨敠之食 a present of food, as a delicacy.

裰 to˒ To mend clothes.
紉針請補丨 thread the needle and ask him to mend this.

鵽 to˒ From *bird* and *connected*; it is also read *choh*˒
A small bird, the 丨鳩 whose cry is *ti-ti*, found in the northern deserts in flocks; it has a crest, a forked tail, and no hind claw or hallux; it is noted for its thieving, and one name is 突厥雀 or Turk's sparrow, because it comes down on the fields like the nomads and devours the crops; it probably belongs to the grouse or plover tribe.

奪 t'o˒ ˏto Formed of 大 *great* 隹 *bird* and 寸 *inch*, but the last part is regarded as a form of 又 or 手 *hand*, united with 奞 to *spread* the *wings*, referring to the fowler's skill in trapping birds.
To take by force; to snatch; to get by striving or anyhow; to carry off, as when a prize is gained; to take away, as when rank is lost; to criticise or expunge.
丨路 to pass another on the road.
刼丨 to rob boldly in bands.
丨取 to carry off, as against one's wishes.
丨標 to take the prize.
丨命金丹 a golden pill that will snatch your life from death.
爭明丨利 to contend for fame and gain.
丨春魁 to get one of the first five places in an examination for *tsintsz'*.
漁丨百姓 to catch and plunder the people.
丨賭籌 to take the gambling reeds; — a mode of playing.
光彩丨目 the dazzling brightness blinded the eye.
察丨 [please] examine and lop off — what is improper; a final phrase in petitions.
酌丨 to deliberate and then fix upon the points.
定丨 finally settled on.
丨胎 to drive off the soul of a fetus and take its place; averred to be done by old Rationalists.
丨倫 discordant, out of place; said of instruments in a band.
丨秀氣 he has carried off all the literary fame.
君子不丨人所好 the princely man does not covet what others prize.

敓, ˏtoh Interchanged with the last.
To take forcibly, to seize; to rob.
丨攘 to appropriate without right.
搶 丨 to plunder.

鐸, ˏto From *metal* and to *peep*.
A square-mouthed, oblong bell, like a cow-bell, usually made of iron, with a long clapper; a kind of jingle or rattle used in the army to convey orders; one who arouses the age; a limit.
木 丨 a wooden-tongued bell.
風 丨 bells hung on eaves to ring with the wind.
司 丨 a native priest in the Roman Catholic churches.
天將以夫子爲木丨 Heaven brings forth a sage to arouse the world.
丨德 to incite to virtue.

澤, t'o' Icicles; a more common name is 氷柱 ice pillars.

㥃, to' Formed of *heart* and *limit*; a synonym of 度, to distinguish it from 度' a rule.
To guess, to calculate.

剫, to' To cut and hew wood, as carpenters do; to divide.
丨木 to work in wood, the joiner's craft.

詑, to' To delude by false representations.
僞 丨 to deceive by falsehoods.

鵽, to' A species of water-bird, the 鶈 丨 which resembles the rail; it is mostly found in the southern provinces.

喥, to' Also read *ch'ah*, and used for *ch'a'* 咤 to grumble.
To gabble; to talk incessantly.
口丨丨無度 a constant stream of talk flows from his mouth.

踱, to' To tread or step on; to walk to and fro.
丨來丨去 to walk back and forth.
任步閒丨 to walk for pleasure.
丨步亭心 walking inside of the arbor.

沰, to' From *water* and *stone*; used for ʿché 赭 ocher.
To let down; to drop, as a line into a well; to drop, as rain.
滴 丨 to drip; leaking by drops.

T'OH.

Old sounds, t'ak *and* t'at. *In Canton*, t'ok *and* t'üt; — *in Swatow*, t'út, t'ak, t'ap, *and* t'o; — *in Amoy*, t'òat *and* t'ok; — *in Fuhchau*, t'auk, tw'ak, *and* nòh; — *in Shanghai*, t'öh, döh, *and* t'ok; — *in Chifu*, t'òa.

脫, ˏt'o From *flesh* and to *arrange*.
The flesh leaving the bones; emaciated, lank; spoiled and dissolving; to undress, to strip; to let go, to escape from, to relinquish; to get out of, to evade, to avoid; to leave; in *rhetoric*, to touch on slightly, to allude to; if, perhaps; when following another verb, often becomes a mere dissyllabic auxiliary, or a form of the perfect tense; as 漏丨 to leak out; 放 丨 to let go; 失 丨 forfeited, lost.
開 丨 to let off, to exonerate.
丨使可行 perhaps it can be done.
丨身 to slip away, to escape.
丨衣服 to undress.
丨皮 to peel; to cast the skin.
解 丨 to deliver from, to rid.
推 丨 to turn over to another.
丨略 liberal; not exacting; to make a résumé.
丨難 to escape trouble.
丨了圈套 slipped out of the noose.
丨然無累 I got away, and was not entangled.
丨俗 elevated, not vulgar; to avoid the world.
灑 丨 in good spirits, well, bright; talented, clever.
丨生爲馬 to be born as a horse, — in the next existence.
金蟬丨殼之計 the spotted cicada is planning how to get rid of its skin; — *i. e.* he is contriving a way to leave.
出 丨 to sell, to part with.
Read *tui'* Leisurely.
丨丨而去 went off very slowly.
In *Cantonese*. A classifier of suits of clothes and messengers.
幾丨人來 several men came one after the other.
一丨衣服 a suit of clothes.

捝, ˏt'o Similar to the last.
To exclude; to remove; to mistake; to leave behind.
Read *shui'* To rub and clean.
坐丨手遂祭酒 on sitting down rub the hands, and then pour the libation.

侻, ˏt'o 人情僣丨 men's dispositions are crafty and guileful.
丨合於敎 education has much to do with the character.

毻, ˏt'o From *hair* and to *fall*.
To molt the hair or feathers, for which 脫 is now generally used.
丨毛 to molt, to shed the hair.

袥, ˏt'o To loosen the neck-cloth or collar; to free the neck; a sort of knee-pad.

天地開闢宇宙丨袓 when heaven and earth were spread out, it was like loosening the bands of the universe; so the Taoists say.

𧘂, ˏt'o To open the dress for air and freedom.

乇, ˏt'o The original form represents ripe *grain* bending down, with the stalk continuing into the *root*, and entering the *ground*, this being represented by the horizontal line; another says it represents the plumule just opening above the ground.

To depend on; to engage one to act for; now written like the next.

In *Fuhchau*. A thing, a matter; articles, goods; an idol, things carried in processions.

骨頭丨 worthless things, no better than old bones.

生丨 to have an eruption.

託, 侘, ˏt'o From *words* and a *shoot*; the second form is little used.

To charge with, to intrust to; to commission, to engage one to do, to ask; to accept a commission and its pay; to trust in, to rely on; to make an excuse of; to use as a pretext.

丨福 by your leave I am well, thank you; or in full, 丨你老人家的福 I have availed myself of your favor to be happy; — a polite phrase, for which 丨賴 is another form.

丨你作事 I beg of you to do this affair.

丨庇 by your auspices.

不可丨 not trustworthy.

丨人情 to engage another's aid and kindness.

寄子丨妻 to commit a son to another, and ask one to care for a wife, — when about to travel.

可以丨六尺之孤 if there be a man who can be intrusted with the charge of an orphan.

丨故 to apologize for, to suggest a reason for; to give as a pretext.

上士可以丨色 only very high minds can resist lust;

中士可以丨辭 inferior ones can carry out others' wishes;

下士可以丨財 and the lowest can use others' property honestly.

受人之丨 I am engaged by some one to do it.

丨音 to play on an instrument.

托, 拓, ˏt'o From *hand* and a *shoot*, though it is regarded as the modified or derived form of the second; it is often erroneously used for the last; the second also means to push away.

To carry on the palm, to bear up, to take on the hand, to take up with the hand; at Canton used for 扛 to carry on the shoulder.

丨子 or 丨盤 a waiter or tray; the first also denotes the satin lining of a sable robe.

丨上膊頭 shoulder it.

丨腮 to lean the head on the hand.

推丨 to equivocate, to dissemble.

丨塔天王 the god who holds the pagoda in his hand.

落落丨丨 unfavorable times, disheartened, unsuccessful.

不丨 what can't be handled; *i. e.* gruel, porridge, &c.

丨落 (also written 魄落) mortified; reduced to poverty.

橐, ˏt'o From 木 *wood* and 囊 *bag* modified, say some; it resembles ˓kao 櫜 a case.

A sack open at both ends; a porte-monnaie or belt worn aronnd the waist.

丨籥 a tube through which to blow the fire; bellows used by potters.

丨粗 a kind of satchel for carrying food and clothes.

椓之丨丨 the continuous sounds of rammers — were heard.

丨駝 the camel; *lit.* a bag-carrier.

裹餱粮于丨于囊 he tied up dried meat and grain in packs and bags.

驝, ˏt'o From *horse* and *bag*; *q. d.* the quadruped who carries bags.

The camel was once known as 丨駝, but the term is now obsolete.

牧丨 a superintendent of camels.

飥, ˏt'o A bun or cake made of wheaten flour; in some places, a cake of any kind.

餺丨 a flour cake.

柝, ˏt'o From *wood* and to *drive off*; but originally the phonetic was the proceding character.

A board with a hole and short handle, used by watchmen to strike the hours.

擊丨 to strike the watches.

更丨 the watchman's clapper.

跅, ˏt'o Negligent; to disregard rules.

丨弛之士 an officer who is remiss, and gives no heed to law.

丨落 heedless, indifferent to restraint, like a bow unstrung, which flies back.

籜, ˏt'o The sheath which envelopes the joints of the bamboo; the first leaves of bamboo shoots; a shoot growing from the roots, like a sucker.

初篁苞綠丨 the first bamboo stalks growing rank with green leaves.

蘀, ˏt'o Fallen, as leaves in autumn; cracked, as the bark of some plants, which peels off.

十月殞丨 in November the vegetation decays and falls.

其下維丨 only withered leaves are below it.

莌, ˏt'o A plant allied to the sarsaparilla, the 活丨 or 寇脫 found in Kiangnan; it grows ten feet high; the leaves are large, and the pith very white; it is the *Aralia edulis*.

TU.

Old sounds, to, tot, tok, do, dot, *and* dok. *In Canton*, tò *and* tu ; — *in Swatow*, tò, tu, *and* chu ; — *in Amoy*, tò ; — *in Fuhchau*, tu, tò, *and* tòk ; — *in Shanghai*, tu *and* du ; — *in Chifu*, tu.

都 ˏtu From 邑 a *city* and 者 *this*.
The place of the palace or imperial ancestral temple; a metropolis or capital; a large city; under the Cheu, a region equivalent to four 縣 districts; a fief granted to princes; an imperial city whose revenue was granted to statesmen; the suburbs of a capital; the state, the country; elegant in manners; abundant, fine, full; an *adjective* of number, all, altogether, usually used after the noun; in general; also, together with; still, possibly, probably; followed by a negative, as 丨不 or 丨沒, has an adversative sense, no, not at all; an exclamation of pleasure, excellent! to occupy, as an office; to dwell; an islet on which birds collect; in some of the cities of Chehkiang, it denotes a ward or a police circuit; elsewhere it often means a group of villages, arranged for fiscal convenience.

京丨 or 丨城 the capital of a country; the court.

洵美且丨 very beautiful and excellent.

丨爲一集 it all formed one collection.

送丨不要 I don't wish it even as a gift.

我丨去 I will go too.

丨督 an old name for a 丨統 or Manchu major-general.

副丨統 a brigadier-general.

一切丨收 all were collected.

陪丨 the double capital; — a term for Mukten.

大丨如是 they are generally like this.

身丨卿相之位 I personally filled the post of prime-minister.

貌雖不丨 she would not be reckoned a great beauty.

丨未去過 I have not been there.

丨察院 the Censorate; its members are commonly called 丨老爺 at Peking.

丨司 or 丨府 or 丨閫 a major; or in the navy, a commander; one is found in each prefecture.

In *Pekingese*. To grumble, to mutter; to be unreasonable and gruff.

丨嚕 or 丨噥 to be dissatisfied and scold unreasonably.

肚 ˏtu A paunch; erroneously used for a beetle or heavy mallet.

胍丨 a big belly.

蔀 ˏtu Name of a plant.

菇丨 a flower bud; it is applied especially to conspicuous ones, like the rose or pomegranate.

覩 ˏ**睹** ˋtu From to *see* or *eye* and *that*.
To look, to observe; perceived, manifested.

目所未丨 what eye hath not seen.

明丨 to be evident.

耳丨之所丨記 what the senses have seen and remembered.

丨而不見 to look and not observe; absent-minded.

堵 ˋtu To obstruct, to guard, to close, to shut or ward off; to fill in; to invest; a wall around a yard, a stretch of wall; 50 cubits length of a wall; at peace, quietly at home.

丨塞 to wall up, to close against.

丨死 to smother to death.

丨口 to gag; to stuff the mouth.

防丨 to defend, to resist.

丨截 to guard, to cut off approach to.

阿丨 pelf, lucre; — an old or poetical term.

觀者如環丨 the spectators were like a wall around him.

巡丨 to patrol and guard, as revenue-cutters.

民皆安丨 the people were all at peace.

百丨皆作 five hundred poles' length of wall rose at once.

丨住寨門口 stopped the doorway to prevent him entering.

In *Fuhchau*. A panel; a compartment; an apartment; a piece of wall.

賭 ˋtu To wager, to risk, to stake; to gamble, to play for money; gaming, play.

丨棍 or 丨鬼 a gambler.

丨博 or 丨錢 to play for stakes.

開丨塲 (or 局) to open a table.

丨彩 try your luck; it depends on luck.

爛丨 a confirmed gambler.

丨呪 to take an oath.

丨當頭 or 丨押賬 a pledge for a gambling debt.

丨命 to risk life, as soldiers do.

久丨無勝家 a gamester in the long run never wins.

丨東道 to bet something, as a dinner.

丨氣 to throw up an affair in disgust, to become angry at.

聚丨 to get gamblers together; to induce men to play.

丨眼力 to get another to decide upon the value of a thing; or between two as to its nature.

花丨 female gamblers involved in a criminal case.

睹 ˋtu The morning, the dawn, when the day begins to grow bright.

丨色 the blush of day.

'肚 From *flesh* and *earth*; the character is rather a modern one, and is sometimes read *tu'*

'tu
tu'

The belly; the stomach; a bellyfull; a good deal; the temper or mind.

兜丨 or 暖丨 a stomacher, a corset.

小丨 the region of the bladder; the pubic region.

有丨子 pregnant.

腸丨 the inwards; entrails.

跑丨的 a looseness, diarrhea.

丨痛 the belly-ache.

一丨火 irascible, fiery; very feverish.

丨腹軟 indigestion, heart-burning.

丨裏明白 of a clear perception, intelligent.

一丨子氣 angry and obstinate.

丨量大 very patient, forbearing.

'⿰土度 From *earth* and *to measure*.

'tu

To stop up, to stuff; to prevent water flowing from a sluice; to obstruct.

丨住 stopped, filled.

丨罐子口 to shut the jar's mouth.

丨窟窿 stuff it into the hole.

把話丨他的嘴 he said what stopped the other's talk.

杜' From *wood* and *earth*.

tu'
'tu

A fruit of a yellowish-red color, called 丨棃子, and regarded by the Chinese as akin to the crab-apple; the wood is used for blocks by printers, and for bows by archers; there is some confusion about this plant, for other details point to a tree resembling the *Euonymus*, but the fruit of that tree is uneatable; to shut out, to restrict, to impede; to allay.

丨門不出 to close the doors, and remain at home — for study.

丨絕文契 a deed in fee simple.

丨絕了 to suspend intercourse with; to cut.

丨伯 a scorpion.

丨鵑花 the Azalea flower.

閉門丨客 to deny one's self to visitors.

丨釁端 to remove causes of strife.

有杕之丨 a solitary spindle-tree.

野丨仲 a vine with black spotted stalks, and leaves shaped like those of the orange; the bark is infused in spirits.

丨仲 the *Euonymus japonicus*, a tree allied to the spindle-tree; the bark is used in medicine.

⿰土鳥' Name of a bird, 丨鵑 which applies best to the cuckoo, but seems also to include the goatsucker or night-jar.

'tu

度' Formed of 庶 *people* contracted, and 又 a *hand* under it: used for the next.

'tu
to'

A measure; a test, a degree, a limit; a degree of latitude or longitude; an interval in music; a rule, a regulation; capacity, endurance; to arrange or spread; to bring under rule; to form by law; to pass, as time; to ford.

丨日 to spend the day.

費用過丨 to spend extravagantly.

丨數 certain times, periods, or distances

丨曲 to keep time in playing.

無丨 illimitable; no restraint; lawless, reckless.

滿丨 and 虧丨 a major and a minor interval in music.

寬宏大丨 liberal-minded and generous.

風丨 courtesy, politeness.

節丨使 special officers in the Ming dynasty sent to see after the revenue of the provinces.

五丨 the five measures of length; *viz.*, 分 line, 寸 inch, 尺 foot, 丈 rod, and 引 fathom.

六丨 the six *paramitas*, or means of reaching *nirvana*, *viz.*, alms, morality, zeal, patience, meditation, and intelligence.

節丨 economy, a definite outlay.

局丨 capacity; enlarged views.

Read *toh*, To guess, to calculate, to estimate; to throw in, as dirt into a caisson or wooden frame, when raising adobie walls.

予忖丨之 I can estimate him fully.

量丨 to reckon the measure of.

諒入丨出 to calculate by what comes in, how much to spend.

以意丨之 to revolve it in the mind; to consider and get an idea of it.

渡' From *water* and *to measure*; interchanged with the last.

tu'

To ford, to cross a stream or sea; to go through, as a road; to pass, as time; to go from one subject to another; a ferry-boat.

丨船 a ferry-boat; a passage-boat.

丨頭 or 擺丨 a ferry.

丨淺 to ford shallows.

人之丨生如客丨海 the life of man is like a voyager crossing the sea.

丨化人 a neophyte, a convert to Budhism.

古丨 an ancient ford.

端陽競丨 to see the races on the Dragon-boat festival.

鍍' To gild, to adorn with gold; to plate.

tu'

丨一層金 washed once with gold.

丨首飾 gilded head ornaments.

丨金作 a goldsmith's shop.

妒' 妬' From 女 *female* and 戶 *inner door*, occasionally changed to 石 *stone*, implying barrenness.

tu'

Jealous, as a wife sometimes is of her husband; envious of another in the heart; averse to.

丨婦 a jealous woman.

丨忌 envy, as seen in actions.

生丨心 to bear envy against.

嫉高者人丨之 men envy the high in rank.

蠹 蝳 tu' } From 虫 *insect* and 橐 *bag* contracted, the second form is more ideographic, but is very seldom met.

Grubs in wood; worms in books or clothes, like the larvæ of the 蛀 or various genera of *Tineites* and *Ptinus;* weevil-grubs; cheese mites.

丨魚 the Lepisma; worms in books; *met.* a close student.

積穀生丨 heaped up grain breeds weevils.

丨吏 or 丨役 extortionate rulers or police.

丨毛虫 hairy caterpillars.

斁 tu' From 攴 *to strike* and 睪 *to peep.*

To destroy; to ruin; fallen in ruins; to besmear; to smudge.

隳丨 ruined, dilapidated; unsuccessful.

耗丨下土 it damages or destroys earthly things; — *i. e.* the inhabitants — as a drought.

Read *yih*, and used for 繹. To discharge; to dislike, to put away; to tire of, to weary of, to loathe; to put an end to, to suffice; to explain.

服之無丨 I have worn this garment without disliking it; — alluding to a concubine of Wăn Wang whom he liked.

解丨甚明 he explained it very clearly.

庸鼓有丨 the drums and bells fill the ear with melody.

殬 tu' Similar to the last.

To break; to ruin, to injure.

丨壞决裂 destroyed and spoiled completely.

事丨垂成 the matter was nearly done when it was ruined.

T'U.

Old sounds, t'o. t'ot, do, *and* dot. *In Canton,* t'ò; — *in Swatow,* t'u, tò, *and* t'ò; — *in Amoy,* tò *and* t'ò; — *in Fuhchau,* t'u, tu, *and* t'ò; — *in Shanghai,* t'u *and* du; — *in Chifu,* t'u.

圖 ˏt'u From 囗 *to surround* and 啚 *difficult; q. d.* how to escape from difficulties.

A plan, drawing, diagram, or chart; to delineate, to sketch an outline; to plan, to scheme; to plot, to intrigue; to reckon on; to remove; to estimate, to calculate; to wish or try for; forethought, care.

貪丨 to earnestly wish; greedy.

丨籍 books and drawings.

丨形 the idea or sketch of, a plate of; the contour; to draw a form.

丨書 a private or personal seal.

丨章 the motto on a seal.

丨名利 to plan how to be famous and rich.

惟懷永丨 he still cherished a fixed resolution.

你丨什麼 what plan have you?

天文丨 a map of the stars.

丨維 plans, propositions, imaginings, schemes.

丨像 a picture of, as a god.

滋蔓難丨 their wide ramifications were not easily extirpated.

我丨爾居 I have consulted about your residence.

丨畫 to draw pictures.

屠 ˏt'u From *body* and *this.*

To butcher, to kill and dress animals for the stall; to rip, to rend in pieces, an ancient town near the capital of Shensi.

丨夫 or 丨戶 a butcher.

禁丨 or 斷丨 to prohibit the slaughter of animals; — it is often ordered to propitiate the gods in times of distress.

鼓刀以丨 he flourished the sword and was about to slay.

瘏 ˏt'u A horse worn out by travel.

我馬丨矣 my horses were quite used up.

予口卒丨 my mouth was all sore.

途 ˏt'u From *to go* and *I;* it is also used with the next two.

A road, a path; a pursuit, a way of doing things.

長丨 a long way or journey.

丨路 a road.

沿丨平安 well and quiet the whole way.

半丨而廢 to fail half-way-in any pursuit.

岐丨 erroneous ways or doctrines.

殊丨同歸 they got home by different roads.

自顧前丨 to see ahead on the road; — to care for the future.

正丨人員 he attained distinction by the right mode.

官丨 officials, those in service.

涂 ˏt'u Name of two streams, branches of the 汾河 in Shansi near Ta-yuen fu; also of one in Shantung which empties into the Gulf; and of another in Sz'-ch'uen; rut of a wheel.

丨月 a classical name for the twelfth moon.

丨丨 a heavy dew.

溝丨 bridge or way over a sluice.

塗 ˏt'u From *earth* and a *stream;* occurs used for the next.

Mud, mire; miry; to daub, to besmear, to dirty; to plaster, to wash; to blot out or efface; to fill cracks; untrustworthy; dull, stupid, pig-headed; a noted hill in Nganhwui.

糊丨 inapt, unready, blundering; to mismanage.

雨雪載 丨 the snow is falling and the roads are muddy.

塵 丨 dirt and dust; *i. e.* the world.

丨 抹 to erase, to scratch out.

丨 牆 to plaster a wall.

丨 飾 to plaster in colors.

丨 面 to daub the face, as actors or burglars do.

丨 鴉 to write badly; said of rude penmanship.

丨 粉 to use cosmetics.

如 丨 丨 附 it is like putting mud on one in the mire.

見豕負 丨 to see a hog and carry dirt; *i. e.* to still more defile one's self.

丨 山 a small fief named from this hill, lying along the River Hwai in Fung-yang fu in Nganhwui.

꜀峹 ꜀嵞 ꜀t'u

Usually written like the last.

Name of a peak, some say in Sheu cheu 壽州, but others put it in Hwai-yuen hien in Fung-yang fu, where Yü the Great married a wife called 丨 山 氏 from the name of the state.

꜀酴 ꜀t'u

Rum or arrack that has not been strained; the mother in spirits.

丨 酥 酒 or 丨 醾 酒 unstrained, whitish, thick liquor, of a sweetish taste, also called 江 米 酒 Kiangnan rice wine; an old custom existed of drinking it on the 15th of the first moon as a prophylactic.

꜀悇 ꜀t'u

Sorrowful looking; distressed.

憚 丨 anxious about, as an event coming to pass.

Read *yü'* Delighted, much gratified.

꜀梌 ꜀t'u

A fine tree allied to the catalpa; sharp-pointed; an old name for thorny trees in Kiangnan.

丨 木 a Canton name for the best kind of pine timber used in making furniture.

꜀荼 ꜀t'u

From *grass* and *I*; not to be confounded with ꜀*ch'a* 茶 tea, with which it was once synonymous.

A bitter herb containing a whitish juice, like the sow-thistle (*Sonchus*) or endive (*Cichorium*); to incroach on prerogatives; weeds; a marsh flower.

丨 毒 noxious weeds; bitter calamities, sorrows.

有女如 丨 the maidens were there like marsh flowers.

丨 苦 afflictions; and the tea-shrub is said to be still known as 苦 丨 in Sz'ch'uen, though this is probably a mistake for some other plant.

倩 丨 to borrow.

丨 蘼 花 a yellow or white rose.

神 丨 and 鬱 壘 the names of two brothers, now deified and worshiped as the wardens of doorways; their names or pictures are pasted on outer gates.

꜀𣘻 ꜀t'u

From *wood* and *weed*; used with the last.

A kind of tree found in Yunnan, an infusion of whose leaves is drunk.

丨 柒 name of a timber tree.

Read ꜀*ch'a*, and used for 茶. Old tea leaves are still called 丨 荈 in some places.

꜀徒 ꜀迏 ꜀t'u

From a *step* and to *walk*, or to *go* and *earth*, the latter being the original form; it resembles *ts'ung* 從 to follow, and ꜀*si* 徙 to move.

A footman, to go afoot; a foot-soldier; in the T'ang dynasty, it often included a bondman or serf; a follower, a disciple; servants about an office; a sensualist, a low fellow, a ruffian, a rowdy; a multitude, a crowd; a cabal; empty, as an open hand; as an initial *adverb*, futile, vainly; only, barely; the punishment of transportation.

丨 弟 an apprentice; a neophyte, a pupil.

丨 步 or 丨 行 to foot it.

無禮之 丨 an unprincipled rascal.

丨 然 to no purpose, uselessly

司 丨 the minister of Education in ancient times.

奸 丨 a brigand, a seditious villain.

丨 勞無益 only trouble, without any advantage.

問 丨 a crime punishable by transportation for three years.

丨 善不足以爲政 mere goodness is not sufficient to carry on a government.

其 丨 數十人 his followers number scores of men.

公 丨 infantry.

實繁有 丨 there is really a large crowd.

꜀跿 ꜀t'u

Barefoot; to stand on one foot.

丨 跔科頭 barefooted and bareheaded.

꜀䖘 ꜀t'u

Composed of *tiger* and *hare*.

In the country of Tsu or Hunan, a tiger was anciently called 烏 丨 probably a local name represented by these characters.

꜀菟 ꜀t'u t'u'

From *grass* and *rabbit*.

A medicinal plant, the 丨' 絲, or 丨' 絲子 *Cuscuta* or dodder.

丨 葵 a kind of Anemone.

伏 丨' another name for China root.

於 丨 an old and local name for the tiger.

丨 瓜 probably another name for the sweet potato.

꜀鵌 ꜀t'u

A yellowish-blackish bird, found in Wéi-yuen hien on the River Wéi in Kansuh, which lives in the same hole with the marmot, keeping watch on the outside; it may be allied to the *Strix cunicularia* or burrowing-owl.

꜀駼 ꜀t'u

A famous palfrey, called 騊 丨; also a wild animal like a horse, perhaps the onager, found in the northern deserts.

稌 *ˏt'u* An old name for a kind of glutinous rice used for making thick liquor; in ancient times it was reckoned as one of the six grains.

豐年多丨 glutinous rice is abundant in fruitful seasons.

土 *ˊt'u* The character is intended to represent two strata of *soil* with *plants* growing up through them; it is defined 地之吐生萬物者 what [the divinity] Earth vomits to produce all things; it is the 32d radical of a large natural group of characters referring to forms and uses of earth.

The fourth of the five elements; the god Earth, Tellus, or Cybele; earth, soil, clods, ground; a region, a place; in commerce often refers to Canton; territory, possessions, lands; earthy; a pale or ochery color; on the ground; local, peculiar, native to the place; in Kiangsi, a designation for a quantity of soil about 12 ft. square by one thick, a ditcher's day's work; to appear, as ground where the water has run off; to till or work the soil.

不服水丨 the climate (or peculiarities of the place) do not agree with me.

丨人 natives, aborigines.

丨絲 Canton raw-silk.

風丨人情 local manners and feelings.

丨房 an adobie house.

丨產 products of a country.

丨工 sextons, undertakers.

丨庫 the ground story; a basement, a cellar; a treasury. (*Cantonese.*)

黑丨 or 丨大 or 小丨 slang names for opium.

脾丨不和 I have no appetite.

破丨 or 探丨 to test the soil, as geomancers do for a grave.

丨神 local deities; in Canton, only the terminalia are usually so denoted.

歸丨 or 入丨 to return to dust, to be buried.

故丨 one's native place.

守丨 the local officials.

丨地神 or 丨地老兒 local divinities, agricultural gods, worshiped on the 丨地誕 second day of the second moon.

告于皇天后丨 I announced it to Imperial Heaven and Sovereign Earth.

爾丨宇昄章 your territory is great and glorious.

面如丨色 very pale-faced, sallow.

丨木偶人 a blockhead, a dolt.

國丨 government lands, the emperor's land.

日居月諸照臨下丨 O sun and moon, which shine on this lower world.

桑丨 mulberry fields; also the white bark of its roots.

丨星 or 煞丨 the planet Saturn; identified by the Budhists with *Sani*, the Hindu regent who rules it; the nose in physiognomy.

雲丨夢作乂 the land of Yun appeared above the surface, and the marsh of Mung was put under cultivation, — after the deluge was drained off.

吐 *ˊt'u* *t'uˋ* From *mouth* and *earth*.

To vomit, to disgorge; to spit out; to open, as flowers; to disclose, to tell all, to make a clean breast.

上丨下瀉 vomiting and purging.

丨出來 to vomit up; to confess everything.

丨舌 to run out the tongue, as when disconcerted.

丨花 to blossom.

一飯三丨哺 thrice he spit out one mouthful; — such was Duke Chen's application to business.

詩人丨屬 a poetical man speaks words like his art.

半吞半丨 he did not tell nearly all.

嘔丨' 淋漓 to vomit continually.

丨血 to bleed at the lungs.

剛則丨之 decline hard tempered, hasty people.

丨氣揚眉 he is contented now that he has reached his degree.

丨番 Tibet or Tangout, a powerful state destroyed by Genghis Khan, north of Lake Koko-nor.

芏 *t'uˋ* A sedge grass, 丨夫 probably a sort of *Scirpus*, found in Chehkiang near the seaside, and used in making mats.

莣丨 the *Cyperus rotundis.*

兔 兎 *t'uˋ* The original form is thought to represent a rabbit squatting with its tail perked up; it is distinguished from ˊ*mien* 免 by the dot; the second form is a common contraction.

A hare or rabbit; to hunt hares; at the North, a hare is called 野猫 the wild cat, because the vulgar name for a bardash has the same sound.

山丨 or 野丨 a hare.

丨子 or 家丨 or 白丨 a rabbit; it was also called 明視 when used in sacrificing on certain occasions, because it is said to look at the full moon or the 玉丨 or 仙丨 in it, at parturition; this refers to a Budhist legend that a hare (*sasi*) once rushed into a fire to furnish its flesh as food for others, when Indra transferred what was left to the moon, calling it 設施 (*sakshi* or *sakti*) one who made a sacrifice.

狡丨有三窟 the wily hare has three holes to his burrow.

守株待丨 he watched the tree for a hare, — refers to a bumpkin who seeing a hare kill himself by running against a tree, watched it for months to get a second.

赤丨 the red rabbit; — the name of Kwanti's horse.

丨穎 or 丨毫 a rabbit's awn or bristle; — *i. e.* a fine elastic pencil.

跳丨 the jumping rabbit, is the *Dipus annulatus* or Siberian jerboa.

TUH.

Old sounds, tot, tok, dot, *and* dok. *In Canton*, tòk *and* tăt; — *in Swatow*, tòk, t'ak, tak, *and* tút; — *in Amoy*, tok, t'ok, tút, *and* ch'út; — *in Fuhchau*, tòk, túk, *and* t'úk; — *in Shanghai*, deh, tòk, dòk, *and* tseh'; — *in Chifu*, tu.

突 *ˏtu* From *cave* and a *dog* putting his head out of it; it is interchanged with *tuh*, 秃 bald, and several of its derivatives.

Abruptly, suddenly; to rush against or out; to bolt; to despise; precipitate, audacious; insolent, offensive; to bore or work through a hole; a bolting horse; bald on the head; a flue.

丨然而來 came on very suddenly.

衝丨 to rush against, to collide.

唐丨 to offend by rude manners, unceremonious.

滑丨 inconsiderate.

丨門 to guard a gate.

丨厥 the Toorks or Turcomans.

未幾見兮丨而弁兮 when you see [the lad] after a short time, lo, he wears the cap!

堗 *ˏtu* From *earth* and *sudden*.

The door or flue of a furnace or range, usually called 竈火門; the grate where the ashes fall.

偠 / **揬** *ˏtu* To offend by assurance or pride; to rush against.

來的偠丨 he came in at an unlucky moment.

鼵 *ˏtu* From *rat* and to *bolt*.

A burrowing animal, probably a kind of marmot, whose habits resemble the prairie-dog of America, and lives in its holes with the bird 鵌, which is regarded as the female; it occurs in Kansuh, and is perhaps the *Arctomys robustus*.

柮 *tu'* The stump of a tree.

榾丨 the leafless, branchless trunk of a tree.

Read *nah*, Cut off; to break off.

咄 *tu'* From *mouth* and to *go out*; *q. d.* words passing to and fro.

To speak to one another, to talk; an exclamation of surprise or of joking.

丨丨 alarmed, surprised; noise of urging.

叱丨 to order to stop; to scold.

In *Pekingese* read *ˏchw'a*. An interjection of displeasure.

我被他丨丨一頓 I got a sharp scolding from him.

椩 *tu'* To set out trees; to fix a door pivot in its socket; a lock-bolt.

踺 *tuh'* Impeded; to make no progress; not advancing; to kneel.

督 *ˏtuh* From 目 *eye* and 叔 a *younger uncle*.

To examine closely; to lead, to encourage, to command; to follow and see how an order has been performed; to warn, to reprove; an overseer, a superior; to set in order, correct; to go in the middle, so as to oversee; weak eyes.

丨人作工 to act as overseer of work.

丨理 to direct.

丨兵 or 丨陣 to head the troops.

總丨 a governor-general.

海關監丨 collector of customs at Canton.

提丨學政 the provincial director of examinations.

家丨 the eldest son.

敎丨 to instruct.

丨率 to act as leader; to take the direction.

丨責 to admonish.

丨辦 to oversee; to manage all the details.

丨催 to urge on.

In *Cantonese*. To prick in, to fork up, to take up on a stick; to point the finger at, to jeer at.

行前丨後 a mark for ridicule.

丨過幾深 pole its depth.

丨我眼人 he is an eyesore to me.

篤 *ˏtu* *ʿtu* From *bamboo* and *horse*, the radical giving the sound; see *chuh*, 竺 India.

A sure, slow-going, or ailing horse; dangerous, as a disease; sincere, honest; firm, stable; generous, magnanimous; unmixed, pure; to give importance to, to be great, to regard seriously; to consolidate; to augment, to establish; in regimen with other adjectives, often makes the superlative.

丨實 in reality, very truly; trustworthy.

丨信 earnest belief.

病丨 or 丨疾 a dangerous illness; a complaint that disables one.

丨學 diligent at study.

丨宗族 pay great regard to ancestors and relatives.

丨行'不倦 to work sedulously without weariness.

危丨 imminently dangerous.

丨厚 very great, as kindness.

丨恭 sincerely respectful.

公劉克丨前烈 Duke Liu was able to consolidate the merits of his predecessors.

丨生武王 [Heaven] made her great in bearing Wu Wang.

㑪 *ˏtu* To shake the head, as when dissatisfied or refusing.

丨倲 an ugly look, irritated.

獨 *ˏtu* From *dog* and a *caterpillar*; "the dog goes by himself, the sheep in flocks."

Solitary, alone; isolated, by one's self, single; widowed or

childless, left alone; one's own consciousness, or what is only felt by himself; one of; only, yet; is it so? a species of baboon or mandrill, not a gregarious kind, which is said to eat the gibbons, and they fly on hearing its cry, as the line says, 丨一鳴而猨散 the baboon cries and the gibbons scatter.
丨自己 only myself.
丨子 an only son.
單丨 only one, by itself.
孤丨 orphan-like, unassisted.
丨有 sole, unequaled, by itself.
丨是這樣 only that sort.
念我丨兮 reflecting on my solitary condition.
丨步 going on alone; a clever man skilled in some art which takes the palm.
不止丨一 not one only.
夫丨無族婣乎 is it that he has neither family nor relatives?
丨斷丨行 to decide and act on his own responsibility.

韣 ꜀tu The covering or case for a bow.
弓丨 a sheath to preserve the bow.
弧丨 a case or wrapper for a flag.

髑 ꜀tu The skull; the bones on the top of the head; used by Roman Catholics in 聖丨 for relics of every kind.
莊子之楚見空丨髏 when Chwangtsz' went to Tsu, he saw a hollow skull.

毒 ꜀tu From 毐 *vicious* and 艸 *plants* contracted above it, alluding to noxious weeds which grow in the way of people.

Noxious, poisonous; hurtful, destructive, baneful, malevolent, cruel, malignant; a poison; a virus, a baneful exudation; an injury; angrily, in hate; to hate, to abominate; to be indignant at.
丨心 malicious, cruel.
丨藥 a poison, a dangerous remedy.
丨手 a flagitious villain.
丨害 to do evil to others.
丨死人 to poison one.
丨氣 a malaria; a noxious vapor or exhalation.
寧爲荼丨 the people prefer bitter and poisonous ways.
服丨 poisoned.
流丨 a pervading, general injury, like opium-smoking.
三丨 the three banes — of the Taoists; *viz.*, cupidity, wrath, and folly.
瘸狠瞎丨 the lame are hateful and the blind dangerous.
便丨 venereal ulcers.
盲精啞丨 the blind are clever and the dumb dangerous.
以丨攻丨 to counteract one poison with another.
五丨 the five poisonous reptiles; *viz.*, the viper, scorpion, centipede, toad, and spider.
蜂蠆小丨 a petty revenge; *lit.* a malicious bee's sting.

纛 ꜀tuh From 縣 *to suspend* and 毒 *noxious;* also read *tao'*

A banner or streamer carrying a feather, used to show the way at a funeral; a large triangular standard, carried before the general-in-chief to mark his presence; it was adorned with red silk tassels, or a tail or feathers.
殺人祭丨 the blood of the slain was offered in sacrifice to the standard.
大丨旂 the general's standard.

启 ꜀tu From *body* and *mouth;* it is regarded as a contraction of ꜀tun 臀 the seat; and is sometimes read *tsien'*

The anus or the rectum; among butchers, the rump; the end of, the bottom, the adit or exit.
丨底 the bottom of, as a long row of houses.
偪丨路 a cul-de-sac; no thoroughfare. (*Cantonese.*)
買豚丨' to buy pork cutlets or steaks.

碡 ꜀tu A stone roller, the 碌丨 used by farmers for rolling down the fields when sown.

瀆 ꜀tu From *water* and *flowing harmoniously;* now written like *mai'* 賣 to *sell;* interchanged with the next.

A ditch, an outlet, a sluice; the large drain of a country, as a great river; foul, muddy; to annoy, to despise.
溝丨 a gutter; dirty, filthy.
四丨 the four great drains of China, *viz.*, the Yangtsz' 江, the Yellow 河, the Hwai 淮, and the Tsi 濟 or New Yellow River 大清河 in Shantung.
嶽丨諸神 the gods of the mountains and streams.

凟 ꜀tu From *ice* and *to sell;* an unauthorized character, commonly used for the last, and with the next.

To annoy; to defile, to profane, to desecrate; to treat contumeliously; to bother by reiterating one's application.
褻丨煩數 to trouble by repeated calls.
丨聽 or 丨聰 you annoy my ears, or abuse my attention; said by officials.
諷丨 I have presumed to annoy you; — a polite phrase.
冒丨 to fail in respect.
上交不諂下交不丨 neither cringe to your superiors, nor insult your inferiors.
干丨 to offend one, to act against propriety.

黷 ꜀tu Analogous to the last and next.
To blacken, to dirty; to annoy, to insult; black, soiled, filthy; a moldy, black color.
丨濁 dirty, begrimed.
蒙丨 to defame, to render opprobrious.
媟丨貴幸 to offend or insult one of the emperor's favorites.
狎丨 rude to; to cause to blush; to betray confidence.

嬻 ꜀tu Analogous to the last two.
Indecent familiarity with; to disgrace a woman.

牘 ꜀tu Boards or tablets for writing on, such as were anciently used; blocks for books; documents, books, archives, registers; a bamboo to keep time on, when beating adobie walls.
尺丨 a note; a brief of; a card or short statement; a model for letters.
案丨 the papers in a law case; the case itself.
取筆丨受之 he gathered the pencil and tablets, and I received them.
長篇累丨 long drawn and tedious documents.
無案丨之勞形 here I have none of the turmoil of a court.

犢 ꜀tu A calf; a heifer, a victim for sacrifice.
老牛舐丨 the old cow licks her calf; — old folks dote on their children.

瓄 ꜀tu A whitish kind of fine jade from the Kwănlun Mts., once used for 丨圭 tablets.

匵 櫝 ꜀tu A case or drawer; a sheath; a coffin; a charger or bowl; a receptacle for books.
劍丨 a scabbard.
啟丨 open the casket.
韞丨而藏 to lay by carefully, as jewels.

殰 殨 ꜀tu An abortion; dead before birth; still-born.
胎生者不丨 females (either women or animals) did not cast their young; *met.* a time of prosperity.

讀 ꜀tuh From *words* and to *flow smoothly* as the phonetic.
To read aloud, to recite, to chant; to read carefully so as to get the meaning; to teach one to read; to study; to divulge; a reader.
丨書 to study, to go to school; in Canton, to read aloud.
丨禮 reading the ritual; — a notice put up at the door, written on blue paper with white ink, declining visits when mourning for parents.
丨出病來 he studied till he became ill.
伴丨 a schoolfellow; a student.
熟丨 to recite perfectly.
丨夜書 to study by night.
默丨 to read to one's self.
侍丨 a reader in waiting; an honorary sinecure at court.
丨賦 to recite irregular meters, to scan.
中冓之言不可丨也 the tattle of the inner chamber need not be recited.
對丨 to read and compare.
著童授丨 let Tung be appointed to teach them to read; — be their tutor.

Read *teu'*. A clause or short sentence, in which the sense is incomplete; a stop like a comma.
點清句丨 punctuate the sentences and clauses distinctly.

讟 ꜀tuh From *wrangling* and *flowing smoothly.*
Discontented, seditious; people slandering one; murmurs against rulers; deep hatred expressed in bitter words.
謗丨 slanders.
怨丨 to hate and rail at.
誹丨 calumnies.

T'UH.

Old sound, t'uk. *In Canton,* t'ŏk; — *in Swatow,* t'ek; — *in Amoy,* t'ut; — *in Fuhchau,* t'ŭk; — *in Shanghai,* t'ŏk; — *in Chifu,* t'u.

禿 ꜀t'u From 禾 *grain* over 人 *man,* said to have been formed by 蒼頡 when he saw a bald-headed man, and hid himself in the grain.
The hair entirely gone; a scald head; bald; stripped, bare; blunt; to make bald; to injure.
老丨 a priest.
丨子 a bald-head.
老丨翁 an old, bald-headed man.
賊丨 you bald-pated rascal!
丨頭光棍 an unscrupulous rascal.
筆丨 a blunt pencil.
丨尾騾 a mule with a hairless tail.
光丨丨 no hair on his head; a leafless tree.
木葉盡丨 stripped of trees and herbage, as a bare hill.
丨巾 to let the cap fall off.
髮丨 the hair is all gone.

In *Shanghai.* All; also.
丨有 also have; all are there.
丨有個 I want it all.
丨勿有 not a single one.
丨拉拉笑 every body laughs at you.

鵚 ꜀t'u The composition of the character denotes the *bald-headed bird.*
A bird when bare of its feathers during molting.
丨梟 an owl.
丨鶖 a long legged bird, perhaps a crane akin to the adjutant, having a bare head.

裻 ꜀t'u The rustling of new garments; the seam down the back of a garment.
偏丨之衣 garments where the back seam is not in the middle, and the sides are of different colors.

瘏꜂ ꜀t'u The scald head; sores covering the scalp.
丨瘖 boils or eruptions on the head.

誂꜂ ꜀t'uh *Bald words*, as the etymology shows.
詆丨 sly, cunning, deceitful; slanderous, recriminating.
併丨之言以污人耳 slanderous insinuations defile men's ears, — as anonymous placards.
丨詐 to deceive, to cheat.

TUI.

Old sounds, tui, dui, tút, *and* dút. *In Canton*, tui; — *in Swatow*, tui, chui, tué, *and* tun; — *in Amoy*, tui *and* toé; — *in Fuhchau*, tòi, toi, *and* tai; — *in Shanghai*, tó *and* dé; — *in Chifu*, téi.

堆 ꜀自 ꜀追 ꜀tui The second and original form delineates a *pile* of *earth*, now changed to 土 *earth* and 隹 *birds;* used with the next, and for ꜀t'ui 推 to push.
A heap, a mass, a mound; a stack, an accumulation of; a guard-house; a crowd; to heap up, to pile, to store; and hence a classifier of piles, heaps, and mounds; to incumber by crowding; to push away.
官丨 a police-station.
草丨 a stack of hay.
丨作一丨 throw it all into a pile.
一丨柴 a heap of firewood.
一丨人 a crowd of people.
一丨煤 a pile of coal.
丨積如山 a great heap like a hill; said of goods in a market.
滿面丨着笑 the face convulsed with laughter.
打灰丨 to pound the ash-hill; — an old sport on newyear's eve by domestic slaves to get luck.
人多丨塞了 the people crowd in and stop the way.
丨房 a storeroom, a warehouse, a wholesale dealer's shop.
丨花燒酒 wine which shows its goodness by the bubbles remaining.

䭔 ꜀tui Interchanged with the last.
Dumplings made of flour and steamed; bait made of flour.
油丨 globular hollow cakes.
隔年前丨 cakes left from last year; *met.* the old stock; not inclined to anger; it has now gone by and so let it go.

䨺 ꜀tui An unauthorized character.
To sit stock still, like a statue.
一邊兒丨着去罷 go away, you statue, sitting here!

磓 ꜀tui To collect stones to build artificial rock-work; to cart stones down from a hill-top.
丨山子石 to pile up rock-work.
Read ꜀chui. The sound of dashing stones.

碓 tui꜄ From *stone* and *birds.*
A foot-pestle, commonly used to hull rice; to pound in a mortar; one beat of the pestle; a heap.
丨架 or 丨牀 the mortar framework.
丨臼 a rice stone mortar.
丨身 the treddle of the pestle.
舂多幾百丨 pound it hundreds of times more.
登丨 to work the pestle.
水丨 mortars worked by water-wheels.
雲丨無人水自舂 where the clouds surround the inaccessible heights, the water does its own pounding, — by cascades.

對꜄ 对꜄ tui꜄ From 寸 an *inch* and a compound of 丵 *luxuriant* and 士 *scholar;* it is defined echoing without rule; the contraction is common.
Parallel sentences on scrolls, hung in Chinese houses for ornament; to front, to correspond to; to suit, to pair; to answer, to respond; to correspond; consistent with, agreeing; opposite; inimical; an opponent; a pair; equal to the occasion; a sign of the dative.
一副丨 or 一丨丨 a pair of scrolls.
丨聯 or 丨子 parallel sentences.
丨他說 speak to him.
我丨儂去 I bid you to go. (*Shanghai.*)
丨頭 a foe, an enemy; hostile.
丨親家 to form a marriage affinity.
其樂無丨 no joy equal to that — of Heaven.
丨數 to compare accounts.
一丨鴿子 a brace of doves.
丨合利 cent. per cent. profit.
丨眼 agreeable to, liking.
丨得住人 not afraid of what men say, equal to men's remarks.
丨一丨 set it over against, as a dial to the sun; see if it fits.
不丨 not correspondent; not on good terms, inconsistent, incongruous.
丨子燈 a pair of lantern-bearers who march opposite each other in a procession.
丨證 eye-witnesses; personal evidence.
丨質 to confront, as opposite parties do in a law-suit.
丨換 to swap, to barter.
In *Cantonese* read ꜂tui. To push towards; to bridge or hand along to another; to make up a lot, to have a batch; to coalesce.
丨埋一起 lump it all in one; — this use seems to be a mistake for 堆 by a change in the tone.

懟 憝 譈 *tui'* From *heart* and *opposed* or *sincere;* also read *chui*; the third is also found in many authors. To dislike, to avoid; to abhor; disliking, displeased, angry with; to cause dissatisfaction; an adversary; inimical.

元惡'大丨 great dislike to the chief criminal.

怨丨紛紛 everybody is scolding and grumbling, as at the officials.

凡民罔不丨 not one of the people but disliked him.

隊 *tui'* From 阜 *place* and 遂 to *follow* contracted; also read *chui'* and used for *sui'* 隧 to follow.

To fall or slide from a higher place, losing one's footing; a dangerous pass through the mountains; a noun of multitude, like a crowd, a group; a military term, a rank, a file, a squad; a company, at first of ten 伍 or fifty men, but now often numbering a hundred men; a platoon; to fall down.

成羣結丨 people gathering in crowds and knots, — ready for a disturbance.

難于歸丨 it will not be easy for me to regain my place, — as a truant clerk.

馬丨 cavalry regiments.

一丨八 a number of people.

兵丨 a detachment, a company.

擺丨 to dress ranks, to fall in.

演丨 to drill; to parade.

丨伍 in ranks; the army; its rank and file.

出丨 to engage the foe.

車按行騎就丨 when the chariots go in their courses, the cavalry will then deploy in rank.

洋鎗丨 foreign drilled troops.

兌 *tui'* From 儿 *man* and 㕣 a *damp place;* but others say from 口 *mouth* and 八 *effluence*, representing the aura of evaporation.

The 58th diagram, to permeate; straight, direct; gratified from having enough; satisfied; to exchange, to barter; to weigh against, to give an equivalent; to be made open or permeable.

丨會 to turn a debt by paying it through another.

丨換 to exchange coin or jewelry.

丨銀子 to weigh silver for exchanging.

出丨 or 發丨 to sell by weight or retail.

七二丨 weighs seven mace two candareens.

松栢斯丨 paths made through the firs and cypresses.

行道丨矣 the roads were all passable or open.

匯丨 to cash an order for money.

薱 *tui'* Abundant vegetation.

丨丨 thick, flourishing.

駾 *tui'* A horse marching out at a rapid pace.

丨突 to rush out in terror.

鐓 *tui'* From *iron* and *substantial;* occurs used for *ˏch'ui* 椎 a mallet.

A spear with a brass ferule which guards the butt; this end must be put forward when presenting the weapon; a beater.

錞 *tui'* From *metal* and to *enjoy;* occurs used for the last.

The brass or gilt butt of a spear.

厹矛鋈丨 the trident spears with their bright ends.

Read *tun'* and *ˏshun,* and used with 淳. A spheric metallic bell, with a piercing sound, called 丨于 intended to accompany a drum, hung upon a frame; to border on.

Read *to'* A pall, a catafalque over a coffin.

T'UI.

Old sounds, t'ui, t'ot, dui, *and* dot. *In Canton,* t'ui; — *in Swatow,* t'ui, t'ué, *and* t'o; — *in Amoy,* tòé, t'ui, *and* ch'ui; — *in Fuhchau,* t'oi, t'òi, *and* chw'i; — *in Shanghai,* dé *and* t'é; — *in Chifu,* t'éi.

穨 *ˏt'ui* From *head* and *bald;* it is interchanged with the next two.

The jowl or under the chin; a bald pate; a rapid gust of wind; submissive, flowing, yielding; to view kindly; to fall; broken down, ruined.

丨然而下 it is gradually decaying or growing worse.

丨壞 ruined, helpless.

玉山丨 a poetical name for a drunkard's rubicund visage.

泰山其丨乎 how is the great mountain falling!

維風及丨 the breeze increases into a whirlwind.

丨惰 lazy and weak, inert.

丨思而就牀 while lazily thinking of him he fell asleep.

𤸎 *ˏt'ui* Jaded, worn out; a disease like broken wind.

我馬虺丨 my steed is utterly broken down.

隤 墤 *ˏt'ui* From *place* or *earth* and *honorable;* it is used for the next; the second, rare form is also a synonym of *k'w'ai'* 塊 a clod.

To fall in ruins; decayed, ruined, lost; to ruin, to overthrow, to involve in ruin; to cause to fall or descend; to push over.

丨名 to blast a reputation.

丨柔 soft; pliable, as a disposition.

傾丨 to tumble down, as a wall.

蓷 ꜀t'ui Also read ꜀chui.

A labiate plant like horehound (*Marrubium*), in appearance, common in the southern provinces; it is now called 白益母 and 茺蔚, but several plants are probably included under these and other names.

中谷有丨嘆其溼矣 the motherwort down in the valleys is scorched by the heat.

蘈 藬 ꜀t'ui A labiate plant called 牛丨, a foot high, with square culms and long pointed leaves, purplish-yellowish flowers in an imbricated head, which furnish a drink when pressed; it seems to be the *Leonurus sibirica*, and the same as the last.

㿗 ꜂t'ui From *disease* and *broken down*.

A pain in the groin, a fit of strangury, or a spasm caused by the stone.

魋 ꜂t'ui From *demon* and *bird*; it is also read ꜀chui.

A supernatural animal, described as like a small bear, with short yellow fur; perhaps a species of wolverene was intended by this goblin.

推 ꜀t'ui From *hand* and *bird*; it is also pronounced ꜀ch'ui, with the same signification, and both sounds are used as correct.

To push away, to expel; to overthrow; to secede from; to keep away, or abstain from; to deny one's self; to shirk, to shift or throw off, as responsibility; to lay to another's charge; to refuse, to decline; to resign, to give up; to arrange or lay out; to elect to fill a post; to select; to infer from, to extend to, to carry out; to succeed to, to applaud or push forward; to include.

丨辭 to decline, as an appointment.

丨出去 to escape from, as a duty; to put off on another.

丨究 to investigate the principles.

丨食 to yield a dainty, to a guest.

丨亡固存邦乃其昌 by abolishing the weakly and strengthening the vigorous, all the states will flourish.

丨磨 to turn a mill.

丨舉 or 丨薦 or 丨陞 to promote higher, to advance in office.

丨開 to have nothing to do with, to evade, to put aside; to change the topic.

丨不開 you can't shirk that.

丨倘 to put off with excuses.

寒暑相丨 cold and heat succeed each other.

三教丨之喇嘛 the three sects, including the lamas.

丨心致腹 I'll put my heart into your belly; — *i. e.* I am all sincerity, guileless.

丨衣 to give clothes to the poor.

丨機 a piston in an engine.

一丨 an inference; an impulse.

丨己及人 to put one's self in the place of others.

丨賢讓能 select the worthy and give place to the able, — that they may fill office.

丨算 to calculate; to reckon; to cast destinies.

丨了他 or 丨却他 I've got rid of him.

丨頭別人 to blame another for one's own misdeeds.

丨他起身 push him to get up.

腿 骽 t'ui˒ From *flesh* and to *retire*; the second form is unusual.

The thigh, the ham; the leg; in *architecture*, the jambs or ends of a piazza or porch, which are formed by the extension of the side walls.

丨子 the leg, divided into 大丨 the thigh, and 小丨 the shank.

後丨 the hind leg.

猪丨 a hog's ham; when cured it is called 火丨 or fire-ham.

快丨 or 飛毛丨 a fast runner.

跑細了丨 I have run myself lean-shanked, — and made nothing.

象丨 a gross fat leg.

狗丨 a dog's shank; *met.* a policeman, who has to run to and fro.

金丨 delicate hams cured in Kinhwa in Chehkiang.

探着丨 to stand at ease.

尵 ꜀t'ui Lame in the legs.

委丨 rheumatism in the legs which disables from walking.

退 t'ui˒ From to *go* and *indignant*; but the first elements were 彳 a *step*, 日 *day* and 夂 *slow*, denoting a slow pace.

To retreat, to retire, to recede, to draw back; to decline, to back out of, to refuse, to excuse, to withdraw; to abate; to yield, to give up to; not to be froward.

丨親 to break a betrothal.

丨貨 to decline a purchase.

丨兵 to retreat.

丨縮 to shrink, as cloth is shrunk by washing; to show the white feather; to draw in, as a snail.

丨色 faded; beauty gone.

丨讓 to cede, to yield to another.

丨不了 you can't back out — of that bargain.

倒丨 to shirk, to back down, to skulk, not to face the music.

丨步 to step backwards.

其身丨然 his body has lost its vigor.

丨汗 it diminishes the perspiration.

丨天之道 to act as Heaven directs.

戎成不丨 war has done its work, but he stays not his hand.

丨却 to decline, to refuse.

毤 t'ui˒ From 毛 *hair* and 蛻 *exuviæ* contracted; an unauthorized character, probably altered from 脫 to cast off.

To cast the hair or feathers.

煺 t'ui˒ From *fire* and to *pursue*.

To scald off the hair or feathers.

丨小鷄 to scald a pullet.

用開水丨毛 use boiling water to get the hair off.

TUN.

Old sounds, tou *and* don. *In Canton*, tun ; — *in Swatow*, tun ; — *in Amoy*, tun ; — *in Fuhchau*, tung, tòng, *and* taung ; — *in Shanghai*, tăng *and* dăng ; — *in Chifu*, tăn.

敦 惇 ˏtun — From 攴 to *strike* or 心 *heart* and 享 to *enjoy* ; it much resembles *shuh*, 孰 who ; the second form is not usual.

Irritated, angry ; to revile ; honest, simple, generous ; firm, solid ; affluent, substantial, big, of consequence ; generously ; to give honor to ; to make a reality, to regard or prove of great importance ; a mass of troops ; to impress upon, to urge ; to station, as pickets ; to impel to do ; who then ?

丨厚 or 丨大 liberal, honest, considerate.

五丨哉 the five generous ways of acting.

丨孝悌 give great weight to filial and fraternal duties.

丨化 transforming influences.

丨請 a sincere invitation.

王事丨我 the king's business presses on me.

丨友於誼 be sincere in dealing with friends.

丨牂 a name for those years which contain the branch 午 *wu*.

Read ˏtwʿan. A succession of, as fruit or plants.

有丨瓜苦 the bitter gourds hung one by one.

丨彼行葦 those patches of springing wayside rushes.

Read ˏtui. To lodge alone ; solitary, one by one ; to regulate ; to cut up, to deal with, to finish up.

丨商之旅 he disposed of or destroyed the forces of Shang.

丨彼獨宿 quietly and solitarily we passed the night.

Read ˏtʿiao. To carve ; ornamented.

丨弓既堅 the ornamented bows are all strong.

噋 ˏtun — Another form of ˏtʿun 啍 the breath.

To swallow down, to gobble, as a bird.

丨得好多 he has gulped down a great deal. (*Cantonese.*)

墩 墪 ˏtun — From *earth* and *solid;* the second unauthorized form is used at Canton.

A heap or tumulus, a mound or barrow of a regular form, while 堆 is one hastily made ; a hillock on a plain ; a square pillar ; a plinth or base ; a block, as of stone or wood ; low, squat ; sometimes used for the English word *ton.*

烟丨 or 烽火丨 a fire signal, a hollow brick cone, in which a lighted fire serves as a signal.

繡丨 low cushions used by favored courtiers to sit on at an audience.

蠟燭丨 a rude candlestick.

五里丨 a five *li* mound, used to mark distances.

丨臺 a beacon terrace.

高丨 a knoll.

In *Cantonese* read tunʾ To shake the dust off a thing by a fillip ; to slap ; to strike on the ground ; a company of boat-people settled ashore.

甈 ˏtun — An earthenware dish shaped like a basin, used in distilling spirits.

驐 ˏtun — To castrate animals ; 鐓 is also used for this.

丨雞 to cut a cock.

蜳 ˏtun — A water insect, the 丨蝺, also called 蟱丨 ; a dytiscus or water beetle (a *Hydrophilus?*) whose larvæ resemble shrimps.

橔 ˏtun — The wooden cover of a coffin ; others define it, a wooden seat or rest.

𧝓 ˏtun — A satchel or bag to put clothes in ; a haversack.

擊 ˏtun — To strike with the fist.

盾 ʿtun — An *eye* with a defense over to guard it, rudely representing a *shield;* also read ʿshun, and used for 遁ʾ to escape.

A buckler ; a shield, such as surround a chariot ; to skulk, to scamper and hide away ; used in the Indian Archipelago to denote a rupee.

龍丨 a shield with dragons painted on it.

掌五丨 to grasp five shields ;—*i. e.* to manage military matters.

櫓丨 the defensive nettings and guards on a junk's poop.

盹 ʿtun — Sometimes read *shun*ʾ

Dull, heavy eyes ; half asleep.

困丨 fast asleep.

打丨兒 to nod, as when asleep.

目丨難分善惡 weak eyes are unable to distinguish the good from the bad.

丨淹心 too sleepy to work.

坉 ʿtun — Water so obstructed by grass and mud that it cannot flow ; marshy places, which like a dike, retain water.

丨子 the north and western sides of a farm ; also a grange.

田丨 fields and plats.

In *Pekingese* used for its primitive. A hamlet, a farmstead.

鄉丨兒 a small village.

不 ˓*tun* Used for 墪 a tumulus in Canton; 白丨子 petuntse, the fine quartz powder which porcelain makers use as an ingredient in the best ware.

債丨 an unlucky day for lending money. (*Cantonese.*)

Read *yeh*˳ The stump of a tree; a sprout.

躉 ˓*tun* An overplus; a dépôt or storehouse; to store, to house.

丨船 hulks, receiving ships.

亞片丨 opium-hulks.

丨家 opium dealers. (*Cantonese.*)

債丨 an insolvent.

In *Cantonese.* To stop when it ought to go; to lie down.

丨在門口 put it in the doorway.

丨貨 goods left on hand.

丨當 to sell goods by wholesale.

沌 *tun*˒ From *water* and *sprouting.*

The rush of a torrent; confused, chaotic, mixed; unable to discover the cause or purpose of; impervious.

渾丨無端 in utter confusion, without any clue.

渾丨 a certain monster, into which 讙兜 a bad man in the days of Shun, was transformed.

扽 *tun*˒ To move, to shake; to rub with the hand.

囤 笹 *tun*˒ From *inclosure* and *resprouting;* occurs used for its primitive.

A kind of round bin like a great hamper, made of coarse matting with an osier bottom, to contain grain; it is prepared in the barn.

丨積 to hoard or collect grain.

米丨 a rice bin.

開丨發粮 open the bin and give out the grain.

頓 *tun*˒ From *head* and sprouting or *turf;* used for the next.

To bow the head, to prostrate, to fall before; to salute; to grieve for; an inn or resting-place; a meal, or the time of a meal; a spell, a turn; a period in a discourse; a rest in music; to rest or put in order, as at a halt; in haste, suddenly; to injure, to impair; to part with, to let go; used in the treaties for the word *ton.*

丨首拜 I respectfully bow the head; — written on cards.

打一丨 gave him one knock.

一丨飯 one meal.

甲兵不丨 not a soldier was lost.

丨改前非 he all at once reformed his ways.

整丨人馬 to get ready troops for war.

句丨 a cæsural stop.

丨丨食黃魚 he ate mango fish every meal.

無一丨飯工夫 a very small job of work.

安丨 to prepare, as a room for a guest; to get ready for.

委丨 ruined.

一氣不丨盡 the breath cannot be stopped in a moment.

丨捨 to suddenly discard in a freak.

In *Cantonese.* To lay down, as one lays aside a burden.

倒丨 turned about; beside himself.

丨穩 place it securely.

鈍 *tun*˒ Dull, blunt; stupid, obtuse, half-witted; superannuated; rude because uneducated.

刀丨 a dull knife.

丨角 an obtuse angle.

頑丨 obstinately stupid; mulish.

吶丨 stammering; a hesitating speech.

遲丨 incapable for business, always behind time.

鋒 and 丨 denote acute or blunt at the point.

忳 *tun*˒ Also read ˳*chun,* when used for 肫 sincere.

Sad, sorrowful, depressed.

惛惛丨丨 altogether out of spirits, heart-sick.

遁 *tun*˒ Formed of to *run* from a *shield; q. d.* a soldier deserting his colors.

To hide away, to skulk, to avoid, to conceal one's self; out of sight, concealed, hid; to vanish, to abscond; in retirement or solitude; hidden.

丨跡山林 to retreat to the wilds, — and live.

奇門丨甲 to skillfully dispose troops in ambush.

丨世無悶 to leave the world without regret.

丨法 rules for becoming invisible.

隱丨 to put one's self out of sight, as by disguising or retiring.

賢人丨 the worthy people secluded themselves.

腯 *tun*˒ From *flesh* and *shield; also read* *tuh,* and similar to ˳*t'un* 豚 fat.

Fat, obese, referring especially to hogs; shielded by fat; full, in good liking.

肥丨 well favored.

充丨 heavy and fat.

泵 In *Cantonese.* From *stone* and *water;* an unauthorized character.

To drool; to drop down; to sound; to hang down, as a weight.

丨魚 to fish with a line.

丨落來 suspended; to hang down.

賺重丨 to make a large fortune.

Read ˓*tăm.* To pound; to strike with the fist, to rap; to thump, to throw at or away; to lower, to let down.

丨錨 to drop anchor.

船打丨 the vessel thumped.

丨印 to stamp or chop, as dollars are certified in Canton.

丨骨 to pommel, to shampoo.

Read *tăm*[2] To stamp, to paw; to press on, to crush; a low, boggy place.

底丨 a low wet spot.

馬丨地 the horse paws the ground.

厚丨丨 very thick.

T'UN.

Old sounds, t'un. *In Canton*, t'un *and* t'ün ; — *in Swatow*, t'un ; — *in Amoy*, t'un, tun, *and* t'ui ; — *in Fuhchau*, t'ong, t'aung, *and* t'oi ; — *in Shanghai*, t'ăng *and* dăng ; — *in Chifu*, t'ăn.

吞 ˛*t'un* From *mouth* and *heaven* above it, giving the sound.

To swallow, to gulp ; to absorb, to seize on and swallow up ; to appropriate, to merge all in one ; to grasp.

丨丸 to bolt down a pill.

丨天 to swallow the sky ; — *met.* inordinate.

丨天下 to seize the empire.

丨并 to engross all ; to seize the whole.

丨騙 to overreach.

忍氣丨聲 to be patient and silent — under obloquy.

半丨半吐 I told only half of it.

丨金 to swallow gold-leaf ; it is a mode of suicide.

丨不下喉 he can't swallow.

丨狗之魚 [grasping as] the fish that gulped down the dog.

啍 ˛*t'un* The breath ; slow-going.

大車丨丨 his great carriage went slowly and heavily.

Read ˛*chun*. Garrulous.

丨丨 to say over and over ; repetition.

暾 ˛*t'un* The sun just appearing above the horizon.

朝丨 sunrise.

涒 ˛*t'un* To vomit after eating ; some say it is a name for the planet Jupiter.

丨灘 a term for the five cyclic years containing 申 in them.

Read ˛*yun*. Meandering.

丨鄰 tortuous, as a serpentine stream.

屯 ˛*t'un* From 屮 a *sprout* rising above 一 a line representing the *earth*, and intended to delineate the struggles of a sprouting shoot.

The beginning of growth ; to collect together ; to bring under one control ; a village, a place where soldiers live ; a resident camp.

草木丨然 vegetation is beginning to start.

丨兵 military colonists, soldiers settled to till the 丨田 fields allotted to them.

丨粮 to hoard up grain.

丨積 to amass ; to prepare stores, as a commissary.

丨蟻 trooping ants.

丨養 to support others on a strike.

人馬丨聚 brought together the men and horses.

分丨要害 detailed garrisons to the important posts.

丨溪 a rivulet near Yen-cheu fu in the west of Chehkiang, whence Twankay green tea comes.

Read ˛*chun*. The third of the 64 diagrams, denoting difficulty or hardship, alluding to the soft and tender radicle coming in contact with the harsh earth ; difficult, hard ; thick ; sparing, avaricious.

丨難' great labors.

丨厚 very gross or thick.

丨其膏 sparing of his favors.

飩 ˛*t'un* A meat cake or ball, rolled in flour and fried in fat called 餛丨 ; a kind of hashed pork-dumpling, simmered in broth.

京丨 cakes used in Fuhkien in ancestral worship.

魨 ˛*t'un* A scaleless fish found in the Yangtsz' R., called 河丨 or 河豚 river pig, shaped like a tadpole, white belly, and striped red and yellow back ; it can distend its throat and wink its eyes, and is regarded as poisonous ; it is probably a species of *Tetraodon*, and not a *Torpedo*, as this power of inflating the body belongs to the former ; it is a foot long, has no gills and no gall ; the 鯸鮐 is the same fish.

軘 ˛*t'un* A war-chariot, used in the Tsin dynasty.

使丨車逆之 he sent a war-chariot to meet and bring him.

豚 豘 ˛*t'un* From *hog* and *flesh*, it is easily confounded with *choh*, 豚 the rump.

A sucking pig, a porker, a shote ; one says, a sow ; to draggle along, and not lift the heels in walking.

肥丨 a fat porkling.

丨蹄 pettitoes.

丨兒 my son ; — a demeaning term.

江丨 a porpoise found in the Yangtsz' River ; one maxim, 拚死吃河丨 if you wish to die eat porpoise, indicates the nature of its flesh when badly prepared ; while the proverb says, when it is well cooked, 一吃河丨百無味 all other food is tasteless after once eating porpoise.

不察于鷄丨 he minds nothing of the pigs and chickens ; — cares not for trifles.

如追放丨 like chasing after a runaway pig.

買利丨 buy my fat pigs ! — a Macao cry.

In *Fuhchau*. Medium in size or age ; half grown, not reached puberty.

臀 ˛*t'un* From *flesh* and *palace*.

The seat, buttocks, or nates ; the lower side, the bottom.

坐丨 to sit down.

後丨 the seat of honor.

丨無膚 his rump has no skin, — the thing has no bottom.

庉 ꜀t'un To dwell : a place of concourse; to come together.

鄉 丨 a village residence.

丨 居 to live in a place.

燉 ꜀t'un A blaze, a raging fire; red, fiery; to boil by putting the dish into that which holds the water; to dress by steam; to stew.

丨 煌 the noise of burning; name of a town and region at the western extreme of the Great Wall in Kansuh in Ngan-si cheu.

丨 飯 to steam rice.

丨 一 丨 熟 cook it properly, as food.

湇 丨 to simmer slowly.

丨 茶 to make tea.

丨 水 to boil water.

丨 鷄 a steamed fowl.

氹 ꜂t'un From *water* and *one* to represent a *hole*; an unauthorized character used at Canton.

A cess-pool; a pit, a tank, a manure reservior.

坭 丨 a hole for setting out trees.

Read ꜀t'ăm. To whirl, to revolve; round, rolling over.

丨 丨 圈 the circuit of, as an islet; a round plat.

氽 ꜂t'un From *water* under a *man*.

Floating on the water, as a drowned body; drifting.

隨 風 飄 丨 drifting at the mercy of the winds.

丨 來 丨 去 floating about on the water.

褪 t'un꜄ From *garment* and to *retire*.

To disrobe, to put off clothes; to pull the arm within the sleeve; flowers falling off; retractile; to take bones out of a fowl; to push along.

花 瓣 丨 了 the petals have fallen.

丨 出 overrun it, as a printer in correcting matter.

倒 丨 一 步 to back a step.

丨 頭 draws in his head, as a turtle.

丨 下 行 drive it into the next line; — a printer's phrase.

丨 甪 to slip out of, as a jacket; (*Cantonese.*)

丨 了 顏 色 the color has faded out.

丨 骨 鷄 a boned chicken.

遯 t'un꜄ From to *go* and a *pig*; it differs but little from *tun*꜄ 遁 to escape.

To hide; to go into obscurity; name of the 33d diagram, denoting invisible.

高 丨 too lofty to leave his seclusion.

昊 天 上 帝 寧 俾 我 丨 O Heavenly Shangti let me retire into obscurity.

丨 跡 to conceal one's retreat.

我 不 顧 行 丨 I do not desire to act in retirement or make my escape.

乃 丨 于 荒 野 then I was concealed in the little settled regions.

TUNG.

Old sounds, tong *and* dong. *In Canton*, tung; — *in Swatow*, tang *and* tung; — *in Amoy*, tong; — *in Fuhchau*, tăng, tung, tong, *and* taing; — *in Shanghai*, tung *and* dung; — *in Chifu*, tung.

東 ꜀tung From 木 *trees* and the 日 *sun* shining through them; in combination it is easily confounded with *kien* 柬 to abridge; the three characters 杲 *kau*꜄ 東 *tung*, and 杳 ꜂*yao*, representing the *sun above*, *through*, and *under* a tree, are instances of ideographic symbols.

The spring of the year, because then all things develop themselves; the east, the place whence light rises; sunrising; eastwards, eastern; towards; in presence of; the place of honor, or the person in it, as a master, a pater-familias; a friend; a feast, a treat; an abbreviation for the province of Shantung.

丨 方 or 丨 邊 the east.

丨 頭 or 我 財 丨 our boss or head-partner.

丨 家 the master of a household.

丨 北 northeast.

向 丨 easterly.

丨 南 不 怕 no fear [of a gale] from the southeast. (*Cantonese.*)

老 丨 a Shantung man.

丨 土 China, a Mohammedan term.

作 丨 to act the 丨 道 manager or host; to spread a feast.

出 丨 to foot the bill; or 我 的 丨 兒 I'll act the host, I'll pay it.

附 之 丨 流 it has gone drifting eastward; — it is no great matter.

丨 道 銀 treating money; presents given to turnkeys to soften an imprisonment.

丨 拉 西 扯 pulling here and hauling there; — *met.* — to borrow money.

丨 西 a thing, — *i. e.* anything between the east and west; it is also a term of reproach, as 什 麽 丨 西 what, that thing!

丨 成 西 就 everything arranged and concluded, all things getting on prosperously.

丨 倒 西 歪 out of line, reeling.

丨 帶 南 east bearing south.

南 丨 其 畝 to cause the land to lie towards the south and east.

平 秩 丨 作 to adjust and arrange the labors of the spring.

涷 ꜀tung From *water* and *east*.

A tributary of the Yellow River; a heavy shower or dew in summer; drenched.

丨 雨 a furious rain in summer.

丨 瀧 wet through with dew.

蝀 ˏtung From *insect* and *east*.

The rainbow.

虹名蝃 丨 the rainbow is called *ti-tung*.

悚 ˏtung Stupid, inapt.

悖 丨 丨 without method, incapable of understanding a subject.

鬃 ˏtung From *hair* and *east*.

Hairy.

丨 鬆 white hair; hairy.

冬 ˏtung From 冫 *ice* and an old form of 終 *end* contracted, referring to the completion of the seasons; used for the next.

The last or winter season; the close, the end; to store up; to fall into the winter torpor; wintry.

丨 天 or 丨 景 天 or 丨 令 or 隆 丨 the winter season.

丨 至 or 丨 節 the winter solstice, known as the 長至節, and observed as one of the popular festivals.

做 丨 or 過 丨 to keep the solstice.

嚴 丨 時 候 snapping cold weather.

丨 藏 winter provision.

三 丨 the winter months.

滬 丨 a rainy solstice.

丨 子 月 or 仲 丨 the eleventh month.

斗 柄 北 指 天 下 皆 丨 when the handle of the Dipper points to the pole, winter prevails.

苳 ˏtung From *plant* and *winter*; *q.d.* the winter vegetable; usually written like the last.

A kind of sow-thistle used for greens, which stands the winter, the 天 門 丨 allied to the *Scorzonera*; also the fleshy translucent tubers of the *Melanthium cochinchinense* found in Chehkiang, and made into a comfit.

蔓 天 門 丨 a trailing plant.

麥 門 丨 a liliaceous plant (*Ophiopogon japonicum*), whose tubers are used in fevers and as a tonic.

倲 ˏtung Weak.

儱 丨 feeble, weary, no vigor.

倯 丨 unmannerly, stupid looking.

董 ˋtung From *plants* and *heavy*; it occurs interchanged with the next.

To rule or lead people on to right ways; to influence for good; firm, made stable; to store up, to hide away; to withdraw.

振 丨 to clap the hands.

紳 丨 the gentry and elders; the latter are also called 丨 事 those who discern wisely.

買 古 丨 to buy curiosities or antiques; old stored-up things.

丨 之 用 威 use dignity in leading them on.

當 丨 其 身 以 自 潔 he then withdrew into retirement in order to preserve his purity — from treason.

丨 勸 to urgently intreat.

丨 蕫 a plant whose synonyms ally it to the *Iris* or orris root.

懂 ˋtung From *heart* and *to lead*.

Disturbed, out of one's wits; to understand, to perceive the meaning clearly.

懞 丨 or 懜 丨 confused, bewildered.

丨 呢 勿 丨 do you understand it?

丨 情 理 to understand the fitness of things.

一 個 字 不 丨 得 I don't know a single word of it.

一 顏 勿 丨 I don't understand it at all. (*Shanghai.*)

你 丨 我 意 思 麼 do you see my meaning?

不 丨 眼 的 not to take a hint.

湩 ˋtung Occurs interchanged with *chwˋang'* 幢 a scroll, and wrongly written like 湅' ice and ˏtung 潼 a place, even in books.

Milk of mares or cows, once used to wash the emperor's feet; muddy water; a noise.

丨 然 the roll or reveille of drums.

丨 容 a kind of carriage curtain.

牛 丨 or 孔 丨 milk.

酪 丨 cream ready for making cheese.

灇 ˋtung The noise of anything falling into the water.

洞 tung' From *water* and *united*; occurs used for ˏtung 峒 a region.

A rapid current; a cave, a grotto; a dell, a gorge, a deep ravine or cañon; a deep recess cut out like a grotto; a cavity, like a cupboard let in a wall; a hole, such as a rat makes; to understand thoroughly, as a mystery; acquainted with; to see through a subject; a territorial division under the Ming dynasty.

丨 庭 湖 Tungting Lake in Hunan.

水 丨 a deep hole in a channel.

丨 悉 to know fully.

丨 識 I see through it all.

仙 丨 a fairy's grotto; — *met.* a beautiful spot.

門 丨 裏 in the gateway, under the portal.

胡 龍 丨 a Mongolian praying-machine.

丨 察 a thorough examination.

丨 燭 其 奸 I see through his villainy.

丨 房 a nuptial chamber, to consummate a marriage.

丨 疑 undecided.

丨 穴 a cavern, a grotto.

丨 然 于 心 my mind is clear on that point.

空 丨 the sky, the canopy.

鴻 丨 connected, bound together.

丨 丨 乎 how reverent and grave!

戙 舩 tung' The first is defined beams and boards used in the construction of a boat; but by others the two are regarded as alike, and defined the beam to which the hawser is secured; a cat-head.

丨 板 pine boards. (*Pekingese.*)

胴 ˀ *tungˀ* The 2d large intestine or colon is 〡䐋; a medical term.
侗〡 honest, straightforward; also, form, appearance.

娴 ˀ *tungˀ* A straight, graceful neck.

衕 ˀ *tungˀ* ꜀*tʻung* From to *go* and *united*, because it connects great streets; it is often contracted to its primitive.
A side street leading from an avenue is 衚〡 in Peking; an alley or cross-street.
穿ˀ 衚〡兒 pass by the cross street. (*Pekingese.*)

凍 ˀ *tungˀ* From *ice* and *east*.
To freeze, to congeal; to cool, to stiffen; to expose to the cold; icy; freezing.
不免〡餒 can't avoid cold and starvation.
〡水 cold icy water. (*Cantonese.*)
〡死 frozen to death.
〡〡的 rather cold. (*Cantonese.*)
攤〡 spread out to cool.
〡瘡 sore from a frost-bite.
凝〡 to freeze.
雪〡 snow and ice.
東風解〡 the east wind melts the ice; — spring is coming.

棟 ˀ *tungˀ* From *wood* and *east*.
The highest beam in a house, the ridge-pole; a large stick, a main support in a building; a leading man in a state, a pillar; the supports of a coffin case; name of a timber tree.
〡梓 a ridge-pole.
〡梁之才 one who has ability to uphold the state.
屋〡 the roof-timbers, the plate or beams.
〡折傷其躬 if the beam split it will crush his body.
In *Cantonese*. To stand on end, to stack.
〡企 to place upright.

動 ˀ *tungˀ* From 力 *strength* and 重 *heavy*, here read ꜀*tʻung*, a kind of grain.
To excite, to move; to affect; to influence, to move the mind; to remove; to shake, to stir; to come out, as a chick from its shell, or leaves in the spring; to set on foot; to take action; momentum, action, working, motion, movement; excited, affected, surprised, agitated; movable, restless; irritable, the opposite of 靜 quiet; when following another verb, 不〡 answers to cannot, indicating that the action cannot be carried out, as 害不〡 he can't (or shall not) hurt you.
起不〡 I cannot lift it.
〡怒 to exasperate.
〡輒 repeatedly, again and again.
〡作 work, workmanship.
日月運〡 the sun and moon revolve in their orbits.
幾時〡身 when do you start?
搖〡 to shake, to joggle.
行〡 or 舉〡 behavior, conduct.
不好〡靜 improper conduct.
〡土 to stir the clods; to commence digging, as when building.
驚〡你 I have annoyed you, or taken your time; a polite phrase.
〡粗 to resort to blows.
〡不〡 whether stirring or at rest, *i. e.* incessantly; without cause; continually moving or acting on.
發〡 to be taken in labor.
亂〡 to take up carelessly.
〡容貌 to change countenance.
性情好〡 a restless disposition.
非禮之〡寧不愧心 if an act be indecent, will it not cause mortification?
走〡不前 unable to advance, as from infirmity.
〡力率 the moving force, as in mechanics.
〡不得 it must not be stirred.
〡聽 to move one's hearing; *i. e.* eloquent.
不必〡 don't be meddling; let things alone.

慟 ˀ *tʻungˀ* The *heart moved* by something affecting and showing it in action; much excited.
〡哭 crying from sorrow.
抱冤哀〡 the feelings aroused at suffering injustice.
心〡 grieved, sympathizing.

TʻUNG.

Old sounds, tʻong *and* dong. *In Canton*, tʻung; — *in Swatow*, tʻong, tang, *and* tʻang; — *in Amoy*, tʻong *and* tong; — *in Fuhchau*, tʻung, tung, tong, *and* tăng; — *in Shanghai*, dung *and* tʻung; — *in Chifu*, tʻung.

通 ꜀*tʻung* From to *go* and *sprouting buds*.
To permeate, to go through; to see clearly, to perceive; to make known to others, to have dealings or political relations with; to communicate with; to interchange, as two characters of the same meaning; to succeed, to bring about; prosperous; pervious, permeable, pervading; clear, as a perspicuous style; current, as money; reaching everywhere; thorough, general; uniform, as a hue; generally, the whole of, complete; entire; illicit, adulterous; a field containing a square league; found in the names of many places.
〡寶 current money or value.
〡曉 he fully understands it.
〡知 to notify, to inform.
〡志 a general topography.
〡風 a thorough draft.
打〡鼓 three taps of the drum.
打〡 to get a thing through; to bribe.
〡道 to open roads.

丨事 an interpreter; a broker who transacts business, once called linguists at Canton, where they were recognized by their rulers, and each had a 丨事館 linguist's hong.
私丨 illicit intercourse; treacherous; to secretly inform.
丨稱 a general designation.
路不丨行 no thoroughfare.
丨書 a calendar, an almanac.
貨不流丨 no sale for the goods.
丨共 the whole of, all.
丨明 perspicuous, intelligible.
未丨中國 it hitherto has had no intercourse with China.
事事變丨 in all things accommodate yourself to circumstances.
丨諭各省 a general order to all the provinces.
丨是我的 all are mine.
丨使 an agent, an envoy.
丨達世情 well versed in the affairs of life.
不丨 obstrŭcted, cŏstive, no outlet; inĕlegant or vŭlgar, as a phrăse.
丨文 elegant language, perspicuous style.
相丨 intercommunicating, interchanging.
丨州 the port of Peking on the Pei-ho.
五神丨 the five supernatural gifts (*pancha-bhidjna*) of the Budhists, which every arhan takes possession of by contemplation.

蓪 ꜀t'ung From *plant* and *permeable*. An herbaceous plant, the 丨草 *Aralia papyrifera*, found in Formosa and Yunnan, whose pith sliced into sheets and ironed out, furnishes the substance wrongly called rice-paper, used in making 丨紙花 or 丨草花 artificial flowers; pith of any kind.
丨紙畫 pith-paper pictures.

烔 ꜀t'ung The aspect of a flame; a furious fire.
丨紅的火苗 a bright red blaze.

恫 ꜀t'ung Pain of body or mind; in pain, aching; moaning from pain; sighing, lamenting.
呻丨 groaning.
奉其丨 he felt the smart.
愢丨 grief and disappointment.
哀丨 to grieve over; alas, alas!
神罔時丨 the spirits [of the ancestors] were not dissatisfied.

痌 ꜀t'ung Interchanged with the preceding. An ulcer suppurating; groaning.
丨聲徹耳 a moan pierces my ear.
丨瘝 sick and pained; grieved for, pained in heart.
丨瘝在抱 [the good ruler] takes the calamities of the people as if they were his own.

同 **仝** ꜀t'ung From 口 *mouth* and 冂 *a covering; q.d.* many talking together and agreeing; the second form is common.
Together, all at once; all, united; identical; same, alike, in time or place; to covenant or give in allegiance; to unite, to harmonize; matched; to equalize; to share in; to assemble; agreeing, as one; joint, joined with another officer who is super-ordinate; a *conjunction*, and, with; in common; the same as; a meeting of feudal princes every twelve years.
丨一塊去 they all went together.
丨居 to live together.
丨一樣 or 丨一般兒 they are of the same sort; just alike.
不丨 different; unusual.
丨知 a joint or sub-prefect.
丨胞兄弟 brothers of the same mother.
會丨 to assemble together.
大丨小異 for the most part alike; the difference is less than the similarity.
丨姓不丨宗 same surname but no relationship.
丨行 partners; fellow travellers.
丨類 same class.
雷丨 to thunder the same, to echo another's words, to corroborate his sayings; it alludes to the popular notion that all nature echoes a clap of thunder.
丨字 characters of the same meaning but having different radicals, as 階 and 堦 steps.
不丨人 eccentric, strange.
丨人 the 11th diagram.
丨心 in accord.
丨年 of the same age; [graduated or appointed] the same year.
丨榜 the same tripos or concours.
丨道 the same profession.
丨甘苦 a fellow in joy and sorrow.
我丨你去 I will go with you, (*Cantonese*).

詷 ꜀t'ung Occurs used with the next. All at once; hasty, hurried, so as to violate etiquette.
輕薄謥丨 she (the queen) was frivolous and hasty in her manners and disposition.

侗 ꜀t'ung From *man* and *as*; *q. d.* like a man. Ignorant and rude; inapt and plain, neither talent nor learning; untrained and unfit.
倥丨 an ignorant boy.
丨然而來 came in his simplicity.

茼 ꜀t'ung A small, wild, syngenesious plant resembling an *Erigeron*, the 丨蒿 having yellow flowers, and the smell like the artemisia,—of which it is probably a species, rather than the camomile or an allied plant.

峒 ꜀t'ung Interchanged with 洞 a cavern, and wrongly replaced by 垌 an earthenware vessel. A territorial division under the Ming dynasty; uneven; up and down, as a defile; a group of islands off Shantung.

挏 ˓t'ung To lead; to draw out; to churn and bring butter from milk.

丨馬 an officer in the Han dynasty who superintended the preparation of quass.

桐 ˓t'ung A large tree belonging to the *Euphorbiacæ*, the 丨樹 or *Elæococca sinensis*, whose light durable wood is used in making musical instruments; the name seems to be applied as a generic term to similar large leaved trees, as the *Catalpa* and *Bignonia;* name of the place where T'ang is said to have been buried, in Yung-ho hien 榮河縣 in the southwest of Shansi.

梧丨(or 井丨 or 孤丨 alluding to its stately appearance,) is the national tree of China, and grows over the central provinces; it is probably the *Elæococca verrucosa*, and its small edible seeds are mixed with the tea given in bridal presents.

油丨 or 罌子丨 cultivated for its large and acrid nut, (*Elæococca vernicifera*) from which the 丨油 oil is pressed for painting and calking, and its soot used for ink; at Canton the oil of the *Curcas purgans* is used under the same name.

海丨 a species (*Elæococca spinosa*) with spinous trunk and branches, whose bark is used medicinally.

臭梧丨 a species of *Clerodendron.*

丨油灰 chunam used in calking; putty.

丨葉灰 fine ashes put in censers.

丨杖 a staff used when a mother dies.

花丨 the *Pawlonia*, so called from its large flowers and stately appearance.

筒 ˓t'ung A tube; a pipe used as a musical instrument, made from a long and knotless bamboo; a duct; a pipe open at both ends.

射丨 a sumpitan.

號丨 a speaking-trumpet.

烟丨 a tobacco-pipe.

萬花丨 a kaleidoscope.

一丨鼻涕 a sniveling booby.

信丨 or 封丨 or 紙丨 an envelop for letters.

筩 ˓t'ung Very similar to the preceding.

A measure made of bamboo; a cup; a pipe; a creel.

箭丨 a quiver.

筆丨 a pencil cup.

十二丨 the twelve reeds of the pandean pipe.

大花丨 a Roman candle in fireworks.

銅 ˓t'ung Copper or 紅丨 is also called the 赤金 red metal; brazen, coppery.

黃丨 brass.

丨箔 brass foil; tinsel.

打丨舖 a brazier's shop.

自然丨 native copper; including also iron and copper pyrites.

白丨 white copper, argentan, or tutenague.

丨綠 verditer or carbonate of copper; verdigris after it is scraped off, but called 丨青 when on the copper.

丨銀錢 copper dollars.

食丨 it eats the copper; — *met.* covetous.

丨燒青 copper enamel or cloisonnée.

滿身丨臭 his whole body smells of copper; — purse-proud.

丨池 water-spouts, gargoyles.

丨板印 printed on copper plates.

化丨 to fuse copper.

廢丨 old copper.

丨葉 brass leaves put at promotion in a graduate's cap.

獞 ˓t'ung A variety of dog.

丨猺 a name of one of the Miaotsz' tribes in Kwéicheu, given to them because they were as savage as dogs.

艟 艟 ˓t'ung A long and swift boat like a galley, called 艨丨 now disused; they were made to board and run down the enemy.

鮦 ˓t'ung A kind of perch, small and resembling a *Labrus.*

丨綠魚 a fresh-water perch, in Peking 20 inches long, color whitish, and flesh good tasted; the 鱧魚 is quoted as another name for this fish, but that is probably a kind of *Ophicephalus* or mullet.

Read *cheu'* Name of an ancient district 丨陽縣 lying in the southern part of Honan in the present Jü-ning fu.

硐 ˓t'ung To rub or smooth.

鎤丨 to trim and pierce the nodes of a bamboo when making a fife.

佟 ˓t'ung Name of T'ai T'ung 台丨 a famous sorcerer in the Han dynasty.

丨萬 T'ung Wan, a scholar of Liaotung.

童 ˓t'ung Composed of 立 to *stand* and 里 a *village;* but others derive it from 辛 a *crime* (like 愆) and 重 *weighty* contracted, referring to the condition of slavery to which some lads were subjected; it is interchanged with the next three.

A boy, a lad under 15 years and unmarried; a slave boy; one who has no house, unprotected; a student, a bachelor; a virgin; undefiled, pure; bare of trees; boyish, youthful; young, said of rams.

成丨 at the age of puberty.

丨女 a spinster, a virgin.

丨子 a boy, a youth.

丨年 youthful, about 14 or 15 years.

頭丨 a bald head.

山丨 a hill bare of trees.

書丨 a schoolboy.

神丨 a bright lad.

文 丨 a young student.
小 丨 a term by which feudal princesses spoke of themselves.
丨心未離 he has not given up his boyish disposition; — said of a man who acts childishly.
反老還 丨 second childhood; in his dotage.
鶴髮 丨 顏 white hair and youthful complexion.
守 丨 貞 to take vows of chastity.
丨 牛 a calf without horns.
丨 叟不欺 no imposition on young or old; — a shop sign.
桑樹 丨 丨 the thrifty, green mulberries.

僮 ˓t'ung A slave boy; a lad who has not yet been capped at marriage; a slave girl or concubine; reverently; rude, unpolished.
家 丨 a waiting-boy.
丨 僕 a young slave.
被之 丨 丨 her head-dress rises high and gracefully.
狂 丨 a wild, crazy fellow.
幼 丨 a youth.

瞳 ˓t'ung From *eye* and *a lad*. The pupil of the eye, which the Chinese say becomes square at the age of 800; to stare at; a vacant look; a silly stare.
丨人 the baby in the eye.
綠水灌 丨 人 or 丨 人轉背 a cataract.
˓重 丨 a double pupil, which Shun is said to have had.

絧 ˓t'ung A sort of cloth.
鴻 丨 緁獵 they hastily went on, following straight ahead in the hunt.

蓳 ˓t'ung The roots of the nelumbium; a kind of sedge or *Scirpus*, the 鄭 丨 from whose stalks sandals are made.
丨 蒿菜 an edible pot-herb like celery.

犝 ˓t'ung A calf whose horns are not yet grown.

羶 ˓t'ung A lamb whose horns have not grown.
彼 丨 而角實訌小子 to say that the lamb has horns, is to deceive the child.

潼 ˓t'ung Also read ˓ch'ung; used for 湩 coagulated milk.
A tributary of the Yellow River which flows into it near
丨 關 the celebrated pass at the elbow of that stream in T'ungcheu fu 同州府 in Shensi; to overflow and destroy a road; damp, wet.
丨 丨 崇麗 a lofty, fine edifice.

橦 ˓t'ung A tree in Yunnan, from whose soft, crisp flowers cloth, called 丨 花布 can be made; it may denote the cotton tree (*Salmalia*), whose stamens are used to stuff quilts.

Read ˓chw'ang. A stick of squared timber; a high staff, from which a pennon 幢 is flown.

氃 ˓t'ung Feathers in confusion is 蒙 丨; it is applied especially to the stork, to one which would not perform its part when its feathers were in disorder.

鶇 ˓t'ung A bird with a yellow bill a foot long, the 鸏 丨 *Buceros* or hornbill; it is described as having a brilliant, variegated plumage, and living on the leaves of trees.

穜 ˓t'ung From *grain* and *lad*; it is also read ˓chung, and used for 種 to sow grain.
Grain which, though sown the first, is gathered last; late, autumnal grain.

曈 ˓t'ung The sun about to rise.
丨 曨 early dawn, the sun just illuminating the sky.

朣 ˓t'ung The moon just rising is 丨 朧, spoken of it as it comes above the horizon.

鼕 鼛 ˓t'ung The rattle of drums.
丨 丨 响 the great clamor of drums.
鼛鼓 丨 丨 the drums are making a loud din.

甋 㼧 ˓t'ung The upper tiles used on roofs, so called because they are like a 筩 tube; also called 覆瓦 covering tiles and 陽瓦 upper tiles.

彤 ˓t'ung From *feathered* and *vermilion*.
Red, rosy; painted with vermilion, brindled; a peach-blossom color.
丨 弓 a bow colored with vermilion; used by ancient emperors.
丨 雲 rose colored clouds.
丨 管 a pencil with a red tube.
丨 伯 the Baron of T'ung, whose ancient principality lay on the River Wéi, not far from the elbow of the Yellow River.

捅 ˓t'ung From *hand* and *a measure*.
To lead on, to advance; to strike against; to stick into, as through a paper window.
丨 一個窟窿 punch a hole in it.
丨 鳥巢 to break up a bird's nest.
不要 丨 佢 don't burst it through.
In *Cantonese*. To baste; to run one thing into another, as two sleeves.
丨 好個件衫 put those jackets into each other.
丨 骨 a basted edge.

桶 ˓t'ung From *wood* and *measure*.
A cask, a tub; a square wooden measure of six pints; a deep wooden case.
水 丨 a pail, a bucket.
丨 梁 the bale or stick to carry it.
櫃 丨 a drawer in a table. (*Cantonese.*)
靴 丨 the leg of a boot.

太平丨 a street tub to hold water for fires.

馬丨 or 恭丨 a close-stool.

傢伙丨 a baggage box.

冰丨 an ice box for cooling rooms.

扶丨 to support a woman in parturition.

襱 ˓t'ung A coat with short sleeves, a kind of waistcoat.

Read ˓*lung* and used for 攏. Overalls worn in winter; outside trowsers; children's trowsers; an apron or petticoat.

統 ˓t'ung From *silk* and to *fill*.

The end of a clue, or beginning of a thread; first of a subject, a hint, a clue; origin, beginning; the whole, general, entire; all under one head; to rule, to control; followers; a classifier of tablets.

一丨 the whole, one entire view.

丨共數目 the total amount, the whole number.

丨領 general control over; a military officer of the second grade.

步軍丨領 the commander-in-chief of the infantry at Peking.

總丨 to oversee the whole.

天下歸一丨 the empire is now under one sway.

丨計多少 how much does it all amount to?

垂丨 to transmit the whole; said of the empire.

丨承 to carry on as it was received, as a doctrine, or the succession to a throne.

一丨碑 one stone tablet.

正丨 central or main governance.

丨屬文武 all civil and military affairs belong to him.

丨緒 a clue to the whole; a succession in the dynasty.

失了體丨 lost his character; disgraced.

痛 t'ung' From *disease* and *common*.

A pain, an ache; disease that causes pain; acute feelings; heartrending, distressed; to commisserate; with energy; a sign of the superlative, extremely, painfully.

丨哭 to weep bitterly.

丨飲 to drink too much.

丨悔 deep repentance.

憐丨 to compassionate.

丨快 extreme joy.

丨心切齒 to gnash with rage.

丨哉 alas, alas!

牙丨 a toothache.

丨改前非 I sincerely regret my past errors.

丨恨 intense hatred.

哀丨不已 incessantly sorrowing for others.

In *Cantonese*. To love, to feel for.

我丨你 I like you.

TWAN.

Old sounds, twan *and* dwan. *In Canton*, tün; — *in Swatow*, túan, to, *and* tǎng; — *in Amoy*, tòan *and* tsòan; — *in Fuhchau*, twang *and* taung; — *in Shanghai*, töⁿ; — *in Chifu*, tan.

耑 ˓twan Designed to represent the *plumule* above a *line* denoting the ground, and the *radical* or rootlets below it; now written like the next, while this is used as a contraction of ˓*chwen* 專 only.

The spring or cause of anything.

端 ˓twan From *standing* and *shoots*.

Springing forth, commencing, sprouting; the origin, the head, elementary principles; strait, direct, correct, upright; modest, grave, decent; to examine into the cause; to bud or commence; an ancient ceremonial robe; a classifier of subjects, a mystery, and a piece of silk; a measure of eighteen cubits in the Cheu dynasty.

丨正 or 丨方 correct; integrity; upright, either physically or morally.

丨整好 all is well arranged.

作丨整 arrange it properly, put it in order.

執其兩丨 [Shun] maintained the two correct extremes.

無丨生有 there is no sufficient reason for it.

用丨命于上帝 having thus the right favoring decree from Shang-ti.

不止一丨 not one affair only.

四丨 the four decorous principles, are 仁 humanity, 義 rectitude, 禮 propriety and 知 knowledge; — to which all 異丨 strange doctrines or heresies are opposed.

丨的 or 丨頭 the cause, the reason of.

造丨 to make a start.

天丨 spring, the time of sprouting.

不丨 improper, immodest, indecent.

丨莊 proper, modest.

丨午 or 丨陽 the dragon-boat festival on the fifth day of the fifth moon.

丨門 the south gate of the palace.

丨人正士 a correct, high principled man.

萬丨 all kinds of causes or affairs.

品行丨方 naturally correct and just.

丨緒 a hint or clue; a means of reaching the subject.

玄丨 an official dress of the Cheu dynasty with enormous sleeves.

剬 ˓twan To cut even; to cut and trim; to arrange; to act a grave, prim deportment.

依仁丨行 to conform his acts to humanity.

丨義 to decide by just rules.

貒 ˏtwan From 豸 *beast* and 耑 to *spring*, for 團 a *lump* or ball, probably alluding to its rolling itself up in its burrow.

A species of small badger, also called 豬貒 the pig badger from the resemblance; found in Shansi and westward; fur of a sandy color, slow in its motions and very fleshy; eats ants and grubs; the description allies this animal to the *teledu* (*Mydaus meliceps*), and its odor is noticed.

短 ˊtwan From *dart* and *dish*, referring to measuring lengths by a bow.

Short; brief, contracted; shortcomings, failures; few, not common or plenty; to shorten, to curtail; to come short, to be in fault.

丨見 not much experience.

丨命 short-lived, died before 16.

丨處 a defect; a mean act, a flaw or shortcoming in one's conduct.

氣丨 short-winded, not strong in the lungs.

丨工 a job; piece-work.

日丨 or 天丨 short days

丨功 short days for work.

丨行 to act overbearingly, to treat rudely.

不長不丨 just right, as a well fitting shoe; 'twill do.

臉丨 testy, quick-tempered.

人各有丨 everybody has his faults.

勿言人之丨 don't talk of people's defects.

志丨 incapable, not much mind.

丨少 few, insufficient; not many.

丨情 without proper feelings, indifferent to other's rights.

丨禮得恨了 I am deficient in civility, don't think me rude; — a polite phrase.

斷 twanˋ From 斤 *hatchet* and an old form of 絕 to *break off*, as silk is parted.

To cut asunder or in pieces; to snap, to break off or in two, to divide; to prohibit, to put a stop to; to discontinue; cut, sundered, broken, snapped; to settle, to give a judicial opinion; a doubt, a dilemma; before a negative, forms an *adverb*, surely, certainly, decidedly.

往來不丨 uninterrupted intercourse.

丨屠 to suspend the slaughter of butcher's meat.

丨路 to break off intercourse.

丨後 to bring up the rear in a retreat.

决丨 to decide, to give sentence.

公丨 a just, open decision.

丨絕 broken, completely disconnected.

丨氣 breath has stopped; dead.

丨水米 to stop the supplies.

丨舟纜 cut the hawser of the boat.

丨然 assuredly, verily, positively.

丨丨不敢 I cannot presume; I dare not do so.

丨得定 it has been finally settled.

丨事 to dispose of a case.

家音已丨 I have no longer news from home.

丨開 to make a division or average, as for losses.

望丨鄉關 I can no longer see my native village.

丨腸人 one who is greatly grieved or afflicted.

丨其疑惑 cleared up all his doubts.

In *Cantonese*. A *preposition*, by, according to.

丨斤賣 sold it by the catty.

段 twanˋ From 殳 to *kill* and 耑 *origin* contracted; not the same as ˊkia 叚 to lend.

To push or lay things apart; a fragment, a piece, a section; a classifier of sections of books, stories or pieces, series or items of regulations, acts of plays, slices of meat, plats of ground, stages in a journey, or other similar portions.

丨半 half of a thing.

一丨地 a patch, a parcel of ground; a lot.

大丨 the largest piece; for the most part.

好手丨 good work, fine performance.

一丨水 a piece of water, a reach in a river.

言無倒丨 to talk incoherently; muddle-headed.

煅 鍛 twanˋ From *fire* or *metal* and *piece*.

To forge metal; to heat and hammer it; to work upon, to practice, to make perfect; mature, practiced.

丨鍊 worked over, wrought, well hammered; well versed in.

丨灰 to calcine, to drive off the moisture, as when preparing drugs; to reduce by analysis.

丨鍊入人罪 to bring a man in guilty by perverting the law.

緞 twanˋ From *silk* and *piece*; also read ˏhia, the heel of a shoe.

Satin, which word is probably itself derived from *sz'-twan* 絲丨; glossy silken or other fabrics.

花丨 or 局丨 brocade.

綢丨犒勞 conferred many silks on him for his valor.

閃丨 changeable satin.

斜文丨 twilled levantine silk.

貢丨 silks made for court.

𣪠 twanˋ Once used for the last.

The heel of a shoe, or the stiffening put in to strengthen the heel, and line the shoe.

腶 twanˋ Meat boiled with ginger and cinnamon put in the pot, called 丨脩; after cooking it was dried.

大饗尙丨脩 at the great feasts the cinnamon-flavored flesh was thought much of.

葮 twanˋ The flower of the *Hibiscus rosa-sinensis*, usually called 木槿花; it is much cultivated.

椴 *twan'* A large tree resembling the aspen in size, and called 白楊; but its timber is like beech, white, with an even grain; it is used for coffins; a beam or pole.

爲丨舁物 to carry things on a pole.

Read *˛hia.* A prison; the stocks.

碬 *twan'* Otherwise read *˛hia.*

A rough coarse stone for whetstones; others say, a term for emery or corundum.

籪 *twan'* An involved weir of bamboo stakes, arranged across a stream or canal to catch crabs or fish; they are common in Kiangnan.

蟹丨 a crab weir.

TW'AN.

Old sounds, tw'an *and* dwan. *In Canton,* t'ün *and* t'un; — *in Swatow,* t'úan *and* chwan; — *in Amoy,* t'òan, hwan, *and* ch'òan; — *in Fuhchau,* tiòng, twòng, *and* tw'ang; — *in Shanghai,* t'ö^n; — *in Chifu,* t'an.

湍 *˛tw'an* Water gushing out; a rapid current; the reflex current or undertow.

丨河 a branch of the River Han in the west of Honan.

急流曰丨 a rapid current is called a torrent.

煓 *˛tw'an* Fire blazing up, red as fire; a statesman in the Han dynasty.

臣入雲丨之幕 the officers entered the ornamented red tent.

團 *˛tw'an* From to *surround* and *condense;* interchanged with the next three.

A globular mass, a lump, an agglomeration; united, agreeing, as a company; a band, as volunteers; the district that furnishes one; a guard; round, lump-like; to collect, to group; to dwell together; to environ, to surround; to round off, to end; the female of crabs; a classifier of pellets and balls, of collections or harmonies.

一丨麪 a lump of dough.

丨圓 full, as the moon; altogether, lumping it; closely united, as husband and wife.

一丨和氣 a harmonious blending of interests; coalescing, as when gases unite.

丨聚 to curl up, to cuddle, as a worm does when touched.

點丨 to review or visit the guard.

此月千古丨圝 this full moon has for ages been just so round.

丨練 to drill bands — of troops; a ward drill or organization.

丨丨的轉着 [the dust is blown up] and whirled round and round in flurries.

丨結 to include in; to condense neatly, as in a resumé; compact.

縮做一丨 all contracted; shrunk into a lump, as a sea anemone does on touching it.

丨龍 a coiled-up dragon, such as are woven on flowered crapes; a sort of gunpowder tea.

丨年 to wind up the year with festivities.

丨丨圍住 hemmed in on all sides.

摶 *˛tw'an* From *hand* and to *condense;* it must not be confounded with *poh,* 搏 to beat.

To roll into a ball; to make round; to pat and roll, as dough or clay; to beat flat; to push or drive together.

毋丨飯 do not roll your food into a ball.

丨合 to roll together.

丨三國之兵 to lead the troops of the three states.

黃土丨人 he worked men out of yellow clay.

Read *chw'n'* A parcel of a hundred feathers; to attend to one thing; to unite; to bind, to roll up.

漙 *˛tw'an* Dew descending in abundance; a river in Shantung.

慱 *˛tw'an* Intense mental emotion; care.

勞心丨丨 in a state of great trouble and anxiety.

糰 糰 *˛tw'an* Dumplings or dough-nuts made of flour or glutinous rice; a round cake.

湯丨 a new year's dumpling.

丨子 small dough cakes.

歡喜丨 crisp rice crullers.

菜中之丨粉名勾汁子 the forced meat balls in a dish are called stir-the-soup-boys.

疃 畽 町 *'tw'an* From *field* and *lad* or *heavy;* it is also read *'tung* and *˛t'un;* the last form is unusual.

Waste land near a city; an alley in a town; a long street in the country, forming a hamlet; paths made and frequented by wild beasts.

丨怨 careless, wayward in conduct; one who does not mind the corners in his traveling.

蘇家丨 the village of the Su family; this usage is common near Pao-ting fu.

彖 *tw'an'* From 彑 a *hog's head* and 豕 a *pig;* in combination it resembles *luh,* 彔 to carve, and *siang'* 象 an elephant.

A hog running; some say, it is the hedgehog; in the Yih King, a summing up of the application of the diagrams, and the good or bad embodied in them.

丨曰 the application thus says.

褖 *tw'an'* Robes anciently worn by the empress, black, with a plain gauze lining; afterwards they were of a yellow color.

TSA.

In Canton, tsa ; — *in Swatow*, cha ; — *in Amoy*, tsa ; — *in Fuhchau*, cha ; — *in Shanghai*, tsa ; — *in Chifu*, tsa.

咱 ꜀*tsa* ꜀*tsan* From *mouth* and *self*; it is properly *tsah*꜆ in Kanghi, and seems to have been formed to indicate the elided pronunciation of ꜀*tsan* 喒.

We, the persons speaking; our, used in the abstract.

丨們 we, our; it includes the speaker and the hearers, and refers to country, occupation, or friends; as 丨們的馬 one of our native horses.

丨兩個 or 丨兩兒 we two.

丨家 I, myself; an expression used by the eunuchs in the Ming dynasty.

丨老子 my father in *Shanghai*; in *Amoy*, used in a plural sense, we, our, as 丨唐人 we Chinese.

TSAH.

Old sounds, tsap *and* dzap. *In Canton*, tsap, sap, *and* ka ; — *in Swatow*, chap ; — *in Amoy*, tsat, tsap, *and* tsan ; — *in Fuhchau*, chak ; — *in Shanghai*, tsah, seh, sah, *and* k'a ; — *in Chifu*, tsa.

匝꜆ **帀**꜆ **迊**꜆ ꜀*tsa* From a *receptacle* and *napkin*; the second unusual form, which is regarded as the obverse of ꜂*fan* 反 to return, is the original one.

To go round, as the heavens do in the course of a year; to perform a circuit or entire revolution; a side, a row; stretching along, as a line of trees; pervading.

周丨 to revolve; to go about everywhere.

三丨 three times around; it curls thrice, as a ram's horn.

一丨 a row; a curl; a circuit.

丨月 a whole month.

彌山丨地 [the crowd] covered the hills and spread over the land.

In *Cantonese*. To please, to delight: lustrous.

不丨眼 does not please the eye.

藍丨丨 a bright blue.

咂꜆ **哂**꜆ ꜀*tsa* To enter the mouth; to suck in; to taste; to lick, to smack; the motion of a fish sucking or moving its gills.

丨丨兒 the nipple.

丨嘴 to put in the mouth and suck, as a child a nursing-bottle.

拿人丨味 taken in by his guile.

丨碎 rubbish; odds and ends.

In *Cantonese*. Deceived, deluded; to coax, to wheedle; trifling, of no importance.

聽人丨 taken in, overreached, diddled.

細丨丨 much cut up; small, minced.

不受人丨 not minding people's blarney.

魳꜆ ꜀*tsa* The motion of a fish's mouth and gills.

Read *hoh*, A kind of reptile, 魶丨 but not defined.

沞꜆ ꜀*tsa* Damp, wet; bubbling up; splashing, as boiling water.

砸꜆ ꜀*tsa* An unauthorized character.

To strike; to rap on, to hit; to knock and shiver.

丨碎 to reduce to fragments.

丨着頭 knocked my head by the fall.

摔丨 to smash by throwing on the ground.

丨爛 shivered by the blow.

噆꜆ ꜀*tsa* Also read ꜂*ts'an*.

To suck up, as a musquito or fly does; to hold in the mouth, as a sweet morsel.

丨乾了 sucked him dry.

丨人的血 to suck the blood from one.

囋꜆ ꜀*tsa* Sound, clamor, noise.

嘈丨 the noise of a drum; a hubbub, as of people talking.

Read ꜀*tsan*. To reiterate tiresomely; to ridicule; to swallow or gulp.

雥꜆ **𡗝**꜆ ꜀*tsa* From *not* or *leek* and *heaven*; both forms are used.

Sordid, vile, evil; irreverent, for which 㒓 is now used, and both these are only employed in combination.

雜꜆ **襍**꜆ ꜀*tsa* From 集 to *flock* together, and 衣 *garments*, altered in combination; the first is commonest.

Mixed, variegated, particolored, streaked; a mixture of colors or ingredients; unassorted, mingled, confused; heterogenous, not alike; to mix confusedly; to bore through; to pervade.

丨貨 all sorts of goods.

丨色 many colored.

丨亂無章 without regulations: in confusion.

佐丨官 official underlings.

心丨 distracted, no perseverance.

打丨 a man of all work; a coolie.

丨種仔 a bastard. (*Cantonese.*)

五方丨處 a place where all kinds of people live.

丨物撰德 to collect or specify the virtues of many things.

閑丨人等 loafers, idlers.

丨紋 irregular veins or streaks.

衆皆丨然曰 they all at once began to cry out and talk.

蘸 ˏtsa A grass from which door-blinds can be woven; a small floating grass, like a *Hippuris*, with linear leaves in whorls, and cultivated in gold fish ponds; it is called 丨草 or 雜草 in Peking, and 金魚茜 at Canton.

磼 ˏtsa A high peak.

磖丨 the sound of things breaking.

卡 ˏtsa ˋchia A guard-house at a pass; a station; the official residence of a military officer; to get stuck, as a bone in the throat.

魚刺丨喉 the fish-bone sticks in his throat.

丨路 or 丨口 a guard-house, a police-station; called 街丨 in Canton, and applied to the men.

丨房 the quarters for the guards.

丨倫 a low post in the maritime customs.

守丨 a frontier station.

潳 ˏtsa Used with *tsien*ˀ 濺 the common form.

To spatter, to scatter water about.

TSʻAH.

Old sound, tsʻat. *In Canton*, tsʻat; — *in Swatow*, chʻat; — *in Amoy*, chʻat; — *in Fuhchau*, chʻak *and* chʻaè; — *in Shanghai*, tsʻah; — *in Chifu*, tsʻa.

擦, **攃** ˏtsʻa The first form is the most common, and the second is also read *sah*ˎ

The action of the feet disturbing the herbage, and making a noise; to scatter; to feel, to rub, to brush; a brush.

丨牙 to brush the teeth.

磨丨 to grind or rub smooth.

丨肥皂 to wash with soap-berries.

丨身過 to brush against one, as when walking.

礤 ˏtsʻa A coarse stone; to rub, to grind.

囃 ˏtsʻa The noise made by spectators in applauding acrobats and mummers.

TSAI.

Old sounds, tsai, tsat, tsap, dzai, *and* dat. *In Canton*, tsoi *and* tsei; — *in Swatow*, chai *and* to; — *in Amoy*, tsai; — *in Fuhchau*, chai *and* chʻai; — *in Shanghai*, tsé *and* dzé; — *in Chifu*, tsai.

哉 ˏtsai From *mouth* and *wounded*.

An exclamation of praise or surprise; an *interrogative* particle implying either doubt or conviction, according to the scope; or often merely a high degree of; an *interjection* placed after important words to draw attention to them; occurs in poetry as an expletive; to begin; to burst forth, as plants in spring.

其故何丨 on what account, pray?

何有於我丨 what, after all, is this to me?

豈可惜丨 would you pity him?

沽之丨沽之丨 sell it! sell it!

仁遠乎丨 has humanity so far gone?

嗚呼哀丨 alas, it is sad indeed!

安得不悲丨 how could I forbear to pity?

大丨孔子 Oh, how great was Confucius!

大丨問 ah! truly an important question.

初三丨生明 in the third moon all nature begins to spring forth.

快丨 how pleased!

至矣丨 Oh, how admirable!

野丨由也 what a clown is Yiu!

有是丨 indeed, is it so!

庶乎丨 what a crowd of people!

何其繆丨 what a wretched blunder!

君子多乎丨 does a wise man ask so much.

何足道丨 should it even be mentioned?

栽 ˏtsai From *tree* and *wounded*.

To set out, to plant trees, to put suckers in the ground; to heap earth about the roots, to hill; a sapling.

丨花 to set out flowers.

花丨 layers of plants, cuttings.

丨種 to plant and sow.

可以丨培 he is worthy of one's patronage.

多丨花少丨刺 plant more flowers than thistles; —*met.* act so as to reap a good reward.

丨樹 to set out trees.

In *Pekingese.* To fall down, to tumble over.

丨折了腿 fell and broke his leg.

丨躺下 stumbled and fell.

丨倒了 fell down.

災 灾 裁 ꜀tsai From *fire* and *water* or *shelter*; the first is most used.

Calamity that comes from above, as floods, pestilence, drought, caterpillars, blight; divine judgments; plagues; miseries, misfortunes; adverse, calamitous, dangerous.

丨害 afflictive, injurious.

丨禍 afflictions, miseries.

降丨 [Heaven] sent them calamities.

救丨 to relieve calamity.

招丨 to bring evil on one's self.

天丨流行 a general visitation, as a pestilence.

送火丨 to dismiss the fire risk, by worshiping the god of Fire.

天丨橫禍 unforeseen judgments from Heaven.

丨難' sufferings, calamities.

丨田 fields that for any reason do not yield full crops.

宰 ꜂𡙈 ꜂tsai From 宀 a *shelter* and 辛 *bitter*; *i. e.* he who has the trouble of affairs in a house; the second form is sometimes used to specially denote the slaughtering of animals.

To govern, to rule; to preside, as at a table; to fashion to one's liking; to slaughter, skin, and dress animals; to fry; a ruler, a head; a steward, a major-domo.

丨相 a prime-minister; once called 太丨 or highest ruler.

主丨 the ruler over all, as a sovereign or general; *met.* the mind.

家丨 anciently an officer of the rites.

邑丨 a district-magistrate.

丨制 to direct, to oversee.

丨殺 to butcher.

丨夫 or 膳丨 the chief cook.

萬靈眞丨 the true lord of all beings.

烹丨 to dress and cook food.

諸丨君婦廢徹不遲 the servants and head-women quickly remove — the dishes.

丨婦 a son's wife.

崽 ꜂tsai From *hill* and to *think*; also read ꜀*shai*; the diminutive 仔 in Cantonese is derived from this.

A common term for a child in Hunan and Kiangsi; to bring forth, said of animals.

狗丨子 the bitch has littered.

下丨子 to bring forth.

猴兒丨子 the monkey has a cub; used in contempt for persons.

燗丨 a rascal, a worthless fellow.

縡 ꜂tsai An affair, a business; what is contained.

上天之丨 that which is doing in the high heavens, the operations of nature or of the gods there.

載 ꜂tsai From a *carriage* and *wounded*; used with the next.

A year; it was so called in early times, because nature having made a revolution, began again.

幾丨 several years.

千丨下 since a thousand years, or handed down that time.

半丨 half a year.

丨記 contemporary annals.

Read *tsai'* To contain; to lade a ship or cart; to fill in, to convey, to carry with one; to load; to bear; to complete; to act, to sustain, to do; to record; to adorn, to beautify; to begin; recorded, written in; an undertaking; acts, doings; filled, loaded; a cargo, a load; an *adverb* of time, then, thereupon; the highest number in numeration, a hundred millions, an incalculable number.

丨滿 stowed full; quite loaded.

丨于何書 in what book is that contained?

不够丨 not enough for a load.

能丨幾擔 [the boat] can carry many peculs.

厚德丨福 good actions are stored up to produce future happiness.

滿丨而回 to return home well laden — with property.

車丨千斤 the cart carries a thousand catties.

丨輸爾丨 what you have loaded will be upset.

上天之丨無聲無臭 the acts of Heaven have neither sound nor smell.

厥聲丨路 their cries filled the road.

丨戢干戈 he thereupon laid up his weapons.

丨籍繁衍 many errors are found in their narratives.

記丨 to record, to note down.

儎 tsai' An unauthorized word, derived from the preceding to indicate the noun.

The cargo, the loading of a boat; the capacity or tonnage of a vessel; to stow cargo; to contain such an amount, as a bank-bill, on the back of which it is stamped.

幾十丨 several scores of cargoes.

船滿丨 the ship is loaded.

丨脚 freight money.

裝百丨 she carries a hundred — peculs.

過丨 to tranship or take out cargo.

在 tsai' From 土 *earth* and 才 the *hand* on it.

To be in or at; present; to belong to, to consist in; to live, to dwell, to reside, to remain; to be preserved or continue; consisting in; involved in, depending on; existing, living, being; a *preposition*, in, on, at, within; and often precedes adverbs of place and time; a place, a home; to examine.

他們不丨家 none of them are at home.

父母不丨 parents are both dead.

丨學堂 at school.

丨何處 where is he living?

不自丨 not feeling well, not very well pleased.

祭如丨 worshiped him (a father) as if he was still alive.

丨下 below; a common man.

罪不丨我 it is not my fault.
丨你 that is your affair.
不丨心上 you need not give yourself a thought about it; no great matter.
敬爾丨公 carefully attend to your public duties.
載丨條約 it is in the treaty.
你丨心 you should remember it.
所丨必有 it is everywhere, in all places.
不丨乎此 it does not consist in this; I don't think it is so.
現丨給銀 you must pay the money now.
住丨那裏 where do you live?
固一世之雄也而今安丨哉 where now are all the heroes of olden time?
丨寬 be gentle, act with lenity.

再 *tsai'* From 一 *one* and 冓 a *frame-work* contracted; *q. v.* as when one stick is added on another; it resembles ˳*yen* 冉 in form and ˳纔 in meaning.

To raise up once and then again; doubled, repeated; twice, a second time; then, again, also, likewise, after all, — and by extension, becomes merely a form of the comparative; continued, longer; to repeat.
明天丨來 come back to-morrow.
丨過幾天 again after some days.
丨三丨四 again and again I—told him.
丨估不中 I should not have guessed it.
丨斯可矣 a second discussion of it will do.
請丨說 please say it again.
丨丨叮嚀 to reiterate the orders.
朕言不丨 We shall not say it a second time.
丨無他人定是他了 it is nobody but he himself.
丨沒得說 they never even had a word between them.
丨看過 I have looked at it again.
我丨不來 I'll never come back.
不丨來 he will not return here.
丨生 restored to life, rescued from death; used for regeneration.
至于丨至于三 they came again and again.
丨者 again, furthermore; used at the beginning of a new subject or a postscript.
丨醮 a remarried widow.
青春不丨來 youthful days never return to one.

TS'AI.

Old sounds, ts'ai, ts'ap, dzai, dzat, *and* dzam. *In Canton*, ts'oi *and* ch'ia; — *in Swatow*, ch'ai; — *in Amoy*, ch'ai *and* tsai; — *in Fuhchau*, ch'ai; — *in Shanghai*, ts'é, dzé, *and* tsa; — *in Chifu*, ts'ai.

猜 ˳*ts'ai* From *dog* and *green*.

To doubt, to dislike, to suspect; to conjecture, to guess; to fear, to apprehend.
丨恨 to cherish hatred, to abhor.
丨疑 to suspect, to doubt of.
丨一丨 guess once.
丨不中 I cannot say at all.
丨不着 he did not guess right.
丨嫌 to suspect and dislike; a suspicious disagreement, as between two statements.
丨謎 to guess riddles.
你拭丨丨 just make a guess.
難以丨量 it is not easy to estimate them, referring to numbers.
丨忌 to envy.
丨丨看 give a guess; divine now!
一丨就着 to divine rightly at once; a shrewd guess.
丨心機 to guess one's thoughts.
胡丨亂想 to fidget and get disturbed.

才 ˳*ts'ai* The upright line 丨 represents the *stem* of a plant forcing its way above 一 the *ground*, and bearing a *root* beneath; it often looks like *tsun'* 寸 an inch.

Materials, the substance of a thing, for which the next is used; mental capacity, power, talents, endowments, or gifts; an educated person, a graduate; genius; to be strong.
丨子 a man of parts.
一表人丨 a fine looking man.
文丨 literary talents.
丨幹 or 丨能 or 丨情 ability to manage; capacity, energy, and tact.
丨也養不丨 let those who have talents train up those who have them not.
天下丨共一石 the gifts of all men may be reckoned at only a pecul — in weight.
偏丨 perverted or useless accomplishments.
三丨 the three Powers, — heaven, earth, and man, who are supposed to rule all things.
丨大于身 his talents exceed (or are not to be judged by) his appearance.
蠢丨 what a goose!
中人之丨 man of common ability.
不丨子 a stupid fellow; this or 不丨 are sometimes used as depreciatory terms by persons speaking of themselves.
無丨不足以濟奸 having no ability he is incompetent to help the rebels.
丨具 executive talent.

材 ˳*ts'ai* From *wood* and *substance*; used with the preceding, and resembles ˳*ts'un* 村 a village.

Materials of which things are made; sticks, timber, lumber, wood; stuff; nature, qualities; abilities; men of parts.
丨木 timber, as for a house.

丨料 materials, ingredients.

頁 丨 good stuff; *met.* upright ministers.

五 丨 the five elements.

六 丨 the six liberal arts; in which the 八 丨 *viz.*, pearls, ivory, gems, stone, earth, metal, skin, and plumes, are materials used.

好身 丨 likely, well-formed, personable.

天之生物必因其丨而篤焉 Heaven, in the production of things, is bountiful according to their qualities.

不成 丨 of no use whatever; superannuated.

丨質 abilities, capacity.

財 **𧵍** ˏ*tsʻai* From *pearl* and *substance;* the old form, composed of 入 to *enter* and 日 *daily*, is more ideographic.

Property, wealth, substance, possessions, goods, whatever men can use; presents, bribes; profits.

發 丨 to get rich; may you make money; — a good wish.

得 丨 to make some profit.

丨禮 complimentary gifts, presents to make way for one.

丨主 or 丨主老 a rich man.

丨東 a capitalist.

天 丨 a windfall; good luck, as a prize in a lottery.

丨神 or 丨帛星君 the god of Wealth, Plutus or Mammon.

你不是丨神 you've given me no custom; you have bought nothing.

破丨擋災 to lavish money to ward off calamity.

偷家 丨 a thief of a cook. (*Cantonese.*)

人為丨死 men lose their lives in the pursuit of wealth.

丨可以通神 money can even move the gods.

丨能壯胆 wealth gives a man courage.

官吏受 丨 officials receiving bribes.

不義之 丨 unjust gains.

裁 ˏ*tsʻai* From *clothes* and *wounded;* occurs used for the preceding.

To cut or fashion garments; to cut, to trim, to tear; to moderate, to diminish, to reduce, to deny; to regulate; to calculate, to plan.

丨縫 a tailor.

丨徹 to disband, to dissolve.

自 丨 to decide for one's self.

丨衣 to cut out garments.

化 丨 to trim and alter.

總 丨 curator of essays at an examination.

大 丨 and 小 丨 a full pattern or a scant one.

聽候丨奪 wait till he has decided.

丨製 to use materials advantageously.

丨其有餘 to cut off superfluity.

丨減些 cut off a little, reduce it some.

𢦏 ˏ*tsʻai* From 戈 a *weapon* and 才 *talent* as the phonetic; it is now used only in combination, but some say it is another form of the preceding.

To wound with weapons; to injure.

纔 ˏ*tsʻai* From *silk* and *crafty;* it resembles 再ʾ in many uses.

An *adverb* of time, near, at hand, thereupon, presently, then, just now, scarcely.

丨來 or 丨到 just arrived.

剛 丨 just then.

丨去了 he has just gone.

丨好 then it will do; at the end of a sentence, answers to just so; that's the case.

方 丨 just now, then, at it.

丨給他 I have given it to him.

辦妥丨說 when it is all arranged, we can then see about it.

這樣丨是 that way will be just the thing.

丨明白了 it is now quite clear.

Read ˏ*san*. A dark gray color, like the top of a sparrow's head.

采 ʻ*tsʻai* Formed of 爪 *claws* on a 木 *tree*, and occurs interchanged with the next three; it much resembles *pien*ʾ 釆 its radical.

To pluck, to take with the hand, to choose; to gather, as flowers; variegated, adorned; cities allotted for revenue to princes; the fifth of the domains of the Cheu dynasty; a business, occupation; to conduct affairs.

丨邑 territory once set apart for grandees in the service of the monarch.

納 丨 to choose and send betrothal presents.

丨丨衣服 splendidly adorned is its dress; said of a pretty fly.

丨丨 to keep gathering.

食 丨 to get a certain allowance as salary from land set apart for the particular officer.

彩 ʻ*tsʻai* Variegated; mixed or ornamented with different colors; elegant, gay, colored; beautiful; lucky, pleased; it is added to some nouns to intensify their meaning.

光 丨 brilliant; animated; glitter or show; smooth, as a shaven head.

好 丨 or 丨頭 fortunate, a lucky hit, a good chance.

無 丨 unprosperous, no chance.

雲 丨 clouded; clouds, a cloud.

丨雲易ʾ散 pretty clouds easily scatter; *met.* human joys soon go.

喝 丨 to clap and encore an actor.

五 丨 the five colors; *viz.*, blue, yellow, carnation, white, and black; variegated, colored.

奪 丨 to win the prize, to reach the goal.

丨錢 the winner's treat, what he gives his competitors.

丨畫 to adorn or paint in colors.

異 丨 unusually beautiful.

金花丨紅 tinsel and fine gay silks, such as are used on joyful occasions.

無精打 丨 no spirit for a game, no relish for the venture.

ʻ啋 ʻtsʻai An exclamation.

In *Cantonese*. An interjection of contempt; tush! pish! to show contempt for.

重唔｜佢 I cared nothing for what he said.

｜瘟你 pox take you!

Read ˏ*hiao*. Agitated, not at ease; moving about; great.

ʻ採 ʻtsʻai To select, to choose; to pick, to pluck, to gather; to take up with the hand; to sip, to suck.

｜桑 to gather mulberry leaves.

｜買 buy the choicest; to buy for government.

｜納 to choose out and take.

｜取 to select.

｜薪之憂 the trouble of gathering fuel; also, a trifling ailment, out of sorts.

｜補者流 one whose breath has been sucked by a fox.

｜訪 to spy out, to get information secretly.

蜂｜花 the bee sips the flower.

｜蓮歌 songs of picking lotuses, sung at the Dragon-boat festival.

ʻ埰 ʻtsʻai Cities or districts allotted for the revenue of princes were anciently termed ｜地, and the lands to maintain their tombs; also, the grave itself.

ʻ寀 ʻtsʻai An officer set over these lands or cities was called ｜官.

寮｜ fellow officers; those in the same office and rank.

ʻ綵 ʻtsʻai Similar to 彩, applied to silks and other fabrics; particolored, variegated.

綾｜ colored sarsnet, used for linings.

挂｜紬 or 結｜ to hang festoons of colored silks, as at festivals.

ʻ䰂 tsʻai Slings for carrying presents, made by four long cords fastened to a ring, called ｜帶 in books, but better known now as 絡子 or slings.

髮｜ a sort of turban.

ʻ棌 ʻtsʻai Name of a tree allied to the oak, the timber of which is suitable for making rafters.

唐虞｜椽 in the days of Shun the oaks furnished rafters.

ʻ睬 ʻtsʻai To notice, to pay attention; to greet.

不｜他 don't mind him.

洋洋不｜ to act like a gawky; to heed nothing.

不偢不｜ to give the cut direct.

菜ʾ tsʻaiʾ From *plants* and *variegated*.

Vegetables; greens, edible herbs; food, viands.

青｜ greens in general.

｜色 cadaverous, emaciated, as if one had lived on pulse only.

好｜ good eating.

美｜ delicacies.

去買｜ he has gone to market.

海｜ what comes from the sea, as fish, seaweed, or prawns.

生｜ raw greens; lettuce.

大｜ the chief dishes; and 小｜ are the smaller and side dishes, condiments, relishes, &c.; the dessert.

野｜ wild greens, as the dandelion.

香｜ celery, or parsley, or sweet-basil.

殼｜ or 淡｜ dried mussels.

葷｜ meats and onions, such as priests should not eat.

｜攤 a vegetable stall.

鹹｜ salt or pickled greens; sourkrout.

送｜ a Canton phrase for the dishes on the table besides rice, called 小｜ elsewhere.

｜花 the rape of Kiangnan, from which the ｜油 or cabbage-oil is expressed.

｜佛 a vegetarian, a herb Budha.

大頭｜ salted turnips.

脢乾｜ dried turnips brought from Hwui-cheu in Kwangtung.

傳家惟有｜根香 in our family we have always lived on greens and roots for generations.

蔡ʾ tsʻaiʾ Weeds, herbs, esculent plants; a species of tortoise, because they were common in ｜國 a small feudal state conferred on ｜叔度 a brother of Wu Wang, B. C. 1122, which held its separate existence till 446, when it was incorporated in Tsu; fifteen rulers only are mentioned; it lay on the River Hwai in the present Jü-ning fu, and 商｜縣 was its capital; the border of a parterre or grass plat; name of a mountain in Ya-cheu fu in Sz'chʻuen.

Read *sah*, as a synonym of [illegible]. To let go, to loose; criminals undergoing a banishment of 500 *li*.

縩ʾ tsʻaiʾ New garments; the noise made in spinning thread; yarn made from hemp.

績｜ to spin linen yarn.

紛綷｜兮紈素聲 behold her new and variegated dress, and hear the rustling of her plain silks.

TSAN.

Old sounds, tsan, tsam, dzan, *and* dzam. *In Canton*, tsan *and* tsam ; — *in Swatow*, cham, chan, *and* chiam ; — *in Amoy*, tsan, tsam, chiam, chim, *and* san ; — *in Fuhchau*, chang *and* chwang ; — *in Shanghai*, tsé^{n}, tsè^{n}, *and* dzè^{n} ; — *in Chifu*, tsan.

簪 ˓tsan From *bamboo* and a phonetic *particle ;* but the original form was 旡, composed of 人 *man* and 匕 a *spoon*, supposed to delineate a hair-pin ; sometimes read *˓chan.*

A clasp, pin, or skewer to confine the hair, or fasten the coiffure ; they are of many shapes and materials ; to stick in the hair, to put on the head ; quick, brisk ; to collect.

丨子 or 丨棒 a hair-pin.

丨花 to wear flowers.

玉丨花 the tuberose.

丨纓世胄 the emperor's descendants, or of a statesman ; alluding to the ball of floss once worn on coronets.

丨筆 to carry a pen in the hair.

In *Cantonese*. To peck, as a fowl.

臢 ˓tsan To boil ; a defect in the lip, a harelip ; dirty.

腌丨 filthy ; dirtied ; this phrase is written several ways.

鐕 ˓tsan A skewer to pass through things, a pin ; to darn garments ; to pierce, to nail.

縫聯補丨 to sew and baste, patch and darn.

用雜金丨 use various metallic nails — to fasten the coffin.

昝 喒 偺 ‘tsan The first also means to vomit ; the second to taste ; and the third is unsanctioned.

A personal pronoun, synonymous with ˓tsa 咱 I, me ; then, a time ; a period.

丨們 we, our's.

多丨 or 多丨子 when ; at the time ; — a word probably adopted from the Manchu.

那丨我還幼 I was then only a boy.

丨不依 I will not yield ; I am set on it.

桚 ‘tsan Strips of wood called 丨子 placed between the fingers of both hands, and pulled together by cords to torture prisoners.

拶 ‘tsan Like the last.

To torture by finger sticks ; to urge, to press.

丨他的手 squeeze his fingers.

排丨 to shake branches, so as to get the snow off.

儹 ‘tsan To accumulate, to hoard up, to collect or bring together.

趲 ‘tsan To hasten, to urge, to quicken, to get on ; to scatter each his own way, to hurry away ; to put to flight.

丨他走 make him go faster.

丨步 walk quicker, hurry your pace.

催丨 to urge on.

丨路 to travel fast.

丨遲 to go very slowly, step by step.

毫無走丨 he never moved a step.

寁 ‘tsan Also read *tsieh*, as a synonym of 捷 quick.

Promptly, quickly ; to accelerate, to hasten one's pace.

無我惡兮不丨故也 do not hate me, for old intercourse should not be hastily broken off.

贊 賛 tsan’ From *pearls* and to *advance ;* the second form is not quite correct, but is much used in combination ; occurs used for the next.

To come before a superior bringing a present ; to assist, to second ; to introduce ; to clear up, to bring to light ; to give evidence ; to praise.

丨助 or 丨佐 to assist.

丨成 to help to bring about.

丨堂 bailiffs in court who aid in keeping order.

丨一辭 helped him by one word.

幽丨于神明 [the sages helped to] make clear the decrees of the gods.

丨理 to help to manage.

少退丨命 the juniors retired and aided in carrying out the orders.

思日丨丨 I wish daily to be helpful.

讚 tsan’ From *words* and to *aid ;* it resembles ˓ts‘an 譖 to slander.

To commend ; to sing praises to ; to record praises or good deeds ; to explain ; to aid.

丨美 to praise, to laud and extol.

稱丨 to speak in praise of.

得人丨 to be praised ; praiseworthy.

丨得過 laudable.

丨頌 to resound one's praises.

丨賞 to commend and reward.

丨嘆不已 praising and lamenting him greatly.

嬻 tsan’ Fair, handsome ; a clear complexion of a female.

巑 tsan’ Mountainous.

丨岏 the lofty summits of mountains.

灒 tsan’ To stir up water, to soil ; to spatter, to splash ; shallow ; turbid water ; to hit one with water.

丨了一點泥 he spattered me a little.

丨出火星 strike sparks out of it.

丨濕身 spattered and wet me.

In *Cantonese*. To recoil, to rebound ; resilient.

丨起 to bound or spring back.

瓚 From *gem* and to *aid;* also read *chanʾ*.

tsanʾ A kind of baton called 圭 丨 or 玉 丨 used in the Cheu dynasty by a marquis during the state worship; others describe it as a sort of stone cup on a handle, shaped like a cythara, holding five pints, and used for libations.

釐爾圭 丨 I give you the large libation cythara.

暫 From *day* and to *cut off*.

tsanʾ *chanʾ* A part of a day; briefly, shortly, for the time being; in the interim, meanwhile; suddenly.

可 丨 不可長 it will only do temporarily.

丨 時 for a little while.

丨 且 for the time being.

丨 忍 be patient a little.

丨 遇 suddenly met him.

丨 住 a temporary lodging.

丨 且燃眉 just escaped singeing my eyebrows; — *i. e.* I was near ruin or starvation.

蹔 撕 From *hand* and to *cut off;* the two characters are usually interchanged.

chanʾ To strike; to raise up; a turn or time; temporarily; to cut in two; to throw into; to exclude; to place planks for crossing water.

Read *shanʾ* for the second form. To cut up plants; to raze.

丨 葛 to cut and gather dolichos stalks.

有 丨 而播之 he mowed the grass and scattered it about.

鏨 From *metal* and to *cut off*.

tsanʾ A fine chisel; a cold chisel; to pierce, as a thorn; to cut out, as characters on stone; to cut in; to pound on the back of a plate of metal so as to raise or enchase on the other side.

丨 字 to enchase letters.

丨 刀 an enchasing graver.

雕 丨 印信 to cut out a brass official seal.

丨 花 to emboss flowers.

細 丨 fine enchasing.

丨 開邊 to split open the edge. (*Cantonese.*)

陽 丨 to enchase flowers, as on silver

禶 *tsanʾ* To implore, to pray.

祝 丨 to supplicate the gods.

鬢 Also read *ʻtswan*.

tsanʾ Black glossy hair; much hair; a woman's chignon or coil of hair.

梳 丨 to do up the hair in a tuft.

TSʻAN.

Old sounds, tsʻan, tsʻam, *and* dzam. *In Canton,* tsʻan, tsʻam, *and* chʻam; — *in Swatow,* chʻan, chʻam, *and* cham — *in Amoy,* chʻan, chʻam, chím, *and* tsan; — *in Fuhchau,* chʻang, chang, chwʻang, *and* chʻéng; — *in Shanghai,* tsʻéⁿ, zéⁿ, dzéⁿ, *and* tsöⁿ; — *in Chifu,* tsʻan.

餐 湌 From to *eat* and *broken;* contracted to *ice;* it is interchanged with ˏ*sun* 飧 supper.

ˏ*tsʻan* To swallow, to eat; a meal; a classifier of meals; a cake; to gather and choose.

一 丨 飯 one meal.

一日二 丨 two meals a day.

聽 丨 食 he works just for his food.

丨 雲臥月 dines in the clouds and sleeps in the moon; *met.* an enthusiast.

維子之故使我不能 丨 兮 but for your sake, Sir, I made myself unable to eat.

早 丨 breakfast.

晚 丨 supper or dinner.

丨 頭飯 a common meal.

丨 粥 丨 飯 a meal of congee and rice; *met.* very poor.

惟加 丨 自愛爲囑 but add a meal that pleases you, is my request; a conclusion to a letter, hoping one's friend is enjoying himself.

秀色堪 丨 she is handsome enough to be eaten.

飽 丨 戰飯 to get a bellyful of rations.

虎嚥狼 丨 to bite like a wolf and swallow like a tiger; — to eat voraciously.

丨 霞客 a water-melon eater.

參 叅 From 晶 *starry light* contracted, and 彡 *streaming hair* or 心 *heart* underneath, referring to three joined, or to Orion; the second form is common.

ˏ*tsʻan* To be concerned with, to stand before; to join with for consultation and advice; to blend, to mix, to form one out of three; to visit or see a superior to be admitted to an audience; to report to the Throne on other officers; a deposition; an impeachment or report against; mixed, confused, as colors; rising in gradation.

丨 奏 to memorialize upon.

打 丨 to make an obeisance.

丨 拜 to visit a superior; to worship.

丨 革 or 丨 處 to degrade a subordinate and report on it.

丨 雜 to throw into confusion.

丨 贊 to advise and aid; to act as adviser to; a joint commissioner.

朝 丨 or 丨 見 to go to a levee; the first also means, to worship or see the Supreme by lower spirits.

丨 將 or 丨 府 a colonel; a post-captain.

丨詳 to consult upon.

丨差 unassorted, incongruous.

丨訂無訛 I have examined it and there are no errors.

丨禪 to sit absorbed in contemplation as Budhists do.

請丨 to request dismissal from office; to resign.

糾丨 to impeach.

轅門聽丨 heard of his accusation at the viceroy's gate.

丨政 councillors in the court of Appeals.

Read ꜀shan. A star, the second zodiacal constellation containing *α β γ δ ε ζ* and *κ* in Orion.

竟若丨商 after all they will be like Orion and Lucifer, — who never see each other.

篸 ꜀tsʻan Bamboos varying in length; the tubes in a pandean pipe; used for 簪 a hair-pin.

籤丨 divining sticks or slips.

In *Cantonese*. An open basket or tray.

抱丨 a wicker scuttle or hod.

灰丨 a mortar hod.

穀斗丨 a winnowing-fan.

𧽍 ꜀tsʻan To run after or to see a sight is 丨趯; said of a crowd of people; to collect, to gather, as at an assembly.

驂 ꜀tsʻan From *horse* and *three*.

The horses outside of the thills, which thus make three abreast.

乘丨 three sitters in a carriage; the left was the seat of honor.

兩丨不猗 the outside horses did not bolt.

脫丨 to unhitch the off-horse.

停丨 to stop the carriage; to reach the lodging.

嵾 ꜀tsʻan Uneven; ascending and descending.

增宮丨嵯 the palaces rising one above the other, like the hills and peaks.

傪 ꜀tsʻan Good, fine-looking.

陸丨 Luh Tsʻan, a noted man in the Tʻang dynasty.

鰺 鰲 ꜀tsʻan From *fish* and *meal*.

A fish otherwise called 鰷魚 the slender fish, whose description shows that is another name for the hairtail or girdle fish (*Trichiurus armatus* and *intermedius*), so common along the coast.

殘 ꜀tsʻan From *evil* and to *wound*; *q. d.* as if 踐 trodden on and hurt.

To ruin, to destroy; to injure, to spoil; to mangle, to kill, to butcher; broken food, leavings; deficient, mischievous, ravening, cruel; pillaged, spoiled; withered; an oppressor.

丨害 to injure, to harry; truculent, savage; to act like brigands.

手足相丨 fraternal strifes.

丨花 a withered flower; a whore.

丨年 an old man, one whose years are failing.

丨忍 cruel, hardhearted.

丨杯 or 酒丨 heel-taps.

食丨 leavings, orts.

丨廢人 or 丨疾 a maimed or deformed person, who has lost an organ, or has an infirmity.

丨廢傢伙 injured, ordinary goods; second-hand.

丨缺 deficient, imperfect.

丨月如弓 the old moon is bow-shaped.

丨賊 to oppress and to do evil.

丨夢 to partly remember a dream.

丨兵敗將 the discomfited troops came scattering back.

譖 ꜀tsʻan From *words* and *impious*; also read *chʻan*꜄ and *tsin*꜄

To slander, to vilify; to exaggerate another's error; calumny, defamation; to discredit.

丨言 unjust aspersions.

誣丨 to defame one; false charges.

丨始竟背 first unbelief and then comes disobedience.

去丨 to dismiss slanderers.

丨言則退 when slandered then you withdraw.

蝎丨 scorpion bites; *i. e.* treacherous vilifyings.

慚 慙 ꜀tsʻan From *heart* and to *cut off*, as if from good or perfection.

Ashamed, mortified, chop-fallen; to blush for, to feel ashamed of; sensible of one's incompetency or failure

丨色 blushing.

丨德 conscious of one's defects.

丨愧 a feeling of shame; said politely when praised.

心內懷丨 lost to all shame.

蠶 蚕 ꜀tsʻan From *insect* and *impious*; the second is a common abbreviation, but is also read ꜀*tʻien*, an earth-worm.

The silkworm (*Bombyx*); applied also to all naked caterpillars which weave cocoons; to tend silkworms.

丨虫乾 or 丨紐 dried silkworms, used for food.

丨眠 the sleep before molting.

丨食 to gnaw as a caterpillar; *met.* to incroach stealthily, as on another's lands.

丨姑 or 丨神 goddess of silk-growers.

餵丨 to feed the worms.

石丨 seems to denote the larvæ of the dragon-fly.

槐丨 the looper caterpillar on the *Sophora* (*Pekingese.*)

慘 ꜀tsʻan Cruel, inhuman, hardhearted; afflicted, injured; wounded or lacerated in feelings; miserable; excessive, as suffering.

傷得丨 horribly wounded.

丨酷 callous, hardfisted.

悲丨 or 心丨丨 extreme grief.

丨遭橫禍 to meet with cruelty and unlooked-for misfortunes.

丨澹經營 a clever plan well written out.

悽丨 sorrowing much.

丨極 very oppressive.

黲 ʻtsʻan A mottled gray; white with black spots or vice versa; turbid; speckled, stained, as a decayed or moldy thing.

黑丨丨的 grimed, blackened, sordid.

丨白鬍子 a grisly beard.

陰陰丨丨 dark, gloomy; clouded, as a dark sky.

憯 ʻ**慘** ʻtsʻan From *heart* and *impious*; the second is regarded as the correct form.

Feeling acutely, distressed for; sickened at and discouraged, because of former sufferings; hardened against; already, even now; also.

胡丨莫懲 how can you be so pained, and not blame yourself?

肢體傷則心丨怛 when the limbs or body are injured, then the heart is grieved.

丨丨日瘁 I am daily sick with grief.

朁 ʻ**朁** ʻtsʻan From 日 to *say* and *tsin* 兟 acute; but others derive it from 竝 *together* and 白 *bright*; it is now superseded by the last.

Not to fear the light; impious; an introductory *particle*, if, supposing.

儳 ʻtsʻan From *man* and *crafty*.

Disorderly, like an undrilled troop; mulish, perverse.

儖丨 ugly, bad.

丨頭 a vile rascal, a worthless fellow; you scamp!

Read ˏchʻan. Uneven, unequal; unsteady; not at once, as a charge in battle; quick, indecorous.

丨信 incoherent, talking at random.

丨互 improper, slightingly, indecent.

粲 tsʻanʾ From *rice* and *broken*; used with the next.

Half a peck 斗 of grain; a meal, a feast; many, much; a multitude; bright, clear; fine white rice; excellent; to laugh; smiling; pure; three women together.

白丨 to pick over rice to get it white; an ancient punishment.

丨丨衣服 elegant apparel.

丨然而笑 he laughed boisterously.

授丨 to give one a feast.

精丨 fine rice; *met.* a gallant fellow.

宴宴丨丨 luxurious living and style.

㛑 tsʻanʾ Used with the last.

Three women (*i. e.* a wife and two concubines,) in one house; beautiful.

今夕何夕見此丨者 this evening, or what evening, shall I see these three women?

謲 tsʻanʾ To rail at, and make people angry or fear one; to provoke; to spy; to satirize.

丨譚 angry speech.

璨 tsʻanʾ The luster of a gem; a beautiful stone.

璀丨 pendent gems; strings of pearls; said also of fine racemes of flowers, like those of the *Vanda* or *Wisteria*.

燦 tsʻanʾ Resplendent, brilliant.

丨爛 bright, lustrous, glittering; applied to a reputation or an action.

星丨漢明 the glittering stars in the luminous Milky Way.

讖 chʻanʾ From *words* and *small*.

To verify; to fulfill; a prognostic, a sybilline hint, an omen.

丨語 a prophecy, a secret intimation or hint.

將來之丨 an unfulfilled prediction.

丨緯 a verification of a prophecy.

圖丨 or 符丨 a diagram or picture indicating future events.

軍丨 a pass-word.

拜丨 to worship wandering spirits; to get prayers said for a long life.

Read chʻanʾ and used with 懺. To confess; to repeat priestly incantations for the dead; masses.

丨願 to annul a vow, which is done with some ceremonies.

In *Cantonese*. Lequacious.

丨氣 silly and talkative, like a dotard.

TSĂN.

Old sounds, tsen *and* tsem. *In Canton*, tsăm; — *in Swatow*, cha *and* chak; — *in Amoy*, chím; — *in Fuhchau*, chéng; — *in Shanghai*, tsăng; — *in Chifu*, tsăn.

怎 ʻtsăn From *heart* and *suddenly*; it is pronounced ʻtsăn, ʻtsăng, ʻtsa, ˏtsun, and ʻtsin, in different parts of the country.

An interrogative word, denoting manner or cause; what? how? why?

丨麼 why is it?

丨敢不低頭 how could I decline assent?

丨樣 how? what is the mode?

丨生是好 what is left then as the best? — *i. e.* there's no help.

丨的 what's the way?

丨得成工 how can we finish the job?

丨麼沒風 why does not the breeze come?

丨說 why does he say so?

丨得 how shall I get it?

不丨麼樣 not anything; no great things; not much.

怕他丨的 or 怕丨麼的 why should I fear him?

你問他丨的不丨的 why do you ask him? no matter.

不知畢竟丨生結果 I cannot tell how it will turn.

TSANG.

Old sound, tsong. *In Canton*, tsong *and* song ; — *in Swatow*, chang *and* chăng ; — *in Amoy*, tsong *and* ch'ong ; — *in Fuhchau*, chòng *and* chaung ; — *in Shanghai*, tsong *and* dzong ; — *in Chifu*, tsang.

臧 ˏ*tsang* From 臣 a *statesman* and 戕 a *spear;* it occurs used for the next, and for 臟ˀ and 藏ˀ but is now chiefly used as a surname.

Good, generous ; virtuous ; dexterous, apt; to approve ; to think good ; to scold.

丨獲 to liberate captives.

何用不丨 how is it that there are none not good !

不丨厥丨 you do not commend what is good in them.

贜 賍 ˏ*tsang* From *value* and to *secrete ;* the contracted form is common.

To receive bribes ; to suborn, to bribe ; to secrete, as plunder; booty, spoil, prizes, loot; stolen goods.

起丨 to recover the plunder.

領丨 to get one's effects back through the yamun.

丨物 spoil, plunder.

繳丨 to restore the stolen things.

坐地分丨 to get a share in the booty, though not going out, as the 窩丨 or custodian does.

作丨 to implicate by secreting a thing.

收買賊丨 to buy stolen goods.

貪丨官 an avaricious, unjust ruler.

牂 ˏ*tsang* A ram ; others say, an ewe.

丨丨 flourishing, as the aspen in full foliage.

丨牁 an extensive principality in the Han dynasty, comprising parts of Sz'ch'uen, Kwéicheu, and Hukwang.

駔 ˊ*tsang* A strong horse ; a stallion ; dirty, ordinary.

丨駭 a fine large horse.

丨儈 a broker or middle-man.

丨子 an epithet of reproach, a scheming rascal.

丨兒貨 poor goods. (*Pekingese.*)

Read ˊ*tsu*. A peculiar insignia of office, called 丨圭 made of stone, and held before the face.

葬 塟 *tsang*ˀ From 艸 *grass* with 死 *dead* under it, and above 土 *earth* or 廾 *hands* supporting.

To bury with decorum ; to inter a coffin ; to lay a body in the tomb.

丨埋 to bury.

送丨 to carry to the grave.

厚丨 to bury in rich dresses and a fine coffin ; a deep grave.

金丨 a coffin suspended in a vault.

火丨 cremation.

槖丨 buried in a mat ; an old custom still observed in the army.

遷丨 or 改丨 to change bodies to another grave, because of the *fung-shui.*

合丨 buried together, as husband and wife.

丨于魚鼈之腹 buried in the fishes' or turtles' bellies.

In *Pekingese*. To spoil ; to rip ; to break accidentally.

髒 *tsang*ˀ ˏ*tsang* Large, obese ; to dirty, to deface.

抗丨 abrupt, churlish.

骯丨 corpulent, fat ; dirty, filthy, like old bones.

別弄丨 mind, don't dirty it.

弄丨了 he has defaced it.

臟 *tsang*ˀ The parenchymatous viscera, what is *stored* in the *body.*

五丨 the five chief organs, *viz.*, the heart, lungs, spleen, liver, and kidneys.

五丨六腑 all the inwards of a body.

神丨 or 靈丨 the viscera put inside of an idol to give it its feelings.

猪肚丨 the entrails of a hog.

TS'ANG.

Old sound, ts'ong. *In Canton*, ts'ong ; — *in Swatow*, ch'ang *and* ch'ăng ; — *in Amoy*, ch'ong *and* ch'iong ; — *in Fuhchau*, ch'òng, *and* chòng ; — *in Shanghai*, ts'ong *and* dzong ; — *in Chifu*, ts'ang.

倉 ˏ*ts'ang* From 口 an *inclosure* and 食 to *eat* contracted ; occurs used for *chw'ang*ˀ 愴 to pity ; and for the next.

A granary of a square shape ; government storehouses ; a box or bin ; a compartment ; to store in a granary ; a pigeon-hole.

穀丨 a storehouse for grain, especially rice.

丨箱 bins in a granary.

丨庫 granary stores.

開丨 to dispense grain to the people ; to give out rations.

貨丨 a pack-house ; a go-down ; a dépôt.

丨兄塡兮 how my pity fills me !

乃求千斯丨 he will seek for a thousand granaries of food.

丨監督 overseer of granaries.

神丨 grain cultivated to offer to the gods.

Read ˊ*ts'ang*. Flurried ; startled, like frightened cattle.

丨皇 fearful, urgent.

丨卒 flurried, quick, bustling.

丨猝之至 excessively hurried.

蒼 From *plants* and *granary;* interchanged with the last.
ts'ang The green tint of plants; the azure of the sky; hasty; hoary, old in one's service; flourishing, prospering.
丨丨者天 the high empyrean.
君丨 Providence.
丨生 the people; sometimes includes all living beings.
彼丨 Heaven.
青丨 a greenish blue color, like the distant hills.
黑丨丨 a dark sallow complexion, as an opium smoker's.
上丨 the firmament, the vault.
丨頭 veterans, so called from their green caps; retainers, old servants, whose hair is grisly gray.
丨老 or 老丨 an old man; waxing effete.
水丨玉 aqua-marine or precious beryl.
丨黃 excited; running here and there; also a greenish yellow.
丨耳 one name for the *Xanthium strumarium* or burweed.

蝽 An unauthorized character, for which the last is probably the correct form.
ts'ang The house fly; flies in general.
丨蠅無縫下蛆 flies will get their eggs in even where there is no crack.

滄 Vast, like the sea; cold.
ts'ang 丨州 a superior district south of Tientsin, near the Canal.
丨海 the deep blue sea.
丨河 and 丨浪 old names of two rivers in or near the present Shantung; the last name was also once applied to the lower portion of the River Han.
丨海之量 [ready to] drink up the sea; said of a wine-bibber.

瑲 The tinkle of stones and bells.
ts'ang 八鸞丨丨 the eight bells on the bits tinkled.
丨丨 color of gems; *i. e.* a pale green.

鶬 A kind of crane, plumage ash-colored and cheeks red.
ts'ang 丨鶏 or 丨鴰 the black crane, called at Canton 田泵鶏 or field puddle hen.
有丨 glittering, as the rings on reins.
丨丨 tinkling like sleigh-bells.

鯧 鱠 From *fish* and *prosperous;* but the second form, though unauthorized has supplanted it at the South; while at Shanghai it refers to a species of herring, and the first is the pomfret.
ts'ang The pomfret, and similar shaped fishes; the 白丨魚 white (*Stromateus argenteus*), and the 黑丨 black (*Stromateus niger*), are most common; 黃蠟丨 yellow pomfret (*Trachinotus auratus*); 瓜子丨 or long-finned pomfret (*Trachinotus asper*); and 花丨 small pomfret (*Caranx malabaricus*); all these sorts are found at Hongkong.

艙 From *boat* and *granary; q.d.* the bin in a vessel.
ts'ang The compartments of a ship or junk; the hold.
船丨 the hold of a ship.
開丨 to begin to unlade.
滿丨 the cargo is all discharged.
封丨 to seal the hatches; to forbid trade at a sea-port.
丨位 the stowage of a vessel.
大肚丨 the main hold.

藏 From 艸 *plants* and 臧 *good;* it is interchanged with 臓 viscera, and was at first identical with its primitive.
ts'ang To hide away, to conceal; to store up, to put aside safely; stores, property; the viscera; to accumulate; to gather, to fix, as a mordant; a classifier of piles or stores of; to store, as a student his knowledge.
一丨箱 a heap of boxes.
收丨 to receive, as in trust.
家丨 heirlooms laid up; family treasures.
包丨 to keep private, not to divulge.
隱丨 to conceal.
丨的影兒都不見了 even of your shadow I saw nothing, — as I looked for you.
丨匿 to hide away.
丨頭露尾 to give a partial account of; to get an inkling.
其葉燒灰以丨所染之色 the ashes of its leaves are used to fix colors in dyeing.
笑裡丨刀 smiled as he grasped his sword; — treacherous.
丨奸 to harbor guile.
丨器待時 to engage the services of an able man against the time they were needed.
無盡丨 insatiably greedy or avaricious.
一丨紙頭 a pile of paper in reams or quires.
厥終智丨瘝在 after these things, wise men kept in obscurity and wicked men ruled.
漫丨誨盜 a careless usage of valuables tempts thieves.
聲丨 a deadened sound.

Read *tsang'*. A storehouse, a receptacle; a retreat; a strong-box; a pile of things laid regularly.
地丨王 a Budha who saves souls.
西丨 Tibet, divided into 前丨 Anterior Tibet, adjoining Sz'ch'uen; and 後丨 Ulterior Tibet, of which Teshi-lombu is the capital.
三丨 the three repositories of Budhistic writings (*tri-pitaka*), *viz.*, aphorisms, disciplines, theology.
入丨 to lie dormant; to keep out of sight.
丨庫 an arsenal, armory, or government storehouse.

剏 From *knife* and *narrow;* it is unauthorized.
ts'ang' To bruise the skin; to bark, rip, or injure the surface.
搬石丨手 barked his hand in moving the stone.
丨破了一塊皮 rubbed off a piece of my skin.
丨臉 bruised his face.

TSĂNG.

Old sound, tseng. *In Canton*, tsăng; — *in Swatow*, cheng *and* chan; — *in Amoy*, cheng; — *in Fuhchau*, chéng *and* chaing; — *in Shanghai*, tsăng; — *in Chifu*, tsăng.

增 ꜀*tsăng* From *earth* and to *add*. To add to, to double, to increase; repeated, more; over, many.

加｜ to augment.

｜價 to raise the price.

不見｜ I don't think there are many.

｜高 to make higher.

戶口歲｜ the population annually increases.

｜減無定 it may be cheaper or dearer, as a price.

｜益 to increase.

｜埋 to throw in; to add to, as price or quantity. (*Cantonese.*)

憎 ꜀*tsăng* To hate, to dislike, to abominate.

可｜ hateful.

得人｜ to be hated.

｜嫌人 to dislike one.

｜愛不同 capricious; now hating, now loving.

取｜於人 to get people's dislike.

譄 ꜀*tsăng* To add to one's words; to increase, to add.

鄫 ꜀*tsăng* A small state anciently situated in the east of Shantung, near the present Yen-cheu fu, not far from the sea; an old place in Ching 鄭, now Sui cheu 睢州 in the east of Honan, on a branch of the River Hwai.

繒 ꜀*tsăng* A general name for common silken fabrics, like pongee, sarsnet, lutestring; ancient name of a place in the south-east of Shantung; used with the next.

以避｜繳 [the goose flies high] so as to avoid the marked arrows.

矰 ꜀*tsăng* A kind of dart or short javelin; an arrow used in hunting birds with the cross-bow, having a mark tied to it.

罾 ꜀*tsăng* A square lifting net, suspended to a frame and let down by a long rope.

罜｜ or 投｜ to let down the net.

拉｜ or 拉掷｜ to raise the net.

鰕｜ a crab-net made of millinet.

扳｜守店 he hauls the net and watches the shop too; — diligent in business.

磳 ꜀*tsăng* Rocky, stony, as the surface of the land; a dangerous stone, one threatening to fall.

橧 ꜀ **竲** ꜀ ꜀*tsăng* A hut in the woods, made of branches and sticks, used by the ancient kings in summer time, before they built palaces; some think the phrase ｜巢 intimates that they lived in booths on the trees, as is done to this day among the Laos and Cambodians; a pig-sty; a watch-tower for the one who watches fields.

䁬 ꜀*tsăng* Dim eyes, small or poor.

瞢｜ indistinctly seen.

睖｜ to stare at; to gaze at half awake, like one collecting his senses.

鏳 ꜀*tsăng* The noise or ring of metal or gems.

｜鎗 a metallic sound; a tinkle given out by metal when struck, as a silver coin.

䏸 ꜀*chăng* From *flesh* and to *wrangle*; perhaps it is oftenest read ꜀*chăng*. The tendon Achilles; the heel; to kick back; to elbow; the elbow.

達｜鞋 to go slipshod.

枕｜ to lean on the 手｜ or elbow.

一｜打過佢 elbowed him off. (*Cantonese.*)

贈 *tsăng*꜄ From *property* and to *add*. To give to another, who is an equal; to make a souvenir; to present, to bestow on; to help; to confer a title; to give a parting gift; to increase.

｜送 to give a present.

餽｜ parting gifts for a journey.

誥｜ or 封｜ to honor an officer's parents when dead for his merits.

待｜ waiting for promotion, as an aged graduate.

｜言 a flattering compliment.

例｜ promoted according to rule, as a scholar when dead is in the ancestral hall.

折柳｜行人 to give a traveler a willow-twig at parting.

｜光前人 to reflect honor on one's ancestors.

無以｜別 I've nothing to give you on going.

何以｜之 what can I give him?

甑 *tsăng*꜄ A boiler used in distilling; an alembic; a still; a boiler for steaming rice, in two parts, the upper one a wooden bucket fitted on an iron dish; to steam; to distil.

飯｜ an earthenware boiler.

以釜｜爨 to steam food in a boiler.

｜上生塵 the dust lies on the boiler; — *met.* extreme poverty.

䵞 *tsăng*꜄ A black face.

奸｜ a swarthy visage, like the Hindoos.

䙢 *tsăng*꜄ A napkin or cloth to wipe the perspiration, so called formerly in Honan.

TS'ĂNG.

Old sounds, dzeng *and* ts'eng. *In Canton*, ts'ăng; — *in Swatow*, chan *and* cheng; — *in Amoy*, cheng'; — *in Fuhchau*, chéng *and* chaing; — *in Shanghai*, tsăng, dzăng, *and* zăng; — *in Chifu*, ts'ăng.

曾 ꜀*ts'ăng* Composed of 曰 to *speak*, 四 a *window*, and 八 to *separate*; it must not be confounded with *hwui*ˀ 會 to meet.

An *adverb* of time, past, already finished, done; a sign of past time; how; at the beginning of a sentence, often implies a strong negative; when in regimen with a negative, it makes an adversative phrase, but yet, still.

丨經 having been, already done.

未丨 not yet; it is often used in reply as a polite form of denial.

丨有 there were some.

丨是以爲孝乎 how can that alone be considered to be filial piety?

何丨 where is it? — *i. e.* there is none.

丨莫惠我師 and still never act kindly to our people.

可丨 or 丨否 is it so or not?

京中可丨下雨 has it rained in Peking or not?

丨是不意 but you have not thought of that.

Read ꜀*tsăng*. To add, for which 增 is more used; to duplicate, said of generations.

丨子 the author of the 大學 or Great Learning.

丨孫 a great-grandson.

丨祖母 a great-grandmother.

層 ꜀*ts'ăng* From *body* and to *add*.

A layer, a tier, a strata, whatever is piled or laid on, as a lamina, a plate; also one behind another; still more, added that; a step, a degree; a classifier of storeys.

一丨 an item, a count, a specification.

上第三丨 go up to the third storey.

加重一丨 it is one degree heavier.

糊兩丨紙 pasted two layers of paper.

丨出不窮 the depths [of this doctrine] cannot be exhausted.

丨次 gradations; series.

丨巒聳翠 see the lofty peaks rising in emerald verdure.

丨丨疊疊 piled up; tier on tier.

三丨房 three series of apartments or buildings.

千丨紙 foliated mica.

嶒 ꜀*ts'ăng* Hills rising one above another.

山勢崚丨 the hills overtop one another in lofty peaks.

蹭 *ts'ăng*ˀ To labor on in a road; not to reach the aim; to miss one's footing; to rub by one, or hit him when passing.

丨蹬不前 not to get on; slow-paced; logy.

磨丨 very slow; fumbling, as when half awake.

木排丨動船 the raft collided with the ship.

噌 *ts'ăng*ˀ The noise and hubbub of a market.

泚丨 a liberal feeling; unprejudiced.

劊 *ts'ăng*ˀ From *knife* and *already*.

To wound by a sudden cut or stroke, as when a knife slips.

丨傷 he has been cut severely.

TSAO.

Old sounds, tso, tsok, tsau, *and* tsop. *In Canton*, tsò; — *in Swatow*, chau, ch'au, cho, *and* cha; — *in Amoy*, tsò, sò, *and* tsau; — *in Fuhchau*, ch'o *and* chau; — *in Shanghai*, tso *and* zo; — *in Chifu*, tsao.

糟 醩 ꜀*tsao* From *rice* or *spirits* and a *class*; the second form is unusual.

The sediment, the dregs; remains of malt; the grains left after distilling spirits.

酒丨 distiller's grains.

醋丨 vinegar grains, made of the spiked millet grain.

丨糕 a dreg-cake; — *i. e.* a bad business, unlucky.

丨燒 a clear mild spirit made from rice.

丨肉 to corn or pickle meat.

丨魚 to put fish in the grains; they are laid in it to cure for a week or more.

褿 ꜀*tsao* A skirt or petticoat; dirty clothes; a knee-pad; to strip up the sleeves; well fitting garments.

慒 ꜀*tsao* In confusion; disordered.

Read ꜀*ts'ung*, and used for 悰 To be anxious about.

遭 蹧 傮 ꜀*tsao* The second form is common but not authorized, and the third is obsolete.

To encounter, to meet, and differs from 遇 in that some trouble is usually implied; to endure, to occur, to happen; to cruise, to go about; to make a revolution; to devolve on; one complete performance; an occasion, a time.

丨賊刧 to be waylaid and robbed.

白走一丨 I went once for nothing, as to make a call, and found nobody at home.
丨逢 to meet.
丨難' to experience troubles.
丨風 to meet bad weather.
丨連夜雨 we had rain all night long.
閔予小子丨家不造 wo is me, a little boy, on whom has devolved this unsettled Realm.
丨塌人 to abuse and treat harshly.
丨塌東西 to waste and misuse things.
丨遇不幸 unlucky; everything goes wrong.
丨然 at last, finally.
丨丨走錯路 every time I went the wrong road.

璪 ʿtsao ʿso Also read ʿso, and sometimes used for 瑣 petty.
A stone like a gem, probably akin to the arragonite; the sound of tinkling gems; a whitish color; the carving over doors.
丨丨 petty, trifling, troublesome.
丨蛣 a name for the hermit crab.
蛇類丨語不可類從者 the kinds of snakes are so numerous that they cannot be minutely classified.

早 ʿtsao From 日 *sun*, and 甲 *first* contracted to 十 *ten; q. d.* the start of the sun.
The early morning; at an early hour, soon; betimes, beforehand, early; just commenced, unskilled; then, presently.
一丨 very early in the morning.
丨晚兒來 early-late come, denotes coming when it is convenient; but 多丨晚兒走 means when will you start?
丨秋 the first month of autumn.
太丨 much too early.
丨飯 breakfast.
趁丨 to start early; to do things in time; to be punctual.

丨年 some years ago.
丨曉得 I knew it before.
丨些回來 come back soon.
丨點 beforehand, earlier, sooner.
丨走丨到 if you start early you will get there early.
丨丨兒的來 come a little earlier.
丨知有此 I knew it was so long ago.
預丨隄防 to take precautions in good time.
丨晨 or 清丨 early dawn, sunrise; the first phrase is used in Cantonese like *Good morning!*
急丨回頭 I will straightway reform — this evil habit.

蚤 蚻 蝨 ʿtsao From 虫 *insect* and 爪 *claws* altered; it occurs used for the preceding.
A sand flea or fly, such as are produced in sandy places; a flea; to scratch; the mortices in the hub for the spokes of a wheel.
虼丨 or 狡丨 or 跳丨 a flea.
丨起施從頁人之所之 she arose early and privately followed her goodman as he went about.
不丨鬋 do not scratch your tresses.
狡丨做事累虱毋 the cunning flea does the deed and leaves the old louse to suffer, as sharpers involve their dull comrades.

棗 ʿtsao From 朿 *thorn* duplicated, referring to its abundance of thorns.
The buck-thorn or jujube tree (*Zizyphus jujuba*), whose fruit is commonly called dates by foreigners, from the resemblance in shape and taste of the 蜜丨 or cured honey date to the true date of Arabia; the 紅丨 and 黑丨 are the common sorts; the date and chestnut are used as metaphors of matronly courtesy to others; to be earnest; prompt; urgently; hazardous.
白丨 fresh dates, just gathered.

波斯丨 Persian date, the fruit of a palm, occasionally brought to China; it has been known as 海丨 and 千年丨 and other names, thus making the same mistake in classifying the two fruits.
酸丨 sour date (*Zizyphus soporifer*); it has a small sourish fruit.
維其丨矣 we must use dispatch.
孔丨且殆 very perilous and full of hazard.
如矢斯丨 like the swift arrow.

澡 ʿtsao From *water* and *many birds on a tree.*
To bathe, to wash the body; covered with icicles; to cleanse the heart.
丨身 to take a bath.
丨盆 or 洗丨盆 a bathing-tub.
丨丨欲沸 it seems as if it would bubble up.
丨瓶 the *kundika* or water-bowl of a Budhist mendicant.

繰 ʿsao Silk of a reddish color like crimson.
丨帛 crimson tinted silk.

藻 ʿtsao Several aquatic grasses which ducks delight in; it seems to include the tussel pondweed (*Ruppia rostellata*), and the *Vallisneria*, and the *Hippuris* or mare's tail; to joy in, to take delight in; elegant, graceful, polished; fine composition, because the leaves of this grass are prettily veined.
覓丨之士 scholars who take delight in literature.
備承丨飾 thanks for your happy commendation — of the house prepared for you.
海丨 algæ; long leaved seaweed.
丨井 a skylight in a house.
丨采紛披 elegant and ample, as a fine composition.
詞丨 apt and elegant expressions.
水丨 applied to an aquatic grass, the *Myriophyllum spicatum.*

璪 ʻtsao Pendents of precious stones or pearls hung like beads around a coronet, so called because they resemble the veins in the 水藻 water grass.
戴冕丨十有二旒 he wore a crown with twelve strings of pendents.

躁 **趮** tsao' Hasty, heedless; to move about, to hurry; dried up by the heat and become light; fierce, harsh.
浮丨 light and irascible; a peppery temper; forward, presuming.
丨動 unsteady, noisy.
丨暴 bustling; cruel; prone to anger.
急丨 techy, hasty.
丨八多辭 a voluble fiery fellow.
In *Pekingese*. Moldy, damp; to tread on.
丨蹋 spoiled by damp.
用脚丨他 stamp on it with your foot.
天氣發丨 the weather is soft and muggy, such as makes people restless and sweaty.

懆 tsao' Chagrined, sad, vexed; uneasy, anxious; affected by.
念子丨丨 I am continually anxious about you.
愁丨 to conceal one's sorrow.
煩丨 troubled, harassed in mind.

皁 **皂** tsao' From *white* and *ten* or *seven*; it is distinguished from ʻ早 early by being usually written like the second.
A black, or very dark gray color; lictors, underlings; runners who execute commands; grain in the milk; very early in the morning; used for 槽 a manger or pen; a stud of twelve horses.
既方既丨 the fruit forms and becomes milky.
衣丨 black dresses.
丨斗 cupules of the acorn.
丨角 legumes of the *Gleditschia sinensis*, used in making the 肥丨 or coarse soap.
丨班 or 丨隸 lictors, criers in a cortége, under-strappers, torturers.
丨裙 a poetical name for a pie.
不分丨白 [the foolish boy] can't tell white from black; said too of unreasonable people.

竈 **灶** tsao' From a *cave* and a *toad*; the contracted form is very common.
A furnace; a place for cooking, a kitchen-range; a bunch of grass or kindlings for fuel; to light the fire.
掌丨的 a cook.
幾丨火 fired up several times.
打丨 or 搭丨 to build a range.
倒丨 he has upset the furnace; — *i. e.* failed, bankrupt.
分丨 to set up housekeeping, to live by one's self.
丨戶 houses, householders.
丨神 or 丨君 or 丨王 the god of the Kitchen, regarded as the arbiter of the family prosperity, whence the phrase 寧媚於丨 you had better not fail to propitiate the Kitchen god.
丨馬 the house cricket, also called 丨雞 the furnace chicken.
送丨 to dismiss the kitchen god to report to Shangti.
上丨下丨 the head-cook and scullions.
觀內無仙丹丨冷 this monastery has no Taoist in it, and the crucible is cold; — deserted.

造 tsao' From to *go* and to *inform*.
To make, to construct, to build; to create, to form; to do, to act; to begin; to seek for; to prosper; established; a party in a cause.
丨化 to create, to form out of.
初丨 to invent, to originate.
好丨化 good fortune; a happy chance.
如同再丨 to rescue from great misery and danger.
巧丨 skillful work.
丨端 to originate, to invent.
起丨 to establish, to begin.
丨冊 to put on the records.
大丨 the great Builder; much the same as 丨物 Maker of things.
改丨 to rebuild or alter a house.
丨言生事 he made words to cause disturbance; an entire fabrication.
兩丨 the plaintiff and defendant.
自丨其禍 he has brought on his own sorrows.
丨舟 to make a bridge of boats.
一錢丨一錢 for one cash spent lay by another.
此才恐爲丨物所忌 such talents might excite the envy of the gods.

Read *tsʻao'* To reach, to arrive; to go to, to advance; to contain.
丨次 in a hurried, thoughtless manner; disorderly.
丨就 to accomplish.
丨府拜候 I came to your palace (or house) to salute you.
小子有丨 the young men made progress.
輕丨 my miserably built hovel.
丨之 to make an advance.
賓客丨焉 the guests all came.

In *Cantonese* read *tsao'* A crop, a harvest.
Also read *tsʻao'* To collect, to lay by or up; to heap up; to pay instalments; to deposit savings.
割禾丨 to cut the rice harvest.
丨當新出 the last of the season is as good as a new crop.
丨埋 to lay up.

TSʻAO.

Old sounds, tsʻo, tsʻok, tsʻau, *and* tsʻop. *In Canton,* tsʻò; — *in Swatow,* chʻau *and* cho; — *in Amoy,* tsò *and* chʻò; — *in Fuhchau,* chʻo *and* cho; — *in Shanghai,* tsʻo *and* zo; — *in Chifu,* tsʻao.

操 ꜀tsʻao To take, to hold; to take in hand, to manage; to exercise, to drill; expert at, used to; to maintain or restrain one's desires, to act moderately; holding one's purpose of mind; in *rhetoric,* to stick to the subject, to keep to the point.

丨演 or 丨練 to drill troops.

看丨 to see a review.

大丨 the triennial review.

丨持 resolute, fixed in holding to the right.

丨心 careworn, anxious.

丨劵而獲 to take the document and get the money — without delay or difficulty.

丨琴 to thrum a lute.

Read *tsʻao*꜄ A principle, a purpose, a design; a self-restraint; moderate, consistent.

節丨 principles; fixed rules of conduct; to maintain them.

風丨 deportment and purpose combined; the air and intention of a man.

氷霜之丨 a pure and stedfast principle, — as of widowhood.

曹 ꜁tsʻao From 日 to *speak* and 東 *east* doubled and contracted, referring to officers who decided in the east halls.

A revisory judge or judge of appeals; a meeting-place of officers; a company or class; those who have fellowship, and thence a sign of the plural; a trough; a place where cattle are kept.

丨國 a small feudal state, conferred on 丨叔振鐸 a brother of Wu Wang, B. C. 1122; it had a separate existence under fifteen rulers from 756 till 486, when it was annexed by Sung; its capital was in the present 丨州府 in the southwest of Shantung, along the Yellow River.

爾丨 you all.

天丨 and 陰丨 gods and devils.

乃造其丨執豕于牢 he sent to the corrals, and took a pig from the pen.

官丨 officials generally.

秋丨 officers of the Board of Punishments.

丨操 the famous general who overthrew the Han dynasty, A. D. 250; his name is used in the phrase 說丨操丨操就到 when you talk of a man he is sure to come.

嘈 **譜** ꜁tsʻao From *mouth* or *words* and *company.*

Noise, clamor, as of birds; a confused din, as of a crowd.

唧丨 an outcry.

丨閙 wrangling, squabbling.

詾丨 to make a din, to make a hubbub.

丨雜 a noise and running together.

丨丨嘲嘲 a tumult; crying and wrangling.

咪丨人耳 don't deafen people with your noise; don't make a row. (*Cantonese.*)

槽 ꜁tsʻao A trough, a manger; a flume, a sluice; a channel, a fissure, a groove for a thing to run in; a trench or ditch; a seam or vein in a mine, a bed; a vat, a tub for spirits; a classifier of frames, doorways, bed-places, &c.

馬丨 a manger.

酒丨 a wine vat.

丨坊 a grog-shop; a distillery.

水丨 a watering trough.

漏丨 an eaves-trough.

擋丨兒的 the boy at an inn.

枸丨子 a kind of sweet fruit.

炮打一條丨 to kill a row of men at one discharge.

鑿丨 to chisel out a trough.

漕 ꜁tsʻao A mill-race, a canal or channel through which water runs and boats go; a gulf, a gorge; to lead on water, to turn a water course; to convey revenue to Peking; revenue junks.

丨運 to transport grain; to take it to the army.

丨河 the Grand Canal.

丨船 transport grain-junks.

丨督 and 丨道 the Imperial Commissioner of Grain and his provincial deputies.

丨粮 grain tax, supposed to be in kind, on which 丨規 grain-tax fees are often demanded.

艚 ꜁tsʻao A junk, a smack.

白丨船 sea-going junks, like those from Amoy.

丨仔 small junks, like a heavy scow. (*Cantonese.*)

膶 ꜁tsʻao Short, crisp, as crust; a rumbling in the stomach; one says, to grease and dirty the dress.

In *Fuhchau* The part above the thigh in a quarter of pork.

螬 ꜁tsʻao From *insect* and a *company.*

Grubs in plums; those in the ground are 蠐丨, and well represented by the grub of the cockchafer.

丨食實者過半矣 the grub has eaten more than half the flesh — of the plum.

髒 ꜁tsʻao Dirty, useless, broken, spoiled; coarse, rough.

丨朽 old, decayed.

丨了 broken, ripped.

丨爛 or 丨舊 spoiled, worn out.

丨壞 broken down, used up.

丨的希髒 this thing is very dirty and worn out.

草 艸 'ts'ao — From 屮 a *sprout* repeated, but the first is now used for plants; it is said to be formed of 艸 *plant* and 皂 *black;* the latter in its contracted form is the 140th radical of a natural group of characters relating to plants.

Plants with herbaceous stems; herbs, grass; vegetation, plants in general; hastily, carelessly; the running hand; a rough copy or original draft; to mow, to cut grass; an acorn used in dyeing black.

丨木 vegetable productions.

禾丨 rice straw.

花丨 flowers; adorned with plants.

青丨 green grass.

丨地 Mongolian pastures.

丨丨了事 to do a job anyhow; to finish it heedlessly.

文書丨 original drafts of documents.

丨創 a rough copy.

丨字 the running hand.

丨丨 careless, lenient, troublesome; in sorrow, cast down.

天造丨昧 Heaven at first made things in the rough.

丨棚 a thatched roof.

勞人丨丨 to trouble people exceedingly; very distressed.

一過丨兒 once get through the grass; — *met.* get it off anyhow.

丨包 an irascible, mulish man.

丨次 precipitately.

丨殲 (or 菅) 人命 to trifle with people's lives, as charlatans do; to look upon the lives of the people as grass, of no account, as harsh officials do.

騲 'ts'ao — A female of equine animals.

丨驢 a she-ass.

丨馬 a mare; — not a common term.

懆 ts'ao' — To stir a thing around with the hand; to stir and mix.

糙 䊂 ts'ao' — Paddy which has only been hulled, and not cleaned; rudely, unworkmanlike; unbleached, darkish, as brown paper or sugar.

太丨 rough, not well done.

丨米 coarse rice, not yet skinned.

粗丨 in a coarse rude manner.

丨貨 poor goods, a bad article.

丨細不同 coarse and fine are not at all the same.

皮膚發丨 the skin is covered with goose pimples, or itches from cold.

慥 ts'ao' — From *heart* and to *act.*

Heartily, sincerely, from the heart.

丨丨爾 verily, honestly, faithfully.

鄵 ts'ao' — The name of a town belonging to the state Ching, not far from Ho-nan fu, where Duke Hi was murdered, B. C. 565.

TSEH.

All these characters are also read CHEH. *Old sounds,* tieh, tek, dek, dzek, *and* dak. *In Canton,* tsăk, ts'ak, chak, *and* chăk; — *in Swatow,* chek, ch'ek, ch'at, ché, cha, *and* tia; — *in Amoy,* chek, cha, *and* t'ek; — *in Fuhchau,* chaik, chék, chah, tek, t'ek, *and* tah; — *in Shanghai,* tsăk, tsah, tsèk, zèk, *and* zăk; — *in Chifu,* tsö.

則 ˏtsö — From 刀 *knife* and 貝 *precious* things, because articles are trimmed for use.

A rule, a precept, a law, a regulation; a pattern; a standard a measure by which to try an act; to conform to rule, to imitate; to be a pattern; to outline, to mark; an illative particle denoting a result, reason, or cause; wherefore, then, and so, immediately; a conditional particle, then, after that, in that case; even then; therefore, next, consequently, — according as the preceding proposition is positive or hypothetical; a *conjunction,* which may be placed either before or after a negative.

法丨 a rule; a pattern to go by.

然丨 if so, then, &c.

丨箇 or 丨可 forms a request, as 恕罪丨箇 Oh, pardon the offense.

皇天可憐垂救丨個 O Heaven, pity and save me.

言而世爲天下丨 he speaks, and the world takes his words for a rule.

丨可 well then; it is possible.

是丨不可無者也 if so then I cannot do without it.

何丨 how then?

一丨 when repeated, answers to either – or, now – then; as — 丨以喜一丨以懼 now it causes joy, and then it excites fear.

準丨 like the pattern, by the rule, as a carpenter's line; at the time.

一丨也 then they are alike.

有物有丨 there is matter and principle, or what is immaterial.

例丨 statutes and regulations; laws and bye-laws.

天下丨 an example to the empire.

天丨 Heaven's unerring rule.

雖丨如是 then I shall do so.

哭丨不歌 he wept without whining.

丨古稱先 to imitate the ancients and do like one's ancestors.

修身丨道立 if the person be cultivated, the principle will be strengthened.

丨其中 the just or middle course.

美丨美矣丨未大也 it is indeed beautiful, but not in the highest degree.

昊天上帝丨不我遺 nor will the Highest Shangti except even me.

閑之維丨 [the horses] were trained into all the rules.

側, ꜀tsö From *man* and *law* as the phonetic; occurs used for the last.

The side; on the sides; lateral, inclining, awry; prejudiced, perverted; mean, low; undistinguished; rebellious, seditious; to incline, to bow, to turn towards; to take a one-sided view; in *penmanship*, a point, usually called 點 a dot.

丨耳而聽 to place the ear and listen.

丨臥 to sleep on the side.

反丨 the rear, the back; a faction; rebellious.

侍我丨 stand at my side.

揚丨陋 to bring forward [one of] the lowly and mean.

不要放丨 don't tip it; don't turn it on the side; this side up, as a box.

丨便 at tho side; aside a little.

歪丨 it leans dangerously.

丨目 sidelong looks, envious glances.

丨身 not erect, lopsided.

時無背無丨 you have now none at your back or side — to guide you.

捑, ꜀tsö To beat, to strike.

丨打 to punish; to ferule a school-boy.

崱, ꜀tsö A sierra or ridge of hills like the spines of a dragon's back.

群巒丨屴 a gallery of hills, a succession of lofty ridges.

一望嶄丨 a view of a lofty peak.

䇥, ꜀tsö The crashing, splitting sound of breaking things to pieces.

賊, ꜀tsö ꜀tséi From 則 a *rule* or transgression of law contracted, and 戈 a *weapon*.

To rob, to plunder; to put to death; to oppress, to maltreat; cruelly; outrageously, murderously; a thief, a bandit, an open robber; those who resist the government, seditious, insurgents; the enemy; a term of contempt, you thief, you wretch; depredations, maraudings of banditti; whatever spoils, as a grub or fly in grain, for which the next is better; rats; to escape, as thieves do.

殘丨 to injure, to ruin.

丨害 to damage another.

丨兵 the enemy's force.

丨頭 or 丨首 a leader of freebooters or rebels.

海丨 a pirate, a dacoit.

丨賢良 to oppress the peaceable.

寇丨 a bandit, a highwayman.

丨性 ungrateful, reprobate.

蟊丨 a grub in grain; a robber, those who, like Cataline, destroy the state.

响馬丨 mounted highwaymen.

窩丨 a retreat of brigands.

做丨 to turn thief.

丨夫人之子 he did evil to that man's son.

丨子 a wicked youngster.

丨贓 booty, loot, pillage.

丨眼 sharp-eyed, suspicious.

木丨 the scouring rush (*Equisetum*), used for polishing wood.

怙終丨刑 those who persisted in transgression were to be capitally punished.

頂着小枷罵丨 one wearing a cangue and railing at the rascals — who got him there, but not blaming himself.

蠈, ꜀tsö The *thief-worm*, is the larva of a kind of Hessian fly which eats the joints of rice; the Cantonese call the fly 黃虫 the yellow insect.

鰂, 鱡, ꜀tsö From *fish* and *then* or *robber*; the first form is most common.

The cuttle-fish (*Sepia*), but the term would include the loligo; it is dried for food, and also known as 墨魚 ink-fish and 烏賊 black thief; it is described as being like a bag without scales, and having two long cirri like straps, and eight legs growing on the sides of the mouth, which is like a horny beak; when it sees men or big fish, it spurts out the ink several feet from the receptacle under the belly; it has one bone on the back, very white and light like pith, called 海鰾鮹 the sea mantis' larva; this fish is supposed to be transformed from the crow, owing to the black fluid in its body; but the Chinese make no india-ink from it.

責, ꜀tsö From 貝 *precious* and 朿 to *bind* contracted.

To ask, to demand; to reprove, to reprimand; to fine, to punish; to sustain, to be responsible for; to impose responsibility; to lay a weight on, to press or crush; charged with; a charge, a duty; a fault.

自丨 self reproaches.

丨罪 to condemn and punish.

丨罰 to beat, to bamboo.

丨問 to put to the question, to torture.

丨成 to charge with, to carry through.

求丨 to exact service of one.

丨善 to incite to good by reproofs.

過丨 punishment for crime.

刻丨 to reprove or punish excessively.

丨望 to reprove in hopes of reform.

丨爛 crushed to pieces, smashed.

丨死 crushed to death.

丨賂 to ask a largess.

丨任 charged with official duties.

丨償 to compel remuneration.

丨載 to ballast a ship.

吾亦無所過丨矣 nor have I done more than I ought.

丨住佢 keep it down. (*Cantonese*).

有言丨者 it is the duty of some to speak.

躬自厚而薄丨於人 he who requires much of himself and little of others, — will prosper.

Read *chai'* and used for 債. A debt; to owe.

聽稱丨以傅別 let [the people] arrange their debts in such ways as they may agree.

嘖 ˏ*tsö* From *mouth* and *to blame* as the phonetic; occurs used with the next.

To cry and bawl; to quarrel, to wrangle; meddlesome; a tumult, an uproar; to praise.

丨丨 note of a bird; the inarticulate expression of the feelings by a hiss or grunt.

讙丨 to speak clearly.

塞丨 to banter with; evasive talk.

丨丨稱善 everybody proclaims his goodness.

丨丨不已 unceasing praise.

賾 ˏ*tsö* Interchanged with the last.

Deep, abstruse, hidden; occult, recondite, so subtle that only sages can perceive it; the secret springs of action.

見天下之丨 to detect the working of principles in the world.

探丨索隱 search out hidden causes, and get at its secret ways.

至丨 very abstruse.

歵 ˏ*tsö* To talk and laugh.

欭丨 the sound of merriment; laughing.

鸅 ˏ*tsö* From 鳥 *bird* and 澤 *marsh*.

A bird that frequents pools, 丨鸆 the white pelican, because it takes in water and fish for its food; it is also called 護田 or guardian of the fields, from its sedentary habits.

幘 ˏ*tsö* From *napkin* and *to bind*.

A soft cap worn in old time, pointed on the top and having ear-flaps to cover the hair; a kerchief to retain the top-knot; a skull-cap; a turban.

介丨 this sort of cap worn by civilians.

喪丨 a mourning cap made of white cloth.

平上丨 the military style of it.

簀 ˏ*tsö* From *bamboo* and *to blame* as the phonetic.

The boards or mat of a bed; a mat used as a seat where an officer was placed in his rank; growing or brought close together; luxuriant; slender reeds for binding; splints or slips.

易丨 changing his mat; — *met.* at the point of death.

大夫之丨 the post or dignity of a grandee.

卽捲以丨 he then rolled up his mat.

綠竹如丨 the green bamboos grow thick as a mat.

Read *chai'* and used with [酉責]. A strainer for spirits; a wine-press.

擇 ˏ*tsö* From *hand* and *to peep*.

To select, to choose, to pick out; to prefer.

取丨 to prefer and take.

丨親 to choose a son-in-law.

丨日 to choose days, especially lucky ones.

揀丨人材 to select and promote talented men.

丨交 to choose one's associates.

丨食 to pick out persons who can be fleeced.

丨鄰處 [Mencius' mother] chose a good neighborhood.

罔有丨言在身 they did not need to choose words in reference to their conduct.

丨其善者而從之 find the good way and follow it.

良禽丨木 good birds choose their roosts; — good men their associates.

澤 ˏ*tsö* A marsh, a fen, a pool; to fertilize, to enrich; to anoint, to cause to shine; to benefit, to show kindness to; to moisten, to cause to grow; humid, smooth; glossy, slippery; fertile; imbued with, redolent of; favor, kindness; lacustrine, marshy; a sword haft; breeches or under-clothes, for which the next is used.

雨丨 moistened with showers; — *met.* heaven's favor.

丨手 to wash or soften the hands.

恩丨 imbued with favor, — from God or the emperor.

潤丨 agreeable, in good order; kindhearted; to enrich by favors; glossy.

大丨 a boggy place — is not fit for troops.

滑丨 or 光丨 glabrous, shining; smooth, as skin.

香丨 to anoint with fragrant oil; to put on cosmetics.

肥丨 fat and sleek.

其耕丨丨 their plows lay open the porous soil.

川丨 streams and pools, such as are made by rain.

丨及枯骨 his kindness extends even to the remains.

丨州 a prefecture in the southwest of Shansi.

丨宮 the damp palace, a Taoist term for the treasury of rain.

白丨 an old name for a lion; applied to the embroidery worn by civilians in the Ming dynasty.

手丨猶存 this relic of him is still kept.

襗 ˏ*tsö* Used for the last; and also read *t'oh*.

Under-garments; breeches which have become dirty; sleeping clothes; a night-gown.

與子同丨 I will give you my under-clothes, — so that you may go to the war.

舴 ˏ*tsö* A boat to paddle about in.

丨艋 a junk's pinnace, a dingey, a punt.

蚱, ˏtsŏ From *insect* and *suddenly* as the phonetic; occurs used for ʻ*cha* 鮓 fish sauce.

A species of locust, the 丨 蜢, which is regarded as edible.

丨 蟬 a small cicada which comes in September.

笮, ˏtsŏ From *bamboo* and *suddenly*; occurs used for the next.

A quiver made of plaited bamboos; the short rafters or ceiling under the tiling of a roof; a hawser to assist boats to cross a river; to brand or tattoo as a punishment; narrow; to squeeze; to strain and clarify spirits; to go out hastily.

丨 錢 an ancient kind of coin.

鑽 丨 to brand or mark a criminal.

門 丨 指 the door caught his fingers.

窄, ˏtsŏ ʻchai From *cave* and *suddenly*.

Narrow, strait, contracted, compressed; insufficient, the opposite of 寬; mean, narrow-minded, illiberal; groveling; unusual, limited; less than the full import or quantity.

太 丨 too narrow, very cramped.

淺 丨 insufficient, straitened.

路 丨 a narrow lane.

肚 量 丨 little-minded, critical, exacting; unable to drink much.

丨 狹 confined, closely hemmed in.

丨 胷 petty, stingy, contracted.

丨 隘 a defile, a narrow pass.

摘, ˏtsŏ ˏchai From 手 *hand* and 適 *to meet* contracted; like the next; also read *tʻih*, but not altogether the same as 擿 to stir up.

To pick; to pull, as fruit; to grasp in the hand; to deprive of, to lay hold of with the fingers; to move on; to start; to point out.

一 丨 one pull, one picking.

丨 頂 to take away the button; the officer's power is often left that he may retrieve his errors.

丨 印 to deprive an officer of his seal.

丨 船 to send off a boat.

指 丨 to point at one as unworthy; to warn him.

丨 根 pull out the root; nip it in the bud, as a bad habit.

丨 茶 女 tea-pickers.

讁, 謫, ˏtsŏ To blame: to remove or suspend officers; to scold, to find fault with; angry at; a flaw, an error; a change in the weather.

丨 罰 to punish by fine.

丨 奸 to disgrace a recreant officer.

無 瑕 丨 no ground for blame; cleared of all imputation.

丨 咎 to find fault with it.

怒 丨 angry at.

罪 丨 criminal, culpable.

室 人 交 徧 丨 我 my family friends are emulous to reproach me.

交 丨 a wife's upbraiding, a curtain lecture.

日 始 有 丨 the sun then showed the change.

仄, ˏtsŏ Composed of 人 *man* stooping under a projecting 厂 *cliff*; regarded as another form of 側, the side.

Inclined, slanting, leaning; oblique; refracted, as a ray of light in passing into another medium.

傾 丨 ready to fall; toppling.

丨 聲 or 丨 韻 the inclined tones, those beside the two 平 聲 even tones.

丨 頭 丨 腦 one who holds his head awry.

赤 丨 a kind of money.

身 不 要 丨 don't loll — in the presence of superiors.

丨 慝 the new moon in the east; — *met.* behindhand.

湢 丨 murmuring, grumbling; grain growing close.

歉 丨 實 深 I am fully conscious of my defects; — a polite phrase.

昃, ˏtsŏ From *sun* and *declining*.

The sun past meridian, the opposite of 昇; afternoon; waning, as the moon; days past the prime, declining, growing sere.

日 丨 而 市 hold the market in the afternoon.

丨 區 geomantic terms for an east and west position.

自 朝 至 于 日 中 丨 from morn till noon and on till eve, — he gave himself no time.

宅, tsŏʼ ˏchai From *shelter* and *springing plants*.

A dwelling; a good situation, a site, a locality; a residence; dwellings, a neighborhood; house of the dead; the location of a house; a position in life; to consolidate, to settle; to reside, to occupy, to dwell; to conform to; to fill an office; to put into office.

丨 門 the door that opens into the rear hall.

大 丨 二 丨 the houses of the eldest and second son.

陰 丨 a grave, a lot in a cemetery; an ancestral shrine.

陽 丨 houses, mansions.

卜 丨 or 丨 兆 to divine for a burial place or day.

田 丨 fields and houses.

丨 園 a court-yard.

內 丨 the inner apartments.

丨 舍 a dwelling-house, a cottage.

丨 眷 inhabited dwellings.

丨 于 天 命 he accepts his fate.

官 丨 an officer's private residence.

朕 丨 帝 位 I have held the imperial dignity.

丨 經 or 丨 鏡 a treatise on geomancy and lucky graves.

乃 用 三 有 丨 克 則 丨 he employed to fill the three posts those who were capable.

丨 是 鎬 京 [he divined] about settling in the capital Hao.

In *Fuhchau.* A village.

馲, tsŏʼ Also read *loh,* and used for 駱 a camel.

A hybrid, 丨 駞 described by the Păn Tsʻao as the offspring of an ass and a cow; but others say more rightly of an ass and a mare.

TSʻEH.

These characters are also read CHʻEH. *Old sounds,* tʻiek, tʻak, kap, *and* tít. *In Canton,* ch'ak *and* chʻăk ; — *in Swatow,* chʻek, tia, chʻé, *and* kʻi ; — *in Amoy,* chʻek *and* chiat ; — *in Fuhchau,* chʻaik ; — *in Shanghai,* tsʻăk ; — *in Chifu,* tsʻö.

測, *tsʻö'* From *water* and *rule* as the phonetic.

A deep place in water; to fathom, to sound; to estimate, to measure; sharp; clear, as fine varnish.

丨度, to conjecture, to calculate; to sound.

不丨 inscrutable, unexpected, unfathomable.

丨量 to measure, as a field; to work out, as a problem.

以本性而推丨 to reason from the nature of the thing; to draw conclusions.

丨字 to dissect characters and recombine the parts in new senses, as fortune-tellers do.

不可丨 it cannot be fathomed; confused in sense; rather unintelligible.

丨丨 sharp, as a keen blade.

惻, *tsʻö'* To pity, to sympathize; acute feelings of pain or grief.

丨仁 to compassionate; humane, kind-hearted.

痛丨 grieved, sorrowing for.

丨隱之心人皆有之 all men have natural sympathies.

心丨 my heart aches for him.

坼, 㡰, *tsʻö'* From *earth* or *slip* and to *eject;* the second form is unusual.

To burst, as buds; to open, to crack from some inward force; split, riven; chapped, as fields in a drought.

甲丨 the buds are bursting.

丨副 a difficult parturition, involving laceration.

不丨不副 neither straining nor rending, as when Heu-tsih was born.

聲喉丨 a cracked or querulous voice; a weazened tone.

砍丨 cracked, as to fracture or break a bowl.

丨口膏藥 a plaster for chapped hands.

龜丨 the earth creased and riven, like the back of a tortoise.

拆, *chʻai* From *hand* and to *eject;* in some of the meanings it is like *cheh,* 折 to bend.

To break up or open, to split by external force; to unrip; to destroy; to pull down, to take away; to take to pieces; to take out the bones; to disgrace, to abase.

丨信 to open a letter.

丨屋 or 丨舍 or 丨毀 to demolish a house, to raze.

丨封 to break a seal; to take off the seals, as from a house.

丨衣裳 to unrip garments.

有丨法 there is a way to get it.

丨散 to take to pieces and scatter.

丨壞 to break up, to spoil utterly.

難以分丨 it will be hard to divide it.

丨開 to tear open, as a package.

皵, *chʻö' chʻai* From *skin* and to *eject.*

The wrinkles on the face.

皺丨 a wrinkle, as on the forehead.

捒, *tsʻö'* To support or assist; to select out a thing; one defines it, a switch for a horse.

策, *tsʻö'* From *bamboo* and *thorn.*

Bamboo slips on which writings were once engraved or etched, and then joined by their edges; they consisted of several 篇 or sections; a book; a plan, a stratagem; a scheme, a proposition; questions proposed to candidates and replies; writings; a means, an expedient; a whip; to switch; a divining-slip; in *penmanship,* a turned-up or sharp stroke.

簡丨 the slips of bamboo books; books, writings.

無丨 without plan, schemeless, no resource.

丨書 a sage's exhortations; the instructions of superiors.

書丨 books; essays.

警丨後人 to warn posterity or one's successors.

籌丨 a stratagem, good at contriving.

良丨 or 神丨 a good plan, one made by a 丨士 clever strategist, which he 獻丨 offers to government.

丨星 the star γ in Cassiopeia.

金丨 a priest's baton, made like a pewter staff.

束手無丨 folded his hands and did nothing.

執丨 a courier or postilion.

丨馬 to whip a horse.

計丨 or 方丨 a plan, an expedient.

對丨 the reply given by the candidate to the 丨問 subjects or inquiries proposed by the examiner.

殿試丨 open replies on subjects proposed to *tsinsz'* at the final examination for Hanlin.

筴, *tsʻö'* From *bamboo* and to *clasp;* it is often interchanged with the last.

To divine by slips or straws.

筮丨 to cast lots.

天授神丨 Heaven gave him a divine pattern or plan.

Read *kiah,* and used 夾. To take under the arm.

丨箸 bamboo chopsticks.

莿, *tsʻö'* From *plant* and *thorn;* a synonym of *tsʻz'* 刺 a thorn.

A prickle, a thorn; to prick; this form is said to have been used in Yen and Corea.

TSEU.

Some of these are read CHEU. *Old sounds*, tsu, dzu, tsup, tsut, *and* dzop. *In Canton*, tsau; — *in Swatow*, chò, chu, jiò, *and* ch'au; — *in Amoy*, tsò *and* tsòk; — *in Fuhchau*, chaiu, chéu, *and* chau; — *in Shanghai*, tsù; — *in Chifu*, tsò.

諏 ꜀tseu From *words* and to *take*.

To consult with others, to inquire into, to take advice in governmental affairs; to choose.

丨吉 to select a lucky day.

共丨其正 to jointly discuss the right of the matter.

周爰咨丨 everywhere consulting or making inquiries.

擇丨 to consult about the best way or man; to hold a caucus.

掫 ꜀tseu To strike the rounds at night, to pace the beat; to take or grasp with the hand.

丨擊 to beat the watches.

賓將丨主人辭 when the guest proposes to leave at night, the host does not detain him.

In *Cantonese*. Tight.

緊丨丨 tie it up very tightly.

棷 ꜀tseu A kind of wood good for fuel; fuel; a shield; a watchman's beater or alarm; a kind of spear.

丨樿 a tree, whose whitish wood is suitable for combs.

陬 ꜀tseu The angle or corner of a city wall, where it is retired or cut off; a nook, a corner; to live together; abashed.

丨隅 a corner, a retreating angle.

列仙之丨 the realm of the genii.

遐丨 a distant place.

偏丨 a secluded spot.

四丨 the four corners or ways, as when looking from a height.

孟丨 or 丨月 a classical term for the first moon of the year.

皐丨 abashed, disconcerted.

丨邑 the village where Confucius was born, and properly written like the next.

郰 郮 ꜀tseu The second form is not commonly used.

The town 丨鄉 in Lu was the birthplace of Confucius; it is now in Kiuh-feu hien in Yen-cheu fu in Shantung.

丨人 a term for the sage.

鄒 ꜀tseu The old name of a small state near Lu, in which Mencius was born, B. C. 371; now the district of 丨縣 in Yen-cheu fu not far from the Grand Canal in the southwest of Shantung.

丨平縣 a district in Tsi-nan fu in the northeast of Shantung.

騶 ꜀tseu From *horse* and *plants*; occurs used, for ꜀ts'ü 趨 to run and the preceding.

A groom or an officer who calls in the horses on a hunt; quick as an arrow or a fleet horse; to go.

虞丨 a fabulous beast from the west, which attracts others to its side by its mildness; it is drawn like a white tiger with a very long tail; its kindness to animals is such that it will not even tread on living grass, and eats only what died of itself; some think that fleet hunters are meant.

因丨從不日 since you, Sir, are to leave at an early day.

謅 ꜀tseu From *words* and *plants*; also read ꜂ch'ao, and interchanged with ꜂訬 and ꜂吵 to disturb.

Sportive or irritating words which annoy; jesting, raillery; to cry out, to halloo; to rail at; to exaggerate.

胡丨 to talk wildly.

丨鬧 rumor, wild stories.

弄丨悅聽 he loves to hear repartees and gibes.

丨讓 to bawl out, to reprimand.

丨心 or 丨經 a fancy story, a wild narrative.

Read ꜀ts'eü. To whisper.

丨諑 to speak in a low tone.

菆 ꜀tseu From *grass* and to *collect* or *gather*.

A tussock, such as grows in a bog; grass and jungle; hemp ready for weaving; a well-made arrow of aspen wood; a mattress; a nest; an overplus.

丨子 a nest of young hawks or eaglets.

左射以丨 on the left side, one shot an aspen arrow.

Read ꜂tswan for 攢. To put wood or poles around a coffin as it lies on the ground, before covering it in the tumulus.

丨塗 to heap earth on a coffin thus protected.

鯫 ꜀tseu Minnows, little white fish that skip over the water; *met.* an artful man.

丨生說我 this scheming fellow is pleased with me.

緅 ꜀tseu Silk first dyed thrice, and then twice dipped in black, making a dark puce color; a purplish tint.

走 ꜂tseu Composed of 夭 to *bend* and 止 to *stop*; *i.e.* to bend the leg and set it down; it is the 156th radical of characters relating to modes of going.

To go, to run, to get on; to sail; to travel; to hasten, to gallop; to get away; to depart, to clear out.

丨過幾省 he has traveled over several provinces.

丨得慢 it goes (or sails) slowly.

鬭鷄丨狗 to fight cocks and race dogs; 丨狗 also means a spy or betrayer.

丨水 to voyage; to raft logs; to leak.

丨不動 unable to walk.

丨脫 to slip off.

丨了水了 hastened the water — to put out the fire; a conflagration. (*Pekingese.*)

丨使 a servant.

牆壁丨動 the wall has cracked.

丨一遭 been there once; I have taken the journey.

丨不過去 the way is impassable, either from robbers or an obstruction.

奔丨事厥考厥長 bustling about in the service of fathers and elders.

不丨樣兒 not to follow the model; to vary from the copy.

丨漏消息 or 丨風 to let out a secret; the news has transpired.

棄甲曳兵而丨 threw off their armor, trailed their weapons, and ran.

丨氣 a crack, a place where water or air leaks out.

丨一個乾淨 all went away leaving a clear space.

不要替他丨攏 do not associate with him; don't cotton to him.

傶 ʻtseu To hire one's self out as a laborer by the day or longer time; one says, a staid, sincere demeanor.

文丨丨 big-sounding, pedantic talk.

奏 tseuʾ Composed of 本 a *paper* held in 廾 *both hands*, and 屮 to *advance*, altered in their combination; it much resembles ˬtsin 秦 grain.

To report to the Throne by a memorial, or by word of mouth; to cause the government to hear or know; to exhibit, to display; success; to celebrate, to congratulate one upon, as a victory; to introduce, to bring forward; to perform the music of a certain part of a piece, like a fugue; songs or tunes.

丨本 or 丨章 a memorial to the throne.

丨上 to send up a report.

片丨 a slip or minute for the sovereign.

暨益丨庶鮮食 with Yih I showed the people how to get food.

准丨 to assent to a memorial.

面丨 to state personally to the emperor.

陳丨 or 敷丨 to state carefully and particularly.

封口丨摺 a sealed memorial.

題丨 a dispatch on one point; and 彙丨 one on several matters.

丨劾 to report against an officer, as a censor.

節丨 to mark the parts.

樂既和丨 the parts were played in harmony, or at proper times.

丨樂 to strike up the band.

䐢 tseuʾ From *eyebrows* and *creaking*; an old form of the next now disused.

To knit the eyebrows is 丨眉, whether in anger or to screen the eye.

縐 tseuʾ cheuʾ From *silk* and *plants*; used with the next.

Fine fibers of hemp; crape; rumpled, wrinkled, crinkled, crisp, frizzled; drawn in; to corrugate; to shrink; to contract.

丨紗 crape; like crape.

綿丨 camlet, sensbaw.

水面風來綠丨 the breeze raises the green wavelets on the water.

丨紬 wrinkled silk.

褰丨 puckered, shriveled.

丨子 or 丨紋 marks of wrinkles; folds; gathers.

線丨 crinkled thread.

縮丨 shrunk, folded, creased.

皺 tseuʾ cheuʾ Regarded by some as an erroneous form of the last.

Wrinkled, as the skin from age; shriveled; furrowed, as the surface of a country with valleys; frowning; creased.

丨眉頭 to scowl, to frown.

面皮丨 an old wrinkled face.

額上堆丨 the wrinkles cover his brow.

丨金 imitation gold leaf.

葉上起丨 corrugated leaves, like the broccoli or kale.

紅丨 dried dates.

㥮 tseuʾ cheuʾ Clothes creased and wrinkled, not laid out or smoothed.

丨摺子 wrinkles, folds, creases; plicatures.

驟 tseuʾ From *horse* and *assembled* for the phonetic.

A horse going swiftly; a racer; to race; quick, urgent; rapidly, suddenly; again and again, frequently.

丨然而來 he came in abruptly.

不可丨得 it cannot be done in an instant.

天丨下雨 it suddenly rained.

馳丨 to ride the horse fast.

足不及丨 he cannot go so fast as the other.

載丨駸駸 they hurried off with speed.

甃 tseuʾ The lining of a well; to repair a well; to lay the brickwork in it.

井丨無咎 the well has now no defect.

TS'EU.

Some of these characters are read CH'EU. *Old sounds,* ts'u *and* dzu. *In Canton,* ts'au *and* shau; — *in Swatow,* ch'o *and* chau; — *in Amoy,* tsò; — *in Fuhchau,* ch'au, ch'éu, *and* chaiu; — *in Shanghai,* ts'ù *and* zù; — *in Chifu,* ts'ò.

篘 *₍ts'eu* A vat or strainer like a basket, made to hold the mash when straining off the liquor.

搊 *₍ts'eu* From *hand* and *plants*.
To hold in the fingers; to curb; to grasp, as a guitar; to crumple up; a local name for a fan; to pull up the skirt or roll up the sleeves; to overhaul; to unloose.

丨金 to crumple gilt paper by rolling and then pressing it.

丨琵琶 a kind of guitar with five strings; it is found in Corea.

兩手丨衣 to hold up the dress with both hands.

櫉 *₍ts'eu* The ring or stick in a bullock's nose to lead it; boards lying unevenly.

愁 *₍ch'eu* From *heart* and *autumn*; not the same as *ts'iao'* 愀 careful.
Mournful, grieved; sad, chagrined; apprehensive, afraid; to assemble.

丨悶 sorrowing, broken-hearted.

消丨 to assuage sorrow.

丨腸百結 my anguished bowels are tied in a hundred knots; — I am utterly cast down.

丨顏 or 丨容 a rueful face.

含丨 gloomy and silent from grief.

丨煞花前月下人 the bard is a doleful man, who writes among the flowers and drinks in the moonshine.

丨佢不要 I fear he won't want it. (*Cantonese*).

丨眉不展 lowering eyebrows.

Read *₍ts'ao*. Confused, in disorder.

牢丨 tangled, weedy; disorderly, troublesome, irregular; a source of grief.

攻破丨城 [the good news] has dispersed all his griefs.

瞅 矁 瞅 *ʿch'eu* From *eye* and *plants* or *grieved*; all are unauthorized, the first is commonest.
To look at steadily; to gaze intently.

丨不見 I cannot see it clearly.

眼丨着 while I was looking around.

丨着字念書 when you read, look closely at your book.

你丨什麼 what are you looking at?

鼈丨蛋 the turtle watches its eggs — till they hatch.

鞪 *ʿcheu* To bind with thongs of hide.
Read *tseu'* and used for 縐. To wrinkle; creases in leather.

㑳 *cheu'* To scold, to blackguard; sad; irritated at, morose.

㑳 abusive, scurrilous language; to rail at.

簉 *cheu'* An attendant, a maid-servant; a concubine, euphuistically called 副倅 or secondary half; equal to.

聽丨弄者 hearing one hum the old ballads, — causes the mind to revert to early times.

凑 湊 *ts'eu'* From *ice* or *water* and to *memorialize*; the first is most common, but is unauthorized; occurs used for the next two.
To collect people on the water, as at a regatta; to gather, to run together; to run into each other; to go with one and take care of; a reunion; a concurrence of circumstances; to estimate the chances of.

丨巧 just as; a fortunate coincidence; a lucky guess.

丨够數 just enough for the occasion.

丨合 people collecting, as to see a show.

丨集 to collect together; to amass, as a library.

時來福丨 a lucky hit, a good chance.

In *Cantonese*. A *preposition*, with, for, together.

唔丨你好 I'll have nothing to do with you.

你去丨我打聽 will you go and learn about it for me?

睇來丨 I'll see about it, or what I had better do.

輳 *ts'eu'* Used with the last.
The center of a wheel; a focus, where things center; to bring together; concentrated.

萬方輻丨之區 [Peking is] the resort of people from all quarters.

腠 *ts'eu'* Flesh next the skin; the muscle.

丨理 the grain of the flesh, the fiber or brawn.

膚丨 the skin of a man; the flesh next to it.

疾在丨理 the disease is in the muscle.

剶 *ts'eu'* To mince or hash meat; to cut up wood into small pieces.

丨斷 to come to pieces, as an old fur; cut fine.

TSI.

Old sounds, tsai, sai, sak, *and* tsat. *In Canton*, tsei; — *in Swatow*, chi; — *in Amoy*, chó; — *in Fuhchau*, chè *and* chie; — *in Shanghai*, tsi; — *in Chifu*, chi.

韲 齏 ˓tsi From *even* and *scallions*, or with *plants* added.

The second form only is a species of leek; to prepare and mix, as condiments; to compound; to blend, as opposite tastes; to make salted preparations, such as the poor use; blended; spoiled, pounded; to compare, as various opinions.

和 丨 to mix, as spices.

斷 丨 畫 粥 a piece of cabbage and a streak of congee; — *i. e.* a poor scholar's fare.

黃 丨 a saffron color.

碎 米 丨 poor fare, broken cakes and pulse.

鹽 丨 菜 salted cabbage, sour-krout.

齎 賫 ˓tsi From *even* and *property*; the contracted form is mostly used.

To take in both hands and offer to; to give, to send a present; to prepare things for a journey; to send, as a dispatch; to supply; to leave behind in store; a sigh of admiration.

親 丨 to give to personally.

丨 送 to present to an equal.

丨 奏 官 a courier of government dispatches.

丨 至 let this be sent to .... part of the address on a dispatch.

丨 賜 to bestow on.

捧 丨 to offer up to.

丨 咨 to sigh, as when thinking of something unattainable.

丨 裝 to pack up to forward, as baggage.

躋 隮 ˓tsi From *foot* or *place* and *even*; the uses of these two words differ slightly.

To ascend, to go up, as stairs; to scale, to climb steep cliffs; to rise, as the clouds; a vapor or rosy clouds; to be ruined, to fall.

攀 丨 to clamber up.

氣 丨 rising vapor or clouds.

丨 升 to go up; to attain high positions.

道 阻 且 丨 the way is difficult and steep.

聖 敬 日 丨 his perfect reverence daily advanced.

告 予 顛 丨 you tell me now of impending ruin.

朝 丨 于 西 the morning [rainbow] rises in the west.

櫅 ˓tsi A fruit tree in Honan, called 白 棗 the white date; it is a variety of jujube, but is sweeter than the common black sort; the wood is good for cart-hubs and felloes.

擠 ˓tsi Also read ˓tsi.

To crowd, to push against or over; to upset; to fall into; to rest against; to press or squeeze, as a boil.

擁 丨 to crowd and press upon; to scrouge.

丨 不 動 I am so crowded that I cannot stir.

丨 上 前 去 pressing to get first.

亂 丨 to crowd tumultuously.

丨 奶 to milk an animal.

丨 水 to pump up water.

Read ˓ts'i. To arrange, to place.

丨 排 八 短 處 to detail and tell over people's shortcomings; detraction.

In *Cantonese*. To put down, to to lay aside; to place.

隨 便 丨 put it where you please.

䍕 ˓tsi From *net* and *even*.

To squeeze out juice or water with the hand; to press and strain out.

丨 手 巾 to wring out a napkin.

丨 蔗 汁 to crush the juice from sugar-cane.

丨 出 汁 來 press the juice out.

濟 tsi˒ From *water* and *even* or *regularly*; also occurs used for the next.

To aid, to succor, to relieve; to furnish gratuitous aid; to cross a stream; to bring about; saddened; to stop, as the rain; to complete, to further; able, clever.

救 丨 to save and relieve; to rescue, as wounded men.

不 丨 事 he won't do; he won't help the matter; insufficient.

以 丨 燃 眉 之 急 to rescue one from imminent danger.

同 舟 共 丨 to cross in the same boat; — *i. e.* fellows in a work.

道 丨 天 下 to reform the world.

丨 涉 to cross or go over.

不 丨 的 貨 物 inferior goods, either second rate or injured.

Read ˓ts'i The river 丨 水 in Shantung, whence Tsi-nan fu 丨 南 府 the capital receives its name.

辟 王 丨 丨 dignified and elegant was our prince and king.

衣 冠 丨 丨 a large concourse of [people in] robes and caps.

四 驪 丨 丨 the four black steeds look beautifully.

霽 tsi˒ The rain holding up; the clouds clearing away, and blue sky appearing.

晴 丨 a clear sky.

丨 色 the clear blue sky.

雨 丨 the rain has stopped.

仰 祈 丨 威 looking up, I implore a mitigation of your sternness.

劑 tsi˒ From *knife* and *even*.

To trim, to pare, to cut even; to equalize, to adjust, to portion out; to compound, as a pill; a dose; a prescription.

一 丨 藥 one dose of medicine.

分' ㄧ 兒 the weight or size of a dose.

藥 ㄧ medicines, drugs.

調 ㄧ to even off; to arrange amicably, to compose differences, to arbitrate between.

質 ㄧ a check in two parts, one of which is the complement and proof of the other; anciently, a sort of counter or token.

救世砭 ㄧ a sovereign remedy against illness, a panacea to relieve mankind.

嚌 tsi' To taste, to sip; to wet the lips.

ㄧ 嘗 to try the taste.

ㄧ 福 to taste the offerings.

Read *˛kiai*. Noise of birds.

鵾鷄 ㄧ ㄧ the jungle fowls cackle and crow.

Read *'chai*. Smiling.

ㄧ 喍 a pleasant countenance.

In *Cantonese*. A superlative, extremely, to the end.

大得 ㄧ far too large.

係得 ㄧ certainly it is so.

齰 tsi' To bite; to take a bite of; some say, irregular teeth.

齧 ㄧ to eat a mouthful of.

癠 tsi' From *disease* and *even; q. d.* sickness disturbs the equilibrium of the body and mind.

Sick, ailing, diseased; in Hunan, a dwarfed, stunted or half developed thing.

親 ㄧ my parents are unwell.

薺 tsi' ˛ts'i The *plant* of *Tsi*.

The shepherd's purse (*Capsella bursa-pastoris*), gathered for greens, as ㄧ 菜; but the term seems to include other small esculent herbs, like cress and pepper-grass.

其甘如 ㄧ sweet as the shepherd's purse; — but as this plant is rather harsh, some natives think the water chestnut is meant in the Book of Odes.

穧 tsi' To cut grain and lay it in a swath by the hand, afterwards to be bound and stacked.

束 ㄧ 而 回 bind up the scattered grain and then return.

此有不斂 ㄧ let this be left ungathered — for the widows.

祭 tsi' From 示 to *declare*, with 肉 *flesh* and 手 *hand* above it contracted; *i. e.* to bring before the gods; occurs used for the next.

To sacrifice, to offer slaughtered victims before the gods or penates, which are now usually cooked beforehand; to bring an oblation, to approach the gods; a sacrifice, an offering; sacrificial; a limit.

ㄧ 祀 to present sacrifices.

ㄧ 文 a prayer, burned after it is offered; an elegy differing from the ㄧ 軸 and hung up before the tablet during the first seven weeks of mourning.

擺路 ㄧ to lay out offerings along the way, — to greet the coffin of a friend or relative.

ㄧ 司 an overseer of sacrifices, a priest.

ㄧ 酒 the title of the two presidents of Kwoh-tsz' kien, because they pour libations to Confucius.

ㄧ 掃 to worship and sweep — the tombs at Tsing-ming term.

ㄧ 神如神在 to sacrifice to the gods as if they were present; *i. e.* reverently.

ㄧ 幽 to appease ghosts by oblations.

上馬 ㄧ offerings made at coffining a body. (*Fuhchau,*).

ㄧ 品 articles used for sacrifices.

際 tsi' From *place* and *sacrifice*, referring to the place where walls join.

A border, a region; a medium or average; a limit, as in time or place; the line of junction or division, as the horizon; the time when something else begins; as an *adverb*, then, since, now; between, the moment of occurring; to begin, to join; among the Taoists, form as distinct from substance.

死生之 ㄧ between life and death.

ㄧ 接 to receive, to blend, to help.

此 ㄧ this occasion.

好 ㄧ 遇 a favorable juncture.

風雲 ㄧ 會 the winds and clouds have met; *met.* to receive a favor.

交 ㄧ intercommunication, blending; associations.

ㄧ 昌 a prosperous time.

事當不 ㄧ 之 ㄧ the affair was then in an untoward way.

無 ㄧ unlimited.

實 ㄧ a real case, true grounds for.

穄 tsi' From *grain* and *sacrifice*, as the phonetic.

A variety of panicled millet (*Panicum miliaceum*) cultivated in Shansi and Chihli; it resembles the 稷 but is not glutinous; this variety has smooth culms, and is not easily distinguished; in some parts of Honan, a small coarse grain resembling sorghum, with a hard or solid stem.

蘆 ㄧ and 木 ㄧ are two sorts of sorghum cultivated in Kiangsu, having sweet juice.

懠 tsi' Angry, irate; used for 猜 suspicious; grieved at.

ㄧ 疑 full of suspicions.

天之方 ㄧ Heaven is now showing its anger.

TSʻI.

Old sounds, tsʻai, dzai, dzak, *and* tsʻit. *In Canton*, tsʻei; — *in Swatow*, chʻi, ché, *and* ki; — *in Amoy*, chʻé *and* ché; — *in Fuhchau*, chʻè, chai, *and* chʻü; — *in Shanghai*, tsʻi; — *in Chifu*, chʻi.

妻 ꜀tsʻi From 女 *woman*, with 又 a *hand* and 屮 a *sprout*, intimating that she enters as an equal.

A wife, a consort who is taken with legal ceremonies, and is equal to the husband; there can be only one at a time, and not while another is living.

丨子 a wife; sometimes wife and children are denoted.

令丨 your wife.

賢丨 my good wife.

平丨 equal to a wife; *i.e.* a concubine.

路頭丨 a wayside wife, one taken while sojourning elsewhere; she is not a 客丨 or courtesan, and the usage is allowed.

丨兒老小 all the family.

嬌丨美妾 an accomplished wife and handsome concubine.

露水夫丨 a dew marriage, one of convenience.

Read *tsʻi*꜄ To give in marriage; to wive.

以女丨之 or 以其子丨之 he married his daughter to him.

凄 淒 ꜀tsʻi From *ice* or *water* and *wife*; the second also means cloudy, windy skies, foreboding storms.

Intense cold; bleak, wintry; shivering, freezing; calamitous; afflicted, sad, in misery.

丨切 bitter suffering.

風雨丨丨 chilly wind and rain.

丨涼景況 in desperate misery.

丨楚甚 in urgent necessity.

美寒烟衰草丨迷 I like the chilly autumnal vapors, and the paths hidden in the high grass.

丨丨 luxuriant or thick, as rushes.

悽 ꜀tsʻi Similar to the last.

Grieved, sorrowing; suffering, pained; indignant from a sense of wrong.

悲丨 pitiable; to feel for.

丨丨 famishing, gaunt.

感時兮丨淸 my sad feelings comport with the gloomy weather.

郪 ꜀tsʻi An old town, named 新丨 in 魏, now 商城縣 in the extreme southeast of Honan, on a branch of the R. Hwai.

丨丘 an ancient place in 齊, towards its eastern border.

丨縣 a former name of 射洪縣 on the River Tao in Sz'chʻuen.

萋 ꜀tsʻi Luxuriant foliage; courtly in one's manner.

丨且敬 stately and respectful.

丨兮斐兮成是貝錦 elegant, waving lines may be made to look like shell tapestry.

有渰丨丨 the clouds roll up in dense masses.

緀 ꜀tsʻi Like the last.

The stripes or shades in silken fabrics; elegant, blended colors; ornamented.

霋 ꜀tsʻi Clouds driving along the sky and clearing up after a storm.

雲丨 the clouds are clearing away.

齊 ꜀tsʻi The character is intended to represent the *even* appearance of a field of ripe rice or wheat; it forms the 210th radical of a few characters, most of which get their meaning from the primitive; it is interchanged with several of its compounds.

Even, equal, uniform; on a level; composed, reverent; exact in doing; to equalize, to tranquillize; to classify or arrange methodically or by ranks; at once, all, alike; quick, smart; good; to discriminate; to happen at the right juncture.

丨州 an old name for China.

丨眉 a married couple.

收丨賬目 collected all the accounts.

整丨 well arranged; all repaired and in order.

丨全 complete throughout.

一丨去 all go at once.

我沒丨截 I have not yet finished it all, as a job of work.

丨心 of one mind.

等丨纔來 wait a little and they will come.

丨備 all are ready, fully arranged.

丨家 to govern a family.

不丨 uneven, incomplete, deficient.

歸丨怎樣 how will it be at last? what will be the end of it?

丨國 an important ancient feudal kingdom, existing just nine centuries down to 224 B.C., and comprising a large part of Northern Shantung and Southern Chihli; the capital was Ying-kiu 營丘 now Lin-tsz' hien; it began B.C. 1122, when it was conferred on Shang-fu 尙父 the marquis of Kiang, by Wu Wang, and its records continue till 265 until King Siang 襄王 under 26 rulers, who always exercised a powerful influence in the empire.

蠐 ꜀tsʻi A large maggot; a grub in the ground or in trees.

領如蝤丨 her neck is as slender as a carpenter grub.

蠙丨 a tumble-dung.

臍 ꜀tsʻi From *flesh* and *even*.

The navel; to cut even, to adjust; the stem or peduncle of a seed or grain.

肚丨 the navel.

噬丨何及 how can a man bite his navel? — *i.e.* it is impossible.

青腰白丨 green body and white stem, said of grain half filled or not well ripened.

丨帶 the umbilical cord.

'臍 'ts'i The peg or pivot for resting the scull on is 艣 丨, so called because it makes a hole in the scull like a navel.

'鱭 鱭 'ts'i Also read 'tsz'; the first form is common; the etymology denotes the *thin fish.*

A thin fish with a silvery belly and sharp back, having barbels and spines; it is also called 刀 魚 or knife fish; a mullet; also applied to some of the mackerel family; the approach of the shoals of mackerel is said to be announced by a drumming sound.

馬 丨 a kind of anchovy. (*Coilia playfairii.*)

黃尾 丨 the yellow tail mullet. (*Mullus xanthurus.*)

白 丨 the greenish mullet. (*Mugil ventricosus.*)

刀 丨 魚 a species of *Thryssa.*

砌 ts'i' From *stone* and *carved;* it is also read *tsié* as a noun.

A stone step; ornamented tiles used in steps; to lay, as tiles or bricks; to pave; to fit in, to lay regularly.

丨 詞 揑 控 to heap up false accusations against one.

丨 牆 to lay a wall.

階 丨 stone-steps.

丨 不 直 this is not laid erect.

玉 丨 a white marble step.

丨 石 路 to pave with slabs of stone.

Read *tseu'* and erroneously used for 甃. To dig a pit.

丨 井 to dig a well. (*Pekingese.*)

粞 ts'i' An unauthorized character.

In *Fuhchau.* Flour made from rice.

送 丨 to send a present of rice-flour to mourners.

丨 丨 白 very white; snowy.

TSIANG.

Old sounds, tsiang *and* dziong. *In Canton,* tséung; — *in Swatow,* chièng *and* chⁿié; — *in Amoy,* chiong; — *in Fuhchau,* chiòng *and* ch'iòng; — *in Shanghai,* tsiang *and* ziang; — *in Chifu,* chiang.

將 敒 ,tsiang Composed of 寸 *inch,* and 醬 *condiment* contracted for the phonetic; the second form is not uncommon; occurs used for ,ts'iang 鏘 to tinkle.

To take, to hold in the hand; taking, considering, regarding, in which use it resembles 把 and becomes a sign of the accusative,— as 丨 金 博 寶 to exchange a rarity for gold; a form of the present participle; a sign of the future, shall, will, about, — as 丨 死 dying; or 丨 如 之 何 how shall we then act? about, ready to do, as 丨 入 門 about to go in the door; a form of the optative, — as 丨 其 來 食 would that he would come and eat; an *adverb,* then, soon, presently; to help, to accommodate; to use, to avail one's self of; to escort, to accompany; to arrange; to present to a superior; to receive and act upon; to follow; to approach, to advance towards a mark; to nourish, to increase; to be endued with; great; to make great; long; passing away, as time; stout; the side, as of a river.

丨 安 丨 樂 to encourage others' peace and happiness.

丨 可 以 走 then he can go.

吾 丨 問 之 I will ask him.

丨 妖 言 傳 布 availed himself of the rumors to make it known.

丨 焉 用 彼 相 矣 how then can we employ this man to help — the blinded king?

輸 丨 to help the government.

丨 軍 a commandant, a captain-general; they are always Manchus, and are stationed in command of garrisons; as an *adjective,* the best, the principal; great, extra, — as 丨 軍 帳 a large awning over a court.

百 輛 丨 之 escorted her with a hundred chariots.

丨 就 it will pass, it must do; passably, let it go; as 幾 分 丨 就 occasionally overlooks things, he is indulgent at times.

日 就 月 丨 the sun comes on and the moon follows; — time flies.

丨 丨 the tinkling of gems; noise of bells; also the frowning look of a high gate; blending, as notes.

丨 來 presently.

丨 近 動 身 nearly ready to start.

不 知 老 之 丨 至 he is unaware that old age is close upon him.

亦 孔 之 丨 it was really very large.

丨 有 爲 也 it will soon be.

Read *tsiang'* To take charge of a force; to lead on men in fight, as a general; a leader; to ask; the white king in chess; and a notice like *check!*

兵 丨 a military leader.

副 丨 chief of staff, a second to the general; a brigadier or commodore.

陛 下 不 善 ,丨 兵 而 善 ,丨 丨 your Majesty is not skilled in leading troops, but you are clever in guiding the generals.

丨 子 無 怒 I beg you not to be angry.

丨 令 general orders.

搬 ,tsiang To lead, as a child; to pierce with a spear.

用 手 丨 他 lead him by the hand.

螿 ,tsiang A small species of locust or cicada, called 寒 丨 having green elytra; it is probably a species allied to *Cicada viridis.*

漿
洲 } A thick fluid like syrup or broth; water in which rice has long been boiled; pus, matter; congee, thick broth; water thickened, as by glue or varnish; gum; to starch.
˛tsiang

汁 丨 gravy.
地 丨 or 泥 丨 slush; mire.
天 丨 or 瓊 丨 a poetical name for dew.
丨 衣服 to starch clothes.
冲 丨 to prepare starch.
酒 丨 a banquet.
太 丨 too pasty; too stiff and sticky.
合 丨 a muscle fish.

獎 'tsiang From *great* and *taking*.
To exhort, to animate, to encourage; to commend, to laud; to vindicate, to give efficacy; to set on, as a dog.
丨 勸 to exhort by praising.
丨 賞 to hold out rewards to; a prize or reward.
何用過 丨 why such extravagant praise!
丨 恤三軍 he enheartened the three divisions with largesses.
請 丨 to request that a testimonial may be conferred.
丨 勵 to stimulate to exertion.

槳
艜 } An oar; a keel-board, in which sense it is also read *ts'iang'*.
'tsiang

打 丨 or 搖 丨 or 掉 丨 to row with oars.
艇子盪雙 丨 the boat was rowed by two oars.
丨 船 a revenue cutter, because it has many oars. (*Cantonese.*)
急水下 丨 let down the keel-board when in swift water; don't be in a premature hurry or fear.

蔣 'tsiang A species of aquatic grass, the *Hydropyrum latifolium*, like the wild rice of Canada, cultivated for its sweet stalks in most parts of China; it is also called 菰 and 茭, and the stalks 茭筍 or 茭白 cane-shoots; its leaves are fed to cattle, and the grain is boiled; an old name for Kwang cheu 光州 in the southeast of Honan, given as a fief to one of Duke Cheu's family.
丨 茅 stubble.

醬 tsiang' A relish made of salt mixed with bean or other kinds of flour, and water, and allowed to remain till cured; it is used as a condiment; relishes, sauces, condiments; salted preparations.
茹 丨 to eat relishes of food.
乾 丨 a dry relish.
丨 坊 or 丨 園 shop for sale of oilman's stores, and condiments.
荳 丨 bean sauce; this is the basis of most of the Chinese relishes.
丨 色 a drab color.
擂 丨 to mix relishes.
枸 丨 tamarind preserves.
丨 小菜 vegetables seasoned in soy.

匠 tsiang' From 匚 an *inclosure* containing an 斤 *ax*, indicative of a workman who uses a square and compass in working.
A mechanic, a workman, an artisan; one who makes things requiring skill.
丨 人 an artificer, a workman.
丨 頭 the overseer, the boss.
瓦 丨 or 泥水 丨 a mason, a bricklayer.
木 丨 a carpenter; a housebuilder.
銀 丨 a silversmith.
頗費 丨 心 rather hard work, as difficult composition.
小爐 丨 a mender of dishes, a tinker.
丨 作主家謀 the workman should follow the master's plans.

TS'IANG.

Old sounds, ts'iong *and* dziong. *In Canton*, ts'éung; — *in Swatow*, ch'ǹg *and* ch'^{n}iè; — *in Amoy*, ch'iong, *and* ch'ong; — *in Fuhchau*, ch'iòng; — *in Shanghai*, ts'iang *and* dziang; — *in Chifu*, ch'iang.

槍 ˛ts'iang From *wood* and *granary*; it is much interchanged with the next, but this is disapproved by the dictionaries.
A spear sharp at both ends; a lance, a boarding-pike; to bend the head to the ground, or very low; to resist; one who is quick and ready.
丨 法 the hand manual; a soldier's profession or discipline.
回馬 丨 to give a back thrust when unhorsed; to leave in the lurch, to outwit.
長 丨 a long spear.
丨 手 a substitute who enters the examination for *siuts'ai*, or who writes themes for another.

鎗 ˛ts'iang A gun, a musket; a spear; an opium pipe; a sort of wine boiler or still; the tinkling of bells, a jingling sound, — in which it is used for the next.
食 丨 糧 to be a soldier.
刀 丨 a musket with a bayonet; also, swords and spears.
鳥 丨 a fowling-piece; a matchlock.
手 丨 a pistol.
風 丨 an air-gun.
服藥丟 丨 take this medicine and throw away the pipe.

鏘 ˛ts'iang Used with the last and its primitive.
The ringing of bells; jingling of stones; a tinkling noise; harmony; musical.
和鳴 丨 丨 jingling in concert, a pleasant tinkle.
音節鏗 丨 harmony of sound, as in singing.

蹌
䠀
˓ts'iang

To walk rapidly; to skip about; to approach a superior quickly.

丨 丨 濟 濟 to move about in a hurried, busy way, as officers do in a court, or people in a crowd.

奔走趨丨 to bustle about, as if obeying orders at a levee; to move quickly.

鳥獸丨丨 the gobbling sound of birds and beasts when feeding; the second form is used in this phrase.

謒 ˓ts'iang

From *word* and *spear* contracted.

To contradict; to oppose; to speak harshly to one.

丨白一頓 scolded him once.

斨 ˓ts'iang

From 斤 *hatchet* and 爿 a *couch*.

A heavy broad-ax, with a square hole for the helve; a pole-ax of a square shape; to hack, to chop.

丨害 to injure one by slander, to defame and libel one.

彼取斧丨 taking their bills and axes.

自相丨賊 to injure and weaken one's own party or friend.

牆
墻
廧
˓ts'iang

From 爿 *couch* or 土 *earth* and 嗇 *frugal*; the second is a contraction of an old form of granary, and the third a synonym of the first.

A wall built of mud, stone, or brick; a defense; the third also means a tribe of red Huns in ancient times, who lived in 丨咎如 before the days of Confucius.

葺丨 or 砌丨 to lay a wall.

泥丨 an adobie wall.

塗丨 or 抹丨 to plaster a wall.

照丨 a screen wall.

在蕭丨之內 within the screen of the court, *i. e.* in the ruler's presence or among his officers.

山丨 or 金字丨 the end wall of a house.

雕丨 a carved or ornamented wall; — one on which carved tiles are faced, often with fine and elaborate painting.

徹我丨屋 he has removed our houses.

禍起蕭丨 an émeute in the household, usually refers to palace intrigues and treason.

幽于園丨之中 hidden in a private house.

嬙 ˓ts'iang

Female officers in the imperial harem; ladies of the bedchamber in the Han dynasty, called 嬪丨; they are not now employed.

王丨 a noted beauty of the Han dynasty.

丨媛 respectfully waiting on, as a maid of honor or concubine.

檣
艢
˓ts'iang

A mast; a spar or mast that sustains the sail.

桅丨 or 女丨 a mast.

帆丨 sails and masts.

薔
蘠
˓ts'iang

A red rose; the 丨薇花 or cinnamon rose, of which there are varieties.

丨薇露 dew of roses, or rose-water, in which a princess of the Han always washed.

Read *seh*, A species of water *polygonum* or smart weed.

戕 ˓ts'iang

From *spear* and *couch*.

A spear, a wooden lance; to do violence, to assault; to kill, as when a soldier kills an officer, or a foreign foe kills the enemy's ruler; to maltreat; to misuse, as by excess; injurious.

丨傷 to wound.

丨暴 cruel, ruthless.

丨官 to rise and kill rulers.

丨賊 to plunder.

自丨 to commit suicide.

丨害生民 to kill and cut up human beings.

曰予不丨禮則然矣 he says I am not misusing you, for the laws order it to be so done.

搶 ˓ts'iang

From *hand* and a *granary*.

To take openly by force; to snatch, to ravish, to rob; to dispute and struggle for; abrupt, rude, sudden.

丨刼之案 a case of plundering.

丨白打丨 going about the country plundering; to make a clean sweep of; to rob all.

丨先 to strive to get first; to thrust one's self forward.

丨奪 to snatch away.

丨白幾句 denounced (or opposed) him in many words.

丨攘 in confusion, disordered.

丨着買 to buy at auction.

Read ˓ts'iang. To withstand, to oppose; to rush against, to thrust at; ahead, as a wind.

以頭丨地 to hit the head on the ground.

丨風 the wind is very scant.

Read ˓ts'ang. To cut up, as a butcher does.

蹡 ts'iang˒

Interchanged with ˓蹌 to skip.

To walk quickly; to go across.

丨 丨 to run together, as a crowd.

趨丨不遑 quick but not at all hurried.

踉踉丨丨 to walk away, to hobble; to reel.

篬 ts'iang˒

To split bamboos without paring away the joints or nodes; a mat.

籮丨 the cross sticks which strengthen the bottom of a basket.

𪍿
漿
ts'iang˒

From *wheat* and *taking*; the second form is unauthorized, but has mostly superseded the first.

Paste made of flour.

打丨子 or 冲丨子 to make paste.

丨糊刷 a paste-brush.

嗆 ʼ *tsʻiangʼ* To peck, as a bird; a coughing caused by an obstruction in the throat, a hacking; foolish looking; idle fear.

丨哼 groundless alarm.

丨着嗓子 he coughed up his uvula; *i. e.* coughed very hard.

丨的出不來氣 he can't cough it up, as a bone in his throat.

喉丨 or 喝丨了 a coughing irritation; to hem and clear the throat.

塵土丨人 the dust irritates the throat.

戧 ʼ *tsʻiangʼ* Another form of ˏ*chʻwang* 創 to wound.

To etch on lacker-ware.

丨金 to paint or gild lacker-ware.

丨花文具 articles on which designs are etched.

TSIAO.

Old sounds, tsio, dzio, tsiok, *and* dzop. *In Canton*, tsiu; — *in Swatow*, chié, chʻau, *and* chio; — *in Amoy*, chiau *and* tsau; — *in Fuhchau*, chiéu; — *in Shanghai*, tsio; — *in Chifu*, chiao.

焦 ˏ*tsiao* From 火 *fire* under 隹 *a bird;* used with the next and ˏ燋 vexed.

Scorched, burned; singed or blackened by fire; dried up; the smell of fire; vexed, anxious, harassed; ancient name of a feudatory state included in the modern prefecture of Shen cheu 陝州 in the west of Honan.

炒丨 to burn in roasting.

飯丨 a crust left after boiling rice.

丨頭爛額 head and face scorched, as by powder; *met.* exposed to great hardships.

丨疤乾 dry as a scorched scab; *met.* at the last gasp; withered.

丨悶 or 丨心 sad at heart; greatly distressed.

丨月 an old term for the sixth moon, because of the great heat.

丨尾 a lute, alluding to a story of one made from a charred log.

丨黑 or 晒丨了 sunburnt.

膲 ˏ*tsiao* The parts of the body between the heart and groin, called 三丨 and regarded as one of the 六腑, are imaginary organs or passages which are supposed to encircle the cavities of the thorax and abdomen, and connect the viscera; Chinese physiologists have used them as a convenient force to explain the obscure operations of digestion and secretion, and say they have no form.

Read *tsiaoʼ* A want of flesh; out of season, as a fish.

癄 ˏ*tsiao* Thin, shriveled, lean; peaked and cadaverous.

丨瘁 emaciated; all dried and shrunken.

蕉 ˏ*tsiao* The plantain or banana, 丨子 of which there are many sorts; fuel, firing; a mere straw.

香牙丨 green-skinned plantains.

鼓槌丨 the triangular plantain.

丨葛 linen made from plantain fiber.

丨酒 a decoction of plantains in spirits.

水丨花 the Indian shot. (*Canna indica.*)

鳳尾丨 the phœnix-tail plantain (*Cycas revoluta*), a sort of palm.

丨薪 fuel of a poor kind.

綠丨葉上作字 he wrote his thoughts on the green plantain leaf, — an ancient incident, whence 種丨學書 denotes a diligent, self-made scholar.

鐎 ˏ*tsiao* A soldier's brass kettle or skillet, holding about a peck.

丨斗 a pan for cooking.

僬 ˏ*tsiao* To understand clearly, to perceive quickly; clever looking.

以己之丨丨受人之掝掝 he thought himself to be acute enough, but he was fooled by the man.

ˏ丨ˏ丨 to hurry along, to walk fast and carelessly.

礁 ˏ*tsiao* An unauthorized character.

Half-tide rocks; rocky islets near the coast; rocks in a stream, or stones placed for fording.

觸丨 to run on a rock.

穛 ˏ*tsiao* Raw fibers of the nettle hemp (*Boehmeria*) not yet rotted.

丨麻 unhatcheled or undressed hemp.

醮 ˏ*tsiao* A faded face, not plump or fresh.

丨顇 careworn and old, as an aged, withered face.

鷦 ˏ*tsiao* A grass warbler; a small bird like a wren.

丨鷯 the little tailor-bird (*Orthotomus*), and other small birds like it.

好丨鷯 frisky, inattentive, playful, skittish. (*Cantonese.*)

龜 ˏ*tsiao* From *tortoise* and *fire;* at present 燋ʼ is more used.

To scorch a terrapin's shell in order to prepare it for divination.

椒 ˏ*tsiao* From *wood* and *uncle*; it is altered from an old form.

Warm, spicy plants like the *Xanthoxylon*, *Capsicum*, *Boymia*, and *Piper*; hot, peppery, burning.

辣丨 or 紅丨 cayenne pepper.

胡丨 black pepper.

花丨 red pepper; also the fruit of the *Xanthoxylon alatum;* the 川丨 Sz'ch'uen pepper is another species.

丨末 ground black pepper.

丨房 the pepper-room; *i. e.* a queen, or a queen's apartments, because an empress of the Han had a room smeared with pepper to keep it warm.

有丨其馨 like pepper is their smell.

丨月 a poetical name of the last moon of the year.

丨花頌 a congratulation presented to the monarch on newyear's day.

山丨 the peak of a hill.

剿 'tsiao From *sword* and *nest.* To attack or fight with rebels; to destroy and scatter them; to put down, to extirpate.

丨絕 to destroy utterly.

丨捕凈盡 to take all, to make a clean sweep.

追丨 to chase, as a flying enemy.

征丨 to make a conquest of.

勦 'tsiao From *strong* and *nest* giving the sound; often wrongly used for the last. To trouble, to annoy; to toil at, to fag; light, nimble.

非丨不能爲 if you are not active you cannot do it.

丨其民 to vex and harass his subjects.

丨勞 to weary.

醮 tsiao' From *spirits* and *to scorch;* occurs used for the next, and resembles *chan'* 蘸 to dip. To sacrifice to ancestors or spirits, by pouring out libations; to pray at an altar by a priest; to make a responsive service for mercies; a requiem, a sacrifice; to give a cup to a son at his marriage; completed, finished, terminated; emptied, all used up.

打丨 or 建丨 or 設丨 to celebrate the All-souls festival, which at Canton is in autumn; also applied to a Taoist worship of their gods to thank them for deliverances.

再丨 to remarry; usually said of widows.

父丨酌子 the father pours out the marriage cup to his son — as he leaves to bring his wife.

丨席 a wedding feast.

水丨 dried, water all gone.

打火星丨 the autumnal festival at Canton to the god of Fire.

平安丨 a Taoist service held in an infected region after the disease has gone.

燋 tsiao' From *fire* and *to scorch.* Properly used for the last. To burn the moxa; to char wood, to scorch; to sear; to scorch a terrapin's shell for divination; to burn over dry grass.

灸三丨 to apply moxa thrice.

丨心 the heart-burn.

丨木 to char wood to bend it.

瞧 tsiao' From *eye* and *nobleman;* some regard this as more correct than 覺 in the phrase 睢覺 to sleep. To close the eyes, as in sleep; an angry look.

丨貝 a strange shell, the sight of which causes miscarriage; others say that it is administered in the form of a powder to produce abortion.

釂 tsiao' From 酉 *spirits* and 嚼 *to bite* contracted. To drain a goblet; to finish the glass.

長者舉未丨少者不敢飲 the juniors did not presume to drink until their elders had drained their uplifted cups.

割鮮飲食舉烽命丨 he dressed the fresh viands for their entertainment, lighted the fire, and ordered them to drink their fill.

TS'IAO.

Old sounds, ts'io, dzio, t'ok, *and* dok. *In Canton,* ts'iu *and* ts'au; — *in Swatow,* chio *and* ch'io; — *in Amoy,* ch'iau, chiau, *and* siau; — *in Fuhchau,* chiéu *and* ch'iu; — *in Shanghai,* dzio *and* ts'io; — *in Chifu,* ch'iao.

鍫 斛 ˏts'iao From *metal* and *autumn;* the second form is rarely met; occurs used with *sao'* 鐰 iron. A shovel, an implement for raising or moving earth; to dig up, to shovel out.

丨塘 to dig a fish-pond.

大動丨 a crowbar.

丨鍤 a spade.

丨泥 to dig the ground.

一丨泥 a shovel of dirt.

帩 ˏts'iao From *kerchief* and *autumn.* A fillet or wrapper for the head, made of unbleached hemp, formerly worn by women as mourning; one defines it, to sew.

幧 ˏts'iao Like the last and used with it. A turban or fillet; a cloth cap once worn by women or musicians to protect the coiffure.

黲 ˏts'iao Hemp spoiled by excessive rain, and turning black; one says, black spots on the face caused by excessive use of cosmetics; they are called 黑丨子 in Peking.

樵 ˏts'iao From *wood* and *scorched* as the phonetic; used with the next. Wood fit for fuel; billets of wood; to cut fuel, to gather fire-wood; a lookout terrace.

丨夫 or 丨子 a woodman.

丨徑 a goat-path, a bridle-path.

丨薪 or 採丨 to cut fuel.

丨青 a servant, a young lad in attendance, a Ganymede.

譙 ˏ*tsʻiao* From *words* and to *scorch;* occurs interchanged with 燋 to parch, and 誚 to blame, and the last.

To reprehend, to scold; to bawl at and blame with a loud cry; to ridicule, to satirize; a lookout tower or loft where drums are beaten on watch; injured, worn.

丨樓 or 丨門 a kind of gallery over a gate or fort to observe the enemy.

丨車 a high turret for archers set on wheels.

丨責 to scold.

丨邑 an old name of 亳州 in the north of Nganhwui.

予羽丨丨 my pinions are broken and frayed.

憔 顦 ˏ*tsʻiao* The heart distressed and pining; mind depressed and body growing thin.

丨悴 becoming thin and haggard, from sorrow or anxiety.

瞧 ˏ*tsʻiao* From *eye* and *scorched.*

To look at hastily, to glance at; to see.

丨一丨 take a look at it.

丨着 I just saw him.

白丨 to have a look at for nothing.

丨了又丨 looked at again and again.

丨不見 I cannot see it well.

東丨西看 looking about carelessly.

丨見麽 have you seen it?

丨不上 or 丨不起 to hold cheap.

丨一個夥計 to engage an assistant.

拭拭丨 taste and see if you like it.

嶕 ˏ*tsʻiao* Mountainous.

丨嶢 lofty ridges and summits rising one above another.

悄 ʻ*tsʻiao* From *heart* and *similar.*

Sad, disheartened, downcast; secretly, unobserved; urgent; quiet, still.

憂心丨丨 sick at heart; sorrowing in secret.

勞心丨兮 how sad is my lacerated heart! bitter disappointment.

靜丨丨的 still, retired, no bustle.

丨沒聲兒的 nobody's voice is heard, no sound at all.

愀 ʻ*tsʻiao* From *heart* and *autumn.*

To blush, to redden, to change color; very careful.

丨然變色 he blushed and colored up.

原野𡼖丨 the wilderness is desolate and dreary.

煍 ʻ*tsʻiao* To change the color of, as to blacken by smoke, to colly; to cure by smoke.

丨黑 smoked quite black.

火燀丨 the fire has blackened it.

被烟丨之 cured [by hanging] in the smoke, as a ham.

俏 *tsʻiao*ʼ From *man* and *similar;* it is often read ˏ*siao*, like its primitive.

Like, as if, similar; appearing; handsome, beautiful, pretty; excellent.

丨皮 pretty; winsome, attractive, as a gaily dressed child.

賣丨 to show off a pretty face, as by standing in the doorway.

丨佳人 a remarkably handsome woman.

丨步 to stretch one's steps; to lope.

丨然 good looking; as if, like.

丨生 life like, as puppets or images.

俊丨 or 丨麗 fine, beautiful.

生得丨 bright, as the eyes; handsome.

面孔丨 a beautiful face.

誚 *tsʻiao*ʼ Sometimes written ˏ譙 but this form is regarded as better.

To blame, to scold and upbraid; to speak harshly at.

譏丨 to ridicule; to jeer.

丨讓 to reprehend.

丨皮人 to rail at one.

背後丨人 to asperse the absent.

峭 陗 *tsʻiao*ʼ The second form is seldom used.

A steep, abrupt hill, a cliff that obstructs the way or separates places; strict, vehement, quick; dangerous, as a cliff.

丨壁 a sheer precipice.

丨直刻深 he is stern and suffers no trifling.

丨風 a biting wind.

劁 *tsʻiao*ʼ To cut off or in two; to mow or reap.

丨禾 to cut the grain.

丨穫 to harvest grain.

偢 *tsʻiao*ʼ From *man* and *autumn.*

Ill, disabled.

僂丨不仁 palsied, unable to use the joints.

Read ˏ*tsʻiu.* To stare at; to look at, as a gawky does; sad, distressed.

不丨不睬 not to regard, to give the cut direct.

佯丨不睬 to seem as if regardless of.

TSIÉ.

Old sounds, tsia, tsap, tsak, *and* tsat. *In Canton*, tsé *and* tsik ; — *in Swatow*, cha, chó, chió, sek, *and* chia ; — *in Amoy*, chia *and* ché ; — *in Fuhchau*, chié *and* chioh ; — *in Shanghai*, tsia, tsíⁿ, *and* zié ; — *in Chifu*, chié.

嗟 ˏtsié ˏtsüé From *mouth* and to *differ*.
To sigh, to lament; an interjection of regret or sorrow, as when one is at a loss for words to express the feelings; painful recollections.

丨嘆 to sigh.

咨丨太息 how very unfortunate it was!

丨丨臣工 alas, alas, this official life!

猗丨昌兮 behold, how he has prospered!

丨來之食 you too have come to get alms; said to an officer of Tsi who resorted to the alms' kitchen.

謯 ˏtsüé Interchanged with the last.
To sigh, to regret; also, strange words.

罝 ˏtsüé From *net* and *moreover*.
A net for catching hares or rabbits.

姐 ˋtsié From a *woman* and *moreover*; see also ˋ*tsu* 毑 a dam.
Formerly applied in Sz'ch'uen to a mother, and now by the Manchus and Mongols, but by the people only to an elder sister; a miss; saucy, pert.

丨妹 sisters.

大丨 my eldest sister; a maid-servant who is marriageable. (*Cantonese.*)

小丨 a young lady.

令丨 your sister.

家丨 my elder sister.

丨夫 or 丨丈 a sister's husband.

丨丨 sister! used in direct address by a brother; women, ladies.

鴨丨 a dwarf duck; — a stupid fellow. (*Fuhchau.*)

亞丨 a sister; in Canton, also denotes a father's concubine; used by the Manchus when calling their mother.

恃愛肆丨 to dote on without restraint.

借 tsié` From *man* and *formerly*, but the primitive was at first like the next.
To assist; to lend, to borrow; to ask for, to beg of; to pretend, to assume, to make a pretext of; supposing, if, for example; fictitious; to use for illustration; to commend.

丨去 to lend.

丨來 or 挪丨 to borrow.

丨單 or 丨約 a borrower's note.

丨水行舟 to get water to float the boat; — *i. e.* to borrow capital.

推窗丨月 open the window to let in the moon.

相丨 to borrow of each other.

丨如 or 假丨 supposing that.

丨名 to use another's name or card.

丨問 to inquire of civilly.

丨勢爲惡 to use power to do wickedly.

丨意 metaphorically, in a figure.

丨路行 or 丨個光 to get aid or introduction of another; to get on by another's influence; to be recommended by another.

丨刀殺人 borrowing a sword to kill one; — *met.* to injure one through a third person.

不丨 not to be borrowed; — a name for straw sandals.

有丨無償 he never pays back his loans.

藉 tsié` From *plant* and *imperial field*; it is much interchanged with the last, and its two sounds of *tsié* and *tsih* are often interchanged.
A kind of mat to hold offerings; to make a means of, to avail of; to help; to borrow; to lean on for aid; to call in aid.

丨神庇佑 he relied on the help of the gods, — or of God.

慰丨良厚 to sympathize heartily with.

枕丨 pillow and mat; mutual aid; to countenance each other; close together, as animals crowded in a field.

醞丨 accomplished, liberal, polite.

丨口 to repeat other's words; to make a pretext; to lay the blame on others.

丨端生事 to make trouble about nothing.

丨故推辭 to excuse one's self for a trifle; to malinger.

丨呈 beg you to take [this note] for me.

Read *tsih*, In confusion, disordered; to lead by a cord; to tread on; to offer, as tribute.

丨田 fields cultivated for the emperor; a kind of scutage service.

口語丨丨 much talking, jabbering.

丨恩 or 丨福 by your kindness I am well; a polite answer to an inquiry for one's health, meaning I have availed myself of your mercy or happiness, and am well.

狼丨 confused, in disorder.

褯 tsié` Children's clothes; mats in which their clothes are wrapped.

TSʻIÉ.

Old sounds, tsʻia *and* tsʻat. *In Canton,* chʻé ; — *in Swatow,* chʻia *and* chʻé ; — *in Amoy,* chʻiaⁿ ; — *in Fuhchau,* chʻié *and* chü ; — *in Shanghai,* tsʻia ; — *in Chifu,* chʻié.

且 ꜀*tsʻié*. The original form is composed of 几 a *stand,* with two inner strokes for the *legs,* and the lower one for the *rung.*

A table used at sacrifices ; a particle implying doubt, if, or, perhaps, should ; also of induction, or the relation of one quality with another ; a copula implying some opposition or inference ; moreover, and, further, and now, still, also, yet ; thus, so, according to the scope of the sentence ; a pronoun, this.

高而丨寬 high and also broad.

相公丨不要哭 I beg you, Sirs, not to weep.

丨信丨疑 half believing, half doubting.

貧丨賤 poor and so is despised.

暫時丨不回去 for the present he will not return.

丨如 supposing that, if.

富丨貴 rich and also honorable.

姑丨 let it go, it is excusable ; for the moment, it may pass.

我丨問大人 let me now ask your honor.

丨夫 or 今丨 now ; furthermore.

丨然 it is also ; it follows.

丨以文王之德 there is also to be still again considered the virtue of Wăn Wang.

丨說 let us further speak of.

不如子之衣安丨吉兮 my dress is not like your's, Sir, so proper and so lucky !

丨別 temporary separation.

Read ꜀*tsü,* a synonym of 趄. To make no progress ; a final affirmative particle ; many, enough ; names of three ancient worthies, called 唐丨 Tʻang-tsü, an orator of the Ching 鄭 state ; 龍丨 Lung-tsü, a warrior under Chu pa-wang ; and 豫丨 Yü-tsü, a fisherman, about A. D. 420.

其樂只丨 his happiness is extreme.

有萋有丨 how reverent and dignified they looked !

乃見狂丨 but see that fool.

趄 *tsʻié*꜆. To stand awry, as when one leg is longer than the other. Read *chʻé.* Angry ; to drag.

TSIEH.

Old sounds, tsit, tit, dzit, tsip, *and* dzip. *In Canton,* tsit *and* tsip ; — *in Swatow,* chat, chiap, chʻip, *and* choi ; — *in Amoy,* chiat, chiet, chiap, chʻip, *and* kiap ; — *in Fuhchau,* chiek *and* chék ; — *in Shanghai,* tsih *and* dzih ; — *in Chifu,* chié.

節 ꜇*tsié*. The nodes or joints of the bamboo ; a joint, a knot ; a verse, section, or article in a composition or writing ; the capital of a pillar ; a limit of time ; a festival, a term ; a time ; a regular interval ; a patent, credentials ; an emergency ; the period or way of doing a thing ; economy, temperance, moderation ; continence in widows in not remarrying ; to keep in limits, to regulate ; to maintain dignity, to restrain one's passions ; to economize ; a tally or token of authority ; to mark, as time in music ; lofty, as a hill ; a classifier of limbs and affairs ; in epitaphs, pure and self-restrained.

丨令 or 時丨 or 二十四丨氣 24 terms or semi-monthly solar periods, which correspond to the day on which the sun enters the first and fifteenth degree of a zodiacal sign ; when an intercalary month occurs, they are reckoned on as in other years, but the intercalation is made so that only one term shall fall in it ; their names and approximate positions in the foreign year are here given.

TWENTY-FOUR SOLAR TERMS.

Feb. 5	立春	spring begins ;	Sun in Aquarius.	August 7	立秋	autumn begins ;	in Leo.
Feb. 19	雨水	rain water ;	} in Pisces	August 23	處暑	limit of heat ;	} in Virgo.
March 5	驚蟄	excited insects ;		Sept. 8	白露	white dew ;	
March 20	春分	vernal equinox ;	} in Aries.	Sept. 23	秋分	autumnal equinox ;	} in Libra.
April 5	清明	clear bright ;		Oct. 8	寒露	cold dew ;	
April 20	穀雨	grain rains ;	} in Taurus.	Oct. 23	霜降	hoar-frost descends ;	} in Scorpio.
May 5	立夏	summer begins ;		Nov. 7	立冬	winter begins ;	
May 21	小滿	grain fills ;	} in Gemini.	Nov. 22	小雪	little snow ;	} in Sagittarius.
June 6	芒種	grain in ear ;		Dec. 7	大雪	heavy snow ;	
June 21	夏至	summer solstice ;	} in Cancer.	Dec. 22	冬至	winter solstice ;	} in Capricorn.
July 7	小暑	slight heat ;		Jan. 6	小寒	little cold ;	
July 23	大暑	great heat ;	in Leo.	Jan. 21	大寒	severe cold ;	Sun enters Aquarius.

八丨 the solstices, equinoxes, and beginning of the four seasons; they are ascribed to Shinnung.

時丨 time, stated times; the terms.

丨飲食 temperate in one's food.

分兩丨 do it two ways; pay it at two payments.

無丨制 no limits to his expenses; lavish.

守丨 and 失丨 refers to widows marrying or not remarrying; also to maintain dignity or lose it.

丨義 chaste, as a continent widow.

過丨 or 做丨 to keep holiday.

天中丨 the dragon-boat festival.

收丨賬 to collect bills at the four terms in a year.

那時丨 at that time or juncture.

買關丨 to get degrees by bribery.

多生枝丨 full of cares and business.

丨丨高 gradually rising higher, in office or wealth, or as storeys.

丨樂 or 丨湊 to mark the time in music.

丨用 or 丨儉 frugal, within one's means.

丨畧 an abridgement, a summary.

小丨 a little affair, a small matter.

臨大丨而不可奪也 on a great emergency he cannot be forced to desert his principles.

名丨攸關 what is said depreciatory of his fame or character.

事分三丨 the affair is divided into three periods.

卩, 㔾, ˏtsié

An original form of the preceding, and intended to represent a *stamp*, each rank having a different kind; it is the 26th radical of a small group, relating mostly to cups, and not unlike 阝 the contracted form of 邑 a city; when placed at the bottom it is written in the second form.

An officer's seal or signet in olden time, made in two parts that tallied, one being kept at court and the other taken away; it was made of stone, horn and metal; a joint, a knot.

信丨 a check or tally.

癤, ˏtsié

A small sore, a pimple.

瘡丨 a boil, an ulcer.

長丨子 to have a little boil.

火丨子 a rash; prickly heat.

櫛, ˏtsié

A comb with the teeth on one side; to comb the hair.

丨風沐雨 combed by the wind and washed by the rain; *i. e.* the hardships of travel.

巾丨 towel and comb; whence a concubine is called 侍巾丨 the waiter with towel and comb.

楶, ˏtsié

The queen or king-posts put in the truss of a roof, called 斗栱 or 短柱; also the cornice or capital of a pillar.

截, ˏtsié

From 戈 *spear* and 雀 *bird* contracted.

To cut in pieces, to cut off or in two; to saw; to amputate; to intercept, to obstruct; to make secure, as a frontier; to make nice distinctions, to discriminate; a portion of.

丨斷 to divide, as a field; to part off, as a room by partitions.

兩丨褂子 a gown or robe whose waist and skirt are of two colors.

惟丨丨善諞言 but as to those who are only skilled in quibbling discriminations and cunning distinctions.

丨路 road infested and the travel stopped, as by robbers.

丨住 to stop one, as in a road.

丨一段去 cut off a piece.

丨選 to divert an officer from the post he was sent to fill another.

有丨其所 those localities were kept in check, or brought under sway.

接, ˏtsié

From *hand* and *concubine*.

To receive in the hand; to succeed to, to take, to connect; to follow on, as in office, or a son his father; to take in, as a workman does a job; to receive, as reflected light on a surface; to interlock; to meet, to associate with; combined with, united to; contiguous, near; spliced, scarfed; to hasten; quick.

迎丨 to greet; to go out and meet a visitor.

丨陪 to conduct a visitor to his seat.

丨到 to receive; come to hand, as a letter.

丨風 to welcome one back.

丨長一尺 one more foot must be added.

無得丨續 nobody takes it; there is no successor.

丨任 or 丨印 to take another's office or seals.

丨待 to wait on a guest.

丨風酒 a feast to welcome a friend.

丨入 or 丨收 or 丨受 to receive, as a package; to get.

承丨 to take orders — for work.

丨骨科 a surgeon.

水光丨天 the water seems to join the sky.

丨手 to take in hand, as doing the duties of another.

丨不上 cannot follow the guiding mark; can't do the job; nothing to match it; cannot equal it.

椄, ˏtsié

To graft trees; to splice; to rabbet on.

丨杏 to graft apricots.

丨槢 a collar for criminals.

丨木爲柱 to insert or scarf in wood to make a pillar.

緁, ˏtsié

To join; to braid in or splice, as a string.

丨續 to splice together.

䀹, 睫, ˏtsié

From *eye* and *to compress*, or quick like a *treddle*.

The eye-lashes, called 眼丨毛 or eye-lash hairs.

忽忽承丨 in a twinkling, only an instant.

眉丨間 very near to, contiguous, as the eyelashes and eyebrows.

交 丨 to wink or close the eyes so as to rest them.

俯 丨 視己 to drop the eye-lashes to see one's self; self-culture.

Read *chah*, and used for 眨 To wink.

不能勿 丨 he cannot help winking.

婕, ˎtsié Handsome; a female officer in the time of the Han called 丨 妤, whose duties were to direct the ceremonies, and oversee the palace hareem.

倢, ˎtsié Similar to the last, and used with the next.

Convenient, like a cross-cut or a side path; a female officer in the palace.

捷, ˎtsié From *hand* and *treddle;* occurs used for 唼, to gabble.

To hunt, which demands quickness; to gain a victory, to overcome, to win the battle; to announce, as a victory or promotion to a degree; to complete; joyful news; prompt, as a herald; anciently, the weight of twelve 銖, which was nearly half a tael; to talk rapidly.

征夫 丨 丨 the traveler or man of business hastens on his way; the combatants were very agile.

紅旗報 丨 the red flag announced the victory.

連 丨 to attain degrees at successive examinations.

直 丨 or 急 丨 prompt, energetic, nimble, ready at.

一月三 丨 three victories in one month.

丨 徑 to take a short cut; to dispatch an affair anyhow.

快 丨 or 丨 丨 quick and spry; clever and smart.

丨 足者先登 the nimble-footed got up first;—the most active will win.

丨 丨 幡幡 clever and unstable.

浹, ˎtsié ˎkiа From *water* and to *compress;* it is often read *kiah*, and interchanged with *kiah*, 挾 to assist.

Water flowing, or moisture penetrating through a body; imbibed, moistened, dampened; to instil into, as by gradual instruction; a complete turn, a circuit.

丨 辰 a whole day of twelve hours in which the twelve branches make a circuit.

丨 日 a decade of days.

周 丨 to extend benefits or aid everywhere; to help all.

丨 洽 fully imbued with; to treat cordially, as friends; to conciliate; blended in views and feelings; converted to entirely.

楫, 艥, tsiˀ An oar, a paddle, or whatever is used to propel a boat; to row; to avail of something to serve one's purpose.

剡木爲 丨 to hew wood into an oar.

若濟巨川用汝作舟 丨 if I cross this big stream, I shall use you as my boat and oars; said of high officers carrying on the state.

統 丨 群元 a term for the emperor, as the chief oar and head of the flock.

烝徒 丨 之 all the rowers pulling at their oars.

林 丨 a thicket, a bosky grove.

岊, ˎtsié From 山 *hill* and 卩 a *knot* altered.

The peaks in a ridge.

夤緣山嶽之 丨 to ascend a high peak at night,—is like going to a high grandee for a favor; *i. e.* a useless effort.

TS'IEH.

Old sounds, ts'it, tit, *and* shap. *In Canton*, ts'ít, sit, *and* ts'ip;—*in Swatow*, ch'iet *and* ch'iap;—*in Amoy*, ch'iap, chiap, *and* ch'iet;—*in Fuhchau*, ch'iek;—*in Shanghai*, ts'ih;—*in Chifu*, ch'ié.

切, ts'iéˀ ˎts'ié From *knife* and *seven* to give the sound.

To cut, to carve, to mince, to slice; to urge, to press; a particle expressing urgency, earnestness; important, pressing, eager; earnestly; in earnest; the chief or important parts of, a résumé; sincere; to feel, as the pulse.

丨 肉 minced meat.

丨 要 very important.

丨 近 nearly related as kinsfolk.

丨 不可去 you must not go.

丨 愛 a warm love for.

反 丨 or 丨 音 the Chinese way to spell by joining the initial of one sound to the final of another to form a third, which expresses the sound of the given character, as *f*-ang 方 and w-*ăn* 文 make *făn* 分.

關 丨 friendly with, intimate, interested in.

確 丨 不疑 unchangeably fixed, irrevocable.

丨 碎 to cut or hash fine.

丨 實 wholly sincere.

丨 諫 urgent remonstrance.

如 丨 如磋者道學也 as we cut and file [to make things,] so is the work of education; also to plead with a friend.

丨 丨 urgent, immediate.

朋友 丨 丨 偲偲 among friends, [a scholar should be] earnest and urgent.

Read *tsi*ˀ All, every, the whole.

一 丨 the entire lot, altogether.

照顧一 丨 I thank you for buying the whole quantity, or for all your custom.

竊, **窃,** Explained as from 穴 a *cave* with 米 *rice* and a kind of *insect* in it, and 廿 *twenty* above them giving the sound; the contraction is very common.
tsie'

To steal, to pilfer; clandestine, underhand, privately; what one does or thinks one's self, I, my; when used alone means my opinion, I did so, I was there; to offer an opinion or assume a place; unfit for, usurped; tinged with light.

丨聞 I have heard.
丨身 I myself.
偷丨 to steal.
丨取 to take slily.
失丨 stolen.
丨意 or 丨思 my humble opinion.
丨位 to neglect one's own official duties; to assume authority.
丨藍 a light blue.
丨脂 a bird like the Java sparrow, fond of fat.
丨謂 I venture to say.
鼠丨 a petty theft.
丨察 my personal observation.
草丨 to lurk, to lie in wait, as a foot-pad.

妾, *ts'ie'* From 女 *woman* and 辛 a *crime* contracted to 立 *to stand*, explained as denoting a woman who has committed an offense and been put to service; it resembles *,kiang* 姜 a name.

A concubine, handmaid, or secondary wife, like Hagar; one who is taken without betrothal or other legal ceremonies, and recommended only when there is no male issue; a demeaning term by which ladies call themselves; female camp-followers.

立丨 or 買丨 or 置丨 to bring a concubine into the family.
丨氏 a concubine.
丨身 I, your handmaid.
小丨 or 賤丨 my concubine.
愛丨 your concubine.
臣丨逋逃 the sutlers and women of the camp absconded.
處丨 a virgin damsel bought for a concubine.
侍丨 waiting-women.

唼, **啑,** From *mouth* and *handmaid*; they are interchanged with 捷, quick, and *shah*, 歃 to smear the mouth; also read *shah*,
ts'ie'

The noise of geese and ducks when feeding is 丨喋; also applied to water fowls swallowing fish; to talk sharply.

丨佞 malicious speech, slander, backbiting.

沏, *ts'ie'* *,ts'i* The noise of water running; the rippling of a rapid current.

In *Pekingese*. To pour water on tea leaves is 丨茶 (in *Cantonese* 局茶); a rapid mode of making tea in covered cups.

TSIEN.

Old sounds, tsen, tsem, tsin *and* dzen. *In Canton*, tsin, tsim, *and* tsím; — *in Swatow*, chian, chiam, ch^{n}wa, *and* chín; — *in Amoy*, chien, chiam, *and* siam; — *in Fuhchau*, chieng *and* chieng; — *in Shanghai*, tsi^{n} *and* dzi^{n}; — *in Chifu*, chien.

煎 *,tsien* From *fire* and *before*.

To fry in fat or oil; to simmer in water or fat in a pan, until the fluid is evaporated; to dry in a pan; to decoct; to vex, to harass.

丨膏 to express lard.
用油丨 fry it in fat.
慢火丨魚 a slow fire fries fish; *met.* small bets drain the purse.
急丨丨不耐煩的二親 anxious and vexed that my husband's parents cannot bear trouble.
丨茶 to prepare brick-tea, as the Mongols do.
熬丨 to fry in much fat; *met.* harassed, annoyed, grieved.
丨炙 to grill by holding over the fire.
丨藥 to simmer medicines.

Read *tsien'* To cover and candy fruit by dipping it in boiling sugar.

蜜丨菓子 to candy fruit, as apples, crabs, &c.

湔 *,tsien* The name of a river north of the capital of Sz'ch'uen; to sprinkle, to spatter.

丨洗 to cleanse thoroughly.

尖 *,tsien* From *small* above and *great* below; it was originally the same as the next, but the two are now distinguished.

Tapering, pointed; acute, sharp; wedge-like, pyramidal, or conical; needle-like; clever, ingenious; the males of crabs.

頂丨 very smart.
丨利 sharp, quick-witted.
玉指丨丨 a woman's tapering fingers.
扮丨鞋 to act female parts at theaters.
丨指頭 a peculator, one who makes a profit unjustly.
打丨 or 打坐丨 to lunch when traveling; to bait at an inn.
筆丨 the tip of the pencil.
丨嘴縮腮 lantern-jawed, hatchet-faced.
發丨寒 to shudder; a shivering.
丨團蟹莫辨 the male and female of this kind of crab could not be distinguished.

鑯 *,tsien* An iron instrument, sharpened like an awl; to cut or sharpen.

丨崚 a slender high peak, an aiguelle.
丨擔 a beam with sharp iron ferules to stick into faggots.

殲 ˎtsien From *bad* and a *slip*.
To destroy, to exterminate; to pierce, to kill.
一刀丨死他 stabbed him dead at a blow.
草丨人命 recklessly destroyed people.
丨厥渠魁 killed the chiefs themselves.
丨除 or 丨滅 to exterminate.

瀸 ˎtsien Occurs used for the last.
To destroy; a spring appearing and disappearing at intervals; an intermittent fountain; to moisten, to soak.
丨漬 to imbue; to soak in the water.

韉 ˎtsien A saddle-cloth or housings.
丨屜 the part or pad placed under the saddle.

戔 ˎtsien From two *spears*, indicating the appearance or danger of marauders; it occurs used for ˎts'an 殘 cruel.
Small, narrow, cramped; prejudiced, contracted.
束帛丨丨 a miserably poor present.
丨狹 straitened.

箋 牋 ˎtsien From *bamboo* or *slip* and *narrow*; the first form is most used.
A tablet or slip on which to make memoranda; note-paper with pictures or water-lines marked on it; a note, a billet; a document or writing.
丨紙 fancy note-paper.
花丨 flowered billet-paper.
蠟丨 glazed or waxed note-paper.
寫在鸞丨方寸紙 he wrote his note to her on a slip of the phœnix billet.
丨幅 a set of four scrolls on fancy paper.

籛 ˎtsien A man, named 丨鏗 who is said to have lived in the Shang and Cheu dynasties to the age of 767 years, and then vanished.

翦 剪 ˎtsien From *feathers* or *knife* and to *advance*; the first is sometimes distinguished as a verb, and the other as the noun; used with ts'ien⁵ 淺 shallow, and the next.
To cut off smooth, to clip even; to intercept, as an army stops the way; to shear; even, regular, as feathers grow; to reduce; to kill or extirpate; light, as a color in dyeing; shears, scissors.
一把丨 or 丨子 or 丨刀 a pair of scissors or shears.
鉸丨 or 裁衣丨 tailor's shears.
能裁能丨的 she can cut and make dresses.
丨地求和 to give up territory and beg for peace.
佞人之心丨丨者 a flatterer's disposition is to be very plausible;— *i. e.* nice at argument.
丨伐 or 丨去 to trim and prune; to clip.
丨斷後隊 the rear regiment was cut off.

戩 ˎtsien From a *spear* and to *advance*; used with the last.
To carry to the utmost; to exhaust, to finish up; to destroy; to kill; to clip, to shear; entirely.
近佳不丨 may your happiness be unlimited.
俾爾丨穀 [I hope that] you may be granted all excellence; the phrase 丨穀 is often placed before gateways as a good wish.

譾 ˎtsien From to *speak* and *shears*.
Superficial, shallow-pated; unskilled; not expert or deep.
丨陋 stupid, inapt.
才識丨淺 his talents and acquirements are very ordinary.
丨劣 feeble, inefficient.

諓 ˎtsien From 言 *words* and 戔 *small*.
Skillful talk, such as will win over people; to adulate, to flatter; sly, artful insinuations.
悅丨丨之言 to be pleased with subtle flattery.

鬋 ˎtsien The hair hanging in tresses on the sides of a woman's face; to dress or cut the hair.

揃 搿 ˎtsien To take from, to cut off; to tie the hands behind the back; to select; to strike, as the watchman does the hours.
倒丨着兩隻手 to tie both hands together.
丨起手來 tied up his hands.

箭 tsien' From *bamboo* and to *advance*.
An arrow; an archer; a bowshot; to dart out quickly; swift as an arrow; bristling; a slender bamboo fit for arrows; the peduncle of certain orchids.
弓丨 bows and arrows.
漏丨 the gauge in a clepsydra.
火丨 a congreve, or other rocket; a fire-dart.
響丨 a whizzing arrow.
好丨 a good shot.
馬丨 mounted bowmen.
一丨一花 each stem bears one flower.
放冷丨 to shoot at a venture, as in battle.
一丨之地 a bowshot, about 120 ch'ih.
光陰似丨 time flies like an arrow.
暗丨 secret and unpropitious influences which come against a house by a narrow lane opposite the door.
暗丨傷人 to injure one with a secret arrow; to slander.
潮流丨至 the tide comes in like a dart.
丨搭上弓 the arrow is on the string;— you cannot draw back.
丨離弦 the arrow has left the string; the time (or the affair) will soon arrive.
穿耳丨 to wear ear-arrows,— as an exposed thief.

嚵 tsien⁵ Without integrity.
丨嗔 avaricious; grasping and greedy.

薦 tsien' From 艸 *grass* and 廌 a *griffon*, denoting the grass that animals eat; used with the next.

Pasture grounds; to lead animals to pasturage; to introduce, to recommend; to repeat; to set forth, to present; to lay out oblations; to honor or worship without offering flesh; repeatedly.

丨祖 to worship ancestors.

寫丨書 to write a letter of introduction.

自丨 to recommend one's self.

草丨 coarse grass matting; straw wrapping.

丨羞之事 religious acts when spreading out sacrifices.

丨菜 take a little something — with your wine; said to a guest.

殷丨之上帝 [his Majesty] brought his offering to Shangti.

丨賢 to bring forward worthy men.

In *Cantonese*. To wedge in.

丨檯脚 wedge the table-leg.

有丨頭 there is an opening.

丨起 raise it up a little.

荐 tsien' From *grass* and to *preserve*; occurs interchanged with the last.

To continue; to keep or do as before; to repeat, to recur often; again, repeatedly.

丨居 to live a nomad life, moving about for pasturage.

丨饑 repeated famines.

洊 tsien' Water flowing out and reaching to a place; to duplicate or come again.

水丨至 the water flowed in again.

丨瀝 successive; continuously, like dropping water.

瀳 tsien Used with the two preceding.

To double; to come again, to repeat.

丨雷震 the diagram for thunder is repeated in the 51st diagram.

踐 tsien' From *foot* and *small*.

To tread upon, to trample on or over; to step, to walk mincingly; to arrange in place; a row, a range.

丨言 to fullfil one's promise.

丨踏 to tread down or in.

毋許坐丨 people are not allowed to squat or stop here.

不丨跡 to disregard precedent; not to follow another's steps.

丨其位 he occupied his rightful throne.

丨人之約 to go to meet an appointment.

作丨 to deface; to injure, as by treading on or soiling a thing.

丨殘 to smash; to spoil an affair.

東門之栗有丨之屋 by the chestnut trees at the east gate is a row of houses.

櫼 tsien' Wood.

竹箭如丨 the bamboo arrow is like wood.

Read *tsin'* An ancient drum, six Chinese feet six inches long.

賤 tsien' From *property* and *small*.

Light in estimation; mean, low, ignoble, worthless; cheap, low-priced; poor in quality; to disesteem, to depreciate, to undervalue, and hence applied to what belongs to one's self.

丨内 or 丨房 my wife.

丨姓張 my surname is Chang.

丨相 a bad physiognomy, a thief's face.

價錢太丨 the price is very low.

丨骨頭 or 丨壞人 a miserable loafer; a shiftless fellow.

丨人 or 丨坯 worthless baggage; said of or to women.

丨格 my poor talents; inferior abilities.

作丨 he disgraced himself.

丨者 people not in office, the plebs.

素貧丨行乎貧丨 in a poor and low condition [the scholar] acts according to it.

下丨 the degraded classes.

輕丨 to depreciate.

丨貨而貴德 you may disesteem riches but you should honor virtue.

餞 tsien' To present food to one about starting on a journey; to give a farewell dinner to a friend; a parting present of money or food; comfits.

丨行 to entertain one going on a journey or traveling.

匆匆丨別 during the hurry of the farewell dinner, — I can't express all my feelings.

丨禮 presents to a traveler.

飲丨 or 丨酌 to present the stirrup cup.

濺 tsien' From *water* and *low*.

A swift current or race-way where the water dashes up; to spatter against, to dash up, to spurt out; to color, to tint.

丨丨 a rapid flow of water.

激丨 to dash up.

丨了一身水 it spattered me all over.

丨泥 to spatter dirt.

請得以頸血丨大王 I beg that my heart's blood may spurt on your Majesty,—to prove my sincerity; — said by Lin Siang-jü of the Han dynasty

雪浪丨衣 the white surf soaked my dress.

丨色 to make of a uniform dusk color, as a fur.

丨的到處 spattered all over.

栫 tsien' A prop to shore up a rickety or leaning house; a sluice or ditch to lead water through.

犂丨 a plough-beam.

丨一丨屋 prop up the leaning house.

漸 tsien' From *water* and to *cut*.

A short affluent of the Yangtsz' River near Nganking fu in Nganhwui; to find its way in, as water does; to advance by degrees, slowly, stealthily, little by little; to flow; to penetrate; to permeate, to be affected; to cross, as a stream.

丨丨來 came on gradually.

丨次 in order, one after another.

丨冷 it is growing colder.

丨丨之石維其高矣 how grandly those frowning crags rise on high.

丨入聖道 he gradually enters the true or holy path.

循序丨進 to follow on regularly; advancing in order.

涕丨 the tears flowed.

丨丨兒的 very gradually.

丨大 growing larger.

丨卦 the 53d diagram, referring to wind and hills.

Read ˏtsien. To tinge, to imbue with; to soak into; to reach.

丨仁摩義 imbued with benevolence and rectitude.

丨染 to tinge, to moisten with.

丨臺 the stars β δ ι in Lyra.

東丨于海 on the east reaching to the sea, — as Yü's influence.

僭 *tsien'* From *man* and *impious*.

To arrogate to one's self, to usurp; to assume what does not belong to one; usurped, despotic, assuming; dubious, confused; disorder; discord in music.

丨位 to aspire to the throne.

丨妄 out of order, not in place.

丨先講 he speaks before his turn.

丨分 to overstep one's powers or position.

丨稱 to arrogate an improper title or rank.

丨尊 to usurp dignity or honor.

Read *tsin'* Slanderous insinuations; to overstep one's place or rank; to be in error.

亂之初生丨始既涵 disorder begins to spring when slanderous suspicions are received in the mind.

覆謂我丨 on the other hand, he says my words are not true.

TS'IEN.

Old sounds, ts'en, ts'em, ts'in, *and* dzen. *In Canton*, ts'in, ts'ím, *and* sín; — *in Swatow*, chian, ch'ⁿoi, ch'iam, chⁿi, ch'ieng, *and* ch'ian; — *in Amoy*, ch'ian, ch'iam, jan, chian, ch'an, *and* ch'eng; — *in Fuhchau*, ch'ieng; — *in Shanghai*, ts'iⁿ *and* dziⁿ; — *in Chifu*, ch'ien.

千 ˏ*ts'ien* The character is described as composed of 十 *ten* with 人 *man* on top of it, but the idea is obscure; this with ˏ*kan* 干 and ˏ*yü* 于 are very liable to be confounded in poorly printed books.

A thousand; many, an indefinite number; very, earnestly; perfect.

丨萬要作 it must by all means be done.

丨方 versatile.

丨年紅 the bachelor's button.

丨金貴體 your good self; said either to a man or woman.

丨祈回來 I earnestly beg you to return.

丨斤 a wrench to draw nails. (*Cantonese.*)

丨奇百怪 exceedingly strange indeed.

丨一不改 a thousand to one he will not reform.

亦服爾耕十丨維耦 look after the plowing with your ten thousand pairs of plowmen.

打丨 to bend one knee.

老丨 name of the winning card; *met.* an old gambler, a blackleg.

大丨世界 the whole universe.

恭祀丨秋 to congratulate the empress or princess on her birthday.

丨繫 a great embarrassment.

丨山萬水 over thousands of hills and streams; — far off.

仟 ˏ*ts'ien* From *man* and a *thousand* whom he rules; it is now chiefly employed as the compound form of the preceding.

A chiliarch, now usually called 千總; anciently a thousand cash.

扦 搟 ˏ*ts'ien* From *hand* and *thousand*; occurs wrongly used for the next.

To graft into; to stick in or between, to put in.

丨脚 a chiropodist.

丨子手 or 丨手 a tide-waiter, an underling in the customs, in which sense it is recent and local.

丨插果木 to graft fruit trees.

杄 ˏ*ts'ien* A *tree* of a *thousand*; a kind of conifera akin to the fir, (*Abies leptolepsis*), a lofty and straight tree found in Shansi and Hunan, whose fruit is edible; there is much discrepancy in the way of writing the name of this tree; its wood serves for making furniture and dwellings

迁 遷 拪 ˏ*ts'ien* From *to go* and a *thousand* or *great*; some distinguish between these two characters, confining the first to moving things; the second occurs used for ˏ*sien* 仙 a fairy; but the third is nearly obsolete.

To move, to remove, to put elsewhere; to ascend; to be promoted, as in rank; to go up; to transpose, to change, to improve; to be removed; to deport, to dismiss.

丨移 or 丨居 to remove, to go elsewhere to live; to change one's lodgings.

帝丨明德 Shangti caused the removal thither of this intelligent and good — ruler.

丨善改過 to reform and become good.

丨移 or 喬丨 to move, as one's residence; to be sent to another post.

丨延時日 to put off the day, to procrastinate and dawdle.

左丨 to degrade to a lower rank; used in former times when the right was the honorable side.

押丨 to eject, to evict, to turn out a tenant.

丨避 to clear out, to skedaddle, to make off.

阡 ˛*tsʻien* A road or way leading north and south through a grove or forest, as 陌 is the old name for a path leading east and west; a path leading up to the grave; occurs used for the next.

嗟丨陌之將蕪 alas, whichever way I look, there is nothing but weeds and rubbish.

谸 ˛*tsʻien* Used with the last.

A road; green, verdant.

望山谷丨丨 see how fresh and green the valleys are!

芊 ˛*tsʻien* From *grass* and a *thousand*.

Exuberant and vigorous foliage; a tint, like the color of topaz.

茂丨 luxuriant.

草色丨丨 the herbage is very green.

韆 ˛*tsʻien* A swing; to swing to and fro.

鞦丨架 a swinging frame.

僉 ˛*tsʻien* Composed of 集 or 亼 to *assemble* over two 口 *mouths*, and two 人 *men*; *q. d.* all the party consulting.

All, the whole; unanimous; the general opinion; a flail.

丨以爲是 all agreed that it was so, or that it was right.

丨不允 all of them were unwilling.

丨言如一 all were of one opinion.

簽 ˛*tsʻien* From *bamboo* and *all*; interchanged with the next.

Bamboo slips used for drawing lots; a sort of cage; the written response of an oracle; to subscribe; to write one's name; to sign.

丨字 a circular, a subscription paper, a round-robin.

丨子 the slip on a letter or box on which the address is written.

丨名 to write one's name; to subscribe. (*Cantonese.*)

丨題 to subscribe for.

丨舘 to join another in engaging a teacher.

剔牙丨 a tooth-pick.

丨押 to stamp a paper, or a pass; a clerk who stamps papers.

丨書 a kind of paper knife; a family register.

籤 ˛*tsʻien* Used with the preceding.

A slip; a lot on which names or characters are written; a label; a warrant, a ticket having an officer's name on it, and answering to a license to sell a thing, as salt; sharp; to pass through a hole, as a thread.

一筒丨 a cup of the 竹丨 or bamboo slips, such as are seen in temples, or before a judge.

求丨問卜 to divine by drawing lots.

火丨 an urgent warrant.

綠頭丨 wooden slips an inch wide and ten long, with the name and lineage and post of officers written on the green end; used as a card to hand into the emperor at a levee.

丨語 the response of the lot.

丨譜 the book of answers.

丨掣 (or 揸丨 in *Cantonese*) to assign officers to a station by lot.

出丨 or 給丨 to issue a permit or warrant.

抽丨 to draw lots.

訣丨靈極 the response of the lot is very intelligible.

插丨的 one who gives the tallies.

籖 ˛*tsʻien* Often, but erroneously used as the contracted form of the last.

A species of wild garlic or onion.

幟 ˛*tsʻien* To signalize; to make a note of, to record; a slip; a form a model; a label; a title of a book.

簿面題丨 write a label on the cover of the blank-book.

貼丨子 paste on a label.

垂丨 a slip pasted to a book or roll, stating the name and price.

法帖丨 label on copy slips.

劗 ˛*tsʻien* To cut; to stick in.

丨佢喉嚨 pierce his weasand. (*Cantonese.*)

丨猪 to stick a pig.

前 ˛*tsʻien* Originally composed of 舟 a *boat* and 止 to *stop* above it, indicating a progress without effort; the 刀 *knife* was afterwards added; occurs used for ˊ剪 to clip.

To advance, to progress; to come before; to lead forward; to present or hand to one, as a sword; in front of, in presence of; before, in advance; the former; the van; formerly, previously, anciently; at the beginning of a sentence, often answers to when, at the time; to clip; a light black color.

丨後 before, after.

丨日 or 丨兒 the day before yesterday.

丨經 already, before done.

丨月 last month; month before last, months ago.

丨頭 ahead; the first.

眼丨 before one's eyes; now, this very time.

丨來 come here; about coming; this coming before me, as a document; on learning this, as a fact.

在丨 before, then, that time.

丨程難料 it is hard to guess how it will turn out; or what rank he may attain.

上丨走 go on, go ahead.

月初丨後可到 he will be here about the first of the month.

丨人打怕後人 I am suspicious of him, — as I have been once deceived.

雨丨茶 hyson tea.

丨人 a predecessor; progenitors.

丨進 to advance.

御丨 in the Imperial presence, as the body guard or chamberlains; also applied to privy councillors.

做事不丨 not to get on in the world; to make no progress.

儘丨先 to advance one over his equals; to overslaugh.

丨路 such an one, as 業已告知丨路 I have already told Mr. So and So.

丨言戲之耳 those words were rather in joke.

媊 ˛ts'ien — From *woman* and *before*.

The planet Venus is 女丨星, applied to it as the morning star; and regarded as the wife of 太白上公, which is the same planet when it is the evening star.

涎 㳄 ˛ts'ien ˛yen ˛nien — From *water* and *to walk* or *to owe*; it is also read ˛*sien*, and perhaps most frequently ˛*yen*.

Spittle; the watering of the mouth; flowing on and over, as water; succeeding, continuously flowing, as a line.

口丨 the mouth watering.

丨衣 a bib.

龍丨 dragon's blood, a medicine or paint; some think that ambergris is or was denoted by this term.

粘丨 viscid saliva.

吐丨沫 frothing at the mouth.

水丨 or 流丨 or 廸丨 drooling.

漫丨 a puddle made by water overflowing.

蝸丨 mucus of snails.

垂丨已久 my mouth has watered for that a long time; he has been greedy for it.

湎丨 water flowing in a channel.

灊 潛 ˛ts'ien — From *water* and *impious* or *for*; the first is the most usual form.

An ancient name for small branches or feeders of the River Han, and now for one of its headwaters near Hanchung fu; to ford or pass over water; to swim or dive; to hide away, to abscond, to secrete one's self; reserved, reticent; underhand, secretly; carefully, heedful, feeling one's way; a cess-pool.

丨步 careful steps.

丨行水中 to walk under water.

沈丨 reserved, reticent, retiring.

丨師 a cautious general, like Fabius.

丨龍無用 a concealed dragon is of no use; — so is a talented man who is kept in retirement.

丨伏 concealed, lying close.

鱗丨 fish hid in the water.

丨身聽 to secretly listen.

丨修 to reform in retirement.

錢 尒 ˛ts'ien — From *metal* and *narrow*; the composition of the character had reference to some implement of husbandry like a pick or bill-hook.

Copper money, coppers; a mace, the tenth part of a 兩 or tael; the only coin of the Chinese now made, called the *sapeque* or *sapeca* and *cash*, — the last from a Moorish word *caixa*, applied to a tin coin made at Malacca A.D. 1500; it originally weighed a full mace, and was once wages for a day's work; the term *mace* is derived from the Malayan word *mas*, abridged from the Hindu *masha*, a weight of 15 grains troy; a coin of any kind; cash, wealth, property, money.

銅丨 copper coins; a cash.

有丨 wealthy, rich.

丨局 a mint.

守丨奴 a miser.

換丨 or 挑丨 to exchange into cash.

紅丨 red paper slips with 福 cut on them hung on doors at newyear.

飄丨 slips of red and white paper placed on graves.

放路丨 to scatter the 白丨 or the 紙丨 paper cash along the road at a funeral.

爛丨 or 小丨 light, bad cash.

丨粮 revenue in cash.

丨落下 or 丨水低 the rate of exchange is low, or has gone down.

値多少丨 what is the price of it?

有丨使得鬼推磨 a rich man can get the devils to grind his mill.

銀丨 silver coins.

丨眼當枷帶 he looks upon the hole in a cash as big enough for a cangue; — he's a niggard.

丨神擺布 money serves for every thing.

丨可通神 money will move the gods.

幾丨重 how many mace does it weigh?

丨一 one mace, one candareen.

丨債細故 a trifling matter to dispute about, as a case at law.

綠丨 a poetical name for a lichen or liverwort. (*Marchantia.*)

青丨萬選 one good cash can be got out of a myriad; — one honest man found in ten thousand.

Read ˓*ts'ien.* A mattock.

以丨鎛發土 they turn over the ground with their mattocks.

淺 ˓ts'ien — Shallow, as shoal water; superficial, not profound; light, as a pale color; easy, simple, as a character having few strokes; short, as fur or pelage; weak, as spectacles; dripping; to sprinkle or dash water.

不知深丨 unacquainted with the difference of things.

丨則揭 if it is shallow then walk through it.

丨學 easy to learn; unlearned, empirical, not profound.

丨近之徒 a superficial scholar.

丨丨可說 he can talk a little, as an infant.
丨率 vulgar and superficial; airy, pretentious, as a composition of little merit.
丨黃 a light yellow.
甚丨 very simple and easy.
眼丨 impatient, testy; not very respectful.
害人不丨 very disastrous to him; a serious injury.
丨而易ʼ見 its meaning is easy; he is easily understood.
丨毛 short fur.
丨丨 rapid, rattling, as a stream.
深人無丨語 deep thinkers never talk shallow words.
擱丨 to run aground; on shore, grounded.
丨陋 vile, lowlive.

俴ʼ *tsʻienʼ* Used with the preceding.

Thin; beaten out, as a plate of metal; shallow.
丨甲 a sort of armor made of plates to put on war horses; the front boot in a chariot.
小戎丨收 the small war chariot boarded in.

茜ʼ *tsʻienʼ* From *plant* and *west*.

A climbing plant with large ovate leaves, found in Shantung, also named 地血 or earth-blood, and 茅蒐, and other names; its roots, collected in May, were used to dye a reddish or carnation hue, which in the Han dynasty was used only for imperial robes; it was also employed as a tonic medicine and in dysmenorrhœa; it is applied to two or three species of madder, perhaps the *Rubia angustissimus* or *cordifolia*, and the *manjista*.

In *Cantonese* read ˛*sai*. A kind of floating grass 金魚丨 with the linear leaves in whorls, grown in goldfish ponds; a *Hippuris*.
芫丨 caraway.

蒨ʼ *tsʻienʼ* The name of a tree; luxuriant and vigorous herbage; fine grain; used for the last.
茂丨 vigorous vegetation.
丨丨嘉穀 a flourishing and rank field of grain.

倩ʼ *tsʻienʼ* From *man* and *azure*; some read it *tsʻingʼ* wrongly.

A commendatory term applied to personable maidens and comely youth, denoting becoming, good, or fair, that they are like beautiful plants; a pretty, smiling mouth; to serve an occasion, to borrow for a purpose.
巧笑丨兮 what a bewitching smile!
美丨 fine-looking, beautiful.
代丨 for, instead of.
離魂丨女 I am quite entranced by the sight of this pretty woman.
僱丨 to hire, to engage to work.

Read *tsʻingʼ*. A daughter's husband was formerly so called in Shantung.

篟ʼ *tsʻienʼ* A sort of basket or cage; a cross-bow of bamboo; fine, delicate bamboos

栫ʼ *tsʻienʼ* A fence or wattle of thorny plants; a palisade across a canal or water-course; a fishing-weir; to fence in or hedge around.

塹ʼ 壍ʼ *tsʻienʼ* The moat or fosse around a town; a ditch to lead water in irrigation; to dig out.
坑丨 a gutter.
掘丨 to dig a sluice.
深丨而守 to guard the place by a deep fosse.

槧ʼ *tsʻienʼ* Boards for cutting inscriptions or books on; tablets for memoranda.
簡丨 a written tablet.
牘丨 blocks for writing or printing on.

輤ʼ *tsʻienʼ* A pall to cover a hearse, now called 棺罩 or coffin cover; that of a prince was of carpeting, an officer's of cloth, and a scholar's of matting; the adornments of a hearse.

綪ʼ *tsʻienʼ* From *silk* and *dark*; also read ˛*tsăng* and ˛*tsʻing*.

A dark reddish color dyed by the Chinese madder (*Rubia*) on silk; a light azure color; to tighten a string that it will not loosen.
丨茷旃旌 banners of a dark red.

TSIH.

Old sounds, tsik, dzik, dzít, dzíp, *and* tsíp. *In Canton*, tsik, tsăt, tsek, tsap, tsʻăp, *and* chíp; — *in Swatow*, chít, chiat, chíp, chek, *and* chia; — *in Amoy*, chít, chek, chíp, *and* siok; — *in Fuhchau*, chík, chék *and* chiéh; — *in Shanghai*, tsih *and* dzih; — *in Chifu*, chi.

疒, ˛*nih* The original form is supposed to resemble a *sick man* propped up in his bed; it is the 104th radical of a group of characters relating to diseases; also read ˛*chwang*.

Disease which makes one take to his bed.

疾, ˛*tsi* From *sickness* and *dart*, intimating the sudden quickness with which disease strikes men; used with the next.

Sickness, disorder, illness; a natural defect; calamities, afflictions; urgent, pressing, prompt; hasty, touchy; infelicitous, unlucky, injurious; to be angry; to envy, to hate or dislike.
丨病 ailments, diseases.
問丨 to go and inquire after an invalid's health.

丨忙 testy, quick, irritable.

並無丨言 still he never spoke impatiently.

染丨 infected by, as malaria.

丨速 in haste, quickly; fast as possible.

丨人 a leper. (*Cantonese.*)

則丨視其長上 the people therefore looked angrily at their superiors.

厥丨弗瘳 he had not recovered from his illness.

丨雷 a crashing clap of thunder.

無言不丨 I never speak but I get hatred.

患丨 to be taken sick.

丨威 impetuous and haughty in temper.

急丨 hurried, urgent.

丨便回來 then immediately come back.

嫉, ˛tsi From *woman* and *sickness*. Envy, jealousy; to dislike, as a competitor; to be grieved at another's prosperity.

丨賢 to envy the good.

同藝者相丨 people of the same craft are usually envious.

丨妬 jealousy.

深懷憤丨 she harbors the most rancorous envy.

丨忌 to repulse one from dislike.

蒺, ˛tsi Gorse, furze.

丨藜 the *Tribulus terrestris* or caltrops, found in Chihli; it is fed to camels, and the seeds are employed in diseases of the eye and coughs.

鉄丨藜 iron caltrops used in war

據于丨藜 like grasping a sprig of caltrops; *met.* the task is very hard to do.

黃丨藜 probably a kind of gorse or furze with yellow flowers.

卽, ˛tsi From 卩 a *seal* and 皀 a sort of *spoon* to take up grain.

Eating, or just about to eat; to go, to approach; an *adverb* of time, now, soon, presently, forthwith, then, when; perhaps; as to, even; this; that is, or, alias, otherwise; the snuff of a candle; to fill.

丨丨充實 an abundance, too much, crammed full.

丨刻 or 立丨 or 丨時 forthwith, presently, instantly, now.

丨事詩 ballads for the times.

丨然 instanter.

丨日 to-day; the same day.

丨是 or 丨係 just that, it is so; the same as.

丨今 just now, meanwhile.

丨使間 supposing that.

丨丨回來 come back immediately.

丨現銀 money on the nail.

丨或 or 丨如 if, supposing.

今我丨命于元龜 I will now seek orders from the great tortoise.

無他丨 no other than

非此丨彼 if it be not this, then it is that.

飛丨 urgently, as speedily as possible.

丨位 to ascend the throne.

丨去丨來 go and come back right away.

年晚在丨 newyear's day comes soon.

大難臨丨 a terrible calamity is very near.

丨速 quickly; hasten him.

苗頑弗丨工 these Miao still refuse to do their work or duty.

胡爲我作不丨我謀 why does he make us act without coming to consult us?

堲, ˛tsi To make bricks of earth and line a grave with them; used for the last, the snuff of a candle; to dislike, to have a horror of; to snuff out.

右手折丨 [hold the candle in the left hand,] and snuff it with the right.

丨除暴行 he utterly extirpated them by his cruelty.

喞, ˛tsi The hum of insects; the noise of a crowd.

丨丨徐來 the sound gradually increases, as of a cicada.

啾丨甚久 groaning a long time.

丨丨復丨丨木蘭當戶織 without the door sat Muhlan, her busy shuttle humming its quick sound.

丨噥 low hum, as people talking.

丨丨呱呱 quick gabble; an earnest talk, which the speakers do not want others to overhear.

楖, ˛tsi Name of a tree, allied to the ash called 丨栗, used to make staffs for old men.

丨人 a workman who makes arrows, or carves gems.

病憐丨栗隨身慣 the weak old man feels kind towards his staff, which he takes with him everywhere.

蝍, ˛tsi The centipede 丨蛆, which is fabled to eat snakes.

丨[illegible] loopers, geometrical worms.

倉丨 a species of beetle.

鯽, ˛tsi A common fish belonging to the carp family.

丨[illegible]魚 a bream (*Cyprinus gibelioides*) with a long dorsal.

縮骨丨 the blunt-headed bream. (*Cyprinus abbreviatus.*)

金丨 the red tailed bream. (*Cyprinus auratus.*)

海丨 a species of perch, 20 inches long, found in the gulf of Chihli.

鮮丨銀絲膾 fresh bream and sliced pork dumplings; *met.* fine eating.

[illegible], ˛tsi The noise of insects; but more commonly the squeak of mice.

老鼠丨的一聲竄入穴 the rat gave one squeak and ran into his hole.

氵匕, ˛tsi From *water* and *spoon*.

Water issuing secretly; ot sprinkle.

集, 亼, ˏtsi } From *birds* on a *tree;* an old form repeats the 隹 thrice; the contracted form of 人 *men* coming into 一 *one* place is common; used with the next, and occurs interchanged with *tsah*, 雜 mixed.

To flock together, as birds; to gather, as clouds; to assemble, to collect; to settle; collected; accomplished; to bring together, to convene; to succeed, to be accomplished; to set down quietly; to mix properly, to blend; to go directly to the mark, to reach at once; to compile, to make a collection, as of writings; a miscellany, ana; a market or fair.

齊 丨 to have a full meeting; all came together.

文 丨 a collection of essays.

我 行 旣 丨 when our expedition was ended, — we said we should return.

一 丨 one division of a book, what is under one head.

終 日 來 丨 many affairs and people came upon me all day.

修 丨 to compile and arrange papers or writings.

丨 會 to convene; to assemble.

安 丨 peacefully gathering, as people in their villages.

丨 成 to collect into a whole.

丨 州 an old name of Shun-king fu in the south of Sz'ch'uen.

赶 丨 to go to the fair.

輯, ˏtsi From *carriage* and a *whisper;* occurs used for the last, and 楫, an oar, and *yih*, 揖 to bow.

To connect and arrange the parts of a carriage, to put every part in its proper place; union, concord; to make everything agreeable; to speak gently and cordially; to look pleasantly; to collect, to assemble; to compile.

丨 要 to bring together the most important; to arrange the best parts, as of writings.

和 丨 in accord; to pacify and arrange.

寧 丨 peaceful.

辭 之 丨 矣 民 之 洽 矣 if your words were affable, the people would become united.

修 丨 隣 邦 to urge neighboring states to be at peace.

丨 斂 to gather.

丨 柔 爾 顏 let your countenance be mild.

潗, ˏtsi A fountain gently bubbling up; the noise of boiling or bubbling.

寂, 宗, ˏtsi } From *cover* and *younger uncle;* the second form is unusual.

Still, silent, as an uninhabited house; quiet, unmoved, like a recluse; lonesome, solitary.

丨 歷 alone, retired, unemployed.

丨 靜 silent, as if dead; nobody to disturb; the Budhists use it for the hermits (*aranyakah*) or strict recluses, of whom there are three classes.

丨 無 人 聲 not a voice heard in the stillness.

丨 然 不 動 sitting still, as a meditative priest; quite inactive.

丨 丨 quiet, as in a settled melancholy; immovable.

啾, ˏtsi Used with the preceding.

Silent, quiet.

念 經 丨 聲 to mumble prayers, as priests do.

空 丨 solitude and silence.

Read *chuh*, To sigh and lament.

丨 丨 sounds of sorrow and grief.

迹, 跡, 蹟, ˏtsi } From to *go* or *foot* and *also;* the last two are common.

A trace, a foot-mark; vestiges, effects, consequences; the results of previous conduct; to trace out, to follow up, as in search for results; examples or words of former great men.

無 形 丨 no clue of him.

形 丨 可 疑 a suspicious appearance or act.

神 丨 or 異 丨 evidences of divine or supernatural power; miracles.

萬 丨 自 身 to pursue one's own course steadily.

足 丨 a footstep; a track.

並 無 蹤 丨 I can find out nothing about him.

痕 丨 a streak, a stain; a grudge, bad feelings left in the mind.

陳 丨 old effects of; examples, influences handed down.

功 丨 insignia of merit.

風 丨 effects of wind; influence of usages.

深 丨 其 道 examine into its nature deeply.

勝 丨 overpowering energy, as of a god.

心 丨 sentiments.

王 丨 royal deeds, or fortunes.

耤, ˏtsi From *plow* and *ancient;* used as another form of *tsié*, 藉 to borrow.

The emperor's field of a thousand *meu*, called the 帝 丨 田 was anciently that on which he began the plowing himself in order to encourage the people; the crops were used in offerings.

藏 帝 丨 於 神 倉 store the crops from the crown lands in the sacred granary.

籍, ˏtsi From *bamboo* and *field;* interchanged with the preceding, and with *tsié*, 藉 to borrow.

A book for records; a list, a register of the people; the place for registration, one's original family seat or village; to enrol.

祖 丨 是 在 his forefathers were of this place.

書 丨 records; books.

狠 丨 violent, savage; destructive.

民 丨 or 戶 丨 or 丨 貫 census; the register of the people; returns of the population.

回 丨 to return to one's birthplace or family seat.

丨 諸 路 兵 he enrolled all the circuits for military service.

原 丨 the original family seat.

無丨遊民 vagrants, gypseys, people that have no home.

在丨養痾 he is at his own village recruiting his health.

丨丨 the sound of much talking.

踖, ꜀tsi From *foot* and *ancient*.

To stride; to step over a thing; to walk reverently, to step formally, with a measured pace.

毋丨席 don't step on the mat; said of those days when chairs were not used.

踧丨如也 thus, go slowly and precisely.

執爨丨丨 they attended to the furnace with dignity or alacrity.

脊, ꜀tsi ꜂tsi The original form delineates the *vertebræ* above 肉 *flesh*, still imperfectly figured in its present form; in common books this character often resembles ꜀*ch'un* 春 the spring.

The spine, the backbone; the back; the ridge of a roof, or on a plant; a sierra, a ridge; the fur on the back of an animal; convergent, as the ribs; a bone; a principle.

背丨骨 or 丨骨 or 丨梁骨 the backbone; the vertebræ.

丨髓 the marrow in bones.

梁丨 the timber in the roof-tree.

山丨 a ridge of hills.

無骨丨 no dependence can be placed on him.

有倫有丨 I have right and reason for it.

窮斷丨梁筋 so poor that his backbone is broken and his muscles twisted, — for want of food.

死丨 dead men's bones.

瘠, ꜀tsi From *disease* and the *spine* as the phonetic.

Lean as a stick, emaciated, reduced to mere bones; poor, as barren land; to make lean; to impoverish; to retrench, to restrict.

損丨 died from his sickness; *lit.* thrown off his leanness.

丨土 meager land.

何必丨人以肥己 why impoverish another to enrich one's self?

丨瘦 thin, lank.

丨馬 a lean horse.

塉, ꜀tsi Poor land, such as is on the tops of ridges and hills; a low ridge.

丨田 lean, unproductive land.

崗丨 the ridge of hills.

蹐, ꜀tsi A short and careful pace; a mincing walk; to step here and there.

跼丨不安 uneasy, oppressed, restrained.

足丨不前 he does not advance.

謂地蓋厚不敢不丨 though we say the earth is so thick, one cannot but tread on it carefully.

鶺, ꜀tsi The *house-top bird*, perhaps alluding to its habits.

A bird, the 丨鴒 or pied wagtail (*Motacilla luzoniensis*), common in southern China; it has a mottled neck, and is called 雪姑 the snow-lady, and sometimes 錢母 or money-mother; it 飛鳴行搖 sings when it flies, and wags when it walks.

丨鴒在原 the wagtail is on the ridge; — a simile for brothers in trouble.

聻, **魙**, ꜀tsi From *ear* or *demon* and *gradual*; they are also read *tsien'*

The death of the ghost of a man; these characters with others are pasted over doors in times of pestilence, under the notion that the devil of this name will drive off sickness.

襀, ꜀tsi The plait or folds of a woman's skirt; the plait in a frill.

勣, ꜀tsi From *strength* and *responsible*; it is nearly synonymous with the next.

Merit, praiseworthy acts; conduct worthy of reward.

績, ꜀tsi From *silk* and *responsible*.

To spin thread, especially of hemp; to splice threads; merit from doing laudable works; duties, services; the place where they are done; an affair; to complete an undertaking; to be achieved; to be operated on; finished; to join or piece.

丨蔴 to twist hemp.

紡丨 to spin and join thread.

丨續 to tie on.

勞丨 meritorious works.

三載考丨 [Yao] triennially examined into their acts.

庶丨咸熙 the worthy deeds of all were quite complete.

敗丨 utterly routed.

積, ꜀tsi To gather, as to store up grain; to hoard, to accumulate, — and spoken chiefly of things; to pile upon, to add, to increase; increasingly.

發丨 to accomplish, to get rich.

丨福 much happiness derived from good works of supererogation, — applauded by the Budhists.

丨年 during many years, for a long time.

丨財 to heap up riches.

丨蓄 or 丨儲 to lay by, to hoard, to amass.

日丨月累 days and months multiply.

禍因惡丨 his misfortunes have been caused by his evil deeds.

氷丨埋 water standing in puddles. (*Cantonese.*)

堆丨 to pile up rubbish.

Read *tsz'* Stores of grain; to pile it in stacks on the floor.

有實其丨 [the reapers] pile up their stacks.

穧, ꜀tsi Also read *tsz'*

Grain piled up on the floor for thrashing, in which sense it is like the last, and is sometimes used with 穡 to reap.

丨之秩秩 the piles of grain are very great and numerous.

磧, ˏ*tsi* From *stone* and *responsible.*
Rocks under water, half-tide rocks; stony places that check the current, were once so called in Honan.
砂 | the desert of Gobi.

畟, ˏ*tsi* From 田 *field* and 人 *man,* with 夂 *to go in.*
A share or plough used at the commencement of spring.
| | 良耜 well sharpened are the good shares.
瓊 | an old local name for dice in the south of Chihli.

Read ˏ*ni.* To point out; used by Budhists as a final particle in writing Sanscrit words.

[illegible], ˏ*tsi* Small, diminutive.
| 民之勞 the toil and labors of the poor people.

稷, ˏ*tsi* Panicled millet (*Panicum miliaceum*), also called 穄, one of the five grains; quick.
| 子 or 黍 | these two are merely varieties of the same species, whose seeds differ in size and colors; it is rather glutinous.

后 | or Prince Tsih was Shun's minister of Agriculture, and the high progenitor of the Cheu emperors; he was made the god of Agriculture.
后 | 教民稼穡 the gods taught people sowing and reaping.
社 | 之臣 a noble statesman, the prop of the realm.
是日下 | the day will soon be done.
| 山 a district in the southwest of Shansi in Kiang cheu on the River Făn.
既齊既 | all ready quickly.

TSʻIH.

Old sounds, tsʻih, tsʻik, tsʻit, *and* tsip. *In Canton,* tsʻik, tsʻat, *and* tsʻăp; — *in Swatow,* chʻèt, chít, *and* chíp; — *in Amoy,* chʻit, chʻíp, *and* chʻek; — *in Fuhchau,* chʻék *and* chók; — *in Shanghai,* tsʻih; — *in Chifu,* chʻi.

戚, ˏ*tsʻi* Composed of 戉 a *hatchet* and 尗 (or 叔) *uncle;* it is interchanged with the next.
A sort of pole-ax; to pity, to commisserate; to cause pity, to distress; mournful, sorry; near, related to, of kin; attached to; angry, vexed, roused; deformed, as a hunchback.
親 | one's relatives not of the same surname.
憂 | 相關 to feel for other's woes, mutually afflicted.
得此 | 施 she has only got this hunchback.
小人長 | | the mean man is always dejected.
| | 兄弟 uterine brothers.
干戈 | 揚 with shields and spears and axes displayed,— he marched out.
未可以 | 我先王 you may not so grieve our former kings.
哀 | sorry, mourning for.

慼, 慽, ˏ*tsʻi* Used for the last.
Grief, sorrow; to be afflicted; sympathizingly; sad, pained, mournful.
自貽伊 | I have involved him in sorrow.

墄, ˏ*tsʻi* The steps of an ascent or stairway, otherwise called 階 | and 階齒 teeth of the stairs.
左 | 右平 on the left a stairway, and a flat place on the right.

鏚, ˏ*tsʻi* A kind of pole-ax, used with spears in war; an ornamental sort of halberd carried in processions.

七, 柒, ˏ*tsʻi* The original form is composed of 一 *one* crossing 中 *middle* deflected; *q.d.* one of the odd numbers; the second character is the complex form used in bills, and like the next.
The number seven.
第 | the seventh.
十 | seventeen.
| 十 seventy.
| 零八落 or 亂 | 八蹧 near destruction, devastated; at sixes and sevens; ruined.
瞎 | 瞎八 to blindly arrange things, to misplace all around.
| 手八脚 too many at it; *met.* too many cooks spoil the broth.
| 巧 or | 夕 the seventh evening of the seventh moon; — a festival for women.

理 | or 做 | to attend to the funeral rites of each seventh day till the 49th day, after which the burial takes place.
| 絕 a verse of four lines pentameters; and | 律 a verse of eight lines.
| 嘴八舌 confused or incoherent talking; a gabble.
| 巧圖 the Chinese puzzle of seven pieces, the tangram.

漆, 桼, 㯃, ˏ*tsʻi* From *water* appearing *to issue* from a *tree;* the second and third forms especially denote the lacker tree, now superseded by the first.
The varnish or lacker tree, (*Rhus vernicifera* or *Vernix vernicia,*) from which the Chinese collect sap for lacker ware; viscid or resinous juices used in varnishing; to paint, to varnish; black, as lacker; adhesive; friendly, doating on; the first form also means a small branch of the River Wéi in Shensi, which flows by Tʻung-kwan, and joins the Tsü before entering the latter; and an ancient city in that region.
油 | paint, varnish; to paint.
油 | 匠 a house-painter.

丨樹 the varnish tree; it is applied to other oil-producing trees, as the *Croton* and *Elæococca.*

雕丨器 Suchau red carved lacker.

火丨 sealing-wax.

火丨片 wafers.

丨食 or 丨咬人 poisoned with lacker.

上丨 to paint.

金丨器 gilded lacker-ware.

丨精 clear varnish.

情如膠丨 his disposition is very affectionate.

丨車 a black carriage.

Read *tsieh*, A staid, composed mien is 丨丨; said of persons engaged in performing ceremonies.

咠, ˏtsʻi From *mouth* over the *ear*.
To whisper in the ear; to asperse, to blame one; the sound of the voice.

無丨丨以悅聽 do not be fond of hearing slander.

緝, ˏtsʻi To twist a cord; to join, to continue, to come after, to succeed; to pursue after, to be on the search for in order to arrest; continuous, successive; occurs used for the last.

丨獲 to pursue and seize.

丨私 to watch smugglers.

丨私船 revenue-cutters.

丨着 he has been caught.

查丨 on the search.

頭丨 a jib set under a junk's bow.

丨丨翩翩謀欲譖人 babbling and talking around, planning how to slander people.

丨熙 to continue the reputation of; lasting brightness.

巡丨 to get on the trail of.

In *Pekingese.* To hem; to sew together; a seam, a hem.

密密的丨 a close-stitched seam.

丨縫子 to sew a seam.

丨邊 to hem or baste.

戢, ˏtsʻi From *spear* and *whisper*.
To store up weapons, to put them back in an arsenal; to gather in; to fold, as wings; to collect one's self; to lay aside, as arms in time of peace; to surcease.

載丨干戈 to lay by arms,—and keep the peace.

兵猶火也弗丨將自焚 war is like fire, those who do not cease from it burn themselves; like Matt. 26: 52.

丨歛 to gather in, to guard.

丨翼 to fold the wings.

較前歛丨 these are fewer in comparison with the former.

In *Cantonese.* To make even or smooth; to press together.

踹到實丨 tread it down solidly or close.

剷丨丨 trim it off evenly, as the edges of sheets.

濈, ˏtsʻi Water rapidly flowing out; rapid; cordial, harmonious, agreeing.

其角丨丨 his horns are harmless as a sheep's.

丨然鳧沒 how quickly the mallard was out of sight!

葺, ˏtsʻi To repair, to put in order; to thatch, to cover; a sort of spinous herb.

丨補 to rebuild, as a wall.

丨累 overlapping, as scales.

丨牆 to put up a wall.

修丨花圃 to fence in and prepare a garden plat.

丨覆 to cover or roof in.

丨理舊址 to repair the old foundations.

蕺, ˏtsʻi From *plant* and *to store* up.
A kind of *Iridæ* growing in damp places in Chehkiang and Hunan, whose leaf is likened to the buckwheat; it preserves fish, and has a sharpish taste.

丨菜 the *Houttuynia cordata*, whose leaves are sometimes eaten.

丨山 a peak in Chehkiang, where this plant is found.

霵, ˏtsʻi From *rain* and *to store*.
The noise of a driving rain; a dash of hard rain; applied to the din and clangor of musical instruments.

TSIN.

Old sounds, tsín, tsím, *and* dzin. *In Canton,* tsun, tsăn, *and* tsʻám; — *in Swatow,* chín *and* chím; — *in Amoy,* chín, chím, *and* sín; — *in Fuhchau,* chíng *and* chéng; — *in Shanghai,* tsing *and* dzing; — *in Chifu,* chin.

津, ˏtsing From *water* and *accordant*.
A ford, a ferry; a place where streams meet; a narrows; a mart where boats stop; to moisten, to imbue, to soften by soaking; saliva; the sap of trees.

迷丨 to miss the fording-place.

關丨 guard-houses or *douanes* at fords.

問丨 to ask the way; *met.* to seek a wife.

丨口 a ferry.

生丨 to produce 丨液 saliva, as acids do.

丨漏 the water oozes in.

丨梁 a bridge over the ford.

問丨過來人 to get hints from other's experience.

丨丨 running over, full and more; as in 丨丨有味 I relish [the study] more and more.

武陵丨 the path to elysium or fairy land.

丨 貼 a *douceur* or something over the regular pay; batta.

天 丨 the port of Tientsin, for which the second character alone is much used in the vicinity; the star γ in Cygnus.

濅 ˏtsin The ancient name of a river in the north of Kiangsu; a place where waters collect, as in a marsh; gradually, increasingly.

丨 以 成 俗 it gradually became a fixed habit.

祲 ˏtsin To influence, to act on; a malign halo around the sun; abundant, full.

氛 丨 noxious, malarious.

陰 陽 相 丨 the powers of nature act and reäct on each other.

妖 丨 an ominous, pernicious influence.

璡 ˏtsin A stone resembling jade; a man's name.

儘 ˋtsin From *man* and *exhausted*; it is often interchanged with the next.

To finish entirely; completely, easily; all; the utmost degree.

丨 夠 quite enough.

丨 可 以 行 it can easily be done.

丨 自 不 來 he has not been here for a long time, — or at all.

丨 下 得 去 it can be easily put in (or go down).

丨 東 the farthest east.

丨 先 拔 補 first on the list for promotion.

丨 敎 蜂 蝶 忙 the bees and butterflies flit about as they please.

盡 尽 tsin' From *dish* and *remains of a fire or cinders*; the contracted form is common; used with the next in some senses.

An empty vessel, as a brazier from which everything is burned out; to exhaust, to use all; to indulge, as excessive grief; a work ended, a quantity finished; ended, as life; the last, as the twelfth moon; finished, empty; achieved; nothing left; all, fully, entirely; to do to the utmost, with the whole energy; the uttermost, extremely.

已 丨 all gone, used up.

丨 我 心 with my whole heart.

有 餘 不 丨 there is still a littl left.

命 丨 his life is ended, his span is run.

家 財 散 丨 his patrimony is all dissipated.

殺 個 丨 絕 he slew them all.

月 丨 給 你 I'll pay you at the month's end.

感 謝 不 丨 I cannot express all my thanks.

丨 人 事 to fulfill the duties of life.

丨 職 to perform well one's official duties.

自 丨 to put an end to one's self.

書 不 丨 言 言 不 丨 意 books do not exhaust words, nor words ideas; — 不 丨 at the end of a note, intimates that the writer has not said all he would or ought.

無 窮 丨 inexhaustible, as reason.

丨 節 died a martyr to chastity.

丨 係 水 漬 all are soaked through.

大 丨 a moon of thirty days.

丨 情 to indulge the feelings, as in acts of kindness.

往 丨 天 涯 to go to the ends of the earth.

丨 頭 at the very end, reached the limit.

一 網 打 丨 took them all at one haul.

丨 在 不 言 中 the idea is not clearly said, — but it is hinted at in the words.

丨 貪 玩 he wishes and thinks of nothing but play.

燼 tsin' From *fire* and *exhausted*.

Ashes, embers, snuff; a residuum after combustion; a quenched brand; the relics, the remnant, as of a conquered people; the remains of.

餘 丨 what is left after the fire.

化 爲 灰 丨 all is turned to ashes.

民 丨 the remnant of the population.

燈 丨 snuff of a lamp.

藎 tsin' Like the preceding.

A plant whose roots afford a yellow dye; a residue; to promote to a high post, as a faithful minister who is 丨 臣 or an officer placed near his sovereign; sincere, attached to.

忠 丨 a loyal officer.

進 思 丨 忠 退 思 補 過 when in office he proved his fidelity, and when he retired to private life he reformed his ways.

濜 tsin' A rapid flow of water; a branch of the River Han in Hupeh, and of a small stream in the south of Shensi; used for ˏ津 saliva.

丨 湏 flowing swiftly.

贐 賮 tsin' Presents given to friends when going on a journey, or exchanged as tokens of remembrance.

丨 儀 parting gifts.

納 丨 to receive presents.

餽 丨 to send some delicacies to a friend going away.

浸 tsin' From *water* and *to sweep* by *hand*.

To soak through, to penetrate; to steep in, to wet, to macerate, to immerse; laid under water, as an inundated field; it has even been used by some for Christian baptism; wet, drenched, imbued with; gently, gradually.

丨 死 drowned.

丨 糖 soaked in syrup.

丨 潤 to imbue with, to bias, to prejudice against.

不 丨 透 not soaked through.

水 丨 街 the water overflowed the street.

汗 丨 紅 顏 the perspiration rolled down her face.

丨 了 幾 次 soaked several times.

丨晝 broad day.

丨一丨透 sprinkle it till it is wet through.

丨在酒 steeped in spirits.

丨濕 wet it, as by immersion.

其說丨淫 his words are insidious and seductive.

In *Cantonese.* A coat, as of paint; a thickness, a skin; callous skin, which can peel off.

漆三丨 varnished it three times.

一丨皮 one envelope, one cover.

縉 *tsin'* From *silk* and to *advance.*

A sort of light red or carnation silk; to wrap or gird, as with a sash.

丨紳 red girdles denote the gentry and officials, whose names are in the 丨紳錄 or 丨紳全書 or 文武丨紳 the government red book.

搢 *tsin'* Interchanged with the last and the next, and also used for *tsien'* 薦 to introduce.

To stick into; to insert, as in a socket; to shake; to strike the watches; to rescue.

丨插 to stick into.

丨笏 to hold the official tablet.

德聲丨鐸 the fame of virtue strikes the bell; *i. e.* animates men.

晋 晉 *tsin'* From 日 *sun* and a contraction of 至 *reaching* to doubled; the second form is common, and not to be confounded with *'pu* 普; it is interchanged with the next.

To increase, as young plants when the sun comes to them; to grow, to flourish; name of the 35th diagram, composed of fire and earth, and referring to the abundance of nature; to stick into; to attach to, as about the person; a drum; to curb a horse; to go to or enter.

丨爵 take another glass; said to a guest.

上丨 to rise in office.

丨謁 to have a personal interview, to visit.

如丨如齊 [their fraternal regard is] like that of the states of Tsin and Tsi.

丨朝 a dynasty which lasted from A. D. 265 to 317, and its successor the 東丨 which continued the name till A. D. 419, in all 154 years.

丨國 a powerful feudal kingdom, in its widest limits occupying the southern half of Shansi and northwest of Honan along the Yellow River; it was conferred on 唐叔虞 a brother of 成王 of Cheu, B. C. 1107, and endured under 26 rulers from 737 till 436, when it was partitioned by Han, Wei, and Cheu; it had several capitals, and is often still used for Shansi province.

進 *tsin'* From to *go* and *birds*, but the primitive is by some regarded as a contraction of *ˏlin* 躙 to tread.

To advance, to enter; to go in, up, or on; to bring in or forward; to exert one's self; to adopt, as a religion; to promote; to make progress in; to come near; a promotion, an advance; a division of a hong or house, in which each has its own entrance.

丨貢香料 the very best sorts of incense; *i. e.* such as are brought as tribute or revenue.

丨達 to be advanced; to promote.

丨退兩難 embarrassed how to act; to advance or retreat is equally difficult.

丨身之計 a scheme to advance one's self.

前丨 to make progress.

沒長丨 he does not improve, he makes no progress.

三揖而丨 he bowed thrice and began to speak.

丨門 come in; beginning to learn as a craft.

丨教 to enter the sect.

中'丨士 to become a *tsinsz'* or graduate of the third degree; these are permitted to erect tablets over their doors; the first on the tripos writes 會元, the next seventeen on the list can write 會魁 chief of the Concours; and the rest merely 丨士 or doctors of Civil Law.

初丨步 to take the first step; *i. e.* to become a *siuts'ai.*

引丨 to bring to notice, to bring forward.

丨香 to worship with a great parade, to go to a temple in style.

先丨 and 後丨 ancients and moderns.

幾丨深 or 幾多丨深 how many divisions or houses is it deep? (*Cantonese.*)

璡 *tsin'* A beautiful grained pebble, like cornelian, regarded as a gem of inferior quality.

鄑 *tsin'* Also read *ˏtsz'.*

A town formerly in the present Ho-kien fu in Chihli, which was taken from 紀 by 齊, and its people moved off; also an old town in the south of Chihli, between the states of Lu and Sung.

蜼 *tsin'* The 蜆丨 is an old name for a *Pinna,* or similar shell which produces a byssus; it is found on the northern coasts.

TSʻIN.

Old sounds, tsʻin *and* tsʻim. *In Canton*, tsʻăn, tsʻăm, tsăm, *and* tsʻun; — *in Swatow*, chʻin *and* chʻim; — *in Amoy*, chʻin, chʻim, *and* sim; — *in Fuhchau*, chʻing, ching *and* chʻeng; — *in Shanghai*, tsʻing, dzing, *and* sing; — *in Chifu*, chin.

親 ꜀tsʻin From to see and *plants* growing together; occurs used for ꜀*sin* 新 new.

To love, to be attached to, as to one's kindred; liking, pleased with; to approach, to place one's self near to; near, intimate; personal, belonging to one's self, myself; a relative; a wife; kin, kith, kindred.

成丨 to consummate a marriage.

嚴丨 or 父丨 a father.

雙丨在堂 both parents are still alive.

迎丨 to receive the bride.

有丨 related to him.

丨派 relatives of the same surname.

內丨 relatives by consanguinity; those derived through the wife or mother.

丨筆寫 I wrote it myself.

丨愛 to love much.

丨近 near to one.

丨熱 very intimate.

遠丨不如近隣 a relative afar off is not like a neighbor near.

一層丨 connected or related by only one tie, as two families.

丨上加丨 to be doubly connected, as to marry a maternal cousin.

貧窮斷六丨 poor people must discard their relatives; the 六丨 are parents, brothers, wife and sons.

丨眷 or 丨串 relatives of another surname.

大人不丨細事 great men do not personally attend to small affairs.

勿躬勿丨 not myself at all.

搥丨 to run against one. (*Canton.*)

丨軍營 the Imperial Guard or Household troops in Peking.

丨身銳任 I myself will take all the responsibility.

Read *tsʻin*꜄ Relationship, affinity.

各有分丨 each person was detailed according to his degree of kindred.

丨家 or 丨翁 the parents of a married couple.

侵 ꜀tsʻin From *man* and to *sweep* by hand.

To usurp, to incroach on others' possessions; to appropriate, to invade, to stealthily advance or enter on; incroaching; rising, as the tide; dwarfed or deformed; possessed, as by a spirit.

大丨 a poor year; bad, as a poor harvest.

丨害 to usurp and injure, as another's functions or property.

丨佔 to occupy another's land unjustly.

丨淩 to intimidate and insult.

丨伐 to invade and chastise a rebel princedom.

丨削 to usurp or pare off by degrees.

丨近 to approach unawares.

丨犯 to sin willfully, to dare the results.

貌丨 low in stature.

丨呑賬目 to falisfy accounts and take the money.

勿使風雨所丨 so as not to let the wind and rain come into — the house.

In *Cantonese*. To put in furtively, to adulterate, to debase the quality of goods.

丨辮牌 to braid in false hair.

丨的入去 stick in a few bad ones.

駸 ꜀tsʻin Occurs used for the preceding.

A fleet horse.

丨丨其馬 the coursers flew over the ground.

載驟丨丨 the charger sped as he felt his rider.

綅 ꜀tsʻin Red fringe of silk worn on the helmet crest as a kind of uniform; it hung down on the neck.

秦 ꜁tsʻin From 禾 *grain* and 舂 to *hull rice* contracted, intimating that good grain was the proper revenue.

A fine kind of rice; a feudal state which arose with Féi-tsz' 非子 B. C. 897, and gradually extended over the whole of Shensi and Kansuh, till, in B. C. 221, under the Emperor First 丨始皇帝 it subdued all China, and was called 丨朝 the Tsʻin dynasty.

丨嶺 the range of mountains which divides the valleys of the rivers Han and Wéi in the south of Shensi.

丨人之弟 he is a brother of Tsʻin; *i. e.* he is not one of my friends; it's none of my business.

不用于丨猶用于楚 if you don't want me, somebody else probably will.

結爲丨晉 to make a marriage alliance.

丨椒 red pepper, which came from the west.

大丨國 the Roman empire.

榛 ꜁tsʻin In the old time, an ox was so called in some parts of the north of China.

螓 ꜁tsʻin A small cicada, which has a square head marked with stripes.

胡丨 a kind of blue-bottle fly.

丨首蛾眉 a cicada's head and a moth's eyebrows; *met.* a fine woman.

寢 ꜀tsʻin From *shelter* and to *sweep* with the *hand*; the addition of 爿 *bedstead* was later.

To lie down to sleep; to desist from, to rest; rest, repose; a bed-chamber; a dwelling-house; a retiring room in a palace; the recess or adytum where the tablets and images are placed, or the rear room of the ancestral temple, used for the purpose; a house or mausoleum near the grave; the resting-place of the dead; the ancient name of Ku-chi hien 固始縣 in the southeast of Honan.

乃安斯丨 he sleeps so quietly.

丨室 a dormitory.

廢丨 to lose one's sleep.

難丨 I cannot finish or stop the affair.

丨兵 to call in troops, to cease from war.

正丨 the apartments behind the hall.

其事遂丨息 the affair was then brought to a close.

丨食不安 no rest either in sleeping or eating.

丨苫枕塊 to sleep on a mat and pillow on a clod, as filial sons do when mourning for a parent.

六丨 an old name for the six offices in the palace for clerks.

載丨之地 put her to sleep on the ground.

鋟 ʻts'in An awl; a graver; a point. Read ˏts'ien. To engrave, to cut, to carve blocks.

濅 ts'in' A noted town in early times in 沈邱縣 in the center of Honan, called then 丨縣; used for 浸 to soak, to moisten; it seems to have been applied to the canals made in the Han dynasty to irrigate that region.

吣 ts'in' From *mouth* and *heart*; this character is sometimes written 唚 as a nearer approach to the sound.

To vomit, said of animals; to spurt out; to belch, as vile talk.

亂丨 or 胡丨 to rail, to talk obscenely.

丨不出好話 to rail is to use bad language.

貓丨 the cat vomits.

沁 ts'in' From *water* and *heart*.

To sound the depth of water; to fathom; to comprehend; to enter into; a large affluent of the Yellow River, near Hwai-king fu, in the southeast of Shansi.

丨州 a small department near it.

凉丨心脾 the cold gets into the heart and stomach.

日丨乎其中 he daily searches and sifts — the mud for things.

香丨鼻端 the fragrance penetrates the nose.

In *Cantonese*. To soak through by rain, to get wet; to let fall.

迷丨濕佢 don't let the rain wet it.

丨入 to get wet through.

一丨落地就爛 if it fall it will be broken.

丨丨吓 try its depth.

篸 ts'in' An implement used in making ink; a marker or pen made of bamboo to draw lines.

TSING.

Old sounds, tsing *and* dzing. *In Canton*, tsing *and* tseng; — *in Swatow*, cheng, chⁿé, *and* chⁿia; — *in Amoy*, chéng, ch'éng, ch'an, *and* séng; — *in Fuhchau*, ching, ch'ing, *and* chéng; — *in Shanghai*, tsing *and* dzing; — *in Chifu*, ching.

精 ˏtsing From *rice* and *pure*; *q. d.* the best of the rice.

Cleaned rice; selected, mature; the best or finest; unmixed; fine, subtle, delicate; accustomed to, devoted to, expert at; skillful, as in strategy; smart, quick, ready; the pure part of a thing, ethereal, essential; the essence of; the germinating principle, semen of males; an apparition, a wraith, a form taken by spirits; before other adjectives sometimes makes an intensive, as 丨巧 very skillful.

丨粗 fine and coarse.

好丨神 in good spirits, vigorous, smart; but 神丨 means an idea, a sentiment, a brilliant conception.

丨工 skilled workman.

題中丨神血脈處 the spirit and scope of the theme or quotation — must first be grasped clearly.

丨兵 the flower of the troops, picked men.

丨氣 animal vigor; the quintessence; subtle air, ether; pure, essential part of a being.

流丨 or 遺丨 involuntary emissions.

業丨于勤 skill in a thing depends mostly on diligence.

丨怪 an elf; one acting strangely; an apparition; prodigies, a portent.

丨靈 fine, spiritual; shrewd, ready at an answer or a plan.

你丨我不呆 if you are cute, I'm not a fool.

丨鬪丨 he has met his match; the one is well pitted against the other.

丨者神之本 the semen is the support of the animal spirits.

丨華 the sun and moon; the real and the ornamental; the spiritual and the substantial.

丨講大話 he's mostly clever at lying. (*Cantonese.*)

丨絕國 a country lying near the Bay of Bengal.

心丨道妙 pure in heart and admirable in doctrine.

圓丨 the round pure; — a poetical name for heaven.

丨衛 a bird resembling a pheasant, fabled to have been the daughter of Shinnung who drowned herself in the eastern sea.

睛 ˌtsing From *eye* and *dark;* it was at first written like the last, bnt early changed.

The ball of the eye; so some say, but more properly the iris; a 方 丨 square iris is regarded as a sign of long life.

眼黑 丨 the iris.

白 丨 the white of the eye.

碧 丨 or 藍 丨 blue eyes, which are supposed to be the color of demon's eyes.

目不轉 丨 to fix the eyes on a thing; eyes set and staring, as when terrified.

畫龍不點 丨 to draw a dragon and leave out the eyes; *met.* to decline to finish a work.

丨 珠 the crystalline lens.

發 丨 光 night-blindness.

不帶眼 丨 not to use one's eyes, not to keep to good manners; a little careless of propriety.

蜻 ˌtsing A dragon-fly, which sips the water; hence 丨 蜓 點 水 the dragon-fly sips water, is said of a style of writing that contains delicate allusions.

丨 蛚 a black field cricket.

豎 丨 蜓 to stand on one's head.

鶄 ˌtsing A wader found in the south, called 鵁 丨 a species of gray heron; the 丨 䳌 is allied to it; a bird like an ibis found in Chehkiang, and sometimes eaten; it feeds on eels, fish, and reptiles.

腈 ˌtsing From *flesh* and *pure.*

Lean meat, having no fat; pieces of lean pork or mutton.

菁 ˌtsing The flower of the leek is 韭 丨, applied also to chives and shallots.

丨 丨 in full leaf; luxuriant.

丨 茅 a large triquetrous sedge found in Honan, used in clearing liquor of sediment.

蕪 丨 a kind of greens resembling turnip, and used like pepper-grass, as an appetizer.

篝 箐 ˌtsing The second is read ʻsing, and is nearly synonymous with the first, and most in use.

Fishing baskets.

筌 丨 a general name in the T'ang dynasty for baskets and creels used in fishing.

Read *tsien'* for the first. A bamboo cross-bow; a small variety of the bamboo.

旌 ˌtsing From *banner* and to *produce.*

A banner, like an oriflamme, having plumes of different colors, which was waved to encourage the troops; a standard of a chieftain; to make signals; notices, signals; to make manifest, to discriminate; to show, a proof.

丨 旗 banners and flags.

銘 丨 banner hung by a corpse; it is sometimes made of paper like a square pillar with the legends written on the sides.

請 丨 to request that a worthy person may be honored with a scroll.

丨 表 insignia or testimonials of merit conferred by the sovereign on deceased persons, as loyal officers or worthy widows; they may consist of flags, inscriptions, and honorary gateways.

丨 別 淑 慝 to mark the difference between good and evil.

丨 節 a kind of ancient way-mark.

丨 郵 a posthumous reward of merit.

悠 悠 旆 丨 slow moved the pennons and banners.

欲 叩 行 丨 I would like to be at your side to salute you.

晶 ˌtsing From *sun* thrice repeated; *q. d.* the essence of light.

Luster, brightness; clear, pure; crystal; stones that are transparent or nearly so, as quartz, fluor-spar, calc-spar, Iceland spar, or beryl; crystalline.

茶 丨 tea-stone, cairngorm stone.

墨 丨 smoky quartz.

水 丨 quartz-crystal.

髮 丨 acicular tourmaline or actinolite in quartz.

紅 丨 rose quartz.

藍 丨 beryl; green flour-spar.

天氣 丨 clear weather.

水 丨 宮 Neptune's palace.

井 ʻtsing Originally designed to represent fields divided among eight families, reserving the middle one for public use and digging a well in it.

A well; a deep pit; the adit or shaft of a mine; an excavation; a plat laid out regularly; arranged or plotted in a regular manner; the 48th diagram, referring to water nourishing people; among masons, the labor on an earthwork is reckoned by the *tsing* or cubic foot measuring 12 *tsun* or inches.

丨 水 well water.

市 丨 人 a loafer; a huckster.

坐 丨 觀 天 [he is like one] looking at the sky in a well; — an inexperienced person.

丨 丨 有 條 arranged in fine order; very regularly, like beds in a garden.

開 丨 or 穿 丨 to dig a well.

一 丨 地 a square rood of land is called 一 丨 田, and anciently measured 900 *meu.*

淘 古 丨 to clear out an old well; *met.* to marry a rich widow.

天 丨 an open court or space between houses.

丨 宿 the 22d constellation, the six stars $\gamma\, \varepsilon\, \zeta\, \lambda\, \mu\, \nu$ in Gemini.

丨 里 a village.

親 操 丨 臼 to bring well-water and [pound in the] mortar; *i. e.* women's work.

臨 渴 掘 丨 he waits till he's thirsty to dig his well, — dilatory beyond endurance.

丨 竹 篙 a shallow well with a bamboo sweep on a frame.

姘 tsing' Female virtue or accomplishments, which induce a quiet, composed way of action.

穽 阱 *tsing'* From *cave* or *place* and a *well*.
A pit-fall, a hole; a pit to catch beasts in; to fall into a hole.

陷 丨 to tumble into a pit; to entrap.

布丨以自陷 he spread a pit-fall and fell into it himself.

爲丨于國中 it will be a snare to the country, as opium is to China.

開金丨 to dig a grave.

凊 *tsing'* To cool, to make cold; fresh, cool.

丨暑 to allay the heat.

丨涼 cool, refreshing.

冬温夏丨 in winter keep warm, and cool in summer.

婧 *tsing'* Female chastity and propriety, exhibited in a retiring demeanor, standing apart from others; slender, lithe, slim, as a girl small-waisted.

丨丨 supple, vigorous; said of a full-grown woman.

圊 *tsing'* A privy, a place which requires constant cleansing, as it receives all sort of things.

靖 *tsing'* From *pure* as the phonetic and to *establish*.
To become quietly settled, as a disturbed region; small fine; peaceful; concord; to tranquillize, to order; to restore peace by destroying the enemy; to clear, as the sea from pirates; to plan, to think on; to regulate, to keep in order; in epitaphs, gentle influence, self-poise and few words.

日丨四方之急務 daily planning for the urgent requirements of every place.

丨逆 to exterminate rebels.

俾予丨之 if I should manage it.

自丨 to make one's self easy by doing the right.

丨共爾位 quietly fulfill the duties of your posts.

地方安丨 the region is at peace.

靜 *tsing'* From *clear* and to *strive*; it is interchanged with the last and the next.
Still, quiet, as a pleasant solitude; quiescence; retiring; imperturbable, impassible; mild, peaceable; silently; pure, as a pool or a sacrifice; at rest, no bustle; to be quiet; to ponder, to think carefully on; to judge or examine; to desist.

心水丨 a contented, patient heart.

丨養 to keep quiet, to nurse one's self.

丨默 silent, not to speak, to hold one's peace.

貞丨 chaste, circumspect.

夜丨 the stilly night.

山丨似太古 these hills are quiet as in the pre-adamite days.

動丨云爲 stirring and quiet; talking and doing; every act; all that one can do or be.

丨極 excessively quiet.

丨坐常思己過 to reflect on one's errors in the quiet of home.

百官丨事毋刑 all officials rested from business and did not punish people.

丨言思之 I moodily think of my case.

丨丨的 be a little quiet, keep still.

靚 *tsing'* From *pure* and to *see*, defined as if it was 請見 to request to see; it is like the last.
To ornament, to bedizen; to paint the face; to allure; to summon, to call.

丨粧 painted and tricked out.

詐丨 false beauty; prinked up.

閃丨 brilliant, splendid.

豐容丨飾 handsomely and prettily adorned; a clear white complexion with black eyebrows, is regarded as beautiful.

曄丨 a flash of lightning.

In *Cantonese*. Handsome, elegant; clear, dazzling, transparent; looks well, becoming.

睇丨唔丨 see if it be pretty.

至丨係此 this is the gayest.

淨 凈 *tsing'* From *water* or *ice* and *quarreling*; one says the meaning is derived from 水 *water* added to 靜 *still*; the second form is much used as a synonym, but properly means cold.
The ancient name of a pond in Lu, and of a rapids in the River Han; actors who personify warriors and paint their faces; pure, spotless, undefiled; limpid, clean, not dirty; to wash, to cleanse; only.

丨重' the net weight.

潔丨其心 to purify his heart.

冷冷丨丨 only myself here; he is quite alone.

丨土 the undefiled land — of bliss, of the Budhists; a pure state of mind.

明窗丨几 a bright room and clean furniture.

丨水符 a cleansing charm, a cabalistic phrase on yellow paper hung in the hall.

乾丨丨 to clean by washing.

丨桶 a close stool.

一個都去乾丨 everybody has gone. (*Cantonese.*)

洗丨 to wash clean; to reform.

竫 *tsing'* From to *stand* and to *quarrel*.
To stand at ease; still, quiet.

惟諓諓善丨言 he delighted in speaking forth his aspersions.

TSʻING.

Old sounds, tsʻing *and* dzing. *In Canton*, tsʻing *and* leng ; — *in Swatow*, chʻeng, chʻⁿé, *and* chʻia ; — *in Amoy*, chʻéng *and* chéng ; — *in Fuhchau*, chʻing ; — *in Shanghai*, tsʻing *and* dzing ; — *in Chifu*, chʻing.

青 ꜀tsʻing Composed of 生 to *bear* above 丹 *red*, alluding to the ground color of plants when starting, on the principle of 木生火 wood produces fire ; it is the 174th radical of a few incongruous characters, and is interchanged with some of its compounds.

The first of the five colors, the color of nature, as the green of sprouting plants, the blue of the sky, and the azure of the ocean ; but especially the dark green of plants ; the green part of a thing ; wan, fading away, pale ; black.

佛頭丨 or 佛丨 ultra-marine, (which some say was the color of Budha's hair,) whence the term 丨石 or 丨金 for lapis-lazuli.

玄丨 or 元丨 black ; usually applied to cloth.

洋丨 or 大丨 smalts.

丨春 or 丨年 juvenile, in the teens ; the spring-time of life.

踏丨 to worship the tombs ; to ramble over the fields.

丨天白日 a clear, bright day.

鷄蛋丨 the white of an egg.

丨丨子衿 that scholar with the bluish collar.

其葉丨丨 tender and green are the leaves ; fresh foliage.

茶丨 a yellowish green.

綠丨 copperas or green vitriol.

燒丨 to burn green wood.

八面丨白 his complexion is very sallow and pale.

丨州府 a prefecture in Shantung, lying in the ancient 丨州 one of Yü's nine divisions.

丨子 or 丨果 a pickled olive.

靘 ꜀tsʻing A dark color ; black ; perhaps the common use of the preceding for black arose from confounding it with this less known character.

淸 ꜀tsʻing From *water* and *green*.

Pure, clear, limpid, unsullied ; incorruptible, right principled, clean ; ringing, clear, as the tone of a fine bell ; applied to drinkables, as being pure ; to settle an account ; to clear out, as a water course ; to settle, to make clear, as turbid water ; to purify ; name of a river in Kiangsi ; Manchu.

家世丨白 a family of unsullied fame.

守丨 to preserve purity ; as a girl refusing to marry, her betrothed having died.

料理丨楚 the whole matter is all well arranged.

數尾未丨 some unbalanced items still remain on the books.

丨了數 cleared off the account.

水洗不丨 it cannot be washed out, — as a bad act.

丨秀 elegant, well-formed, manly.

丨見毛髮 it is clear enough to see a hair through it.

丨理積案以靖災沴 let the courts clear off their long protracted cases in order to eliminate the discords which have caused this calamity.

大丨朝 the Pure or Manchu dynasty ; the following list gives the names of the eight sovereigns, both in Chinese and Manchu.

EMPERORS OF THE TSʻING OR MANCHU DYNASTY.

STYLE OF REIGN.	TEMPLE NAME.	ACCESSION A. D.	REIGNED YEARS.	GENEALOGY.
Shunchi 順治 Ichishōn dasan.	世祖章皇帝 Shitsu eltembughe hoangdi.	1644	18	Son of Tsung-teh.
Kʻanghi 康熙 Elghe taifin.	聖祖仁皇帝 Shengtsu gosin hoangdi.	1662	61	Son of the last.
Yungching 雍正 Hōwaliyasun top.	世宗憲皇帝 Shitsung temgetoleghe hoangdi.	1723	13	Son of the last.
Kienlung 乾隆 Apkai weghiyeghe.	高宗純皇帝 Geotsung yonggiyangga hoangdi.	1736	60	Son of the last.
Kiakʻing 嘉慶 Saitchungga fengshen.	仁宗睿皇帝 Jintsung sunggiyen hoangdi.	1796	25	Son of the last.
Taokwang 道光 Toro eltengge.	宣宗成皇帝 Sioantsung shangyan hoangdi.	1821	30	Son of the last.
Hienfung 咸豐 Guptchi elgiyengge.	文宗顯皇帝 Wentsung ilado hoangdi.	1851	11	Son of the last.
Tungchi 同治 Yauningga dasan.		1862		Son of the last.

丨字 or 丨文 Manchu writing.
丨心 to purify the heart.
丨規 Budhist rules, referring to their living on vegetables.
丨凈 undefiled, pure.
丨涼世界 a retired, clean situation, as for a temple.
丨單 a clear, correct account.
丨官 a clean-handed ruler, a just officer.
丨風徐來 the balmy breeze comes in gently.
暫且丨閒 just now I have some leisure.

Read *tsing'* and used for 凈. To make cool.

In *Cantonese.* All, as things; made clean away with.
擰丨 taken all away.
捉丨 seized every one.
丨丨的 take a little.
丨頭佬 an old bachelor.

鯖 *ˏts'ing* The *green fish*, from its color; and applied to some kinds of mackerel and mullets.
海丨魚 a species of mackerel of a greenish color which comes up the Pei-ho in spring; it has a depression in the neck.
丨魚 a fresh water fish, two to three feet long, and prettily marbled, reared in the central provinces.
丨鯶 a variety of the last, with deeper tints; both are akin to the surmullets. (*Upeneus.*)

Read *ˏching*, and used for 脏. To fry fish.

情 *ˏts'ing* From *heart* and *green*.
Human passions, of which there are seven, *viz.*, 喜 joy, 怒 anger, 哀 sorrow, 懼 fear, 愛 love, 惡' hatred, and 欲 concupiscence; the feelings, the desires; temper, passion, affection; lust; kindliness, jollity; the facts or circumstances of a matter; an affair, a case.

用丨 to assist or treat one heartily.
薄丨 or 無丨 ungrateful.
多丨 or 丨重' grateful.
不知丨 or 情丨 indifferent to kindness.
事丨沒完 the affair is not yet finished.
實丨 the real facts or incidents.
無才丨 inapt, stolid.
丨由 or 丨節 the causes; and 丨形 the aspects of a matter, as of a law case or charge.
丨理 reasonable, common sense; as 出夫丨理之外 this is beyond all explanation; it is unreasonable.
我丨願作 I am willing to do it.
有丨 having affections; a Budhist term (*pudgala*) for reasonable beings, man as subject to metempsychosis.
丨所不甘 I do not want to do it; it is not agreeable.
丨投 a mutual liking or friendship.
留丨 to remember a kindness.
說丨 to plead with or for people, as a lawyer or a friend.
以丨還丨 to pay him in his own coin.

晴 *ˏts'ing* From *sun* and *azure*.
The weather clearing up after a storm; the clear, blue sky; the stars coming out; to cease, as falling snow.
雨丨 the rain has ceased.
丨雲 red or fair-weather clouds.
春丨 a bright, spring day.
丨天 or 丨日 a fair day.
雲歛丨空冰輪乍擁 the clouds rolled away from the sky, and the silver moon suddenly came forth.
陰丨 cloudy and clear.

睛 *ˏts'ing* To receive, as a present; to come into possession of.
丨家產 to receive one's patrimony.

丨受若干銀 how much money did you get?
盡丨多少 how much did you get altogether?

請 *ˊts'ing* To request, to ask courteously; to beg of, to ask liberty to do, to request orders; to beg leave; by your leave; to propose; to promise; to invite, to bid, to engage, — and by extension, to hire, to call; to confess, to acknowledge.
丨坐 please sit down.
丨酒帖 an invitation to dine.
丨告 please tell me.
丨期 to request that a time may be appointed, as for a wedding.
丨便 don't let me incommode you; take your own time.
丨先生 to engage a teacher.
丨駕 will your lordship return? often used as equivalent to Please go, Sir.
丨命 will you let me know your wishes? — said to a high officer.
丨旨 to ask for orders — from the Throne.
丨罪 to confess, to beg pardon; to acknowledge a thing.
丨問 to request, to ask another.
丨丨 thank you; good-bye; the word *chin-chin* is a corruption of this phrase.
丨去 you are requested to go there.
丨呀丨呀 a salutation at meeting or parting.
丨益 please explain it again.
丨受而甘心焉 how happy I should be if you would give me that!
丨用點 please take a bit; please sit at the table.

Read *tsing'* A term for autumn, because anciently feudal princes brought presents at that season.
朝丨大夫 chamberlains in the palace in old times,
丨酒 rules for drinking at a banquet.

TSIOH.

Old sound, tsiak. *In Canton*, tséuk ; — *in Swatow*, chiak ; — *in Amoy*, chiok ; — *in Fuhchau*, chiók, chièh, *and* chioh ; — *in Shanghai*, tsiĕk *and* ziĕk ; — *in Chifu*, chŏa.

爵 ˏtsioh ˏchüé Supposed to represent a *cup* with its *contents* held in the *hand* ; the lower part is composed of 鬯 *wine* and 又 a *hand*, and the upper originally resembled a *goblet*.

A cyathus with three legs, a cup for libations ; a bamboo wine bottle ; a bird, birds ; a degree of nobility, of which there are now nine, *viz.* 親王 and 郡王 princes of the blood ; 貝子 beisse and 貝勒 beile, palatine princes ; 公 duke, 侯 marquis, 伯 earl, 子 viscount, 男 baron, each of the last five arranged in three classes ; in addition to these there are four inferior ranks, two of which 輕車都尉 and 騎都尉 are conferred mostly on soldiers, and the others 雲騎尉 and 恩騎尉 on all deemed to be worthy ; rank, station ; to estimate one's ability.

丨杯 a wine goblet.

丨位 of noble rank, one of the nine grades of nobility.

錫丨 to confer noble rank.

丨祿 rank and salary.

襲丨 hereditary rank.

古之人修其天丨而人丨從之 the ancients practiced heavenly nobility, and honors from man followed in its train.

人丨 human nobility conferred for merit, is contrasted by Mencius with 天丨 heaven's nobility, the love and practice of the five virtues.

嚼 ˏtsioh ˏchiao From *mouth* and a *goblet*.

To chew ; to ruminate, "which cows can do, but fishes, having no crop, cannot do ;" to craunch, to bite, to masticate ; a mouthful, a bite, a morsel ; to drink.

噬丨 or 咀丨 to chew.

倒丨 to chew the cud.

丨爛 chewed fine.

咬文丨字 to bite phrases and chew characters ; — a pedantic style of writing.

丨不動 too tough to chew.

丨蠟無味 tasteless as chewing beeswax ; said of a disagreeable job.

丨舌頭 to chew the tongue ; *met.* to deceive, to cajole.

In *Pekingese*. The bit of a bridle is 丨子 ; the headstall is 丨帽 or hat of the bit.

雀 tsʻiohʾ ʿtsiao From *bird* and *tender*, because it attaches itself to man; often wrongly interchanged with 鵲, a magpie.

A bird ; small birds like the finch, lark, tomtit, &c., but especially the sparrow, which is also called 家賓 the family guest ; a variety of wheat.

丨弁 a kind of leather cap, resembling a helmet.

孔丨 the peacock.

麻丨 or 瓦丨 the house-sparrow.

靈丨 and 山麻丨 two kinds of larks.

麻丨王 sparrow king or shrike. (*Lanius schach.*)

時辰丨 the canary.

筆丨 the munia.

禾花丨 rice-birds or ortolans.

丨舌花 the *Gardenia radicans*.

燕丨安知鴻鵠志 what do the swallow and sparrow know of the plans of the stork ?

丨立 to hop, to skip, as a sparrow ; to move promptly.

丨舌茶 a kind of fine tea.

飛啼丨 a species of surmullet. (*Upeneus biaculeatus*).

誰謂丨無角 who says the sparrow has no horns — and can't fight ? hence the phrase 丨角 for litigation, quarreling.

黃丨 a goldfinch.

丨皇 the bird of paradise.

梅花丨 the avedavat.

燕丨 a small gray finch at Peking, taught to play tricks.

暗丨 the night-heron. (*Nycticorax griseus.*)

爝 ˏtsioh A flambeau, a torch or link ; a lighted match burned at night on a cry of alarm.

日出矣而丨火不息 the sun and moon go out indeed, yet the light of man's torches is not put out.

皭 ˏtsioh A pure white ; clean, nice, fair.

丨然不滓 white, without the least blemish ; said of snow or a liquid.

穱 ˏtsioh Also read *tsuh*,

To sow wheat between the rice, as is done on uplands ; small ; early ripe.

冬稌夏丨 the winter rice and summer wheat.

瀺 ˏtsioh The rippling rush of water caused by stones ; the noise of waves.

遊鱗瀺丨 the darting fish show their [bright] scales.

TSʻIOH.

Old sounds, tsʻiak *and* dziak. *In Canton*, tsʻéuk ; — *in Swatow*, chʻiak ; — *in Amoy*, chʻiok ; — *in Fuhchau*, chʻiòk ; — *in Shanghai*, tsʻièk ; — *in Chifu*, chʻòa.

鵲, *tsʻioh*ˀ From *bird* and *ancient*, but some give the original primitive as a contraction of 雜, particolored.

A term for the pie, jackdaw, jay, and similar birds.

喜 丨 the magpie, *lit.* the joyous bird, so named from its incessant bowing ; also called 乾 丨 from its nest being in dry places, and its delight in dry weather ; and 駁 鳥 from its piebald plumage.

練 丨 the longtailed blue jay of Formosa (*Urocissa cerulea*) ; also the blue magpie (*Cyanopica cyana*) of the North.

山 喜 丨 a magpie (*Pica caudata*) with a long gradated tail.

蝟 孱 于 丨 the hedgehog yields disgracefully to the magpie ; — the legend is that he turns over on his back to be killed by it.

扁 丨 a famous physician of the San Kwoh.

七 夕 丨 成 橋 the magpies make a bridge on the 7th evening of the 7th moon — for the Herd-boy to see the Weaveress ; some say that this alludes to the migration of this bird.

烏 丨 a raven.

碏, *tsʻioh*ˀ Stones of many colors, a variegated stone ; to respect.

石 丨 an officer of Wéi.

Read *sih*, A stumbling-block.

猎, **猩**, *tsʻioh*ˀ A docile, well-trained dog in the state of Sung, and like *Gelert*, it has come to designate such an animal.

檓, *tsʻioh*ˀ Like the next.

The rough bark of a tree, full of cracks and furrows, like that of the oak (*Quercus sinensis*) or fir.

皵, *tsʻioh*ˀ The *old bark* of tree ; a rough, corrugated bark, like the hemlock or fir ; applied to the wrinkled skin of old men.

皮 皴 丨 以 龍 驚 take a wrinkled bark to scare away the dragon.

丨 皺 有 緻 this mottled rough surface is beautiful.

鯌, *tso*ˀ From *fish* and *old*, but defined as *blended* stripes.

A species of shark allied to the saw-fish (*Pristis*) ; the saw snout is six inches long and two wide, the teeth slender ; the body is over three feet long, of a sandy brown color ; the Chinese say the young go out in the morning to feed, and return into their mother at evening ; the skin is good for scabbards ; this species occurs along the coast of Chehkiang, and is eaten by the people.

TSIU.

Old sounds, tsiu, dziu, tsiak, *and* dziok. *In Canton*, tsau, tsʻau, *and* tsò ; — *in Swatow*, chiu *and* chʻiu ; — *in Amoy*, chʻiu, chiu, *and* iu ; — *in Fuhchau*, chʻiu, iu, chʻéu *and* chʻiu ; — *in Shanghai*, tsiù *and* dziù ; — *in Chifu*, chiu.

湫, ˏ*tsiu* From *water* and *autumn*.

A pool, a pond ; a branch of the Yellow River in Lin hien in the northwest of Shansi, famed for its clear, pure water ; cool, refreshing, as a breeze ; to distress, to sadden.

丨 丨 mournful, sorrowing.

觀 斯 景 也 好 不 丨 人 I regard these circumstances as not calculated to make men sad.

龍 丨 a waterfall.

丨 兮 如 風 a chilly, moaning wind.

敝 居 丨 隘 my residence is small and contracted ; — a depreciatory phrase.

Read ˊ*tsiao*. To be stopped, as water by a dike, or in a tank.

啾, ˏ*tsiu* The wailing of infants.

丨 唧 the hum of insects, the buzz of flies ; a low murmur.

丨 丨 the moaning of infants.

揫, **揪**, ˏ*tsiu* From *hand* and *autumn* ; there is a slight difference in these two characters ; and the second is most commonly used.

The first is to collect, to gather ; to bring up, as a sheaf and bind it ; the second is to clutch, to grasp, to gripe ; to pinch and pull, as the skin ; to take hold of forcibly.

丨 心 anxious about the result.

丨 歛 to make up into bundle.

丨 住 to seize fast.

丨 辮 子 take him by the cue.

丨 着 不 撒 手 they won't let go their hold of each other.

丨 耳 nabbed him by the ears.

丨 束 to bind in a sheaf.

丨 皮 to rub and pull the skin ; done as a counter-irritant.

丨 着 心 繫 兒 去 做 tie your heart to your hand and go do it ; — *i. e.* be very careful.

瞅, ˏ*tsiu* A ringing in the ears.

丨 的 一 聲 or 耳 中 丨 丨 a humming noise in the ear.

䨂 *ts'iu* A pullet.
丨子 a chicken.

鰽 *'tsiu* A herring, which the Chinese fable to be transformed from a bird, and therefore it has a gizzard in its body.
黑丨 a perch with an emarginate dorsal. (*Lates calcarifer.*)
丨魚 a silvery perch, ventral and pectoral opposite. (*Lates nobilis.*)
杭丨白 a yellowish herring at Macao (*Megalops setipinnis*), with yellow fins.
丨白 a leek-green herring at Macao, (*Ilisha abnormis*), with a long swallow tail.

酋 *tsiu* From 酉 *must* or *mash* and half of 水 *water* above it, denoting the water which collects on liquor when settling.

Liquor after the fermentation is over, spirits that have settled; to finish, to come to perfection; cooked thoroughly, well-boiled; a chief butler; a headman, a brave or chief of tribes of people; the season for gathering when things are ripe.
丨雄 warlike, valiant.
丨長 a headman of foreign tribes; a leader.
似先公丨矣 to carry on the work of the late prince.
大丨 a chief cup-bearer.

鬌 *tsiu* A false cue or wig, a chignon; the hair, especially of girls, done up in a coil on the side; the cue coiled on the back of the head.
挽 (or 梳) 一個丨兒 tie up her hair in a [side] coil.
正髻丨 a coil or knot in the middle.
牛屎丨 the cue coiled up.

醔 *tsiu* The oily scum which is found on rich spirits and adheres to the cup; occurs used for 糟, the rice cake or refuse left after making spirits.

湭 *tsiu* Same as 泅 to swim.
丨丨 dregs, secretions.
丨河 a small affluent of the River Wéi in the southeast of Shensi, near where it joins the Yellow River.

遒 *ch'iu* From *to go* and *liquor*.

To urge, to constrain; a crowd, a throng; to exhaust, to end, to carry to the utmost; firm, as a well governed state; to collect, to consolidate, to call in; concentrated; strong, unyielding; sudden.
丨人 a policeman; a herald.
四國是丨 the four states were firm in their power.
百祿是丨 all happiness and riches were concentred in him.
丨健 vigorous.
歲忽忽而丨盡 how rapidly has the year come to an end!

蝤 *tsiu* The long white larvæ of a beetle, resembling the carpenter beetle, called 丨蠐 to which a lady's neck is likened; occurs used for 蝣 the ephemera fly.
丨蛑 a large marine crab.

酒 *'tsiu* From *must* and *water*; it is liable to be mistaken for *'sha* 洒 to sprinkle.

Liquor, defined as "that which perfects the good or the evil in men's natures, or makes fortune or misfortune to them;" it includes spirits, wine, beer, and other drinks; the Chinese make no wine, and chiefly distil their liquors, and say that Tu K'ang 杜康 a woman of the Tih 狄 tribes first made it; given to drink.
賣丨不說丨酸 he who sells grog, never tells you it is sour.
燒丨 samshew, saki, arrack.
丨席 a banquet.
旨丨 fine, generous liquor.
無丨量 I have no ability to drink.
發丨瘋 drunk, maudlin, raving.
陳丨 old wine.
黃丨 sweet spirits, usually applied to the best which comes from Shaohing.
丨中 boozy, tipsy.
丨瘋脚 gouty, rheumatism in the feet.
丨坊 or 丨局 a grog-shop, a wine-cellar.
紅丨 claret; 白丨 sherry; 啤丨 beer, with others, are terms of foreign origin.
丨脚 a heel-tap.
水丨 weak or poor wine; used to depreciate one's own liquor.
天丨 a poetical name for dew, as 玄丨 is for water.
色丨 mulled wine.
丨神降 to relish the flavor of the wine.
美丨 good liquor; a fine flavor.
祭丨 the head of the Kwoh-tsz'-kien; he is cup-bearer at the state worship of Confucius; an ancient title of honor, like that of a judge of wines; to pour out a libation.
丨仙 or 醉丨佬 or 丨囊 a drunkard, a wine-bibber.
丨保 a waiter, a servant in a restaurant.

䅵 *tsiu'* From *grain* and *color* of wine; it resembles 穐 to fast.

To shrink up small; to divide or sort.
丨丨了 all shriveled up, withered.
丨短 contracted, as dry timber.
丨分'兩 to shrink in weight.
丨一半 shrunk one half.
丨縮 shrunk, as cloth in washing.
丨旗 a group of stars partly in Leo and partly in Cancer.

就 *tsiu'* From 尤 more and 京 a *capital* city; *q. d.* the place to which things tend or culminate.

To go towards, to approach; to accompany, to follow; to complete, to make a circuit; accommodated to, agreeable to; completed, finished, met; to come near in point of time; able, willing; an *adverb* of time, then, immediately, just now, presently, forthwith; in a little while, coming; a *conjunction*, then, if, as if.

丨來 he has just come.

丨來丨去 he has just come and gone.

丨先 just now, only a little while ago.

成丨 to bring about, to finish up.

丨手 handily, just at this time it is convenient.

不能將丨 this will not do at all; I don't like it so.

東不成西不丨 everything is out of order; all is in confusion or at cross-purposes.

丨地辦理 to settle it (or judge a case) off-hand.

丨地取材 this will serve the purpose; he will perhaps do for the place.

丨近 to choose the near, as an official for his post; to prefer the most convenient; to be near.

丨是了 just so, let it rest; that is it; very well.

丨好 this is right; it will do so.

百姓丨了他來 the people all came to him.

丨手去做 go and do it at your early convenience; do it soon.

將計丨計 to meet one scheme with another; to give a Rowland for an Oliver.

丨知明白 I shall understand it presently.

丨他的車 I availed myself of his carriage.

你丨搭他 (in *Cantonese*, 丨埋佢) bear with him.

領伊丨來 bring him directly. (*Shanghai.*)

丨要去 go directly.

丨是伊 that is the man. (*Shanghai.*)

鷲 *tsiuʼ* A large accipitrine bird, of a black plumage, described as having a yellow head and piercing sight; it is probably the condor or lammergeir, found in Manchuria.

丨悍 rapacious, grasping.

借梵宮而爲丨室 he uses the hall of Budha to make it a harpy's nest; *i. e.* a den of thieves.

靈丨山 a peak in India, called Gridhrakuta, now Giddore, where Pisuna assumed a vulture's shape, or on which vultures had their nests; many ascetics lived there in caves.

僦 *tsiuʼ* To *draw near* to a *man*, to hire, to employ; to procure.

丨屋 to rent a house.

丨傭 to engage, as a workman.

丨載者 to hire a conveyance for carrying things.

瘷 *tsiuʼ* From *disease* and *autumn*.

To shrivel and heal up, as a sore.

癤子消瘇丨了 the pimple has healed and the swelling gone down.

稩 粙 *tsiuʼ* From *grain* or *rice* and a *helmet*; the second form is unusual.

The rice fully ripe, and ready to cut.

割丨 to reap the rice.

丨出穗 the rice has headed.

丨楻 and 丨馬 frames on which grain is beaten out by hand.

TSʻIU.

Old sounds, tsʻiu, tsʻiok, dziu, *and* dok. *In Canton*, tsʻau; — *in Swatow*, chʻiu; — *in Amoy*, chʻiu — *in Fuhchau*, chʻiu; — *in Shanghai*, tsʻiù *and* dziù; — *in Chifu*, chʻiu.

秋 龝 *tsʻiu* From 禾 *grain* and 火 *fire* indicating ripeness, but also regarded as a contraction of 龜 *scorched*, as the second form intimates.

The season of ripe grain, autumn; autumnal; harvest time; the return of the year; a season, a time, a period; unhappy, sorrowful, feelings saddened by seeing the seasons depart.

晚立丨熱死牛 the evening that autumn comes in, it is hot enough to kill the kine.

丨天 or 丨季 autumn.

麥丨 the wheat harvest in May; also the 4th moon.

丨氣 cool, autumnal weather.

丨後扇 a fan after autumn; — *met* a useless thing.

丨官 or 丨曹 the officers of the Board of Punishments, because cases are decided at the 丨審 autumnal assizes.

丨毫無犯 not the error of an autumn's down.

竹丨 the third moon.

三丨 or 九丨 the ninth moon.

蘭丨 the seventh moon.

丨收 the harvest.

多事之丨 a time of trouble and anxiety.

丨成之事 the time of ripe grain.

丨石 urea, obtained always from the human secretion.

其能無一日三丨之感 how can the feelings of one day be made to appear like those of three years?

乃亦有丨 there is still time for a crop.

丨水共長天一色 the blue water reflects the hue of heaven.

鳳凰丨丨 the sprightly movements of the phœnix.

令肅丨霜 the general is stern and strict as the fall frost.

遊子悲丨 the trials of a traveler.

楸 ˏtsʻiu The *autumn tree*, because its leaves are shed *early;* the character 榎 which some regard as a synonym, means the *summer-tree*, alluding to the same thing.

A forest tree, the *Catalpa Bungei*, with a rough bark; it resembles a chestnut in its foliage, but the timber is like the beech.

刺丨樹 a tall spinous tree with palmate leaves, found in Honan.

丨枰 a chess-board.

萩 ˏtsʻiu From *plant* and *autumn;* it is also used for the last.

A syngenesious plant like the may-weed (*Antennaria* and *Anthemis*), having fragrant leaves, and burned to dispel noxious vapors.

丨苴 a Corean term for the sons of titled statesmen.

輶 ˏtsʻiu The spokes of a wheel.

丨轉如風 the wheels roll around swiftly.

緧 ˏtsʻiu From *silk* and *chief;* occurs interchanged with the next.

To put on a crupper.

丨䪇 the crupper and the bridle or reins.

鞦 ˏtsʻiu The traces of a carriage; a crupper; a breast-strap.

打丨韆 to swing on a gallows-swing; the 丨韆 was a whirlwheel like the Russian.

後丨 a crupper of wood.

鰍 鰌 ˏtsʻiu An eel, the large mud or conger eel.

泥丨 a fresh-water eel; it is shorter and darker colored than the 鱓 yellow eel.

丨魚骨 whale-bone.

山泥丨 a small brown lizard.

海丨 a sea-dragon of immense length, whose movements cause the ebb and flood tides; a sort of long, narrow boat.

鶖 ˏtsʻiu From *bird* and *autumn*, because it sheds its head feathers in autumn, and looks like a bald head.

A long legged bird, 鵚丨 like the marabou stork or adjutant (*Ciconia*) which eats snakes; it is five feet high, has red eyes and a bare neck; the bill is yellowish, plumage grayish, and a pouch is under the bill.

烏丨 the black adjutant or the drongo (*Dicrurus macrocercus*), a small hen-harrier in Formosa.

有丨在梁 the marabou stands on the dam.

丨鷺鳥 a long-legged bird, like the secretary falcon in many of its traits; Sariputtra, one of the leading disciples of Sakyamuni, is called 丨鷺子 from his mother.

煪 ˏtsʻiu To scorch, to roast, to dry; fiery, fire.

TSʻIÜN.

Old sounds, tsien *and* dzien. *In Canton*, tsun; — *in Swatow*, chun; — *in Amoy*, chwʻan *and* tsun; — *in Fuhchau*, chòng; — *in Shanghai*, tsing *and* tsăng; — *in Chifu*, tsăn.

皴 ˏtsʻun The skin wrinkled or hardened, as from labor; chapped, shriveled; a mode of painting in raised figures or coarse outline.

丨裂 cracked skin.

凍丨了 chapped from cold.

丨皮 rough, cracked skin; a fanciful name for the lichi fruit.

斧劈丨 chopped, riven; said of overhanging, jagged cliffs.

丨法 rules for painting in the rough.

䨿 ˏtsʻün A cunning hare.

竣 ˏtsʻun From to *stand* and a *proud* gait.

To stop work from having finished the task; to complete, to finish; to stand still, to wait aside; to retire after ending the affair; completed, done.

告丨 to report the completion.

諸事已丨 everything has been done.

完丨 to complete; to bring a job to its full end.

勢不能按限報丨 it seems to me that we cannot report its completion within the set time.

夋 ˏtsʻün From 夊 to *saunter* and 允 *permitting;* now used only in combination as a primitive, the next taking its place.

To dawdle and drag along, so as to show one's pride by not really advancing; a name of Yao's father.

行丨丨 to walk mincingly.

逡 ˏtsʻün To retire, to recede; to act as if returning; to feel abashed, self-humiliated; a revolution of the moon.

丨巡退縮 to shrink back, from fear or diffidence; not to go forward, to hesitate and skulk.

丨次 in file; proceeding in order, as troops advancing.

丨行 to boggle, to shirk danger.

踆 ˏtsʻün Similar to the two preceding, and interchanged with ˏtsʻun 蹲 to squat.

To retire, to fall back, to retreat; to kick back or run against backwards; to perch, as birds; to crouch.

丨丨 hopping like a magpie.

已事而丨 to finish the affair and then step aside.

壿 ˏtsʻun From *scholar* and *honored.*

Joyful, happy.

丨丨舞我 I can caper from very happiness, as when over a stoup of wine.

TSO.

Old sounds, tsa, dza, tsap, *and* dzat. *In Canton*, tso *and* tsò ; — *in Swatow*, cho ; — *in Amoy*, tsò ; — *in Fuhchau*, cho ; — *in Shanghai*, tsu *and* zu ; — *in Chifu*, tsò *and* tsòa.

㑴 ꜀tso ꜀tso From *man* and to *take out*.

To make believe, to simulate, to put on appearances.

Read *tsü*ʾ To hasten; pressing, urgent; near to.

丨近 to crowd, to press upon.

迫丨心忙 in a desperate hurry and flutter.

𡯴 ꜀tso ꜂tso One leg injured and crippled.

跛丨 to walk irregularly and lamely.

左 ꜀tso ꜂tso The original form was merely ナ respresenting the *left hand* (as 又 does the right), to which 工 *work* was afterwards added.

The left side, the left hand, now the seat of honor; second to, an assistant or deputy, only used when there are two of them, as the 正, the 左, the 右, or the principal, the vice, and the substitute; to degrade, to lower, because in former dynasties, the left was the less honorable side; depraved, bad; to witness to, to verify; used for the east in speaking of the coast of China.

丨驗 to prove; to corroborate, as a coadjutor can.

丨右 near to, in that region; this and that.

丨性 crotchety, set in his way, whimsical.

丨道 erroneous or heretical doctrines.

相丨 a mutual mistake; not to suit; disagreeing.

丨思右想 thinking of this and of that way.

丨手交右手 to exchange from hand to hand; — *i. e.* not to give credit.

轉灣丨邊 turn to the left.

兩丨 both missed each other, as in making calls.

面丨丨 to dislike one's looks.

不差丨右 not very much unlike.

列於丨 written below; it is as follows.

天子居明堂丨個 the emperor lives in the side-room, near the great hall.

丨不過 most probably, on the whole, very likely.

山丨 and 山右 terms for Shantung and Shansi, having reference to Peking.

佐 tsoʾ tsoʾ From *man* and the *left*; but originally the same as the last.

To assist, to second; an assistant, a coadjutor, a vice, a deputy; a captain in the Manchu Banner force; they often hold civil functions in the colonies, and are either 世管 hereditary, or 公中 of common grade; the former are divided into original 勳舊 *lit.* enduring merits, and promoted 優異 *lit.* singularly advanced; these officers rule a sort of constabulary force.

王丨之才 the talents of [Wăn Wang's] prime ministers.

丨雜官 officers in a district magistrate's yamun under the grade of 右堂 second deputy.

爲義以丨善 to do right aids good principles.

相丨 an aid to a prime minister; an under-secretary.

丨君布化 to second the prince in carrying on his mild sway.

坐 tsoʾ tsoʾ From 土 *ground* and 留 *to rest*, contracted to two 人 *men* above it.

To sit in a crouching way or on a seat; to squat; sitting, remaining, and by extension, doing nothing, unemployed, idle; a seat, a place; to sit in judgment on; to maintain, to hold; involved in, implicated, as one who is in the criminal's seat; in Budhism, to pass a season in devotional exercises; anciently meant to kneel; to place, to put in a seat.

請丨 please sit down; to which the guest, in cases of much formality, replies 告丨 I beg leave to sit.

你丨 keep your seat; *i. e.* good bye, said by the visitor.

丨車 to ride in a cart.

丨月 the month of a woman's confinement.

丨罪于你 brought the punishment on yourself.

丨位 a seat; *met.* to fill a station.

無丨位 having no seat, not entitled to a seat.

丨實 the affair or thing is securely arranged.

丨向 or 丨落 the aspect, as of a tomb; the position of a house.

丨索 to demand with urgency, as the payment of a debt; to quarter on one to get it.

正丨 and 傍丨 to sit in the chief or inferior seats; to give the first or second seat to one.

丨船 to command a ship; to go on a voyage.

打丨參禪 to meditate in a retreat; the Budhists also say 丨臘 to retreat (*varchas*) during the twelfth moon.

反丨 to bring the crime on one's self, as a false accuser does.

丨牢 in prison.

丨黨死者數百人 several hundreds belonging to that faction were killed.

趺丨 to squat on the ground.

‘舍其丨遷 they leave their seats to go elsewhere.

丨食山空 (or 崩) doing nothing but eat till even the mountain is emptied (or fallen); — indolent.

丨席 to partake of a feast.

丨子 a stand for a jar.

其文內丨日係初七日 the date of the letter was the 7th.

小子禮當侍丨 a youth should wait till asked to be seated.

丨守無期 to fulfill the duties for a time.

丨贓 to charge another with having the plunder.

In *Cantonese.* To lower, as a sail of a boat.

In *Pekingese.* The recoil of a gun.

座 *tso*ʾ From *shelter* and *seat.* A raised seat, a throne, a dais; a shrine; a classifier of hills, walls, towers, buildings, pagodas, movable pavilions, encampments, &c.

寶丨 a throne, a shrine.

開光陞丨 to vivify and enshrine an idol.

一丨城 one wall.

公丨椅 a large chair, like a magistrate's; an easy chair.

法丨 the seat of law; *i. e.* the throne or a judge's bench.

八丨 eight bearers who carry the governor's chair. (*Cantonese.*)

丨右 [let this letter come] to the right side of your seat.

矬 *tso*ʾ A hill that appears ready to fall.

袏 *tso*ʾ A bag to carry clothes in; a haversack; a clothes-bag.

丨衣 a garment without a lining.

做 *tsu*ʾ From *man* and *old;* also read *tsu*ʾ and *tsoh*, in many places; it is regarded as another form of *tsoh*, 作 to do, and resembles *tsao*ʾ 造 in some meanings.

To do, to act; to perform the duties of; it differs from 作 in referring to mental as well as physical acts.

丨不了 not yet done; occasionally means, I won't do it.

丨官 to be in office.

丨酒 to prepare a feast. (*Cantonese.*)

會丨人 he understands the world, he is popular.

丨人 be a man, act as a man.

你名叫丨甚麽 what is your name? in this sentence it is the passive voice of the previous verb.

不想丨 I do not want to do it; I don't think of doing it.

丨得唔丨得 (like 行不行) can you do or undertake this? will it do or not? (*Cantonese.*)

丨不來 it cannot be brought about or done.

一股氣兒丨 do it at once, keep on to the end without stopping.

TSʻO.

Old sounds, tsʻa, tsʻap, tsʻat, *and* tsʻak. *In Canton,* tsʻo; — *in Swatow,* chʻo tsò; — *in Amoy,* chʻò, tsʻò, *and* chia; — *in Fuhchau,* chʻo *and* chʻauk; — *in Shanghai,* tsʻu; — *in Chifu,* tsʻòa.

搓 ꜀*tsʻo* From *hand* and *to differ.* To twist, as thread by rubbing on the knee; to rub between the hands; to scrub and rub; to lay on paint with a wad of tow; bent, hanging down, as a pendent branch.

丨挪 to roll round, as a pill.

丨線 to twist thread.

丨香 to roll incense sticks.

丨作一團 roll it into a ball.

柳細丨難似花新染未乾 [the threads] are not even as delicate as the drooping willow twigs, or fresh as the newly opened petals.

丨紙條 to roll allumettes or paper strings.

Read ꜀*chʻai.* To strike and push against.

蹉 ꜀*tsʻo* To slip, to slide in walking; to miss, to err; to pass; to go by; to cross.

渡丨 passed over.

跌丨 slipped and fell.

孟公結重關賓客不得丨 Lord Măng had the gates firmly barred, so that his guests could not get out.

見事當辦無得丨跎 when an affair is in a good train, do not let the favorable moment to conclude it slip by.

磋 ꜀*tsʻo* To polish, to work on, as bones or ivory; to rub and polish; to correct carefully, to work at, the *labor limæ* of composing.

切丨 to cut and polish, as ivory.

丨磨 carving and polishing.

切而復丨 to trim and then still polish, as a carefully written essay.

嵯 ꜀*tsʻo* From *hill* and *to differ.* The uneven outline of hills.

山岳丨峨而連岡 the undulating tops of the high hills run along like a sierra.

Read ꜀*tsz*ʾ. Irregular.

嵾丨 uneven, as the peaks of hills.

瘥 ꜀*tsʻo* ꜀*chʻa* From *disease* and *to differ;* it is also read ꜀*chʻai* and ꜀*chʻa.* A disease, like an influenza; a slight epidemic; to get well of an indisposition.

札丨 epidemics of any kind.

天方薦丨 heaven visits the people with many epidemics.

丨愈 convalescent.

病丨些 his complaint is a little better.

病已就丨 he had then recovered from his illness.

鹺 ꜀ts'o Also read ꜀tso.

Briny, salt.

鹹丨 salted.

丨味 a very salt taste.

矬 ꜀ts'o From a *javelin* and to *sit*.

Short, squat, stunted.

丨陋 stunted and ugly looking, as a boor.

丨峒塲 a salt marsh in Kwangtung.

短丨丨兒 dwarfed, short of stature.

丨子 a short fellow.

我不能比人家丨下去 I am not to be regarded as inferior in rank to that person.

身材很丨 his body is very small.

瑳 ʿts'o Interchanged with 磋 to polish.

A stone of a brilliant white color like fine milky quartz; white, fresh; gay, adorned; to smile; smiling, as when one shows white teeth; to look fascinating.

巧笑之丨 the white teeth showed finely through her smile.

丨兮丨兮其之展也 how white and splendid is her robe of state!

矬 ʿts'o Broken stones; the rubbish of rocks; the best kind of orpiment or hartall.

脞 ts'o' Minced meat, hashed; broken to bits, ruined, spoiled; to attend to trifles; crisp, brittle.

叢丨 to manage an affair badly, to interfere and spoil things; trifling, fussy, vexatious.

剉 ts'o' From *knife* and to *sit*; occurs used for the next.

To cut, to lop off the points and corners; to trim and prune; to file; to cut in pieces, as criminals are sometimes executed.

丨折 file it in two.

丨光 to file a thing bright.

丨平 smooth it even.

丨屍 to cut the [criminal's] corpse in pieces.

丨角 file off the corners.

銼 ts'o' Used with the preceding.

A file, a rasp; an iron pan or boiler; to file, to trim; to make small.

鉄丨 an iron file.

斧丨 a broad iron pan or boiler.

一把丨 one file.

雞糯丨 or 芝蔴丨 one who files eggs or rasps sesamum seeds; a skin-flint. (*Cantonese.*)

挫 ts'o' From *hand* and to *sit*; it occurs wrongly used for the two last.

To come down on harshly, to oppress; to break or wound; to dislocate a joint; to push off or over; to retire from the field defeated; to humble, to take down one's pride; a close in music; to chasten, to purify.

折丨 to try, as by adversity; to polish in manners; chastened, as people who improve under trials.

摧丨 to impose on, to thrust at, to be impudent to.

丨了銳氣 brought down his bravado.

丨後 to be pushed back, as a defeated army.

一毫不丨 I will not take any of his insults.

丨浄心思 to chasten the will.

抑揚頓丨 diminuendo and crescendo, rest and close, in music.

莝 ts'o' To chop straw fine for animals; to cut fine.

丨之秣之 chop the straw to feed it to them.

斫丨 to cut fine.

蹉 ts'o' Like the next.

To mistake in making an obeisance; to deceive.

躍丨 impeded, not advancing.

夎 **䂳** ts'o' From 夂 to *trip* and 坐 to *sit*; the second form is unusual.

To slip or stumble when making an obeisance, and not perform it, either by catching the dress, or from stiff knees, is 丨拜; those who wore mail were excused from doing it; to deceive.

諎 ts'o' From *words* and *ancient*; also read *tsoh*, and occurs used for the next.

To reply; to mistake; to crow, to cry.

丨話 improper language.

説丨了 to take wrongly, to mislead.

Read *cha'* To deceive.

錯 ts'o' From *metal* and *old*; it is also pronounced *ts'u'* and interchanged with the next.

In disorder, confused; to mistake, to err; wrong, mixed; be wrong; perverse, offensive; as a *conjunction*, excepting; then; to polish; a polishing stone.

不丨 right, correct; no mistake.

丨脚難返 it is hard to regain the right path; a faux-pas is not easily recovered.

丨然 respectful, obeisant.

丨過必改 the wrong or error must be retracted.

丨悞 erroneous, mismanaged.

不認丨 he will not confess the wrong.

丨不了 he will not mistake.

丨亂 or 丨雜 confused, mixed up.

丨骨縫 to dislocate a joint.

午丨時 or 晌午丨 about noon, it was then noontide.

茍丨諸地則可矣 to put it on the ground will do.

差丨 not exact, wanting, not according to rule.

他山之石可以攻丨 a stone from another hill can be here polished and worked; — *i.e.* you, Sir, can much improve and teach me.

Read *ts'oh*, To wash or plate with gold; the veins, striæ, or streaks in stones or wood; to file or polish; to tattoo; a lapidary's stone.

丨刀 a copper knife-shaped coin washed with gold, issued by Wang Mang, B. C. 2.

丨臂 to tattoo the arm.

In *Cantonese* like 噦 *yueh*, A hacking in the throat; a difficulty or stoppage in the throat.

丨氣 the heart up in the throat.

抽丨 a retching cough.

厝 *ts'o'* Interchanged with the last, and with 措 to place; also read *ts'oh*, A large smooth stone fit for a gravestone or tablet; to put away a corpse properly; to carve, to engrave.

安丨 quietly placed, as a coffin in its grave or lararium.

浮丨 temporarily placed on the ground, to await a proper interment.

丨注 to cut an epitaph.

TSOH.

Old sounds, tsak, dzak, *and* tsot. *In Canton*, tsok *and* ts'üt; — *in Swatow*, chak, cha, chek, *and* ch'o; — *in Amoy*, tsok, tsa, ch'ok, *and* tswat; — *in Fuhchau*, chauk *and* chŏk; — *in Shanghai*, tsoh, zok, ts'üh, *and* ts'u; — *in Chifu*, tsòa.

作 *tso'* *tso* From 人 *man* and 乍 to *excite*; regarded as a synonym of *tso'* 做 with which it is continually interchanged, but the former rather refers to making, and the latter to doing things.

To act, to do, to make; to discover, to invent; to become; to arise, to appear; to stimulate, to arouse, as to a reformation; operations, work, workmanship; a workman.

丨爲 acts, conduct, doings.

振丨 to stir up to diligence, to excite; one who makes a stir, a heroic man.

丨福 to implore blessings.

病發丨 my ailment has returned.

下丨 mean acts; stingy or close-fisted.

好丨家 very fine writing; beautiful work.

丨家 an essayist, a writer; an inventor or originator; applied to fine work, a thing well set off.

丨文章 to write essays.

丨死 you murder it I think; you'll kill yourself; murderous, savagely done, — said to careless or obstinate people.

丨反 to turn rebel.

丨新民 to stir up the people to amend their ways.

丨得很好 done extremely well.

有王者丨 a hero has appeared.

東丨 agricultural labors in spring.

丨歹 to do wickedly.

天丨 of heavenly origin.

丨疾 tricky, treacherous; virulent, as an eruption.

丨頭 or 木丨 a carpenter; a head-carpenter, a house-builder.

何必改丨 what need is there of changing or rebuilding?

五行八丨 all sorts of arts and crafts.

丨房 to act as an importer, or one who makes the goods, and sells them by wholesale.

瓦丨 or 水丨 a mason; masons, bricklayers.

In *Shanghai*. A coffin.

丨鋪店 a coffin shop.

昨 *tso* From *sun* and *hasty*. Yesterday; time gone; recently.

丨聞 I recently heard it.

丨者 some days ago.

丨日 or 丨天 or 丨兒 yesterday.

丨宵 or 丨晚 last evening.

千年如丨 a thousand years have gone like yesterday.

怍 *tso'* From *heart* and to *arouse*. Fluttered, disconcerted; to blush, to be put out of countenance; shamefaced, confused.

言不丨 he spoke without hesitation; sometimes means he spoke glibly or falsely.

容毋丨 do not blush — when you speak.

俯不丨于人 do not blush before men.

愧丨 mortified.

Read *cha'* Deceitful.

忓丨 malicious.

柞 *tso'* An evergreen oak on which silkworms feed, the *Quercus mongolica* and *dentata*; its foliage is like the chestnut oak; the wood is very firm, and used for combs; found in Manchuria and Shantung.

小葉丨樹 the *Quercus mongolica*, mostly used for feeding worms.

五丨宮 a palace of Han Wu-ti.

丨樹 a spinous tree in Kiangsi, with obovate leaves, reddish black seeds like large peas, and an inflorescence like the ash; it is used for hedges.

瑟彼丨棫民所燎矣 thick grow the oaks and scrubs which the people get for fuel.

Read *tseh*, To fell timber; to clear away the bushes; contracted, narrow; clumpy, too big for its length.

載芟載丨 to go out to cut grass and fuel.

Read *choh*, A spring 丨㮫 inside of a trap which closes on the animals.

酢, *tso'* From *spirits* and to *rouse;* it is also written 醋 in this sense, and the two are capriciously interchanged.

To pledge a host, and return his health; to recompense; a pickle; a sour taste.

是故可與酬丨 we therefore can pledge ourselves in a glass.

君子有酒酌言丨之 the princely man having wine ever thinks to ask others to pledge him in it.

鑿, *tso'* *ˎtsao* From *metal* and pounded *rice*.

A chisel, a punch; a cold chisel for cutting stones; to bore into; to dig, as a well; to sift, as evidence; to commence; to do; to open out, as a road; to brand, to mark, to tattoo; solid, secure; to cleanse rice.

蛾眉丨 a half-moon gouge.

丨井而飲 to dig a well and drink of it.

丨冰冲冲 the click of people at work cutting out ice.

斧打丨丨入木 the hammer hits the chisel, and the chisel enters the wood; if you press me, then I must force him.

穿丨 to bore a hole, as through a wall; to pervert, to corrupt, as doctrine; to bore the cheeks, as devotees do for penance.

石丨 a stone chisel.

丨丨可據 indisputable proof of the assertion.

丨通 to open a way, as a tunnel; to bore a hole.

白石丨丨 the white rocks rise up grandly in the stream.

言之丨丨可聽 he will believe it when he learns the full proofs.

精丨 fine clean rice.

事甚確丨 the thing is very certain or sure, or can be thoroughly ascertained.

丨死卯兒 a stupid fellow, one who can infer nothing.

丨齒 to knock out the teeth, as some tribes of Miaotsz' do; name of a wild beast.

撮, *tso'* *ˎts'o* From *hand* and *very*.

To take a pinch with two or three fingers, to pinch up a little; to take in the hand; a pinch, a pugil, a little, a handful; a term of depreciation; a measure of 60 (some say 256) grains of millet or 10 圭; to snatch for a short time; to bring together, to gather up; to make a resumé; to pull.

丨要 to select the most important things, as in excerptæ.

一丨土 a bit of land, a small plat.

丨合 to unite by equalizing; to bring about a reconciliation; to make a match, or form a partnership.

丨箕 a refuse-basket.

丨起灰塵 [the gust] whirls the dust up in the air.

丨上轎 to force into a sedan.

行險以丨 to run into danger by taking things.

丨糞土 to gather refuse and dung.

丨借點錢財 to lend money for a very short period.

暫丨 a very little while.

Read ˎ*tsui*. An apex; a peaked cap.

緇丨 a black cap.

繓, *ˎtso* The end of a thread left in after sewing or mending, without being tied.

結丨 fasten the raveling.

棤, *ˎtso* The coarse, split bark on some trees, as the hemlock or oak.

籗, *tsu'* To spear or hook up terrapins in the mud with fish-grains.

以時丨魚 to spear fish [or turtles] at the right time.

牢丨 a corral to gather the stock into.

TS'OH.

Old sound, ts'ak. *In Canton*, tsòk; — *in Swatow*, ch'ak; — *in Amoy*, ch'iok — *in Fuhchau*, ch'òk; — *in Shanghai* ts'òk; — *in Chifu*, ts'òa.

𠝤, *ts'o'* Regarded as another form of 錯, inexact.

To dress the horn of the rhinoceros, and make it into cups; to carve wood into things.

娖, 婡, *ˎts'o* From 女 *woman* and 足 *foot* or 束 *restrained;* the second form is obsolete; both are also read *chioh*, and interchanged with *tsuh*, 捉 to grasp.

Attentive, cautious, respectful; discreet; regular, doing the duties of.

丨丨廉謹 economical and diligent at their posts.

守丨 continually watchful, as in doing duty.

TSU.

Old sounds, tso, tsot, *and* tsak. *In Canton,* tsò *and* na; — *in Swatow,* chò *and* chu; — *in Amoy,* tsò, tsu, *and* tsui; — *in Fuhchau,* chu; — *in Shanghai,* tsu, dzò, zu, *and* 'm; — *in Chifu,* tsu.

租 *tsu* From 禾 *grain* and 組 a sacrificial *dish* contracted.

Rent or tax in kind from fields; rental, rent; income; taxes; to rent; to lease.

丨銀 or 丨子 rent in money, sometimes called 乾丨 to distinguish it from 濕丨 rent in kind.

納丨 to pay in rent; and 收丨 to collect the rent.

減丨 or 割丨 to reduce or deduct from the rent.

丨賃 to rent or lease.

丨米 rent-rice; *i. e.* grain paid in.

加丨 or 增丨 or 起丨 to raise the rent.

包丨人 or 擔丨 the security for rent.

丨業 to rent one's property.

丨屋住 to rent a house to live in.

丨地造屋 to lease a lot for building on.

小丨 bonus to a tax-gatherer.

丨地界 leased lands; lands for which ground-rent is paid.

祖 *'tsu* From *worship* and *sacrificial* vessel contracted.

A grandfather; a progenitor; ancestors; the founder, as of a family; to imitate an ancestor; the first, the origin or beginning, as of a family; to do like; to begin; to be accustomed to; to honor or propitiate wayside gods.

家丨 or 丨父 my grandfather.

先丨 my late grandfather.

曾丨 my great-grandfather.

高丨 a great-great grandfather.

元丨 or 世丨 a remote, or the first ancestor.

太丨 the first emperor of a dynasty.

丨廟 an ancestral temple; a temple of Shangti in Canton.

丨識地德 he well knew the qualities of the land.

數典不忘丨 in doing the various rules and modes, do not forget whence they came.

法丨 to imitate the originator.

丨述堯舜 he first held up Yao and Shun, as examples.

公丨大人 your excellency my grandfather; a term by which to address a prefect or intendant.

組 *'tsu* A band, fillet, tape, or braid, with which to tie the dress or hair; a fringe or tuft of silk, occasionally appended to coronets, bridles, &c.

織丨 to weave a band.

解丨歸田 to untie the girdle and return home; — to retire from office.

丨甲 the cords to fasten armor.

璣丨 strings of pearls.

素絲丨之 bound with plain-silk ribbons.

俎 *'tsu* From two 人 *men*, which is really a contraction of 肉 *flesh* upon 且 a sacrificial *dish*; not the same as 徂 to go on.

A basin or bowl on three legs, used to hold flesh in sacrifices.

丨豆之事 the affairs of worship; things relating to bowls and censers.

丨鼎 bowls and tripods, for worship.

起謀于樽丨 to concoct a conspiracy in one's cups; — *i. e.* at one's table.

樽丨之地 a little bit of land.

毑 㛗 *'tsu* From *mother* and *also;* also read *'tsié* and *'tso,* and regarded as another form of *'tsié* 姐 sister.

A dam; a granny; among the Manchus, 亞丨 is a term for mother.

丨嬰 a girlish boy; effeminate.

丨婢 a mother.

In *Cantonese* read *'na.* The female of animals.

阿丨 an old granny, a grandam.

猪丨帶耳環 a sow wearing an earring; — out of all taste, incongruous.

祚 *tsu'* From *worship* and to *excite.*

The happiness derived from wealth, emoluments, or office; felicity; a year of one's life; to confer, to bestow.

帝丨 the length of a monarch's reign.

國丨 or 年丨 the long happy duration of a dynasty.

福丨 happy and noted.

永綏王丨 may his Majesty live forever.

天丨明德 Heaven conferred illustrious virtue on him.

佐天子之丨 the happiness of helping the Emperor.

保年丨 to conserve [the monarch's] health and long life.

冲齡踐丨 the reign of a minor; a minority reign.

胙 *tsu'* From *flesh* and to *excite;* occurs used with the last.

Roast flesh offered to gods and ancestors; to set up or care for the altar to 社稷 or Ceres; blessings, rank, happiness; a seat, a place.

丨肉 sacrificial flesh.

食丨 to feast on sacrifices.

復丨 an old name for summer.

反丨 to resume a place or dignity.

分茅丨土 he divided to him land for grass and sacrifices; *i. e.* made him a feudal prince.

丨城 a city near Wei-hwui fu in Honan.

阼 tsu' The steps leading to the eastern door called 丨階, by which the guest entered; the landing-place, where the host stood to receive him.

丨席 the stair-way and seat appropriated to the chief guest.

踐丨臨祭 he passed up the steps on his way to worship.

東丨 the eastern steps.

殂 tsu' To pass away; to die, said of the decease of King Yao.

丨落 to fall and die.

草容丨謝 the beauty of the flowers fades.

徂 tsu' To advance, to go up; to travel; to go to; able to go; to preserve or lay up; name of a mall state subdued by Wăn Wang, and of a hill in Lu; henceforth.

征東丨西 to attack on the east by taking the western route, — good strategy.

我丨東山 I go to the eastern hills.

我丨維求定 I shall now only desire the security of the state.

丨征 to reduce refractory states.

TS'U.

Old sounds, ts'o, ts'ok, ts'ot, *and* dzút. *In Canton,* ts'ò; — *in Swatow,* ch'ò *and* ch'u; — *in Amoy,* ch'u; — *in Fuhchau,* ch'u *and* ch'o; — *in Shanghai,* ts'u; — *in Chifu,* ts'u.

粗 麤 麄 觕 ts'u From *rice* and *moreover;* the other two forms are now regarded as identical with it, but originally they represented *three deer* opposed to an enemy, and were defined the leaps of deer; on the lookout, as timid deer are, which stand back to back; the fourth form also means an ox's horn bending down.

Rough, uncleaned; dirty, as rice just thrashed; large, open, coarse, as a texture; rude, vulgar, boisterous; indecent, gross; vile; harsh, as a stern voice; partially, heedlessly, as in doing things.

丨細 coarse and fine, as cloth.

丨俗人 a rude, uncultivated man.

丨話 obscene language; vile talk.

精丨 delicate and coarse, as feelings.

丨完 hurried the work through.

丨知 partly learned it; some knowledge of a study or duty.

手丨 a rough hand-writing.

丨心浮氣 light and giddy; rascally and treacherous.

丨風暴雨 a sudden rain-storm.

丨大 too broad and big, as a big table in a closet.

丨疏 heedless, careless in doing things.

動丨 to resort to violence, instead of keeping the temper.

丨鹵 vulgar, unpolished.

聲丨以厲 boisterous harsh tones, as of anger.

丨食丨肥 coarse and poor food.

丨糙塞蹇的様 he looked wretchedly dirty and starved.

皻 ts'u The skin chapped and cracked, as in winter.

麆 ts'u The fawn of an antelope; great; in Shansi, a boy was once fondly so called.

怚 ts'u Proud and suspicious; unable to comprehend character fully; exceedingly.

秦王丨而不信人 Tsin Chi-hwang was so proud that he trusted nobody.

醋 ts'u' From *spirits* and *formerly;* once a synonym of *tsoh,* 酢 to pledge, but now confined chiefly to this meaning.

Vinegar; pickle; pickled.

高丨 best vinegar, of which the 黑丨 or black vinegar, and 白丨 white vinegar are two sorts.

丨拌 to serve or dress in vinegar, as cucumbers.

食丨 or 呷丨 to sip vinegar; *met.* bickering between the wife and concubine.

丨炒 to fry with vinegar.

做丨不酸 your vinegar has no sourness; — *i. e. you* can do nothing effectual.

喫丨生妬 to listen to surmises and become jealous.

一酹一丨都非偶 not even to give a bumper or a pledge happens fortuitously.

吃薑丨 to eat ginger vinegar; *met.* to have a child. (*Cantonese.*)

丨螺子 a kind of marine medusa or polypus, from which good vinegar is made; also called 明服魚 the bright bellied fish.

措 ts'u' ts'oh' From *hand* and *formerly.*

To place, to put; to relinquish, to cast away or throw down; to show abroad or make known; to employ, to use; to arrange, to set in order.

故時丨之宜也 it is therefore proper always to use it.

無所丨手足 no place to put my hands and feet; *i. e.* perplexed, at a loss.

丨施 to publish; to give out; to distribute.

丨理 to adjust.

學之弗能弗丨也 if you learn it, you must certainly practice it.

借丨無罪 no means of action; no way of flight.

設丨 to propose a plan; to open and arrange, as a shop.

何以丨詞 what phraseology will you use for this purpose?

Read *cheh,* To pursue after in order to seize; to chase; to ferret out, as robbers.

追丨 to follow and seize.

TSŬ.

Old sounds, tsio, ts'it, dzi, *and* dzit. *In Canton*, tsü; — *in Swatow*, chu; — *in Amoy*, tsò *and* tsa; — *in Fuhchau*, chü *and* chéu; — *in Shanghai*, tsü *and* dzü; — *in Chifu*, tsü *and* chü.

疽 ˏtsü From *disease* and *moreover*.

A deep-seated ulcer, like a carbuncle or anthrax.

吮 丨 to suck out a boil.

丨 爛 the abscess has opened.

而主'癰 丨 he went and lived with a curer of abscesses and cancers.

乳 丨 cancer of the breast.

趄 **跙** ˏtsü From *to go* and *moreover*; occurs used with the primitive.

Weak; unable to get on fast, from illness or lameness; to be impeded in going.

其行趦 丨 his walking is slow and hobbling.

丨 阻 impeded; stumbling along.

就成了個 丨 條子了 you'll become then only a country booby!

岨 **砠** ˏtsü Rocks thinly covered with earth; a road full of small stones and rough for traveling.

陟彼 丨 矣 they slowly toiled up that rocky slope.

狙 ˏtsü A species of monkey, the 丨 猿, also called 丨 猴 the waiting monkey, because it lies in covert, and is artful in seizing its prey; to peep, to spy, to watch for.

丨 伺 to lie in wait for.

丨 察 to examine too minutely.

丨 伏 to lie in ambush.

駿 丨 詐之兵 to detail a squad to lie in cover.

其人 丨 詐不測 this man's tricks are unfathomable.

苴 ˏtsü The female plant of the nettle hemp (*Boehmeria nivea*); some erroneously call this the male plant, and 枲 the female; sackcloth; a rush, a sedge used in making sandals; a kind of mat; coarse, rustic, unpolished; occurs used for Pa 巴 the southern part of Sz'ch'uen.

丨 布 sackcloth, mourning apparel.

丨 杖 the chief mourner's staff.

丨 麻 the female plant of the common hemp.

補 丨 to make notes on; to improve or correct bad composition, which, like mending silk with hemp, often costs more than it comes to.

苞 丨 to wrap articles in mats, paper, or other things.

履 丨 sandal or straw-shoe grass.

狄 丨 an ancient place near the Gulf of Chihli.

Read ˊcha. Drift grass, the washings that float on rivers; weeds and rotten heaps fit for manure.

邋 丨 refuse; dirt, foul stuff.

如彼棲 丨 like water drift of grass caught on trees, — so this country is in confusion.

菹 ˏtsü Fruits pickled whole or in pieces, not mashed; greens, as melons or cabbage; gherkins, sour-krout; pickles; to put in salt or brine; to impede, to interrupt.

丨 菜 salted vegetables.

Read ˏtsié. A morass full of sedge.

驅蛇龍而放之 丨 drive off the dragons and snakes, and let them loose in the swamp.

雎 ˏtsü From 隹 *birds* and 且 *moreover*; it is unlike ˏ*sui* 睢 to stare at.

A skua or gull, called 丨 鳩 which, like the mandarin duck, is said to observe conjugal fidelity in its pairings; its cry is called 關關; it is also called 王 丨 the royal duck, because it understands the civil relations of 君臣 prince and minister; it is found along the Yangtsz' River.

次 丨 for 趦趄 to go with difficulty.

娵 ˏtsü From *woman* and *to take*; it is not the same as 娶' to marry.

The name of certain stars called 丨 訾 which lie near Pegasus and Andromeda; perhaps named from the wife of 帝嚳 B. C. 2420.

閭 丨 a famous beauty in the state of 魏 Wéi.

沮 ˊtsü An affluent of the Yangtsz' River west of K'ingchau fu in Hupeh; a branch of the River Han, and the name of an ancient district near their basins, now the extreme south of Shensi in Han-chung fu; also a branch of the River Wéi in western Shensi, which it joins near Lin-tung hien.

Read ˊtsü. To stop, to prohibit; to pass over bounds, to destroy, to injure; to divulge; to threaten; to spoil, stopped; to leak or waste.

丨 止 to stop, to quash; to intrigue against.

地氣 丨 洩 the malaria escapes.

丨 洩 to blab.

濕 丨 dank, damp.

何日斯 丨 when will he stop — his evil course?

丨 之以兵 to intimidate him by his troops.

彼汾 丨 洳 in those low marshy places near the River Făn.

丨 人是非 to stop backbiting others.

Read ˏtsien. Ripples.
涓 丨 leaking; a slight rippling flow.

齟 From *teeth* and *moreover*; it is also read ˊ*chu*.
ˊtsü Irregular and unmatched, as the teeth of a saw; discordant, as opposite opinions; incongruous; to bite, to chew.
丨 齬 irregular, not in harmony; at cross purposes, as in managing an affair.

咀 From *mouth* and *moreover*.
ˊtsü To suck; to get the taste of by biting or sucking.
丨 片 bits of medicine for chewing; lozenges.
丨 嚼 to suck and bite at; to chew a little in order to get the taste.
含英 丨 華 to study and relish the beauties of a style.

商量哎 丨 to think over a matter by one's self, or after a public discussion or proposal.

In *Cantonese*. A suffix to a verb denoting the past tense.
去 丨 he has gone.

聚 冣 From 取 to *take* and three 人 *men* (*i.e.* many) underneath; the old form from 冖 a *vail* and 取 to *take*, is now unused.
tsü' To assemble, to gather, to call or invite an assembly; to collect, to bring together, to make a collection; to dwell together; to converge, as to a focus; popular; to tend to, to concur; a dwelling-place or hamlet; a meeting, the place of meeting.
丨 首 a reunion or gathering of friends or relatives.

不 丨 財 not a fortunate place; no money to be made here; a ne'er-do-well.
丨 寶堂 the shrine of the god of Wealth. (*Cantonese*.)
丨 會堂 a synagogue; a meeting-house.
丨 會 to call a meeting.
丨 議 to meet and deliberate.
丨 歛 to collect specimens; to amass property.
一家團 丨 the entire family live together.
丨 珍 collected pearls, a name given to movable copper types.
君子學以 丨 之 the princely man studies in order to combine all learning.
鄉 丨 or 丨 落 a collection of villages; — *i. e.* a city and its suburbs or dependent hamlets.

TS'Ü.

Old sounds, ts'u *and* ts'ut. *In Canton*, ts'ü; — *in Swatow*, ch'u; — *in Amoy*, ch'ò *and* chu; — *in Fuhchau*, ch'ü, chu, *and* chéu; — *in Shanghai*, ts'ü *and* tsi; — *in Chifu*, ch'ü.

趨 趋 From to *run* and *grass* as the phonetic; *q. d.* go on the grass; the contracted form is common.
ˏts'ü To run, to hasten to one's place; to stride off, as when in the presence of a superior to obey his orders; to walk quickly towards; to follow hastily.
丨 蹌 to run quickly; to sidle away politely.
亦步亦 丨 to follow step by step, as a servant.
盡 丨 謁之忱 I have an earnest desire to come and see you.
丨 向 to dwell on fondly, to long for.
丨 時 to follow the times or fashion.
丨 炎附勢 to approach the bustling place and cleave to the strong; — said of a parasite.
宇內之道各擇所 丨 amidst all the ways (doctrines) in the world, each chooses the one he goes in.

丨 步 to straddle off rapidly.
丨 赴逢迎 I hurry to receive your requests, as a sycophant.
Read ts'uhˏ To urge to constrain.
丨 民牧歛 to hasten on the people to get in the harvest.

蛆 蠦 From *insect* and *moreover*.
ˏts'ü Maggots in putrid flesh.
下 丨 or 發 丨 it has bred worms.
雪 丨 a worm in snow found in Sz'ch'uen, perhaps a species of *Protococcus* or *Philodena*.
無縫生 丨 the worms came without a crack — for the flies to enter; *i. e.* no cause for the result.
水 丨 larvæ in water like maggots; probably a kind of bloodsucker.
Read ˏtsü. The centipede, 蝍 丨 which is fabled to eat serpent's brains.

取 From 又 *hand* and 耳 *ear*, explained as referring to taking the 聝 or left ears of captives to present to the general; used for the next.
ˊts'ü To lay hold on, to take or use; to exact, to seize on or take away; to appropriate, to assume another's things or place; to take in hand and finish; to receive, as an offering; to apply to one's use; to get, to induce, to bring upon; taken, applied, selected for use; to take a wife.
收 丨 to receive; come to hand.
丨 不ˊ上 not selected or chosen; he was unsuccessful in the competition.
丨 中' chosen, selected, promoted.
大有可 丨 estimable, suitable.
一無可 丨 unfit, incapable; unlovely.
丨 出 taken out, as from a box; chosen, appropriated.

索丨 to beg earnestly for, as a loan.

自丨之禍 he brought the misery on himself.

就地丨才 happily I just then turned it up, — as something that was wanted.

不必可丨 I don't want it very much.

公丨 and 私丨 to take publicly and fairly, or illegally and secretly.

丨信 to exhibit or give evidence of faith; a trustworthy act or man.

上' 丨, and 中' 丨 and 次丨 chosen the highest on the list of graduates, near it, and lower down.

丨城池 they have taken the walls and moat.

丨名 to strive for a name; aspiring for fame.

丨來 and 丨去 to bring and take away.

丨笑他 he got the laugh on him.

丨樂 to pursue pleasure.

ʻ娶 *ʻts'ü* From *woman* and *to take.*

To take a wife; to marry a woman with the legal ceremonies; a marriage.

丨二婚婆 to marry a widow.

續丨 to marry a second wife.

丨妻 or 丨新婦 or 丨親 marrying a wife; but in order to dignify the practice, the terms 丨妾 or 丨偏房 are used for taking a concubine.

榮丨 and 貧丨 are terms used by friends when speaking of a man's marriage and by himself of it.

趣' *ts'ü'* From *to run* and *to take;* it is similar to ˏ趨 to stride.

To advance quickly; to run, to show alacrity in doing anything; to perceive what will please, and do the proper things with readiness; to regard pleasurably; jolly, pleasant, graceful; amusing, sprightly.

丨女人 a beautiful woman.

不識丨 unaccommodating, harsh, grouty.

打丨人家 to joke others, to make sport of them.

好丨 or 狠丨 very lively, gleesome; joyous.

丨味 an agreeable relish, as a pleasant drink, friends, or attractive books.

丨舍萬殊 agreeable or repulsive, makes all the difference in the world.

六丨 the six paths (*gati*) of transmigration.

意丨 brilliant, clever.

頗有興丨 this is rather jolly.

丨話 or 丨兒 a jest, a quip.

疾丨王事 to hasten the completion of public affairs.

丨向 the direction of; to go towards; — as 心之丨向不同 their views and feelings are unlike.

左右丨之 the attendants bustled about to serve — the king.

Read *ʻtseu.* To breed.

丨馬 to rear or take care of horses; an ancient office like an equerry.

Read *tsuh,* To hasten, to urge.

使丨齊兵 to hurry on the preparation of the troops.

局丨 cramped, confined; small room.

覷' 覰' *ts'ü'* From 見 *to see* and 虛 *a dish* altered.

To espy, to peep; to descry; to reconnoiter; to watch for.

丨便而行 to be on the lookout for a chance.

北寇丨邊 the northern hordes are spying our frontiers.

拘丨 to let be known, to divulge; not to keep secret.

近丨眼 very near-sighted.

TSÜEH.

Old sounds, dzit *and* tsit. *In Canton,* tsüt; — *in Swatow,* cho *and* chúat; — *in Amoy,* tswat; — *in Fuhchau,* chiòk; — *in Shanghai,* dzih; — *in Chifu,* chié.

絕ˎ *ˏtsüeh* From 絲 *silk,* 刀 *knife,* and 卩 a *knot; q. d.* cutting a knot or line of silk.

To cut short a thread, to interrupt the connection of; to sunder, to break off, to interrupt; to sever; to exterminate, to utterly destroy; to bring on ruin; to renounce, to abjure; terminated, ended; alienated; to overpass, as difficulties or a ridge; to cross a river; shooting athwart, like a meteor; a *superlative,* very, extremely, entirely, most; really, decidedly; stanzas of four lines.

丨後 or 丨嗣 or 丨戶 posterity all cut off; no heir left, as by violence or death.

斷丨 to stop; ceased, as a ration or a correspondence.

丨無好處 no luck at all; not at all a good place.

罵不丨口 he never ceases to rail and scold.

丨路 the road is broken up, the way is shut up; our resources are all cut off.

丨對 a pun on words; as 不丨對 not to be able to guess the quip or charade.

自丨于天結怨于民 he has cut himself off from heaven, and brought anger on his people.

丨賣 a final sale, as of land never to be redeemed.

五丨 stanzas in pentameters.

妙 丨 superior to all, the finest.

丨 色 very beautiful or alluring.

丨 而 不 離 separated and yet not sundered, as characters in the running hand which are slightly joined.

丨 代 佳 人 she is the belle of the age.

丨 無 更 改 it cannot be changed or retracted.

自 丨 deprive one's self of.

殺 丨 killed every one.

丨 交 the acquaintance is broken off; to cut one.

天 無 丨 人 之 路 Heaven never stops a man's ways; — *i. e.* his ills are chiefly from his own doings; like Proverbs 26 : 2.

丨 流 the flow is stopped, as a stream without an outlet.

丨 粒 自 盡 starved himself to death.

[絕+力] *ˎtsüeh* From *strength* and *cut off*. To break a thing asunder.

一 丨 兩 節 at one snap it broke in two.

蕝 *ˎtsüeh* From *grass* and *cut off*; it is also used as a synonym of *tsuiˀ* 蕞 small.

A bundle or sheaf of coarse grass, called 茅 丨, used to strain spirits through, which retains the coarse dregs.

TSÜEN.

Old sound, tsín. *In Canton*, tsun, sün, *and* shün ; — *in Swatow*, chun *and* jun ; — *in Amoy*, ˋtsun, chwʻan, *and* bún ; — *in Fuhchau*, chòng *and* chièng ; — *in Shanghai*, tsíⁿ *and* tsing ; — *in Chifu*, chien.

鐫 鋑 *ˏtsün* *ˏtsien* The second form is rather obsolete ; when read, *ˏtsien*, it also means an awl, a knife.

To engrave; to cut, as an epitaph on stone; to carve blocks for printing or ornamental work ; to censure, to degrade.

丨 石 to cut in stone.

丨 級 to degrade to a lower rank.

丨 鑿 to chisel out.

能 者 丨 勳 the able man's merits are chiseled — on the libation cups.

新 丨 a new edition, as of a set of blocks.

雋 *ˋtsün* From 隹 *birds* and 弓 a *bow*, with which they are shot.

Fat, fleshy, as a bird in good season; *met.* racy, pleasant discourse.

肥 丨 fat fleshed.

丨 縣 the name in the Tʻang dynasty of Chʻung-yang hien 崇 陽 縣 in the south of Hupeh, a part of the more ancient 下 丨 in the same region.

Read *tsunˀ* a synonym of 儁. Valiant, heroic.

英 丨 a brave man.

賢 丨 wise and brave.

吮 *ˋtsün* From *mouth* and to *permit*; it is also read *ˏshun*.

To suck, as infants do; to lick, as dogs sometimes do a sore.

丨 乾 净 sucked quite dry.

丨 味 to test the flavor.

丨 癰 to lick an ulcer; *met.* to toady to; a lick-spittle.

TSʻÜEN.

Old sounds, tsʻüen *and* dzien. *In Canton*, tsʻün ; — *in Swatow*, chwʻan *and* chwⁿa ; — *in Amoy*, chwʻan, tswan, *and* chwan ; — *in Fuhchau*, chwʻang *and* chiòng ; — *in Shanghai*, tsʻíⁿ *and* dzíⁿ ; — *in Chifu*, chʻien.

銓 *ˏchʻüen* From *metal* and *all*; occurs used for the next.

To estimate the quantity or quality; to weigh, to measure; to assort, to select according to merit and capacity, whence 丨 部 is one term for the Board of Civil Office; to value aright; a carpenter's plane.

丨 度ˀ to estimate, as a quantity; to weigh.

丨 選 to select, as proper men.

丨 衡 to put in the balance.

丨 量 to judge of.

丨 才 諷 說 之 徒 a foolish, reckless defamer.

輇 *ˏchʻüen* From *carriage* and *entire*; interchanged with the last.

A wagon with a mat or screen, and low solid wheels.

丨 車 a rude cart to truck grain.

詮 *ˏchʻüen* From *words* and *complete*.

To explain, to comment on; to illustrate or expound; to make a résumé; to discourse upon and enforce; allusions, comparisons.

註 丨 explanatory notes.

丨 義 to open out the meaning.

言 丨 to explain fully.

丨 證 full proof.

未 奉 丨 論 I have not yet received your full discourse, — referring to a letter.

痊 *ˏchʻüen* Recovered from sickness; cured, convalescent, well.

病 丨 quite recovered.

醫 丨 quite strong again.

未 能 大 丨 not thoroughly recovered.

筌 ꜀*chʻüen* A bamboo trap or creel for catching fish or crabs; the entrance is guarded by points converging inwards.

得魚忘丨 to get the fish and forget the trap; — ungrateful for benefits.

佺 ꜀*chʻüen* The *man* who is *complete;* the name of 偓丨, one of the genii who gave pine seeds to Yao, and he refusing to eat them, his attendants did so, and lived hundreds of years.

荃 ꜀*tsʻüen* A fragrant plant; spicery, seasoning; fine grasscloth; used for you, in polite address among friends; — as 丨照 or 丨鑒 your observation, your care of; your information.

丨蕪香 a perfume found in the 波弋 country, which makes even the earth and stones fragrant wherever it is buried, and causes flesh to grow on old bones if burned under them.

悛 ꜀*chʻüen* From *heart* and to *strut.* To change, to alter; to trust to one's opinion; presumptuous; willful; next in order; to rest.

怙惡不丨 wickedly obdurate and irreclaimable.

不速丨改 refusing to reform.

丨心 penitent, heartily sorry.

Read ꜀*sün,* a synonym of 恂. Sincere, honest.

丨從 to rely on another.

跧 ꜀*chʻüen* To kick; to tread on, as if to try the weight; to sit on the heels; decrepit, bowed; to meander.

丨莊 to crawl; to go stooping over.

全 仝 ꜀*chʻüen* The common form from 入 to *enter* and 玉 *gem*, refers to a scepter; the antique form of 入 to *enter* and 工 *work*, shows that the work is done; but another old form is composed of 入 and 弄 a probable derivation; the first is easily mistaken for ꜀*kin* 金 metal.

Completed, finished; entire in all its parts; unbroken, perfect; all, the whole; to do all that is required; to complete.

完丨 all done; all in order.

兼丨 to lump all together.

丨智丨能 almighty and omniscient.

丨家利市 may your whole family prosper.

丨副精神 with undivided energies.

以丨和好 in order to render complete our peaceful relations.

丨仗着冬天的雪 everything depends on the winter's snow.

丨 and 不丨 and 丨加 are foreign grammatical terms for the perfect, imperfect, and pluperfect tenses.

萬丨無弊 not the least defect — or misfortune.

大丨 complete, as the works of an author.

丨權大臣 a plenipotentiary or envoy with full powers; — a foreign term.

不能丨盤交出 the whole matter (or all the facts) has not been made known.

丨肯 all are willing.

完丨的事體 a perfect organization; a business entirely settled.

才貌雙丨的人 his mind and body are equally perfect.

丨要來個 all of them must come.

牷 ꜀*chʻüen* A *bullock* that is *perfect,* one which is complete in all its parts, having no spot or blemish, and uniform in color, called 丨牲, required in sacrifice.

牲丨肥腯 a fat and unblemished victim.

泉 洤 ꜀*chʻüen* From 水 *water* and 白 *white,* as if denoting pure water; but the original form represents a *covering* and a *line,* the aspect of a spring and its rill; the second form is not uncommon.

A fountain, a spring; the head-waters of a river; money, riches.

井丨 a well at a spring.

立丨 or 飛丨 a water-fall, a cascade.

貨丨 the money or coin of the usurper Wang Mang.

黃丨 or 九丨 the grave, hades, or elysium.

黃丨路上 he has gone to the shades.

歸丨養老 to lay up a fountain (*i. e.* a fortune) for old age.

丨水 spring water.

TSUH.

Old sounds, tsot, tsok, *and* dzut. *In Canton,* tsȯk, tsut, *and* tsʻüt; — *in Swatow,* chȯk, chut, chui, *and* chʻȯk; — *in Amoy,* tsut, chiok, siok, tsok, *and* chʻek; — *in Fuhchau,* chȯk *and* chʻéuk; — *in Shanghai,* tsăh, tsʻok *and* dzȯk; — *in Chifu,* tsu.

卒 卆 ꜀*tsu* Originally composed of 十 *ten* under 衣 *clothes,* because retainers wore dyed garments; the first form is the common one, and is interchanged with several of its derivatives.

Those who execute a chief's orders, as lictors, underlings, menials, retainers; to conclude, to finish; soldiers, privates; to have a sequel; the end; to die, to come to an end; white pawn in chess; an *adverb,* hurriedly, suddenly; quite, entirely; then, when all was over.

兵丨 soldiers.

士丨 officers and men.

小丨 camp-followers.
倉丨至此 why are you in such a haste?
丨爲善士 he was a good man to the last.
終丨 died, gone.
病丨 a mortal disease.
讀書丨時 the time for study is over or past.
丨然問 suddenly asked him.
丨急 in a great hurry.
丨然來到 he all at once came on him.
丨于任內 died in the service of government.
無名小丨 an unknown private; a fellow of no account.
監丨 turnkeys.

𣨛, ˏtsu Interchanged with the last.
To die, to end; said of officials of an inferior rank.
丨歿 to die.

捽, ˏtsu To grasp, to clutch, to seize; to throttle; to clinch in the hand; to run against, to butt; to snatch or take out, as a drowning person.
丨住頭髮 seized him by the hair.
丨頸 grasped him by the nape.
撞丨鐘聲 the wind clangs the tongues of the bells.
一丨 a very little, a handful.

椊, ˏtsu To put a handle in a socket, as a helve into the eye of an ax; the protruding top of a pillar above the cross beam.
丨杌 to put in a helve.

𣯲, ˏtsu Also read *suh*,
Short hair, as on an ox; hairy.
一丨毛兒 a hair-mole.

足, ˏtsu Composed of 口 *mouth* and 止 to *stop*, but another says the upper part really represents the thigh; it is the 157th radical of characters referring to motions.

The leg; the foot; enough, full, sufficient; no deficiency or debasement; to satisfy, to make up what is wanting; entirely, in full; pure, as unalloyed silver; actions, conduct; to move; to connect.
十丨 complete in all respects.
手丨不相爭 the hands and feet (*i. e.* brothers) should not quarrel.
丨够用 there is plenty for all our uses.
自丨 self-sufficient, conceited.
丨丨找你半天 I've greatly annoyed you a long time.
丨丨有一百兩 a full hundred taels.
失丨 to slip up, to make a blunder; a faux-pas.
丨下 your presence, your honor, you, Sir.
不知丨 unsatisfied, never contented.
不我丨 does not meet my wishes.
不丨道 not worth talking about; a trifling affair.
丨數不丨 is the number (or length) just right?
滿丨 quite right; full.
不一而丨 not one occasion by any means.
丨色銀兩 silver of standard purity.
丨可以行 it can be done.
豐丨 abounding, as a plentiful harvest; well supplied, abundant.
不丨以當大事 he is unfit to undertake a large business.
何丨怪 what is there wonderful in that?
維日不丨 the days are not enough to enjoy it all.

Read ʻtsü. To treat others with respect for the furtherance of one's ends is 丨恭; to increase; to benefit; to push along.
丨言丨容 to be careful of one's words and actions.

踧, ˏtsu From *foot* and *uncle*; occurs interchanged with the next.
To walk with great care, as when carrying a precious thing, or in the presence of a ruler.
丨縮縮 to advance step by step.

Read *tʻih*, To walk with ease on a level road.
丨丨周道 to go along pleasantly on the high road.

蹙, ˏtsu From *foot* and to *pity*; used with the last, and occurs interchanged with 蹴, to kick.
To press, to urge forward, to hasten; impelled; urgent; cramped, embarrassed; wrinkled, contracted; to trouble; anxious, careworn; to draw in, to retract.
今也日丨國百里 the borders of the state are now pushed in a hundred *li* a day.
近丨 pressed upon closely, as by a creditor.
丨丨 cramped for room; hampered; contracted; distressed.
丨額 or 頻丨 to contract the eyebrows, as when angry or anxious.
丨然 imminently.
促丨 to impel, to drive.

顣, ˏtsu Interchanged with the last.
To frown, to wrinkle the forehead.
丨頞 to knit the eyebrows.
愁丨 careworn; a furrowed brow.

嘁, ˏtsu Grieved, ashamed; to redden, to color up.
丨吝 mortified, sorry.

In *Pekingese*. A subdued or indistinct sound.
丨丨 whispering, in a low voice.

噈, ˏtsu Also read *tsah*,
To smack the lips; to draw in the breath; to kiss another; to bring the lips of two persons together.
嗚丨 to smack the lips, and purse up the mouth.

槭, ˏtsu A tree found in Shansi, furnishing good timber for thills; its flowers are white, shaped like the cotton flower, and the leaves are quinary, on long petioles; to shed leaves; to reach; bare, leafless branches.

族 ˏtsu From a *flag* and a *dart*, referring to the head of a javelin where a pennon is tied to recognize it afterward.

To collect into one place, as a banner signalizes men to do; a clan, a tribe; a family, which traces its descent from one ancestor, and has one surname; kindred, relatives; a class, a kind.

宗 丨 of the same clan.

丨 譜 the clan register of names.

出 丨 to disown, to turn out of the family.

丨 ʻ長 or 丨 老 the senior of the clan.

三 丨 father, son, and grandson; also, father, mother, and wife's kindred.

水 丨 aquatic animals.

百 丨 creation; animated nature.

累及同 丨 compromised all his clan or family.

言歸復我邦 丨 then back to my country and kin.

鏃 ˏtsu The head or barb of an arrow or a javelin; the point of a dart.

利 丨 sharp barbs.

去其 丨 knocked off the barbs.

TSʻUH.

Old sounds, tsʻok, tsʻut, *and* dzut. *In Canton*, tsʻŏk, tsŏk, *and* tsʻüt; — *in Swatow*, chʻŏk; — *in Amoy*, tsut, tsok, *and* chʻiok; — *in Fuhchau*, chʻóuk, chúk, *and* chŏk; — *in Shanghai*, tsʻŏk *and* tsʻăh; — *in Chifu*, tsʻu.

促 tsʻuʾ From *man* and *foot*; this and the next are interchanged with *tsuh*, 蹙 to urge.

To constrain, to urge; urgent, driven, pressed on; near, close; shortened, contracted.

局 丨 hampered; a narrow space.

丨 膝談心 to cross knees and talk upon matters, as long absent friends.

丨 之太甚 to urge one overmuch, to constantly talk to one.

時候短 丨 the time is very short.

追 丨 to hurry on, to stimulate.

丨 織 the house-cricket, because it incites the goodwife to weaving; its chirp is supposed to resemble the sound made by a rapid shuttle.

蹴 ˏtsʻu From *foot* and *then*; also read *tsʻuh*, and interchanged with 蹙 to urge.

To tread on; to press on with the foot; to kick.

丨 然 carefully, seriously.

丨 踼 to tread on.

踤 tsʻuʾ To butt, to run against, to kick the shin.

Read *tsuiʾ* To huddle, to flock together; treading on one another.

鷺 丨 於林 the egrets gather in flocks in the wood.

猝 tsʻuʾ From *beast* and *lictor*; it is interchanged with its primitive.

A dog rushing from a cover; to rush out and drive people away; abrupt, precipitate.

倉 丨 impetuous; perplexed and hurried by affairs.

丨 然 soon; readily; abruptly.

崒 tsʻuʾ High; hazardous, as the summit of a peak like the Matterhorn.

山冢 丨 崩 the peak came crashing down.

簇 tsʻuʾ tseuʾ From *bamboo* and *clan*; it is nearly synonymous with the next.

Small bamboos; a framework or whisk, on which silkworms spin their cocoons; an arrow-head or barb; a crowd of people, a group; a mold for making cakes; in *botany*, a round corymb, like the snowball; a cyme.

丨 擁前來 they came pressing on in a crowd.

修成蠶 丨 to attend to the silkworms laying.

數百朵成 丨 several hundred flowrets making one tuft.

花團錦 丨 like heads of flowers and colored groups; — said of fine embroidery or a well written essay.

丨 丨 新 bran new; fine; clean and all new, as a dress.

Read *tsʻeuʾ* Things budding in the spring, said of grass in tussocks; thick, vigorous growth.

萬物 丨 生 all nature springing into life.

律中ʾ太 丨 a great springing forth among the tubes; *i. e.* the spring is coming on; — the 太 丨 or 泰 丨 was a pipe anciently played in the first moon.

蔟 tsʻuʾ Like the last.

A nest; to collect, to call together; a crowd; a silkworm whisk.

風如 丨 a strong gust of wind.

泎 tsʻuʾ The noise of splashing or bubbling waters; an old name of the Chehkiang 浙江 river; occurs used for 酌 to plan.

瀱 丨 intermittent, as a fountain; outside of the capital of Kwéicheu, there is an intermittent well which rises and falls a hundred times a day, going regularly like a clepsydra.

邦 丨 to spy into the plans of a state in order to surprise it.

In *Cantonese*. Soft, like thin mud or fresh mortar; thin, fluid, as milk; lean; careless of one's reputation.

炷 丨 的 cook it very soft.

TSUI.

Old sounds, tsui, dzui, tsut. *and* dzut. *In Canton*, tsui *and* tsúi ; — *in Swatow*, chué *and* chui ; — *in Amoy*, tsui, tsòé, ch'ui, *and* tswat ; — *in Fuhchau*, choi, chòi, *and* ch'òi ; — *in Shanghai*, ts', tsüé *and* dzüé ; — *in Chifu*, tsói.

嗺 ˏtsui To purse up the mouth, as when about to sip or to kiss.

丨口 to pucker the mouth.

丨酒逐歌 to guzzle wine and blurt out songs.

丨頹 depressed, complaining, weakened.

Read ˏsui. To urge to drink when singing and playing.

𣐈 ˏtsui From 束 to *bind* and 此 *this*; it is regarded as another form of the next.

To know; to store up, to conceal; the mouth, the beak; stone needles used in acupuncture.

嘴 ˋtsui From *mouth* and to *bristle up*.

A bird's bill; the lips; a beak, a snout; a mouth; a muzzle, a spout, an aperture, a nozzle; to wrangle, to talk much and impudently, to give lip.

親丨 to kiss.

烟筒丨 mouth-piece of a pipe.

油丨光棍 glib-tongued; a specious rascal.

丨臊 vile upbraidings, scurrilous, apt at reviling.

你莫多丨 don't chatter so much.

不答丨 do not interfere; don't reply to it.

賣丨乖 to boast of one's eloquence.

丨說易ˋ it's all easy enough to talk.

打丨巴 to beat the lips, a cruel mode of torture.

丨碎 loquacious, garrulous.

水丨 a reckless talker.

丨饞的狠 or 好ˋ食丨頭 my mouth waters much for it; to love good eating.

接丨 or 幫丨 to take the part of; to side with, as in a dispute.

利丨 a skillful pleader.

貪丨 or 爲丨 gluttonous.

撒丨 or 闘丨 to wrangle, to bicker, to raise a dispute.

一丨官話 he has learned to speak the court dialect, — intimating that it is another language than his mother tongue.

蠵 ˏtsui Also read ˏtsz'

A species of tortoise, called 丨龜 or 丨蠵 and found near the mouth of the Yellow River; its shell is fine enough for ornaments, but much inferior to tortoise-shell.

醉 tsuiˋ From *spirits* and come to the *end* of, as of the ability to drink.

Exhilirated with drink; happy, fuddled, intoxicated, drunk; a debauch; fascinated with, stupefied with, devoted to; unconscious, as a man of his danger; engrossed with.

喝丨 or 飲丨 drunken.

不知丨 not affected by liquor.

丨漢 (or 丨酒佬 in *Cantonese*) a drunkard, a sot.

丨鄉 intoxicated, maudlin.

丨八仙 a drunken lout, a winebibber.

詐丨 or 裝丨的 one who feigns to be drunk.

丨眼 sleepy from drink; also, a term of railing for a man's inattentive looking.

心丨六經 the mind wrapped up in the classics.

丨如泥 drunk as a clod.

酒不丨人人自丨 if you make yourself drunk, it is not [the fault of] the wine.

無酒三分丨 he's half drunk and yet has drunk nothing; *i. e.* he acts like a simpleton.

神具丨止 the spirits have drunk to the full.

檇 tsuiˋ A clothes' beater.

丨李 an old name for Kiahing fu in Chehkiang.

罪 辠 tsuiˋ From 网 *net* and 非 *wrong*; *q. d.* crime entangles men into the net of the law; the ancient form, which was changed by Tsin because it resembled 皇 emperor, is composed of 自 *self* and 辛 *bitter*, and refers to the offender, but the 自 is also a contraction of 鼻 *origin*, as transgression is the origin of sorrow.

A bamboo net for fish; to become involved, as a law-breaker; trespass, crime, sin, fault; injury, damage; a violation of order, law, or decorum; to give occasion for blame; to criminate, to regard one as guilty; to deal with him so; punishment, retribution.

丨犯 or 丨人 a criminal.

得丨你 I have offended you; I beg your pardon.

犯了小丨 a venial sin, a peccadillo.

丨上加丨 a repeated offense.

問丨 to examine a criminal.

定丨 to sentence for crime.

王子犯法與民同丨 violation of law is the same crime in prince as people.

受丨 got his demerits; he has been punished; received damage; alluding to the idea of transmigration and its sanctions.

死丨 a capital crime.

丨所應得 a well deserved fate.

丨惡貫盈 the measure of his iniquity is full.

丨之 to criminate one.

庶無丨悔以迄于今 no one has caused blame or regret to the present time.

負荊請丨 to take a rod and request punishment, — as is said to the emperor by officials.

無丨以富貴 the innocent are the really honorable.

天討有丨 Heaven reckons with the guilty.

最 tsui' From 日 to *speak*, (but really changed from 冐 to *offend*) and 取 to *take*; *i. e.* to come in contact with and take away.

To assemble the whole company; to carry anything to the extreme; a high grade of military merit; an intensive *adverb*, which precedes its subject, exceedingly, extremely.

丨善 excellent and good.

投丨 to come together, as to a fair.

丨美 the handsomest of all.

丨要緊 the most important.

丨先 in the front, very first of all.

以此爲丨 this is the most so of all, as high, or good, or fit, &c.

丨便當 the most convenient; the handiest.

丨不中用 not of the least use.

丨早 too early, by far.

報丨 reported for promotion, — by one's superiors.

丨難 very difficult, the most difficult.

蕞 tsui' Small, insignificant, as a country; vile, contemptible; to collect; an ancient place near Si-ngan fu.

丨芮 to assemble.

丨爾之國 a small unimportant country.

嶵 tsui' Hilly, rough country; mountainous.

上林岑以壘丨 the range is not only very steep, but rugged also.

TS'UI.

Old sounds, ts'ui, dzui, ts'ut, *and* dzut. *In Canton*, ts'ui *and* ts'úi; — *in Swatow*, ch'ui, kúi, *and* chui; — *in Amoy*, ch'ui, tsoé, soé, tsui, *and* tsut; — *in Fuhchau*, ch'oi, chw'ói, chw'i, *and* sòi; — *in Shanghai*, ts'üé; — *in Chifu*, ts'éi.

催 ˛ts'ui To urge, to press, to importune; to hasten, as the payment of a debt; to dun; to egg on; to reiterate.

丨討 to demand urgently.

乏价走丨 I have no servant to send to hasten you; — written on invitation notes.

丨請 to repeat the invitation; to hurry — the guest.

丨得我 he is pressing me for it.

丨促 or 丨迫 to press, to expedite, to drive forward.

丨科 to urge the payment of land taxes.

崔 確 ˛ts'ui From 山 *hill* and 隹 *good*; the second form is unusual.

A high mountain; a town in the kingdom of Tsi, whence the surname was derived.

丨嵬 high, rocky summits.

摧 ˛ts'ui From *hand* and *lofty*.

To repress, to stop, to drive back; to force into a certain way or to obey; to overpower; to push, to impel, to thrust at, to scorn; to destroy, as a family; to reach, to arrive; to break, as wind does the trees; to feed, as with forage.

丨折 to break off.

丨剛爲柔 to oblige the obstinate to become yielding, or the stiff to be supple.

丨倒 to push over.

交徧丨我 everybody scolds and rails at me.

丨烷了箍 you've pounded the hoop till it has burst.

先祖于丨 the departed sire has now come — to partake of the sacrifice.

丨抑 to restrain the temper; to repress, to abate.

丨之秣之 feed him with forage and grain.

縗 ˛ts'ui From *silk* and *frayed*; also read ˛*shwai*, and interchanged with its primitive.

A strip of sackcloth anciently worn on the breast as a badge of mourning, six inches long and four wide; the unhemmed frayed edges of mourning apparel.

斬丨 in deep mourning, referring to this raveled coarse dress.

榱 ˛ts'ui Also read ˛*shwai*.

The small rafters which project from the eaves like a frayed edge, and support the tiling; they were formerly called 丨桷 but now are usually termed ˛*ch'wen* 椽; the 華丨 are often ornamented or carved.

璀 ˋts'ui The luster of gems; pearls hanging down.

戈甲丨錯 the spears and arms lay mixed in confusion; *i. e.* like gems on a dress.

漼 ˋts'ui Deep, clear water; fresh, clean; tears trickling down; spoiled, destroyed; frozen drifts of snow, for which the next is also used.

有丨者淵 there was a deep place in the stream.

漼 ˋts'ui Sleet and snow together.

丨溰 hoar-frost coming with snow.

倅 ts'ui' From *man* and *soldier*; it occurs used for 卒 a cohort of a hundred men.

A substitute, a vice; secondary or supplementary, an aid.

丨車 the second grade of *küjin*.

郡丨 a deputy sub-prefect.

遊丨 a circuit examiner.

啐 ts'ui' To alarm, to call; to taste, to put in the mouth, to sip.

驚丨 to terrify by bawling.

丨嘗 to get the flavor of.
咄丨 to slobber in eating.
丨唾沫 to spit at one.
丨了一口 I took one taste.

Read *tsuh*, To craunch; to suck and smack the lips.
嘈丨 a hubbub, a row and clamor.
丨乾淨 sucked it dry.

悴 *ts'ui'* From *heart* and *dead*.
Sad, downcast, chagrined.
哀丨 distressed, grieved.
憔丨容顏 a cadaverous countenance; distressed, fallen.
困丨 in extremity, disheartened.

顇 *ts'ui'* Like the preceding, and used with the next.
Wearied; sad; worn out, decrepit.
Read *tsuh*, A short face.

瘁 *ts'ui'* Diseased; wearied; decrepit by age, service, or ailments; the infirmities of age.
僕夫況丨 his postman was worn out.
癄丨之音 melancholy sad notes, as of the lute.
勞丨 full of cares, exhausted by toil.
鞠躬盡丨 the whole body entirely worn out; in a state of decrepitude.

淬 *ts'ui'* Interchanged with the next.
To harden iron by plunging it in water; to temper; to dye to come into contact with, as fire with water; to flow.
寒丨 chilly.
丨鉄 to harden iron.
丨布 to dye cloth.

焠 *ts'ui'* Nearly the same as the preceding.
An extinguisher; to plunge and put out fire; to temper; to burn.
有子臥而丨掌 Yiutsz' (a disciple of Confucius) scorched his palm to prevent nodding.

清水丨其鋒 harden its point by dipping it in clear water; *met.* to stimulate people by promotion or promises.

翠 *ts'ui'* The feathers of the turquoise kingfisher, the 翡丨 or 丨碧鳥 which are used in plumagery; the name is said to be an imitation of the whirring sound of the wings; applied also to the humming bird.
丨微 lying on a hill-side.
點丨 to put on feathers; to imitate feather-work in enamel.
丨毛 the kingfisher's feathers.
丨轎 a bridal chair adorned with plumagery.
丨館 a brothel.
丨色 a purplish blue.
丨雀花 the larkspur.
丨花 a head ornament of ladies.
珠圍丨繞 bound around with pearls and clasped with feathers; — richly dressed.

臎 *ts'ui'* The tail of a bird, called 尾巴 in common discourse; the bones of the pelvis.
丨肉 the flesh of a bird's tail.

脆 **脃** *ts'ui'* The original and second form is 肉 *flesh* and 絕 *to break off*, contracted to 色 *color*, but the first form is most used.
Delicate, easily broken; brittle, crackling, easily shivered; short, light, as pastry; trifling, unsteady in character.
柔丨 or 輭丨 mellow and soft as a ripe apple; crisp.
乾丨 dry and crisp, as hard baked cakes.
鹹丨花生 ground-nuts baked in salt very crisp.
作事爽丨 to do things quickly and smartly.
油炸的很丨 fried in fat very crisp.
爽丨 delicate, as pie-crust.
丨森森的 to crackle when eating, as ginger snaps.

膬 *ts'ui'* Almost the same as the last.
Tender; crisp and sweetish, yet firm, as well cooked meat.
肥美甘丨 fat and delicious, as a tender capon.

篧 *ts'ui'* A bamboo brush or scrub, called 丨箒; a whisk used by cooks to clean pans.

毳 *ts'ui'* From *hair* thrice repeated, to denote its fineness.
The down on birds; the fine fur next the skin; furry, downy; soft, velvety; crisp; delicate; fragile, easily broken.
丨冕 a plush cap worn in old times.
火丨 asbestos cloth.
甘養丨親 to get delicate food for parents.
綿丨 cotton staple, raw cotton.
丨布 cloth with a nap; plush.
丨衣如菼 his court robes glitter like the rushes in seed.

萃 *ts'ui'* Grassy, tussocky; a collection, a selection; to be with; collected together, to congregate, as people into towns; to roost on; used for 倅 an aid.
羣丨而州處 to come and dwell together in a town.
森丨 a thicket; thick and leafy like jungle.
丨蔡 a rustling sound, as of bushes.
出類拔丨 to select the meritorious out of the crowd.
王命所在理所丨也 wherever the imperial orders reach, there men of principle gather.
丨錦 books of elegant extracts.
丨於一堂 brought together in the same school.

稡 *tsui'* Similar to the preceding.
To collect, to bring together.
會丨舊說 to make a collection of old sayings.
百貨出處不如丨處 it is better to gather all commodities than to have them go abroad; — protection of native industry.
Read *tsuh*, Grain in the milk.

TSUN.

See also under TSIUN. *Old sounds,* tsun *and* dzun. *In Canton,* tsün *and* tsun ; — *in Swatow,* chun ; — *in Amoy,* tsun ; — *in Fuhchau,* chòng *and* chw'ang ; — *in Shanghai,* tsăng *and* tsing ; — *in Chifu,* tsăn.

尊 ˏtsun From 廾 *two hands* contracted to 寸 an *inch,* under 酋 *chief,* to represent handing a cup to a man ; occurs used for the next two.

High, honorable, eminent, respected ; noble ; you, your, in direct address ; to honor, to venerate ; to dignify ; a wine vessel.

令 丨 your father.

丨 駕 your honor ; you, Sir.

丨 夫 人 your wife.

丨 敬 to venerate and esteem.

丨 者 an appellation of Budhas and arhans, answering to *arya* or venerable ; given to those who have mastered the four spiritual truths ; the term 世 丨 honored by the world, is a title given to every Budha ; and by an easy transition, 一 丨 菩 薩 comes to mean a Budhist idol.

至 丨 the emperor.

丨 ˋ長 elderly, honored persons.

府 丨 the prefect.

丨 榮 respectable ; good family and character.

丨 德 樂 道 to honor virtue and delight in philosophy.

一 丨 砲 one cannon ; a local use, perhaps derived from the respect it demands.

天 下 有 達 丨 三 there are three classes in the world to be honored ; — the noble, the aged, and the virtuous.

元 始 天 丨 Laotsz', the honored in heaven.

屈 丨 你 I have given you trouble ; I beg your pardon.

禮 者 自 卑 而 丨 人 the well bred disesteem themselves and honor others.

繜 ˏtsun Drawers for women reaching to the knees ; used for the last in the phrase 丨 紺 to be careful.

樽 罇 墫 ˏtsun From *wood* or *vase* or *earth* and to *honor.*

A vase or goblet for libations ; a glass or cup ; a wine-jar or amphora ; a decanter ; the last forms are commonly used at Canton for bottle, phial, flask, or small jug, whether of stone or glass ; to drink from a bottle ; luxuriant foliage.

一 丨 酒 a bottle (or cup) of spirits.

把 丨 對 飲 to take a glass with one.

花 丨 a flower vase.

開 丨 open the bottle or jar.

遵 ˏtsun From to *go* and to *honor ; e. g.* to follow the honorable ; occurs used for *chwen'* 僎 a headman.

To follow orders, to obey, to comply with, to conform to ; to act as required, as an officer in carrying out instructions ; to induce to follow, or influence to obedience ; to accord with times ; obedience, acquiescence ; as an *adverb,* accordingly, consequently ; had no other way to act.

丨 旨 to follow the emperor's behests.

丨 法 to obey laws.

具 丨 carried out every order.

丨 王 之 路 to walk in the ways of the ancient kings.

丨 守 to keep in obedience.

丨 者 those who honor and keep the precepts.

丨 行 儒 教 to become (or act as) a literary man.

撙 ˏtsun To adjust, to regulate ; to observe rule and order, and thus restrain others.

丨 不 下 we cannot be more sparing.

丨 節 to economize ; to keep within the rules.

丨 丨 to call together.

日 用 要 丨 着 you must daily use a little less.

嶟 ˏtsun Lofty, grand, as a mountain peak.

丨 丨 elevated ; peering one above another, as mountain peaks.

噂 譐 ˋtsun The first character is the most in use, and both are often read ˏtsun.

Many persons conversing amicably without real friendship ; to talk agreeably ; unitedly, as a chorus.

丨 沓 背 憎 to speak fair words, and then backbite each other.

In *Cantonese.* To have a thing ready, as an ax to cut a tree.

丨 沓 埋 嚨 lay them all by carefully.

僔 ˋtsun Like the last.

To assemble ; to respect, to have a regard for.

丨 集 to come together.

丨 敬 有 德 to show respect to the virtuous.

鐏 ˋtsun The copper ferule or place to grasp, on the handle of a spear.

進 戈 者 前 其 丨 when handing a dart present it by the handle.

駿 tsün' From *horse* and to *walk slowly ;* it occurs used for the next, and for *siün'* 峻 lofty.

A stately, fine shaped horse ; a noble steed, of which Mah-wang 穆 王 of Cheu had eight ; dignified, reserved without being proud ; excelling ; great ; lofty ; swift ; rapid.

丨馬 a majestic horse.

丨速 fleet, as a racer or ship.

精丨 a hero.

丨命不易' the great appointment will be hard — to carry out.

追風丨 a courser fleet as the wind.

丨極于天 [these mountains] reach to the skies.

丨丨 very exalted, like a sage.

丨發其私 altogether express or make clear his private opinions.

俊' *tsün'* From *man* and to *walk*; it is also used with the last and the next.

Superior, remarkable, one of a thousand; talent or ability of such; eminent.

丨士 a fine scholar.

丨傑在位 to have brave and sterling men in office.

羣歸丨秀 all were distinguished for their high accomplishments.

丨俏龐兒 an elegant lady.

他的模樣很丨 her form is very handsome.

千人曰丨 he is one of a thousand.

丨人物 a fine-looking man.

曰三有丨克則丨 those who were termed having the three grades of talent, could exhibit their powers — in proper stations.

儁' *tsün'* Used for its primitive, and also like the last.

Valiant, brave; able, pre-eminent in force or wisdom; to overcome; to raise.

丨異 extraordinary, unrivaled; strange.

英丨 a brave hero.

儶' *tsün'* Intelligent, quick of apprehension.

心思靈丨 a bright mind and lively imagination.

慧丨 perspicuous, clever, astute.

晙' *tsün'* To look at carefully.

丨晉灼 a hero in the Han dynasty.

餕' *tsün'* The remains of a sacrifice; the fragments left after a meal; to eat the remnants; dressed food.

佐丨 to eat at the second table; *i. e.* to urge parents to eat more, and then for children to eat their leavings.

丨旣盡也 every thing has been eaten up.

丨餘不祭 leavings cannot be used for offerings.

日中而丨 at noon eat what was left at breakfast.

畯' *tsün'* The *chief* of the *fields*, a landlord, a proprietor; an officer who had oversight of the fields; a sort of bailiff was anciently called 田丨 because he was 田之俊 the great man of the fields.

寒丨 a clown, a rude peasant.

焌' *tsün'* A fire burning; to put out a fire; to scorch or prick shell in divination.

丨了香火 to put out the incense and candles; it is done by the acolytes to save them.

捘' *tsün'* To pinch the flesh with the fingers; to put the nails together, as when killing a flea; to push away; to lay the hand on.

丨蝨 to crack a louse.

丨衛侯之手 he pinched the arm of the prince of Wéi.

鼨' *tsün'* A kind of marmot found in the hilly parts of Sz'ch'uen, 丨鼠 or 鼫鼠 whose tail furnishes hairs for pencils; it eats chestnuts and roots, and destroys fields like the mole; its cry is musical.

TS'UN.

Old sounds, ts'un *and* dzun. *In Canton*, ts'ün; — *in Swatow*, ch'un *and* ch'ăng; — *in Amoy*, ch'un, tsun, *and* chw'an; — *in Fuhchau*, ch'òng, ch'aung, *and* chòng; — *in Shanghai*, ts'ăng *and* dzăng; — *in Chifu*, ts'ăn.

村 邨 *˛ts'un* From *wood* and *inch*; the second and obsolete form, composed of 屯 to *collect* and 邑 *town*, is regarded as more authentic; it resembles *˛ts'ai* 材 material.

The beginning of a town; a hamlet, a village.

丨俗 rustic, unpolished; gross, paganish.

丨子 or 鄉丨 a village; country places.

丨夫 a villager, a countryman

丨莊 or 丨落 villages and farmsteads.

丨墟 a market village.

撒丨 to scatter village abuse; to blackguard people.

存 *˛ts'un* From 子 *child* and 手 or 才 *hand*; *q. d.* the latter protects the former.

To preserve or defend from injury; to maintain, to retain, as a purpose or principle; to take care of, as one's health; to inquire after, to heedfully look after, to watch; to lay by, to let remain, to put away, to place on deposit; left over, as a balance of account; extant, alive; to exist.

丨沒 and 丨亡 are correlatives, — as alive or dead; to preserve and to ruin, as a dynasty; to continue or to destroy; saved or lost.

告丨 to inform the emperor of one's recovery or health, as aged officers should do; also, to make kind inquiries about.

以仁丨心 to preserve the heart in humane feelings, *i. e.* pure from vice or error.

保 丨 to conserve; to keep warily.

丨 厚道 to maintain cordial relations with; to uphold good principles of conduct.

丨 一點後裔 only one of his descendants remained.

丨 留 to detain or keep back.

尙 丨 it still remains, it is still extant.

丨 養 to nurture goodness in the heart.

丨 身 to take care of one's self, to keep out of danger.

丨 下 to lay aside carefully.

收 丨 to gather or store carefully.

意 丨 a settled purpose.

無 丨 nobody spared alive or escaped; nothing was saved.

丨 了食 undigested, indigestible.

蹲 ꜀ts'un ꜀tun From *foot* and *honor;* this is used for a colloquial word (occasionally written 蹾) ꜀*tun*, having this meaning, whence this too is sometimes read ꜀*tun*.

To sit on the heels, to set couchant, to squat; to place close to each other, as men in line.

丨 丨 有節 to walk in measured steps.

‘丨 甲而射之 to set up the mailed dresses and shoot at them.

丨 不住 unable to squat.

踞 丨 to crouch, as a tiger; to occupy by force.

丨 到腿痠 squatted till my legs are stiff.

自己 丨 在戥盤裏 he squats on his own scales; — said of a man praising himself.

鱒 ‘ts'un From *fish* and *honorable*, because it leads others.

A fish like the rudd, with red eyes, round and long body, small scales, and reddish marks; it is also called 赤目魚 red eyed fish, and is probably a kind of roach, perhaps the same as the 紅眼筭 (*Leuciscus homospilotus,*) at Canton; in Japan, the salmon.

九罭之魚 丨 魴 in the nine-pouched net are rudds and bream.

忖 ‘ts'un From *heart* and *inch*.

To guess, to surmise; to consider, to reflect on.

丨 思 to ponder on.

自 丨 無能 I think that I have not the ability or power.

他人有心予 丨 度之 what others have in their minds, I can measure by reflection.

寸 ts'un’ Formed of 又 the *hand* and 一 *one* under it, to denote the pulse of the wrist, an inch from the hand; it is the 41st radical of a small heterogeneous group of characters; in accounts it is often used as a contraction of *swan*’ 算 to reckon.

The Chinese inch or punto, which is regarded as equal to the middle joint of the finger; it measures one-tenth of a cubit 尺 or foot, and like it varies in length; a very little.

丨 心 or 方 丨 or 丨 衷 the heart.

丨 口 the pulse at the wrist.

惜 丨 陰 improve every inch or moment of time.

丨 步難行 I cannot move a step; I cannot alter.

得失 丨 心知 a man's heart knows when he swerves from the right.

一 丨 眉擔萬 丨 愁 an inch of eyebrows often bears a myriad inches of sorrow.

若有 丨 進 I have got on about an inch, *i. e.* a very little; a depreciating phrase.

尺 丨 feet and inches, dimensions, the measure of a thing; also etiquette, respect, regard according to station.

特修 丨 字 I have just written a short note.

三 丨 小金蓮 my little daughter, — referring to her tiny feet.

得尺則尺得 丨 則 丨 if you can get (or learn) much then get it; if not, then a little; — even anything is good.

刌 ts'un’ To *cut* into *inches;* to cut small, to cut up; to part, to divide.

丨 切 to cut fine.

分 丨 節度 distinguish clearly the stops and meter, — in making and singing verses.

TSUNG.

Old sound, tsong. *In Canton,* tsung; — *in Swatow,* chong *and* chang; — *in Amoy,* tsong, ch'iong, *and* ch'ong; — *in Fuhchau,* chung, ch'ung, *and* chüng; — *in Shanghai,* tsung; — *in Chifu,* tsung.

宗 ꜀tsung From *shelter* and to *proclaim*.

An ancestral hall, where the honored ones are present to hear and answer prayers; an ancestral tablet; sacrificial, used in worship; to honor, to revere; that which men resort to or recur to; to appear at court; to revert or turn to, as the water of the Yangtsz' flows to the sea, or people turn to the throne; to agree with or follow, as an authority; to honor; the natural focus, origin, or center; honorable; a clan, those who bear the same surname, and are derived from the same ancestor; a matter, a manner, a sort; among Budhists, a school, a sect.

天 丨 the heavenly bodies.

丨 丨 件件 each sort and manner; every kind.

丨 廟 a temple where the tablets of kings or forefathers stand.

丨 周 the honored place of Cheu; — *i. e.* the metropolis.

丨 人府 the Board of the Imperial Kindred which regulates the 丨 室 Imperial Clan.

祖 丨 family ancestors.
同 丨 clansmen.
地 丨 rivers, seas and mountains.
丨 族 or 丨 親 all one's kindred.
丨 子 the lineal descendant in the eldest son.
一 丨 美 事 a noble act.
大 丨 貨 a great lot of goods.
你 丨 那 一 家 to what family (or sect) do you belong?
亦 可 丨 也 he can be relied on.
學 者 丨 之 all scholars honor — Confucius as their master in doctrine.
一 丨 秉 性 the whole disposition of the man.
丨 原 to recur to the origin.

鯼 ꜀tsung A large fish which comes in from the sea and returns at proper times; it appears to be allied to the sturgeon, and is sometimes wrongly called 石首魚, from its large ear bones; its body is round, nose very long, and has a hollow in its neck; it weighs sometimes 30 catties.

棕 椶 ꜀tsung The first form is a contraction of the second which is derived from 木 *wood* and 嵕 *a mane*, referring to the fibers.
A kind of gomuti palm, the *Chamærops*, whose sheaths and scapes both furnish coir for rain-cloaks, ropes, mats, &c.; its wood 丨 櫚 木 is used for posts; coir obtained from palms, like the *Borassus gomutus*, the *Caryota*, and other plants.
鐵 丨 a dark brown, umber color.
丨 毯 or 丨 簟 a coir mat.
丨 竹 a variety of black bamboo whose roots furnish canes.
丨 筍 clusters of the flower buds of palms, used for food.
丨 箱 a coir trunk.
丨 簑 a coir rain-cloak.

緫 ꜀tsung A dark green color, like dried up leaves; said only of silk; a classifier of threads of silk.

騣 騌 ꜀tsung From *horse* and *gathered up* or *ancestors*.
A mane; the bristles on a hog's nape; long, disheveled hair.
猪 丨 毛 hog's bristles.
丨 刷 a brush of bristles.
拉 住 馬 丨 hold the horse by his mane.
打 丨 or 翦 丨 to trim the mane.
編 丨 to braid the mane into ringlets.

鬉 ꜀tsung Similar to and interchanged with the last.
A high head-dress; the back lappet of a Chinese lady's head-dress, sometimes likened to a rudder, and also called 燕 尾 a swallow's tail; a wig, peruke; a cue.
假 丨 a false coiffure, a lady's periwig.
抆 丨 to rub the lappet with gum.
頭 丨 尾 票 a ticket given in Batavia for the tax paid on cues by Chinese.

稯 ꜀tsung From *grain* and *gathered up*.
A cock of grain containing forty 秉 or handfuls; a run of thread of eighty 縷 hanks; the comment on the Lun Yü says 640 斛 or 3,200 斗 make one ꜀*tsung*, which would make it equal to about 320 peculs; to collect or assemble together.
丨 束 a great sheaf, as of sorghum.

嵏 ꜀tsung From 夊 to *step* and 兇 *unlucky*.
To gather the feet under the body, as a sparrow or hawk does in its flight; ornaments on a horse's head; a small feudal state called 三 丨 國 lying in the present Ting-tau hien 定 陶 縣 in the southwest of Shantung, near the Yellow River.

猣 ꜀tsung Like the preceding.
The short uneven flight of a magpie, up and down, but not far or swift in its course.

鍐 ꜀tsung A bridle or head-stall ornamented with metal, and set off with a plume of feathers between the horse's ears.

葼 ꜀tsung Small twigs at the end of branches; a plant used for dyeing.
猶 折 丨 笞 之 [a kind mother when offended] breaks off a twig to punish her child.

賨 ꜀tsung Certain presents of cloth, called 丨 布 offered by tribes on the south and west in the Han dynasty.
巴 丨 綫 cotton cloth presented from Pa, the south of Sz'ch'uen.

艐 ꜀tsung To run aground in a boat; to get upon the sands; to arrive at, and in this sense used with *kiai'* 屆 a limit of time.

搜 稯 ꜀tsung Both are also read *chw'ang*.
To sow seed without first ploughing the ground.

㯶 ꜀tsung An edible mushroom (*Agaricus*) called 雞 丨; it is found in Yunnan, and is also known as 土 菌 earth agaric; and in Kiangsu as 鬼 涼 傘 the devil's parasol.
鷄 丨 also a kind of hand brasier made by weaving an earthen basin in a bamboo basket.

縱 ꜀tsung From *silk* and *accordant*.
Perpendicular, downward; a meridian line; a vestige; a step.
丨 生 者 人 mankind alone are made erect.
有 丨 有 横 there are parallel and cross-lines; up and down and across; *met.* pettish; versatile or unaccountable acts.
Read *tsung'* Remiss, careless; wild, extravagant talking; to allow; to wrongfully permit, to connive at; to let go, to indulge, to over-

look, to let things take their course; to let fly; as a *conjunction*, although, allowing, perhaps; in *rhetoric*, a concession, admitting.

丨容 to connive at, not to check, unrestrained.

故丨 purposely conniving at.

丨然 allowing it to be, supposing.

一擒一丨 caught them once, and then let them escape.

丨丨 hastily, busily, as in ordering a funeral.

丨慣 over indulgence; heedless of other's evil-deeds.

丨臾 to encourage, to praise and stimulate.

丨步 to take long strides.

丨使 an illative phrase used in regimen with 也 or 亦, seeing that, though, if, and implies a positive fact; as 丨使你飛上天去我也會跟你的 though you should fly up to the sky I will follow you; or 丨使爾爲乞丐我亦願嫁爾 even if you are a beggar, I am going to marry you.

丨子行兇 to let a child act wickedly.

蹤 蹤 ꜀tsung From *foot* and *accordant*.

A vestige, a trace, a footstep; to follow in another's track; to imitate.

無丨無影 no trace at all of it.

來丨去跡 to ask the course and objects of one, as a traveler at a pass; to learn his line of travel.

追丨 to follow a trail; to pursue a clue, to hunt up the traces of.

萍丨無定 going about without any fixed purpose or residence, as a tramp.

緵 ꜀tsung A caldron or boiler; a run or hank, as of hempen threads; to reckon these hanks; name of 三丨 a small feudal state in Shantung.

豵 ꜀tsung A shote six months old; a pig; the last of a litter, a litter; *met.* a large family.

引丨 a bristle to stiffen a waxed-end.

豵 ꜀tsung Very similar to the last.

A pig a year old; to have only three at a litter.

一發五丨 to hit five pigs at one shot.

總 摠 捴 ꜂tsung From *silk* or *hand* and *bustling;* the third form is a common contraction.

To collect and tie up, as in a sheaf; to unite under one rule or in a whole; to comprehend in one or under one; all, the whole, altogether; a general or generic term; a supervisor or controller; generally; still, yet; before a negative, it makes a strong assertion; a tuft of hair; a sheaf.

丨共 or 攏丨 the whole, all.

丨不行 he utterly refused to do it.

丨要 still I must; it is yet necessary.

丨計 reckon them all; in all.

丨頭 or 管丨的 or 亞丨 a boss, a head driver; the foreman of workmen.

一丨多少 how many in all?

丨督 a governor-general.

丨兵 a major-general in command of a division.

千丨 a chiliarch, a lieutenant in a regiment; the next grade to a 守備 captain; and next to him is a 把丨 or ensign.

丨之 to sum up, to bring together.

偶來丨角之童 two little children came on together.

丨不能應日子 he could not come at all on the promised day.

一丨都是 the whole are of the same sort.

丨然 although, nevertheless.

丨賸 the whole, including everything.

一丨拉勻 to make an average of all.

丨理 general supervision of.

丨該有的 it is so no doubt; very likely it is there.

穗 ꜂tsung Similar to the last, but regarded as a synonym of 稯 a sheaf.

A bundle or sheaf of grain.

納丨 to present the tax of grain.

慫 ꜂tsung To alarm, to arouse.

丨動 to stir one up, to rouse his feelings.

聞發火無不丨然 who would not be startled at hearing the cry of fire!

憁 ꜂tsung Disappointed.

生不逢辰殊覺丨恫 if things do not succeed as you wish, you are exceedingly dissatisfied.

綜 tsung꜄ The harness of a loom; to work the slaie, and arrange the patterns in weaving; to hold the threads; to keep the reins of authority; to collect.

丨核名實 to inquire into what is nominal and real of all.

錯丨其數 to make an error in reckoning the number.

粽 糉 tsung꜄ Dumplings, with meat, fruit, or sweetmeats inside, made by boiling panicled millet or glutinous rice wrapped in leaves; a piece of sapan wood is often put in to color it, and the grain is sometimes first soaked in weak lye; they are called 端陽丨 and eaten on the 5th day of the 5th moon in memory of Kiüh Yuen.

假丨 false dumplings; — a peculiar flower head-ornament worn on this festival.

狗啖丨 a dog bolting a dumpling; — a fool misunderstanding or not relishing an allusion.

丨子 or 三角丨 a three-cornered dumpling.

丨葉 the tough leaves of rushes used to wrap the dumpling.

猔 tsung꜄ A bitch having one at a litter.

丨生猫 puss has only one kitten.

傯 傯 tsung' } Careworn, wearied out; having no leisure.

倥 丨 oppressed with much and varied business, and quite exhausted with one's duties.

戎馬 丨 丨 the unceasing marches of troopers.

瘲 tsung' A disease of young children like fits or convulsions, caused by indigestion.

瘛 丨 a spasm, a convulsion.

從 从 tsung' } The second, denoting *two men* listening side by side, is the original form, afterwards increased to the first; it is like *si'* 徙 to move; the next is interchanged with ˊ總 generally and 縱ˋ loose.

A clan, a family, a succession of, as posterity; to be second to or subordinate; attached to, to follow, as one of secondary rank; followers; to plough lengthwise.

丨然如此 I am inclined to think it is so.

丨者 followers or attendants.

不分首 丨 make no distinction between a chief and his adherents.

丨三品 of the secondary third grade.

丨堂兄弟 second cousins of the same surname.

丨我者其由歟 my only follower is this Yiu.

隨 丨 an aid, a waiting-man.

Read *ˊtsung.* Very high; too high, as a head-dress.

爾無 丨 丨 爾 you do not want your hair dressed up so high.

TS'UNG.

Old sounds, ts'ong *and* dzong. *In Canton,* ts'ung; — *in Swatow,* ch'ong *and* ch'ang; — *in Amoy,* ch'ong, tsong, *and* ch'iong; — *in Fuhchau,* ch'ung, ch'üng, *and* chung; — *in Shanghai,* ts'ung *and* dzung; — *in Chifu,* ts'ung.

從 ˏts'ung To follow, to listen to and comply with; to agree with, to believe in; to employ as before; to be made to follow; to pursue; to finish, as a duty; compliance, accord; the way a thing comes, the point or place of its origin; a *preposition,* from, by, through, in; since, whence; consequently; a way, a manner; hunting grounds.

丨心所欲 what I much desire.

丨來 heretofore, hitherto.

無丨入手 there is no way to begin.

不得冒昧丨事 so that he will not blindly carry out the affair.

任丨你 do as you choose; as you like.

依 丨 according with, to agree to.

曲 丨 and 順 丨 and 願 丨 compliance by constraint, from a sense of duty, or from a willing heart

于何丨祿 whence shall I henceforth get my living?

丨遊 to follow, as a pupil his teacher.

丨自 from this place or time.

丨今而後 hereafter, henceforth.

丨不 or 丨未 never so; it was not so at all.

丨小 since childhood.

三 丨 the three obediences — of a woman to her father, husband, or son.

丨容 an easy, unembarrassed manner; dignified and complaisant.

月之丨星 the moon's course among the stars.

丨良 a reformed or married prostitute.

丨重ˋ論罪 to judge the crime with severity.

刑法一丨庶民多犯 if you excuse crimes lightly, the people will increasingly break the laws.

天不丨人願 Heaven does not comply with human wishes.

悤 怱 匆 ˏts'ung } From *heart* and a *window* or *aperture;* the second form is most common, and the third is unauthorized.

To feel alarm or agitation; excited, hurried.

丨丨不及 too much hurried to do (or attend to) it.

丨忙 urgent and unceasing; precipitate.

行色丨猝 seems to be in a desperate hurry to go.

丨遽 impelled by some cause to be in haste, urged to speed.

葱 ˏts'ung A general term for alliaceous plants with fistular leaves; onions, garlics; a leek green,

丨頭 an onion.

丨白 the bulb of the onion

丨鬚 the rootlets.

丨綠 a light green.

丨靈 a kind of ancient baggage wagon.

丨嶺 the Karakorum Mts. of Turkestan.

佳氣丨丨 the fresh wind has a free draught, in allusion to the tubular leaves of the onion.

胡丨 scallions. (*Allium ascalonicum.*)

細香丨 chives. (*Allium schœnoprasum.*)

聰 聦 ˏts'ung } From *ear* and *quick.*

Ready, astute, quick at hearing; sharpwitted; to perceive clearly, to discriminate intelligently.

天 丨 natural gifts.

丨明 or 丨慧 apt, clever, quick at catching an idea.

耳丨目不明 having good hearing but dim eye-sight.

聽斯丨 to understand as soon as heard; perspicacious.

冒瀆聖丨 I venture to importune your Majesty's ear.

驄 驄 ꜀tsʻung From *horse* and *quick*. A piebald, black and white horse; a dapple black; a fine steed.

五花丨 a fancy, piebald steed.

陌上游丨 a dappled charger is galloping along the far edge of the plain.

後話雖多玉丨難繫 though you may have many words, do not say my steed cannot be longer held in.

青丨馬 a gray speckled horse.

蓯 ꜀tsʻung Grassy.

苯丨 tender grass.

草丨蓉 the fleshy roots of a plant allied to the *Cynomorium*, a fungoid plant used as a remedy in colic.

肉丨蓉 is another sort more esteemed, and sometimes used in soups.

Read ʻsung. Choking, filling up.

騷擾衝丨 many people crowded and pressed to get in.

樅 ꜀tsʻung The larch or spruce (*Larix orientalis*); a trunk like a cedar, used for pillars; a swinging mallet or drum-stick, to beat bells or drums; to beat a bell; straight, like teeth sticking out.

丨金鼓 to rap the bells or gongs and the drums.

蠑 ꜀tsʻung A species of gadfly or breeze, which deposits its eggs in the skin of cattle.

瑽 ꜀tsʻung The tinkling of gems or trinkets hanging from the girdle.

鏦 ꜀tsʻung A small spear or javelin; to stab with a spear, as an assassin.

使人丨殺吳王 he employed a man to spear the king of Wu.

Read ꜀chwʻang. To beat a drum or bell.

琮 ꜀tsʻung An ancient badge used in the Cheu dynasty, to denote princely rank, made of jade, and of different sizes; it had eight corners with a round hole in the center, and looked like a wheel; its component parts denote the *gem* of the eight *venerated* regions, (the whole empire,) and its shape was thought to resemble the earth.

瑞丨 the propitious signet.

悰 ꜀tsʻung Delight, joy; to rejoice.

樂丨 great pleasure.

常戚戚而無丨 he is continually sad, and no gleam of joy comes to his mind.

楤 樬 ꜀tsʻung A sharp-pointed carrying-beam.

丨木 a small tree, (*Aralia canescens*,) cultivated as an ornamental shrub.

璁 ꜀tsʻung From *gem* and *quick*; but the primitive is a contraction of *onion*, referring to the *leek* color.

A stone of a fine kind, probably the massive turquoise, though that is usually called 松兒石, from the color being like pine leaves.

賨 ꜀tsʻung A tribute of cloth anciently brought to court by the people of Yunnan and south of Sz'chʻuen.

淙 ꜀tsʻung The noise of flowing water; murmuring, bubbling, rippling, as a brook or fountain.

山岋岋水丨丨 the rugged cliffs and rushing waters.

潀 ꜀tsʻung From *water* and *many*; it occurs used for the last.

Smaller streams flowing into a large one; the place where the waters meet.

鳧鷖在丨 the ducks and gulls are in the center of the streams.

叢 藂 ꜀tsʻung Formed of 丵 *bushy* or 林 *forest*, and 取 to *gather together*, intimating the tussocky growth of some plants; the second form is unusual, and rather denotes a clump growing from one root.

A bushy place, a copse or coppice; crowded, as shrubs; collected thickly; assembled in a crowded manner.

丨林 a wood or grove; a place of concourse, usually refers to a number of priests or a monastery.

生丨這樣 jammed, crowded as possible.

書丨 a bookstore; a library room; a street like Paternoster Row.

臨老入花丨 to become depraved when old.

一丨數本 one tussock contains many stalks.

爲丨毆爵 to drive the birds into the copse.

愁思丨集 overwhelmed with sorrows.

丨生 growing free and luxuriant.

篆 ꜀tsʻung From *bamboo* and to *gather*.

A wicker basket or creel, called 篭丨, shaped like a pot, with a small mouth.

TSWAN.

Old sounds, tsan, tsam, tswan, *and* dzan. *In Canton*, tsün; — *in Swatow*, chăng, chan, jwan, *and* chuan; — *in Amoy*, chw'an, ch'iang, ch'iam, *and* tsan; — *in Fuhchau*, chwang *and* chòng; — *in Shanghai*, tsöⁿ, tsiⁿ *and* tsèⁿ; — *in Chifu*, tsan.

鑽 鑚 ˏtswan tswanˀ From *metal* and *to advance.* To bore, to make a hole through a thing; to pierce, as a thing; to worm one's self into, as one who pries into secrets; to control the mental powers, as a master passion does; to employ intrigue.

丨之彌堅 the deeper you bore the harder it is; — *met.* the more you study this, the more difficult it is to comprehend.

丨眼 or 丨竅窿 to bore a hole.

丨謀 or 丨營 to seek and plan, as for a living.

丨頭覓縫 to put one's self everywhere, seeking for a chance or opening.

丨過去 to bore through.

無隙可丨 there's no crack for [the wind] to enter; — no ground for trouble.

Read *tswan*ˀ A bit, a gimlet, augur, or borer; an instrument for perforating; the point of a weapon; among furriers, the fur on the top of the neck.

丨子 or 縄丨 a center-bit; of which 丨頭 is the borer, and 丨把 is the handle.

金鋼丨 a diamond or corundrum borer; this gem is fabled to be produced under water.

鉄丨 a bit; an iron borer.

丨心釘 a jack of all trades.

蚊子丨 a musquito's proboscis; *met.* a ruthless villain.

丨木取火 to bore wood to raise a flame.

儹 ˏtswan To lose one's way.

丨行 to wander about, like one who has lost his way.

躦 躜 ˏtswan Also read ˏ*tso.* To jump with the feet together; to tread on.

丨踞 to squat, to crouch.

好跳好丨 fond of hopping and skipping; he likes to cut capers.

纂 ˋtswan From 糸 *silk* and 算 to *reckon;* occurs used for the next, and ˋ攢 to collect.

A kind of carnation band or cord to tie on a coronet; to collect materials; to compile a work, to edit or abridge; a résumé, a digest or compend; a compilation, a collection of writings; to hand them down.

新丨 a new edition.

丨修 to prepare materials for publication.

丨集 to make a collectanea.

御丨 an Imperial edition or compilation.

錄丨 to copy out writings for editing.

自丨 to strike out a new path, as in writing or an invention.

撮丨 to make a précis of papers.

丨組 floss balls worn of old on hats.

纘 ˋtswan From *silk* and *to advance.* To tie things together; to carry on, to take up where others left off; to imitate, as to copy one's virtues.

丨繼 to continue the hereditary succession.

丨禹舊服 to take up Yü's old mantle; —*i. e.* imitate his virtues.

丨武功 to record the detail of his valorous deeds.

丨述 to extract, as a record, or the sayings of a man.

丨緒 to continue the succession or business.

臇 燽 ˏtswan From *flesh* or *fire* and *fat*; the second form is unauthorized; the first is also defined fat, rich.

A chowder or porridge with little fluid in it, made of fish and crabs.

揝 攢 攢 tswanˀ From *hand* and *I* or *to advance.* To hold in the hand, to carry in one hand; to move with the hand; hasty, quick; entirely; to select.

丨籌 to draw lots.

丨不住 I can't hold it.

兩手丨空拳 both hands are quite empty.

丨着不撒手 hold it fast, and do not open your hands

丨着筆據 he has the papers and evidence, — as in a lawsuit.

身丨萬箭 his body was pierced with a thousand darts.

謙 tswanˀ From *words* and *frugal;* also read ˏ*lien,* meaning vile talk, impudence.

Deception; a swindle, a sell; to deceive; to be taken in; it is nearly synonymous with *chan*ˀ 賺 to palm off goods, one referring to deception in words, the other in trading, and in these last senses both characters are pronounced *tswan*ˀ

受人丨 to be deluded or hoaxed.

丨謀 a confidence game, a way to raise the wind.

人丨我 people deceived me.

丨戳 to palm off bad goods.

TSWʻAN.

Old sounds, tswʻan *and* dzan. *In Canton*, tsʻün *and* chʻün ; — *in Swatow*, chwan *and* chwʻan ; — *in Amoy*, chwʻan *and* tsan ; — *in Fuhchau*, chwʻang ; — *in Shanghai*, tsʻö^{n} *and* tsö^{n} ; — *in Chifu*, tsʻan.

攛 From *hand* and to *skulk*.
ˏ*tswʻan* To fling away; to part with; to cause divisions; to cajole one to consent.

丨掇 to rouse, as by misrepresentation; to excite to a certain course; to stir up; to inveigle, to entice; an intreaty.

丨梭引線 to throw the shuttle and pass the thread.

丨籠 shelves and cases for goods in a shop.

丨ˏ行 to sell to the trade.

丨貨 to sell wholesale.

攢 From *hand* and to *advance*; occurs interchanged with the next.
ˏ*tswʻan* To collect things of the same sort; to assemble, to come together; to lay a coffin under a shed.

丨聚 to gather materials.

丨基 a brick tomb on the ground like a house; common in Kiangnan.

丨賬 to reckon the total of accounts.

丨羅列聚 to collect and arrange in order.

丨盒 a box with partitions, used for sweetmeats.

欑 ʻ*tswʻan* To collect bamboos; a slight shed or hearse to contain a coffin, which is daubed with mud; a spear handle.

君殯用輴丨 they use a covered wain or hearse in burying the prince.

丨木 a kind of palisade under a a bridge to guard the bank.

穳 ʻ*tswʻan* To gather grain and stack it, or make it into cocks, as is done with sorghum.

酇 ˏ*tswʻan* A hamlet, a place where people assemble to reside; a few houses in a spot.

Read ˏ*tso*. The ancient name of a district in Péi hien 沛縣 in the north of Kiangsu; and of another in the southwest of Honan.

爨 From 火 *fire*, 大 *great*, 林 *forest*, all under 興 to *rise*, which however here denotes 臼 a *mortar*.
tsʻwanʼ A furnace for cooking; a mess, a table; to cook by steam.

炊丨 to light the furnace.

分丨 or 各丨 each has his own table; they eat separately.

同丨 messmates.

搭丨 a boarder; sometimes applied to a sorner.

滅火更丨 to put out the fire and then light it again; — beholden to nobody.

自已開丨 to eat by himself.

粒食鄉丨 he gets his kernels at the village furnace; — *i. e.* lives privately and frugally.

竄 From *cave* and *rat*, *i. e.* a rat in his hole.
tswʻanʼ To sneak away, to hide; to skulk, as rebels and banditti do; to seduce, to beguile into evil; to kill; to secrete or store away; to change, to correct; privily, stealthily, furtively; petty, weak, pusillanimous.

改丨 changed his course and escaped.

丨匿他方 skulked away and hid in another place.

大股分丨 the great body of the rebels separated and got away.

丨竊 to pilfer; to steal, as a rat does.

逃丨 to escape and hide.

丨俗 to corrupt others.

敏能丨謀 he clearly understands the minutest plan.

丨藥 to fumigate by burning herbs.

抱頭鼠丨 to cover the head and skulk off.

點丨 to correct the style of a writing.

躥 An unauthorized character, sometimes written under the radical 足 a foot.
tswʻanʼ To leap, to jump; to prance; to eject, to spurt out.

丨山跳澗 to leap over hills and jump ravines, as a gazelle.

丨不過去 he cannot jump over it.

老馬學丨 can an old horse learn to jump? — I am too old for that.

TSZʼ.

Old sounds, tsai, tsi, dzai, tsít, dzít, ti, *and* tip. *In Canton*, tszʼ ; — *in Swatow*, chù, chè, *and* chek ; — *in Amoy*, tsu, chʻu, tʻu, chè, *and* tsai ; — *in Fuhchau*, chū, chi, *and* chè ; — *in Shanghai*, tszʼ, tsʼ, szʼ, *and* tsi ; — *in Chifu*, tszʼ.

資 From *property* and a *time*; occurs used for the next two.
ˏ*tszʼ* Property, riches, valuable things; necessaries, articles wanted; a fee, a douceur, a treat; to take or employ, to avail of, to trust to, to help, to depend on another; what is part of one's self, as a disposition; to lament.

丨貨 stock, goods.

分丨 a subscription to a friend's exigencies; quota due from one, as the present at a marriage.

吾山丨已足 my country property is quite enough.

丨本 capital in trade.

丨斧 what is necessary to carry out an object, as things for a journey.

丨質 or 丨稟 the natural disposition or talents.

酒丨 or 檳丨 postage money; a drink fee.

以丨保護 I depend on it for protection and safety, — as a traveler on a passport.

始丨生 the buds are all starting.

香丨 presents given to priests; cash for a festival, or for repairing a temple.

懷其丨 he doats on his wealth.

丨格 capabilities, efficiency; talents, — said of officers.

問歲月之丨 ask for the outlay for the year or the month.

薪水之丨 necessaries of life.

丨江 a large tributary of the Tung-ting Lake in the center of Hunan; its basin measures about 10,000 square miles.

咨 諮 嗞 ꜀tsz' From *mouth* and a *time*; the second and unusual form is used only in the first sense of to plan, and the third in that of sighing.

To deliberate, to consult about, to plan; to inquire and find; to state in writing; to report, as among officers of nearly equal rank; a minute, a dispatch; to sigh; an interjection, ah! oh!

丨文 an official dispatch among equals; the letter from the king of Corea is so called by the Board of Rites.

丨會 to inform; to move an equal in rank to do.

丨稱 he reported to me, saying.

丨行 to notify; to inform the next below one.

丨謀 to consult upon.

丨稟 to state to a high superior.

何爲丨嗟 why do you lament so?

移丨 to forward a dispatch.

丨問 or 丨訪 to write to inquire about any point.

怨丨 grieving over wrong received.

姿 ꜀tsz' Manner, gait, form, carriage, especially of women; fascinating, beautiful, graceful; agreeable parts, fine endowments; a beauty.

丰丨 a fine, plump figure.

仙丨 or 丨色 a beauty.

天丨 natural beauty or gifts.

性丨 disposition, temper.

天丨國色 a peerless beauty; bewitching grace and beauty, such as 楊貴妃 of the T'ang dynasty had.

龍鳳之丨 the air of a dragon and a phœnix; — *i. e.* majestic.

丨態 carriage, manner.

粢 ꜀tsz' A term for clean millet (*Milium*), but includes also glutinous rice, as sacrificial cakes are made of both, by steaming the grain.

六丨 the six kinds of common grain; *viz.* three varieties of millet, rice, pulse, and wheat.

明丨 boiled rice offered to ancestors.

丨盛既潔 the offering of cakes should be clean.

齍 ꜀tsz' From *even* and *dish*, referring to the orderly arrangement in the dish; it is like the preceding.

Sacrificial dishes for holding grain.

丨盛必潔 the dishes for offerings must be clean.

奉玉丨 to offer up the precious or jade dishes.

趑 ꜀tsz' From *to go* and *next*.

Unable to get on easily or quickly, either from the crowd, or fatigue, or other causes.

足將進而丨趄 he wished to get on but was much hindered.

貲 ꜀tsz' From *property* and *this*; occurs interchanged with ꜀資 property.

A fine paid to redeem one's self from punishment; mulct money; riches, property.

家丨 a family estate.

丨贖 to ransom one's self.

丨財 valuables; wealth.

輕丨好'義 to disesteem money and love justice.

訾 ꜀tsz' From *to speak* and *this*; occurs used for 恣' and for the last, but its meaning is modified by the context.

To speak sharply and unadvisedly; to detract, to slander; to consult, to think upon; to restrict, to limit; faulty, loose, dissipated; evil, defective.

不苟丨 don't revile people.

丨毀 to backbite others.

翕翕丨丨 to defame, to cast out from a company.

禮之丨也 a want of politeness.

丨限難窮 it is hard to say what such ability cannot accomplish.

丨食 fastidious; dainty as to one's food.

不丨而得 I got it without much thought, it was obtained unexpectedly.

眥 ꜀tsz' The canthus or corner of the eye, called 內丨 for the inner canthus, and 外丨 or 銳丨 for the outer corner.

衣丨 the lapel of the coat.

內丨肉 caruncula in the eyes of aged people.

拭丨揚目 to rub the eyes and stretch the eyebrows, — and have a good look.

Read ꜀chai. To look at fixedly, to regard angrily.

睚丨之怨必報 a fierce glance of hatred will surely beget reprisals.

齜 ꜀tsz' Also read ꜀ch'ai and ꜀ch'a.

To show the teeth; to snarl at; various teeth; irregular teeth.

丨牙露齒 teeth which project from the mouth.

丨着牙 teeth which show.

觜 From *horn* and *this*; it is interchanged with ʻ*tsui* 嘴 a beak.
ˌ*tsz'* The 21st zodiacal constellation, consisting of the stars λ and 2 π in Orion's head.
娵 丨 a lunar mansion.

Read ʻ*tsui*. To erect the feathers or egret on the head, as an owl does; to bristle up, to look incensed, to pout; a beak, a bill; the curved corners on a roof or ridge-pole.
厲其丨吻 he is bitter with his tongue at reviling; — referring to the pecking of a bird.

髭 The mustaches, usually called 髯丨 or 丨鬚, which
ˌ*tsz'* the Chinese usually wear long, except the Mohammedans, who trim them evenly; occurs used for 姿 beautiful, engaging.

茲 茲 From 艸 *grass* and 絲 *silk* contracted; the second form is generally used; occurs used for the next.
ˌ*tsz'* Herbs and grass growing thickly; rich underbrush; a coarse mat; a *pronoun*, this, this one; an *adverb*, now, here, still; a *conjunction*, for.
丨者 the following, this time; — a phrase used at the beginning of a notice.
丨今 now, at present.
念丨在丨 think of this here, *i. e.* attend to the affair, or subject without distraction; be careful what you are about.
丨將貨八官 now confiscating the goods.
如丨 hereupon, now, then.
負丨 to carry the mat; an old term for the illness of a prince.
挹彼注丨 pour it out of that into this; *met.* to supply the want of one with another's fullness.

滋 Occurs used for the last.
ˌ*tsz'* Names of several rivers, one of which is in the south of Shensi; humid, soft; juicy, rich, thick; muddy; moisture, juice, sap; numerous, many; to enrich, to fertilize, to moisten; to grow, to increase; to stir up evil, to cause ill-will and riot; old name of a part of Lu cheu 瀘州 in the south of Sz'ch'uen.
丨事 to make trouble, to get up a row.
丨擾 to disturb the peace, to excite a rising.
丨ʻ長 to grow larger.
丨生 to sprout; to multiply, as the increase of population.
好丨味 a fine flavor.
丨潤 to mollify; to soften down, as coloring; to fertilize, to increase the juices.
丨補 to strengthen, as a tonic.
丨蔓 a sprouting tendril; something left, as of a seditious band.

嵫 Name of a hill in Tsz'yang
ˌ*tsz'* hien 滋陽縣 in the south of Shantung, which gives its name to the district.

鎡 A hoe for opening the soil;
ˌ*tsz'* a mattock with a long narrow blade.
雖有丨基不如待時 it is better to wait till the proper season, even if you have all your farming tools; — *i. e.* watch the right moment.

鼒 A black color.
ˌ*tsz'* 染丨 to dye black.

鰦 A small slender fish, probably
ˌ*tsz'* one of the mackerel family, that delights in gamboling on the surface of the water.
黑丨 a sort of goby or loche, on mud shores, shaped like an eel.

厜 A peak of a hill.
ˌ*tsz'* 丨㕒 the summit of a hill.

孶 From *child* and *growing*; used with the next.
ˌ*tsz'* To bear; to produce and suckle, as animals; to grow gradually; affectionate, strong love, like a mother's; diligent, unwearied in.
日有丨丨 daily be zealous in your duties.
丨息 to care for her young, as a ewe.
鳥獸丨尾 mammals suckle and birds tread.
萬物丨生 all things gradually increase.

孜 From *child* and to *strike*; it is nearly synonymous with the preceding.
ˌ*tsz'* Unceasing, unwearied effort; self-denying attachment and sacrifice for.
丨丨爲善 to strive after goodness.

耔 秄 From to *plow* or *grain* and *son*; the second form is unusual.
ˌ*tsz'* To hoe up earth around the roots of plants.
今適南畝或耘或丨 let us go to the southern fields to weed and to hoe.

齋 From *raiment* and to *even*.
ˌ*tsz'* The hem or border of a garment.
丨縗 mourning apparel.
裳丨 a hem, a selvage.

鼒 From *tripod* and *talent*.
ˌ*tsz'* A round lid or cover of a kettle or tripod, with a hole in it; a small kettle.

菑 甾 From 田 *field*, 巛 *obstructed*, and 艸 *plants*; *q. d.* weeds choke the ground; occurs used for *ts'ai* 災 calamity.
ˌ*tsz'* An uncultivated field; waste, untilled land; overgrown, as a jungle; to clear new land; ground under cultivation one year; to open a new road; to cut; a dead tree still standing; old name of a place in the south of Shantung.
無丨無害 no calamity or trouble.
治丨爇之地 to look after the old fields.

緇 ˓tsz' Like the last.
To plow; fields which have been cultivated a year.
耕 丨 to cultivate the ground.

淄 ˓tsz' A small river of Shantung which flows northeast into the gulf of Chihli; a dark color.
忘 丨 蠢 overlooked his being such a black (or vile) fellow.
丨 川 and 臨 丨 are two districts in Shantung near the River Tsz'.

緇 ˓tsz' From *silk* and *waste*.
Very black silk dyed many times, and used anciently by high officers; dark, as a sediment.
泥 丨 black mud, like alluvial.
丨 衣 之 宜 兮 how becoming to you are the black robes!

輜 ˓tsz' The end of the axle within the nave; baggage wagons with a boot to carry arms and spoils; large traveling wains.
丨 重 or 丨 車 traveling store-wagons used in armies.
庫 丨 provision carts.

錙 ˓tsz' An ancient weight equal to six 銖, about the fourth part of a tael; though others make it equal to eight taels, or less than half the present catty; trifling, petty.
丨 銖 計 較 you must look after the pennies and mites; — care for even trifling things.

鯔 ˓tsz' A marine fish allied to the *Cyprinidæ*, found in Kiangsu and northerly, with a round body, greenish back, tender bones, and flat head; it is reputed to be excellent eating, and one description says it is very prolific, and that otters like it.

孖 ˓tsz' From 子 *child* repeated; it is regarded as an old form of ˓lwan 孿 twins.
Twins; two of a sort.
生 丨 or 生 丨 仔 to bear twins.
丨 生 a twin.

In *Cantonese*. To go halves, to divide equally; a half; to take equal responsibility; to duplicate.
丨 貨 本 to go equal shares.
丨 指 a double thumb.
丨 字 a repetition, a duplicated expression.
丨 埋 去 they have gone off together.
丨 佢 做 join him in doing it.
黑 丨 丨 very dark or obscure.

子 ˋtsz' The original form is said by one to represent a *baby* strapped on the back, its legs looking as one; it is the 39th radical of characters most of which relate to children.
Anciently a child, but now confined to a son; a boy, a lad, a person; the people, in distinction from the prince; a sage, a teacher, a venerable and worthy man, especially Confucius; to act in a filial manner as a son; to treat as a son; an heir, issue, posterity; a seed, a kernel; a term of respect, you, Sir; or more familiarly, a comrade; an officer; officers; the fourth order of nobility, a viscount; the first of the twelve stems, related to water, and denoted by the rat; it is applied to the eleventh moon, and to the third watch from 11 o'clock P. M. to 1 A. M.; north, on the compass card; a spot, as of dirt or the points on dice; subordinate; added to nouns it sometimes indicates that they are smaller than others of the same kind, as 書 丨 a letter, a little book; but more often like 兒 as a mere dissyllabic particle in speaking; added to verbs, it makes them nouns, and has the function of *er* in English as 揚 丨 an extender, a stretcher.
太 丨 or 元 丨 the heir-apparent.
ˋ長 丨 the eldest son.
丨 孫 sons and grandsons; it is also used to denote big and little things together, as 丨 孫 石 conglomerate stone, breccia.
丨 孫 餑 餑 large cakes with little cakes inside, a kind given to brides at their marriage, intimating a wish that they may have many children.
小 丨 I the Emperor, — an old term; my pupil; my son.
冢 丨 the oldest sons of gentry.
丨 息 children, posterity.
別 丨 or 公 丨 or 世 丨 old names for sons of noblemen.
赤 丨 an infant.
支 丨 sons of concubines.
丨 母 錢 interest and principal.
丨 嫩 tender, as veal or shoots.
庶 民 丨 來 the people came up like sons.
丨 弟 young people.
黑 丨 a black spot.
聖 丨 a name given the Savior as the second Person.
丨 來 幾 日 矣 how long since you came?
諸 丨 百 家 all the authors and sages.
三 小 丨 a servant of servants; attendants on official servants.
丨 口 a barrier station, *i. e.* one subordinate to the maritime port, and situated in the interior.
丨 丨 small seeds, as those of the grape, pomegranate, &c.
打 丨 to embroider in threads.

仔 ˋtsz' To bear, to carry, as a nurse does a child; to undertake.
丨 細 attentive and careful; to discriminate.
丨 肩 重 任 able to sustain important duties.

In *Cantonese*. A word added to nouns as a diminutive; a little thing, the smaller of the two; a boy.
丨 女 sons and daughters.
細 蚊 丨 children; lads.
狗 丨 a puppy.
事 丨 a servant, a shop-boy, a waiting lad.
公 丨 pictures, images, playthings.
冇 丨 佬 a childless man.

ʿ呰 ʿ訾 ʿtsz'
Similar to ʿ訾 to revile.
To be too strict; to molest; to slander; to chide; weak; a defect, a flaw.
丨短 a deficiency.
丨窳偷生 he let those escape who should have been punished.

ʿ紫 ʿtsz'
A purple color, passing into a clay color, or the tint of nankeen, and even browner hues; a fictitious, undecided color, a fugacious tint, which Confucius disliked.
丨檀色 a dark complexion, sunburnt, weather-beaten face.
丨粉 or 丨紅 a purple color.
丨標 a violet; the dye made with sapan-wood, and mixed with betle-nut.
丨黑肉 black and blue, as a bruise.
丨宸 a poetical name for the rising sun; *met.* the court.
丨禁城 the Forbidden City in Peking.
丨微星拱照 may the royal stars (in the Dipper, and other circumpolar stars,) illumine this house.
丨草 denotes several plants which furnish a red dye, as alkanet, bugloss, and *Rubia*, but particularly the *Tournefortia arguzina* in north China.
丨微神 a god worshiped for protection against malaria.

ʿ梓 ʿtsz'
From 木 *wood* and 辛 *bitter*, but the primitive is 宰 *to rule*; contracted.
A durable and stately tree considered to be so valuable that it is called 木王 the king of trees; it is *Rottlera japonica*, the one of the *Euphorbiæ*; to engrave characters; a graver, a burin; bowls, cups.
丨里 one's native village or country.
桑丨必敬 greatly regard one's birthplace.

丨州 an old name for a part of Tung-ch'uen fu 東川府 in the northeast of Yunnan.
活板行丨 printed with movable types.
丨宮 the coffin of an emperor.

ʿ耔 ʿtsz'
An unauthorized character.
The seeds of rice, wheat, and other grains, the 五穀丨 which does not include pulse, melons, or fruit.
丨粒枯𪏭 the grain is shriveled and dry.
丨花五包 five bales of seed cotton.

ʿ滓 ʿtsz'
From *water* and to *rule*.
Sediment; dregs, grounds, settlings, lees.
醋渣丨 grains of vinegar.
泥丨 dirt settled at the bottom.
消丨 to settle a liquid, as river water by alum.
汁丨相將 he then handed him the broth and settlings.

ʿ𠂔 ʿtsz'
A primitive, explained as a plant coming up, and passing by something which is represented by the cross line.
To stop.

ʿ姊 ʿ姉 ʿtsz'
From *female* and *market* or to *stop*; the second form is seldom used.
An elder sister; a woman who has experience; an old term for mother; a schoolmistress.
丨丈 an elder sister's husband.
丨妹 sisters generally; in Cantonese 八丨妹 includes all the young children of a family, referring to the eight genii.
七丨妹 or 十丨妹 a monthly climbing rose.
大丨 an old name for a father's concubine, now applied to the eldest sister.

ʿ胏 ʿtsz'
The fragments left after eating; meat with bones in it.
乾丨 cold victuals.

ʿ秭 ʿtsz'
To number up, to multiply greatly; a bundle of 200 handfuls of grain; a great weight, reckoned to be over 3809 tons; the ninth place in notation, or a hundred millions.
萬億及丨 millions upon millions; numberless.

ʿ泲 ʿtsz'
An old form of *tsi'* 濟 to help.
To flow; a river, the 丨水 flowing into the sea near the Yellow River.
丨酒 the best of spirits; probably from a place in the kingdom of Lu, which produced it.

ʿ第 ʿtsz'
A bed-mat; applied to the boards also, and to the bedstead.
牀丨之言不踰閾 do not let what you say in the bedchamber pass the threshold.

自ʾ tsz'ʾ
The original is thought to resemble the nose 鼻 of which it forms the upper part, considered as the embryo from which the rest of the body grows; it is the 132d radical of a few incongruous characters, many of them formatives of *ch'eu'* 臭 stinking.
A *preposition*, from, commencing at, referring to time or place, when it is usually in regimen with 至; a *pronoun*, self, I; my own, personally; to use, to serve; to lead.
丨己 or 丨家 myself; yourself, the second phrase is common in Kiangsu.
你丨己 yourself.
丨做 or 丨爲 I did it.
丨然 natural, spontaneous; willingly, certainly, of course, to be sure.
丨然銅 native copper.
丨從去年 since last year.
丨滿 or 丨用 or 丨是 self-confident, self-trusting; presumptuous; conceited, lofty ideas; haughty in his opinion.
不丨由 I cannot do as I would.
丨然而然 by degrees to become used to a thing, to get confident.

不請丨來 he came uninvited or of his own accord; it also sometimes involves the meaning that he must take the responsibility of it; run his own risk.

丨造 made by the man who sells; our own manufacture.

丨京至上海 from Peking to Shanghai.

好去丨 you had better not go away.

丨己稱丨己 to praise one's self unduly.

丨若 or 丨在 or 丨丨在在 in good health or spirits; — but 丨在 also means independent, self-existing, and the Budhists call the god Siva 大丨在 the Great Independent (*Mahesvara*).

丨食丨 I find my own food.

丨作丨受 he gets what he gave, he is only paid for his evil.

丨後 henceforth.

丨斟丨飲 helping themselves to drink as they liked.

来丨何處 whence did you come?

不我丨先 he is not before me, or older than I.

丨易以及難 to advance from the easy to the difficult.

丨彼成康 they used those [principles of the rulers] Ch'ing and K'ang — to guide their government; *i. e.* the successors of these sovereigns imitated them.

豈非丨外 do not they exceed their proper station? is he not out of his place?

字 *tsz'* From *child* under a *shelter*.

To love and shelter; to bear and nurse, as a mother does; used with the next, a female; a character or symbol in writing, a letter; lettered, marked, written on; a writing, a letter; a word or symbol of thought; a name, a designation; a style or title taken by educated people at marriage; to betroth a daughter.

一張丨 a writing, a document, an order.

丨典 a dictionary.

丨母 the initials: and 丨韻 or 丨頭 the finals in Chinese spelling; they are combined to indicate the sound of a character.

無丨願 no mind for learning.

花碼丨 or 畫碼丨 the contracted forms of the numerals.

丨眼 a set phrase, an expression.

活丨 or 丨粒 or 鉛丨 movable types.

尊丨 what is your respected style?

別丨 the familiar style taken at marriage.

立丨 to write out an agreement.

丨格 black lines.

印丨格 to copy by laying slips under paper, as when learning to write.

未丨 not yet betrothed.

父不能丨厥子 the father cannot be partial to his own son.

丨之 deal kindly with him.

拆丨 to dissect characters, as is done by fortune-tellers; to explain their meaning and construction.

捉丨虱 to pick flaws in a writing; to find fault uselessly.

一個丨號 a chop, as of tea; a lot of things with the same label.

蠅頭小丨 very small characters.

丨丨有意 every word in it has a meaning.

丨兒 the reverse of a coin.

牸 *tsz'* A cow, but also includes the females of domestic animals.

丨馬 a mare.

畜丨牛 to keep cows for their milk.

漬 *tsz'* From *water* and to *blame*; also read *tsih*.

To soak, to steep; to dye; to tint; water-soaked, moldy, damaged by water; the death of a brute; in *medicine*, a cold infusion or percolation.

浸丨 laid under water, to drench.

漸丨失教 he has gradually lost all regard for his profession or faith.

水丨 damaged, as cargo by water.

痕丨 or 印丨 spotted; marks of watering; stained.

恣 *tsz'* From *heart* and *next*; also read ˛*tsz'*.

Dissipation, gaiety; licentious, loose; to throw off restraint, to let the passions have sway.

放丨 to cast off scruples; profligate.

縱丨 unrestrained indulgence.

丨行無忌 to care for nobody; a rude manner.

丨意 to do as one likes, to disregard rules; lustful.

骴 胔 髊 *tsz'* From *bone* or *flesh* and *this*; the first is most common, and the third a mere alteration.

The bones of animals or human beings lying exposed, with putrid flesh still attached to them; to make things out of bone or teeth.

掌除丨 he attended to the removal of the putrid remains.

腐丨 putrid flesh and bones.

胾 *tsz'* To cut meat into steaks or cutlets; slices; morsels or bits of meats.

大丨 a large slice.

丨羹 meat soups, thick and rich.

肴丨 meat cooked with or without the bones.

[此/皮] *tsz'* The skin shriveled and furrowed by age.

剚 倳 *tsz'* To stick into, as a share in the soil, or when driving down a stake; to put a knife into or between; to stab, to stick; to erect, as a pole; to establish.

[此/衣] *tsz'* The garments crumpled or doubled in, as the Chinese long sleeves are often worn.

Read *tsi'* To double the lapels one over the other on the breast.

TSʻZʼ.

Old sounds, tsʻi, tsʻai, dzi, dzai, tsʻit, tsʻat, *and* dzat. *In Canton*, tsʻzʼ ; — *in Swatow*, chʻù, si, sù, *and* chʻó ; — *in Amoy*, tsu, chʻu, su, chʻi, *and* chʻó ; — *in Fuhchau*, chʻü, chü, chʻi, *and* chʻóü — *in Shanghai*, tsʻzʼ, szʼ, *and* tsʼ ; — *in Chifu*, tsʻzʼ.

雌 *꜀tsʻzʼ* From *bird* and *this*. The female of birds; *met.* weak, inferior.

丨伏 to lie perdu or skulk.

丨雄劍 a pair of swords.

見個丨雄 see which of the two will beat, or is the strongest.

誰知烏之丨雄 who can tell (or who cares to know) hens from cocks among crows? — useless knowledge.

丨鷄啼鳴 the hen is crowing in the morning; — the wife rules.

砒 *꜀tsʻz* The native trisulphide of arsenic or orpiment is called 雌黃, and this character is only another form of the last in this sense; when pulverized, 雄黃 is the name given it.

姕 *꜀tsʻzʼ* A slatternly, worthless woman.

丨妓 a drab, an ugly woman; an awkward rough woman.

疵 *꜀tsʻzʼ* Scab of a sore; a malady, an infirmity; an imperfection, as a hair-mole; a failing, an eccentricity; petty jealousy.

丨病 bad habits, a fault.

小丨 a little fault, a blemish in a character.

吹毛求丨 to seek for defects under the fur; — petty cavilling at men's faults; a mean fault-finder.

玼 *꜀tsʻzʼ* Used for the last and for 泚 new. A flaw in a gem; the luster of a gem; fresh, vigorous.

盛丨 abundant, fresh.

鮮丨 new; bright and clean.

誰孰無丨 who of us is perfect?

丨兮丨兮 how rich and splendid — is her robe!

茈 *꜀tsʻzʼ* A plant yielding a red dye, called 丨草 or 丨蒗, and perhaps allied to the *Rubia*; the Caladium 丨菰 is sometimes thus written.

丨魚 a cuttle-fish, or a marine animal resembling it.

茨 *꜀tsʻzʼ* From *grass* and a *time*. Thatch; to thatch a roof; a prickly plant growing on city walls and roofs, said by the comments to be the *Tribulus*.

丨以生草 to thatch with fresh grass.

茅丨 a thatched cabin or cottage.

丨菰 the *Caladium sagittifolium* or small arum, is sometimes thus written.

牆丨貽羞 my roof full of thistles makes me ashamed; — my family is not a great one.

牆有丨不可襄也 tribulus grows on the wall, but it cannot be removed.

瓷 磁 *꜀tsʻzʼ* From *tile* and a *time*, or *stone* and *grass*; the second is the most common, and alone used for loadstone. Crockery, china-ware.

丨器 porcelain.

洋丨 foreign ware.

縹丨 translucent, fine porcelain.

丨石吸鉄 the magnet draws iron.

官窰丨 ware from the government furnaces; it always has the reign stamped on it.

慈 𢙐 *꜀tsʻzʼ* From *heart* and *grass*, but the primitive is said to be 玄 *somber* doubled; the second form is unusual. Maternal affection; a mother, to act like a mother; love; kindness and compassion, mercy; gentle, tender to, soft.

家丨 my mother.

丨母 indulgent mothers — often spoil their children.

丨竹 a bamboo with many suckers.

令丨 your mother.

承丨命 I have received my mother's orders.

丨悲 compassionate, forbearing.

丨悲大士 a term for Kwanyin.

丨愛 loving affection.

丨祥 merciful and propitious.

丨心 a kind heart.

丨菰 or 丨姑 a water vegetable (*Caladium*), which the Chinese say bears thirteen tubers every intercalated year.

山丨姑 the tuber of an *Amaryllis*.

鷀 *꜀tsʻzʼ* The fishing cormorant, much used to catch fish.

鸕丨 the cormorant; also called 水老鴉 water crow.

辭 辞 辤 *꜀tsʻzʼ* From 辛 *acrid* contracted from 辠 *crime*, and 亂 to *confuse* contracted; similar to the next. In *grammar*, an expression, word, or particle; applied to a kind of irregular verse, something between prose and poetry, where the rhyme recurs at the end of lines of various lengths; evidence, words; orders, instructions; to refuse, to decline respectfully; to resign, to leave; to go, to retire, to depart; fame; a plea, an argument; an apology.

推丨 to decline, as an office.

丨去 to leave, as one's service.

告丨 or 丨別 to take leave; to announce, as a visitor his departure.

各執一丨 each one held to his own opinion.

心丨to dislike, averse to.

明清于單丨be intelligent and pure in the single pleas; *i. e.* the arguments brought up on the plaintiff's side.

丨帖 to send a regret, as when invited to dine.

丨行帖 a card sent at leaving; a *p. p. c.* card.

虛丨a falsehood, a wrong statement, a formal word.

不丨勞苦 he never thinks of his toils.

嘆語丨an interjection.

說丨a rejoinder, a plea in reply.

丨謝 to decline with thanks.

固丨to firmly decline.

不丨而行 to go off without bidding good-bye.

丨說分明 he talks clearly and intelligently.

好丨句 a good style.

不丨遠近來 he will not mind coming, whether it is near or distant; *i. e.* he will undoubtedly come.

詞 ꜀tsʻzʻ From *words* and to *direct;* used with the preceding.

An expression, a word or phrase; a poetical composition in rhyme, like a roundelay; a writing, an official paper; style, phraseology; to speak out the real thoughts; to accuse; to ask, to request.

言丨an expression.

丨不達意 the sentence does not fully convey the idea.

文丨or 丨章 composition, style.

狀丨an accusation or reply; a petition.

砌丨sophisticated arguments.

丨林 the Hanlin Academy.

口丨utterance, speech.

情見乎丨my feelings are expressed in my words.

祠 ꜀tsʻzʻ From *worship* and to *direct.*

To offer a sacrifice in the spring to one's ancestors, since the opening spring suggests that as life then exhibits itself, so their progenitors formerly gave them their birth; the building where they are worshiped; the spring; to obtain the request prayed for.

丨堂 the ancestral hall of a family.

生丨to make an image of a man, and worship it while he is still living, as of a powerful ruler.

神丨an old name for the ancestral tablet.

此 ʻtsʻzʻ From 止 to *stop* and 匕 or 比 to *compare, q. d.* to rest and arrange what comes next.

This, the last spoken of, the thing in hand; here, now.

去彼就丨to come from there to this place; to leave there and come here.

如丨like this; thus, so.

在丨he is here.

丨等小人 this sort of worthless men.

丨生 in life, during life.

只丨告止 enter no farther than this spot; he is just so always.

以丨or 丨是 by, or on this account; therefore.

丨恩丨德 for this very kindness.

專丨for this end or reason; the why, the only cause.

丨謂知本 this may be termed knowing the basis of it.

跐 ʻtsʻzʻ To use *this foot, i. e.* to tread on; to trample; to step.

一步丨空 to step on nothing or on uncertain ground, as to miss a step in coming down a stairs, or to step into the mud.

丨穩 to step carefully; look well to your footing.

丨不下了 he cannot get on or do any better.

脚丨兩頭船 to step on two boats; *i. e.* fall between two stools.

丨蹈 to step, to walk.

用脚丨着 put your foot on it.

佌 ʻtsʻzʻ Small; diminutive; of little capacity or talents.

丨丨之物 a very little mind or thing.

丨丨彼有屋 these little mean people have their dwellings.

泚 ʻtsʻzʻ Also read ʻtsʻi.

Clear, as water; an old name of a stream in Hunan; fresh, new; perspiring; to sweat.

其顙有丨his forehead was wet with perspiration.

新臺有丨the new terrace is bran new.

次 tsʻzʻ꜄ From to *breatne* and *two.*

Neither the first nor the best; coming after, second in order; next, secondary, succeeding to; a time, a trial; a halting-place, an encampment; a stated post to halt at; an inn, a stall; a rest-house, a shed; a lunar mansion or position of the moon among the stars; to put in the order of; to pitch tents where one halts; to braid in false hair.

丨第 regularly, in a sequence.

一丨once.

頭丨the first time.

途丨一晤 passed each other on the road.

在其丨in that (or its own) place; next in order.

層層丨丨rising gradually, as a gallery or a climax.

丨早 the next morning.

位丨a seat, a position.

草丨or 造丨flurried, immethodical, rash, flighty.

客丨or 旅丨an inn, a traveler's lodging-house, a hotel.

張大丨to erect a large shed or halting-lodge.

胸丨in the mind; as 不入胸丨he cares very little about it; also he does not imitate or attend to such things.

丨骨 enters even to the bones, as a bad cold.

丨玉 an inferior gem.
王丨于河朔 the king halted north of the Yellow River.
世丨 a genealogical record.
舟丨上海 the ship reached Shanghai.
是又其丨也 this is still one time more, as the third or after.
丨硝 refuse saltpetre.

佽 ts'z' From *man* and *next to.*

Light, nimble, sprightly; to assist, to relieve; to fit on; to close the fingers in drawing the bow; for, instead of.
丨助 to help.
丨飛 the name of an ancient archer; used in the Han dynasty as the name of an office, whence 丨飛勇士 means valorous, skillful troops.

諫 ts'z' From *words* and a *thorn*; interchanged with the next in this sense.

To criticise, to reprove sharply; to satirize or ridicule, in order to an amendment.
諷丨 to ridicule one.
丨諫 to earnestly expostulate with.

刺 ts'z' From *knife* and *thorn*; it is also read *ts'ih*, in many of these senses, especially those relating to pricking; and is not to be confounded with *lah*, 刺 sharp.

A thorn, a sting, a spine; to wound by a direct thrust, as officers were executed in old times; to prick; to brand by sharp points, to tattoo, to cut into; to stab and kill; to spade up, as plants with a trowel; to pole a boat; to criticise, to lampoon; to blame; an innuendo, a sly sarcasm; to pry into, to overhear, to examine.

行丨 to kill or stab a superior; to assassinate him, as a 丨客 or assassin does.
投丨 to send in a card, alluding to the days when visiting-cards were cut on blocks of wood.
毛丨 one name for the hedgehog.
挑丨, to prick and baste, as in sewing.
丨, 繡 to embroider.
丨地 to dig up the ground, to hoe.
丨船 to pole a boat.
說丨 or 譏丨 to taunt, to ridicule; to speak in raillery.
丨字 to write with a stylus; to brand a criminal by tattooing, for which 丨臉 is also used.
蜂丨 a bee's sting.
丨探 to pry into and criticise.
丨, 丨, 不休 to talk incessantly.
丨史 now used as a term for a 知州 or sub-prefect, but in the Han applied to an intendant.
丨責 to blame, to scold.
丨撓 uneasy; skin irritated, as by prickly heat.

莿 朿 ts'z' Interchanged with the last; the second is the original form of both, intended to delineate a bramble like the *Zizyphus*; it must not be confounded with *shuh*, 束 a sheaf.

A prickle, a thorn on plants; to be sarcastic.
芒丨 the beard or awn of barley.
丨玫花 a prickly rose.
荆棘之丨 the thorns on brambles.
丨兒松 the juniper.
挑丨爲好肉 he took out the thorn and let the flesh heal;— said of a peacemaker.
丨菓兒 a hooked seed, like the bur-marygold (*Bidens*); — *met.* a captious man.

蛓 蠀 蚝 ts'z' The last form is rarely used.

Caterpillars which have stiff or spiny hairs that are regarded as poisonous, such as the tiger-moth (*Euprepia*) and others.
丨蝟 the hedgehog.
毛丨 hairy caterpillars
丨毛 to ruffle up the feathers
龍丨 a name for the telini fly or cantharides. (*Mylabris.*)

In *Cantonese.* A nit, a louse; insects which irritate the skin; an itching, a prickling.
一身丨 the whole person is frowzy.
生丨狗 a mangy dog.
生丨狗咁聲 like a whining dog, said of a peevish child.
花丨 plant lice.
水丨 water spiders and such like insects.

廁 厠 ts'z' tsö sz' From *shelter* and *rule.*

A place which needs to be constantly cleansed, a privy; to cleanse; a gorge where a stream forces its way; to arrange guests in order; a high brink; the edge of a bed.
丨所 or 丨坑 or 茅丨 or 東丨 a necessary; a jakes.
倒丨 to empty night soil.
上丨 to go to stool.
踞丨視之 to see one in bed.
丨之賓客之中 mix him among the guests.

庛 ts'z' The wooden part of the share of a plow, the 耒丨, to which the iron was formerly attached; others say it was the brace of the share

WA.

Old sounds, wa *and* ngwa. *In Canton*, wa *and* nga; — *in Swatow*, wa *or* úa; — *in Amoy*, wa; — *in Fuhchau*, wa *and* ngwa; — *in Shanghai*, wò *and* ngò; — *in Chifu*, wa.

蛙 鼃 ˓wa } A green and striped frog, with a broad line down the back; used with the next, wanton, exciting tones.

怒 丨 the enraged frog, refers to a story of the king of Tso.

井底 丨 like a frog in a well; — inexperienced and ignorant.

紫色 丨 聲 a painted face and wanton song.

丨 鼓六更天 the frog's croak serves as the drum of the sixth watch.

哇 ˓wa Wanton, enticing sounds; lascivious music; to wheedle, to coax; sobbing, whining; to retch or vomit.

丨 吐 to vomit, to spit out.

出而 丨 之 he went out and threw it up.

丨 咬 lewd songs.

娃 ˓wa A beautiful woman; a fine, pretty girl.

女 丨 子 pretty girls.

小 丨 丨 a baby; small children.

女嬌 丨 a fine elegant woman.

洼 ˓wa Name of a river in Kansuh; used with the next, a puddle; deep and winding, as a stream.

漥 ˓wa The footsteps of an ox, in which dirty water collects; a puddle; a hollow.

丨 水 clear water.

丨 深 a deep pool in a stream.

丨 子 a bog, a swamp.

丨 田 or 丨 地 low ground.

窊 ˓wa From *cave* and *melon*; also read *wa*˒ and used with the preceding; 凹 is regarded as a synonym.

The bottom of a cavity; a depression in a level place, a spot where the ground is low; a puddle; a hoof-print.

丨 地墊高 fill in the hollow.

丨 隆是若 like low shrill notes, as the tones of a fife.

地卑 丨 the spot is very low.

草 丨 a grassy plateau; applied to Mongolia.

菀 丨 the god of silkworms.

坑坑 丨 丨 的 ups and downs, as in a rough road; not plane.

哾 ˓wa From *mouth* and *child*.

The prattle of children.

丨 嘔 the sound of children talking and playing.

Read ˓*'rh*. A forced laugh, 嚅 丨 denoting that the compliance is compulsory.

瓦 ˊwa The original is supposed to have resembled a tile; it is the 98th radical of a few homogeneous characters relating to pottery.

A general name for earthenware, tiles, flags, encaustic tiles, glazed bricks, pottery, &c.; a roof, from its covering of tiling.

鋪 丨 to lay tiles.

丨 版 or 仰 丨 or 看 丨 the flat tiles laid on the bottom.

䨻 丨 the cylindrical tiles laid at the eaves.

牡 丨 or 覆 丨 or 丨 筒 the convex tiles.

丨 桁 or 丨 隴 a row of tiles.

丨 頂 or 丨 背 a tiled roof.

弄 丨 之慶 the joy of having a daughter.

丨 盤 a glazed earthen dish.

丨 器 coarse earthenware, as water jars.

氷消 丨 解 the ice is melted and the tile is broken; — gone, destroyed, the glory departed.

丨 松 the house-leek (*Umbilicus* or *Sempevrivum*), also called 屋游 or house vagrant.

丨 稜子 shells like the *Arca*, referring to their ribbed valves.

搲 ˊwa To seize with the hand, to grasp, to hold on; to pull towards one, as a lot of little things.

丨 荳 draw the beans — into the basket.

踠 ˊwa To tread on the ground.

丨 踏 to stamp the feet; to patter along, as a child who is beginning to walk.

宼 wa˒ From *covering* and a *tile*.

A mud house; to build a mud hovel.

丨 屋 a mud or adobie house.

嗁 呱 wa˒ ˓ku } The second form is also read ˓*ku*.

The wailing of an infant; to sob and moan.

丨 的一聲哭了 loud screaming of a child.

鳥乃去矣后稷 丨 矣 when the bird went off, Heu-tsih began to wail.

丨 丨 的哭 a long continued wail.

小兒遺毋 丨 丨 載道 children who have lost their mothers go sobbing through the streets.

In *Cantonese*. A final particle like 咩 implying doubt.

WAH

Old sounds, wot *and* met. *In Canton*, wat *and* mat ; — *in Swatow*, wat, bué, *and* mít ; — *in Amoy*, wat *and* biat ; — *in Fuhchau*, wak ; — *in Shanghai*, wĕh *and* mĕh ; — *in Chifu*, wa.

窊 wa' A deep, cavernous hollow, a large hole, as in a hill; to explore with the hand in a dark hole.

挖 ˏwa To scoop out, to excavate; to stir up, as an old grudge; to dig out, to hollow out; to gouge; to clean out, to dredge.

丨金砂 to dig gold dust.

丨耳 to pick the ears.

丨井 to dig a well.

爬丨 to scratch a hole.

如丨眼睛 like plucking out the eye, — I am so disappointed.

要丨荷包 you must fork out the money.

丨斷路 to break up and destroy the road, as a retreating army.

丨補 to take out and replace or mend with another.

挑丨 to open out, as a choked-up channel.

丨剢人語 to find fault with others' words, to criticise people's talk.

丨窟人 to annoy others, to ridicule people, to rake up old scores.

韤 韈 wa' Stockings, hose, socks; whatever covers the feet.

一對丨子 a pair of stockings.

棉丨 quilted stockings.

袷丨 lined socks.

大筒丨 a stocking big enough for all; — a generally useful thing.

插在丨筒 put it in the stocking, — which is often used for a pocket.

WAI.

Old sounds, ngat *and* yat. *In Canton*, wai *and* ngoi ; — *in Swatow*, chw'a *and* gwa ; — *in Amoy*, wai, goé, *and* oé ; — *in Fuhchau*, wai, ngwoi, *and* ngié ; — *in Shanghai*, hwah *and* nga ; — *in Chifu*, wai.

歪 ˏwai From *correct* and *not* above it.

Deflected from the perpendicular, aslant, asquint, askew, awry; deflected, as a bent ray of light; depraved, wicked; to lay obliquely, to put down awry.

丨嘴 a wry mouth.

丨戴帽子 to wear a hat awry.

船丨着 the boat heels over.

丨頭 a crooked neck; also applied to tipsy people.

坐丨 to sit awkwardly or slovenly.

丨心 a wicked heart.

晌午丨了 it is past noon.

企丨的 to loll, to lean against.

咪放丨 don't lay it crookedly. (*Cantonese.*)

崴 ˏwai Uneven, rugged; a goat path going up a hill-side in a crooked manner; lofty.

喎 ˏwa A distorted mouth, caused by palsy, or a contortion of muscles.

眼丨斜 mouth and eyes awry.

外 wai' From *evening* and to *divine*; *q. d.* to cast lots at evening is beyond or aside from the business of the day.

Outside, without, beyond; not native; moreover, another; extraneous, over and above; foreign, beyond the house, village, or empire; relatives by marriage; to exclude, to reject; to put aside or outside.

丨國 foreign countries.

丨省 another province.

丨江佬 people from beyond the River; a Northerner. (*Cantonese.*)

丨父 a wife's father.

除此之丨 excluding this; besides these; moreover.

丨面 or 丨頭 outside, in the streets; not included.

格丨之好 extraordinarily good.

意丨 unexpectedly.

丨馬 a postman, a courier.

出丨 to go abroad, to leave home.

自丨來 from abroad, not native.

內文明而丨柔順 when the principles are intelligent, the conduct will be gentle and courteous.

有丨才 he has a knowledge of the world, not of books only.

丨人 not one of our set; an outsider, an alien.

丨感 affected by the weather, out of sorts.

舉頭天丨 he stretches his head beyond the skies; very haughty.

方丨 wandering, gipsey people; tramps.

丨方 remote places, desolate regions.

丨行 a raw hand; unskilled. (*Shanghai.*)

其大無丨 nothing greater than this.

聵 wai' Deaf, arising from defect in the ear or age; born deaf.

聾丨 deaf.

昏丨 stupid and deaf, as one in a fit.

歹 wai' From *not* and *good*; an ideographic character, but like some others of the same construction with 不 on top, regarded as vulgar by native lexicographers.

A synonym of 歹 similar to 歪 and used in contrast with 好 good; ill looking, defective.

WAN.

Old sounds, wan, ngwan, *and* man. *In Canton*, man, wan, *and* ún, ; — *in Swatow*, wan, măng, mien, *and* búan ; — *in Amoy*, wan, gwan, bwan, ban, *and* bien ; — *in Fuhchau*, wang, mang, *and* mwang ; — *in Shanghai*, wèⁿ, èⁿ, mèⁿ *and* wèh ; — *in Chifu*, wan.

彎 *wan* From *bow* and *connected;* interchanged with the next.

To draw a bow, to bend anything to a curve; bent, bowed, curved; arched.

丨弓 to draw and shoot a bow.

木頭丨了 the stick is bent or warped.

一丨新月 the crescent moon.

拐丨 crooked and circuitous, as a serpentine road.

灣 *wan* From *water* and to *curve;* often wrongly written 瓌, and interchanged with the preceding.

A winding bank, a cove, a bay; a low retiring beach; an anchorage; a bend, an indentation in a coast-line; to enter a cove, as a vessel; to moor.

河丨 a river bend.

南丨 the Praya Grande at Macao.

丨丨曲曲 winding, tortuous, serpentine.

丨着的船 a vessel at anchor.

丨泊 to anchor.

轉丨 to turn a corner.

沙丨 a sandy beach.

萬重丨 full of bends, as a river or coast-line.

丨一秋水 one arch of autumnal water; — *met.* a liquid, beautiful eye.

剜 *wan* To pare, to cut down; to make thinner; to gouge out, as in cutting characters; to pull out, as an eye; to excavate.

丨補 to cut out and patch.

丨骨上的肉 to cut away the flesh from the bones.

雕丨 to carve, as on wood.

丨心待人 diligent and earnest in his service.

丨割 to cut out, as a tumor.

有洞若神丨 caves are doubtless dug out by the gods.

捥 *wan* Used with the last 腕 and wrist.

To bend the wrist; to curve with the hand; the wrist; to lift and carry a thing.

帵 *wan* From *napkin* and to *yield.*

Remnants, cabbage, cuttings.

丨子 fragments left from making clothes.

豌 *wan* From *pulse* and *flexible*, referring to its stalk.

A species of pea, common at Peking, the 丨豆 or 淮豆 which is probably the *lablab*, and said to have been introduced; the pod is round, and usually contains four round white and large peas; it resembles the marrowfat pea.

糖丨豆 sugared bean soup.

黎丨豆 a spotted bean fed to beasts.

頑 *wan* From *head* and *original;* sometimes wrongly used for 翫 to sport.

A thick-headed stupid person; heedless; inconsiderate; immovable, passive, mulish; to push or butt with the head.

丨疲 stupid and weak; trifling and inattentive to his duty.

奸丨 a sly rascal.

丨梗 obstinate, cross-grained.

丨民 the stupid, unlettered people.

丨夫廉 a man of integrity but rather simple.

冥丨不靈 a dull mind which does not readily catch an idea.

疎丨 careless and inattentive.

丨石 a shapeless, useless stone.

丨劣 an inefficient, useless man.

岏 *wan* The peak of a mountain; sharp summit of a mountain.

刓 园 *wan* To pare off the corners, to cut or round off, to trim; to equalize, to make out a report without sticking to facts.

丨角 to clip and round the corners.

痽 *wan* Numbness in the hands or feet; another defines it, a running sore or ring-worm that will not heal.

晚 *wan* From *day* and *without.*

Evening, sun-set, but not after dark; time of twilight, the gloaming; late in life; behind, tardy, late; the last, the latter; afterwards.

昨丨 last evening.

今丨 this evening.

傍丨 or 挨丨 towards evening.

丨上 or 丨間 in the evening, towards nine or ten o'clock.

不丨 it is not late; I am not behind time.

丨半晌 at sunset; the sun is down.

丨年 old, advanced, over sixty.

丨弟 or 丨生 a junior; your pupil, your servant; — a polite term for one's self.

歲丨 late in the year.

享丨福 to enjoy a happy end of life.

相見恨丨 I regret that I did not know you before.

丨燒晴 a promising evening for a fair day.

丨禾 or 丨造 a late crop, as of rice or wheat.

悔之丨矣 it is now too late to regret it, or repent of it.

丨運 succeeded at last, as a student in getting a degree.

婉 *'wan* — From *woman* and *without*; also read *'mien*, and used for 挽 to bear.

Complaisant, agreeable, winning; trying to please, obliging.

丨順 accommodating, kind.

婉丨聽從 condescending and ready to hear favorably.

挽 *'wan* — To lead, as a child; to draw, to pull along; to turn over, as a cuff; to regain, as favor; to revert to the previous sentence or argument; to restore, to make good; to carry on the arm; to turn round, to bend.

丨住 to grasp in the hand.

丨頹風 to reform a degenerate age or manners.

丨回不得 they cannot be restored; the first state cannot be brought back.

丨髻 to dress the hair.

丨手同行 to walk arm in arm.

丨袖 the broad-faced, embroidered sleeves of women; to roll up the cuffs.

丨歌 funereal dirges chanted by pall-bearers.

丨柩 to bear a coffin; to weep over it, as a son.

丨油瓶 to carry the oil-jar; *i. e.* to go with a father's widow when she is married.

丨留 to detain, to draw back.

丨救 to save from disaster, to rescue, to prevent evils.

丨長耳籃 to carry a long-baled basket, *i. e.* to beg, referring to the basket for food. (*Cantonese.*)

輓 *'wan* — To pull a wheeled barrow or an easy-chair carriage; to draw a hearse; ropes for it.

丨詩 a monody.

祭丨 elegiac prayers or sayings.

丨祝 funeral scrolls hung in the hall.

丨歌喪車執紼者相和聲 the hearse-carriers and they who held the ropes, both chanted in union.

晼 *'wan* — The declining sun.

白日丨晚其將入兮 the bright sun declines to the evening, and soon will be gone from us!

碗 盌 椀 *'wan* — From *wood* or *dish* and to *cover*; the first and now the common form is unauthorized.

A bowl, a deep dish; a wooden trencher; a bowl-full.

飯丨 a rice-bowl.

鉒丨 or 馬丨 to clamp and mend bowls.

大海丨 a punch bowl.

施捨丨發財飯 give me a bowl of your surplus rice; — a beggar's cry.

擺九大丨 lay out the nine big dishes; — *met.* to give a large entertainment.

火丨 a dish with a heater to keep things warm.

吃人丨半由人使喚 if you eat of a man's dish, you must come at his call, — as a servant on wages.

丨盞杯盆 crockery-ware.

破丨詛嘴 to take an oath by breaking a bowl.

涴 *'wan* — From *water* and *cover*.

Eddying water is 丨演; to run in eddies.

Read *ngoh*, To spatter mud on one, as a carriage in passing.

綰 綄 *'wan* — From *silk* and *officer* or *finished*; the second form is obsolete, but is sometimes used to denote a weather-cock.

To hate, to dislike; a crimson color; lustring, a cheap sort of silk; to run through, as in stringing cash, or as a pin through the hair; to perforate; to tie up.

忨 *wan'* — Like the next.

To desire, to covet, to long for; to waste away.

丨忽 heedless, forgetful.

丨歲愒日 to idle away the years and waste the days.

翫 *wan'* — From to *practice* and *origin*; *q.d.* as if one had gone to the bottom of a subject; used with the next.

To study till weary of a thing, to get tired of doing a thing, or being with a person.

習丨 to be perfect in, to get thoroughly.

玩 *wan'* — Interchanged with the last.

Trinkets or gems for playing with; to toy or play with; to ramble and divert one's self; to linger and dawdle; to enjoy, as an agreeable author; to test, to try, to practice with; valuable, rare, fine; child's play.

細丨 to carefully examine, as a book.

丨法 to despise or set lightly by the laws.

遊丨 to ramble, to take recreation.

古丨 articles of virtu; rarities.

丨味 to try the taste of; to relish, as a book.

丨器 or 丨物 toys; desirable, highly prized things.

丨人喪德 familiar license destroys one's virtue; like I. Cor. xv. 33.

丨耍 to trifle, to dally with; to tempt to vice.

丨月 to enjoy the moonlight.

丨藝 playthings, toys; to take delight in.

丨弄 trifling play; to toy with.

丨景 to enjoy scenery.

妧 *wan'* — A handsome, beautiful woman.

腕 𦛗 *wan'* — The wrist; a flexible, easy-moving, universal joint; to grasp, to twist.

手丨 the wrist.

肘丨 the elbow.

扼丨太息 to clasp and wring the hands in great grief.

丨力 strength in wrist-work, as penmanship or archery.

活動丨子 a flexible or skilled wrist.

惋 wan' Alarmed and dreading something; startled, as at meeting a foe.
悵 丨 surprised.
丨 恨 angry at.
不 勝 丨 惜 exceedingly grieved for.

腕 wan' The knee-pan or knee-joint.
膝 丨 the knee.

萬 万 wan' From *plants* and *monkey*, but originally the lower part was formed of 禸 a *track*, and the *gyrations* of a swarm of musquitoes or bees; the contracted form is common.

Like bees swarming under a queen for number; a number, ten thousand or a myriad, the highest number usually employed in notation; an indefinite number, many, every one, all; before a negative, forms a strong superlative.
丨 歲 爺 the emperor; *lit.* the lord of all ages.
丨 壽 his Majesty's birthday.
丨 民 all people.
巨 丨 a millionare.
丨 不 能 it cannot be done.
丨 無 此 理 there is no such principle.
丨 一 死 ten thousand to one he will live; most probably he will not die.
百 丨 a million.
十 千 丨 a hundred millions.
丨 不 及 一 not one equals him; unsurpassed.
丨 丨 ten thousand myriads, innumerable.
丨 人 綠 everybody's interest; a term used by priests when asking funds for festivals.
丨 不 失 一 wholly correct; nothing lost or missed
丨 勿 復 言 on no account return an answer.
出 于 尋 常 丨 丨 it is beyond expression extraordinary.
丨 福 every blessing.

卍 wan' A form of the last, but usually used for an ornament like the character.

A mystic emblem of high antiquity, the Indian *swastika* drawn on the breasts of Budhistic idols, and the special mark of the deities worshiped by the Lotus School, and explained to be the symbol of Budha's heart; it ist he hammer of Thor, and is common in Norse mythology.
丨 字 菓 the *Hovenia dulcis*, so called from the angular peduncles of the fruit.
丨 字 欄 杆 a balustrade with a convoluted lattice.
丨 字 錦 the Vitruvian scroll.

蔓 wan' From *plants* and *lengthened*.
To shoot forth, to ramify, to creep; a vine; a creeping, trailing plant; tangled, intricate; obscure, verbose.
葛 丨 a species of bean (*Dolichos?*) that furnishes fibers for cloth.
不 丨 不 枝 it has neither vines nor branches; — as an essay, which sticks to the argument.
延 丨 to spread abroad, to break out, as robbers; diffusive, irrelevant; to expatiate largely.
瓜 丨 a melon-vine.
爬 丨 子 a climbing vine; ivy.
打 丨 子 to break off the tendrils, as of a vine.
丨 丨 日 茂 every day it spreads more vigorously.
方 出 丨 子 the tendrils started right out.
無 使 滋 丨 do not introduce irrelevant matters.

Read ˏ*man*. A root, the 丨 菁 a kind of round turnip, whose tuber is above ground and green colored, common at Peking; a second sort, the 芥 丨 菁 has its white tuber under ground.

鄤 wan' A town in the feudal state of Ching 鄭 not far from the present Tʻung-chʻuen fu in Sz'chʻuen, where its troops suffered a great defeat.

WĂN.

Old sounds, wen, men, mún, *and* won. *In Canton,* wăn *and* măn; — *in Swatow,* ún, bún, mút, *and* măng; — *in Amoy,* ún *and* bún; — *in Fuhchau,* ung *and* òng; — *in Shanghai,* wăng, măng, văng, *and* ming; — *in Chifu,* wăn.

溫 ˏwăn From *water* and *benevolent*.
Name of a river and district in the northwest of Honan, north of the Yellow River; warm, genial; tepid, lukewarm; placid, mild, kind, gentle; soothing, bland; matured, acquainted with; to warm, to revive.
丨 書 to review a lesson.
丨 風 a genial breeze.
丨 和 mild, as weather; tepid; benign, gracious.
丨 補 tonics, aphrodisiacs.
丨 丨 恭 人 a goodly gentleman.
丨 故 而 知 新 be thorough in what you learn, then you can know what is new.
敍 寒 丨 to talk about the weather; to chat and gossip.
丨 舊 情 to revive the old affection.
丨 飽 warm and fed; as 可 以 丨 飽 in good circumstances, above want.

瘟 ˏwăn A pestilential or widespread sickness, an epidemic; a giddiness; to wish the plague on one, as in anger.
丨 疫 or 丨 病 a prevailing sickness.
解 丨 to remove the epidemic.

丨鬼 the demon of a pestilence.

丨對頭 plague take him; blast him.

丨氣 malaria.

丨牛 a murrian among cattle, a rhinderpest.

活遭丨 to get a pommeling; lynch law.

Read *wuh*, Melancholy, reserved.

情思丨丨眼不開 he was so downcast he would not open his eyes.

𥁕 ꜀*wăn* From *dish* and *prisoner*.

To feed a prisoner; benevolent, kind, compassionate.

榲 ꜀*wăn* From *wood* and *mild*; it is correctly read *wuh*, but the primitive gives it this sound.

A small acid fruit, the 丨桲 like the *Cratægus*, the size of a bullace, and red like a cherry, found in northern China; the prepared sweetmeat is like cranberry in taste; a timber like pine; a root; a pillar; fine foliage.

文 ꜀*wăn* Considered to be originally a form or alteration of 爻 to *blend*, now restricted to the *lines* and marks of things; it forms the 67th radical of a few characters mostly relating to ornamenting.

Strokes, lines, veins, or bands, in wood, skins, or stones; ripples, markings, striæ; clouded, brindled; what is variegated, symmetrically marked; genteel, stylish, beautiful; elegant, accomplished, scholarly; the pursuits of peace; literary, literature; civil, endowed with political qualities; the literary class, civilians, the gentry; what is extraneous or ornamental and not essential; ceremonial; blazonry of flags; a form, as of prayer; a classifier of cash and coins; a dispatch.

丨彩 literary in taste, critically elegant; scientific.

丨墨事件 literary pursuits, correspondence.

丨法 grammar, rules of composition.

一丨 or 一丨錢 a cash; any coin, as a dollar or rupee.

丨理 style in writing; book expressions; classical, polished.

古丨 the ancient classical style.

斯丨 or 丨雅 scholarly, genteel, stylish.

原丨 the original text.

白丨 the plain text; no glosses.

不丨 inelegant, rustic.

投丨 to deliver a dispatch.

丨王課 to inquire of Wăn Wang, *i. e.* to toss up three cash together and count the chances.

丨不加點 the style is unimprovable.

他識丨章 he is a judge of composition and style.

丨昌帝君 the god of Literature, to whose worship the 丨筆塔 three-storeyed literary pagodas are erected in southern China; the star Dubhe in Ursa Major is consecrated to him.

洋丨 foreign writing or book.

説丨 to discuss characters; *i. e.* to explain their etymology.

通丨 a high bookish style of conversation, not using colloquialisms.

丨草 a rough draft, an original copy of a writing.

丨元 the style of a *küjin*, *q. d.* the head of letters.

Read *wăn'* To gloss over, to moderate.

丨過 to conceal a fault; to disguise one's evil conduct.

丨飾 to trump up, to impose on, to falsify.

紋 ꜀*wăn* From *silk* and *mark*.

The pattern, figures or marks in weaving; a mark, line, or trace.

丨銀 sycee, pure silver.

水波丨 the ripples on water.

縐丨 puckered, crinkled, corrugated.

横丨 the cross lines, as in wood or on the hand; across the grain.

丨亂 the pattern is awry.

並無丨跡 there is not the least trace.

花丨 the figure in cloth or silks.

陰騭丨 the lines under the eyes.

羅丨 the striæ on the finger ends.

魰 ꜀*wăn* The *pictured fish*; a fish beautifully striped with blue, and having a white head, called 丨鰩魚 found in the West Sea (Koko-nor?); it is remarkable for its large pectoral fins which enable it to fly, and is perhaps allied to the gurnards.

丨魚 a gold fish. (*Shanghai.*)

蚊 蟁 𧈧 ꜀*wăn* From *insect* and *streaks*, referring to the banded wings of musquitoes; but the other two forms, alluding to their gregarious habits like *people*, are more ancient.

A musquito, a gnat.

丨雷 buzz of musquitoes.

丨口 a musquito bite.

丨市 a swarm of musquitoes.

丨拂 a musquito-whip.

虎丨 or 花丨 the tiger musquito.

避丨香 or 丨烟香 pastiles or plants burned to drive them off.

雯 ꜀*wăn* From *rain* and *streaks*.

The coloring in the clouds.

丨錦 colored clouds.

月雲素丨 the moon clouds are plain white, [the sun clouds] are 赤丨 red-veined.

聞 ꜀*wăn* From *ear* and *door*; the *ear* is the *door* of knowledge.

To hear; to learn by report, hearing; to smell; fame, news; small; a scent.

聽丨 to hear.

傳丨 to repeat a report; a legend, a tradition.

風丨 a rumor.

昨兒丨得 I heard it yesterday.

丨香 smell the fragrance.

難丨 hard of hearing.
多丨 of great information.
不忍丨 distressing to hear; heart-rending.

Read *wăn'* To state to; where the voice reaches; character, fame; a noise.
丨於王 told it to the king.
令丨 famous reputation; of good report.
其尙顯丨于天 their report goes so manifestly to heaven.
舉賢以丨 he promoted good men in order that they might state — all to the king.
丨于四國 he is famed throughout the whole kingdom.

閿 / 闅 ꜀*wăn* Old forms of the preceding.
To look down and stoop, as one sees a thing; to look closely at.
丨鄉縣 a district in the extreme west of Honan on the south bank of the Yellow river.

刎 ‘*wăn* From *knife* and *not*.
To cut cross-wise; to divide.
自丨 or 丨喉 to cut one's throat.
丨頸交 a friendship that would lead persons to die for each other.
丨頸以見志 [I am ready] to cut my throat to show that I am in earnest.

吻 / 肳 / 呡 ‘*wăn* The second also means to contract the eyes, as near-sighted people do to see further.
The corners of the mouth; the lips; speech, talk.
接丨 to join the lips, to kiss.
吐脣丨 to pout, to thrust out the lips.
莫輕決丨 don't be too facile with your lips.
口丨不合 your mouths and lips do not match; your evidence is contradictory.
丨猶黃 your bill is yellow; *met.* you are very inexperienced.

In *Cantonese*, for which only the third form is used. Near; the edge; close; the last moment.
企得太丨 you stand too near the brink.
割好丨 trimmed it too close.

脗 ‘*wăn* From *flesh* and *lips*; originally a form of the last.
To join, to match, to blend as one; mingling and blending, as the sky and sea.
丨合 harmoniously blended.

伆 ‘*wăn* To separate, to cut asunder; to divide or break.

抆 ‘*wăn* From *hand* and *marks*.
To rub, to smooth off; to wipe off, to dry by rubbing.
丨拭 to brush and wipe off.
丨淚 to brush away the tears.
丨摩 to stroke down.

In *Cantonese*. To rub in; to fill up.
油丨 a horn spatula used to dress the hair.
丨磚口 to point bricks.
丨頭髮 to rub pomatum in the hair.
丨密 rub (or fill) it in tight, as a crack with putty.

搵 ‘*wăn* From *hand* and *genial*; also read *wuh*,
To place the hand on; to wipe; to dip or thrust into the water, as hot iron; to immerse, as when dyeing; to souse in.
丨抦 to sprout beans for greens.
丨染 to dye, to stain.
丨抩 to put anything into the water; to rinse.

In *Cantonese*. To search, to look for, to hunt up, to seek what is lost.
丨着 found it.
丨疋點 get me another piece.
丨倒監 to hale to prison, to put in the lockup.
丨計 seeking for employment.

媼 ‘*wăn* From *woman* and *genial*; also read ‘*ngao* and *uh*,
An old dame, an old woman; I, the old lady.
丨神 a name for the goddess of Earth.
老丨 a dame.
丨婆 a midwife; an herb-doctress.
丨娘 an old maid.
丨、妠 a fat baby.

穩 / 㒚 ‘*wăn* From 禾 *grain* and 隱 *small* contracted; the second form is unusual; it is also read *yin'* to follow, to rely on another.
To heap up grain on the thrashing-floor to be thrashed out; a sheaf or faggot of grass for fuel; firm, constant; firm, well placed, safe, secure, stable, immovable; to rest, to put down steadily or securely; repose, confidence; assured, implicit.
安丨 placed securely; at rest about a thing, composed.
站丨 or 企丨 to stand firmly.
丨當' out of danger; no fear now; quite safe.
不多丨 not very solvent or safe, as a firm; dubious, risky.
踏丨地步 stand firm on your feet; get good backers.
拿不丨 I can't tell how it will be, I cannot venture to say.
丨重 grave, reserved; formal in manners.
不得丨 it cannot be made safe; it is insecure.
丨妥 steady, uniform, as a motion.

問 *wăn'* From *mouth* and *door*.
To ask, to inquire of or about; to demand, to exact of; to investigate, to try, to examine a case; to convict, to give sentence; to clear up a doubt; a command, a mandate; to send presents when asking after one; an examiner in a court; fame.
丨對 or 丨答 a dialogue, a conversation.
丨[illegible] to inquire after, to send friendly messages to.

丨細底 to search into the truth of; a thorough investigation, in distinction to 泛丨 a superficial inquiry.
丨明白 to ask distinctly.
丨斬 to sentence to decapitation.
請丨 I beg to ask you.
公丨不至 the prince's orders have not yet come.
丨俗 to learn the usages of a country.
借丨 give me leave to ask you.
不恥下丨 don't be ashamed to ask your inferiors.
好丨決疑 it is well to ask about things if you are in doubt.
丨難 to get abstruse points cleared up, to learn the reasons for.

紊 *wăn'* From *silk* and *lines;* not the same as ˏ紋 ripples.
Raveled, as tangled thread; confused, involved; to embroil.
有條而不丨 the lines are very distinct.
丨亂 confused, anarchical.

不容丨 don't suffer the least disorder.

汶 *wăn'* The name of a river, the 丨河 in Shantung, rising southwest of T'aishan and running west into the Grand Canal, near 丨上縣 in Yen-cheu fu; it was the boundary between Tsi and Lu in old times; a large affluent of the Yangtsz', now also known as the River Min in the south of Sz'-ch'uen.
丨水湯湯 the waters of the Wăn flow ever on.

Read ˏ*măn.* To dishonor, to grieve.
受物之丨丨者乎 can I thus receive the reproaches of such a man?
丨濛 dirtied, defiled.

璺 *wăn'* From *gem* and *rising.*
A cracked porcelain or stone dish; a crack; a flaw.
碎丨 much cracked.
打破一道丨 he has cracked it.
驚丨 a very dangerous crack.

絻 *wăn'* Mourning clothes; the ropes held by mourners, which hang from the bier or catafalque.
丨服 mourning apparel.
執丨 to hold the cords of the pall.
袒丨 the arms exposed in mourning; a sign of great grief.

Read *mien'* and used for 冕' A crown.
麻丨 a hempen or sackcloth cap.

慍 *wăn'* Suppressed anger, indignant feelings; wrathy; rage; to be hated.
丨怒 irritated.
丨色 flushed with anger.
人不知而不丨不亦君子乎 not to feel angry at another's slight, is not this to be truly great or princely?
喜丨無常 now glad now vexed, as a freaky, irritable person.
丨于羣小 I am hated by the mean.
肆不殄厥丨 though he could not prevent their rage,—he kept his fame.

WANG.

Old sounds, wung *and* mung. *In Canton,* wong *and* mong; — *in Swatow,* wang, mang, buang, *and* mo; — *in Amoy,* ong, ang, *and* bong; — *in Fuhchau,* wòng; — *in Shanghai,* wong, vong, mong, *and* yong; — *in Chifu,* wang.

ˏ汪 *ˏwang* A deep and wide expanse of water; vast and still, as the deep; a lake, pool, or pond; great.
丨洋 the wide open sea.
大量丨容 of great patience and consideration.
藍丨丨的天 the clear blue sky.

ˏ尩 ˏ尪 ˏ尢 ˏ尣 *ˏwang* The last two are different forms of the 43d radical of contorted things, derived from 大 *great* made crooked; to make the first, 王 *king* is added as a phonetic, the others not being used.
Weak, feeble, or crooked, especially in the legs; deformed, in the breast; emaciated.

吾欲暴丨而奚若 I wish to expose a poor crooked fellow to the sun on account of the drought, but how will it do?
賤之如丨 to disregard (or depreciate) him as you would a weakling.

ˏ王 *ˏwang* Composed of 三 representing *heaven, earth,* and *man;* whoever joins them is a 王 *ruler;* the middle line is written nearest the top to show that a ruler should imitate heaven.
A king; a ruler, who is looked up to by all; to acknowledge him, as a feudal prince does; a title for monarchs before B. C. 220; royal, regal, princely; to be a king; a regulus, a beg.

親丨 and 君丨 the uncles or brothers and cousins of the emperor, like Prince Imperial and Prince Royal, who are addressed as 丨爺 my Lord King.
番丨 Mongol begs.
法丨 or 象丨 Budha.
丨聖轉輪 a Budhist term for universal and holy monarch; applied to Budha, it indicates the highest power and sovereignty, and suggests an analogy to the wheels of Ezekiel's vision.
丨父 a grandfather in the ancestral hall.
莫敢不來丨 [the chiefs] did not dare to withhold their fealty.
丨法 the laws of the land.

議政丨 a Prince Regent.
山大丨 a bandit chief; a blackamoor in theaters.
丨春 the first month of the year.
丨耶 a chief god of rivers, the object of fishermen and boatmen's fear and worship; his temples are called 紫雲宮 palace of the effulgent cloud.

Read *wang'* To rule as a king, to govern, to bear sway; to rule properly, or by law, as distinguished from 覇 a rule by force; a reign; occurs used for 往 to go, to resort to.

丨天下 to rule the world.
無以則丨乎 if you will not desist, then let us speak of the rights of ruling.
尤丨 it overtops others of the sort, it superabounds; exceeding.

亡 亾 *꜀wang* Originally formed of 入 to *enter* and ㄴ a contraction of 隱 *obscurity*, which is now altered to the first form.

Lost, destroyed; gone, no trace left; going to ruin; extinct, as a dynasty; dead; forgotten, out of mind; to go to ruin; in poverty; to escape, to abscond.

死丨 or 丨故 dead, exterminated.
丨失 lost, utterly gone.
丨人 a fugitive, like Cain; one dead or supposed to be.
未丨人 I, a widow.
陣丨 died in battle.
敗丨 discomfited, utterly defeated.
出丨 to skulk off, to go to other lands, as a fugitive prince or refugee nobleman.
人之云丨邦國殄瘁 noblemen are going away, and the country is ruining.

Read *꜀wu*; used for 無 or 毋. Without.

貧丨 very poor, without anything.
丨而爲有 having nothing and yet professing to have.

忘 *꜀wang* *wang'* From *heart* and *lost;* not the same as *꜀mang* 忙 busy.

To forget, to escape the mind; to neglect, to leave undone; to disregard.

丨恩思小怨 ungrateful, and yet always remembering his petty spites.
坐丨 to sit vacantly, to dawdle.
丨記 or 丨了 or 丨却 to forget, to slip one's recollection; out of mind.
丨本 to forget one's benefactor or parent.
丨食 he forgot to eat, from excess of business.
不能丨情 I can never forget your kindness and affection.
守此丨彼 to observe this and neglect that.
見丨 loss of memory, very absent-minded.

往 徃 *ʻwang* From *step* and a *lord;* but the other unauthorized form, composed of *step* and *born*, is now most in use.

To go, to pass; to go away, to depart; formerly, gone, past; the future; to send a present to.

無丨來 no acquaintance with him, I do not know him.
有來丨 there is some intercourse with him.
丨常 or 丨日 constantly, usually, formerly.
丨反 he has gone and come back.
丨丨如此 it is often so; it frequently happens.
丨罪 past offenses
何丨 or 丨那裏去 where are you going?
無丨不利 he makes money with everything; everything prospers with him.
向丨 the intention; a design.
其丨 henceforward.
丨事休題 don't bring up past deeds, let the past go.
已丨 gone, time is past.
丨好裏學 walk with the good and you'll learn good things; like Prov. xiii. 20.

枉 *ʻwang* From *wood* and to *rule; q.d.* to rule with club-law.

To force, to put a constraint on; bad, illegal, enforced; a wrong, a grievance; distorted, awry, crooked; to act crookedly or underhand; needlessly, to no purpose.

直丨 the right and the wrong of.
丨駕 or 丨臨 you must force or abase yourself to come; — a polite phrase.
大冤大丨 extreme suffering and persecution.
丨廢心機 lost all your pains.
丨居人世 you are of no use in the world.
舉直錯諸丨 employ the upright and remove the crooked.
呼丨 to complain of one's wrongs.
屈丨 to suffer wrong unjustly, to oppress.
丨矢 a crooked or deflected javelin; a malign or shooting star.
不丨了一番工夫 not lost your time altogether.

罔 网 *ʻwang* From 网 *net* and 亡 *lost*, originally derived from 冂 a *covering* and intercrossed *lines* inside to represent netting; the second original form, contracted to 罒 on the top of the primitive, is the 122d radical of characters concerning nets; differs from *꜀kang* 剛 stiff, and is interchanged with the next two.

A net, both literally and metaphorically; stopped, hindered, deceived, entangled; an *adverb* of negation, without, having none, nothing; to weave or twist; to do wrong, to impose upon, to deceive.

丨見 I saw nothing of it.
天之降丨 Heaven is letting down its net — of calamity to punish them.
丨有攸赦 there can be no forgiveness for him.
丨上 to scoff at superiors.
丨極 boundless, great, as kindness; also to offend extremely.
丨然 useless, undecided.
姦丨 treacherous, crooked ways.

網 ʻwang From *silk* and *net;* it looks like ˏ*kang* 綱 a rope.

A net of any kind, a web; to net, to catch, to entrap; a net, that which arrests people, a law that catches one; to implicate people.

一張丨 one net.

塵丨 the dusty entanglements; a Budhistic term for this life.

天丨 the government of Heaven; fate, what cannot be evaded.

丨魚 to catch fish.

設丨 or 張丨 to set a decoy net.

撒丨 to throw a net for fish.

漏丨 to escape the net, to avoid arrest.

丨開三面 he opened three holes in the net, — to let the birds have a chance to get out.

拍丨 a trap for birds.

一丨打盡 bagged them all at one haul; said of vigilant policemen, or a successful general.

醬丨 to bait a net with the white of eggs, as is done off Canton.

脫了羅丨 escaped from the net, got clear, taken himself off.

誷 ʻwang To scoff at, to accuse falsely; accusations.

欺丨 to disesteem, to revile.

誣丨 to calumniate.

高歌返故室自丨非所欣 to return singing to one's old home, it must be without any self-compulsion.

輞 棢 ʻwang The second form is obsolete; it is used by the Cantonese for the mango 丨菓 fruit.

The tire of a wheel; the emperor's chariot had double tires.

牙丨 the spokes and felly.

車丨子 a wheel's felly.

魍 ʻwang An undine or nyx.

民知神姦故丨魎魑魅莫能害 when people know the gods, the naiads and dryads will never harm them.

惘 ʻwang To lose one's self-possession; perturbed, disconcerted; forgetful.

意丨丨 or 丨然 irresolute, not knowing exactly what to do.

丨惝 fluttered, not able to collect one's wits.

旺 wangʼ From *sun* and *to rule* as the phonetic.

The sun brightening into full day; rising, prosperous; violent, fervid; glorious, brilliant; good, in a high degree of; to lustrate a house with fire.

丁財兩丨 prosperous both in family and purse.

血氣丨 or 健丨 or 壯丨 vigorous health; fat and hearty.

火丨 or 火苗丨 the fire blazes high, a very bright fire.

燈心丨 the wick is too high.

丨屋 to purify a house by certain rites.

丨月 the best part of the year for business.

丨相堂 the shrine of Plutus in a shop. (*Cantonese.*)

生意興丨 business is now brisk.

好丨 or 丨極 very prosperous; bright and splendid.

發丨 vigorous, as a fine tree.

妄 wangʼ From *woman* and *defunct* or *fugitive.*

Disorderly, brutish, unmannerly; false, incoherent; absurd, wild; abandoned, reckless; not existing; occurs used for ʻ凡 in 諸丨 all.

丨作丨爲 unseemly behavior.

丨證 false witness; perjury or talebearing.

狂丨 half crazy, disorderly, immoral; acting like a mad-cap.

丨自尊大 to wildly boast of one's self; as a drunkard or a crazy man.

丨殺 to give no quarter.

丨誕 incoherent, fabulous stories.

眞實無丨 a really honest heart.

丨對 to answer before the time.

諺 wangʼ Incoherent words, wild statements; to talk without regard to facts.

僞丨 hypocritical, wild talk.

望 朢 wangʼ From 月 *moon,* 壬 *court* and 亡 *fugitive;* the second ancient form with 臣 *officer,* now obsolete, denoted the visit of officers to court at full moon.

The moon in opposition, the fifteenth day or full of the moon; to hope for, to expect; to observe, to look at, or forward, or towards; to espy from afar; hopes, expectations, desire; near to, about fronting; that which can be seen, open to sight; a sacrifice to hills and streams.

今天丨日 to-day is full moon.

丨小山而去 went away towards the hill.

令聞令丨 it raises people's praises and hopes.

喜出丨外 joy beyond all expectation.

掛丨 to live in hopes of.

無所丨 nothing to hope for.

失丨 or 絕丨 lost all hope.

盼丨赦到 still expecting pardon; hoping for forgiveness.

丨丨然去 staring and gaping, he went off; he left in disgust.

丨六 or 丨花甲 nearly sixty years old.

丨穿雙眼 nearly bored my eyes through — expecting you.

民丨 the hope of the people; very popular, as Kanghi was.

怨丨 to feel a grudge towards; to look for impatiently.

引領而丨 or 企丨 to stretch the neck and look; on the tiptoe of expectation.

探丨 an informal visit.

迋 wangʼ To go, to travel; to deceive, to treat badly; to be afraid of, to be terrified.

魂丨丨 half scared to death.

子無我丨 you need not be afraid of me, Sir.

WĂNG.

Old sounds, wung *and* yung. *In Canton,* yung ; — *in Swatow,* ong, eng, *and* ang ; — *in Amoy,* ong ; — *in Fuhchau,* ung, éung, *and* éūng ; — *in Shanghai,* ăng ; — *in Chifu,* wung.

翁 ꜀wăng From *feathers* and *lord.*

The feathers on the neck, a ruff, like that on some birds; flying ; venerable ; an old man, a graybeard, one whose locks cover his neck ; a husband.

老 丨 an old gentleman.

堂 丨 a term of honor for a *chi-hien,* who in turn applies it to the prefect, and he to his superior.

尊 丨 your honored father.

家 丨 my husband ; and 丨 姑 denotes one's parents.

魚 丨 a fisherman.

賀新 丨 to congratulate a bridegroom.

丨 仲 statues of officers and animals before the tombs of great men.

吾 丨 卽 若 丨 my father is like yours ; — *i. e.* we friends have, as it were, but one father.

鶲 ꜀wăng Used with the last.

The ruff or neck feathers on a bird.

雁 丨 the neck of the wild goose.

嗡 ꜀wăng The lowing of cattle.

丨 丨 the hum of insects, as musquitoes.

丨 吼 the grunting of cattle.

In *Cantonese.* Over-ripe, as fruit.

爛 丨 丨 this fruit is rotten.

鞰 ꜀wăng The upper part of a boot or stocking.

鞋 丨 the vamp of a shoe.

螉 ꜀wăng The slender waisted wasp or *Sphex.*

牛 丨 nits in the skin of cattle, laid by the 丨 蜨 a kind of gad-fly.

蓊 ꜀wăng From *plant* and *old.*

The footstalk of a flower ; a plant that dyes yellow.

丨 鬱 luxuriant, bushy.

丨 薹 plants which grow in tufted heads with slender peduncles.

滃 ʻwăng To rise and float, as clouds and mist ; the drizzling look of a fog.

丨 渤 a rising fog ; the mist rising, when it looks like a sea.

塕 ʻwăng The dust rising in clouds ; the gust of wind.

丨 然 起 於 窮 巷 之 間 the blast whistles through the deserted lanes.

丨 城 the enciente of a city gate.

飛 塵 丨 起 the flying dust rises in noisy gusts.

甕 瓮 罋 wăngʼ From *pottery* and *harmonious* or *lord.*

An earthen jar ; a water amphora, having no handles or spout, sometimes used to draw water ; a skylight or orifice.

丨 缸 a water jar.

丨 圈 a small arched gate.

打 滿 丨 水 fill up the jar with water.

丨 牖 a round window like a jar's mouth ; some say one made of a broken jar.

古 丨 old narrow flower jars.

丨 洞 the entrance of a city-gate at Peking, so called from its depth.

齆 wăngʼ A stoppage of the nose, caused by a cold ; nasal, as a tone.

丨 噥 thick speech, from a cold.

伊 個 話 說 話 是 丨 頭 個 he speaks through his nose. (*Shanghai.*)

膉 wăngʼ Smelling ; fetid, rank, stinking.

一 股 丨 氣 a great stink.

WÉI OR WI.

Old sounds, wéi, hwéi, ngwéi, hwat, wat, ngek, nget, mi, *and* mít. *In Canton,* wei, úi, *and* mi ; — *in Swatow,* úi, úé, jui, ngui, mui, bué, *and* lui ; — *in Amoy,* úi, i, oé, gúi, bi, húi, *and* lui ; — *in Fuhchau,* wi, úi, òi, mi, é, mwi, ngui, *and* loi ; — *in Shanghai,* wé, vi, ni, *and* mi ; — *in Chifu,* wéi.

威 ꜀wéi Explained as denoting the *earth* (which belongs to the branch 戌) being flourishing, and *woman* as 陰之主 chief of the female principle.

The stern composure suitable to an officer's dignity ; majesty, pomp ; august, imposing, solemn, lordly ; grave, awful, intimidating ; imperious ; terrible ; to overawe, to impress ; to be violent ; the dread of an occasion ; to be awed by majesty.

死 喪 之 丨 the dreaded times of death and burial.

丨 勢 authority, the exercise of power.

丨 而 不 猛 stern but not ferocious ; rigorously just.

下 馬 丨 prompt reprisals ; instant severity.

丨 風 凜 凜 awfully overawing.

丨儀 dignity of demeanor, majesty.
虎丨 awful majesty.
發丨 threatening; to sternly repress levity.
丨嚴 majestic severity or dignity.
作丨 to assume a stern manner; to play the tyrant.
官丨不如牙爪丨 officers themselves are not as fearful as their lictors and minions.
懷德畏丨 to cherish virtue while respecting dignity.
丨州 an old district in Ching-tʻu fu in Sz'chu'en
丨之 overawe him, scare him.
丨侮五行 to waste and misuse the five elements.

In *Cantonese*. The bravery of fine apparel.
好丨 an imposing attire, a new dress.
丨過頭 much too fine for me to wear; it is above his situation.

楲 ˏwéi The young of a tiger.
丨窬 a close chair, a jakes.

蝛 ˏwéi The sowbug; an insect that is found under stones and in damp places, called also 鼠姑 mouse girl.

葳 ˏwéi Flourishing, luxuriant.
丨蕤 a medicinal root, sweetish and white like iris-root.
紫丨花 a reddish species of *Bignonia*.
丨靈仙 a remedy for boils and ulcers, said to be *Clematis sinensis;* a decoction of the twigs is used.

煨 ˏwéi To cook or roast in the ashes; to burn under ashes; to bake; to put fire into to warm things; to warm before the fire.
丨黃 or 丨焦 to roast brown.
丨炭 the brown or peat coal found in the north of Chihli; also, to burn pit charcoal.

炭丨 to roast before a charcoal fire.
蹈丨炭 to jump through burning coals, as the Taoists do.

偎 ˏwéi From *man* and to *fear*.
To hug; loving; to lean on one; to love women, attached to females.
丨近 to lie together, as children in bed.
丨臉 to hug up, to embrace, as a mother her child.
丨暖衾 to hug the warm coverlet.
相丨 to dally and fondle.
丨傍 going together; lovingly.

椳 ˏwéi The pivots at the top and bottom of a Chinese door on which it turns.
丨鳴 the creaking pivot.

隈 **渨** ˏwéi From *place* or *water* and to *fear;* the second is also read *wéi*ˀ
A bend or cove in a shore; the winding of a shore; a corner or bluff; the curve of a bow.
隅丨 a retired cove.
丨ˀ灅 dashing waves.

碨 ˏwéi Uneven, rough ground caused by stones.
丨柍 a shrill clear tone, as is that of a fife.

逶 ˏwéi From to *go*, and *bent down;* used with its primitive.
To walk deviously; to reel, to roll in walking; long and tortuous.
丨蛇 to swagger in a supercilious way when walking.

痿 ˏwéi ʻwéi From *disease* and *bent*.
Paralysis of the legs, arising from dampness; stiffness of the extremities; weak, lame, impotent.
陰丨 loss of virility.
下丨 or 足丨 weakness of the legs by rheumatism.
丨痺 no use of the limbs, as from gout.

[illegible] ʻwéi Like the last.
Diseased, weak.
鹿丨 venison which has been buried, or kept till it becomes high.

萎 ˏwéi Plants wilted and hanging down, blasted, drying up, drooping; rotten, dying.
哲人其丨乎 how the clever men are dying away!
無木不丨 all the trees are withering away — because of the snow.
丨仁 a dried kernel of a nut used in medicine.
枯丨 withering, dead from cold.
丨腇 drooping, weak, delicate.
零丨 or 丨落 falling off, decaying.

[illegible] ˏwéi The best cut of 鹿丨 venison, referring to the sirloin.

爲 ˏwéi wéiˀ The original has 爪 *claws* drawn on the top, and the rest is supposed to represent the belly and limbs of a female monkey, which is always playing with its paws.
To do, to make, to effect, to act; at the beginning of a sentence, it is often the substantive verb is or to have; to be in the place of, to play the part of; to manage, to attend to; when in regimen with 以, to consider as, to take to be, to regard; wherewith to make; to study or attend to for the purpose of doing; a *conjunction*, for, on account of; because, for the sake of; as an initial, it can also be rendered if, in case of; to cause, to induce; to say, to declare.
丨人在世 he leads an active life.
未必無丨 don't think that there was no reason for it.
不以丨恥 he deems it no disgrace.
無所不丨 he recks at nothing; he's ready for anything.
無能丨 there's no way of effecting it; it can't be brought about.
何丨 what will he do?

所丨 or 所丨者 what is done; acts, deeds.

惟士丨能 only scholars are able to do so.

丨官 to act as an officer, to have authority.

丨臣不易' it is not easy to be a magistrate or statesman.

丨非作歹 the wicked still act wickedly.

任其所丨 let him do as he pleases; don't interfere with him.

丨我葬必以魏子丨殉 if I am buried, the prince of Wéi must be laid with me.

丨今之計 a plan for the present juncture.

欲以宋丨君 they desired to make Sung their king.

我不丨 I'll not do it, I'll not act.

朝丨天子 to render homage to the emperor.

以此丨先 to regard this as the most important.

大無丨 surely there's no occasion for it.

何以伐丨 why has he attacked him?

丨言 explained by, defined to be.

有丨 to have power, to act energetically.

Read *wéi*' To help, to give; for, owing to, because, wherefore, in the interest of, — and thus a sign of the dative; to receive or suffer, and thus a sign of the passive; serves sometimes merely as a redundant word; reputed, regarded as; to cover or protect.

丨何 or 丨甚麽 why, for what reason?

丨王誦之 he rehearsed it to the king.

何丨來꜀丨 why has he come?

丨國致命 to risk life for one's country.

丨着何故 what is the reason?

福祿來丨 may happiness and emolument come to your aid.

丨公丨私 both public and private affairs.

丨人꜀丨 I do it for others.

不知者以꜀丨丨肉 those who were unaware of the cause, thought it was on account of the flesh.

丨顧人 to take interest in other's welfare.

所丨何事 what are you now doing? what business are you at?

丨照會事 [I, the minister] on this account (or hereby) communicate to you on the [following] business.

韋 ꜀*wéi* Composed of 舛 *refractory* one above other, and 囗 to *surround* in the center; it forms the 178th radical of characters relating to hides.

The perverse and ungovernable must be restrained by thongs, hence the character denotes the straps or thongs with which persons are bound; tanned and soft leather; refractory, insubordinate.

依丨 accordant, as two instruments; harmonious, because soft leather fits a thing.

丨陀 or 丨馱 the Vedas; a guardian deity found in Budhist temples.

佩丨 a girdle of leather.

不丨 old name of Yung-chang fu in the southwest of Yunnan.

石丨 or stone straps, the fronds of the *Niphobolus lingua*, a fern used in medicine.

圍 ꜀*wéi* From to *surround* and *perverse.*

To invest, to surround; to besiege, to hem in; to circumscribe, to limit; to inclose, as at a hunt; to confine, as a mold does its castings; to curtain in; an inclosure, a snare; a fortified village or *pah*, into which the people flee against robbers; a measure of half a cubit; an embankment around fields, a dike; the periphery, a circumference or measure, as of the span of the fingers, or arms around a thing; a circle of people.

丨困 besieged, environed.

四丨 four points of compass.

丨墻 an inclosing wall.

重重丨住 to keep him very close, as a prisoner; around, everywhere, as trees and copses; to besiege closely.

棘丨 the thistle gate, or examination hall, from the thorns often placed at the entrance.

打丨 to drive in animals for a battue.

崩丨 the embankments are broken away.

丨環 to inclose in a ring, to environ.

下丨棊 to have a game of chess.

九丨 the nine inclosures, *i. e.* the empire.

殺出꜁重丨 they valiantly burst through the investing force.

打飯丨 to make one of a party to eat, to sorn on.

親自合丨 to be one of a circle.

十丨 ten spans of, (*i.e.* fifty inches around,) is a large tree or log.

In *Cantonese.* A party around a table, usually four.

開幾丨 how many tables shall I spread?

囗 ꜀*hwui* Regarded as an old form of the last, and like 回 to revolve, both depicting a turning; it is the 31st radical of words relating to inclosures.

An inclosure; occurs used for 某 or 厶, to denote that something is omitted; an old form of 國 a kingdom.

湋 ꜀*wéi* To return; to flow back.

丨源 a small lake in Hupeh, not far from the Yangtsz' River.

褘 ꜀*wéi* Also read ꜀*hwui.*

A queen's garment embroidered with pheasants, worn when sacrificing to ancestors; a scent bag carried by ladies; pads to cover the knees, garter fronts; admirable, said of virtue; mourning garments.

侯其丨而 in what did the excellence of Wu-ti's virtue consist?

꜀闈 From *door* and *insubordinate.*
꜀*wéi* The doors of the harem; side doors of the palace, where candidates once underwent their examination.

入丨 to compete at the examination.

出丨 the officers leaving the hall after they have decided on the essays, and announced the names.

舉鄕丨 to lift the village gate; *met.* to become a *küjin.*

春丨 the examination for *tsinsz'* at Peking; as 秋丨 is for *küjin* in the provinces.

買丨姓 to buy graduates' names, a mode of gambling at Canton by betting on the surnames of successful candidates.

丨墨 essays of the successful candidate.

꜀幃 From *cloth* and *perverse;* it is interchanged with the next and last.
꜀*wéi* A perfume bag, 香丨 worn on the lapel; a curtain or valance; the rooms for women.

慈丨 the loving curtain; *met.* a mother.

闈丨之中 in the female apartments.

丨帳隱千金之體 in the curtained room is a body worth a thousand taels; — *i. e.* a sister or daughter.

꜀帷 From *cloth* and *bird;* used with the last.
꜀*wéi* A curtain, a cloth screen; a tent; an apron, a skirt; a veil.

床丨 a tester to a bed.

丨幙 a cloth partition.

車丨 the curtain of a carriage.

丨薄不修 the neglected curtain became thin; — *i. e.* women lost their modesty.

丨房 the bedchamber.

꜀違 From to *go* and *insubordinate.*
꜀*wéi* To oppose, to go against, to disobey; not to heed, to disregard; to leave, to take leg-bail; to relinquish, to vacate; to avoid; to be distant; perverse, seditious, intractable.

丨背 to turn the back on.

毋丨 let none disregard — these commands.

陽奉陰丨 to agree before one's face, but to oppose behind his back.

丨和 run down, indisposed, out of sorts; — a phrase used in letters.

君子如夷惡'怒是丨 if good men were just, hatred and anger would disappear.

丨教許久 or 久丨芝顏 I have long neglected you, Sir; I have not seen you for a good while.

丨怨 to cherish resentment against.

三丨 thrice threw up his appointment.

依丨 or 從丨 undetermined; in doubt how to act, *i. e.* whether to agree with or oppose.

丨心之論 to talk against the heart or conscience.

不丨農時 don't let the time for planting slip by.

꜀惟 From *heart* and *bird*; sometimes written ꜀唯 and also used with the next.
꜀*wéi* To consider, to think on, to plan; to care for; is or has, to consist in, to do or to be; just so, precisely; an adversative particle, but, only; in a series it denotes and, with; and so, only that; also, further; just so, precisely; certainly; it is often a redundant word for euphony.

豈丨 only one! not only that.

丨是 but that.

丨當 but it ought; indispensable; it is proper.

丨一 but one.

丨獨 there's only one; only it alone.

視遠丨明 looking afar I think I have a clear idea of it.

丨查 I have examined it.

亦丨女'故 this is just for your interests alone.

我聞丨曰 I have heard it said.

齒革羽毛丨木 elephant's tusks, hides, feathers, hair, with timber also.

꜀維 From *silk* and *bird;* used with the last in ancient books.
꜀*wéi* The curtain of a carriage; tied to; connected with, as a horse in a cart; to hold together, to hold fast; tied up, as a boat to a wharf; a particle like the last, but, only; as a copula, also, and so; as an initial word, whereas, seeing that, referring to; a net; one says, a corner or angle.

丨繫 to fasten together; to connect with, as effects with causes.

丨持 to aid, to have united action.

丨今 now; just at this time.

四丨 the four cardinal points; also four virtues, as 禮義廉恥 propriety, right, integrity and modesty.

再四思丨 to ponder a subject on all points.

行動丨難 it seems to be difficult to act in any way.

四方是丨 they were linked together all around.

꜀蜼 Also read ꜂*léi.*
꜀*wéi* A long tailed monkey, described as having a yellowish gray head, a forked tail and turned-up nose; it suspends itself from trees during rain, stopping its nose with the forked tail; it may refer to the Wanderoo or a *Rhinopithecus* from the southwest of China, as it is said to associate with the rhinoceros, elephant, and bear.

丨彝 goblets with monkeys carved on them.

꜀濰 A river in the northern part of the promontory of Shantung, west of Lai-cheu fu, from whence Wéi hien 丨縣 takes its name.
꜀*wéi*

危 ꜀wéi From 卩 a *limit* or whatever stops, and ⺈ a *man* on top of a *ledge*.

High, precipitous, dangerous, imminent ; hazardous, unsteady ; not upright, inclined ; an uneasy place ; sick, dangerously ill ; peril, danger ; to feel in danger ; to rush into danger ; to hazard, to ruin ; a beam in a roof ; used for the next ; the twelfth constellation, comprising α Aquarius and η ϑ Pegasus, or more accurately 35 Arietis.

臨丨 near death ; dangerous, to approach danger.

丨乎其丨 how awfully perilous it is !

丨篤 very dangerous, as a disease.

丨言 words of warning.

國丨 the dangers, (*i. e.* the enemies) of a country.

丨邦不入 don't go into a disturbed country.

不自知丨 he does not know his danger.

丨在旦夕 near dissolution ; ready to perish, as between a night and morning.

丨難之間 in times of danger.

桅 ꜀wéi From *wood* and *dangerous*.

A tree that furnishes a yellow dye-wood ; the mast of a vessel ; a short spear.

丨竿 a mast, when it is one stick.

三枝丨 three masts.

大丨 the mainmast.

丨尾 the mast-head.

起丨 step the mast, which is done in junks in the 丨夾艙 or main-hold between two cheeks.

丨盤 or 丨斗 the tops on a mast.

丨頭旂 a pennant.

眠丨 to lower the mast.

丨牆 the steering plank on the side of the vessel.

豎丨 to step the mast.

溎 ꜀wéi Also read ʿkwéi.

A small branch of the River Tsü near King-cheu fu in the southeast of Hupeh.

鮠 ꜀wéi A fish allied to the silures, whose fins are fleshy, but its mouth and head like a sturgeon ; the color on the back is yellow and on the belly whitish ; it is common in the Yangtsz' River, and may possibly be a member of the sturgeon family.

峗 ꜀wéi A noted peak in Kansuh near 沙州 at the West end of the Great Wall, called 三丨山 ; one of the same name is in Sz'chʿuen.

嵬 ꜀wéi From *hill* and *demon* ; it is now regarded a synonym of the next.

A high rugged rock is 崔丨, referring to its hazardous, bare appearance.

維山崔丨 on the rocky tops of the hills.

巍 ꜀wéi Like the last.

Lofty ; conspicuous and sublime, like a towering cliff ; exalted, as virtue.

丨丨乎 how grand and excellent !

道高德丨 his doctrine is sublime and virtue superior.

㕒 ꜀wéi A peak, the distant summit of a hill, peering into the sky ; it is regarded as another form of ʿi 嶬 a peak.

微 ꜀wéi From a *step* and *original germ*.

Small, trifling, insignificant, mean ; minute, fine ; in a slight degree, too, rather ; hidden, subtle ; obscure, recondite, abstruse ; to fade or dwindle away, to diminish in extent or value ; to conceal ; to hide away ; reduced to obscurity ; waning ; to repress, as grief ; not, without, have not ; an ulcer on the leg ; an old state lying eastward from Pa cheu in Sz'chʿuen.

丨妙 minute, very small, atomic ; an exclamation of admiration, exactly the thing ! capital !

丨細 very small and fine, as work.

丨毫 trifling, unimportant.

丨薄 rather thin.

丨風 a little breeze.

丨賤 or 輕丨 vulgar ; inferior.

丨臣 subordinates, low grade officers, as of the 6th or 7th rank.

丨物 trifling, of no value, said of a present ; a thing of little use.

三丨 the incipient germs of things.

丨小 the least bit of, very little.

丨丨笑 a passing smile, a grace.

寧適不來丨我弗顧 it is better that they come not, than that I should fail in caring for them.

丨行 or 丨服而去 to go disguised or in a strange dress.

些丨看見 I can see it just a little.

丨我無酒 it's not I that have no drink ; — *i. e.* I have a little.

丨乎其丨 how subtle are its mysteries, how abstruse !

隱丨 occult, hidden, esoteric.

恨無丨情以效愛 I regret that I have not a trifling present with which to testify my love.

旣丨且尰 their legs were both ulcerated and dropsical.

丨明 moonshine.

溦 ꜀wéi The last is also used for this.

A slight shower of rain 丨丨雨, alluding to its quickness.

浽丨 a sprinkle of a shower.

Read *wi'* A torrent in a gorge.

薇 ꜀wéi A kind of pot-herb, growing in damp places, producing a small pea, sometimes used for food ; herbs ; a kind of fern which has sharp points, and is also occasionally eaten.

言采其丨 there I picked the coarse ferns.

採丨而食 to gather greens and roots for food.

紫丨花 the crape myrtle (*Lagerstræmia indica*) of which three varieties are common.

白丨 the *Vincetoxicum* ; a small trailing plant allied to the swallow-wort ; also a white rose.

尾 ʿwéi ʿi

From a *body* which has *hair* behind it.

The tail of animals; the end, the extreme part, the last of, the tail of; remnants, driblets; a spit, a sandy point; the hinder part of; a stern; the bottom of; a classifier of fishes; copulation of animals.

丨宿 the sixth constellation, the stars ε μ in Scorpio.

首丨 or 頭丨 head to the tail; first and last; beginning — end.

跟丨 to follow one, as a lackey.

擺丨 to wag the tail.

夾丨 to put the tail between the legs.

數丨 unsettled items of an account.

話帶土丨子 his speech has a local drawl.

丨後 afterwards; after that.

二丨魚 two fish.

收買銀丨 broken and bad money bought here; — a sign.

不知首丨 I don't know about the matter; I dont know where it was put.

瑣兮丨兮 how trifling and unimportant these things are!

丨底 the end of, the finality, the very last; the results of.

娓 ʿwéi

From *woman* and *tail*; now changed for the next.

To comply with, attentive to; handsome.

丨順 accommodating.

丨勉 to exert one's self.

亹 ʿwéi

From 亠 *head* and [illegible] or 釁 a *cause* of offense; it is the same as the preceding.

Indefatigable, unwearied; fixed in mind, resolved.

丨丨文王 earnest and energetic was Wăn Wang.

丨丨不倦 willing and unwearied in one's duties.

浩丨水 a stream in the west of Shensi, and an old district.

Read ˓man. A narrow gorge in a stream caused by jutting rocks.

委 ʿwéi

From *woman* and *grain*, alluding to the bending heads of ripe grain.

Bowing under a burden; to sustain, to bear a responsibility; to infer, to alledge; to send off, to confide to, to put in charge of, to commit to, to trouble; to reject; to depute, to delegate; commissioned on public service; a wrong; a grievance; the end, the last; really, indeed.

奉丨 to receive orders to go.

丨員 a deputy or special agent of an officer; a special commissioner.

丨實好 very good, the best of.

外丨 a sergeant in the army, under whom is a 外外丨 a lance-sergeant or corporal.

丨驗 sent him to inspect goods, or hold an inquest.

盡悉原丨 I know it from the first to last; I am aware of the circumstances.

丨曲 hardship, a wrong, a grievance; whatever one suffers.

端丨 an ancient dress of ceremony worn by princes at worship; the circumstances, the rise and progress of an affair.

丨棄 to throw away a thing.

丨係 it is really so.

丨託 to give a commission to an underling, to engage the services of an inferior.

差丨 to delegate, to send.

丨丨佗佗 elegant, as a brocade dress; stylish, easy, handsome.

丨宛其說 to speak in metaphor, to allude to indirectly.

蜲 ʿwéi

The sow-bug or wood-louse (*Oniscus*) 丨蝛; also called 鼠婦 or 鼠負 from the notion that mice carry it on their backs; this and ˓蝛 are synonymous.

⿱吅尹 ʿwéi

The noise made in calling ducks, probably in Honan, as the call is unlike in different places.

瑋 ʿwéi

From *gem* and *perverse*.

A gem of a red color; a rare or curious relic of former days.

瑰丨 a precious thing which illustrates former times.

丨重 valuable and rare.

偉 ʿwéi

Admirable, rare, extraordinary, as one famed for beauty or skill; fine-looking, powerful.

丨男子 a brave clever man.

人材傀丨 a powerful, gigantic man.

俊丨 personable and handsome.

英丨 a brave, gallant man.

葦 ʿwéi

Grass which grows in the bottoms of rivers; a hollow rush or reed smaller than the 蘆; tall grass, woven into ropes, or dried for fuel and thatch.

丨蓆 rush mats, like those woven from the *Phragmites*.

丨錐 the sprouts of the rush.

一丨航之 he crossed [the river] on one reed.

縱一丨之所如 [as little as] the space that one rush occupies.

蘆丨 a reed common in Kiangsu (*Arundo indica*); these also denote two kinds of rushes.

丨子 reed stalks, cane stalks.

煒 ʿwéi

A *fire* that is *insubordinate*; a great, raging fire; lurid, blazing, glowing.

光丨 a great light.

赤丨 a glowing red blaze.

青丨 a low flame, like that of a spirit lamp.

丨盛 a nice bright fire; a fervid sun.

壝 ʿwéi

From *earth* and *to leave behind*.

A low wall which protects the border of the terrace on which an altar is built.

社丨 the low wall around an altar of earth.

丨宮 a sort of mud-wall shrine.

ʿ骫 ʿwéi From *bone* and *all* or *a ball*.
A distorted bone; to crook, to bend; to intertwine, as branches; to bend to or agree with.
丨天下正法 to pervert the just laws of the land.
林木茷丨 the trees interlaced their branches.
丨靡 to appear as if assenting to a thing.
丨曲 to suffer injustice.
福兮禍所丨 Ah! happiness must bend to infelicity, — and joy give place to sadness.

ʿ唯 ʿwéi ˏwéi Also read ˏwéi, when synonymous with ˏ惟 to think.
To answer smartly; to echo, as in replying; an answer.
丨而起 he answered and instantly arose.
莫不丨丨 every one directly replied.
其魚丨丨 the fish move in and out of the creel.
男丨女俞 boys [are to] reply, aye, aye! girls to drawl, y-e-s; so the Book of Rites directs.
丨丨諾諾 aye, aye! to be sure; I promise you.

ʿ䦱 ʿwéi From *door* and to *act*.
A door half open, as when a woman stands within the threshold and talks with a man outside; a door ajar.
丨門而與之言 she opened the gate a little and spoke with him.

猥 ˏwéi From *dog* and *fearing*.
The yelp of a terrified dog; a slut whelping three pups; many, plentiful; very, exceedingly; mixed up, ill assorted; rustic, low; to cause to submit.
丨鄙 rustic, unpolished, coarse.
丨承獎譽 I am deeply obliged for your commendation.
丨來就之 came in numbers and quickly.
自云卑丨 I call myself vile and despised.
水丨盛則放溢 when the water rises it runs over the bank.

ʿ磈 ʿwéi Name of a peak and a god; dangerous; rough and stony, as a road.
丨硊 perilously steep.
丨礧 stony and rough, as a road gullied out by rains.

ʿ隗 ʿwéi From *place* and *demon*.
A small state which was destroyed B. C. 633, by Tsu; it was in the south of the present Shansi; lofty and grand.
嵔丨 rising in a high peak.
高丨 imposing and lofty.

ʿ洧 ʿwéi From *water* and to *have*.
A small river in the state of Ching, now in Honan fu in that province, at which there was a ford; the district of Wéi-chʻuen 丨川 retains the name.
丨之外洵訏且樂 beyond the Wéi, the ground is broad and pleasant.

ʿ痏 ʿwéi A bruise, a contusion.
瘡丨 a swelling, such as is caused by a blow from a club, which turns the skin black and blue; used for 胃 the stomach, in the phrase 翻丨 to turn the stomach, to disagree with one.

ʿ鮪 ʿwéi A synonym of ˏsün 鱘 in some books.
A singular fish found in the Yangtsz' River, having a long snout and a gaping mouth, called the mud or snouted sturgeon; the large sort is called 王丨 and the small 叔丨, but there may be two species; the flesh is good, but inferior to the 鱣 or sturgeon, with which it is grouped; it seems to be sometimes confounded with the porpoise by the Chinese; ancient name of a river in Kung hien 鞏縣 in the west of Honan.
匪鱣匪丨潛逃於淵 I am not a sturgeon that I can dive and hide in the deep.

ʿ㕒 ʿwéi Elegant, fine looking.
丨美 handsome, personable.

寪 ʿwéi Arranged or looking like a house; uneasy, disconcerted.
隍丨 unsettled, uneasy.

ʿ蔿 ʿwéi Plants, grass; name of a place in Tsin 晉 now the south of Shansi.
千丨 the thousand plants, a noted poem of the Tʻang dynasty.

ʿ薳 ʿwéi Similar to the last.
Grass, herbage; name of a place.
Read ʿyuen. A bud, especially a leaf-bud.
桑丨 mulberry buds, a medicine.
出丨 the buds are swelling.

ʿ暐 ʿwéi From *sun* and *perverse*.
The sun shining in his strength.
光丨 the bright sunlight.

ʿ韙 ʿwéi From *skin* and *is*, but the primitive gives the idea, and the radical the sound.
Right, proper; what is correct, like the five virtues.
五丨 all the excellencies of conduct and character.
犯五不丨 he five ways committed improprieties; — *i. e.* he offended every principle.
昭丨見戒 to illustrate what is right and define what is wrong.

未ʾ wéiʾ From 木 a *tree* and a *line*, showing abundance of leaves and its full vigor in the sixth moon; not to be confounded with *muh*, 末 the end.
The eighth of the twelve branches, symbolized by a goat; the hour from 1 to 3 o'clock P. M, towards evening; the sixth moon; an *adverb* of negation and doubt, not yet, not now, never; in combination answers to *in*, *un*, as 丨足 incomplete; 丨成 unfinished; sometimes denotes that an order or obligation previously required the act.
丨有 none; never has been any.
丨曾 not yet; often intimates an impossibility.

吾丨嘗無誨 I have never failed to give instruction.

丨定 it is uncertain.

丨必 probably not; not at all.

丨免 cannot be prevented.

丨知其詳 I don't know the particulars truly; I am not intimate with the affair.

丨然 not so; it cannot be.

丨幾 not long after, not a great while.

丨入流 clerks about courts who are not in the line of promotion.

丨可擅便 should not assume what is merely convenient, — but study to do what is right.

丨若貧而樂 this is not so good as to be poor, and still to be contented.

丨是丨拉哩 the set time has not yet expired. (*Shanghai.*)

味 *wéi'* From *mouth* and *not yet.*

Taste, flavor, smell; relish, seasoning; a dainty, a delicacy; the style or beauties of a composition; to relish, to take pleasure, to solace, to recreate in.

五丨 the five tastes, *viz.*, acrid, sour, salt, bitter, sweet, — which the Chinese doctors suppose to reside in the 五丨子 or red berries of the *Kadsura Chinensis.*

好丨道 delicious, nice.

野丨 game, delicacies from the forest.

更加一丨 add one more taste, *i. e.* season it a little more.

丨類 aromatics, spices, seasonings.

丨其言 relished his talk.

滋丨 very toothsome.

走丨 lost its taste, insipid.

未入丨 it is not well seasoned; he cannot yet relish the beauties — of his lessons.

合丨 palatable, well tasted.

仍屬一丨延擱 he still persists in his delay; 一丨 is also used for uniformly, still, only; as 一丨好'寫字 he only likes to copy letters.

詩之丨 the allusions or beauties of an ode.

丨濃 or 丨淡 a rich or slight taste; a ripe or raw flavor.

氣丨 a smell; a puff or odor.

殊無丨 it is very insipid; this is very dull work; it does not interest me at all.

一丨藥 a dose of medicine.

菋 *wéi'* From *plant* and *taste*, as it is supposed to possess the quintessence of all tastes.

A trailing medicinal plant (*Kadsura Chinensis*), found in many parts, noted for the viscid mucus on the fruit and branches; the seeds, called 五丨子 are used as a tonic, lenitive, and stimulant; the vine produces a yellow flower, and the red berries are wrinkled and reniform, containing two yellowish seeds.

位 *wéi'* From *man* and *standing*, referring to the servants appointed on the sides of the hall.

Those who sit erect, as in a hall, or are arranged there in rank; the place, the seat; the throne; a post, a trust, a position, a dignity; right, proper, correct; established, arranged; to arrange in proper rank; to enthrone; to assume regal sway, to begin to reign; the room a thing takes up, the place it ought to be in; a classifier of persons, dignifying them.

失丨 to lose the throne.

龍丨 and occasionally 天丨 the throne, intimating its divine character and source.

幾丨客人 how many guests?

客丨 the guest's seat — is on the host's left or west.

諸丨 or 列丨 you, Sirs; Gentlemen! used in direct address.

大地丨 or 高丨 a high situation or office.

在丨 or 坐丨 reigning; a reign.

三丨一體 three persons in one; triune, the Trinity.

讓丨 to resign or abdicate the throne; to yield one's seat.

買艙丨 get freight in the ship.

女正丨乎內 the proper place for women is in domestic affairs.

各歸丨所 each went to his own seat.

無可丨置 we have no position for him; no berth suitable.

胃 *wéi'* From 肉 *flesh* and 田 a *field*, altered from 㘚 to represent the rugous coating of the stomach; it closely resembles *cheu'* 冑 a helmet.

The stomach, defined as the 穀府 or grain store-room; it is also defined by 圍 because it incloses the food; the appetite; the digestion; the 17th constellation of three large stars in Musca Borealis.

翻丨 turns the stomach.

丨脈 the pulse in the right wrist.

無丨口 having no appetite.

開丨 to excite the appetite, as by bitters.

丨火盛 a morbid, foul, or offensive stomach and breath.

去'丨火 to cool or cleanse the blood, to remove bad humors.

丨寒 a weak stomach.

丨氣疼 a gripe in the stomach, a belly-ache.

猬 **蝟** *wéi'* From *dog* or *insect* and *stomach*, because its skin is exhibited in diseases of the stomach; others say because its coat resembles tripe.

The hedge-hog (*Erinaceus dealbatus*), and will include also the tenrec and porcupine.

刺丨 the small hedgehog, common in Chihli, also called 丨鼠 in books; the spines are described as forked.

事如丨集 my affairs are numerous as porcupine's quills.

捲踡如丨 to roll up like a hedgehog.

悁 *wéi'* From *heart* and *stomach.*

Disquieted.

怫丨 anxious and perturbed; some say, resolute; to bear up against.

謂 wéi˺ From *words* and *stomach*.
To address, to inform; to speak to or report on something to another; to suppose, to instance; to say, to speak of; to call, to denominate; designated, termed, styled; means, meaning; to send on a message; diligent, careful; also, with; to; how? occurs used for 爲 to be.
此之丨也 this is the purport of it.
此丨知本 this can be called knowing one's origin.
丨之曰 addressing him, he said.
何丨 why? what do you say? what is it called? how is this explained?
甚無丨 really inexcusable; you are of no kind of use.
無所丨 nothing can be said in your favor; I have no excuse to offer.
不丨 at the beginning of a sentence, unexpectedly; who would have said it?
有丨 something can be said for it; commendable, reasonable, excusable.
自丨無愧 I say that I have nothing to be ashamed of.
誰丨爲之 who can say who did this?
丨天蓋高 it may be said of the sky that it is very lofty.
遐不丨矣 [I love him heartily,] but when he is far away I am not so careful to think of him.
天實爲之丨之何哉 heaven really made this, but how indeed!
夫子之丨也 this was, Sir, speaking of you.

渭 wéi˺ A large tributary of the Yellow River, famous for its turbid waters, which joins it near the elbow in Shensi, and drains the southern half of that province; roaring, hurrying, as rapids.
涇以丨濁 the River King shows its turbidness by contrast with the Wéi.
沸丨 anxious, unquiet.

娟 wéi˺ From *woman* and *stomach*.
An old name for a younger sister.
姊丨 sisters.

䮹 wéi˺ An unauthorized character.
An ass.

畏 wéi˺ Composed of 田 a *field*, which is here a contraction of 鬼 *demon*, and 爪 *claws* of a tiger underneath, — both to be feared.
To dread, to venerate, to stand in awe of; to awe; what one dreads; to respect; a right fear, a humble awe; devotion for, weighed down by; the carefulness of respect and fear; dread, awfulness; timidity; to put to death judicially.
深丨 very dreadful.
丨首丨尾 I want nothing to do with it.
丨天命 to fear Heaven's commands.
君子有三丨 the good man venerates three things, — heaven, the words of the sages, and good men.
丨多風 it is hurt by much wind, as a plant.
丨縮 hesitating, timid, indolent.
丨懼 apprehension, great dread.
望而生丨 afraid when they see him, as truants do a teacher.
丨葸無能 useless and cowardly; incapacitated through fear.
丨語兒字 Wigour letters.
無丨 fearless, unappalled; this term is applied to every Budha.
丨羞 bashful, sensitive to shame.
丨凊 shrinking from the cold.
雖丨勿丨 though I would put them to death, do you not do so.

餧 喂 wéi˺ From to *eat* and to *bend*; or *mouth* and to *dread*; the second also is read ˛*wéi*, to fear, but is now chiefly used as a synonym of the first.
To feed, to give food to, especially to animals; to rear.
丨馬 to fodder a horse.
丨飽他 give it all it can eat.
丨仔 to feed the baby. (*Cantonese.*)
丨牲口 or 丨頭貨 feed the animals or stock.
The first read *néi*. Hungry.
魚丨 stinking fish.
In *Cantonese*. A word of address when calling out to a man.
呀，丨 halloo, there!
丨咯 get out! get away, clear out! often heard among sailors as *wylo!*

衛 衞 wéi˺ From 行 to *walk*, and 韋 *opposed*, and 帀 *around* under it; the first form is most common.
To escort, to go with, as a protection or in honor of; to guard, to defend, to restrain; a military station, an outpost, a frontier town and garrison; a local name for Tientsin.
丨身 or 丨生 to take care of one's health.
丨千總 an officer who escorts the grain-junks.
護丨一方 the protecting shield of this region, as a god.
防丨 to guard the place.
榮丨 vigorous animal spirits.
丨生丸 life preserving pills.
臣丨 we, [your majesty's] defenders.
營丨 a garrison or cantonment.
相丨 mutual aid and protection.
丨國 an important feudal state occupying southern Chihli and eastern Honan, in the valley of the 丨河; its capital was the present Ki hien 淇縣; it existed 781 years, till it was absorbed by Tsin B. C. 241, at which time it joined three others to resist it; 22 rulers are enumerated down to B. C. 469.

懲 wéi˺ To talk wildly in one's sleep.
丨道其實 people tell the truth in their sleep.

讆 wéi˺ Too much; to exaggerate.
丨言 to tell big stories, incredible statements.

魏› *wéi›* From *demon* and *to delegate*.

Formerly used for 巍 high; lofty, sublime, as a towering peak.

丨闕 the gate of the palace where edicts are published; as 象丨 is the gate of the capital where they are issued.

丨丨 said of a small portion of a thing that is completed.

丨國 a small feudal state which existed B. C. 403–241, under six or eight rulers, when it was absorbed by Tsin; it lay in the southern part of Shansi and north of Honan, occupying nearly the region where Yao and Shun ruled; Ts'ao Tsao of the 三國 called his state the 丨國, which lasted from A. D. 220–264, and included the provinces of Honan and Shansi.

丨朝 a dynasty of Hunnish origin established in northern Shansi A. D. 386, which lasted till 536, and at one time ruled over half the empire in the north and west, under twelve sovereigns.

⿱魏香› *wéi›* From *fragrant* and the *country* of Wéi.

Assafætida, 阿丨 or 丨魏 brought from Persia and Cashmere, and used for plasters; it is also burnt as a deodorizer.

蘶› *wéi›* The sprouts growing on plants that have been plucked; to sprout again, as a willow stump.

僞› *wéi›* From *man* and *to do*; *q. d.* that it is the doing of man, and did not come of itself.

False, hypocritical; counterfeit, simulated; pretended, so called, as officers among rebels; to put on, to deceive.

低丨 counterfeit, adulterated.

作丨 to act hypocritically.

至誠而無丨 not the least deception in any way.

丨念 guileful designs, underhand plans.

虛丨 or 忘丨 wholly false.

丨爲不知 pretended not to know anything of it.

丨充官長 to pretend and act as officials or gentry.

In *Cantonese*. To dun, to importune; to solicit.

꜀丨來꜀丨去 to beg and weary people.

細꜀丨 mean; a very little; stingy.

丨菩薩 to weary the gods.

尉› 熨› *wéi›* From *fire* and *to smooth*; it is now in the North much superseded by *yun›* 熅; also read *yuh*,

To smooth cloth with a hot iron; a flat-iron or smoothing-iron that holds coals; to rub and push, as in ironing.

丨斗 a flat-iron.

丨衣服 to iron out clothes.

丨手 to feel for gently, as in the dark. (*Cantonese.*)

毒丨 to rub hot applications on a sore.

尉› *wéi› yü›* From 寸 *inch* and 𡰥 an old form of 仁 *humanity*; it is regarded as a synonym or derivative of the last, for which it is sometimes incorrectly used.

Tranquil, calm; to still, to quiet; to settle disagreements, to harmonize feuds, — in which senses the next has mostly taken its place; a military officer.

校丨 chair-bearers of the emperor, retinue of the emperor.

廷丨 palace guards in old times.

太丨 an ancient officer like a governor.

Read *yü›* A military officer in the palace or capital.

協丨 a corporal of police in Peking.

雲騎丨 and 恩騎丨 hereditary titular officers of the fifth and seventh ranks in Peking, who are supposed to ride to keep the peace.

防守丨 a garrison major among Manchu Bannermen.

慰› *wéi›* Like the last, and now used for it in this sense.

To soothe, to console, to comfort; to tranquillize the feelings.

安丨 to appease, to calm.

丨冥 to quiet the manes, as by burning incense or offerings.

弔丨 to condole aud mourn with.

受丨 comforted, to be calmed and resigned.

有子七人莫丨母心 we are seven sons and cannot comfort our mother.

丨愜其心 refreshed his heart, as by hearty counsel.

以丨我願望 it has fully gratified my wishes.

今爾罔不由丨日勤 now it will be only by daily diligence that you will not fail to tread the path of satisfaction.

蔚› *wéi›* From *plant* and *soothing*.

An odorous plant akin to the *Stachys* or *Vitex*, having purplish blossoms; luxuriant, rank, as foliage; elegant, classic, fine, as style; numerous, as population.

丨茂 growing vigorously.

丨藍天 a pure blue sky.

丨丨 or 薈丨 flourishing finely.

人民丨起 the people increase rapidly.

Read *yuh*, A city 丨州 in Süen-hwa fu, lying nearly west of Peking near Shansi.

罻› *wéi›* A small net, the 丨羅 which was directed to be set in the autumn.

霨› *wéi›* Clouds rising.

丨然雲起 how rapidly the clouds have come up.

螱› *wéi›* The perfect ant, when it has its wings, usually called 飛蟻 or 飛螞 winged ants; they are supposed to proceed from rotten wood.

濊ʾ wéiʾ From *water* and a *year;* often interchanged with the next.

Deep, vast, like the ocean; name of a river in Honan; thick, turbid.

汪 ┃ deep, extensive; numerous.

Read *hwah*, The gurgling of water.

施罛 ┃ ┃ throw the nets in with a splashing sound.

穢ʾ wéiʾ hwuiʾ From *grain* and a *year;* it is used with the preceding.

Weeds growing disorderly among grain; dirty, unclean; filthiness; wickedness; obscene, indecent; noisome, vile, rank, detestable; to defile, to debauch.

┃ 氣 a stinking savor.

┃ 亂宮中 the seraglio was full of lewdness and disorder.

┃ 言 vile talk, lewd speech.

┃ 事 improper things, illegal doings, disgraceful affairs.

無起 ┃ 以自臭 nobody makes dirt for himself to get a stink.

污 ┃ 不堪 I cannot endure this filth and dirt.

┃ 德彰聞 its rank odor smells even to heaven.

薉ʾ wéiʾ Like the last.

Overgrown with weeds; jungly.

┃ 行 to do things slovenly.

彙ʾ wéiʾ hwuiʾ From 彐 a contraction of a *pig* and 胃 the *stomach* altered; it is also read ʿ*léi*.

An animal like the hedgehog, but also resembling the pig; a class, a series, many of the same sort; to sort, to classify.

字 ┃ a collection of characters, like a manual dictionary; name of a lexicon.

┃ 核 to examine all of the same sort at once.

等 ┃ all those kinds or classes.

薈ʾ wéiʾ From *plants* and *assembled.*

To screen, to intercept; a species of leek or squills (*Allium porrum*), called 鴻 ┃ used as a pot-herb.

┃ 蔚 to rise and float, as mist or clouds; vapors floating upward.

緯ʾ wéiʾ From *silk* and *perverse.*

The transverse threads of cloth, the woof; parallels of latitude; transverse lines, those which cross the breadth of a thing; to weave, to twine in.

┃ 帽 a fringed official summer cap.

道 ┃ degrees of latitude.

五 ┃ the five planets, which, as it were, wind through the zodiac.

地 ┃ geographical divisions.

農 ┃ 厥耒 the husbandman binds on his plow, — and shoulders it to go to work in the early spring time.

有經 ┃ he has the classics woven into him.

蟦ʾ wéiʾ A generic name for small apterous insects.

蛒 ┃ an insect allied to the *Cermatia*, but the species is uncertain.

颹ʾ wéiʾ A fresh breeze.

長風 ┃ 以增扇 this constant breeze will serve as another fan — to cool us.

韡ʾ wéiʾ Full, gorgeous, as the flowers of the crab-apple.

鄂不 ┃ ┃ are they not very splendid!

WO.

Old sounds, kwa, wa, nga, *and* kap. *In Canton,* wo, ngo, *and* lo; — *in Swatow,* ùi *and* o; — *in Amoy,* ò, oé, *and* gò; — *in Fuhchau,* wo *and* ngwò; — *in Shanghai,* u *and* ngu; — *in Chifu,* wòa.

ˏ窩 ˏwo From *cave* and *distorted mouth;* nearly synonymous with ˏk'o 窠.

A nest on the ground or in a hole; a grot or hole; a depression on the body; a warm, nest-like thing; occurs used for a shrine or small oratory; a nook or retired corner; a lonely house; a den, a retreat for bandits; to shelter thieves; a peculiar right, a goodwill.

┃ 賍 to receive plunder, as a ┃ 家 or receiver does.

心 ┃ a place over the breast bone.

鬼 ┃ a devil's nest; an owl-hole.

毛 ┃ a pair of lined warm shoes.

┃ ┃ a hollow millet-bun.

一 ┃ 八代 eight generations (a large family) in one household.

胳肢 ┃ the arm-pits.

酒 ┃ a dimple in the cheek.

一 ┃ 蜂 [people are coming in like] a nest of bees.

止赦安樂之 ┃ I only wish to get a quiet retreat — for my age.

爭嘴 ┃ 子 the hollow on the neck between two great muscles; it is fancied to be connected with the appetite.

┃ 子ˏ行 a cook.

挪臊 ┃ a woman's visit to her mother one month after child-birth.

┃ 留 or ┃ 藏 to shelter runaways, to harbor people.

In *Pekingese.* A class of workmen.

井 ┃ the class of water-carriers.

ˏ渦 ˏwo A whirlpool, an eddy.

旋 ┃ a deep pool in a stream where the water revolves.

Read ˏ*ko.* A large branch of the River Hwai, which flows into it in the north of Nganhwui.

萵 ˏwo A term for plants used as salads, either raw or cooked, as lettuce, endive, succory, the sow thistle, and other similar plants.

丨苣菜 lettuce.

丨苣乾 dried endive stalks, a salted vegetable.

丨苣筍 or 丨筍 young stalks of a kind of Cichorium (?) boiled as a vegetable.

猧 ˏwo The pet spaniels or lap-dogs found in Peking.

嬌丨睡猶怒 the lap-dog snarls even in its sleep.

倭 ˏwo From *man* and *bent.*

The Japanese.

丨國 Japan; a term used by themselves, as the equivalent of Yamato; it is defined by Chinese, as the country of dwarfs.

Read ˏ*wéi.* Yielding, trimming, — even to countenancing vice.

周道丨遲 the long and winding highway from Cheu.

涹 ˏwo Muddy, roiled, as water; used with 漚 a reservoir, a pool; to steep

丨濁 turbid, dirty water.

踒 ˏwo To slip and fall; to sprain one's leg or arm, to double it under when falling; curly.

丨足 slipped on his leg.

丨着腿 sprained his leg or ankle.

鬚都丨了 his beard is curled — into the bag, for dyeing it.

婐 ˊwo From *female* and *really;* for the second meaning, it is often pronounced ˊ*lo.*

Delicate, fine figure; winning, alluring; a servant, a waiting woman, a maid.

珠佩丨妮戲金闕 two elegant females, finely adorned with jewels, played in the hareem.

二女丨 two women servants.

妮 ˊwo Also read ˊ*ngo.*

Attractive, elegant; weak, delicate.

煥赫婐丨 resplendently beautiful.

不宜燮且丨 it is not so brilliant and effulgent — as the full moon.

臥 woˋ From *officer* and *man,* alluding to the position he is in when making his prostration.

To rest, to desist from toil; to put to sleep; to cease, to lie down, to repose; to doze; the place one sleeps on.

坐丨不寧 no ease, sitting or lying.

丨月明 to sleep in the moonshine.

高丨 to sleep high; *met.* to keep aloof from official cares, to let the world wag.

丨名利 to cease from pursuit of fame or wealth.

丨內 in the bedchamber.

睡丨 to sleep, to repose.

倒丨 died in the streets, as a beggar.

丨房 a bedroom.

丨兔 a fur-lined cap, used by northern people.

丨息 to rest, to lie down.

丨孩子 put the children to bed.

WOH.

Old sounds, wak *and* ngak. *In Canton,* wok *and* òk; — *in Swatow,* wok *and* òk; — *in Amoy,* ak *and* hoé; — *in Fuhchau,* hò *and* auk; — *in Shanghai,* hòk *and* òk; — *in Chifu,* u *and* woh.

⿰食蒦 hwoˋ From *to eat* and *to measure.*

Insipid, tasteless.

肥而不丨 fat and unsavory, as biche-de-mer.

鸌 hwoˋ A kind of water bird; when it cries, the rain is said to fall; perhaps the petrel.

籆 hwoˋ A four-sided reel for winding silk, now called 線框; it is sometimes made with jointed legs.

蠖 hwoˋ From *insect* and *to measure.*

Geometrical worms or loopers; turbid, restrained; to span with the fingers.

蚇丨之屈以求伸也 the looper curls up only that he may stretch out again.

尺丨 to span with the fingers.

溫丨 unfeeling, perverse, as the world.

丨畧 to move regularly.

曲丨 a squirming worm.

齷 / **⿰𧾷屋** uˋ From *teeth* or *foot* and *house.*

The teeth crowding each other in the mouth; small, little-minded.

丨齒 crowded teeth.

丨齪 crowded on; pushing, as teeth.

ˏ爲人丨齪 a narrow-minded, prejudiced man; in Shanghai, this phrase means sordid, dirty; and the Cantonese phrase 汚粗 is probably derived from it.

WU.

Old sounds, ngo, wo, wok, wot, mo, *and* mot. *In Canton*, u, 'ng, *and* mò ; — *in Swatow*, u, ò, bo, bu, wa, ak, ngò, *and* gò ; — *in Amoy*, u, ò, ngò, bu, bò, *and* wa ; — *in Fuhchau*, u, mwò, ngu, ngü, *and* ngwò ; — *in Shanghai*, u, vu, 'm, 'ng, *and* ngu ; — *in Chifu*, u.

烏 *꜀wu* The character is supposed to represent the *crow*, and differs from ʿ*niao* 鳥 a bird by omitting the stroke in the middle, which represents the eyes; occurs used for the next.

A crow; but the raven, chough, and blackbird are all included, though it specially means the crow, noted for its filial duty, as it is supposed to feed its aged dam sixty days out of its own crop, — hence the phrase 能學丨哺 he must learn to exhibit filial duty; black, inky, dark; to render black; an exclamation, what! how, in what way? not reduced to order, promiscuous; the obverse of a coin.

丨鴉 a crow.

丨鴉命 unlucky people; *lit.* a raven's fate. (*Cantonese.*)

丨頭虫 an unshaven lout.

丨有 all gone, none.

歸之丨有 it brought me in nothing, as an adventure; it was an entire loss.

丨鬚藥 a dye to blacken the beard.

丨黑 black as ink.

丨衣 the swallow, because it winters in the Wu-i country.

丨有此事 how can this be?

丨魚 the black fish (*Philypnus sinensis*), akin to the blenny.

丨私念切 filial duty imposes its bonds upon me.

丨合之衆 a set of lawless fellows; roughs and vagabonds.

莫黑匪丨 if it be not black, it is not a crow.

丨乎 alas, how sad!

慈丨 and 孝丨 two names for the white throated blackbird common about Peking.

金丨 or 三足丨 the golden crow or the three legged raven; a term for the sun, whose disk is supposed to be thus marked.

嗚 *꜀wu* An exclamation of regret; a sigh, a groan; well-a-day, ah!

丨呼 alas! wo worth the day.

噫丨 sobbing, whimpering.

歍 *꜀wu* To nauseate, to loathe and vomit; the sound made in doing so; to bring mouths together, as birds do in feeding their young.

歐丨 to vomit.

Read *꜀yang*. To lose the voice.

丨唈 to choke with emotion, and be unable to speak.

鴮 *꜀wu* An implement like a bill-hook, the 丨刀 with which to cut grass or weeds.

圬 杇 *꜀wu* From *earth* or *wood* and *vapor*; these two are not the same as 圩 and 杅 but they are often wrongly used for them.

To cover walls with plaster; to stucco, to adorn walls; a mason's trowel.

丨人 a plasterer, a mason.

丨鏝 a trowel.

丨墻 to plaster or whitewash a wall.

糞土之墻不可丨也 a dung wall can't be plastered; — *i. e.* you can't make a purse out of a sow's ear.

汚 汙 洿 *꜀wu* From *water* and *vapor*; the first two are the same, but the third is sometimes regarded as different.

Stagnant water, dirty pools; deep, as a pool or puddle; foul, filthy, muddy; impure, unclean; obscene, vile, depraved, abominable; to defile, to insult; to stain; to dig down or excavate; to bale out, as when irrigating; to become dirty by hard work; to wash out dirt.

丨辱 to debauch; to blackguard, to insult.

同流合丨 to go with the vulgar into their sinks.

丨池 a dirty puddle; also to scoop out a hole.

丨穢 to dirty; filthy, impure.

丨名 a blasted name.

田卒丨萊 our fields have become nothing but pools and jungle.

丨下 a low-lying place.

舊染丨俗 a long time used to vile habits.

ʻ處不避丨 I have no way to avoid this kind of work.

薄丨我私 I will wash my own [clothes] clean.

貪官丨吏 he covets office only for the spoils.

Read *꜀yü*. An old name of a branch of the Wéi River in the northern part of Honan, and a town of the same name on it.

Read *꜀wa*. To scoop out, to dig a hole.

丨樽而抔飲 scoop out a goblet in the ground, and drink out of your hands.

弙 *꜀wu* To draw a bow, and aim the arrow is 丨弓; but one defines it the whirr of the arrow.

鄔 *꜀wu* Often written like its primitive.

The district Wu-ching 丨程縣 in the northwest of Chehkiang, the city of Hu-cheu fu.

故丨城 a famous place in ancient Tsin, now Kiai-hiu hien 介休縣 on the River Fǎn in Shansi.

槝 *꜀wu* A wood suitable for arrows; a tree producing a sort of crab, the 丨棒 found in Hunan.

無 无 橆 ˓wu

The third and original form represents a luxuriant forest, with 亾 *lost* between the trees, but the lower portion of 林 and 亾 are now contracted to 火 *fire* under *foliage;* the second form is the 71st radical, and regarded as identical, but its etymology is doubtful, and it is explained as being the vacancy which existed in the northwest part of the sky before Nü-wa mended it.

An *adverb* of negation, none, not, not having, destitute of, without, wanting; joined to 不 forms a strong affirmation; in combination answers to the termination *less,* as 無形 formless; 丨度 limitless, excessive; occurs interchanged with 不 and 非 and 未, and takes their shades of meaning; as an initial, is sometimes redundant, as 丨念爾祖 think upon your grandparents; not extant, a state between emptiness and annihilation.

丨用人 a useless fellow.

丨爲之事 an unimportant matter.

丨可如何 there is no help for it; no matter how or in what way.

丨事 at leisure, not busy; no annoyance.

有 and 丨 are opposites, — to have and not to have, to exist and to be annihilated.

丨常 a demon regarded as the messenger of Yen-lo wang, — as in 丨常到 death has come.

丨所見聞 no one ever saw or heard of it.

丨爲 no use, doing nothing; the Budhists use it for the absolute, a nonentity; there is a small sect of them, the 丨爲敎 whose chief feature is mystic contemplation and idealism.

丨爲自然 not made, but self existing.

上德丨爲而丨以爲 truly virtuous men do not act, nor have they wherewith to act.

丨中生有 it grew out of nothing; made out of whole cloth; unfounded.

丨限期 no time set, not limited.

丨一不曉 there's nothing he does not understand.

丨一可用 it is of very little use.

丨我 a Budhist metaphysical term (*anatma*), inanition, having no vitality, nothing in me.

丨則言丨 if it be not then say so; don't prevaricate.

初出于丨而還于丨 it sprung from nothing and returns at last to nothing.

未免丨故 there cannot but be a reason.

丨乃 or 丨寧 often answers to perhaps, rather, if that; — as 丨寧以爲宗羞 it seems to be rather a disgrace to his ancestors.

丨如 that is the best way, nothing like this way.

丨意中買 bought it without thinking.

丨法可治 there's no way to arrange it; remediless.

丨妄 the 25th diagram, denoting sincerity.

天之所生地之所養丨人爲大 among the beings which earth nourishes, there is none greater than man.

‘有

An unauthorized character, used like the last, but applied chiefly to things, as the character (有 without a *heart*) indicates.

In *Cantonese.* None, nothing, not yet.

有丨呢 is there any or not?

丨心得 unintentional.

丨去過 I have never been there.

你丨畀我 you have not yet given it to me.

In *Fuhchau.* Empty, open; light, porous; coarse grained, as timber.

丨談 chitchat, gossip.

蕪 ˓wu

A vigorous growth of weeds and jungle; neglected; fertile.

丨湖 a lake in Tan-yang hien in Kiangsu, which gives name to the city of Wu-hu.

丨穢 full of weeds, as a neglected garden.

丨雜 obscure, as a vague style; inelegant.

草苞丨茂 abundant, fine grass.

丨札 my poor letter or epistle.

巫 ˓wu

From 工 *labor* and 人 *man* or 又 *hand* repeated in it; but the ancient complicated form is intended to represent gesticulating with hands, mouth, and sleeves, as a witch does.

A sorceress or enchantress, a spiritual medium; one on whom the gods descend; to perform incantations, as women do who call on the dead; fetishism, magic.

丨術 divination arts; gramarye, enchantments.

男丨 a wizard.

女丨 a witch; an enchantress.

丨醫 medical treatment by magic, like that used by the Shamans.

丨山 a mountain and a district in Kwéi-cheu fu in the east of Sz'ch'uen, where the Yangtsz' enters the province; the twelve peaks of this mountain are fabled to have been twelve sisters.

暴丨而奚若 I will broil the witch in the sun, and see whether it will bring rain.

誣 ˓wu

From *words* and *witch.*

To affirm what does not exist with malicious intentions; to invent and add to a statement; to inculpate falsely, to calumniate; visionary, false, superstitious; calumny.

丨陷 to ruin by slander, to involve unjustly.

丨賴人 to implicate people.

丨告反坐 a lying charge brings down its punishment on the accuser.

丨罔善人 to accuse an innocent man.

丨良爲娼 to malign an honest woman.

虛丨惑世 slanderous charges trouble society.

毋 ꜀wu From an old form of 女 *woman* with a line drawn across it to indicate a prohibition of illicit conduct; it is the 80th radical of a few characters, and is distinguished from ˊmu 母 mother by the prolongation of the middle stroke.

A prohibitive negative *adverb* like 莫 do not, don't do; used for 無 without; an interrogative particle like 否 intimating a doubt or denial.

丨不敬 do not fail in respect.

丨違特示 don't oppose this special edict.

坐乎將丨 may I sit down?

丨庸掛慮 do not be anxious for me.

丨爲小人儒 no, I will not be a pretended philosopher.

Read ꜀meu. A black cloth cap, 丨追 used in the Hia dynasty.

吳 ꜀wu From 口 *mouth* and 大 *great,* altered so as to resemble 天 *heaven.*

To talk loud, to bawl; to brag, to put on airs,— in which senses it is now read *hwa'*.

丨國 eastern of the Three States, A. D. 250, comprising Chehkiang and extending north and west; Su-chau, which is still called 丨縣 was the capital.

不丨不敖 [when talking with your inferiors,] do not vociferate nor browbeat them.

蜈 ꜀wu The *insect* of *Wu*, the centipede, called 丨蚣 and 百足 and other names.

峿 ꜀wu A hill 崛丨 in Tsi-nan fu in Shantung; also a town.

岨丨 hilly, uneven.

岨丨而不安 ups and downs, unsettled, alluding to the look of a row of hills.

郚 ꜀wu An ancient place in the 紀 state near the center of Shantung in I-shui 沂水縣; also a town in Lu, near its second capital, now in Sz'-shui in the south of Shantung.

吾 ꜀wu From 口 *mouth* and 五 *five.*

A personal pronoun, I, my; to impede, to excuse and delay; to guard, to defend, to resist.

丨等 we, us.

丨非某人 I am not that man.

可與丨輩相並 they can rank with us on equal terms.

支丨了事 to hurry through a business carelessly.

金丨不禁 the feast of lanterns.

執金丨 an officer in the Han dynasty like a captain-general.

丨與汝弗如也 my intercourse with you is such, because you are not like others, *i. e.* proud and presuming.

梧 ꜀wu A tree noted for the even grain of its wood 丨桐 the *Eleococca verrucosa;* the fall of its leaf denotes autumn.

碧丨 the topaz tree. (*Sterculia tomentosa.*)

枝丨 a pillar or support out of the perpendicular.

魁丨 brave, valiant, one fit to lead.

捂 ꜀wu From *hand* and *I;* interchanged with the last two.

To oppose, to contradict, to resist; a lean to, a brace; to shore up, as a prop does a wall.

支丨 to guard against, as anarchy or vice.

抵丨 to resist; *q. d.* to set a pole against one.

搘丨 forced to do a thing, as a subaltern by his superior.

唔 ꜀wu A sound in singing.

咿ˊ丨 a refrain at the end of a line.

In *Cantonese.* A simple negative like 不; no, not, do not.

佢丨肯 he won't.

丨曾 not yet.

你寫丨喺呢 did you write this?

浯 ꜀wu Name of a river in Yung-cheu fu in the south of Hunan; also the 丨江 in the south of Fuhkien, and another 丨水 in the southwest of Shantung.

鼯 ꜀wu The flying squirrel, 丨鼠 or 夷由 the *Pteromys volans,* common in Siberia; it is also called 飛生 because it is thought to bear its young while on the wing.

鋙 ꜀wu Fine iron from the hill 錕丨; a 錕丨之劍 is a good sword made of ore from this hill, a Toledo blade.

Read ˊyü. A hoe or its handle.

鉏丨 unsuitable, uncongenial.

五 伍 ˊwu } The original form is composed of 二 *two* strokes, representing the dual powers of heaven and earth connected by crossing *lines;* the second, more complex form is used in bills, &c.

A perfect number, five; the whole, all of a kind, applied to many things, as the planets, the tastes, &c.

第丨 the fifth.

初丨 fifth day of the moon.

丨丨爲廿丨 5 times 5 is 25.

丨陰 the five hidden things, or 丨衆 five aggregates, or 丨蘊 five sheaves, are Budhist terms (*skandha*) for the elements or constituents of a human being, *viz.*, form, perception, consciousness, action, knowledge.

不宜丨方民人雜處 did not allow them to live everywhere among the people.

丨車書 a great collection of books.

不與汝丨 I will have nothing to do with you.

四分丨裂 out of order, confused, scattered, irregular.

丨出 a five-petaled flower.

丨分像 a profile or half likeness.

ʿ伍 ʿwu A file of soldiers, which had its leader; *men* arranged by *fives*, a squad, a corporal's guard; a company; a comrade, an associate; a fellow soldier; to associate with.

行丨 a file of men; the rank and file.

擺隊丨 to parade troops, to draw up in rank.

羞與爲丨 ashamed to own him as a companion.

行丨出身 to be born into, or enter on life in the army.

閭丨之中 [living] among the hamlets without regard to rank.

ʿ仵 ʿwu A *man opposed* to one; a match, a pair, an equal in rank; occurs used for the last, and for 忤.

丨作 certain persons attached to the courts whose decision at inquests is relied on, and their report taken; at *Canton*, also applied to those who enshroud the dead.

以不丨之辭相應 to make statements harmonize which really do not match at all.

ʿ午 ʿwu Defined as expressing the resistance which the earthy vapors of the 5th moon (hence called 丨月) oppose to the skyey influences, covering the earth with fog.

The seventh of the twelve stems, symbolized by the horse; consequently every 12th day is termed 丨日, referring to this cyclic notation; the time between 11 A.M. and 1 P.M. or noon; midday; south, and marks that point on the compass; used with 迕, to oppose, to stand up, to resist; crosswise, transverse.

交丨 11 o'clock.

正丨 or 中丨 or 丨時 noon; midday, meridian.

下丨 afternoon; 上丨 forenoon.

停丨 or 歇丨 to rest at noon, a nooning.

過丨 or 丨飯 a luncheon.

使者旁丨 the messengers spread out in various directions.

丨割 to cut crosswise.

正子丨 due north and south; whence the palace is called 丨門, because the emperor is supposed to sit in that position.

ʿ㠸 ʿwu A turban or a napkin to cover the head.

ʿ旿 ʿwu The brightness of the sun at noontide; clear and bright.

ʿ塢 ʿ隖 ʿwu A bank, a low wall thrown up for defense; barracks, intrenchments; a walledor fortified camp; a village defended by a wall; winding roads among cultivated hills.

村丨 a walled village.

營丨 an intrenchment.

花丨 a raised parterre for flowers.

ʿ熓 ʿwu *Fire* that has been *blacked*, *i. e.* embers covered or smothered over; to cook.

ʿ摀 ʿwu An unauthorized character, a synonym of ʿ*yen* 掩 to close.

To screen or hide a thing with the hand; to put the hand over a place, or press it as when aching.

拿手丨着 put your hand over it.

丨着耳朶搖核桃 like shutting the ears and rattling a walnut; *i. e.* to care nothing for the matter.

ʿ武 ʿwu From 止 to *stop* and 戈 a *spear* or fighting, as the king of Tsu said, ʿ*wu* means to stop fighting and withdraw the troops.

Military; martial, strong, warlike, brave; firm, majestic, decided, stern; fierce-looking; to stop disorder by force; to take two steps; a vestige, the traces of; a footstep, an example; to connect; in epitaphs indicates the highest qualities.

丨官 or 丨將 military officers.

丨童 military students; cadets.

棄文就丨 to discard the civil service and enter the military.

學丨藝 to study tactics.

丨夫 a hero, a soldierly man.

一元大丨 one head and a great track, *i. e.* an ox, referring to its heavy tread.

丨斷 to threaten; to intimidate.

丨家 a cadet.

丨牛 a stupid cadet, a lout of a calf; — an epithet of obloquy.

繩其祖丨 to emulate and carry on his forefathers' deeds.

丨火 a great heat.

丨則天 a celebrated empress of the T'ang dynasty, A. D. 640; *met.* a prostitute, a Messalina.

無用丨之地 he has no fields to use his troops in, — and make conquests.

丨塲 arena for military trials.

丨彝山 or 丨夷山 the hills in in the north of Fuhkien, whence Bohea tea was first brought.

ʿ珷 ʿ碔 ʿwu A stone, the 丨玞, which like veined jasper, resembles a gem, but is inferior in hardness and luster.

ʿ鵡 ʿwu From *bird* and *martial*.

A large parrot that can talk, 鸚丨 the cockatoo or the macaw; it is sacred to Kwanyin; "when stroked it becomes dumb," say the books, referring to its stillness when its head is scratched.

ʿ㑄 ʿ侮 ʿwu From *man* and *do not*, *q.d.* to make nothing of a man; the second is the more common form.

To insult, to despise; to ridicule, to make fun of good things; contempt of; neglect, disrespect; chagrined, disappointed; to deal summarily with.

丨弄 to make game of; humbugged.

丨慢 to lord it over one.

啟寵納丨 to show kindness and receive neglect; to be treated with ingratitude.

不狎丨 not to treat things with levity; to show complaisance.

ʿ潕 ʿ㵲 } A river in the west of Hunan, a branch of the Yuen River, which gave its name in the days of Han to Wu-yang hien 丨陽縣 (or 舞陽) in Shăn-cheu fu.
ʿwu

ʿ廡 From *shelter* and *unoccupied*.
ʿwu The open porch or vestibule placed between the gatehouse and the main hall, of which there are sometimes three, making a shelter like a piazza; the rooms on the sides are sometimes inclosed; it resembles the *propylon* of the Greeks; side piazzas or galleries; an open vacant hall.

廊丨之下 at the emperor's gate.

Read ˏwu, and used with 蕪. Luxuriant, overgrown.

庶草蕃丨 how vigorous and rich is the vegetation.

荒丨 uncultivated, waste.

ʿ甒 An earthen jar for holding spirits, shaped like a gallipot; it has a bulging body and small neck; some contain five pecks, others five gills.
ʿwu

一丨醴 one jar of rich wine.

ʿ嫵 To flatter, to try to win another's affections.
ʿwu

丨媚 delicate, insinuating, fascinating.

ʿ憮 Also read ˏwu, meaning empty.
ʿwu To flatter or caress; to soothe, to comfort; to express great affection for.

愛丨 to love fondly.

撫丨 to protect and cherish.

丨言相及 I earnestly plead with him.

夫子丨然曰 the Master, sighing, said.

Read *hu*. Great.

亂如此丨 to suffer from such great disorders.

ʿ煤 To love, to soothe; it is regarded as nearly the same as ʿfu 撫, to care for tenderly.
ʿwu

ʿ舞 From 舛 *opposing* and 無 *without* contracted, explained as alluding to placing the foot on the back.
ʿwu

To play with the body, as the posture-makers and harlequins do, holding something in the hand; to gesture, to act tableaux-vivants; pantomime, fencing, sleight-of-hand, masker's play; to flourish, to brandish.

跳丨 to dance, to tumble; to play, as acrobats.

打丨 boxing.

丨劍 fencing; to play with swords.

丨弄 to play a double part, to play a trick.

丨手弄脚 to play games of agility.

鼓丨成仇 intriguing with people makes them enemies.

藉勢丨權 to affect power by assuming another's authority.

顛狂柳絮隨風丨 the willow catkins are tossed by every breeze; — so is a giddy woman.

丨弊 surreptitiously; an officer winking at delinquencies.

丨文弄墨 to employ fine words and good writing.

歌兒丨女 singing boys and dancing girls; singers and actors.

丨技勇 to try feats of strength.

ʿ儛 To skip and dance, as when highly elated; to excite.
ʿwu

朝丨山 a mountain in the north of Shantung.

務ʾ Composed of 力 *strength* and 敄 *to encourage* one.
wuʾ

To use great effort and bend the mind to a subject; to strive after; what is thus attended to, business, function, duty, concerns, whatever comes under one's eye; an important post near the Great Wall, because there the officers and men are to encourage each other; an affirmative or intensive particle, must, certainly; used for 侮 to insult.

丨需要 it is absolutely required.

事丨 business; what one's functions require him to do.

丨必 indispensable.

丨本 what a station requires; the important thing.

本丨 my own affairs.

丨心 an intention, a project.

小人丨于利 petty minds are bent on gain.

丨農 agricultural affairs.

專丨讀書 devoted to study.

公丨 and 家丨 public affairs, and domestic or private concerns.

外禦其丨 they will oppose insult from without, or those not in the family.

霧ʾ From *rain* and *business*.
wuʾ Fog, mist; vapor rising from the earth and condensing.

雲丨 a fog.

滿天丨氣 a misty sky.

霞丨 a smoky, misty vapor; confused, unintelligible.

黃丨 a thick, dense mist.

一頭丨水 it is all foggy — to me; I don't understand it.

臭丨 a noisome vapor or malaria.

打丨 to go with a paramour. (*Cantonese.*)

丨鳥 the fog bird, or the bird of paradise, so called in the Archipelago, from its supposed aërial life among the clouds.

騖ʾ To prance and race a horse, to gallop furiously; boisterous, violent.
wuʾ

騖丨 prancing; headstrong, furious.

趨之如丨 they gather together there very rapidly, as traders at a port.

婺ʾ A star 丨女, said to be near the middle of Capricorn, but others say in Hercules.
wuʾ

丨州 an old name for part of Kin-hwa fu 金華府 in Chehkiang, and now partly retained in Wu-yuen hien 丨源縣 in the south of Nganhwui.

戊 *wu'* From 戈 a *spear*, but the original form is likened to a *man's ribs*, as it follows 丁 in the ten stems; also read *meu'*

The fifth or middle of the ten stems, relating to earth, and answering to 茂 luxuriant, when all things are flourishing.

吉日維丨 a lucky day has *wu'* in it.

迕 *wu'* From to *go* and *noon*; it is like the next.

To meet in opposition, to run counter to; a rencontre; to thwart, to resist; opposing, disobedient; disordered, contrary, confused.

相丨 conflicting views, opposing factions.

丨旨 to oppose the imperial will.

錯丨 confused, blended incongruously; wrongly done.

忤 捂 *wu'* From *heart* and *noon*; or *my* and *noon*; they are both used with the last and next.

Stiff in holding to one's opinions, especially against superiors; obstinately adhering to what one deems to be right; disobedient, intractable, untoward, froward.

丨意 to hold to one's views.

丨丨然 irritated at, displeased.

牾 *wu'* Like the two last.

A bovine wild beast; to oppose, to meet as an enemy.

牴丨 to butt; to resist.

丨戾 intractable, pig-headed.

悟 *wu'* From *heart* and *myself*.

To arouse to a sense of one's situation; to awake, to perceive clearly, to understand fully; to recover; aware of, discerning, alive to.

丨道 to comprehend the doctrine.

有丨性 he has a good perception of things.

覺丨 to catch the idea.

自丨 to bethink one's self of.

執迷不丨 he adheres to his stupid way and will not arouse.

丨出 to see the bearing of; to appreciate a position.

醒丨 startled; aroused to a consideration of one's position.

殆弗興弗丨 it seems as if I could not again rise or recover.

晤 *wu'* Light, clear; to see face to face; to meet; to explain, to clear up; to perceive what another says.

久不相丨 we have not seen each other for a long time.

把丨有期 I am sure we shall meet again.

丨會 or 面丨 a personal interview.

丨別之時 since the time I left you.

丨解 to perceive, as after an explanation.

寤 *wu'* To awake from sleep or indifference; to rouse up.

獨寐丨言 to start from slumber and begin to talk.

驚丨 to be startled from sleep, as by a clap of thunder.

契契丨嘆 I wake and sigh in my sorrow.

丨寐思服 waking and sleeping he thought about her.

惡 *wu'* *öh'* From *heart* and *second to*; *q. d.* one who is specious and guileful.

To hate, to dislike; to blush, ashamed of; to dread; averse to, repulsive.

可丨 detestable, hateful.

羞丨 to feel compunction for; shame-faced, sensitive.

丨利口 to dislike fine talkers.

衆丨之必察焉 when everybody speaks evil of a thing, then it must be examined, — to see whether the odium is just.

憎丨 or 恨丨 to hate, to harbor ill-will.

丨不善 to loathe evil persons.

如丨'丨, 臭 [he disliked him] as he abominated a noisome thing.

Read *꜀wu*. Why, how; an interjection of regret.

丨乎 how; where? wherein?

丨是何言也 why, what kind of talk is this?

丨得賢 how can a worthy man be got? who then is worthy?

丨在其爲民父毋也 wherein can he be called the people's parent? — *i.e.* acting as a parent.

Read *ngoh*, Bad intentionally; vicious, evil; vile, ugly, deformed; filthy, sordid; unlucky; the evil; wickedness.

丨衣 tattered raiment.

兇丨 savage, malicious.

元丨 chief criminals.

先丨 to set an evil example.

丨有丨報 wickedness brings its own retribution.

丨棍 an unscrupulous fellow.

丨疾 an incurable complaint; it usually denotes leprosy, and is a reason for divorce.

醜丨不食 [Confucius] would not eat disagreeable food.

歳丨 a year of dearth.

苦丨 beggared, sad, miserable.

十丨 ten kinds of capital crimes.

In *Cantonese*. Hard to do, difficult, unpleasant.

丨行 not easy to go.

做丨 very difficult.

丨講 under constraint in speaking.

噁 *wu'* From *mouth* and *hate*; also read *hu'* in 丨丨 the cooing of doves, which the phrase imitates.

To scowl, to look displeased.

唶丨 to appear angry.

In *Cantonese*. To stoop, to bend the head, when entering a low place.

丨低頭 stoop down to it.

誤 *wu'* From *words* and to *talk big*; interchanged with the next.

To mistake, to be in error; to hinder by mistaking, to thwart, to hamper; an unintentional wrong; faulty, unauthorized, as a wrong character.

丨害好人 you have wrongly destroyed good men.

丨傳 to report erroneously.
丨會意 to misapprehend one's ideas or designs.
貽丨 to bring evil or disaster upon others.
一丨豈容再丨 if you have made one mistake, now can I allow you to make another?
躭丨 to hinder, to dawdle, to put obstacles in the way.
故丨 to purposely hinder.
丨了時刻 you have missed the hour; to pass the hour.
失丨 to miss, to fail to do, to overlook, to forget.

悮, wu' Like the last, and the two are continually interchanged.

To deceive, to make a pretext; false, designedly wrong.
丨大事 to neglect important business.
臨期不丨 he did not fail to come at the time.
丨信 a mistaken confidence.
主顧(or 固)不丨 my goods are well made, and no mistake; meaning that the shopkeeper will make no error in the goods furnished to his patrons.

WUH.

Old sounds, wok, wot, ok, ot, *and* mot. *In Canton*, ȯk, măt, ngăt, *and* yȯk; — *in Swatow*, ȯk, ngùt, mué, *and* mút; — *in Amoy*, ak, ȯk, *and* gút, ; — *in Fuhchau*, ȯk, wok, auk, woh, *and* úk; — *in Shanghai*, ȯk, wok, ngéh, veh, feh, *and* meh; — *in Chifu*, u and wu.

屋, ˏuh From 尸 a *body* or person and 至 to *reach*; *q. d.* the place one gets to.

A house, a room in a house; in the South it usually denotes the former, at the North, the latter; a state-room, a cabin, a cell; a covering or tent of a carriage; a roof; to stop at, to remain at.
房丨 a building; dwelling-houses.
盖丨 or 起丨 to build a house.
一間丨 a house.
一間丨子 one room in a house.
外丨 the outer (not sleeping) apartment.
丨址 or 丨塲 a house-lot; the ground on which the building stands.
夏丨渠渠 an imposing, extensive edifice.
同丨住 to live in the same house, room, or cabin.
白丨 a private dwelling.
神丨 a poetical name for tortoise-shell, from its use in divining.
丨漏無欺 do not irritate or despise [the god in] the southeast corner of the house.

喔, uh' The crowing or cackling of fowls; *q. d.* the *voice* of a *household*.
雞丨咿 or 雞丨丨 the crowing of cocks.

剭, uh' To execute one in his house or near it, and not on the public square.

偓, uh' woh' Restrained; kept in order.
丨促 hampered, interfering.
爲法所丨制 the laws curb such things as that.
丨佺 name of an elf or fairy

握, ˏuh wo' From *hand* and *house*.

To hold fast in the hand, to grasp; as much as the hand can hold, a little; small; a handful.
丨定 to hold tight, to grasp firmly.
把丨 a hold; to have sway over.
毫無把丨 not the least evidence.
丨手 to shake hands.
在丨 under one's control, as a seal; in one's power.
丨要 what is necessary, the essential powers or things.

渥, ˏuh wuh' Name of a river in Kiangsi; to water, to moisten, to tinge; to irrigate; to enrich with favors; to benefit; to cover or daub thick; shining, rich.
丨蒙 to be deeply grateful for.
恩丨 imperial (or divine) favor.
既優既丨 [the land] has been fully soaked; *met.* to be greatly favored or blessed.
丨丹 a deep red; to dye deep red.
丨澤 enriched with favors.

幄, uh' woh' A *cloth house*, a markee, the general's tent; a temporary tent for worshiping in, a cover or protection; to shelter.
丨幕 a common tent.
覆丨之恩 the benefit of his protection.
帷丨 the chief's tent.

兀, uh' From 儿 *man* and 一 *one*, denoting level; *i. e.* high and level on the top.

To cut off the feet as a punishment; stable, decided, persistent; an exclamation of surprise.
下丨 to descend from a high place.
丨者 the maimed, those whose feet have 丨趾 been cut off.
丨然不動 fixed in purpose.
丨丨以窮年 decided in his resolution to the end of his days.
丨高 to stand on tiptoe. (*Cantonese.*)
天阿丨的 oh, Heavens! a sort of theatrical phrase.

矹, uh' Similar to the last.

A stone that is insecurely placed.
硉丨 gravel and silt carried down by a torrent; anything piled up in a dangerous heap.

屼, *uh'* A bare hill.
五 | a peak in the range lying east of Kien-wéi hien in the south of Sz'ch'uen, famous for five plateaux.

卼, **仉,** *uh'* From 危 *dangerous* or 人 *man* and 兀 *high.*
Disquieted; hazardous.
| 困 wearied out.
臲 | alarmed, as when on a giddy height; apprehensive, anxious.
跛 | to limp, to halt in walking.

扤, *uh'* Like the preceding.
To move, to sway to and fro; to rack; to stuff in, to fill a gap.
| 開的 move off a little.
| | 下 to rock; to swing from side to side; to work in a socket.
搖 | inconstant, uncertain, as the wind.
| 滿 stuff it full.
| 膝 stingy, giving the least trifle.
In *Cantonese.* Uneasy, fidgetty.

杌, *uh'* A stump or trunk of a tree having no leaves or branches; a sprout just appearing; unquiet.
| 子 a square and large stool.
桌 | a table and stool.

膃, *uh'* Fat, fleshy.
| 肭 corpulent, obese.
| 脖 sick, infirm.
| 肭獸 a seal, whose testicles are brought from Koko-nor for medicine, perhaps also obtained from the *Phoca annellata* in Lake Baikal.

嗢, *uh'* To hem and clear the throat; to hawk.
| 噦 to clear the phlegm, as when beginning to sing.

鋈, *uh'* From *metal* and *to wet;* also read *woh,*
To wash or plate inferior metal with silver or gold; to overlay with finer metal, as the ornaments of a harness.
| 錞 iron plated with silver.

沃, *wuh'* *wo'* From *water* and *weird;* also read *woh,*
To water or irrigate; to soften with water; to enrich, to cleanse; to reform; fat, fertile, rich; abundant, luxuriant; glossy.
| 壤 fertile loam.
| 若 rich and glossy — as silken reins.
| 手 to wash the hands.
| 雨 wet by the rain.
衍 | fine rich soil.
灌 | 我心 [truth] purifies my heart.
夭之 | | vigorous and handsome, as a young tree; strong, manly beauty.
深資啟 | I entirely relied on him to expand and cleanse my mind.

勿, *wuh'* The original form is supposed to represent a *flag* with three *pennons* attached, which in the days of Cheu was hoisted by officials to call the people of a commune together; it resembles ꜀*ts'ung* 匆 hurried.
An adverb of negation, like 莫, not having, do not; it is much used in Kiangnan for 不 not.
手 | 動 do not touch this; let this alone.
| 謂言不預也 do not say you have not been forewarned.
| 畏難 be not afraid of difficulties.
夨來話 | 得 unspeakably great.
| | 乎其欲饗之也 how earnest he is! he wishes the fragrance of the sacrifices to come up — before his ancestors.

沕, *wu'* Abstruse; distant.
| 穆 recondite and vague, inexhaustible and limitless.
Read *mih,* Covered with dust, dirty and dusty; to dive or hide deep.
| 深潛以自珍 he dived to the depth, to show the estimation he held himself in,— speaking of Kiüh Yuen's drowning himself.

物, *wuh'* From *ox* and *flag,* because the ox is one of the largest of things.
A thing, matter, or substance, anything between heaven and earth; an article, goods; affairs of life; a creature, a being; persons; to distinguish by appearance, to have a knowledge of; a flag.
| 件 or | 事 a thing, an article.
萬 | all things, creation.
人 | a human being; the sort of person.
| 故 deceased.
大 | a buffalo or ox.
三 | denote the cock, dog and hog, from a line in the Trimetrical Classic; also three duties of life, called 正德 cultivating virtue; 利用 getting a living; and 厚生 preserving health.
神 | strange things, a lusus naturæ.
食 | eatables.
| 色 to judge by the looks.
多招 | 議 which led many persons to reflect or judge about it.
| 各有主 everything has its maker.
空洞無 | empty, nothing at all.
不 | lawless, eccentric, reckless.
蠢然一 | just a stupid block.
| 業 patrimony, property.
| 格 to learn the nature of things.
In *Cantonese.* A day.
昨 | yesterday.
今 | to-day.

岉, *uh'* High, as a hill or house, mountain or tower.
崛 | lofty, imposing.

芴, *uh'* A tuber regarded as like the 菲 having thick leaves and a woody stem; it may be a variety of the Chinese yam.
軋 | minute, fine and delicate.

YA.

Old sounds, ya, nga, yat, ngat, *and* ak. *In Canton*, ya, nga, *and* a; — *in Swatow*, a, é, gé, ngé, gia, ngia, *and* o; — *in Amoy*, a, ga, *and* nga; — *in Fuhchau*, a *and* nga; — *in Shanghai*, ya, nga, ah, o, *and* èh; — *in Chifu*, ya.

鴉 ꜀ya From *bird* and *tooth*.

A raven with a white streak on its neck; but the name 老丨 or 烏丨 is also applied to the crow.

丨陣 crows flying in flocks.

塗丨 written out roughly; a very rough copy of a thing.

丨片 black flakes, *i. e.* opium, an imitation of the foreign word.

丨知反哺 the crow can disgorge its food — to feed its young or its dam; *met.* filial duty.

陽丨 or 陽烏 a small black bodied crane, with a long white neck, found in Fuhkien.

慈丨 or 寒丨 a species of blackbird common about Peking, having a white breast and neck.

呀 ꜀ya From *mouth* and *tooth*; also read ꜀hia in many cases.

To gape or open the mouth wide, as 丨丨 is to imitate opening the mouth as if to bite or gape; a final particle finishing the sense; a gaping hole; appearance of the moon partly eclipsed.

牙角何丨丨 why are the toothed horns so like a crack? alluding to the moon's disk almost eclipsed.

Read ꜀ya. To wrangle; the bickering of children.

丨的一聲 the creaking of an opening door.

In *Cantonese*, read ꜀a and a꜄. A final particle giving force to the expression; a term for ten after a higher number, as 四丨錢 forty cash.

丫 ꜀ya From 丨 a *stick* with *prongs* on it to delineate the forking of branches; it is used with the next.

A fork; a crotch; the place where a thing forks; fingers, tines.

丨杈 a rest, a crotch, a fork.

丨頭 or 丨鬟 a young slave girl, alluding to the two tufts of hair.

手丨巴 the fork of the fingers.

In *Cantonese* also written 吖. An interrogative particle; a word denoting that an affirmation is indisputable; a tone indicating the end of a sentence.

好丨 well; very well.

椏 ꜀ya A fork in a tree.

丨枝 or 丨杈 a crotch in trees, the fork of branches.

一丨枝 one tree. (*Chehkiang.*)

一副丨棍 a pair of crutches.

刭 ꜀ya To cut the throat, as of a sheep.

丨猪 to stick a pig.

丨頸 he cut his thoat.

窒 ꜀ya Awry; suspended.

丨窣 not perpendicular; also defined elegant, lady-like.

砑 ꜀ya Rough ground.

地形硍丨 the surface is uneven; a rough country.

啞 ꜀ya Used as a synonym of ꜂瘂 dumb.

The confused noise of boys' studying; dumb; to keep silent.

丨嘔 the clamor of a school-room.

情難丨忍 it is hard to bear it patiently.

推聾妝丨 to pretend not to hear.

咿丨 the creaking of a scull on its pivot.

丨吧車 a baggage cart.

Read *oh*, Laughter.

笑言丨丨 laughing and talking greatly.

牙 ꜀ya The original was a rude delineation of the upper and lower molars and the under jaw, now contracted to represent a single molar; it is the 93d radical of a few characters relating to teeth.

The molar teeth or grinders; the teeth; a tusk; a toothlike process, as a tenon; jagged, scored, toothed; used for the next, a bud; ivory; to gnaw; an agent, a farmer of the revenue, as if he were one who bit the people.

丨色 a buff or salmon color.

丨疼 or 丨痛 the toothache.

丨力 strong teeth; *i. e.* convincing, able to convince.

敖丨 a protruding tooth.

丨工 a worker in ivory.

一副丨 a set of teeth.

丨灰 tooth-powder.

丨關緊閉 the jaws immovable, the teeth set; *i.e.* dying.

丨交 or 丨髈骨 the jaw-bone.

花丨利嘴 specious talk; a glib-tongued talker.

鼠丨雀角 rats' teeth and birds' bills; *met.* litigation in courts; squabbles, skirmishes.

丨婆 a woman who acts as a broker.

丨旗繽紛 the scollop-fringed flags were all elegantly displayed.

丨爪 an agent of others; people who frighten or annoy others.

咬丨 to grit the teeth; to dispute with, to annoy another.

君丨 an ancient Minister of Instruction.

丨齒打鼓 the teeth beating a tattoo, *i. e.* chattering with cold.

丨虫 carious teeth, supposed to be caused by worms.

奶丨未脫 his first set of teeth is unchanged, he is still verdant.

丨牌 ivory counters, slips or tablets.

丨釐總局 an office for levying the transit or local duties.

磨丨 to beat down the price.

丨行 or 丨儈 a broker or middle-man; in Peking they farm the revenues derived from various octroi laws.

芽 ꜀ya From *plant* and *tooth.*

A germ, a shoot; a plumule; to bud; the beginning, the budding forth.

發丨 or 冒丨 to bud forth.

丨菜 bean sprouts, used as food.

丨笴 sprouts, shoots; a tenon.

黃丨白 Shantung cabbage. (*Brassica sinensis.*)

月丨 the moon three days' old.

枒 ꜀ya Used for ꜀yé 椰 the cocoa-nut.

The felloe of a wheel 輪丨 clamped with big spikes.

丨葉無陰 the cocoa-nut gives no shade.

丨槎 a dried up, dying tree.

衙 ꜀ya From to *walk* and *I.*

The markee of a general, distinguished by a standard; anciently called 牙旗; the house or office of a ruler; a court; a bureau, an office; a tribunal or department; to exercise official functions, to open court.

早丨 an early court.

丨門 a *yamun* or Chinese official establishment; a public court; government offices.

丨署 the buildings of a court.

排丨 to open a court.

上丨 to visit an official superior at new and full moon.

早晚丨集 morning and evening he held his court.

二丨 and 四丨 the two assistant magistrates of a district.

丨吏 clerks in a court.

犽 ꜀ya From *tooth* and *child.*

A child whose teeth are not shed is called 亞丨 in Chehkiang.

丨兒梨 the winter pear. (*Pekingese.*)

齖 ꜀ya Composed of *teeth* of both kinds.

Uneven teeth.

齟丨 uneven, distorted teeth.

礬丨 indifferent to others' criticisms, as a well balanced mind; heedless of carping.

瘂 ʻya From *disease* and *second.*

Dumb, unable to speak; dull, faded, as a pale color; a cracked sound, as of a bell; hoarse, wheezing.

丨門 the depression at the nape of the neck.

丨巴 or 丨子 or 丨仔 a dumb person; a deaf mute.

丨口無言 he's dumb and won't speak; — sulky, mute.

音太丨 the sound is too indistinct.

嗓子丨 throat swelled so as to be unable to speak.

丨毒 dumb people are revengeful.

丨喉 lost his voice.

雅 ʻya From *bird* and *tooth;* it was at first read ꜀yá, and regarded as a form of 鴉 a crow.

Elegant, genteel, correct, decorous; unadorned, plain, polished, refined; continual; to rectify, to make thoroughly correct; the music of wind instruments; a cup for wine.

丨致 stylish, elegant; soft, winning, gentle.

不文丨 harsh, unrefined, lowbred.

子所丨言 what the Sage constantly said.

丨淡 plain but stylish.

閒丨 elegant leisure.

丨座 the best rooms in an inn; the private rooms.

幽丨 retired, studious, not mixing with the world.

丨儀 courteous manners, dignified.

佳丨 a charming place, a fine view.

面斥不丨 it is impolite to reprimand people to their faces.

In *Suchau.* A superlative like 狠 very.

好的丨嗒 exceedingly fine.

庌 ʻya A piazza or lodge near the great hall; a verandah that goes around the house; a rough shed for sheltering horses.

厊 ʻya Uneven; unmatched.

厏丨莫可結構 these uneven tenons will not dovetail closely.

砑 ya˒ From *stone* and *toothed.*

To grind; to polish, as by a calendering stone.

碾丨麥子 to grind wheat.

丨光 to brighten, to make smooth.

丨紙 to roll paper.

丨螺 beautiful mottled cowrie shells.

丨坊 a calendering shop.

迓 ya˒ From to *go* and a *tooth;* occurs used with 御 in the classics, and is interchanged with the next.

To go out to receive one; to descend and greet; to see with respect.

敬丨 to respectfully greet; to politely wait for.

拈香以丨時暘 burn incense till fair weather appears.

以丨田祖 for greeting the gods of the land — to get a harvest.

未能迎丨 I am unable to go and meet you; I cannot now call on you.

訝 ya˒ Interchanged with the last.

To meet and receive, as a guest; to express surprise at, to exclaim.

嗟丨 to admire, to wonder at.

無丨無訾 he neither wondered at him nor scolded him.

一驚丨 a great fright, a surprise.

怪丨 to be astonished, as at a lusus naturæ.

丨于道左 he waited on the left of the road.

是亦一丨觀也 it was also a fine sight.

In *Cantonese.* To stop the road, to obstruct the way.

霸丨個笪地 to occupy a spot while others want it.

丨定 to block up a place or passage.

亞 阿 *ya* *a* The original is said to represent two hunchbacked men looking at each other; another says it is made of 八 to *separate* above 日 *day*, because the sun goes with the brightness of the day; used with the next.

Deformed, ugly, as a hunchback; to regard as inferior, to esteem lightly; second; the second form is employed as a sound before proper names, and to impersonate epithets or nicknames; next to, inferior, junior.

丨初 a raw hand. (*Cantonese.*)

不丨于人 not inferior to other people.

花枝低丨 the branch of flowers drooped to the ground.

丨次 the second in order or quality.

婭 *ya* The *woman* who is *second*; the last is also used for it.

Brothers-in-law.

並無姻丨 I am not related to him by any marriage.

丨婿 so husbands of two sisters call each other.

掗 *ya* To shake; to take up; to urge one to take.

丨賣 to press one to buy.

丨搖 to shake, to rattle.

丨目 to pluck out the eyes.

稏 *ya* A variety of rice 罷丨, but one authority defines this as the ear of grain.

𠲘 *ya* The braying of an ass is 𠲘丨 intended to represent its melancholy tone.

YAH.

Old sounds, yet, ap, *and* at. *In Canton*, ap, at, chat, *and* ngăt; — *in Swatow*, a, yap, *and* ap; — *in Amoy*, ap, at, *and* tsat; — *in Fuhchau*, ak, tah, *and* chak; — *in Shanghai*, wėh, ėh, ngėh, *and* k'ėh; — *in Chifu*, ya.

押 *ya* *yah* From *hand* and *mail-armor*.

To sign, to stamp or affix a seal; to escort; to control, to guard; to detain, to arrest; to compel, to force; a lockup, the room where people are detained; to suppress; an unlicensed pawnshop; to reserve, to keep back; to pawn.

丨冬 kept over winter; left over the season.

不敢丨你 I'll not detain you; I would not hinder you.

丨他作 I will make him do it, I'll force it out of him.

丨賬 to leave a thing as security for a loan.

丨住不放 still detained in custody.

小丨 a pawn-shop, where small things are pawned.

九五丨 a pawnbroker who charges only five per cent.

丨貨 to escort or convoy goods.

丨送人 the guard of a prisoner.

丨陣 to go into battle; to join battle.

看丨在班館 watch him while detained in the lockup.

丨歲錢 money given the evening before newyear.

丨韻 to make rhymes.

管丨 to keep in custody.

丨字 to write a running hand.

丨表 to shave a pawn-ticket, to pledge it for something else.

按丨 to keep a letter before replying to it; to keep, as a security.

丨令 to compel, to enjoin on.

簽丨 to authenticate a paper, as by stamping or signing it; to endorse, as by dating an edict in red ink; hence 簽丨房 is the signet office in a yamun.

畫花丨 to make one's mark, to write a device · the 花丨 or 花碼 is a composite paraph, composed of several characters in a cypher, which learned men or officials use instead of their signature; as in the combination 𢡟 for the phrase 正大光明, which thus forms the person's motto.

鴨 *ya* From *bird* and *mail-armor* for the phonetic, in imitation of the quack.

A duck; a mallard; any species of the genus *Anser*.

丨子 or 水丨 a duck.

雛丨 or 丨苗 ducklings.

焙丨子 or 數丨 to hatch ducks' eggs artificially.

臘丨 or 板丨 dried salted ducks.

麻丨 a speckled duck.

野丨 or 水丨 wild ducks.

我伴雜鵝丨 my companions were geese and ducks.

龍頭丨 the muscovy duck. (*Cairina moschata.*)

軋 *ya* From 車 a *cart* and 乙 *one*.

The creaking roll of a wheel; a creaking, crushing sound.

淜丨 the roaring of a torrent.

丨刑 an ancient punishment of crushing the bones under a wheel.

清風丨忽 the balmy breeze blows a long time.

勢相磨丨 they used their strength to distress and injure each other.

丨丨 the sound of creaking or crushing, as of a loom or wheel.

魟 *ya* A scaleless, slimy fish, 鱙丨 having a yellow belly, blackish back, two cirri, and two plates joining the pectoral fins; it is the goby, of which family of fishes many species occur along the coast.

扎 *ya*ͻ Fine dust hardening or agglutinating.
块 丨 a vast, illimitable aspect; a foggy boundless appearance, like clouds and mist coalescing; or as chaos, undefinable and inscrutable.

揠 *ya*ͻ Used with *chah*, 扎 to prick.
To pull up weeds or plants; to eradicate.
丨 拔 to pull up.
丨 出 to pull out.
丨 苗 to pull up shoots for transplanting.

壓 ꜀*ya* From *earth* and to *dislike;* occurs used for its primitive.
To press down, to steady, to settle; to subject or conquer, to bend to one's will; to overthrow or level; to crush, to stop up; to supply a want; to repress, to quiet an alarm; to suppress, to intimidate; to dislike.
丨 壞 to injure by lying on or pressing.
丨 害百姓 to oppress the people.
鎮 丨 or 彈 丨 or 丨 住 to suppress; to stop, as a riot; to remove evils; to keep down, as public opinion; to steady.
丨 驚 to calm one's fears.
一福丨百禍 one happy thing will neutralize a hundred sorrows.
丨 邪 to drive away evils.
丨 死人 crushed a man to death.
丨 服 to subject to one's rule; to control.
丨 守 to keep in one's hands, to maintain by force; to defend.
丨 實 to press down solid.
丨 住運 to remove unlucky influences.
丨 倒 to upset, to throw down.
丨 班不能超升 if you are the last on the list of candidates, you cannot rise fast in rank.
丨 紙 to keep paper from flying about; to put a long slip of white paper on a grave as a sign it has been worshiped.

In *Pekingese.* To build.
丨 一間房 to erect a house.

齾 ꜀*yeh* From *teeth* and to *offer.*
Fragmentary things; an article with a nick or flaw in it; remnants left after a beast has eaten; a sherd or broken utensil; a tooth lost from the row.

YAI.

See also under AI *and* NGAI. *Old sounds,* ngai *and* ngat. *In Canton,* ngai; — *in Swatow,* ngai; — *in Amoy,* gai; — *in Fuhchau,* ngai; — *in Shanghai,* ya; — *in Chifu,* yai.

厓 崖 ꜀*yai* From an *overhanging cliff* and a *baton;* the second form with *hill* is most used.
The sheer side of a hill; a cliff, a precipice; a bank, a shore.
山 丨 a ledge, a high bank.
丨 際 the edge of a cliff.
丨 岸 a steep bank; *met.* a discrepancy, a disagreement of views.
丨 茶 rare (*i. e.* cliff) tea.
上 丨 to go ashore.
懸 丨 an overhanging cliff.
丨 門 a place in Sin-hwui hien in Kwangtung, where Ti-ping, the last emperor of the Sung dynasty, died A. D. 1279.
剛介不屈與物乖丨 he has a stiff, unbending disposition, and cannot accommodate himself to other's tempers.

涯 ꜀*yai* From *water* and *cliff;* it is interchanged with the preceding.
The margin of a river, a bank; a water-line; a limit, a shore.
津 丨 the ford on a stream; the moat near it.
無 丨 illimitable, shoreless.
走天丨 to go to the ends of the earth.
水 丨 a bank or shore.
吾生也有丨 my life also has its limit.
閣下作何生丨 what, Sir, is your occupation?

捱 ꜀*yai* From *hand* and *bank.*
To lean against; to loiter, to put off, to procrastinate; to trifle with; to suffer, to bear with.
丨 世界 to suffer the ills of life, or the hard usage of the world.
丨 苦 to endure sorrows and ills.
不能延丨 it cannot be delayed, it must not be put off.
丨 了打 I've had a beating.
丨 不住 I cannot endure it; I won't stand it.
丨 了一會是一會 wait for a chance, it will come.
丨 到晚間 put it off till the evening.
丨 丨 躓躓 dilatory, slow, hesitating.
丨 死 in great danger of death, as a man who has fallen overboard.

啀 ꜀*yai* A dog snarling and wishing to bite people.

涯 ꜀*yai* Stupid, silly-looking.
丨 笨 stupid and heedless.
魚都丨了 the fish are all dead. (*Kiangsu.*)

YANG.

Old sound, yung. *In Canton,* yéung; — *in Swatow,* yang, y^{n}é, *and* yòng; — *in Amoy,* jong, giong, *and* siong; — *in Fuhchau,* yòng *and* ngiòng; — *in Shanghai,* yang *and* mang; — *in Chifu,* yang.

央 ˌ*yang* From 大 *great* within 冂 a *space*, defined as denoting one who is standing at one's side, having the same opinion; it occurs used with the next.

In the midst; the middle or center; the half of; to finish, to conclude; to press earnestly or to the utmost; urgently.

丨浼 or 丨求 or 丨及 to solicit, to strongly intercede for, as a favor; to beg alms.

丨丨 ample, spacious; fresh; splendid, said of banners; tinkling, jingling, as bells.

夜未丨 the night is not yet spent; hence applied to the 未丨宮 a famous seraglio in the days of Han where revelries were prolonged.

泱 ˌ*yang* From *water* and *center.*

Moving, agitated, as the clouds; wide, boundless; babbling, impetuous, as a stream; violent, as a wind.

瞻彼洛矣維水丨丨 look at the Loh with its wide and deep waters.

雲山丨丨 the clouds are whirling around the hill-tops.

丨漭 disturbed, tossed, as water rushing over rocks.

坱 ˌ*yang* Fine dust; to fill.

氣丨然太虛 the air fills the heavens above.

塵丨 dust, fine sand.

殃 **䄃** ˌ*yang* From *evil* or *omen* and *wide.*

A misfortune from above; a punitive calamity, a visitation, a judgment, a retribution; to punish; unhappily, unluckily.

遭丨 to meet with a mishap.

以除疾丨 to remove the general sickness, to drive off trouble.

丨及于身 the evil has come upon me.

災丨 a plague, a common calamity.

作不善降之百丨 he who does wickedly will be visited with every misfortune.

丨盡必昌 when judgment has done its work, prosperity will come; — after evil there must be an improvement.

丨榜 a license for carrying a coffin out of the gates of Peking.

丨咎 crime worthy of punishment.

出丨 the soul leaving the coffin about the third day.

秧 ˌ*yang* Grain in the blade; shoots, young plants, especially of rice; country, rural.

打丨 to bind up shoots.

揷丨 or 蒔丨 to transplant shoots or sprouts.

撒丨 to sow for shoots; done by thickly sowing a manured bed.

瓜丨 melon sprouts.

稻丨 or 禾丨 rice shoots.

ˊ丨穰 grain standing thickly.

魚丨 small fish, fish fry.

拉丨 pull up old vines, as beans or cucumbers.

唱丨歌 to sing a country song.

起丨 in heat, said of dogs or cats.

鴦 ˌ*yang* The hen of the mandarin duck (*Anas galericulata*) or Chinese teal, also called 節木鳥 the constant virtuous bird and 匹鳥 the pairing bird, both referring to its conjugal fidelity for which it is celebrated.

兄之恩活我鴦丨厚矣 your great kindness, Sir, has as it were given life to our consorts.

[魚央] ˌ*yang* A small fish, the 丨[魚乙] also called 黃顙魚 yellow forehead fish; it is probably the long goby, which can jump on dry land, and is also said to make a noise.

咉 ˌ*yang* A reply or echo, intimating attention.

丨咽 an uninterrupted flow, as of water.

In *Pekingese.* To throw up; to gag.

丨奶 to throw up milk, as infants.

[犭雍] ˌ*yang* A dog that refuses to be led is called 丨[犭夅]; an obstinate brute.

昜 ˌ*yang* From 日 *sun,* 一 *one* and 勿 *flying* combined, referring to the cheering influence of the rising sun; to be distinguished from *yih,* 易 to alter.

To open out; to fly abroad; to expand; bright, glorious; energetic.

揚 ˌ*yang* From *hand* and *expanding.*

To rise and dash up, as waves; to impede and fret them; to splash; to display, to spread out, to extend widely; to render famous, to publish abroad; to scatter; to divulge; to applaud; to winnow; to raise, to lift up, as the voice; high and spreading, as branches; to open the eyebrows; a high forehead; to stare, to spread the wings in flying; a battle-ax.

發丨 in good spirits, smart; loquacious and impulsive.

止步丨聲 stop and cry out — when you approach the private apartments.

一抑一丨 now a loss and then a gain; now up, then down; high and low, as musical notes.

海不丨波 the sea raised no waves — in Yao and Shun's time.

丨鞭 to flourish the whip.

張丨於外 to report it abroad, to tell private affairs.

丨塵 to raise the dust.

丨丨得意 everything to one's liking.

丨于王庭 [his fame] has reached even to the palace.

丨名 to become celebrated.

時維鷹丨 then like a falcon pouncing — on its prey.

丨之水不流束薪 a dash of water won't float a bundle of faggots.

讚丨 to praise, to commend.

隱惡而丨善 to conceal the evil (or disreputable), but publish the good (or fair) side.

毋任遠丨 don't let [the robbers] escape far away.

其貌不丨 an ill-favored countenance.

丨州府 a prefecture in Kiangsu, north of the Yangtsz', within the ancient 丨州 one of Yü's nine divisions, lying south of the Yangtsz' and Hwai rivers along the sea to Fuhchau, including most of Kiangsi, Chehkiang, and Fuhkien.

颺 ˏyang Similar to the last.

Driven to and fro by the wind; tossed, whirled; vagrant, at large; sailing; to winnow; presuming and loud; to set forth, to publish; to fly.

舟遙遙以輕丨 the boat rocks and rolls as it flies along.

稽首丨言 he prostrated himself [before the throne] and spoke.

鷹飽則丨去 when the falcon has been fed he will fly off.

飛丨 to make a bluster, to swell and boast.

車丨 to winnow and clean, as grain.

楊 ˏyang From *tree* and *expanding*.

A name applied in different parts of the country, to several trees very unlike; the aspen or poplar of the north of China, also called the rain tree from the rustling of its leaves; there is the 大葉丨 large leaved aspen and the 白丨 white-barked aspen; at Shanghai this name is given to the white willow.

丨柳 the common willow; so called south of the Yangtsz' River, where the aspen is seldom seen.

赤丨 the alder, a species with red bark.

丨梅 the *Myrica*, which produces a tart fruit like the arbutus; also a bubo.

丨桃 the sweet carambola. (*Averrhoa.*)

黃丨木 boxwood (*Buxus*) used by carvers for images, &c.; there is a softer kind, called mango wood, which may be taken from another plant.

野黃丨 the elder. (*Sambucus.*)

暘 ˏyang From *sun* and to *expand*.

The rising sun; clear, shining weather; serene; to dry in the sun.

丨谷 the valley of sunshine in the extreme east, probably in Corea, where Yao worshiped the sun at the vernal equinox; *met.* the orient; the spring.

雨丨時若 rainy and fair weather come each in their season.

煬 烊 ˏyang To roast, to scorch; to warm at the fire; to refine or purify, as beeswax; to assay, to fuse; hot, blazing; to put or stand before a fire.

丨火 to put before the fire.

丨炙 to toast; to cook by roasting.

丨金 to melt metals, to cast.

丨暴 quick, impetuous, zealous.

瘍 ˏyang From *disease* and to *spread*.

An ulcer, a sore.

頭丨 or 爛頭丨 a scald head.

傷丨 a bad sore, that destroys the skin.

身有丨則浴 bathe when sores come on the body.

崵 ˏyang A celebrated mountain in Loh-yang in Honan, the 首丨 where 伯夷 and 叔齊 starved themselves to death.

禓 ˏyang Also read ˏ*shang*.

Wayside gods; spirits which infest roads and highways; used with 儺, to drive out demons or noxious influences from the house at newyear, — an ancient service, which the Board of Rites now performs ten days before it.

鄉人丨 the villagers exorcised the goblins.

陽 氜 阳 ˏyang From *place* and *spreading*; the forms which contain the *sun* are common contractions.

Lofty, clear, manifest; the superior of the dual powers, which united Chinese philosophers regard as forming, directing, and modifying all things; this is defined "that which does Heaven's good work and shows forth all things;" matter in motion; the pure, ethereal, subtle parts of matter, out of which gods and souls are formed; the superior of two things in contrast, as the sun, day, heaven; openly; a bright spot; brilliant, as color; the front; sunny, light; and opposed to moon, night, earth, &c., &c.; much used in names of places; the male of animals, virility; north of a river; a south side exposure.

當丨 in the sun; towards the south.

正丨 due south.

太丨 the sun, sometimes called 老丨; the 兩太丨 are the two temples on the forehead.

丨間 or 丨世 in this world, during this life.

ˏ重丨節 the 9th day of the 9th moon, when people ramble.

君子丨丨 my husband looks so satisfied.

赴丨臺 gone to the land of dreams.

ˏ朝丨 the morning sun.

夕丨 declining day, eventide.

丨物 the virile member.

丨事 sexual intercourse.

壯丨 to strengthen the animal powers.

辭丨 to depart this life.

丨手 the palm upwards.

雲丨 hamadryads, elfins in trees.

丨壽永 a long life, as living till eighty.

丨月 the tenth moon, because the heats are all over.

丨衰 the heat of the season is diminishing; *met.* the powers of the body are decaying.

丨雀 poetical name for the cuckoo.

丨鳥攸居 the wild geese had places to roost on.

鍚 ˏyang Not the same as *sih*, 錫 tin.

Ornaments on a bridle near the forehead 丨鸞鈴 which jingle as the horse moves; bells have now taken their place; an ancient place in Shantung.

羊 ˏyang The original form was designed to represent the *horns, head, feet* and *tail* of a sheep; it is the 123d radical of words relating to ovine animals; used with the next.

A sheep, a goat; some think the latter was first known; animals of this family, as the antilope or gazelle; to roam, to saunter.

棉丨 or 丨咩 a sheep.

丁丨 and 母丨 are names sometimes used for ram and ewe.

山丨 or 羱丨 a goat.

丨羔 or 丨羔子 a lamb.

黃丨 the *Antilope gutturosa* or dzeron of Mongolia.

丨酒 a sheep and a jar of wine — are wedding presents.

丨欄 or 丨圈 a sheep-cote.

丨脂玉 sheep's suet jade, the whitest variety.

擲 (or 赶) 棉丨 to throw dice.

丨角風 a whirlwind, a spiral gust.

地丨 a poetical name for a dog.

丨腿 a hind quarter of mutton.

丨齒 a large fern or brake. (*Pteris.*)

白丨 the Mongols, so termed from their numerous flocks.

駝丨 or 封丨 the humped goat said to be in Kansuh, probably denotes a variety of the zebu.

徉 ˏyang To ramble, to rove; to stray off, as a sheep.

彷丨無所倚 in a state of doubt, with nothing to rely on.

徜丨天下 to travel and see the whole empire.

佯 ˏyang From *man* and *sheep*; occurs interchanged with ˏ陽 in the sense professing.

To feign, to simulate, to profess; false, unreal, pretended; a feint, a ruse, a dodge.

丨爲不知 he affected not to know.

丨醉 appeared to be drunk.

丨善 hypocritical.

此善爲詐丨者也 this man is a skillful deceiver.

丨狂 made believe that he was mad.

垟 ˏyang From *earth* and *sheep*.

The elf or sprite that guards a spot; Confucius was asked the meaning of a sheep found in digging a well, when he said it was a 羵丨 or local brownie.

洋 ˏyang The name of two small streams in the north of Shantung, which run into the sea; also of a river in the southeast of Kansuh; the ocean, denoting a larger body of water than 海; vast, wide, overspreading; extensive; foreign, from over the sea, European; a voyage by sea, a passage.

丨海 vast oceans; seas; the sea.

外丨 the outer seas, beyond the coast; foreign parts; at Canton it denotes beyond the Bogue.

丨面 an offing, a roadstead; when placed after a place, refers to the waters or anchorage near it.

東丨 the eastern sea; Japanese.

遠涉重丨 to go back and forth on long sea voyages.

丨烟 usually means snuff; it first denoted opium, now more usually known as 丨藥 foreign medicine.

丨丨入耳 [the music] wholly fills my ears.

西丨人 western ocean men; this at first included all foreigners, but is now confined to the Portuguese, though 大西丨 still means Europe.

河水丨丨 how wide is the river! 丨丨 is also applied to a vast plain and many dancers.

丨錢 dollars, rupees, or rubles, for which 洋 alone is occasionally used, where the context is clear.

丨溢乎中國 overflowed from China, — into wild regions; said of fame or influence.

養 ʿyang From to *eat* and *sheep*, perhaps intimating the common food given to people.

To nourish, to rear, to bring up, to provide for, to support; to pay regard to; to take care of, to preserve the health; to tame; to improve, as a breed; to raise, as plants; to educate, to mature, as a virtue by practice; to develop, as a talent; aliments; a support, a living; a cook; to itch.

丨生 to nourish one's health; to support one's parents.

丨育 to rear, as one's own young.

丨神 to refresh the spirits.

丨身 to strengthen the health, as by resting or taking a trip.

丨眼神 to rest the eyes.

丨得熟 tame, very docile.

丨老 to give a pension to old men.

敎丨 to educate and support.

奉丨 to obey and take care of.

都丨 to be a servant of all work.

丨身工夫 certain gymnastic exercises used by Taoists to promote health.

中心丨丨 my mind is harassed with sorrow; distracted.

丨不住 not enough to live on.

Read *yang'* To attend on one's parents.

供丨' 父母 to wait on and support one's parents.

告終丨' to retire from office to spend one's days in quiet.

蛘 ᶜ蝆 ᶜyang } The second is regarded as the most correct, and is often read ꜀mé from the primitive.

The 丨 丨 is another name for the mantis.

Read ᶜmi. The black weevil found in rice, called 强 丨 and other names.

ᶜ癢 ᶜyang To itch; to scratch.

痕 丨 it itches. (*Cantonese.*)

無關痛 丨 not worth a scratch, of no importance.

怕 丨 花 the sensitive plant; and other species of *Mimosa.*

痛 丨 相關 I sympathize in all your trials.

ᶜ痒 ᶜyang Used for the last; also read ꜀yang.

A sore, an ulcer; to be ill; in a bad plight.

瘡 丨 a boil.

癙憂以 丨 my hidden sorrow makes me ill.

Read ꜀siang. A wound or pain in the head.

ᶜ懩 ᶜyang From *heart* and *to nourish.*

What the heart longs for; to have an itching for.

心 丨 難撈 it is not always easy to get what one desires.

徒心煩而技 丨 the uneasy heart still longs for it.

ᶜ仰 ᶜyang From *man* and *high.*

To look up, to look towards heaven; to look to, to regard with respect; to think of kindly; to direct a subordinate, to transmit orders to an inferior; used in official papers as a form of the imperative, let; to wait on, to rely.

丨 望 to expect, to long for, to look up at.

丨 頭 to raise the head.

久 丨 or 素 丨 or 久 丨 了 I have long admired or respected you, — for your talents; *i. e.* I have long wished to see you.

丨 伏 to look up to and confide in, to take as a guide.

丨 而思之 puzzled, in a brown study, to cast about for the best way.

丨 慕 to look up to admiringly.

丨 給 let it be given him; I hope he will give it to me, said by a superior; I shall expect it.

右 丨 知悉 let these orders be all fully understood; — a phrase appended to proclamations.

爲此票 丨 having this warrant, I (the magistrate) expect you will — secure the criminal.

ᶜ抰 ᶜyang To whip with a strap; to slap and beat, as a horse with the reins.

In *Cantonese.* To dust, to clear from dust; to shake, as a cloth.

丨 蓆角 to shake the corner of the mat; *i. e.* to lose a wager.

丨 乾淨 shake it clean.

ᶜ鞅 ᶜyang A martingale on a bridle; the trappings and tassels attached to it; a halter; traces to draw a cart; to tie, to halter; used with the next.

牛 丨 a cow's tether or halter.

丨 掌 perplexed, harassed and wearied with many cares, like a horse under a heavy load, and restrained by his bridle.

丨 罔 flurried, entangled, as in a net.

怏 yangᵓ From *heart* and *wide;* also read ᶜyang, and occurs used with the last.

Discontented, uneasy; restive under others' treatment.

塞其 丨 丨 心 to satisfy his discontented heart.

實深 丨 丨 excessively disgusted and dissatisfied with.

Read ꜀yang. Great.

丨 然 self-complacent, satisfied.

羕 yangᵓ From *sheep* with *perpetual* under it, referring to the unceasing flow of water; the next has now taken its place.

A rising of water.

江之 丨 矣 the rising of the Great River.

漾 瀁 yangᵓ } From *water* and *rising,* or to *nourish;* the second is unusual.

The ancient name of a small river in the southeast of Kansuh, or the southwest of Shensi, one of the headwaters of the River Han, a name it retains almost to Han-chung fu; water in commotion, ripples, rapids; vast and large, as rising waves.

盪 丨 之見 an indistinct vision of; *met.* vast but vague ideas.

搖 丨 roughened into waves; rocked on the water.

輕 丨 微風 light waves and gentle breezes.

河水 丨 到岸上 the river is rising over the banks.

In *Fuhchau.* To talk about, to make known; to shake.

丨 盪清 cleared by shaking it.

㨾 yangᵓ A rule, a pattern; for which the next is now most commonly used.

式 丨 a model or guide.

樣 yangᵓ From *wood* and *rising.*

A model, rule, or pattern; a muster; manner, style, way, mode; a kind of oak with pointed acorns.

丨 子 a pattern, a fashion.

照 丨 作 do it like the pattern.

柳家新 丨 the new style of writing of Mr. Liu (of the T'ang dynasty); — *i. e.* beautiful penmanship.

出花 丨 to draw a pattern of a thing.

走 丨 failed of reaching the model; lost the impression, said of a photograph when blurred.

裝模作 丨 to put on airs, to mimic; to burlesque others.

依 丨 葫蘆 to copy another man's plan.

丨 丨 的事 all kinds of business and affairs.

怎 丨 or 怎麼 丨 how, in what way?

都是一 丨 they are all alike; it is all the same.

儀 *yang'* A fidgety manner, as when one cannot stand still.
竹 丨 the waving of the bamboos in the wind.

訷 *yang'* To stop talking; words ceasing to flow.
聲 丨 the sound has stopped.

恙 *yang'* From *heart* and *sheep* as the phonetic.
Out of sorts, nervous, low-spirited; ailments, complaints, sickness; grief; chagrined; a carking care, as if worms were gnawing at the heart.
貴 丨 or 尊 丨 your complaint.
別來無 丨 have you been well since I saw you?
賤 丨 my indisposition.
奈 丨 何 I have to bear it.
抱 丨 to have an illness.
有 丨 在身 he has a bodily complaint.

YAO.

Old sounds, yo, ngo, ok, ngok, ngot, *and* ot. *In Canton*, iu, ngao, *and* ao; — *in Swatow*, yò, hiò, ngiò, au, *and* ka; — *in Amoy*, jau, giau, au, hiau, ju, *and* ka; — *in Fuhchau*, yéu, miu, au, ngéu, *and* ngiu; — *in Shanghai*, yo, o, *and* ngo; — *in Chifu*, yao.

腰 *˛yao* From *flesh* and *important*; *q. d.* the vital part of the body.
The loins, the waist, the region above the hips, or between the ribs and pelvis; the middle of a thing, or act; the bulge of a kernel of wheat; an isthmus or strip of land.
丨 子 the kidneys of animals.
丨 部 in or around the loins; a medical phrase.
努着 丨 it hurt my back, as a heavy weight.
半中 丨 half done, as an unfinished journey or job.
丨 背 the lower backbone.
書 丨 the back of a book.
無 丨 骨 a witless, inefficient fellow. (*Cantonese.*)
柳 丨 a slender waist.
丨 骨頭痕 your back itches — for me to thrash you. (*Cantonese.*)
折 丨 to make a prostration, to bend the head very low.
點頭躬 丨 to nod and bow, as polite people do.
弓 丨 bent over; a hunch-back.
丨 截 cut it in the middle.
閃了 丨 a stitch in the side.
圍 丨 a waist-band, as of flannel.
山 丨 half-way up the hill.
丨 裏沒錢 no money in his waist (or purse); beggared, indigent; referring to the fob when worn behind.

褄 *˛yao* From *clothes* and *necessary*.
The part of a garment which folds or laps over; a plait.
裙 丨 the plaits on a skirt.
褲 丨 the waist-band of trowsers.
壓 丨 to fold over a collar or cuff.

夭 *˛yao* From 大 *great*, the top being added like a broken *point*, to denote something born incomplete; another says the character represents a crooked neck; its shape resembles ˛t'ien 天 heaven.
Pleasing, winning; the freshness of youth; delicate, tender as a flower; long and thin, as grass; gentle; used for ʻ殀 broken off, an untimely death; ominous; to beguile; to disgrace; a calamity.
丨 壽 an early death.
桃之 丨 丨 the delicate peach-blossom.
丨 冶之容 a wanton, enticing look and aspect; ogling ways.
丨 嬌 unusual, not like others, remarkable; — used in a good sense.
天 丨 是椓 Heaven's retributions are beating upon them.

妖 *˛yao* From *woman* and *winning*.
Strange, bewitching, beautiful; ominous, unaccountable; monstrous, a *lusus naturæ*; not according to usage, heretical, magical, silly, and used by officials to stigmatize things or people which they dislike; a phantom, kelpie, sprite, or transformed being; an imp, a fiend; to flatter, to enchant, to entice to ruin.
丨 怪 supernatural, a warning omen.
丨 精 a metamorphosis; an elf, a fay; an animal possessed.
丨 書 magical books; charmed writing or spells.
丨 言 strange legends; stories of apparitions.
丨 孽 prodigies, signs of impending woe, retributive portents.
土木 丨 bogies which dwell on trees or in the ground.
丨 氣 or 丨 氛 apparitions; a spook, a ghost; applied to rebels and robbers.
˛降 丨 to call for the spirits to come, to exhibit a prodigy.

吆 *˛yao* A confused discord of sounds.
丨 咋 the yelps and howls of many dogs.
In *Shanghai*. A word of assent, yes; I understand; lookout! be careful, take heed.
當心 丨 mind yourself!

芺 *˛yao* Also read ˛*ngao*.
The *strange plant*, a species of thistle, found in Kiangsu, having a bitter taste, called 鉤 丨 and 苦 丨; the stalk is tubular, and the flower flat on top; the young plants are eaten as a preventive of flatulence.

祅 ˏyao Supernatural sights and ominous prodigies sent by the gods for crimes.

幺 么 ˏyao The original is deemed to resemble a *new-born child*, and usually contracted to the second form in common books; it is the 52d radical of a few unusual characters.

Small; tender.

骰 丨 the face of a dice.

丨 豚 the last of a litter of pigs.

六 丨 曲 a tune on the guitar.

丨 小 diminutive, puny.

丨 麽 minute, atomic, microscopic.

吆 ˏyao The bawling of peddlers.

丨 喝 to scold people; to talk to one harshly; to cry wares; to animate, to inspirit by cries.

In *Cantonese*. A word used by women to still children.

丨 丨 咯 be still; keep quiet.

喓 ˏyao The chirping of grasshoppers.

丨 丨 聒 耳 the stridulous racket [of the cicadas and crickets] dins the ears.

丨 丨 草 虫 the noisy insects sing in the grass.

邀 ˏyao From to *go* and *gliding*.

To interrupt when in the way, to stop; to intercept; to invite, to send for, to engage, to go with or in one's service; to salute; to seek, to look for.

丨 于 路 met him in the way and went with him.

相 丨 a mutual invitation.

丨 我 去 逛 asked me to go and take a stroll.

虛 丨 a formal invitation to eat, one which means nothing.

丨 福 to induce blessings, to seek prosperity, as by worshiping the gods.

丨 賓 or 丨 客 to invite guests.

丨 駕 I invite you, Sir.

丨 接 to go out and meet one.

丨 明 月 he saluted the moon.

葽 ˏyao From *grass* and *necessary*.

The fresh and vigorous vegetation of summer; a medicinal plant (*Polygala tenuifolia*), now known as the 遠 志 or seek further; its roots are used in coughs.

丨 丨 luxuriant.

四 月 秀 丨 in May the *Polygala* is in flower.

䚻 ˏyao From to *speak* and *flesh*, *i. e.* words proceeding from the mouth.

To hum or chant, unaccompanied by any instrument, and speaking no words.

歌 丨 to hum a strain.

缶 ˏyao From 缶 *earthenware* and 月 *flesh* over it; but others say it is the preceding contracted, which gives a better phonetic.

A jar or vase; a crockery or earthenware vessel or pitcher.

嗂 ˏyao Delighted, happy, jolly.

咏 斯 丨 singing for very joy.

媱 ˏyao Handsome; to play and make people happy.

戲 丨 to play and make antics for entertainment.

姑 丨 a celebrated fountain where a princess was turned into a flower.

徭 傜 ˏyao From to *walk* and *dish*; the second form is unusual, and also means not uniform in size, mixed, adulterated.

Feudal vassalage or labor of a serf; socage; a villein's service.

差 丨 service of government officers or workmen when sent abroad.

丨 役 scutage or escuage, a service or work done by retainers.

丨 粮 food given to government workmen on their way.

愮 ˏyao From *heart* and *dish*.

Sad; tempted; deluded.

丨 亂 greatly perturbed, out of one's wits, flurried.

中 心 丨 丨 disheartened, and having no one to unburden to.

搖 ˏyao From *hand* and a *jar*.

To move, to shake, to wag; to sway to and fro; agitated, tossed, vibrating; disturbed, discomposed.

丨 櫓 to work a scull.

丨 動 to joggle; to shake; waving to and fro, fluttering; unsteady; amazed, perturbed.

風 雨 所 漂 丨 [my nest] is tossed by the wind and rain.

丨 頭 to shake the head, to refuse.

扶 丨 直 上 rose directly to high rank, as if on a roc's back.

丨 丨 擺 擺 swaggering, proud.

丨 鈴 to ring a hand-bell.

丨 光 a revolving light; a twinkling, as of the stars.

丨 丨 欲 墜 it shakes as if just about to fall.

招 丨 誘 騙 者 those who have tried to pass themselves off [as rich men] by bragging.

瑤 ˏyao A precious kind of green jasper, or quartz colored green; emerald-like, green.

丨 臺 a grassy terrace.

丨 光 the star η Benetsnach in the Dipper.

丨 箋 your gem of a letter; a complimentary term.

丨 池 a pool in fairy land where 王 母 rules.

維 玉 及 丨 pieces of jade and green crystal.

丨 琴 a lute with jasper mountings.

窰 窯 ˏyao From *pit* and a *jar* or *lamb*; the second form is least used.

A pit for burning bricks, a kiln; a furnace for porcelain or pottery; a brothel; a den of a place.

煤 丨 a coal-mine.

瓦 丨 a kiln for tiles or pottery.

官 丨 governmental porcelain furnaces; their ware has a 丨 印 or furnace stamp on it.

丨 館 a barracoon.

丨 門 the mouth of the furnace.

丨口 an opium shop. (*Cantonese.*)
丨子 a brothel.
打丨 or 遊丨 to frequent one.
住破丨 vagrant, beggarly, those who live in old kilns.

猺 ˎyao A wild dog or jackal called 獏丨; applied by the Cantonese to the 丨民 or 丨人 a tribe of aborigines still living in Lien cheu 連州 in the northwest of the province, who are reputed to have tails.

鰩 ˎyao The 鮫丨魚 or flying fish, found along the coast; its body is bluish white, with stripes; the Chinese liken it to the carp; the flying gurnard seems also to be referred to.

謠 ˎyao From *words* and a *jar*.
To sing when unoccupied; a ballad or rustic ditty, called 丨歌 made impromptu by peasants; a rumor; a report circulated to stir up people.
造丨 a made-up tale.
童丨 childish songs; ballads.
布散丨言 (or 丨傳) to tell fish stories, to spread seditious or wild rumors.
這話是老丨 that's the talk of the old liar.
丨謊山 his lies are big as hills; he is a great liar.
我歌且丨 I play and sing—to ease my sadness.

軺 軺 ˎyao Also read ˎshao.
An open cart of light construction, from which a sight can be had all around.
星丨 the traveling carriage of an imperial envoy; the allusion is to the emperor's favor shining on his path.
丨車而傳 may the post-cart hasten this letter to you.

䠛 ˎyao To leap, to jump.
跳丨 to go by leaps, to jump and pace, as boys in play.

遙 ˎyao Distant, far, remote.
丨望 to look off afar.
丨遠 very remote.
丨丨無期 entirely undeterminate, not possible to fix a time.
路丨知馬力 a long journey tests a horse's strength.

颻 ˎyao Floating in the air, as down; waving in the wind, floated by the wind.
縱步飄丨 wandering about at pleasure; roaming.
隨諸風而任丨颺之逸 blown along by favorable winds, I am going where my fancy calls me.

堯 ˎyao From 土 *earth* heaped up on 兀 a *high* base.
High, eminent; lofty,—for which the next is now used; a celebrated sovereign, called 帝丨 and sometimes 唐丨, who is said to have reigned 103 years from B. C. 2357–2255; in epitaphs, eminent for justice and virtue.
孔子曰唯天爲大唯丨則之 Confucius said, Heaven alone is great, and only Yao imitated it.

嶢 ˎyao The *hill* of *Yao*; towering, high; lofty, as a peak.
岧丨岑立 it (the palace) stands so lofty and grand.

僥 ˎyao Deceitful, false, pretended; a nation of pigmies, said to be three feet in height, called 丨丨 found on the southwest of China; the negritos or papuans of New Guinea may be intended.
僬丨 a pigmy, a dwarf.
Read ˏkiao and used for 儌. Fortunate, lucky.
小人行險以丨倖 the foolish man acts recklessly and then trusts to luck.

篚 ˎyao The laths or scantling laid on the top of rafters to retain the mud in which the tiles are laid.

In *Cantonese*. Divining blocks, otherwise called 珓杯 made from bamboo roots.

姚 ˎyao From *woman* and *omen*; it is like 嬈 in its meanings.
Handsome, elegant; a descendant of Shun.
丨冶 beautiful, winsome.
Read ˏtiao. Undisciplined, not drilled.
楚師輕丨 the troops of Tsu were quite heady and ungovernable.

珧 ˎyao The iridiscent naker of certain shells (*Pinna*, *Mya*, or *Unio*) used in inlaid work, and for ornamenting bows; a bow thus adorned.
江丨 or 玉丨 naker-shells from the Yangtsz' R.; also called 海月 or sea-moon, from the shape of one sort; probably a species of *Pinna* was first used.

杳 ˋyao ˋmiao From *tree* and *sun* under it, indicating the decline of the day; it is to be distinguished from ˎch'a 查 to search, and *tah*, 沓 to pile.
Obscure, dark, somber; mysterious; unintelligible; far off.
丨冥 dark; cloudy; indistinct, as a bird flying away.
丨無音信 no answer has been received for a long time.
丨丨無踪 not the least traces or tidings.
丨遠 far distant and obscure.
日方丨矣 the sun had then gone down.

舀 抌 ˋyao From 臼 *mortar* and 爪 *claws* or hand; the second and unusual form refers alone to cleaning; not the same as ˋhien 臽 a pit.
To bale out water into another vessel; to lade from one vessel into another; to clean a rice mortar.
丨酒 to lade out spirits.
丨一大碗 bale out a big bowl full.
丨不乾 you can't bale it dry.

ʿ窈 ʿyao From *cave* and *young*.
Obscure, because deep and retired from public gaze; tranquil, easy; composed, said of high-bred ladies.

生而丨窕 they who are naturally retiring and refined, — are desired for wives.

舒丨糾兮 how quiet and composed she is!

幽丨 retired, as a retreat.

ʿ拗 ʿyao From *hand* and *tender* as the phonetic.
To pull and snap a thing in two; to break off, to drag along; to pluck, as a flower.

丨折 to break; to twist off.

丨碎 to snap in shivers.

丨節 the day after the festival.

丨轉說 badinage, irony, raillery; to chaff one.

丨魚 to catch fish in a lifting net.

丨手把 to test strength by seizing each other's wrists.

丨九節 29th day of the 1st moon, when offerings are made to idols and tablets. (*Fuhchau.*)

Read *ngao'* Obstinate, self-willed; unyielding; to rush against madly.

丨頸 perverse, stiff-necked.

丨强 mulish, disobliging.

丨當 disputatious, bickering.

丨執 set in his way, fixed.

丨子 a pig-headed man.

In *Pekingese*. To buy meat.

丨羊肉 to buy mutton.

In *Cantonese*. Warped, bent; curved.

丨丨的 rather crooked; not flat.

ʿ窅 ʿyao From *cavern* and *eye*.
Deep, sunken eyes; extensive; deep, as a house.

丨一目 blind of one eye.

曠丨 extensive, as a plain.

丨然喪其所守 mortified and inconsolable at having lost what he guarded, as a priest his vows through heedlessness.

ʿ眑 ʿyao Used for the last in the meaning of sunken eyes; a vacant look, lost in a brown study; deep, as a large house; any blemish on the face.

二目丨丨 hollow eyes.

淸思丨丨 in deep thought, abstracted.

ʿ殀 ʿyao From *evil* and *tender*.
To die before entering office, to die young; short-lived, an untimely end; to cut off or kill the young.

丨折 or 丨亡 to die young, or under thirty.

不丨夭 do not kill young or immature animals.

命丨 a short life.

丨壽不貳 neither early death nor long life may lead one to hesitate — in duty.

ʿ咬 }
ʿ齩 } ʿyao From *mouth* or *teeth* and to *join*; the latter form is unusual; also read ˏngao.
To bite, to gnaw; to chew, to masticate; to set the teeth, as in pain; wailing, tones of suffering; to ruminate on, to con over.

丨一口 or 丨一啖 to bite off a mouthful.

丨不動 I can't bite it through, — it is too tough.

丨穿 to bite or tear a hole.

賊丨一口 the thief (or accused person) involved me wrongly in the crime.

丨恨 to gnash the teeth in rage.

丨唇 to bite the lips.

丨文嚼字 to chew phrases and gnaw books; —*i. e.* to study carefully.

証供丨實 the evidence quite condemns him.

丨住牙 to set the teeth.

Read ˏ*kiao*, and used for 交, as if for 叫ʾ to call. The voice of the oriole or yellow bird.

In *Pekingese*. To bark at.

狗丨人 the dog barks at the man.

In *Cantonese*. To trim off the ends even; to read.

丨錯字音 you have read that tone wrongly.

ʿ嫋 ʿyao Delicate, slender, as a female.
丨嬈 lithe, lissome, as a young girl.

ʿ㛂 ʿyao Like the last, and also read *miao'*
Small-waisted; agile, like an acrobat.

柔腰丨㛂 slim waisted and very lithe.

ʿ騕 ʿyao A fleet or divine steed, the 丨褭 fabled to go a myriad *li* in a day.

ʿ淼 ʿyao Boundless.
浩丨 limitless, as when the ocean meets the horizon.

皛丨 the lustrous brightness of water reflected in the sun.

ʿ鷕 ʿyao From *bird* and a *cry*.
The note of the hen of the Tartar pheasant.

有丨雉鳴 the cry of the hen pheasant was there.

要ʾ yao' From *west* and *woman*; but the upper part is now regarded as a contraction of 臼 *mortar*, and the under as 交 to *join* much altered; the two representing the pelvis and hips of the body, for which ˏ腰 is now used.

To want, to need; the things required; necessary, important; an abstract, a digest, the essentials, the best parts of; to intend, to design; before a verb it denotes that the action is about taking place, or makes a present participle; and thus becomes a sign of the future.

至丨 the most important.

不丨 unnecessary, needless; I do not wish it.

丨死 dying, as when dangerously sick.

丨活 reviving, as parched plants in a rain.

不丨緊 no matter, unimportant; by and by will do.

至德丨道 important virtues and necessary doctrines.

隘丨 important defiles or passes.

天可就丨晴 the sky will then be clear.

並不是丨死 he certainly will not die.

丨信 an important letter.

定丨 very necessary.

將丨到天津 I design to go to Tientsin.

握丨 maintain the important points.

Read ˏyao. To make an agreement, to be bound; to restrict; to seek for; to win to; to expostulate with, to importune; carefully; diligent; to assemble, to try, to examine into; to receive in the lap.

丨求 to require, to seek.

丨約 to contract with.

久丨不忘 don't forget the old agreement.

丨之以禮 to treat with courtesy.

丨勒 to demand with threats.

丨服 the fief of restraint; it was the fourth of Yü's tenures.

丨會 to meet in conclave.

皇太后固丨上 the empress dowager earnestly expostulated with her son.

艞 yao˒ t'iao˒ Large scow-like boats on the Yangtsz' River, the 對丨 which are used for freighting.

Read t'iao˒. The 丨板 is a board used to pass from a boat to the shore.

鞠 yao˒ From *leather* and *tender;* used with the next.

The upper part or leg of a boot.

靴丨子 the leg or body of a boot.

曲丨 curved, bent over.

袎 yao˒ The upper leather or vamp of a shoe.

襪丨子 the leg of a stocking.

詏 yao˒ Opposing, contradictory talk.

曜 yao˒ yüé˒ From *sun* and *feathered robes.*

The effulgence of the sun; the splendor of heavenly bodies.

照丨 dazzling, bright.

日丨 rays of the sun.

七丨 the sun, moon, and five planets; to which some add four more, making 十一丨 eleven rulers of the sky.

金光丨眼 the brilliant brightness dazzles the eyes; said of much gilding.

顯丨于人間 his fame is illustrious among men.

耀 燿 yao˒ yüé˒ From *bright* or *fire* and *feathered;* similar to the last.

To illumine, to shine on; lustrous, glorious, shining, bright.

光丨 magnificent.

榮丨 luster; glory.

熠丨宵行 the beautiful sparkle of the fire-flies.

福丨 the happy star's brightness.

鷂 yao˒ A general name for harriers (*Circus*), and for a small gray kestrel trained for hawking; a paper kite.

老丨鷹 a falcon common at Peking. (*Milvus melanotus.*)

海丨魚 a sting-ray, because it is supposed to be transformed from the fish-hawk.

丨子 the hawking kestrel; applied also to the sparrow-hawk.

鷹鼻丨眼不可交 don't trust a man who has a hawk's nose and a kite's eyes.

放丨子 to fly paper kites.

Read ˏyao. A gay francolin with a crest, the 丨雉 resembling the medallion pheasant in its markings.

𩍘 yao˒ A very rough way, making it hard to get along.

丨𩍑 uneasy; irksome; applied chiefly to the walking.

撽 yao˒ Another form of 拗 obstinate, perverse.

In *Cantonese.* To scratch; to collect, to scrape together, to pick up things.

多少都丨反的 get together as much (or many) as you can.

隔壁丨癢 [as well] scratch one through a wall; — a useless attempt.

趭 yao˒ Also read tsiao˒

To flee; to bolt and run.

神騰鬼丨 [the torrent made noise enough to make] the gods and sprites all run away.

YÉ.

Old sounds, ya, yap, yat, *and* yak. *In Canton,* yé *and* ya; — *in Swatow,* é, ya, *and* mé; — *in Amoy,* ya *and* gia; — *in Fuhchau,* yè; — *in Shanghai,* ya *and* yé; — *in Chifu,* yié.

耶 ˏyé From *ear* and *city;* the ancient form was 邪 now meaning heretical.

An interrogative particle, usually in regimen with 豈, and implying a doubt; it is placed at the end of a sentence; an appellation of a father.

是丨非丨 is it so or not? is it true?

丨穌 Jesus, a name of early date, meaning the Lord of the Resurrection.

此豈近於人情丨 how does this accord with human feelings?

何丨 what does it mean?
果不樂丨 am I not much pleased?
然則所謂心者爲一丨爲二丨 is then that which we call mind, simple or complex?
其信然丨 can this be believed?
丨婆提 an old Budhist name for Java (*Yawa dwipa*), described by Fah-hien.

爺 ꜀yé From *father* and *sire*, the 父 having been added to the last in order to limit it to this sense.

A father, a sire; a title used in addressing divinities, officers, noblemen, princes, and gentlemen.
丨媽 my grandparents.
丨孃 my parents.
公丨 your Grace,—to a duke; a title of the municipal god; in *Cantonese*, a grandfather.
丨丨 my grandfather; and 丨丨兒 my husband. (*Pekingese.*)
師丨 a scholar; a private secretary.
丨們 an officer's servants; clerks or attachés in a yamun.
太丨 your worship, when speaking to the *chihien* or district magistrate.
大老丨 your honor, the prefect.
二丨 a servant, an official hanger-on, an attendant; as 三丨 is his servant.
天老丨 the highest god, whoever he may be, the Ruler of the sky.
父子丨兒們 belongs to my father's own family.

椰 梛 ꜀yé A cocoa-nut is 丨子; and a poetical name is 越王頭 from a legend that it was transformed from the head of a king of Annam, whose eyes can still be seen on it.
丨肉 cocoa-nut pulp.
丨殼 cocoa-nut shells.
丨花酒 toddy or arrack.
丨菜 a savoy cabbage.
丨衣簑 a coir rain-cloak.
丨子瓢 a cocoa-nut dipper.

鎁 釾 ꜀yé From *metal* and *lord*.
A celebrated two-edged claymore, called 鏌丨 from its maker's wife, who lived in Wu about B. C. 300.

琊 ꜀yé A place, 琅丨 an ancient district, now Tsing-cheu fu in the eastern part of Shantung, and still often applied to the whole promontory.

挪 揶 ꜀yé To gesticulate; to play antics.
丨揄 to mimic, to make people laugh by motions.
市人皆大笑舉手丨揄之 the market-people all burst into a loud laugh, and began to make fun and caper about.

也 ꜂yé A final particle akin to an exclamation, and not usually needing to be translated, serving to limit the idea or round the period; after a noun, it often puts it in an adverbial form, as 古丨 formerly; after a proper name, it also makes the vocative; and after verbs, often merely arrests the attention; in colloquial, as an initial, it implies without doubt, even, and, also, likewise; before a negative, implies an alternative or a question; before 是 it intensifies the assertion; and with 有 denotes also, likewise.
看他行丨不行 see whether he is willing or not?
未之有丨 there never was such a thing.
丨未可定 it is also undecided, uncertain; still unsettled.
丨不說丨不寫 he neither would speak nor write.
一些丨不差 there's not the least error.
丨罷 after an assertion denotes a modified assent, "that's all."
一丨 all alike; they are the same.
大不可丨 it truly will not be permitted.

他丨無可如何 nor can he do any better.
丨曾來過 they have already come.
無異丨一丨 there is not the least difference.
丨好 very well; that will do.
丨下得去 you can get along down.
今丨每食無餘 now-a-days, there's nothing left over at each meal.
着驚丨無 are you afraid or not?

In *Cantonese*. An exclamation of surprise or pain.
嘜丨痛喇 Oh, you hurt me! it hurts!

野 埜 ꜂yé From *village* and to *give*; the second form is rather pedantic.

A waste, a moor, a neglected place outside of a city; a common, a wild; a desert, a wilderness; savage, wild; uncultivated, as plants; rustic, rude; away from court, as 在丨 in obscurity.
丨人 a rustic, a clod-hopper; a savage, a wild man.
丨生 growing spontaneously, as wild flowers.
丨性 skittish, restive; a wild disposition.
丨味 a game flavor.
丨外 savage wilds, a desert.
丨仔 a bastard. (*Cantonese.*)
撒丨 to exhibit rudeness or violence.
丨干 an animal whose description answers best to the jackal.
朴丨 uncouth, plain, rustic.
浪子丨心 a foolish, reckless fellow.

In *Cantonese*. A thing, an object; a subject or topic.
好丨 a good article.
叫做乜丨 what is this called? what does [he] wish [me] to do?

In *Shanghai*. A form of the superlative.
大來丨箇 very large, immense.

冶 ˓yé From *ice* and *I*; explained as including in its meaning both liquefying and congealing, and is therefore placed under the radical *ice;* it is very like ˓*chi* 治 to rule.

To fuse metals, to smelt; a founder; a furnace; bedizened, a false glitter; enticing.
銷 丨 to melt metals, especially iron or copper.
丨 匠 a smelter, a founder.
妖 丨 mincing, bewitching, as a courtesan.
丨 容誨淫 meretricious arts incite to lust.
艷 丨 an elegant, enticing manner.
丨 城 an old name of Nanking, and of a place near Fuhchau.

夜ˀ yéˀ From 夕 *evening* and 亦 *also* abridged; others derive it from *evening* and a line to show the *horizon* above it.

Night, darkness; after daylight.
今 丨 this night.
昨 丨 last night.
終 丨 or 成 丨 the whole night.
丨 臺 the dark terrace, *i. e.* the grave, because spirits gambol there at that hour; it is also called 長 丨 the long night.
丨 行人 or 丨 摩 a thief, a night prowler.
丨 不收 night never stops him, as a courier.
丨 深 late at night.
入 丨 by night, as when belated or at work.
丨 以繼日 the night runs on into the day; *i. e.* the night is not used for sleep.
坐 丨 to sit up at night.
下 丨 or 查 丨 to patrol at night.
半 丨 midnight.
星 丨 而來 came in by night.
不能隔 丨 it will not keep over night.
丨 义 in Sanscrit *yaksha,* demons who are said to shed a glare of light, which makes them shine like 流星 shooting stars when they go swiftly; the usual notion of them is that they are messengers of Yama in hell, but specially of the Dragon King, his guard which patrols the sea; they have red hair, green faces, bare legs, and carry a tripod on their shoulders.

In *Cantonese.* Late at night.
好 丨 very late.
行 丨 abroad late at night.

㖡ˀ yéˀ From *mouth* and *night.*

The cry of birds at night, especially of herons and gulls.
丨 鳴 a night-bird's song.
水鳥夜 丨 the water birds cry at night.

YEH.

Old sounds, yet, nget, yep, *and* ngep. *In Canton,* íp, ít, ngít, ím, *and* ngăt; — *in Swatow,* hié, ngiak, ngièt, ngièp, *and* hat; — *in Amoy,* yet, giet, yap, giap, *and* íp; — *in Fuhchau,* ngiek, yek, hiòk, ngak, *and* ié; — *in Shanghai,* ih, níh, yih, *and* yiⁿ; — *in Chifu,* yié.

謁ˀ yéˀ From to *speak* and *why.*

To visit a superior or a gentleman; to have an audience; to signify to, to intimate; to declare or state; a guest; a card.
請 丨 to request an interview.
丨 見 to visit an official superior.
丨 貴 to see great personages.
丨 舍 a guest-house, such as are used by officials; a choultry; a visitor's room.
報 丨 to announce a guest.
能典 丨 矣 you can then entertain my guests; said to a young son.
拜 丨 to visit a friend.

暍ˀ yéˀ From *sun* and *why.*

Injured by the sun; a sunstroke.
丨 死 died by heat apoplexy.
丨 暑 injured by the heat.

噎ˀ ˓yé From *mouth* and *one;* occurs interchanged with *yin*ˀ 咽 in this sense.

A stoppage in the throat; a sobbing; a hiccough; a choking which hinders swallowing.
丨 喉 the throat obstructed.
丨 塞 unable to swallow.
中心如 丨 inconsolable from grief, as if the heart was in the throat.
打息 丨 to hiccough. (*Cantonese.*)
流水鳴聲幽 丨 the gentle ripple and purling of water.
食不下 丨 if I eat I cannot swallow for grief.
乾 丨 to swallow dry flour.

臲ˀ niehˀ Unsteady, not well based.
丨 卼 unsettled, movable; uneasy, anxious; restless, as one on a giddy height.

齧ˀ 囓ˀ niehˀ From *teeth* and to *cut into.*

To gnaw, to craunch; to seize with the teeth.
丨 牙 to grit the teeth.
毋 丨 骨 don't gnaw your bones — at table.
丨 嗑 to eat; to bite a thing.
丨 桑 a grub that eats mulberries.

臬ˀ niehˀ From 自 *self,* which is regarded by some as a contraction of 劓 to cut off the *nose,* and 木 *wood;* first used for the next.

A target, a mark; a rule, a precedent; a post which anciently served for the gnomon of a dial; a threshold; to hit the target.
丨 司 or 丨 臺 the magistrate who administers the law, known as the provincial judge, he whose doors should be shut when he decides cases.

丨法 a law, a statute.
丨限 an impediment.
爾罔不克丨 you must carefully regard the laws.

闑, *nieh'* The threshold, which is often so high as to obstruct the entrance; a small door cut in the large gateway for convenience; a side door; a post in a gateway; an impediment.
門丨 a threshold.
丨西 the west postern gate.
拂丨 to brush the threshold; — *met.* to do menial services.
丨以內寡人制之 I (the emperor) will manage my domestic affairs myself.

枼, *yeh'* From *wood* and *age*, but this last is altered from 卉 thirty.
A flat piece of wood, a slip, a leaf, a slat, a cleat.

葉, *yeh'* From *plants* and a *thin slip.*
The leaves of plants; a thin plate of gold or metal; a leaf of a book, for which 頁 is now used; a lobe of the lung or liver; a clamp, a hinge; posterity, ages; an age; to collect, to assemble.
駕一丨之扁舟 he embarked on a flat punt.
明中丨 during the Ming dynasty.
荷丨 the lily leaf; — a door hinge.
後丨 or 奕丨 posterity.
開枝散丨 to have numerous posterity.
木丨盡脫 the leaves are gone from the trees.
丨落歸根 the falling leaves seek their root; — a man desires to be buried with his fathers.
秋丨 a jade ear-ring like a leaf.

楪, *yeh'* Interchanged with the last two.
A window, a sky-light; used sometimes in 丨榆 an old name of Ta-li fu in Yunnan.
Read *tieh,* A bed mat.
Read *sieh,* A small door-post.

鍱, *yeh'* A thin plate of iron, such as are used in the scales of armor.
Read *hieh,* The plate of metal on the shaft of an arrow; a ring.

偞, 僷, *yeh'* From *man* and *leaf; q.d.* a man volatile as a leaf.
A gay, jolly, light-hearted manner; a handsome face.
衣攝丨 the dress rumpled and creased.
微風蕩兮烟丨丨 the gentle breeze whisks the smoke to and fro.

䭟, *yeh'* A color that has lost its luster; faded; a brindled or striped black.
紅色不丨 the red color is not stained.
敗丨 faded, blanched.

嶭, *yeh'* Elevated; lofty.
旗亭之巋丨 the high pavilion which bears the flags.

孼, 孽, *nieh'* From 子 *son* and 薛 *sin* altered; the second form is most common, but not quite correct.
A son of a concubine; the child of an illicit connection; the consequences of sin, retribution for crime; sorrow, evils; neat.
罪丨 the result or evils of sin.
下民多丨匪降自天 the ills of the common people do not come from Heaven.
丨賬 a retribution for undutiful acts by the evil conduct of one's own children.
自作丨 the recompense brought on by one's sins.
丨子 a concubine's son.
庶姜丨丨 finely adorned were her sister ladies.
蘊利生丨 hoarded wealth produces trouble.

槷, *yeh'* A stick of timber; to plant a post in the ground; a post to fasten two doors together.
危丨 the felloe of a wheel.

櫱, 欁, *nieh'* First composed of 木 *wood* and 獻 *to offer,* now changed to either of these two forms, and also contracted to 不.
The stock or stump of a tree; the bole remaining in the ground after the tree is cut down.
萌丨 suckers, sprouts, shoots.
生丨 the shoots from a root.
丨木 the *Pterocarpus flavus,* a large leguminous tree whose bark furnishes a yellow dye.

糱, 蘖, *nieh* From *rice* or *wheat* and *sprout.*
Grain which has sprouted; leaven or barm used in making spirits.
猶酒之有丨 [politeness is as necessary among men] as yeast in making spirits.

擫, *yeh'* From *hand* and *to restrain.*
To stow away, to put aside; to press down with the hand, to hold firmly with the finger.
丨在懷中 to put into the bosom.
丨起了找不着 it is put away so that you cannot find it.
藏藏丨丨 to stealthily put out of sight.

靨, *yeh'* A dimpled cheek; a pretty plump cheek.
丨輔奇牙宜笑嗎只 one who has a handsome face and fine teeth can afford to smile.
Read *'yen.* A spot or pimple on the face; a mole or black mark; a freckle.
痘丨 a pock-mark.

饁, *yeh'* From *to eat* and a *box.*
To carry food to field laborers; provisions for workmen; to supply with food.
田丨 provisions for the fields.
丨彼南畝 she took food to [the laborers in] the south fields.
丨獸 to offer game — to the spirits of the wilderness.
有饋丨 the stores for the field hands.

曄, *yeh'* The brilliancy of a flash.
丨丨 abundant.
丨丨震電 the brilliant flash and rolling peal.
光丨 dazzling brightness, as of the sun.

業, *yeh'* Originally intended to represent the well mortised *frame of boards* and *beams* that uphold a bell.

That which a person ought to do, his employment; a calling, an occupation; pursuit, office, profession, art, or trade; an estate, a patrimony, that which has been acquired by a calling; merit, or a title to reward for what has been done; to transmit a calling or post; deserving, meritorious; in peril and anxiety; a sign of the past tense, done, a finished toothed board on a bell-stand.
事丨 an occupation; affairs.
基丨 a foundation; what was done before, the original work.
丨已 or 丨經 already done, past.
功丨 eligible for reward.
丨精于勤 diligent in business.
四牡丨丨 the four steeds are very strong.
藝丨 a handicraft; an art.
臺駘丨能其官 T'ai T'ai can hand down his office to his son.
圖大丨有何不可 do you think that I shall ever get to be emperor?
本丨 the family or original calling.
家丨 family estate, patrimony.
丨歸原主 the property reverted to its real owner.
建丨 a name for Nanking, A.D. 250.

鄴, *yeh'* An unimportant principality in the state of Wéi, which lay in Lin-chang hien 臨漳縣 in the north of Honan.
丨架 a complimentary term for a library, referring to Li Pi 李泌 the learned prince of Yeh.

⿰魚邑, 腌, *yeh'* The first is the name of a fish; to salt down fish; to salt flesh.
丨酸 pickled in brine.
丨魚 salted fish.

YEN.

Old sounds, yìn, ngin, ngim, ngien, an, am, yam, *and* ngam. *In Canton*, ín, ím, ün, ngam, *and* ngan; — *in Swatow*, yam, ín, yien, ngan, ngam, *and* am; — *in Amoy*, yen, yam, giam, gan, am, an, *and* hien; — *in Fuhchau*, yeng, yòng, ngiòng, ngang, ngieng, *and* sièng; — *in Shanghai*, í^{n}, ní^{n}, yí^{n}, ngè^{n}, é^{n}, *and* yè^{n}; — *in Chifu*, yen.

烟, 煙, 菸, *yen* From *fire* and *cause*; the third is used, because of similarity of sound with the others, only to denote tobacco; it is also read *yü*, sick; faded; rotting, as leaves or compost.

Smoke; misty vapor; modern names for tobacco and opium, because they are smoked; india ink.
生丨 or 水丨 smoking tobacco.
頂丨 the best kind of ink.
明丨 excellent tobacco.
呂宋丨 or 孖姑丨 cigars; cigarettes, cheroots.
丨筒 a pipe; a stove-pipe; a chimney.
丨火 smoke; *met.* daily expenses.
丨葉 tobacco in the leaf.
放丨火 or 燒丨火 to let off fireworks.
抽丨 or 食丨 or 吸丨 to smoke; to take a pipe.
丨塵 dust or motes in the air; *met.* banditti.
暮丨 sunset, evening drawing on.
冒丨 the chimney smokes.
聞丨 to take snuff.
人丨稠密 a place very thickly settled.
丨花浪子 a brothel-goer.
熟丨 prepared opium.
丨頭 a volume of smoke; also, twist tobacco.
丨霧 or 濕丨 exhalations, fog, mist.
香丨 perfume from pastilles.
得意在丨波 to delight in going to sea.
烏丨 opium; also lamp-black.
丨槍 an opium pipe.

咽, 嚥, *yen* From *flesh* and *cause*; the second form is seldom used.

The throat; a cosmetic like rouge.
點丨脂 to rouge; to use vermilion cosmetic.
丨喉 the throat; *met.* a gorge, an important pass or place.
丨脂花 the *Mirabilis dichotoma* or four-o'-clock, from the seeds of which the Japanese manufacture a soft, pure white powder.

渰, *yen* From *water* and to *hide*.

Clouds rising and spreading.
有丨淒淒 the clouds will distill their showers, — and all nature spring forth.

焉, *yen* The character originally delineated a yellow spotted bird found in central China, the golden pheasant?

A final affirmative particle; after an adjective this word often forms the comparative, as 大丨 greater than; used in regimen with 如, as 如天丨 as it is in heaven; after adjectives makes them *adverbs*, as 正丨 really, truly; 少丨 presently; an elegant euphonic particle adding emphasis to the previous word; thereupon, after that.

游丨息丨 take a turn and rest a little, as from study.

道不傳丨 the truth is really not taught.

設此有人丨 supposing there was a man.

已丨哉 it is already settled.

Read ˏyen. An initial *interrogative*, how, who is, why, according to the scope, and conveying some doubtfulness; also a final *adverb*, denoting that the sense is complete, and affirming the fact; in some cases, it has the sense of is, being; as 安定國家必大丨先 to solidly pacify a state, its high position must first be secured.

丨知 how should I know?

丨用殺他 why kill him?

忻忻丨 with great joy.

丨得富貴 how can I be rich and honorable?

丨能 how can it be? unable.

丨其從之 how can he (*i. e.* should he) follow him?

丨逢 (properly written 閼逢) the first year of the cycle; sometimes used for the first year of creation.

[illegible]丨而逝 hereupon he disappeared.

人丨廋哉 how can the man get off, or out of the way so?

嫣 ˏyen Sometimes read ˏhien.

The winning smile of a beautiful woman; tall and handsome, gracious; to connect.

丨紅 a deep red; crimson.

丨然一笑傾國傾城 the smile of beauty has destroyed states and cities.

蔫 ˏyen Plants drooping; decayed vegetables; not fresh, corrupt, changed, stinking; faded, old.

色丨 the color is faded.

丨臭 stinking, as decayed flesh.

丨舊 old, worn out; shop-worn, second-hand.

丨丨味 a noisome odor.

閹 **剦** ˏyen From *door* or *knife* and *to conceal*; the second, unauthorized form is used as the verb.

Doorkeepers in the harem; persons who stand as guard; eunuchs; to geld.

丨猪 to castrate a pig.

內丨 or 丨人 palace eunuchs.

天丨 eunuchs from birth.

淹 ˏyen From *water* and *to conceal*.

To soak, to saturate; to spoil by soaking; to overflow; to detain, to tarry away long, to stay away; margin of a stream.

丨久 long delayed, as a case in court.

丨留 to tarry long.

丨貫 to thoroughly understand; to permeate.

眡丨心 very drowsy.

丨斃 or 丨沒 or 丨溺 lost under the water; suffocated, drowned.

丨纏 said of one sick a good while; a long fit of illness.

丨跡 lost the trace of, no clue.

丨丨一息 he is at his last gasp.

丨滯 hindered, hampered, as by unforeseen contingencies.

醃 ˏyen To lay in salt, to salt down; to pickle.

丨漬 to cover with salt.

丨腿 smoked hams.

俺 ˏyen Pleased; full of thoughts; joyful of heart; to like.

丨憸 much thought about, and so to look pleased with.

懕 ˏyen From *heart* and *full*; used with its primitive.

To be filled; satiated, glutted; to remain long at the wine.

飲後思丨 one feels sleepy after drinking much.

孆 ˏyen Also read *yen*ˋ.

Placable, good-tempered, mild.

丨婆 handsome, beautiful, voluptuous, enticing.

Read *yeh*, Well-dressed, finely trimmed up.

顏 ˏyen From *head* and *accomplished*.

The space between the eyebrow and eye; a fine forehead; the countenance, the visage; color, hue.

容丨 the expression of the face.

丨料 paints; materials for painting, not including the oil.

丨色 the color of.

亢丨 angry, displeased.

無丨相見 I have no face to call on him.

忞丨 dislike expressed in the face; to be at enmity.

朱丨 a rosy face.

和丨悅色 a pleasing, gracious face.

不會尊丨已經數載 I have not seen you, Sir, for many years.

丨之厚矣 his face is thick; *i. e.* he has no shame.

囒 ˏyen Quarreling, wrangling.

丨丨而爭 scolding and fighting.

言 ˏyen Composed of 口 *mouth* and *lines* to express the *words* issuing; but others derive the upper part from 辛, an old form of 愆 *crime*; it is the 149th radical of characters relating to speech.

A word, a sentence; a remark; an assertion, a phrase; speech, talk; sayings, reports, rumor; an order; to discourse, to say, to address; to talk, to express an opinion; to mean, meaning; to deliberate; I myself, the speaker; to ask; a designation; a sort of flageolet; an initial euphonic particle; a term in syntax for an expression, as 大丨 hyperbole, 設丨 a hypothesis or example, 醒丨 prosopopœia, or 寓丨 allegory.

花丨 exaggeration, brag, talking big.

丨語 words, talk.

失丨 a slip of the tongue, an error, a mis-statement.

人丨 arsenic, so called from its making an anagram of the first character in 信石.

豫丨 a prediction, a prophecy.

丨官 a term for 御史 or censors.
開丨路 to request the candid reproof and opinion of officers, by the emperor.
藥石丨 a word of exhortation and warning.
與余成丨 you must consult with me.
城垣丨丨 the city wall is high and great.
寤丨不寐 I am in bed and yet cannot sleep.
丨行 words and acts; biography.
一丨已畢之 one word is enough.
造丨 to make up a story.
口出大丨 to boast, to deceive by bragging.
丨旋丨歸 I am decided to go home.
納丨 an officer to transmit the emperor's words.
丨外之意 an implied meaning, an idea beyond the literal words.
丨已盡于今日 I have declared everything to-day.
大丨不慚 a liar knows no shame.
巧丨 smooth talk.
爲丨 means so; to regard the words of others.
甚丨也 an exaggerated way of speaking; blarney, bathos.

䇾 ꜀yen — From *bamboo* and *words*; it has been altered from the last.

A kind of clarinet eighteen inches long, having 23 holes.
簫聲丨丨 the shrill note of the clarinet.

閻 閆 ꜀yen — From *door* and *pitfall* or *three*; the second form is only used for the surname.

The gate in the village, or at its border; a hamlet; a lane.
食丨 to advise, to dissuade.
閭丨 the villages and hamlets; the country people.
里丨 country-places, villages.
丨浮樹 the triangular-leaf tree (*Jambu*) of the Budhists, whence 丨浮洲 denotes *Jambu-dwipa* or the universe.
丨羅王 or 丨君 or 丨摩羅社 the king of Hell, the Rhadamanthus of the Chinese Budhists, answering to the *Yama* of the Hindus; he was brought into notice in the Sung dynasty.
丨苦 an old phrase, to open a door.

嚴 ꜀yen — From 吅 to *bawl out*, and 厰 a *rock* for the phonetic.

Severe, stern, rigorous, unrelenting; rigid, the opposite of 寬; strict, as a father; *met.* a father; reserved, dour, austere; solemn, majestic, dignified, awe-inspiring, as a god or sovereign; a beat or tap of a drum; an *adverb* denoting the superlative, as 丨寒 excessively cold; close, tight, as a door; a night-watch or guard; in Budhist books, glorious.
丨拿 to strictly seize.
丨密 very secret, strictly private.
尊丨 your revered father.
先丨 my late father.
家丨 or 丨父 my father.
師丨 a severe teacher.
丨肅 or 威丨 dignified, sedate; of a staid, solemn demeanor.
丨重之 respected and esteemed him.
丨加管束 bind and detain them with increased rigor.
夜丨 the night drum.
擂鼓一丨 strike the drum once.
功課丨 to strictly finish the regular duties of an office.
有丨天子 an Emperor who is just and majestic.
丨州 an ancient region in Kwangsi now Liu-cheu fu; a department in the west of Chehkiang.
丨闔 the door fits very tightly.

巖 岩 ꜀yen — From *hill* and *strict*; the contracted form is common.

A high bank; a precipice, a rocky cliff or hill; lofty, steep; hazardous, dangerous; a terrace or ledge on hill-sides.
丨茶爲上品 the cliffs [in Fuhkien] produce the best tea.
丨谷 a gorge between hills.
不立乎丨墻之下 don't stand near a dangerous wall.
丨廊 the edge of a verandah.
乳丨 a cancerous or hard breast.

In *Cantonese* for the second form. Agreeing, exact, just, and refers to time, place, form, quantity, or other particulars.
丨丨出去 he has just gone out.
唔多丨 they don't exactly suit, spoken of persons or things.

喦 ꜀yen — Like the last and next.

Hazardous.
嶃丨 high and steep, as a beetling peak.

碞 ꜀yen — Like the preceding; both are intended to represent piled up rocks.

Hazardous, like rocks in danger of falling; critical, imminent; to fit; agreeing, exact; happily, lofty.
用顧畏于民丨 [let the king] regard and fear for the perils of the people.

⿱𥫗嚴 ꜀yen — A temporary breast-work designed to protect archers or spearmen; a fence or wattle to prevent trespassers.

延 ꜀yen — From 廴 to *stretch* and 正 *correct;* but etymologists derive it from 㢟 to *go steadily* and 丿 a *stroke;* it is to be distinguished from ꜀*t'ing* 廷 a hall.

To reach far; to extend to, to lengthen out; to protract, to prolong in time; to involve; to extend to, as distant ages; slow, dilatory; long, distant; to invite, to call together; to conduct; to arrange in order; to spread like a vine or from one to another; an interval, a crevice; occurs in proper names denoting a large area.
丨長 a long time.
丨遲 slow, dilatory.
丨擱 to neglect, to procrastinate, to dilly-dally; to lay aside.
丨緩 to lag, to be behindhand.

丨賓 to invite guests.

丨及他人 he compromised another man.

丨入內庭 to introduce him at court.

俗丨 old, long known, as a custom or fashion.

永丨帝祚 may the gods prolong His Majesty's dynasty for ever.

遷丨歲月 delayed it months and years.

毋任蔓丨以致滋事 do not let the matter drag on, lest it produce trouble by and by.

丨州 the ancient name of Yenngan fu 丨安府 in the north of Shansi.

莚 ꜀yen

Trailing and climbing as plants.

枝葉蔓丨 the branches and leaves run — over the frame.

筵 ꜀yen

From *bamboo* and *long;* it is not the same as ꜀*tʻing* 筳 a moving frame on a spinning-wheel.

A bamboo or grass mat spread out; a mat nicely prepared for a feast, used before tables and chairs were introduced; a feast, a banquet.

丨席 a meal, an entertainment.

經丨 the hall where the emperor meets academicians; the oratory where priests recite prayers.

酒丨 a dining-hall.

華丨 your sumptuous feast.

設丨 or 擺丨 to give an entertainment.

綖 ꜀yen

The strings or tassels which in ancient times held the pendent gems before and behind a crown; they covered the board which formed its top.

冕丨 the tassels of a crown.

郔 ꜀yen

A place in the state Ching north of the Yellow River near Kʻai-fung fu; also one in Tsu, near the southeast of Hupeh.

梴 ꜀ ‘chʻan

Not the same as ꜀*tʻing* 梃 a club.

A long piece of timber; in some places the pivot of a rice pestle is so called.

松桷有丨 the fir beam is very long.

蜒 ꜀yen

From *insect* and *long;* not to be confounded with *tan’* 蜑 an egg, or ꜀*tʻing* 蜓 a dragon-fly.

An insect allied to the centipede having many legs, called 蚰丨; it is a *Scutigera* or spider-millipede, which is supposed to get into the ear; two or three species are known, and it has many names; the same term is applied to the garden slug (*Limax*) in Kiangsu.

祝丨 a local name for a lizard.

埏 ꜀yen

Limits of a plat of ground; the road up to a sepulcher.

九垓八丨 the wide universe, that is the 9 corners and the 8 points; all around.

墓丨 a path to a grave.

遐丨 a far-off region.

Read ꜀*shen.* Water mixed with earth, mud; to ascend; square.

炎 ꜀yen

From 火 *fire* doubled, to represent flame rising; it is nearly synonymous with *yen’* 燄 fire.

To flame, to blaze; glorious, brilliant, what draws the eyes of men; hot, ardent.

火丨 the fire blazes up; a flame.

丨丨赫赫 growing hot; fierce and fiery, as a drought.

丨風 a hot wind; a sirocco.

丨涼世態 the inconstant world; fickle friends; hot and cold.

丨帝 the god Shinnung, because he rules the south.

天氣丨暑 the weather is very hot.

Read ꜀*tan.* To argue well.

大言丨丨 he speaks finely, with an *ore rotundo.*

妍 ꜀nien

From *woman* and *level.*

Beautiful, elegant, handsome; accomplished, versed in, skilled; in Shensi used for good.

丨美 fine, excellent, pretty.

貌丨 a fine face and figure.

鮮丨 fresh and elegant.

爭丨 to dispute which is prettiest.

研 揅 ꜀yen

From *stone* and *level;* the second form is unusual, and always used as the verb.

To grind or triturate, to rub fine, to powder; to calendar cloth; to search into carefully, to grind out; thoroughly, fully, earnestly.

丨末 to rub fine, as paints.

丨船 a narrow iron mortar, in which drugs are 丨細 triturated.

丨究 or 丨訊 to search out the truth, as officials do, and usually implies the use of torture; but 丨審 would rather imply patient inquiry; both denoting a thorough examination.

Read *yen’* An ink-stone.

耕丨田 to be a scholar, to teach.

In *Cantonese.* To draw a fiddle bow; to polish; to roll out, as dough by the rolling-pin.

丨二絃 to play on a rebeck.

丨薄 roll it thin.

沿 㳂 沿 ꜀yen

From *water* and a *pass* or *swampy* place between hills; the second, unusual form is regarded the same as 沇 ꜀*yuen;* the third is now interchanged with the others, but is in the dictionary read ‘*yen*, and defined to go; the first is also read ꜀*yuen.*

To follow a stream, to flow along a course; to sail along or go along a shore; to perpetuate, to hand down; continuous, successive; along or by, as a road or coast; to conform to others' wishes.

丨途州縣 to go over the districts; to make a thorough tour.

丨路 by or through the way.

風俗相丨 this custom has been handed down.

丨海一帶地方 the whole coast region.

丨革 successive changes, as in a government or country.

鹽 盐 ˎyen — From 鹵 *salt land* and 監 to *supervise*; the contraction is very common.

Salt; saltish, saline; it is applied to other salts than the common salt.

白 丨 white salt.

丨 田 salt vats or fields.

丨 商 official salt merchants.

丨 灘 salt pans, or manufactory.

晒 丨 to evaporate salt.

丨 運 司 the official salt commissioner, who superintends its manufacture and sale.

官 丨 salt that has paid duty, and not 私 丨 smuggled salt.

生 丨 dirty, raw salt; plumbago.

丨 罌 出 蛆 the salt-jar has produced worms; — said of reprobate sons.

魚 丨 之 利 the business of fishing and making salt.

青 丨 soda.

Read *yen'* and used for 醃. To salt.

屑 其 肉 丨 而 藏 之 cut up the flesh, salt it, and lay it by.

簷 檐 櫩 ˎyen — From *bamboo* or *wood* and *extreme*; the third form is unusual.

The eaves of a roof; the boards or beams which uphold the eaves; a star in the Milky Way.

丨 頭 beyond the eaves.

丨 口 or 房 丨 the eaves.

丨 下 under the eaves; tropically used for those in low life.

四 丨 a four-eaved house, an arbor.

飛 丨 the turned-up corners of a hipped roof; in *Peking*, the side awnings of a cart.

雕 丨 or 彩 丨 carved or ornamented eaves.

Read *tan'* when used for 擔 to carry; also read *chan* in Budhistic writings, denoting the 丨 木 or rose apple, jambu fruit (*Eugenia jambos*); and 丨 木 山 the Jambu mountain (*karavika*) which surrounds the earth.

阽 ˎyen — From *place* and *to rest;* also read *t'ien'*

A wall just ready to fall; imminent, dangerous; to fall; in danger of falling over a precipice.

丨 於 死 亡 in danger of death.

丨 危 之 聲 a horrid sound, as a squealing pig.

眼 ʿyen — From *eye* and *firm*.

The eye, whose color indicates the condition of the viscera; a small space; a hole; an opening; a square in a chess-board; a port-hole; a limit; adit of a mine.

有 丨 無 珠 not to discriminate persons, as to their merits.

丨 皮 or 丨 蓋 the eyelids.

丨 睛 or 丨 胞 the eyeball, the eye.

丨 眶 the socket.

丨 花 eyes blurred; motes in eye.

鳳 丨 a phœnix eye, the long narrow eye, peculiarly Chinese.

不 覺 丨 or 不 在 丨 裏 to overlook, not to perceive; gave no attention to it.

一 丨 針 one needle.

好 丨 力 to see at a glance; to judge of a thing accurately.

翻 篩 丨 a hoop which recoils or uncoils; to deny one's promise.

斜 丨 or 遐 丨 cross-eyed.

打 丨 作 to drill holes.

丨 發 亂 the eyes strained, as from reading in the twight.

看 不 上 丨 to look with contempt upon, to disrespect, to disesteem.

受 人 白 丨 despised, neglected.

不 懂 丨 兒 not to understand one's intentions.

丨 熱 a hot eye, *i. e.* covetous or longing; to desire greatly.

丨 中 釘 to take a prejudice against, to be angry at one.

丨 看 着 in a little while, as one is looking; presently.

丨 線 an informer, a tale-bearer.

買 丨 線 to employ a detective.

丨 界 大 the prospect is very wide and grand.

丨 口 相 引 the eyes leading the mouth; *i.e.* telling a thing vividly as one has seen it.

青 丨 to eye kindly; sympathizing.

丨 光 如 炬 sharp-sighted; an intelligent, quick eye.

總 要 帶 雙 丨 睛 you must carry your eyes with you; use your wits and see what is going on.

Read *ʿkun*. Protuberant, bulging, as a cart hub.

In *Shanghai*. A term of comparison.

高 大 一 丨 let it be higher and bigger, or better and more of it.

一 丨 勿 疑 心 not the least incredulous.

偃 ʿyen — From *man* and *to lie on*.

To cease, to desist from; to sleep, to recline; to make to lie down; to still, to hush; to throw or push over; to bend, as a wind the grass; to fall along; prostrated.

丨 息 to rest; to take a nap.

丨 蹇 undecided, as one from having his plans frustrated; irresolute; obstinate, disobedient.

丨 臥 to lie down for a rest.

丨 仆 to fall over, as by a push.

丨 武 修 文 to leave the military and follow the civil service.

能 丨 氷 it can go under the water, *i. e.* to hide itself.

匽 ʿyen — From *to conceal* and *repose;* it resembles the last.

To hide away, to secrete one's self; to repress; a wayside privy.

興 文 丨 武 to advance the literati and repress the military.

蝘 ʿyen — From *insect* and *to lie on*.

A species of livid lizard common about walls, called 丨 蜓 which changes its color; the chameleon; a cicada with a horn or crest, also called 冠 蟬 or capped cicada, which may perhaps denote a *Fulgora*.

鄢 *ʿyen* A region, now 丨城縣 in Hü chau in the east of Honan, formerly a petty principality at the junction of the Jü and Sha rivers.

褗 *ʿyen* A collar or band on the neck of a coat, called 丨領 which was embroidered in the times of the Tʻang and Sung dynasties.

鼴 *ʿyen* From *rat* and to *hide*, alluding to its habit of lying in streams.

An animal, having a white back, a rat's nose, elephant's feet, and hard hide, as large as an ox, and fond of lying in the water; it is the Malacca tapir, and bears the names of 丨鼠 and 鼠母 or 鼠王, and 隱鼠 referring to its supposed habit of burrowing and concealing itself; this term is also incorrectly applied to the mole 鼢 or 田鼠, and the two animals are confounded by the Chinese.

鰋 *ʿyen* From *fish* and to *lie on*.

A cat-fish, mudfish, or silure, which lies flat on the ground; it has a white head.

丨鯉之爲美美人之飴 the delicate taste of the carp and bull-head [are comparable to] the sweetness of a pretty woman.

鶠 *ʿyen* The female of the phœnix, same as the 凰 so called in early times because it was 偃伏鳥, the bird before which all others bowed.

丨鳳 a phœnix.

鄢 *ʿyen* A district, 丨陵縣 in Kʻai-fung fu in Honan south of the Yellow River; also anciently a place in the south of Honan near I-yang.

巘 *ʿyen* From *hill* and to *offer up*.

The top of a mountain, likened to a boiler; perhaps referring especially to hills with concave tops, which are like burnt-out volcanoes.

陟則在丨 he ascended the hill-tops.

演 *ʿyen* From *water* and to *fear*, one of the horary characters.

A stream flowing far; long, ample, extended; widely; to practice, to exercise, as a craft or art; to perform; to moisten, to permeate, to lead; occurs used for the next.

丨習 to learn, and become a proficient in; to practice.

丨武 to drill in military exercises.

丨戲 to act plays.

丨拳棒 to learn boxing and fencing.

涴丨 an eddy in the water; to whirl round and round.

衍 *ʿyen* From to *go* and *water*.

To overflow, to inundate; to enlarge, to spread out, to amplify; superfluous, abundant, much; prolix, turgid; beautiful, elegant; fertile, rich, as a level field.

繁丨 abundant; numerous, as many descendants.

游丨 to relax, to overpass; to give loose to one's passions.

沙丨 a sand-spit or bank.

丨聖公 the very Holy Duke, a title of the lineal descendant of Confucius, conferred A. D. 1055, and still held by him.

推丨聖德 to make known widely his perfect virtue.

敷丨其詞 to write a thing carelessly, without regard to style or accuracy.

丨丨清風爛 a cool breeze comes by in the heated day.

蜒 *ʿyen* A centipede, 蚰丨 another mode of writing 蚰蜒 the *Cermatia* or *Scutigera*.

谷 *ʿyen* From *mouth* and to *enter*; contracted from an old form representing a ravine down which water and mud poured, making a morass at its mouth; it is used only as a primitive, and as an old form of ˏ*yuen* 沇, a district in Shantung, and also of the next.

A marshy place at the foot of hills; mud and water debris.

兗 *ʿyen* A large prefecture, 丨州府 in the south of Shantung, which belonged to Lu, and was the scene of important historical events; but it is not included in the ancient 丨州, the smallest of Yü's nine divisions, which comprised the region lying between the rivers Péi-ho and Tsi and the Gulf of Chihli, afterwards the state of Tsi; correct, trustworthy, which is explained as having been applied to this region.

黯 *ʿyen* From *black* and *sound*.

Black; pitchy black, as the sky, which makes a background for stars.

深丨 inky dark, as the heavens.

雲山丨淡 the piled-up clouds are very dark.

丨然消魂者 his face was gloomy, as if his spirits had melted, — at the parting.

广 *ʿyen* Supposed to represent the projecting end of the plate under the eaves; others say it is like a house or the slope of the roof; it is the 53d radical of characters relating to dwellings.

A spacious covering or shelter, capable of protecting people.

琰 琰 *ʿyen* From *gem* and *flame*; it was the personal name of the Emperor Kiaking, and only the second form is now used.

A gem of great brilliancy like the topaz.

丨圭 a tablet or mace held as a warrant by the emperor's envoys, who were sent to punish refractory princes; it was nine inches long and sharp-pointed; bright, beautiful, as a gem.

扊 *ʿyen* The upright bar which shuts the door inside is 丨扅; it laps over the two leaves and fits into sockets.

掞 *ʿyen* Also read *shenʾ*

Luminous, bright; easy, quiet, smoothed out; to cover.

丨舒 at leisure and in health.

ˎ剡 ˎyen Sharp, having a sharp point; to sharpen, to point; to cut off or in two.

丨銳 sharp-pointed.

丨丨起屨 he rose up and went away.

丨丨 glorious, bright; said of the emperor's discernment.

丨木爲矢 he sharpened the stick for a dart.

丨孚州 one form of *Jambu-dwipa*, the Budhistic universe.

ˎ儼 ˎyen From *man* and *stern*.

Of a commanding presence, carrying the head high; majestic, stern, severe-looking; as before, like.

丨若 like as.

回看則封金丨然 he came back to see and there was the package of money as before (*i. e.* untouched).

丨恭 very precise and formal, particular in etiquette, like a martinet.

丨然一色 just the same color.

ˎ奄 ˎyen From 大 *great* and 申 *to extend out, i. e.* large overmuch; also read ˏyen.

To remain, to stop awhile; to cover, to hide from; a surplus, an excess; as an *adverb*, forthwith, erelong, hastily, quickly; entirely; grandly.

丨里 a town near where Confucius lived.

丨有四方 [Wăn Wang] erelong got possession of the whole land.

氣息丨丨 gasping, fainting, expiring.

ˏ丨觀 to look at a long time.

丨留 to seek a refuge; to stay long, or as it were hidden.

ˎ崦 ˎyen Some say, the shadow of a hill; a mountain in the west, called 丨嵫 fabled to contain the cave where the sun goes at night; perhaps alluding to some of the lofty peaks in Kansuh or the Koulkun range.

ˎ晻 ˎyen The sun obscured by clouds; indistinct, from something intervening and obstructing the sight; obscure, as twilight.

日丨丨而下頹 the sun is darkening and will soon be down.

丨昧 obscured, dimmed; said of the sun or moon.

丨障 to intercept the light, as a curtain.

丨丨而沒于世 [the hero who can save it] is hidden and unknown to the world.

ˎ腌 ˎyen From *piece* and *to hide*.

The boards or screen, called 丨雀 placed over the plate beneath the eaves to prevent birds from nestling there.

ˎ裺 ˎyen The selvage or border of a dress.

丨囊 in Shensi a bag or bucket for horses to drink from; a very wide and large dress.

ˎ埯 ˎyen To cover a thing with earth.

丨埋 to bury.

土丨墳山 to pile or heap up earth over a grave.

水來土丨 bank up earth and stop the water.

丨藏 to conceal by burying; said of money or bodies.

ˎ掩 ˎ揜 ˎyen From *hand* and *to cover;* the second form is the least used.

To gather in order to cover; to screen, to shade from view, especially with the hand; to close; to hide from observation; to soothe; to stroke; to catch at a disadvantage; to surprise and cover, as a net does birds.

丨袂 to screen the face with the sleeves.

丨面 to hide the face.

丨鼻 to hold the nose.

丨飾 or 丨惡 to act hypocritically; to conceal one's bad deeds.

半丨 half concealed or shut; amphibology, meaning half said.

丨門 to shut or close the door.

丨蔽 or 遮丨 to hide from view, to shade.

丨不住 it won't remain closed, as a door.

瑕不丨瑜瑜不丨瑕 the flaw cannot hide the gem, nor the gem cover up its defects; — each one must stand on his own merits.

ˎ弇 ˎyen From 廾 *to raise the hands* and 合 *to join;* it resembles the last in its meanings.

To cover over; to hide, as a star at an occultation; a narrow path; to intervene and shade; bell-shaped, or like a vase with a large belly and small mouth.

丨中 in a narrow path, as an alley or a pass in the mountains.

丨蓋 to put a cover over.

蔽雲丨日 the clouds obscure the sun.

ˎ魘 ˎyen From *demon* and *to hate*.

Disturbed in sleep by horrid dreams, and to cry out in distress; to have the nightmare.

丨着 oppressed by nightmare.

夢丨 or 睡丨 in a nightmare.

丨魔 the nightmare demon.

發丨 infatuated, bewitched, as by a vile beauty.

ˎ厴 ˎyen From *a scale* and *to dislike*.

The operculum of a snail, whelk, winkle, or other spiral univalve, also called 螺丨錢 or snail's cash.

蟹丨 the sternum or thorax of a crab.

ˎ檿 ˎyen From *tree* and *to dislike*.

The wild mulberry, (*Morus sylvestris,*) whose wood is veined, and used for making bows and hubs.

丨絲 wild silk from this tree, good for guitar strings, cords, and traces.

其丨其柘 there was the wild and cultivated mulberry.

‘厴 ‘yen Armor for the breast like a cuirass or breast-plate.

‘⿰礻厭 ‘yen To pray for happiness; to implore the gods.
丨 禳 to ask for blessings.

‘⿱厭皮 ‘yen The scar of a wound or sore.

‘黶 ‘yen Black pimples or scars on the face or body.
丨 斑 dark spots; a nævus.
丨 痕 a dark scar.

厭’ yen’ From a *precipice* and *sufficient*; this character is used to illustrate the four tones; it has the meanings of several of its compounds.

Sufficient, filled; satiated; distasteful, disagreeable; to dislike, to reject; to loathe, to sicken at; wearied with; quietly, steady.
百 丨 hated or avoided by all.
討人 丨 to get people's dislike; to bore others.
不知 丨 足 he is never satisfied.
丨 惡’ or 憎 丨 to hate, to avoid a person.
丨 煩 to dislike being troubled.
可 丨 loathsome, disagreeable.

Read ꜀yen. Satisfied, gratified.
貪得無 丨 the avaricious can never be satisfied.
丨 丨 夜飲不醉無歸 let us have a quiet, jolly time to-night, and not go home till we get drunk.

Read ‘yen and used for 掩. To cover, to shade; to retreat from bustle; a nightmare, a bad dream.
丨 目 to shade the eyes.
見君子而后 丨 然 [when the fool] sees the princely man, he skulks away for shame.

Read *yeh*, Constrained, narrow; to bring under subjection, to restrict; obedient; to unite as one, united; to injure; to beckon in, as at a door-way.
丨 然 submissive looking.
丨 衆 to keep down the people.
丨 絕 to destroy entirely.
於是因東游以 丨 之 he thereupon for this reason went eastward to oppose them.

Read *yah*, and used for 壓. To press.
鎮 丨 to subdue, as rebels.
丨 伏 to bring again under control.

Read *yih*, Wet, damp.

饜’ yen’ From to *eat* and *enough* for the phonetic; like the last.

Eaten to repletion; satiated, even to loathing; to satisfy desires.
丨 飽 or 丨 飫 having eaten to the full; satiated.
無 丨 unsatisfied, covetous.
不奪不 丨 if he does not grab all he is never satisfied.
丨 口 or 丨 腹 a bellyful.
終日營營以求有 丨 于一身 I am busy as I can be all the day, and can yet get hardly enough for my own living.

鴳’ 鷃’ yen’ These two forms are by most books regarded as the same, but their descriptions differ.

A small bird like the quail, that breeds on the ground and never settles on trees; it is speckled brown and has a crest; crows in the time of wheat harvest.
以效 丨 之不木處安 to imitate the quail which never rests on trees and yet is quiet.

鴈’ 雁’ yen’ From *bird* and *man* and a *cliff*; the second form is also used as a contraction of ꜀*ying* 鷹 a hawk.

A wild goose, white and smaller than the common brown goose; its annual flight determines seasons; it was anciently offered to the emperor; in a series, in order, alluding to its mode of flight; a marriage ceremony, from the usage of carrying a pair at weddings.
水 丨 or 丨 鵝 a wild goose.
丨 行 to go a little behind another, as brothers should; *met.* brethren.
奠 丨 to pour out a libation to the goose, intimating that the new couple should cordially agree.
丨 來 the geese have come; — a term for the 9th moon.
丨 來紅 the *Plumbago zeylanica*, because it blooms in that moon.
嫁 丨 a married pair.
鴻 丨 來賓 the large and small wild goose treat each other according to politeness.
丨 帛 a family letter.
天 丨 a poetical term for a comet.
家 丨 the household wild goose, a name for the common goose.

贗’ 贋’ 偐’ yen’ From *precious* and a *goose* or *man* and *elegant*; the third form is rarely used, and the second is not altogether correct, though most in use.

False, counterfeit, as goods; spurious, adulterated; deceitful; harsh and selfish.
丨 僞 cheating, false.
眞 丨 true and false.
圖外 丨 忻失內眞愉 when a man puts on a joyful exterior, he loses the verity of his inward peace.
作 丨 to act the hypocrite; to counterfeit goods.

⿰火閹’ ⿰火奄’ yié’ öh’ From *fire* and to *geld*; the second is read *ngoh*, and the first seems to have been changed from it in order to conform the primitive to the colloquial sound of *yen*, *im*, or *aing* in the southern dialects.

A dull fire; one half extinguished; to bank a fire; to smother a fire, — for which the second form is most proper.

晏’ yen’ From *sun* and *quiet*; also read *ngan*’

A serene clear sky; towards evening, afternoon; tardy, late, behindhand; quiet, peaceful, gentle; new, rich, as a fur robe.
何 丨 也 why are you so late?

早丨 morning, evening; early, late.
丨丨 peaceful, quiet times, prosperous days; harmoniously.
海丨 peaceful seas, no pirates or storms.

In *Cantonese*. A lunch.
食丨 to eat tiffin.
放丨學 to take a recess in school.
丨晝 noon-time.

燕ˋ *yen*ˋ The four points represent the *tail*, the sides the *wings*, and with the *mouth* and *head*, furnish a faint likeness to the *swallow*.

The house swallow, or the martin, including all kinds of these birds; in *Canton*, a shuttlecock; used for the last, a feast; to give a feast; to please; pleased; to soothe; to rest, as when retired from official life; leisurely, easy, peaceful; alone; to disgrace, to bring reproach on.
丨子 a swallow.
石丨 or 土丨 cliff or bank martin.
丨雀 a Peking species of gray finch.
丨剪 a swallow's tail.
夜丨 a bat.
丨丨于飛 swallows flitting about.
或丨丨居息 some enjoy their peaceful rest.
踢丨 to kick the shuttlecock.
丨語呢喃 the swallows twitter and chirp.
丨居 to live at ease and leisure.
用丨 for pleasure's sake.
飲丨 to give a feast.
丨天子 to entertain the emperor at a banquet, as a feudal prince.
丨器 the paraphernalia of a bride.

Read ˏ*yen*. A principality established by Wǎn Wang, which continued from B. C. 1122 to 265, but only six rulers are mentioned from 333 to 278; its capital was at or near the present Peking, still called 丨都 or 丨京, but its territory often extended north and east to the Desert and Songari River.
丨州 an old district in the south of Kwangsi.

咽ˋ **嚥**ˋ *yen*ˋ From *mouth* and *because* or a *swallow;* they are not quite synonymous, and the latter is rarely met; the first is also used with *yeh*ˎ 噎 to hiccough.

To swallow down, to gulp.
丨不下去 I can't swallow.
丨水 to drink.
丨一大口 to gulp a huge swallow.
丨氣 to give up the ghost.
三丨 [for a starving man to take] three bites — of a plum, denotes a temperate man.

Read ˏ*yen*. The throat or larynx; the gullet; a narrow and important pass.
丨喉地方 a straight, throat-like passage, as the Nan-kʻau 南口 pass near Peking.

Read ˏ*yin*. A sound imitating the roll of drums.
淵淵丨丨 [like the] distant réveille.

宴ˋ **讌**ˋ *yen*ˋ From a *shelter* and *rest;* the second form is nearly synonymous with 燕ˋ but is not much used.

A feast, a banquet, such as is given to graduates; rest, repose; merriment.
丨坐 to sit and converse.
賜丨 to confer a banquet, as on a high officer.
丨樂嘉賓 to get merry at a feast of friends.
丨會 to invite guests.
丨賀 a congratulatory feast.
春丨 to give a spring-tide feast.
賜瓊林丨 an imperial banquet given to the *tsinsz*ˋ graduates.
鹿鳴丨 and 鷹揚丨 the feasts given to the civil and military *küjin* graduates by the provincial authorities.
何能如是之丨丨 what makes you look so happy?

堰ˋ *yen*ˋ From *earth* and *to hide*.

A bank of earth which prevents an overflow; a moat, a dike.
築丨 to build dikes.
柳丨 a bank lined with willows.
隄丨 a bund, a levee, a dike.

彥ˋ *yen*ˋ From 彣 *mixed colors* and 厂 a *covert*.

An elegant and handsome person, a fine figure; excellent, accomplished.
俊丨 a personable and clever man.
美丨 or 丨士 a fine, portly looking man.
碩丨 a distinguished scholar.
邦之丨兮 he is the finest one, *i. e.* the very Bayard of the state.

諺ˋ *yen*ˋ From *words* and *elegant*.

A proverb, a common saying; traditionary or legendary talk; village stories.
俗丨 a vulgar saying.
俚丨 the sayings of low people.
故丨有之曰 as the old proverb hath it.

Read *ngan*ˋ and used for the next. A blunt and menacing talk, boastful; brusque in manner.
叛丨 disrespectful.

喭ˋ **唁**ˋ *yen*ˋ The first of these when read *ngan*ˋ is like the preceding, but otherwise it is most frequently used with the second.

To moan with one for the loss of one's country; to condole with the miserable, or those disgraced from office.
丨弔 to condole with.
丨失國者 to go and mourn with one whose country is destroyed.
不入丨我 he never came to condole with me.

硯ˋ *yen*ˋ From *stone* and *to appear*.

The smooth stone on which the Chinese rub their ink.
丨耕 to get one's living by writing, *i. e.* plowing the ink-stones.
同丨 or 丨兄 or 丨友 fellow-students; schoolmates, who use the same ink-stone.
鐵丨磨穿 he ground a hole in his ink-stone by his application.

讞 yen' From *words* and to *offer up;* it is also read *yeh*,

To decide on judicial cases, and give a sentence; to pronounce judgment; to adjudge the decision.

丨獄 to sentence.

丨典 a legal decision.

秋丨 the autumnal assize.

有信丨 an equitable decision.

成丨 a final decision.

艷 豔 豓 yen' From 豐 *abundant* and 盇 to *cover over;* the first unauthorized form is most common, but not considered to be so correct as the last two.

Beautiful, captivating, handsome; plump; voluptuous and winsome, as a fine face; bedizened, wanton, dissipated; tall, well-shaped.

美而丨 incomparably beautiful.

羣芳鬪丨 [in the spring] the flowers emulate each other's beauty.

丨粧 handsomely dressed.

光丨 gorgeous and beautiful, as an illumination.

嬌丨 bright, enticing; winsome, as a pretty face.

淫丨 wanton; seductive and lascivious.

丨色動人 beauty excites men.

丨口爲禍 a ready tongue is an evil — or brings trouble.

丨陽天 the balmy days of spring.

丨慕 to admire and desire, as great learning or wealth.

釅 yen' From *spirit* and *severe;* used with ꜀*nung* 濃 rich.

Vinegar or spirits of a strong, sharp taste.

丨茶 strong tea.

酒丨 this drink is very strong.

灩 yen' *Water* moving *beautifully*, as the boisterous, rolling sea.

瀲丨池中水 the bubbling waters fill up the pool.

燄 焰 爓 焱 yen' From *flame* and to *involve;* it is nearly synonymous with ꜀炎; the first form is preferred, and the last two are rather pedantic.

Brilliant, drawing the gaze of men; the fury of a fire.

火丨 a flame, the blaze.

青丨 a blue flame.

烈丨 a roaring high blaze.

燈光碧丨 the flames of the lamp are very bright.

接三放丨口 to say mass on the third day after death and open the door of hell to release a soul.

丨光直冲霄漢 the lurid flames shot up to the heavens.

丨丨 the leaping tongues of flame.

狂丨日長 the pestilent fire [of heresy] daily spreads.

驗 騐 yen' From *horse* and the *whole;* the second form is rather vulgar.

Name of a horse; to verify, to examine officially for purposes of verification; to prove by inspection; to examine into, as the cause of a death; proof, evidence; a testimony or examination which proves a thing.

丨屍 to hold an inquest.

相丨 to hold an official inquest or examination, as of wounds received, or of a corpse.

丨貨 to inspect and pass goods.

丨放 to ascertain the personal efficiency of officers before sending them to their posts.

丨單 a permit.

照丨 to examine if genuine.

丨箕斗 to test a man's identity by his fingers' ends.

丨艙 to examine a vessel.

丨看 to examine an officer or candidate as to his qualifications; it is done monthly in the Board of Civil Office by special commissioners.

丨夢 the fulfillment of a dream.

效丨 a satisfactory proof of; an examination approved by a superior.

應丨了 the proofs are complete; it was verified.

丨明斤兩 look sharp after the catties and taels; a shop notice.

考丨明白 to examine into carefully.

試丨 to try or test.

何以爲丨 what proof will suffice?

丨河 the river of verification, in Budhism, Sindhu 信度 or the River Indus, which rises in the Himalaya Mts.

噞 yen' The action of a fish's mouth when it comes to the top of the water.

魚口丨喁 the fish is gasping and panting.

傿 yen' From *man* and *settled;* it is another form of 鄢 a district.

To settle or arrange the prices of articles, as a broker.

丨綠 names of two gods or genii.

揜 擫 yen' To pare, to clip, to even off; to bale out, as grain.

丨米 or 丨斛糧米 to ladle or pour out rice.

猏 猏 yen' A hunting dog of great strength used in hunting tigers; probably allied to the Mongolian or Tibetan mastiff.

YIH.

Od sounds, yik, yit, yip, *and* ngik. *In Canton*, yik, yat, üt, *and* yăp ; — *in Swatow*, ék, ia, íp, ít, *and* at ; — *in Amoy*, ek, giet, íp, ít, *and* gek ; — *in Fuhchau*, ek, ík, yèh, *and* è ; — *in Shanghai*, yăk, niăk, yih, ih, yȯk, *and* ngéh ; — *in Chifu*, i.

益 *yi'* From *water* and *vessel* ; *q. d.* a dish filling with water ; occurs used for the next.

To pour in more ; to increase ; to advance, to promote ; to benefit ; advantageous, beneficial ; full, superabundant ; strengthening, restorative, as a tonic ; a term of comparison, more, in a higher degree ; the 42d diagram, denoting to augment.

好大丨處 it will be highly advantageous.

有損無丨 it will only be injurious, and not beneficial.

謙受丨 humility advances one's interests.

進丨 gradual progress, as in learning.

請丨 to ask again about ; to ask further, to inquire more.

丨遠而丨薄 the further [from the times of the sages] the worse — the customs.

丨多 more and more ; worse and worse.

丨州 an old name for the capital of Sz'ch'uen.

丨智 a poetical name for the *lung-yen.* (*Nephelium longan.*)

深荷教丨 I am deeply obliged for your kindness.

溢 *yi'* From *water* and to *augment* ; occurs used for the last.

A vessel full to the brim ; ready to overflow, to run over ; abundant ; to spread abroad, to diffuse ; still, as water in a vessel ; a handful ; a measure or weight.

滿丨 full and sufficient.

丨出 an overplus, good measure.

無得丨 nothing over, just enough.

丨數 what was over or more than enough.

聲音四丨 this noise (or music) was heard on all sides.

流丨 to overflow.

嗌 *yi'* From *mouth* and to *add* ; but the seal character represents the veins of the throat ; used for *yen'* 咽 the throat.

The throat, the organs of eating and speaking ; to hiccough.

終日號而丨不嗄 he cried the whole day without getting hoarse.

丨不容粒 not a grain of rice can stay in the throat.

Read *wuh*, To laugh ; the noise of laughing.

疾笑丨丨 laughed convulsively.

In *Cantonese*. To call after one ; to quarrel, to scold, to bawl ; crowded, thronged ; near to.

丨交 to wrangle about.

丨鬧 brawling, making a row ; a hubbub.

十丨九爭銀 ten to one but it is a quarrel about money.

鎰 *yi'* A piece of gold of 20 taels weight in the Cheu dynasty, but in the state 鄭 it weighed 30 ; in the 秦 dynasty, a catty of gold of 24 taels ; and in the Han dynasty, of 16 taels ; it was sometimes used to weigh rice.

萬丨 great wealth, much gold.

艗 *yi'* The open bow or prow of a junk, called 丨艏 from its being thought to resemble a monstrous sea bird, and thereby to terrify the spirits.

丨舟 a handsomely carved boat.

鷁 *yi'* From *bird* and *increasing* ; it is used for the last.

A kind of sea bird that flies high, whose figure is gaily painted on the sterns of junks, to denote their swift sailing ; the descriptions are contradictory, but its picture rudely resembles a heron.

龍舟丨首 a dragon-boat with a heron's figure-head.

鶂 *yi'* Regarded as the same, and a more correct form than the preceding.

A bird of the heron kind ; the hen is fabled to conceive by looking at the cock.

六丨退飛過宋都 six herons flew back and forth over the capital of Sung ; — a good omen.

丨鸛 the tiger bittern or chestnut heron (*Gorsachius goisaki*), found in Formosa.

鶃 *yi'* Another form of the last ; also the cackling of geese.

惡用是丨丨者爲哉 pray, what is the use of this cackling ?

鷊 *yi'* Seems to be interchanged with the last, but this is probably an error.

A species of gallinaceous bird, the medallion pheasant (*Tragopan satyrus*) or Nipal horned pheasant, called 吐綬鷄 or cock that ejects the comb.

邛有旨丨 on the height is the ribbed grass ; probably alluding to its markings which resemble the bird's.

億 *yi'* From *man* and *thought* ; *q. d.* a number beyond his thought.

A hundred thousand, or a lakh of ten myriads ; the Budhists use it for a *koti*, or ten thousand millions ; quiet, repose of mind ; to contrive ; to guess, to bet.

丨度 to calculate, to plan, as whether the means are enough.

心丨則樂 when the heart is quiet, then it is pleased.

丨兆之衆 myriads and millions of people.

不能供丨 he could not make him at ease ; not satisfy his desires.

繶 *yi*ˋ Red or yellow binding inserted around the upper leather above the sole.

憶 *yi*ˋ From *heart* and to *think*.
To recall, to bring to mind; to reflect on, to think upon.
丨起 to recall to mind.
不能復丨 I cannot recollect it.
丨着 recollected it.
追丨 to bring up to mind, as by a strong effort.
丨恨 to cherish ill-will.
相丨 a mutual remembrance.

檍 *yi*ˋ A tough kind of wood like the ash or wild cherry, suitable for making bows or arrows.
杻丨 a kind of wild plum.
取榦之道丨次于柘 in getting out rods for arrows, the ash is next in goodness to the wild mulberry.

臆 *yi*ˋ The breast, the pit of the stomach; the heart or bosom; full; used for its primitive, the thoughts, the feelings.
丨見 my opinion; I think so, — implying some conceit in it.
胸丨 the breast; the desires.
丨斷 your decided views; your prejudices.
愁懷滿丨 the mind filled with anxious feelings.
丨說 prejudices, notions.
丨撰之文 an original composition.
丨對 to get a judgment or opinion from another.
愊丨 the breast swollen a little; asthmatic.

抑 *yi*ˋ From *hand* and to *look up*; but the original primitive is 印 *seal*; *q.d.* turned by the hand.
A *conjunction*, else, or; either or better; moreover, further; to press down with the hand, to settle; to stop, to repress, to keep back or down; to rule; to keep one's self-possession, to curb; close; handsome.
丨或 or else; otherwise.
丨或無歟 or is it so that there are none?
丨鬱 grieved, desponding from being held back; irked, vexed.
丨之 repress it; keep it down.
丨亦可矣 however, this may also be.
威儀丨丨 his air is very careful and reserved.
丨遏 to abate or restrain; to press down.
求之與丨與之與 shall we seek it, or will it be better to give it to him?

亦 *yi*ˋ The original is described as formed from 大 *great* with a *line* each side to represent a man's *arms*; in which sense the character 腋 is now used.
A *copula*, and, also, moreover, too; likewise, further, involving a measure of qualification of the idea; after 不 it has no particular meaning, but rounds the period; an adversative particle, as not, or.
丨足以成 I can also do as well; I can likewise effect it.
如無丨可 either will do, to have it or not.
丨無如何 then in fact there's no help for it.
丨係 it is also that.
不丨君子乎 is he not also a good man?
丨若是 it is also just that.
丨不必問丨不敢言 don't ask, for I dare not tell.
丨既見止丨既覯止 I have seen and likewise met him.
丨運而已矣 it will do quite as well if he goes another way.

奕 *yi*ˋ From *great* and *also*; it is constantly used for the next.
Very large; great; abundant; adorned, beautiful; grand looking; unsettled; enduring, as generations or a family; following in order; to play chess.
丨葉 abundant leaves, or 丨世 many ages, *i. e.* an old family, many generations.
憂心丨丨 gloomy and of a sad heart.
四牡丨丨 the double tandem chariots came on in line.
王室丨丨 the magnificent palace of the Sovereign.
丨秋 name of a great chess player, B. C. 450; the Philidor of China.

弈 *yi*ˋ Confounded with the last.
A game where the men number 180 white and black men each, to represent days and nights; the aim of the player is to surround his opponent's man as in our game of fox and geese; to play a game, as chess; the mien or air; a tent.
博丨 to play chess.

帟 *yi*ˋ From *napkin* and *also*.
A very small tent, chiefly used, according to one, to protect a coffin from the dust.

㑊 *yi*ˋ A very slow pulse is called 解丨 in medical books.
食丨 a disease of a voracious appetite, and yet the patient grows thin; caused probably by tape-worm.

翌 *yi*ˋ From *wings* and to *stand* — as if ready for *flight*, in which sense alone it is used with the next.
Bright, as it will be on the morrow.
俟之丨日 wait for him till to-morrow.
丨朝 to-morrow morning.

翼 *yi*ˋ From *wings* and *separated*.
The wings of a bird; sails of a vessel; flanks or wings of an army; applied to side horses, houses, or rooms; to serve as wings; to assist, as a councillor; to append, as a wing; to brood over, to shelter and defend; to be reverent; leisure; cordial; vigorous, daring; well-ordered; exuberant, flourishing; next.
扶丨 to help; to give succor, as to the center corps.
小心丨丨 very careful and respectful.

羽丨 wings; helps, adherents, accomplices; aids to study, as comments, glossaries.

丨丨 leisurely, like four horses abreast; regular, as marching troops.

左丨長 a Manchu major-general.

伏丨 or 服丨 the bat, from its folding the wings during the day.

ʻ長齊毛丨 his feathers and wings are all grown, said of a lad of 16 years.

拍丨 or 撲丨 or 振丨 to clap the wings.

無丨上天嗎 can you fly to heaven without wings?

丨宿 the 27th zodiacal constellation, including the Crater.

折丨 the wing is broken; *met.* the death of a brother.

丨以爲食 placed [this tuber] as a side dish, or to fill out the table.

翊 *yi*ˋ Like the two preceding.

To assist; standing ready to fly.

輔丨 an assistant; to help.

共丨丨合所思 their notions are the same, just as two wings fly in unison.

瀷 *yi*ˋ A small branch of the 潁水 in Mih-hien in the north of Honan, one of the headwaters of the River Hwai; a boiling current caused by a rock in a stream.

睪 *yi*ˋ From 目 *eye* written transversely and 幸 *happily*, denoting the eye of an officer motioning to the lictors to seize a criminal.

To spy, to be on the lookout for offenders; to lead on.

丨丨 pleased; alive, growing; good.

Read *nieh*, To stop and see what one will do.

圛 *yi*ˋ Mists and vapors ascending in thin revolving flecks; to revolve and return upon; for which the next is now used.

驛 *yi*ˋ From *horse* and to *spy*; like the next, and often contracted to it.

A government post, a fixed station where couriers rest or exchange; a stage; a courier or express; to praise, to extol a person; uninterrupted, incessant, as passing postmen; a want of sequence, said of divination tokens.

丨亭 a wayside rest-house.

丨舍 or 丨館 a station house; the official stations.

丨傳 or 丨遞 the courier, the post.

丨馬性 fidgety, in a hurry, flighty.

丨丨其達 the blades are springing up rapidly.

丨馬星進命 born under a wandering star; — never at rest

馹 *yi*ˋ From *horse* and *day*, because postmen ride a day; interchanged with the last.

A post-horse, a fleet steed for carrying dispatches; a courier sent with letters.

丨馬 a post-horse.

郵丨 post-houses and couriers.

傳ˋ丨 to forward the courier.

繹 *yi*ˋ From *silk* and to *spy*; it occurs interchanged with the last and next.

To draw out or unravel silk, to get the clue; to unfold, as a subject in the mind; to state in order, to lay before one; to explain; uninterruptedly, unceasing; long; great; at the last extreme.

紬丨 to get at the clue, to unravel or extricate an affair.

絡丨不斷 constant and incessant, as intercourse.

各丨己志 each man stated his opinion.

丨如也 [the sound] kept on just that way; incessantly.

克由丨之 able to draw them out, as the talents of officers.

丨續 unceasing, continuous.

譯 *yi*ˋ To explain, to make clear; to interpret, and make parties understand each other; to translate from one language to another.

傳丨 to interpret.

丨官 an official interpreter.

重丨 far off regions, people who live so remote that repeated interpretings from mouth to mouth are necessary to understand them.

丨出漢文 translated it into Chinese.

懌 *yi*ˋ To like, to rejoice in; to please; happy, contented, jovial.

丨然 delighted, gleefully.

丨悅 pleased with.

不丨 sick, indisposed.

嶧 *yi*ˋ A hill in Tsʻao hien 曹縣 in Shantung; and of another, the 葛丨山 in Pei hien 邳縣 in the north of Kiangsu.

弋 *yi*ˋ The original form represents a short *stake* with a *hook* to hang things; it is the 56th radical of eight characters, and resembles ˏ*kwo* 戈 a spear; used with the next.

An arrow with a string tied to it; a perch or roost; to appropriate; to seize or take, because the bird shot with this arrow was drawn in to one; to aim at; to let fly an arrow; black.

丨取 to take or seize without order or erroneously.

丨獲 to arrest criminals.

丨彼在穴 drag him out of his den or hole.

非我小國敢丨殷命 it is not that our small state ventured to aim at the appointment of the Yin dynasty.

黓 *yi*ˋ Used for the last.

Black.

皂丨 black.

身衣ˋ丨綈 he wore a black silk.

釴 *yi*ˋ The ears or side ornaments of a tripod.

杙 yi' A post to tether animals; a pillar; in *Cantonese*, a spike or hook; a fruit from Annam like a pear.

石 丨 a stone which divides lands.

長釘 丨 a long spike or peg.

䴬 yi' Wheat from which the chaff or glume has been taken or thrashed out.

䘸 yé' From *clothes* and *night*.

The part of the dress under the arms.

丨縫 the seam on the side of the dress.

Read *chih*, A sleeve.

液 yé' From *water* and *night*.

That which shows exhaustion of the powers, *viz.*, fluid secretions, as saliva, sweat, pus, milk, sap; thick dregs; to disperse, as water thrown down.

膏 丨 rich juices, applied to dew and genial rains.

雲 丨 sweat of the clouds, *i. e.* dew.

玉 丨 the pearly secretion; *met.* spring water.

潤 丨 humid, moist.

淫 丨 continued sound, as of one humming or groaning.

太丨池 name of a pool within the palace at Peking.

腋 yé' The arm-pits, the side of the body; the part under the fore legs of animals.

丨下 under the arms.

集丨成裘 he collects the bits of fur under foxes' legs to make his robe;—he asks aid from everybody.

丨臭 fetor of the arm-pits.

掖 yé' From *hand* and *night*; but the primitive is rather the preceding contracted, which occurs interchanged with it.

To sustain one by his arms; to raise up or lead by the arm; to seize one by the arm and throw him down; the side-houses or apartments in the palace, used for retiring-rooms.

扶 丨 to uphold, to protect.

誘 丨 to lead on and encourage one, as in a good course.

左右丨門 the gates on the sides of the palace entrance.

縫 丨 sides of a long robe.

蜴 yih' The *insect* that *changes*, referring to its different hues or its celerity; a small eft or chameleon common in Hu-kwang, called 蜥 丨 and 草龍 or grass dragon; it is fed to larks.

焬, **焲** yi' Also read *sih*,

A blaze, a light; bright, brilliant; dry, dried up; rancid, not fresh, said of walnuts and chestnuts.

丨乾 dry, withered.

埸 yi' From *earth* and *to change*; very similar to ₍ch'ang 塲 an arena.

A border, a limit; a raised fence or dike between fields; to dike off fields.

田 丨 edge of a field.

疆 丨 frontiers and dikes, the bounds of states and fields.

封 丨 to confer a territory on one.

坄 yi' The door of a furnace where pottery is burned; the opening of a fire-place.

役 yi' From *to go* and a *javelin*.

Men sent to guard the frontier; to send on service; work for a feudal prince; government service; to minister to; official underlings and attendants; policemen; to set in rows, as when transplanting grain.

衙 丨 a runner about the public courts; of whom there are 頭 丨 and 捕 丨 head sergeants and constables, 門 丨 and 茶 丨 door-keepers and waiters, 牢 頭 丨 head jailers, &c.

人丨而恥爲丨 when I am a servant I perform its duties, even when disagreeable.

夫 丨 a servant, an employé, a coolie.

丨使 to employ, as a servant.

行 丨 to go to the wars.

賤 丨 or 下 丨 the lowest class of menials; scavengers, runners.

職 丨 occupation, calling.

世 丨 servants who are bought for life.

終身丨丨 to work incessantly to the end of life.

疫 yi' From *disease* and a *javelin*.

A prevalent disease, or one attended with unusual symptoms; an epidemic, a pestilence.

丨氣傳染 the pestilential vapor passed on and infected others.

逐丨鬼 to expel the demon of the contagion.

避丨丹 an amulet against the epidemic.

一, **壹**, **弌** yi' The dividing stroke between heaven and earth is represented by this beginning of numbers; it is the 1st radical of a few characters; the two other forms are used on bills for safety.

One; the first; any one of; the same, as one, alike; once, at once; a, an; a few; the whole of; honest, perfect; one and undivided; unchanging; to consider as one; to harmonize, to unite, to render uniform; after a numeral sometimes means one out of it, as 二十 丨 the twentieth; used like *item*, when giving a series of articles; before verbs often makes a participial form, as 丨去 having gone, or as soon as he had gone; when repeated, it has the force of this and that, each, one by one; as 丨 丨說出 tell the facts one by one.

丨直走 go straight on.

丨早 very early, still earlier.

不 丨 or 不丨樣 unlike.

畫 丨 make them alike; all must conform to the same rule.

丨句是丨句 a word is a word, there must be no shuffling or retracting.

專丨 devoted to, a single calling; earnest in pursuit of.

丨五丨十 complete, as a narration; honest.

丨還丨二還二 let one be one and two be two; the two things are not alike.

不丨而足 not one by any means, a great many.

德丨 sincere virtue.

丨二 one or two; we; a few.

丨聽卽答 he replied as soon as he heard.

那丨個人 which man?

丨來二來 firstly, secondly.

去看丨看 go and take a look.

丨面飲丨面想 while drinking he was pondering.

丨而再 once and again, repeatedly.

丨俟 the whole matter should wait; after a while, then.

第丨 the first of; the best.

丨之爲甚其可再乎 once is too much, why do you want it again?

丨成丨敗在天 man proposes and God disposes.

太陽丨照又風丨颺 the sun comes out and then the wind whistles.

壹, yi' From 吉 *happy* under 壺 a *vase*, both contracted; it is usually used for the complex form of the last.

To join into one; honest, pure; to close or stop up.

丨切 the whole of.

志丨則動氣 when the determination is sincere, then the powers can be moved; — an energetic will can move others.

統丨 to make all alike, to reduce to uniformity.

丨是皆以修身爲本 self-culture is the foundation of all honesty and sincerity.

妷, yi' A class of women officers in the Cheu dynasty, whose duty was to aid at the worship of the goddess of silkworms.

乙, 'yi yüeh' The original form of this character, now used as the 5th radical of a score of incongruous characters, represents a curling *sprout* or bud just coming out of the darkness and seclusion of winter.

The second of the ten stems, relating to the east and to wood; often used as a pedantic form of 一 one; bent, curved; to mark the end of a topic; to erase or check off, as erroneous characters by a catch line; a fish's bowels, from a supposed similarity in shape.

太丨 the primordial cause; the ground or reason of; a star in Draco.

未定甲丨 we have not decided yet who is best.

得虎如挾丨 he was got up like the stripes on a tiger's flanks, — the bands on the tiger being likened to this character.

丨謂甲曰 this man said to that.

鳦, yi' Once interchanged with the last.

A house martin with bluish plumage, having two or three names, all apparently given in imitation of its twitter; the granddaughter of 顓頊 B. C. 2300 is fabled to have swallowed a 丨子 and bore a son, who was the great progenitor of the monarchs of the Shang dynasty.

屹, yi' An isolated, imposing mountain.

丨崒 a grand peak; firm, imposing, like a mountain.

仡, yi' From 人 *man* and 气 *vapor* contracted.

Strong, tall, robust; martial, like the prancing of a steed; suddenly, abruptly.

丨然而入 he rushed in unexpectedly.

丨丨公羊 a stately he-goat.

舟之丨丨不安 the vessel rocked uneasily to and fro.

巍丨 lofty and imposing, like a high terrace.

崇墉丨丨 the ramparts of Ts'ung are strong and stout.

邑, 阝, yi' From 口 an *inclosure* and 卩 a *seal*, referring to the patents given to feudal princes; it is the 163d radical of a natural group of characters denoting towns, and in the contracted form is placed on the right of the primitive; occurs interchanged with the next two.

A city, a fortified place of great concourse; a capital; the fief or domain of which it is the capital, now applied chiefly to a 縣 district; the royal domain; the principality of a prince; to have one's capital; a camp; a stoppage of the breath, a shortness of breathing.

丨宰 the district magistrate.

首丨 the chief district in a prefecture.

敝丨 my district; and 盛丨 your city or town.

封丨 to confer a country on a prince; a fief, a princedom.

丨人 citizens, towns-folk.

氣於丨而不可止 he could not stop his panting and hiccough.

丨豪 a village elder or headman.

四井爲丨 four hamlets made a village — of 32 houses in the Cheu dynasty.

同丨 from the same district.

通都大丨 a great place of trade and concourse, as Canton.

母丨 the female sex (*matrigrama*), used in Budhist books.

唈, yi' A short or interrupted breathing, a catching of the breath.

嗚丨 an asthmatic or hesitating breathing.

沁丨 palpitation of the heart.

悒, yi' Disquieted, sorrowful; a feeling of being neglected.

丨丨 sad looking.

于心何所丨 what heart-grief have you?

俋, yi' Strong, robust; exerting one's strength.

丨丨乎耕而不顧 going on diligently, like the ploughman who never looks back.

浥, *yi'* Damp, as from dew; moist, soaked; to steep.
丨潤 humid, wet.
丨濕 soaked through.
厭丨行露 thick dew lay on the path.

Read *yah,* To fall into a pit or ditch; water running down, as from a hillside.

裛, *yi'* A bag or satchel to hold books; a wrapper in which to preserve them; perfumed; to wind around.
丨香 a scent-bag hung on the dress.
丨以藻綉 bind it on the embroidered dress.
丨衣 perfumed garments.

挹, *yi'* From *hand* and *city*; occurs interchanged with the next.

To bale out; to pour or lade out, to transfer or decant liquids; to take up; to retire from, to repress.
丨酌 pour out a glass or cup.
丨彼酒漿 draw off some wine for him.
捐丨 to injure and get out of, as an affair.

揖, *˛yi* From *hand* and a *whisper*.

To make a bow with the hands joined upon the breast, *à la Chinoise*; to cede, to yield politely; to give way to; a bow, a salutation; to bow in.
作丨 to make a bow by bending the knee.
長丨不拜 a low bow is not worship.
拱丨 a very formal bow, the hands raised to the eyes.
還丨 to return a bow.
三丨而進 enter the house after the third bow; an old custom.
丨讓而升 they bowed to each other as they went up.

Read *ts'ih,* Multitudinous.
螽斯羽丨丨兮 how thick the locusts are!

撎, *˛yi* A synonym of the last, and now superseded by it; also read *˛i*; and by some defined to make a bow, dropping the hands to the ground.

Read *ki'* To receive an imperial order with deep respect, and immediately obey it, as a general should.

逸, *yi'* From *to go* and a *rabbit*, it being wily in escaping; like the next two.

To get away, to get off; to let loose; to retire, as into quiet; to enjoy ease; to run to excess, to throw off restraint; ease, leisure, idleness; unambitious; kind, easy, careless about.
隱丨 in retirement, out of office.
丨囚 to release prisoners.
丨民 cultivated persons living in retirement.
安丨 retired leisure; *otium cum dignitate*.
丨勞 fresh or worn-out, as troops; confident — dispirited.
縱丨 to let loose, to give rein to.
而何能如是之丨丨 how can you lead such a reckless life?
飄丨 bright and agile; not easy to catch, sprightly.
丨志 an easy, gentle manner; modest, not desirous of fame.
丨厥丨 carried his dissipation to an extreme.

佚, *yi'* From *man* and to *lose*; it is nearly a synonym of the preceding.

Ease; idle leisure; sinful luxury; retirement; to fail in, to omit, as a duty; the people; suddenly.
淫丨 vicious indulgence.
遺丨而不怨 he willingly remained in retirement.
樂丨遊 delights in roaming.
遁丨 to escape from danger.

Read *tieh,* and used for 迭. Carefully, gently, surely; successively.
四國丨興 the four states one after another raised their troops.

泆, *yi'* From *water* and to *lose*; it is nearly synonymous with the last, and also interchanged with 溢, to overrun.

To overflow; to rise, as a flood; to be dissipated; licentious, immoral; excessive.
蕩丨 driven as the water by wind; dissipated, libidinous.
丨陽 a fabulous animal of the leopard kind; name of a god.

佾, *yi'* From *man* and *sacrificial articles*.

A band of eight dancers or mummers who performed set figures at sacrifices during the worship of ancestors.
八丨舞于庭 the eight bands are performing in the hall.
丨生 a mummer; a scholar who fails to reach the rank of *siuts'ai*, and is reserved for a new trial.

溹, *yi'* From 水 *water*, 天 *heaven*, and 井 a *well*, the primitive being explained to mean *man's mouth*.

To add to; to fill up, as saliva does the mouth; the spittle; another defines it a medicine made by the Taoists to preserve life, who say that a man dies if he secretes no saliva for seven day.

熠, *yi'* From *fire* and to *practise*; it is also read *sih,*

Brilliant, glorious; glistening, sparkling.
丨燿 a name for the fire-fly.
倉庚于飛丨燿其羽 how the orioles are flying about; see their bright wings!

匜, *yi'* An iron agricultural implement; some say an incense burner; others, a large kettle.

軼, *yi'* From *carriage* and to *lose*; it is also used for *tieh,* 迭 a succession.

A number of carriages rushing out together; to rush by another; to rush on, as in battle.
侵丨 to invade.
散丨 to scatter; to disperse.

齸, yi' The paunch or first stomach of a deer; to ruminate.
咽 〡 to chew the cud.

In *Cantonese.* To bite hard on, to craunch; to chew on, as tobacco.

虉, yi' A small grassy plant having stripes and colors on it like a ribbon; perhaps it refers to a species of *Phalaris* or canary-grass; it is used with its primitive.

圛, yi' The shrill note of a flute is 窊 〡 referring to its alternate high and low tones.
窳 〡 窴 窾 the prolonged and diminishing notes — as of a distant flute.

YIN.

Old sounds. yin, yim, *and* ngin. *In Canton,* yăn, yăm, *and* ngăn; — *in Swatow,* ín, ím, am, hùn, ùn, ngun, éng, *and* ngím; — *in Amoy,* ien, ín, ím, gím, gún, *and* ún; — *in Fuhchau,* íng, ngüng, üng, *and* éng; — *in Shanghai,* yăng, niăng, *and* iⁿ; — *in Chifu,* yin.

因 yin From an *inclosure* with *great* inside; *q. d.* that which is great when comprehended includes all.

A cause, a reason; to avail of, to take occasion from; a foundation or base; to proceed; to conform to what exists, to rely on, to continue on, to allow according to a precedent; the conduct of a person as being the cause of his reward or punishment; as a *preposition,* because, for, wherefore, why, on account of; by means of; owing to, in consequence of; often makes a participial form of the following verb, or forms the ablative absolute; an illative *particle,* then, next, and, so; in *mathematics,* to multiply by one figure; in Budhist literature, monographs or particular treatises explaining one subject.

有 〡 there is a reason.

〡 由 a cause, a reason.

〡 此 識 彼 to infer that from this, learn one from the other.

〡 乘 to multiply, as in arithmetic.

〡 小 失 大 to lose the great for the less.

未 必 無 〡 doubtless there is a reason for it.

〡 爲 because of, on that account.

何 〡 or 〡 何 why? what's the reason?

〡 時 制 宜 to do the right thing at its proper time.

〡 and 革 are legal terms, to follow precedent or to disregard it; to continue on or to reject usage.

〡 之 inferring from this, availing myself of this.

〡 何 緣 由 owing to what original reasons or circumstances?

〡 循 怠 緩 to heedlessly follow a routine without regard to the exigency.

〡 心 則 友 for his heart led him to friendly duty.

〡 果 不 昧 the consequences of these acts will be made manifest — in your retribution.

〡 思 I infer from the above; to conclude from; as an initial phrase, owing to, in consequence of, from this.

〡 緣 a cause (*nidana*), of which Budhists enumerate twelve; this fundamental dogma of their metaphysics is used to solve the riddle of life and show its inanity.

〡 陀 羅 Indra, the god of Brahmins and Budhists, and sometimes used for India, the country under his sway.

姻 婣 yin From *woman* and *because* of; explained that when the bridegroom comes at dusk for her, it is for his sake she leaves her home, and the purpose for which she was formed is then accomplished.

A bride; a girl who has been betrothed; connection, relationship, affinity on the female side.

結 成 婚 〡 to arrange the betrothal; to have a wedding.

〡 親 a wife's relatives.

〡 弟 or 〡 兄 your relative; the two expressions are used in reference to the ages of a person.

〡 緣 the fate or influence which brings lovers together.

各 有 〡 緣 莫 羨 人 every one has his lot or fate, don't therefore envy another.

氤 絪 yin From *vapor* or *silk* and *because of;* the second form is less used, and also defined hempen cloth.

A warm, genial aura.

〡 氳 the generative influences of heaven and earth, through whose stimulus all things are produced.

茵 yin The padded mats anciently laid on floors, and still used in Japan; cushions or mats, such as are on chairs or in a carriage; a commodious seat.

文 〡 a tiger's skin used for a seat.

細 草 如 〡 a cushion-like turf, thick greensward.

〡 芋 the *Skimmia japonica,* an evergreen shrub, bearing red berries.

乘 〡 to take a place of honor.

裀 鞇 yin Like the last; the second form is rare, and specially denotes those covered with leather.

A mat or mattress; the lining of a garment; a plait; the under garments next the skin.

〡 褥 a mat or mattress.

拂 〡 to sweep the mat, as before sitting down.

累 〡 而 坐 列 鼎 而 食 they lie on double mattresses, and eat from dishes laid in rows; — *met.* the rich.

麔 ˏyin A female deer; a doe, a roe.

駰 ˏyin A cream-colored mare, but having gray spots mixing the colors.

我馬維丨 my horses are all gray.

垔 堙 陻 ˏyin From *earth* and the *west*; *q. d.* the nature of water is to flow east, and earth must be used to make it flow west.

To raise an earth-work to restrain water; to close; to turn a water-course.

距丨 a mound raised before a wall to escalade it.

丨塞 to dike, to raise a dam.

鯀丨洪水 Kwun dammed up the waters of the deluge.

湮 ˏyin Also read ˏyen, and occurs interchanged with the last.

To fall into the water, to sink and be lost; to dam up; to stain; to wet thoroughly; to ooze or soak, as water through a porous dish; to spread, as a spot of water on paper; bibulous; a stain; name of a river.

丨沒 to be drowned.

丨沒不彰 he is lost among the crowd, he has never attained any eminence.

油丨了紙 the oil stained the paper.

雨丨透衣服 the rain has soaked my clothes.

丨濕 wet through.

墨丨 ink spots.

闉 ˏyin From *gate* and *dam*; it is like the two preceding.

The circular wall which incloses the gates of cities, sometimes within, and sometimes outside of the main wall; to stop; to shut off or to hem in.

丨門 the gate in this side wall.

窮困丨厄 impeded, in straits; oppressed by poverty; unlucky in everything.

丨遮各路 to stop all the roads.

諲 ˏyin To respect, to reverence.

丨恭 to esteem, to hold in great regard.

禋 ˏyin From *worship* and to *dike*.

To worship with a pure intention and clean sacrifices, such as the Emperor alone makes.

丨享 to worship and be accepted.

丨于上帝 [the emperor] worshiped Shangti.

丨祀 a pure and proper sacrifice, a sweet-smelling offering.

明丨 a pure sacrificial gift.

陰 隂 阴 侌 ˏyin The primitive itself was the old form, but is now disused; the last two forms, containing *moon*, are common contractions.

A shadow, the shady side of a hill, for which 蔭ʼ is also used; obscure, dark, somber; the shades, hades; the inferior of the dual powers in Chinese philosophy; the female or the receptive in nature; matter when quiescent; the inferior of two things contrasted, as when the moon, the earth, night, or water, are compared with the 陽 *yang* or sun, the heavens, day, or fire; underhand, secret; the back, in the rear; privately; concealed, masked; cloudy, darkly; north side of a hill; the grosser or opaque, as of matter; that of which things are made, as opposed to their anima; to cover over; obscured by clouds.

太丨 the moon.

丨符 a subtle charm against disease.

光丨 time, duration; a day, the length of a day.

丨間 or 丨曹 or 丨司 or 丨府 the abode of the dead; the house or court in the unseen; phrases that may be compared with the *beth olam*, long home or hidden house of Ecc. xii. 5.

丨手 secretly, underhand.

過丨 to visit hades, to consult the souls, to act as a necromancer.

丨涼 a shade; cool, shady.

天丨 a cloudy day; dull, dark sky.

丨禮 female propriety.

下丨 or 丨物 or 丨戶 the female organ of women or animals.

丨德 unostentatious virtue; secret, kind acts.

丨毒 to injure slyly, to secretly wrong another.

寸丨是競 to improve every moment.

丨陽生 a man who calculates the destiny of a person from the horoscope of the moment of his death; but 丨陽家 is rather a necromancer or magician.

連丨了幾天 it has been cloudy for several days.

Read ˏngan. The hut or house erected in olden time over the emperor's tomb, was called 諒丨 or the shed to meditate in.

Read ˏyung. An ice-house.

三之日納于淩丨 in the third moon they take it to the ice-houses.

Read yinʼ To benefit indirectly.

旣之丨ʻ女反予來赫 I went to do you good, but you were angry at me.

殷 ˏyin From a *spear* and to *revert* to virtue; used with the next.

An *adjective*, as a superlative, the highest degree of; full, flourishing, abundant, many; to regulate; regulated; a full band of musicians; a rolling of thunder; correct, in the middle; substantial, rich; to sustain.

丨實 substantial, having property, well off.

丨人以柏 the men of Yin planted the juniper — near their altars.

丨盛 affluent, abundant.

憂心丨丨 my grieved heart is full of sorrow.

丨當盛世 it is but proper that the times be flourishing.

閣下丨拳照拂 I am greatly indebted, Sir, for your great and continued kindness and hospitality.

丨然 to hope ardently for.

丨朝 the Yin dynasty, a name given to the last part of the Shang, from B. C. 1401 to 1137, in consequence of the monarch Pan-kăng removing his capital to Yin, a town north of the Yellow River, now Hwoh-kia hien 獲嘉縣 in Honan.

慇 ‹yin From *heart* and *full;* interchanged with the last.

Mournful, sorry; careful, particular about, anxious.

假丨懃 a pretended interest in one, a flattering kindness to.

丨心 anxious, feeling for.

丨丨懃懃 very careful of, to exhibit sincere regard for one.

音 ‹yin Formed of 言 *words* placed over 含 to *hold* in the mouth, both contracted to their present form; it is the 180th radical of a small natural group of characters.

A sound of any kind, but more especially a musical note or tone; in the Chinese way of spelling, the initial sound or letter; news; a reply; an intimation or order; occurs used for 蔭' a shade.

牙丨 a dental tone or word.

失丨 speechless.

丨韻 a rhyme, the word that makes the rhyme.

丨韻淸楚 clear and harmonious musical sounds.

口丨 pronunciation, enunciation.

八丨 the eight things (silk, bamboo, metal, stone, gourd, crockery, leather, and wood) of which musical instruments are made; *met.* music, melody.

八丨班 a band of musicians.

回丨 a reply, an echo, an answer.

正丨 the true sound, the correct or ancient pronunciation.

土丨 local pronunciation or dialect.

字丨 initial sounds.

佳丨 sweet words; your kind greetings or congratulations.

杳無丨信 no news or reply from you for a long time.

丨號 a note in music.

唱南丨 歌丨 to chant southern ditties or as ballads or vocal music are called.

餘丨 in *rhetoric*, a final reflection.

鹿死不擇丨' the deer when dying does not seek for a shade.

喑 ‹yin The incessant sobbing and wailing of infants; dumb, unable to speak from great grief or an accident.

丨啞 dumb from any cause.

丨不能言 not able to speak, as from paralysis.

瘖 ‹yin Like the last.

Dumb, whether born so or become so by disease; a disease which prevents one talking.

丨聾 deaf and dumb.

口丨 mouth crippled so that the person cannot speak.

愔 ‹yin Also read ‹ngan.

Quiet, peaceful, good-natured; still, composed; solemn, as plaintive music.

丨丨度日 to spend the day in silence, as a priest.

醅 ‹yin Drunk; the noise of drunken fellows; a coarse, sour ragout or hash made by some Miaotsz' of bones mixed with flesh, rice, lime, and fish, and stored as a condiment; to cover a vessel so closely that no smell shall escape.

丨菜 this stinking preparation.

蓄丨桶幾世矣 how many generations have you had these tubs of bone ragouts? — is asked of the better classes of the Miaotsz' to inquire of their riches.

吟 唫 ‹yin From *mouth* and *now* or *gold;* the second is not much used as a variant for the first.

To hum, to intone; to read fast, as when half singing a ballad; to sigh; to moan.

沉丨 to ponder; to hum to one's self.

笑口丨丨 smiling and humming.

丨秋 to make sonnets upon the autumn.

水底龍丨 the dragon howls under the deep.

鸞丨 the notes of a phœnix; *met.* a concert of music.

丨風弄月 to sing and play in the evening breeze.

丨詩 to hum poetry.

The second is also read ‘k‘in. To close, to shut; congealed, dormant; to speak very fast, as when humming.

陰陽丨閉 the moon and sun have shut up (or withdrawn) their influences, as in winter, when 萬物各丨 everything is torpid.

崟 崯 ‹yin From *hill* or *stone* and *metal.*

High and dangerous cliffs, running along one after the other; a ridge.

岑丨 a high, dangerous peak standing out like an *aiguille.*

崎丨 projecting cliffs.

寅 ‹yin From 宀 a *covering*, which is likened to the knee-pan that prevents the humors from ascending the body; these humors are depicted by 臼 a *mortar* as coming out of the ground, and include the stimulus of nature in the spring which the frost hinders.

The ancient punishment of cutting off the kneepan; the third of the twelve branches, which is symbolized by a tiger, and connected with wood, and denotes the hour 3 to 5 A. M.; to reverence, to respect; respectfully; a fellow-officer, a colleague; vigorous, strong.

丨時 in early morning.

丨恭 to show great regard to.

同丨 or 丨兄 a colleague in the same yamun, and of the same rank.

丨賓 to treat a guest with consideration.

弗永丨念于祀 you did not constantly and reverently reflect upon the sacrifices — to ancestors.

丨畏 to regard with dread.

夤 ˏyin From 夕 *evening* and 寅 *to respect;* similar to the last.

To respect; to advance; a distant place; eventide; to be leagued with; a colleague; a money girdle; one rib.

八丨 eight places beyond the frontier.

丨夜 late in the evening.

丨緣 to give bribes to get into office, to have secret relationships with officials, to intrigue for office.

淫 ˏyin From *water* and *approaching near;* it is constantly interchanged with the next.

The rising of waters; to soak, to drench; to give loose to; excesses of any kind, but especially in licentiousness; lewd, immoral; to debauch; as an *adjective*, extraordinary, excessive, very, great; the bad; to incroach, as on another's functions or place; a long time; to overpass, said of the stars when their motions do not agree with the calculations.

丨風 lewd manners; the fashion of dissipation.

丨亂 debauchery.

飽暖思丨慾 fullness of bread and ease beget lustful desires.

丨祀無福 no advantage is to be derived from excessive worship, or worshiping what does not exist.

浸丨 soaked too much.

鄭聲丨 the music of the Chʻing people was licentious.

天道福善而禍丨 Heaven annexes happiness to goodness and woes to lewdness.

日丨于書史 daily confined to his books; *i. e.* excessive study.

既有丨威 he was possessed of great dignity.

婬 ˏyin Similar to the last.

Lewd, obscene; to debauch, to whore; to seek for pleasure; theatrical amusements.

丨婦 a loose woman.

姦丨 adultery and fornication.

丨人妻女 to debauch others' wives and daughters.

丨戲 lewd amusements and shows.

貞丨 chastity and lewdness.

霪 ˏyin From *rain* and *excessive.*

Rain for more than ten days without ceasing; a long and drenching rain.

連丨雨 continuous rains.

晝夜丨霖 incessant rain day and night.

丨雨連綿 uninterrupted rains.

听 ˏyin From *mouth* and a *hatchet;* it is also a contraction of ˏtʻing 聽 to hear.

To open the mouth wide and laugh immoderately.

丨然而笑 he laughed loudly.

誾 ˏyin From *words* and *door.*

To speak gently, as people who ask at the doorway; to speak mildly, as when reproving; an agreeable, respectful manner.

丨丨如也 so gentle and courteous.

丨悅 to speak pleasantly.

狺 ˏyin From *dog* and a *word;* it also occurs read ˏshăn.

The barking and snarling of one or many dogs.

猛犬丨丨以迎吠 a furious dog came rushing out, barking at him as he came up.

銀 ˏyin From *metal* and *perverse;* it is contracted to 艮 in common books.

Silver; the 白金 or white gold, as gold is known as the 黃丨 yellow silver; money, cash, wealth.

水丨 quicksilver, mercury.

碎丨 broken silver.

丨子 or 丨錢 money, bullion, specie, silver.

丨兩 the money, *i. e.* the weight of a piece of silver.

鷹丨 a Mexican dollar.

紋丨 or 細絲丨 sycee silver.

補丨色 or 補丨水 make up the difference in value between the various sorts of silver.

花紅丨 a reward offered; the notice is called 花紅帖 or the red card.

丨單 or 匯丨單 an order, a bill or draft.

銅丨 silver alloyed with copper.

丨鈎 the silver hook, *i. e.* the new moon when first seen.

丨東 a man of means.

丨海 the silver sea, a Taoist name for the eye.

有筆無丨僅屬虛文 when one is learned but is poor, his talk is like empty words,—not much listened to.

丨河 the Milky Way.

丨魚 the white-bait. (*Leucosoma.*)

丨樹開花 [can] a silver tree blossom?—an impossibility.

祭丨 or 丨錠 silvered paper shaped like ingots; used in worship.

垠 ˏyin From *earth* and *limit*

A bank; a boundary, a limit.

丨岸 a shore, a beach.

門丨 a threshold.

一望無丨 no bound anywhere to the prospect.

地丨開 to open a road through.

九丨 the nine bounds, *i. e.* the empyrean; the high heavens.

齗 ˏyin From *teeth* and *ax.*

The gums of the teeth; dogs snarling and fighting.

丨肉 the gums.

丨丨 quarreling; anarchy and contention.

Read ʻkin. The palate.

嚚 ˏyin From *four mouths* and *officer,* denoting the hum of voices.

The sound of conversation; without any conscience, to say things unworthy of belief; stupid.

父頑母丨 [Shun's] father was perverse and his mother stupid.

丨訟可乎 will it do to perjure or say anything in the trial?

鄞 ˏyin The district in which Ningpo city lies is 丨縣, a name given it during the Cheu dynasty.

蟫 ˏyin From *insect* and *sharp*; also read ˏ*tan*.

The book moth (*Lepisma*), the 蠹魚 or 白魚 from its shape and mealy color; two species are common, which injure books and clothing, by eating the paste and sizing.

Read ˏ*sin*. Wriggling.

丨丨 moving and squirming.

訢 ˏh'in From *words* and *ax*; it resembles *su* ˊ訴 to tell, and is used as a synonym of *hin* 欣 or 忻 pleased.

An affable, respectful manner; pleasant and gracious.

僮僕丨丨如也 his attendants were so very attentive and courteous.

Read ˏ*hi*. The vapor which rises from the ground.

引 ˊyin From *bow* and a *line*; intended to figure a drawn bow.

To draw a bow; prolonged, carried on for a long time, as descendants; to lead on, to show; to induce, to point out; to bring forward, to recommend; to lead into evil; used for ˊ癮 victimized, confirmed, as in a habit; to perpetuate; to decline, to retire; to quote, as in proof of; a preface or argument of a book; a fuse or match; the efficacious principle of; a measure in the Han dynasty of 100 *ch'ih*; a weight of 2 *kin*; in the gabel, a lot of 8 bags of salt, which weigh 6⅗ peculs net.

丨水 to lead water, as into fields.

丨水人 a pilot.

丨水于井 to draw well-water.

小丨 a preface.

丨火 to light or strike a fire.

指丨 to point at.

丨頭 a leader, one who shows the way, or heads a subscription.

丨書 to quote authors or books.

丨線 a spy, a guide; to furnish a clue.

丨導 to lead, to induce to go in a way.

導丨 to hold in the breath, as the Taoists or jugglers do.

丨見 to introduce to the imperial presence.

曲丨 the subject of a ballad or song.

播丨 to cure disease by shampooing.

互相牽丨 one thing induces (or involves) another.

丨而伸之 developed or carried out the hint or clue.

藥丨子 the active or leading principle of a preparation.

丨動 to influence, to urge on.

殷乃丨考 let [the people of] Yin long enjoy prosperity.

Read *yin*ˋ A halter, a drag rope.

弔于葬必執丨 one should hold the rope when going with the hearse; — do your part.

廴 ˊyin Originally formed of 彳 a *step* led on and on; it is the 54th radical of a few unusual characters.

To journey; to move on.

蚓 螾 ˊyin From *insect* and *to lead* or *to respect*.

The earthworm (*Lumbricus*), the 蚯丨 also called 土龍 earth-dragon; it is used as a remedy in urinary complaints.

山丨 a singular snake resembling a *Cecilia*.

尹 ˊyin From *body* and a *stroke*, but the original composition is from 又 a *hand* and 丿 *holding* on; *q. d.* to manage things.

To grasp in the hand; to govern, to rule; to direct; true, earnest; to introduce, to advance; an old term for chief, principal or first; a director or overseer of other officers.

丨祭 square pieces of dried meat, once used in sacrifices.

府丨 the mayor of Peking, a high officer, whose jurisdiction is independent of the provincial governor, and restricted within the metropolitan prefecture.

庶丨 all the directors of high rank.

飲 ˊyin From *to eat* and *to breathe*.

To drink; it is by some confined to animals, as 喝 is to persons; to suck in the breath; to rinse the mouth; drink, drinking; used like 吃 as a sign of the passive, to receive; to cherish: concealed, secret.

丨杯 drink a glass.

濫丨 drinking to excess.

請丨 please drink.

丨片 a slice of medicine.

痛丨一塲 a mad drinking bout.

丨水知源 we know the fountain by drinking the water.

丨恨 to have a cause for dislike.

丨新娘酒 to attend a wedding feast.

丨於鄉 to drink in the village, an appellation for a village elder.

丨箭 hit by the arrow.

丨章 an anonymous or secret document.

好丨 good to drink.

一丨而盡 he quaffed it off at a draft.

Read *yin*ˋ To give to drink.

丨馬投錢 he watered the horse and threw down some cash.

食ˋ之丨之 to furnish food and drink.

In *Cantonese*, used for 醮. To dip.

丨臘燭 to dip candles.

丨豉油 dip it in the soy.

縯 纆 ˊyin To lead on; long, drawn out; to sew and stitch; to stitch, to quilt.

丨線 to sew across, as when quilting.

丨衣邊 to stitch the selvage of a garment.

先丨後緝 first baste and then sew it.

戭 ʿyin. A long spear or pointed weapon.

Read ʿyü. A long shield.

矛莫丨陷 the spears did not rattle against the shields; *i. e.* peaceful times.

隱 乚 ʿyin. From a *place* and *compassionate*; but the original form, like a right-angle, is supposed to imitate something hidden.

Retired, private; small, minute; screened, covered, put away, obscured; in private life, not in office; to keep out of view, to avoid, to keep back, to withdraw; fixed, settled; to lean on; tranquil, mournful; painful; suffering, worthy of compassion; the contracted form is used in *musical* books for 挑 to snap the string of the lute in playing.

丨遁山林 to hide away in the country.

丨語 an elliptical sentence.

丨士 a retired scholar, one never in office.

丨沒 one unknown to fame.

歸丨 retired from active official life.

丨禍 an unexpected calamity, a causeless affliction.

丨惜 to restrain one's compassion, *i.e.* to keep secret something useful to others.

丨藏 to keep perdu or out of the way; to hide a thing.

丨惡而揚善 to hide the evil and make known the good deeds of one, as Yao and Shun did.

丨微 obscure, from its minuteness; abstruse.

有丨憂 a secret grief.

吾無丨乎爾 I have kept nothing back from you.

丨身法 modes of rendering one's self invisible, as the Taoists do.

費而丨 vast and still, minute; reaches to the widest and the smallest, as the principles of Confucius.

欲欹非丨ˀ I want to doze but I have nothing to lean on.

㥯 ʿyin. Careful, compassionate; taking an interest in, loving.

檼 ʿyin. From *wood* and *hidden*.

The ridge-pole of a roof, the beam which is out of sight.

丨脊 the ridge of a house.

丨棟 the beams of the roof.

櫽 ʿyin. Like the last.

A kind of measure used by carpenters, called 丨栝 for making chords and angles when building walls; to bend wood by fire or steam for building boats or carts.

嶾 ʿyin. Lofty and mountainous.

丨嶙 the lofty and rugged mountains.

⿰車隱 ʿyin. The rattling of carts.

丨丨車來 the thumping, rolling carriages are coming.

磤 ʿyin. The sound of thunder; and used with ˛殷 in this sense.

丨其雷 how loud is that thunder.

丨丨霹靂 clap upon clap of loud thunder.

癮 ʿyin. From *disease* and *hidden*.

A blister, a pimple; confirmed in, victimized, craving, longing for, bound by a habit, especially of using opium,—in which sense 引 is also used.

亞片烟丨 a besotted opium-smoker.

上丨 besotted by, habituated to.

丨起 or 丨發 beginning to be a slave to the pipe.

過丨 the craving satisfied.

戒丨 to cure the habit.

丨疹 little sores or boils.

看見好有丨 he has a craving [for the pipe] when he sees it.

癊 ʿyin. A disease of the heart; sometimes erroneously used for the last; besotted with.

蔭 廕 yinˀ. From *plants* or *shelter* and *obscure*.

Shady, umbrageous; a shade, a covert, a shadow; to overshadow, to hide; to shelter, to protect; hereditary honors in the state, intimating that they protect the realm.

庇丨 to protect, to countenance and aid.

丨生員外 and 丨生主事 honorary titles conferred on the sons of high officers at an accession; 丨生 indicates that they are nobly born.

丨凉 a shade.

日丨 the sun's shadow.

茂樹丨蔚 the shady tree screens the plants.

In *Cantonese*. To fill up a hollow.

丨地 to raise the land.

靷 yinˀ. From *leather* and to *lead*

A collar or poitrel which goes around the breast of the leading horses to draw the cart, and holds the traces which are fastened to the axle, called 套包子 in Peking; the term sometimes includes the ropes.

我兩丨將絕 both my collars are likely to break.

窨 yinˀ. From *cave* and a *sound*.

A cellar; a store-room or treasury entered from the cellar, and often extending beyond the house.

酒丨 a wine-cellar.

丨室 the dark room where silk-worms are reared.

˛丨窔 dark, unable to see things.

印 yinˀ. From 卩 a *check* and 爪 *claws*; *q. d.* the hand holding something worth believing.

A seal or official signet; a stamp, but especially the device or legend on it; to seal, to affix the credentials; to print, to take off an impression; to trace or write over

copy, as boys in learning to write; on addresses of letters, often used for the *ming* of the person to whom it is sent; a spot, a stain, a mark.
一顆 丨 one seal.
官 丨 the official seal.
盖 丨 or 用 丨 to seal, to affix a stamp.
打 丨 to chop or stamp, as dollars.
封 丨 and 開 丨 to close the offices ten days before, and open them twenty days after new-year.
丨 書 to print books.
丨 房 the bureau in a yamun where the seal is kept.
月 丨 萬川 the moon prints itself on myriads of streams.
丨 色 the red ink used in sealing.
丨 堂 the frontal sinus.
丨 跡 a dirty spot.
掛帥 丨 to act as generalissimo.
丨 信 or 符 丨 a particular seal.
丨 送 to print and give away books.
火 丨 or 烙 丨 to burn or sear a mark, as on a horse.
佛心 丨 or 佛 丨 the seal on Budha's heart, the *swastika* 卐 often depicted on images; it is the symbol of the esoteric or secret doctrines of Budha.

孕 *yün'* From 子 *child* and 儿 *man* infolding it.
Pregnant.
懷 丨 to be with child.
丨 育 to be with young, said of animals.
四胎怪 丨 a monstrous birth, a malformed child, an abortion.
受 丨 to conceive.
丨 十月 went her full time.
牲 丨 弗食 pregnant animals should not be eaten.

媵 㑤 *yin'* From 女 *woman* and 朕 *We*; but others say it is altered from 人 *man*, 火 *fire* and 廾 *two hands*, which form is better retained in the second; it is sometimes read *ying'*
A woman who accompanies the bride, a concubine; afterwards, a maid of honor; a bridesmaid; to escort, to accompany; to offer a cup to one; to send anything, to forward goods.
丨 觴 urge him to take another cup.
丨 婦 a waiting-maid.
丨 妾 a concubine.
丨 送 to send on to one.

胤 *yin'* From 肉 *flesh*, 八 *eight*, and 幺 to *duplicate*.
The succession in a family of one generation after another; a line of posterity; heirs, generations; to imitate, to inherit, to succeed in; a fief, whose ruler 丨 后 was sent by Chung-kăng to punish Hi and Ho.
承 丨 to continue the rule, to take the succession.
乃 丨 文武安天下之道 I have followed the rules of Wăn Wang and Wu Wang in pacifying the empire.
永錫祚 丨 honor and posterity will evermore be granted.
天 丨 a divinely ordained succession.

酳 *yin'* From *spirits* and to *nourish*.
To rinse the mouth with spirits, as the king anciently did after eating, or as a bridal pair when pledging each other in the marriage-cup.
丨 尸 to pledge the dead, refers to an ancient custom of a father making his son personate his own deceased father, and worshiping him with a libation.

垽 *yin'* Slime, mire; dregs, leavings.
丨 泥 滓 viscid mud and mire.

濥 *yin'* Water-courses running under ground like veins in the body, and forming fountains; the geomancers call them 水門 or water doors.

㓹 *yin'* Also read *ˌying*.
To cut down the high trees on the hills.
丨 剎林木 to fell the forests.

憖 慭 *yin'* From *heart* and a *dog growling;* the second form is regarded as incorrect.
To inquire of, to ask respectfully, to speak; pleased with; further, moreover; a particle like an interjection; willing, to desire; deficient; to force one's self to do a thing; grieved, wounded.
不 丨 遺一老 he could bear to leave one old minister.
皆未 丨 也 not one of them was wanting.
敬 丨 to inquire politely of.

YING.

Old sounds, ying, yang, yeng, *and* ngung. *In Canton*, ying, wing, *and* yéung; — *in Swatow*, éng, yⁿa, yong, *and* yang; — *in Amoy*, eng, geng, seng, *and* jong; — *in Fuhchau*, ing, yèng, *and* yòng; — *in Shanghai*, yăng, ang, kiăng, *and* ngan; — *in Chifu*, ying.

英 *ˌying* From *plants* and *fresh-looking*.
A flower whose fruit is not yet formed; flourishing, luxuriant; excellent, superior, beautiful; eminent, high, commanding talent; brave, virtuous, noble; a crystal; a tassel; ornament on a spear.
丨 雄 a hero; a manly, noble person.
丨 才 superior talents and accomplishments.
丨 國 an ancient petty state lying in the present Jü-ning fu in the southeast of Honan; the term is now applied in 大 丨 國 to Great Britain or England.
重 丨 a double tassel on a spear.

丨生丨子 a hero's son will be a hero.

丨主 a ruler of heroes, one who sets them the example.

白石丨 a fine quartz crystal.

丨石 blue limestone used for artificial rock-work, which occurs in Ying-teh hien 丨德縣 north of Canton.

丨丨 elegant and flowery; said of fleecy clouds, or a parterre of flowers.

丨華 comely, beautiful; also used for the English and Chinese.

丨氣勃勃 a noble, commanding presence.

華采衣兮若丨 how gorgeous is her dress!

丨明 talented and clear-headed.

丨銳 clever, shrewd, smart; used in a good sense.

顏如舜丨 her face is like an Althea.

吸露餐丨 drinks dew and eats flowers, said of ascétics.

瑛 *ying* Like the last, applied to stones.

The luster of gems; a crystal, especially a well formed one.

紫石丨 amethystine quartz; rose quartz.

玉丨仁寶不斵自成 the crystals of quartz and the pearls of humanity, perfect themselves without any polishing.

鍈 *ying* The sound of jingling bells is 鈴丨 referring to the round ones worn by mules.

霙 *ying* From *rain* and *beautiful*.

Rain and sleet falling together; the crystals of snow, which fall in flowery flakes when the weather is not very cold.

雪丨 crystals of snow.

祥丨 a fortunate fall of snow.

霰丨 sleety snow.

丨丨 snow-white clouds.

賏 *ying* Two *pearls* strung together; an ornament for the neck, as a necklace of shells or beads.

罌 甖 罃 *ying* From *jar* or *tile* and a *necklace*; the third form is rather restricted to flower vases.

Earthenware jars with small mouths, and two or four ears, through which a cord is run to carry them by; a vase, a jar; a gallipot, a pitcher.

瓶丨 jars and vases.

糖菓丨 a jar of sweetmeats.

水丨 a water gurglet or ewer.

丨粟 or 丨子菓 the poppy, so called from the jar-like shape of the capsules.

木丨渡軍 [Han Sin, B. C. 210] used wooden tubs to transport his troops over the river.

嬰 孆 *ying* From *woman* and *necklace*; the second form means only a child.

An infant, a babe, a suckling, especially a new-born girl; used for some of its compounds; to rush against; to encircle, to surround; to inclose, to entangle; hampered, restrained; to add to; head ornaments.

丨兒 a baby.

育丨堂 a foundling-hospital, an orphanage.

抱丨 a babe in arms.

丨累 senility, the weakness of age.

丨痾 attacked by disease.

世網丨吾身 the entanglements and temptations of this world have got me fast.

嚶 *ying* From *mouth* and *infant*.

The melody of many birds; birds calling.

鳥鳴丨丨 the birds are caroling melodiously.

丨其鳴矣 she is singing her best.

丨丨 the rivalries and emulations of friends.

瓔 *ying* A fine pebble suitable to put in a lady's necklace.

擺丨珞 to spread out curiosities and jewels for sale.

丨珞我身 he put a necklace on my person.

攖 *ying* From *hand* and *infant*.

To take in the hand, to finger and put into disorder; to run against; to assail, to excite the ire of; audacious, provoking.

虎負嵎莫之敢丨 when the tiger backs against a hill, nobody durst attack him.

丨其鋒 rushed against the spears; *met.* a close fight.

櫻 *ying* The cherry, called 丨桃 and 含桃; the common varieties are the 朱丨 red cherry, and 臘丨 yellow cherry.

丨桃口 cherry lips.

金丨子 the seeds of the *Rosa hystrix*.

鸚 *ying* The *bird* for *infants*, because it learns to talk as infants do by listening to their mothers.

A parrot; the macaw or cockatoo.

白丨鵡 the white cockatoo, brought from the Archipelago.

丨哥 a parrot.

丨鵡螺 a *Buccinum;* a nautilus shell; and applied to other shells resembling these.

丨哥鼻 a Roman or crooked nose.

鶯 鸎 *ying* From 鳥 *bird* and 榮 *splendid* contracted; these two characters may perhaps refer to different birds; the first is used erroneously for the preceding, when meaning a parrot.

A species of warbler that nestles on the willow, having many names, one of which, the 黃鸝 seems to identify it with the mango bird; but the common one 黃丨 refers to the Chinese oriole. (*Oriolus sinensis.*)

有丨其羽 its plumes are beautifully variegated; *i. e.* like an oriole's.

丨梭織柳絲 the oriole flits through the willows like a shuttle.

燕侶丨儔 the swallow and the oriole have made a match;—referring to a marriage.

In *Cantonese*. A knot in wood.

應 From *heart* and *obeying man's call*, as a trained falcon.
ˏying That which is right and should be; ought to be; suitable, proper; therefore, accordingly; that which is likely to take place; in ancient times, the fourth gate of the palace.

丨當 or 丨該 or 丨分ˋ ought, must, should, certainly, necessary,— according to the scope.

丨得 due to him or suitable for; belongs to.

本丨該怎麽作 that's the proper way to do it.

不丨 unsuitable, unnecessary.

一丨俱全 everything needed is supplied; all completely furnished.

難丨重ˋ任 he cannot well fill so important an office.

未達丨 or 未丨承 I have not (or do not) promise.

丨門 the Imperial palace.

丨斬死 [a deed] worthy of death by decapitation.

丨國 a petty princedom in the present Yeh hien 葉縣 in the southwest of Honan.

Read *ying*ˋ in which it is similar to the next. An answer, a response; an echo; to fulfill, to come up to expectation; to respond; responded to, correspondent, answering to; correlative, proportionate, retributive; in divination, denotes the diagrams which refer to others; a small drum.

答丨 to reply, to answer.

丨驗頁方 a specific, a good prescription.

丨令 an order of the heir-apparent.

接丨 to reinforce, as in battle.

同聲相丨 the echo answers; *met.* people of kindred tastes, birds of a feather.

供丨 to entertain a high officer on his route.

不能丨手 not to be able to meet my hand, *i.e.* answer my request.

丨天順人 to please heaven and be kind to men.

叫到丨爲止 when you get a response then stop,— and not call again.

In *Cantonese*. A lot; a number of things.

一副丨當ˋ the whole lot together.

譍 Like the preceding.
ˏying To answer, to reply to a call verbally.

丨門 to come to, or answer the door, when a visitor calls.

叫不丨 he does not answer.

膺 From *flesh* and *to respond*; used with ˏ應 and also read *ying*ˋ to answer.
ˏying The breast; personally, self; to strike; to bear, to sustain; to stand up against; to receive, as a duty; a belly-band, a surcingle; ornaments on the martingale; to fasten.

丨受 to undertake, as an office.

則拳拳服丨 he carefully took and clasped it to his breast.

丨塞 stifled, half suffocated.

戎狄是丨 he attacked the Jung and Tih tribes.

莫之敢丨 how can I undertake such a heavy charge!

鷹 The *bird* that *answers* to man's *pointing*, which is exhibited in the ancient form 雁; others say it is from *bird* and *breast*, because it strikes its prey there.
ˏying The falcon; a term for all accipitrine birds, as the eagle, hawk, owl, kite, &c.

神丨 the golden eagle, the barkoot used to capture animals.

鳸丨 or 魚丨 an osprey or fish-eagle.

猫兒頭丨 the common owl.

丨隼出風塵 the eagle soars above the wind and dust.

角丨 the harpy eagle.

丨眼猴手 an eagle eye and a monkey's hand;— sharp, clever.

丨揚 the falcon soars on his swoop; applied to warriors who at first were in low, private life.

纓 From *silk* and a *babe*.
ˏying A throat-band to hold the hat; the dyed hair or silk which covers official hats; tassels, tufts or fringes; tassels on the breast collar.

紅丨帽 the red fringed hats.

馬丨 the tassels or pendents on a bridle.

女子許嫁丨 the girl has promised her bridal tassel.

釁起摘丨 the insult and strife arose from merely seizing a tassel.

絨丨 round balls of floss worn by girls in the hair.

丨繫 the band to hold the button.

蘡 A vine like the grape, which produces berries or grapes.
ˏying 金丨糕 a preparation of candy at Canton.

盈 From *dish* and *overmuch*, referring to purchasing more than is necessary.
ˏying A full vessel; completed, overflowing, replenished; arrogant, audacious; to fill; to be full; to overpass, to stretch beyond; more than is wanted.

虛而爲丨 though ignorant he still thinks he is quite capable.

丨滿 full; self-satisfied; a complacent conceit.

丨缺 waxing and waning.

罪惡貫丨 he has filled the sum of his iniquities.

器小易丨 his abilities are small and he is soon exhausted.

丰神情態丨丨獨立 her animated appearance and sprightly ways were admirable and well sustained.

輕丨 dainty and elegant, as the step of a lady.

朝丨 the court or levee is full.

丨縮 to increase and to decrease; to overpass and retract; sufficient and insufficient, as expenses and receipts.

丨川 an ancient city in K'ü-cheu fu in southwest of Chehkiang.

丨把 a full handful.

楹 From *wood* and *full* as the phonetic.

ˏ*ying* A column which is seen; a pillar in the center upholding the roof; a tree whose heart-wood is red and the outer gray.

奠在兩丨之間 he poured out the libation between the columns.

丨帖 sentences put upon pillars before the door.

瀯 An eddy; a rivulet.

ˏ*ying* 丨丨 the murmur of running water.

澴丨 a whirlpool.

渟丨 a small stream, a brook.

絜丨 clever and glib in talking.

堂有三丨 the hall was three 間 or divisions wide,—for each one required a pillar.

營 From 熒 *bright* and 宮 *mansion*, both contracted.

ˏ*ying* To live in a market; to measure, to lay out; to scheme, to plan, to cast about or attend to a business; to regulate, to define, to get a living; to build or make a dwelling-place; a cantonment, an intrenched camp; military; the division or corps of an army, especially infantry; troops of the line, not volunteers.

六丨 the Chinese army, not including the Bannermen, or the 親軍丨 the household guards, and other corps.

經丨 to seek a living, to calculate the ways and means; to attend to from first to last.

經之丨之 he measured it and built it.

丨汛 an outpost, a guard-house.

丨盤 or 丨房 a cantonment, a garrison; a dépôt of troops.

軍丨 or 丨伍 the army.

投丨 or 入丨 to enlist.

武丨 military officers.

偷丨劫寨 to surprise and plunder a camp.

丨室 to build a dwelling-house; a star near Aquila.

丨謀 or 丨生 to trade, to get a living.

丨惑 to circumvent and cozen; to carry away; to enrapture, as fine music does the feelings.

丨丨 going to and fro, to travail in, as a peddler; buzzing, flitting, as flies.

塋 From 土 *earth* and 熒 *bright*.

ˏ*ying* A tomb, the grounds belonging to a family sepulcher.

墳丨 a burial-ground.

先丨 the family grave-yard.

寶丨 your family tombs.

未開丨穴 (or 丨窟) the grave is not yet dug.

丨界 or 丨域 the limits of the grounds, where stone pillars are erected.

萌 The opening year clear and flourishing, as the composi-

ˏ*ying* tion of the character indicates.

丨橋 a bridge in Kwăn-shan in Kiangsu.

嬴 From *woman* and the next character contracted; it occurs interchanged with ˏ盈 full.

ˏ*ying* The family surname of Tsin Chi Hwangti, derived from Shaohao (B.C. 2597); full; an overplus; to open out; to loosen, as nature in spring; to originate, to produce what is new.

丨女 or 丨氏 a famous belle.

丨滿 to fill up.

夏爲ʻ長丨 summer develops things.

贏 From *precious* and a nondescript beast like a tiger.

ˏ*ying* An overplus left after selling a thing; gain, profit; superfluity, abundance,—which is obtained after much clamor and haggling; to beat, to win, to excel, to conquer; slow; very full, as a vessel; to carry on a beam; three day's rations for a prisoner.

我丨你輸 I have won and you have lost.

丨餘 an abundance, excessive; more than just enough.

丨錢 to win by gaming.

丨熟 over-ripe.

丨東道 to win the bet,—which must not be money.

丨了他 I have beaten him; I won it of him.

奇丨 a high price for really good things.

丨利 profits, gain.

昭假無丨 you have come to my help with all your powers.

瀛 From *water* and to *fill*.

ˏ*ying* The ocean, the circuit of the seas; a pool in a marsh; an ancient name for Chao-cheu fu in the east of Kwangtung.

丨州 fairy land.

登丨洲 to go to (or to reach) the capital, referring to an ancient name of Ho-kien fu in Chihli.

丨海 all the wide oceans.

籯 A basket or hamper, also called 筷籠子 hung up in a

ˏ*ying* kitchen to hold the chopsticks.

籝 Often confounded with the last.

ˏ*ying* A strong box or safe, made of bamboo.

黃金滿丨 the yellow gold fills the safe.

蠅 From 虫 *insect* and 繩 *string* contracted, referring to the spinning-like action of the fore-legs.

ˏ*ying* A house-fly; a dipterous fly of any sort or color; *met.* specious flatterers who confound good and evil, as flies dirty things both black and white.

蒼丨 or 烏丨 house-flies.

丨虎 a spider which catches flies.

丨鑽 a fly-borer, *i. e.* flies will find their way through the smallest hole; *met.* traders who watch for the smallest profits.

丨頭微利 petty gains like a fly's head.

丨箒子 a fly-switch of horse-hair.

營營青丨 the blue flies buzz merrily.

狗丨 a dog tick, reputed to live in a dog's ears during the winter.

迎 From to go and one's self.

ˏying To go out and receive, as a guest; to meet; to occur; to calculate, as a lucky day; to acknowledge; a meeting, a reception, an interview.

丨春花 the yellow jasmine.

失丨 to miss a visit; not to be at the door to receive a guest.

丨着頭 to meet one, as in the streets.

丨接上憲 to meet and escort a superior officer.

丨風而去 to go on, even with a head-wind.

不丨不送 to treat without any particular ceremony, as an intimate friend, or as a rude fellow ought to be treated.

逢丨 to receive with excessive civility; sycophantic.

Read *ying'* To meet a bride.

親丨'則得妻 when the groom went himself to receive her, then she became his wife.

影 From *variegated* and *sunlight*.

ʻying A shadow; a picture or image of a thing; a vanishing appearance, a dissolving view.

丨響 shadow and echo; *met.* obedient, attentive to.

有一點丨響 I have some hint of it; there is an inkling of him.

日丨 a shadow.

丨射朦混 to delude with false statements and get one thing when specifying another.

畫丨 to paint a portrait.

丨丨綽綽 vague outlines, shadows moving; indistinct, no clear apprehension of.

倒丨 to explain one thing by another, to illustrate aptly.

一魚幾丨 several images of one fish; *met.* great exaggeration.

照丨 to throw a reflection, as by a mirror.

仄丨 a poetical name for a fan.

瓀 璟 The second form is usually read *ʻking*, and is chiefly used in proper names.

ʻying ʻching The luster of precious stones.

寶玉騰丨 this rare gem sparkles.

玉丨 the brilliancy of gems.

癭 From *disease* and *babe*.

ʻying Bronchocele or goitre; a wen or ganglionic swelling on the neck, of which five sorts are distinguished.

丨袋 a goitre, common in Chihli.

氣丨 glandular swellings, which swell when one is in a passion.

血丨 a tumor on the neck with turgid veins.

丨瘤 a tumor on the neck.

郢 From *city* and to *state* to a superior.

ʻying The ancient capital of Tsu, just north of Kiang-ling hien 江陵縣 in King-cheu fu in the south of Hupeh.

丨州 an old name of Wu-chang fu, the capital of Hupeh.

穎 頴 From 禾 *grain* or 示 *omen*, and 頃 *leaning*, referring to the ripe head of grain; the second is not quite correct.

ʻying A full head or spike of grain, which then bends over; a sharp point, as of a pencil or an awl; a ring on a scabbard; a fine critical taste.

毛丨 a sharp pen; *met.* a well-read scholar.

丨悟 versatile, quick parts.

聰丨 intelligent, ready, apt.

脫丨而出 the awl has forced its way through [the bag]; *i. e.* talent will find its way to distinction.

禾丨 the awn of grain.

實丨實栗 the ripe grain bowed over in its full ear.

潁 This character is often written like the preceding.

ʻying An ancient district 丨川, now 丨州府 in the northwest of Nganhwui, occupying the valleys of the River Hwai and its affluents, named after the 丨水, a noted stream in its borders, now in Honan; a man of 丨川郡 is one whose surname is Chin 陳, because many of that surname came from that region.

映 暎 From *sun* and *midst* or *luxuriant*.

ying' The sun beginning to decline; to shine on; to reflect, as a ray of light; to favor, to countenance; to show, not to hide or retire; the sunlight, the bright glare; a reflection or image; open, apparent, in sight.

掩丨 to screen from the sun's glare.

日丨 it is past noontide; the sun shines on you.

丨日 a bright sunlight.

丨雪 the reflection of the snow.

丨眼 [the glare] shines in my eyes.

丨帶左右 [I carry] the brightness of the sun on both hands, referring to a poem of the Tsin 晉 dynasty.

後先輝丨 the new incumbent reflects the brightness of his predecessor; said of one good ruler who succeeds another.

Read *ang'* Obscure.

丨睐 not bright, not light enough.

硬 鞕 From *stone* or *hide* and to *change*; the second form is not common.

ying' Hard; not soft but solid; stiff, not pliable; unbending; obstinate, perverse; sharp, stiff, as a bad handwriting; to stiffen, to harden; powerful and willful.

堅丨 hard, impenetrable, inflexible.

手丨 strong, brawny, hardfisted.

丨直 mulish, willful, set.

丨郎 muscular, vigorous, as a hale old man.

說 丨 話 to speak hard words; *i. e.* to frighten.

恣 丨 如 鉄 hard-hearted, impervious to the truth.

書 貴 瘦 丨 方 通 神 the best style of character is slim and stiff, and arresting the attention.

丨 砍 實 鑿 I will exert all my efforts to do it.

In *Cantonese*. A particle denoting a fixed purpose, certainly, still, surely, only, indeed, in fact; dear, in price.

丨 好 食 it is really good-tasted.

丨 到 底 good pluck to the last; it died game.

丨 要 多 I will and must have more.

丨 頸 人 an obstinate, pig-headed fellow.

丨 自 做 it was I alone who did it.

冷 丨 stiff from cold.

揸 丨 hold it firmly in your hand.

丨 得 噃 domineering; too stiff.

丨 口 foul-mouthed.

賸 *ying'* Same as 媵 to give an escort of maid-servants to a bride or a princess, when going to her husband; to exchange presents, to give douceurs.

副 丨 the maid servants.

Read *shing'* for 剩. An overplus.

餘 丨 what is left over.

嫈 *ying'* A good style in a woman.

丨 媖 a country woman, a village wench or goodwife.

丨 媔 a young wife.

YIU.

Old sounds, wu, yiu, u, ok, ot, ak, *and* at. *In Canton*, yau; — *in Swatow*, iu, iⁿu, u, *and* hiu; — *in Amoy*, iu *and* u; — *in Fuhchau*, iu, éu, *and* hiu; — *in Shanghai*, yù; — *in Chifu*, yiu.

幽 *yiu* From 幺 *small* and 山 *hill*.

In a shady dell, darkish, umbrageous; retired, solitary, secret; hidden from view, far back; to be of a dark color, obscure, mysterious, occult; the ignorant, idle; the shades or spirits who are in obscure places; to go or be sent into retirement, to be kept out of sight, half banished; to rusticate one.

丨 雅 clean and tasteful; in elegant retirement; retired and tasteful, as a copse or garden retreat.

丨 暗 dark; obscure, as a ravine.

丨 都 the north extreme of Yao's realm.

丨 居 to live retired, out of public life.

丨 深 wild, remote; dismal, as a deep gorge.

超 丨 to deliver spirits by a mass.

祭 丨 風 a gust that scatters the paper garments burned to clothe ghosts; *met.* an object of contempt, a wretch. (*Cantonese.*)

丨 門 the gates of hades; also, the pylorus.

丨 丨 南 山 the far off calm southern mountains.

黜 退 其 丨 升 進 其 明 dismiss the scheming officers, and advance the intelligent.

丨 冥 教 主 the judge of souls in hades; a Budhist god.

丨 微 subtle, abstruse; infinitesmal, fine, delicate.

丨 囚 to imprison, to confine.

丨 閒 貞 靜 之 德 the accomplishments of lady-like reserve and maiden quiet.

丨 峭 in *rhetoric*, emphasis.

麀 *yiu* From 鹿 *deer* and 牝 *female* contracted.

A roe or doe; the female of the stag or axis.

鄾 *yiu* A place anciently belonging to the state 鄧, now occupied by that district in the southwest part of Honan, on the headwaters of the River Han.

憂 *yiu* From 心 *heart* and 頁 *head*, which some regard as a contraction of 顏 the *face*, because grief shows itself in the countenance.

Grieved, mournful, sad; in mourning for parents; anxious, careworn; sorrow that is kept to one's self, heart-sick; to think of with sorrow; melancholy; low spirited, nervous; nauseated, as pregnant women; to sympathize with; to act so as to bring disgrace.

丨 悶 disappointed, sorry, grieved.

丨 愁 or 丨 心 cast down, heart-sick, of a sad countenance.

談 丨 to sympathize and condole with one.

居 丨 or 宅 丨 sorrowing, mourning.

不 丨 careless what grief may be given to others.

不 丨 不 好 do not be anxious lest they be bad; *i. e.* they will probably be good.

不 知 丨 stolid, light-hearted.

高 枕 無 丨 you can go to sleep without any anxiety; the last two words in 無 丨 王 refer to king Asoka, *i. e.* the untroubled or sorrowless king.

丨 民 之 丨 者 民 亦 丨 其 丨 if you take to heart the sorrows of the people, they will also bear yours in mind.

王 宅 丨 the emperor's time of mourning.

採 薪 之 丨 a slight indisposition; *i. e.* sorrow because he could not shoulder a faggot.

小 人 道 丨 也 the ways of a mean man bring disgrace on him.

嚘 *yiu* To grow hoarse; to hesitate and stammer in talking; to sigh.

佇 立 久 咿 丨 he stood a long while talking slowly.

優 From *man* and *sorrowful*, but explained as from 夂 to *step off* and 憂 *grief; q.d.* a man relieves his grief by rambling.
ˌyiu

Abundant, excessive, as rains; redundant, overmuch, extra; satisfied, tranquil; unconcerned, easy about; very, fully, more than able for; to excel; those who excel; to play with or before; to dally, to trifle; a mime.

丨人 or 丨伶 a juggler, a mimic, a mountebank.

學丨則仕 he can be an officer when he is fully learned.

敷政丨丨 wisely and gently he managed the affairs of state.

丨游 to relieve care by a stroll.

丨劣宜分 their fitness and unfitness should be fairly tested.

丨禮相待 to treat with unusual politeness.

未見所丨 I have never seen anything remarkable in him.

丨孟衣冠 [antiquated as] the robes and caps of Yiu and Măng, two actors of the T'ang dynasty.

丨丨有餘 more than enough, too much, in excess.

櫌 耰 A harrow or roller to cover in the grain when sown; a beetle for breaking clods; to cover in seed.
ˌyiu

鋤丨 to follow agriculture.

深其耕而熟丨之 plow deep and harrow the seed in thoroughly.

丨而不輟 they kept on breaking the clods without stopping — to listen to Confucius asking the way.

攸 逌 From 攴 to *tap* and 水 *water* altered, which is explained as referring to a pole to sound the depth of water; the second ancient form is composed of *vapor* or *spirit* issuing, and hanging *fruit*, and defined to be moving vapor; used for the next.
ˌyiu

To go on the water, or dart through it; a place; a relative *pronoun* like 所, what, that which, who; an initial particle; distant.

丨然而逝 how suddenly [the fish] darted away!

君子丨行 that which the good man does.

利有丨往 it is for your advantage wherever you go.

丨丨外寓 to dwell very far from one's home.

福祿丨歸 whence the blessings and emoluments come to me.

為韓姞相丨 he sought everywhere [for a son-in-law] for Han's daughter.

四方丨同 [the people] were alike [obedient] in every part.

監罔丨辟 an inspector should not use punishments.

丨水 a stream near Yiu hien 丨縣 in the north of Honan.

悠 Interchanged with the last.
ˌyiu

To think of with sorrow; discontented, sorry; far-reaching, as a plan; remote, far off; reiterated, frequent; leisurely.

丨丨我里 I am grieved for my village and household.

丨丨蒼天 the illimitable heavens.

丨丨 slow moving of banners; waving of trees in a breeze; long and anxious thinking; horses going far.

丨哉丨哉 think of it! think of it! — *i. e.* so sad, so grievous.

丨遠 far, a long stretch.

丨丨之論 common talk.

滺 Used for the last.
ˌyiu

Water flowing along rapidly.

淇水丨丨 how swiftly run the waters of the Ki!

呦 From *mouth* and *young*.
ˌyiu

A harmonious sound.

丨丨 the bleating of deer, an imitation of their cry; also a cry of pain.

人語呷丨 the singing hum or gabble of a number of people.

怮 To restrain one's anger by saying nothing; morose.
ˌyiu

丨丨 sad and unhappy.

ˌ重丨 sorrow and grief multiplied.

尤 From 尢 *lame*, some say changed into this form by combining 乙 the *beginning* and 又 *hand*; others that it is the odd walk of a person with a long and a short leg; interchanged with the next.
ˌyiu

An *adverb* of comparison, more, very, still more; odd, different from; evils, calamities; to blame; to exceed, to surpass; error; to dislike, to murmur, to bear a grudge.

丨異 singular; surprisingly unlike.

效丨 to surpass one's example; to go beyond, as in crime.

丨物 a rare and beautiful thing; a beautiful woman.

丨人 to hate, to blame people; there is a proverb 京丨子衛嘴子 Peking people are haters, Tientsin people janglers.

丨甚 vastly more or greater.

則寡丨 then his error is less criminal.

懷怨丨之念 I bear him an old grudge; to harbor resentment.

丨可怪 still more surprising.

殊丨之才 remarkable talent.

莫知其丨 I know not the evil cause.

訧 Used with the last; a fault or error; a crime.
ˌyiu

惡丨 guilt; wickedness.

俾無丨兮 do not cause him to transgress.

報以庶丨 reported all their misdeeds.

疣 肬 A swelling or gathering; a wen or big wart; ganglionic swellings in the neck.
ˌyiu

皮上結丨 a tumor has come on the skin.

豆渣丨 a ripe boil or pimple.

贅懸丨 hanging on, as a wen; said of a son-in-law who lives at his wife's home.

魷 An unauthorized character, employed along the coast to denote the 丨魚 or cuttle fish; the right name is probably 鰌魚, as the characters are read alike.
ˌyiu

逌 ꜀yiu Used as synonym for ꜀攸 and the next.

Breathing fast, as when laughing.

丨爾而笑 laughing and jolly, as when convivial.

丨然 pleased, as when showing it in the face.

由 ꜀yiu The etymology is lost; occurs written like the last, and used for ꜀猶 still.

The antecedents of a thing; a *preposition*, through, by, from; a way, a means; the cause or instrument for effecting a thing; from or by permission of; depending on; to let, to permit; to enter by; to pass through, as one's hand; to proceed to; to serve of; to follow; still, still further; the sprouts of a felled tree.

不知其丨 I do not know the reason for it, or its original.

丨此門進 go in by this door.

丨來 heretofore, from the first.

來丨 origin of; as in 怎麽來丨 why was it so? how came it about? what were the reasons?

沒有來丨 there was really no cause for it.

丨有妖乎 are there more goblins?

丨他去作 let him go and do it.

丨我自便 let me do as I like.

丨你 as you please.

經丨此門 it passed by this door.

丨此而來 from this and after, or to the next; thenceforth.

丨天不丨人 it depends on Heaven, not on man.

丨丨自得 delighted with, very well satisfied; self-possessed.

無丨自達 no way of getting to see you.

等丨 such and such reasons; &c.

事有因丨 the affair has a cause.

丨京而來 I (or it) came from the capital.

胥丨 the capital or metropolis, *i.e.* whither all roads tend.

率丨 to observe and follow, as a precedent.

君子無易丨言 the princely man should not lightly utter his words.

不丨詭道 he did not resort to mean stratagems — in waging war.

我骸不丨我作主 my sore leg will not let me do as I would like.

繇 ꜀yiu This is usually regarded as another form of the last; it is also used with ꜀猶 and ꜀悠.

To follow; to resemble or try to be like.

Read *cheu'* The enigmatical interpretation of the fourteen diagrams, as given in the Book of Changes under each, is called 丨辭; they are of different lengths.

Read ꜀*yao*, and used for 謠 and 傜. To tell wild stories; luxuriant, as herbage; a retainer.

蘨 ꜀yiu Used with the last.

Luxuriant vegetation.

厥草惟丨 that grass grows very rank and thick.

油 ꜀yiu From *water* and *from* as the phonetic.

A branch of the River Pa, an affluent of the Yangtsz' east of Wu-chang in Hupeh; a small tributary of the Tungting Lake near Chang-teh fu in Hunan; oil; fluid fat; paint; oily, unctuous, greasy; fat, shining, sleek; glazed, glossy; easy, gliding; cordial, agreeing.

香丨 sesamum, gingilie or benne oil, also known as 清丨 clear oil; made from the seeds of the *Sesamum orientale*.

丨嘴光棍 an oily-tongued sharper.

桐丨炭 chunam, such as is prepared for calking.

丨漆 oil paints; varnishes ready for use.

天丨然作雲 the sky is dark, and clouds are rising.

丨頭粉面 to oil the hair and rouge the face.

石丨 or 煤丨 petroleum, kerosine.

猛火丨 naphtha.

丨然 slippery, oily, smooth.

丨丨 a mild and scrupulous disposition.

上丨 to paint, to oil.

Read *yiu'* To oil, to paint.

丨顏色 to paint or varnish a thing in color.

蚰 ꜀yiu An apterous insect allied to the millipedes, the 丨蜒 or cermatia (*Scutigera*), common in eastern China; a harmless insect, known by many names, as 錢龍 cash-dragon; 蓑衣虫 rain-cloak bug, and 錢串虫 cash-threading insect; 丨蜑 is another form of it; the *Julus*, or galley-worm is sometimes wrongly called by this name.

庮 ꜀yiu An old building whose timbers are decayed; a dank, rotten smell.

牛夜鳴則丨 if an ox lows at night, then [his flesh] is rank.

木丨臭 rotten wood smells bad.

囮 **[illegible]** ꜀yiu From *inclosure* and to *transform* or a *bird*, alluding to the purpose of a decoy; often read ꜀*ngo*.

To interpret the cries of birds or beasts; to tell the meaning of foreign speech or gibberish; to decoy, to inveigle; to improve, to change for the better; stool-pigeons, also called 鳥媒 or bird go-betweens.

群類丨育 everything is transformed and nourished.

做丨人 one who seduces into evil or trouble.

鳥丨 or 丨子 a decoy-bird

斿 ꜀yiu From *flag* and *child*; it occurs used with the next.

The scollops along the lower edge of a flag; in old time, the king's pennon had twelve scollops, his fiefs nine, and others less; a fluttering, as of a pennon.

Read ꜀*liu*, and used for 旒. A pendent on a crown.

游 From *water* and a fluttering *pennon*; interchanged with the next.

ˎyiu Old name of a tributary of the River Hwai; to float, to drift; to swim; to travel, to rove or idle about; to enjoy one's self, to go with the crowd; to take pleasure in; satisfied, pleased; an air of contentment.

丨民 or 丨手 an idler; lazy people, those having no calling.

丨蕩 dissipated; reckless and vicious.

泳之丨之 to enjoy swimming; to dabble and play in the water.

丨戲 to enjoy sports, to frequent theaters.

丨波 the petrel; it is said to 興波祈雨 ride on the waves, and pray for rain.

溯丨從之 to drift with the current.

上下丨 wherever found, all parts, all belonging to.

上丨 and 下丨 above and below the elbow of the Yellow River in Shensi near Tung-kwan; it is extended to places north and south of one, wherever he is.

依于德丨于藝 to apply one's self to virtue and divert one's self with art.

丨水 to swim; to take a water excursion.

蛇丨 the snake crawls.

遊 Often interchanged with the last.

ˎyiu To saunter idly; to ramble, to roam, to travel for amusement or information; to go on a circuit; scattering, as troops on a march; voyaging, traveling; friendly, as two traveling mates.

丨歷各省 to travel through the provinces.

丨玩 to take a holiday, and have a ramble.

丨方僧 a begging, itinerant priest.

丨魂 wandering, hungry ghosts.

菩薩出丨 the idol is taking an airing, *i.e.* carried in a procession.

丨手好'閒 the idle love to waste their time.

丨擊 or 丨府 a lieutenant-colonel.

丨子 traveling merchant or scholar.

丨學 to travel for information.

丨子思親 the absent son remembers his parents.

秉燭夜丨 to trim the midnight lamp.

交丨 a chum, an intimate friend.

蝣 From *insect* and fluttering *pennon;* interchanged with 蝤 a cermatia.

ˎyiu A species of the ephemera fly (*Tipulidæ*), the 蜉丨 (derived from 浮遊 to flit over the water) which, like man 寄蜉丨于天地 is only a sojourner in the world; the description of this insect is so confused as to show that two or three kinds are confounded under the same name, one of which is probably a *Scarabeus* or dungchaffer.

郵 From *city* and *border*, because posts were established there; interchanged with 尤 very.

ˎyiu A post-house, an establishment for changing horses and sending on letters; a lodge for watching fields; very, much more; an error, mistake.

丨亭 a government lodge once raised to watch the farmers.

丨舍 a lodge for the postmaster.

魯君迷丨 the prince of Lu blundered greatly.

督丨 an ancient officer, whose duties resembled those of a circuit judge on the borders.

猶 From *dog* and *wine;* it is interchanged with the next.

ˎyiu A monkey, which climbs the tree when man is near, and descends after he is out of sight; an old name in Shensi for a puppy; doubtful, suspicious of; still, even; as if, like, rather, somewhat, resembling, same, alike; if; thus, so; a rule, a way; to plan, to scheme; ought, can; a map or sketch of.

丨可 it probably can be done; it is likely to be so.

丨且 still further.

丨有 there are more to be had.

寫字吾丨人也 I can write as well as others.

丨若 as if.

丨言 it may be said.

丨未定 it is rather undecided.

作事丨豫 undecided in all he does.

丨子 like a son; *i. e.* a nephew.

君子盖丨丨爾 the princely man is calm at all times.

五丨 the kind of soil that is lowest down, regarded as very poor.

克壯其丨 the plan proved to be the best one possible.

丨來無止 he ought to come without stopping.

Read *ˎyao*, and used for 搖 To move.

咏斯丨丨斯舞 he sung as he moved, and then skipped and gesticulated.

猷 Like the last.

ˎyiu A scheme, a plan; to contrive, to plot; to consult with; to draw, to make a likeness; an exclamation, ho! oh! a mode, a way of action, such as is adopted after wise counsel; cheerful.

嘉丨 a fine, excellent scheme.

謀丨 a device; to scheme.

大丨 the great doctrine or plan of ordering the universe; fate.

以丨鬼神祗 to draw the effigies of the demons, gods, and terminalia, — to be worshiped.

丨大誥爾多邦 Ah! I make a great announcement to you, [the princes] of all the states.

建勳丨 a careful plan for defending the state.

有丨 wise in counsel.

楢 A soft wood easily ignited by friction; others say, a hard wood good for axles; to collect.

ˎyiu

冬取柞丨之火 in winter they procured fire from the scrub oak and the hornbeam (?)

槱 Composed of *wood*, *fire*, and *spirits*; used with and for the last.
ˏyiu *ˊyiu* To lay in fire-wood to burn the sacrifice of a heifer or sheep, when worshiping the highest gods.

薪之丨之 heap up the faggots, lay in a supply of fire-wood.

莤 A trailing plant growing in shallow water.
ˏyiu Read *shuh*, and used for 蕭 A grass formerly used in making filters, through which wine used in sacrifices was strained; to strain, to defecate.

蕕 A trailing plant growing in the water, having a fetid smell, perhaps akin to a *Potamogeton*; but others say it is a stinking vine (*Smilax?*) found along the edge of the water; noisome, dank, like rotten wood.
ˏyiu

薰丨不同器而處 do not put fragrant and stinking things into the same vessel; — do not mix up good and bad things.

輶 A light carriage, like a curricle or chaise; light, trifling.
ˏyiu 丨軒 a gig or cabriolet.

德丨如毛 merit light as a feather.

丨儀 a trifling present; — said in depreciation.

冘 From 凵 a *desert* and 人 *man* coming out of it.
ˏyiu Doubtful, not quite certain.

丨豫不决 this is not at all sure.

Read *ˏyin*. Walking on, as one traveling afoot.

有 From 月 the *moon*, and 又 the right *hand*, said to refer to its appearance in an eclipse as if seized.
ˊyiu

To have, to possess; the opposite of 無 without; to be, or in possession of; to exist; in Budhist writings, a being, existence (*bhava*); often is merely a form of the past tense; before the name of a state often denotes the holder of it or of an office; in replies, yes, I have, it is so; often has the sense of farther, and, also, more; used before names and in lists of things to individualize them; to get, to attain.

丨限 or 丨數目 there are not many; a limited number.

沒丨 there are none.

所丨的貨物 every kind of goods.

無所不丨 to have everything; without exception.

丨事 or 丨事幹 busy, occupied.

何難之丨 what difficulty is there about it?

大丨之年 a fertile or abundant year.

自丨 self-originating; *i. e.* grew or come itself.

丨無違禁 whether this violates the prohibition or not?

富丨 possessing everything.

克國得妃其丨吉孰大焉 to conquer a kingdom and obtain a princess to wife, what great luck you have?

丨理 reasonable, has some right.

九丨 or 九州 the nine divisions of the empire by Yü.

少丨 there are few such.

十丨三 thirteen.

丨德此丨人 he who has the virtue will draw men to him, — and thus get the empire.

大丨 the fourteenth diagram, referring to fire rising.

丨意來 I came on purposely; 丨意 among Budhists, a rational being (*manushya*), a man or god in human form; the term 丨智慧 is another similar term.

大丨爲之君 a prince of great deeds.

丨身家人 a man of honor and wealth, a very respectable man.

丨則言丨 if it is so, then say it is; if it exists, then assert it.

丨在嗎。不丨在 is he alive or not? no, he's dead; is he still here? no, he has gone off.

丨沒丨。丨的 have you any? yes, some.

丨以利我 it will be of some benefit to me.

期盡所丨 to have all I hoped for, to realize one's desires.

一切丨 all things; — a Budhist term; 一切丨根本 the origin of all things (*mula sarvastivada*).

友 Composed of two 又 *hands* joined.
ˊyiu One of the same mind; a companion, a friend, an associate; attached to, friendly, fraternal, cordial, hearty; to act as a friend; to blend with, to cotton with; friendship; by twos.

尙丨古人 to be fond of the ancients, partial to their writings.

酒肉朋丨 wine and flesh friends; selfish associates.

老丨 an old friend.

同志爲丨 a friend is one who is of the same disposition.

會丨 a fellow-member, as of an association, club, or church.

弗丨 unfriendly, disobedient.

丨愛 fraternal, cordial love.

益丨 or 良丨 or 好丨 a dear or good friend, one who is of advantage; a moral friend.

交丨 or 相丨 to make an acquaintance with one, to associate with one.

或羣或丨 by threes and by twos; said of deer.

丨直丨諒丨多聞益矣 to make friends with the upright, the earnest, and the intelligent, is of great advantage.

丨也者丨其德 he whom I have for my friend, is one whose virtue I blend with.

同年丨 a friend of about the same age; opposed to 忘年丨 one who is much younger, whose age is disregarded.

丨道 rules regulating the intercourse of friends.

天地相丨 when heaven and earth accord, — then all things grow.

ʻ酉 ʻyiu The original form resembles a vessel for distilling; it refers too to the closing up of nature in the eighth moon, when crops are ripe; it is the 164th radical of characters relating to liquors.

Ripe, finished; matured; mellow, as ripe millet fit for making spirits; the ripeness of crops; the tenth of the twelve branches, denotes west on the compass-card, and is represented by the cock.

丨時 the hours from 5 to 7 o'clock P.M.

五丨 a goblin, such as Confucius once saw.

請你說個子午卯丨 please tell me more of the particulars; give me the details.

書探二丨 he has handled the books in the two hills; *i. e.* is a well read scholar; it refers to two peaks called 大丨 and 小丨 situated in Shin-cheu fu in Hunan, in whose caves the legend says that thousands of books were hidden.

丨水 a branch of the River Yuen 沅河 near these mountains.

ʻ卣 ʻyiu An ancient sacrificial tankard of copper, with a cover and a bail, used to hold the fragrant spirits employed in worship.

秬鬯二丨 two goblets of flavored millet wine, for libations.

ʻ羑 ʻyiu From *sheep* and *long;* occurs used for ʻ誘 to entice.

To lead on in the right way; right, reason.

誕受丨若 they fully accorded with the highest laws of Heaven.

丨里 a place, now T'ang-yin hien 湯陰縣 in the north of Honan, where Wu Wang was imprisoned, B. C. 1130.

ʻ䱂 ʻyiu A yellowish black fish, 黃丨魚 four inches long, which from its habit of burying itself in the mud, is also called 船矴魚 or grapnel fish; it has a forked tail, large head, wide mouth, and many sharp dorsal spines; perhaps akin to the stickle-back.

ʻ蜏 ʻyiu A short-lived fly, also called 孳母 produced from eggs laid in rotten wood; it resembles a silkworm moth.

ʻ莠 ʻyiu From *plant* and *elegant.*

A kind of useless grass resembling the panicled millet growing among grain; weeds; tares, darnel; the riffraff of society; vicious, mischievous.

丨言自口 their offensive words are just from the mouth.

除丨安良 to extirpate the wicked, that the good may be quiet.

馬餘不過稂丨 weeds are the only return the horse gets.

丨似苗而非苗 darnel resembles grain [when young], but it still is not grain.

維丨驕驕 the weeds grow rank and high.

ʻ黝 ʻyiu From *black* and *young;* also read ʻ*yao.*

A color like invisible green, almost a black; also an ashy color; to smear and blacken; black earth.

丨牲 black bullocks, fit for sacrificing.

塗丨其面 he smeared his face darkly.

丨青 a blue-black.

丨堊 to plaster with black mortar.

晒的起丨 he is much tanned or sun-burnt.

ʻ懮 ʻyiu An indolent, sans-souci way; to relax from labor and take one's ease; used for 憂, sorrow, grief; anxious longings.

傷余心之丨丨 the misery and grief that rends my heart.

ʻ牖 ʻyiu From 片 *slip,* 戶 *door* and 甫 *bored; i. e.* to open a hole as a door.

A hole in a wall or roof, as a window to see the sun; a lattice window; to slide or open; to lead on, to instruct; towards.

甕丨 a window made of a jar.

自丨執其手 to grasp the hand put through the window, as when visiting an invalid.

開丨通光 open the lattice to let in the light.

戶丨 doors and windows; glass or lattice doors.

天之丨民 the leading guidance of the people by Heaven.

丨上有業屨 a finished pair of shoes lay on the window-sill.

ʻ誘 ʻ誧 ʻyiu From *words* and *elegant;* the second form is unusual.

To speak to affably, to advise kindly; to allure, to draw on, to entice; to tempt, to mislead; drawn towards, attracted; to encourage, as a teacher his pupils.

引丨 to entice — to evil.

丨我友邦君 he urged me to treat the neighboring princes kindly.

循循善丨 to lead one gradually on from good to better.

喜貪者可丨以利 the covetous are easily enticed with the prospect of gain.

丨惑 to tempt to sin, to seduce to evil.

丨射 to teach archery.

哄丨 to befool, to lead into error.

丨導其迷 to lead the ignorant and wayward into good ways.

又ˀ yiuˀ Originally the same as the next, and intended to represent *three fingers* of the hand when tortured; it is the 29th radical of a few incongruous characters, mostly relating to managing affairs; also occurs read *yih,*

The hand; a *copula,* more, also, furthermore, moreover, and, and then, again, still again, in a higher degree; before a negative, makes a disjunctive sense, as but, while, not yet; placed between two verbs, it makes the former a present participle.

罵了丨打打了丨罵 he scolds and then beats me, and then beats and scolds again.

丨一天 there's another day coming; *i. e.* why hurry so?
得而丨失 he obtained it and after that he lost it.
問過丨問 he asked and then asked again.
丨來了 there, you have come again! see, you bring up that matter again!
丨要出門 he wishes to go out again.
丨冷丨下雨 it is cold and raining too.
丨其次也 again this sort also; again this third sort.
丨換一個生手 we have only changed him for another raw hand.
丨要馬兒好丨要馬兒不吃草 there are good horses, and there are horses which won't eat their straw; *i. e.* some things are cheap and good, while others are too dear.
坐丨不安 he could not sit easy.
丨有客來 still one more guest has come.
況丨 furthermore.
丨不可 still more improper or impossible.
且丨 still more.

右 *yiu'* Derived from 口 *mouth* with 又 the right *hand* added, because they mutually assist each other; when language fails the hand helps; it is interchanged with the next two as a verb.

The right hand; on the right; to honor, to give precedence to, as the right side was once the highest seat; to aid, to support; to turn to the right, as in driving; high, noble, honorable; a spearman on the right of the driver; violent, high tempered; when added to official designations, it denotes a second or deputy, the lower rank of, as 丨侍郎 a junior vice-president.
丨手 the right hand.
在丨首 or 在丨邊 on the right hand.
丨僧 a nun.
吩咐左丨 ordered his attendants.
既丨烈考亦丨文毋 I honor my meritorious father and my accomplished mother—with this sacrifice.
不離左丨 he never leaves her side, as a child its mother.
無出其丨 no one excelled him.
開列于丨 it is explained above; as above written.
座丨 let this come to the right of your seat;—said in letters.
丨照會 let the above communication [come to such an officer];—a concluding phrase in dispatches.
道路婦人由丨 in going on the highway, women should take the right hand.
左之丨之 they turned the horses to the right and left.
豪丨 a valiant or clever man, a leading mind.
尊文曰丨文 to honor literary pursuits is called right-ing letters.
左丨綏之 I will comfort him every way.
丨旋 a diagram of a conch whose spirals turn to the right (*nandavartaya*), regarded as fortunate.

佑 *yiu'* From *man* and *right* hand; used with the next.

To aid, to help, to countenance.
助丨 to lend a hand.
上天孚丨下民 high Heaven sees and cares for the people.

祐 *yiu'* To protect, to shield; to defend, as the gods or spirits; divine care and protection, heavenly kindness.
神靈庇丨 may the divine spirits protect you.
受天之丨 to enjoy the favor of Heaven.
皇天眷丨 high Heaven oversees and assists.
神恩默丨 the secret blessings of the gods.

宥 *yiu'* From a *shelter* and *having*; occurs used with the next.

To be lenient towards, to be indulgent, to forbear with; to relax, to excuse; to give scope to; an inadvertence, a sin of ignorance; a permanent, far-reaching benefit.
丨罪 to remit or forbear an offence.
恕丨 or 赦丨 to excuse, to forgive an error; to reprieve.
三丨 three reasons for leniency, *viz.*, ignorance, inadvertence and forgetfulness.
祈爲原丨 I beg you to excuse the fault;—a polite phrase.
法所難丨 the law does not allow this to be excused.
丨州 ancient name for part of Yü-lin fu in Shensi.
賄丨 bribed to remit punishment.

侑 *yiu'* To urge one to eat; to wait on, to do the honors of the table, to entertain guests with music; to help; to stimulate.
丨卮 an ancient drinking cup.
以妥以丨 to seat [the personators of the dead] and invite them to eat.
丨食尊客 he urged the noble guests to eat.
奏樂丨食 to divert and animate guests by music.
丨酒 to press a guest to drink.

姷 *yiu'* It seems to be a mere variety of the last.

To assist, as a fellow does; a pair, a couple.

囿 *yiu'* A park or paddock for rearing animals; an aviary; a menagerie; a walled garden, as distinguished from a hedged one; to inclose, to pen up, to restrain; a limited, superficial knowledge of.
鹿丨 a deer-park.
禁丨 a prohibited garden, one not open to all.
淺丨 superficial, as a shallow scholar.
丨于風俗 bound down by the usage; hampered by custom.

丨苑 or 園丨 gardens and parks.

丨𡤼見聞不廣 limited in his knowledge of the world.

幼 From *slender* and *strength*.
yiu'

Young, immature, tender, delicate; growing, as grain; youthful, from ten to nineteen years of age.

慈丨 to treat kindly, as young people; tender affection for.

丨學 scholars, young pupils; boy's studies.

丨視 to look upon as juvenile; supercilious.

丨主 a youthful monarch.

'長丨 or 老丨 old and young, mature and growing.

丨童 a young lad, under ten.

丨婦 a young wife or bride.

年丨無知 he is still young and inexperienced.

丨嫩 tender and smooth; sleek and delicate, as nestlings.

丨細 delicate; fine as lace; pretty.

丨吾丨以及人之丨 as I pity my young children, so let me pity others' children.

棄爾丨志 put aside your boyish, childish notions.

Read ,*yao*, and used for 杳. Delicate, subtle, abstruse.

丨眇 recondite, metaphysical.

疻 A shaking of the head, caused by old age or palsy.
yiu'

顫丨 a quivering; trembling of the body.

丨子 the ague; the shivering or cold fit.

柚 The pumelo or shaddock, the 丨子 (*Citrus decumanus*), also known at Canton as 碌丨 and 文朋 at Shanghai.
yiu'

厥包橘丨 those pumelos and oranges must be rolled up.

Read *chuh*, and used for 軸. The reed or slaie of a loom.

鼬 From *rat* and the last contracted, from the color of the skin.
yiu'

A species of the weasel family, which is described as near the size of the sable, of a reddish-yellow color, large bushy tail, and runs up trees and eats mice; it is also called 地猴 earth monkey; it is probably an animal akin to the stoat, but one synonym is 黃鼠狼 the common weasel.

釉 Used with ,油 oil.
yiu'

Glossy, glazed; the glazing on porcelain.

挂丨 to glaze things.

狖 貁 From *beast* and *cave*.
yiu'

A species of black monkey, called 狨丨 probably allied to the douc; it is very suspicious and restless in its motions; has many colors, a long tail, thick whiskers, and is described as partly resembling a squirrel, a badger, a fox, and a monkey.

猿啾啾兮丨夜鳴 how the gibbons howl and the doucs cry by night.

褎 An obsolete form of *siu'* 袖 a cuff, for which it is sometimes used.
yiu'

Elegantly dressed, with embroidery; a cuff of a sleeve; the blade of grain; easy, quiet enjoyment and plenty; to promote.

丨然盛服 he was beautifully dressed indeed, — but he knew nothing.

實種實丨 the seed was used and it sprang up.

丨如充耳 well dressed and yet as if his ears were stuffed.

YOH.

Old sounds, yak, ngak, *and* wak. *In Canton*, yéuk *and* ngok; — *in Swatow*, yiak, ngak, *and* ié; — *in Amoy*, iok, ak, gak, *and* giok; — *in Fuhchau*, yòh, ngòk, *and* yòk; — *in Shanghai*, yak, yü, *and* ngòk; — *in Chifu*, yòa.

藥 葯 From *plant* and *music* or *contract*; the second and common contracted form properly means the leaves of the orris root (*Iris*); it is also read *tih*, to bind or bandage; to entwine about and cover.
yao'

Medicinal herbs; medicine, physic; remedial or chemical preparations; to give medicines to; to remedy; medical healing.

丨材 medicines.

開丨方 to write a prescription for the 丨家 or apothecaries, who 抓丨 or 合丨 put it up.

丨鋪 or 丨局 an apothecary's shop; a dispensary.

生丨 the raw, and 熟丨 the prepared opium.

丨引 a disguise given with a dose.

一劑丨 one dose of medicine.

丨酒 medicated spirits.

山丨 the Chinese yam.

甫疾易'丨 a malady is easily cured if treated at the first.

多將熇熇不可救丨 the troubles flame out till they are beyond help or remedy.

食丨 or 服丨 to take medicine.

丨性有君臣 medicines are necessarily divided into principal and subordinate remedies.

丨王廟 a temple to the Chinese Esculapius.

良丨 or 妙丨 or 聖丨 an effectual or excellent remedy.

爚 From *fire* and *measure*.
yoh'

Fiery, hot; bright, by flashes.

震震丨丨 the flashes of lightning and thunder — came in a wonderful manner.

禴, 礿, *yoh'* From *worship* and *thin* or a *measure*, because at the vernal sacrifice the offerings were scant, as nature had not fully expanded. A worship held by the emperors of the Hia dynasty near the vernal equinox, in the ancestral temple, but in the summer by the Cheu sovereigns; hence some use the first character for the vernal, and the second for the summer sacrifice.

約, *yoh'* From *silk* and *ladle* for the sound. To bind, to cord up; to bind by contract, to agree with; to form a treaty or compact; to retrench, to moderate, to spare, to economize; to restrain, to restrict; to stoop, to bend down; to cause to submit; bound, corded; a part of a city like a ward, associated under an eldership,— and sometimes, a single neighborhood in it; it varies in different provinces; a confederation; a treaty, contract, or agreement; in *arithmetic*, to divide; agreeing with; brief, condensed; restricted, meager; an *adverb*, about, nearly.

丨我同他去 he agreed that I should go with him.

丨束 to restrain, to keep in bounds.

儉丨 frugal, not extravagant.

立合丨 to make an indenture or contract.

丨單 the agreement; a compact.

丨摸六百個 about six hundred of them.

大丨 or 丨略 for the most part, on the whole.

丨酌 about, near to; ready for; as 丨酌三點鐘 about three o'clock; 丨酌要話 just going to speak. (*Shanghai.*)

丨信 to make a promise.

丨定他來 he certainly agreed to come.

退丨 to withdraw from the engagement.

背丨 violated a contract.

符丨 to fulfill an agreement

未如丨 or 失丨 unable to complete an engagement.

不丨而同 to agree undesignedly, to happen to coincide in act or opinion; to meet accidentally.

君子丨言 the princely man is sparing of his words.

八丨以二爲四 eight divided by two is four.

潮如有丨 the tide comes in as if it had a contract; *i. e.* is trustworthy.

貧丨 poor, in straitened circumstances.

In *Pekingese.* An interjection, 哎丨 or 噯丨 expressing dislike to the trouble of; dissatisfaction with.

龠, *yoh'* Intended to delineate a *pipe*; composed of 品 and 侖 one representing the *holes*, and the other the *unison* or rhythm of their sounds; it is the 214th radical of pandean pipes and similar instruments.

An ancient reed with three or seven holes, shaped like a flute, but shorter and played with one hand; a measure anciently reckoned as 1200 grains of millet; five 勺 now make one *yoh*, and two of them make one 合 or gill.

管丨 a pipe, a fife.

籥, *yoh'* Like the preceding, and sometimes used for the next.

A satchel or basket; a fife or flute.

啟丨見書 open the case and you'll see the books.

天丨 a group of seven stars near the handle of the Dipper.

以丨不僭 moving to the sound of the flutes in even measure.

鑰, *yao'* From *metal* and *pipe* as the phonetic.

The bolt or catch of a lock; to enter, to get in at.

丨匙 a key.

投丨 to put the key in the lock.

管丨 a cross-bolt to fasten gates.

闖丨 to force one's way in.

酒丨 a kind of tankard.

籲, 顲, *yoh'* From a *pipe* or *reed* and *head* contracted.

To cry with loud intreaty; to invoke in prayer; to implore; to groan from pain in the head.

呼丨 to pray with loud cries.

懇丨 to importune urgently.

丨禱 to pray to.

Read *yü'* Together with, and. 率丨衆戚 [the prince] went out with the crowd to vent his anger.

瀹, *yoh'* To boil; to cook with water, as a soup or stew; to wash, to cleanse out; to soak, to wet through.

疏丨而心 cleanse and reform your hearts.

潭丨 moving; agitated, as water.

丨沸 bubbling, gurgling.

𤂋, *yoh'* From to *divide* and *extreme.* Bubbling of boiling water.

In *Fuhchau* read ˳*lo.* To scald in boiling water, to cook hastily.

丨鷄 to scald a fowl, so as to pluck it easily.

丨麪 to scald vermicelli.

嶽, *yo'* From *hill* and *prison.* The highest peaks of mountains, a lofty summit; the 五丨 are high mountains worshiped by the ancient emperors, and venerated to this day; the 東丨 is 泰山 in Shantung; 西丨 is 華山 in Shensi, south of Si-ngan fu; 北丨 is 恒山 in the southwest of Chihli; 南丨 is 衡山 in the western-center of Hunan; 中丨 is 嵩山 or 泰室 in the west of Honan, near the Yellow River.

四丨 a president of the princes in the days of Yao.

丨丨 antler-like; projecting like deer's horns.

太丨 a peak ten miles east of Hoh cheu in Shansi.

岳, yo' Regarded as a contraction of the preceding, but now chiefly used for a wife's parents, intimating the respect due to them.

丨父 or 丨丈 a wife's father.

鸑, yo' From *bird* and a *prison*.

A felicitous bird, 丨鷟 described as larger than a mallard, with red eyes; its description allies it to the rails; it appeared when Wăn Wang got the empire.

丨鷟鳴於岐陽 the mallard-phœnix sung in K'i-yang.

躍, 趯, yo' From *foot* and *feathered garments;* both are also read *t'ih*,

To skip and caper, to leap for joy; to sport, to frisk and gambol; the second also denotes the hooked perpendicular stroke of a character.

魚丨龍門 the carp has leaped through the dragon gate;—rapid advancement in the tripos.

踴丨用兵 leaping and brandishing weapons, as when joining battle.

不勝雀丨 to jump and hop like a magpie for joy.

丨丨 quickly, instantly, as an arrow on the string.

丨丨蟲螽 the grasshoppers skip merrily.

超丨 to excel, to surpass.

YÜ.

Old sounds, ngo, yo, ngop, ngot, yop, yot, yok, *and* ngu. *In Canton*, ü; — *in Swatow*, i, u, ù, gù, *and* ngo; — *in Amoy*, u, ju, gu, i, *and* ngò; — *in Fuhchau*, ü, ngü, wò, éü, *and* ngéü; — *in Shanghai*, ü, nü, *and* 'ng; — *in Chifu*, yü.

꜀於, ꜀亐, ꜀于, ꜀扵 ꜀yü Etymologists regard the first as an abbreviated form of 烏 a *raven*, as it occurs of the same sound and meaning in the phrase 丨呼哀哉 alas, how sad and piteous! The other is intended to represent vapor rising in successive strata or expanding itself evenly over the earth; the last is a common contraction of the first.

A *preposition* in, at, on, with, by, upon; to be in, to occupy a position; as, so, to become; at the beginning of a sentence, or after 之 it means respecting, in case, relating to; often marks the *accusative* case, and at other times emphasizes the object of the verb and completes the rhythm; after 莫 forms the comparative degree, more, than; before pronouns, it may be rendered as, as to, referring to; it sometimes reverses the position of the object and subject, as 室丨怒市丨色 if you are angry at home, it will manifest itself in the market.

丨三年 in the third year.

不求丨人 ask advice or help of no man.

醫者致丨病也 doctors only increase the disease.

問丨我 he asked me; learned it from me.

丨傳'有之 it is in the record

丨今 at this present, now.

莫大丨天父 none is greater than God.

丨此有人焉 supposing there is a man.

丨民也仁之 he treats the people with humanity.

丨是乎 how with regard to this? thereupon.

丨心何忍 where is your patience?

止丨至善 to rest in the highest good.

有益丨君 it is advantageous to the prince.

死之丨刀 he died by the sword.

如此而成丨孝子也 try acting in this manner, he will show that he is a dutiful son.

不丨其事 do not mix in that affair.

魚在丨沼 the fish are in that pond.

易'丨消化 easy of digestion.

丨斯三者何先 which is the first of these three?

Read ꜀*yü* for only the form 于. To speak, to say; to go, to proceed; resembling.

丨丨 going along, as a person in the distance; also self-satisfied.

王丨出征 the king went to subdue them.

丨民生之不易' he said the subsistence of the people was not an easy thing.

Read ꜀*hü* or ꜀*yü;* same as the next. Wide, vast; also occurs used for 吁, as 丨嗟麟兮 Ah, behold, [such sons are the real] unicorn!—meaning Wăn Wang's sons.

迂 ꜀yü From to *go* and *curling vapor* as the phonetic.

Vague, vast, distant; not exact or clear; to misinterpret, to pervert, to distort; very; to avoid, to escape from; wide, spacious.

丨久 a very long time.

丨乃心 to distort another's intentions.

言丨效近 the proposition is very general, but it is applicable to present times.

丨腐 inapt, doltish.

丨拘 precise, too particular.

丨遠而闊于事情 a vague and indistinct thing; no certainty, no tact in doing things.

紆 ꜀yü To wind or twist; to distort; to pervert justice; foolish, inexpert; a cord; crooked, bent; weak in the middle, said of an arrow whose shaft is too small.

冤結丨軫兮 alas, my wrongs are deep and must be kept down.

丨廻 circuitous, indirect.

丨曲 vague, indistinct, not perspicuous in meaning or intention.

扵 ꜀yü Mud, silt, deposit; to silt up a gutter, or the channel of a river.

泥丨了河 the mud has silted up the stream.

風丨住子 the wind has raised a dust-heap.

淤 ꜀yü Like the last.

A sedgy bank deposited in a stream; a bar in a channel; to silt up.

丨濁 dirty, turbid, muddy.

丨塞不通 the mud stops the water flowing.

出于丨泥而不染 it came out of the mire, but can't be dyed; *met.* I came from a sink, but nobody can now corrupt me.

Read ꜀yü, when used for 飫. Satiated.

棜 ꜀yü A tray for holding sacrificial meats, supported on long handles, by which it was carried to the worship.

魚 ꜁yü The original rudely represented a fish, the four lower points being the *tail*, the upper two the *head*, with the scaly *body* between; it forms the 195th radical of names and parts of fishes.

A fish, classed with 鱗蟲 scaly beings, 水蟲 aquatic beings, and 蟲之隱者 those beings which are hidden; fishy; a horse with eyes like a fish, for which the next is also used.

一尾丨 or 一條丨 one fish.

捕丨 or 打丨 to fish.

丨服 fish-skin clothes worn by the 丨皮韃子 or Ghiliaks in Manchuria.

木丨 the wooden fish; it is a skull-shaped block on which priests beat time when chanting.

丨杈 a fizgig or fish-spear.

壁丨 or 衣丨 and 白丨 the lepisma found in clothes.

唱木丨 to sing ditties and ballads, as blind women do. (*Cantonese.*)

敲卜丨 to beat the divining-fish, as is done by Taoists.

丨子 or 丨穚 spawn of fish.

丨苗 or 丨秧 the young fry, minnows.

丨書 or 丨函 or 丨素 a letter or note; referring to an ancient story.

出丨燈 a procession of fancy lanterns at Canton, many of them shaped like fish.

走了丨兒是大的 the fish that ran off was a big one; said of anticipated profits, or things lost which are hard to prove.

丨水和諧 as closely dependent as water and fish; said of married people, or a ruler and his ministers.

佩金丨 a prince royal among the Kitans, because he wore a fish made of gold.

脚丨 a turtle, emys, or other kind of water *Chelonia*.

坐丨 and 蛤丨 the frog, from its habit of sitting, and in imitation of its croak.

䁩 ꜁yü A horse with white rings around the eyes, like a fish's eye, at the edge of the cornea.

漁 / 𢿢 ꜁yü From *water* and *fish*; the second form is only used in the classics.

To fish; to take indiscriminately whatever comes; to seize; immoderate.

丨色 inordinate lust.

丨翁 or 丨夫 a fisherman.

丨婆 a fishwife.

丨其利 seeking nothing but his own gain.

丨取 to incroach on and seize.

丨陽 an old name for Ki cheu 薊州 in Chihli from the 丨水 a branch of the Peh-tang River.

丨樵耕讀 fishermen, foresters, farmers, and scholars.

魰 ꜁yü From *fish* and to *strike*; it differs from ꜀wăn 魰; like the last.

To fish; to catch fish.

畋丨逸樂 to take recreation in hunting and fishing.

禺 ꜁yü From 禸 a *paw* and 甶 a *demon*.

A term for quadrumanous animals, more particularly those like spider monkeys; to start, as an affair; the space of a *li* in the Cheu dynasty; occurs used for 虞 in 丨淵 the place where the sun goes down.

丨中 the sun in 巳 from 9 to 11 A.M.

端丨 incipient stages of a matter.

嵎 ꜁yü From *hill* and *monkey*.

A mountain or region in the east, called 丨夷 the extreme east of Yao's sway, where the sun rises; it probably refers to 東夷 or Yesso Island, though others think it denotes Shantung Promontary or Corea.

山丨 a covert or dell in hills, protected from the bleak winds.

負丨死守 resting on the hill he held out to the last; *i.e.* he stood at bay, made a last stand.

隅 ꜁yü From *place* and *monkey*.

A corner, a nook, a secluded spot; a cove, inlet, or small bay; a part, a little; rigid, precise, as an angle; in *mathematics*, the unit or lowest term of a cube root.

一丨之地 a lot, a parcel of land.

海丨 isles of the sea, an islet; a bay or place on the coast.

童子丨坐 boys should sit at a corner [table].

砥礪廉丨 this will prove his integrity and firmness of principle.

角丨 a corner.

舉一丨不以三丨反 to point to a corner and not to understand that there are three corners more; *i.e.* dull, not to take a hint.

趨 丨 to enter on the corner mat; *i. e.* to come to the table.

向 丨 獨 抱 I will stand aside and bear the trouble (or responsibility) alone.

方 丨 a right angle or square corner; between the cardinal points, as northeast or northwest.

齵 ˏyü Uneven teeth, or those interfering with each other; many tenons entering one piece, as felloes in the hub of a wheel; perplexed, in confusion, as the affairs of a state.

丨 差 discrepant, irreconcilable.

In *Fuhchau.* Warped, twisted; obstinate, mulish.

蝺 ˏyü A water-beetle, the [illegible] 丨 or 青蚨 whose appearance is described like a cicada, and the eggs are glued by the mother to leaves, especially of the sweet-flag, in rows of eights and nines; it is also called 魚父 and answers to a *Hydrophilus.*

髃 腢 ˏyü The clavicle or collar-bone; usually known as 鎖子骨 the key-bone.

愚 ˏyü From *heart* and *monkey.*

Having a monkey's wit, which animal the Chinese regard as a silly brute; simple, uninstructed, rude, unpolished; confounding right and wrong; stupid, unwise, and in this sense used for one's self in writing letters; to deceive, to befool.

丨 弟 or 丨 者 "your stupid brother;" like "your humble servant."

丨 拙 or 丨 笨 foolish, unskilled, awkward.

鄉 丨 rustics, clodhoppers, village swains.

丨 民 the silly people, the canaille, the mob; — a phrase used by the rulers for their subjects.

丨 見 in my humble opinion.

大 智 若 丨 a very clever man with a doltish expression.

丨 弄 人 to deceive; to gammon.

丨 昧 stupid, unenlightened.

丨 狂 conceited and foolish, a vaporing simpleton.

余 予 ˏyü From 人 *man* and 舍 *house* contracted, alluding to the freedom of conversation in the house; it nearly resembles ˏshé 佘; the second is also read ˊyü.

The first personal *pronoun,* I; we, our, myself; mostly used in writing, and often printed in a smaller type at the side.

其 如 丨 何 what can he do to me?

丨 所 否 者 I am one who has done a thing rather out of the way.

比 丨 the head-dress of a Mongol princess.

丨 一 人 our Emperor.

Read ˏtu. Name of a mountain, 檮 丨 in Mongolia.

妤 伃 ˏyü From *woman* or *man* and *I;* the first is easily mistaken for ˊhao 好 good.

Fair, handsome; in the Tsu state, a very tall and portly man.

婕 丨 in the T'ang dynasty, a kind of chamberlain housekeeper.

邘 ˏyü Not the same as ˏhan 邗 a town.

A small fief conferred on Wu Wang's son, lying somewhere in the present Hwai-ngan fu, just south of the Yellow River; also a town in the state Ching 鄭, now K'ai-fung fu.

圩 ˏyü From *earth* and *in;* it is often but erroneously used as a contracted form of ˏhü 墟 a *market.*

A dike or levee, raised to restrain the waters; a bund, a bank; a low place.

丨 頜 a sluice cut through a dike.

丨 岸 an overseer of dikes.

丨 長 a dike.

丨 田 fields guarded by dikes, as in Hwai-ngan fu in Kiangsu.

蕩 平 賊 丨 cleared the dike country of robbers.

貐 ˏyü An animal whose voice is like a child's; it is applied to 壁 the constellation in γ Pegasus, which when seen great rain follows; the 豲 丨 or the great porcupine, also called 豪豬 or bristled hog, found in Shensi and westerly; its quills are sold for chopsticks; the body is about three feet long, white belly, black head, and banded quills.

盂 盓 ˏyü From *dish* and *vapor.*

Originally denoted a wooden dish, but now includes those of any material; a basin; a porringer, a large cup.

漱 口 丨 a cup to rinse the mouth at table.

盤 丨 wooden dishes or bowls.

丨 方 則 水 方 if the dish be square the water in it will be square too; —denoting the great influence of the prince in molding the people; as 君 猶 丨 也 he is like the dish.

硯 水 丨 a cup for watering the ink-stone.

痰 丨 a small spittoon for the sick.

丨 縣 in Ping-ting cheu in the east of Shansi.

杅 ˏyü Used with the preceding, but referring more to tubs large enough to wash or bathe in.

水 丨 a wash-tub.

Used for its primitive; 丨 丨 a self-satisfied look and manner.

竽 ˏyü An ancient reed organ like the 笙 having 36 tubes, meeting in a bulb, and blown through the mouth-piece; it is called 盜 丨 because it leads other instruments, and a chief of banditti is also metaphorically called by the same term.

濫厠吹丨 an awkward performer blowing the organ; *i. e.* a charlatan, one who gets paid for what he cannot do; used also in self-depreciation when complimented.

雩 ˏyü From *rain* and *alas*, the primitive here denoting 吁嗟 or the cry of suppliants.

The summer sacrifice for rain; to pray for rain in the second month of summer; distant, because in this service, the answer was not obtained until the grain was ripe months after; in Honan, an old name for the rainbow.

丨雨 to pray for rain.

丨都縣 in the south of Kiangsi.

龍見而丨 when the dragon-star (Sirius?) rises, pray for rain.

畬 ˏyü From *field* and *my*; it is also read ˏshé, meaning tinder.

A field which has been plowed three successive seasons (some say two); to cultivate a field; a field newly opened was called 菑, in the second year it was 新, and the third year 丨 or 田 field, being by that time subdued.

如何新丨 how are you going to plow up this field?

丨客 the "field guests," or squatters, refers to a settlement of Canton people in Kin-hwa fu in Chehkiang.

餘 ˏyü From *to eat* and *my*.

What is left after eating; remnants, overplus; the rest, the remainder; superabundant; moreover, as well as; after a period.

丨地 vacant ground, unused space.

留丨地 spare a portion; lay by the surplus, as of wages.

有丨 more than enough.

丨賸 enough and to spare.

丨坭 rubbish left after building; debris; earth for filling.

丨暇 or 丨閒 leisure days, spare time after necessary duties.

丨力 spare moments and energy.

其丨 as to the rest; what remains.

丨黨 the rest of the banditti.

捧讀之丨 after I had read your letter.

丨姚 a district in Shao-hing fu, not far from Ningpo.

丨子 children who are not the eldest or direct heirs, as sons of concubines; supernumeraries.

丨夫 extra hands on a farm, referring to the youngest sons of feudal retainers who tilled the land.

丨羨 or 富丨 an abundance of.

忠厚留有丨地 may your faithful kindness be more than rewarded to your descendants.

虎口丨生 just escaped with his life, as from the tiger's mouth.

悲悼之丨 in addition to my own sorrow.

舁 ˏyü From 臼 *hands* and 廾 *bearing up*, as two hands or two men raising a weight, and holding it secure with their hands and nails.

To raise a thing; to lift it for presentation.

丨拱 or 丨舉 to raise up; to bring or offer to one.

丨夫 a porter, a bearer of burdens.

二人共丨 two men brought it.

丨扛 to bear on a pole.

臾 ˏyü From the old form of 申 a horary character and 乙 *crooked*.

A moment, a little while.

不可須丨離也 [right] must not be neglected even for a moment.

顓丨 a small state in Lu, now Mung-yin hien 蒙陰縣 in the south of Shantung.

Read *kw'éi'* and used for 蕢. A hamper or basket to carry grass, which this character is thought to resemble.

Read ˋ*yung*, and used for 慂. To arouse, to excite.

㥚 ˏyü Sorrowful, grieved at; alarmed, in terror.

心丨 sick at heart.

憂丨 sad; in much misery.

諛 ˏyü From *words* and a *moment*.

To flatter, to praise to one's face; to adulate; a flatterer, a sycophant.

面丨 personal, direct flattery; to say pleasing things.

富貴多丨言 high people hear much flattery.

丨色 a simpering, smirking countenance.

僕臣丨厥后自聖 when an officer bepraises his master, he soon thinks himself something wonderful.

孝子不丨其親 a filial son never adulates his parents.

何言之丨 why speak such flattering (or untrue) words.

萸 **茰** ˏyü The second form presents a common abbreviation of this primitive.

A medicinal plant of several varieties.

山茱丨 is probably the dogwood; its sub-acid drupes are dried to use as an astringent.

茱丨江 a stream in Yih-tu hien in central Shantung.

噳 ˏyü Herds of deer gathering in one spot; laughing, frolicking.

麀鹿丨丨 multitudes of happy deer and does.

腴 ˏyü From *flesh* and a *moment*.

The fat on the belly; big-bellied, like some fishes; corpulent, obese; soft and flabby fat; rich, as productive soil; entrails of dogs and swine.

肥丨 fat, in good condition for killing.

膏丨 fertile, rich, as soil.

進魚冬右丨 when presenting fish in winter, place the belly on the right hand.

丨濃之味 a rich luscious taste.

味道之丨 the choicest, richest dainties.

道丨 the gist or essence of a doctrine.

百畝膏丨 a very fertile piece of land.

虞 騶虞 ˏyü From *tiger* and to *talk big*; the second form denotes only the animal; occurs used for the next.

A fabulous beast of a mild disposition, the 騶〡 which is said to have appeared in the days of Wu Wang; anxious for, and therefore prepared; to sympathize with, to think upon, to expect; to estimate; an impediment, mishap, accident; vigilant, ready, provided against; to understand; to help; to select; to possess; to quiet a spirit; a period of seven days' mourning; a place where the Great Yü lived, now 安邑縣 in the southwest of Shansi.

士〡禮 the scholar performs the rites of appeasing — the ghost.

無〡 nothing to apprehend.

不〡 an unexpected accident.

防〡 watching, on the lookout.

疎〡 careless, remiss, unready.

以備不〡 to guard against contingencies.

〡人 a warden of the parks and ponds in the Cheu, now called 〡衡司.

無貳無〡上帝臨女 you need have no doubts, no anxieties, for Shangti will approach or bless you.

〡樂 blessed, delighted.

娛 ˏyü Joy, pleasure; to amuse, to divert one's self or others; relaxation, diversion.

歡〡 delight, pleasure.

自〡 to enjoy one's self.

戲彩〡親 with sports and gay dresses, he diverted his parents; said of Lao Laitsz'.

〡順 to take pleasure in obliging others.

極〡 ecstatic joy, extreme delight.

璵 ˏyü A striped stone, 〡璠 resembling cornelian, or more probably the cat's-eye; found in Shantung.

美哉〡璠煥若也 beautiful indeed is the brilliant cat's-eye!

澞 ˏyü A rivulet running between two hillocks or rising banks.

歟 ˏyü From to *breathe* and *giving*; it was at first written without the radical, but the two are now usually distinguished.

A final particle indicative of relief or admiration, but mostly used after questions expressing doubt, surprise, affirmation, or irony; to breathe easier, as after a sudden start or excitement.

君子人〡 is that man a good man?

可不愼〡 must we not be very careful?

故有此言〡 does not this expression (or phrase) therefore arise?

歸〡歸〡 shall we not go home? go home now? — said Confucius to his disciples.

猗〡 excellent! fine!

嗟〡 alas, how sad!

若是之難〡 does not this look as if it was rather difficult?

求之〡抑與之〡 did he ask for it, or was it given to him?

豈非天〡 is this your work, or did Heaven assist you?

譽 ˏyü From *words* and *give*; it is similar to 諛 to flatter.

To eulogize, to praise to the utmost, to extol; to overpraise, to flatter.

面〡背毀 to praise one to his face and then defame him.

稱〡 or 揚〡 to eulogize, to greatly commend.

〡之不喜 he is not pleased with such flattery.

〡善 to commend goodness.

Read *yü*' Fame, credit, praise.

沽名釣〡 to buy fame and fish for praise.

令聞廣〡 his fame and praise are everywhere heard.

〡處 pleasure, a feeling of gratification.

含〡 a certain felicitous star.

旟 ˏyü From *flag* and to *give*.

A triangular flag, the 革〡 having a scolloped border of a stiff material, with falcons drawn on it, and suspended on a staff; given to valiant and successful officers; to fly abroad, as loose hair.

孑孑干〡 high rise the falcon-pictured banners.

〡〡 a large number of people.

匪伊卷之髮則有〡 she did not roll it up, and her hair spread over her shoulders.

彼〡旐斯胡不旆旆 how grandly flaunted the banners, showing their tortoises and falcons!

輿 ˏyü From 車 *carriage* contained in 舁 to *bear*; the radical is sometimes written underneath.

The box or body of a cart or chariot; a carriage; to hold, to sustain; to contain and bear, as the earth does its inhabitants; *met.* the earth; a foundation, a basis; many.

〡人 a carriage-maker or cartwright; a cartman.

地〡圖 a map of the world, or of the Chinese empire.

皇〡 the imperial city, the palace.

〡宅 a tomb, a sepulcher.

國母〡瘍之實 the reality of the empress dowager's illness.

乘〡 the traveling equipage and carts of the emperor.

〡論 the public or general opinion.

權〡 the first, the introduction or starting of, as an enterprise, referring to making a cart by beginning at the base boards.

百人〡瓢兒趨 a hundred men carrying gourds ran off.

扶〡 a kind, genial manner.

籃〡 a basket litter in which sick persons are carried.

敬禮之〡 respect is the beginning of courtesy.

肩〡 a small sedan chair.

洞察〡情 he has thoroughly examined its deep meaning.

鸒 鷽 ˏyü — A bird of the crow family, with a white belly and breast, which assembles in flocks; it is probably a species of jay or blackbird, but others say it is the crow.

鍝 ˏyü — A saw; a fine awl, the 鏤 丨 with which the ears of women are bored.

俞 ˏyü — Composed of 亼 an old form of 集 *to bring together*, 舟 *a boat*, and 巛 *water*, denoting to scoop out a boat from a log; it occurs used for 愈ˋ more.

To respond, to answer, as a maid-servant; to assent; yes, so, certainly, well; to agree to willingly.

如蒙丨允 if you ask for a favor, [the emperor will] no doubt accord it.

都丨吁咈 sighing, he replied, it cannot be.

Read *yü*ˋ Mild.

丨丨 an easy, courteous manner.

Read ˏ*shu*. A fief in the Han dynasty.

丨元 old name for Ching-kiang fu in Yunnan, north of L. Sien.

媮 ˏyü — From *woman* and *to consent*; occurs interchanged with the next.

Wasteful, careless, like one belonging to a rich family; delicate and pleasure-seeking; to despise or set light by, to depreciate; joyfully.

富貴以丨生乎 the rich and grand pass their lives in one long pleasure.

不敢丨生 do not presume to trifle with life.

Read ˏ*t'eu*. Clandestine, illicit; deceptive, crafty.

惟丨合以取容 they tried to conceal their designs by assuming an easy manner.

愉 ˏyü — A contented, pleased countenance; happy, self-satisfied; joyfully, willingly; to please; good style, well brought up.

丨色 a jolly, glad face.

他人是丨 others are happy, — but not I.

丨悅 joyful, rejoiced, glad.

我有嘉賓其樂丨丨 I entertain these friends, and their happy contentment is great.

丨丨如也 see how joyful.

萮 ˏyü — A wild plant, the 山丨菜 resembling the skunk-cabbage (*Symplocarpus*) in its growth, but the flowers are malvaceous; found in Honan.

丨茈 a boletus, the punk mushroom.

渝 ˏyü — A river near the east end of the Great Wall; to change; to exchange, as sides; to deteriorate, to grow worse.

丨州 an old name for Chung-king fu in the south of Sz'ch'uen.

丨變 to retract, as a promise.

舍命不丨 if I lose my life, I will not change.

至死不丨其所守 he will not yield up his charge even to save his life.

闟 ˏyü — To spy and peep; to get aside, so as to see a person.

闟丨門內 he hid inside of the gate, — so as get a sly look at her.

榆 ˏyü — The elm (*Ulmus*), of which ten sorts are described; one of them is a species of *Microptelea*, another a kind of hornbeam or *Carpinus*.

丨莢 or 丨錢 elm seeds and their winged seed-vessels.

失之東隅收之桑丨 if I have lost the east plat, I have got my village home.

丨皮 slippery elm bark, a tonic medicine.

白丨 a star which guides the husbandman in his planting.

啖丨 to take a decoction of elm seeds in order to sleep.

地丨 ground elm, the *Hypericum* or St. John's wort.

瑜 ˏyü — Luster of gems; a beautiful stone, like jasper, worn by the sons of noblemen; excellencies, good qualities.

瑕丨互見 the defects and excellencies are well contrasted.

披褐懷丨 under a plain dress he cherished the highest virtues.

羭 ˏyü — In the Hia dynasty, a black ram; credit, reputation; the name of a god of the hills.

窬 ˏyü — A small door or hole cut in a wainscot, a lattice partition or side wall; a small door for daily use, within a large gateway, the latter being opened on great occasions; to bore a hole in a wall, as burglars do.

穿丨or 丨牆 to cut through a wall.

Read ˏ*teu*. Low; depressed below the level.

甌丨 a deep depression or excavation in the ground.

In *Cantonse.* The thickness of a brick in a wall, when laid edgewise.

三丨磚 a wall, a brick and a half thick.

五丨厚 a wall two and a half bricks thick.

褕 ˏyü — Sleeves of a woman's robes adorned with feathers; elegant, as a costly dress.

短丨 a short sleeve.

貂襜丨 a sleeve trimmed with sable fur.

丨衣甘食 fine clothes and good eating.

Read ˏ*yao*. Dresses with pheasants drawn on them.

丨狄后衣 the queen's dress with painted pheasants on it.

廠 ˏyü — Interchanged with the next.

To mimic and make sport of.

揶丨 to clap the hands and laugh at one.

邪丨 to act in a pantomime, to throw the hands about.

揄 揄 ˏyü — From *hand* and to *assent*. A long sleeve reaching to the feet; to lead, to draw forth and show the merits of, to bring out merit; to praise.

丨然 laughing and clapping.

雍容丨揚 everywhere extolled his grace and worthy acts.

揶丨 a "devil's laugh;" — to mimic and make sport of.

Read ˏyao, and used for 褕. To draw pheasants on the dress, as was the fashion in the Cheu dynasty.

Read ˏt'eu. To draw out.

丨文竿出比目 he lifted up the painted rod and drew out a sole fish.

Read ˏyiu. To scoop grain out of a mortar.

或舂或丨 some hulled it with the stone pestle, and some scooped it out.

Read ˏch'eu and ˏt'eu. To walk with the hands hanging and swinging.

丨手徐行 to saunter along with hands hanging carelessly.

被髮丨袂 with disheveled hair and hanging sleeves.

覦 ˏyü From to *look at* and *assent;* used with ˏ窬 to cut through.

To desire, to long earnestly for; to covet and spy how to obtain.

窺丨 to spy and peep, in order to plunder; to lurk about.

無覬丨以求幸 having no inordinate desires, you will thus get happiness.

無丨心 pureminded, not covetous.

敵人丨我 my enemy watches privily.

蝓 ˏyü A garden slug, 蜲丨 a *Limax*, called also 蝸牛 the snail-cow; the name is also given to a large garden spider.

逾 踰 ˏyü — From to *go* or *foot* and to *wish; q.d.* to get where one wishes.

To pass over, to cross; to get over, as a wall; or beyond, as a time; to exceed; to pass by, to omit.

丨牆 to leap a wall.

丨節 to exceed the limit or margin, as in an outlay.

丨限 to overpass the mark or time.

丨月 to pass over the month.

丨遠 to travel far.

丨于洛 it flowed into the River Loh.

丨城 to get over the city wall.

丨分' to forget one's proper place.

日月丨邁 the days and months have passed away.

堬 ˏyü A grave; in the Tsin dynasty, the tumulus raised over it.

歈 ˏyü To clap the hands; in the state of Wu 吳 a song.

丨歌 a tune or song.

舞丨 to sport and sing; to carouse.

颶 ˏyü A sudden tempest, like a tornado.

颹丨 a violent blast.

燸 ˏyü Also read ˏjü; fiery.

The flames of fire; color faded out.

火苗青丨丨 the bluish flames of the fire.

雨 ˊyü Intended to represent *rain*, the upper line being the *sky*, the sides the *clouds*, and the *drops* within; it forms the 173d radical of characters relating to meteorology.

Rain; a shower; to come fast and furious, like rain.

下丨 or 落丨 to rain.

雲行丨施 when the clouds move the rain is given down.

微絲丨 a drizzling, misty rain.

苦丨 a rain which spoils the crops, a very long rain.

平田丨 a widely extended rain.

過雲丨 a passing shower.

白撞丨 a sun shower.

暴丨 or 疾丨 a terrible gust of a shower; a squall which is dangerous.

夏丨丨'人 the summer rain falls on man; *met.* the emperor's kindness reaches all.

舊丨 old rain; *met.* an old friend.

今丨 a recent acquaintance.

丨風不更 no alteration on account of the weather, as a race.

丨露恩 the kindness of rain and dew; *i. e.* the Emperor's favor.

握丨携雲 to hold the rain and guide the clouds, as a god; *met.* to embrace a woman.

Read yü' To rain; to fall from the sky.

丨金三日 it rained gold three days — in the days of Fuhhi; this may be a legend of a great fall of ærolites.

丨雪紛紛 a great fall of rain.

矢石丨下 the darts and stones came raining down.

隨車甘丨 the sweet showers follow his carriage.

紅丨 the peach blossoms are falling.

羽 ˊyü Intended to represent the long *wing* primaries and the large quill *feathers* of birds; it is the 124th radical of characters relating to plumagery and feathers.

Wings, plumes; made of or having feathers; feathered; winged tribes; a banner or signal of feathers; cloth having a rough feel, as bunting; quick, flying; the fifth of the five kinds of musical sounds, that are made by smacking.

丨族 or 丨類 the feathered tribes.

黨丨 deatchments from a force; foraging or predatory bands.

舞干丨 a sort of panache used by mummers.

丨儀 what reflects honor on a ruler, as a good envoy sent by him.

丨布 bunting.

丨綢 bombasin.

丨紗 English camlets.

丨士 a Taoist priest; he is called 丨化而登仙 referring to the flight of the soul after death.

丨林軍 the Imperial body-guard of about 300 men.

丨林天軍 a group of 35 stars in Aquarius, including δ τ χ ψ and others.

ʻ禹 ʻyü — Combined of 禸 a *paw* and 虫 *insect*; it once denoted a certain insect, now unknown.

Loose, free; the reputed founder of the Hia dynasty, called 大丨 and also 神丨 who reigned at Ping-yang fu in Shansi; in epitaphs, one who receives a kingdom and perfects its work.

丨惡ʼ旨酒 Yü detested even the best liquor.

丨餘糧 concretions of brown hæmatite, supposed to be petrified crumbs from Yü's table.

ʻ萭 ʻyü — Grass; a kind of tree, whence the character was used as a surname.

Read ˏkü. A kind of dividers, called 丨蔞 used to mark off the spokes in a wheel when making it.

ʻ楀 ʻyü — A kind of tree.

丨維師氏 Yü is the captain of the guards.

ʻ瑀 ʻyü — A pebble with stripes and coloring, which make it almost as valuable as a gem; probably a variety of cornelian.

ʻ鄅 ʻyü — A small ancient state in the present department of Tsing cheu in Shantung, whence the descendants of Shin-nung, named 妘 came.

ʻ與 ʻ与 ʻyü — The second form, composed of 一 *one* and 勹 *spoonful*, (for 酌) denoting equal consultation, is the oldest; afterwards 舁 to *hold up* was combined with it, making it denote *one debate held in a mortar*; the contraction is common.

As a *preposition*, nearly synonymous with 于, by, with, to; as a *copula*, and, together with; as, as if; but when repeated it has a disjunctive sense, either, or; when followed by 寧 denotes a comparison; before a verb it often denotes the dative; after a verb it expresses merely a transitive action; to give, to commit to, to transfer; to make known to, to represent; to consort or associate with; a band, a company or combination; to accept, to allow; to agree, to comply with, to promise; to give in to, to submit; to grant or concede; to approve; to wait, to delay for; to use, to employ.

丨人不同 unlike other men.

丨你走 I'll go with you.

好相丨 a good friend; intimate. (*Cantonese.*)

黨丨 connected or linked with, as in a club or band; a company, an association.

歲不我丨 the years will not wait for me.

孰丨我 who is like me or equal to me?

丨我無干涉 it is none of my business, it does not concern me.

天丨之 Heaven gave it.

甲丨乙孰美 which is the best of them 甲 or 乙, this or that?

喪丨其易也寧戚 in mourning true grief is better than show.

容丨 at ease, careless about, self-indulgent.

則王丨之乎 would the king then grant it?

丨助 to give aid, to help.

之子歸不我丨 when that gentleman returns, he will not take me with him.

鄙夫可ʻ丨事君ˏ丨哉 can one serve his prince when associated with a mean fellow?

Read *yü*ʼ. To take part in; to assist at, to be concerned in; used for ˏ歟 as an exclamation.

我黍丨丨 our millet is flourishing.

不丨問 I will not ask him.

猶丨無決 as if he was undecided in his mind.

吾不丨祭如不祭 if I am not at the sacrifice, it is as if I did not sacrifice.

ʻ瘐 ʻyü — From *disease* and a *moment*.

A prisoner dying from cold and hunger; sick; weak; to treat prisoners badly.

憂丨 melancholy and diseased; hypochondriac.

丨死獄中 starved to death in the prison.

身丨丨而未起 I am very weak and unable to rise.

丨斃水手人 they maltreated the sailors so that they died under their hands.

ʻ庾 ʻ㔱 ʻ匬 ʻ斞 ʻyü — From *shelter* or *receptacle* and *momentary*; all four are nearly synonymous, but the two last especially mean the measure.

An extemporaneous cover; a temporary granary or stack for the crops in the field, or when waiting to be transported; a pile, a stack; abundant, affluent; a measure of 16 斗 or pecks, not now used.

客有丨積 shocks of grain are piled up in the fields.

我丨維億 my stacks are numbered by the myriad.

大丨嶺 the Great Stack Mts., which lie east of the Méi-ling, between Kwangtung, Kwangsi, and Hunan.

露丨 open uncovered stacks.

ʻ楰 ʻyü — Also read ˏyü.

A tree, also called 鼠梓木 or rat *Rottlera*, whose wood is said to be tough in dry weather, and brittle in wet weather; the description allies it to the ash (*Fraxinæ*), or perhaps to a *Catalpa*.

ʻ惥 ʻyü — To walk rapidly; to walk in a dignified respectful manner.

趨步丨丨 he hastened his steps, walking fast.

ʿ窳 ʿyü From *hole* and a *melon vine.*

A vase with a crack or hole; filthy, dirty; listless, inefficient, useless; weak, sickly.

器不苦丨 the vase is perfect.

手足惰丨 my hands and feet cannot be used; *i. e.* have been rendered useless.

呰丨苟且 he is heedless and negligent, good for nothing.

ʿ傴 ʿyü From *man* and a *corner.*

Hunchbacked; the body inclining, stooping; to show great respect, to bend forward as if hearing orders.

丨者使之塗 [stooping like] a man cleaning up the dirt.

丨者不袒 a hunchback should not strip, — for his back is not comely.

ʿ雓 ʿyü A chicken just fledged; out of the shell.

ʿ愈 ʿyü From *heart* and *assent;* interchanged with its primitive and the next, and occasionally with ʿ愉 happy.

To surpass, to exceed; to overcome, to get the better of; to get well; healed, convalescent, cured; a sign of the comparative, more, better, in a further degree.

憂心丨丨 grieved at more and more.

此丨于彼 this is better than that.

今病小丨 his disease is now a little better.

丨好 mending, recovered, nearly or quite well.

丹之治水丨于禹 [Tan said to Mencius,] I could have drained the flood better than Yü.

立丨 it is an immediate cure.

丨多不丨足 the more he has the more dissatisfied he is.

丕丨受謝 no cure no pay.

丨甚 much more, more serious, greatly increased.

昨已粗丨 he is rather better than he was yesterday.

ʿ瘉 ʿyü Like the preceding.

To be cured; convalescent; disease, a functional disorder of the body; clever, upright.

不令兄弟交相爲丨 do not let it be a cause of strife between these offended brothers.

東方之士孰爲丨 who is the bright one among these scholars?

父母生我胡俾我丨 my parents bore me, and whence then have I so much illness?

ʿ噢 ʿyü From *mouth* and *profound;* it is sometimes read *yuh,*

Sorrow or remorse expressed by groans; the cry of pain.

丨咻 groans and moans.

丨咿 sick at heart, full of sorrow.

ʿ俁 ʿyü Large features, a person with a large face.

碩人丨丨 a man of large size; a stalwart man.

ʿ麌 ʿyü A male deer, a stag; to herd.

麀鹿丨丨 the does and bucks were numerous.

ʿ宇 ʿyü From *covering* and *in* as the phonetic.

The part of the house covered by the eaves; to cover, to shelter; to brood over, as a bird; to regard, to countenance; wide, vast, reaching everywhere; territory; the canopy of heaven; to choose a site.

丨宙 the universe, all ages; one character refers to space, and the other to time.

上棟下丨 the ridge-pole is above, and the eaves below.

屋丨 the place under the eaves.

丨下 or 丨內 under the vault or in the world; *i. e.* within the empire; the wide world.

託人丨下 to obtain the aid of a person.

多蒙仁丨庇廕 I am greatly indebted for your humane protection.

公男器丨不凡 the young man's talents and countenance are unusual.

ʿ圄 ʿyü From 口 *inclosure* and 悟 to *reflect* contracted; occurs used for the next.

To detain, to imprison a criminal, in order that he may reform.

拘罪人于丨中 he held the criminals in the prison.

省囹丨 to examine into the prisons.

ʿ圉 ʿyü From *inclosure* and *lucky;* occurs interchanged with the next and the last.

A stable or place where horses are reared; a groom, a hostler; a prison; to guard, to defend; used for the next, a wooden image of a tiger; the borders of the country, a frontier where flocks are kept.

丨師 the master of the sovereign's stud.

丨守 to guard the frontiers.

丨官 a kind of steward or bailiff.

始舍之丨丨焉 how lively [the fish] are when you first let them go.

丨鄉 an ancient town near Lohyang in the west of Honan.

誰捍牧丨 who will guard the shepherds on the borders?

疆丨 the frontier of a state; cyclic years with 丁 in them.

朱丨 a mountain, southwest of Fuhkiang in Kung-chʻang fu in Kansuh.

ʿ敔 ʿyü From 攴 to *strike* and 吾 *I;* interchanged with the last.

To stop the music; an ancient musical instrument carved to resemble a recumbent tiger, having 27 notches along its back, and when a rod was rapidly drawn over it, the musical instruments stopped.

合止柷丨 they arranged and used the signals for starting and stopping the orchestra.

ʿ語 ʿyü From *words* and *I;* the verb is sometimes read *yü*ʾ

To talk with, to converse; to tell, to inform; to warn, to

speak with; words, conversation, discourse; expressions, phrases; a sentence; language.

言丨 conversation, words; discussion.

交頭接丨 to whisper something in his ear.

細丨 whispering, low words.

丨言粗俗 low, vulgar expressions; a low patois.

愼言丨 be careful of what you say.

一丨道破 cleared up the matter in a single sentence, as a clever judge does a dispute.

簽丨 oracular sentences, phrases written on bamboos, which worshipers draw out of a cup to learn their fate.

轉丨 words, which like disjunctive conjunctions, give a turn to the meaning.

起丨 initial phrases or particles in a sentence.

成丨 proverbs, sayings, trite expressions.

居吾丨汝 sit down and I will tell you plainly.

言三丨四 loquacious, chattering.

小丨 chitchat, gossip.

于時言言于時丨丨 at one time he spake his mind, and at another he began to deliberate.

隱丨 a dark saying.

傾蓋而丨終日 just to open the umbrella [as they met], and yet they talked the whole day.

齬 ʿyü A row of irregular teeth, with some wanting.

其志齟丨 his designs were opposed (or did not agree) with the others.

Read ˏngo. Uneven.

山勢巖丨 the peaks of the mountains are of many heights.

御 yü' From 彳 to *go* and 卸 to *lay aside*; *i.e.* to unharness horses; interchanged with the two next.

To drive, as a charioteer; any place where the sovereign stops; to manage, to superintend, to rule; to break in, as a horse; to provide against; to extend everywhere, as imperial power; to condescend to, as a sovereign; imperial, royal, whatever belongs to the monarch; rule, government; to wait on, to help; to have at one's side; to offer, as a cup to a guest; to advance, to bring in; an attendant.

丨前 in the emperor's presence; *met.* the guards, chamberlains, or servants of the palace.

丨書 the imperial autograph.

臨丨 to take the reins of government.

統丨 to govern the whole empire.

丨事 manager of affairs; an office in the Cheu dynasty.

丨駕 the imperial carriage; *i. e.* the monarch himself.

飲丨諸友 he entertained all his friends.

不能丨冬 I cannot endure the winter.

丨門辦事 to attend at the palace-gate; *i. e.* to act as a minister of state.

丨河 the Imperial Canal; name given to it at the North.

Read *ya'* To meet, to go out to receive; to invoke.

以丨田祖 to invoke the father of husbandry, probably Shin-nung.

馭 yü' Like the last.

To have the *hand* over a *horse*, *i. e.* to curb and drive him; to oversee; a charioteer.

丨藝 the art of driving or managing horses.

丨車 or 丨馬 to drive a chariot.

駕丨有方 there are rules for managing and curbing the horse; *met.* there is a right way to rule the people.

若朽索之丨六馬 [it is as ineffectual] as to try to curb six steeds with a rotten rope.

駛丨 to sail or manage a vessel; to go a sailing.

丨萬民 to rule the people.

仙丨 or 鶴丨 the fairy ride, or to ride a crane; — euphemisms for dying.

丨侍 to wait on, to serve.

禦 yü' From *worship* and to *rule;* partly synonymous with the last.

To withstand, to resist; to stop by satisfying, to bring to an end; to cause to desist, to prevent; to worship.

丨饑 to appease hunger.

防丨 or 抵丨 or 扞丨 to guard against; to watch and protect.

孰能丨之 who can withstand him?

莫之敢丨也 nobody ventured (or was able) to oppose him.

丨止 to stop further progress.

以言乎遠則不丨 though you discourse about such a far off and mysterious thing, yet you cannot guard against it.

籞 yü' From *bamboo* and to *fend off*.

To stretch a bamboo rope along the street where the emperor goes, to restrain the crowd; weirs to inclose a place to rear fish.

苑丨 to rope off a garden for the emperor's use.

竹丨 a bamboo withe.

嫗 yü' From *woman* and a *corner*.

A mother; a dame, a hag; to cherish, to brood over; to warm, as nature does.

煦丨覆育萬物 the vapors [of the earth] warm, and the canopy nourishes all things into life.

老丨 a granny, an old dame.

萬石丨 the matron of myriads of revenue, was the honorable name given to the mother of Yen Yen-nien 嚴延年 of the Han dynasty, one of five brothers who all attained high rank.

巫丨 an old witch.

窳 yü' A cave in a hill; a hole or den.

寓' yü' From a *covert* and a *monkey*; *q. d.* to hang on as a monkey to a tree.

To lodge, to sojourn, to dwell in; to attach or hang on; to pertain, to belong to; to borrow, as a metaphor; a residence, a home; a shelter, a lodging, a temporary residence.

暫丨 living at or with for a while.

丨次 or 丨所 a dwelling, a lodging to sojourn in.

尊丨何處 where is your abode?

客丨 or 店丨 an inn, a hotel.

移丨別處 to move one's residence.

留丨 people who are not yet entered as citizens, their register being in another prefecture.

丨言 metaphorical, by metonymy.

借丨 to live without rent or as a guest.

寄丨 to stick to, as a parasite or hanger-on; also, an invited guest.

丨兵于民 to make a levy of troops.

安丨客商 pleasant lodgings for visitors and traders; — a sign on an inn.

旅丨 a lodger, a guest.

天地丨萬物丨我丨道 heaven and earth exist in the universe, in me, in true doctrine as well.

遇' yü' To meet, to come unexpectedly upon one; to occur, to happen, denoting rather what is pleasant; whenever, at the time of; to intreat, to entertain or act towards; to agree together.

不約而丨 to meet without previous arrangement.

丨着 it happened, it came to pass.

丨時大吉 happened at a lucky moment; a fortunate meeting.

丨難'成祥 to turn hardships into blessings.

丨見 or 丨面 to see unexpectedly.

丨我厚 he treated me well.

丨有事 I happen to be busy.

百年不丨 one would hardly meet such a thing once in a century.

接丨 to receive, as a visitor.

丨豐年 to have a bountiful harvest.

丨合難期 I cannot at all tell when they (the prince and his ministers) will be in accord.

丨緣 it happened well; lucky.

不丨 unlucky, mal-apropos.

丨時一肚氣 he is always cross when I see him.

裕' yü' From *garment* and *valley*.

Rich in clothes and chattels; plenty, superabundant; to enrich, to leave to; liberal; overmuch; supererogation.

豐丨 an abundance of, as crops.

寬丨 noble-minded and generous.

布施優丨 to distribute with an open hand; *i. e.* enough for all.

丨國便民 to benefit the state and accommodate the people; — a pawnbroker's sign.

丨足 sufficient, a full supply.

光于前丨于後 honored his ancestors and enriched his posterity.

Read *yiu'* Easy with, gentle.

天姿玉丨 his heavenly gifts of disposition were perfect.

飫' 饇' yü' From to *eat* and *incomplete*; but one etymologist derives it from 食 to *eat* and 芺 an edible *thistle*; the second form is unusual.

To eat much, to fill one's belly; to confer, to give; filled, surfeited; gluttonous, glutted.

如食宜丨 in eating, see that you take just enough.

立丨坐晏 sit at a feast and stand at a lunch; — an ancient usage.

食到丨 eaten to the full.

丨賜 to confer on, to bestow, as food on troops.

俗物不丨目綺語莫饜靈 vulgar things cannot satisfy the eye, nor fancy phrases fill the soul.

好丨喉 to loathe food; eaten to the gorge.

瘀' yü' Extravasated blood, like that settled in a bruise or sore; a bruise, a contusion.

丨血 effused blood.

丨傷 sores or bruises, which do not heal; inert sores.

丨肉 proud or gangrenous flesh.

去丨生新 removed the old flesh to let the new grow.

In *Cantonese*: A dull color, no luster.

色澤好丨 there's no luster in it; it is very dull.

丨黑色 a black and blue color.

芋' yü' From 艸 *plant* and 吁 *moaning sound*, as if its solid root startled people.

The taro; also applied to other edible tubers; flourishing.

丨頭 the taro (*Arum aquaticum*); the small size is the best.

丨葉 taro leaves, fed to pigs.

雀丨 a tuber or corm which is regarded as so poisonous, that birds fall down after pecking it; it is used to make spirits more intoxicating; it is perhaps allied to the wild-turnip (*Arisæma*), or some other species of *Araceæ*.

春及草丨 when spring arrives the grass becomes flourishing.

煨丨 to roast taro, as priests do.

海丨 said to be a kind of sow-bread (*Cyclamen*) dedicated to Kwan-yin.

豫' 預' 忬' yü' From 象 *elephant* and 予 to *give*; the second and perverted form is not much used, and the third is still more uncommon.

A large and docile elephant; easy, contented, indulgent, taking one's pleasure; satisfied with what comes; dissipation; to pre-arrange to get ready for; to be comfortable, as in illness; prepared for, ready, provided; beforehand, already; the 16th diagram, referring to thunder

秋丨 a jaunt, an excursion in the summer.

丨章 an old name for Kiangsi.

丨州 the province of Honan; derived from the central of Yü's nine divisions, which had nearly the same limits.

悅丨 pleased, delighted.

丨備 ready, all arranged; fixed up.

猶丨未决 irresolute, undecided, not settled upon a course; the phrase refers to the monkey and elephant, which are mistrustful and timid.

丨定 well settled, decided on.

丨聞 I will let you know in time.

無時丨怠 do not at any time indulge in idleness.

丨機務 to deliberate on state affairs.

丨禁 to forbid beforehand.

一遊一丨爲諸侯度 one visit [to court in spring] and one [in autumn] was the rule for all the princes.

丨公家之任 he gave them office in the public service.

凡事丨則立 whenever a matter is arranged, let it stand.

灩 *yü'* A tributary of the Yangtsz' River, the 灩丨水 in the eastern part of Sz'ch'uen in Wu-shan hien, made the subject of a poem by Tu Fu; there is a high isolated and dangerous rock, the 灩丨堆 in the Yangtsz' near its embouchure.

蕷 *yü'* An edible tuber, 薯丨 the Chinese yam, more commonly known as 山藥 or hill medicine.

喻 *yü'* From *mouth* and to *assent*; used with the next.

To make known by authority; to explain, to instruct, to declare; to admonish and enforce, as a rule; to illustrate, to compare; to understand, to comprehend the import of; instruction, explanation; informed of.

教丨 to instruct, as by explanations and illustrations.

勸丨 or 諫丨 to exhort, to warn, to expostulate with.

借丨 or 譬丨 or 丨言 a metaphor, an illustration, a comparison; to make a supposition.

丨義丨利君子小人之趨向不同 the princely man speaks of justice, differing much from the mean man who talks of gain.

丨以利害 he explained its advantages and disadvantages.

嘔丨受之 he received him with kind and affable words.

審丨之 examined it thoroughly and explained it fully.

善丨 skilled in teaching.

家丨戶曉 let all families and people fully understand — these orders.

諭 *yü'* Used with the last.

An order, edict, or official notification or command from a superior; to signify, to proclaim, to order; to advise or instruct those under one; politely used for another's wishes and requests; a comparison.

丨旨 or 上丨 or 聖丨 his Majesty's commands.

明丨 your instructions.

教丨 a district superintendent of instruction.

不言而丨 I see you understand it without further explanation.

劄丨 an order from one's superior.

手丨 or 來丨 your letter, your commands.

理丨勢禁 to explain reasonably but to forbid with decision.

我已丨爾之意 I fully understand your views.

曉丨志意告于鬼神 when you really know your own wishes then inform the gods of them.

礜 *yü'* A white ore of arsenic found in Hupeh, which kills rats and fattens silkworms.

穥 *yü'* The waving, fine appearance of a thick field of grain; the crop of grain.

我黍丨丨 what a fine field of millet I have.

YUEH.

Old sounds, nget *and* yet. *In Canton*, üt; — *in Swatow*, gué, wat, yet, ngiak, jwat, *and* sút; — *in Amoy*, goat, wat, yet, *and* oé; — *in Fuhchau*, ngwȯk, wȯk, wak, *and* yȯk; — *in Shanghai*, yüeh *and* nüeh; — *in Chifu*, yüé.

月 *yueh'* The original form represents the moon in her quarter; it is the 74th radical of a few characters relating to her times.

The moon, the ancestor of all *yin* things, and the mate of the sun; a moon or lunar month; monthly; the Budhist employ it to designate India, whose holy men illumine and guide the dark world; they also speak of a 丨王 or regent of the moon (*Chandra*) of enormous bulk.

丨亮 the moon; moonlight.

丨大 a moon of thirty days; 丨小 one of twenty-nine days.

蛾眉丨 or 丨芽 the moon when a few days old.

丨餅 cakes made to worship at the full of the eighth moon.

丨水 or 丨經 or 丨信 the monthly courses.

好不丨 the girl's menses are obstructed, she has none.

做滿丨 to receive congratulations a month after confinement.

按丨 or 論丨 monthly; by the month.

丨弦 the moon's quarters.

好丨色 bright moonlight.

玩丨 or 步丨 to ramble in the moonlight.

丨氐 the Getæ or ancient Scythians near the sea of Aral.

輪丨 took it in monthly turns.

氷丨宮 a temple dedicated to Kwanyin.

先個丨 or 上丨 last month.

下丨 or 第二丨 next moon.

丨丨 or 各丨 monthly.

丨丨紅 or 丨季 the monthly rose.

丨白縐 bluish white crape.

丨老 or 丨下老人 a god, called the Old Man of the Moon, who is said to make matches; a marriage broker.

莫負丨華明 do not frustrate the glorious beauty of the moonlight.

掬水丨在手 one may even see the moon in a handful of water; — appearances deceive.

The months of each season are designated by 孟 and 仲 and 季 placed before the season; besides its numerative and cyclic name, each moon has also a poetical or allusive name, which are given in the following list:

1.	正月	元月	三陽	春王
2.	中和	杏月	如月	
3.	桃月	上巳	寒食	
4.	淸和	麥秋		
5.	榴月	天中	滿月	端月
6.	荷月	天貺		
7.	桐月	巧月		
8.	桂月	中秋		
9.	菊秋	菊月	重陽	
10.	陽春	小陽		
11.	葭月	仲冬月		
12.	臘月	嘉平	淸祀	

刖, 跀, *yueh'* From *knife* and *moon;* the other pictures the punishment, and is made from the first.

To cut off the feet at the ankles, an ancient punishment.

兩丨其足 cut off both feet.

丨辟疑赦 if there be any doubt about the propriety of cutting off the feet, pardon the man.

In *Cantonese.* The second form is sometimes used for *küeh,* 觖 to cock up, to perk.

抈, *yueh'* To bend into a crescent, as a bow, or the tire of a wheel; to bend back and straighten; to move; to take in the fingers.

丨折了 to snap in bending.

把木丨彎 to bend a stick.

丨一個蛋 bring me an egg. (*Shanghai.*)

曰, *yueh* From 口 *mouth* and 一 denoting *breath* issuing; it is easily mistaken for *jih,* 日 sun; it is the 73d radical of a few characters, into which it enters by combination.

To speak, to utter; said, spoken; to call or name; is said, designated, called, termed; an expletive particle separating sentences.

對丨 or 答丨 answering, said.

一丨 one says; one is called, as in a list.

詩丨 the Book of Odes says.

其湛丨樂 they are happy and delighted.

然丨否 then say so, will you?

不丨如之何 if you do not say how it should be.

居則丨不吾知也 if I live in quiet, then it will be said nobody knows me.

丨若 an initial phrase, therefore.

汩, *yueh* From *water* and *speaking;* it resembles *kuh,* 汨 noise of waves.

Flowing fast and silently, as a stream; quick; limpid, pure.

流丨 a rapid flow.

丨越 bright and sunny.

拂丨 moving about with celerity, as troops in a camp when breaking up.

奔丨 quickly, hastily.

蚏, *yueh* A small crab, 蟚丨 which is found on sandy beaches.

䏳, *yueh* Analagous to [illegible]; a disease like a stiff joint or blighted limb, which prevents its free use.

粵, *yueh'* From 丂 *breath* issuing combined with 宷 a *recess,* referring to the careful utterances of the mind at beginning a declaration.

An initial particle; to examine; verily, really; behold, now then, implying the desire to call attention to the subject; occurs used for 曰 to say; kind, liberal, as Heaven in giving life to plants and fruitful seasons; the region south of the Méi-ling, early subdued by the Han dynasty, and for which the next is sometimes wrongly used.

丨考 to examine.

丨東 Kwangtung.

丨西 Kwangsi, in which K'ing-yuen fu was called 丨州 in the T'ang dynasty.

丨稽上古 to investigate ancient things.

越, *yueh'* From *to go* and a *battle-ax.*

To overstep, to exceed, to pass over; to go out of or beyond one's place, to transgress; to assault, to throw down; far, remote; to waste, as one's bodily powers; to frustrate; to give out orders; a sign of the comparative; a *copula* of continuance, then, and, reaching on, moreover; the holes in a lute through which the strings pass to the nuts.

丨禮 to overstep propriety.

超丨 or 卓丨 to surpass, to excel.

丨宿不候 I'll not wait for you beyond to-night.

丨境 to incroach on another's possessions.

丨訴 to pass by a court in an appeal to a higher, as to go to the intendant from the district-magistrate.

丨發好 still better.

丨快丨好 the quicker the better.

踰丨節 a name for the passover.

於我楚丨 he is to me like the states Tsu and Yueh; *i.e.* I will have nothing to do with him, these two kingdoms being always fighting.

不聞丨宿之言 no one hears a word of passing the night; — he never delays to fulfill his promise.

丨氣 to get out of breath.

丨若來 and then.

隕丨於下 reduced to a low condition, deprived of all rank.

丨席 to leave one's place at table, and take a higher.

風不丨而殺 [the plants] were killed though the wind did not pass over them.

丨以 an initial phrase, hereupon.

丨哉 alas, too much! too dear!

丨國 a feudal state in the north and east of Chehkiang, conferred (B. C. 2066) on Wu-yü by his father Shao-kang; the records give two rulers B. C. 537 and 496, who swayed all Kiangnan and south till 334, when it was reduced by Tsu.

丨南 Annam or Tonquin, called Vietnam by that people.

丨王鳥 the royal bird of the king of Vietnam; *i. e.* the hornbill or *Buceros*.

鉞, 戉, *yueh'* From 戈 *spear* and 亅 a *catch;* the second form is now obsolete.

A battle-ax, whose blade is crescent shape; a sort of lictor's ax, borne as a sign of authority; the star η in Gemini.

不怒而民威于鈇丨 if you are not angry, the people will dread you as they do battle-axes.

樾, *yueh'* The shade caused by trees interlacing their branches.

蔭丨 a good shade.

道丨爲枯 the shade along the road has failed, — by the death of the trees.

悅, *yueh'* From *heart* and *pleased;* it occurs written 説 in this sense, but is now disused.

Contented, gratified; delightful, gladsome; to agree to willingly.

丨服 to listen to terms.

不亦丨乎 will not that also be pleasant!

丨目 pleasing to the eye.

人丨之 the people like him.

喜丨 delighted with.

不丨 distasteful, displeased with.

無圖丨聽 don't covet the applause (or ready ear) of people.

閱, *yueh'* From 門 *door* and 説 to *speak* contracted.

To take a look at the things or papers at the door, as when memorials were handed in at the palace-gate; to examine, to inspect, to pass in review; to look over, to compare, in order to vouch for; to read carefully; to abate, as a price; to allow.

丨卷 or 評丨 to revise an essay.

大丨三軍 a general review of the army.

丨歷深 passed through it all, well-versed in, thoroughly up in the matter.

披丨 to look over, as a book.

頃丨來示 I have just looked over your letter.

丨看 to examine a work.

丨實其罪 ascertained the real facts of his offenses.

我躬不丨 I myself cannot go to see into it.

軏, *yueh'* Originally composed of 車 *carriage* and 元 *first* contracted.

The bar on the tongue of a carriage to which the horses are fastened.

小車無丨 small carts need no brace.

妜, *yueh'* The space between the nose and eyes, the inner canthus of the eye; another says, the space between the eye-brow and the eye, called 憂妒 or sad-envy.

Read *küeh*, Beautiful.

噦, *yué'* Also read *hwui'* a hum of people.

To retch, to gag, to belch; to keck, to bring up the food.

乾丨 to gag and bring up nothing.

丨氣 to eructate, as when nauseated.

丨出水來 to throw up water.

狘, *yué'* To scamper away, as terrified animals do.

麟以爲畜故獸不丨 if the unicorn can be once tamed, the other beasts will certainly show no terror.

YUEN.

Old sounds, yien, yen, yuen, ngon, yon, *and* won. *In Canton*, ūn *and* ún; — *in Swatow*, wan, yien, í^{n}, *and* ngwan; — *in Amoy*, oan, gwan, yen, yong, hwan, *and* swan; — *in Fuhchau*, yòng, wong, hwong, wang, *and* ngwòng; — *in Shanghai*, yū^{n}, nū^{n}, ní^{n}, í^{n}, *and* wó; — *in Chifu*, yuen.

淵, *yuen* From *water* flowing between two *banks;* it was first written without this radical, the inner horizontal line denoting the current; it occurs used with the last.

An eddy, a whirlpool or place where the back water seems to stop; deep hole, a gulf; an abyss: it has been applied to the gulf of Chihli.

天丨相隔 as far apart as the sky and sea.

深丨 deep, unfathomable.

丨潭 a lake or pool in Shantung.

魂欲上天魄入丨 as the soul ascends the skies, the effigy (*eidolon*) goes down to the abyss.

丨博 having great and varied learning.

丨海 the vast deep.

鼘 ꜀yuen Used with the preceding.
The sound of drums.
伐鼓丨丨 strike the drums, tantarara.

弲 ꜀yuen The curvature of a bow near its two ends, the place where it begins to taper.

寃 冤 ꜀yuen From a *covert* and a *rabbit*, whence it is unable to run, and forced to crouch and submit; the second form is old and least used.
To injure, oppress, or ill-use without cause; to make one stoop or submit; ill usage, wrong, grievance, oppression, injustice; to vex, to ridicule, to annoy.
訴丨 or 鳴丨 to state one's wrongs.
含丨 to bear a grudge, to cherish enmity for some wrong.
丨枉 or 丨屈 an injustice, whatever wrongs or prejudices one; to falsely implicate.
伸丨 to obtain redress, to get one's wrongs avenged.
結丨 to become enemies, to get up a quarrel and incur hatred.
丨魂不息 the injured ghost will not be quiet.
你想丨我嗎 are you trying to fool me?
洗丨 or 雪丨 or 解丨 to be revenged; to wipe out a grudge.
我不受你的丨 I won't be insulted by you.
丨孽 the retribution of Heaven; a sudden destruction on one's enemy.
覆盆之丨 an unredressed wrong, an injury that is concealed.
撒丨 or 花丨錢 to spend money on rarities, as a 丨大頭 virtuoso does. (*Pekingese.*)
賙恤丨陷諸臣 he befriended and helped all the officers who had been oppressed.
不白之丨 a hidden wrong that cannot be divulged.
丨丨相報 their mutual injuries were revenged on each other.
慘丨 inhuman oppression.

惌 ꜀yuen Similar to the last; also read ꜂yuen and used for its primitive; read *yuh*, grief; vexed.
Ill treatment, which leads to revenge; to have a grudge; to sigh, to regret; surprised at; small, as a hole; an orifice.
覘其鑽空欲其丨也 I see him boring a hole [in the armor], but let it be very small.
丨屈 a wrong.

夗 ꜀yuen From *evening* and *seal*, alluding to the form showing where one has slept.
To turn over as when asleep; a curling, snake-like motion; to yield, to give away.
臥丨 to turn in bed.

眢 ꜀yuen An eye without expression or brightness; empty, vacant.
丨井 an old and dry well.
丨目 a vacant, dull eye.

蜿 ꜀yuen The squirming motion of a snake, a stealthy gliding step of a cat; tortuous; stealthy.
丨蜒 the tortuous motion of a serpent; applied to the undulating ridge of a range of mountains.
虎豹丨只 the gliding, circuitous approach of a tiger or leopard.
丨蟮 a crawling worm or eel.
蟠丨 to wriggle and squirm.

鴛 ꜀yuen The drake of the 丨鴦 or mandarin duck; also of the falcated teal.
鵲好'外反丨好'內思 the magpie likes to gad abroad, but the drake loves home.
丨鴦枕 a kind of double pillow used by a newly married couple.

鵷 ꜀yuen A gallinaceous bird found in the South, the 丨雛 which, from the description is intended for the young of the argus pheasant.

肙 ꜀yuen From 肉 *flesh* and 口 to *surround*; now used only as a primitive in combination.
A small worm; to twist or wrench; to surround; empty.

員 ꜀yuen From *mouth* and *pearl* or value; *q.d.* the mouth stating the valuable things; it was once written 云 and is used for *yun*꜄ 隕 a border and the next.
A classifier of officers, and of round things; round; to reach all around, to circulate; to be of use to.
官丨 officers, grandees, soldiers.
一丨官 one official.
生丨 a *siuts'ai* graduate.
能丨 an efficient officer.
大丨 a high statesman.
廢丨 an officer who has been disgraced.
備丨朝廷之上 to fill up the number of the king's officers.
丨外郎 an officer in a Board who reports to its Vice President.

Read ꜀*yun* and used for 云. To add to; to speak.
丨于爾輻 I will enlarge your territory.
聊樂我丨 I think you are pleased with what I say.
伍丨 a celebrated warrior of the Yueh state, B.C. 520.

圓 ꜀yuen From to *inclose* and *officer*; it is interchanged with the last, and with ꜀*hwan* 圜 to go around.
Round, circular; a globe, a ball, a sphere, a globular lump; to interpret; to make round, to cut off corners; to accommodate; a dollar; a rupee.
方丨 square and round; *met.* particular and precise; lax and accommodating.
丨圈 a ring, a circle.
搓丨 to roll round, as a pill.
丨滿 finished; done up, as a job.
一大丨 a whole dollar.
半丨 or 中丨 half a dollar.
丨夢 to explain dreams.
頂上丨光 an aureola around the head, as on divine personages.
丨而神 [the virtue of a lot is that it] can divine and bring about what will come to pass.

志欲丨而行欲方 the resolution should be accommodating, but the performance should be firm.

處' 世丨通 in life be accommodating, and take things practically.

盂丨而水丨 if the cup be round the water will be round.

丨扁子 a runner in the courts, a constable or watchman. (*Pekingese.*)

丨寂 the death of a Budhist priest.

洹 ˏyuen A small branch of the River Wéi, the 丨水 near Changteh fu in Honan; an ancient district in that region.

泥丨 nirvana or nigban.

丨丨 flowing.

鳶 ˏyuen From *bird* and *javelin;* but the primitive is regarded as a contraction of 屰 *opposing.*

The kite (*Milvus melanotis*), common in Eastern China; its scream portends wind; the term is also applicable to the family of kites.

風丨 or 紙丨 a paper kite.

載鳴丨 expose [the pennon] with a screaming kite, — to indicate wind and dust ahead of the troops.

木丨 a sort of machine kite made by Meh-tsz' 墨子 in three years, when it flew away.

鳶 ˏyuen Regarded by some as another form of the last, but others separate them.

丨韞 a celebrated warrior of the Cheu dynasty; name of a district in Cochinchina.

原 ˏyuen From 厂 *cliff* and 泉 a *fountain* contracted; but the next form is oldest, and the two were afterwards distinguished.

A plateau or a high and level field, a terrace; a waste, a common; an origin, a source, a beginning; natural, proper, innate; originally, primarily, really, honestly; the original condition of; before another verb is often merely a form of the pluperfect tense; to trace a matter to its source; to retrace, to repeat; to remit, to forgive; again, a repetition, another.

高丨下隰 above are the terraces, and below are the meadows.

田丨 fields and plains.

本丨 origin of, at first.

推丨 to analyze, as a chemist; to infer from premises, to trace back to a cause.

丨主 the first owner or proprietor.

丨舊 like the old way.

丨不想作 I really did not think then of doing it.

一線可丨 there is the least reason for pardoning him.

丨來如此 it was so at first; it has been so always.

丨由 or 丨故 the causes, the circumstances, the first occasion.

丨來頭 the genuine article; of the original lot; it is from the maker.

情由可丨 the extenuating circumstances.

中丨 at first denoted Honan, but now means all China.

丨諒 to be lenient to; excusing.

丨州 an old name of 濟源縣 in the northwest of Honan.

丨委 the head and tail, the origin and end of a matter.

丨不該 by rights it should not be so; it properly is not so.

故事尋丨 to investigate the origin of things or history.

道之大丨 the great principles of virtue.

丨丨本本 to search out all the details.

源 ˏyuen From *water* and *origin.*

A fountain, a spring; used with the last, a source.

水丨頭 the headwaters, as of a river.

丨丨而來 incessantly coming, as customers.

飲水思丨 when you drink the water, think of the fountain.

塞丨 stop the fountain or source.

財丨輻輳 money rapidly coming in, growing rich.

星丨 the source of the Yellow River.

萬派同丨 all the streams have one source.

嫄 ˏyuen The name of 姜丨, a concubine of the sovereign Ti-kuh B. C. 4200, and mother of Heutsih, the ancestor of Wăn Wang.

赫赫姜丨 how widely known was Kiang-yuen!

羱 ˏyuen A species of sheep found west of China with large horns, of which things can be made; it is fond of fighting, and resembles an ass in size; grass is said to grow on the horns in summer; the *Ovis argali* or *naghor*?

騵 ˏyuen A bay horse with a white belly.

駟丨彭彭 four bays came rushing along.

縓 ˏyuen Also read ˏtsüen.

Silk of a reddish yellow or orange; a light red color.

丨緣 a red neck-tie or collar.

袁 ˏyuen From 衣 *clothes* and 長 *long* contracted.

A robe; dressed in long garments.

丨州府 a prefecture in Kiangsi, bordering on Hunan.

園 ˏyuen From an *inclosure* and *long.*

An inclosed place for planting flowers or vegetables; imperial tombs; a yard, a court; a park; a garden, an orchard; a fine shop, a saloon; an inclosure for a public purpose.

花丨 a flower garden.

丨丁 or 丨工 a gardener; a florist.

戲丨 a play-garden, a place for amusements.

樂丨 a foreign term for paradise.

醬丨 a soy or condiment shop.

梨丨 the pear-garden; a theater.

文丨 or 寢丨 imperial sepulchers.

何人不起故丨思 what man is there whose heart does not rise at the thought of the old garden, — *i.e.* his native place.

轅 ˛*yuen* From *carriage* and *long*.

The thills of a carriage; the tongue or shaft; a whippletree; the side-gates into the court of a yamun or general's marquee; the head-quarters, office, or post of a general.

車丨 or 丨木 the thills.

丨門 gates of a public office; hence 丨門報 a provincial governor's court-circular.

赴丨聽調 to go into court to hear and decide public business.

跼促如丨下駒 a mulish man is like a colt between the thills.

元 ˛*yuen* From 儿 *man* and 二 *two*, referring to heaven and earth over man, producing all things; others derive it from 兀 *high* and 一 *first*, *i.e.* superior, the best of all; used for ˛圓 a dollar and for ˛*hüen* 玄 black.

The commencement, the first cause, the incipient steps; the first, the head, the principal; the eldest; original, primary; among Taoists, a vast period of time, like a geological epoch; one writer estimates it at 24,192, 000 years, another at 129,600; it is subdivided into 12 revolutions called 會 or cycles.

改丨 changed or fixed the style of the reign.

丨年 the first year of a reign.

丨旦 or 丨日 new-year's day.

丨駒 black colts, a term for ants, from their quickness and going in lines.

丨首明哉 how intelligent is our monarch!

丨寶 large ingots of sycee; gilt paper folded like ingots, to be burned in worship.

上丨 and 中丨 and 下丨 three festivals on the 15th of the 1st, 7th and 10th moons, of which the second is the most observed.

一丨復始 the spring has come again.

一褭丨 a robe that is not open or slit before or behind, regarded as not dress for company.

丨始 the beginning of a thing.

丨子 the eldest son.

在德丨 first in virtue, surpassing others.

丨氣不足 his constitution is not sound; his stamina is gone.

丨神 a Budhist term for the soul going out of the body as in a trance; also the animal spirits.

三丨及第 three senior graduates are the 狀丨, the 解丨 and the 會丨 the three senior wranglers among the successful candidates for the degrees of *Hanlin*, *tsinsz'* and *küjin*; there is also a 案丨 or senior *siuts'ai*, but he is not reckoned.

丨亨利貞 a phrase from the Yih-king, often used to denote 1, 2, 3, 4.

丨丨 the mass of people; from the idea that they are all good.

丨丨本本 the very first of a thing or time.

丨朝 the Original or Mongol dynasty; it swayed China and central Asia from A.D 1278 to 1369, under nine sovereigns, whose Chinese and Mongolian names are given in this list.

EMPERORS OF THE YUEN OR MONGOL DYNASTY.

TEMPLE NAME.	STYLE OF REIGN.	ACCESSION A. D.	REIGNED YEARS.	GENEALOGY.
世祖文武皇帝 Kublai 忽必烈 or Sitchen 薛禪	Chung-tung 中統 Chi-yuen 至元	1260 1264	35	Grandson of Genghis 成吉思
成宗皇帝 Temur 鐵木耳 or Olcheitu.	Yuen-ching 元貞 Ta-teh 大德	1295 1297	13	Grandson of the last.
武宗皇帝 Kaisun 海山 or Guluk 曲律	Chi-ta 至大	1308	4	Nephew of the last.
仁宗皇帝 Ayuli Palpata 愛育黎拔力八達	Hwang-king 皇慶 Yen-yiu 延祐	1312 1314	9	Brother of the last.
英宗皇帝 Kotpala 碩德八剌	Chi-chi 至治	1321	3	Son of the last.
泰定皇帝 Yesun Timur 也孫鐵木兒	Tai-ting 泰定 Chi-ho 致和	1324 1328	5	Grand-nephew of Kublai.
幼主 Achakpa 阿速吉八	Tien-shun 天順	1328		Son of the last.
明宗皇帝 Hosila 和世㻋.	Tien-lih 天歷	1328	2	Son of Wu-tsung.
文宗皇帝 Tup-temur 圖帖睦爾	Chi-shun 至順	1330	3	Brother of the last.
寧宗皇帝 Ile-chepe 懿璘質班		1332		Son of Ming-tsung.
順帝 or 惠宗皇帝 Tohan Temur 妥歡帖睦爾	Yuen-tung 元統 Chi-yuen 至元 Chi-ching 至正	1333 1335 1341	36	Brother of the last.

沅 ˌyuen A large river in the west of Hunan, flowing into the Tungting Lake; its basin occupies the western half of the province, and measures about 34,300 square miles; along its valley lies Yuen-cheu fu.

丨有芷兮 what fine orris root comes from the River Yuen!

芫 ˌyuen A plant, found in Kiangsu, the *Daphne genkwa* or *Passerina chamœdaphne*, whose flower, when boiled and thrown into the water, stupefies and kills fish; it is also called 魚毒 fish poison, and an infusion is said to be good for coughs and lumbago.

丨青 a beetle found on this plant, dried like the Cantharides; the colors are green, black, and yellow; perhaps a kind of *Cetonia*.

丨荽 coriander.

胡荽 caraway.

杬 ˌyuen Sometimes used for the last.

A tall tree in Kiangsi, with a thick, red, bitter bark, a decoction of which preserves fruit from spoiling; the bark is also destructive of fish; perhaps it is allied to a *Piscidia*.

黿 ˌyuen From *tortoise* and *great; i.e.* the *tortoise originally* made.

The great sea turtle, 丨鼈 said to be twenty feet around.

元丨 the first tortoise from which all scaly animals were derived.

老丨 a god worshiped in Cheh-kiang to preserve dikes.

蚖 ˌyuen Sometimes wrongly written like the last.

A small venemous snake, a foot long.

蠑丨 a lizard found in damp places.

龍蟠於泥丨其肆矣 when the dragon curls up in the mud, then the boa disports itself; *i. e.* when the cat's away, the mice will play.

蝮丨 vipers and asps.

螈 ˌyuen Sometimes written for the preceding.

A silkworm, called 丨蠶 which produces silk very late and only once in the season.

爰 ˌyuen Originally formed of 爫 to *claw hold* and 于 *in*, combined together, like "the thills of a carriage."

To lead from one place or thing on to another, for which the next is also used; therefore, on this account; as an initial particle like 於 for, at, to, up to, even to; thereupon; to say; to consist in; to change; mournful, sad.

丨丨 slow progress, said of a hare.

丨居丨處丨笑丨語 then they lived and dwelt there, and there they laughed and talked.

作丨書 to arrange a book of punishments.

丨及我朝 from the time that our dynasty began.

援 ˌyuen To lead or take by the hand; to cling to; to pull up higher, to drag out; to put forward; to relieve, to rescue, to assist, to restrain.

丨引 to lead on, to urge and guide.

丨兵 auxiliary troops, for succor or relief.

救丨 to come to the rescue; to deliver from ruin.

丨結 to mutually assist, to bring one forward; log-rolling.

舉賢丨能 promote the worthy and bring forward the talented.

丨溺 to rescue the drowning.

丨助 to assist, to relieve.

以爾鉤丨 get ready your scaling-ladders.

無然畔丨 do not let other influences draw you aside.

丨之以手 lend him a hand, help him.

爲四隣之丨' they are my four nighbors.

扳丨 to help; to aid, as in going up hills.

媛 ˌyuen From 女 *woman* and the last contracted; also read *yuen*'

A beauty, a Hebe, one who draws admirers; winning, attractive; unsteady, flighty.

淑丨 a chaste, modest woman.

名丨' a celebrated, talented woman.

嬋丨而不定 volatile; unwilling to fix the mind on.

令丨 your daughter.

篤生哲丨 favored the world by producing this clever beauty.

英丨 a very clever woman.

褑 ˌyuen A second girdle to which ornaments are hung, worn with the other.

佩丨 the girdle for ornaments.

猿 猨 蝯 ˌyuen From *beast* and to *lead* or *grasp*, from its habit; the name is also said to imitate their cry.

The gibbons, as distinct from apes, baboons, or monkeys, for which family, including the hooluck, this term is applicable; the Chinese include apes under it.

烏丨 the black gibboon.

通臂丨 a gibbon, said to have no elbow in its arm, whose bone can be used for flutes.

白丨 the white gibbon.

鶢 ˌyuen A sea-shore bird, the 丨鶋 which seems to be a sandpiper, though it may denote the tern.

垣 ˌyuen From *earth* and *perpetual*.

A low wall of brick, which may be relied on, or which protects.

井丨 a well-curb.

城丨 a city wall.

大師維丨 a great statesman is as a wall — to the country.

踰丨而避之 leaped the wall and avoided him; as 段干木 did when he was asked to take office in Lu.

掖丨 a low wall, breast high, built within a palace.

上丨 and 中丨 and 下丨 three groups of stars in the Galaxy.

丨縣 old name of Yuen-kiuh hien 丨曲縣 in the south of Shansi.

蝝 The young of locusts, before their wings have grown.
ˏyuen 蠹丨仆柱梁 the lepisma and grasshopper knocked the pillar and beam; *i. e.* like the frog triying to swell bigger than the bull.

櫞 From *wood* and *cause;* it is sometimes wrongly written 橼.
ˏyuen A tree similar to a palm, the 枸丨 found in Annam, whose bark can be used for coir; but now denotes a large orange, the 香丨 or citron (*Sarcodactylis*), otherwise called Budha's hand; in Peking these two names are applied to two fruits, the first of which is a large acid orange with a thick wrinkled peel.

野香丨 a lofty flowering tree in Yunnan of the myrtle family, resembling the guava in its foliage; the white flowers are fragrant and short-lived.

掾 Also read *ˏyin* and *yen'*
ˏyüen A principal officer, the one who properly holds the post.

吏丨 officials, magnates.

丨屬 an officer and his subordinates.

緣 From *silk* and a *pig;* it much resembles *luh*, 綠 green.
ˏyuen A binding on the hem, a facing or trimming; a collar; to harmonize or correspond with something that existed previously; a recondite, subtle sympathy; an inexplicable attraction; a connection; an affinity, a relationship; to climb; as a *conjunction*, because, since, therefore; on this account.

丨分' or 有丨 there is some reason; it is so ordained; in sympathy with.

丨故 or 丨由 the causes which brought it about, the reason, the circumstances.

無丨 they cannot agree, there's no luck in it, unfortunate; — Budhistic ideas, all referring to an unknown operation of fate in human affairs.

機丨 a casual, pleasant contingency.

天丨湊巧 a providential meeting, a lucky coincidence.

頁丨 a harmonious union, a happy match.

丨分'淺 not much intimacy.

丨木求魚 climb a tree to catch a fish; — a useless search.

丨飾以儒術 to make a hypocritical parade of learning for the sake of gain.

丨此未必無丨 it is not so certain that because of this you will have no luck.

爲何丨故 why? what is the reason of it?

他與我投丨 he and I are on the best of terms, or agree very well.

鉛 鈆 From *metal* and *passing;* the second form is not common; it is also read *ˏyen.*
ˏch'ien Lead, called 青金 the azure metal, but more commonly 黑丨 or 黑錫; the Chinese mention many sorts of it; leaden; to protect, to countenance.

丨罐 lead canisters, used to hold tea.

丨粉 or 丨華 white lead, ceruse.

白丨 pewter; also tutenague.

釘丨 or 夾丨 dollars which have been bored or leaded.

丨子 or 丨碼 leaden bullets.

丨之ˏ重之 he soothed him often and helped him.

縋丨 or 貫丨 to adulterate sycee with lead.

丨片 leads, used by printers.

沇 Also read *ˏyen*, and considered as another form of 沿 to flow by.
ʻyuen An ancient name of the 濟, one of the small streams in Hwai-king fu in the northwest of Honan, which flows into the Yellow River; often wrongly used for *ʻyen* 兗 a department in Shantung.

阮 Name of a mountain; a small feudal state of Wăn Wang,
ʻjwan lying in the southeast of Kansuh, in which was afterwards the 五丨關 a famous post.

小丨 a nephew.

劉丨入天臺 Liu and Yuen of the Han went up into heavenly regions; — *met.* extatic happiness.

宛 From a *shelter* and to *turn over;* it is also read *ʻwan.*
ʻwan To hide one's self by bending over the thickets and grass; to yield, to give in; courteously; used with the next, obliging, accommodating, yielding; unexpected.

丨然 or 丨若 adverbial phrases, as if, same as, according to.

丨轉 yielding to circumstances; trimming.

丨平縣 the western district of Peking city.

丨邱 or 丨丘 an old name for part of 陳州府 in the southeast of Honan.

丨然左辟 he courteously stood aside.

Read *ˏyuen*, in 大丨國 an ancient country in the region of the Aral Sea, thought to answer to the present Kokand.

Read *yuen'* Small, as a diminutive hole or retreat.

丨彼鳴鳩 small is that cooing dove.

婉 Like the last, and also read *ʻwan.*
ʻwan Yielding, docile; complaisant, obliging; genial; lovely, winning.

丨容 a pleasant mild countenance.

丨順 to condescend to, agreeable.

駕八龍之丨丨 went up [on a chariot] with eight squirming dragons; *i. e.* became as a god or fairy.

燕丨之求 a joyous, gracious mate she sought.

苑 ʽwan From *plants* and *yielding*; occurs used for the next, and for 院ʼ a court-yard.

A pasture, a field for horses; a park or menagerie; a book of extracts, a collectanea; applied to some kinds of houses; young, soft; fine, luxuriant herbage.

文丨 a library-room; an encyclopædia.

丨風 a high wind.

內丨 the imperial parks.

說丨 a collection of dialogues or phrases.

天丨 a group of stars in Eridanus.

沙丨子 the officinal name of the seeds of the caltrops (*Tribulus*).

Read *yuh*, Grieved.

我心丨結 my heart is ill at ease.

菀 ʽwan Also read *yuh*, by some.

Luxuriant, tender; soft, fresh.

丨彼柳斯 how delicate and fresh are those willows!

有丨其特 luxuriant springs the grain.

紫丨 a medicinal plant used in coughs, having slender, red rootlets, with yellowish white flowers, producing black seeds with a white woolly envelope.

筦ʼ ʽjwan A bamboo basket or utensil; the thing in which articles are weighed; the case, the tare.

刨丨子 take off the tare.

幾重丨 how much is the tare?

除丨無鱓 there are no eels when the basket is gone; *i. e.* I have nothing left, I've no profit.

琬 ʽwan A round baton-like scepter of jade, called 丨圭 held by the sovereign to indicate his willingness to rule according to virtue; it was nine inches long with a rounded top.

畹 ʽwan A long field measuring twenty or thirty *meu*.

田丨 a field.

戚丨 imperial kindred.

滋蘭九丨 to support your progeny [you will need] nine plots.

遠 ʽyuen From to *go* and *long*.

Distant, far off; remote, either in time or place; from afar; to become distant or alienated; to consider as distant.

路丨 it is very far away.

日子丨 the time is long; the day is unknown.

永丨 for ever; always.

不大丨 it is not very far away.

差得丨 very much unlike; they are entirely different.

不丨千里 he does not regard a thousand miles as very distant.

丨年 many years ago.

丨大的話 heard far and wide.

離丨的 keep far away from it; take it away.

遙丨 remote, in the far distance.

丨丨跟隨 to follow afar off.

丨望弗及 see, he is too far off to be overtaken.

丨近不同 the distance makes all the difference.

丨及兒孫 [may my calamity] reach your children and grandchildren; — an imprecation.

Read *yuen*ʼ To keep at a distance; to remove, to send away.

敬鬼神丨之 respect demons and gods, but keep them at a distance.

丨別 to absent one's self from; to hold aloof.

應令回避以丨嫌疑 it will be best that she should retire in order to remove all suspicion.

院ʼ yuenʼ From *place* and *perfect*; occurs used with ʽ苑 a collectanea.

A walled and secure inclosure in which houses are placed; a court-yard; a public establishment, such as a court; a hall, a college, an asylum, a hospital, a monastery, a museum, &c.; the body of officials connected with an office.

本部丨 I, the governor-general.

丨子 a court-yard.

書丨 a college, a school.

進貢丨 to enter the examination-hall, to compete for a degree.

寺丨 monastic establishments, as convents, nunneries, &c.

學丨 the literary chancellor.

一宅分為兩丨 one house or compound divided into two yards.

勾欄丨 or 娼丨 a brothel.

發瘋丨 a lazaretto. (*Cantonese.*)

丨宇深大 a great and splendid establishment.

愿ʼ yuenʼ From *heart* and *original*; *q.d.* the mind as it was first made; often interchanged with the next.

Sincere, respectful, honest, pure; bluntness; faithful, virtuous; thankful, sensible of mercies.

許丨 to vow and promise, as when in distress.

還丨 to fulfill a vow.

平安貞丨 [thankful for] peace and virtue.

丨而恭 virtuous and reverential.

鄉丨德之賊也 one who assumes the semblance of good is the thief of all virtue.

願ʼ yuenʼ From *head* and *original*; *q.d.* the first or great head, looking out in expectation of a thing.

A large head; to desire, to wish, to hope; a wish, a preference; the object of desire; a vow, a sincere promise; every, each; a short face.

情丨 voluntary, willing.

甘丨 a willing, hearty promise.

情丨死 I had rather die.

完了心丨 it has gratified my heart's wish.

自丨作 my own free wish or act.

遂丨 favorable to my wishes; as I like.

了丨心 to summarily pay a vow; to do things without any method.

不丨意 I do not wish it; I disapprove of it.

丨欲 a strong desire for.

丨言思子 each time we talked together, we thought of these two sons.

夙丨已酧 my long cherished wish is gratified.

怨' *yuen'* From *heart* and to *turn over*.
To hate, to dislike; to feel bitter against; to murmur, at; to abhor; hating, inimical, bitter; averse to; repining, dissatisfied; murmuring against rulers; ill-will, hatred, malice; wrong, a cause of hatred or murmuring; ashamed, regretful.

抱丨 to keep a grudge against, to feel indignant at.

結丨 a mutual animosity.

招丨 to get people's hatred.

報丨人 to be revenged on.

以德報丨 to requite injury with kindness.

埋丨 or 懷丨 to cherish enmity against.

好'大丨聲 he likes to grumble at people.

丨得 very likely there was a cause; perhaps 'twas your fault.

無作丨 do not give occasion for murmurings.

丨貧 to repine at poverty.

丨命 or 丨天 disgusted with one's fate, murmuring at one's luck.

丨言 bitter, malignant words.

不避嫌丨 do not be afraid of the envy and ill-will of others, — but do right.

Read ˛*yun.* To hoard up, as property.

傆' *yuen'* An unprincipled, clever man, who is ready to help in wicked or underhand cabals.

瑗' *yuen'* A large ring of fine jade, which a prince held in his hands as he approached the throne, to show his rank.

衏 ˛*yuen* An old term for musicians, 衏丨 denoting those who play on instruments.

YUH.

Old sounds, yok, ngok, *and* yik. *In Canton*, yok, wăt, *and* wik; — *in Swatow*, yòk, gek, út, hiòk, *and* hòk; — *in Amoy*, yok, út, lút, hiok, giok, *and* hek; — *in Fuhchau*, ngŭk, ngwŏh, ŏk, ük, mík, éük, *and* o; — *in Shanghai*, niòk, yòk, yüh, yüeh; — *in Chifu*, yü.

玉˛ *yü'* It is explained as being three horizontal lines, denoting three stones connected by a cross line, and the dot denotes certain appendages, as on a chatelaine; it is the 96th radical of a natural group relating to gems.
A gem; a stone fit for a lapidary; clear white jade was originally designated; beautiful, delightsome, precious; pearly, gemmeous; happily, pleasantly, agreeably; perfect, immaculate, highest and best; *met.* you, your's; imperial; to perfect, to bring about.

丨器 articles of jade and quartz.

青丨 or 碧丨 noble serpentine.

丨成其事 complete this important affair.

丨女 your daughter.

丨人 a lovely girl.

丨石俱焚 gems and stones were all burned together; — indiscriminate destruction.

望其移丨 I hope you will come yourself.

丨樓 the shoulder; a Taoist term.

丨鏡 or 丨盤 the full moon.

丨體 your precious self.

丨披 open [this letter] yourself.

金丨其心 he has a pure and good heart.

丨屑 a term for falling snow and white sugar.

氷丨 quartz crystal.

丨食 his Majesty's provisions; the revenues of his domain.

漢丨 jade ornaments obtained from old graves.

丨燭 the harmony of the seasons.

金口言丨 a golden mouth and pearly words; *met.* the Emperor's speech.

客丨 spare your steps! — *i. e.* I regret you could not have come.

丨衡 the star Alioth ε in Ursa Major.

拋磚引丨 he threw a brick and got a gem; to get an unexpected reward.

丨食 your delicate viands.

丨帝 the perfect, highest Shangti.

鈺˛ *yü'* Pure hard gold; precious, valuable; chiefly used in names of persons.

鳿˛ *yü'* A fresh water bird, one of the waders, the 鸑丨; it is larger than a duck, with a long neck, and dark red variegated plumage; akin to the rail or jacana.

聿˛ *yü'* Intended to depict a *hand* holding a *pencil;* it forms the 129th radical of a few incongruous characters.
A thing to write with, as a style, pen, or pencil; to narrate, to declare; to obey, to follow; an initial particle, forthwith, thereon, then, straightway; suddenly.

歲丨其莫' the year then was near its close.

武騎丨惶 the cavalry were fleet and nimble.

丨台小子 therefore, I the little child.

我征丨至 we suddenly came in from the raid.

丨越 fleet, as a wild beast.

昱, *yü'* From *sun* and *to establish.*
The full glory of the sun; the bright light.
日 | 乎晝月 | 乎夜 the sun is the glory of the day, and the moon of the night.

煜, *yü'* From *fire* and *effulgence.*
The bright blaze of fire; glorious, shining, full; lustrous; unsullied, as a good name.
管絃曄 | full and gorgeous was [the orchestra] of wind and stringed instruments.
其道德 | 耀于世者不可勝載 it is impossible fully to record the glory of his doctrine and virtue throughout the world.

峪, *yü'* A pool in a ravine; but it seems to be another form of 谷 a dry gully or ravine; it occurs in the names of many valleys east of Peking, crossed by the Great Wall.
平 | 縣 an old form of 平谷縣 a district northeast of Peking.

浴, *yü'* From *water* and *ravine.*
To bathe, to make ablution; to purify, to cleanse the heart, and has been used by some foreigners for baptism; to flit or skim up and down, as swallows or butterflies.
洗 | take a bath.
| 堂 or | 室 a bathing-house.
| 潔其身 washed the body thoroughly clean.
江中日 | the sun bathed itself [at sunrise] in the river.
澡身 | 德 to bathe the person and reform the heart.
| 佛誕 the festival of bathing Budha and the arhans on the 8th day of the 4th moon, observed by priests.

欲, *yü'* To long for, to desire, to wish for, to breathe after; to seek ardently, to covet; aspirations, desires; wishes, ambition; strong hopes; used with the next, passion, lust, appetite; as a gerundive particle, about to be, ready to, on the point of, in order that, for the purpose.
私 | private ends, selfish views.
隨心所 | it is just what I desire.
| 往 | 來 undecided as to going; in a quandary.
頗有 | 雨之意 it looks rather as if it would rain.
| 速不達 undue haste will hinder you.
人之大 | the ruling appetites of mankind.
口 | 受而心 | 辭 though the mouth receives it, the heart rejects it.
我 | 仁斯 | 至矣 when I long for benevolence, then it is presently here.
| 不可縱 the desires must not be too far gratified.
將 | 去 I was on the point of going.

慾, *yü'* From *heart* and *to desire*; the radical was added because all passion proceeds from the heart.
Inordinate desire, covetous; concupiscence, appetite; lascivious, lustful.
嗜 | to relish and hanker after.
| 情 passion, lust.
| 火焚身 the fires of lust consume the body.
| 海 the sea of passion.
無厭 | 壑 the ditch of lust is insatiable.
| 想 lascivious desires.
滌 | to chasten the lusts.

鵒, *yü'* The mainah, 鴝 | a species of singing thrush; it is classed among the pies by the Chinese.

鋊, *yü'* A poker or pincers to stir coals in a furnace or remove them; to sweat money in order to get the filings; also the copper dust thus obtained.
磨 | to polish and file, as cash.

獄, *yü'* From two 犬 *dogs* 言 *speaking,* referring to their acting as guardians.
That which decides who is right in a strife; a prison, a jail.
折 | or 斷 | to decide criminal cases; a jail delivery.
訟 | a litigation, a case in court.
監 | or 牢 | a prison.
煉 | or 練 | purgatory; a Roman Catholic term.
司 | a jailor; one who has | 卒 turnkeys under him.
下 | or | 中 or 坐 | in prison.
打落九重地 | he deserves the deepest hell.
地 | or 冥府 (*naraka*) the abode of the damned, of which the Budhists speak of hot, cold, and vivifying hells, eight of each, from whose sufferings the priests can alone deliver souls of men.
牛頭 | 卒 the lictors of Rhadamanthus.
片言折 | a few words would have settled the quarrel.

鬰, 鬱, 欝, *yü'* It is combined from 鬯 *millet,* 臼 *a mortar,* 冖 *a cover,* 彡 *adorned,* and 缶 *a dish,* indicating the prepared and fragrant libation of a sacrifice; the second contracted form, with 林 *a forest,* to denote *herbs,* is the one commonly used.
Bushy, thicket-like; a wild plum or cherry, sweet and red; a fragrant herb (turmeric?) anciently mixed with spirits in sacrificing; irritated, worked upon; vexed, surly and sullen; careworn; kinked, snarled, as a tangled string; desponding; mildewed, putrid; bent, as a stick.
| 氣 repressed, pent up feeling; the steam kept down, vapor smothered.
| 結 aggrieved, sullen, brooding over a wrong.
| 蔥 flourishing, like a fine crop.
| 陶乎予心 my heart is harassed with grief.

抑丨不伸 a secret grief which is not divulged.

肝丨不舒 the liver is torpid.

丨金 the yellow aromatic root of a sort of *Curcuma* or turmeric; but the 丨金香 seems to be the sumbul root or musk-root, a fragrant root from western China.

丨林州 a prefecture in the southwest of Kwangsi, which perhaps gives its name to the two preceding plants.

樹木須從小時丨 trees must be bent when young.

薁, *yü'* Seems to be interchanged with the last.

A species of wild vine, the 蘡丨 (*Vitis ficifolia*), smaller than the cultivated.

六月食鬱及丨 in the sixth moon they eat the wild plums and blue grapes.

燠, 暵, *yü'* From *fire* and *secret;* it is also read *ngao'*

A hot sun; warm; latent heat; warmed by sunshine.

寒丨 cold and warm.

暖丨 comfortable and warm.

衣歌安丨 this dress sings out how warm and nice it is?

丨休 the noise of sorrow and regret.

膜, *yü'* The crop of birds; the lower ribs of an animal.

鴇丨鹿胃 the crop of the bustard and stomach of the deer.

矞, *yü'* From 矛 a *javelin* and 冏 *stuttering;* it occurs interchanged with *küeh,* 獝 to stampede.

To bore through with an awl; over full; flying, fluttering, agitated; hurrying about, as horses.

丨丨皇皇 all things bursting into life, as by the vernal breezes.

捧讀丨雲 I have received and read the felicitous cloud; *i. e.* your letter.

遙瞻丨采 I anxiously long to see your face.

噊, *yü'* Also read *shuh,*

Dangerous; the note of a bird.

遹, *yü'* From to *go* and *bored.*

To follow in another's work; to take up and carry on; to transmit; an initial particle, that, this very one.

紹丨 to continue another's book or writing.

祗丨乃文考 you (Wu Wang) can properly continue the writings of your ancestor Wăn Wang.

Read *shuh,* Deceitful, wicked.

謀猶回丨 the scheme looks like a very malicious one.

繘, *yü'* A well rope.

丨索 a rope used in drawing water.

霱, *yü'* Particolored clouds which are regarded as felicitous, having three colors in them.

鱊, *yü'* A slender, tiny fish likened to a bodkin, and called 鵝毛脡 or goose-quill slice; it is found in Kwangtung, and reckoned a delicacy; when cured the taste resembles shrimps; it is perhaps a kind of goby (*Tœnioides*).

鷸, *yü'* A water-bird, perhaps a lapwing, named from its note, *yuh yŭh;* it knows the approach of rain, and is thought by the Chinese to be akin to the quail.

冠丨 the oyster-catcher, or perhaps a species of *Tringa.*

蚌丨相持 when the oyster-catcher and clam caught each other, — the fisherman profited.

翠丨 the variegated kingfisher; to dart, as a kingfisher on its prey.

鴥, *yü'* From *bird* and *cave.*

To dart down, as a falcon on its prey; to fly swiftly and high.

丨風之逸响方傳 the rushing whirr of the hawks was heard on all sides.

彧, *yü'* Literary; elegant and accomplished, as a finished scholar.

文丨 clever and learned; adorned.

Read *yih,* and used with the next; colored, brilliant.

黍稷丨丨 the rich and flourishing fields of millet.

郁, *yü'* Used with the last.

Elegant; adorned; variegated, as silks; ancient name of a region in the south of Shensi and Kansuh.

丨丨紛紛 brilliant and beautiful, as clouds.

丨丨乎文哉 how courteous and elegant were all their ways! — said of the Cheu dynasty.

In *Cantonese.* To move, to shake, to joggle; to quiver, to vibrate.

丨手指 to reckon with the fingers; to shake one's finger at, to talk with the fingers.

丨動 to shake.

莫丨手丨脚 don't fidget and squirm so; don't touch me.

鬻, *yü'* From a *boiler* and *congee;* interchanged with the next.

Nature's food; to sell; to nourish, to rear.

丨女 to sell daughters.

自丨 I sold myself.

賣官丨爵 to sell office and and trade in titles.

Read *chuh,* and used with its primitive; rice gruel.

饘于是丨于是 I ate my rice here, and got my congee too; *i. e.* I lived here.

育, *yü'* From *flesh* and *child* in labor.

To bear and bring up; to rear, to support, to nurture; to educate in virtue; to bring forward and increase; to have the means of living.

養丨 to rear and maintain.

丨德 to add to one's virtue, by good works.

發 丨 萬 物 [God] produces and rears all things.

丨 才 bring forward the talented.

覆 丨 to overspread and shelter, as the heavens do.

孕 丨 to conceive and rear young.

昔 丨 恐 丨 鞠 at first I feared that our means of living would be spent.

唷, *yué* To vomit; the noise of vomiting; to belch; food rising on the stomach.

淯, *yü'* A stream, the 丨 水 one of the headwaters of an affluent of the River Han in Nan-yang fu in the southwest of Honan, formerly giving its name to 丨 陽 縣 district in that region.

蜟, *yü'* The larvæ of the cicada, 腹 丨 before the wings are grown or the pupa-skin is cast off; the skin itself.

閾, *yü'* From *door* and *border.*

The sill or threshold of the door, the 門 丨 which Confucius said 行 不 履 丨 should not be troddenon when walking through it.

思 不 出 乎 門 丨 I do not trouble myself with what is going on out of doors.

域, 畡, *yü'* From *earth* and *perhaps; q.d.* a dorbtful, unknown place.

A frontier, a border; a region, a country, a far off territory; lands, states; to limit, to make a border; the border of a grave.

西 丨 western regions; foreign countries.

兆 丨 the limits of a grave, marked by pillars.

聖 丨 the tomb of Confucius.

丨 中 之 土 地 甚 廣 the limits of the country are very wide.

絕 丨 far distant lands.

自 丨 to keep one's self within a certain limit.

身 居 異 丨 to live in foreign lands.

棫, *yü'* Thorny bushes, like scrub oaks, which make thickets and chapparal; a species of *Rhamnus* or hawthorn, the 白 桵, which is associated with the scrub oak.

柞 丨 拔 矣 thin out the oak and date bushes.

蜮, *yü'* A marine animal, also called 射 工 the archer, and 水 弩 the water crossbow; it is fabled to spurt sand at people or to bite their shadow to injure them; it is drawn like a small turtle (*Emys*), but is more probably a gigantic kind of beetle or *Dytiscus; met.* a masked enemy, underhand dealings.

鬼 丨 之 人 a subtle, hypocritical enemy.

爲 鬼 爲 丨 if you were an imp or a water-bug.

緎, *yü'* A seam.

裘 丨 the seam in a fur dress.

素 絲 五 丨 [lambskin coats] are usually sewed five seams with silk.

罭, *yü'* A fine drag-net, the 九 丨 having nine satchels or bags woven inside of it, used to catch dace and tench.

丨 網 or 丨 罟 a fine-meshed drag net.

In *Cantonese.* To twirl, as a stone tied to a string; to shake the cue; to lift the dress in walking.

淢, *yü'* From *water* and *if;* also read *siüh,* and interchanged with 洫.

To flow rapidly; a swift current; the moat of a city.

水 波 淢 丨 the rippling waves flowed on — like a fish's scales.

一 帆 隨 丨 如 飛 the boat flew along with the current.

毓, *yü'* From *mother* and *flowing;* an old form of 育, from which the primitive is altered.

To nurture, to educate a child in good habits; to rear, to bring up; to bring forward plants.

郁 丨 abundant, luxuriant; growing, as one's garden.

鍾 靈 丨 秀 the protecting spirit [of this region] has raised up a man of talent.

瑞 徵 已 卜 丨 麟 the felicitous conjunctions have now allotted you to nourish a unicorn; — a congratulation on the birth of a son.

儥, *yü'* To sell, to hawk or peddle; to move; to increase.

衒 丨 to expose wares for sale.

軉, *yü'* From *body* and *precious.*

The pearl of the body, the collected purity of the soul and virility.

丨 注 two pure tears, which upon death proceed from the nostrils of a Budhist priest, who has always been chaste, thus showing his real character.

颶, *yü'* A high gale.

謝 丨 a name given by Wu Tsih-tien to a subdued state.

雷 霆 逼 颶 丨 the claps of thunder followed quick on the gust.

噎, *yü'* A noise in the throat, a guttural sound or word.

YUN.

Old sounds, yun, wun, yin, *and* yon. *In Canton*, wăn; — *in Swatow*, ún, hún, jun, *and* ín; — *in Amoy*, ín, hún, ún, oan, *and* kún; — *in Fuhchau*, ŭng, úng, hung, *and* ŏng; — *in Shanghai*, yün; — *in Chifu*, yüin.

氳 ꜀yun From *breath* and *genial*.
The genial, life-giving influences of nature, a procreative aura or power.
氛 ｜ 蕭索 the vivifying breaths of nature are chilled, — there may be snow.

鰛 ꜀yun An unauthorized character, used to denote the 天 ｜ a small fish like a minnow taken in the shallow waters near Canton.

蝹 ꜀yun The motion of snakes; to squirm and writhe.
｜ ｜ the wriggling motion of eels, — when swimming.
Read ʿngao. A strange ghoul like an ape, that eats men's brains in the ground.

澐 ꜀yun A *vast* and deep *abyss* of water.
聖德至深兮 ｜ ｜ 如淵 his perfect virtue how deep it was! vast as the mighty deep!
泓澄 ｜ 潏 pure and illimitable, as the ocean.

云 ꜀yun Originally designed to represent *vapors curling* and rising, for which the next is now employed.
To speak, to say; to move and return, to circulate; occurs used with 紜 abundant; an initial particle, now, then; and used in connection with an interrogation; a final particle.
古語 ｜ the old saying is.
胡不 ｜ why don't you say so?
人 ｜ 我亦 ｜ what people say, that also will I speak; I'll not dispute.
盍記時也 ｜ why do you not note the epoch?
胡 ｜ to speak foolishly; why so?
不更 ｜ don't you reply again.
以俟君子 ｜ to wait for the good man.
道之 ｜ 遠曷 ｜ 能來 the road is long; how could he come?
如此 ｜ ｜ they all say so and so; all talk in this manner; thus and thus.
萬物 ｜ ｜ the vast variety in the universe.
｜ 如之何 now in what way?
不知老之將至 ｜ 爾 he did not perceive that age was creeping on.

雲 ꜀yun From *rain* and *revolving*; it was at first written like the last.
Clouds; a fog or cloud, which comes from the dragon; cloudy; shaded; numerous, gathering like the clouds; a fructifying principle; enters into the names of many places, among which was the lake country, north of the Yangtsz' and west of the River Han, which Yü drained, but now applied to Yunnan province.
｜ 彩 or 浮 ｜ a cloud.
滿天 ｜ the sky is all overcast.
｜ 頭 a thunder-cloud; a threatening cloud.
打 ｜ 板 to strike the cloudy board; — to announce visitors at a yamun or monastery by tapping an iron plate.
｜ 衣 a name for a priest's robes.
｜ 集 to assemble in crowds.
｜ 肩 a shoulder ornament embroidered on lady's dresses.
上天同 ｜ the sky is covered with clouds.
祥 ｜ rosy, propitious clouds.
｜ 師 the god of Rain.
朶 ｜ your epistle, your favor.
｜ 雨 sexual intercourse.
浮 ｜ 的人 a pompous or unreliable man, like a vapory cloud.

紜 ꜀yun Raveled, confused; perturbed; perplexing; mixed up, embroiled with.
萬騎紛 ｜ a myriad horses all in confusion.

耘 秐 頛 ꜀yun Only the first form is in common use.
To weed, to remove grass and other plants from fields; to take harmful things away.
不戰而 ｜ let alone war and attend to agriculture.
｜ 草 to root up weeds.

芸 ꜀yun Used for the last.
A fragrant herb, the ｜ 草 perhaps a species of rue; it will sprout when seemingly dead, and the leaves are put under mats and in books to drive away fleas or insects.
｜ 臺 or ｜ 牕 a study; *met.* a student.
夫物 ｜ ｜ 各復歸其根 Ah! all things will return to their origin, — alluding to the apparent dying and reviving of this plant.
｜ 香 a perfume like gum sandarac, perhaps obtained from the resin of a conifer (*Callitris?*)
｜ 芝 fragrant flowers.

蕓 ꜀yun A vegetable common in Hupeh, the ｜ 薹菜 which grows up rapidly, and becomes very bushy; its seeds furnish oil, and the stalks are eaten; the oil-cabbage.

澐 ꜀yun The waves rising high, applied especially to those on the River Yangtsz'.

勻 ꜀yun From 勹 to *infold* and 二 *two* or to *divide*, referring to the management of affairs.
Equal, even, alike; a little; to divide or allot equally.

分贓不丨 they did not share the plunder fairly.

丨不開 I cannot divide with you, as when one has not enough.

大小要丨 the large and small should be proportionate.

搽不丨 it is not rubbed on evenly.

調丨 or 攪丨 stir it up thoroughly; mixed fully.

骨肉停丨 his bones and flesh are well proportioned.

分丨 or 均丨 equally apportioned, fairly divided, proportionate.

In *Cantonese.* A time, an occasion.

一丨 once; on one occasion.

畇 ˏyun From *field* and *evenly.*

Cultivated land laid out in regular plats.

丨田 to clear land.

丨丨原隰 marshes and plains parceled out and prepared for tillage.

筠 ˏyun From *bamboo* and *evenly.*

The hard siliceous skin of the bamboo.

丨籃 splint baskets.

竹丨 or 青丨 bamboo skin or peel.

丨冲 a name in Chinese books for Arabia in the Yuen dynasty.

溳 ˏyun A small branch of the River Han in Sui-cheu in Hupeh, (joining it near its mouth,) once giving name to 丨州 in Teh-ngan fu.

潐丨 waves following each other.

鄖 ˏyun A small feudatory in the Cheu dynasty, which lay near the present 丨縣 in Yun-yang fu in the east of Hupeh.

篔 ˏyun From *bamboo* and *round.*

A variety of bamboo, 丨簹 cultivated for its large, long-jointed culms, twenty inches around, suitable for making machines and shields.

鋆 ˏyun From *metal* and *evenly.*

Gold; it is used in proper names.

抎 ʻyun Similar to the next.

To lose, as a fortress; to fall; to conquer, to overcome.

不戰而丨 not to fight, and still to beat him, — will not the advantage be great?

隕 ʻyun
磒 From *place* or *stone* and *round;* the second form is unusual.

To roll down, to fall with a crash; to fall from a height, or from the sky.

丨落 to fall, as an ærolite.

丨墮 to fall into ruin.

星丨如雨 the stars fell like rain; mentioned B. C. 685.

從高丨下 it fell down from above.

丨越貽羞 a breach of politeness hurts one's bashfulness.

十月丨蘀 the falling foliage in the autumn.

丨涕 to shed tears.

丨于深淵 to fall into the abyss; to go to utter ruin.

殞 ʻyun Similar to the last.

To perish, to die; to fail, to become extinct; to fall, as a withered leaf at even.

丨命 to die, to perish.

未曾身丨 [though wounded,] he is not yet dead.

全家丨滅 the whole family perished or was destroyed.

忽聞令先君星丨 I have just heard that your late father's star has fallen; — *i. e.* dead.

壽丨 died in a good old age.

絕粒丨命 starved himself to death.

允 ʻyun From 儿 *man* and 㠯 or 以 *by* contracted.

To permit, to assent; promised, allowed; true, loyal; sincerity; really, honestly; according to the facts; without guile; truly; to be believed.

丨准 granted; acceded to.

丨諾 yes, it can be allowed.

不丨 forbidden, disallowed.

應丨 liberty granted; conceded, promised.

丨協 to coöperate, as after a strife; cordiality restored.

蒙丨 thankful for the permission.

丨矣君子 sincere indeed is the princely man.

中丨 an ancient palace-officer like a chief butler.

丨州 old name of Hwai-yuen hien 懷遠縣 in the north of Kwangsi.

丨文丨武 loyal and great in peace and war.

狁 ʻyun A tribe of Scythian nomads, the 玁丨 which opposed the Cheu dynasty; afterwards called Hiung-nu.

惲 ʻyun From *heart* and *army.*

Liberal, kind in feeling; hearty goodwill; to deliberate upon the best way.

丨議 to consult upon.

丨謀 to make plans and schemes.

愪 ʻyun Grieved, sad; moved by.

懷丨莫伸 to keep one's grief in the breast.

心丨如結 the mind tortured with griefs, — which cannot be divulged.

韻
韵 yun' From *sound* and *round* or *equally.*

Sounds which rhyme in their tone as well as termination; an even and oblique tone are not regarded as rhyming; the final word or rhyme, the rhyming tone; a musical chord; a line of rhyme; in the native mode of spelling, the initial characters; a harmony of tone; dulcet, sweet.

平丨 rhymes in the even tone.

押丨 to make a rhyme.

八丨 eight rhymes, *i. e.* sixteen lines with alternate rhymes on the second, fourth and even ones.

仄丨 oblique rhymes.

風丨之人 an elegant, cultivated man.

丨書 small dictionaries arranged by their finals.

正丨 the authorized tone and sound of a character.

風發丨流 [his style is like] a harmonious breeze and a gently flowing stream.

人作丨事 an honorable person will do a creditable thing; an act that does him honor, such as patronizing letters.

不合丨 a discord; unlike in disposition.

縕' *yun'* Interchanged with 氳 genial vapor, and the next.

Raveled silk; a dark red or orange color; confused, disordered; flaxen, hempen.

丨袍 a wadded robe.

紛丨 abundant, as the productions of nature.

丨枲 raveled hemp thread or string.

自丨 to hang one's self.

束丨 a hank or skein of yarn.

'韞' *yun'* From *leather* and *mild;* interchanged with the next in some senses.

An orange color; a lining or inside of anything; a bowcase; to guard carefully, to lay up; to keep quiet, to conceal; to contain, as a lode the ore.

包丨 to hold, to contain, to store.

丨秘 to keep close, as a recipe or secret.

丨匱而藏 hide it away in the case.

石丨玉而山輝 if the stones contain gems, the hills will sparkle; — good acts will be known.

才華內丨 he has great talents and learning in him.

In *Cantonese.* To shut up, to entrap; to catch and lock-up.

丨住 keep him fast.

丨埋 to drive in, as sheep for the night.

蘊' *yun'* Occurs used for the last two.

To collect, to heap together; abstruse, recondite, mysterious; to pile up, as straw; a sort of water vegetable.

丨結 not at ease, oppressed, sad.

底丨 the secret reason for; the real cause, as for a person's conduct.

含丨 to repress ill feelings, to keep one's temper.

丨隆蟲蟲 multiplying, numerous as insects; — *met.* getting rich.

丨寶 it contains gems, as a stone.

丨積如堆 pile it up in a heap.

丨蓄 to collect and lay up, as rarities.

海丨 sea conferva, growing in long branches like tangle-weed.

熅' *yun'* From *fire* and *genial;* interchanged with the last.

Smoke without a blaze, a smothered fire; a warm vapor or steam, such as imparts a genial feeling in spring; to smooth out things by heat; thick smoke.

丨斗 a smoothing iron.

丨衣服 to iron clothes.

丨黃了 you have scorched — the clothes.

In *Fuhchau.* To heats spirit in a jar.

薀' *yun'* This and 蘊' are often interchangeably used, but this is the correct form for the plant, and is the least used.

An aquatic plant, whose leaves grow from the joints; to gather, to heap up, to accumulate; to practice.

丨藻 a *Hippuris* or mare's tail.

醞' *yun'* From *spirit* and *warm.*

Fermented liquor; spirit made from fruit, or by allowing the must to ferment a hundred days.

良丨一瓻 one jar of good beer.

丨酒 or 丨釀 to brew liquor, by fermenting it.

丨藉自持 to think over a matter carefully till one is master of it.

運' *yun'* From to *go* and *army.*

To revolve, to turn in a circuit, to move in an orbit; to travel around; to transport, to carry from place to place; a circuit, a revolution; what is done in succession, as the course of nature; a period of five or ten years; turn, chance; calculations or a conjunction, as in a horoscope; luck, lot, a run; times, a chapter of accidents.

丨動 to move about, to exercise; to use one's powers.

丨氣 hap, luck, fortunes.

倒丨 bad luck, unpropitious.

家丨 the fortunes of a family.

奉天承丨 to succeed to the throne by Heaven's order.

丨不佳 the prospects are not flattering; has been unfortunate.

日月丨行 the regular movements of the sun and moon.

丨脚 the cost of 丨米糧 transporting grain, on the 丨河 Grand Canal.

應丨而興 to take advantage of a turn and get on or forward.

入丨 or 交丨 had a turn of affairs; a contingency arose.

地丨 the nature or luck of land.

字丨 the times, the fate of one's horoscope.

不好時丨 hard times; unfortunate, as from sickness; an unpropitious time.

行大丨 to get through a long (ten years) period.

治天下可丨於掌上 governing the country [in Yao's day] was as easy as turning a thing in the palm of the hand.

丨用 to exercise upon; to make anything one's own by practice.

五丨 the reciprocal action of the five elements.

流年丨限 the conjunctions and times as years run on; said of one's horoscope.

丨籌幃幄 the head-quarters of the general; his powers.

丨柩 to carry a coffin home.

海丨 to send grain by sea.

暈 *yun'* From *sun* and *army*.
A halo around the sun or moon; vapors condensing towards them; thick, as smoke; obscure, as a fog; fuddled.
酒 丨 flushed and red with drink.
丨死復甦 fainted away and then revived.
曚 丨 殊 甚 an extraordinary obscurity, as a dense fog.
丨 氣 foggy vapors, in which the 月 丨 lunar halo shows.
頭 丨 dizzy; vertigo.

䲰 *yun'* A bird said to resemble a raven; but in the Păn Ts'ao, the 丨日 is a synonym of the 䳄 a bird that eats snakes, found in Annam and southern China; it is called 同力鳥 from its note resembling those words, and is probably a bird more allied to the heron or bittern.

鄆 *yun'* An ancient city in Lu, now Yun-ch'ing hien 丨城縣 in the southwest of Shantung.
丨邑 a large town and region there, which was 丨州 in A. D. 500; also, a village in the east of Shansi in Tsin cheu.

韗 韗 *yun'* A worker in leather; one who makes saddles or boots, and drums.
丨人爲臯陶 the leather-dresser also makes the wooden part of the drum.
丨韋裘 he made skin and fur garments.

YUNG.

Old sounds, yong *and* ngong. *In Canton*, yung *and* wing; — *in Swatow*, yong *and* eng; — *in Amoy*, yong, eng, gong, *and* hiong; — *in Fuhchau*, ŭng, éüng, íng, *and* éng; — *in Shanghai*, yung; — *in Chifu*, yung.

邕 雝 *yung* From 邑 *city* and 巛 *water* or a moat; the second form (once written like the next) is a contraction, and has since superseded it.
A four-square city with a moat around it, well protected; harmony, union; concord, as of sound; living at peace, as a well-governed people; to collect together, to stop, as a water-course.
丨丨 affable, courteous, easy with.
丨和 or 丨熙 harmony and peace in a state; to appease.
時 丨 the times were halcyon.
丨容下問乃爲愷悌之誠 to treat inferiors affably is to carry out the principles of commiseration.
列辟丨 a graduate of the rank of *kien-săng*, — referring to the hall of this name in Peking.
丨州 the largest and western of the nine divisions of Yü, comprising the country lying west of the Yellow River, and north of the River Wéi.

雝 *yung* Like the last, and used for 擁 to cover.
The singing of birds; to obscure; a marsh or pool.
丨合 agreeable, pacified.
丨丨 the cry of wild geese; the tinkling of bells.
有來丨丨 they came agreeable and affable.
維塵所丨 you will get covered with dust.
肅丨和鳴 harmoniously blend their sounds.

廱 *yung* Similar to the last.
Once used for 雍 in the name 辟丨 the imperial gymnasium where the highest scholars studied.

蘿 *yung* A trailing plant, 丨菜 the *Convolvulus reptans*, whose stem and leaves are mucilaginous, and eaten as a vegetable; a decoction of the leaves is regarded as a remedy against opium before the habit is fixed.

癰 *yung* From *disease* and *to stop*.
A malignant boil; an imposthume caused by the stoppage of the humors, which then discharge offensively.
丨疽 a sluggish ulcer, a cancer.
背 丨 a carbuncle on the back.
砍頭 丨 an abscess in the neck.
丨瘡 a severe abscess.

饔 *yung* From *to eat* and *harmony*, referring to the agreeable noises and scents of a kitchen.
Breakfast, the first meal; to dress food.
丨人 a cook.
丨飧不斷 breakfast and dinner always keep coming.
丨餼 cooked and raw meats offered to gods.

噰 噰 *yung* The harmonious singing of birds; the cry of birds.
丨丨 caroling of many birds in a pleasing concert.
怒氣丨喉 his passion chokes his voice.

搣 *yung* In *Cantonese*. To throw away as useless, to throw aside; to throw down.
丨開 heave it away.
丨來丨去 taking it up and throwing it down again.

灉 灉 *yung* A sluice or waste-weir opened along the banks of the Yellow River to receive the waters which then ran into it farther on; a small stream which anciently flowed into a marsh in Puh cheu in the southwest of Shantung.

榮 ₍yung ₍rung From 木 *wood* and 熒 *lustrous*. Beams of the *wu-t'ung* (*Elæococca*) tree; the king-posts in the turned-up corners of temples; glory, splendor; prosperous, honored; beautiful, as flowers; used for your in direct address; blood.

丨華富貴 prosperous, rich, and honorable.

丨 and 辱 or 枯 are opposites,—flourishing and fading; honored and disgraced; prosperity and adversity?

丨歸 or 丨旋 returning home in honor, as a retiring statesman.

丨任何處 where is your official post?

丨行 [when are] you going your journey.

秀丨 flourishing and beautiful, as a rose in bloom.

丨衞 blood and breath; a medical term for life.

恩丨 honored, distingushed by the emperor.

蠑 ₍yung A lizard found in damp places, the 丨螈 otherwise called 守宮 or palace guard; its body is blackish, smooth, and sometimes spotted.

熒 ₍rung From three *fires* under a *cover*. The light of many lamps in a house; sparkling, twinkling; shimmering; a doubtful, intermittent light; to lighten up.

丨臺 a volcano.

丨惑星 the glimmering star; a name for the planet Mars.

聽丨 to hear indistinctly.

丨丨鬼火 the glimmering will-o'-the-wisps.

丨丨燈火 the bright blazing lamps.

瑩 ₍rung From 玉 *gem* and 榮 *beautiful* contracted, referring to an idea that gems grow like plants.

Luster of gems; a bright quartzose pebble like a precious stone, once used to plug the ears, or cover the orifice; to brighten; lustrous; intelligent, bright.

晶丨 brilliant, shining, as a diamond.

瓊丨 an elegant gem, such as were used for ear-stoppers.

心地精丨 a mind clear and intelligent, a very clear head.

丨潔 pure, as a crystal.

滎 ₍rung Small rills of water; little brooks.

丨水 rivulets, streams.

丨波旣豬 the waves of the river Yung all remain within their banks.

丨陽縣 and 丨澤縣 in K'ai-fung fu in Honan, were the ancient borders of Tsu and Ching.

濴 ₍rung Like the preceding.

To revolve; to run around, as eddies in the water.

池水瀠丨 the rippling waters flow from the pool.

縈 ₍rung To wind, to tie around; to reel; to entwine, to coil around; to go around.

丨繞 to bind or cord around; to encompass.

丨回 to go round and round.

時丨夢穀 sleeping and eating, I am always thinking of you.

慚歉交丨 my unworthiness and defects surround me; my shortcomings embarrass me.

螢 ₍ying A glow-worm; a fire-fly, called 丹鳥 the red bird, and 夜炤 night brightness; luminous insects of any kind.

丨火虫 a lightning-bug.

腐草化爲丨 fire-flies are transformed from rotten plants.

丨窓雪案 the fire-flies [shining] in the window, and the snow [reflected] on the table,—helped him to study.

肜 ₍yung From *flesh* and *adorned*, but the original radical was 舟 referring to the gliding motion of a vessel; not the same as ₍t'ung 彤 rosy.

To sacrifice two days in succession; a continual sacrifice, the one offered on the second day.

丨魚氏 a concubine of Hwangti, the Yellow Emperor.

Read ₍ch'ăn. A vessel sailing quickly.

容 ₍rung From *covering* and *ravine*; *q. d.* a gully is empty, until it receives rain.

To receive; to contain, as a house its inmates; to endure, to tolerate, to bear with; forbearing; to nourish; the way in which one takes things, the air, manner, conduct; the face, countenance, looks, or attitude; perfumed amulets; gauzes; a screen before a privy.

丨貌 the presence of a person, his style and looks.

不丨 or 難丨 inexcusable, unendurable.

包丨 affable, patient, long-enduring; to comprehend.

華丨 pretty, graceful, as a girl.

笑丨 simpering, always smiling.

從丨幾日 I'll allow a few days.

丨納 to contain; to behave kindly towards.

聖丨 an imperial portrait.

輕丨 light plain gauze silks.

無以自丨 no way to hide his mortification.

丨易' easy, not difficult; used ironically and interrogatively, as 好丨易'嗎 was it so easy?—*i. e.* it was not easy

丨忍 patient, meek.

屋小丨膝 the house is small, but it will hold our knees;—just enough, in narrow circumstances, we can get on.

失丨 to lose one's self-possession, disconcerted; to blush.

不丨於死 death even cannot excuse the offense.

僅可丨身 it just holds me, as a chair; just big enough to hold it.

丨讓 to kindly yield, to pass by, to give in.

丨顏好 a handsome face.

榕 ₍rung The bastard banian, (*Ficus pyrifolia* and *F. indica*,) worshiped in southern China for long life; one name is 不死木 the deathless tree; the wood is used for chopping-blocks; though it closely resembles the Indian banian (*F. religiosa*), the Budhists have not called it 菩提 or *bo* tree.
丨城 the Banian city, *i. e.* Fuhchau; as 丨談 or 丨腔 is the local dialect of that city.
丨樹公 or 丨鬚 the pendent rootlets of the banian.

溶 ₍rung Water flowing full and gently within its banks; leisurely; a deep current.
丨盛 abundantly.
月色丨丨 the moon is shining brightly.

蓉 ₍rung A flower, 芙丨花 the *Hibiscus mutabilis*; but this name is applied to several plants in different places.

傛 ₍rung Uneasy, not at rest.
丨丨抱恙 the disease is still violent.
武藝丨丨 well skilled in warlike accomplishments.

瑢 ₍rung Gems attached to the girdle.
瑽丨 the tinkling of gems hanging to the girdle.

鎔 ₍rung From *metal* and *to contain.*
A mold in which to pour castings; a die for coins; to smelt, to fuse metals; to forge; to influence, as doctrine.
丨化 to smelt and separate dross from ore, and then 丨鑄 pour the metal into a mold; to transform and alter.
金之在丨 [as] metal takes to the mold, — so do people to a ruler.

鱅 鰫 ₍yung Some regard these two as essentially different.
A dace or tench (*Leuciscus*) common at Canton, of a greenish yellowish tint; there are two different sorts; the *Păn Ts'ao* speaks of a common freshwater fish under this name, with a very large head, and weighing as much as fifty catties, which is probably a species of *Percidæ*.

喁 ₍yung From *mouth* and *monkey.*
The motion of a fish's mouth when breathing; gasping, as a fish.
水濁則魚丨 when the water is turbid, the fishes gasp.
延頸舉踵丨丨然 with outstretched necks they all stood on tiptoe, mouths all agape.
小語丨丨 many voices talking in a low tone.
Read *₍yü.* To respond, as in singing.
丨丨唱和 they sang in response harmoniously.

顒 ₍yung From *head* and *monkey*; this character being the private name of the emperor Kiaking, is usually avoided, or contracted to 顒; when it is possible 永 is used instead, and has nearly superseded the other.
A large head; a dignified, serene presence; portly and imposing, but benign and agreeable.
丨仰 to look up to.
丨丨卬卬 amiable and courtly, as the emperor.
其大有丨 his great bulk is imposing, as an elephant.

融 ₍yung From *insect* and *a caldron.*
Vapor blending as it rises in the air, and cannot be repressed; melting, thawing; harmonizing, combining, interpenetrating; clear, bright, intelligent.
丨駿 tall, stately, as a fine steed.
天氣丨和 a pleasant spring temperature.
水乳交丨 [as intimate as] milk mingled with water.
丨會貫通 well versed in, made it thoroughly my own.
通丨辦理 to make an arrangement for the time, to get the use of awhile; to borrow, as services.
丨散 or 丨化 to dissipate or arrest, as malaria; to absorb or liquefy, and make new combinations.
丨洽 to understand fully; to instil into; to blend or unite with.
其樂也丨丨 his satisfaction and joy were complete.
昭明有丨 let his clear intelligence become perfect.
丨縣 in the north of Kwangsi.

瀜 ₍yung Wide and deep, as a vast expanse of water, 沖丨 applied to the lakes of China, and its great rivers.

庸 ₍yung From 庚 to *change* and 用 to *use* combined.
To employ, as servants; constant, common, usual; laborious, and therefore deserving; meritorious; on purpose, therefore, to have use for; cordial, obliging, accomodating; merit, services; simple, unpolished, having no parts; joined with an interrogative, how? labor paid instead of taxes; a state or region; a kind of bell, and used with the next.
丨才 trivial talents, said by officers of themselves.
丨丨 to employ those who are fit.
丨常 or 平丨 ordinary, common, not of the best sort.
務丨 (or 無丨) 遠慮 do not be anxious about the distant or doubtful.
靜言丨違 when unemployed he brags [what he could do]; when set at work, he disobeys.
碌碌丨人 ordinary people, laborers.
丨民 or 丨愚 the commonalty; rude, unlearned people.
丨合 if, premising.
丨惡陋劣 the worthless and degraded.
丨醫 a quack, a charlatan.
丨何 or 丨安 how; as 丨何傷 what harm was it, or came of it?
丨非貳乎 did [the two princes] not have different intentions?

鏞 ˏyung A large bell.
笙丨以間' to separate the pieces of music by the pan-dean-pipes and bell.
鳴丨 to sound the bell.

傭 ˏyung From *man* and *common*.
To hire, to engage one's self as a laborer; to serve; hired.
丨工 to hire laborers.
丨人 workmen; a hireling; to hire men.
家丨 hired men.
丨役 hired attendants.
Read ʽ*chung*. To treat equally; impartial; alike; to do.
昊天不丨 Heaven is not impartial.

墉 ˏyung A wall of dirt thrown up for defense; a low wall, a redoubt, an adobie wall; the north wall of a hall.
丨垣 a mud wall around a village.
其崇如丨 [the sheaves] were high as a wall; — an abundant harvest.
以伐崇丨 he destroyed the city walls of Tsung.
我丨宮 a palace built by Han Wu-ti.

鄘 ˏyung A small feudatory in the Cheu dynasty, now Wéi-hwui fu 衛輝府 in Honan; a place among the southern tribes.

甬 ʽyung Composed of 用 to *use* and 弓 a *bow*; used with its compounds.
Bursting forth, as plants or a fountain; a measure of ten 斗 or pecks; middle, passing through, as a raised path; the ear by which a bell is upheld.

埇 ʽyung Used for the last.
A raised walk up to a house is 丨道; applied at first to that leading up to the palace, which was walled in.
In *Cantonese*. A pit; the hole into which the coffin is laid.
開丨 to dig a grave.
山丨 a grave, usually on a hill.

衕 ʽyung Like the last.
A narrow raised or paved walk in a yard, 丨路 or 丨衕 leading up to the main entrance; a paved road; a highway.

勇 ʽyung From *strong* and *rising-up*; it is embroidered on the breasts and backs of soldiers' uniforms.
Bravery, courage; fearless, daring; brawny, soldierly; to advance fearlessly or resist manfully; to exert one's strength.
丨人 an intrepid man.
丨猛 fearless, resolute.
丨士 a brave, lusty fellow.
小丨 hasty, testy, ready to fly into a passion.
仁者必有丨 a humane man is always brave.
奮丨向前 the most valiant take the lead.
丨號 a title of military honor, indicating a low grade of the Manchu patulu.
大丨若怯 a self-possessed, resolute determination is like fear — in its outward manifestation.
打技丨 to exhibit feats of strength.
好'丨 fond of brave deeds; liking to show off one's prowess.
爾丨伊何 how can you exhibit your valor?
血氣之丨 the assurance and daring of youth.
告奮丨 I tell you that I will lead the van.
丨敢 imprudent daring.

俑 ʽyung From *man* and *through*, because it could jump; others derive the phonetic from the next to leap.
A wooden puppet made like a man, anciently buried with chiefs; afterwards exchanged for straw effigies, and then living men were immolated.
作丨 an inventor, one who discovers new things.
丨人 a human effigy, a statuette.
Read ˏ*tung*, and used for 痛. Pain; to feel for.

踊 ʽyung To exult, to leap; to stamp; to excite by hopping about.
跳丨 to dance, to jump.
一丨過河 he leaped the stream at one jump.
辟丨 to beat the breast and stamp, as hired mourners.
丨躍踢毬 to jump up and hit the ball; to bestir one's self.

蛹 蜎 ʽyung The second form is nearly disused.
The pupa or chrysalis of the silkworm, 繭丨 also applied to those of the bee, wasp, and other insects.
土丨 a small grub found in rotten grain.

恿 慂 ʽyung Having a brave heart; bold, adventurous, animated.
慫丨 to urge on, to stir up, to inspirit; to seduce into evil ways.

涌 湧 ʽyung From *water* and *rising*; but the second form with *strong* is most used.
To bubble and run off, as a fountain; rising, rushing on, filling and running over; an affluent of the Yangtsz' in the north of Hupeh.
潮丨 the tide is coming in.
月丨大江流 the [reflection of the] moon rolls on with the rushing waters of the Yangtsz'.
一丨而進 it rushed in at a gush.
淚如泉丨 her tears ran like a bubbling fountain.
痰丨 phlegm rising in the throat.
In *Cantonese*. A creek; a side stream coming into a river; to wash out.
丨滘 a side canal or creek.
丨乾淨 rinse it clean.

壅 ʽyung ʽyung From *earth* and a *wall*.
To stop with earth; to dam, to close up; to hinder, to prevent; to heap earth around plants; to conceal, to suppress.

丨塞 to obstruct, to block up; to stuff in.
奸臣丨蔽 a bad minister conceals things.
丨上 or 丨于上聞 to prevent superiors (or the emperor) knowing it.
丨培 to put mold and dung to the roots of plants; to mulch.

擁 'yung Like the preceding.
To embrace or clasp to the bosom, to carry in the arms or hold in the lap; to gird the loins, as a runner; to conceal from; to intercept; to crowd, to push and run together, to throng.
丨上前 to crowd on those before.
前呼後丨 those who go before halloo, and those behind crowd up, as when an officer goes out.
丨抱 to hug, to clasp.
樹丨濤聲 the gust roars through the trees.
一丨 a great rush, at one push.
丨兒而睡 she took the child in her arms and slept.
丨面 to screen the face.

臃 'yung To swell, as a boil; swelling.
丨腫 fat, pursy; bulging, as a barrel; a swelling, a boil.
發丨 it has swollen.

鞾 'yung The upper leather or leg of a boot.

永 'yung Represents *water flowing* on in streams; this character is considered as embodying the eight strokes used in writing Chinese characters.
Ever-flowing; perpetual, eternal, everlasting; final, complete, as a permanent cure; distant in time; long continued; to prolong, as a tone.
日丨 long midsummer days.
丨不要 I never shall want it.
丨別 a final separation.
壽不丨矣 his days will not last much longer.
享丨福 to enjoy eternal bliss.

丨止 it will entirely stop — the cough.
丨古不壞 it will never wear out or spoil.
以丨上帝之恩 to perpetuate the favor of Shangti.
以丨終夜 to make a night of it, as roistering fellows do.
丨不錄用 never again write him down to be employed.
圍爐丨夜 they sat around the furnace all night.

咏 詠 yung' From *mouth* or *words* and *flowing* on.
To sing or hum in a drawling tone; to chant or intone the words; a chant.
丨詩 to chant verses.
丨嘆 to sigh and sing.
唱丨 to sing hymns.
丨歸 returned home singing as they went.
歌丨 hymns and chants; also a Budhist name for the *Sama-Veda*, a prayer and hymn book, out of which some are sung or chanted by choristers at public sacrifices.

泳 yung' To dive and go under water.
丨之游之 dive into it and swim in it.
丨水 to dive and swim.
漢之廣矣不可丨思 the country of the Han River is broad, and I cannot fully comprehend — its people's manners.

醟 yung' From 酉 *spirits* and 熒 *fiery* contracted.
To lose one's head by drinking, which foolish people soon do.
酗丨 boisterous and happy under the influence of wine.

禜 yung' From *worship* and *brilliant*.
A sacrifice offered to the gods of the hills and fountains, and to the heavenly bodies, in times of drought and pestilence.

瑩 yung' From *heart* and *bright*.
To dislike.
灯丨 to hate, to abhor.

嗡 yung' To retch; to choke.
嚏丨欲吐而難道 he could not speak it out fully for his emotion.

用 yung' Composed of 卜 to *divine* and 中 to hit the *center*; *i.e.* if the lot is right it can be used; another old form makes it a union of 片 a *splinter* and 刀 a *knife*; it is the 101st radical of a few incongruous characters.
To use, to give out for use; to put forth, to employ, to avail of; to cause; useful, available; as a *preposition*, by, with, from, because of; thereby, hence; what is needed for use; expenses, outlays; useful things; emanation, action of a 體 or principle; the exercise of a function, or the acting out of principle or law.
勿丨 do not use it.
無丨 or 不中丨 or 丨不着 useless, not useful for the purpose; used up, worn out.
費丨 or 使丨 necessary outlays.
焉丨佞 how can I use deception?
喜怒之丨 the exercise of joy and anger.
禮之丨 for the use of ceremony; *i.e.* what propriety requires.
作爲何丨 of what service will this be?
抱奇謀而不丨 he devised an excellent plan, but it was discarded.
丨意 to give attention to a thing, to study closely.
天地無全功萬物無全丨 heaven and earth do not contain all kinds of merit, nor does everything useful exist among created things.
丨刀自殺 killed himself with a sword.
我信丨他 I put great confidence in him.

功 丨 meritorious services.
不受 丨 indisposed, out of sorts.
不勝 丨 more than can be used.
你 丨 朝嗎 have you breakfasted?
試 丨 a trial of, an experimental use.
不曉 丨 人 ignorant of human nature.
以道員升 丨 let him be promoted to the post of intendant.
妄 丨 improper use of, as a phrase or tool.

節 丨 or 儉 丨 frugal; a careful use of.
有財此有 丨 money is profitable for all things; it can be done with money.
閒時置下忙時 丨 make it ready when you have leisure, and it will be available at the time it is needed.
好便當 丨 very convenient and useful.
丨 錢 a commission or contingent expenses.
丨 是 therefore, for this cause.

何 丨 弗受 why has he not received that?
故謀 丨 是作 therefore stratagems arose from this.
足 丨 爲善 quite capable (or adequate) of doing the right thing.
丨 上 and 丨 下 superiors and inferiors.
有 丨 頭 it is of some use; it will be of service.
不忮不求何 丨 不臧 as he neither dislikes nor covets, what good quality does he not exhibit fully?

LIST OF THE RADICALS.

In this list, the number, sound, and leading signification of each radical are given; the letter C attached to some of them denotes that such are generally used in combination; the contractions placed after the full form of others are always found in combination. The figures which follow the meaning show firstly, the number of characters following each radical in the K'anghi Tsz'-tien; and secondly, the number given in this dictionary, which comprise all those in common use.

RADICALS FORMED OF ONE STROKE.

1.	*Yih*		一	one, unity	42–26
2.	*Kwun*	C	丨	to pass through	21–11
3.	*Chu*	C	丶	a point	10–3
4.	*P'ieh*	C	丿	a left stroke	33–17
5.	*Yih*	C	乙	one, a hook	42–12
6.	*Küeh*	C	亅	a barb	19–4

OF TWO STROKES.

7.	*'Rh*		二	two	29–14
8.	*T'eu*	C	亠	cover, head	38–14
9.	*Jăn*		人 亻	man	794–436
10.	*Jăn*	C	儿	a man	52–21
11.	*Juh*		入	to enter	28–8
12.	*Pah*		八	eight	44–11
13.	*K'iüng*	C	冂	a limit	50–17
14.	*Mih*	C	冖	to cover	30–11
15.	*Ping*	C	冫	ice, icicle	115–39
16.	*Ki*	C	几	a bench	38–8
17.	*K'an*	C	凵	a receptacle	23–6
18.	*Tao*		刀 刂	a sword	377–140
19.	*Lih*		力	strength	163–54
20.	*Pao*	C	勹	to wrap	64–19
21.	*Pi*	C	匕	a ladle	19–5
22.	*Fang*	C	匚	a basket, case	64–19
23.	*Hi*	C	匸	to conceal	17–7
24.	*Shih*		十	ten; perfect	55–17
25.	*Puh*		卜	to divine	45–11
26.	*Tsieh*	C	卩 㔾	a stamp	40–18
27.	*Han*	C	厂	a cliff	129–29
28.	*Sz'*	C	厶	selfish, perverse	40–8
29.	*Yiu*		又	hand, also	91–23

OF THREE STROKES.

30.	*K'eu*		口	mouth	1146–478
31.	*Hwui*	C	囗	an inclosure	118–41
32.	*T'u*		土	earth, land	580–251
33	*Sz'*		士	scholar, sage	24–10
34.	*Chi*	C	夂	to follow	11–2
35.	*Sui*	C	夊	walking slow	23–7
36.	*Sih*		夕	evening, dusk	34–12
37.	*Ta*		大	great	132–45
38.	*Nü*		女	daughter	681–231
39.	*Tsz'*		子	son, child	83–29
40.	*Mien*	C	宀	a roof	246–90
41.	*Ts'un*		寸	an inch	40–15
42.	*Siao*		小	small, petty	41–11
43.	*Wang*	C	尢 尤 兀	lame	66–14
44.	*Shi*	C	尸	a corpse	148–45
45.	*Ch'eh*	C	屮	a sprout	38–2
46.	*Shan*		山	hill; wild	636–144
47.	*Chw'en*		巛 川 巜	streams	26–8
48.	*Kung*		工	laborer, art	17–6
49.	*Ki*		己	self, private	20–6
50.	*Kin*		巾	napkin, cap	295–92
51.	*Kan*		干	to oppose	17–7
52.	*Yao*	C	幺	immature	20–6
53.	*Yen*	C	广	a covering	285–80
54.	*Yin*	C	廴	to move on	9–8
55.	*Kung*	C	廾	hands joined	50–9
56.	*Yih*		弋	a dart	15–5
57.	*Kung*		弓	archery	165–40
58.	*Ki*	C	彐 彑	hog's head	25–7
59.	*San*	C	彡	pelage	52–12
60.	*Ch'ih*	C	彳	a step	215–57

OF FOUR STROKES.

61.	*Sin*		心 忄 ⺗	heart	1115–431
62.	*Kwo*		戈	a spear	116–31
63.	*Hu*		戶	a door	44–19
64.	*Sheu*		手 扌	hand	1203–566
65.	*Chi*		支	branch	26–2
66.	*Puh*	C	攴 攵	to rap	296–59
67.	*Wăn*		文	literature	20–8
68.	*Teu*		斗	a peck	32–12
69.	*Kin*		斤	hatchet	55–12
70.	*Fang*		方	square	92–30
71.	*Wu*	C	无 旡	without	12–2
72.	*Jih*		日	sun, day	435–144
73.	*Yueh*		曰	speaking	37–14
74.	*Yueh*		月	moon; month	69–18
75.	*Muh*		木	wood, tree	1369–573
76.	*K'ien*		欠	owe; to pant	235–51
77.	*Chi*		止	to stop	99–12
78.	*Tai*		歹 歺	vicious	231–36
79.	*Shu*	C	殳	to kill	93–16
80.	*Wu*		毋	to deny; not	16–7
81.	*Pi*		比	to compare	21–5

82.	*Mao*		毛	hair, wool	211–34
83.	*Shi*		氏	surname	10–4
84.	*Kʻi*	C	气	breath, aura	17–6
85.	*Shui*		水氵氺	water	1595–595
86.	*Hwo*		火灬	fire	639–190
87.	*Chao*		爪爫	claws	36–6
88.	*Fu*		父	father, senior	10–3
89.	*Hiao*	C	爻	blending	16–2
90.	*Chwʻang*	C	爿	a frame, couch	48–9
91.	*Pʻien*		片	a splinter	77–15
92.	*Ya*		牙	a tooth	9–2
93.	*Niu*		牛	cattle	233–51
94.	*Kʻüen*		犬犭	a dog	444–120

OF FIVE STROKES.

95.	*Hüen*		玄	somber, deep	6–4
96.	*Yuh*		玉王	a gem	473–161
97.	*Kwa*		瓜	a melon	55–8
98.	*Wa*		瓦	a tile, brick	174–34
99.	*Kan*		甘	pleasant	22–3
100.	*Shăng*		生	to produce	22–5
101.	*Yung*		用	to use; useful	10–5
102.	*Tʻien*		田	a field; to till	192–60
103.	*Pʻih*		疋	a roll of cloth	15–4
104.	*Nih*	C	疒	disease	526–180
105.	*Poh*	C	癶	back to back	15–3
106.	*Poh*		白	white; freely	109–23
107.	*Pʻi*		皮	skin, bark	94–42
108.	*Ming*		皿	dish; platter	129–41
109.	*Muh*		目罒	eye	647–150
110.	*Meu*		矛	a halberd	65–3
111.	*Shi*		矢	a dart	64–11
112.	*Shih*		石	stone	499–171
113.	*Shi*		示示礻	omen	213–82
114.	*Jeu*	C	禸	a footprint	12–5
115.	*Hwo*		禾	grain	431–131
116.	*Hüeh*		穴	a cave	298–61
117.	*Lih*		立	to set up	101–20

OF SIX STROKES.

118.	*Chuh*		竹	bamboo	953–232
119.	*Mi*		米	rice	318–77
120.	*Mih*		糸糹	silk	823–288
121.	*Feu*		缶	crockery	77–19
122.	*Wang*	C	网罒⺳	net	163–42
123.	*Yang*		羊	a sheep	156–39
124.	*Yü*		羽	wing, plume	220–47
125.	*Lao*		老	old, senior	22–7
126.	*'Rh*		而	and, still, yet	22–5
127.	*Léi*		耒	a plow	84–19
128.	*'Rh*		耳	the ear; side	72–36
129.	*Yuh*	C	聿	a stile, a pencil	19–6
130.	*Juh*		肉月	meat	674–256
131.	*Chʻăn*		臣	a statesman	16–4
132.	*Tsz'*		自	self, from	34–4
133.	*Chi*		至	to reach; very	24–4
134.	*Kiu*		臼	a mortar	71–13
135.	*Sheh*		舌	tongue, taste	31–12
136.	*Chwʻen*		舛	opposing	10–3
137.	*Cheu*	C	舟	to transport	197–53
138.	*Kăn*	C	艮	perverse; fixed	5–2
139.	*Seh*		色	color; vice	21–2
140.	*Tsʻao*	C	艸艹	herbs	1902–559
141.	*Hu*		虍	a tiger	114–21
142.	*Chʻung*		虫	insects	1067–301
143.	*Hüeh*		血	blood	60–9
144.	*Hing*		行	to do; a row	53–22
145.	*I*		衣衤	clothes	607–199
146.	*Hia*	C	襾西	cover; west	29–7

OF SEVEN STROKES.

147.	*Kien*		見	to see	161–30
148.	*Kioh*		角	horn; corner	158–27
149.	*Yen*		言	to speak	861–303
150.	*Kuh*		谷	gully, valley	54–5
151.	*Teu*		豆	pulse; a plate	68–14
152.	*Shi*		豕	swine	148–24
153.	*Chai*	C	豸	reptiles	140–29
154.	*Péi*		貝	precious	277–99
155.	*Chʻih*		赤	flesh color	31–8
156.	*Tseu*		走	to run	285–34
157.	*Tsuh*		足	foot; enough	580–174
158.	*Shăn*		身	the body	97–21
159.	*Ché*		車	a carriage	361–102
160.	*Sin*		辛	distressing	36–11
161.	*Chʻăn*		辰	time	15–2
162.	*Choh*	C	辵辶	going	381–138
163.	*Yih*		邑阝	a region	350–105
164.	*Yiu*		酉	new wine	290–80
165.	*Pien*	C	釆	to separate	14–3
166.	*Li*		里	a Chinese mile	14–4

OF EIGHT STROKES.

167.	*Kin*		金	gold	806–257
168.	*Chʻang*		長镸	long	55–1
169.	*Măn*		門	a door	246–73
170.	*Feu*	C	阜阝	a mound	348–94
171.	*Tai*	C	隶	to reach to	12–2
172.	*Chui*	C	隹	birds	233–35
173.	*Yü*		雨	rain	298–70
174.	*Tsʻing*		青	azure color	17–6
175.	*Féi*		非	wrong	25–4

OF NINE STROKES.

176.	*Mien*		面	the face	66–5
177.	*Koh*		革	raw hide	305–75
178.	*Wéi*	C	韋	leather	100–20
179.	*Kiu*		韭	leeks	20–4
180.	*Yin*		音	sound; news	43–8
181.	*Hieh*		頁	a page	372–77
182.	*Fung*		風	wind	182–30
183.	*Féi*		飛	to fly	12–1
184.	*Shih*		食	to eat	403–108
185.	*Sheu*		首	head; first	20–3
186.	*Hiang*		香	incense	37–10

OF TEN STROKES.

187.	*Ma*		馬	horse	472–132
188.	*Kuh*		骨	a bone	185–43
189.	*Kao*		高	high, eminent	34–1
190.	*Piao*	C	髟	hair	243–59
191.	*Teu*		鬥	to quarrel	23–10
192.	*Chʻang*	C	鬯	fragrant herbs	8–2
193.	*Lih*	C	鬲	a tripod	73–5
194.	*Kwéi*		鬼	ghost	141–22

OF ELEVEN STROKES.

195.	*Yü*		魚	a fish	571–154
196.	*Niao*		鳥	a bird	750–174

197. *Lu* 鹵 salt land 44-9
198. *Luh* 鹿 a deer 104-32
199. *Meh* 麥 wheat 131-19
200. *Ma* 麻 textile fiber 34-4

OF TWELVE STROKES.

201. *Hwang* 黃 yellow 42-4
202. *Shu* 黍 panicled millet 46-8
203 *Hoh* 黑 black 172-30
204. *Chi* 黹 embroidery 8-3

OF THIRTEEN STROKES.

205. *Min* 黽 frogs 40-7
206. *Ting* 鼎 a tripod 14-4
207. *Ku* 鼓 a drum 46-12
208. *Shu* 鼠 mouse; rat 92-18

OF FOURTEEN STROKES.

209. *Pi* 鼻 the nose 49-14
210. *Ts'i* 齊 even, correct 18-4

OF FIFTEEN STROKES.

211. *Ch'i* 齒 front teeth 162-31

OF SIXTEEN STROKES.

212. *Lung* 龍 dragon; awful 14-4
213. *Kwéi* 龜 the tortoise 24-1

OF SEVENTEEN STROKES.

214. *Yoh* 龠 a musical reed 19-5

A CLASSIFICATION OF THE RADICALS BY A NATURAL METHOD LIKE THE FOLLOWING, WILL ASSIST IN REMEMBERING THE LEADING GROUPS.

Parts of a Body.—Body 身; corpse 尸; head 首; parts of a skull 頁; hair 髟; down 毛; whiskers 而; face 面; eye 目; ear 耳; nose 鼻; mouth 口; teeth 齒; tusk 牙; tongue 舌; hand 手; right hand 又; heart 心; foot 足; hide 革; leather 韋; skin 皮; wings 羽; feathers 彡; blood 血; flesh 肉; talons 爪; horn 角; bone 骨; a bear's footprint 禸.

Zoological Radicals.—Man 人; woman 女; child 子; horse 馬; sheep 羊; tiger 虍; dog 犬; ox 牛; hog 豕; hog's head 彑; deer 鹿; tortoise 龜; dragon 龍; reptile 豸; rodents 鼠; toad 黽; bird 鳥; gallinaceous fowls 隹; fish 魚; insect 虫.

Botanical Radicals.—Herb 艸; grain 禾; rice 米; wheat 麥; millet 黍; hemp 麻; leeks 韭; melon 瓜; pulse 豆; bamboo 竹; sacrificial herbs 鬯; wood 木; branch 支; sprout 屮; petal 片.

Mineral Radicals.—Metal 金; stone 石; gems 玉; salt 鹵; earth 土.

Meteorological Radicals.—Rain 雨; wind 風; fire 火; water 水; icicle 冫; vapor 气; sound 音; sun 日; moon 月, evening 夕; time 辰.

Utensils.—A chest 匚; a measure 斗; a mortar 臼; spoon 匕; knife 刀; bench 几; couch 爿; clothes 衣; a head-covering 冖; crockery 缶; tile 瓦; dish 皿; napkin 巾; net 网; plow 耒; vase 鬲; tripod 鼎; boat 舟; carriage 車; pencil 聿; bow 弓; shield 干; halberd 矛; javelin 弋; arrow 矢; spear 戈; ax 斤; musical-reed 龠; drum 鼓; seal 卩.

Qualities.—Color 色; black 黑; white 白; yellow 黃; azure 青; carnation 赤; somber 玄; high 高; long 長, sweet 甘; square 方; large 大; small 小; slender 幺; strong 力; feeble 尢; old 老; fragrant 香; acrid, 辛; vicious, 歹; perverse, 艮; selfish, 厶; opposed 舛; blending 爻; even 齊.

Actions.—To enter 入; to follow 夂; to walk slowly 夊; to arrive at 至; to stride 走; to walk 行; to reach to 隶; to move on 廴; to step 彳; to go swiftly 辵; to stop 止; to fly 飛; to conceal 匸; to envelop 勹; to encircle 囗; to establish 立; to overshadow 襾; to distinguish 釆; to divine 卜; to see 見; to eat 食; to say 言; to speak 曰; to kill 殳; to quarrel 鬥; to rap 攴; to embroider 黹; to owe 欠; to compare 比; to bring forth 生; to use 用; to promulge 示; to straddle 癶.

Parts of the World and Dwellings.—A desert 冂; cave 穴; field 田; mound 阜; hill 山; valley 谷; rivulet 川; cliff 厂; receptacle 凵; a city 邑; roof 宀; gate 門; door 戶; portico 广.

Figures.—One 一; two 二; eight 八; ten 十.

Miscellaneous.—A demon 鬼; an inch 寸; a mile 里; without 无; not 非; not having 毋; a scholar 士; a statesman 臣; letters 文; art 工; wealth 貝; self 自; myself 己; father 父; a point 丶; a hook 亅; new wine 酉; silk 糸; joined hands 廾; disease 疒; a surname 氏; a classifier of cloth 疋.

CHARACTERS IN THIS DICTIONARY

ARRANGED BY THEIR RADICALS.

In this Index, the figures placed above each character show the page on which it occurs; and these numbers are arranged so that the characters under each radical, having the same number of strokes, follow each other in alphabetical order; the figures on the right side of the column in heavy type, shows how many strokes, not including the radical itself, are in each character following it. The sound of each character, where it is known, is given in the Canton, Amoy, and Shanghai dialects in that order, according to a uniform system of spelling.

Radicals: 1 一; 2 丨; 3 丶; 4 丿; 5 乙

1095 一 yăt, ít, ih

1

874 丂 hao, ch'o

903 丁 ting, téng, ting

987 七 ts'ăt, ch'ít, ts'ih

2

25 丈 chéung, tiong, dzang

83 下 ha, ha, 'o

723 三 sam, sam, sè^{n}

741 上 shéung, siong, zong

1040 万 man, ban, mè^{n}

3

307 丐 k'oi, kai, ké

594 丏 mín, bian, mí^{n}

717 不 păt, pút, peh

1125 与 ü, u, ü

52 丑 ch'au, t'iu, ts'ù

516 丽 li, li, li

4

416 丘 yau, k'iu, chù

671 丕 p'i, p'i, p'é

699 丙 ping, péng, ping

763 世 shei, sé, sz'

974 且 ch'é, ch'ia^{n}, ts'ia

5

78 丞 shing, séng, dzăng

526 両 léung, léong, liang

899 㐁 'ím, t'iam, t'i^{n}

909 丢 tiu, tiu, tiù

6

526 两 léung, léong, liang

7

700 並 ping, péng, bing

10

876 亜 t'au, tòé, dù

494 丨 kwăn, k'un, kw'ăng

1

413 丩 kau, k'iu, kiù

2

423 个 ko, kò, ku

1066 丫 a, a, o

3

105 中 chung, tiong, tsung

156 丰 fung, hong, fung

261 丯 kai, kai, kia

378 㠯 i, i, i

476 丱 kwan, kwan, kwè^{n}

6

121 串 ch'ün, chwàn, ts'é^{n}

7

14 丳 ch'an, san, ts'é^{n}

8

342 亝 k'i, k'i, ch'i

87 丶 chü, tsu, dzö

2

246 丸 ün, wan, wè^{n}

3

849 丹 tan, tan, té^{n}

4

87 主 chü, tsu, tsö

686 丿 p'ít, p'iat, p'ih

284 乂 ngai, ngai^{n}, ni

612 乃 nai, nai, né^{n}

2

915 乇 t'ok, t'ék, t'ok

982 尒 ts'ín, chian, dzi^{n}

413 久 kau, kiu, kiù

3

53 之 chi, chi, tsz'

4 乍 cha, tsa, zò

122 乏 fat, hwat, vèh

224 乎 u, ho, u

1031 朿 tsz', ché, tsz'

5

108 重 chung, chiong, tsung

650 𠂢 p'ai, p'ai, p'a

924 𠂤 túi, túi, té

7

470 乖 kwai, kwai, kwa

9

772 乘 shing, séng, zăng

10

102 𠂹 shui, sui, dzüé

12

924 𨸏 túi, té

1096 乙 üt, ít, ih

1

1103 乚 yăn, un, yăng

431 九 kau, kiu, kiù

583 乜 măt, moh, mi

2

395 乞 hăt, k'it, chih

1079 也 ya, ya, ya

4

274 乤 i, i, i

5

335 乩 ki, ki, ki

6

570 乱 lün, lwan, lö^{n}

7

298 乳 ü, ju, sö, sü

8

481 亀 kwei, kúi, kwé

10

311 乾 kon, kan, kü^{n}

12

570 亂 lün, lwan, lö^{n}

6 亅 7 二 8 亠 9 人 亻

9 人 亻 10 儿

17 凵 18 刀刂

26 卩 卫 27 厂 28 厶 29 又 30 口

30 口

30 口

32 土

37 大

38 女

38 女 39 子 40 宀

47 川 巛 巜 48 工 49 己 50 巾 51 干

61 心忄⺗

61 心忄⺗

61 心小忄 62 戈 63 戶 64 手才

64 手 扌

64 手扌

75 木

75 木 76 欠

85 水氵氺

85 水氵氺

86 火 灬

87 爪 爫

130 肉 月

800 肉 yàk jiok niòk

2

334 肌 ki ki ki
509 肋 lăk lék lăk
695 [illegible] pʻăt pʻít pʻih

3

49 肘 chau tiu tsù
204 肐 yăt gut hih
250 肓 fong hong hwong
288 肕 ngăn jím zăng
310 肝 kon kan kō^{n}
319 肛 kong kong kong
795 肖 tsʻiu siau sio
916 [illegible] tò tò tu
917 肚 tò tʻò du
1132 肙 ün wan yü^{n}
1146 肜 yung yung
192 肴 ngao ngau^{n} yo
204 肸 yăt hćk hih
288 [illegible] yăm jím zăng
324 肯 hăng kʻéng kăng
346 肵 kʻi ki dji
380 肩 kín kam ki^{n}
390 肷 kím kiam chi^{n}
433 股 ku ko ku
460 肱 kwăng kéng kung
486 [illegible] kwei kwó
640 肭 năt neh
651 肦 pan pʻan pè^{n}
658 肨 pʻong pʻong bong
671 肧 pʻúi pʻi pʻó

4

55 肢 chi chi tsz'
103 肫 chun tun tsăng
133 肪 fong hong fong
137 肥 fi hui vi
139 肺 feř hui fi
1042 肳 măn bún văng
1110 肬 yau iu yù
1140 育 yòk yok yòk

5

2 胦 yéung jong yang
17 胗 chʻăn chín tsăng
49 冑 chau tiu zù
55 胑 chi chi tsz'
55 胝 chi chi tsz'
74 [illegible] ching chéng tsăng
198 胘 ín hian yi^{n}
221 胡 u o u
356 胛 kap ka kăh
431 胍 ku ko ku
433 胋 ku ko ku
443 胊 kʻü kʻu kʻü
443 胠 kʻü kʻu kʻü
455 胐 wăt kʻút djüih
584 脉 măk bék mak
641 胬 nò nu
647 胈 pat pwat pèh
659 胖 pʻún pwʻan pʻong
663 胞 pao pau po
669 背 púi pòó pó
671 胚 pʻui pʻi pʻó
818 胥 sü su sü
847 胎 tʻoi tʻai tʻó
851 胆 tam tam tè^{n}
1007 胙 tsò tsa dzò
1031 胏 tsz' chó tsz'
1032 胔 tsʻz' tsu tsz'
1039 [illegible] ún wan wè^{n}
1053 胃 wei úi wé
1104 胤 yăn in yăng

6

55 脂 chi chi tsz'
63 胵 chʻi chi tsʻz
74 脀 ching chéng tsăng
86 [illegible] chü tsü
192 胶 ngao yo
195 脇 híp hiap hih
195 脅 híp hiap hih
214 胷 hung hiong hʻiung
214 胸 hung hiong hʻiung
276 胰 i i i
276 [illegible] i i i
302 [illegible] yun zăng
306 胲 koi kai kó
427 胳 kok kok kăk
468 胯 kwa kwʻa kwʻò
478 胱 kwang kong kwong
584 脈 măk bék mak
616 能 năng léng năng
629 胺 at at ùh
659 胮 pʻong pʻong
687 胼 pín pian pí^{n}
719 胹 i ji 'ıh
888 脁 tʻiu tʻiau tʻio
932 胴 tung tong dung
986 脊 tsik chék tsih
1018 脆 tsʻui chʻui tsʻüó
1018 脃 tsʻui chʻui tsʻüó
1032 胾 tsz' tsu tsz'
1082 胭 ín yen i^{n}
1130 [illegible] ngo ngu

7

146 脯 fu hu fu
169 脝 hăng héng hăng
205 脪 yăn hun hʻiăng
209 脛 king kéng yăng
288 [illegible] yăn jím zăng
410 脚 kéuk kʻiok kièk
475 脘 kún kwan kwé^{n}
584 脢 múi múi^{n} mé
666 脬 pʻò pʻau, hu pʻo
718 脖 pút pút peh
783 脣 shun tun zăng
784 脤 shun sun săng
811 脩 sau siu siù
821 脧 tsun chʻwan tsí^{n}
875 脰 tau tò dù
882 [illegible] tʻei tʻé tʻi
908 脡 tʻing tʻéng tʻing
914 脫 tʻüt twʻat tʻöh
1004 脞 tsʻo tsʻò tsʻu
1042 脗 măn bún văng

8

24 脹 chéung tiong tsang
70 [illegible] chik chít tseh
103 腄 shui sui dzüó
137 腓 fi hui fi
145 腐 fu hu vu
145 腑 fu hu fu
163 [illegible] ham ham yé^{n}
205 [illegible] hín hím hʻiăng
288 腍 năm jím săng
351 [illegible] ka ka
365 腔 hong kʻong chʻiang
438 腒 kü ku kü
455 [illegible] wat kʻút djüih
475 [illegible] kún kwan kwé^{n}
680 脾 pʻi pi bi
738 腎 shăn sín zăng
781 脽 shui sui tsüé
802 腊 sik sek sih
899 腆 tʻín tian tʻi^{n}
951 [illegible] chăng chéng tsăng
993 腈 tsing chʻéng tsing
1039 腕 ún wan wé^{n}
1082 腌 íp íp yi^{n}
1095 腋 yăt ék yăk
1121 腴 ü yu ü

9

3 [illegible] cha hai tso
27 腸 chʻéung tiong dzang
41 [illegible] chíp siap tseh
105 [illegible] chʻun chʻun tsʻăng
107 腫 chung chiong tsung
151 腹 fòk hok fòk
268 腪 fán hun hwăng
295 腬 yau jiu zù
305 腝 ün jwan niō^{n}
390 腱 kín kian djé^{n}
410 腳 kéuk kiok kièk
551 腡 wo lò lu
552 [illegible] lo lò lu
585 腜 múi múi^{n} mé
615 腩 nam lam né^{n}
617 腦 nò nau, lò no
621 腤 òm am é^{n}
628 腭 ngok gok ngok
689 [illegible] pín pian pí^{n}
722 腮 soi su só
809 腥 seng séng sing
856 [illegible] tʻam tam té^{n}
928 腯 tʻun tun dăng
937 腶 tün tö^{n}
963 腠 tsʻau tsò tsʻù
1074 腰 iu yau yo
1120 腢 ü gu ü

10

11 [illegible] chʻa chʻa tsʻah
15 [illegible] chăn yan tsăng
101 膇 chui tui, dzüé

135 舌 136 舛 137 舟 138 艮 139 色 140 艸 艹

140 艸 艹

140 艸 艹

140 艸 艹

142 虫

142 虫
143 血
144 行
145 衣 衤

593 蠛 mít biat mih
16
93 蠩 ch'ü su dzú
568 蠪 lung long lung
918 蠧 tò tò tu
17
156 蠭 fung hong fung
272 蠮 i i i
434 蠱 ku ko ku
450 蠲 kün kwan kün
660 蠯 păng péng ping
1055 螱 wei óó wé
18
179 蠵 kw'ei hé i
947 蠶 ts'am ch'am zén
19
574 蠻 man ban mèn
614 ⿱難虫 nan lan nèn
789 ⿰虫麗 li, sei si
21
97 蠾 chòk chiok tsòk

230 血 hüt hiat hüih
4
640 衄 nòk lok no
671 衃 p'úi p'ó
5
205 衅 yăn hun h'iăng
584 衇 măk bék mak
6
108 衆 chung chiong tsung
429 衉 hak keh
721 衈 i ji 'rh
15
593 衊 mít biat mih
18
203 衋 nik gék hih

207 行 hăng héng yăng
3
316 衎 hon k'an kén
1087 衍 ín yan in
4
168 衖 hong hong hong
1138 衏 ün gwan nün
5
232 衒 ün hian yön
778 術 shut sut zeh
6
238 衖 hung hang lung
359 街 kai ké ka
412 ⿲彳谷亍 k'éuk k'òk
932 衕 tung tong dung
7
1067 衙 nga ga nga
1148 ⿲彳甬亍 yung yong yung
9
109 衝 ch'ung ch'iong ts'ung
222 衚 u o u
867 衜 tò tò do
10
1054 衛 wei óó wó
103 衠 chun tsun tsăng
169 衡 hăng héng 'ăng
1054 衞 wei óó wé
169 衡 hăng héng 'ăng
12
109 衝 ch'ung ch'iong ts'ung
18
444 衢 k'ü ku kü

270 衣 i i i
2
284 𧘇 yui é i
520 ⿰衤了 liu liau lio
1013 卒 tsut tsut tsăh
3
5 衩 ch'a ch'a ts'ò
682 表 piu piau pio
733 衫 sham san sèn
915 ⿰衤乇 t'ok t'ok t'ok
4
106 衷 ch'ung t'iong tsung
129 衯 făn hun făng
142 衭 fu hu fu
285 衻 ím jiam zé
289 衽 yăm jím zăng
294 衵 yăt jit nih
361 衸 kai kai ka
394 衱 k'ăp kíp kiăk
398 衿 k'ăm k'ím kiăng
402 衾 k'ăm k'ím chăng
418 袀 kwăn kun kün
494 衮 kw'ăn kun kw'ăng
586 袂 mei main mó
612 衲 nap lap neh
785 衰 shui sòó sé
796 衺 ts'ó sia sia
874 ⿰衤斗 tau tò tù
1133 袁 ün wan yün
5
17 袗 ch'ăn chín tsăng
69 袠 tít ék zeh
155 袚 fát hut feh
233 袨 ün hian yön
350 袈 ka ka ka
443 袪 k'ü k'u k'ü
494 袞 kw'ăn kun kw'ăng
498 ⿰衤立 lap liap lèh
546 袊 ling léng ling
573 袜 mút biat meh
588 袤 mao bò mù
647 袙 p'a p'a p'ò
654 袢 p'ún pw'an p'én
667 袍 p'ò pau bo
669 被 pi p'i pí
746 袑 shiu siau dzo
812 袖 tsau siu ziù
845 袋 toi tai dó
856 袒 t'an t'an tò
915 袥 t'ok t'ok t'ck
1032 ⿱此衣 tsz' ch'u tsz'
1078 袎 ao yu o
6
86 袾 chü tsu tsü
152 袱 fök hok vòk
283 袣 yei é i
289 袵 yăm jím zăng
299 袽 ū, na ju sü
318 裉 ngăn k'ăng
357 袷 kap kiap kăh
370 ⿰衤交 kao kau kio
379 袺 kít k'iat kih
427 袼 kak kek kăk
437 袴 fu k'o k'u
481 袿 kwei kúi kwé
531 裂 lít liat lih
610 ⿱如衣 na na nò
673 袌 pau p'ò pù
909 ⿰衤朵 tò tò tu
936 ⿰衤同 t'ung t'ong dung
943 裁 ts'oi ch'ai dzé
1098 裀 yăn ín yăng
7
79 裎 ch'ing t'óng dzăng
113 裝 chong tsong tsong
284 裔 yui é i
416 裘 k'au kiu djù
420 裙 kw'ăn kun k'üin
496 裍 kw'ăn k'un kw'ăng
519 裡 li li li
519 裏 li li li
632 裊 niu niau nio
712 補 pò pò pu
730 裟 sha sa sò
745 ⿰衤肖 shao sau so
778 裋 shū su sü
1097 裛 yăp ék ih
1003 ⿰衤坐 tso tsò zu
1128 裕 ü yu ü
8
12 ⿰衤定 chan téng zan
26 裮 ch'éung ch'iong ts'ang
46 裧 chím ch'ian ts'én
51 裯 ch'au tiu dzù
59 製 chei chó tsz
136 裶 fi hui fi
163 ⿰衤函 ham ham yèn
438 裾 kü ku kü
468 褂 kwa kwa kwò
490 裹 kwo kò ku
551 裸 lo lò lu
660 ⿰衤并 ping péng ping
672 裴 p'úi pòé bé

145 衣 衤

146 襾 西

147 見

149 言

INDEX OF CHARACTERS.

167 金

168 長镸

846 隶 toi tai dé
7
837 肆 sz' su sz'
9
524 隸 tei lé tí

100 隹 chui tsui tsö
2
69 隻 chek chék tsèk
219 隺 hok hok ngòk
614 难 nan lan nè^{n}
813 隼 sun tsun sing
3
997 雀 tséuk ch'iok ts'iòk
4
214 雄 hung hiong yung
435 雇 ku ko ku
482 推 kwei kwé
985 集 tsap chíp dzih
1067 雅 nga nga ya
1089 雁 ngan gan ngè^{n}
5
60 雉 chi ti sz'
330 雊 kau ko kù
1009 雎 tsü tsu tsü
1012 雋 tsun ch'wan tsí^{n}
1033 雌 ts'z' ch'u ts'z'
1145 雍 yung yong yung
6
553 雒 lok lok lok
7
1126 [illegible] ü ü

8
52 雔 ch'au siu dzù
885 雕 tiu tiau tio
9
826 雖 sui sui süé
999 [illegible] ts'au ch'iu tsiù
10
93 雛 ch'o ch'u dzu
166 雗 han han 'ö^{n}
179 巂 kw'ei i
258 雘 wok hòk
334 雞 kei ki ki
476 雚 kún kwan kwé^{n}
787 雙 shéung song song
939 雜 tsap tsap seh
1145 雝 yung yong yung
11
517 離 li li li
614 難 nan lan nè^{n}
14
1123 雤 ü u ü

1124 雨 ü u ü
3
734 [illegible] sham san sè^{n}
820 雪 süt swat sih
1121 雩 ü u ü
4
129 雰 făn hun făng
658 雱 p'ong pong p'ong
1041 雯 măn bún ming
1142 雲 wăn hun yün
5
311 雸 kòm kam kó^{n}
510 雷 lúi lui lé
545 零 ling léng ling
708 雹 pòk p'auh bo
719 [illegible] p'út peh
896 電 tín tian dí^{n}
6
818 需 sü su sü
884 [illegible] t'ei té di
7
8 霅 chap sap sèh
18 震 chăn chín tsăng
20 霃 ch'ăm tím dzăng
584 霉 múi múi^{n} mé

607 霂 mòk bok mòk
673 霈 p'úi p'ai p'é
794 霄 síu siau sio
802 [illegible] sín san sí^{n}
907 霆 t'ing téng ding
8
43 霑 chím tiam tsé^{n}
89 霔 chü tsu dzö
116 [illegible] ch'ong ch'ong zong
136 霏 fi hui fi
273 霓 ngei gé ni
257 霍 fok hok hok
498 [illegible] lap lat lèh
540 霖 lăm lím ling
732 霎 sap siap sèh
966 霋 ts'ei ch'é ts'i
9
182 霞 ha ha ya
543 霝 ling léng ling
583 霡 măk bék măk
787 霜 séung song song

1105 霙 ying éng yăng
10
550 霤 lau liu liù
11
1055 霨 wei ói wé
1062 霧 mò bu vu
493 霩 kwok kok kw'ok
502 [illegible] lam lam lè^{n}
696 霦 păn pín ping
805 霫 tsap síp zih
1101 霪 yăm ím yăng
12
569 霳 lung liong lung
802 霰 sín san sí^{n}
865 霯 t'ăng téng dăng
1140 霱 lut yüh
13
557 露 lò lò lu
643 [illegible] nung long nung
645 霸 pa pa pò
658 霶 p'ong pong p'ong
694 霹 p'ik p'ék p'ih
988 霵 ts'ăp ch'ip ts'ih

14
181 霼 hi k'ai i
573 霾 mei bai ma
608 靀 mung bong mung
618 [illegible] nau nù
833 [illegible] sün swan sö^{n}
964 霽 tsei chó tsi
16
1 靄 oi ai é
537 靂 lik lék lih
543 靈 ling léng ling
846 靆 toi tai dé
17
1 靉 oi ai é
83 [illegible] chok tsok tsoh
31
702 靐 p'ing p'éng p'ing

995 青 ts'ing ch'éng ts'ing
5
994 靖 tsing chéng dzing
6
965 靘 ts'ing ch'éng ts'ing
7
994 靚 leng ch'éng dzing
8
897 靛 tín téng dí^{n}
994 靜 tsing chéng dzing
10
897 靝 t'ín t'ian t'í^{n}

136 非 hus fi
3
649 啡 p'ai pai p'a
4
939 [illegible] sap sèh
7
327 靠 k'ao k'ò k'o
11
591 靡 mi bi mi

171 隶
172 隹
173 雨
174 青
175 非

190 髟
191 鬥
192 鬯
193 鬲
194 鬼

196 鳥
197 鹵
198 鹿
199 麥
200 麻
201 黃
202 黍
203 黑

211 齒
212 龍
213 龜
21 龠

LIST OF DIFFICULT CHARACTERS.

THE following table contains a selection of all the characters occurring in the preceding Index whose radicals are not very obvious, being combined with other parts or placed in unusual positions. They are arranged in classes by the whole number of their strokes in a regular series; the figures after each one denote its radical and additional strokes in the Index. Characters in which the difficulty of finding their place chiefly consists in the choice of the right radical out of two or three, as 攷 or 刱, are not often inserted.

Characters of **3 STROKES.**	亡 8—1	丑 1—3	內 11—2	午 24—2	尹 44—1	世 1—4	以 9—3	匃 20—3
七 1—1	亾 11—1	丹 3—3	公 12—2	卞 25—2	尺 44—1	丘 1—4	兄 10—3	北 21—3
万 1—2	凡 16—1	之 4—3	六 12—2	卬 26—2	屯 45—1	丙 1—4	充 10—3	卉 24—3
丈 1—2	刁 18—1	予 6—3	兮 12—2	厄 27—2	巴 49—1	丱 2—4	仝 11—3	半 24—3
个 2—2	千 24—1	云 7—2	有 13—2	及 29—2	市 50—1	㠯 2—4	冉 13—3	占 25—3
丫 2—2	叉 29—1	互 7—2	冘 14—2	収 29—2	廿 55—1	主 3—4	有 13—3	卡 25—3
丸 3—2	才 64—1	五 7—2	办 18—2	友 29—2	弔 57—1	乐 4—4	冊 13—3	卯 26—3
乃 4—2	**4 STROKES.**	井 7—2	切 18—2	反 29—2	引 57—1	乍 4—4	冬 15—3	去 28—3
不 4—2	丆 1—3	从 9—2	分 18—2	壬 32—1	朩 75—1	乎 4—4	処 16—3	只 30—2
乞 5—2	不 1—3	今 9—2	勿 20—2	壬 33—1	不 75—1	乏 4—4	凸 17—3	史 30—2
也 5—2	与 1—3	介 9—2	化 21—2	夭 37—1	**5 STROKES**	乪 5—4	凹 17—3	右 30—2
了 6—1	丐 1—3	允 10—2	匹 23—2	孔 39—1	且 1—4	仝 9—3	出 17—3	叵 30—2
于 7—1	丏 1—3	元 10—2	升 24—2	少 42—1	丕 1—4	令 9—3	匆 20—3	司 30—2

農 161—6	朅 73—10	**15 STROKES.**	賡 154—8	燕 86—12	糞 119—11	[illegible] 109—13	辮 120—14	變 149—16
雍 172—5	朢 74—10	勰 1—913	輝 159—8	瞢 109—11	糜 119—11	[illegible] 114—13	躉 157—13	驘 187—13
飱 184—3	榮 75—10	壿 33—12	辤 160—8	穎 115—11	繇 120—11	舊 134—12	**21 STROKES.**	黴 203—11
14 STROKES.	歰 77—10	奭 37—12	黎 202—3	禦 113—11	羹 123—11	虩 141—12	亹 8—19	**24 STROKES.**
僰 9—12	毓 80—10	慕 61—11	**16 STROKES.**	縣 120—10	[illegible] 130—11	隳 170—15	囂 30—18	矗 109—19
凳 16—12	爾 89—10	慶 61—11	冀 12—14	羲 123—10	舉 134—11	雘 172—10	纇 120—15	衋 143—18
凴 16—12	疑 103—9	憂 61—11	噩 30—13	臲 132—10	謄 149—10	雚 172—10	臝 130—17	贛 154—17
[illegible] 28—12	疐 103—9	暴 72—11	[illegible] 30—13	舘 135—10	豳 152—10	巂 172—10	[illegible] 195—10	靆 173—16
叠 29—12	睿 105—9	樊 75—11	奮 37—13	虤 141—10	賸 154—10	**19 STROKES.**	**22 STROKES.**	鹽 197—13
嘉 30—11	粼 119—8	標 75—11	[illegible] 37—13	螣 142—10	賾 154—10	厴 27—17	囅 30—19	**25 STROKES.**
嘏 30—11	肅 129—8	熲 86—11	嬴 38—13	豎 151—9	輿 159—10	嚮 30—16	囊 30—19	糶 119—19
嘗 30—11	肇 129—8	[illegible] 109—10	學 39—13	豫 152—9	隸 171—9	繭 120—13	懿 61—18	纛 120—19
壽 33—11	膏 130—10	睘 109—10	嶲 46—13	販 154—9	韱 179—8	羸 123—11	糴 119—16	釁 164—18
夐 35—11	臧 131—8	緜 120—9	憲 61—12	賴 154—9	**18 STROKES.**	蘷 140—15	聽 128—16	靉 173—17
夢 36—11	臺 133—8	膚 130—11	整 66—12	**17 STROKES.**	叢 29—16	**20 STROKES.**	轡 159—15	**26 STROKES.**
夤 36—11	與 134—8	鋪 132—9	暹 72—12	嚭 30—14	彝 58—15	嚲 30—17	**23 STROKES.**	豔 151—20
夥 36—11	舞 136—8	虢 141—9	暨 72—12	徽 60—14	擊 64—14	嚳 30—17	夔 36—20	鑿 167—17
搴 64—10	蒙 140—10	魯 195—4	槷 75—12	應 61—13	歸 77—14	嚴 30—17	虋 140—19	**27 STROKES.**
暢 72—10	養 184—6	興 134—9	橐 75—12	毚 81—13	瞿 109—13	競 117—15	蠲 142—17	鬱 192—16

LIST OF THE FAMILY SURNAMES OF THE CHINESE,

BOTH SINGLE AND DOUBLE.

THE following list has been collected from the common school-book known as the 百家姓 or Family Surnames, and from K'ang-hi's Dictionary; those contained in the former, numbering 408 單姓 or single surnames, and 30 複姓 or 雙姓 double surnames, are distinguished by being printed in italics. Probably four-fifths of the people are called by these surnames, the rest being seldom used or extinct. Native authors have carefully investigated their origin, and traced them back, in some cases more than three thousand years, to the time when they are first mentioned. A few tens of those contained in this list are characters not found in this Dictionary, their use being almost confined to that of a proper name; a few others, like *Feu* 不 or *Hang* 汻, take a different sound when used as surnames. All are arranged alphabetically on the same plan as the Dictionary. When mentioning their surnames, the Chinese have a custom of dissecting the parts, so as the better to define it when there is any doubt; 二馬馮 *two-horse Fung*; 木子李 *wooden-son Li*; 弓長張 *bow-long Chang*; 立早章 *stand-early Chang*; 文武武 *Wăn-Wu Wu*; &c.

In writing Chinese proper names in Roman letters, the *sing* and *ming* should be carefully distinguished as two names, as noted on page 810, and not printed as one word, as is often done to their utter confusion. The Manchus were required by the Emperor K‘anghi to use only their *ming* in writing their names in Chinese, so that the *sing* is known only among themselves, like a kind of clan sign; such names, therefore, as *Yuen-yuen* or *O-keh-tun-pu* are properly written in one word, as much as *Benjamin* or *Christopher*, though the syllables may be separated for convenience of pronunciation.

藹 ai	臣 ch‘ăn	超 ch‘ao	讐 ch‘eu	直 chih	成 ch‘ing	竹 chuh	崇 ch‘ung	奮 făn
盎 ang	塵 ch‘ăn	抄 ch‘ao	犨 ch‘eu	植 chih	城 ch‘ing	竺 chuh	蟲 ch‘ung	方 fang
查 cha	張 chang	巢 ch‘ao	釗 ch‘eu	質 chih	祋 ch‘o	策 chuh	寵 ch‘ung	坊 fang
諎 cha	章 chang	蓢 ch‘ao	醜 ch‘eu	執 chih	妁 choh	燭 chuh	揣 chwai	芳 fang
霅 chah	黨 chang	鼂 ch‘ao	胄 ch‘eu	職 chih	卓 choh	祝 chuh	莊 chwang	房 fang
察 ch‘ah	仉 chang	鈔 ch‘ao	窌 ch‘eu	袠 chih	斫 choh	觸 ch‘uh	顓 chwen	魴 fang
柴 ch‘ai	掌 chang	柘 ché	脂 chi	帙 chih	濁 choh	畜 ch‘uh	鱄 chwen	防 fang
棧 chan	昌 ch‘ang	車 ch‘e	知 chi	秩 chih	諸 chu	鄐 ch‘uh	專 chwen	訪 fang
湛 chan	長 ch‘ang	折 cheh	之 chi	蛭 chih	朱 chu	騅 chui	歂 chw‘en	非 féi
産 ch‘an	萇 ch‘ang	輒 ch‘eh	支 chi	郅 chih	洙 chu	諄 chun	船 chw‘en	棐 féi
甄 chăn	嘗 ch‘ang	詹 chen	枝 chi	卣 ch‘ih	邾 chu	準 chun	釧 chw‘en	肥 féi
箴 chăn	暢 ch‘ang	瞻 chen	只 chi	斥 ch‘ih	銖 chu	春 ch‘un	法 fah	賁 féi
葴 chăn	爭 chăng	苫 chen	紙 chi	赤 ch‘ih	住 chu	鍾 chung	髮 fah	斐 féi
眞 chăn	朝 chao	展 chen	彘 chi	征 ching	鑄 chu	東 chung	發 fah	費 féi
枕 chăn	炤 chao	戰 chen	雉 chi	徵 ching	初 ch‘u	中 chung	樊 fan	不 feu
軫 chăn	釗 chao	纏 ch‘en	稚 chi	稱 ching	儲 ch‘u	終 chung	凡 fan	芣 feu
針 chăn	招 chao	周 cheu	智 chi	正 ching	鉏 ch‘u	重 chung	蕃 fan	旉 foh
鎮 chăn	昭 chao	舟 cheu	蚩 ch‘i	鄭 ching	芻 ch‘u	仲 chung	氾 fan	夫 fu
斟 chăn	晁 chao	州 cheu	絺 ch‘i	政 ching	褚 ch‘u	衆 chung	范 fan	扶 fu
郴 ch‘ăn	肁 chao	晝 cheu	遲 ch‘i	呈 ch‘ing	楚 ch‘u	种 ch‘ung	範 fan	鳧 fu
岑 ch‘ăn	狣 chao	稠 ch‘eu	馳 ch‘i	程 ch‘ing	處 ch‘u	充 ch‘ung	芬 făn	苻 fu
陳 ch‘ăn	趙 chao	疇 ch‘eu	池 ch‘i	承 ch‘ing	粥 chuh	沖 ch‘ung	紛 făn	符 fu

府 fu
甫 fu
輔 fu
付 fu
傅 fu
富 fuh
幅 fuh
福 fuh
佛 fuh
鄜 fuh
復 fuh
腹 fuh
蝮 fuh
服 fuh
虙 fuh
伏 fuh
風 fung
豐 *fung*
酆 *fung*
封 *fung*
馮 *fung*
逢 *fung*
奉 fung
鳳 *fung*
海 hai
譀 han
函 han
寒 han
韓 *han*
罕 han
僕 han

翰 han
漢 han
杭 *hang*
汻 hang
恒 hăng
衡 *hăng*
蒿 hao
豪 hao
毫 hao
郝 *hao*
好 hao
皓 hao
昊 hao
浩 hao
侯 *heu*
後 *heu*
后 heu
郈 heu
厚 heu
稀 hi
毒 hi
郗 *hi*
僖 hi
嵐 hi
羲 hi
攜 hi
希 hi
喜 hi
系 hi
戲 hi
叚 hia

瑕 hia
夏 *hia*
解 *hiai*
香 hiang
鄉 hiang
向 *hiang*
項 *hiang*
梟 hiao
孝 hiao
頡 hieh
軒 hien
賢 hien
咸 *hien*
瞯 hien
縣 hien
弦 hien
㬎 hien
顯 hien
獻 hien
憲 hien
訢 hin
忻 hih
欣 hin
釁 hin
興 hing
邢 *hing*
刑 hing
陘 hing
涬 hing
行 hing
荇 hing

幸 *hing*
杏 hing
學 hioh
休 hiu
訓 hiün
熊 *hiung*
何 *ho*
河 ho
賀 *ho*
合 hoh
哈 hoh
郃 hoh
頜 hoh
霍 *hoh*
鶴 hoh
紇 hoh
黑 hoh
盍 hoh
盇 hoh
赫 hoh
居 hoh
滸 hu
呼 hu
嘑 hu
壺 hu
狐 hu
胡 *hu*
虎 hu
扈 *hu*
戶 hu
謼 hu

邘 hü
盱 hü
虛 hü
許 *hü*
禤 hüen
玹 hüen
玄 hüen
斛 huh
鴻 hung
紅 *hung*
弘 *hung*
閎 hung
雄 hung
橫 hung
洪 *hung*
訇 hung
閧 hung
花 *hwa*
華 hwa
滑 *hwah*
淮 hwai
懷 *hwai*
槐 hwai
讙 hwan
桓 *hwan*
丸 hwan
環 hwan
瞏 hwan
奐 hwan
宦 *hwan*
患 hwan

荒 hwang
黃 *hwang*
皇 hwang
況 hwang
禾 hwo
和 *hwo*
火 hwo
獲 hwoh
舩 hwoh
忽 hwuh
回 hwui
虺 hwui
惠 *hwui*
繪 hwui
會 hwui
倱 hwun
昏 hwun
渾 hwun
衣 i
依 i
沂 i
伊 *i*
移 i
倪 *i or* ni
儀 i
遺 i
宜 i
怡 i
夷 i
倚 i
綺 i

錡 i
齮 i
猗 i
扆 i
懿 i
羿 *i*
藝 i
異 i
裔 i
義 i
燃 jan
然 jan
蚺 jan
染 jan
冉 *jan*
仁 jăn
人 jăn
任 *jăn*
忍 jăn
穰 jang
壤 jang
仍 jăng
扔 jăng
饒 *jao*
繞 jao
偌 joh
若 joh
挐 jü
如 jü
茹 *jü*
汝 jü

辱 juh
蓐 juh
擩 jui
芮 *jui*
銳 jui
絨 jung
戎 *jung*
茙 jung
阮 *jwan*
該 kai
改 kai
蓋 *kai*
開 k'ai
甘 *kan*
干 *kan*
幹 kan
堪 k'ăn
看 k'an
闞 *k'an*
坎 k'an
根 kăn
艮 kăn
阬 k'ang
坑 k'ang
康 *k'ang*
亢 k'ang
伉 k'ang
庚 kăng
耿 *kăng*
亙 kăng
高 *kao*

咎 kao
臯 kao
告 kao
郜 *kao*
考 k'ao
革 keh
勾 *keu*
鉤 keu
緱 keu
狗 keu
茍 keu
詬 keu
彄 k'eu
口 k'eu
寇 *k'eu*
姬 *ki*
稽 *ki*
飢 ki
箕 ki
雞 ki
奚 *ki*
騏 ki
己 ki
紀 *ki*
忌 ki
季 *ki*
薊 ki
暨 *ki*
計 *ki*
冀 *ki*
谿 k'i

˛其 k'i
˛綦 k'i
˛旗 k'i
˛祁 k'i
˛蘄 k'i
˛奇 k'i
˛岐 k'i
ʻ杞 k'i
ʻ啓 k'i
ʻ啓 k'i
ʻ起 k'i
器ʼ k'i
契ʼ k'i
肐ʼ k'i
˛家 *kia*
˛乩 kia
˛嘉 kia
ʻ賈 *kia*
˛佉 k'ia
甲ˏ kiah
鵊ˏ kiah
莢ˏ kiah
介ʼ kiai
˛江 *kiang*
˛姜 *kiang*
˛羌 k'iang
˛强 *k'iang*
˛膠 kiao
˛橋 kiao
ʻ蟜 kiao
ʻ皎 kiao
ʻ儌 kiao
ʻ矯 kiao
ʻ佼 kiao
ʻ姣 kiao
ʻ絞 kiao
校ʼ kiao
鄗ʼ k'iao
˛喬 *k'iao*
˛僑 k'iao
孑ˏ kieh
揭ˏ kieh
桀ˏ kieh
˛肩 kien
˛蕑 kien
˛兼 kien
˛堅 kien
˛开 kien
˛菅 kien
ʻ簡 *kien*
ʻ檢 kien
ʻ儉 kien
ʻ蹇 kien
ʻ謇 kien
ʻ減 kien
ʻ寋 kien
監ʼ kien
健ʼ kien
見ʼ kien
諫ʼ kien
建ʼ kien
˛謙 k'ien
˛牽 k'ien
˛騫 k'ien
˛鉗 k'ien
˛乾 k'ien
˛搴 k'ien
˛虔 k'ien
ʻ譴 k'ien
ʻ掀 k'ien
劇ˏ kih
棘ˏ kih
激ˏ kih
吉ˏ *kih*
姞ˏ kih
汲ˏ *kih*
乞ˏ k'ih
郄ˏ k'ih
郤ˏ *k'ih*
˛金 *kin*
˛筋 kin
ʻ謹 kin
ʻ錦 kin
靳ʼ *kin*
禁ʼ kin
˛欽 k'in
˛懃 k'in
˛禽 k'in
˛琴 k'in
˛黔 k'in
˛荆 *king*
˛經 king
˛京 king
ʻ景 *king*
鏡ʼ king
竟ʼ king
敬ʼ king
˛卿 k'ing
˛黥 k'ing
慶ʼ k'ing
角ˏ kioh
覺ˏ kioh
郟ˏ *kioh*
矍ˏ kioh
˛摎 kiu
˛樛 kiu
ʻ九 kiu
ʻ雂 kiu
ʻ灸 kiu
廄ʼ kiu
臼ʼ kiu
舊ʼ kiu
救ʼ kiu
˛盚 k'iu
˛裘 k'iu
˛仇 *k'iu*
˛求 k'iu
˛邱 *k'iu*
糗ʼ k'iu
舅ʼ k'iu
˛君 kiün
˛軍 kiün
˛鈞 kiün
˛柯 *k'o*
˛苛 k'o
ʻ可 k'o
佫ˏ koh
格ˏ koh
閣ˏ koh
葛ˏ *koh*
佮ˏ koh
鬲ˏ koh
恪ˏ k'oh
客ˏ k'oh
˛辜 ku
˛姑 ku
ʻ古 *ku*
固ʼ ku
顧ʼ *ku*
˛軲 k'u
ʻ苦 k'u
庫ʼ *k'u*
˛居 *kü*
˛俱 kü
˛駒 kü
ʻ禑 kü
ʻ莒 kü
ʻ舉 kü
遽ʼ kü
璩ʼ *kü*
具ʼ kü
巨ʼ kü
˛朐 k'ü
˛曜 k'ü
˛瞿 *k'ü*
˛衢 k'ü
˛蘧 k'ü
厥ˏ küeh
蹶ˏ küeh
闕ˏ k'üeh
˛涓 küen
˛蜎 küen
圈ʼ küen
眷ʼ küen
˛權 *k'üen*
˛拳 k'üen
谷ˏ *kuh*
穀ˏ kuh
鵠ˏ kuh
骨ˏ kuh
麯ˏ k'uh
䏱ˏ küh
鞠ˏ *küh*
肮ˏ küh
麴ˏ *k'üh*
曲ˏ k'üh
詘ˏ k'üh
屈ˏ *k'üh*
˛共 kung
˛供 kung
˛龔 *kung*
˛弓 *kung*
˛躬 kung
˛恭 kung
˛公 *kung*
˛攻 kung
˛宮 *kung*
ʻ拱 kung
ʻ舉 kung
ʻ嚳 kung
ʻ鞏 *kung*
貢ʼ *kung*
˛空 k'ung
ʻ孔 *k'ung*
˛媧 kwa
ʻ冎 kwa
˛夸 kw'a
怪ʼ kwai
ʻ蒯 *kw'ai*
鄶ʼ kw'ai
噲ʼ kw'ai
快ʼ kw'ai
˛關 *kwan*
˛官 kwan
˛淪 kwan
˛莞 kwan
ʻ管 *kwan*
ʻ筦 kwan
貫ʼ kwan
觀ʼ kwan
冠ʼ kwan
˛寬 kw'an
˛光 kwang
ʻ廣 *kwang*
ʻ鄺 kwang
˛匡 *kw'ang*
曠ʼ kw'ang
˛邽 kwéi
˛歸 kwéi
˛規 kwéi
ʻ鬼 kwéi
ʻ癸 kwéi
ʻ詭 kwéi
鄶ʼ kwéi
貴ʼ kwéi
桂ʼ *kwéi*
炔ʼ kwéi
炅ʼ kwéi
˛葵 kw'éi
˛魁 kw'éi
˛夔 kw'éi
餽ʼ kw'éi
匱ʼ kw'éi
蕢ʼ kw'éi
˛戈 *kwo*
˛過 kwo
ʻ果 kwo
郭ˏ *kwoh*
虢ˏ kwoh
國ˏ *kwoh*
˛昆 kwun
˛來 lai
˛萊 lai
˛郲 lai
賴ʼ *lai*
˛藍 *lan*
˛蘭 lan
ʻ覽 lan
˛狼 lang
˛琅 lang
˛郎 *lang*
浪ʼ lang
ʻ冷 *lăng*
˛牢 lao
˛勞 *lao*
ʻ嫪 lao
ʻ老 lao
˛雷 *léi*
˛嫘 léi
˛纍 léi
ʻ壘 léi
類ʼ léi
˛鏤 leu
˛婁 *leu*
˛樓 leu
˛莉 li
˛孋 li
˛離 li
˛劦 li
˛黎 *li*
˛藜 li
˛釐 li
ʻ理 li
ʻ里 li
ʻ禮 li
ʻ李 *li*
ʻ履 li
利ʼ *li*
吏ʼ li

厲 *li*	綾 ling	逯 *luh*	陌 meh	謬 miu	甌 ngeu	霸 pa	悖 péi	邲 pih
荔 li	陵 ling	鹿 luh	眉 mei	莫 *moh*	歐 ngeu	怕 pa	貝 *péi*	豳 pin
隸 li	伶 ling	戀 lüen	梅 *méi*	鄚 moh	謳 ngeu	仈 pah	丕 p'éi	斌 pin
麗 li	泠 ling	倫 lun	枚 méi	末 moh	耦 ngeu	班 *pan*	邳 p'éi	賓 pin
酈 *li*	零 ling	綸 lun	每 méi	默 moh	偶 ngeu	盤 p'an	裴 *p'éi*	頻 p'in
涼 liang	靈 ling	論 lun	牟 meu	牧 *muh*	娥 ngo	繁 p'an	掊 p'éi	品 p'in
梁 *liang*	令 ling	龍 *lung*	謀 meu	慕 *muh*	蛾 ngo	潘 *p'an*	棓 p'éi	幷 ping
良 liang	畧 lioh	隆 *lung*	瞀 meu	穆 *muh*	訛 ngo	盼 p'an	沛 p'éi	邴 *ping*
亮 liang	劉 *liu*	隴 lung	茂 meu	沐 muh	鄂 *ngoh*	奔 păn	裨 pi	秉 ping
諒 liang	留 liu	欒 *lwan*	貿 meu	睦 muh	郳 ni	盆 p'ăn	婄 pi	平 *p'ing*
僚 liao	瞟 liu	麻 *ma*	糜 *mi*	幕 muh	泥 ni	邦 pang	敝 pi	評 p'ing
聊 liao	柳 *liu*	馬 *ma*	彌 mi	目 muh	齧 nieh	逄 p'ang	被 p'i	瓶 p'ing
蓼 liao	飂 liu	買 mai	芈 mi	木 muh	聶 *nieh*	龎 p'ang	皮 *p'i*	凴 p'ing
廖 liao	羅 *lo*	蠻 man	米 *mi*	蒙 *mung*	蘖 nieh	龐 *p'ang*	郫 p'i	彪 piu
列 lieh	絡 loh	瞞 man	苗 *miao*	夢 mung	揑 nieh	傍 p'ang	表 piao	播 po
烈 lieh	落 loh	蔄 man	妙 miao	那 *na*	年 nien	崩 păng	別 *pieh*	番 p'o
連 *lien*	駱 *loh*	滿 *man*	繆 *miao*	納 nah	念 nien	朋 p'ăng	鼈 pieh	白 *poh*
廉 *lien*	雒 loh	曼 man	乜 *mieh*	難 nan	甯 *ning*	倗 p'ăng	鱉 pieh	伯 poh
輦 lien	盧 *lu*	門 măn	綿 mien	鷬 nan	牛 *niu*	彭 *p'ăng*	邊 *pien*	柏 *poh*
斂 lien	鹵 lu	芒 mang	眠 mien	男 nan	妞 niu	蓬 p'ăng	便 pien	帛 poh
練 lien	魯 *lu*	忙 mang	免 mien	南 nan	紐 niu	褒 pao	扁 pien	百 poh
栗 lih	露 lu	莽 mang	宓 *mih*	弇 nan	鈕 *niu*	包 *pao*	卞 *pien*	薄 *poh*
立 lih	路 *lu*	萌 măng	密 mih	囊 nang	諾 noh	郇 pao	辨 pien	跋 poh
力 lih	閭 lü	黽 măng	祕 mih	能 *năng*	女 nü	保 pao	變 pien	璞 p'oh
林 *lin*	呂 *lü*	猛 măng	覓 mih	淖 nao	農 *nung*	鮑 pao	弁 pien	捕 pu
遴 lin	旅 lü	孟 *măng*	民 min	哀 ngai	儂 nung	寶 pao	篇 p'ien	普 pu
鱗 lin	慮 lü	茅 *mao*	閔 *min*	艾 *ngai*	莀 nung	鮑 *pao*	偏 p'ien	補 pu
臨 lin	鑢 lü	毛 *mao*	明 *ming*	安 *ngan*	阿 o *or* ngo	暴 *pao*	碧 pih	步 *pu*
藺 *lin*	祿 *luh*	貌 mao	鳴 ming	恩 ngăn	婀 o	豹 pao	畢 *pih*	布 pu
凌 *ling*	錄 luh	墨 meh	瞑 ming	敖 *ngao*	巴 *pa*	雹 pao	辟 pih	蒲 *p'u*
淩 ling	陸 *luh*	麥 meh	名 ming	區 ngeu	把 pa	卑 péi	萆 pih	浦 *p'u*

卜 *puh*	傷 shang	施 *shi*	竪 shu	鮮 sien	秀 siu	恤 süh	亶 tan	斗 *teu*
孛 puh	常 *shang*	時 *shi*	樹 shu	彡 sien	荀 *siün*	睢 sui	膽 tan	逗 teu
僕 puh	賞 shang	茬 shi	述 shuh	先 sien	郇 siün	隋 sui	笪 tan	竇 teu
勃 puh	尚 *shang*	矢 shi	束 *shuh*	洗 sien	瑣 so	隨 sui	炭 tan	稻 teu
濮 *puh*	上 shang	史 *shi*	叔 shuh	羨 sien	索 *soh*	眭 sui	啖 tan	鬬 teu
耏 'rh	生 shăng	亓 shi	贖 shuh	線 sien	索 soh	孫 *sun*	淡 tan	豆 teu
尒 'rh	甥 shăng	士 shi	續 shuh	席 *sih*	率 soh	松 *sung*	但 tan	鬭 teu
耳 'rh	省 shăng	是 shi	誰 shui	習 *sih*	蘇 *su*	嵩 sung	談 *t'an*	鍮 t'eu
佴 'rh	韶 *shao*	氏 shi	水 *shui*	隰 sih	所 su	頌 sung	檀 t'an	投 t'eu
貳 'rh	召 shao	世 shi	瑞 shui	襲 sih	素 su	宋 *sung*	覃 t'an	醍 ti
撒 sah	邵 *shao*	視 shi	稅 shui	錫 sih	須 *sü*	師 *sz'*	譚 *t'an*	邸 ti
薩 sah	少 shao	試 shi	舜 shun	昔 sih	需 sü	司 *sz'*	覃 t'an	第 ti
散 san	紹 shao	石 *shih*	帥 shwai	息 sih	蒪 sü	思 sz'	坦 t'an	棣 ti
桑 *sang*	佘 shé	室 shih	霜 shwang	夕 sih	胥 *sü*	私 sz'	當 tang	刁 *tiao*
丧 sang	荼 shé	實 shih	雙 *shwang*	辛 *sin*	徐 *sü*	斯 sz'	黨 tang	貂 tiao
塞 seh	蛇 shé	釋 shih	說 shwoh	莘 *sin*	緒 sü	四 sz'	党 *tang*	雕 tiao
僿 seh	捨 shé	食 shih	西 si	新 sin	絮 sü	肆 sz'	蕩 tang	調 tiao
薔 seh	赦 shé	式 shih	璽 si	侁 sin	序 sü	嗣 sz'	湯 *tang*	條 t'iao
沙 *sha*	厙 *shé*	識 shih	襄 siang	尋 sin	杼 sü	姒 sz'	堂 t'ang	糶 t'iao
歃 shah	涉 sheh	奭 shih	相 *siang*	鄩 sin	雪 süeh	俟 sz'	棠 t'ang	鐵 t'ieh
山 *shan*	設 sheh	聲 shing	象 siang	鄩 sin	亘 süen	沓 t'ah	唐 *t'ang*	顛 tien
申 *shăn*	舌 sheh	陞 shing	蛸 siao	鐔 sin	宣 *süen*	塔 t'ah	登 tăng	吞 t'ien
宷 shăn	閃 shen	乘 shing	霄 siao	𩇕 sin	宿 *suh*	戴 tai	滕 t'ăng	田 *t'ien*
神 shăn	善 shen	聖 shing	銷 siao	信 sin	縮 suh	台 t'ai	騰 t'ăng	銛 t'ien
諶 shăn	單 *shen*	盛 *shing*	蕭 *siao*	星 sing	肅 suh	咍 t'ai	鄧 *tăng*	翟 *tih*
瞫 shăn	守 sheu	殳 *shu*	謝 *sié*	渻 sing	潚 suh	邰 *t'ai*	道 tao	狄 *tih*
審 shăn	首 sheu	舒 *shu*	薛 *sieh*	性 sing	夙 suh	臺 t'ai	到 tao	丁 *ting*
沈 *shăn*	授 sheu	疋 shu	偰 sieh	姓 sing	㝛 suh	太 t'ai	陶 *t'ao*	鼎 ting
慎 *shăn*	壽 sheu	疏 shu	泄 sieh	脩 siu	粟 suh	儋 tan	桃 t'ao	多 to
眘 shăn	詩 shi	豎 shu	渫 sieh	修 siu	蔌 suh	聃 tan	耀 t'ao	佗 t'o
商 shang	尸 shi	庶 shu	燮 sieh	繡 siu	玉 suh	丹 tan	特 teh	鐸 toh

敓 toh	仝 t'ung	笮 tseh	籍 tsih	鎡 tsuh	文 wăn	烏 wu	冶 yé	亦 yih
都 tu	同 t'ung	鄹 tseu	戢 tsih	足 tsuh	聞 wăn	毋 wu	也 yé	翼 yih
覩 tu	彤 t'ung	郰 tseu	戚 ts'ih	鉐 tsuh	問 wăn	巫 wu	夜 yé	壹 yih
堵 tu	統 t'ung	鯫 tseu	緝 ts'ih	崔 ts'ui	汪 wang	吳 wu	葉 yeh	佚 yih
杜 tu	垌 t'ung	聚 tseu	盡 tsin	毳 ts'ui	王 wang	無 wu	業 yeh	液 yih
度 tu	痛 t'ung	[illegible] tseu	晉 tsin	翠 ts'ui	枉 wang	吾 wu	鄴 yeh	陰 yin
屠 t'u	端 twan	騶 tseu	親 ts'in	尊 tsun	望 wang	五 wu	蘖 yeh	殷 yin
塗 t'u	段 twan	齊 tsi	秦 ts'in	忖 ts'un	翁 wăng	伍 wu	謁 yeh	音 yin
涂 t'u	歪 tsah	祭 tsi	井 tsing	寸 ts'un	嶲 wéi	武 wu	燕 yen	誾 yin
荼 t'u	宰 tsai	蔣 tsiang	靖 tsing	宗 tsung	媯 wéi	舞 wu	鄢 yen	闉 yin
土 t'u	在 tsai	匠 tsiang	青 ts'ing	琮 tsung	爲 wéi	鄔 wu	閼 yen	因 yin
吐 t'u	載 tsai	槍 ts'iang	清 ts'ing	鬷 tsung	韋 wéi	務 wu	顏 yen	銀 yin
督 tuh	才 ts'ai	椒 tsiao	酒 tsiu	叢 ts'ung	惟 wéi	沃 wuh	閻 yen	吟 yin
獨 tuh	采 ts'ai	焦 tsiao	秋 ts'iu	從 ts'ung	維 wéi	偓 wuh	嚴 yen	霒 yin
讀 tuh	蔡 ts'ai	譙 ts'iao	左 tso	樅 ts'ung	微 wéi	兀 wuh	言 yen	隱 yin
秃 t'uh	昝 tsan	且 ts'ié	坐 tso	茲 tsz'	危 wéi	衙 ya	郔 yen	尹 yin
敦 tun	粲 tsan	節 tsieh	[illegible] tsoh	菑 tsz	蔿 wéi	牙 ya	鹽 yen	胤 yin
頓 tun	臧 tsang	接 tsieh	稓 tsoh	資 tsz'	偉 wéi	雅 ya	閆 yen	印 yin
豚 t'un	蒼 ts'ang	捷 tsieh	作 tsoh	訾 tsz'	尾 wéi	軋 yah	延 yen	英 ying
屯 t'un	藏 ts'ang	妾 ts'ieh	昨 tsoh	紫 tsz'	薳 wéi	楊 yang	兗 yen	郢 ying
東 tung	倉 ts'ang	籛 tsien	錯 ts'oh	子 tsz'	隗 wéi	楊 yang	眼 yen	嬰 ying
冬 tung	鄫 tsăng	賤 tsien	狙 tsu	字 tsz'	骫 wéi	陽 yang	偃 yen	嬴 ying
箽 tung	繒 tsăng	阡 ts'ien	祖 tsu	賜 tsz'	衛 wéi	羊 yang	衍 yen	盈 ying
董 tung	曾 ts'ăng	遷 ts'ien	沮 tsü	茨 ts'z'	魏 wéi	仰 yang	鴈 yen	營 ying
凍 tung	糟 tsao	錢 ts'ien	睢 tsü	慈 ts'z'	尉 wéi	養 yang	晏 yen	潁 ying
通 t'ung	藻 tsao	潛 ts'ien	苴 tsü	次 ts'z'	蔚 wéi	要 yao	硯 yen	應 ying
桐 t'ung	棗 tsao	瘠 tsih	[illegible] ts'ü	爨 tsw'an	位 wéi	幺 yao	易 yih	幽 yiu
[illegible] t'ung	操 ts'ao	藉 tsih	全 tsüen	萬 wan	謂 wéi	姚 yao	乙 yih	優 yiu
僮 t'ung	漕 ts'ao	疾 tsih	雋 tsüen	嫚 wan	闈 wéi	銚 yao	弋 yih	攸 yiu
童 t'ung	曹 ts'ao	即 tsih	泉 ts'üen	蔓 wan	渦 wo	傜 yao	益 yih	游 yiu
佟 t'ung	草 ts'ao	稷 tsih	銓 ts'üen	溫 wăn	我 wo	搖 yao	驛 yih	憂 yiu

猶 yiu	鼬 yiu	漁 yü	楀 yü	御 yü	淵 yuen	苑 yuen	覞 yun	容 *yung*
繇 yiu	宥 yiu	余 *yü*	鄅 yü	圉 yü	元 *yuen*	員 yuen	惲 yun	融 *yung*
由 yiu	樂 *yoh*	餘 yü	羽 yü	喩 *yü*	原 yuen	郁 *yuh*	鄆 yun	榮 *yung*
攸 yiu	岳 yoh	俞 *yü*	與 yü	諭 yü	源 yuen	鬱 *yuh*	鄖 yun	永 yung
尤 *yiu*	約 yoh	榆 yü	庾 *yü*	衙 yü	垣 yuen	玉 yuh	雍 *yung*	用 yung
郵 yiu	紆 yü	禺 yü	禹 *yü*	越 *yueh*	爰 yuen	遹 yuh	庸 yung	
酉 yiu	輿 yü	愚 yü	萬 yü	月 yueh	袁 *yuen*	郥 yüh	鄘 yung	
有 yiu	於 *yü*	盂 yü	遇 yü	嶽 yueh	榬 yuen	鬻 yüh	雝 yung	
右 yiu	臾 yü	虞 *yü*	譽 yü	藥 yueh	轅 yuen	雲 *yun*	夐 yung	
羑 yiu	魚 yü	于 *yü*	豫 yü	宛 yuen	遠 yuen	妘 yun	彤 yung	

LIST OF THE 複姓 OR DOUBLE SURNAMES.

臧巫 chăn-wu	主父 chu-fu	豐將 fung-tsiang	獯鬻 hiün-yuh	解律 huh-lüh	臯落 kao-loh	鸜鵒 k'ü ts'ioh	瓜田 kwa-tien
章仇 chang-cheu	中行 chung-hing	函治 han-chi	熊率 hiung-shwai	豢龍 hwan-lung	庚桑 kăng-sang	轂梁 kuh-liang	鮭陽 kw'ei-yang
長孫 *chang-sun*	鍾離 *chung-li*	浩生 hao-shăng	褐扶 hoh-fu	皇甫 *hwang-fu*	鉤弋 keu-yih	屈突 k'üh-t'uh	荔菲 li-féi
常壽 ch'ang-sheu	仲長 chung-ch'ang	豨韋 hi-wéi	紇骨 hoh-tuh	惠牆 hwui-ts'iang	解枇 kiai-p'i	公山 kung-shan	令狐 *ling-hu*
長盧 ch'ang-lu	仲孫 *chung-sun*	夏侯 *hia-heu*	黑齒 hoh-ch'i	伊秩 i-chih	茄羅 k'ié-lo	公孫 *kung-sun*	泠淪 ling-lun
醜門 ch'eu-măn	顓頊 chwen-süh	瑕丘 hia-k'iu	赫連 *hoh-lien*	伊祈 i-k'i	幵官 kien-kwan	公羊 *kung-yang*	龍逢 lung-p'ăng
成功 ch'ing-kung	顓孫 chwen-sun	霞露 hia-lu	壺丘 hu-k'iu	茙眷 jung-küen	乞伏 k'ih-fuh	公冶 *kung-yé*	攣鞮 lwan-ti
斫胥 choh-sü	穿封 chw'en fung	軒丘 hien-k'iu	胡母 hu-mu	高唐 kao-t'ang	九百 kiu-poh	空桐 k'ung-t'ung	秘邦 mih-pang
諸葛 *chu-koh*	夫餘 fu-yü	軒轅 *hien-yuen*	呼延 hu-yen	高陽 kao-yang	古冶 ku-yé	咼哈 kwa-hoh	万俟 *moh-ki*

慕容	*mu-yung*
目夷	muh-i
鳥俗	niao-suh
歐陽	*ngeu-yang*
女媧	nü-kwa
豹皮	pao-pʻi
庖犧	pʻao-ki
佛肸	pih-hih
賓牟	pin-meu
病坊	ping-fang
百里	poh-li
不第	puh-ti
僕固	puh-ku
濮陽	*puh-yang*
彡姐	shan-tsié
申屠	*shăn-tu*
商瞿	shang-kʻü
上官	*shang-kwan*
社北	shé-poh
單于	*shen-yü*
矢宮	shi-kung
侍其	shi-kʻi
豕韋	shi-wéi
士孫	shi-sun
石作	shih-tsoh
勝屠	shing-tʻu
淳于	*shun-yü*
爽鳩	shwang-kiu
相里	siang-li
鮮于	sien-yü
息夫	sih-fu
信都	sin-tu
徐吾	sü-wu
宣于	süen-yü
宿沙	suh-sha
燧人	sui-jăn
司城	sz'-chʻing
司禍	sz'-hoh
司空	*sz'-kung*
司馬	*sz'-ma*
司徒	*sz'-tu*
荅祿	tah-luh
太史	tʻai-shi
太叔	*tʻai-suh*
澹臺	*tʻan-tʻai*
棠谿	tʻang-kʻi
豆盧	teu-lu
第五	ti-wu
鐵伐	tʻieh-fah
拓跋	tʻoh-pah
覩斯	tu-sz'
吐奚	tʻu-hi
獨孤	tuh-hu
禿髮	tʻuh-fah
東野	tung-yé
東方	*tung-fang*
端木	twan-muh
宰父	tsai-fu
匠麗	tsiang-li
芊尹	tsʻien-yin
卽墨	tsih-moh
青陽	tsʻing-yang
左人	tso-jăn
左丘	tso-kʻiu
昨和	tsoh-hwo
沮渠	tsü-kʻü
宗政	*tsung-ching*
訾辱	tsz'-juh
子言	tsz'-yen
梓愼	tsz'-shăn
次第	tsʻz'-ti
聞人	*wăn-jăn*
微生	wéi-shăng
未央	wéi-yang
巫陽	wu-yang
毋鹽	wu-yen
無庸	wu-yung
五京	wu-king
五鹿	wu-luh
武安	wu-ngan
屋盧	wuh-lu
羊舌	yang-sheh
耶律	yé-lüh
邑由	yih-yiu
由吾	yiu-wu
有熊	yiu-hiung
有仍	yiu-jăng
有㜪	yiu-sin
右行	yiu-hing
右師	yiu-shi
樂毅	yoh-i
於陵	yü-ling
宇文	*yü-wăn*
原褚	yuen-chʻu
尉遲	*yuh-chi*
尉千	yuh-tsʻien
執失代	chih-shih-tai
侯莫陳	heu-moh-chʻăn
盱母萬	hü-mu-wan
奚斗盧	kʻi-teu-lu
阿伏于	o-fuh-yü
步隲又	pu-chih-yiu
勿忸于	wuh-niu-yü
壹斗眷	yih-teu-küen

ERRATA AND CORRECTIONS.

SINCE the issue of the first edition of this book in 1874, its merits have been fairly discussed, its deficiencies pointed out, and its errors set forth by several friendly critics and scholars. Their suggestions will by useful to those who may, by and by, undertake a similar work. From their remarks the following list has been mostly selected, as containing the errors most desirable to be corrected. As their notices are scattered here and there, their intentions in making them will be promoted by bringing them together. In respect to the explanation of the construction of characters, a reference may be made to page xlviii. of the Introduction, where the object is stated; some mistakes were made in discriminating the component parts, but the main design was to aid beginners to remember the leading portions of characters, rather than to give all their etymologies. In addition to the dialects given in the Index, Miss A. M. FIELDE, of the American Baptist Mission at Swatow, has published a complete list of the sounds of all the characters in that dialect, including many variants; and Mr. JAMES ACHESON, of the Imperial Customs, has issued another list giving the Peking sounds according to Sir T. F. WADE's *Progressive Course.* All sinologues will be thankful for these lists. A full collection of the vocables in the best defined and leading dialects in the empire will furnish accurate materials for comparisons and deductions, which may enable some philologist, like GRIMM or WHITNEY, to ascertain the genesis of Chinese pronunciation, and the laws which govern its perplexing changes.

SHANGHAI, *March* 1*st*, 1883

Page	116,	col.	1, top,	for	霔	read	霖
,,	163,	,,	1, ,,	,,	凾	,,	函
,,	116,	,,	3, bottom	,,	悽	,,	悽
,,	130,	,,	2, ,,	,,	仲春	,,	仲春
,,	145,	,,	3, near top,	,,	丨巡	,,	巡丨
,,	152,	,,	2, ,,	,,	既丨其幸	,,	既丨其幸
,,	157,	,,	1, middle,	,,	不何	,,	不合
,,	167,	,,	3, near bottom	for	不懇	read	不肯

,, 309, ,, 3, line 17 for 佛 read 拂

,, 320, ,, 1, ,, 34 ,, 遭 read 糟

,, 336, ,, 3, ,, 20 ,, *Boreas* and *Eolus.*

,, 536, ,, 1, ,, 26 ,, 雀 read 鵲

,, 543, ,, 1, ,, at bottom, for *tact* read *versatility.*

,, 611, ,, 2, ,, 26 for *Tanki's* read *Ta-ki's.*

,, 667, ,, 3, ,, 4 ,, *knight* read *castle.*

,, 680, ,, 2, ,, 19 ,, *Manchuria* read *Koko-nor.*

,, 906, ,, 2, ,, 14 ,, 王 read 壬

,, 911, ,, 3, ,, 17 ,, *double* read *swollen.*

,, 941, ,, 3, ,, 28 ,, *month* read *year.*

,, 948, ,, 1, ,, 24 ,, *to advance* read *tsin* 疹 *acute.*

148^{2} The 鮒 is a carp; the name includes similar species of soft finned fish, of which some sorts are known as 鯽魚; they are served up at wedding feasts.

155^{3} The expression 馬牛風 is said of persons who avoid meeting, or who cannot see each other; 風流 is also used in the sense of accomplished, elegant.

182^{3} The 蝦 is the toad; it is often eaten.

210^{1} The 鸒 is the book name of the Chinese blue jay (*Urocissa sinensis*), also called blue magpie.

217^{2} The composition of 合 is 口 *mouth* and 亼 *triangle*, indicating *union*; the latter element also occurs in 侖 on page 565^{1}; in 會 on page 264^{2}; in 舍 on page 748^{1}; in it is explained on page 985^{1} under 集 to *assemble*.

217^{1} The 鶡鷄 is the eared pheasant (*Crossoptilon auritus*) or Pallas' pheasant; the name is commonly written 火鷄 fire cock, which may be a mistake of the proper characters from the similarity of sound.

220^{1} The 貉 is the raccoon dog (*Nyctereutes procyonoides*) also known as 菓子狸 or fruit cat and 窩狐 or cave fox; the primitive in 貉 is simply phonetic.

224^{3} A 虎臂 or tiger's shoulder, also means a hidden ledge or rocks in a rapid.

225^{2} The 桑扈 or 扈鳥 is a general term for finches, bull-finches, Java sparrows, &c. (*Eophona* and *Coccothraustes*), otherwise called 蜡嘴鳥 or wax-bills, as a general designation.

228^{1} Erase, under 栩, soft, pliable; flexible wood easily bent. A misprinted character in *Kanghi* caused the mistake.

246^{3} The character 丸 is the reversed form of 仄 the side of.

297^{2} The example in the 10th line is better rendered, Though you have it, you would be better without it.

320^{1} The 13th line is better rendered, The wife of my poverty shall not leave the hall.

330^{1} The 雊嘍兒 is a name for the curlew (*Numenius*) in Chihli province.

337^{3} The 麃 of Kiangnan is the river deer (*Hydropotes inermis*) which has tusks similar to the musk deer.

340^{3} The 花鯚魚 is the mandarin fish (*Siniperca chua-tsi*) a kind of perch; another species, the 黃鯚魚 is the *Siniperca chuan-tsi*; both found in Chihli.

340^{3} The 記室 is also a secretary in an office.

348^{3} At bottom. The phrase 習氣 is applied to habit, custom, temper, manner; nature of, as a soil.

349^{1} The expression 棄市 is a euphuism for decollation; the execution-ground in Peking is in a vegetable market.

503^{2} A synonym of 懶 is 嬾; both forms are common.

563^{3} Under 趢, the last phrase is also written 打一個轂轆, referring to the turns of a pulley.

518^{1} The 野狸 is the tarai (*Felis viverrina*), which resembles the wild cat; but in Chihli, the 野狸子 is the cat of the steppes (*Felis manul*).

546^{3} The phrase 酒令 denotes a rule imposed at a feast in respect of drinking.

574^{1} The 蠻夷 are also known as 八蠻 because eight tribes were reckoned on all sides of China; 蠻悍 also means rowdy; rude, as a bully.

590^{1} The 麋 is more probably the tailed deer (*Elaphurus Davidianus*), once common in northern China, and called 四不像 at Peking.

613^{2} The phrase 奈不過 rather means, Unable to bear it.

619^{1} The term 哀子 is properly applied to motherless sons.

628^{3} The 鱷魚 is the alligator found in the Yangtsz' River; but the term has been extended as generic to include other great saurians.

633^{2} line 16. The whole sentence from the *Analects* will make this clearer:--不曰白乎涅而不緇 Is it not said, that if a thing be white, it may be muddied, and still not be blackened?

639^{1} bottom. For 挼沙 read 挼挲 to crumple up; see page 814^{1} bottom. Under 狃 after a fox's footsteps, add the fox, from its being wry-footed.

647^{1} The 八仙桌子 is a table for eight persons to dine at, sometimes square, sometimes octagonal.

650^{2} middle. The phrase 班師 also means to deploy a force; to withdraw troops and avoid a battle. The expression just below, 班行天下 is likewise written 頒行天下 with the same meaning.

664^{2} The composition of 保 is apparently from *man* and *stupid;* but the primitive is altered from 孚 to *trust to.*

665^{1} The 抱 is more than an arm's length; it is a fathom or the extended arms. The 豹 also denotes the *Felis Fontanierii* or North China panther. The proverb quoted under it is better rendered, You've looked at the leopard through a tube, — and saw only one spot; *i. e.* you have a partial acquaintance with the matter.

684^{1} bottom. Correct to, To see one off, as to his chair.

685^{2} The 鼈 popularly includes sea turtles along the Kwangtung coast, but there and in the north it properly denotes soft-shelled Cheloniæ (*Emys*, *Trionyx*, &c.), the turtle sometimes called 玳瑁 in books.

688[2] The phrase 便衣 also denotes in undress, unrobed; applied to officials.

692[1] The composition of 畢 is 田 a *field* above 革 a *refuse-basket;* it is supposed to delineate a *field-basket;* some explain the upper part as altered from 由 giving the sound *fuh.*

697[1] middle. The phrase 認你所爲 should read 認憑你所爲 and transferred to page 702[2].

693[1] middle. The phrase 筆氣壯勁 means a bold hand, a vigorous style. — The fish 鮅 on the same page is a rudd or [illegible] (*[illegible]*), and common all over China.

706[3] middle. The phrase 磅礴 is similar to the one here quoted, in its form, and means easy, unconstrained.

613[1] The composition of 步 is 止 to *stop* and 少 the same reversed, indicating a quick stride.

714[3] The last sentence under 哺 reads in full 羊羔跪乳烏鴉反哺, lambs kneel to suckle, crows disgorge for their dams;—nature herself teaches filial piety.

717[3] The composition of 僕 is 人 *man* and 丵 *thick underbrush* altered, denoting troublesome; it is sometimes wrongly written like 業 an *estate.*

733[1] The term 山人 also means a priest; as 山門 does a temple.

736[1] The character 申 is formed of 臼 *two hands* with 丨 a *down stroke,* as if one braced himself; it is supposed to represent the *yin* principle in full action in the seventh moon.

740[3] The phrase 無常鬼, the unusual demon, refers to a human soul which arrests wicked spirits on earth, while its own body is inanimate; this explanation is given as the reason of a cataleptic fit. The 鱨 is referred to the *Pseudobagrus fulvidraco,* a kind of silure or sheatfish with two cirri, also called 黃頰魚 yellow cheek fish and 黃顙魚 yellow temples fish; it makes a curious creaking sound like 軋軋 ya-ya.

741[3] The character 尙 is composed of 向 *towards* and 八 *eight* above.

746[1] The phrase 韶華 is better, Splendid, as the fading life of man and its glories.

750[1] The 䅎 denotes the third gathering of tea leaves. Under 涉 on same page, the phrase 跋涉勿動 is better rendered, I have never traveled much.

754[3] To play chess or other games like it, is a metaphorical meaning of 手談, as well as to teach or talk with the fingers.

766[2] near top. C[illegible]rect 打把丨 to 打把式 and put it on the [illegible]t page.

770[3] The 鼪 inclu[illegible] the striped *squirrel* (*Sciurus Davidianus*) and the North China squirrel (*Sc. striatus*).

778[2] The 術家 also includes geomancers, magicians, soothsayers, clairvoyants, &c.

779[2] The expression 不自檢束 means, He puts no restraint on himself; reckless, lost to decency.

785[3] The character 帥 is formed of 巾 *napkin* and an old form of 堆 to *pile up,* which refer to putting the handkerchief in the girdle.

789[1] bottom A better version is, Either they are twice, or they are five times [as many.]

790[3] top. The terms 細小 and 細君 are both also used for a wife by her husband only.

791[2] The name 湘妃竹 given to the speckled bamboo alludes to the tears wept at Shun's grave by his two sister wives. See Mayers' *Manual,* page 165.

835[3] The composition of 虒 is 虎 a *tiger* and 厂 to *drag,* which gives the sound.

843[2] The primitive 曷 is formed of 羽 *wings* under 日 to *cover* contracted to resemble 曰 to *speak.*

861[3] bottom. The phrase 儻來之物 indicates that the thing came by a wrong road; ill-gotten gains.

876[1] bottom. The phrase 無頭公案 also means a charge against some person unknown.

876[3] top. The third example is better rendered, Half a sentence is too much if not spoken to the point.

884[1] The 鮧 is recognized as the sheatfish (*Silurus asotus*) of European rivers, sometimes seen five feet long in China.

896[3] The components of 奠 are 大 altered from 丌 an old form of 基 a *foundation,* with 酋 a form of 酒 *spirits* above it for worship.

905[2] The lower half of 定 is 正 *correct* reduced to an earlier form 疋 with a straight top line.

912[1] The 鮀 and 鼉 are synonyms, and especially denote the *Alligator sinensis* found in the Yang-tsz' river.

113[2] The 鵽 is the 沙鷄 sand grouse (*Syrrhaptes paradoxus*) of the northern Desert.

917[2] near top. For spindle-tree read, A solitary russet pear tree.

922[2] The 五毒 likewise denote the five legal punishments.

928[1] top. The bricks are also called 白不子 by potters; see Julien's *Porcelaine,* page 251. In col. 2, line 21, the phrase also means in mandarin, The time of a meal, a short space; indicating that one has no leisure at all. The other signification is common at Canton.

934[3] The two parts of 童 are really derived from 辛 a *crime* and 重 *heavy* contracted; and from 立 and 里 only in appearance.

937[1] The expression 短見 is a euphuism for suicide; as is also 自裁 on page 943[2] near top.

939[1] The character 丏 is the original form of 之 to *sprout* turned upside down.

945[1] Under 簪 the character 匕 a *spoon* should be 匕 to *change*, which is 化 contracted.

962[1] Under 奏, the character 本 should be 夲 *to enter hastily*.

992[1] Under 正寢 which properly means a man's death chamber, add 內寢 which denotes more strictly that of a woman's.

1001[2] The 鰍 is the loach *(Cobitis)*, call· also 泥魚 mud fish; it somewhat resembles a.ı eel, and is called 鰼 in books, and 泥毬兒; the latter a northern name.

1020[3] The 鼪 is a striped ground squirrel (*Sciurus striatus*) common in Chihli.

1027[2] The character 爨 is composed of 火 *fire* at bottom with 廾 *two hands* pushing 林 *wood* beneath 冂 a *furnace mouth* over which is an 𦥑 *earthern pot* or stove held by *two hands*; it is one of the most complicated ideographs in the language, and has two modified, simpler forms.

1044[2] The primitive of 往 is not really 主 *lord*, but a modified form of 㞷 *underbrush*, which gives the sound.

1057[2] The phrase 二女媟 means, Two women waited [on Shun]; they were the daughters of Yao.

1058[1] bottom. The example 莫黑匪烏 should be rendered, Nothing black besides crows [are seen].

1059[2] The sixth example should be rendered, There really was no reason [for the act].

1065[3] middle. The phrase 物色 has a wider application; to detect, to find, to search out.

1071[2] The first example under 陽 also means, On the throne, when he was reigning.

1073[1] The sentence 無關痛癢 is rather, His pains and itchings don't hurt me; we've no common interests.

1074[3] top. The phrase 奈恙何 is used by doctors for, I fear it is all over with him: *lit.* remedy the disease how?

1077[3] The character 要 is apparently formed of *west* and *woman*; but the original form is derived from 臼 the *hands* clasping the body above 交 to *join* contracted, giving the sound.

1083[3] The composition of 言 is from 口 *mouth* with 辛 a *fault* above it, much contracted.

1087[1] The 鼹 is the 地拍 or 地拍鼠 the ground rat, (*Scaptochirus moschatus*) a small mole common in Chihli and North China.

1092[2] bottom. The 鴗 has also been defined the chough (*Fregilus graculus*), for which 紅嘴鴉 or red billed raven is the Peking raven.

1094[1] The composition of 睪 is apparently 目 *eye* over 幸 *lucky*; but the primitive is an old form of 夲 *to scare*. See also 圉 on page 1126[3].

1093[3] The game referred to under 弈 is the 圍碁 or game of war or blockade, here incorrectly called chess; Mr. Giles has given an account of it in *Temple Bar*, January, 1877.

1100[1] The component parts of 音 are 言 *words* with *one* in mouth, alluding to modulations in music.

1106[2] The tassel on an official hat is 馬纓; and the silk tree 絨花樹 (*Julibrissin*) seems to have the fitting name of 馬纓花 tassel flower sometimes applied to it.

1115[1] The phrase 坐又不安 is better rendered, Neither could he sit easy.

1116[2] The 鼬 probably denotes the polecat (*Putorius Fontanierii* and *sebiricus)* for which 鼪鼠 is another name.

1120[2] The second form 予 is also used as a common synonym of 與 to *give*.

1122[3] bottom. A better version is, To thoroughly ascertain the feeling of the people.

1123[1] top. This bird is the eastern jackdaw (*Lycos daurica*.

1125 bottom. Correct the italics to *One debate between two men*.

1133[1] Under 原, instead of "but the next form is oldest," read, It is the orig of the next, which is now confined to a spring, and had another form of *three fountains* under a *cliff*, now disused.

1135[2] The 爰書 is the record of a case appealed to a higher court, and sent with the prisoner.

1140[1] top. The phrase 抑鬱不伸 is better rendered, Oppressed without remedy; no relief from my misery.

1141 Confucius is said in the *Lun-yü* not to have trodden on the threshold when entering the court.